2004

WRITER'S MARKET *ONLINE*

Welcome to WRITERSMARKET.COM

THE ULTIMATE MARKET RESEARCH TOOL FOR WRITERS

Inside this booklet, you'll discover how to use the tools that make *Writer's Market Online* your best book buy for the buck!

- EASY-TO-USE SEARCHABLE DATABASE
- SUBMISSION TRACKER
- PERSONALIZED MARKET LISTS
- 5,600+ LISTINGS
- QUICK-CLICK CONNECTIONS
- DAILY UPDATES
- INDUSTRY NEWS
- AND MORE!

OPEN HERE

REMOVE ABOVE BOOKLET TO REVEAL INSTRUCTIONS FOR STARTING YOUR ONE-YEAR SUBSCRIPTION TO WRITERSMARKET.COM!

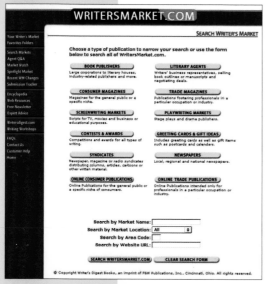

2004

WRITER'S MARKET®

8,000+ BOOK AND MAGAZINE EDITORS WHO BUY WHAT YOU WRITE

EDITOR
KATHRYN S. BROGAN

ASSISTANT EDITOR
ROBERT LEE BREWER

WRITER'S DIGEST BOOKS
CINCINNATI, OH

Praise for *Writer's Market*

"No writer should be without the *Writer's Market* . . . This is the biggest and best book in the industry for American markets."
—American Markets Newsletter

"The *Writer's Market* is by far and away the premier source for [finding a publication or publisher] for writers in all stages in ther career(s)."
—John Austin, Book of the Month

"The *Writer's Market* is another must-have book for writers seeking to profit from their writing endeavors."
—Writer's Write, The Internet Writing Journal

"An invaluable resource that lays out the nuts and bolts of getting published."
—Library Journal

"The writer's bible and best friend. If you're serious about selling what you write and submit material regularly, you need a new copy every year."
—Freelance Writer's Report

"This volume is a freelancer's working tool, as important as the basic computer or typewriter."
—The Bloomsbury Review

If your company or contest would like to be considered for a listing in the next edition of *Writer's Market* or on WritersMarket.com, send a message specifying which section of the book you wish to be in by e-mail to writersmarket@fwpubs.com or by mail to Writer's Market—Questionnaire, 4700 East Galbraith Rd., Cincinnati OH 45236.

All listings in *Writer's Market* are paying markets.

Editorial Director, Writer's Digest Books: Barbara Kuroff
Managing Editor, Writer's Digest Books: Alice Pope

Writer's Market Website: www.writersmarket.com

Writer's Digest Website: www.writersdigest.com

Library of Congress Catalog Number 31-20772
International Standard Serial Number 0084-2729
International Standard Book Number 1-58297-189-7
International Standard Book Number 1-58297-190-0 (*Writer's Market Online*)

Attention Booksellers: This is an annual directory of F&W Publications. Return deadline for this edition is December 31, 2004.

contents at a glance

Contents

THE BUSINESS OF WRITING

LITERARY & SCRIPT AGENTS

THE MARKETS

COMPLAINT PROCEDURE

If you feel you have not been treated fairly by a listing in ***Writer's Market***, we advise you to take the following steps:

- First try to contact the listing. Sometimes one phone call or a letter can quickly clear up the matter.
- Document all your correspondence with the listing. When you write to us with a complaint, provide the details of your submission, the date of your first contact with the listing, and the nature of your subsequent correspondence.
- We will enter your letter into our files and attempt to contact the listing.
- The number and severity of complaints will be considered in our decision whether to delete the listing from the next edition.

From the Editor

In a period of four days, I was asked the same questions by two different people: Do publishing houses change much, and how long do editors stay at any given house? One of these people is a successful entrepreneur living in New Hampshire (who knows very little, if anything, about the publishing industry); the other is a writer living in Montana who still uses his *1999 Writer's Market* (Word to the wise: Don't use any edition except for the current edition—as you continue to read on, you'll learn why!). The best answer I could provide each of them was: Constantly.

Like everything in life, the publishing industry changes on a daily basis. For example, if you compare last year's Publishers and Their Imprints feature with this year's feature (page 79), you will notice significant changes at each of the major houses. Some imprints no longer exist, while new imprints have been added as the houses have acquired new titles and authors. Accompanying those shifts is a new barrage of editors with new e-mail addresses and telephone numbers—that's why I told the writer from Montana not to use his *1999 Writer's Market*!

Anyone who has a copy of *Writer's Market* from years past will notice significant changes to the book. One of the biggest changes in this edition is there are now more than 250 listings for literary and script agents compared to the 75 of years past. There is also a new section of articles dealing with the basics of finding and working with agents. We've made these changes with you, the writer, in mind. We've taken everything once offered in *Guide to Literary Agents* and combined it with the always up-to-date content in *Writer's Market* to give you one resource that contains all the information you need to get published.

In order to facilitate these new markets and articles, we've moved the greeting card listings and the syndicate listings from *Writer's Market* to *Writer's Market Online*. These two sections are now online-exclusive sections, along with newspapers and online publications, found only on WritersMarket.com. In addition to these new sections, we've also made it easier for you to search for markets on the website. Not only can you search for markets by name, you can also search for them by keywords. These two search methods allow you to refine your search and find the exact markets for which you are looking.

Again, it is with you, the writer, in mind that we've made the changes to this edition and to our website. Whether you're yet-to-be-published or regularly published, I think you'll find the changes both beneficial and refreshing.

Since the publishing industry is constantly changing we will too, to make sure you have access to the most comprehensive, accurate, and useful resource. And to those of you still holding on to your old, tattered *1999 Writer's Market*—remember, change is good!

Kathryn Struckel Brogan

Kathryn Struckel Brogan, Editor, *Writer's Market*
writersmarket@fwpubs.com

Writer's Market
Feedback Form

If you have a suggestion for improving *Writer's Market*, or would like to take part in a reader survey we conduct from time to time, please make a photocopy of this form (or cut it out of the book), fill it out, and return it to:

Writer's Market Feedback
4700 E. Galbraith Rd.
Cincinnati OH 45236
Fax: (513)531-2686

☐ Yes! I'm willing to fill out a short survey by mail or online to provide feedback on *Writer's Market* or other books on writing.

☐ Yes! I have a suggestion to improve *Writer's Market* (attach a second sheet if more room is necessary):

____

____

____

____

____

____

____

Name: ________________________________

Address: ______________________________

City: __________ State: ________ Zip: ________

Phone: ________________ Fax: ________________

E-mail: ________________ Website: ________________

I am
☐ a beginning writer (not-yet published)
☐ a published writer

I write
☐ fiction
☐ nonfiction
☐ both

Using Your *Writer's Market* to Sell Your Writing

Writer's Market is here to help you decide where and how to submit your writing to appropriate markets. Each listing contains information about the editorial focus of the market, how it prefers material to be submitted, payment information, and other helpful tips.

WHAT'S INSIDE?

Since 1921, *Writer's Market* has been giving you the important information you need to know in order to approach a market knowledgeably. We've continued to search out improvements to help you access that information more efficiently.

Symbols. There are a variety of symbols that appear before each listing. A key to all of the symbols appears on the front and back inside covers. However, there are a few symbols we'd like to point out. In book publishers, the ⊶ quickly sums up a publisher's interests. In Consumer Magazines the ⊶ zeroes in on what areas of that market are particularly open to freelancers to help you break in to that market. Other symbols let you know whether a listing is new to the book (N), a book publisher accepts only agented writers (A), comparative pay rates for a magazine (**$-$$$$**), and more.

Acquisition names, royalty rates, and advances. In the Book Publishers section we identify acquisition editors with the boldface word **Acquisitions** to help you get your manuscript to the right person. Royalty rates and advances are highlighted in boldface, as well as other important information on the percentage of first-time writers and unagented writers the company publishes, the number of books published, and the number of manuscripts received each year.

Editors, pay rates, and percentage of material written by freelance writers. In Consumer Magazines and Trade, Technical & Professional Journal sections, we identify who to send your query or article to by the boldface word **Contact**. The amount (percentage) of material accepted from freelance writers, and the pay rates for features, columns and departments, and fillers are also highlighted in boldface to help you quickly identify the information you need to know when considering whether to submit your work.

Query formats. We asked editors how they prefer to receive queries and have indicated in the listings whether they prefer queries by mail, e-mail, fax, or phone. Be sure to check an editor's individual preference before sending your query.

Articles. All of the articles, with the exception of a few standard pieces, are new to this edition. Newer, unpublished writers should be sure to read the articles in the Getting Published section, while more experienced writers should focus on those in The Business of Writing section. In addition to these sections, there is also a section of interviews, Personal Views, with industry professionals and other career-oriented professionals. Also new to this edition is the Literary and Script Agents section of articles. The articles in this section will help you determine whether you need an agent and, if you do, how to find the right agent and then contact him.

How Much Should I Charge? is back! This popular feature has been resurveyed and is 100 percent updated! You can use the information in this feature as a guide to determine appropriate pay rates for a variety of freelance opportunities.

IF *WRITER'S MARKET* IS NEW TO YOU . . .

A quick look at the Table of Contents will familiarize you with the arrangement of *Writer's Market*. The three largest sections of the book are the market listings of Book Publishers; Consumer Magazines; and Trade, Technical & Professional Journals. You will also find other sections of market listings for Literary Agents, Script Agents, Scriptwriting, and Contests & Awards. The section introductions contain specific information about trends, submission methods, and other helpful resources for the material included in that section (which are indicated by the For More Information boxes).

Important Listing Information

- Listings are based on editorial questionnaires and interviews. They are not advertisements; publishers do not pay for their listings. The markets are not endorsed by *Writer's Market* editors. F&W Publications, Inc., Writer's Digest Books, and its employees go to great effort to ascertain the validity of information in this book. However, transactions between users of the information and individuals and/or companies are strictly between those parties.
- All listings have been verified before publication of this book. If a listing has not changed from last year, then the editor told us the market's needs have not changed and the previous listing continues to accurately reflect its policies.
- *Writer's Market* reserves the right to exclude any listing.
- When looking for a specific market, check the index. A market may not be listed for one of these reasons:
    1. It doesn't solicit freelance material.
    2. It doesn't pay for material.
    3. It has gone out of business.
    4. It has failed to verify or update its listing for this edition.
    5. It hasn't answered *Writer's Market* inquiries satisfactorily. (To the best of our ability, and with our readers' help, we try to screen fraudulent listings.)
- Individual markets that appeared in last year's edition but are not listed in this edition are included in the General Index, with a notation giving the reason for their exclusion.

Narrowing your search

After you've identified the market categories you're interested in, you can begin researching specific markets within each section.

Book Publishers are categorized, in the Book Publishers Subject Index, according to types of books they are interested in. If, for example, you plan to write a book on a religious topic, simply turn to the Book Publishers Subject Index and look under the Religion subhead in Nonfiction for the names and page numbers of companies that publish such books.

Consumer Magazines and Trade, Technical & Professional Journals are categorized by subject to make it easier for you to identify markets for your work. If you want to publish an article dealing with some aspect of retirement, you could look under the Retirement category of Consumer Magazines to find an appropriate market. You would want to keep in mind, however, that magazines in other categories might also be interested in your article (for example, women's magazines publish such material as well). Keep your antennae up while studying the markets: Less obvious markets often offer the best opportunities.

Interpreting the markets

Once you've identified companies or publications that cover the subjects you're interested in, you can begin evaluating specific listings to pinpoint the markets most receptive to your work and most beneficial to you.

In evaluating an individual listing, first check the location of the company, the types of material it is interested in seeing, submission requirements, and rights and payment policies.

Depending upon your personal concerns, any of these items could be a deciding factor as you determine which markets you plan to approach. Many listings also include a reporting time, which lets you know how long it will typically take for the publisher to respond to your initial query or submission. (We suggest that you allow an additional two months for a response, just in case your submission is under further review or the publisher is backlogged.)

Check the Glossary at the back of the book for unfamiliar words. Specific symbols and abbreviations are explained in the key appearing on the front and back inside covers. The most important abbreviation is SASE—self-addressed, stamped envelope. Always enclose a SASE when you send unsolicited queries, proposals, or manuscripts. This requirement is not included in most of the individual market listings because it is a "given" you must follow if you expect to receive a reply.

A careful reading of the listings will reveal that many editors are very specific about their needs. Your chances of success increase if you follow directions to the letter. Often companies do not accept unsolicited manuscripts and return them unread. If a company does not accept unsolicited manuscripts (⊘), it is indicated in the listing. Read each listing closely, heed the tips given, and follow the instructions.

Whenever possible, obtain writer's guidelines before submitting material. You can usually obtain guidelines by sending a SASE to the address in the listing. Magazines often post their guidelines on their website as well. Most of the listings indicate how writer's guidelines are made available. You should also familiarize yourself with the company's publications. Many of the listings contain instructions on how to obtain sample copies, catalogs, or market lists. The more research you do upfront, the better your chances of acceptance, publication, and payment.

Guide to Listing Features

Below is an example of the market listings you'll find in each of the listing sections in *Writer's Market*. Note the callouts that identify various format features of the listing. The front and back covers of the book contain a key to the symbols used at the beginning of all listings.

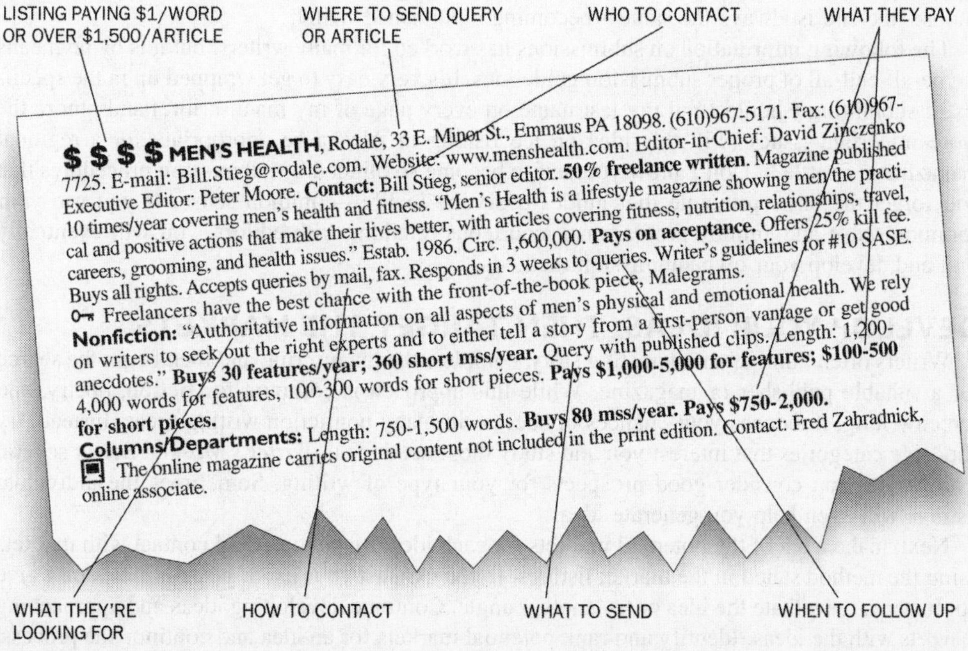

$ $ $ $ MEN'S HEALTH, Rodale, 33 E. Minor St., Emmaus PA 18098. (610)967-5171. Fax: (610)967-7725. E-mail: Bill.Stieg@rodale.com. Website: www.menshealth.com. Editor-in-Chief: David Zinczenko Executive Editor: Peter Moore. **Contact:** Bill Stieg, senior editor. **50% freelance written.** Magazine published 10 times/year covering men's health and fitness. "Men's Health is a lifestyle magazine showing men the practical and positive actions that make their lives better, with articles covering fitness, nutrition, relationships, travel, careers, grooming, and health issues." Estab. 1986. Circ. 1,600,000. **Pays on acceptance.** Offers 25% kill fee. Buys all rights. Accepts queries by mail, fax. Responds in 3 weeks to queries. Writer's guidelines for #10 SASE.

0→ Freelancers have the best chance with the front-of-the-book piece, Malegrams.

Nonfiction: "Authoritative information on all aspects of men's physical and emotional health. We rely on writers to seek out the right experts and to either tell a story from a first-person vantage or get good anecdotes." **Buys 30 features/year; 360 short mss/year.** Query with published clips. Length: 1,200-4,000 words for features, 100-300 words for short pieces. **Pays $1,000-5,000 for features; $100-500 for short pieces.**

Columns/Departments: Length: 750-1,500 words. **Buys 80 mss/year. Pays $750-2,000.**

The online magazine carries original content not included in the print edition. Contact: Fred Zahradnick, online associate.

Getting Published

Before Your First Sale

Everything in life has to start somewhere and that somewhere is always at the beginning. The same is true for writers. Stephen King, J.K. Rowling, John Grisham, Nora Roberts—they all had to start at the beginning. It would be great to say that becoming a writer is as easy as waving a magic wand over your manuscript and "Poof!" you're a published writer, but that's not how it happens. There's no magic potion or one true "key" to a successful writing career. However, a long, successful, well-paid writing career *can* happen when you combine four elements:

- Good writing
- Knowledge of writing markets (magazines and book publishers)
- Professionalism
- Persistence

Good writing is useless if you don't know which markets will buy your work or how to pitch and sell your writing. If you aren't professional and persistent in your contact with editors, your writing is just that—your writing. But if you are a writer who possesses, and can manipulate, the above four elements, then you have a good chance at becoming a paid, published writer who will reap the benefits of a long and successful career.

As you become more involved with writing, you may read new articles or talk with editors and writers with conflicting opinions about the right way to submit your work. The truth is there are many different routes a writer can follow to get published, but no matter which route you choose, the end is always the same—becoming a published writer.

The following information on submissions has worked for many writers, but it is by no means the be-all-end-all of proper submission guidelines. It's very easy to get wrapped up in the specifics of submitting (should I put my last name on every page of my manuscript?) and ignore the more important issues (will this idea on ice fishing in Alaska be appropriate for a regional magazine in Seattle?). Don't allow yourself to become so blinded by submission procedures that you forget the basic principle that guides everyone in life—common sense. If you use your common sense and employ professional, courteous relations with editors, you will eventually find and develop your own submission methods.

DEVELOP YOUR IDEAS, THEN TARGET THE MARKETS

Writers often think of an interesting story, complete the manuscript, and then begin the search for a suitable publisher or magazine. While this approach is common for fiction, poetry, and screenwriting, it reduces your chances of success in many nonfiction writing areas. Instead, try choosing categories that interest you and study those sections in *Writer's Market*. Select several listings that you consider good prospects for your type of writing. Sometimes the individual listings will even help you generate ideas.

Next, make a list of the potential markets for each idea. Make the initial contact with markets using the method stated in the market listings. If you exhaust your list of possibilities, don't give up. Instead, reevaluate the idea or try another angle. Continue developing ideas and approaching markets with the ideas. Identify and rank potential markets for an idea and continue the process.

As you submit to the various publications listed in *Writer's Market*, it's important to remember that every magazine is published with a particular audience and slant in mind. Probably the number one complaint we receive from editors is that the submissions they receive are completely wrong for their magazines. The first mark of professionalism is to know your market well. That knowledge starts in *Writer's Market*, but you should also do your own detective work. Search out back issues of the magazines you wish to write for, pick up recent issues at your local newsstand, or visit magazines' websites—anything that will help you figure out what subjects specific magazines publish. This research is also helpful in learning what topics have been covered ad nauseum—the topics that you should stay away from or approach in a fresh, new way. Magazine's websites are invaluable as most websites post the current issue of the magazine as well as back issues of the magazine, and most offer writer's guidelines.

Prepare for rejection and the sometimes lengthy wait. When a submission is returned, check your file folder of potential markets for that idea. Cross off the market that rejected the idea. If the editor has given you suggestions or reasons why the manuscript was not accepted, you might want to incorporate these suggestions when revising your manuscript. After revising your manuscript mail it to the next market on your list.

Take rejection with a grain of salt

Rejection is a way of life in the publishing world. It's inevitable in a business that deals with such an overwhelming number of applicants for such a limited number of positions. Anyone who has published has lived through many rejections, and writers with thin skin are at a distinct disadvantage. A rejection letter is not a personal attack. It simply indicates that your submission is not appropriate for that one specific market. Writers who let rejection dissuade them from pursuing their dream or who react to an editor's "No" with indignation or fury do themselves a disservice. Writers who let rejection stop them do not publish. Resign yourself to facing rejection now. You will live through it, and you'll eventually overcome it.

QUERY AND COVER LETTERS

A query letter is a brief, one-page letter used as a tool to hook an editor and get him interested in your idea. When you send a query letter to a magazine, you are trying to get an editor to buy your idea or article. When you query a book publisher, you are attempting to get an editor interested enough in your idea to request your book proposal or your entire manuscript. (*Note:* Some book editors prefer to receive book proposals on first contact. Check individual listings for which method editors prefer.)

While there are no set-in-stone rules for writing query letters, there are some basic guidelines to help you write a polished, well-organized query:

- Limit it to one page, single-spaced, and address the editor by name (Mr. or Ms. and the surname). *Note:* Do not assume that a person is a Mr. or Ms. unless it is obvious from the name listed. For example, if you are contacting a D.J. Smith, do not assume that D.J. should be preceded by Mr. or Ms. Instead, address the letter to D.J. Smith.
- Grab the editor's interest with a strong opening. Some magazine queries begin with a paragraph meant to approximate the lead of the intended article.
- Indicate how you intend to develop the article or book. Give the editor some idea of the work's structure and content.
- Let the editor know if you have photos or illustrations available to accompany your magazine article.
- Mention any expertise or training that qualifies you to write the article or book. If you've been published before, mention it; if not, don't.
- End with a direct request to write the article (or, if you're pitching a book, ask for the go-ahead to send in a full proposal or the entire manuscript). Give the editor an idea of the expected length and delivery date of your manuscript.

Another question that arises is: If I don't hear from an editor in the reported response time, how do I know when I can safely send the query to another market? Many writers find it helpful to indicate in their query that if they don't receive a response from the editor (slightly after the listed reporting time), they will assume the editor is not interested. It's best to take this approach, particularly if your topic is timely.

A brief, single-spaced cover letter is helpful when sending a manuscript as it helps personalize the submission. However, if you have previously queried the editor, use the cover letter to politely and briefly remind the editor of that query—when it was sent, what it contained, etc. "Here is the piece on low-fat cooking that I queried you about on December 12. I look forward to hearing from you at your earliest convenience." Do not use the cover letter as a sales pitch.

If you are submitting to a market that accepts unsolicited manuscripts, a cover letter is useful in that it personalizes your submission. You can, and should, include information about the manuscript, yourself, your publishing history, and your qualifications.

The Query Letter Clinic on page 23 offers six different query letters, some that work and some that don't, as well as editors' comments on why the letters were either successful or failed to garner an assignment.

Write Great Query Letters, Cover Letters, and Book Proposals

Books on the following list provide you with more detailed information on writing query letters, cover letters, and book proposals. All titles are published by Writer's Digest Books.

- *How to Write Irresistible Query Letters*, by Lisa Collier Cool.
- *How to Write Attention-Grabbing Query & Cover Letters*, by John Wood.
- *The Marshall Plan for Novel Writing*, by Evan Marshall.
- *Your Novel Proposal From Creation to Contract*, by Blythe Camenson and Marshall J. Cook.
- *How to Write a Book Proposal*, by Michael Larsen.
- *Formatting & Submitting Your Manuscript*, by Jack and Glenda Neff and Don Prues.

Querying for fiction

Fiction is sometimes queried, but more often not. Many fiction editors won't decide on a submission until they have seen the complete manuscript. When submitting a fiction book idea, most editors prefer to see at least a synopsis and sample chapters (usually the first three). For fiction that is published in magazines, most editors want to see the complete short story manuscript. If an editor does request a query for fiction, it should include a description of the main theme and story line, including the conflict and resolution. Take a look at individual listings to see what editors prefer to receive.

NONFICTION BOOK PROPOSALS

Most nonfiction books are sold by a book proposal, a package of materials that details what your book is about, who its intended audience is, and how you intend to write the book. It includes some combination of a cover or query letter, an overview, an outline, author's information sheet, and sample chapters. Editors also want to see information about the audience for your book and about titles that compete with your proposed book.

Submitting a nonfiction book proposal

When sending a proposal package you should include:

☑ The cover or query letter should be a short introduction to the material you include in the proposal.

- ☑ An overview is a brief summary of your book. For nonfiction, it should detail your book's subject and give an idea of how that subject will be developed. If you're sending a synopsis of a novel, cover the basic plot.

- ☑ An outline covers your book chapter by chapter. The outline should include all major points covered in each chapter. Some outlines are done in traditional outline form, but most are written in paragraph form.

- ☑ An author's information sheet should—as succinctly and clearly as possible—acquaint the editor with your writing background and convince her of your qualifications to write about the subject of your book.

- ☑ Many editors like to see sample chapters, especially for a first book. Sample chapters show the editor how well you write and develop the ideas from your outline.

- ☑ Marketing information—i.e., facts about how and to whom your book can be successfully marketed—is now expected to accompany every book proposal. If you can provide information about the audience for your book and suggest ways the book publisher can reach those people, you will increase your chances of acceptance.

- ☑ Competitive title analysis is an integral part of the marketing information. Check the *Subject Guide to Books in Print* for other titles on your topic. Write a one- or two-sentence synopsis of each. Point out how your book differs and improves upon existing topics.

A WORD ABOUT AGENTS

An agent represents a writer's work to buyers, negotiates contracts, follows up to see that contracts are fulfilled, and generally handles a writer's business affairs, leaving the writer free to write. Effective agents are valued for their contacts in the publishing industry, their savvy about which publishers and editors to approach with which ideas, their ability to guide an author's career, and their business sense.

While most book publishers listed in *Writer's Market* publish books by unagented writers, some of the larger houses are reluctant to consider submissions that have not reached them through a literary agent. Companies with such a policy are noted by a symbol (Ⓐ) at the beginning of the listing, as well as in the submission information within the listing.

PROFESSIONALISM AND COURTESY

An editor's time is precious. Between struggling to meet deadlines, maintain budgets, and deal with hundreds of submissions on a daily basis, it's only natural that an editor's communication with writers is limited.

To help advance your communication with editors and receive professional communication in return, there are a few things you can do. Keep all correspondence, whether written or spoken, short and to the point. Don't hound an editor with follow up e-mails, letters, or phone calls to find out the status of your submission. Honor all agreements that you make with an editor. This includes deadlines, payment, and rewrites. Give all of your efforts 100 percent. As with all things in life, try to remain pleasant, keep your sense of humor, and be honest and reliable. If you keep these things in mind when dealing with an editor, your communication with most editors will be a pleasant and rewarding experience.

MANUSCRIPT FORMAT

You can increase your chances of publication by following a few standard guidelines regarding the physical format of your manuscript. It should be your goal to make your manuscript readable. Use these suggestions as you would any other suggestions: Use what works for you and discard what doesn't.

In general, when submitting a manuscript, you should use white, 8½×11, 20 lb. bond paper, and you should also choose a legible, professional looking font (i.e., Times New Roman)—no all-italic or artsy fonts. Your entire manuscript should be double-spaced with a 1½-inch margin on all sides of the page. Once you are ready to print your manuscript, you should print either on a laser printer or an ink-jet printer.

A five-step checklist for articles and short story manuscripts

- ☑ In the upper left corner, place your name, address, phone number, and e-mail address, on separate lines, single-spaced. Even if you write under a pseudonym, your name must appear here.
- ☑ In the upper right corner, place the estimated word count and the rights you are offering.
- ☑ One-third of the way down the first page, center the title in capital letters. Then, double-space and type "by," double-space again and center your name/pseudonym.
- ☑ Double-space two more times, paragraph indent and begin typing your manuscript.
- ☑ On every subsequent page, type your name, a dash, and the page number in the upper left or right corner.

A six-step checklist for articles and short story manuscripts

- ☑ On a separate cover sheet, place your name, address, phone number, and e-mail address in the upper left corner.
- ☑ In the upper right corner of the cover sheet, place the estimated word count.
- ☑ If you have an agent, you may place the agent's name in the upper right corner of the cover sheet and place word count in the bottom center.
- ☑ Halfway down the cover sheet, center your title in all capital letters. Then, double-space and type "by," double-space again, and center your name/pseudonym.
- ☑ On the next page, center your chapter number and title (if there is one) in capital letters one-third of the way down the page. Double-space twice, paragraph indent, and begin typing your chapter.
- ☑ In the upper left or right corner of each subsequent page, place your last name (followed by a dash), the page number (followed by another dash) and a shortened version of your manuscript title.

ESTIMATING WORD COUNT

Many computers will provide you with a word count of your manuscript. Your editor will count again after editing the manuscript. Although your computer is counting characters, an editor or production editor is more concerned about the amount of space the text will occupy on a page. Several small headlines or subheads, for instance, will be counted the same by your computer as any other word of text. However, headlines and subheads usually employ a different font size than the body text, so an editor may count them differently to be sure enough space has been estimated for larger type.

For short manuscripts, it's often quickest to count each word on a representative page and multiply by the number of pages. You can get a very rough count by multiplying the number of pages in your manuscript by 250 (the average number of words on a double-spaced typewritten page). Do not count words for a poetry manuscript or put the word count at the top of the manuscript because most poems are "counted" by lines, not words.

PHOTOGRAPHS AND SLIDES

In some cases, the availability of photographs and slides can be the deciding factor as to whether an editor will accept your submission. This is especially true when querying a publication that relies heavily on photographs, illustrations, or artwork to enhance the article (i.e., craft magazines, hobby magazines, etc.). In some instances, the publication may offer additional payment for photographs or illustrations.

Check the individual listings for photograph submission guidelines and to find out which magazines review photographs. Most publications prefer that you do not send photographs with your submission. However, if photographs or illustrations are available, you should indicate as such in your query. As with manuscripts, never send the originals of your photographs or illustrations. Instead, send prints or duplicates of slides and transparencies.

On all your photographs and slides, you should stamp or print your copyright notice and "Return to:" followed by your name, address, phone number, and e-mail address. Rubber stamps (which can be ordered from stationery or office supply stores) are preferred for labeling photos since they are less likely to cause damage. If you use a pen to write this information on the back of your photos, be careful not to damage the print by pressing too hard or by allowing ink to bleed through the paper. A felt tip pen is best, but you should take care not to put photos or copy together before the ink dries.

Captions can be typed on adhesive labels and affixed to the back of the prints. Some writers, when submitting several transparencies or photos, number the photos and type captions (numbered accordingly) on a separate 8½ × 11 sheet of paper.

SEND PHOTOCOPIES

If there is one hard-and-fast rule in publishing, it's this: *Never* send the original (or only) copy of your manuscript. Most editors cringe when they find out that a writer has sent the only copy of their manuscript. You should always send photocopies of your manuscript.

Some writers choose to send a self-addressed, stamped postcard with a photocopied submission. In their cover letter they suggest that if the editor is not interested in their manuscript, it may be tossed out and a reply sent on the postcard. This method is particularly helpful when sending your submissions to international markets.

MAILING SUBMISSIONS

No matter what size manuscript you're mailing, always include a self-addressed, stamped envelope (SASE) with sufficient return postage. The website for the U.S. Postal Service (www.usps.gov) and the website for the Canadian Postal Service (www.canadapost.ca) both have postage calculators if you are unsure of how much postage you'll need to affix.

A book manuscript should be mailed in a sturdy, well-wrapped box. Enclose a self-addressed mailing label and paper clip your return postage to the label. However, be aware that some book publishers do not return unsolicited manuscripts, so make sure that you know the practice of the publisher before sending any unsolicited material.

Mailing Short Correspondence or Short Manuscripts

- Fold manuscripts under five pages into thirds, and send in a #10 SASE.
- Mail manuscripts five pages or more unfolded in a 9×12 or 10×13 SASE.
- Mark envelopes in all caps, FIRST CLASS MAIL or SPECIAL FOURTH CLASS MANUSCRIPT RATE.
- For return envelope, fold the envelope in half, address it to yourself, and add a stamp or, if going to Canada or another international destination, International Reply Coupons (available at most main branches of your local post office).
- Don't send by Certified mail—this is a sign of an amateur.

Always mail photos and slides First Class. The rougher handling received by Standard Mail could damage the photos and slides. If you are concerned about losing prints or slides, send them Certified or Registered Mail. For any photo submission that is mailed separately from a manuscript, enclose a short cover letter of explanation, separate self-addressed label, adequate return postage, and an envelope. Never submit photos or slides in mounted glass.

Types of mail service

There are many different mailing service options available to you whether you are sending a query letter, complete manuscript, or photos. You can work with the U.S. Postal Service, United Parcel Service, Federal Express, or any number of private mailing companies. The following are the five most common types of mailing services offered by the U.S. Postal Service.

- **First Class** is an expensive way to mail a manuscript, but many writers prefer it. First-Class mail generally receives better handling and is delivered more quickly than Standard mail. First Class is only available for packages that weigh 13 ounces or less. Mail sent First Class is also forwarded for one year if the addressee has moved, and is returned if it is undeliverable.
- **Priority mail** reaches its destination within two or three days.
- **Standard mail** rates are available for packages, but be sure to pack your materials carefully because they will be handled roughly. To make sure your package will be returned to you if it is undeliverable, print "Return Postage Guaranteed" under your address.
- **Certified mail** must be signed for when it reaches its destination.
- **Registered mail** is a high-security method of mailing where the contents are insured. The package is signed in and out of every office it passes through, and a receipt is returned to the sender when the package reaches its destination.

RECORD SUBMISSIONS

Once you begin sending out queries and manuscripts you will find that it becomes a business. As with any business, organization and management are essential. You should always keep records of any correspondence you have with editors as well as the dates relating to the correspondence.

Many writers find it helpful to set up spreadsheets for queries and manuscripts. You can easily set up two types of tracking systems for your work: one for materials sent and one for materials received. When setting up a system for materials sent, it is best to include dates, materials sent, enclosures, editors' names, titles of manuscripts, etc. The system for materials received should log dates of responses, rejection letters, whether the material was accepted, and if it was accepted, any rewrites completed, deadlines, publication dates, and pay rates.

Some writers find it helpful to keep a separate calendar just for dates. You can use the calendar to mark the dates material is sent, when you plan on following up, when you plan on sending to new markets, etc. The Query Letter Clinic on page 23 includes important information about how and when you should follow up on queries.

WritersMarket.com, the online edition of *Writer's Market*, has taken recording submissions to another level. The site contains a special feature called the Submission Tracker. This feature has been set up to allow you to record all of the above mentioned information in an easy-to-understand electronic format—all you have to do is enter your personal submission information.

Nine Habits of Frequently Published Authors

BY STEPHEN BLAKE METTEE

As I go about my vocation of publishing books and my avocation of reading everything I can get my hands on, I am often struck with the thought that writers who consistently get published share common traits. These traits can be distilled down to nine simple principles.

1. Widely published authors develop a sense of what the market requires.

This is the part, as creative artists, we don't want to hear. "I'm a writer, not a businessman," we protest. Alas, if you want to be published regularly, you're going to have to grasp the fact that publishing is a business. At the most basic level, publishers simply supply products to consumers. In turn, you, as the writer, supply the product to the publisher. That's the business.

OK, now pay attention; here's the key part: You must supply product that a publisher can use to satisfy the demands of its consumers, and you must do it in a businesslike way.

"Too simple," you say. Yes, it is simple, but the business basics are all too often ignored by us creative folk. Here are a few simple strategies you can use to help make the business of publishing your business.

- Put on your professional persona when contacting editors. Spell the editor's name correctly (double-check this!). Use crisp, clean paper for your letterhead. Never handwrite letters or manuscripts. Always be polite, concise, and nondemanding when talking on the phone to an editor. Always include a SASE (self-addressed, stamped envelope) with each query or unsolicited submission.
- Always know who it is that you're contacting. Use guides such as *Writer's Market* to find the appropriate editor's name and precise title, then phone to verify that this editor is still employed with that particular company and is still the correct editor to contact.
- Use standard format (8½ × 11 white paper, double-spaced, numbered pages, etc.) for manuscripts and book proposals.
- Let queries and other short correspondences sit overnight, then reread them before sending them out. For manuscripts or book proposals, make it at least a week.
- Learn as much as you can about the demographics of the potential reader for whatever it is you are writing. What gender is he or she? What age? Income and education level? Conservative or liberal? Likes and dislikes? What else is this person likely to read? Keep this reader in mind as you pitch your idea to the editor and when you write the article, short story, or book.
- If you plan on submitting to a magazine, obtain a copy of the magazine's writer's guidelines—the tip sheet prepared for potential contributors by the magazine's editors. (These guidelines are often available on the Internet or by sending a SASE to the publisher.) After perusing the guidelines, pore over six to eight issues of the magazine, analyzing the nuances of content and tone before submitting a story or suggesting an idea.

STEPHEN BLAKE METTEE *is founder and publisher of Quill Driver Books/Word Dancer Press and author of* The Fast-Track Course on How to Write a Nonfiction Book Proposal *(Word Dancer Press, 2001).*

- If it is a book you're proposing, be sure the book publisher you are contacting publishes books of the type and genre you're proposing. (Like magazines, many book publishers prepare writer's guidelines.) In your query or cover letter, explain why you selected this publisher.
- Synchronize your book, short story, or article's length to your prospective market. If novels in your genre rarely exceed 150,000 words, it is unlikely that a publisher will be interested in one that runs 300,000 words. This holds true with nonfiction books. If a magazine's upper limit for short stories or articles is 2,500 words, 5,000 words will get a rejection slip.
- Pitch one idea to a publisher at a time, but tweak the idea and pitch it to other publishers at the same time.
- Watch for birthing trends and try to be on the front edge of the wave. In publishing, new and fresh is good.

2. Oft-published writers always write their best.

I know writers who always seem to be saving their best for later. Sometimes, it's because they don't allow themselves enough time to do the job right. They tell themselves the next piece will get the attention it deserves. Other times, it's because they don't feel they are being paid enough for what they are writing. "This is good enough for what they're paying me," is a common refrain.

Yet, while a writer who turns in shoddy work may get it published, the editor certainly won't put that author at the top of his call list. And, although low pay is ubiquitous in this industry, poor quality writing does not build a reputation that attracts higher paying offers.

Some writers suffer from a sort of depression mentality. They feel that if they put their best effort into what they are writing now, when the big break comes along, they won't have anything left in their creative reserves. The truth is, however, good writing begets good writing. The better you write today, the better you will write tomorrow.

3. Writers who know the rules and break them, break into print more often.

Don't try this at home: In *Chasing Eights* (Donald I. Fine), a Dan Fortune mystery, adroit novelist Michael Collins switches between points of view and from first person to third person. That's the literary equivalent of trying to juggle six china plates while threading a needle. The mostly likely outcome is disaster.

Michael Collins, a pseudonym for Dennis Lynds, not only pulled off this bit of legerdemain, but *Chasing Eights* is all the better for it. Collins had been writing for years. He knew the rules. And, he knew how to break them.

Neophyte writers often weaken their writing—and pick up rejection slips—by breaking rules in ways they feel are clever but in reality are just inappropriate. Step one: Learn the rules. Step two: Break them.

You can get published regularly with good, sound prose that follows the beaten path, and that's what I suggest you do until you are accomplished at staying on the path. But then! Reach out, stretch for the virgin, the rare, the wonderful. Titillate the mind, the senses, the intellect with your unique form of brilliance, and then revel in your successes as your publishing credits roll in.

4. Frequently published writers exploit their passions.

Two things dominated my life in the 1980s, raising my son and developing my printing business. When I look back at the articles I wrote during those years, I'm not surprised to discover that they ran in publications with names such as *Indy's Child* and *Quick Printing Magazine*.

I remember bragging to less-fortunate writers that I was batting 1000—everything I wrote got published. In retrospect, I now realize that wasn't very kind or modest of me, but I was young and brash. (Over the years I've changed; now I'm middle-aged and brash.) The point is, the reason I was getting published was because I was writing on subjects about which I was deeply passionate.

Answer this question: What are the two or three things you are most passionate about? Whatever your answer, these are the things about which you will write best. Follow your passions, and editors will be passionate about publishing you.

5. Writers who hook readers with strong leads hook more editors.

Try this sometime. Go into a bookstore and pull down five novels. Read the first three paragraphs of each, then ask yourself which book most entices you to read onward. Chances are that book's author knows the value of writing strong leads.

The lead—sometimes called the "hook," because it hooks the reader—is the first few sentences or paragraphs of whatever you're writing. The job of the lead is to get the reader interested in reading more. Use strong leads with everything you write, from query letters to book proposals, from romance novels to nonfiction articles.

Use a strong lead at the beginning of every chapter in both fiction and nonfiction. If you are writing an article, write a compelling lead each time you transition to a new concept. A strong lead for a short story may make the difference between selling it to an editor and finding it back in your mailbox.

What kind of leads work? Creative ones. Anecdotes that set a scene or mood and intriguing or startling facts are common components of strong leads. Posing a question in your lead entices the reader to read on to learn the answer and often works well. I tried to write a strong lead for each section of this piece. How did I do?

6. Writers who don't add to workloads get published more often.

If you were in the auto parts business, would you expect to supply a garage with parts that needed fixing before they could be used? Of course not. But many authors send out work that obviously needs rewriting or is filled with grammar or spelling errors.

Today's editors are busy multi-taskers. I know a senior editor at one of the big New York book publishing houses who says he doesn't mind he has a two-hour-each-way commute to work. He says the time on the train is the only time he has to read and edit manuscripts. If you make an editor rewrite portions of your work or correct your spelling or double-check your facts or chase something you promised to have to him a week ago, he's not likely to smile with pleasant anticipation the next time you suggest a project to him.

Make life easier for editors and watch your acceptance rate soar.

The Following Tips Will Help You Become a Frequently Published Author

- Learn the business as well as the craft.
- Write your best.
- Know the rules and break them.
- Follow your passions.
- Make life easier for editors.
- Read, read, read.
- Never stop learning your craft.
- Submit, submit, submit.

7. All great writers are great readers.

Last year, when a local TV anchorman approached me about publishing his book, I asked him a trick question. I asked what he liked to read. His answer, as is so often the case when I ask this question, was, "Oh, I don't have much time to read."

Because I'm such a swell fellow, I took a look at his book proposal anyway, even though I already knew it wasn't going to be very good. I wasn't disappointed.

Am I prescient? No, I just subscribe to the theory that you'll never be a great writer until you're a great reader. It may be magic, or perhaps it's some kind of osmosis, but, somehow, reading other peoples' work makes you a better writer.

Certainly, if you write mysteries, read mysteries, or if you write technical pieces, read technical pieces, but don't just stick to your genre; read a broad range of literature. Read fiction, read poetry, read news magazines, read cereal boxes.

8. Regularly published authors never stop cultivating their skills.

When I present at writers' conferences, where I'm supposed to be promoting the books I publish via which I make my living, I suggest attendees buy one book that I don't publish. The book? *The Elements of Style* by William Strunk, Jr. and E. B. White (Allyn & Bacon). I tell them to read Strunk and White's delightful treatise before they write anything else, and to reread it at least once a year.

What I am actually telling them is to continually hone their craft. *Elements of Style* is a thin volume that provides concise instruction in the essence of good writing. Reading it and rereading it is an excellent way to keep the basics of superior writing at the front of your mind as your fingers dance on the keyboard.

What else can you do? Peruse the information in books like this one, read magazines such as *Writer's Digest*, go to writers' conferences, join a critique group, take classes, listen to feedback from those whose opinions you have reason to respect (but beware of well-intentioned family and friends), and analyze what other writers are doing.

If you never stop learning your craft, you'll never stop hearing editors saying, "Yes!"

9. People who collect bylines spend money on postage.

Wouldn't it be great if you could write the Great American Novel, leave it on a park bench where an (apparently bored) editor would happen by, recognize it for the brilliant work it is, then hunt you down to get a contract signed? Fame and fortune would follow. Best of all, your mother's doubts would dissipate forever.

OK, so, since real life isn't the movies, submit to submitting. If you don't submit your work to publishers, it isn't going to get published. That's a given.

And, when your work comes back with that little note that starts, "Thank you for letting us see this, but . . ." send it out again. And again.

While the first article, short story, or book proposal is out, write something else and send it off, then write another and another until you have ten, 15, 20 making the rounds. Soon one will get picked up, then another, and then another. Eventually, editors will be contacting you.

Four Top Editors Offer Tips and Insights on Breaking into City and Regional Magazines

BY WILL ALLISON

Sometimes the best freelance opportunities can be found right in your own backyard. City and regional magazines—publications with a local focus—represent one of the fastest-growing segments of the magazine industry. In 2001, 86 new city magazines were launched, tops among all categories of start-ups. Most of these magazines rely heavily upon local freelancers, writers who know and understand their city or region.

Traditionally, the purview of city and regional magazines has been at once very narrow and very broad. They typically have a strict geographical focus (usually a city, sometimes a state or region), but within that focus, the coverage is wide-ranging, encompassing sports, crime, business, politics, arts, lifestyles, health, food and drink, home and garden—anything you might find in a national general-interest publication.

A city magazine often serves as the primary cultural and lifestyle guide to its town, catering to a readership that is educated, affluent, and predominantly female. Popular staples include annual "Best of" issues, restaurant awards, and service packages highlighting top doctors, lawyers, schools, and neighborhoods. Frequently, city magazines also boast the most influential restaurant reviews in town.

While a general-interest format is favored by most of the best-known city and regional magazines, such as *Texas Monthly*, *Los Angeles*, and *New York*, many recent local start-ups reflect a trend seen in national magazines: niche marketing. Instead of taking a general-interest approach, the start-ups are targeting particular segments of the local readership. In addition to *San Francisco* magazine, for instance, the Bay City is now served by more specialized publications such as *San Francisco Gourmet*, *San Francisco Socialite*, *Paper City* (geared toward the social jet set), and the urban glossy *7×7*. Such start-ups have resulted in more assignments for freelancers who are willing to do their homework and carefully craft story pitches to meet the unique needs of each magazine.

Writing for city and regional magazines can also offer more prestige than one might think. In addition to competing for the annual slate of awards presented by the City and Regional Magazine Association (CRMA), city magazines have been making a run at the most coveted national prizes as well. In 2002, *New York* won a National Magazine Award, and several others—including *Cincinnati Magazine*, *Los Angeles*, *New York*, *Philadelphia*, *San Francisco*, *Texas Monthly*, and *Yankee*—were National Magazine Award finalists.

The following roundtable interview features editors from four of the most-respected general-interest city and regional magazines—*Atlanta Magazine*, *Cincinnati Magazine*, *HOUR Detroit*, and *Yankee*. For more information on these and others, please see the individual listings in this book and visit the CRMA's website (www.citymag.org), which provides contact information for more than 75 member publications.

WILL ALLISON*'s (willalliso@aol.com) columns, sports profiles, and news features have appeared in* Indianapolis Monthly *and* Indianapolis at Home.

Ric Bohy is *HOUR Detroit*'s editor, and chief food and restaurant critic. He's been with the magazine since it started in 1997. He spent the first half of his 30-year career in Detroit journalism as a daily newspaper reporter before moving to magazines in 1988. He also has been a full-time freelancer and on-camera commentator for Detroit's WDIV-TV.

Rebecca Poynor Burns is the editor-in-chief of *Atlanta Magazine*. She previously was editor of *Indianapolis Monthly* and has written for the *Atlanta Journal-Constitution* and other Southern regional publications.

Michael Carlton is the editor of *Yankee* magazine. Before he joined *Yankee* in 2001, he was editor of *Coastal Living* and editorial director of *Southern Living*. He has also worked at a number of newspapers, including the *Philadelphia Inquirer, Dallas Times Herald, Denver Post*, and *Atlanta Journal-Constitution*.

Kitty Morgan is the editor of *Cincinnati Magazine*, which during her five years at the helm has won numerous regional and national awards for writing, design, and photography, including the Gold Award for General Excellence in 2001 from the CRMA. Morgan has also worked at the *Orange County Register, Cincinnati Enquirer*, and *Sunset Magazine*.

Give us an overview of your magazine.

Bohy: We have a fairly standard city magazine editorial mix focusing on the greater metro Detroit area, with some attention to outstate areas of Michigan as well as occasional pieces on out-of-state events, issues, or people with impact on or ties to our readership area. What sets us apart in particular is our oversize glossy format with the highest possible production values. It's a city magazine done coffee-table-book style.

Burns: *Atlanta Magazine*, at 41, is one of the oldest city/regional titles in the country. The magazine's historical strength has been publishing literary, narrative journalism. The magazine has garnered more than 80 national awards. A number of writers got their start with the magazine, including Tom Junod, Anne Rivers Siddons, and Pat Conroy.

Carlton: *Yankee* is somewhat unusual in that it is a lifestyle magazine with regular departments on homes and gardens, food, and travel. Unlike many such magazines, however, we also do important investigative journalism, which has resulted in our being a finalist four times in the National Magazine Awards. We are unusual as well for our size. Our 6×9 format provides many design challenges, as we try to give it a big look even though we are small in physical size. It seems to be working; we won this year's CRMA award for design.

Morgan: We follow the standard city magazine formula: A backbone of service stories, serious journalism examining the region's issues, a laser focus on the local. We have, however, made excellent writing and photography a hallmark, and have published memoirs, photo essays, and even fiction that captures a sense of this place.

Who are your readers, and what aspects of your magazine are most important to them?

Bohy: When *HOUR Detroit* started in the spring of 1997, we thought more in terms of reader psychographics than demographics. At its simplest, we assumed a reader with a high degree of intellectual curiosity not bound by age, geography, race, or income level. Of course, like any city magazine, we have since refined that to focus more than before on affluent readers in the suburbs, especially in lifestyle coverage. They, like all our readers, come to *HOUR Detroit* not only for its expert insight into the area, but because our staff offers institutional memory that's increasingly rare in Detroit journalism.

Burns: Our readers are primarily (70 percent) women. They are educated, affluent professionals (80 percent of them work full time). They rely on the magazine's coverage of lifestyle subjects (dining, travel, real estate) but also care about our viewpoint on issues that have an impact on their family, friends, and others. *Atlanta Magazine* serves as a 'must read' for citizens who want to stay on top of what's happening in the city.

Carlton: Our typical reader is female between 35 and 55. She is affluent, college educated, and lives in a city or the suburbs. All aspects of the magazine appear to be of importance, although we have had a growing demand for more 'home and hearth' stories, particularly decorating.

Morgan: It's easy to map out our readers' demographic, the same one shared by most city magazines: Age ranging from 35 to 65, educated, affluent, homeowners, great targets for the sellers of high-end cars and cosmetic surgery, etc. Our readers are also hungry for information on their city (at the same time, they're quite knowledgeable, and don't brook the obvious) and eager to take pride in the city (though they're not averse to criticizing it—a 'tough love' stance). At the same time, they're well-traveled, sophisticated readers. They know what's going on in the world and are engaged in the world, as civic leaders, volunteers, professionals.

What parts of your magazine are most open to freelance writers?

Bohy: Any part of the magazine—politics and issues, profiles, arts and entertainment, home and fashion—except food and restaurants, which I write every month.

Burns: Personal essays (which *must* have an Atlanta focus), and short, front-of-the-book pieces.

Carlton: All areas are equally open to freelancers.

Morgan: A writer who can pitch an only-for-Cincinnati feature, whose clips show stylish writing, good reporting skills, and strong grasp of story, has the best chance of scoring. We also look for first-person essays that reveal something surprising about Cincinnati.

How do you decide if a story will be written by a staff member or assigned to a freelance writer?

Bohy: It really is a question of matching the requirements of the piece with the abilities of the writer. While we've worked in the past couple of years to bring more assignments in-house, if a particular piece demands expertise better met by one of our regular contributors, that's who we'll get.

Burns: Most front-of-the-book items are written by freelancers. Most features are staff written or done by our contributing editors. We will assign freelance features to writers who have particular experiences or viewpoints that they can bring to the stories. For instance, we recently ran a first-person narrative recalling the rise of black political power in Atlanta in the 1960s from a person who was intimately involved.

Carlton: Such decisions are made by the senior editorial committee. If we have the expertise on staff, we generally assign a staff person. If not, we look for an outside expert.

Morgan: I've learned that most freelancers can either write with style or do the hard work required for skeptical reporting—but hardly anyone can do both. So for our big stories, for the backbone of the magazine, I rely on the staff writers. To be honest, freelancers bring us the lagniappe.

City magazines often publish the most influential restaurant reviews in town. Is this true in your city, and are there opportunities for freelancers in your dining coverage?

Bohy: Our restaurant coverage has earned two national Gold Awards from the CRMA and, yes, we'd like to think it is the most influential in town, but currently isn't open to freelancers.

Burns: That is true in our case. Our reviewer has won the James Beard award for dining coverage along with other national awards. She has a national reputation. Our expertise in dining is important to us, and we keep that knowledge in-house, so unfortunately there is no dining freelance work.

Carlton: *Yankee* does food reviews as part of its travel coverage. We also feature restaurants in the feature well on occasion.

Morgan: We have contributing editors for food and restaurants. But feature stories that drill deep into a local foodie phenomenon—I'll listen to those pitches any day.

What are the most common reasons you reject story proposals?

Bohy: By far the most common is the pitch for a story that has no conceivable place in *HOUR Detroit*, clearly because the writer has little or no knowledge of our content and editorial needs. Next is the pitch that itself is badly made, badly written, and riddled with errors, including misspelled names and errata that could and should have been caught in spell-checking. These are not niggling peeves. They show sloppiness and lack of even basic research.

Burns: The ideas are not tailored to *Atlanta Magazine*. We get a lot of generic proposals on topics that could run anywhere. Writers who understand Atlanta and the peculiar dynamics of the city have a better chance of crafting good proposals for us. We also get a lot of sloppy proposals. If a freelancer has not taken the time to get the editor's name (spelling is key) and title correct in a query, our assumption is that the freelancer will not put in the effort to write a story at the level we want.

Carlton: Subject failure. We always want to see some previously published work. The story must appeal to New Englanders.

Morgan: We've done them already. They're not focused on Cincinnati. They're really just souped-up press releases. For instance, I hate being pitched a story profile on a person who sounds in the query to be a saint. A saint with guts, personality, and a real story to tell—bring me that. And finally, we reject proposals that sound like medicine—stories we should do because they'd be good for our readers. Generally, those stories are only good for the subject and the writer.

What kinds of stories or coverage are you most in need of?

Bohy: Profiles and features that show particular insight into metro Detroit's people, issues, government, business, and politics.

Burns: Compelling, gutsy features with a strong viewpoint.

Carlton: Interiors and homes; gardens.

Morgan: Great narratives, with subjects, regardless of whether they're high-profile or not, who have lived through an ordeal, changed their lives or those of others, who've started at point A and ended up at point Z. Told without sappiness. Plus, we're always grappling with the problem of writing stories that take place in our suburbs.

How do you typically find writers?

Bohy: First, through other writers and seeing especially good and interesting work in other publications. We very rarely find high-caliber writers through résumé-and-clips submissions or by mining writing seminars and conferences.

Burns: We woo them from other publications, or they rise through the ranks of our freelance pool. Patient writers can make it. I personally started as a freelancer for *Atlanta Magazine* and wrote short front-of-the-book items for 18 months before landing a feature assignment.

Carlton: Through networking and long experience in the business; mostly, they find us.

Morgan: There's no typical way. Sometimes one pitches a story, writes it, and it's marvelous—that happens, oh, once a year. Other times a writer pitches, the pitch is wrong, but the attitude, the clips, and the eagerness says to me, "There's something here." And I approach writers all the time—ex-newspaper reporters, fiction writers, poets, ad copywriters. Sometimes they write and they stick.

What's your best piece of advice for a freelancer who wants to write for your magazine?

Bohy: Know how to write, make your pitch as interesting as the story you're proposing, be sure you're thoroughly familiar with our editorial needs, be persistent, then make some sacrifice to the gods of freelancing, a very surly bunch.

Burns: Read the magazine. Know what we publish and what we don't, and send ideas that fit what we do.

Carlton: Read the magazine. See what makes us tick. Be aware of the New England sensibility.

Morgan: Please read the magazine so you know what we've already covered—and you find the holes, you see what we're missing in the big story that is Cincinnati. Then find me some fascinating subculture, with a central character, and spend lots and lots of time learning everything about that person. Then write the heck out of the story, filled with dialogue and keen observations.

Query Letter Clinic

BY KATHRYN S. BROGAN AND CYNTHIA LAUFENBERG

The query letter is the catalyst in the chemical reaction of publishing. Overall, writing a query letter is a fairly simple process that serves one purpose—selling an article.

There are two types of queries, a query for a finished manuscript, and a query for an idea that has yet to be developed into an article. Either way, a query letter is the tool that sells an idea using brief, attention-getting prose.

WHAT SHOULD I INCLUDE IN A QUERY LETTER?

A query should tell an editor how you plan to handle and develop the proposed article. Many writers even include the lead of the article as the first sentence of their query as a sales pitch to the editor. A query letter should also show that you are familiar with the publication and tell the editor why you are the most qualified person to write the article.

Beyond the information mentioned above, a query letter is also the appropriate place to state the availability of photographs or artwork. Do not send photographs with your query. You can also include a working title and a projected word count. Some writers also indicate whether a sidebar or other accompanying short would be appropriate, and the type of research they plan to conduct. It is also appropriate to include a tentative deadline and to indicate if the query is being simultaneously submitted.

WHAT SHOULD I *NOT* INCLUDE IN A QUERY LETTER?

The query letter is not the place to discuss pay rates. By mentioning what you would like to be paid, you are prematurely assuming that the editor is going to buy your article. Plus, if you are really just looking to get published and get paid some amount of money, you could be doing yourself a disservice. If you offer a rate that is higher than what the editor is willing to pay, you could lose the assignment. And, if you offer a figure that's too low, you are short-changing yourself on what could possibly be a lucrative assignment.

Another thing you should avoid is requesting writer's guidelines or a sample copy of the publication. This is a red flag to the editor because it indicates that you are not familiar with the magazine or its content. Don't use the query letter to list pages of qualifications. Only list those qualifications that you feel would best help you land the gig. If you have too many qualifications that you still feel would convince the editor to give you the assignment, include them as a separate page. Finally, never admit if five other editors rejected the query. This is your chance to shine, and sell the best article ever written.

HOW DO I FORMAT A QUERY LETTER?

There are no hard-and-fast rules when it comes to formatting your query letter. But there are some general, widely accepted guidelines like those listed below from *Formatting & Submitting Your Manuscript*, by Jack and Glenda Neff, and Don Prues (Writer's Digest Books).

KATHRYN S. BROGAN *is the editor of* Writer's Market *and* Writer's Market Online.

CYNTHIA LAUFENBERG *is editor-in-chief of* HealthyPet *magazine and former managing editor of Writer's Digest Books. She lives in Princeton, New Jersey.*

Fourteen Things Not to Do In Your Query Letter

1. Don't try any cute attention-getting devices, like marking the envelope "Personal." This also includes fancy stationery that lists every publication you've ever sold to, or "clever" slogans.
2. Don't talk about fees.
3. Keep your opinions to yourself.
4. Don't tell the editors what others you've shown the idea to think of it. ("Several of my friends have read this and think it's marvelous . . ." is a certain sign of the amateur writer.) The same goes for comments from other editors.
5. Don't name drop. However, if you do know somebody who works for that magazine, or writes for it, or if you know an editor on another magazine who has bought your work and likes it, say so.
6. Don't try to soft soap the editor by telling him or her how great the magazine is, but definitely make it clear that you read it.
7. Don't send in any unnecessary enclosures, such as a picture of yourself (or your prize-winning Labrador Retriever).
8. Don't offer irrelevant information about yourself. Simply tell the editor what there might be in your background that qualifies you to write this story.
9. Don't offer such comments as, "I never read your magazine, but this seems to be a natural . . ." or "I know you don't usually publish articles about mountain-climbing, but . . ." Know the magazine, and send only those ideas that fit the format.
10. Don't ask for a meeting to discuss your idea further. If the editor feels this is necessary, he or she will suggest it.
11. Don't ask for advice, such as, "If you don't think you can use this, could you suggest another magazine that could?"
12. Don't offer to rewrite, as this implies you know it's not good enough as you've submitted it. Again, editors will ask for rewrites, if necessary, and they usually are.
13. Don't make such threats as, "If I don't hear from you within four weeks I'll submit it elsewhere."
14. Don't include a multiple-choice reply card, letting the editor check a box to indicate whether he likes it.

From Magazine Writing That Sells, *by Don McKinney (Writer's Digest Books).*

- Use a standard font or typeface (avoid bold, script, or italics, except for publication titles).
- Your name, address, and phone number (plus e-mail and fax, if possible) should appear in the top right corner or on your letterhead.
- Use a 1-inch margin on all sides.
- Address the query to a specific editor, preferably the editor assigned to handle freelance submissions or who handles the section you're writing for. Note: The listings in *Writer's Market* provide a contact name for most submissions.
- Keep it to one page. If necessary, use a résumé or list of credits attached separately to provide additional information.
- Include a SASE or postcard for reply; state you have done so, either in the body of the letter or in a listing of enclosures.
- Use block format (no indentations).
- Single-space the body of the letter and double-space between paragraphs.
- When possible, mention that you can send the manuscript on disk or via e-mail.
- Thank the editor for considering your proposal.

How to Include Clips with E-Mail Queries

When you send an e-mail query, you can provide clips five ways. There are no generally accepted standards yet for which is best, but the pros and cons of each method are described below:

1. Include a line telling the editor that clips are available on request. Then, mail, fax, or e-mail clips according to the editor's preference. This is a convenient solution for the writer, but not necessarily for the editor. The clips aren't available immediately, so you potentially slow the decision process by adding an additional step, and you lose any speed you've gained by e-mailing the query in the first place.
2. Include electronic versions of the clips in the body of the e-mail message. This can make for an awfully long e-mail, and it doesn't look as presentable as other alternatives, but it may be better than making the editor wait to download attachments or log on to a website.
3. Include electronic versions of the articles as attachments. The disadvantage here is the editor has to download the clips, which can take several minutes. Also, if there's a format disparity, the editor may not be able to read the attachment. The safest bet is to attach the documents as ".rtf" or ".txt" files, which should be readable with any word processing software, although you will lose formatting.
4. Send the clips as a separate e-mail message. This cuts the download time and eliminates software-related glitches, but it clutters the editor's e-mail queue.
5. Set up a personal web page and include your clips as hypertext links in or at the end of the e-mail (e.g., www.aolmembers.com/jackneff/smallbusinessclips). Setting up and maintaining the page takes a considerable amount of effort, but it may be the most convenient and reliable way for editors to access your clips electronically.

From Formatting & Submitting Your Manuscript, *by Jack and Glenda Neff, and Don Prues (Writer's Digest Books).*

WHEN SHOULD I FOLLOW UP?

Sometimes things happen to your query and it never reaches the editor's hands. Problems can arise with the mail delivery, the query may have been sent to a different department, or the editor may have inadvertently thrown the query away. Whatever the reason, there are a few simple guidelines you should use when you send a follow-up letter.

You should wait to follow up on your query at least until after the reported response time in the *Writer's Market* listing for that publication. If, after two months, you have not received a response to your query, you should compose a brief follow-up letter. The letter should describe the original query sent, the date the query was sent, and a reply postcard or a SASE. Some writers find it helpful to include a photocopy of the original query to help jog the editor's memory.

Above all, though, be polite and businesslike when following up. Don't take the lack of response personal. Editors are only human—situations can arise that are beyond their control.

WHAT THE CLINIC SHOWS YOU

Unpublished writers wonder how published writers break into print. It's not a matter of luck. Published writers know how to craft a well-written, hard-hitting query. What follows are six actual queries submitted to editors (names and addresses have been altered). Three queries are strong; three are not. Detailed comments from the editors show what the writer did and did not do to secure a sale. As you'll see, there is not a cut-and-dry "good" query format; every strong query works because of its own merit.

Good

I actually prefer e-mail queries to any other kind. And I like it that the subject line identifies that this e-mail is a query.

To: editor@aspca.org
Subject: article query

I'm not put off by the informal salutation, and while I prefer a strong lead that takes me right into the story, in this case it actually worked well for the author to get my attention up front with the quality of the magazines that have published her work.

Hi. I'm a professional writer whose articles have appeared in many national magazines and newspapers, including *The New York Times*, *Woman's Day*, *New Choices*, *BrainWork*, *The Philadelphia Inquirer Magazine*, *ActiveTimes*, *MidAtlantic Country*, and others. For more details about my work, please visit my website at www.wandawriter.com.

I respond negatively to being sent to a website. That's work for me, and I think the author should take responsibility for selecting the salient facts about herself and her work.

Last year, I discovered a children's book about a little pig who lives on a farm for homeless animals (*Skippy and Gavin*, by Linda Taylor). Our then-five-year-old daughter was enchanted by the book and its illustrations (by Susan Simcox), as were we. The storyline centered on the little pig's loneliness, his joy at the arrival of an aging donkey, and how the pig ("Gavin" in the title) wins over the bigger animal to be his friend.

I had never heard of the author, but the book jacket explained that she based the book on the formerly homeless animals at the farm she and her husband share in Bucks County, Pennsylvania.

Paragraphs 2, 3, and 4 reassure me that the author knows what she wants to write about and knows that it's a good fit for Animal Watch.

A second "Gavin" book was published earlier this year, dealing with the little pig's journey to self-acceptance with the help of his barnyard friends. According to the author's website, a third "Gavin" book will be published later this year. All of the "Gavin" books center on the rescued animals and explore important concepts about friendship, caring, and kindness.

In proposing a profile specifically, I see that the author really has a particular story and angle in mind. This is an element of professionalism.

I've never seen another children's book series featuring rescued farm animals. Knowing that improving children's awareness of humane concerns and issues is important to the ASPCA, I thought that *ASPCA Animal Watch* might be interested in a profile of this author, her farm, and her books.

Let's talk about this idea. You may reach me anytime by e-mail at wandawriter@email.com or by phone at (555)517-6857.

Her closing could be stronger. I'd prefer to see all the author's contact information in a block, including her mailing address, which isn't even given.

Best wishes,
Wanda Writer
www.wandawriter.com
member: ASJA (American Society of Journalists and Authors), Author's Guild

Comments provided by Marion Lane, editor of *ASPCA Animal Watch* magazine.

Bad

March 3, 2003

ASPCA Animal Watch
Attn: Marion Lane, Editor
315 East 62nd St.
New York, NY 10021

We moved from this address in May 2002. Not a big deal, but suggests lack of careful attention to detail.

Three years ago, I witnessed first-hand the aftermath of a dog attack on a herd of goats. As a reporter for a daily newspaper, I was able to retell the story of the attack to 15,000 readers. Since then, I realized many more people could benefit from this story, and so, I ask you to consider allowing me to publish a similar story in *ASPCA Animal Watch*.

This is not a subject we've covered before, and due to the growth in "backyard barnyards," I'm interested. On the other hand, the author's use of language ("allowing me to publish") is sloppy enough to send up a red flag regarding her basic writing skills.

Using the Osbourne family's experience of having seven of their goats die as a result of the attack, I would like to inform your readers about this occurrence. The article would benefit readers on both sides. Owners of livestock will be informed on how to protect their animals from such an attack, and dog owners will learn the repercussions of allowing their pets to roam free, which may result in an attack on area farm animals.

The assignment is lost in this paragraph. The author is unfamiliar with our magazine and our readers.

I have already established contacts with the Kansas State University's veterinary practice and school, which were used in the original article. However, a new, expanded version of the article would include advice as given by the ASPCA and laws or fines that aim at providing accountability to dog owners who allow these attacks to take place.

These references confirm the article would not be appropriate for Animal Watch. We hardly need veterinary opinion to persuade us that dogs can maim goats and lambs. I'm pleased to see that the author realizes it would be good to interview ASPCA legal and legislative experts, but I'd rather see evidence that she has done some research first.

While I am no longer employed with the newspaper in which this story was first printed, I have permission to use the information contained within it. I have included the article, but remind you I do not intend to republish this piece. I would like to use the information contained within it and write an informational piece for a national.

I have also included an additional article, which was published in *Nebraska Today* — a quarterly consumer magazine — to show the variety of topics I have covered in the five years I have been employed in the journalism field. I am currently the editor of a weekly newspaper, *The Kansas Gazette*. As someone who thoroughly enjoys writing, I have begun pursuing ways to publish freelance work aside from my full-time job.

Paragraphs 4 and 5 contain irrelevant information that reinforces my impression that this individual is inexperienced.

Thank you for your consideration. A SASE is enclosed, and I look forward to hearing from you.

Sincerely,

Nathan Neophyte
27 Uphill St.
Needshelp, KS 45682
(555) 356-8182

Comments provided by Marion Lane, editor of *ASPCA Animal Watch* magazine.

Good

Contact information provided; however, she should also include her phone number and e-mail address, if applicable.

Barbara Best
836 Fine Lane
Efficient, CT 56424

February 22, 2003

Bayard, editor
Happy Magazine
240 E. 35th St., Suite 11A
New York, NY 10016

Proper greeting format especially since she doesn't know the sex of the editor from the contact name provided.

Dear Sir or Madam,

I am pleased to enclose the manuscript of my story, "Can't Stand Up for Falling Down," offered to your magazine for publication. It runs 2,200 words in length.

She's read our writer's guidelines.

This paragraph summarizes the author's credentials well.

I am a writer whose work has been published on multiple occasions by *Ex Libris Nocturnis*, and I currently have a story awaiting publication by *Antietam Review Magazine*. A previous story of mine, "Crazy," received the Sonya Blate Award for Creative Writing.

I am a lifelong resident of Connecticut. Currently, I am attending Yale University, with a declared major of English literature.

Thank you for considering "Can't Stand Up for Falling Down."

Sincerely,

Barbara Best

Enclosures:
Manuscript
SASE

This is a good letter. It is so bland nothing about it offends.

Comments provided by Bayard, editor of *Happy Magazine*.

Bad

Subj: RE: FICTION SUBMISSION ON SPEC
"Awkward Movements"
Date: June 15, 2003
From: Neil Novice
To: BayardX
File: Awkward Movements

We don't accept e-mail submissions.

Neil Novice
Freelance Writer
67 North Street
Lacking, MD 53841
Fax: (555)569-5697
Phone: (555)975-5961
neilnovice@email.com

This shows the stamp of an amateur.

Are you sure?

Dear Mr. Bayard:

Robert's day begins with great joy but then he has to deal with his co-worker who sees the world through very different lenses. She's an evangelist eager to spread the good news, he's a private person who feels that his religious beliefs are too precious to discuss in an elevator. Together they have a near-death experience — each approaching the moment in their own way.

Don't tell me about the story. Let the story speak for itself.

I'd like to submit a 4,000-word short story called, "Awkward Movements," which explores the relationship between men and women, conservative and liberal, religious and secular, workers and politicians, co-workers, and employers.

You'd like to submit or are submitting? Is this a submission or a query?

My writing credentials include features, reviews, essays, humor, and fiction. I've had articles published in *Gasoline News*, *Pilots Today*, and *Etchings*. Additional articles are scheduled for publication this year in magazines like *Byline* and *the Writer*. I am a regular contributor to *At Home with a Good Book*, and I've had several short stories published. I have a collection for short stories entitled *Winning Passion* and I am currently seeking representation for two novels: *Downplay* which is a historical piece about the women who worked on battleships for the military during World War II, and *Screen Name* which is a thriller about a psychopath and a computer hacker.

Is any of this relevant?

Thanks for your time and attention. The manuscript is attached to this e-mail as a Word Document.

A query wouldn't have the story attached.

Neil Novice

Comments provided by Bayard, editor of *Happy Magazine*.

Good

638 S. Good St.
Experience, UT 59786
(518)654-6854
pattyperfect@email.com

Thomas Lavoie, Associate Publisher
Dufour Editions
P.O. Box 7
Chester Springs, PA 19425

All the basic letterhead information is there, and my name is spelled correctly.

August 31, 2003

Dear Mr. Lavoie,

She gets right to the point with what kind of manuscript it is, and points out specific information about this collection that might help it rise above all the others—why it is better than most. And, as it is a short story collection, it provides that very important information about where some of the stories have been previously published.

I'm writing to inquire whether Dufour would be interested in considering for publication my short story collection manuscript entitled *Observing Trust*. The manuscript has recently been named a finalist or runner-up in several prominent publication competitions including the Flannery O'Connor Award, the Breadloaf Prize, Ohio State University Press' Sandstone Prize, and the Mid-List Press Award. In addition, ten of the 11 stories have appeared or are slated to appear in such literary journals as *American Literary Review*, *Ascent*, *High Plains Literary Review*, *Image*, *Third Coast*, and *Whetstone*, and three of the stories have recently been nominated for Pushcart Prizes.

A summary of the stories is almost as difficult as giving a novel's summary. Here there are many separate pieces. This summary does the job, although I might actually have liked to see more information here.

It's nice to see a list of protagonists, the variety. It's a clean and direct summary.

While individual stories in the collection are not linked in terms of plot, they share several characteristics. Humor is an important thematic and stylistic element in the collection, and in many of the stories, the day-to-day occupations of the characters serve to clarify their crises and conflicts. Among the protagonists in the collection are a priest, a college hockey player, a pharmacist, a daycare worker, a painter, and a basketball team mascot.

This paragraph nicely summarizes the author's credentials, which, in this case, are primarily academic and emphasize her writing experience.

By way of a brief biography, I've received graduate degrees in Creative Writing/English from Iowa State University and Syracuse University. Last year, I served as Visiting Writer-in-Residence at Moorhead College in Concordia, Utah, and I've just begun working as a member of the permanent creative writing faculty at Utah State University.

The final paragraph brings things together nicely in a brief manner, and it's good to see that they've given us the option of receiving the manuscript electronically. And the author provided her e-mail address above so we can get in touch with them quickly and economically.

I've enclosed a SASE for your reply. Should you decide you'd like to see a sample story or the entire manuscript, I'd be glad to send the work immediately, either electronically or through standard mail. Thanks for your time and attention.

Best,

Patricia Perfect

Comments provided by Thomas Lavoie, associate publisher of Dufour Editions.

Bad

January 1, 2003

My name is Amy Amateur, and I have just finished a timely dark comedy novel called *The Conglomerate Cookies*. I refer to it as timely because I finished it on New Year's Day, and it's about a woman, Theresa Monroe, who realizes that she's neglected her family her whole life. Only through a miserable self-destruction can she communicate her feelings to her family, and even then, they don't understand any of her actions.

It starts out with Theresa being interviewed by a reporter from her hometown newspaper, the *Newton Post Gazette*. Theresa has "made it big" in New York, and she'll be front page news (few Newtonites leave the small-town confines). But the reporter, Mike Gilmore, is alarmed by Theresa's nervous tics and habitual over-emphasizing of words and phrases. Theresa especially seems to hate all of the cookies that are brought to her big corporate office building, whereby she has gotten fat. After the interview, Mike takes a perilous highway journey back to Newton, during which he accidentally loses all of his notes from the interview. So, piecing the story together from memory, the story falsely reveals that Theresa's biggest concern in the big city is that she is too far from all the cookies.

Theresa's mental state slowly deteriorates at work to the point where she yells out loud at a Tony Robbins-style motivational speaker. She is forced to take three weeks of vacation, which she uses to revisit her hometown. In a flashback, it is revealed that Theresa was constantly tortured by neighborhood bullies because she was a bookworm. Her parents were unloving, and her visit to her father's for Christmas ends with her silently murdering him after he suffers a grand-mal seizure.

Theresa leaves her family and disappears into the Amazon forest (according to the FBI). She resurfaces ten years later as a maniacal super-villain who wishes to destroy the world's sugar supply so no more cookies can be manufactured, and she insists that the work week be shortened so everyone can spend more quality time with their families. Of course, the ending is tragic, because the CIA and FBI assault her secret base and destroy her and her plans. But the President of the U.S.A. declares a national Cookie Day in honor of the brave CIA and FBI agents.

With your permission, I would ecstatically send you a copy of the manuscript for your perusal in hopes that you will represent or publish it. Please respond via SASE, phone, or e-mail. *The Conglomerate Cookies* is my first full-length novel; I have several short-stories published in literary journals, and a screenplay about depression-era Oklahoma City which is being produced sometime next year.

Fantastically Yours,
Amy Amateur
5741 Main St.
Average, OK 68523
965-854-9587
amya@email.net

This isn't a terrible query letter, but it does have enough wrong with it to hurt the query and cause an editor to think that the quality of the work itself will be weak as well.

This letter is totally over the top. There's no salutation at all, no dear me, and it's written January 1, the same day the novel in question, we're told, was finished.

The first paragraph has awkward phrases and reads rough-warning signs. Don't plunge into the novel's contents so soon. This is the kind of summary that could come at the end. Who is this author, and where are the credentials?

In all, there are basically four paragraphs of summary about the novel—this is too much. The summary needs more balance. Paragraphs 2-4 could be reduced to one.

Material in this paragraph should have come sooner. No need to "ecstatically" send a copy, and we don't "represent" works, agents do. This undermines the author's credibility. This paragraph has some glaring grammatical errors. It can't be stressed enough that a query letter should be well written; if it isn't it will probably automatically damn itself by what it says (or doesn't say).

It's not really a good idea to end query letters with "fantastically yours." These are the kinds of things that undermine the professionalism of the writer.

Comments provided by Thomas Lavoie, associate publisher of Dufour Editions.

E-Wrongs About E-Rights: How to Counter the Most-Repeated Cyberfables

ADAPTED BY ANTHONY TEDESCO

These days, contracts for freelance articles can be super-dense, high-legalese documents longer than the articles they commission. Rights clauses—in particular, those pertaining to electronic rights—cause the most consternation, especially when the publisher wants those rights for free. Often they cause the most confusion, too. The discussions frequently include certain basic information about electronic publishing in the world of periodicals. The problem is, much of that information is wrong.

Here are the most-repeated cyberfables, each accompanied by what you should know to correct them.

Databases like Lexis-Nexis are just another way of distributing our publication. You wouldn't expect more money if we signed up 1,000 more newsstands, would you?

A database is not simply another means of distributing a publication, because a database doesn't distribute publications at all; it distributes individual articles. Online services usually collect a per-article fee from database users; publishers collect a piece of the pie in regular royalty payments. It's as if a reader could go to a newsstand, slice an article out of a magazine, and pay for the clipping alone. It is, in effect, an electronic delivery system for a reprint service.

We don't "cherry-pick." We use the article only as part of the whole issue in which it appears. It's simple archiving.

In a text-only database, there are no graphics and no ads, and frequently the database is missing some editorial matter, such as letters to the editor, short items, and articles by authors who have insisted that their work not be included. Hardly "the whole issue."

This is just like microfilm.

Microfilm, which replaced bound volumes, was a new form of archiving, containing each issue in its entirety, page after page, just as it appears on paper. But an electronic database, online or CD-ROM, is an archive of articles, not of issues. The publisher's copyright covers the collective work—the articles, graphics, and ads as strung together—but not the individual constituent parts. (Just as a writer's copyright in an article is for the stringing together of words; the writer doesn't own the individual words.) In the case of online databases, the reader generally pays the online service per hit, the database producer takes a cut, and the publisher gets a royalty.

Prepared by the ASJA Contracts Committee (www.asja.org), and adapted by Anthony Tedesco with permission. ASJA's Contracts Committee serves as a clearinghouse of information on terms being offered and contract changes being accepted by many periodicals. It offers this information to members and nonmembers alike, in the belief that better-informed negotiators help us all.

The only party in the chain who doesn't keep making money is the author—unless the author-publisher agreement calls for sharing the revenue.

But no publisher is making a dime at this.

Wrong. With databases, publishers profit from the first sale on because they have no startup costs; they sign a deal and collect royalties. Some heavily researched publications, like *The New York Times*, already make millions a year from electronic products, others make peanuts. But whatever they make from these databases is pure profit. On the other hand, publishers' own online efforts, including sites on the World Wide Web, may have high startup costs and bring little initial income (although major advertisers are starting to sign up for some prominent magazines' sites). But while bottom line is what it's all about, in a print venture no publisher expects profits from day one, and no publisher expects freebies from freelancers. In electronic publishing, even before they start turning a profit, publishers pay everyone from their computer programmers to the electric company. Why should they get content for free?

We don't charge download fees on our website. If we start charging, then we'll pay authors.

Download fees are just one of several ways online publishers profit. They sell ads, products and services, and mailing lists. They gain increased paper subscriptions and general promotion. In deals with commercial services, like America Online, they may earn finders' fees for bringing new subscribers to the service. Some of the most profitable print publications are controlled-circulation giveaways with heavy advertising; should writers provide them with free articles because they don't charge for subscriptions?

We don't know which articles are accessed. It would be too expensive to keep track.

Untrue. Per-article tracking is not only doable but also common.

It would be too expensive to write a lot of small checks.

It might have been, but writers and agents have joined in the Authors Registry (www.authorsregistry.org), which will keep accounts and conglomerate those small checks for authors. "The bookkeeping is difficult, so we'll keep all the money" was always undesirable; now it's also indefensible. Such major publications as *Cooking Light*, *Food & Wine*, *Harper's*, *The Nation*, *Publishers Weekly*, *Travel & Leisure*, and *Yankee* have already begun arrangements with the Registry to get payments to authors.

The exposure will be good for you. It'll get your name around. In the case of books, it's free publicity.

By that reasoning, authors shouldn't be paid for print publication either and should give away first serial rights to books. Even it if seems that an online appearance can help a new book with extra exposure, how will it help in a couple of years, when the book is out of print? The chapter excerpted in a magazine or newspaper may continue to earn royalties for that publication . . . but not for the author.

We can't delete one article.

Standard agreements with database producers allow for removal of any material as requested by the publisher, before compilation or after. If a publisher won't pay, a piece can be left out.

If you make us delete this article, you'll be interfering with the flow of information, research, scholarship, the future of the world.

In other words, when it comes to aiding research, publishers should be allowed to profit, but authors should do it as a public service?

We ask for only nonexclusive e-rights; the author can relicense the work too.

Should an author have to compete with Condé Nast or Hearst in marketing? And what happens when a potential purchaser asks for territory or category exclusivity? The author has to say no, because the original publisher may be selling to the competition. But even more basic is this question: Should a publisher be able to make continuing use of a freelancer's property and keep all the proceeds?

The business is new. Let it shake down a few years, then renegotiate.

Ever try to push the toothpaste back into the tube? Industry standards of the future are being established now. Publishers and freelancers should build them together. Fairly.

All the other writers are signing.

Oldest line in the book of publisher-speak, and rarely true.

Our lawyer won't allow any changes.

Best response: "Neither will mine."

A Multi-Dimensional Approach to Building a Writing Career

BY SEAN MURPHY

When I was younger, I imagined the writer's existence to be a calm, contemplative one. Lots of time to spin scenarios while staring out the window, long walks in the woods with the dogs, that sort of thing. I dreamed of having a life where no one bothered me much, other people handled my business affairs, and the bulk of each day was devoted to creative work. I had plenty of time to dream in this fashion, since my first novel, *The Hope Valley Hubcap King* (Bantam/Dell, 2002), took me 12 years to complete—sandwiched between making a living and going to graduate school.

I received a big wake-up call, however, with the publication of my first two books, six months apart from one another. Not only were my publishers, to my surprise, busy with *other* books, and not solely occupied with promoting mine—but the advances I'd received had been spent in the writing, and there were no royalties in sight for at least six months. I had to come to grips with the fact that no one was going to make sure that my books sold if I didn't do it—and certainly no one else was going to bring in an income. Clearly, a broader approach was necessary if I was to make a life as a writer.

Realize this: You're no Hemingway

I'm speaking largely here of the book business, but the general principles apply to writers in any field, whether published or unpublished. In today's competitive market, we don't have the leisure enjoyed by a Hemingway or Faulkner of gradually building up a career under the patient guidance of a beneficent publisher. In any case, this hallowed status enjoyed by authors of old is, at least partly, a myth. T.S. Eliot worked for years as a banker. Faulkner and Fitzgerald wrote for the movies. Wallace Stevens was an insurance executive, and William Carlos Williams a family physician—in both cases, for the majority of their adult lives.

In the last few years, I've been taking my own personal crash course in how to build a writing career from the ground up, from selling my first book to placing follow-up articles, dealing with promotion and marketing, public events, the media—an array of activities I'd never imagined myself doing. I've learned that it's important to use every resource available in my life to develop my career. The reason for this is simple, if sobering: Most of us, unless we're extremely lucky, are unlikely to make enough income from our writing alone to support ourselves. To truly live the writing life requires a broad-based, multi-dimensional approach—building a platform for our work—that includes many activities other than sitting in front of the keyboard, slipping into the seductive dream of the story. If we view the whole project, including placement, marketing, promotion—in fact, our entire career as a writer—as a creative act, our efforts not only become more effective; the process is also more enjoyable.

SEAN MURPHY's The Hope Valley Hubcap King *(Bantam/Dell, 2002) won the Hemingway Award for a First Novel and was featured on the American Booksellers Association Book Sense 76 list of recommended titles. He is also the author of* One Bird, One Stone: 108 American Zen Stories *(Renaissance/St. Martin's, 2002), and has signed a contract with Bantam/Dell for his next two novels,* The Finished Man *and* Tiny Miracles.

So how do we go about building a life in which every element supports and enhances our goal of becoming a successful writer? I'm going to lead you through some areas worth considering, in roughly the order I encountered them.

Enter the fray: Take advantage of awards and writing contests

When I finished *The Hope Valley Hubcap King*, I faced the universal challenge of all unknown novelists: getting the manuscript before an agent or publisher. I reasoned that submitting it for competitions might be a starting point. That way I was sure someone would read it in its entirety (something I suspect rarely happens in the case of unknown authors), and I'd receive feedback that could improve it. Even if I didn't win, I might place in the finals or semifinals, and could mention this in my query letter, which would make it stand out from the masses of correspondence editors and agents receive.

I decided to enter every novel contest available. I ended up placing in three of these, which would probably have been enough on its own to attract an agent's interest. Then I won the Hemingway Award for a First Novel, which included an agent as part of the prize, thereby solving part of my problem. I always encourage my writing students to enter competitions. There are many available, in fields ranging from nonfiction to short stories to poetry. If you submit work on a diligent, thorough basis, you'll tend to get results, no matter how minor, that may help in acquiring an agent or publisher. If not, this tells you that you need to go back to the drawing board and hone your craft—either that, or you're ahead of your time, in which case it won't hurt to work on your craft some more anyway! And you'll get advance warning of the obstacles you may face in placing your work.

For More Information

GRANTS, FELLOWSHIPS, & RESIDENCY PROGRAMS

- See page 992 of the Contests & Awards section of *Writer's Market* for more information on various writing grants and fellowships in a variety of genres and disciplines.
- PEN publishes an extremely useful publication titled, *Grants and Awards Available to American Writers*. It can be ordered through the PEN American Center, 568 Broadway, New York NY 10012 (www.pen.org).

Be flexible: Use success in one arena to open doors in another

One of the first questions my agent asked, to my surprise, was whether I had any ideas for nonfiction books. As it turned out, I did have an idea I'd been nursing for some time. Being a practitioner of Zen meditation, I'd noticed that every few years a collection of Zen teaching stories was published, and met with some success. However, most of these assemblages of enlightening quotes and anecdotes (you might call them "Miso Soup for the Soul") depended on ancient tales of Asian Zen masters for their material. Despite the fact that there were an estimated 1 million or more Zen practitioners in the United States, no one had yet written a book of Zen wisdom drawn from contemporary American sources.

My agent thought this was a saleable idea. We decided it would be a good strategy to try to sell this book before selling the novel, as a nonfiction book with a built-in audience would be easier to place than a novel by an unknown author, prize-winning or not. The proposal went to auction, and within a month we'd sold *One Bird, One Stone: 108 American Zen Stories* (Renaissance/St. Martin's, 2002), based on a 25-page synopsis. Oddly, I'd sold the book I *hadn't* written before selling the novel I'd already finished! This is an example of how being creative in one's marketing approach, and thinking "outside the box" can yield results. And having one book contract under my belt made placing the novel an easier task.

I find in working with writing students that they often have more resources at their disposal than they are aware of. Learning how to take advantage of these can be a key aspect in developing your career. For instance, I have a student who raises purebred dogs, belongs to various related organizations, and uses these contacts in pitching articles and securing speaking engagements. It is worthwhile to consider what areas of knowledge or expertise you've developed that might lend themselves to a book or series of articles. Classic automobiles? Jazz music? African violets?

If you write books, these can provide material for articles; and many a successful article has been expanded to a book-length project. Broadening your scope can be an important element of career building. I've been able to spin off from my books to write articles for publications including *Yoga Journal* and *Tricycle*. These have not only helped promote my books, but have provided valuable contacts with editors who later published reviews and excerpts from my work. This is better than free publicity—you can publicize your work and actually get paid for it!

Consider This! Quick Tips to Help You Develop a Multi-Dimensional Approach

- Diligently submit your work to writing contests, if only to walk away with feedback to help you improve your manuscript and resubmit it to another contest at a later date.
- Consider the areas of knowledge or expertise that you have, and use those areas to develop a book or series of articles.
- Attend events, writers' conferences, book signings, book clubs, readings, etc., that allow you to interact and "rub shoulders" with other members of the writing community.
- Join a community of writers who share your thoughts and goals, and allow that group to help you develop your work and morale.
- Garner local media coverage by sending out press releases, making phone calls, and networking with members of your writing community.
- Become an active writer, not a passive one. If you want to make writing your career, you must make it a priority in your life.

Give help and take it: The importance of creative networking

Bantam/Dell expressed a strong interest in buying *The Hope Valley Hubcap King*, but were hesitant because its unusual mix of dark comedy, social satire, and the protagonist's quest for meaning didn't fall clearly into an existing genre (in publishing lingo, this means they weren't exactly sure how they were going to sell it!). They asked me to come up with a well-known author to provide a cover blurb. Two years earlier I'd met Malachy McCourt, author of *A Monk Swimming*, at the Southwest Writers Workshop conference in Albuquerque. I'd prepared for the conference by printing postcards to publicize my novel. These featured a picture of a hubcap on the front, and mock, humorous blurbs from "authorities" as diverse as Bill Clinton, Julia Child, and Winnie-the-Pooh on the back. McCourt got such a kick out of the card that he gave me his phone number and told me to call him if I ever needed anything. I did call, two years later. He read the manuscript, loved it, and provided me with a full page of praise—and Bantam/Dell bought the novel.

Successful authors, however, often have so many demands upon them that they may find it difficult even to find the time to write. If you go after these people hungrily, with the attitude of wanting something, they are unlikely to respond well. The important thing is to attend events where you can rub shoulders with members of the writing community, to be friendly and open, and especially, to help others. When I was finishing *The Hope Valley Hubcap King*, I met periodically with two friends, Daniel Villasenor, who was writing his novel *The Lake* (Viking Press, 2000), and Mirabai Starr, who was working on a new translation of St. John of the Cross' *Dark Night of the Soul*. We read each other's work, providing encouragement and suggestions for improvement. When Daniel's novel was published, he shared his lists of agents and other contacts, and after my book was sold I referred Mirabai to my agent, who placed her translation with Riverhead. Our first books ended up coming out within 18 months of each other.

I cannot over-emphasize how important it is to be part of a community of writers who can help and encourage one another. One of the most common ways agents and publications acquire new talent is through referrals from authors they already know. And friendship with fellow writers is one of the joys of the creative life.

Broaden your platform: Teaching, conferences, and public speaking

Although you may not realize it, publishing a book or article makes you an instant expert. Teaching or giving talks on your subject can be an invaluable way of broadening the platform for your writing career, sharpening up your own craft, and building an audience. For the past five years I've taught writing and literature for the University of New Mexico in Taos, as well as the Taos Institute of Arts. I also taught for four years with Natalie Goldberg, author of *Writing Down the Bones* (Shambhala, 1986), in her writing seminars, and now conduct my own workshops at locations throughout the United States.

I have assembled an extensive contact list of all my students. When my books come out, there is a built-in audience waiting, and I know how to spread the word. On the basis of teaching and publications, I've secured speaking engagements at conferences and on radio programs. These, in turn, have helped publicize the books. And the books attract more students, in a self-reinforcing circle. While not everyone has a degree that allows them to teach university courses, most communities have organizations that sponsor adult education courses. These may be a perfect venue for your talents. Churches and recreation centers may be interested in sponsoring you for a weekend writing workshop. Or you can set up your own events, and publicize them through putting up posters and through the local media.

Be a joiner: Group memberships and affiliations

Personally, I've never been much of a "joiner." I've always hated meetings, elections, committees, and other such elements associated with organizations. Nevertheless, I've found that joining a few select groups has been invaluable, not only in terms of networking, but in practical areas such as health insurance, contract negotiations, and opportunities for readings and workshops. There are many writers' organizations available, but just to provide an idea, here are the ones to which I belong *(Editor's note: For a complete list of writer's organizations, see page 1004)*:

- **Associated Writing Programs (www.awpwriter.org).** They publish a monthly list of residencies, fellowships, and academic appointments. They also sponsor a dossier service, which submits recommendations, school transcripts, etc., on your behalf to any positions for which you'd like to apply. And their magazine, *The Writer's Chronicle*, is one of the smartest writers' publications around.
- **Authors Guild (www.authorsguild.org).** I signed up to get on their medical insurance plan, which is reasonably priced and, in general, excellent. I've since discovered that they provide contract consultations, legal services, and low-cost, easy-to-maintain websites. Their *Bulletin* is an excellent resource for keeping abreast of such issues as copyright, e-books, and freedom of speech.
- **Local Writers Organizations.** I belong to two of these, the Southwest Writers Workshop (www.southwestwriters.com), and The Society of the Muse of the Southwest (SOMOS) (www.somotaos.org); their equivalent can be found in most metropolitan areas. Both organizations have sponsored me for readings and workshops. And they'll print free announce-

ments of member publications and other events in their newsletters. Groups such as these provide a built-in audience for your work, as well as a strong base for networking with other writers. Making an inquiry at a local library is a good place to start looking for one in your area.

Another good resource is that venerable writer's organization and advocacy group, PEN (www.pen.org). And don't forget alumni and religious organizations; they'll generally print publication announcements for members in their newsletters. Remember, every group to which you belong helps build community; and every community provides valuable contacts and an audience for your work.

Apply yourself: Grants, fellowships, and residency programs

The U.S. government, as well as many states and local communities, has arts boards and grants councils, private organizations, and residency programs that provide financial assistance to writers. These often-overlooked resources were of tremendous help to me in the early stages of my writing career. Community organizations in California and Colorado awarded me grants when I was living there. Aside from the financial benefits, I found the application process enormously helpful, as it required that I focus and delineate my project clearly in the proposal. I also developed skills in presenting and marketing my work which have served me well ever since.

Many writers have made their start, and in some case sustained themselves for years, through such programs. Although these can be competitive and time-consuming to enter, the rewards are enormous. A fellowship, grant, or residency can provide the freedom to write, while removing the financial pressure that makes it necessary to do something else for a living. What more does an author need?

Make the news: Using the media creatively

It's taken me a while to catch on to this. Why give readings, I wondered, when your average bookstore event might only attract a dozen listeners? It doesn't take a rocket scientist to figure that royalties from the handful of books sold is hardly adequate compensation for your time. So why do it?

Building good will among readers and positive relationships with bookstores are worthy goals in themselves—particularly because hand-selling by booksellers is of central importance in getting the word out to readers. Word of mouth continues to be the single most important factor in book sales. People who enjoy your work are likely to recommend it to their friends, creating an ever-expanding web of readership. For these reasons, it's not only worthwhile to schedule readings, but to visit booksellers and sign copies of your books whenever you have the opportunity.

But there's another quite compelling reason to schedule such events, whether or not you currently have any books in print: the media coverage they generate. This not only promotes books, but also raises your profile in terms of getting public speaking engagements, teaching opportunities, and requests to write articles.

When *One Bird, One Stone* came out, I did five readings in my area, which provided a "news hook" for me to contact local media. The result was three radio interviews, and reviews or features in four publications. When *The Hope Valley Hubcap King* was published, I had my media contacts already in place, and they were eager to hear more from me—particularly since a new author publishing his first two books in the same year provided a newsworthy angle. I did four readings in New Mexico for *Hubcap King*, which generated six articles and a half-dozen radio interviews. I spoke to dozens of people afterward who mentioned: "I heard you on the radio" or "I saw that article in the paper." Local bookstores couldn't keep up with the demand.

Regional media coverage can be achieved through press releases, phone calls, and referrals from members of your writing community. Everybody's fascinated by writers and wants to read about our glamorous lives (no one seems to realize we spend most of our time alone in small rooms staring at computer screens!). And many of these readers may go on to buy our work.

Keep faith and focus: Staying on track

When I began sending out my first manuscript I was teaching part time, and working as an audiovisual technician and projectionist for a local theater. Although these were interesting arts-related occupations, they were not directly allied to my goal of becoming a writer. In recent years I've realized the need to streamline my work activities so that they reinforce one key area: my writing.

Sometimes giving up a peripheral activity requires a leap of faith. When I quit working for the theater I wasn't sure how I was going to make ends meet. But I soon made up the lost income by writing articles and giving workshops, activities that more closely supported my goals. Simply put, if you want your writing career to work, you have to make it a priority.

It's important to remember that when creativity is applied to business and promotion, it enlivens it. The multi-dimensional approach described in this article is one I've seen used successfully by many writing friends and colleagues. There are other benefits too: Agents and editors are more likely to take on authors who will actively promote their work. It's simple economics. They realize that such authors are motivated toward success and will ultimately sell more books.

All of this may sound like hard work, but it's part of the package, particularly in today's increasingly profit-driven publishing world. Remember that, in the largest sense, there is nothing in your life that *isn't* a part of your career.

Who knows? You may just find yourself enjoying the process. If not—well, if going through a little bother allows you to realize your dream of succeeding as a writer, isn't it worth it?

After all, it beats working in a bank. Ask T.S. Eliot. He got out of there and never looked back.

Marcela Landres: A Real-Life *Charlie's Angel* Inside Simon & Schuster

BY KATHRYN S. BROGAN

"What personal life? Am I supposed to have one?" jokingly replies Marcela Landres, an associate editor in the Touchstone/Fireside division of Simon & Schuster, when asked how she balances her work with her personal life. Landres, who's been at Simon & Schuster for over six years, says that like most editors, she has to prove herself every day of her career—which isn't easy given that Landres is one of the few Latinos in the industry. "It can be lonely, but it's all how you look at it, like anything in life," she says. "The fact that I'm one of the few Latinas makes me stand out, so it's easier for people to find me to talk about the Latino market because I am, by default, an expert." Landres feels that she is somehow "pioneering this kind of publishing"—this kind of publishing being that which is representative of Latino authors.

Landres makes it clear, though, that publishing is not a job or a career, it's a lifestyle. "Every time you read a magazine or a newspaper, or every time you watch TV or listen to the radio, there's a part of you, if you're a true editor, that says, 'Is there a book here?'" Beyond searching for the next Latino author, Landres also focuses on literate, commercial women's fiction, pop culture, self-help, New Age, spirituality, sexuality, women's studies, inspiration, relationships, movie tie-ins, and multicultural content in general (not just for Latinos). However, the proposals for all these kinds of books usually never get touched until after regular business hours and on weekends. "In the office, you're answering the phone, you're responding to e-mail, you're dealing with paperwork, and you work long hours," she says. "Then, you go home, and the work of actually reading things for consideration for publication begins."

Here Landres shares her opinion on only being a virgin once, *Charlie's Angels*, and the number one mistake most writers make.

How open are you to first-time writers?

They are my favorite kind. I think a lot of people assume that it's easier if you've already been published as if that gives you some Good Housekeeping Stamp of Approval. But the opposite is true, particularly for fiction writers. You are only a virgin once, meaning you have no reputation as a writer—good, bad, or otherwise. Once your first book is published, you have a reputation. You could be a best-selling author, or you could be out of print. Also, everyone who chooses a career in book publishing—editors, publicists, booksellers, etc.—does so because they love books, usually novels. And book lovers love to discover the next new talent. They love to share their discoveries, to tell everyone they know, "I've just read this amazing novel, you must read it too." You can't do that with a second, third, or fourth novel, and it's not quite the same with nonfiction.

I also prefer first-time authors because there's a greater chance we'll be able to properly publish them. It's one thing to be published; it's another to be happily published. I like to get a

---

KATHRYN S. BROGAN *is the editor of* Writer's Market *and* Writer's Market Online, *and co-editor of WritersMarket.com.*

hold of first-time authors and say, "This is how the system really works, and now that you know how the system works, you can make the system work for you." That's a much better situation than working with someone who's been unhappily published and who feels burnt. When the burnt authors come to me, they will have to unlearn the lessons from their past bad love affair, and learn that, yes, love can be good.

How do you prefer potential authors approach you?

I prefer writers submit complete, polished, professional proposals. I am very willing to look at a proposal from an unagented author but I insist they follow my submission guidelines. This is especially true for Latinos because there are very few agents who represent Latino writers. Currently there are only two Latino agents that I know of, and they've only recently become agents. If there's one thing I've learned from being a Latina editor at a major publishing house it's that we live in a segregated society. Agents who are not Latino, don't know Latinos, much less talented Latino writers. In order to connect with the Latino writing community, I have to function as an agent as well as an editor, because if I sit and wait for agents to deliver Latino writers to me, I'm going to be waiting a very long time.

What is your involvement with women writers?

I am a girly-girl, so I prefer female voices, particularly strong, smart, and sexy women because you don't always find those three qualities in one voice. So much of what I see from female writers is writing from the wound, or Lifetime Television-for-women type stories. There is a place for that, and it's certainly a legitimate aspect of the female experience, but to obsess about one's weight or a man is something I just don't find appealing. What I do find appealing is the sensibility I see in film and television, but not very much in books: that is strong, smart, and sexy women who literally and metaphorically kick butt—the *Charlie's Angels*, the *Crouching Tiger Hidden Dragon*'s, *Alias*, the Buffy's of the world. It's rare when the protagonist is a strong woman, and she's not killed off at the end. In fact, much of our storytelling seems to involve a dead woman. It seems almost every Mel Gibson film involves a dead wife, and nearly every episode of *Law and Order* or *CSI* begins with a dead woman. Dead women, particularly mothers, abound in fairy tales and Disney films, as well as in literature, like Dickens or Edgar Allen Poe.

As cheesy and fluffy as the film *Charlie's Angels* is—and it is—it makes a legitimate feminist statement. The women are strong, they have their own jobs, they drive cool cars, and, most importantly, they do not die at the end. In American film iconography, whoever owns and drives the cool car usually owns and drives the story. Invariably, the drivers tend to be men. The only movie previous to *Charlie's Angels* that I can recall featuring strong, smart, and sexy women who drove cars is *Thelma and Louise*—but they die at the end. This is not a feminist statement. It's rare to see a film or TV show where women aren't punished for being powerful. Similarly, it's a challenge to find manuscripts which feature powerful women. By powerful I mean a female character to whom things don't just happen, instead she makes things happen. She's responsible for the choices she makes, and though she may make mistakes, she learns from them and moves on.

What's the biggest mistake new writers make?

The number one mistake most writers make, even published ones, is thinking that their only job is to be the best writer they can, and that everything else—the boring marketing/publicity/sales part—is the publisher's job. Writers who think this way tend to be either unpublished or unhappily published because they are abdicating responsibility for their own success. It's the equivalent of creating a small business and turning it over to a stranger to run. It's very unlikely other people will care about your writing career as much as you do, so writers must master and manage the publishing process. Many writers don't understand this, which is why many writers are unhappy.

Ghostwriter Rusty Fischer Cashes in Under Other People's Bylines

BY JENNA GLATZER

Rusty Fischer has done it all—he's written books and articles; worked as an on-site and freelance editor for some of the biggest names in the publishing industry, including McGraw-Hill, Harcourt Brace School Publishers, and Simon & Schuster; had stories published in countless anthologies (such as the Chicken Soup series); and worked as a publicist for individual authors and publishers.

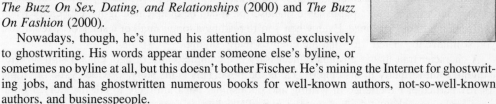

Some of Fischer's best-known books include *Creative Writing Made Easy* (McGraw-Hill) and several books in the popular Buzz On series of reference guides for Lebhar-Friedman Books, including *The Buzz On Sex, Dating, and Relationships* (2000) and *The Buzz On Fashion* (2000).

Nowadays, though, he's turned his attention almost exclusively to ghostwriting. His words appear under someone else's byline, or sometimes no byline at all, but this doesn't bother Fischer. He's mining the Internet for ghostwriting jobs, and has ghostwritten numerous books for well-known authors, not-so-well-known authors, and businesspeople.

How did you get your start as a ghostwriter?

You could call it a "happy accident." As a staff writer at a local book packager several years ago, I was always looking to pick up extra freelance writing work. Looking through the classified section one Sunday, I noticed an ad seeking a professional writer for a "history project." I called and set up an interview. In the interim, my job at the book packager was "downsized"—the series I had been hired to write wasn't selling as well as the publisher had hoped—and I suddenly found myself unemployed!

When I got to the interview, I found that it was for something called "ghostwriting." I had always assumed ghostwriters wrote celebrity bios, but that was about it. Instead, this was a prominent real estate professional who had always wanted to write a business book based on the teaching principles of Robert E. Lee. He wanted someone to help him research and write it. He asked me how long I thought it would take and what it might cost.

What did you tell him?

I had no idea how to answer either question, so I asked him how long he thought the book might be. He wanted to write about 200 pages, which was roughly the page count of the reference series I had been working on at the book packager. Generally, those took about four months to research, compile, write, rewrite, and fine-tune. So, I quoted him four months and, trying not to sound too hopeful, asked for the equivalent of my monthly salary at the time. Amazingly, he agreed!

JENNA GLATZER *is the editor-in-chief of Absolute Write (www.absolutewrite.com), a popular website for writers. She is also the editor of* Conquering Panic and Anxiety Disorders (*Hunter House,* 2000).

What kind of qualifications does a writer need to become a ghostwriter?

I have an English degree from a state university. No journalism degree or MA in creative writing. I have since found it is what you've done professionally that really matters in this business. It helps to already have published books. I had published about ten books under my own name by the time I got my first ghostwriting gig. That helped a lot!

How can you prove that you've done ghostwriting work?

That's the old catch-22: How can I prove to you I'm a ghostwriter when my name's not on anything? What I try to do with each new client is finagle my name on—or at least *in*—the book somewhere. Often all I get is a nod as "the editor" in the acknowledgements section. That's fine. The main goal is to get permission from the client to use the book in my portfolio. Most people don't care. Others want it stated clearly in the contract that I only show the book to "potential clients." I think ghostwriting is getting less stigmatized as the years go by, and more and more ghostwriters are getting their names on the book. Some clients even *want* my name on the book, if for no other reasons than mere cross-promotional purposes. I think that's smart—I'm much more inclined to promote a book carrying my byline than one without!

What skills do you need as a ghostwriter?

The ability to listen is paramount. That is the ghostwriter's first job because you are translating a nonwriter's words into a publishable manuscript. It can be quite challenging, especially when you're doing it long distance. Even when you're reading a long e-mail or a stack of faxed notes, you still have to "listen" to what the client is really saying.

A character trait that is absolutely necessary is a complete lack of ego. Once I sign on with a client, I am formally in his employ. He is the boss. This is his story. Obviously, he hired me for my particular experience in writing and publishing, but I am there to tell his story. I often warn my clients about "the honeymoon period" ending as soon as they get that first stack of pages from me. Talking about the concept, fleshing it out, chatting on the phone—that's all fine and good. But when I turn in my first pages, that's where the rubber hits the road. They have to be able to say, "This is not what I expected," or "Close, but no cigar," or even "Great! I loved it! Except for this one small part on page 16." At that point, you have to say to yourself, "OK. My instinct says this, but he wants to do that. Breathe deeply. So the line was beautiful and he wants to cut it. He's the boss. I'll use the line in my *own* book someday." It sounds simple, but it can be very challenging.

Do you have a certain number of rewrites built into your contract?

In general, my contract stipulates a rough draft, a rough final draft, and a final draft.

How do you determine what to charge?

I would love to say that I have a bottom-line flat fee, but the reality is that I charge on a case-by-case basis. There are some things I simply can't do, like write for "royalties only." But, barring that "walk away point," I take into account that I have to pay rent, cover the bills, and take my wife out to the occasional dinner. I listen very carefully when my clients are first talking about themselves, then I throw out a number I think they'll like. Generally, they take my first offer. (Which, as any good negotiator will tell you, means I bid too low.) But that's OK: I know what I need to make it through each month, and by now I'm a pretty good judge about how much work each project will take. It usually evens out in the wash or at least the client load. For instance, rarely do I have one "big" client who pays me enough to be my only client. Therefore, the less each client pays me, the more clients I have to have to make the business run. *(Editor's note: For more information on pay rates for ghostwriters, see How Much Should I Charge? on page 71.)*

What do you do to "sell yourself" to clients?

I carefully tailor a cover letter to each potential client's needs, and I'm not afraid to do "extra work." In addition to ghostwriting, I often act as a literary agent, publicist, self-publishing scout, etc. Every client comes to the table needing something different. I mention this because the field of ghostwriting is very competitive, and these additional services—finding a publisher, marketing the finished product, even finding a designer for the book cover—all help to supplement my income, which now comes solely from ghostwriting. In other words, potential ghostwriters should be prepared to do things other than merely "write."

How do you find ghostwriting jobs?

I generally find clients over the Internet. I have several trusted freelance writing websites bookmarked and check them on a daily basis. My favorites are www.absolutewrite.com, www.freelancewriting.com, www.writing-world.com, and www.writers-editors.com. Ten to 12 times a month someone will post a classified requesting a ghostwriter. I then send out a letter listing my qualifications and contact information, and offering published samples should they so desire.

How do you communicate with clients?

Once a contract is signed, I generally e-mail material back and forth each week. Other clients are more "old-fashioned," however, and prefer to talk by phone, or receive copies of my work by snail mail. Occasionally, I have a local client and we can meet on a regular basis to go over things. I am also fortunate in that I live in Orlando, Florida, so that many clients mix business with pleasure and ask to meet me at their hotel while they're on vacation! I try to accommodate the clients as much as possible—short of flying up to see them every weekend.

Six Authors Share Their Secrets on How They Make Time to Write

BY WILL ALLISON

Sooner or later, all successful writers learn that you can't go through life expecting to find time to write—you have to *make* time. This inevitably involves sacrifice, taking time away from the other important things in life: your family, your friends, your day job. Sometimes it also involves self-imposed exile, bargains with the devil, strange rituals, and other writer's tricks best not discussed in polite company. Here, six authors discuss how they get themselves to the keyboard and how they stay there long enough to finish the job.

ALDO ALVAREZ

Photo by Ric Cradick

Aldo Alvarez is the author of *Interesting Monsters: Fictions* (Graywolf Press), which was featured as one of the best short-story collections of the fall 2001 book season by *The Washington Post Book World* and nominated for the 2002 Violet Quill Award.

"It's easy to make writing a priority when I'm in the composition phase of a story. I can usually manage to complete a 1,000- to 5,000-word story in about two to four, four-hour stretches. But it takes me a month or three to think through a story before I write it. My problem, in other words, is making time to think about what I am writing.

"Writing the same kind of story over and over bores me. I need 'creative leisure time' to browse for a character, an idea, or a narrative strategy that will take my writing to a new place. I can't chart unexplored territory if I haven't found it, and, more often than not, I stumble into it by mistake. I need time to get lost in pursuit of a story. If I don't have time to wander, I don't produce at all.

"I spent most of my free time this summer researching a popular folkloric hero from Puerto Rican history. Naturally, I ended up straying off my research topic; I read about his particular time period and scanned material on folkloric figures of similar stripe in other sea-faring cultures. I wound up with a pile of research on folkloric heroes in general, real or imaginary. The funny thing is, I didn't find the character, and the narrative and metaphorical core of the story, until I read something that had no direct connection with my research. I read an interview with Billy Wilder where he discussed how he navigated subject-matter restrictions in Hollywood. And it all fell into place.

This is how I work best. My short stories smell like MFA McFiction if I don't think about them in a leisurely, playful manner before I sit down to write."

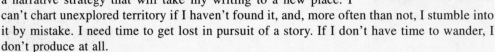

WILL ALLISON*'s (willalliso@aol.com) short stories have appeared in* American Short Fiction, Shenandoah, Kenyon Review, *and other magazines.*

DAN BARDEN

Dan Barden is the author of *John Wayne: A Novel* (Anchor Books, 1998). He has written personal essays for *GQ*, *Details*, *Indy Men's Magazine*, and *Organic Style*.

"For the last few years, I've turned my life over to a Timex Ironman Triathlon digital watch that I found in a drawer of the first apartment I shared with my wife. She's never getting it back. I set a daily schedule for myself, and I break up the schedule into chunks of time that I can manage between everything else I do with my life. For a while now, I've been working in terms of 90-minute chunks that I time on that lovely little watch. I also give myself half-hour chunks for freewriting and brainstorming ideas for articles and whatnot, and lately I have promised myself that no matter what I will spend at least two, 90-minute chunks on my novel every day. Most days it's three chunks. When I'm not teaching, it can be as many as six. Ninety minutes is a nice amount of time, though. It's deep enough to find my way back into any project, but short enough to insert into even the most harried days. On days when I have nothing to do but write, I take ten- to 15-minute breaks between each 90-minute chunk. I enjoy my little watch extravagantly. I think of the time it contains as a big gift that I give myself. The numbers are spinning right now."

JAMES BROWN

James Brown is the author of several novels and the memoir, *The Los Angeles Diaries* (Morrow/HarperCollins, 2003). He received the Nelson Algren Award in Short Fiction and a National Endowment for the Arts fellowship in creative writing.

"Most serious writers hold down two jobs: their writing and that other one, whatever it is, that pays the bills. When I'm writing I get up very early and spend three or four hours at it until it's time to go off to my other job. I do it in the morning instead of the evening because I'm fresh then, because I have more energy, and because my mind isn't cluttered yet with the day's problems. I used to think that it was talent that made a writer, but over the years I've come to believe that it has mostly to do with discipline and a certain urgency, a certain need to tell a story honestly and well."

JANET FITCH

Photo by Jerry Bauer

Janet Fitch is the author of the best-selling novel *White Oleander* (Little, Brown, 1999), which has been translated into 22 languages. Her short stories have appeared in such journals as *Room of One's Own*, *Black Warrior Review*, and *Rain City Review*; her nonfiction in magazines such as *Vogue*, the *Los Angeles Times Magazine*, *Speakeasy*, and *Writer's Digest*. She teaches fiction writing in Los Angeles.

"I'm selfish. Basically, that's it. I put myself, or rather my writing, ahead of my husband, my kid, my friends, family, neighbors, the school, worthy causes, and all of the rest. Because I learned long ago that the truth is, nobody gives a damn whether you write, only you. The most important words in a writer's vocabulary are these: 'Bugger off' (which can be phrased more nicely—'I'll be free in just a few minutes, dear'—but whose inviolability stands).

"Unfortunately, selfishness is regularly tested by a gregarious nature. After 20 years of writing at home, I rented a studio—just four walls and no phone. Now I go to work every morning, sit there until five, nothing to do except read, sleep, or write. It's unalloyed bliss."

JENNY OFFILL

Photo by Gasper Tringale

Jenny Offill is the author of the novel *Last Things* (Farrar, Straus and Giroux, 1999). Her stories and book reviews have appeared in *Story*, *Epoch*, *Boulevard*, and the *Washington Post*. She lives in Brooklyn.

"The way to make time for writing is to steal time from everything else. Don't answer the phone. Forget the mail. Let the houseplants die a lonely death. Call in sick to Thanksgiving and send Christmas cards in January. Do not fix the toaster. Do not fix the broken chair. Do not replace the batteries in anything. Live off the change that has fallen beneath the sofa cushions. Cultivate kind friends and patient landlords. Master the art of the charming refusal. Master the art of the early exit. And when you've finally alienated everyone you know, throw a big party and ply them with liquor and food. Play loud music and put tiny umbrellas in everyone's drinks. When they ask about the book, say, 'Soon, soon.' "

FREDERICK REIKEN

Photo by Nancy Crampton

Frederick Reiken is the author of two novels, *The Odd Sea* (Harcourt, 1998) and *The Lost Legends of New Jersey* (Harcourt, 2000). His short stories have appeared in *The New Yorker* and other publications. He teaches writing and literature at Emerson College and lives in western Massachusetts.

"I am someone who is easily distracted by things like e-mails, phone calls, lunch invitations, or whatever procrastination option is available. So, in order to make the time to write, I have to do two things. The first is to block out six-hour periods in my daily planner (the preferred block is 10 a.m. to 4 p.m., five days a week). Anything less than six hours for me is pointless, as I need time to settle in, focus, take long ruminative walks, etc., and with a shorter period I'm likely to just spend most of it worrying that my writing time will soon expire. I find it crucial to block out the time because so many people have difficulty seeing the internally motivated, solitary act of writing as 'work' and, therefore, feel no qualms about interrupting and/or suggesting alternate plans. Not only am I suggestible, I too sometimes have a hard time seeing the act of sitting around dreaming up strange situations for fictional people as 'work,' and so it helps to create at least the illusion of an externally motivated schedule. That way when someone invites me to lunch I can say, 'Sorry, I'm scheduled to write. A six-hour block from ten to four'—and if they don't believe me I can show them my daily planner.

"Many writers find it important to have some sort of little ritual that brings them into the so-called writing trance. In my case, this constitutes the second part of making time and consists of getting myself out of the house and driving down to the Westfield River. I have found that sitting by the river in my car offers very few procrastination incentives. What I usually do is read for a bit. Then, I'll read over some of what I wrote the day before, and after that I'll hopefully start writing (I write longhand). In winter the combination of the heat blasting and my hound dog Boz snoring in the passenger seat seems to create a sort of protected space. In spring and summer—when I don't need to blast the heat—the singing wood warblers and vireos and my snoring dog suffice. The length of time I stay by the river varies. I'll usually stay until I've gotten focused on something. Then I'll race back home and continue working at my desk. If I don't go through this ritual, there's a good chance I'll never get around to writing (or at least waste half of my blocked-out time returning e-mails). If I do go through with it, there's about an 80-percent chance I'll get something done. When I'm not at home (i.e., with a river five minutes away), taking a walk can serve the same anti-procrastination/focusing purpose. I take a lot of walks, even on days I've sat by the river. To get even more complicated, I'll sometimes take a walk *along* the river."

Sex Writer Katy Terrega Says Business is a Pleasure

BY JENNA GLATZER

If you met Katy Terrega, you'd see a typical wife and mother. But as her family knows, she makes her living as a sex writer. "My son (12) thinks that what I write about is the grossest thing in the world; my daughter (13) takes a more pragmatic view," she says. "My husband is very supportive."

Besides her family, very few other people know Terrega's writing has filled the pages of *Score*, *Gallery*, *Swank*, *Penthouse Variations*, *Hustler Fantasies*, *Nugget*, *Playgirl*, "and many others with names too gross to print." Working from a little corner in her living room, Terrega writes while her kids are at school. She has more than 300 sex-writing credits, and her work includes a sex-advice column for the magazine *Naughty Neighbors*, and a column about sex writing for AbsoluteWrite.com.

Terrega is also the author of the book *It's A Dirty Job . . . Writing Porn for Fun and Profit* (Booklocker.com) and runs a free newsletter for sex writers (www.KatyTerrega.com/newsletter.html) with more than a thousand subscribers, "many of whom have gone on to publishing success."

How did you become a sex writer?

I had lots of hurdles to overcome in my quest to become a published writer, not the least of which was the ingrained belief that I *couldn't* write. That negative thinking was reinforced over the years as I sent out personal essays to the big markets, only to be resoundingly rejected. I enjoyed reading erotica, but it didn't occur to me to write it, until I happened to read a porn story in a national magazine. It was like an epiphany—I realized, hey, I can do better than this! It occurred to me that I'd had a lot of experience (as a reader) with the genre over the years and that I'd kind of absorbed the format by osmosis.

How did you make your first sale?

I bought a *Writer's Market* and found likely markets, then I bought and devoured several magazines. One of the magazines, *Naughty Neighbors*, seemed to be the likeliest candidate, so I tailored a story to them. I was very surprised when I received an acceptance letter, and soon another.

I decided I could make enough money by writing several stories a month. Of course, reality soon set in; unfortunately, I hadn't factored in all of the variables, like the fact that you don't get accepted every time. Plus, I had no way of knowing then that a lot of markets are less than professional about their dealings with writers: About half of my early submissions went unacknowledged. It took me several years to sell regularly and several more to make decent money. But I made it a point early on to be as professional as possible both in my writing and in my dealings with editors.

JENNA GLATZER *is the author of several books, including* Outwitting Writer's Block *(Lyons Press, 2003) and* Words You Thought You Knew *(Adams Media, 2003). She is also the editor-in-chief of Absolute Write (www.absolutewrite.com). Get a free e-book when you subscribe.*

How do you increase your chances of acceptance?

Being professional is the surest way to increase your chances of success. Writing for money is a job, and has to be approached that way, whether you're writing about sex or mutual funds. Sex writing is not about the writer's personal fantasies (although tapping into those can certainly be helpful); it's about doing your job. That means being courteous in your dealings with editors, and it means learning your markets and your craft (researching genres and subniches) and figuring out how best to present yourself.

Developing strong characters can also increase your sales potential. Let's face it: Sex writing is not always terribly plot driven, and well-written, personable characters can make a world of difference. Your audience wants to identify with these people, and the more you can draw them into your world, the better. I really get into my characters; I enjoy becoming them. It's almost like acting for me.

I understand that most erotic stories have to be written on speculation.

It's an unfortunate part of this genre, at least at first. Since fiction is often the easiest way to break into this market, you must put out a lot of unsolicited stories. But you increase your sales odds by knowing exactly what each market wants—how many words, what perspective, what slant, etc., before you submit.

Do most sex writers only write particular types of stories?

The more subgenres you can write about, the more sales you can make. As a matter of fact, you're not going to make very much money if you stick to one category of sex writing—the genres are just too limited. But diversifying is not about your own personal experience; it's mostly about research. I'm not a gay man or an 18-year-old girl, but I write a lot of stories from those perspectives.

Do you advise writing a story and then picking a market, or do you write each story based on a market's guidelines?

You have to pick your market first if you want to sell; there really is no way around that. Sex writing, even more so than other types of writing, is so specific. Word length, category, slant, tone, attitude, level of explicitness, readership, all those factors vary wildly from one market to another. A really fantastic story won't stand a chance if it doesn't fit the editor's exact specs, and you're wasting time if you write before you research.

Is there any formula for writing sex stories?

Sometimes. A "standard" porn story is around 3,000 words, and most markets like the sex to start within the first 1,000 words, although earlier is better. And a lot of markets like two sex scenes per full-length story. But those are just basics. Markets are fairly flexible as long as you stay within their style guidelines. For example, you could start a 2,500-word story with 750 words of sex, then segue into 500 words of background, and then finish with a long sex scene at the end. Letters often follow certain formats; the sex usually starts in the second paragraph, for example.

Aside from erotic stories, what other opportunities exist for sex writers?

Letters, picture copy, nonfiction articles, and even columns are all often open to freelancers.

Do most magazines pay for the erotic letters that are supposedly true confessions from readers?

I get asked that question a lot when people find out what I do for a living, and nonwriters are often very disappointed to find out that most published erotic letters are written by professionals.

(As is the copy beside the photographs.) One notable exception is *Penthouse Variations*: All of the letters are reader generated. But yes, the majority of the "letter to the editor" market is either staff or freelance written.

Letters are great for beginners, partly because they're shorter and usually have a more easily understood format. They don't always pay well, but they're a good way to get your foot in the door. A lot of editors will consider letter submissions from an unknown writer before they'll consider a full-length story. Picture copy—where you write a storyline to photos—is fun, and similar to letters, but you generally have to be on good terms with an editor to get those assignments.

Must the letters be true?

No. As a matter of fact, very little of what's written in this genre is true.

You write under a pen name. Do editors know your real name?

Most of the editors I deal with know my real name. But for various reasons, one of which is privacy, I sometimes find it easier to just use my pen name. It's possible to use a pen name exclusively.

Can you get paid under your pen name?

Yes. I got a state business license, which costs about $50, and I used my pseudonym as a DBA, which stands for "Doing Business As." That means that my pseudonym is considered a business name. Using that documentation, I opened a checking account under the pen name, and checks can legally be made out to either name.

Do you primarily write fiction?

When I first started, I only wrote fiction; mostly full-length stories. An editor who I sold to often asked if I'd be willing to try some nonfiction. Now nonfiction accounts for well over half of my writing income.

The Business of Writing

Minding the Details

Writers who have been successful in getting their work published know that publishing requires two different mind-sets. The first is the actual act of writing the manuscript. The second is the business of writing—the marketing and selling of the manuscript. This shift in perspective is necessary if you want to become a successful career writer. That said, you need to keep the business side of writing in mind as you continually develop your writing.

Each of the following sections and accompanying sidebars discusses a writing business topic that affects anyone selling a manuscript. Our treatment of the business topics that follow is necessarily limited, so look for short blocks of information and resources throughout this section to help you further research the content mentioned.

CONTRACTS AND AGREEMENTS

If you've been freelancing, you know that contracts and agreements vary from publisher to publisher. Very rarely will you find two contracts that are exactly the same. Some magazine editors work only by verbal agreement, as do many agents; others have elaborate documents you must sign in duplicate and return to the editor before you even begin the assignment. It is essential that you consider all of the elements involved in a contract, whether verbal or written, and know what you stand to gain and lose by agreeing to the contract. Maybe you want to repurpose the article and resell it to a market that is different from the first publication to which you sold the article. If that's the case, then you need to know what rights you want to sell.

In contract negotiations, the writer is usually interested in licensing the work for a particular use, but limiting the publisher's ability to make other uses of the work in the future. It's in the publisher's best interest, however, to secure as many rights as possible, both now and later on. Those are the basic positions of both parties. The negotiation is a process of compromise on questions relating to those basic points—and the amount of compensation to be given the writer for his work. If at any time you are unsure about any portion of the contract, it is best to consult a lawyer who specializes in media law and contract negotiation.

A contract is rarely a take-it-or-leave-it proposition. If an editor tells you that his company

For More Information

CONTRACTS AND CONTRACT NEGOTIATION

- **The Authors Guild** (www.authorsguild.org), 31 E. 28th St., 10th Floor, New York NY 10016-7923. (212)563-5904. E-mail: staff@authorsguild.org.
- **The National Writers Union** (www.nwu.org), 113 University Place, 6th Floor, New York NY 10003. (212)254-0279. E-mail: nwu@wu.org.

will allow no changes to the contract, you will then have to decide how important the assignment is to you. However, most editors are open to negotiations, so you need to learn how to compromise on points that don't matter to you, and stand your ground on those that do matter.

RIGHTS AND THE WRITER

A creative work can be used in many different ways. As the author of the work, you hold all rights to the work in question. When you agree to have your work published, you are granting a publisher the right to use your work in any number of ways. Whether that right is to publish the manuscript for the first time in a publication or to publish it as many times and in many different ways as a publisher wishes is up to you—it all depends on the agreed upon terms. As a general rule, the more rights you license away, the less control you have over your work and the money you're paid. You should strive to keep as many rights to your work as you can.

Writers and editors sometimes define rights in a number of different ways. Below you will find a classification of terms as they relate to rights.

- **First Serial Rights**—Rights that the writer offers a newspaper or magazine to publish the manuscript for the first time in any periodical. All other rights remain with the writer. Sometimes the qualifier "North American" is added to these rights to specify a geographical limitation to the license.

  When content is excerpted from a book scheduled to be published, and it appears in a magazine or newspaper prior to book publication, this is also called first serial rights.
- **One-Time Rights**—Nonexclusive rights (rights that can be licensed to more than one market) purchased by a periodical to publish the work once (also known as simultaneous rights). That is, there is nothing to stop the author from selling the work to other publications at the same time.
- **Second Serial (Reprint) Rights**—Nonexclusive rights given to a newspaper or magazine to publish a manuscript after it has already appeared in another newspaper or magazine.
- **All Rights**—This is exactly what it sounds like. All rights mean that an author is selling every right they have to a work. If you license all rights to your work, you forfeit the right to ever use the work again. If you think you may want to use the article again, you should avoid submitting to such markets or refuse payment and withdraw your material.
- **Electronic Rights**—Rights that cover a broad range of electronic media, from online magazines and databases to CD-ROM magazine anthologies and interactive games. The contract should specify if—and which—electronic rights are included. The presumption is that unspecified rights remain with the writer.
- **Subsidiary Rights**—Rights, other than book publication rights, that should be covered in a book contract. These may include various serial rights; movie, TV, audiotape, and other electronic rights; translation rights, etc. The book contract should specify who controls the rights (author or publisher) and what percentage of sales from the licensing of these rights goes to the author.
- **Dramatic, TV, and Motion Picture Rights**—Rights for use of material on the stage, in TV, or in the movies. Often a one-year option to buy such rights is offered (generally for 10 percent of the total price). The party interested in the rights then tries to sell the idea to other people—actors, directors, studios, or TV networks. Some properties are optioned numerous times, but most fail to become full productions. In those cases, the writer can sell the rights again and again.

Sometimes editors don't take the time to specify the rights they are buying. If you sense that an editor is interested in getting stories, but doesn't seem to know what his and the writer's responsibilities are, be wary. In such a case, you'll want to explain what rights you're offering (preferably one-time or first serial rights only) and that you expect additional payment for subsequent use of your work.

The Copyright Law that went into effect January 1, 1978, states that writers are primarily selling one-time rights to their work unless they—and the publisher—agree otherwise in writing. Book rights are covered fully by contract between the writer and the book publisher.

SELLING SUBSIDIARY RIGHTS

The primary right in book publishing is the right to publish the book itself. All other rights (movie rights, audio rights, book club rights, etc.) are considered secondary, or subsidiary, to the right to print publication. In contract negotiations, authors and their agents traditionally try to avoid granting the publisher subsidiary rights that they feel comfortable marketing themselves. Publishers, on the other hand, want to obtain as many of the subsidiary rights as they can.

Larger agencies have experience selling subsidiary rights, and many authors represented by such agents prefer to retain those rights and let their agents do the selling. On the other hand, book publishers have subsidiary rights departments whose sole job is to exploit the subsidiary rights the publisher was able to retain during the contract negotiation.

The marketing of electronic rights can be tricky. With the proliferation of electronic and multimedia formats, publishers, agents, and authors are going to great lengths to make sure contracts specify exactly which electronic rights are being conveyed (or retained). Compensation for these rights is a major source of conflict because many book publishers seek control of them, and many magazines routinely include electronic rights in the purchase of all rights, often with no additional payment.

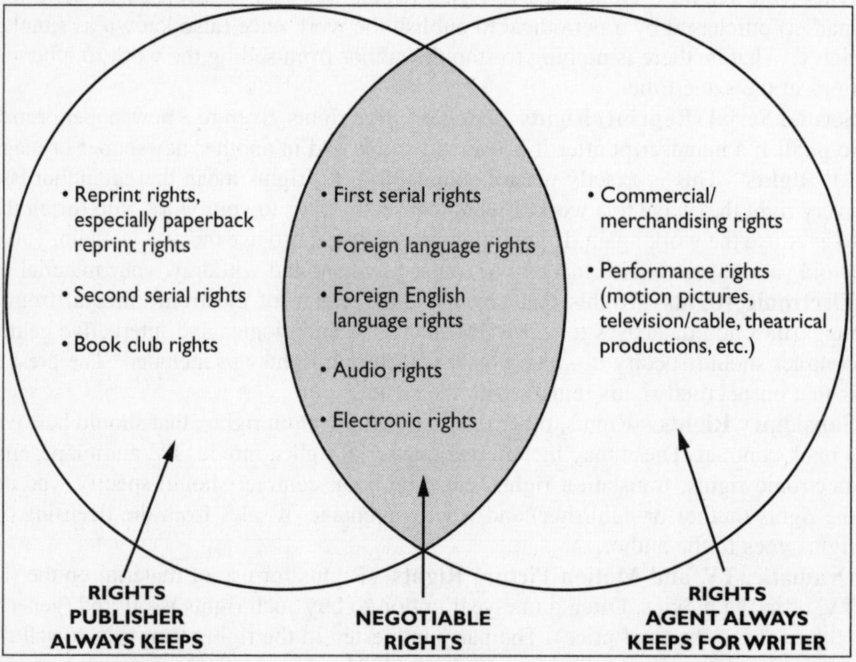

Some subsidiary rights are always granted to the publisher. Some should always be retained by the author. The remainder are negotiable, and require knowledgeable advice from a literary agent or attorney in deciding whether it is more advantageous to grant the rights to the publisher or to reserve them.

COPYRIGHT

Copyright law exists to protect creators of original works. Copyright law is designed to encourage the production of creative works by ensuring that artists and writers hold the rights by which they can profit from their hard work.

The moment you finish a piece of writing—or in fact, the second you begin to pen the manuscript—the law recognizes that only you can decide how the work is used. Copyright protects your writing, recognizes you (its sole creator) as its owner, and grants you all the rights and benefits that accompany ownership. With very few exceptions, anything you write today will enjoy copyright protection for your lifetime, plus 70 years. Copyright protects "original works of authorship" that are fixed in a tangible form of expression. *Copyright law cannot protect titles, ideas, and facts.*

Some writers are under the mistaken impression that a registered copyright with the Library of Congress Copyright Office is necessary to protect their work, and that their work is not protected until they "receive" their copyright paperwork from the government. *This is not true.* You don't have to register your work with the Copyright Office for it to be protected. Registration for your work does, however, offer some additional protection (specifically, the possibility of recovering punitive damages in an infringement suit) as well as legal proof of the date of copyright.

Most magazines are registered with the Copyright Office as single collective entities themselves; that is, the individual works that make up the magazine are *not* copyrighted individually in the names of the authors. You'll need to register your article yourself if you wish to have the additional protection of copyright (your name, the year of first publication, and the copyright symbol ©) appended to any published version of your work. You may use the copyright notice regardless of whether your work has been registered with the Copyright Office.

One thing you need to pay particular attention to is work-for-hire arrangements. If you sign a work-for-hire agreement, you are agreeing that your writing will be done as a work for hire, you will not control the copyright of the completed work—the person or organization who hired you will be the copyright owner. These agreements and transfers of exclusive rights must appear in writing to be legal. However, it's a good idea to get every publishing agreement you negotiate in writing before the sale.

For More Information

COPYRIGHT

- To learn more about general copyright information, filling out copyright forms, and links to other websites related to copyright issues, contact the Copyright Office (www.copyright.gov), Library of Congress, 101 Independence Ave. SE, Washington DC 20559-6000. (202)707-3000.
- If you want to register your work with the U.S. Copyright Office you need to fill out an application form (Form TX) which is available by calling (202)707-9100 or by downloading from www.copyright.gov/forms. Send the completed form, a nonreturnable copy of the work in question, and a check for $30 to the Library of Congress, Copyright Office, Register of Copyrights, 101 Independence Ave. SE, Washington DC 20559-6000.

FINANCES AND TAXES

You will find that as your writing business expands, so will your need to keep track of writing-related expenses and incomes. Keeping a close eye on these details will prove very helpful when it comes time to report your income to the IRS. It will also help you pay as little tax as possible and keep you aware of the state of your freelance writing as a business. It's essential that you maintain your writing business as any other business. This means that you need to set up a detailed tracking and organizing system to log all expenses and income. Without such a system, your writing as a business will eventually fold. If you dislike handling finance-related tasks, you can always hire a professional to oversee these duties for you. However, even if you do hire a professional, you still need to keep all original records.

Important Tax Information

While we cannot offer you tax advice or interpretations, we can suggest several sources for the most current information.

- Check the IRS website (www.irs.gov).
- Call your local IRS office.
- Obtain the basic IRS publications by phone or by mail; most are available at libraries and some post offices.

The following tips will help you keep track of the finance-related tasks associated with your freelance business.

- Keep accurate records.
- Separate your writing income and expenses from your personal income and expenses.
- Maintain a separate bank account and credit card for business-related expenses.
- Record every transaction (expenses and earnings) related to your writing.
- Begin keeping records when you make your first writing-related purchase.
- Establish a working, detailed system of tracking expenses and income. Include the date; the source of income (or the vendor of your purchase); a description of what was sold or bought; how the payment was rendered (cash, check, credit card); and the amount of the transaction.
- Keep all check stubs and receipts (cash purchases and credit cards).
- Set up a record-keeping system, such as a file folder system, to store all receipts.

Writing for Trade and Business Publications

BY ROB SPIEGEL

Pity the poor trade editor who never receives queries. When her staff is cut to trim expenses, she turns to freelancers to fill the pages. But what freelancers will she use? Unlike her counterparts at consumer publications, she doesn't have a stack of queries that have been reviewed carefully by an assistant. She doesn't have an assistant. She's not particularly interested in queries. She already knows what stories need to be covered. But she certainly needs a competent group of professional freelance journalists to write gripping stories for next week's issue, and for the week after and the week after that.

When I began freelancing, I scoured the newsstands for potential markets. I was aware that I was missing tons of potential magazines, since trade publications seldom appear on magazine racks, but the notion of selling to a trade magazine was intimidating. What kind of story would I pitch to the editor of *Electronic Business* magazine? Even if I perused recent articles on the website, the publication's future needs are still a mystery.

When I finally decided to turn my attention to trade publishers, I quickly learned you don't have to create and pitch stories to the trades. And surprisingly, you don't have to know much about the particular subject in order to cover the assignment. Most trade editors willingly give you the names of potential sources. From there, you simply do your journalistic best: follow the story; ask sources for more sources; check in with the editor if you're getting lost; and produce an article that builds your sources' comments into a credible story.

Take a quick look at the number of trade publications listed here in *Writer's Market (Editor's note: Listings for Trade, Technical & Professional Journals begin on page 768)*. The market is robust, and even in hard times these publications need freelancers. Yet they receive few queries or inquiries from freelancers. Take *Sound & Video Contractor*. This monthly magazine is 60 percent freelance written. Topics in a typical issue cover techniques for pulling cable, the use of subwoofers, and the unique challenges of stage rigging. It certainly helps if you know something about the business of sound and video contracting, but it isn't critical if you're willing to learn and you have some understanding of how trade publications develop stories.

The market: Writers wanted

The competition you're up against with trade and business publications tends to be educated, well-trained, experienced journalists. But don't fear: Though the competition is fierce in credentials, it is weak in numbers compared with consumer magazines. Since trade editors don't receive mailbags full of queries, they are much less likely to casually dismiss inquires from freelancers seeking work. Their rejections are typically individual and polite. If you're turned down, you can be assured that your cover letter, writing samples, and résumé were reviewed carefully.

If you have a degree in English, journalism, or communication, and if you also have a track record of published articles, especially in trade or business publications, your inquiry will be taken seriously. You will still get your share of rejections, since freelance needs come and go,

---

ROB SPIEGEL *is senior editor at* Electronic News. *He also has freelanced extensively with a wide range of business and trade publishers over his 25-year writing career.*

but at least you won't be pushed away without consideration. And more likely than not, if you have the educational background and published track record, the editor saying no to your inquiry will suggest you check back at a later date. With hundreds of trade and business titles on the market, you can take a fair amount of rejection and still find plenty of lucrative work.

Compensation: Good pay

When I started freelancing in the late 1970s, I was warned by other freelancers that trade publications didn't pay well. They were easier to break into, but their rates were slight compared with the well-known, mass-market consumer publications. That has changed in the past decade. A small handful of the largest consumer magazines still pay more than most trade publications, but the average consumer publication no longer pays significantly more than trade publications. Plus, trade publishers seek a small group of freelancers who write for most issues, which is rare among consumer magazines. When you freelance for consumer magazines, you're always seeking new markets. When you freelance with the trades, you can fill all your time with a small group of client publications.

Most freelancers who make a living selling to consumer magazines sell to the largest markets, which include the top women's titles, *Reader's Digest*, *Rolling Stone*, and a few others. Yet trade reporters can make a healthy living freelancing for a handful of publications with unknown titles such as *Food Manufacturing*, *Global Design News*, or *Furniture Today*. You won't be able to tell your mom to go out and pick up the new issue with your cover story, but you also won't have to hit her up for a loan.

Distinction: Weeklies vs. monthlies

What is the difference between trade *papers* (weeklies) and trade *magazines* (monthlies)? These two types of publications vary greatly in both style and content. Most weeklies view themselves as trade papers, which usually means they are very news-oriented and typically follow the Associated Press style. In addition to news, they present sections where editors report in industry beats. Weeklies tend to seek journalists who have logged time in the trenches of daily newspapers. Attributions at weeklies follow the news style of "she said," while most monthlies tend to write in a more feature-oriented presentation, using the less newsy "he says."

Trade monthlies put a smaller emphasis on news, since breaking news can't be covered effectively on a monthly basis. Instead, monthlies present highly researched features that delve into long-term trends. The stories in monthlies go into much greater depth and include more sources and background research. A writer at a monthly may spend six weeks on an article, while the reporter at a weekly rarely spends more than two or three days on a story. Both are good bets for freelancing. With a weekly, you'll get small assignments due in a week. At a monthly you'll get six weeks to write a much longer article.

Business publications differ greatly from trade publications. Business magazines or papers such as the *Wall Street Journal*, *Business Week*, and *Fortune* use plenty of freelancers, but they tend to behave more like consumer publications than trade titles. They are generally more responsive to the query approach, and the writing style they present is more like a newsmagazine than a trade paper. Even though the audience is made up of business professionals, they come from a wide range of industries, so the writing style resembles that of a well-written consumer publication.

The readership for a trade publication is very specific. Most trade magazines have controlled circulation, which means the publisher sends the issues at no charge to all of the professionals it can identify with specific positions in a particular industry. This makes for an inside audience. Business publications behave more like consumer titles in their circulation makeup. They are sold by subscription to anyone with the interest and subscription fee, which usually makes for a general audience.

Internet: Web news and e-mail newsletters

The Internet has presented new opportunities for trade and business freelancers. These publications have discovered that many of their readers want a daily dose of breaking news from their industry, and they can't wait for print. Thus, most publications send out a daily e-mail of short items that are posted to the website as they're written. I recently spent a year writing two daily web stories for an Internet-based news service that tracked developments in Internet-based business. I had a 9 a.m. deadline and a 3 p.m. deadline each weekday. The stories had to be 250-350 words. I had to come up with the story ideas by plowing through hundreds of press releases that began hitting the wire around 5 a.m.

For other trades, I've written longer stories, about 800-900 words for weekly e-mail newsletters that carried more in-depth stories. One of the style features common to trade Web stories is the inclusion of hyperlinks that allow the reader to click through to the website of any company mentioned in the story. Freelancers don't typically need to know html language to deliver these stories. Typically, the publication asks for freelancers to include the company's website next to the first mention of the company. Then the Web editor creates the hyperlink.

One of the great advantages of writing Web stories for a freelance client is that it becomes habit forming. Trade editors don't want to go to the trouble of making assignments on a daily basis. They prefer to work with reliable freelancers who have demonstrated the ability and dependability to take on the task of delivering reliable Web assignments. If you pass a few initial trials, there is a good chance you'll get assigned to writing a handful of Web stories each week. For some freelancers, the regularity of the work is welcome. For those who find daily work too confining, trade editors are often happy to save feature assignments for those who prefer working on in-depth stories.

Ideas: Editors make assignments

One of the monumental differences between trade and consumer titles is that you don't have to send queries to trade editors. Even on short-notice Web stories, trade editors usually assign story ideas. They typically work from editorial calendars that have been planned months ahead of time. You can go to the publication's website and peruse the editorial calendar. Since the editors have to cover particular subjects that are tied to advertising sales strategies, they are not inclined to welcome story ideas presented by freelancers. Though trade publications follow an editorial calendar that is designed to attract specific groups of advertisers, the advertising community does not dictate the treatment of those subjects. Most trade publishers have a very strong division between editorial and advertising.

In addition to working from editorial calendars, trade publishers also follow specific industry beats, covering product announcements, mergers, layoffs, and other business news. Editors will often scour the wires for relevant business stories, then assign them to freelancers tagged to cover a particular type of company. Since it isn't practical for a freelancer to anticipate this type of story, it will come directly as an assignment from the editor. In an environment of editorial calendars and breaking news, the practice of pitching a story via query is simply not practical.

Clients: Develop relationships

Don't approach a trade publication with the idea of writing a one-off story, unless the experience is unpleasant. At consumer magazines, it's common for freelancers to write only occasionally. At trade publishers, editors seek regular contributors. They like to create a small core of very reliable freelancers who can deliver stories on a regular basis, often for every issue. These regular freelancers are sometimes listed on the publication's masthead as contributing editors, even including contact information. Many of these freelance contributors work year-in and year-out for the same publications.

It's not unusual for these regular contributors to earn the equivalent of a full-time salary from just one publication. An editor I know hired one of his long-time freelancers at a lower rate than the freelancer earned in an average year. The freelancer wanted to take advantage of the company's generous retirement contributions as well as the health benefit package that makes a salaried position attractive even though the monthly paychecks were lower than the average freelance payments.

Most successful freelancers work with a small collection of editors who offer regular work. Trade publications are particularly well-suited clients for full-time freelancers since trade editors value regular contributions. Professional freelancers tend to work much like accountants or attorneys. Their first goal is to create enough work to fill the workweek, then they concentrate on replacing their weaker clients (low pay or slow pay) with stronger ones (high pay and repeat work).

The final advantage of working with a small number of editors is that you learn the subject matter well enough to establish sources you can call on again and again. Working with a new publication is very inefficient, since you have to dig deep to find credible sources, and those sources may not be responsive, since they don't know you and have no reason to trust you. If you work repeatedly for a publication, you get to know your sources, and once you gain their trust, their help can be immeasurable in finding the real story behind the story you originally intended to write.

Credentials: What it takes

Trade editors like their writers to have a degree in journalism, English, or communication. They like it even better if you have additional degrees. Publications that rely heavily on financial analysis prefer writers who have a master's degree in business administration. Trades that cover biotech, genome development, or pharmaceuticals look for writers with life science degrees. The closer the degree is to the magazine's subject, the better. If you're a pharmacist with a journalism degree, you're a shoe-in for a publication like *Drug Discovery and Development*. At the biweekly, *Design News*, which targets the engineers who design products and technology, the editor-in-chief looks for journalists with an engineering degree.

Though it may seem peculiar for someone with a technical degree to pursue journalism, there are professionals in many fields who like to research and write about the developments in their profession or industry. Though editors prefer double degrees for specialized reporting, they will always choose writing abilities over technical education. They are not interested in engineers who are not trained and adept at reporting. If your writing samples display sharp, incisive reporting, you can often lure an editor away from a preference for a technical degree. As a former *Wall Street Journal* executive editor, Frederick Taylor, once said, "It's easier to make a reporter into an economist than an economist into a reporter."

Trade editors who seek journalists with advanced degrees are usually willing to pay for the specialized knowledge. A publication that covers the construction industry, fashion market, or other industries that don't require writers to have specialized education, typically pay from 50¢ to 80¢ per word. Those covering design engineering or the life sciences tend to pay 80¢ to $1.25 per word.

Contact: No gatekeepers here

One of the challenges of breaking into consumer magazines is getting through the gatekeepers, those editorial assistants whose job it is to keep their editor bosses free from the calls, e-mails, and stacks of mail flooding in from prospective freelancers. Not so with trade editors. They don't have gatekeepers because they don't need to filter a flood of queries. They check their own e-mail, and they generally respond personally to each one. With postal mail, your chances of receiving a personal response are not as great as your chances by e-mail. Don't bother with phone calls. Unsolicited phone calls are viewed as intrusive.

Trade editors prefer to communicate by e-mail, which is great news for freelancers, since e-mail responses come within a few quick days, while postal mail responses take two or three weeks. When approaching an editor with questions about freelance opportunities, include your résumé and writing samples in the e-mail itself. Attachments of résumés and sample writings will go unopened, since most trade publishers discourage their editors from opening unsolicited attachments due to the risk of viruses.

Links to published and Web-posted articles is the preferred way to show sample writing. If this is not possible, paste short samples following your résumé and paste it in the e-mail itself. If your article is longer than 200 or 300 words, just include the first few paragraphs, and explain that it has been trimmed. Above each sample indicate the publication and date the article ran. Three samples is optimum, and the more recent the better. Try to include a variety of styles such as news, feature, and column. If possible, match the subject of your samples with the subject of the publication you're addressing.

Make sure you reach the right editor. Most websites list e-mail addresses for editorial staff members, though you may have to poke around to find the staff list. If the publication has a small group of ten or fewer editors, send your e-mail to the top editor. The lead editor's title varies from editor-in-chief to editorial director or simply editor. It will always be the top editorial name on the masthead. If the publication has a larger staff, send your package to the second-ranked editor, with a title such as managing editor or executive editor.

Potential: You may get a job offer

Freelancing for trade magazines can get to be a habit. Some freelancers work with the same group of magazines for many years. When an editorial position comes open at a trade publisher, the editors will often look to their freelance staff for potential employees. One of the great allures to freelancing is the freedom to work from your home during the hours you choose. Many trade publishers have embraced the virtual office and have become quite comfortable allowing staff editors to work from home, so employee editors at trade publications can now have it both ways, living the freedom of a freelancer while receiving regular paychecks, health benefits, vacations, sick leave, and a retirement plan.

I spent a few years on the editorial staff of a very large trade publisher. I worked in Albuquerque while my boss worked in Boston. Her boss worked in San Jose and his boss worked in Chicago. Other team members worked in San Francisco, Los Angeles, and Greensboro, North Carolina. The art director worked in New York. I generally have earned more income freelancing with trade publishers than working on staff, but holding a staff position for a few years bolsters your résumé, making freelancing easier and more lucrative when you cut the strings and go back to the freedom of the self-employed.

Strategies for Negotiating Electronic Rights and Rates

BY ANTHONY TEDESCO

Welcome to the most potentially profitable time for writers in history. Nearly every traditional media venue, whether rooted in print or radio or television, has also launched a companion online magazine. Many of those venues not only pay for online use of your work, they also purchase original material geared specifically for the Internet medium. Add those markets to the throng of new Internet-only magazines, custom corporate online publications, and e-mail newsletters, and you can begin to see the potential for online income. Like many of my fellow writers, I started writing for online markets as an explorative foray, but soon found that what I thought might be a novel supplement to my print income soon surpassed my print income altogether.

My freelancer's e-boon, however, hasn't been solely rooted in churning out more articles for more markets. I've also been selling more electronic uses of the same articles, and securing more money for each of those sales. With help from the National Writers Union (NWU), the American Society of Journalists and Authors (ASJA), and the tight-knit community of writers pioneering this field, I've learned to navigate the legally binding hieroglyphics of electronic rights clauses and negotiate top online rights and rates. You can too. To learn how to counter the most-repeated contract cyberfables, see ASJA's "E-Wrongs About E-Rights" on page 32. For a downloadable text file of the NWU's "Standard Journalism Contract for Online Markets," go to www.nwu.org/journ/jsjcweb.txt. Writers worldwide are hoping you do. The most potentially profitable time in history is also the most precarious time. Future standards in this new medium are being negotiated by writers today. Better-informed negotiators are better for all of us.

Print basics apply

Don't go shredding your notes from print negotiations. Many of those basic skills and principles still apply to electronic rights and rates. Always read your contract carefully; don't lose your professionalism by getting personal or taking things personally. Before you start negotiating, know what you want, know what you're willing to accept, and know what you're willing to walk away from. Do your market research, figure out what you deserve for your article, and then ask for what you deserve. If necessary, politely insist on what you deserve, and explain why you deserve it. Build trust, foster good relationships. Leave bad ones.

E-clauses in print contracts

You can start negotiating money for electronic uses before you've even sold a piece to an electronic market. Most print contracts include clauses for future electronic uses and sales, usually within two categories.

ANTHONY TEDESCO *(anthony@marketsforwriters.com) is co-author of* 2004 Online Markets for Writers: How and Where to Make Money by Selling Your Writing on the Internet *(MarketsForWriters.com Press), and co-author of* Top 250 Free Resources for Writers*, which is available free of charge at Top250FreeResourcesForWriters.org. He's also publisher of MarketsForWriters.com and co-founder of the Student Publishing Program (www.225pm.org).*

1. **Database sales.** Whether the database is online or on CD-ROM or Lexis-Nexis-style, print publications usually offer writers a not-so-glorious 25 percent of any fees they receive from these sales. The ASJA reports that 50/50 is becoming the standard split, similar to the standard 50/50 split of subsidiary rights for print books and periodicals, but you need to decide on your own standard, based mostly on how much you could get elsewhere. Personally, I often ask for a 50/50 split, but I rarely push for it. The concession is almost built-in for me, a peace offering made mostly because, as of this minute in my career, these sales aren't my specialty.
2. **Online publication sales.** AKA, my specialty. I rarely—like, two steps from never—accept the ubiquitous, boilerplate clause of print contracts, which offers 25 percent of the print fee for online use. NWU recommends that writers be compensated 100 percent of the print fee for online use because "licensing to a World Wide Web site is similar to first print rights in different geographic regions, i.e., first U.K., first French." I agree. But I also justify the 100 percent by humbly explaining that I have online markets that will pay me that equivalent.

Actually, I've found this immediate, tangible case of "what I could get elsewhere" to be one of my most effective bargaining chips. "What writers should be getting" is an important cause to advocate toward as an industry, but it often falls on deaf editorial ears. Even the most benevolent, hearing-abled editors are often, unfortunately, too deadline-riddled and policy-restricted to stage an industry coup in the name of fair treatment for writers. So, I work hard to keep apprised of current online market rates.

Know your online market rates

Even if online publication sales aren't your specialty, you can still negotiate specialty-worthy rates. Negotiation is done with what money you *could* get elsewhere, not necessarily what you *are* getting elsewhere.

Keep researching and stockpiling specific market rates for your negotiations. It's the same strategy that applies in print. You just have to seek pay-and-policy info for online markets in different places.

Don't forget to cite market rates delicately. It's hard for editors to hear you're not happy with their offer, and even harder to hear their competitors are able to pay writers better. Consider

For More Information

RESOURCES

The following list of books is designed to help you receive better negotiation results:

- *A Writer's Guide To Contract Negotiations*, by Richard Balkin (Writer's Digest Books)
- *National Writers Union Freelance Writers' Guide*, edited by James Waller (Writer's Digest Books)
- *The Writer's Legal Guide: An Authors Guild Desk Reference*, by Tad Crawford and Kay Murray (Allworth Press)
- *The Writer's Lawyer: Essential Legal Advice For Writers And Editors In All Media*, by Ronald L. Goldfarb and Gail E. Ross (Times Books)
- *2004 Online Markets For Writers: How and Where to Make Money by Selling Your Writing on the Internet* by Anthony and Paul Tedesco (MarketsForWriters.com Press)
- *Writing.com: Creative Internet Strategies to Advance Your Writing Career*, Second Edition, by Moira Allen (Allworth Press)

putting something like this into your own voice: "I completely understand your budget restrictions, but you've got to understand that it's really hard for me to accept YourMarket.com's $1,000 fee, when I know I could get $1,500 for the article from ThisOtherMarket.com. But I'd really like to work with you (if you do). Is there any way you could possibly get $500 more for the piece?" Give the editor some quiet time to consider your offer. If he still can't get the extra $500, but you really want to work with this market, consider reiterating the fact that you want to write for this publication, then add that you'd be willing to do the article for only another $250, as long as after the editor saw the professionalism of your work, he might agree to pay you the market rate for your next article.

Bulk e-sales

Online publications need more writing than print publications because Net readers have come to expect daily, if not hourly, updates. Fortunately for online publishers, more content doesn't mean more printing costs or more delivery costs. Fortunately for writers, more content demand means more online editors looking to buy your writing in bulk. Instead of selling one 5,000-word piece, serialize and sell it as 10 much more Web-friendly and money-worthy 500-word articles that are intertwined but able to stand alone, or find themes in your past writing and present your work as a year's worth of a column. Present, for example, 12 evergreen career-related articles as a year's worth of monthly career columns. The articles will have the added bonus of being delivered up front, easing the production process not just for the editor but for the programmers who can often just crib columns to be updated automatically on a certain day of the month.

The multiple pieces don't even have to run as niche columns. Again, without the limitations of printing or distribution costs, many online publications are open to mass surges in content related to their entire magazine as opposed to individual sections or themes. When asked to write a short, $250 career-related article for a post-college website, I instead negotiated the sale of 15 reprints on life after college in general—career-related articles, dating-related articles, travel-related articles, etc. The site got an instant content boost for their publication, and I got $3,750 for 500-word articles that I had already written and already sold to print markets. (I had retained electronic rights for most of them. The others were under older contracts that didn't include electronic clauses. Thanks to a recent, NWU-lead Supreme Court victory, writers own electronic rights to their work unless a contract clause specifically gives up those rights.) In addition to the money, I also saved time by negotiating 15 sales all at once. The Web is conducive enough to bulk buys that I've opted not to work with online syndicates, instead making (and keeping) the sales myself.

Word counts count less

One of the most important differences between online writing and print writing is that online writing, which is of course read on small computer screens, needs to be effective in far fewer words. Consequently, one of the most important differences in negotiating online rates is making certain to get paid for your time and not for your word count. "You have to work harder to write shorter," advises Lisa Price, author of *Hot Text: Web Writing that Works* (New Riders Publishing). "So add up your hours per piece, set a reasonable hourly rate, given your budget, and calculate how much, total, the piece ought to earn."

Your online time is money

Online publications also differ from print publications in that they can give their readers dramatically greater access to their writers, often at the expense of writers' schedules. I usually agree to have my e-mail address published with my articles, and I always, eventually, answer my e-mails. But when a high-profile online magazine put a clause into my contract binding me to being online during certain hours to discuss my article and the magazine in a live online chat—without compensating me, I politely said that I'd prefer to provide just my writing services and not my PR services. I politely didn't say, "You're supposed to be my publisher, not my pimp." They were quick to let me scratch out the clause. You'll find that often the most odious contract points are masterminded by the publication's lawyers and loathed by the publication's editors, who have to deliver them but are happy to remove them—if you ask.

Add-ons for additional money

Similar to print, the more value-added elements you can include with your online article, the more valuables you can request from the editor. Only the online medium provides you with far more options for supplementary materials than print's staple photos and illustrations. An article about the best restaurants in Rome could include audio clips so readers actually hear how to order the local specialties in Italian. Fashion articles could include short video clips so readers see how the clothing moves on the body. Even links can be packaged as a comprehensive sidebar of resources, warranting comprehensive side money for your supplementary work.

Limit the genre of use

I've always tried to resell my print articles to publications with noncompeting readerships, but it took a while before I thought of doing it with my online articles. I had mistakenly assumed that every online publication shared the same readership: "People using the Internet." Then I read an article on negotiating by Todd Pitock, a print and online writer who formerly served as the chairperson of the NWU's Journalism Division. He explained the importance of defining the specific online market in your contract. "For instance," he wrote, "you might give Todays Angler.com a three-month license that's exclusive to all *fishing-related* websites only." I finally realized that online readerships are as distinct as print readerships, and that I could negotiate genre limitations into my online market contracts—and bring in extra freelance money from multiple e-sales to noncompeting publications.

Limit the duration of use

Another way to bump up your online income is by restricting the duration of the rights you grant. A disturbing number of online market contracts ask for rights to use your article online "in perpetuity." That's forever and that's a mighty long time. They often refer to this use as "archiving" your article on their website. I often refer to this use as "unfair," and instead suggest a use limited to three months, six months, nine months or, at most, one year, with the option to renew each subsequent year at a certain price, if they still want the article. I've found most publications extremely flexible about this clause. They recognize the inequity of making a lifetime of money on your article when you got paid for it once, the same way you would've been paid for a one-time print article. Worst-case scenario, you can always diffuse the situation and secure your rights with the catch phrase "on terms to be negotiated." No one's bound to anything, and you get to negotiate with an editor who has later decided that he really wants to use your work.

The annual renewal fee for subsequent online use is usually lower than the original fee. For example, after the agreed-upon one year of use expired on the bulk sale I had made to that post-college website, I then secured an additional $125 each for eight of the 15 short reprints I had originally sold for $250 a piece.

What happened to the other seven pieces? I chose to have their electronic rights revert back to me. I knew the marketplace well enough to know that I could sell the online use of them for more than $125 each to other online publications. And who knows what I might make from negotiating the sale of each additional use after that?

Negotiating electronic rights and rates isn't easy. But it gets easy. Whether you're advocating for fair compensation in your next print contract's e-clause or your next online market contract, your future of better money and fairer treatment will make it far worth your while.

For More Information

ONLINE RESOURCES

This list of articles was designed to help you receive better negotiation results.

- "A Brief Primer on Electronic Rights for Authors" from Adler & Robin Books, Inc. (www.adlerbooks.com/erights.html)
- "Contract Advice: Electronic Rights" by The Authors Guild (www.authorsguild.org/?p=103&PHPSESSID=2b58365c8fb82e6eea215e15030b46e0)
- "Contract Issues: Books Published Online" by the National Writers Union (www.nwu.org/docs/online-p.htm)
- "Contracts: Top Ten Things to Negotiate and What's Not Worth Your Time" by Laura Resnick for Novelists, Inc. (www.ninc.com/tips/cntrt.asp)
- "Creating Your Future Through the Fine Art of Negotiation" by Toni and Daniel Will-Harris for EFuse.com (www.efuse.com/Plan/get_what_you_want.html)
- "Electronic Issues in Publishing Contracts" by Ivan Hoffman, B.A., J.D. (ivanhoffman.com/electronic.html)
- "Getting E-Screwed: Exploitation of Writers on the Internet" by Morris Rosenthal, for Foner Books (www.fonerbooks.com/escrewed.htm)
- "How To Negotiate Freelance Writing Rates" by Russ Naymark for WetFeet.com (www.wetfeet.com/asp/article.asp?aid=306&atype=Freelancing)
- "Protecting Your Electronic Rights" by Moira Allen for Writing-World.com (www.writing-world.com/rights/erights.shtml)
- "Sample Electronic Reprint Contract" by Peanut Press for Mystery Writers of America (www.mysterywriters.org/library/sample_electronic_reprint.html)
- "SFWA Statement on Electronic Rights" by a subcommittee of the Science Fiction and Fantasy Writers of America's Contracts Committee, composed of Greg Bear, Richard Curtis, Bud Sparhawk, and Sarah Smith (www.sfwa.org/contracts/ELEC.htm)
- "The Art of Negotiation" by S.C. Giles (www.thepauper.com/article/Paupermill/ArtOfNegotiation.shtml)
- "The Electronic Rights Clause In Magazine and Newspaper Contracts" prepared by the ASJA Contracts Committee (www.asja.org/pubtips/cometerm.php)
- "Top 50 Free Negotiation Resources for Writers" by Jake Cooney, for MarketsForWriters.com (www.marketsforwriters.com/business/resources.html)
- "Watch Out: Dangerous Clauses!" by the ASJA Contracts Committee (www.asja.org/pubtips/clauses.php)
- "When is a Contract a Contract?" by Alex Pendrite for FreeAgent.com (www.freeagent.com/advice/legal/makesacontract.asp)

Excerpted from the book Top 250 Free Resources for Writers, *which is available free of charge at Top250FreeResourcesForWriters.org. Adapted by Jake Cooney with permission.*

Books—and Authors—for Sale

BY KELLY MILNER HALLS

"Writers should be read, but neither seen nor heard," according to the late Daphne Du Maurier, best known for her novel *Rebecca* and her short story, *The Birds* (both adapted to film by Alfred Hitchcock). Sound advice, perhaps, in its day. But the times, they are rapidly changing.

More and more publishing insiders believe the salability of an author is almost as important as the strength of his or her book. "After an editor reads a manuscript and likes it," said one anonymous expert, "her next question is, 'What is this guy like? What does he look like? Can I put him on tour?'"

Nicholas Sparks takes a gamble

Best-selling novelist Nicholas Sparks (*The Notebook, Message in a Bottle, A Walk to Remember, Nights in Rodanthe*) concurs. "Writing and publishing has changed dramatically, especially within the last ten years. It used to be about the story. But now, they look at the total package."

Sparks' perspective is experiential. After Warner Books shelled out a cool million for his first published novel, *The Notebook* (1996), New York buzz said the staggering advance won the then-unknown-author an unprecedented 45-city, three-month book tour. But Sparks begs to differ.

"When the fall sales catalog came out in March or April," Sparks says, "publicity was planning a five-city tour. My agent said, 'No way. We've got to get you out there more.'" How did the author win ten times the original promotional reach? He crashed a party.

"My agent knew and worked with the head of a well-known foreign rights literary agency who was well-connected at Warner," Sparks remembers. "She [my agent] was invited to his house-warming party in Arizona, and knew Larry Kirshbaum, the CEO of Warner Books, was also going to be there. She said, 'You have to go to that party.' So I bought a plane ticket and went to Arizona.

"It was a gamble," Sparks continues. "I had to pay my own way. I had to leave my wife in South Carolina. I had to be back at work when the weekend was over. But it paid off. Monday morning, Larry walked into the publicity office and said, 'He looks just like Tom Cruise. I want at least 20 cities on that book tour.' What I looked like and how I handled myself were absolutely crucial."

Sparks' personal power also secured him a spot on the CBS prime-time news magazine show, *48 Hours*. "My publicist Jennifer Romanelli was talking to Andrew Cohen, the show's producer at Book Expo [America], and handed him a copy of *The Notebook* to read on the plane. He had a lot of books to choose from after being at BEA, of course," Sparks admits. "But mine was the short one."

Intrigued by back-flap copy that said the story was loosely based on Sparks' grandparents' romance and struggle with Alzheimer's, Cohen headed for South Carolina to document a real-life drama.

"Sounds great," Sparks says, "except *The Notebook* was a novel. It was fiction. My grandpar-

---

KELLY MILNER HALLS *is a Spokane-based freelance writer. Her work has appeared in the* Washington Post, Chicago Tribune, Atlanta-Journal Constitution, Denver Post, Booklist, Teen People, *and* Family Fun. *She has written 10 books, and her latest is* Dinosaur Mummies: Beyond Bare Bone Fossils *(Darby Creek Publishing, 2003).*

Ten Tips for Selling Your Personality (No Matter What Your Personality Might Be)

Nicholas Sparks and Chris Crutcher may be natural born speakers—magnetic personalities who also successfully write. But what if your knees knock when you face a crowd? Is there hope for the terminally awkward? These ten tips will guide even the most reluctant authors to public glory.

1. **Be yourself.** Too often, a new writer slips under the spell of illusion. He starts to think he's got to present a public lecture precisely like somebody else's. Wrong. The best way to miss your target audience is to try and duplicate somebody else. Be true to who you are.
2. **Be prepared.** Writing a speech in advance of your public engagement is very often a good idea. It sets your mind at the ready for presenting the ideas you most want to convey and keeps you on task. But whenever possible, use that written speech as a guidepost, not a straight jacket. Trust yourself to express those thoughts spontaneously, whenever possible.
3. **Prepare handouts.** Make copies of the speech you wrote out in the calm of your home or office as a handout to distribute to your speaking event guests. Be sure your name, contact information, book titles, and website are prominently featured at the top of the page. Follow-up invitations could be no more than a post-engagement phone call away.
4. **Get plenty of rest.** The night before you plan to greet your reading public, be sure you get plenty of good old-fashioned rest. A groggy speaker is very often a boring speaker.
5. **Plan your wardrobe.** Wear the outfit that makes you feel like a million bucks, not the outfit your best friend says makes you look smart. Comfort shows like a lighthouse beacon when you're speaking to a crowd. Make sure your clothing helps you say you're comfortable with exactly who you are.
6. **Bring a friend.** Never underestimate the power of a friendly face—or the welcome nature of a question from an audience member you know is on your side. When at all possible, bring a trusted friend to your author events.
7. **Show up early.** Early is always more confidence inspiring than late—for you and for your speaking engagement host. So show up at least 15 minutes early for each event.
8. **Breathe.** It sounds too simple. But when we are uneasy, we frequently forget to breathe. And when our minds slip into oxygen deprivation, it's very hard to intelligently speak. Don't forget to breathe while you're speaking on stage.
9. **Have fun.** Who said you had to seem self-important? If you want your audience to enjoy their lecture experience, try to enjoy yours. Fun is contagious, and experts say it sells books.
10. **Bring water.** Be sure to bring a bottle of cool water to every event, just in case your host is running a little dry. It's tough to speak with power and authority when your throat is scratchy and dry.

ents didn't even live in the same state. He came down with expectations I couldn't fulfill. So I said, 'This isn't exactly what happened to my grandparents, but let me tell you another story.'"

Sold! So instead of documenting what he thought was a real-life drama, Cohen produced a segment on the making of a bestseller—with Sparks as the primary focus. "And it was largely because we hit it off," Sparks admits. "Personality matters. It can be your first impression—get your foot in the door. Then you have to deliver a story that won't let your readers down."

Chris Crutcher on the road again

HarperCollins author and humorist Chris Crutcher's human factor required a lengthier gestation. "Neither my agent nor my publisher knew how amazingly charming I was," Crutcher says of his first publication, with tongue firmly in cheek. "They had to go on the strength of the story." But, he admits, cultivating a robust crop of professional relationships has enhanced his career.

Trained as both an educator and a family therapist, Crutcher's eight novels—including *Whale Talk*, *Ironman*, and *Staying Fat for Sarah Byrnes* (which will soon be a major motion picture)—address topical elements (including physical and sexual abuse, racism and school violence) that appeal to mature readers of all ages. His ability to convey the diversity of his expertise has made Crutcher vastly popular on the lecture circuit.

How popular is popular? According to his website appearances (www.christcrutcher.com), Crutcher visited 26 cities from April to December of 2002, speaking to approximately 50 full-capacity audiences in that nine-month period. The spring 2003 release of his critically acclaimed autobiography, *King of the Mild Frontier* sent Crutcher on a 20-city, two-week book tour where he lectured at libraries and academic facilities, *and* signed for loyal booksellers.

"I can't say for sure," Crutcher says, "but I believe that my ability to present well to teenagers in middle and high schools, along with my ability to talk with parents, teachers, and librarians about kids in tough situations helps get me and my books extra exposure. We explore alternative strategies to work with their challenges, much as do some of the adult characters in my books. It keeps me in touch with my readers."

HarperCollins publicist Josette Kurey is less modest about Crutcher's personal magnetism. "He's a whole different animal," she says. "Once you meet him and hear him talk, it makes what he writes more important. He's out at least 100 days a year, but he doesn't come off as an arrogant, 'famous writer.' He's more like every man. He's real, so people listen."

According to Kurey, once an audience hears Crutcher speak, they're hooked on his books for life. "When he tells an anecdotal story from his work as a therapist, the origin of his fiction becomes obvious. He's able to convey that authenticity to the general public so naturally and comfortably, he's impossible to resist. Crutcher knows who he is—a therapist first, a writer second. His readers passionately respond."

Does reader response really matter to Crutcher, or is it a clever marketing ploy? "It matters," Crutcher says. "If I've successfully connected with my readers, it's because I am sincere about making that connection. I like hearing what people think about my stories and about things in general. And I think keeping myself as personally linked as I can be with the public has helped sell a lot of books, too."

Joseph Marshall III uses his voice

Sicangu Lakota Sioux author Joseph Marshall III (*The Lakota Way*) echoes Crutcher's devotion to authenticity. That truthful ring and personal credibility is what secured Marshall's six-figure, two-book deal at Viking Compass.

After developing a top-notch book proposal, Marshall's agent sent him to Manhattan. "I spent two days talking to publishers," he says. "I explained my idea for the book, my plan to tell not only traditional stories but also to show how they serve a purpose today."

Marshall wasn't sure his quiet sophistication would play in the Big Apple. "I was intimidated, to a certain extent," he admits, "by the environment of the city. But once I walked into an office, once I looked an individual in the eye, any sense of intimidation vanished. Then it was up to me."

Marshall admits his personal voice empowers him as an author. "If someone is interested to begin with and invites you to speak, that's a big open door," he says. "But then it's up to you to sell yourself. Eye-to-eye, one-on-one, the floor is yours. You make your project special by showing how you feel about it. If you're passionate, that's something they can see."

Even Marshall's agent admits, face-time isn't right for every would-be author. But if a writer is secure and adept at personal interaction, it's hard to resist playing that powerful card. "There are so many people out there with unique, interesting, even outrageous things to say," Marshall says. "It's become an 'in-your-face' kind of business. You have to find a way to capture a reader's attention. Being a good speaker is good for your book."

Simon & Schuster publicity manager Tracy van Straaten agrees, a powerful author or illustrator presence can make selling merchandise a lot easier. "Toni DiTerlizzi who illustrated *The Spider and the Fly* (2002) is perhaps the perfect example," she says. "He's amazing, a natural. He's creative and hilarious and great with adults and kids. Even when he was on the cusp of breaking out, we felt confident saying he'd be a good speaker. We knew once anybody met him, they'd fall instantly in love."

Beyond Public Speaking

Are there public marketing alternatives to large crowds? Absolutely. Here are four of the most popular alternatives for creative inspiration.

1. **Radio.** How can you reach millions of potential readers with a one-on-one conversation? Live radio. According to publicity master Rick Frishman, radio is one of the most effective and yet most overlooked marketing options.
2. **Websites.** Literally millions of computer literate readers surf the Internet each day. Creating a website that creatively presents and celebrates your books can help you dazzle the book-buying public without setting foot outside your front door.
3. **Book clubs.** More and more libraries, classrooms, and social clubs are sponsoring public readings and organized book clubs, thanks to Oprah and NBC's *Today*. By speaking to a local book club, you face a small group of people already familiar with your work, not a room full of strangers who may or may not know who you are.
4. **Private workshops.** Are you gifted when it comes to research? Character development? Settings or plot? Hold a private workshop, advertised in your local newspaper or community publication. Word of mouth will expand your author visibility, a few individuals at a time.

Pop-up book master Robert Sabuda author of *The Night Before Christmas*, is another example of Simon & Schuster's prize personalities. "He has done the *Today* show," van Straaten says, "and he's among the best—well-spoken, articulate, charming, and a genius at creating incredible books. For so many years, he'd go on book tours, and only a few people would show up. But he fine-tuned his presentation, his pop-up demonstration. Now whether he's at a bookstore talking to a group of kids or on NBC with Matt Lauer, he's got the same, natural presence. It's just who he is."

Are shy authors and illustrators shut out of the book-selling competition? "Absolutely not," according to van Straaten. "I can't imagine not marketing a wonderful book just because the author is publicly uneasy. We know some professionals are painfully shy and don't like making appearances," she says. "We won't force them if they're not interested. But touring can impact sales. And shy can be endearing on camera. So we offer media training to prepare people who are uneasy, but willing to try."

After the marketing dust has settled, Marshall says, "It's still about the story. I still write books mainly for the non-Indian community so they will learn more about us—where we're coming from, what we've had to do to survive. These stories aren't just entertainment. They are life lessons. They are timeless."

Crutcher agrees. "As a speaker, you must always know your audience and address the issues they are most likely to be interested in. One audience might simply be interested in your stories. Another might be more interested in how you go about telling them. Making the connection as a speaker is mostly about knowing which things people want to hear. Making a connection as a writer, is about telling the truth as you see it, even in the fictional stories you're trying to tell."

How Much Should I Charge?

BY LYNN WASNAK

It may seem strange to open a chapter on freelance pay rates by saying there are few "standard rates"—but if you look at the data, it's true. In this latest rate survey, as in surveys past, almost every category shows wide variation. Freelancers in general are an independent bunch—no groupthink for us! No matter how long and hard full-time freelancers beg their part-time and beginning counterparts to *not* write for free or for cheap—freelance writers and editors do what they've always done about rates. They charge whatever they please. They guess what the market will bear. Sometimes they get the rate they want, sometimes not, but decisions on rates are made individually.

Freelancers are not interchangeable widgets. What you as a freelancer offer for sale is simply *yourself*. The teeming contents of your brain—skills, abilities, personality, experience—form a unique combination that no one else can duplicate. It's no secret the pros make money writing by finding outlets where their special qualities meet needs for which others are willing to pay. Factors affecting pay range include product complexity (technology and medical writing pay higher rates than general topics) and geographic location (rates tend to be higher on the coasts than the Midwest, while urban rates are higher than small towns or rural areas).

Overall pay rates and volume were down the past two years, yet some freelancers enjoyed gains despite the economic downturn. Those with improved income found new markets when old ones collapsed. They made the choice to keep going despite the difficulty. You can too. Becoming a well-paid writer takes a little study, a lot of networking, and plenty of practice.

WHERE DO YOU FIT IN?

Three variables can help you determine where you fit on the freelance pay scale:

1. **Expertise and experience.** How well can you craft the results a publisher or client expects in the given category? Have you done it before? Can you demonstrate your skill with clips or samples?
2. **Special knowledge.** How thoroughly do you know this subject area?
3. **Chutzpah, courage, confidence—or just plain nerve.** Aside from basic writing skills, this may be the most important quality any freelancer can develop. From contacting new markets to negotiating rates and contract terms, you must believe in yourself.

Next, develop a sound pricing strategy. Monitor your personal writing, research and editing speed on typical assignments to convert per word or per page rates to a targeted hourly range. (Rates of production vary, but one rule of thumb is to plan for about three hours per page of copy.)

HOW DO YOU DETERMINE YOUR RATES?

To choose the income target you want from freelancing, remember that as an independent business person you must pay all your overhead, health benefits, vacation pay, retirement savings and taxes. Also, you must set aside regular time for marketing, accounting, and other nonbillable work. Total cost of living, expenses, and overhead are then divided by billable hours to figure

---

LYNN WASNAK *has experienced the highs and lows of full-time freelance writing for 25 years. She specializes in medical and business topics, and chases rainbows at every opportunity.*

the minimum per-hour rate you need to stay afloat. Billable hour estimates range from 1,000 to 1,500 hours per year. A quick ballpark estimate takes hourly rate × 1,000 hours to project potential annual income: i.e., $55/hour × 1,000 hours = annual income of $55,000. (To fulfill this goal, though, you need 1,000 hours of billable work!)

Once you have determined your estimated hourly rate, you can use it to decide if you'll earn more than the average fast-food employee on a particular assignment. You can also use the rate to prepare project rates—a single all-inclusive fee where Project X is delivered for Y amount by Z deadline. Many clients and publishers prefer project rates, since they know the total cost in advance. It's good for the freelancer who works fast, too. If a given assignment pays $500, but takes 40 hours to complete, you've earned $10.50 an hour. But if you do that same assignment in 10 hours, you've earned $50 an hour—and have 30 hours left over to devote to another paying project. Some freelancers add an extra "hassle factor" charge for difficult clients or rush jobs.

For More Information

RESOURCES

For more information on determining freelance pay rates, negotiating contracts, etc., you can visit the following organizations. *(Editor's note: A special thank you to the organizations listed below who each contributed responses to our survey.)*

- American Society of Journalists & Authors (ASJA): www.asja.org
- American Translators Association (ATA): www.atanet.org
- American Literary Translators Association (ALTA): www.literarytranslators.org
- Association of Personal Historians (APH): www.personalhistorians.org
- Editorial Freelancers Association (EFA): www.the-efa.org
- Freelance Success (FLX): www.freelancesuccess.com
- Independent Writers of Chicago (IWOC): www.iwoc.org
- International Association of Business Communicators (IABC): www.iabc.com
- Investigative Reporters & Editors, Inc. (IRE): www.ire.org
- Media Communicators Association International (MCA-I): www.mca-i.org
- National Writers Union (NWU): www.nwu.org
- Washington Independent Writers (WIW): www.washwriter.org
- Society of Professional Journalists (SPJ): www.spj.org
- Society for Technical Communication (STC): www.stc.org
- Women in Film (WIF): www.wif.org
- Writer's Guild of America, East (WGAE): www.wgae.org
- Writer's Guild of America, West (WGA): www.wga.org/top.html

The following rates are generic basics to get you started in setting a personal fee. Learn the going market rates for specific projects of interest by networking with other writers in your region and joining professional writers' organizations. The benefits received from membership in professional writers' organizations—learning to thrive as a writer—will more than offset the annual fees.

ADVERTISING, COPYWRITING & PR

Copywriting: $300/half day, $500/full day on-site in agency.

Advertising copywriting: $120 high/hour, $33 low/hour, $66 average/hour; $750 high/project, $250 low/project, $525 average/project; $1.50/word.

Book jacket copywriting: $100 high/hour, $30 low/hour, $65 average/hour; $500 high/project, $75 low/project, $300 average/project.

Campaign development or product launch: $150 high/hour, $60 low/hour, $82 average/hour; $7,500 high/project, $1,500 low/project, $3,740 average/project.

Catalog copywriting: $85 high/hour, $30 low/hour, $60 average/hour.

Copyediting for advertising: $120 high/hour, $25 low/hour, $60 average/hour; $120/project for 1,000 words.

Direct-mail copywriting: $150 high/hour, $35 low/hour, $78 average/hour; $15,000 high/project, $500 low/project, $5,000 average/product.

E-mail ad copywriting: $100 high/hour, $35 low/hour, $70 average/hour; $2,500/project.

Event promotions/publicity: $100 high/hour, $45 low/hour, $67 average/hour.

Fund-raising campaign brochure: $75 high/hour, $23 low/hour, $58 average/hour; $2,000 high/project, $1,000 low/project, $1,500 average/project.

Political campaigns, public relations: $75 high/hour, $23 low/hour, $49 average/hour.

Press kits: $125 high/hour, $53 low/hour, $85 average/hour; $5,000 high/project, $1,000 low/project, $2,334 average/project.

Press/news release: $100 high/hour, $23 low/hour, $62 average/hour; $1,000 high/project, $75 low/project, $305 average/project.

Public relations for businesses: $115 high/hour, $25 low/hour, $76 average/hour.

Public relations for government: $60 high/hour, $40 low/hour, $49 average/hour.

Public relations for organizations or nonprofits: $95 high/hour, $25 low/hour, $56 average/hour.

Public relations for schools or libraries: $75 high/hour, $50 low/hour, $65 average/hour.

Speechwriting/editing (general): $100 high/hour, $65 low/hour, $83 average/hour; $6,000 high/30-minute speech, $2,700 low/30-minute speech, $4,064 average/30-minute speech.

Speechwriting for government officials: $90 high/hour, $30 low/hour, $52 average/hour.

Speechwriting for political candidates: $60/hour.

AUDIOVISUALS & ELECTRONIC COMMUNICATIONS

Copyediting audiovisual: $85 high/hour, $40 low/hour, $58 average/hour.

Business film scripts (training and information): $125 high/hour, $40 low/hour, $82 average/hour; $500 high/run minute, $200 low/run minute, $325 average/run minute; $550 day rate (with discount up to 20% for multiple-day project); $3,500 high/project, $1,500 low/project, $2,500 average/project.

Educational/training film scripts: $100 high/hour, $30 low/hour, $77 average/hour; $6,000 high/project, $1,500 low/project, $3,500 average/project; $500 high/run minute, $200 low/run minute, $325 average/run minute; $500 high day rate, $300 low day rate, $400 average day rate.

Corporate product film: $100 high/hour, $30 low/hour, $70 average/hour; $500 high/run minute, $200 low/run minute, $325 average/run minute.

Movie novelization: $10,000 high, $5,000 low, $7,000 average.

Options (feature films): First 180 days, 5% WGA minimum; 10% minimum each 180-day period thereafter.

Radio editorials: $70/hour, $50 low/hour, $60 average/hour.

Radio interviews: $1,500 high, $35 low, $100 average (rates depend on who you are and how badly the radio station wants you); $100 high/run minute (produced pieces over 2 minutes), $65 low/run minute (produced pieces over 2 minutes), $75 average/run minute (produced pieces over 2 minutes).

Radio commercials/PSAs: $85 high/hour, $70 low/hour, $72 average/hour.

Script synopsis for business: $70/hour; $20/news show.

Screenwriting (original screenplay): $91,495 high, $48,738 low, $70,117 average.

Script synopsis for agent or film producer: $2,000 or $500/day.

Scripts for nontheatrical films for education, business, industry: $100 high/hour, $55 low/hour, $80 average/hour; $500 high/run minute, $200 low/run minute, $325 average/run minute; $5,000/script (starting point).

TV news story/feature: $100 high/hour, $70 low/hour, $90 average/hour.

TV scripts (nontheatrical): $150 high/hour, $70 low/hour, $100 average/hour; $1,000 high/day, $550 low/day, $800 average/day; $250/page; $1,200 (minimum)/project.

TV scripts (teleplay/MOW): $500 high/run minute, $200 low/run minute, $350 average/run minute; $6,567 story only (30 minutes or less); $19,699 (plus teleplay); $11,560 (story only); $28,974 (plus teleplay).

TV commercials/PSAs: $85 high/hour, $60 low/hour, $73 average/hour.

BOOK PUBLISHING

Abstracting and abridging: $35 high/hour, $30 low/hour, $33 average/hour.

Anthology editing: $60 high/hour, $25 low/hour, $39 average/hour.

Book proposal consultation: $60 high/hour, $35 low/hour, $48 average/hour; $500/project.

Book proposal writing: $60 high/hour, $35 low/hour, $47 average/hour; $5,000 high/project, $500 low/project, $2,300 average/project.

Book query critique: $55 high/hour, $45 low/hour, $51 average/hour; $30/page.

Book query writing: $500 high/project, $120 low/project, $200 average/project.

Children's book writing: Advance against royalties: $10,000 high, $200 low, $4,900 average.

Content editing (scholarly): $80 high/hour, $20 low/hour, $40 average/hour; $3-$5/page; $850-$2,000/project.

Content editing (textbook): $65 high/hour, $20 low/hour, $36 average/hour.

Content editing (trade): $75 high/hour, $20 low/hour, $46 average/hour.

Copyediting: $75 high/hour, $17 low/hour, $38 average/hour; $3,000 high/project, $1,000 low/project, $1,875 average/project.

Fiction book writing (own): $7,500 advance against royalties.

Ghostwriting, as told to: $55 high/hour, $25 low/hour, $40 average/hour; $55,000 (one report)/project.

Ghostwriting, no credit: $80 high/hour, $25 low/hour, $55 average/hour; $20,000 (one report)/project.

Indexing: $8 high/page, $2.35 low/page, $3.50 average/page.

Manuscript evaluation and critique: $65 high/hour, $45 low/hour, $55 average/hour; $1,500 high/project, $350 low/project, $950 average/project.

Movie novelization: $7,000.

Nonfiction book writing (own): Advance against royalties: $150,000 high, $5,000 low, $25,500 average; (textbook) $60/hour.

Nonfiction books (collaborative): Advance against royalties: $30,000 high, $5,000 low, $15,700 average; $65 high/hour, $35 low/hour, $50 average/hour.

Novel synopsis (general): $60 high/hour, $45 low/hour, $51 average/hour.

Proofreading: $45 high/hour, $16 low/hour, $26 average/hour; $3 high/page, $1 low/page, $2 average/page.

Research for writers or book publishers: $75 high/hour, $30/hour, $49 average/hour; $500/day.

Rewriting: $75 high/hour, $30 low/hour, $46 average/hour.

Translation: (fiction) 12¢ high/target word, 6¢ low/target word, 9¢ average/target word; $10,000 high/book, $7,000 low/book, $8,500 average/book; (nonfiction) 15¢ high/target word, 8¢ low/target word, 10¢ average/target word; (poetry) $15 high/page, $0 low/page, $7.50 average/page.

Work for hire (flat fee, no royalties): $10,000 high, $1,000 low, $2,484 average.

BUSINESS

Annual reports: $150 high/hour, $40 low/hour, $65 average/hour; $15,000 high/project, $3,000 low/project, $8,334 average/project.

Associations and organizations (writing for): $100 high/hour, $25 low/hour, $62 average/hour; $20,000 high/project, $2,500 low/project, $7,500 average/project.

Brochures, fliers, booklets for business: $150 high/hour, $28 low/hour, $75 average/hour; $100/page; $5,000 high/project, $500 low/project, $3,125 average/project.

Business editing (general): $100 high/hour, $35 low/hour, $57 average/hour.

Business letters: $150 high/hour, $30 low/hour, $70 average/hour; $1,200 (minimum) high/project, $200 low/project, $500 average/project.

Business plan: $150 high/hour, $35 low/hour, $80 average/hour.

Business writing seminars: $200 high/hour, $65 low/hour, $83 average/hour; $3,500 high/project, $1,000 low/project, $2,250 average/project.

Catalogs for businesses: $150 high/hour, $30 low/hour, $73 average/hour; $2,500 high/project, $2,000 low/project, $2,250 average/project.

Consultation on communications: $150 high/hour, $28 low/hour, $84 average/hour; $500/half day; $1,200 (minimum)/project.

Copyediting for business: $100 high/hour, $27 low/hour, $57 average/hour; $4/page.

Corporate histories: $115 high/hour, $28 low/hour, $71 average/hour; $200/printed page.

Corporate periodicals, editing: $100 high/hour, $27 low/hour, $56 average/hour.

Corporate periodicals, writing: $125 high/hour, $40 low/hour, $72 average/hour; $2/word.

Corporate profile: $115 high/hour, $80 low/hour, $98 average/hour; $350/project (200 words); $1.40/word.

Ghostwriting for business (usually trade magazine articles for business columns): $115 high/hour, $50 low/hour, $82 average/hour.

Government research: $100 high/hour, $30 low/hour, $65 average/hour.

Government writing: $100 high/hour, $30 low/hour, $64 average/hour.

Grant proposal writing for nonprofits: $100 high/hour, $15 low/hour, $49 average/hour.

Newsletters, desktop publishing/production: $100 high/hour, $23 low/hour, $54 average/hour; $3,800 high/project (4 pages), $1,000 low/project (4 pages), $2,520 average/project (4 pages); $750/page.

Newsletters, editing: $100 high/hour, $25 low/hour, $53 average/hour.

Newsletters, writing: $150 high/hour, $23 low/hour, $63 average/hour; $1 high/word, 30¢ low/word, 69¢ average/word.

Translation (commercial, for government agencies, technical): Rates for translating vary widely, from 12¢ to 20¢/target word, depending on language combination (source and target) and area of specialization. (Example: Spanish is inexpensive, Chinese is expensive.) Also may charge by target line ($1.20 line) or $90-$120/1,000 words.

COMPUTER, SCIENTIFIC & TECHNICAL

Computer-related manual writing: $125 high/hour, $40 low/hour, $75 average/hour.

Copyediting scientific journals: $18/hour (one report).

E-mail copywriting: $150 high/hour, $50 low/hour, $77 average/hour; $1,200/project (minimum).

Medical and science editing: $100 high/hour, $16 low/hour, $54 average/hour.

Medical and science proofreading: $75 high/hour, $16 low/hour, $35 average/hour.

Medical and science writing: $200 high/hour, $40 low/hour, $86 average/hour; $5,000/project.

Online editing: $120 high/hour, $28 low/hour, $58 average/hour.

Technical editing: $100 high/hour, $25 low/hour, $51 average/hour.

Technical writing: $110 high/hour, $40 low/hour, $66 average/hour.

Web page design: $75 high/hour, $40 low/hour, $59 average/hour; $4,000 high/project, $500 low/project, $2,000 average/project.

Web page editing: $120 high/hour, $35 low/hour, $65 average/hour.

Web page writing: $120 high/hour, $25 low/hour, $75 average/hour; $1 high/word, 50¢ low/word, 69¢ average/word; $300 high/page, $50 low/page, $150 average/page.

White Papers: $120 high/hour, $45 low/hour, $80 average/hour.

EDITORIAL/DESIGN PACKAGES

(Editor's note: For more information about photography rates, please see 2004 Photographer's Market.*)*

Desktop publishing: $150 high/hour, $25 low/hour, $61 average/hour.

Greeting card ideas: $60/hour; $125 high/card, $25 low/card, $77 average/card.

Photo brochures: $75 high/hour, $65 low/hour, $70 average/hour.

Photo research: $75 high/hour, $60 low/hour, $69 average/hour.

Photography: $125 high/hour, $60 low/hour, $83 average/hour; $100 high/photo, $10 low/photo, $35 average/photo.

Picture editing: $150 high/hour, $40 low/hour, $60 average/hour.

EDUCATIONAL & LITERARY SERVICES

Educational consulting and designing courses for business or adult education: $50 high/hour, $30 low/hour, $45 average/hour; $2,500 high/project, $600 low/project, $1,213 average/project.

Educational grant and proposal writing: $50 high/hour, $35 low/hour, $43 average/hour. $2,500 high/project, $600 low/project, $1,550 average/project.

Manuscript evaluation for theses/dissertations: $95 high/hour, $20 low/hour, $46 average/hour; $1550 high/project, $250 low/project, $700 average/project.

Poetry manuscript critique: $200 high/hour, $75 low/hour, $100 average/hour.

Presentations at national conventions by well-known authors: $30,000 high/event, $1,000 low/event, $5,000 average/event. (Note: Celebrity authors may earn much higher rates. Some presentations are given for travel expenses only or honorarium.)

Presentations at regional writers' conferences: $10,000 high/event, $50 low/event (or expenses only), $1,180 average/event.

Presentations to local groups, librarians, or teachers: $50/hour; $250 high/event, $35 low/event, $129 average/event.

Presentations to school classes: $900/day; $500/half day; $3,400 high/five-day visiting artist program, $2,500 low/five-day visiting artist program, $2,750 average/five-day visiting artist program. (Note: Some presentations to local groups and school classes given free or for a very nominal fee.)

Readings by poets, fiction writers: $3,000 high/event, $50 low/event, $200 average/event (highest fees for celebrity writers).

Short story manuscript critique: $200 high/hour, $53 low/hour, $75 average/hour; $5/page.

Teaching college course/seminar (includes adult education): $4,500 high/course, $500 low/course, $1,827 average/course.

Writer's workshop: $1,000 high/event, $100 low/event, $606 average/event.

Writing for scholarly journals: 14¢/word (one report); $450/article. (Most scholarly writing is authored free as a "career enhancer.")

MAGAZINES & TRADE JOURNALS

(Editor's note: For specific pay rate information for feature articles, columns/departments, fillers, etc., please see individual market listings.)

Article manuscript critique: $35 high/hour, $25 low/hour, $30 average/hour.

Arts reviewing: $300 high/project, $25 low/project, $125 average/project; $1.25 high/word, 25¢ low/word, 75¢ average/word.

Book reviews: $650 high/project, $20 low/project, $150 average/project; $1 high/word, 5¢ low/word, 44¢/word.

Consultation on magazine editorial: $200 high/hour, $35 low/hour, $95 average/hour.

Content editing: $55 high/hour, $35 low/hour, $46 average/hour; $6,500 high/issue, $2,000 low/issue, $4,250 average/issue.

Copyediting: $55 high/hour, $18 low/hour, $40 average/hour.

Fact checking: $20 high/hour, $15 low/hour, $18 average/hour.

Ghostwriting articles (general): $100 high/hour, $55 low/hour, $77 average/hour; $3,500 high/project, $2,000 low/project, $2,750 average/project; $1.50 high/word, 75¢ low/word, $1.25 average/word.

City magazine, calendar of events column: $150 high/column, $50 low/column, $75 average/column.

Consumer magazine column: $575 high/project, $200 low/project, $350 average/project.

Consumer magazine feature articles: $4 high/word, 30¢ low/word, $1.19 average/word; $3,000 high/project, $100 low/project, $822 average/project.

Magazine research: $100 high/hour, $25 low/hour, $52 average/hour; $150 high/topic, $100 low/topic, $125 average/topic.

Proofreading: $40 high/hour, $25 low/hour, $32 average/hour; $7/page.

Reprint fees: $700 high/project, $20 low/project, $200 average/project.

Rewriting: $50 high/hour, $35 low/hour, $45 average/hour.

Trade journal column: $1 high/word, 50¢ low/word, 74¢ average/word; $550 high/column, $75 low/column, $219 average/column; $50/hour.

Trade journal feature article: $1 high/word, 15¢ low/word, 61¢ average/word; $90 high/hour, $50 low/hour, $70 average/hour.

NEWSPAPERS

Arts reviewing: 60¢ high/word, 10¢ low/word, 36¢ average/word; $200 high/review, $20 low/review, $80 average/review.

Book reviews: 60¢ high/word, 25¢ low/word, 40¢ average/word; $250 high/review, $50 low/review, $100 average/review.

Column, local: $175 high/column, $10 low/column, $100 average/column.

Copyediting: $35 high/hour, $17.50 low/hour, $26 average/hour.

Editing/manuscript evaluation: $35/hour.

Feature: 50¢ high/word, 8¢ low/word, 22¢ average/word; $1,500 high/project, $50 low/project, $276 average/project.

Obituary copy: $75 high/story, $35 low/story, $50 average/story.

Proofreading: $22 high/hour, $18 low/hour, $20 average/hour.

Stringing: $300 high/story, $150 low/story, $225 average/story.

Syndicated column, self-promoted (rate depends on circulation): $35 high/insertion; $4 low/insertion, $8 average/insertion.

MISCELLANEOUS

Comedy writing for nightclub entertainers: $50 high/joke, $5 low/joke, $33 average/joke; $500/group of jokes.

Comic book or strip writing: $35 for short back-up script.

Craft projects with instructions: $350 high/project, $75 low/project, $212 average/project.

Encyclopedia articles: $200 high/article, $50 low/article, $125 average/article; 30¢/word.

Family histories: $80 high/hour, $30 low/hour, $65 average/hour; $20,000 high/project, $5,000 low/project, $9,500 average/project (plus expenses).

Gag writing for cartoonists: $40/gag.

Institutional (church, school) history: $125/printed page.

Manuscript typing: $2.50 high/page, 95¢ low/page, $1.27 average/page.

Original prose story for comic book: $200.

Playwriting for the stage: 10% box office revenue (if any).

Published plays: $100/10 minutes; $300/one-act; $400/three-act.

Résumés: $500 high/project, $200 low/project, $300 average/project.

Story set in publisher's comic universe: $500. (Some write for percentage of profit, which may be $0.)

Writing contest judging: $250 high, $0 low, $50 average (includes some gift certificates or books. Judging of finalists may be duty included in speaker's fee.).

Publishers and Their Imprints

The publishing world is constantly changing and evolving. With all of the buying, selling, reorganizing, consolidating, and dissolving, it's hard to keep publishers and their imprints straight. To help you make sense of these changes, we offer this breakdown of major publishers (and their divisions)—who owns whom and which imprints are under each company umbrella. Keep in mind that this information is constantly changing. We have provided the websites to each of the publishers so you can continue to keep an eye on this ever-evolving business.

SIMON & SCHUSTER
(Viacom, Inc.)
www.simonsays.com

Simon & Schuster Audio
Pimsleur
Simon & Schuster Audioworks
Simon & Schuster Sound Ideas

Simon & Schuster Adult Publishing
Atria Books
The Free Press
Kaplan
Pocket Books
Scribner
Simon & Schuster
Simon & Schuster Trade Paperback

Simon & Schuster Children's Publishing
Aladdin Paperbacks
Atheneum Books for Young Readers
Little Simon®
Margaret K. McElderry Books
Simon & Schuster Books for Young Readers
Simon Pulse
Simon Spotlight®

Simon & Schuster Interactive

Simon & Schuster International
Simon & Schuster Australia
Simon & Schuster Canada
Simon & Schuster UK

HARPERCOLLINS
(subsidiary of News Corp.)
www.harpercollins.com

HarperCollins General Books Group
Access Press
Amistad Press
Avon
Ecco
Eos
Fourth Estate
Harper Design International
HarperAudio
HarperBusiness
HarperCollins
HarperEntertainment
HarperLargePrint
HarperResource
HarperSanFrancisco
HarperTorch
Perennial
PerfectBound
Quill
Rayo
ReganBooks
William Morrow

HarperCollins Children's Books Group
Avon
Greenwillow Books
HarperCollins Children's Books
HarperFestival
HarperTrophy
Joanna Cotler Books

Laura Geringer Books
Tempest

HarperCollins Australia
Angus & Robertson
Flamingo
4th Estate
HarperBusiness
HarperCollins
HarperReligious
HarperSports
Voyager

HarperCollins Canada
HarperFlamingoCanada
Perennial Canada

HarperCollins UK
Collins
Collins Education
4th Estate
Thorsons/Element
Voyager Books

Zondervan
Inspirio
Vida Publishers
Zonderkidz

RANDOM HOUSE, INC.
(Bertelsmann AG)
www.randomhouse.com

Ballantine Publishing Group
Ballantine Books
Ballantine Reader's Circle
Del Rey
Del Rey/Lucas Books
Fawcett
Ivy
One World
Wellspring

Bantam Dell Publishing Group
Bantam Hardcover
Bantam Mass Market
Bantam Trade Paperback
Crimeline
Delacorte Press
Dell
Delta
The Dial Press
Domain
DTP
Fanfare
Island
Spectra

Crown Publishing Group
Bell Tower
Clarkson Potter
Crown Business
Crown Publishers, Inc.
Harmony Books
Prima
Shaye Areheart Books
Three Rivers Press

Doubleday Broadway Publishing Group
Broadway Books
Currency
Doubleday
Doubleday Image
Doubleday Religious Publishing
Main Street Books
Nan A. Talese

Knopf Publishing Group
Alfred A. Knopf
Anchor
Everyman's Library
Pantheon Books
Schocken Books
Vintage Anchor Publishing

Random House Adult Trade Publishing Group
The Modern Library
Random House Trade Group
Random House Trade Paperbacks
Strivers Row Books
Villard Books

Random House Audio Publishing Group
Listening Library
Random House Audible
Random House Audio
Random House Audio Assets
Random House Audio Dimensions
Random House Audio Price-less

Random House Audio Roads
Random House Audio Voices

Random House Children's Books
BooksReportsNow.com
GoldenBooks.com
Junie B. Jones
Kids@Random
Magic Tree House
Parents@Random
Seussville
Teachers@Random
Teens@Random

Knopf/Delacorte/Dell Young Readers Group
Alfred A. Knopf
Bantam
Crown
David Fickling Books
Delacorte Press
Dell Dragonfly
Dell Laurel-Leaf
Dell Yearling Books
Doubleday
Wendy Lamb Books

Random House Young Readers Group
Akiko
Arthur
Barbie
Beginner Books
The Berenstain Bears
Bob the Builder
Disney
Dragon Tales
First Time Books
Golden Books
Landmark Books
Little Golden Books
Lucas Books
Mercer Mayer
Nickelodeon
Nick, Jr.
pat the bunny
Picturebacks
Precious Moments
Richard Scarry
Sesame Street Books
Step into Reading
Stepping Stones
Star Wars
Thomas the Tank Engine and Friends

Random House Direct, Inc.
Bon Appétit
Gourmet Books
Pillsbury

Random House Information Group
Fodor's Travel Publications
Living Language
Prima Games
Princeton Review
Random House Español
Random House Puzzles & Games
Random House Reference Publishing

Random House Large Print Publishing

Random House Value Publishing

Random House International
Areté
McClelland & Stewart Ltd.
Plaza & Janés
Random House Australia
Random House of Canada Ltd.
Random House Mondadori
Random House South America
Random House United Kingdom
Transworld UK
Verlagsgruppe Random House

Waterbrook Press
Fisherman Bible Study Guides
Shaw Books
Waterbrook Press

PENGUIN GROUP (USA), INC.
(Pearson plc)
www.penguinputnam.com

Penguin Putnam, Inc. (Adult)
Ace Books
Avery
Berkley Books
 Diamond Books
 Jam

Prime Crime
Boulevard
Dutton
Gotham
G.P. Putnam's Sons
Blue Hen Putnam
HPBooks
Jeremy P. Tarcher
Jove
NAL
New American Library
Penguin
Perigee
Plume
Portfolio
Riverhead Books (paperback)
Viking

Penguin Putnam Books for Young Readers (Children)
AlloyBooks
Dial Books for Young Readers
Dutton Children's Books
Firebird
Frederick Warne
G.P. Putnam's Sons
Grosset & Dunlap
Planet Dexter
Platt & Munk
Philomel
Phyllis Fogelman Books
PaperStar
Planet Dexter
Platt & Munk
Playskool
Price Stern Sloan
PSS
Puffin Books
Viking Children's Books

AOL TIME WARNER BOOK GROUP
www.twbookmark.com

Warner Books
Aspect
Mysterious Press
Time Warner AudioBooks
Warner Business Books
Warner Faith
Warner Forever
Warner Vision

Little, Brown and Co. Adult Trade Books
Back Bay Books
Bulfinch Press

Little, Brown and Co. Children's Publishing
Megan Tingley Books

HOLTZBRINCK PUBLISHERS (Germany)
www.vhpsva.com/bookseller/HBGenInfo.html

St. Martin's Press
Griffin
Minotaur
St. Martin's Press Paperback & Reference
St. Martin's Press Trade Division
Thomas Dunne Books
Truman Talley Books
Whitman Coin Books & Products

Tor Books
Forge Books
Orb Books

Henry Holt & Co.
Henry Holt Books for Young Readers
John Macrae Books
Metropolitan Books
Owl Books
Picador USA
Times Books

Farrar, Straus & Giroux
Faber and Faber
FSG Books for Young Readers
Hill and Wang
Mirasol/libros
North Point Press
Sunburst Paperback

Do I Need an Agent?

If you have a book ready to be published, you may be wondering if you need a literary agent. If you're not sure whether you want to work with an agent, consider the following factors.

WHAT CAN AN AGENT DO FOR YOU?

An agent will believe in your writing and know an audience interested in what you write exists somewhere. As the representative for your work, your agent will tell editors your manuscript is the best thing to land on her desk this year. But beyond being enthusiastic about your book, there are a lot of benefits to using an agent.

For starters, today's competitive marketplace can be difficult to break into, especially for previously unpublished writers. Many larger publishing houses will only look at manuscripts from agents. In fact, approximately 80 percent of books published by the major houses are sold to them by agents.

But an agent's job isn't just getting your book through a publisher's door. That's only a small part of what an agent can do for you. The following describes the various jobs agents do for their clients, many of which would be difficult for a writer to do without outside help.

Agents know editors' tastes and needs

An agent possesses information on a complex web of publishing houses and a multitude of editors to make sure her clients' manuscripts are placed in the hands of the right editors. This knowledge is gathered through relationships she cultivates with acquisition editors—the people who decide which books to present to their publisher for possible publication. Through her industry connections, an agent becomes aware of the specializations of publishing houses and their imprints, knowing that one publisher only wants contemporary romances while another is interested solely in nonfiction books about the military. By networking with editors over lunch, an agent also learns more specialized information—which editor is looking for a crafty Agatha Christie-style mystery for the fall catalog, for example.

Agents track changes in publishing

Being attentive to constant market changes and vacillating trends is also a major requirement of an agent's job. He understands what it may mean for clients when publisher A merges with publisher B, and when an editor from house C moves to house D. Or what it means when readers—and therefore editors—are no longer interested in westerns, but instead can't get their hands on enough Stephen King-style suspense novels.

Agents get your manuscript read faster

Although it may seem like an extra step to send your manuscript to an agent instead of directly to a publishing house, the truth is an agent can prevent writers from wasting months sending manuscripts to the wrong places or being buried in someone's slush pile. Editors rely on agents to save them time as well. With little time to sift through the hundreds of unsolicited submissions arriving weekly in the mail, an editor is naturally going to prefer a manuscript that has already been approved by a qualified reader. For this reason, many of the larger publishers accept agented submissions only.

Agents understand contracts

When publishers write contracts, they are primarily interested in their own bottom line rather than the best interests of the author. Writers unfamiliar with contractual language may find themselves bound to a publisher with whom they no longer want to work or prevented them from getting royalties on their first book until they have written several. An agent uses her experience to negotiate a contract that benefits the writer while still respecting some of the publisher's needs.

Agents negotiate—and exploit—subsidiary rights

Beyond publication, a savvy agent keeps in mind other opportunities for your manuscript. If your agent believes your book will also be successful as an audio book, a Book-of-the-Month club selection, or even a blockbuster movie, he will take these options into consideration when shopping your manuscript. These additional mediums for your writing are called "subsidiary rights." Part of an agent's job is to keep track of the strengths and weaknesses of different publishers's subsidiary rights offices to determine the deposition of these rights to your work. After the contract is negotiated, the agent will seek additional money-making opportunities for the rights he kept for his client.

Agents get escalators

An escalator is a bonus that an agent can negotiate as part of the book contract. It is commonly given when a book appears on a bestseller list or if a client appears on a popular television show. For example, a publisher might give a writer a $50,000 bonus if she is picked for a book club. Both the agent and the editor know such media attention will sell more books, and the agent negotiates an escalator to ensure the writer benefits from this increase in sales.

Agents track payments

Because an agent only receives payment when the publisher pays the writer, it is in her best interest to make sure the writer is paid on schedule. Some publishing houses are notorious for late payments. Having an agent distances you from any conflict over payment and allows you to spend your time writing instead of on the phone.

Agents are strong advocates

Besides standing up for your right to be paid on time, agents can ensure your book gets more attention from the publisher's marketing department, a better cover design, or other benefits you may not know to ask for during the publishing process. An agent can also provide advice during each step of this process as well as guidance about your long-term writing career.

WHEN MIGHT YOU NOT NEED AN AGENT?

Although there are many reasons to work with an agent, an author can benefit from submitting his own work. For example, if your writing focuses on a very specific area, you may want to work with a small or specialized publisher. These houses are usually open to receiving material directly from writers. Smaller houses can often give more attention to a writer than a large house, providing editorial help, marketing expertise, and other advice directly to the writer.

Some writers use a lawyer or entertainment attorney instead of an agent. If a lawyer specializes in intellectual property, he can help a writer with contract negotiations. Instead of giving the lawyer a commission, the lawyer is paid for his time only.

And, of course, some people prefer working independently instead of relying on others to do their work. If you are one of these people, it is probably better to shop your own work instead of constantly butting heads with an agent. And despite the benefits of working with an agent, it is possible to sell your work directly to a publisher—people do it all the time!

How to Know When You are Ready for an Agent

BY DEBBIE MACOMBER

You need an agent to sell a book—don't you? I was convinced of it before I sold my first book. During the early part of my five-year sojourn in the desert of no sales, I sought a high-powered agent. All right, *any* agent. First, I had to locate one willing to read my work which—as those of you lingering in the desert will recognize—is no easy task.

Once I did manage to catch an agent's attention, I was under pressure to convince this person I was an undiscovered literary genius. At the time I was eager to do anything, pay anything, sign anything, if only I could find an agent who'd agree to represent me.

Twenty years and dozens of published books later, I'm here to tell you something shocking. Contrary to popular belief, agents don't sell books. What *does* persuade an editor to offer a contract with your name on it—excellent writing, powerful characterization, and scintillating dialogue.

KNOW WHY YOU NEED AN AGENT

Many writers want agents. I know I did, and I had good reasons for feeling that way. First, I have a real talent when it comes to storytelling, but about negotiating a contract I know next to nothing. I felt I needed representation in order to get the best terms and the highest advance. Having an agent is often part of the publishing process, and I wanted in as quickly as possible. I was convinced an agent would smooth the way for me, that he or she would be my foot in the proverbial door. After all, agents are interested in acquiring writers whose books they can sell, so knowing the market, the editors, and the publishing houses is their business.

There's another reason an agent made sense to me. My mother and my husband assured me I was a good writer. So did anyone else I could talk or manipulate into reading my stories. That's all well and good, but these people are my family and friends. The approval of an agent, a real publishing professional, said so much more. Having an agent validated me as a writer. That was an important stage in my development and it bolstered my confidence tremendously.

I wrote for five years before I sold a word of fiction. Five long years filled with struggles and doubt! I felt like Moses headed for the Promised Land, encountering one discouragement after another, and I could only pray it wouldn't take me 40 years to sell. Every day when I sat down to write, I faced a blank page and the fear of an equally blank future. I was investing my heart, my ego, my time—everything—in getting published, and there was a very real possibility it might never happen. Having an agent assured me that what I wrote was worthy of publication. It gave me faith that my dream would be realized.

This, however, was only one side of that particular coin. Having an agent validated me to others, too. Talking about my agent during those bleak early years was my favorite response to any nonbelievers I met. As with any worthwhile endeavor, there are plenty of naysayers who consider it their personal responsibility to disillusion us dreamers. It sounded so good to say,

---

DEBBIE MACOMBER *is a* New York Times *best-selling author with more than 60 million copies of her novels in print worldwide. Residing in Washington state, Debbie is dedicated to her craft and to her readers. Visit Debbie's website at www.debbiemacomber.com.*

"Well, my agent says . . ." That was usually all it took to silence their pessimism.

Having an agent said in bright, bold letters that someone other than my mother and my husband thought I had talent. I loved to say it as much as I loved to hear it. "My agent."

DETERMINE THE RIGHT TIME

As you can tell, getting an agent was my first priority when I finished my novel. I wanted to be ready when that all-important phone call came. For that reason, I didn't submit to a publisher. I was convinced I needed an agent before I could do that, so I searched until I found one willing to take me on as a client. As a result, I wasted precious time. Eventually, I did find an agent willing to represent me—but for a hefty reading fee. A fee, moreover, that continued to escalate on top of accumulating expenses.

Naturally, she told me what I wanted to hear. She never ceased to praise my work and repeatedly told me how talented I was. I was bound to sell soon, she assured me. Later, to my horror, I discovered she hadn't submitted any of my work to a publisher.

Herein lies one of the pitfalls of hiring an agent *before* you sell. In essence, the agent chooses you. I was so grateful this woman had accepted me as her client, I willingly dug into my weekly grocery money in order to pay her fees. She was my big chance at selling, my one hope. I took delight in dropping her name at the slightest excuse. "Hi, my name is Debbie, and my agent's name is . . ."

I don't mean to imply that every agent who takes on an unpublished writer is running a scam, although please be careful. No reputable agent charges reading fees. When we're pursuing our dreams we can be incredibly naïve. We so badly want to believe our work is worthy of publication that we become prey to unscrupulous people.

The point I want to make is how fortunate I felt to have an agent, any agent, represent me, how excited I was. But there's a real problem with this kind of thinking. Agents are employed by the writer. Remember that. In other words, the agent is your employee. You pay him or her a percentage of your earnings, not the other way around. If you were hiring, you wouldn't choose just any employee; you'd look carefully at the qualifications of all your candidates. As inexperienced writers, we're often far too eager to overlook what should be obvious. We're too ready to accept questionable situations in exchange for an agent's representation.

When we're willing to take on an agent, *any agent*, we risk confusing the whole "who employs whom" issue. Because an unpublished novelist isn't bringing funds into the agency, that writer is often at the bottom of the list as far as receiving attention is concerned. Phone calls go unanswered, reports aren't made—for one practical reason. Agents invest their time and expertise on the clients who pay the bills. As an unpublished writer, that isn't you.

An agent will sometimes ask a writer to do revisions. I've known a number of authors who have rewritten their manuscripts for their agents, spending literally weeks on reconstructing their plots. The outcome of that rewrite depends on the agent's vision of the book, and there's a risk in that. Sometimes an author will get so caught up in giving the agent the story he or she wants that they lose sight of whose story it really is—who the author really is. The lesson here is simple. Revise your work for the people who write the check! If an editor asks for a rewrite, do it. If an agent does, think about it. The agent could be right on track, but the decision on whether to rewrite should be up to the author.

Over the years, I've met a number of writers who did find an agent to represent them early in their writing careers, before the sale of their first books. Eventually they did manage to sell, but I'm convinced the vast majority would have gotten that publishing contract with or without representation (especially those submitting genre fiction). Soon after that initial sale, problems arose with the agents. As their careers progressed, these writers discovered, with time and publishing experience, that the agents were no longer a good fit for them—and in some cases, never had been.

After several sales, a writer often feels obligated to stick with the agent. Staying with or leaving an agent should be considered a business decision, but emotions, personal feelings and subtle pressure often make the writer reluctant to walk away from the original agent. It's easy to understand why. That first agent believed in the writer before anyone else did. The agent was there in the beginning. Now, what should be a straightforward business decision has become tangled in emotions and feelings of guilt.

Unfortunately, many publishers are no longer willing to accept unagented material. Talk about a catch-22! You need an agent to sell, and you have to sell before you can get an agent. However, there are a number of inventive solutions to that dilemma. I have a couple of suggestions, but I urge you to be creative and come up with your own ideas.

Ask the experts for advice

The best way to learn about marketing your book is to network with other authors. Most of the published authors I'm acquainted with are happy to share the knowledge they've gained. You can meet authors at writers' conferences. Ask and you shall receive. Knock and the door shall be opened. I've made this suggestion before, and I'm amazed at how few people actually seek an author's advice.

Target editors first, not agents

Published authors are the best source of information about editors. However, as I've already said, remember the key to publishing is submitting your work to the person who writes the check. If you're at a conference, make it your goal to learn as much about the editors as you can. You can do this by attending their workshops and, if the opportunity presents itself, sitting at their tables during meals. If an editor is speaking, be there, take good notes, and listen. Make a point of meeting editors whenever possible, but always be polite and respectful of their time. Sign up for editor appointments if the conference offers them. If that can't be arranged, write a letter after the conference, and let the editor know what you learned from him or her at the workshop you attended. Then, ask if it would be permissible to submit a query. In essence, this is a query on a query. If the response to your letter is positive, a submission would then be sent to the publisher as requested material. Now you have your manuscript in front of an editor without an agent—at a house that states it will only consider manuscripts represented by agents. Remember there are exceptions to every rule.

Another method is to enter writing contests. Many authors have received publishing contracts as the result of entering writing competitions. However, before you plunk down your hard-earned dollars for the entry fee, make sure an editor is the final judge. Writing organizations such as RWA and magazines such as *Writer's Digest* are good resources of such contests *(Editor's note: Contest & Awards listing begin on page 924.)*. (And be aware that there are frequently contests associated with conferences.) Recently, publishing houses have started running contests themselves, seeking out new talent. Check a publisher's website for details.

To summarize, you don't need an agent to get your manuscript read by an editor. Be smart. Where there's a will and a brain, there's a way. Don't stand in front of a closed door; pound on it!

Consider the attorney route

Hire a literary attorney to submit on your behalf. While there are attorneys who specialize in publishing contracts, they aren't as common. Still they do exist, especially in Los Angeles and New York. *The Yellow Pages* are available online, and it's a simple matter of making contact and querying them about submissions on your behalf.

I'm sure you can understand that after the fiasco with my first agent, I was gun shy. I wasted two years filling an unscrupulous agent's coffers, and I wasn't about to trust just anybody again. Nor would I fall prey to agents who offered to "doctor" manuscripts for an outrageous fee. From that point forward, I submitted my own work.

I don't think anyone was more shocked than I was when I sold my first book. I'd grown so accustomed to rejection that when the editor phoned on September 29, 1982, at 4:29 p.m., I was speechless. Because I'd been writing for almost five years and had four completed manuscripts, I quickly sold a number of books to that same editor. Suddenly, my career as a novelist was promising.

Far be it from me to hire an agent when I no longer thought I needed one. Why pay an agent 15 percent, when I was perfectly capable of selling books on my own? As far as I was concerned, it would be a waste of money. Besides, I had a good working relationship with my editor.

The negative experience with that first agent, in addition to pure stubbornness, prevented me from seeking out representation for several years after that. Truth be known, paying an agent a percentage of my advances rubbed me the wrong way. When I'd needed one, nary an agent could be found. Now I was easy money. An agent wouldn't have to work to sell my books, so why hand over a commission he or she had done nothing to earn?

Then, I happened to meet with a group of writers who had sold to my publisher. While discussing foreign sales, I learned I was collecting only half of what they were receiving. Their agent had gotten them a higher royalty rate on foreign sales. I didn't know those rates were negotiable. If I was getting 50 percent less on foreign royalty rates I wanted to know what else I wasn't receiving. That was a daunting question only an agent could answer.

Play good cop, bad cop

In addition, I discovered I was uncomfortable talking money with my editor—such as when too much time had elapsed between the delivery of my manuscript and the receipt of my advance check. I found it embarrassing and a bit humiliating to ask if she'd put in a payment request. I needed someone to step in and deal with the awkward questions, someone who knew far more about a publishing contract than I did! My goal was to preserve the delicate author-editor relationship.

I knew it was time to get an agent. I talked it over with my editor and sought her advice. She gave me the names of five or six agents she liked and worked well with and thought I would, too. I compiled a list of questions and booked my first trip to New York, where I met a number of reputable agents face to face. After selling 23 books on my own, I hired a real agent. I admit it now: I waited too long. I'd let pride stand in my way, and I paid for that foolishness.

I discovered agents do far more than negotiate contracts. That's merely the first step. Agents are also involved in subsidiary rights, such as film and foreign sales. Agents offer ideas, suggestions, and guidance when it comes to plot lines. My first *New York Times* bestseller, *Promise, Texas* (MIRA Books, 1999), was based on an idea that came directly from my agent.

So when is the best time to hire an agent? If I had it to do over again, I'd hire an agent after selling a couple of books. By that time, I'd learned from other authors and knew a lot more about the publishing process. I would have recognized what I wanted and what I was looking for in an agent.

When is the time right for you? That's a decision you'll need to make on your own. Don't leap in too quickly, and don't wait too long.

How to Find the Right Agent

A writer's job is to write. A literary agent's job is to find publishers for her clients' books. Any writer who has endeavored to attract the attention of a publishing house knows this is no easy task. But beyond selling manuscripts, an agent must keep track of the ever-changing industry, writers' royalty statements, fluctuating reading habits, and the list continues.

Because publishing houses receive more unsolicited manuscripts each year, securing an agent is becoming more of a necessity. Nevertheless, finding an eager *and* reputable agent is a difficult task. Even the most patient of writers can become frustrated, even disillusioned. Therefore, as a writer seeking agent representation, you should prepare yourself before starting your search. By learning effective strategies for approaching agents, as well as what to expect from an author/agent relationship, you will save yourself time—and quite possibly, heartache.

Make sure you are ready for an agent

With an agent's job in mind, you should ask yourself if you and your work are at a stage where you need an agent. Look at the "Ten Step Checklists for Fiction and Nonfiction Writers," and judge how prepared you are for contacting an agent. Have you spent enough time researching or polishing your manuscript? Sending an agent an incomplete project not only wastes your time but may turn him off in the process. Literary agents are not magicians. An agent cannot sell an unsalable property.

Moreover, your material may not be appropriate for an agent. Most agents do not represent poetry, magazine articles, short stories, or material suitable for academic or small presses—the agents' commission earned does not justify spending time submitting these type of works. Those agents who do take on such material generally represent authors on larger projects first, and then represent these smaller items only as a favor for their clients.

If you strongly believe your work is ready to be placed with an agent, make sure you are personally ready to be represented. In other words, before you contact an agent, consider the direction in which your writing career is headed. Besides skillful writers, agencies want clients with the ability to produce more than one book. Most agents will say they represent careers, not books. So as you compose your query letter—your initial contact with an agent—briefly mention your potential. Let an agent know if you've already started drafting your second novel. Let him know that for you writing is more than a half-hearted hobby.

The importance of research

Nobody would buy a used car without at least checking the odometer, and the savvy shopper would consult the blue books, take a test drive, and even ask for a mechanic's opinion. Because you want to obtain the best possible agent for your writing, you should do some research on the business of agents before sending out query letters. Understanding how agents operate will help you find an agent appropriate for your work.

The best way to educate yourself is to read all you can about agents and other authors. Organizations such as the Association of Authors' Representatives (AAR), the National Writers Union (NWU), American Society of Journalists and Authors (ASJA), and Poets & Writers, Inc. all have informational material on agenting. (These, along with other helpful organizations, are listed in the back of this book.) *Publishers Weekly* covers publishing news affecting agents and others in the publishing industry in general; discusses specific events in the "Hot Deals" and "Behind the Bestsellers" columns; and occasionally lists individual author's agents in the "Fore-

Before You Contact an Agent: A Nine-step Checklist for Fiction Writers

- ☑ **Finish your novel** or short story collection.
- ☑ **Revise your novel.** Have other writers offer criticism to ensure your manuscript is as finished as you believe possible.
- ☑ **Proofread.** Don't let your hard work go to waste by turning off an agent with typos.
- ☑ **Publish** short stories or novel excerpts in literary journals, proving to potential agents that editors see quality in your writing.
- ☑ **Research** to find the agents of writers you admire or whose work is similar to your own.
- ☑ **Rank your list.** Use the listings in this book to determine the agents most suitable for you and your work, and to eliminate inappropriate agencies.
- ☑ **Write your synopsis.** Completing this step early will help you write your query letter and save you time later when agents contact you.
- ☑ **Compose your query letter.** This brief letter should be polished and to the point.
- ☑ **Read about the business** of agents so you are knowledgeable and prepared to act on any offer.

casts" section. Their website, www.publishersweekly.com, also offers a wealth of information about specific agents.

Even the Internet has a wide range of sites devoted to agents. Through the different forums provided on the Web, you can learn basic information about preparing for your initial contact or more specific material about individual agents. Keep in mind, however, not everything printed on the Web is a solid fact; you may come across the site of a writer who is bitter because an agent rejected his manuscript. Your best bet is to use the Internet to supplement your other research.

Through your research, you will discover the need to be wary of some agents. Anybody can go to the neighborhood copy center and order business cards which say she is a literary agent. But that title does not mean she can sell your book. She may ask for a large sum of money, then disappear from society. Becoming knowledgeable about the different types of fees agents may charge is a *crucial* step to take before contacting any agent.

An agent also may not have any connections with others in the publishing industry. An agent's reputation with editors can be her major strength or weakness. While it's true that even top agents are not able to sell every book they represent, an inexperienced agent who submits too many inappropriate submissions will quickly lose her standing with any editor. It is acceptable to ask an agent for recent sales before he agrees to represent you, but keep in mind that some agents consider this information confidential. If an agent does give you a list of recent sales, you can call the publishers' contracts department to ensure the sale was actually made by that agent.

The pros and cons of location

For years, the major editors and agents were located in New York. If a writer wanted to be published with a big-name house, he had to contact a New York agency. But this has changed over time for many reasons. For starters, publishing companies are appearing all over the country—San Francisco, Seattle, Chicago, Minneapolis. And naturally, agents are locating closer to these smaller publishing hubs.

The recent advances in technology have also had an impact on the importance of location. Thanks to fax machines, the Internet, e-mail, express mail, and inexpensive long-distance tele-

Before You Contact an Agent: An Eight-step Checklist for Nonfiction Writers

- ☑ **Formulate a concrete idea** for your book.
- ☑ **Research** works on similar topics to understand the competition and determine how yours is unique.
- ☑ **Compose sample chapters.**
- ☑ **Publish** completed chapters in journals.
- ☑ **Polish your outline** to refer to while drafting a query letter and avoid wasting time when agents contact you.
- ☑ **Brainstorm** three to four subject categories that best describe your material.
- ☑ **Write your query.** Describe your premise and your experience professionally and succinctly, to give an agent an excellent first impression of you.
- ☑ **Read about the business** of agents so you are knowledgeable and prepared to act on any offer.

phone rates, an agent no longer needs to live in New York to work closely with a New York publisher.

Nevertheless, there are simply more opportunities for agents located in New York to network with editors. They are able to meet face-to-face over lunch. The editor can share his specific needs, and the agent can promote her newest talent. As long as New York remains the publishing capital of the world, the majority of agents will be found there, too.

Contacting agents

Once your manuscript is prepared and you have a solid understanding of how literary agents work, the time is right to contact an agent. Your initial contact is the first impression you make on an agent; therefore, you want to be professional and brief.

Again, research plays an important role in getting an agent's attention. You'll want to show her you've done your homework. Read the listings in this book to learn her areas of interest, check out her website to learn more details about how she operates business, and find out the names of some of her clients. If there is an author whose book is similar to yours, call the author's publisher. Someone in the contracts department can tell you the name of the agent who sold the title, provided an agent was used. Contact that agent, and impress her with your knowledge of her agency.)*Editor's note: For more on contacting agents, see The Basics of Contacting Literary Agents on page 93.*)

Evaluate any offer

Once you've received an offer of representation, you must determine if the agent is right for you. As flattering as any offer may be, you need to be confident that you are going to work well with this person and that this person is going to work hard to sell your manuscript.

You need to know what you should expect once you enter into a business relationship. You should know how much editorial input to expect from your agent; how often he gives updates about where your manuscript has been and who has seen it; and what subsidiary rights the agent represents.

More importantly, you should know when you will be paid. The publisher will send your advance and any subsequent royalty checks directly to the agent. After deducting his commission—usually 10 to 15 percent—your agent will send you the remaining balance. Most agents charge a higher commission of 20 to 25 percent when using a co-agent for foreign, dramatic, or other specialized rights. As you enter into a relationship with an agent, have him explain his specific commission rates and payment policy.

As your potential partner, you have the right to ask an agent for information that convinces you she knows what she's doing. Be reasonable about what you ask, however. Asking for recent sales is okay; asking for the average size of clients' advances is not. Remember, agents are very busy. Often asking a general question like, "How do you work?" or requesting a sample contract, can quickly answer your concerns.

Evaluate the agent's level of experience. Agents who have been in the business awhile have a larger number of contacts, but new agents may be hungrier, as well as more open to previously unpublished writers. Talk to other writers about their interactions with specific agents. Writers' organizations such as the National Writers Association (NWA), the American Society of Journalists and Authors (ASJA), and the National Writers Union (NWU) maintain files on agents their members have dealt with, and can share this information by written request or through their membership newsletters.

Understand any contract before you sign

Some agents offer written contracts, some do not. If your prospective agent does not, at least ask for a "memorandum of understanding" that details the basic relationship of expenses and commissions. If your agent does offer a contract, be sure to read it carefully, and keep a copy for yourself. Because contracts can be confusing, you may want to have a lawyer or knowledgeable writer friend check it out before you sign anything.

The National Writers Union (NWU) has drafted a Preferred Literary Agent Agreement and a pamphlet, *Understand the Author-Agent Relationship*, which is available to members. The union suggests clauses that delineate such issues as:

- the scope of representation (One work? One work with the right of refusal on the next? All work completed in the coming year? All work completed until the agreement is terminated?)
- the extension of authority to the agent to negotiate on behalf of the author
- compensation for the agent, and any co-agent, if used
- manner and time frame for forwarding monies received by the agent on behalf of the client
- termination clause, allowing client to give about thirty days to terminate the agreement
- the effect of termination on concluded agreements as well as ongoing negotiations
- arbitration in the event of a dispute between agent and client

If things don't work out

Because this is a business relationship, a time may come when it is beneficial for you and your agent to part ways. Unlike a marriage, you don't need to go through counseling to keep the relationship together. Instead, you end it professionally on terms upon which you both agree.

First check to see if your written agreement spells out any specific procedures. If not, write a brief, businesslike letter, stating that you no longer think the relationship is advantageous and you wish to terminate it. Instruct the agent not to make any new submissions and give her a 30- to 60-day limit to continue as representative on submissions already under consideration. You can ask for a list of all publishers who have rejected your unsold work, as well as a list of those who are currently considering it. If your agent charges for office expenses, you will have to reimburse him upon terminating the contract. For this reason, you may want to ask for a cap on expenses when you originally enter into an agency agreement. If your agent has made sales for you, he will continue to receive those monies from the publisher, deduct his commission and remit the balance to you. A statement and your share of the money should be sent to you within thirty days. You can also ask that all manuscripts in his possession be returned to you.

The Basics of Contacting Literary Agents

Once you and your manuscript are thoroughly prepared, the time is right to contact an agent. Finding an agent can often be as difficult as finding a publisher. Nevertheless, there are four ways to maximize your chances of finding the right agent: Obtain a referral from someone who knows the agent; meet the agent in person at a writers' conference; submit a query letter or proposal; or attract the agent's attention with your own published writing.

Referrals

The best way to get your foot in an agent's door is to be referred by one of his clients, or by an editor or another agent he has worked with in the past. Because an agent trusts his clients, he will usually read referred work before over-the-transom submissions. If you are friends with anyone in the publishing business who has connections with agents, ask politely for a referral. However, don't be offended if another writer will not share the name of his agent.

If you don't have a wide network of publishing professionals, use the resources you do have to get an agent's attention.

Conferences

Going to a conference is your best bet for meeting an agent in person. Many conferences invite agents to either give a speech or simply be available for meetings with authors. Agents view conferences as a way to find writers. Often agents set aside time for one-to-one discussions with writers, and occasionally they may even look at material writers bring to the conference. If an agent is impressed with you and your work, she may ask for writing samples after the conference. When you send your query, be sure to mention the specific conference where you met and that she asked to see your work.

Because this is an effective way to connect with agents, we've asked agents to indicate in their listings which conferences they regularly attend.

Submissions

The most common way to contact an agent is by a query letter or a proposal package. Most agents will accept unsolicited queries. Some will also look at outlines and sample chapters. Almost none want unsolicited complete manuscripts. Check the **How to Contact** subhead in each listing to learn exactly how an agent prefers to be solicited. Never call—let the writing in your query letter speak for itself.

Because a query letter is your first impression on an agent, it should be professional and to the point. As a brief introduction to your manuscript, a query letter should only be one page in length.

- The first paragraph should quickly state your purpose—you want representation.
- In the second paragraph, mention why you have specifically chosen to query him. Perhaps he specializes in your areas of interest or represents authors you admire. Show him you have done your homework.
- In the next paragraph or two, describe the project, the proposed audience, why your book will sell, etc. Be sure to mention the approximate length and any special features.
- Then discuss why you are the perfect person to write this book, listing your professional

credentials or relative experience.

- Close your query with an offer to send either an outline, sample chapters, or the complete manuscript—depending on your type of book.

Agents agree to be listed in directories such as *Writer's Market* to indicate to writers what they want to see, and how they wish to receive submissions. As you start to query agents, make sure you follow their individual submission directions. This, too, shows an agent you've done your research. Like publishers, agencies have specialties. Some are only interested in novel-length works. Others are open to a wide variety of subjects and may actually have member agents within the agency who specialize in only a handful of the topics covered by the entire agency.

Publishing credits

Some agents read magazines or journals to find writers to represent. If you have had an outstanding piece published in a periodical, you may be contacted by an agent wishing to represent you. In such cases, make sure the agent has read your work. Some agents send form letters to writers, and such agents often make their living entirely from charging reading fees, not from commissions on sales.

However, many reputable and respected agents do contact potential clients in this way. For them, you already possess attributes of a good client: you have publishing credits, and an editor has validated your work. To receive a letter from a reputable agent who has read your material and wants to represent you is an honor.

Occasionally, writers who have self-published or who have had their work published electronically may attract an agent's attention, especially if the self-published book has sold well or received a lot of positive reviews.

Recently, writers have been posting their work on the Internet in hope of attracting an agent's eye. With all the submissions most agents receive, they likely have little time to peruse writer's websites. Nevertheless, there are agents who do consider the Internet a resource for finding fresh voices. Only the future will show how often writers are discovered through this medium.

The Markets

Literary Agents

Agents listed in this section generate 98 to 100 percent of their income from commission on sales. They do not charge for reading, critiquing, or editing. Sending a query to a nonfee-charging agent means you pay only the cost of postage to have your work considered by an agent with an imperative to find salable manuscripts: Her income depends on finding the best publisher for your manuscript.

Because her time is more profitably spent meeting with editors, she will have little or no time to critique your writing. Agents who don't charge fees must be selective and often prefer to work with established authors, celebrities, or those with professional credentials in a particular field.

Some agents in this section may charge clients for office expenses such as photocopying, foreign postage, long distance phone calls, or express mail services. Make sure you have a clear understanding of what these expenses are before signing any agency agreement.

Canadian and international agents are also included in this section. Canadian agents have a ( ) preceding their listing while international agents (those located outside of the U.S. and Canada) have a ( ) preceding their listing. Remember to include an International Reply Coupon (IRC) with your self-addressed envelope when contacting Canadian and international agents.

Level of Openness

Each agency has an icon indicating its openness to submissions. Before contacting any agency, check the listing to make sure it is open to new clients.

- Newer agency actively seeking clients.
- Agency seeking both new and established writers.
- Agency prefers to work with established writers, mostly obtains new clients through referrals.
- Agency handling only certain types of work or work by writers under certain circumstances.
- Agency not currently seeking new clients. We include these agencies to let you know they are currently not open to new clients. *Unless you have a strong recommendation from someone well respected in the field, our advice is to avoid approaching these agents.*

SUBHEADS

Each listing is broken down into subheads to make locating specific information easier. In the first section, you'll find contact information for each agency. You'll also learn if they belong to any professional organizations which can tell you a lot about an agency. For example, members of the Association of Authors' Representatives (AAR) are prohibited from charging reading or evaluating fees. Further information is provided which indicates an agency's size, its willingness to work with a new or previously unpublished writer, and its general areas of interest.

Member Agents: Agencies comprised of more than one agent list member agents and their

individual specialties to help you determine the most appropriate person for your query letter.
Represents: Here agencies specify what nonfiction and fiction subjects they consider. Make sure you query only agents who represent the type of material you write.

O‑ Look for the key icon to quickly learn an agent's areas of specialization or specific strengths (i.e., editorial or marketing experience, sub-rights expertise, etc.). Agents mention here what specific areas they are currently seeking as well as subjects they do *not* wish to receive.

How to Contact: Most agents open to submissions prefer initially to receive a query letter briefly describing your work. Some agents ask for an outline and a number of sample chapters, but you should send these only if requested to do so. Here agents also mention if they accept queries by fax or e-mail, if they consider simultaneous submissions, and their preferred way of meeting new clients.

Recent Sales: To give a sense of the types of material they represent, agents provide specific titles they've sold as well as a sampling of clients' names. Some agents consider their client list confidential and may only share names once they agree to represent you.

Terms: Provided here are details of an agent's commission, whether a contract is offered and for how long, and what additional office expenses you might have to pay if the agent agrees to represent you. Standard commissions range from 10 to 15 percent for domestic sales, and 15 to 20 percent for foreign or dramatic sales with the difference going to the co-agent who places the work.

Writers' Conferences: A great way to meet an agent is at a writers' conference. Here agents list the ones they attend.

Tips: Agents offer advice and additional instructions for writers looking for representation.

For More Information

For more information on approaching agents, read "The Basics of Contacting Literary Agents." Be sure to read the informative articles at the beginning of this book to fully understand the process a writer should go through when finding a literary agent.

ACACIA HOUSE PUBLISHING SERVICES, LTD., 51 Acacia Rd., Toronto ON M4S 2K6, Canada. (416)484-8356. Fax: (416)484-8356. E-mail: fhanna.acacia@rogers.com. **Contact:** (Ms.) Frances Hanna. Estab. 1985. Represents 50 clients. Works with a small number of new/unpublished writers. Currently handles: 30% nonfiction books; 70% novels.

- Ms. Hanna has been in the publishing business for 30 years, first in London (UK) as a fiction editor with Barrie & Jenkins and Pan Books, and as a senior editor with a packager of mainly illustrated books. She was condensed books editor for 6 years for *Reader's Digest* in Montreal, senior editor and foreign rights manager for (the then) William Collins & Sons (now HarperCollins) in Toronto. Her husband, Vice President Bill Hanna, has over 40 years experience in the publishing business.

Member Agents: Bill Hanna, vice president (business, self-help, modern history).

Represents: Nonfiction books, novels. **Considers these nonfiction areas:** Animals; biography/autobiography; language/literature/criticism; memoirs; military/war; music/dance; nature/environment; theater/film; travel. **Considers these fiction areas:** Action/adventure; detective/police/crime; literary; mainstream/contemporary; mystery/suspense; thriller.

O‑ This agency specializes in contemporary fiction: literary or commercial. Actively seeking "outstanding first novels with literary merit." Does not want to receive horror, occult, science fiction.

How to Contact: Query with outline and SASE. *No unsolicited mss.* No e-mail or fax queries. Responds in 6 weeks to queries. Returns materials only with SASE.

Recent Sales: Sold over 50 titles in the last year. Also made numerous international rights sales. This agency prefers not to share information on specific sales or clients.

Terms: Agent receives 15% commission on English language sales, 20% on dramatic sales, 25% commission on foreign sales. Charges clients for photocopying, postage and courier, as necessary.

Tips: "We prefer that writers be previously published, with at least a few short stories or articles to their credit. Strongest consideration will be given to those with, say, three or more published books. However, we *would* take on an unpublished writer of outstanding talent."

N **AGENTS, INC., FOR MEDICAL AND MENTAL HEALTH PROFESSIONALS**, P.O. Box 4956, Fresno CA 93744. (559)438-8289. **Contact:** Sydney H. Harriet, Ph.D., Psy. D., director. Estab. 1987. Member of APA. Represents 49 clients. 70% of clients are new/unpublished writers. Currently handles: 80% nonfiction books; 20% novels; multimedia.

- Prior to opening his agency, Dr. Harriet was a professor of English, psychologist, and radio and television reporter.

Member Agents: Sydney Harriet, Ph.D., director.

Represents: Nonfiction books, novels. **Considers these nonfiction areas:** Cooking/foods/nutrition; health/medicine (mind-body healing); psychology; science/technology; self-help/personal improvement; sociology; sports (medicine, psychology); law. **Considers these fiction areas:** *Currently representing previously published novelists only.*

O‑ This agency specializes in writers who have education and experience in the business, legal and health professions. It is helpful if the writer is licensed but not necessary. Prior nonfiction book publication not necessary. For fiction, previously published fiction is prerequisite for representation. Does not want memoirs, autobiographies, stories about overcoming an illness, science fiction, fantasy, religious materials and children's books.

How to Contact: Query with SASE. Considers simultaneous queries. Responds in 1 month to queries; 1 month to mss.

Recent Sales: Sold 5 titles in the last year. *Infantry Soldier*, by George Neil (University of Oklahoma Press); *SAMe, The European Arthritis and Depression Breakthrough*, by Sol Grazi, M.D. and Maria Costa (Prima); *What to Eat if You Have Diabetes*, by Danielle Chase M.S. (Contemporary); *How to Turn Your Fat Husband Into a Lean Lover*, by Maureen Keane (Random House).

Terms: Agent receives 15% commission on domestic sales; 20% commission on foreign sales. Offers written contract, binding for 6-12 months (negotiable). Writers reimbursed for office fees after the sale of ms.

Writers' Conferences: "Scheduled as a speaker at a number of conferences across the country in 2001-2002. Contact agency to book authors and agents for conferences."

Tips: "Remember, query first. Do not call to pitch an idea. The only way we can judge the quality of your idea is to see how you write. Please, unsolicited manuscripts will not be read if they arrive without a SASE. Currently we are receving more than 200 query letters and proposals each month. Send complete proposal/manuscript only if requested. Please, please ask yourself why someone would be compelled to buy your book. If you think the idea is unique, spend the time to create a query and then a proposal where every word counts. Fiction writers need to understand that the craft is just as important as the idea. 99% of the fiction is rejected because of sloppy overwritten dialogue, wooden characters, predictable plotting and lifeless narrative. Once you finish your novel, put it away and let it percolate, then take it out and work on fine-tuning it some more. A novel is never finished until you stop working on it. Would love to represent more fiction writers and probably will when we read a manuscript that has gone through a dozen or more drafts. Because of rising costs, we no longer can respond to queries, proposals, and/or complete manuscripts without receiving a return envelope and sufficient postage."

N **THE AHEARN AGENCY, INC.**, 2021 Pine St., New Orleans LA 70118-5456. (504)861-8395. Fax: (504)866-6434. E-mail: pahearn@aol.com. **Contact:** Pamela G. Ahearn. Estab. 1992. Member of RWA. Represents 25 clients. 20% of clients are new/unpublished writers. Currently handles: 10% nonfiction books; 90% novels.

- Prior to opening her agency, Ms. Ahearn was an agent for eight years and an editor with Bantam Books.

Represents: Nonfiction books, novels, short story collections (if stories previously published). **Considers these nonfiction areas:** Animals; biography/autobiography; child guidance/parenting; current affairs; ethnic/cultural interests; gay/lesbian issues; health/medicine; history; music/dance; popular culture; self-help/personal improvement; theater/film; true crime/investigative; women's issues/studies. **Considers these fiction areas:** Action/adventure; contemporary issues; detective/police/crime; ethnic; family saga; feminist; gay/lesbian; glitz; historical; humor/satire; literary; mainstream/contemporary; mystery/suspense; psychic/supernatural; regional; romance; thriller.

O‑ This agency specializes in historical romance; also very interested in mysteries and suspense fiction. Does not want to receive category romance, science fiction or fantasy.

How to Contact: Query with SASE. Accepts e-mail queries, no attachments. Considers simultaneous queries. Responds in 6 weeks to queries; 10 weeks to mss. Obtains most new clients through recommendations from others, solicitations, conferences.

Recent Sales: *The Amber Room*, by Steve Berry (Balantine); *The Dragon King's Palace*, by Laura Joh Rowland (St. Martin's); *Dance of Seduction*, by Sabrina Jeffries (Avon).

Terms: Agent receives 15% commission on domestic sales; 20% commission on foreign sales. Offers written contract, binding for 1 year; renewable by mutual consent.

Writers' Conferences: Moonlight & Magnolias; RWA National Conference (Orlando); Virginia Romance Writers (Williamsburg VA); Florida Romance Writers (Ft. Lauderdale FL); Golden Triangle Writers Conference; Bouchercon (Monterey, November); Malice Domestic (DC, May).

Tips: "Be professional! Always send in exactly what an agent/editor asks for, no more, no less. Keep query letters brief and to the point, giving your writing credentials and a very brief summary of your book. If one agent rejects you, keep trying—there are a lot of us out there!"

N **ALIVE COMMUNICATIONS, INC.**, 7680 Goddard St., Suite 200, Colorado Springs CO 80920. (719)260-7080. Fax: (719)260-8223. Website: www.alivecom.com. Estab. 1989. Member of CBA. Represents 200+ clients. 5% of clients are new/unpublished writers. Currently handles: 50% nonfiction books; 30% novels; 4% story collections; 5% novellas; 10% juvenile books; 1% syndicated material.

Member Agents: Rick Christian, president (blockbusters, bestsellers); Greg Johnson, vice president (popular/commercial nonfiction and fiction, Christian organizations); Jerry "Chip" MacGregor (popular/commercial nonfiction and fiction, new authors with breakout potential); Andrea Christian (gift, women's fiction/nonfiction, Christian living); Lee Hough (popular/commercial nonfiction and fiction, thoughtful spirituality, children's).

Represents: Nonfiction books, novels, short story collections, novellas, juvenile books. **Considers these nonfiction areas:** Biography/autobiography; business/economics; child guidance/parenting; how-to; memoir; religious/inspirational; self-help/personal improvement; sports; women's issues. **Considers these fiction areas:** Action/adventure; contemporary issues; detective/police/crime; family saga; historical; humor/satire; juvenile; literary; mainstream/contemporary; mystery/suspense; religious/inspirational; thriller; western/frontier; young adult.

This agency specializes in fiction, Christian living, how-to, children's and commercial nonfiction. Actively seeking inspirational/literary/mainstream fiction and work from authors with established track record and platforms. Does not want poetry, young adult paperback, scripts, dark themes.

How to Contact: Works primarily with well-established, best-selling and career authors. Returns materials only with SASE. Obtains most new clients through recommendations from others, "On rare occasions accepts new clients through referrals."

Recent Sales: Sold 300 titles in the last year. *Left Behind series*, by Tim LaHaye and Jerry B. Jenkins (Tyndale); *Let's Roll*, by Lisa Beamer (Tyndale); *The Message*, by Eugene Peterson (NavPress); *Every Man Series*, by Stephen Arterburn (Waterbrook); *Cafe Refuge*, by Terri Blackstock (Zondervan).

Terms: Agent receives 15% commission on domestic sales; 10% commission on foreign sales. Offers written contract; 60-day written notice to terminate contract.

Tips: "Rewrite and polish until the words on the page shine. Endorsements and great connections may help, provided you can write with power and passion. Network with publishing professionals by making contacts, joining citique groups, and attending writers' conferences in order to make personal connections in publishing and to get feedback. Alive Communications, Inc. has established itself as a premiere literary agency. Based in Colorado Springs, we serve an elite group of authors who are critically acclaimed and commercially successful in both Christian and general markets."

LINDA ALLEN LITERARY AGENCY, 1949 Green St., Suite 5, San Francisco CA 94123-4829. (415)921-6437. **Contact:** Linda Allen. Estab. 1982. Member of AAR. Represents 35-40 clients.

Represents: Nonfiction books (adult), novels (adult). **Considers these nonfiction areas:** Current affairs; health/medicine; history; multicultural; food/wine, narrative. **Considers these fiction areas:** Historical; multicultural; narrative, current affairs, food/wine, health.

How to Contact: Query with SASE. Considers simultaneous queries. Responds in 3 weeks to queries. Returns materials only with SASE. Obtains most new clients through recommendations from others.

Recent Sales: This agency prefers not to share information on specific sales.

Terms: Agent receives 15% commission on domestic sales. Charges for photocopying.

ALLRED AND ALLRED LITERARY AGENTS, 7834 Alabama Ave., Canoga Park CA 91304-4905. (818)346-4313. **Contact:** Robert Allred. Estab. 1991. Represents 5 clients. 100% of clients are new/unpublished writers. Currently handles: nonfiction books; novels; movie scripts; TV scripts.

- Prior to opening his agency, Mr. Allred was a writer, assistant producer, associate director and editorial assistant.

Member Agents: Robert Allred (all); Kim Allred (all).

Represents: Nonfiction books, novels, short story collections, juvenile books, scholarly books, textbooks. **Considers these nonfiction areas:** Anthropology/archaeology; art/architecture/design; biography/autobiography; cooking/foods/nutrition; crafts/hobbies; current affairs; education; ethnic/cultural interests; health/medicine; history; how-to; humor/satire; interior design/decorating; juvenile nonfiction; language/literature/criticism; military/war; music/dance; New Age/metaphysics; photography; popular culture; psychology; religious/inspirational; science/technology; self-help/personal improvement; sociology; sports; theater/film; true crime/investigative; women's issues/studies. **Considers these fiction areas:** Action/adventure; confession; detective/police/crime; ethnic; family saga; fantasy; feminist; gay/lesbian; glitz; historical; horror; humor/satire; juvenile; literary; mainstream/contemporary; mystery/suspense; psychic/supernatural; regional; religious/inspirational; romance (contemporary, gothic, historical, regency); science fiction; sports; thriller; western/frontier; young adult. **Considers these script subject areas:** Action/adventure; biography/autobiography; cartoon/animation; comedy; contemporary issues; detective/police/crime; erotica; ethnic; experimental; family saga; fantasy; feminist; gay/lesbian; glitz; historical; horror; juvenile; mainstream; multicultural; multimedia; mystery/suspense; psychic/supernatural; regional; religious/inspirational; romantic comedy; romantic drama; science fiction; sports; teen; thriller; western/frontier.

How to Contact: Query with SASE. Submit first 25 pages for book submissions. For scripts, send entire ms. Include 1-2 page synopsis and SASE. No e-mail or fax queries. Considers simultaneous queries. Responds in 3 weeks to queries; 2 months to mss. Returns materials only with SASE. Obtains most new clients through recommendations from others, solicitations.

Recent Sales: Sold 1 title in the last year. *Diamond in the Rough*, by Richard Blacke (Wide Western); *Red Rose, White Rose*, Betty Stuart (Sunset Publications); *Way Out West*, by V. West (Golden West).

Terms: Agent receives 10% commission on domestic sales; 10% commission on foreign sales. Offers written contract, binding for 1 year; 100% of business is derived from commissions on ms sales.

Tips: "Be professional."

ALTAIR LITERARY AGENCY, P.O. Box 11656, Washington DC 20008. (212)505-3320. Estab. 1996. Member of AAR. Represents 60 clients. Currently handles: 90% nonfiction books; 5% novels.

Member Agents: Andrea Pedolsky, partner; Nicholas Smith, partner.

Represents: Nonfiction and fiction books. **Considers these nonfiction areas:** Biography (no person currently alive);

history; current events/contemporary issues; popular culture (esp. pre-1970s music); science/technology (history of). **Considers these fiction areas:** Historical (pre-20th century).

O→ This agency specializes in nonfiction with an emphasis on authors who have credentials and professional recognition for their topic, and a high level of public exposure. Actively seeking solid, well-informed authors who have a public platform for the subject specialty.

How to Contact: Query with SASE. See website for more specific query information. Considers simultaneous queries. Responds in 4 weeks to queries; 1 month to mss. Obtains most new clients through recommendations from others, solicitations, author queries.

Recent Sales: *Stillpoint Dhammapada*, by Geri Larkin (Harper SF); *Cross-Training for Runners*, by Matt Fitzgerald (Rodale); *Rules for a Pretty Woman*, by Suzette Francis (Avon).

Terms: Agent receives 15% commission on domestic sales; 20% commission on foreign sales. Offers written contract, binding for 1 year; 60-day notice must be given to terminate contract. Charges clients for postage, copying, messengers and Fedex and UPS.

MIRIAM ALTSHULER LITERARY AGENCY, 53 Old Post Rd. N., Red Hook NY 12571. (845)758-9408. Fax: (845)758-3118. **Contact:** Miriam Altshuler. Estab. 1994. Member of AAR. Represents 40 clients. Currently handles: 45% nonfiction books; 45% novels; 5% story collections; 5% juvenile books.

- Ms. Altshuler has been an agent since 1982.

Represents: Nonfiction books, novels, short story collections, juvenile books. **Considers these nonfiction areas:** Biography/autobiography; ethnic/cultural interests; history; language/literature/criticism; memoirs; multicultural; music/dance; nature/environment; popular culture; psychology; sociology; theater/film; women's issues/studies. **Considers these fiction areas:** Literary; mainstream/contemporary; multicultural; thriller.

How to Contact: Query with SASE. Prefers to read materials exclusively. No e-mail or fax queries. Considers simultaneous queries. Responds in 2 weeks to queries; 3 weeks to mss. Returns materials only with SASE. Obtains most new clients through recommendations from others.

Terms: Agent receives 15% commission on domestic sales; 20% commission on foreign sales. No written contract. Charges clients for overseas mailing, photocopies, overnight mail when requested by author.

Writers' Conferences: Bread Loaf Writers' Conference (Middlebury VT, August).

BETSY AMSTER LITERARY ENTERPRISES, P.O. Box 27788, Los Angeles CA 90027-0788. **Contact:** Betsy Amster. Estab. 1992. Member of AAR. Represents over 65 clients. 35% of clients are new/unpublished writers. Currently handles: 65% nonfiction books; 35% novels.

- Prior to opening her agency, Ms. Amster was an editor at Pantheon and Vintage for 10 years and served as editorial director for the Globe Pequot Press for 2 years. "This experience gives me a wider perspective on the business and the ability to give focused editorial feedback to my clients."

Represents: Nonfiction books, novels. **Considers these nonfiction areas:** Biography/autobiography; business/economics; child guidance/parenting; ethnic/cultural interests; gardening; health/medicine; history; money/finance; psychology; sociology; women's issues/studies. **Considers these fiction areas:** Ethnic; literary.

O→ Actively seeking "strong narrative nonfiction, particularly by journalists; outstanding literary fiction (the next Michael Chabon or Jhumpa Lahiri); and high profile self-help and psychology, preferably research-based." Does not want to receive poetry, children's books, romances, westerns, science fiction.

How to Contact: For fiction send query, first 3 pages and SASE. For nonfiction send query or proposal with SASE. No e-mail or fax queries. Considers simultaneous queries. Responds in 1 month to queries; 2 months to mss. Obtains most new clients through recommendations from others, solicitations, conferences.

Recent Sales: *I Was Howard Hughes*, by Steven Carter (Bloomsbury); *AgeLess*, by Edward Schneider, M.D., and Elizabeth Miles (Rodale); *I Know I'm in There Somewhere: A Woman's Guide to Finding Her Inner Voice and Living a Life of Authenticity*, by Helene Brenner, Ph.D. (Gotham). Other clients include Dwight Allen, Elaine N. Aron, Lynette Brasfield, Robin Chotzinoff, Frank Clifford, Rob Cohen & David Wollock, Jan DeBlieu, Maria Amparo Escandon, Wendy Mogel, Sharon Montrose, Joy Nicholson, Katie Singer, Louise Steinman, Diana Wells.

Terms: Agent receives 15% commission on domestic sales; 20% commission on foreign sales. Offers written contract, binding for 1-2 years; 60-day notice must be given to terminate contract. Charges for photocopying, postage, long distance phone calls, messengers and galleys and books used in submissions to foreign and film agents and to magazines for first serial rights.

Writers' Conferences: Squaw Valley; Pacific Northwest Conference; San Diego Writers Conference; UCLA Writers Conference.

N **MARCIA AMSTERDAM AGENCY**, 41 W. 82nd St., New York NY 10024-5613. (212)873-4945. **Contact:** Marcia Amsterdam. Estab. 1970. Signatory of WGA. Currently handles: 15% nonfiction books; 70% novels; 5% movie scripts; 10% TV scripts.

- Prior to opening her agency, Ms. Amsterdam was an editor.

Represents: Nonfiction books, novels, feature film, TV movie of the week, sitcom. **Considers these nonfiction areas:** Child guidance/parenting; popular culture; self-help/personal improvement. **Considers these fiction areas:** Action/adventure; detective/police/crime; horror; mainstream/contemporary; mystery/suspense; romance (contemporary, historical); science fiction; thriller; western/frontier; young adult. **Considers these script subject areas:** Comedy; mainstream; mystery/suspense; romantic comedy; romantic drama.

How to Contact: Submit outline, 3 sample chapter(s), SASE. Responds in 1 month to queries.

Recent Sales: *Rosey in the Present Tense*, by Louise Hawes (Walker); *Flash Factor*, by William H. Lovejoy (Kensington).

Terms: Agent receives 15% commission on domestic sales; 20% commission on foreign sales; 10% commission on dramatic rights sales. Offers written contract, binding for 1 year. Charges clients for extra office expenses, foreign postage, copying, legal fees (when agreed upon).

Tips: "We are always looking for interesting literary voices."

BART ANDREWS & ASSOCIATES, 7510 Sunset Blvd., Suite 100, Los Angeles CA 90046. (310)271-9916. **Contact:** Bart Andrews. Estab. 1982. Represents 25 clients. 25% of clients are new/unpublished writers. Currently handles: 100% nonfiction books.

Represents: Nonfiction books. **Considers these nonfiction areas:** Biography/autobiography; music/dance; theater/film; TV.

This agency specializes in nonfiction only, and in the general category of entertainment (movies, TV, biographies, autobiographies).

How to Contact: Query with SASE. Considers simultaneous queries. Responds in 1 week to queries; 1 month to mss.

Recent Sales: Sold 25 titles in the last year. *Roseanne*, by J. Randy Taraborrelli (G.P. Putnam's Sons); *Out of the Madness*, by Rose Books packaging firm (HarperCollins).

Terms: Agent receives 15% commission on domestic sales; 15% (after subagent takes his 10%) commission on foreign sales. Offers written contract. Charges clients for all photocopying, mailing, phone calls, postage, etc; Writers reimbursed for office fees after the sale of ms.

Writers' Conferences: Frequently lectures at UCLA in Los Angeles.

Tips: "Recommendations from existing clients or professionals are best, although I find a lot of new clients by seeking them out myself. I rarely find a new client through the mail. Spend time writing a query letter. Sell yourself like a product. The bottom line is writing ability, and then the idea itself. It takes a lot to convince me. I've seen it all! I hear from too many first-time authors who don't do their homework. They're trying to get a book published and they haven't the faintest idea what is required of them. There are plenty of good books on the subject and, in my opinion, it's their responsibility—not mine—to educate themselves before they try to find an agent to represent their work. When I ask an author to see a manuscript or even a partial manuscript. I really must be convinced I want to read it—based on a strong query letter—because of wasting my time reading just for the fun of it."

APPLESEEDS MANAGEMENT, 200 E. 30th St., Suite 302, San Bernardino CA 92404. (909)882-1667. **Contact:** S. James Foiles. Estab. 1988. 40% of clients are new/unpublished writers. Currently handles: 15% nonfiction books; 85% novels.

Represents: Nonfiction books, novels. **Considers these nonfiction areas:** True crime/investigative. **Considers these fiction areas:** Detective/police/crime; mystery/suspense.

How to Contact: Query with SASE. Responds in 2 weeks to queries; 2 months to mss.

Recent Sales: This agency prefers not to share information on specific sales.

Terms: Agent receives 10-15% commission on domestic sales; 20% commission on foreign sales. Offers written contract, binding for 1-7 years.

Tips: "Appleseeds specializes in mysteries with a detective who could be in a continuing series because readership of mysteries is expanding."

AUTHENTIC CREATIONS LITERARY AGENCY, 875 Lawrenceville-Suwanee Rd., Suite 310-306, Lawrenceville GA 30043. (770)339-3774. Fax: (770)339-7126. E-mail: ron@authenticcreations.com. Website: www.authenticcreations.com. **Contact:** Mary Lee Laitsch. Estab. 1993. Represents 70 clients. 30% of clients are new/unpublished writers. Currently handles: 60% nonfiction books; 40% novels.

- Prior to becoming agents, Ms. Laitsch was a librarian and elementary school teacher; Mr. Laitsch was an attorney and a writer.

Member Agents: Mary Lee Laitsch; Ronald Laitsch; Jason Laitsch.

Represents: Nonfiction books, novels, scholarly books. **Considers these nonfiction areas:** Anthropology/archaeology; biography/autobiography; child guidance/parenting; crafts/hobbies; current affairs; history; how-to; science/technology; self-help/personal improvement; sports; true crime/investigative; women's issues/studies. **Considers these fiction areas:** Action/adventure; contemporary issues; detective/police/crime; family saga; literary; mainstream/contemporary; mystery/suspense; romance; sports; thriller.

How to Contact: Query with SASE. No e-mail or fax queries. Considers simultaneous queries. Responds in 2 weeks to queries; 2 months to mss.

Recent Sales: Sold 15 titles in the last year. *Frankenstein—The Legacy*, by Christopher Schildt (Simon & Schuster); *Night of Dracula*, by Christopher Schildt (Simon & Schuster).

Terms: Agent receives 15% commission on domestic sales; 15% commission on foreign sales. Charges clients for photocopying.

Tips: "The tragic events of September 11 followed by the anthrax scare has changed the nature of the marketplace. Agents need to be aware of these changes and guide their authors into new directions that tap into this new market."

AUTHORS & ARTISTS GROUP, INC., (Specialized: celebrity autobiographies), 41 E. 11th St., 11th Floor, New York NY 10003. (212)944-9898. Fax: (212)944-6484. **Contact:** Al Lowman, president. Estab. 1984. Represents 50 clients. 25% of clients are new/unpublished writers. Currently handles: 95% nonfiction books; 5% novels.

- Prior to becoming an agent, Mr. Lowman was an advertising executive.

Member Agents: B.G. Dilworth (nonfiction); Al Lowman (president nonfiction).

Represents: Nonfiction books, novels. **Considers these nonfiction areas:** Art/architecture/design; biography/autobiography; business/economics; child guidance/parenting; computers/electronic; cooking/foods/nutrition; crafts/hobbies; current affairs; education; ethnic/cultural interests; gay/lesbian issues; health/medicine; history; how-to; humor/satire; interior design/decorating; memoirs; money/finance; music/dance; nature/environment; New Age/metaphysics; photography; popular culture; psychology; religious/inspirational; science/technology; self-help/personal improvement; sociology; sports; true crime/investigative; women's issues/studies. **Considers these fiction areas:** Action/adventure; contemporary issues; detective/police/crime; erotica; ethnic; gay/lesbian; horror; humor/satire; mainstream/contemporary; psychic/supernatural; religious/inspirational; thriller.

O→ This agency specializes in celebrity-based autobiographies and self-help books; and any books that bring its readers to "higher ground." Actively seeking fresh full-length, adult nonfiction ideas and established novelists. Does not want to receive film and TV scripts, children's stories, poetry or short stories.

How to Contact: Fax 1 page query. Considers simultaneous queries. Responds in 3 weeks to queries. Obtains most new clients through recommendations from others.

Recent Sales: Sold 20 titles in the last year. *Labelle Cuisine*, by Patti Labelle (Broadway); *Get Skinny on Fabulous Food*, by Suzanne Somers (Crown); *Forgive or Forget*, by Mother Love (HarperCollins). Other clients include Sarah, Duchess of York, Diana Ross, Mary Lou Retton.

Terms: Agent receives 15% commission on domestic sales; 20% commission on foreign sales. Charges clients for office expenses, postage, photocopying not to exceed $1,000 without permission of author.

THE AXELROD AGENCY, 49 Main St., P.O. Box 357, Chatham NY 12037. (518)392-2100. Fax: (518)392-2944. E-mail: steve@axelrodagency.com. **Contact:** Steven Axelrod. Estab. 1983. Member of AAR. Represents 20-30 clients. 1% of clients are new/unpublished writers. Currently handles: 5% nonfiction books; 95% novels.

- Prior to becoming an agent, Mr. Axelrod was a book club editor.

Represents: Nonfiction books, novels. **Considers these fiction areas:** Mystery/suspense; romance; women's.

How to Contact: Query with SASE. Considers simultaneous queries. Responds in 3 weeks to queries; 6 weeks to mss. Returns materials only with SASE. Obtains most new clients through recommendations from others.

Recent Sales: This agency prefers not to share information on specific sales.

Terms: Agent receives 15% commission on domestic sales; 20% commission on foreign sales. No written contract.

Writers' Conferences: Romance Writers of America (July).

BALKIN AGENCY, INC., P.O. Box 222, Amherst MA 01004. (413)548-9835. Fax: (413)548-9836. **Contact:** Rick Balkin, president. Estab. 1972. Member of AAR. Represents 50 clients. 10% of clients are new/unpublished writers. Currently handles: 85% nonfiction books; 5% scholarly books; 5% textbooks; 5% reference books.

- Prior to opening his agency, Mr. Balkin served as executive editor with Bobbs-Merrill Company.

Represents: Nonfiction books, scholarly books, textbooks. **Considers these nonfiction areas:** Animals; anthropology/archaeology; biography/autobiography; current affairs; health/medicine; history; how-to; language/literature/criticism; music/dance; nature/environment; popular culture; science/technology; sociology; translation; travel; true crime/investigative.

O→ This agency specializes in adult nonfiction. Does not want to receive fiction, poetry, screenplays, computer books.

How to Contact: Query with SASE, proposal package, outline. No e-mail or fax queries. Responds in 1 week to queries; 2 weeks to mss. Returns materials only with SASE. Obtains most new clients through recommendations from others.

Recent Sales: Sold 30 titles in the last year. *The Liar's Tale* (W.W. Norton Co.); *Adolescent Depression* (Henry Holt); *Eliz. Van Lew: A Union Spy in the Heart of the Confederacy*, (biography, Oxford U.P.).

Terms: Agent receives 15% commission on domestic sales; 20% commission on foreign sales. Offers written contract, binding for 1 year. Charges clients for photocopying and express or foreign mail.

Tips: "I do not take on books described as bestsellers or potential bestsellers. Any nonfiction work that is either unique, paradigmatic, a contribution, truly witty or a labor of love is grist for my mill."

LORETTA BARRETT BOOKS, INC., 101 Fifth Ave., New York NY 10003. (212)242-3420. Fax: (212)807-9579. E-mail: mail@lorettabarrettbooks.com. **Contact:** Loretta A. Barrett or Nick Mullendore. Estab. 1990. Member of AAR. Represents 90 clients. Currently handles: 60% nonfiction books; 40% novels.

- Prior to opening her agency, Ms. Barrett was vice president and executive editor at Doubleday for 25 years.

Represents: Nonfiction books, novels. **Considers these nonfiction areas:** Americana; animals; anthropology/archaeology; art/architecture/design; biography/autobiography; business/economics; child guidance/parenting; computers/electronic; cooking/foods/nutrition; crafts/hobbies; creative nonfiction; current affairs; education; ethnic/cultural interests; gay/lesbian issues; government/politics/law; health/medicine; history; how-to; humor/satire; interior design/decorating; language/literature/criticism; memoirs; military/war; money/finance; multicultural; music/dance; nature/environment; New Age/metaphysics; philosophy; photography; popular culture; psychology; recreation; regional; religious/inspirational; science/technology; self-help/personal improvement; sex; sociology; spirituality; sports; theater/film; travel; true crime/investigative; women's issues/studies. **Considers these fiction areas:** Action/adventure; confession; contemporary issues; detective/police/crime; ethnic; family saga; feminist; gay/lesbian; glitz; historical; humor/satire; literary; mainstream/contemporary; mystery/suspense; psychic/supernatural; religious/inspirational; romance; spiritual; sports; thriller.

O→ This agency specializes in general interest books. No children's or juvenile.

How to Contact: Query with SASE. No e-mail or fax queries. Considers simultaneous queries. Responds in 4 weeks to queries. Returns materials only with SASE.

Recent Sales: *A Lady First*, by Letitia Baldrige (Viking); *The Singularity is Near*, by Ray Kurzweil (Viking); *Flesh Tones*, by MJ Rose (Ballantine Books); *The Lake of Dead Languages*, by Carol Goodman (Ballantine Books); *The Bad Witness*, by Laura Van Wormer (Mira Books).

Terms: Agent receives 15% commission on domestic sales; 20% commission on foreign sales. Offers written contract. Charges clients for shipping and photocopying.

Writers' Conferences: San Diego State University Writer's Conference; Maui Writer's Conference.

THE BARRY-SWAYNE AGENCY, LLC, 4 Manitou Rd., Garrison NY 10524. (845)424-2448. E-mail: proposals@barry-swayneagency.com. Website: www.barry-swayneagency.com. Estab. 1997. Represents 80 clients. Currently handles: 100% nonfiction books; 10% fiction.

Member Agents: Susan Barry (history, biography, business, business narrative, finance, memoir, narrative nonfiction and equine-related topics).

Represents: Nonfiction books. **Considers these nonfiction areas:** Business/economics; current affairs; ethnic/cultural interests; history; popular culture; women's issues/studies.

This agency specializes in authors who are journalists or participate in multimedia: book publishing, radio, movies and television, and information technology. Does not want to receive westerns, romance novels, science fiction, children's books, or erotica.

How to Contact: Query with SASE, proposal package, outline. No fax queries. Accepts e-mail queries, no attachments. Considers simultaneous queries. Responds in 2 months to mss. Obtains most new clients through recommendations from colleagues and clients.

Recent Sales: *Library: A Unique History*, by Matthew Battles (W.W. Norton); *Predicting the Present*, by Kenneth McGee, The Gartner Group (Harvard Business School Press).

Terms: Agent receives 15% commission on domestic sales; 20% commission on foreign sales. Offers written contract, binding for 1 year; 60-day notice must be given to terminate contract.

MARGARET BASCH, 850 E. Higgins, #125, Schaumburg IL 60173. (847)240-1199. Fax: (847)240-1845. E-mail: lawlady@aol.com. **Contact:** Margaret Basch. Represents 100 clients. 5% of clients are new/unpublished writers. Currently not accepting new clients. Currently handles: 40% nonfiction books; 40% novels; 20% juvenile books.

- Prior to becoming an agent, Ms. Bach was a trial lawyer.

Recent Sales: This agency prefers not to share information about specific sales.

Terms: Agent receives 10% commission on domestic sales; 10% commission on foreign sales. Offers written contract.

Tips: "All of our clients are published and most came from other agents to be with us."

JENNY BENT, HARVEY KLINGER, INC., 301 W. 53rd St., New York NY 10019. (212)581-7068. Fax: (212)315-3823. E-mail: jenlbent@aol.com. Website: www.jennybent.com. **Contact:** Jenny Bent. Member of AAR. Represents 60 clients. 40% of clients are new/unpublished writers. Currently handles: 70% nonfiction books; 30% novels.

- Prior to joining her agency, Ms. Bent worked as an editor in book publishing and magazines.

Represents: Nonfiction books, novels. **Considers these nonfiction areas:** Animals; biography/autobiography; ethnic/cultural interests; health/medicine; history; popular culture; psychology; self-help/personal improvement; women's issues/studies. **Considers these fiction areas:** Ethnic; literary; mainstream/contemporary; romance.

Actively seeking quality fiction and nonfiction from well-credentialed authors. Does not want to receive science fiction, New Age fiction, mysteries, thrillers, children's, self-help from non-credentialed writers.

How to Contact: Query with SASE, submit proposal package, outline, résumé, publishing history, author bio. Please always include a bio or résumé with submissions or queries. Accepts e-mail queries, but no attachments. Considers simultaneous queries. Responds in 1 month to queries; 2 months to mss. Returns materials only with SASE. Obtains most new clients through recommendations from others, solicitations, conferences.

Recent Sales: Sold 20 titles in the last year. *Red Ant House*, by Ann Cummins (Houghton Mifflin); *Makeover Moms Meal Club*, by Liz Weiss and Janice N. Bissey (Broadway).

Terms: Agent receives 15% commission on domestic sales; 25% commission on foreign sales. Offers written contract; 30 days notice must be given to terminate contract. Charges for overnight mail, out-of-office photocopies (deducted from advance).

MEREDITH BERNSTEIN LITERARY AGENCY, 2112 Broadway, Suite 503A, New York NY 10023. (212)799-1007. Fax: (212)799-1145. Estab. 1981. Member of AAR. Represents 85 clients. 20% of clients are new/unpublished writers. Currently handles: 50% nonfiction books; 50% fiction.

- Prior to opening her agency, Ms. Bernstein served in another agency for 5 years.

Member Agents: Meredith Bernstein; Elizabeth Cavanaugh.

Represents: Nonfiction books, fiction of all kinds. **Considers these nonfiction areas:** Any area of nonfiction in which the author has an established "platform" or track record. Narrative nonfiction is considered as well. **Considers these fiction areas:** Literary; mystery/suspense; romance; thriller; women's fiction.

This agency does not specialize, "very eclectic."

How to Contact: Query with SASE. No e-mail or fax queries. Considers simultaneous queries. Obtains most new clients through recommendations from others, conferences, also develops and packages own ideas.

Recent Sales: *The Giftionary*, by Robyn Spizman (St. Martins); *Women for Hire*, by Tony Johnson and Robyn Spizman (Perigee); *365 Days of Dressing Well*, by Mary Lou Andre (Perigee).

Terms: Agent receives 15% commission on domestic sales; 20% commission on foreign sales. Charges clients $75 disbursement fee/year.

Writers' Conferences: Southwest Writers Conference (Albuquereque, August); Rocky Moutnain Writers' Conference (Denver, September); Golden Triangle (Beaumont TX, October); Pacific Northwest Writers Conference; Austin League Writers Conference; Willamette Writers Conference (Portland, OR); Lafayette Writers Conference (Lafayette, LA); Surrey

Writers Conference (Surrey, BC.); San Diego State University Writers Conference (San Diego, CA).

DANIEL BIAL AGENCY, 41 W. 83rd St., Suite 5-C, New York NY 10024-5246. (212)721-1786. Fax: (309)213-0230. E-mail: dbialagency@juno.com. **Contact:** Daniel Bial. Estab. 1992. Represents under 50 clients. 15% of clients are new/unpublished writers. Currently handles: 95% nonfiction books; 5% novels.

- Prior to opening his agency, Mr. Bial was an editor for 15 years.

Represents: Nonfiction books, novels. **Considers these nonfiction areas:** Animals; anthropology/archaeology; biography/autobiography; business/economics; child guidance/parenting; cooking/foods/nutrition; current affairs; ethnic/cultural interests; gay/lesbian issues; government/politics/law; history; how-to; humor/satire; language/literature/criticism; memoirs; military/war; money/finance; music/dance; nature/environment; New Age/metaphysics; popular culture; psychology; religious/inspirational; science/technology; self-help/personal improvement; sociology; spirituality; sports; theater/film; travel; true crime/investigative; women's issues/studies. **Considers these fiction areas:** Action/adventure; contemporary issues; detective/police/crime; erotica; ethnic; feminist; gay/lesbian; humor/satire; literary.

How to Contact: Submit proposal package, outline. Responds in 2 weeks to queries. Returns materials only with SASE. Obtains most new clients through recommendations from others, solicitations, "good rolodex"

Recent Sales: This agency recently had a number one New York Times bestseller with *Osama Bin Ladin: The Man Who Delcared War on America*, by Yossef Bodansky.

Terms: Agent receives 15% commission on domestic sales; 25% commission on foreign sales. Offers written contract, binding for 1 year with cancellation clause. Charges clients for overseas calls, overnight mailing, photocopying, messenger expenses.

Tips: "Publishers are looking for authors with platforms—that is, people who already have positioned themselves in order to get their books heard...and sold."

BIGSCORE PRODUCTIONS, INC., P.O. Box 4575, Lancaster PA 17604. (717)293-0247. Fax: (717)293-1945. E-mail: bigscore@bigscoreproductions.com. Website: www.bigscoreproductions.com. **Contact:** David A. Robie, agent; Sharon Hanby-Robie, agent; Deb Strubel, associate. Estab. 1995. Represents 50-75 clients. 25% of clients are new/unpublished writers.

Represents: Nonfiction and fiction (see website for categories of interest).

This agency specializes in inspirational and self-help nonfiction and fiction and has over 40 years in the publishing and agenting business.

How to Contact: See website for submission guidelines. Query by e-mail or mail. No fax queries. Considers simultaneous queries. Responds in 1 month to proposals.

Terms: Agent receives 15% commission on domestic sales. Offers written contract, binding for 6 months. Charges clients for expedited shipping, ms photocopying and preparation, and books for subsidiary rights submissions.

Tips: "Very open to taking on new clients. Submit a well-prepared proposal that will take minimal fine-tuning for presentation to publishers. Nonfiction writers must be highly marketable and media savvy—the more established in speaking or in your profession, the better. Bigscore Productions works with all major general and Christian publishers"

DAVID BLACK LITERARY AGENCY, 156 Fifth Ave., New York NY 10010. (212)242-5080. Fax: (212)924-6609. **Contact:** David Black, owner. Estab. 1990. Member of AAR. Represents 150 clients. Currently handles: 90% nonfiction books; 10% novels.

Member Agents: Susan Raihofer (general nonfiction to literary fiction); Gary Morris (commercial fiction to psychology); Joy E. Tutela (general nonfiction to literary fiction); Laureen Rowland (business, health).

Represents: Nonfiction books, novels. **Considers these nonfiction areas:** Biography/autobiography; business/economics; government/politics/law; history; memoirs; military/war; money/finance; multicultural; sports. **Considers these fiction areas:** Literary; mainstream/contemporary; commercial.

This agency specializes in business, sports, politics, and novels.

How to Contact: Query with SASE, outline. No e-mail or fax queries. Considers simultaneous queries. Responds in 2 months to queries. Returns materials only with SASE.

Recent Sales: *Body for Life*, by Bill Phillips with Mike D'Orso (HarperCollins); *Walking with the Wind*, by John Lewis with Micke D'Orso (Simon & Schuster).

Terms: Agent receives 15% commission on domestic sales. Charges clients for photocopying and books purchased for sale of foreign rights.

BLEECKER STREET ASSOCIATES, INC., 532 LaGuardia Place, #617, New York NY 10012. (212)677-4492. Fax: (212)388-0001. **Contact:** Agnes Birnbaum. Estab. 1984. Member of AAR, RWA, MWA. Represents 60 clients. 20% of clients are new/unpublished writers. Currently handles: 75% nonfiction books; 25% novels.

- Prior to becoming an agent, Ms. Birnbaum was a senior editor at Simon & Schuster, Dutton/Signet and other publishing houses.

Represents: Nonfiction books, novels. **Considers these nonfiction areas:** Animals; biography/autobiography; business/economics; child guidance/parenting; computers/electronic; cooking/foods/nutrition; current affairs; ethnic/cultural interests; government/politics/law; health/medicine; history; how-to; memoirs; military/war; money/finance; nature/environment; New Age/metaphysics; popular culture; psychology; religious/inspirational; science/technology; self-help/personal improvement; sociology; sports; true crime/investigative; women's issues/studies. **Considers these fiction areas:** Ethnic; historical; literary; mystery/suspense; romance; thriller; women's (interest).

"We're very hands-on and accessible. We try to be truly creative in our submission approaches. We've had especially good luck with first-time authors." Does not want to receive science fiction, westerns, poetry, children's books, academic/scholarly/professional books, plays, scripts, short stories.

How to Contact: Query with SASE. No email, phone or fax queries. Considers simultaneous queries. Responds in 2 weeks to queries; 1 month to mss. Returns materials only with SASE. Obtains most new clients through recommendations from others, solicitations, conferences, "plus, I will approach someone with a letter if his/her work impresses me."

Recent Sales: Sold 30 titles in the last year. *The Art of War*, by Bevin Alexander (Crown); *The Dim Sum of All Things*, by Kim Wong Keltner (Morrow/Avon); *Healing Miracles*, by Brad & Sherry Steiger (Adams Media).

Terms: Agent receives 15% commission on domestic sales; 25% commission on foreign sales. Offers written contract; 30 days notice must be given to terminate contract. Charges for postage, long distance, fax, messengers, photocopies, not to exceed $200.

Tips: "Keep query letters short and to the point; include only information pertaining to book or background as writer. Try to avoid superlatives in description. Work needs to stand on its own, so how much editing it may have received has no place in a query letter."

N ⊘ **REID BOATES LITERARY AGENCY**, 69 Cooks Crossroad, Pittstown NJ 08867. (908)730-8523. Fax: (908)730-8931. E-mail: boatesliterary@att.net. **Contact:** Reid Boates. Estab. 1985. Represents 45 clients. 5% of clients are new/unpublished writers. Currently handles: 85% nonfiction books; 15% novels; very rarely story collections.

How to Contact: No unsolicited queries of any kind. Obtains most new clients through recommendations from others, new clients by personal referral only.

Recent Sales: Sold 20 titles in the last year. This agency prefers not to share information on specific sales.

Terms: Agent receives 15% commission on domestic sales; 20% commission on foreign sales.

BOOK DEALS, INC., 244 Fifth Ave., Suite 2164, New York NY 10001-7604. (212)252-2701. Fax: (212)591-6211. E-mail: submissions@bookdealsinc.com. Website: www.bookdealsinc.com. **Contact:** Caroline Francis Carney. Estab. 1996. Member of AAR. Represents 40 clients. 15% of clients are new/unpublished writers. Currently handles: 85% nonfiction books; 15% novels.

- Prior to opening her agency, Ms. Carney was editorial director for a consumer book imprint within Times Mirror and held senior editorial positions in McGraw-Hill and NYIF/Simon & Schuster.

Represents: Nonfiction books, novels (commercial and literary). **Considers these nonfiction areas:** Business/economics; child guidance/parenting; ethnic/cultural interests; health/medicine (nutrition); history; how-to; money/finance; multicultural; popular culture; psychology (popular); religious/inspirational; science/technology; self-help/personal improvement; spirituality. **Considers these fiction areas:** Ethnic; literary; mainstream/contemporary; women's (contemporary); urban literature.

This agency specializes in highly commercial nonfiction and books for African-American readers and women. Actively seeking well-crafted fiction and nonfiction from authors with engaging voices and impeccable credentials.

How to Contact: Query with SASE. Considers simultaneous queries.

Recent Sales: Sold 25 titles in the last year. *Eat Right for Your Personality Type*, by Dr. Robert Kushner & Nancy Kushner (St. Martin's Press); *Self-Proclaimed*, by Rochelle Shapiro (Simon & Schuster); *Par for the Course*, by Alice Dye and Mark Shaw (HarperCollins).

Terms: Agent receives 15% commission on domestic sales; 20% commission on foreign sales. Offers written contract. Charges clients for photocopying and postage.

Tips: "If you have Internet access, please visit our website before submitting a query letter. It has a lot of insider tips to assist you in your search."

N **BOOKENDS, LLC**, 136 Long Hill Rd., Gillette NJ 07933. (908)604-2652. E-mail: editor@bookends-inc.com. Website: www.bookends-inc.com. **Contact:** Jessica Faust or Jacky Sach. Estab. 1999. Represents 50 clients. 60% of clients are new/unpublished writers. Currently handles: 50% nonfiction books; 50% novels.

- Prior to opening their agency, Ms. Faust and Ms. Sach worked at such publishing houses as Berkley, Penguin Putnam, Macmillan and IDG.

Member Agents: Jessica Faust (mysteries, romance, relationships, business, finance, pets, general self-help); Jacky Sach (suspense thrillers, mysteries, literary fiction, spirituality, pets, general self-help)

Represents: Nonfiction books, novels. **Considers these nonfiction areas:** Animals; biography/autobiography; business/economics; child guidance/parenting; cooking/foods/nutrition; crafts/hobbies; current affairs; ethnic/cultural interests; gay/lesbian issues; health/medicine; how-to; humor/satire; memoirs; money/finance; New Age/metaphysics; psychology; religious/inspirational; self-help/personal improvement; women's issues/studies. **Considers these fiction areas:** Contemporary issues; detective/police/crime; ethnic; family saga; feminist; glitz; historical; literary; mainstream/contemporary; mystery/suspense; romance; thriller.

BookEnds specializes in genre fiction and personality driven nonfiction. Actively seeking romance, mystery, women's fiction, literary fiction and suspense thrillers. For nonfiction, relationships, business, general self-help, women's interest, parenting, pets, spirituality, health and psychology. Does not want to receive children's books, screenplays, science fiction, poetry, technical/military thrillers.

How to Contact: Submit outline, 3 sample chapter(s). Considers simultaneous queries. Responds in 4-6 weeks to queries; 8-10 to mss. Returns materials only with SASE. Obtains most new clients through recommendations from others, solicitations, conferences.

Recent Sales: Sold 55 titles in the last year. *Parrot Fish Don't Talk*, by Kathy Brandt (NAL); *Summer Wind*, by Barbara Gale (Harlequin); *The Art of Smoothies*, by Dela Quigley (Adams Media).

Terms: Agent receives 15% commission on domestic sales; 20% commission on foreign sales. Offers written contract.

Charges clients for photocopying, messenger, cables, overseas postage, long-distance phone calls, copies of the published book when purchases for subsidiary rights submissions. Expenses will not exceed $150.
Writers' Conferences: Central Florida Romance Writers Conference (Orlando FL, September); Emerald Coast Writers Conference (Seattle WA, October); Panhandle Professional Writer's Conference (Amarillo TX, June); Washington Romance Writers' (Harper's Ferry Retreat, April).
Tips: "When submitting material be sure to include any information that might be helpful to the agent. In your query letter you should include the title of the book, your name, your publishing history and a brief 1 or 2 sentence description of the book. Also be sure to let the agent know if you see this book as part of a series and if you've already begun work on other books. Once an agent has expressed interest in representing you it is crucial to let her know who has seen your book and even supply copies of any correspondence you've had with prospective editors."

BOOKS & SUCH, (Specialized: Christian market), 4788 Carissa Ave., Santa Rosa CA 94505. (707)538-4184. Fax: (707)538-3937. E-mail: jkgbooks@aol.com. Website: janetgrant.com. **Contact:** Janet Kobobel Grant. Estab. 1996. Member of CBA (associate). Represents 40 clients. 20% of clients are new/unpublished writers. Currently handles: 42% nonfiction books; 46% novels; 2% juvenile books; 10% children's picture books.

- Before becoming an agent, Ms. Grant was an editor for Zondervan and managing editor for Focus on the Family.

Represents: Nonfiction books, novels, juvenile books. **Considers these nonfiction areas:** Child guidance/parenting; humor/satire; juvenile nonfiction; religious/inspirational; self-help/personal improvement; women's issues/studies. **Considers these fiction areas:** Contemporary issues; family saga; historical; juvenile; mainstream/contemporary; picture books; religious/inspirational; romance; young adult.

This agency specializes in "general and inspirational fiction, romance, and in the Christian booksellers market." Actively seeking "material appropriate to the Christian market."

How to Contact: Query with SASE. Considers simultaneous queries. Responds in 1 month to queries; 2 months to mss. Returns materials only with SASE. Obtains most new clients through recommendations from others, conferences.
Recent Sales: Sold 31 titles in the last year. *Gentle Passages*, by Robin Jones Gunn (Multnomah Publishers); *Fair Haven*, by BJ Hoff (W Publishing). Other clients include Janet McHenry, Jane Orcutt, Gayle Roper, Stephanie Grace Whitson.
Terms: Agent receives 15% commission on domestic sales; 15% commission on foreign sales. Offers written contract; 2 months notice must be given to terminate contract. Charges clients for postage, photocopying, telephone calls, fax and express mail.
Writers' Conferences: Romance Writers of America; Mt. Hermon Writers Conference (Mt. Hermon CA, March 22-26); Glorieta Writers Conference (Santa Fe NM, October).
Tips: "The heart of my motivation is to develop relationships with the authors I serve, to do what I can to shine the light of success on them, and to help be a caretaker of their gifts and time."

GEORGES BORCHARDT, INC., 136 E. 57th St., New York NY 10022. (212)753-5785. Fax: (212)838-6518. Estab. 1967. Member of AAR. Represents 200 clients. 10% of clients are new/unpublished writers. Currently handles: 60% nonfiction books; 37% novels; 1% novellas; 1% juvenile books; 1% poetry.
Member Agents: Anne Borchardt; Georges Borchardt; DeAnna Heindel; Valerie Borchardt.
Represents: Nonfiction books, novels. **Considers these nonfiction areas:** Anthropology/archaeology; biography/autobiography; current affairs; history; memoirs; travel; women's issues/studies. **Considers these fiction areas:** Literary.

This agency specializes in literary fiction and outstanding nonfiction.

How to Contact: Responds in 1 week to queries; 1 month to mss. Obtains most new clients through recommendations from others.
Recent Sales: Sold 100 titles in the last year. *Drop City*, by T. Coraghessan Boyle (Viking/Penguin); *Any Human Heart*, by William Boyd (Knopf); *Friendship*, by Joseph Epstein (Houghton Mifflin).
Terms: Agent receives 15% commission on domestic sales; 20% commission on foreign sales. Offers written contract. "We charge clients cost of outside photocopying and shipping manuscripts or books overseas."

THE BOSTON LITERARY GROUP, 156 Mount Auburn St., Cambridge MA 02138-4875. (617)547-0800. Fax: (617)876-8474. E-mail: agent@bostonliterary.com. **Contact:** Elizabeth Mack. Estab. 1994. Member of PEN New England. Represents 30 clients. 25% of clients are new/unpublished writers. Currently handles: 100% nonfiction books.
Member Agents: Kirsten Wainwright (psychology, biography, health, current events, memoir, business); Heather Moehn (science, history, fiction).
Represents: Nonfiction books. **Considers these nonfiction areas:** Animals; anthropology/archaeology; art/architecture/design; biography/autobiography; business/economics; child guidance/parenting; current affairs; ethnic/cultural interests; government/politics/law; health/medicine; history; military/war; money/finance; nature/environment; photography; psychology; science/technology; sociology; true crime/investigative; women's issues/studies.

Actively seeking "nonfiction manuscripts that have something new and fascinating to say. Good writing skills are essential." Does not want to receive poetry, cookbooks, children's literature or fiction.

How to Contact: Query with SASE. Prefers to read materials exclusively. Accepts e-mail and fax queries. Responds in 6 weeks to queries. Returns materials only with SASE. Obtains most new clients through recommendations from others, journal articles.
Recent Sales: Sold 10 titles in the last year. *Zero: The Biography of a Dangerous Idea*, by Charles Seife (Viking Penguin); *The Skin We're In: Teaching Our Children to be Emotionally Strong*, by Janie Ward (Free Press); *The Change Monster*, by Jeannie Daniel Dock (Crown Business).
Terms: Agent receives 15% commission on domestic sales; 10% commission on foreign sales. Offers written contract, binding for 1 year; 60-day notice must be given to terminate contract. Charges clients for expenses associated with

manuscript submissions (postage, photocopy); Makes referrals to editing service. "We match-make with development editors on promising projects."

THE BARBARA BOVA LITERARY AGENCY, 3951 Gulfshore Blvd. N., PH1-B, Naples FL 34103. (941)649-7237. Fax: (239)649-7263. E-mail: bovabefore@aol.com. **Contact:** Barbara Bova. Estab. 1974. Represents 30 clients. Currently handles: 20% nonfiction books; 80% novels.

Represents: Nonfiction books, novels. **Considers these nonfiction areas:** Biography/autobiography; science/technology; self-help/personal improvement; true crime/investigative; women's issues/studies; social sciences. **Considers these fiction areas:** Action/adventure; detective/police/crime; glitz; mystery/suspense; science fiction; thriller.

This agency specializes in fiction and nonfiction, hard and soft science.

How to Contact: Query with SASE. Obtains most new clients through recommendations from others.

Recent Sales: Sold 6 titles in the last year. *Saturn*, by Ben Bova; *Crystal City*, by Orson Scott Card; *Bone Cold*, by Rick Wilber.

Terms: Agent receives 15% commission on domestic sales; 20% commission on foreign sales.

Tips: This agency also handles foreign rights, movies, television, audio.

BRADY LITERARY MANAGEMENT, P.O. Box 164, Hartland Four Corners VT 05049. **Contact:** Upton Brady. Estab. 1988. Represents 100 clients.

Represents: Nonfiction books, novels, short story collections, novellas. **Considers these fiction areas:** Literary; mainstream/contemporary.

How to Contact: Query with SASE, submit outline, 2 sample chapters for nonfiction; first 50 pages for fiction. Responds in 2 months to queries.

Recent Sales: This agency prefers not to share information on specific sales.

Terms: Agent receives 15% commission on domestic sales; 20% commission on foreign sales. Charges clients for extensive international postage and photocopying.

BRANDT & HOCHMAN LITERARY AGENTS, INC., 1501 Broadway, New York NY 10036. (212)840-5760. Fax: (212)840-5776. **Contact:** Carl Brandt; Gail Hochman; Marianne Merola; Charles Schlessiger; Bill Contardi. Estab. 1913. Member of AAR. Represents 200 clients.

Represents: Nonfiction books, novels, short story collections, juvenile books, journalism. **Considers these nonfiction areas:** Biography/autobiography; current affairs; ethnic/cultural interests; government/politics/law; history; theater/film; women's issues/studies. **Considers these fiction areas:** Contemporary issues; ethnic; family saga; historical; literary; mainstream/contemporary; mystery/suspense; romance; thriller; young adult.

How to Contact: Query with SASE. No fax queries. Considers simultaneous queries. Responds in 1 month to queries. Returns materials only with SASE. Obtains most new clients through recommendations from others.

Recent Sales: Sold 50 titles in the last year. This agency prefers not to share information on specific sales. Other clients include Scott Turow, Carlos Fuentes, Ursula Hegi, Michael Cunningham, Mary Pope Osborne.

Terms: Agent receives 15% commission on domestic sales; 20% commission on foreign sales. Charges clients for "manuscript duplication or other special expenses agreed to in advance."

Tips: "Write a letter which will give the agent a sense of you as a professional writer, your long-term interests as well as a short description of the work at hand."

THE JOAN BRANDT AGENCY, 788 Wesley Dr., Atlanta GA 30305-3933. (404)351-8877. **Contact:** Joan Brandt. Estab. 1980. Represents 30 clients. 50% of clients are new/unpublished writers. Currently handles: 45% nonfiction books; 45% novels; 10% juvenile books.

Represents: Nonfiction books, novels, short story collections. **Considers these fiction areas:** Contemporary issues; detective/police/crime; family saga; literary; mainstream/contemporary; mystery/suspense; thriller.

How to Contact: Query with SASE. No e-mail or fax queries. Considers simultaneous queries. Returns materials only with SASE. Obtains most new clients through solicitations.

Recent Sales: This agency prefers not to share information on specific sales.

Terms: Agent receives 15% commission on domestic sales; 20% commission on foreign sales. No written contract.

M. COURTNEY BRIGGS, 100 N. Broadway Ave., 20th Floor, Oklahoma City OK 73102-8806. **Contact:** M. Courtney Briggs. Estab. 1994. 25% of clients are new/unpublished writers. Currently handles: 5% nonfiction books; 10% novels; 80% juvenile books; 5% multimedia.

- Prior to becoming an agent, Ms. Briggs was in subsidiary rights at Random House for 3 years; an associate agent and film rights associate with Curtis Brown, Ltd.; also an attorney for 12 years.

Represents: Nonfiction books, novels, juvenile books. **Considers these nonfiction areas:** Animals; biography/autobiography; health/medicine; juvenile nonfiction; self-help/personal improvement; young adult. **Considers these fiction areas:** Juvenile; mainstream/contemporary; picture books; young adult.

M. Courtney Briggs is an agent and an attorney. "I work primarily, but not exclusively, with children's book authors and illustrators. I will also consult or review a contract on an hourly basis." Actively seeking children's fiction, children's picture books (illustrations and text), young adult novels, fiction, nonfiction.

How to Contact: Query with SASE. No e-mail or fax queries. Responds in 2 weeks to queries; 6 weeks to mss. Returns materials only with SASE. Obtains most new clients through recommendations from others.

Recent Sales: This agency prefers not to share information on specific sales.

Terms: Agent receives 15% commission on domestic sales; 25% commission on foreign sales. Offers written contract; 60—day notice must be given to terminate contract.

Writers' Conferences: National Conference on Writing & Illustrating for Children (August).

MARIE BROWN ASSOCIATES, INC., 412 W. 154th St., New York NY 10032. (212)939-9725. Fax: (212)939-9728. E-mail: mbrownlit@aol.com. **Contact:** Marie Brown. Estab. 1984. Represents 60 clients. Currently handles: 75% nonfiction books; 10% juvenile books; 15% other.

Member Agents: Janell Walden Agyeman.

Represents: Nonfiction books, juvenile books. **Considers these nonfiction areas:** Art/architecture/design; biography/autobiography; business/economics; ethnic/cultural interests; history; juvenile nonfiction; music/dance; religious/inspirational; self-help/personal improvement; theater/film; women's issues/studies. **Considers these fiction areas:** Contemporary issues; ethnic; juvenile; literary; mainstream/contemporary.

O→ This agency specializes in multicultural and African-American writers.

How to Contact: Query with SASE. Prefers to read materials exclusively. Responds in 6 weeks to queries. Obtains most new clients through recommendations from others.

Recent Sales: *Finding Venus Finding*, by Trisha Thomas; *When the Spirit Speaks Mambo*, by Marta Moreno Vega; *Cosmopolitan Girls*, by Lyah LeFlore and Charlotte Burley.

Terms: Agent receives 15% commission on domestic sales; 20% commission on foreign sales. Offers written contract.

ANDREA BROWN LITERARY AGENCY, INC., (Specialized: juvenile), 1076 Eagle Dr., Salinas CA 93905. (831)422-5925. Fax: (831)422-5915. E-mail: ablitag@netzer.net. **Contact:** Andrea Brown, president. Estab. 1981. Member of WNBA, SCBWI. 10% of clients are new/unpublished writers. Currently handles: 95% juvenile nonfiction; 5% adult nonfiction books.

- Prior to opening her agency, Ms. Brown served as an editorial assistant at Random House and Dell Publishing and as an editor with Alfred A. Knopf.

Member Agents: Andrea Brown; Laura Rennert; Laurel Newby

Represents: Nonfiction books (juvenile). **Considers these nonfiction areas:** Animals; anthropology/archaeology; art/architecture/design; biography/autobiography; current affairs; ethnic/cultural interests; history; how-to; juvenile nonfiction; nature/environment; photography; popular culture; science/technology; sociology; sports; all nonfiction subjects for juveniles and adults. **Considers these fiction areas:** Juvenile; young adult; all fiction genres for juveniles.

O→ This agency specializes in "all kinds fo children's books—illustrators and authors." Considers all juvenile fiction areas; all genres of nonfiction.

How to Contact: Query with SASE. Accepts e-mail queries. No fax queries. Considers simultaneous queries. Responds in 3 to 4 to queries. Obtains most new clients through recommendations from others, referrals from editors, clients and agents.

Recent Sales: *Not So Scary Monster Handbook*, by Dave Ross (HarperCollins); *Mercedes and the Candy Bomber*, by Margot Raven (Sleeping Bear Press).

Terms: Agent receives 15% commission on domestic sales; 20% commission on foreign sales. Offers written contract. Charges clients for shipping costs.

Writers' Conferences: Austin Writers League; SCBWI, Orange County Conferences; Mills College Childrens Literature Conference (Oakland CA); Asilomar (Pacific Grove CA); Maui Writers Conference; Southwest Writers Conference; San Diego State University Writer's Conference; Big Sur Children's Writing Workshop (Director); William Saroyan Conference; Columbus Writers Conference; Willamette Writers Conference.

Tips: "Query first—so many submissions come in it takes three to four months to get a response. Taking on very few picture books. Must be unique—no rhyme, no anthropomorphism. Handling some adult historical fiction."

CURTIS BROWN, LTD., 10 Astor Place, New York NY 10003-6935. (212)473-5400. Also: 1750 Montgomery St., San Fancisco CA 94111. (415)954-8566. **Contact:** Perry Knowlton, chairman; Timothy Knowlton, CEO; Peter L. Ginsberg, president. Member of AAR; signatory of WGA.

Member Agents: Laura Blake Peterson; Ellen Geiger; Emilie Jacobson, vice president; Maureen Walters, vice president; Virginia Knowlton (literary, adult, children's); Timothy Knowlton (film, screenplays, plays; Marilyn Marlow, executive vice president; Ed Wintle (film, screenplays, plays); Mitchell Waters; Elizabeth Harding; Douglas Stewart; Kristen Manges; Dave Barber (translation rights).

Represents: Nonfiction books, novels, short story collections, novellas, juvenile books, poetry books, movie scripts, feature film, TV scripts, TV movie of the week, stage plays. **Considers these nonfiction areas:** Agriculture/horticulture; americana; animals; anthropology/archaeology; art/architecture/design; biography/autobiography; business/economics; child guidance/parenting; computers/electronic; cooking/foods/nutrition; crafts/hobbies; creative nonfiction; current affairs; education; ethnic/cultural interests; gardening; gay/lesbian issues; government/politics/law; health/medicine; history; how-to; humor/satire; interior design/decorating; juvenile nonfiction; language/literature/criticism; memoirs; military/war; money/finance; multicultural; music/dance; nature/environment; New Age/metaphysics; philosophy; photography; popular culture; psychology; recreation; regional; religious/inspirational; science/technology; self-help/personal improvement; sex; sociology; software; spirituality; sports; theater/film; translation; travel; true crime/investigative; women's issues/studies; young adult. **Considers these fiction areas:** Action/adventure; comic books/cartoon; confession; contemporary issues; detective/police/crime; erotica; ethnic; experimental; family saga; fantasy; feminist; gay/lesbian; glitz; gothic; hi-lo; historical; horror; humor/satire; juvenile; literary; mainstream/contemporary; military/war; multicultural; multimedia; mystery/suspense; New Age; occult; picture books; plays; poetry; poetry in translation; psychic/supernatural; regional; religious/inspirational; romance; science fiction; short story collections; spiritual; sports; thriller; translation; western/frontier; young adult; women's. **Considers these script subject areas:** Action/adventure; comedy; detective/police/crime; ethnic; feminist;

gay/lesbian; historical; horror; mainstream; mystery/suspense; psychic/supernatural; romantic comedy; romantic drama; thriller; western/frontier.

How to Contact: Query with SASE. Prefers to read materials exclusively. No unsolicited mss. No e-mail or fax queries. Responds in 3 weeks to queries; 5 weeks to mss. Obtains most new clients through recommendations from others, solicitations, conferences.

Recent Sales: This agency prefers not to share information on specific sales.

Terms: Offers written contract. Charges for photocopying, some postage.

SHEREE BYKOFSKY ASSOCIATES, INC., 16 W. 36th St., 13th Floor, New York NY 10018. E-mail: shereebee@aol.com. Website: www.shereebee.com. **Contact:** Sheree Bykofsky. Estab. 1984, incorporated 1991. Member of AAR, ASJA, WNBA. Currently handles: 80% nonfiction books; 20% novels.

- Prior to opening her agency, Ms. Bykofsky served as executive editor of The Stonesong Press and managing editor of Chiron Press. She is also the author or co-author of more than 17 books, including *The Complete Idiot's Guide to Getting Published*. Ms. Bykofsky teaches publishing at NYU and The 92nd St. Y.

Member Agents: Janet Rosen, associate; Megan Buckley, associate.

Represents: Nonfiction books, novels. **Considers these nonfiction areas:** Americana; animals; anthropology/archaeology; art/architecture/design; biography/autobiography; business/economics; child guidance/parenting; computers/electronic; cooking/foods/nutrition; crafts/hobbies; creative nonfiction; current affairs; education; ethnic/cultural interests; gardening; gay/lesbian issues; government/politics/law; health/medicine; history; how-to; humor/satire; interior design/decorating; language/literature/criticism; memoirs; military/war; money/finance (personal finance); multicultural; music/dance; nature/environment; New Age/metaphysics; philosophy; photography; popular culture; psychology; recreation; regional; religious/inspirational; science/technology; self-help/personal improvement; sex; sociology; software; spirituality; sports; theater/film; translation; travel; true crime/investigative; women's issues/studies. **Considers these fiction areas:** Literary; mainstream/contemporary.

O→ This agency specializes in popular reference nonfiction, commercial fiction with a literary quality and mysteries. "I have wide-ranging interests, but it really depends on quality of writing, originality, and how a particular project appeals to me (or not). I take on fiction when I completely love it—it doesn't matter what area or genre." Does not want to receive poetry, material for children, screenplays, westerns, horror, sci-fi or fantasy.

How to Contact: Query with SASE. No unsolicited mss or phone calls. Considers simultaneous queries. Responds in 1 week to queries; 1 month to mss. Returns materials only with SASE. Obtains most new clients through recommendations from others.

Recent Sales: Sold 100 titles in the last year. *10 Sure Signs a Movie Character Is Doomed and Other Surprising Movie Lists*, by Richard Roeper (Hyperion); *Open Your Mind, Open Your Life*, by Taro Gold (Andrews & McMeel).

Terms: Agent receives 15% commission on domestic sales; 20% commission on foreign sales. Offers written contract, binding for 1 year. Charges for postage, photocopying and fax.

Writers' Conferences: ASJA (New York City); Asilomar (Pacific Grove CA); St. Petersburg; Whidbey Island; Jacksonville; Albuquerque; Austin; Columbus; Southwestern Writers; Willamette (Portland); Dorothy Canfield Fisher (San Diego); Writers Union (Maui); Pacific NW; IWWG; and many others.

Tips: "Read the agent listing carefully, and comply with guidelines."

CARLISLE & CO., 24 E. 64th St., New York NY 10021. (212)813-1881. Fax: (212)813-9567. E-mail: mtessler@carlisleco.com. Website: www.carlisleco.com. **Contact:** Michelle Tessler. Estab. 1998. Member of AAR. Represents 200 clients. Currently handles: 70% nonfiction books; 30% novels.

- Prior to opening his agency, Mr. Carlisle was the Vice President of William Morris for 18 years.

Member Agents: Michael Carlisle; Christy Fletcher; Emma Parry; Michelle Tessler; Joe Veltre. Affiliates: Donald S. Lamm, Robert Bernstein, Paul Bresnick, Diane Gedymin, Kathy Green.

Represents: Nonfiction books, fiction. **Considers these nonfiction areas:** Biography/autobiography; business/economics; cooking/foods/nutrition; health/medicine; history; memoirs; popular culture; psychology; science/technology; lifestyle; military history. **Considers these fiction areas:** Literary; mainstream/contemporary; mystery/thriller/adventure.

O→ This agency has "expertise in nonfiction and literary fiction. We have a strong focus on editorial input before submission." Does not want to receive science fiction, fantasy, or romance.

How to Contact: Query with SASE. Responds in 10 days to queries; 3 weeks to mss. Obtains most new clients through recommendations from others.

Recent Sales: Sold 100 titles in the last year. *Our Inner Ape*, by Frans de Wall (Riverhead); *The Commissariat of Enlightenment*, by Ken Kalfus (Ecco/Scribner UK); *The Man I Should Have Married*, by Pamela Satran (Pocket Books).

Terms: Agent receives 15% commission on domestic sales; 20% commission on foreign sales. Offers written contract, binding for 1 book only.

Writers' Conferences: Squaw Valley Community Conference (California).

Tips: "Be sure to write as original a story as possible. Remember, you're asking the public to pay $25 for your book."

MARIA CARVAINIS AGENCY, INC., 1350 Avenue of the Americas, Suite 2905, New York NY 10019. (212)245-6365. Fax: (212)245-7196. E-mail: mca@mariacarvainisagency.com. **Contact:** Maria Carvainis, president; Frances Kuffel, executive vice president. Estab. 1977. Member of AAR, Authors Guild, Women's Media Group, ABA, MWA, RWA; signatory of WGA. Represents 70 clients. 10% of clients are new/unpublished writers. Currently handles: 34% nonfiction books; 65% novels; 1% poetry.

- Prior to opening her agency, Ms. Carvainis spent more than 10 years in the publishing industry as a senior editor with Macmillan Publishing, Basic Books, Avon Books (where she worked closely with Peter Mayer), and Crown

Publishers. Ms. Carvainis has served as a member of the AAR Board of Directors and AAR Treasurer, as well as serving as chair of the AAR Contracts Committee. She presently serves on the AAR Royalty Committee.

Member Agents: Frances Kuffel (Executive Vice President); Anna Del Vecchio (Contracts Associate); Moira Sullivan (Editorial Associate); David Harvey (Literary Assistant).

Represents: Nonfiction books, novels. **Considers these nonfiction areas:** Biography/autobiography; business/economics; health/medicine; history; memoirs; science/technology (pop science); women's issues/studies. **Considers these fiction areas:** Literary; mainstream/contemporary; mystery/suspense; romance; thriller; young adult; middle grade, women's fiction.

O→ Does not want to receive science fiction or children's picture books.

How to Contact: Query with SASE. Responds in 1 week to queries; 3 months to mss. Obtains most new clients through recommendations from others, conferences, 60% from conferences/referrals; 40% from query letters.

Recent Sales: *The Bedwyn Series*, by Mary Balogh (Delacorte); *The Guru Guide to Money Management*, by Joseph H. Boyett and Jimmie T. Boyett (John Wiley and Sons); *Hello, Darkness*, by Sandra Brown (Simon & Schuster). Other clients include Sue Erikson Boland, Pam Conrad, Phillip DePoy, Carlos Dews, Fred Haefle, Hugo Mager, Ellen Newmark, David Saxe, Kristine Rolofson, Janet Mansfield Soares, Peter Stark, Ernest Suarez.

Terms: Agent receives 15% commission on domestic sales; 20% commission on foreign sales. Offers written contract, binding for 2 years on a book-by-book basis. Charges clients for foreign postage, bulk copying.

Writers' Conferences: BEA.

MARTHA CASSELMAN LITERARY AGENCY, (Specialized: cookbooks), P.O. Box 342, Calistoga CA 94515-0342. (707)942-4341. Fax: (707)942-4358. **Contact:** Martha Casselman. Estab. 1978. Member of IACP. Represents 30 clients. Currently handles: 100% nonfiction books.

Represents: Nonfiction books (food-related proposals and cookbooks). **Considers these nonfiction areas:** Agriculture/horticulture; anthropology/archaeology; biography/autobiography; cooking/foods/nutrition; health/medicine; women's issues/studies.

O→ This agency specializes in "nonfiction, especially food books." Does not want to receive children's book material or fiction.

How to Contact: Query with SASE, proposal package, outline, 3 sample chapter(s). Do not send any submission without querying first. Considers simultaneous queries. Responds in 3 weeks to queries. Obtains most new clients through recommendations from others.

Recent Sales: Sold 10 titles in the last year.

Terms: Agent receives 15% commission on domestic sales; 20% commission on foreign sales. Charges clients for photocopying, overnight and overseas mailings.

Writers' Conferences: IACP; other food-writers' conferences.

Tips: "No tricky letters; no gimmicks; always include SASE or mailer, or we can't contact you."

CASTIGLIA LITERARY AGENCY, 1155 Camino Del Mar, Suite 510, Del Mar CA 92014. (858)755-8761. Fax: (858)755-7063. **Contact:** Julie Castiglia. Estab. 1993. Member of AAR, PEN. Represents 50 clients. Currently handles: 55% nonfiction books; 45% novels.

Member Agents: Winifred Golden; Julie Castiglia.

Represents: Nonfiction books, novels. **Considers these nonfiction areas:** Animals; anthropology/archaeology; biography/autobiography; business/economics; child guidance/parenting; cooking/foods/nutrition; current affairs; ethnic/cultural interests; health/medicine; history; language/literature/criticism; money/finance; nature/environment; New Age/metaphysics; psychology; religious/inspirational; science/technology; self-help/personal improvement; sociology; women's issues/studies. **Considers these fiction areas:** Contemporary issues; ethnic; literary; mainstream/contemporary; mystery/suspense; women's (especially).

O→ Does not want to receive horror, screenplays or academic nonfiction.

How to Contact: Query with SASE. No fax queries. Responds in 2 months to mss. Returns materials only with SASE. Obtains most new clients through recommendations from others, solicitations, conferences.

Recent Sales: Sold 21 titles in the last year. *Outwit Your Genes and Lose Weight Now*, by Dr. Catherine Christie & Dr. Susan Mitchell; *One Foot in Love*, by Bil Wright.

Terms: Agent receives 15% commission on domestic sales; 25% commission on foreign sales. Offers written contract; 6-week notice must be given to terminate contract. Charges clients for Fed Ex or Messenger.

Writers' Conferences: Southwestern Writers Conference (Albuquerque NM, August); National Writers Conference; Willamette Writers Conference (OR); San Diego State University (CA); Writers at Work (Utah); Austin Conference (TX).

Tips: "Be professional with submissions. Attend workshops and conferences before you approach an agent."

WM CLARK ASSOCIATES, 355 W. 22nd St., New York NY 10011. (212)675-2784. Fax: (646)349-1658. E-mail: query@wmclark.com. Website: www.wmclark.com. **Contact:** William Clark. Estab. 1999. Member of AAR. 4.25% of clients are new/unpublished writers. Currently handles: 50% nonfiction books; 50% novels.

• Prior to opening WCA, Mr. Clark was an agent at the Virginia Barber Literary Agency and William Morris Agency.

Represents: Nonfiction books, novels, short story collections. **Considers these nonfiction areas:** Art/architecture/design; biography/autobiography; current affairs; ethnic/cultural interests; history; memoirs; music/dance; popular culture; religious/inspirational (Eastern philosophy only); science/technology; sociology; theater/film; translation. **Considers these fiction areas:** Contemporary issues; ethnic; historical; literary; mainstream/contemporary; Southern fiction.

O→ "As one of the new breed of media agents recognizing their expanded roles in today's ever-changing media landscape, William Clark represents a diverse range of commercial and literary fiction and quality nonfiction to the book publishing, motion picture, television, and new media fields."

How to Contact: Prefers to read materials exclusively. E-mail queries only. Responds in 1 month to queries.

Recent Sales: Sold 25 titles in the last year. *Fallingwater Rising: E.J. Kaufman and Frank Lloyd Wright Create the Most Exciting House in the World*, by Franklin Toker (Alfred A. Knopf); *Behind Deep Blue: Building the Computer that Defeated the World Chess Champion*, by Feng-hsiung Hsu (Princeton University Pess); *Hungry Ghost*, by Keith Kachtick (HarperCollins). Other clients include Russell Martin, Mian Mian, Jonathan Stone, Jocko Weyland, Carolin Young, Rev. Billy (aka Billy Talen).

Terms: Agent receives 15% commission on domestic sales; 20% commission on foreign sales. Offers written contract.

Tips: "E-mail queries should include a general description of the work, a synopsis/outline if available, biographical information, and publishing history, if any."

N **CLAUSEN, MAYS & TAHAN, LLC**, 249 W. 34th St., Suite 605, New York NY 10001-2815. (212)239-4343. Fax: (212)239-5248. E-mail: cmtassist@aol.com. **Contact:** Stedman Mays, Mary M. Tahan. Estab. 1976. 10% of clients are new/unpublished writers. Currently handles: nonfiction books; novels.

Member Agents: Stedman Mays; Mary M. Tahan; Jena Anderson.

Represents: Nonfiction books, novels. **Considers these nonfiction areas:** Biography/autobiography; cooking/foods/nutrition; health/medicine; history; how-to; humor/satire; memoirs; money/finance; psychology; religious/inspirational; spirituality; women's issues/studies; fashion/beauty/style; relationships; also rights for books optioned for TV movies and feature films.

How to Contact: Query with SASE, proposal package, outline. No e-mail or fax queries. Considers simultaneous queries. Responds in 3 weeks to queries; 1 month to mss. Returns materials only with SASE.

Recent Sales: *And If I Perish*, by Evelyn Monahan and Rosemary Neidle-Greenlee (Knopf); *The Rules for Online Dating*, by Ellen Fein and Sherrie Schneider (Pocket Books); *The Anti-Inflammation Diet*, by Richard Fleming, M.D. with Tom Monte (Putnam).

Terms: Agent receives 15% commission on domestic sales; 20% commission on foreign sales. Charges clients for postage, shipping, and photocopying.

Tips: "Research proposal writing and the publishing process. Always study your book's competition. Send a proposal and outline instead of complete manuscript for faster response. Always pitch books in writing, not over the phone."

N **RUTH COHEN, INC., LITERARY AGENCY**, P.O. Box 2244, La Jolla CA 92038-2244. (858)456-5805. **Contact:** Ruth Cohen. Estab. 1982. Member of AAR, Authors Guild, Sisters in Crime, RWA, SCBWI. Represents 45 clients. 15% of clients are new/unpublished writers. Currently handles: 60% novels; 40% juvenile books.

- Prior to becoming an agent, Ms. Cohen served as directing editor at Scott Foresman & Company (now HarperCollins).

Represents: Novels (adult), juvenile books. **Considers these fiction areas:** Ethnic; historical; juvenile; literary; mainstream/contemporary; mystery/suspense; picture books; young adult.

This agency specializes in "quality writing in contemporary fiction, women's fiction, mysteries, thrillers and juvenile fiction." Does not want to receive poetry, westerns, film scripts or how-to books.

How to Contact: Submit outline, 1 sample chapter(s). Responds in 3 weeks to queries. Returns materials only with SASE. Obtains most new clients through recommendations from others, solicitations.

Recent Sales: This agency prefers not to share information on specific sales.

Terms: Agent receives 15% commission on domestic sales; 20% commission on foreign sales. Offers written contract, binding for 1 year. Charges for foreign postage, phone calls, photocopying submissions and overnight delivery of mss when appropriate.

Tips: "As the publishing world merges and changes, there seem to be fewer opportunities for new writers to succeed in the work that they love. We urge you to develop the patience, persistence and preseverance that have made this agency so successful. Prepare a well-written and well-crafted manuscript, and our combined best efforts can help advance both our careers."

N **FRANCES COLLIN, LITERARY AGENT**, P.O. Box 33, Wayne PA 19087-0033. **Contact:** Frances Collin. Estab. 1948. Member of AAR. Represents 90 clients. 1% of clients are new/unpublished writers. Currently handles: 50% nonfiction books; 48% novels; 1% textbooks; 1% poetry.

Represents: Nonfiction books, novels. **Considers these nonfiction areas:** Anthropology/archaeology; biography/autobiography; health/medicine; history; nature/environment; true crime/investigative. **Considers these fiction areas:** Detective/police/crime; ethnic; family saga; fantasy; historical; literary; mainstream/contemporary; mystery/suspense; psychic/supernatural; regional; romance (historical); science fiction.

How to Contact: Query with SASE. Considers simultaneous queries. Responds in 1 week to queries; 2 months to mss. Obtains most new clients through recommendations from others.

Recent Sales: This agency prefers not to share information on specific sales.

Terms: Agent receives 15% commission on domestic sales; 20% commission on foreign sales. Offers written contract. Charges clients for overseas postage for books mailed to foreign agents; photocopying of mss, books, proposals; copyright registration fees; registered mail fees; passes along cost of any books purchased.

N **CONNOR LITERARY AGENCY**, 2911 W. 71st St., Minneapolis MN 55423. (612)866-1426. Fax: (612)869-4074. E-mail: coolmkc@aol.com. **Contact:** Marlene Connor Lynch. Estab. 1985. Represents 50 clients. 30% of clients are new/unpublished writers. Currently handles: 50% nonfiction books; 50% novels.

- Prior to opening her agency, Ms. Connor served at the Literary Guild of America, Simon and Schuster and Random

House. She is author of *What is Cool: Understanding Black Manhood in America* (Crown).

Member Agents: Deborah Coker (children's books)

Represents: Nonfiction books, novels, especially with a minority slant. **Considers these nonfiction areas:** Child guidance/parenting; cooking/foods/nutrition; crafts/hobbies; current affairs; ethnic/cultural interests; government/politics/law; health/medicine; how-to; humor/satire; interior design/decorating; language/literature/criticism; money/finance; photography; popular culture; self-help/personal improvement; sports; true crime/investigative; women's issues/studies; relationships. **Considers these fiction areas:** Historical; horror; literary; mainstream/contemporary; multicultural; thriller; women's; suspense.

How to Contact: Query with SASE. Obtains most new clients through recommendations from others, conferences, grapevine.

Recent Sales: *Outrageous Commitments*, by Dr. Ronn Elmore (HarperCollins); *Seductions*, by Snow Starborn (Sourcebooks); *Simplicitys Simply the Best Sewing Book, Revised Edition.*

Terms: Agent receives 15% commission on domestic sales; 25% commission on foreign sales. Offers written contract, binding for 1 year.

Writers' Conferences: National Writers Union, Midwest Chapter; Agents, Agents, Agents; Texas Writer's Conference; Detroit Writer's Conference.

Tips: "Seeking previously published writers with good sales records and new writers with real talent."

THE DOE COOVER AGENCY, P.O. Box 668, Winchester MA 01890. (781)721-6000. Fax: (781)721-6727. **Contact:** Doe Coover, president. Estab. 1985. Represents over 100 clients. Currently handles: 80% nonfiction books; 20% novels.

- Prior to becoming agents, Ms. Coover and Ms. Mohyde were editors for over a decade.

Member Agents: Doe Coover (cooking, general nonfiction); Colleen Mohyde (literary and commercial fiction, general nonfiction and journalism) Frances Kennedy (assistant)

Represents: Nonfiction books, novels. **Considers these nonfiction areas:** Anthropology/archaeology; biography/autobiography; business/economics; child guidance/parenting; cooking/foods/nutrition; ethnic/cultural interests; health/medicine; history; language/literature/criticism; memoirs; money/finance; nature/environment; psychology; sociology; travel; true crime/investigative; women's issues/studies. **Considers these fiction areas:** Literary; mainstream/contemporary (commercial).

This agency specializes in cookbooks, serious nonfiction—particularly books on social issues—as well as fiction (literary and commercial), journalism and general nonfiction. Does not want children's books.

How to Contact: Query with SASE, outline. No e-mail or fax queries. Considers simultaneous queries. Returns materials only with SASE. Obtains most new clients through recommendations from others, solicitations.

Recent Sales: Sold 25-30 titles in the last year. *The Gourmet Cookbook*, by Gourmet Magazine (W.W. Norton); *The Cradle of Flavor*, by James Oseland (W.W. Norton); *Seven Things Your Teenager Doesn't Want You to Know*, by Jennifer Lippincott and Robin Deutsch (Random House). ***Movie/TV MOW script(s) optioned/sold:*** *Drinking: A Love Story*, by Caroline Knapp; *Danville*, by Robin McCorquodale; *Mr. White's Confession*, by Robert Clark. Other clients include WGBH, Peter Lynch, Jacques Pepin, Deborah Madison, Rick Bayless, Adria Bernardi, Suzanne Berne and Thrity Umrigar.

Terms: Agent receives 15% commission on domestic sales; 15% commission on foreign sales.

Writers' Conferences: BEA.

CORE CREATIONS, LLC, 9024 S. Sanderling Way, Littleton CO 80126. (303)683-6792. E-mail: agent@eoncity.com. Website: www.eoncity.com/agent. **Contact:** Calvin Rex. Estab. 1994. Represents 10 clients. 70% of clients are new/unpublished writers. Currently handles: 30% nonfiction books; 60% novels; 5% novellas; 5% games.

- Prior to becoming an agent, Mr. Rex managed a small publishing house.

Member Agents: Calvin Rex.

Represents: Nonfiction books, novels, novellas. **Considers these nonfiction areas:** Gay/lesbian issues; how-to; humor/satire; psychology; true crime/investigative. **Considers these fiction areas:** Detective/police/crime; horror; science fiction.

This agency specializes in "bold, daring literature." Agency has strong "experience with royalty contracts and licensing agreements."

How to Contact: Query with SASE, outline/proposal. Responds in 3 weeks to queries; 3 months to mss. Obtains most new clients through recommendations from others, solicitations, through the Internet.

Terms: Agent receives 15% commission on domestic sales; 20% commission on foreign sales. Offers written contract. Charges clients for postage (applicable mailing costs).

Writers' Conferences: Steamboat Springs Writers Group (Colorado, July); Rocky Mountain Fiction Writers Colorado Gold Conference.

Tips: "Have all material proofread. Visit our webpage before sending anything. We want books that dare to be different. Give us a unique angle, a new style of writing, something that stands out from the crowd!"

CORNERSTONE LITERARY, INC., 4500 Wilshire Blvd., 3rd floor, Los Angeles CA 90010. (323)930-6039. Fax: (323)930-0407. Website: www.cornerstoneliterary.com. **Contact:** Helen Breitwieser. Estab. 1998. Member of AAR; Author's Guild. Represents 40 clients. 75% of clients are new/unpublished writers.

- Prior to founding her own boutique agency, Ms. Breitwieser was a literary agent at The William Morris Agency.

Represents: Novels. **Considers these fiction areas:** Detective/police/crime; erotica; ethnic; family saga; glitz; historical; literary; mainstream/contemporary; multicultural; mystery/suspense; romance; thriller.

Actively seeking first fiction, literary. Does not want to receive science fiction, westerns, children's books, poetry, screenplays, fantasy, gay/lesbian, horror, self-help, psychology, business.

How to Contact: Query with SASE. Responds in 2 weeks to queries; 2 months to mss. Returns materials only with SASE. Obtains most new clients through recommendations from others.
Recent Sales: Sold 42 titles in the last year. *Last Breath*, by Rachel Lee (Warner); *Cold Silence*, by Danielle Girard (NAL); *Bare Necessity*, by Carole Matthews (HarperCollins). Other clients include Stan Diehl, Elaine Coffman, R.J. Kaiser, Kayla Perrin, Candice Proctor.
Terms: Agent receives 15% commission on domestic sales; 20% commission on foreign sales. Offers written contract, binding for 1 year; 60-day notice must be given to terminate contract.
Tips: "Don't query about more than one manuscript. Do not e-mail queries/submissions."

CRAWFORD LITERARY AGENCY, 94 Evans Rd., Barnstead NH 03218. (603)269-5851. Fax: (603)269-2533. E-mail: crawfordlit@att.net. **Contact:** Susan Crawford. Winter Office: 3920 Bayside Rd., Fort Myers Beach FL 33931. (239)463-4651. Fax: (239)463-0125. Estab. 1988. Represents 45 clients. 10% of clients are new/unpublished writers. Currently handles: 50% nonfiction books; 50% novels.
Member Agents: Susan Crawford; Lorne Crawford (commercial fiction and nonfiction); Scott Neister (scientific/techno thrillers).
Represents: Considers these nonfiction areas: Psychology; religious/inspirational; self-help/personal improvement; women's issues/studies; celebrity/media. **Considers these fiction areas:** Action/adventure; mystery/suspense; thriller (medical).

This agency specializes in celebrity and/or media-based books and authors. Actively seeking action/adventure stories, medical thrillers, self-help, inspirational, how-to and women's issues. Does not want to receive short stories, poetry.

How to Contact: Query with SASE. Considers simultaneous queries. Responds in 3 weeks to queries. Returns materials only with SASE. Obtains most new clients through recommendations from others, solicitations, conferences.
Recent Sales: Sold 42 titles in the last year. *Excelsior! The Amazing Life of Stan Lee*, by Stan Lee (Simon & Schuster); *Web Thinking*, by Dr. Linda Seger (Inner Ocean Publishing); *Gray Matter*, by Gary Braven. Other clients include John Travolta, Cal Morris,MD, Mimi Donaldson, Ruby Dee, Ossie Davis.
Terms: Agent receives 15% commission on domestic sales; 20% commission on foreign sales. Offers written contract, binding for 90 days; 100% of business is derived from commissions on ms sales.
Writers' Conferences: International Film & Television Workshops (Rockport ME); Maui Writers Conference.
Tips: "Keep learning to improve your craft. Attend conferences and network."

RICHARD CURTIS ASSOCIATES, INC., 171 E. 74th St., New York NY 10021. (212)772-7363. Fax: (212)772-7393. Website: www.curtisagency.com. Estab. 1979. Member of RWA, MWA, WWA, SFWA; signatory of WGA. Represents 100 clients. 1% of clients are new/unpublished writers. Currently handles: 75% nonfiction books; 25% novels.

- Prior to opening his agency, Mr. Curtis was an agent with the Scott Meredith Literary Agency for 7 years and has authored over 50 published books.

Member Agents: Richard Curtis; Pamela Valvera.
Represents: Commercial nonfiction, commercial and literary fiction. **Considers these nonfiction areas:** Popular culture; young adult. **Considers these fiction areas:** Fantasy; romance; science fiction; thriller; young adult.
How to Contact: One-page query letter, plus no more than a one-page synopsis of proposed submission. No submission of mss unless specifically requested. If requested, submission must be accompanied by a SASE or we will assume you don't want your submission back. No e-mail or fax queries. Returns materials only with SASE.
Recent Sales: Sold 150 titles in the last year. *Ilium*, by Dan Simmons; *Suspicion of Vengeance*, by Barbara Parker; *Darwin's Children*, by Greg Bear. Other clients include Jennifer Blake, Leonard Maltin, Earl Mindell and Barbara Parker.
Terms: Agent receives 15% commission on domestic sales; 25% commission on foreign sales. Offers written contract, binding for book-by-book basis. Charges for photocopying, express, international freight, book orders.
Writers' Conferences: Science Fiction Writers of America; Horror Writers of America; Romance Writers of America; World Fantasy Conference.

JAMES R. CYPHER, THE CYPHER AGENCY, 816 Wolcott Ave., Beacon NY 12508-4261. (845)831-5677. Fax: (845)831-5677. E-mail: jimcypher@prodigy.net. Website: pages.prodigy.net/jimcypher/. **Contact:** James R. Cypher. Estab. 1993. Member of AAR, Authors Guild. Represents 40 clients. 40% of clients are new/unpublished writers. Currently handles: 100% nonfiction books.

- Prior to opening his agency, Mr. Cypher worked as a corporate public relations manager for a Fortune 500 multinational computer company for 28 years.

Represents: Nonfiction books. **Considers these nonfiction areas:** Biography/autobiography; current affairs; ethnic/cultural interests; gay/lesbian issues; government/politics/law; health/medicine; history; how-to; language/literature/criticism; memoirs (travel); money/finance; music/dance; nature/environment; popular culture; psychology; science/technology; self-help/personal improvement; sociology; sports; theater/film; travel (memoirs); true crime/investigative; women's issues/studies.

Actively seeking a wide variety of topical nonfiction. Does not want to receive humor; pets; gardening; cooking books; crafts; spiritual; religious or New Age topics.

How to Contact: Query with SASE, proposal package, outline, 2 sample chapter(s). Accepts e-mail and fax queries. Considers simultaneous queries. Responds in 2 weeks to queries; 6 weeks to mss. Obtains most new clients through recommendations from others, conferences, networking on online computer service.
Recent Sales: Sold 5 titles in the last year. *The Night the Defeos Died: Reinvestigating the Amityville Murders*, by Ric Osuna (Katco Literary & Media); *Revolution in Zanzibar: An American's Cold War Tale*, by Donald Petterson (Westview

Press); *Once Upon a Word: True Tales of Word Origins*, by Rob Kyff (Tapestry Press).
Terms: Agent receives 15% commission on domestic sales; 20% commission on foreign sales. Offers written contract; 30-day cancellation clause notice must be given to terminate contract. 100% of business is derived from commissions on ms sales. Charges clients for postage, photocopying, overseas phone calls and faxes.

DARHANSOFF, VERRILL, FELDMAN LITERARY AGENTS, 236 W. 26th St., Suite 802, New York NY 10001. (917)305-1300. Fax: (917)305-1400. Estab. 1975. Member of AAR. Represents 120 clients. 10% of clients are new/unpublished writers. Currently handles: 25% nonfiction books; 60% novels; 15% story collections.
Member Agents: Liz Darhansoff; Charles Verrill; Leigh Feldman.
Represents: Novels, short story collections. **Considers these nonfiction areas:** Narrative nonfiction.
- Specializes in literary fiction.

How to Contact: Obtains most new clients through recommendations from others.

LIZA DAWSON ASSOCIATES, 240 W. 35th St., Suite 500, New York NY 10001. (212)465-9071. **Contact:** Liza Dawson, Caitlin Blasdell. Member of AAR, MWA, Women's Media Group. Represents 50 clients. 10% of clients are new/unpublished writers. Currently handles: 60% nonfiction books; 40% novels.
- Prior to becoming an agent, Ms. Dawson was an editor for 20 years, spending 11 years at William Morrow as vice president and 2 at Putnam as executive editor. Ms. Blasdell was a senior editor at HarperCollins and Avon.

Member Agents: Liza Dawson; Caitlin Blasdell.
Represents: Nonfiction books, novels, scholarly books. **Considers these nonfiction areas:** Biography/autobiography; business/economics; child guidance/parenting; health/medicine; history; memoirs; psychology; sociology; women's issues/studies. **Considers these fiction areas:** Ethnic; family saga; historical; literary; mystery/suspense; regional; science fiction (Blasdell only); thriller.
- This agency specializes in readable literary fiction, thrillers, mainstream historicals and women's fiction, academics, historians, business, journalists and psychology. Does not want to receive westerns, sports, computers, juvenile.

How to Contact: Query with SASE. Responds in 3 weeks to queries; 6 weeks to mss. Obtains most new clients through recommendations from others, conferences.
Recent Sales: Sold 40 titles in the last year. *Pastries*, by Bharti Kirchner (St. Martin's); *Using What You Got*, by Karen E. Quinones Miller (Simon and Schuster); *Seven Days of Possibilities*, by Anemona Hartocollis (Public Affairs).
Terms: Agent receives 15% commission on domestic sales; 20% commission on foreign sales. Offers written contract. Charges clients for photocopying and overseas postage.
Writers' Conferences: Pacific Northwest Book Conference (Seattle, July).

DeFIORE AND CO., 72 Spring St., Suite 304, New York NY 10012. (212)925-7744. Fax: (212)925-9803. E-mail: info@defioreandco.com. Website: www.defioreandco.com. **Contact:** Brian DeFiore. Estab. 1999. Represents 35 clients. 50% of clients are new/unpublished writers. Currently handles: 70% nonfiction books; 30% novels.
- Prior to becoming an agent, Mr. DeFiore was Publisher of Villard Books 1997-1998; Editor-in-Chief of Hyperion 1992-1997; Editorial Director of Delacorte Press 1988-1992.

Member Agents: Brian DeFiore (popular nonfiction, business, pop culture, parenting, commercial fiction); Kate Garrick (literary fiction, crime, pop culture, politics, history, psychology, narrative nonfiction).
Represents: Nonfiction books, novels. **Considers these nonfiction areas:** Biography/autobiography; business/economics; child guidance/parenting; cooking/foods/nutrition; gay/lesbian issues; health/medicine; money/finance; multicultural; popular culture; psychology; religious/inspirational; self-help/personal improvement; sports. **Considers these fiction areas:** Ethnic; gay/lesbian; literary; mainstream/contemporary; mystery/suspense; thriller.
How to Contact: Query with SASE. Considers simultaneous queries. Responds in 3 weeks to queries; 2 months to mss. Returns materials only with SASE. Obtains most new clients through recommendations from others.
Recent Sales: Sold 20 titles in the last year. *The Money Is the Gravy*, by John Clark (Warner Books); *The Birdwatcher*, by Norm Green (HarperCollins); *So Five Minutes Ago*, by Hilary De Vries (Random House). Other clients include David Rensin, Loretta LaRoche, Jason Starr, Joel Engel, Christopher Keane, Robin McMillan, Jessica Teich, Ronna Lichtenberg, Fran Sorin, Christine Dimmick, Jimmy Lerner, Lou Mantredini, Dan Hays.
Terms: Agent receives 15% commission on domestic sales; 20% commission on foreign sales. Offers written contract; 10-day notice must be given to terminate contract. Charges clients for photocopying, overnight delivery (deducted only after a sale is made).
Writers' Conferences: Maui Writers Conference (Maui HI, September); Pacific Northwest Writers Association Conference; North Carolina Writer's Network Conference.

DHS LITERARY, INC., 2528 Elm St., Suite 350, Dallas TX 75226. (214)363-4422. Fax: (214)363-4423. E-mail: submissions@dhsliterary.com. Website: www.dhsliterary.com. **Contact:** David Hale Smith, president. Estab. 1994. Represents 35 clients. 15% of clients are new/unpublished writers. Currently handles: 60% nonfiction books; 40% novels.
- Prior to opening his agency, Mr. Smith was an editor at a newswire service.

Represents: Nonfiction books, novels. **Considers these nonfiction areas:** Biography/autobiography; business/economics; child guidance/parenting; cooking/foods/nutrition; current affairs; ethnic/cultural interests; popular culture; sports; true crime/investigative. **Considers these fiction areas:** Detective/police/crime; ethnic; literary; mainstream/contemporary; mystery/suspense; thriller; western/frontier.
- This agency specializes in commercial fiction and nonfiction for adult trade market. Actively seeking thrillers, mysteries, suspense, etc., and narrative nonfiction. Does not want to receive poetry, short fiction, children's books.

How to Contact: "We no longer accept unsolicited queries. We only accept 1-page queries by e-mail from publisher professionals, authors and contacts." No paper queries accepted unless requested by agency. Will request more material if appropriate. Considers simultaneous queries. Responds in 1 month to queries. Obtains most new clients through recommendations from others, editors and agents.

Recent Sales: Sold 35 titles in the last year. *The Curve of the World*, by Marcus Stevens (Algonquin); *City on Fire*, by Bill Minutaglio (Morrow).

Terms: Agent receives 15% commission on domestic sales; 25% commission on foreign sales. Offers written contract; 10-day notice must be given to terminate contract. Charges for client expenses, i.e., postage, photocopying. 100% of business is derived from commissions on sales.

Tips: "Remember to be courteous and professional, and to treat marketing your work and approaching an agent as you would any formal business matter. When in doubt, always query first via e-mail.Visit our website for more information."

N ⊘ **SANDRA DIJKSTRA LITERARY AGENCY**, 1155 Camino del Mar, PMB 515, Del Mar CA 92014-2605. (858)755-3115. Fax: (858) 794-2822. E-mail: sdla@dijkstraagency.com. **Contact:** Jill Marr. Estab. 1981. Member of AAR, Authors Guild, PEN West, Poets and Editors, MWA. Represents 200 clients. 30% of clients are new/unpublished writers. Currently handles: 50% nonfiction books; 45% novels; 5% juvenile books.

- We specialize in a number of fields.

Member Agents: Sandra Dijkstra.

Represents: Nonfiction books, novels. **Considers these nonfiction areas:** Anthropology/archaeology; business/economics; child guidance/parenting; cooking/foods/nutrition; ethnic/cultural interests; government/politics/law; health/medicine; history; language/literature/criticism; military/war; money/finance; nature/environment; psychology; science/technology; sociology; women's issues/studies. **Considers these fiction areas:** Ethnic; literary; mainstream/contemporary; mystery/suspense; thriller.

How to Contact: Submit proposal package, outline, sample chapter(s), author bio, SASE. No e-mail or fax queries. Responds in 1 month to queries; 6 weeks to mss. Obtains most new clients through recommendations from others, solicitations, conferences.

Recent Sales: Sold over 40 titles in the last year. *The Hottentot Venus*, by Barbara Chase-Riboud (Doubleday); *The Lady, The Chef and the Lover*, by Marisol Konczal (Harper Collins); *End of Adolescence*, by Robert Epstein (Harcourt).

Terms: Agent receives 15% commission on domestic sales; 20% commission on foreign sales. Offers written contract. Charges clients for expenses "to cover domestic costs so that we can spend time selling books instead of accounting expenses. We also charge for the photocopying of the full ms or nonfiction proposal and for foreign postage."

Writers' Conferences: "Have attended Squaw Valley, Santa Barbara, Asilomar, Southern California Writers Conference, Rocky Mountain Fiction Writers, to name a few. We also speak regularly for writers groups such as PEN West and the Independent Writers Association."

Tips: "Be professional and learn the standard procedures for submitting your work. Give full biographical information on yourself, especially for a nonfiction project. Send no more than 50 pages of your manuscript, a very brief synopsis, detailed author bio (awards, publications, accomplishments) and a SASE. We will not respond to submissions without a SASE. Nine page letters telling us your life story, or your book's, are unprofessional and usually not read. Tell us about your book and write your query well. It's our first introduction to who you are and what you can do! Call if you don't hear within six weeks. Be a regular patron of bookstores and study what kind of books are being published. READ. Check out your local library and bookstores—you'll find lots of books on writing and the publishing industry that will help you! At conferences, ask published writers about their agents. Don't believe the myth that an agent has to be in New York to be successful—we've already disproved it!"

JANIS A. DONNAUD & ASSOCIATES, INC., 525 Broadway, 2nd Floor, New York NY 10012. (212)431-2664. Fax: (212)431-2667. E-mail: jdonnaud@aol.com. **Contact:** Janis A. Donnaud. Member of AAR; signatory of WGA. Represents 40 clients. 5% of clients are new/unpublished writers. Currently handles: 100% nonfiction books.

- Prior to opening her agency, Ms. Donnaud was Vice President, Associate Publisher, Random House Adult Trade group.

Represents: Nonfiction books. **Considers these nonfiction areas:** Art/architecture/design; biography/autobiography; child guidance/parenting; cooking/foods/nutrition; creative nonfiction; current affairs; health/medicine; humor/satire; psychology (pop).

This agency specializes in health, medical, cooking, humor, pop psychology, narrative nonfiction, photography, biography, parenting, current affairs. "We give a lot of service and attention to clients." Actively seeking serious narrative nonfiction; cookbooks; health and medical all written by experts with an already established platform in their area of specialty. Does not want to receive fiction, poetry, mysteries, juvenile books, romances, science fiction, young adult, religious, fantasy.

How to Contact: Query with SASE, description of book and 2-3 pages of sample material. Prefers to read materials exclusively. Accepts e-mail queries. Responds in 1 month to queries; 1 month to mss. Obtains most new clients through recommendations from others.

Recent Sales: Sold 25 titles in the last year. *Made for Each Other: Fashion and the Oscars*, by Bronwyn Cosgrave (Bloomsbury); *Sunday Suppers from Lucques*, by Suzanne Goin (Wiley).

Terms: Agent receives 15% commission on domestic sales; 20% commission on foreign sales; 20% commission on dramatic rights sales. Offers written contract; 30-day notice must be given to terminate contract. Charges clients for messengers, photocopying, purchase of books.

JIM DONOVAN LITERARY, 4515 Prentice St., Suite 109, Dallas TX 75206. **Contact:** Jim Donovan, president; Kathryn Lindsey. Estab. 1993. Represents 35 clients. 20% of clients are new/unpublished writers. Currently handles: 75% nonfiction books; 25% novels.

Member Agents: Jim Donovan (president); Kathryn Lindsey.

Represents: Nonfiction books, novels. **Considers these nonfiction areas:** Biography/autobiography; business/economics; child guidance/parenting; current affairs; health/medicine; history; military/war; money/finance; music/dance; nature/environment; popular culture; sports; true crime/investigative. **Considers these fiction areas:** Action/adventure; detective/police/crime; historical; horror; literary; mainstream/contemporary; mystery/suspense; sports; thriller; western/frontier.

This agency specializes in commercial fiction and nonfiction. Does not want to receive poetry, humor, short stories, juvenile, romance or religious work.

How to Contact: Query with SASE. For nonfiction, send query letter. For fiction, send 2- to 5-page outline and 3 sample chapters. No e-mail or fax queries. Considers simultaneous queries. Responds in 1 month to queries; 1 month to mss. Obtains most new clients through recommendations from others, solicitations.

Recent Sales: Sold 24 titles in the last year. *Given Up for Dead*, by Bill Sloan (Bantam); *Duel in the Sun*, by Curt Sampson (Pocket/Atria); *Streetcar: Blanche Dubois, Marlon Brando, and the Movie that Outraged America*, by Sam Staggs (St. Martin's).

Terms: Agent receives 15% commission on domestic sales; 20% commission on foreign sales. Offers written contract, binding for 1 year; written notice must be given to terminate contract.

Tips: "The vast majority of material I receive, particularly fiction, is not ready for publication. Do everything you can to get your fiction work in top shape before you try to find an agent. I've been in the book business since 1981, in retail (as a chain buyer), as an editor, and as a published author. I'm open to working with new writers if they're serious about their writing and are prepared to put in the work necessary—the rewriting—to become publishable."

DOYEN LITERARY SERVICES, INC., 1931 660th St., Newell IA 50568-7613. (712)272-3300. Website: www.barbaradoyen.com. **Contact:** (Ms.) B.J. Doyen, president. Estab. 1988. Represents 60 clients. 20% of clients are new/unpublished writers. Currently handles: 90% nonfiction books; 10% novels.

- Prior to opening her agency, Ms. Doyen worked as a published author, teacher, guest speaker and wrote and appeared in her own weekly TV show airing in 7 states.

Represents: Nonfiction books, novels. **Considers these nonfiction areas:** Agriculture/horticulture; americana; animals; anthropology/archaeology; art/architecture/design; biography/autobiography; business/economics; child guidance/parenting; computers/electronic; cooking/foods/nutrition; crafts/hobbies; creative nonfiction; current affairs; education; ethnic/cultural interests; gardening; government/politics/law; health/medicine; history; how-to; humor/satire; interior design/decorating; juvenile nonfiction; language/literature/criticism; memoirs; military/war; money/finance; multicultural; music/dance; nature/environment; New Age/metaphysics; philosophy; photography; popular culture; psychology; recreation; regional; religious/inspirational; science/technology; self-help/personal improvement; sex; sociology; software; spirituality; sports; theater/film; translation; travel; true crime/investigative; women's issues/studies; young adult. **Considers these fiction areas:** Contemporary issues; family saga; historical; literary; mainstream/contemporary; occult; psychic/supernatural.

This agency specializes in nonfiction and occasionally handles genre and mainstream fiction for adults. Actively seeking business, health, how-to, psychology; all kinds of adult nonfiction suitable for the major trade publishers. Prefers fiction from published novelists only. Does not want to receive pornography, children's, poetry.

How to Contact: Query with SASE. No e-mail or fax queries. Considers simultaneous queries. Responds in 2 weeks to mss. Responds immediately to queries. Returns materials only with SASE.

Terms: Agent receives 15% commission on domestic sales; 20% commission on foreign sales. Offers written contract, binding for 1 year.

Tips: "Our authors receive personalized attention. We market aggressively, undeterred by rejection. We get the best possible publishing contracts. We are very interested in nonfiction book ideas at this time; will consider most topics. Many writers come to us from referrals, but we also get quite a few who initially approach us with query letters. Do not use phone queries unless you are successfully published or a celebrity. It is best if you do not collect editorial rejections prior to seeking an agent, but if you do, be up-front and honest about it. Do not submit your manuscript to more than one agent at a time—querying first can save you (and us) much time. We're open to established or beginning writers—just send us a terrific letter with SASE!"

DUNHAM LITERARY, INC., 156 Fifth Ave., Suite 625, New York NY 10010-7002. (212)929-0994. Website: www.dunhamlit.com. **Contact:** Jennie Dunham. Estab. 2000. Member of AAR. Represents 50 clients. 15% of clients are new/unpublished writers. Currently handles: 25% nonfiction books; 25% novels; 50% juvenile books.

- Prior to opening her agency, Ms. Dunham worked as a literary agent for Russell & Volkening. The Rhoda Weyr Agency is now a division of Dunham Literary, Inc.

Member Agents: Donna Lieberman (mainstream fiction and nonfiction, mysteries, suspense, thrillers).

Represents: Nonfiction books, novels, short story collections, juvenile books. **Considers these nonfiction areas:** Anthropology/archaeology; art/architecture/design; biography/autobiography; business/economics; current affairs; education; ethnic/cultural interests; gay/lesbian issues; government/politics/law; health/medicine; history; juvenile nonfiction; language/literature/criticism; music/dance; nature/environment; photography; popular culture; psychology; science/technology; sociology; sports; women's issues/studies. **Considers these fiction areas:** Ethnic; juvenile; literary; mainstream/contemporary; mystery/suspense; picture books; thriller; young adult.

How to Contact: Query with SASE. No e-mail or fax queries. Responds in 1 week to queries; 2 months to mss. Obtains most new clients through recommendations from others, solicitations.

Recent Sales: *Black Hawk Down*, by Mark Bowden; *Look Back All the Green Valley*, by Fred Chappell; *Even Now*, by Susan S. Kelly.

Terms: Agent receives 15% commission on domestic sales; 20% commission on foreign sales. Writers reimbursed for office fees after the sale of ms.

DWYER & O'GRADY, INC., (Specialized: children's books), P.O. Box 790, Cedar Key FL 32625. (352)543-9307. **Contact:** Elizabeth O'Grady. Estab. 1990. Member of SCBWI. Represents 20 clients. Currently handles: 100% juvenile books.

- Prior to opening their agency, Mr. Dwyer and Ms. Grady were booksellers and publishers.

Member Agents: Elizabeth O'Grady (children's books); Jeff Dwyer (children's books).

Represents: Juvenile books. **Considers these nonfiction areas:** Juvenile nonfiction. **Considers these fiction areas:** Juvenile; picture books; young adult.

O→ This agency represents only writers and illustrators of children's books. Does not want to receive submissions that are not for juvenile audiences.

How to Contact: Not accepting new clients. No unsolicited mss. Obtains most new clients through recommendations from others, direct approach by agent to writer whose work they've read.

Recent Sales: Sold 22 titles in the last year. Clients include Kim Ablon, Mary Azarian, Tom Bodett, Odds Bodkin, Donna Clair, Leonard Jenkins, E.B. Lewis, Steve Schuch, Virginia Stroud, Natasha Tarpley, Zong-Zhou Wang, Rashida Watson, Rich Michelson, Barry Moser, Peter Sycuada.

Terms: Agent receives 15% commission on domestic sales; 20% commission on foreign sales. Offers written contract; 30-day notice must be given to terminate contract. Charges clients for "photocopying of longer manuscripts or mutually agreed upon marketing expenses."

Writers' Conferences: Book Expo; American Library Association; Society of Children's Book Writers & Illustrators.

DYSTEL & GODERICH LITERARY MANAGEMENT, 1 Union Square W., Suite 904, New York NY 10003. (212)627-9100. Fax: (212)627-9313. E-mail: miriam@dystel.com. Website: www.dystel.com. **Contact:** Miriam Goderich. Estab. 1994. Member of AAR. Represents 300 clients. 50% of clients are new/unpublished writers. Currently handles: 65% nonfiction books; 25% novels; 10% cookbooks.

- Dystel & Goderich Literary Management recently acquired the client list of Bedford Book Works.

Member Agents: Stacey Glick; Jane Dystel; Miriam Goderich; Michael Bourret; Jessica Papin; Jim McCarthy.

Represents: Nonfiction books, novels, cookbooks. **Considers these nonfiction areas:** Animals; anthropology/archaeology; biography/autobiography; business/economics; child guidance/parenting; cooking/foods/nutrition; current affairs; education; ethnic/cultural interests; gay/lesbian issues; government/politics/law; health/medicine; history; humor/satire; military/war; money/finance; New Age/metaphysics; popular culture; psychology; religious/inspirational; science/technology; true crime/investigative; women's issues/studies. **Considers these fiction areas:** Action/adventure; contemporary issues; detective/police/crime; ethnic; family saga; gay/lesbian; literary; mainstream/contemporary; mystery/suspense; thriller (especially).

O→ This agency specializes in commercial and literary fiction and nonfiction plus cookbooks.

How to Contact: Query with SASE. Considers simultaneous queries. Responds in 1 month to queries; 6 weeks to mss. Obtains most new clients through recommendations from others, solicitations, conferences.

Recent Sales: *The Sparrow*, by Mary Russell; *Lidia's Italian-American Kitchen*, by Lidia Bastianich; *Leaving Atlanta*, by Tayari Jones.

Terms: Agent receives 15% commission on domestic sales; 19% commission on foreign sales. Offers written contract, binding for book to book basis. Charges for photocopying. Galley charges and book charges from the publisher are passed on to the author.

Writers' Conferences: West Coast Writers Conference (Whidbey Island WA, Columbus Day weekend); University of Iowa Writer's Conference; Pacific Northwest Writer's Conference; Pike's Peak Writer's Conference; Santa Barbara Writer's Conference; Harriette Austin's Writer's Conference; Sandhills Writers Conference; ASU Writers Conference.

Tips: "Work on sending professional, well written queries that are concise and addressed to the specific agent the author is contacting. No dear Sirs/Madam."

ETHAN ELLENBERG LITERARY AGENCY, 548 Broadway, #5-E, New York NY 10012. (212)431-4554. Fax: (212)941-4652. E-mail: agent@ethanellenberg.com. Website: www.ethanellenberg.com. **Contact:** Ethan Ellenberg, Michael Psaltis. Estab. 1983. Represents 80 clients. 10% of clients are new/unpublished writers. Currently handles: 25% nonfiction books; 75% novels.

- Prior to opening his agency, Mr. Ellenberg was contracts manager of Berkley/Jove and associate contracts manager for Bantam.

Member Agents: Michael Psaltis (serious and commercial nonfiction, including science, health, popular culture, cooking, current events, politics, business, memoir and other unique projects; and commercial and literary fiction); Ethan Ellenberg

Represents: Nonfiction books, novels. **Considers these nonfiction areas:** Biography/autobiography; health/medicine; history; military/war; New Age/metaphysics; religious/inspirational; science/technology. **Considers these fiction areas:** Fantasy; romance; science fiction; thriller; women's.

O→ This agency specializes in commercial fiction, especially thrillers, romance/women's fiction and specialized nonfiction. "We also do a lot of children's books." For children's books: Send introductory letter (with credits, if any), up to 3 picture book mss, outline and first 3 chapters for longer projects, SASE. Actively seeking commercial and literary fiction, children's books, break-through nonfiction. Does not want to receive poetry, short stories, westerns, autobiographies.

How to Contact: For fiction: Send introductory letter (with credits, if any), outline, first 3 chapters and SASE. For nonfiction: Send query letter and/or proposal, 1 sample chapter if written and SASE. No fax queries. Accepts e-mail queries, no attachments. Considers simultaneous queries. Responds in 2 weeks to queries; 4-6 weeks to mss. Returns materials only with SASE.

Recent Sales: Has sold over 100 titles in the last 3 years. *After Sundown*, by Madeline Baker (Kensington); *The Keys to the Universe*, by Richard Morris (Joseph Henry Press); *Grosbeck Creek*, by Clay Reynolds (Berkley).

Terms: Agent receives 15% commission on domestic sales; 10% commission on foreign sales. Offers written contract. Charges clients for "direct expenses only limited to photocopying, postage, by writer's consent only."

Writers' Conferences: RWA National; Novelists, Inc.; and other regional conferences.

Tips: "We do consider new material from unsolicited authors. Write a good clear letter with a succinct description of your book. We prefer the first three chapters when we consider fiction. For all submissions you must include SASE for return or the material is discarded. It's always hard to break in, but talent will find a home. Check our website for complete submission guidelines. We continue to see natural storytellers and nonfiction writers with important books."

N **NICHOLAS ELLISON, INC.**, affiliated with Sanford J. Greenburger Associates, 55 Fifth Ave., 15th Floor, New York NY 10003. (212)206-6050. Fax: (212)436-8718. **Contact:** Jennifer Cayea. Estab. 1983. Represents 70 clients. Currently handles: 50% nonfiction books; 50% novels.

- Prior to becoming an agent, Mr. Ellison was an editor at Minerva Editions, Harper & Row and editor-in-chief at Delacorte.

Member Agents: Jennifer Cayea.

Represents: Nonfiction books, novels. **Considers these nonfiction areas:** Considers most nonfiction areas. **Considers these fiction areas:** Literary; mainstream/contemporary.

O→ Does not want to receive self-help.

How to Contact: Query with SASE. Responds in 6 weeks to queries.

Recent Sales: *Up Country*, by Nelson DeMille (Warner); *The Anniversary*, by Amy Gutman (Little, Brown); *The Big Love*, by Sarah Dunn (Little, Brown). Other clients include Olivia Goldsmith, P.T. Deutermann, Nancy Geary.

Terms: Agent receives 15% commission on domestic sales; 20% commission on foreign sales.

ANN ELMO AGENCY, INC., 60 E. 42nd St., New York NY 10165. (212)661-2880, 2881. Fax: (212)661-2883. **Contact:** Lettie Lee. Estab. 1959. Member of AAR, MWA, Authors Guild.

Member Agents: Lettie Lee; Mari Cronin (plays); A.L. Abecassis (nonfiction).

Represents: Nonfiction books, novels. **Considers these nonfiction areas:** Biography/autobiography; business/economics; cooking/foods/nutrition; current affairs; health/medicine; history; how-to; money/finance; music/dance; popular culture; psychology; science/technology; self-help/personal improvement; theater/film. **Considers these fiction areas:** Contemporary issues; detective/police/crime; ethnic; family saga; historical; literary; mainstream/contemporary; mystery/suspense; regional; romance (contemporary, gothic, historical, regency); thriller.

How to Contact: Letter queries *only* with SASE. No fax queries. Responds in 3 months to queries. Obtains most new clients through recommendations from others.

Recent Sales: This agency prefers not to share information on specific sales.

Terms: Agent receives 15% commission on domestic sales; 20% commission on foreign sales. Offers written contract. Charges clients for "special mailings or shipping considerations or multiple international calls. No charge for usual cost of doing business."

Tips: "Query first, and when asked only please send properly prepared manuscript. A double-spaced, readable manuscript is the best recommendation. Include SASE, of course."

N **ELAINE P. ENGLISH**, Graybill & English, LLC, 1875 Connecticut Ave. NW, Suite 712, Washington DC 20009. (202)588-9798, ext. 143. Fax: (202)457-0662. E-mail: elaineengl@aol.com. Website: www.graybillandenglish.com. **Contact:** Elaine English. Member of AAR. Represents 12 clients. 50% of clients are new/unpublished writers. Currently handles: 100% novels.

- Ms. English is also an attorney specializing in media and publishing law.

Member Agents: Elaine English (women's fiction, including romance and mysteries).

Represents: Novels. **Considers these fiction areas:** Historical; mainstream/contemporary; multicultural; mystery/suspense; romance (including single titles); thriller; women's.

O→ "While not as an agent, per se, I have been working in publishing for over fifteen years. Also, I'm affiliated with other agents who represent a broad spectrum of projects." Actively seeking women's fiction, including single title romances. Does not want to receive anything other than above.

How to Contact: Submit outline, 3 sample chapter(s), SASE. Responds in 6 weeks to queries; 6 months to mss. Returns materials only with SASE. Obtains most new clients through solicitations.

Terms: Agent receives 15% commission on domestic sales; 20% commission on foreign sales. Offers written contract; 30-day notice must be given to terminate contract. Charges only for expenses directly related to sales of manuscript (long distance, postage, copying).

Writers' Conferences: Washington Romance Writers (Harpers Ferry VA, April); RWA Nationals (New York NY, July); Georgia Romance Writers (Atlanta GA, November); Ohio Fiction Writers (October); SEAK Medical Fiction Writing for Physcians (Cape Cod, September).

FELICIA ETH LITERARY REPRESENTATION, 555 Bryant St., Suite 350, Palo Alto CA 94301-1700. (650)375-1276. Fax: (650)401-8892. E-mail: feliciaeth@aol.com. **Contact:** Felicia Eth. Estab. 1988. Member of AAR. Represents

25-35 clients. Works with established and new writers. Currently handles: 85% nonfiction books; 15% adult novels.

Represents: Nonfiction books, novels. **Considers these nonfiction areas:** Animals; anthropology/archaeology; biography/autobiography; business/economics; child guidance/parenting; current affairs; ethnic/cultural interests; gay/lesbian issues; government/politics/law; health/medicine; history; nature/environment; popular culture; psychology; science/technology; sociology; true crime/investigative; women's issues/studies. **Considers these fiction areas:** Ethnic; feminist; gay/lesbian; literary; mainstream/contemporary; thriller.

O→ This agency specializes in "provocative, intelligent, thoughtful nonfiction on a wide array of subjects which are commercial and high-quality fiction; preferably mainstream and contemporary."

How to Contact: Query with SASE, outline. Considers simultaneous queries. Responds in 3 weeks to queries; 4-6 weeks to mss which are requested.

Recent Sales: Sold 7-10 titles in the last year. *Jane Austen in Boca*, by Paula Marantz Cohen (St. Martin's Press); *Beyond Pink and Blue*, by Dr. Leonard Sax (Doubleday/Random House); *Lavendar Road to Success*, by Kirk Snyder (Ten Speed Press).

Terms: Agent receives 15% commission on domestic sales; 20% commission on foreign sales; 20% commission on dramatic rights sales. Charges clients for photocopying, express mail service—extraordinary expenses.

Writers' Conferences: Independent Writers of LA (Los Angeles); Conference of National Coalition of Independent Scholars (Berkley CA); Writers Guild.

Tips: "For nonfiction, established expertise is certainly a plus, as is magazine publication—though not a prerequisite. I am highly dedicated to those projects I represent, but highly selective in what I choose."

FARBER LITERARY AGENCY, INC., 14 E. 75th St., #2E, New York NY 10021. (212)861-7075. Fax: (212)861-7076. E-mail: farberlit@aol.com. Website: www.donaldfarber.com. **Contact:** Ann Farber; Dr. Seth Farber. Estab. 1989. Represents 40 clients. 50% of clients are new/unpublished writers. Currently handles: 40% nonfiction books; 15% scholarly books; 45% stage plays.

Member Agents: Ann Farber (novels); Seth Farber (plays, scholarly books, novels); Donald C. Farber (attourney, all entertainment media).

Represents: Nonfiction books, novels, juvenile books, textbooks, stage plays. **Considers these nonfiction areas:** Child guidance/parenting; cooking/foods/nutrition; music/dance; psychology; theater/film. **Considers these fiction areas:** Action/adventure; contemporary issues; humor/satire; juvenile; literary; mainstream/contemporary; mystery/suspense; thriller; young adult.

How to Contact: Submit outline, 3 sample chapter(s), SASE. Prefers to read materials exclusively. Responds in 1 month to queries; 2 month to mss. Obtains most new clients through recommendations from others.

Recent Sales: Sold 5 titles in the last year. *The Eden Express*, by Mark Vonnegut (Seven Stories-Eden); *The Gardens of Frau Hess*, by Milton Marcus; *Hot Feat*, by Ed Bullins; *Bright Freedom Song*, by Gloria Houston (Harcourt Brace & Co.).

Terms: Agent receives 15% commission on domestic sales; 20% commission on foreign sales. Offers written contract, binding for 1 year. Client must furnish copies of ms, treatments and any other items for submission.

Tips: "Our attorney, Donald C. Farber, is the author of many books. His services are available to the agency's clients as part of the agency service at no additional charge."

FLAMING STAR LITERARY ENTERPRISES, 320 Riverside Dr., New York NY 10025. **Contact:** Joseph B. Vallely or Janis C. Vallely. Estab. 1985. Represents 100 clients. 25% of clients are new/unpublished writers. Currently handles: 100% nonfiction books.

- Prior to opening the agency, Joseph Vallely served as national sales manager for Dell; Janis Vallely was vice president of Doubleday.

Represents: Nonfiction books. **Considers these nonfiction areas:** Current affairs; government/politics/law; health/medicine; nature/environment; New Age/metaphysics; science/technology; self-help/personal improvement; spirituality; sports.

O→ This agency specializes in upscale commercial nonfiction.

How to Contact: Query with SASE. Obtains most new clients through recommendations from others, solicitations.

Terms: Agent receives 15% commission on domestic sales; 20% commission on foreign sales. Offers written contract. Charges clients for photocopying, postage only.

FLANNERY LITERARY, (Specialized: juvenile books), 1140 Wickfield Court, Naperville IL 60563-3300. (630)428-2682. Fax: (630)428-2683. **Contact:** Jennifer Flannery. Estab. 1992. Represents 33 clients. 90% of clients are new/unpublished writers. Currently handles: 100% juvenile books.

- Prior to opening her agency, Ms. Flannery was an editorial assistant.

Represents: Juvenile books. **Considers these nonfiction areas:** Juvenile nonfiction; young adult. **Considers these fiction areas:** Juvenile; picture books; young adult.

O→ This agency specializes in children's and young adult, juvenile fiction and nonfiction.

How to Contact: Query with SASE. Responds in 3 weeks to queries; 1 month to mss. Obtains most new clients through recommendations from others, solicitations.

Recent Sales: Sold 20 titles in the last year. This agency prefers not to share information on specific sales.

Terms: Agent receives 15% commission on domestic sales; 20% commission on foreign sales. Offers written contract, binding for life of book in print; 30-day notice must be given to terminate contract. 100% of business is derived from commissions on ms sales.

Writers' Conferences: SCBWI Fall Conference.

Tips: "Write an engrossing, succinct query describing your work."

PETER FLEMING AGENCY, P.O. Box 458, Pacific Palisades CA 90272. (310)454-1373. **Contact:** Peter Fleming. Estab. 1962. Currently handles: 100% nonfiction books.

Represents: Nonfiction books.

O→ This agency specializes in "nonfiction books that unearth innovative and uncomfortable truths with bestseller potential."

How to Contact: Query with SASE. Obtains most new clients through "through a different, one-of-a-kind idea for a book often backed by the writer's experience in that area of expertise."

Recent Sales: *Rulers of Evil*, by F. Tupper Saussy (HarperCollins); *Why Is It Always About You-Saving Yourself from the Narcissists in Your Life*, by Sandy Hotchkiss (Free Press).

Terms: Agent receives 15% commission on domestic sales; 25% commission on foreign sales. Offers written contract, binding for 1 year. Charges clients "only those fees agreed to in writing, i.e., NY-ABA expenses shared. We may ask for a TV contract, too."

Tips: "You can begin by self-publishing, test marketing with direct sales, starting your own website."

B.R. FLEURY AGENCY, P.O. Box 149352, Orlando FL 32814-9352. (407)895-8494. Fax: (407)898-3923 or (888)310-8142. E-mail: brfleuryagency@juno.com. **Contact:** Blanche or Margaret. Estab. 1994. Signatory of WGA. Currently handles: 30% nonfiction books; 60% novels; 10% movie scripts.

Represents: Nonfiction books, novels, feature film, TV movie of the week. **Considers these nonfiction areas:** Health/medicine; how-to; humor/satire; money/finance; New Age/metaphysics; self-help/personal improvement; spirituality; true crime/investigative. **Considers these fiction areas:** Fantasy; horror; humor/satire; literary; psychic/supernatural; thriller. **Considers these script subject areas:** Detective/police/crime; fantasy; horror; mystery/suspense; psychic/supernatural; thriller.

O→ Only accepts scripts "if adapted from manuscripts by writers whom we represent."

How to Contact: Prefers to read materials exclusively. Query with one-page letter, SASE; or call for information. Accepts 1-page e-mail queries, no attachments and snail mail with no enclosures. Responds in 3 months to mss. Responds immediately to queries.

Recent Sales: Sold 5 manuscripts and 1 screenplay in the last year. This agency prefers not to share information on specific sales.

Terms: Agent receives 15% commission on domestic sales. Offers written contract, binding for as per contract. Receives screenplay commission according to WGA guidelines. Charges clients for business expenses directly related to work represented.

Tips: "Read your work aloud with someone who is not in love with you before you send it to us." E-mail queries should be 1 page maximum, no attachments. Queries with attachments or additional information will be returned unread.

THE FOGELMAN LITERARY AGENCY, 7515 Greenville, Suite 712, Dallas TX 75231. (214)361-9956. Fax: (214)361-9553. E-mail: foglit@aol.com. Website: www.fogelman.com. Also: 599 Lexington Ave., Suite 2300; New York NY 10022; (212)836-4803. **Contact:** Evan Fogelman. Estab. 1990. Member of AAR. Represents 100 clients. 2% of clients are new/unpublished writers. Currently handles: 40% nonfiction books; 40% novels; 10% scholarly books; 10% TV scripts.

- Prior to opening his agency, Mr. Fogelman was an entertainment lawyer. He is still active in the field and serves as chairman of the Texas Entertainment and Sports Lawyers Association.

Member Agents: Evan Fogelman (nonfiction, women's fiction); Linda Kruger (women's fiction, nonfiction); Helen Brown (literary fiction).

Represents: Nonfiction books, novels. **Considers these nonfiction areas:** Biography/autobiography; business/economics; child guidance/parenting; current affairs; education; ethnic/cultural interests; government/politics/law; health/medicine; popular culture; psychology; sports; true crime/investigative; women's issues/studies. **Considers these fiction areas:** Historical; literary; mainstream/contemporary; romance (all sub-genres).

O→ This agency specializes in women's fiction and nonfiction. "Zealous advocacy" makes this agency stand apart from others. Actively seeking "nonfiction of all types; romance fiction." Does not want to receive children's/juvenile.

How to Contact: Query with SASE. Considers simultaneous queries. Responds in 3 months to mss. Responds 'next business day' to queries. Returns materials only with SASE. Obtains most new clients through recommendations from others.

Recent Sales: Sold 60 titles in the last year. Other clients include Caroline Hunt, Katherine Sutcliffe, Crystal Stovall.

Terms: Agent receives 15% commission on domestic sales; 10% commission on foreign sales. Offers written contract, binding for project-to-project.

Writers' Conferences: Romance Writers of America; Novelists, Inc.

Tips: "Finish your manuscript, and see our website."

THE FOLEY LITERARY AGENCY, 34 E. 38th St., New York NY 10016-2508. (212)686-6930. **Contact:** Joan Foley or Joseph Foley. Estab. 1961. Represents 10 clients. Rarely takes on new clients. Currently handles: 75% nonfiction books; 25% novels.

Represents: Nonfiction books, novels.

How to Contact: Query with letter, brief outline, SASE. Responds promptly to queries. Obtains most new clients through recommendations from others, taking on new clients rarely.

Recent Sales: This agency prefers not to share information on specific sales.

Terms: Agent receives 10% commission on domestic sales; 15% commission on foreign sales. 100% of business is derived from commissions on ms sales.

Tips: Desires brevity in querying.

FORT ROSS, INC., RUSSIAN-AMERICAN PUBLISHING PROJECTS, 26 Arthur Place, Yonkers NY 10701-1703. (914)375-6448. Fax: (914)375-6439. E-mail: ftross@ix.netcom.com. Website: www.fortross.net. **Contact:** Dr. Vladimir P. Karsev. Estab. 1992. Represents about 100 clients. 2% of clients are new/unpublished writers. Currently handles: 50% nonfiction books; 40% novels; 10% juvenile books.

Member Agents: Ms. Olga Borodyanskaya, St. Petersburg, Russia, phone: 7-812-1738607 (fiction, nonfiction); Mr. Konstantin Paltchikov, Moscow, Russia, phone: 7-095-2035280 (romance, science fiction, fantasy, thriller); Kristin Olson, Prague, Czech Republic, phone: 420-2 2251-9639.

Represents: Nonfiction books, novels, juvenile books. **Considers these nonfiction areas:** Biography/autobiography; history; memoirs; psychology; self-help/personal improvement; true crime/investigative. **Considers these fiction areas:** Action/adventure; detective/police/crime; fantasy; horror; juvenile; mystery/suspense; romance (contemporary, gothic, historical, regency); science fiction; thriller; young adult.

This agency specializes in selling rights for Russian books and illustrations (covers) to American publishers and American books and illustrations for Europe; also Russian-English and English-Russian translations. Actively seeking adventure, fiction, mystery, romance, science fiction, thriller from established authors and illustrators for Russian and European markets.

How to Contact: Send published book or galleys. Accepts e-mail and fax queries. Considers simultaneous queries. Returns materials only with SASE.

Recent Sales: Sold 12 titles in the last year. *Mastering Judo with Vladimir Putin*, by Vladimir Putin et al (North Atlantic Books [USA]); *Max*, by Howard Fast (Baronet [Czech Republic]); *Kiss of Midas*, by George Vainer (Neri [Italy]); *Redemption*, by Howard Fast (Oram [Israel]); *Billion Dollars Cash*, by Anatoly Romov (Amber [Poland]).

Terms: Agent receives 10% commission on domestic sales; 20% commission on foreign sales. Offers written contract, binding for 2 years; 2-month notice must be given to terminate contract.

Tips: "Established authors and book illustrators (especially cover art) are welcome for the following genres: romance, fantasy, science fiction, mystery and adventure."

LYNN C. FRANKLIN ASSOCIATES, LTD., 1350 Broadway, Suite 2015, New York NY 10018. (212)868-6311. Fax: (212)868-6312. **Contact:** Lynn Franklin and Claudia Nys. Estab. 1987. Member of PEN America. Represents 30-35 clients. 50% of clients are new/unpublished writers. Currently handles: 90% nonfiction books; 10% novels.

Represents: Nonfiction books, novels. **Considers these nonfiction areas:** Biography/autobiography; current affairs; health/medicine; history; memoirs; New Age/metaphysics; psychology; religious/inspirational (inspirational); self-help/personal improvement; spirituality. **Considers these fiction areas:** Literary; mainstream/contemporary (commercial).

This agency specializes in general nonfiction with a special interest in health, biography, international affairs, and spirituality.

How to Contact: Query with SASE. No unsolicited mss. Considers simultaneous queries. Responds in 2 weeks to queries; 6 weeks to mss. Obtains most new clients through recommendations from others, solicitations.

Recent Sales: *The Rich Part of Life*, by Jim Kokoris (St. Martin's Press/film rights secured by Columbia Pictures); *Total Renewal: 7 Key Steps to Resilience, Vitality, Long-Term Health*, by Frank Lipman, M.D. (Tarcher/Putnam); *After Breast Cancer Treatment: A Survivor's Guide to Renewed Health and Happiness*, by Hester Hill Schnipper (Bantam/Dell); *Meeting Faith: the Forest Journals of a Black Buddhist Nun in Thailand*, by Faith Adiele (W.W. Norton).

Terms: Agent receives 15% commission on domestic sales; 20% commission on foreign sales. Offers written contract; 60-day notice must be given to terminate contract. 100% of business is derived from commissions on ms sales. Charges clients for postage, photocopying, long distance telephone if significant.

JEANNE FREDERICKS LITERARY AGENCY, INC., 221 Benedict Hill Rd., New Canaan CT 06840. (203)972-3011. Fax: (203)972-3011. E-mail: jfredrks@optonline.net. **Contact:** Jeanne Fredericks. Estab. 1997. Member of AAR, Authors Guild. Represents 90 clients. 10% of clients are new/unpublished writers. Currently handles: 100% nonfiction books.

- Prior to opening her agency, Ms. Fredericks was an agent and acting director with the Susan P. Urstadt Inc. Agency. In an earlier career she held editorial positions in trade publishing, most recently as editorial director of Ziff-Davis Books.

Represents: Nonfiction books. **Considers these nonfiction areas:** Animals; biography/autobiography; child guidance/parenting; cooking/foods/nutrition; gardening; health/medicine (and alternative health); history; how-to; interior design/decorating; money/finance; nature/environment; psychology; self-help/personal improvement; sports; women's issues.

This agency specializes in quality adult nonfiction by authorities in their fields. Does not want to receive children's books or fiction.

How to Contact: Query first with SASE. Then send outline/proposal, 1-2 sample chapters and SASE. No fax queries. Accepts e-mail queries if short; no attachments. Considers simultaneous queries. Responds in 3 weeks to queries; 2 months to mss. Returns materials only with SASE. Obtains most new clients through recommendations from others, solicitations, conferences.

Recent Sales: Sold 20 titles in the last year. *Yoga for Men*, by Tom Claire (Career Press); *Cowboys and Dragons: Achieving Successful American-Chinese Business Relations*, by Charles Lee (Dearborn); *Creating Optimism: The Uplift Program for Healing Past Trauma and Current Depression*, by Bob Murray, Ph.D., and Alice Fortinberry, M.S.

Terms: Agent receives 15% commission on domestic sales; 25% commission on foreign sales with co-agent; without co-agent receives 20% commission on foreign sales. Offers written contract, binding for 9 months; 2 months notice must be given to terminate contract. Charges client for photocopying of whole proposals and mss, overseas postage, priority mail and express mail services.

Writers' Conferences: PEN Women Conference (Williamsburg VA, February); Connecticut Press Club Biennial Writer's Conference (Stamford CT, April); ASJA Annual Writers' Conference East (New York NY, May); BEA (New York, May); Garden Writers of America Conference (New York, November).

Tips: "Be sure to research the competition for your work and be able to justify why there's a need for it. I enjoy building an author's career, particularly if s(he) is professional, hardworking, and courteous. Aside from ten years of agenting experience, I've had ten years of editorial experience in adult trade book publishing that enables me to help an author polish a proposal so that it's more appealing to prospective editors. My MBA in marketing also distinguishes me from other agents."

SARAH JANE FREYMANN LITERARY AGENCY, 59 W. 71st St., Suite 9B, New York NY 10023. (212)362-9277. Fax: (212)501-8240. E-mail: sjfs@aol.com. **Contact:** Sarah Jane Freymann. Represents 100 clients. 20% of clients are new/unpublished writers. Currently handles: 75% nonfiction books; 23% novels; 2% juvenile books.

Represents: Nonfiction books, novels, illustrated books. **Considers these nonfiction areas:** Animals; anthropology/archaeology; art/architecture/design; biography/autobiography; business/economics; child guidance/parenting; cooking/foods/nutrition; current affairs; ethnic/cultural interests; health/medicine; history; interior design/decorating; memoirs (narrative, nonfiction); nature/environment; psychology; religious/inspirational; self-help/personal improvement; women's issues/studies; lifestyle. **Considers these fiction areas:** Contemporary issues; ethnic; literary; mainstream/contemporary; mystery/suspense; thriller.

How to Contact: Query with SASE. Responds in 2 weeks to queries; 6 weeks to mss. Obtains most new clients through recommendations from others.

Recent Sales: *Serenity in Motion*, by Nancy O'Hara (Harmony 2003); *Vagabonding: The Uncommon Guide to the Art of Long-Term Travel*, by Rolf Potts (Villard); *How to Share a Meal*, by Pam Anderson (Houghton Mifflin).

Terms: Agent receives 15% commission on domestic sales; 20% commission on foreign sales. Offers written contract. Charges clients for long distance, overseas postage, photocopying. 100% of business is derived from commissions on ms sales.

Tips: "I love fresh new passionate works by authors who love what they are doing and have both natural talent and carefully honed skill."

MAX GARTENBERG, LITERARY AGENT, 521 Fifth Ave., Suite 1700, New York NY 10175. (212)292-4354. E-mail: gartenbook@att.net. **Contact:** Max Gartenberg. Estab. 1954. Represents 30 clients. 5% of clients are new/unpublished writers. Currently handles: 90% nonfiction books; 10% novels.

Represents: Nonfiction books, novels. **Considers these nonfiction areas:** Agriculture/horticulture; animals; art/architecture/design; biography/autobiography; child guidance/parenting; current affairs; health/medicine; history; military/war; money/finance; music/dance; nature/environment; psychology; science/technology; self-help/personal improvement; sports; theater/film; true crime/investigative; women's issues/studies.

How to Contact: Query with SASE. Considers simultaneous queries. Responds in 2 weeks to queries; 6 weeks to mss. Obtains most new clients through recommendations from others, occasionally by "following up on good query letters"

Recent Sales: *The Tao of War*, by Ralph D. Sawyer (Westview Press); *Passing Gas and Other Towns Along the American Highway*, by Gary Gladstone (Ten Speed Press); *Ogallala Blue*, by William Ashworth (W.W. Norton).

Terms: Agent receives 15% commission on first domestic sales; 10% subsequent commission on domestic sales; 15-20% commission on foreign sales.

Tips: "This is a small agency serving established writers; new writers whose work it is able to handle are few and far between. Nonfiction is more likely to be of interest here than fiction, and category fiction not at all."

GELFMAN SCHNEIDER LITERARY AGENTS, INC., 250 W. 57th St., New York NY 10107. (212)245-1993. Fax: (212)245-8678. **Contact:** Jane Gelfman, Deborah Schneider. Estab. 1981. Member of AAR. Represents 150 clients. 10% of clients are new/unpublished writers.

Represents: Nonfiction books, novels, 'We represent adult, general, hardcover fiction and nonfiction, literary and commercial, and some mysteries. **Considers these fiction areas:** Literary; mainstream/contemporary; mystery/suspense.

Does not want to receive romances, science fiction, westerns or children's books.

How to Contact: Query with SASE. Responds in 1 month to queries; 2 months to mss. Obtains most new clients through recommendations from others.

Terms: Agent receives 15% commission on domestic sales; 20% commission on foreign sales. Offers written contract. Charges clients for photocopying, messengers and couriers.

GHOSTS & COLLABORATORS INTERNATIONAL, (Specialized: ghostwriting), division of James Peter Associates, Inc., P.O. Box 358, New Canaan CT 06840. (203)972-1070. E-mail: gene_brissie@msn.com. **Contact:** Gene Brissie. Estab. 1971. Represents 75 clients. Currently handles: 100% nonfiction books.

Represents: Nonfiction collaborations and ghost writing assignments.

This agency specializes in representing only published ghost writers and collaborators, nonfiction only.

How to Contact: Prefers to read materials exclusively.

Recent Sales: Sold 50 titles in the last year. Clients include Alan Axelrod, Carol Turkington, George Mair, Brandon Toropov, Richard Marek, Susan Shelly, Carol Devito.

Terms: Agent receives 15% commission on domestic sales; 20% commission on foreign sales. Offers written contract.

Tips: "We would like to hear from professional writers who are looking for ghosting and collaboration projects. We invite inquiries from book publishers who are seeking writers to develop house-generated ideas and to work with their authors who need professional assistance."

THE GISLASON AGENCY, 219 Main St. SE, Suite 506, Minneapolis MN 55414-2160. (612)331-8033. Fax: (612)331-8115. E-mail: gislasonbj@aol.com. Website: www.thegislasonagency.com. **Contact:** Barbara J. Gislason, literary agent. Estab. 1992. Member of Minnesota State Bar Association, Art & Entertainment Law Section (former chair), Internet Committee, Minnesota Intellectual Property Law Association Copyright Committee (former chair); also a member of SFWA, MWA, RWA, Sisters in Crime, Oak Street Arts Board (board member), Icelandic Association of Minnesota (president) and American Academy of Acupuncture and Oriental Medicine (advisory board member). 80% of clients are new/unpublished writers. Currently handles: 25% nonfiction books; 75% novels.

- Ms. Gislason became an attorney in 1980, and continues to practice Art & Entertainment Law. She has been nationally recognized as a Leading American Attorney and a Super Lawyer.

Member Agents: Deborah Sweeney (fantasy, science fiction); Kellie Hultgren (fantasy, science fiction); Lisa Higgs (Romance); Kris Olson (mystery).

Represents: Nonfiction books, novels. **Considers these nonfiction areas:** Animals (behavior/communications); health/medicine (alternative); New Age/metaphysics; psychology (popular); science/technology; self-help/personal improvement; sociology; spirituality. **Considers these fiction areas:** Fantasy; mainstream/contemporary; mystery/suspense; romance; science fiction; thriller (legal).

O━ Do not send personal memoirs, poetry, short stories, screenplays or children's books.

How to Contact: Fiction: Query with synopsis, first 3 chapters and SASE. Nonfiction: Query with proposal and sample chapters; published authors may submit complete ms. No e-mail or fax queries. Responds in 2 months to queries; 3 months to mss. Obtains most new clients through recommendations from others, conferences, *Guide to Literary Agents, Literary Market Place* and other reference books.

Recent Sales: *Historical Romance # 4*, by Linda Cook (Kensington); *Dancing Dead*, by Deborah Woodworth (HarperCollins); *Autumn World*, by Joan Verba, et. al. (Dragon Stone Press).

Terms: Agent receives 15 commission on domestic sales; 20 commission on foreign sales. Offers written contract, binding for 1 year with option to renew. Charges clients for photocopying and postage.

Writers' Conferences: Romance Writers of America; Midwest Fiction Writers; University of Wisconsin Writer's Institute. Also attend state and regional writers conferences.

Tips: "Cover letter should be well written and include a detailed synopsis (if fiction) or proposal (if nonfiction), the first three chapters and author bio. Appropriate SASE required. We are looking for a great writer with a poetic, lyrical or quirky writing style who can create intriguing ambiguities. We expect a well-researched, imaginative and fresh plot that reflects a familiarity with the applicable genre. If submitting nonfiction work, explain how the submission differs from and adds to previously published works in the field. Scenes with sex and violence must be intrinsic to the plot. Remember to proofread, proofread, proofread. If the work was written with a specific publisher in mind, this should be communicated. In addition to owning an agency, Ms. Gislason practices law in the area of Art and Entertainment and has a broad spectrum of entertainment industry contacts."

GOLDFARB & ASSOCIATES, 1501 M St. NW, Washington DC 20005-2902. (202)466-3030. Fax: (202)293-3187. E-mail: rglawlit@aol.com. **Contact:** Ronald Goldfarb. Estab. 1966. Currently handles: 75% nonfiction books; 25% novels; increasing TV and movie deals.

- Ron Goldfarb's book (his ninth), *Perfect Villains, Imperfect Heroes*, was published by Random House. His tenth, *TV or not TV: Courts, Television, and Justice* (NYU Press), 1998. His *RFK* book is coming out in paper this year and is about to be optioned for dramatic development.

Member Agents: B. Farley Chase (New York office); Robbie Anna Hare; Kimberlee Damen, Esq.; Louise Wheatley.

Represents: Nonfiction books, novels. **Considers these nonfiction areas:** Art/architecture/design; biography/autobiography; business/economics; cooking/foods/nutrition; creative nonfiction; current affairs; education; ethnic/cultural interests; government/politics/law; health/medicine; history; language/literature/criticism; memoirs; military/war; money/finance; multicultural; nature/environment; popular culture; sociology; sports; theater/film; travel; true crime/investigative; women's issues/studies. **Considers these fiction areas:** Action/adventure; contemporary issues; detective/police/crime; ethnic; literary; mainstream/contemporary; mystery/suspense; thriller.

O━ This agency specializes primarily in nonfiction but has a growing interest in well-written fiction. "Given our D.C. location, we represent many journalists, politicians and former federal officials. We arrange collaborations. We also represent a broad range of nonfiction writers and novelists." Actively seeking "fiction with literary overtones; strong nonfiction ideas." Does very little children's fiction or poetry.

How to Contact: No fax queries. Responds in 1 month to queries; 2 months to mss. Obtains most new clients through recommendations from others.

Recent Sales: Sold 35 titles in the last year. *Imperfect Justice*, by Stuart Eizenstat; *Sargent Shriver*, by Scott Stossell. Other clients include former Congressman John Kasich, Diane Rehm, Susan Eisenhower, Dan Moldea, Roy Gutman, Leonard Garment, United States Holocaust Memorial Museum, Harlem Jazz Museum.

Terms: Charges clients for photocopying, long distance phone calls, postage.

Writers' Conferences: Washington Independent Writers Conference ; Medical Writers Conference; VCCA; participates in many ad hoc writers' and publishers' groups and events each year.

Tips: "We are a law firm which can help writers with related legal problems, Freedom of Information Act requests, libel, copyright, contracts, etc. As published authors ourselves, we understand the creative process."

ASHLEY GRAYSON LITERARY AGENCY, 1342 18th St., San Pedro CA 90732. Fax: (310)514-1148. Member of AAR. Represents 100 clients. 5% of clients are new/unpublished writers. Currently handles: 20% nonfiction books; 50% novels; 30% juvenile books.

Member Agents: Ashley Grayson (commercial and literary fiction, historical novels, mysteries, science fiction, thrillers, young adult); Carolyn Grayson (mainstream commercial fiction, mainstream women's fiction, romance, crime fiction, suspense, thrillers, fantasy, horror, true crime, children's and young adult, gardening, science, medical, health, self-help, how-to, pop culture, travel, creative nonfiction); Dan Hooker (commercial fiction, mysteries, thrillers, suspense, hard science fiction, contemporary and dark fantasy, horror, young adult and middle-grade, popular subjects and treatment with high commercial potential).

"We prefer to work with published (traditional print publishing), established authors. We will give first consideration to authors who come recommended to us by our clients or other publishing professionals. We accept a very small number of new, previously unpublished authors."

How to Contact: Published authors: "We would prefer you send us a written letter with SASE to introduce yourself. If you need a fast response, you may call."

Recent Sales: Sold more than 100 titles in the last year. *Dreaming Pachinko*, by Isaac Adamson (HarperCollins); *The Sky So Big and Black*, by John Barnes (Tor); *Move Your Stuff, Change Your Life*, by Karen Rauch Carter (Simon & Schuster).

Terms: Agent receives 15% commission on domestic sales; 20% commission on foreign sales.

SANFORD J. GREENBURGER ASSOCIATES, INC., 55 Fifth Ave., New York NY 10003. (212)206-5600. Fax: (212)463-8718. Website: www.greenburger.com. **Contact:** Heide Lange. Estab. 1945. Member of AAR. Represents 500 clients.

Member Agents: Heide Lange; Faith Hamlin; Theresa Park; Elyse Cheney; Dan Mandel; Julie Barer.

Represents: Nonfiction books, novels. **Considers these nonfiction areas:** Agriculture/horticulture; americana; animals; anthropology/archaeology; art/architecture/design; biography/autobiography; business/economics; child guidance/parenting; computers/electronic; cooking/foods/nutrition; crafts/hobbies; creative nonfiction; current affairs; education; ethnic/cultural interests; gardening; gay/lesbian issues; government/politics/law; health/medicine; history; how-to; humor/satire; interior design/decorating; juvenile nonfiction; language/literature/criticism; memoirs; military/war; money/finance; multicultural; music/dance; nature/environment; New Age/metaphysics; philosophy; photography; popular culture; psychology; recreation; regional; religious/inspirational; science/technology; self-help/personal improvement; sex; sociology; software; spirituality; sports; theater/film; translation; travel; true crime/investigative; women's issues/studies; young adult. **Considers these fiction areas:** Action/adventure; contemporary issues; detective/police/crime; ethnic; family saga; feminist; gay/lesbian; glitz; historical; humor/satire; literary; mainstream/contemporary; mystery/suspense; psychic/supernatural; regional; sports; thriller.

Does not want to receive romances or westerns.

How to Contact: Query with SASE. Considers simultaneous queries. Responds in 3 weeks to queries; 2 months to mss.

Recent Sales: Sold 200 titles in the last year. This agency prefers not to share information on specific sales. Clients include Andrew Ross, Margaret Cuthbert, Nicholas Sparks, Mary Kurcinka, Linda Nichols, Edy Clarke and Peggy Claude Pierre, Brad Thor, Dan Brown, Sallie Bissell.

Terms: Agent receives 15% commission on domestic sales; 20% commission on foreign sales. Charges for photocopying, books for foreign and subsidiary rights submissions.

GREGORY AND CO. AUTHORS' AGENTS, 3 Barb Mews, London W6 7PA, England. 020-7610-4676. Fax: 020-7610-4686. E-mail: info@gregoryandcompany.co.uk. Website: www.gregoryandcompany.co.uk. **Contact:** Jane Gregory, sales; Broo Doherty, editorial; Jane Barlow/Claire Morris rights. Estab. 1987. Member of Association of Authors' Agents. Represents 60 clients. Currently handles: 10% nonfiction books; 90% novels.

- Prior to becoming an agent, Ms. Gregory was Rights Director for Chatto & Windus.

Member Agents: Jane Gregory (sales); Broo Doherty (editorial); Jane Barlow/Claire Morris (rights).

Represents: Nonfiction and fiction books. **Considers these nonfiction areas:** Biography/autobiography; history. **Considers these fiction areas:** Action/adventure; contemporary women's fiction; detective/police/crime; historical; humor/satire; literary; mainstream/contemporary; multicultural; thriller.

"Jane Gregory is successful at selling rights all over the world, including film and television rights. As a British agency we do not generally take on American authors." Actively seeking well-written, accessible modern novels. Does not want to receive horror, science fiction, fantasy, mind/body/spirit, children's books, screenplays and plays, short stories, poetry.

How to Contact: Query with SASE, or submit outline, 3 sample chapters, SASE. Considers simultaneous queries. Returns materials only with SASE. Obtains most new clients through recommendations from others, conferences.

Recent Sales: Sold 100 titles in the last year. *Tokyo*, by Mo Hayder (Bantam UK/Doubleday USA); *Distant Echo*, by Val McDermid (HarperCollins UK/St. Martin's Press NY); *Fox Evil*, by Minette Walters (McMillan UK/Putnam USA); *Hello, Bunny Alice*, by Laura Wilson (Orion UK/Bantam USA); *A Place of Safety*, by Natasha Cooper (Simon & Schuster UK/St. Martin's Press USA).

Terms: Agent receives 15% commission on domestic sales; 20% commission on foreign sales. Offers written contract; 3-month notice must be given to terminate contract. Charges clients for photocopying of whole typescripts and copies of book for submissions.

Writers' Conferences: CWA Conference (United Kingdom, Spring); Dead on Deansgate (Manchester, Autumn); Harrogate Literary Festival (United Kingdom, Summer); Bouchercon (location varies, Autumn).

JILL GROSJEAN LITERARY AGENCY, 1390 Millstone Rd., Sag Harbor NY 11963-2214. (631)725-7419. Fax: (631)725-8632. E-mail: jill6981@aol.com. Website: www.hometown.aol.com/jill6981/myhomepage/index.html. **Con-**

tact: Jill Grosjean. Estab. 1999. Represents 21 clients. 100% of clients are new/unpublished writers. Currently handles: 1% nonfiction books; 99% novels.

- Prior to becoming an agent, Ms. Grosjean was manager of an independent bookstore. She also worked in publishing and advertising.

Represents: Nonfiction books (few), novels (almost entirely). **Considers these nonfiction areas:** Art/architecture/design; gardening; humor/satire; interior design/decorating; nature/environment; travel; women's issues/studies. **Considers these fiction areas:** Contemporary issues; historical; humor/satire; literary; mainstream/contemporary; mystery/suspense; regional; romance; thriller.

O→ This agency offers some editorial assistance (i.e., line-by-line edits). Actively seeking literary novels and mysteries. Does not want to receive any nonfiction subjects not indicated above.

How to Contact: Query with SASE. Considers simultaneous queries. Responds in 1 week to queries; 1 month to mss. Returns materials only with SASE. Obtains most new clients through recommendations from others, solicitations.

Recent Sales: *I Love You Like a Tomato*, by Marie Giordano (Forge Books); *Nectar*, by David C. Fickett (Forge Books); *Cycling*, by Greg Garrett (Kensington).

Terms: Agent receives 15% commission on domestic sales; 20% commission on foreign sales. No written contract. Charges clients for photocopying, mailing expenses; Writers reimbursed for office fees after the sale of ms.

Writers' Conferences: Book Passages Mystery Writer's Conference (Corte Madera CA, July); Writers' League of Texas Conference (Austin TX, July).

THE GROSVENOR LITERARY AGENCY, 5510 Grosvenor Lane, Bethesda MD 20814. Phone/Fax: (301)564-6231. E-mail: dcgrosveno@aol.com. **Contact:** Deborah C. Grosvenor. Estab. 1995. Member of National Press Club. Represents 30 clients. 10% of clients are new/unpublished writers. Currently handles: 80% nonfiction books; 20% novels.

- Prior to opening her agency, Ms. Grosvenor was a book editor for 18 years.

Represents: Nonfiction books, novels. **Considers these nonfiction areas:** Animals; anthropology/archaeology; art/architecture/design; biography/autobiography; business/economics; child guidance/parenting; current affairs; government/politics/law; health/medicine; history; how-to; language/literature/criticism; military/war; money/finance; music/dance; nature/environment; photography; popular culture; psychology; religious/inspirational; science/technology; self-help/personal improvement; sociology; spirituality; theater/film; translation; true crime/investigative; women's issues/studies. **Considers these fiction areas:** Contemporary issues; detective/police/crime; family saga; historical; literary; mainstream/contemporary; mystery/suspense; romance (contemporary, gothic, historical); thriller.

How to Contact: Send outline/proposal for nonfiction; send query and 3 sample chapters for fiction. No e-mail or fax queries. Responds in 1 month to queries; 2 months to mss. Returns materials only with SASE. Obtains most new clients through recommendations from others.

Recent Sales: *The Greatest Moment: The Year the Brooklyn Dodgers Won the World Series*, by Thomas Oliphant (Thomas Dunn Books); *Radical Innocent: Upton Sinclair, A Biography.*

Terms: Agent receives 15% commission on domestic sales; 20% commission on foreign sales. Offers written contract; 10-day notice must be given to terminate contract.

REECE HALSEY AGENCY, 8733 Sunset Blvd., Suite 101, Los Angeles CA 90069. Fax: (310)652-7595. **Contact:** Kimberley Cameron (all queries) at Reece Halsey North. Estab. 1957. Member of AAR. Represents 40 clients. 30% of clients are new/unpublished writers. Currently handles: 30% nonfiction books; 60% novels; 10% movie scripts.

- The Reece Halsey Agency has an illustrious client list largely of established writers, including the estate of Aldous Huxley and has represented Upton Sinclair, William Faulkner and Henry Miller. Ms. Cameron has recently opened a Northern California office and all queries should be addressed to her at the Reece Halsey North office.

Member Agents: Dorris Halsey; Kimberley Cameron.

Represents: Nonfiction books, novels. **Considers these nonfiction areas:** Biography/autobiography; current affairs; history; language/literature/criticism; popular culture; true crime/investigative; women's issues/studies. **Considers these fiction areas:** Action/adventure; contemporary issues; detective/police/crime; ethnic; family saga; historical; literary; mainstream/contemporary; mystery/suspense; science fiction; thriller; women's.

O→ This agency specializes mostly in books/excellent writing.

How to Contact: Query with SASE. Prefers to read materials exclusively. No e-mail or fax queries. Responds in 3 weeks to queries; 3 months to mss. Obtains most new clients through recommendations from others, solicitations.

Terms: Agent receives 15% commission on domestic sales; 10% commission on dramatic rights sales. Offers written contract, binding for 1 year. Requests 6 copies of ms if representing an author.

Writers' Conferences: Maui Writers Conference; ABA.

Tips: "Always send a well-written query and include a SASE with it!"

REECE HALSEY NORTH, 98 Main St., #704, Tiburon CA 94920. (415)789-9191. E-mail: info@reecehalseynorth.com. Website: www.reecehalseynorth.com or www.kimberleycameron.com. **Contact:** Kimberley Cameron. Estab. 1995. Member of AAR. Represents 40 clients. 30% of clients are new/unpublished writers. Currently handles: 30% nonfiction books; 70% fiction.

Member Agents: Kimberley Cameron (Reece Halsey North); Dorris Halsey (by referral only, LA office).

Represents: Nonfiction and fiction books. **Considers these nonfiction areas:** Biography/autobiography; health/medicine; history; science/technology; spirituality. **Considers these fiction areas:** Action/adventure; comic books/cartoon; detective/police/crime; ethnic; family saga; historical; horror; literary; mainstream/contemporary; mystery/suspense; science fiction; thriller; women's.

O→ This agency specializes in mystery, literary and mainstream fiction, excellent writing. The Reece Halsey Agency has an illustrious client list largely of established writers, including the estate of Aldous Huxley and has represented Upton Sinclair, William Faulkner and Henry Miller. Ms. Cameron has a Northern California office and all queries should be addressed to her at the Tiburon address.

How to Contact: Query with SASE. No e-mail or fax queries. Considers simultaneous queries. Responds in 1 month to queries; 3 months to mss. Obtains most new clients through recommendations from others, solicitations.

Recent Sales: *Jinn*, by Matthew Delaney (St. Martin's Press); *Final Epidemic*, by Earl Merkel (Dutton-NAL); *Sea Room*, by Norman Gautreau; *The Modern Gentleman*, by Phineas Mollod and Jason Tesauro.

Terms: Agent receives 15% commission on domestic sales. Offers written contract, binding for 1 year. Requests 8 copies of ms if representing an author.

Writers' Conferences: BEA; Maui Writers Conference; San Diego State University; Pacific Northwest; Cape Cod.

Tips: "Please send a polite, well-written query and include a SASE with it! You may also include the first ten pages of the manuscript."

THE JOY HARRIS LITERARY AGENCY, INC., 156 Fifth Ave., Suite 617, New York NY 10010. (212)924-6269. Fax: (212)924-6609. E-mail: gen.office@jhlitagent.com. **Contact:** Joy Harris. Member of AAR. Represents over 100 clients. Currently handles: 50% nonfiction books; 50% novels.

Member Agents: Leslie Daniels; Stéphanie Abou; Alexia Paul.

Represents: Nonfiction books, novels. **Considers these fiction areas:** Contemporary issues; ethnic; experimental; family saga; feminist; gay/lesbian; glitz; hi-lo; historical; humor/satire; literary; mainstream/contemporary; multicultural; multimedia; mystery/suspense; picture books; regional; short story collections; spiritual; translation; women's.

Does not want to receive screenplays.

How to Contact: Query with sample chapter, outline/proposal, SASE. Considers simultaneous queries. Responds in 2 months to queries. Obtains most new clients through recommendations from clients and editors.

Recent Sales: Sold 15 titles in the last year. This agency prefers not to share information on specific sales.

Terms: Agent receives 15% commission on domestic sales; 20% commission on foreign sales. Charges clients for some office expenses.

HARTLINE LITERARY AGENCY, 123 Queenston Dr., Pittsburgh PA 15235-5429. (412)829-2495 or 2483. Fax: (412)829-2450. E-mail: joyce@hartlineliterary.com. Website: www.hartlineliterary.com. **Contact:** Joyce A. Hart. Estab. 1990. Represents 40 clients. 30% of clients are new/unpublished writers. Currently handles: 40% nonfiction books; 60% novels.

Member Agents: Joyce A. Hart, principal agent; Janet Benrey; Tamela Hancock Murray; Andrea Boeshaar.

Represents: Nonfiction books, novels. **Considers these nonfiction areas:** Business/economics; child guidance/parenting; cooking/foods/nutrition; money/finance; religious/inspirational; self-help/personal improvement; women's issues/studies. **Considers these fiction areas:** Action/adventure; contemporary issues; family saga; historical; literary; mystery/suspense (amateur sleuth, cozy); regional; religious/inspirational; romance (contemporary, gothic, historical, regency); thriller.

This agency specializes in the Christian bookseller market. Actively seeking adult fiction, self-help, nutritional books, devotional, business. Does not want to receive science fiction, erotica, gay/lesbian, fantasy, horror, etc.

How to Contact: Submit outline, 3 sample chapter(s). Accepts e-mail and fax queries. Considers simultaneous queries. Responds in 2 months to queries; 3 months to mss. Returns materials only with SASE. Obtains most new clients through recommendations from others.

Recent Sales: *Every Fixed Star*, by Jane Kirkpatrick (Waterbrook); *Daughter of Liberty*, by H.M. Hostetter (Zondervan); *Happily Ever After*, by Susan Warren (Tyndale House).

Terms: Agent receives 15% commission on domestic sales. Offers written contract.

JOHN HAWKINS & ASSOCIATES, INC., 71 W. 23rd St., Suite 1600, New York NY 10010. (212)807-7040. Fax: (212)807-9555. E-mail: jha@jhaliterary.com. Website: jhaliterary.com. **Contact:** John Hawkins, William Reiss. Estab. 1893. Member of AAR. Represents over 100 clients. 5-10% of clients are new/unpublished writers. Currently handles: 40% nonfiction books; 40% novels; 20% juvenile books.

Member Agents: Moses Cardona; Warren Frazier; Anne Hawkins; John Hawkins; William Reiss; Elly Sidel.

Represents: Nonfiction books, novels, juvenile books. **Considers these nonfiction areas:** Agriculture/horticulture; americana; animals; anthropology/archaeology; art/architecture/design; biography/autobiography; business/economics; child guidance/parenting; cooking/foods/nutrition; crafts/hobbies; creative nonfiction; current affairs; education; ethnic/cultural interests; gardening; gay/lesbian issues; government/politics/law; health/medicine; history; how-to; humor/satire; interior design/decorating; juvenile nonfiction; language/literature/criticism; memoirs; military/war; money/finance; multicultural; music/dance; nature/environment; New Age/metaphysics; philosophy; photography; popular culture; psychology; recreation; regional; science/technology; self-help/personal improvement; sex; sociology; software; spirituality; sports; theater/film; travel; true crime/investigative; women's issues/studies; young adult. **Considers these fiction areas:** Action/adventure; comic books/cartoon; contemporary issues; detective/police/crime; ethnic; experimental; family saga; fantasy; feminist; gay/lesbian; glitz; gothic; hi-lo; historical; horror; humor/satire; juvenile; literary; mainstream/contemporary; military/war; multicultural; multimedia; mystery/suspense; New Age; occult; picture books; plays; poetry; poetry in translation; psychic/supernatural; regional; religious/inspirational; science fiction; short story collections; spiritual; sports; thriller; translation; western/frontier; young adult; women's.

How to Contact: Query with SASE, submit proposal package, outline. Considers simultaneous queries. Responds in 1 month to queries. Returns materials only with SASE. Obtains most new clients through recommendations from others.

Recent Sales: *Dead Halt on the Lunatic Line*, by Sarah Rose (Random House); *Empire of Light*, by David Czuchlewski (Putnam).

Terms: Agent receives 15% commission on domestic sales; 20% commission on foreign sales. Charges clients for photocopying.

RICHARD HENSHAW GROUP, 127 W. 24th St., 4th Floor, New York NY 10011. (212)414-1172. Fax: (435)417-5208. E-mail: submissions@henshaw.com. Website: www.rich.henshaw.com. **Contact:** Rich Henshaw. Estab. 1995. Member of AAR, SinC, MWA, HWA, SFWA. Represents 35 clients. 20% of clients are new/unpublished writers. Currently handles: 30% nonfiction books; 70% novels.

- Prior to opening his agency, Mr. Henshaw served as an agent with Richard Curtis Associates, Inc.

Represents: Nonfiction books, novels. **Considers these nonfiction areas:** Animals; biography/autobiography; business/economics; child guidance/parenting; computers/electronic; cooking/foods/nutrition; current affairs; gay/lesbian issues; government/politics/law; health/medicine; how-to; humor/satire; military/war; money/finance; music/dance; nature/environment; New Age/metaphysics; popular culture; psychology; science/technology; self-help/personal improvement; sociology; sports; true crime/investigative; women's issues/studies. **Considers these fiction areas:** Action/adventure; detective/police/crime; ethnic; family saga; fantasy; glitz; historical; horror; humor/satire; literary; mainstream/contemporary; mystery/suspense; psychic/supernatural; romance; science fiction; sports; thriller.

This agency specializes in thrillers, mysteries, science fiction, fantasy and horror.

How to Contact: Query with SASE. Responds in 3 weeks to queries; 6 weeks to mss. Obtains most new clients through recommendations from others, solicitations, conferences.

Recent Sales: *The Clueless Grooms Guide*, by Peter van Dijk; *Dead Soul*, by James D. Doss (St. Martin's). Other clients include Susan Wise Bauer, Jessie Wise.

Terms: Agent receives 15% commission on domestic sales; 20% commission on foreign sales. No written contract. 100% of business is derived from commissions on ms sales. Charges clients for photocopying mss and book orders.

Tips: "While we do not have any reason to believe that our submission guidelines will change in the near future, writers can find up-to-date submission policy information on our website. Always include SASE with correct return postage."

THE JEFF HERMAN AGENCY, LLC, P.O. Box 1522, Stockbridge MA 01262. (413)298-0077. Fax: (413)298-8188. E-mail: jeff@jeffherman.com. Website: www.jeffherman.com. **Contact:** Jeffrey H. Herman. Estab. 1985. Represents 100 clients. 10% of clients are new/unpublished writers. Currently handles: 85% nonfiction books; 5% novels; 5% scholarly books; 5% textbooks.

- Prior to opening his agency, Mr. Herman served as a public relations executive.

Member Agents: Deborah Levine (vice president, nonfiction book doctor); Jeff Herman.

Represents: Nonfiction books. **Considers these nonfiction areas:** Business/economics; computers/electronic; government/politics/law; health/medicine (and recovery issues); history; how-to; psychology (pop); self-help/personal improvement; spirituality; popular reference.

This agency specializes in adult nonfiction.

How to Contact: Query with SASE. Accepts e-mail and fax queries. Considers simultaneous queries.

Recent Sales: Sold 35 titles in the last year. This agency prefers not to share information on specific sales.

Terms: Agent receives 15% commission on domestic sales. Offers written contract. Charges clients for copying, postage.

SUSAN HERNER RIGHTS AGENCY, P.O. Box 303, Scarsdale NY 10583-0303. (914)725-8967. Fax: (914)725-8969. **Contact:** Susan Herner. Estab. 1987. Represents 100 clients. 30% of clients are new/unpublished writers. Currently handles: 60% nonfiction books; 40% novels.

Member Agents: Susan Herner, president (nonfiction, thriller, mystery, strong women's fiction).

Represents: Nonfiction books (adult), novels (adult). **Considers these nonfiction areas:** Anthropology/archaeology; biography/autobiography; business/economics; child guidance/parenting; current affairs; ethnic/cultural interests; gay/lesbian issues; government/politics/law; health/medicine; history; how-to; language/literature/criticism; nature/environment; New Age/metaphysics; popular culture; psychology; religious/inspirational; science/technology; self-help/personal improvement; sociology; spirituality; true crime/investigative; women's issues/studies. **Considers these fiction areas:** Action/adventure; contemporary issues; detective/police/crime; ethnic; family saga; feminist; glitz; historical; horror; literary; mainstream/contemporary; mystery/suspense; thriller.

"I'm particularly looking for strong women's fiction and thrillers. I'm particularly interested in women's issues, popular science, and feminist spirituality."

How to Contact: Query with SASE, outline, sample chapter(s). Considers simultaneous queries. Responds in 1 month to queries. Returns materials only with SASE.

Recent Sales: *If Cooks Could Kill*, by Joanne Pence (Avon); *Our Improble Universe*, by Michael Mallary (4 Walls 8 Windows); *Everything You Need to Know About Latino History*, by Hemilce Novas (Plume).

Terms: Agent receives 15% commission on domestic sales; 20% commission on foreign sales; 20% commission on dramatic rights sales. Charges clients for extraordinary postage and photocopying. "Agency has two divisions: one represents writers on a commission-only basis; the other represents the rights for small publishers and packagers who do not have in-house subsidiary rights representation. Percentage of income derived from each division is currently 80-20."

FREDERICK HILL BONNIE NADELL, INC., 1842 Union St., San Francisco CA 94123. (415)921-2910. Fax: (415)921-2802. **Contact:** Irene Moore. Estab. 1979. Represents 100 clients.

Member Agents: Fred Hill (president); Bonnie Nadell (vice president); Irene Moore (associate).

Represents: Nonfiction books, novels. **Considers these nonfiction areas:** Biography/autobiography; cooking/foods/nutrition (cookbooks); current affairs; government/politics/law; language/literature/criticism; women's issues/studies. **Considers these fiction areas:** Literary; mainstream/contemporary.

How to Contact: Query with SASE. No e-mail or fax queries. Considers simultaneous queries. Returns materials only with SASE.
Recent Sales: *River of Shadows: Eadweard Muybridge and the Technological Wild West*, by Rebecca Solnit; *The Country Under My Skin*, by Gioconda Belli; *Fear Itself*, by Jonathan Nasaw.
Terms: Agent receives 15% commission on domestic sales; 20% commission on foreign sales; 15% commission on dramatic rights sales. Charges clients for photocopying.

JOHN L. HOCHMANN BOOKS, 320 E. 58th St., New York NY 10022-2220. (212)319-0505. **Contact:** Theadora Eagle. Director: John L. Hochman. Estab. 1976. Member of PEN. Represents 23 clients. Prefers to work with previously published/established authors. Currently handles: 100% nonfiction books.
Member Agents: Theodora Eagle (popular medical and nutrition books).
Represents: Nonfiction books, textbooks (college). **Considers these nonfiction areas:** Anthropology/archaeology; art/architecture/design; biography/autobiography; cooking/foods/nutrition; current affairs; gay/lesbian issues; government/politics/law; health/medicine; history; military/war; music/dance; sociology; theater/film.

- This agency specializes in nonfiction books. "Writers must have demonstrable eminence in field or previous publications."

How to Contact: Query first with detailed chapter outline, titles and sample reviews of previously published books. Responds in 1 week to queries. Reports in one month to solicited manuscripts. Obtains most new clients through recommendations from authors and editors.
Recent Sales: Sold 6 titles in the last year. *Granite and Rainbow: The Life of Virginia Woolf*, by Mitchell Leaska (Farrar, Straus & Giroux); *Manuel Puig and the Spider Woman*, by Suzanne Jill Levine (Farrar, Straus & Giroux); *Part-Time Vegetarian*, by Louise Lambert-Lagasse (Stoddart).
Terms: Agent receives 15% commission on domestic sales.
Tips: "Detailed outlines are read carefully; letters and proposals written like flap copy get chucked. We make multiple submissions to editors, but we do not accept multiple submissions from authors. Why? Editors are on salary, but we work for commission, and do not have time to read manuscripts on spec."

HOPKINS LITERARY ASSOCIATES, 2117 Buffalo Rd., Suite 327, Rochester NY 14624-1507. (585)352-6268. Fax: (585)352-6270. **Contact:** Pam Hopkins. Estab. 1996. Member of AAR, RWA. Represents 30 clients. 5% of clients are new/unpublished writers. Currently handles: 100% novels.
Represents: Novels. **Considers these fiction areas:** Historical; mainstream/contemporary; romance; women's.

- This agency specializes in women's fiction, particularly historical, contemporary and category romance as well as mainstream work.

How to Contact: Submit outline, 3 sample chapter(s). No e-mail or fax queries. Considers simultaneous queries. Responds in 2 weeks to queries; 1 month to mss. Returns materials only with SASE. Obtains most new clients through recommendations from others, solicitations, conferences.
Recent Sales: Sold 50 titles in the last year. *The Napolean Gates*, by Merline Lovelace (Mira); *The Charmer*, by Madeline Hunter (Bantam); *Knock Me Off My Feet*, by Susan Donovan (St. Martin's).
Terms: Agent receives 15% commission on domestic sales; 20% commission on foreign sales. No written contract.
Writers' Conferences: Romance Writers of America.

HORNFISCHER LITERARY MANAGEMENT, INC., P.O. Box 50067, Austin TX 78763-0067. E-mail: jim@hornfischerliterarymanagement.com. Website: www.hornfischerliterarymanagement.com. **Contact:** James D. Hornfischer, president. Estab. 2001. Represents 45 clients. 20% of clients are new/unpublished writers. Currently handles: 90% nonfiction books; 10% novels.

- Prior to opening his agency, Mr. Hornfischer was an agent with Literary Group International and held editorial positions at HarperCollins and McGraw-Hill. "I work hard to make an author's first trip to market a successful one. That means closely working with my clients prior to submission to produce the strongest possible book proposal or manuscript. My New York editorial background, at HarperCollins and McGraw-Hill, where I worked on books by a variety of bestselling authors such as Erma Bombeck, Jared Diamond and Erica Jong among others, is useful in this regard. In eight years as an agent I've handled two number 1 *New York Times* nonfiction bestsellers, and in 2001 one of my clients was a finalist for the Pulitzer Prize."

Represents: Nonfiction books, novels, feature film, TV movie of the week. **Considers these nonfiction areas:** Anthropology/archaeology; biography/autobiography; business/economics; child guidance/parenting; current affairs; government/politics/law; health/medicine; history; how-to; humor/satire; memoirs; military/war; money/finance; multicultural; nature/environment; popular culture; psychology; religious/inspirational; science/technology; self-help/personal improvement; sociology; sports; true crime/investigative. **Considers these fiction areas:** Historical; literary; mainstream/contemporary; thriller.

- Actively seeking the best work of terrific writers. Does not want poetry, genre mysteries, romance or science fiction.

How to Contact: Submit proposal package, outline, 2 sample chapter(s). Considers simultaneous queries. Responds in 1 month to queries. Returns materials only with SASE. Obtains most new clients through referrals from clients; reading books and magazines; pursuing ideas with New York editors.
Recent Sales: *A Good Forest for Dying*, by Patrick Beach (Doubleday); *Pacific Alamo*, by John Wukovits (NAL); *Kings of Texas*, by Don Graham (Wiley).
Terms: Agent receives 15% commission on domestic sales; 20% commission on foreign sales. Offers written contract. Reasonable expenses deducted from proceeds after book is sold.

Tips: "When you query agents and send out proposals, present yourself as someone who's in command of his material and comfortable in his own skin. Too many writers have a palpable sense of anxiety and insecurity. Take a deep breath and realize that—if you're good—someone in the publishing world will want you."

IMG LITERARY, 825 Seventh Ave., 9th Floor, New York NY 10019. **Contact:** Lisa Queen, Sophia Seidner.

INTERNATIONAL CREATIVE MANAGEMENT, 40 W. 57th St., New York NY 10019. (212)556-5600. Fax: (212)556-5665. **Contact:** Literary Department. Member of AAR; signatory of WGA.

Member Agents: Esther Newberg and Amanda Urban, department heads; Richard Abate; Lisa Bankoff; Sam Cohn; Kristine Dahl; Mitch Douglas; Liz Farrell; Sloan Harris; Heather Schroeder; Denise Shannon; Amy Williams.

How to Contact: Not currently accepting submissions. Obtains most new clients through recommendations from others.

Terms: Agent receives 10% commission on domestic sales; 15% commission on foreign sales.

J DE S ASSOCIATES, INC., 9 Shagbark Rd., Wilson Point, South Norwalk CT 06854. (203)838-7571. **Contact:** Jacques de Spoelberch. Estab. 1975. Represents 50 clients. Currently handles: 50% nonfiction books; 50% novels.

- Prior to opening his agency, Mr. de Spoelberch was an editor with Houghton Mifflin.

Represents: Nonfiction books, novels. **Considers these nonfiction areas:** Biography/autobiography; business/economics; current affairs; ethnic/cultural interests; government/politics/law; health/medicine; history; military/war; New Age/metaphysics; self-help/personal improvement; sociology; sports; translation. **Considers these fiction areas:** Detective/police/crime; historical; juvenile; literary; mainstream/contemporary; mystery/suspense; New Age; western/frontier; young adult.

How to Contact: Query with SASE. Responds in 2 months to queries. Obtains most new clients through recommendations from authors and other clients.

Terms: Agent receives 15% commission on domestic sales; 20% commission on foreign sales. Charges clients for foreign postage and photocopying.

JABBERWOCKY LITERARY AGENCY, P.O. Box 4558, Sunnyside NY 11104-0558. (718)392-5985. Fax: (718)392-5985. **Contact:** Joshua Bilmes. Estab. 1994. Member of SFWA. Represents 40 clients. 25% of clients are new/unpublished writers. Currently handles: 15% nonfiction books; 75% novels; 5% scholarly books; 5% other.

Represents: Nonfiction books, novels, scholarly books. **Considers these nonfiction areas:** Biography/autobiography; business/economics; cooking/foods/nutrition; current affairs; gay/lesbian issues; government/politics/law; health/medicine; history; humor/satire; language/literature/criticism; military/war; money/finance; music/dance; nature/environment; popular culture; science/technology; sociology; sports; theater/film; true crime/investigative; women's issues/studies. **Considers these fiction areas:** Action/adventure; comic books/cartoon; contemporary issues; detective/police/crime; ethnic; family saga; fantasy; gay/lesbian; glitz; historical; horror; humor/satire; literary; mainstream/contemporary; psychic/supernatural; regional; science fiction; sports; thriller.

This agency represents quite a lot of genre fiction and is actively seeking to increase amount of nonfiction projects. It does not handle juvenile or young adult. Book-length material only; no poetry, articles or short fiction.

How to Contact: Query with SASE. No mss unless requested. No e-mail or fax queries. Considers simultaneous queries. Responds in 2 weeks to queries. Returns materials only with SASE. Obtains most new clients through solicitations, recommendation by current clients.

Recent Sales: Sold 20 titles in the last year. *Club Dead*, by Charlaine Harris (ACE); *The Speed of Dark*, by Elizabeth Moon (Ballantine); *Deathstalker Return*, by Simon Green (ROC); *Follow Me and Die*, by Ceil Currey (Cooper Square). Other clients include Tanya Huff, Kristine Smith, Edo Van Belkom.

Terms: Agent receives 12.5% commission on domestic sales; 20% commission on foreign sales. Offers written contract, binding for 1 year. Charges clients for book purchases, photocopying, international book/ms mailing, international long distance.

Writers' Conferences: Malice Domestic (Washington DC, May); World SF Convention (Boston, August); Icon (Stony Brook NY, April).

Tips: "In approaching with a query, the most important things to me are your credits and your biographical background to the extent it's relevant to your work. I (and most agents) will ignore the adjectives you may choose to describe your own work."

JAMES PETER ASSOCIATES, INC., P.O. Box 358, New Canaan CT 06840. (203)972-1070. E-mail: gene_brissie@msn.com. **Contact:** Gene Brissie. Estab. 1971. Represents 75 individual and 6 corporate clients. 15% of clients are new/unpublished writers. Currently handles: 100% nonfiction books.

Member Agents: Gene Brissie.

Represents: Nonfiction books. **Considers these nonfiction areas:** Anthropology/archaeology; art/architecture/design; biography/autobiography; business/economics; child guidance/parenting; current affairs; ethnic/cultural interests; gay/lesbian issues; government/politics/law; health/medicine; history; language/literature/criticism; memoirs (political or business); military/war; money/finance; music/dance; popular culture; psychology; self-help/personal improvement; theater/film; travel; women's issues/studies.

This agency specializes in nonfiction, all categories. "We are especially interested in general, trade and reference." Actively seeking "good ideas in all areas of adult nonfiction." Does not want to receive "children's and young adult books, poetry, fiction."

How to Contact: Submit proposal package, outline, SASE. Prefers to read materials exclusively. No e-mail or fax queries. Responds in 1 month to queries. Returns materials only with SASE. Obtains most new clients through recommendations from others, solicitations, contact "with people who are doing interesting things."

Recent Sales: Sold 50 titles in the last year. *Nothing to Fear*, by Dr. Alan Axelrod (Prentice-Hall); *The Subject Is Left-*

Handed, by Barney Rosset (Algonquin Books); *It's OK to Be Neurotic*, by Dr. Frank Bruno (Adams Media).
Terms: Agent receives 15% commission on domestic sales; 20% commission on foreign sales. Offers written contract.

N JCA LITERARY AGENCY, 27 W. 20th St., Suite 1103, New York NY 10011. (212)807-0888. Fax: (212)807-0461. Website: www.jcalit.com. **Contact:** Jeff Gerecke, Tony Outhwaite. Estab. 1978. Member of AAR. Represents 100 clients. 10% of clients are new/unpublished writers. Currently handles: 20% nonfiction books; 75% novels; 5% scholarly books.
Member Agents: Jeff Gerecke; Tony Outhwaite; Peter Steinberg.
Represents: Nonfiction books, novels. **Considers these nonfiction areas:** Anthropology/archaeology; biography/autobiography; business/economics; current affairs; government/politics/law; health/medicine; history; language/literature/criticism; memoirs; military/war; money/finance; music/dance; nature/environment; popular culture; science/technology; sociology; sports; theater/film; translation; true crime/investigative; women's issues/studies. **Considers these fiction areas:** Action/adventure; contemporary issues; detective/police/crime; family saga; historical; literary; mainstream/contemporary; mystery/suspense; sports; thriller.

O— Does not want to receive screenplays, poetry, children's books, science fiction/fantasy, genre romance.

How to Contact: Query with SASE. No e-mail or fax queries. Considers simultaneous queries. Responds in 2 weeks to queries; 10 weeks to mss. Returns materials only with SASE. Obtains most new clients through recommendations from others, solicitations, conferences.
Recent Sales: *Life Sentence*, by David Ellis (Putnam); *The Heaven of Mercury*, by Brad Watson (Norton); *The Rope Eater*, by Ben Jones. Other clients include Ernest J. Gaines, Gwen Hunter, Cathy Dal.
Terms: Agent receives 15% commission on domestic sales; 20% commission on foreign sales. No written contract. "We work with our clients on a handshake basis." Charges for postage on overseas submissions, photocopying, mss for submission, books purchased for subrights submission, and bank charges, where applicable. "We deduct the cost from payments received from publishers."
Tips: "We do not ourselves provide legal, accounting, or public relations services for our clients, although some of the advice we give falls somewhat into these realms. In cases where it seems necessary we will recommend obtaining outside advice or assistance in these areas from professionals who are not in any way connected to the agency."

N JELLINEK & MURRAY LITERARY AGENCY, 3623 Kumu St., Honolulu HI 96822. (808)988-8461. Fax: (808)988-8462. E-mail: jellinek@lava.net. **Contact:** Roger Jellinek. Estab. 1995. Represents 65 clients. 90% of clients are new/unpublished writers. Currently handles: 60% nonfiction books; 40% novels.

- Prior to becoming an agent, Mr. Jellinek was deputy editor, *New York Times Book Review* (1966-74); Editor-in-Chief, New York Times Book Company (1975-1981); editor/packager book/TV projects (1981-1995).

Member Agents: Roger Jellinek (general fiction, nonfiction); Eden Lee Murray (general fiction, nonfiction).
Represents: Nonfiction books, novels, textbooks, movie scripts (from book clients), TV scripts (from book clients). **Considers these nonfiction areas:** Animals; anthropology/archaeology; art/architecture/design; biography/autobiography; business/economics; child guidance/parenting; computers/electronic; cooking/foods/nutrition; current affairs; ethnic/cultural interests; gay/lesbian issues; government/politics/law; health/medicine; history; how-to; memoirs; military/war; money/finance; nature/environment; New Age/metaphysics; popular culture; psychology; religious/inspirational; science/technology; self-help/personal improvement; travel; true crime/investigative; women's issues/studies. **Considers these fiction areas:** Action/adventure; confession; contemporary issues; detective/police/crime; erotica; ethnic; family saga; feminist; gay/lesbian; glitz; historical; horror; humor/satire; literary; mainstream/contemporary; multicultural; mystery/suspense; New Age; picture books; psychic/supernatural; regional; thriller; western/frontier.

O— This agency is the only literary agency in Hawaii. "Half our clients are based in Hawaii, half from all over the world. We accept submissions (after a query) via e-mail attachment; we only send out fully-edited proposals and manuscripts." Actively seeking first-rate writing.

How to Contact: Query with SASE, submit outline, 2 sample chapter(s), if requested. Accepts e-mail and fax queries. Considers simultaneous queries. Responds in 2 weeks to queries; 2 months to mss. Returns materials only with SASE. Obtains most new clients through recommendations from others, solicitations, conferences.
Recent Sales: Sold 10 titles and sold 1 scripts in the last year. *God's Photo Album*, by Shelly Mecum (HarperSanFrancisco); *The Cookie Never Crumbles*, by Wally Amos (St. Martin's Press).
Terms: Agent receives 15% commission on domestic sales; 25% commission on foreign sales. Offers written contract, binding for indefinite period; 30-day notice must be given to terminate contract. Charges clients for photocopies and postage. May refer to editing services occasionally, if author asks for recommendation. "We have no income deriving from our referrals. Referrals to editors do not imply representation."
Tips: "Would-be authors should be well read and knowledgeable about their field and genre."

N LAWRENCE JORDAN LITERARY AGENCY, a Morning Star Communications, LLC company, 345 W. 121st St., New York NY 10027. (212)662-7871. Fax: (212)662-8138. E-mail: ljlagency@aol.com. **Contact:** President: Lawrence Jordan. Estab. 1978. Represents 50 clients. 25% of clients are new/unpublished writers. Works with a small number of new/previously unpublished authors. Currently handles: 70% nonfiction books; 30% novels.

- Prior to opening his agency, Mr. Jordan served as an editor with Doubleday & Co.

Represents: Nonfiction books, novels. **Considers these nonfiction areas:** Biography/autobiography; business/economics; cooking/foods/nutrition (cookbooks); health/medicine; memoirs; religious/inspirational; science/technology; self-help/personal improvement; sports; travel.

O— This agency specializes in general adult fiction and nonfiction. Actively seeking spiritual and religious books, mystery novels, action suspense, thrillers, biographies, autobiographies, celebrity books. Does not want to receive poetry, movie scripts, stage plays, juvenile books, fantasy novels, science fiction.

How to Contact: Query with SASE, outline. Responds in 3 weeks to queries; 6 weeks to mss.

Recent Sales: *Broken Silence: Black Women and Therapy*, by Dr. D. Kim Singleton (One World/Ballantine); *The Undiscovered Paul Robeson, Vol. II*, by Paul Robeson, Jr. (Wiley); *A View from the Wreckage: A Black Political Perspective*, by Paul Robeson, Jr. (Seven Stories Press).

Terms: Agent receives 15% commission on domestic sales; 20% commission on foreign sales; 20% commission on dramatic rights sales. 99% of business is derived from commissions on ms sales. Charges long-distance calls, photocopying, foreign submission costs, postage, cables and messengers.

NATASHA KERN LITERARY AGENCY, P.O. Box 2908, Portland OR 97208-2908. (503)297-6190. Website: www.natashakern.com. **Contact:** Natasha Kern. Estab. 1986. Member of RWA, MWA, SinC.

- Prior to opening her agency, Ms. Kern worked as an editor and publicist for New York publishers (Simon & Schuster, Bantam, Ballantine). "This agency has sold over 500 books."

Member Agents: Natasha Kern; Ruth Widener.

Represents: Adult commercial nonfiction and fiction. **Considers these nonfiction areas:** Animals; anthropology/archaeology; business/economics; child guidance/parenting; current affairs; ethnic/cultural interests; gardening; health/medicine; nature/environment; New Age/metaphysics; popular culture; psychology; religious/inspirational; science/technology; self-help/personal improvement; spirituality; women's issues/studies; investigative journalism. **Considers these fiction areas:** Ethnic; feminist; historical; mainstream/contemporary; mystery/suspense; religious/inspirational; romance (contemporary, historical); thriller (medical, scientific, historical).

This agency specializes in commercial fiction and nonfiction for adults. "A full service agency." Does not represent sports, true crime, scholarly works, coffee table books, war memoirs, software, scripts, literary fiction, photography, poetry, short stories, children's, horror, fantasy, genre science fiction, stage plays or traditional Westerns.

How to Contact: Query with SASE, include submission history, writing credits, how long ms is. For fiction: send 2-3 page synopsis and 3-5 first pages. For nonfiction: overview, describe market and how ms is different/better than similar works, author bio and ms length. See Web site before querying. No e-mail or fax queries. Considers simultaneous queries. Responds in 3 weeks to queries.

Recent Sales: Sold 53 titles in the last year. *Firstborn*, by Robin Lee Hatcher (Tyndale); *The Waiting Child*, by Cindy Champnella; *The Power of Losing Control*, by Joe Caruso (Penguin/Putnam).

Terms: Agent receives 15% commission on domestic sales; 20% commission on foreign sales; 15% commission on dramatic rights sales.

Writers' Conferences: RWA National Conference, MWA National Conference and many regional conferences.

Tips: "Our idea of a Dream Client is someone who participates in a mutually respectful business relationship, is clear about needs and goals, and communicates about career planning. If we know what you need and want, we can help you achieve it. A dream client has a storytelling gift, a commitment to a writing career, a desire to learn and grow, and a passion for excellence. We want clients who are expressing their own unique voice and truly have something of their own to communicate. This client understands that many people have to work together for a book to succeed and that everything in publishing takes far longer than one imagines. Trust and communication are truly essential."

LOUISE B. KETZ AGENCY, 1485 First Ave., Suite 4B, New York NY 10021-1363. (212)535-9259. Fax: (212)249-3103. E-mail: ketzagency@aol.com. **Contact:** Louise B. Ketz. Estab. 1983. Represents 25 clients. 15% of clients are new/unpublished writers. Currently handles: 100% nonfiction books.

Represents: Nonfiction books. **Considers these nonfiction areas:** Business/economics; current affairs; history; military/war; science/technology; sports.

This agency specializes in science, business, sports, history and reference.

How to Contact: Submit outline, 2 sample chapter(s), author bio, with qualifications for authorship of work. Responds in 6 weeks to mss. Obtains most new clients through recommendations from others, idea development.

Terms: Agent receives 15% commission on domestic sales.

VIRGINIA KIDD AGENCY, INC., (Specialized: science fiction/fantasy), 538 E. Harford St., P.O. Box 278, Milford PA 18337-0278. (570)296-6205. Fax: (570)296-7266. E-mail: vkagency@ptd.net. **Contact:** Linn Prentis, Nanci McCloskey. Estab. 1965. Member of SFWA, SFRA. Represents 80 clients.

Member Agents: Nanci McCloskey; Linn Prentis; Christine Cohen; Vaughne Hansen.

Represents: Novels. **Considers these fiction areas:** Fantasy (special interest in non-traditional fantasy); glitz; historical; literary; mainstream/contemporary; mystery/suspense; science fiction; young adult; speculative fiction.

This agency specializes in "science fiction but we do not limit ourselves to it."

How to Contact: Submit synopsis, cover letter, SASE. Prefers to read materials exclusively. Considers simultaneous queries. Responds in 1 month to queries. Obtains most new clients through recommendations.

Recent Sales: Sold 75 titles in the last year. *Changing Planes*, by Ursula K. Le Guin (Harcourt Brace); *Stories of Your Life and Others*, by Ted Chiang (Tor Books); *The Knight*, by Gene Wolfe (Tor Books). Other clients include Alan Dean Foster, Kage Baker, Wen Spencer, Eleanor Arnason, Katie Waitman, Margaret Ball.

Terms: Agent receives 15% commission on domestic sales; 20-25% commission on foreign sales; 20% commission on dramatic rights sales. Offers written contract; 60-day notice must be given to terminate contract. Charges clients occasionally for extraordinary expenses.

Tips: "If you have a novel of speculative fiction, romance, or mainstream that is really extraordinary, please query me, including a synopsis, publishing credits and a SASE."

N **JEFFREY M. KLEINMAN, ESQ.**, Graybill & English L.L.C, 1875 Connecticut Ave. NW, Suite 712, Washington DC 20009. (202)588-9798. Fax: (202)457-0662. E-mail: jmkagent@aol.com. Website: www.graybillandenglish.com/jmk. **Contact:** Jeff Kleinman. Estab. 1998. 50% of clients are new/unpublished writers.

- Mr. Kleinman is a literary agent and attorney.

Represents: Nonfiction books (particularly narrative nonfiction), novels. **Considers these nonfiction areas:** Agriculture/horticulture; animals; anthropology/archaeology; art/architecture/design; biography/autobiography; business/economics; child guidance/parenting; computers/electronic; cooking/foods/nutrition; crafts/hobbies; creative nonfiction; current affairs; education; ethnic/cultural interests; gay/lesbian issues; government/politics/law; health/medicine; history; how-to; humor/satire; interior design/decorating; language/literature/criticism; money/finance; music/dance; nature/environment; photography; popular culture; psychology; science/technology; self-help/personal improvement; sociology; theater/film; translation; true crime/investigative; women's issues/studies. **Considers these fiction areas:** Action/adventure; contemporary issues; ethnic; family saga; fantasy; feminist; gay/lesbian; glitz; historical; horror; humor/satire; literary; mainstream/contemporary; multimedia (tie-ins with literary projects); psychic/supernatural; regional; science fiction; thriller.

O→ This agency specializes in narrative nonfiction, nonfiction, fiction. Does not want to receive children's literature, romances, westerns or poetry.

How to Contact: Query with SASE, or send outline, 3 sample chapters, SASE. Accepts e-mail queries, no attachments. Considers simultaneous queries. Responds in 2 weeks to queries; 1 month to mss. Returns materials only with SASE. Obtains most new clients through recommendations from others, solicitations.

Recent Sales: Sold 12 titles in the last year. *Gentelmen's Blood*, by Barbara Holland (Bloomsbury); *Teasing Secrets from the Dead*, by Dr. Emily Craig (Crown); *The Lost Pet Chronicles*, by Kat Albrecht (Bloomsbury).

Terms: Agent receives 15% commission on domestic sales; 20% commission on foreign sales. Offers written contract; 30-day notice must be given to terminate contract. Charges clients for postage, long distance, photocopying.

Writers' Conferences: Wrangling on Writing (Tucson, January); Mid-Atlantic Creative Nonfiction Summer Writer's Conference (Baltimore MD, August); Baltimore Writers (Baltimore MD, September).

HARVEY KLINGER, INC., 301 W. 53rd St., Suite 21-A, New York NY 10019. (212)581-7068. Fax: (212)315-3823. E-mail: queries@harveyklinger.com. Website: www.harveyklinger.com. **Contact:** Harvey Klinger. Estab. 1977. Member of AAR. Represents 100 clients. 25% of clients are new/unpublished writers. Currently handles: 50% nonfiction books; 50% novels.

Member Agents: Jenny Bent (literary fiction; commercial women's fiction; memoir; narrative nonfiction; self help/pop psychology); David Dunton (popular culture, with a speciality in music-related books; literary fiction; crime novels; thrillers); Wendy Silbert (narrative nonfiction; historical narrative nonfiction; politics; history; biographies; memoir; literary ficiton; business books; culinary narratives).

Represents: Nonfiction books, novels. **Considers these nonfiction areas:** Biography/autobiography; cooking/foods/nutrition; health/medicine; psychology; science/technology; self-help/personal improvement; spirituality; sports; true crime/investigative; women's issues/studies. **Considers these fiction areas:** Action/adventure; detective/police/crime; family saga; glitz; literary; mainstream/contemporary; mystery/suspense; thriller.

O→ This agency specializes in "big, mainstream contemporary fiction and nonfiction."

How to Contact: Query with SASE. No phone queries. Accepts e-mail queries. No fax queries. Responds in 2 months to queries; 2 months to mss. Obtains most new clients through recommendations from others.

Recent Sales: Sold 30 titles in the last year. *Swan Place*, by Augusta Trobaugh (Dutton); *Fund Your Future*, by Julie Stav (Berkley); *Auriel Rising*, by Elizabeth Redfern (Putnam); *A Love Supreme*, by Ashley Kahn (Viking); *Idiot Girls' Action Adventure Guide*, by Laurie Notaro; *Inside Medicine*, by Kevin Soden and Christine Dumas; *Where I work and Other Stories*, by Ann Cummins (Houghton Mifflin); *Thirty Years of Shame*, by Mark Kemp (Free Press). Other clients include Barbara Wood, Terry Kay, Barbara De Angelis, Jill Conner Browne, Michael Farquhar, Greg Bottoms, Jeremy Jackson, Pamela Berkman, Jonetta Rose Barras, Paul Russell.

Terms: Agent receives 15% commission on domestic sales; 25% commission on foreign sales. Offers written contract. Charges for photocopying mss, overseas postage for mss.

THE KNIGHT AGENCY, P.O. Box 550648, Atlanta GA 30355. (404)816-9620. E-mail: knightagency@msn.com. Website: www.knightagency.net. **Contact:** Deidre Knight. Estab. 1996. Member of AAR, RWA, Authors Guild. Represents 65 clients. 40% of clients are new/unpublished writers. Currently handles: 50% nonfiction books; 50% novels.

Member Agents: Deidre Knight (president, agent); Pamela Harty (agent).

Represents: Nonfiction books, novels. **Considers these nonfiction areas:** Business/economics; child guidance/parenting; current affairs; ethnic/cultural interests; health/medicine; history; how-to; money/finance; popular culture; psychology; religious/inspirational; self-help/personal improvement; theater/film. **Considers these fiction areas:** Literary; mainstream/contemporary (commercial); romance (contemporary, paranormal, romantic suspense, historical, inspirational); women's.

O→ "We are looking for a wide variety of fiction and nonfiction. In the nonfiction area, we're particularly eager to find personal finance, business investment, pop culture, self-help/motivational and popular reference books. In fiction, we're always looking for romance; women's fiction; commercial fiction."

How to Contact: Query with SASE. Accepts e-mail queries; no attachments. No phone queries please. Considers simultaneous queries. Responds in 3 weeks to queries; 3 months to mss.

Recent Sales: Sold approximately 65 titles in the last year. *Dark Highlander*, by Karen Marie Moning (Bantam Dell); *The Healing Quilt*, by Lauraine Snelling (WaterBrook Press).

Terms: Agent receives 15% commission on domestic sales; 20-25% commission on foreign sales. Offers written contract, binding for 1 year; 30-day notice must be given to terminate contract. Charges clients for photocopying, postage, overnight

courier expenses. "These are deducted from the sale of the work, not billed upfront."
Tips: "At the Knight Agency, a client usually ends up becoming a friend."

LINDA KONNER LITERARY AGENCY, 10 W. 15th St., Suite 1918, New York NY 10011-6829. (212)691-3419. E-mail: ldkonner@cs.com. **Contact:** Linda Konner. Estab. 1996. Member of AAR, ASJA; signatory of WGA. Represents 65 clients. 5-10% of clients are new/unpublished writers. Currently handles: 100% nonfiction books.

Represents: Nonfiction books (adult only). **Considers these nonfiction areas:** Business/economics; child guidance/parenting; gay/lesbian issues; health/medicine (diet/nutrition/fitness); how-to; money/finance (personal finance); popular culture; psychology; self-help/personal improvement; women's issues/studies; relationships.

O→ This agency specializes in health, self-help and how-to books.

How to Contact: Query with SASE, outline, sufficient return postage. Prefers to read materials exclusively for 2 weeks. Considers simultaneous queries. Obtains most new clients through recommendations from others, occasional solicitation among established authors/journalists.

Recent Sales: Sold 26 titles in the last year. *The Ultimate Body*, by Liz Neporent (Ballantine); *Stength for Their Journey: The Five Disciplines Every African-American Parent Must Teach Her Child*, by Robert Johnson, MD, and Paula Stanford, MD, (Doubleday).

Terms: Agent receives 15% commission on domestic sales; 25% commission on foreign sales. Offers written contract. Charges $85 one-time fee for domestic expenses; additional expenses may be incurred for foreign sales.

Writers' Conferences: American Society of Journalists and Authors (New York City, Spring).

ELAINE KOSTER LITERARY AGENCY, LLC, 55 Central Park West, Suite 6, New York NY 10023. (212)362-9488. Fax: (212)712-0164. **Contact:** Elaine Koster. Member of AAR, MWA. Represents 50 clients. 10% of clients are new/unpublished writers. Currently handles: 30% nonfiction books; 70% novels.

- Prior to opening her agency, Ms. Koster was president and publisher of Dutton NAL.

Represents: Nonfiction books, novels. **Considers these nonfiction areas:** Biography/autobiography; business/economics; child guidance/parenting; cooking/foods/nutrition; current affairs; ethnic/cultural interests; health/medicine; history; how-to; money/finance; nature/environment; New Age/metaphysics; popular culture; psychology; self-help/personal improvement; spirituality; women's issues/studies. **Considers these fiction areas:** Chick lit; contemporary issues; detective/police/crime; ethnic; family saga; feminist; historical; literary; mainstream/contemporary; mystery/suspense (amateur sleuth, cozy, culinary, malice domestic); regional; thriller.

O→ This agency specializes in quality fiction and nonfiction. Does not want to receive juvenile, screenplays, or science fiction.

How to Contact: Query with SASE, outline, 3 sample chapter(s). Prefers to read materials exclusively. No e-mail or fax queries. Responds in 3 weeks to queries; 1 month to mss. Returns materials only with SASE. Obtains most new clients through recommendations from others.

Recent Sales: Sold over 30 titles in the last year. *Tastes Like Chicken*, by Lolita Files (Simon & Schuster); *The Kite Runner*, by Khaled Hosseini (Riverhead); *Farewell Angelina*, by Virginia Swift (HarperCollins).

Terms: Agent receives 15% commission on domestic sales. Bills back specific expenses incurred doing business for a client.

Tips: "We prefer exclusive submissions. Don't e-mail or fax submissions. Please include biographical information and publishing history."

KRAAS LITERARY AGENCY, 256 Rancho Alegre Rd., Santa Fe NM 87508. (505)438-7715. Fax: (505)438-7783. Address Other: Ashley Kraas, Associate, 507 NW 22nd Ave., Suite 104, Portland OR 97210. (503)721-7442. Estab. 1990. Represents 40 clients. 75% of clients are new/unpublished writers. Currently handles: 5% nonfiction books; 95% novels.

Represents: Nonfiction books, novels, young adult.

O→ This agency specializes in adult fiction. Actively seeking "books that are well written with commercial potential." Does not want to receive short stories, plays or poetry.

How to Contact: Submit cover letter, first 50 pages of a completed ms, SASE; must include return postage and/or SASE. No e-mail or fax queries. Considers simultaneous queries. Returns materials only with SASE.

Recent Sales: *No Place Like the Chevy*, by Janet Lee Carey (Antheneum); *Night Terror*, by Chandler McGrew (Bantam); *Patriots in Petticoats*, by Shirley Raye Redmond (Random).

Terms: Agent receives 15% commission on domestic sales. Offers written contract. Charges clients for photocopying and postage.

Writers' Conferences: Southwest Writers Conference (Albuquerque NM); Durango Writers Conference (Durango CO); Wrangling with Writing (Tucson AZ); Surrey Writers Conference (Surrey BC); Schuwap Writers Conference (Schuwap BC); Willamette Writers Group (Portland OR).

PETER LAMPACK AGENCY, INC., 551 Fifth Ave., Suite 1613, New York NY 10176-0187. (212)687-9106. Fax: (212)687-9109. E-mail: renbopla@aol.com. **Contact:** Loren G. Soeiro. Estab. 1977. Represents 50 clients. 10% of clients are new/unpublished writers. Currently handles: 20% nonfiction books; 80% novels.

Member Agents: Peter Lampack (psychological suspense, action/adventure, literary fiction, nonfiction, contemporary relationships); Sandra Blanton (foreign rights); Loren G. Soeiro (literary and commercial fiction, mystery, suspense, nonfiction, narrative nonfiction).

Represents: Nonfiction books, novels. **Considers these fiction areas:** Action/adventure; detective/police/crime; family saga; historical; literary; mainstream/contemporary; mystery/suspense; thriller; contemporary relationships.

O-ₙ This agency specializes in commercial fiction, nonfiction by recognized experts. Actively seeking literary and commercial fiction, thrillers, mysteries, suspense, psychological thrillers. Does not want to receive horror, romance, science fiction, western, academic material.

How to Contact: Query with SASE. No unsolicited mss. Accepts e-mail queries. No fax queries. Considers simultaneous queries. Responds in 3 weeks to queries; 2 months to mss. Obtains most new clients through referrals made by clients.

Recent Sales: *The Grave Maurice*, by Martha Grimes (Viking); *The Widow's Defense*, by Stephen Horn (HarperCollins); *The Sea Hunters 2*, by Clive Cussler (Putnam).

Terms: Agent receives 15% commission on domestic sales; 20% commission on foreign sales.

Writers' Conferences: BEA (Chicago, June).

Tips: "Submit only your best work for consideration. Have a very specific agenda of goals you wish your prospective agent to accomplish for you. Provide the agent with a comprehensive statement of your credentials: educational and professional."

MICHAEL LARSEN/ELIZABETH POMADA LITERARY AGENTS, 1029 Jones St., San Francisco CA 94109-5023. (415)673-0939. E-mail: larsenpoma@aol.com. Website: www.larsen-pomada.com. **Contact:** Mike Larsen or Elizabeth Pomada. Estab. 1972. Member of AAR, Authors Guild, ASJA, PEN, WNBA, California Writers Club. Represents 100 clients. 40-45% of clients are new/unpublished writers. Currently handles: 70% nonfiction books; 30% novels.

- Prior to opening their agency, Mr. Larsen and Ms. Pomada were promotion executives for major publishing houses. Mr. Larsen worked for Morrow, Bantam and Pyramid (now part of Berkley), Ms. Pomada worked at Holt, David McKay, and The Dial Press.

Member Agents: Michael Larsen (nonfiction); Elizabeth Pomada (narrative nonfiction, books of interest to women).

Represents: Nonfiction books (adult), novels. **Considers these nonfiction areas:** Anthropology/archaeology; art/architecture/design; biography/autobiography; business/economics; cooking/foods/nutrition; current affairs; ethnic/cultural interests; gay/lesbian issues; government/politics/law; health/medicine; history; how-to; humor/satire; interior design/decorating; memoirs; money/finance; music/dance; nature/environment; New Age/metaphysics; photography; popular culture; psychology; religious/inspirational; science/technology; self-help/personal improvement; sociology; sports; theater/film; travel; true crime/investigative; women's issues/studies; futurism. **Considers these fiction areas:** Action/adventure; contemporary issues; detective/police/crime; ethnic; experimental; family saga; fantasy; feminist; gay/lesbian; glitz; historical; humor/satire; literary; mainstream/contemporary; mystery/suspense; religious/inspirational; romance (contemporary, gothic, historical).

O-ₙ "We have very diverse tastes. We look for fresh voices and new ideas. We handle literary, commercial and genre fiction, and the full range of nonfiction books." Actively seeking commercial and literary fiction. Does not want to receive children's books, plays, short stories, screenplays, pornography, poetry or stories of abuse.

How to Contact: Query with SASE, first 10 pages of completed novel and two page synopsis, SASE. For nonfiction, send title, promotion plan and proposal done according to our plan (See brochure and website.). No e-mail or fax queries. Responds in 2 months to queries.

Recent Sales: Sold 15 titles in the last year. *Night Whispers*, by Pam Chun (Sourcebooks); *Marketing for Free*, by Jay C. Levinson (Houghton Mifflin); *Snoopy's Guide to the Writing Life*, introduction by Barnaby Conrad and foreward by Monte Schulz (Writer's Digest); *Fox on the Rhine*, by Michael Dobson and Doug Niles (Tor)

Terms: Agent receives 15% commission on domestic sales; 20% (30% for Asia) commission on foreign sales. May charge for printing, postage for multiple submissions, foreign mail, foreign phone calls, galleys, books, and legal fees.

Writers' Conferences: Book Expo America; Santa Barbara Writers Conference (Santa Barbara); Maui Writers Conference (Maui); ASJA.

Tips: "If you can write books that meet the needs of the marketplace, and you can promote your books, now is the best time ever to be a writer. We must find new writers to make a living so we are very eager to hear from new writers whose work will interest large houses and nonfiction writers who can promote their books. Please send a SASE for a free 16-page brochure and a list of recent sales."

N ◙ **LAZEAR AGENCY, INC.**, 800 Washington Ave. N., Suite 660, Minneapolis MN 55401. (612)332-8640. Fax: (612)332-4648. E-mail: info@lazear.com. Website: www.lazear.com. **Contact:** Editorial Board. Estab. 1984. Represents 250 clients. Currently handles: 60% nonfiction books; 30% novels; 10% juvenile books.

- The Lazear Agency opened a New York Office in September 1997.

Member Agents: Jonathon Lazear; Wendy Lazear; Christi Cardenas; Anne Blackstone; Julie Mayo.

Represents: Nonfiction books, novels, juvenile books, feature film, TV scripts, syndicated material, licensing; new media with connection to book project. **Considers these nonfiction areas:** Agriculture/horticulture; americana; animals; anthropology/archaeology; art/architecture/design; biography/autobiography; business/economics; child guidance/parenting; computers/electronic; cooking/foods/nutrition; crafts/hobbies; creative nonfiction; current affairs; education; ethnic/cultural interests; gardening; gay/lesbian issues; government/politics/law; health/medicine; history; how-to; humor/satire; interior design/decorating; juvenile nonfiction; language/literature/criticism; memoirs; military/war; money/finance; multicultural; music/dance; nature/environment; New Age/metaphysics; philosophy; photography; popular culture; psychology; recreation; regional; religious/inspirational; science/technology; self-help/personal improvement; sex; sociology; software; spirituality; sports; theater/film; translation; travel; true crime/investigative; women's issues/studies; young adult. **Considers these fiction areas:** Action/adventure; comic books/cartoon; confession; contemporary issues; detective/police/crime; erotica; ethnic; experimental; family saga; fantasy; feminist; gay/lesbian; glitz; gothic; hi-lo; historical; horror; humor/satire; juvenile; literary; mainstream/contemporary; military/war; multicultural; multimedia; mystery/suspense; New Age; occult; picture books; plays; poetry; poetry in translation; psychic/supernatural; regional; religious/inspirational; romance; science

fiction; short story collections; spiritual; sports; thriller; translation; western/frontier; young adult; women's.
How to Contact: Query with SASE, outline/proposal. Highly selective. No phone calls or faxes. No e-mail or fax queries. Responds in 3 weeks to queries; 1 month to mss. Returns materials only with SASE. Obtains most new clients through recommendations from others, "through the bestseller lists, word-of-mouth."
Recent Sales: Sold over 50 titles in the last year. *Oh, The Things I Know*, by Al Franken (Dutton); *You Ain't Got no Easter Clothes*, by Laura Love (Hyperion).
Terms: Agent receives 15% commission on domestic sales; 20% commission on foreign sales. Offers written contract. Charges clients for photocopying, international express mail, bound galleys and finished books used for subsidiary rights sales. "No fees charged if book is not sold."
Tips: "The writer should first view himself as a salesperson in order to obtain an agent. Sell yourself, your idea, your concept. Do your homework. Notice what is in the marketplace. Be sophisticated about the arena in which you are writing."

N **LESCHER & LESCHER, LTD.**, 47 E. 19th St., New York NY 10003. (212)529-1790. Fax: (212)529-2716. **Contact:** Robert Lescher, Susan Lescher, Michael Choate. Estab. 1966. Member of AAR. Represents 150 clients. Currently handles: 80% nonfiction books; 20% novels.
Represents: Nonfiction books, novels. **Considers these nonfiction areas:** Biography/autobiography; cooking/foods/nutrition (cookbooks); current affairs; government/politics/law; history; memoirs; popular culture; contemporary issues; narrative nonfiction. **Considers these fiction areas:** Literary; mystery/suspense; commercial fiction.

O→ Does not want to receive screenplays or science fiction.

How to Contact: Query with SASE. Obtains most new clients through recommendations from others.
Recent Sales: Sold 35 titles in the last year. This agency prefers not to share information on specific sales. Clients include Neil Sheehan, Madeleine L'Engle, Calvin Trillin, Judith Viorst, Thomas Perry, Anne Fadiman, Frances FitzGerald, Paula Fox and Robert M. Parker, Jr.
Terms: Agent receives 15% commission on domestic sales; 20-25% commission on foreign sales.

N **LEVINE GREENBERG LITERARY AGENCY, INC.**, 307 7th Ave., Suite 1906, New York NY 10001. (212)337-0934. Fax: (212)337-0948. Website: www.jameslevine.com. Estab. 1989. Member of AAR. Represents 250 clients. 33% of clients are new/unpublished writers. Currently handles: 70% nonfiction books; 30% novels.

- Prior to opening his agency, Mr. Levine served as vice president of the Bank Street College of Education.

Member Agents: James Levine; Arielle Eckstut; Daniel Greenberg; Stephanie Kip Roston.
Represents: Nonfiction books, novels. **Considers these nonfiction areas:** Animals; art/architecture/design; biography/autobiography; business/economics; child guidance/parenting; computers/electronic; cooking/foods/nutrition; gardening; gay/lesbian issues; health/medicine; money/finance; nature/environment; New Age/metaphysics; psychology; religious/inspirational; science/technology; self-help/personal improvement; sociology; spirituality; sports; women's issues/studies. **Considers these fiction areas:** Contemporary issues; literary; mainstream/contemporary; mystery/suspense; thriller (psychological); women's.

O→ This agency specializes in business, psychology, parenting, health/medicine, narrative nonfiction, psychology, spirituality, religion, women's issues and commercial fiction.

How to Contact: See www.jameslevine.com for full submission procedure. Prefers e-mail queries. Obtains most new clients through recommendations from others.
Recent Sales: *Queen Bees Wannabes: Helping Your Daughter Survive Cliques, Gossip, Boyfriends, and Other Realities of Adolescence*, by Rosalind Wiseman (Crown); *Chicken: A Self-Portrait*, by David Sterry (Regan Books/HarperCollins); *Raising Fences: A Black Man's Love Story*, by Michael Datcher (Riverhead/Penguin Putnam); *21 Dog Years: Doing Time*, by Mike Daisey (Free Press/Simon and Schuster).
Terms: Agent receives 15% commission on domestic sales; 20% commission on foreign sales. Offers written contract, binding for variable length of time. Charges clients for out-of-pocket expenses—telephone, fax, postage and photocopying—directly connected to the project.
Writers' Conferences: ASJA Annual Conference (New York City, May).
Tips: "We work closely with clients on editorial development and promotion. We work to place our clients as magazine columnists and have created columnists for *McCall's* (renamed *Rosie's*) and *Child*. We work with clients to develop their projects across various media—video, software, and audio."

N **PAUL S. LEVINE LITERARY AGENCY**, 1054 Superba Ave., Venice CA 90291-3940. (310)450-6711. Fax: (310)450-0181. E-mail: pslevine@ix.netcom.com. Website: www.netcom.com/~pslevine/lawliterary.html. **Contact:** Paul S. Levine. Estab. 1996. Member of the State Bar of California. Represents over 100 clients. 75% of clients are new/unpublished writers. Currently handles: 30% nonfiction books; 30% novels; 10% movie scripts; 30% TV scripts.
Represents: Nonfiction books, novels, movie scripts, feature film, TV scripts, TV movie of the week, episodic drama, sitcom, animation, documentary, miniseries, syndicated material. **Considers these nonfiction areas:** Art/architecture/design; biography/autobiography; business/economics; child guidance/parenting; computers/electronic; cooking/foods/nutrition; crafts/hobbies; creative nonfiction; current affairs; education; ethnic/cultural interests; gay/lesbian issues; government/politics/law; health/medicine; history; how-to; humor/satire; interior design/decorating; language/literature/criticism; memoirs; military/war; money/finance; music/dance; nature/environment; New Age/metaphysics; photography; popular culture; psychology; religious/inspirational; science/technology; self-help/personal improvement; sociology; sports; theater/film; true crime/investigative; women's issues/studies. **Considers these fiction areas:** Action/adventure; comic books/cartoon; confession; contemporary issues; detective/police/crime; erotica; ethnic; experimental; family saga; feminist; gay/lesbian; glitz; historical; humor/satire; literary; mainstream/contemporary; mystery/suspense; regional; religious/inspirational; romance; sports; thriller; western/frontier. **Considers these script subject areas:** Action/adventure; biography/autobiography;

cartoon/animation; comedy; contemporary issues; detective/police/crime; erotica; ethnic; experimental; family saga; feminist; gay/lesbian; glitz; historical; horror; juvenile; mainstream; multimedia; mystery/suspense; religious/inspirational; romantic comedy; romantic drama; sports; teen; thriller; western/frontier.

O→ Actively seeking commercial fiction and nonfiction. Also handles children's and young adult fiction and nonfiction. Does not want to receive science fiction, fantasy or horror.

How to Contact: Query with SASE. Accepts e-mail and fax queries. Considers simultaneous queries. Responds in 1 day to queries; 2 months to mss. Returns materials only with SASE. Obtains most new clients through conferences, referrals, listings on various websites and through listings in directories.

Recent Sales: Sold 25 titles in the last year. This agency prefers not to share information on specific sales.

Terms: Agent receives 15% commission on domestic sales; 20% commission on foreign sales. Offers written contract. Charges clients for messengers, long distance, postage. "Only when incurred. No advance payment necessary."

Writers' Conferences: California Lawyers for the Arts (Los Angeles CA); National Writers Club (Los Angeles CA); "Selling to Hollywood" Writer's Connection (Glendale CA); "Spotlight on Craft" Willamette Writers Conference (Portland OR); Women in Animation (Los Angeles CA); and many others.

N **ROBERT LIEBERMAN ASSOCIATES**, 400 Nelson Rd., Ithaca NY 14850-9440. (607)273-8801. Fax: (801)749-9682. E-mail: rhl10@cornell.edu. Website: www.people.cornell.edu/pages/rhl10/. **Contact:** Robert Lieberman. Estab. 1993. Represents 30 clients. 50% of clients are new/unpublished writers. Currently handles: 20% nonfiction books; 80% textbooks.

Represents: Nonfiction books (trade), scholarly books, textbooks (college, high school and middle school level). **Considers these nonfiction areas:** Agriculture/horticulture; anthropology/archaeology; art/architecture/design; business/economics; computers/electronic; education; health/medicine; memoirs (by authors with high public recognition); money/finance; music/dance; nature/environment; psychology; science/technology; sociology; theater/film.

O→ This agency specializes in university/college level textbooks, CD-ROM/software and popular tradebooks in science, math, engineering, economics and other subjects. Does not want to receive fiction, self-help or screenplays.

How to Contact: Query with SASE or by e-mail. Prefers to read materials exclusively. Prefers e-mail queries. Considers simultaneous queries. Responds in 2 weeks to queries; 1 month to mss. Returns materials only with SASE. Obtains most new clients through referrals.

Recent Sales: Sold 15 titles in the last year. *Conflict Resolution*, by Baltos and Weir (Cambridge University Press).

Terms: Agent receives 15% commission on domestic sales; 20% commission on foreign sales. Offers written contract, binding for open-ended length of time; 30-day notice must be given to terminate contract. 100% of business is derived from commissions on ms sales. "Fees are sometimes charged to clients for shipping and when special reviewers are required."

Tips: "The trade books we handle are by authors who are highly recognized in their fields of expertise. Client list includes Nobel Prize winners and others with high name recognition, either by the public or within a given area of expertise."

N **RAY LINCOLN LITERARY AGENCY**, Elkins Park House, Suite 107-B, 7900 Old York Rd., Elkins Park PA 19027. (215)782-8882. Fax: (215)782-8882. **Contact:** Mrs. Ray Lincoln. Estab. 1974. Represents 30 clients. 35% of clients are new/unpublished writers. Currently handles: 30% nonfiction books; 50% novels; 20% juvenile books.

Member Agents: Jerome A. Lincoln; Mrs. Ray Lincoln.

Represents: Nonfiction books, novels, juvenile books, scholarly books. **Considers these nonfiction areas:** Animals; anthropology/archaeology; art/architecture/design; biography/autobiography; business/economics; child guidance/parenting; cooking/foods/nutrition; crafts/hobbies; creative nonfiction; current affairs; ethnic/cultural interests; gardening; gay/lesbian issues; government/politics/law; health/medicine; history; interior design/decorating; juvenile nonfiction; language/literature/criticism; money/finance; music/dance; nature/environment; psychology; science/technology; self-help/personal improvement; sociology; sports; theater/film; women's issues/studies. **Considers these fiction areas:** Action/adventure; contemporary issues; detective/police/crime; ethnic; family saga; fantasy; feminist; gay/lesbian; historical; humor/satire; juvenile; literary; mainstream/contemporary; mystery/suspense; psychic/supernatural; regional; romance (contemporary, gothic, historical); sports; thriller; young adult.

O→ This agency specializes in biography, nature, the sciences, fiction in both adult and chilren's categories.

How to Contact: Query with SASE. Prefers to read materials exclusively. If requested, send an outline, 2 sample chapters, SASE. No e-mail or fax queries. Responds in 2 weeks to queries. Obtains most new clients through recommendations from others.

Recent Sales: *Alexander Hamilton: A Life*, by Willard Sterne Randall (HarperCollins); *The Laser*, by Jerry Spinelli (HarperCollins); *Planet Walk*, by John Francis (Chelsea Green).

Terms: Agent receives 15% commission on domestic sales; 20% commission on foreign sales. Offers written contract. Charges clients for overseas telephone calls; upfront postage fee for unpublished authors only. "I request authors to do manuscript photocopying themselves."

Tips: "I always look for polished writing style, fresh points of view and professional attitudes. I send for balance of manuscript if it is a likely project."

N **LINDSEY'S LITERARY SERVICES**, 7502 Greenville Ave., Suite 500, Dallas TX 75231. (214)890-9262. Fax: (214)890-9265. E-mail: bonedges001@aol.com. **Contact:** Bonnie James; Emily Armenta. Estab. 2002. Represents 10 clients. 60% of clients are new/unpublished writers. Currently handles: 70% nonfiction books; 30% novels.

- Prior to becoming an agent, Bonnie James was a drama instructor and magazine editor, while Emily Armenta was an independent film editor and magazine editor.

Member Agents: Bonnie James (nonfiction: New Age/metaphysics, self-help, psychology, women's issues; fiction:

mystery/suspense, thriller, horror, literary, mainstream, romance); Emily Armenta (nonfiction: New Age/metaphysics, self-help, psychology, women's issues; fiction: mystery/suspense, thriller, horror, literary, mainstream, romance).

Represents: Nonfiction books, novels. **Considers these nonfiction areas:** Animals; biography/autobiography; ethnic/cultural interests; gay/lesbian issues; health/medicine; history; memoirs; multicultural; psychology; self-help/personal improvement; true crime/investigative; women's issues/studies. **Considers these fiction areas:** Action/adventure; detective/police/crime; ethnic; historical; horror; literary; mainstream/contemporary; multicultural; mystery/suspense; religious/inspirational; romance; science fiction; thriller.

O→ "We are a new agency with a clear vision and will aggressively represent our clients." Actively seeking nonfiction self-help, metaphysical, psychology, and women's issues; for fiction seeking exceptionally written books. Does not want poetry, children's books, text books.

How to Contact: Query with SASE, submit proposal package, synopsis, sample chapter(s), author bio. Considers simultaneous queries. Responds in 6 weeks to queries; 3 months to mss. Returns materials only with SASE. Obtains most new clients through recommendations from others, solicitations.

Terms: Agent receives 15% commission on domestic sales; 20% commission on foreign sales. Offers written contract, binding for 1 year; cancelable by either party with 30 days written notice notice must be given to terminate contract.

Tips: "Write a clear, concise query describing your project. Pay attention to the craft of writing. Provide complete package, including education, profession, writing credits and what you want to accomplish."

N **WENDY LIPKIND AGENCY**, 120 E. 81st St., New York NY 10028. (212)628-9653. Fax: (212)585-1306. **Contact:** Wendy Lipkind. Estab. 1977. Member of AAR. Represents 60 clients. Currently handles: 80% nonfiction books; 20% novels.

Represents: Nonfiction books, novels. **Considers these nonfiction areas:** Biography/autobiography; current affairs; health/medicine; history; science/technology; women's issues/studies; social history. **Considers these fiction areas:** Mainstream/contemporary; mystery/suspense (psychological suspense).

O→ This agency specializes in adult nonfiction. Does not want to receive mass market originals.

How to Contact: Prefers to read materials exclusively. For nonfiction, query with outline/proposal. For fiction, query with SASE only. Responds in 1 month to queries. Returns materials only with SASE. Obtains most new clients through recommendations from others.

Recent Sales: Sold 10 titles in the last year. *One Small Step*, by Robert Mauner (Workman); *In the Land of Lyme*, by Pamela Weintraub (Scribner).

Terms: Agent receives 15% commission on domestic sales; 20% commission on foreign sales. Sometimes offers written contract. Charges clients for foreign postage, messenger service, photocopying, transatlantic calls, faxes.

Tips: "Send intelligent query letter first. Let me know if you sent to other agents."

N **LITERARY AND CREATIVE ARTISTS, INC.**, 3543 Albemarle St. NW, Washington DC 20008-4213. (202)362-4688. Fax: (202)362-362-8875. E-mail: query@lcadc.com. Website: www.lcadc.com. **Contact:** Muriel Nellis, Jane Roberts. Estab. 1981. Member of AAR, Authors Guild, associate member of American Bar Association. Represents 75 clients. Currently handles: 70% nonfiction books; 15% novels; 15% audio/video/film/TV.

Member Agents: Muriel Nellis; Jane Roberts; Stephen Ruwe.

Represents: Nonfiction books, novels, audio, film/TV rights. **Considers these nonfiction areas:** Biography/autobiography; business/economics; cooking/foods/nutrition; government/politics/law; health/medicine; how-to; memoirs; philosophy; human drama; lifestyle.

How to Contact: Query with SASE, outline, author bio. No unsolicited mss. Responds in 3 weeks to queries.

Recent Sales: *Seasons of Grace*, by John O'Neil and Alan Jones (John Wiley and Sons); *Lady Cottington's Fairy Album*, by Brian Froud (Harry N. Abrams); *The Origin of Minds*, by Peggy La Cerra and Roger Bingham (Harmony Books).

Terms: Agent receives 15% commission on domestic sales; 20% commission on foreign sales; 25% commission on dramatic rights sales. Charges clients for long-distance phone and fax, photocopying, shipping.

Tips: "While we prefer published writers, it is not required if the proposed work has great merit."

N **THE LITERARY GROUP**, 270 Lafayette St., 1505, New York NY 10012. (212)274-1616. Fax: (212)274-9876. E-mail: fweimann@theliterarygroup.com. Website: www.theliterarygroup.com. **Contact:** Frank Weimann. Estab. 1985. Represents 200 clients. 65% of clients are new/unpublished writers. Currently handles: 50% nonfiction books; 50% fiction.

Member Agents: Frank Weimann (fiction, nonfiction); Ian Kleinert (nonfiction); Priya Ratneshwar (fiction).

Represents: Nonfiction and fiction books. **Considers these nonfiction areas:** Animals; anthropology/archaeology; biography/autobiography; business/economics; child guidance/parenting; cooking/foods/nutrition; crafts/hobbies; creative nonfiction; current affairs; education; ethnic/cultural interests; government/politics/law; health/medicine; history; how-to; humor/satire; juvenile nonfiction; language/literature/criticism; memoirs; military/war; money/finance; multicultural; music/dance; nature/environment; popular culture; psychology; religious/inspirational; science/technology; self-help/personal improvement; sociology; sports; theater/film; true crime/investigative; women's issues/studies. **Considers these fiction areas:** Action/adventure; contemporary issues; detective/police/crime; ethnic; family saga; fantasy; feminist; horror; humor/satire; mystery/suspense; psychic/supernatural; romance (contemporary, gothic, historical, regency); sports; thriller; western/frontier.

O→ This agency specializes in nonfiction (true crime, military, history, biography, sports, how-to).

How to Contact: Query with SASE, outline, 3 sample chapter(s). Prefers to read materials exclusively. Responds in 1 week to queries; 1 month to mss. Returns materials only with SASE. Obtains most new clients through referrals, writers' conferences, query letters.

Recent Sales: Sold 100 titles in the last year. *Keep It Simple*, by Terry Bradshaw; *Cry Me a River*, by Ernest Hill; *Double*

Deal, by Michael Corbitt and Sam Giancana. Other clients include Tommy Chong, Dr. Peter Salgo, Homer Hickman.

Terms: Agent receives 15% commission on domestic sales; 15% commission on foreign sales. Offers written contract; 30-day notice must be given to terminate contract.

Writers' Conferences: Detroit Women's Writers (MI); Kent State University (OH); San Diego Writers Conference (CA); Maui Writers Conference (HI); Austin Writers' Conference (TX).

LITWEST GROUP, LLC, Website: www.litwest.com. Represents 160 clients. 45% of clients are new/unpublished writers. Currently handles: 75% nonfiction books; 25% novels; TV, movie, Internet projects revolving around the book.

- Prior to opening the agency, Ms. Ellis was in academia, Mr. Preskill was in law and Ms. Mead and Ms. Boyle were in publishing.

Member Agents: Linda Mead (business, personal improvement, memoir, historical fiction/nonfiction steeped in research, ethnic/multicultural fiction/nonfiction, cozy mysteries); Nancy Ellis (mystery/suspense, religion/spiritual, parenting, psychology, science, women's literary/commercial, coming of age); Rob Preskill (men's, thrillers and mysteries where the writing is subtle, sports, travel, leisure, lifestyle, fitness, male health, business, design/architecture/art, politics, subculture, graphic novels, narrative nonfiction, literary); Katie Boyle (literary fiction, surreal, avant-garde, narrative nonfiction/memoir, contemporary culture/politics, art/music bios, graphic novels/subculture, psychology, women's issues, pop-culture, religion/spirituality).

Represents: Nonfiction books, novels, scholarly books. **Considers these nonfiction areas:** Biography/autobiography; business/economics; child guidance/parenting; current affairs; ethnic/cultural interests; health/medicine; history; how-to; humor/satire; memoirs; military/war; money/finance; multicultural; popular culture; psychology; religious/inspirational; self-help/personal improvement; sociology; sports; true crime/investigative; women's issues/studies. **Considers these fiction areas:** Contemporary issues; detective/police/crime; ethnic; family saga; feminist; historical; humor/satire; literary; mainstream/contemporary; multicultural; mystery/suspense; religious/inspirational; sports; thriller.

"We are multi-faceted." Actively seeking all subjects. Does not want to receive science fiction, horror, western, cookbooks.

How to Contact: Query with SASE, outline, 3 sample chapter(s). Considers simultaneous queries. Responds in 1 month to queries. Response time varies. Returns materials only with SASE. Obtains most new clients through recommendations from others, solicitations, conferences.

Recent Sales: *Winners Are Driven*, by Bobby Unser with Paul Pease (Wiley); *The Elegant Gathering of White Snows*, by Kris Radish (Bantam); *Sickened: The Memoir of a Munchausen by Proxy Childhood*, by Julie Gregory (Bantam). Other clients include Woodleigh Marx Hubbard, Jennifer Openshaw, Jed Diamond, Dr. Jay Gordon, Dr. Arthur White, Eric Harr, Brad Herzog, Martin Yan, Lyn Webster-Wilde, Larraine Segil.

Terms: Agent receives 15% commission on domestic sales; 20% commission on foreign sales. Offers written contract. Charges for postage and photocopying.

Writers' Conferences: Maui Writers Conference (Maui HI, Labor Day); San Diego State University Writers' Conference (San Diego CA, January); William Saroyan Writers Conference (Fresno CA, March); Santa Barbara (June) and many others.

Tips: "Clarity and precision about your work also helps the agent process."

LIVINGSTON COOKE, 278 Bloor St. E., Suite 305, Toronto ON M4W 3M4, Canada. (416)406-3390. Fax: (416)406-3389. E-mail: livcooke@idirect.ca. **Contact:** Elizabeth Griffen. Estab. 1992. Represents 200 clients. 30% of clients are new/unpublished writers. Currently handles: 50% nonfiction books; 50% novels.

- Prior to becoming an agent, Mr. Cooke was the publisher of Seal Bantam Books Canada.

Member Agents: David Johnston (film rights, literary fiction/nonfiction); Dean Cooke (literary fiction, nonfiction).

Represents: Nonfiction books, novels, juvenile books. **Considers these nonfiction areas:** Biography/autobiography; business/economics; child guidance/parenting; current affairs; gay/lesbian issues; health/medicine; popular culture; science/technology; young adult. **Considers these fiction areas:** Juvenile; literary.

Livingston Cooke represents some of the best Canadian writers in the world. "Through our contacts and subagents, we are building an international reputation for quality. Curtis Brown Canada is jointly owned by Dean Cooke and Curtis Brown New York. It represents Curtis Brown New York authors in Canada." Does not want to receive how-to, self-help, spirituality, genre fiction (science fiction, fantasy, mystery, thriller, horror).

How to Contact: Query with SASE. Accepts e-mail and fax queries. Considers simultaneous queries. Responds in 1 month to queries; 6 weeks to mss. Returns materials only with SASE. Obtains most new clients through recommendations from others.

Recent Sales: Sold 40 titles and sold 4 scripts in the last year. *Clara Callan*, by Richard B. Wright (Harperflamingo Canada); *Stanley Park*, by Timothy Taylor (Knopf Canada); *Your Mouth is Lovely*, by Nancy Richler (Harper Collins); *Spirit Cabinet*, by Paul Quarrinton (Grove/Atlantic); *Lazarus and the Hurricane*, by S. Charton/T. Swinton (St. Martin's Press); *Latitudes of Melt*, by Joan Clark (Knopf Canada); *Possesing Genius: The Bizarre Odyssey of Eintein's Brain*, by Caroline Abraham (Penguin Canada, St. Martin's Press); *Englishman's Boy*, by Guy Vanderhaeghe (Minds Eye); *Lazarus and the Hurricane*, by T. Swinton and S. Chaiton (Universal/Beacon). Other clients include Margaret Gibson, Richard Scrimger, Tony Hillerman, Robertson Davies, Brian Moore.

Terms: Agent receives 15% commission on domestic sales; 20% commission on foreign sales. Offers written contract. Charges clients for postage, photocopying, courier.

LOS BRAVOS LITERARY MANAGEMENT, 1811 N. Whitley Ave., Suite 1003, Los Angeles CA 90028. (323)461-5589. Fax: (323)417-4879. E-mail: marc@losbravosmanagement.com. **Contact:** Marc Gerald. Estab. 2002. Represents 25 clients. 50% of clients are new/unpublished writers. Currently handles: 70% nonfiction books; 20% novels; 10% movie scripts.

- Prior to becoming an agent, Mr. Gerald found and ran *The Syndicate*, an urban oriented publishing and entertainment company, co-owned with Wesley Snipes; found and edited W.W. Norton's Old School Books imprint; wrote and produced America's Most Wanted and numerous specials for Fox Television.

Represents: Nonfiction books, novels, feature film. **Considers these nonfiction areas:** Biography/autobiography; business/economics; child guidance/parenting; current affairs; ethnic/cultural interests; health/medicine; history; how-to; memoirs; music/dance; popular culture; self-help/personal improvement; sports; true crime/investigative; juvenile nonfiction, New Age. **Considers these fiction areas:** Action/adventure; confession; detective/police/crime; erotica; ethnic; horror; literary; mystery/suspense; thriller; young adult; glitz. **Considers these script subject areas:** Action/adventure; biography/autobiography; comedy; contemporary issues; detective/police/crime; ethnic; horror; mystery/suspense; romantic comedy; romantic drama; teen; thriller.

O-→ "We represent a free-ranging roster of largely pop culture-leaning clients across platform. While we represent story-tellers of all stripes, the majority of our clients are artists and athletes looking to tell their story in book form, and pop culture brands seeking to impact in the publishing space."

How to Contact: Submit outline, 2 sample chapter(s). Considers simultaneous queries. Responds in 1 month to queries; 2 months to mss. Returns materials only with SASE. Obtains most new clients through recommendations from others.

Recent Sales: Sold 20 titles and sold 1 script in the last year. Other clients include Lil' Kim, *Gearhead Magazine*, SuicideGirls.com.

Terms: Agent receives 15% commission on domestic sales; 20% commission on foreign sales. Offers written contract. Charges clients for postage and photocopying.

NANCY LOVE LITERARY AGENCY, 250 E. 65th St., New York NY 10021-6614. (212)980-3499. Fax: (212)308-6405. **Contact:** Nancy Love. Estab. 1984. Member of AAR. Represents 60-80 clients. Currently handles: 90% nonfiction books; 10% novels.

Member Agents: Nancy Love.

Represents: Nonfiction books, novels (mysteries and thrillers only). **Considers these nonfiction areas:** Biography/autobiography; child guidance/parenting; cooking/foods/nutrition; current affairs; ethnic/cultural interests; government/politics/law; health/medicine; history; how-to; memoirs; nature/environment; New Age/metaphysics; popular culture; psychology; religious/inspirational; science/technology; self-help/personal improvement; sociology; spirituality; travel (armchair only, no how-to travel); true crime/investigative; women's issues/studies. **Considers these fiction areas:** Mystery/suspense; thriller.

O-→ This agency specializes in adult nonfiction and mysteries. Actively seeking health and medicine (including alternative medicine), parenting, spiritual and inspirational. Does not want to receive novels other than mysteries and thrillers.

How to Contact: For nonfiction, send a proposal, chapter summary and sample chapter. For fiction, query first. Fiction is only read on an exclusive basis. No e-mail or fax queries. Considers simultaneous queries. Responds in 3 weeks to queries; 6 weeks to mss. Returns materials only with SASE. Obtains most new clients through recommendations from others, solicitations.

Recent Sales: Sold 20 titles in the last year. *The Tools People Use to Quit Addictions*, by Stanton Peele, Ph.D. (Crown); *All the Shah's Men: The Hidden Story of the CIA's Coup in Iran*, by Steven Kinzer (John Wiley).

Terms: Agent receives 15% commission on domestic sales; 20% commission on foreign sales. Offers written contract. Charges clients for photocopying "if it runs over $20."

Tips: "Nonfiction author and/or collaborator must be an authority in subject area and have a platform. Send a SASE if you want a response."

N **ANDREW LOWNIE LITERARY AGENCY, LTD.**, 17 Sutherland St., London SW1V4JU, England. (0207)828 1274. Fax: (0207)828 7608. E-mail: lownie@globalnet.co.uk. Website: www.andrewlownie.co.uk. **Contact:** Andrew Lownie. Estab. 1988. Member of Association of Author's Agents. Represents 130 clients. 20% of clients are new/unpublished writers. Currently handles: 90% nonfiction books; 10% novels.

- Prior to becoming an agent, Mr. Lownie was a journalist, bookseller, publisher, author of 12 books, and previously a director of the Curtis Brown Agency.

Represents: Nonfiction books. **Considers these nonfiction areas:** Anthropology/archaeology; biography/autobiography; current affairs; government/politics/law; history; memoirs; military/war; music/dance; popular culture; theater/film; true crime/investigative.

O-→ This agent has wide publishing experience, extensive journalistic contacts, and a specialty in showbiz memoir and celebrities. Actively seeking showbiz memoirs, narrative histories and biographies. Does not want to receive poetry, short stories, children's fiction, scripts, academic.

How to Contact: Query with SASE and/or IRCs. Submit outline, 1 sample chapter(s). Accepts e-mail and fax queries. Considers simultaneous queries. Responds in 1 week to queries; 1 month to mss. Returns materials only with SASE. Obtains most new clients through recommendations from others.

Recent Sales: Sold 50 titles in the last year. *Henry Cooper: The Authorised Biography*, by Robert Edwards (BBC Books); *The Disappearing Duke*, by Andrew Crofts (Carroll & Graf); *Jihad*, by Tom Carew (Mainstream); *Warrior Race* (St. Martin's). Other clients include Norma Major, Guy Bellamy, Joyce Cary estate, Lawrence James, Juliet Barker, Patrick McNee, Sir John Mills, Peter Evans, Desmond Seward, Laurence Gardner, Richard Rudgley.

Terms: Agent receives 15% commission on domestic sales; 15% commission on foreign sales. Offers written contract,

binding for until author chooses to break it but contract valid while book in print; 30-day notice must be given to terminate contract. Charges clients for some copying, postage, copies of books for submission.

Tips: "I prefer submissions in writing by letter."

DONALD MAASS LITERARY AGENCY, 160 W. 95th St., Suite 1B, New York NY 10025. (212)866-8200. **Contact:** Donald Maass, Jennifer Jackson or Michelle Brummer. Estab. 1980. Member of AAR, SFWA, MWA, RWA. Represents over 100 clients. 5% of clients are new/unpublished writers. Currently handles: 100% novels.

- Prior to opening his agency, Mr. Maass served as an editor at Dell Publishing (NY) and as a reader at Gollancz (London). He is the current president of AAR.

Member Agents: Donald Maass (mainstream, literary, mystery/suspense, science fiction); Jennifer Jackson (commercial fiction, especially romance, science fiction, fantasy, mystery/suspense); Michelle Brummer (fiction: literary, contemporary, feminist, science fiction, fantasy, romance).

Represents: Novels. **Considers these fiction areas:** Detective/police/crime; fantasy; historical; horror; literary; mainstream/contemporary; mystery/suspense; psychic/supernatural; romance (historical, paranormal, time travel); science fiction; thriller; women's.

This agency specializes in commercial fiction, especially science fiction, fantasy, mystery, romance, suspense. Actively seeking "to expand the literary portion of our list and expand in romance and women's fiction." Does not want to receive nonfiction, children's or poetry.

How to Contact: Query with SASE. Returns material only with SASE. Considers simultaneous queries. Responds in 2 weeks to queries; 3 months to mss.

Recent Sales: Sold over 100 titles in the last year. *No Graves as Yet*, by Anne Perry (Ballantine); *Griffone*, by Nalo Hopkinson (Warner Aspect).

Terms: Agent receives 15% commission on domestic sales; 20% commission on foreign sales.

Writers' Conferences: *Donald Maass*: World Science Fiction Convention; Frankfurt Book Fair; Pacific Northwest Writers Conference; Bouchercon and others; *Jennifer Jackson*: World Science Fiction and Fantasy Convention; RWA National and others; *Michelle Brummer*: ReaderCon; Luna Con; Frankfurt.

Tips: "We are fiction specialists, also noted for our innovative approach to career planning. Few new clients are accepted, but interested authors should query with SASE. Subagents in all principle foreign countries and Hollywood. No nonfiction or juvenile works considered."

N **GINA MACCOBY AGENCY**, P.O. Box 60, Chappaqua NY 10514. (914)238-5630. **Contact:** Gina Maccoby. Estab. 1986. Represents 35 clients. Currently handles: 33% nonfiction books; 33% novels; 33% juvenile books. Represents illustrators of children's books.

Represents: Nonfiction books, novels, juvenile books. **Considers these nonfiction areas:** Biography/autobiography; current affairs; ethnic/cultural interests; history; juvenile nonfiction; popular culture; women's issues/studies. **Considers these fiction areas:** Juvenile; literary; mainstream/contemporary; mystery/suspense; thriller; young adult.

How to Contact: Query with SASE. Considers simultaneous queries. Responds in 2 months to queries. Returns materials only with SASE. Obtains most new clients through recommendations from own clients.

Recent Sales: Sold 26 titles in the last year. *The Lost Colony*, by Jean Fritz; *Successful Television Writing*, by Lee Goldberg and William Rabkin; *Eaglestrike*, by Anthony Horowitz.

Terms: Agent receives 15% commission on domestic sales; 25% commission on foreign sales. Charges clients for photocopying. May recover certain costs such as the cost of shipping books by air to Europe or Japan or legal fees.

CAROL MANN AGENCY, 55 Fifth Ave., New York NY 10003. (212)206-5635. Fax: (212)675-4809. E-mail: kim@carolmannagency.com. **Contact:** Kim Goldstein. Estab. 1977. Member of AAR. Represents 200 clients. 25% of clients are new/unpublished writers. Currently handles: 70% nonfiction books; 30% novels.

Member Agents: Jim Fitzgerald (fiction, popular culture, biography); Carol Mann (literary fiction, nonfiction); Leylha Ahuile (Spanish and Latin American fiction and nonfiction); Kim Goldstein (fiction, nonfiction).

Represents: Nonfiction books, novels. **Considers these nonfiction areas:** Anthropology/archaeology; art/architecture/design; biography/autobiography; business/economics; child guidance/parenting; current affairs; ethnic/cultural interests; government/politics/law; health/medicine; history; money/finance; psychology; self-help/personal improvement; sociology; women's issues/studies. **Considers these fiction areas:** Literary.

This agency specializes in current affairs; self-help; popular culture; psychology; parenting; history. Does not want to receive "genre fiction (romance, mystery, etc.)."

How to Contact: Query with outline/proposal and SASE. Responds in 3 weeks to queries.

Recent Sales: *America 24/7*, by Rick Smolen and David Cohen (DK); *White Guilt*, by Shelby Steele (HarperCollins); *Eminem*, by Anthony Borza (Crown). Other clients include novelist Marita Golden; journalists Tim Egan, Elizabeth Mehren, Pulitzer Prize winner Fox Butterfield and National Book Critic Award winner James Tobin; essayist Shelby Steele; sociologist Dr. William Julius Wilson; economist Thomas Sowell; and Tufts University's Elliot Pearson School of Education.

Terms: Agent receives 15% commission on domestic sales; 20% commission on foreign sales. Offers written contract.

MANUS & ASSOCIATES LITERARY AGENCY, INC., 375 Forest Ave., Palo Alto CA 94301. (650)470-5151. Fax: (650)470-5159. E-mail: manuslit@manuslit.com. Website: www.manuslit.com. **Contact:** Jillian Manus. Also: 445 Park Ave., New York NY 10022. (212)644-8020. Fax (212)644-3374. **Contact:** Janet Manus. Estab. 1985. Member of AAR. Represents 75 clients. 30% of clients are new/unpublished writers. Currently handles: 55% nonfiction books; 40% novels; 5% juvenile books.

- Prior to becoming agents, Jillian Manus was associate publisher of two national magazines and director of development at Warner Bros. and Universal Studios; Janet Manus has been a literary agent for 20 years.

Member Agents: Jandy Nelson (self-help, health, memoirs, narrative nonfiction, women's fiction, literary fiction, multicultural fiction, thrillers); Stephanie Lee (self-help, narrative nonfiction, commercial literary fiction, quirky/edgy fiction, pop culture, pop science); Christine Cummings (history, biography, science, literary fiction, mystery/suspense, pop philosophy).

Represents: Nonfiction books, novels. **Considers these nonfiction areas:** Biography/autobiography; business/economics; child guidance/parenting; creative nonfiction; current affairs; ethnic/cultural interests; health/medicine; how-to; memoirs; money/finance; nature/environment; popular culture; psychology; science/technology; self-help/personal improvement; women's issues/studies; Gen X and Gen Y issues. **Considers these fiction areas:** Literary; mainstream/contemporary; multicultural; mystery/suspense; thriller; women's; quirky/edgy fiction.

This agency specializes in commercial literary fiction, narrative nonfiction, thrillers, health, pop psychology, women's empowerment. "Our agency is unique in the way that we not only sell the material, but we edit, develop concepts and participate in the marketing effort. We specialize in large, conceptual fiction and nonfiction, and always value a project that can be sold in the TV/feature film market." Actively seeking high-concept thrillers, commercial literary fiction, women's fiction, celebrity biographies, memoirs, multicultural fiction, popular health, women's empowerment, mysteries. Does not want to receive horror, romance, science fiction/fantasy, westerns, young adult, children's, poetry, cookbooks, magazine articles. Usually obtains new clients through recommendations from editors, clients and others; conferences; and unsolicited materials.

How to Contact: Query with SASE. If requested, submit outline, 2-3 sample chapter(s). Accepts e-mail and fax queries. Considers simultaneous queries. Responds in 2 months to queries; 6 weeks to mss. Returns materials only with SASE. Obtains most new clients through recommendations from others, solicitations, conferences.

Recent Sales: *Under Control: Stories About Women, Guns and Family*, by Laurie Lynn Drummond (HarperCollins); *Gettysburg: A Novel of the Civil War*, by Newt Gingrich (St. Martin's/Thomas Dunne); *All the President's Children*, by Doug Wead (Atria Books).

Terms: Agent receives 15% commission on domestic sales; 20-25% commission on foreign sales. Offers written contract, binding for 2 years; 60 days notice must be given to terminate contract. Charges for photocopying and postage.

Writers' Conferences: Maui Writers Conference (Maui HI, Labor Day); San Diego Writer's Conference (San Diego CA, January); Willamette Writers Conference (Willamette OR, July).

Tips: "Research agents using a variety of sources, including *LMP*, guides, *Publishers Weekly*, conferences and even acknowledgements in books similar in tone to yours."

MARCH TENTH, INC., 4 Myrtle St., Haworth NJ 07641-1740. (201)387-6551. Fax: (201)387-6552. E-mail: hchoron@aol.com. **Contact:** Harry Choron, vice president. Estab. 1982. Represents 40 clients. 30% of clients are new/unpublished writers. Currently handles: 75% nonfiction books; 25% novels.

Represents: Nonfiction books, novels. **Considers these nonfiction areas:** Biography/autobiography; current affairs; health/medicine; history; humor/satire; language/literature/criticism; music/dance; popular culture; theater/film. **Considers these fiction areas:** Confession; ethnic; family saga; historical; humor/satire; literary; mainstream/contemporary.

"Writers must have professional expertise in their field. Pefer to work with published/established writers."

How to Contact: Query with SASE. Considers simultaneous queries. Responds in 1 month to queries. Returns materials only with SASE.

Recent Sales: Sold 12 titles in the last year. *The Case for Zionism*, by Rabbi Arthur Hertzberg; *Learning Sickness*, by James Lang; *The 100 Simple Secrets of Happy Families*, by David Niven.

Terms: Agent receives 15% commission on domestic sales; 20% commission on foreign sales; 20% commission on dramatic rights sales. Charges clients for postage, photocopying, overseas phone expenses. "Does not require expense money upfront." Writers reimbursed for office fees after the sale of ms.

THE DENISE MARCIL LITERARY AGENCY, INC., 685 West End Ave., New York NY 10025. (212)932-3110. **Contact:** Denise Marcil. Estab. 1977. Member of AAR. Represents 35 clients. 40% of clients are new/unpublished writers. Currently handles: Commercial fiction and nonfiction.

- Prior to opening her agency, Ms. Marcil served as an editorial assistant with Avon Books and as an editor with Simon & Schuster.

Represents: Nonfiction books (commercial), novels (commercial).

This agency specializes in thrillers, suspense, women's commercial fiction, business books, popular reference, how-to, self-help, and spirituality. "We are looking for fresh new voices in commercial women's fiction: chick lit, mom-lit, stories that capture women's experiences today. We are especially seeking well-written thrillers with the potential to break out."

How to Contact: Query with SASE.

Recent Sales: Sold 43 titles in the last year. *Black Maps*, by Peter Spiegalman (Knopf); *Flamingo Diner*, by Sheryl Woods (Mira); *Tarmac*, by Lynne Heitman (NAL).

Terms: Agent receives 15% commission on domestic sales; 20% commission on foreign sales. Offers written contract, binding for 2 years; 100% of business is derived from commissions on ms sales. Charges $100/year for postage, photocopying, long-distance calls, etc.

Writers' Conferences: Pacific Northwest Writers Conference; RWA.

THE EVAN MARSHALL AGENCY, 6 Tristam Place, Pine Brook NJ 07058-9445. (973)882-1122. Fax: (973)882-3099. E-mail: evanmarshall@thenovelist.com. Website: www.thenovelist.com. **Contact:** Evan Marshall. Estab. 1987. Member of AAR, MWA. Currently handles: 100% novels.

• Prior to opening his agency, Mr. Marshall served as an editor with New American Library, Everest House, and Dodd, Mead & Co., and then worked as a literary agent at The Sterling Lord Agency.

Represents: Novels. **Considers these fiction areas:** Action/adventure; erotica; ethnic; historical; horror; humor/satire; literary; mainstream/contemporary; mystery/suspense; religious/inspirational; romance (contemporary, gothic, historical, Regency); science fiction; western/frontier.

How to Contact: Query first with SASE; do not enclose material. Responds in 1 week to queries; 2 months to mss. Obtains most new clients through recommendations from others.

Recent Sales: *In Silence*, by Erica Spindlev (Mira); *Dreaming of You*, by Dixie Kane (Kensington); *Hunter's Moon*, by Bobbi Smith (Dorchester).

Terms: Agent receives 15% commission on domestic sales; 20% commission on foreign sales. Offers written contract.

N **MARGRET McBRIDE LITERARY AGENCY**, 7744 Fay Ave., Suite 201, La Jolla CA 92037. (858)454-1550. Fax: (858)454-2156. Estab. 1980. Member of AAR, Authors Guild.

• Prior to opening her agency, Ms. McBride worked at Random House, Ballantine Books and Warner Books.

Represents: Nonfiction books, novels, audio, video film rights. **Considers these nonfiction areas:** Biography/autobiography; business/economics; cooking/foods/nutrition; current affairs; ethnic/cultural interests; government/politics/law; health/medicine; history; how-to; money/finance; music/dance; popular culture; psychology; science/technology; self-help/personal improvement; sociology; women's issues/studies; style. **Considers these fiction areas:** Action/adventure; detective/police/crime; ethnic; historical; humor/satire; literary; mainstream/contemporary; mystery/suspense; thriller; western/frontier.

This agency specializes in mainstream fiction and nonfiction. Does not want to receive screenplays. Does not represent romance, poetry or children's/young adult.

How to Contact: Query with synopsis or outline and SASE. Considers simultaneous queries. Will not respond/read e-mail queries. Responds in 2 months to queries. Returns materials only with SASE.

Recent Sales: Sold 22 titles in the last year. *Incriminating Evidence*, by Sheldon Siegel (Bantam); *Fierce Conversations*, by Susan Scott (Viking); *Dinner After Dark*, by Colin Cowie (Clarkson Potter).

Terms: Agent receives 15% commission on domestic sales; 25% commission on foreign sales. Charges for overnight delivery and photocopying.

N **GERARD McCAULEY**, P.O. Box 844, Katonah NY 10536. (914)232-5700. Fax: (914)232-1506. Estab. 1970. Member of AAR. Represents 60 clients. 5% of clients are new/unpublished writers. Currently not accepting new clients. Currently handles: 65% nonfiction books; 15% scholarly books; 20% textbooks.

This agency specializes in history, biography and general nonfiction.

How to Contact: Obtains most new clients through recommendations from others.

Recent Sales: Sold 30 titles in the last year. *Jack Johnson*, by Ken Burns(Knopf); *At War at Sea*, by Ronald Spector (Viking).

Terms: Agent receives 15% commission on domestic sales; 20% commission on foreign sales.

N **HELEN McGRATH**, 1406 Idaho Ct., Concord CA 94521. (925)672-6211. Fax: (925)672-6383. E-mail: hmcgrath_lit@yahoo.com. **Contact:** Helen McGrath. Estab. 1977. Currently handles: 50% nonfiction books; 50% novels.

Represents: Nonfiction books, novels. **Considers these nonfiction areas:** Biography/autobiography; business/economics; current affairs; health/medicine; history; how-to; military/war; psychology; self-help/personal improvement; sports; women's issues/studies. **Considers these fiction areas:** Contemporary issues; detective/police/crime; literary; mainstream/contemporary; mystery/suspense; psychic/supernatural; romance; science fiction; thriller.

How to Contact: Submit proposal with SASE. *No unsolicited mss.* Responds in 2 months to queries. Obtains most new clients through recommendations from others.

Terms: Agent receives 15% commission on domestic sales. Offers written contract. Charges clients for photocopying.

N **McHUGH LITERARY AGENCY**, 1033 Lyon Rd., Moscow ID 83843-9167. (208)882-0107. Fax: (847)628-0146. E-mail: elisabetmch@turbonet.com. **Contact:** Elisabet McHugh. Estab. 1994. Represents 49 clients. 30% of clients are new/unpublished writers. Currently handles: 25% nonfiction books; 75% fiction.

Represents: Nonfiction books, novels. **Considers these nonfiction areas:** Animals; anthropology/archaeology; biography/autobiography; child guidance/parenting; cooking/foods/nutrition; current affairs; education; gardening; health/medicine; history; how-to; memoirs; military/war; money/finance; multicultural; nature/environment; popular culture; recreation; religious/inspirational; science/technology; self-help/personal improvement; travel; true crime/investigative; women's issues/studies; young adult; alternative medicine. **Considers these fiction areas:** Historical; literary; mainstream/contemporary; mystery/suspense; romance; thriller; western/frontier.

Does not handle children's books, poetry, science fiction, fantasy, horror.

How to Contact: Query by e-mail. Considers simultaneous queries. Returns materials only with SASE.

Recent Sales: *The Beginning of Children's Right in America* (McFarland & Co.); *Family Secrets* (Bantam); *Divided Loyalty* (Harlequin).

Terms: Agent receives 15% commission on domestic sales; 20% commission on foreign sales. Does not charge any upfront fees. Offers written contract. "Client must provide all copies of manuscripts needed for submissions."

Tips: "Be professional."

CLAUDIA MENZA LITERARY AGENCY, 1170 Broadway, Suite 807, New York NY 10001. (212)889-6850. **Contact:** Claudia Menza. Estab. 1983. Member of AAR. Represents 111 clients. 50% of clients are new/unpublished writers.

• Prior to becoming an agent, Ms. Menza was an editor/managing editor at a publishing company.

Represents: Nonfiction books, novels. **Considers these nonfiction areas:** Current affairs; education; ethnic/cultural interests (especially African-American); health/medicine; history; multicultural; music/dance; photography; psychology; self-help/personal improvement; theater/film.

O→ This agency specializes in African-American fiction and nonfiction, and editorial assistance.

How to Contact: Submit outline, 1 sample chapter(s). Prefers to read materials exclusively. Responds in 2 weeks to queries; 4 months to mss. Returns materials only with SASE. Obtains most new clients through recommendations from others.

Recent Sales: This agency prefers not to share information on specific sales.

Terms: Agent receives 15% commission on domestic sales; 20% (if co-agent is used) commission on foreign sales; 20% commission on dramatic rights sales. Offers written contract.

N **DORIS S. MICHAELS LITERARY AGENCY, INC.**, 1841 Broadway, Suite #903, New York NY 10023. Website: www.dsmagency.com. **Contact:** Doris S. Michaels, president. Estab. 1994. Member of AAR, WNBA.

Member Agents: Faye Bender.

Represents: Novels. **Considers these fiction areas:** Literary (with commercial appeal and strong screen potential).

How to Contact: All unsolicited mss returned unopened. Query by e-mail; see submission guidelines on website. Returns materials only with SASE. Obtains most new clients through recommendations from others, conferences.

Recent Sales: Sold over 30 titles in the last year. *Cycles: How We'll Live, Work and Buy*, by Maddy Dychtwald (The Free Press); *In the River Sweet*, by Patricia Henley (Knopf); *Healing Conversations: What to Say When You Don't Know What to Say*, by Nance Guilmartin (Jossey-Bass); *The Mushroom Man*, by Sophie Powell (Peguin Putnam); *How to Become a Marketing Superstar*, by Jeff Fox (Hyperion).

Terms: Agent receives 15% commission on domestic sales; 20% commission on foreign sales. Offers written contract, binding for 1 year; 30-day notice must be given to terminate contract. 100% of business is derived from commissions on ms sales. Charges clients for office expenses, not to exceed $150 without written permission.

Writers' Conferences: BEA; Frankfurt Book Fair (Germany, October); London Book Fair; Maui Writers Conference.

N **MARTHA MILLARD LITERARY AGENCY**, 145 W. 71st St. #8A, New York NY 10023. (973)593-9233. Fax: (973)593-9235. E-mail: marmillink@aol.com. **Contact:** Martha Millard. Estab. 1980. Member of AAR, SFWA. Represents 50 clients. Currently handles: 25% nonfiction books; 65% novels; 10% story collections.

• Prior to becoming an agent, Ms. Millard worked in editorial departments of several publishers and was vice president at another agency for four and a half years.

Represents: Nonfiction books, novels. **Considers these nonfiction areas:** Art/architecture/design; biography/autobiography; business/economics; child guidance/parenting; cooking/foods/nutrition; current affairs; education; ethnic/cultural interests; health/medicine; history; how-to; juvenile nonfiction; memoirs; money/finance; music/dance; New Age/metaphysics; photography; popular culture; psychology; self-help/personal improvement; theater/film; true crime/investigative; women's issues/studies. **Considers these fiction areas:** Considers fiction depending on writer's credits and skills.

How to Contact: No unsolicited queries. No e-mail or fax queries. Returns materials only with SASE. Obtains most new clients through recommendations from others.

Recent Sales: *Backfire*, by Peter Burrows (Wiley); *Fallen Star*, by Nancy Herkness (Berkley Sensation); *The Rosetta Codex*, by Richard Paul Russ (Penguin).

Terms: Agent receives 15% commission on domestic sales; 20% commission on foreign sales. Offers written contract.

N **THE MILLER AGENCY**, 1 Sheridan Square, 7B, #32, New York NY 10014. (212) 206-0913. Fax: (212) 206-1473. E-mail: angela@milleragency.net. Website: www.milleragency.net. **Contact:** Angela Miller. Estab. 1990. Represents 100 clients. 5% of clients are new/unpublished writers.

Represents: Nonfiction books. **Considers these nonfiction areas:** Anthropology/archaeology; art/architecture/design; biography/autobiography; business/economics; child guidance/parenting; cooking/foods/nutrition; current affairs; ethnic/cultural interests; gay/lesbian issues; health/medicine; language/literature/criticism; New Age/metaphysics; psychology; self-help/personal improvement; sports; women's issues/studies.

O→ This agency specializes in nonfiction, multicultural arts, psychology, self-help, cookbooks, biography, travel, memoir, sports.

How to Contact: Query with SASE, submit outline, a few sample chapter(s). Considers simultaneous queries. Responds in 1 week to queries. Obtains most new clients through referrals.

Recent Sales: Sold 25 titles in the last year.

Terms: Agent receives 15% commission on domestic sales; 20-25% commission on foreign sales. Offers written contract, binding for 2-3 years; 60-day notice must be given to terminate contract. 100% of business is derived from commissions on ms sales. Charges clients for postage (express mail or messenger services) and photocopying.

N **MOORE LITERARY AGENCY**, 83 High St., Newburyport MA 01950-3047. (978)465-9015. Fax: (978)465-8817. E-mail: cmoore@moorelit.com; mmeehan@moorelit.com; dmckenna@moorelit.com. **Contact:** Claudette Moore, Mike Meehan, Deborah McKenna. Estab. 1989. 10% of clients are new/unpublished writers. Currently handles: 100% nonfiction books.

Represents: Nonfiction books. **Considers these nonfiction areas:** Business/economics; computers/electronic; technology.

O→ This agency specializes in trade computer books (90% of titles); also handles business/hi-tech/general trade nonfiction.

How to Contact: Submit outline. Obtains most new clients through recommendations from others, conferences.

Recent Sales: *Programming Windows With C#*, by Charles Petzold (Microsoft Press); *Microsoft XP Inside Out Deluxe Edition*, by Ed Bott, Carl Siechert and Craig Stinson; *C# for Dummies*, by Stephen R. Davis (Hungry Minds); *Lessons Learned in Software Testing*, by Cem Kaner, et. al. (John Wiley & Sons).

Terms: Agent receives 15% commission on domestic sales; 15% commission on foreign sales; 15% commission on dramatic rights sales. Offers written contract.

MAUREEN MORAN AGENCY, P.O. Box 20191, Park West Station, New York NY 10025-1518. (212)222-3838. Fax: (212)531-3464. E-mail: maureenm@erols.com. **Contact:** Maureen Moran. Represents 30 clients. Currently handles: 100% novels.

Represents: Novels. **Considers these fiction areas:** Women's.

This agency specializes in women's fiction, principally romance and mystery. Does not want to receive science fiction, fantasy or juvenile books.

How to Contact: Query with SASE, Will accept email query without attachments. Does not read unsolicited mss. Considers simultaneous queries. Responds in 1 week to queries. Returns materials only with SASE.

Recent Sales: *Silver Scream*, by Mary Daheim; *The Older Woman*, by Cheryl Reavis.

Terms: Agent receives 10% commission on domestic sales; 15-20% commission on foreign sales. Charges clients for extraordinary expenses such as courier, messanger and bank wire fees by prior arrangement.

Tips: "This agency does not handle unpublished writers."

WILLIAM MORRIS AGENCY, INC., 1325 Ave. of the Americas, New York NY 10019. (212)586-5100. Fax: (212)903-1418. Website: www.wma.com. California office: 151 El Camino Dr., Beverly Hills CA 90212. Member of AAR.

Member Agents: Owen Laster; Jennifer Rudolph Walsh; Suzanne Gluck; Joni Evans; Tracy Fisher; Mel Berger; Virginia Barber; Jay Mandel; Manie Barron.

Represents: Nonfiction books, novels.

How to Contact: Query with SASE. Considers simultaneous queries.

Recent Sales: This agency prefers not to share information on specific sales.

Terms: Agent receives 15% commission on domestic sales; 20% commission on foreign sales.

HENRY MORRISON, INC., 105 S. Bedford Rd., Suite 306A, Mt. Kisco NY 10549. (914)666-3500. Fax: (914)241-7846. **Contact:** Henry Morrison. Estab. 1965. Signatory of WGA. Represents 49 clients. 5% of clients are new/unpublished writers. Currently handles: 5% nonfiction books; 90% novels; 5% juvenile books.

Represents: Nonfiction books, novels. **Considers these nonfiction areas:** Anthropology/archaeology; biography/autobiography; government/politics/law; history; juvenile nonfiction. **Considers these fiction areas:** Action/adventure; detective/police/crime; family saga; historical.

How to Contact: Query with SASE. Responds in 2 weeks to queries; 3 months to mss. Obtains most new clients through recommendations from others.

Recent Sales: Sold 18 titles in the last year. *The Altman Code*, by Robert Ludlum and Gayle Lynds (St. Martin's Press); *Truman on Leadership*, by Alan Axelrod (Putnam); *Drift Glass*, by Samuel R. Delany (Vintage). Other clients include Daniel Cohen, Molly Katz, Steve Samuel, Sol Stein, Beverly Swerling.

Terms: Agent receives 15% commission on domestic sales; 25% commission on foreign sales. Charges clients for ms copies, bound galleys and finished books for submissions to publishers, movie producers, foreign publishers.

MULTIMEDIA PRODUCT DEVELOPMENT, INC., 410 S. Michigan Ave., Suite 724, Chicago IL 60605-1465. (312)922-3063. E-mail: mpd@mpdinc.net. **Contact:** Danielle Egan-Miller. Estab. 1971. Member of AAR, RWA, MWA, SCBWI. Represents 150 clients. 2% of clients are new/unpublished writers. Currently handles: 60% nonfiction books; 40% novels.

Member Agents: Nik Vargas (generalist).

Represents: Nonfiction books, novels. **Considers these nonfiction areas:** Agriculture/horticulture; animals; anthropology/archaeology; biography/autobiography; business/economics; child guidance/parenting; cooking/foods/nutrition; crafts/hobbies; creative nonfiction; current affairs; ethnic/cultural interests; health/medicine; how-to; humor/satire; juvenile nonfiction; memoirs; money/finance; nature/environment; popular culture; psychology; religious/inspirational; science/technology; self-help/personal improvement; sociology; sports; travel; true crime/investigative; women's issues/studies. **Considers these fiction areas:** Contemporary issues; detective/police/crime; ethnic; family saga; glitz; historical; juvenile; literary; mainstream/contemporary; mystery/suspense; picture books; religious/inspirational; romance (contemporary, gothic, historical, regency, western); sports; thriller.

"We are generalists looking for professional writers with finely honed skill in writing. We are partial to authors with promotion savvy. We work closely with our authors through the entire publishing process, from proposal to after publication." Actively seeking highly commercial mainstream fiction and nonfiction. Does not want to receive poetry, short stories, plays, screenplays, articles.

How to Contact: Query by mail, SASE required. Accepts e-mail queries. No unsolicited mss accepted. Prefers to read material exclusively. Responds in 1 month to queries. Returns materials only with SASE. Obtains most new clients through "referrals, queries by professional, marketable authors."

Recent Sales: Sold 50 titles in the last year. *The Chili Queen*, by Sandra Dallas (St. Martin's Press); *The Procrastinating Child: A Handbook for Adults to Help Children Stop Putting Things Off*, by Rita Emmett (Walker); *In the Castle of hte Flynns*, by Michael Raleigh (Sourcebooks); *Remembered Prisoners of a Forgotten War*, by Lewis H. Carlson (St. Martin's Press).

Terms: Agent receives 15% commission on domestic sales; 20% commission on foreign sales. Offers written contract,

binding for 2 years. Charges clients for photocopying, overseas postage, faxes, phone calls.

Writers' Conferences: BEA (June); Frankfurt Book Fair (October); RWA (July); CBA (July); London International Book Fair (March); Boucheron (October).

Tips: "If interested in agency representation, be well informed."

DEE MURA LITERARY, 269 West Shore Dr., Massapequa NY 11758-8225. (516)795-1616. Fax: (516)795-8797. E-mail: samurai5@ix.netcom.com. **Contact:** Dee Mura, Karen Roberts, Frank Nakamura. Estab. 1987. Signatory of WGA. 50% of clients are new/unpublished writers.

- Prior to opening her agency, Ms. Mura was a public relations executive with a roster of film and entertainment clients; and worked in editorial for major weekly news magazines.

Represents: Nonfiction books, juvenile books, scholarly books, feature film, TV scripts, episodic drama, sitcom, animation, documentary, miniseries, variety show. **Considers these nonfiction areas:** Agriculture/horticulture; animals; anthropology/archaeology; biography/autobiography; business/economics; child guidance/parenting; computers/electronic; current affairs; education; ethnic/cultural interests; gay/lesbian issues; government/politics/law; health/medicine; history; how-to; humor/satire; juvenile nonfiction; memoirs; military/war; money/finance; nature/environment; science/technology; self-help/personal improvement; sociology; sports; travel; true crime/investigative; women's issues/studies. **Considers these fiction areas:** Action/adventure; contemporary issues; detective/police/crime; ethnic; experimental; family saga; fantasy; feminist; gay/lesbian; glitz; historical; humor/satire; juvenile; literary; mainstream/contemporary; mystery/suspense; psychic/supernatural; regional; romance (contemporary, gothic, historical, regency); science fiction; sports; thriller (medical thrillers); western/frontier; young adult; espionage; political. **Considers these script subject areas:** Action/adventure; cartoon/animation; comedy; contemporary issues; detective/police/crime; family saga; fantasy; feminist; gay/lesbian; glitz; historical; horror; juvenile; mainstream; mystery/suspense; psychic/supernatural; religious/inspirational; romantic comedy; romantic drama; science fiction; sports; teen; thriller; western/frontier.

"We work on everything, but are especially interested in literary fiction, commercial fiction and nonfiction, thrillers and espionage, self-help, inspirational, medical, scholarly, true life stories, true crime, women's stories and issues." Actively seeking "unique nonfiction manuscripts and proposals; novelists who are great storytellers; contemporary writers with distinct voices and passion." Does not want to receive "ideas for sitcoms, novels, film, etc. or queries without SASEs."

How to Contact: Query with SASE. No fax queries. Accepts queries by e-mail without attachments. Considers simultaneous queries. Responds in 2 weeks to queries. Returns materials only with SASE. Obtains most new clients through recommendations from others, queries.

Recent Sales: Sold over 40 titles and sold 35 scripts in the last year.

Terms: Agent receives 15% commission on domestic sales; 20% commission on foreign sales. Offers written contract. Charges clients for photocopying, mailing expenses, overseas and long distance phone calls and faxes.

Tips: "Please include a paragraph on writer's background even if writer has no literary background and a brief synopsis of the project. We enjoy well-written query letters that tell us about the project and the author."

JEAN V. NAGGAR LITERARY AGENCY, 216 E. 75th St., Suite 1E, New York NY 10021. (212)794-1082. **Contact:** Jean Naggar. Estab. 1978. Member of AAR, Women's Media Group and Women's Forum. Represents 100 clients. 20% of clients are new/unpublished writers. Currently handles: 35% nonfiction books; 45% novels; 15% juvenile books; 5% scholarly books.

- Ms. Naggar served as president of AAR.

Member Agents: Alice Tasman (Senior Agent, narrative nonfiction, commercial/literary fiction, thrillers); Anne Engel (academic-based nonfiction for general readership) ; Jennifer Weltz (Director, Subsidiary Rights).

Represents: Nonfiction books, novels. **Considers these nonfiction areas:** Biography/autobiography; child guidance/parenting; current affairs; government/politics/law; health/medicine; history; juvenile nonfiction; memoirs; New Age/metaphysics; psychology; religious/inspirational; self-help/personal improvement; sociology; travel; women's issues/studies. **Considers these fiction areas:** Action/adventure; contemporary issues; detective/police/crime; ethnic; family saga; feminist; historical; literary; mainstream/contemporary; mystery/suspense; psychic/supernatural; thriller.

This agency specializes in mainstream fiction and nonfiction, literary fiction with commercial potential.

How to Contact: Query with SASE. Prefers to read materials exclusively. No e-mail or fax queries. Responds in 1 day to queries; 2 months to mss. Returns materials only with SASE. Obtains most new clients through recommendations from others, solicitations, conferences.

Recent Sales: *Leaving Ireland*, by Ann Moore (NAL); *The Associate*, by Phillip Margolin (HarperCollins); *Quantico Rules*, by Gene Riehl (St. Martin's Press). Other clients include Jean M. Auel, Robert Pollack, Mary McGarry Morris, Lily Prior, Susan Fromberg Schaeffer, David Ball, Elizabeth Crane, Maud Casey.

Terms: Agent receives 15% commission on domestic sales; 20% commission on foreign sales. Offers written contract. Charges for overseas mailing; messenger services; book purchases; long-distance telephone; photocopying. "These are deductible from royalties received."

Writers' Conferences: Willamette Writers Conference; Pacific Northwest Writers Conference; Breadloaf Writers Conference; Virginia Women's Press Conference (Richmond VA); Marymount Manhattan Writers Conference.

Tips: "Use a professional presentation. Because of the avalanche of unsolicited queries that flood the agency every week, we have had to modify our policy. We will now only guarantee to read and respond to queries from writers who come recommended by someone we know. Our areas are general fiction and nonfiction, no children's books by unpublished writers, no multimedia, no screenplays, no formula fiction, no mysteries by unpublished writers. We recommend patience and fortitude: the courage to be true to your own vision, the fortitude to finish a novel and polish and polish again before sending it out, and the patience to accept rejection gracefully and wait for the stars to align themselves appropriately for success."

N ☑ **NATIONAL WRITERS LITERARY AGENCY**, division of GTR, Inc., 3140 S. Peoria #295, Aurora CO 80014. (720)851-1959. Fax: (720)851-1960. E-mail: aajwiii@aol.com or nationalwriters@aol.com. **Contact:** Andrew J. Whelchel III. Estab. 1987. Represents 52 clients. 20% of clients are new/unpublished writers. Currently handles: 40% nonfiction books; 34% novels; 20% juvenile books; 6% scripts.
Member Agents: Andrew J. Whelchel III (screenplays, nonfiction, mystery, thriller); Jason S. Cangialosi (nonfiction); Shayne Sharpe (novels, screenplays, fantasy).
Represents: Nonfiction and fiction books. **Considers these nonfiction areas:** Animals; biography/autobiography; child guidance/parenting; education; government/politics/law; how-to; popular culture; science/technology; sports; travel. **Considers these fiction areas:** Action/adventure; juvenile; mainstream/contemporary; mystery/suspense; science fiction; sports; young adult.

　　○┐ Actively seeking "mystery/thrillers, music, business, cutting edge novels; pop culture, compelling true stories, science and technology." Does not want to receive "concept books, westerns, over-published self-help topics."
How to Contact: Query with outline and SASE. Accepts e-mail queries. No fax queries. Considers simultaneous queries. Responds in 6 weeks to queries; 2 months to mss. Returns materials only with SASE. Obtains most new clients through solicitations, conferences, or over the transom.
Recent Sales: Sold 22 titles in the last year. *Final Cut: Business Plans for Independent Films*, by Reed Martin (Faber & Faber); *Open Season* (Warner Brothers Pictures) *Your Air Force Academy* (feature documentary).
Terms: Agent receives 15% commission on domestic sales; 20% commission on foreign sales; 10% commission on dramatic rights sales. Offers written contract; 30-day notice must be given to terminate contract.
Tips: "Query letters should include a great hook just as if you only had a few seconds to impress us. A professional package gets professional attention. Always include return postage!"

N ☑ **KAREN NAZOR LITERARY AGENCY**, 100 Powdermill Rd., PMB 182, Acton MA 01720. (978) 266-3792. Fax: (978) 263-6230. E-mail: query@nazor.org. **Contact:** Karen Nazor. Estab. 1991. Represents 35 clients. 15% of clients are new/unpublished writers. Currently handles: 75% nonfiction books; 10% novels; 10% electronic multimedia.

　　● Prior to opening her agency, Ms. Nazor served a brief apprenticeship with Raines & Raines and was assistant to Peter Ginsberg, president of Curtis Brown Ltd.
Member Agents: Kris Ashley (literary and commercial fiction).
Represents: Nonfiction books, novels, novellas. **Considers these nonfiction areas:** Biography/autobiography; business/economics; child guidance/parenting; computers/electronic; current affairs; ethnic/cultural interests; government/politics/law; history; how-to; music/dance; nature/environment; photography; popular culture; science/technology; sociology; sports; travel; women's issues/studies. **Considers these fiction areas:** Feminist; literary; multicultural; regional; women's.

　　○┐ This agency specializes in "good writers! Mostly nonfiction—arts, culture, politics, technology, civil rights, etc."
How to Contact: Query (preferred) or send outline/proposal (accepted). No unsolicited mss. Responds in 2 weeks to queries; 2 months to mss. Returns materials only with SASE.
Recent Sales: Sold 12 titles in the last year. *The Secret Life of Dust*, by Hannah Holmes (John Wiley & Sons); *Childhood and Adolescent Obsessive Compulsive Disorder*, by Mitzi Waltz (O'Reilly).
Terms: Agent receives 15% commission on domestic sales; 20% commission on foreign sales. Offers written contract. Charges clients for express mail services, photocopying costs.
Tips: "I'm interested in good writers who want a long term, long haul relationship. Not a one-book writer, but a writer who has many ideas, is productive, professional, passionate and meets deadlines!"

N ☑ **NEW BRAND AGENCY GROUP, LLC**, Website: www.literaryagent.net. **Contact:** Mark Ryan, Ingrid Elfver-Ryan. Estab. 1994. Represents 30 clients. 40% of clients are new/unpublished writers. Currently handles: 50% nonfiction books; 30% novels; 20% juvenile books.

　　● New Brand Agency is currently closed to submissions. Check out website for more details.
Member Agents: Mark Ryan and Ingrid Elfver-Ryan (fiction and nonfiction with bestseller or high commercial potential..-..projects with national and/or international appeal likely to sell at least 100,000 copies.)
Represents: Nonfiction books, novels, juvenile books (books for younger readers). **Considers these nonfiction areas:** Biography/autobiography; business/economics; health/medicine; humor/satire; juvenile nonfiction; memoirs; New Age/metaphysics; popular culture; psychology; religious/inspirational; self-help/personal improvement; sex; spirituality; women's issues/studies; body and soul, celebrity, family, finance, fitness, gift/novelty, leadership, men's issues, parenting, personal growth, relationships, success. **Considers these fiction areas:** Erotica (mainstream); fantasy; historical; horror; juvenile; literary; mainstream/contemporary; mystery/suspense; romance (mainstream); science fiction; thriller; western/frontier (mainstream); cross-genre, magical realism, supernatural, suspense.

　　○┐ "We only work with authors we are passionate about on three levels: The financial promise of the work and its ability to entertain, educate, and inspire; the personality and character of the author; and the potential career of the author (future books and willingness and ability to promote). We don't represent books we wouldn't buy ourselves and pull all-nighters to read. Actively seeking the stories and voices that no one else can share but you. Genuine. Authentic. Genre-bending okay. Does not want to receive Star Trek, personal manifestos, knitting, rowing, things defined by genre rather than having some elements of a genre."
How to Contact: Accepts e-mail queries only; submit electronic query at www.literaryagent.net. Responds in 1 day to queries; 1 week to mss. Obtains most new clients through queries and conferences.

Recent Sales: *24/7*, by Jim Brown (Ballantine); *The Marriage Plan*, by Aggie Jordan, Ph.D. (Broadway/Bantam); *The Father to Daughter*, by Harry Harrison (Workman).
Terms: Agent receives 15% commission on domestic sales. Offers written contract, binding for 6 months; 30 days notice must be given to terminate contract. 20% commission for subsidiary rights; Charges for postage and phone costs out of proceeds from the project; Writers reimbursed for office fees after the sale of ms.
Writers' Conferences: Sleuthfest (Ft. Lauderdale, March 15-17); Moving the Borders (Lexington, April 3); Author's Venue (Mesa, May 9-12); First Coast Festival (Jacksonville, May 16-18); Writing the Region (Gainesville, July 25-29); Rocky Mountain Fiction Writers' Conference (Denver, September 12-15); Missouri Writers' Conference (Kansas City, October 3-5), and many more.

NEW ENGLAND PUBLISHING ASSOCIATES, INC., P.O. Box 5, Chester CT 06412-0645. (860)345-READ and (860)345-4976. Fax: (860)345-3660. E-mail: nepa@nepa.com. Website: www.nepa.com. **Contact:** Elizabeth Frost-Knappman, Edward W. Knappman, Kristine Schiavi, Ron Formica, or Victoria Harlow. Estab. 1983. Member of AAR, ASJA, Authors Guild, Connecticut Press Club. Represents 125-150 clients. 15% of clients are new/unpublished writers.
Member Agents: Elizabeth Frost-Knappman; Edward W. Knappman; Kristine Schiavi; Ron Formica; Victoria Harlow.
Represents: Nonfiction books. **Considers these nonfiction areas:** Biography/autobiography; business/economics; child guidance/parenting; government/politics/law; health/medicine; history; language/literature/criticism; military/war; money/finance; nature/environment; psychology; science/technology; self-help/personal improvement; true crime/investigative; women's issues/studies; Reference.

This agency specializes in adult nonfiction of serious purpose.

How to Contact: Send outline/proposal, SASE. Accepts e-mail and fax queries. Considers simultaneous queries. Responds in 1 month to queries; 5 weeks to mss. Returns materials only with SASE.
Recent Sales: Sold over 70 titles in the last year. *Swimming with Sharks*, by Peter Klimley(Simon and Schuster); *Turnaround: How Carlos Ghosn Rescued Nissan*, by David Magee (HarperCollins); *The Princeton Murder Project*, by Ann Waldron (Berkeley); *Elementary, My Dear: Thinking Logically*, by Deborah Bennett (Norton).
Terms: Agent receives 15% commission on domestic sales; 20% commission on foreign sales. Offers written contract, binding for 6 months. Charges clients for copying.
Writers' Conferences: BEA (Chicago, June); ALA (San Antonio, January); ALA (New York, July); ASJA (May); Frankfurt (October).
Tips: "Send us a well-written proposal that clearly identifies your audience—who will buy this book and why. Check our website for tips on proposals and advice on how to market your books. Revise, revise, revise, but never give up. We don't."

N NINE MUSES AND APOLLO, INC., 525 Broadway, Suite 201, New York NY 10012. (212)431-2665. **Contact:** Ling Lucas. Estab. 1991. Represents 50 clients. 10% of clients are new/unpublished writers. Currently handles: 90% nonfiction books; 10% novels.

• Ms. Lucas formerly served as vice president, sales & marketing director and associate publisher of Warner Books.

Represents: Nonfiction books. **Considers these nonfiction areas:** Animals; biography/autobiography; business/economics; current affairs; ethnic/cultural interests; health/medicine; language/literature/criticism; psychology; spirituality; women's issues/studies. **Considers these fiction areas:** Ethnic; literary; mainstream/contemporary (commercial).

This agency specializes in nonfiction. Does not want to receive children's and young adult material.

How to Contact: Submit outline, 2 sample chapter(s), SASE. Prefers to read materials exclusively. Responds in 1 month to mss.
Recent Sales: Sold 20 titles in the last year. *Baron Baptiste Yoga*, by Baron Baptiste (Simon & Schuster/Fireside); *The Twelve Gifts of Birth*, by Charlene Costanzo (HarperCollins).
Terms: Agent receives 15% commission on domestic sales; 20-25% commission on foreign sales. Offers written contract. Charges clients for photocopying, postage.
Tips: "Your outline should already be well developed, cogent, and reveal clarity of thought about the general structure and direction of your project."

N THE NORMA-LEWIS AGENCY, 311 W. 43rd St., Suite 602, New York NY 10036. (212)664-0807. **Contact:** Norma Liebert. Estab. 1980. 50% of clients are new/unpublished writers. Currently handles: 60% juvenile books; 40% adult books.
Represents: Movie scripts, TV scripts, documentary, miniseries, stage plays, juvenile and adult nonfiction and fiction. **Considers these nonfiction areas:** Art/architecture/design; biography/autobiography; child guidance/parenting; cooking/foods/nutrition; crafts/hobbies; current affairs; ethnic/cultural interests; government/politics/law; health/medicine; history; juvenile nonfiction; music/dance; nature/environment; photography; popular culture; self-help/personal improvement; theater/film; true crime/investigative; women's issues/studies. **Considers these fiction areas:** Action/adventure; detective/police/crime; family saga; historical; horror; humor/satire; juvenile; mainstream/contemporary; mystery/suspense; picture books; romance (contemporary, gothic, historical, regency); thriller; western/frontier; young adult.

This agency specializes in juvenile books (pre-school to high school).

How to Contact: Query with SASE. Prefers to read materials exclusively. Considers simultaneous queries Responds in 6 weeks to queries. Returns materials only with SASE.
Recent Sales: *Viper Quarry*, by Dean Feldmeyer (Pocket Books); *Pitchfork Hollow*, by Dean Feldmeyer (Pocket Books).
Terms: Agent receives 15% commission on domestic sales; 20% commission on foreign sales.

N HAROLD OBER ASSOCIATES, 425 Madison Ave., New York NY 10017. (212)759-8600. Fax: (212)759-9428. Estab. 1929. Member of AAR. Represents 250 clients. 10% of clients are new/unpublished writers. Currently handles: 35% nonfiction books; 50% novels; 15% juvenile books.

Member Agents: Phyllis Westberg; Pamela Malpas; Emma Sweeney; Knox Burger; Craig Tenney (not accepting new clients); Alexander C. Smithline.

Represents: Nonfiction books, novels, juvenile books. **Considers these nonfiction areas:** Considers all nonfiction areas. **Considers these fiction areas:** Considers all fiction subjects.

How to Contact: Query letter only with SASE. No e-mail or fax queries. Responds as promptly as possible. Obtains most new clients through recommendations from others.

Terms: Agent receives 15% commission on domestic sales; 20% commission on foreign sales. Charges clients for photocopying and express mail or package services.

FIFI OSCARD AGENCY, INC., 110 W. 40th St., New York NY 10018. (212)764-1100. **Contact:** Literary Department. Estab. 1956. Member of AAR; signatory of WGA. Represents 108 clients. 5% of clients are new/unpublished writers. Currently handles: 60% nonfiction books; 10% novels; 30% stage plays.

Member Agents: Fifi Oscard; Peter Sawyer; Carmen La Via; Kevin McShane; Ivy Fischer Stone; Carolyn French; Lindley Kirksey; Jerry Rudes.

Represents: Nonfiction books, novels (by referral only), stage plays.

O→ This agency specializes in history, celebrity biography and autobiography, pop culture, travel/adventure, performing arts, fine arts/design.

How to Contact: Query with outline. No unsolicited mss.

Recent Sales: *My Father Had a Daughter: Judith Shakespeare's Tale*, by Grace Tiffany (Berkeley); *The Gospel According to Martin: The Spiritual Biography of Martin Luther King*, by Stewart Burns (Harper San Francisco); *Colored Lights*, by Kander and Ebb (Farrar, Strauss, & Giroux).

Terms: Agent receives 15% commission on domestic sales; 20% commission on foreign sales; 10% commission on dramatic rights sales. Charges clients for photocopying expenses.

Tips: "Writer must have published articles or books in major markets or have screen credits if movie scripts, etc."

N **PARAVIEW, INC., (Specialized: spiritual/New Age, self help)**, 191 7th Ave., Suite 2F, New York NY 10011. (212)989-3616. Fax: (212)989-3662. E-mail: lhagan@paraview.com. Website: www.paraview.com. **Contact:** Lisa Hagan. Estab. Paraview, Inc. was established in 1988. Represents 75 clients. 50% of clients are new/unpublished writers. Currently handles: 80% nonfiction books; 10% novels; 10% scholarly books.

- Ms. Hagan has agented since 1995.

Member Agents: Lisa Hagan (fiction and nonfiction self-help).

Represents: Nonfiction books, novels. **Considers these nonfiction areas:** Agriculture/horticulture; americana; animals; anthropology/archaeology; art/architecture/design; biography/autobiography; business/economics; child guidance/parenting; computers/electronic; cooking/foods/nutrition; crafts/hobbies; creative nonfiction; current affairs; education; ethnic/cultural interests; gardening; gay/lesbian issues; government/politics/law; health/medicine; history; how-to; humor/satire; interior design/decorating; juvenile nonfiction; language/literature/criticism; memoirs; military/war; money/finance; multicultural; music/dance; nature/environment; New Age/metaphysics; philosophy; photography; popular culture; psychology; recreation; regional; religious/inspirational; science/technology; self-help/personal improvement; sex; sociology; software; spirituality; sports; theater/film; translation; travel; true crime/investigative; women's issues/studies; young adult. **Considers these fiction areas:** Action/adventure; contemporary issues; ethnic; feminist; literary; mainstream/contemporary; regional; romance; women's.

O→ This agency specializes in spiritual, New Age and self-help.

How to Contact: Query including, synopsis, author, bio via email. Responds in 1 month to queries; 3 months to mss. Obtains most new clients through recommendations from editors and current clients.

Recent Sales: Sold 40 titles in the last year. *Poetry*, by Jewel Kilcher (Pocket Books); *King of the Cowboys*, by Ty Muarry (Pocket Books); *Angel Signs*, by Albert Haldane and Simha Seryaru (HarperCollins).

Terms: Agent receives 15% commission on domestic sales; 20% commission on foreign sales.

Writers' Conferences: BEA (Chicago, June); London Book Fair; E3—Electronic Entertainment Exposition.

Tips: "New writers should have their work edited, critiqued, and carefully reworked prior to submission. First contact should be via e-mail to lhagan@paraview.com."

THE RICHARD PARKS AGENCY, 138 E. 16th St., 5th Floor, New York NY 10003. (212)254-9067. Website: www.richardparksagency.com. **Contact:** Richard Parks. Estab. 1988. Member of AAR. Currently handles: 55% nonfiction books; 40% novels; 5% story collections.

- Prior to opening his agency, Mr. Parks served as an agent with Curtis Brown, Ltd.

Represents: Nonfiction books, novels. **Considers these nonfiction areas:** Animals; anthropology/archaeology; art/architecture/design; biography/autobiography; business/economics; child guidance/parenting; cooking/foods/nutrition; crafts/hobbies; current affairs; ethnic/cultural interests; gardening; gay/lesbian issues; government/politics/law; health/medicine; history; how-to; humor/satire; language/literature/criticism; memoirs; military/war; money/finance; music/dance; nature/environment; popular culture; psychology; science/technology; self-help/personal improvement; sociology; theater/film; travel; women's issues/studies. **Considers these fiction areas:** Considers fiction by referral only.

O→ Actively seeking nonfiction. Does not want to receive unsolicited material.

How to Contact: Query by mail only with SASE. No e-mail or fax queries. Considers simultaneous queries Responds in 2 weeks to queries. Returns materials only with SASE. Obtains most new clients through recommendations and referrals.

Terms: Agent receives 15% commission on domestic sales; 20% commission on foreign sales. Charges clients for photocopying or any unusual expense incurred at the writer's request.

L. PERKINS ASSOCIATES, 5800 Arlington Ave., Riverdale NY 10471. (718)543-5344. Fax: (718)543-5354. E-mail: lperkinsagency@yahoo.com. **Contact:** Lori Perkins. Estab. 1990. Member of AAR. Represents 50 clients. 10% of clients are new/unpublished writers.

- Ms. Perkins has been an agent for 18 years. Her agency has an affiliate agency, Southern Literary Group. She is also the author of *The Insider's Guide to Getting an Agent* (Writer's Digest Books).

Represents: Nonfiction books, novels. **Considers these nonfiction areas:** Popular culture. **Considers these fiction areas:** Fantasy; horror; literary (dark); science fiction.

All of Ms. Perkins's clients write both fiction and nonfiction. "This combination keeps my clients publishing for years. I am also a published author so I know what it takes to write a book." Actively seeking a Latino *Gone With the Wind* and *Waiting to Exhale,* and urban ethnic horror. Does not want to receive "anything outside of the above categories, i.e., westerns, romance."

How to Contact: Query with SASE. Considers simultaneous queries. Responds in 6 weeks to queries; 3 months to mss. Returns materials only with SASE. Obtains most new clients through recommendations from others, solicitations, conferences.

Recent Sales: Sold 100 titles in the last year. *The Illustrated Ray Bradbury*, by Jerry Weist (Avon); *The Poet in Exile*, by Ray Manzarek (Avalon); *Behind Sad Eyes: The Life of George Harrison*, (St. Martin's Press).

Terms: Agent receives 15% commission on domestic sales; 20% commission on foreign sales. No written contract. Charges clients for photocopying.

Writers' Conferences: San Diego Writer's Conference; NECON; BEA; World Fantasy.

Tips: "Research your field and contact professional writers' organizations to see who is looking for what. Finish your novel before querying agents. Read my book, *An Insider's Guide to Getting an Agent* to get a sense of how agents operate."

STEPHEN PEVNER, INC., 382 Lafayette Street, 8th Floor, New York NY 10003. (212)674-8403. Fax: (212)529-3692. E-mail: spevner@aol.com. **Contact:** Stephen Pevner.

Represents: Nonfiction books, novels, feature film, TV scripts, TV movie of the week, episodic drama, animation, documentary, miniseries. **Considers these nonfiction areas:** Biography/autobiography; ethnic/cultural interests; gay/lesbian issues; history; humor/satire; language/literature/criticism; memoirs; music/dance; New Age/metaphysics; photography; popular culture; religious/inspirational; sociology; travel. **Considers these fiction areas:** Comic books/cartoon; contemporary issues; erotica; ethnic; experimental; gay/lesbian; glitz; horror; humor/satire; literary; mainstream/contemporary; psychic/supernatural; thriller; urban. **Considers these script subject areas:** Comedy; contemporary issues; detective/police/crime; gay/lesbian; glitz; horror; romantic comedy; romantic drama; thriller.

This agency specializes in motion pictures, novels, humor, pop culture, urban fiction, independent filmmakers. Actively seeking urban fiction, popular culture, screenplays and film proposals.

How to Contact: Query with SASE, outline/proposal. Prefers to read materials exclusively. No e-mail or fax queries. Responds in 2 weeks to queries; 1 month to mss. Obtains most new clients through recommendations from others.

Recent Sales: *In the Company of Men* and *Bash: Latterday Plays*, by Neil Labote; *The Vagina Monologues*, by Eve Ensler; *Guide to Life*, by The Five Lesbian Brothers; *Noise From Underground*, by Michael Levine. Other clients include Richard Linklater, Gregg Araki, Tom DiCillo, Genvieve Turner/Rose Troche, Todd Solondz, Neil LaBute.

Terms: Agent receives 15% commission on domestic sales; 20% commission on foreign sales. Offers written contract, binding for 1 year; 6-week notice must be given to terminate contract. 100% of business is derived from commissions on ms sales.

Tips: "Be persistent but civilized."

ALISON J. PICARD, LITERARY AGENT, P.O. Box 2000, Cotuit MA 02635. (508)477-7192. Fax: (508)477-7192 (Please contact before faxing.). E-mail: ajpicard@aol.com. **Contact:** Alison Picard. Estab. 1985. Represents 48 clients. 30% of clients are new/unpublished writers. Currently handles: 40% nonfiction books; 40% novels; 20% juvenile books.

- Prior to becoming an agent, Ms. Picard was an assistant at an NYC literary agency.

Member Agents: Alison Picard (mysteries/suspense/thriller, romance, literary fiction, adult nonfiction, juvenile books).

Represents: Nonfiction books, novels, short story collections, novellas, juvenile books. **Considers these nonfiction areas:** Animals; anthropology/archaeology; art/architecture/design; biography/autobiography; business/economics; child guidance/parenting; cooking/foods/nutrition; current affairs; education; ethnic/cultural interests; gay/lesbian issues; government/politics/law; health/medicine; history; how-to; humor/satire; juvenile nonfiction; memoirs; military/war; money/finance; multicultural; music/dance; nature/environment; New Age/metaphysics; popular culture; psychology; religious/inspirational; science/technology; self-help/personal improvement; translation; travel; true crime/investigative; women's issues/studies; young adult. **Considers these fiction areas:** Action/adventure; contemporary issues; detective/police/crime; erotica; ethnic; experimental; family saga; feminist; gay/lesbian; glitz; historical; horror; humor/satire; juvenile; literary; mainstream/contemporary; multicultural; mystery/suspense; New Age; picture books; psychic/supernatural; regional; religious/inspirational; romance; sports; thriller; young adult.

"Many of my clients have come to me from big agencies, where they felt overlooked or ignored. I communicate freely with my clients, and offer a lot of career advice, suggestions for revising manuscripts, etc. If I believe in a project, I will submit it to a dozen or more publishers, unlike some agents who give up after 4 or 5 rejections." Actively seeking commercial adult fiction and nonfiction, middle grade juvenile fiction. Does not want to receive sci-fi/fantasy, westerns, poetry, plays, articles.

How to Contact: Query with SASE. Considers simultaneous queries. Responds in 1 week to queries; 6 weeks to mss. Returns materials only with SASE. Obtains most new clients through recommendations from others, solicitations.

Recent Sales: Sold 27 titles in the last year. *The Shade of My Own Tree*, by Sheila Williams (Ballantine); *The Boldness* *of Boys*, by Susan Strong (Andrews McMeel); *The Complete Bridal Shower Planner*, by Sharon Naylor (Prima); *Nicole Kidman*, by James Dickerson (Kensington/Citadel); *Pierce Brosnan*, by Peter Carrick (Kensington/Citadel). Other clients include Caryl Rivers, Osha Gray Davidson, Amy Dean, David Housewright, Nancy Means Wright.

Terms: Agent receives 15% commission on domestic sales; 20% commission on foreign sales. Offers written contract, binding for 1 year; 1 week notice must be given to terminate contract.

Tips: "Please don't send material without sending a query first via mail or e-mail. I don't accept phone or fax queries. Always enclose a SASE with a query."

PINDER LANE & GARON-BROOKE ASSOCIATES, LTD., 159 W. 53rd St., Suite 14E, New York NY 10019-6005. (212)489-0880. E-mail: pinderl@interport.net. **Contact:** Robert Thixton. Member of AAR; signatory of WGA. Represents 30 clients. 20% of clients are new/unpublished writers. Currently handles: 25% nonfiction books; 75% novels.

Member Agents: Nancy Coffey (contributing agent); Dick Duane; Robert Thixton.

Represents: Nonfiction books, novels. **Considers these fiction areas:** Contemporary issues; detective/police/crime; family saga; fantasy; gay/lesbian; literary; mainstream/contemporary; mystery/suspense; romance; science fiction.

This agency specializes in mainstream fiction and nonfiction. Does not want to receive screenplays, TV series teleplays or dramatic plays.

How to Contact: Query with SASE. No unsolicited mss. Responds in 3 weeks to queries; 2 months to mss. Obtains most new clients through referrals, queries.

Recent Sales: Sold 20 titles in the last year. *Diana & Jackie - Maidens, Mothers & Myths*, by Jay Mulvaney (St. Martin's Press); *The Sixth Fleet* (series), by David Meadows (Berkley); *Dark Fires*, by Rosemary Rogers (Mira Books).

Terms: Agent receives 15% commission on domestic sales; 30% commission on foreign sales. Offers written contract, binding for 3-5 years.

Tips: "With our literary and media experience, our agency is uniquely positioned for the current and future direction publishing is taking. Send query letter first giving the essence of the ms and a personal or career bio with SASE."

ARTHUR PINE ASSOCIATES, INC., 250 W. 57th St., Suite 417, New York NY 10019. (215)265-7330. Fax: (212)265-4650. Estab. 1966. Represents 100 clients. 25% of clients are new/unpublished writers. Currently handles: 60% nonfiction books; 40% novels.

Member Agents: Richard Pine; Catherine Drayton; Lori Andiman; Matthew Guma.

Represents: Nonfiction books, novels. **Considers these nonfiction areas:** Business/economics; current affairs; health/medicine; money/finance; psychology; self-help/personal improvement. **Considers these fiction areas:** Detective/police/crime; family saga; historical; literary; mainstream/contemporary; thriller.

How to Contact: Query with SASE, outline/proposal. Prefers to read materials exclusively. No e-mail or fax queries. Responds in 1 month to queries. Obtains most new clients through recommendations from others.

Recent Sales: Sold 60 titles in the last year.

Terms: Agent receives 15% commission on domestic sales; 15% commission on foreign sales. Offers written contract.

Tips: "Our agency will consider exclusive submissions only. All submissions must be accompanied by postage or SASE. Will not read manuscripts before receiving a letter of inquiry."

JULIE POPKIN, 15340 Albright St., #204, Pacific Palisades CA 90272-2520. (310)459-2834. **Contact:** Julie Popkin. Estab. 1989. Represents 35 clients. 30% of clients are new/unpublished writers. Currently handles: 70% nonfiction books; 30% novels.

- Prior to opening her agency, Ms. Popkin taught at the university level and did freelance editing and writing.

Member Agents: Julie Popkin; Margaret McCord (fiction, memoirs, biography); Linda Schubert (nonfiction).

Represents: Nonfiction books, novels, translations. **Considers these nonfiction areas:** Art/architecture/design; ethnic/cultural interests; government/politics/law; history; memoirs; philosophy; women's issues/studies (feminist); criticism. **Considers these fiction areas:** Literary; mainstream/contemporary; mystery/suspense.

This agency specializes in selling book-length mss including fiction and nonfiction. Especially interested in social issues, ethnic and minority subjects, Latin American authors. Does not want to receive New Age, spiritual, romance, science fiction.

How to Contact: Query with SASE. No e-mail or fax queries. Responds in 1 month to queries; 2 months to mss. Obtains most new clients through "Mostly clients find me through guides and personal contacts."

Recent Sales: Sold 8 titles in the last year. *Two Worlds in One*, by Virginia Li (Prometheus); *The Red and the Blacklist*, by Norma Barzman (Nation Books); *Planet Earth*, by P.K. Page (Godine).

Terms: Agent receives 15% commission on domestic sales; 20% commission on foreign sales; 10% commission on dramatic rights sales. Sometimes asks for fee if ms requires extensive copying and mailing.

Writers' Conferences: BEA (Los Angeles, June); Santa Barbara (June).

Tips: "Keep your eyes on the current market. Publishing responds to changes very quickly and often works toward perceived and fresh subject matter. Historical fiction seems to be rising in interest after a long quiet period."

ROBERT PRESKILL LITERARY AGENCY, Lit West Group LLC, 2130 Fillmore St., #313, San Francisco CA 94115. (415)346-9449. Fax: (415)820-7745. E-mail: literaryagent.geo@yahoo.com. Website: www.litwest.com. **Contact:** Robert Preskill, Esq. Member of Illinois Bar; Authors Guild. 10% of clients are new/unpublished writers. Currently handles: 50% nonfiction books; 40% novels; 10% story collections.

- Mr. Preskill formerly worked for McGraw-Hill Companies.

Member Agents: Agents of Lit West Group LLC: Robert Preskill (literary fiction, relevant nonfiction by "experts"); Katherine Boyle (pop-culture, psychology, literary fiction); Linda Mead (business, self-help, general nonfiction, selected works of fiction); Nancy Ellis (general nonfiction, reference, self-help, young adult, fiction).

Represents: Nonfiction books, novels, short story collections, novellas. **Considers these nonfiction areas:** Art/architecture/design; biography/autobiography; business/economics; current affairs; government/politics/law; history; how-to; humor/satire; interior design/decorating; language/literature/criticism; memoirs; military/war; money/finance; multicultural; music/dance; nature/environment; popular culture; psychology; self-help/personal improvement; sports; travel; true crime/investigative. **Considers these fiction areas:** Comic books/cartoon; detective/police/crime; literary; thriller.

O-ᴿ RPLA spends extra time editing and reviewing a work once it is chosen. Much of the time we will help chart a course toward publication by assisting with marketing ideas, submitting to literary magazines and other appropriate publications and through pursuit of sub-rights. Regarding fiction, looks for things grounded in personal storytelling, subtle and powerful action, politics, issues that illuminate a deeper layer of imagery; things that take dialog and the negative space of good dialog somewhere beyond the simple experience. There are plenty of stories that pass us by on a daily basis, but we fail to see them. I am interested in those stories in the world as it exists. Does not want fantasy, romance.

How to Contact: Query with SASE. *After* query, send 3 sample chapters with SASE. Considers simultaneous queries. Responds in 1 week to queries; 10 weeks to mss. Returns materials only with SASE. Obtains most new clients through recommendations from others, solicitations.

Recent Sales: Sold 10 titles and sold 2 options on scripts in the last year. *Instant Karma*, by Mark Swartz (City Lights Publishers); *Indigenous*, personal essays by Cris Mazza (City Lights Publishers); *Unititled Sports/Lifestyle Narrative*, by world class athelete Marla Streb (Plume); *Westerfield's Chain*, by Jack Clark(St. Martin's Press); *On the Homefront*, by Jack Clark and Mary Jo Clark (Plume); *Murder for Christmas*, (Morrow); *Esther Stories*, by Peter Orner (Houghton Mifflin); *Small World* (travel), by Brad Herzog (Simon & Schuster). Other clients include Dan Whipple, Robley Wilson, Alvin Greenberg, Robert Goldberg, Alexai Galaviz-Budzlszewski.

Terms: Agent receives 15% commission on domestic sales; 20% commission on foreign sales. Offers written contract; 30-day notice must be given to terminate contract. Charges clients for project related expenses only (such as postage and photocopying).

Writers' Conferences: Maui Writers Conference (Maui HI); Asilomar Writers Conference (Pacific Grove CA); Saroyan Writers Conferance (Fresno CA); Willamet Writers Conference (Portland OR).

Tips: "I was trained through the wonderful program at University of Illinois and learned from the writing of Mark Costello, William Gass, William Maxwell, Joy Williams, Grace Paley, Richard Ford, Joan Didion, Alice Munro, Mary Gaitskill, Nathaniel West, Steve Erickson and Thoms McGuane."

N **SUSAN ANN PROTTER, LITERARY AGENT**, 110 W. 40th St., Suite 1408, New York NY 10018. (212)840-0480. **Contact:** Susan Protter. Estab. 1971. Member of AAR. Represents 40 clients. 5% of clients are new/unpublished writers. Works with a very small number of new/previously unpublished authors Currently handles: 50% nonfiction books; 50% novels; occasional magazine article or short story (for established clients only).

- Prior to opening her agency, Ms. Protter was associate director of subsidiary rights at Harper & Row Publishers.

Represents: Nonfiction books, novels. **Considers these nonfiction areas:** Biography/autobiography; current affairs; health/medicine; memoirs; psychology; science/technology; international. **Considers these fiction areas:** Detective/police/crime; mystery/suspense; science fiction; thriller.

O-ᴿ Writers must have book-length project or manuscript that is ready to be sold. Does not want to receive westerns, romance, fantasy, children's books, young adult novels, screenplays, plays, poetry, Star Wars or Star Trek.

How to Contact: Currently looking for limited number of new clients. Send short query with SASE. No unsolicited manuscripts. Responds in 3 weeks to queries; 2 months to mss.

Recent Sales: *As Above, So Below*, by Rudy Rucker (Forge); *The Light Ages*, by Ian R. Macleod (Ace); *The Hard SF Renaissance*, edited by David G. Hartwell and Kathryn Cramer (Tor).

Terms: Agent receives 15% commission on domestic sales; 15% commission on dramatic rights sales. "If, after seeing your query, we request to see your manuscript, there will be a small shipping and handling fee requested to cover cost of returning materials should they not be suitable." Charges clients for photocopying, messenger, express mail, airmail and overseas shipping expenses.

Tips: "Please send neat and professionally organized queries. Make sure to include a SASE or we cannot reply. We receive approximately 200 queries a week and read them in the order they arrive. We usually reply within two weeks to any query. Please, do not call or email queries. If you are sending a multiple query, make sure to note that in your letter. I am looking for something outstanding in a large, difficult market."

N **QUICKSILVER BOOKS—LITERARY AGENTS**, 50 Wilson St., Hartsdale NY 10530-2542. (914)946-8748. Fax: (914)946-8748. Website: www.quicksilverbooks.com. **Contact:** Bob Silverstein. Estab. 1973 as packager; 1987 as literary agency. Represents 50 clients. 50% of clients are new/unpublished writers. Currently handles: 75% nonfiction books; 25% novels.

- Prior to opening his agency, Mr. Silverstein served as senior editor at Bantam Books and Dell Books/Delacorte Press.

Represents: Nonfiction books, novels. **Considers these nonfiction areas:** Anthropology/archaeology; biography/autobiography; business/economics; child guidance/parenting; cooking/foods/nutrition; current affairs; ethnic/cultural interests; health/medicine; history; how-to; language/literature/criticism; memoirs; nature/environment; New Age/metaphysics; popular culture; psychology; religious/inspirational; science/technology; self-help/personal improvement; sociology; sports; true crime/investigative; women's issues/studies. **Considers these fiction areas:** Action/adventure; glitz; mystery/suspense; thriller.

O-ᴿ This agency specializes in literary and commercial mainstream fiction and nonfiction (especially psychology, New

Age, holistic healing, consciousness, ecology, environment, spirituality, reference, cookbooks, narrative nonfiction). Actively seeking commercial mainstream fiction and nonfiction in most categories. Does not want to receive science fiction, pornography, poetry, or single-spaced manuscripts.

How to Contact: Query with SASE. Authors are expected to supply SASE for return of mss and for query letter responses. No e-mail or fax queries. Considers simultaneous queries. Responds in 2 weeks to queries; 1 month to mss. Returns materials only with SASE. Obtains most new clients through recommendations, listings in sourcebooks, solicitations, workshop participation.

Recent Sales: Sold over 20 titles in the last year. *The Look Great Naked Diet*, by Brad Schoenfeld (Putnam/Avery); *Zainabu's African Cookbook*, by Zainabu Kpaka Kallon (Dafina Books); *Tarot D'Amour*, by Kooch and Victor Daniels (Red Wheel/Weiser).

Terms: Agent receives 15% commission on domestic sales; 20% commission on foreign sales. Offers written contract. Charges clients for photocopying of mss and proposals, but prefers authors provide actual copies; foreign mailings of books and mss.

Writers' Conferences: National Writers Union Conference (Dobbs Ferry NY, April).

Tips: "Write what you know. Write from the heart. Publishers print. Authors sell."

SUSAN RABINER, LITERARY AGENT, INC., 240 W. 35 St., Suite 500, New York NY 10001-2506. (212)279-0316. Fax: (212)279-0932. E-mail: susan@rabiner.net. **Contact:** Susan Rabiner.

- Prior to becoming an agent, Susan Rabiner was editorial director of Basic Books, then the serious nonfiction division of HarperCollins Publishers. She is the co-author of *Thinking Like Your Editor: How to Write Great Serious Nonfiction and Get it Published* (W.W. Norton).

Member Agents: Susan Rabiner, Susan Arellano (formerly senior editor Basic Books, The Free Press).

Represents: Nonfiction books, textbooks. **Considers these nonfiction areas:** Biography/autobiography; business/economics; education; history; memoirs; psychology; science/technology.

Does not want to receive fiction, self-help.

How to Contact: Submit outline/proposal, SASE. Accepts e-mail queries. No fax queries. Considers simultaneous queries. Responds in 3 weeks to queries. Returns materials only with SASE. Obtains most new clients through recommendations from others.

Recent Sales: Sold 10-20 titles in the last year. *The Seduction of Difference*, by Roz Barnett and Caryl Rivers (Basic Books); *The Guns of June*, by Constantine Pleshakov (Houghton-Mifflin); *Trapped*, by Elizabeth Warren and Amelia Tyagi Warren (Basic Books). Other clients include Iris Chang, Lawrence Krauss, Daniel Schacter, Herbert Bix, Bruce Tulgan, Stephanie Coontz.

Terms: Agent receives 15% commission on domestic sales; 20% commission on foreign sales. Offers written contract; 30-day notice must be given to terminate contract.

HELEN REES LITERARY AGENCY, 123 N. Washington St., Boston MA 02114-2113. (617)227-9014, ext. 233 or 222. **Contact:** Joan Mazmanian, Ann Collette, Helen Rees. Estab. 1983. Member of AAR. Represents 80 clients. 50% of clients are new/unpublished writers. Currently handles: 60% nonfiction books; 40% novels.

Member Agents: Ann Collette (literary fiction, women's studies, health, biography, history); Helen Rees (business, money/finance/economics, government/politics/law, contemporary issues, literary fiction).

Represents: Nonfiction books, novels. **Considers these nonfiction areas:** Biography/autobiography; business/economics; current affairs; government/politics/law; health/medicine; history; money/finance; women's issues/studies. **Considers these fiction areas:** Contemporary issues; historical; literary; mainstream/contemporary; mystery/suspense; thriller.

How to Contact: Query with SASE, outline, 2 sample chapter(s). No e-mail or fax queries. Responds in 2-3 weeks to queries. Obtains most new clients through recommendations from others, solicitations, conferences.

Recent Sales: Sold 28 titles in the last year. *The Case for Israel*, by Alan Dershowitz (Wiley); *Why Businesses Fail*, by Sydney Finkelstein (Viking); *Remember Who You Are: Harvard Business Professors on Life and Leadership*, by Daisy Wademan (HBSP).

Terms: Agent receives 15% commission on domestic sales; 20% commission on foreign sales.

JODY REIN BOOKS, INC., 7741 S. Ash Court, Centennial CO 80122. (303)694-4430. Fax: (303)694-0687. Website: jodyreinbooks.com. **Contact:** Winnefred Dollar. Estab. 1994. Member of AAR, Authors Guild. Currently handles: 70% nonfiction books; 30% novels.

- Prior to opening her agency, Jody Rein worked for 13 years as an acquisitions editor for Contemporary Books, Bantam/Doubleday/Dell (executive editor) and Morrow/Avon (executive editor).

Member Agents: Jody Rein; Johnna Hietala.

Represents: Nonfiction books (primarily narrative and commercial nonfiction), novels (select literary novels, commercial mainstream and mystery). **Considers these nonfiction areas:** Business/economics; child guidance/parenting; current affairs; ethnic/cultural interests; government/politics/law; health/medicine; history; how-to; humor/satire; music/dance; nature/environment; popular culture; psychology; religious/inspirational; science/technology; self-help/personal improvement; sociology; theater/film; women's issues/studies. **Considers these fiction areas:** Literary; mainstream/contemporary; mystery/suspense.

This agency specializes in commercial and narrative nonfiction.

How to Contact: Query with SASE. No e-mail or fax queries. Considers simultaneous queries. Responds in 6 weeks to queries; 2 months to mss. Obtains most new clients through recommendations from others, solicitations.

Recent Sales: *8 Simple Rules for Dating My Teenage Daughter*, by Bruce Cameron (ABC/Disney); *The Lakota Way*, by Joseph Marshall III (Viking Penguin); *The Big Year*, by Mark Obmascik (The Free Press).

Terms: Agent receives 15% commission on domestic sales; 25% commission on foreign sales; 20% commission on dramatic rights sales. Offers written contract. Charges clients for express mail, overseas expenses, photocopying ms.
Tips: "Do your homework before submitting. Make sure you have a marketable topic and the credentials to write about it. Well-written books on fresh and original nonfiction topics that have broad appeal. Novels written by authors who have spent years developing their craft. Authors must be well established in their fields and have strong media experience."

JODIE RHODES LITERARY AGENCY, 8840 Villa La Jolla Dr., Suite 315, La Jolla CA 92037-1957. (858)625-0544. Fax: (858)625-0544. Website: www.writers.net and www.literaryagent.com. **Contact:** Jodie Rhodes, president. Estab. 1998. Member of AAR. Represents 50 clients. 60% of clients are new/unpublished writers. Currently handles: 60% nonfiction books; 35% novels; 5% middle to young adult books.

• Prior to opening her agency, Ms. Rhodes was a university level creative writing teacher, workshop director, published novelist and Vice President Media Director at the N.W. Ayer Advertising Agency.

Member Agents: Jodie Rhodes, president; Clark McCutcheon (fiction); Bob McCarter (nonfiction).
Represents: Nonfiction books, novels, juvenile books. **Considers these nonfiction areas:** Biography/autobiography; child guidance/parenting; ethnic/cultural interests; government/politics/law; health/medicine; history; memoirs; military/war; science/technology; women's issues/studies. **Considers these fiction areas:** Contemporary issues; ethnic; family saga; historical; juvenile; literary; mainstream/contemporary; mystery/suspense; thriller; young adult; women's.

O┳ Actively seeking "writers passionate about their books with a talent for richly textured narrative, an eye for details, and a nose for research." Nonfiction writers must have recognized credentials and expert knowledge of their subject matter. Does not want to receive erotica, horror, fantasy, romance, science fiction, children's books.

How to Contact: Query with brief synopsis, first 30 to 50 pages and SASE. No e-mail or fax queries. Considers simultaneous queries. Responds in 10 days to queries. Returns materials only with SASE. Obtains most new clients through recommendations from others, agent sourcebooks.
Recent Sales: Sold 25 titles in the last year. *For Material Purposes*, by Kavita Daswani (Putnam); *Tamina of the Chew*, by Denise Lamothe (Penguin); *Living in a Black & White World*, by Ann Pearlman (John Wiley & Sons).
Terms: Agent receives 15% commission on domestic sales; 20% commission on foreign sales. Offers written contract; 30-day notice must be given to terminate contract. Charges clients for fax, photocopying, phone calls and postage. "Charges are itemized and approved by writers upfront."
Writers' Conferences: Southern California Writers Conference (San Diego, mid-February); SDSU Writers Conference (San Diego, mid-January); Los Angeles Writers' Conference (Los Angeles, mid-October).
Tips: "Think your book out before you write it. Do your research, know your subject matter intimately, write vivid specifics, not bland generalities. Care deeply about your book. Don't imitate other writers. Find your own voice. We never take on a book we don't believe in, and we go the extra mile for our writers. We welcome talented new writers. We hold monthly weekend clinics on how to write a query letter and weekly writing workshops for area writers."

ANGELA RINALDI LITERARY AGENCY, P.O. Box 7877, Beverly Hills CA 90212-7877. (310)842-7665. Fax: (310)837-8143. E-mail: mail@rinaldiliterary.com. Estab. 1994. Member of AAR. Represents 50 clients. Currently handles: 40% nonfiction books; 60% novels.

• Prior to opening her agency, Ms. Rinaldi was an editor at NAL/Signet, Pocket Books and Bantam, and the Manager of Book Development for *The Los Angeles Times*.

Represents: Nonfiction books, novels, TV and motion picture rights for clients only. **Considers these nonfiction areas:** Biography/autobiography; business/economics; health/medicine; money/finance; self-help/personal improvement; true crime/investigative; women's issues/studies; books by journalists and academics. **Considers these fiction areas:** Literary; commercial; upmarket women's fiction; suspense.

O┳ Actively seeking commercial and literary fiction. Does not want to receive scripts, poetry, category romances, children's books, westerns, science fiction/fantasy, technothrillers and cookbooks.

How to Contact: For fiction: Send the first 3 chapters, brief synopsis, SASE. For nonfiction: Query with SASE first or send outline/proposal, SASE. Do not send metered mail as SASE. Considers simultaneous queries. Please advise if this is a multiple submission. Responds in 6 weeks to queries. Returns materials only with SASE.
Recent Sales: *Calling in the One You Love*, by Katherine Woodward Thomas (Ballantine); *Carrying a Little Extra: A Guide to Healthy Pregnancy for the Plus-Size Woman*, by Bernstein, Clark and Levine (Berkley); *Letters in the Attic*, by Bonnie Shimko (Academy).
Terms: Agent receives 15% commission on domestic sales; 20% commission on foreign sales. Offers written contract. Charges clients for photocopying if not provided by client.

N **ANN RITTENBERG LITERARY AGENCY, INC.**, 1201 Broadway, Suite 708, New York NY 10001. (212)684-6936. Fax: (212)684-6929. **Contact:** Ann Rittenberg, president. Agent: Ted Gideonse. Estab. 1992. Member of AAR. Represents 35 clients. 40% of clients are new/unpublished writers. Currently handles: 50% nonfiction books; 50% novels.
Represents: Nonfiction books, novels. **Considers these nonfiction areas:** Biography/autobiography; gay/lesbian issues; history (social/cultural); memoirs; women's issues/studies. **Considers these fiction areas:** Literary.

O┳ This agent specializes in literary fiction and literary nonfiction.

How to Contact: Submit outline, 3 sample chapter(s), SASE. Considers simultaneous queries. Responds in 6 weeks to queries; 2 months to mss. Obtains most new clients through referrals from established writers and editors.
Recent Sales: Sold 20 titles in the last year. *Seven Blessings*, by Ruchama King (St. Martin's Press 2003); *All Hat*, by Brad Smith (Holt 2003); *Meena, Heroine of Afghanistan* (St. Martin's Press 2003).
Terms: Agent receives 15% commission on domestic sales; 20% commission on foreign sales. Offers written contract. Charges clients for photocopying only.

RIVERSIDE LITERARY AGENCY, 1052 Weatherhead Hollow, Guilford VT 05301. (802)257-2677. Fax: (802)257-8907. E-mail: rivlit@sover.net. **Contact:** Susan Lee Cohen. Estab. 1991. Represents 40 clients. 20% of clients are new/unpublished writers.

Represents: Nonfiction books (adult), novels (adult), very selective.

How to Contact: Query with SASE, outline. Accepts e-mail queries. No fax queries. Considers simultaneous queries. Responds in 1 month to queries. Obtains most new clients through referrals.

Recent Sales: Sold 14 titles in the last year. *Letters to a Young Therapist*, by Mary Pipher, Ph.D. (Basic Books); *The Devil You Know*, by Martha Stout, Ph.D. (Broadway); *Letting Go of the Person You Used to Be*, by Lama Surya Das (Doubleday Broadway).

Terms: Agent receives 15% commission on domestic sales. Offers written contract. Charges clients for foreign postage, photocopying large manuscripts, express mail deliveries, etc.

RLR ASSOCIATES, LTD., Literary Department, 7 W. 51st St., New York NY 10019. (212)541-8641. Fax: (212)541-6052. Website: www.rlrassociates.net/literary. **Contact:** Jennifer Unter, Ezra Fitz. Represents 50 clients. 25% of clients are new/unpublished writers. Currently handles: 70% nonfiction books; 25% novels; 5% story collections.

Member Agents: Jennifer Unter, Ezra Fitz.

Represents: Nonfiction books, novels, short story collections, scholarly books. **Considers these nonfiction areas:** Animals; anthropology/archaeology; art/architecture/design; biography/autobiography; business/economics; child guidance/parenting; cooking/foods/nutrition; current affairs; education; ethnic/cultural interests; gay/lesbian issues; government/politics/law; health/medicine; history; humor/satire; interior design/decorating; language/literature/criticism; memoirs; money/finance; multicultural; music/dance; nature/environment; photography; popular culture; psychology; religious/inspirational; science/technology; self-help/personal improvement; sociology; sports; translation; travel; true crime/investigative; women's issues/studies. **Considers these fiction areas:** Action/adventure; comic books/cartoon; contemporary issues; detective/police/crime; ethnic; experimental; family saga; feminist; gay/lesbian; historical; horror; humor/satire; literary; mainstream/contemporary; multicultural; mystery/suspense; sports; thriller.

"We provide a lot of editorial assistance to our clients and have connections." Actively seeking fiction (all types except for romance and fantasy), current affairs, history, art, popular culture, health, business. Does not want to receive romance or fantasy; screenplays.

How to Contact: Query with SASE. Considers simultaneous queries. Responds in 5 weeks to queries; 5 weeks to mss. Returns materials only with SASE. Obtains most new clients through recommendations from others.

Recent Sales: Sold 20 titles in the last year. Clients include Shelby Foote, The Grief Recovery Institute, Don Wade, Don Zimmer, The Knot.com, David Plowder, PGA of America, Danny Peary, Jahnna Beecham & Malcolm Hillgartner.

Terms: Agent receives 15% commission on domestic sales; 20% commission on foreign sales. Offers written contract.

Tips: "Please check out our website for more details on our agency. No e-mail submissions please."

B.J. ROBBINS LITERARY AGENCY, 5130 Bellaire Ave., North Hollywood CA 91607-2908. (818)760-6602. Fax: (818)760-6616. E-mail: robbinsliterary@aol.com. **Contact:** (Ms.) B.J. Robbins. Estab. 1992. Member of Board of Directors, PEN American Center West. Represents 40 clients. 50% of clients are new/unpublished writers. Currently handles: 50% nonfiction books; 50% novels.

Member Agents: Rob McAndrews (commercial fiction).

Represents: Nonfiction books, novels. **Considers these nonfiction areas:** Biography/autobiography; child guidance/parenting; current affairs; ethnic/cultural interests; health/medicine; how-to; humor/satire; memoirs; music/dance; popular culture; psychology; self-help/personal improvement; sociology; sports; theater/film; true crime/investigative; women's issues/studies. **Considers these fiction areas:** Contemporary issues; detective/police/crime; ethnic; literary; mainstream/contemporary; mystery/suspense; sports; thriller.

How to Contact: Submit 3 sample chapter(s), outline/proposal, SASE. No e-mail or fax queries. Considers simultaneous queries. Responds in 2 weeks to queries; 6 weeks to mss. Returns materials only with SASE. Obtains most new clients through conferences, referrals.

Recent Sales: Sold 15 titles in the last year. *Please, Please, Please*, by Renee Swindle (Dial Press); *Katie.com*, by Katherine Tarbox (Dutton); *Quickening*, by Laura Catherine Brown (Random House/Ballantine); *Snow Mountain Passage*, by James D. Houston (Knopf); *The Last Summer*, by John Hough, Jr. (Simon & Schuster).

Terms: Agent receives 15% commission on domestic sales; 20% commission on foreign sales. Offers written contract; 3-month notice must be given to terminate contract. 100% of business is derived from commissions on ms sales. Charges clients for postage and photocopying only. Writers charged for fees only after the sale of ms.

Writers' Conferences: Squaw Valley Fiction Writers Workshop (Squaw Valley CA, August); Maui Writers Conference (Maui HI); SDSU Writers Conference (San Diego CA, January).

LINDA ROGHAAR LITERARY AGENCY, INC., 133 High Point Dr., Amherst MA 01002. (413)256-1921. Fax: (413)256-2636. E-mail: contact@lindaroghaar.com. Website: www.lindaroghaar.com. **Contact:** Linda L. Roghaar. Estab. 1996. Represents 50 clients. 40% of clients are new/unpublished writers. Currently handles: 90% nonfiction books; 10% novels.

- Prior to opening her agency, Ms. Roghaar worked in retail bookselling for 5 years and as a publishers' sales rep for 15 years.

Represents: Nonfiction books, novels. **Considers these nonfiction areas:** Animals; anthropology/archaeology; biography/autobiography; education; history; nature/environment; popular culture; religious/inspirational; self-help/personal improvement; women's issues/studies. **Considers these fiction areas:** Mystery/suspense (amateur sleuth, cozy, culinary, malice domestic).

How to Contact: Query with SASE. Accepts e-mail queries. No fax queries. Considers simultaneous queries. Responds in 2 months to queries; 4 months to mss.

Recent Sales: *Refrigerator Rights*, by Dr. Will Miller (Penguin Putnam/Perigee); *White China*, by Molly Wolf (Jossey-Bass); *Crooked Heart*, by Cristina Sumners (Bantam).

Terms: Agent receives 15% commission on domestic sales; negotiable commission on foreign sales. Offers written contract, binding for negotiable time.

THE ROSENBERG GROUP, 23 Lincoln Ave., Marblehead MA 01945. (781)990-1341. Fax: (781)990-1344. Website: www.rosenberggroup.com. **Contact:** Barbara Collins Rosenberg. Estab. 1998. Member of AAR, Recognized agent of the RWA. Represents 32 clients. 50% of clients are new/unpublished writers. Currently handles: 30% nonfiction books; 30% novels; 10% scholarly books; 30% textbooks.

- Prior to becoming an agent, Barbara was a senior editor for Harcourt.

Member Agents: Barbara Collins Rosenberg.

Represents: Nonfiction books, novels, textbooks. **Considers these nonfiction areas:** Current affairs; memoirs; popular culture; psychology; women's issues/studies; women's health, food/wine/beverages, autobiography. **Considers these fiction areas:** Literary; romance; women's.

"Barbara is well versed in the romance market (both category and single title). She is a frequent speaker at romance conferences. Actively seeking romance category or single title in contemporary "chick-lit," romantic suspense and the historical sub-genres. Does not want to receive time-travel, paranormal, or inspirational/spiritual romances.

How to Contact: Query with SASE. No e-mail or fax queries. Responds in 2 weeks to queries; 4-6 weeks to mss. Returns materials only with SASE. Obtains most new clients through recommendations from others, solicitations, conferences.

Recent Sales: Sold 26 titles in the last year.

Terms: Agent receives 15% commission on domestic sales; 15% commission on foreign sales. Offers written contract; 30 days notice must be given to terminate contract. Postage and photocopying limit of $350 per year.

Writers' Conferences: RWA Annual Conference (New York City, July 2003); Silicon Valley Romance Writers of America (October 2003).

RITA ROSENKRANZ LITERARY AGENCY, 440 West End Ave., Suite 15D, New York NY 10024-5358. (212)873-6333. **Contact:** Rita Rosenkranz. Estab. 1990. Member of AAR. Represents 30 clients. 20% of clients are new/unpublished writers. Currently handles: 98% nonfiction books; 2% novels.

- Prior to opening her agency, Rita Rosenkranz worked as an editor in major New York publishing houses.

Represents: Nonfiction books. **Considers these nonfiction areas:** Animals; anthropology/archaeology; art/architecture/design; biography/autobiography; business/economics; child guidance/parenting; computers/electronic; cooking/foods/nutrition; crafts/hobbies; current affairs; ethnic/cultural interests; gay/lesbian issues; government/politics/law; health/medicine; history; how-to; humor/satire; interior design/decorating; language/literature/criticism; military/war; money/finance; music/dance; nature/environment; New Age/metaphysics; photography; popular culture; psychology; religious/inspirational; science/technology; self-help/personal improvement; sports; theater/film; women's issues/studies.

"This agency focuses on adult nonfiction. Stresses strong editorial development and refinement before submitting to publishers, and brainstorms ideas with authors." Actively seeking authors "who are well paired with their subject, either for professional or personal reasons."

How to Contact: Submit proposal package, outline, SASE. No e-mail or fax queries. Considers simultaneous queries. Responds in 2 weeks to queries. Obtains most new clients through solicitations, conferences, word of mouth.

Recent Sales: Sold 35 titles in the last year. *Life in a Bowl of Soup*, by Pat Solley (Three Rivers/Crown); *Inside Songwriting*, by Jason Blume (Billboard Books); *Wolf Pack*, by Steven T. Smith (Wiley).

Terms: Agent receives 15% commission on domestic sales; 20% commission on foreign sales. Offers written contract, binding for 3 years; 60-day written notice must be given to terminate contract. 100% of business is derived from commissions on ms sales. Charges clients for photocopying. Makes referrals to editing service.

Tips: "Identify the current competition for your project to make sure the project is valid. A strong cover letter is very important."

THE GAIL ROSS LITERARY AGENCY, 1666 Connecticut Ave. NW, #500, Washington DC 20009. (202)328-3282. Fax: (202)328-9162. E-mail: jennifer@gailross.com. Website: www.gailross.com. **Contact:** Jennifer Manguera. Estab. 1988. Member of AAR. Represents 200 clients. 75% of clients are new/unpublished writers. Currently handles: 95% nonfiction books; 5% novels.

Member Agents: Gail Ross.

Represents: Nonfiction books, novels. **Considers these nonfiction areas:** Anthropology/archaeology; biography/autobiography; business/economics; education; ethnic/cultural interests; gay/lesbian issues; government/politics/law; health/medicine; money/finance; nature/environment; psychology; religious/inspirational; science/technology; self-help/personal improvement; sociology; sports; true crime/investigative. **Considers these fiction areas:** Literary.

This agency specializes in adult trade nonfiction.

How to Contact: Query with SASE. Considers simultaneous queries. Responds in 1 month to queries. Obtains most new clients through recommendations from others.

Recent Sales: Sold 50 titles in the last year. This agency prefers not to share information on specific sales.

Terms: Agent receives 15% commission on domestic sales; 25% commission on foreign sales. Charges for office expenses (i.e., postage, copying).

CAROL SUSAN ROTH, LITERARY, (Specialized: health, business, spirituality, self-help), PO Box 620337, Woodside CA 94062. (650)323-3795. E-mail: carol@authorsbest.com. **Contact:** Carol Susan Roth. Estab. 1995. Represents 40 clients. 50% of clients are new/unpublished writers. Currently handles: 100% nonfiction books.

- Prior to becoming and agent, Ms. Roth was trained as a psychotherapist and worked as a motivational coach, conference producer and promoter for bestselling authors (e.g. Scott Peck, Bernie Siegal, John Gray) and the Heart of Business conference.

Represents: Nonfiction books. **Considers these nonfiction areas:** Business/economics; health/medicine; money/finance (personal finance/investing); religious/inspirational; self-help/personal improvement; spirituality; yoga; Buddhism.

This agency specializes in spirituality, health, personal growth, personal finance, business. Actively seeking previously published authors—experts in health, spirituality, personal growth, business with an established audience. Does not want to receive fiction.

How to Contact: Submit proposal package, media kit, promotional video, SASE. Accepts e-mail queries, no attachments please. Considers simultaneous queries. Responds in 1 week to queries. Returns materials only with SASE. Obtains most new clients through recommendations from others, solicitations.

Recent Sales: Sold 15 titles in the last year. *The Infertility Cure*, by Randine Lewis (Little, Brown); *Dojo Wisdom*, by Jennifer Lawler (Viking); *Pilates Fusion*, by Shirely Archer (Chronicle Books).

Terms: Agent receives 15% commission on domestic sales; 15% commission on foreign sales. Offers written contract, binding for 3 years; 60-day notice must be given to terminate contract. This agency "asks the client to provide postage and do copying." Offers a proposal development and marketing consulting service on request. Service is separate from agenting services.

Writers' Conferences: Maui Writer's Conference (Maui HI, September).

Tips: "Have charisma, content, and credentials—solve an old problem in a new way. I prefer clients with extensive seminar and media experience."

THE PETER RUBIE LITERARY AGENCY, 240 W. 35th St., Suite 500, New York NY 10001. (212)279-1776. Fax: (212)279-0927. E-mail: peterrubie@prlit.com. Website: www.prlit.com. **Contact:** Peter Rubie or June Clark (pralit@aol.com). Estab. 2000. Member of AAR. Represents 130 clients. 30% of clients are new/unpublished writers.

- Prior to opening his agency, Mr. Rubie was a founding partner of another literary agency at Perkins, Rubie & Associates and the fiction editor at Walker and Co.

Member Agents: June Clark (nonfiction consisting of celebrity biographies, commercial, traditional, alternative health, parenting pets, women's issues, teen nonfiction, how-to, self-help, offbeat business, food/wine, New Age, pop culture, gay issues); Peter Rubie (crime, science fiction, fantasy, literary fiction, thrillers, narrative nonfiction, business, self-help, how-to, popular, food/wine, history, commercial science, music).

Represents: Nonfiction books, novels. **Considers these nonfiction areas:** Cooking/foods/nutrition; creative nonfiction; current affairs; ethnic/cultural interests; music/dance; popular culture; science/technology; theater/film; commercial academic material; TV business; self-help; how-to; pop culture; food/wine. **Considers these fiction areas:** Action/adventure; detective/police/crime; ethnic; fantasy; gay/lesbian; historical; literary; science fiction; thriller.

How to Contact: Query with SASE. Responds in 2 months to queries; 3 months to mss. Returns materials only with SASE. Obtains most new clients through recommendations from others.

Recent Sales: Sold 30 titles in the last year. *The Emperor and the Wolf*, by Stuart Galbraith (Faber and Faber); *The Maquisarde*, by Louise Marley; *An Askew View: The Films of Kevin Smith*, by John Muir (Applause).

Terms: Agent receives 15% commission on domestic sales; 20% commission on foreign sales. Offers written contract. Charges clients for photocopying and some foreign mailings.

Tips: "We look for writers who are experts, have a strong platform and reputation in their field and have an outstanding prose style. Be professional. Subscribe to PublishersLunch.com. Read *Publishers Weekly* and genre-related magazines. Join writers' organizations. Go to conferences. Know your market, and learn your craft. Read Rubie's books *The Elements of Storytelling* (Wiley) and *The Writer's Market FAQs* (Writer's Digest Books). Go to our Web site for up-to-date information on clients and sales."

REGINA RYAN PUBLISHING ENTERPRISES, INC., 251 Central Park W., 7D, New York NY 10024. (212)787-5589. E-mail: queryreginaryanbooks@rcn.com. **Contact:** Regina Ryan. Estab. 1976. Currently handles: 90% nonfiction books; 5% novels; 5% juvenile books.

- Prior to becoming an agent, Ms. Ryan was an editor at Alfred A. Knopf, editor-in-chief of Macmillan Adult Trade, and a book producer.

Represents: Nonfiction books, novels, short story collections, juvenile books.

How to Contact: Query only by e-mail or mail with SASE. No telephone queries. Considers simultaneous queries. Responds in 1 month to queries. Returns materials only with SASE. Obtains most new clients through recommendations from others.

Recent Sales: *The Altruist*, by Walter Keady (Macadam/Cage); *Surviving Hitler*, by Andrea Warren (HarperCollins Books for Young Readers); *The Harlem Renaissance*, by Lionel Bascom (Sourcebooks/A Mediafusion Book).

Terms: Agent receives 15% commission on domestic sales; 15% commission on foreign sales. Offers written contract; 1 month, negotiable notice must be given to terminate contract. Charges clients for all out of pocket expenses, such as long distance, messengers, freight, copying, "if it's more than just a nominal amount."

Tips: "For nonfiction proposals, an analysis of the competition is essential; a sample chapter is helpful. For a fiction query, the first 10 pages are essential."

THE SAGALYN AGENCY, 7201 Bethesda Ave., Suite 675, Bethesda MD 20814. (301)718-6440. Fax: (310)718-6444. E-mail: agency@sagalyn.com. Website: sagalyn.com. **Contact:** Rebeca Sagalyn. Estab. 1980. Member of AAR. Currently handles: 85% nonfiction books; 5% novels; 10% scholarly books.
Member Agents: Raphael Sagalyn, Rebeca Sagalyn.
Represents: Nonfiction books (history, science, business).
Does not want to receive stage plays, screenplays, poetry, science fiction, romance, children's books or young adult books.
How to Contact: Please send e-mail queries only, no attachments. Include one of these words in subject line: Query, submission, inquiry. Response time depends on number of current queries, generally within 3 weeks.
Recent Sales: See website for sales information.
Tips: "We receive between 1,000-1,200 queries a year, which in turn lead to two or three new clients."

VICTORIA SANDERS & ASSOCIATES, 241 Ave. of the Americas, New York NY 10014-4822. (212)633-8811. Fax: (212)633-0525. E-mail: queriesvsa@hotmail.com. Website: www.victoriasanders.com. **Contact:** Victoria Sanders or Diane Dickensheid. Estab. 1993. Member of AAR; signatory of WGA. Represents 75 clients. 25% of clients are new/unpublished writers. Currently handles: 50% nonfiction books; 50% novels.
Member Agents: Imani Wilson (assistant literary agent).
Represents: Nonfiction books, novels. **Considers these nonfiction areas:** Biography/autobiography; current affairs; ethnic/cultural interests; gay/lesbian issues; government/politics/law; history; humor/satire; language/literature/criticism; music/dance; popular culture; psychology; theater/film; translation; women's issues/studies. **Considers these fiction areas:** Action/adventure; contemporary issues; ethnic; family saga; feminist; gay/lesbian; literary; thriller.
How to Contact: Query with SASE. Considers simultaneous queries. Responds in 3 weeks to queries; 1 month to mss. Returns materials only with SASE. Obtains most new clients through recommendations from others, or "I find them through my reading and pursue."
Recent Sales: Sold 20 titles in the last year. *Incredible*, by Karin Slaughter (Morrow); *When Love Calls, You Better Answer*, by Bertice Berry (Doubleday).
Terms: Agent receives 15% commission on domestic sales; 20% commission on foreign sales. Offers written contract. Charges for photocopying, ms, messenger, express mail and extraordinary fees. If in excess of $100, client approval is required.
Tips: "Limit query to letter, no calls, and give it your best shot. A good query is going to get a good response."

SANDUM & ASSOCIATES, 144 E. 84th St., New York NY 10028-2035. (212)737-2011. Fax: (on request). **Contact:** Howard E. Sandum, managing director. Estab. 1987. Represents 35 clients. 20% of clients are new/unpublished writers. Currently handles: 80% nonfiction books; 20% novels.
Represents: Nonfiction books, novels (literary). **Considers these fiction areas:** Literary.
This agency specializes in general nonfiction.
How to Contact: Query with proposal, sample pages and SASE. Do not send full ms unless requested. Responds in 2 weeks to queries.
Terms: Agent receives 15% commission on domestic sales; adjustable commission on foreign sales; adjustable commission on dramatic rights sales. Charges clients for photocopying, air express, long-distance telephone/fax.

SCHIAVONE LITERARY AGENCY, INC., 236 Trails End, West Palm Beach FL 33413-2135. (561)966-9294. Fax: (561)966-9294. E-mail: profschia@aol.com. Website: www.freeyellow.com/members8/schiavone/index.html. **Contact:** James Schiavone, Ed.D. Estab. 1996. Member of National Education Association. Represents 40 clients. 2% of clients are new/unpublished writers. Currently handles: 50% nonfiction books; 49% novels; 1% textbooks.
- Prior to opening his agency, Dr. Schiavone was a full professor of development skills at the City University of New York and author of 5 trade books and 3 textbooks.

Represents: Nonfiction books, novels, juvenile books, scholarly books, textbooks, movie scripts, feature film, TV movie of the week. **Considers these nonfiction areas:** Animals; anthropology/archaeology; biography/autobiography; child guidance/parenting; current affairs; education; ethnic/cultural interests; gay/lesbian issues; government/politics/law; health/medicine; history; how-to; humor/satire; juvenile nonfiction; language/literature/criticism; military/war; nature/environment; popular culture; psychology; science/technology; self-help/personal improvement; sociology; true crime/investigative. **Considers these fiction areas:** Contemporary issues; ethnic; family saga; historical; horror; humor/satire; juvenile; literary; mainstream/contemporary; science fiction; young adult.
This agency specializes in celebrity biography and autobiography. "We have a management division that handles motion picture and TV rights." Actively seeking serious nonfiction, literary fiction and celebrity biography. Does not want to receive poetry.
How to Contact: Query with SASE. Considers one page e-mail queries with no attachments. Does not accept phone or fax queries. Considers simultaneous queries. Responds in 2 weeks to queries; 6 weeks to mss. Returns materials only with SASE. Obtains most new clients through recommendations from others, solicitations, conferences.
Terms: Agent receives 15% commission on domestic sales; 20% commission on foreign sales. Offers written contract, binding for project period; written notice must be given to terminate contract. Charges clients for long distance, photocopying, postage, special handling. Dollar amount varies with each project depending on level of activity.
Writers' Conferences: Key West Literary Seminar (Key West FL, January); South Florida Writer's Conference (Miami FL, May).
Tips: "I prefer to work with established authors published by major houses in New York. I will consider marketable proposals from new/previously unpublished writers."

N **SUSAN SCHULMAN, A LITERARY AGENCY, (Specialized: health, business, public policy, self-help, women's issues)**, 454 W. 44th St., New York NY 10036-5205. (212)713-1633/4/5. Fax: (212)581-8830. E-mail: schulman@aol.com. Website: www.susanschulmanagency.com. **Contact:** Susan Schulman, president. Estab. 1979. Member of AAR, Dramatists Guild, Women's Media Group; signatory of WGA. 10-15% of clients are new/unpublished writers. Currently handles: 70% nonfiction books; 20% novels; 10% stage plays.

Member Agents: Susan Schulman (self-help, health, business, spirituality); Christine Morin (children's books, ecology, natural sciences and business books); Bryan Leifert (plays and pitches for films).

Represents: Nonfiction books, novels. **Considers these nonfiction areas:** Anthropology/archaeology; biography/autobiography; child guidance/parenting; current affairs; education; ethnic/cultural interests; gay/lesbian issues; government/politics/law; health/medicine; history; how-to; juvenile nonfiction; money/finance; music/dance; nature/environment; popular culture; psychology; self-help/personal improvement; sociology; theater/film; translation; true crime/investigative; women's issues/studies. **Considers these fiction areas:** Contemporary issues; detective/police/crime; gay/lesbian; historical; literary; mainstream/contemporary; mystery/suspense; young adult. **Considers these script subject areas:** Comedy; contemporary issues; detective/police/crime; feminist; historical; mainstream; mystery/suspense; psychic/supernatural; teen.

O→ This agency specializes in books for, by and about women's issues including family, careers, health and spiritual development, business and sociology, history and economics. Emphasizing contemporary women's fiction and nonfiction books of interest to women.

How to Contact: Query with SASE, outline/proposal, SASE. Accepts e-mail and fax queries. Considers simultaneous queries. Responds in 1 week to queries; 6 weeks to mss. Returns materials only with SASE.

Recent Sales: Sold 30 titles in the last year. *Prayers for a Non-Believer*, by Julia Cameron (Putnam); *The Half-Empty Heart*, by Alan Downs (St. Martin's Press); *The Walls Around Us*, by David Owen (Simon & Schuster). ***Movie/TV MOW script(s) optioned/sold:*** *In the Skin of a Lion*, by Michael Ondaatje (Serendipity Parent Productions); *Holes*, by Louis Sachar (Phoenix Pictures); *Sideways Stories from Wayside School*, by Louis Sachar (Len Oliver Productions).

Terms: Agent receives 15% commission on domestic sales; 7½-10% (plus 7½-10% to co-agent) commission on foreign sales; 10-20% commission on dramatic rights sales. Charges client for special messenger or copying services, foreign mail and any other service requested by client.

N **LAURENS R. SCHWARTZ AGENCY**, 5 E. 22nd St., Suite 15D, New York NY 10010-5325. (212)228-2614. **Contact:** Laurens R. Schwartz. Estab. 1984. Represents 100 clients.

Represents: Nonfiction books, novels, general mix of nonfiction and fiction. Also handles movie and TV tie-ins, licensing and merchandising.

How to Contact: Query with SASE. No unsolicited mss. Responds in 1 month to queries. "Have had 18 best-sellers."

Terms: Agent receives 15% commission on domestic sales; 25% commission on foreign sales. "No client fees except for photocopying, and that fee is avoided by an author providing necessary copies or, in certain instances, transferring files on diskette or by e-mail attachment." Where necessary to bring a project into publishing form, editorial work and some rewriting provided as part of service. Works with authors on long-term career goals and promotion.

Tips: "I do not like receiving mass mailings sent to all agents. I am extremely selective—only take on one to three new clients a year. Do not send everything you have ever written. Choose one work and promote that. Always include an SASE. Never send your only copy. Always include a background sheet on yourself and a one-page synopsis of the work (too many summaries end up being as long as the work)."

SCOVIL CHICHAK GALEN LITERARY AGENCY, 381 Park Ave. S., Suite 1020, New York NY 10016. (212)679-8686. Fax: (212)679-6710. E-mail: mailroom@scglit.com. **Contact:** Russell Galen. Estab. 1993. Member of AAR. Represents 300 clients. Currently handles: 70% nonfiction books; 30% novels.

Member Agents: Russell Galen; Jack Scovil; Anna Ghosh.

How to Contact: Accepts e-mail and fax queries. Considers simultaneous queries.

Recent Sales: Sold 100 titles in the last year. *Across the Black Waters*, by Minai Hajratwala (Houghton Mifflin); *The Secret*, by Walter Anderson (HarperCollins); *The Pillars of Creation*, by Terry Goodkind (Tor); *In The Hand of Dante*, by Nick Tosches (Little, Brown).

Terms: Charges clients for photocopying and postage.

N **SEDGEBAND LITERARY ASSOCIATES**, 7312 Martha Lane, Fort Worth TX 76112. (817)496-3652. Fax: (425)952-9518. E-mail: queries@sedgeband.com. Website: www.sedgeband.com. **Contact:** David Duperre or Ginger Norton. Estab. 1997. 50% of clients are new/unpublished writers. Currently handles: 50% nonfiction books; 50% fiction novels.

Member Agents: David Duperre (literary, scripts, mystery, suspense); Ginger Norton (romance, horror, nonfiction, mainstream/contemporary).

Represents: Nonfiction books, novels, novellas. **Considers these nonfiction areas:** Biography/autobiography; ethnic/cultural interests; history; true crime/investigative. **Considers these fiction areas:** Action/adventure; experimental; horror; literary; mainstream/contemporary; mystery/suspense; romance.

O→ This agency is looking for talented writers who have patience and are willing to work hard. Actively seeking new nonfiction writers, some fiction.

How to Contact: Query with SASE. No phone queries accepted. No full mss. Accepts e-mail queries with no attachments; repsonds in 1 week. Responds in 4 months to written queries Responds in 4 months to requested mss. Returns materials only with SASE. Obtains most new clients through queries, the Internet, referrals.

Recent Sales: Sold 28 titles in the last year. *The Torso Murders of Victorian London*, (Mcfarland); *Kiss Me, Kat*, (Lionhearted); *Silent Screams* (Gardenia Press).

Terms: Agent receives 15% commission on domestic sales; 20% commission on foreign sales. Offers written contract,

binding for 1 year; 30-day written notice must be given to terminate contract. Charges clients for postage, photocopies, long distance calls, etc., "until we make a sale to an established publisher. We do not charge any reading or retainer fees."

Tips: "We care about writers and books, not just money, but we care about the industry as well. We will not represent anyone who might hurt our clients or our reputation. We expect our writers to work hard and to be patient. Do not send a rude query, it will get you nowhere. If we ask to see your book, send it as soon as possible. Don't wait around or ask a bunch of irrelevant questions about movie rights and so forth, *(at this point we haven't even offered to represent you!)*. If you can't write a synopsis, don't bother to query us. Don't handwrite your query or send us samples of your writing that are handwritten - we won't read any of it. Be professional."

LYNN SELIGMAN, LITERARY AGENT, 400 Highland Ave., Upper Montclair NJ 07043. (973)783-3631. **Contact:** Lynn Seligman. Estab. 1985. Member of Women's Media Group. Represents 32 clients. 15% of clients are new/unpublished writers. Currently handles: 85% nonfiction books; 15% novels.

- Prior to opening her agency, Ms. Seligman worked in the subsidiary rights department of Doubleday and Simon & Schuster, and served as an agent with Julian Bach Literary Agency (now IMG Literary Agency).

Represents: Nonfiction books, novels. **Considers these nonfiction areas:** Anthropology/archaeology; art/architecture/design; biography/autobiography; business/economics; child guidance/parenting; cooking/foods/nutrition; current affairs; education; ethnic/cultural interests; government/politics/law; health/medicine; history; how-to; humor/satire; interior design/decorating; language/literature/criticism; money/finance; music/dance; nature/environment; photography; popular culture; psychology; science/technology; self-help/personal improvement; sociology; theater/film; true crime/investigative; women's issues/studies. **Considers these fiction areas:** Detective/police/crime; ethnic; fantasy; feminist; gay/lesbian; historical; horror; humor/satire; literary; mainstream/contemporary; mystery/suspense; romance (contemporary, gothic, historical, regency); science fiction.

This agency specializes in "general nonfiction and fiction. I do illustrated and photography books and represent several photographers for books." This agency does not handle children or young adult books.

How to Contact: Query with SASE, 1 sample chapter(s), outline/proposal. Prefers to read materials exclusively. No e-mail or fax queries. Considers simultaneous queries. Responds in 2 weeks to queries; 2 months to mss. Returns materials only with SASE. Obtains most new clients through referrals from other writers or editors.

Recent Sales: Sold 10 titles in the last year. *Tempting a Lady and a Lady's Heart*, by Barbara Pierce; *Treating Children in Their Family Contexts*, by Dr. Peter Goldenthal.

Terms: Agent receives 15% commission on domestic sales; 25% commission on foreign sales. Charges clients for photocopying, unusual postage or telephone expenses (checking first with the author), express mail.

SERENDIPITY LITERARY AGENCY, LLC, 732 Fulton St., Suite 3, Brooklyn NY 11238. (718)230-7689. Fax: (718)230-7689. E-mail: rbrooks@serendipitylit.com. Website: www.serendipitylit.com. **Contact:** Regina Brooks. Estab. 2000. Represents 30 clients. 20% of clients are new/unpublished writers. Currently handles: 60% nonfiction books; 40% novels.

- Prior to becoming an agent, Ms. Brooks was an acquisitions editor for John Wiley & Sons, Inc. and McGraw-Hill Companies.

Represents: Nonfiction books, novels, children's/juvenile books, scholarly books, textbooks. **Considers these nonfiction areas:** Business/economics; computers/electronic; education; ethnic/cultural interests; how-to; juvenile nonfiction; memoirs; money/finance; multicultural; New Age/metaphysics; popular culture; psychology; religious/inspirational; science/technology; self-help/personal improvement; sports; women's issues/studies. **Considers these fiction areas:** Action/adventure; confession; ethnic; historical; juvenile; literary; multicultural; mystery; picture books; romance; thriller. **Considers these script subject areas:** Ethnic; fantasy; juvenile; multimedia; also interested in children's CD/video projects.

Serendipity provides developmental editing. "We help build marketing plans for nontraditional outlets." Actively seeking African-American nonfiction, computer books (nonfiction), juvenile books. Does not want to receive poetry.

How to Contact: Submit outline, 1 sample chapter(s), SASE. Prefers to read materials exclusively. Responds in 2 months to queries; 3 months to mss. Obtains most new clients through recommendations from others, conferences.

Recent Sales: This agency prefers not to share information on specific sales. Recent sales available upon request by prospective client.

Terms: Agent receives 15% commission on domestic sales; 20% commission on foreign sales. Offers written contract; 60-day notice notice must be given to terminate contract. Charges clients $200 upon signing for office fees or office fees will be taken from any advance. "If author requests editing services, I can offer a list of potential services." 0% of business is derived from referral to editing services.

Tips: "Looking for African-American children's books. We also represent illustrators."

THE SEYMOUR AGENCY, 475 Miner St., Canton NY 13617. (315)386-1831. Fax: (315)386-1037. E-mail: marysue@slic.com. Website: www.theseymouragency.com. **Contact:** Mary Sue Seymour. Estab. 1992. Represents 100 clients. 20% of clients are new/unpublished writers. Currently handles: 70% nonfiction books; 30% novels.

- Ms. Seymour is a retired New York State certified teacher.

Represents: Nonfiction books, novels (romance). **Considers these nonfiction areas:** Agriculture/horticulture; americana; animals; anthropology/archaeology; art/architecture/design; biography/autobiography; business/economics; child guidance/parenting; computers/electronic; cooking/foods/nutrition; crafts/hobbies; creative nonfiction; current affairs; education; ethnic/cultural interests; gardening; government/politics/law; health/medicine; history; how-to; interior design/decorating; juvenile nonfiction; language/literature/criticism; memoirs; military/war; money/finance; multicultural; music/dance; nature/environment; philosophy; photography; popular culture; psychology; recreation; religious/inspirational; science/technology; self-help/personal improvement; sex; sociology; sports; theater/film; travel; true crime/investigative; women's issues/studies; young adult. **Considers these fiction areas:** Religious/inspirational; romance (contemporary, gothic, historical, medieval, regency); western/frontier.

O→ Actively seeking nonfiction and well-written romance. Does not want to receive screenplays, short stories, poetry, general novels, New Age.

How to Contact: Query with SASE, synopsis, first 50 pages for romance. Accepts e-mail queries. No fax queries. Considers simultaneous queries. Responds in 1 month to queries; 3 months to mss. Returns materials only with SASE.

Recent Sales: *The Everything Golf Instruction Book* , by Rob Plumer, Ph.D. (Adams Media Corp.); *Heart of a Hunter*, by Betty Davidson (Berkley); *Weddings on a Budget*, by Barbara Cameron (Adams Media Corp.); *Smart Baby, Clever Child*, by Val Dmitrieu, Ph.D.

Terms: Agent receives 15% commission on domestic sales; 20% commission on foreign sales. Offers written contract, binding for 1 year; Takes 12 and½% of published author% of business is derived from commissions on ms sales. This agency charges unpublished authors $4.97 for sending out a copy of a manuscript; Writers reimbursed for office fees after the sale of ms.

Writers' Conferences: RWA conferences.

Tips: "Send query, synopsis and first 50 pages. If you don't hear from us, you didn't send SASE. We are looking for nonfiction and romance—women in jeopardy, suspense, contemporary, historical, regency and any well-written fiction and nonfiction by credentialed authors."

N ◪ THE ROBERT E. SHEPARD AGENCY, 1608 Dwight Way, Berkeley CA 94703-1804. (510)849-3999. E-mail: query@shepardagency.com. Website: www.shepardagency.com. **Contact:** Robert Shepard. Estab. 1994. Member of Authors Guild (associate). Represents 30 clients. 25% of clients are new/unpublished writers. Currently handles: 90% nonfiction books; 10% scholarly books.

- Prior to opening his agency, Mr. Shepard "spent eight and a half years in trade publishing (both editorial and sales/marketing management). I also consulted to a number of major publishers on related subjects."

Represents: Nonfiction books, scholarly books (appropriate for trade publishers). **Considers these nonfiction areas:** Business/economics; current affairs; ethnic/cultural interests; gay/lesbian issues; government/politics/law; history; money/finance; narrative nonfiction; popular culture; science/technology; sociology; sports; women's issues/studies.

O→ This agency specializes in nonfiction, particularly key issues facing society and culture. Actively seeking "works by experts recognized in their fields whether or not they're well-known to the general public and books that offer fresh perspectives or new information even when the subject is familiar." Does not want to receive autobiography, highly visual works, fiction.

How to Contact: Query with SASE. E-mail queries encouraged. Fax and phone queries strongly discouraged. Considers simultaneous queries. Responds in 1 month to queries; 6 weeks to mss. Returns materials only with SASE. Obtains most new clients through recommendations from others, solicitations.

Recent Sales: Sold 10 titles in the last year. Recent titles include the bestselling *Word Freak: Heartbreak, Triumph, Genius, and Obsession in the World of Competitive Scrabble Players*, by Stefan Fatsis (Houghton Mifflin HC, Penguin PB); *Wine & War: The French, the Nazis, and the Battle for France's Greatest Treasure*, by Don and Petie Kladstrup (Broadway Books); *Coal: A Human History*, by Barbara Freese (Perseus).

Terms: Agent receives 15% commission on domestic sales; 20% commission on foreign sales. Offers written contract, binding for term of project or until canceled; 30-day notice must be given to terminate contract. Charges clients "actual expenses for phone/fax, photocopying, and postage only if and when project sells, against advance."

Tips: "We pay attention to detail. We believe in close working relationships between author and agent and between author and editor. Regular communication is key. Please do your homework! There's no substitute for learning all you can about similar or directly competing books and presenting a well-reasoned competitive analysis. Don't work in a vacuum; visit bookstores, and talk to other writers about their own experiences."

N ◪ WENDY SHERMAN ASSOCIATES, INC., 450 Seventh Ave., Suite 3004, New York NY 10123. (212)279-9027. Fax: (212)279-8863. E-mail: wendy@wsherman.com. **Contact:** Wendy Sherman. Estab. 1999. Member of AAR. Represents 30 clients. 30% of clients are new/unpublished writers. Currently handles: 50% nonfiction books; 50% novels.

- Prior to opening the agency, Ms. Sherman worked for The Aaron Priest agency and was vice president, executive director of Henry Holt, associate publisher, subsidary rights director, sales and marketing director.

Member Agents: Jessica Lichtenstein; Wendy Sherman.

Represents: Nonfiction books, novels. **Considers these nonfiction areas:** Psychology; narrative nonfiction, practical. **Considers these fiction areas:** Literary; women's.

O→ "We specialize in developing new writers as well as working with more established writers. My experience as a publisher has proven to be a great asset to my clients."

How to Contact: Query with SASE, or send outline/proposal, 1 sample chapter. All unsolicited mss returned unopened. Considers simultaneous queries. Responds in 1 month to queries. Returns materials only with SASE. Obtains most new clients through recommendations from others.

Recent Sales: Sold 14 titles in the last year. *Real Love* , by Greg Baer, M.D. (Penguin Putnam); *The Cloud Atlas*, by Liam Callanan (Delacorte); *Alvin Ailey, Dance Moves!*, by Lise Friedman (Stewart Tabori and Chang); *The Holy Thief*, by Rabbi Mark Borowitz and Alan Eisenstock (William Morrow). Other clients include D.W. Buffa, William Lashner, Nani Power, Sarah Stonich, American Dance Foundation, Howard Bahr, Lundy Bancroft, Tom Schweich, Suzanne Chazin.

Terms: Agent receives 15% commission on domestic sales; 20% commission on foreign sales. Offers written contract. Charges for photocopying of ms, messengers, express mail services, etc. (reasonable, standard expenses).

ROSALIE SIEGEL, INTERNATIONAL LITERARY AGENCY, INC., 1 Abey Dr., Pennington NJ 08534. (609)737-1007. Fax: (609)737-3708. **Contact:** Rosalie Siegel. Estab. 1977. Member of AAR. Represents 35 clients. 10% of clients are new/unpublished writers. Currently handles: 45% nonfiction books; 45% novels; 10% young adult books and short story collections for current clients.

Represents: Nonfiction books, novels, short story collections, young adult books.

How to Contact: Obtains most new clients through referrals from writers and friends.

Terms: Agent receives 15% commission on domestic sales; 20% commission on foreign sales. Offers written contract; 60-day notice must be given to terminate contract. Charges clients for photocopying.

Tips: "I'm not looking for new authors in an active way."

JEFFREY SIMMONS LITERARY AGENCY, 10 Lowndes Square, London SWIX 9HA, England. (020)7235 8852. Fax: (020)7235 9733. **Contact:** Jeffrey Simmons. Estab. 1978. Represents 43 clients. 40% of clients are new/unpublished writers. Currently handles: 60% nonfiction books; 40% novels.

- Prior to becoming an agent, Mr. Simmons was a publisher and he is also an author.

Represents: Nonfiction books, novels. **Considers these nonfiction areas:** Biography/autobiography; current affairs; government/politics/law; history; language/literature/criticism; memoirs; music/dance; popular culture; sociology; sports; theater/film; translation; true crime/investigative. **Considers these fiction areas:** Action/adventure; confession; detective/police/crime; family saga; literary; mainstream/contemporary; mystery/suspense; thriller.

This agency seeks to handle good books and promising young writers. "My long experience in publishing and as an author and ghostwriter means I can offer an excellent service all round, especially in terms of editorial experience where appropriate." Actively seeking quality fiction, biography, autobiography, showbiz, personality books, law, crime, politics, world affairs. Does not want to receive science fiction, horror, fantasy, juvenile, academic books, specialist subjects (i.e., cooking, gardening, religious).

How to Contact: Submit sample chapter, outline/proposal, IRCs if necessary, SASE. Prefers to read materials exclusively. Responds in 1 week to queries; 1 month to mss. Obtains most new clients through recommendations from others, solicitations.

Recent Sales: Sold 18 titles in the last year. *Friendly Fire*, by Picknett, Prince & Prior (mainstream); *Nelson: Love and Fame* (Yale); *Burmese Secrets* (Murray).

Terms: Agent receives 10-15% commission on domestic sales; 15% commission on foreign sales. Offers written contract, binding for lifetime of book in question or until it becomes out of print.

Tips: "When contacting us with an outline/proposal, include a brief biographical note (listing any previous publications, with publishers and dates). Preferably tell us if the book has already been offered elsewhere."

IRENE SKOLNICK LITERARY AGENCY, 22 W. 23rd St., 5th Floor, New York NY 10010. (212)727-3648. Fax: (212)727-1024. E-mail: sirene35@aol.com. **Contact:** Irene Skolnick. Estab. 1993. Member of AAR. Represents 45 clients. 75% of clients are new/unpublished writers.

Member Agents: Irene Skolnick; Laura Friedman Williams.

Represents: Nonfiction books (adult), novels (adult). **Considers these nonfiction areas:** Biography/autobiography; current affairs; cultural history. **Considers these fiction areas:** Contemporary issues; literary; mainstream/contemporary.

How to Contact: Query with SASE, outline, sample chapter(s). Accepts e-mail and fax queries. Considers simultaneous queries. Responds in 1 month to queries. Returns materials only with SASE.

Recent Sales: *In Vivo*, by Allegra Goodman (Dial); *Don't Get Too Comfortable*, by David Rakoff (Doubleday); *The Pieces from Berlin*, by Michael Pye (Knopf).

Terms: Agent receives 15% commission on domestic sales; 20% commission on foreign sales. Sometimes offers criticism service; Charges for international postage, photocopying over 40 pages.

BEVERLEY SLOPEN LITERARY AGENCY, 131 Bloor St. W., Suite 711, Toronto ON M5S 1S3, Canada. (416)964-9598. Fax: (416)921-7726. E-mail: slopen@inforamp.net. Website: www.slopenagency.on.ca. **Contact:** Beverley Slopen. Estab. 1974. Represents 60 clients. 40% of clients are new/unpublished writers. Currently handles: 60% nonfiction books; 40% novels.

- Prior to opening her agency, Ms. Slopen worked in publishing and as a journalist.

Represents: Nonfiction books, novels, scholarly books, textbooks (college). **Considers these nonfiction areas:** Anthropology/archaeology; biography/autobiography; business/economics; current affairs; psychology; sociology; true crime/investigative; women's issues/studies. **Considers these fiction areas:** Literary; mystery/suspense.

This agency has a "strong bent towards Canadian writers." Actively seeking "serious nonfiction that is accessible and appealing to the general reader." Does not want to receive fantasy, science fiction or children's.

How to Contact: Query with SAE and IRCs. Returns materials only with SASE (Canadian postage). Accepts short e-mail queries. Considers simultaneous queries. Responds in 2 months to queries.

Recent Sales: Sold 25 titles in the last year. *Baroque-a-nova*, by Kevin Chong (Penguin Putnam); *The Rescue of Jerusalem*, by Henry T. Aubin (Doubleday Canada, Soho Press US); *Midnight Cab*, by James W. Nichol (Knopf Canada); *Fatal Passage*, by Ken McGoogan (Carroll & Graf US, Bantam Press UK). Other clients include historians Modris Eksteins, Michael Marrus, Timothy Brook, critic Robert Fulford, novelists Donna Morrissey (*Kit's Law* and *Downhill Chance*), Howard Engel, Morley Torgov.

Terms: Agent receives 15% commission on domestic sales; 10% commission on foreign sales. Offers written contract, binding for 2 years; 90-day notice must be given to terminate contract.

Tips: "Please no unsolicited manuscripts."

ROBERT SMITH LITERARY AGENCY, LTD., 12 Bridge Wharf, 156 Caledonian Road, London NI 9UU, England. (020) 7278 2444. Fax: (020) 7833 5680. E-mail: robertsmith.literaryagency@virgin.net. **Contact:** Robert Smith. Estab. 1997. Member of Association of Authors' Agents. Represents 25 clients. 10% of clients are new/unpublished writers. Currently handles: 80% nonfiction books; 20% syndicated material.

- Prior to becoming an agent, Mr. Smith was a book publisher.

Member Agents: Robert Smith (all nonfiction).

Represents: Nonfiction books, syndicated material. **Considers these nonfiction areas:** Biography/autobiography; cooking/foods/nutrition; health/medicine; memoirs; music/dance; New Age/metaphysics; popular culture; self-help/personal improvement; theater/film; true crime/investigative.

O→ This agency offers clients full management service in all media. Clients are not necessarily book authors. "Our special expertise is in placing newspaper series internationally." Actively seeking autobiographies.

How to Contact: Submit outline/proposal, IRCs if necessary, SASE. Prefers to read materials exclusively. Accepts e-mail and fax queries. Responds in 1 week to queries. Returns materials only with SASE. Obtains most new clients through recommendations from others, direct approaches to prospective authors.

Recent Sales: Sold 25 titles in the last year. *Carry That Weight*, by Geoffrey Giuliano (Sidgwick & Jackson); *Hughie & Paula*, by Christopher Green (Robson Books); *Reg Kray*, by Robert Kray (Sidgwick & Jackson). ***Movie/TV MOW script(s) optioned/sold:*** *The Guv'nor*, by Lenny McLean and Peter Gerrard (Arrival Films); *The Lottery Liar*, by Howard and Kathy Walmsley (Hewland International). Other clients include Neil & Christine Hamilton, James Haspiel, Geoffrey Guiliano, Norman Parker, Mike Reid, Rochelle Morton.

Terms: Agent receives 15% commission on domestic sales; 20% commission on foreign sales. Offers written contract, binding for 3 months; 3-month notice must be given to terminate contract. Charges clients for couriers, photocopying and postage, overseas mailings of mss, subject to client authorization.

MICHAEL SNELL LITERARY AGENCY, P.O. Box 1206, Truro MA 02666-1206. (508)349-3718. **Contact:** Michael Snell. Estab. 1978. Represents 200 clients. 25% of clients are new/unpublished writers. Currently handles: 90% nonfiction books; 10% novels.

- Prior to opening his agency, Mr. Snell served as an editor at Wadsworth and Addison-Wesley for 13 years.

Member Agents: Michael Snell (all catergories); Patricia Smith (nonfiction, all categories).

Represents: Nonfiction books. **Considers these nonfiction areas:** Agriculture/horticulture; animals (pets); anthropology/archaeology; art/architecture/design; business/economics; child guidance/parenting; computers/electronic; cooking/foods/nutrition; crafts/hobbies; creative nonfiction; current affairs; education; ethnic/cultural interests; gardening; gay/lesbian issues; government/politics/law; health/medicine; history; how-to; humor/satire; interior design/decorating; language/literature/criticism; military/war; money/finance; music/dance; nature/environment; New Age/metaphysics; photography; popular culture; psychology; recreation; religious/inspirational; science/technology; self-help/personal improvement; sex; spirituality; sports (fitness); theater/film; travel; true crime/investigative; women's issues/studies.

O→ This agency specializes in how-to, self-help and all types of business and computer books, from low-level how-to to professional and reference. Especially interested in business, health, law, medicine, psychology, science, women's issues. Actively seeking "strong book proposals in any nonfiction area where a clear need exists for a new book. Especially self-help, how-to books on all subjects, from business to personal well-being." Does not want to receive "complete manuscripts; considers proposals only. No fiction. No children's books."

How to Contact: Query with SASE. Prefers to read materials exclusively. Responds in 1 week to queries; 2 weeks to mss. Obtains most new clients through unsolicited mss, word-of-mouth and directories.

Recent Sales: *Complete Idiot's Guide to Economics*, by Tom Gorman (Macmillan/Alpha); *How to Talk to Your Horse*, by Ginen Bucklin (Howell); *Do-It-Yourself Advertising*, by Fred Hohn (Wiley).

Terms: Agent receives 15% commission on domestic sales; 15% commission on foreign sales.

Tips: "Send a half- to full-page query, with SASE. Brochure 'How to Write a Book Proposal' available on request and SASE. We suggest prospective clients read Michael Snell's book, *From Book Idea to Bestseller* (Prima, 1997)."

SPECTRUM LITERARY AGENCY, 320 Central Park W., Suite 1-D, New York NY 10025. Website: www.spectrumliteraryagency.com. **Contact:** Eleanor Wood, president. Represents 80 clients. Currently handles: 10% nonfiction books; 90% novels.

Member Agents: Lucienne Diver.

Represents: Nonfiction books, novels. **Considers these nonfiction areas:** Considers select nonfiction. **Considers these fiction areas:** Contemporary issues; fantasy; historical; mainstream/contemporary; mystery/suspense; romance; science fiction.

How to Contact: Query with SASE. No e-mail or fax queries. Responds in 2 months to queries. Obtains most new clients through recommendations from authors and others.

Recent Sales: Sold over 100 titles in the last year. This agency prefers not to share information on specific sales.

Terms: Agent receives 15% commission on domestic sales. Deducts for photocopying and book orders.

THE SPIELER AGENCY, 154 W. 57th St., 13th Floor, Room 135, New York NY 10019. (212)757-4439. Fax: (212)333-2019. **Contact:** Katya Batter. Estab. 1981. Represents 160 clients. 2% of clients are new/unpublished writers.

- Prior to opening his agency, Mr. Spieler was a magazine editor.

Member Agents: Joe Spieler; John Thornton (nonfiction); Lisa M. Ross (fiction/nonfiction); Deirdre Mullane (nonfiction/fiction); Eric Myers. Spieler Agency West (Oakland, CA): Victoria Shoemaker.

Represents: Nonfiction books, literary fiction, children's books. **Considers these nonfiction areas:** Biography/autobiography; business/economics; child guidance/parenting; cooking/foods/nutrition; current affairs; gay/lesbian issues; government/politics/law; history; memoirs; money/finance; music/dance; nature/environment (environmental issues); sociology; theater/film; travel; women's issues/studies. **Considers these fiction areas:** Experimental; family saga; feminist; gay/lesbian; humor/satire; literary.

How to Contact: Query with SASE. Prefers to read materials exclusively. No fax queries. Considers simultaneous queries. Responds in 2 weeks to queries; 5 weeks to mss. Returns materials only with SASE. Obtains most new clients through recommendations and occasionally through listing in *Guide to Literary Agents.*

Recent Sales: *A Needle to the Heart: Special Military Operations from the Heroic to the Nuclear Age*, by Derek Leebaert (Little, Brown); *Natural History of the Rich*, by Richard Conniff (W.W. Norton); *The Clothes They Stood Up In*, by Alan Bennett (Random House).

Terms: Agent receives 15% commission on domestic sales. Charges clients for messenger bills, photocopying, postage.

Writers' Conferences: London Bookfair.

PHILIP G. SPITZER LITERARY AGENCY, 50 Talmage Farm Lane, East Hampton NY 11937. (631)329-3650. Fax: (631)329-3651. E-mail: spitzer516@aol.com. **Contact:** Philip Spitzer. Estab. 1969. Member of AAR. Represents 60 clients. 10% of clients are new/unpublished writers. Currently handles: 50% nonfiction books; 50% novels.

- Prior to opening his agency, Mr. Spitzer served at New York University Press, McGraw-Hill and the John Cushman Associates literary agency.

Represents: Nonfiction books, novels. **Considers these nonfiction areas:** Biography/autobiography; business/economics; current affairs; ethnic/cultural interests; government/politics/law; health/medicine; history; language/literature/criticism; military/war; music/dance; nature/environment; popular culture; psychology; sociology; sports; theater/film; true crime/investigative. **Considers these fiction areas:** Contemporary issues; detective/police/crime; literary; mainstream/contemporary; mystery/suspense; sports; thriller.

This agency specializes in mystery/suspense, literary fiction, sports, general nonfiction (no how-to).

How to Contact: Query with SASE, outline, 1 sample chapter(s). Responds in 1 week to queries; 6 weeks to mss. Obtains most new clients through recommendations from others.

Recent Sales: *Chasing the Dime*, by Michael Connelly (Little, Brown); *White Doves at Morning*, by James Lee Burke (Hyperion); *Eleanora Duse*, by Helen Sheehy (Knopf); *Air Burial*, by Jean Shields (Carroll and Graff).

Terms: Agent receives 15% commission on domestic sales; 20% commission on foreign sales. Charges clients for photocopying.

Writers' Conferences: BEA (Chicago).

N **NANCY STAUFFER ASSOCIATES**, P.O. Box 1203, Darien CT 06820. (203)655-3717. Fax: (203)655-3704. E-mail: nanstauf@optonline.net. **Contact:** Nancy Stauffer Cahoon. Estab. 1989. Member of the Authors Guild. 5% of clients are new/unpublished writers. Currently handles: 15% nonfiction books; 85% novels.

Represents: Nonfiction books, novels (literary fiction). **Considers these nonfiction areas:** Creative nonfiction; current affairs; ethnic/cultural interests. **Considers these fiction areas:** Contemporary issues; literary; mainstream/contemporary; regional.

How to Contact: Obtains most new clients through referrals from existing clients.

Recent Sales: *Ten Little Indians*, by Sherman Alexie (Grove/Atlantic); *No Enemy But Time*, by William C. Harris (St. Martin's Press); *An Unfinished Life*, by Mark Spragg.

Terms: Agent receives 15% commission on domestic sales; 20% commission on foreign sales; 20% commission on dramatic rights sales.

N **STEELE-PERKINS LITERARY AGENCY**, 26 Island Lane, Canandaigua NY 14424. (585)396-9290. Fax: (585)396-3579. E-mail: pattiesp@aol.com. **Contact:** Pattie Steele-Perkins. Member of AAR, RWA. Currently handles: 100% Romance and mainstream women's fiction.

Represents: Novels. **Considers these fiction areas:** Mainstream/contemporary; multicultural; romance; women's.

Actively seeking romance, women's fiction and multicultural works.

How to Contact: Submit outline, 3 sample chapter(s), SASE. Considers simultaneous queries. Responds in 6 weeks to queries. Returns materials only with SASE. Obtains most new clients through recommendations from others, queries/solicitations.

Recent Sales: This agency prefers not to share information on specific sales.

Terms: Agent receives 15% commission on domestic sales. Offers written contract, binding for 1 year; 30-day notice must be given to terminate contract.

Writers' Conferences: National Conference of Romance Writers of America; Book Expo America Writers' Conferences.

Tips: "Be patient. E-mail rather than call. Make sure what you are sending is the best it can be."

N **STERLING LORD LITERISTIC, INC.**, 65 Bleecker St., New York NY 10012. (212)780-6050. Fax: (212)780-6095. **Contact:** Philippa Brophy. Estab. 1952. Signatory of WGA. Represents 600 clients. Currently handles: 50% nonfiction books; 50% novels.

Member Agents: Philippa Brophy; Laurie Liss; Chris Calhoun; Peter Matson; Sterling Lord; Claudia Cross; Neeti Madan; George Nicholson; Jim Rutman; Charlotte Sheedy.

Represents: Nonfiction books, novels, literary value considered first.

How to Contact: Query with SASE. Responds in 1 month to mss. Obtains most new clients through recommendations from others.

Recent Sales: This agency prefers not to share information on specific sales. Clients include Kent Haruf, Dick Fancis, Mary Gordon, Sen. John McCain, Simon Winchester, James McBride, Billy Collins, Richard Paul Evans, Dave Pelzer.

Terms: Agent receives 15% commission on domestic sales; 20% commission on foreign sales. Offers written contract. Charges clients for photocopying.

[N] [●] STERNIG & BYRNE LITERARY AGENCY, 3209 S. 55, Milwaukee WI 53219-4433. (414)328-8034. Fax: (414)328-8034. E-mail: jackbyrne@hotmail.com. Website: www.sff.net/people/jackbyrne. **Contact:** Jack Byrne. Estab. 1950s. Member of SFWA, MWA. Represents 30 clients. 10% of clients are new/unpublished writers. Accepting few new clients. Currently handles: 5% nonfiction books; 85% novels; 10% juvenile books.
Member Agents: Jack Byrne.
Represents: Nonfiction books, novels, juvenile books. **Considers these fiction areas:** Fantasy; horror; mystery/suspense; science fiction.
   O— "Our client list is comfortably full and our current needs are therefore quite limited." Actively seeking science fiction/fantasy by established writers. Does not want to receive romance, poetry, textbooks, highly specialized nonfiction.
How to Contact: Query with SASE. Accepts e-mail queries, no attachments. Responds in 3 weeks to queries; 3 months to mss. Returns materials only with SASE.
Recent Sales: Sold 16 titles in the last year. *When the Beast Ravens*, by E. Rose Sabin; *Stone of the Stars Trilogy*, by Alison Baird. Other clients include Jane Routley, Gerard Hourner, Betty Ren Wright, and Andre Norton.
Terms: Agent receives 15% commission on domestic sales; 20% commission on foreign sales. Offers written contract; 60-day notice must be given to terminate contract.
Tips: "Don't send first drafts; have a professional presentation...including cover letter; know your field. Read what's been done...good and bad."

[N] STIMOLA LITERARY STUDIO, 210 Crescent Ave., Leonia NJ 07605. Phone/fax: (201)944-9886. E-mail: ltrystudio@aol.com. **Contact:** Rosemary B. Stimola. Member of AAR.
Member Agents: Rosemary B. Stimola.
Represents: Preschool through young adult fiction/nonfiction.
How to Contact: Query with SASE, or via e-mail. Responds in 3 weeks to queries; 2 months to mss. Obtains most new clients through recommendations from others, solicitations.
Recent Sales: *Gregor the Overlander*, by Suzanne Collins; *Beacon Hill Boys*, by Ken Mochizuki; *Johnny Mutton, He's So Him!*, by James Proimos.
Terms: Agent receives 15% commission on domestic sales; 20% commission on foreign sales. Offers written contract, binding for 1 year; Covers all children's literary work not previously published or under agreement. Notice must be given to terminate contract.
Tips: "No phone inquiries."

[●] ROBIN STRAUS AGENCY, INC., 229 E. 79th St., New York NY 10021. (212)472-3282. Fax: (212)472-3833. E-mail: springbird@aol.com. **Contact:** Ms. Robin Straus. Estab. 1983. Member of AAR. Currently handles: 65% nonfiction books; 35% novels.
   ● Prior to becoming an agent, Robin Straus served as a subsidary rights manager at Random House and Doubleday and worked in editorial at Little, Brown.
Represents: Nonfiction books, novels. **Considers these nonfiction areas:** Animals; anthropology/archaeology; art/architecture/design; biography/autobiography; child guidance/parenting; cooking/foods/nutrition; current affairs; ethnic/cultural interests; government/politics/law; health/medicine; history; language/literature/criticism; music/dance; nature/environment; popular culture; psychology; sociology; theater/film; women's issues/studies. **Considers these fiction areas:** Contemporary issues; family saga; historical; literary; mainstream/contemporary.
   O— This agency specializes in high quality fiction and nonfiction for adults (no genre fiction; no screenplays; no books for children). Takes on very few new clients.
How to Contact: For nonfiction: Query with proposal and sample pages. For fiction: Query with brief synopsis and opening chapter or 2. Responds and returns materials only with SASE. We do not download **any** submissions. Responds in 1 month to queries; 1 month to mss. Obtains most new clients through recommendations from others.
Recent Sales: This agency prefers not to share information on specific sales.
Terms: Agent receives 15% commission on domestic sales; 20% commission on foreign sales. Offers written contract. Charges for "photocopying, express mail services, messenger and foreign postage, etc. as incurred."

[N] [●] [●] THE SUSIJN AGENCY, 3rd Floor, 64 Great Titchfield St., London W1W 7QH, England. 0044 (207)580-6341. Fax: 0044 (207)580-8626. E-mail: info@thesusijnagency.com. Website: www.thesusijnagency.com. **Contact:** Laura Susijn, Charles Buchau. Estab. 1998. Currently handles: 15% nonfiction books; 85% novels.
   ● Prior to becoming an agent, Ms. Susijn was a rights director at Sheil Land Associates and at Fourth Estate Ltd.
Member Agents: Laura Susijn.
Represents: Nonfiction books, novels. **Considers these nonfiction areas:** Biography/autobiography; memoirs; multicultural; popular culture; science/technology; travel. **Considers these fiction areas:** Literary.
   O— This agency specializes in international works, selling world rights, representing non-English language writing as well as English. Emphasis on cross-cultural subjects. Self-help, romance, sagas, science fiction, screenplays.
How to Contact: Submit outline, 2 sample chapter(s). Accepts e-mail and fax queries. Considers simultaneous queries. Responds in 2 months to queries. Returns materials only with SASE. Obtains most new clients through recommendations from others, via publishers in Europe and beyond.
Recent Sales: Sold 120 titles in the last year. *Gone*, by Helena Echlin (Secker and Warburg, UK); *Daalder*, by Philibert

Schogt (4 Walls 8 Windows); *Prisoner in a Red Rose Chain*, by Jeffrey Moore (Weidenfeld & Nicholson); *Smell*, by Radhika Jha (Quartet Books); *The Formula One Fanatic*, by Koen Vergeer (Bloomsbury); *A Mouthful of Glass*, by Henk Van Woerden (Granta); *Fragile Science*, by Robin Baker (Macmillan); *East of Acre Lane*, by Alex Wheatle (Fourth Estate). Other clients include Vassallucci, Podium, Atlas, De Arbeiderspers, Tiderne Skifter, MB Agency, Van Oorschot

Terms: Agent receives 15% commission on domestic sales; 15-20% commission on foreign sales. Offers written contract; 6 weeks notice must be given to terminate contract. Charges clients for photocopying, buying copies only if sale is made.

THE JOHN TALBOT AGENCY, INC., 540 W. Boston Post Rd., PMB 266, Mamaroneck NY 10543-3437. (914)381-9463. Fax: (914)381-0507. E-mail: talbotagency@mac.com. Website: www.johntalbotagency.com. **Contact:** John Talbot. Estab. 1998. Member of Authors Guild. Represents 50 clients. 15% of clients are new/unpublished writers. Currently handles: 35% nonfiction books; 65% novels.

- Prior to becoming an agent, Mr. Talbot was a book editor at Simon & Schuster and Putnam Berkley.

Represents: Nonfiction books, novels. **Considers these nonfiction areas:** General and narrative nonfiction. **Considers these fiction areas:** Literary; mystery/suspense.

This agency specializes in commercial suspense and literary fiction "by writers who are beginning to publish in magazines and literary journals." Also narrative nonfiction, especially outdoor adventure and spirituality. Does not want to receive children's books, science fiction, fantasy, westerns, poetry, screenplays.

How to Contact: Query via e-mail only. See website for instructions.

Recent Sales: Sold 30 titles in the last year. *The Edge of Justice*, by Clinton McKinzie (Delacorte/Dell); *Crush Depth*, by Joe Buff (Morrow); *Burden*, by Tony Walters (St. Martin's Press); *Around Again*, by Suzanne Strempek Shea (Pocket Books). Other clients include Doris Meredith, Peter Telep, Clarence Major.

Terms: Agent receives 15% commission on domestic sales; 20% commission on foreign sales. Offers written contract; 60 days notice must be given to terminate contract. Charges clients for photocopying, overnight delivery, additional copies of books needed for use in sale of subsidiary rights, and fees incurred for submitting mss or books overseas.

ROSLYN TARG LITERARY AGENCY, INC., 105 W. 13th St., New York NY 10011. (212)206-9390. Fax: (212)989-6233. E-mail: roslyntarg@aol.com. **Contact:** Roslyn Targ. Estab. 1945. Member of AAR. Represents 100 clients.

Member Agents: Roslyn Targ.

How to Contact: Query with SASE, outline/proposal, curriculum vitae. Prefers to read materials exclusively. No mss without query first. Obtains most new clients through recommendations from others, solicitations.

Terms: Agent receives 15% commission on domestic sales; 20% commission on foreign sales. Charges standard agency fees (bank charges, long distance, postage, photocopying, shipping of books, overseas long distance and shipping, etc.).

Tips: "This agency reads on an exclusive basis only."

PATRICIA TEAL LITERARY AGENCY, 2036 Vista Del Rosa, Fullerton CA 92831-1336. Phone/fax: (714)738-8333. **Contact:** Patricia Teal. Estab. 1978. Member of AAR. Represents 20 clients. Currently handles: 10% nonfiction books; 90% novels.

Represents: Nonfiction books, novels. **Considers these nonfiction areas:** Animals; biography/autobiography; child guidance/parenting; health/medicine; how-to; psychology; self-help/personal improvement; true crime/investigative; women's issues/studies. **Considers these fiction areas:** Glitz; mainstream/contemporary; mystery/suspense; romance (contemporary, historical).

This agency specializes in women's fiction and commercial how-to and self-help nonfiction. Does not want to receive poetry, short stories, articles, science fiction, fantasy, regency romance.

How to Contact: *Published authors only.* Query with SASE. No e-mail or fax queries. Considers simultaneous queries. Responds in 10 days to queries; 6 weeks to mss. Returns materials only with SASE. Obtains most new clients through conferences, recommendations from authors and editors.

Recent Sales: Sold 20 titles in the last year. *The Black Sheep's Baby*, by Kathleen Creighton (Silhouette); *Man with a Message*, by Muriel Jensen (Harlequin).

Terms: Agent receives 10-15% commission on domestic sales; 20% commission on foreign sales. Offers written contract, binding for 1 year. Charges clients for postage and phone calls.

Writers' Conferences: Romance Writers of America conferences; Asilomar (California Writers Club); BEA; Bouchercon; Hawaii Writers Conference (Maui).

Tips: "Include SASE with all correspondence. Taking on very few authors."

3 SEAS LITERARY AGENCY, P.O. Box 8571, Madison WI 53708. (608)221-4306. E-mail: threeseaslit@aol.com. Website: www.threeseaslit.com. **Contact:** Michelle Grajkowski. Estab. 2000. Member of Romance Writers of America, Society of Children's Books Writers and Illustrators. Represents 40 clients. 50% of clients are new/unpublished writers. Currently handles: 30% nonfiction books; 60% novels; 10% juvenile books.

- Prior to becoming an agent, Ms. Grajkowski worked in both sales and in purchasing for a medical facility. She has a degree in journalism from the University of Wisconsin-Madison.

Represents: Nonfiction books, novels, juvenile books, scholarly books. **Considers these nonfiction areas:** Agriculture/horticulture; animals; biography/autobiography; business/economics; child guidance/parenting; computers/electronic; cooking/foods/nutrition; current affairs; education; ethnic/cultural interests; government/politics/law; health/medicine; history; how-to; humor/satire; memoirs; military/war; money/finance; music/dance; nature/environment; popular culture; psychology; religious/inspirational; science/technology; self-help/personal improvement; sociology; sports; true crime/investigative; women's issues/studies; interior design/decorating, juvenile nonfiction. **Considers these fiction areas:** Action/adventure; detective/police/crime; family saga; fantasy (only if there is romance in the story); historical; horror; humor/satire;

juvenile; literary; mainstream/contemporary; mystery/suspense; picture books; religious/inspirational; romance; science fiction (only if there is romance in the story); thriller; western/frontier; young adult; psychic/supernatural.

O→ 3 Seas focuses on romance and women's fiction. "We also handle a variety of nonfiction and children's stories. We believe in working with our clients to help plan their careers." Actively seeking authors who are committed to their careers and are determined to make it in this business. "We typically represent our clients as a whole, not just on a project by project basis." Does not want to receive science fiction and fantasy, unless the mss have a romance flair.

How to Contact: For fiction: Please query with first 3 chapters, a synopsis and your bio. For nonfiction: Please query with your complete proposal and first 3 chapters. Considers simultaneous queries. Responds in 2 months to queries; 3 months to mss. Returns materials only with SASE. Obtains most new clients through recommendations from others, conferences.

Recent Sales: Sold 20 titles in the last year. Clients include Marshall Cook, Winnie Griggs, Diane Amos, Rebekah Shardy, Ellen Browning, Lisa Mondello, Natalie Damschroder, Juliet Blackett, Jessica Barkley, Chris deSmet, Donna Smith.

Terms: Agent receives 15% commission on domestic sales; 20% commission on foreign sales. Offers written contract, binding for 30 days.

Writers' Conferences: RWA National Conference (New York, July); Romantic Times Conference (Kansas City, October); Rocky Mountain Fiction Writers (Denver, April); New England RWA Conference (Boston, April).

LYNDA TOLLS LITERARY AGENCY, P.O. Box 1785, Bend OR 97709. (541)388-3510. E-mail: blswarts@juno.com. **Contact:** Lynda Tolls Swarts. Estab. 1995. Represents 8 clients. 20% of clients are new/unpublished writers. Currently handles: 70% nonfiction books; 30% novels.

Represents: Nonfiction books, novels. **Considers these nonfiction areas:** Biography/autobiography; education; ethnic/cultural interests (cultural, global interests); health/medicine; history; popular culture; religious/inspirational (inspirational); self-help/personal improvement; sociology; travel; current affairs, investigative. **Considers these fiction areas:** Ethnic (multicultural); historical; literary; mystery/suspense; romance; contemporary, inspirational, women's.

How to Contact: Query with SASE, Nonfiction: send query including the concept of your book, market, competing titles, and your expertise. Fiction: query with synopsis and first 30 pages.

Writers' Conferences: Williamette Writers' Conference; Surrey Writers' Conference; Idaho Writers' Conference.

S©OTT TREIMEL NY, (Specialized: children's books), 434 Lafayette St., New York NY 10003. (212)505-8353. Fax: (212)505-0664. E-mail: st.ny@verizon.net. Estab. 1995. Member of AAR. Represents 38 clients. 15% of clients are new/unpublished writers. Currently handles: 100% juvenile books.

- Prior to becoming an agent, Mr. Treimel was an assistant at Curtis Brown, Ltd. (for Marilyn E. Marlow); a rights agent for Scholastic, Inc.; a book packager and rights agent for United Feature Syndicate; a freelance editor, a rights consultant for HarperCollins Children's Books; and the founding director of Warner Bros. Worldwide Publishing.

Member Agents: Ari Hopkins.

Represents: Children's book authors and illustrators.

O→ This agency specializes in children's books: tightly focused segments of the trade and institutional markets. Interested in seeing author-illustrators, first chapter books, middle-grade and teen fiction. Does not consider activity or coloring books.

How to Contact: Two complete picture books may be submitted. For longer work, query with SASE. No fax queries.

Recent Sales: Sold 19 titles in the last year. *Dust*, by Arthur Slade (Harper Collins Canada and Random House); *Ollie*, by Olivier Dunrea (Houghton Mifflin).

Terms: Agent receives 15-20% commission on domestic sales; 20-25% commission on foreign sales. Offers verbal or written contract, "binding on a book contract by contract basis." Charges clients for photocopying, express postage, messengers, and books ordered to sell foreign, film, etc. rights.

Writers' Conferences: Can You Make a Living from Children's Books, Society of Children's Book Writers & Illustrators (Los Angeles, August); Society of Children's Book Writers & Illustrators (Los Angeles, August); "Understanding Book Contracts," SCBWI (Watertown NY); "Creating Believable Teen Characters," SCBWI; Picture Book Judge for Tassie Walden Award; New Voices in Children's Literature; "Craft" SCBWI (North Carolina); "Understanding Book Contracts" SCBWI (North Dakota); The Professionals Panel.

Tips: "Keep cover letters short and include publishing credits. Manuscripts and illustration smaples received without a SASE are recycled on receipt."

2M COMMUNICATIONS, LTD., 121 W. 27 St., #601, New York NY 10001. (212)741-1509. Fax: (212)691-4460. E-mail: morel@bookhaven.com. **Contact:** Madeleine Morel. Estab. 1982. Represents 50 clients. 20% of clients are new/unpublished writers. Currently handles: 100% nonfiction books.

- Prior to becoming an agent, Madeleine Morel worked at a publishing company.

Represents: Nonfiction books. **Considers these nonfiction areas:** Biography/autobiography; child guidance/parenting; ethnic/cultural interests; gay/lesbian issues; health/medicine; memoirs; music/dance; self-help/personal improvement; theater/film; travel; women's issues/studies.

O→ This agency specializes in adult nonfiction.

How to Contact: Query with SASE, submit outline, 3 sample chapter(s). Considers simultaneous queries. Responds in 1 week to queries; 1 month to mss. Obtains most new clients through recommendations from others, solicitations.

Recent Sales: Sold 10 titles in the last year. *Botox*, by Terri Malloy (Berkley); *Patriotic Songs*, by Ale Collins (HarperCollins).

Terms: Agent receives 15% commission on domestic sales; 20% commission on foreign sales. Offers written contract, binding for 2 years. Charges clients for postage, photocopying, long distance calls, faxes.

UNITED TRIBES MEDIA, INC., 240 W. 35th St., Suite 500, New York NY 10001. (212)534-7646. E-mail: janguerth@aol.com. **Contact:** Jan-Erik Guerth. Estab. 1998. Currently handles: 100% nonfiction books.

- Prior to becoming an agent, Mr. Guerth was a comedian, journalist, radio producer and film distributor.

Represents: Nonfiction books. **Considers these nonfiction areas:** Anthropology/archaeology; art/architecture/design; biography/autobiography; business/economics; child guidance/parenting; cooking/foods/nutrition; current affairs; education; ethnic/cultural interests; gay/lesbian issues; government/politics/law; health/medicine; history; how-to; language/literature/criticism; memoirs; money/finance; music/dance; nature/environment; popular culture; psychology; religious/inspirational; science/technology (popular); self-help/personal improvement; sociology; theater/film; translation; women's issues/studies.

O→ This agency represents serious nonfiction; and ethnic, social, gender and cultural issues, comparative religions, self-help, spirituality and wellness, science and arts, history and politics, nature and travel, and any fascinating future trends.

How to Contact: Submit outline, résumé, SASE. Agent prefers email queries. Considers simultaneous queries. Responds in 1 month to queries. Returns materials only with SASE. Obtains most new clients through recommendations from others, solicitations, conferences.

Recent Sales: *Squatting in the City of Tomorrow*, by Robert Neuwirth (Routledge); *The Green Desert*, by Rita Winters (Wildcat Canyon Press); *Into the Melting Pot*, by James McWilliams (Columbia University Press).

Terms: Agent receives 15% commission on domestic sales; 20% commission on foreign sales.

THE RICHARD R. VALCOURT AGENCY, INC., (Specialized: government issues), 177 E. 77th St., PHC, New York NY 10021-1934. Phone/fax: (212)570-2340. **Contact:** Richard R. Valcourt, president. Estab. 1995. Represents 25 clients. 20% of clients are new/unpublished writers. Currently handles: 100% nonfiction books.

- Prior to opening his agency, Mr. Valcourt was a journalist, editor and college political science instructor. He is also editor-in-chief of the International Journal of Intelligence and faculty member at American Military University in Virginia.

Represents: Scholarly books.

O→ This agency specializes in intelligence and other national security affairs. Represents exclusively academics, journalists and professionals in the categories listed.

How to Contact: Query with SASE. Prefers to read materials exclusively. No e-mail or fax queries. Responds in 1 week to queries; 1 month to mss. Returns materials only with SASE. Obtains most new clients through recommendations from others.

Terms: Agent receives 15% commission on domestic sales; 20% commission on foreign sales. Offers written contract. Charges clients for excessive photocopying, express mail, overseas telephone expenses.

VENTURE LITERARY, 8895 Towne Centre Dr., Suite 105, #141, San Diego CA 92122. (619)807-1887. E-mail: agents@ventureliterary.com. Website: www.ventureliterary.com. **Contact:** Frank R. Scatoni. Estab. 1999. Represents 30 clients. 50% of clients are new/unpublished writers. Currently handles: 95% nonfiction books; 5% novels.

- Prior to becoming an agent, Mr. Scatoni worked as an editor at Simon & Schuster.

Member Agents: Frank R. Scatoni (general nonfiction, including biography, memoir, narrative nonfiction, sports and serious nonfiction); Greg Dinkin (general nonfiction/business, gambling).

Represents: Considers these nonfiction areas: Animals; anthropology/archaeology; biography/autobiography; business/economics; current affairs; ethnic/cultural interests; government/politics/law; history; memoirs; military/war; money/finance; multicultural; music/dance; nature/environment; popular culture; psychology; science/technology; sports; true crime/investigative; gambling. **Considers these fiction areas:** Action/adventure; detective/police/crime; literary; mainstream/contemporary; mystery/suspense; sports; thriller.

O→ Specializes in nonfiction, sports, business, natural history, biography, gambling. Actively seeking nonfiction.

How to Contact: Nonfiction: submit proposal with 3 sample chapters. Considers simultaneous queries. Responds in 3 months to queries; 6 months to mss. Returns materials only with SASE. Obtains most new clients through recommendations from others.

Recent Sales: *Amarillo Slim in a World Full of Fat People*, by Amarillo Slim Preston (HarperCollins); *Stocking Up on Sin*, by Caroline Waxler (Wiley); *The Last True Cowboys*, by Erich Krauss (Ken Singleton).

Terms: Agent receives 15% commission on domestic sales; 20% commission on foreign sales. Offers written contract. Charges clients for photocopying and postage only.

Writers' Conferences: San Diego State University Writers Conference (San Diego CA); Southern California Writers Conference (Los Angeles and San Diego).

THE VINES AGENCY, INC., 648 Broadway, Suite 901, New York NY 10012. (212)777-5522. Fax: (212)777-5978. E-mail: jv@vinesagency.com. Website: www.vinesagency.com. **Contact:** James C. Vines, Paul Surdi, Ali Ryan, Gary Neuwirth. Estab. 1995. Signatory of WGA; Author's Guild. Represents 52 clients. 20% of clients are new/unpublished writers. Currently handles: 50% nonfiction books; 50% novels.

- Prior to opening his agency, Mr. Vines served as an agent with the Virginia Barber Literary Agency.

Member Agents: James C. Vines (quality and commercial fiction and nonfiction); Gary Neuwirth; Paul Surdi (women's fiction, ethnic fiction, quality nonfiction); Ali Ryan (women's fiction and nonfiction, mainstream).

Represents: Nonfiction books, novels, feature film, TV scripts. **Considers these nonfiction areas:** Biography/autobiography; business/economics; current affairs; ethnic/cultural interests; history; how-to; humor/satire; memoirs; military/war; money/finance; nature/environment; New Age/metaphysics; photography; popular culture; psychology; religious/inspirational; science/technology; self-help/personal improvement; sociology; spirituality; sports; translation; travel; true crime/investigative; women's issues/studies. **Considers these fiction areas:** Action/adventure; contemporary issues; detective/police/crime; ethnic; experimental; family saga; feminist; gay/lesbian; historical; horror; humor/satire; literary; mainstream/

contemporary; mystery/suspense; occult; psychic/supernatural; regional; romance (contemporary, historical); science fiction; sports; thriller; western/frontier; women's. **Considers these script subject areas:** Action/adventure; comedy; detective/police/crime; ethnic; experimental; feminist; gay/lesbian; historical; horror; mainstream; mystery/suspense; romantic comedy; romantic drama; science fiction; teen; thriller; western/frontier.

O→ This agency specializes in mystery, suspense, science fiction, women's fiction, ethnic fiction, mainstream novels, screenplays, teleplays.

How to Contact: Submit outline, 3 sample chapter(s), SASE. Accepts e-mail and fax queries. Considers simultaneous queries. Responds in 2 weeks to queries; 1 month to mss. Returns materials only with SASE. Obtains most new clients through query letters, recommendations from others, reading short stories in magazines, soliciting conferences.

Recent Sales: Sold 48 titles and sold 5 scripts in the last year. *A Fine Dark Line*, by Joe R. Lansdale; *Loving Donovan*, by Bernice McFadden; *Bad Seed*, by Beth Saulnier.

Terms: Agent receives 15% commission on domestic sales; 25% commission on foreign sales. Offers written contract, binding for 1 year; 30 days notice must be given to terminate contract. 100% of business is derived from commissions on ms sales. Charges clients for foreign postage, messenger services, photocopying.

Writers' Conferences: Maui Writer's Conference.

Tips: "Do not follow up on submissions with phone calls to the agency. The agency will read and respond by mail only. Do not pack your manuscript in plastic 'peanuts' that will make us have to vacuum the office after opening the package containing your manuscript. Always enclose return postage."

MARY JACK WALD ASSOCIATES, INC., 111 E. 14th St., New York NY 10003. (212)254-7842. **Contact:** Danis Sher. Estab. 1985. Member of AAR, Authors Guild, SCBWI. Represents 35 clients. 5% of clients are new/unpublished writers. Currently handles: nonfiction books; novels; story collections; novellas; juvenile books.

- This agency is not accepting mss at this time.

Member Agents: Mary Jack Wald; Danis Sher; Lynne Rabinoff Agency (assoc. represents our foreign rights); Alvin Wald.

Represents: Nonfiction books, novels, short story collections, novellas, juvenile books, movie and TV scripts by our authors. **Considers these nonfiction areas:** Biography/autobiography; current affairs; ethnic/cultural interests; history; juvenile nonfiction; language/literature/criticism; music/dance; nature/environment; photography; sociology; theater/film; translation; true crime/investigative. **Considers these fiction areas:** Action/adventure; contemporary issues; detective/police/crime; ethnic; experimental; family saga; feminist; gay/lesbian; glitz; historical; juvenile; literary; mainstream/contemporary; mystery/suspense; picture books; thriller; young adult; satire.

O→ This agency specializes in literary works, juvenile.

How to Contact: Not accepting new clients at this time.

Recent Sales: *Horseshoes, Cowsocks & Duckfeet*, by Baxter Black; 3 novels by Richie Tankensley Cusick.

Terms: Agent receives 15% commission on domestic sales; 15-30% commission on foreign sales. Offers written contract, binding for 1 year.

WALES LITERARY AGENCY, INC., P.O. Box 9428, Seattle WA 98109-0428. (206)284-7114. E-mail: waleslit@aol.com. **Contact:** Elizabeth Wales, Meg Lemke. Estab. 1988. Member of AAR, Book Publishers' Northwest, Pacific Northwest Booksellers Association, PEN. Represents 65 clients. 10% of clients are new/unpublished writers. Currently handles: 60% nonfiction books; 40% fiction.

- Prior to becoming an agent, Ms. Wales worked at Oxford University Press and Viking Penguin.

Member Agents: Elizabeth Wales.

O→ This agency specializes in narrative nonfiction and quality, mainstream and literary fiction. Does not handle screenplays, children's literature, genre fiction, most category nonfiction.

How to Contact: Query with cover letter, writing sample (approx. 30 pages) and SASE. No phone or fax queries. Prefers regular mail queries, but accepts one-page e-mail queries with no attachments. Considers simultaneous queries. Responds in 3 weeks to queries; 6 weeks to mss. Returns materials only with SASE.

Recent Sales: *Windfalls*, by Jean Hegland (Atria/Simon & Schuster); *The Bathhouse*, by Farnoosh Moshiri Scigliano (Houghton-Mifflin); *Excerpts from a Family Medical Dictionary*, by Rebecca Brown (U. of Wisconsin Press).

Terms: Agent receives 15% commission on domestic sales; 20% commission on foreign sales.

Writers' Conferences: Pacific NW Writers Conference (Seattle); Writers at Work (Salt Lake City); Writing Rendezvous (Anchorage); Willamette Writers (Portland).

Tips: "Especially interested in work that espouses a progressive cultural or political view, projects a new voice, or simply shares an important, compelling story. Encourages writers living in the Pacific Northwest, West Coast, Alaska and Pacific Rim countries, and writers from historically underrepresented groups, such as gay and lesbian writers and writers of color, to submit work (but does not discourage writers outside these areas). Most importantly, whether in fiction or nonfiction, the agency is looking for talented storytellers."

JOHN A. WARE LITERARY AGENCY, 392 Central Park West, New York NY 10025-5801. (212)866-4733. Fax: (212)866-4734. **Contact:** John Ware. Estab. 1978. Represents 60 clients. 40% of clients are new/unpublished writers. Currently handles: 75% nonfiction books; 25% novels.

- Prior to opening his agency, Mr. Ware served as a literary agency with James Brown Associates/Curtis Brown, Ltd. and as an editor for Doubleday & Company.

Represents: Nonfiction books, novels. **Considers these nonfiction areas:** Animals; anthropology/archaeology; biography/autobiography; current affairs; health/medicine (academic credentials reqired); history (including oral history, Americana and folklore); language/literature; music/dance; nature/environment; popular culture; psychology (academic credentials required); science/technology; sports; travel; true crime/investigative; women's issues/studies; social commentary; investigative journalism; 'bird's eye' views of phenomena. **Considers these fiction areas:** Detective/police/crime; mystery/suspense; thriller; accessible literate noncategory fiction.

How to Contact: Query first by letter only, including SASE. No e-mail or fax queries. Considers simultaneous queries Responds in 2 weeks to queries.

Recent Sales: *Under the Banner of Heaven*, by Jon Krakauer (Doubleday); *The Traveller: A Biography of John Ledyard*, by Bill Gifford (St. Martin's); *Stealing Convenience: A Memoir of Simplicity*, by Eric Brende (HarperCollins).

Terms: Agent receives 15% commission on domestic sales; 20% commission on foreign sales; 15% commission on dramatic rights sales. Charges clients for messenger service, photocopying.

Tips: "Writers must have appropriate credentials for authorship of proposal (nonfiction) or manuscript (fiction); no publishing track record required. Open to good writing and interesting ideas by new or veteran writers."

N **◎** **WATERSIDE PRODUCTIONS, INC.**, 2187 Newcastle Ave., Suite 204, Cardiff-by-the-Sea CA 92007. (760)632-9190. Fax: (760)632-9295. E-mail: admin@waterside.com. Website: www.waterside.com. **Contact:** Matt Wagner, Margot Maley, David Fugate. President: Bill Gladstone. Estab. 1982. Represents 300 clients. 20% of clients are new/unpublished writers. Currently handles: 100% nonfiction books.

Member Agents: Bill Gladstone (trade computer titles, business); Margot Maley Hutchison (trade computer titles, nonfiction); Matthew Wagner (trade computer titles, nonfiction); Carole McClendon (trade computer titles); David Fugate (trade computer titles, business, general nonfiction, sports books); Christian Crumlish (trade computer titles); Danielle Jatlow; Neil Gudovitz; Jawahara K. Saidullah; Kimberly Valentini.

Represents: Nonfiction books. **Considers these nonfiction areas:** Art/architecture/design; biography/autobiography; business/economics; child guidance/parenting; computers/electronic; ethnic/cultural interests; health/medicine; humor/satire; money/finance; nature/environment; popular culture; psychology; sociology; sports.

How to Contact: Prefers to read materials exclusively. Query with outline/proposal and SASE. Considers simultaneous queries. Responds in 2 weeks to queries; 2 months to mss. Obtains most new clients through recommendations from others.

Recent Sales: Sold 300 titles in the last year. *Dan Gookin's Naked Windows*, by Dan Gookin (Sybex); *Battlebots: The Official Guide*, by Mark Clarkson (Osborne McGraw-Hill); *Opening the XBox: Inside Microsoft's Effort to Unleash an Entertainment Revolution*, by Dean Takahashi (Prima); *Just for Fun*, by Linus Torvalds and David Diamond (Harper Collins).

Terms: Agent receives 15% commission on domestic sales; 25% commission on foreign sales. Offers written contract. Charges clients for photocopying and other unusual expenses.

Writers' Conferences: "We host the Waterside Publishing Conference each spring. Please check our website at www.waterside.com for details."

Tips: "For new writers, a quality proposal and a strong knowledge of the market you're writing for goes a long way towards helping us turn you into a published author."

N **◎** **WATKINS LOOMIS AGENCY, INC.**, 133 E. 35th St., Suite 1, New York NY 10016. (212)532-0080. Fax: (212)889-0506. **Contact:** Katherine Fausset. Estab. 1908. Represents 150 clients.

Member Agents: Gloria Loomis (president); Katherine Fausset (agent).

Represents: Nonfiction books, novels, short story collections. **Considers these nonfiction areas:** Art/architecture/design; biography/autobiography; current affairs; ethnic/cultural interests; history; nature/environment; popular culture; science/technology; true crime/investigative; journalism. **Considers these fiction areas:** Literary.

O— This agency specializes in literary fiction, nonfiction.

How to Contact: Query with SASE, by standard mail only. Responds in 1 month to queries.

Recent Sales: This agency prefers not to share information on specific sales. Clients include Walter Mosley and Cornel West.

Terms: Agent receives 15% commission on domestic sales; 20% commission on foreign sales.

N **◎** **WAXMAN LITERARY AGENCY, INC.**, 80 Fifth Ave., Suite 1101, New York NY 10011. Website: www.waxmanagency.com. Estab. 1997. Member of AAR. Represents 60 clients. 50% of clients are new/unpublished writers. Currently handles: 60% nonfiction books; 40% novels.

● Prior to opening his agency, Mr. Waxman was editor for five years at HarperCollins.

Member Agents: Scott Waxman (all categories of nonfiction, commercial fiction). **Considers these nonfiction areas:** Narrative nonfiction. **Considers these fiction areas:** Literary.

O— "Looking for serious journalists and novelists with published works."

How to Contact: Query through Web site. All unsolicited mss returned unopened. Considers simultaneous queries. Responds in 2 weeks to queries; 6 weeks to mss. Returns materials only with SASE. Obtains most new clients through recommendations from others, solicitations, conferences.

Terms: Agent receives 15% commission on domestic sales; 25% commission on foreign sales. Offers written contract; 60 days notice must be given to terminate contract. Charges for photocopying, express mail, fax, international postage, book orders. Refers to editing services for clients only. 0% of business is derived from editing services.

N **◎** **CHERRY WEINER LITERARY AGENCY**, 28 Kipling Way, Manalapan NJ 07726-3711. (732)446-2096. Fax: (732)792-0506. E-mail: cherry8486@aol.com. **Contact:** Cherry Weiner. Estab. 1977. Represents 40 clients. 10% of clients are new/unpublished writers. Currently handles: 10-20% nonfiction books; 80-90% novels.

● This agency is currently not looking for new clients except by referral or by personal contact at writers' conferences.

Represents: Nonfiction books, novels. **Considers these nonfiction areas:** Self-help/personal improvement; sociology. **Considers these fiction areas:** Action/adventure; contemporary issues; detective/police/crime; family saga; fantasy; glitz; historical;

mainstream/contemporary; mystery/suspense; psychic/supernatural; romance; science fiction; thriller; western/frontier.

O→ This agency specializes in science fiction, fantasy, westerns, mysteries (both contemporary and historical), historical novels, Native American works, mainstream, all the genre romances.

How to Contact: Query with SASE. Prefers to read materials exclusively. No e-mail or fax queries. Responds in 1 week to queries; 2 months to mss. Returns materials only with SASE.

Recent Sales: Sold 50 titles in the last year.

Terms: Agent receives 15% commission on domestic sales; 15% commission on foreign sales. Offers written contract. Charges clients for extra copies of mss "but would prefer author do it"; 1st class postage for author's copies of books; Express Mail for important document/manuscripts.

Writers' Conferences: Western writers convention; science fiction conventions; fantasy conventions.

Tips: "Meet agents and publishers at conferences. Establish a relationship, then get in touch with them reminding them of meetings and conference."

THE WEINGEL-FIDEL AGENCY, 310 E. 46th St., 21E, New York NY 10017. (212)599-2959. **Contact:** Loretta Weingel-Fidel. Estab. 1989. Currently handles: 75% nonfiction books; 25% novels.

- Prior to opening her agency, Ms. Weingel-Fidel was a psychoeducational diagnostician.

Represents: Nonfiction books, novels. **Considers these nonfiction areas:** Art/architecture/design; biography/autobiography; memoirs; music/dance; psychology; science/technology; sociology; women's issues/studies; investigative. **Considers these fiction areas:** Literary; mainstream/contemporary.

O→ This agency specializes in commercial, literary fiction and nonfiction. Actively seeking investigative journalism. Does not want to receive genre fiction, self-help, science fiction, fantasy.

How to Contact: Referred writers only. No unsolicited mss. Obtains most new clients through referrals.

Recent Sales: *The New Rabbi*, by Stephen Fried (Bantam); *Love, Greg & Lauren*, by Greg Manning (Bantam); *The V Book*, by Elizabeth G. Stewart, M.D. and Paula Spencer (Bantam).

Terms: Agent receives 15% commission on domestic sales; 20% commission on foreign sales. Offers written contract, binding for 1 year; automatic renewal. Bills sent back to clients all reasonable expenses such as UPS, express mail, photocopying, etc.

Tips: "A very small, selective list enables me to work very closely with my clients to develop and nurture talent. I only take on projects and writers about which I am extremely enthusiastic."

TED WEINSTEIN LITERARY MANAGEMENT, 287 Duncan St., San Francisco CA 94131-2019. Website: www.twliterary.com. **Contact:** Ted Weinstein. Estab. 2001. Represents 30 clients. 75% of clients are new/unpublished writers. Currently handles: 100% nonfiction books.

Represents: Nonfiction books. **Considers these nonfiction areas:** Biography/autobiography; business/economics; current affairs; government/politics/law; health/medicine; history; popular culture; science/technology; self-help/personal improvement; travel; environment, lifestyle.

How to Contact: Query with SASE, submit proposal package, outline, 1 sample chapter(s). No full mss. See website for detailed submission guidelines. Considers simultaneous queries. Responds in 3 weeks to queries. Returns materials only with SASE.

Terms: Agent receives 15% commission on domestic sales; 20-30% commission on foreign sales. Offers written contract, binding for 1 year. Charges clients for photocopying and express shipping.

LYNN WHITTAKER, LITERARY AGENT, Graybill & English, LLC, 1875 Connecticut Ave. NW, Suite 712, Washington DC 20009. (202)588-9798, ext. 127. Fax: (202)457-0662. E-mail: lynnwhittaker@aol.com. Website: www.graybillandenglish.com. Estab. 1998. Member of AAR. Represents 24 clients. 10% of clients are new/unpublished writers. Currently handles: 85% nonfiction books; 15% novels.

- Prior to becoming an agent, Ms. Whittaker was an editor, owner of a small press, and taught at the college level.

Represents: Nonfiction books, novels, short story collections. **Considers these nonfiction areas:** Animals; biography/autobiography; current affairs; ethnic/cultural interests; health/medicine; history; memoirs; money/finance; multicultural; nature/environment; popular culture; science/technology; sports; women's issues/studies. **Considers these fiction areas:** Detective/police/crime; ethnic; historical; literary; multicultural; mystery/suspense; sports.

O→ "As a former editor, I especially enjoy working closely with writers to develop and polish their proposals and manuscripts." Actively seeking literary fiction, sports, history, creative nonfiction of all kinds, ethnic/multicultural, women's stories & issues. Does not want to receive romance/women's commercial fiction, children's/young adult, religious, fantasy/horror.

How to Contact: Query with SASE, submit proposal package, outline, 2 sample chapter(s). Responds in 2 weeks to queries; 1 month to mss. Returns materials only with SASE. Obtains most new clients through recommendations from others.

Recent Sales: *Never Say Never: When Others Say You Can't and You Know You Can*, by Phyllis George (McGraw-Hill); *Leadership the Eleanor Roosevelt Way*, by Robin Gerber. Other clients include Michael Wilbon, Mariah Burton Nelson, Leonard Shapiro, John Tallmadge, Dorothy Sucher, Brooke Foster, James McGregor Burns.

Terms: Agent receives 15% commission on domestic sales; 20% commission on foreign sales. Offers written contract; 30 days notice must be given to terminate contract. Direct expenses for photocopying of proposals and mss, UPS/FedEx.

Writers' Conferences: Creative Nonfiction Conference, (Goucher College MD, August); Washington Independent Writers, (Washington DC, May); Hariette Austin Writers Conference, (Athens GA, July).

WIESER & WIESER, INC., 25 E. 21 St., 6th Floor, New York NY 10010. (212)260-0860. **Contact:** Olga Wieser. Estab. 1975. 30% of clients are new/unpublished writers. Currently handles: 50% nonfiction books; 50% novels.

Member Agents: Jake Elwell (history, military, mysteries, romance, sports, thrillers); Olga Wieser (psychology, fiction, pop medical, literary fiction).

Represents: Nonfiction books, novels. **Considers these nonfiction areas:** Business/economics; cooking/foods/nutrition; current affairs; health/medicine; history; money/finance; nature/environment; psychology; sports; true crime/investigative. **Considers these fiction areas:** Contemporary issues; detective/police/crime; historical; literary; mainstream/contemporary; mystery/suspense; romance; thriller.

O→ This agency specializes in mainstream fiction and nonfiction.

How to Contact: Query with outline/proposal and SASE. Responds in 2 weeks to queries. Obtains most new clients through queries, authors' recommendations and industry professionals.

Recent Sales: *Mary: The Chosen One*, by Roberta Kells Dorr (Revell); *Eddie Rickenbacker*, by H. Paul Jeffers (Presidio); *Sea of Grey*, by Dewey Lambdin (St. Martin's Press); *The Voyage of the Hunley*, by Edwin P. Hoyt (Burford Books); *Cyclops*, by Jim DeFelice (Pocket); *Fire Flight*, by John Nance (Simon & Schuster).

Terms: Agent receives 15% commission on domestic sales; 20% commission on foreign sales. Offers written contract. Charges clients for photocopying and overseas mailing.

Writers' Conferences: BEA; Frankfurt Book Fair.

WILLIAMS LITERARY AGENCY, RI Box 109H, Kosciusko MS 39090-9706. (662)674-5703. Fax: (305)489-2329. E-mail: submissions@williamsliteraryagency.com. Website: williamsliteraryagency.com. **Contact:** Sheri Homan Williams. Estab. 1997. Represents 64 clients.

- Prior to becoming an agent, Sheri Homan Williams was a freelance writer and literary assistant.

Member Agents: Sheri Homan Williams, owner, literary agent (fiction, nonfiction, novels, scripts); Ann Rought, literary assistant, editor (fiction, nonfiction, novels, juvenile); Kathie Erwin, associate agent (nonfiction, scholarly); Shannon Edwards, associate agent (fiction, nonfiction, novels).

Represents: Nonfiction books, novels, juvenile books, movie scripts, feature film, TV scripts, animation, miniseries.

O→ "Looks for well-written books with a strong plot and consistency throughout." No longer works with first-time writers.

How to Contact: Query with SASE or submit cover letter, outline/proposal, and bio. Considers simultaneous queries. Reports in 3-6 months, depending on the number of submissions in-house. Returns materials only with SASE.

WRITERS HOUSE, 21 W. 26th St., New York NY 10010. (212)685-2400. Fax: (212)685-6550. Estab. 1974. Member of AAR. Represents 440 clients. 50% of clients are new/unpublished writers. Currently handles: 25% nonfiction books; 40% novels; 35% juvenile books.

Member Agents: Albert Zuckerman (major novels, thrillers, women's fiction, important nonfiction); Amy Berkower (major juvenile authors, women's fiction, art and decorating, psychology); Merrilee Heifetz (quality children's fiction, science fiction and fantasy, popular culture, literary fiction); Susan Cohen (juvenile and young adult fiction and nonfiction, Judaism, women's issues); Susan Ginsburg (serious and popular fiction, true crime, narrative nonfiction, personality books, cookbooks); Michele Rubin (serious nonfiction); Robin Rue (commercial fiction and nonfiction, YA fiction); Jennifer Lyons (literary, commercial fiction, international fiction, nonfiction and illustrated); Jodi Reamer (juvenile and young adult fiction and nonfiction, adult commercial fiction, popular culture); Simon Lipskar (literary and commercial fiction, narrative nonfiction); Nicole Pitesa (juvenile and young adult fiction, literary fiction); Steven Malk (juvenile and young adult fiction and nonfiction).

Represents: Nonfiction books, novels, juvenile books. **Considers these nonfiction areas:** Animals; art/architecture/design; biography/autobiography; business/economics; child guidance/parenting; cooking/foods/nutrition; health/medicine; history; interior design/decorating; juvenile nonfiction; military/war; money/finance; music/dance; nature/environment; psychology; science/technology; self-help/personal improvement; theater/film; true crime/investigative; women's issues/studies. **Considers these fiction areas:** Action/adventure; comic books/cartoon; confession; contemporary issues; detective/police/crime; erotica; ethnic; experimental; family saga; fantasy; feminist; gay/lesbian; glitz; gothic; hi-lo; historical; horror; humor/satire; juvenile; literary; mainstream/contemporary; military/war; multicultural; multimedia; mystery/suspense; New Age; occult; picture books; plays; poetry; poetry in translation; psychic/supernatural; regional; religious/inspirational; romance; science fiction; short story collections; spiritual; sports; thriller; translation; western/frontier; young adult; women's.

O→ This agency specializes in all types of popular fiction and nonfiction. Does not want to receive scholarly, professional, poetry, plays or screenplays.

How to Contact: Query with SASE. No e-mail or fax queries. Responds in 1 month to queries. Obtains most new clients through recommendations from others.

Recent Sales: Sold 200-300 titles in the last year. *Next*, by Michael Lewis (Norton); *Art of Deception*, by Ridley Pearson (Hyperion); *Report from Ground Zero*, by Dennis Smith (Viking); *The Villa*, by Nora Roberts (Penguin/Putnam); *Captain Underpants*, by Dan Pilkey (Scholastic). Other clients include Francine Pascal, Ken Follett, Stephen Hawking, Linda Howard, F. Paul Wilson, Neil Gaiman and Laurel Hamilton.

Terms: Agent receives 15% commission on domestic sales; 20% commission on foreign sales. Offers written contract, binding for 1 year. Agency charges fees for copying manuscripts and proposals and overseas airmail of books.

Tips: "Do not send mss. Write a compelling letter. If you do, we'll ask to see your work."

WRITERS' PRODUCTIONS, P.O. Box 630, Westport CT 06881-0630. (203)227-8199. Fax: (203)227-6349. E-mail: dlm67@worldnet.att.net. **Contact:** David L. Meth. Estab. 1982. Represents 25 clients. Currently handles: 40% nonfiction books; 60% novels.

- "I am not taking on new clients at this time."

Represents: Nonfiction books, novels, literary quality fiction.

How to Contact: No new clients accepted at this time. No e-mail or fax queries. Obtains most new clients through recommendations from others.

Recent Sales: This agency prefers not to share information on specific sales.

Terms: Agent receives 15% commission on domestic sales; 25% commission on foreign sales. Offers written contract. Charges clients for electronic transmissions, long-distance phone calls, express or overnight mail, courier service, etc.

Tips: "Send only your best, most professionally prepared work. Do not send it before it is ready. We must have SASE for all correspondence and return of manuscripts. Do not waste time sending work to agencies or editors who are not accepting new clients."

WRITERS' REPRESENTATIVES, INC., 116 W. 14th St., 11th Floor, New York NY 10011-7305. (212)620-0023. E-mail: transom@writersreps.com. Website: www.writersreps.com. **Contact:** Glen Hartley or Lynn Chu. Estab. 1985. Represents 130 clients. 5% of clients are new/unpublished writers. Currently handles: 90% nonfiction books; 10% novels.

- Prior to becoming agents, Ms. Chu was a lawyer, and Mr. Hartley worked at Simon & Schuster, Harper & Row and Cornell University Press.

Member Agents: Lynn Chu; Glen Hartley; Catharine Sprinkel.

Represents: Nonfiction books, novels. **Considers these fiction areas:** Literary.

This agency specializes in serious nonfiction. Actively seeking serious nonfiction and quality fiction. Does not want to receive motion picture/television screenplays.

How to Contact: Prefers to read materials exclusively. Considers simultaneous queries. Obtains most new clients through "recommendations from our clients."

Recent Sales: Sold 30 titles in the last year. *The Shield of Achilles*, by Philip Bobbitt; *Sisters of Salome*, by Toni Bentley; *World on Fire*, by Amy Chua; *Genius*, by Harold Bloom.

Terms: Agent receives 15% commission on domestic sales; 20% commission on foreign sales.

Tips: "Always include a SASE that will ensure a response from the agent and the return of material submitted."

WYLIE-MERRICK LITERARY AGENCY, 1138 S. Webster St., Kokomo IN 46902-6357. (765)459-8258 or (765)457-3783. E-mail: smartin@wylie-merrick.com; rbrown@wylie-merrick.com. Website: www.wylie-merrick.com. **Contact:** S.A. Martin, Robert Brown. Estab. 1999. Member of SCBWI. Currently handles: 25% nonfiction books; 25% novels; 50% juvenile books.

- Ms. Martin holds a Master's degree in Language Education and is a writing and technology curriculum specialist.

Member Agents: S.A. Martin (juvenile/middle grade/young adult); Robert Brown (adult fiction/nonfiction, young adult).

Represents: Nonfiction books (adult and juvenile), novels (adult and juvenile), juvenile books. **Considers these nonfiction areas:** How-to; juvenile nonfiction; self-help/personal improvement. **Considers these fiction areas:** Action/adventure; fantasy; historical; mystery/suspense; picture books; religious/inspirational; romance; science fiction; thriller; young adult (middle grade).

This agency specializes in children's and young adult literary as well as mainstream adult fiction. Actively seeking middle-grade/young adult fiction and nonfiction; picture books; adult fiction and nonfiction.

How to Contact: Query with SASE, Include first 10 pages for novels, complete mss for picturebooks. No e-mail or fax queries. Considers simultaneous queries. Responds in 1 month to queries; 3 months to mss. Returns materials only with SASE. Obtains most new clients through recommendations from others, queries and conferences.

Recent Sales: *Full Court Pressure*, by Jon Ripslinger (Roaring Brook).

Terms: Agent receives 15% commission on domestic sales; 20% commission on foreign sales. Offers written contract. Charges clients for postage, photocopying, handling.

Tips: "We work with a small, select group of writers. We are highly selective when considering new clients, so your work must be the best it can possibly be for us to consider it. We only work with serious professionals who know their craft and the publishing industry. Anything less we reject."

ZACHARY SHUSTER HARMSWORTH, 1776 Broadway, Suite 1405, New York NY 10019. (212)765-6900. Fax: (212)765-6490. E-mail: eharmsworth@zshliterary.com. Website: www.zshliterary.com. Also: Boston Office: 729 Boylston St., 5th Floor. Phone: (617)262-2400, Fax: (617)262-2468. **Contact:** Esmond Harmsworth; Scott Gold (NY). Estab. 1996. Represents 125 clients. 20% of clients are new/unpublished writers. Currently handles: 45% nonfiction books; 45% novels; 5% story collections; 5% scholarly books.

- "Our principals include two former publishing and entertainment lawyers, a journalist and an editor/agent." Lane Zachary was an editor at Random House before becoming an agent.

Member Agents: Esmond Harmsworth (commercial and literary fiction, history, science, adventure); Todd Shuster (narrative and prescriptive nonfiction, biography, memoirs); Lane Zachary (biography, memoirs, literary fiction); Jennifer Gates (literary fiction, nonfiction).

Represents: Nonfiction books, novels. **Considers these nonfiction areas:** Animals; biography/autobiography; business/economics; current affairs; gay/lesbian issues; government/politics/law; health/medicine; history; how-to; language/literature/criticism; memoirs; money/finance; music/dance; psychology; science/technology; self-help/personal improvement; sports; true crime/investigative; women's issues/studies. **Considers these fiction areas:** Contemporary issues; detective/police/crime; ethnic; feminist; gay/lesbian; historical; literary; mainstream/contemporary; mystery/suspense; thriller.

This agency specializes in journalist-driven narrative nonfiction, literary and commercial fiction. Actively seeking narrative nonfiction, mystery, commercial and literary fiction, memoirs, history, biographies. Does not want to receive poetry.

How to Contact: Query with SASE, submit 50 page sample of ms. No e-mail or fax queries. Considers simultaneous queries. Responds in 3 months to mss. Obtains most new clients through recommendations from others, solicitations, conferences.

Recent Sales: Sold 40-50 titles in the last year. *All Kinds of Minds*, by Mel Levine (Simon & Schuster). Other clients include Leslie Epstein, David Mixner.

Terms: Agent receives 15% commission on domestic sales; 20% commission on foreign sales. Offers written contract, binding for 1 work only; 30 days notice must be given to terminate contract. Charges clients for postage, copying, courier, telephone. "We only charge expenses if the manuscript is sold."

Tips: "We work closely with all our clients on all editorial and promotional aspects of their works."

SUSAN ZECKENDORF ASSOC., INC., 171 W. 57th St., New York NY 10019. (212)245-2928. **Contact:** Susan Zeckendorf. Estab. 1979. Member of AAR. Represents 15 clients. 25% of clients are new/unpublished writers. Currently handles: 50% nonfiction books; 50% novels.

- Prior to opening her agency, Ms. Zeckendorf was a counseling psychologist.

Represents: Nonfiction books, novels. **Considers these nonfiction areas:** Biography/autobiography; child guidance/parenting; health/medicine; history; music/dance; psychology; science/technology; sociology; women's issues/studies. **Considers these fiction areas:** Detective/police/crime; ethnic; historical; literary; mainstream/contemporary; mystery/suspense; thriller.

Actively seeking mysteries, literary fiction, mainstream fiction, thrillers, social history, parenting, classical music, biography. Does not want to receive science fiction, romance. "No children's books."

How to Contact: Query with SASE. No e-mail or fax queries. Considers simultaneous queries. Responds in 10 days to queries; 3 weeks to mss. Returns materials only with SASE.

Recent Sales: *How to Write a Damn Good Mystery*, by James N. Frey (St. Martin's); *Moment of Madness*, by Una-Mary Parker (Headline).

Terms: Agent receives 15% commission on domestic sales; 20% commission on foreign sales. Charges for photocopying, messenger services.

Writers' Conferences: Central Valley Writers Conference; The Tucson Publishers Association Conference; Writer's Connection; Frontiers in Writing Conference (Amarillo TX); Golden Triangle Writers Conference (Beaumont TX); Oklahoma Festival of Books (Claremont OK); SMU Writers Conference (NYC).

Tips: "We are a small agency giving lots of individual attention. We respond quickly to submissions."

Script Agents

This section contains agents who sell feature film scripts, television scripts, and theatrical stage plays. A breakdown of the types of scripts each agency handles is included in the listing.

Many of the script agents listed here are signatories to the Writers Guild of America Artists' Manager Basic Agreement. They have paid a membership fee and agreed to abide by the WGA's standard code of behavior. Agents who are WGA signatories are not permitted to charge a reading fee to WGA members, but are allowed to do so to nonmembers. They are permitted to charge for critiques and other services, but they may not refer you to a particular script doctor. Enforcement is uneven, however. Although a signatory can, theoretically, be stripped of its signatory status, this rarely happens.

A few of the listings in this section are actually management companies. The role of managers is quickly changing in Hollywood—they were once only used by actors, or "talent," and the occasional writer. Now many managers are actually selling scripts to producers.

It's a good idea to register your script before sending it out, and the WGA offers a registration service to members and nonmembers alike. Membership in the WGA is earned through the accumulation of professional credits and carries a number of significant benefits. Write the Guild for more information on specific agencies, script registration, and membership requirements, or visit their website at www.wga.org.

Like the literary agents listed in this book, some script agencies ask that clients pay for some or all of the office fees accrued when sending out scripts. Some agents ask for a one-time "handling" fee up front, while others deduct office expenses after a script has been sold. Always have a clear understanding of any fee an agent asks you to pay.

Canadian and international agents are included in this section. Canadian agents have a ( ) preceding their listing, while international agents (those located outside of the U.S. and Canada) have a ( ) preceding their listing. Remember to include an International Reply Coupon (IRC) with your self-addressed envelope when contacting Canadian and international agents.

SUBHEADS

Each listing is broken down into subheads to make locating specific information easier. In the first section, you'll find contact information for each agency. You'll also learn if the agent

Level of Openness

Each agency has an icon indicating its openness to submissions. Before contacting any agency, check the listing to make sure it is open to new clients.

- Newer agency actively seeking clients.
- Agency seeking both new and established writers.
- Agency prefers to work with established writers, mostly obtains new clients through referrals.
- Agency handling only certain types of work or work by writers under certain circumstances.
- Agency not currently seeking new clients. We include these agencies to let you know they are currently not open to new clients. *Unless you have a strong recommendation from someone well-respected in the field, our advice is to avoid approaching these agents.*

is a WGA signatory or a member of any other professional organizations. Further information is provided which indicates an agency's size, its willingness to work with a new or previously unpublished writer, and a percentage breakdown of the general types of scripts the agency will consider.

Member Agents: Agencies comprised of more than one agent list member agents and their individual specialties to help you determine the most appropriate person for your query letter.

Represents: Make sure you query only agents who represent the type of material you write.

O-ᵣ Look for the key icon to quickly learn an agent's areas of specializations and individual strengths. Agents also mention here what specific areas they are currently seeking as well as subjects they do *not* wish to receive.

How to Contact: Most agents open to submissions prefer initially to receive a query letter briefly describing your work. Script agents usually discard material sent without a SASE. Here agents also indicate if they accept queries by fax or e-mail, if they consider simultaneous submissi ons, and their preferred way of meeting new clients.

Recent Sales: Reflecting the different ways scriptwriters work, agents list scripts optioned or sold, and scripting assignments procured for clients. The film industry is very secretive about sales, but you may be able to get a list of clients or other references upon request—especially if the agency is interested in representing your work.

Terms: Most agents' commissions range from 10 to 15 percent, and WGA signatories may not earn over 10 percent from WGA members.

Writers' Conferences: For screenwriters unable to move to Los Angeles, writers' conferences provide another venue for meeting agents.

Tips: Agents offer advice and additional instructions for writers looking for representation.

For More Information

For more information on approaching agents, read "The Basics of Contacting Literary Agents" on page 93.

ABOVE THE LINE AGENCY, 9200 Sunset Blvd., #804, Los Angeles CA 90069. (310)859-6115. Fax: (310)859-6119. **Contact:** Bruce Bartlett. Owner: Rima Bauer Greer. Estab. 1994. Signatory of WGA. Represents 35 clients. 10% of clients are new/unpublished writers. Currently handles: 95% movie scripts; 5% TV scripts.

- Prior to opening her agency, Ms. Greer served as president with Writers & Artists Agency.

Represents: Feature film, TV MOW. **Considers these script subject areas:** Cartoon/animation; writers and directors.

How to Contact: Query with SASE, This agency does not guarantee a response.

Recent Sales: ***Movie/TV MOW script(s) optioned/sold:*** *The Great Cookie Wars*, by Greg Taylor and Jim Strain (Fox); *Velveteen Rabbit*, by Greg Taylor (Disney); *Wing and a Prayer*, by David Engelbach and John Wolff (franchise). ***Scripting Assignment(s):*** *Constantine*, by Frank Capello (Warner Brothers); *Rainbow Six*, by Frank Capello (Paramount); *Duke Nukem*, by Ryan Rowe (Miramax).

Terms: Agent receives 10% commission on domestic sales; 10% commission on foreign sales.

ABRAMS ARTISTS AGENCY, 275 Seventh Ave., 26th Floor, New York NY 10001. (646)486-4600. Fax: (646)486-2358. **Contact:** Jack Tantleff. Estab. 1986. Member of AAR; signatory of WGA.

Member Agents: Jack Tantleff (theater, TV, film); Maura E. Teitelbaum (film, TV, publishing); John Santoianni (TV, film, theater).

Represents: Feature film, episodic drama, sitcom, animation (TV), soap opera, musical. **Considers these script subject areas:** Comedy; contemporary issues; mainstream; mystery/suspense; romantic comedy; romantic drama.

O-ᵣ This agency specializes in theater, film, TV.

How to Contact: Query with SASE, outline. Returns material only with SASE.

Recent Sales: This agency prefers not to share information on specific sales.

Terms: Agent receives 10% commission on domestic sales; 10% commission on foreign sales; 10% commission on dramatic rights sales.

MICHAEL AMATO AGENCY, 1650 Broadway, Suite 307, New York NY 10019. (212)247-4456 or (212)247-4457. Website: www.amatoagency.tv.heaven.com. **Contact:** Michael Amato. Estab. 1970.; Member of SAG, AFTRA. Represents 6 clients. 2% of clients are new/unpublished writers.

Represents: Feature film, TV MOW, episodic drama, animation, documentary, miniseries. **Considers these script subject areas:** Action/adventure.

This agency specializes in action/adventure scripts.

How to Contact: Query with SASE. Responds in 1 month to queries. Obtains most new clients through recommendations from others.

Recent Sales: This agency prefers not to share information on specific sales.

BASKOW AGENCY, 2948 E. Russell Rd., Las Vegas NV 89120. (702)733-7818. Fax: (702)733-2052. E-mail: jaki@baskow.com. **Contact:** Jaki Baskow. Estab. 1976. Represents 8 clients. 40% of clients are new/unpublished writers. Currently handles: 5% nonfiction books; 5% novels; 20% movie scripts; 70% TV scripts.

Member Agents: Crivolus Sarulus (scripts), Jaki Baskow.

Represents: Feature film, TV MOW, episodic drama, sitcom, documentary, miniseries, variety show. **Considers these script subject areas:** Action/adventure; biography/autobiography; comedy; contemporary issues; family saga; glitz; mystery/suspense; religious/inspirational; romantic comedy; romantic drama; science fiction (juvenile only); thriller.

Actively seeking unique scripts/all-American true stories, kids projects and movies of the week. Does not want to receive heavy violence.

How to Contact: Submit outline, proposal and treatments. Accepts e-mail and fax queries. Responds in 1 month to queries. Obtains most new clients through recommendations from others.

Recent Sales: Sold 3 movie/TV MOW scripts in the last year. *Malpractice*, by Larry Leirketen (Blakely); *Angel of Death*, (CBS). Other clients include Cheryl Anderson, Camisole Prods, Michael Store.

Terms: Agent receives 10% commission on domestic sales; 10% commission on foreign sales. Offers written contract.

THE BOHRMAN AGENCY, 8899 Beverly Blvd., Suite 811, Los Angeles CA 90048. (310)550-5444. **Contact:** Michael Hruska, Caren Bohrman. Signatory of WGA.

Represents: Novels, feature film, TV scripts. **Considers these script subject areas:** Action/adventure; biography/autobiography; cartoon/animation; comedy; contemporary issues; detective/police/crime; erotica; ethnic; experimental; family saga; fantasy; feminist; gay/lesbian; glitz; historical; horror; juvenile; mainstream; multicultural; multimedia; mystery/suspense; psychic/supernatural; regional; religious/inspirational; romantic comedy; romantic drama; science fiction; sports; teen; thriller; western/frontier.

How to Contact: Query with SASE. No unsolicited mss. Obtains most new clients through recommendations from others.

Recent Sales: This agency prefers not to share information on specific sales.

ALAN BRODIE REPRESENTATION, 211 Piccadilly, London W1J 9HF, England. 0207-917-2871. Fax: 0207-917-2872. E-mail: info@alanbrodie.com. Website: www.alanbrodie.com. **Contact:** Alan Brodie, Sarah McNair or Ali Howarth. Member of PMA. 10% of clients are new/unpublished writers.

Member Agents: Alan Brodie (theater, film, TV); Sarah McNair (theater); Ali Howarth (new writing-theater and TV)

This agency specializes in stage, film and television.

How to Contact: All unsolicited mss returned unopened. North American writers are only accepted in exceptional circumstances. Accepts e-mail and fax queries. Obtains most new clients through recommendations from others.

Recent Sales: This agency prefers not to share information on specific sales.

Terms: Agent receives 10-15% commission on domestic sales. Charges clients for photocopying.

Tips: "Biographical details can be helpful. Generally only playwrights whose work has been performed will be considered, provided they come recommended by an industry professional."

CEDAR GROVE AGENCY ENTERTAINMENT, P.O. Box 1692, Issaquah WA 98027-0068. (425)837-1687. E-mail: cedargroveagency@juno.com. Website: freeyellow.com/members/cedargrove/index.html. **Contact:** Renee MacKenzie, Samantha Powers. Estab. 1995. Member of Cinema Seattle. Represents 7 clients. 100% of clients are new/unpublished writers. Currently handles: 90% movie scripts; 10% TV scripts.

- Prior to becoming agents, Ms. Taylor worked for the stock brokerage firm, Morgan Stanley Dean Witter; Ms. Powers was a customer service/office manager; Ms. MacKenzie was an office manager and recently a Production Manager.

Member Agents: Amy Taylor (Senior Vice President-Motion Picture Division), Samantha Powers (Executive Vice President-Motion Picture Division), Renee MacKenzie (Story Editor).

Represents: Feature film, TV MOW, sitcom. **Considers these script subject areas:** Action/adventure; biography/autobiography; comedy; detective/police/crime; family saga; juvenile; mystery/suspense; romantic comedy; science fiction; sports; thriller; western/frontier.

Cedar Grove Agency Entertainment was formed in the Pacific Northwest to take advantage of the rich and diverse culture as well as the many writers who reside there. Does not want period pieces, horror genres, children scripts dealing with illness, or scripts with excessive substance abuse.

How to Contact: Query with SASE, 1-page synopsis. No phone calls please. Mail, email or fax. No attachments if emailed. Accepts e-mail and fax queries. Responds in 10 days to queries; 2 months to mss. Obtains most new clients through referrals and website.

Recent Sales: This agency prefers not to share information on specific sales.

Terms: Agent receives 10% commission on domestic sales. Offers written contract, binding for 6-12 months; 30-day notice must be given to terminate contract.

Tips: "We focus on finding that rare gem, the undiscovered, multi-talented writer, no matter where they live. Write, write, write! Find time everyday to write. Network with other writers when possible, and write what you know. Learn the craft through books. Read scripts of your favorite movies. Enjoy what you write!"

CHADWICK & GROS LITERARY AGENCY, Garden District Branch, Belleview Dr. Palazzo 226, Baton Rouge LA 70806-5049. (225)338-9521. Fax: (225)338-9521. E-mail: apiazza@peoplepc.com or cguk@peoplepc.com. Website: colorpro.com/chadwick-gros/. **Contact:** Tony Seigan,associate director/overseas officer; Anna Piazza, director. Estab. 1998. Represents 30 clients. 95% of clients are new/unpublished writers. Currently handles: 90% movie scripts; 10% TV scripts.

- Prior to becoming an agent, Ms. Piazza was a talent scout for Rinehart & Associates.

Member Agents: Anna Piazza (director), Tony Seigan (associate director/overseas officer), David J. Carubba (business manager), C.J. Myerson (president of Institute of Baton Rouge Oxford Writers [I-BROWS] Colony), Theron T. Jacks (business advisor).

Represents: Feature film, TV MOW, sitcom. **Considers these script subject areas:** Action/adventure; biography/autobiography; comedy; detective/police/crime; family saga; juvenile; mystery/suspense; romantic comedy; science fiction; sports; thriller; western/frontier.

Actively seeking "good attitudes; tough-minded, sure-footed, potential pros." This agency will not be signing new clients until July 2007. "Presently, our plate is full."

How to Contact: Query with SASE, 1-page synopsis. Accepts queries during February, July and October, but will not be signing new clients until July 2007. Considers simultaneous queries. Responds in 10 days to queries; 2 months to mss. Returns materials only with SASE. Obtains most new clients through recommendations from others, website.

Recent Sales: Sold 17 scripts in the last year. *Carrot Tips*, by J. Seivers (Generation X); *The Author*; *The Ouida Link*; *WhorehouseRoux*; *The Fine and the Wicked*, by Sam Goldwyn, Jr.

Terms: Agent receives 10% commission on domestic sales; 15% commission on foreign sales. Offers written contract, binding for 1-2 years; 6-month notice must be given to terminate contract. Charges clients for all communications with C&G - phone, fax, postage and handling - fees fall to queries/clients; that is, office expenses, postage, photocopying, but *no marketing fee*.

Tips: "Be most businesslike when you tap on an agency's door. Agencies are business offices, and every exchange costs money, time, effort, grief or joy."

CIRCLE OF CONFUSION, LTD., 107-23 71st Rd., Suite 30, Forest Hills NY 11375. E-mail: circlequeries@aol.com. **Contact:** Shelly Narine. Estab. 1990. Represents 30 clients. 40% of clients are new/unpublished writers. Currently handles: 95% movie scripts.

Member Agents: Lawrence Mattis; David Mattis; Trisha Smith.

Represents: Nonfiction books, novels, novellas, feature film, TV scripts. **Considers these nonfiction areas:** Agriculture/horticulture; americana; animals; anthropology/archaeology; art/architecture/design; biography/autobiography; business/economics; child guidance/parenting; computers/electronic; cooking/foods/nutrition; crafts/hobbies; creative nonfiction; current affairs; education; ethnic/cultural interests; gardening; gay/lesbian issues; government/politics/law; health/medicine; history; how-to; humor/satire; interior design/decorating; juvenile nonfiction; language/literature/criticism; memoirs; military/war; money/finance; multicultural; music/dance; nature/environment; New Age/metaphysics; philosophy; photography; popular culture; psychology; recreation; regional; religious/inspirational; science/technology; self-help/personal improvement; sex; sociology; software; spirituality; sports; theater/film; translation; travel; true crime/investigative; women's issues/studies; young adult. **Considers these fiction areas:** Action/adventure; comic books/cartoon; confession; contemporary issues; detective/police/crime; erotica; ethnic; experimental; family saga; fantasy; feminist; gay/lesbian; glitz; gothic; hi-lo; historical; horror; humor/satire; juvenile; literary; mainstream/contemporary; military/war; multicultural; multimedia; mystery/suspense; New Age; occult; picture books; plays; poetry; poetry in translation; psychic/supernatural; regional; religious/inspirational; romance; science fiction; short story collections; spiritual; sports; thriller; translation; western/frontier; young adult; women's. **Considers these script subject areas:** Action/adventure; biography/autobiography; cartoon/animation; comedy; contemporary issues; detective/police/crime; erotica; ethnic; experimental; family saga; fantasy; feminist; gay/lesbian; glitz; historical; horror; juvenile; mainstream; multicultural; multimedia; mystery/suspense; psychic/supernatural; regional; religious/inspirational; romantic comedy; romantic drama; science fiction; sports; teen; thriller; western/frontier.

Specializes in screenplays for film and TV.

How to Contact: Query with SASE. Responds in 1 month to queries; 2 months to mss. Obtains most new clients through recommendations from others, solicitations, writing contests and queries.

Recent Sales: ***Movie/TV MOW script(s) optioned/sold:*** *The Matrix*, by Wachowski Brothers (Warner Brothers); *Reign of Fire*, by Chabot/Peterka (Dreamworks); *Mr. & Mrs. Smith*, by Simon Kinberg. Other clients include Jaswinki, Massa, Ferrer.

Terms: Agent receives 10% commission on domestic sales; 10% commission on foreign sales. Offers written contract, binding for 1 year.

Tips: "We look for writing that shows a unique voice, especially one which puts a fresh spin on commercial Hollywood genres."

CLIENT FIRST-A/K/A LEO P. HAFFEY AGENCY, P.O.Box 128049, Nashville TN 37212-8049. (615)463-2388. E-mail: c1st@nashville.net. Website: www.c-1st.com or www.nashville.net/~cl. **Contact:** Robin Swensen. Estab. 1990.

Signatory of WGA. Represents 21 clients. 25% of clients are new/unpublished writers. Currently handles: 40% novels; 60% movie scripts.
Member Agents: Leo Haffey (attorney/agent in the motion picture industry).
Represents: Nonfiction books (self-help), novels, short story collections, novellas, feature film, animation. **Considers these script subject areas:** Action/adventure; cartoon/animation; comedy; contemporary issues; detective/police/crime; family saga; historical; mystery/suspense; romantic drama (contemporary, historical); science fiction; sports; thriller; western/frontier.

O→ This agency specializes in movie scripts and novels for sale to motion picture industry.

How to Contact: Query with SASE, synopsis, treatment or summary. Do not send scripts/screenplays unless requested. Considers simultaneous queries. Responds in 1 week to queries; 2 months to mss. Returns materials only with SASE. Obtains most new clients through recommendations from others.
Recent Sales: This agency prefers not to share information on specific sales.
Terms: Offers written contract, binding for negotiable length of time.
Tips: "The motion picture business is a numbers game like any other. The more you write the better your chances are of success. Please send a SASE along with your query letter."

COMMUNICATIONS MANAGEMENT ASSOCIATES, 1129 Sixth Ave., #1, Rockford IL 61104-3147. Fax: (815)964-3061. **Contact:** Thomas R. Lee. Estab. 1989. Represents 30 clients. 50% of clients are new/unpublished writers. Currently handles: 5% nonfiction books; 10% novels; 80% movie scripts; 5% TV scripts.
Member Agents: Jack Young.
Represents: Novels, short story collections, novellas, juvenile books, scholarly books, poetry books, feature film, TV MOW, animation, documentary, miniseries. **Considers these fiction areas:** Action/adventure (adventure); detective/police/crime; erotica; fantasy; historical; horror; juvenile; mainstream/contemporary; mystery/suspense; picture books; romance (historical, regency); science fiction; thriller; western/frontier; young adult. **Considers these script subject areas:** Action/adventure; biography/autobiography; cartoon/animation; comedy; contemporary issues; detective/police/crime; erotica; fantasy; historical; horror; juvenile; mainstream; psychic/supernatural; religious/inspirational; romantic comedy; romantic drama; science fiction; teen; thriller; western/frontier.

O→ This agency specializes in research, editing and financing.

How to Contact: Query with SASE, proposal package, outline, 3 sample chapter(s). Discards unwanted material. Considers simultaneous queries. Obtains most new clients through recommendations from others.
Recent Sales: Sold 2 scripts in the last year. This agency prefers not to share information on specific sales. Send query for list of credits.
Terms: Agent receives 10% commission on domestic sales; 15% commission on foreign sales. Offers written contract, binding for 2-4 months; 60 days notice must be given to terminate contract. Charges clients for postage, photocopying and office expenses; Writers reimbursed for office fees after the sale of ms.
Writers' Conferences: BEA.
Tips: "Don't let greed or fame-seeking, or anything but a sincere love of writing push you into this business."

THE COPPAGE CO., 5411 Carmellia Ave., North Hollywood CA 91601. (818)980-8806. Fax: (818)980-8824. **Contact:** Judy Coppage; Celeste Cooley-Mitchell. Estab. 1985. Signatory of WGA; Member of DGA, SAG, AFTRA.
Represents: Feature film, TV scripts (original).

O→ This agency specializes in "writers who also produce, direct and act."

How to Contact: Obtains most new clients through recommendation only.
Recent Sales: This agency prefers not to share information on specific sales.

DOUGLAS & KOPELMAN ARTISTS, INC., 393 W. 49th St., Suite 5G, New York NY, 10019. (212)445-0160. Fax: (212)246-7138. **Contact:** Sarah Douglas. Member of AAR.
Member Agents: Sarah Douglas; Charles Kopelman; Cheryl Andrews.
Represents: Stage plays. **Considers these script subject areas:** Action/adventure; biography/autobiography; cartoon/animation; comedy; contemporary issues; detective/police/crime; erotica; ethnic; experimental; family saga; fantasy; feminist; gay/lesbian; glitz; historical; horror; juvenile; mainstream; multicultural; multimedia; mystery/suspense; psychic/supernatural; regional; religious/inspirational; romantic comedy; romantic drama; science fiction; sports; teen; thriller; western/frontier.

O→ This agency specializes in musical stage plays.

How to Contact: Query with SASE. Prefers to read materials exclusively. No e-mail or fax queries.

DRAMATIC PUBLISHING, (Specialized: theatrical works), 311 Washington St., Woodstock IL 60098. (815)338-7170. Fax: (815)338-8981. E-mail: plays@dramaticpublishing.com. Website: www.dramaticpublishing.com. **Contact:** Linda Habjan. Estab. 1885. Currently handles: 2% textbooks; 98% stage plays.
Represents: Stage plays.

O→ This agency specializes in a full range of stage plays, musicals, adaptations, and instructional books about theater.

How to Contact: Submit complete ms, SASE. Responds in 10-12 to mss.
Recent Sales: This agency prefers not to share information on specific sales.

DIANE DURRETT AGENCY, 727 22nd St., Sacramento CA 95818-4011. (916)492-9003. Fax: (916)444-5436. E-mail: diane_durrett@pacbell.net. **Contact:** Diane Durrett. Signatory of WGA. Currently handles: 10% novels; 90% movie scripts.

• Prior to becoming an agent, Ms. Durrett worked in print and online publishing for 10 years and served as president of the Northern California Writers & Artists association.

Represents: Novels, movie scripts, feature film. **Considers these fiction areas:** Action/adventure; detective/police/crime; historical; horror; humor/satire; literary; mainstream/contemporary; romance; science fiction; thriller. **Considers these script subject areas:** Action/adventure; biography/autobiography; comedy; contemporary issues; detective/police/crime; historical; horror; mystery/suspense; romantic comedy; romantic drama; science fiction; thriller.

How to Contact: Query with SASE. Responds in 2 months to queries; 2 months to mss. Returns materials only with SASE.

Terms: Agent receives 10% commission on domestic sales; 10% commission on foreign sales. Offers written contract. Charges for photocopies and postage.

Tips: "Please be sure you understand the craft of screenwriting and are using the proper format. Scripts and manuscripts should be free of spelling and grammatical errors."

THE E S AGENCY, 6612 Pacheco Way, Citrus Heights CA 95610. (916)723-2794. Fax: (916)723-2796. E-mail: edley07@cs.com. **Contact:** Ed Silver, president. Estab. 1995. Represents 50-75 clients. 70% of clients are new/unpublished writers. Currently handles: 50% nonfiction books; 25% novels; 25% movie scripts.

• Prior to becoming an agent, Mr. Silver was an entertainment business manager.

Member Agents: Ed Silver.

Represents: Nonfiction books, novels, movie scripts, feature film, TV MOW. **Considers these nonfiction areas:** Considers general nonfiction areas. **Considers these fiction areas:** Action/adventure; detective/police/crime; erotica; experimental; historical; humor/satire; literary; mainstream/contemporary; mystery/suspense; thriller; young adult. **Considers these script subject areas:** Action/adventure; comedy; contemporary issues; detective/police/crime; erotica; ethnic; experimental; family saga; mainstream; mystery/suspense; romantic comedy; romantic drama; sports; thriller.

This agency specializes in theatrical screenplays, MOW and miniseries. Actively seeking "anything good and distinctive."

How to Contact: Query with SASE. Considers simultaneous queries. Responds in 1 month to queries. Returns materials only with SASE. Obtains most new clients through recommendations from others, queries from WGA agency list.

Recent Sales: *The Cannabible*, by Jason King; *How to Read Maya Hieroglyphs*, by John Montgomery; *Dictionary of Maya Hieroglyphs*, by John Montgomery.

Terms: Agent receives 15% commission on domestic sales; 20% commission on foreign sales; 10% commission on dramatic rights sales. Offers written contract; 30 days notice must be given to terminate contract.

FILMWRITERS LITERARY AGENCY, 4932 Long Shadow Dr., Midlothian VA 23112. (804)744-1718. **Contact:** Helene Wagner. Signatory of WGA. Currently not accepting clients.

• Prior to opening her agency, Ms. Wagner was director of the Virginia Screenwriter's Forum for 7 years and taught college level screenwriting classes. "As a writer myself, I have won or been a finalist in most major screenwriting competitions throughout the country and have a number of my screenplays optioned. Through the years I have enjoyed helping and working with other writers. Some have gone on to have their movies made, their work optioned, and won national contests."

Represents: Feature film, TV MOW, miniseries. **Considers these script subject areas:** Action/adventure; comedy; contemporary issues; detective/police/crime; historical; juvenile; mystery/suspense; psychic/supernatural; romantic comedy; romantic drama; teen; thriller.

This agency does not accept unsolicited queries.

How to Contact: No e-mail or fax queries. Obtains most new clients only through recommendations.

Recent Sales: ***Movie/TV MOW script(s) optioned/sold:*** *Woman of His Dreams*, by Jeff Rubin (Ellenfreyer Productions).

Terms: Agent receives 10% commission on domestic sales; 10% commission on foreign sales. Offers written contract. Clients supply photocopying and postage. Writers reimbursed for office fees after the sale of ms.

Tips: "Professional writers should wait until they have at least four drafts done before they send out their work because they know it takes that much hard work to make a story and characters work. Show me something I haven't seen before with characters that I care about, that jump off the page. I not only look at writer's work, I look at the writer's talent. If I believe in a writer, even though a piece may not sell, I'll stay with the writer and help nurture that talent which a lot of the big agencies won't do."

FITZGERALD LITERARY MANAGEMENT, 84 Monte Alto Rd., Santa Fe NM 87505. (505)466-1186. **Contact:** Lisa FitzGerald. Estab. 1994. Represents 12 clients. 75% of clients are new/unpublished writers. Currently handles: 15% film rights novels; 85% movie scripts.

• Ms. FitzGerald headed development at Universal Studios for Bruce Evans and Raynold Gideon, Oscar-nominated writer-producers. She also served as Executive Story Analyst at CBS, and held positions at Curtis Brown Agency in New York and Adams, Ray & Rosenberg Talent Agency in Los Angeles.

Represents: Novels (film rights to), feature film, TV MOW. **Considers these fiction areas:** Mainstream/contemporary (novels with film potential). **Considers these script subject areas:** Action/adventure; biography/autobiography; comedy; contemporary issues; detective/police/crime; ethnic; family saga; fantasy; historical; horror; mainstream; mystery/suspense; psychic/supernatural; romantic comedy; romantic drama; science fiction; sports; teen; thriller; western/frontier.

This agency specializes in screenwriters and selling film rights to novels. Actively seeking mainstream feature film scripts. Does not want to receive true stories.

How to Contact: We are not accepting new clients except by referral.

Recent Sales: Sold 7 titles and sold 5 scripts in the last year.

Terms: Agent receives 15% commission on domestic sales. Offers written contract, binding for 1-2 years. Charges clients for photocopying and postage.
Tips: "Know your craft. Read produced screenplays. Enter screenplay contests. Educate yourself on the business in general (read The Hollywood Reporter or Daily Variety). Learn how to pitch. Keep writing and don't be afraid to get your work out there."

THE BARRY FREED CO., 468 N. Camden Dr., #201, Beverly Hills CA 90210. (310)860-5627. Fax: (310)474-1087. E-mail: blfreed@aol.com. **Contact:** Barry Freed. Signatory of WGA. Represents 15 clients. 95% of clients are new/unpublished writers. Currently handles: 100% movie scripts.
- Prior to opening his agency, Mr. Freed worked for ICM.

Represents: Feature film, TV MOW. **Considers these script subject areas:** Action/adventure; comedy; contemporary issues; detective/police/crime; ethnic; family saga.
Actively seeking adult drama, comedy, romantic comedy. Does not want to receive period, science fiction.
How to Contact: Query with SASE. Prefers to read materials exclusively. Accepts e-mail and fax queries. Responds in 3 months to mss. Responds immediately to queries. Obtains most new clients through recommendations from others.
Recent Sales: This agency prefers not to share information on specific sales.
Terms: Offers written contract, binding for 2 years.
Tips: "Our clients are a high qualified small roster of writers who write comedy, action adventure/thrillers, adult drama, romantic comedy."

ROBERT A. FREEDMAN DRAMATIC AGENCY, INC., 1501 Broadway, Suite 2310, New York NY 10036. (212)840-5760. **Contact:** Robert A. Freedman. Estab. 1928. Member of AAR; signatory of WGA.
- Mr. Freedman has served as vice president of the dramatic division of AAR.

Member Agents: Robert A. Freedman, president; Selma Luttinger, vice president; Marta Praeger (stage plays) and Robin Kaver (movie and TV scripts), associates.
Represents: Movie scripts, TV scripts, stage plays.
This agency works with both established and new authors. Specializes in plays, movie scripts and TV scripts.
How to Contact: Query with SASE. All unsolicited mss returned unopened. Responds in 2 weeks to queries; 3 months to mss.
Recent Sales: "We will speak directly with any prospective client concerning sales that are relevant to his/her specific script."
Terms: Agent receives 10% commission on domestic sales. Charges clients for photocopying.

SAMUEL FRENCH, INC., 45 W. 25th St., New York NY 10010-2751. (212)206-8990. Fax: (212)206-1429. E-mail: samuelfrench@earthlink.net. Website: www.samuelfrench.com. **Contact:** Lawrence Harbison, senior editor. Estab. 1830. Member of AAR.
Member Agents: Alleen Hussung; Brad Lorenz; Linda Kirland; Charles R. Van Nostrand
Represents: Theatrical stage plays, musicals. **Considers these script subject areas:** Comedy; contemporary issues; detective/police/crime; ethnic; fantasy; horror; mystery/suspense; thriller.
This agency specializes in publishing plays which they also license for production.
How to Contact: Query with SASE, or submit complete ms. to Lawrence Harbison. Accepts e-mail and fax queries. Considers simultaneous queries. Responds in 2-8 months to mss. Responds immediately to queries.
Recent Sales: This agency prefers not to share information on specific sales.
Terms: Agent receives variable commission on domestic sales.

GRAHAM AGENCY, 311 W. 43rd St., New York NY 10036. **Contact:** Earl Graham. Estab. 1971. Represents 40 clients. 30% of clients are new/unpublished writers. Currently handles: stage plays; musicals.
Represents: Theatrical stage plays, musicals.
This agency specializes in playwrights. "We're interested in commercial material of quality." Does not want to receive one-acts or material for children.
How to Contact: Query with SASE. No e-mail or fax queries. Responds in 3 months to queries; 6 weeks to mss. Obtains most new clients through recommendations from others, solicitations.
Recent Sales: This agency prefers not to share information on specific sales.
Terms: Agent receives 10% commission on dramatic rights sales.
Tips: "Write a concise, intelligent letter giving the gist of what you are offering."

HART LITERARY MANAGEMENT, 5686 Antelope Trail, Orcutt CA 93455-6066. E-mail: tibicen@silcom.com. Website: hartliterary.com. **Contact:** Susan Hart. Estab. 1997. Signatory of WGA. Represents 25 clients. 95% of clients are new/unpublished writers. Currently handles: 100% movie scripts.
- Prior to opening the agency, Ms. Hart was a screenwriter.

Represents: Movie scripts, feature film, TV MOW, mostly PG-13. **Considers these script subject areas:** Biography/autobiography; family saga; horror; juvenile; mainstream; science fiction; teen.
How to Contact: E-mail queries only. Considers simultaneous queries. Responds in 2 days to queries. Returns materials only with SASE. Obtains most new clients through solicitations.
Recent Sales: Sold 1 script in the last year. *Encrypt*, by Richard Taylor (Sci-Fi Channel).
Terms: Agent receives 10% domestic or worldwide sales on gross income written any source from the screenplays commission on domestic sales. Offers written contract, binding for 1 year but may be cancelled at any time by both parties in writing. Charges clients for photocopies and postage; $7 domestic, $10 Canadian and $12 international (currently). This

is the same as WGA requirement that screenwriters send copies of all screenplays to their agents and is cheaper than that in most cases.

Tips: "I want a great story spell-checked, formatted, and "typed" in industry standard 12 point Courier or Courier New only, between 95-120 pages maximum. No overt gore, sex, violence. See website for genres I may look at."

CAROLYN HODGES AGENCY, 1980 Glenwood Dr., Boulder CO 80304-2329. (303)443-4636. Fax: (303)443-4636. E-mail: hodgesc@earthlink.net. **Contact:** Carolyn Hodges. Estab. 1989. Signatory of WGA. Represents 15 clients. 75% of clients are new/unpublished writers. Currently handles: 15% movie scripts; 45% TV scripts.

- Prior to opening her agency, Ms. Hodges was a freelance writer and founded the Writers in the Rockies Screenwriting Conference.

Represents: Feature film, TV MOW. **Considers these script subject areas:** Comedy (light, black); romantic comedy; thriller (suspense, psychological).

This agency represents screenwriters for film and TV MOW. Does not want TV sitcom, drama or episodics.

How to Contact: Query with SASE. Accepts e-mail and fax queries. Considers simultaneous queries. Responds in 1 week to queries; 10 weeks to mss. Returns materials only with SASE. Obtains most new clients through recommendations from others.

Recent Sales: Available upon request.

Terms: Agent receives 10% commission on domestic sales; 10% commission on foreign sales. Offers written contract. No charge for criticism. "I always try to offer concrete feedback, even when rejecting a piece of material."

Tips: "Become proficient at your craft. Attend all workshops accessible to you. Read all the books applicable to your area of interest. Read as many 'produced' screenplays as possible. Live a full, vital and rewarding life so your writing will have something to say. Get involved in a writer's support group. Network with other writers. Receive 'critiques' from your peers and consider merit of suggestions. Don't be afraid to re-examine your perspective. Do yourself a favor and don't submit the 'first draft' of 'first script' to agents. Immature writing is obvious and will hurt your chance of later submissions."

BARBARA HOGENSON AGENCY, 165 West End Ave., Suite 19-C, New York NY 10023. (212)874-8084. Fax: (212)362-3011. **Contact:** Barbara Hogenson. Estab. 1994. Member of AAR; signatory of WGA. Represents 60 clients. 5% of clients are new/unpublished writers. Currently handles: 35% nonfiction books; 15% novels; 50% stage plays.

- Prior to opening her agency, Ms. Hogenson was with the prestigious Lucy Kroll Agency for 10 years.

Represents: Nonfiction books, novels, theatrical stage play. **Considers these nonfiction areas:** Biography/autobiography; history; interior design/decorating; music/dance; popular culture; theater/film. **Considers these fiction areas:** Action/adventure; detective/police/crime; ethnic; historical; humor/satire; literary; mainstream/contemporary; mystery/suspense; romance (contemporary); thriller.

How to Contact: Query with SASE, outline. No unsolicited mss. Responds in 1 month to queries. Obtains most new clients through recommendations from others.

Recent Sales: *Letters of James Thurber*, by Harrison Kinney and Rosemary Thurber; *Ghosts of McDougal Street*, by Hesper Anderson; *Learning to Swim*, by Penelope Niven.

Terms: Agent receives 15% commission on domestic sales; 20% commission on foreign sales; 10% commission on dramatic rights sales. Offers written contract.

HUDSON AGENCY, 3 Travis Lane, Montrose NY 10548. (914)737-1475. Fax: (914)736-3064. Website: www.hudsonagency.net. Estab. 1994. Signatory of WGA. Represents 20 clients. Currently handles: 100% movie scripts.

Represents: Feature film, TV MOW, animation, miniseries. **Considers these script subject areas:** Action/adventure; cartoon/animation; comedy; contemporary issues; detective/police/crime; family saga; fantasy; juvenile; mystery/suspense; romantic comedy; romantic drama; teen; western/frontier.

This agency specializes in feature film. Actively seeking "writers with screenwriting education or workshops under their belts." Does not want to receive "R-rated material, no occult, no one that hasn't taken at least one screenwriting workshop."

How to Contact: Query with email only. Considers simultaneous queries. Responds in 1 week to queries; 3 weeks to mss. Returns materials only with SASE. Obtains most new clients through recommendations from others.

Terms: Agent receives 10% commission on domestic sales; 10% commission on foreign sales.

Tips: "Yes, we may be small, but we work very hard for our clients. Any script we are representing gets excellent exposure to producers. Our network has over 1,000 contacts in the business and growing rapidly. We are GOOD salespeople. Ultimately it all depends on the quality of the writing and the market for the subject matter. Do not query unless you have taken at least one screenwriting course and read all of Syd Field's books. Check out our Web site for our staff member list, the appropriate e-mail addresses to send queries to, or view our client list. We specialize in features of all genres but will not handle anything associated with the occult or anything containing gratuitous violence, sex or language."

INTERNATIONAL LEONARDS CORP., 3612 N. Washington Blvd., Indianapolis IN 46205-3534. (317)926-7566. **Contact:** David Leonards. Estab. 1972. Signatory of WGA. Currently handles: 50% movie scripts; 50% TV scripts.

Represents: Feature film, TV MOW, sitcom, animation, variety show. **Considers these script subject areas:** Action/adventure; cartoon/animation; comedy; contemporary issues; detective/police/crime; horror; mystery/suspense; romantic comedy; science fiction; sports; thriller.

How to Contact: All unsolicited mss returned unopened.

Recent Sales: This agency prefers not to share information on specific sales.

Terms: Agent receives 10% commission on domestic sales; 10% commission on foreign sales. Offers written contract, binding for WGA standard terms, which vary.

JARET ENTERTAINMENT, 6973 Birdview Ave., Malibu CA 90265. (310) 589-9600. Fax: (310) 589-9602. E-mail: info@jaretentertainment.com. Website: www.jaretentertainment.com. **Contact:** Nathan Santell. Represents 20 clients. 70% of clients are new/unpublished writers. Currently handles: 75% movie scripts; 25% TV scripts.

Member Agents: Nathan Santell (senior assistant/junior manager).

Represents: Movie scripts, TV scripts, TV MOW, animation. **Considers these script subject areas:** Action/adventure; biography/autobiography; cartoon/animation; comedy; mystery/suspense; psychic/supernatural; romantic comedy; romantic drama; science fiction; sports; thriller.

This management company specializes in creative, out-of-the-box thinking. "We're willing to take a chance on well-written materials." Actively seeking "high concept science fiction, thrillers, mysteries and smart romantic comedies." Does not want "any projects with unnecessary violence, westerns, or antyhing you've seen before-studio programmers, black comedy or period pieces that drag out and are boring."

How to Contact: Query with SASE. Discards unwanted material. Accepts e-mail and fax queries. Considers simultaneous queries. Obtains most new clients through recommendations from others.

Recent Sales: Sold 5 scripts in the last year. *Bumper to Bumper*, (Fox); *The Fraud Prince*, (Warner Brothers). ***Scripting Assignment(s):*** *Girl in the Curl*, (Paramount).

Terms: Agent receives 10% commission on domestic sales. Offers written contract, binding for 10-24 months.

LESLIE KALLEN AGENCY, 15760 Ventura Blvd., Suite #700, Encino CA 91436. (800)755-2785. Fax: (818)906-8931. E-mail: kallengroup@earthlink.net. Website: www.lesliekallen.com. Estab. 2001.

Represents: Feature film, TV MOW.

This agency specializes in feature film, gamers, animators and MOWs.

How to Contact: Referral only.

Recent Sales: This agency prefers not to share information on specific sales.

Terms: Agent receives 10% commission on domestic sales.

CHARLENE KAY AGENCY, 901 Beaudry St., Suite 6, St.Jean/Richelieu QC J3A 1C6, Canada. (450)348-5296. **Contact:** Louise Meyers, director of development. Estab. 1992. Member of BMI; signatory of WGA. 100% of clients are new/unpublished writers. Currently handles: 50% movie scripts; 50% TV scripts.

- Prior to opening her agency, Ms. Kay was a screenwriter.

Member Agents: Louise Meyers; Karen Forsyth.

Represents: Feature film, TV scripts, TV MOW, episodic drama, sitcom. **Considers these script subject areas:** Action/adventure; biography/autobiography; family saga; fantasy; psychic/supernatural; romantic comedy; romantic drama; science fiction.

This agency specializes in teleplays and screenplays. "We seek stories that are out of the ordinary, something we don't see too often. A well-written and well-constructed script is important." Does not want to receive "thrillers or barbaric and erotic films. No novels, books, or manuscripts."

How to Contact: Query with SASE, outline/proposal, IRCs for submissions outside of Canada. No e-mail or fax queries. Considers simultaneous queries. Responds in 1 month to queries; 10 weeks to mss. Returns materials only with SASE.

Recent Sales: This agency prefers not to share information on specific sales.

Terms: Agent receives 10% commission on domestic sales; 10% commission on foreign sales. Offers written contract, binding for 1 year.

Tips: "This agency is listed on the WGA lists and query letters arrive by the dozens every week. As our present clients understand, success comes with patience. A sale rarely happens overnight, especially when you are dealing with totally unknown writers. We are not impressed by the credentials of a writer, amateur or professional or by his or her pitching techniques, but by his or her story ideas and ability to build a well-crafted script."

LEGACIES, 501 Woodstork Circle, Bradenton FL 34209-7393. (941)792-9159. E-mail: legaciesliterary@hotmail.com. **Contact:** Mary Ann Amato, executive director. Estab. 1992. Member Florida Motion Picture & Television Association, Board of Talent Agents, Dept. of Professional Regulations License No. TA 0000404; signatory of WGA. 50% of clients are new/unpublished writers. Currently handles: 10% novels; 80% movie scripts; 10% stage plays.

Represents: Feature film. **Considers these script subject areas:** Comedy; contemporary issues; family saga; feminist; historical.

This agency specializes in screenplays.

How to Contact: Query with SASE. Considers simultaneous queries. Responds in 2 weeks to queries; 6 weeks to mss.

Recent Sales: *Death's Parallel*, by Dr. Oakley Jordan (Rainbow Books). ***Movie/TV MOW script(s) optioned/sold:*** *A Bench On Which To Rest*, by Maria Phillips; *Progress of the Sun*, by Patricia Friedberg; *Elsie Venner & Aurora Leigh*, by Raleigh Marcell.

Terms: Agent receives 10% commission on domestic sales; 15% commission on foreign sales. Offers written contract.

Tips: "New writers should purchase script writing computer programs, or read and apply screenplay format before submitting."

THE LUEDTKE AGENCY, 1674 Broadway, Suite 7A, New York NY 10019. (212)765-9564. Fax: (212)765-9582. **Contact:** Elaine Devlin. Estab. 1997. Signatory of WGA. Represents 35 clients. 20% of clients are new/unpublished writers. Currently handles: 50% movie scripts; 10% TV scripts; 40% stage plays.

- Prior to becoming an agent, Penny Luedtke was in classical music management; Elaine Devlin was in film development, story editing.

Member Agents: Penny Luedtke (primarily represents talent-some special project writers); Elaine Devlin (screenwriters, playwrights, television).

Represents: Movie scripts, feature film, TV scripts, TV MOW, sitcom, miniseries, soap opera, theatrical stage play, stage plays. **Considers these script subject areas:** Action/adventure; biography/autobiography; cartoon/animation; comedy; contemporary issues; detective/police/crime; ethnic; family saga; fantasy; feminist; gay/lesbian; historical; horror; juvenile; mainstream; multicultural; multimedia; mystery/suspense; psychic/supernatural; regional; religious/inspirational; romantic comedy; romantic drama; science fiction; sports; teen; thriller; western/frontier.

"We are a small shop and like it that way. We work closely with our writers developing projets and offer extensive editorial assistance." Actively seeking well-written material. Does not want any project with graphic or explicit violence against women or children.

How to Contact: Query with SASE. No e-mail or fax queries. Considers simultaneous queries. Responds in 1 month to queries; 6 months to mss. Returns materials only with SASE. Obtains most new clients through recommendations from others.

Recent Sales: This agency prefers not to share information on specific sales.

Terms: Agent receives 10% commission on domestic sales; 15% commission on foreign sales. Offers written contract, binding for WGA standard terms. Charges clients for reimbursement of expenses for couriers, messengers, international telephone and photocopying.

THE MANAGEMENT CO., 1337 Ocean Ave., Suite F, Santa Monica CA 90401. (310)990-5602. **Contact:** Tom Klassen. Represents 15 clients.

- Prior to starting his agency Mr. Klassen was an agent with International Creative Management (ICM).

Member Agents: Tom Klassen; F. Miguel Valenti; Helene Taber; Paul Davis; Steve Gamber.

Represents: Feature film (scripts), TV scripts, episodic drama, sitcom, miniseries.

Actively seeking "studio quality action-drama scripts and really good comedies." Does not want horror scripts.

How to Contact: Submit query letter with synopsis. No e-mail or fax queries. Responds in 2-3 weeks to queries. Returns materials only with SASE. Obtains most new clients through recommendations from others, conferences.

Recent Sales: Sold 11 scripts in the last year.

Terms: Agent receives 10% commission on domestic sales; 10% commission on foreign sales. Offers written contract, binding for 2 years.

Writers' Conferences: Sundance Film Festival; New York Film Festival; Telluride; Atlanta; Chicago; Minnesota.

Tips: "We only accept query letters with a short, one-page synopsis. We will request full manuscript with a SASE if interested. We rarely take on nonreferred material, but do review query letters and occasionally take on new writers. We have done very well with those we have taken on."

THE MARTON AGENCY, INC., One Union Square W., Suite 612, New York NY 10003-3303. Fax: (212)691-9061. E-mail: info@martonagency.com. **Contact:** Tonda Marton. Member of AAR.

Member Agents: Tonda Marton; Anne Reingold.

This agency specializes in foreign language licensing.

HELEN MERRILL, LTD., 295 Lafayatte St., Suite 915, New York NY 10012-2700. **Contact:** Patrick Herold. Member of AAR.

Member Agents: Patrick Herold (AAR); Beth Blickers (AAR); Morgan Jenness.

THE STUART M. MILLER, CO., 11684 Ventura Blvd., #225, Studio City CA 91604-2699. (818)506-6067. Fax: (818)506-4079. E-mail: smmco@aol.com. **Contact:** Stuart Miller. Estab. 1977. Signatory of WGA; Signatory of DGA. Currently handles: 50% movie scripts; 40% multimedia; 10% books.

Represents: Nonfiction books, novels, movie scripts. **Considers these nonfiction areas:** Biography/autobiography; computers/electronic; current affairs; government/politics/law; health/medicine; history; how-to; memoirs; military/war; self-help/personal improvement; true crime/investigative. **Considers these fiction areas:** Action/adventure; detective/police/crime; historical; literary; mainstream/contemporary; mystery/suspense; science fiction; sports; thriller. **Considers these script subject areas:** Action/adventure; biography/autobiography; cartoon/animation; comedy; contemporary issues; detective/police/crime; family saga; historical; mainstream; multimedia; mystery/suspense; romantic comedy; romantic drama; science fiction; sports; teen; thriller.

How to Contact: Query with SASE, 2-3 page narrative and outline/proposal. Accepts e-mail and fax queries. Considers simultaneous queries. Responds in 3 days to queries; 6 weeks to mss. Returns materials only with SASE.

Recent Sales: This agency prefers not to share information on specific sales.

Terms: Agent receives 10% for movie/TV commission on domestic sales; 15-25% for books commission on foreign sales. Offers written contract, binding for 2 years; WGA standard notice must be given to terminate contract.

Tips: "Always include SASE, e-mail address, or fax number with query letters. Make it easy to respond."

MONTEIRO ROSE DRAVIS AGENCY, (formerly Monteiro Rose Agency), 17514 Ventura Blvd., Suite 205, Encino CA 91316. (818)501-1177. Fax: (818)501-1194. Website: www.monteiro-rose.com. **Contact:** Candy Monteiro. Estab. 1987. Signatory of WGA. Represents 50 clients. Currently handles: 40% movie scripts; 20% TV scripts; 40% animation.

Member Agents: Candace Monteiro (literary); Fredda Rose (literary); Jason Dravis (literary).

Represents: Feature film, TV MOW, episodic drama, animation. **Considers these script subject areas:** Action/adventure; cartoon/animation; comedy; contemporary issues; detective/police/crime; ethnic; family saga; historical; juvenile; mainstream; mystery/suspense; psychic/supernatural; romantic comedy; romantic drama; science fiction; teen; thriller.

O-ᴿ This agency specializes in scripts for animation, TV and film.

How to Contact: Query with SASE. Responds in 1 week to queries; 2 months to mss. Returns materials only with SASE. Obtains most new clients through recommendations from others, solicitations.

Recent Sales: This agency prefers not to share information on specific sales.

Terms: Agent receives 10% commission on domestic sales. Offers written contract, binding for 2 years; 90 days notice must be given to terminate contract. Charges for photocopying.

Tips: "It does no good to call and try to speak to an agent before they have read your material, unless referred by someone we know. The best and only way, if you're a new writer, is to send a query letter with a SASE. If agents are interested, they will request to read it. Also enclose a SASE with the script if you want it back."

NIAD MANAGEMENT, 3465 Coy Dr., Sherman Oaks CA 91423. (818)981-2505. Fax: (818)386-2082. E-mail: query@niadmanagement.com. Website: www.niadmanagement.com. Estab. 1997. Represents 20 clients. 2% of clients are new/unpublished writers. Currently handles: 1% novels; 98% movie scripts; 1% stage plays.

Represents: Movie scripts, feature film, TV MOW, miniseries, stage plays. **Considers these nonfiction areas:** Biography/autobiography. **Considers these fiction areas:** Action/adventure; detective/police/crime; family saga; literary; mainstream/contemporary; multicultural; mystery/suspense; psychic/supernatural; romance; thriller. **Considers these script subject areas:** Action/adventure; biography/autobiography; comedy; contemporary issues; detective/police/crime; ethnic; family saga; historical; horror; mainstream; multicultural; mystery/suspense; psychic/supernatural; romantic comedy; romantic drama; sports; teen; thriller.

How to Contact: Query with SASE. Accepts e-mail and fax queries. Considers simultaneous queries. Responds in 1 week to queries; 3 months to mss. Returns materials only with SASE. Obtains most new clients through recommendations from others.

Recent Sales: Sold 5 scripts in the last year. *The Dan Gable Story*, by Lee Zlotoff (Charles Hirschorn/Disney); *Insider Trading*, by Claudia Salter (USA Network); *Killing the People Upstairs*, by Bruce Griffiths (Max Media). Other clients include Neil Cohen, Julian Grant, Susan Sandler, Michael Lazarou, Jim McGlynn, Don Most, Fernando Fragata.

Terms: Agent receives 15% commission on domestic sales. Offers written contract, binding for 1 year; 30-day notice must be given to terminate contract.

DOROTHY PALMER, 235 W. 56 St., New York NY 10019. (212)765-4280. Fax: (212)977-9801. Estab. 1990. Signatory of WGA. Represents 12 clients. 0% of clients are new/unpublished writers. Currently handles: 70% movie scripts; 30% TV scripts.

- In addition to being a literary agent, Ms. Palmer has worked as a talent agent for 30 years.

Represents: Feature film, TV MOW, episodic drama, sitcom, miniseries. **Considers these script subject areas:** Action/adventure; comedy; contemporary issues; detective/police/crime; family saga; feminist; mainstream; mystery/suspense; romantic comedy; romantic drama; thriller.

O-ᴿ This agency specializes in screenplays, TV. Actively seeking successful, published writers (screenplays only). Does not want to receive work from new or unpublished writers.

How to Contact: Query with SASE. Prefers to read materials exclusively. Published writers *only*. Returns materials only with SASE. Obtains most new clients through recommendations from others.

Recent Sales: This agency prefers not to share information on specific sales.

Terms: Agent receives 10% commission on domestic sales; 10% commission on foreign sales. Offers written contract, binding for 1 year. Charges clients for postage, photocopies.

Tips: "Do *not* telephone. When I find a script that interests me, I call the writer. Calls to me are a turn-off because they cut into my reading time. The only ones who can call are serious investors of independent films."

BARRY PERELMAN AGENCY, 1155 N. Laeceniga, #412, W. Hollywood CA 90069. (310)659-1122. Fax: (310)659-1122. Estab. 1982. Member of DGA; signatory of WGA. Represents 40 clients. 15% of clients are new/unpublished writers. Currently handles: 100% movie scripts.

Member Agents: Barry Perelman (motion picture/packaging).

Represents: Movie scripts. **Considers these script subject areas:** Action/adventure; biography/autobiography; contemporary issues; detective/police/crime; historical; horror; mystery/suspense; romantic comedy; romantic drama; science fiction; thriller.

O-ᴿ This agency specializes in motion pictures/packaging.

How to Contact: Query with SASE, proposal package, outline. Responds in 1 month to queries. Obtains most new clients through recommendations from others, solicitations.

Recent Sales: This agency prefers not to share information on specific sales.

Terms: Agent receives 10% commission on domestic sales; 10% commission on foreign sales. Offers written contract, binding for 1-2 years. Charges clients for postage and photocopying.

A PICTURE OF YOU, 1176 Elizabeth Dr., Hamilton OH 45013-3507. (513)863-1108. Fax: (513)863-1108. E-mail: apoy1@aol.com. **Contact:** Lenny Minelli. Estab. 1993. Signatory of WGA. Represents 45 clients. 50% of clients are new/unpublished writers. Currently handles: 80% movie scripts; 10% TV scripts; 10% syndicated material.

- Prior to opening his agency, Mr. Minelli was an actor/producer for 10 years. Also owned and directed a talent agency and represented actors and actresses from around the world.

Member Agents: Michelle Chang (fiction/nonfiction books).

Represents: Nonfiction books, novels, short story collections, novellas, feature film, TV MOW, episodic drama, sitcom, animation, documentary, miniseries, syndicated material. **Considers these nonfiction areas:** Gay/lesbian issues; history;

juvenile nonfiction; music/dance; religious/inspirational; self-help/personal improvement; theater/film. **Considers these fiction areas:** Action/adventure; detective/police/crime; erotica; ethnic; family saga; fantasy; gay/lesbian; glitz; historical; horror; literary; mainstream/contemporary; mystery/suspense; religious/inspirational; romance (contemporary, gothic, historical); thriller; western/frontier; young adult. **Considers these script subject areas:** Action/adventure; biography/autobiography; cartoon/animation; comedy; contemporary issues; detective/police/crime; erotica; ethnic; experimental; family saga; fantasy; feminist; gay/lesbian; glitz; historical; horror; juvenile; mainstream; multicultural; multimedia; mystery/suspense; psychic/supernatural; regional; religious/inspirational; romantic comedy; romantic drama; science fiction; sports; teen; thriller; western/frontier.

O→ This agency specializes in screenplays and TV scripts.

How to Contact: Query with SASE. Accepts e-mail and fax queries. Considers simultaneous queries. Responds in 3 weeks to queries; 1 month to mss. Obtains most new clients through recommendations from others, solicitations.

Recent Sales: *Lost and Found*, by J.P. Brice; *So Long*, by Patrick Cappella. ***Scripting Assignment(s):*** *The Governor*, by Gary M. Cappetta.

Terms: Agent receives 10% commission on domestic sales; 15% commission on foreign sales. Offers written contract, binding for 1 year; 90-day notice must be given to terminate contract. Charges clients for postage/express mail and long distance calls.

Tips: "Make sure that the script is the best it can be before seeking an agent."

N ⊘ **THE QUILLCO AGENCY**, 3104 W. Cumberland Court, Westlake Village CA 91362. (805)495-8436. Fax: (805)373-9868. E-mail: quillco2@aol.com. **Contact:** Sandy Mackey (owner). Estab. 1993. Signatory of WGA. Represents 7 clients.

Represents: Feature film, TV MOW, animation, documentary.

How to Contact: Prefers to read materials exclusively. Not accepting query letters at this time. Returns materials only with SASE.

Recent Sales: This agency prefers not to share information on specific sales.

Terms: Agent receives 10% commission on domestic sales; 10% commission on foreign sales.

N ✓ **DAN REDLER ENTERTAINMENT**, 5303 Pearfield Ave., Woodland Hills CA 91364. **Contact:** Dan Redler. Represents 10 clients. Currently handles: 100% movie scripts.

Represents: Movie scripts, feature film. **Considers these script subject areas:** Action/adventure; biography/autobiography; comedy; contemporary issues; detective/police/crime; ethnic; family saga; fantasy; feminist; historical; horror; juvenile; mainstream; mystery/suspense; psychic/supernatural; romantic comedy; romantic drama; science fiction; sports; teen; thriller.

O→ Actively seeking mainstream and contemporary scripts. Does not want to receive small noncommercial stories.

How to Contact: Query with SASE. Prefers to read materials exclusively. Returns materials only with SASE.

Recent Sales: This agency prefers not to share information on specific sales.

Terms: Agent receives 10% commission on domestic sales; 10% commission on foreign sales. Offers written contract, binding for 2 years. Client must supply all copies of scripts.

Tips: "We offer personal service, indepth career guidance, and aggressive sales efforts."

N ✓ **MICHAEL D. ROBINS & ASSOCIATES**, 23241 Ventura Blvd., #300, Woodland Hills CA 91364. (818)343-1755. Fax: (818)343-7355. E-mail: mdr2@msn.com. **Contact:** Michael D. Robins. Estab. 1991. Member of DGA; signatory of WGA. 10% of clients are new/unpublished writers. Currently handles: 5% nonfiction books; 5% novels; 20% movie scripts; 60% TV scripts; 10% syndicated material.

- Prior to opening his agency, Mr. Robins was a literary agent at a mid-sized agency.

Represents: Nonfiction books, novels, movie scripts, feature film, TV scripts, TV MOW, episodic drama, animation, miniseries, syndicated material, stage plays. **Considers these nonfiction areas:** History; humor/satire; memoirs; military/war; popular culture; science/technology; true crime/investigative; urban lifestyle. **Considers these fiction areas:** Action/adventure; comic books/cartoon; detective/police/crime; family saga; fantasy; gay/lesbian; mainstream/contemporary; western/frontier (frontier); young adult. **Considers these script subject areas:** Action/adventure; biography/autobiography; cartoon/animation; comedy; contemporary issues; detective/police/crime; erotica; ethnic; experimental; family saga; fantasy; feminist; gay/lesbian; glitz; historical; horror; juvenile; mainstream; multicultural; multimedia; mystery/suspense; psychic/supernatural; regional; religious/inspirational; romantic comedy; romantic drama; science fiction; sports; teen; thriller; western/frontier.

How to Contact: Query with SASE. Accepts e-mail and fax queries. Considers simultaneous queries. Responds in 1 week to queries; 1 month to mss. Obtains most new clients through recommendations from others.

Recent Sales: This agency prefers not to share information on specific sales.

Terms: Agent receives 10% commission on domestic sales; 10% commission on foreign sales. Offers written contract, binding for 2 years; 4 months notice must be given to terminate contract.

✓ **SHAPIRO-LICHTMAN**, Shapiro-Lichtman Building, 8827 Beverly Blvd., Los Angeles CA 90048. (310)859-8877. Fax: (310)859-7153. **Contact:** Martin Shapiro. Estab. 1969. Signatory of WGA.

Represents: Nonfiction books, novels, novellas, feature film, TV MOW, episodic drama, sitcom, animation (movie, TV), miniseries, soap opera, variety show. **Considers these nonfiction areas:** Americana; animals; art/architecture/design; biography/autobiography; business/economics; child guidance/parenting; computers/electronic; creative nonfiction; current affairs; education; ethnic/cultural interests; gay/lesbian issues; government/politics/law; health/medicine; history; humor/satire; juvenile nonfiction; language/literature/criticism; memoirs; military/war; money/finance; multicultural; music/dance;

nature/environment; photography; popular culture; psychology; science/technology; self-help/personal improvement; sex; sociology; software; spirituality; sports; theater/film; translation; travel; true crime/investigative; women's issues/studies; young adult. **Considers these fiction areas:** Action/adventure; comic books/cartoon; confession; contemporary issues; detective/police/crime; erotica; ethnic; experimental; family saga; fantasy; feminist; gay/lesbian; glitz; gothic; hi-lo; historical; horror; humor/satire; juvenile; literary; mainstream/contemporary; military/war; multicultural; multimedia; mystery/suspense; New Age; occult; picture books; plays; romance; science fiction; short story collections; spiritual; sports; thriller; translation; western/frontier; young adult. **Considers these script subject areas:** Action/adventure; cartoon/animation; comedy; contemporary issues; detective/police/crime; ethnic; family saga; historical; horror; mainstream; mystery/suspense; romantic comedy; romantic drama; science fiction; teen; thriller; western/frontier.

How to Contact: Query with SASE. Responds in 10 days to queries. Returns materials only with SASE. Obtains most new clients through recommendations from others.

Recent Sales: This agency prefers not to share information on specific sales.

Terms: Agent receives 10% commission on domestic sales; 20% commission on foreign sales. Offers written contract, binding for 2 years.

KEN SHERMAN & ASSOCIATES, 9507 Santa Monica Blvd., Beverly Hills CA 90210. (310)273-3840. Fax: (310)271-2875. **Contact:** Ken Sherman. Estab. 1989. Member of BAFTA, PEN Int'l; signatory of WGA; DGA. Represents approximately 50 clients. 10% of clients are new/unpublished writers. Currently handles: nonfiction books; novels; juvenile books; movie scripts; TV scripts; video games/fiction.

- Prior to opening his agency, Mr. Sherman was with The William Morris Agency, The Lantz Office, and Paul Kohner, Inc.

Represents: Nonfiction books, novels, movie scripts, TV scripts, film, television and life rights to books. **Considers these nonfiction areas:** Agriculture/horticulture; americana; animals; anthropology/archaeology; art/architecture/design; biography/autobiography; business/economics; child guidance/parenting; computers/electronic; cooking/foods/nutrition; crafts/hobbies; creative nonfiction; current affairs; education; ethnic/cultural interests; gardening; gay/lesbian issues; government/politics/law; health/medicine; history; how-to; humor/satire; interior design/decorating; juvenile nonfiction; language/literature/criticism; memoirs; military/war; money/finance; multicultural; music/dance; nature/environment; New Age/metaphysics; philosophy; photography; popular culture; psychology; recreation; regional; religious/inspirational; science/technology; self-help/personal improvement; sex; sociology; software; spirituality; sports; theater/film; translation; travel; true crime/investigative; women's issues/studies; young adult. **Considers these fiction areas:** Action/adventure; comic books/cartoon; confession; contemporary issues; detective/police/crime; erotica; ethnic; experimental; family saga; fantasy; feminist; gay/lesbian; glitz; gothic; hi-lo; historical; horror; humor/satire; juvenile; literary; mainstream/contemporary; military/war; multicultural; multimedia; mystery/suspense; New Age; occult; picture books; plays; poetry; poetry in translation; psychic/supernatural; regional; religious/inspirational; romance; science fiction; short story collections; spiritual; sports; thriller; translation; western/frontier; young adult. **Considers these script subject areas:** Action/adventure; biography/autobiography; cartoon/animation; comedy; contemporary issues; detective/police/crime; erotica; ethnic; experimental; family saga; fantasy; feminist; gay/lesbian; glitz; historical; horror; juvenile; mainstream; multicultural; multimedia; mystery/suspense; psychic/supernatural; regional; religious/inspirational; romantic comedy; romantic drama; science fiction; sports; teen; thriller; western/frontier.

This agency specializes in solid writers for film TV, books and rights to books for film and TV.

How to Contact: Contact by referral only please. Responds in 1 month to mss. Obtains most new clients through recommendations from others.

Recent Sales: Sold over 20 scripts in the last year. *Priscilla Salyers Story*, produced by Andrea Baynes (ABC); *Toys of Glass*, by Martin Booth (ABC/Saban Ent.); *Brazil*, by John Updike (film rights to Glaucia Carmagos); *Fifth Sacred Thing*, by Starhawk (Bantam); *Questions From Dad*, by Dwight Twilly (Tuttle); *Snow Falling on Cedars*, by David Guterson (Universal Pictures); *The Witches of Eastwick-The Musical*, by John Updike (Cameron Macintosh, Ltd.).

Terms: Agent receives 15% commission on domestic sales; 15% commission on foreign sales; 15% commission on dramatic rights sales. Offers written contract. Charges clients for reasonable office expenses, postage, photocopying, and other negotiable expenses.

Writers' Conferences: Maui; Squaw Valley; Santa Barbara; Santa Fe; Aspen Institute; Aspen Writers Foundation, etc.

N **SILVER SCREEN PLACEMENTS**, 602 65th St., Downers Grove IL 60516-3020. (630)963-2124. Fax: (630)963-1998. E-mail: silverscreen11@yahoo.com. **Contact:** William Levin. Estab. 1989. Signatory of WGA. Represents 14 clients. 80% of clients are new/unpublished writers.

- Prior to opening his agency, Mr. Levin did product placement for motion pictures/TV.

Member Agents: Bernadette LaHaie, Jeff Dudley.

Represents: Novels, movie and feature film scripts. **Considers these nonfiction areas:** All genres. **Considers these fiction areas:** All genres. **Considers these script subject areas:** All genres except religious, x-rated, and horror.

How to Contact: Brief. Accepts e-mail queries. No fax queries. Responds in 2 weeks to queries. Obtains most new clients through recommendations from others, listings with WGA and directories.

Recent Sales: Sold 2 titles; 3 scripts in the last year. This agency prefers not to share information on specific sales. Other clients include C. Geier, N. Melamed, R. Melley, and N. Russell.

Terms: Agent receives 15% (manuscript) commission on domestic sales; 10% (screenplay) commission on dramatic rights sales. May make referrals to freelance editors. Use of said editors does not ensure representation.

Tips: "No 'cute' queries please."

SUITE A MANAGEMENT TALENT & LITERARY AGENCY, (formerly Robinson Talent and Literary Management), 1101 S. Robertson Blvd., Suite 210, Los Angeles CA 90035. (310)278-0801. Fax: (310)278-0807. **Contact:** Lloyd Robinson. Estab. 1996. Member of DGA; signatory of WGA. Represents 76 clients. 10% of clients are new/unpublished writers. Currently handles: 15% novels; 40% movie scripts; 40% TV scripts; 5% stage plays.

- Prior to becoming an agent, Mr. Robinson worked as a manager.

Member Agents: Lloyd Robinson (adaptation of books and plays for development as features or TV MOW); Kevin Douglas (scripts for film and TV); Judy Jacobs (feature development).

Represents: Feature film, TV MOW, episodic drama, documentary, miniseries, variety show, stage plays, CD-ROM. **Considers these script subject areas:** Action/adventure; cartoon/animation; comedy; contemporary issues; detective/police/crime; erotica; ethnic; experimental; family saga; fantasy; mainstream; mystery/suspense; psychic/supernatural; religious/inspirational; romantic comedy; romantic drama; science fiction; sports; teen; thriller; western/frontier.

O— "We represent screenwriters, playwrights, novelists and producers, directors."

How to Contact: Submit synopsis, outline/proposal, log line. Obtains most new clients through recommendations from others.

Recent Sales: This agency prefers not to share information on specific sales or client names.

Terms: Agent receives 10% commission on domestic sales; 10% commission on foreign sales. Offers written contract, binding for 1 year minimum. Charges clients for photocopying, messenger, FedEx, and postage when required.

Tips: "We are a talent agency specializing in the copyright business. Fifty percent of our clients generate copyright-screenwriters, playrights and novelists. Fifty percent of our clients service copyright—producers and directors. We represent produced, published and/or WGA writers who are eligible for staff TV positions as well as novelists and playwrights whose works may be adapted for film on television."

TALENT SOURCE, 107 E. Hall St., P.O. Box 14120, Savannah GA 31416-1120. (912)232-9390. Fax: (912)232-8213. E-mail: michael@talentsource.com. Website: www.talentsource.com. **Contact:** Michael L. Shortt. Estab. 1991. Signatory of WGA. 35% of clients are new/unpublished writers. Currently handles: 85% movie scripts; 15% TV scripts.

- Prior to becoming an agent, Mr. Shortt was a television program producer/director.

Represents: Feature film, TV MOW, episodic drama, sitcom. **Considers these script subject areas:** Comedy; contemporary issues; detective/police/crime; erotica; family saga; juvenile; mainstream; mystery/suspense; romantic comedy; romantic drama; teen.

O— Actively seeking "character-driven stories (e.g., *Sling Blade*, *Sex Lies & Videotape*)." Does not want to receive "big budget special effects science fiction."

How to Contact: Query with SASE, Include a proper synopsis, please see the literary button on our website for complete submission details. No e-mail or fax queries. Responds in 10 weeks to queries. Obtains most new clients through recommendations from others.

Recent Sales: This agency prefers not to share information on specific sales.

Terms: Agent receives 10% commission on domestic sales; 15% commission on foreign sales. Offers written contract.

TALESMYTH ENTERTAINMENT, INC., 312 St. John St., Suite #69, Portland ME 04102. **Contact:** Thomas Burgess. Estab. 2000. Signatory of WGA. Represents 7 clients. 100% of clients are new/unpublished writers. Currently handles: 10% novels; 10% story collections; 80% movie scripts.

- Prior to becoming an agent, Mr. Burgess produced short films and managed a restaurant.

Member Agents: Thomas "TJ" Burgess (screenplays/book-length fiction).

Represents: Novels, short story collections, movie scripts, feature film. **Considers these fiction areas:** Action/adventure; detective/police/crime; fantasy; historical; horror; humor/satire; mainstream/contemporary; mystery/suspense; New Age; psychic/supernatural; thriller; western/frontier. **Considers these script subject areas:** Action/adventure; comedy; detective/police/crime; fantasy; historical; horror; mystery/suspense; psychic/supernatural; romantic comedy; romantic drama; science fiction; thriller; western/frontier.

O— "As a writer and producer myself I have a keen eye for industry trends and an amazing way to have the right ear hear the right pitch. I work to develop writers to marketable levels as well as represent authors that are ready for publication." Recently focusing on mainstream and genre novels with strong character and thematic development throughout. Screenplays with a strong driving plot and meaningful character/plot development. Does not want romance, juvenile, children or young adult-oriented stories, and also do not want new clients if not referred by an existing client.

How to Contact: Query with SASE. Talesmyth Entertainment accepts new submissions from July 1-December 31 only. Responds in 1 month to queries; 2 months to mss. Obtains most new clients through recommendations from others, we will not be accepting any new clients in 2004 without a referral from an existing client. Productivity of current clients does not allow for allocation of resources to numerous "new" clients at this time.

Recent Sales: Clients include Gary Hauger, Kevin Brown, F. Allen Farnham, Christopher Cairnduff, Michael Lewin, Lawrence Climo, MD., and Peter Borregine.

Terms: Agent receives 10% commission on domestic sales; 15% commission on foreign sales. Offers written contract, binding for 1 year; 60 days notice must be given to terminate contract. "Submissions of appropriate genre, if requested, received during our acceptance period, whether accepted or rejected, will receive a one-page critique penned by the agent that reviewed the material. At this time all reviews are completed by T.J. Burgess, president of Talesmyth Entertainment. No fee is charged for this critique."

Tips: "Be sure to submit only your best work for consideration. I don't want to see something you just want to get rid of, because I will probably respond in kind. Be certain that your query does a good job of selling me the story and characters and is not just a playful enticement with a "quirky twist." A solid query should summarize the plot and character development in an interesting fashion in one page or less as well as briefly address your expertise in the area or other relevant facts about the market for the story presented, anything else is a waste of your and my time."

PEREGRINE WHITTLESEY AGENCY, 345 E. 80 St., New York NY 10021. (212)737-0153. Fax: (212)734-5176. E-mail: pwwagy@aol.com. **Contact:** Peregrine Whittlesey. Estab. 1986. Signatory of WGA. Represents 30 clients. 50% of clients are new/unpublished writers. Currently handles: 10% movie scripts; 90% stage plays.

Represents: Feature film, stage plays.

O→ This agency specializes in playwrights who also write for screen and TV.

How to Contact: Query with SASE. Prefers to read materials exclusively. Accepts e-mail and fax queries. Responds in 1 week to queries; 1 month to mss. Obtains most new clients through recommendations from others.

Recent Sales: Sold 20 scripts in the last year. *Christmas Movie*, by Darrah Cloud (CBS). Productions at Arena Stage in Washinton, New Theatre in Miami, La Jolla Playhouse, Seattle Rep., Oregon Shakespeare Festival, South Coast Rep.

Terms: Agent receives 10% commission on domestic sales; 15% commission on foreign sales. Offers written contract, binding for 2 years.

WRITERS & ARTISTS AGENCY, 19 W. 44th St., Suite 1000, New York NY 10036. (212)391-1112. Fax: (212)575-6397. West Coast location: 8383 Wilshire Blvd., Suite 550, Beverly Hills CA 90211. (323)866-0900. Fax: (323)866-1899 **Contact:** William Craver, Christopher Till. Estab. 1970. Member of AAR; signatory of WGA. Represents 100 clients.

Represents: Movie scripts, feature film, TV scripts, TV MOW, episodic drama, miniseries, stage plays, stage musicals. **Considers these script subject areas:** Action/adventure; biography/autobiography; cartoon/animation; comedy; contemporary issues; detective/police/crime; erotica; ethnic; experimental; family saga; fantasy; feminist; gay/lesbian; glitz; historical; horror; juvenile; mainstream; multicultural; multimedia; mystery/suspense; psychic/supernatural; regional; romantic comedy; romantic drama; sports; teen; thriller; western/frontier.

How to Contact: Query with SASE, author bio, brief description of the project. No unsolicited mss. Responds in 1 month to queries only when accompanied by SASE. Obtains most new clients through professional recommendation preferred.

Recent Sales: This agency prefers not to share information on specific sales.

Book Publishers

The book business, for the most part, runs on hunches. Whether the idea for a book comes from a writer, an agent, or the imagination of an acquiring editor, it is generally expressed in these terms: "This is a book that I *think* people will like. People will *probably* want to buy it." The decision to publish is mainly a matter of the right person, or persons, agreeing that those hunches are sound.

THE PATH TO PUBLICATION

Ideas reach editors in a variety of ways. They arrive unsolicited every day through the mail. They come by phone, sometimes from writers but most often from agents. They arise in the editor's mind because of his daily traffic with the culture in which he lives. The acquisitions editor, so named because he is responsible for securing manuscripts for his company to publish, sifts through the deluge of possibilities, waiting for a book idea to strike him as extraordinary, inevitable, or profitable.

In some companies, acquisitions editors possess the authority required to say, "Yes, we will publish this book." In most publishing houses, though, the acquisitions editor must prepare and present the idea to a proposal committee made up of marketing and administrative personnel. Proposal committees are usually less interested in questions of extraordinariness and inevitability than they are in profitability. The editor has to convince the committees that it makes good business sense to publish this book.

Once a contract is signed, several different wheels are set in motion. The author, of course, writes the book if he hasn't done so already. While the editor is helping to assure that the author is making the book the best it can be, promotion and publicity people are planning mailings of review copies to influential newspapers and review periodicals, writing catalog copy that will help sales representatives push the book to bookstores, and plotting a multitude of other promotional efforts (including interview tours and book signings by the author) designed to dangle the book attractively before the reading public's eye.

When the book is published, it usually receives a concerted promotional push for a month or two. After that, the fate of the book—whether it will "grow legs" and set sales records, or sit untouched on bookstore shelves—rests in the hands of the public. Publishers have to compete with all of the other entertainment industries vying for the consumer's money and limited leisure time.

THE STATE OF THE BUSINESS

Publishers sell their products to bookstores on a returnable basis, which means the stores usually have 120 days to either pay the bill or return the order. With independent bookstores continuing to close and superstores experiencing setbacks as well, many publishers were hit with staggering returns. This has slowed somewhat but continues to be a concern. While there are many more outlets to *buy* books, including online bookstores such as Amazon.com and Barnesandnoble.com, this doesn't necessarily translate into more books being *bought*. Some feel the superstore phenomenon has proved a mixed blessing. The greater shelf area means there are more materials available, but also drives a need for books as "wallpaper" that is continually refreshed by returning older books and restocking with newer ones.

But that's not to say publishers are rushing to bring esoteric or highly experimental material to the marketplace. The blockbuster mentality—publishing's penchant for sticking with "name brand" novelists—still drives most large publishers. It's simply a less risky venture to continue publishing authors whom they know readers like. On the other hand, the prospects for nonfiction authors are perhaps better than they have been for years. The boom in available shelf space has provided entry to the marketplace for books on niche topics that heretofore would not have seen the light of day in most bookstores. The superstores position themselves as one-stop shopping centers for readers of every stripe. As such, they must carry books on a wide range of subjects.

HOW TO PUBLISH YOUR BOOK

The markets in this year's Book Publishers section offer opportunities in nearly every area of publishing. Large, commercial houses are here as are their smaller counterparts; large and small "literary" houses are represented as well. In addition, you'll find university presses, industry-related publishers, textbook houses, and more.

The Book Publishers Subject Index is the place to start. You'll find it in the back of the book, before the General Index. Subject areas for both fiction and nonfiction are broken out for the over 1,100 total book publisher listings. Not all of them buy the kind of book you've written, but this Index will tell you which ones do.

When you have compiled a list of publishers interested in books in your subject area, read the detailed listings. Pare down your list by cross-referencing two or three subject areas and eliminating the listings only marginally suited to your book. When you have a good list, send for those publishers' catalogs and any manuscript guidelines available, or check publishers' websites, which often contain catalog listings, manuscript preparation guidelines, current contact names, and other information helpful to prospective authors. You want to make sure your book idea is in line with a publisher's list but is not a duplicate of something already published.

Visit bookstores and libraries to see if the publisher's books are well represented. When you find a couple of books the house has published that are similar to yours, write or call the company to find out who edited those books. This last, extra bit of research could be the key to getting your proposal to precisely the right editor.

Publishers prefer different methods of submission on first contact. Most like to see a one-page query with SASE, especially for nonfiction. Others will accept a brief proposal package that might include an outline and/or a sample chapter. Some publishers will accept submissions from agents only. Virtually no publisher wants to see a complete manuscript on initial contact, and sending one when they prefer another method will signal to the publisher, "this is an amateur's submission." Editors do not have the time to read an entire manuscript, even editors at small presses who receive fewer submissions.

In your one-page query, give an overview of your book, mention the intended audience, the competition (check *Books in Print* and local bookstore shelves), and what sets your book apart. Detail any previous publishing experience or special training relevant to the subject of your book. All of this information will help your cause; it's the professional approach.

For More Information

RESOURCES

- *Books in Print* (R.R. Bowker).
- The Association of Authors' Representatives (www.aar-online.org), P.O. Box 237201, Ansonia Station, New York NY 10003.
- Volunteer Lawyers for the Arts (www.vlany.org), 1 E. 53rd St., 6th Floor, New York NY 10022-4201. (212)319-2787, ext. 1.

Only one in a thousand writers will sell a book to the first publisher they query, especially if the book is the writer's first effort. Make a list of a dozen or so publishers that might be interested in your book. Try to learn as much about the books they publish and their editors as you can. Research, knowing the specifics of your subject area, and a professional approach are often the difference between acceptance and rejection.

Personalize your queries by addressing them individually and mentioning what you know about a company from its catalog or books you've seen. Never send a form letter as a query. Envelopes addressed to "Editor" or "Editorial Department" end up in the dreaded slush pile.

If a publisher offers you a contract, you may want to seek advice from either a lawyer or an agent before signing and returning it. An author's agent will likely take 15 percent if you employ one, but you could be making 85 percent of a larger amount. Some literary agents are available on an hourly basis for contract negotiations only.

AUTHOR-SUBSIDY PUBLISHERS' LISTINGS NOT INCLUDED

Writer's Market is a reference tool to help you sell your writing, and we encourage you to work with publishers that pay a royalty. Subsidy publishing involves paying money to a publishing house to publish a book. The source of the money could be a government, foundation, or university grant, or it could be the author of the book. If one of the publishers listed here offers you an author-subsidy arrangement (sometimes called "cooperative publishing," "co-publishing," or "joint venture"), asks you to pay for part or all of the cost of any aspect of publishing (editing services, manuscript critiques, printing, advertising, etc.), or to guarantee the purchase of any number of the books yourself, we would like you to let us know about that company immediately.

Sometimes new publishers will offer author-subsidy contracts to get a leg up in the business and plan to become royalty-only publishers once they've reached a firm financial footing. Some publishers feel they must offer subsidy contracts to expand their lists beyond the capabilities of their limited resources. This may be true, and you may be willing to agree to it, but we choose to list only those publishers paying a royalty without requiring a financial investment from the author.

INFORMATION AT-A-GLANCE

There are a number of symbols at the beginning of each listing to quickly convey certain information at a glance. In the Book Publisher sections, these symbols identify new listings (N), Canadian markets (🍁), publishers located outside of the U.S. and Canada (🌐), and publishers that accept agented submissions only (A). Different sections of *Writer's Market* include other symbols; check the front and back inside covers for an explanation of all the symbols used throughout the book.

How much money? What are my odds?

We've also highlighted important information in boldface, the "quick facts" you won't find in any other market guide but should know before you submit your work. This includes: how many manuscripts a publisher buys per year; how many manuscripts from first-time authors; how many manuscripts from unagented writers; the royalty rate a publisher pays; and how large an advance is offered.

Publishers, their imprints, and how they are related

In this era of big publishing—and big mergers—the world of publishing has grown even more intertwined. A "family tree" on page 79 lists the imprints and often confusing divisions of the largest conglomerate publishers.

In the listings, "umbrella" listings for these larger houses list the imprints under the information about the company.

Most listings include a summary of the editorial mission of the house, an overarching principle that ties together what they publish. Under the heading **Acquisitions:** we list many more editors, often with their specific areas of expertise. We have also included the royalty rates for those publishers willing to disclose them, but contract details are closely guarded and a number of larger publishers are reluctant to publicly state these terms. Standard royalty rates for paperbacks generally range from 7½ to 12½ percent, for hardcovers from 10 to 15 percent. Royalty rates for children's books are often lower, generally ranging from 5 to 10 percent; 10 percent for picture books (split between the author and the illustrator).

For a list of publishers according to their subjects of interest, see the nonfiction and fiction sections of the Book Publishers Subject Index. Information on book publishers listed in the previous edition of *Writer's Market* but not included in this edition can be found in the General Index.

A-R EDITIONS, INC., 8551 Research Way, Suite 180, Middleton WI 53562. (608)836-9000. Fax: (608)831-8200. Website: www.areditions.com. **Acquisitions:** Paul L. Ranzini, managing editor (Recent Researches music editions); James L. Zychowicz, managing editor (Computer Music and Digital Audio Series). Estab. 1962. **Publishes 30 titles/year. Receives 40 queries and 30 mss/year. 75% of books from first-time authors; 100% from unagented writers. Pays royalty or honoraria.** Does not accept simultaneous submissions. Responds in 1 month to queries; 3 months to proposals; 6 months to mss. Book catalog and ms guidelines online; ms guidelines online.

O-→ A-R Editions publishes modern critical editions of music based on current musicological research. Each edition is devoted to works by a single composer or to a single genre of composition. The contents are chosen for their potential interest to scholars and performers, then prepared for publication according to the standards that govern the making of all reliable, historical editions.

Nonfiction: Subjects include computers/electronic music, software, historical music editions. Computer Music and Digital Audio titles deal with issues tied to digital and electronic media, and include both textbooks and handbooks in this area. Query with SASE or submit outline.

Recent Title(s): *Audio Recording Handbook*, by Alan P. Kefauver; *Orlando di Lasso: The Complete Motets 19*, edited by Peter Bergquist.

ABI PROFESSIONAL PUBLICATIONS, P.O. Box 17446, Clearwater FL 33762. (727)556-0950. Fax: (727)556-2560. E-mail: abipropub@vandamere.com. Website: www.abipropub.com. **Acquisitions:** Art Brown, publisher/editor-in-chief (prosthetics, rehabilitation, dental/medical research). Publishes hardcover and trade paperback originals. **Publishes 10 titles/year. Receives 20-30 queries and 5-10 mss/year. 25% of books from first-time authors; 100% from unagented writers. Pays royalty on revenues generated. Offers small advance.** Publishes book 1+ years after acceptance of ms. Accepts simultaneous submissions. Responds in 3 months to queries. Book catalog and ms guidelines online.

- "No registered, certified, return receipt submissions accepted!"

Nonfiction: Reference, technical, textbook. Subjects include health/medicine. Submit proposal package including outline, representative sample chapter(s), author bio or submit complete ms. Reviews artwork/photos as part of ms package. Send photocopies.

Recent Title(s): *Cleft Palate Dentistry*, by Robert McKinstry (dental text); *Managing Stroke*, by Paul R. Rao and John E. Toerge (rehabilitation).

Tips: Audience is allied health professionals, dentists, researchers, patients undergoing physical rehabilitation. "We will not review electronic submissions."

ABINGDON PRESS, The United Methodist Publishing House, 201 Eighth Ave. S., Nashville TN 37203. (615)749-6000. Fax: (615)749-6512. Website: www.abingdon.org. President/Publisher: Neil M. Alexander. Senior Vice President/Publishing: Harriett Jane Olson. **Acquisitions:** Robert Ratcliff, editor (professional clergy and academic); Peg Augustine, editor (children's); Joseph A. Crowe, editor (general interest). Estab. 1789. Publishes hardcover and paperback originals; church supplies. **Publishes 120 titles/year. Receives 3,000 queries and 250 mss/year. Small% of books from first-time authors; 85% from unagented writers. Pays 7½% royalty on retail price.** Publishes book 2 years after acceptance of ms. Does not accept simultaneous submissions. Responds in 3 months to queries. Book catalog free; ms guidelines online.

Imprints: Dimensions for Living, Cokesbury, Abingdon Press.

O-→ Abingdon Press, America's oldest theological publisher, provides an ecumenical publishing program dedicated to serving the Christian community—clergy, scholars, church leaders, musicians and general readers—with quality resources in the areas of Bible study, the practice of ministry, theology, devotion, spirituality, inspiration, prayer, music and worship, reference, Christian education and church supplies.

Nonfiction: Children's/juvenile, gift book, reference, textbook, religious-lay and professional; scholarly. Subjects include education, music/dance, religion. Query with outline and samples only.

Recent Title(s): *St. Benediction the Freeway: A Rule of Life for the 21st Century*, by Ware; *The Delaney Sisters Reach High*, by Hearth (children's).

HARRY N. ABRAMS, INC., La Martiniere Groupe, 100 Fifth Ave., New York NY 10011. (212)206-7715. Fax: (212)645-8437. Website: www.abramsbooks.com. President: Steven Parr. **Acquisitions:** Eric Himmel, editor-in-chief. Estab. 1949. Publishes hardcover and "a few" paperback originals. **Publishes 150 titles/year. Pays royalty. Offers variable advance.** Publishes book 2 years after acceptance of ms. Does not accept simultaneous submissions. Responds in 6-8 weeks to queries. Book catalog for $5.

O━ "We publish *only* high-quality illustrated art books, i.e., art, art history, museum exhibition catalogs, written by specialists and scholars in the field."

Nonfiction: Illustrated book. Subjects include art/architecture, nature/environment, recreation (outdoor). Requires illustrated material for art and art history, museums. Submit outline, sample chapter(s), illustrations. Reviews artwork/photos as part of ms package.

Tips: "We are one of the few publishers who publish almost exclusively illustrated books. We consider ourselves the leading publishers of art books and high-quality artwork in the U.S. Once the author has signed a contract to write a book for our firm the author must finish the manuscript to agreed-upon high standards within the schedule agreed upon in the contract."

ABSEY & CO., 23011 Northcrest Dr., Spring TX 77389. (281)257-2340. Fax: (281)251-4676. E-mail: abseyandco@aol.com. Website: www.absey.com. **Acquisitions:** Edward Wilson, editor-in-chief. Publishes hardcover, trade paperback and mass market paperback originals. **Publishes 6-10 titles/year. 50% of books from first-time authors; 50% from unagented writers. Royalty and advance vary.** Publishes book 1 year after acceptance of ms. Does not accept simultaneous submissions. Responds in 3 months to queries; 9 months to mss. Ms guidelines online.

O━ "Our goal is to publish original, creative works of literary merit." Currently emphasizing educational, young adult literature. De-emphasizing self-help.

Nonfiction: Subjects include education, language/literature (language arts), general nonfiction. "We will not open anything without a return address. All submissions sent without return or insufficient postage are discarded." Query with SASE.

Fiction: Juvenile, mainstream/contemporary, short story collections. "Since we are a small, new press, we are looking for book-length manuscripts with a firm intended audience." Query with SASE.

Poetry: Publishes the "Writers and Young Writers Series." Interested in thematic poetry collections of literary merit. Query.

Recent Title(s): *Dragonfly*, by Alice McLerran (fiction); *Where I'm From*, by George Ella Lyon (poetry).

Tips: "We work closely and attentively with authors and their work." Does not accept e-mail submissions.

ACADEMY CHICAGO PUBLISHERS, 363 W. Erie St., Chicago IL 60610-3125. (312)751-7300. Fax: (312)751-7306. E-mail: info@academychicago.com. Website: www.academychicago.com. **Acquisitions:** Anita Miller, editorial director/senior editor. Estab. 1975. Publishes hardcover originals and trade paperback reprints. **Publishes 15 titles/year. Receives 2,000 submissions/year. Pays 7-10% royalty on wholesale price. Offers modest advance.** Publishes book 18 months after acceptance of ms. Responds in 3 months to queries. Book catalog online; ms guidelines online.

O━ "We publish quality fiction and nonfiction. Our audience is literate and discriminating. No novelized biography, history or science fiction."

Nonfiction: Biography. Subjects include history, travel. No religion or self-help. Submit proposal package including outline, 3 sample chapter(s), author bio.

Fiction: Historical, mainstream/contemporary, military/war, mystery. "We look for quality work, but we do not publish experimental, avant garde novels." Submit proposal package including 3 sample chapter(s), synopsis.

Recent Title(s): *Letters in the Attic*, by Bonnie Shimko; *Tinder Box: The Iroquois Theatre Disaster 1903*, by Anthony Hatch.

Tips: "At the moment, we are looking for good nonfiction; we certainly want excellent original fiction, but we are swamped. No fax queries, no disks. No electronic submissions. We are always interested in reprinting good out-of-print books."

[A] **ACE SCIENCE FICTION AND FANTASY**, The Berkley Publishing Group, Penguin Putnam, Inc., 375 Hudson St., New York NY 10014. (212)366-2000. Website: www.penguinputnam.com. **Acquisitions:** Anne Sowards, editor. Estab. 1953. Publishes hardcover, paperback and trade paperback originals and reprints. **Publishes 75 titles/year. Pays royalty. Offers advance.** Publishes book 18 months after acceptance of ms. Does not accept simultaneous submissions. Responds in 6 months to queries; 2 months to mss. Ms guidelines for #10 SASE.

O━ Ace publishes science fiction and fantasy exclusively.

Fiction: Fantasy, science fiction. No other genre accepted. No short stories. *Agented submissions only.* Query first with SASE.

Recent Title(s): *King Kelson's Bride*, by Katherine Kurtz; *All Tomorrow's Parties*, by William Gibson.

ACEN PRESS, DNA Press, P.O. Box 572, Eagleville PA 19408. (610)489-8404. Fax: (208)692-2855. E-mail: dnapress@yahoo.com. **Acquisitions:** Alexander Kuklin, Ph.D., managing editor (popular science and children scientific books); Xela Schenk, operations manager (New Age). Estab. 1998. Publishes trade paperback originals. **Publishes 10 titles/year; imprint publishes 5 titles/year. Receives 75 queries and 20 mss/year. 90% of books from first-time authors; 100% from unagented writers. Pays 10-20% royalty.** Publishes book 4 months after acceptance of ms. Accepts simultaneous submissions. Responds in 2 weeks to queries; 1 month to proposals; 6 weeks to mss. Book catalog free; ms guidelines free.

O━ Book publisher for young adults, children and adults.

Nonfiction: Children's/juvenile (explaining science), how-to. Subjects include education, New Age, science. "We publish books for children or how-to for adults which carry scientific knowledge and contribute to learning." Submit complete ms. Reviews artwork/photos as part of ms package. Send photocopies.

Fiction: Juvenile, science fiction, young adult. "All books should be oriented to explaining science even if they do not fall 100% under the category of science fiction." Submit complete ms.

Recent Title(s): *How to DNA Test Our Family Relationships?*, by Terrence Carmichael and Alexander Kuklin; *How Do Witches Fly?*, by Alexander Kuklin; *DNA Array Image Analysis*.

Tips: "Quick response, great relationships, high commission/royalty."

ACTA PUBLICATIONS, 4848 N. Clark St., Chicago IL 60640-4711. Fax: (773)271-7399. E-mail: actapublications@aol.com. **Acquisitions:** Gregory F. Augustine Pierce. Estab. 1958. Publishes trade paperback originals. **Publishes 12 titles/year. Receives 100 queries and 25 mss/year. 50% of books from first-time authors; 90% from unagented writers. Pays 10-12% royalty on wholesale price.** Publishes book 1 year after acceptance of ms. Does not accept simultaneous submissions. Responds in 1 month to proposals. Book catalog and ms guidelines for #10 SASE.

O→ ACTA publishes non-academic, practical books aimed at the mainline religious market.

Nonfiction: Self-help. Subjects include religion, spirituality. Submit outline, 1 sample chapter(s). Reviews artwork/photos as part of ms package. Send photocopies.

Recent Title(s): *Invitation to Catholicism*, by Alice Camille (religious education); *Protect Us from All Anxiety: Meditations for the Depressed*, by William Burke (self-help).

Tips: "Don't send a submission unless you have read our catalog or one of our books."

N **ADAMS MEDIA CORP.**, 57 Littlefield St., Avon MA 02322. (508)427-7100. Fax: (800)872-5628. E-mail: editors@adamsmedia.com. Website: www.adamsmedia.com. **Acquisitions:** Gary M. Krebs, publishing director; Jill Alexander, editor; Tracy Quinn McLennan, associate editor; Danielle Chiotti, project editor; Kate Epstein, assistant editor; Courtney Nolan, editorial assistant; Bethany Brown, associate editor; Eric Hall, project editor. Estab. 1980. Publishes hardcover originals, trade paperback originals and reprints. **Publishes 160 titles/year. Receives 5,000 queries and 1,500 mss/year. 40% of books from first-time authors; 40% from unagented writers. Pays standard royalty or makes outright purchase. Offers variable advance.** Publishes book 1 year after acceptance of ms. Accepts simultaneous submissions. Responds in 3 months to queries. Ms guidelines online.

O→ Adams Media publishes commercial nonfiction, including self-help, inspiration, women's issues, pop psychology, relationships, business, parenting, New Age, gift books, cookbooks, how-to, reference. Does not return unsolicited materials. Submit outline. Does not return unsolicited materials.

Recent Title(s): *Why Men Love Bitches*, by Sherry Argov; *Small Miracles for the Jewish Heart*, by Yitta Halberstam and Judith Leventhal; *God Is My CEO*, by Larry Julian.

ADDICUS BOOKS, INC., P.O. Box 45327, Omaha NE 68145. (402)330-7493. Website: www.addicusbooks.com. **Acquisitions:** Rod Colvin, president. Estab. 1994. Publishes trade paperback originals. **Publishes 8-10 titles/year. 70% of books from first-time authors; 60% from unagented writers. Pays royalty on retail price. Offers advance.** Publishes book 9 months after acceptance of ms. Accepts simultaneous submissions. Responds in 1 month to proposals. Ms guidelines online.

O→ Addicus Books, Inc. seeks mss with strong national or regional appeal.

Nonfiction: How-to, self-help. Subjects include Americana, business/economics, health/medicine, psychology, regional, true crime, true crime. "We are expanding our line of consumer health titles." Query with SASE. Do not send entire ms unless requested. No electronic submissions.

Recent Title(s): *A Simple Guide to Thyroid Disorders*, by Paul Ruggieri, M.D.; *Understanding Lumpectomy—A Guide to Breast Cancer Treatment*, by Rosalind Benedet, R.N. and Mark Rounsaville, M.D.

Tips: "We are looking for quick-reference books on health topics. Do some market research to make sure the market is not already flooded with similar books. We're also looking for good true-crime manuscripts, with an interesting story, with twists and turns, behind the crime."

ADIRONDACK MOUNTAIN CLUB, INC., 814 Goggins Rd., Lake George NY 12845-4117. (518)668-4447. Fax: (518)668-3746. E-mail: pubs@adk.org. Website: www.adk.org. **Acquisitions:** John Kettlewell, editor (all titles); Neal Burdick, editor (*Adirondack* magazine, published quarterly). Publishes hardcover and trade paperback originals and reprints. **Publishes 34 titles/year. Receives 36 queries and 12 mss/year. 95% of books from first-time authors; 95% from unagented writers. Pays 6-10% royalty on retail price. Offers $250-1,000 advance.** Publishes book 1 year after acceptance of ms. Does not accept simultaneous submissions. Responds in 3 months to queries; 4 months to proposals; 4 months to mss. Book catalog free and online; ms guidelines free.

O→ "Our main focus is recreational guides to the Adirondack and Catskill Parks; however, our titles continue to include natural, cultural and literary histories of these regions. Our main interest is in protecting the resource through environmental education. This is the focus of our magazine, *Adirondac*, as well."

Nonfiction: Reference. Subjects include nature/environment, recreation, regional, sports, travel, trail maps. Query with SASE or submit proposal package including outline, 1-2 sample chapter(s), with proposed illustrations and visuals. Reviews artwork/photos as part of ms package. Send photocopies.

Recent Title(s): *Ski and Snowshoe Trails in the Adirondacks*; *Catskill Day Hikes for All Seasons*.

Tips: "Our audience consists of outdoors people interested in muscle-powered recreation, natural history, and 'armchair traveling' in the Adirondacks and Catskills. Bear in mind the educational mandate implicit in our organization's mission. Note range of current ADK titles."

AERONAUTICAL PUBLISHERS, (formerly Aviation Publishers), 1 Oakglade Circle, Hummelstown PA 17036-9525. (717)566-0468. Fax: (717)566-6423. E-mail: aeronauticalpubs@aol.com. Website: www.aeronauticalpublishers.com. **Ac-**

quisitions: Mike Markowski, publisher; Marjie Markowski, editor-in-chief. Estab. 1981. Publishes trade paperback originals. **Pays variable royalty.** Responds in 2 months to queries. Ms guidelines online.
Imprints: American Aeronautical Archives, Aviation Publishers.

O⊸ "Our mission is to help people learn more about aviation and model aviation through the written word."

Nonfiction: How-to, technical, general. Subjects include history (aviation), hobbies, recreation, radio control, free flight, indoor models, micro radio control, homebuilt aircraft, ultralights and hang gliders. Prefers submission by e-mail.
Recent Title(s): *Flying Models*, by Don Ross.
Tips: "Our focus is on books of short to medium length that will serve the emerging needs of the hobby. We also want to help youth get started, while enhancing everyone's enjoyment of the hobby. We are looking for authors that are passionate about the hobby, and will champion the messages of their books."

AFRIMAX, INC., 703 Shannon Lane, Kirksville MO 63501. (660)665-0757. **Acquisitions:** Emmanuel Nnadozie, president. Publishes trade paperback originals. **Publishes 4 titles/year. Pays 8% royalty.** Responds in 5 months to queries; 1 month to proposals; 3 months to mss. Ms guidelines free.
Nonfiction: How-to, textbook. Subjects include business/economics, ethnic, money/finance, regional, travel. "International business and African business related interests." Query.
Recent Title(s): *African Culture & American Business in Africa*, by Emmanuel Nnadozie (business/how-to).
Tips: Audience includes business managers, busines educations, students.

AKTRIN FURNITURE INFORMATION CENTER, 164 S. Main St., P.O. Box 898, High Point NC 27261. (336)841-8535. Fax: (336)841-5435. E-mail: aktrin@aktrin.com. Website: www.furniture-info.com. **Acquisitions:** Donna Fincher, director of operations. Estab. 1985. Publishes trade paperback originals. **Publishes 8 titles/year. Receives 5 queries/year. 20% of books from first-time authors; 20% from unagented writers. Makes outright purchase of $1,500 minimum. Offers $300-600 advance.** Publishes book 2 months after acceptance of ms. Accepts simultaneous submissions. Responds in 1 month. *Writer's Market* recommends allowing 2 months for reply to queries. Book catalog free.
Imprints: AKTRIN Furniture Information Center-Canada (151 Randall St., Oakville ON L6J 1P5 Canada. (905)845-3474. Contact: Stefan Wille).

O⊸ AKTRIN is a full-service organization dedicated to the furniture industry. "Our focus is on determining trends, challenges and opportunities, while also identifying problems and weak spots." Currently emphasizing the wood industry.

Nonfiction: Reference. Subjects include business/economics. "We are writing only about the furniture industry. Have an understanding of business/economics." Query.
Recent Title(s): *The American Demand for Household Furniture and Trends*, by Thomas McCormick (in-depth analysis of American household furniture market).
Tips: Audience is executives of furniture companies (manufacturers and retailers) and suppliers and consultants to the furniture industry.

ALASKA NORTHWEST BOOKS, Graphic Arts Center Publishing, P.O. Box 10306, Portland OR 97296-0306. (503)226-2402. Fax: (503)223-1410. Website: www.gacpc.com. **Acquisitions:** Tricia Brown. Estab. 1959. Publishes hardcover and trade paperback originals and reprints. **Publishes 12 titles/year. Receives hundreds of submissions/year. 10% of books from first-time authors; 90% from unagented writers. Pays 10-14% royalty on net revenues. Buys mss outright (rarely). Offers advance.** Publishes book an average of 2 years after acceptance of ms. Accepts simultaneous submissions. Responds in 6 months to queries. Book catalog for 9×12 SAE with 6 first-class stamps; ms guidelines online.
Nonfiction: Children's/juvenile, cookbook. Subjects include nature/environment, recreation, sports, travel, Native American culture, adventure, the arts. "All written for a general readership, not for experts in the subject." Submit outline, sample chapter(s).
Recent Title(s): *One Wing's Gift: Rescuing Alaska's Wild Birds*; *Kumak's House: A Tale of the Far North.*
Tips: "Book proposals that are professionally written and polished with a clear market receive our most careful consideration. We are looking for originality. We publish a wide range of books for a wide audience. Some of our books are clearly for travelers, others for those interested in outdoor recreation or various regional subjects. If I were a writer trying to market a book today, I would research the competition (existing books) for what I have in mind, and clearly (and concisely) express why my idea is different and better. I would describe the book buyers (and readers)—where they are, how many of them are there, how they can be reached (organizations, publications), why they would want or need my book."

[N] **ALBA HOUSE**, 2187 Victory Blvd., Staten Island NY 10314-6603. (718)761-0047. Fax: (718)761-0057. E-mail: albabooks@aol.com. Website: www.albahouse.org. **Acquisitions:** Edmund C. Lane, S.S.P., editor. Estab. 1961. Publishes hardcover, trade paperback and mass market paperback originals. **Publishes 24 titles/year. Receives 300 queries and 150 mss/year. 20% of books from first-time authors; 100% from unagented writers. Pays 7-10% royalty.** Publishes book 9 months after acceptance of ms. Does not accept simultaneous submissions. Responds in 1 month to queries; 1 month to proposals; 2 months to mss. Book catalog and ms guidelines free.

O⊸ Alba House is the North American publishing division of the Society of St. Paul, an International Roman Catholic Missionary Religious Congregation dedicated to spreading the Gospel message.

Nonfiction: Manuscripts which contribute, from a Roman Catholic perspective, to the personal, intellectual and spiritual growth of individuals in the following areas: Scripture, theology and the Church, saints (their lives and teachings), spirituality and prayer, religious life, marriage and family life, liturgy and homily preparation, pastoral concerns, religious education, bereavement, moral and ethical concerns. Reference, textbook. Subjects include education, philosophy, psychology, religion, spirituality. Reviews artwork/photos as part of ms package. Send photocopies.

Recent Title(s): *Christian Spirituality*, by Charles J. Healey, S.J.

ALBION PRESS, 4532 W. Kennedy Blvd., Suite 233, Tampa FL 33609. (813)805-2665 or (888)405-2665. Fax: (813)832-6777. **Acquisitions:** Lonnie Herman, managing editor. Publishes hardcover and trade paperback orginals. **Publishes 20-25 titles/year. Receives 200 queries and 40 mss/year. 50% of books from first-time authors; 80% from unagented writers. 10% royalty on retail price for hardcover and 8% royalty on retail price for trade paperback. Advance varies.** Publishes book 16 months after acceptance of ms. Accepts simultaneous submissions. Responds in 2 months to queries; 2 months to proposals; 3 months to mss. Book catalog free; ms guidelines free.

Nonfiction: "We're always looking for regional nonfiction titles, and especially for sports, biographies, true crime and how-to books." Biography, how-to. Subjects include business/economics, ethnic, history, regional, sports, true crime. "We specialize in nonfiction books that 'tell the story behind the story.' " Query with SASE or submit outline, 2 sample chapter(s).

Recent Title(s): *Nightmare on 33rd Street: A Long Season With the New York Rangers*, by Rick Carpiniello.

Tips: "We pride ourselves on working closely with an author and producing a quality product with strong promotional campaigns. Best to have a strong point of view."

ALEXANDER BOOKS, Creativity, Inc., 65 Macedonia Rd., Alexander NC 28701. (828)252-9515. Fax: (828)255-8719. E-mail: sales@abooks.com. Website: abooks.com. **Acquisitions:** Pat Roberts, acquisitions editor. Publishes hardcover originals and trade and mass market paperback originals and reprints. **Publishes 15-20 titles/year. Receives 200 queries and 100 mss/year. 10% of books from first-time authors; 75% from unagented writers. Pays 12-15% royalty on wholesale price. Offers rare (minimum $100) advance.** Publishes book 18 months after acceptance of ms. Book catalog online; ms guidelines online.

Imprints: Farthest Star (classic science fiction, very few new titles), Mountain Church (mainline Protestant material).

O━ Alexander Books publishes mostly nonfiction national titles, both new and reprints.

Nonfiction: Biography, how-to, reference, self-help. Subjects include computers/electronic, government/politics, history, regional, religion, travel, collectibles. "We are interested in large niche markets." Query or submit 3 sample chapters and proposal package, including marketing plans with SASE. Reviews artwork/photos as part of ms package. Send photocopies.

Fiction: Mainstream/contemporary, mystery, science fiction, western. "We prefer local or well-known authors or local interest settings." Query with SASE or submit 3 sample chapter(s), synopsis.

Recent Title(s): *Sanders Price Guide to Autographs, 5th ed*, by Sanders and Roberts; *Birthright*, by Mike Resnick.

Tips: "Send well-proofed manuscripts in final form. We will not read first rough drafts. Know your market."

ALGONQUIN BOOKS OF CHAPEL HILL, Workman Publishing, P.O. Box 2225, Chapel Hill NC 27515-2225. (919)967-0108. Website: www.algonquin.com. **Acquisitions:** Editorial Department. Publishes hardcover originals. **Publishes 24 titles/year.** Query by mail before submitting work. No phone, e-mail or fax queries or submissions. Visit our website for full submission policy to queries. Ms guidelines online.

O━ Algonquin Books publishes quality literary fiction and literary nonfiction.

ALGORA PUBLISHING, 222 Riverside Dr., 16th Floor, New York NY 10025-6809. (212)678-0232. Fax: (212)663-9805. E-mail: editors@algora.com. Website: www.algora.com. **Acquisitions:** Martin DeMers, editor (sociology/philosophy/economics); Claudiu A. Secara, publisher (philosophy/international affairs). Publishes hardcover and trade paperback originals and reprints. **Publishes 25 titles/year. Receives 1,500 queries and 800 mss/year. 20% of books from first-time authors; 85% from unagented writers. Pays 7½-12% royalty on net receipts. Offers $0-1,000 advance.** Publishes book 10 months after acceptance of ms. Accepts simultaneous submissions. Responds in 1 month to queries; 1 month to proposals; 2 months to mss. Book catalog and ms guidelines online; ms guidelines online.

O━ Algora Publishing is an academic-type press, focusing on works by American, European or Asian authors for the educated general reader.

Nonfiction: General nonfiction for the educated reader. Subjects include anthropology/archeology, business/economics, creative nonfiction, education, government/politics, history, language/literature, military/war, money/finance, music/dance, nature/environment, philosophy, psychology, religion, science, sociology, translation, women's issues/studies. Query by e-mail (preferred) or submit proposal package including outline, 3 sample chapters or complete ms.

Recent Title(s): *Soul Snatchers—The Mechanics of Cults*, by Jean-Marie Abgrall (sociology); *Russian Intelligence Services*, by Vladimir Plougin (history).

Tips: "We welcome first-time writers; we help them outline their project, crafting an author's raw manuscript into a literary work."

N ALL ABOUT KIDS PUBLISHING, 6280 San Ignacio Ave., Suite D, San Jose CA 95119. (408)578-4026. Fax: (408)578-4029. E-mail: lguevara@aakp.com. Website: www.aakp.com. **Acquisitions:** Linda Guevara, editor. Publishes hardcover originals. **Publishes 10-12 titles/year. Receives 250 queries and 7,500 mss/year. 80% of books from first-time authors; 75% from unagented writers. Pays 3-5% royalty. Offers $1,000 advance.** Publishes book 2 years after acceptance of ms. Accepts simultaneous submissions. Responds in 3 months to mss. Book catalog for $3.50 or on website; ms guidelines online.

• "Due to overwhelming response, we will not be accepting submissions until after December 31, 2003."

Nonfiction: Children's/juvenile, cookbook (fall 2004). Subjects include animals, art/architecture, cooking/foods/nutrition, education, ethnic. Submit complete ms. No queries, please. Reviews artwork/photos as part of ms package. Send photocopies.

Fiction: Adventure, ethnic, fantasy, humor, juvenile, picture books, young adult (in 2002). Submit complete ms. No queries please.

ALLIGATOR PRESS, INC., P.O. Box 7908, Austin TX 78713-7908. Fax: (512)371-7541. E-mail: kkimball@alligatorpress.com. Website: www.alligatorpress.com.

O→ Publisher of books in Spanish and their translations.

Nonfiction: Query with SASE.

Recent Title(s): *When Alligators Sing*, by Miguel Santana (historical romance); *Cloven*, by Chae Waters (mystery/suspense).

ALLWORTH PRESS, 10 E. 23rd St., Suite 510, New York NY 10010-4402. Fax: (212)777-8261. E-mail: pub@allworth.com. Website: www.allworth.com. Publisher: Tad Crawford. **Acquisitions:** Nicole Potter, senior editor. Estab. 1989. Publishes hardcover and trade paperback originals. **Publishes 36-40 titles/year. Offers advance.** Does not accept simultaneous submissions. Responds in 1 month to queries; 1 month to proposals. Book catalog and ms guidelines free; ms guidelines online.

O→ Allworth Press publishes business and self-help information for artists, designers, photographers, authors and film and performing artists, as well as books about business, money and the law for the general public. The press also publishes the best of classic and contemporary writing in art and graphic design. Currently emphasizing photography, film, video, music and theater.

Nonfiction: How-to, reference. Subjects include art/architecture, business/economics, film/cinema/stage, music/dance, photography, film, television, graphic design, performing arts, writing, as well as business and legal guides for the public. Query.

Recent Title(s): *Citizen Brand*, by Marc Gobé; *Talking Photography*, by Frank Van Riper; *Hollywood Dealmaking*, by Dina Appleton and Daniel Yankelevits.

Tips: "We are trying to give ordinary people advice to better themselves in practical ways—as well as helping creative people in the fine and commercial arts."

ALPHOS PUBLISHING, (formerly APDG Publishing, Inc.), 404 Wake Chapel Rd., Fuguay-Varina NC 27526-1936. (919)557-2260. Fax: (919)557-2261. E-mail: info@alphos.com. Website: www.alphos.com. Publisher: Lawrence Harte. **Acquisitions:** Karen Bunn. Publishes hardcover and trade paperback originals. **Publishes 20 titles/year. Receives 50 queries/year. Pays 5-15% royalty on sales.** Publishes book 3-6 months after acceptance of ms. Responds in 3 months to proposals; 6 months to mss. Book catalog online; ms guidelines free.

O→ Alphos Publishing supplies expertise and services to telecommunications and consumer electronics companies not only through publishing but consulting, research, training and techno-media as well.

Nonfiction: Textbook. Subjects include telecommunications. Query with SASE. Reviews artwork/photos as part of ms package. Send photocopies.

ALPINE PUBLICATIONS, 225 S. Madison Ave., Loveland CO 80537. (970)667-9317. Fax: (970)667-9157. E-mail: alpinepubl@aol.com. Website: alpinepub.com. **Acquisitions:** Ms. B.J. McKinney, publisher. Estab. 1975. Publishes hardcover and trade paperback originals and reprints. **Publishes 6-10 titles/year. 40% of books from first-time authors; 95% from unagented writers. Pays 8-15% royalty on wholesale price. Offers advance.** Publishes book 18 months after acceptance of ms. Accepts simultaneous submissions. Responds in 1-3 months to queries; 1 month to proposals; 1 month to mss. Book catalog free; ms guidelines online.

Imprints: Blue Ribbon Books.

Nonfiction: How-to, illustrated book, reference. Subjects include animals. "Alpine specializes in books that promote the enjoyment of and responsibility for companion animals with emphasis on dogs and horses." Reviews artwork/photos as part of ms package. Send photocopies.

Recent Title(s): *New Secrets of Successful Show Dog Handling*, by Peter Green and Mario Migliorini (dog); *Training for Trail Horse Classes*, by Laurie Truskauskas (horse); *The Japanese Chin*, by Elisabeth Legl (dogs).

Tips: "Our audience is pet owners, breeders and exhibitors, veterinarians, animal trainers, animal care specialists and judges. Look up some of our titles before you submit. See what is unique about our books. Write your proposal to suit our guidelines."

ALYSON PUBLICATIONS, INC., 6922 Hollywood Blvd., Suite 1000, Los Angeles CA 90028. (323)860-6065. Fax: (323)467-0152. E-mail: mail@alyson.com. Website: www.alyson.com. **Acquisitions:** Angela Brown, editor-in-chief. Estab. 1979. Publishes hardcover and trade paperback originals and reprints. **Publishes 60 titles/year. Receives 1,500 submissions/year. 40% of books from first-time authors; 70% from unagented writers. Pays 8-15% royalty on net receipts. Offers $1,500-15,000 advance.** Accepts simultaneous submissions. Responds in 4 months to queries. Book catalog and ms guidelines for 6×9 SAE with 3 first-class stamps; ms guidelines online.

Imprints: Advocate Books.

O→ Alyson Publications publishes books for and about gay men and lesbians from all economic and social segments of society, and explores the political, legal, financial, medical, spiritual, social and sexual aspects of gay and lesbian life, and contributions to society. They also consider bisexual and transgender material. Emphasizing self-help, humor, and popular culture nonfiction titles.

Nonfiction: Subjects include gay/lesbian. "We are especially interested in nonfiction providing a positive approach to gay/lesbian/bisexual issues." Accepts nonfiction translations. No dissertations. Submit 2-page outline with SASE. Reviews artwork/photos as part of ms package.

Fiction: "We are interested in all categories; *all* materials must be geared toward lesbian and/or gay readers." No poetry. Query with SASE.

Recent Title(s): *The Greatest Taboo*, by Delroy Constantine-Simms; *Under the Mink*, by Lisa Davis.

Tips: "We publish many books by new authors. The writer has the best chance of selling to our firm well-researched, popularly written nonfiction on a subject (e.g., some aspect of gay history) that has not yet been written about much. With fiction, create a strong storyline that makes the reader want to find out what happens. With nonfiction, write in a popular style for a nonacademic audience."

AMACOM BOOKS, American Management Association, 1601 Broadway, New York NY 10019-7406. (212)903-8417. Fax: (212)903-8083. Website: www.amanet.org. President and Publisher: Hank Kennedy. **Acquisitions:** Adrienne Hickey, executive editor (management, human resources development, organizational effectiveness, strategic planning); Ellen Kadin, senior acquisitions editor (marketing, sales, customer service); Ray O'Connell, senior acquisitions editor (finance, project management, real estate); Jacquie Flynn, senior acquisitions editor (personal development training); Neil Levine, senior acquisitions editor (manufacturing, technology applications, supply chain management, facilities management). Estab. 1923. Publishes hardcover and trade paperback originals, professional books in various formats. **Publishes 80-90 titles/year. Receives 800 submissions/year. 50% of books from first-time authors; 70% from unagented writers. Pays 10-15% royalty on net receipts. Offers advance.** Publishes book 6-9 months after acceptance of ms. Responds in 2 months to queries. Book catalog and ms guidelines free; ms guidelines online.

O→ Amacom is the publishing arm of the American Management Association, the world's largest training organization for managers and executives. Amacom publishes books on business issues, strategies and tasks to enhance organizational and individual effectiveness, as well as self-help books for more personal and professional growth. Currently emphasizing leadership/management skills, real estate, self-help. De-emphasizing small-business management, job-finding.

Nonfiction: Biography. Publishes business books of all types, including management, business strategy, organizational effectiveness, sales, marketing, training, technology applications, finance, career, professional skills for retail, direct mail, college and corporate markets. Query or submit outline/synopsis, sample chapters, résumé.

Recent Title(s): *Victory*, by Brian Tracy; *Partnering: The New Face of Leadership*, edited by Larraine Segil, Marshall Goldsmith and James Belasco; *Laugh and Learn*, by Doni Tamblyn.

AMERICA WEST PUBLISHERS, P.O. Box 2208, Carson City NV 89702-2208. (775)885-0700. Fax: (877)726-2632. E-mail: global@nohoax.com. Website: www.nohoax.com. **Acquisitions:** George Green, president. Estab. 1985. Publishes hardcover and trade paperback originals and reprints. **Publishes 20 titles/year. Receives 150 submissions/year. 90% of books from first-time authors; 90% from unagented writers. Pays 10% royalty on wholesale price. Offers $300 average advance.** Publishes book 6 months after acceptance of ms. Accepts simultaneous submissions. Responds in 1 month to queries. Book catalog and ms guidelines free.

Imprints: Bridger House Publishers, Inc.

O→ America West seeks the "other side of the picture," political cover-ups and new health alternatives.

Nonfiction: Subjects include business/economics, government/politics, health/medicine (holistic self-help), New Age, UFO-metaphysical. Submit outline, sample chapter(s). Reviews artwork/photos as part of ms package.

Recent Title(s): *Psychokinesiology*, by Dr. Alec Halub.

Tips: "We currently have materials in all bookstores that have areas of UFOs; also political and economic nonfiction."

AMERICAN BAR ASSOCIATION BOOK PUBLISHING, 750 N. Lake Shore Dr., Chicago IL 60611. (312)988-5000. Fax: (312)988-6030. E-mail: kayb@staff.abanet.org. Website: www.ababooks.org. **Acquisitions:** Bryan Kay, Esq., publisher/director; Adrienne Cook, Esq., director of new product development. Estab. 1878. Publishes hardcover and trade paperback originals. **Publishes 100 titles/year. Receives 50 queries/year. 20% of books from first-time authors; 95% from unagented writers. Pays 5-15% royalty on net receipts.** Publishes book 6 months after acceptance of ms. Accepts simultaneous submissions. Responds in 1 month to queries; 1 month to proposals; 3 months to mss. Book catalog and ms guidelines on website; ms guidelines online.

O→ "We are interested in books that will help lawyers practice law more effectively whether it's help in handling clients, structuring a real estate deal or taking an antitrust case to court."

Nonfiction: All areas of legal practice. How-to (in the legal market), reference, technical. Subjects include business/economics, computers/electronic, money/finance, software, legal practice. "Our market is not, generally, the public. Books need to be targeted to lawyers who are seeking solutions to their practice problems. We rarely publish scholarly treatises." Query with SASE.

Recent Title(s): *The Attorney-Client Privilege and the Work-Product Doctrine*; *A Practical Guide to Real Estate Transactions*; *The Spine at Trial*.

Tips: "ABA books are written for busy, practicing lawyers. The most successful books have a practical, reader-friendly voice. If you can build in features like checklists, exhibits, sample contracts, flow charts, and tables of cases, please do so." The Association also publishes over 50 major national periodicals in a variety of legal areas. Contact Kathleen Welton, director of book publishing, at the above address for guidelines.

AMERICAN CATHOLIC PRESS, 16565 S. State St., South Holland IL 60473. (312)331-5845. Fax: (708)331-5484. E-mail: acp@acpress.org. Website: www.acpress.org. **Acquisitions:** Rev. Michael Gilligan, Ph.D., editorial director. Estab. 1967. Publishes hardcover originals and hardcover and paperback reprints. **Publishes 4 titles/year. Makes outright purchase of $25-100.** Does not accept simultaneous submissions. Ms guidelines online.

Nonfiction: Subjects include education, music/dance, religion, spirituality. "We publish books on the Roman Catholic liturgy—for the most part, books on religious music and educational books and pamphlets. We also publish religious songs for church use, including Psalms, as well as choral and instrumental arrangements. We are interested in new music, meant for use in church services. Books, or even pamphlets, on the Roman Catholic Mass are especially welcome. We have no interest in secular topics and are not interested in religious poetry of any kind."

Tips: "Most of our sales are by direct mail, although we do work through retail outlets."

AMERICAN CORRECTIONAL ASSOCIATION, 4380 Forbes Blvd., Lanham MD 20706. (301)918-1800. Fax: (301)918-1896. E-mail: aliceh@aca.org. Website: www.corrections.com/aca. **Acquisitions:** Alice Heiserman, manager of publications. Estab. 1870. Publishes hardcover and trade paperback originals. **Publishes 18 titles/year. Receives 40 submissions/year. 90% of books from first-time authors; 100% from unagented writers. Pays 10% royalty on net receipts.** Publishes book 1 year after acceptance of ms. Responds in 4 months to queries. Book catalog and ms guidelines free; ms guidelines online.

O━ American Correctional Association provides practical information on jails, prisons, boot camps, probation, parole, community corrections, juvenile facilities and rehabilitation programs, substance abuse programs and other areas of corrections.

Nonfiction: "We are looking for practical, how-to texts or training materials written for the corrections profession." How-to, reference, technical, textbook, correspondence courses. Subjects include corrections and criminal justice. No autobiographies or true-life accounts by current or former inmates or correctional officers, theses, or dissertations. No fiction or poetry. Query with SASE. Reviews artwork/photos as part of ms package.

Recent Title(s): *Recess Is Over: Managing Youthful Offenders in Adult Correctional Systems*, by Barry Glick, Ph.D., William Sturgeon; *Arresting Addictions: Drug Education and Relapse Prevention in Corrections*, by Robert Alexander, Ph.D., George J. Pratsinak, Ph.D.

Tips: Authors are professionals in the field and corrections. "Our audience is made up of corrections professionals and criminal justice students. No books by inmates or former inmates." This publisher advises out-of-town freelance editors, indexers and proofreaders to refrain from requesting work from them.

AMERICAN COUNSELING ASSOCIATION, 5999 Stevenson Ave., Alexandria VA 22304-3300. (703)823-9800. **Acquisitions:** Carolyn C. Baker, director of publications. Estab. 1952. Publishes paperback originals. **Publishes 10-15 titles/year. Receives 75 submissions/year. 5% of books from first-time authors; 90% from unagented writers. Pays 10-15% royalty on net receipts.** Publishes book 7 months after acceptance of ms. Accepts simultaneous submissions. Responds in 2 months to queries; 2 months to proposals; 4 months to mss. Ms guidelines free.

O━ The American Counseling Association is dedicated to promoting public confidence and trust in the counseling profession. "We publish scholarly texts for graduate level students and mental health professionals. We do not publish books for the general public."

Nonfiction: Reference, scholarly, textbook (for professional counselors). Subjects include education, gay/lesbian, health/medicine, multicultural, psychology, religion, sociology, spirituality, women's issues/studies. ACA does not publish self-help books or autobiographies. Query with SASE or submit proposal package including outline, 2 sample chapter(s), vitae.

Recent Title(s): *Assessment in Counseling, 3rd ed*, by Albert Hood and Richard Johnson; *Documentation in Counseling Records, 2nd ed*, by Robert Mitchell.

Tips: "Target your market. Your books will not be appropriate for everyone across all disciplines."

AMERICAN FEDERATION OF ASTROLOGERS, P.O. Box 22040, Tempe AZ 85285. (480)838-1751. Fax: (480)838-8293. E-mail: afa@msn.com. Website: www.astrologers.com. **Acquisitions:** Kris Brandt Riske, publications manager. Estab. 1938. Publishes trade paperback originals and reprints. **Publishes 10-15 titles/year. Receives 10 queries and 20 mss/year. 50% of books from first-time authors; 100% from unagented writers. Pays 10% royalty. Offers advance.** Publishes book 10 months after acceptance of ms. Accepts simultaneous submissions. Responds in 6 months to mss. Book catalog for $2; ms guidelines free.

O━ American Federation of Astrologers publishes astrology books, calendars, charts and related aids.

Nonfiction: Subjects include astrology. Submit complete ms.

Recent Title(s): *Road Map to Your Future*, by Bernie Ashman.

AMERICAN NURSES PUBLISHING, American Nurses Association, 600 Maryland Ave. SW, #100 West, Washington DC 20024-2571. (202)651-7212. Fax: (202)651-7003. **Acquisitions:** Rosanne O'Connor, publisher; Eric Wurzbacher, editor/project manager. Publishes professional paperback originals and reprints. **Publishes 15 titles/year. Receives 300 queries and 8-10 mss/year. 75% of books from first-time authors; 100% from unagented writers. Pays 12% royalty on net receipts. Offers negotiable advance.** Publishes book 4 months after acceptance of ms. Does not accept simultaneous submissions. Responds in 3 months to proposals; 3 months to mss. Book catalog online; ms guidelines free.

O━ ANP publishes books designed to help professional nurses in their work and careers. Through the publishing program, ANP provides nurses in all practice settings with publications that address cutting-edge issues and form a basis for debate and exploration of this century's most critical health care trends.

Nonfiction: Reference, technical, textbook, handbooks; resource guides. Subjects include health/medicine. Subjects include advanced practice, computers, continuing education, ethics, human rights, health care policy, managed care, nursing administration, psychiatric and mental health, quality, research, workplace issues, key clinical topics. Submit outline, 1 sample chapter, cv. Reviews artwork/photos as part of ms package. Send photocopies.

Recent Title(s): *Nursing and the Law*; *End-of-Life Care*; *Critical Practice Management Strategies*.

AMERICAN PRESS, 28 State St., Suite 1100, Boston MA 02109. (617)247-0022. Fax: (617)247-0022. **Acquisitions:** Jana Kirk, editor. Estab. 1911. Publishes college textbooks. **Publishes 25 titles/year. Receives 350 queries and 100 mss/year. 50% of books from first-time authors; 90% from unagented writers. Pays 5-15% royalty on wholesale price.**

Publishes book 9 months after acceptance of ms. Does not accept simultaneous submissions. Responds in 3 months to queries. Book catalog free.

Nonfiction: Technical, textbook. Subjects include agriculture/horticulture, anthropology/archeology, art/architecture, business/economics, education, government/politics, health/medicine, history, music/dance, psychology, science, sociology, sports. "We prefer that our authors actually teach courses for which the manuscripts are designed." Query or submit outline with tentative table of contents. No complete mss.

Recent Title(s): *Sexuality Counseling*, by Weinstein.

AMERICAN QUILTER'S SOCIETY, Schroeder Publishing, P.O. Box 3290, Paducah KY 42002-3290. (270)898-7903. Fax: (270)898-1173. E-mail: meredith@aqsquilt.com; editor@aqsquilt.com. Website: www.aqsquilt.com. **Acquisitions:** Barbara Smith, executive book editor (primarily how-to and patterns, but other quilting books sometimes published). Estab. 1984. Publishes hardcover and trade paperback originals. **Publishes 20 titles/year. Receives 300 queries/year. 60% of books from first-time authors; 100% from unagented writers. Pays 5% royalty on retail price.** Publishes book 11 months after acceptance of ms. Accepts simultaneous submissions. Responds in same day to queries; 2 months to proposals. Book catalog and ms guidelines free; ms guidelines online.

- American Quilter's Society publishes how-to and pattern books for quilters (beginners through intermediate skill level).

Nonfiction: Coffee table book, how-to, reference, technical (about quilting). Subjects include creative nonfiction, hobbies (about quilting). Query with SASE or submit proposal package including outline, 2 sample chapter(s), photos and patterns (if available). Reviews artwork/photos as part of ms package. Send photocopies; slides and drawings are also acceptable for a proposal.

Recent Title(s): *Guide to Machine Quilting*, by Diane Gaudynski; *Quiltscapes*, by Rebecca Barker; *Birds and Flowers Album*, by Bea Oglesby.

AMERICAN SOCIETY FOR TRAINING AND DEVELOPMENT, 1640 King St., Alexandria VA 22313. (800)628-2783. Fax: (703)683-9591. E-mail: mmorrow@astd.org. Website: www.astd.org. **Acquisitions:** Mark Morrow, manager (acquisitions and development). Estab. 1944. Publishes trade paperback originals. **Publishes 15-20 titles/year. Receives 50-100 queries and 25-50 mss/year. 50% of books from first-time authors; 95% from unagented writers. Pays 10% royalty on net receipts. Offers $500-1,000 advance.** Publishes book up to 1 year after acceptance of ms. Accepts simultaneous submissions. Responds in 1 month to queries; 1 month to proposals; 1 month to mss. Book catalog free; ms guidelines free.

Nonfiction: Trade Books for training and performance improvement professionals. Subjects include training and development. Submit proposal package including outline, 1 sample chapter(s). Reviews artwork/photos as part of ms package.

Recent Title(s): *Leading E-Learning*, by William Horton; *Training on the Job*, by Diane Walter; *Return on Investment, Vol. 3*, by Jack Phillips.

Tips: Audience includes training professionals including frontline trainers, training managers and executives; performance professionals, including performance consultants; organizational development and human resource development professionals. "Send a good proposal targeted to our audience providing how-to advice that readers can apply now!"

N AMERICAN SOCIETY OF CIVIL ENGINEERS PRESS, 1801 Alexander Bell Dr., Reston VA 20191-4400. (703)295-6275. Fax: (703)295-6278. E-mail: ascepress@asce.org. Website: www.pubs.asce.org. **Acquisitions:** Jack Bruggeman, acquisitions editor. Estab. 1988. **Publishes 15-20 titles/year. 50% of books from first-time authors; 100% from unagented writers. Pays 10% royalty.** Accepts simultaneous submissions. Request ASCE book proposal submission guidelines; ms guidelines online.

- ASCE Press publishes technical volumes that are useful to both practicing civil engineers and graduate level civil engineering students. "We publish books by individual authors and editors to advance the civil engineering profession." Currently emphasizing geotechnical, hydrology, structural engineering and bridge engineering. De-emphasizing highly specialized areas with narrow scope.

Nonfiction: "We are looking for topics that are useful and instructive to the engineering practitioner." Subjects include civil engineering. Query with outline, sample chapters and cv.

Recent Title(s): *Degrees of Belief: Subjective Probability and Engineering Judgement*, by Steven G. Vick.

Tips: "ASCE Press is a book publishing imprint of ASCE and produces authored and edited applications-oriented books for practicing civil engineers and graduate level civil engineering students. All proposals and manuscripts undergo a vigorous review process."

N AMERICAN WATER WORKS ASSOCIATION, 6666 W. Quincy Ave., Denver CO 80235. (303)794-7711. Fax: (303)794-7310. E-mail: cmurcray@awwa.org. Website: www.awwa.org. **Acquisitions:** Colin Murcray, senior acquisitions editor; Mindy Burke, senior technical editor. Estab. 1881. Publishes hardcover and trade paperback originals. **Publishes 100 titles/year. Receives 200 queries and 35 mss/year. 30% of books from first-time authors; 100% from unagented writers. Pays 15% royalty on wholesale or retail price.** Publishes book 1 year after acceptance of ms. Does not accept simultaneous submissions. Responds in 4 months to queries. Book catalog and ms guidelines free.

- AWWA strives to advance and promote the safety and knowledge of drinking water and related issues to all audiences—from kindergarten through post-doctorate.

Nonfiction: Subjects include nature/environment, science, software, drinking water-related topics. Query with SASE or submit outline, 3 sample chapter(s), author bio. Reviews artwork/photos as part of ms package. Send photocopies.

Recent Title(s): *Handbook of CCL Microbes*, by Martha Embrey, et. al.

N AMERICANA PUBLISHING, INC., 303 San Mateo N.E., Suite 104 A, Albuquerque NM 87108. (505)265-6121. Fax: (505)255-6189. E-mail: editor@americanabooks.com. Website: www.americanabooks.com. **Acquisitions:** Patricia Woods, managing editor. Publishes trade paperback and electronic originals. **Publishes 6 titles/year. Receives 500+ queries and 300+ mss/year. 50% of books from first-time authors; 50% from unagented writers. Pays 10% royalty.** Publishes book 1-2 years after acceptance of ms. Accepts simultaneous submissions. Responds in 2 months to queries; 2 months to proposals; 2 months to mss. Book catalog free; ms guidelines free.

Nonfiction: Audiocassettes, children's/juvenile, cookbook, how-to, illustrated book, self-help. Subjects include history, military/war, regional, religion, spirituality. Submit complete ms.

Fiction: Adventure, fantasy (space fantasy), historical, literary, mainstream/contemporary, military/war, mystery (amateur, sleuth, cozy, police procedural, private eye/hardboiled), regional, religious (general religious, inspirational), romance (contemporary, historical, romanitc suspense), science fiction (soft/sociological), spiritual, western, young adult (fantasy/science fiction, mystery/suspense). Does not want children's, poetry, sexually explicit (soft or hard porn), autobiographies. Query with SASE or submit proposal package including 3 sample chapter(s), synopsis.

Recent Title(s): *Beloved Beau*, by Cynthia Davis (historical fiction).

Tips: "Get an agent."

N AMG PUBLISHERS, 6815 Shallowford Rd., Chattanooga TN 37421-1755. (423)894-6060. Fax: (423)894-9511. E-mail: danp@amginternational.org. Website: www.amgpublishers.com. **Acquisitions:** Dr. Warren Baker, senior editor; Richard Steele, Jr., associate editor; Dan Penwell, acquisition manager. Publishes hardcover and trade paperback originals and trade paperback reprints. **Publishes 25-30 titles/year. Receives 1,000 queries and 500 mss/year. 25% of books from first-time authors; 75% from unagented writers. Pays 10-15% royalty on wholesale price.** Publishes book 1 year after acceptance of ms. Accepts simultaneous submissions. Responds in 1-2 weeks to queries; 2 months to proposals; 4 months to mss. Book catalog online; ms guidelines online.

Nonfiction: Reference, textbook, workbook; Bibles; commentaries. Looking for books that facilitate interaction with bible, encourage and facilitate spiritual growth. Subjects include Christian living, women's, men's and family issues, single and divorce issues, devotionals, inspirationals, prayer, contemporary issues, Biblical reference, applied theology and apologetics, Christian ministry and Bible study in the "Following God" series format. Note our *Following God* series (www.followinggod.com) which provides a personal look at the lives of key characters found in the Bible. This Bible study is designed in an interactive format. Prefer queries by e-mail.

Recent Title(s): *Hungry for More God*, by Dr. Rob Currie; *Dear God Send Me a Soul Mate*, by Rose Sweet; *A Guide Book for New Believers*, by Bette Nordberg.

Tips: "The AMG readership consists largely of adults involved in personal Bible study. We rarely accept books outside of our current genres, so be sure what you're submitting will fit in with our current works."

AMHERST MEDIA, INC., 155 Rano St., Suite 300, Buffalo NY 14207. (716)874-4450. Fax: (716)874-4508. E-mail: amherstmed@aol.com. Website: www.AmherstMedia.com. **Acquisitions:** Craig Alesse, publisher. Estab. 1974. Publishes trade paperback originals and reprints. **Publishes 30 titles/year. Receives 100 submissions/year. 60% of books from first-time authors; 90% from unagented writers. Pays 6-8% royalty on retail price. Offers advance.** Publishes book 1 year after acceptance of ms. Accepts simultaneous submissions. Responds in 2 months to queries. Book catalog and ms guidelines free.

O→ Amherst Media publishes how-to photography books.

Nonfiction: How-to. Subjects include photography. "Looking for well-written and illustrated photo books." Query with outline, 2 sample chapters and SASE. Reviews artwork/photos as part of ms package.

Recent Title(s): *Portrait Photographer's Handbook*, by Bill Hurter.

Tips: "Our audience is made up of beginning to advanced photographers. If I were a writer trying to market a book today, I would fill the need of a specific audience and self-edit in a tight manner."

THE AMWELL PRESS, P.O. Box 5385, Clinton NJ 08809-0385. (908)638-9033. Fax: (908)638-4728. President: James Rikhoff. Corporate Secretary: Genevieve Symonds. **Acquisitions:** Monica Sullivan, vice president. Estab. 1976. Publishes hardcover originals. **Publishes 4 titles/year.** Publishes book 18 months after acceptance of ms. Responds in 2 months to queries.

O→ The Amwell Press publishes hunting and fishing nonfiction, but not how-to books on these subjects.

Nonfiction: Subjects include hunting and fishing stories/literature (not how-to). Mostly limited editions. No fiction. Query with SASE.

Recent Title(s): *Handy to Home*, by Tom Hennessey; *Beyond Hill Country*, by Rikhoff and Sullivan; *Timber and Tide*, by Bob Elman.

ANCESTRY PUBLISHING, imprint of MyFamily.com, Inc., 360 W. 4800 North, Provo UT 84604. (801)705-7000. Fax: (801)705-7120. E-mail: mwright@ancestry.com. Loretto Szucs, executive editor. **Acquisitions:** Matthew Wright, book editor; Jennifer Utley, *Ancestry* magazine editor. Estab. 1983. Publishes hardcover, trade and paperback originals and *Ancestry* magazine. **Publishes 12-20 titles/year. Receives over 100 submissions/year. 70% of books from first-time authors; 100% from unagented writers. Pays 8-12% royalty or makes outright purchase.** Accepts simultaneous submissions. Responds in 2 months to queries. Book catalog for 9×12 SAE with 2 first-class stamps.

O→ "Our publications are aimed exclusively at the genealogist. We consider everything from short monographs to book length works on topics such as immigration, migration, record collections and heraldic topics, among others."

Nonfiction: How-to, reference, genealogy. Subjects include Americana, hobbies, historcial methodology and genealogical

research techniques. No mss that are not genealogical or historical. Query with SASE or submit outline, sample chapter(s). Reviews artwork/photos as part of ms package.
Recent Title(s): *Finding Your African-American Ancestors*; *Finding Answers in U.S. Census Records*.
Tips: "Genealogical and historical reference, how-to, and descriptions of source collections have the best chance of selling to our firm. Be precise in your description. Please, no family histories or genealogies."

ANCHORAGE PRESS PLAYS, INC., P.O. Box 2901, Louisville KY 40201. (502)583-2288. Fax: (502)583-2281. E-mail: applays@bellsouth.net. Website: www.applays.com. **Acquisitions:** Marilee Miller, publisher. Estab. 1935. Publishes hardcover and trade paperback originals. **Publishes 10 titles/year. Receives 45-90 submissions/year. 50% of books from first-time authors; 80% from unagented writers. Pays 10-15% royalty. Playwrights also receive 50-75% royalties.** Publishes book 1-2 years after acceptance of ms. Accepts simultaneous submissions. Responds in 1 month to queries; 6 months to mss. Book catalog online; ms guidelines online.

O→ "We are an international agency for plays for young people. First in the field since 1935."

Nonfiction: Textbook, plays. Subjects include education, theatre, child drama, plays. "We are looking for texts for teachers of drama/theater." Query. Reviews artwork/photos as part of ms package.
Recent Title(s): *Eziqbo The Spirit Child*, by Max Bush; *Amy Crockett*, by Frumi Cohen; *Paper Lanterns, Paper Cranes*, by Brian Kral.

[N] **WILLIAM ANDREW/NOYES PUBLISHING**, 13 Eaton Ave., Norwich NY 13815. (607)337-5000. Fax: (607)337-5090. E-mail: editorial@williamandrew.com. Website: www.williamandrew.com. **Acquisitions:** Millicent Treloar, senior editor (plastics, chemical safety, adhesives, manufacturing). Estab. 1989. Publishes hardcover originals. **Publishes 15 titles/year. Receives 100 queries and 20 mss/year. 40% of books from first-time authors; 100% from unagented writers. Pays 12% royalty on net receipts. Pays $1,000-5,000 advance, depending on author's reputation and nature of book.** Publishes book 1 year after acceptance of ms. Accepts simultaneous submissions. Responds in 1 month to queries; 2 months to proposals; 2 months to mss. Book catalog online; ms guidelines online.

O→ William Andrew/Noyes publishes post-baccalaureate references for practicing engineers and technologists with particular emphasis on practical aspects. Currently emphasizing advanced materials for electronics, plastics and polymers, technical communication.

Nonfiction: Reference, scholarly, technical, textbook. Subjects include computers/electronic, military/war, science. Specific subject areas include industrial processing, science, engineering, materials science, economic books pertaining to chemistry, chemical engineering food, textiles, energy electronics, pollution control, semiconductor material, process technology and electronics. Submit outline. SASE. Reviews artwork/photos as part of ms package. Send photocopies.
Recent Title(s): *Nanostructured Materials*, by Koch; *Horse Behaviour, 2nd Ed*, by Waring.

[A] **ANDREWS McMEEL UNIVERSAL**, 4520 Main St., Kansas City MO 64111-7701. (816)932-6700. **Acquisitions:** Christine Schillig, vice president/editorial director. Estab. 1973. Publishes hardcover and paperback originals. **Publishes 200 titles/year. Pays royalty on retail price or net receipts. Offers advance.**

O→ Andrews McMeel publishes general trade books, humor books, miniature gift books, calendars, and stationery products.

Nonfiction: How-to, humor, inspirational. Subjects include contemporary culture, general trade, relationships. Also produces gift books. *Agented submissions only.*
Recent Title(s): *The Blue Day Book*, by Bradley Trevor Greive.

ANKER PUBLISHING CO., INC., 176 Ballville Rd., P.O. Box 249, Bolton MA 01740-0249. (978)779-6190. E-mail: info@ankerpub.com. Website: www.ankerpub.com. **Acquisitions:** James D. Anker, president and publisher. Publishes hardcover and paperback professional books. **Publishes 6 titles/year. Pays royalty. Offers advance.** Publishes book 4 months after acceptance of ms. Accepts simultaneous submissions.

O→ Publishes professional development books for higher education faculty and administrators.

Nonfiction: Professional development. Subjects include education. Query with SASE or submit proposal package including outline, 3 sample chapter(s).

APPALACHIAN MOUNTAIN CLUB BOOKS, 5 Joy St., Boston MA 02108. Fax: (617)523-0722. Website: www.outdoors.org. **Acquisitions:** Beth Krusi, publisher/editor. Estab. 1897. Publishes hardcover and trade paperback originals. **Publishes 10-15 titles/year. Receives 100 queries and 30 mss/year. 30% of books from first-time authors; 90% from unagented writers. Pays 7-10% royalty on retail price. Offers modest advance.** Publishes book 12-18 months after acceptance of ms. Accepts simultaneous submissions. Responds in 3 months to proposals. Ms guidelines online.

O→ Appalachian Mountain Club publishes hiking guides, paddling guides, nature, conservation and mountain-subject guides for America's Northeast. "We connect recreation to conservation and education."

Nonfiction: Subjects include nature/environment, recreation, regional (Northeast outdoor recreation), literary nonfiction, guidebooks. "Writers should avoid submitting: proposals on Appalachia (rural southern mountains)." Query. Accepts electronic submissions. Reviews artwork/photos as part of ms package. Send photocopies or transparencies.
Recent Title(s): *Women on High*; *Northeastern Wilds*.
Tips: "Our audience is outdoor recreationalists, conservation-minded hikers and canoeists, family outdoor lovers, armchair enthusiasts. Our guidebooks have a strong conservation message. Visit our website for proposal submission guidelines and more information."

[N] ⊘ **ARABESQUE**, BET Books, 850 Third Ave., 16th Floor, New York NY 10022. (212)407-1500. Website: www.bet.com. **Acquisitions:** Karen Thomas, editorial director; Chandra Taylor, consulting editor. Publishes mass market paperback originals. **Publishes 60 titles/year. 30-50% of books from first-time authors; 50% from unagented writers. Pays**

royalty on retail price, varies by author. Offers varying advance. Publishes book 18 months after acceptance of ms. Accepts simultaneous submissions. Responds in 3 months to mss. Book catalog for #10 SASE.

Arabesque publishes contemporary romances about African-American couples.

Fiction: Multicultural (romance). Query with synopsis and SASE. *No unsolicited mss.*

Recent Title(s): *His 1-800 Wife*, by Shirley Hailstock.

[N] [A] **ARCADE PUBLISHING**, 141 Fifth Ave., New York NY 10010. (212)475-2633. President/editor-in-chief: Richard Seaver. Publisher/executive editor: Jeannette Seaver. **Acquisitions:** Cal Barksdale, senior editor. Estab. 1988. Publishes hardcover originals, trade paperback reprints. **Publishes 50 titles/year. 5% of books from first-time authors. Pays royalty on retail price. 10 author's copies. Offers advance.** Publishes book within 18 months after acceptance of ms. Responds in 2 weeks to queries; 4 months to mss. Book catalog for #10 SASE; ms guidelines for #10 SASE.

Arcade prides itself on publishing top-notch literary nonfiction and fiction, with a significant proportion of foreign writers.

Nonfiction: Biography, general nonfiction. Subjects include general nonfiction, government/politics, history, nature/environment, travel. *Agented submissions only.* Reviews artwork/photos as part of ms package. Send photocopies.

Fiction: Ethnic, historical, humor, literary, mainstream/contemporary, mystery, short story collections, suspense, translation. No romance, science fiction. *Agented submissions only.*

Recent Title(s): *Napoleon*, by Frank McLyon.

ARDEN PRESS, INC., P.O. Box 418, Denver CO 80201-0418. (303)697-6766. Fax: (303)697-3443. **Acquisitions:** Susan Conley, publisher. Estab. 1980. Publishes hardcover and trade paperback originals and reprints. **Publishes 4-6 titles/year. Receives 600 submissions/year. 20% of books from first-time authors; 80% from unagented writers. Pays 8-15% royalty on wholesale price. Offers $2,000 average advance.** Publishes book 6 months after acceptance of ms. Accepts simultaneous submissions. Responds in 2 months to queries. Ms guidelines free.

Arden Press publishes nonfiction on women's history and women's issues. "We sell to general and women's bookstores as well as public and academic libraries. Many of our titles are adopted as texts for use in college courses."

Nonfiction: Subjects include women's issues/studies. No personal memoirs or autobiographies. Query with outline/synopsis and sample chapters.

Recent Title(s): *Whatever Happened to the Year of the Woman?*, by Amy Handlin.

Tips: "Writers have the best chance selling us nonfiction on women's subjects. If I were a writer trying to market a book today, I would learn as much as I could about publishers' profiles *then* contact those who publish similar works."

ARDSLEY HOUSE PUBLISHERS, INC., Rowman & Littlefield, 4501 Forbes Blvd., Lanham MD 20706. (301)459-3366. Fax: (301)429-5748. Website: www.rowmanlittlefield.com. **Acquisitions:** Jon Sisk. Estab. 1982. Publishes hardcover and trade paperback originals and reprints. **Publishes 5-8 titles/year. 25% of books from first-time authors; 100% from unagented writers. Pays generally by royalty. Offers advance.** Publishes book 1 year after acceptance of ms. Does not accept simultaneous submissions. Responds in 1 month to queries; 2 months to proposals; 3 months to mss. Ms guidelines online.

Ardsley House publishes only college-level textbooks in mathematics and economics.

Nonfiction: Textbook (college). Subjects include business/economics, mathematics. "We don't accept any other type of manuscript." Query with SASE or submit proposal package including outline, 2-3 sample chapter(s), résumé, author bio, prospectus. Send photocopies.

Recent Title(s): *A Mathemataics Sampler*; *Invention and the Rise of Techno-Capitalism*, by Suarez-Villa.

ARKANSAS RESEARCH, INC., P.O. Box 303, Conway AR 72033. (501)470-1120. Fax: (501)470-1120. E-mail: desmond@ipa.net. **Acquisitions:** Desmond Walls Allen, owner. Estab. 1985. Publishes hardcover originals and trade paperback originals and reprints. **Publishes 20 titles/year. 90% of books from first-time authors; 100% from unagented writers. Pays 5-10% royalty on retail price.** Publishes book 6 months after acceptance of ms. Does not accept simultaneous submissions. Responds in 1 month to queries. Book catalog for $1; ms guidelines free.

Imprints: Research Associates.

"Our company opens a world of information to researchers interested in the history of Arkansas."

Nonfiction: All Arkansas-related subjects. How-to (genealogy), reference, self-help. Subjects include Americana, ethnic, history, hobbies (genealogy), military/war, regional. "We don't print autobiographies or genealogies about one family." Query with SASE. Reviews artwork/photos as part of ms package. Send photocopies.

Recent Title(s): *Life & Times from The Clay County Courier Newspaper Published at Corning, Arkansas, 1893-1900.*

JASON ARONSON, INC., 230 Livingston St., Northvale NJ 07647-1726. (201)767-4093. Fax: (201)767-4330. Website: www.aronson.com. Editor-in-chief: Jason Aronson. **Acquisitions:** Jason Aronson. Estab. 1967. Publishes hardcover and trade paperback originals and reprints. **Publishes 100 titles/year. 50% of books from first-time authors; 95% from unagented writers. Pays 10-15% royalty on retail price.** Publishes book an average of 2 years after acceptance of ms. Does not accept simultaneous submissions. Responds in 1 month to queries. Book catalog and ms guidelines free; ms guidelines online.

"We are looking for high quality, serious, scholarly books in two fields: psychotherapy and Judaica."

Nonfiction: Subjects include history, philosophy, psychology, religion, translation. Query or submit outline and sample chapters. Reviews artwork/photos as part of ms package. Send photocopies.

Recent Title(s): *Parent Therapy: A Relational Alternative to Working With Children*, by Linda Jacobs and Carol Wachs;

Play Therapy Techniques, 2nd Edition, by Charles E. Schaefer and Donna Cangelosi, Eds.; *Understanding the Borderline Mother*, by Christine Lawson.

ART DIRECTION BOOK CO., INC., 456 Glenbrook Rd., Glenbrook CT 06096-1800. (203)353-1441. Fax: (203)353-1371. **Acquisitions:** Don Barron, editorial director. Estab. 1959. Publishes hardcover and paperback originals. **Publishes 8 titles/year. Pays 10% royalty on retail price. Offers average $1,000 advance.** Publishes book 1 year after acceptance of ms. Does not accept simultaneous submissions. Responds in 3 months to queries. Book catalog for 6×9 SAE.

Imprints: Infosource Publications.

O→ Art Direction Book Company is interested in books for the professional advertising art field—books for art directors, designers, etc.; also entry level books for commercial and advertising art students in such fields as typography, photography, paste-up, illustration, clip-art, design, layout and graphic arts.

Nonfiction: Textbook, commercial art; ad art how-to. Subjects include art/architecture. Query with outline and 1 sample chapter. Reviews artwork/photos as part of ms package.

Recent Title(s): *The Write Book.*

ARTE PUBLICO PRESS, University of Houston, 452 Cullen Performance Hall, Houston TX 77204-2174. (713)743-2841. Fax: (713)743-2847. Website: www.artepublicopress.com. **Acquisitions:** Nicolas Kanellos, editor. Estab. 1979. Publishes hardcover originals, trade paperback originals and reprints. **Publishes 36 titles/year. Receives 1,000 queries and 2,000 mss/year. 50% of books from first-time authors; 80% from unagented writers. Pays 10% royalty on wholesale price. Provides 20 author's copies; 40% discount on subsequent copies. Offers $1,000-3,000 advance.** Publishes book 2 years after acceptance of ms. Accepts simultaneous submissions. Responds in 1 month to queries; 1 month to proposals; 4 months to mss. Book catalog free; ms guidelines online.

Imprints: Piñata Books

O→ "We are a showcase for Hispanic literary creativity, arts and culture. Our endeavor is to provide a national forum for Hispanic literature."

Nonfiction: Children's/juvenile, reference. Subjects include ethnic, language/literature, regional, translation, women's issues/studies. Hispanic civil rights issues for new series: "The Hispanic Civil Rights Series." Query with SASE or submit outline, 2 sample chapter(s).

Fiction: Ethnic, literary, mainstream/contemporary, Written by U.S.-Hispanic authors. Query with SASE or submit outline/proposal, 2 sample chapter(s), synopsis or submit complete ms.

Poetry: Submit 10 sample poems.

Recent Title(s): *Shadows and Supposes*, by Gloria Vando (poetry); *Home Killings*, by Marcos McPeek Villatoro (mystery); *Message to Aztlár*, by Rodolfo "Corky" Gonzales (Hispanic Civil Rights Series book).

ARTEMIS CREATIONS PUBLISHING, 3395 Nostrand Ave., 2-J, Brooklyn NY 11229. **Acquisitions:** President: Shirley Oliveira. Publishes trade paperback and mass market paperback originals. **Publishes 4 titles/year. Pays 50% royalty on retail price for eBooks only.**

Imprints: FemSuprem Books.

O→ "Our publications explore femme supremacy, matriarchy, sex, gender, relationships, etc., masochism (male only)."

Nonfiction: Subjects include language/literature, religion (pagan), science, sex, women's issues/studies. "Strong feminine archetypes, subjects only." Query with SASE or submit outline, 3 sample chapter(s). author bio; marketing plan.

Fiction: Erotica, experimental, fantasy, feminist, gothic, horror, mystery, occult, religious, science fiction. Submit synopsis, SASE.

Recent Title(s): *Lady Killer: Tale of Horror and the Erotic*, by Tony Malo.; *Gospel of Goddess*, by Bond and Suffield (metaphysical).

Tips: "Our readers are looking for strong, powerful feminine archetypes in fiction and nonfiction. Graphic sex and language are OK."

ASA, AVIATION SUPPLIES & ACADEMICS, 7005 132nd Pl. SE, Newcastle WA 98059. (425)235-1500. Fax: (425)235-0128. Website: www.asa2fly.com. Director of Operations: Mike Lorden. Editor: Jennifer Trerise. **Acquisitions:** Fred Boyns, controller; Jacqueline Spanitz, curriculum director and technical advisor (pilot and aviation educator). **Publishes 25-40 titles/year. 100% from unagented writers.** Publishes book 9 months or more after acceptance of ms. Does not accept simultaneous submissions. Book catalog free.

O→ ASA is an industry leader in the development and sales of aviation supplies, publications, and software for pilots, flight instructors, flight engineers and aviation technicians. All ASA products are developed by a team of researchers, authors and editors.

Nonfiction: All subjects must be related to aviation education and training. How-to, technical. Subjects include education. "We are primarily an aviation publisher. Educational books in this area are our specialty; other aviation books will be considered." Query with outline. Send photocopies.

Recent Title(s): *The Savvy Flight Instructor: Secrets of the Successful CFI*, by Greg Brown.

Tips: "Two of our specialty series include ASA's *Focus Series*, and ASA *Aviator's Library.* Books in our *Focus Series* concentrate on single-subject areas of aviation knowledge, curriculum and practice. The *Aviator's Library* is comprised of titles of known and/or classic aviation authors or established instructor/authors in the industry, and other aviation specialty titles."

ASIAN HUMANITIES PRESS, Jain Publishing Co., P.O. Box 3523, Fremont CA 94539. (510)659-8272. Fax: (510)659-0501. E-mail: mail@jainpub.com. Website: www.jainpub.com. **Acquisitions:** M.K. Jain, editor-in-chief. Estab. 1989. Publishes hardcover and trade paperback originals and reprints. **Publishes 6 titles/year. Receives 200 submissions/year. 100%**

from unagented writers. Pays 5-15% royalty on net receipts. Publishes book 1-2 years after acceptance of ms. Does not return proposal material. Responds in 3 months to mss. Book catalog and ms guidelines online; ms guidelines online.

O→ Asian Humanities Press publishes in the areas of humanities and social sciences pertaining to Asia, commonly categorized as "Asian Studies." Currently emphasizing undergraduate-level textbooks.

Nonfiction: Reference, textbook, general trade books. Subjects include language/literature, philosophy, psychology, religion, spirituality, Asian classics, social sciences, art/culture. Submit proposal package including vita, list of prior publications. Reviews artwork/photos as part of ms package. Send photocopies.

Recent Title(s): *Adhidharma Samuccaya*, by Walpola Rahula.

ASM INTERNATIONAL, 9639 Kinsman Rd., Materials Park OH 44073-0002. (440)338-5151. Fax: (440)338-4634. E-mail: cust-srv@asminternational.org. Website: www.asminternational.org. **Acquisitions:** Scott D. Henry, assistant director of reference publications (metallurgy/materials). Publishes hardcover originals. **Publishes 15-20 titles/year. Receives 50 queries and 10 mss/year. 50% of books from first-time authors; 100% from unagented writers. Pays royalty on wholesale price or makes outright purchase.** Does not accept simultaneous submissions. Responds in 1 month to queries; 4 months to proposals; 2 months to mss. Book catalog free or online at website; ms guidelines free.

O→ "We focus on practical information related to materials selection and processing."

Nonfiction: Reference, technical, textbook. Subjects include engineering reference. Submit proposal package including outline, 1 sample chapter(s), author credentials. Reviews artwork/photos as part of ms package. Send photocopies.

Recent Title(s): *Introduction to Aluminum Alloys and Tempers*, by J.G. Kaufman; *Titanium: A Technical Guide, 2nd edition*, by M.J. Donachie, Jr.

Tips: "Our audience consists of technically trained people seeking practical information on metals and materials to help them solve problems on the job."

ASSOCIATION FOR SUPERVISION AND CURRICULUM DEVELOPMENT, 1703 N. Beauregard St., Alexandria VA 22311. (703)578-9600. Fax: (703)575-5400. E-mail: swillis@ascd.org. Website: www.ascd.org. **Acquisitions:** Scott Willis, acquisitions director. Estab. 1943. Publishes trade paperback originals. **Publishes 24-30 titles/year. Receives 100 queries and 100 mss/year. 50% of books from first-time authors; 95% from unagented writers. Pays negotiable royalty on actual monies received.** Publishes book 1 year after acceptance of ms. Accepts simultaneous submissions. Responds in 3 months to proposals. Book catalog and ms guidelines free or online.

O→ ASCD publishes high-quality professional books for educators.

Nonfiction: Subjects include education (for professional educators). Submit outline, 2 sample chapter(s). Reviews artwork/photos as part of ms package. Send photocopies.

Recent Title(s): *Leadership for the Learning: How to Help Students Succeed*, by Carl Glickman; *The Multiple Intelligences of Reading and Writing*, by Thomas Armstrong; *Educating Oppositional and Defiant Children*, by Philip S. Hall, Nancy D. Hall.

ASTRAGAL PRESS, P.O. Box 239, Mendham NJ 07945. (973)543-3045. Fax: (973)543-3044. E-mail: info@astragalpress.com. Website: www.astragalpress.com. Estab. 1983. Publishes hardcover and trade paperback originals and reprints. **Publishes 4-6 titles/year. Receives 50 queries/year. Pays 10% royalty on net receipts.** Publishes book 1 year after acceptance of ms. Does not accept simultaneous submissions. Responds in 1 month to queries. Book catalog and ms guidelines free.

O→ "Our primary audience includes those interested in collecting and working with old tools (hand tools especially) and working in traditional early trades. We also publish books on railroads."

Nonfiction: Books on early tools, trades & technology, and railroads. Query. Send photocopies.

Recent Title(s): *A Price Guide to Antique Tools, 3rd ed*, by Herbert P. Kean.

Tips: "We sell to niche markets. We are happy to work with knowledgeable amateur authors in developing titles."

N ⊘ **ATHENEUM BOOKS FOR YOUNG READERS**, Simon & Schuster, 1230 Avenue of the Americas, New York NY 10020. (212)698-2715. Fax: (212)698-2796. Website: www.simonsayskids.com. Associate Publisher/Vice President: Ginee Seo. **Acquisitions:** Anne Schwartz, editorial director, Anne Schwartz Books; Caitlyn Dlouhy, senior editor; Richard Jackson, editorial director(Richard Jackson Books). Estab. 1960. Publishes hardcover originals. **Publishes 70 titles/year. Receives 15,000 submissions/year. 8-12% of books from first-time authors; 50% from unagented writers. Pays 10% royalty on retail price. Offers $2,000-3,000 average advance.** Publishes book 18 months after acceptance of ms. Accepts simultaneous submissions. Responds in 3 months to queries. Ms guidelines for #10 SASE.

O→ Atheneum Books for Young Readers publishes books aimed at children from pre-school age, up through high school.

Nonfiction: Biography, children's/juvenile, humor, self-help. Subjects include Americana, animals, art/architecture, business/economics, government/politics, health/medicine, history, music/dance, nature/environment, photography, psychology, recreation, religion, science, sociology, sports, travel. "Do remember, most publishers plan their lists as much as two years in advance. So if a topic is 'hot' right now, it may be 'old hat' by the time we could bring it out. It's better to steer clear of fads. Some writers assume juvenile books are for 'practice' until you get good enough to write adult books. Not so. Books for young readers demand just as much professionalism in writing as adult books. So save those 'practice' manuscripts for class, or polish them before sending them. *Query letter only for all submissions. We do not accept unsolicited mss.*"

Fiction: All in juvenile versions. Adventure, ethnic, experimental, fantasy, gothic, historical, horror, humor, mainstream/contemporary, mystery, science fiction, sports, suspense, western, Animal. "We have few specific needs except for books that are fresh, interesting and well written. Again, fad topics are dangerous, as are works you haven't polished to the best of your ability. (The competition is fierce.) Other things we don't need at this time are safety pamphlets, ABC books, coloring books and board books. In writing picture book texts, avoid the coy and 'cutesy,' such as stories about characters with alliterative names. *Query letter only for all submissions.* We do not accept unsolicited mss." No "paperback romance type" fiction. Query with SASE. Send art samples under separate cover to Ann Bobco at the above address.

Recent Title(s): *Beautiful Blackbird*, by Ashley Bryan; *Olivia Saves the Circus*, by Ian Falconer; *The House of the Scorpion*, by Nancy Farmer.

ATHENOS PUBLISHING, P.O. Box 782054, Wichita KS 67278-2054. E-mail: athenos_info@lycos.com. Website: www.athenospublishing.com. **Acquisitions:** Quinn Aubrey, editor. Estab. 2000. Publishes hardcover and trade paperback originals. **Publishes 5-10 titles/year. 99% of books from first-time authors; 100% from unagented writers. Pays 5-10% royalty on retail price. Offers $500-1,000 advance.** Publishes book 1 year after acceptance of ms. Accepts simultaneous submissions. Responds in 1 month to queries; 2 months to proposals. Book catalog for #10 SASE; ms guidelines online.

Nonfiction: Biography, children's/juvenile, self-help. Subjects include alternative lifestyles, anthropology/archeology, community, contemporary culture, creative nonfiction, ethnic, gay/lesbian, general nonfiction, government/politics, history, humanities, multicultural, religion, sex, social sciences, women's issues/studies, world affairs. The current publishing program emphasizes multicultural interests, anthropology, current events, gay/lesbian/gender issues, religious interests and societal concerns, and women's studies/interests. Query with SASE. *All unsolicited mss returned unopened.* Reviews artwork/photos as part of ms package. Send photocopies or If color, send color photocopies.

Recent Title(s): *Natural Blues*, by Jheri Shayler; *The World I Know*, by Melanie Price; *Southern Ritual*, by Nella Banks.

Tips: "Query with a short overview of the book's main theme(s), also include some background on the author or contributors. If we like the sound of a proposal, we will contact you to request sample sections or a completed manuscript."

AUGSBURG BOOKS, Augsburg Fortress Publishers, P.O. Box 1209, Minneapolis MN 55440-1209. (612)330-3300. Website: www.augsburgbooks.com. Director of Publications: Roy Harrisville. **Acquisitions:** Michael Wilt, acquisitions editor. Publishes trade and mass market paperback originals and reprints, hardcover picture books. **Publishes 40 titles/year. 2-3% of books from first-time authors. Pays royalty.** Publishes book 18 months after acceptance of ms. Responds in 3 months to queries. Book catalog for 9×12 SAE with 3 first-class stamps; ms guidelines online.

Augsburg Books publishes for the mainline Christian market.

Nonfiction: Children's/juvenile, self-help. Subjects include religion, spirituality (adult), grief/healing/wholeness, parenting, interactive books for children and families, seasonal and picture books. Submit outline, 1-2 sample chapters (if requested).

Recent Title(s): *Angels & All Children: A Nativity Story in Words, Music, and Art*, by Walter Wangerin, Jr.; *Violence in Families: What Every Christian Needs to Know*, by Rev. Al Miles.

AUTONOMEDIA, P.O. Box 568, Williamsburgh Station, Brooklyn NY 11211. (718)963-2603. Fax: (718)963-2603. E-mail: info@autonomedia.org. Website: www.autonomedia.org. **Acquisitions:** Jim Fleming, acquisitions editor. Estab. 1984. Publishes trade paperback originals and reprints. **Publishes 25 titles/year. Receives 350 queries/year. 30% of books from first-time authors; 90% from unagented writers. Pays variable royalty. Offers $100 advance.** Publishes book 6 months after acceptance of ms. Accepts simultaneous submissions. Responds in 2 months to queries. Book catalog for $1; ms guidelines online.

Autonomedia publishes radical and marginal books on culture, media and politics.

Nonfiction: Subjects include anthropology/archeology, art/architecture, business/economics, computers/electronic, gay/lesbian, government/politics, history, multicultural, nature/environment, philosophy, religion, sex, translation, women's issues/studies, world affairs, general nonfiction. Submit outline, SASE. Reviews artwork/photos as part of ms package. Send photocopies.

Fiction: Erotica, experimental, feminist, gay/lesbian, literary, mainstream/contemporary, occult, science fiction, short story collections. Submit synopsis, SASE.

Recent Title(s): *The Anarchists*, by John Henry MacKay.

AVALON BOOKS, Thomas Bouregy & Co., Inc., 160 Madison Ave., 5th Floor, New York NY 10016. (212)598-0222. Fax: (212)979-1862. E-mail: avalon@avalonbooks.com. Website: www.avalonbooks.com. **Acquisitions:** Erin Cartwright, senior editor; Mira Son, editor. Estab. 1950. Publishes hardcover originals. **Publishes 60 titles/year. Receives 2,000 queries and 1,200 mss/year. 65% of books from first-time authors; 80% from unagented writers. Pays 5-15% royalty. Offers $1,000+ advance.** Publishes book 6-10 months after acceptance of ms. Responds in 1 month to queries; 4 months to mss. Book catalog online; ms guidelines online.

"We publish wholesome fiction. We're the 'Family Channel' of publishing. We try to make what we publish suitable for anybody in the family." Currently seeking contemporary romances, career romances, mysteries, series, westerns, good writing, developed characters, interesting story lines. De-emphasizing romantic suspense.

Fiction: Historical (romance), mystery, romance, western. "We publish wholesome contemporary romances, mysteries, historical romances and westerns. Our books are read by adults as well as teenagers, and the characters are all adults. All mysteries are contemporary. We publish: hardcover career romances (two every two months); contemporary romances (four every two months—changing in 2002 to two every two months), mysteries (two every two months) and westerns (two every two months). Submit first 3 sample chapters, a 2-3 page synopsis and SASE. The manuscripts should be between 50,000 to 60,000 words. Manuscripts that are too long will not be considered. Time period and setting are the author's preference. The historical romances will maintain the high level of reading expected by our readers. The books shall be wholesome fiction, without graphic sex, violence or strong language." Query with SASE.

Recent Title(s): *A Wanted Man*, by Nancy J. Parra (historical romance); *Outlaw's Quarry*, by S.J. Stewart; *Death on a Cellular Level*, by Vicky Hunnings (mystery).

Tips: "We are looking for love stories, heroines who have interesting professions, and we are actively seeking new authors. We do accept unagented manuscripts, and we do publish first novels. Right now we are concentrating on finding talented new mystery and historical romance writers with solid story-telling skills. Read our guidelines carefully before submitting."

AVANYU PUBLISHING, INC., P.O. Box 27134, Albuquerque NM 87125. (505)341-1280. Fax: (505)341-1281. Website: www.avanyu-publishing.com. **Acquisitions:** J. Brent Ricks, president. Estab. 1984. Publishes hardcover and trade paperback originals and reprints. **Publishes 4 titles/year. Receives 40 submissions/year. 30% of books from first-time authors; 90% from unagented writers. Pays 8% maximum royalty on wholesale price. Offers advance.** Publishes book 1 year after acceptance of ms. Does not accept simultaneous submissions. Responds in 2 months to queries. Book catalog for #10 SASE.

O‑ Avanyu publishes highly-illustrated, history-oriented books on American Indians and adventures in the Southwest.

Nonfiction: Biography, children's/juvenile, coffee table book, illustrated book, reference, scholarly. Subjects include Americana (Southwest), anthropology/archeology, art/architecture, ethnic, history, multicultural, photography, regional, sociology, spirituality. Query with SASE. Reviews artwork/photos as part of ms package.

Recent Title(s): *Kachinas Spirit Beings of the Hopi*; *Mesa Verde Ancient Architecture*; *Hopi Snake Ceremonies*.

Tips: "Our audience consists of libraries, art collectors and history students. We publish subjects dealing with modern and historic American Indian matters of all kinds."

AVERY, Penguin Putnam, 375 Hudson St., New York NY 10014. (212)366-2000. Fax: (212)366-2365. Website: www.penguinputnam.com. John Duff, publisher. Estab. 1976. Publishes hardcover and trade paperback originals. **Publishes 25 titles/year. 50% of books from first-time authors; 25% from unagented writers. Pays royalty. Offers advance.** Publishes book 1 year after acceptance of ms. Accepts simultaneous submissions. Responds in 1 month to queries; 1 month to proposals; 6 weeks to mss. Book catalog free; ms guidelines free.

O‑ Avery specializes in health, nutrition, alternative medicine, and fitness.

Nonfiction: "We generally do not publish personal accounts of health topics unless they outline a specific plan that covers all areas of the topic." Submit proposal package including outline, author bio, cover letter, table of contents, preface, SASE.

Recent Title(s): *Natural Highs*, by Hyla Cass, M.D. and Patrick Holford; *Dare to Lose*, by Shari Lieberman, Ph.D.; *Prescription for Nutritional Healing*, by Phyllis A. Balch, CNC.

Tips: "Our mission is to enable people to improve their health through clear and up-to-date information."

AVISSON PRESS, INC., 3007 Taliaferro Rd., Greensboro NC 27408. Fax: (336)288-6989. **Acquisitions:** M.L. Hester, editor. Estab. 1994. Publishes hardcover originals and trade paperback originals and reprints. **Publishes 5-6 titles/year. Receives 600 queries and 400 mss/year. 5% of books from first-time authors; 90% from unagented writers. Pays 8-10% royalty on wholesale price. Offers occasional small advance.** Publishes book 15 months after acceptance of ms. Accepts simultaneous submissions. Responds in 1 week to queries; 1 week to proposals; 3 months to mss. Book catalog for #10 SASE.

O‑ Currently emphasizing young-adult biography only. No fiction or poetry.

Nonfiction: Biography. Subjects include ethnic, sports, women's issues/studies. Query with SASE or submit outline, 1-3 sample chapter(s).

Recent Title(s): *Go, Girl!: Young Women Superstars of Pop Music*, by Jacqueline Robb; *The Experimenters: Eleven Great Chemists*, by Margery Everden.

Tips: Audience is primarily public and school libraries.

AZTEX CORP., P.O. Box 50046, Tucson AZ 85703-1046. (520)882-4656. Website: www.aztexcorp.com. **Acquisitions:** Elaine Jordan, editor. Estab. 1976. Publishes hardcover and paperback originals. **Publishes 5 titles/year. Receives 250 submissions/year. 100% from unagented writers. Pays 10% royalty.** Publishes book 18 months after acceptance of ms. Responds in 3 months to queries. Ms guidelines online.

Nonfiction: How-to. Subjects include history, transportation, motor sports, automobiles. "We specialize in transportation subjects (how-to and history)." Biographies and autobiographies are of less interest. Accepts nonfiction translations. Submit outline, 2 sample chapter(s). Reviews artwork/photos as part of ms package.

Tips: "We look for accuracy, thoroughness and interesting presentation."

BACKCOUNTRY GUIDES, The Countryman Press, P. O. Box 748, Woodstock VT 05091-0748. (802)457-4826. Fax: (802)457-1678. E-mail: countrymanpress@wwnorton.com. Website: www.countrymanpress.com. **Acquisitions:** Kermit Hummell, editorial director. Publishes trade paperback originals. **Publishes 15 titles/year. Receives 1,000 queries and a few mss/year. 25% of books from first-time authors; 75% from unagented writers. Pays 6-8% royalty on retail price. Offers $1,500-2,500 advance.** Publishes book 18 months after acceptance of ms. Accepts simultaneous submissions. Responds in 2 months to proposals. Book catalog free; ms guidelines online.

O‑ Backcountry Guides publishes guidebooks that encourage physical fitness and appreciation for and understanding of the natural world, self-sufficiency and adventure. "We publish several series of regional destination guidebooks to outdoor recreation. They include: the 50 Hikes series; Backroad Bicycling series; Trout Streams series; Bicycling America's National Parks series; and a paddling (canoeing and kayaking) series."

Nonfiction: Subjects include nature/environment, recreation (bicycling, hiking, canoeing, kayaking, fly fishing, walking, guidebooks and series), sports. Query with SASE or submit proposal package including outline, market analysis, 50 sample pages.

Recent Title(s): *Bicycling America's National Parks: California*, by David Story; *Kayaking the Maine Coast*, by Dorcas Miller.

Tips: "Look at our existing series of guidebooks to see how your proposal fits in."

BAEN PUBLISHING ENTERPRISES, P.O. Box 1403, Riverdale NY 10471-0671. (718)548-3100. Website: www.baen.com. **Acquisitions:** Jim Baen, editor-in-chief; Toni Weisskopf, executive editor. Estab. 1983. Publishes hardcover, trade paperback and mass market paperback originals and reprints. **Publishes 120 titles/year. Receives 5,000 submissions/year. 5% of books from first-time authors; 50% from unagented writers. Pays royalty on retail price. Offers advance.** Does not accept simultaneous submissions. Responds in 8 months to queries; 8 months to proposals; 1 year to mss. Book catalog free; ms guidelines online.

"We publish books at the heart of science fiction and fantasy."

Fiction: Fantasy, science fiction. Interested in science fiction novels (based on real science) and fantasy novels "that at least strive for originality." Submit outline, 3 consecutive sample chapter(s), synopsis or submit complete ms.

Recent Title(s): *War of Honor*, by David Weber.

Tips: "See our books before submitting. Send for our writers' guidelines. We recommend *Writing to the Point*, by Algis Budrys."

BAKER BOOK HOUSE CO., P.O. Box 6287, Grand Rapids MI 49516-6287. (616)676-9185. Fax: (616)676-2315. Website: www.bakerbooks.com.

Imprints: Baker Academic, Baker Books, Bethany House, Brazos Press, Chosen, Fleming H. Revell.

BAKER BOOKS, Baker Book House Company, P.O. Box 6287, Grand Rapids MI 49516-6287. (616)676-9185. Fax: (616)676-9573. Website: www.bakerbooks.com. Director of Publications: Don Stephenson. Estab. 1939. Publishes hardcover and trade paperback originals and trade paperback reprints. **Publishes 80 titles/year. 10% of books from first-time authors; 85% from unagented writers. Pays 14% royalty on net receipts. Offers advance.** Publishes book within 1 year after acceptance of ms. Does not accept unsolicited proposals. Book catalog for 9½ x 12½ SAE with 3 first-class stamps; ms guidelines for #10 SASE.

"Baker Books publishes popular religious nonfiction and fiction, children's books, academic and reference books, and professional books for church leaders. Most of our authors and readers are evangelical Christians, and our books are purchased from Christian bookstores, mail-order retailers, and school bookstores." Does not accept unsolicited proposals.

Nonfiction: Biography, children's/juvenile, gift book, illustrated book, multimedia, reference, self-help, textbook, CD-ROM. Subjects include anthropology/archeology, child guidance/parenting, psychology, religion, women's issues/studies, Christian doctrine, books for pastors and church leaders, seniors' concerns, singleness, contemporary issues.

Fiction: Juvenile, literary, mainstream/contemporary, mystery, picture books, religious, young adult. "We are mainly seeking fiction of two genres: contemporary women's fiction and mystery." No fiction that is not written from a Christian world view or of a genre not specified.

Recent Title(s): *The Last Days According to Jesus*, by R.C. Sproul (theology); *Resting in the Bosom of the Lamb*, by Augusta Trobaugh (southern fiction).

BALCONY PRESS, 512 E. Wilson, Suite 213, Glendale CA 91206. (818)956-5313. E-mail: ann@balconypress.com. **Acquisitions:** Ann Gray, publisher. Publishes hardcover and trade paperback originals. **Publishes 6-8 titles/year. Pays 10% royalty on wholesale price.** Accepts simultaneous submissions. Responds in 1 month to queries; 1 month to proposals; 3 months to mss. Book catalog free.

- "We also now publish *LA Architect* magazine focusing on contemporary architecture and design in Southern California. Editor: Laura Hull."

Nonfiction: Subjects include art/architecture, ethnic, gardening, history (relative to design, art and architecture), regional. "We are interested in the human side of design as opposed to technical or how-to. We like to think our books will be interesting to the general public who might not otherwise select an architecture or design book." Query by e-mail or letter. Submit outline and 2 sample chapters with introduction if applicable.

Recent Title(s): *Iron: Erecting the Walt Disney Concert Hall*, by Gil Garcetti.

Tips: Audience consists of architects, designers and the general public who enjoy those fields. "Our books typically cover California subjects but that is not a restriction. It's always nice when an author has strong ideas about how the book can be effectively marketed. We are not afraid of small niches if a good sales plan can be devised."

BALE BOOKS, Bale Publications, 5121 St. Charles Ave., Suite #13, New Orleans LA 70115. **Acquisitions:** Don Bale, Jr, editor-in-chief. Estab. 1963. Publishes hardcover and paperback originals and reprints. **Publishes 10 titles/year. Receives 25 submissions/year. 50% of books from first-time authors; 90% from unagented writers. Offers standard 10-12½% royalty contract on wholesale or retail price; sometimes makes outright purchases of $500.** Publishes book 3 years after acceptance of ms. Does not accept simultaneous submissions. Responds in 3 months to queries. Book catalog for #10 SAE with 2 first-class stamps.

"Our mission is to educate numismatists about coins, coin collecting and investing opportunities."

Nonfiction: Numismatics. Subjects include hobbies, money/finance. "Our specialties are coin and stock market investment books; especially coin investment books and coin price guides." Submit outline, 3 sample chapter(s).

Recent Title(s): *How to Find Valuable Old & Scarce Coins*, by Jules Penn.

Tips: "Most of our books are sold through publicity and ads in the coin newspapers. We are open to any new ideas in the area of numismatics. Write for a teenage through adult level. Lead the reader by the hand like a teacher, building chapter by chapter. Our books sometimes have a light, humorous treatment, but not necessarily. We look for good English, construction and content, and sales potential."

BALL PUBLISHING, 335 N. River St., Batavia IL 60510. (630)208-9080. Fax: (630)208-9350. E-mail: info@ballpublishing.com. Website: www.ballpublishing.com. **Acquisitions:** Rick Blanchette, managing editor (floriculture, horticulture, agriculture). Publishes hardcover and trade paperback originals. **Publishes 4-6 titles/year. Receives 25 queries and 10 mss/year. 20% of books from first-time authors; 95% from unagented writers. Pays 10-15% royalty on wholesale price, makes outright purchase of $500. Offers up to $3,000 advance.** Publishes book 1 year after acceptance of ms. Accepts simultaneous submissions. Responds in 2 months to queries. Book catalog for 8½×11 SAE with 3 first-class stamps.

O⁻ "Our books have been primarily published for professionals in the floriculture and horticulture fields. We are open to books on gardening for the consumer, but that is not our primary focus."

Nonfiction: How-to, reference, technical, textbook. Subjects include agriculture/horticulture, gardening, floriculture. Query with SASE or submit proposal package including outline, 2 sample chapter(s). Reviews artwork/photos as part of ms package. Send photocopies.

Recent Title(s): *Contain Yourself*, by Kerstin Ouellet; *The Ball Redbook, 17th Ed.*

Tips: "Professional growers and retailers in floriculture and horticulture make up the majority of our audience. Serious gardeners are a secondary audience. Make sure you know your subject well and present the material in a way that will be of interest to professionals. We do not publish for the inexperienced gardener. Include photos if they are critical to your proposal."

[A] **BALLANTINE BOOKS**, Random House, Inc., 1540 Broadway, New York NY 10036. (212)782-9000. Website: www.randomhouse.com/bb. Publisher: Gina Centrello. Senior VP/Editor-in-Chief: Nancy Miller. VP/Editorial Director: Linda Marrow. **Acquisitions:** Joe Blades, vice president/executive editor (*fiction*: suspense, mystery, *nonfiction*: pop culture, film history and criticism, travel); Tracy Brown, senior editor (*fiction*: literary, quality commerical, paperback reprint *nonfiction*: history, travel, issue-oriented, nature, narrative, biography, paperback reprint); Allison Dickens, assistant editor (*fiction*: literary, women's fiction, commercial, *nonfiction*: biography, narrative, history (art, culinary, travel); Charlotte Herscher, associate editor (*fiction*: historical and contemporary romance); Linda Marrow, vice president/editorial director (*fiction*: suspense, women's, crime); Nancy Miller, senior vice president/editor-in-chief (*nonfiction*: serious commercial, narrative, memoirs, issue-oriented health, parenting); Maureen O'Neal, vice president/editorial director (*nonfiction*: health, childcare, parenting, narrative, diet, *fiction*: women's, quality commercial, Southern fictiom, Ballantine Reader's Circle, trade paperback); Patricia Peters, assistant editor (*nonfiction*: biography, history, travel, narrative, *fiction*: commercial, literary, mysteries); Dan Smetanka, senior editor (*nonfiction*: adventure, narrative, science, religion, *fiction*: literary, quality commercial paperback reprint, story collections); Shauna Summers, senior editor (*fiction*: historical and contemporary romance, general women's fiction, thrillers, suspense); Zach Schisgal, senior editor (*nonfiction*: pop culture, health/fitness, self-help, military history, celebrity/media tie-in). Estab. 1952. Publishes hardcover, trade paperback, mass market paperback originals. **Pays 8-15% royalty. Offers variable advance.** Ms guidelines online.

O⁻ Ballantine Books publishes a wide variety of nonfiction and fiction.

Nonfiction: Biography, gift book, how-to, humor, self-help. Subjects include animals, child guidance/parenting, community, cooking/foods/nutrition, creative nonfiction, education, gay/lesbian, general nonfiction, health/medicine, history, language/literature, memoirs, military/war, recreation, religion, sex, spirituality, travel, true crime, women's issues/studies. *Agented submissions only.* Reviews artwork/photos as part of ms package. Send photocopies.

Fiction: Confession, ethnic, fantasy, feminist, gay/lesbian, historical, humor, literary, mainstream/contemporary (women's), military/war, multicultural, mystery, romance, short story collections, spiritual, suspense, translation, general fiction. *Agented submissions only.*

BANCROFT PRESS, P.O. Box 65360, Baltimore MD 21209-9945. (410)358-0658. Fax: (410)764-1967. E-mail: bruceb@bancroftpress.com. Website: www.bancroftpress.com. **Acquisitions:** Bruce Bortz, publisher (health, investments, politics, history, humor); Fiction Editor (literary novels, mystery/thrillers, young adult). Publishes hardcover and trade paperback originals. Also packages books for other publishers (no fee to authors). **Publishes 4 titles/year. Pays 6-8% royalty. Pays various royalties on retail price. Offers $750 advance.** Publishes book up to 3 years after acceptance of ms. Accepts simultaneous submissions. Responds in 6 months to queries; 4-8 months to proposals; 6 months to mss. Ms guidelines online.

O⁻ Bancroft Press is a general trade publisher. Currently emphasizing young adult nonfiction and fiction (single titles and series) and humorous mysteries. De-emphasizing celebrity fiction.

Nonfiction: Biography, how-to, humor, self-help. Subjects include business/economics, government/politics, health/medicine, money/finance, regional, sports, women's issues/studies, popular culture, essays. "We advise writers to visit the website." Submit proposal package including outline, 2 sample chapter(s), competition/market survey.

Fiction: Ethnic (general), feminist, gay/lesbian, historical, humor, literary, mainstream/contemporary, military/war, mystery (amateur sleuth, cozy, police procedural, private eye/harboiled), regional, science fiction (hard science/technological, soft/sociological), young adult (historical, problem novels, series), thrillers, translation. Query with SASE or submit outline, 2 sample chapter(s), synopsis, by mail or e-mail or submit complete ms.

Recent Title(s): *Finn: A Novel*, by Matthew Olshan; *The Reappearance of Sam Webber*, by Jonathon Scott Fuqua; *For Whom the Minivan Rolls: An Aaron Tucker Suburban Mystery*, by Jeffrey Cohen.

BANTAM DELL PUBLISHING GROUP, Random House, Inc., 1745 Broadway, New York NY 10019. (212)782-9000. Fax: (212)302-7985. Website: www.bantamdell.com. Executive Vice President/Deputy Publisher: Nita Taublib. **Acquisitions:** Toni Burbank (nonfiction: self-help, health/medicine, nature, spirituality, philosophy); Jackie Cantor (fiction: general commercial, literary, women's fiction, memoir); Kara Cesare (fiction: romance, women's fiction); Tracy Devine (fiction and nonfiction: narrative nonfiction, history, adventure, military, science, women's fiction, general upscale commercial fiction, suspense); Anne Groell (fiction: fantasy, science fiction); Jackie Farber (fiction: women's fiction, general commercial fiction); Susan Kamil (The Dial Press, fiction and nonfiction: literary, memoir, sociological, historical); Kathleen Jayes (fiction and nonfiction: literary, self-help, sociological, philosophy, mythology); Robin Michaelson (nonfiction: self-help, child care/parenting, psychology); Kate Miciak (fiction: mystery, suspense, historical fiction); Wendy McCurdy (fiction: romance, women's fiction); Daniel Perez (nonfiction: Americana, self-help, health/medicine); Beth Rashbaum (nonfiction: health, psychology, self-help, women's issues, Judaica, history, memoir); Tom Spain (fiction and nonfiction: Americana, memoir, sociology, historical). Estab. 1945. Publishes hardcover, trade paperback and mass market paperback originals; mass market paperback reprints. **Publishes 350 titles/year. Offers advance.** Publishes book 1 year after acceptance of ms. Accepts simultaneous submissions.

Imprints: Bantam Hardcover; Bantam Mass Market; Bantam Trade Paperback; Delacorte Press; Dell; Delta; DTP; The Dial Press; Fanfare; Island; Spectra.

Bantam Dell is a division of Random House, publishing both fiction and nonfiction. No unsolicited mss; send one-page queries.

Nonfiction: Biography, how-to, humor, self-help. Subjects include Americana, business/economics, child guidance/parenting, cooking/foods/nutrition, government/politics, health/medicine, history, humor, language/literature, military/war, nature/environment, New Age, philosophy, psychology, religion, science, sociology, spirituality, sports, true crime, women's issues/studies, Diet fitness, Mysticism/astrology, True crime. Agent submissions or single-page query letter briefly describing the work (including category and subject matter) and author biography. SASE a must.

Fiction: Adventure, fantasy, horror.

Recent Title(s): *Irresistible Forces*, by Danielle Steel (Delacorte, fiction); *The Testament*, by John Grisham (Dell, fiction); *The Plutonium Files*, by Eileen Welsom (The Dial Press, nonfiction).

BANTAM DOUBLEDAY DELL BOOKS FOR YOUNG READERS, Random House Children's Publishing, Random House, Inc., 1745 Broadway, New York NY 10019. (212)782-9000. Fax: (212)782-8234. Website: www.randomhouse.com/kids. Vice President/Publisher: Beverly Horowitz. **Acquisitions:** Michelle Poploff, editorial director. Publishes hardcover, trade paperback and mass market paperback series originals, trade paperback reprints. **Publishes 300 titles/year. Receives thousands queries/year. 10% of books from first-time authors; small% from unagented writers. Pays royalty. Offers varied advance.** Publishes book 2 years after acceptance of ms. Does not accept simultaneous submissions. Responds in 2 months to queries; 4 months to mss. Book catalog for 9×12 SASE.

Imprints: Delacorte Press Books for Young Readers, Doubleday Books for Young Readers, Dell Laurel Leaf (ya), Yearling (middle grade).

"Bantam Doubleday Dell Books for Young Readers publishes award-winning books by distinguished authors and the most promising new writers." The best way to break in to this market is through its two contests, the Marguerite de Angeli Contest and the Delacorte Press Contest for a First Young Adult Novel, listed in the Contests & Awards section of this book.

Nonfiction: Children's/juvenile. "Bantam Doubleday Dell Books for Young Readers publishes a very limited number of nonfiction titles."

Fiction: Adventure, fantasy, historical, humor, juvenile, mainstream/contemporary, mystery, picture books, suspense, young adult, chapter books, middle-grade. *Agented submissions only. No unsolicited mss. Accepts unsolicited queries only.*

Recent Title(s): *Bud, Not Buddy*, by Christopher Paul Curtis (Newbery Award winner); *Ties That Bind, Ties That Break*, by Lensey Namiska (fiction).

BARBOUR PUBLISHING, INC., P.O. Box 719, Uhrichsville OH 44683. (740)922-6045. Fax: (740)922-5948. Website: www.barbourpublishing.com. **Acquisitions:** Paul Muckley, senior editor (all areas); Rebecca Germany, managing editor (fiction). Estab. 1981. Publishes hardcover, trade paperback and mass market paperback originals and reprints. **Publishes 200 titles/year. Receives 500 queries and 1000 mss/year. 40% of books from first-time authors; 95% from unagented writers. Pays 0-12% royalty on net price or makes outright purchase of $500-5,000. Offers $500-2,500 advance.** Publishes book 2 years after acceptance of ms. Accepts simultaneous submissions. Responds in 1 month to queries; 3 months to proposals; 3 months to mss. Book catalog online or for 9×12 SAE with 2 first-class stamps; ms guidelines for #10 SASE or online; ms guidelines online.

Imprints: Heartsong Presents (contact Rebecca Germany, managing editor).

Barbour Books publishes mostly devotional material that is non-denominational and evangelical in nature; Heartsong Presents publishes Christian romance. "We're a Christian evangelical publisher."

Nonfiction: Biography, gift book, humor, reference, devotional, Bible Trivia. Subjects include child guidance/parenting, cooking/foods/nutrition, money/finance, religion (evangelical Christian), women's issues/studies. "We look for book ideas with mass appeal - nothing in narrowly-defined niches. If you can appeal to a wide audience with an important message, creatively presented, we'd be interested to see your proposal." Submit outline, 3 sample chapter(s), SASE. Reviews artwork/photos as part of ms package. Send photocopies.

Fiction: Historical, mainstream/contemporary, religious, romance, western. "All of our fiction is 'sweet' romance. No sex, no bad language, etc. Audience is evangelical/Christian, and we're looking for wholesome material for young as well as old. Common writer's mistakes are a sketchy proposal, an unbelievable story and a story that doesn't fit our guidelines for inspirational romances." Submit 3 sample chapter(s), synopsis, SASE.

Recent Title(s): *Faith that Breathes*, by Michael Ross (devotional); *A Treasure Deep*, by Alton Gansky (fiction); *You're Late Again Lord*, by Karon Phillips Goodman (women's issues).

Tips: "Audience is evangelical/Christian conservative, non-denominational, young and old. We're looking for *great concepts*, not necessarily a big name author or agent. We want to publish books that will sell millions, not just 'flash in the pan' releases. Send us your ideas!"

BAREFOOT BOOKS, PO Box 382207, Cambridge MA 02238-2207. (617)576-0660. Fax: (617)576-0049. E-mail: alison.keehn@barefootbooks.com. Website: www.barefootbooks.com. **Acquisitions:** Alison Keehn, U.S. editor (picture books and anthologies of folktales). Publishes hardcover and trade paperback originals. **Publishes 30 titles/year. Receives 2,000 queries and 3,000 mss/year. 35% of books from first-time authors; 60% from unagented writers. Pays 2½-5% royalty on retail price or makes outright purchase of $5.99-19.99. Offers advance.** Publishes book 2 years after acceptance of ms. Accepts simultaneous submissions. Responds in 2 months to queries; 2 months to proposals; 3 months to mss. Book catalog for #10 SASE; ms guidelines online.

O→ We are a small, independent publishing company that publishes high-quality picture books for children of all ages and specializes in the work of artists and writers from many cultures. We focus on themes that support independence of spirit, encourage openness to others, and foster a life-long love of learning. Does not accept unsolicited mss, but does accept query letters and first pages of mss.

Fiction: Juvenile. Barefoot Books only publishes children's picture books and anthologies of folktales. "We do not publish novels. We are no longer accepting unsolicited manuscripts. We do accept query letters, and we encourage authors to send the first page of their manuscript with the query letter." Query with SASE or submit first page of ms. Anthology collection with SASE and one sample story.

Recent Title(s): *We All Went on Safari: A Counting Journey through Tanzania*, by Laurie Krebs (early learning picture book); *The Fairie's Gift*, by Tanya Robyn Batt (picture book); *The Lady of Ten Thousand Names: Goddess Stories from Many Cultures*, by Borleigh Mutein (illustrated anthology).

Tips: "Our audience is made up of children and parents, teachers and students, of many different ages and cultures. Since we are a small publisher, and we definitely publish for a 'niche' market, it is helpful to look at our books and our website before submitting, to see if your book would fit into the type of book we publish."

BARNEGAT LIGHT PRESS, Pine Barrens Press, P.O. Box 607, 3959 Rt. 563, Chatsworth NJ 08019-0607. (609)894-4415. Fax: (609)894-2350. **Acquisitions:** R. Marilyn Schmidt, publisher. Publishes trade paperback originals. **Publishes 4 titles/year. Receives 50 queries and 30 mss/year. 0% of books from first-time authors; 100% from unagented writers. Makes outright purchase.** Publishes book 6 months after acceptance of ms. Responds in 1 month to queries. Book catalog free or online at website.

Imprints: Pine Barrens Press.

O→ "We are a regional publisher emphasizing the mid-Atlantic region. Areas concerned are gardening, cooking and travel."

Nonfiction: Cookbook, how-to, illustrated book. Subjects include agriculture/horticulture, cooking/foods/nutrition, gardening, regional, travel. Query with SASE. Reviews artwork/photos as part of ms package. Send photocopies.

Recent Title(s): *Churches and Graveyards of the Pine Gardens*, R. Marilyn Schmidt.

BARRICADE BOOKS, INC., 185 Bridge Plaza N., Suite 308A, Fort Lee NJ 07024-5900. (201)944-7600. Fax: (201)944-6363. **Acquisitions:** Carole Stuart, publisher. Estab. 1991. Publishes hardcover and trade paperback originals, trade paperback reprints. **Publishes 30 titles/year. Receives 200 queries and 100 mss/year. 80% of books from first-time authors; 50% from unagented writers. Pays 10-12% royalty on retail price for hardcover. Offers advance.** Publishes book 18 months after acceptance of ms. Responds in 1 month to queries. Book catalog for $3.

O→ Barricade Books publishes nonfiction, "mostly of the controversial type, and books we can promote with authors who can talk about their topics on radio and television and to the press."

Nonfiction: Biography, how-to, reference, self-help. Subjects include business/economics, ethnic, gay/lesbian, government/politics, health/medicine, history, nature/environment, psychology, sociology, women's issues/studies. Query with SASE or submit outline, 1-2 sample chapter(s). Material will not be returned without SASE. Reviews artwork/photos as part of ms package. Send photocopies.

Recent Title(s): *Murder at the Conspiracy Convention*, by Paul Riessner; *A German Tale*, by Erika Rarres.

Tips: "Do your homework. Visit bookshops to find publishers who are doing the kinds of books you want to write. Always submit to a *person*—not just 'Editor.' Always enclose SASE or you may not get a response."

BARRON'S EDUCATIONAL SERIES, INC., 250 Wireless Blvd., Hauppauge NY 11788. (631)434-3311. Fax: (631)434-3394. Website: barronseduc.com. **Acquisitions:** Wayne Barr, acquisitions editor. Estab. 1941. Publishes hardcover, paperback and mass market originals and software. **Publishes 400 titles/year. Receives 2,000 queries and 1,000 submissions/year. 40% of books from first-time authors; 75% from unagented writers. Pays 12-14% royalty on net receipts. Offers $3-4,000 advance.** Publishes book 18 months after acceptance of ms. Accepts simultaneous submissions. Responds in 3 months to queries; 8 months to mss. Book catalog free; ms guidelines online.

O→ Barron's tends to publish series of books, both for adults and children. "We are always on the lookout for creative nonfiction ideas for children and adults."

Nonfiction: Children's/juvenile, cookbook, textbook, student test prep guides. Subjects include art/architecture, business/economics, child guidance/parenting, cooking/foods/nutrition, education, health/medicine, hobbies, language/literature, New Age, sports, translation, travel, adult education, foreign language, review books, guidance, pets, literary guides. Query with SASE or submit outline, 2-3 sample chapter(s). Reviews artwork/photos as part of ms package.

Fiction: Juvenile. Submit sample chapter(s), synopsis.

Recent Title(s): *A Book of Magical Herbs*, by Margaret Picton; *Family Gardener*, by Lucy Peel.

Tips: "Audience is mostly educated self-learners and hobbyists. The writer has the best chance of selling us a book that will fit into one of our series. Children's books have less chance for acceptance because of the glut of submissions. SASE must be included for the return of all materials. Please be patient for replies."

BASIC BOOKS, Perseus Books, 387 Park Ave. S., 12th Floor, New York NY 10016. (212)340-8100. Website: www.basicbooks.com. **Acquisitions:** Elizabeth Maguire, VP, associate publisher, editorial director; Jo Ann Miller, executive editor; Bill Frucht, senior editor; Jessica Mobley, editor. Publishes hardcover originals and reprints, trade paperback originals and reprints. **Publishes 100 titles/year. Receives 500 queries and 300 mss/year. 5% of books from first-time authors; 10% from unagented writers. Pays 10-15% royalty on retail price. Offers less than $10,000 advance.** Publishes book 1 year after acceptance of ms. Accepts simultaneous submissions. Responds in 3 months to queries; 3 months to proposals; 6 months to mss. Book catalog free; ms guidelines free.

Nonfiction: Biography, serious adult trade. Subjects include Americana, anthropology/archeology, business/economics, child guidance/parenting, computers/electronic, creative nonfiction, education, ethnic, gay/lesbian, government/politics, health/medicine, history, language/literature, memoirs, military/war, money/finance, multicultural, music/dance, nature/environment, philosophy, psychology, regional, religion, science, sex, sociology, spirituality, translation, women's issues/studies. "Because of the current post 9/11 situation, we are not currently accepting any unsolicited submissions. This is subject to change without notice." Query with SASE or submit proposal package including outline, 3 sample chapter(s), author bio, TOC. **All unsolicited mss returned unopened.** Reviews artwork/photos as part of ms package. Send photocopies.

Recent Title(s): *The Mystery of Capital*, by Hernando de Soto (economics); *The Hidden Hitler*, by Lothar Machton (history/biography); *The Truth Will Set You Free*, by Alice Miller (psychology).

[N] **BASIC HEALTH PUBLICATIONS, INC.**, 8200 Boulevard E., 25F, North Bergen NJ 07047. (201)868-8336. Fax: (201)868-2842. E-mail: ngoldfind@basichealthpub.com. Website: www.letsliveonline.com. **Acquisitions:** Norman Goldfind, publisher (health, alternative medicine, nutrition, fitness). Estab. 2001. Publishes trade paperback and mass market paperback originals and reprints. **Publishes 30 titles/year; imprint publishes 30 titles/year. Receives 100 queries and 75 mss/year. 10% of books from first-time authors; 10% from unagented writers. Pays 10-20% royalty on wholesale price. Offers $2,500-25,000 advance.** Publishes book 1 year after acceptance of ms. Accepts simultaneous submissions. Responds in 1 month to queries; 1 month to proposals; 2 months to mss. Book catalog online; ms guidelines for #10 SASE.

Nonfiction: Booklets, trade paperback, mass market paperback. Subjects include health/medicine. "We are very highly focused on health, alternative medicine, nutrition, and fitness. Must be well researched and documented with appropriate references. Writing should be aimed at lay audience but also be able to cross over to professional market." Submit proposal package including outline, 2-3 sample chapter(s), introduction.

Recent Title(s): *Stopping the Clock: Longevity for the New Millennium*, by Ronald Klatz, M.D., D.O. & Robert Goldman, M.D., D.O., Ph.D.; *Dr. Earl Mindell's Natural Remedies for 101 Ailments*, by Earl Mindell, R.Ph., Ph.D.

Tips: "Our audience is over 30, well educated, middle to upper income." "We prefer writers with professional credentials (M.D.s, Ph.D.s, N.D.s, etc.) or writers with backgrounds in health and medicine."

BATTELLE PRESS, Battelle Memorial Institute, 505 King Ave., Columbus OH 43201. (614)424-6393. Fax: (614)424-3819. E-mail: press@battelle.org. Website: www.battelle.org/bookstore. **Acquisitions:** Joe Sheldrick. Estab. 1980. Publishes hardcover and paperback originals and markets primarily by direct mail. **Publishes 15 titles/year. Pays 10% royalty on wholesale price.** Publishes book 6 months after acceptance of ms. Accepts simultaneous submissions. Responds in 1 month to queries. Book catalog free; ms guidelines online.

Battelle Press strives to be a primary source of books and software on science and technology management.

Nonfiction: Subjects include science. "We are looking for management, leadership, project management and communication books specifically targeted to engineers and scientists." Query with SASE. Returns submissions with SASE only by writer's request. Reviews artwork/photos as part of ms package. Send photocopies.

Recent Title(s): *Managing the Industry/University Cooperative Research Center*; *Project Manager's Survival Guide.*

Tips: Audience consists of engineers, researchers, scientists and corporate researchers and developers.

BAY/SOMA PUBLISHING, INC., 444 DeHaro St., Suite 130, San Francisco CA 94107. (415)252-4350 and (415)252-4360. Fax: (415)252-4352. E-mail: info@baybooks.com. Website: www.baybooks.com. **Acquisitions:** James Connolly, editorial director. Publishes hardcover originals, trade paperback originals and reprints. **Publishes 20 titles/year. Receives 300 queries/year. 10% of books from first-time authors. Royalties vary substantially. Offers $0-25,000 advance.** Publishes book 6 months-1 year after acceptance of ms. Accepts simultaneous submissions. Responds in 3 months to queries. Book catalog for 9×12 SAE with 3 first-class stamps or see website.

Nonfiction: Coffee table book, cookbook, gift book, how-to, humor, illustrated book. Subjects include cooking/foods/nutrition, gardening, health/medicine, nature/environment, interior design. Query with SASE.

Recent Title(s): *Savor the Southwest*, by Barbara Fenzl (cooking); *Low-Carb Meals in Minutes*, by Linda Gassenheimer; *Designs for a Healthy Home*, by Dan Phillips.

[N] **BAYCREST BOOKS**, P.O. Box 2009, Monroe MI 48161. E-mail: ceo@baycrestbooks.com.Submissions E-mail: submissions@baycrestbooks.com. Website: www.baycrestbooks.com. **Acquisitions:** Nadine Meeker, CEO/publisher; Kate Orlando, senior editor. Estab. 2002. Publishes trade paperback originals. **Publishes 6 titles/year; imprint publishes 1 titles/year. 100% of books from first-time authors. Pays 7-10% royalty on retail price.** Publishes book 12-18 months after acceptance of ms. Accepts simultaneous submissions. Responds in 2 months to queries; 2 months to proposals; 4 months to mss. Book catalog online; ms guidelines online.

Imprints: Finger Print (mystery); One in Ten (gay/lesbian fiction); Storm Front (action); Orange Moon (young adult); Sunset Rapids (mainstream/romance); StarPoint (sci-fi).

Fiction: Adventure, erotica, fantasy, feminist, gay/lesbian, historical, horror, literary, mainstream/contemporary, mystery, romance, science fiction, suspense, western, young adult. "Writers seeking to publish with us should visit our website to see which divisions we carry and what we are looking for in each division. In short, we are looking for fiction that captivates readers and 're-writes' the genre, taking it to a new level. We seek character driven pieces with characters you love or love to hate. Think pulp fiction with a literary edge. We want stories from fresh new authors (or published authors) who can think 'outside the box' and marketplace. We don't want a re-manufactured version of the hottest trends. We look for books that set the trends and engage the readers. Give us something that hasn't 'been done' before." Submit proposal package including synopsis.

Recent Title(s): *One Belief Away*, by C.N. Winters (historical lesbian fiction); *Inferno*, by Trish Shields (contemporary lesbian fiction).

Tips: "We want our books to appeal to the 'common man' yet have characters and plots which grab the literature reader as well. If your query doesn't capture our attention, we feel your books will bore us as well. We're not interested in what your neighbor or best friend thinks about your book. We'll be the judge. Prior publishing experience is welcome but not an automatic ticket to publish with us. Be sure to carefully proof everything you send and be sure to follow our guidelines to the letter."

BAYLOR UNIVERSITY PRESS, P.O. Box 97363, Waco TX 76798. (254)710-3164. Fax: (254)710-3440. Website: www.baylorpress.com. **Acquisitions:** Carey C. Newman, editor. Publishes hardcover and trade paperback originals. **Publishes 5 titles/year. Pays 10% royalty on wholesale price.** Publishes book 6 months after acceptance of ms. Does not accept simultaneous submissions. Responds in 2 months to proposals. Ms guidelines online.

Imprints: Markham Press Fund.

- "We publish contemporary and historical scholarly works on religion, ethics, church-state studies, and oral history, particularly as these relate to Texas and the Southwest." Currently emphasizing religious studies, history. De-emphasizing art, archaeology.

Nonfiction: Subjects include anthropology/archeology, history, regional, religion, women's issues/studies. Submit outline, 1-3 sample chapter(s).

Recent Title(s): *A Year at the Catholic Worker: A Spiritual Journey Among the Poor*, by Marc H. Ellis (Literature and the Religious Spirit Series).

Tips: "We publish contemporary and historical scholarly works on religion, ethics, church-state studies, and oral history, particularly as these relate to Texas and the Southwest." Currently emphasizing religious studies, history. De-emphasizing art, archaeology.

BAYWOOD PUBLISHING CO., INC., 26 Austin Ave., Amityville NY 11701. (631)691-1270. Fax: (631)691-1770. E-mail: baywood@baywood.com. Website: www.baywood.com. **Acquisitions:** Stuart Cohen, managing editor. Estab. 1964. **Publishes 25 titles/year. Pays 7-15% royalty on retail price. Offers advance.** Publishes book within 1 year after acceptance of ms. Does not accept simultaneous submissions. Book catalog and ms guidelines free; ms guidelines online.

- Baywood Publishing publishes original and innovative books in the humanities and social sciences, including areas such as health sciences, gerontology, death and bereavement, psychology, technical communications and archaeology.

Nonfiction: Scholarly, technical, scholarly. Subjects include anthropology/archeology, computers/electronic, education, health/medicine, nature/environment, psychology, sociology, women's issues/studies, gerontology, imagery, labor relations, death/dying, drugs. Submit outline, sample chapter(s).

Recent Title(s): *Common Threads: Nine Widows' Journeys Through Love, Loss and Healing*, by Diane S. Kaimann; *Invitation to the Life Course: Toward New Understandings of Later Life*, edited by Richard A. Settersten, Jr.; *Exploding Steamboats, Senate Debates and Technical Reports: The Convergence of Technology, Politics and Rhetoric in the Steamboat Bill of 1838*, by R. John Brockmann.

BEACON HILL PRESS OF KANSAS CITY, Nazarene Publishing House, P.O. Box 419527, Kansas City KS 64141. (816)931-1900. Fax: (816)753-4071. **Acquisitions:** Bonnie Perry, director. Estab. 1912. Publishes hardcover and paperback originals. **Publishes 30 titles/year. Pays 12% royalty on net sales for first 10,000 copies and 14% on subsequent copies. Sometimes makes flat rate purchase.** Publishes book 1 year after acceptance of ms. Responds in 3 months to queries.

- "Beacon Hill Press is a Christ-centered publisher that provides authentically Christian resources faithful to God's word and relevant to life."

Nonfiction: Doctrinally must conform to the evangelical, Wesleyan tradition. Accent on holy living; encouragement in daily Christian life. Subjects include applied Christianity, spiritual formation, leadership resources, contemporary issues and Christian care. No fiction, autobiography, poetry, short stories or children's picture books. Query with SASE or submit proposal package. Average ms length: 30,000-60,000.

Recent Title(s): *Unshakeable Faith in Shaky Times*, by Joyce Williams.

BEACON PRESS, 25 Beacon St., Boston MA 02108-2892. (617)742-2110. Fax: (617)723-3097. E-mail: cvyce@beacon.org. Website: www.beacon.org. Director: Helene Atwan. **Acquisitions:** Gayatri Patnaik, senior editor (African-American, Asian-American, Latino, Native American, Jewish and gay and lesbian studies, anthropology); Joanne Wyckoff, executive editor (child and family issues, environmental concerns); Amy Caldwell, associate editor (poetry, gender studies, gay/lesbian studies and Cuban studies); Christopher Vyce, assistant editor. Estab. 1854. Publishes hardcover originals and paperback reprints. **Publishes 60 titles/year. Receives 4,000 submissions/year. 10% of books from first-time authors. Pays royalty. Offers advance.** Accepts simultaneous submissions. Responds in 3 months to queries.

Imprints: Bluestreak Series (innovative literary writing by women of color).

O→ Beacon Press publishes general interest books that promote the following values: the inherent worth and dignity of every person; justice, equity, and compassion in human relations; acceptance of one another; a free and responsible search for truth and meaning; the goal of world community with peace, liberty and justice for all; respect for the interdependent web of all existence. Currently emphasizing innovative nonfiction writing by people of all colors. De-emphasizing poetry, children's stories, art books, self-help.

Nonfiction: Scholarly. Subjects include anthropology/archeology, child guidance/parenting, education, ethnic, gay/lesbian, nature/environment, philosophy, religion, women's issues/studies, world affairs. General nonfiction including works of original scholarship, religion, women's studies, philosophy, current affairs, anthropology, environmental concerns, African-American, Asian-American, Native American, Latino and Jewish studies, gay and lesbian studies, education, legal studies, child and family issues, Irish studies. *Strongly prefers agented submissions.* Query with SASE or submit outline, sample chapter(s), résumé, CV. *Strongly prefers referred submissions, on exclusive.*

Recent Title(s): *Radical Equation*, by Robert Moses and Charles Cobb; *All Souls*, by Michael Patrick McDonald; *Speak to Me*, by Marcie Hershman.

Tips: "We probably accept only one or two manuscripts from an unpublished pool of 4,000 submissions per year. No fiction, children's book, or poetry submissions invited. An academic affiliation is helpful."

[N] **BEARMANOR MEDIA**, P.O. Box 750, Boalsburg PA 16827. E-mail: benohmart@yahoo.com. Website: www.bearmanormedia.com. Estab. 2001. Publishes trade paperback originals and reprints. **Publishes 6 titles/year. 50% of books from first-time authors; 100% from unagented writers. Pays 20% royalty on retail price.** Publishes book 8 months after acceptance of ms. Accepts simultaneous submissions. Responds in 1 month to queries; 1 month to proposals; 2 months to mss. Book catalog for #10 SASE; ms guidelines by email.

Nonfiction: Autobiography, biography. Subjects include general nonfiction, old time radio, voice actors, old movies. Query with SASE or submit proposal package including outline, list of credits on the subject.

Recent Title(s): *The Great Gildersleeve*, by Charles Stumpf (radio biography); *Hollywood's Golden Age*, by Edward Dmytryk (Hollywood biography); *It's That Time Again!*, by various writers (radio short stories).

Tips: "My readers love the past. Radio, old movies, old television. My own tastes include voice actors and scripts, especially of radio and television no longer available. I prefer books on subjects that haven't previously been covered as full books. Doesn't matter to me if you're a first-time author or have a track record. Just know your subject!"

[N] **BEARPAW PUBLISHING**, 9120 Thorton Rd., #343, Stockton CA 95209. (800)books04. Website: www.bearpawpublishing.com. **Acquisitions:** Jiana Behr, owner (gay fiction). Estab. 2002. Publishes trade paperback originals. **Publishes 5 titles/year. Receives 30 queries and 20 mss/year. 50% of books from first-time authors; 100% from unagented writers. Pays 10% royalty on wholesale price.** Publishes book 10 months after acceptance of ms. Does not accept simultaneous submissions. Responds in 1 month to queries; 2 months to mss. Book catalog online; ms guidelines online.

Fiction: Adventure, confession, erotica, ethnic, fantasy, gay/lesbian, gothic, historical, horror, humor, mainstream/contemporary, military/war, multicultural, mystery, occult, romance, science fiction, short story collections, spiritual, sports, suspense, western. All submissions should include gay characters as the main characters. Sex in the book is requested but not required. Submit complete ms.

Recent Title(s): *Cost of Love*, by Alexis Rogers (contemporary).

Tips: "Audience is gay men. I prefer submissions via e-mail in text format. I will accept attachments and large loads."

[N] **BEAVER POND PUBLISHING**, P.O. Box 224, Greenville PA 16125. (724)588-3492. Fax: (724)588-2486. E-mail: oj@zoominternet.net. Website: www.beaverpondpublishing.com. **Acquisitions:** Rich Faler, publications director. Estab. 1990. Publishes trade paperback originals and reprints. **Publishes 4 titles/year. Receives 30 queries and 20 mss/year. 50% of books from first-time authors; 100% from unagented writers. On most contracts, pays 8-10% royalty on net sales or makes outright purchase.** Publishes book 1 year after acceptance of ms. Accepts simultaneous submissions. Responds in 1 month to queries. Book catalog free; ms guidelines online.

O→ Beaver Pond publishes primarily outdoor-oriented books and magazines.

Nonfiction: How-to. Subjects include nature/environment, photography (outdoor), sports, Hunting, Fishing. "We are actively seeking shorter length manuscripts suitable for 20-40 page booklets, in addition to longer length books. Don't offer too general a title with no 'meat.' ". Query with SASE or submit outline, 2 sample chapter(s). Reviews artwork/photos as part of ms package.

Recent Title(s): *Allegheny Angler: Fifty Years a Fly Fisher*, by John Buch; *Crow Shooting Secrets #2*, by Dick Mermon.

Tips: "Audience is active outdoor people that want to excel at their craft. Write the book that you would have wanted when you first began a specific outdoor activity. The manuscript needs to completely cover a narrow topic indepth."

BEEMAN JORGENSEN, INC., 7510 Allisonville Rd., Indianapolis IN 46250. (317)841-7677. Fax: (317)849-2001. **Acquisitions:** Brett Johnson, president (automotive/auto racing). Publishes hardcover and trade paperback originals and hardcover reprints. **Publishes 4 titles/year. Receives 10 queries/year. 50% of books from first-time authors; 100% from unagented writers. Pays 15-30% royalty on wholesale price. Offers up to $1,000 advance.** Publishes book 8 months after acceptance of ms. Responds in 1 month to queries; 2 months to proposals. Book catalog free.

Nonfiction: Publishes books on automobiles and auto racing. Coffee table book, illustrated book, reference. Subjects include sports (auto racing). Query with SASE or submit proposal package including outline, 1 sample chapter(s).

Recent Title(s): *Porsche Speedster*, by Michel Thiriar (coffee table); *Road America*, by Tom Schultz (illustrated book); *Volkswagon KdF, 1934-1945*, by Terry Shuler (illustrated book).

Tips: Audience is automotive enthusiasts, specific marque owners/enthusiasts, auto racing fans and participants.

BEHRMAN HOUSE, INC., 11 Edison Place, Springfield NJ 07081. (973)379-7200. Fax: (973)379-7280. E-mail: webmaster@behrmanhouse.com. Website: www.behrmanhouse.com. **Acquisitions:** David Behrman. Estab. 1921. **Publishes 20 titles/year. Receives 200 submissions/year. 20% of books from first-time authors; 95% from unagented writers. Pays 2-10% on wholesale price or retail price or makes outright purchase of $500-10,000. Offers $1,000 average advance.** Publishes book 18 months after acceptance of ms. Accepts simultaneous submissions. Responds in 2 months to queries. Book catalog free; ms guidelines online.

O- "Behrman House publishes quality books of Jewish content—history, Bible, philosophy, holidays, ethics, Israel, Hebrew—for children and adults."

Nonfiction: Children's/juvenile (ages 1-18), reference, textbook. Subjects include ethnic, philosophy, religion. "We want Jewish textbooks for the el-hi market." Query with SASE.

Recent Title(s): *Great Israel Scavenger Hunt*, by Scott Blumenthal (Israel); *Rediscovering the Jewish Holidays*, by Nina Beth Cardin and Gila Gevirtz (Jewish Holidays).

FREDERIC C. BEIL, PUBLISHER, INC., 609 Whitaker St., Savannah GA 31401. (912)233-2446. Fax: (912)233-6456. E-mail: beilbook@beil.com. Website: www.beil.com. **Acquisitions:** Mary Ann Bowman, editor. Estab. 1982. Publishes hardcover originals and reprints. **Publishes 13 titles/year. Receives 3,500 queries and 13 mss/year. 80% of books from first-time authors; 100% from unagented writers. Pays 7½% royalty on retail price.** Publishes book 20 months after acceptance of ms. Accepts simultaneous submissions. Responds in 2 weeks to queries. Book catalog free.

Imprints: The Sandstone Press, Hypermedia, Inc.

O- Frederic C. Beil publishes in the fields of history, literature, biography, books about books, and the book arts.

Nonfiction: Biography, children's/juvenile, illustrated book, reference, general trade. Subjects include art/architecture, general nonfiction, history, language/literature, book arts. Query with SASE. Reviews artwork/photos as part of ms package. Send photocopies.

Fiction: Historical, literary, regional, short story collections, translation, biography. Query with SASE.

Recent Title(s): *Joseph Jefferson: Dean of the American Theatre*, by Arthur Bloom; *Goya, Are You With Me Now?*, by H.E. Francis.

Tips: "Our objectives are (1) to offer to the reading public carefully selected texts of lasting value; (2) to adhere to high standards in the choice of materials and in bookmaking craftsmanship; (3) to produce books that exemplify good taste in format and design; and (4) to maintain the lowest cost consistent with quality."

BELLWETHER-CROSS PUBLISHING, 18319 Highway 20 W., East Dubuque IL 61025. (815)747-6255 or (888)516-5096. Fax: (815)747-3770. E-mail: jsheldon@bellwethercross.com. **Acquisitions:** Jana Sheldon, acquisitions editor. Publishes college textbooks. **Publishes 18 titles/year. Receives 100 mss/year. 80% of books from first-time authors; 100% from unagented writers. Pays 10% royalty on wholesale price.** Publishes book 6 months after acceptance of ms. Does not accept simultaneous submissions. Responds in 1 month to queries. Ms guidelines available.

O- Bellwether-Cross concentrates on college environmental books and nontraditional textbooks with mainstream possibilities.

Nonfiction: Textbook. Submit cover letter and complete ms with SASE. Reviews artwork/photos as part of ms package. Send photocopies.

Recent Title(s): *Transitional Science*, by H. Sue Way and Gaines B. Jackson; *Daring to Be Different: A Manager's Ascent to Leadership*, by James A. Hatherley.

N **BENOY PUBLISHING**, Imprint of P&D, 735 Bragg Dr., Unit H, Wilmington NC 28412. (910)796-0424. Fax: (910)796-0424. E-mail: buzzy@benoypublishing.com. Website: www.benoypublishing.com. **Acquisitions:** Buzzy Benoy, senior editor (fiction). Estab. 2001. Publishes hardcover, trade paperback, and mass market paperback originals. **Publishes 15-20 titles/year; imprint publishes 12-15 titles/year. Receives 300 queries and 300 mss/year. 95% of books from first-time authors; 100% from unagented writers. Pays 15-25% royalty on retail price.** Publishes book 12-15 months after acceptance of ms. Accepts simultaneous submissions. Responds in 2 months to queries; 2 months to proposals. Book catalog for #10 SASE or online at website; ms guidelines online.

Imprints: P&D Books, AZM Books.

Nonfiction: Autobiography, biography, coffee table book, cookbook, how-to, illustrated book, multimedia, reference, self-help. Subjects include Americana (collectibles), animals, anthropology/archeology, art/architecture, community (public affairs), contemporary culture, cooking/foods/nutrition, creative nonfiction, general nonfiction, health/medicine, history, hobbies, language/literature, memoirs, military/war, music/dance, nature/environment (environment), photography, regional (North Carolina), spirituality, sports (limited), travel (in North Carolina). "Hardback coffee table books published 1 year after acceptance. Others published 9 months after acceptance." Query with SASE or submit proposal package including outline, 2 sample chapter(s), SASE. **All unsolicited mss returned unopened.** Reviews artwork/photos as part of ms package. Send photocopies.

Fiction: Adventure, historical, humor, juvenile, mainstream/contemporary, military/war, multimedia, mystery, picture books, regional (North Carolina), short story collections, spiritual, sports, suspense, young adult. "Paperbacks published within 6 months of acceptance. Hardbacks within 9 months of acceptance." Query with SASE or submit 2 sample chapter(s), synopsis, SASE. **All unsolicited mss returned unopened.**

Recent Title(s): *Three Grunts and a Water Buffalo*, by John Montalbano (nonfiction war); *Pepsi*, by Buzzy Benoy (nonfiction North Carolina history); *Lazarus Milkshake*, by Steven Gibbs (short story collection).

Tips: "Our audience is adult readers with a high school education and above. Our interests include cookbooks, how-to, self-help, biography, autobiography, coffee table books, and history." "No unsolicited manuscripts, query appropriately, SASE, North Carolina history, and North Carolina authors welcome. Guidelines available by request and Internet."

BENTLEY PUBLISHERS, Automotive Publishers, 1734 Massachusetts Ave., Cambridge MA 02138-1804. (617)547-4170. **Acquisitions:** Janet Barnes, director of publishing; Jonathan Stein, editor. Estab. 1949. Publishes hardcover and trade paperback originals and reprints. **Publishes 15-20 titles/year. 20% of books from first-time authors; 95% from unagented writers. Pays 10-15% royalty on net price or makes outright purchase. Offers negotiable advance.** Publishes book 1 year after acceptance of ms. Does not accept simultaneous submissions. Responds in 6 weeks to queries. Book catalog and ms guidelines for 9×12 SAE with 4 first-class stamps.

O- Bentley Publishers publishes books for automotive enthusiasts.

Nonfiction: Automotive subjects only. How-to, technical, theory of operation. Subjects include sports (motor sports). Query with SASE or submit outline, sample chapter(s). Reviews artwork/photos as part of ms package.

Recent Title(s): *Corvette from the Inside*, by Dave McLellan (reference); *Zora Arkus-Duntov: The Legend Behind the Corvette*, by Jerry Burton (biography); *Mercedes-Benz E-class (W124) Owner's Bible™: 1986-1995* (how-to).

Tips: "Our audience is composed of serious, intelligent automobile, sports car, and racing enthusiasts, automotive technicians and high-performance tuners."

BERKSHIRE HOUSE PUBLISHERS, INC., 480 Pleasant St., Suite #5, Lee MA 01238. (413)243-0303. Fax: (413)243-4737. E-mail: info@berkshirehouse.com. Website: www.berkshirehouse.com. President: Jean J. Rousseau. **Acquisitions:** Philip Rich, editorial director. Estab. 1966. **Publishes 10-15 titles/year. Receives 100 queries and 6 mss/year. 50% of books from first-time authors; 80% from unagented writers. Pays 5-10% royalty on retail price. Offers $500-5,000 advance.** Publishes book 18 months after acceptance of ms. Accepts simultaneous submissions. Responds in 1 month to proposals. Book catalog free.

O- "We publish a series of travel guides, the Great Destinations Series, about specific U.S. destinations, guides to appeal to discerning travelers. We also specialize in books about our own region (the Berkshires and New England), especially recreational activities such as outdoor exploration. We publish cookbooks related to New England, country living and the northeast. We offer books of historical interest in our American Classics Series." Currently emphasizing Great Destinations series, outdoor recreation, cookbooks related to our region/country living. Please refer to website for more information.

Nonfiction: Cookbook (relating to country inns, travel, especially in New England). Subjects include Americana, history, nature/environment, recreation, regional, travel. "To a great extent, we choose our topics then commission the authors, but we don't discourage speculative submissions. We just don't accept many. Don't overdo it; a well-written outline/proposal is more useful than a full manuscript. Also, include a c.v. with writing credits."

Recent Title(s): *The Finger Lakes Book: A Complete Guide*, by Katherine Delavan Dyson; *New England Cooking*; *Adirondack Cuisine*.

Tips: "Our readers are literate, active and interested in travel, especially in selected 'Great Destinations' areas and outdoor activities and cooking."

BETHANY HOUSE PUBLISHERS, 11400 Hampshire Ave. S., Minneapolis MN 55438. (952)829-2500. Fax: (952)829-2768. Website: www.bethanyhouse.com. Estab. 1956. Publishes hardcover and trade paperback originals, mass market paperback reprints. **Publishes 120-150 titles/year. 2% of books from first-time authors; 93% from unagented writers. Pays negotiable royalty on net price. Offers negotiable advance.** Publishes book 1 year after acceptance of ms. Accepts simultaneous submissions. Responds in 3 months to queries. Book catalog for 9×12 SAE with 5 first-class stamps; ms guidelines online.

O- Bethany House Publishers specializes in books that communicate Biblical truth and assist people in both spiritual and practical areas of life. New interest in contemporary fiction.

Nonfiction: Biography, gift book, how-to, reference, self-help. Subjects include child guidance/parenting, ethnic, psychology, religion, sociology, women's issues/studies, personal growth, devotional, contemporary issues, marriage and family, applied theology, inspirational. "While we do not accept unsolicited queries or proposals via telephone or e-mail, we will consider one-page queries sent by facsimile to (952)996-1304 and directed to Adult Nonfiction, Adult Fiction or Young Adult/Children. Queries of interest to us should receive a reply in four to six weeks." **All unsolicited mss returned unopened.** Reviews artwork/photos as part of ms package. Send photocopies.

Fiction: Adventure, historical, juvenile, young adult, children's fiction series (ages 8-12) and Bethany Backyard (ages 6-12). New interest in contemporary fiction. Query with SASE. Send SASE for guidelines.

Recent Title(s): *Heroes at Home*, by Ellie Kay (Christian living); *Swan House*, by Elizabeth Musser (fiction).

Tips: "Bethany House Publishers' publishing program relates Biblical truth to all areas of life—whether in the framework of a well-told story, of a challenging book for spiritual growth, or of a Bible reference work. We are seeking high quality fiction and nonfiction that will inspire and challenge our audience."

BETTERWAY BOOKS, F&W Publications, 4700 E. Galbraith Rd., Cincinnati OH 45236. Fax: (513)531-7107. **Acquisitions:** Alice Pope (small business; home organization, time management); Sharon Carmack (genealogy), P.O. Box 338, Simla CO 80835. Estab. 1982. Publishes hardcover and trade paperback originals, trade paperback reprints. **Publishes 10 titles/year. Pays 10-20% royalty on net receipts. Offers $3,000-5,000 advance.** Publishes book an average of 18 months after acceptance of ms. Accepts simultaneous submissions. Responds in 6 weeks to queries. Book catalog for 9×12 SAE with 6 first-class stamps.

O- Betterway books are practical instructional books that are to be *used*. "We like specific step-by-step advice, charts, illustrations, and clear explanations of the activities and projects the books describe."

Nonfiction: How-to, illustrated book, reference. Subjects include business/economics, money/finance, family history, time management/home organization. "We publish 6 how-to family history/genealogy books per year. We are interested mostly in original material, but we will consider republishing self-published nonfiction books and good instructional or reference books that have gone out of print before their time. Send a sample copy, sales information, and reviews, if available. If you have a good idea for a reference book that can be updated annually, try us. We're willing to consider freelance compilers of such works." No cookbooks, diet/exercise, psychology self-help, health or parenting books. Submit outline, sample chapter(s). Reviews artwork/photos as part of ms package.

Recent Title(s): *Jump Start Your Business Brain*, by Doug Hall (business); *The Genealogist's Question & Answer Book*, by Marcia Yannizze Melnyk.

Tips: "Keep the imprint name well in mind when submitting ideas to us. What is the 'better way' you're proposing? How will readers benefit *immediately* from the instruction and information you're giving them?"

BEYOND WORDS PUBLISHING, INC., 20827 NW Cornell Rd., Suite 500, Hillsboro OR 97124. (503)531-8700. Fax: (503)531-8773. E-mail: info@beyondword.com. Website: www.beyondword.com. **Acquisitions:** Cynthia Black, editor-in-chief (adult books); Barbara Mann, acquisitions editor (children's books). Publishes hardcover and trade paperback originals. **Publishes 20-25 titles/year. Receives 4,000 queries and 2,000 mss/year. 65% of books from first-time authors; 50% from unagented writers. Pays 10-15% royalty on publishers proceeds. Offers advance.** Publishes book 12-18 months after acceptance of ms. Accepts simultaneous submissions. Responds in 4 months to queries; 4 months to proposals; 4 months to mss. Book catalog and ms guidelines for #10 SASE or online; ms guidelines online.

Nonfiction: Children's/juvenile, coffee table book, gift book, how-to, self-help. Subjects include animals, child guidance/parenting, health/medicine, photography (selectively), psychology, spirituality, women's issues/studies. Query with SASE or submit proposal package including outline, 3 sample chapter(s). Reviews artwork/photos as part of ms package. Send photocopies.

Tips: "*Beyond Words* markets to cultural, creative people, mostly women ages 30-60. Study our list before you submit and check out our website to make sure your book is a good fit for our list."

BICK PUBLISHING HOUSE, 307 Neck Rd., Madison CT 06443. (203)245-0073. Fax: (203)245-5990. E-mail: bickpubhse@aol.com. Website: www.bickpubhouse.com. **Acquisitions:** Dale Carlson, president (psychology); Hannah Carlson (special needs, disabilities); Irene Ruth (wildlife). Estab. 1994. Publishes trade paperback originals. **Publishes 4 titles/year. Receives 100 queries and 100 mss/year. 55% of books from first-time authors; 55% from unagented writers. Pays 10% royalty on net receipts. Offers $500-1,000 advance.** Publishes book 1 year after acceptance of ms. Responds in 1 month to queries; 2 months to proposals; 3 months to mss. Book catalog free; ms guidelines for #10 SASE.

- Bick Publishing House publishes step-by-step, easy-to-read professional information for the general adult public about physical, psychological and emotional disabilities or special needs. Currently emphasizing teen psychology for teens.

Nonfiction: Subjects include health/medicine (disability/special needs), psychology, young adult or teen science, psychology, wildlife rehabilitation. Query with SASE or submit proposal package including outline, 3 sample chapter(s), résumé.

Recent Title(s): *The Courage to Lead Support Groups: Mental Illnesses and Addictions*, by Hannah Carlson; *In and Out of Your Mind Teen Science*, by Dale Carlson.

BKMK PRESS, University of Missouri-Kansas City, 5101 Rockhill Rd., Kansas City MO 64110-2499. (816)235-2558. Fax: (816)235-2611. E-mail: bkmk@umkc.edu. Website: www.umkc.edu/bkmk. **Acquisitions:** Ben Furnish, managing editor. Estab. 1971. Publishes trade paperback originals. **Publishes 5-6 titles/year. Receives 450-500 queries and 250 mss/year. 20% of books from first-time authors; 70% from unagented writers. Pays 10% royalty on wholesale price.** Publishes book 1 year after acceptance of ms. Accepts simultaneous submissions. Responds in 8 months to queries; 8 months to mss. Ms guidelines online.

- BkMk Press publishes fine literature.

Nonfiction: Subjects include creative nonfiction. Query with SASE.

Fiction: Literary, short story collections. Query with SASE.

Poetry: Submit 10 sample poems.

Recent Title(s): *Father's Mechanical Universe*, by Steve Heller (fiction); *Beyond the Reach*, by Deborah Cummins (poetry).

Tips: "We skew toward readers of literature, particularly contemporary writing. Because of our limited number of titles published per year, we discourage apprentice writers or 'scattershot' submissions."

BLACK HERON PRESS, P.O. Box 95676, Seattle WA 98145. Fax: (206)363-5210. **Acquisitions:** Jerry Gold, publisher. Estab. 1984. Publishes hardcover and trade paperback originals. **Publishes 4 titles/year. Pays 8-9% royalty on retail price.** Accepts simultaneous submissions. Responds in 3 months to queries; 6 months to proposals; 6 months to mss.

- "Black Heron Press publishes literary fiction—lately we've tended toward surrealism/science fiction (not fantasy) and social fiction; writers should look at some of our titles. We're especially interested in books on the social or historical significances of independent publishing. We've already done 2 titles."

Fiction: High quality, innovative fiction. Adventure, experimental, humor, literary, mainstream/contemporary, science fiction (surrealism), Vietnam war novel - literary. "We don't want to see fiction written for the mass market. If it sells to the mass market, fine, but we don't see ourselves as a commercial press." Query with SASE.

Recent Title(s): *Obscure in the Shade of the Giants*, by Jerome Gold; *The Bathhouse*, by Farnoosh Moshiri.

Tips: "Readers should look at some of our books before submitting—they are easily available. Most submissions we see are done competently but have been sent to the wrong place. We do not publish self-help books or romances."

JOHN F. BLAIR, PUBLISHER, 1406 Plaza Dr., Winston-Salem NC 27103-1470. (336)768-1374. Fax: (336)768-9194. Website: www.blairpub.com. President: Carolyn Sakowski. **Acquisitions:** Acquisitions Committee. Estab. 1954. Publishes hardcover originals and trade paperbacks. **Publishes 20 titles/year. Receives 2,000 submissions/year. 20-30% of books**

from first-time authors; 90% from unagented writers. Royalty negotiable. Offers advance. Publishes book 18 months after acceptance of ms. Accepts simultaneous submissions. Responds in 3 months to queries. Book catalog for 9×12 SAE with 5 first-class stamps; ms guidelines online.

O⇁ John F. Blair publishes in the areas of travel, history, folklore and the outdoors for a general trade audience, most of whom live or travel in the Southeastern U.S.

Nonfiction: Subjects include Americana, history, nature/environment, regional, travel, women's issues/studies. Especially interested in travel guides dealing with the Southeastern U.S. Also interested in Civil War, outdoors, travel and Americana; query on other nonfiction topics. Looks for utility and significance. Submit outline, 3 sample chapter(s). Reviews artwork/photos as part of ms package.

Fiction: Prefers regional material dealing with southeastern U.S. "We publish one work of fiction per season relating to the Southeastern U.S." "Our editorial focus concentrates mostly on nonfiction." No category fiction, juvenile fiction, picture books, short story collections or poetry. No confessions or erotica. Query with SASE or submit complete ms.

BLOOMBERG PRESS, Bloomberg L.P., 100 Business Park Dr., P.O. Box 888, Princeton NJ 08542-0888. Website: www.bloomberg.com/books. **Acquisitions:** Kathleen Peterson, senior acquisitions editor. Estab. 1995. Publishes hardcover and trade paperback originals. **Publishes 18-22 titles/year. Receives 200 queries and 20 mss/year. 45% from unagented writers. Pays negotiable, competitive royalty. Offers negotiable advance.** Publishes book 9 months after acceptance of ms. Accepts simultaneous submissions. Responds in 1 month to queries. Book catalog for 10×13 SAE with 5 first-class stamps.

Imprints: Bloomberg Personal Bookshelf, Bloomberg Professional Library.

O⇁ Bloomberg Press publishes professional books for practitioners in the financial markets, and finance and investing books for informed personal investors, entrepreneurs, and consumers. "We publish commercially successful, very high-quality books that stand out clearly from the competition by their brevity, ease of use, sophistication, and abundance of practical tips and strategies; books readers need, will use and appreciate."

Nonfiction: How-to, reference, technical. Subjects include business/economics, money/finance, small business, current affairs, personal finance and investing for consumers, professional books on finance, investment and financial services. "We are looking for authorities and for experienced service journalists. We are looking for original solutions to widespread problems and books offering fresh investment opportunities. Do not send us unfocused books containing general information already covered by books in the marketplace." Submit outline, sample chapter(s), SAE with sufficient postage or submit complete ms.

Tips: "*Bloomberg Professional Library*: Audience is upscale financial professionals—traders, dealers, brokers, planners and advisors, financial managers, money managers, company executives, sophisticated investors. *Bloomberg Personal Bookshelf:* audience is upscale consumers and individual investors. Authors are experienced business and financial journalists and/or financial professionals nationally prominent in their specialty for some time who have proven an ability to write a successful book. Research Bloomberg and look at our books in a library or bookstore, read *Bloomberg Personal Finance* magazine and peruse our website."

⊘ **BLUE MOON BOOKS, INC.**, Avalon Publishing Group, 161 William St., New York NY 10038. (646)375-2570. Fax: (646)375-2571. E-mail: tmpress@aol.com. Website: www.avalonpub.com. **Acquisitions:** Gayle Watkins, editor. Estab. 1987. Publishes trade paperback and mass market paperback originals. **Publishes 50-60 titles/year. Receives 1,000 queries and 500 mss/year. Pays 7½% royalty on retail price. Offers $500 and up advance.** Publishes book 1 year after acceptance of ms. Responds in 2 months to queries. Book catalog free.

O⇁ "Blue Moon Books is strictly an erotic press; largely fetish-oriented material, B&D, S&M, etc."

Nonfiction: Subjects include sex. Trade erotic and sexual nonfiction. *No unsolicited mss.*

Fiction: Erotica. *No unsolicited mss.*

Recent Title(s): *Sex Practice*, by Ray Gordon; *66 Chapters About 33 Women*, by Michael Hemmingson.

BLUE/GRAY BOOKS, Creativity, Inc., 65 Macedonia Rd., Alexander NC 28701. (828)252-9515. Fax: (828)255-8719. Website: blue-gray.com. **Acquisitions:** Pat Roberts, acquisitions editor. Publishes trade paperback originals and reprints. **Publishes 4 titles/year. Pays negotiable royalty on wholesale price. Offers advance.** Publishes book 18 months after acceptance of ms.

O⇁ Blue/Gray Books specializes in Civil War history.

Nonfiction: Biography. Subjects include military/war (Civil War). Query with SASE or submit proposal package including 3 sample chapter(s), original book if wanting reprint. Reviews artwork/photos as part of ms package. Send photocopies.

Recent Title(s): *Deo Vindice: Heroes in Gray Forever*, by Lee Jacobs.

BLUEWOOD BOOKS, The Siyeh Group, Inc., P.O. Box 689, San Mateo CA 94401. (650)548-0754. Fax: (650)548-0654. E-mail: bluewoodb@aol.com. **Acquisitions:** Richard Michaels, director. Publishes trade paperback originals. **Publishes 8 titles/year. 20% of books from first-time authors; 100% from unagented writers. Makes work for hire assignments—fee depends upon book and writer's expertise. Offers ⅓ fee advance.** Does not accept simultaneous submissions.

O⇁ "We are looking for qualified writers for nonfiction series—history and biography oriented."

Nonfiction: Biography, illustrated book. Subjects include Americana, anthropology/archeology, art/architecture, business/economics, government/politics, health/medicine, history, military/war, multicultural, science, sports, women's issues/studies. Query with SASE.

Recent Title(s): *American Politics in the 20th Century*, by J. Bonasia (political history); *100 Families Who Shaped World History*, by Samuel Crompton (world history).

Tips: "Our audience consists of adults and young adults. Our books are written on a newspaper level—clear, concise, well organized and easy to understand. We encourage potential writers to send us a résumé, providing background, qualifications and references."

BNA BOOKS, The Bureau of National Affairs, Inc., 1231 25th St. NW, Washington DC 20037-1165. (202)452-4343. Fax: (202)452-4997. E-mail: books@bna.com. Website: www.bnabooks.com. **Acquisitions:** Jim Fattibene, acquisitions manager. Estab. 1929. Publishes hardcover and softcover originals. **Publishes 35 titles/year. Receives 50 submissions/year. 20% of books from first-time authors; 95% from unagented writers. Pays 10-15% royalty on net receipts. Offers $500 average advance.** Publishes book 1 year after acceptance of ms. Accepts simultaneous submissions. Responds in 3 months to queries. Book catalog online; ms guidelines online.

O- BNA Books publishes professional reference books written by lawyers, for lawyers. Currently emphasizing employment, intellectual property, and health law.

Nonfiction: Reference, scholarly. Subjects include labor and employment law, health law, legal practice, labor relations law, intellectual property law. No fiction, biographies, bibliographies, cookbooks, religion books, humor or trade books. Submit detailed table of contents or outline.

Recent Title(s): *Fair Labor Standards Act; Intellectual Property Law in Cyberspace*; *Health Care Fraud and Abuse*.

Tips: "Our audience is made up of practicing lawyers and law librarians. We look for authoritative and comprehensive works that can be supplemented or revised every year or two on subjects of interest to those audiences."

BOA EDITIONS, LTD., 260 East Ave., Rochester NY 14604. (585)546-3410. Fax: (585)546-3913. E-mail: boaedit@frontiernet.net. Website: www.boaeditions.org. **Acquisitions:** Steven Huff, publisher/managing editor; Thom Ward, editor. Estab. 1976. Publishes hardcover and trade paperback originals. **Publishes 10 titles/year. Receives 1,000 queries and 700 mss/year. 15% of books from first-time authors; 90% from unagented writers. Pays 8-10% royalty on retail price. Offers variable advance.** Publishes book 18 months after acceptance of ms. Accepts simultaneous submissions. Responds in 1 week to queries; 5 months to mss. Ms guidelines online.

O- BOA Editions publishes distinguished collections of poetry and poetry in translation. "Our goal is to publish the finest American contemporary poetry and poetry in translation."

Poetry: Query by mail or e-mail after January 1, 2004. Boa offers a first book poetry prize of $1,500 and book publication for the winner. For guidelines, see the home page of our website.

Recent Title(s): *Tell Me*, by Kim Addonizio; *Blessing the Boats*, by Lucille Clifton.

Tips: "Readers who, like Whitman, expect of the poet to 'indicate more than the beauty and dignity which always attach to dumb real objects... They expect him to indicate the path between reality and their souls,' are the audience of BOA's books."

[N] **BONUS BOOKS, INC.**, Precept Press, 160 E. Illinois St., Chicago IL 60611. (312)467-0580. Fax: (312)467-9271. E-mail: acquisitions@bonusbooks.com. Website: www.bonusbooks.com. **Acquisitions:** Kelley Thornton, acquisitions editor. Estab. 1985. Publishes hardcover and trade paperback originals and reprints. **Publishes 30 titles/year. Receives 400-500 submissions/year. 40% of books from first-time authors; 50% from unagented writers. Royalties vary.** Publishes book 8 months after acceptance of ms. Accepts simultaneous submissions. Responds in 2 months to queries. Book catalog for 9x11 SAE; ms guidelines for #10 SASE.

O- Bonus Books is a publishing company featuring subjects ranging from human interest to sports to gambling.

Nonfiction: Biography, self-help. Subjects include business/economics, cooking/foods/nutrition, education, health/medicine, hobbies, money/finance, regional, sports (gambling), women's issues/studies, pop culture, automotive/self-help, current affairs, broadcasting, business/self-help, Chicago people and places, collectibles, education/self-help, fundraising, handicapping winners, home and health, entertainment. Query with SASE or submit outline, sample chapter(s), SASE. All submissions and queries must include SASE. Reviews artwork/photos as part of ms package.

Recent Title(s): *TVParty: Television's Untold Tales*, by Billy Ingram.

[N] **BOOKWORLD, INC./BLUE STAR PRODUCTIONS**, 9666 E. Riggs Rd., #194, Sun Lakes AZ 85248. (480)895-7995. Fax: (480)895-6991. E-mail: bookworldinc@earthlink.net. Website: bluestarproductions.net. **Acquisitions:** Barbara DeBolt, editor. Publishes trade paperback originals. **Publishes 10-12 titles/year. Receives thousands of submissions/year. 75% of books from first-time authors; 90% from unagented writers. Pays royalty.** Does not accept simultaneous submissions. Responds in 8 months to queries; 16 or more months to mss. Book catalog online.

O- "We focus on UFOs, the paranormal, metaphysical, angels, psychic phenomena, visionary fiction, spiritual—both fiction and nonfiction."

Nonfiction: "To save time and reduce the amount of paper submissions, we are encouraging e-mail queries and submissions (no downloads or attachments), or disk submissions formatted for Windows 95, using Word Perfect or Microsoft Word. Our response will be via e-mail so no SASE will be needed in these instances, unless the disk needs to be returned. For those without computer access, a SASE is a must and we prefer seeing the actual manuscript, a query letter. *No phone queries.*"

Tips: "Authors selected for publication must be prepared to promote their books via public appearances and/or work with a publicist."

BOYDS MILLS PRESS, *Highlights for Children*, 815 Church St., Honesdale PA 18431-1895. (570)253-1164. Website: www.boydsmillspress.com. Publisher: Kent L. Brown. **Acquisitions:** Larry Rosler, editorial director. Estab. 1990. Publishes hardcover originals and trade paperback reprints. **Publishes 50 titles/year. Receives 10,000 queries and 7,500 mss/year. 40% of books from first-time authors; 60% from unagented writers. Pays royalty on retail price. Offers variable advance.** Publishes book Time between acceptance and publication depends on "what season it is scheduled for." after acceptance of ms. Accepts simultaneous submissions. Responds in 1 month to mss. Book catalog online; ms guidelines online.

Imprints: Wordsong (poetry).

O→ Boyds Mill Press, the book publishing arm of *Highlights for Children*, publishes a wide range of children's books of literary merit, from preschool to young adult. Currently emphasizing picture books and novels (but no fantasy, romance or horror).

Nonfiction: Children's/juvenile. Subjects include agriculture/horticulture, animals, ethnic, history, nature/environment, sports, travel. "Nonfiction should be accurate, tailored to young audience. Prefer simple, narrative style, but in compelling, evocative language. Too many authors overwrite for the young audience and get bogged down in minutiae. Boyds Mills Press is not interested in mss depicting violence, explicit sexuality, racism of any kind or which promote hatred. We also are not the right market for self-help books." Query with SASE or submit proposal package including outline. Reviews artwork/photos as part of ms package.

Fiction: Adventure, ethnic, historical, humor, juvenile, mystery, picture books, young adult (adventure, animal, contemporary, ethnic, historical, humor, mystery, sports). "Don't let a personal agenda dominate to the detriment of plot. In short, tell a good story. Too many writers miss the essence of a good story: beginning, middle, end; conflict and resolution because they're more interested in making a sociological statement." No fantasy, romance, horror. Query with SASE. Submit outline/synopsis and 3 sample chapters for novel or complete ms.

Poetry: "Poetry should be appropriate for young audiences, clever, fun language, with easily understood meaning. Too much poetry is either too simple and static in meaning or too obscure." Collections should have a unifying theme.

Recent Title(s): *Rat*, by Jan Cheripko (novel); *The Alligator in the Closet*, by David Harrison (poetry).

Tips: "Our audience is pre-school to young adult. Concentrate first on your writing. Polish it. Then—and only then—select a market. We need primarily picture books with fresh ideas and characters—avoid worn themes of 'coming-of-age,' 'new sibling,' and self-help ideas. We are always interested in multicultural settings. Please—no anthropomorphic characters."

[N] BRANCH AND VINE PUBLISHERS, LLC, P.O. Box 1297, Radford VA 24143-1297. (540)639-3096. Fax: (540)639-3096. E-mail: branchandvine@aol.com. Website: www.branchandvinepublishers.com. **Acquisitions:** Steven Macon and James Armentrout, editors (science fiction, fantasy, alternate history). Estab. 1995. Publishes hardcover and trade paperback originals, as well as electronic originals and reprints. **Publishes 10 titles/year. Receives 50-100 queries and 70+ mss/year. 50% of books from first-time authors; 75% from unagented writers. Pays 10% royalty on retail price.** Publishes book 6-12 months after acceptance of ms. Does not accept simultaneous submissions. Responds in 4-6 months to queries; 4-6 months to proposals; 4-6 months to mss. Book catalog online; ms guidelines online.

Nonfiction: Booklets, children's/juvenile, how-to, humor, reference, scholarly, self-help, textbook. Subjects include Americana, art/architecture, child guidance/parenting, computers/electronic, cooking/foods/nutrition, creative nonfiction, education, gardening, general nonfiction, government/politics, health/medicine, history, hobbies, military/war, nature/environment, psychology, religion, science, spirituality, sports, travel, world affairs. Submit proposal package including outline, 3 sample chapter(s). Reviews artwork/photos as part of ms package. Send photocopies.

Fiction: Adventure, fantasy, historical, horror, humor, juvenile, literary, mainstream/contemporary, military/war, mystery, poetry, religious, science fiction, short story collections, spiritual, suspense, western, alternate history, plays and dramatic subjects. "Follow guidelines on our website." Submit 3 sample chapter(s), synopsis.

Tips: "Audience is anyone that appreciates good fiction and likes to be surprised by plot twists and living characters. Know your market. Here's a secret: Editors are concerned about only one thing, 'Will this manuscript make money!' Other than that, know how to tell a story. Don't be afraid of revisions and read, read, read!"

⊘ BRANDEN PUBLISHING CO., INC., P.O. Box 812094, Wellesley MA 02482. (781)235-3634. Fax: (781)790-1056. Website: www.branden.com. **Acquisitions:** Adolph Caso, editor. Estab. 1965. Publishes hardcover and trade paperback originals, reprints and software. **Publishes 15 titles/year. Receives 1,000 submissions/year. 80% of books from first-time authors; 90% from unagented writers. Pays 5-10% royalty on net receipts. 10 author's copies. Offers $1,000 maximum advance.** Publishes book 10 months after acceptance of ms. Responds in 1 month to queries.

Imprints: International Pocket Library and Popular Technology, Four Seas and Brashear.

O→ Branden publishes books by or about women, children, military, Italian-American or African-American themes.

Nonfiction: Biography, children's/juvenile, illustrated book, reference, technical, textbook. Subjects include Americana, art/architecture, computers/electronic, contemporary culture, education, ethnic, general nonfiction, government/politics, health/medicine, history, military/war, music/dance, photography, sociology, software, classics. Especially looking for "about 10 manuscripts on national and international subjects, including biographies of well-known individuals. Currently specializing in Americana, Italian-American, African-American." No religion or philosophy. *No unsolicited mss.* Paragraph query only with author's vita and SASE. No telephone inquiries, e-mail or fax inquiries. Reviews artwork/photos as part of ms package.

Fiction: Ethnic (histories, integration), historical, literary, military/war, religious (historical-reconstructive), short story collections, translation. Looking for "contemporary, fast pace, modern society." No science, mystery, experimental, horor or pornography. *No unsolicited mss.* Query with SASE. Paragraph query only with author's vita and SASE. No telephone inquiries, e-mail or fax inquiries.

Recent Title(s): *Quilt of America*, by Carole Gariepy; *The Wisdom of Angels*, by Martha Cummings; *Water and Life*, by Adolph Caso.

BRASSEY'S, INC., 22841 Quicksilver Dr., Dulles VA 20166. (703)661-1548. Fax: (703)661-1547. E-mail: djacobs@booksintl.com. Website: www.brasseysinc.com. **Acquisitions:** Don McKeon, vice president/publisher; Don Jacobs, senior assistant editor (general inquiries). Estab. 1984. Publishes hardcover and trade paperback originals and reprints. **Publishes 100 titles/year. Receives 900 queries/year. 20% of books from first-time authors; 70% from unagented writers. Pays 8-12% royalty on wholesale price. Offers $30,000 maximum advance.** Publishes book 1 year after acceptance of ms. Accepts simultaneous submissions. Responds in 2 months to queries. Book catalog free; ms guidelines for 9×12 SAE with 4 first-class stamps.

Imprints: Brassey's Sports.

O→ Brassey's specializes in national and international affairs, history (military), biography, intelligence, foreign policy, defense, transportation, reference and sports. "We are seeking to build our history and international affairs college textbook lists."

Nonfiction: Biography, coffee table book, reference, textbook. Subjects include government/politics, history, military/war, sports, world affairs, national and international affairs, intelligence studies. When submitting nonfiction, be sure to include sufficient biographical information (e.g., track records of previous publications), and "make clear in the proposal how your work might differ from other such works already published and with which yours might compete." Query with SASE or submit proposal package including outline, 2 sample chapter(s), author bio, analysis of book's competition. Reviews artwork/photos as part of ms package. Send photocopies.

Recent Title(s): *Nerve Center: Inside the White House Situation Room*, by Michael K. Bohn; *Through Our Enemies' Eyes: Osama Bin Laden, Radical Islam, and the Future of America*, by Anonymous; *Mickey Mantle: America's Prodigal Son*, by Tony Castro.

Tips: "Our audience consists of military personnel, government policymakers, professors, undergraduate and graduate students, and general readers with an interest in our subjects."

[N] **BREAKAWAY BOOKS**, P.O. Box 24, Halcottsville NY 12438. (212)898-0408. E-mail: mail@breakawaybooks.com. Website: www.breakawaybooks.com. **Acquisitions:** Garth Battista, publisher. Estab. 1994. Publishes hardcover and trade paperback originals. **Publishes 8-10 titles/year. Receives 400 queries and 100 mss/year. 35% of books from first-time authors; 75% from unagented writers. Pays 6-15% royalty on retail price. Offers $2,000-3,000 advance.** Publishes book 9 months after acceptance of ms. Accepts simultaneous submissions. Responds in 1 month to queries; 1 month to proposals; 2 months to mss. Book catalog and ms guidelines free; ms guidelines online.

O→ "Breakaway Books is a sports literature specialty publisher—only fiction and narrative nonfiction. No how-tos."

Nonfiction: Subjects include sports (narrative only, not how-to). Query with SASE or by e-mail.

Fiction: Short story collections (sports stories), sports, translation. Query with SASE or submit complete ms.

Recent Title(s): *The Runner and the Path*, by Dean Ottati; *Becoming an Ironman*, by Kara Douglass Thom; *Running Through the Wall*, by Neal Jamison.

Tips: Audience is intelligent, passionately committed to athletes. "We're starting a new children's book line—only children's books dealing with running, cycling, swimming, triathlon, plus boating (canoes, kayaks and sailboats). First title due out in September 2003."

BREAKOUT PRODUCTIONS, P.O. Box 1643, Port Townsend WA 98368. (360)379-1965. Fax: (360)379-3794. **Acquisitions:** Gia Cosindas, editor. Publishes trade paperback originals and reprints. **Publishes 6 titles/year. Pays 10-15% royalty on wholesale price. Offers $500-1,500 advance.** Publishes book 6 months after acceptance of ms. Accepts simultaneous submissions. Responds in 1 month to queries; 3 months to proposals; 3 months to mss. Ms guidelines free.

Nonfiction: How-to, self-help (off-beat), technical. Subjects include agriculture/horticulture, Americana, anthropology/archeology, computers/electronic, creative nonfiction, education, gardening, health/medicine (alternative), history, hobbies, military/war, philosophy, psychology, science, travel, unusual jobs, privacy. No electronic submissions or phone calls. Query with SASE or submit proposal package including outline, sample chapter(s) or submit complete ms. Reviews artwork/photos as part of ms package. Send photocopies.

Recent Title(s): *Be Your Own Dick—Private Investigation Made Easy*, by John Newman (how-to); *Think Free to Be Free*, by Claire Wolfe (self help).

Tips: "We like the unusual 'take' on things. The author who presents his ideas from an unusual 'road less taken' viewpoint has a better chance than someone who recycles old ideas. We never publish fiction or poetry."

[N] **BREVET PRESS, INC.**, P.O. Box 1404, Sioux Falls SD 57101. **Acquisitions:** Donald P. Mackintosh, publisher (business); Peter E. Reid, managing editor (technical); A. Melton, editor (Americana); B. Mackintosh, editor (history). Estab. 1972. Publishes hardcover and paperback originals and reprints. **Publishes 15 titles/year. Receives 40 submissions/year. 50% of books from first-time authors; 100% from unagented writers. Pays 5% royalty. Offers $1,000 average advance.** Publishes book 1 year after acceptance of ms. Accepts simultaneous submissions. Responds in 2 months to queries. Book catalog free.

O→ Brevet Books seeks nonfiction with "market potential and literary excellence."

Nonfiction: Technical. Subjects include Americana, business/economics, history. Query with SASE. Reviews artwork/photos as part of ms package. Send photocopies.

Tips: "Keep sexism out of the manuscripts."

[N] **BREWERS PUBLICATIONS**, Association of Brewers, 736 Pearl St., Boulder CO 80302. (303)447-0816. Fax: (303)447-2825. E-mail: ray@aob.org. Website: beertown.org. **Acquisitions:** Ray Daniels, publisher. Estab. 1986. Publishes hardcover and trade paperback originals. **Publishes 4 titles/year. 50% of books from first-time authors; 50% from unagented writers. Pays royalty on net receipts. Offers negotiated advance.** Publishes book 18 months after acceptance of ms. Accepts simultaneous submissions. Responds in 3 months to queries. Ms guidelines online.

O→ Brewers Publications is the largest publisher of books on beer-related subjects.

Nonfiction: Biography, humor. Subjects include art/architecture, community, cooking/foods/nutrition, health/medicine, history, hobbies, language/literature, science. "We publish books on history, art, culture, literature, brewing and science of beer. In a broad sense, this also includes biographies, humor, cooking." Query first with brief proposal and SASE.
Recent Title(s): *Standards of Brewing*, by Dr. Charles Bamforth; *The Compleat Meadmaker*, by Ken Schramm.

N **BRIDGE WORKS PUBLISHING CO.**, Box 1798, 221 Bridge Lane, Bridgehampton NY 11932. (516)537-3418. Fax: (516)537-5092. E-mail: bap@hamptons.com. **Acquisitions:** Barbara Phillips, editor/publisher. Estab. 1992. Publishes hardcover originals and reprints. **Publishes 6-9 titles/year. Receives 1,000 queries and 1,000 mss/year. 50% of books from first-time authors; 50% from unagented writers. Pays 10% royalty on retail price. Offers $1,000 advance.** Publishes book 1 year after acceptance of ms. Responds in 1 month to queries; 1 month to proposals; 2 months to mss. Book catalog and ms guidelines for #10 SASE.

O→ "Bridge Works is a small press dedicated to mainstream quality fiction. Also mysteries and short story collections. A first-time author should have manuscript vetted by freelance editor before submitting."

Nonfiction: Biography. Subjects include history, language/literature, public policy. "We do not accept multiple submissions. We prefer a query first." Query with SASE or submit proposal package including outline.
Fiction: Humor, literary, mystery, short story collections, translation. "Query with SASE before submitting ms. First-time authors should have manuscripts vetted by freelance editors before submitting. We do not accept or read multiple submissions." Query with SASE or submit 2 sample chapter(s), synopsis.
Poetry: "We publish only *one* collection every five years." Query.
Recent Title(s): *Dirt Under My Nails*, by Marilee Foster; *The Cost of Doing Business*, by John S. Tarlton.
Tips: "Query letters should be one page, giving general subject or plot of the book and stating who the writer feels is the audience for the work. In the case of novels or poetry, a portion of the work could be enclosed. We *do not* publish how-to's, self-help, romances or cookbooks."

BRIGHT MOUNTAIN BOOKS, INC., 206 Riva Ridge Dr., Fairview NC 28730. (828)628-1768. Fax: (828)628-1755. E-mail: booksbmb@charter.net. **Acquisitions:** Cynthia F. Bright, editor. Publishes hardcover originals and trade paperback originals and reprints. **Publishes 6 titles/year. Pays 5-10% royalty on retail price.** Responds in 1 month to queries; 3 months to mss.
Imprints: Historical Images.
Nonfiction: Biography. Subjects include history, regional. "Our current emphasis is on regional titles set in the Southern Appalachians and Carolinas, which can include nonfiction by local writers." Query with SASE.
Recent Title(s): *Présumed Dead: A Civil War Mystery*, by Howard Alley; *Lucy's Recipes for Mountain Living*, by Eva McCall and Emma Edsall.

BRISTOL FASHION PUBLICATIONS, INC., P.O. Box 4676, Harrisburg PA 17111-4676. Website: www.bfpbooks.com. **Acquisitions:** John Kaufman, publisher. Publishes trade paperback originals. **Publishes 25 titles/year. Receives 250 queries and 200 mss/year. 50% of books from first-time authors; 100% from unagented writers. Pays 7-11% royalty on retail price.** Publishes book 3 months after acceptance of ms. Responds in 1 month to queries. Ms guidelines online.

O→ Bristol Fashion publishes books on boats and boating.

Nonfiction: General interest relating to boats and boating. How-to, reference. Subjects include history. "We are interested in any title which relates to these fields. Query with a list of ideas. Include phone number. This is a fast changing market. Our title plans rarely extend past 6 months, although we know the type and quantity of books we will publish over the next 2 years. We prefer good knowledge with simple to understand writing style containing a well-rounded vocabulary." Query with SASE. Reviews artwork/photos as part of ms package. Send photocopies or JPEG files on CD.
Recent Title(s): *Scuttlebutt, After 40 Years*; *Electronics Aboard*; *Practical Seamanship*.
Tips: "All of our staff and editors are boaters. As such, we publish what we would want to read relating to boats. Our audience is generally boat owners or expected owners who are interested in learning about boats, boat repair and boating. Keep it easy and simple to follow. Use nautical terms where appropriate. Do not use complicated technical jargon, terms or formulas without a detailed explanation of same. Use experienced craftsmen as a resource for knowledge."

BRISTOL PUBLISHING ENTERPRISES, 2714 McCone Ave., Hayward CA 94545. Fax: (510)895-4459. Website: bristolcookbooks.com. **Acquisitions:** Aidan Wylde. Estab. 1988. Publishes trade paperback originals. **Publishes 10-20 titles/year. Receives 100-200 queries/year. 25% of books from first-time authors; 100% from unagented writers. Pays 6% royalty on net proceeds or makes outright purchase. Offers small advance.** Publishes book 1 year after acceptance of ms. Accepts simultaneous submissions. Responds in 4 months to queries. Book catalog online.
Imprints: Nitty Gritty cookbooks, The Best 50 Recipe Series, Pet Care Series.
Nonfiction: Cookbook, craft books, pet care books. Subjects include cooking/foods/nutrition. Send a proposal or query with possible outline, brief note about author's background, sample of writing or chapter from ms.
Recent Title(s): *Cooking on the Indoor Grill*, by Catherine Fulde; *Vegetarian Slow Cooker*, by Joanna White; *Best 50 Bar Drinks*, by Dona Z. Mellach.
Tips: Readers of cookbooks are novice cooks. "Our books educate without intimidating. We require our authors to have some form of background in the food industry."

BROADMAN & HOLMAN, LifeWay Christian Resources, 127 Ninth Ave. N., Nashville TN 37234. (615)251-2392. Fax: (615)251-3752. Publisher: David Shepherd. **Acquisitions:** Leonard G. Goss, editorial director. Estab. 1934. Publishes hardcover and paperback originals. **Publishes 90 titles/year. Pays negotiable royalty.** Publishes book 10 months after acceptance of ms. Accepts simultaneous submissions. Responds in 3 months to queries; 2 months to mss. Book catalog free; ms guidelines for #10 SASE.

O-- Broadman & Holman publishes books that provide biblical solutions that spiritually transform individuals and cultures. Currently emphasizing inspirational/gift books, general Christian living and books on Christianity and society.

Nonfiction: Children's/juvenile, gift book, illustrated book, reference, textbook, devotional journals. Subjects include religion, spirituality. Christian living, devotionals, prayer, women, youth, spiritual growth, Christian history, parenting, home school, biblical studies, science and faith, current events, marriage and family concerns, church life, pastoral helps, preaching, evangelism. "We are open to freelance submissions in all areas. Materials in these areas must be suited for an evangelical Christian readership." No poetry, biography or sermons. Query with SASE.

Fiction: Adventure, mystery, religious (general religious, inspirational, religious fantasy, religious mystery/suspense, religious thriller, religious romance), western. "We publish fiction in all the main genres. We want not only a very good story, but also one that sets forth Christian values. Nothing that lacks a positive Christian emphasis (but do NOT preach, however); nothing that fails to sustain reader interest." Query with SASE.

Recent Title(s): *Payne Stewart: The Authorized Biography*, by Tracey Stewart (nonfiction); *To Live is Christ*, by Beth Moore; *In the Shadow of the Cross*, by Ray Pritchard.

[A] **BROADWAY BOOKS**, Doubleday Broadway Publishing Group, Random House, Inc., 1745 Broadway, New York NY 10019. (212)782-9000. Fax: (212)782-8338. Website: www.broadwaybooks.com. **Acquisitions:** Gerald Howard, editor-at-large; Kristine Puopolo, senior editor (general nonfiction, health, self-help); Patricia Medved, senior editor (parenting, self-help); Becky Cole, associate editor (nonfiction, popular culture); Charles Conrad, vice president and executive editor (general nonfiction); Jennifer Josephy (cookbooks); Ann Campbell, editor (psychology/self-help, parenting, health). Estab. 1995. Publishes hardcover and trade paperback originals and reprints.

O-- Broadway publishes general interest nonfiction and fiction for adults.

Nonfiction: Biography, cookbook, illustrated book, reference, General interest adult books. Subjects include business/economics, child guidance/parenting, contemporary culture, cooking/foods/nutrition, gay/lesbian, general nonfiction, government/politics, health/medicine, history, memoirs, money/finance, multicultural, New Age, psychology, sex, spirituality, sports, travel (narrative), women's issues/studies, current affairs, motivational/inspirational, popular culture, consumer reference. *Agented submissions only.*

Fiction: Publishes a limited list of commercial literary fiction. *Agented submissions only.*

Recent Title(s): *I'm a Stranger Here Myself*, by Bill Bryson; *Bella Tuscany*, by Frances Mayes.

BUCKNELL UNIVERSITY PRESS, Lewisburg PA 17837. (570)577-3674. Fax: (570)577-3797. E-mail: clingham@bucknell.edu. Website: www.departments.bucknell.edu/univ_press. **Acquisitions:** Greg Clingham, director. Estab. 1969. Publishes hardcover originals. **Publishes 35-40 titles/year. Receives 400 submissions/year. 20% of books from first-time authors; 99% from unagented writers. Pays royalty.** Publishes book 12-18 months after acceptance of ms. Does not accept simultaneous submissions. Responds in 1 month to queries. Book catalog free; ms guidelines online.

O-- "In all fields, our criteria are scholarly excellence, critical originality, and interdisciplinary and theoretical expertise and sensitivity."

Nonfiction: Scholarly. Subjects include art/architecture, history, language/literature, philosophy, religion, sociology, English and American literary criticism, literary theory and cultural studies, historiography, art history, modern languages, classics, anthropology, ethnology, cultural and political geography, Hispanic and Latin American studies. Series: Bucknell Studies in Eighteenth-Century Literature and Culture, Bucknell Studies in Latin American Literature and Theory, Eighteenth-Century Scotland. Query with SASE.

Recent Title(s): *Modes of Discipline: Women, Conservatism, and the Novel after the French Revolution*, by Lisa Wood; *Helen Maria Williams adn the Age of Revolution*, by Deborah Kennedy; *The Routes of Modernity: Spanish American Poetry from the Early Eighteenth to Mid-Nineteenth Century*, by Andrew Bush.

BUILDERBOOKS, National Association of Home Builders, 1201 15th St. NW, Washington DC 20005-2800. (800)368-5242 ext. 8368. Fax: (202)266-8559. E-mail: publishing@nahb.com. Website: www.builderbooks.com. Publisher: Eric Johnson. **Acquisitions:** Doris M. Tennyson, acquisitions editor (business and construction management for remodelers; computerization, marketing and selling for builders, remodelers, developers, suppliers, manufacturers, and their sales and marketing directors; customer relations; legal issues; seniors housing); Thersa Minch (business and construction management for builders, developers, and others; construction how-to; computerization, multifamily, safety). Publishes "educated books and electronic products for builders, remodelers, developers, sales & marketing professionals & consumers in the residential construction industry. Writers must be experts." **Publishes 24 titles/year. 33% of books from first-time authors; 99% from unagented writers. Pays royalty.** Publishes book 6-9 months after acceptance of ms. Does not accept simultaneous submissions. Responds in 1-2 months to queries. Book catalog free or on website; ms guidelines by email.

Nonfiction: "We prefer a detailed outline on a strong industry topic. Our readers like step-by-step, how-to books and other products, no history or philosophy of the industry." How-to, reference, technical. Subjects include home building, remodeling, light construction industry and related topics such as business and construction management, sales and marketing, legal issues, customer service, computerization, electronic templates, multifamily, safety. Query first. E-mail queries accepted. Include electronic and hard copy artwork/photos as part of ms package. Send photocopies.

Recent Title(s): *Warranty Service for Homebuilders*, by Carol Smith; *The Scaffold Safety Handbook: English-Spanish Edition*; *Financing and Cash Management*, by Dennis J. Rourke.

Tips: "Ask for a sample outline." Audience is primarily small-, medium-, and high-volume home builders; remodelers; developers; sales and marketing directors; multifamily builders; light commercial and institutional builders (not skyscrapers), providers of services and materials for the industry employees of industry businesses; attorneys; and others in the industry.

BULFINCH PRESS, AOL Time Warner Book Group, Time Life Building, 1271 Avenue of the Americas, New York NY 10020. (212)522-8700. Website: www.bulfinchpress.com. VP/Publisher: Jill Cohen. **Acquisitions:** Jared Silverman, assistant to the publisher. Publishes hardcover and trade paperback originals. **Publishes 70-80 titles/year. Receives 600 queries/year. Pays variable royalty on wholesale price. Offers variable advance.** Publishes book 18 months after acceptance of ms. Accepts simultaneous submissions. Responds in 2 months to proposals.

O→ Bulfinch Press publishes large format art books. "We are the home of Ansel Adams and Irving Penn."

Nonfiction: Coffee table book, cookbook, gift book, illustrated book. Subjects include art/architecture, cooking/foods/nutrition, gardening, photography, interior design, lifestyle. Query with SASE or submit sample artwork, outline. Reviews artwork/photos as part of ms package. Send color photocopies, slides or laser prints.

Recent Title(s): *The Architecture of Philip Johnson*, by Hilary Lewis, Philip Johnson and photography by Richard Payne; *Preston Bailey's Design for Entertaining*, by Preston Bailey; *100 Years of Harley Davidson*, by Willie G. Davidson.

THE BUREAU FOR AT-RISK YOUTH, P.O. Box 760, Plainview NY 11803-0760. (516)349-5520. Fax: (516)349-5521. E-mail: info@at-risk.com. Website: www.at-risk.com. **Acquisitions:** Sally Germain, editor-in-chief. Estab. 1988. **Publishes 25-50 titles/year. Receives hundreds submissions/year. 100% from unagented writers. Pays 10% maximum royalty on selling price. Offers variable advance.** Publishes book 1 year after acceptance of ms. Accepts simultaneous submissions. Responds in 8 months to queries. Book catalog free if appropriate after communication with author.

O→ Publishes materials on youth guidance topics, such as drugs and violence prevention, character education and life skills for young people in grades K-12, and the educators, parents, mental health and juvenile justice professionals who work with them. "We prefer a workbook/activity book, curriculum, or book/booklet series format."

Nonfiction: Educational materials for parents, educators and other professionals who work with youth. Booklets. Subjects include child guidance/parenting, education. "The materials we publish are curriculum, book series, workbook/activity books or how-to-oriented pieces tailored to our audience. They are generally not single book titles and our series are rarely book length." Query with SASE.

Recent Title(s): *The Emotional Recovery Resource Kit*, by Debra Alexander.

Tips: "Publications are sold through direct mail catalogs and Internet. Writers whose expertise is a fit with our customers' interests should send query or proposals since we tailor everything very specifically to meet our audience's needs."

BURFORD BOOKS, 32 Morris Ave., Springfield NJ 07081. (973)258-0960. Fax: (973)258-0113. **Acquisitions:** Peter Burford, publisher. Estab. 1997. Publishes hardcover originals, trade paperback originals and reprints. **Publishes 25 titles/year. Receives 300 queries and 200 mss/year. 30% of books from first-time authors; 60% from unagented writers. Pays royalty on wholesale price.** Publishes book 18 months after acceptance of ms. Accepts simultaneous submissions. Responds in 1 month to queries; 1 month to proposals; 2 months to mss. Book catalog and ms guidelines free.

O→ Burford Books publishes books on all aspects of the outdoors, from gardening to sports, practical and literary.

Nonfiction: How-to, illustrated book. Subjects include agriculture/horticulture, animals, cooking/foods/nutrition, gardening, hobbies, military/war, nature/environment, recreation, sports, travel. Query with SASE or submit outline. Reviews artwork/photos as part of ms package. Send photocopies.

Recent Title(s): *Gettysburg: You Are There*, by Robert Clasby; *The GPS Handbook*, by Bob Egbert and Joe King.

BUTTE PUBLICATIONS, INC., P.O. Box 1328, Hillsboro OR 97123-1328. (503)648-9791. Fax: (503)693-9526. Website: www.buttepublications.com. **Acquisitions:** M. Brink, president. Estab. 1992. **Publishes 6-8 titles/year. Receives 30 queries and 20 mss/year. 50% of books from first-time authors; 100% from unagented writers. Pays 8-12% royalty on net receipts.** Publishes book 1 year after acceptance of ms. Accepts simultaneous submissions. Responds in (usually) 1 month to queries; 4 months to proposals; 6 months to mss. Book catalog and ms guidelines for #10 SASE or online; ms guidelines online.

O→ Butte publishes classroom books related to deafness and language.

Nonfiction: Children's/juvenile, textbook. Subjects include education (all related to field of deafness and education). Submit proposal package, including author bio, synopsis, market survey and complete ms, if completed. Reviews artwork/photos as part of ms package. Send photocopies.

Recent Title(s): *Myths*, by Paris and Tracy; *Lessons In Syntax*, by McCarr; *El Jardin Silencioso*, by Ogden.

Tips: "Audience is students, teachers, parents and professionals in the arena dealing with deafness and hearing loss. We are not seeking autobiographies or novels."

C&T PUBLISHING, 1651 Challenge Dr., Concord CA 94520. (925)677-0377. Fax: (925)677-0374. E-mail: ctinfo@ctpub.com. Website: www.ctpub.com. **Acquisitions:** Jan Grigsby, editor. Estab. 1983. Publishes hardcover and trade paperback originals. **Publishes 32 titles/year. Receives 120 submissions/year. 20% of books from first-time authors; 100% from unagented writers. Pays 5-10% royalty on retail price.** Accepts simultaneous submissions. Responds in 3 months to queries. Book catalog and proposal guidelines free; ms guidelines online.

O→ "C&T publishes well-written, beautifully designed books on quilting, dollmaking, fiber arts and ribbonwork."

Nonfiction: How-to (quilting), illustrated book. Subjects include art/architecture, hobbies, quilting books, primarily how-to, occasional quilt picture books, quilt-related crafts, wearable art, needlework, fiber and surface embellishments, other books relating to fabric crafting. "Please call or write for proposal guidelines." Extensive proposal guidelines are also available on their website.

Recent Title(s): *Laurel Burch Quilts*, by Laurel Burch; *Machine Embroidery and More*, by Kristen Dibbs.

Tips: "In our industry, we find that how-to books have the longest selling life. Quiltmakers, sewing enthusiasts, needle artists and fiber artists are our audience. We like to see new concepts or techniques. Include some great examples and you'll get our attention quickly. Dynamic design is hard to resist, and if that's your forte, show us what you've done."

CADENCE JAZZ BOOKS, Cadence Building, Redwood NY 13679. (315)287-2852. Fax: (315)287-2860. E-mail: cjb@cadencebuilding.com. Website: www.cadencebuilding.com. **Acquisitions:** Bob Rusch, Larry Raye. Estab. 1992. Publishes trade paperback and mass market paperback originals. **Publishes 5 titles/year. 90% of books from first-time authors; 100% from unagented writers. Pays royalty or makes outright purchase. Offers advance.** Publishes book 6-12 months after acceptance of ms. Responds in 1 month to queries.

O-- Cadence publishes jazz histories and discographies.

Nonfiction: Biography, reference. Subjects include music/dance, jazz music biographies, discographies and reference works. Submit outline, sample chapter(s), SASE. Reviews artwork/photos as part of ms package. Send photocopies.

Recent Title(s): *The Earthly Recordings of Sun Ra*, by Robert L. Campbell (discography).

[N] **CAMBRIDGE EDUCATIONAL**, 12 Perrine Rd., Monmouth Junction NJ 08852-0931. (609)520-6117. Fax: (609)419-8072. Website: www.cambridgeeducational.com. President: Betsy Sherer. Subsidiaries include: Cambridge Parenting and Cambridge Job Search. **Acquisitions:** Julian Chiabella, manager of acquisitions. Estab. 1981. Publishes supplemental educational products. **Publishes 30-40 titles/year. Receives 200 submissions/year. 20% of books from first-time authors; 90% from unagented writers. Makes outright purchase of $1,500-4,000. Occasional royalty arrangement.** Publishes book 8 months after acceptance of ms. Accepts simultaneous submissions.

O-- "We are known in the education industry for guidance-related and career search programs." Currently emphasizing social studies and science.

Nonfiction: Subjects include child guidance/parenting, cooking/foods/nutrition, education, health/medicine, money/finance, science, social sciences, career guidance, social studies. "We are looking for scriptwriters in the same subject areas and age group. We only publish books written for young adults and primarily sold to libraries, schools, etc. We do not seek books targeted to adults or written at high readability levels." Query or submit outline/synopsis and sample chapters. Does not respond unless interested. Reviews artwork/photos as part of ms package.

Recent Title(s): *6 Steps to Getting a Job for People with Disabilities*, by Wayne Forster.

Tips: "We encourage the submission of high-quality books on timely topics written for young adult audiences at moderate to low readibility levels. Call and request a copy of all our current catalogs, talk to the management about what is timely in the areas you wish to write on, thoroughly research the topic, and write a manuscript that will be read by young adults without being overly technical. Low to moderate readibility yet entertaining, informative and accurate."

CAMINO BOOKS, INC., P.O. Box 59026, Philadelphia PA 19102. (215)413-1917. Fax: (215)413-3255. Website: www.caminobooks.com. **Acquisitions:** E. Jutkowitz, publisher. Estab. 1987. Publishes hardcover and trade paperback originals. **Publishes 8 titles/year. Receives 500 submissions/year. 20% of books from first-time authors. Pays 6-12% royalty on net receipts. Offers $1,000 average advance.** Publishes book 1 year after acceptance of ms. Responds in 2 weeks to queries. Ms guidelines online.

O-- Camino publishes nonfiction of regional interest to the Mid-Atlantic states.

Nonfiction: Biography, children's/juvenile, cookbook, how-to. Subjects include agriculture/horticulture, Americana, art/architecture, child guidance/parenting, cooking/foods/nutrition, ethnic, gardening, government/politics, history, regional, travel. Query with SASE or submit outline, sample chapter(s).

Tips: "The books must be of interest to readers in the Middle Atlantic states, or they should have a clearly defined niche, such as cookbooks."

[⊘] **CANDLEWICK PRESS**, Subsidiary of Walker Books Ltd. (London), 2067 Massachusetts Ave., Cambridge MA 02140. (617)661-3330. Fax: (617)661-0565. Website: www.candlewick.com. President/Publisher: Karen Lotz. **Acquisitions:** Jamie Michalak, editor; Joan Powers, editor-at-large (novelty); Liz Bicknell, editorial director/associate publisher (poetry, picture books, fiction); Mary Lee Donovan, executive editor (picture books, fiction); Kara LaReau, senior editor; Cynthia Platt, editor (nonfiction); Sarah Ketchersid, editor (board, toddler). Estab. 1991. Publishes hardcover originals, trade paperback originals and reprints. **Publishes 200 titles/year. Receives 12,000-15,000 submissions/year. 5% of books from first-time authors; 40% from unagented writers. Pays 10% royalty on retail price. Offers varying advance.** Publishes book 1-3 years after acceptance of ms. Accepts simultaneous submissions. Responds in 10 weeks to mss.

O-- Candlewick Press publishes high-quality, illustrated children's books for ages infant through young adult. "We are a truly child-centered publisher."

Nonfiction: Children's/juvenile. "Good writing is essential; specific topics are less important than strong, clear writing."

Fiction: Juvenile, picture books.

Recent Title(s): *Fairieality*, by Ellwand, Downtou, and Bird; *Feed*, by M.T. Anderson (National Book Award finalist); *Judy Moody*, by Megan McDonald.

Tips: "We no longer accept unsolicited mss. See our website for further information about us."

[N] **CANDYCANE PRESS**, Ideals Publications, Inc., 535 Metroplex Dr., Suite 250, Nashville TN 37211. (615)333-0478. Publisher: Patricia Pingry. **Acquisitions:** Assistant Editor. **Publishes 20 titles/year. Offers varied advance.** Does not accept simultaneous submissions. Responds in 2 months to queries.

O-- CandyCane publishes board books for children ages 3-5.

Fiction: Juvenile, religious, holiday, patriotic themes. Submit complete ms with SASE.

Recent Title(s): *The Story of the Ten Commandments*; *I'm Thankful Each Day*; *My Mommy and I*.

CAPITAL BOOKS, 22841 Quicksilver Dr., Dulles VA 20166. (703)661-1571. Fax: (703)661-1547. E-mail: jennifer@booksintl.com. Website: www.capital-books.com. **Acquisitions:** Kathleen Hughes, publisher (self-help, memoirs); Noemi Taylor, acquisitions editor (travel, pets, lifestyle); Judy Karpinski, senior acquisitions editor (business, cooking, health). Estab. 1998. Publishes hardcover, trade paperback, mass market paperback and electronic originals, and trade paperback and mass market paperback reprints. **Publishes 50 titles/year. Receives 200 queries and 200 mss/year. 50% of books from first-time authors; 50% from unagented writers. Pays 1-10% royalty on net receipts. Offers $1,000-10,000 advance.** Publishes book 9 months after acceptance of ms. Accepts simultaneous submissions. Responds in 1 month to queries; 2 months to proposals; 3 months to mss. Book catalog and ms guidelines free; ms guidelines online.

Nonfiction: Autobiography, cookbook, how-to, reference, self-help. Subjects include animals, business/economics, child guidance/parenting, computers/electronic, contemporary culture, cooking/foods/nutrition, gardening, general nonfiction, health/medicine, money/finance, multicultural, nature/environment, psychology, regional, social sciences, software, travel, women's issues/studies. "We are looking for lifestyle and business books by experts with their own marketing and sales outlets." No religious titles, fiction or children's books. Submit proposal package including outline, 3 sample chapter(s), Query Letter. Reviews artwork/photos as part of ms package. Send photocopies.

Recent Title(s): *Mangia Bene*, by Kate DeVivo; *Mrs. Ike*, by Susan Eisenhower; *There's a Porcupine in My Outhouse*, by Michael Touglas.

Tips: "Our audience is comprised of enthusiastic readers who look to books for answers and information. Do not send fiction or religious titles. Please tell us how you, the author, can help market and sell the book."

CAPSTONE PRESS, P.O. Box 669, Mankato MN 56002. (507)388-6650. Fax: (507)625-4662. Website: www.capstone-press.com. **Acquisitions:** Eric Kudalis, product planning manager (nonfiction for students grades K-12). Publishes hardcover originals. **Publishes 400 titles/year. Receives 100 queries/year. 5% of books from first-time authors. Makes outright purchase; payment varies by imprint. Offers advance.** Responds in 3 months to queries. Book catalog online; ms guidelines online.

Imprints: Capstone Books, Blue Earth Books, Bridgestone Books, Pebble Books, LifeMatters.

O-ᴿ Capstone publishes nonfiction children's books for schools and libraries.

Nonfiction: Children's/juvenile. Subjects include Americana, animals, child guidance/parenting, cooking/foods/nutrition, health/medicine, history, military/war, multicultural, nature/environment, recreation, science, sports. "We do not accept proposals or manuscripts. Authors interested in writing for Capstone Press can request an author's brochure." Query via website.

Recent Title(s): *Downhill In-Line Skating*, by Nick Cook; *The Nez Perce Tribe*, by Allison Lassieur.

Tips: Audience is made up of elementary, middle school, and high school students who are just learning how to read, who are experiencing reading difficulties, or who are learning English. Capstone Press does not publish unsolicited mss submitted by authors, and it rarely entertains proposals. Instead, Capstone hires freelance authors to write on nonfiction topics selected by the company. Authors may request a brochure via website.

[N] **CARDOZA PUBLISHING**, 857 Broadway, 3rd Floor, New York NY 10003. E-mail: carissa@cardozapub.com. Website: www.cardozapub.com. **Acquisitions:** Carissa Alden, acquisitions editor (gaming, gambling, card and casino games); Michelle Knoetgen, acquisitions editor (chess, board games). Estab. 1981. Publishes trade paperback originals and reprints. **Publishes 35-40 titles/year. Receives 20-30 queries and 20-30 mss/year. 50% of books from first-time authors; 90% from unagented writers. Pays 5-6% royalty on retail price. Offers $1,000-10,000 advance.** Publishes book 7 months after acceptance of ms. Accepts simultaneous submissions. Responds in 1-2 months to queries; 1-2 months to proposals; 2-3 months to mss. Book catalog online; ms guidelines by email.

Nonfiction: How-to. Subjects include hobbies, gaming, gambling, backgammon chess, card games. "Cardoza Publishing publishes exclusively gaming and gambling titles. In the past, we have specialized in poker and chess titles. While we always need more of those, we are currently seeking more books on various non-casino card games, such as bridge, hearts, spades, gin rummy or canasta." Query with SASE or submit complete ms. Reviews artwork/photos as part of ms package. Send photocopies.

Recent Title(s): *Ken Warren Teaches Texas Hold 'Em*, by Ken Warren (poker); *Master Checkmate Strategy*, by Bill Robertie (chess); *Winning Casino Play*, by Avery Cardoza (gambling).

Tips: Audience is professional and recreational gamblers, chess players, card players. "We prefer not to deal with agents whenever possible. We publish only titles in a very specific niche market; please do not send us material that will not be relevant to our business."

THE CAREER PRESS, INC., Box 687, 3 Tice Rd., Franklin Lakes NJ 07417. (201)848-0310. Fax: (201)848-1727. Website: www.careerpress.com; www.newpagebooks.com. President: Ronald Fry. **Acquisitions:** Michael Lewis, senior acquisitions editor. Estab. 1985. Publishes hardcover and paperback originals. **Publishes 70 titles/year. Receives 300 queries and 1,000 mss/year. 10% of books from first-time authors; 10% from unagented writers. Offers advance.** Publishes book up to 6 months after acceptance of ms. Does not accept simultaneous submissions. Ms guidelines online.

Imprints: New Page Books.

O-ᴿ Career Press publishes books for adult readers seeking practical information to improve themselves in careers, college, finance, parenting, retirement, spirituality and other related topics, as well as management philosophy titles for a small business and management audience. New Page Books publishes in the areas of New Age, health, parenting, and weddings/entertaining. Currently de-emphasizing Judaica.

Nonfiction: How-to, reference, self-help. Subjects include business/economics, money/finance, recreation, nutrition. "Look through our catalog; become familiar with our publications. We like to select authors who are specialists on their topic." Query with SASE or submit outline, 1-2 sample chapter(s).

Recent Title(s): *Hollywood Urban Legends*, by Richard Roeper; *100 Ways to Motivate Yourself*, by Steve Chandler.

CAROLRHODA BOOKS, INC., Lerner Publishing Group, 241 First Ave. N., Minneapolis MN 55401. (612)332-3344. *No phone calls*. Fax: (612)332-7615. Website: www.lernerbooks.com. **Acquisitions:** Zelda Wagner, fiction submissions editor. Estab. 1969. Publishes hardcover originals. **Publishes 50-60 titles/year. Receives 2,000 submissions/year. 10% of books from first-time authors; 90% from unagented writers. Pays royalty on wholesale price or makes outright purchase. Negotiates payments of advance against royalty. Offers varied advance.** Accepts simultaneous submissions. Responds in 6 months to queries. Book catalog for 9×12 SAE with $3.50 postage; ms guidelines online.

- Accepts submissions from March 1-31 and October 1-31 only. Submission received at other times of the year will be returned to sender.

O‑ Carolrhoda Books is a children's publisher focused on producing high-quality, socially conscious nonfiction and fiction books with unique and well-developed ideas and angles for young readers that help them learn about and explore the world around them.

Nonfiction: Carolrhoda Books seeks creative children's nonfiction. Biography. Subjects include ethnic, nature/environment, science. "We are always interested in adding to our biography series. Books on the natural and hard sciences are also of interest." Query with SASE. Reviews artwork/photos as part of ms package. Send photocopies.

Fiction: Historical, juvenile, multicultural, picture books, young reader, middle grade and young adult fiction. "We continue to add fiction for middle grades and 8-10 picture books per year. Not looking for folktales or anthropomorphic animal stories." Carolrhoda does not publish alphabet books, puzzle books, song books, textbooks, workbooks, religious subject matter or plays. Query with SASE or submit complete ms. Query with SASE, send complete ms for picture books.

Recent Title(s): *The War*, by Anais Vaugelade; *Little Wolf's Haunted Hall for Small Horrors*, by Ian Whybrow.

Tips: Carolrhoda does not publish alphabet books, puzzle books, songbooks, textbooks, workbooks, religious subject matter or plays.

CARROLL & GRAF PUBLISHERS, INC., Avalon Publishing Group, 161 William St., New York NY 10038. (646)375-2570. Fax: (646)375-2571. Website: www.avalonpub.com. **Acquisitions:** Herman Graf, publisher; Phillip Turner, executive editor; Tina Pohlman, senior editor. Estab. 1982. Publishes hardcover and trade paperback originals. **Publishes 120 titles/year. 10% of books from first-time authors. Pays 10-15% royalty on retail price for hardcover, 6-7½% for paperback. Offers advance commensurate with the work.** Publishes book 9-18 months after acceptance of ms. Responds in a timely fashion to queries. Book catalog free.

O‑ Carroll and Graf Publishers offers quality fiction and nonfiction for a general readership.

Nonfiction: Publish general trade books; interested in developing long term relations with authors. Biography, reference, self-help. Subjects include business/economics, contemporary culture, health/medicine, history, memoirs, military/war, psychology, sports, true crime, adventure/exploration. *Agented submissions only.*

Fiction: Literary, mainstream/contemporary, mystery, science fiction, suspense, thriller. No romance. *Agented submissions only.* Query with SASE.

Recent Title(s): *Ziff: A Life?*, by Alan Lelchuk; *Hell Hath No Fury: Women's Letters from the End of the Affair*, edited by Anna Holmes; *Robert Maxwell: Israel's Superspy*, by Gordon Thomas and Martin Dillon.

CARSON-DELLOSA PUBLISHING CO., INC., P.O. Box 35665, Greensboro NC 27425-5665. (336)632-0084. Fax: (336)856-9414. Website: www.carson-dellosa.com. **Acquisitions:** Wolfgang D. Hoelscher, senior editor. **Publishes 20-30 titles/year. Receives 100-150 submissions/year. 50% of books from first-time authors; 95% from unagented writers. Makes outright purchase.** Accepts simultaneous submissions. Responds in 2 months to proposals. Book catalog online; ms guidelines free.

Nonfiction: We publish supplementary educational materials, such as teacher resource books, workbooks, and activity books. Subjects include education. No textbooks or trade children's books, please. Submit proposal package including sample chapters or pages, SASE. Reviews artwork/photos as part of ms package. Send photocopies.

Tips: "Our audience consists of pre-K through 8 educators, parents and students. Ask for our submission guidelines and a catalog before you send us your materials. We do not publish fiction or nonfiction storybooks."

CARSTENS PUBLICATIONS, INC., Hobby Book Division, P.O. Box 700, Newton NJ 07860-0700. (973)383-3355. Fax: (973)383-4064. Website: www.carstens-publications.com. **Acquisitions:** Harold H. Carstens, publisher. Estab. 1933. Publishes paperback originals. **Publishes 8 titles/year. 100% from unagented writers. Pays 10% royalty on retail price. Offers advance.** Publishes book 1 year after acceptance of ms. Responds in 2 months to queries. Book catalog for #10 SASE.

O‑ Carstens specializes in books about railroads, model railroads and airplanes for hobbyists.

Nonfiction: Subjects include hobbies, model railroading, toy trains, model aviation, railroads and model hobbies. "Authors must know their field intimately because our readers are active modelers. Writers cannot write about somebody else's hobby with authority. If they do, we can't use them. Our railroad books presently are primarily photographic essays on specific railroads." Query with SASE. Reviews artwork/photos as part of ms package.

Recent Title(s): *150 Years of Train Models*, by Harold H. Carstens; *B&O Thunder on the Alleghenies*, by Dean Mellander.

Tips: "We need lots of good photos. Material must be in model, hobby, railroad and transportation field only."

CARTWHEEL BOOKS, Scholastic, Inc., 557 Broadway, New York NY 10012. (212)343-6200. Website: www.scholastic.com. Vice President/Editorial Director: Ken Geist. **Acquisitions:** Grace Maccarone, executive editor; Sonia Black, senior editor; Jane Gerver, executive editor. Estab. 1991. Publishes novelty books, easy readers, board books, hardcover and trade paperback originals. **Publishes 85-100 titles/year. Receives 1,200 mss/year. Pays royalty on retail price. or flat fee. Offers advance.** Publishes book 2 years after acceptance of ms. Accepts simultaneous submissions. Responds in 1-4 months to queries; 6 months to mss. 9×12 SASE; ms guidelines free.

O‑ Cartwheel Books publishes innovative books for children, up to age 8. "We are looking for 'novelties' that are books first, play objects second. Even without its gimmick, a Cartwheel Book should stand alone as a valid piece of children's literature."

Nonfiction: Children's/juvenile. Subjects include animals, history, music/dance, nature/environment, recreation, science, sports. "Cartwheel Books publishes for the very young, therefore nonfiction should be written in a manner that is accessible to preschoolers through 2nd grade. Often writers choose topics that are too narrow or 'special' and do not appeal to the mass market. Also, the text and vocabulary are frequently too difficult for our young audience." Accepts mss from agents, previously published authors only. Do not send queries. Reviews artwork/photos as part of ms package. Please do not send original artwork.

Fiction: Humor, juvenile, mystery, picture books. "Again, the subject should have mass market appeal for very young children. Humor can be helpful, but not necessary. Mistakes writers make are a reading level that is too difficult, a topic of no interest or too narrow, or manuscripts that are too long." Accepts mss from agents, previously published authors only. Do not send queries.

Tips: Audience is young children, ages 0-8. "Know what types of books the publisher does. Some manuscripts that don't work for one house may be perfect for another. Check out bookstores or catalogs to see where your writing would 'fit' best."

CATHOLIC UNIVERSITY OF AMERICA PRESS, 620 Michigan Ave. NE, Washington DC 20064. (202)319-5052. Fax: (202)319-4985. E-mail: cua-press@cua.edu. Website: cuapress.cua.edu. **Acquisitions:** Dr. Gregory F. Lanave, acquisitions editor (philosophy, theology); Dr. David J. McGonagle, director (all other fields). Estab. 1939. **Publishes 20-25 titles/year. Receives 100 submissions/year. 50% of books from first-time authors; 100% from unagented writers. Pays variable royalty on net receipts.** Publishes book 2 years after acceptance of ms. Responds in 6 months to queries. Book catalog for #10 SASE; ms guidelines online.

O→ The Catholic University of America Press publishes in the fields of history (ecclesiastical and secular), literature and languages, philosophy, political theory, social studies, and theology. "We have interdisciplinary emphasis on patristics, medieval studies and Irish studies. Our principal interest is in works of original scholarship intended for scholars and other professionals and for academic libraries, but we will also consider manuscripts whose chief contribution is to offer a synthesis of knowledge of the subject which may be of interest to a wider audience or suitable for use as supplementary reading material in courses."

Nonfiction: Scholarly. Subjects include government/politics, history, language/literature, philosophy, religion, Church-state relations. No unrevised doctoral dissertations. Length: 80,000-200,000 words. Query with outline, sample chapter, cv and list of previous publications.

Recent Title(s): *Mediapolitik: How the Mass Media Have Transformed World Politics*, by Lee Edwards.

Tips: "Scholarly monographs and works suitable for adoption as supplementary reading material in courses have the best chance."

CATO INSTITUTE, 1000 Massachusetts Ave. NW, Washington DC 20001. (202)842-0200. Website: www.cato.org. **Acquisitions:** Gene Healy, senior editor. Estab. 1977. Publishes hardcover originals, trade paperback originals and reprints. **Publishes 12 titles/year. Receives 50 submissions/year. 25% of books from first-time authors; 90% from unagented writers. Makes outright purchase of $1,000-10,000. Offers advance.** Publishes book 9 months after acceptance of ms. Accepts simultaneous submissions. Responds in 3 months to queries. Book catalog online.

O→ Cato Institute publishes books on public policy issues from a free-market or libertarian perspective.

Nonfiction: Scholarly. Subjects include business/economics, education, government/politics, health/medicine, money/finance, sociology, public policy, foreign policy, monetary policy. Query with SASE.

Recent Title(s): *Toward Liberty*, edited by David Boaz; *Voucher Wars*, by Clint Bolick.

CAXTON PRESS, 312 Main St., Caldwell ID 83605-3299. (208)459-7421. Fax: (208)459-7450. Website: caxtonpress.com. President: Scott Gipson. **Acquisitions:** Wayne Cornell, managing acquisitions editor (Western Americana, regional nonfiction). Estab. 1907. Publishes hardcover and trade paperback originals. **Publishes 6-10 titles/year. Receives 250/year submissions/year. 50% of books from first-time authors; 60% from unagented writers. Pays royalty. Offers advance.** Publishes book 18 months after acceptance of ms. Accepts simultaneous submissions. Responds in 3 months to queries. Book catalog for 9×12 SAE; ms guidelines online.

O→ "Western Americana nonfiction remains our focus. We define Western Americana as almost any topic that deals with the people or culture of the west, past and present." Currently emphasizing regional issues—primarily Pacific Northwest. De-emphasizing "coffee table" or photographic intensive books.

Nonfiction: Biography, children's/juvenile, cookbook, scholarly. Subjects include Americana, history, regional. "We need good Western Americana, especially the Northwest, emphasis on serious, narrative nonfiction." Query. Reviews artwork/photos as part of ms package.

Recent Title(s): *Rotting Face: Smallpox & the American Indian*, by R.G. Robertson; *Cool North Wind: Morley Nelson and His Life with Birds of Prey*, by Stephen Stuebner; *Holy Rollers: Murder and Madness in Oregon's Love Cult*, by T. McCracken and Robert Blodgett.

Tips: "Books to us never can or will be primarily articles of merchandise to be produced as cheaply as possible and to be sold like slabs of bacon or packages of cereal over the counter. If there is anything that is really worthwhile in this mad jumble we call the twenty-first century, it should be books."

CCC PUBLICATIONS, LLC, 9725 Lurline Ave., Chatsworth CA 91311. (818)718-0507. **Acquisitions:** Cliff Carle, editorial director. Estab. 1983. Publishes trade paperback originals. **Publishes 40 titles/year. Receives 1,000 mss/year. 30% of books from first-time authors; 50% from unagented writers. Pays 8-12% royalty on wholesale price. Offers**

variable advance. Publishes book 8 months after acceptance of ms. Accepts simultaneous submissions. Responds in 3 months to queries. Book catalog for 10×13 SAE with 2 first-class stamps.

O→ CCC publishes humor that is "today" and will appeal to a wide demographic. Currently emphasizing "short, punchy pieces with *lots* of cartoon illustrations, or very well-written text if long form."

Nonfiction: How-to, humor, self-help. "We are looking for *original*, *clever* and *current* humor that is not too limited in audience appeal or that will have a limited shelf life. All of our titles are as marketable five years from now as they are today. No rip-offs of previously published books, or too special interest manuscripts." Query with SASE or submit complete ms. Reviews artwork/photos as part of ms package.

Recent Title(s): *If Men Had Babies.*, by Karen Rostoker-Gruber.

Tips: "Humor—we specialize in the subject and have a good reputation with retailers and wholesalers for publishing super-impulse titles. SASE is a must!"

CELESTIAL ARTS, Ten Speed Press, P.O. Box 7123, Berkeley CA 94707. (510)559-1600. Fax: (510)524-1052. Website: www.tenspeed.com. **Acquisitions:** Jo Ann Deck, publisher; Veronica Randall, managing editor. Estab. 1966. Publishes trade paperback originals and reprints. **Publishes 40 titles/year. Receives 500 queries and 200 mss/year. 30% of books from first-time authors; 10% from unagented writers. Pays 15% royalty on wholesale price. Offers modest advance.** Accepts simultaneous submissions. Responds in 2 months to queries. Book catalog and ms guidelines free.

O→ Celestial Arts publishes nonfiction for a forward-thinking, open-minded audience interested in psychology, self-help, spirituality, health and parenting.

Nonfiction: Cookbook, how-to, reference, self-help. Subjects include child guidance/parenting, cooking/foods/nutrition, education, health/medicine, New Age, psychology, women's issues/studies. "We specialize in parenting, alternative health, how-to and spirituality. And please, no poetry!" Submit proposal package including outline, 1-2 sample chapter(s), author bio, SASE. Reviews artwork/photos as part of ms package. Send photocopies.

Recent Title(s): *How to Be Happy, Dammit: A Cynic's Guide to Enlightenment*, by Karen Salmansohn.

Tips: Audience is fairly well-informed, interested in psychology and sociology-related topics, open-minded, innovative, forward-thinking. "The most completely thought-out (developed) proposals earn the most consideration."

[N] **CENTERSTREAM PUBLICATIONS**, P.O. Box 17878, Anaheim Hills CA 92807. (714)779-9390. Fax: (714)779-9390. E-mail: centerstrm@aol.com. Website: www.centerstream-usa.com. **Acquisitions:** Ron Middlebrook, Cindy Middlebrook, owners. Estab. 1980. Publishes hardcover and mass market paperback originals, trade paperback and mass market paperback reprints. **Publishes 12 titles/year. Receives 15 queries and 15 mss/year. 80% of books from first-time authors; 100% from unagented writers. Pays 10-15% royalty on wholesale price. Offers $300-3,000 advance.** Publishes book 8 months after acceptance of ms. Accepts simultaneous submissions. Responds in 3 months to queries. Book catalog and ms guidelines for #10 SASE.

O→ Centerstream publishes music history and instructional books.

Nonfiction: How-to. Subjects include history, music/dance. Query with SASE.

Recent Title(s): *History of Dobro Guitars.*

CHALICE PRESS, P.O. Box 179, St. Louis MO 63166. (314)231-8500. Fax: (314)231-8524. E-mail: chalice@cbp21.com. Website: www.chalicepress.com. **Acquisitions:** Dr. David P. Polk, editor-in-chief (religion: general); Dr. Jon L. Berquist, senior academic editor (religion: academic). Publishes hardcover and trade paperback originals. **Publishes 40 titles/year. Receives 500 queries and 400 mss/year. 15% of books from first-time authors; 100% from unagented writers. Pays 14% royalty on wholesale price.** Publishes book 1 year after acceptance of ms. Accepts simultaneous submissions. Responds in 2 months to queries; 3 months to proposals; 4 months to mss. Book catalog online; ms guidelines online.

Nonfiction: Textbook. Subjects include religion, spirituality. Submit proposal package including outline, 1-2 sample chapter(s).

Recent Title(s): *Embracing a Beautiful God*, by Patricia Farmer; *The Process Perspective*, by John B. Cobb, Jr.; *Strike Terror No More*, edited by Jon Berquist.

Tips: "We publish for both professional and lay Christian readers."

CHARISMA HOUSE, Strang Communications, 600 Rinehart Rd., Lake Mary FL 32746. (407)333-0600. Fax: (407)333-7100. Website: www.charismahouse.com. **Acquisitions:** Atalie Anderson, acquisitions assistant. Publishes hardcover and trade paperback originals. **Publishes 40-50 titles/year. Receives 600 mss/year. 2% of books from first-time authors; 95% from unagented writers. Pays 4-18% royalty on retail price. Offers $1,500-5,000 advance.** Publishes book 9 months after acceptance of ms. Accepts simultaneous submissions. Allow 1 year for review to proposals. Ms guidelines online.

Imprints: Creation House Press (customized publications of Christian fiction and nonfiction); Siloam (emphasizing healthy living in mind, body and spirit).

O→ "Charisma House publishes books for the Pentecostal/Charismatic Christian market to inspire and equip people to live a Christian life and to walk in the divine purpose for which they were created. We are interested in fiction but have not yet begun a fiction line."

Nonfiction: Biography, cookbook, gift book, self-help. Subjects include child guidance/parenting, cooking/foods/nutrition, health/medicine, religion (Christian), sex, spirituality (charismatic), women's issues/studies, spirit-filled interest. Request ms guidelines to receive Project Appraisal Form Questionnaire.

Recent Title(s): *Gatekeeper*, by Terry Craig (fiction); *Matters of the Heart*, by Juanita Bynum, Ph.D. (nonfiction).

Tips: "For all book submission requests, we send a Project Appraisal Questionnaire Form to all who want to submit a manuscript. They must complete and return the form. This allows a thorough review without weeding through excess information."

THE CHARLES PRESS, PUBLISHERS, 117 S. 17th St., Suite 310, Philadelphia PA 19103. (215)496-9616. Fax: (215)496-9637. E-mail: mailbox@charlespresspub.com. Website: www.charlespresspub.com. **Acquisitions:** Lauren Meltzer, publisher. Estab. 1982. Publishes hardcover and trade paperback originals. **Publishes 10-16 titles/year. Receives 1,500 queries and 500 mss/year. Pays 7½-12% royalty. Advances commensurate with first year sales potential.** Publishes book 4-12 months after acceptance of ms. Accepts simultaneous submissions. Responds in 1 month to queries; 2 months to proposals; 3 months to mss. Book catalog online; ms guidelines online.

O⊸ Currently emphasizing true crime, criminology, psychology (including suicide, anger and violence).

Nonfiction: Subjects include child guidance/parenting, health/medicine (allied), psychology, counseling, criminology, true crime. No fiction or poetry. Query or submit proposal package that includes a description of the book, a few representative sample chapters, intended audience, author's qualifications/background and SASE. No e-mailed submissions. Reviews artwork/photos as part of ms package. Send photocopies or transparencies.

Recent Title(s): *The Golden Age of Medical Science and the Dark Age of Healthcare Delivery*, by Sylvan Weinberg, M.D.

CHARLES RIVER MEDIA, 20 Downer Ave., Suite 3, Hingham MA 02043-1132. (781)740-0400. Fax: (781)740-8816. E-mail: info@charlesriver.com. Website: www.charlesriver.com. **Acquisitions:** David Pallai, president (networking, Internet related); Jennifer Niles, publisher (computer graphics, animation, game programming). Publishes hardcover and trade paperback originals. **Publishes 50 titles/year. Receives 1,000 queries and 250 mss/year. 20% of books from first-time authors; 90% from unagented writers. Pays 5-20% royalty on wholesale price. Offers $3,000-20,000 advance.** Publishes book 4 months after acceptance of ms. Accepts simultaneous submissions. Responds in 1 month to queries. Book catalog for #10 SASE; ms guidelines online.

O⊸ "Our publishing program concentrates on 3 major areas: Internet, networking, and graphics. The majority of our titles are considered intermediate, not high level research monographs, and not for lowest-level general users."

Nonfiction: Multimedia (Win/Mac format), reference, technical. Subjects include computers/electronic. Query with SASE or submit proposal package including outline, 2 sample chapter(s), résumé. Reviews artwork/photos as part of ms package. Send photocopies or GIF, TIFF or PDF files.

Recent Title(s): *Game Programming Gems 3*, edited by Dante Treglia; *Security+ Exam Guide*, by C. Crayton.

Tips: "We are very receptive to detailed proposals by first-time or non-agented authors. Consult our website for proposal outlines. Manuscripts must be completed within 6 months of contract signing."

CHARLESBRIDGE PUBLISHING, School Division, 85 Main St., Watertown MA 02472. (617)926-0329. Fax: (617)926-5720. E-mail: schooleditorial@charlesbridge.com. Website: www.charlesbridge.com/school. **Acquisitions:** Elena Dworkin Wright, vice president school division. Estab. 1980. Publishes educational curricula and hardcover and paperback nonfiction and fiction children's picture books. **Publishes 20 titles/year. Receives 1,000 submissions/year. 10-20% of books from first-time authors; 80% from unagented writers. Royalty and advance vary.** Publishes book 2 years after acceptance of ms. Ms guidelines online.

O⊸ "We're looking for compelling story lines, humor and strong educational content."

Nonfiction: Children's/juvenile, textbook. Subjects include education, multicultural, nature/environment, science, math, astronomy, physical science, problem solving. Submit complete ms.

Fiction: Non-rhyming stories.

Recent Title(s): *A Place for Zero*, by Angeline Spraivagna Lo Presti; *Sir Cumference and the Sword in the Cone*, by Cindy Neuschwander.

CHARLESBRIDGE PUBLISHING, Trade Division, 85 Main St., Watertown MA 02472. (617)926-0329. Fax: (617)926-5720. E-mail: tradeeditorial@charlesbridge.com. Website: www.charlesbridge.com. **Acquisitions:** Submission Editor. Estab. 1980. Publishes hardcover and trade paperback nonfiction children's picture picture books (80%) and fiction picture books for the trade and library markets. **Publishes 30 titles/year. Receives 2,500 submissions/year. 10-20% of books from first-time authors; 80% from unagented writers. Pays royalty. Offers advance.** Publishes book 2-4 years after acceptance of ms. Ms guidelines online.

Imprints: Charlesbridge (8 nonfiction titles/season); Talewinds (2 fiction titles/season); Whispering Coyote (3 fiction titles/season)

O⊸ "We're always interested in innovative approaches to a difficult genre, the nonfiction picture book. No novels or books for older children." Currently emphasizing nature, science, multiculturalism.

Nonfiction: Children's/juvenile. Subjects include animals, creative nonfiction, history, multicultural, nature/environment, science, social science. Strong interest in nature, environment, social studies and other topics for trade and library markets. *Exclusive submissions only.*

Fiction: "Strong stories with enduring themes." *Exclusive submissions only.*

Recent Title(s): *First Year Letters*, by Julie Dannenberg; *Don't Say Ain't*, by Irene Smalls; *The Deep-Sea Floor*, by Sneed B. Collard III.

CHATHAM PRESS, Box A, Greenwich CT 06870. **Acquisitions:** Jane Andrassi. Estab. 1971. Publishes hardcover and paperback originals, reprints and anthologies. **Publishes 10 titles/year. Receives 50 submissions/year. 25% of books from first-time authors; 75% from unagented writers.** Publishes book 6 months after acceptance of ms. Responds in 2 months to queries. Book catalog and ms guidelines for 6×9 SAE with 6 first-class stamps.

O‑ Chatham Press publishes "books that relate to the U.S. coastline from Maine to the Carolinas and which bring a new insight, visual or verbal, to the nonfiction topic."

Nonfiction: Illustrated book. Subjects include history, nature/environment, regional (Northeast seaboard), translation (from French and German), natural history. Query with SASE. Reviews artwork/photos as part of ms package.

Recent Title(s): *Exploring Old Martha's Vineyard.*

Tips: "Illustrated New England-relevant titles have the best chance of being sold to our firm. We have a slightly greater (15%) skew towards cooking and travel titles."

CHELSEA GREEN PUBLISHING CO., P.O. Box 428, #205 Gates-Briggs Bldg., White River Junction VT 05001-0428. (802)295-6300. Fax: (802)295-6444. Website: www.chelseagreen.com. **Acquisitions:** Ben Watson, senior editor. Estab. 1984. Publishes hardcover and trade paperback originals and reprints. **Publishes 8-12 titles/year. Receives 300-400 queries and 200-300 mss/year. 30% of books from first-time authors; 80% from unagented writers. Pays royalty on publisher's net. Offers $2,500-10,000 advance.** Publishes book 18 months after acceptance of ms. Responds in 1 week to queries; 1 month to proposals; 1 month to mss. Book catalog and ms guidelines free or online; ms guidelines online.

O‑ Chelsea Green publishes and distributes books relating to issues of sustainability with a special concentration on books about nature, the environment, independent living and enterprise, organic gardening, renewable energy and alternative or natural building techniques. The books reflect positive options in a world of environmental turmoil. Emphasizing food/agriculture/gardening, innovative shelter and natural building, renewable energy, sustainable business and enterprise. De-emphasizing nature/natural history.

Nonfiction: Cookbook, how-to, reference, self-help, technical. Subjects include agriculture/horticulture, art/architecture, cooking/foods/nutrition, gardening, health/medicine, memoirs, money/finance, nature/environment, forestry. Query with SASE or submit proposal package including outline, 1-2 sample chapter(s). Reviews artwork/photos as part of ms package.

Recent Title(s): *The Slow Food Guide to New York City*, by Slow Food USA; *The Straw Bale House*, by Steen, Steen, Bainbridge; *Gaia's Garden*, by Toby Henerway.

Tips: "Our readers are passionately enthusiastic about ecological solutions for contemporary challenges in construction, energy harvesting, agriculture and forestry. Our books are also carefully and handsomely produced to give pleasure to bibliophiles of a practical bent. It would be very helpful for prospective authors to have a look at several of our current books, as well as our catalog and website. For certain types of book, we are the perfect publisher, but we are exceedingly focused on particular areas."

CHELSEA HOUSE PUBLISHERS, Haights Cross Communications, 1974 Sproul Rd., Suite 400, Broomall PA 19008-0914. (610)353-5166. Fax: (610)353-5191. E-mail: editorial@chelseahouse.com. Website: www.chelseahouse.com. **Acquisitions:** Editorial Assistant. Publishes hardcover originals and reprints. **Publishes 350 titles/year. Receives 1,000 queries and 500 mss/year. 25% of books from first-time authors; 98% from unagented writers. Makes outright purchase of $1,500-3,500.** Publishes book 16 months after acceptance of ms. Accepts simultaneous submissions. Responds in 1 month to queries; 3 months to proposals; 3 months to mss. Book catalog online; ms guidelines for #10 SASE.

O‑ "We publish a nonfiction education series primarily for the library market/schools."

Nonfiction: Biography (must be common format, fitting under a series umbreальа), children's/juvenile. Subjects include Americana, animals, anthropology/archeology, ethnic, gay/lesbian, government/politics, health/medicine, history, hobbies, language/literature, military/war, multicultural, music/dance, nature/environment, recreation, regional, religion, science, sociology, sports, travel, women's issues/studies. "We are interested in expanding our topics to include more on the physical, life and environmental sciences." Query with SASE or submit proposal package including outline, 2-3 sample chapter(s), résumé. Reviews artwork/photos as part of ms package. Send photocopies.

Recent Title(s): *Ireland* (Modern World Nation Series—geography); *Moliere* (Bloom's Major Dramatists Series—literary criticism); *Right to Privacy* (Point/Counterpoint Series).

Tips: "Know our product. Do not waste your time or ours by sending something that does not fit our market. Be professional. Send clean, clear submissions that show you read the preferred submission format. Always include SASE."

CHEMICAL PUBLISHING CO., INC., 527 Third Ave., #427, New York NY 10016-4168. (212)779-0090. Fax: (212)889-1537. E-mail: chempub@aol.com. Website: www.chemicalpublishing.com. **Acquisitions:** Ms. S. Soto-Galicia, publisher. Estab. 1934. Publishes hardcover originals. **Publishes 8 titles/year. Receives 20 queries/year. 50% of books from first-time authors; 100% from unagented writers. Pays 10% royalty on retail price or makes negotiable outright purchase. Offers negotiable advance.** Publishes book 8 months after acceptance of ms. Does not accept simultaneous submissions. Responds in 3 weeks to queries; 5 weeks to proposals; 2 months to mss. Book catalog and ms guidelines free; ms guidelines online.

O‑ Chemical publishes professional chemistry-technical titles aimed at people employed in the chemical industry, libraries and graduate courses.

Nonfiction: "We request a fax letter with an introduction of the author and the kind of book written. Afterwards, we will reply. If the title is of interest, then we will request samples of the ms." How-to, reference, applied chemical technology (cosmetics, cement, textiles). Subjects include agriculture/horticulture, cooking/foods/nutrition, health/medicine, nature/environment, science, analytical methods, chemical technology, cosmetics, dictionaries, engineering, environmental science, food technology, formularies, industrial technology, medical, metallurgy, textiles. Submit outline, few pages of 3 sample chapter(s), SASE. Reviews artwork/photos as part of ms package.

Recent Title(s): *Cooling Water Treatment, Principles and Practice*; *Harry's Cosmeticology, 8th Edition*; *Library Handbook for Organic Chemists.*

Tips: Audience is professionals in various fields of chemistry, corporate and public libraries, college libraries. "We request a fax letter with an introduction of the author and the kind of book written. Afterwards, we will reply. If the title is of interest, then we will request samples of the ms."

CHICAGO REVIEW PRESS, 814 N. Franklin, Chicago IL 60610-3109. (312)337-0747. Fax: (312)337-5110. E-mail: csherry@ipgbook.com.Submissions E-mail: yuval@ipgbook.com. Website: www.ipgbook.com. **Acquisitions:** Cynthia Sherry, executive editor (general nonfiction, children's); Yuval Taylor, editor (African, African-American and performing arts). Estab. 1973. Publishes hardcover and trade paperback originals and trade paperback reprints. **Publishes 30-35 titles/year. Receives 200 queries and 600 mss/year. 50% of books from first-time authors; 50% from unagented writers. Pays 7-12½% royalty. Offers $1,500-5,000 average advance.** Publishes book 18 months after acceptance of ms. Accepts simultaneous submissions. Responds in 3 months to queries. Book catalog for $3.50; ms guidelines for #10 SASE or online at website.

Imprints: Lawrence Hill Books, A Capella Books (contact Yuval Taylor).

O→ Chicago Review Press publishes intelligent nonfiction on timely subjects for educated readers with special interests.

Nonfiction: Children's/juvenile (activity books only), cookbook (specialty only), how-to. Subjects include art/architecture, child guidance/parenting, cooking/foods/nutrition, creative nonfiction, education, ethnic, gardening (regional), health/medicine, history, hobbies, memoirs, multicultural, music/dance, nature/environment, recreation, regional. Query with outline, toc and 1-2 sample chapters. Reviews artwork/photos as part of ms package.

Recent Title(s): *The Civil War for Kids*, by Janis Herbert.

Tips: "Along with a table of contents and 1-2 sample chapters, also send a cover letter and a list of credentials with your proposal. Also, provide the following information in your cover letter: audience, market and competition—who is the book written for and what sets it apart from what's already out there."

CHILD WELFARE LEAGUE OF AMERICA, 440 First St. NW, 3rd Floor, Washington DC 20001. (202)638-2952. Fax: (202)638-4004. E-mail: books@cwla.org. Website: www.cwla.org. **Acquisitions:** Acquisitions Editor. Publishes hardcover and trade paperback originals. **Publishes 30-50 titles/year. Receives 300 submissions/year. 95% from unagented writers. Pays 0-10% royalty on net domestic sales.** Publishes book 1 year after acceptance of ms. Responds in 3 months to queries. Book catalog and ms guidelines free; ms guidelines online.

Imprints: CWLA Press (child welfare professional publications), Child & Family Press (children's books and parenting books for the general public).

O→ CWLA is a privately supported, nonprofit, membership-based organization committed to preserving, protecting and promoting the well-being of all children and their families.

Nonfiction: Children's/juvenile. Subjects include child guidance/parenting, sociology. Submit complete ms.

Recent Title(s): *The Coffee Can Kid* (children's); *Respectful Parenting* (parenting).

Tips: "We are looking for positive, kid friendly books for ages 3-9. We are looking for books that have a positive message... a feel-good book."

[N] **CHILDREN'S PRESS/FRANKLIN WATTS**, Scholastic, Inc., 90 Old Sherman Turnpike, Danbury CT 06816. (203)797-3500. Fax: (203)797-6986. Website: publishing.grolier.com. **Acquisitions:** Kate Nunn, editor-in-chief; Wendy Mead, editor; Eileen Robinson, executive editor; Christine Florie, associate editor. Estab. 1946. Publishes nonfiction hardcover originals. **Publishes 350 titles/year. Pays 5-8% royalty on net receipts or makes outright purchase.** Publishes book 20 months after acceptance of ms. Book catalog for #10 SASE.

O→ Children's Press publishes 90% nonfiction for the school and library market, and 10% early reader fiction and nonfiction. "Our books support textbooks and closely relate to the elementary and middle-school curriculum." Franklin Watts publishes nonfiction for middle and high school curriculum.

Nonfiction: Biography, children's/juvenile, reference. Subjects include animals, anthropology/archeology, art/architecture, ethnic, health/medicine, history, hobbies, multicultural, music/dance, nature/environment, science, sports, general children's nonfiction. "We publish nonfiction books that supplement the school curriculum." No fiction, poetry, folktales, cookbooks or novelty books. Query with SASE.

Recent Title(s): *Extraordinary People of the Harlem Renaissance*, by Hardy and Hardy; *My Book of Me*, by Dana Meachen Rau.

Tips: Most of this publisher's books are developed inhouse; less than 5% come from unsolicited submissions. However, they publish several series for which they always need new books. Study catalogs to discover possible needs.

CHILDSWORK/CHILDSPLAY, LLC, The Guidance Channel, 135 Dupont St., P.O. Box 760, Plainview NY 11803-0760. (516)349-5520. Website: www.childswork.com. **Acquisitions:** Karen Schader, editor (psychological books and games for use with children). Publishes trade paperback originals and reprints. **Publishes 10-12 titles/year. Receives 250 queries and 50 mss/year. 5% of books from first-time authors; 100% from unagented writers. Makes outright purchase of $500-3,000.** Publishes book 9 months after acceptance of ms. Accepts simultaneous submissions. Responds in 1 month to queries; 1 month to proposals; 3 months to mss. Book catalog and ms guidelines for 9×12 SAE with 4 first-class stamps.

O→ Our target market includes therapists, counselors and teachers working with children who are experiencing behavioral, emotional and social difficulties.

Nonfiction: Psychological storybooks and workbooks, psychological games. Subjects include child guidance/parenting, education, health/medicine, psychology. All books and games are psychologically based and well researched. Query with SASE.

Fiction: Children's storybooks must deal with some aspect of psychological development or difficulty (e.g., ADHD, anger management, social skills, OCD, etc.). "Be in our files (résumé, writing samples) and we will contact you when we develop new projects." Submit complete ms.

Recent Title(s): *The Stop, Relax & Think Scriptbook.*

Tips: "Our market is comprised of mental health and education professionals who are primarily therapists, guidance counselors and teachers. A majority of our projects are assignments rather than submissions. Impress us with your writing ability and your background in psychology and education. If submitting rather seeking work on assignment, demonstrate that your work is marketable and profitable."

CHINA BOOKS, (formerly China Books & Periodicals, Inc.), Long River Press, 2929 24th St., San Francisco CA 94110-4126. (415)282-2994. Fax: (415)282-0994. Website: www.chinabooks.com. **Acquisitions:** Greg Jones, editor (language study, health, history). Estab. 1960. Publishes hardcover and trade paperback originals. **Publishes 5 titles/year. Receives 300 submissions/year. 10% of books from first-time authors; 95% from unagented writers. Pays 6-8% royalty on net receipts. Offers negotiable advance.** Publishes book 1 year after acceptance of ms. Accepts simultaneous submissions. Responds in 3 months to queries. Book catalog free; ms guidelines online.

O→ China Books is the main importer and distributor of books and magazines from China, providing an ever-changing variety of useful tools for travelers, scholars and others interested in China and Chinese culture. "We are looking for original book ideas, especially in the areas of language study, children's books, history and culture, all relating to China." Currently emphasizing language study. De-emphasizing art, fiction, poetry.

Nonfiction: "*Important*: *All* books *must* be on topics related to China or Chinese-Americans. Books on China's history, politics, environment, women, art/architecture; language textbooks, acupuncture and folklore." Biography, children's/juvenile, coffee table book, how-to, self-help, textbook. Subjects include agriculture/horticulture, art/architecture, business/economics, cooking/foods/nutrition, education, ethnic, gardening, government/politics, health/medicine, history, language/literature, music/dance, nature/environment, religion, sociology, translation, travel, women's issues/studies. Reviews artwork/photos as part of ms package.

Recent Title(s): *Rise of Digital China*, by Lid Wong; *Healing Energy*, by Virginia Newton.

Tips: "We are looking for original ideas, especially in language study, children's education, adoption of Chinese babies, or health issues relating to traditional Chinese medicine."

CHITRA PUBLICATIONS, 2 Public Ave., Montrose PA 18801. (570)278-1984. Fax: (570)278-2223. E-mail: chitraed@epix.net. Website: www.quilttownusa.com. **Acquisitions:** Acquisitions Editors. Publishes trade paperback originals. **Publishes 6 titles/year. Receives 70-80 queries and 10-20 mss/year. Pays royalty.** Publishes book 6-12 months after acceptance of ms. Does not accept simultaneous submissions. Responds in 2 weeks to queries; 3 weeks to proposals; 1 month to mss. Book catalog and ms quidelines for #10 SASE; ms guidelines online.

O→ "We publish quality quilting magazines and pattern books that recognize, promote, and inspire self expression."

Nonfiction: How-to. Subjects include quilting. Query with SASE. Reviews artwork/photos as part of ms package. Send photocopies or transparencies.

CHOSEN BOOKS PUBLISHING CO., LTD., 3985 Bradwater St., Fairfax VA 22031-3702. (703)764-8250. Fax: (703)764-3995. E-mail: jecampbell@aol.com. Website: www.bakerbooks.com. **Acquisitions:** Jane Campbell, editorial director. Estab. 1971. Publishes hardcover and trade paperback originals. **Publishes 16 titles/year. Receives 500 submissions/year. 15% of books from first-time authors; 99% from unagented writers. Offers small advance.** Publishes book 12-18 months after acceptance of ms. Accepts simultaneous submissions. Responds in 3 months to queries. Ms guidelines for #10 SASE.

O→ "We publish well-crafted books that recognize the gifts and ministry of the Holy Spirit, and help the reader live a more empowered and effective life for Jesus Christ."

Nonfiction: Subjects include religion (Christianity). "We publish books reflecting the current acts of the Holy Spirit in the world, books with a charismatic Christian orientation." No New Age, poetry, fiction, autobiographies, biographies, compilations, Bible studies, booklets, academic or children's books. Submit synopsis, chapter outline, résumé, 2 chapters and SASE. No computer disks or e-mail attachments; brief query only by e-mail.

Recent Title(s): *Healing the Nations: A Call to Global Intercession*, by John Sandford.

Tips: "We look for solid, practical advice for the growing and maturing Christian from authors with professional or personal experience platforms. No conversion accounts or chronicling of life events, please. State the topic or theme of your book clearly in your cover letter."

CHRISTIAN ED. PUBLISHERS, P.O. Box 26639, San Diego CA 92196. (858)578-4700. Fax: (858)578-2431. Website: www.christianedwarehouse.com. **Acquisitions:** Janet Ackelson, assistant editor. **Publishes 64 titles/year. Makes outright purchase of 3¢/word.** Responds in 3 months on assigned material to mss. Book catalog for 9×12 SAE with 4 first-class stamps; ms guidelines for #10 SASE.

O→ Christian Ed. Publishers is an independent, non-denominational, evangelical company founded nearly 50 years ago to produce Christ-centered curriculum materials based on the Word of God for thousands of churches of different denominations throughout the world. "Our mission is to introduce children, teens, and adults to a personal faith in Jesus Christ and to help them grow in their faith and service to the Lord. We publish materials that teach moral and spiritual values while training individuals for a lifetime of Christian service." Currently emphasizing Bible curriculum for preschool through preteen ages.

Nonfiction: Children's/juvenile. Subjects include education (Christian), religion. "All subjects are on assignment." Query with SASE.

Fiction: "All writing is done on assignment." Query with SASE.

Recent Title(s): *All-Stars for Jesus: Bible Curriculum for Preteens.*

Tips: "Read our guidelines carefully before sending us a manuscript. All writing is done on assignment only and must be age appropriate (preschool-6th grade)."

CHRISTIAN PUBLICATIONS, INC., (formerly included Horizon Books), 3825 Hartzdale Dr., Camp Hill PA 17011. (717)761-7044. Fax: (717)761-7273. E-mail: dfessenden@christianpublications.com. Website: www.christianpublications.com. **Acquisitions:** David E. Fessenden, senior editor. Estab. 1883. Publishes hardcover, mass market and trade paperback originals. **Publishes 25 titles/year. Receives 600 queries and 600 mss/year. 25% of books from first-time authors; 90% from unagented writers. Pays 5-10% royalty on retail price or makes outright purchase. Offers varying advance.** Publishes book 14-18 months after acceptance of ms. Accepts simultaneous submissions. Responds in 1 month to queries; 3 months to proposals; 3 months to mss. Book catalog for 9×12 SAE with 7 first-class stamps; ms guidelines online.
Imprints: Horizon Books.

O→ "Our purpose is to exalt God and impact lives by producing and distributing biblically faithful resources."

Nonfiction: Biblical studies, Christian living, homeschooling, deeper life/classics, missions, church resources/pastoral helps. Subjects include Americana, religion (Evangelical Christian perspective), spirituality, devotionals, bible studies (with practical application), family/marriage, children's books. Full proposal must accompany ms. Does not want fiction, poetry. Query with SASE or submit proposal package, including chapter synopsis, 2 sample chapters (including chapter 1), audience and market ideas, author bio. Reviews artwork/photos as part of ms package. Send photocopies.
Recent Title(s): *Leaving a Legacy: How to Make Your Marriage Outlive You*, by Phil and Suzy Downer, with Ken Walker (marriage/family); *Show Me Your Glory: 52 Weekly Meditations on the Majesty of God*, by Ethel Herr (devotional).
Tips: "Please do not send manuscripts without a complete proposal. We do *not* reprint other publishers' material. We are owned by The Christian and Missionary Alliance denomination; while we welcome and publish authors from various denominations, their theological perspective must be compatible with The Christian and Missionary Alliance. We are especially interested in fresh, practical approaches to deeper life—sanctification with running shoes on. Readers are evangelical, regular church-goers, mostly female, usually leaders in their church. Your book should grow out of a thorough and faithful study of Scripture. You need not be a 'Bible scholar,' but you should be a devoted student of the Bible."

CHRONICLE BOOKS, 85 Second St., 6th Floor, San Francisco CA 94105. (415)537-4200. Fax: (415)537-4440. E-mail: frontdesk@chroniclebooks.com. Website: www.chroniclebooks.com. President: Jack Jensen. **Acquisitions:** Jay Schaefer (fiction); Bill LeBlond (cookbooks); Leslie Jonath (lifestyle); Alan Rapp (art and design); Sarah Malarky (licensing and popular culture); Mikyla Bruder (crafts and lifestyle); Steve Mockus (popular culture); Debra Lande (gift books); Victoria Rock (children's). Estab. 1966. Publishes hardcover and trade paperback originals. **Publishes 200 titles/year.** Publishes book 18 months after acceptance of ms. Accepts simultaneous submissions. Responds in 3 months to queries. Book catalog for 11x14 SAE with 5 first-class stamps; ms guidelines online.
Imprints: Chronicle Books for Children, GiftWorks (ancillary products, such as stationery, gift books).

O→ "Inspired by the enduring magic and importance of books, our objective is to create and distribute exceptional publishing that is instantly recognizable for its spirit, creativity and value. This objective informs our business relationships and endeavors, be they with customers, authors, suppliers or colleagues."

Nonfiction: Coffee table book, cookbook, gift book. Subjects include art/architecture, cooking/foods/nutrition, gardening, nature/environment, photography, recreation, regional, design, pop culture, interior design. Query or submit outline/synopsis with artwork and sample chapters.
Fiction: Submit complete ms.
Recent Title(s): *The Beatles Anthology*, by The Beatles; *Worst-Case Scenario Survival Handbook*, by David Borgenicht and Joshua Piven.

CHRONICLE BOOKS FOR CHILDREN, 85 Second St., 6th Floor, San Francisco CA 94105. (415)537-4200. Fax: (415)537-4420. E-mail: frontdesk@chroniclebooks.com. Website: www.chroniclekids.com. **Acquisitions:** Victoria Rock, associate publisher; Beth Weber, managing editor; Jennifer Vetter, editor; Susan Pearson, editor-at-large; Samantha McFerrin, assistant editor. Publishes hardcover and trade paperback originals. **Publishes 40-50 titles/year. Receives 20,000 submissions/year. 5% of books from first-time authors; 25% from unagented writers. Pays 8% royalty. Offers variable advance.** Publishes book 18 months after acceptance of ms. Accepts simultaneous submissions. Responds in 2-18 weeks to queries; 6 months to mss. Book catalog for 9×12 SAE with 3 first-class stamps; ms guidelines online.

O→ Chronicle Books for Children publishes an eclectic mixture of traditional and innovative children's books. "Our aim is to publish books that inspire young readers to learn and grow creatively while helping them discover the joy of reading. We're looking for quirky, bold artwork and subject matter." Currently emphasizing picture books. De-emphasizing young adult.

Nonfiction: Biography, children's/juvenile (for ages 8-12), illustrated book, picture books (for ages up to 8 years). Subjects include animals, art/architecture, multicultural, nature/environment, science. Query with synopsis and SASE. Reviews artwork/photos as part of ms package.
Fiction: Mainstream/contemporary, multicultural, young adult, picture books; middle grade fiction; young adult projects. "We do not accept proposals by fax, via e-mail, or on disk. When submitting artwork, either as a part of a project or as samples for review, do not send original art. Please be sure to include an SASE large enough to hold your materials. Projects submitted without an appropriate SASE will be recycled." Query with SASE. Query with synopsis and SASE. Send complete ms for picture books.
Recent Title(s): *Ghost Wings*; *Dream Carver*; *Star in the Darkness*.
Tips: "We are interested in projects that have a unique bent to them—be it in subject matter, writing style, or illustrative technique. As a small list, we are looking for books that will lend our list a distinctive flavor. Primarily we are interested in fiction and nonfiction picture books for children ages up to eight years, and nonfiction books for children ages up to

twelve years. We publish board, pop-up, and other novelty formats as well as picture books. We are also interested in early chapter books, middle grade fiction, and young adult projects."

CHURCH GROWTH INSTITUTE, P.O. Box 7, Elkton MD 21922-0007. (434)525-0022. Fax: (434)525-0608. E-mail: cgimail@churchgrowth.org. Website: www.churchgrowth.org. **Acquisitions:** Cindy Spear, administrator/resource development director. Estab. 1978. Publishes trade paperback originals, 3-ring-bound manuals, mixed media resource packets. **Publishes 4 titles/year. Pays 6% royalty on retail price.** Publishes book 1 year after acceptance of ms. Accepts simultaneous submissions. Responds in 3 months to queries. Book catalog for 9×12 SAE with 4 first-class stamps; ms guidelines given after query and outline is received.

"Our mission is to provide practical resources to help pastors, churches and individuals reach their potential for Christ; to promote spiritual and numerical growth in churches, thereby leading Christians to maturity and lost people to Christ; and to equip pastors so they can equip their church members to do the work of the ministry."

Nonfiction: "Material should originate from a conservative Christian view and cover topics that will help churches grow, through leadership training, self-evaluation, and new or unique ministries, or enhancing existing ministries. Self-discovery inventories regarding spiritual growth, relationship improvement, etc., are hot items." How-to. Subjects include education, religion (church-growth related), ministry, how-to manuals, spiritual growth, relationship-building, evangelism. "Accepted manuscripts will be adapted to our resource packet, manual or inventory format. All material must be practical and easy for the *average* Christian to understand." Query or submit outline and brief explanation of what the packet will accomplish in the local church and whether it is leadership or lay-oriented. Queries accepted by mail or e-mail. No phone queries. Reviews artwork/photos as part of ms package. Send photocopies or transparencies.

Recent Title(s): *Ministry Descriptions: Identifying Opportunities and Clarifying Expectations*; *Sunday School Growth for Rookies*; *Marriage Communication Assessment.*

Tips: "We are not publishing many *textbooks*. Concentrate on how-to manuals and ministry evaluation and diagnostic tools and spiritual or relationship-oriented 'inventories' for individual Christians."

CIRCLET PRESS, INC., 1770 Massachusetts Ave., #278, Cambridge MA 02140. (617)864-0492. Fax: (617)864-0663. E-mail: circlet-info@circlet.com. Website: www.circlet.com. **Acquisitions:** Cecilia Tan, publisher/editor. Estab. 1992. Publishes hardcover and trade paperback originals. **Publishes 4-6 titles/year. Receives 50-100 queries and 500 mss/year. 90% from unagented writers. Pays 4-12% royalty on retail price or makes outright purchase. Also pays in books, if author prefers.** Publishes book 18 months after acceptance of ms. Accepts simultaneous submissions. Responds in 1 months to queries; 6-18 months to mss. Book catalog for 10 SAE with 2 first-class stamps; ms guidelines online.

Imprints: The Ultra Violet Library (gay and lesbian science fiction and fantasy "these books will not be as erotic as our others"); Circumflex (erotic and sexual nonfiction titles, how-to and essays).

"Circlet Press publishes science fiction/fantasy short stories which are too erotic for the mainstream and to promote literature with a positive view of sex and sexuality, which celebrates pleasure and diversity. We also publish other books celebrating sexuality and imagination with our imprints: The Ultra Violet Library and Circumflex."

Fiction: Erotica, fantasy, gay/lesbian, science fiction, short story collections. "Fiction must combine both the erotic and the fantastic. The erotic content needs to be an integral part of a science fiction story, and vice versa. Writers should not assume that any sex is the same as erotica." "No horror! No exploitative sex, murder or rape. No degradation." No novels. Query with SASE. Submit full short stories up to 10,000 words between April 15 and August 31. Manuscripts received outside this reading period are discarded. Queries only via e-mail.

Recent Title(s): *Nymph*, by Francesca Lia Block; *The Darker Passions: Dracula*, by Amarantha Knight.

Tips: "Our audience is adults who enjoy science fiction and fantasy, especially the works of Anne Rice, Storm Constantine, Samuel Delany, who enjoy vivid storytelling and erotic content. Seize your most vivid fantasy, your deepest dream and set it free onto paper. That is at the heart of all good speculative fiction. Then if it has an erotic theme as well as a science fiction one, send it to me. No horror, rape, death or mutilation! I want to see stories that *celebrate* sex and sexuality in a positive manner. Please write for our guidelines as each year we have a specific list of topics we seek. Short stories only, *no* novels."

CLARION BOOKS, Houghton Mifflin Co., 215 Park Ave. S., New York NY 10003. Website: www.houghtonmifflinbook.com. **Acquisitions:** Dinah Stevenson, editorial director; Jennifer B. Greene, editor (contemporary fiction, picture books for all ages, nonfiction); Jennifer Wingertzahn, editor (fiction, picture books); Lynne Polvino, associate editor (fiction, nonfiction, picture books). Estab. 1965. Publishes hardcover originals for children. **Publishes 50 titles/year. Pays 5-10% royalty on retail price. Offers minimum of $4,000 advance.** Publishes book 2 years after acceptance of ms. Responds in 2 months to queries Prefers no multiple submissions to mss. Ms guidelines for #10 SASE.

Clarion Books publishes picture books, nonfiction, and fiction for infants through grade 12. Avoid telling your stories in verse unless you are a professional poet.

Nonfiction: Biography, children's/juvenile, photo essay. Subjects include Americana, history, language/literature, nature/environment, photography, holiday. No unsolicited mss. Query with SASE or submit proposal package including sample chapter(s), SASE. Reviews artwork/photos as part of ms package. Send photocopies.

Fiction: Adventure, historical, humor, mystery, suspense, strong character studies. Clarion is highly selective in the areas of historical fiction, fantasy, and science fiction. A novel must be superlatively written in order to find a place on the list. Mss that arrive without an SASE of adequate size will *not* be responded to or returned. Accepts fiction translations. No unsolicited mss. Submit complete ms. No queries, please. Send to only *one* Clarion editor.

Recent Title(s): *Opera Cat*, by Tess Weaver; *The Same Stuff as Stars*, by Katherine Paterson.

Tips: Looks for "freshness, enthusiasm—in short, life."

CLARITY PRESS, INC., 3277 Roswell Rd. NE, #469, Atlanta GA 30305. (877)613-1495. Fax: (404)231-3899 and (877)613-7868. E-mail: claritypress@usa.net. Website: www.claritypress.com. **Acquisitions:** Diana G. Collier, editorial director (contemporary justice issues). Estab. 1984. Publishes hardcover and trade paperback originals. **Publishes 4 titles/year.** Does not accept simultaneous submissions. Responds in 3 months to queries.

Nonfiction: Publishes books on contemporary issues in U.S., Middle East and Africa. Subjects include ethnic, world affairs, human rights/socio-economic and minority issues. No fiction. Query with synopsis, annotated outline, résumé, publishing history.

Recent Title(s): *The Criminality of Nuclear Deterrence*, by Francis A. Boyle.

Tips: "Check our titles on website."

CLEAR LIGHT PUBLISHERS, 823 Don Diego, Santa Fe NM 87505-4224. (505)989-9590. E-mail: publish@clearlightbooks.com. **Acquisitions:** Harmon Houghton, publisher. Estab. 1981. Publishes hardcover and trade paperback originals. **Publishes 20-24 titles/year. Receives 100 queries/year. 10% of books from first-time authors; 50% from unagented writers. Pays 10% royalty on wholesale price. Offers advance, a percent of gross potential.** Publishes book 1 year after acceptance of ms. Accepts simultaneous submissions. Responds in 3 months to queries. Book catalog free.

O→ Clear Light publishes books that "accurately depict the positive side of human experience and inspire the spirit."

Nonfiction: Biography, coffee table book, cookbook. Subjects include Americana, anthropology/archeology, art/architecture, cooking/foods/nutrition, ethnic, history, nature/environment, philosophy, photography, regional (Southwest). Query with SASE. Reviews artwork/photos as part of ms package. Send photocopies.

Recent Title(s): *Fourteen Dalai Lamas*, by Glenn H. Mullin; *When Technology Fails*, by Matthew Stein; *Cape Cod Wampanoag Cook Book*, by Chief Earl Mills & Betty Breen.

CLEIS PRESS, P.O. Box 14684, San Francisco CA 94114-0684. (415)575-4700. Fax: (415)575-4705. Website: www.cleispress.com. **Acquisitions:** Frederique Delacoste. Estab. 1980. Publishes trade paperback originals and reprints. **Publishes 20 titles/year. 10% of books from first-time authors; 90% from unagented writers. Pays variable royalty on retail price.** Publishes book 2 years after acceptance of ms. Responds in 1 month to queries. Book catalog for #10 SAE with 2 first-class stamps.

O→ Cleis Press specializes in feminist and gay/lesbian fiction and nonfiction.

Nonfiction: Subjects include gay/lesbian, women's issues/studies, sexual politics, erotica, human rights, African-American studies. "We are interested in books on topics of sexuality, human rights and women's and gay and lesbian literature. Please consult our website first to be certain that your book fits our list." Query or submit outline and sample chapters.

Fiction: Feminist, gay/lesbian, literary. "We are looking for high quality fiction by women and men." No romances. Submit complete ms. *Writer's Market* recommends sending a query with SASE first.

Recent Title(s): *Black Like Us* (fiction); *Whole Lesbian Sex Book* (nonfiction); *No Place Like Home: Echoes from Kosovo* (nonfiction).

Tips: "Be familiar with publishers' catalogs; be absolutely aware of your audience; research potential markets; present fresh new ways of looking at your topic; avoid 'PR' language and include publishing history in query letter."

CLEVELAND STATE UNIVERSITY POETRY CENTER, R.T. 1841, Cleveland State University, 2121 Euclid Ave., Cleveland OH 44115-2214. (216)687-3986. Fax: (216)687-6943. E-mail: poetrycenter@csuohio.edu. Website: www.csuohio.edu/poetrycenter. **Acquisitions:** Rita Grabowski, coordinator; Ted Lardner, director. Estab. 1962. Publishes trade paperback originals. **Publishes 4 titles/year. Receives 500 queries and up to 1,000 mss/year. 60% of books from first-time authors; 100% from unagented writers. CSU Poetry Series pays one-time, lump-sum royalty of $300, plus 50 copies; Cleveland Poets Series (Ohio poets only) pays 100 copies. $1,000 prize for best full-length ms each year in 2 categories.** Accepts simultaneous submissions. Responds in 1 month to queries; 8 months to mss. Manuscript guidelines for SASE. Manuscripts are not returned.

Poetry: Send SASE for guidelines or check website. Submit only November-January. Charges $20 reading fee. Reviews artwork/photos only if applicable (e.g., concrete poetry). No light verse, inspirational, or greeting card verse. ("This does not mean that we do not consider poetry with humor or philosophical/religious import.").

Recent Title(s): *The Saint of Letting Small Fish Go*, by Eliot Khabil Wilson; *Double Exposure*, by Sarah Kennedy.

Tips: "Our books are for serious readers of poetry, i.e. poets, critics, academics, students, people who read *Poetry, Field, American Poetry Review*, etc. Trends include movement away from 'confessional' poetry; greater attention to form and craftsmanship. Project an interesting, coherent personality; link poems so as to make coherent unity, not just a miscellaneous collection. Especially need poems with *mystery*, i.e., poems that suggest much, but do not tell all."

⊘ **CLOUD PEAK**, 730 W. 51st St., Casper WY 82601. **Acquisitions:** Paul Harwitz. Publishes hardcover, trade paperback and mass market paperback originals and reprints. **Publishes 36 titles/year. Receives 200 queries and 80 mss/year. 10% of books from first-time authors; 50% from unagented writers. Pays 10% royalty for nonfiction; percentage for fiction varies.** Publishes book 1-2 years after acceptance of ms. Accepts simultaneous submissions. Responds in 2 months to queries; 3 months to proposals; 2 months to mss. Book catalog for #10 SASE; ms guidelines for #10 SASE.

O→ Cloud Peak is currently emphasizing nonfiction books about Indians, African-Americans, Asians, Hispanics and other "minorities" in the West.

Nonfiction: Biography, children's/juvenile, how-to, humor. Subjects include Americana (Western), education, history, humor, military/war, multicultural, sports, women's issues/studies. "Submissions to our 'Women of the West' line of nonfiction will receive special consideration." Query with SASE. **All unsolicited mss returned unopened.** Reviews artwork/photos as part of ms package. Send photocopies, transparencies or computer files on 3.5-inch disk.

Fiction: Adventure, fantasy, historical, horror, humor, juvenile, military/war, multicultural, multimedia, mystery, poetry, science fiction, suspense, western, Native American. "Do everything you can to make the book a real 'page-turner,' Plots and sub-plots must be plausible and suited to the locale(s). Main and secondary characters must speak dialog which matches their respective personality traits. Blacks, Spanish-speaking people and other 'minorities' must *not* be portrayed stereotypically. Historical accuracy is important." Query with SASE. *All unsolicited mss returned unopened.*

Poetry: "We publish Western/cowboy/Indian poetry in single-author collections and multi-author anthologies." Query or submit 3 sample poems or submit complete ms.

Recent Title(s): *Soldiers Falling Into Camp: The Battles at the Rosebud and Little Bighorn*, by Robert Kammen, Frederick Lefthand and Joe Marshall (military history); *The Watcher*, by Robert Kammen (Western/supernatural/ecological); *Riders of the Leafy Spurge*, by Bill Lowman (cowboy poetry).

Tips: "Buy, read and study the *Writer's Market* each year. Writing must flow. Imagine you are a reader visiting a bookstore. Write the first page of the book in such a way that the reader feels *compelled* to buy it. It helps a writer to work from an outline. When we solicit a manuscript for consideration, we like to receive a floppy disk, in order to conserve trees."

[N] COACHES CHOICE, P.O. Box 1828, Monterey CA 93942. (888)229-5745. Fax: (831)372-6075. E-mail: info@healthylearning.com. Website: www.coacheschoice.com. **Acquisitions:** Sue Peterson, general manager (sports). Publishes trade paperback originals and reprints. **Publishes 75 titles/year. Receives 100 queries and 60 mss/year. 50% of books from first-time authors; 95% from unagented writers. Pays 10-15% royalty.** Publishes book 1 year after acceptance of ms. Accepts simultaneous submissions. Responds in 2 months to queries. Book catalog free; ms guidelines online.

"We publish books for anyone who coaches a sport or has an interest in coaching a sport—all levels of competition."

Nonfiction: How-to, reference. Subjects include sports, sports specific training, general physical conditioning. Submit proposal package including outline, 2 sample chapter(s), résumé. Reviews artwork/photos as part of ms package. Send photocopies or diagrams.

Recent Title(s): *Coaching the Multiple West Coast Offense*, by Ron Jenkins.

COASTAL CAROLINA PRESS, 2231 Wrightsville Ave., Wilmington NC 28403. Website: www.coastalcarolinapress.org. Hardcover, trade paperback and mass market paperback originals and trade paperback reprints. **Publishes 6-8 titles/year. 70% of books from first-time authors; 100% from unagented writers. Pays royalty.** Publishes book 1 year after acceptance of ms. Book catalog online; ms guidelines online.

"We are a nonprofit corporation dedicated to publishing materials about the history, culture and activities of coastal North & South Carolina. We do not publish poetry or religious titles."

Nonfiction: Coffee table book, cookbook, how-to, humor. Subjects include agriculture/horticulture, art/architecture, cooking/foods/nutrition, creative nonfiction, education, ethnic, gardening, history, language/literature, memoirs, military/war, multicultural, music/dance, nature/environment, photography, recreation, regional, sociology, travel, women's issues/studies. Publishes books with regional niche. Query with SASE.

Fiction: Adventure, ethnic, historical, humor, juvenile, literary, mainstream/contemporary, military/war, multicultural, mystery, regional, short story collections, suspense, young adult. Publishes books with regional niche. Query with SASE.

Recent Title(s): *Searching for Virginia Dave: A Fool's Errand*, by Marjorie Hudson (historical nonfiction/memoir); *Island Murders*, by Wanda Campbell (fiction).

[N] COASTAL PUBLISHING INTERNATIONAL, P.O. Box 910, Queen Creek AZ 85242. E-mail: acquisitions@coastalpublishingintl.com. Website: www.coastalpublishingintl.com. **Acquisitions:** Acquisitions Editor. Estab. 2001. Publishes trade paperback, mass market paperback, and electronic originals, and trade paperback, mass market paperback, and electronic reprints. **Publishes 4-6 titles/year. 75% of books from first-time authors; 98% from unagented writers. Pays 10-40% royalty on wholesale price.** Publishes book 6-12 months after acceptance of ms. Accepts simultaneous submissions. Responds in 1 month to queries; 2 months to mss.

Nonfiction: Audiocassettes, biography, cookbook, gift book, how-to, humor, multimedia, reference, scholarly, self-help, technical, textbook. Subjects include agriculture/horticulture, alternative lifestyles, Americana, animals, anthropology/archeology, art/architecture, business/economics, child guidance/parenting, cooking/foods/nutrition, creative nonfiction, education, gardening, general nonfiction, health/medicine, hobbies, humanities, money/finance, music/dance, nature/environment, New Age, philosophy, photography, psychology, recreation, science, sex, social sciences, sociology, software, spirituality, sports, travel, women's issues/studies. "We're open to most subjects, but we expect the author to actively participate in promotion." Submit 3 sample chapter(s), author bio, query, promotion plans and availability. Reviews artwork/photos as part of ms package. Send photocopies.

Tips: "We help our authors with as much promotion as possible. We believe in rewarding with higher royalties when the author actively participates in book sales."

[N] COFFEE HOUSE PRESS, 27 N. Fourth St., Suite 400, Minneapolis MN 55401. Fax: (612)338-4004. Publisher: Allan Kornblum. **Acquisitions:** Chris Fischbach, senior editor. Estab. 1984. Publishes hardcover and trade paperback originals. **Publishes 14 titles/year. Receives 5,000 queries and 3,000 mss/year. 75% from unagented writers. Pays 8% royalty on retail price. Provides 15 author's copies.** Publishes book 18 months after acceptance of ms. Responds in 1 month to queries; up to 6 months to mss. Book catalog and ms guidelines for #10 SASE with 2 first-class stamps; ms guidelines for #10 SAE with 55¢ first-class stamps.

Fiction: Ethnic, experimental, literary, mainstream/contemporary, short story collections, novels. No genre. Query with SASE. Query first with samples and SASE.

Poetry: Full-length collections.

Recent Title(s): *Our Sometime Sister*, by Norah Labiner (fiction); *Avalanche*, by Quincy Troupe (poetry).

Tips: "Look for our books at stores and libraries to get a feel for what we like to publish. No phone calls, e-mails, or faxes."

COLLECTORS PRESS, INC., P.O. Box 230986, Portland OR 97281-0986. (503)684-3030. Fax: (503)684-3777. Website: www.collectorspress.com. **Acquisitions:** Richard Perry, publisher. Estab. 1992. Publishes hardcover and trade paperback originals. **Publishes 20 titles/year. Receives 500 queries and 200 mss/year. 75% of books from first-time authors; 75% from unagented writers. Pays royalty.** Publishes book 1 year after acceptance of ms. Responds in 1 month to queries. Book catalog and ms guidelines free.

O→ Collectors Press Inc. publishes award-winning popular-culture coffee table and gift books on 20th century and modern collections and interests.

Nonfiction: Illustrated book, reference. Subjects include art/architecture, photography, nostalgic pop culture, science-fiction art, fantasy art, graphic design, comic art, magazine art, historical art, poster art, genre specific art. Submit proposal package, including market research, outline, 2 sample chapters and SASE. Reviews artwork/photos as part of ms package. Send transparencies or *very* clear photos.

Recent Title(s): *Science Fiction of the 20th Century: An Illustrated History.*

Tips: "Your professional package must be typed. No computer disks accepted."

COLLEGE PRESS PUBLISHING CO., P.O. Box 1132, Joplin MO 64802. (417)623-6280. Website: www.collegepress.com. **Acquisitions:** Acquisitions Editor. Estab. 1959. Publishes hardcover and trade paperback originals and reprints. **Publishes 15-20 titles/year. Receives 400 queries and 300 mss/year. 25% of books from first-time authors; 90% from unagented writers. Pays 5-15% royalty on wholesale price.** Publishes book 6 months after acceptance of ms. Accepts simultaneous submissions. Responds in 3 months to proposals. Book catalog for 9×12 SAE with 5 first-class stamps; ms guidelines online.

Imprints: HeartSpring Publishing (nonacademic Christian, inspirational, devotional and Christian fiction).

O→ "College Press is an evangelical Christian publishing house primarily associated with the Christian churches/Church of Christ."

Nonfiction: "We seek textbooks used in Christian colleges and universities—leaning toward an Arminian and an amillennial mindset." Textbook (Christian textbooks and small group studies). Subjects include religion, Christian apologetics. Query with SASE or submit proposal package including 3 sample chapter(s), author bio, synopsis.

Recent Title(s): *Encounters with Christ*, by Mark E. Moore.

Tips: "Our core market is Christian Churches/Churches of Christ and conservative evangelical Christians. Have your material critically reviewed prior to sending it. Make sure that it is non-Calvinistic and that it leans more amillennial (if it is apocalyptic writing)."

COMMON COURAGE PRESS, One Red Barn Rd. Box 702, Monroe ME 04951. (207)525-0900 or (800)497-3207. Fax: (207)525-3068. E-mail: orders-info@commoncouragepress.com. Website: www.commoncouragepress.com. **Acquisitions:** Ms. Flic Shooter, publisher (leftist political literature). Publishes hardcover and trade paperback originals and trade paperback reprints. **Publishes 12 titles/year. Receives 50 queries and 200 mss/year. 50% of books from first-time authors; 100% from unagented writers. Pays 10% royalty on wholesale price.** Publishes book 9 months after acceptance of ms. Accepts simultaneous submissions. Responds in 1 month to queries. Book catalog online; ms guidelines online.

O→ "Nonfiction leftist, activist, political, history, feminist, media issues are our niche."

Nonfiction: Reference, textbook. Subjects include anthropology/archeology, creative nonfiction, ethnic, gay/lesbian, government/politics, health/medicine, history, military/war, multicultural, nature/environment, science. Query with SASE or submit proposal package, including outline or submit completed ms. Reviews artwork/photos as part of ms package.

Recent Title(s): *New Military Humanism*, by Noam Chomsky (leftist political); *Rogue State*, by William Blum (leftist political).

Tips: Audience consists of left-wing activists, college audiences.

[N] **COMMUTERS LIBRARY**, Sound Room Publishers, P.O. Box 3168, Falls Church VA 22043. (703)790-8250. Fax: (703)790-8234. E-mail: jlangenfeld@commuterslibrary.com. Website: www.commuterslibrary.com. **Acquisitions:** Joe Langenfeld, editor. Estab. 1991. Publishes audiobooks. **Publishes 80 titles/year. Pays 5-10% royalty. Offers $200-1,000 advance.** Publishes book 1 year after acceptance of ms. Accepts simultaneous submissions. Responds in 3 months to queries; 6 months to mss. Ms guidelines online.

Imprints: Inaudio.

O→ "Small publisher of audiobooks (many classics) with plans to publish new works of fiction and nonfiction, primarily novellas."

Nonfiction: Audiocassettes, children's/juvenile, humor. Subjects include government/politics, current affairs, environment. Query with SASE or submit outline, 1 sample chapter(s), Synopsis; Estimated Word Count. Does not accept unsolicited mss. Responds only with SASE.

Fiction: Adventure, fantasy, historical, horror, humor, literary, mainstream/contemporary, military/war, mystery, suspense, western, young adult. Does not accept unsolicited mss. Responds only with SASE. Query with SASE or submit outline, 1 sample chapter(s), synopsis.

Tips: "Audiobooks are growing in popularity. Authors should consider going directly to audio for special works. Give us good writing 10,000 to 20,000 words in length."

CONCORDIA PUBLISHING HOUSE, 3558 S. Jefferson Ave., St. Louis MO 63118-3968. (314)268-1187. Fax: (314)268-1329. E-mail: Brandy.overton@cph.org. Website: www.cph.org. **Acquisitions:** Peggy Kuethe, production editor (children's product, adult devotional, teaching resources); Mark Sell, senior editor (adult nonfiction on Christian spirituality and culture, academic works of interest in Lutheran markets). Estab. 1869. Publishes hardcover and trade paperback originals. **Publishes 50 titles/year.** Ms guidelines online.

O→ Concordia publishes Protestant, inspirational, theological, family and juvenile material. All manuscripts must conform to the doctrinal tenets of The Lutheran Church—Missouri Synod. No longer publishes fiction.

Nonfiction: Children's/juvenile, adult. Subjects include child guidance/parenting (in Christian context), religion, inspirational.

Recent Title(s): *Seasons Under the Son*, by Tim Wesemann (inspirational); *Right from the Start*, by Shirley Morgentha (parenting).

Tips: "We are no longer accepting freelance submissions."

CONSORTIUM PUBLISHING, 640 Weaver Hill Rd., West Greenwich RI 02817-2261. (401)397-9838. Fax: (401)392-1926. John M. Carlevale, chief of publications. Estab. 1990. Publishes trade paperback originals and reprints. **Publishes 12 titles/year. Receives 150 queries and 50 mss/year. 50% of books from first-time authors; 95% from unagented writers. Pays 10-15% royalty.** Publishes book 3 months after acceptance of ms. Responds in 2 months to queries. Book catalog and ms guidelines for #10 SASE.

O→ Consortium publishes books for all levels of the education market.

Nonfiction: Autobiography, how-to, humor, illustrated book, reference, self-help, technical, textbook. Subjects include business/economics, child guidance/parenting, education, government/politics, health/medicine, history, music/dance, nature/environment, psychology, science, sociology, women's issues/studies. Query or submit proposal package, including table of contents, outline, 1 sample chapter and SASE. Reviews artwork/photos as part of ms package. Send photocopies.

Recent Title(s): *Teaching the Child Under Six, 4th edition*, by James L. Hymes, Jr. (education).

Tips: Audience is college and high school students and instructors, elementary school teachers and other trainers.

CONTEMPORARY BOOKS, McGraw-Hill Company, 130 E. Randolph St., Suite 900, Chicago IL 60601. (312)233-6500. Fax: (312)233-7570. Website: www.books.mcgraw-hill.com. Vice President: Philip Ruppel. **Acquisitions:** Denise Betts, associate editor; Monica Stoll, editorial assistant (general trade); Christopher Brown, senior editor; Garret Lemoi, associate editor (world languages). Estab. 1947. Publishes hardcover originals and trade paperback originals and reprints. **Publishes 300 titles/year. Receives 5,000 submissions/year. 10% of books from first-time authors; 25% from unagented writers. Pays 6-15% royalty on retail price. Offers advance.** Publishes book 1 year after acceptance of ms. Accepts simultaneous submissions. Responds in 2 months to queries. Ms guidelines for #10 SASE.

Imprints: Contemporary Books, VGM Career Books, McGraw-Hill.

O→ "We are a midsize, niche-oriented, backlist-oriented publisher. We publish exclusively nonfiction in general interest trade categories."

Nonfiction: How-to, reference (popular and general), self-help. Subjects include child guidance/parenting, cooking/foods/nutrition, health/medicine, psychology, sports, careers, foreign languages. Query with SASE or submit outline, sample chapter(s). Reviews artwork/photos as part of ms package.

Recent Title(s): *Raising Resilient Children*, by Robert Brooks and Sam Goldstein; *The Last-Minute Party Girl*, by Erika Lenkert.

COOK COMMUNICATIONS MINISTRIES, 4050 Lee Vance View, Colorado Springs CO 80918. (719)536-3271. Fax: (719)536-3265. Website: www.cookministries/proposals.com. **Acquisitions:** Karen Athen, editorial assistant. Estab. 1875. Publishes hardcover and trade paperback originals. **Publishes 130 titles/year. 10% of books from first-time authors; 50% from unagented writers. Pays variable royalty on net price. Offers varied advance.** Publishes book 1-2 years after acceptance of ms. Accepts simultaneous submissions. Responds in 3-4 months to queries. Ms guidelines online.

Imprints: Faith Kidz Books (children), Victor (church resources), Next Gen, River Oak (fiction), Honor (inspiration).

O→ Cook Communications publishes children's and family spiritual growth books. Books "must have strong, overt Christian themes or clearly stated biblical value."

Nonfiction: Biography, children's/juvenile, reference (Bible). Subjects include child guidance/parenting, history, religion. Submit proposal package including outline, 1 sample chapter(s), cover letter, SASE.

Fiction: Juvenile, adult.

Recent Title(s): *Taking the High Ground*, by Col. Jeff O'Leary, USAF (nonfiction); *Understanding the Heartbeat of Jesus*, by Jill Briscoe (women/spiritual growth); *Tale of Three Trees*, by Angela Elwell Hunt (children's picture book).

Tips: "All books must in some way be Bible-related and written by authors who themselves are evangelical Christians with a platform. Only a small fraction of the manuscripts received can be seriously considered for publication. Most books result from contacts that acquisitions editors make with qualified authors, though from time to time an unsolicited proposal triggers enough excitement to result in a contract. A writer has the best chance of selling Cook a well-conceived and imaginative manuscript that helps the reader apply Christianity to her life in practical ways. Christians active in the local church and their children are our audience."

COOPER SQUARE PRESS, Rowman and Littlefield Publishing Group, 200 Park Ave. S., Suite 1109, New York NY 10003. (212)529-3888. Fax: (212)529-4223. **Acquisitions:** Ross Plotkin, acquisitions editor. Estab. 1984. Publishes hardcover originals, trade paperback originals and reprints. **Publishes 40 titles/year. Receives 1,200 submissions/year. 15% of books from first-time authors; 65% from unagented writers. Pays 10-15% royalty on net receipts.** Publishes book 1 year after acceptance of ms. Responds in 2 months to queries. Book catalog and ms guidelines for 9×12 SAE with 4 first-class stamps.

Nonfiction: Biography, reference (trade). Subjects include contemporary culture, history, contemporary affairs. No unsolicited mss. Query with SASE or submit outline, sample chapter(s).

COPPER CANYON PRESS, P.O. Box 271, Port Townsend WA 98368. (360)385-4925. E-mail: poetry@coppercanyonpress.org. Website: www.coppercanyonpress.org. **Acquisitions:** Sam Hamill, editor. Estab. 1972. Publishes trade paperback originals and occasional clothbound editions. **Publishes 18 titles/year. Receives 2,000 queries and 1,500 mss/year. 10% of books from first-time authors; 95% from unagented writers. Pays royalty.** Publishes book 2 years after acceptance of ms. Responds in 4 months to queries. Book catalog free; ms guidelines online.

- Copper Canyon Press is dedicated to publishing poetry in a wide range of styles and from a full range of the world's many cultures.

Poetry: "First and second book manuscripts are considered only for our Hayden Carruth Awards, presented annually." Send SASE for entry form in September of each year. *No unsolicited mss.*

Recent Title(s): *Steal Away*, by C.D. Wright; *Nightworks*, by Marvin Bell; *The Complete Poems of Kenneth Rexroth.*

CORNELL MARITIME PRESS, INC., P.O. Box 456, Centreville MD 21617-0456. (410)758-1075. Fax: (410)758-6849. E-mail: cornell@crosslink.net. **Acquisitions:** Charlotte Kurst, managing editor. Estab. 1938. Publishes hardcover originals and quality paperbacks. **Publishes 7-9 titles/year. Receives 150 submissions/year. 80% of books from first-time authors; 99% from unagented writers.** Publishes book 1 year after acceptance of ms. Responds in 2 months to queries. Book catalog for 10×13 SAE with 5 first-class stamps.

Imprints: Tidewater (regional history, folklore and wildlife of the Chesapeake Bay and the Delmarva Peninsula).

- Cornell Maritime Press publishes books for the merchant marine and a few recreational boating books for professional mariners and yachtsmen.

Nonfiction: How-to (on maritime subjects), technical, manuals. Subjects include marine subjects (highly technical). Query first, with writing samples and outlines of book ideas.

Recent Title(s): *Amphibians and Reptiles of Delmarva*, by James F. White, Jr. and Amy Wendt White; *Perry's Baltimore Adventure*, by Peter Dans; *Handbook of Rights and Concerns for Mariners*, by Roberto Tiangco and Russ Jackson.

CORNELL UNIVERSITY PRESS, Sage House, 512 E. State St., Ithaca NY 14850. (607)277-2338. Fax: (607)277-2374. Website: www.cornellpress.cornell.edu. Estab. 1869. Publishes hardcover and paperback originals. **Publishes 150 titles/year. Pays royalty. Offers $0-5,000 advance.** Publishes book 1 year after acceptance of ms. Accepts simultaneous submissions. Book catalog and ms guidelines online; ms guidelines online.

Imprints: Comstock (contact Peter J. Prescott, science editor), ILR Press (contact Frances Benson).

- Cornell Press is an academic publisher of nonfiction with particular strengths in anthropology, Asian studies, biological sciences, classics, history, labor and business, literary criticism, politics and international relations, psychology, women's studies, Slavic studies, philosophy. Currently emphasizing sound scholarship that appeals beyond the academic community.

Nonfiction: Biography, reference, scholarly, textbook. Subjects include agriculture/horticulture, anthropology/archeology, art/architecture, business/economics, education, ethnic, gay/lesbian, government/politics, history, language/literature, military/war, music/dance, philosophy, psychology, regional, religion, science, sociology, translation, women's issues/studies. Submit résumé, cover letter and prospectus.

Recent Title(s): *Ermengard of Narbonne and the World of the Troubadours*, by Fredric L. Cheyette; *Russia's Unfinished Revolution*, by Michael McFaul; *The Birds of Ecuador*, by Robert S. Ridgely and Paul J. Greenfield.

CORWIN PRESS, INC., 2455 Teller Rd., Thousand Oaks CA 91320. (805)499-9734. Fax: (805)499-2692. E-mail: faye.zucker@corwinpress.com. **Acquisitions:** Faye Zucker, executive editor (teaching, learning, assessment); Robb Clouse, senior acquisitions editor (administration, special education, leadership); Rachel Livsey, acquisitions editor (staff development, diversity, research, school reform); Kylee Liegl, acquisitions editor (curriculum and content, gifted education, technology). Estab. 1990. Publishes hardcover and paperback originals. **Publishes 90 titles/year.** Publishes book 7 months after acceptance of ms. Responds in 1 month to queries. Ms guidelines for #10 SASE.

- Corwin Press, Inc. publishes leading-edge, user-friendly publications for education professionals.

Nonfiction: Professional-level publications for administrators, teachers, school specialists, policymakers, researchers and others involved with K-12 education. Subjects include education. Seeking fresh insights, conclusions, and recommendations for action. Prefers theory or research based books that provide real-world examples and practical, hands-on strategies to help busy educators be successful. No textbooks that simply summarize existing knowledge or mass-market books. Query with SASE.

Recent Title(s): *Differentiated Instructional Strategies*, by Gayle H. Gregory and Carolyn Chapman; *Evaluating Professional Development*, by Thomas R. Guskey; *Refaming the Path to School Leadership*, by Lee G. Bolman and Terrence E. Deal.

COUNCIL OAK BOOKS/WILDCAT CANYON PRESS, 2105 E. 15th St., Suite B, Tulsa OK 74104. (918)743-BOOK. Fax: (918)583-4995. E-mail: pmillichap@bigplanet.com. **Acquisitions:** Paulette Millichap, publisher (stories about women and relationships, Native American history and spirituality, memoir, small inspirational gift books, Americana). Estab. 1984. Publishes hardcover originals, trade paperback originals and reprints. **Publishes 10-12 titles/year. Receives 1,000 queries/year. 35% of books from first-time authors; 75% from unagented writers. Pays 10-20% royalty on net receipts.** Publishes book 9-12 months after acceptance of ms. Accepts simultaneous submissions. Responds in 1 month to queries; 1 month to proposals. Book catalog for #10 SASE; ms guidelines for #10 SASE.

Nonfiction: Autobiography, gift book, illustrated book. Subjects include Americana, memoirs, Native American studies. Query with SASE. Reviews artwork/photos as part of ms package. Send photocopies.

Recent Title(s): *Native New Yorkers*, by Evan Pritchard.

COUNCIL ON SOCIAL WORK EDUCATION, 1725 Duke St., Suite 500, Alexandria VA 22314-3457. (703)683-8080. Fax: (703)683-8099. E-mail: publications@cswe.org. Website: www.cswe.org. **Acquisitions:** Michael J. Monti, director of publications. Estab. 1952. Publishes trade paperback originals. **Publishes 4 titles/year. Receives 12 queries and 8 mss/year. 25% of books from first-time authors; 100% from unagented writers. Pays sliding royalty scale, starting at 10%.** Publishes book 1 year after acceptance of ms. Responds in 2 months to queries; 3 months to proposals; 3 months to mss. Book catalog and ms guidelines free via website or with SASE.

O→ Council on Social Work Education produces books and resources for social work educators, students and practitioners.

Nonfiction: Subjects include education, sociology, social work. Books for social work and other educators. Query with proposal package, including cv, outline, 2 sample chapters and SASE. Reviews artwork/photos as part of ms package. Send photocopies.

Recent Title(s): *Group Work Education in the Field*, by Julianne Wayne and Carol S. Cohen; *Ethics Education in Social Work*, by Frederic G. Reamer.

Tips: Audience is "Social work educators and students and others in the helping professions. Check areas of publication interest on website."

THE COUNTRYMAN PRESS, P.O. Box 748, Woodstock VT 05091-0748. (802)457-4826. Fax: (802)457-1678. E-mail: countrymanpress@wwnorton.com. Website: www.countrymanpress.com. Editorial Director: Kermit Hummel. **Acquisitions:** Ann Kraybill, managing editor. Estab. 1973. Publishes hardcover originals, trade paperback originals and reprints. **Publishes 35 titles/year. Receives 1,000 queries/year. 30% of books from first-time authors; 70% from unagented writers. Pays 5-15% royalty on retail price. Offers $1,000-5,000 advance.** Publishes book 18 months after acceptance of ms. Accepts simultaneous submissions. Responds in 2 months to proposals. Book catalog free; ms guidelines online.

Imprints: Backcountry Guides.

O→ Countryman Press publishes books that encourage physical fitness and appreciation for and understanding of the natural world, self-sufficiency and adventure.

Nonfiction: "We publish several series of regional recreation guidebooks—hiking, bicycling, walking, fly-fishing, canoeing, kayaking—and are looking to expand them. We're also looking for books of national interest on travel, gardening, rural living, nature and fly-fishing." How-to, guidebooks; general nonfiction. Subjects include cooking/foods/nutrition, gardening, general nonfiction, history (New England), nature/environment, recreation, regional (New England), travel, country living. Submit proposal package including outline, 3 sample chapter(s), author bio, market information, SASE. Reviews artwork/photos as part of ms package. Send photocopies.

Recent Title(s): *The King Arthur Flour Baker's Companion: The All-Purpose Baking Cookbook*; *Tying Contemporary Saltwater Flies*, by Klausmeyer/Largay; *Maine: An Explorer's Guide*, by Tree.

COVENANT COMMUNICATIONS, INC., Box 416, American Fork UT 84003-0416. (801)756-1041. Website: www.covenant-lds.com. **Publishes 50+ titles/year. 35% of books from first-time authors; 100% from unagented writers. Pays 6½-15% royalty on retail price.** Publishes book 6-12 months after acceptance of ms. Responds in 4 months to mss. Ms guidelines online.

O→ Currently emphasizing inspirational, devotional, historical, biography. Our fiction is also expanding, and we are looking for new approaches to LDS literature and storytelling.

Nonfiction: Biography, children's/juvenile, coffee table book, gift book, humor, illustrated book, multimedia (CD-ROM), reference, scholarly. Subjects include child guidance/parenting, creative nonfiction, history, memoirs, religion (LDS or Mormon), spirituality. Submit completed manuscript with synopsis and one-page cover letter.

Fiction: "We publish exclusively to the 'Mormon' (The Church of Jesus Christ of Latter-Day Saints) market. All work must appeal to that audience." Adventure, fantasy, historical, humor, juvenile, literary, mainstream/contemporary, mystery, picture books, regional, religious, romance, science fiction, spiritual, suspense, young adult. Submit completed manuscript with synopsis and one-page cover letter.

Recent Title(s): *Between Husband and Wife*, by Brinley and Lamb (marriage/self-help); *On Holy Ground: Old Testament Lands*, by S. Michael Wilcox; *Saints at War*, by Robert Freeman and Dennis Wright.

Tips: Our audience is exclusively LDS (Latter-Day Saints, "Mormon").

CRAFTSMAN BOOK CO., 6058 Corte Del Cedro, Carlsbad CA 92009-9974. (760)438-7828 or (800)829-8123. Fax: (760)438-0398. E-mail: jacobs@costbook.com. Website: www.craftsman-book.com. **Acquisitions:** Laurence D. Jacobs, editorial manager. Estab. 1957. Publishes paperback originals. **Publishes 12 titles/year. Receives 50 submissions/year. 85% of books from first-time authors; 98% from unagented writers. Pays 7½-12½% royalty on wholesale price or retail price.** Publishes book 2 years after acceptance of ms. Accepts simultaneous submissions. Responds in 2 months to queries. Book catalog and ms guidelines free.

O→ Publishes how-to manuals for professional builders. Currently emphasizing construction software.

Nonfiction: All titles are related to construction for professional builders. How-to, technical. Subjects include building, construction. Query with SASE. Reviews artwork/photos as part of ms package.

Recent Title(s): *Steel-Frame House Construction*, by Tim Waite.

Tips: "The book should be loaded with step-by-step instructions, illustrations, charts, reference data, forms, samples, cost estimates, rules of thumb, and examples that solve actual problems in the builder's office and in the field. The book must cover the subject completely, become the owner's primary reference on the subject, have a high utility-to-cost ratio, and help the owner make a better living in his chosen field."

N **CRANE HILL PUBLISHERS**, Southern Lights Custom Publishing, 3608 Clairmont Ave., Birmingham AL 35222. (205)714-3007. Fax: (205)714-3008. Estab. 1992. Publishes hardcover and trade paperback originals. **Publishes 8-12 titles/year. Receives 200-300 queries and 100 mss/year. 65% of books from first-time authors; 95% from unagented writers. Pays royalty.** Publishes book 2 years after acceptance of ms. Accepts simultaneous submissions. Responds in 2-3 months to queries; 6 months to proposals. Book catalog free; ms guidelines by email.

"Crane Hill Publishers is dedicated to the publication of America's indigenous cultural traditions. Our mission is to build a tradition of quality books that reflect the history, perceptions, experience, and customs of people in regional locales around the United States."

Nonfiction: Biography, coffee table book, cookbook, gift book, reference, self-help. Subjects include Americana, art/architecture, cooking/foods/nutrition, creative nonfiction, gardening, general nonfiction, history, travel. Query with SASE. Reviews artwork/photos as part of ms package. Send photocopies.

Fiction: Literary, mainstream/contemporary. Query with SASE.

CREATIVE HOMEOWNER, 24 Park Way, Upper Saddle River NJ 07458. (201)934-7100. Fax: (201)934-7541. E-mail: sharon.ranftle@creativehomeowner.com. Website: www.creativehomeowner.com. **Acquisitions:** Tim Bakke, editorial director; Fran Donegan, senior editor (home improvement/repair); Kathie Robitz, senior editor (home decorating/design). Estab. 1978. Publishes trade paperback originals. **Publishes 12-16 titles/year. Receives dozens of queries mss/year. 50% of books from first-time authors; 98% from unagented writers. Pays royalty or makes outright purchase of $8,000-35,000.** Publishes book 16 months after acceptance of ms. Responds in 6 months to queries. Book catalog free.

Creative Homeowner is the one source for the largest selection of quality how-to books, booklets and project plans.

Nonfiction: How-to, illustrated book. Subjects include gardening, hobbies, home remodeling/building, home repairs, home decorating/design, ideas, inspiration. Query or submit proposal package, including competitive books (short analysis) and outline and SASE. Reviews artwork/photos as part of ms package.

Recent Title(s): *The New Smart Approach to Kitchen Design*, by Susan Maney; *The New Smart Approach to Bath Design*, by Susan Maney; *Trellises & Arbors*, by Bill Hylton.

CRICKET BOOKS, Carus Publishing, 332 S. Michigan Ave., #1100, Chicago IL 60604. (312)939-1500. Fax: (312)939-8150. Website: www.cricketbooks.net. **Acquisitions:** Submissions Editor. Estab. 1999. Publishes hardcover and paperback originals. **Publishes 20 titles/year. Receives 1,500 queries and 5,000 mss/year. Pays 10% royalty on net receipts. Open to first-time and unagented authors. Pays up to 10% royalty on retail price. Offers $1,500 and up advance.** Publishes book 18 months after acceptance of ms. Accepts simultaneous submissions. Responds in 4 months to queries; 4 months to proposals; 6 months to mss. Ms guidelines online.

- Currently not accepting queries or ms. Check website for submissions details and updates.

Cricket Books publishes picture books, chapter books and middle-grade novels and young adult fiction and nonfiction.

Nonfiction: Children's/juvenile, young adult. Send proposal, including sample chapters, table of contents, and description of competition.

Fiction: Juvenile, young adult (adventure, easy-to-read, fantasy/science fiction, historical, horror, mystery/suspense, problem novels, romance, sports, western), Early chapter books and middle-grade fiction. Submit complete ms.

Recent Title(s): *Seek*, by Paul Fleischman; *Robert and the Lemming Problem*, by Barbar Seuling; *The Power of Un*, by Nancy Etchemendy.

Tips: "Take a look at the recent titles to see what sort of materials we're interested in, especially for nonfiction. Please note that we aren't doing the sort of strictly educational nonfiction that other publishers specialize in."

CROSSQUARTER PUBLISHING GROUP, P.O. Box 8756, Santa Fe NM 87504. (505)438-9846. Website: www.crossquarter.com. **Acquisitions:** Anthony Ravenscroft. Publishes case and trade paperback originals and reprints. **Publishes 5-10 titles/year. Receives 250 queries/year. 90% of books from first-time authors. Pays 8-10% royalty on wholesale or retail price.** Publishes book 1 year after acceptance of ms. Accepts simultaneous submissions. Responds in 3 months to queries. Book catalog for $1.75; ms guidelines online.

"We emphasize personal sovereignty, self responsibility and growth with pagan or pagan-friendly emphasis for young adults and adults."

Nonfiction: Biography, how-to, self-help. Subjects include health/medicine, nature/environment, New Age, philosophy, psychology, religion (pagan only), spirituality, autobiography. Query with SASE. Reviews artwork/photos as part of ms package. Send photocopies.

Fiction: Science fiction, visionary fiction. Query with SASE.

Recent Title(s): *Dead as I'll Ever Be: Psychic Adventures that Changed My Life*, by Pamela Evans; *Beyond One's Own*, by Gabriel Constans; *The Shamrock and The Feather*, by Dori Dalton.

Tips: "Audience is earth-conscious people looking to grow into balance of body, mind, heart and spirit."

CROSSWAY BOOKS, Division of Good News Publishers, 1300 Crescent St., Wheaton IL 60187-5800. (630)682-4300. Fax: (630)682-4785. Website: www.crosswaybooks.org. Vice President: Marvin Padgett. **Acquisitions:** Jill Carter. Estab. 1938. Publishes hardcover and trade paperback originals. **Publishes 85 titles/year. Receives 2,500 submissions/year. 2% of books from first-time authors; 75% from unagented writers. Pays negotiable royalty. Offers negotiable advance.** Publishes book 18 months after acceptance of ms. Accepts simultaneous submissions. Responds in up to 3 months to queries; 3 months to mss. Book catalog for 9×12 SAE with 7 first-class stamps; ms guidelines online.

"With 'making a difference in people's lives for Christ' as its maxim, Crossway Books lists titles written from an evangelical Christian worldview."

Nonfiction: Subjects include religion, spirituality. "Books that provide fresh understanding and a distinctively Christian examination of questions confronting Christians and non-Christians in their personal lives, families, churches, communities and the wider culture. The main types include: (1) Issues books that typically address critical issues facing Christians today; (2) Books on the deeper Christian life that provide a deeper understanding of Christianity and its application to daily life; and, (3) Christian academic and professional books directed at an audience of religious professionals. Books must be written from an evangelical Christian worldview. Writers often give sketchy information on their book's content." Query with SASE. No phone queries.

Fiction: Historical, literary, western, Christian. "We publish fiction that falls into these categories: (1) Christian realism, or novels set in modern, true-to-life settings as a means of telling stories about Christians today in an increasingly post-Christian era; (2) Supernatural fiction, or stories typically set in the 'real world' but that bring supernatural reality into it in a way that heightens our spiritual dimension; (3) Historical fiction, using historical characters, times and places of interest as a mirror for our own times; (4) Some genre-technique fiction (mystery, western); and (5) Children's fiction. We are not interested in romance novels, horror novels, biblical novels (i.e., stories set in Bible times that fictionalize events in the lives of prominent biblical characters), issues novels (i.e., fictionalized treatments of contemporary issues), and end times/prophecy novels. We do not accept full manuscripts or electronic submissions." Query with SASE. Submit book summary, chapter by chapter synopsis with 2 sample chapters and SASE.

Recent Title(s): *The Hidden Smile of God*, by John Piper (nonfiction); *Cry Freedom*, by Marlo Schalesky (fiction).

Tips: "All of our books must have 'Christian' content—combine the Truth of God's Word with a passion to live it out. Writers often submit without thinking about what a publisher actually publishes. They also send full manuscripts without a synopsis. Without a synopsis, the manuscript does not get read."

N **CROWN BUSINESS**, Random House, Inc., 1745 Broadway, New York NY 10019. (212)572-2275. Fax: (212)572-6192. E-mail: jmahaney@randomhouse.com. Website: www.crownbusiness.com. **Acquisitions:** John Mahaney, executive editor. Estab. 1995. Publishes hardcover and trade paperback originals. **Publishes 20-25 titles/year. 50% of books from first-time authors; 15% from unagented writers. Pays standard hardcover and trade paperback royalties. Offers negotiable advance.** Publishes book 9 months after acceptance of ms. Accepts simultaneous submissions. Responds in 1 month to proposals. Book catalog online.

Nonfiction: Subjects include business/economics, money/finance, management, technology. Query with proposal package including outline, 1-2 sample chapters, market analysis and SASE.

Recent Title(s): *Execution: The Discipline of Getting Things Done*, by Larry Bossidy and Ram Charan.

CSLI PUBLICATIONS, Ventura Hall, Stanford University, Stanford CA 94305-4115. (650)723-1839. Fax: (650)725-2166. E-mail: pubs@csli.stanford.edu. Website: cslipublications.stanford.edu. **Acquisitions:** Dikran Karagueuzian, director (linguistics, philosophy, logic, computer science). Publishes hardcover and scholarly paperback originals. **Publishes 40 titles/year. Receives 200 queries and 50 mss/year. Pays 3-10% royalty; honorarium.** Publishes book 1 year after acceptance of ms. Does not accept simultaneous submissions. Responds in 1 month to queries; 4 months to proposals; 6 months to mss. Book catalog free; ms guidelines online.

"CSLI Publications, part of the Center for the Study of Language and Information, specializes in books in the areas of formal linguistics, logic, philosophy, computer science and human-computer interaction." Currently emphasizing human-computer interaction, computers and media, voice technology, pragmatic linguistics.

Nonfiction: Reference, technical, textbook, scholarly. Subjects include anthropology/archeology, computers/electronic, language/literature (linguistics), science, logic, cognitive science. Query with SASE or by email.

Recent Title(s): *Computer Prediction*, by Stefan Muller; *On the Formal Way to Chinese Languages*, edited by Sao-Wing Zang and Chen-Sheng Luthan Liu; *Collaborative Language Engineering*, edited by Stephan Oepen, et. al.

CUMBERLAND HOUSE PUBLISHING, 431 Harding Industrial Dr., Nashville TN 37211. (615)832-1171. Fax: (615)832-0633. E-mail: info@cumberlandhouse.com. Website: www.cumberlandhouse.com. **Acquisitions:** Tilly Katz, acquisitions editor. Estab. 1996. Publishes hardcover, trade paperback and mass market originals and reprints. **Publishes 60 titles/year; imprint publishes 5 titles/year. Receives 3,000 queries and 500 mss/year. 30% of books from first-time authors; 80% from unagented writers. Pays 10-15% royalty on net receipts. Offers $500-5,000 advance.** Publishes book an average of 12 months after acceptance of ms. Accepts simultaneous submissions. Responds in 6 months to queries; 6 months to proposals; 1 year to mss. Book catalog for 8×10 SAE with 4 first-class stamps; ms guidelines online.

Imprints: Cumberland House Hearthside, Highland Books.

Cumberland House publishes "market specific books. We evaluate in terms of how sure we are that we can publish the book successfully and then the quality or uniqueness of a project." Currently emphasizing nonfiction. Deemphasizing nonfiction and mystery.

Nonfiction: Cookbook, gift book, how-to, humor, reference. Subjects include Americana, cooking/foods/nutrition, government/politics, history, military/war, recreation, regional, sports, travel, popular culture, civil war. Query or submit outline. Reviews artwork/photos as part of ms package. Send photocopies only; not original copies.

Fiction: Historical, mystery. Writers should know "the odds are really stacked against them." Query with SASE.

Recent Title(s): *Why a Daughter Needs a Dad*, by Greg Lang.

Tips: Audience is "adventuresome people who like a fresh approach to things. Writers should tell what their idea is, why it's unique and why somebody would want to buy it—but don't pester us."

N A **CURRENCY**, 1540 Broadway, New York NY 10036. (212)782-9730. Fax: (212)782-8911. E-mail: rscholl@randomhouse.com. **Acquisitions:** Roger Scholl, editorial director. Estab. 1989. **Pays 7½-15% royalty on retail price. Offers advance.** Publishes book 1 year after acceptance of ms.

Currency publishes "business books for people who want to make a difference, not just a living."

Nonfiction: Subjects include marketing, investment. *Agented submissions only.*

Recent Title(s): *Managing Up*; *Don't Mess with My Money.*

CURRENT CLINICAL STRATEGIES PUBLISHING, 27071 Cabot Rd., Suite 126, Laguna Hills CA 92653. Fax: (949)348-8405. E-mail: info@ccspublishing.com. Website: www.ccspublishing.com. **Acquisitions:** Camille deTonnancour, editor. Estab. 1988. Publishes trade paperback originals. **Publishes 20 titles/year. Receives 10 queries and 10 mss/year. 30% of books from first-time authors; 20% from unagented writers. Pays royalty.** Publishes book 6 months after acceptance of ms.

Current Clinical Strategies is a medical publisher for healthcare professionals.

Nonfiction: Technical. Subjects include health/medicine. *Physician authors only.* Submit 6 sample chapter(s). Reviews artwork/photos as part of ms package. Send ms by e-mail only.

Recent Title(s): *Psychiatry*, by Rhoda Hahn, M.D.; *Anesthesiology*, by Mark Ezekiel, M.D.

CYCLE PUBLISHING, (formerly Van Der Plas Publications), 1282 Seventh Ave., San Francisco CA 94122-2526. (415)665-8214. Fax: (415)753-8572. **Acquisitions:** Rob van der Plas, publisher/editor. Estab. 1997. Publishes hardcover and trade paperback originals. **Publishes 6 titles/year. Receives 15 submissions/year. 10% of books from first-time authors; 100% from unagented writers. Pays 12% royalty on net receipts.** Publishes book an average of 1 year after acceptance of ms. Accepts simultaneous submissions. Responds in 3 months to queries. Book catalog and ms guidelines for #10 SASE.

Nonfiction: How-to, technical. Subjects include recreation, sports, travel. Submit complete ms. Reviews artwork/photos as part of ms package.

Recent Title(s): *Lance Armstrong's Comeback from Cancer*; *Buying a Manufactured Home.*

Tips: "Writers have a good chance selling us books with better and more illustrations and a systematic treatment of the subject. First check what is on the market and ask yourself whether you are writing something that is not yet available and wanted."

N **DA CAPO PRESS**, Perseus Books Group, 11 Cambridge Center, Cambridge MA 02142. Website: www.dacapopress.com. Estab. 1975. Publishes hardcover originals and trade paperback originals and reprints. **Publishes 200 titles/year; imprint publishes 60 titles/year. Receives 500 queries and 300 mss/year. 25% of books from first-time authors; 1% from unagented writers. Pays 7-10% royalty. Offers $1,000-100,000 advance.** Publishes book 3-6 months after acceptance of ms. Accepts simultaneous submissions. Responds in 6 months to queries; 6 months to proposals; 6 months to mss. Book catalog online; ms guidelines online.

Nonfiction: Autobiography, biography, coffee table book, gift book. Subjects include art/architecture, contemporary culture, creative nonfiction, general nonfiction, government/politics, history, language/literature, memoirs, military/war, social sciences, sports, translation, travel, world affairs. Does not accept electronic submissions or take phone calls regarding submissions. Query with SASE or submit proposal package including outline, 3 sample chapter(s), c.v. Reviews artwork/photos as part of ms package. Send photocopies.

Recent Title(s): *My Turf*, by William Nack; *The Man Behind the Guns*, by Edward G. Longacre; *How to Lose Friends & Alienate People*, by Toby Young.

N **DAN RIVER PRESS**, Conservatory of American Letters, P.O. Box 298, Thomaston ME 04861-0298. (207)354-0998. Fax: (207)354-0998. E-mail: cal@americanletters.org. Website: www.americanletters.org. **Acquisitions:** Richard S. Danbury, fiction editor. Estab. 1977. Publishes hardcover and paperback originals. **Publishes 8-10 titles/year. Pays 10-15% royalty. Offers occassional advance.** Publishes book 3-4 months after acceptance of ms. Accepts simultaneous submissions. Responds in 2-3 days to queries. Book catalog for 6 X 9 SAE with 60¢ postage affixed; ms guidelines online.

"Small press publisher of fiction and biographies owned by a nonprofit foundation."

Fiction: Fantasy (space fantasy, sword and sorcery), historical (general), horror (dark fantasy, futuristic, psychological, supernatural), humor, literary, mainstream/contemporary, mystery (amateur sleuth, police procedural, private eye/hard-boiled), regional, religious (general religious, inspirational, religious mystery/suspense, religious thriller, religious romance), romance (contemporary, futuristic/time travel, gothic, historical, romantic suspense), science fiction (hard science/technological, soft/sociological), short story collections, suspense (amateur sleuth, police procedural, private eye/hardboiled), western (frontier saga, traditional), outdoors/fishing/hunting/camping/trapping. Submit publishing history, synopsis, author bio. Cover Letter or query should include estimated word count, brief bio and brief publishing history. Query should also deal with marketing ideas. Be specific ("All Women" is not a marketing idea we can work with) and social security number, #10 SASE.

Poetry: Publishes poetry and fiction anthology (submission guidelines to *Dan River Anthology* on the Web or send #10 SASE).

Recent Title(s): *Dan River Anthology 2003*, by R.S. Danbury III, editor (poetry and short stories); *Wytopitloc: Tales of a Deer Hunter*, by Ed Rau Jr. (hunting stories).

Tips: "Spend some time developing a following. Forget the advice as 'Your first job is to find a publisher!' That's nonsense. Your first job as a writer is to develop an audience. Do that and a publisher will find you."

THE DANA PRESS, 900 15th St. NW, Washington DC 20005. (202)737-9200. Fax: (202)737-9204. Website: www.dana.org/books/press. **Acquisitions:** Jane Nevins, editor-in-chief. Publishes hardcover and trade paperback originals. **Publishes**

4 titles/year. Receives 10 queries and 3 mss/year. 50% of books from first-time authors; 90% from unagented writers. Pays 14-20% royalty on wholesale price. Offers $10,000-35,000 advance. Publishes book 1 year after acceptance of ms. Accepts simultaneous submissions. Responds in 2 weeks to queries; 1 month to proposals; 2 months to mss. Book catalog and ms guidelines online; ms guidelines online.

Nonfiction: Biography, coffee table book, self-help, brain-related health books. Subjects include health/medicine, memoirs, psychology, science. "We focus almost exclusively on the brain." Reviews artwork/photos as part of ms package. Send photocopies.

Recent Title(s): *The Dana Guide to Brain Health*, edited by Floyd E. Bloom, M.D., M. Flint Beal, M.D., and David J. Kupfer, M.D.

Tips: "Coherent, thought-out proposals are key. What is the scope of the book? Who is the reader? It's important to have an angle."

JOHN DANIEL AND CO., Daniel & Daniel, Publishers, Inc., P.O. Box 2790, McKinleyville CA 95519. (707)839-3495. Fax: (805)962-8835. E-mail: jd@danielpublishing.com. Website: www.danielpublishing.com. **Acquisitions:** John Daniel, publisher. Estab. 1980. Publishes hardcover originals and trade paperback originals. Publishes poetry, fiction and nonfiction. **Publishes 4 titles/year. Pays 10% royalty on wholesale price. Offers $0-500 advance.** Publishes book 1 year after acceptance of ms. Accepts simultaneous submissions. Responds in 1 month to queries; 1 month to proposals; 2 months to mss. Book catalog free or online; ms guidelines online.

Nonfiction: Biography, essay. Subjects include creative nonfiction, memoirs. "We seldom publish books over 70,000 words. Other than that, we're looking for books that are important and well-written." Query with SASE or submit proposal package including outline, 50 pages.

Fiction: Literary, poetry, short story collections. Publishes poetry, fiction and nonfiction; specializes in belles lettres, literary memoir. Query with SASE or submit proposal package including synopsis, 50 pages.

Poetry: "We publish very little poetry, I'm sorry to say." Query or submit complete ms.

Recent Title(s): *Home Is Where the Bus Is*, by Anne Beck with Johnson (travel memoir); *The House on Q Street*, by Ann L. McLaughlin (novel); *Shot with Eros*, by Glenna Luschei (poetry).

Tips: "Literate, intelligent general readers. We are very small and very cautious, so any submission to us is a long shot. But we welcome your submissions. By mail only, please. We don't want submissions by phone, fax, disk, or e-mail."

DANTE UNIVERSITY OF AMERICA PRESS, INC., P.O. Box 812158, Wellesley MA 02482. Fax: (781)790-1056. E-mail: danteu@danteuniversity.org. Website: www.danteuniversity.org/dpress.html. **Acquisitions:** Adolph Caso, president. Estab. 1975. Publishes hardcover and trade paperback originals and reprints. **Publishes 5 titles/year. Receives 50 submissions/year. 50% of books from first-time authors; 50% from unagented writers. Pays royalty. Offers negotiable advance.** Publishes book 10 months after acceptance of ms. Responds in 2 months to queries.

O→ "The Dante University Press exists to bring quality, educational books pertaining to our Italian heritage as well as the historical and political studies of America. Profits from the sale of these publications benefit the Foundation, bringing Dante University closer to a reality."

Nonfiction: Biography, reference, scholarly, reprints. Subjects include history (Italian-American), humanities, translation (from Italian and latin), general scholarly nonfiction, Renaissance thought and letter, Italian language and linguistics, Italian-American culture, bilingual education. Query with SASE. Reviews artwork/photos as part of ms package.

Fiction: Translations from Italian and Latin. Query with SASE.

Poetry: "There is a chance that we would use Renaissance poetry translations."

Recent Title(s): *The Prince*, by Machiavelli (social sciences); *The Kaso Dictionary—English-Italian* (reference).

MAY DAVENPORT, PUBLISHERS, 26313 Purissima Rd., Los Altos Hills CA 94022. (650)947-1275. Fax: (650)947-1373. E-mail: mdbooks@earthlink.net. Website: www.maydavenportpublishers.com. **Acquisitions:** May Davenport, editor/publisher. Estab. 1976. Publishes hardcover and paperback originals. **Publishes 4 titles/year. Receives 1,500 submissions/year. 95% of books from first-time authors; 100% from unagented writers. Pays 15% royalty on retail price. Offers no advance.** Publishes book 1 year after acceptance of ms. Responds in 1 month to queries. Book catalog for #10 SASE; ms guidelines for #10 SASE.

Imprints: md Books (nonfiction and fiction).

O→ May Davenport publishes "literature for teenagers (before they graduate from high schools) as supplementary literary material in English courses nationwide." Looking particularly for authors able to write for the "teen Internet" generation who don't like to read in-depth. Currently emphasizing more upper-level subjects for teens.

Nonfiction: Subjects include Americana, language/literature, humorous memoirs for chldren/young adults. "For children ages 6-8: stories to read with pictures to color in 500 words. For preteens and young adults: exhibit your writing skills and entertain them with your literary tools." Query with SASE.

Fiction: Humor, literary. "We want to focus on novels junior and senior high school teachers can share with their reluctant readers in their classrooms." Query with SASE.

Recent Title(s): *The Runaway Game*, by Kevin Casey (nonfiction); *Significant Footsteps*, by Ashleigh E. Grange (fiction); *The Lesson Plan*, by Irvin Gay (fiction).

Tips: "If you have to write only about the ills of today's society of incest, murders, homelessness, divorce, one-parent families, just write your fictional novel humorously. If you can't write that way, create youthful characters so teachers, as well as 15-18 year-old high school readers, will laugh at your descriptive passages and contemporary dialogue. Avoid one-sentence paragraphs. The audience we want to reach is past Nancy Drew and Hardy Boy readers."

JONATHAN DAVID PUBLISHERS, INC., 68-22 Eliot Ave., Middle Village NY 11379-1194. (718)456-8611. Fax: (718)894-2818. E-mail: info@jdbooks.com. Website: www.jdbooks.com. **Acquisitions:** Alfred J. Kolatch, editor-in-chief. Estab. 1948. Publishes hardcover and trade paperback originals and reprints. **Publishes 20-25 titles/year. 50% of books from first-time authors; 90% from unagented writers. Pays royalty or makes outright purchase.** Publishes book 18 months after acceptance of ms. Responds in 1 month to queries; 1 month to proposals; 2 months to mss. Book catalog online; ms guidelines online.

O➛ Jonathan David publishes "popular Judaica." Currently emphasizing projects geared toward children.

Nonfiction: Biography, children's/juvenile, coffee table book, cookbook, gift book, how-to, humor, illustrated book, reference, self-help. Subjects include cooking/foods/nutrition, creative nonfiction, ethnic, humor, multicultural, religion, sex, sports. Query with SASE or submit proposal package including outline, 3 sample chapter(s), résumé. Reviews artwork/photos as part of ms package. Send photocopies.

Recent Title(s): *Drawing a Crowd*, by Bill Gallo (sports cartoons/memoir).

DAVIS PUBLICATIONS, INC., 50 Portland St., Worcester MA 01608. (508)754-7201. Fax: (508)753-3834. **Acquisitions:** Claire M. Golding, editor-in-chief. Estab. 1901. **Publishes 5-10 titles/year. Pays 10-12% royalty. Offers advance.** Publishes book 1 year after acceptance of ms. Does not accept simultaneous submissions. Book catalog for 9×12 SAE with $2 U.S. postage; ms guidelines for #10 SASE.

O➛ Davis publishes art, design and craft books for the elementary through high school art education markets. Our mission is to produce materials that help art teachers do their job better.

Nonfiction: Illustrated book. Subjects include art/architecture, education, history. Submit outline, sample chapter(s). Reviews artwork/photos as part of ms package.

Recent Title(s): *From Ordinary to Extraordinary, Art and Design Problem-Solving*, by Ken Vieth; *Creative Coloring*, by Art Sherwyn; *You Can Weave!*, by Kathleen Monaghan.

Tips: "Keep in mind the intended audience. Our readers are visually oriented. Photos should be good quality transparencies and black and white photographs. Well-selected illustrations should explain, amplify, and enhance the text. We average 2-4 photos/page. We like to see technique photos as well as illustrations of finished artwork, by a variety of artists, including students. Recent books have been on using technology in art teaching, printmaking, art education profession, history through art timeline. We do not publish fiction or poetry in any form!"

DAW BOOKS, INC., Penguin Putnam, Inc., 375 Hudson St., 3rd Floor, New York NY 10014-3658. (212)366-2096. Fax: (212)366-2090. E-mail: daw@penguinputnam.com. Website: www.dawbooks.com. Publishers: Elizabeth Wollheim and Sheila Gilbert. **Acquisitions:** Peter Stampfel, submissions editor. Estab. 1971. Publishes hardcover and paperback originals and reprints. **Publishes 60-80 titles/year. Pays in royalties with an advance negotiable on a book-by-book basis.** Book catalog free; ms guidelines online.

- Simultaneous submissions "returned unread at once, unless prior arrangements are made by agent."

O➛ DAW Books publishes science fiction and fantasy.

Fiction: Fantasy, science fiction. "We are interested in science fiction and fantasy novels. We need science fiction more than fantasy right now, but we're still looking for both. We like character-driven books with attractive characters. We accept both agented and unagented manuscripts. Long books are absolutely not a problem. We are not seeking collections of short stories or ideas for anthologies. We do not want any nonfiction manuscripts." Query with SASE. Simultaneous submissions "returned unread at once unless prior arrangements are made by agent."

Recent Title(s): *The Joust*, by Mercedes Lacky (fantasy); *The War of the Flowers*, by Tad Williams (fantasy).

DAWN PUBLICATIONS, P.O. Box 2010, Nevada City CA 95959. (530)478-0111. Fax: (530)478-0112. E-mail: nature@dawnpub.com. Website: www.dawnpub.com. **Acquisitions:** Glenn Hovemann, editor. Estab. 1979. Publishes hardcover and trade paperback originals. **Publishes 6 titles/year. Receives 550 queries and 2,500 mss/year. 15% of books from first-time authors; 90% from unagented writers. Pays royalty on net receipts. Offers advance.** Publishes book 1 to 2 years after acceptance of ms. Accepts simultaneous submissions. Responds in 2 months to queries. Book catalog online; ms guidelines online.

O➛ Dawn Publications is dedicated to inspiring in children a sense of appreciation for all life on earth. Dawn looks for nature awareness and appreciation titles that promote a relationship with the natural world and specific habitats, usually through inspiring treatment and nonfiction.

Nonfiction: Children's/juvenile. Subjects include animals, nature/environment. Query with SASE.

Recent Title(s): *Salmon Stream*, by Carol Reed-Jones; *In One Tidepool*, by Anthony Fredericks; *The Okomi Series*, with Jane Goodall.

Tips: Publishes mostly nonfiction with lightness and inspiration.

[N] **DBS PRODUCTIONS**, P.O. Box 1894, Charlottesville VA 22903. (800)745-1581. Fax: (434)293-5502. E-mail: robert@dbs-sar.com. Website: www.dbs-sar.com. **Acquisitions:** Bob Adams, publisher. Estab. 1989. Publishes hardcover and trade paperback originals. **Publishes 6 titles/year. Receives 5 queries/year. 5% of books from first-time authors; 100% from unagented writers. Pays 5-20% royalty on retail price.** Publishes book 1 year after acceptance of ms. Does not accept simultaneous submissions. Responds in 2 months to queries. Book catalog on request or on website; ms guidelines for #10 SASE.

O➛ dbs Productions produces search and rescue and outdoor first-aid related materials and courses. It offers a selection of publications, videotapes, management kits and tools and instructional modules.

Nonfiction: Technical, textbook. Subjects include health/medicine. Submit proposal package including outline, 2 sample chapter(s). Reviews artwork/photos as part of ms package. Send photocopies.

Recent Title(s): *Field Operations Guide for Search and Rescue, 2nd Edition*, by R. Koester.

N **DEAD END STREET, LLC**, 813 Third St., Hoquiam WA 98550. (415)378-7401. E-mail: submissions@deadendstreet.com. Website: deadendstreet.com. Director of Publications: Ivan Black. **Acquisitions:** John Rutledge, director of submissions. Estab. 1997. Publishes all genres and seeks "cutting edge authors who represent the world's dead end streets." **Pays 10-40% royalties, and 10 author's copies.** Publishes book 6 months after acceptance of ms. Accepts simultaneous submissions. Responds in 1 month to submissions to queries. Book catalog online; ms guidelines online.

Poetry: Accepts poetry written by children. Sample books available on website. "We require electonic submissions via e-mail in MS Word or Word Perfect." Cover letter required.

DEARBORN, Trade Publishing, 30 S. Wacker Dr., Suite 2500, Chicago IL 60606-1719. (312)836-4400. Fax: (312)836-1021. E-mail: posek@dearborn.com. Website: www.dearborntrade.com. **Acquisitions:** Cynthia Zigmund, VP/publisher/editorial director; Jonathan Malysiak, senior acquisitions editor (general business/management); Mary Good, acquisitions editor (consumer real estate, personal finance); Michael Cunningham, acquisitions editor (sales & marketing). Estab. 1959. Publishes hardcover and paperback originals. **Publishes 50 titles/year. Receives 400 submissions/year. 30% of books from first-time authors; 50% from unagented writers. Pays 10-15% royalty on wholesale price. Offers advance.** Publishes book 6 months after acceptance of ms. Accepts simultaneous submissions. Responds in 1 month to queries. Book catalog and ms guidelines free.

O→ The trade division of Dearborn publishes practical, solutions-oriented books for individuals and corporations on the subjects of finance, consumer real estate, business and entrepreneurship. Currently emphasizing finance, general business/management, consumer real estate. De-emphasizing small business.

Nonfiction: How-to, reference, textbook. Subjects include business/economics, money/finance. Query with SASE.

Recent Title(s): *The Power of Six Sigma*, by Subir Chowdhury; *Flipping Properties*, by William Bronchick; *Millionaire Real Estate Mentor*, by Russ Whitney.

IVAN R. DEE, PUBLISHER, The Rowman & Littlefield Publishing Group, 1332 N. Halsted St., Chicago IL 60622-2694. (312)787-6262. Fax: (312)787-6269. E-mail: elephant@ivanrdee.com. Website: www.ivanrdee.com. **Acquisitions:** Ivan R. Dee, president; Hilary Schaefer, associate editor. Estab. 1988. Publishes hardcover originals and trade paperback originals and reprints. **Publishes 60 titles/year. 10% of books from first-time authors; 80% from unagented writers. Pays royalty. Offers advance.** Publishes book 8 months after acceptance of ms. Accepts simultaneous submissions. Responds in 1 month to queries; 1 month to proposals; 1 month to mss. Book catalog free.

Imprints: Elephant Paperbacks, New Amsterdam Books, J.S. Sanders Books.

O→ Ivan R. Dee publishes serious nonfiction for general informed readers.

Nonfiction: Biography. Subjects include art/architecture, film/cinema/stage, government/politics, history, language/literature, world affairs, contemporary culture, film/cinema/stage, baseball. Submit outline, sample chapter(s). Reviews artwork/photos as part of ms package.

Recent Title(s): *Good Morning, Mr. Zip Zip Zip*, by Richard Schickel; *Are Cops Racist?*, by Heather MacDonald; *A History of the Dora Camp*, by Andre Sellier.

Tips: "We publish for an intelligent lay audience and college course adoptions."

A **DEL REY BOOKS**, Ballantine Publishing Group, Random House, Inc., 1745 Broadway, 18th Floor, New York NY 10019. (212)782-8393. E-mail: delrey@randomhouse.com. Website: www.randomhouse.com/delrey. **Acquisitions:** Betsy Mitchell, VP & editor-in-chief (science fiction, fantasy); Shelly Shapiro, editorial director (science fiction, fantasy); Steve Saffel, executive editor (fantasy, alternate history, media tie-ins); Chris Schluep, editor (science fiction, fantasy). Estab. 1977. Publishes hardcover, trade paperback, and mass market originals and mass market paperback reprints. **Publishes 140 titles/year. Receives 1,900 submissions/year. 10% of books from first-time authors; 0% from unagented writers. Pays royalty on retail price. Offers competitive advance.** Publishes book 1 year after acceptance of ms. Does not accept simultaneous submissions. Responds in 6 months to queries. Ms guidelines online.

O→ Del Rey publishes top level fantasy, alternate history, and science fiction.

Fiction: Fantasy (should have the practice of magic as an essential element of the plot), science fiction (well-plotted novels with good characterizations, exotic locales and detailed alien creatures), alternate history ("novels that take major historical events, such as the Civil War, and bend history in a new direction sometimes through science fiction and fantasy devices.") *Agented submissions only.*

Recent Title(s): *Vitals*, by Greg Bear; *Morgawr*, by Terry Brooks; *The Scar*, by China Miéville.

Tips: "Del Rey is a reader's house. Pay particular attention to plotting, strong characters, and dramatic, satisfactory conclusions. It must be/feel believable. That's what the readers like. In terms of mass market, we basically created the field of fantasy bestsellers. Not that it didn't exist before, but we put the mass into mass market."

THE DENALI PRESS, P.O. Box 021535, Juneau AK 99802-1535. (907)586-6014. Fax: (907)463-6780. E-mail: denalipress@alaska.com. Website: www.denalipress.com. **Acquisitions:** Alan Schorr, editorial director; Sally Silvas-Ottumwa, editorial associate. Estab. 1986. Publishes trade paperback originals. **Publishes 5 titles/year. Receives 120 submissions/year. 50% of books from first-time authors; 80% from unagented writers. Pays 10% royalty on wholesale price or makes outright purchase. Offers advance.** Publishes book 1 year after acceptance of ms. Accepts simultaneous submissions. Responds in 1 month to queries.

O→ The Denali Press looks for reference works suitable for the educational, professional and library market. "Though we publish books on a variety of topics, our focus is most broadly centered on multiculturalism, public policy, Alaskana, and general reference works."

Nonfiction: Reference. Subjects include Americana, anthropology/archeology, ethnic, government/politics, history, multicultural, recreation, regional. "We need reference books—ethnic, refugee and minority concerns." Query with SASE or submit outline, sample chapter(s). **All unsolicited mss returned unopened.**

Recent Title(s): *Winning Political Campaigns: A Comprehensive Guide to Electoral Success*, by William S. Bike.

DESCANT PUBLISHING, P.O. Box 12973, Mill Creek WA 98082. (206)235-3357. Fax: (646)365-7513. Website: www.descantpub.com. **Acquisitions:** Bret Sable, senior editor (nonfiction); Alex Royal, editor (fiction). Estab. 2001. Publishes hardcover, trade paperback, mass market paperback, and electronic originals. **Publishes 10-12 titles/year. Receives 1,200 queries/year. 50% of books from first-time authors; 50% from unagented writers. Pays 6-15% royalty.** Publishes book 18 months after acceptance of ms. Accepts simultaneous submissions. Responds in 3 months to queries; 3 months to proposals; 3 months to mss. Ms guidelines for #10 SASE.

Nonfiction: Children's/juvenile, how-to, self-help. Subjects include community, contemporary culture, creative nonfiction, education, general nonfiction, humanities, memoirs, music/dance, religion, spirituality. Submissions should be original and timely. "Our nonfiction must capture a known audience." Query with SASE.

Fiction: Fantasy, horror, mainstream/contemporary, mystery, religious, science fiction, suspense. Fresh storylines are critical. Query with SASE.

Recent Title(s): *From White House to Crack House*, by Nancy Dudley (current affairs); *At the Manger: The Stories of Those Who Were There*, by Peter Orullian (historical fiction).

N **DEVORSS & CO.**, DeVorss Publications, P.O. Box 1389, Camarillo CA 93011-1389. E-mail: editorial@devorss.com. Website: www.devorss.com. Publishes hardcover and trade paperback originals and reprints. **Receives 700 queries and 300 mss/year. 95% of books from first-time authors; 100% from unagented writers. 10% maximum royalty on retail price.** Publishes book 6 months after acceptance of ms. Accepts simultaneous submissions. Responds in 1 month to mss. Book catalog for #10 SASE; ms guidelines for #10 SASE.

Nonfiction: Children's/juvenile, gift book, self-help, Body, Mind, and Spirit. Subjects include creative nonfiction, philosophy, psychology, spirituality, Body, Mind, and Spirit. Query with SASE. Reviews artwork/photos as part of ms package. Send photocopies.

Recent Title(s): *Little Green Apples*, by O.C. Smith and James Shaw.

Tips: "Our audience is people using their mind to improve health, finances, relationships, life changes, etc. Ask for guidelines first. Don't submit outlines, proposals, or manuscripts. Don't call. Please send submissions and inquiries by mail only."

A **DIAL BOOKS FOR YOUNG READERS**, Penguin Group USA, 345 Hudson St., 14th Floor, New York NY 10014. (212)366-2000. Website: www.penguinputnam.com. President/Publisher: Nancy Paulsen. Associate Publisher/Editorial Director: Lauri Hornik. **Acquisitions:** Submissions Editor. Estab. 1961. Publishes hardcover originals. **Publishes 50 titles/year. Receives 5,000 queries/year. 20% of books from first-time authors. Pays royalty. Offers varies advance.** Does not accept simultaneous submissions. Responds in 3 months to queries. Book catalog for 9 x12 SAE with 4 first-class stamps.

O━ Dial Books for Young Readers publishes quality picture books for ages 18 months-8 years, lively, believable novels for middle readers and young adults, and occasional nonfiction for middle readers and young adults.

Nonfiction: Children's/juvenile, illustrated book. Accepts unsolicited queries.

Fiction: Adventure, fantasy, juvenile, picture books, young adult. Especially looking for "lively and well-written novels for middle grade and young adult children involving a convincing plot and believable characters. The subject matter or theme should not already be overworked in previously published books. The approach must not be demeaning to any minority group, nor should the roles of female characters (or others) be stereotyped, though we don't think books should be didactic, or in any way message-y. No topics inappropriate for the juvenile, young adult, and middle grade audiences. No plays." Query with SASE. Accepts unsolicited queries for longer works and unsolicited mss for picture books.

Recent Title(s): *Asteroid Impact*, by Doug Henderson; *A Year Down Yonder*, by Richard Peck; *The Missing Mitten Mystery*, by Steven Kellogg.

Tips: "Our readers are anywhere from preschool age to teenage. Picture books must have strong plots, lots of action, unusual premises, or universal themes treated with freshness and originality. Humor works well in these books. A very well thought out and intelligently presented book has the best chance of being taken on. Genre isn't as much of a factor as presentation."

A **DIAL PRESS**, Bantam Dell Publishing Group, Random House, Inc., 1745 Broadway, New York NY 10019. (212)782-9000. Fax: (212)782-9523. Website: www.randomhouse.com/bantamdell/. **Acquisitions:** Susan Kamil, vice president, editorial director. Estab. 1924. **Publishes 6-12 titles/year. Receives 200 queries and 450 mss/year. 75% of books from first-time authors. Pays royalty on retail price. Offers advance.** Publishes book 18 months after acceptance of ms. Accepts simultaneous submissions.

O━ Dial Press publishes quality fiction and nonfiction. *Agented submissions only.*

Nonfiction: Biography. Subjects include contemporary culture, history, memoirs. *Agented submissions only.*

Fiction: Literary (general). *Agented submissions only.*

Recent Title(s): *American Chica* (nonfiction); *Mary and O'Neil* (stories); *Niagara Falls All Over Again* (novel).

DIMI PRESS, 3820 Oak Hollow Lane, SE, Salem OR 97302-4774. (503)364-7698. Fax: (503)364-9727. E-mail: dickbook @earthlink.net. Website: www.home.earthlink.net/~dickbook. **Acquisitions:** Dick Lutz, president. Publishes trade paperback originals. **Publishes 5 titles/year. Receives 100-150 queries and 20-25 mss/year. 80% of books from first-time authors; 90% from unagented writers. Pays 10% royalty on net receipts.** Publishes book 9 months after acceptance of ms. Accepts simultaneous submissions. Responds in 1 month to queries. Book catalog online; ms guidelines online.

"We provide accurate information about unusual things in nature." Currently de-emphasizing self-help books. No mss until requested.

Nonfiction: Subjects include animals, nature/environment, science. "Soliciting manuscripts on unusual things in nature, such as unusual animals or natural formations. Also natural disasters such as volcanic eruptions, earthquakes, or floods. Preferably of the world's 'worst.' Also related manuscripts on nature/travel/environment. No travel guides." Query with SASE or submit outline, 1 sample chapter(s). Reviews artwork/photos as part of ms package. Send photocopies.

Recent Title(s): *The Running Indians*; *Komodo, The Living Dragon*; *Hidden Amazon.*

Tips: "Audience is adults who wish to learn something and are interested in unusual travel excursions. Also assists self-publishers in producing their book. Please check guidelines before submitting."

DISCOVERY ENTERPRISES, LTD., 31 Laurelwood Dr., Carlisle MA 07141. (978)287-5401. Fax: (978)287-5402. E-mail: ushistorydocs@aol.com. **Acquisitions:** JoAnne W. Deitch, president (plays for Readers Theatre, on American history). Publishes trade paperback originals. **Publishes 10 titles/year. Receives 50 queries and 20 mss/year. 5% of books from first-time authors; 90% from unagented writers. Pays 20-20% royalty.** Publishes book 3 months after acceptance of ms. Accepts simultaneous submissions. Responds in 1 month to queries. Book catalog for 6×9 SAE with 3 first-class stamps.

Fiction: "We're interested in 40-minute plays (reading time) for students in grades 4-10 on topics in U.S. history." Historical, plays. Query with SASE or submit complete ms.

Recent Title(s): *Life on the Road to Freedom: Sojourner Truth*, by Sharon Fennessey; *Salem Witch Hunt*, by Hilary Weisman; *Lewis and Clark: Across a Vast Land*, by Harold Torrance.

Tips: "Call or send query letter on topic prior to sending ms for plays. We currently need a play on early colonists in Jamestown or Plymouth; a play on post-Civil War South; a play on the Revolutionary War, focusing on George Washington; and a play on the early Spanish explorers in America."

DO-IT-YOURSELF LEGAL PUBLISHERS, 60 Park Place, Suite 103, Newark NJ 07102. (973)639-0400. Fax: (973)639-1801. **Acquisitions:** Dan Benjamin, associate editor; Anne Torrey, editorial director. Estab. 1978. Publishes trade paperback originals. **Publishes 6 titles/year; imprint publishes 2 titles/year. Receives 25 queries/year. Pays 15-20% royalty on wholesale price.** Publishes book 6 months after acceptance of ms. Accepts simultaneous submissions. Responds in 1 month to queries; 1 month to proposals; 3 months to mss.

Imprints: Selfhelper Law Press of America.

"The fundamental premise underlying our works is that the simplest problems can be effectively handled by anyone with average common sense and a competent guidebook."

Nonfiction: Subject matter should deal with self-help law topics that instruct the lay person on how to undertake legal tasks without the use of attorney or other high cost experts. How-to, self-help. Subjects include law. Query with SASE.

Recent Title(s): *The National Mortgage Qualification Kit*, by Benji O. Anosike, Ph.D.

DORAL PUBLISHING, INC., 2501 W. Behrend Dr. #43, Phoenix AZ 85027. (623)875-2057. Fax: (623)875-2059. E-mail: doralpub@mindspring.com. Website: www.doralpub.com. **Acquisitions:** Alvin Grossman, publisher; Luana Luther, editor-in-chief (purebred dogs). Estab. 1986. Publishes hardcover and trade paperback originals. **Publishes 7 titles/year. Receives 30 queries and 15 mss/year. 85% from unagented writers. Pays 10% royalty on wholesale price.** Publishes book 6 months after acceptance of ms. Does not accept simultaneous submissions. Responds in 2 months to queries. Book catalog free; ms guidelines for #10 SASE.

Doral Publishing publishes only books about dogs and dog-related topics, mostly geared for pure-bred dog owners and showing. Currently emphasizing breed books. De-emphasizing children's work.

Nonfiction: Children's/juvenile, how-to, reference. Subjects include animals, health/medicine. "We are looking for new ideas. No flowery prose. Manuscripts should be literate, intelligent, but easy to read." Subjects must be dog-related. Query with SASE or submit outline, 2 sample chapter(s). Reviews artwork/photos as part of ms package. Send photocopies.

Fiction: Juvenile. Subjects must center around dogs. Either the main character should be a dog or a dog should play an integral role. Query with SASE.

Recent Title(s): *The Mastiff*; *The Welsh Terrier.*

Tips: "We are currently expanding and are looking for new topics and fresh ideas while staying true to our niche. While we will steadfastly maintain that market—we are always looking for excellent breed books—we also want to explore more 'mainstream' topics."

DORCHESTER PUBLISHING CO., INC., 276 Fifth Ave., Suite 1008, New York NY 10001-0112. (212)725-8811. Fax: (212)532-1054. **Offers advance.** Does not accept simultaneous submissions.

Imprints: Love Spell (romance), Leisure Books (romance, westerns, horror), Smooch (young adult).

[A] **DOUBLEDAY**, Doubleday Broadway Publishing Group, Random House, Inc., 1745 Broadway, New York NY 10019. (212)782-9000. Fax: (212)782-9700. Website: www.randomhouse.com. Vice President/Editor-in-Chief: William Thomas. Estab. 1897. Publishes hardcover originals. **Publishes 70 titles/year. Receives thousands of queries and thousands of mss/year. 30% of books from first-time authors. Pays royalty on retail price. Offers advance.** Publishes book 1 year after acceptance of ms. Does not accept simultaneous submissions.

Imprints: Currency; Doubleday Religious Division; Image Books; Nan A. Talese.

- Does not accept any unagented submissions. No exceptions.

Doubleday publishes high-quality fiction and nonfiction.

Nonfiction: Biography. Subjects include Americana, anthropology/archeology, business/economics, computers/electronic, education, ethnic, government/politics, health/medicine, history, language/literature, money/finance, nature/environment,

philosophy, religion, science, sociology, software, sports, translation, women's issues/studies. *Agented submissions only.*
Fiction: Adventure, confession, ethnic, experimental, feminist, gay/lesbian, historical, humor, literary, mainstream/contemporary, religious, short story collections. *Agented submissions only.*
Recent Title(s): *The Street Lawyer*, by John Grisham (fiction).

DOUBLEDAY RELIGIOUS PUBLISHING, Doubleday Broadway Publishing Group, Random House, Inc., 1540 Broadway, New York NY 10036. (212)354-6500. Fax: (212)782-3735. Website: www.randomhouse.com. **Acquisitions:** Michelle Rapkin, vice president, religious division; Trace Murphy, executive editor; Andrew Corbin, editor. Estab. 1897. Publishes hardcover and trade paperback originals and reprints. **Publishes 45-50 titles/year; imprint publishes 12 titles/year. Receives 1,000 queries and 500 mss/year. 3% from unagented writers. Pays 7½-15% royalty. Offers advance.** Publishes book 1 year after acceptance of ms. Accepts simultaneous submissions. Responds in 3 months to proposals. Book catalog for SAE with 3 first-class stamps.
Imprints: Image Books, Anchor Bible Commentary, Anchor Bible Reference, Galilee, New Jerusalem Bible.
Nonfiction: Biography, cookbook, gift book, reference, self-help. Subjects include child guidance/parenting, cooking/foods/nutrition, money/finance, religion, sex, spirituality. *Agented submissions only.*
Fiction: Religious. *Agented submissions only.*
Recent Title(s): *First Comes Love*, by Scott Hahn; *Religions for Peace*, by Cardinal Arinze.

DOUBLEDAY/IMAGE, Doubleday Broadway Publishing Group, Random House, Inc., 1745 Broadway, New York NY 10019. (212)782-9000. Fax: (212)302-7985. Website: www.randomhouse.com. **Acquisitions:** Trace Murphy, executive editor. Estab. 1956. Publishes hardcover, trade and mass market paperback originals and reprints. **Publishes 12 titles/year. Receives 500 queries and 300 mss/year. 10% of books from first-time authors. Pays royalty on retail price. Offers varied advance.** Publishes book 18 months after acceptance of ms. Accepts simultaneous submissions. Responds in 3 months to proposals.

Image Books has grown from a classic Catholic list to include a variety of current and future classics, maintaining a high standard of quality as the finest in religious paperbacks. Also publishes Doubleday paperbacks/hardcovers for general religion, spirituality, including works based in Buddhism, Islam, Judaism.

Nonfiction: Biography, gift book, how-to, illustrated book, reference, self-help. Subjects include philosophy, psychology, religion, women's issues/studies. Query with SASE. Reviews artwork/photos as part of ms package. Send photocopies.
Recent Title(s): *Papal Sin*, by Garry Wills; *Soul Survivor*, by Philip Yancey; *The Lamb's Supper*, by Scott Hahn.

DOVER PUBLICATIONS, INC., 31 E. 2nd St., Mineola NY 11501. (516)294-7000. Fax: (516)873-1401. Website: www.doverpublications.com. **Acquisitions:** Paul Negri, editor-in-chief; John Grafton (math/science reprints). Estab. 1941. Publishes trade paperback originals and reprints. **Publishes 660 titles/year. Makes outright purchase.** Accepts simultaneous submissions. Book catalog online.
Nonfiction: Biography, children's/juvenile, cookbook, how-to, humor, illustrated book, textbook. Subjects include agriculture/horticulture, Americana, animals, anthropology/archeology, art/architecture, cooking/foods/nutrition, health/medicine, history, hobbies, language/literature, music/dance, nature/environment, philosophy, photography, religion, science, sports, translation, travel. Publishes mostly reprints. Accepts original paper doll collections, game books, coloring books (juvenile). Query with SASE. Reviews artwork/photos as part of ms package.
Recent Title(s): *The Waning of the Middle Ages*, by John Huizenga.

DOWN THE SHORE PUBLISHING, Box 3100, Harvey Cedars NJ 08008. (609)978-1233. Website: www.down-the-shore.com. **Acquisitions:** Leslee Ganss, associate editor. Publishes hardcover and trade paperback originals and reprints. **Publishes 5-8 titles/year. Receives 200 queries and 20 mss/year. 80% of books from first-time authors; 100% from unagented writers. Pays royalty on wholesale price or retail price, or makes outright purchase. Offers occasional advance.** Publishes book 1-2 years after acceptance of ms. Accepts simultaneous submissions. Responds in 3 months to queries. Book catalog for 8×10 SAE with 2 first-class stamps or on website; ms guidelines online.

"Bear in mind that our market is regional—New Jersey, the Jersey Shore, the mid-Atlantic, and seashore and coastal subjects."

Nonfiction: Children's/juvenile, coffee table book, gift book, illustrated book. Subjects include Americana, art/architecture, history, nature/environment, regional. Query with SASE or submit proposal package including outline, 1 sample chapter(s). Reviews artwork/photos as part of ms package. Send photocopies.
Fiction: Regional. Query with SASE or submit proposal package including 1 sample chapter(s), synopsis.
Poetry: "We do not publish poetry, unless it is to be included as part of an anthology."
Recent Title(s): *Shore Chronicles: Diaries and Travelers' Tales from the Jersey Shore 1764-1955*, by Margaret Thomas Buchholz, editor (nonfiction); *Shore Stories: An Anthology of the Jersey Shore*, edited by Rich Youmans (fiction).
Tips: "Carefully consider whether your proposal is a good fit for our established market."

LISA DREW BOOKS, Scribner, 1230 Avenue of the Americas, New York NY 10020. (212)698-7000. Website: www.simonsays.com. **Acquisitions:** Lisa Drew, publisher. Publishes hardcover originals. **Publishes 10-14 titles/year. Receives 600 queries/year. 10% of books from first-time authors. Pays royalty on retail price. Offers variable advance.** Publishes book 1 year after acceptance of ms. Accepts simultaneous submissions. Responds in 1 month to queries. Book catalog free.

"We publish *reading* books; nonfiction that tells a story, not 'Fourteen Ways to Improve Your Marriage.'"

Nonfiction: Subjects include government/politics, history, women's issues/studies. No unsolicited material. *Agented submissions only.*

THOMAS DUNNE BOOKS, St. Martin's Press, 175 Fifth Ave., New York NY 10010. (212)674-5151. Website: www.stmartins.com. **Acquisitions:** Tom Dunne, publisher; Peter J. Wolverton, associate publisher; Ruth Cavin, associate publisher (mysteries). Publishes hardcover originals, trade paperback originals and reprints. **Publishes 210 titles/year. Receives 1,000 queries/year. 20% of books from first-time authors. Pays royalty. Pays 10-15% royalty on retail price for hardcover, 7½% for paperback. Offers varying advance.** Publishes book 1 year after acceptance of ms. Accepts simultaneous submissions. Responds in 2 months to queries. Book catalog free; ms guidelines free.

Thomas Dunne publishes a wide range of fiction and nonfiction. Accepts submissions from agents only.

Nonfiction: Biography. Subjects include government/politics, history, political commentary. "Author's attention to detail is important. We get a lot of manuscripts that are poorly proofread and just can't be considered." Agents submit query or an outline and 100 sample pages. Reviews artwork/photos as part of ms package. Send photocopies.

Fiction: Mainstream/contemporary, mystery, suspense, thrillers; women's. Agents submit query or submit synopsis and 100 sample pages.

Recent Title(s): *Knight: My Story*, by Bob Knight; *Death of the West*, by Patrick J. Buchanan.

DUQUESNE UNIVERSITY PRESS, 600 Forbes Ave., Pittsburgh PA 15282-0101. (412)396-6610. Fax: (412)396-5984. Website: www.dupress.duq.edu. **Acquisitions:** Susan Wadsworth-Booth, director. Estab. 1927. Publishes hardcover and trade paperback originals. **Publishes 8-12 titles/year. Receives 500 queries and 75 mss/year. 30% of books from first-time authors; 95% from unagented writers. Pays royalty on net price. Offers (some) advance.** Publishes book 1 year after acceptance of ms. Responds in 1 month to proposals; 3 months to mss. Book catalog and ms guidelines for #10 SASE; ms guidelines online.

Duquesne publishes scholarly monographs in the fields of literary studies (medieval & Renaissance), continental philosophy, ethics, religious studies and existential psychology. "We also publish a series, *Emerging Writers in Creative Nonfiction*, for first-time authors of creative nonfiction for a general readership."

Nonfiction: Scholarly (academic). Subjects include creative nonfiction, language/literature, philosophy (continental), psychology (existential), religion. "We look for quality of scholarship." For scholarly books, query or submit outline, 1 sample chapter and SASE. For creative nonfiction, submit 1 copy of ms.

Recent Title(s): *Walking My Dog, Jane*, by Ned Rozell; *The Last Settler*, by Jennifer Brice and Charles Mason.

DURBAN HOUSE PUBLISHING CO., 7502 Greenville Ave., Suite 500, Dallas TX 75231. (214)890-4050. Fax: (214)890-9295. E-mail: info@durbanhouse.com. Website: www.durbanhouse.com. **Acquisitions:** Robert Middlemiss, acquisitions editor (all areas consistent with house interest). Estab. 2000. Publishes hardcover and trade paperback originals. **Publishes 8-12 titles/year. 50% of books from first-time authors; 60% from unagented writers. Pays 8-15% royalty on wholesale price. Offers up to $2,000 advance.** Publishes book 1 year-15 months after acceptance of ms. Accepts simultaneous submissions. Book catalog online; ms guidelines online.

Nonfiction: Autobiography, biography, how-to, self-help. Subjects include alternative lifestyles, ethnic, gay/lesbian, general nonfiction, health/medicine, New Age, psychology, sex, spirituality. "We are actively looking for titles consistent with house interests. Writers should have established platform and appropriate credentials before querying. Query only. No phone queries." Query with SASE or submit proposal package including outline, 3 sample chapter(s), author bio.

Fiction: Adventure, historical, horror, literary, mainstream/contemporary, mystery, suspense. "We are concentrating on mystery/thriller/suspense titles. Query only. No phone queries." Query with SASE or submit 3 sample chapter(s), synopsis, author bio.

Recent Title(s): *Middle Essence: Women of Wonder Years*, by Landy Reed (nonfiction); *Basha*, by John Hamilton Lewis (fiction); *Private Justice*, by Richard Sand (fiction).

Tips: "Readers look for quality in writing, story and plot."

DUTTON (ADULT TRADE), Penguin Putnam, Inc., 375 Hudson St., New York NY 10014. (212)366-2000. Website: www.penguinputnam.com. Editorial Director: Brian Tart. Editor: Michelle Coppola. Estab. 1852. Publishers hardcover originals. **Publishes 40 titles/year. Pays royalty. Offers negotiable advance.** Publishes book 12-18 months after acceptance of ms. Accepts simultaneous submissions. Responds in 6 months to queries. Book catalog for #10 SASE.

Dutton publishes hardcover, original, mainstream, and contemporary fiction and nonfiction in the areas of memoir, self-help, politics, psychology, and science for a general readership.

Nonfiction: Humor, reference, self-help, Memoir. Subjects include general nonfiction. *Agented submissions only. No unsolicited mss.*

Fiction: Adventure, historical, literary, mainstream/contemporary, mystery, short story collections, suspense. *Agented submissions only. No unsolicited mss.*

Recent Title(s): *The Darwin Awards II*, by Wendy Northcutt (humor); *The Oath*, by John Lescroart (fiction); *Falling Angels*, by Tracy Chevalier (fiction).

Tips: "Write the complete manuscript and submit it to an agent or agents. They will know exactly which editor will be interested in a project."

DUTTON CHILDREN'S BOOKS, Penguin Putman, Inc., 345 Hudson St., New York NY 10014. (212)414-3700. Fax: (212)414-3397. Website: www.penguinputnam.com. **Acquisitions:** Stephanie Owens Lurie, president and publisher (picture books and fiction); Donna Brooks, editorial director (books for all ages with distinctive narrative style); Lucia Monfried, senior editor (picture books, easy-to-read books, fiction); Michele Coppola, editor (picture books and fiction); Julie Strauss-Gabel, editor (picture books and fiction); Alissa Heyman, associate editor (fiction, poetry, picture books); Meredith Mundy Wasinger, editor (picture books, fiction and nonfiction). Estab. 1852. Publishes hardcover originals as well as novelty formats. **Publishes 100 titles/year. 15% of books from first-time authors. Pays royalty on retail price. Offers advance.**

O→ Dutton Children's Books publishes high-quality fiction and nonfiction for readers ranging from preschoolers to young adults on a variety of subjects. Currently emphasizing picture books and middle-grade and young adult novels that offer a fresh perspective. De-emphasizing photographic nonfiction and picture books that teach a lesson.

Nonfiction: Children's/juvenile, for preschoolers to young adults. Subjects include animals, history (U.S.), nature/environment, science. Query with SASE.

Fiction: Dutton Children's Books has a diverse, general interest list that includes picture books; easy-to-read books; and fiction for all ages, from "first chapter" books to young adult readers. Query with SASE. Query with SASE and letter only.

Recent Title(s): *Even Firefighters Hug Their Moms*, by Christine MacLean, illustrated by Mike Reed (picture book); *Double Fudge*, by Judy Blume (novel); *The Viper*, by Lisa Thiesing (easy-to-read).

EAGLE'S VIEW PUBLISHING, 6756 N. Fork Rd., Liberty UT 84310. Fax: (801)745-0903. E-mail: eglcrafts@aol.com. Website: www.eaglesviewpub.com. **Acquisitions:** Denise Knight, editor-in-chief. Estab. 1982. Publishes trade paperback originals. **Publishes 4-6 titles/year. Receives 40 queries and 20 mss/year. 90% of books from first-time authors; 100% from unagented writers. Pays 8-10% royalty on net selling price.** Publishes book 1 year or more after acceptance of ms. Accepts simultaneous submissions. Responds in 1 year to proposals. Book catalog and ms guidelines for $4.

O→ Eagle's View publishes primarily how-to craft books with a subject related to historical or contemporary Native American/Mountain Man/frontier crafts/bead crafts. Currently emphasizing bead-related craft books. De-emphasizing history except for historical Indian crafts.

Nonfiction: How-to, Indian, mountain man and American frontier (history and craft). Subjects include anthropology/archeology (Native American crafts), ethnic (Native American), history (American frontier historical patterns and books), hobbies (crafts, especially beadwork). "We are expanding from our Indian craft base to more general but related crafts. We prefer to do photography in house." Submit outline, 1-2 sample chapter(s). Reviews artwork/photos as part of ms package. Send photocopies or sample illustrations.

Recent Title(s): *Treasury of Beaded Jewelry*, by Mary Ellen Harte; *Beads and Beadwork of the American Indian*, by William C. Orchard.

Tips: "We will not be publishing any new beaded earrings books for 1-2 years. We are interested in other craft projects using seed beads, especially books that feature a variety of items, not just different designs for one item."

EAKIN PRESS/SUNBELT MEDIA, INC., P.O. Box 90159, Austin TX 78709-0159. (512)288-1771. Fax: (512)288-1813. E-mail: sales@eakinpress.com. Website: www.eakinpress.com. **Acquisitions:** Virginia Messer, publisher. Estab. 1978. Publishes hardcover and paperback originals and reprints. **Publishes 60 titles/year. Receives 1,500 submissions/year. 50% of books from first-time authors; 90% from unagented writers. Pays royalty. Pays 10-12-15% royalty on net sales.** Publishes book 18 months after acceptance of ms. Accepts simultaneous submissions. Responds in 3 months to queries. Book catalog for $1.25; ms guidelines online.

Imprints: Eakin Press, Nortex Press, Sunbelt Eakin.

O→ Eakin specializes in Texana and Western Americana for adults and juveniles. Currently emphasizing women's studies.

Nonfiction: Biography, cookbook (regional). Subjects include Americana (Western), business/economics, cooking/foods/nutrition, ethnic, history, military/war, regional, sports, African American studies, Civil War, Texas history. Juvenile nonfiction: includes biographies of historic personalities, prefer with Texas or regional interest, or nature studies; and easy-read illustrated books for grades 1-3. Query with SASE.

Fiction: Historical, juvenile. Juvenile fiction for grades K-12, preferably relating to Texas and the Southwest or contemporary. Nonfiction adult with Texas or Southwest theme. No adult fiction. Query or submit outline/synopsis and sample chapters.

Recent Title(s): *The Golden Bay*, by John J. Nance; *Red Zone*, by Red McCombs.

[N] **ECLIPSE PRESS**, The Blood-Horse, Inc., 1736 Alexandria Dr., Lexington KY 40504. Website: www.eclipsepress.com. **Acquisitions:** Jacqueline Duke, editor (equine). Estab. 1916. Publishes hardcover and trade paperback originals. **Publishes 12-15 titles/year. Receives 100 queries and 50 mss/year. 50% of books from first-time authors; 40% from unagented writers. Pays 10-15% royalty on net receipts or makes outright purchase. Offers $3,000-12,000 advance.** Publishes book 18 months after acceptance of ms. Accepts simultaneous submissions. Responds in 2-3 months to queries; 2-3 months to proposals; 2-3 months to mss. Book catalog free.

Nonfiction: Subjects include sports (equine, equestrian). "We only accept nonfiction works on equine and equestrian topics." Query with SASE or submit outline, sample chapter(s). Reviews artwork/photos as part of ms package.

Tips: "Our audience is sports, horse, and racing enthusiasts."

EDUCATORS PUBLISHING SERVICE, 31 Smith Place, Cambridge MA 02138-1089. (617)547-6706. Fax: (617)547-3805. Website: www.epsbooks.com and www.lessonlogic.com. **Acquisitions:** Charles H. Heinle, vice president, Publishing Group. Estab. 1952. **Publishes 26 titles/year. Receives 400 queries and 400 mss/year. 50% of books from first-time authors; 100% from unagented writers. Pays 5-12% royalty on retail price.** Publishes book 8 months minimum after acceptance of ms. Accepts simultaneous submissions. Responds in 1 month to queries; 3 months to proposals; 3 months to mss. Book catalog and ms guidelines free; ms guidelines online.

O→ EPS is looking for supplementary materials for the regular K-12 and special education classroom. "We are particularly interested in workbook and text series, but will gladly consider any proposals for high-quality material that is useful to teachers and students." Currently emphasizing reading language arts material for K-8.

Nonfiction: Workbooks (language arts) and some professional books. Subjects include education (reading comprehension, phonics vocabulary development and writing). supplementary texts and workbooks (reading and language arts). Query with SASE. Reviews artwork/photos as part of ms package. Send photocopies.

Recent Title(s): *Words Are Wonderful*, by Dorothy Grant Hennings; *Game Plan*, by Joanna Kennedy; *Educational Care*, by Mel Levine.

Tips: Teacher, students (K-adult) audiences.

EDUPRESS, INC., 208 Avenida Fabricante #200, San Clemente CA 92672. (949)366-9499. Fax: (949)366-9441. E-mail: info@edupressinc.com. Website: www.edupressinc.com. **Acquisitions:** Amanda Meinke, product coordinator. Estab. 1979. Publishes trade paperback originals. **Publishes 40 titles/year. Receives 20 queries and 100 mss/year. 25% of books from first-time authors. Makes outright purchase.** Publishes book 1 year after acceptance of ms. Responds in 2 months to queries; 5 months to mss. Book catalog and ms guidelines free.

O→ Edupress publishes supplemental resources for classroom curriculum. Currently emphasizing more science, math, language arts emphasis than in the past.

Nonfiction: Subjects include education (resources for pre-school through middle school). Submit proposal package, including ms copy, outline, 1 sample chapter and SASE. Reviews artwork/photos as part of ms package. Send photocopies.

Recent Title(s): *Two Can Read* (two level readers); *Crossnumber Puzzles*.

Tips: Audience is classroom teachers and homeschool parents.

EERDMANS BOOKS FOR YOUNG READERS, William B. Eerdmans Publishing Co., 255 Jefferson Ave. SE, Grand Rapids MI 49503. (616)459-4591. Fax: (616)459-6540. **Acquisitions:** Judy Zylstra, editor. Publishes picture books and middle reader and young adult fiction and nonfiction. **Publishes 12-15 titles/year. Receives 3,000 submissions/year. Pays 5-7½% royalty on retail price.** Publishes book Publishes middle reader and YA books in 1 year; publishes picture books in 2-3 years after acceptance of ms. Accepts simultaneous submissions. Responds in 6 weeks to queries. Book catalog for #10 SASE.

O→ "We publish books for children and young adults that deal with spiritual themes—but never in a preachy or heavy-handed way. Some of our books are clearly religious, while others (especially our novels) look at spiritual issues in very subtle ways. We look for books that are honest, wise and hopeful." Currently emphasizing general picture books (also picture book biographies), novels (middle reader and YA). De-emphasizing retellings of Bible stories.

Nonfiction: Children's/juvenile, picture books, middle reader, young adult nonfiction. "Do not send illustrations unless you are a professional illustrator." Submit complete mss for picture books and novels or biographies under 200 pages with SASE. For longer books, send query letter and 3 or 4 sample chapters with SASE. Reviews artwork/photos as part of ms package. Send color photocopies rather than original art.

Fiction: Juvenile, picture books, young adult, middle reader. "Do not send illustrations unless you are a professional illustrator." Submit complete mss for picture books and novels or biographies under 200 pages with SASE. For longer books, send query letter and 3 or 4 sample chapters with SASE.

Recent Title(s): *A Bird or Two: A Story about Henri Matisse*, written and illustrated by Bijou Le Tord; *When Daddy Prays*, written by Nikki Grimes, illustrated by Tim Ladwig; *Secrets in the House of Delgado*, by Gloria Miklowitz.

WILLIAM B. EERDMANS PUBLISHING CO., 255 Jefferson Ave. SE, Grand Rapids MI 49503. (616)459-4591. Fax: (616)459-6540. E-mail: sales@eerdmans.com. Website: www.eerdmans.com. **Acquisitions:** Jon Pott, editor-in-chief; Charles Van Hof, managing editor (history); Judy Zylstra, children's book editor. Estab. 1911. Publishes hardcover and paperback originals and reprints. **Publishes 120-130 titles/year. Receives 3,000-4,000 submissions/year. 10% of books from first-time authors; 95% from unagented writers. Pays 7% royalty. Offers occasional advance.** Publishes book usually within 1 year after acceptance of ms. Accepts simultaneous submissions. Responds in 6 weeks to queries. Book catalog free; ms guidelines free.

Imprints: Eerdmans Books for Young Readers (Judy Zylstra, editor).

O→ "Approximately 80% of our adult publications are religious and most of these are academic or semi-academic in character (as opposed to inspirational or celebrity books), though we also publish general trade books on the Christian life. Our nonreligious titles, most of them in regional history or on social issues, aim, similarly, at an educated audience."

Nonfiction: Children's/juvenile, reference, textbook, monographs. Subjects include history (religious), language/literature, philosophy (of religion), psychology, regional (history), religion, sociology, translation, Biblical studies, theology, ethics. "We prefer that writers take the time to notice if we have published anything at all in the same category as their manuscript before sending it to us." Query with outline, 2-3 sample chapter and SASE for return of ms. Reviews artwork/photos as part of ms package.

Fiction: Religious (children's, general, fantasy). Query with SASE.

Recent Title(s): *Scarred by Struggle, Transformed by Hope*, by Joan Chittister; *Living Next Door to the Death House*, by Virginia Stem Owens and David Owens; *Who Were the Early Israelites and Where Did They Come From*, by William G. Dever.

ELECTRIC WORKS PUBLISHING, 605 Ave. C.E., Bismarck ND 58501. (701)255-0356. E-mail: editors@electricpublishing.com. Website: www.electricpublishing.com. **Acquisitions:** James R. Bohe, editor-in-chief. Publishes digital books. **Publishes 15 titles/year. Receives 80 queries and 250 mss/year. 90% of books from first-time authors; 95% from unagented writers. Pays 36-40% royalty on wholesale price.** Publishes book 3 months after acceptance of ms. Accepts simultaneous submissions. Responds in 5 months to queries. Book catalog and ms guidelines online; ms guidelines online.

O→ Digital publisher offering a wide range of subjects.

Nonfiction: Biography, children's/juvenile, cookbook, how-to, humor, self-help, technical. Subjects include child guidance/parenting, computers/electronic, cooking/foods/nutrition, creative nonfiction, education, history, hobbies, military/war, money/finance, multicultural, nature/environment, recreation, regional, religion, science, sociology, spirituality, women's issues/studies. *Electronic submissions only.* Submit entire ms in digital format. Reviews artwork/photos as part of ms package.
Fiction: Adventure, ethnic, experimental, fantasy, gothic, historical, horror, humor, juvenile, literary, mainstream/contemporary, military/war, multicultural, multimedia, mystery, occult, plays, poetry in translation, regional, religious, romance, science fiction, short story collections, spiritual, sports, suspense, translation, western, young adult. *Electronic submissions only.* Submit ms in digital format.
Recent Title(s): *A Season of Dragons*, by Terry Leatherwood; *Lightning Strikes Twice*, by Gary and Sheila Gewirtzman; *The Mark of Cain*, by Margaret Dupier.

ELEPHANT BOOKS, 65 Macedonia Rd., Alexander NC 28701. (828)252-9515. Fax: (828)255-8719. E-mail: sales@abooks.com. Website: abooks.com. **Acquisitions:** Pat Roberts, acquisitions editor. Publishes trade paperback originals and reprints. **Publishes 8 titles/year. Receives 100 queries and 50 mss/year. 90% of books from first-time authors; 80% from unagented writers. Pays 12-15% royalty on wholesale price. Seldom offers advance.** Publishes book 18 months after acceptance of ms. Book catalog online; ms guidelines online.
Imprints: Blue/Gray Books (contact Ralph Roberts, Civil War history).
Nonfiction: Cookbook. Subjects include cooking/foods/nutrition, history, military/war (Civil War). Query or submit outline with 3 sample chapters and proposal package, including potential marketing plans with SASE. Reviews artwork/photos as part of ms package. Send photocopies.
Recent Title(s): *Rebel Boast*, by Manly Wade Wellman.

EMIS, INC., P.O. Box 820062, Dallas TX 75382-0062. Website: www.emispub.com. **Acquisitions:** Lynda Blake, president. Publishes trade paperback originals. **Publishes 4 titles/year. Pays 12% royalty on retail price.** Responds in 3 months to queries. Book catalog free; ms guidelines free.

O→ "Our books are published as a medical text designed for physicians to fit in the lab coat pocket as a quick means of locating information." Currently emphasizing infectious diseases. De-emphasizing medical program management.

Nonfiction: Reference. Subjects include health/medicine, psychology, Women's health/medicine. Submit 3 sample chapters with SASE.
Recent Title(s): *Managing Contraceptive Pill Patients.*
Tips: Audience is medical professionals and medical product manufacturers and distributors.

EMPEROR'S NEW CLOTHES PRESS. E-mail: info@encpress.com. Submissions E-mail: publisher@encpress.com. Website: www.encpress.com. **Acquisitions:** Olga Gardner Galvin, publisher/editor-in-chief. Estab. 2003. Publishes trade paperback originals and reprints. **Publishes 4-6 titles/year. 75% of books from first-time authors; 100% from unagented writers. Pays 50-60% royalty on retail price.** Publishes book 9 months after acceptance of ms. Accepts simultaneous submissions. Responds in 1 week to queries; 1 month to proposals; 3 months to mss. Book catalog online; ms guidelines online.
Fiction: Adventure, fantasy, humor, literary, mainstream/contemporary, mystery, science fiction, suspense, political satire, utopias/dystopias, social satire, translation, picaresque novel. Query through e-mail to publisher@encpress.com.
Recent Title(s): *Don't Call It "Virtual"*, by Beth Elliott (political satire/utopia/lesbian); *Vodka for Breakfast*, by David Gurevich (existential thriller/love story).
Tips: Audience is well-informed, socially liberal, fiscally conservative, decidedly not politically correct readers. "Don't be afraid to offend: we're not publishing for the 'broadest possible audience.' We're publishing for the politically incorrect audience with a good sense of humor. And: if it's not at all funny, we don't want to read it."

EMPIRE PUBLISHING SERVICE, P.O. Box 1344, Studio City CA 91614-0344. **Acquisitions:** Joseph Witt. Estab. 1960. Publishes hardcover reprints and trade paperback originals and reprints. **Publishes 40 titles/year; imprint publishes 15 titles/year. Receives 500 queries and 85 mss/year. 50% of books from first-time authors; 95% from unagented writers. Pays 6-10% royalty on retail price. Offers variable advance.** Publishes book up to 2 years after acceptance of ms. Does not accept simultaneous submissions. Responds in 1 month to queries; 2 months to proposals; up to 1 year to mss. Book catalog for #10 SASE; ms guidelines for $1 or #10 SASE.
Imprints: Gaslight Publications, Gaslight Books, Empire Publications, Empire Books, Empire Music.

O→ "Submit only Sherlock Holmes, performing arts and health."

Nonfiction: How-to, humor, reference, technical, textbook. Subjects include health/medicine, humor, music/dance, Sherlock Holmes. Query with SASE. Reviews artwork/photos as part of ms package. Send photocopies.
Fiction: Historical (pre-18th century), mystery (Sherlock Holmes). Query with SASE.
Recent Title(s): *On the Scent with Sherlock Holmes*, by Jacy Tracy; *Elementary My Dear Watson*, by William Alan Landes; *The Magic of Food*, by James Cohen.

ENCOUNTER BOOKS, 665 Third St., Suite 330, San Francisco CA 94107-1951. (415)538-1460. Fax: (415)538-1461. Website: www.encounterbooks.com. **Acquisitions:** Peter Collier, publisher. Hardcover originals and trade paperback reprints. **Publishes 12-20 titles/year. Receives 500 queries and 200 mss/year. 10% of books from first-time authors; 40% from unagented writers. Pays 7-10% royalty on retail price. Offers $2,000-25,000 advance.** Publishes book 18 months after acceptance of ms. Accepts simultaneous submissions. Responds in 3 months to queries; 4 months to proposals; 4 months to mss. Book catalog and ms guidelines free or online; ms guidelines online.

Encounter Books publishes serious nonfiction—books that can alter our society, challenge our morality, stimulate our imaginations. Currently emphasizing history, culture, social criticism and politics.

Nonfiction: Biography, reference. Subjects include child guidance/parenting, education, ethnic, government/politics, health/medicine, history, language/literature, memoirs, military/war, multicultural, philosophy, psychology, religion, science, sociology, women's issues/studies, gender studies. Submit proposal package, including outline and 1 sample chapter.

Recent Title(s): *Islam Unveiled: Disturbing Questions about the World's Fastest Growing Faith*; *Code Name KINDRED SPIRIT: Inside the Chinese Nuclear Espionage Scandal*, by Notra Trulock.

ENSLOW PUBLISHERS, INC., 40 Industrial Rd., Box 398, Berkeley Heights NJ 07922. (973)771-9400. Website: www.enslow.com. **Acquisitions:** Brian D. Enslow, editor. Estab. 1977. Publishes hardcover originals. 10% require freelance illustration. **Publishes 250 titles/year. Pays royalty on net price. Offers advance.** Publishes book 1 year after acceptance of ms. Responds in 1 month to queries. Ms guidelines for #10 SASE.

Enslow publishes hardcover nonfiction books for young adults and school-age children, mostly as part of a series.

Nonfiction: Biography, children's/juvenile, reference. Subjects include health/medicine, history, recreation (Sports), science, sociology. Interested in new ideas for series of books for young people. No fiction, fictionalized history or dialog.

Recent Title(s): *Advertising*, by Nancy Day; *Holocaust Rescuers*, by David Lyman.

Tips: "We love to receive résumés from experienced writers with good research skills who can think like young people."

ENTREPRENEUR PRESS, 2445 McCabe Way, Irvine CA 92614. (949)261-2325. Fax: (949)261-7729. Website: www.smallbizbooks.com. **Acquisitions:** Jere Calmes, editorial director; Leanne Harvey, director of marketing. Publishes hardcover and trade paperback originals and trade paperback reprints. **Publishes 35-40 titles/year. Receives 1,200 queries and 600 mss/year. 40% of books from first-time authors; 60% from unagented writers. Pays 2-30% royalty or makes $2,000-15,000 outright purchase.** Accepts simultaneous submissions. Book catalog and ms guidelines free.

Nonfiction: Subjects include business/economics, small business, leadership, management, accounting, human resources, finance and marketing, economics. Query with SASE or submit proposal package including outline, 2 sample chapter(s), author bio, detailed TOC, preface or executive summary, competition. Reviews artwork/photos as part of ms package. Send transparencies.

Recent Title(s): *Start Your Own Business*, by Lesonsky; *Many Miles to Go*, by Brian Tracy; *E2: Using the Powers of Ethics & Ettiquette in American Business*, by Phyllis Davis.

Tips: Audience is "general business skills, including finance, marketing, presentation, leadership, etc."

[N] [A] [⊘] **EOS**, HarperCollins, 10 E. 53rd St., New York NY 10022. (212)207-7000.Submissions E-mail: eossubs@harpercollins.com. Website: www.eosbooks.com. Publishes hardcover originals, trade and mass market paperback originals and reprints. **Publishes 40-46 titles/year. 10% of books from first-time authors. Pays royalty on retail price. Offers variable advance.** Publishes book 18-24 months after acceptance of ms. Responds in 6 months to queries. Ms guidelines for #10 SASE.

Eos publishes "quality science fiction/fantasy with broad appeal."

Fiction: Fantasy, science fiction. No horror or juvenile. *Agented submissions only.* **All unsolicited mss returned unopened.** *No unsolicited submissions.*

Recent Title(s): *The Visitor*, by Sheri S. Tepper; *Ascending*, by James Alan Gardner; *The Curse of Chalcum*, by Lois McMaster Bujold.

Tips: "The official HarperCollins submissions policy has changed, and we can no longer accept unsolicited submissions. To submit your science fiction or fantasy novel to Eos, please query first. We strongly urge you to query via e-mail. Your query should be brief—no more than a 2-page description of your book. Do not send chapters or full synopsis at this time. You will receive a response—either a decline or a request for more material—in approximately 1-2 months."

EPICENTER PRESS, INC., P.O. Box 82368, Kenmore WA 98028. (425)485-6822. Fax: (425)481-8253. E-mail: info@epicenterpress.com. Website: www.epicenterpress.com. **Acquisitions:** Kent Sturgis, publisher. Estab. 1987. Publishes hardcover and trade paperback originals. **Publishes 10 titles/year. Receives 200 queries and 100 mss/year. 75% of books from first-time authors; 90% from unagented writers.** Publishes book 1-2 years after acceptance of ms. Responds in 2 months to queries. Book catalog and ms guidelines on website; ms guidelines online.

"We are a regional press founded in Alaska whose interests include but are not limited to the arts, history, environment, and diverse cultures and lifestyles of the North Pacific and high latitudes.

Nonfiction: "Our focus is Alaska. We do not encourage nonfiction titles from outside Alaska." Biography, coffee table book, gift book, humor. Subjects include animals, art/architecture, ethnic, history, humor, nature/environment, photography, recreation, regional, women's issues/studies. Submit outline and 3 sample chapters. Reviews artwork/photos as part of ms package. Send photocopies.

Recent Title(s): *Raising Ourselves*, by Velma Wallis.

ETC PUBLICATIONS, 700 E. Vereda Sur, Palm Springs CA 92262-4816. (760)325-5352. Fax: (760)325-8841. **Acquisitions:** Dr. Richard W. Hostrop, publisher (education and social sciences); Lee Ona S. Hostrop, editorial director (history and works suitable below the college level). Estab. 1972. Publishes hardcover and paperback originals. **Publishes 6-12 titles/year. Receives 100 submissions/year. 75% of books from first-time authors; 90% from unagented writers. Offers 5-15% royalty, based on wholesale and retail price.** Publishes book 9 months after acceptance of ms. *Writer's Market* recommends allowing 2 months for reply to queries.

ETC publishes works that "further learning as opposed to entertainment."

Nonfiction: Textbook, educational management; gifted education; futuristics. Subjects include education, translation (in above areas). Submit complete ms with SASE. *Writer's Market* recommends query first with SASE. Reviews artwork/ photos as part of ms package.

Recent Title(s): *The Internet for Educators and Homeschoolers*, by Steve Jones, Ph.D.

Tips: "Special consideration is given to those authors who are capable and willing to submit their completed work in camera-ready, typeset form. We are particularly interested in works suitable for *both* the Christian school market and homeschoolers; e.g., state history texts below the high school level with a Christian-oriented slant."

EVAN-MOOR EDUCATIONAL PUBLISHERS, 18 Lower Ragsdale Dr., Monterey CA 93940-5746. (831)649-5901. Fax: (831)649-6256. E-mail: editorial@evan-moor.com. Website: www.evan-moor.com. **Acquisitions:** Marilyn Evans, senior editor. Estab. 1979. Publishes teaching materials. **Publishes 50-60 titles/year. Receives 50 queries and 100 mss/ year. 1% of books from first-time authors; 100% from unagented writers. Makes outright purchase.** Publishes book 1 year after acceptance of ms. Accepts simultaneous submissions. Responds in 3 months to queries. Book catalog and ms guidelines free or on website; ms guidelines online.

O→ "Our books are teaching ideas, lesson plans, and blackline reproducibles for grades PreK-6 in all curriculum areas except music and bilingual." Currently emphasizing writing/language arts, practice materials for home use. De-emphasizing thematic materials. We do not publish children's literary fiction or literary nonfiction.

Nonfiction: Subjects include education, teaching materials, grade pre-K-6. No children's fiction or nonfiction literature. Submit proposal package, including outline and 3 sample chapters.

Recent Title(s): *Reader's Theatre* (6 book series); *Literacy Centers* (full color books, grades 1-6); *Basic Math Skills* (6 book series).

Tips: "Writers should know how classroom/educational materials differ from trade publications. They should request catalogs and submissions guidelines before sending queries or manuscripts. Visiting our website will give writers a clear picture of the type of materials we publish."

EXCALIBUR PUBLICATIONS, P.O. Box 35369, Tucson AZ 85740-5369. E-mail: excalibureditor@earthlink.net. **Acquisitions:** Alan M. Petrillo, editor. Publishes trade paperback originals. **Publishes 4-6 titles/year. Pays royalty or makes outright purchase.** Responds in 1 month to queries; 1 month to mss.

O→ Excalibur publishes historical and military works from all time periods.

Nonfiction: Subjects include history (military), military/war (strategy and tactics, as well as the history of battles, firearms, arms and armour), historical personalities. "We are seeking well-researched and documented works. Unpublished writers are welcome." Query with outline, first 3 chapters, SASE. Include notes on photos, illustrations and maps.

Recent Title(s): *Famous Faces of World War II*, by Robert Van Osdol; *Present Sabers: A History of the U.S. Horse Cavalry*, by Allan Heninger.

Tips: "Know your subject matter, and present it in a clear and precise manner. Please give us a brief description of your background or experience as it relates to your submission, as well as any marketing insight you might have on your subject."

EXCELSIOR CEE PUBLISHING, P.O. Box 5861, Norman OK 73070. (405)329-3909. Fax: (405)329-6886. **Acquisitions:** J.C. Marshall. Estab. 1989. Publishes hardcover and trade paperback originals. **Publishes 15 titles/year. Receives 400 queries/year. Pays royalty or makes outright purchase (both negotiable); will consider co-op publishing some titles.** Publishes book 1 year after acceptance of ms. Accepts simultaneous submissions. Responds in 1 month to queries. Book catalog for #10 SASE.

O→ "All of our books speak to the reader through words of feeling—whether they are how-to, educational, humor or whatever genre, the reader comes away with feeling, truth and inspiration." Currently emphasizing how-to, family history, memoirs, inspiration. De-emphasizing childrens.

Nonfiction: Biography, coffee table book, gift book, how-to, humor, self-help. Subjects include Americana, education, history, hobbies, language/literature, memoirs, women's issues/studies, general nonfiction, writing. Query with SASE.

Recent Title(s): *Goodbye Kite*, by Lois Redpath; *Coming Full Circle*, by Loretta Hamilton-Geary; *Living with Cancer—A Story of Hope and Survival.*

Tips: "We have a general audience, book store browsers interested in nonfiction reading. We publish titles that have a mass appeal and can be enjoyed by a large reading public. We publish very few unsolicited manuscripts, and our publishing calendar is 75% full up to 1 year in advance."

EXECUTIVE EXCELLENCE PUBLISHING, 1366 E. 1120 S., Provo UT 84606. (800)304-9782. Fax: (801)377-5960. E-mail: info@eep.com. Website: www.eep.com. **Acquisitions:** Ken Shelton, editor in chief. Estab. 1984. Publishes hardcover and trade paperback originals and trade paperback reprints. **Publishes 10 titles/year. Receives 300 queries and 150 mss/year. 35% of books from first-time authors; 95% from unagented writers. Pays 15% on cash received and 50% of subsidary right proceeds.** Publishes book 6-9 months after acceptance of ms. Accepts simultaneous submissions. Responds in 1 month to queries; 1 month to proposals; 1 month to mss. Book catalog free or on website.

O→ Executive Excellence publishes business and self-help titles. "We help you—the busy person, executive or entrepreneur—to find a wiser, better way to live your life and lead your organization." Currently emphasizing business innovations for general management and leadership (from the personal perspective). De-emphasizing technical or scholarly textbooks on operational processes and financial management or workbooks.

Nonfiction: Self-help. Subjects include business/economics, leadership/management, entrepreneurship, career, motivational. Submit proposal package, including outline, 1-2 sample chapters and author bio, company information.

Recent Title(s): *Spirit of Leadership*, by Robert J. Spitzer; *Traits of Champions*, by Andrew Wood and Brian Tracy.

Tips: "Executive Excellence Publishing is an established publishing house with a strong niche in the marketplace. Our magazines, *Executive Excellence*, *Sales and Marketing Excellence* and *Personal Excellence*, are distributed monthly in countries across the world. Our authors are on the cutting edge in their fields of leadership, self-help and business and organizational development. We are always looking for strong new talent with something to say, and a burning desire to say it."

FACTS ON FILE, INC., 132 W. 31st St., 17th Floor, New York NY 10001. (212)967-8800. Fax: (212)967-9196. E-mail: llikoff@factsonfile.com. Website: www.factsonfile.com. **Acquisitions:** Laurie Likoff, editorial director (science, fashion, natural history); Frank Darmstadt (science & technology, nature, reference); Nicole Bowen, senior editor (American history, women's studies, young adult reference); James Chambers, trade editor (health, pop culture, true crime, sports); Jeff Soloway, acquisitions editor (language/literature). Estab. 1941. Publishes hardcover originals and reprints. **Publishes 135 titles/year. 25% from unagented writers. Pays 10% royalty on retail price. Offers $5,000-10,000 advance.** Accepts simultaneous submissions. Responds in 2 months to queries. Book catalog free; ms guidelines online.

Imprints: Checkmark Books.

O→ Facts on File produces high-quality reference materials on a broad range of subjects for the school library market and the general nonfiction trade.

Nonfiction: "We publish serious, informational books for a targeted audience. All our books must have strong library interest, but we also distribute books effectively to the trade. Our library books fit the junior and senior high school curriculum." Reference. Subjects include contemporary culture, education, health/medicine, history, language/literature, multicultural, recreation, religion, sports, careers, entertainment, natural history, popular culture. No computer books, technical books, cookbooks, biographies (except YA), pop psychology, humor, fiction or poetry. Query or submit outline and sample chapter with SASE. No submissions returned without SASE.

Tips: "Our audience is school and public libraries for our more reference-oriented books and libraries, schools and bookstores for our less reference-oriented informational titles."

FAIRLEIGH DICKINSON UNIVERSITY PRESS, 285 Madison Ave., Madison NJ 07940. (973)443-8564. Fax: (973)443-8364. E-mail: fdupress@fdu.edu. **Acquisitions:** Harry Keyishian, director. Estab. 1967. Publishes hardcover originals. **Publishes 45 titles/year. Receives 300 submissions/year. 33% of books from first-time authors; 95% from unagented writers.** Publishes book 1 year after acceptance of ms. Responds in 2 weeks to queries. *Writer's Market* recommends allowing 2 months for reply.

- "Contract is arranged through Associated University Presses of Cranbury, New Jersey. We are a *selection* committee only." Nonauthor subsidy publishes 2% of books.

O→ Fairleigh Dickinson publishes scholarly books for the academic market.

Nonfiction: Biography, reference, scholarly, scholarly books. Subjects include art/architecture, business/economics, ethnic, film/cinema/stage, gay/lesbian, government/politics, history, music/dance, philosophy, psychology, sociology, women's issues/studies, Civil War, film, Jewish studies, literary criticism, scholarly editions. Looking for scholarly books in all fields; no nonscholarly books. Query with outline and sample chapters. Reviews artwork/photos as part of ms package.

Recent Title(s): *The Carlyle Encyclopedia*, edited by Mark Cummings; *Sleuthing Ethnicity: The Detective in Multiethnic Crime Fiction*, edited by D. Fischer-Hornung and Monika Mueller; *Whig's Progress: Tom Wharton Between Revolutions*, by J. Kent Clark.

Tips: "Research must be up to date. Poor reviews result when bibliographies and notes don't reflect current research. We follow *Chicago Manual of Style* (14th edition) style in scholarly citations. We welcome collections of unpublished conference papers or essay collections, if they relate to a strong central theme and have scholarly merit."

FAIRVIEW PRESS, 2450 Riverside Ave., Minneapolis MN 55454. (800)544-8207. Fax: (612)672-4980. E-mail: press@fairview.org. Website: www.fairviewpress.org. **Acquisitions:** Lane Stiles, director; Stephanie Billecke, senior editor. Estab. 1988. Publishes hardcover and trade paperback originals and reprints. **Publishes 8-12 titles/year. Receives 3,000 queries and 1,500 mss/year. 40% of books from first-time authors; 65% from unagented writers. Advance and royalties negotiable.** Publishes book 1 year after acceptance of ms. Accepts simultaneous submissions. Responds in 6 months to proposals. Book catalog and ms guidelines free; ms guidelines online.

O→ Fairview Press currently publishes books and related materials emphasizing aging, end-of-life issues, caregiving, grief and bereavement.

Nonfiction: Reference, self-help. Subjects include health/medicine, women's issues/studies, aging, grief and bereavement, patient education, nutrition. "Manuscripts that are essentially one person's story are rarely salable." Submit proposal package including outline, 2 sample chapter(s), author bio, marketing ideas, SASE. Reviews artwork/photos as part of ms package. Send photocopies.

Tips: Audience is general reader, especially families. "Tell us what void your book fills in the market; give us an angle. Tell us who will buy your book. We have moved away from recovery books and have focused on health and medical issues."

FAITH KIDS BOOKS, Cook Communications Ministries, 4050 Lee Vance View, Colorado Springs CO 80918. (719)536-3271. Fax: (719)536-3265. Website: www.faithkids.com. **Acquisitions:** Heather Gemmen, associate acquisitions editor. Publishes hardcover and paperback originals. **Publishes 40-50 titles/year. Receives 1,000-1,500 mss/year. Pays variable royalty on retail price or flat fee, depending on project. Offers advance.** Publishes book 18 months after acceptance of ms. Accepts simultaneous submissions. Responds in 6 months to queries. Ms guidelines online.

O→ Faith Kids Books publishes inspirational works for children, ages 1-12, with a strong underlying Christian theme or clearly stated biblical value, designed to foster spiritual growth in children and positive interaction between parent and child. Currently emphasizing Bible storybooks, Christian living books, life issue books, early readers, and picture books.

Nonfiction: Biography, children's/juvenile. Subjects include religion (Bible stories, devotionals), picture books on nonfiction subjects. Submit proposal package including cover letter, SASE.
Fiction: Historical, juvenile, picture books, religious, toddler books. "Picture books, devotionals, Bible storybooks, for an age range of 1-12. We're particularly interested in materials for beginning readers." No teen fiction. Query with SASE. Accepts proposals with SASE. Previously published or agented authors preferred.
Recent Title(s): *Tale of Three Trees*, by Angela Hunt (fiction).

N **FANTAGRAPHICS BOOKS**, 7563 Lake City Way NE, Seattle WA 98115. Website: www.fantagraphics.com. Co-owners: Gary Groth, Kim Thompson. **Acquisitions:** Submissions Editor. Estab. 1976. Publishes original trade paperbacks. Responds in 3 months to queries; 3 months to proposals; 3 months to mss. Book catalog online; ms guidelines online.
Fiction: Comic books. "Fantagraphics is an independent company with a modus operandi different from larger, factory-like corporate comics publishers. If your talents are limited to a specific area of expertise (i.e. inking, writing, etc.), then you will need to develop your own team before submitting a project to us. We want to see an idea that is fully fleshed-out in your mind, at least, if not on paper." "Submit a minimum of 5 fully-inked pages of art, a synopsis, and a brief note stating approximately how many issues you have in mind."
Recent Title(s): *Zippy Annual*, by Bill Griffith; *Don't Call Me Stupid*, by Steve Weissman; *Hey, Wait.*, by Jason.
Tips: "Take note of the originality and diversity of the themes and approaches to drawing in such Fantagraphics titles as *Love & Rockets* (stories of life in Latin America and Chicano L.A.), *Palestine* (journalistic autobiography in the Middle East), *Eightball* (surrealism mixed with kitsch culture in stories alternately humorous and painfully personal), and *Naughty Bits* (feminist humor and short stories which both attack and commiserate). Try to develop your own, equally individual voice; originality, aesthetic maturity, and graphic storytelling skill are the signs by which Fantagraphics judges whether or not your submission is ripe for publication."

A **FARRAR, STRAUS & GIROUX**, 19 Union Square W., New York NY 10003. (212)741-6900. Publishes hardcover and trade paperback books. **Publishes 170 titles/year. Receives 1,500-2,000 queries and mss/year.** Responds in 2 months to queries; 2 months to proposals. Ms guidelines free.
Imprints: Northpoint Press; Hill and Wang; Faber and Faber Inc.
Nonfiction: Subjects include literary.
Fiction: Literary.

FARRAR, STRAUS & GIROUX BOOKS FOR YOUNG READERS, Farrar Straus Giroux, Inc., 19 Union Square W., New York NY 10003. (212)741-6900. Fax: (212)633-2427. **Acquisitions:** Margaret Ferguson, editorial director. Estab. 1946. Publishes hardcover originals and trade paperback reprints. **Publishes 75 titles/year. Receives 6,000 queries and mss/year. 5% of books from first-time authors; 50% from unagented writers. Pays royalty. Pays 2-6% royalty on retail price for paperbacks, 3-10% for hardcovers. Offers $3,000-25,000 advance.** Publishes book 18 months after acceptance of ms. Accepts simultaneous submissions. Responds in 2 months to queries; 4 months to mss. Book catalog for 9×12 SAE with $1.87 postage; ms guidelines for #10 SASE.
Imprints: Frances Foster Books, Melanie Kroupa Books.

"We publish original and well-written material for all ages."

Fiction: Juvenile, picture books, young adult, nonfiction. "Do not query picture books; just send manuscript. Do not fax queries or manuscripts." Query with SASE.
Recent Title(s): *A Hole in My Life*, by Jack Gautos (ages 12 up); *Everything on a Waffle*, by Polly Horvath (Newberry Honor Book, 10-14); *Madlenka's Dog*, by Peter Sis (ages 4-8).
Tips: Audience is full age range, preschool to young adult. Specializes in literary fiction.

N **FC2**, Department of English, FSU, Tallahassee FL 32306-1580. (850)644-2260. E-mail: fc2@english.fsu.edu. Website: fc2.org. **Acquisitions:** R.M. Berry, publisher (fiction). Estab. 1974. Publishes hardcover and paperback originals. **Publishes 6 titles/year. 95% from unagented writers. Pays 10% royalty.** Publishes book 1-3 years after acceptance of ms. Accepts simultaneous submissions. Responds in 3 weeks to queries; 2-6 months to mss. Ms guidelines online.

Publisher of innovative fiction.

Fiction: Experimental, feminist, gay/lesbian, Innovative; Modernist/Postmodern; Avant-Garde; Anarchist; Minority; Cyberpunk. Query with SASE or submit outline, publishing history, synopsis, author bio. Send queries to: FC2, Unit for Contemporary Literature, Illinois State University, 109 Fairchild Hall, Normal IL 61790-4241.
Recent Title(s): *Book of Lazarus*, by Richard Grossman; *Is It Sexual Harassment Yet?*, by Cris Mazza; *Liberty's Excess*, by Lidia Yuknavitch.
Tips: "Be familiar with our list."

FREDERICK FELL PUBLISHERS, INC., 2131 Hollywood Blvd., Suite 305, Hollywood FL 33020. (954)925-5242. Fax: (954)925-5244. E-mail: fellpub@aol.com. Website: www.fellpub.com. **Acquisitions:** Barnara Newman, senior editor. Publishes hardcover and trade paperback originals. **Publishes 40 titles/year. Receives 4,000 queries and 1,000 mss/year. 95% of books from first-time authors; 95% from unagented writers. Pays negotiable royalty on retail price. Offers up to $10,000 advance.** Publishes book 1 year after acceptance of ms. Accepts simultaneous submissions. Responds in 1 month to queries; 3 months to proposals. Ms guidelines for #10 SASE.

"Fell has just launched 25 titles in the *Know-It-All* series. We will be publishing over 125 titles in all genres. Prove to us that your title is the best in this new exciting format."

Nonfiction: "We are reviewing in all categories. Advise us of the top three competitive titles for your work and the reasons why the public would benefit by having your book published." How-to, reference, self-help. Subjects include business/economics, child guidance/parenting, education, ethnic, film/cinema/stage, health/medicine, hobbies, money/finance, spirituality. Submit proposal package, including outline, 3 sample chapters, author bio, publicity ideas, market analysis. Reviews artwork/photos as part of ms package. Send photocopies.

Recent Title(s): *Venus & Serena: My Seven Years as Hitting Coach for the Williams Sisters.*

Tips: "We are most interested in well-written, timely nonfiction with strong sales potential. We will not consider topics that appeal to a small, select audience. Learn markets and be prepared to help with sales and promotion. Show us how your book is unique or better than the competition."

FILTER PRESS, LLC, P.O. Box 95, Palmer Lake CO 80133-0095. (719)481-2420. Fax: (719)481-2420. E-mail: filter.press@prodigy.net. Website: www.filterpressbooks.com. **Acquisitions:** Doris Baker, president. Estab. 1956. Publishes trade paperback originals and reprints. **Publishes 4-6 titles/year. Pays 10-12% royalty on wholesale price.** Publishes book 1 year after acceptance of ms.

O→ Filter Press specializes in nonfiction of the West. De-emphasizing cooking, foods and nutrition.

Nonfiction: Subjects include Americana, anthropology/archeology, cooking/foods/nutrition, ethnic, history, memoirs, nature/environment, regional, crafts and crafts people of the Southwest. "We're interested in the history and natural history of the West." Query with outline and SASE. Reviews artwork/photos as part of ms package.

Recent Title(s): *First Governor, First Lady-John and Eliza Raitt of Colorado*, by Joyce Lohse (biography); *Bent's Fort: Crossroads of Cultures on the Santa Fe Trail*, by Mel Bacon and Dan Blegen (history).

FIRE ENGINEERING BOOKS & VIDEOS, PennWell Corp., 1421 S. Sheridan Rd., Tulsa OK 74112-6600. (918)831-9420. Fax: (918)832-9319. E-mail: jaredw@pennwell.com. Website: www.pennwellbooks.com. **Acquisitions:** Jared Wicklund, supervising editor. Publishes hardcover and softcover originals. **Publishes 10 titles/year. Receives 24 queries/year. 75% of books from first-time authors; 100% from unagented writers. Pays variable royalty on net sales.** Publishes book 1 year after acceptance of ms. Does not accept simultaneous submissions. Responds in 3 months to proposals. Book catalog free.

O→ Fire Engineering publishes textbooks relevant to firefighting and training. Training firefighters and other emergency responders. Currently emphasizing strategy and tactics, reserve training, preparedness for terrorist threats, natural disasters, first response to fires and emergencies.

Nonfiction: Reference, technical, textbook. Subjects include firefighter training, public safety. Submit outline, 2 sample chapter(s), résumé, author bio, table of contents, SASE.

Recent Title(s): *The Fire Chief's Handbook, 6th Ed*, edited by Robert C. Barr and John Eversole.

Tips: "No human interest stories, technical training only."

FLORIDA ACADEMIC PRESS, P.O. Box 540, Gainesville FL 32602. (352)332-5104. Fax: (352)331-6003. E-mail: fapress@worldnet.att.net. **Acquisitions:** Max Vargas, CEO and managing editor; Sam Decalo, acquisitions editor (scholarly, self-help); Florence Dusek, assistant editor (fiction). Publishes hardcover and trade paperback originals. **Publishes 6 titles/year. Receives 300+ queries and 100+ mss/year. 50% of books from first-time authors; 100% from unagented writers. Pays 5-8% royalty on retail price, depending if paperback or hardcover.** Publishes book 3-5 months after acceptance of ms. Responds in 2-6 months to mss.

O→ "We are primarily an academic/scholarly publisher. We do publish self-help books if assessed as original. Our interest in serious fiction is secondary, and our criteria is strict. No poetry, science fiction, religious, autobiography, polemical, children's books or collections of stories."

Nonfiction: Reference, scholarly, self-help. Subjects include government/politics, history, third world. Submit complete ms. Reviews artwork/photos as part of ms package. Send photocopies.

Fiction: Literary, criticism. Submit complete ms.

Recent Title(s): *Complete Publishers Resource Manual*, by Linda Able (reference); *Civil-Military Relations in Africa*, by Samuel Decalo (history); *Orpheus in Brooklyn*, by Bertrand Mathieu (literary criticism).

Tips: Considers complete mss only. "Manuscripts we decide to publish must be re-submitted in camera-ready form."

FOCUS PUBLISHING, INC., P.O. Box 665, Bemidji MN 56619. (218)759-9817. Fax: (218)751-7210. Website: www.focuspublishing.com. **Acquisitions:** Jan Haley, president. Estab. 1993. Publishes hardcover and trade paperback originals and reprints. **Publishes 4-6 titles/year. Receives 300 queries and 200 mss/year. 90% of books from first-time authors; 100% from unagented writers. Pays 7-10% royalty on retail price.** Publishes book 1 year after acceptance of ms. Responds in less than 20 months to queries. Book catalog free.

O→ "Focus Publishing is a small press primarily devoted to adult Christian books with a Bible study emphasis."

Nonfiction: Subjects include religion, Christian living, Bible studies for men and women. Submit proposal package, including marketing ideas with SASE. Reviews artwork/photos as part of ms package. Send photocopies.

Recent Title(s): *Pure Freedom: Breaking the Addiction to Pornography*, by Mike Cleveland; *The Fruit of the Spirit Is...Self-Control*, by Lynn Stanley.

FORDHAM UNIVERSITY PRESS, University Box L, Bronx NY 10458. Fax: (718)807-4785. Website: www.fordhampress.com. **Acquisitions:** Mary Beatrice Schulte, executive editor. Publishes hardcover and trade paperback originals and reprints. **Publishes 30 titles/year. Receives 450 queries and 100 mss/year. 25% of books from first-time authors; 100% from unagented writers. Pays 4-7% royalty on retail price.** Publishes book 6-24 months after acceptance of ms. Responds in 2 months to proposals; 2 months to mss. Book catalog and ms guidelines free.

O→ "We are a publisher in humanities, accepting scholarly monographs, collections, occasional reprints and general interest titles for consideration."

Nonfiction: Biography, textbook, scholarly. Subjects include Americana, anthropology/archeology, art/architecture, gov-

ernment/politics, history, language/literature, military/war (World War II), philosophy, regional (New York), religion, sociology, translation. No fiction. Submit outline, 2-5 sample chapter(s).
Recent Title(s): *Palisades: 100,000 Acres in 100 years*, by Robert Binnewies.
Tips: "We have an academic and general audience."

FOREIGN POLICY ASSOCIATION, 470 Park Ave. S., New York NY 10016. (212)481-8100. Fax: (212)481-9275. Website: www.fpa.org. **Acquisitions:** Karen Rohan, editor-in-chief. Publishes 2 periodicals and an occasional hardcover and trade paperback original. **Publishes 5-6 titles/year. Receives 12 queries and 6 mss/year. 99% from unagented writers. Makes outright purchase of $2,500-4,000.** Publishes book 9 months after acceptance of ms. Accepts simultaneous submissions. Responds in 2 months to queries. Book catalog free.
Imprints: Headline Series (quarterly), Great Decisions (annual).
O‑ "The Foreign Policy Association, a nonpartisan, not-for-profit educational organization founded in 1918, is a catalyst for developing awareness, understanding of and informed opinion on U.S. foreign policy and global issues. Through its balanced, nonpartisan publications, FPA seeks to encourage individuals in schools, communities and the workplace to participate in the foreign policy process."
Nonfiction: Reference, textbook. Subjects include government/politics, history, foreign policy, social studies. Query, submit outline.
Recent Title(s): *NATO and Transatlantic Relations in the Twenty-First Century*, by Stanley R. Sloan.
Tips: Audience is students and people with an interest, but not necessarily any expertise, in foreign policy and international relations.

FORT ROSS, INC., RUSSIAN-AMERICAN PUBLISHING PROJECTS, 26 Arthur Place, Yonkers NY 10701. (914)375-6448. Fax: (914)375-6439. E-mail: ftross@ix.netcom.com. Website: www.fortross.net. **Acquisitions:** Dr. Vladimir P. Kartsev, executive director. Estab. 1992. Publishes paperback originals. **Publishes 12 titles/year. Receives 100 queries and 100 mss/year. Pays 4-7% royalty on wholesale price or makes outright purchase of $500-1,500. Offers $500-$1,000; negotiable advance.** Publishes book 1 year after acceptance of ms. Accepts simultaneous submissions. Responds in 1 month to queries; 1 month to proposals; 3 months to mss.
O‑ "Generally, we publish Russia-related books in English or Russian. Sometimes we publish various fiction and nonfiction books in collaboration with the East European publishers in translation. We are looking mainly for well-established authors."
Nonfiction: Biography, illustrated book (for adults and children), reference.
Fiction: Adventure, fantasy (space fantasy, sword and sorcery), horror, mainstream/contemporary, mystery (amateur sleuth, police procedural, private eye/hardboiled), romance (contemporary, futuristic/time travel), science fiction (hard science/technological, soft/sociological), suspense. Query with SASE.
Recent Title(s): *Cosack Galloped Far Away*, by Nikolas Feodoroff; *Verses*, by Filip Novikov; *Bay of Cross*, by Yury Egorov (in Russian).

FORTRESS PRESS, Box 1209, Minneapolis MN 55440-1209. (612)330-3300. Website: www.fortresspress.com. **Acquisitions:** J. Michael West, editor-in-chief; Dr. K.C. Hanson, editor. Publishes hardcover and trade paperback originals. **Publishes 60 titles/year. Receives 1,000 queries/year. 5-10% of books from first-time authors. Pays royalty on retail price.** Publishes book within 1 year after acceptance of ms. Accepts simultaneous submissions. Responds in 3 months to proposals. Book catalog free (call 1-800-328-4648); ms guidelines online.
O‑ Fortress Press publishes academic books in Biblical studies, theology, Christian ethics, church history, and professional books in pastoral care and counseling.
Nonfiction: Subjects include religion, women's issues/studies, church history, African-American studies. Query with annotated toc, brief cv, sample chapter (introduction) and SASE. Please study guidelines before submitting.
Recent Title(s): *The Writings of The New Testament*, by Luke Timothy Johnson; *The Wrath of Jonah: The Crisis of Religious Nationalism in the Israli-Palestinian Conflict*, by Rosemary Radford Ruether and Herman J. Ruether.

FORUM PUBLISHING CO., 383 E. Main St., Centerport NY 11721. (631)754-5000. Fax: (631)754-0630. Website: www.forum123.com. **Acquisitions:** Martin Stevens. Estab. 1981. Publishes trade paperback originals. **Publishes 12 titles/year. Receives 200 queries and 25 mss/year. 75% of books from first-time authors; 75% from unagented writers. Makes outright purchase of $250-750.** Publishes book 4 months after acceptance of ms. Accepts simultaneous submissions. Responds in 1 month to mss. Book catalog free.
O‑ "Forum publishes only business titles."
Nonfiction: Subjects include business/economics, money/finance. Submit outline. Reviews artwork/photos as part of ms package. Send photocopies.
Recent Title(s): *Selling Information By Mail*, by Glen Gilcrest.

FORWARD MOVEMENT PUBLICATIONS, 412 Sycamore St., Cincinnati OH 45202. (513)721-6659. Fax: (513)721-0729. E-mail: esgleason@forwarddaybyday.com. Website: www.forwardmovement.org. **Acquisitions:** The Reverend Dr. Edward S. Gleason, editor and director. Estab. 1934. Publishes trade and mass market paperback originals, trade paperback reprints and tracts. **Publishes 6 titles/year. Receives 1,000 queries and 300 mss/year. 30% of books from first-time authors; 100% from unagented writers. Pays one-time honorarium.** Responds in 1 month to queries; 1 month to proposals; 2 months to mss. Book catalog and ms guidelines free.
O‑ "Forward Movement was established 'to help reinvigorate the life of the church.' Many titles focus on the life of prayer, where our relationship with God is centered, death, marriage, baptism, recovery, joy, the Episcopal Church and more." Currently emphasizing prayer/spirituality.

Nonfiction: "We publish a variety of types of books, but they all relate to the lives of Christians. We are an agency of the Episcopal Church." Biography, children's/juvenile, reference, self-help (about religion and prayer). Subjects include religion. Query with SASE or submit complete ms.
Fiction: Episcopal for middle school (ages 8-12) readers. Juvenile. Query with SASE.
Recent Title(s): *God Is Not in the Thesaurus*, by Bo Don Cox (nonfiction); *Dare to Imagine*, by Sydney Vom Lehn (fiction).
Tips: Audience is primarily Episcopalians and other Christians.

FOUR WALLS EIGHT WINDOWS, 39 W. 14th St., Room 503, New York NY 10011. (212)206-8965. Fax: (212)206-8799. Website: www.4w8w.com. Publisher: John Oakes. **Acquisitions:** Acquistions Editor. Estab. 1987. Publishes hardcover originals, trade paperback originals and reprints. **Publishes 35 titles/year. Receives 3,000 submissions/year. 15% of books from first-time authors; 50% from unagented writers. Pays royalty on retail or net price, depending on contract. Offers variable advance.** Publishes book 1-2 years after acceptance of ms. Accepts simultaneous submissions. Responds in 2 months to queries. Book catalog for 6 X 9 SAE with 3 first-class stamps.
Imprints: No Exit, Axoplasm.

O→ Emphasizing fine literature and quality nonfiction, Four Walls Eight Windows has a reputation for carefully edited and distinctive books.

Nonfiction: Subjects include history, nature/environment, science. No New Age. Query with outline and SASE. All mss without SASE discarded.
Fiction: Feminist, gay/lesbian, nonfiction. "No romance, popular." Query with SASE. "Query letter accompanied by sample chapter, outline and SASE is best. Useful to know if writer has published elsewhere, and if so, where."
Recent Title(s): *The Mystery of the Aleph*, by Amir D. Aczel (science); *Valentine*, by Lucius Shepard (fiction); *Sizzling Chops, Dazzling Spins: Ping-Pong and the Art of Staying Alive*, by Jerome Charyn (history/memoir).

FOX CHAPEL PUBLISHING, 1970 Broad St., East Petersburg PA 17520. (717)560-4703. Fax: (717)560-4702. E-mail: editors@carvingworld.com. Website: www.foxchapelpublishing.com. **Acquisitions:** Alan Giagnocavo, publisher; Ayleen Stellhorn, editor. Publishes hardcover and trade paperback originals and trade paperback reprints. **Publishes 20-30 titles/year. 80% of books from first-time authors; 100% from unagented writers. Pays royalty or makes outright purchase. Offers variable advance.** Publishes book 6-18 months after acceptance of ms. Accepts simultaneous submissions. Responds in 2 months to queries.

O→ Fox Chapel publishes woodworking and woodcarving titles for professionals and hobbyists.

Nonfiction: Subjects include woodworking, wood carving, scroll saw and woodturning. Write for query submission guidelines. Reviews artwork/photos as part of ms package. Send photocopies.
Recent Title(s): *Carving the Human Face*, by Jeff Phares; *Scroll Saw Workbook*.
Tips: "We're looking for knowledgeable artists, woodworkers first, writers second to write for us. Our market is for avid woodworking hobbyists and professionals."

[N] **FPMI/STAR MOUNTAIN, INC.**, 4901 University Square, Suite 3, Huntsville AL 35816. (256)539-1850. Fax: (256)539-0911. E-mail: johns@fpmi.com. Website: www.fpmi.com. **Acquisitions:** John Sutherland, publications director. Estab. 1985. Publishes trade paperback originals. **Publishes 4-6 titles/year. Receives 4-5 submissions/year. 60% of books from first-time authors; 100% from unagented writers. Pays 15% on retail price.** Publishes book an average of 1 year after acceptance of ms. Accepts simultaneous submissions. Responds in 3 weeks to queries; 2 months to mss. Book catalog free or online.

O→ "Our primary audience is federal managers and supervisors—particularly first and second level."

Nonfiction: Technical. Subjects include government/politics, labor relations, personnel issues. "We will be publishing books for government and business on topics such as sexual harassment, human resources, and how to deal with leave abuse by employees. Our books are practical, how-to books for a supervisor or manager. Scholarly theoretical works do not interest our audience." Submit outline/synopsis and sample chapters or send complete ms.
Recent Title(s): *Building the Optimum Organization for Federal Agencies*, by C. Robert Nelson, DPA; *Workplace Harassment: A Handbook for Supervisors, Managers and EEO and Human Resources Professions*, by Marilyn L. (Teplitz) Mattingly.
Tips: "We are interested in books that are practical, easy-to-read and less than 150 pages. If I were a writer trying to market a book today, I would emphasize practical topics with plenty of examples in succinct, concrete language."

FRANCISCAN UNIVERSITY PRESS, 1235 University Blvd., Steubenville OH 43852. (888)333-0381 or (740)283-6357. Fax: (740)284-5454. Website: www.franciscan.edu. **Acquisitions:** Dreama Thompson. Publishes trade paperback originals and reprints. **Publishes 4 titles/year. 5% of books from first-time authors; 100% from unagented writers. Pays 5-15% royalty on retail price.** Publishes book 1 year after acceptance of ms. Responds in 3 months to proposals. Book catalog free; ms guidelines free.

O→ "We seek to further the Catholic and Franciscan mission of Franciscan University of Steubenville by publishing books in the areas of theology, biblical studies, religious education, youth ministry and prayer with a particular focus on Apologetics."

Nonfiction: Subjects include religion. Publications that will teach the Catholic faith and lend to a deeper understanding of Christian living. Query with cv and SASE or send complete ms.
Recent Title(s): *The Holy Spirit*, by Fr. Michael Scanlan, TOR; *Loving Abba*, by Fr. Sam Tiesi, TOR.

[A] **FREE PRESS**, Simon & Schuster, 1230 Avenue of the Americas, New York NY 10020. (212)698-7000. Fax: (212)632-4989. Website: www.simonsays.com. Publisher: Martha Levin. **Acquisitions:** Bruce Nichols, vice president/senior editor (history/serious nonfiction); Leslie Meredith, vice president/senior editor (psychology/sprituality/self-help); Fred Hills (business/serious nonfiction); Bill Rosen, vice president/executive editor (serious nonfiction/illustrated/reference); Amy Scheibe, senior editor (literary fiction); Elizabeth Stein, senior editor (history, current events, biography, memoir); Dominick Anfuso, vice president/editorial director (self-help/literary fiction). Estab. 1947. **Publishes 120 titles/year. Receives 3,000 submissions/year. 15% of books from first-time authors; 50% from unagented writers. Pays variable royalty. Offers advance.** Publishes book 1 year after acceptance of ms. Responds in 2 months to queries.

O→ The Free Press publishes a wide variety of fiction and nonfiction.

Nonfiction: Does not accept unagented submissions. Query with 1-3 sample chapters, outline before submitting mss.

Recent Title(s): *Self Matters*, by Phil McGraw; *American Jihad*, by Steven Emerson.

FREE SPIRIT PUBLISHING, INC., 217 Fifth Ave. N., Suite 200, Minneapolis MN 55401-1260. (612)338-2068. Fax: (612)337-5050. E-mail: help4kids@freespirit.com. Website: www.freespirit.com. Publisher: Judy Galbraith. **Acquisitions:** Acquisitions Editor. Estab. 1983. Publishes trade paperback originals and reprints. **Publishes 20 titles/year. 25% of books from first-time authors; 50% from unagented writers. Offers advance.** Book catalog and ms guidelines free; ms guidelines online.

Imprints: Self-Help for Kids, Learning to Get Along Series, Self-Help for Teens.

O→ "We believe passionately in empowering kids to learn to think for themselves and make their own good choices."

Nonfiction: Children's/juvenile (young adult), self-help (parenting). Subjects include child guidance/parenting, education (pre-K-12, study and social skills, special needs, differentiation but not textbooks or basic skills books like reading, counting, etc.), health/medicine (mental/emotional health for/about children), psychology (for/about children), sociology (for/about children). "Many of our authors are educators, mental health professionals, and youth workers involved in helping kids and teens." No fiction or picture storybooks, poetry, single biographies or autobiographies, books with mythical or animal characters, or books with religious or New Age content. Query with cover letter stating qualifications, intent, and intended audience and how your book stands out from the field, along with outline, 2 sample chapters, résumé, SASE. Do not send original copies of work.

Recent Title(s): *See Jane Win for Girls*; *Life Lists for Teens*; *How to Take the Grrrr Out of Anger.*

Tips: "Our books are issue-oriented, jargon-free, and solution-focused. Our audience is children, teens, teachers, parents and youth counselors. We are especially concerned with kids' social and emotional well-being and look for books with ready-to-use strategies for coping with today's issues at home or in school—written in every-day language. We are not looking for academic or religious materials, or books that analyze problem's with the nation's school systems. Instead, we want books that offer practical, positive advice so kids can help themselves and parents and teachers can help kids succeed."

FRONT STREET, 20 Battery Park Ave., #403, Asheville NC 28801. (828)236-3097. Fax: (828)236-3098. E-mail: contactus@frontstreetbooks.com. Website: www.frontstreetbooks.com. **Acquisitions:** Joy Neaves, editor. Estab. 1994. Publishes hardcover originals. **Publishes 10-15 titles/year; imprint publishes 6-12 titles/year. Receives 1,000 queries and 2,000 mss/year. 75% of books from first-time authors; 90% from unagented writers. Pays royalty on retail price. Offers advance.** Publishes book 1 year after acceptance of ms. Accepts simultaneous submissions. Responds in 1 month to queries; 2 months to proposals; 3 months to mss. Book catalog online; ms guidelines online.

Imprints: Front Street/Lemniscant Books.

O→ "We are an independent publisher of books for children and young adults."

Nonfiction: Biography, children's/juvenile, humor, illustrated book. Subjects include animals, creative nonfiction, ethnic, history, language/literature, memoirs, spirituality. Reviews artwork/photos as part of ms package. Send photocopies.

Fiction: Adventure, fantasy, feminist, historical, humor, juvenile, literary, picture books, science fiction, young adult (adventure, fantasy/science fiction, historical, mystery/suspense, problem novels, sports). Query with SASE or submit complete ms.

Poetry: Submit 25 sample poems.

Recent Title(s): *Marika*, by Andrea Cheng (YA novel); *Stray Voltage*, by Eugenie Doyle; *Many Stones*, by Carolyn Coman (YA novel).

FUTURE HORIZONS, 721 W. Abram St., Arlington TX 76013. (817)277-0727. Fax: (817)277-2270. E-mail: info@futurehorizons-autism.com. Website: www.futurehorizons-autism.com. **Acquisitions:** R. Wayne Gilpin, president (autism/Asperger's syndrome). Publishes hardcover originals, trade paperback originals and reprints. **Publishes 10 titles/year. Receives 250 queries and 125 mss/year. 75% of books from first-time authors; 95% from unagented writers. Pays 10% royalty or makes outright purchase.** Publishes book 2 months after acceptance of ms. Accepts simultaneous submissions. Responds in 1 month to queries; 2 months to proposals. Book catalog and ms guidelines free on request.

Nonfiction: Children's/juvenile (pertaining to autism), cookbook (for autistic individuals), humor (about autism), self-help (detailing with autism/Asperger's syndrome). Subjects include education (about autism/Asperger's syndrome), autism. Submit proposal package including outline. Reviews artwork/photos as part of ms package. Send photocopies.

Recent Title(s): *Diagnosing Jefferson*, by Norm Ledgin (nonfiction); *Tobin Learns to Make Friends*, by Diane Murrell (childrens fiction).

Tips: Audience is parents, teachers, professionals dealing with individuals with autism or Asperger's syndrome. "Books that sell well, have practical and useful information on how to help individuals and/or care givers of individuals with autism. Personal stories, even success stories, are usually not helpful to others in a practical way."

GATFPress, Graphic Arts Technical Foundation, 200 Deer Run Rd., Sewickley PA 15143-2600. (412)741-6860. Fax: (412)741-2311. E-mail: poresick@gatf.org. Website: www.gain.net. **Acquisitions:** Peter Oresick, director of publications; Tom Destree, editor in chief; Amy Woodall, managing editor (graphic arts, communication, book publishing, printing).

Estab. 1924. Publishes trade paperback originals and hardcover reference texts. **Publishes 15 titles/year. Receives 25 submissions/year. 50% of books from first-time authors; 100% from unagented writers. Pays 5-15% royalty on retail price.** Publishes book 6 months after acceptance of ms. Responds in 1 month. *Writer's Market* recommends allowing 2 months for reply to queries. Book catalog for 9×12 SAE with 2 first-class stamps; ms guidelines for #10 SASE.

O→ "GATF's mission is to serve the graphic communications community as the major resource for technical information and services through research and education." Currrently emphasizing career guides for graphic communications.

Nonfiction: How-to, reference, technical, textbook. Subjects include printing/graphic communications, electronic publishing. "We primarily want textbook/reference books about printing and related technologies. However, we are expanding our reach into electronic communications." Query with SASE or submit outline, sample chapters and SASE. Reviews artwork/photos as part of ms package.

Recent Title(s): *Practical Proofreading*, by Matthew Willen; *Understanding Graphic Communication*, by Harvey Levenson; *Chemistry for the Graphic Arts*, by Nelson Eldred.

Tips: "We are publishing titles that are updated more frequently, such as *On-Demand Publishing*. Our scope now includes reference titles geared toward general audiences interested in computers, imaging, and Internet as well as print publishing."

GEM GUIDES BOOK CO., 315 Cloverleaf Dr., Suite F, Baldwin Park CA 91706-6510. (626)855-1611. Fax: (626)855-1610. E-mail: gembooks@aol.com. Website: www.gemguidesbooks.com. **Acquisitions:** Kathy Mayerski, editor. Estab. 1965. **Publishes 6-8 titles/year. Receives 20 submissions/year. 60% of books from first-time authors; 100% from unagented writers. Pays 6-10% royalty on retail price.** Publishes book 1 year after acceptance of ms. Accepts simultaneous submissions. Responds in 5 months to queries.

Imprints: Gembooks.

O→ "Gem Guides prefers nonfiction books for the hobbyist in rocks and minerals; lapidary and jewelry-making; travel and recreation guide books for the West and Southwest; and other regional local interest." Currently emphasizing how-to, field guides, West/Southwest regional interest. De-emphasizing stories, history, poetry.

Nonfiction: Subjects include history (Western), hobbies (lapidary and jewelry-making), nature/environment, recreation, regional (Western US), science (earth), travel. Query with outline/synopsis and sample chapters with SASE. Reviews artwork/photos as part of ms package.

Recent Title(s): *Fee Mining and Rockhounding Adventures in the West*, by James Martin Monaco and Jeannette Hathaway Monaco; *The GPS Guide to Western Gem Trails*, by David Kelty; *The Toddler's Guide to Southern California*, by Jobea Way.

Tips: "We have a general audience of people interested in recreational activities. Publishers plan and have specific book lines in which they specialize. Learn about the publisher and submit materials compatible with that publisher's product line."

GGC, INC./PUBLISHING, 2545 Sandbourne Lane, Herndon VA 20171. (703)793-8604. Fax: (703)793-8830. E-mail: gardner@ggcinc.com. Website: www.gogardner.com. **Acquisitions:** Garth Gardner, publisher (computer graphics, animation cartoons); Bonney Ford, editor (GGC, art, animation). Publishes trade paperback reprints. **Publishes 10 titles/year; imprint publishes 2 titles/year. Receives 50 queries and 25 mss/year. 80% of books from first-time authors; 70% from unagented writers. Pays 10-15% royalty on wholesale price or makes outright purchase.** Publishes book 3 months after acceptance of ms. Accepts simultaneous submissions. Responds in 1 month to queries. Book catalog online; ms guidelines online.

O→ GGC publishes books on the subjects of computer graphics, animation, new media, multimedia, art, cartoons, drawing.

Nonfiction: How-to, multimedia, reference, self-help, technical, textbook. Subjects include art/architecture, education, history, computer graphics. Submit proposal package including 2 sample chapter(s), résumé, cover letter. Reviews artwork/photos as part of ms package. Send photocopies.

Recent Title(s): *Career Diary of an Animation Studio Owner*, by Joseph L. Daniels; *Career Diary of an Animation Producer*, by Sue Riedl.

GLENBRIDGE PUBLISHING, LTD., 19923 E. Long Ave., Centennial CO 80016. (720)870-8381. Fax: (720)870-5598. E-mail: glenbr@eazy.net. **Acquisitions:** James A. Keene, editor. Estab. 1986. Publishes hardcover originals and reprints, trade paperback originals. **Publishes 6-8 titles/year. Pays 10% royalty.** Publishes book 1 year after acceptance of ms. Accepts simultaneous submissions. Responds in 2 months to queries. Book catalog online; ms guidelines for #10 SASE.

O→ "Glenbridge has an eclectic approach to publishing. We look for titles that have long-term capabilities."

Nonfiction: Subjects include Americana, business/economics, cooking/foods/nutrition, history, philosophy, psychology, sociology, music. Query with outline/synopsis, sample chapters and SASE.

Recent Title(s): *Three Minute Therapy: Change Your Thinking/Change Your Life*, by Dr. Michael Edelstein with David R. Steele.

THE GLOBE PEQUOT PRESS, INC., P.O. Box 480, Guilford CT 06437. (203)458-4500. Fax: (203)458-4604. Website: www.globe-pequot.com. President/Publisher: Linda Kennedy. **Acquisitions:** Shelley Wolf, submissions editor. Estab. 1947. Publishes paperback originals, hardcover originals and reprints. **Publishes 500 titles/year. Receives 2,500 submissions/year. 30% of books from first-time authors; 70% from unagented writers. Average print order for a first book is 4,000-7,500. Makes an outright purchase or pays 10% royalty on net price. Offers advance.** Publishes book 1 year after acceptance of ms. Accepts simultaneous submissions. Responds in 3 months to queries. Ms guidelines online.

O⸺ Globe Pequot is the largest publisher of regional travel books and outdoor recreation in the United States and offers the broadest selection of travel titles of any vendor in this market.

Nonfiction: Humor (regional), regional travel guidebooks, outdoor recreation guides, natural history field guides. Subjects include cooking/foods/nutrition (regional), history (popular, regional), nature/environment, recreation, regional, travel. No doctoral theses, fiction, genealogies, poetry, or textbooks. Submit brief synopsis of work, table of contents or outline, sample chapter, résumé/vita, definition of target audience, and an analysis of competing titles. Reviews artwork/photos as part of ms package.

Recent Title(s): *Exploring Glacier National Park*; *Hiking Wisconsin*; *Kansas Curiosities*.

DAVID R. GODINE, PUBLISHER, INC., 9 Hamilton Place, Boston MA 02108. (617)451-9600. Fax: (617)350-0250. E-mail: info@godine.com. Website: www.godine.com. Estab. 1970. Publishes hardcover and trade paperback originals and reprints. **Publishes 35 titles/year. Pays royalty on retail price.** Publishes book 3 years after acceptance of ms. Book catalog for 5×8 SAE with 3 first-class stamps.

O⸺ "Our particular strengths are books about the history and design of the written word, literary essays, and the best of world fiction in translation. We also have an unusually strong list of children's books, all of them printed in their entirety with no cuts, deletions, or side-stepping to keep the political watchdogs happy."

Nonfiction: Biography, children's/juvenile, coffee table book, cookbook, illustrated book. Subjects include Americana, art/architecture, gardening, nature/environment, photography, literary criticism, book arts, typography. *No unsolicited mss.* Query with SASE.

Fiction: Historical, literary, translation. *No unsolicited mss.* Query with SASE.

Recent Title(s): *The Penelopeia*, by Jane Rawlings; *A Year with Emerson*, selected and edited by Richard Grossman; *Henrietta & the Golden Eggs*, by Hanna Johansen, pictures by Kaethi Bhend.

Tips: "Please visit our website for more information about our books and detailed submission policy. No phone calls, please."

THE GRADUATE GROUP, P.O. Box 370351, West Hartford CT 06137-0351. (860)233-2330. Fax: (860)233-2330. E-mail: graduategroup@hotmail.com. Website: www.graduategroup.com. **Acquisitions:** Mara Whitman, president; Robert Whitman, vice president. Estab. 1964. Publishes trade paperback originals. **Publishes 50 titles/year. Receives 100 queries and 70 mss/year. 60% of books from first-time authors; 85% from unagented writers. Pays 20% royalty on retail price.** Publishes book 3 months after acceptance of ms. Accepts simultaneous submissions. Responds in 1 month to queries. Book catalog and ms guidelines free; ms guidelines online.

O⸺ "The Graduate Group helps college and graduate students better prepare themselves for rewarding careers and helps people advance in the workplace." Currently emphasizing test preparation, career advancement and materials for prisoners, law enforcement, books on unique careers.

Nonfiction: Reference. Subjects include business/economics, education, government/politics, health/medicine, money/finance, law enforcement. Submit complete ms and SASE with sufficient postage.

Recent Title(s): *Real Life 101: Winning Secrets You Won't Find in Class*, by Debra Yergen; *Getting In: Applicant's Guide to Graduate School Admissions*, by David Burrell.

Tips: Audience is career planning offices; college, graduate school and public libraries. "We are open to all submissions, especially those involving career planning, internships and other nonfiction titles. Looking for books on law enforcement, books for prisoners and reference books on subjects/fields students would be interested in. We want books on helping students and others to interview, pass tests, gain opportunity, understand the world of work, networking, building experience, preparing for advancement, preparing to enter business, improving personality and building relationships."

GRAND CANYON ASSOCIATION, P.O. Box 399, 1 Tonto St., Grand Canyon AZ 86023. (928)638-2481. Fax: (928)638-2484. E-mail: tberger@grandcanyon.org. Website: www.grandcanyon.org. **Acquisitions:** Todd R. Berger, managing editor (Grand Canyon-related geology, natural history, outdoor activities, human history, photography, ecology, etc., posters and other non-book products). Estab. 1932. Publishes hardcover originals and reprints and trade paperback originals and reprints. **Publishes 6 titles/year. Receives 100 queries and 100 submissions/year. 70% of books from first-time authors; 99% from unagented writers. Pays royalty on wholesale price or makes outright purchase.** Publishes book 1 month-1 year after acceptance of ms. Accepts simultaneous submissions. Responds in 2 months to queries; 2 months to proposals; 2 months to mss. Book catalog online; ms guidelines by email.

Nonfiction: Autobiography, biography, booklets, children's/juvenile, coffee table book, gift book, how-to, illustrated book, scholarly. Subjects include animals, anthropology/archeology, art/architecture, creative nonfiction, general nonfiction, history, nature/environment, photography, recreation, regional, science, sports, travel, geology. Grand Canyon Association (GCA) is a nonprofit organization established in 1932 to support education, research, and other programs for the benefit of Grand Canyon National Park and its visitors. GCA operates bookstores throughout the park, publishes books and other materials related to the Grand Canyon region, supports wildlife surveys and other research, funds acquisitions for the park's research library, and produces a wide variety of free publications and exhibits for park visitors. Since 1932 GCA has provided Grand Canyon National Park with over $15 million in aid. All publications and other products are related to Grand Canyon National Park and the surrounding region. Query with SASE or submit proposal package including outline, 3-4 sample chapter(s), list of publication credits and samples of previous work or submit complete ms. Reviews artwork/photos as part of ms package. Send transparencies or color or b&w prints are okay, as are digital scans of images.

Recent Title(s): *Phantom Ranch*, by Scott Thybony (illustrated history); *Grand Canyon: The Vault of Heaven*, by Susan Lamb (photograhic scenic book); *An Introduction to Grand Canyon Geology*, by L. Greer Price (illustrated geology).

Tips: "All books, articles, and other products must be about the Grand Canyon. We also publish some things, to a much lesser extent, on the surrounding region, particularly geology-related titles with a connection to the Grand Canyon."

GRAYWOLF PRESS, 2402 University Ave., Suite 203, St. Paul MN 55114. (651)641-0077. Fax: (651)641-0036. Website: www.graywolfpress.org. Editor/Publisher: Fiona McCrae. Executive Editor: Anne Czarniecki. Poetry Editor: Jeffrey Shotts. **Acquisitions:** Katie Dublinski, editor (nonfiction, fiction). Estab. 1974. Publishes trade cloth and paperback originals. **Publishes 16 titles/year. Receives 2,500 queries/year. 20% of books from first-time authors; 50% from unagented writers. Pays royalty on retail price. author's copies. Offers $1,000-6,000 advance.** Publishes book 18 months after acceptance of ms. Does not accept simultaneous submissions. Responds in 3 months to queries. Book catalog free; ms guidelines online.

O→ Graywolf Press is an independent, nonprofit publisher dedicated to the creation and promotion of thoughtful and imaginative contemporary literature essential to a vital and diverse culture.

Nonfiction: Subjects include contemporary culture, language/literature, culture. Query with SASE.

Fiction: Literary, short story collections. "Familiarize yourself with our list first." No genre books (romance, western, science fiction, suspense). Query with SASE. "Please do not fax or e-mail queries or submissions."

Poetry: "We are interested in linguistically challenging work." Query with SASE.

Recent Title(s): *Blind Huber*, by Nick Flynn; *The House on Eccles Road*, by Judith Kitchen; *Famous Builder*, by Paul Lisickey.

[N] **GREAT POTENTIAL PRESS**, P.O. Box 5057, Scottsdale AZ 85261. (602)954-4200. Fax: (602)954-0185. E-mail: info@giftedbooks.com. Website: www.giftedbooks.com. **Acquisitions:** Janet Gore, editor (gifted curriculum in schools); James Webb, president (parenting and social and emotional needs). Estab. 1986. Publishes trade paperback originals. **Publishes 4-5 titles/year. Receives 10 queries and 10-15 mss/year. 25% of books from first-time authors; 100% from unagented writers. Pays 10% royalty on retail price.** Publishes book 6-12 months after acceptance of ms. Accepts simultaneous submissions. Responds in 2 months to queries; 3 months to proposals; 4 months to mss. Book catalog free or on website; ms guidelines online.

O→ Great Potential Press publishes books on the social/emotional/interpersonal/creative needs of gifted and talented children and adults for parents and teachers of gifted and talented youngsters. Currently emphasizing books regarding gifted and talented children, their parents and teachers. De-emphasizing research-based books.

Nonfiction: Biography, children's/juvenile, humor, reference, self-help, textbook, assessment scales, advocacy, parenting tips. Subjects include child guidance/parenting, education, multicultural, psychology, translation, travel, women's issues/studies, gifted/talented children and adults. No research-based books, dissertations. Submit proposal package, including preface or introduction, TOC, outline, 3 sample chapters and an explanation of how work differs from similar published books.

Recent Title(s): *Helping Gifted Children Soar*, by Carol Strip, Ph.D.; *Raisin' Brains: Surviving My Smart Family*, by Karen Isaacson; *Some of My Best Friends Are Books, 2nd Ed*, by Judith Halste.

Tips: "Manuscripts should be clear, cogent, and well-written and should pertain to gifted, talented, and creative persons and/or issues."

GREAT QUOTATIONS PUBLISHING, 8102 Lemont Rd., #300, Woodridge IL 60517. (630)390-3580. **Acquisitions:** Diane Voreis, acquisitions editor (humor, relationships, Christian); Jan Stob, acquisitions editor (children's). Estab. 1991. **Publishes 30 titles/year. Receives 1,500 queries and 1,200 mss/year. 50% of books from first-time authors; 80% from unagented writers. Pays 3-8% royalty on net receipts.** Publishes book 6 months after acceptance of ms. Accepts simultaneous submissions. Responds in 6 months with SASE to queries. Book catalog for $2; ms guidelines for #10 SASE.

O→ Great Quotations seeks original material for the following general categories: children, humor, inspiration, motivation, success, romance, tributes to mom/dad/grandma/grandpa, etc. Currently emphasizing humor, relationships. De-emphasizing poetry, self-help. We publish new books twice a year, in July and in January.

Nonfiction: Humor, illustrated book, self-help. Subjects include business/economics, child guidance/parenting, nature/environment, religion, sports, women's issues/studies. "We look for subjects with identifiable markets, appealing to the general public. We publish humorous books or others requiring multicolor illustration on the inside. We don't publish highly controversial subject matter." Submit outline, 2 sample chapter(s). Reviews artwork/photos as part of ms package. Send photocopies or transparencies.

Poetry: "We would be most interested in upbeat and humorous poetry."

Recent Title(s): *Secret Language of Men*; *Astrology for Cat.*

Tips: "Our books are physically small and generally a very quick read. They are available at gift shops and book shops throughout the country. We are aware that most of our books are bought on impulse and given as gifts. We need strong, clever, descriptive titles; beautiful cover art and brief, positive, upbeat text. Be prepared to submit final manuscript on computer disk, according to our specifications. (It is not necessary to try to format the typesetting of your manuscript to look like a finished book.)"

[N] ⊘ **GREEN BEAN PRESS**, P.O. Box 237, New York NY 10013. (718)965-2076. Fax: (718)965-2076. E-mail: gbpress@earthlink.net. Website: www.greenbeanpress.com. **Acquisitions:** Ian Griffin, editor. Estab. 1993. Publishes paperback originals. **Publishes 6 titles/year. 90% from unagented writers. Pays 10-15% royalty.** Publishes book 6-12 months after acceptance of ms. Does not accept simultaneous submissions. Responds in 2 weeks to queries; 2 months to mss. Book catalog online; ms guidelines online.

O→ "Small independent press dedicated to publishing gritty, unique, distinctive authors."

Fiction: Humor, literary, mystery (private eye/hardboiled), short story collections. Prefers "shorter works, averaging between 80 and 175 pages." Query with SASE or submit outline, 2-4 sample chapter(s), synopsis, author bio. **All unsolicited mss returned unopened.**

Recent Title(s): *Frostbite*, by Nathan Graziano; *Do Not Look Directly Into Me*, by Daniel Crocker (short story); *Wing-Ding at Uncle Tug's*, by Jeff Grimshaw (humor/short story).

Tips: "Green Bean Press is not currently considering new mss, so please do not query us about your ms until 2004. We are sorry for this inconvenience, but we are a very small company and our schedule is completely booked."

GREENE BARK PRESS, P.O. Box 1108, Bridgeport CT 06601. (203)372-4861. Fax: (203)371-5856. Website: www.greenebarkpress.com. **Acquisitions:** Thomas J. Greene, publisher; Michele Hofbauer, associate publisher. Estab. 1991. Publishes hardcover originals. **Publishes 5 titles/year. Receives 100 queries and 6,000 mss/year. 60% of books from first-time authors; 100% from unagented writers. Pays 10-15% royalty on wholesale price.** Publishes book 1 year after acceptance of ms. Accepts simultaneous submissions. Responds in 1 month to queries; 6 months to mss. Book catalog for $2; ms guidelines for SASE.

Greene Bark Press only publishes books for children and young adults, mainly picture and read-to books. "All of our titles appeal to the imagination and encourage children to read and explore the world through books. We only publish children's fiction—all subjects—but in reading picture book format appealing to ages 3-9 or all ages."

Fiction: Juvenile. Submit complete ms. No queries or ms by e-mail.

Recent Title(s): *The Magical Trunk*, by Gigi Tegge; *Hey! There's a Goblin Under My Throne!*, by Rhett Ransom Pennell.

Tips: Audience is "children who read to themselves and others. Mothers, fathers, grandparents, godparents who read to their respective children, grandchildren. Include SASE, be prepared to wait, do not inquire by telephone."

GREENHAVEN PRESS, INC., 10911 Technology Place, San Diego CA 92127. Website: www.greenhaven.com. **Acquisitions:** Chandra Howard, aquisitions editor. Estab. 1970. Publishes approximately 135 anthologies/year; all anthologies are works for hire. **Makes outright purchase of $1,000-3,000.** Send query letter and résumé. No unsolicited ms to queries. Book catalog for 9×12 SAE with 3 first-class stamps or online.

Greenhaven Press publishes hard and softcover educational supplementary materials and (nontrade) nonfiction anthologies on contemporary issues, literary criticism and history for high school and college readers. These anthologies serve as supplementary educational material for high school and college libraries and classrooms. Currently emphasizing historical topics, and social-issue anthologies.

Nonfiction: Children's/juvenile. Subjects include education, history. "We produce tightly formatted anthologies on contemporary issues, literary criticism, and history for high school and college-level readers. We are looking for freelance book editors to research and compile these anthologies; we are not interested in submissions of single-author manuscripts. Each series has specific requirements. Potential book editors should familiarize themselves with our catalog and anthologies." Query. No unsolicited ms.

Recent Title(s): *Opposing Viewpoints: Abortion*; *Examining Pop Culture: Violence in Film and TV*; *At Issue in History: The Cuban Missle Crisis*.

GREENLINE PUBLICATIONS, P.O. Box 590780, San Francisco CA 94159-0780. (415)386-8646, ext. 39. Fax: (415)386-8049. E-mail: funrises2@aol.com. Website: www.greenlinepub.com. **Acquisitions:** Chuck Thompson, executive editor (travel publications); Roger Migdow, associate publisher. Estab. 1998. Publishes trade paperback originals. **Publishes 6 titles/year; imprint publishes 4 (Fun); 2 (Historic) titles/year. Makes outright purchase of $15,000-20,000. Offers $5,000 advance.** Does not accept simultaneous submissions. Responds in 2 months to queries; 2 months to proposals; 2 months to mss. Book catalog free.

Imprints: Fun Seeker's Guides; Greenline Historical Travel Guides.

Nonfiction: Subjects include history, travel. Submit proposal package including outline. Reviews artwork/photos as part of ms package.

Recent Title(s): *The 25 Best World War II Sites: Pacific Theater*, by Chuck Thompson (travel); *The Fun Seeker's North America*, by Alan S. Davis (travel).

Tips: Adult travelers.

GREENWILLOW BOOKS, HarperCollins Publishers, 1350 Avenue of the Americas, New York NY 10019. (212)261-6500. Website: www.harperchildrens.com. Senior Editor: Rebecca Davis. Estab. 1974. Publishes hardcover originals and reprints. **Publishes 50-60 titles/year. 1% of books from first-time authors; 30% from unagented writers. Pays 10% royalty. on wholesale price for first-time authors. Offers variable advance.** Publishes book 2 years after acceptance of ms.

Greenwillow Books publishes quality picture books and fiction for young readers of all ages, and nonfiction primarily for children under seven years of age.

Fiction: Juvenile. Fantasy, humor, literary, mystery, picture books.

Recent Title(s): *Whale Talk*, by Chris Crutcher.

Tips: "Currently not accepting unsolicited mail, mss or queries. Please call (212)261-6627 for an update."

GREENWOOD PRESS, Greenwood Publishing Group, 88 Post Rd. W., Westport CT 06881. (203)226-3571. Fax: (203)222-1502. Website: www.greenwood.com. **Acquisitions:** Gary Kuris, editorial director; Emily Birch, managing editor. Publishes hardcover originals. **Publishes 200 titles/year. Receives 1,000 queries/year. 25% of books from first-time authors. Pays variable royalty on net price. Offers rare advance.** Publishes book 1 year after acceptance of ms. Accepts simultaneous submissions. Responds in 6 months to queries. Book catalog and ms guidelines online; ms guidelines online.

Greenwood Press publishes reference materials for high school, public and academic libraries in the humanities and the social and hard sciences.

Nonfiction: Reference, scholarly. Subjects include humanities, social sciences, humanities and the social and hard sciences.

Query with proposal package, including scope, organization, length of project, whether complete ms is available or when it will be, cv or résumé and SASE. *No unsolicited mss.*

Recent Title(s): *All Things Shakespeare*, by Kirstin Olsen.

GREENWOOD PUBLISHING GROUP, Reed-Elsevier (USA) Inc., 88 Post Rd. W, Westport CT 06881. (203)226-3571. Fax: (203)222-1502. Website: www.greenwood.com. **Acquisitions:** Reference—George Butler (literature, drama, gbutler@greenwood.com); Debbie Carvalko (psychology); Eric Levy (art and architecture, music and dance, popular culture, elevy@greenwood.com). Secondary School Reference—Heather Staines (history and military studies, hstaines@-greenwood.com). **Publishes 700 titles/year. Pays variable royalty on net price. Offers advance rarely. Offers rare advance.** Publishes book 1 year after acceptance of ms. Accepts simultaneous submissions. Book catalog online; ms guidelines online.

Imprints: Praeger, Greenwood Press.

The Greenwood Publishing Group consists of two distinguished imprints with one unifying purpose: to provide the best possible reference and general interest resources in the humanities and the social and hard sciences.

Nonfiction: Reference, scholarly. Subjects include business/economics, child guidance/parenting, education, government/politics, history, humanities, language/literature, music/dance, psychology, religion, social sciences, sociology, sports, women's issues/studies. Query with proposal package, including scope, organization, length of project, whether a complete ms is available or when it will be, cv or résumé and SASE. *No unsolicited mss.*

Tips: "No interest in fiction, drama, poetry—looking for reference materials and materials for educated general readers. Most of our authors are college professors who have distinguished credentialsa and who have published research widely in their fields." Greenwood Publishing maintains an excellent website, providing complete catalog, ms guidelines and editorial contacts.

GROSSET & DUNLAP PUBLISHERS, Penguin Putnam Inc., 345 Hudson St., New York NY 10014. President/Publisher: Debra Dorfman. Estab. 1898. Publishes hardcover (few) and paperback originals. **Publishes 175 titles/year. Pays royalty. Offers advance.** Publishes book 18 months after acceptance of ms. Does not accept simultaneous submissions. Responds in 2 months to queries.

Grosset & Dunlap publishes children's books that show children that reading is fun, with books that speak to their interests, and that are affordable so that children can build a home library of their own. Focus on licensed properties, series and readers.

Nonfiction: Children's/juvenile. Subjects include nature/environment, science. *Agented submissions only.*

Fiction: Juvenile. *Agented submissions only.*

Recent Title(s): *Katie Kazoo* (series); *Dish* (series); *Strawberry Shortcake* (license).

Tips: "Nonfiction that is particularly topical or of wide interest in the mass market; new concepts for novelty format for preschoolers; and very well-written easy readers on topics that appeal to primary graders have the best chance of selling to our firm."

GROUP PUBLISHING, INC., 1515 Cascade Ave., Loveland CO 80538. (970)669-3836. Fax: (970)679-4370. E-mail: kloesche@grouppublishing.com. Website: www.grouppublishing.com. **Acquisitions:** Kerri Loesche, editorial assistant. Estab. 1974. Publishes trade paperback originals. **Publishes 24 titles/year. Receives 200 queries and 50 mss/year. 40% of books from first-time authors; 95% from unagented writers. Pays up to 10% royalty on wholesale price or makes outright purchase or work for hire. Offers up to $1,000 advance.** Publishes book 18 months after acceptance of ms. Accepts simultaneous submissions. Responds in 1 month to queries; 6 months to proposals; 6 months to mss. Book catalog for 9×12 SAE with 2 first-class stamps; ms guidelines online.

"Our mission is to encourage Christian growth in children, youth and adults."

Nonfiction: Children's/juvenile, how-to, multimedia, textbook. Subjects include education, religion. "We're an interdenominational publisher of resource materials for people who work with adults, youth or children in a Christian church setting. We also publish materials for use directly by youth or children (such as devotional books, workbooks or Bibles stories). Everything we do is based on concepts of active and interactive learning as described in *Why Nobody Learns Much of Anything at Church: And How to Fix It*, by Thom and Joani Schultz. We need new, practical, hands-on, innovative, out-of-the-box ideas—things that no one's doing... yet." Query with SASE or submit proposal package including outline, 3 sample chapter(s), cover letter, introduction to book, and sample activities if appropriate.

Recent Title(s): *Aqua Church*, by Leonard Sweet (church leadership); *The Dirt on Learning*, by Thom and Joani Schultz (effective teaching and learning).

Tips: "Our audience consists of pastors, Christian education directors and Sunday school teachers."

ALDINE DE GRUYTER, Walter de Gruyter, Inc., 200 Saw Mill River Rd., Hawthorne NY 10532. (914)747-0110, ext. 19. Fax: (914)747-1326. E-mail: rkoffler@degruyterny.com. Website: www.degruyter.de. **Acquisitions:** Dr. Richard Koffler, executive editor. Publishes hardcover and academic paperback originals. **Publishes 15-25 titles/year. Receives several hundred queries and 100 mss/year. 15% of books from first-time authors; 99% from unagented writers. Pays 7½-10% royalty on net receipts.** Publishes book 9 months after acceptance of ms. Accepts simultaneous submissions. Responds in 2 months to proposals. Book catalog free; ms guidelines only after contract.

Aldine de Gruyter is an academic nonfiction publisher.

Nonfiction: Scholarly, textbook (rare), course-related monographs; edited volumes. Subjects include anthropology/archeology, humanities, psychology (evolutionary), sociology, social psychology (not clinical), human services. "Aldine's authors are academics with Ph.D.'s and strong publication records. No poetry or fiction." Submit proposal package including 1-2 sample chapter(s), cv; market; competing texts; reviews of early work.

Recent Title(s): *The Politics of Medicare, 2nd Ed*, by Theodore R. Marmor.

Tips: Audience is professors and upper level and graduate students. "Never send unsolicited mss; always query before sending anything."

GRYPHON HOUSE, INC., P.O. Box 207, Beltsville MD 20704. (301)595-9500. Fax: (301)595-0051. Website: www.gryphonhouse.com. **Acquisitions:** Kathy Charner, editor-in-chief. Estab. 1971. Publishes trade paperback originals. **Publishes 12-15 titles/year. Pays royalty on wholesale price.** Does not accept simultaneous submissions. Responds in 3-6 months to queries. Ms guidelines online.

O⊸ Gryphon House publishes books that teachers and parents of young children (birth to age 8) consider essential to their daily lives.

Nonfiction: Children's/juvenile, how-to. Subjects include child guidance/parenting, education (early childhood). Currently emphasizing reading; de-emphasizing after-school activities. Submit outline, 2-3 sample chapter(s), SASE.

Recent Title(s): *The Big Messy Art Book*, by Maryann Kohl; *Games to Play with Babies, 3rd ed*, by Jackie Silberg; *Creating Readers*, by Pam Schiller.

GRYPHON PUBLICATIONS, P.O. Box 209, Brooklyn NY 11228. **Acquisitions:** Gary Lovisi, owner/publisher. Publishes trade paperback originals and reprints. **Publishes 10 titles/year. Receives 500 queries and 1,000 mss/year. 20% of books from first-time authors; 90% from unagented writers. Makes outright purchase by contract, price varies. Offers no advance.** Publishes book 1-2 years after acceptance of ms. Responds in 1 month to queries. *Writer's Market* recommends allowing 2 months for reply to queries. Book catalog and ms guidelines for #10 SASE.

Imprints: Paperback Parade Magazine, Hardboiled Magazine, Gryphon Books, Gryphon Doubles.

O⊸ "I publish very genre oriented work (science fiction, crime, pulps) and nonfiction on these topics, authors and artists. It's best to query with an idea first."

Nonfiction: Reference, scholarly, bibliography. Subjects include hobbies, language/literature, book collecting. "We need well-written, well-researched articles, but query first on topic and length. Writers should not submit material that is not fully developed/researched." Query with SASE. Reviews artwork/photos as part of ms package. Send photocopies; slides, transparencies may be necessary later.

Fiction: Crime, hard-boiled fiction. "We want cutting-edge fiction, under 3,000 words with impact!" For short stories, query or submit complete ms. For novels, send 1-page query letter with SASE.

Recent Title(s): *Barsom: Edgar Rice Burroughs & the Martian Myth*, by Richard A. Lysoff; *Sherlock Holmes & the Terror Out of Time*, by Ralph Vaughan; *A Trunk Full of Murder*, by Julius Fast.

Tips: "We are very particular about novels and book-length work. A first-timer has a better chance with a short story or article. On anything over 4,000 words *do not* send manuscript, send *only* query letter with SASE."

HACHAI PUBLISHING, 156 Chester Ave., Brooklyn NY 11218. (718)633-0100. Website: www.hachai.com. **Acquisitions:** Devorah Leah Rosenfeld, editor. Estab. 1988. Publishes hardcover originals. **Publishes 4 titles/year. Makes outright purchase of $600 and up.** Accepts simultaneous submissions. Responds in 2 months to mss. Book catalog free; ms guidelines online.

O⊸ "Hachai is dedicated to producing high quality Jewish children's literature, ages 2 through 10. Story should promote universal values such as sharing, kindness, etc."

Nonfiction: Children's/juvenile. Subjects include ethnic, religion. Submit complete ms, SASE. Reviews artwork/photos as part of ms package. Send photocopies.

Recent Title(s): *Five Alive!*, by Dina Rosenfield; *Once Upon a Time*, by Draizy Zelcer.

Tips: "We are looking for books that convey the traditional Jewish experience in modern times or long ago; traditional Jewish observance such as Sabbath and Holidays and mitzvos such as mezuzah, blessings etc.; positive character traits (middos) such as honesty, charity, respect, sharing, etc. We are also interested in historical fiction for young readers (7-10) written with a traditional Jewish perspective and highlighting the relevance of Torah in making important choices. Please, no animal stories, romance, violence, preachy sermonizing."

HALF HALT PRESS, INC., P.O. Box 67, Boonsboro MD 21713. (301)733-7119. Fax: (301)733-7408. E-mail: hhpress@aol.com. Website: www.halfhaltpress.com. **Acquisitions:** Elizabeth Carnes, publisher. Estab. 1986. Publishes 90% hardcover and trade paperback originals and 10% reprints. **Publishes 15 titles/year. Receives 150 submissions/year. 25% of books from first-time authors; 50% from unagented writers. Pays 10-12½% royalty on retail price.** Publishes book 1 year after acceptance of ms. Does not accept simultaneous submissions. Responds in 1 month. *Writer's Market* suggests allowing 2 months for reply to queries. Book catalog for 6×9 SAE 2 first-class stamps.

O⊸ "We publish high-quality nonfiction on equestrian topics, books that help riders and trainers do something better."

Nonfiction: How-to. Subjects include animals (horses), sports. "We need serious instructional works by authorities in the field on horse-related topics, broadly defined." Query with SASE. Reviews artwork/photos as part of ms package.

Recent Title(s): *Dressage in Harmony*, by Walter Zettl.

Tips: "Writers have the best chance selling us well-written, unique works that teach serious horse people how to do something better. If I were a writer trying to market a book today, I would offer a straightforward presentation, letting the work speak for itself, without hype or hard sell. Allow publisher to contact writer, without frequent calling to check status. They haven't forgotten the writer but may have many different proposals at hand; frequent calls to 'touch base,' multiplied by the number of submissions, become an annoyance. As the publisher/author relationship becomes close and is based on working well together, early impressions may be important, even to the point of being a consideration in acceptance for publication."

ALEXANDER HAMILTON INSTITUTE, 70 Hilltop Rd., Ramsey NJ 07446-1119. (201)825-3377. Fax: (201)825-8696. Website: www.ahipubs.com. **Acquisitions:** Brian L.P. Zevnik, editor-in-chief; Gloria Ju, editor. Estab. 1909. Publishes 3-ring binder and paperback originals. **Publishes 5-10 titles/year. Receives 50 queries and 10 mss/year. 25% of books from first-time authors; 95% from unagented writers. Pays 5-8% royalty on retail price or makes outright purchase of $3,500-7,000. Offers $3,500-7,000 advance.** Publishes book 10 months after acceptance of ms. Accepts simultaneous submissions. Responds in 1 month to queries; 2 months to mss.

O⊸ Alexander Hamilton Institute publishes management books for upper-level managers and executives. Currently emphasizing legal issues for HR/personnel.

Nonfiction: The main audience is US personnel executives and high-level management. Subjects include legal personnel matters. "These books combine court case research and practical application of defensible programs."

Recent Title(s): *Employer's Guide to Record-Keeping Requirements.*

Tips: "We sell exclusively by direct mail or through electronic means to managers and executives. A writer must know his/her field and be able to communicate legal and practical systems and programs."

HAMPTON ROADS PUBLISHING CO., INC., 1125 Stoney Ridge Rd., Charlottesville VA 22902. (434)296-2772. Fax: (434)296-5096. E-mail: hrpc@hrpub.com. Website: www.hrpub.com. **Acquisitions:** Frank DeMarco, chief editor (metaphysical/visionary fiction); Robert S. Friedman, president (metaphysical, spiritual, inspirational, self-help); Ken Smith, marketing director (spiritual paths/Toltec); Richard Leviton, senior editor (alternative medicine). Estab. 1989. Publishes hardcover and trade paperback originals. Publishes and distributes hardcover and paperback originals on subjects including metaphysics, health, complementary medicine, visionary fiction and other related topics. **Publishes 35-40 titles/year. Receives 1,000 queries and 1,500 mss/year. 50% of books from first-time authors; 70% from unagented writers. Pays royalty. Offers $1,000-100,000 advance.** Publishes book 1 year after acceptance of ms. Accepts simultaneous submissions. Responds in 2 months to queries; 2 months to proposals; 6 months to mss. Ms guidelines online.

Imprints: Young Spirit (children's spiritual).

O⊸ "Our reason for being is to impact, uplift and contribute to positive change in the world. We publish books that will enrich and empower the evolving consciousness of mankind."

Nonfiction: How-to, illustrated book, self-help. Subjects include New Age, spirituality. Query with SASE or submit synopsis, SASE. Reviews artwork/photos as part of ms package. Send photocopies.

Fiction: Literary, spiritual, Visionary fiction, past-life fiction, based on actual memories. "Fiction should have one or more of the following themes: spiritual, inspirational, metaphysical, i.e., past life recall, out-of-body experiences, near death experience, paranormal." Query with SASE or submit outline, 2 sample chapter(s), synopsis or submit complete ms.

Recent Title(s): *The Beethoven Factor*, by Paul Pearsall; *The Fifth Harmonica*, by F. Paul Wilson.

HANCOCK HOUSE PUBLISHERS, 1431 Harrison Ave., Blaine WA 98230-5005. (604)538-1114. Fax: (604)538-2262. E-mail: david@hancockwildlife.org. Website: www.hancockwildlife.org. David Hancock, publisher. **Acquisitions:** Yvonne Lund, promotional manager. Estab. 1971. Publishes hardcover and trade paperback originals and reprints. **Publishes 12-20 titles/year. Receives 300 submissions/year. 50% of books from first-time authors; 90% from unagented writers. Pays 10% royalty.** Publishes book up to 1 year after acceptance of ms. Accepts simultaneous submissions. Book catalog free; ms guidelines online.

O⊸ Hancock House Publishers is the largest North American publisher of wildlife, and Native Indian titles. "We also cover Pacific Northwest, fishing, history, Canadiana, biographies. We are seeking agriculture, natural history, animal husbandry, conservation and popular science titles with a regional (Pacific Northwest), national or international focus." Currently emphasizing non-fiction wildlife, cryptozoology, guide books, native history, biography, fishing.

Nonfiction: "Centered around Pacific Northwest, local history, nature guide books, international ornithology and Native Americans." Biography, how-to, reference, technical, Pacific Northwest history and biography. Subjects include agriculture/horticulture, animals, ethnic, history, nature/environment, regional. Submit proposal package including outline, 3 sample chapter(s), selling points, SASE. Reviews artwork/photos as part of ms package. Send photocopies.

Recent Title(s): *Arabian Falconry*, by Roger Upton; *Estrildid Finches*, by Matthew Vriends.

HANSER GARDNER PUBLICATIONS, 6915 Valley Ave., Cincinnati OH 45244. (513)527-8977. Fax: (513)527-8950. Website: www.hansergardner.com. **Acquisitions:** Woody Chapman. Estab. 1993. Publishes hardcover and paperback originals and reprints. **Publishes 5-10 titles/year. Receives 40-50 queries and 5-10 mss/year. 75% of books from first-time authors; 100% from unagented writers. Pays 10-15% royalty on net receipts.** Publishes book 10 months after acceptance of ms. Accepts simultaneous submissions. Responds in 2 weeks to queries; 1 month to proposals; 1 month to mss. Book catalog and ms guidelines free; ms guidelines online.

O⊸ Hanser Gardner publishes training and practical application titles for metalworking, machining and finishing shops/plants.

Nonfiction: "Our books are primarily basic introductory-level training books and books that emphasize practical applications. Strictly deal with subjects shown above." How-to, technical, textbook. Subjects include metalworking, machining and finishing shops/plants. Submit outline, sample chapter(s), résumé, preface and comparison to competing or similar titles. Reviews artwork/photos as part of ms package. Send photocopies.

Recent Title(s): *Industrial Painting*, by Norman R. Roobol (industrial reference).

Tips: "Our readers and authors occupy various positions within small and large metalworking, machining and finishing shops/plants. We prefer that interested individuals write, call, or fax us with their queries first, so we can send them our proposal guideline form."

HARBOR PRESS, 5713 Wollochet Dr. NW, Gig Harbor WA 98335. Fax: (253)851-5191. E-mail: info@harborpress.com. Website: www.harborpress.com. President/Publisher: Harry R. Lynn. **Acquisitions:** Deborah Young, senior editor (please direct submissions to Harbor Press, 5 Glen Dr., Plainview NY 11803). Estab. 1985. Publishes hardcover and trade paperback originals and reprints. **Publishes 4-6 titles/year. Negotiates competitive royalties on wholesale price or makes outright purchase.** Does not accept simultaneous submissions.

- Harbor Press publishes books that will help readers achieve better health and more successful lives. Currently emphasizing diet and weight loss, parenting, psychology/human relationships, successful living books. Credentialed authors only.

Nonfiction: How-to, self-help. Subjects include child guidance/parenting, cooking/foods/nutrition (diet and weight loss only), health/medicine, psychology. Query with SASE or submit proposal package including outline, 3 sample chapter(s), synopsis. Reviews artwork/photos as part of ms package. Send photocopies.

Recent Title(s): *The Prostate Diet Cookbook*, by Buffy Sanders; *Yes! Your Teen Is Crazy: Loving Your Kid Without Losing Your Mind*, by Michael Bradley.

[A] **HARCOURT, INC.**, Trade Division, 525 B St., Suite 1900, San Diego CA 92101. (619)699-6560. Fax: (619)699-5555. Website: www.harcourtbooks.com. **Acquisitions:** David Hough, managing editor; Jane Isay, editor-in-chief (science, math, history, language); Drenka Willen, senior editor (poetry, fiction in translation, history); Andrea Schulz (nonfiction, American fiction, history, science); Ann Patty (American fiction). Publishes hardcover and trade paperback originals and trade paperback reprints. **Publishes 120 titles/year. 5% of books from first-time authors; 5% from unagented writers. Pays 6-15% royalty on retail price. Offers $2,000 minimum advance.** Accepts simultaneous submissions. Book catalog for 9×12 SAE; ms guidelines online.

Imprints: Harvest Books (contact Andre Bernard).

- Harcourt Inc. owns some of the world's most prestigious publishing imprints—imprints which distinguish quality products for the juvenile, educational, scientific, technical, medical, professional and trade markets worldwide. Currently emphasizing science and math.

Nonfiction: Biography, children's/juvenile, coffee table book, gift book, illustrated book, multimedia, reference, technical. Subjects include anthropology/archeology, art/architecture, child guidance/parenting, creative nonfiction, education, ethnic, gay/lesbian, general nonfiction, government/politics, health/medicine, history, language/literature, memoirs, military/war, multicultural, philosophy, psychology, religion, science, sociology, spirituality, sports, translation, travel, women's issues/studies. Published all categories *except* business/finance (university texts), cookbooks, self-help, sex. No unsolicited mss. *Agented submissions only.*Historical, mystery, picture books, Nonfiction. *Agented submissions only.*

Recent Title(s): *Life of Pi*, by Yann Martel (fiction); *Baudolino*, by Umberto Eco (fiction); *Odd Girl Out*, by Rachel Simmons (nonfiction).

[N] [⊘] **HARCOURT, INC.**, Children's Books Division, 525 B St., Suite 1900, San Diego CA 92101. (619)281-6616. Fax: (619)699-6777. Website: www.harcourtbooks.com/htm/childrens_index.asp. Estab. 1919. Publishes hardcover originals and trade paperback reprints.

Imprints: Harcourt Children's Books, Gulliver Books, Silver Whistle, Red Wagon Books, Harcourt Young Classics, Green Light Readers, Voyager Books/Libros Viajeros, Harcourt Paperbacks, Odyssey Classics, Magic Carpet Books.

- Harcourt Inc., owns some of the world's most prestigious publishing imprints—imprints which distinguish quality products for the juvenile, educational, scientific, technical, medical, professional and trade markets worldwide.

Nonfiction: No unsolicited mss or queries accepted. No phone calls.

Fiction: Young adult. No unsolicited mss or queries accepted. No phone calls.

Recent Title(s): *In My World*, by Lois Ehlert; *The Magic Hat*, by Mem Fox.

[A] **HARPERCOLLINS CHILDREN'S BOOKS**, HarperCollins Publishers, 1350 Avenue of the Americas, New York NY 10019. (212)261-6500. Fax: (212)261-6689. Website: www.harperchildrens.com. Editor-in-Chief: Kate Morgan Jackson. **Acquisitions:** Alix Reid, editorial director; Barbara Lalichi, senior VP & editorial director; Phoebe Yeh, editorial director; Maria Modugno, editorial director; Margaret Anastos, editorial director. Publishes hardcover originals. **Publishes 350 titles/year. Receives 200 queries and 5,000 mss/year. 5% of books from first-time authors. Pays 10-12½% royalty on retail price. Offers variable advance.** Publishes book 1 year (novels) or 2 years (picture books) after acceptance of ms.

Imprints: Joanna Cotler Books (Joanna Cotler, Senior VP, publisher); Laura Geringer Books(Laura Geringer, senior VP, publisher); Greenwillow Books (Virginia Duncan, vice president & publisher); Harper Festival (Emily Brenner, editorial director); Avon; Katherine Tegon Books (Katherine Tegon, editorial director at large); Harper Trophy; Harper Tempest (Elise Howard, VP/paperback publishing director).

Fiction: Adventure, fantasy, historical, humor, juvenile, literary, picture books, young adult. *Agented submissions only.* No unsolicited mss.

Recent Title(s): *Mary Engelbreit's The Night Before Christmas* (picture book); *A Series of Unfortunate Events*, by Lemony Snicket (novel).

[N] **HARPERENTERTAINMENT**, HarperCollins Publishers, 10 E. 53rd St., New York NY 10022. (212)207-7000. E-mail: jeffery.mcgraw@harpercollins.com. Website: www.harpercollins.com. Editorial Director/Vice President: Hope Innelli. **Acquisitions:** Jeffrey McGraw, editor; Susan Kitzen, editor. Estab. 1997. **20% of books from first-time authors. Write-for-hire arrangements mostly. Fees vary.** Responds in 3-12 months to mss.

- "A newly formed imprint, HarperEntertainment is dedicated to publishing sports, movie and TV tie-ins, celebrity bios and books reflecting trends in popular culture."

Nonfiction: Biography, children's/juvenile, humor, Movie and TV tie-ins. Subjects include film/cinema/stage, humor. "The bulk of our work is done by experienced writers for hire, but we are open to original ideas." Query with SASE.
Fiction: Humor, juvenile, Movie and TV tie-ins. Query with SASE.
Recent Title(s): *Mary-Kate & Ashley's New Adventures.*
Tips: "We are demanding about the quality of proposals; in addition to strong writing skills and thorough knowledge of the subject matter, we require a detailed analysis of the competition."

HARPERINFORMATION, HarperCollins Publishers, 10 East 53rd St., New York NY 10022. (212)207-7000. Fax: (212)207-6961. Website: www.harpercollins.com. **Acquisitions:** Megan Newman, editorial director (resource); Marion Maneker, editorial director (business). Publishes hardcover originals, trade paperback originals and reprints. **10% of books from first-time authors; 0% from unagented writers.** Publishes book 18 months after acceptance of ms. Accepts simultaneous submissions. Responds in 1 month to queries; 1 month to proposals; 1 month to mss. Book catalog online.
Imprints: HarperBusiness (Marion Maneker); HarperResource (Megan Newman).
Nonfiction: Coffee table book, gift book, how-to, reference, self-help. Subjects include business/economics, child guidance/parenting, computers/electronic, cooking/foods/nutrition, health/medicine, hobbies, language/literature, money/finance, sex, sociology, spirituality. *Agented submissions only.*
Recent Title(s): *Good to Great*, by Jim Collins (business); *The Perricone Prescription*, by Nicholas V. Perricone, M.D. (resource).

HARPERSANFRANCISCO, Harper Collins Publishers, 353 Sacramento St., Suite 500, San Francisco CA 94111-3653. (415)477-4400. Fax: (415)477-4444. E-mail: hcsanfrancisco@harpercollins.com. **Acquisitions:** Stephen Hanselman, senior vice president/publisher (Christian spirituality, history, biography); Liz Perle, editor-at-large (general nonfiction, women's studies, psychology, personal growth, inspiration); John Loudon, executive editor (religious studies, biblical studies, psychology/personal growth, Eastern religions, Catholic, spirituality, inspiration); Gideon Weil, editor (general nonfiction, spiritual fiction, self-help, inspiration, Judaica); Renee Sedliar, associate editor (general nonfiction, spiritual fiction, inspiration). Estab. 1977. Publishes hardcover originals, trade paperback originals and reprints. **Publishes 75 titles/year. Receives about 10,000 submissions/year. 5% of books from first-time authors. Pays royalty. Offers advance.** Publishes book within 18 months after acceptance of ms.

O→ HarperSanFrancisco "strives to be the preeminent publisher of the most important books across the full spectrum of religion and spiritual literature, adding to the wealth of the world's wisdom by respecting all traditions."

Nonfiction: Biography, how-to, reference, self-help. Subjects include psychology (inspiration), religion, spirituality. No unsolicited mss.
Recent Title(s): *Why Religion Matters*, by Huston Smith; *The Dance*, by Oriah Mountain Dreamer; *Touching My Father's Soul*, by Jamling Tenzing Norgay.

HARTMAN PUBLISHING, INC., 8529-A Indian School NE, Albuquerque NM 87112. (505)291-1274. Fax: (505)291-1284. E-mail: susan@hartmanonline.com. Website: www.hartmanonline.com. **Acquisitions:** Susan Alvare, managing editor (healthcare education). Publishes trade paperback originals. **Publishes 5-10 titles/year. Receives 50 queries and 25 mss/year. 50% of books from first-time authors; 100% from unagented writers. Pays 6-12% royalty on wholesale or retail price or makes outright purchase of $200-600.** Publishes book 4-12 months after acceptance of ms. Accepts simultaneous submissions. Responds in 2 months to proposals; 3 months to mss. Book catalog and ms guidelines free; ms guidelines online.
Imprints: Care Spring (Mark Hartman, publisher).

O→ We publish educational and inspirational books for employees of nursing homes, home health agencies, hospitals, and providers of eldercare.

Nonfiction: Textbook. Subjects include health/medicine. "Writers should request our books wanted list, as well as view samples of our published material." Query with SASE or submit proposal package including outline, 1 sample chapter(s) or submit complete ms. Reviews artwork/photos as part of ms package. Send photocopies or transparencies.

HARVARD BUSINESS SCHOOL PRESS, Harvard Business School Publishing Corp., 60 Harvard Way, Boston MA 02163. (617)783-7400. Fax: (617)783-7489. E-mail: bookpublisher@hbsp.harvard.edu. Website: www.hbsp.harvard.edu. Director: Carol Franco. **Acquisitions:** Hollis Heinbouch, editorial director; Kirsten Sandberg, executive editor; Melinda Adams Merino, executive editor; Jeff Kehoe, senior editor. Estab. 1984. Publishes hardcover originals. **Publishes 35-45 titles/year. Pays escalating royalty on retail price. Advances vary widely depending on author and market for the book.** Accepts simultaneous submissions. Responds in 1 month to proposals; 1 month to mss. Book catalog and ms guidelines online; ms guidelines online.

O→ The Harvard Business School Press publishes books for an audience of senior and general managers and business scholars. HBS Press is the source of the most influential ideas and conversations that shape business worldwide.

Nonfiction: Scholarly. Subjects include business/economics, general management, marketing, finance, digital economy, technology and innovation, human resources. Submit proposal package including outline, sample chapter(s).
Recent Title(s): *The Strategy Focused Organization*, by Robert Kaplan and David P. Norton; *The Heart of Change*, by John Kotler.
Tips: "Take care to really look into the type of business books we publish. They are generally not policy-oriented, dissertations, or edited collections."

THE HARVARD COMMON PRESS, 535 Albany St., Boston MA 02118-2500. (617)423-5803. Fax: (617)695-9794. Website: www.harvardcommonpress.com. Publisher/President: Bruce P. Shaw. **Acquisitions:** Pamela Hoenig, executive editor. Estab. 1976. Publishes hardcover and trade paperback originals and reprints. **Publishes 16 titles/year. Receives**

1,000 submissions/year. 20% of books from first-time authors; 40% from unagented writers. Pays royalty. Offers average $4,000 advance. Publishes book 1 year after acceptance of ms. Accepts simultaneous submissions. Responds in 2 months to queries. Book catalog for 9×12 SAE with 3 first-class stamps; ms guidelines for #10 SASE.

Imprints: Gambit Books.

O‒ "We want strong, practical books that help people gain control over a particular area of their lives." Currently emphasizing cooking, child care/parenting, health. De-emphasizing general instructional books, travel.

Nonfiction: Subjects include child guidance/parenting, cooking/foods/nutrition, health/medicine. "A large percentage of our list is made up of books about cooking, child care, and parenting; in these areas we are looking for authors who are knowledgeable, if not experts, and who can offer a different approach to the subject. We are open to good nonfiction proposals that show evidence of strong organization and writing, and clearly demonstrate a need in the marketplace. First-time authors are welcome." Submit outline, 1-3 sample chapter(s). Reviews artwork/photos as part of ms package.

Recent Title(s): *Icebox Pies*, by Lauren Chattman; *Real Stew*, by Clifford A. Wright.

Tips: "We are demanding about the quality of proposals; in addition to strong writing skills and thorough knowledge of the subject matter, we require a detailed analysis of the competition."

HARVEST HOUSE PUBLISHERS, 990 Owen Loop N., Eugene OR 97402. (541)343-0123. Fax: (541)302-0731. Website: www.harvesthousepublishers.com. Estab. 1974. Publishes hardcover originals and reprints, trade paperback originals and reprints, and mass market paperback originals and reprints. **Publishes 160 titles/year. Receives 1,500 queries and 1,000 mss/year. 1% of books from first-time authors; 5% from unagented writers. Pays royalty.** Publishes book 6 months after acceptance of ms. Responds in 1 month to queries; 2 months to proposals; 3 months to mss. Book catalog free; ms guidelines free.

- Harvest House is no longer accepting unsolicited manuscripts.

Nonfiction: Audiocassettes, autobiography, children's/juvenile, gift book, humor, illustrated book, reference, self-help. Subjects include anthropology/archeology, business/economics, child guidance/parenting, general nonfiction, health/medicine, money/finance, religion, women's issues/studies, Bible studies. **No longer accepts unsolicited material.** *Agented submissions only.*

Recent Title(s): *Power of a Praying Husband*, by Stormie Omartial (Christian living); *Life Management for Busy Women*, by Elizabeth George (Christian living); *After Anne*, by Roxanne Henke (relationship).

Tips: "For first time/nonpublished authors we suggest building their literary résumé by submitting to magazines, or perhaps accruing book contributions. First: Build slowly."

HASTINGS HOUSE, Daytrips Publishers, LINI LLC, 2601 Wells Ave., Suite 161, Fern Park FL 32730-2000. (407)339-3600. Fax: (407)339-5900. E-mail: hastings_daytrips@earthlink.net. Website: www.hastingshousebooks.com. Publisher: Peter Leers. **Acquisitions:** Earl Steinbicker, senior travel editor (edits Daytrips series of guides). Publishes trade paperback originals and reprints. **Publishes 20 titles/year. Receives 600 queries and 900 mss/year. 10% of books from first-time authors; 40% from unagented writers. Pays 8-10% royalty on net receipts.** Publishes book 6-10 months after acceptance of ms. Responds in 2 months to queries.

O‒ "We are primarily focused on expanding our Daytrips Travel Series (facts/guide) nationally and internationally." Currently de-emphasizing all other subjects.

Nonfiction: Subjects include travel. Submit outline. Query.

Recent Title(s): *The Complete Book of Baseball's Negro Leagues*, by John Holway; *Extraordinary Places...Close to London*, by Elizabeth Wallace; *Revitalize Your Life*, by Jack LaLanne.

HAWK PUBLISHING GROUP, 7107 S. Yale Ave., #345, Tulsa OK 74136. (918)492-3677. Fax: (918)492-2120. Website: www.hawkpub.com. Estab. 1999. Publishes hardcover and trade paperback originals. **Publishes 10-12 titles/year. 25% of books from first-time authors; 50% from unagented writers. Pays royalty.** Publishes book 9-12 months after acceptance of ms. Accepts simultaneous submissions. Ms guidelines online.

O‒ "Please visit our website and read the submission guidelines before sending anything to us. The best way to learn what might interest us is to visit the website, read the information there, look at the books, and perhaps even read a few of them."

Nonfiction: Looking for subjects of broad appeal and interest. Queries by e-mail are welcome.

Fiction: Looking for good books of all kinds. Does not want childrens or young adult books. Submissions will not be returned, so send only copies. No SASE. No submissions by email or by "certified mail or any other service that requires a signature." Replies "only if interested. If you have not heard from us within three months after the receipt of your submission, you may safely assume that we were not able to find a place for it in our list."

Recent Title(s): *Who Really Cares?*, by Janis Ian (poetry and essays); *Goddess by Mistake*, by P.C. Cast (women's fiction); *Inside Trek*, by Susan Sackett (Star Trek nonfiction).

THE HAWORTH PRESS, INC., 10 Alice St., Binghamton NY 13904. (607)722-5857. Fax: (607)722-8465. Website: www.haworthpress.com. **Acquisitions:** Bill Palmer, vice president, publications. Estab. 1973. Publishes hardcover and trade paperback originals. **Publishes 100 titles/year. Receives 500 queries and 250 mss/year. 60% of books from first-time authors; 98% from unagented writers. Pays 7½-15% royalty on wholesale price.** Publishes book 1 year after acceptance of ms. Responds in 2 months to proposals. Ms guidelines online.

Imprints: Best Business Books; Food Products Press; Harrington Park Press; Alice Street Editions; Southern Tier Editions; International Business Press; Pharmaceutical Products Press; The Haworth Clinical Practice Press; The Haworth Hispanic/Latino Press; The Haworth Herbal Press; The Haworth Hospitality Press; The Haworth Information Press; The Haworth Integrative Healing Press; The Haworth Maltreatment & Trauma Press; The Haworth Medical Press; The Haworth Pastoral

Press; The Haworth Social Work Practice Press; The Haworth Reference Press; The Haworth Political Press; The Haworth Judaic Press.

O→ The Haworth Press is primarily a scholarly press.

Nonfiction: Reference, scholarly, textbook. Subjects include agriculture/horticulture, business/economics, child guidance/parenting, cooking/foods/nutrition, gay/lesbian, health/medicine, money/finance, psychology, sociology, women's issues/studies. Submit proposal package including outline, 1-3 sample chapter(s), author bio. Reviews artwork/photos as part of ms package. Send photocopies.

Recent Title(s): *The Body Bears the Burden: Trauma, Dissociation, and Disease*; *The Mental Health Diagnostic Desk Reference: Visual Guides and More for Learning to Use the Diagnostic and Statistical Manual (DSM-IV-TR), 2nd Ed*; *Handbook of Psychotropic Herbs: A Scientific Analysis of Herbal Remedies for Psychiatric Conditions.*

[A] **HAY HOUSE, INC.**, P.O. Box 5100, Carlsbad CA 92018-5100. (760)431-7695. Fax: (760)431-6948. E-mail: slittrell@hayhouse.com. Website: www.hayhouse.com. Editorial Director: Jill Kramer. **Acquisitions:** Shannon Littrell, acquisitions editor. Estab. 1985. Publishes hardcover and trade paperback originals. **Publishes 50 titles/year. Receives 1,200 submissions/year. 5% of books from first-time authors. Pays standard royalty.** Publishes book 12-15 months after acceptance of ms. Accepts simultaneous submissions. Responds in 2 months to mss. No e-mail submissions; ms guidelines online.

Imprints: Astro Room, Hay House Lifestyles, Mountain Movers Press.

- Hay House will not accept submissions of any kind until January 2004, and then, only from agents.

O→ "We publish books, audios and videos that help heal the planet."

Nonfiction: Biography, self-help. Subjects include cooking/foods/nutrition, education, health/medicine, money/finance, nature/environment, New Age, philosophy, psychology, sociology, women's issues/studies. "Hay House is interested in a variety of subjects as long as they have a positive self-help slant to them. No poetry, children's books or negative concepts that are not conducive to helping/healing ourselves or our planet." *Agented submissions only.*

Recent Title(s): *10 Secrets for Success and Inner Peace*, by Wayne Dyer.

Tips: "Our audience is concerned with our planet, the healing properties of love, and general self-help principles. If I were a writer trying to market a book today, I would research the market thoroughly to make sure there weren't already too many books on the subject I was interested in writing about. Then I would make sure I had a unique slant on my idea. SASE a must! Simultaneous submissions from agents must include SASEs. No e-mail submissions."

[N] **HAZELDEN PUBLISHING AND EDUCATIONAL SERVICES**, P.O. Box 176, Center City MN 55012. (651)257-4010. Website: www.hazelden.org. Rebecca Post, executive editor. Estab. 1954. Publishes hardcover and trade paperback originals and trade paperback reprints. **Publishes 100 titles/year. Receives 2,500 queries and 2,000 mss/year. 30% of books from first-time authors; 50% from unagented writers. Pays 8% royalty on retail price. Offers variable advance.** Publishes book 1 year after acceptance of ms. Accepts simultaneous submissions. Responds in 6 months to queries. Book catalog and ms guidelines online; ms guidelines online.

O→ Hazelden is a trade, educational and professional publisher specializing is psychology, self-help, and spiritual books that help enhance the quality of people's lives. Products include gift books, curriculum, workbooks, audio and video, computer-based products and wellness products. "We specialize in books on addiction/recovery, spirituality/personal growth and prevention topics related to chemical and mental health."

Nonfiction: Gift book, how-to, multimedia, self-help. Subjects include child guidance/parenting, gay/lesbian, health/medicine, memoirs, psychology, sex (sexual addiction), spirituality. Query with SASE.

Recent Title(s): *Alchohol Cradel to Grave*, by Eric Newhouse; *It Will Never Happen to Me*, by Claudia Black.

Tips: Audience includes "consumers and professionals interested in the range of topics related to chemical and emotional health, including spirituality, self-help and addiction recovery."

HEALTH COMMUNICATIONS, INC., 3201 SW 15th St., Deerfield Beach FL 33442. (954)360-0909. Fax: (954)360-0034. Website: www.hci-online.com. **Acquisitions:** Christine Belleris, editorial director; Susan Tobias, editor; Allison Janse, senior editor; Lisa Drucker, senior editor. Estab. 1976. Publishes hardcover and trade paperback originals. **Publishes 50 titles/year. 20% of books from first-time authors; 50% from unagented writers. Pays 15% royalty on net price.** Publishes book 9 months after acceptance of ms. Accepts simultaneous submissions. Responds in 1 month to queries; 3 months to proposals; 3 months to mss. Book catalog for 8½×11 SASE; ms guidelines online.

O→ "We are the Life Issues Publisher. Health Communications, Inc., strives to help people grow and improve their lives, from physical and emotional health to finances and interpersonal relationships." Currently emphasizing books for a teenage audience with a new interest in books for active senior citizens.

Nonfiction: Gift book, self-help. Subjects include child guidance/parenting, health/medicine, psychology, sex, women's issues/studies. Submit proposal package including outline, 2 sample chapter(s), vitae, marketing study. *No phone calls*, SASE. Reviews artwork/photos as part of ms package. Send photocopies.

Recent Title(s): *How to Be Like Mike*, by Pat Williams; *The Schwarzbein Principle II*, by Diana Schwarzbein, M.D.; *My Soul Said to Me*, by Robert E. Roberts, Ph.D.

Tips: Audience is composed primarily of women, aged 25-60, interested in personal growth and self-improvement. "Please do your research in your subject area. We publish general self-help books and are expanding to include new subjects such as alternative healing. We need to know why there is a need for your book, how it might differ from other books on the market and what you have to offer to promote your work."

[N] **HEALTH INFORMATION PRESS (HIP)**, PMIC (Practice Management Information Corp.), 4727 Wilshire Blvd., Los Angeles CA 90010. (323)954-0224. Fax: (323)954-0253. Website: www.pmiconline.com. **Acquisitions:** Kathryn Swanson, managing editor. Publishes hardcover originals, trade paperback originals and reprints. **Publishes 8-10 titles/year.**

Receives 1,000 queries and 50 mss/year. 10% of books from first-time authors; 90% from unagented writers. Pays 10-15% royalty on net receipts. Offers $3,000 average advance. Publishes book 18 months after acceptance of ms. Does not accept simultaneous submissions. Responds in 6 months to queries. Book catalog for #10 SASE; ms guidelines for #10 SASE.

O‒ Health Information Press publishes books for consumers who are interested in taking an active role in their health care.

Nonfiction: How-to, illustrated book, reference, self-help. Subjects include health/medicine, psychology, science. "We seek to simplify health and medicine for consumers." Submit proposal package including outline, 3-5 sample chapter(s), résumé. Letter detailing who would by the book and the market/need for the book. Reviews artwork/photos as part of ms package.

Recent Title(s): *Living Longer with Heart Disease*, Howard Wayne, M.D.; *A Spy in the Nursing Home*, Eileen Kraatz.

HEALTH PRESS, P.O. Box 37470, Albuquerque NM 87176. (505)888-1394. Fax: (505)888-1521. E-mail: goodbooks@healthpress.com. Website: www.healthpress.com. **Acquisitions:** K. Frazer, editor. Estab. 1988. Publishes hardcover and trade paperback originals. **Publishes 8 titles/year. 90% of books from first-time authors; 90% from unagented writers. Pays standard royalty on wholesale price.** Publishes book 1 year after acceptance of ms. Accepts simultaneous submissions. Responds in 3 months to proposals. Book catalog free; ms guidelines online.

O‒ Health Press publishes books by health care professionals on cutting-edge patient education topics.

Nonfiction: How-to, reference, self-help, textbook. Subjects include education, health/medicine. Submit proposal package including outline, 3 complete sample chapter(s), résumé. Reviews artwork/photos as part of ms package. Send photocopies.

Recent Title(s): *Keeping a Secret: A Story about Juvenile Rheumatoid Arthritis*; *Peanut Butter Jam: A Story about Peanut Allergy*; *Health and Nutrition Secrets*.

HEALTH PROFESSIONS PRESS, P.O. Box 10624, Baltimore MD 21285-0624. (410)337-9585. Fax: (410)337-8539. E-mail: acquis@healthpropress.com. Website: www.healthpropress.com. **Acquisitions:** Mary Magnus, director of publications (aging, long-term care, health administration). Publishes hardcover and trade paperback originals. **Publishes 6-8 titles/year. Receives 70 queries and 12 mss/year. 50% of books from first-time authors; 100% from unagented writers. Pays 8-18% royalty on wholesale price.** Publishes book 10 months after acceptance of ms. Accepts simultaneous submissions. Responds in 1 month to queries; 3 months to proposals; 4 months to mss. Book catalog and ms guidelines free or online; ms guidelines online.

O‒ "We are a specialty publisher. Our primary audiences are professionals, students and educated consumers interested in topics related to aging and eldercare."

Nonfiction: How-to, reference, self-help, textbook. Subjects include health/medicine, psychology. Query with SASE or submit proposal package including outline, 1-2 sample chapter(s), résumé, cover letter.

Recent Title(s): *Mental Wellness in Aging: Strengths-Based Approaches*, by Ronch & Goldfield; *Managing & Treating Urinary Incontinence*, by Newman; *Becoming an Effective Health Care Manager: The Essential Skills of Leadership*, by Sperry.

HEALTHWISE PUBLICATIONS, Piccadilly Books Ltd., P.O. Box 25203, Colorado Springs CO 80936-5203. (719)550-9887. Website: www.piccadillybooks.com. Publisher: Bruce Fife. **Acquisitions:** Submissions Department. Publishes hardcover and trade paperback originals and trade paperback reprints. **Pays 10% royalty on retail price.** Publishes book within 1 year after acceptance of ms. Accepts simultaneous submissions.

O‒ Healthwise specializes in the publication of books on health and fitness written with a holistic or natural health viewpoint.

Nonfiction: Subjects include cooking/foods/nutrition, health/medicine. Query with sample chapters. Responds only if interested, unless accompanied by a SASE.

Recent Title(s): *The Healing Miracles of Coconut Oil*, by Bruce Fife, N.D.

WILLIAM S. HEIN & CO., INC., 1285 Main St., Buffalo NY 14209-1987. (716)882-2600. Fax: (716)883-8100. E-mail: mail@wshein.com. Website: www.wshein.com. **Acquisitions:** Sheila Jarrett, publications manager. Estab. 1961. **Publishes 50 titles/year. Receives 80 queries and 40 mss/year. 20% of books from first-time authors; 100% from unagented writers. Pays 10-20% royalty on net price.** Publishes book 9 months after acceptance of ms. Accepts simultaneous submissions. Responds in 2 months to queries. Book catalog online; ms guidelines for #10 SASE.

O‒ William S. Hein & Co. publishes reference books for law librarians, legal researchers and those interested in legal writing. Currently emphasizing legal research, legal writing and legal education.

Nonfiction: Law. Reference, scholarly. Subjects include education, government/politics, women's issues/studies, world affairs, legislative histories.

Recent Title(s): *Landmark Indian Law Cases*, by Native American Rights Fund; *Leadership Role for Librarians*, by Herb Cihak.

HELLGATE PRESS, PSI Research, P.O. Box 3727, Central Point OR 97502-0032. (541)245-6502. Fax: (541)245-6505. Website: www.hellgatepress.com. **Acquisitions:** Emmett Ramey, president. Estab. 1996. **Publishes 20-25 titles/year. Pays royalty.** Publishes book 6 months after acceptance of ms. Responds in 2 months to queries. Book catalog for catalog envelope with SASE; ms guidelines online.

O‒ Hellgate Press specializes in military history, other military topics and travel.

Nonfiction: Subjects include history, memoirs, military/war, travel. Query with SASE or submit outline, sample chapter(s). Reviews artwork/photos as part of ms package. Send photocopies.

Recent Title(s): *Code to Keep*, by Ernest Brace.

HENDRICK-LONG PUBLISHING CO., INC., P.O. Box 1247, Friendswood TX 77549. (281)482-6187. Fax: (281)482-6169. E-mail: hendrick-long@worldnet.att.net. Website: hendricklongpublishing.com. **Acquisitions:** Vilma Long. Estab. 1969. Publishes hardcover and trade paperback originals and hardcover reprints. **Publishes 4 titles/year. Receives 500 submissions/year. 90% from unagented writers. Pays royalty. Pays royalty on selling price. Offers advance.** Publishes book 18 months after acceptance of ms. Does not accept simultaneous submissions. 1 month to queries, 2 months if more than one query is sent to queries. Book catalog for 8½ x11 or 9×12 SASE with 4 first-class stamps; ms guidelines online.

O-→ Hendrick-Long publishes historical fiction and nonfiction primarily about Texas and the Southwest for children and young adults.

Nonfiction: Biography, children's/juvenile. Subjects include history, regional. Query or submit outline and 2 sample chapters. Reviews artwork/photos as part of ms package. Send photocopies or No original art.

Fiction: Juvenile, young adult. Query with SASE or submit outline, 2 sample chapter(s), synopsis.

Recent Title(s): *Pioneer Children*, by Betsy Warren; *Maggie Houston*, by Jane Cook; *The Official TASP Study Guide*.

HENSLEY PUBLISHING, 6116 E. 32nd St., Tulsa OK 74135-5494. (918)664-8520. E-mail: editorial@hensleypublishing.com. Website: www.hensleypublishing.com. **Acquisitions:** Acquisitions Department. Publishes trade paperback originals. **Publishes 5-10 titles/year. Receives 800 submissions/year. 50% of books from first-time authors; 50% from unagented writers.** Publishes book 18 months after acceptance of ms. Responds in 2 months to queries. Ms guidelines online.

O-→ Hensley Publishing publishes Bible studies and curriculum that offer the reader a wide range of topics. Currently emphasizing 192-page workbook studies.

Nonfiction: Subjects include child guidance/parenting, money/finance, religion, women's issues/studies, marriage/family. "We do not want to see anything non-Christian." No New Age, poetry, plays, sermon collections. Query with synopsis and sample chapters.

Recent Title(s): *The Fear Factor*, by Dr. Wayne Mack and Joshua Mack; *Embracing Grace*, by Judy Baker.

Tips: "Submit something that crosses denominational lines directed toward the large Christian market, not small specialized groups. We serve an interdenominational market—all Christian persuasions. Our goal is to get readers back into studying their Bible instead of studying about the Bible."

HERITAGE BOOKS, INC., 1540-E Pointer Ridge Place, Bowie MD 20716-1859. (301)390-7708. Fax: (301)390-7153.Submissions E-mail: submissions@heritagebooks.com. **Acquisitions:** Editorial Director. Estab. 1978. Publishes hardcover and paperback originals and reprints. **Publishes 200 titles/year. Receives 300 submissions/year. 25% of books from first-time authors; 100% from unagented writers. Pays 10% royalty on list price.** Accepts simultaneous submissions. Responds in 1 month. Book catalog free; ms guidelines free.

O-→ "Our goal is to celebrate life by exploring all aspects of American life: settlement, development, wars and other significant events, including family histories, memoirs, etc." Currently emphasizing early American life, early wars and conflicts, ethnic studies.

Nonfiction: Biography, how-to (genealogical, historical), reference, scholarly. Subjects include Americana, ethnic (origins and research guides), history, memoirs, military/war, regional (history). Query with SASE. Submit outline to submissions@heritagebooks.com. Reviews artwork/photos as part of ms package.

Fiction: Historical (relating to early American life, 1600-1900). Query with SASE. Submit outline to submissions@heritagebooks.com.

Tips: "The quality of the book is of prime importance; next is its relevance to our fields of interest."

[N] **HEYDAY BOOKS**, Box 9145, Berkeley CA 94709-9145. Fax: (510)549-1889. E-mail: heyday@heydaybooks.com. Website: www.heydaybooks.com. **Acquisitions:** Jeannine Gendar, managing editor. Estab. 1974. Publishes hardcover originals, trade paperback originals and reprints. **Publishes 12-15 titles/year. Receives 200 submissions/year. 50% of books from first-time authors; 90% from unagented writers. Pays 8% royalty on net price.** Publishes book 10 months after acceptance of ms. Does not accept simultaneous submissions. Responds in 2 months to queries; 2 months to mss. Book catalog for 7×9 SAE with 3 first-class stamps.

O-→ Heyday Books publishes nonfiction books and literary anthologies with a strong California focus. "We publish books about Native Americans, natural history, history, literature, and recreation, with a strong California focus."

Nonfiction: Books about California only. Subjects include Americana, ethnic, history, nature/environment, recreation, regional, travel. Query with outline and synopsis. Reviews artwork/photos as part of ms package.

Recent Title(s): *Dark God of Eros: A William Everson Reader*, edited by Albert Gelpi; *The High Sierra of California*, by Gary Snyder and Tom Killion; *Under the Fifth Sun: Latino Literature from California*, edited by Rick Heidre.

HIDDENSPRING, 997 Macarthur Blvd., Mahwah NJ 07430. (201)825-7300. Fax: (201)825-8345. Website: www.hiddenspringbooks.com. **Acquisitions:** Jan-Erik Guerth, editorial director (nonfiction/spirituality). Publishes hardcover and trade paperback originals and reprints. **Publishes 10-12 titles/year. 5% of books from first-time authors; 10% from unagented writers. Royalty varies. Offers variable advance.** Accepts simultaneous submissions. Responds in 1 month to queries.

O-→ "Books should always have a spiritual angle—nonfiction with a spiritual twist."

Nonfiction: Biography, self-help. Subjects include Americana, anthropology/archeology, art/architecture, business/economics, child guidance/parenting, cooking/foods/nutrition, creative nonfiction, ethnic, gardening, gay/lesbian, government/politics, health/medicine, history, money/finance, multicultural, music/dance, nature/environment, philosophy, psychology, regional, religion, science, sex, sociology, travel, women's issues/studies. Submit proposal package including outline, 1 sample chapter(s), SASE.

Recent Title(s): *The Spiritual Traveler: Boston and New England*, by Jana Riess; *The Little Tern*, by Brooke Newman; *Francis of Assisi*, by Adrian House.

HIGH PLAINS PRESS, P.O. Box 123, 539 Cassa Rd., Glendo WY 82213. (307)735-4370. Fax: (307)735-4590. E-mail: editor@highplainspress.com. Website: www.highplainspress.com. **Acquisitions:** Nancy Curtis, publisher. Estab. 1986. Publishes hardcover and trade paperback originals. **Publishes 4 titles/year. Receives 300 queries and 200 mss/year. 80% of books from first-time authors; 95% from unagented writers. Pays 10% royalty on wholesale price. Offers $100-600 advance.** Publishes book 2 years after acceptance of ms. Accepts simultaneous submissions. Responds in 1 month to queries; 1 month to proposals; 3 months to mss. Book catalog and ms guidelines for 9×12 SASE; ms guidelines online.

O→ "What we sell best is history of the Old West, particularly things relating to Wyoming. We also publish one book of poetry a year in our Poetry of the American West series."

Nonfiction: "We focus on books of the American West, mainly history." Biography. Subjects include Americana, art/architecture, history, nature/environment, regional. Submit outline, 3 sample chapter(s). Reviews artwork/photos as part of ms package. Send photocopies.

Poetry: "We only seek poetry closely tied to the Rockies. Do not submit single poems." Query or submit complete ms.

Recent Title(s): *Tom Horn: Blood on the Moon*, by Chip Carlson; *Sheepwagon: Home on the Range*, by Nancy Weidel; *Drybone: A History of Fort Fetterman, Wyoming*.

HIGH TIDE PRESS, 3650 W. 183rd St., Homewood IL 60430-2603. (708)206-2054. Fax: (708)206-2044. E-mail: managing.editor@hightidepress.com. Website: www.hightidepress.com. **Acquisitions:** Diane J. Bell, managing editor. Publishes hardcover and trade paperback originals. **Publishes 8 titles/year. Receives 200 queries and 100 mss/year. 50% of books from first-time authors; 80% from unagented writers. Offers $500-1,000 advance.** Publishes book 1 year after acceptance of ms. Accepts simultaneous submissions. Responds in 1-3 months to queries; 1-3 months to proposals; 1-3 months to mss. Book catalog free or on website.

Nonfiction: Subjects include business/economics, psychology, mental illness and developmental disabilities. Reviews artwork/photos as part of ms package.

Recent Title(s): *Managed Care & Developmental Disabilities*, by Dale Mitchell, Ph.D.; *Making Money While Making a Difference*, by Richard Steckel, Ph.D.

Tips: "Our audience consists of professionals in these fields: mental health/psychology, disabilities, business, marketing, nonprofit leadership and management. You should send us a one-page query with SASE, giving a brief overview of the book, its market and your background. If we are interested, we will request a book proposal. The book proposal outlines the nature of your work, who your market is, and information about your background. Please do not send a complete manuscript unless we request one."

HILL AND WANG, Farrar Straus & Giroux, Inc., 19 Union Square W., New York NY 10003. (212)741-6900. Fax: (212)633-9385. **Acquisitions:** Elisabeth Sifton, publisher; Thomas LeBien, editor. Estab. 1956. Publishes hardcover and trade paperbacks. **Publishes 12 titles/year. Receives 1,500 queries/year. 50% of books from first-time authors; 50% from unagented writers. Pays 10% royalty on retail price to 5,000 copies sold, 12½% to 10,000 copies, 15% thereafter on hardcover; 7½% on retail price for paperback.** Publishes book 1 year after acceptance of ms. Accepts simultaneous submissions. Book catalog free.

O→ Hill and Wang publishes serious nonfiction books, primarily in history and the social sciences.

Nonfiction: Subjects include government/politics, history (American), women's issues/studies. Submit outline, sample chapter(s). SASE and a letter explaining rationale for book.

Fiction: Not considering new fiction, drama or poetry.

Recent Title(s): *Pox Americana: The Great Smallpox Epidemic of 1775-82*, by Elizabeth A. Fenn; *1831: Year of Eclipse*, by Louis P. Masur.

HILL STREET PRESS, 191 E. Broad St., Suite 209, Athens GA 30601-2848. (706)613-7200. Fax: (706)613-7204. E-mail: editorial@hillstreetpress.com. Website: www.hillstreetpress.com. **Acquisitions:** Judy Long, editor-in-chief. Estab. 1998. Publishes hardcover originals, trade paperback originals and reprints. **Publishes 20 titles/year. Receives 300 queries/year. 5% of books from first-time authors; 2% from unagented writers. Pays 9-12½% royalty on wholesale price.** Publishes book 1 year after acceptance of ms. Accepts simultaneous submissions. Responds in 1 month to queries; 3 months to proposals; 6 months to mss. Book catalog and ms guidelines online.

O→ "HSP is a Southern regional press. While we are not a scholarly or academic press, our nonfiction titles must meet the standards of research for an exacting general audience."

Nonfiction: Biography, coffee table book, cookbook, gift book, humor, illustrated book. Subjects include Americana, cooking/foods/nutrition, creative nonfiction, gardening, gay/lesbian, history, memoirs, nature/environment, recreation, regional (Southern), sports, travel. Submit proposal package including outline, 3 sample chapter(s), résumé.

Fiction: Must have a strong connection with the American South. Gay/lesbian, historical, humor, literary, mainstream/contemporary, military/war, regional (southern uS), religious, sports, African American. "Reasonable length projects (50,000-85,000 words) stand a far better chance of review. Do not submit proposals for works in excess of 125,000 words in length." No short stories. "No cornball moonlight-and-magnolia stuff." Query with SASE or submit proposal package including 3 sample chapter(s), résumé, synopsis, press clips. "Let us know at the point of submission if you are represented by an agent."

Recent Title(s): *Strange Birds in the Tree of Heaven*, by Karen Salyer McElmurray (literary fiction); *The Worst Day of My Life, So Far*, by M.A. Harper (literary fiction); *How I Learned to Snap* (memoir).

Tips: "Audience is discerning with an interest in the fiction, history, current issues and food of the American South"

HIPPOCRENE BOOKS, INC., 171 Madison Ave., New York NY 10016. (212)685-4371. Fax: (212)779-9338. E-mail: hippocrene.books@verizon.net. Website: www.hippocrenebooks.com. President/Publisher: George Blagowidow. **Acquisitions:** Anne E. McBride, editor-in-chief (food and wine, nonfiction reference); Nicholas Williams, associate editor (foreign language, dictionaries, language guides); Anne Kemper, associate editor (history). Estab. 1971. Publishes hardcover and trade paperback originals. **Publishes 100 titles/year. Receives 250 submissions/year. 10% of books from first-time authors; 95% from unagented writers. Pays 6-10% royalty on retail price. Offers $2,000 advance.** Publishes book 16 months after acceptance of ms. Accepts simultaneous submissions. Responds in 2 months to queries. Book catalog for 9 x12 SAE with 5 first-class stamps; ms guidelines for #10 SASE.

"We focus on ethnic-interest and language-related titles, particularly on lesser published and often overlooked ones." Currently emphasizing concise foreign language dictionaries. De-emphasizing military history.

Nonfiction: Biography, cookbook, reference. Subjects include cooking/foods/nutrition, ethnic, history, language/literature, multicultural, travel. Submit proposal package including outline, 2 sample chapter(s), table of contents.

Recent Title(s): *Chinese Frequency Dictionary*; *Cuisines of Portuguese Encounters*.

Tips: "Our recent successes in publishing general books considered midlist by larger publishers is making us more of a general trade publisher. We continue to do well with reference books like dictionaries, atlases and language studies. We ask for proposal, sample chapter, and table of contents. We then ask for material if we are interested."

HOBAR PUBLICATIONS, Finney Company, 3943 Meadowbrook Rd., Minneapolis MN 55426. (952)938-9330. Fax: (952)938-7353. E-mail: feedback@finney-hobar.com. Website: www.finney-hobar.com. **Acquisitions:** Alan E. Krysan, president. Publishes trade paperback originals. **Publishes 4-6 titles/year. Receives 30 queries and 10 mss/year. 35% of books from first-time authors; 100% from unagented writers. Pays 10% royalty on wholesale price. Offers advance.** Publishes book 6-12 months after acceptance of ms. Accepts simultaneous submissions. Responds in 3 weeks to queries.

Hobar publishes agricultural and industrial technology educational materials.

Nonfiction: How-to, illustrated book, reference, technical, textbook, handbooks, field guides. Subjects include agriculture/horticulture, animals, business/economics, education, gardening, nature/environment, science, building trades. Query with SASE. Reviews artwork/photos as part of ms package.

Recent Title(s): *Reading a Ruler*, by Susan Resch.

HOBBY HOUSE PRESS, 1 Corporate Dr., Grantsville MD 21536. (301)895-3792. Fax: (301)895-5029. Website: www.hobbyhouse.com. Publishes hardcover and trade paperback originals. **Publishes 20 titles/year. Receives 50 queries and 25 mss/year. 85% of books from first-time authors; 95% from unagented writers. Pays 10% royalty on net receipts.** Publishes book 6 months after acceptance of ms. Accepts simultaneous submissions. Responds in 2 weeks to queries; 1 month to proposals. Book catalog and ms guidelines free.

Nonfiction: Gift book, how-to, reference, price guides. Subjects include gardening, hobbies (collecting/antiques). Query with SASE or submit outline, 1 sample chapter(s), photos. Reviews artwork/photos as part of ms package. Send prints.

Recent Title(s): *A Century of Crayola Collectibles*; *Comic Book Survival and Price Guide*; *Teddy Bear Artist Pattern Book*.

HOLIDAY HOUSE, INC., 425 Madison Ave., New York NY 10017. (212)688-0085. Fax: (212)421-6134. Editor-in-Chief: Regina Griffin. **Acquisitions:** Suzanne Reinoehl, editor. Estab. 1935. Publishes hardcover originals and paperback reprints. **Publishes 60 titles/year. Receives 3,000 submissions/year. 2-5% of books from first-time authors; 50% from unagented writers. Pays royalty on list price, range varies. Offers Flexible, depending on whether the book is illustrated. advance.** Publishes book 1-2 years after acceptance of ms. Does not accept simultaneous submissions. Ms guidelines for #10 SASE.

Holiday House publishes children's and young adult books for the school and library markets. "We have a commitment to publishing first-time authors and illustrators. We specialize in quality hardcovers from picture books to young adult, both fiction and nonfiction, primarily for the school and library market." Currently emphasizing literary middle-grade novels.

Nonfiction: Biography, humor. Subjects include Americana, history, science, Judaica. Query with SASE. Reviews artwork/photos as part of ms package. Send photocopies—no originals—to Claire Counihan, art director.

Fiction: Adventure, historical, humor, literary, mainstream/contemporary, Judaica and holiday, animal stories for young readers. Children's books only. Query with SASE. "No phone calls, please."

Recent Title(s): *John and Abigail Adams*, by Judith St. George; *A Child's Calendar*, by John Updike, illustrated by Trina Schart Hyman.

Tips: "We are not geared toward the mass market, but toward school and library markets. We need picture book texts with strong stories and writing. We do not publish board books or novelties."

N **HOLLIS PUBLISHING CO.**, Puritan Press, Inc., 95 Runnells Bridge Rd., Hollis NH 03049. (603)889-4500. Fax: (603)889-6551. E-mail: books@hollispublishing.com. Website: www.hollispublishing.com. **Acquisitions:** Frederick Lyford, editor. Publishes hardcover and trade paperback originals. **Publishes 5 titles/year. Receives 25 queries and 15 mss/year. 50% of books from first-time authors; 100% from unagented writers. Pays 5-10% royalty on retail price.** Publishes book 6 months after acceptance of ms. Does not accept simultaneous submissions. Responds in 1 month to queries; 2 months to mss. Book catalog free; ms guidelines for #10 SASE.

Hollis publishes books on social policy, government, politics, and current and recent events intended for use by professors and their students, college and university libraries and the general reader. Currently emphasizing works about education, the Internet, government, history-in-the-making, social values and politics.

Nonfiction: Biography. Subjects include Americana, anthropology/archeology, education, ethnic, government/politics, health/medicine, history, memoirs, nature/environment, regional, sociology, travel. Query with SASE or submit outline, 2 sample chapter(s).

Recent Title(s): *Lymphatic Filariasis: The Quest to Eliminate a 4,000-Year-Old Disease*, by Malcolm Dean; *Campaign for President: The Managers Look at 2000*, by Institute of Politics, Harvard University.

HOLMES & MEIER PUBLISHERS, INC., East Building, 160 Broadway, New York NY 10038. (212)374-0100. Fax: (212)374-1313. E-mail: info@holmesandmeier.com. Website: www.holmesandmeier.com. Publisher: Miriam H. Holmes. **Acquisitions:** Maggie Kennedy, managing editor. Estab. 1969. Publishes hardcover and paperback originals. **Publishes 20 titles/year. Pays royalty.** Publishes book an average of 18 months after acceptance of ms. Does not accept simultaneous submissions. Responds in 6 months to queries. Book catalog free.

Imprints: Africana Publishing Co.

"We are noted as an academic publishing house and are pleased with our reputation for excellence in the field. However, we are also expanding our list to include books of more general interest."

Nonfiction: Biography, reference. Subjects include art/architecture, business/economics, ethnic, government/politics, history, regional, translation, women's issues/studies. Query first with outline, sample chapters, cv and idea of intended market/audience.

HENRY HOLT & CO. BOOKS FOR YOUNG READERS, Henry Holt & Co., LLC, 115 W. 18th St., New York NY 10011. (212)886-9200. Fax: (212)645-5832. Website: www.henryholt.com. **Acquisitions:** Laura Godwin, associate publisher and editorial director; Christy Ottaviano, executive editor; Nina Ignatowicz, senior editor; Reka Simonsen, editor; Adriane Fry, associate editor; Kate Farrell, associate editor. Estab. 1866 (Holt). Publishes hardcover originals of picture books, chapter books, middle grade and young adult novels. **Publishes 70-80 titles/year. 10% of books from first-time authors; 50% from unagented writers. Pays royalty on retail price. Offers $3,000 and up advance.** Publishes book 18 months after acceptance of ms. Does not accept simultaneous submissions. Responds in 3-4 months to queries. Book catalog for 8 1/2X11 SAE with $1.75 postage; ms guidelines online.

"Henry Holt Books for Young Readers publishes highly original and cutting-edge fiction and nonfiction for all ages, from the very young to the young adult."

Nonfiction: Children's/juvenile, illustrated book. Submit complete ms, attention: Submissions Editor.

Fiction: Adventure, fantasy, historical, humor, juvenile, mainstream/contemporary, multicultural, mystery, picture books, sports, suspense, young adult. Juvenile: adventure, animal, contemporary, fantasy, history, humor, multicultural, sports, suspense/mystery. Picture books: animal, concept, history, humor, mulitcultural, sports. Young adult: contemporary, fantasy, history, multicultural, nature/environment, problem novels, sports. Submit complete ms, attention: Submissions Editor.

Recent Title(s): *Hondo and Fabian*, by Peter McCarty; *Keeper of the Night*, by Kimberly Willis Holt.

HENRY HOLT & CO., INC., 115 W. 18th St., New York NY 10011. (212)886-9200. Fax: (212)633-0748. Website: www.henryholt.com. President and Publisher: John Sterling. **Acquisitions:** Jennifer Barth, editor-in-chief (adult literary fiction, narrative nonfiction); Sara Bershtel, associate publisher of Metropolitan Books (literary fiction, politics, history); Vanessa Mobley, editor, adult trade; David Sobel, editorial director, Times Books (science, culture, history, health); Deb Brody, senior editor, adult trade (lifestyle, health, self help, parenting). Estab. 1866. Does not accept simultaneous submissions.

Imprints: Edge Books; Henry Holt for Young Readers; Henry Holt Reference; John Macrae Books; Metropolitan Books; Owl Books; Owlets Paperbacks; Redfeather Books; Times Books; 21st Century Books.

- Does not accept unsolicited queries or mss.

Holt is a general interest publisher of quality fiction and nonfiction. Currently emphasizing narrative nonfiction. De-emphasizing cooking, gardening.

Recent Title(s): *M: The Man Who Became Caravaggio*; *Wild Minds*, Marc Hanser.

N **HOMA & SEKEY BOOKS**, P.O. Box 103, Dumont NJ 07628. (201)384-6692. Fax: (201)384-6055. E-mail: info@homabooks.com. Submissions E-mail: submission@homabooks.com. Website: www.homabooks.com. **Acquisitions:** Shawn Ye, editor (fiction and nonfiction). Estab. 1997. Publishes hardcover originals and trade paperback originals and reprints. **Publishes 10 titles/year. Receives 300-500 queries and 100-200 mss/year. 50% of books from first-time authors; 90% from unagented writers. Pays 5-10% royalty on retail price.** Publishes book 1 year after acceptance of ms. Accepts simultaneous submissions. Responds in 2 months to queries; 3 months to proposals; 4 months to mss. Book catalog online; ms guidelines online.

Nonfiction: Autobiography, biography, coffee table book, illustrated book, reference, scholarly, textbook. Subjects include alternative lifestyles, art/architecture, business/economics, contemporary culture, creative nonfiction, ethnic, general nonfiction, health/medicine, history, language/literature, memoirs, multicultural, New Age, photography, social sciences, translation, travel, world affairs. "We publish books on Asian topics. Books should have something to do with Asia." Submit proposal package including outline, 2 sample chapter(s) or submit complete ms. Reviews artwork/photos as part of ms package. Send photocopies.

Fiction: Adventure, ethnic, feminist, historical, literary, multicultural, mystery, plays, poetry, poetry in translation, romance, short story collections, translation, young adult. "We publish books on Asian topics. Books should be Asia-related." Submit proposal package including 2 sample chapter(s), synopsis or submit complete ms.

Poetry: "We publish books on Asian topics. Poetry should have things to do with Asia." Submit complete ms.

Recent Title(s): *The Haier Way: The Making of a Chinese Business Leader and a Global Brand*, by Dr. Jeannie Yi; *Father and Son*, by Han Sung-won (novel); *Selected Short Stories*, by Korean women writers (Korean translation).

Tips: General readership with a leaning on Asian cultures. "Authors should be willing to participate in publicity and promotion activities."

N **HOT JAVA PRODUCTIONS, INC.**, P.O. Box 354, Kirkland WA 98083-0354. (425)820-6848. Fax: (253)875-1719. E-mail: rom.author@juno.com.Submissions E-mail: rom.author@juno.com. Website: www.hotjavaproductions.com. **Acquisitions:** Nancy Radke, executive editor; Nolan Radke, senior editor. Estab. 2002. Publishes electronic originals. **Publishes 100 titles/year. 98% of books from first-time authors; 90% from unagented writers. Pays 2% royalty on retail price. Offers $5,000 advance.** Publishes book 10 months after acceptance of ms. Accepts simultaneous submissions. Responds in 1 month to queries; 1 month to proposals; 2 months to mss. Ms guidelines for #10 SASE.

Fiction: Adventure, fantasy, gothic, historical, horror, humor, juvenile, mainstream/contemporary, military/war, mystery, picture books, regional, religious, romance, science fiction, short story collections, spiritual, sports, suspense, western, young adult. "We are looking for good books from new authors. We are also acquiring books from established authors which have 'fallen through the cracks' and rejected by companies with strict guidelines. We will look at partials of a manuscript not finished and are willing to work to develop new authors. Hot Java will look at all fiction, especially romance of all types." Submit proposal package including 2 sample chapter(s), synopsis.

Tips: "We are looking at a wide range of readers, all ages, but especially women. This is an international endeavor, so the books will go out in several languages. We already have authors, editors, and readers in several countries—need more of all of these." "Write the best book you can. We'd like to see stories that come close to 60,000 words. Top range is 100,000, low is 55,000. We will probably do some cutting on the 100,000 word books."

HOUGHTON MIFFLIN BOOKS FOR CHILDREN, Houghton Mifflin Company, 222 Berkeley St., Boston MA 02116. (617)351-5959. Fax: (617)351-1111. E-mail: children's_books@hmco.com. Website: www.houghtonmifflinbooks.com. **Acquisitions:** Hannah Rodgers, submissions coordinator; Ann Rider, Margaret Raymo, senior editors; Kate O'Sullivan, assistant editor. Publishes hardcover originals and trade paperback originals and reprints. **Publishes 100 titles/year. Receives 5,000 queries and 14,000 mss/year. 10% of books from first-time authors; 60% from unagented writers. Pays 5-10% royalty on retail price. Offers variable advance.** Publishes book 18-24 months after acceptance of ms. Accepts simultaneous submissions. Responds in 4 months to queries; 3 months to mss. Book catalog for 9×12 SASE with 3 first-class stamps; ms guidelines online.

Imprints: Sandpiper Paperback Books (Eden Edwards, editor).

O‑ "Houghton Mifflin gives shape to ideas that educate, inform, and above all, delight."

Nonfiction: Biography, children's/juvenile, humor, illustrated book. Subjects include animals, anthropology/archeology, art/architecture, ethnic, history, language/literature, music/dance, nature/environment, science, sports. Interested in innovative books and subjects about which the author is passionate. Query with SASE or submit sample chapter(s), synopsis. **Note:** Mss not returned without appropriate-sized SASE. Reviews artwork/photos as part of ms package. Send photocopies.

Fiction: Adventure, ethnic, historical, humor, juvenile (early readers), literary, mystery, picture books, suspense, young adult, board books. Submit complete ms with appropriate-sized SASE.

Recent Title(s): *Henry Builds a Cabin*, by D.B. Johnson; *Angelo*, by David Macaulay; *Phineas Gage: A Gruesome but True Story about Brain Science*, by John Fleischman (poetry).

Tips: "Faxed or e-mailed manuscripts and proposals are not considered."

A **HOUGHTON MIFFLIN CO.**, 222 Berkeley St., Boston MA 02116. Website: www.hmco.com. Executive Vice President: Theresa D. Kelly. Editor-in-Chief/Publisher, Adult Books: Janet Silver. **Acquisitions:** Submissions Editor. Estab. 1832. Publishes hardcover originals and trade paperback originals and reprints. **Publishes 250 titles/year; imprint publishes 25 titles/year. Receives 1,000 queries and 2,000 mss/year. 10% of books from first-time authors. Hardcover: pays 10-15% royalty on retail price, sliding scale or flat rate based on sales; paperback: 7½% flat fee, but negotiable. Offers variable advance.** Publishes book 3 years after acceptance of ms. Accepts simultaneous submissions. Book catalog online.

Imprints: American Heritage Dictionaries; Clarion Books; Great Source; Houghton Mifflin; Houghton Mifflin Books for Children; Houghton Mifflin Paperbacks; Mariner Books; McDougal Littell; Peterson Field Guides; Riverside Publishing Company; Sunburst Technology; Taylor's Gardening Guides.

O‑ "Houghton Mifflin gives shape to ideas that educate, inform and delight. In a new era of publishing, our legacy of quality thrives as we combine imagination with technology, bringing you new ways to know."

Nonfiction: Audiocassettes, autobiography, biography, children's/juvenile, cookbook, gift book, how-to, illustrated book, reference, self-help. Subjects include agriculture/horticulture, animals, anthropology/archeology, cooking/foods/nutrition, ethnic, gardening, gay/lesbian, general nonfiction, health/medicine, history, memoirs, military/war, social sciences. "We are not a mass market publisher. Our main focus is serious nonfiction. We do practical self-help but not pop psychology self-help." *Agented submissions only.*

Fiction: Literary. "We are not a mass market publisher. Study the current list." *Agented submissions only.*

Recent Title(s): *Fast Food Nation*, by Eric Schlosser (nonfiction); *Why I Am Catholic*, by Garry Wills (nonfiction); *The Best American Short Stories*.

Tips: "Our audience is high end literary."

HOUSE OF COLLECTIBLES, Random House, Inc., 1745 Broadway, New York NY 10019. Website: www.houseofcollectibles.com. **Acquisitions:** Dorothy Harris, director. Publishes trade and mass market paperback originals. **Publishes 25-28 titles/year. Receives 200 queries/year. 7% of books from first-time authors; 75% from unagented writers. Royalty on retail price varies. Offers varied advance.** Publishes book 1 year after acceptance of ms. Does not accept simultaneous submissions. Book catalog free.

Imprints: Official Price Guide series.

O→ "One of the premier publishing companies devoted to books on a wide range of antiques and collectibles, House of Collectibles publishes books for the seasoned expert and the beginning collector alike."

Nonfiction: How-to (related to collecting antiques and coins), reference. Subjects include art/architecture (fine art), sports, comic books, American patriotic memorabilia, clocks, character toys, coins, stamps, costume jewelry, knives, books, military, glassware, records, arts and crafts, Native American collectibles, pottery, fleamarkets. Accepts unsolicited proposals only.

Recent Title(s): *The Official Price Guide to Vintage Fashion and Fabrics*, by Pamela Smith.

Tips: "We have been publishing price guides and other books on antiques and collectibles for over 35 years and plan to meet the needs of collectors, dealers and appraisers well into the 21st century."

HOWELL PRESS, INC., 1713-2D Allied Lane, Charlottesville VA 22903. (434)977-4006. Fax: (434)971-7204. E-mail: rhowell@howellpress.com. Website: www.howellpress.com. **Acquisitions:** Ross A. Howell, president; Dara Parker, editor. Estab. 1985. **Publishes 10-13 titles/year. Receives 500 submissions/year. 10% of books from first-time authors; 80% from unagented writers. Pays 5-10% royalty. Offers advance.** Publishes book 18 months after acceptance of ms. Book catalog for 9×12 SAE with 4 first-class stamps; ms guidelines online.

O→ "While our aviation, history and transportation titles are produced for the enthusiast market, writing must be accessible to the general adult reader." Currently emphasizing regional (Mid-Atlantic and Southeast), travel, ghost stories, gardens, quilts and quilt history. De-emphasizing general garden guides.

Nonfiction: Illustrated book. Subjects include history, regional, aviation, transportation, gourmet, quilts. "Generally open to most ideas, as long as writing is accessible to average adult reader. Our line is targeted, so it would be advisable to look over our catalog before querying to better understand what Howell Press does." Query with SASE or submit outline, sample chapter(s). Does not return mss without SASE. Reviews artwork/photos as part of ms package.

Recent Title(s): *The Virginia Landscape*, by James Kelly and William Rasmussen.

Tips: "Focus of our program has been illustrated books, but we will also consider nonfiction manuscripts that would not be illustrated."

HOWELLS HOUSE, P.O. Box 9546, Washington DC 20016-9546. (202)333-2182. **Acquisitions:** W.D. Howells, publisher. Estab. 1988. Publishes hardcover and trade paperback originals and reprints. **Publishes 4 titles/year; imprint publishes 2-3 titles/year. Receives 2,000 queries and 300 mss/year. 50% of books from first-time authors; 60% from unagented writers. Pays 15% net royalty or makes outright purchase. May offer advance.** Publishes book 8 months after acceptance of ms. Does not accept simultaneous submissions. Responds in 2 months to proposals.

Imprints: The Compass Press, Whalesback Books.

O→ "Our interests are institutions and institutional change."

Nonfiction: Biography, illustrated book, textbook. Subjects include Americana, anthropology/archeology, art/architecture, business/economics, education, government/politics, history, photography, science, sociology, translation, women's issues/studies. Query.

Fiction: Historical, literary, mainstream/contemporary. Query.

HUDSON HILLS PRESS, INC., 74-2 Union St., Box 205, Manchester VT 05254. (802)362-6450. Fax: (802)362-6459. E-mail: sbutterfield@hudsonhills.com. Website: www.hudsonhills.com. **Acquisitions:** Sarah Butterfield, assistant to publisher. Estab. 1978. Publishes hardcover and paperback originals. **Publishes 15+ titles/year. Receives 50-100 submissions/year. 15% of books from first-time authors; 90% from unagented writers. Pays 4-6% royalty on retail price. Offers $3,500 average advance.** Publishes book 1 year after acceptance of ms. Accepts simultaneous submissions. Responds in 2 months to queries. Book catalog for 6×9 SAE with 2 first-class stamps.

O→ Hudson Hills Press publishes books about art and photography, including monographs.

Nonfiction: Subjects include art/architecture, photography. Query first, then submit outline and sample chapters. Reviews artwork/photos as part of ms package.

Recent Title(s): *Splendid Pages: The Molly & Walter Bareiss Collection of Modern Illustrated Books*, by Julie Mellby, et. al.

HUMAN KINETICS PUBLISHERS, INC., P.O. Box 5076, Champaign IL 61825-5076. (217)351-5076. Fax: (217)351-2674. E-mail: webmaster@hkusa.com. Website: www.humankinetics.com. CEO: Brian Holding. President: Rainer Martens. **Acquisitions:** Ted Miller, vice president and director (trade); Martin Barnard, trade senior acquisitions editor (fitness, running, golf, tennis); Ed McNeely, trade acquisitions editor (strength training, cycling, martial arts, minor spa); Scott Wikgren, HPERD director (health, physical education, recreation, dance); Bonnie Pettifor, acquisitions editor, HPERD; Gayle Kassing, acquisitions editor, HPERD; Mike Bahrke, STM acquisitions editor (scientific, technical, medical); Loarn Robertson, STM acquisitions editor (biomechanics, anatomy, athletic training, cardiac rehab, test/measurement); Judy Wright, HPERD acquisitions editor (dance, motor, learning/behavior/performance/development, gymnastics, adapted physical education, older adults); Amy Clocksin, acquisitions editor. Estab. 1974. Publishes hardcover and paperback text and reference books, trade paperback originals, software and audiovisual. **Publishes 120 titles/year. Receives 300 submissions/year. 30% of books from first-time authors; 90% from unagented writers. Pays 10-15% royalty on net income.** Publishes book up to 18 months after acceptance of ms. Accepts simultaneous submissions. Responds in 2 months to queries. Book catalog free; ms guidelines online.

Imprints: HK.

O→ Human Kinetics publishes books which provide expert knowledge in sport and fitness training and techniques, physical education, sports sciences and sports medicine for coaches, athletes and fitness enthusiasts and professionals in the physical action field.

Nonfiction: How-to, multimedia, reference, self-help, technical, textbook. Subjects include education, health/medicine, psychology, recreation, sports (sciences). Submit outline, sample chapter(s). Reviews artwork/photos as part of ms package.

Recent Title(s): *Fitness and Health*, by Brian J. Sharkey; *Artistry on Ice*, by Nancy Kerrigan.

HUMANICS LEARNING, Humanics Publishing Group, P.O. Box 7400, Atlanta GA 30357. (404)874-2176. Fax: (404)874-1976. Website: www.humanicspub.com. **Acquisitions:** Arthur Blye, editor. Estab. 1976. Publishes hardcover and trade paperback originals and reprints. **Publishes 20 titles/year. Receives 1,500 queries and 1,300 mss/year. 90% from unagented writers. Pays 5-13% royalty on net receipts. Offers $500-1,000 advance.** Publishes book 6 months after acceptance of ms. Accepts simultaneous submissions. Responds in 3 months to queries. Book catalog for 9×12 SAE and 1 55¢ stamp; ms guidelines online.

- Charges $50 one-time, non-refundable submission fee. Approach such fees with caution.

O→ "Our goal is to furnish teachers, home schoolers, day care facilitators and other instructors with the best teacher resource guides available to help improve the education of the child."

Nonfiction: How-to (teacher resource guides). Subjects include child guidance/parenting, education, ethnic, health/medicine, language/literature, music/dance, nature/environment, psychology, science, self esteem. "Know our focus. Request a catalog." Query with SASE or submit outline, 3 sample chapter(s). Reviews artwork/photos as part of ms package. Send photocopies.

Recent Title(s): *Peace in Any Language*, by Jeanine Perez.

HUNTER HOUSE, P.O. Box 2914, Alameda CA 94501. (510)865-5282. Fax: (510)865-4295. E-mail: acquisitions@hunterhouse.com. Website: www.hunterhouse.com. **Acquisitions:** Jeanne Brondino, acquisitions editor; Kiran S. Rana, publisher. Estab. 1978. Publishes hardcover and trade paperback originals and reprints. **Publishes 24 titles/year. Receives 200-300 queries and 100 mss/year. 50% of books from first-time authors; 80% from unagented writers. Pays 12% royalty on net receipts, defined as selling price. Offers $500-3,000 advance.** Publishes book 1-2 years after acceptance of ms. Accepts simultaneous submissions. Responds in 2 months to queries; 3 months to proposals; 6 months to mss. Book catalog and ms guidelines for 8½×11 SAE with 3 first-class stamps; ms guidelines online.

O→ Hunter House publishes health books (especially women's health), self-help health, sexuality and couple relationships, violence prevention and intervention. De-emphasizing reference, self-help psychology.

Nonfiction: Subjects include alternative lifestyles, health/medicine, self-help, women's health, fitness, relationships, sexuality, personal growth, and violence prevention. "Health books (especially women's health) should focus on emerging health issues or current issues that are inadequately covered and be written for the general population. Family books: Our current focus is sexuality and couple relationships, and alternative lifestyles to high stress. Community topics include violence prevention/violence intervention. We also publish specialized curricula for counselors and educators in the areas of violence prevention and trauma in children." Query with proposal package, including synopsis, table of contents and chapter outline, sample chapter, target audience information, competition and what distinguishes the book. Reviews artwork/photos as part of ms package. Send photocopies, proposals generally not returned, requested mss returned with SASE. Reviews artwork/photos as part of ms package.

Recent Title(s): *The Complete Guide to Joseph H. Pilates' Techniques of Physical Conditioning*, by Allan Menezes; *Pocket Book of Foreplay*, Richard Craze; *Living Beyond Multiple Sclerosis—A Women's Guide*, by Judith Lynn Nichols.

Tips: Audience is concerned people who are looking to educate themselves and their community about real-life issues that affect them. "Please send as much information as possible about *who* your audience is, *how* your book addresses their needs, and *how* you reach that audience in your ongoing work."

HUNTER PUBLISHING, INC., 130 Campus Dr., Edison NJ 08818. Fax: (772)546-8040. E-mail: hunterp@bellsouth.net. Website: www.hunterpublishing.com. President: Michael Hunter. **Acquisitions:** Kim Andre, editor; Lissa Dailey. Estab. 1985. **Publishes 100 titles/year. Receives 300 submissions/year. 10% of books from first-time authors; 75% from unagented writers. Pays royalty. Offers negotiable advance.** Publishes book 5 months after acceptance of ms. Accepts simultaneous submissions. Responds in 3 weeks to queries; 1 month to mss. Book catalog for #10 SAE with 4 first-class stamps.

Imprints: Adventure Guides, Romantic Weekends Guides, Alive Guides.

O→ Hunter Publishing publishes practical guides for travelers going to the Caribbean, U.S., Europe, South America, and the far reaches of the globe.

Nonfiction: Reference. Subjects include regional, travel (travel guides). "We need travel guides to areas covered by few competitors: Caribbean Islands, South and Central America, Europe, Australia, New Zealand from an active 'adventure' perspective." No personal travel stories or books not directed to travelers. Query or submit outline/synopsis and sample chapters. Reviews artwork/photos as part of ms package.

Recent Title(s): *Adventure Guide to Canada's Atlantic Provinces*, by Barbara Radcliffe-Rogers.

Tips: "Guides should be destination-specific, rather than theme-based alone. Thus, 'travel with kids' is too broad; 'Florida with Kids' is OK. Make sure the guide doesn't duplicate what other guide publishers do."

IBEX PUBLISHERS, P.O. Box 30087, Bethesda MD 20824. (301)718-8188. Fax: (301)907-8707. E-mail: info@ibexpub.com. Website: www.ibexpub.com. Publishes hardcover and trade paperback originals and reprints. **Publishes 6-10 titles/year. Payment varies.** Accepts simultaneous submissions. Book catalog free.

Imprints: Iranbooks Press.

O→ IBEX publishes books about Iran and the Middle East.

Nonfiction: Biography, cookbook, reference, textbook. Subjects include cooking/foods/nutrition, language/literature. Query with SASE or submit propsal package, including outline and 2 sample chapters.
Poetry: Translations of Persian poets will be considered.

THE ICON EDITIONS, Westview Press, Perseus Books Group, 5500 Central Ave., Boulder CO 80301-2877. (720)562-3281. Fax: (720)406-7337. Website: www.westviewpress.com. **Acquisitions:** Sarah Warner. Estab. 1973. Publishes hardcover and trade paperback originals. **Publishes 5 titles/year. Receives hundreds of queries/year. 10% of books from first-time authors; 50% from unagented writers. Royalty and advance vary.** Publishes book 6-9 months after acceptance of ms. Accepts simultaneous submissions. Book catalog free.

O→ The Icon Editions focus on books in art history, art criticism and architecture for the textbook and trade markets.

Nonfiction: Textbook, general readership titles. Subjects include art/architecture, art history, art criticism. Query with SASE. Reviews artwork/photos as part of ms package.
Recent Title(s): *Italian Renaissance Art*, by Laurie Schneider Adams; *Matisse and Picasso*, by Jack Flam.

ICONOGRAFIX, INC., 1830A Hanley Rd., P.O. Box 446, Hudson WI 54016. (715)381-9755. Fax: (715)381-9756. E-mail: iconogfx@spacestar.net. **Acquisitions:** Dylan Frautschi, acquisitions manager (transportation). Estab. 1992. Publishes trade paperback originals. **Publishes 24 titles/year. Receives 100 queries and 20 mss/year. 50% of books from first-time authors; 100% from unagented writers. Pays 8-12½% royalty on wholesale price or makes outright purchase of $1,000-3,000. Offers $1,000-3,500 advance.** Publishes book 1 year after acceptance of ms. Accepts simultaneous submissions. Responds in 1 month to queries; 3 months to proposals; 3 months to mss. Book catalog and ms guidelines free.

O→ Iconografix publishes special historical interest photographic books for transportation equipment enthusiasts. Currently emphasizing emergency vehicles, buses, trucks, railroads, automobiles, auto racing, construction equipment.

Nonfiction: Interested in photo archives. Coffee table book, illustrated book (photographic), photo albums. Subjects include Americana (photos from archives of historic places, objects, people), history, hobbies, military/war, transportation (older photos of specific vehicles). Query with SASE or submit proposal package, including outline. Reviews artwork/photos as part of ms package. Send photocopies.
Recent Title(s): *Greyhound Buses 1914-2000 Photo Archive*, by William A. Luke; *Indianapolis Racing Cars of Frank Kurtis, 1941-1963 Photo Archive*, by Gordon Eliot White; *The American Ambulance 1900-2002: An Illustrated History*, by Walter M.P. McCall.

ICS PUBLICATIONS, Institute of Carmelite Studies, 2131 Lincoln Rd. NE, Washington DC 20002. (202)832-8489. Fax: (202)832-8967. Website: www.icspublications.org. **Acquisitions:** John Sullivan, O.C.D. Publishes hardcover and trade paperback originals and reprints. **Publishes 6 titles/year. Receives 10-20 queries and 10 mss/year. 10% of books from first-time authors; 90-100% from unagented writers. Pays 2-6% royalty on retail price or makes outright purchase. Offers $500 advance.** Publishes book 2 years after acceptance of ms. Responds in 4 months to proposals. Book catalog for 7x10 SAE with 2 first-class stamps; ms guidelines for #10 SASE.

O→ "Our audience consists of those interested in the Carmelite tradition and in developing their life of prayer and spirituality."

Nonfiction: "We are looking for significant works on Carmelite history, spirituality, and main figures (Saints Teresa, John of the Cross, Therese of Lisieux, etc.)." Religious (should relate to Carmelite spirituality and prayer). "Too often we receive proposals for works that merely repeat what has already been done, are too technical for a general audience, or have little to do with the Carmelite tradition and spirit." Query or submit outline and 1 sample chapter.
Recent Title(s): *The Science of the Cross*, by St. Edith Stein.

[N] **IDEALS CHILDRENS BOOKS**, Ideals Publications, Inc., 535 Metroplex Dr., Suite 250, Nashville TN 37211. (615)333-0478. Publisher: Patricia Pingry. **Acquisitions:** Copy Editor. Estab. 1944. Publishes 8-10 hardbound books, 25-30 childrens titles. **Publishes 15-20 titles/year. Offers varied advance.** Publishes book 18 months after acceptance of ms. Accepts simultaneous submissions. Responds in 2 months only with SASE to queries. Ms guidelines for #10 SASE.

O→ Ideals Childrens Books publishes picture books for children ages 5-8.

Nonfiction: Biography, religious, holiday. Subjects include history, travel, inspirational, nostalgic, patriotic.
Recent Title(s): *Meet Abraham Lincoln*; *Conversations on the Ark*; *Seaman's Journal*.

IDYLL ARBOR, INC., P.O. Box 720, Ravensdale WA 98051. (425)432-3231. Fax: (425)432-3726. E-mail: editors@idyllarbor.com. Website: www.idyllarbor.com. **Acquisitions:** Tom Blaschko. Publishes hardcover and trade paperback originals and trade paperback reprints. **Publishes 6 titles/year. 50% of books from first-time authors; 100% from unagented writers. Pays 8-15% royalty on wholesale price or retail price.** Publishes book 1 year after acceptance of ms. Accepts simultaneous submissions. Responds in 1 month to queries; 2 months to proposals; 4 months to mss. Book catalog and ms guidelines free.
Imprints: Issues Press, Pine Woods Winds Press.

O→ Idyll Arbor publishes practical information on the current state and art of health care practice. Currently emphasizing therapies (recreational, occupational, music, horticultural), activity directors in long term care facilities, and social service professionals.

Nonfiction: Reference, technical, textbook. Subjects include agriculture/horticulture (used in long-term care activities or health care-therapy), health/medicine (for therapists, social service providers and activity directors), psychology, recreation (as therapy). "Idyll Arbor is currently developing a line of books under the imprint Issues Press, which treats emotional issues in a clear-headed manner. The first books are *Female Sex Offenders: What Therapists, Law Enforcement and Child Protective Services Need to Know* and *Sexual Addiction: My Journey from Shame to Grace*. Another series of *Personal*

Health books explains a condition or a closely related set of medical or psychological conditions. The target audience is the person or the family of the person with the condition. We want to publish a book that explains a condition at the level of detail expected of the average primary care physician so that our readers can address the situation intelligently with specialists. We look for manuscripts from authors with recent clinical experience. Good grounding in theory is required, but practical experience is more important." Query preferred with outline and 1 sample chapter. Reviews artwork/photos as part of ms package. Send photocopies.

Recent Title(s): *Eating Disorders: Providing Recreational Therapy Interventions*, by Dayna Miller and Laurie Jake; *Assessment Tools for Recreational Therapy, 3rd ed*, by Joan Burlingame and Tom Blaschko.

Tips: "The books must be useful for the health practitioner who meets face to face with patients *or* the books must be useful for teaching undergraduate and graduate level classes. We are especially looking for therapists with a solid clinical background to write on their area of expertise."

ILLUMINATION ARTS, P.O. Box 1865, Bellevue WA 98009. (425)644-7185. Fax: (425)644-9274. E-mail: liteinfo@illumin.com. Website: www.illumin.com. **Acquisitions:** Ruth Thompson, editorial director, (children's books); Terri Cohlene, creative director (artwork). Publishes hardcover originals. **Publishes 4-5 titles/year. Pays royalty on wholesale price. Offers advance for artists.** Book catalog online; ms guidelines online.

O→ Illumination Arts publishes inspirational/spiritual (not religious), children's picture books.

Nonfiction: Children's/juvenile. "Our books are all high quality. Send for our guidelines. Stories need to be exciting and inspirational for children." Submit complete ms with SASE. Reviews artwork/photos as part of ms package. Send photocopies.

Fiction: Picture books (children's), prefer under 1,000 words; 1,500 words max. "All are inspirational/spiritual. Be sure story is geared toward children and has an inspirational message." No electronic submissions.

Recent Title(s): *The Tree*.

Tips: "A smart writer researches publishing companies first and then follows submission guidelines."

ILR PRESS, Cornell University Press, Sage House, 512 E. State St., Ithaca NY 14850. (607)277-2338 ext. 222. Fax: (607)277-2374. **Acquisitions:** F. Benson, editor. Estab. 1945. Publishes hardcover and trade paperback originals and reprints. **Publishes 10-12 titles/year. Pays royalty.** Does not accept simultaneous submissions. Responds in 2 months to queries. Book catalog free.

O→ "We are interested in manuscripts with innovative perspectives on current workplace issues that concern both academics and the general public."

Nonfiction: Subjects include business/economics, government/politics, history, sociology. All titles relate to industrial relations and/or workplace issues including relevant work in the fields of history, sociology, political science, economics, human resources, and organizational behavior. Developing a new series on the work of health care. Query with SASE or submit outline, sample chapter(s), cv.

Recent Title(s): *Code Green: Money-driven Hospitals and the Dismantling of Nursing*, by Dana Beth Weinberg; *The Working Class Majority: America's Best Kept Secret*, by Michael Zweig; *State of Working America*, by Lawrence Mishel, et. al.

Tips: "Manuscripts must be well documented to pass our editorial evaluation, which includes review by academics in related fields."

IMAGES SI, INC., Images Publishing, 39 Seneca Loop, Staten Island NY 10314. (718)698-8305. Fax: (718)982-6145. E-mail: gina@imagesco.com. Website: www.imagesco.com. **Acquisitions:** Gina McNeil, vice president (science and tech); Dan Bianco, vice president (science fiction). Estab. 1990. Publishes hardcover originals, trade paperback originals and audio. **Publishes 5 titles/year. 10% of books from first-time authors; 75% from unagented writers. Pays 10-20% royalty on wholesale price. Offers $1,000-5,000 advance.** Publishes book 6 months after acceptance of ms. Accepts simultaneous submissions. Responds in 2 months to queries; 2 months to proposals; 2 months to mss. Book catalog online.

Nonfiction: Audiocassettes, booklets, how-to, technical. Subjects include computers/electronic, photography, science, software. Query with SASE.

Fiction: Fantasy, science fiction. "We are looking for short stories as well as full-length novels." Query with SASE.

Recent Title(s): *Kirlian Photography*, by John Iovine (photo/how-to); *Nova-Audio*, by Hoyt, Franklin, Schoen (science fiction).

IMAJINN BOOKS, P.O. Box 162, Hickory Corners MI 49060-0162. (269)671-4633. Fax: (269)671-4535. E-mail: editors@imajinnbooks.com. Website: www.imajinnbooks.com. **Acquisitions:** Linda Kichline, senior editor. Estab. 1998. Publishes trade paperback originals and reprints. **Publishes 24-36 titles/year. Receives 2,500 queries and 300 submissions/year. 70% of books from first-time authors; 80% from unagented writers. Pays 6-10% royalty on retail price. Offers 25-100 advance.** Publishes book 1-3 years after acceptance of ms. Responds in 3 months to queries; 6 months to proposals; 9-12 months to mss. Book catalog and ms guidelines for #10 SASE or online; ms guidelines online.

Fiction: "We publish only alternative reality romance, i.e., paranormal, supernatural, futuristic, fantasy, time travel, romance, with a word length of 70,000-90,000 words. We also publish children's and young adult science fiction and fantasy, ages 9-12 and 13-17, with a word length of 50,000+ words." Fantasy (romance), horror (romance), romance (futuristic/time travel), science fiction (romance), young adult (fantasy/science fiction). "We look for specific story lines based on what the readers are asking for and what story lines in which we're short. We post our current needs on our website." Query with SASE. Query with SASE and synopsis. On request only, proposal package, including 5 sample chapters and synopsis. Unsolicited submissions will not be read.

Recent Title(s): *Afterimage*, by Jaye Roycraft; *Chasing the Shadows*, by Keri Arthur; *Penelope Quagmire*, by Hal Lanse.

Tips: "We require certain elements to be in our books. Read several of them to determine how to ensure your book meets our needs."

IMPACT PUBLISHERS, INC., P.O. Box 6016, Atascadero CA 93423-6016. (805)466-5917. Fax: (805)466-5919. E-mail: info@impactpublishers.com. Website: www.impactpublishers.com. **Acquisitions:** Freeman Porter, acquisitions editor. Estab. 1970. Publishes trade paperback originals. **Publishes 6-10 titles/year. Receives 250 queries and 250 mss/year. 20% of books from first-time authors; 60% from unagented writers. Pays 10% royalty on net receipts. Offers advance.** Publishes book 12-18 months after acceptance of ms. Accepts simultaneous submissions. Responds in 5 months to proposals. Book catalog and ms guidelines free; ms guidelines online.

Imprints: American Source Books, Little Imp Books, Rebuilding Books, Practical Therapist series.

"Our purpose is to make the best human services expertise available to the widest possible audience: children, teens, parents, couples, individuals seeking self-help and personal growth, and human service professionals." Currently emphasizing books on divorce recovery for "The Rebuilding Books Series." De-emphasizing children's books.

Nonfiction: "All our books are written by qualified human service professionals and are in the fields of mental health, personal growth, relationships, aging, families, children and professional psychology." Children's/juvenile, self-help. Subjects include child guidance/parenting, health/medicine, psychology (professional), caregiving/eldercare. "We do not publish general fiction for children. We do not publish poetry." Submit proposal package, including short résumé or vita, book description, audience description, outline, 1-3 sample chapters and SASE.

Recent Title(s): *Time for a Better Marriage: Training in Marriage Enrichment*, by Jon Carlson, Ph.D. and Don Dinkmeyer, Sr., Ph.D.

Tips: "Don't call to see if we have received your submission. Include a self-addressed, stamped postcard if you want to know if manuscript arrived safely. We prefer a non-academic, readable style. We publish only popular psychology and self-help materials written in 'everyday language' by professionals with advanced degrees and significant experience in the human services."

INCENTIVE PUBLICATIONS, INC., 3835 Cleghorn Ave., Nashville TN 37215-2532. (615)385-2934. Fax: (615)385-2967. E-mail: comments@incentivepublications.com. Website: www.incentivepublications.com. **Acquisitions:** Charlotte Bosarge, editor. Estab. 1970. Publishes paperback originals. **Publishes 25-30 titles/year. Receives 350 submissions/year. 25% of books from first-time authors; 100% from unagented writers. Pays royalty or makes outright purchase.** Publishes book an average of 1 year after acceptance of ms. Responds in 1 month to queries. Ms guidelines online.

Incentive publishes developmentally appropriate teacher/parent resource materials and educational workbooks for children in grades K-12. Currently emphasizing primary material. Also interested in character education, English as a second language programs, early learning, current technology, related materials.

Nonfiction: Subjects include education. Teacher resource books in pre-K through 12th grade. Query with synopsis and detailed outline.

Recent Title(s): *The Ready to Learn Book Series*, by Imogene Forte (Grades pre K-K); *Drumming to the Beat of a Different Marcher*, by Debbie Silver; *As Reading Programs Come and Go, This Is What You Need to Know*, by Judith Cochran.

INFO NET PUBLISHING, 21142 Canada Rd., Unit 1-C, Lake Forest CA 92630. (949)458-9292. Fax: (949)462-9595. E-mail: herb@infonetpublishing.com. Website: www.infonetpublishing.com. **Acquisitions:** Herb Wetenkamp, president. Estab. 1987. Publishes hardcover and trade paperback originals. **Publishes 6 titles/year. Receives 50 queries and 20 mss/year. 80% of books from first-time authors; 85% from unagented writers. Pays 7-10% royalty on wholesale price or makes outright purchase of $1,000-5,000. Offers $1,000-2,000 advance in some cases.** Publishes book 10 months after acceptance of ms. Accepts simultaneous submissions. Responds in 2 months to queries. Book catalog for 10×12 SAE with 2 first-class stamps; ms guidelines for #10 SASE.

Info Net publishes for easily identified niche markets; specific markets with some sort of special interest, hobby, avocation, profession, sport or lifestyle. New emphasis on collectibles and a series of books on retailing with CD-Roms.

Nonfiction: Biography, children's/juvenile, gift book, how-to, reference, self-help, technical. Subjects include Americana (and collectibles), business/economics (retailing), history, hobbies, military/war, nature/environment (and environment), recreation, regional, sports, travel, women's issues/studies, aviation/aircraft archaeology. "We are looking for specific niche market books, not general titles, other than self-help. Do not repeat same formula as other books. Offer something new, in other words." Submit outline, 3 sample chapters, proposal package, including demographics, marketing plans/data with SASE. Reviews artwork/photos as part of ms package. Send photocopies.

Recent Title(s): *Aircraft Wrecks in the Mountains and Deserts of California, 3rd Ed.*

Tips: "Please check to be sure similar titles are not already published covering the exact same subject matter. Research the book you are proposing."

INFORMATION TODAY, INC., 143 Old Marlton Pike, Medford NJ 08055. (609)654-6266. Fax: (609)654-4309. E-mail: jbryans@infotoday.com. Website: www.infotoday.com. **Acquisitions:** John B. Bryans, editor-in-chief. Publishes hardcover and trade paperback originals. **Publishes 15-20 titles/year. Receives 100 queries and 30 mss/year. 30% of books from first-time authors; 90% from unagented writers. Pays 10-15% royalty on wholesale price. Offers $500-2,500 advance.** Publishes book 9 months after acceptance of ms. Accepts simultaneous submissions. Responds in 1 month to queries; 2 months to proposals; 3 months to mss. Book catalog free or on website; ms guidelines free or via e-mail as attachment.

Imprints: ITI (academic, scholarly, library science); CyberAge Books (high-end consumer and business technology books—emphasis on Internet/www topics including online research).

- "We look for highly-focused coverage of cutting-edge technology topics, written by established experts and targeted to a tech-savvy readership. Virtually all our titles focus on how information is accessed, used, shared and transformed into knowledge that can benefit people, business and society." Currently emphasizing Internet/online technologies, including their social significance; biography, how-to, technical, reference. De-emphasizing fiction.

Nonfiction: Biography, how-to, multimedia, reference, self-help, technical, scholarly. Subjects include business/economics, computers/electronic, education, science, Internet and cyberculture, library and information science. Query with SASE. Reviews artwork/photos as part of ms package. Send photocopies.

Recent Title(s): *Web Deception: Misinformation on the Internet*, edited by Anne P. Mintz; *Naked in Cyberspace: How to Find Personal Information Online, 2nd ed*, by Carole A. Lane.

Tips: "Our readers include scholars, academics, indexers, librarians, information professionals (ITI imprint) as well as high-end consumer and business users of Internet/www/online technologies, and people interested in the marriage of technology with issues of social significance (i.e., cyberculture)."

INNER OCEAN PUBLISHING, INC., 1037 Makawao Ave., P.O. Box 1239, Makawao HI 96768. (808)573-8000. Fax: (808)573-0700. E-mail: info@innerocean.com. Website: www.innerocean.com. **Acquisitions:** John Nelson (New Age) and Roger Jellinek (general nonfiction), co-editorial directors. Estab. 1999. Publishes hardcover originals and trade paperback originals and reprints. **Publishes 10 titles/year. Receives 300-400 queries and 50-100 mss/year. 50% of books from first-time authors; 60% from unagented writers. Pays 10-15% royalty on wholesale price. Offers $2,500+ advance.** Publishes book 1 year after acceptance of ms. Accepts simultaneous submissions. Responds in 1 month to queries; 3 months to proposals; 3-6 months to mss. Book catalog free; ms guidelines online.

Nonfiction: Self-help. Subjects include animals, child guidance/parenting, education, gardening, general nonfiction, multicultural, nature/environment, New Age, psychology, religion, science, spirituality, women's issues/studies, personal growth. Looking for original voices in the genres of self-help, personal growth and alternative medicine with a strong element of personal experience by writers with ongoing seminars and workshops. Submit proposal package including outline, 3 sample chapter(s), SASE.

Recent Title(s): *Mystical Dogs*, by Jean Houston (New Age/psychology).

Tips: Audience is a wide range of readers interested in improving their lives by deepening their psycho/spiritual search and making healthy lifestyle choices. "Submit work in our genres, do your homework on comparable titles, be patient with our acquisition process, and be willing to meet sometimes short deadlines."

INNER TRADITIONS, Bear & Co., P.O. Box 388, 1 Park St., Rochester VT 05767. (802)767-3174. Fax: (802)767-3726. E-mail: info@innertraditions.com. Website: www.innertraditions.com. Managing Editor: Jennie Levitan. **Acquisitions:** Jon Graham, editor . Estab. 1975. Publishes hardcover and trade paperback originals and reprints. **Publishes 60 titles/year. Receives 3,000 submissions/year. 10% of books from first-time authors; 20% from unagented writers. Pays 8-10% royalty on net receipts. Offers $1,000 average advance.** Publishes book 1 year after acceptance of ms. Responds in 3 months to queries; 6 months to mss. Book catalog and ms guidelines free; ms guidelines online.

Imprints: Destiny Audio Editions, Destiny Books, Destiny Recordings, Healing Arts Press, Inner Traditions, Inner Traditions En Espanol, Inner Traditions India, Park Street Press, Bear & Company, Bear Cub, Bindu Books.

- Inner Traditions publishes works representing the spiritual, cultural and mythic traditions of the world and works on alternative medicine and holistic health that combine contemporary thought with the knowledge of the world's great healing traditions. Currently emphasizing sacred sexuality, indigenous spirituality, ancient history.

Nonfiction: "We are interested in the relationship of the spiritual and transformative aspects of world cultures." Children's/juvenile, self-help. Subjects include animals, art/architecture, child guidance/parenting, contemporary culture, ethnic, fashion/beauty, health/medicine (alternative medicine), history (ancient history and mythology), music/dance, nature/environment (and environment), New Age, philosophy (esoteric), psychology, religion (world religions), sex, spirituality, women's issues/studies, indigenous cultures, ethnobotany business. No fiction. Query or submit outline and sample chapters with SASE. Does not return mss without SASE. Reviews artwork/photos as part of ms package.

Recent Title(s): *Pilates on the Ball*, by Colleen Craig; *The Biology of Transcendence*, by Joseph Chilton Pearce; *The Templars and the Assassins*, by James Wasserman.

Tips: "We are not interested in autobiographical stories of self-transformation. We do accept electronic submissions (via e-mail). We are not currently looking at fiction."

INNISFREE PRESS, 136 Roumfort Rd., Philadelphia PA 19119. (215)247-4085. Fax: (215)247-2343. E-mail: InnisfreeP@aol.com. Website: www.innisfreepress.com. **Acquisitions:** Marcia Broucek, publisher. Estab. 1996. Publishes trade paperback originals. **Publishes 6-8 titles/year. Receives 500 queries and 300 mss/year. 50% of books from first-time authors; 90% from unagented writers. Pays 10% royalty on wholesale price.** Publishes book 1 year after acceptance of ms. Accepts simultaneous submissions. Responds in 2 months to queries; 3 months to proposals; 4 months to mss. Book catalog and ms guidelines free; ms guidelines online.

- "Innisfree's mission is to publish spiritual classics that 'call to the deep heart's core.'" Currently emphasizing women's issues, spirituality. De-emphasizing self-help books.

Nonfiction: Spiritually focused. Subjects include religion, women's issues/studies. No poetry or children's material or fiction please. Query with proposal package, including outline, 2 sample chapters, potential audience, and what makes the book unique, with SASE. Reviews artwork/photos as part of ms package. Send photocopies.

Recent Title(s): *Stumbling Toward God*, by Margaret McGee; *The Haunt of Grace*, by Ted Loder; *Mending the World*, by Rev. Bruce Epperly and Rabbi Lewis Solomon.

Tips: "Our books respond to the needs of today's seekers—people who are looking for deeper meaning and purpose in their lives, for ways to integrate spiritual depth with religious traditions."

INSTITUTE OF POLICE TECHNOLOGY AND MANAGEMENT, University of North Florida, 12000 Alumni Dr., Jacksonville FL 32224-2678. (904)620-4786. Fax: (904)620-2453. E-mail: rhodge@unf.edu. Website: www.iptm.org. **Acquisitions:** Richard C. Hodge, editor. Estab. 1980. Publishes trade paperback originals. **Publishes 8 titles/year. Receives 30 queries and 12 mss/year. 50% of books from first-time authors; 100% from unagented writers. Pays 25% royalty on actual sale price or makes outright purchase of $300-2,000.** Publishes book 6 months after acceptance of ms. Does not accept simultaneous submissions. Responds in 3 weeks to queries.

O→ "Our publications are principally for law enforcement. Will consider works in nearly every area of law enforcement."

Nonfiction: Illustrated book, reference, technical, textbook. Subjects include law enforcement, criminal investigations, security. "Our authors are mostly active or retired law enforcement officers with excellent, up-to-date knowledge of their particular areas. However, some authors are highly regarded professionals in other specialized fields that in some way intersect with law enforcement." Reviews artwork/photos as part of ms package.

Tips: "Manuscripts should not be submitted before the author has contacted IPTM's editor by e-mail or telephone. It is best to make this contact before completing a lengthy work such as a manual."

[N] **INTEL PRESS**, 5200 NE Elam Young Parkway, Hillsboro OR 97124-6461. E-mail: intelpress@intel.com. Website: www.intel.com/intelpress. **Acquisitions:** David B. Spencer, managing editor (computer technology). Estab. 1999. Publishes hardcover and trade paperback originals. **Publishes 10 titles/year. Receives 200 queries and 6 mss/year. 80% of books from first-time authors; 100% from unagented writers. Pays 7-10% royalty on retail price.** Publishes book 1 year after acceptance of ms. Accepts simultaneous submissions. Responds in 2 months to queries; 1 month to proposals; 1 month to mss. Ms guidelines online.

Nonfiction: Reference, technical. Subjects include computers/electronic, software. "We publish books about technologies, initiatives or products in which Intel Corporation has an interest." Submit proposal package including outline, form from website. Reviews artwork/photos as part of ms package. Send photocopies.

Recent Title(s): *The Software Optimization Cookbook*, by Richard Gerber (software engineering); *Infiniband Architecture Development & Deployment*, by William T. Futral (computer architecture).

Tips: "Our books are written by engineers for engineers. They should solve a commonly recognized problem faced by computer developers. Review the information on our website. Submit a clear 25-word summary of the book concept via e-mail."

INTERCULTURAL PRESS, INC., P.O. Box 700, Yarmouth ME 04096. (207)846-5168. Fax: (207)846-5181. E-mail: books@interculturalpress.com. Website: www.interculturalpress.com. **Acquisitions:** Ms. Toby Frank, president. Estab. 1980. Publishes hardcover and paperback originals. **Publishes 8-12 titles/year. Receives 50-80 submissions/year. 50% of books from first-time authors; 95% from unagented writers. Pays royalty. Offers small advance occasionally.** Publishes book within 18 months after acceptance of ms. Accepts simultaneous submissions. Responds in 1 month to queries. Book catalog and ms guidelines free; ms guidelines online.

O→ Intercultural Press publishes materials related to intercultural relations, including the practical concerns of living and working in foreign countries, the impact of cultural differences on personal and professional relationships and the challenges of interacting with people from unfamiliar cultures, whether at home or abroad. Currently emphasizing international business.

Nonfiction: "We want books with an international or domestic intercultural or multicultural focus, including those on business operations (how to be effective in intercultural business activities), education (textbooks for teaching intercultural subjects, for instance) and training (for Americans abroad or foreign nationals coming to the United States)." Reference, textbooks, theory. Subjects include world affairs, business, education, diversity and multicultural, relocation and cultural adaptation, culture learning, training materials, country-specific guides. "Our books are published for educators in the intercultural field, business people engaged in international business, managers concerned with cultural diversity in the workplace, and anyone who works in an occupation where cross-cultural communication and adaptation are important skills. No manuscripts that don't have an intercultural focus." Accepts nonfiction translations. Submit proposals, outline.

Recent Title(s): *The Cultural Imperative: Global Trends in the 21st Century*, by Richard D. Lewis; *Exploring Culture: Excercises, Stories and Synthetic Cultures*, by Gert Jan Hofstede, Paul B. Pedersen and Geert Hofstede.

INTERLINK PUBLISHING GROUP, INC., 46 Crosby St., Northampton MA 01060. (413)582-7054. Fax: (413)582-7057. E-mail: info@interlinkbooks.com. Website: www.interlinkbooks.com. **Acquisitions:** Michel Moushabeck, publisher. Estab. 1987. Publishes hardcover and trade paperback originals. **Publishes 50 titles/year. Receives 600 submissions/year. 30% of books from first-time authors; 50% from unagented writers. Pays 6-8% royalty on retail price. Offers small advance.** Publishes book 18 months after acceptance of ms. Accepts simultaneous submissions. Responds in 1 month to queries. Book catalog free; ms guidelines online.

Imprints: Crocodile Books, USA; Interlink Books; Olive Branch Press.

O→ Interlink publishes a general trade list of adult fiction and nonfiction with an emphasis on books that have a wide appeal while also meeting high intellectual and literary standards.

Nonfiction: Subjects include world travel, world history and politics, ethnic cooking, world music. Submit outline and sample chapters.

Fiction: Ethnic, international. "Adult—We are looking for translated works relating to the Middle East, Africa or Latin

America. Juvenile/Picture Books—Our list is full for the next two years." No science fiction, romance, plays, erotica, fantasy, horror. Query with SASE or submit outline, sample chapter(s).
Recent Title(s): *House of the Winds*, by Mia Yun.
Tips: "Any submissions that fit well in our publishing program will receive careful attention. A visit to our website, your local bookstore, or library to look at some of our books before you send in your submission is recommended."

INTERNATIONAL FOUNDATION OF EMPLOYEE BENEFIT PLANS, P.O. Box 69, Brookfield WI 53008-0069. (262)786-6700. Fax: (262)786-8780. E-mail: books@ifebp.org. Website: www.ifebp.org. **Acquisitions:** Dee Birschel, senior director of publications. Estab. 1954. Publishes trade paperback originals. **Publishes 10 titles/year. Receives 20 submissions/year. 15% of books from first-time authors; 80% from unagented writers. Pays 5-15% royalty on wholesale and retail price.** Publishes book 1 year after acceptance of ms. Responds in 3 months to queries. Book catalog free; ms guidelines for #10 SASE.

O→ IFEBP publishes general and technical monographs on all aspects of employee benefits—pension plans, health insurance, etc.

Nonfiction: Subjects limited to health care, pensions, retirement planning and employee benefits and compensation. Reference, technical, textbook. Subjects include consumer information. Query with outline.
Recent Title(s): *Integrated Disability Management: An Employers Guide*, by Janet R. Douglas.
Tips: "Be aware of interests of employers and the marketplace in benefits topics, for example, how AIDS affects employers, health care cost containment."

INTERNATIONAL MARINE, The McGraw-Hill Companies, P.O. Box 220, Camden ME 04843-0220. (207)236-4838. Fax: (207)236-6314. Website: www.internationalmarine.com. Jonathan Eaton, editorial director (boating, marine nonfiction). Estab. 1969. Publishes hardcover and paperback originals. **Publishes 50 titles/year. Receives 500-700 mss/year. 30% of books from first-time authors; 60% from unagented writers. Pays standard royalties based on net price. Offers advance.** Publishes book 1 year after acceptance of ms. Responds in 2 months to queries. Ms guidelines online.
Imprints: Ragged Mountain Press (sports and outdoor books that take you off the beaten path).

O→ International Marine publishes "good books about boats."

Nonfiction: Publishes "a wide range of subjects include: sea stories, seamanship, boat maintenance, etc." Subjects include marine and outdoor nonfiction. All books are illustrated. "Material in all stages welcome." Query first with outline and 2-3 sample chapters. Reviews artwork/photos as part of ms package.
Recent Title(s): *How to Read a Nautical Chart*, by Nigel Caulder; *By the Grace of the Sea: A Woman's Solo Odyssey Around the World*, by Pat Henry; *Coaching Girls' Lacrosse: A Baffled Parent's Guide*, by Janine Tucker.
Tips: "Writers should be aware of the need for clarity, accuracy and interest. Many progress too far in the actual writing."

INTERNATIONAL MEDICAL PUBLISHING, 1313 Dolley Madison Blvd., Suite 302, McLean VA 22101. (703)356-2037. Fax: (703)734-8987. E-mail: contact@medicalpublishing.com. Website: www.medicalpublishing.com. **Acquisitions:** Thomas Masterson, MD, editor. Estab. 1991. Publishes mass market paperback originals. **Publishes 30 titles/year. Receives 100 queries and 20 mss/year. 5% of books from first-time authors; 100% from unagented writers. Pays royalty on gross receipts.** Publishes book 8 months after acceptance of ms. Responds in 2 months to queries.

O→ IMP publishes books to make life easier for doctors in training. "We're branching out to also make life easier for people with chronic medical problems."

Nonfiction: Reference, textbook. Subjects include health/medicine. "We distribute only through medical and scientific bookstores. Think about practical material for doctors-in-training. We are interested in handbooks. Online projects are of interest." Query with outline.
Recent Title(s): *Healthy People 2010*, by the US Department of Health and Human Services; *Day-by-Day Diabetes*, by Resa Levetan.

INTERNATIONAL PUBLISHERS CO., INC., 239 W. 23 St., New York NY 10011. (212)366-9816. Fax: (212)366-9820. E-mail: service@intpubnyc.com. Website: www.intpubnyc.com. **Acquisitions:** Betty Smith, president. Estab. 1924. Publishes hardcover originals, trade paperback originals and reprints. **Publishes 5-6 titles/year. Receives 50-100 mss/year. 10% of books from first-time authors. Pays 5-7½% royalty on paperbacks; 10% royalty on cloth.** Publishes book 6 months after acceptance of ms. Accepts simultaneous submissions. Responds in 1 month to queries with SASE to queries; 6 months to mss. Book catalog and ms guidelines for SAE with 60¢ postage.

O→ International Publishers Co., Inc. emphasizes books based on Marxist science.

Nonfiction: Subjects include art/architecture, government/politics, history, philosophy, economics, social sciences, Marxist-Leninist classics. "Books on labor, black studies and women's studies based on Marxist science have high priority." Query or submit outline, sample chapters and SASE. Reviews artwork/photos as part of ms package.
Recent Title(s): *Fiddle and Fight: A Memoir*, by Russell V. Brodine; *Afghanistan: Washington's Secret War*, by Phillip Bonosky.
Tips: No fiction or poetry.

INTERNATIONAL SOCIETY FOR TECHNOLOGY IN EDUCATION (ISTE), 480 Charnelton St., Eugene OR 97401. (541)434-8928. E-mail: mmanweller@iste.org. Website: www.iste.org. **Acquisitions:** Mathew Manweller, acquisitions editor. Publishes trade paperback originals. **Publishes 20 titles/year. Receives 150 queries and 50 mss/year. 75% of books from first-time authors; 95% from unagented writers. Pays 12-15% royalty on retail price.** Publishes book 5 months after acceptance of ms. Accepts simultaneous submissions. Responds in 1 month to queries; 1 month to proposals; 1 month to mss. Book catalog and ms guidelines free.

O→ Currently emphasizing curriculum and project development books. De-emphasizing how-to books.

Nonfiction: Reference, technical, curriculum. Subjects include computers/electronic, education, software, technology. Submit proposal package including outline, 1 sample chapter(s). Reviews artwork/photos as part of ms package. Send photocopies.
Recent Title(s): *The Best Web Sites for Teachers*, by Vicki Sharp.
Tips: "Our audience is teachers, technology coordinators, administrators."

INTERNATIONAL WEALTH SUCCESS, P.O. Box 186, Merrick NY 11570-0186. (516)766-5850. Fax: (516)766-5919. **Acquisitions:** Tyler G. Hicks, editor. Estab. 1967. **Publishes 10 titles/year. Receives 100 submissions/year. 100% of books from first-time authors; 100% from unagented writers. Pays 10% royalty on wholesale or retail price. Offers usual advance of $1,000, but this varies depending on author's reputation and nature of book. Buys all rights.** Publishes book 4 months after acceptance of ms. Responds in 1 month to queries. Book catalog and ms guidelines for 9×12 SAE with 3 first-class stamps.

O→ "Our mission is to publish books, newsletters and self-study courses aimed at helping beginners and experienced business people start, and succeed in, their own small business in the fields of real estate, import-export, mail order, licensing, venture capital, financial brokerage, etc. The large number of layoffs and downsizings have made our publications of greater importance to people seeking financial independence in their own business, free of layoff threats and snarling bosses."

Nonfiction: How-to, self-help. Subjects include business/economics, financing, business success, venture capital, etc. "Techniques, methods, sources for building wealth. Highly personal, how-to-do-it with plenty of case histories. Books are aimed at wealth builders and are highly sympathetic to their problems. These publications present a wide range of business opportunities while providing practical, hands-on, step-by-step instructions aimed at helping readers achieve their personal goals in as short a time as possible while adhering to ethical and professional business standards." Length: 60,000-70,000 words. Query. Reviews artwork/photos as part of ms package.
Recent Title(s): *How to Buy and Flip Real Estate for a Profit*, by Rod L. Griffin.
Tips: "With the mass layoffs in large and medium-size companies there is an increasing interest in owning your own business. So we focus on more how-to hands-on material on owning—and becoming successful in—one's own business of any kind. Our market is the BWB—Beginning Wealth Builder. This person has so little money that financial planning is something they never think of. Instead, they want to know what kind of a business they can get into to make some money without a large investment. Write for this market and you have millions of potential readers. Remember—there are a lot more people *without* money than *with* money."

⊘ **INTERVARSITY PRESS**, P.O. Box 1400, Downers Grove IL 60515. (630)734-4000. Fax: (630)734-4200. E-mail: mail@ivpress.com. Website: www.ivpress.com. **Acquisitions:** David Zimmerman, assistant editor; Andy Le Peau, editorial director; Jim Hoover, associate editorial director (academic, reference); Cindy Bunch, editor (Bible study, Christian living); Gary Deddo, associate editor (academic); Dan Reid, editor (reference, academic); Al Hsu, associate editor (general). Estab. 1947. Publishes hardcover originals, trade paperback and mass market paperback originals. **Publishes 70-80 titles/year. Receives 1,500 queries and 1,000 mss/year. 15% of books from first-time authors; 85% from unagented writers. Pays negotiable flat fee or royalty on retail price. Offers negotiable advance.** Publishes book 1 year after acceptance of ms. Accepts simultaneous submissions. Responds in 3 months to proposals. Book catalog for 9×12 SAE and 5 first-class stamps; ms guidelines online.
Imprints: Academic (contact Gary Deddo); Bible Study (contact Cindy Bunch); General (contact Al Hsu); Reference (contact Dan Reid).

O→ InterVarsity Press publishes a full line of books from an evangelical Christian perspective targeted to an open-minded audience. "We serve those in the university, the church and the world, by publishing books from an evangelical Christian perspective."

Nonfiction: Subjects include religion. Query with SASE. *No unsolicited mss.*
Recent Title(s): *Habits of the Mind*, by James Sire; *Spritual Mentoring*, by Keith Anderson and Randy Reese.

INTERWEAVE PRESS, 201 E. 4th St., Loveland CO 80537. (970)669-7672. Fax: (970)667-8317. Website: www.interweave.com. **Acquisitions:** Betsy Armstrong, book editorial director. Estab. 1975. Publishes hardcover and trade paperback originals. **Publishes 16-20 titles/year. Receives 50 submissions/year. 60% of books from first-time authors; 98% from unagented writers. Pays 10% royalty on net receipts.** Publishes book 1-3 years after acceptance of ms. Accepts simultaneous submissions. Responds in 2 months to queries. Book catalog and ms guidelines free.

O→ Interweave Press publishes instructive and inspirational titles relating to the fiber arts and beadwork topics.

Nonfiction: Subjects limited to fiber arts—basketry, spinning, knitting, dyeing and weaving—and beadwork topics. How-to, technical. Submit outline, sample chapter(s). Reviews artwork/photos as part of ms package.
Recent Title(s): *Beading in the Native American Tradition*, by David Dean.
Tips: "We are looking for very clear, informally written, technically correct manuscripts, generally of a how-to nature, in our specific fiber and beadwork fields only. Our audience includes a variety of creative self-starters who appreciate inspiration and clear instruction. They are often well educated and skillful in many areas."

[N] **THE INVISIBLE COLLEGE PRESS**, P.O. Box 209, Woodbridge VA 22194-0209. (703)590-4005. E-mail: submissions@invispress.com. Website: www.invispress.com. **Acquisitions:** Dr. Phillip Reynolds, editor (nonfiction); Paul Mossinger, submissions editor (fiction). Publishes trade paperback originals and reprints. **Publishes 12 titles/year. Receives 120 queries and 30 mss/year. 75% of books from first-time authors; 75% from unagented writers. Pays 10-25% royalty on wholesale price. Offers $100 advance.** Publishes book 4 months after acceptance of ms. Accepts simultaneous submissions. Responds in 1 month to queries; 1 month to proposals; 3 months to mss. Book catalog online; ms guidelines online.

Nonfiction: Reference. Subjects include creative nonfiction, government/politics, religion, spirituality, conspiracy. "We only publish nonfiction related to conspiracies, UFOs, government cover-ups, and the paranormal." Query with SASE or submit proposal package including outline, 1 sample chapter(s).

Fiction: Experimental, fantasy, gothic, horror, literary, mainstream/contemporary, occult, religious, science fiction, spiritual, suspense, Conspiracy. "We only publish fiction related to conspiracies, UFOs, government cover-ups, and the paranormal." Query with SASE or submit proposal package including 1 sample chapter(s), synopsis.

Recent Title(s): *UFO Politics at the White House*, by Larry Bryant (nonfiction); *City of Pillars*, by Dominic Peloso (fiction); *The Third Day*, by Mark Graham (fiction).

Tips: "Our audience tends to be fans of conspiracies and UFO mythology. They go to UFO conventions, they research who shot JFK, they believe that they are being followed by Men in Black, they wear aluminum-foil hats to stop the CIA from beaming them thought-control rays." "We are only interested in work dealing with established conspiracy/UFO mythology. Rosicrucians, Illuminatti, Men in Black, Area 51, Atlantis, etc. If your book doesn't sound like an episode of the X-Files, we probably won't consider it."

IRON GATE PUBLISHING, P.O. Box 999, Niwot CO 80544-0999. (303)530-2551. Fax: (303)530-5273. E-mail: editor@irongate.com. Website: www.irongate.com; www.reunionsolutions.com. **Acquisitions:** Dina C. Carson, publisher (how-to, genealogy). Publishes hardcover and trade paperback originals. **Publishes 6-10 titles/year; imprint publishes 2-6 titles/year. Receives 100 queries and 20 mss/year. 30% of books from first-time authors; 10% from unagented writers. Pays royalty on a case-by-case basis.** Publishes book 1 year after acceptance of ms. Accepts simultaneous submissions. Responds in 2 months to proposals. Book catalog free or on website; ms guidelines online.

Imprints: Reunion Solutions Press, KinderMed Press.

O→ "Our readers are people who are looking for solid, how-to advice on planning reunions or self-publishing a genealogy."

Nonfiction: How-to, multimedia, reference. Subjects include child guidance/parenting, health/medicine, hobbies. Query with SASE or submit proposal package, including outline, 2 sample chapters and marketing summary. Reviews artwork/photos as part of ms package. Send photocopies.

Recent Title(s): *The Genealogy and Local History Researcher's Self-Publishing Guide*; *Reunion Solutions: Everything You Need to Know to Plan a Family, Class, Military, Association or Corporate Reunion*.

Tips: "Please look at the other books we publish and tell us in your query letter why your book would fit into our line of books."

ITALICA PRESS, 595 Main St., Suite 605, New York NY 10044-0047. (212)935-4230. Fax: (212)838-7812. E-mail: inquiries@italicapress.com. Website: www.italicapress.com. **Acquisitions:** Ronald G. Musto and Eileen Gardiner, publishers. Estab. 1985. Publishes trade paperback originals. **Publishes 6 titles/year. Receives 600 queries and 60 mss/year. 5% of books from first-time authors; 100% from unagented writers. Pays 7-15% royalty on wholesale price. author's copies.** Publishes book 1 year after acceptance of ms. Accepts simultaneous submissions. Responds in 1 month to queries; 2 months to mss. Book catalog free; ms guidelines online.

O→ Italica Press publishes English translations of modern Italian fiction and medieval and Renaissance nonfiction.

Nonfiction: Subjects include translation. "We publish English translations of medieval and Renaissance source materials and English translations of modern Italian fiction." Query with SASE. Reviews artwork/photos as part of ms package. Send photocopies.

Fiction: Translations of 20th century Italian fiction. Query with SASE.

Poetry: Poetry titles are generally dual language.

Tips: "We are interested in considering a wide variety of medieval and Renaissance topics (not historical fiction), and for modern works we are only interested in translations from Italian fiction by well-known Italian authors."

JAIN PUBLISHING CO., P.O. Box 3523, Fremont CA 94539. (510)659-8272. Fax: (510)659-0501. E-mail: mail@jainpub.com. Website: www.jainpub.com. **Acquisitions:** M.K. Jain, editor-in-chief. Estab. 1989. Publishes hardcover and paperback originals and reprints. **Publishes 6 titles/year. Receives 300 queries/year. 100% from unagented writers. Pays 5-15% royalty on net sales.** Publishes book 1-2 years after acceptance of ms. Responds in 3 months to mss. Book catalog and ms guidelines online; ms guidelines online.

Imprints: Asian Humanities Press.

O→ Jain Publishing Co. is a college textbook publisher with a diversified list. Continued emphasis on undergraduate textbooks.

Nonfiction: Reference, textbook. Subjects include humanities, social sciences, communication, English & literature, religious studies, business, scientific/technical. Submit proposal package including publishing history. Reviews artwork/photos as part of ms package. Send photocopies.

Recent Title(s): *A Student Guide to College Composition*, by William Murdiek.

ALICE JAMES BOOKS, 238 Main St., Farmington ME 04938. (207)778-7071. Fax: (207)778-7071. E-mail: ajb@umf.maine.edu. Website: www.alicejamesbooks.org. **Acquisitions:** April Ossmann, director (poetry). Publishes trade paperback originals. **Publishes 4 titles/year. Receives 800 mss/year. 75% of books from first-time authors; 99% from unagented writers. Pays through competition awards.** Publishes book 1 year after acceptance of ms. Accepts simultaneous submissions. Responds in 1 month to queries; 4 months to mss. Book catalog for free or on website; ms guidelines for #10 SASE or on website.

O→ Alice James Books is a nonprofit poetry press.

Poetry: Query.

Recent Title(s): *The Art of the Lathe*, by B.H. Fairchild; *The River at Wolf*, by Jean Valentine; *Pity the Bathtub Its Forced Embrace of the Human Form*, by Matthea Harvey.

Tips: "Send SASE for contest guidelines or check website. Do not send work without consulting current guidelines."

JAMESON BOOKS, INC., 722 Columbus St., P.O. Box 738, Ottawa IL 61350. (815)434-7905. Fax: (815)434-7907. **Acquisitions:** Jameson G. Campaigne, publisher/editor. Estab. 1986. Publishes hardcover originals. **Publishes 6 titles/year. Receives 500 queries and 300 mss/year. 33% of books from first-time authors; 33% from unagented writers. Pays 6-15% royalty on retail price. Offers $1,000-25,000 advance.** Publishes book 1 year after acceptance of ms. Accepts simultaneous submissions. Responds in 6 months to queries.

O→ Jameson Books publishes conservative politics and economics; Chicago area history; and biographies.

Nonfiction: Biography. Subjects include business/economics, government/politics, history, regional (Chicago area). Query with SASE or submit 1 sample chapter(s). Submissions not returned without SASE.

Fiction: Very well researched western (frontier pre 1850). Interested in pre-cowboy "mountain men" in American west, before 1820 in east frontier fiction. No cowboys, no science fiction, mystery, poetry, et al. Query with SASE or submit outline, 1 sample chapter(s), synopsis.

Recent Title(s): *Politics as a Noble Calling*, by F. Clifton White (memoirs); *Yellowstone Kelly: Gentleman and Scout*, by Peter Bowen (fiction).

JAYJO BOOKS, LLC, The Guidance Channel, P.O. Box 760, 135 Dupont St., Plainview NY 11803-0769. (516)349-5520. Fax: (516)349-5521. **Acquisitions:** Sally Germain, editor-in-chief (for elementary school age youth). Publishes trade paperback originals. **Publishes 8-12 titles/year. Receives 100 queries/year. 25% of books from first-time authors; 100% from unagented writers. Makes outright purchase of $500-1,000.** Publishes book 9 months after acceptance of ms. Accepts simultaneous submissions. Responds in 2 months to queries; 2 months to proposals; 2 months to mss. Book catalog and writer's guidelines for #10 SASE.

Imprints: Each book published is for a specific series. Series include: Special Family and Friends, Health Habits for Kids, Substance Free Kids, Special Kids in School. Series publish 1-5 titles/year.

Nonfiction: Children's/juvenile, illustrated book. Subjects include health/medicine (issues for children). "JayJo Books is a publisher of nonfiction books to help teachers, parents, and children cope with chronic illnesses, special needs, and health education in classroom, family, and social settings. Each JayJo series has a particular style and format it must follow. Writers should send query letter with areas of expertise or interest and suggested focus of book." No animal character books or illustrated books. Query with SASE.

Tips: "Send query letter—since we only publish books adapted to our special formats—we contact appropriate potential authors and work with them to customize manuscript."

JEWISH LIGHTS PUBLISHING, LongHill Partners, Inc., P.O. Box 237, Sunset Farm Offices, Rt. 4, Woodstock VT 05091. (802)457-4000. Editor: Stuart Matlins. **Acquisitions:** Acquisitions Editor. Estab. 1990. Publishes hardcover and trade paperback originals, trade paperback reprints. **Publishes 30 titles/year. Receives 1,000 submissions/year. 30% of books from first-time authors; 99% from unagented writers. Pays royalty on net sales, 10% on first printing, then increases.** Publishes book 1 year after acceptance of ms. Accepts simultaneous submissions. Responds in 3 months to queries. Book catalog and ms guidelines free.

O→ "People of all faiths and backgrounds yearn for books that attract, engage, educate and spiritually inspire. Our principal goal is to stimulate thought and help all people learn about who the Jewish people are, where they come from, and what the future can be made to hold."

Nonfiction: Children's/juvenile, illustrated book, reference, self-help. Subjects include business/economics (with spiritual slant, finding spiritual meaning in one's work), health/medicine (healing/recovery, wellness, aging, life cycle), history, nature/environment, philosophy, religion (theology), spirituality (and inspiration), women's issues/studies. "We do *not* publish haggadot, biography, poetry, or cookbooks." Submit proposal package, including cover letter, table of contents, 2 sample chapters and SASE (postage must cover weight of ms). Reviews artwork/photos as part of ms package. Send photocopies.

Recent Title(s): *The Rituals and Practices of a Jewish Life: A Handbook for Personal Spiritual Renewal*, by Kerry M. Olitzky and Daniel Judson; *The Jewish Prophet: Visionary Words from Moses and Miriam to Henrietta Szold and A.J. Heschel*, by Michael J. Shire; *Noah's Wife: The Story of Naamah*, by Sandy Eisenberg Sasso.

Tips: "We publish books for all faiths and backgrounds that also reflect the Jewish wisdom tradition."

JIST PUBLISHING, INC., (formerly Jist Works, Inc.), 8902 Otis Ave., Indianapolis IN 46216-1033. (317)613-4200. Fax: (317)613-4304. E-mail: info@jist.com. Website: www.jist.com. **Acquisitions:** Susan Pines, associate publisher (institutional and educational mss). Estab. 1981. Publishes trade and instructional hardcover and paperback originals and reprints. **Publishes 40 titles/year. Receives 150 submissions/year. 25% of books from first-time authors. Pays 5-10% royalty on wholesale price or makes outright purchase (negotiable).** Publishes book 1-2 years after acceptance of ms. Accepts simultaneous submissions. Responds in 5-6 months to queries. Book catalog online; ms guidelines online.

Imprints: JIST Works (job search, career development, and occupational information titles); Park Avenue (education, business, self-help, and life skills titles); Your Domain Publishing (public domain and government agency data and information titles); JIST Life (adults); KIDSRIGHTS (children).

O→ "Our purpose is to provide quality job search, career development, and occupational information, and other life skills information, products, and services that help people manage and improve their lives and careers—and the lives of others." Will consider books for professional staff and educators, appropriate career-related software, and videos.

Nonfiction: How-to, multimedia, reference, self-help, textbook, video. Subjects include business/economics, computers/electronic, software, careers. Specializes in job search, self-help and career-related topics. "We want text/workbook formats that would be useful in a school or other institutional setting. We also publish trade titles for all reading levels. Will consider books for professional staff and educators, appropriate software and videos." Query with SASE. Reviews artwork/photos as part of ms package.
Recent Title(s): *Getting the Job You Really Want, 4th ed*, by J. Michael Farr.
Tips: "Our primary audience is institutions and staff who work with people of all reading and academic skill levels, making career and life decisions, and people who are looking for jobs."

JOHNSON BOOKS, Johnson Publishing Co., 1880 S. 57th Court., Boulder CO 80301. (303)443-9766. Fax: (303)998-7594. E-mail: books@jpcolorado.com. **Acquisitions:** Stephen Topping, editorial director. Estab. 1979. Publishes hardcover and paperback originals and reprints. **Publishes 10-12 titles/year. Receives 500 submissions/year. 30% of books from first-time authors; 90% from unagented writers. Royalties vary.** Publishes book 1 year after acceptance of ms. Responds in 3 months to queries. Book catalog for 9×12 SAE with 5 first-class stamps.
Imprints: Spring Creek Press.

O→ Johnson Books specializes in books on the American West, primarily outdoor, "useful" titles that will have strong national appeal.

Nonfiction: Subjects include anthropology/archeology, history, nature/environment (environmental subjects), recreation (outdoor), regional, science, travel (regional), general nonfiction, books on the West, natural history, paleontology, geology. "We are primarily interested in books for the informed popular market, though we will consider vividly written scholarly works." Looks for "good writing, thorough research, professional presentation and appropriate style. Marketing suggestions from writers are helpful." Submit outline/synopsis and 3 sample chapters.
Recent Title(s): *Life Lessons from a Ranch Horse*, by Mark Roshid (horses); *Libby, Montana*, by Andrea Peacock (environment); *Denver's Glitch Gardens*, by Betty Hull (local history).

[N] **JONA BOOKS**, P.O. Box 336, Bedford IN 47421. (812)278-9512. Fax: (812)278-9518. E-mail: jonabook@kiva.net. Website: www.kiva.net/~jonabook. **Acquisitions:** Joe Glasgow, publisher (nonfiction); Maizyna Guba, managing editor (fiction). Estab. 1996. Publishes hardcover and trade paperback originals. **Publishes 12 titles/year. Receives 200 queries and 500 mss/year. 40% of books from first-time authors. Pays 6-15% royalty.** Publishes book 16 months after acceptance of ms. Accepts simultaneous submissions. Responds in 1 month to queries; 1 month to proposals; 3 months to mss. Book catalog free; ms guidelines for #10 SASE.
Nonfiction: Autobiography, biography, reference. Subjects include history, military/war, sports. "We are always looking for military titles, old West, Native American. Query with SASE or submit proposal package including outline, 3 sample chapter(s). Reviews artwork/photos as part of ms package. Send photocopies.
Fiction: Adventure, historical, military/war, mystery, science fiction. "We are expanding our mystery titles for 2003 and beyond." Submit complete ms.
Recent Title(s): *Lawman to Outlaw: Verne Miller and the Kansas City Massacre*, by Brad Smith (true crime); *Raid at Inclon: Left Behind the Lines*, by Katherine Jones (military history); *Bones of the Cross*, by Jeffrey Denhart (mystery).

JOURNEYFORTH, BJU Press, 1700 Wade Hampton Blvd., Greenville SC 29614-0001. (864)242-5100, ext. 4350. E-mail: jb@bjup.com. Website: www.bjup.com. **Acquisitions:** Nancy Lohr, manuscript editor (juvenile fiction). Estab. 1974. Publishes paperback original and reprints. **Publishes 10 titles/year. Pays royalty.** Publishes book 12-18 months after acceptance of ms. Accepts simultaneous submissions. Responds in 1 month to queries; 3 months to mss. Book catalog free; ms guidelines online.

O→ "Small independent publisher of excellent, trustworthy novels, information books, audio tapes and ancillary materials for readers pre-school through high school. We desire to develop in our children a love for and understanding of the written word, ultimately helping them love and understand God's word."

Fiction: Adventure (children's/juvenile, young adult), historical (children's/juvenile, young adult), juvenile (animal, easy-to-read, series), mystery (children's/juvenile, young adult), sports (children's/juvenile, young adult), suspense (young adult), western (young adult), young adult (series). "Our fiction is all based on a moral and Christian word-view." Query with SASE or submit outline, 5 sample chapter(s) or submit complete ms.
Recent Title(s): *Case of the Sassy Parrot*, by Milly Howard (fiction, ages 7-9); *Daniel Colton Kid Knapped*, by Elaine Schulte (historical nonfiction, ages 9-12); *Children of the Storm: The Autobiography of Natasha Vins* (young adult).
Tips: "Study the publisher's guidelines. Make sure your work is suitable or you waste time for you and the publisher."

JUDAICA PRESS, 123 Ditmas Ave., Brooklyn NY 11218. (718)972-6200. Fax: (718)972-6204. E-mail: info@judaicapress.com. Website: www.judaicapress.com. **Acquisitions:** Nachum Shapiro, managing editor. Estab. 1963. Publishes hardcover and trade paperback originals and reprints. **Publishes 12 titles/year.** Responds in 3 months to queries. Book catalog online.

O→ "We cater to the traditional, Orthodox Jewish market."

Nonfiction: "Looking for very traditional Judaica, especially children's books." Children's/juvenile, cookbook, textbook. Subjects include history, religion (Bible commentary). Submit ms with SASE.
Recent Title(s): *Facing the Music*, by Eva Vogiel; *Taking Care of Mom, Taking Care of Me*, by Sima Schloss; *Too Big, Too Little...Just Right!*, by Loren Hodes.

JUSTICE HOUSE PUBLISHING, INC., P.O. Box 4233, Spanaway WA 98387. (253)262-0205. Fax: (253)475-2158. E-mail: submissions@justicehouse.com. Website: www.justicehouse.com. Publishes trade paperback originals. **Publishes 20-30 titles/year. Receives 5-10 queries and 1-5 mss/year. 100% of books from first-time authors; 100% from unagented writers. Pays 10-15% royalty on wholesale price.** Publishes book 2 years after acceptance of ms. Does not accept simultaneous submissions. Responds in 2-3 months to queries; 2-3 months to proposals; 3-6 months to mss. Book catalog free; ms guidelines online.

Fiction: Fantasy, feminist, gay/lesbian, mystery, romance, science fiction, short story collections. "We specialize in lesbian fiction." Submit complete ms.

Recent Title(s): *Tropical Storm*, by Melissa Good (lesbian fiction); *The Deal*, by Maggie Ryan (lesbian fiction); *Kona Dreams*, by Shari J. Berman.

Tips: Audience is comprised of 18 and older eductated lesbian females.

[N] KAEDEN BOOKS, P.O. Box 16190, Rocky River OH 44116-0190. (440)356-0030. Fax: (440)356-5081. E-mail: jhoyer@kaeden.com. Website: www.kaeden.com. **Acquisitions:** Craig Urmston, fiction editor (children's grades preK-3); Karen Todak, fiction editor (children's K-2). Estab. 1990. Publishes paperback originals. **Publishes 8-16 titles/year. Pays royalty. Negotiable, either royalties or flat fee by individual arrangement with author depending on book.** Publishes book 6-24 months after acceptance of ms. Ms guidelines online.

O→ "Children's book publisher for education K-3 market: reading stories, science, math and social studies materials, also poetry."

Nonfiction: Needs all subjects. Query with SASE or submit outline, publishing history, author bio, Synopsis, SASE. Send a disposable copy of ms and SASE for reply only. Responds only "if interested."

Fiction: Adventure (children's/juvenile), ethnic, fantasy, historical (children's/juvenile; general), humor, mystery (children's/juvenile, amatuer sleuth), science fiction (soft/sociological), short story collections, sports (children's/juvenile), suspense (amateur sleuth), Children's/Juvenile; Animal; Series; Thriller/Espionage. Query with SASE or submit outline, publishing history, synopsis, author bio, SASE. Send a disposable copy of ms and SASE for reply only. Responds only "if interested."

Tips: "Our line is expanding with particular interest in fiction/nonfiction for grades two to six. Material must be suitable for use in the public school classroom, be multicultural and be high interest with appropriate word usage and a positive tone for the respective grade."

KALMBACH PUBLISHING CO., 21027 Crossroads Circle, P.O. Box 1612, Waukesha WI 53187-1612. (262)796-8776. Fax: (262)798-6468. E-mail: books@kalmbach.com. Website: corporate.kalmbach.com. **Acquisitions:** Cedric St. Jacques, editor-in-chief; Kent Johnson, senior acquisitions editor (hobby books); Philip Martin, acquisitions editor (writing books). Estab. 1934. Publishes hardcover and paperback originals, paperback reprints. **Publishes 15-20 titles/year. Receives 100 submissions/year. 75% of books from first-time authors; 99% from unagented writers. Pays 7% royalty on net receipts (hobby); 10% royalty on net receipts (writing). Offers $1,500 (writing); $2,500 (hobby) advance.** Publishes book 18 months after acceptance of ms. Responds in 2 months to queries.

O→ Kalmbach publishes reference materials and how-to publications for serious hobbyists in the railfan, model railroading, plastic modeling and toy train collecting/operating hobbies. Also publishes titles on business and craft of writing under The Writer Books imprint.

Nonfiction: How-to, illustrated book. Subjects include hobbies, science, amateur astronomy, railroading, writing. "Our book publishing effort is in railroading and similar hobby how-to-do-it titles. However, we are expanding our line to include books for the trade on creative and freelance writing. In the near future, we will be looking to acquire how-to titles on beading and fashionable jewelry making." Hobby: Query with 2-3 page detailed outline, sample chapter with photos, drawings and how-to text. Writing: Query or send formal proposal. Reviews artwork/photos as part of ms package.

Recent Title(s): *Toy Train Memories*, by John Grams; *Toy Train Layout from Start to Finish*, by Stan Trzoniec; *The Writer's Handbook*, by Elfrieda Abbe.

Tips: "Our hobby books are about half text and half illustrations. Any hobby author who wants to publish with us must be able to furnish good photographs and rough drawings before we'll consider his or her book."

[N] KAR-BEN PUBLISHING, 6800 Tildenwood Lane, Rockville MD 20852. (301)984-8826. Fax: (301)881-9195. E-mail: karben@aol.com. Website: www.karben.com. **Acquisitions:** Madeline Wikler, editor (juvenile Judaica). Estab. 1976. Publishes hardcover and trade paperback originals. **Publishes 8-10 titles/year. Receives 50-100 queries and 300-400 mss/year. 5% of books from first-time authors; 100% from unagented writers. Pays 5-8% royalty on net receipts. Offers $500-2,500 advance.** Publishes book 10 months after acceptance of ms. Accepts simultaneous submissions. Responds in 1 month to queries. Book catalog free or on website; ms guidelines online.

O→ Kar-Ben Copies publishes high-quality materials on Jewish themes for young children and families.

Nonfiction: "Jewish themes only!" Children's/juvenile (Judaica only). Subjects include religion. Submit complete ms.

Fiction: "Jewish themes and young kids only!" Juvenile, religious.

Recent Title(s): *The Hardest Word*; *Mitzvah Magic*; *It's Challah Time*.

Tips: "Do a literature search to make sure similar title doesn't already exist."

[N] KAYA PRODUCTION, 373 Broadway #F3, New York NY 10013. (212)343-9503. E-mail: kaya@kaya.com. Website: www.kaya.com. **Acquisitions:** Sunyoung Lee, editor. Publishes hardcover originals and trade paperback originals and reprints. Accepts simultaneous submissions. Responds in 6 months to mss. Book catalog free; ms guidelines online.

O→ "Kaya is an independent literary press dedicated to the publication of innovative literature from the Asian diaspora."

Nonfiction: Subjects include multicultural. "Kaya publishes Asian, Asian American and Asian diasporic materials. We are looking for innovative writers with a commitment to quality literature." Submit proposal package including outline, sample chapter(s), previous publications, SASE. Reviews artwork/photos as part of ms package. Send photocopies.

Fiction: "Kaya publishes Asian, Asian-American and Asian diasporic materials. We are looking for innovative writers with a commitment to quality literature." Submit 2-4 sample chapter(s), synopsis, SASE.

Poetry: Submit complete ms.

Recent Title(s): *Where We Once Belonged*, by Sia Figiel (novel); *The Anchored Angel: Selected Writings*, by Jose Garcia Villa, edited by Gileen Tabios.

Tips: Audience is people interested in a high standard of literature and who are interested in breaking down easy approaches to multicultural literature.

KENSINGTON PUBLISHING CORP., 850 Third Ave., 16th Floor, New York NY 10022. (212)407-1500. Fax: (212)935-0699. Website: www.kensingtonbooks.com. **Acquisitions:** Michaela Hamilton, editor-in-chief (thrillers, mysteries, mainstream fiction, true crime, current events); Kate Duffy, editorial director, romance and women's fiction (historical romance, Regency romance, Brava erotic romance, women's contemporary fiction); John Scognamiglio, editorial director, fiction (historical romance, Regency romance, women's contemporary fiction, gay and lesbian fiction and nonfiction, mysteries, suspense, mainstream fiction); Karen Thomas, editorial director, Dafina Books/Arabesque romances (African-American fiction and nonfiction); Bruce Bender, managing director, Citadel Press (popular nonfiction, film, television, wicca, gambling, current events); Ann LaFarge, executive editor, Zebra Books and Citadel Press (women's fiction, thrillers, westerns, commercial nonfiction); Bob Shuman, senior editor, Citadel Press (politics, military, wicca, business, Judaica, sports); Elaine Sparber, senior editor (health, alternative health, pets, New Age, self-help); Margaret Wolf, senior editor, Citadel Press (psychology, women's issues, women's health, entertainment, current events, cookbooks); Jeremie Ruby-Strauss, senior editor (nonfiction, pop culture, pop reference, true crime); Richard Ember, editor, Citadel Press (biography, film, sports, New Age, spirituality); Miles Lott, assistant editor (mainstream fiction, thrillers, horror, women's fiction, general nonfiction, popular culture, entertainment); Hilary Sares, consulting editor (historical romance, Regency romance, women's fiction); Lisa Filippattos, consulting editor (contemporary and historical romance, Regency romances, Brava erotic romance, women's fiction, thrillers); Lee Heiman, consulting editor (alternative health). Estab. 1975. Publishes hardcover and trade paperback originals, mass market paperback originals and reprints. **Publishes over 500 titles/year. Receives 5,000 queries and 2,000 mss/year. 10% of books from first-time authors; 30% from unagented writers. Pays 8-15% royalty on retail price or makes outright purchase. Offers $2,000 and up advance.** Publishes book 9-12 months after acceptance of ms. Accepts simultaneous submissions. Responds in 1 month to queries; 1 month to proposals; 4 months to mss. Book catalog online.

Imprints: Kensington Books; Brava Books; Citadel Press; Dafina Books; Pinnacle Books; Zebra Books.

- Kensington recently purchased the assets of Carol Publishing Group.

O→ Kensington focuses on profitable niches and uses aggressive marketing techniques to support its books.

Nonfiction: Biography, cookbook, gift book, how-to, humor, illustrated book, reference, self-help. Subjects include Americana, animals, business/economics, child guidance/parenting, contemporary culture, cooking/foods/nutrition, gay/lesbian, health/medicine (alternative), history, hobbies, memoirs, military/war, money/finance, multicultural, nature/environment, philosophy, psychology, recreation, regional, sex, sports, travel, true crime, women's issues/studies, pop culture, true crime, current events. *Agented submissions only. No unsolicited mss.* Reviews artwork/photos as part of ms package. Send photocopies.

Fiction: Erotica, ethnic, gay/lesbian, historical, horror, mainstream/contemporary, multicultural, mystery, occult, romance (contemporary, historical, regency, erotica), suspense, western (epic), thrillers; women's, biographies, paranormal, self-help, alternative health, pop culture nonfiction. No science fiction/fantasy, experimental fiction, business texts or children's titles. *Agented submissions only. No unsolicited mss.*

Recent Title(s): *Green Calder Grass*, by Janet Dailey (fiction); *Unfinished Business*, by Harlan Ullman (nonfiction).

Tips: Agented submissions only, except for submissions to Arabesque, Ballad, Bouquet, Encanto and Precious Gems. For those imprints, query with SASE or submit proposal package including 3 sample chapter(s), synopsis.

KENT STATE UNIVERSITY PRESS, P.O. Box 5190, Kent OH 44242-0001. (330)672-7913. Fax: (330)672-3104. **Acquisitions:** Joanna H. Craig, editor-in-chief. Estab. 1965. Publishes hardcover and paperback originals and some reprints. **Publishes 30-35 titles/year. Nonauthor subsidy publishes 20% of books. Standard minimum book contract on net sales.** Responds in 3 months to queries. Book catalog free.

O→ Kent State publishes primarily scholarly works and titles of regional interest. Currently emphasizing US history, literary criticism. De-emphasizing European history.

Nonfiction: Biography, scholarly. Subjects include anthropology/archeology, art/architecture, general nonfiction, history, language/literature, regional, true crime, literary criticism, material culture, textile/fashion studies. Especially interested in "scholarly works in history and literary studies of high quality, any titles of regional interest for Ohio, scholarly biographies, the arts, and general nonfiction. Always write a letter of inquiry before submitting manuscripts. We can publish only a limited number of titles each year and can frequently tell in advance whether or not we would be interested in a particular manuscript. This practice saves both our time and that of the author, not to mention postage costs. If interested we will ask for complete manuscript. Decisions based on inhouse readings and 2 by outside scholars in the field of study." Enclose return postage.

DENIS KITCHEN PUBLISHING, P.O. Box 9514, North Amherst MA 01059-9514. (413)259-1627. Fax: (413)259-1812. E-mail: publishing@deniskitchen.com. Website: www.deniskitchen.com. **Acquisitions:** Denis Kitchen, publisher (graphic novels, classic comic strips, postcard books, graphics, pop culture, alternative culture). Publishes hardcover and trade paperback originals and reprints. **Publishes 4 titles/year. 15% of books from first-time authors; 50% from unagented writers. Pays 6-10% royalty on retail price. Occasionally makes deals based on percentage of wholesale if idea and/or bulk of work is done in-house. Offers $1-5,000 advance.** Publishes book 9 months after acceptance of ms.

Accepts simultaneous submissions. Responds in 1 month to queries; 1 month to proposals; 1 month to mss. Book catalog and ms guidelines on website.

- This publisher strongly discourages e-mail submissions.

Nonfiction: Coffee table book, illustrated book, graphic novels. Subjects include art, comic art, pop culture, alternative culture, graphic novels. Query with SASE or submit proposal package including outline, illustrative matter or submit complete ms. Reviews artwork/photos as part of ms package. Send photocopies or transparencies.
Fiction: Adventure, comic books, erotica, historical, horror, humor, literary, mystery, occult, picture books, science fiction. "We do not want pure fiction. We seek cartoonists or writer/illustrator teams who can tell compelling stories with a combination of words and pictures." No pure fiction. Query with SASE or submit sample illustrations/comic pages or submit complete ms.
Recent Title(s): *The Unsyndicated Kurtzman*, by Harvey Kurtzman; *The Grasshopper and the Ant*, by Harvey Kurtzman; *Heroes of the Blues*, by R. Crumb.
Tips: "Readers who embrace the graphic novel revolution, who appreciate historical comic strips and books, and those who follow popular and alternative culture. Readers who supported Kitchen Sink Press for three decades will find that Denis Kitchen Publishing continues the tradition and precedents established by KSP. We like to discover new talent. The artist who has a day job but a great idea is encouraged to contact us. The pop culture historian who has a new take on an important figure is likewise encouraged. We have few preconceived notions about manuscripts or ideas though we are decidedly selective. Historically we have published many first-time authors and artists, some of whom developed into award-winning creators with substantial followings. Artists or illustrators who do not have confidence in their writing should send us self-promotional postcards (our favorite way of spotting new talent)."

B. KLEIN PUBLICATIONS, P.O. Box 6578, Delray Beach FL 33482. (561)496-3316. Fax: (561)496-5546. **Acquisitions:** Bernard Klein, editor-in-chief. Estab. 1946. Publishes hardcover and paperback originals. **Publishes 5 titles/year. Pays 10% royalty on wholesale price.** Accepts simultaneous submissions. Responds in 2 months to queries. Book catalog for #10 SASE.

O‑ B. Klein Publications specializes in directories, annuals, who's who books, bibliography, business opportunity, reference books. Markets books by direct mail and mail order.

Nonfiction: How-to, reference, self-help, directories; bibliographies. Subjects include business/economics, hobbies. Query with SASE or submit outline, sample chapter(s).
Recent Title(s): *Guide to American Directories*, by Bernard Klein.

ALFRED A. KNOPF, Knopf Publishing Group, Random House, Inc., 1745 Broadway, New York NY 10019. (212)751-2600. Website: www.aaknopf.com. **Acquisitions:** Senior Editor. Estab. 1915. Publishes hardcover and paperback originals. **Publishes 200 titles/year. 15% of books from first-time authors; 30% from unagented writers. Pays 10-15% royalty. Royalty and advance vary. Offers advance.** Publishes book 1 year after acceptance of ms. Accepts simultaneous submissions. Responds in 3 months to queries. Book catalog for 7½×10½ SAE with 5 first-class stamps; ms guidelines online.

O‑ Knopf is a general publisher of quality nonfiction and fiction.

Nonfiction: Scholarly, Book-length nonfiction, including books of scholarly merit. Subjects include general nonfiction, general scholarly nonfiction. "A good nonfiction writer should be able to follow the latest scholarship in any field of human knowledge, and fill in the abstractions of scholarship for the benefit of the general reader by means of good, concrete, sensory reporting." **Preferred length: 50,000-150,000 words.** Query with SASE. Reviews artwork/photos as part of ms package.
Fiction: Publishes book-length fiction of literary merit by known or unknown writers. **Length: 40,000-150,000 words.** Query with SASE or submit sample chapter(s).
Recent Title(s): *The Emperor of Ocean Park*, by Stephen Carter (first novel); *Master of the Senate*, by Robert A. Caro; *Balzac and the Little Chinese Seamstress*, by Dai Sijie.

KOENISHA PUBLICATIONS, 3196 53rd St., Hamilton MI 49419-9626. (269)751-4100. Fax: (269)751-4100. E-mail: koenisha@macatawa.org. Website: www.koenisha.com. **Acquisitions:** Sharolett Koenig, publisher; Flavia Crowner, proof editor; Earl Leon, acquisition editor. Publishes trade paperback originals. **Publishes 10-12 titles/year. Receives 50 queries and 50 mss/year. 95% of books from first-time authors; 100% from unagented writers. Pays 15-25% royalty on net receipts.** Publishes book 1 year after acceptance of ms. Accepts simultaneous submissions. Responds in 2 months to queries; 3 months to proposals; 3 months to mss. Book catalog and ms guidelines free or on website; ms guidelines online.
Nonfiction: Autobiography, children's/juvenile, cookbook, how-to. Subjects include gardening, hobbies, memoirs, nature/environment. Query with SASE or submit complete ms. Reviews artwork/photos as part of ms package. Send photocopies.
Fiction: Humor, mainstream/contemporary, mystery, romance, suspense, young adult. "We do not accept manuscripts that contain unnecessary foul language, explicit sex or gratuitous violence." Query with SASE or submit proposal package including 3 sample chapter(s), synopsis.
Poetry: Submit 3 sample poems.
Recent Title(s): *Lake of Spies*, by Sherri Bigbee and Steve Hicok (spy thriller); *The Mad Season*, by Al Blanchard (mystery); *The Friend Factory*, by Gary Crow and Marissa Crow (children's nonfiction self-help).
Tips: "We're NOT interested in books written to suit a particular line or house or because it's trendy. Instead write a book from your heart—the inspiration or idea that kept you going through the writing process."

H.J. KRAMER, INC., New World Library, P.O. Box 1082, Tiburon CA 94920. (415)435-5367. Fax: (415)435-5364. E-mail: hjkramer@jps.net. **Acquisitions:** Jan Phillips, managing editor. Estab. 1984. Publishes hardcover and trade paperback originals. **Publishes 5 titles/year. Receives 1,000 queries and 500 mss/year. 20% of books from first-time authors.**

Advance varies. Publishes book 18 months after acceptance of ms. Book catalog free.

Imprints: Starseed Press Children's Illustrated Books.

Nonfiction: Children's/juvenile, illustrated book, spiritual themes. Subjects include health/medicine (holistic), spirituality, metaphysical.

Fiction: Juvenile, picture books. Prospective authors please note: Kramer's list is selective and is normally fully slated several seasons in advance.

Recent Title(s): *No Regrets*, by Barry Neil Kaufman (nonfiction); *Thank You God*, by Holly Bea, illustrated by Kim Howard (fiction).

Tips: "Our books are for people who are interested in personal growth and consciousness-raising. We are not interested in personal stories unless it has universal appeal. We do not accept e-mail submissions of mss although queries will be answered."

KRAUSE PUBLICATIONS, 700 E. State, Iola WI 54990. (715)445-2214. Fax: (715)445-4087. E-mail: info@krause.com. Website: www.krause.com. **Acquisitions:** Acquisitions Editor. Publishes hardcover and trade paperback originals. **Publishes 170 titles/year. Receives 400 queries and 40 mss/year. 10% of books from first-time authors; 90% from unagented writers. Pays 9-12% royalty on net or makes outright purchase of $2,000-10,000. Offers $1,500-4,000 advance.** Publishes book 1 year after acceptance of ms. Does not accept simultaneous submissions. Responds in 2 months to proposals; 2 months to mss. Book catalog for free or on website; ms guidelines free.

O→ "We are the world's largest hobby and collectibles publisher."

Nonfiction: How-to, illustrated book, reference, technical, price guides. Subjects include hobbies (antiques, collectibles, toys), sports (outdoors, hunting, fishing), coins, stamps, firearms, knives, records, sewing, quilting, ceramics. Submit proposal package, including outline, 1-3 sample chapters and letter explaining your project's unique contributions. Reviews artwork/photos as part of ms package. Send sample photos.

Recent Title(s): *Encyclopedia of Pepsi-Cola Collectibles*, by Bob Stoddard (reference/price guide); *The Basic Guide to Dyeing and Painting Fabric*, by Cindy Walter and Jennifer Priestly (how-to); *Tying Trout Flies*, by C. Boyd Pfeiffer (how-to/reference).

Tips: Audience consists of serious hobbyists. "Your work should provide a unique contribution to the special interest."

KREGEL PUBLICATIONS, Kregel, Inc., P.O. Box 2607, Grand Rapids MI 49501. (616)451-4775. Fax: (616)451-9330. E-mail: acquisitions@kregel.com. Website: www.kregel.com. **Acquisitions:** Dennis R. Hillman, publisher. Estab. 1949. Publishes hardcover and trade paperback originals and reprints. **Publishes 90 titles/year. Receives 1,000 queries and 300 mss/year. 10% of books from first-time authors; 90% from unagented writers. Pays 8-16% royalty on wholesale price. Offers $200-2,000 advance.** Publishes book 14 months after acceptance of ms. Accepts simultaneous submissions. Responds in 3 months to queries. Book catalog for #10 SASE; ms guidelines online.

Imprints: Editorial Portavoz, Kregel Academic, Kregel Kidzone.

O→ "Our mission as an evangelical Christian publisher is to provide—with integrity and excellence—trusted, biblically-based resources that challenge and encourage individuals in their Christian lives. Works in theology and biblical studies should reflect the historic, orthodox Protestant tradition."

Nonfiction: "We serve evangelical Christian readers and those in career Christian service." Biography (Christian), gift book, reference. Subjects include religion, spirituality. Query with SASE.

Fiction: Adventure, historical, mystery, religious (children's, general, inspirational, fantasy/sci-fi, mystery/suspense, religious thriller, relationships), young adult (adventure). Fiction should be geared toward the evangelical Christian market. Wants "books with fast-paced, contemporary storylines&#151strong Christian message presented in engaging, entertaining style as well as books for juvenile and young adults, especially young women." Query with SASE.

Recent Title(s): *Unveiling Islam*, by Ergun Caner and Emir Caner (missions); *Praying the Attributes of God*, by Rosemary Jensen (devotional); *Romance Rustlers and Thunderbird Thieves*, by Sharon Dunn (mystery).

Tips: "Our audience consists of conservative, evangelical Christians, including pastors and ministry students. Think through very clearly the intended audience for the work."

KRIEGER PUBLISHING CO., P.O. Box 9542, Melbourne FL 32902-9542. (321)724-9542. Fax: (321)951-3671. E-mail: info@krieger-publishing.com. Website: www.krieger-publishing.com. **Acquisitions:** Sharan B. Merriam and Ronald M. Cervero, series editor (adult education); Donald M. Waltz, series editor (space sciences); David E. Kyvig, series director (local history); Hans Trefousse, series editor (history); James B. Gardner, series editor (public history). Estab. 1969. Publishes hardcover and paperback originals and reprints. **Publishes 30 titles/year. Receives 100 submissions/year. 30% of books from first-time authors; 100% from unagented writers. Pays royalty on net price.** Publishes book 18 months after acceptance of ms. Responds in 3 months to queries. Book catalog free.

Imprints: Anvil Series, Orbit Series, Public History, Professional Practices in Adult Education and Lifelong Learning Series.

O→ "We are a short-run niche publisher providing accurate and well-documented scientific and technical titles for text and reference use, college level and higher."

Nonfiction: Reference, technical, textbook, scholarly. Subjects include agriculture/horticulture, animals, education (adult), history, nature/environment, science (space), herpetology, chemistry, physics, engineering, veterinary medicine, natural history, math. Query with SASE. Reviews artwork/photos as part of ms package.

Recent Title(s): *Amphibian Medicine & Captive Husbandry*, edited by Kevin R. Wright and Brent R. Whitaker; *A History of Christian Education: Protestant, Catholic, and Orthodox Perspectives*, by John L. Elias.

LAKE CLAREMONT PRESS, 4650 N. Rockwell St., Chicago IL 60625. (773)583-7800. Fax: (773)583-7877. E-mail: sharon@lakeclaremont.com. Website: www.lakeclaremont.com. **Acquisitions:** Sharon Woodhouse, publisher. Publishes trade paperback originals. **Publishes 5-7 titles/year. Receives 300 queries and 50 mss/year. 50% of books from first-time authors; 100% from unagented writers. Pays 10-15% royalty on wholesale price. Offers $250-2,000 advance.** Publishes book 8 months after acceptance of ms. Accepts simultaneous submissions. Responds in 1 month to queries; 2 months to proposals; 2-6 months to mss. Book catalog online.

O→ "We specialize in books on the Chicago area and its history, and may consider regional titles for the Midwest. We also like nonfiction books on ghosts and cemeteries."

Nonfiction: Subjects include Americana, ethnic, history, nature/environment (regional), regional, travel, women's issues/studies, film/cinema/stage (regional), urban studies. Query with SASE or submit proposal package, including outline and 2 sample chapters, or submit complete ms (e-mail queries and proposals preferred).

Recent Title(s): *The Chicago River: A Natural and Unnatural History*, by Libby Hill; *Chicago's Midway Airport: The First Seventy-Five Years*, by Christopher Lynch.

Tips: "Please include a market analysis in proposals (who would buy this book & where?) and an analysis of similar books available for different regions. Please know what else is out there."

N **WENDY LAMB BOOKS**, Random House Children's Books Group, 1745 Broadway, New York NY 10019. **Acquisitions:** Wendy Lamb, VP/publicity director (fiction & nonfiction, ages 2-18). Estab. 2001. Publishes hardcover originals. **Publishes 10-12 titles/year. Receives 500-600 queries and 500 mss/year. 20% of books from first-time authors; 25% from unagented writers. Pays royalty on retail price.** Accepts simultaneous submissions. Responds in 1 month to queries. Ms guidelines for #10 SASE.

Nonfiction: Children's/juvenile. Query with SASE.

Fiction: Juvenile (ages 2-18). Query with SASE.

Poetry: Submit 4 sample poems.

Recent Title(s): *Bud, Not Buddy*, by Christopher Paul Curtis; *The Beet Fields*, by Gary Paulsen; *Nory Ryan's Song*, by Patricia Reilly Cliff.

Tips: Young readers.

LANGENSCHEIDT PUBLISHING GROUP, 46-35 54th Rd., Maspeth NY 11378. (800)432-MAPS. Fax: (718)784-0640. E-mail: spohja@langenscheidt.com. **Acquisitions:** Sue Pohja, acquisitions; Christine Cardone, editor. Estab. 1983. Publishes hardcover and trade paperback originals. **Publishes 350 titles/year. Receives 125 queries and 50 mss/year. 100% from unagented writers. Pays royalty or makes outright purchase.** Publishes book 6 months after acceptance of ms. Accepts simultaneous submissions. Responds in 1 month to proposals. Book catalog free.

Imprints: ADC Map, American Map, Arrow Map, Creative Sales, Hagstrom Map, Hammond Map, Insight Guides, Hammond World Atlas Corp., Trakker Map, Langenscheidt Trade, Berlitz Publishing.

O→ Langenscheidt Publishing Group publishes maps, travel guides, foreign language reference and dictionary titles, world atlases, educational materials and foreign language audio products.

Nonfiction: Reference. Subjects include education, travel, foreign language. "Any potential title that fills a gap in our line is welcome." Submit outline and 2 sample chapters (complete ms preferred).

Recent Title(s): *European Phrasebook*; *Insight Guide to Museums of London*; *Pocket Chinese Dictionary.*

Tips: "Any item related to our map, foreign language dictionary, atlas and travel lines could have potential for us. Of particular interest are titles that have a sizeable potential customer base and have little in the way of good competition."

LARK, Sterling Publishing, 67 Broadway, Asheville NC 28801. (828)253-0467. Fax: (828)253-7952. Website: www.larkbooks.com. Director of Publishing: Carol Taylor. **Acquisitions:** Nicole Tuggle, submissions coordinator. Estab. 1976. Publishes hardcover and trade paperback originals and reprints. **Publishes 50 titles/year. Receives 300 queries and 100 mss/year. 80% of books from first-time authors; 90% from unagented writers. Offers up to $4,000 advance.** Publishes book 1 year after acceptance of ms. Accepts simultaneous submissions. Responds in 3 months to queries. Ms guidelines online.

O→ Lark Books publishes high quality, highly illustrated books, primarily in the crafts/leisure markets celebrating the creative spirit. We work closely with bookclubs. Our books are either how-to, 'gallery' or combination books."

Nonfiction: Children's/juvenile, coffee table book, how-to, illustrated book. Subjects include gardening, hobbies, nature/environment, crafts. Query first. If asked, submit outline and 1 sample chapter, sample projects, table of contents, visuals. Reviews artwork/photos as part of ms package. Send transparencies.

Recent Title(s): *Gorgeous Leather Crafts.*

Tips: "We publish both first-time and seasoned authors. In either case, we need to know that you have substantial expertise on the topic of the proposed book—that we can trust you to know what you're talking about. If you're great at your craft but not so great as a writer, you might want to work with us as a coauthor or as a creative consultant."

LARSON PUBLICATIONS/PBPF, 4936 Rt. 414, Burdett NY 14818-9729. E-mail: larson@lightlink.com. Website: www.larsonpublications.org. **Acquisitions:** Paul Cash, director. Estab. 1982. Publishes hardcover and trade paperback originals. **Publishes 4-5 titles/year. Receives 1,000 submissions/year. 5% of books from first-time authors. Pays variable royalty. Seldom offers advance.** Publishes book 1-2 years after acceptance of ms. Accepts simultaneous submissions. Responds in 4-6 months to queries. Visit website for book catalog.

Nonfiction: Subjects include philosophy, psychology, religion, spirituality. Query with SASE and outline.

Recent Title(s): *Astonoesis*, by Anthony Damiani.

Tips: "We look for original studies of comparative spiritual philosophy or personal fruits of independent (transsectarian viewpoint) spiritual research/practice."

N **MERLOYD LAWRENCE BOOKS**, Perseus Book Group, 102 Chestnut St., Boston MA 02108. **Acquisitions:** Merloyd Lawrence, president. Estab. 1982. Publishes hardcover and trade paperback originals. **Publishes 7-8 titles/year. Receives 400 submissions/year. 25% of books from first-time authors; 20% from unagented writers. Pays royalty on retail price. Offers advance.** Accepts simultaneous submissions.

Nonfiction: Subjects include health/medicine, nature/environment, psychology, social sciences, child development. *No unsolicited mss.* Query with SASE. **All unsolicited mss returned unopened.**

Recent Title(s): *The Wildest Place on Earth*, by John Hanson Mitchell.

LAWYERS & JUDGES PUBLISHING CO., P.O. Box 30040, Tucson AZ 85751-0040. (520)323-1500. Fax: (520)323-0055. E-mail: sales@lawyersandjudges.com. Website: www.lawyersandjudges.com. **Acquisitions:** Steve Weintraub, president. Estab. 1963. Publishes professional hardcover and trade paperback originals. **Publishes 15 titles/year. Receives 200 queries and 30 mss/year. 15% of books from first-time authors; 100% from unagented writers. Pays 7-10% royalty on net receipts.** Publishes book 5 months after acceptance of ms. Accepts simultaneous submissions. Responds in 2 months to queries. Book catalog free; ms guidelines online.

O→ Lawyers & Judges is a highly specific publishing company, reaching the legal and insurance fields and accident reconstruction.

Nonfiction: Reference. Subjects include law, insurance, forensics, accident reconstruction. "Unless a writer is an expert in the forensics/legal/insurance areas, we are not interested." Submit proposal package including outline, sample chapter(s).

Recent Title(s): *Human Factors in Traffic Safety.*

LEARNING PUBLICATIONS, INC., 5351 Gulf Dr., Holmes Beach FL 34217. (941)778-6651. Fax: (941)778-6818. E-mail: info@learningpublications.com. Website: www.learningpublications.com. **Acquisitions:** Ruth Erickson, editor. Estab. 1975. Publishes trade paperback originals and reprints. **Publishes 10-15 titles/year. Receives 150 queries and 50 mss/year. 50% of books from first-time authors; 100% from unagented writers. Pays 5-10% royalty.** Publishes book 1 year after acceptance of ms. Accepts simultaneous submissions. Responds in 1 month to queries; 1 month to proposals; 4 months to mss. Book catalog and ms guidelines online; ms guidelines online.

O→ "We specifically market by direct mail to education and human service professionals materials to use with students and clients."

Nonfiction: Reference, textbook. Subjects include education, humanities, psychology, sociology, women's issues/studies. "Writers interested in submitting mss should request our guidelines first." Query with SASE or submit proposal package including outline, 1 sample chapter(s), résumé. Reviews artwork/photos as part of ms package. Send photocopies.

Tips: "Learning Publications has a limited, specific market. Writers should be familiar with who buys our books."

LEE & LOW BOOKS, 95 Madison Ave., New York NY 10016. (212)779-4400. Fax: (212)683-1894. Website: www.leeandlow.com. **Acquisitions:** Louise May, executive editor. Estab. 1991. Publishes hardcover originals—picture books only. **Publishes 12-16 titles/year. Pays royalty. Offers advance.** Accepts simultaneous submissions. Responds in 2-4 months to queries; 2-4 months to mss. Book catalog for SASE with $1.75 postage; ms guidelines online.

O→ "Our goals are to meet a growing need for books that address children of color, and to present literature that all children can identify with. We only consider multicultural children's picture books." Currently emphasizing material for 2-10 year olds. Sponsors a yearly New Voices Award for first-time picture book authors of color. Contest rules online at website or for SASE.

Nonfiction: Children's/juvenile, illustrated book. Subjects include ethnic, multicultural.

Fiction: Ethnic, juvenile, multicultural, illustrated. "We do not consider folktales, fairy tales or animal stories." Send complete ms with cover letter or through an agent.

Recent Title(s): *The Pot that Juan Built*, by Nancy Andrews-Goebel; *Summer Sun Risin'*, by W. Nikola-Lisa.

Tips: "Of special interest are stories set in contemporary America. We are interested in fiction as well as nonfiction. We do not consider folktales, fairy tales or animal stories."

J & L LEE CO., P.O. Box 5575, Lincoln NE 68505. **Acquisitions:** Jim McKee, acquisitions editor. Publishes trade paperback originals and reprints. **Publishes 5 titles/year. Receives 25 queries and 5-10 mss/year. 20% of books from first-time authors; 60% from unagented writers. Pays 10% royalty on retail price or makes outright purchase. Offers advance.** Publishes book 18 months after acceptance of ms. Accepts simultaneous submissions. Responds in 6 months to queries; 1 month to proposals; 6 months to mss. Book catalog free.

Imprints: Salt Creek Press, Young Hearts.

O→ "Virtually everything we publish is of a Great Plains nature."

Nonfiction: Biography, reference. Subjects include Americana, history, regional. Query with SASE.

Recent Title(s): *The Good Old Days*, by Van Duling; *Bipartisan Efforts and Other Mutations*, by Paul Fell.

Tips: "We do not publish poetry."

LEGACY PRESS, Rainbow Publishers, P.O. Box 261129, San Diego CA 92196. (858)271-7600. **Acquisitions:** Christy Scannell, editor,. Estab. 1997. **Publishes 20 titles/year. Receives 250 queries and 100 mss/year. 50% of books from first-time authors. Pays royalty based on wholesale price. Offers negotiable advance.** Publishes book 1-3 years after acceptance of ms. Accepts simultaneous submissions. Book catalog for 9×12 SAE with 2 first-class stamps; ms guidelines for #10 SASE.

O→ "Legacy Press strives to publish Bible-based materials that inspire Christian spiritual growth and development in children." Currently emphasizing nonfiction for kids, particularly pre-teens and more specifically girls, although we are publishing boys and girls 2-12. No picture books, fiction without additional activities, poetry or plays.

Nonfiction: Subjects include creative nonfiction, education, hobbies, religion. Query with SASE or submit outline, 3-5 sample chapter(s), market analysis.

Recent Title(s): *The Official Christian Babysitting Guide*, by Rebecca P. Totilo; *The Ponytails*, by Bonnie Compton Hanson (5-book series).

Tips: "We are looking for Christian versions of general market nonfiction for kids, as well as original ideas."

LEGEND BOOKS, 69 Lansing St., Auburn NY 13021. (315)258-8012. **Acquisitions:** Joseph P. Berry, editor. Publishes paperback monographs, scholarly books and college textbooks. **Publishes 15 titles/year. Receives 100 queries and 60 mss/year. 50% of books from first-time authors; 100% from unagented writers. Pays 20% royalty on net sales.** Publishes book 9 months after acceptance of ms. Accepts simultaneous submissions. Responds in 2 months to queries; 2 months to proposals; 2 months to mss.

O→ Legend Books publishes a variety of books used in the college classroom, including workbooks. However, it does not publish any books on mathematics or hard sciences.

Nonfiction: Biography, scholarly, textbook, community/public affairs, speech/mass communication. Subjects include business/economics, child guidance/parenting, community, education, government/politics, health/medicine, history, humanities, philosophy, psychology, recreation, social sciences, sociology, sports, journalism, public relations, television. Query with SASE or submit complete ms (include SASE if ms is to be returned). Reviews artwork/photos as part of ms package. Send photocopies.

Recent Title(s): *The Conversion of the King of Bissau*, by Timothy Coates, Ph.D. (world history); *Values, Society & Evolution*, by H. James Birx, Ph.D. (anthropology and sociology).

Tips: "We seek college professors who actually teach courses for which their books are designed."

LEHIGH UNIVERSITY PRESS, Linderman Library, 30 Library Dr., Lehigh University, Bethlehem PA 18015-3067. (610)758-3933. Fax: (610)758-6331. E-mail: inlup@lehigh.edu. **Acquisitions:** Philip A. Metzger, director. Estab. 1985. Publishes hardcover originals. **Publishes 10 titles/year. Receives 90-100 queries and 50-60 mss/year. 70% of books from first-time authors; 100% from unagented writers. Pays royalty.** Publishes book 18 months after acceptance of ms. Accepts simultaneous submissions. Responds in 3 months to queries. Book catalog and ms guidelines free.

O→ "Currently emphasizing works on 18th-century studies, East-Asian studies and literary criticism. Accepts all subjects of academic merit."

Nonfiction: Lehigh University Press is a conduit for nonfiction works of scholarly interest to the academic community. Biography, reference, scholarly. Subjects include Americana, art/architecture, history, language/literature, science. Submit proposal package including 1 sample chapter(s).

Recent Title(s): *The Terror of Our Days: Four American Poets Respond to the Holocaust*, by Harriet L. Parmet; *One Woman Determined to Make a Difference: The Life of Madeleine Zabruskie Doty*, by Alice Duffy Rinehart.

LEISURE BOOKS, Dorchester Publishing Co., 276 Fifth Ave., Suite 1008, New York NY 10001-0112. (212)725-8811. Fax: (212)532-1054. E-mail: dorchesterpub@dorchesterpub.com. Website: www.dorchesterpub.com. **Acquisitions:** Ashley Kuehl, editorial assistant; Kate Seaver, associate editor; Alicia Condon, editorial director; Don D'Auria, executive editor (westerns, technothrillers, horror); Christopher Keeslar, editor. Estab. 1970. Publishes mass market paperback originals and reprints. Publishes romances, westerns, horrors and technothrillers only. **Publishes 160 titles/year. Receives thousands submissions/year. 20% of books from first-time authors; 20% from unagented writers. Pays royalty on retail price. Offers negotiable advance.** Publishes book 18 months after acceptance of ms. Does not accept simultaneous submissions. Responds in 6 months to queries. Book catalog for free (800)481-9191; ms guidelines online.

Imprints: Love Spell (romance), Leisure (romance, western, techno, horror).

O→ Leisure Books/Love Spell is seeking historical, contemporary and time travel romances.

Fiction: Historical (romance), horror, romance, western, technothrillers. "We are strongly backing historical romance (90,000-100,000 words). All historical romance should be set pre-1900. Horrors and westerns are growing as well. No sweet romance, science fiction, erotica, contemporary women's fiction, mainstream or action/adventure." Query with SASE or submit outline, first 3 sample chapter(s), synopsis. "All mss must be typed, double-spaced on one side and left unbound."

Recent Title(s): *Dark Guardian*, by Christine Feehan (romance).

LERNER PUBLISHING GROUP, 241 First Ave. N., Minneapolis MN 55401. (612)332-3344. Fax: (612)332-7615. Website: www.lernerbooks.com. **Acquisitions:** Jennifer Zimian, nonfiction submissions editor. Estab. 1959. Publishes hardcover originals, trade paperback originals and reprints. **Publishes 200 titles/year. Receives 1,000 queries and 300 mss/year. 20% of books from first-time authors; 95% from unagented writers. Offers varied advance.** Accepts simultaneous submissions. Book catalog for 9×12 SAE with $3.50 postage; ms guidelines online.

Imprints: Carolrhoda Books; First Avenue Editions (paperback reprints for hard/soft deals only); Lerner Publications; LernerSports; LernerClassroom.

O→ "Our goal is to publish children's books that educate, stimulate and stretch the imagination, foster global awareness, encourage critical thinking and inform, inspire and entertain."

Nonfiction: Biography, children's/juvenile. Subjects include art/architecture, ethnic, history, nature/environment, science, sports. Query with SASE or submit outline, 1-2 sample chapter(s), during March or October.

Recent Title(s): *Your Travel Guide to Ancient Greece*, by Nancy Day; *Alice Walker*, by Caroline Lazo.

Tips: "No alphabet, puzzle, song or text books, religious subject matter or plays. Submissions are accepted in the months of March and October only. Work received in any other month will be returned unopened. SASE required for authors who wish to have their material returned or business-sized SASE for response only. Submissions without an SASE will receive no reply. Please allow 4-6 months for a response. No phone calls."

ARTHUR A. LEVINE BOOKS, Scholastic Inc., 557 Broadway, New York NY 10012. (212)343-4436. Website: www.scholastic.com. **Acquisitions:** Arthur Levine, editorial director. **Publishes 10-14 titles/year. Pays variable royalty on retail price. Offers variable advance.** Book catalog for 9×12 SASE.

Fiction: Juvenile, picture books, young adult, middle grade novels. Query with SASE. "We are willing to work with first-time authors, with or without agent."

Recent Title(s): *Frida*, by Jonah Winter; *The World Before This One*, by Rafe Martin; *St. Michael's Scales*, by Neil Connelly.

LIBRARIES UNLIMITED, INC., 88 Post Rd. W., Westport CT 06881. (800)225-5800. Fax: (203)222-1502. E-mail: mdillon@lu.com. Website: www.lu.com. **Acquisitions:** Martin Dillon, director of acquisitions; Barbara Ittner, acquisitions editor (public library titles); Sharon Coatney (school library titles); Suzanne Barchers (teacher resources); Edward Kurdyla, general manager (academic/reference titles). Estab. 1964. Publishes hardcover originals. **Publishes 100 titles/year. Receives 400 queries and 100 mss/year. 50% of books from first-time authors; 100% from unagented writers. Pays 8-15% royalty on wholesale price. Offers advance.** Publishes book 1 year after acceptance of ms. Accepts simultaneous submissions. Responds in 1 month to queries; 2 months to proposals; 2 months to mss. Book catalog and ms guidelines available via website or with SASE; ms guidelines online.

Imprints: Teacher Ideas Press.

O┳ Libraries Unlimited publishes resources for libraries, librarians and educators. "We are currently emphasizing readers' advisory guides, academic reference works, readers' theatre, storytelling, biographical dictionary, and de-emphasizing teacher books."

Nonfiction: Biography (collections), reference, textbook. Subjects include agriculture/horticulture, anthropology/archeology, art/architecture, business/economics, education, ethnic, health/medicine, history, language/literature, music/dance, philosophy, psychology, religion, science, sociology, women's issues/studies, technology. "We are interested in library applications and tools for all subject areas." Submit proposal package including outline, 1 sample chapter(s), résumé. Reviews artwork/photos as part of ms package. Send photocopies.

Recent Title(s): *Women in U.S. History*, by Lyda Mary Hardy; *The Eagle on the Cactus: Traditional Stories from Mexico*, by Angel Vigil.

Tips: "We welcome any ideas that combine professional expertise, writing ability, and innovative thinking. Audience is librarians (school, public, academic and special) and teachers (K-12)."

LIGUORI PUBLICATIONS, One Liguori Dr., Liguori MO 63057. (636)464-2500. Fax: (636)464-8449. Website: www.liguori.org. Publisher: Harry Grile. Editorial Director: Hans Christoffesen. **Acquisitions:** Judith A. Bauer, managing editor (Trade Group); Lisa Miller, managing editor (Pastorlink, electronic publishing). Estab. 1947. Publishes paperback originals and reprints under the Ligouri and Libros Ligouri imprints. **Publishes 30 titles/year. Pays royalty or makes outright purchase. Offers varied advance.** Publishes book 2 years after acceptance of ms. Does not accept simultaneous submissions. Responds in 2 months to queries; 2 months to proposals; 3 months to mss. Ms guidelines online.

Imprints: Faithwarerg, Libros Liguori, Liguori Books, Liguori/Triumph, Liguori Lithspan.

O┳ Liguori Publications, faithful to the charism of Saint Alphonsus, is an apostolate within the mission of the Denver Province. Its mission, a collaborative effort of Redemptorists and laity, is to spread the gospel of Jesus Christ primarily through the print and electronic media. It shares in the Redemptorist priority of giving special attention to the poor and the most abandoned. Currently emphasizing practical spirituality, prayers and devotions, "how-to" spirituality.

Nonfiction: Manuscripts with Catholic sensibility. Self-help. Subjects include computers/electronic, religion, spirituality. Mostly adult audience; limited children/juvenile. Query with SASE or submit outline, 1 sample chapter(s).

LIMELIGHT EDITIONS, Proscenium Publishers, Inc., 118 E. 30th St., New York NY 10016. Fax: (212)532-5526. E-mail: limelighteditions@earthlink.net. Website: www.limelighteditions.com. **Acquisitions:** Melvyn B. Zerman, president; Jenna Young, art director. Estab. 1983. Publishes hardcover and trade paperback originals, trade paperback reprints. **Publishes 14 titles/year. Receives 150 queries and 40 mss/year. 15% of books from first-time authors; 20% from unagented writers. Pays 7½-10% royalty on retail price. Offers $500-2,000 advance.** Publishes book 10 months after acceptance of ms. Does not accept simultaneous submissions. Responds in 1 month to queries; 1 month to proposals; 3 months to mss. Book catalog and ms guidelines free.

O┳ Limelight Editions publishes books on film, theater, music and dance history. "Our books make a strong contribution to their fields and deserve to remain in print for many years."

Nonfiction: "All books are on the performing arts *exclusively*." Biography, how-to (instructional), humor, illustrated book. Subjects include film/cinema/stage, history, multicultural, music/dance. Query with SASE or submit proposal package including outline, 2-3 sample chapter(s). Reviews artwork/photos as part of ms package. Send photocopies.

Recent Title(s): *Transformational Acting*, by Sande Shurin; *The Spy Who Thrilled Us*, by Mike Di Leo; *The Nashville Chronicles*, by Jan Stuart.

N **LIMITLESS DARE 2 DREAM PUBLISHING**, 100 Pin Oak Ct., Lexington SC 29073. (803)356-8231. Fax: (803)356-8231. E-mail: limitlessd2d@aol.com. Website: www.limitlessd2d.net. **Acquisitions:** Samantha E. Ruskin, CEO; Anne M. Clarkson, CIO (purchasing and marketing). Estab. 2002. Publishes trade paperback originals and reprints. **Publishes 35-50 titles/year; imprint publishes 35-50 titles/year. Receives 400-600 queries and 800-1,200 mss/year. Pays 12-20% royalty on retail price.** Publishes book 1-4 months after acceptance of ms. Does not accept simultaneous submissions.

Responds in 1 month to queries; 3 months to mss. Book catalog for #10 SASE; ms guidelines for #10 SASE.
Imprints: Dare 2 Dream.
Nonfiction: Audiocassettes, reference. Subjects include alternative lifestyles, animals, creative nonfiction, general nonfiction, history, hobbies, humanities, memoirs, military/war, philosophy, photography, psychology, regional, spirituality, women's issues/studies. "We do not do books that demean women in any way or books where the women are helpless females waiting to be rescued. Other than that writers will find us quite open minded and willing to read and consider their manuscripts. The criteria at D2D is good stories, good writing, and hold the reader's interest." Query with SASE or submit complete ms. Reviews artwork/photos as part of ms package. Send photocopies or e-mail attachments or burned onto a CD.
Fiction: Adventure, erotica, fantasy, feminist, gay/lesbian, historical, horror, humor, mainstream/contemporary, military/war, multimedia, mystery, occult, poetry, regional, romance, science fiction, short story collections, spiritual, suspense, western. "We do not do books that demean women in any way or books where women are helpless females waiting to be rescued. Other than that, writers will find us quite open minded and willing to read and consider their manuscripts. The criteria at D2D is good stories, good writing, and hold the reader's interest." Query with SASE or submit complete ms.
Poetry: "Poetry can be a tough market, but we do publish volumes of poetry. All we can say is try us. If it is very good poetry, you have a good chance with us." Nothing that demeans women in any way or books where the women are helpless females waiting to be rescued. Query or submit any number of poems sample poems or submit complete ms.
Recent Title(s): *The Amazon Nation*, by Carla Osborne (research and entertainment); *Desert Hawk*, by Archangel (lesbian fiction); *Fatal Impressions*, by Jeanne Foguth (manistream suspense/romance).
Tips: "Our audience is primarily women in all walks of life and from all educational levels. This company was created by 2 women who know the struggle to get into print, so our best advice is to just go ahead and do it—send the manuscript to us and give it a try. We promise to treat it with honor and respect."

[N] **LION BOOKS**, 210 Nelson Rd., Scarsdale NY 10583. (914)725-2280. Fax: (914)725-3572. **Acquisitions:** Harriet Ross, editor. Estab. 1966. Publishes hardcover originals and reprints, trade paperback reprints. **Publishes 12 titles/year. Receives 60-150 queries and 100 mss/year. 60% of books from first-time authors. Pays 7-15% royalty on wholesale price. Offers advance.** Publishes book 9 months after acceptance of ms. Does not accept simultaneous submissions. Responds in 1 week to queries; 1 month to mss.
Nonfiction: Biography, how-to. Subjects include Americana, ethnic, government/politics, history, recreation, sports. No fiction. Submit complete manuscript with SASE.

[N] **LIONHEARTED PUBLISHING, INC.**, P.O. Box 618, Zephyr Cove NV 89448-0618. (775)588-1388. E-mail: admin@lionhearted.com. Website: www.lionhearted.com. **Acquisitions:** Historical or Contemporary Acquistions Editor. Estab. 1994. Publishes mass market paperback originals and ebooks. Also expanded romance into e-book formats. **Publishes 12-72 titles/year. 90% from unagented writers. Royalties of 10% maximum on paperbacks; 30% on electronic books. Offers $100 advance.** Publishes book 18-24 months after acceptance of ms. Does not accept simultaneous submissions. Responds in 1 month to queries; 3 months to mss. Book catalog for #10 SASE; ms guidelines online.

- "Multiple award-winning, independent publisher of single title, mass market paperback and ebook, romance novels."

Fiction: Romance (contemporary, futuristic/time travel, historical, regency period, romantic suspense; over 65,000 words only). Query with SASE or submit outline, 3 sample chapter(s), publishing history, synopsis, Estimated Word Count, Cover Letter and 1 Paragraph Story Summary in Cover Letter, SASE. Do not send ms by regular mail unless invited by editor.
Recent Title(s): *The Only One*, by Karen Woods (contemporary romance); *The Magic Token*, by Susan Christina (Regency romance); *Suddenly Love*, by Catherine Sellers (contemporary).
Tips: "If you are not an avid reader of romance, don't attempt to write romance, and don't waste your time or an editor's by submitting to a publisher of romance. Please read a few of our single title releases (they are a bit different) before submitting your romance novel."

[N] [A] **LISTEN & LIVE AUDIO, INC.**, P.O. Box 817, Roseland NJ 07068. (973)781-1444. Fax: (973)781-0333. E-mail: alfred@listenandlive.com. Website: www.listenandlive.com. **Acquisitions:** Alisa Weberman, publisher (manuscripts for audiobook consideration). **Publishes 20 titles/year. Receives 200 mss/year. Offers advance.** Publishes book 3-6 months after acceptance of ms. Accepts simultaneous submissions. Responds in 1 month to mss. Book catalog online.
Imprints: Defiance Audio, Appleseed Audio, South Bay Entertainment.

- Listen & Live publishes fiction and nonfiction books on audio cassette/CD.

Nonfiction: Multimedia (audio format), self-help, true life. Subjects include business/economics, relationships. *Agented submissions only.*
Fiction: Young adult. *Agented submissions only.*
Recent Title(s): *The Darwin Awards I & II*; *Jump the Shark*; *No One Left Behind.*
Tips: Agents/publishers only may submit books.

[A] **LITTLE, BROWN AND CO., ADULT TRADE BOOKS**, Division of AOL Time Warner Book Group, 1271 Avenue of the Americas, New York NY 10020. (212)522-8700. Fax: (212)522-2067. Website: www.twbookmark.com. Estab. 1837. Publishes hardcover originals and paperback originals and reprints.

[A] **LITTLE, BROWN AND CO., CHILDREN'S PUBLISHING**, Division of AOL Time Warner Books Group, Time Life Building, 1271 Avenue of the Americas, 11th Floor, New York NY 10020. (212)522-8700. Website: www.littlebrown.com. Editor-in-Chief/V-P, Associate Publisher: Megan Tingley. Marketing Director VP/Associate Publisher: Bill Boedeker. Senior Editor: Cindy Eagan. Editor: Jennifer Hunt. Estab. 1837. Publishes hardcover originals, trade paperback reprints.

Publishes 70-100 titles/year. Pays royalty on retail price. Offers negotiable advance. Publishes book 2 years after acceptance of ms. Accepts simultaneous submissions. Responds in 1 month to queries; 2 months to proposals; 2 months to mss. Ms guidelines online.

Imprints: Megan Tingley Books (Megan Tingley, editorial director).

O-- Little, Brown and Co., Children's Publishing publishes board books, picture books, middle grade fiction and nonfiction YA titles. "We are looking for strong writing and presentation, but no predetermined topics."

Nonfiction: Children's/juvenile. Subjects include animals, art/architecture, ethnic, gay/lesbian, history, hobbies, nature/environment, recreation, science, sports. Writers should avoid "looking for the 'issue' they think publishers want to see, choosing instead topics they know best and are most enthusiastic about/inspired by." *Agented submissions only.*

Fiction: Adventure, ethnic, fantasy, feminist, gay/lesbian, historical, humor, juvenile, mystery, picture books, science fiction, suspense, young adult. "We are looking for strong fiction for children of all ages in any area, including multicultural. We always prefer full manuscripts for fiction." *Agented submissions only.*

Recent Title(s): *Gossip Girl*, by Cecily von Ziegesar; *Little Brown Bear Won't Take a Nap*, by Jane Dyer; *The Feel Good Book*, by Todd Parr.

Tips: "Our audience is children of all ages, from preschool through young adult. We are looking for quality material that will work in hardcover—send us your best."

LITTLE SIMON, Simon & Schuster Children's Publishing Division, Simon & Schuster, 1230 Avenue of the Americas, New York NY 10020. (212)698-1295. Fax: (212)698-2794. Website: www.simonsayskids.com. Executive Vice President/Publisher: Robin Corey. **Acquisitions:** Cindy Alvarez, vice president/editorial director; Erin Molta, senior editor. Publishes novelty books only. **Publishes 65 titles/year. 5% of books from first-time authors. Offers advance and royalties.** Publishes book 2 years after acceptance of ms. Does not accept simultaneous submissions. Responds in 8 months to queries.

O-- "Our goal is to provide fresh material in an innovative format for preschool to age eight. Our books are often, if not exclusively, format driven."

Nonfiction: "We publish very few nonfiction titles." Children's/juvenile. No picture books. Query with SASE.

Fiction: "Novelty books include many things that do not fit in the traditional hardcover or paperback format, such as pop-up, board book, scratch and sniff, glow in the dark, lift the flap, etc." Children's/juvenile. No picture books. Large part of the list is holiday-themed.

Recent Title(s): *The Night Before Christmas*, by Robert Sabuda; *Chanukah Bugs*, by David Carter; *It's the Great Pumpkin, Charlie Brown*, by Charles M. Schultz.

LIVINGSTON PRESS, University of West Alabama, Station 22, Livingston AL 35470. E-mail: jwt@uwa.edu. Website: www.livingstonpress.uwa.edu. **Acquisitions:** Joe Taylor, director. Estab. 1984. Publishes hardcover and trade paperback originals. **Publishes 8-10 titles/year. 50% of books from first-time authors; 99% from unagented writers. Pays a choice of 12% of initial run or a combination of contributor's copies and 10% royalty of net.** Publishes book 18 months after acceptance of ms. Accepts simultaneous submissions. Responds in 1 month to queries; 1 year to mss. Book catalog for SASE; ms guidelines online.

Imprints: Swallow's Tale Press.

O-- Livingston Press publishes topics such as Southern literature and quirky fiction. Currently emphasizing short stories. De-emphasizing poetry.

Fiction: Experimental, literary, short story collections, off-beat or southern. "We are interested in form and, of course style." Query with SASE.

Poetry: "We publish very little poetry, mostly books we have asked to see." Query.

Recent Title(s): *Partita In Venice*, by Curt Leviant; *Flight From Valhalla*, by Michael Bugeja (poetry); *B. Horror and Other Stories*, by Wendell Mayo.

Tips: "Our readers are interested in literature, often quirky literature that emphasizes form and style. Please visit our website for current needs." Reads manuscripts from Dec. 1st to Jan. 15th only.

LLEWELLYN ESPAÑOL, P.O. Box 64383, St. Paul MN 55164-0383. (651)291-1970. Fax: (651)291-1908. E-mail: lwlpc@llewellyn.com. Website: www.llewellyn.com. **Acquisitions:** Maria Bloomberg, manager. Estab. 1993. Publishes mass market and trade paperback originals and reprints. **Publishes 24 titles/year. Receives 50 queries and 100 mss/year. 25% of books from first-time authors; 90% from unagented writers. Pays 10% royalty.** Publishes book 1 year after acceptance of ms. Accepts simultaneous submissions. Responds in 3 months to queries; 3 months to proposals; 1 month to mss. Book catalog online; ms guidelines online.

O-- Publishes Spanish-language books for people of any age interested in material discussing "mind, body and spirit."

Nonfiction: Gift book, how-to, self-help, teen/young adult. Subjects include general nonfiction, health/medicine, New Age, psychology, sex, spirituality, foods/nutrition; angels; magic. "Have it edited, including all ortographic punctuation and accents." Query with SASE or submit proposal package including outline, 4 sample chapter(s) or submit complete ms. Reviews artwork/photos as part of ms package. Send photocopies.

Recent Title(s): *Diccionario de los Suenos*, by Mario Jimenez Castillo; *Tao del Amente Perfecto*, by Mabel Iam.

LLEWELLYN PUBLICATIONS, Llewellyn Worldwide, Ltd., P.O. Box 64383, St. Paul MN 55164-0383. (651)291-1970. Fax: (651)291-1908. E-mail: lwlpc@llewellyn.com. Website: www.llewellyn.com. **Acquisitions:** Nancy J. Mostad, acquisitions manager (New Age, metaphysical, occult, astrology, tarot, wicca, pagan, magick, alternative health, self-help, how-to books). Estab. 1901. Publishes trade and mass market paperback originals. **Publishes 100 titles/year. Receives 2,000 submissions/year. 30% of books from first-time authors; 90% from unagented writers. Pays 10% royalty on**

wholesale price or retail price. Accepts simultaneous submissions. Responds in 3 months to queries. Book catalog for 9×12 SAE with 4 first-class stamps; ms guidelines online.

O→ Llewellyn publishes New Age fiction and nonfiction exploring "new worlds of mind and spirit." Currently emphasizing astrology, wicca, alternative health and healing, tarot. De-emphasizing fiction, channeling.

Nonfiction: How-to, self-help. Subjects include cooking/foods/nutrition, health/medicine, nature/environment, New Age, psychology, women's issues/studies. Submit outline, sample chapter(s). Reviews artwork/photos as part of ms package.

Fiction: "Authentic and educational, yet entertaining." Occult, spiritual (metaphysical). "Authentic and educational, yet entertaining."

Recent Title(s): *10 Spiritual Steps to a Magic Life*, by Adrian Calabrese, Ph.D.; *The Inner Temple of Witchcraft*, by Christopher Penczak.

LOCUST HILL PRESS, P.O. Box 260, West Cornwall CT 06796-0260. (860)672-0060. Fax: (860)672-4968. E-mail: locusthill@optonline.net. **Acquisitions:** Thomas C. Bechtle, publisher. Estab. 1985. Publishes hardcover originals. **Publishes 12 titles/year. Receives 150 queries and 20 mss/year. 100% from unagented writers. Pays 12% royalty on retail price. Offers advance.** Publishes book 6 months after acceptance of ms. Accepts simultaneous submissions. Responds in 2 months to queries. Book catalog free.

O→ Locust Hill Press specializes in essay collections on literary subjects but also publishes a small number of reference works as well.

Nonfiction: Reference. Subjects include ethnic, language/literature, women's issues/studies. "Since our audience is exclusively college and university libraries (and the occasional specialist), we are less inclined to accept manuscripts in 'popular' (i.e., public library) fields. Our Locust Hill Literary Studies is gaining popularity as a series of essay collections and monographs in a wide variety of literary topics." Query with SASE.

Recent Title(s): *A Companion to Brian Friel*, edited by Richard Harp and Robert Evans; *Prophetic Character: Essays on William Blake in Honor of John E. Grant*, edited by Alexander S. Gourlay; *In Their Own Words: An Index of Interviews with American Authors, 1945-2000*, by Jim McWilliams.

Tips: "Remember that this is a small, very specialized academic publisher with no distribution network other than mail contact with most academic libraries worldwide. Please shape your expectations accordingly. If your aim is to reach the world's scholarly community by way of its libraries, we are the correct firm to contact. But *please*: no fiction, poetry, popular religion, or personal memoirs."

LOFT PRESS, INC., P.O. Box 150, Fort Valley VA 22652. (540)933-6210. Website: www.loftpress.com. **Acquisitions:** Ann A. Hunter, editor-in-chief. Publishes hardcover and trade paperback originals and reprints. **Publishes 12-20 titles/year; imprint publishes 6-8 titles/year. Receives 200 queries and 150 mss/year. 50% of books from first-time authors; 100% from unagented writers. Pays royalty on net receipts.** Publishes book 6 months after acceptance of ms. Ms guidelines online.

Imprints: Punch Press, Eschat Press, Far Muse Press (for all contact Stephen R. Hunter, publisher).

Nonfiction: Biography, coffee table book, how-to, technical, textbook. Subjects include Americana, art/architecture, business/economics, computers/electronic, government/politics, history, language/literature, memoirs, philosophy, regional, religion, science. Submit proposal package including outline, 1 sample chapter(s). Reviews artwork/photos as part of ms package. Send photocopies.

Fiction: Literary, plays, poetry, poetry in translation, regional, short story collections. Submit proposal package including 1 sample chapter(s), synopsis.

Poetry: Submit 5 sample poems.

Recent Title(s): *Who Is God*, by Mohan Rao; *Light Ruck*, by Tom Lacombe.

LONE EAGLE PUBLISHING CO., 1024 N. Orange Dr., Hollywood CA 90038. (323)308-3411; (800)815-0503. E-mail: jblack@ifilm.com. Website: www.hdconline.com. **Acquisitions:** Jeff Black, editor. Estab. 1982. Publishes perfectbound and trade paperback originals. **Publishes 15 titles/year. Receives 100 submissions/year. 50% from unagented writers. Pays 10% royalty. Offers $2,500-5,000 average advance.** Publishes book 1 year after acceptance of ms. Accepts simultaneous submissions. Responds quarterly to queries. Book catalog free.

O→ Lone Eagle Publishing Company publishes reference directories that contain comprehensive and accurate credits, personal data and contact information for every major entertainment industry craft. Lone Eagle also publishes many 'how-to' books for the film production business, including books on screenwriting, directing, budgeting and producing, acting, editing, etc. Lone Eagle is broadening its base to include general entertainment titles.

Nonfiction: Biography, how-to, reference, technical. Subjects include film/cinema/stage, entertainment. "We are looking for books in film and television, related topics or biographies." Submit outline, sample chapter(s). Reviews artwork/photos as part of ms package.

Recent Title(s): *Elements of Style for Screenwriters*, by Paul Argentina; *1001: A Video Odyssey*, by Steve Tathan.

Tips: "A well-written, well-thought-out book on some technical aspect of the motion picture (or video) industry has the best chance. Pick a subject that has not been done to death, make sure you know what you're talking about, get someone well-known in that area to endorse the book and prepare to spend a lot of time publicizing the book. Completed manuscripts have the best chance for acceptance."

N **LONELY PLANET PUBLICATIONS**, 150 Linden St., Oakland CA 94607-2538. (510)893-8556. Fax: (510)893-8572. E-mail: info@lonelyplanet.com. Website: www.lonelyplanet.com. Estab. 1973. Publishes trade paperback originals. **Publishes 60 titles/year. Receives 500 queries and 100 mss/year. 5% of books from first-time authors; 100% from**

unagented writers. Work-for-hire: ⅓ on contract, ⅓ on submission, ⅓ on approval. Offers advance. Accepts simultaneous submissions. Responds in 3 months to queries. Ms guidelines online.

O→ Lonely Planet publishes travel guides, atlases, travel literature, diving and snorkeling guides.

Nonfiction: "We only work with contract writers on book ideas that we originate. We do not accept original proposals. Request our writer's guidelines. Send résumé and clips of travel writing." Subjects include travel. "Request our catalog first to make sure we don't already have a similar book or call and see if a similar book is on our production schedule."

Recent Title(s): *Las Vegas Condensed*; *Yosemite National Park*.

LOOMPANICS UNLIMITED, P.O. Box 1197, Port Townsend WA 98368-0997. Fax: (360)385-7785. E-mail: editorial@loompanics.com. Website: www.loompanics.com. President: Michael Hoy. **Acquisitions:** Gia Cosindas, editor. Estab. 1975. Publishes trade paperback originals. **Publishes 15 titles/year. Receives 500 submissions/year. 40% of books from first-time authors; 100% from unagented writers. Pays 10-15% royalty on wholesale price or retail price or makes outright purchase of $100-1,200. Offers $500 average advance.** Publishes book 1 year after acceptance of ms. Accepts simultaneous submissions. Responds in 3 months to queries. Book catalog for $5, postage paid; ms guidelines online.

O→ "Our motto 'No more secrets-no more excuses-no more limits' says it all, whatever the subject. Our books are somewhat 'edgy'. From computer hacking to gardening to tax avoision, we are the name in beat-the-system books." Currently emphasizing unusual takes on subjects that are controversial and how-to books. Does not want anything that's already been done or New Age.

Nonfiction: "In general, we like works about outrageous topics or obscure-but-useful technology written authoritatively in a matter-of-fact way. We are looking for how-to books in the fields of espionage, investigation, the underground economy, police methods, how to beat the system, crime and criminal techniques." How-to, reference, self-help, technical. Subjects include agriculture/horticulture, Americana, anthropology/archeology, computers/electronic, government/politics, health/medicine, money/finance, psychology, science, film/cinema/stage. "We are also looking for articles on similar subjects for our catalog and its supplements." Query with SASE or submit outline, sample chapter(s). Reviews artwork/photos as part of ms package.

Recent Title(s): *Don't Be a Victim*, by Michael Chesbro; *Guns Save Lives!*, by Robert A. Waters; *I Am Not a Number!*, by Claire Wolfe.

Tips: "Our audience is primarily young males looking for hard-to-find information on alternatives to 'The System.' Your chances for success are greatly improved if you can show us how your proposal fits in with our catalog."

[N] **LOST HORSE PRESS**, 105 Lost Horse Lane, Sandpoint ID 83864. (208)255-4410. Fax: (208)255-1560. E-mail: losthorsepress@mindspring.com. **Acquisitions:** Christine Holbert, editor (novels, novellas). Estab. 1998. Publishes hardcover and paperback originals. **Publishes 4 titles/year.** Publishes book 1-2 years after acceptance of ms. Responds in 3 months to queries; 6 months to mss. Book catalog free; ms guidelines for #10 SASE.

Fiction: Ethnic, experimental, literary, regional (Pacific NW), short story collections, translation. Accepts queries by e-mail. Accepts submissions on disk. Query with SASE or submit publishing history, author bio, SASE or submit complete ms. Submit cover letter.

Recent Title(s): *Woman on the Cross*, by Pierre Delattre (novel); *Iron Fever*, by Stephan Torre (poetry); *Hiding from Salesmen*, by Scott Poole (poetry).

LOUISIANA STATE UNIVERSITY PRESS, P.O. Box 25053, Baton Rouge LA 70894-5053. (225)578-6294. Fax: (225)578-6461. **Acquisitions:** Sylvia Frank, editor-in-chief. Estab. 1935. Publishes hardcover originals, hardcover and trade paperback reprints. **Publishes 70-80 titles/year. Receives 800 submissions/year. 33% of books from first-time authors; 95% from unagented writers. Pays royalty.** Publishes book 1 year after acceptance of ms. Does not accept simultaneous submissions. Responds in 1 month to queries. Book catalog and ms guidelines free.

Nonfiction: Biography. Subjects include art/architecture, ethnic, government/politics, history, language/literature, music/dance, photography, regional, women's issues/studies. Query with SASE or submit outline, sample chapter(s).

Poetry: Literary.

Recent Title(s): *The Collected Poems of Robert Penn Warren* (poetry); *Lee and His Generals in War and Memory*, by Gary W. Gallagher (history).

Tips: "Our audience includes scholars, intelligent laymen, general audience."

LOVE SPELL, Dorchester Publishing Co., Inc., 276 Fifth Ave., Suite 1008, New York NY 10001-0112. (212)725-8811. Fax: (212)532-1054. Website: www.dorchesterpub.com. **Acquisitions:** Ashley Kuehl, editorial assistant; Kate Seaver, editor; Christopher Keeslar, senior editor. Publishes mass market paperback originals. **Publishes 48 titles/year. Receives 1,500-2,000 queries and 150-500 mss/year. 30% of books from first-time authors; 25-30% from unagented writers. Pays 4% royalty on retail price. Offers $2,000 average advance.** Publishes book 1 year after acceptance of ms. Does not accept simultaneous submissions. Responds in 6 months to mss. Book catalog for free (800)481-9191; ms guidelines online.

O→ Love Spell publishes the quirky sub-genres of romance: time-travel, paranormal, futuristic. "Despite the exotic settings, we are still interested in character-driven plots." Love Spell has 2 humor lines including both contemporary and historical romances.

Fiction: Romance (futuristic, time travel, paranormal, historical), science fiction, futuristic, time travel, whimsical contemporaries. "Books industry-wide are getting shorter; we're interested in 90,000 words." Query with SASE or submit 3 sample chapter(s), synopsis. No material will be returned without SASE. Query first. No queries by fax. "All mss must be typed, double-spaced on one side and left unbound."

Recent Title(s): *Dr. Yes*, by Lisa Cach; *Improper English*, by Katie MacAlister.

LOYOLA PRESS, 3441 N. Ashland Ave., Chicago IL 60657-1397. (773)281-1818. Fax: (773)281-0152. E-mail: editorial@loyolapress.com. Website: www.loyolapress.org. **Acquisitions:** Joseph Durepos, acquisitions editor (religion, spirituality). Estab. 1912. Publishes hardcover and trade paperback originals. **Publishes 30 titles/year. Receives 500 queries/year. 5% of books from first-time authors; 50% from unagented writers. Pays 15-18% royalty on wholesale price. Offers reasonable advance.** Publishes book 1 year after acceptance of ms. Accepts simultaneous submissions. Responds in 1 month to queries; 3 months to proposals. Book catalog and ms guidelines online; ms guidelines online.

Imprints: Jesuit Way

Nonfiction: Subjects include religion, spirituality, inspirational, prayer, Catholic life, grief and loss, marriage and family. *Jesuit Way* books focus on Jesuit life and history as well as on Ignatian spirituality and ministry. Query with SASE.

Recent Title(s): *Go in Peace*, by Pope John Paul II; *The New Faithful*, by Colleen Carroll; *Waiting with Gabriel*, by Amy Kuebelbeck.

Tips: "We're looking for authors who have a fresh approach to religion and spirituality, especially for readers looking for a way to respond to God in their daily lives. We are a trade publisher of religious books for a broad market of readers with Catholic or sacramental interests. We do not publish academic books, fiction or poetry, or books for religious professionals. We do publish in the area of Catholic faith formation. Study our guidelines."

LRP PUBLICATIONS, INC., P.O. Box 980, Horsham PA 19044-0980. (215)784-0860. Fax: (215)784-9639. E-mail: custserve@lrp.com. Website: www.lrp.com. **Acquisitions:** Claude Werder, VP of editorial. Estab. 1977. Publishes hardcover and trade paperback originals. **Publishes 50 titles/year. Receives 15 queries and 12 mss/year. 95% of books from first-time authors; 100% from unagented writers. Pays royalty. Offers $0-1,000 advance.** Publishes book 9 months after acceptance of ms. Does not accept simultaneous submissions. Responds in 1 month to queries; 2 months to proposals; 3 months to mss. Book catalog free; ms guidelines free.

Nonfiction: Reference. Subjects include business/economics, education. Submit proposal package including outline.

Recent Title(s): *Preventing and Responding to Workplace Sexual Harassment*, Christopher McNeill.

LUCENT BOOKS, 10911 Technology Place, San Diego CA 92127. **Acquisitions:** Chandra Howard, acquisitions editor. Estab. 1988. **Publishes 200 titles/year. 10% of books from first-time authors; 90% from unagented writers. Makes outright purchase of $2,500-3,000.** Query with cover letter, résumé, list of publications, and 9×12 SAE with 3 first-class stamps for book catalog and ms guidelines.

Lucent Books is a non-trade publisher of nonfiction for the middle school audience providing students with resource material for academic studies and for independent learning.

Nonfiction: Children's/juvenile. Subjects include history, world affairs, cultural and social issues. "We produce tightly formatted books for middle grade readers. Each series has specific requirements. Potential writers should familiarize themselves with our material." All are works for hire, by assignment only. No unsolicited mss accepted.

Recent Title(s): *J.K. Rowling*, by Bradley Steffans; *Life in the Trenches*, by Stephen Currie; *Women of the American Revolution*, by Louise Chipley Slavicek.

Tips: "We expect writers to do thorough research using books, magazines and newspapers. Biased writing, whether liberal or conservative, has no place in our books. We prefer to work with writers who have experience writing nonfiction for middle grade students. We are looking for experienced writers, especially those who have written nonfiction books at young adult level."

THE LYONS PRESS, an imprint of The Globe Pequot Press, Inc., 246 Goose Lane, Guilford CT 06437. (203)458-4500. Fax: (203)458-4668. Website: www.lyonspress.com. Publisher/Editorial Director: Tony Lyons. **Acquisitions:** Lilly Golden, editor-at-large (fiction, memoirs, narrative nonfiction); Jay Cassell, senior editor (fishing, hunting, survival, military, history, gardening); Jay McCullough, editor (narrative nonfiction, travelogues, adventure, military, espionage, international current events, fishing); Tom McCarthy, senior editor (sports & fitness, history, outdoor adventure, memoirs); Ann Treistman, editor (narrative nonfiction, travelogues, adventure, sports, animals, cooking); Lisa Purcell, editor-at-large (history, adventure, narrative nonfiction, cooking, gardening); George Donahue, senior editor; Enrica Gadler, editor-at-large; Alicia Solis. Estab. 1984 (Lyons & Burford), 1997 (The Lyons Press). Publishes hardcover and trade paperback originals and reprints. **Publishes 240 titles/year. 50% of books from first-time authors; 30% from unagented writers. Pays 5-10% royalty on wholesale price. Offers $2,000-7,000 advance.** Publishes book 1 year after acceptance of ms. Accepts simultaneous submissions. Responds in 1 month to queries; 1 month to proposals; 2 months to mss. Book catalog online; ms guidelines online.

- The Lyons Press has teamed up to develop books with L.L. Bean, *Field & Stream*, Orvis, Outward Bound, Buckmasters and *Golf Magazine*. It was recently purchased by Globe Pequot Press.

The Lyons Press publishes practical and literary books, chiefly centered on outdoor subjects—natural history, all sports, gardening, horses, fishing. Currently emphasizing adventure, sports. De-emphasizing hobbies, travel.

Nonfiction: Biography, cookbook, how-to, reference. Subjects include agriculture/horticulture, Americana, animals, anthropology/archeology, cooking/foods/nutrition, gardening, health/medicine, history, hobbies, military/war, nature/environment (environment), recreation, science, sports, travel. "Visit our website and note the featured categories." Query with SASE or submit proposal package including outline, 3 sample chapter(s). and marketing description. Reviews artwork/photos as part of ms package. Send photocopies or non-original prints.

Fiction: Historical, military/war, short story collections (fishing, hunting, outdoor, nature), sports. Query with SASE or submit proposal package including outline, 3-5 sample chapter(s).

Recent Title(s): *Facing Ali*, by Stephen Brunt (sports); *Zane Grey on Fishing* (fishing); *The Faraway Horses*, by Buck Brannaman (horses).

MACADAM/CAGE PUBLISHING, INC., 155 Sansome St., Suite 550, San Francisco CA 94104. (415)986-7502. Fax: (415)986-7414. E-mail: info@macadamcage.com. Website: www.macadamcage.com. Publisher: David Poindexter. **Acquisitions:** Patrick Walsh, editor; Anika Streitfeld, editor. Estab. 1999. Publishes hardcover and trade paperback originals. **Publishes 25 titles/year. Receives 5,000 queries and 1,500 mss/year. 75% of books from first-time authors; 50% from unagented writers. Pays negotiable royalties. Offers negotiable advance.** Publishes book up to 1 year after acceptance of ms. Accepts simultaneous submissions. Responds in 4 months to queries; 4 months to mss. Ms guidelines for SASE or on website.

O→ MacAdam/Cage publishes quality works of literary fiction that are carefully crafted and tell a bold story. De-emphasizing romance, poetry, Christian or New Age mss.

Nonfiction: Biography. Subjects include history, memoirs, science, social sciences. "Narrative nonfiction that reads like fiction." No self-help or New Age. Submit proposal package including outline, up to 3 sample chapter(s), SASE.

Fiction: Historical, literary, mainstream/contemporary. No electronic or faxed submissions. No romance, science fiction, Christian, New Age. Submit proposal package including up to 3 sample chapter(s), synopsis, SASE.

Recent Title(s): *Ella Minnow Pea*, by Mark Dunn (fiction); *The Time Traveler's Wife*, by Audrey Niffenegger (fiction).

Tips: "We like to keep in close contact with writers. We publish for readers of quality fiction and nonfiction."

N **MADE E-Z PRODUCTS, INC.**, 384 S. Military Trail, Deerfield Beach FL 33442. (954)480-8933. Fax: (954)480-8906. E-mail: acquisitions@madee-z.com. Website: www.madee-z.com. **Acquisitions:** Janet Trakin, director of rights, licensing, and acquisitions (business, legal, financial, self-help); Dr. Arnold Goldstein, chairman (business, legal, financial, self-help). Publishes trade paperback and electronic originals. **Publishes 8 titles/year. Receives 20 queries and 35 mss/year. 15% of books from first-time authors; 50% from unagented writers. Pays 10% royalty on wholesale price.** Publishes book 6 months after acceptance of ms. Accepts simultaneous submissions. Responds in 1 month to queries; 1 month to proposals; 1 month to mss. Book catalog free.

Nonfiction: How-to. Subjects include business/economics, money/finance. "We require 200 pages minimum in the self-help, business, financial, and legal fields." Submit complete ms. Reviews artwork/photos as part of ms package. Send photocopies.

Recent Title(s): *Organizing Your Home Business*, by Lisa Kanarek (self-help); *Teleworking & Telecommuting*, by Jeff Zbar (self-help).

Tips: "Our audience is interested in business, legal, and financial matters."

MAGE PUBLISHERS, INC., 1032 29th St. NW, Washington DC 20007. (202)342-1642. Fax: (202)342-9269. E-mail: info@mage.com. Website: www.mage.com. **Acquisitions:** Amin Sepehri, assistant to publisher. Estab. 1985. Publishes hardcover originals and reprints, trade paperback originals. **Publishes 4 titles/year. Receives 40 queries and 20 mss/year. 10% of books from first-time authors; 95% from unagented writers. Pays royalty. Offers $250-1,500 advance.** Publishes book 8-16 months after acceptance of ms. Accepts simultaneous submissions. Responds in 1 month to queries; 1 month to proposals; 3 months to mss. Book catalog free; ms guidelines online.

O→ Mage publishes books relating to Persian/Iranian culture.

Nonfiction: Biography, children's/juvenile, coffee table book, cookbook, gift book, illustrated book. Subjects include anthropology/archeology, art/architecture, cooking/foods/nutrition, ethnic, history, language/literature, music/dance, sociology, translation. Query with SASE. Reviews artwork/photos as part of ms package. Send photocopies.

Fiction: Ethnic, feminist, historical, literary, mainstream/contemporary, short story collections. Must relate to Persian/Iranian culture. Query with SASE.

Poetry: Must relate to Persian/Iranian culture. Query.

Recent Title(s): *A Taste of Persia*, N. Batmanglis (cooking); *The Lion and the Throne*, Ferdowsi (mythology).

Tips: Audience is the Iranian-American community in America and Americans interested in Persian culture.

THE MAGNI GROUP, INC., 7106 Wellington Point Rd., McKinney TX 75070. (972)540-2050. Fax: (972)540-1057. E-mail: info@magnico.com. Website: www.magnico.com. **Acquisitions:** Evan Reynolds, president. Publishes hardcover originals and trade paperback reprints. **Publishes 5-10 titles/year. Receives 20 queries and 10-20 mss/year. 50% of books from first-time authors; 80% from unagented writers. Pays royalty on wholesale price or makes outright purchase. Offers advance.** Publishes book 6 months after acceptance of ms. Does not accept simultaneous submissions. Responds in 2 months to queries. Book catalog and ms guidelines online.

Imprints: Magni Publishing.

Nonfiction: Cookbook, how-to, self-help. Subjects include child guidance/parenting, cooking/foods/nutrition, health/medicine, money/finance, sex. Submit complete ms. Reviews artwork/photos as part of ms package. Send photocopies.

Recent Title(s): *Eat Like the Stars Cookbook*; *Holiday Planner*; *Birthday Planner*.

MAISONNEUVE PRESS, P.O. Box 2980, Washington DC 20013-2980. (301)277-7505. Fax: (301)277-2467. E-mail: editors@maisonneuvepress.com. Website: www.maisonneuvepress.com. **Acquisitions:** Robert Merrill, editor (politics, literature, philosophy); Dennis Crow, editor (architecture, urban studies, sociology). Publishes hardcover and trade paperback originals. **Publishes 6 titles/year. 5% of books from first-time authors; 100% from unagented writers. Pays 5% royalty on cover price or $2,000 maximum outright purchase.** Publishes book 1 year after acceptance of ms. Accepts simultaneous submissions. Responds in 1 month to queries; 1 month to proposals; 1 month to mss. Book catalog free; Send letter for guidelines, individual response.

O→ "Maisonneuve provides solid, first-hand information for serious adult readers: academics and political activists."

Nonfiction: Biography. Subjects include education, ethnic, gay/lesbian, government/politics, history, language/literature, military/war, philosophy, psychology, sociology, translation, women's issues/studies, literary criticism, social theory, economics, essay collections. "We make decisions on completed mss only. Will correspond on work in progress. Some books submitted are too narrowly focused; not marketable enough. We are eager to read mss on the current crisis and war. The commercial media—TV and newspapers—are not doing a very good job of cutting through the government propaganda." Query with SASE or submit complete ms. Reviews artwork/photos as part of ms package. Send photocopies.

Recent Title(s): *Morse Peckham, Man's Rage for Chaos: Biology, Behavior and the Arts.*

[N] **MANDALEY PRESS**, subsidiary of Solution Resources, 720 Rio Grande Dr., Suite 100, Alpharetta GA 30022. (770)643-8455. E-mail: msatt@mindspring.com. **Acquisitions:** Mark Satterfield, president (business books with a particular interest in sales training). Estab. 2001. Publishes hardcover, trade paperback, and mass market paperback originals. **Publishes 10 titles/year; imprint publishes 10 titles/year. Receives 50 queries and 50 mss/year. 80% of books from first-time authors; 100% from unagented writers. Pays 10-20% royalty on wholesale price.** Publishes book 6 months after acceptance of ms. Accepts simultaneous submissions. Responds in 1 month to queries; 2 months to proposals; 2 months to mss.

Nonfiction: Audiocassettes, booklets, how-to, self-help. Subjects include business/economics. "We are looking for authors in the sales marketing arena with a value-added message. There are many books currently available that focus on 'what' successful sales professionals do. We are interested in 'how' specifically to achieve success." No books on a "winning attitude." Query with SASE. Reviews artwork/photos as part of ms package.

[A] **MARINER BOOKS**, Houghton Mifflin, 222 Berkeley St., Boston MA 02116. (617)351-5000. Fax: (617)351-1202. Website: www.hmco.com. **Acquisitions:** Susan Canavan, managing director. Estab. 1997. Publishes trade paperback originals and reprints. **Pays royalty on retail price or makes outright purchase. Offers variable advance.** Responds in 4 months to mss. Book catalog free.

O→ Houghton Mifflin books give shape to ideas that educate, inform and delight. Mariner has an eclectic list that notably embraces fiction.

Nonfiction: Biography. Subjects include education, government/politics, history, nature/environment, philosophy, sociology, women's issues/studies, political thought. *Agented submissions only.*

Fiction: Literary, mainstream/contemporary. *Agented submissions only.*

Recent Title(s): *Red Ant House*, by Ann Cummins; *Atomic Farm Girl*, by Teri Hein.

MARLOR PRESS, INC., 4304 Brigadoon Dr., St. Paul MN 55126. (651)484-4600. E-mail: marlin.marlor@minn.net. **Acquisitions:** Marlin Bree, publisher. Estab. 1981. Publishes trade paperback originals. **Publishes 6 titles/year. Receives 100 queries and 25 mss/year. Pays 8-10% royalty on wholesale price.** Publishes book 1 year after acceptance of ms. Does not accept simultaneous submissions. Responds in 3-6 weeks to queries. Ms guidelines for #10 SASE.

O→ Currently emphasizing general interest nonfiction children's books and nonfiction boating books. De-emphasizing travel.

Nonfiction: Children's/juvenile, how-to. Subjects include travel, boating. "Primarily how-to stuff." No unsolicited mss. No anecdotal reminiscences or biographical materials. No fiction or poetry. Query first; submit outline with sample chapters only when requested. Do not send full ms. Reviews artwork/photos as part of ms package.

Recent Title(s): *Going Abroad: The Bathroom Survival Guide*, by Eva Newman; *Wake of the Green Storm: A Survivor's Tale*, by Marlin Bree.

McBOOKS PRESS, 1D Booth Building, 520 N. Meadow St., Ithaca NY 14850. (607)272-2114. Fax: (607)273-6068. E-mail: mcbooks@mcbooks.com. Website: www.mcbooks.com. Publisher: Alexander G. Skutt. **Acquisitions:** Ellen Porter, editorial director. Estab. 1979. Publishes trade paperback and hardcover originals and reprints. **Publishes 20 titles/year. Pays 5-10% royalty on retail price. Offers $1,000-5,000 advance.** Accepts simultaneous submissions. Responds in 1 month to queries; 2 months to proposals. Ms guidelines online.

- "We are booked nearly solid for the next few years. We can only consider the highest quality projects in our narrow interest areas."

O→ Currently emphasizing nautical and military historical fiction.

Nonfiction: Subjects include regional (New York state), vegetarianism and veganism. "Authors' ability to promote a plus." No unsolicited mss. Query with SASE.

Fiction: Historical (nautical), nautical and military historical. Query with SASE.

Recent Title(s): *Motoo Eetee*, by Irv C. Rogers; *The Boxing Register, 3rd Ed*, by James B. Roberts and Alexander G. Skutt; *Between Two Fires*, by Nicholas Nicastro.

McDONALD & WOODWARD PUBLISHING CO., 431-B E. Broadway, Granville OH 43023-1310. (740)321-1140. Fax: (740)321-1141. Website: www.mwpubco.com. **Acquisitions:** Jerry N. McDonald, managing partner/publisher. Estab. 1986. Publishes hardcover and trade paperback originals. **Publishes 8 titles/year. Receives 100 queries and 20 mss/year. 50% of books from first-time authors; 100% from unagented writers. Pays 10% royalty on net receipts.** Publishes book 1 year after acceptance of ms. Accepts simultaneous submissions. Responds in 2 weeks to queries. Book catalog free.

O→ "McDonald & Woodward publishes books in natural and cultural history." Currently emphasizing travel, natural and cultural history. De-emphasizing self-help.

Nonfiction: Biography, coffee table book, illustrated book. Subjects include Americana, animals, anthropology/archeology, ethnic, history, nature/environment, science, travel. Query with SASE or submit outline, sample chapter(s). Reviews artwork/photos as part of ms package. Send photocopies.

Recent Title(s): *The Carousel Keepers: An Oral History of American Carousels*, by Carrie Papa; *A Guide to Common Freshwater Invertebrates of North America*, by J. Reese Voshell; *Juan Ponce de Leon and the Spanish Discovery of Puerto Rico and Florida*, by Robert H. Fuson.

Tips: "We are especially interested in additional titles in our 'Guides to the American Landscape' series. Should consult titles in print for guidance. We want well-organized, clearly written, substantive material."

MARGARET K. McELDERRY BOOKS, Simon & Schuster Children's Publishing Division, Simon & Schuster, 1230 Sixth Ave., New York NY 10020. (212)698-2761. Fax: (212)698-2796. Website: www.simonsayskids.com. Vice President/Publisher: Brenda Bowen. **Acquisitions:** Emma D. Dryden, vice president/editorial director (books for preschoolers to 16-year-olds); Sarah Nielsen, assistant editor. Estab. 1971. Publishes quality material for preschoolers to 18-year-olds. Publishes hardcover originals. **Publishes 25-30 titles/year. Receives 4,000 queries/year. 15% of books from first-time authors; 50% from unagented writers. Average print order is 4,000-6,000 for a first middle grade or young adult book; 7,500-15,000 for a first picture book. Pays royalty on hardcover retail price: 10% fiction, picture book; 5% author; 5% illustrator. Offers $5,000-8,000 advance for new authors.** Publishes book up to 3 years after acceptance of ms. Ms guidelines for #10 SASE.

- "We are more interested in superior writing and illustration than in a particular 'type' of book." Currently emphasizing young picture books and funny middle grade fiction.

Nonfiction: Biography, children's/juvenile. Subjects include history, adventure. "Read. The field is competitive. See what's been done and what's out there before submitting. Looks for originality of ideas, clarity and felicity of expression, well-organized plot and strong characterization (fiction) or clear exposition (nonfiction); quality. Accept query letters with SASE only." *No unsolicited mss.*

Fiction: Adventure, fantasy, historical, mainstream/contemporary, mystery, picture books, young adult (or middle grade), All categories (fiction and nonfiction) for juvenile and young adult. "We will consider any category. Results depend on the quality of the imagination, the artwork and the writing." No unsolicited mss. Send query letter with SASE only for picture books; query letter with first 3 chapters, SASE for middle grade and young adult novels.

Poetry: *No unsolicited mss.* Query or submit 3 sample poems.

Recent Title(s): *Bear Wants More*, by Karma Wilson and Jane Chapman (picture book); *Shout, Sister, Shout!*, by Roxane Orgill (nonfiction); *Saffy's Angel*, by Hilary McKay (middle grade fiction).

Tips: "Read! The children's book field is competitive. See what's been done and what's out there before submitting. We look for high quality: an originality of ideas, clarity and felicity of expression, a well-organized plot and strong character-driven stories."

McFARLAND & CO, INC., PUBLISHERS, Box 611, Jefferson NC 28640. (336)246-4460. Fax: (336)246-5018. E-mail: info@mcfarlandpub.com. Website: www.mcfarlandpub.com. **Acquisitions:** Steve Wilson, senior editor (automotive, general); Virginia Tobiassen, editorial development chief (general, medieval history, bilingual works); Gary Mitchem, assistant editor (genreral, baseball). Estab. 1979. Publishes hardcover and "quality" paperback originals; a "non-trade" publisher. **Publishes 250 titles/year. Receives 1,400 submissions/year. 70% of books from first-time authors; 95% from unagented writers. Pays 10-12½% royalty on net receipts.** Publishes book 10 months after acceptance of ms. Responds in 1 month to queries. Ms guidelines online.

- McFarland publishes serious nonfiction in a variety of fields, including general reference, performing arts, sports (particularly baseball); women's studies, librarianship, literature, Civil War, history and international studies. Currently emphasizing medieval history, automotive history, Spanish-English bilingual works. De-emphasizing memoirs.

Nonfiction: Reference (and scholarly), scholarly, technical, professional monographs. Subjects include art/architecture, business/economics, contemporary culture, ethnic, film/cinema/stage, health/medicine, history, music/dance, recreation, sociology, sports (very strong), women's issues/studies (very strong), world affairs, African-American studies (very strong), chess, Civil War, drama/theater, cinema/radio/TV (very strong), librarianship (very strong), pop culture, world affairs (very strong). Reference books are particularly wanted—fresh material (i.e., not in head-to-head competition with an established title). "We prefer manuscripts of 250 or more double-spaced pages." No fiction, New Age, exposés, poetry, children's books, devotional/inspirational works, Bible studies or personal essays. Query with SASE or submit outline, sample chapter(s). Reviews artwork/photos as part of ms package.

Recent Title(s): *Encyclopedia of Abortion in the United States*, by Louis J. Palmer; *The Women of Afghanistan Under the Taliban*, by Rosemarie Skaine.

Tips: "We want well-organized knowledge of an area in which there is not information coverage at present, plus reliability so we don't feel we have to check absolutely everything. Our market is worldwide and libraries are an important part." McFarland also publishes the *Journal of Information Ethics*.

McGAVICK FIELD PUBLISHING, 118 N. Cherry, Olathe KS 66061. (913)780-1973. Fax: (913)782-1765. E-mail: fhernan@prodigy.net. Website: www.abcnanny.com. **Publishes 4 titles/year.** Does not accept simultaneous submissions. Fax or e-mail for ms guidelines.

- McGavick Field publishes handbooks dealing with life situations, parent care, child care. "We are looking for books that can be published in the format of *The ABCs of Hiring a Nanny*, accompanied by a companion disk and website."

Nonfiction: Biography, how-to, humor, reference, self-help. Subjects include business/economics, child guidance/parenting, computers/electronic, government/politics, humor, women's issues/studies.

Recent Title(s): *The ABCs of Credit*; *Too Much Information, not enough time to read the small print.*

Tips: "We are looking for manuscripts that deal with life style issues and the various government agencies that are set up to protect us as consumers."

N **McGRAW-HILL TRADE**, The McGraw-Hill Companies, 2 Penn Plaza, 11th Floor, New York NY 10121. (212)904-2000. Fax: (212)904-6096. Website: www.books.mcgraw-hill.com/business/contact.html. Publisher: Philip Ruppel. **Publishes 550 titles/year. Receives 1,200 queries and 1,200 mss/year. Offers advance.** Publishes book 1 year after acceptance of ms. Accepts simultaneous submissions. Responds in 3 months to queries. Ms guidelines online.

O→ "McGraw Hill Trade is a major nonfiction reference publisher in three distinct areas: business reference, self-help, sports/fitness, education, and consumer reference."

Nonfiction: How-to, reference, self-help, technical. Subjects include business/economics, child guidance/parenting, education (study guides), health/medicine, money/finance, sports (fitness), management, consumer reference, English and foreign language reference. "Current, up-to-date, original ideas are needed. Good self-promotion is key." Submit proposal package including outline, TOC, concept of book.

Recent Title(s): *More than a Pink Cadillac*, by Jim Underwood; *Leadership Secrets of Colin Powell*, by Oren Harari; *Fat Flush Plan*, by Anne Louise Gittleman.

MCGRAW-HILL/OSBORNE, The McGraw-Hill Companies, 2100 Powell St., 10th Floor, Emeryville CA 94608. (800)227-0900. Website: www.osborne.com. **Acquisitions:** Scott Rogers, editor-in-chief/vice president; Wendy Rinaldi, editorial director (programming, databases and web development); Gareth Hancock, editorial director (certification); Roger Stewart, editorial director (consumer technology); Tracey Dunkelberger, editorial director of networking. Estab. 1979. Publishes computer trade paperback originals. **Publishes 200 titles/year. Receives 500 submissions/year. 25% of books from first-time authors; 50% from unagented writers. Pays 7½-12% royalty on net receipts. Offers varying advance.** Publishes book 4-8 months after acceptance of ms. Responds in 2 weeks to proposals. Book catalog online; ms guidelines online.

O→ Publishes technical computer books and software with an emphasis on emerging technologies.

Nonfiction: Reference, technical. Subjects include computers/electronic, software (and hardware). Query with SASE or submit proposal package including outline, sample chapter(s), SASE. Reviews artwork/photos as part of ms package.

Recent Title(s): *All-in-One A+ Exam Guide*, by Meyers; *Hacking Exposéd*, by McClure, Scambray and Kurtz.

Tips: "A leader in self-paced training and skills development tools on information technology and computers."

McGREGOR PUBLISHING, 4532 W. Kennedy Blvd., Suite 233, Tampa FL 33609. (813)805-2665 or (888)405-2665. Fax: (813)832-6777. E-mail: mcgregpub@aol.com. **Acquisitions:** Dave Rosenbaum, acquisitions editor. Publishes hardcover and trade paperback originals. **Publishes 15-20 titles/year. Receives 150 queries and 40 mss/year. 75% of books from first-time authors; 80% from unagented writers. Pays 10-12% royalty on retail price; 13-16% on wholesale price. Offers variable advance.** Publishes book 1 year after acceptance of ms. Accepts simultaneous submissions. Responds in 2 months to queries; 2 months to proposals; 3 months to mss. Book catalog and ms guidelines free.

- McGregor no longer publishes fiction.

O→ "We specialize in nonfiction books that 'tell the story behind the story.' " Currently emphasizing true crime, sports. De-emphasizing self-help.

Nonfiction: "We're always looking for regional nonfiction titles, and especially for sports, biographies, true crime and how-to books." Biography, how-to. Subjects include business/economics, ethnic, history, money/finance, regional, sports, true crime. Query with SASE or submit outline, 2 sample chapter(s).

Recent Title(s): *Home Ice: Reflections on Frozen Ponds and Backyard Rinks*, by Jack Falls (nonfiction).

Tips: "We pride ourselves on working closely with an author and producing a quality product with strong promotional campaigns."

MEADOWBROOK PRESS, 5451 Smetana Dr., Minnetonka MN 55343. (952)930-1100. Fax: (952)930-1940. Website: www.meadowbrookpress.com. **Acquisitions:** Submissions Editor. Estab. 1975. Publishes trade paperback originals and reprints. **Publishes 12 titles/year. Receives 1,500 queries/year. 10% of books from first-time authors. Pays 10% royalty. Offers small advance.** Publishes book 1 year after acceptance of ms. Accepts simultaneous submissions. Responds in 4 months to queries. Book catalog and ms guidelines for #10 SASE; ms guidelines online.

O→ Meadowbrook is a family-oriented press which specializes in parenting and pregnancy books, party planning books.

Nonfiction: How-to, reference. Subjects include child guidance/parenting, cooking/foods/nutrition, pregnancy, childbirth, party planning, children's activities, relationships. "We prefer a query first; then we will request an outline and/or sample material." Send for guidelines. No children's fiction, poetry, academic or biography. Query with SASE or submit outline, sample chapter(s).

Recent Title(s): *365 Baby Care Tips*, by Penny Warner (parenting); *Themed Baby Showers*, by Becky Long (party planning).

Tips: "Always send for guidelines before submitting material. We do not accept unsolicited picture book submissions."

MEDICAL PHYSICS PUBLISHING, 4513 Vernon Blvd., Madison WI 53705. (608)262-4021. Fax: (608)265-2121. E-mail: mpp@medicalphysics.org. Website: www.medicalphysics.org. **Acquisitions:** John Cameron, president; Betsey Phelps, managing editor. Estab. 1985. Publishes hardcover and paperback originals and reprints. **Publishes 10-12 titles/year. Receives 10-20 queries/year. 100% from unagented writers. Pays 10% royalty on wholesale price.** Publishes book 6 months after acceptance of ms. Accepts simultaneous submissions. Responds in 6 months to mss. Book catalog available via website or upon request.

O→ "We are a nonprofit, membership organization publishing affordable books in medical physics and related fields." Currently emphasizing biomedical engineering. De-emphasizing books for the general public.

Nonfiction: Reference, technical, textbook. Subjects include health/medicine, symposium proceedings in the fields of medical physics and radiology. Submit complete ms. Reviews artwork/photos as part of ms package. Send disposable copies.

Recent Title(s): *The Modern Technology of Radiation Oncology*, edited by Jacob Van Dyk; *Physics of the Body*, by John R. Cameron, James G. Skofronick and Roderick M. Grant.

N **MENASHA RIDGE PRESS**, P.O. Box 43059, Birmingham AL 35243. (205)322-0439. E-mail: rhelms@menasharidge.com. Website: www.menasharidge.com. **Acquisitions:** Bud Zehmer, senior acquisitions editor (outdoors); Molly Merkle, associate publisher (travel, reference); Russell Helms, senior acquisitions editor. Publishes hardcover and trade paperback originals. **Publishes 20 titles/year. Receives 600-800 submissions/year. 30% of books from first-time authors; 85% from unagented writers. Pays varying royalty. Offers varying advance.** Publishes book 1 year after acceptance of ms. Accepts simultaneous submissions. Responds in 2 months to queries. Book catalog for 9×12 SAE with 4 first-class stamps.

- Menasha Ridge Press publishes "distinctive books in the areas of outdoor sports, travel and diving. Our authors are among the best in their fields."

Nonfiction: How-to, humor, travel guides. Subjects include recreation (outdoor), sports (adventure), travel, outdoors. "Most concepts are generated in-house, but a few come from outside submissions." Submit proposal package including résumé, synopsis. Reviews artwork/photos as part of ms package.

Recent Title(s): *Land Between the Lakes Recreation Guide*, by Johnny Molloy.

Tips: Audience is 25-60, 14-18 years' education, white collar and professional, $30,000 median income, 75% male, 55% east of the Mississippi River.

MERIWETHER PUBLISHING, LTD., 885 Elkton Dr., Colorado Springs CO 80907-3557. (719)594-4422. Fax: (719)594-9916. E-mail: merpeds@aol.com. Website: www.meriwetherpublishing.com; www.contemporarydrama.com. **Acquisitions:** Arthur Zapel, Theodore Zapel, Rhonda Wray, editors. Estab. 1969. Publishes paperback originals and reprints. **Receives 1,200 submissions/year. 50% of books from first-time authors; 90% from unagented writers. Pays 10% royalty on retail price or makes outright purchase.** Publishes book 6-12 months after acceptance of ms. Accepts simultaneous submissions. Responds in 3 weeks to queries; 2 months to mss. Book catalog and ms guidelines for $2 postage.

- Meriwether publishes theater books, games and videos; speech resources; plays, skits and musicals; and resources for gifted students. "We specialize in books on the theatre arts and religious plays for Christmas, Easter and youth activities. We also publish musicals for high school performers and churches." Currently emphasizing how-to books for theatrical arts and church youth activities.

Nonfiction: "We publish unusual textbooks or trade books related to the communication or performing arts and how-to books on staging, costuming, lighting, etc." How-to, humor, reference, textbook. Subjects include performing arts, theater/drama. "We prefer mainstream religion theatre titles." Query or submit outline/synopsis and sample chapters.

Fiction: Plays and musicals for middle grades through college only. Humor, mainstream/contemporary, mystery, plays (and musicals), religious (children's plays and religious Christmas and Easter plays), suspense, all in playscript format. Query with SASE.

Recent Title(s): *International Plays for Young Audiences*, by Roger Ellis; *Spontaneous Performance*, by Marsh Cassady.

Tips: "Our educational books are sold to teachers and students at college, high school and middle school levels. Our religious books are sold to youth activity directors, pastors and choir directors. Our trade books are directed at the public with a tie to the performing arts. Another group of buyers is the professional theatre, radio and TV category. We focus more on books of plays and short scenes and textbooks on directing, staging, make-up, lighting, etc."

MERRIAM PRESS, 218 Beech St., Bennington VT 05201-2611. (802)447-0313. Fax: (305)847-5978. E-mail: ray@merriam-press.com. Website: www.merriam-press.com. Publishes hardcover and trade paperback originals and reprints. **Publishes 12 titles/year. Receives 100 queries and 50 mss/year. 70-90% of books from first-time authors; 95% from unagented writers. Pays 10% royalty on retail price.** Publishes book 1 year or less after acceptance of ms. Does not accept simultaneous submissions. Responds quickly to queries; e-mail preferred to queries. Book catalog for $1 or on website; ms guidelines online.

- Merriam Press publishes only World War II military history.

Nonfiction: Biography, illustrated book, reference, technical. Subjects include military/war (World War II). Query with SASE or by e-mail first. Reviews artwork/photos as part of ms package. Send photocopies or on floppy disk/CD.

Recent Title(s): *Valor Without Arms: A History of the 316th Troop Carrier Group, 1942-1945*, by Michael N. Ingrisano, Jr.; *The Fighting Bob: A Wartime History of the USS Robely D. Evans, DD-552*, by Michael Staton; *Riflemen: On the Cutting Edge of World War II*, by Earl A. Reitan.

Tips: "Our books are geared for WWII historians, collectors, model kit builders, wargamers, veterans, general enthusiasts. We do not publish any fiction or poetry, only WWII military history."

METAL POWDER INDUSTRIES FEDERATION, 105 College Rd. E., Princeton NJ 08540. (609)452-7700. Fax: (609)987-8523. E-mail: info@mpif.org. Website: www.mpif.org. **Acquisitions:** Cindy Jablonowski, publications manager; Peggy Lebedz, assistant publications manager. Estab. 1946. Publishes hardcover originals. **Publishes 10 titles/year. Pays 3-12½% royalty on wholesale or retail price. Offers $3,000-5,000 advance.** Responds in 1 month to queries.

- Metal Powder Industries publishes monographs, textbooks, handbooks, design guides, conference proceedings, standards, and general titles in the field of powder metallurgy or particulate materials.

Nonfiction: Work must relate to powder metallurgy or particulate materials. Technical, textbook.

Recent Title(s): *Advances in Powder Metallurgy and Particulate Materials* (conference proceeding).

MEYERBOOKS, PUBLISHER, P.O. Box 427, Glenwood IL 60425-0427. (708)757-4950. **Acquisitions:** David Meyer, publisher. Estab. 1976. Publishes hardcover and trade paperback originals and reprints. **Publishes 5 titles/year. Pays 10-15% royalty on wholesale or retail price.** Responds in 3 months to queries.

Imprints: David Meyer Magic Books, Waltham Street Press.

O━ "We are currently publishing books on stage magic history. We only consider subjects which have never been presented in book form before. We are not currently considering books on health, herbs, cookery or general Americana."

Nonfiction: Reference. Subjects include history of stage magic. Query with SASE.

Recent Title(s): *Inclined Toward Magic: Encounters with Books, Collectors and Conjurors' Lives*, by David Meyer; *Houdini and the Indescribable Phenomenon*, by Robert Lund.

MICHIGAN STATE UNIVERSITY PRESS, 1405 S. Harrison Rd., Manly Miles Bldg., Suite 25, East Lansing MI 48823-5202. (517)355-9543. Fax: (517)432-2611. E-mail: msupress@msu.edu. Website: www.msupress.msu.edu. **Acquisitions:** Martha Bates, acquisitions editor. Estab. 1947. Publishes hardcover and softcover originals. **Publishes 35 titles/year. Receives 2,400 submissions/year. 75% of books from first-time authors; 100% from unagented writers. Pays variable royalty.** Publishes book 18 months after acceptance of ms. Does not accept simultaneous submissions. Book catalog and manuscript guidelines for 9×12 SASE; ms guidelines online.

Imprints: Lotus/Colleagues; University of Calgary Press; Penumbra; National Museum of Science and Industry, UK; Lynx House; African Books Collective.

O━ Michigan State University publishes scholarly books that further scholarship in their particular field. In addition they publish nonfiction that addresses, in a more contemporary way, social concerns, such as diversity, civil rights, the environment.

Nonfiction: Scholarly. Subjects include Americana (American studies), business/economics, creative nonfiction, ethnic (Afro-American studies), government/politics, history (contemporary civil rights), language/literature, regional (Great Lakes regional, Canadian studies), women's issues/studies. Reviews artwork/photos as part of ms package.

Recent Title(s): *My Grandfather's Book: Generations of an American Family*, by Gary Gildner (memoir); *The Blue Yonder Inn*, by Helen Campbell (fiction); *Mes Confitures: The Jams and Jellies of Christine Ferber* (English translation, cookbook).

MID-LIST PRESS, 4324 12th Ave S., Minneapolis MN 55407-3218. (612)822-3733. Fax: (612)823-8387. Website: www.midlist.org. Publisher: Lane Stiles. Estab. 1989. Publishes hardcover and trade paperback originals. **Publishes 4 titles/year. Pays 40-50% royalty on net receipts. Offers $1,000 advance.** Publishes book 12-18 months after acceptance of ms. Accepts simultaneous submissions. Responds in 3 weeks to queries; 3 months to mss. Ms guidelines online.

O━ Mid-List Press publishes books of high literary merit and fresh artistic vision by new and emerging writers.

Fiction: General fiction. No children's/juvenile, romance, young adult. Send query letter first.

Recent Title(s): *Objects and Empathy*, by Arthur Saltzman (nonfiction); *Wonderful Tricks*, by Gregory Spatz (short fiction); *Tip to Rump*, by Katherine Starke (poetry).

Tips: Mid-List Press is an independent press. In addition to publishing the annual winners of the Mid-List Press First Series Awards, Mid-List Press publishes fiction, poetry, and creative nonfiction by established writers.

[N] **MIGHTYBOOK**, Guardian Press, 10924 Grant Rd., #225, Houston TX 77070. (281)955-9855. Fax: (281)890-4818. E-mail: reaves@mightybook.com. Website: www.mightybook.com. **Acquisitions:** Richard Eaves, acquisitions editor. Estab. 1991. Publishes electronic books. **Publishes 30-50 titles/year. Pays royalties of 20% gross.** Publishes book 3-9 months after acceptance of ms. Accepts simultaneous submissions. Responds in 6 weeks to queries; 6 weeks to mss. Book catalog online; ms guidelines online.

O━ "Small independent publisher of electronic, read aloud picture books, books on audiocassette/CD. Much of our marketing and sales are done on the Internet."

Fiction: Very short children's picture books (100-200 words). Submit complete ms with cover letter (include estimated word count and brief bio).

Recent Title(s): *When I Find Courage*, by Robin McKay Pimental; *A Bug Time Story*, by Naomi Tola.

Tips: "Write really good, very short stories for children."

MILKWEED EDITIONS, 1011 Washington Ave. S., Suite 300, Minneapolis MN 55415. (612)332-3192. Fax: (612)215-2550. Website: www.milkweed.org and www.worldashome.org. **Acquisitions:** Emilie Buchwald, publisher; Elisabeth Fitz, first reader (fiction, nonfiction, children's fiction, poetry). Estab. 1980. Publishes hardcover originals and paperback originals and reprints. **Publishes 15 titles/year. Receives 3,000 submissions/year. 30% of books from first-time authors; 70% from unagented writers. Pays 7½% royalty on retail price. Offers varied advance.** Publishes book 1-2 years after acceptance of ms. Accepts simultaneous submissions. Responds in 2 months to queries; 6 months to mss. Book catalog for $1.50 postage; ms guidelines online.

Imprints: Milkweeds for Young Readers.

O━ Milkweed Editions publishes literary fiction for adults and middle grade readers, nonfiction, memoir and poetry. "Our vision is focused on giving voice to writers whose work is of the highest literary quality and whose ideas engender personal reflection and cultural action." Currently emphasizing nonfiction about the natural world.

Nonfiction: Literary. Subjects include nature/environment, human community. Submit complete ms. with SASE.

Fiction: Literary. Novels for adults and for readers 8-13. High literary quality. For adult readers: literary fiction, nonfiction, poetry, essays; for children (ages 8-12): literary novels. Translations welcome for both audiences. No romance, mysteries, science fiction. Submit complete ms. Send for guidelines first, then submit complete ms.

Recent Title(s): *The Book of the Everglades*, edited by Susan Cerulean (nonfiction); *Roofwalkers*, by Susan Power (fiction); *The Porcelain Apes of Moses Mendelssohn*, by Jean Nordhaus (poetry).

Tips: "We are looking for excellent writing in fiction, nonfiction, poetry, and children's novels, with the intent of making a humane impact on society. Send for guidelines. Acquaint yourself with our books in terms of style and quality before submitting. Many factors influence our selection process, so don't get discouraged. Nonfiction is focused on literary writing about the natural world, including living well in urban environments. We no longer publish children's biographies. We read poetry in January and June only."

THE MILLBROOK PRESS, INC., 2 Old New Milford Rd., Brookfield CT 06804. Fax: (203)775-5643. Website: www.millbrookpress.com. Executive Vice President/Publisher: Jean Reynolds. Editor in Chief: Amy Shields. Senior Editors: Kristen Bettcher. **Acquisitions:** Ben Tomek, manuscript coordinator. Estab. 1989. Publishes hardcover and paperback originals. **Publishes 200 titles/year. Pays varying royalty on wholesale price or makes outright purchase. Offers variable advance.** Publishes book 1 year after acceptance of ms. Does not accept simultaneous submissions. Ms guidelines online.

Imprints: Twenty-First Century Books, Roaring Brook.

Millbrook Press publishes quality children's books of curriculum-related nonfiction for the school/library market.

Nonfiction: Children's/juvenile. Subjects include animals, anthropology/archeology, ethnic, government/politics, health/medicine, history, hobbies, multicultural, nature/environment, science, sports. Specializes in general reference, social studies, science, arts and crafts, multicultural and picutre books. *Agented submissions only. No unsolicited mss.*

Recent Title(s): *Air Force One*; *Nature Did It First*; *Jobs for Kids*.

MINNESOTA HISTORICAL SOCIETY PRESS, Minnesota Historical Society, 345 Kellogg Blvd. W., St. Paul MN 55102-1906. (651)296-2264. Fax: (651)297-1345. Website: www.mnhs.org/mhspress. **Acquisitions:** Gregory M. Britton, director; Ann Regan, managing editor. Estab. 1849. Publishes hardcover and trade paperback originals, trade paperback reprints. **Publishes 20 titles/year; imprint publishes 1-4 titles/year. Receives 100 queries and 25 mss/year. 50% of books from first-time authors; 85% from unagented writers. Royalties are negotiated. Offers advance.** Publishes book 14 months after acceptance of ms. Accepts simultaneous submissions. Responds in 1 month. *Writer's Market* recommends allowing 2 months for reply to queries. Book catalog free.

Imprints: Borealis Books; Midwest Reflections (memoir and personal history); Native Voices (works by American Indians).

Minnesota Historical Society Press publishes both scholarly and general interest books that contribute to the understanding of the Midwest.

Nonfiction: Regional works only. Biography, coffee table book, cookbook, illustrated book, reference, scholarly. Subjects include anthropology/archeology, art/architecture, cooking/foods/nutrition, ethnic, history, memoirs, photography, regional, women's issues/studies. Query with SASE or submit proposal package including outline, 1 sample chapter(s). Reviews artwork/photos as part of ms package. Send photocopies.

Recent Title(s): *Bamboo Among the Oaks: Contemporary Writing by Hmong Americans*, edited by Mai Neng Moua; *Baghdad Express: A Gulf War Memoir*, by Joel Turnipseed; *Forgetting Ireland*, by Bridget Connelly.

Tips: A regional connection is required.

MITCHELL LANE PUBLISHERS, INC., P.O. Box 619, Bear DE 19701. (302)834-9646. Fax: (302)834-4164. **Acquisitions:** Barbara Mitchell, publisher. Estab. 1993. Publishes hardcover and library bound originals. **Publishes 45 titles/year. Receives 100 queries and 5 mss/year. 0% of books from first-time authors; 90% from unagented writers. Makes outright purchase on work-for-hire basis.** Publishes book 1 year after acceptance of ms. Does not accept simultaneous submissions. Responds only if interested to queries. Book catalog free.

"Mitchell Lane publishes multicultural biographies for children and young adults."

Nonfiction: Biography, children's/juvenile. Subjects include ethnic, multicultural. Query with SASE. **All unsolicited mss returned unopened.**

Recent Title(s): *Mary-Kate and Ashley Olsen*, by Kathleen Tracy (Real-Life Reader Biography); *Albert Einstein and the Theory of Relativity*, by John Bankston (Unlocking the Secrets of Science); *Juan Ponce de Leon*, by Jim Whiting (Latinos in American History).

Tips: "We hire writers on a 'work-for-hire' basis to complete book projects we assign. Send résumé and writing samples that do not need to be returned."

MODERN LANGUAGE ASSOCIATION OF AMERICA, 26 Broadway, 3rd Floor, New York NY 10004-1789. (646)576-5000. Fax: (646)458-0030. Director of MLA Book Publications: David G. Nicholls. **Acquisitions:** Joseph Gibaldi, director of book acquisitions and development; Sonia Kane, acquisitions editor. Estab. 1883. Publishes hardcover and paperback originals. **Publishes 15 titles/year. Receives 125 submissions/year. 100% from unagented writers. Pays 4-8% royalty on net receipts.** Publishes book 1 year after acceptance of ms. Does not accept simultaneous submissions. Responds in 2 months to mss. Book catalog free.

The MLA publishes on current issues in literary and linguistic research and teaching of language and literature at postsecondary level.

Nonfiction: Reference, scholarly, professional. Subjects include education, language/literature, translation (with companion volume in foreign language, for classroom use). No critical monographs. Query with SASE or submit outline.

Recent Title(s): *Recovering Spain's Feminist Tradition*, edited by Lisa Vollendorf; *Nihilist Girl*, by Sofya Kovalevskaya.

MOMENTUM BOOKS, LLC, 117 W. Third St., Royal Oak MI 48067. (800)758-1870. Fax: (248)691-4531. E-mail: momentumbooks@glis.net. Website: www.momentumbooks.com. **Acquisitions:** Franklin Foxx, editor. Estab. 1987. **Pub-**

lishes 6 titles/year. Receives 100 queries and 30 mss/year. 95% of books from first-time authors; 100% from unagented writers. Pays 10-15% royalty. Does not accept simultaneous submissions. Ms guidelines online.

O╖ Momentum Books publishes regional books and general interest nonfiction.

Nonfiction: Biography, cookbook, guides. Subjects include cooking/foods/nutrition, government/politics, history, memoirs, military/war, sports, travel, women's issues/studies. Submit proposal package including outline, 3 sample chapter(s), marketing outline.

Recent Title(s): *Thus Spake David E*, by David E. Davis, Sr. (automotive); *Rockin' Down the Dial*, by David Carson (regional history); *Offbeat Cruises & Excursions*, by Len Barnes (travel).

[A] **MOODY PUBLISHERS**, (formerly Moody Press), Moody Bible Institute, 820 N. LaSalle Blvd., Chicago IL 60610. (312)329-8047. Fax: (312)329-2019. Website: www.moodypublishers.org. Vice President/Executive Editor: Greg Thornton. **Acquisitions:** Acquisitions Coordinator. Estab. 1894. Publishes hardcover, trade and mass market paperback originals. **Publishes 60 titles/year; imprint publishes 5-10 titles/year. Receives 1,500 queries and 2,000 mss/year. 1% of books from first-time authors; 80% from unagented writers. Royalty varies. Offers $1,000-10,000 advance.** Publishes book 9-12 months after acceptance of ms. Does not accept simultaneous submissions. Responds in 2-3 months to queries. Book catalog for 9×12 SAE with 4 first-class stamps; ms guidelines for SASE and on website.

Imprints: Northfield Publishing, Lift Every Voice (African American interest).

O╖ "The mission of Moody Publishers is to educate and edify the Christian and to evangelize the non-Christian by ethically publishing conservative, evangelical Christian literature and other media for all ages around the world; and to help provide resources for Moody Bible Institute in its training of future Christian leaders."

Nonfiction: Children's/juvenile, gift book, general Christian living. Subjects include child guidance/parenting, money/finance, religion, spirituality, women's issues/studies. "We are no longer reviewing queries or unsolicited manuscripts unless they come to us through an agent. Unsolicited proposals will be returned only if proper postage is included. We are not able to acknowledge the receipt of your unsolicited proposal." *Agented submissions only.*

Fiction: Fantasy, historical, mystery, religious (children's religious, inspirational, religious mystery/suspense), science fiction, young adult (adventure, fantasy/science fiction, historical, mystery/suspense, series). Query with SASE.

Recent Title(s): *Nothing to Fear*, by Larry Burkett; *Daughters of Faith series*, by Wendy Lawton; *The Second Thief*, by Travis Thrasher.

Tips: "Our audience consists of general, average Christian readers, not scholars. Know the market and publishers. Spend time in bookstores researching."

THOMAS MORE PUBLISHING, Resources for Christian Living, 200 E. Bethany Dr., Allen TX 75002. (972)390-6923. Fax: (972)390-6620. E-mail: dhampton@rcl-enterprises.com. Website: www.thomasmore.com. **Acquisitions:** Debra Hampton, marketing and acquisitions director (religious publishing). Publishes hardcover, trade paperback and mass market paperback originals and reprints. **Publishes 25 titles/year. Receives 250 queries and 150 mss/year. 25% of books from first-time authors; 50% from unagented writers. Pays 8-12% royalty on wholesale price. Offers $2-10,000 advance.** Publishes book 8 months after acceptance of ms. Accepts simultaneous submissions. Responds in 3 months to proposals; 3 months to mss. Book catalog free; ms guidelines online.

Imprints: Christian Classics (contact: Debra Hampton).

O╖ Thomas More specializes in self-help and religious titles.

Nonfiction: Self-help. Subjects include religion, spirituality, women's issues/studies. Submit proposal package including outline, 3 sample chapter(s). Reviews artwork/photos as part of ms package. Send photocopies.

Recent Title(s): *Forever Young: The Authorized Biography of Loretta Young*, by Joan Webster-Anderson; *Good Marriages Don't Just Happen*, by Catherine Musco Garcia-Prats and Joseph A. Garcia-Prats, M.D.

[N] **MOREHOUSE PUBLISHING CO.**, 4475 Linglestown Rd., Harrisburg PA 17112. (717)541-8130. Fax: (717)541-8136. E-mail: morehouse@morehousegroup.com. Website: www.morehousepublishing.com. **Acquisitions:** Debra Farrington, editorial director. Estab. 1884. Publishes hardcover and paperback originals. **Publishes 35 titles/year. 50% of books from first-time authors. Pays 10% royalty on net receipts. Offers small advance.** Publishes book 18 months after acceptance of ms. Accepts simultaneous submissions. Responds in 2 months to queries. Ms guidelines online.

O╖ Morehouse Publishing publishes mainline Christian books, primarily Episcopal/Anglican works. Currently emphasizing Christian spiritual direction.

Nonfiction: Subjects include religion (Christian), women's issues/studies, Christian spirituality, Liturgies, congregational resources, issues around Christian life. Submit outline, 1-2 sample chapter(s), résumé, market analysis.

Recent Title(s): *Welcome to Sunday*, by Christopher Webber; *101 Reasons to Be Episcopalian*, by Louie Crew.

MORNINGSIDE HOUSE, INC., Morningside Bookshop, 260 Oak St., Dayton OH 45410. (937)461-6736. Fax: (937)461-4260. E-mail: msbooks@erinet.com. Website: www.morningsidebooks.com. **Acquisitions:** Robert J. Younger, publisher. Publishes hardcover and trade paperback originals. **Publishes 10 titles/year; imprint publishes 5 titles/year. Receives 30 queries and 10 mss/year. 20% of books from first-time authors; 80% from unagented writers. Pays 10% royalty on retail price. Offers $1,000-2,000 advance.** Publishes book 15 months after acceptance of ms. Accepts simultaneous submissions. Book catalog for $5 or on website.

Imprints: Morningside Press, Press of Morningside Bookshop.

O╖ Morningside publishes books for readers interested in the history of the American Civil War.

Nonfiction: Subjects include history, military/war. Query with SASE or submit complete ms. Reviews artwork/photos as part of ms package. Send photocopies.

Recent Title(s): *The Mississippi Brigade of Brig. Gen. Joseph R. Davis*, by T.P. Williams; *The 16th Michigan Infantry*, by Kim Crawford.

Tips: "We are only interested in previously unpublished material."

[N] MORROW/AVON BOOKS, HarperCollins, 10 E. 53rd St., New York NY 10022. E-mail: avonromance@harpercollins.com. Website: www.avonbooks.com. **Acquisitions:** Editorial Submissions. Estab. 1941. Publishes hardover and mass market paperback originals and reprints. **Publishes 400 titles/year. Royalty negotiable. Offers advance.** Publishes book 2 years after acceptance of ms. Accepts simultaneous submissions. Responds in 3 months to queries. Ms guidelines for #10 SASE.

Imprints: Avon Eos, HarperEntertainment, HarperTorch

Nonfiction: Biography, how-to, self-help. Subjects include business/economics, government/politics, health/medicine, history, military/war, psychology (popular), sports. No textbooks. Query with SASE.

Fiction: Fantasy, mystery, romance (contemporary, historical), science fiction, suspense. Query with SASE.

Recent Title(s): *Joining*, by Johanna Lindsey.

[N] MOUNT OLIVE COLLEGE PRESS, Mount Olive College, 634 Henderson St., Mount Olive NC 28365. (919)658-2502. **Acquisitions:** Dr. Pepper Worthington, director (nonfiction, fiction, poetry, children's stories). Estab. 1990. Publishes trade paperback originals. **Publishes 5 titles/year. Receives 2,500 queries/year. 75% of books from first-time authors.** Does not accept simultaneous submissions. with 2 first-class stamps.

Nonfiction: Biography, children's/juvenile, scholarly, self-help. Subjects include creative nonfiction, general nonfiction, history, humanities, language/literature, memoirs, philosophy, psychology, religion, sociology, travel, women's issues/studies. Submit 3 sample chapter(s). Reviews artwork/photos as part of ms package. Send photocopies.

Fiction: Literary, poetry, religious, short story collections, spiritual. Submit 3 sample chapter(s).

Poetry: Submit 10 sample poems.

MOUNTAIN N'AIR BOOKS, P.O. Box 12540, La Crescenta CA 91224. (818)248-9345. Website: www.mountain-n-air.com. **Acquisitions:** Gilberto d'Urso, owner. Publishes trade paperback originals. **Publishes 6 titles/year. Receives 50 queries and 35 mss/year. 75% of books from first-time authors; 100% from unagented writers. Pays 5-10% royalty on retail price or makes outright purchase.** Publishes book 6 months after acceptance of ms. Does not accept simultaneous submissions. Responds in 2 weeks to queries; 2 months to mss. Ms guidelines online.

Imprints: Bearly Cooking.

O-- Mountain N'Air publishes books for those generally interested in the outdoors and travel.

Nonfiction: Biography, cookbook, how-to. Subjects include cooking/foods/nutrition, nature/environment, recreation, travel. Submit outline, 2 sample chapter(s). Reviews artwork/photos as part of ms package. Send photocopies.

Recent Title(s): *Thinking Out Loud Through the American West*; *An Explorer's Adventures in Tibet: An 1897 Epic*; *Hiking With Your Dog*.

MOUNTAIN PRESS PUBLISHING CO., P.O. Box 2399, Missoula MT 59806-2399. (406)728-1900 or (800)234-5308. Fax: (406)728-1635. E-mail: info@mtnpress.com. Website: www.mountain-press.com. **Acquisitions:** Kathleen Ort, editor (natural history/science/outdoors); Gwen McKenna, editor (history); Jennifer Carey, editor (Roadside Geology, Field Guides and Tumblweed Series). Estab. 1948. Publishes hardcover and trade paperback originals. **Publishes 15 titles/year. Receives 250 submissions/year. 50% of books from first-time authors; 90% from unagented writers. Pays 7-12% royalty on wholesale price.** Publishes book 2 years after acceptance of ms. Responds in 3 months to queries. Book catalog online.

- Expanding children's/juvenile nonfiction titles.

O-- "We are expanding our Roadside Geology, Geology Underfoot and Roadside History series (done on a state by state basis). We are interested in well-written regional field guides—plants and flowers—and readable history and natural history."

Nonfiction: How-to. Subjects include animals, history (Western), nature/environment, regional, science (Earth science). "No personal histories or journals." Query with SASE or submit outline, sample chapter(s). Reviews artwork/photos as part of ms package.

Recent Title(s): *Wild Berries of the West*, by Betty Derig and Margaret Fuller; *Dinosaurs Under the Big Sky*, by Jack Horner; *Sacagawea's Son*, by Marion Tinling.

Tips: "Find out what kind of books a publisher is interested in and tailor your writing to them; research markets and target your audience. Research other books on the same subjects. Make yours different. Don't present your manuscript to a publisher—*sell* it to him. Give him the information he needs to make a decision on a title. Please learn what we publish before sending your proposal. We are a 'niche' publisher."

THE MOUNTAINEERS BOOKS, 1001 SW Klickitat Way, Suite 201, Seattle WA 98134-1162. (206)223-6303. Fax: (206)223-6306. E-mail: mbooks@mountaineersbooks.org. Website: www.mountaineersbooks.org. **Acquisitions:** Cassandra Conyers, acquisitions editor. Estab. 1961. Publishes 95% hardcover and trade paperback originals and 5% reprints. **Publishes 40 titles/year. Receives 150-250 submissions/year. 25% of books from first-time authors; 98% from unagented writers. Pays royalty on net receipts. Offers advance.** Publishes book 1 year after acceptance of ms. Does not accept simultaneous submissions. Responds in 3 months to queries. Book catalog for 9×12 SAE with $1.33 postage first-class stamps; ms guidelines online.

- See the Contests and Awards section for information on the Barbara Savage/'Miles From Nowhere' Memorial Award for outstanding adventure narratives offered by Mountaineers Books.

O-- Mountaineers Books specializes in expert, authoritative books dealing with mountaineering, hiking, backpacking, skiing, snowshoeing, etc. These can be either how-to-do-it or where-to-do-it (guidebooks). Currently emphasizing regional conservation and natural history.

Nonfiction: How-to (outdoor), guidebooks for national and international adventure travel. Subjects include nature/environment, recreation, regional, sports (non-competitive self-propelled), translation, travel, natural history, conservation. Accepts nonfiction translations. Looks for "expert knowledge, good organization." Also interested in nonfiction adventure narratives. Does *not* want to see "anything dealing with hunting, fishing or motorized travel." Submit outline, 2 sample chapter(s), author bio.

Recent Title(s): *Best Hikes with Dogs: Western Washington*, by Nelson; *Backpacker: More Everyday Wisdom*, by Berger; *Detectives on Everest*, by Hemmleb and Simonson.

Tips: "The type of book the writer has the best chance of selling to our firm is an authoritative guidebook (*in our field*) to a specific area not otherwise covered; or a how-to that is better than existing competition (again, *in our field*)."

MOYER BELL, LTD., 549 Old North Rd., Kingston RI 02881. (401)783-5480. Fax: (401)284-0959. Website: www.moyerbellbooks.com. **Publishes 15 titles/year; imprint publishes 5 titles/year. Pays 6-10% royalty on retail price.** Book catalog online.

Imprints: Asphodel Press, Papier-Mache Press, Albion Press, Olmstead Press.

Nonfiction: Biography, reference. Subjects include government/politics, memoirs, women's issues/studies. Query with SASE.

Fiction: Literary. Query with SASE.

[N] [A] **MULTNOMAH PUBLISHERS, INC.**, P.O. Box 1720, Sisters OR 97759. (541)549-1144. Fax: (541)549-8048. Website: www.multnomahbooks.com. **Acquisitions:** Rod Morris, senior editor (general fiction). Estab. 1987. Publishes hardcover and trade paperback originals. **Publishes 100 titles/year. 2% of books from first-time authors; 50% from unagented writers. Pays royalty on wholesale price. Provides 100 author's copies. Offers advance.** Publishes book 1-2 years after acceptance of ms. Accepts simultaneous submissions. Ms guidelines online.

Imprints: Multnomah Books, Multnomah Gifts, Multnomah Fiction.

- Multnomah is currently not accepting unsolicited queries, proposals or manuscripts. Queries will be accepted through agents and at writers' conferences at which a Multnomah representative is present.

O→ Multnomah publishes books on Christian living, family enrichment, devotional and gift books and fiction.

Nonfiction: Subjects include child guidance/parenting, religion, Christian living. *Agented submissions only.*

Fiction: Adventure, historical, humor, literary, mystery, religious, romance, suspense, western. *Agented submissions only.*

Recent Title(s): *The Prayer of Jabez*, by Bruce Wilkinson (nonfiction); *The Healer*, by Dee Henderson (fiction); *Night Light*, by James Dobson (nonfiction).

MUSTANG PUBLISHING CO., P.O. Box 770426, Memphis TN 38177-0426. Website: www.mustangpublishing.com. **Acquisitions:** Rollin Riggs, editor. Estab. 1983. Publishes hardcover and trade paperback originals. **Publishes 10 titles/year. Receives 1,000 submissions/year. 50% of books from first-time authors; 90% from unagented writers. Pays 6-8% royalty on retail price. Offers advance.** Publishes book 1 year after acceptance of ms. Accepts simultaneous submissions. Responds in 1 month. *Writer's Market* recommends allowing 2 months for reply to queries. Book catalog for $2 and #10 SASE. No phone calls, please.

O→ Mustang publishes general interest nonfiction for an adult audience.

Nonfiction: How-to, humor, self-help. Subjects include Americana, general nonfiction, hobbies, humor, recreation, sports, travel. "Our needs are very general—humor, travel, how-to, etc.—for the 18-to 60-year-old market." Query with SASE or submit outline, sample chapter(s). Reviews artwork/photos as part of ms package. Send photocopies.

Recent Title(s): *Medical School Admissions: The Insider's Guide*, by Zebala (career); *The Complete Book of Golf Games*, by Johnston (sports).

Tips: "From the proposals we receive, it seems that many writers never go to bookstores and have no idea what sells. Before you waste a lot of time on a nonfiction book idea, ask yourself, 'How often have my friends and I actually *bought* a book like this?' We are not interested in first-person travel accounts or memoirs."

[A] **THE MYSTERIOUS PRESS**, Warner Books, 1271 Avenue of the Americas, New York NY 10020. (212)522-7200. Fax: (212)522-7990. Website: www.twbookmark.com. **Acquisitions:** Sara Ann Freed, editor-in-chief. Estab. 1976. Publishes hardcover, trade paperback and mass market editions. **Publishes 36-45 titles/year. Pays standard, but negotiable, royalty on retail price. Offers negotiable advance.** Publishes book an average of 1 year after acceptance of ms. Responds in 2 months to queries. Ms guidelines online.

O→ The Mysterious Press publishes well-written crime/mystery/suspense fiction.

Fiction: Mystery, suspense, Crime/detective novels. No short stories. *Agented submissions only.*

Recent Title(s): *Bad News*, by Donald Westlake; *The Red Room*, by Nicci French.

THE NARRATIVE PRESS, P.O. Box 2487, Santa Barbara CA 93120. (805)966-2186. Fax: (805)456-3915. E-mail: admin@narrativepress.com. Website: www.narrativepress.com. **Acquisitions:** William Urschel, publisher (true first-person adventure and exploration). Publishes trade paperback originals and reprints and electronic originals and reprints. **Publishes 30 titles/year; imprint publishes 78 titles/year. Receives 100 queries and 20 submissions/year. 10% of books from first-time authors; 50% from unagented writers.** Publishes book 2 months after acceptance of ms. Accepts simultaneous submissions. Responds in 1 month to queries; 1 month to proposals; 3 months to mss. Book catalog online; ms guidelines free.

Nonfiction: Biography. Subjects include anthropology/archeology, creative nonfiction, history, memoirs, military/war, travel. Query with SASE. Reviews artwork/photos as part of ms package.

THE NAUTICAL & AVIATION PUBLISHING CO., 1250 Fairmont Ave., Mt. Pleasant SC 29464. (843)856-0561. Fax: (843)856-3164. **Acquisitions:** Melissa A. Pluta, acquisitions editor. Estab. 1979. Publishes hardcover originals and reprints. **Publishes 10-12 titles/year. Receives 500 submissions/year. Pays 10-12% royalty on net receipts. Offers rare advance.** Accepts simultaneous submissions. Responds in 3 weeks to queries. Book catalog free.

O¬ The Nautical & Aviation Publishing Co. publishes naval and military history fiction and reference.

Nonfiction: Reference. Subjects include military/war (American), naval history. Query with SASE or submit 3 sample chapter(s), synopsis. Reviews artwork/photos as part of ms package.

Fiction: Historical, military/war (Revolutionary War, War of 1812, Civil War, WW I and II, Persian Gulf and Marine Corps history). Looks for "novels with a strong military history orientation." Submit complete ms. with cover letter and brief synopsis.

Recent Title(s): *The Civil War in the Carolinas*, by Dan L. Morrill; *Christopher and the Quasi War with France*, by William P. Mack; *The Independence Light Aircraft Carriers*, by Andrew Faltum.

Tips: "We are primarily a nonfiction publisher, but we will review historical fiction of military interest with strong literary merit."

NAVAL INSTITUTE PRESS, U.S. Naval Institute, 291 Wood Ave., Annapolis MD 21402-5035. (410)268-6110. Fax: (410)295-1084. E-mail: esecunda@usni.org. Website: www.usni.org; www.nip.org. Press Director: Ronald Chambers. **Acquisitions:** Paul Wilderson, executive editor; Tom Cutler, senior acquisitions editor; Eric Mills, acquisitions editor. Estab. 1873. **Publishes 80-90 titles/year. Receives 700-800 submissions/year. 50% of books from first-time authors; 90% from unagented writers. Pays 5-10% royalty on net receipts.** Publishes book 1 year after acceptance of ms. Accepts simultaneous submissions. Book catalog for 9×12 SASE; ms guidelines online.

Imprints: Bluejacket Books (paperback reprints).

O¬ The U.S. Naval Institute Press publishes general and scholarly books of professional, scientific, historical and literary interest to the naval and maritime community.

Nonfiction: "We are interested in naval and maritime subjects and in broad military topics, including government policy and funding." Biography. Subjects include government/politics, history, science, women's issues/studies, tactics, strategy, navigation, aviation, technology and others. Submit proposal package including outline, sample chapter(s), author bio, synopsis or submit complete ms.

Fiction: Historical, military/war. Limited to fiction on military and naval themes. Very small proportion of publishing program. Submit outline, sample chapter(s), synopsis, author bio.

Recent Title(s): *Punk's War*, by Ward Carroll (fiction); *Nelson Speaks*, by Joseph Callo (nonfiction).

⊘ **NAVPRESS PUBLISHING GROUP**, P.O. Box 35001, Colorado Springs CO 80935. Website: www.navpress.com. Publishes hardcover, trade paperback and mass market paperback originals and reprints. **Publishes 45 titles/year. 25% of books from first-time authors; 90% from unagented writers. Pays royalty.** Book catalog free.

Imprints: Pinion Press, Think Books.

Nonfiction: Reference, self-help, inspirational, Christian living, Bible studies. Subjects include business/economics, child guidance/parenting, religion, spirituality, marriage. "We do not accept unsolicited mss. Unsolicited mss will not be acknowledged without an SASE."

NEAL-SCHUMAN PUBLISHERS, INC., 100 Varick St., New York NY 10013. (212)925-8650. Fax: (212)219-8916. E-mail: charles@neal-schuman.com. Website: www.neal-schuman.com. **Acquisitions:** Charles Harmon, director of publishing. Estab. 1976. Publishes trade paperback originals. **Publishes 30 titles/year. Receives 500 submissions/year. 75% of books from first-time authors; 90% from unagented writers. Pays 10% royalty on net receipts. Offers infrequent advance.** Publishes book 4 months after acceptance of ms. Does not accept simultaneous submissions. Responds in 1 month to proposals. Book catalog and ms guidelines free.

O¬ "Neal-Schuman publishes books about libraries, information science and the use of information technology, especially in education and libraries." Especially soliciting proposals for undergraduate information studios, knowledge management textbooks.

Nonfiction: Reference, technical, textbook, professional. Subjects include computers/electronic, education, software, Internet guides, library and information science. "We are looking for many books about the Internet." Submit proposal package including outline, sample chapter(s), résumé, preface.

Recent Title(s): *Fundamentals of Information Studies*, by June Lester and Wallace C. Koehler, Jr.; *Digital Futures*, by Marilyn Deegan and Simon Tanner.

THOMAS NELSON, INC., Box 141000, Nashville TN 37214-1000. (615)889-9000. Website: www.thomasnelson.com. **Acquisitions:** Acquisitions Editor. Publishes hardcover and paperback orginals. **Publishes 100-150 titles/year. Pays royalty on net receipts. Rates negotiated for each project. Offers advance.** Publishes book 1-2 years after acceptance of ms. Accepts simultaneous submissions. Responds in 3 months to queries. Ms guidelines online.

Imprints: Thomas Nelson Publishers, W Publishing, Rutledge Hill, J. Countryman, Cool Springs Press, Reference and Electronic Publishing, Editorial Caribe, Nelson Multimedia Group, Tommy Nelson, WND Books.

- Corporate address does not accept unsolicited mss; no phone queires.

O¬ Thomas Nelson publishes Christian lifestyle nonfiction and fiction.

Nonfiction: Reference, self-help. Subjects include business/economics (business development), health/medicine (and fitness), religion, spirituality, adult inspirational, motivational, devotional, Christian living, prayer and evangelism, Bible study, personal development. Query with SASE or submit 1 sample chapter(s), résumé, 1-page synopsis.

Fiction: Publishes commercial fiction authors who write for adults from a Christian perspective.

Recent Title(s): *The Savage Nation*, by Michael Savage; *21 Irrefutable Laws of Leadership*, by John C. Maxwell; *Traveling Light*, by Max Lucado.

TOMMY NELSON, Thomas Nelson, Inc., P.O. Box 141000, Nashville TN 37214-1000. (615)889-9000. Fax: (615)902-2219. Website: www.tommynelson.com. Publishes hardcover and trade paperback originals. **Publishes 50-75 titles/year.** Does not accept simultaneous submissions. *No unsolicited submissions.* Ms guidelines online.

Imprints: Word Kids.

Tommy Nelson publishes children's Christian nonfiction and fiction for boys and girls up to age 14. "We honor God and serve people through books, videos, software and Bibles for children that improve the lives of our customers."

Nonfiction: Children's/juvenile. Subjects include religion (Christian evangelical).

Fiction: Adventure, juvenile, mystery, picture books, religious. "No stereotypical characters."

Recent Title(s): *Hangman's Curse*, by Frank Paretti; *Prayer of Jabez for Kids*, by Bruce Wilkinson.

Tips: "Know the CBA market. Check out the Christian bookstores to see what sells and what is needed."

NETIMPRESS PUBLISHING, INC., 3186 Michael's Ct., Green Cove Springs FL 32043. (513)464-2082. E-mail: rtrent@netimpress.com. Submissions E-mail: acquisitions@netimpress.com. Website: www.netimpress.com. **Acquisitions:** Rod Trent, owner (technology); Brian Knight, owner (technology). Estab. 2002. Publishes trade paperback and electronic originals. **Publishes 50 titles/year; imprint publishes 25 titles/year. Receives 150 queries and 50 mss/year. 50% of books from first-time authors; 80% from unagented writers. Pays 50% royalty on retail price.** Publishes book 4 months after acceptance of ms. Accepts simultaneous submissions. Responds in 1 month to queries; 1 month to proposals; 1 month to mss. Book catalog online; ms guidelines by email.

Imprints: Start To Finish Guide, Just the FAQs.

Nonfiction: Booklets, how-to, reference, self-help, technical. Subjects include computers/electronic, software. "Our goal is to publish e-books that are 50-150 pages in length. These books should be a no-frills technical guide or how-to for a specific subject in the technology industry." Query with SASE or submit proposal package including outline, 1 sample chapter(s). Reviews artwork/photos as part of ms package. Electronic Images.

Recent Title(s): *Start To Finish Guide To SMS Delivery*, by Dana Daugherty (technology); *Start To Finish Guide To SQL Server Performance*, by Brian Kelley (technology); *Just the FAQs for SMS*, by Cliff Hobbs (technology).

Tips: "Our audience is a group of people heavily involved in technology and technology support for companies for which they are employed. These include consultants and IT." "Writers must understand the proposed topic very well. They must also be able to communicate technical expertise into easy-to-understand text."

NEW AMERICAN LIBRARY, Penguin Putnam, Inc., 375 Hudson St., New York NY 10014. (212)366-2000. Fax: (212)366-2889. Website: www.penguinputnam.com. Publisher: Kara Welsh. Editorial Director: Claire Zion. **Acquisitions:** Ellen Edwards, executive editor (commercial women's fiction—chicklit and contemporary romances; mysteries in a series and single title suspense); Laura Anne Gilman, executive editor (science fiction/fantasy/horror, mystery series); Jennifer Heddle, associate editor (science fiction/fantasy, pop culture and general nonfiction, erotica); Audrey LaFehr, executive editor (contemporary and historical romance, women's suspense, multicultural fiction); Hilary Ross, associate executive editor (romances, Regencies); Doug Grad, senior editor (thrillers, suspense novels, international intrigue, technothrillers, military fiction and nonfiction, adventure nonfiction); Genny Ostertag, senior editor (mysteries, suspense, commerical women's fiction); Dan Slater, senior editor (westerns, thrillers, military fiction and nonfiction, true crime, media tie-ins); Laura Cifelli, senior editor (commercial women's fiction, historical and contemporary romance). Estab. 1948. Publishes mass market and trade paperback originals and reprints. **Publishes 500 titles/year. Receives 20,000 queries and 10,000 mss/year. 30-40% of books from first-time authors; 5% from unagented writers. Pays negotiable royalty. Offers negotiable advance.** Publishes book 1-2 years after acceptance of ms. Does not accept simultaneous submissions. Responds in 6 months to queries. Book catalog for SASE.

Imprints: Onyx, ROC, Signet, Signet Classic, NAL trade paperback, Accent.

NAL publishes commercial fiction and nonfiction for the popular audience.

Nonfiction: How-to, reference, self-help. Subjects include animals, child guidance/parenting, ethnic, health/medicine, military/war, psychology, sports, movie tie-in. *Agented submissions only.*

Fiction: Erotica, ethnic, fantasy, historical, horror, mainstream/contemporary, mystery, romance, science fiction, suspense, western, chicklit. "All kinds of commercial fiction." *Agented submissions only.* Query with SASE. "State type of book and past publishing projects."

Recent Title(s): *Suspicion of Betrayal*, by Barbara Parker; *The Medusa Stone*, by Jack DuBrul.

NEW CANAAN PUBLISHING CO., INC., P.O. Box 752, New Canaan CT 06840. (203)966-3408. Fax: (203)966-3408. E-mail: info@newcanaanpublishing.com. Website: www.newcanaanpublishing.com. **Acquisitions:** Kathy Mittelstadt, vice president (children's fiction). Publishes hardcover trade and paperback originals and reprints. **Publishes 4 titles/year. Receives 500 queries and 500 mss/year. 25% of books from first-time authors; 90% from unagented writers. Pays 8-10% royalty on wholesale price. Offers occasional advance.** Publishes book 1 year after acceptance of ms. Does not accept simultaneous submissions. Responds in 3 months to queries; 3 months to proposals; 4 months to mss. Book catalog and ms guidelines available via website or #10 SASE; ms guidelines online.

New Canaan publishes children's, young adult, and Christian titles. "We are developing two lists (1)children's/young adult titles, fiction or educational (science/history/religion); and (2) Christian titles (fiction or nonfiction)."

Nonfiction: Children's/juvenile. Subjects include education, religion, science. Submit proposal package including outline,

2 sample chapter(s) or submit complete ms. "We no longer return submissions." Reviews artwork/photos as part of ms package. Send photocopies.

Fiction: Juvenile, religious (Christian), young adult. Query with SASE or submit proposal package including 2 sample chapter(s), synopsis, or submit complete ms, SASE.

Recent Title(s): *My Daddy Is a Guardsman*, by Kirk Hilbrecht; *The Grundilini*, by Benjamin Doolittle.

N **NEW ENGLAND LEAGUE OF MIDDLE SCHOOLS (NELMS)**, 460 Boston St., Suite #4, Topsfield MA 01983-1223. (978)887-6263. Fax: (978)887-6504. E-mail: nelms@nelms.org. Website: www.nelms.org. Estab. 1974. Publishes trade paperback originals and reprints. **Publishes 4 titles/year. Receives 30 queries and 25 mss/year. 50% of books from first-time authors; 100% from unagented writers. Pays 0-20% royalty on wholesale price.** Publishes book 1 year after acceptance of ms. Does not accept simultaneous submissions. Responds in 2 months to mss. Book catalog online; ms guidelines online.

Nonfiction: Scholarly. Subjects include education. "We have a juried review and offer an educational journal. Our focus is on middle level education." Submit complete ms. Reviews artwork/photos as part of ms package. Send photos only.

Recent Title(s): *NELMS Journal, Vol. 15 #1*, by multiple authors; *NELMS Journal, Vol. 14 #2*, by multiple authors.

Tips: Educators.

THE NEW ENGLAND PRESS, INC., P.O. Box 575, Shelburne VT 05482. (802)863-2520. Fax: (802)863-1510. E-mail: nep@together.net. Website: www.nepress.com. **Acquisitions:** Christopher A. Bray, managing editor. Estab. 1978. Publishes hardcover and trade paperback originals. **Publishes 6-8 titles/year. Receives 500 queries and 200 mss/year. 20% of books from first-time authors; 90% from unagented writers. Pays royalty on wholesale price.** Publishes book 15 months after acceptance of ms. Accepts simultaneous submissions. Responds in 6-9 months to queries. Book catalog free; ms guidelines online.

O→ The New England Press publishes high-quality trade books of regional northern New England interest. Currently emphasizing young adult biography. De-emphasizing railroading.

Nonfiction: Biography, illustrated book, young adult. Subjects include history, nature/environment, regional, world affairs, Vermontiana. "Nonfiction submissions must be based in Vermont and have northern New England topics. No memoirs or family histories. Identify potential markets and ways to reach them in cover letter." Query with SASE or submit outline, 2 sample chapter(s). Reviews artwork/photos as part of ms package. Send photocopies.

Fiction: Historical (Vermont, New Hampshire, Maine). "We look for very specific subject matters based on Vermont history and heritage. We are also interested in historical novels for young adults based in New Hampshire and Maine. We do not publish contemporary adult fiction of any kind." Query with SASE or submit 2 sample chapter(s), synopsis.

Recent Title(s): *Rumrunners and Revenuers: Prohibition in Vermont* (history); *Vermont Quiz Book*, by Melissa and Frank Bryan.

Tips: "Our readers are interested in all aspects of Vermont and northern New England, including hobbyists (railroad books) and students (young adult fiction and biography). No agent is needed, but our market is extremely specific and our volume is low, so send a query or outline and writing samples first. Sending the whole manuscript is discouraged. We will not accept projects that are still under development or give advances."

NEW HARBINGER PUBLICATIONS, 5674 Shattuck Ave., Oakland CA 94609. (510)652-0215. Fax: (510)652-5472. E-mail: proposals@newharbinger.com. Website: www.newharbinger.com. **Acquisitions:** Catharine Sutker, acquisitions manager; Jueli Gastwirth, senior acquisitions editor. Estab. 1979. **Publishes 50 titles/year. Receives 1,000 queries and 300 mss/year. 60% of books from first-time authors; 75% from unagented writers. Pays 10% royalty on net receipts.** Publishes book 1 year after acceptance of ms. Accepts simultaneous submissions. Responds in 1 month to queries; 1 month to proposals; 2 months to mss. Book catalog and ms guidelines free; ms guidelines online.

O→ "We look for step-by-step self-help titles on psychology, health and balanced living titles that teach the average reader how to master essential skills. Our books are also read by mental health professionals who want simple, clear explanations of important psychological techniques and health issues."

Nonfiction: Self-help (psychology/health). Subjects include health/medicine, psychology, women's issues/studies, balanced living, anger management, anxiety, coping. "Authors need to be a qualified psychotherapist or health practitioner to publish with us." Submit proposal package including outline, 2 sample chapter(s), competing titles and a compelling, supported reason why the book is unique.

Recent Title(s): *The Anxiety & Phobia Workbook, 3rd ed*, by Edmund J. Bourne; *Rosacea: A Self-Help Guide*, by Arlen Brownstein; *Brave New You*, by Mary and John Valentis.

Tips: Audience includes psychotherapists and lay readers wanting step-by-step strategies to solve specific problems. "Our definition of a self-help psychology or health book is one that teaches essential life skills. The primary goal is to train the reader so that, after reading the book, he or she can deal more effectively with health and/or psychological challenges."

NEW HOPE PUBLISHERS, Woman's Missionary Union, P.O. Box 12065, Birmingham AL 35202-2065. (205)991-8100. Fax: (205)991-4015. E-mail: new_hope@wmu.org. Website: www.newhopepubl.com. **Acquisitions:** Acquisitions Editor. **Publishes 24-27 titles/year. Receives several hundred queries/year. 25% of books from first-time authors; large% from unagented writers. Pays royalty on net receipts.** Publishes book 2 years after acceptance of ms. Responds in 6 weeks to mss. Book catalog for 9×12 SAE with 3 first-class stamps; ms guidelines online.

Imprints: New Hope.

O→ "Our goal is to create unique books that help women and families to grow in Christ and share His hope."

Nonfiction: "We publish books dealing with all facets of Christian life for women and families, including health, discipleship, missions, ministry, Bible studies, spiritual development, parenting, and marriage. We currently do not accept adult fiction or children's picture books. We are particularly interested in niche categories and books on lifestyle development and change." Children's/juvenile (religion). Subjects include child guidance/parenting (from Christian perspective), education (Christian church), health/medicine (Christian), multicultural, religion (spiritual development, Bible study, life situations from Christian perspective, ministry), women's issues/studies (Christian), church leadership, evangelism. Prefers a query and prospectus but will evaluate a complete ms.

Recent Title(s): *Called and Accountable*, by Henry Blackaby; *Getting Better, Not Bitter: A Spiritual Prescription for Breast Cancer*, by Brenda Ladun; *The Gospel Truth About Money Management*, by Judy Woodward Bates.

NEW HORIZON PRESS, P.O. Box 669, Far Hills NJ 07931. (908)604-6311. Fax: (908)604-6330. E-mail: nhp@newhorizonpressbooks.com. Website: www.newhorizonpressbooks.com. **Acquisitions:** Dr. Joan S. Dunphy, publisher (nonfiction, social cause, true crime). Estab. 1983. Publishes hardcover and trade paperback originals. **Publishes 12 titles/year. 90% of books from first-time authors; 50% from unagented writers. Pays standard royalty on net receipts. Offers advance.** Publishes book 2 years after acceptance of ms. Accepts simultaneous submissions. Book catalog and ms guidelines free; ms guidelines online.

Imprints: Small Horizons.

O→ New Horizon publishes adult nonfiction featuring true stories of uncommon heroes, true crime, social issues and self help. Introducing a new line of children's self-help.

Nonfiction: Biography, children's/juvenile, how-to, self-help. Subjects include child guidance/parenting, creative nonfiction, government/politics, health/medicine, nature/environment, psychology, women's issues/studies, true crime. Submit proposal package including outline, 3 sample chapter(s), résumé, author bio, photo, marketing information.

Recent Title(s): *Shattered Bonds*, by Cindy Band and Julie Malear; *Perilous Journey*, by Patricia Sutherland; *Race Against Evil*, by David Race Bannon.

Tips: "We are a small publisher, thus it is important that the author/publisher have a good working relationship. The author must be willing to promote his book."

NEW VICTORIA PUBLISHERS, P.O. Box 27, Norwich VT 05055-0027. (802)649-5297. Fax: (802)649-5297. E-mail: newvic@aol.com. Website: www.newvictoria.com. Editor: ReBecca Beguin. **Acquisitions:** Claudia Lamperti, editor. Estab. 1976. Publishes trade paperback originals. **Publishes 4-6 titles/year. Receives 100 submissions/year. 50% of books from first-time authors; large% from unagented writers. Pays 10% royalty.** Publishes book 1 year after acceptance of ms. Does not accept simultaneous submissions. Book catalog free; ms guidelines for SASE.

O→ "New Victoria is a nonprofit literary and cultural organization producing the finest in lesbian fiction and nonfiction." Emphasizing mystery. De-emphasizing coming-of-age stories.

Nonfiction: Biography. Subjects include gay/lesbian, history (feminist), women's issues/studies. "We are interested in feminist history or biography and interviews with or topics relating to lesbians." No poetry. Submit outline, sample chapter(s).

Fiction: Adventure, erotica, fantasy, feminist, historical, humor, mystery (amateur sleuth), romance, science fiction, western. "Looking for strong feminist characters, also strong plot and action. We will consider most anything if it is well written and appeals to lesbian/feminist audience. Hard copy only—no disks." Submit outline, sample chapter(s), synopsis.

Recent Title(s): *Theoretically Dead*, by Tinker Marks (mystery); *Circles of Power*, by Barbara Summerhawk.

Tips: "Try to appeal to a specific audience and not write for the general market. We're still looking for well-written, hopefully humorous, lesbian fiction and well-researched biography or nonfiction."

NEW VOICES PUBLISHING, KidsTerrain, Inc., P.O. Box 560, Wilmington MA 01887. (978)658-2131. Fax: (978)988-8833. E-mail: rschiano@kidsterrain.com. Website: www.kidsterrain.com. **Acquisitions:** Rita Schiano, executive editor (children's books). Estab. 2000. Publishes hardcover and trade paperback originals. **Publishes 5 titles/year. Receives 30 queries and 20 mss/year. 95% of books from first-time authors; 95% from unagented writers. Pays 10-15% royalty on wholesale price.** Publishes book 1 year after acceptance of ms. Does not accept simultaneous submissions. Responds in 1 month to queries; 3 months to proposals; 3 months to mss. Book catalog online; ms guidelines online.

O→ The audience for this company is children ages 4-9.

Nonfiction: Children's/juvenile, illustrated book. Subjects include child guidance/parenting. Query with SASE. Reviews artwork/photos as part of ms package. Send photocopies.

Fiction: Juvenile. Query with SASE.

Recent Title(s): *The Magic in Me*, by Maggie Moran (children's fiction); *Aunt Rosa's House*, by Maggie Moran (children's fiction); *Last Night I Left Earth for Awhile*, by Natalie Brown-Douglas (children's fiction).

Tips: "Know, specifically, what your story/book is about."

NEW WORLD LIBRARY, 14 Pamaron Way, Novato CA 94949. (415)884-2100. Fax: (415)884-2199. E-mail: escort@nwlib.com. Website: www.newworldlibrary.com. Publisher: Marc Allen. Senior Editor: Jason Gardner. **Acquisitions:** Georgia Hughes, editorial director. Estab. 1979. Publishes hardcover and trade paperback originals and reprints. **Publishes 40 titles/year. 20% of books from first-time authors; 50% from unagented writers. Pays 12-20% royalty on wholesale price for hardcover. Offers $0-30,000 advance.** Publishes book 12-18 months after acceptance of ms. Accepts simultaneous submissions. Responds in 3 months to queries. Book catalog and ms guidelines free; ms guidelines online.

Imprints: Nataraj, H.J. Kramer

O→ NWL is dedicated to publishing books and audio projects that inspire and challenge us to improve the quality of our lives and our world.

Nonfiction: Gift book, self-help. Subjects include alternative lifestyles (health), business/economics (prosperity), ethnic (African/American, Native American), health/medicine (natural), money/finance, nature/environment, psychology, religion,

spirituality, women's issues/studies, nutrition, personal growth, parenting. Query with SASE or submit outline, 1 sample chapter(s), author bio, SASE. Reviews artwork/photos as part of ms package. Send photocopies.
Recent Title(s): *The Seven Whispers*, by Christina Baldwin; *The Power of Now*, by Eckhart Tolle; *The Power of Partnership*, by Riane Eisler.

NEW YORK UNIVERSITY PRESS, 838 Broadway, New York NY 10003. (212)998-2575. Fax: (212)995-3833. Website: www.nyupress.org. **Acquisitions:** Eric Zinner (cultural studies, literature, media, history); Jennifer Hammer (Jewish studies, psychology, religion, women's studies); Stephen Magro (social sciences); Deborah Gershenowitz (law, American history). Estab. 1916. Hardcover and trade paperback originals. **Publishes 100 titles/year. Receives 800-1,000 queries/year. 30% of books from first-time authors; 90% from unagented writers. Pays royalty on net receipts.** Publishes book 9-11 months after acceptance of ms. Accepts simultaneous submissions. Responds in 1-4 months (peer reviewed) to proposals. Ms guidelines online.

O→ New York University Press embraces ideological diversity. "We often publish books on the same issue from different poles to generate dialogue, engender and resist pat categorizations."

Nonfiction: Subjects include anthropology/archeology, business/economics, ethnic, gay/lesbian, government/politics, history, language/literature, military/war, psychology, regional, religion, sociology, sports, women's issues/studies. Query with SASE or submit proposal package including outline, 1 sample chapter(s). Reviews artwork/photos as part of ms package. Send photocopies.

NEWMARKET PRESS, 18 E. 48th St., New York NY 10017. (212)832-3575. Fax: (212)832-3629. E-mail: mailbox@newmarketpress.com. President/Publisher: Esther Margolis. **Acquisitions:** Keith Hollaman, executive editor; Shannon Berning, assistant editor. Publishes hardcover and trade paperback originals and reprints. **Publishes 25-30 titles/year. 10% of books from first-time authors; 20% from unagented writers. Pays royalty. Offers varied advance.** Publishes book 1 year after acceptance of ms. Accepts simultaneous submissions. Responds in 3 months to queries; 3 months to proposals; 3 months to mss. Ms guidelines for #10 SASE.

O→ Currently emphasizing movie tie-in/companion books, health, psychology, parenting. De-emphasizing fiction.

Nonfiction: "Our focus is on parenting and health titles, and on finance books." Biography, coffee table book, self-help. Subjects include child guidance/parenting, cooking/foods/nutrition, general nonfiction, health/medicine, history, memoirs, personal finance, film/performing arts. Query with SASE or submit proposal package including outline, 1-3 sample chapter(s), author info explaining why you're the best person to write this book.
Recent Title(s): *Kids & Sports: Everything You and Your Child Need to Know About Sports, Physical Activity, and Good Health*, by Eric Small, M.D., F.A.A.P. (health and fitness/parenting); *E.T.: The Extra-Terrestrial from Concept to Classic: The Illustrated Story of the Film and Filmmakers*, by Stephen Spielberg and Melissa Mathison (film).

NO STARCH PRESS, INC., 555 De Haro St., Suite 250, San Francisco CA 94107. (415)863-9900. Fax: (415)863-9950. E-mail: info@nostarch.com. Website: www.nostarch.com. **Acquisitions:** William Pollock, publisher. Estab. 1994. Publishes trade paperback originals. **Publishes 10-12 titles/year. Receives 100 queries and 5 mss/year. 80% of books from first-time authors; 90% from unagented writers. Pays 10-15% royalty on wholesale price. Offers advance.** Publishes book 4 months after acceptance of ms. Accepts simultaneous submissions. Book catalog free.
Imprints: Linux Journal Press.

O→ No Starch Press Inc. is an independent publishing company committed to producing easy-to-read and information-packed computer books. Currently emphasizing open source, Web development, computer security issues, programming tools, and robotics. "More stuff, less fluff."

Nonfiction: How-to, reference, technical. Subjects include computers/electronic, hobbies, software (Open Source). Submit outline, 1 sample chapter(s), author bio, market rationale. Reviews artwork/photos as part of ms package. Send photocopies.
Recent Title(s): *The Art of Interactive Design*, by Chris Crawford; *The Book of Wi-Fi*, by John Ross.
Tips: "No fluff—content, content, content or just plain fun. Understand how your book fits into the market. Tell us why someone, anyone, will buy your book. Be enthusiastic."

[N] **NODIN PRESS**, Micawber's Inc., 530 N. Third St., Suite 120, Minneapolis MN 55401. (612)333-6300. Fax: (612)333-6303. E-mail: nstill4402@aol.com. **Acquisitions:** Norton Stillman, publisher. Publishes hardcover and trade paperback originals. **Publishes 4 titles/year. Receives 20 queries and 20 mss/year. 75% of books from first-time authors; 100% from unagented writers. Pays 10% royalty. Offers $250-1,000 advance.** Publishes book 20 months after acceptance of ms. Accepts simultaneous submissions. Responds in 6 months to queries. Book catalog and ms guidelines free.

O→ Nodin Press publishes Minnesota regional titles: nonfiction, memoir, sports, poetry.

Nonfiction: Biography, regional guide book. Subjects include history (ethnic), regional, sports, travel. Query with SASE.
Poetry: Regional (Minnesota poets). Submit 10 sample poems.
Recent Title(s): *Mountain Upside Down*, by John Toren; *Batter Up: Century of Minnesota Baseball*, by Ross Bernstein; *26 Minnesota Writers*, by D.E. Grazi (anthology).

NOLO, (formerly Nolo.com), 950 Parker St., Berkeley CA 94710. (510)549-1976. Fax: (510)548-5902. E-mail: info@nolo.com. Website: www.nolo.com. **Acquisitions:** Janet Portman, managing editor; Marcia Stewart, acquisitions editor. Estab. 1971. Publishes trade paperback originals. **Publishes 25 titles/year. 10% of books from first-time authors; 98% from unagented writers. Pays 10-12% royalty on net receipts.** Accepts simultaneous submissions. Responds in 2 weeks to proposals.

O→ "Our goal is to publish 'plain English' self-help law books, software and various electronic products for our consumers."

Nonfiction: How-to, reference, self-help. Subjects include business/economics, general nonfiction, money/finance, legal guides in various topics including employment, consumer, small business, intellectual property landlord/tenant and estate planning. "We do some business and finance titles, but always from a legal perspective, i.e., bankruptcy law." Query with SASE or submit outline, 1 sample chapter(s). Welcome queries but majority of titles are produced inhouse.

Recent Title(s): *Create Your Own Employee Handbook*, by Amy Del Po and Lisa Guerin; *Using Divorce Mediation*, by Katherine E. Stoner.

NOMAD PRESS, Nomad Communications, P.O. Box 875, Route 5 South, Norwich VT 05055. (802)649-1995. Fax: (802)649-2667. E-mail: info@nomadpress.net. Website: www.nomadpress.net. Publisher: Alex Kahan. **Acquisitions:** Lauri Berkenkamp, acquisitions editor. Publishes trade paperback originals. **Publishes 6+ titles/year. 60% of books from first-time authors; 90% from unagented writers. Pays royalty on retail price or makes outright purchase. Offers negotiable advance.** Publishes book 1 year after acceptance of ms. Does not accept simultaneous submissions. Responds in 1-2 months to mss. Book catalog online; ms guidelines online.

Nonfiction: Coffee table book, how-to, humor. Subjects include Americana, child guidance/parenting, creative nonfiction, hobbies, memoirs, money/finance, recreation, sports, travel. Actively seeking well-written nonfiction. No disorder-specific parenting mss, cookbooks, poetry, or technical manuals. Submit complete ms. Reviews artwork/photos as part of ms package. Send photocopies.

Recent Title(s): *Fighting Finish: The Volvo Ocean Race Round the World 2001-2002*, by Gary Jobson (sports); *The Risk in Being Alive: One Man's Adventures Around the Planet*, by Brian Hancock (adventure travel); *The New Teacher's Handbook*, by Yvonne Bender (teaching).

N **NONETHELESS PRESS**, 20332 W. 98th St., Lenexa KS 66220. (913)254-7266. Fax: (913)393-3245. E-mail: info@nonethelesspress.com. Website: www.nonethelesspress.com. **Acquisitions:** Morten Nilsen, acquisitions. Estab. 2002. Publishes hardcover, trade paperback and electronic originals and reprints. **Publishes 10-16 titles/year. Receives 400 queries and 100 mss/year. 50% of books from first-time authors; 60% from unagented writers. Pays 20% royalty on wholesale price.** Publishes book 8 months after acceptance of ms. Accepts simultaneous submissions. Responds in 3 months to queries; 3 months to proposals; 3 months to mss. Book catalog online; ms guidelines online.

Nonfiction: Audiocassettes, biography, children's/juvenile, coffee table book, gift book, illustrated book, scholarly, textbook. Subjects include alternative lifestyles, anthropology/archeology, art/architecture, contemporary culture, creative nonfiction, general nonfiction, history, humanities, language/literature, multicultural, New Age, philosophy, regional, social sciences, sociology, spirituality, translation, women's issues/studies, world affairs. Nonetheless Press is a new publisher that is following the best traditions of the small press movement, with an ambitious initial list. At a time when most independent publishers are crowding their titles into ever smaller niches, Nonetheless defies that convention and chooses manuscripts for the best of all possible reasons—because they are good. Query with SASE or submit proposal package including outline, 1-3 sample chapter(s). **All unsolicited mss returned unopened.** Reviews artwork/photos as part of ms package. Send photocopies.

Fiction: Adventure, comic books, experimental, historical, literary, mainstream/contemporary, mystery, picture books, poetry, poetry in translation, science fiction, short story collections, spiritual, suspense, translation, western, young adult. Query with SASE or send proposal with 1-3 sample chapter(s), synopsis. **All unsolicited mss returned unopened.**

Poetry: Query or submit 1-3 sample poems.

Recent Title(s): *Xenophilia*, by Robin Sathoff (art/spirituality); *The New Wife: The Evolving Role of the American Wife*, by Susan Shapiro Barash (women's studies); *The Reincarnation of Bennett McKinney*, by Steve From (western).

Tips: "Provide a detailed, specific proposal. Don't waste your time or ours with half-formed ideas vaguely expressed."

NORTH CAROLINA OFFICE OF ARCHIVES AND HISTORY, Historical Publications Section, 4622 Mail Service Center, Raleigh NC 27699-4622. (919)733-7442. Fax: (919)733-1439. E-mail: donna.kelly@ncmail.net. Website: www.ah.dcr.state.nc.us/sections/hp. **Acquisitions:** Donna E. Kelly, administrator (North Carolina and southern history). Publishes hardcover and trade paperback originals. **Publishes 4 titles/year. Receives 20 queries and 25 mss/year. 5% of books from first-time authors; 100% from unagented writers. Makes one-time payment upon delivery of completed ms.** Publishes book 2 years after acceptance of ms. Accepts simultaneous submissions. Responds in 1 week to queries; 1 week to proposals; 2 months to mss. Ms guidelines for $3.

O→ "We publish *only* titles that relate to North Carolina. The North Carolina Office of Archives and History also publishes the *North Carolina Historical Review*, a scholarly journal of history."

Nonfiction: Hardcover and trade paperback books relating to North Carolina. Subjects include history (related to NC), military/war (related to NC), regional (NC and southern history). Query with SASE. Reviews artwork/photos as part of ms package. Send photocopies.

Recent Title(s): *Tar Heels: How North Carolinians Got Their Nickname*, by Michael Taylor; *The Civil War in Coastal North Carolina*, by John S. Carbone; *A History of African Americans in North Carolina*, by Crow, Escott and Hatley.

Tips: Audience is public school and college teachers and students, librarians, historians, genealogists, NC citizens, tourists.

NORTH LIGHT BOOKS, F&W Publications, 4700 Galbraith Rd., Cincinnati OH 45236. Editorial Director: Greg Albert. **Acquisitions:** Acquisitions Coordinator. Publishes hardcover and trade paperback how-to books. **Publishes 40-45 titles/year. Pays 10% royalty on net receipts. Offers $4,000 advance.** Accepts simultaneous submissions. Responds in 1 month to queries. Book catalog for 9×12 SAE with 6 first-class stamps.

O→ North Light Books publishes art, craft and design books, including watercolor, drawing, colored pencil and decorative painting titles that emphasize illustrated how-to art instruction. Currently emphasizing table-top crafts using materials found in craft stores like Michael's, Hobby Lobby.

Nonfiction: Art. How-to. Subjects include computers/electronic, hobbies, watercolor, drawing, colored pencil, decorative painting, comics, craft and graphic design instruction books. Interested in books on watercolor painting, basic drawing, pen and ink, colored pencil, decorative painting, table-top crafts, basic design, computer graphics, layout and typograpy. Do not submit coffee table art books without how-to art instruction. Query with SASE or submit outline. Send photocopies or duplicate transparencies.

Recent Title(s): *Mastering the Watercolor Wash*, by Joe Garcia; *Rubber Stamp Extravaganza*, by Vesta Abel; *Easy Christmas Projects You Can Paint*, by Margaret Wilson and Robyn Thomas.

NORTH POINT PRESS, Farrar Straus & Giroux, Inc., 19 Union Square W., New York NY 10003. (212)741-6900. Fax: (212)633-9385. **Acquisitions:** Rebecca Saletan, editorial director; Ethan Nosowsky, editor; Shacra Decker, editorial assistant. Estab. 1980. Publishes hardcover and paperback originals. **Publishes 25 titles/year. Receives 100 queries and 100 mss/year. 20% of books from first-time authors. Payhes 10 titles/year. Receives 100 queries and 20 mss/year. 10% of books from first-time authors; 100% from unagented writers.** Publishes book up to 2 years after acceptance of ms. Accepts simultaneous submissions. Responds in 6 months to queries. Book catalog for 9×12 SAE with 4 first-class stamps; ms guidelines online.

O→ "We publish collective biographies for ages 10 and up. Although we cover a wide array of subjects, all are published in this format. We are looking for titles for our Innovators series (history of technology) and Business Builders series."

Nonfiction: Collective biographies only. Children's/juvenile. Subjects include business/economics, ethnic, government/politics, health/medicine, history (history of technology), military/war, nature/environment, science. Query with SASE.

Recent Title(s): *Business Builders in Fast Food*, by Nathan Aaseng; *Women with Wings*, by Jacqueline McLean.

Tips: "Audience is primarily junior and senior high school students writing reports."

NORTHEASTERN UNIVERSITY PRESS, 360 Huntington Ave., 416CP, Boston MA 02115. (617)373-5480. Fax: (617)373-5483. Website: www.neu.edu/nupress. **Acquisitions:** William Frohlich, director (music, criminal justice); Robert Gormley, senior editor (history, political science, law and society); Elizabeth Swayze, editor (women's studies, American studies). Estab. 1977. Publishes hardcover originals and trade paperback originals and reprints. **Publishes 40 titles/year. Receives 500 queries and 100 mss/year. 50% of books from first-time authors; 90% from unagented writers. Pays 5-15% royalty on wholesale price. Offers $500-20,000 advance.** Publishes book 1 year after acceptance of ms. Accepts simultaneous submissions. Book catalog and ms guidelines free; ms guidelines online.

O→ Northeastern University Press publishes scholarly and general interest titles in the areas of American history, political science, criminal justice, women's studies, music and reprints of African-American literature. Currently emphasizing American studies. De-emphasizing literary studies.

Nonfiction: Biography, scholarly, adult trade, scholarly monographs. Subjects include Americana, history, regional, women's issues/studies, music, criminal justice. Query with SASE or submit proposal package including outline, 1-2 sample chapter(s). Reviews artwork/photos as part of ms package. Send photocopies.

Recent Title(s): *Rosie's Mom*, by Carrie Brown; *Puccini*, by Mary Jane Phillips-Matz; *Beacon Hill*, by Moying Li-Marcus.

NORTHERN ILLINOIS UNIVERSITY PRESS, 310 N. Fifth St., DeKalb IL 60115-2854. (815)753-1826. Fax: (815)753-1845. Director/Editor-in-Chief: Mary L. Lincoln. **Acquisitions:** Martin Johnson, acquisitions editor (history, politics); Kevin Batterfield, acquisitions editor (sports history, early American history). Estab. 1965. **Publishes 18-20 titles/year. Pays 10-15% royalty on wholesale price. Offers advance.** Does not accept simultaneous submissions. Book catalog free.

O→ NIU Press publishes scholarly work and books of general interest to the informed public. "We publish mainly history, politics, anthropology, and other social sciences. We are interested also in studies on the Chicago area and Midwest and in literature in translation." Currently emphasizing history, the social sciences and cultural studies.

Nonfiction: "Publishes mainly history, political science, social sciences, philosophy, literary and cultural studies, and regional studies." Subjects include anthropology/archeology, government/politics, history, language/literature, philosophy, regional, social sciences, translation, cultural studies. No collections of previously published essays, no unsolicited poetry. Query with SASE or submit outline, 1-3 sample chapter(s).

Recent Title(s): *Possessed: Women, Witches and Demons in Imperial Russia.*

[A] **NORTHFIELD PUBLISHING**, Moody Publishers, 215 W. Locust St., Chicago IL 60610. (800)678-8001. Fax: (312)329-2019. E-mail: acquisitions@moody.edu. Website: www.moodypublishers.org. **Acquisitions:** Acquisitions Coordinator. **Publishes 5-10 titles/year. 1% of books from first-time authors. Pays royalty on net receipts. Offers $500-50,000 advance.** Publishes book 1 year after acceptance of ms. Does not accept simultaneous submissions. Book catalog for 9×12 SAE with 2 first-class stamps.

O→ "Northfield publishes a line of books for non-Christians or those exploring the Christian faith. While staying true to Biblical principles, we eliminate some of the Christian wording and Scriptual references to avoid confusion."

Nonfiction: Biography (classic). Subjects include business/economics, child guidance/parenting, money/finance, religion. *Agented submissions only.*

Recent Title(s): *The World's Easiest Guide to Finances*, by Larry Burkett with Randy Southern.

NORTHLAND PUBLISHING, LLC, P.O. Box 1389, Flagstaff AZ 86002-1389. (928)774-5251. Fax: (928)774-0592. Website: www.northlandpub.com. **Acquisitions:** Tammy Gales, adult editor; Theresa Howell, kids editor (picture books, especially with wide appeal). Estab. 1958. Publishes hardcover and trade paperback originals. **Publishes 8-10 titles/year; imprint publishes 8-10 titles/year. Receives 2,000 submissions/year. 20% of books from first-time authors; 20% from unagented writers. Pays royalty. Offers advance.** Publishes book 1-2 years after acceptance of ms. Accepts simultaneous

submissions. Responds in 3 months to queries. Call for book catalog; ms guidelines online.
Imprints: Rising Moon (books for children).

- Rising Moon has temporarily suspended consideration of unsolicited manuscripts.

O⊸ "Northland Publishing acquires nonfiction books intended for general trade audiences on the American West and Southwest, including Native American arts, crafts, and culture; Mexican culture; regional cookery; Western lifestyle; and interior design and architecture. Northland is also accepting samples from entertaining travel writers and photographers from around the U.S. Samples will be considered on a work-for-hire basis for Northland's new visual tour series. Northland is not accepting poetry or fiction at this time."

Nonfiction: Query with SASE or submit outline, 2-3 sample chapter(s). No fax or e-mail submissions. Reviews artwork/photos as part of ms package. Picture books. Submit complete ms.
Recent Title(s): *The Desert Home*, by Tamara Hawkinson; *Fiesta Mexicali*, by Kelley Coffeen; *Sedona: Treasure of the Southwest*, by Kathleen Bryant.
Tips: "Our audience is composed of general interest readers."

[N] **W.W. NORTON CO., INC.**, 500 Fifth Ave., New York NY 10110. Fax: (212)869-0856. E-mail: manuscripts@wwnorton.com. Website: www.wwnorton.com. **Acquisitions:** Starling Lawrence, editor-in-chief; Robert Weil, executive editor; Edwin Barber; Jill Bialosky (literary fiction, biography, memoirs); Amy Cherry (history, biography, women's issues, African-American, health); Carol Houck-Smith (literary fiction, travel memoirs, behavioral sciences, nature); Angela von der Leppe (trade nonfiction, behavioral sciences, earth sciences, astronomy, neuro-science, education); Jim Mairs (history, biography, illustrated books); Alane Mason (serious nonfiction cultural and intellectual history, illustrated books, literary fiction and memoir); W. Drake McFeely, president (nonfiction, particularly science and social science). Estab. 1923. Publishes hardcover and paperback originals and reprints. **Publishes 300 titles/year. Pays royalty. Offers advance.** Does not accept simultaneous submissions. Responds in 2 months to queries. Ms guidelines online.
Imprints: Backcountry Publication, Countryman Press, W.W. Norton.

O⊸ General trade publisher of fiction, poetry and nonfiction, educational and professional books. "W. W. Norton Co. strives to carry out the imperative of its founder to 'publish books not for a single season, but for the years' in the areas of fiction, nonfiction and poetry."

Nonfiction: Autobiography, biography, reference, self-help. Subjects include agriculture/horticulture, art/architecture, business/economics, child guidance/parenting, community, computers/electronic, cooking/foods/nutrition, government/politics, health/medicine, history, hobbies, language/literature, memoirs, music/dance, nature/environment, photography, psychology, religion, science, sports, travel, antiques and collectibles, current affairs, family, games, law, mystery, nautical subjects, poetry, political science, sailing, transportation. College Department: Subjects include biological sciences, economics, psychology, political science and computer science. Professional Books specializes in psychotherapy. "We are not interested in considering books from the following categories: juvenile or young adult, religious, occult or paranormal, and arts and crafts." Query with SASE or submit 2-3, one of which should be the first chapter sample chapter(s). Please give a brief description of your submission, your writing credentials, and any experience, professional or otherwise, which is relevant to your submission. No phone calls. Address envelope and letter to The Editors.
Fiction: Literary, poetry, poetry in translation, religious. High-qulity literary fiction. "We are not interested in considering books from the following categories: juvenile or young adult, religious, occult or paranormal, genre fiction (formula romances, sci-fi or westerns)." Query with SASE or submit 2-3, one of which should be the first chapter sample chapter(s). Please give a brief description of your submission, your writing credentials, and any experience, professional or otherwise, which is relevant to your submission. No phone calls. Address envelope and letter to The Editors.
Recent Title(s): *Guns, Germs and Steel*, by Jared Diamond; *Island*, by Alistir MacLeod.

NOVA PRESS, 11659 Mayfield Ave., Suite 1, Los Angeles CA 90049. (310)207-4078. Fax: (310)571-0908. E-mail: novapress@aol.com. Website: www.novapress.net. **Acquisitions:** Jeff Kolby, president. Estab. 1993. Publishes trade paperback originals. **Publishes 4 titles/year. Pays 10-22½% royalty on net receipts. Offers advance.** Publishes book 6 months after acceptance of ms. Does not accept simultaneous submissions. Book catalog free.

O⊸ Nova Press publishes only test prep books for college entrance exams (SAT, GRE, GMAT, LSAT, etc.), and closely related reference books, such as college guides and vocabulary books.

Nonfiction: How-to, self-help, technical, test prep books for college entrance exams. Subjects include education, software.
Recent Title(s): *The MCAT Chemistry Book*, by Ajikumar Aryangat.

NW WRITERS' CORP., NSpirit Cultural Newsmagazine, Ogun Books, P.O. Box 24873, Federal Way WA 98093. (253)839-3177. Fax: (253)839-3207. E-mail: nwwriterscorp@aol.com. Website: www.nwwriterscorp.com. **Acquisitions:** Book Review Committee; Orisade Awodola, editor (nonfiction, genealogy, history, spiritual, empowerment, black, cultural studies). Estab. 1998. Publishes hardcover and trade paperback originals and reprints. **Publishes 6-8 titles/year; imprint publishes 2-3 titles/year. Receives 600 queries and 200 mss/year. 100% of books from first-time authors; 100% from unagented writers. Pays 20-25% royalty or makes outright purchase of $1,000-2,000.** Publishes book 1 year after acceptance of ms. Accepts simultaneous submissions. Responds in 1 month to queries; 1 month to proposals; 3 months to mss. Book catalog online; ms guidelines online.
Nonfiction: Autobiography, biography, booklets, multimedia. Subjects include creative nonfiction, education, ethnic, general nonfiction, history, multicultural, psychology, religion, social sciences, sociology, spirituality, women's issues/studies, world affairs, metaphysics. Query with SASE or submit proposal package including outline, 4 sample chapter(s). Reviews artwork/photos as part of ms package. Send photocopies.
Fiction: Ethnic, historical, multicultural, multimedia, religious, spiritual. "We accept fiction mss based on marketability and review for filming potential." Query with SASE.

Recent Title(s): *Millenium Trials of Black History*, by Lemuel Israel; *Ema Jane Whose Rib Am I*, by Della Westerfield.
Tips: Audience consists of educators, business leaders, college students.

OAK KNOLL PRESS, 310 Delaware St., New Castle DE 19720. (302)328-7232. Fax: (302)328-7274. E-mail: oakknoll@oakknoll.com. Website: www.oakknoll.com. **Acquisitions:** John Von Hoelle, director of publishing. Estab. 1976. Publishes hardcover and trade paperback originals and reprints. **Publishes 40 titles/year. Receives 250 queries and 100 mss/year. 50% of books from first-time authors; 100% from unagented writers.** Publishes book 12 months after acceptance of ms. Accepts simultaneous submissions. Ms guidelines online.

O- Oak Knoll specializes in books about books—preserving the art and lore of the printed word.

Nonfiction: How-to. Subjects include book arts, printing, papermaking, bookbinding, book collecting, etc. Reviews artwork/photos as part of ms package. Send photocopies.
Recent Title(s): *Historical Scripts*, by Stan Knight; *The Great Libraries*, by Stan Staikos.

OAK TREE PRESS, 2743 S. Veterans Pkwy., Suite 135, Springfield IL 62704-6402. (217)824-8001. Fax: (217)824-3424. E-mail: oaktreepub@aol.com. Website: www.oaktreebooks.com. **Acquisitions:** Sarah Wasson, acquisitions editor; Billie Johnson, publisher. Estab. 1998. Publishes hardcover, trade paperback and mass market paperback originals and reprints. **Publishes 8-10 titles/year; imprint publishes 3-4 titles/year. Receives 5,000 queries and 300 mss/year. 99% of books from first-time authors; 99% from unagented writers. Pays 10-20% royalty on wholesale price. Offers negotiable advance.** Publishes book 9-18 months after acceptance of ms. Accepts simultaneous submissions. Responds in 4-6 weeks to queries; 2 months to proposals; 2-3 months to mss. Book catalog for SASE or on website; ms guidelines for SASE or on website.

Imprints: Dark Oak Mysteries, Timeless Love.

O- "Oak Tree books primarily target readers of commercial, rather than literary fiction, and our nonfiction targets mainstream rather than academic readers."

Nonfiction: Biography, coffee table book, gift book, how-to, humor, self-help. Subjects include Americana, art/architecture, business/economics, creative nonfiction, ethnic, health/medicine, history, memoirs, philosophy, photography, regional, sociology, travel. Query with SASE. Reviews artwork/photos as part of ms package. Send photocopies.
Fiction: Adventure, confession, ethnic, fantasy (romance), feminist, humor, mainstream/contemporary, mystery (amateur sleuth, cozy, police procedural, private eye/hardboiled), picture books, romance (contemporary, futuristic/time travel, romantic suspense), suspense, young adult (adventure, mystery/suspense, romance). Small independent publisher with emphasis on mystery and romance novels. Query with SASE.
Recent Title(s): *Midlife Mojo*, by Robert M. Davis, Ph.D. (self-help); *Hearts Across Forever*, by Mary Montague Sikes (romance); *Callie & the Dealer & A Dog Named Jake*, by Wendy H. Mills (mystery).
Tips: "Spell everything correctly in the query letter! Understand the business side of book publishing—or at least be willing to learn a few basics. Be eager and enthusiastic about participating in the marketing and promotion of the title."

THE OAKLEA PRESS, 6912-B Three Chopt Rd., Richmond VA 23226. (804)281-5872. Fax: (804)281-5686. E-mail: info@oakleapress.com. Website: www.oakleapress.com. **Acquisitions:** John Gotschalk, editor; S.H. Martin, publisher. Publishes hardcover and trade paperback originals. **Receives 150 queries and 50 mss/year. 25% of books from first-time authors; 100% from unagented writers. Pays 10-20% royalty on wholesale price.** Publishes book 6 months after acceptance of ms. Accepts simultaneous submissions. Responds in 1 month to queries; 1 month to proposals; 3 months to mss. Book catalog online.
Nonfiction: How-to, self-help. Subjects include business/economics, psychology, spirituality, self-actualization, lean manufacturing, marketing. "Currently we are looking for books on self-improvement." Submit proposal package including outline, 1 sample chapter(s).
Recent Title(s): *Keys to the Kingdom and the Life You Want*, by Stephen Hawley Martin; *How to Grow a Second Skin for Your Soul*, by Alisa S. Burgess, Ph.D.

OCTAMERON ASSOCIATES, 1900 Mount Vernon Ave., Alexandria VA 22301. (703)836-5480. Website: www.octameron.com. **Acquisitions:** Karen Stokstad, editor. Publishes trade paperback originals. **Publishes 17 titles/year. Receives 100 submissions/year. 15% of books from first-time authors; 100% from unagented writers. Pays 7½% royalty on retail price. Offers $500-1,000 advance.** Publishes book 9 months after acceptance of ms. Accepts simultaneous submissions. Responds in 2 months to proposals. Book catalog free.
Nonfiction: Reference. Subjects include education. Submit proposal package including 2 sample chapter(s), table of contents.
Recent Title(s): *Majoring in Success*, by Anthony Arcieri and Marianne Green; *Great Colleges for the Real World*, by Michael Viollt.
Tips: Audience is high school students and their parents, high school guidance counselors. "Keep the tone light."

N **OHIO STATE UNIVERSITY PRESS**, 1070 Carmack Rd., Columbus OH 43210-1002. (614)292-6930. Fax: (614)292-2065. E-mail: ohiostatepress@osu.edu. Website: www.ohiostatepress.org. **Acquisitions:** Malcolm Litchfield, director; Heather Miller, acquisitions editor. Estab. 1957. **Publishes 30 titles/year. Pays royalty. Offers advance.** Responds in 3 months to queries. Ms guidelines online.

O- Ohio State University Press publishes scholarly nonfiction, and offers short fiction and short poetry prizes. Currently emphasizing history, literary studies, political science, women's health.

Nonfiction: Scholarly, scholarly. Subjects include business/economics, education, general nonfiction, government/politics, history (American), language/literature, multicultural, regional, sociology, women's issues/studies, criminology, literary criticism, women's health. Query with SASE.

Recent Title(s): *Saving Lives*, by Albert Goldbarth (poetry); *Visions of Place: The City, Neighborhoods, Suburbs, and Cincinnati's Clifton 1850-2000*, by Zane L. Miller (nonfiction).

OHIO UNIVERSITY PRESS, Scott Quadrangle, Athens OH 45701. (740)593-1155. Fax: (740)593-4536. Website: www.ohio.edu/oupress/. **Acquisitions:** Gillian Berchowitz, senior editor (American history and popular culture, legal history, African studies, Appalachian studies); David Sanders, director (literature, literary criticism, midwest and frontier studies, Ohioana). Estab. 1964. Publishes hardcover and trade paperback originals and reprints. **Publishes 45-50 titles/year. Receives 500 queries and 50 mss/year. 20% of books from first-time authors; 95% from unagented writers. Pays 7-10% royalty on net receipts.** Publishes book 1 year after acceptance of ms. Responds in 1 month to queries; 1 month to proposals; 2 months to mss. Book catalog free; ms guidelines online.

Imprints: Ohio University Research in International Studies (Gillian Berchowitz); Swallow Press (David Sanders, director).

O→ Ohio University Press publishes and disseminates the fruits of research and creative endeavor, specifically in the areas of literary studies, regional works, philosophy, contemporary history, African studies and frontier Americana. Its charge to produce books of value in service to the academic community and for the enrichment of the broader culture is in keeping with the university's mission of teaching, research and service to its constituents.

Nonfiction: Reference, scholarly. Subjects include Americana, anthropology/archeology, art/architecture, ethnic, gardening, government/politics, history, language/literature, military/war, nature/environment, philosophy, regional, sociology, travel, women's issues/studies, African studies. "We prefer queries or detailed proposals, rather than manuscripts, pertaining to scholarly projects that might have a general interest. Proposals should explain the thesis and details of the subject matter, not just sell a title." Query with SASE. Reviews artwork/photos as part of ms package. Send photocopies.

Recent Title(s): *Acquamarine Blue Five: Personal Stories of College Students with Autism*, edited by Dawn Prince-Hughes; *John Reed and the Writing of a Revolution*, by Daniel W. Lehman; *The Inclusive Corporation: The Disability Handbook for Business Professionals*, edited by Griff Hogan.

Tips: "Rather than trying to hook the editor on your work, let the material be compelling enough and well-presented enough to do it for you."

THE OLIVER PRESS, INC., 5707 W. 36th St., Minneapolis MN 55416-2510. (952)926-8981. Fax: (952)926-8965. E-mail: queries@oliverpress.com. Website: www.oliverpress.com. **Acquisitions:** Denise Sterling, editor. Estab. 1991. Publishes hardcover originals. **Publishes 10 titles/year. Receives 100 queries and 20 mss/year. 10% of books from first-time authors; 100% from unagented writers.** Publishes book up to 2 years after acceptance of ms. Accepts simultaneous submissions. Responds in 6 months to queries. Book catalog for 9×12 SAE with 4 first-class stamps; ms guidelines online.

O→ "We publish collective biographies for ages 10 and up. Although we cover a wide array of subjects, all are published in this format. We are looking for titles for our Innovators series (history of technology) and Business Builders series."

Nonfiction: Collective biographies only. Children's/juvenile. Subjects include business/economics, ethnic, government/politics, health/medicine, history (history of technology), military/war, nature/environment, science. Query with SASE.

Recent Title(s): *Business Builders in Fast Food*, by Nathan Aaseng; *Women with Wings*, by Jacqueline McLean.

Tips: "Audience is primarily junior and senior high school students writing reports."

ONE ON ONE COMPUTER TRAINING, Mosaic Media, 2055 Army Trail Rd., Suite 100, Addison IL 60101. (630)628-0500. Fax: (630)628-0550. E-mail: oneonone@pincom.com. Website: www.oootraining.com. **Acquisitions:** Natalie Young, manager product development. Estab. 1976. **Publishes 10-20 titles/year. 100% from unagented writers. Makes outright purchase of $3,500-10,000. Pays 5-10% royalty (rarely). Advance offer depends on purchase contract.** Publishes book 3 months after acceptance of ms. Does not accept simultaneous submissions. Responds in 1 month to queries. Book catalog free.

Imprints: OneOnOne Computer Training, Working Smarter, Professional Training Associates.

O→ One On One Computer Training publishes ongoing computer training and soft skills training for computer users and office professionals.

Nonfiction: How-to, self-help, technical. Subjects include computers/electronic, software, soft skills for businesses and creative use of digital media, Internet. **All unsolicited mss returned unopened.** Query.

Recent Title(s): *Problem Solving with Visual Basic*; *Managing People at Work.*

[A] **ONE WORLD BOOKS**, Ballantine Publishing Group, Inc., 1745 Broadway, New York NY 10019. (212)782-8378. Fax: (212)782-8442. **Acquisitions:** Melody Guy, senior editor. Publishes hardcover, trade and mass market paperback originals and trade paperback reprints. **Publishes 24 titles/year. Receives 350 queries and 500 submissions/year. 50% of books from first-time authors; 5% from unagented writers. Pays 7½-15% royalty on retail price. Offers $40,000-200,000 advance.** Publishes book 18 months after acceptance of ms. Accepts simultaneous submissions. Responds in 1 month to queries; 1 month to proposals; 2 months to mss.

Nonfiction: "All One World Books must be specifically written for either an African-American, Asian or Hispanic audience. Absolutely no exceptions!" Biography, cookbook, how-to, humor, self-help. Subjects include Americana, cooking/foods/nutrition, creative nonfiction, ethnic, government/politics, history, memoirs, multicultural, philosophy, psychology, recreation, travel, women's issues/studies, African-American studies. *Agented submissions only.*

Fiction: "All One World Books must be specifically written for either an African-American, Asian or Hispanic audience. Absolutely no exceptions!" Adventure, comic books, confession, erotica, ethnic, historical, humor, literary, mainstream/contemporary, multicultural, mystery, regional, romance, suspense, strong need for commercial women's fiction. "All One World Books must be specifically written for either an African-American, Asian or Hispanic audience. Absolutely no exceptions!" No poetry. *Agented submissions only.*

Recent Title(s): *Bill Clinton and Black America*, by Dewayne Wickham; *Bittersweet*, by Freddie Lee Johnson III.
Tips: Targets African-American, Asian and Hispanic readers. All books must be written in English.

N **ONSTAGE PUBLISHING**, 214 E. Moulton St. NE, Decatur AL 35601. (256)308-2300. Website: www.onstagebooks.com. **Acquisitions:** Dianne Hamilton, senior editor. Estab. 1999. Publishes hardcover and mass market paperback originals. **Publishes 5 titles/year. Receives 100 queries and 300 mss/year. 80% of books from first-time authors; 95% from unagented writers. Pays royalty on wholesale price. Offers variable advance.** Publishes book 1-2 years after acceptance of ms. Accepts simultaneous submissions. Responds in 1-2 months to queries; 1-2 months to proposals; 2-4 months to mss. Book catalog for 9×12 SASE with 3 first-class stamps or online at website; ms guidelines for #10 SASE or online at website.
Nonfiction: Biography, children's/juvenile, coffee table book. Subjects include education, history, music/dance, photography, sports. "We want nonfiction that reads like a story and is well referenced." Submit proposal package including outline, 3 sample chapter(s) or submit complete ms. Reviews artwork/photos as part of ms package. Send photocopies.
Fiction: Adventure, fantasy, historical, humor, juvenile, literary, mainstream/contemporary, mystery, picture books, regional, romance, science fiction, short story collections, sports, suspense, young adult. "We pride ourselves in scouting out new talent and publishing works by new writers. We publish mainly children's titles." Submit proposal package including 3 sample chapter(s), synopsis. Submit complete manuscript, if less than 50 pages. Submit art work to Senior Editor, copies only.
Recent Title(s): *Miracle at the Pump*, by Darren Butler (activity book for ages 5-8 based on the early life of Helen Keller); *Write Away*, by Laurel Griffith (educational instruction book designed by an elementary teacher that lays out a series of creative writing exercises for grades 1-6); *Secret of Crybaby Hollow*, by Darren Butler (middle-grade mystery book, ages 8-12, the third book in the Abbie Girl Spy Adventures).
Tips: "Our audience is pre-K to young adult." "Study our catalog and get a sense of the kind of books we publish, so that you know whether your project is likely to be right for us."

N **OPEN COURT PUBLISHING CO.**, Carus Publishing Company, 332 S. Michigan Ave., Suite 1100, Chicago IL 60604-9968. Fax: (312)939-8150. Estab. 1887. Publishes hardcover and trade paperback originals. **Publishes 20 titles/year. Pays 5-15% royalty on wholesale price.** Publishes book 8 months after acceptance of ms. Does not accept simultaneous submissions. Book catalog online; ms guidelines free.
Nonfiction: Scholarly. Subjects include contemporary culture (popular culture), education, general nonfiction, history, philosophy, psychology, religion. Query with SASE or submit proposal package including outline, 1 sample chapter(s), TOC, author's VITA, cover letter, intended audience.
Recent Title(s): *The Matrix and Philosophy*, edited by William Irwin (philosophy); *Tool-Being*, by Graham Harman (philosophy).
Tips: Philosophers and intelligent general readers.

OPEN ROAD PUBLISHING, P.O. Box 284, Cold Spring Harbor NY 11724. (631)692-7172. Fax: (631)692-7193. E-mail: Jopenroad@aol.com. Website: openroadpub.com. Publisher: Jonathan Stein. Publishes trade paperback originals. **Publishes 22-27 titles/year. Receives 200 queries and 75 mss/year. 30% of books from first-time authors; 98% from unagented writers. Pays 5-6% royalty on retail price. Offers $1,000-5,000 advance.** Publishes book 3 months after acceptance of ms. Accepts simultaneous submissions. Responds in 1 month to queries; 2 months to proposals. Book catalog and ms guidelines free.

- Open Road publishes travel guides and has expanded into other areas with its new imprint, Cold Spring Press, particularly sports/fitness, topical, biographies, history, fantasy.

Nonfiction: How-to. Subjects include travel. Query with SASE.
Recent Title(s): *Tahiti & French Polynesia Guide*, by Jon Prince; *Arizona Guide*, by Larry Ludmer; *Caribbean with Kids*, by Paris Permenter & John Bigley.

OPTIMA BOOKS, 2820 Eighth St., Berkeley CA 94710. (510)848-8708. Fax: (510)848-8737. E-mail: esl@optimabooks.com. Website: www.optimabooks.com. **Acquisitions:** Robert Graul, editor (ESL, remedial reading, writing). Estab. 1988. Publishes books for English as a second language. **Publishes 4 titles/year. Receives 8 queries and 5 mss/year. 20% of books from first-time authors; 100% from unagented writers. Makes outright purchase.** Publishes book 8 months after acceptance of ms. Accepts simultaneous submissions. Responds in 2 months to mss.

- Optima publishes books dealing with English as a second language. Currently emphasizing remedial reading, remedial writing and reading training. Discontinuing foreign language products. Also interested in remedial arithmetic and math.

Nonfiction: Textbook, self teaching. Subjects include language/literature, ESL (English as a second language), remedial reading, writing and math. "Books should be usable in the classroom or by the individual in a self-teaching capacity. Should be written for the non-native speaker desiring knowledge of American slang and jargon." Query with SASE. Reviews artwork/photos as part of ms package. Send photocopies.
Recent Title(s): *Raising Reading Scores*, by Allan Sack; *Real Stories*, by Toni Ortner; *The Street Talk Dictionary*, by R.E. Goodman.

ORANGE FRAZER PRESS, INC., P.O. Box 214, Wilmington OH 45177. (937)382-3196. Fax: (937)383-3159. Website: www.orangefrazer.com. **Acquisitions:** Marcy Hawley, editor. Publishes hardcover and trade paperback originals and reprints. **Publishes 20 titles/year. Receives 50 queries and 40 mss/year. 50% of books from first-time authors; 99% from unagented writers. Pays 10-12% royalty on wholesale price. Offers advance.** Publishes book 18 months after acceptance of ms. Accepts simultaneous submissions. Responds in 2 months to queries; 1 month to proposals; 1 month to mss. Book catalog free.

O‐ Orange Frazer Press accepts Ohio-related nonfiction only; corporate histories.

Nonfiction: Accepts Ohio nonfiction only! Biography, coffee table book, cookbook, gift book, humor, illustrated book, reference, textbook. Subjects include art/architecture, cooking/foods/nutrition, education, history, memoirs, nature/environment, photography, recreation, regional (Ohio), sports, travel, women's issues/studies. Submit proposal package including outline, 1 sample chapter(s), SASE. Reviews artwork/photos as part of ms package. Send photocopies or transparencies.

Recent Title(s): *Party Animals, Washington, D.C*; *Building Ohio, A Traveler's Guide to Rural Ohio.*

Tips: "We do many high-end company and corporate histories."

OREGON STATE UNIVERSITY PRESS, 101 Waldo Hall, Corvallis OR 97331-6407. (541)737-3166. Fax: (541)737-3170. Website: osu.orst.edu/dept/press. **Acquisitions:** Mary Elizabeth Braun, acquiring editor. Estab. 1962. Publishes hardcover and paperback originals. **Publishes 15-20 titles/year. Receives 400 submissions/year. 75% of books from first-time authors; 100% from unagented writers. Pays royalty on net receipts.** Publishes book 1 year after acceptance of ms. Does not accept simultaneous submissions. Responds in 3 months to queries. Book catalog and ms guidelines online or for 6×9 SAE with 2 first-class stamps; ms guidelines online.

O‐ Oregon State University Press publishes several scholarly and specialized books and books of particular importance to the Pacific Northwest. "OSU Press plays an essential role by publishing books that may not have a large audience, but are important to scholars, students and librarians in the region."

Nonfiction: Publishes scholarly books in history, biography, geography, literature, natural resource management, with strong emphasis on Pacific or Northwestern topics. Reference, scholarly. Subjects include regional, science. Submit outline, sample chapter(s).

Recent Title(s): *Frigid Embrace: Politics, Economics, & Environment in Alaska*, by Stephen Haycox; *Elegant Arches, Soaring Spans: C.B. McCullough, Oregon's Master Bridge Builder*, by Robert W. Hadlow; *Crater Lake National Park: A History*, by Rick Harmon.

[A] **THE OVERLOOK PRESS**, Distributed by Penguin Putnam, 141 Wooster St., New York NY 10012. (212)673-2210. Fax: (212)673-2296. Publisher: Peter Mayer. **Acquisitions:** (Ms.) Tracy Carns, publishing director. Estab. 1971. Publishes hardcover and trade paperback originals and hardcover reprints. **Publishes 40 titles/year. Receives 300 submissions/year. Pays 3-15% royalty on wholesale price or retail price. Offers advance.** Does not accept simultaneous submissions. Responds in 5 months to queries. Book catalog free.

Imprints: Elephant's Eye, Tusk Books.

O‐ Overlook Press publishes fiction, children's books and nonfiction.

Nonfiction: Biography. Subjects include art/architecture, film/cinema/stage, history, regional (New York State), current events, design, health/fitness, how-to, lifestyle, martial arts. No pornography. *Agented submissions only.*

Fiction: Literary, some commercial, foreign literature in translation. *Agented submissions only.*

THE OVERMOUNTAIN PRESS, P.O. Box 1261, Johnson City TN 37605. (423)926-2691. Fax: (423)929-2464. E-mail: submissions@overmtn.com. Website: www.overmountainpress.com. **Acquisitions:** Jason Weems, editor. Estab. 1970. Publishes hardcover and trade paperback originals and reprints. **Publishes 15-20 titles/year. Receives 500 queries and 100 mss/year. 50% of books from first-time authors; 100% from unagented writers. Pays 7½-15% royalty on wholesale price.** Publishes book 1 year after acceptance of ms. Accepts simultaneous submissions. Responds in 6 months to proposals; 6 months to mss. Book catalog and ms guidelines free; ms guidelines online.

Imprints: Silver Dagger Mysteries.

O‐ The Overmountain Press publishes primarily Appalachian history. Audience is people interested in history of Tennessee, Virginia, North Carolina, Kentucky, and all aspects of this region—Revolutionary War, Civil War, county histories, historical biographies, etc. Currently reviewing only regional. De-emphasizing general interest children's fiction, poetry.

Nonfiction: Regional works only. Biography, children's/juvenile, coffee table book, cookbook. Subjects include Americana, cooking/foods/nutrition, ethnic, history, military/war, nature/environment, photography, regional, women's issues/studies, Native American. Submit proposal package including outline, 3 sample chapter(s), marketing suggestions. Reviews artwork/photos as part of ms package. Send photocopies.

Fiction: Picture books.

Recent Title(s): *Apple Doll*, by Kathleen Phillips Poulsen (children's picture books); *Southwest Virginia Crossroads*, by Joe Tennis.

Tips: "Please submit a proposal. Please no phone calls."

RICHARD C. OWEN PUBLISHERS, INC., P.O. Box 585, Katonah NY 10536. (914)232-3903. Website: www.rcowen.com. **Acquisitions:** Janice Boland, director, children's books; Amy Finney, project editor (professional development, teacher-oriented books). Estab. 1982. Publishes hardcover and paperback originals. **Publishes 23 titles/year. Receives 50 queries and 1,000 mss/year. 99% of books from first-time authors; 100% from unagented writers. Pays 5% royalty on wholesale price. Books for Young Learners Anthologies and picture storybooks: flat fee for all rights.** Publishes book 2-5 years after acceptance of ms. Accepts simultaneous submissions. Responds in 1 month to queries; 1 month to proposals; 5 months to mss. Ms guidelines online.

O‐ "In addition to publishing good literature, stories for 5-7-year-old children, we are also seeking mss for short, snappy stories to be included in anthologies for 7-8-year-old children. Subjects include humor, careers, mysteries, science fiction, folktales, women, fashion trends, sports, music, myths, journalism, history, inventions, planets, architecture, plays, adventure, technology, vehicles."

Nonfiction: Children's/juvenile. Subjects include animals, art/architecture, fashion/beauty, gardening, history, music/dance, nature/environment, recreation, science, sports, women's issues/studies, contemporary culture. "Our books are for kindergarten, first and second grade children to read on their own. The stories are very brief—under 1,000 words—yet well structured and crafted with memorable characters, language and plots." Send for ms guidelines, then submit complete ms with SASE via mail only or visit website.

Fiction: Picture books. "Brief, strong story line, believable characters, natural language, exciting—child-appealing stories with a twist. No lists books, alphabet or counting books." Also seeking mss for upcoming anthologies of short, snappy stories and articles for 7-8-year-old children (2nd grade). Subjects include humor, careers, mysteries, science fiction, folktales, women, fashion trends, sports, music, mysteries, myths, journalism, history, inventions, planets, architecture, plays, adventure, technology, vehicles. Send for ms guidelines, then submit full ms with SASE via mail only. No e-mail submissions please.

Poetry: "Poems that excite children are fun, humorous, fresh and interesting. If rhyming, must be without force or contrivance. Poems should tell a story or evoke a mood or atmostphere and have rhythmic language." No jingles. Submit complete ms.

Recent Title(s): *Powwow*, by Rhonda Cox (nonfiction); *Concrete*, by Ellen Javernich (fiction); *Bunny Magic*, by Suzanne Hardin (humor).

Tips: "We don't respond to queries or e-mails. Please do *not* fax or e-mail us. Because our books are so brief it is better to send entire ms. We publish story books with inherent educational value for young readers—books they can read with enjoyment and success. We believe students become enthusiastic, independent, life-long learners when supported and guided by skillful teachers using good books. The professional development work we do and the books we publish support these beliefs."

OWL BOOKS, Henry Holt & Co., Inc., 115 W. 18th St., New York NY 10011. (212)886-9200. Fax: (212)633-0748. Website: www.henryholt.com. **Acquisitions:** Deborah Brody, senior editor. Estab. 1996. **Publishes 135-140 titles/year; imprint publishes 50-60 titles/year. 30% of books from first-time authors. Pays 6-7½% royalty on retail price. Offers variable advance.** Publishes book 1 year after acceptance of ms. Accepts simultaneous submissions. Responds in 3 months to proposals. Ms guidelines online.

- "This publisher accepts agented submissions only."

"We are looking for original, great ideas that have commercial appeal, but that you can respect."

Nonfiction: Subjects include art/architecture, cooking/foods/nutrition, gardening, health/medicine, history, language/literature, nature/environment (and Environment), regional, sociology, sports, travel, biography. "Broad range." *Agented submissions only.* Query with outline, 1 sample chapter and SASE.

Fiction: Literary, mainstream/contemporary. *Agented submissions only.* Query with synopsis, 1 sample chapter and SASE.

Recent Title(s): *White Boy Shuffle*, by Paul Beatty; *The Debt to Pleasure*, by John Lanchester.

OXFORD UNIVERSITY PRESS, 198 Madison Ave., New York NY 10016. (212)726-6000. Website: www.oupusa.org. **Acquisitions:** Joan Bossert, vice president/editorial director; Laura Brown, president. Publishes hardcover and trade paperback originals and reprints. **Publishes 1,500 titles/year. 40% of books from first-time authors; 80% from unagented writers. Pays 0-15% royalty on wholesale price or retail price. Offers $0-40,000 advance.** Publishes book 10 months after acceptance of ms. Accepts simultaneous submissions. Responds in at least 3 months to proposals. Book catalog free; ms guidelines online.

"We publish books that make a significant contribution to the literature and research in a number of disciplines, which reflect the departments at the University of Oxford."

Nonfiction: Oxford is an academic, scholarly press. Biography, children's/juvenile, reference, technical, textbook. Subjects include anthropology/archeology, art/architecture, business/economics, computers/electronic, gay/lesbian, government/politics, health/medicine, history, language/literature, military/war, money/finance, music/dance, nature/environment, philosophy, psychology (and psychiatry), religion, science, sociology, women's issues/studies, law. Submit outline, sample chapter(s), cv. Reviews artwork/photos as part of ms package.

PACIFIC BOOKS, PUBLISHERS, P.O. Box 558, Palo Alto CA 94302-0558. Phone/Fax: (650)856-6400. **Acquisitions:** Henry Ponleithner, editor. Estab. 1945. **Publishes 6-12 titles/year. Pays 7½-15% royalty.** Does not accept simultaneous submissions. Responds in 1 month to queries. Book catalog for 9×12 SAE; ms guidelines for 9×12 SAE.

Pacific Books publishes general interest and scholarly nonfiction including professional and technical books, and college textbooks.

Nonfiction: General interest, professional, technical and scholarly nonfiction trade books. Reference, scholarly, technical, textbook. Subjects include Americana (western), general nonfiction, regional, translation, Hawaiiana. Looks for "well-written, documented material of interest to a significant audience." Also considers text and reference books for high school and college. Query with SASE or submit outline. Reviews artwork/photos as part of ms package.

Recent Title(s): *How to Choose a Nursery School: A Parents' Guide to Preschool Education*, by Ada Anbar.

PACIFIC PRESS PUBLISHING ASSOCIATION, Trade Book Division, P.O. Box 5353, Nampa ID 83653-5353. (208)465-2570. Fax: (208)465-2531. E-mail: booksubmissions@pacificpress.com. Website: www.pacificpress.com. **Acquisitions:** Tim Lale (children's stories, inspirational, biography, lifestyle, biblical, doctrinal). Estab. 1874. Publishes hardcover and trade paperback originals and reprints. **Publishes 35 titles/year. Receives 600 submissions/year. 35% of books from first-time authors; 100% from unagented writers. Pays 8-16% royalty. Offers $300-1,500 advance depending on**

length. Publishes book up to 2 years after acceptance of ms. Does not accept simultaneous submissions. Responds in 3 months to queries. Ms guidelines online.

- Pacific Press is an exclusively religious publisher of the Seventh-day Adventist denomination. "We are looking for practical, how-to oriented manuscripts on religion, health, and family life that speak to human needs, interests and problems from a biblical perspective. We publish books that promote a stronger relationship with God, deeper Bible study, and a healthy, helping lifestyle."

Nonfiction: Biography, children's/juvenile, cookbook (vegetarian), how-to, humor, self-help. Subjects include child guidance/parenting, cooking/foods/nutrition (vegetarian only), health/medicine, history, nature/environment, philosophy, religion, women's issues/studies, family living, Christian lifestyle, bible study, Christian doctrine, eschatology. "We can't use anything totally secular or written from other than a Christian perspective." No fiction accepted. Query or request information on how to submit a proposal. Reviews artwork/photos as part of ms package.

Recent Title(s): *Under the Shadow of the Rising Sun*, by Don Mansell; *100 Creative Prayer Ideas for Kids*, by Karen Holford.

Tips: "Our primary audience is members of the Seventh-day Adventist denomination. Almost all are written by Seventh-day Adventists. Books that are doing well for us are those that relate the biblical message to practical human concerns and those that focus more on the experiential rather than theoretical aspects of Christianity. We are assigning more titles, using less unsolicited material—although we still publish manuscripts from freelance submissions and proposals."

PALADIN PRESS, P.O. Box 1307, Boulder CO 80306-1307. (303)443-7250. Fax: (303)442-8741. E-mail: editorial@paladin-press.com. Website: www.paladin-press.com. President/Publisher: Peder C. Lund. **Acquisitions:** Jon Ford, editorial director. Estab. 1970. Publishes hardcover originals and paperback originals and reprints. **Publishes 50 titles/year. 50% of books from first-time authors; 100% from unagented writers. Pays 10-15% royalty on net receipts. Offers advance.** Publishes book 1 year after acceptance of ms. Accepts simultaneous submissions. Responds in 2 months to proposals. Book catalog free.

Imprints: Sycamore Island Books, Flying Machines Press, Outer Limits Press.

- Paladin Press publishes the "action library" of nonfiction in military science, police science, weapons, combat, personal freedom, self-defense, survival.

Nonfiction: "Paladin Press primarily publishes original manuscripts on military science, weaponry, self-defense, personal privacy, financial freedom, espionage, police science, action careers, guerrilla warfare and fieldcraft." How-to, reference. Subjects include government/politics, military/war, money/finance, science. "If applicable, send sample photographs and line drawings with complete outline and sample chapters." Query with SASE.

Recent Title(s): *Techniques of Medieval Armour Reproduction*, by Brian Price.

Tips: "We need lucid, instructive material aimed at our market and accompanied by sharp, relevant illustrations and photos. As we are primarily a publisher of 'how-to' books, a manuscript that has step-by-step instructions, written in a clear and concise manner (but not strictly outline form) is desirable. No fiction, first-person accounts, children's, religious or joke books. We are also interested in serious, professional videos and video ideas (contact Michael Janich)."

N **PALGRAVE MACMILLAN**, St. Martin's Press, 175 Fifth Ave., New York NY 10010. (212)982-3900. Fax: (212)777-6359. **Acquisitions:** Michael Flamini, vice president and editorial director (history, education, theater); Anthony Wahl, senior editor (political economy, political theory, business, Asian studies); David Pervin, editor (political science, Middle East studies, Slavic studies); Brendan O'Malley, editor (American history, popular culture); Farideh Koohi-Kamali, editor (literary criticism, anthropology, cultural studies); Amanda Johnson, associate editor (education, religion, women's history); Ella Pearce, associate editor (African studies, Latin American studies, popular culture); Roee Raz, assistant editor (anthropology). Publishes hardcover and trade paperback originals. **Publishes 700 titles/year; imprint publishes 500 titles/year. Receives 500 queries and 600 mss/year. 25% of books from first-time authors; 50% from unagented writers. Pays royalty: trade, 10-15% list; other, 7-10% net. Offers variable advance.** Publishes book 9 months after acceptance of ms. Accepts simultaneous submissions. Responds in 1 month to proposals. Book catalog and ms guidelines free.

- St. Martin's Press, Scholarly and Reference Division joined with Macmillan UK and is now called Palgrave Macmillan.
- Palgrave wishes to "expand on our already successful academic, trade, and reference programs so that we will remain at the forefront of publishing in the global information economy of the 21st century. We publish high-quality academic works and a distinguished range of reference titles, and we expect to see many of our works available in electronic form. We do not accept fiction or poetry."

Nonfiction: Biography, reference, scholarly. Subjects include business/economics, creative nonfiction, education, ethnic, gay/lesbian, government/politics, history, language/literature, military/war, money/finance, multicultural, music/dance, philosophy, regional, religion, sociology, spirituality, translation, women's issues/studies, humanities, social studies, film/cinema/stage, contemporary culture, general nonfiction, world affairs. "We are looking for good solid scholarship." Query with proposal package including outline, 3-4 sample chapters, prospectus, cv and SASE. Reviews artwork/photos as part of ms package.

Recent Title(s): *Hobbits, Elves and Wizards*, by Michael Stanton; *Open a New Window*, by Ethan Mordden; *Social Security Under the Gun*, by Arthur Benavie.

PARACLETE PRESS, P.O. Box 1568, Orleans MA 02653. (508)255-4685. Fax: (508)255-5705. **Acquisitions:** Editorial Review Committee. Estab. 1981. Publishes hardcover and trade paperback originals. **Publishes 16 titles/year. Receives 250 mss/year.** Publishes book up to 2 years after acceptance of ms. Accepts simultaneous submissions. Responds in 2 months to queries; 2 months to mss. Book catalog for 8½×11 SASE; ms guidelines for #10 SASE.

O→ Publisher of Christian classics, personal testimonies, devotionals, new editions of classics, compact discs and videos.

Nonfiction: Subjects include religion. No poetry or children's books. Query with SASE or submit 2-3 sample chapter(s), table of contents, chapter summaries.

Recent Title(s): *The Illumined Heart*, by Frederica Mathewes-Green; *Seeking His Mind*, by M. Basil Pennington, O.C.S.O.; *Radical Hospitality*, by Lonni Collins Pratt and Daniel Homan, O.S.B.

PARADISE CAY PUBLICATIONS, P.O. Box 29, Arcata CA 95518-0029. (707)822-9063. Fax: (707)822-9163. E-mail: paracay@humboldt1.com. Website: www.paracay.com. **Acquisitions:** Matt Morehouse, publisher (nautical). Publishes hardcover and trade paperback originals and reprints. **Publishes 5 titles/year; imprint publishes 2 titles/year. Receives 30-40 queries and 20-30 mss/year. 10% of books from first-time authors; 100% from unagented writers. Pays 10-15% royalty on wholesale price or makes outright purchase of $1,000-10,000. Offers $0-2,000 advance.** Publishes book 4 months after acceptance of ms. Responds in 1 month to queries; 1 month to proposals; 2 months to mss. Book catalog and ms guidelines free on request or online.

Imprints: Pardey Books.

Nonfiction: Cookbook, how-to, illustrated book, reference, technical, textbook. Subjects include cooking/foods/nutrition, recreation, sports, travel. Query with SASE or submit proposal package including 2-3 sample chapter(s), call first. Reviews artwork/photos as part of ms package. Send photocopies.

Fiction: Adventure (nautical, sailing). All fiction must have a nautical theme. Query with SASE or submit proposal package including 2-3 sample chapter(s), synopsis.

Recent Title(s): *Heavy Weather Tactics Using Sea Anchors and Drogues*, by Earl R. Hinz (nonfiction); *Easing Sheets*, by L.M. Lawson; *American Practical Navigator*, by Nathaniel Bowden.

Tips: Audience is recreational sailors and powerboaters. Call Matt Morehouse (publisher) before submitting anything.

PARAGON HOUSE PUBLISHERS, 2285 University Ave. W., Suite 200, St. Paul MN 55114-1635. (651)644-3087. Fax: (651)644-0997. E-mail: paragon@paragonhouse.com. Website: www.paragonhouse.com. **Acquisitions:** Rosemary Yokoi, acquisitions editor. Estab. 1962. Publishes hardcover and trade paperback originals and trade paperback reprints. **Publishes 12-15 titles/year; imprint publishes 2-5 titles/year. Receives 1,500 queries and 150 mss/year. 7% of books from first-time authors; 90% from unagented writers. Offers $500-1,500 advance.** Publishes book 1 year after acceptance of ms. Accepts simultaneous submissions. Ms guidelines online.

Imprints: PWPA Books (Dr. Gordon L. Anderson); Althena Books; New Era Books; ICUS Books

O→ "We publish general interest titles and textbooks that provide the readers greater understanding of society and the world." Currently emphasizing religion, philosophy.

Nonfiction: Biography, reference, textbook. Subjects include child guidance/parenting, government/politics, memoirs, multicultural, nature/environment, philosophy, religion, sex, sociology, women's issues/studies, world affairs. Submit proposal package including outline, 2 sample chapter(s), market breakdown, SASE.

Recent Title(s): *Personal Character and National Destiny*, by Harold B. Jones; *The Woman Who Defied Kings*, by Andree Aelion Brooks; *Infinity and the Brain*, by Dudley Gould.

N **PARALLAX PRESS**, United Buddhist Church, Inc., P.O. Box 7355, Berkeley CA 94707. (510)525-0101, ext. 113. Fax: (510)525-7129. E-mail: rachel@parallax.org. Website: www.parallax.org. **Acquisitions:** Rachel Neumann, senior editor (Buddhism, engaged Buddhism, social responsibility, spirituality). Estab. 1985. Publishes hardcover and trade paperback originals. **Publishes 8 titles/year. Receives 200-6,000 queries and 200 mss/year. 2% of books from first-time authors; 10% from unagented writers. Pays 20-30% royalty on wholesale price or makes outright purchase of $500-2,000.** Publishes book 6-9 months after acceptance of ms. Does not accept simultaneous submissions. Responds in 1 month to queries; 3 months to proposals; 3 months to mss. Book catalog for 1 SAE with 3 first-class stamps; ms guidelines for #10 SASE.

Nonfiction: Children's/juvenile, coffee table book, self-help. Subjects include multicultural, religion, spirituality. Query with SASE or submit proposal package including outline, 2 sample chapter(s). Reviews artwork/photos as part of ms package. Send photocopies.

Recent Title(s): *Mindfulness in the Marketplace*, by Allan Hunt Badiner (collection of essays); *Be Free Where You Are*, by Thich Nhat Hanh (nonfiction); *Thomas Merton and Thich Nhat Hanh*, by Robert H. King (nonfiction).

PARKWAY PUBLISHERS, INC., Box 3678, Boone NC 28607. (828)265-3993. Fax: (828)265-3993. E-mail: parkwaypub@hotmail.com. Website: www.parkwaypublishers.com. **Acquisitions:** Rao Aluri, president. Publishes hardcover and trade paperback originals. **Publishes 4-6 titles/year. Receives 15-20 queries and 10 mss/year. 75% of books from first-time authors; 100% from unagented writers.** Publishes book 8 months after acceptance of ms. Does not accept simultaneous submissions.

O→ Parkway publishes books on the local history and culture of Western North Carolina. "We are located on Blue Ridge Parkway and our primary industry is tourism. We are interested in books which present the history and culture of western North Carolina to the tourist market." Will consider fiction if it highlights the region. De-emphasizing academic books and poetry books.

Nonfiction: Technical. Subjects include history, psychology, regional. Query with SASE or submit complete ms.

Recent Title(s): *Letter from James*, by Ruth Layng (historical fiction).

PASSPORT PRESS, P.O. Box 1346, Champlain NY 12919-1346. **Acquisitions:** Jack Levesque, publisher. Estab. 1975. Publishes trade paperback originals. **Publishes 4 titles/year. 25% of books from first-time authors; 100% from un-**

agented writers. Pays 6% royalty on retail price. Offers advance. Publishes book 9 months after acceptance of ms. Does not accept simultaneous submissions.

Imprints: Travel Line Press.

O━ Passport Press publishes practical travel guides on specific countries. Currently emphasizing offbeat countries.

Nonfiction: Subjects include travel. Especially looking for mss on practical travel subjects and travel guides on specific countries. No travelogues. Send 1-page query only. Reviews artwork/photos as part of ms package.

Recent Title(s): *Costa Rica Guide: New Authorized Edition*, by Paul Glassman.

PATHFINDER PUBLISHING OF CALIFORNIA, 3600 Harbor Blvd., #82, Oxnard CA 93035. (805)984-7756. Fax: (805)985-3267. E-mail: bmosbrook@earthlink.net. Website: www.pathfinderpublishing.com. Publishes hardcover and trade paperback originals. **Publishes 4 titles/year. Receives 100 queries and 75 mss/year. 80% of books from first-time authors; 70% from unagented writers. Pays 9-15% royalty on wholesale price. Offers $200-1,000 advance.** Publishes book 4 months after acceptance of ms. Does not accept simultaneous submissions. Responds in 1 month to queries. Book catalog free or on website.

O━ Pathfinder Publishing of California was founded to seek new ways to help people cope with psychological and health problems resulting from illness, accidents, losses or crime.

Nonfiction: Self-help. Subjects include creative nonfiction, health/medicine, hobbies, psychology, sociology. Submit complete ms. "We do not open envelopes from people we do not know. We require e-mail proposals or mss now." Reviews artwork/photos as part of ms package. Send photocopies.

Recent Title(s): *When Our Parents Need Us*; *Coffee in the Cereal.*

PAULINE BOOKS & MEDIA, Daughters of St. Paul, 50 St. Paul's Ave., Jamaica Plain MA 02130-3491. (617)522-8911. Fax: (617)541-9805. Website: www.pauline.org. **Acquisitions:** Sister Patricia Edward Jablonski, acquisitions (children); Sister Madonna Ratliff, FSP, acquisitions editor (adult). Estab. 1948. Publishes trade paperback originals and reprints. **Publishes 25-35 titles/year. Receives 1,300 submissions/year. Pays 8-12% royalty on net receipts. Offers advance.** Publishes book 2-3 years after acceptance of ms. Does not accept simultaneous submissions. Responds in 3 months to queries. Book catalog for 9×12 SAE with 4 first-class stamps.

O━ "As a Catholic publishing house, Pauline Books and Media publishes in the areas of faith and moral values, family formation, spiritual growth and development, children's faith formation, instruction in the Catholic faith for young adults and adults. Works consonant with Catholic theology are sought." Currently emphasizing adult faith formation. De-emphasizing teacher resources.

Nonfiction: Biography (saints), children's/juvenile, self-help, spiritual growth; faith development. Subjects include child guidance/parenting, religion (teacher resources), Scripture. No strictly secular mss. No unsolicited mss. Query with SASE.

Fiction: Juvenile. No unsolicited mss. Query only with SASE.

Recent Title(s): *Vatican II Weekday Missal, Millenium Edition*; *Lights, Camera...Faith: A Movie Lectionary*, by Peter Malone and Rose Pacatte; *The Miracle of Hope: Life of Cardinal Francis X*, by Van Thuan.

PEACHTREE CHILDREN'S BOOKS, Peachtree Publishers, Ltd., 1700 Chattahoochee Avenue, Atlanta GA 30318-2112. (404)876-8761. Fax: (404)875-2578. E-mail: hello@peachtree-online.com. Website: www.peachtree-online.com. **Acquisitions:** Helen Harriss, submissions editor. Publishes hardcover and trade paperback originals. **Publishes 20 titles/year. 25% of books from first-time authors; 25% from unagented writers. Pays royalty on retail price.; Advance varies.** Publishes book 1 year or more after acceptance of ms. Accepts simultaneous submissions. Responds in 6 months to queries; 6 months to mss. Book catalog for 6 first-class stamps; ms guidelines online.

Imprints: Freestone, Peachtree Jr.

O━ "We publish a broad range of subjects and perspectives, with emphasis on innovative plots and strong writing."

Nonfiction: Children's/juvenile. Subjects include animals, child guidance/parenting, creative nonfiction, education, ethnic, gardening, health/medicine, history, language/literature, multicultural, music/dance, nature/environment, recreation, regional, science, social sciences, sports, travel. No e-mail or fax queries of mss. Submit complete ms. with SASE.

Fiction: Juvenile, picture books, young adult. No collections of poetry or short stories; no romance or sci-fi. Submit complete ms. with SASE.

Recent Title(s): *About Amphibians*, Cathryn Sill (children's picture book); *Yellow Star*, by Carmen Agra Deedy; *My Life and Death by Alexandra Ganarsie*, by Susan Heyboer O'Keefe.

PEACHTREE PUBLISHERS, LTD., 1700 Chattahoochee Ave., Atlanta GA 30318-2112. (404)876-8761. Fax: (404)875-2578. E-mail: hello@peachtree-online.com. Website: www.peachtree-online.com. **Acquisitions:** Helen Harriss, submissions editor. Estab. 1978. Publishes hardcover and trade paperback originals. **Publishes 20-25 titles/year. Receives 18,000 submissions/year. 25% of books from first-time authors; 75% from unagented writers. Pays royalty. Royalty varies. Offers advance.** Publishes book 1 year or more after acceptance of ms. Accepts simultaneous submissions. Responds in 6 months to queries; 6 months to mss. Book catalog for 9×12 SAE with 6 first-class stamps; ms guidelines online.

Imprints: Peachtree Children's Books (Peachtree Jr., FreeStone).

O━ Peachtree Publishers specializes in children's books, middle reader and books, young adult, regional guidebooks, parenting and self-help.

Nonfiction: Children's/juvenile, self-help, regional guides. Subjects include general nonfiction, health/medicine, recreation. No technical or reference. No e-mail or fax submissions or queries. Submit outline, 4 sample chapter(s) or submit complete ms. Include SASE for response.

Fiction: Juvenile, young adult. "Absolutely no adult fiction! We are seeking YA and juvenile works including mystery and historical fiction, of high literary merit." No adult fiction, fantasy, science fiction or romance. No collections of poetry or short stories. Query with SASE. Query, submit outline/synopsis and 3 sample chapters, or submit complete ms with SASE. Inquires/submissions by US Mail only. E-mail and fax will not be answered.

Recent Title(s): *Around Atlanta with Children*, by Denise Black and Janet Schwartz; *Yellow Star*, by Carhen Agra Deedy; *Surviving Jamestown: The Adventures of Young Sam Collier*, by Gail Langer Karwoski.

PEARSON PROFESSIONAL DEVELOPMENT, (formerly Skylight Professional Development), 1900 E. Lake Ave., Glenview IL 60025. (800)348-4474. Website: www.pearsonpd.com. **Publishes 10-15 titles/year. 100% from unagented writers. Pays 5% royalty on net receipts.** Publishes book 1 year after acceptance of ms. Responds in 1-2 months to queries. Book catalog and ms guidelines free.

"We seek books that provide a bridge from the theory to practice in the classroom."

Nonfiction: Subjects include education. Educational how-to for K-12 classroom practitioners. Teaching strategies, mentoring and coaching, assessment and standards, classroom management, school leadership and literacy. Submit outline, sample chapter(s), brief synopsis of each chapter. Reviews artwork/photos as part of ms package. Send photocopies.

Recent Title(s): *Bully Prevention: Tips and Strategies for School Leaders and Classroom Teachers*, by Elizabeth A. Barton.

Tips: "Target K-12 classroom practitioners, staff developers, school administrators. We are interested in research-based books that tell teachers in a clear, friendly, direct manner how to apply educational best practices to their classrooms."

PELICAN PUBLISHING CO., P.O. Box 3110, Gretna LA 70054. (504)368-1175. Website: www.pelicanpub.com. **Acquisitions:** Nina Kooij, editor-in-chief. Estab. 1926. Publishes hardcover, trade paperback and mass market paperback originals and reprints. **Publishes 90 titles/year. Receives 5,000 submissions/year. 15% of books from first-time authors; 80% from unagented writers. Pays royalty on actual receipts. Offers considered advance.** Publishes book 9-18 months after acceptance of ms. Does not accept simultaneous submissions. Responds in 1 month to queries; 3 months to mss. Book catalog for SASE; Writer's guidelines for SASE or on website.

"We believe ideas have consequences. One of the consequences is that they lead to a bestselling book. We publish books to improve and uplift the reader." Currently emphasizing business titles.

Nonfiction: Biography, children's/juvenile, coffee table book (limited), cookbook, gift book, illustrated book, self-help. Subjects include Americana (especially Southern regional, Ozarks, Texas, Florida and Southwest), art/architecture, contemporary culture, ethnic, government/politics, history (popular), multicultural, regional, religion (for popular audience mostly, but will consider others), sports, travel (regional and international), motivational (with business slant), inspirational (author must be someone with potential for large audience), Scottish, Irish, editorial cartoon. "We look for authors who can promote successfully. We require that a query be made first. This greatly expedites the review process and can save the writer additional postage expenses." No multiple queries or submissions. Query with SASE. Reviews artwork/photos as part of ms package.

Fiction: Historical, juvenile (regional or historical focus). "We publish maybe one novel a year, usually by an author we already have. Almost all proposals are returned. We are most interested in historical Southern novels." No young adult, romance, science fiction, fantasy, gothic, mystery, erotica, confession, horror, sex or violence. Also no "psychological" novels. Query with SASE or submit outline, 2 sample chapter(s), synopsis, SASE. "Not responsible if writer's only copy is sent."

Recent Title(s): *Douglas Southall Freeman*, by David E. Johnson (biography).

Tips: "We do extremely well with cookbooks, travel, popular histories, and some business. We will continue to build in these areas. The writer must have a clear sense of the market and knowledge of the competition. A query letter should describe the project briefly, give the author's writing and professional credentials, and promotional ideas."

PENGUIN PUTNAM, INC., 375 Hudson St., New York NY 10014. (212)366-2717. Website: www.penguinputnam.com. General interest publisher of both fiction and nonfiction. Ms guidelines online.

Imprints: ***Adult Division***: Ace Books; Avery; Berkley Books; Dutton; G.P. Putnam's Sons; HPBooks; Jeremy P. Tarcher; Jove; New American Library [Mentor, Onyx, Signet, Signet Classics, Signet Reference]; Penguin; Putnam; Perigee; Plume; Riverhead Books; Viking. ***Children's Division***: AlloyBooks; Dial Books for Young Readers; Dutton Children's Books; Firebird; Frederick Warne; G.P. Putnam's Sons; Grosset & Dunlap; Philomel; Phyllis Fogelman Books; Price Stern Sloan; Puffin Books; Viking Children's Books.

PENNSYLVANIA HISTORICAL AND MUSEUM COMMISSION, Commonwealth of Pennsylvania, Keystone Building, 400 North St., Harrisburg PA 17120-0053. (717)787-8099. Fax: (717)787-8312. Website: www.phmc.state.pa.us. **Acquisitions:** Diane B. Reed, chief, publications and sales division. Estab. 1913. Publishes hardcover and paperback originals and reprints. **Publishes 6-8 titles/year. Receives 25 submissions/year. Pays 5-10% royalty on retail price or makes outright purchase.** Publishes book 18-24 months after acceptance of ms. Accepts simultaneous submissions. Responds in 4 months to queries. Prepare ms according to the *Chicago Manual of Style*.

"We are a public history agency and have a tradition of publishing scholarly and reference works, as well as more popularly styled books that reach an even broader audience interested in some aspect of Pennsylvania's history and heritage."

Nonfiction: All books must be related to Pennsylvania, its history or culture. "The Commission considers manuscripts on Pennsylvania, specifically on archaeology, history, art (decorative and fine), politics and biography." Illustrated book, reference, technical. Subjects include anthropology/archeology, art/architecture, government/politics, history, travel (historic). Guidelines and proposal forms available. No fiction. Query with SASE or submit outline, sample chapter(s).

Recent Title(s): *Classification Guide for Arrowheads and Spearpoints of Eastern Pennsylvania and the Central Middle Atlantic*, by Jay Custer.

Tips: "Our audience is diverse—students, specialists and generalists—all of them interested in one or more aspects of Pennsylvania's history and culture. Manuscripts must be well researched and documented (footnotes not necessarily required depending on the nature of the manuscript) and interestingly written. Manuscripts must be factually accurate, but in being so, writers must not sacrifice style."

N A **PERENNIAL/QUILL**, HarperCollins Publishers, 10 E. 53rd St., New York NY 10022. (212)207-7000. Website: www.harpercollins.com. **Acquisitions:** Acquisitions Editor. Estab. 1963. Publishes trade paperback originals and reprints. **Publishes 220 titles/year. Receives 500 queries/year. 5% of books from first-time authors. Pays 5-7½% royalty. Offers variable advance.** Publishes book 6 months after acceptance of ms. Book catalog free.

O→ Perennial publishes a broad range of adult literary fiction and nonfiction paperbacks.

Nonfiction: Subjects include Americana, animals, business/economics, child guidance/parenting, cooking/foods/nutrition, education, ethnic, gay/lesbian, history, language/literature, military/war, money/finance, music/dance, nature/environment (and environment), philosophy, psychology (self-help psychotherapy), recreation, regional, religion (spirituality), science, sociology, sports, translation, travel, women's issues/studies, mental health, health, classic literature. "Our focus is ever-changing, adjusting to the marketplace. Mistakes writers often make are not giving their background and credentials - why they are qualified to write the book. A proposal should explain why the author wants to write this book; why it will sell; and why it is better or different from others of its kind." *Agented submissions only.*

Fiction: Ethnic, feminist, literary. *Agented submissions only.*

Poetry: "Don't send poetry unless you have been published in several established literary magazines already." *Agented submissions only.* Query or submit 10 sample poems.

Tips: "See our website for a list of titles or write to us for a free catalog."

PERFECTION LEARNING CORP., 10520 New York Ave., Des Moines IA 50322-3775. (515)278-0133. Fax: (515)278-2980. Website: perfectionlearning.com. **Acquisitions:** Sue Thies, editorial director (books division); Rebecca Christian, senior editor (curriculum division). Estab. 1926. Publishes hardcover and trade paperback originals. **Publishes 50-100 fiction and informational; 25 workbooks titles/year. Pays 5-7% royalty on net receipts. Offers $300-500 advance.** Publishes book 6-8 months after acceptance of ms. Accepts simultaneous submissions. Responds in 2 months to proposals; 3 months to mss. Book catalog for 9X12 SASE with $2.31 postage; ms guidelines online.

Imprints: Cover-to-Cover, Summit Books.

O→ "Perfection Learning is dedicated to publishing books and literature-based materials that enhance teaching and learning in pre-K-12 classrooms and libraries." Emphasizing hi/lo fiction and nonfiction books for reluctant readers (extreme sports, adventure fiction, etc.), high-interest novels with male protagonists.

Nonfiction: Publishes nonfiction. "We are publishing hi-lo informational books for students in grades 2-12, reading levels 1-6." Biography. Subjects include science, social studies, high-interest topics. Query with SASE or submit outline. For curriculum books, submit proposal and writing sample with SASE.

Fiction: "We are publishing hi-lo chapter books and novels as well as curriculum books, including workbooks, literature anthologies, teacher guides, literature tests, and niche textbooks for grades 3-12." Readability of ms should be at least two grade levels below interest level. "Please do not submit mss with fewer that 4,000 words or more than 30,000 words." No picture books. Query with SASE or submit outline, 2-3 sample chapter(s), synopsis, SASE. or submit complete manuscript with a cover letter.

Recent Title(s): *Into the Abyss: A Tour of Inner Space*, by Ellen Hopkins.

PERIGEE BOOKS, Penguin Putnam, Inc., 375 Hudson St., New York NY 10014. (212)366-2000. Publisher: John Duff. **Acquisitions:** Sheila Curry Oakes, executive editor (child care, health); Michelle Howry, editor (personal growth, personal finance, women's issues). Publishes hardcover and trade paperback originals and reprints. **Publishes 55-60 titles/year. Receives hundreds queries and 300+ submissions/year. 30% of books from first-time authors; 10% from unagented writers. Pays 6-7½% royalty. Offers $5,000-150,000 advance.** Publishes book within 18 months after acceptance of ms. Accepts simultaneous submissions. Responds in 2 months to queries. Book catalog free; ms guidelines given on contract.

O→ Publishes in all areas of self-help and how-to with particular interest in health and child care. Currently emphasizing popular psychology, women's issues in health, fitness, and careers and lifestyles.

Nonfiction: How-to, reference (popular), self-help, prescriptive books. Subjects include animals, child guidance/parenting, cooking/foods/nutrition, health/medicine, hobbies, money/finance (personal finance), psychology, sex, sports, women's issues/studies, fashion/beauty. Prefers agented mss, but accepts unsolicited queries. Query with SASE or submit outline.

THE PERMANENT PRESS/SECOND CHANCE PRESS, 4170 Noyac Rd., Sag Harbor NY 11963. (631)725-1101. Fax: (631)725-8215. Website: www.thepermanentpress.com. **Acquisitions:** Judith Shepard, editor. Estab. 1978. Publishes hardcover originals. **Publishes 12 titles/year. Receives 7,000 submissions/year. 60% of books from first-time authors; 60% from unagented writers. Pays 10-15% royalty on wholesale price. Offers $1,000 advance for Permanent Press books; royalty only on Second Chance Press titles.** Publishes book 18 months after acceptance of ms. Accepts simultaneous submissions. Responds in 3 weeks to queries; 6 months to mss. Book catalog for 8×10 SAE with 7 first-class stamps; ms guidelines for #10 SASE.

O→ Permanent Press publishes literary fiction. Second Chance Press devotes itself exclusively to re-publishing fine books that are out of print and deserve continued recognition. "We endeavor to publish quality writing—primarily fiction—without regard to authors' reputations or track records." Currently emphasizing literary fiction. No poetry, short story collections.

Nonfiction: Autobiography, biography. Subjects include history, memoirs. No scientific and technical material, academic studies. Query with SASE.

Fiction: Literary, mainstream/contemporary, mystery. Especially looking for high line literary fiction, "artful, original and arresting." Accepts any fiction category as long as it is a "well-written, original full-length novel." Query with SASE or submit. Query with first 20 pages. No queries by fax.

Recent Title(s): *Lydia Cassatt Reading the Morning Paper*, by Harriett Scott Chessman; *Walking the Perfect Square*, by Reed Coleman.

Tips: "Audience is the silent minority—people with good taste. We are interested in the writing more than anything and dislike long outlines. The SASE is vital to keep track of things, as we are receiving ever more submissions. No fax queries will be answered. We aren't looking for genre fiction but a compelling, well-written story." Permanent Press does not employ readers and the number of submissions it receives has grown. If the writer sends a query or ms that the press is not interested in, a reply may take six weeks. If there is interest, it may take 3 to 6 months.

[N] **PETER PAUPER PRESS, INC.**, 202 Mamaroneck Ave., White Plains NY 10601-5376. E-mail: nbeilenson@peterpauper.com. **Acquisitions:** Neil Beilenson, editorial director. Estab. 1928. Publishes hardcover originals. **Publishes 40-50 titles/year. Receives 100 queries and 150 mss/year. 5% from unagented writers. Makes outright purchase only. Offers advance.** Publishes book 1 year after acceptance of ms. Does not accept simultaneous submissions. Responds in 1 month to queries. Manuscript guidelines for #10 SASE or may request via e-mail for a faxed copy (include fax number in e-mail request).

> PPP publishes small and medium format, illustrated gift books for occasions and in celebration of specific relationships such as Mom, sister, friend, teacher, grandmother, granddaughter. PPP has expanded into the following areas: books for teens and tweens, books on popular topics of nonfiction for adults and licensed books by bestselling authors.

Nonfiction: Gift book. Subjects include specific relationships or special occasions (graduation, Mother's Day, Christmas, etc.). "We do publish interactive journals and workbooks but not narrative manuscripts or fiction. We publish brief, original quotes, aphorisms, and wise sayings. *Please do not send us other people's quotes*." Query with SASE.

Recent Title(s): *The Essential Writer's Notebook*, by Natalie Goldberg; *The Feng Shui Journal*, by Teresa Polanco; *My Llife as a Baby.*

Tips: "Our readers are primarily female, age 10 and over, who are likely to buy a 'gift' book or gift book set in a stationery, gift, book or boutique store or national book chain. Writers should become familiar with our previously published work. We publish only small- and medium-format illustrated hardcover gift books and sets of between 1,000-4,000 words. We have no interest in work aimed at men."

[N] **PETERSON'S**, 2000 Lenox Dr., Princeton Pike Corporate Center, Lawrenceville NJ 08648. (800)338-3282. Fax: (609)896-1800. Website: www.petersons.com. **Acquisitions:** Denise Rance, executive assistant, editorial. Estab. 1966. Publishes trade and reference books. **Publishes over 200 titles/year. Receives 250-300 submissions/year. 60% of books from first-time authors; 90% from unagented writers. Pays royalty. Offers advance.** Publishes book 1 year after acceptance of ms. Does not accept simultaneous submissions. Responds in 3 months to queries. Book catalog free.

> "Peterson's publishes guides to graduate and professional programs, colleges and universities, financial aid, distance learning, private schools, summer programs, international study, executive education, job hunting and career opportunities, educational and career test prep, as well as online products and services offering educational and career guidance and information for adult learners and workplace solutions for education professionals."

Nonfiction: Authored titles; education directories; career directories. Subjects include business/economics, education, careers. Looks for "appropriateness of contents to our markets, author's credentials, and writing style suitable for audience." Submit complete ms or table of contents, introduction and 2 sample chapters with SASE.

Recent Title(s): *The Insider's Guide to Study Abroad*, by Ann M. Moore.

Tips: Many of Peterson's reference works are updated annually. Peterson's markets strongly to libraries and institutions, as well as to the corporate sector.

PFLAUM PUBLISHING GROUP, N90 W16890 Roosevelt Dr., Menomonee Falls WI 53051-7933. (262)502-4222. Fax: (262)502-4224. E-mail: kcannizzo@pflaum.com. **Acquisitions:** Karen A. Cannizzo, co-publisher. **Publishes 20 titles/year. Payment may be outright purchase, royalty or down payment plus royalty.** Book catalog and ms guidelines free.

> "Pflaum Publishing Group, a division of Peter Li, Inc., serves the specialized market of religious education, primarily Roman Catholic. We provide high quality, theologically sound, practical, and affordable resources that assist religious educators of and ministers to children from preschool through senior high school."

Nonfiction: Religious education programs and catechetical resources. Query with SASE.

Recent Title(s): *Reaching Teens through Film, Volume 10*; *Ready Resources for Catholic Teens.*

PHI DELTA KAPPA EDUCATIONAL FOUNDATION, P.O. Box 789, Bloomington IN 47402. (812)339-1156. Fax: (812)339-0018. E-mail: special.pubs@pdkintl.org. Website: www.pdkintl.org. **Acquisitions:** Donovan R. Walling, director of publications and research. Estab. 1906. Publishes hardcover and trade paperback originals. **Publishes 24-30 titles/year. Receives 100 queries and 50-60 mss/year. 50% of books from first-time authors; 100% from unagented writers. Pays honorarium of $500-5,000.** Publishes book 9 months after acceptance of ms. Does not accept simultaneous submissions. Responds in 3 months to proposals. Book catalog and ms guidelines free.

> "We publish books for educators—K-12 and higher education. Our professional books are often used in college courses but are never specifically designed as textbooks."

Nonfiction: How-to, reference, scholarly, essay collections. Subjects include child guidance/parenting, education, legal issues. Query with SASE or submit outline, 1 sample chapter(s). Reviews artwork/photos as part of ms package.

Recent Title(s): *The ABC's of Behavior Change*, by Frank J. Sparzo; *American Overseas Schools*, edited by Robert J. Simpson and Charles R. Duke.

PHILOMEL BOOKS, Penguin Putnam Inc., 345 Hudson St., New York NY 10014. (212)414-3610. **Acquisitions:** Patricia Lee Gauch, editorial director; Michael Green, senior editor. Estab. 1980. Publishes hardcover originals. **Publishes 20-25 titles/year. Receives 2,600 submissions/year. 15% of books from first-time authors; 30% from unagented writers. Pays royalty. author's copies. Offers negotiable advance.** Publishes book 1-2 years after acceptance of ms. Accepts simultaneous submissions. Responds in 3 months to queries; 4 months to mss. Book catalog for 9×12 SAE with 4 first-class stamps; ms guidelines for #10 SASE.

O→ "We look for beautifully written, engaging manuscripts for children and young adults."

Fiction: Adventure, ethnic, fantasy, historical, juvenile (5-9 years), literary, picture books, regional, short story collections, translation, western (young adult), young adult (10-18 years). Children's picture books (ages 3-8); middle-grade fiction and illustrated chapter books (ages 7-10); young adult novels (ages 10-15). Particularly interested in picture book mss with original stories and regional fiction with a distinct voice. Looking for "story-driven novels with a strong cultural voice but which speak universally." No series or activity books. No "generic, mass-market oriented fiction." Query with SASE or submit outline, 3 sample chapter(s), synopsis. *No unsolicited mss*,.

Recent Title(s): *Triss*, by Brian Jacques; *Gisfor Goat*, by Patricia Palacco; *Slowly Slowly Slowly Said the Sloth*, by Eric Carle.

Tips: "We prefer a very brief synopsis that states the basic premise of the story. This will help us determine whether or not the manuscript is suited to our list. If applicable, we'd be interested in knowing the author's writing experience or background knowledge. We try to be less influenced by the swings of the market than in the power, value, essence of the manuscript itself."

PHILOSOPHY DOCUMENTATION CENTER, P.O. Box 7147, Charlottesville VA 22906-7147. (434)220-3300. Fax: (434)220-3301. E-mail: order@pdcnet.org. Website: www.pdcnet.org. **Acquisitions:** Dr. George Leaman, director. Estab. 1966. **Publishes 4 titles/year. Receives 4-6 queries and 4-6 mss/year. 50% of books from first-time authors. Pays 2½-10% royalty. Offers advance.** Publishes book 1 year after acceptance of ms. Does not accept simultaneous submissions. Responds in 2 months to queries. Book catalog free.

O→ The Philosophy Documentation Center works in cooperation with publishers, database producers, software developers, journal editors, authors, librarians and philosophers to create an electronic clearinghouse for philosophical publishing.

Nonfiction: Reference, textbook, guidebooks; directories in the field of philosophy. Subjects include philosophy, software. "We want to increase our range of philosophical titles and are especially interested in electronic publishing." Query with SASE or submit outline.

Recent Title(s): *Proceedings of the World Congress of Philosophy*; *2002-2003 Directory of American Philosophers*.

N A **PICADOR USA**, St. Martin's Press, 175 Fifth Ave., New York NY 10010. Website: www.picadorusa.com. Estab. 1994. Publishes hardcover originals and trade paperback originals and reprints. **Publishes 70-80 titles/year. 30% of books from first-time authors. Pays 7½-15% royalty on retail price. Offers varies advance.** Publishes book 18 months after acceptance of ms. Accepts simultaneous submissions. Responds in 2 months to queries. Book catalog for 9×12 SASE and $2.60 postage; ms guidelines for #10 SASE or online.

O→ Picador publishes high-quality literary fiction and nonfiction. "We are open to a broad range of subjects, well written by authoritative authors."

Nonfiction: Biography, illustrated book. Subjects include contemporary culture, language/literature, philosophy, cultural history, narrative books with a point of view on a particular subject. "When submitting queries, be aware of things outside the book, including credentials, that may affect our decision." *Agented submissions only.*

Fiction: Literary. *Agented submissions only.*

Recent Title(s): *The Amazing Adventures of Kavalier and Cly*, by Michael Chabon; *The Hours*, by Michael Cunningham.

PICCADILLY BOOKS, LTD., P.O. Box 25203, Colorado Springs CO 80936-5203. (719)550-9887. Website: www.piccadillybooks.com. Publisher: Bruce Fife. **Acquisitions:** Submissions Department. Estab. 1985. Publishes hardcover originals and trade paperback originals and reprints. **Publishes 5-8 titles/year. Receives 120 submissions/year. 70% of books from first-time authors; 95% from unagented writers. Pays 10% royalty on retail price.** Publishes book 1 year after acceptance of ms. Accepts simultaneous submissions. Responds only if interested, unless accompanied by a SASE to queries.

O→ Picadilly publishes books on humor, entertainment, performing arts, skits and sketches, and writing.

Nonfiction: How-to (on entertainment), humor. Subjects include film/cinema/stage, performing arts, writing, small business. "We have a strong interest in subjects on clowning, magic, puppetry and related arts, including comedy skits and dialogs." Query with SASE or submit sample chapter(s).

Recent Title(s): *The Sherlock Holmes Book of Magic*, by Jeff Brown.

Tips: "Experience has shown that those who order our books are either kooky or highly intelligent or both. If you like to laugh, have fun, enjoy games, or have a desire to act like a jolly buffoon, we've got the books for you."

PICTON PRESS, Picton Corp., P.O. Box 250, Rockport ME 04856-0250. (207)236-6565. Fax: (207)236-6713. E-mail: sales@pictonpress.com. Website: www.pictonpress.com. Publishes hardcover and mass market paperback originals and reprints. **Publishes 30 titles/year. Receives 30 queries and 15 mss/year. 50% of books from first-time authors; 100% from unagented writers. Pays 0-10% royalty on wholesale price or makes outright purchase. Offers advance.** Publishes book 6 months after acceptance of ms. Does not accept simultaneous submissions. Responds in 2 months to queries; 2 months to proposals; 3 months to mss. Book catalog free.

Imprints: Cricketfield Press, New England History Press, Penobscot Press, Picton Press.

O— "Picton Press is one of America's oldest, largest and most respected publishers of genealogical and historical books specializing in research tools for the 17th, 18th and 19th centuries."

Nonfiction: Reference, textbook. Subjects include Americana, history, hobbies, genealogy, vital records. Query with SASE or submit outline.

Recent Title(s): *Nemesis At Potsdam*, by Alfred de Zayas.

THE PILGRIM PRESS, 700 Prospect Ave. E., Cleveland OH 44115-1100. (216)736-3755. Fax: (216)736-2207. E-mail: stavetet@ucc.org. Website: www.pilgrimpress.com. **Acquisitions:** Timothy G. Staveteig, publisher. Publishes hardcover and trade paperback originals. **Publishes 55 titles/year. 60% of books from first-time authors; 80% from unagented writers. Pays standard royalties. Offers advance.** Publishes book an average of 18 months after acceptance of ms. Does not accept simultaneous submissions. Responds in 3 months to queries. Book catalog and ms guidelines online.

Nonfiction: Scholarly. Subjects include business/economics, gay/lesbian, government/politics, health/medicine, nature/environment, religion, social sciences, ethics, social issues with a strong commitment to justice—addressing such topics as public policy, sexuality and gender, human rights and minority liberation—primarily in a Christian context, but not exclusively.

Recent Title(s): *Coming Out Young and Faithful*, by Leanne McCall and Timothy Brown.

Tips: "We are concentrating more on academic and trade submissions. Writers should send books about contemporary social issues. Our audience is liberal, open-minded, socially aware, feminist, church members and clergy, teachers and seminary professors."

PIÑATA BOOKS, Arte Publico Press, University of Houston, Houston TX 77204-2004. (713)743-2841. Fax: (713)743-3080. Website: www.artepublicopress.com. **Acquisitions:** Nicolas Kanellos, director. Estab. 1994. Publishes hardcover and trade paperback originals. **Publishes 10-15 titles/year. 60% of books from first-time authors. Pays 10% royalty on wholesale price. Offers $1,000-3,000 advance.** Publishes book 2 years after acceptance of ms. Accepts simultaneous submissions. Responds in 1 month to queries; 6 months to mss. Book catalog and ms guidelines available via website or with #10 SASE.

O— Pinata Books is dedicated to the publication of children's and young adult literature focusing on US Hispanic culture by U.S. Hispanic authors.

Nonfiction: "Piñata Books specializes in publication of children's and young adult literature that authentically portrays themes, characters and customs unique to U.S. Hispanic culture." Children's/juvenile. Subjects include ethnic. Query with SASE or submit outline, 2 sample chapter(s), synopsis.

Fiction: Adventure, juvenile, picture books, young adult. Query with SASE or submit 2 sample chapter(s), synopsis, SASE. Query with synopsis, 2 sample chapters and SASE.

Poetry: Appropriate to Hispanic theme. Submit 10 sample poems.

Recent Title(s): *Walking Stars*, by Victor Villasenor; *The Bakery Lady*, by Pat Mora.

Tips: "Include cover letter with submission explaining why your manuscript is unique and important, why we should publish it, who will buy it, etc."

PINEAPPLE PRESS, INC., P.O. Box 3889, Sarasota FL 34230. (941)359-0886. Fax: (941)351-9988. Website: www.pineapplepress.com. **Acquisitions:** June Cussen, editor. Estab. 1982. Publishes hardcover and trade paperback originals. **Publishes 20 titles/year. Receives 1,500 submissions/year. 20% of books from first-time authors; 80% from unagented writers. Pays 6½-15% royalty on net receipts. Offers rare advance.** Publishes book 18 months after acceptance of ms. Accepts simultaneous submissions. Responds in 3 months to queries. Book catalog for 9×12 SAE with $1.25 postage.

O— "We are seeking quality nonfiction on diverse topics for the library and book trade markets."

Nonfiction: Biography, how-to, reference. Subjects include animals, gardening, history, nature/environment, regional (Florida). "We will consider most nonfiction topics. Most, though not all, of our fiction and nonfiction deals with Florida." No pop psychology or autobiographies. Query or submit outline/brief synopsis, sample chapters and SASE.

Fiction: Historical, literary, mainstream/contemporary, regional (Florida). No romance or science fiction. Query with SASE or submit outline, sample chapter(s), synopsis. Submit outline/brief synopsis and sample chapters.

Recent Title(s): *Ornamental Tropical Shrubs*, by Amanda Jarrett.

Tips: "Learn everything you can about book publishing and publicity and agree to actively participate in promoting your book. A query on a novel without a brief sample seems useless."

PIPPIN PRESS, 229 E. 85th St., P.O. Box 1347, Gracie Station, New York NY 10028. (212)288-4920. Fax: (732)225-1562. **Acquisitions:** Barbara Francis, president and editor-in-chief; Joyce Segal, senior editor. Estab. 1987. Publishes hardcover originals. **Publishes 4-6 titles/year. Receives 1,500 queries/year. 80% from unagented writers. Pays royalty. Offers advance.** Publishes book 2 years after acceptance of ms. Does not accept simultaneous submissions. Responds in 3 weeks to queries. Book catalog for 6×9 SASE; ms guidelines for #10 SASE.

O— Pippin publishes general nonfiction and fiction for children ages 4-12.

Nonfiction: Biography, children's/juvenile, humor, autobiography. Subjects include animals, history (American), language/literature, memoirs, nature/environment, science, general nonfiction for children ages 4-12. No unsolicited mss. Query with SASE only. Reviews artwork/photos as part of ms package. Send photocopies.

Fiction: Historical, humor, mystery, picture books. "We're especially looking for small chapter books for 7- to 11-year olds, especially by people of many cultures." Also interested in humorous fiction for ages 7-11. "At this time, we are especially interested in historical novels, 'autobiographical' novels, historical and literary biographies and humor." Query with SASE. Query with SASE only.

Recent Title(s): *A Visit from the Leopard: Memories of a Ugandan Childhood*, by Catherine Mudiko-Piwang and Edward Frascino; *Abigail's Drum*, by John A. Minahan, illustrated by Robert Quackenbush (historical fiction).

Tips: "Read as many of the best children's books published in the last five years as you can. We are looking for multi-ethnic fiction and nonfiction for ages 7-10, as well as general fiction for this age group. I would pay particular attention to children's books favorably reviewed in *School Library Journal*, *The Booklist*, *The New York Times Book Review*, and *Publishers Weekly*."

PLANNERS PRESS, American Planning Association, 122 S. Michigan Ave., Chicago IL 60603. Fax: (312)431-9985. E-mail: slewis@planning.org. Website: www.planning.org. **Acquisitions:** Sylvia Lewis, director of publications. Estab. 1978. Publishes hardcover and trade paperback originals. **Publishes 4-6 titles/year. Receives 20 queries and 6-8 mss/year. 50% of books from first-time authors; 100% from unagented writers. Pays 7½-12% royalty on retail price. Offers advance.** Publishes book 1 year after acceptance of ms. Does not accept simultaneous submissions. Responds in 1 month to queries; 2 months to proposals; 2 months to mss. Book catalog and ms guidelines free.

O→ "Our books have a narrow audience of city planners and often focus on the tools of city planning."

Nonfiction: Technical (public policy and city planning). Subjects include government/politics. Submit 2 sample chapters and table of contents. Reviews artwork/photos as part of ms package. Send photocopies.

Recent Title(s): *Redesigning Cities—Principles, Practice, Implementation*; *Making Places Special—Stories of Real Places Made Better by Planning*; *Above and Beyond—Visualizing Change in Small Towns and Rural Areas*.

PLAYERS PRESS, INC., P.O. Box 1132, Studio City CA 91614-0132. (818)789-4980. **Acquisitions:** Robert W. Gordon, vice president, editorial. Estab. 1965. Publishes hardcover originals and trade paperback originals and reprints. **Publishes 35-70 titles/year. Receives 200-1,000 submissions/year. 15% of books from first-time authors; 80% from unagented writers. Pays royalty on wholesale price. Offers advance.** Publishes book 3 months-2 years after acceptance of ms. Does not accept simultaneous submissions. Book catalog for 9×12 SAE with 5 first-class stamps; ms guidelines for #10 SASE.

O→ Players Press publishes support books for the entertainment industries: theater, film, television, dance and technical. Currently emphasizing plays for all ages, theatre crafts, monologues and short scenes for ages 5-9, 11-15, and musicals.

Nonfiction: Children's/juvenile, theatrical drama/entertainment industry. Subjects include film/cinema/stage, performing arts, costume, theater crafts, film crafts, dance. Needs quality plays and musicals, adult or juvenile. Query with SASE. Reviews music as part of ms package.

Fiction: Plays: Subject matter includes adventure, confession, ethnic, experimental, fantasy, historical, horror, humor, mainstream, mystery, religious romance, science fiction, suspense, western. Submit complete ms for theatrical plays only. Plays must be previously produced. "No novels or story books are accepted."

Recent Title(s): *Women's Wear of the 1930's*, by Hopper/Countryman; *Rhyme Tyme*, by William-Alan Landes; *Borrowed Plumage*, by David Crawford.

Tips: "Plays, entertainment industry texts, theater, film and TV books have the only chances of selling to our firm."

PLAYHOUSE PUBLISHING, 1566 Akron-Peninsula Rd., Akron OH 44313. (330)926-1313. Fax: (330)926-1315. E-mail: webmaster@playhousepublishing.com. Website: www.playhousepublishing.com. **Acquisitions:** Children's Acquisitions Editor. Publishes hardcover originals and novelty board books. **Publishes 10-15 titles/year; imprint publishes 3-5 titles/year. Work-for-hire. Makes outright purchase.** Publishes book 18-24 months after acceptance of ms. Accepts simultaneous submissions. Responds in 2 months to proposals. Book catalog online; ms guidelines online.

Imprints: Picture Me Books (board books with photos) and Nibble Me Books (board books with edibles).

- Playhouse Publishing will no longer accept unsolicited mss sent for review in the mail. The company will not open or review any material not addressed to an individual or from a known source. Any items sent in the mail will be returned to sender or destroyed. The company encourages writers to submit query letters/book proposals electronically to webmaster@playhousepublishing.com. All copy must be contained in the body of an e-mail. Attachments will not be opened.

O→ "We publish juvenile fiction appropriate for children from pre-school to third grade. All Picture Me Books titles incorporate the 'picture me' concept. All Nibble Me Books titles incorporate an edible that completes the illustrations."

Fiction: Juvenile. Query with SASE.

Recent Title(s): *My Family*, by Merry North; *Sparkle Purse*, by Cathy Hapka; *Sparkle Basket*, by Jackie Wolf.

PLEASANT COMPANY PUBLICATIONS, 8400 Fairway Pl., Middleton WI 53562. Fax: (608)828-4768. Website: www.americangirl.com. **Acquisitions:** Submissions Editor. Estab. 1986. Publishes hardcover and trade paperback originals. **Publishes 50-60 titles/year. Receives 500 queries and 800 mss/year. 90% from unagented writers. Offers varying advance.** Publishes book 3-12 months after acceptance of ms. Accepts simultaneous submissions. Responds in 3 months to queries; 4 months to mss. Book catalog for #10 SASE; ms guidelines for for SASE or on the website.

Imprints: The American Girls Collection, American Girl Library, AG Fiction, History Mysteries, Girls of Many Lands.

O→ Pleasant Company publishes fiction and nonfiction for girls 7-12.

Nonfiction: Children's/juvenile (for girls 7-12), how-to. Subjects include Americana, history, contemporary lifestyle, activities. Query with SASE.

Fiction: Contemporary. "Contemporary fiction submissions should capture the spirit of contemporary American girls and also illuminate the ways in which their lives are personally touched by issues and concerns affecting America today. We are seeking strong, well-written fiction, historical and contemporary, told from the perspective of a middle-school-age girl. No romance, picture books, poetry." Stories must feature an American girl, aged 10-13; reading level 4th-6th grade. No picture book submissions. Query with SASE or submit complete ms. Submit complete ms with cover letter for contemporary fiction.

Recent Title(s): *Smoke Screen*, by Amy Goldman Koss; *Nowhere, Now Here*, by Ann Howard Creel.

PLEXUS PUBLISHING, INC., 143 Old Marlton Pike, Medford NJ 08055-8750. (609)654-6500. Fax: (609)654-4309. E-mail: jbryans@infotoday.com. **Acquisitions:** John B. Bryans, editor-in-chief. Estab. 1977. Publishes hardcover and paperback originals. **Publishes 4-5 titles/year. Receives 30-60 submissions/year. 70% of books from first-time authors; 90% from unagented writers. Pays 10-15% royalty on net receipts. Offers $500-1,000 advance.** Accepts simultaneous submissions. Responds in 3 months to proposals. Book catalog and ms guidelines for 10×13 SAE with 4 first-class stamps.

O→ Plexus publishes mainly regional-interest (southern NJ) fiction and nonfiction including mysteries, field guides, history. Also health/medicine, biology, botany, ecology, botony, astronomy.

Nonfiction: How-to, illustrated book, reference, textbook, natural, historical references, and scholarly. Subjects include agriculture/horticulture, education, gardening, health/medicine, history (southern New Jersey), nature/environment, recreation, regional (southern NJ), science, botany, medicine, biology, ecology, astronomy. "We will consider any book on a nature/biology subject, particularly those of a reference (permanent) nature that would be of lasting value to high school and college audiences, and/or the general reading public (ages 14 and up). Authors should have authentic qualifications in their subject area, but qualifications may be by experience as well as academic training." Also interested in mss of about 20-40 pages in length for feature articles in *Biology Digest* (guidelines available for SASE). No gardening, philosophy or psychology; generally not interested in travel but will consider travel that gives sound ecological information. Query with SASE. Reviews artwork/photos as part of ms package. Send photocopies.

Fiction: Mysteries and literary novels with a strong regional (southern NJ) angle. Query with SASE.

Recent Title(s): *Boardwalk Empire: The Birth, High Times, and Corruption of Atlantic City*, by Nelson Johnson; *Wildflowers of the Pine Barrens of New Jersey*, by Howard P. Boyd.

N A **POCKET BOOKS**, Simon & Schuster, 1230 Avenue of the Americas, New York NY 10020. (212)698-7000. Website: www.simonsays.com. Vice President/Editorial Director: Maggie Crawford. Publishes paperback originals and reprints, mass market and trade paperbacks. **Publishes 250 titles/year. Receives 2,500 submissions/year. 25% of books from first-time authors; 5% from unagented writers. Pays 6-8% royalty on retail price. Offers advance.** Publishes book an average of 2 years after acceptance of ms. Does not accept simultaneous submissions. Responds in 1 month to queries. Book catalog free; ms guidelines online.

O→ Pocket Books publishes commercial fiction and genre fiction (WWE, Downtown Press, Star Trek).

Nonfiction: Reference. Subjects include cooking/foods/nutrition. *Agented submissions only.*

Fiction: Mystery, romance, suspense (psychological suspense, thriller), western, *Star Trek* novels. *Agented submissions only.*

Recent Title(s): *Forever*, by Jude Deveraux.

POLYCHROME PUBLISHING CORP., 4509 N. Francisco, Chicago IL 60625. (773)478-4455. Fax: (773)478-0786. E-mail: polypub@earthlink.net. Website: www.polychromebooks.com. Estab. 1990. Publishes hardcover originals and reprints. **Publishes 4 titles/year. Receives 3,000 queries and 7,500-8,000 mss/year. 50% of books from first-time authors; 100% from unagented writers. Pays royalty,. Offers advance.** Publishes book 2 years after acceptance of ms. Accepts simultaneous submissions. Responds in 8 months to mss. Book catalog for #10 SASE; ms guidelines for #10 SASE or on the website.

Nonfiction: Children's/juvenile. Subjects include ethnic. Subjects emphasize ethnic, particularly multicultural/Asian-American. Submit outline, 3 sample chapter(s). Reviews artwork/photos as part of ms package. Send photocopies.

Fiction: Ethnic, juvenile, multicultural (particularly Asian-American), picture books, young adult. "We do not publish fables, folktales, fairytales or anthropomorphic animal stories." Submit synopsis and 3 sample chapters, for picture books submit whole ms.

Recent Title(s): *Striking It Rich: Treasures from Gold Mountain*; *Char Siu Bao Boy*.

POPULAR WOODWORKING BOOKS, F&W Publications, 4700 Galbraith Rd., Cincinnati OH 45236. (513)531-2690. **Acquisitions:** Jim Stack, acquisitions editor. Publishes trade paperback originals and reprints. **Publishes 10-12 titles/year. Receives 30 queries and 10 mss/year. 50% of books from first-time authors; 95% from unagented writers. Pays 10-20% royalty on net receipts. Offers $3,000-5,000 advance.** Publishes book 1 year after acceptance of ms. Accepts simultaneous submissions. Responds in 1 month to queries. Book catalog for 9×12 SAE with 6 first-class stamps; ms guidelines for 9×12 SAE with 6 first-class stamps.

O→ Popular Woodworking publishes how-to woodworking books that use photos with captions to show and tell the reader how to build projects. Technical illustrations and materials lists supply all the rest of the information needed. Currently emphasizing woodworking jigs and fixtures, furniture and cabinet projects, smaller finely crafted boxes, all styles of furniture. De-emphasizing woodturning, woodcarving, scroll saw projects.

Nonfiction: "We publish heavily illustrated how-to woodworking books that show, rather than tell, our readers how to accomplish their woodworking goals." How-to, illustrated book. Subjects include hobbies, woodworking/wood crafts. Query with SASE or submit proposal package including outline, transparencies. Reviews artwork/photos as part of ms package.

Recent Title(s): *Jigs & Fixtures Bible*, by R.J. DeCristoforo; *Build Your Own Home Office Furniture*, by Danny Proulx; *Jim Tolpin's Table Saw Magic, 2nd Ed*, by Jim Toplin.

Tips: "Our books are for beginners to advanced woodworking enthusiasts."

POSSIBILITY PRESS, One Oakglade Circle, Hummelstown PA 17036-9525. (717)566-0468. Fax: (717)566-6423. E-mail: possibilitypress@aol.com. Website: www.possibilitypress.com. **Acquisitions:** Mike Markowski, publisher; Marjie Markowski, editor-in-chief. Estab. 1981. Publishes trade paperback originals. **Publishes 5-10 titles/year. Receives 1,000 submissions/year. 90% of books from first-time authors; 95% from unagented writers. Royalties vary.** Responds in 2 months to queries. Ms guidelines online.

Imprints: Aeronautical Publishers, Possibility Press.

O┱ "Our mission is to help the people of the world grow and become the best they can be, through the written and spoken word."

Nonfiction: How-to, self-help, inspirational. Subjects include business/economics, psychology (pop psychology), current significant events, success/motivation, inspiration, entrepreneurship, sales marketing, network, MLM and homebased business topics, and human interest success stories. Prefers submissions to be mailed.

Fiction: Parables that teach lessons about life and success.

Recent Title(s): *The Power of 2*, by Anthony C. Scire; *What Choice Do I Have*, by Michael Kerrigan; *The Millionaire Mentor*, by Greg S. Reid.

Tips: "Our focus is on creating and publishing short to medium length bestsellers written by authors who speak and consult. We're looking for kind and compassionate authors who are passionate about making a difference in the world, and on a mission to do so."

THE POST-APOLLO PRESS, 35 Marie St., Sausalito CA 94965. (415)332-1458. Fax: (415)332-8045. Website: www.dnai.com/~tpapress/. **Acquisitions:** Simone Fattal, publisher,. Estab. 1982. Publishes trade paperback originals and reprints. **Publishes 4 titles/year. Pays 5-7% royalty on wholesale price.** Publishes book 1½ years after acceptance of ms. Responds in 3 months to queries. Book catalog free; Book catalog and ms guidelines for #10 SASE.

- "We are not accepting new manuscripts for the time being."

Nonfiction: Essay; letters. Subjects include art/architecture, language/literature, translation, women's issues/studies. Query.

Fiction: Experimental, literary (plays), spiritual, translation. "Many of our books are first translations into English." No juvenile, horror, sports or romance. Submit 1 sample chapter(s), SASE. "The Post-Apollo Press is not accepting manuscripts or queries currently due to a full publishing schedule."

Poetry: Experimental/translations.

Recent Title(s): *Happily*, by Lyn Hejinian; *Some Life*, by Joanne Kyger; *Where the Rocks Started*, by Marc Atherton.

Tips: "We are interested in writers with a fresh and original vision. We often publish foreign literature that is already well-known in its original country, but new to the American reader."

N **PRACTICE MANAGEMENT INFORMATION CORP. (PMIC)**, 4727 Wilshire Blvd., #300, Los Angeles CA 90010. (323)954-0224. Fax: (323)954-0253. E-mail: kathy.swanson@pmicmail.com. Website: www.medicalbookstore.com. **Acquisitions:** Kathryn Swanson, managing editor. Estab. 1986. Publishes hardcover originals. **Publishes 21 titles/year. Receives 100 queries and 50 mss/year. 10% of books from first-time authors; 90% from unagented writers. Pays 12½% royalty on net receipts. Offers $1,000-5,000 advance.** Publishes book 18 months after acceptance of ms. Does not accept simultaneous submissions. Responds in 6 months to queries. Book catalog for #10 SASE; ms guidelines for #10 SASE.

Imprints: PMIC, Health Information Press (HIP).

O┱ PMIC helps health care workers understand the business of medicine by publishing books for doctors, medical office and hospital staff, medical managers, insurance coding/billing personnel. HIP seeks to simplify health care for consumers.

Nonfiction: Reference, technical, textbook, medical practice management, clinical. Subjects include business/economics, health/medicine, science. Submit proposal package including outline, 3-5 sample chapter(s). Letter stating who is the intended audience, the need/market for such a book, as well as outline, curriculum vitae/résumé.

Recent Title(s): *ICD-9-CM Coding Made Easy*, by James Davis; *Medicare Rules & Regulations*, by Maxine Lewis; *Medical Practice Forms*, by Keith Borglum.

PRB PRODUCTIONS, 963 Peralta Ave., Albany CA 94706-2144. (510)526-0722. Fax: (510)527-4763. E-mail: prbprdns@aol.com. Website: www.prbpro.com; www.prbmusic.com. **Acquisitions:** Peter R. Ballinger, publisher (early and contemporary music for instruments and voices). **Publishes 10-15 titles/year. Pays 10% royalty on retail price.** Accepts simultaneous submissions. Responds in 1 month to queries; 3 months to mss. Book catalog free on request or on website.

Nonfiction: Textbook, sheet music. Subjects include music/dance. Query with SASE or submit complete ms.

Recent Title(s): *Six Sonatas for Violoncello and Basso Continuo*, by Francesco Guerini, edited by Sarah Freiberg (music score and parts); *G.P. Telemann, Fortsetzung des Harmonischen Gottesdienstes, Vol. V*, edited by Jeanne Swack (hardcover score, vocal score and 4 instrumental parts).

Tips: Audience is music schools, universities, libraries, professional music educators, and amateur/professional musicians.

THE PRESS AT THE MARYLAND HISTORICAL SOCIETY, 201 W. Monument St., Baltimore MD 21201. (410)685-3750. Fax: (410)385-2105. E-mail: rcottom@mdhs.org. Website: www.mdhs.org. **Acquisitions:** Robert I. Cottom, publisher (Maryland-Chesapeake history); Donna B. Shear, senior editor (Maryland-Chesapeake history). Publishes hardcover and trade paperback originals and trade paperback reprints. **Publishes 4-6 titles/year. Receives 15-20 queries and 8-10 mss/year. 50% of books from first-time authors; 100% from unagented writers. Pays 6-10% royalty on retail price.** Publishes book 1-2 years after acceptance of ms. Accepts simultaneous submissions. Responds in 2 months to queries; 2 months to proposals; 6 months to mss. Book catalog online.

O⌐ The Press at the Maryland Historical Society specializes in Maryland state and Chesapeake regional subjects.

Nonfiction: Biography, children's/juvenile, illustrated book, scholarly textbook. Subjects include anthropology/archeology, art/architecture, history. Query with SASE or submit proposal package including outline, 1-2 sample chapter(s).

Recent Title(s): *The Chesapeake: An Environmental Biography*, by John R. Wennersten; *The Patapsco Valley: Cradle of the Industrial Revolution in Maryland*, by Henry K. Sharp.

Tips: "Our audience consists of intelligent readers of Maryland/Chesapeake regional history and biography."

PRESTWICK HOUSE, INC., 605 Forest St., Dover DE 19904. (302)736-5614. Website: www.prestwickhouse.com. **Acquisitions:** Paul Moliken, editor. **Publishes 50+ titles/year. Makes outright purchase of $200-1,500.**

Nonfiction: Reference, textbook, teaching supplements. Subjects include grammar, writing, test taking. Submit proposal package including outline, 1 sample chapter(s), résumé, table of contents.

Recent Title(s): *Vocabulary from Latin and Greek Roots*; *Notetaking and Outlining*.

Tips: "We market our books primarily for middle and high school English teachers. Submissions should address a direct need of grades 7-12 language arts teachers. Current and former English teachers are encouraged to submit materials developed and used by them successfully in the classroom."

PRICE STERN SLOAN, INC., Penguin Putnam, Inc., 345 Hudson, New York NY 10014. (212)414-3590. Fax: (212)414-3396. **Acquisitions:** Debra Dorfman, publisher. Estab. 1963. **Publishes 80 titles/year. Makes outright purchase. Offers advance.** Does not accept simultaneous submissions. Responds in 3 months to queries. Book catalog for 9×12 SAE with 5 first-class stamps; ms guidelines for #10 SASE. Address to Book Catalog or Manuscript Guidelines.

Imprints: Doodle Art, Mad Libs, Mr. Men & Little Miss, Serendipity, Troubador Press, Wee Sing.

O⌐ Price Stern Sloan publishes quirky mass market novelty series for children.

Nonfiction: Children's/juvenile, humor. "Most of our titles are unique in concept as well as execution." Do not send *original* artwork or ms. *No unsolicited mss.*

Fiction: "We publish very little in the way of fiction."

Recent Title(s): *Who's Got Mail?*, by Charles Reasoner (preschool); *What Do You Want On Your Pizza?*, by William Boniface (preschool); *Growing-Money*, by Gail Karlitz (nonfiction).

Tips: "Price Stern Sloan has a unique, humorous, off-the-wall feel."

PROFESSIONAL PUBLICATIONS, INC., 1250 Fifth Ave., Belmont CA 94002-3863. (650)593-9119. Fax: (650)592-4519. E-mail: talent2@ppi2pass.com. **Acquisitions:** Sarah Hubbard, acquisitions manager. Estab. 1975. Publishes hardcover, electronic and paperback originals, video and audio cassettes, CD-ROMs. **Publishes 30 titles/year. Receives 100-200 submissions/year. Offers advance.** Publishes book 18 months after acceptance of ms. Accepts simultaneous submissions. Responds in 2 weeks to queries. Book catalog free; ms guidelines free.

O⌐ PPI publishes for engineering, architecture, land surveying, and interior design professionals preparing to take examinations for national licensing. Professional Publications wants only professionals practicing in the field to submit material. Currently emphasizing engineering exam review.

Nonfiction: Multimedia, reference, technical, textbook. Subjects include art/architecture, science, engineering mathematics, engineering, land surveying, interior design. Especially needs "review books for all professional licensing examinations." Query with SASE or submit sample chapter(s). Reviews artwork/photos as part of ms package.

Recent Title(s): *Civil Engineering Reference Manual for the PE Exam*, Michael R. Lindeburg, PE.

Tips: "We specialize in books for working professionals: engineers, architects, land surveyors, interior designers, etc. The more technically complex the manuscript is the happier we are. We love equations, tables of data, complex illustrations, mathematics, etc. In technical/professional book publishing, it isn't always obvious to us if a market exists. We can judge the quality of a manuscript, but the author should make some effort to convince us that a market exists. Facts, figures, and estimates about the market—and marketing ideas from the author—will help sell us on the work."

PROMETHEUS BOOKS, 59 John Glenn Dr., Amherst NY 14228-2197. (716)691-0133 ext. 207. Fax: (716)564-2711. E-mail: editorial@prometheusmail.com. Website: www.prometheusbooks.com. **Acquisitions:** Steven L. Mitchell, editor-in-chief (Prometheus/Humanity Books, philosophy, social science, political science, general nonfiction); Dr. Ann O'Hear, acquisitions editor (Humanity Books, scholarly and professional works in philosophy, social science); Linda Greenspan Regan, executive editor (Prometheus, popular science, health, psychology, criminology); Matt Cravatta, editorial assistant (permissions). Estab. 1969. Publishes hardcover originals, trade paperback originals and reprints. **Publishes 85-100 titles/year. Receives 2,500 submissions/year. 25% of books from first-time authors; 50% from unagented writers. Pays 10-15% royalty on wholesale price. Offers $0-3,000 advance.** Publishes book 18 months after acceptance of ms. Accepts simultaneous submissions. Responds in 1 month to queries; 2 months to proposals; 4 months to mss. Book catalog free or online; ms guidelines for #10 SASE.

Imprints: Humanity Books (scholarly and professionals monographs in philosophy, social science, sociology, archaeology, Marxist studies, etc.).

O⌐ "Prometheus Books is a leading independent publisher in philosophy, popular science and critical thinking. We publish authoritative and thoughtful books by distinguished authors in many categories. We are a niche, or specialized, publisher that features *critiques* of the paranormal and pseudoscience, critiques of religious extremism and right wing fundamentalism and creationism; Biblical and Koranic criticism: human sexuality, etc. Currently emphasizing popular science, health, psychology, social science."

Nonfiction: Biography, children's/juvenile, reference, self-help. Subjects include education, government/politics, health/medicine, history, language/literature, New Age, philosophy, psychology, religion (not religious, but critiquing), contemporary issues, current events, Islamic studies, law, popular science, critiques of the paranormal and UFO sightings, sexuality.

"Ask for a catalog, go to the library or our website, look at our books and others like them to get an idea of what our focus is." Submit proposal package including outline, synopsis and a well-developed query letter with SASE. Reviews artwork/photos as part of ms package. Send photocopies.

Recent Title(s): *The Erotic History of Advertising*, by Tom Reichert; *Science and Religion: Are They Compatible*, edited by Paul Kurtz and Barry Karr.

Tips: "Audience is highly literate with multiple degrees; an audience that is intellectually mature and knows what it wants. They are aware, and we try to provide them with new information on topics of interest to them in mainstream and related areas."

PROSTAR PUBLICATIONS, INC., 3 Church Circle, #109, Annapolis MD 21401. (800)481-6277. Fax: (800)487-6277. Website: www.nauticalbooks.com. **Acquisitions:** Peter Griffes, president (marine-related/how-to/business/technical); Susan Willson, editor (history/memoirs). Estab. 1965. Publishes trade paperback originals. **Publishes 150 titles/year; imprint publishes 10-15 titles/year. Receives 120 queries and 50 submissions and 25 mss/year. 50% of books from first-time authors; 100% from unagented writers. Pays 15% royalty on wholesale price. Rarely offers advance.** Publishes book 1 year after acceptance of ms. Accepts simultaneous submissions. Responds in 3 months to queries; 3 months to proposals. Book catalog online.

Imprints: Lighthouse Press (Peter Griffes).

O→ "Originally, ProStar published only nautical books. At present, however, we are expanding. Any quality nonfiction book would be of interest."

Nonfiction: Coffee table book, how-to, illustrated book, technical. Subjects include history, memoirs, nature/environment, travel, nautical. Query with SASE. Reviews artwork/photos as part of ms package. Send photocopies.

Recent Title(s): *The Media Shaping the Image of a People*, by Bill Overton; *Rock Roll & Reminisce*, by Joe Andrews; *Little Known Adventures Under Sale*, by Jeff Markell.

Tips: "We prefer to work directly with the author and seldom work with agents. Please send in a well-written query letter, and we will give your book serious consideration."

PRUETT PUBLISHING, 7464 Arapahoe Rd., Suite A-9, Boulder CO 80303. (303)449-4919. Fax: (303)443-9019. E-mail: pruettbks@aol.com. **Acquisitions:** Jim Pruett, publisher. Estab. 1959. Publishes hardcover and trade paperback originals and reprints. **Publishes 10-15 titles/year. 60% of books from first-time authors; 95% from unagented writers. Pays 10-12% royalty on net receipts. Offers advance.** Publishes book 18 months after acceptance of ms. Accepts simultaneous submissions. Responds in 2 months to queries. Book catalog and ms guidelines free.

O→ "Pruett Publishing strives to convey to our customers and readers a respect of the American West, in particular the spirit, traditions, and attitude of the region. We publish books in the following subject areas: outdoor recreation, regional history, environment and nature, travel and culture. We especially need books on outdoor recreation."

Nonfiction: "We are looking for nonfiction manuscripts and guides that focus on the Rocky Mountain West." Guidebooks. Subjects include Americana (Western), anthropology/archeology (Native American), cooking/foods/nutrition (Native American, Mexican, Spanish), ethnic, history (Western), nature/environment, recreation (outdoor), regional, sports (cycling, hiking, fly fishing), travel. Submit proposal package. Reviews artwork/photos as part of ms package.

Recent Title(s): *Flyfishing the Texas Coast: Back Country Flats to Bluewater*, by Chuck Scales and Phil Shook, photography by David J. Sams; *Trout Country: Reflections on Rivers, Flyfishing & Related Addictions*, by Bob Saile; *Rocky Mountain Christmas*, by John H. Monnett.

Tips: "There has been a movement away from large publisher's mass market books and towards small publisher's regional interest books, and in turn distributors and retail outlets are more interested in small publishers. Authors don't need to have a big name to have a good publisher. Look for similar books that you feel are well produced—consider design, editing, overall quality and contact those publishers. Get to know several publishers, and find the one that feels right—trust your instincts."

[N] **PRUFROCK PRESS, INC.**, P.O. Box 8813, Waco TX 76714. (254)756-3337. Fax: (254)756-3339. E-mail: prufrock@prufrock.com. Website: www.prufrock.com. **Acquisitions:** Joel McIntosh, publisher. Publishes trade paperback originals and reprints. **Publishes 10 titles/year. Receives 150 queries and 50 mss/year. 50% of books from first-time authors; 100% from unagented writers. Pays 10% royalty on sale price. Offers advance.** Publishes book 9 months after acceptance of ms. Does not accept simultaneous submissions. Responds in 2 months to queries. Book catalog and ms guidelines free.

O→ "Prufrock Press publishes exciting, innovative and current resources supporting the education of gifted and talented learners."

Nonfiction: How-to, textbook, scholarly. Subjects include child guidance/parenting, education. "We publish for the education market. Our readers are typically teachers or parents of gifted and talented children. Our product line is built around professional development books for teachers and activity books for gifted children. Our products support innovative ways of making learning more fun and exciting for gifted and talented children." Request query package from publisher.

Recent Title(s): *Early Gifts: Recognizing and Nurturing Children's Talent*, edited by Paula Olszewski-Kubilius, Ph.D., Lisa Limburg-Weber, Ph.D., Steven Pfeiffer, Ph.D.; *The Ultimate Guide to Getting Money for Your Classroom & School*, by Frances A. Karnes and Kristen R. Stephens; *Content-Based Curriculum for High-Ability Learners*, edited by Joyce Van Tassel-Baska, Ed.D. and Catherine A. Little, Ph.D.

Tips: "We are looking for practical, classroom-ready materials that encourage children to creatively learn and think."

[N] **PURDUE UNIVERSITY PRESS**, South Campus Courts, Bldg. E, 509 Harrison St., West Lafayette IN 47907-2025. (765)494-2038. Website: www.thepress.purdue.edu. **Acquisitions:** Thomas Bacher, director (technology, business, veterinary medicine, health, philosophy); Margaret Hunt, managing editor (Central European studies, regional, literature). Estab. 1960. Publishes hardcover and trade paperback originals and trade paperback reprints. **Publishes 14-20 titles/year. Receives 600 submissions/year. Pays 7½-15% royalty. Offers advance.** Publishes book 9 months after acceptance of ms. Does not accept simultaneous submissions. Responds in 2 months to queries. Book catalog and ms guidelines for 9×12 SASE.

"We look for books that look at the world as a whole and offer new thoughts and insights into the standard debate." Currently emphasizing technology, human-animal issues, business. De-emphasizing literary studies.

Nonfiction: "We publish work of quality scholarship and titles with regional (Midwest) flair. Especially interested in innovative contributions to the social sciences and humanities that break new barriers and provide unique views on current topics. Expanding into veterinary medicine, engineering and business topics." Biography, scholarly. Subjects include agriculture/horticulture, Americana, business/economics, government/politics, health/medicine, history, language/literature, philosophy, regional, science, social sciences, sociology. "Always looking for new authors who show creativity and thoroughness of research." Print and electronic projects accepted. Query before submitting.

Recent Title(s): *Route Across the Rocky Mountains*, edited by Angela Firkus; *Bitter Prerequisites: A Faculty for Survival from Nazi Terror*, by Laird Kleine-Ahlbrandt; *Feeding the Media Beast: An Easy Recipe for Great Publicity*, by Mark Mathis.

G.P. PUTNAM'S SONS, (Adult Trade), Penguin Putnam, Inc., 375 Hudson, New York NY 10014. (212)366-2000. Fax: (212)366-2666. Website: www.penguinputnam.com. Publisher: Neil Nyren. Publishes hardcover and trade paperback originals. **Pays variable royalties on retail price. Offers varies advance.** Accepts simultaneous submissions. Responds in 6 months to queries. Request book catalog through mail order department; ms guidelines free.

Nonfiction: Biography, cookbook, self-help. Subjects include animals, business/economics, child guidance/parenting, contemporary culture, cooking/foods/nutrition, health/medicine, military/war, nature/environment, religion, science, sports, travel, women's issues/studies, celebrity-related topics. *Agented submissions only. No unsolicited mss.*

Fiction: Adventure, literary, mainstream/contemporary, mystery, suspense, Women's. Prefers agented submissions. *Agented submissions only. No unsolicited mss.*

Recent Title(s): *Portrait of a Killer*, by Patricia Cornwell (nonfiction); *Red Rabbit*, by Tom Clancy (fiction).

G.P. PUTNAM'S SONS BOOKS FOR YOUNG READERS, Penguin Young Readers Group, Penguin Group USA, 345 Hudson St., 14th Floor, New York NY 10014. (212)414-3610. Website: www.penguin.com. Publishes hardcover originals. **Publishes 45 titles/year. Receives 8,000 submissions/year. 20% of books from first-time authors; 30% from unagented writers. Pays standard royalty. Offers negotiable advance.** Publishes book 2 years after acceptance of ms. Accepts simultaneous submissions. Responds in 2 months to queries; 2 months to mss. Manuscript guidelines for SASE.

Fiction: Children's picture books (ages 0-8); middle-grade fiction and illustrated chapter books (ages 7-10); older middle-grade fiction (ages 10-14); some young adult (14-18). Particularly interested in middle-grade fiction with strong voice, literary quality, high interest for audience, poignancy, humor, unusual settings or plots. Historical fiction OK. No series or activity books, no board books. Query with SASE or submit proposal package including outline, 3 sample chapter(s), table of contents, SASE. No response without SASE.

Recent Title(s): *Hope Was Here*, by Joan Bauer; *What a Trip, Amber Brown*, by Paula Danziger; *Car Wash*, by Susan Steen and Sandra Steen.

QUE, Pearson Education, Indianapolis IN 46290. (317)581-3500. Website: www.quepublishing.com. Publisher: Paul Boger. **Acquisitions:** Angelina Ward, Jeff Riley, Loretta Yates, Rick Kughen, Stephanie McComb, acquisitions editors. Publishes hardcover, trade paperback and mass market paperback originals and reprints. **Publishes 100 titles/year. 80% from unagented writers. Pays variable royalty on wholesale price or makes work-for-hire arrangements. Offers varying advance.** Accepts simultaneous submissions. Responds in 1 month to proposals. Book catalog and ms guidelines online; ms guidelines online.

Nonfiction: Subjects include computers/electronic.

Recent Title(s): *Upgrading and Repairing PCs, 14th edition*, by Scott Mueller.

QUEST BOOKS, Theosophical Publishing House, 306 West Geneva Rd., Wheaton IL 60187. (630)665-0130. Fax: (630)665-8791. E-mail: questbooks@theosmail.net. Website: www.questbooks.net. **Acquisitions:** Brenda Rosen. Publishes hardcover originals and trade paperback originals and reprints. **Publishes 12-15 titles/year. Receives 500 submissions/year. 75% of books from first-time authors; 90% from unagented writers. Pays royalty. Offers varying advance.** Publishes book 20 months after acceptance of ms. Accepts simultaneous submissions. Responds in 1 month to queries. Book catalog free; ms guidelines online.

"Quest Books is the imprint of the Theosophical Publishing House, the publishing arm of the Theosophical Society of America. Since 1965, Quest books has sold millions of books by leading cultural thinkers on such increasingly popular subjects as transpersonal psychology, comparative religion, deep ecology, spiritual growth, the development of creativity and alternative health practices."

Nonfiction: Biography, illustrated book, self-help. Subjects include anthropology/archeology, art/architecture, health/medicine, music/dance, nature/environment, New Age, philosophy (holistic), psychology (transpersonal), religion (Eastern and Western), science, sex, spirituality (men, women, Native American), travel, women's issues/studies, theosophy, comparative religion, men's and women's spirituality, holistic implications in science, health and healing, yoga, meditation, astrology. "Our speciality is high-quality spiritual nonfiction with a self-help aspect. Great writing is a must. We seldom publish 'personal spiritual awakening' stories. No submissions accepted that do not fit the needs outlined above." Accepts nonfiction translations. No fiction, poetry, children's books or any literature based on channeling or personal psychic impressions.

Query with SASE or submit proposal package including sample chapter(s), author bio, toc. Reviews artwork/photos as part of ms package. Send photocopies.

Recent Title(s): *The Feminine Face of Christianity*; *The Real St. Nicholas*; *The Templars and the Grail*.

Tips: "Our audience includes the 'New Age' community, seekers in all religions, general public, professors, and health professionals. Read a few recent Quest titles. Know our books and our company goals. Explain how your book or proposal relates to other Quest titles. Quest gives preference to writers with established reputations/successful publications."

QUILL DRIVER BOOKS/WORD DANCER PRESS, 1831 Industrial Way #101, Sanger CA 93657. (559)876-2170. Fax: (559)876-2180. **Acquisitions:** Stephen Blake Mettee, publisher. Publishes hardcover and trade paperback originals and reprints. **Publishes 10-12 (Quill Driver Books: 4/year, Word Dancer Press: 6-8/year) titles/year. 50% of books from first-time authors; 95% from unagented writers. Pays 4-10% royalty on retail price. Offers $500-5,000 advance.** Publishes book 9 months after acceptance of ms. Accepts simultaneous submissions. Responds in 1 month to queries; 1 month to proposals; 3 months to mss. Book catalog and ms guidelines for #10 SASE.

O→ "We publish a modest number of books per year, each of which, we hope, makes a worthwhile contribution to the human community, and we have a little fun along the way. We are strongly emphasizing our two new book series: The Best Half of Life series—on subjects which will serve to enhance the lifestyles, life skills, and pleasures of living for those over 50. The Fast Track Course series—short how-to or explanatory books on any subject."

Nonfiction: Biography, how-to, reference, general. Subjects include general nonfiction, regional (California), writing, aging. Query with SASE or submit proposal package. Reviews artwork/photos as part of ms package. Send photocopies.

Recent Title(s): *If You Want It Done Right, You Don't Have to Do It Yourself*, by Donna M. Genett, Ph.D.; *The Fast Track Course on How to Write a Nonfiction Book Proposal*, by Stephen Blake Mettee.

QUITE SPECIFIC MEDIA GROUP, LTD., 7 Old Fulton St., Brooklyn Heights NY 11201. (212)725-5377. Fax: (212)725-8506. E-mail: info@quitespecificmedia.com. Website: www.quitespecificmedia.com. **Acquisitions:** Ralph Pine, editor-in-chief. Editorial Office: 7373 Pyramid Place, Hollywood CA 90046. Estab. 1967. Publishes hardcover originals, trade paperback originals and reprints. **Publishes 12 titles/year. Receives 300 queries and 100 mss/year. 75% of books from first-time authors; 85% from unagented writers. Pays royalty on wholesale price. Offers varies advance.** Publishes book 18 months after acceptance of ms. Accepts simultaneous submissions. Responds to queries. Book catalog online; ms guidelines free.

Imprints: Costume & Fashion Press, Drama Publishers, By Design Press, Entertainment Pro, Jade Rabbit.

O→ Quite Specific Media Group is an umbrella company of five imprints specializing in costume and fashion, theater and design.

Nonfiction: For and about performing arts theory and practice: acting, directing; voice, speech, movement; makeup, masks, wits; costumes, sets, lighting, sound; design and execution; technical theater, stagecraft, equipment; stage management; producing; arts management, all varieties; business and legal aspects; film, radio, television, cable, video; theory, criticism, reference; theater and performance history; costume and fashion. How-to, multimedia, reference, textbook, guides; manuals; directories. Subjects include fashion/beauty, film/cinema/stage, history, translation. Accepts nonfiction and technical works in translations also. Query with SASE or submit 1-3 sample chapter(s). No complete ms. Reviews artwork/photos as part of ms package.

RAGGED MOUNTAIN PRESS, The McGraw Hill Companies, P.O. Box 220, Camden ME 04843-0220. (207)236-4837. Fax: (207)236-6314. Website: www.raggedmountainpress.com. **Acquisitions:** Jonathan Eaton, editorial director. Estab. 1993. Publishes hardcover and trade paperback originals and reprints. **Publishes 50 titles/year; imprint publishes 25 titles/year. Receives 200 queries and 100 mss/year. 30% of books from first-time authors; 60% from unagented writers. Pays 10-15% royalty on net receipts. Offers advance.** Publishes book 1 year after acceptance of ms. Accepts simultaneous submissions. Responds in 1 month to queries. Ms guidelines online.

Imprints: International Marine (books about boats and the sea).

O→ Ragged Mountain Press publishes books that take you off the beaten path.

Nonfiction: "Ragged Mountain publishes nonconsumptive outdoor and environmental issues books of literary merit or unique appeal." How-to (outdoor-related), humor, guidebooks; essays. Subjects include cooking/foods/nutrition, nature/environment, recreation, sports, team sports, adventure, camping, fly fishing, snowshoeing, backpacking, canoeing, outdoor cookery, skiing, snowboarding, survival skills, wilderness know-how, birdwatching, natural history, climbing, kayaking. "Be familiar with the existing literature. Find a subject that hasn't been done or has been done poorly, then explore it in detail and from all angles." Query with SASE or submit outline, 1 sample chapter(s). Reviews artwork/photos as part of ms package. Send photocopies.

Recent Title(s): *Coaching Tee-Ball: The Baffled Parents Guide*, by Bing Braido; *Sea Kayaking Illustrated*, by John Robison.

[N] **RAMSEY BOOKS**, Nor-Cal Builders, Inc., 500 Industrial Way #8, Dixon CA 95620-9220. (707)678-4006. Fax: (707)678-0355. E-mail: leon@ramseybooks.com. Submissions E-mail: submissions@ramseybooks.com. Website: www.ramseybooks.com. **Acquisitions:** Leon Portelance, editor (fiction, nonfiction); Debi Williams, assistant editor (fashion, sewing). Estab. 2002. Publishes trade paperback and electronic originals. **Publishes 8-10 titles/year. 100% of books from first-time authors; 100% from unagented writers. Pays 10-15% for trade paperback; 25-30% for electronic. Offers $500-2,000 advance.** Publishes book 1 year after acceptance of ms. Accepts simultaneous submissions. "We only accept electronic submissions." Responds in 1 month to queries; 1 month to proposals; 2 months to mss. Book catalog online; ms guidelines online.

Nonfiction: How-to, illustrated book. Subjects include music/dance, construction, home improvement/woodworking, music, songwriting/home recording, fashion design, sewing, quilting. "We are most interested in 'how-to' and other instructional books." Submit complete ms via website in worddoc orpdf. Reviews artwork/photos as part of ms package. Writers should send via website aspdf orjpg file.

Fiction: Adventure, fantasy, horror, mystery, science fiction, suspense, crime/detective. "We are looking for fast paced books, mixing the description in with the dialogue and action. No unneccesary pornography, violence or profanity. Make us laugh or cry." Submit proposal package including 3 sample chapter(s), synopsis, via website in Worddoc orpdf.

Recent Title(s): *Portable Studios*, by Leon Portelance (how-to); *Slumach: The Lost Mine*, by Edgar Ramsey (horror).

Tips: Audience is either hands on people who like to do things for themselves (nonfiction) or adventure, mystery, horror junkies (fiction). "Self-edit carefully using a spell check or have someone edit your work for you."

N A **RANDOM HOUSE/GOLDEN BOOKS FOR YOUNG READERS GROUP**, 1745 Broadway, New York NY 10019. (212)782-9000. Website: www.randomhouse.com/kids. Vice President/Publisher: Kate Klimo. Vice President/Associate Publisher (Random House): Mallory Loehr. Associate Publisher (Golden Books): Amy Jarashow. **Acquisitions:** Shana Corey, assistant editorial director (Step into Reading); Jennifer Dussling, senior editor (Stepping Stones); Alice Jonaitis, senior editor (nonfiction); Heidi Kilgras, editorial director (picture books); Diane Muldrow, editorial director (Little Golden Books); Dennis Shealy, editorial director (novelty and media tie-ins); Jim Thomas, senior editor (middle grade, YA). Estab. 1935. Publishes hardcover, trade paperback, and mass market paperback originals and reprints. **Publishes 375 titles/year. Receives 1,000 queries/year. Pays 1-6% royalty or makes outright purchase. Offers variable advance.** Accepts simultaneous submissions. Book catalog free.

Imprints: Beginner Books; Disney; First Time Books; Landmark Books; Picturebacks; Sesame Workshop; Step into Reading; Stepping Stones; Little Golden Books.

- "Our aim is to create books that nurture the hearts and minds of children, providing and promoting quality books and a rich variety of media that entertain and educate readers from birth to 16 years."

Nonfiction: Children's/juvenile. Subjects include animals, history, nature/environment, science, sports, popular culture. No unsolicited manuscripts. *Agented submissions only.*

Fiction: Horror, juvenile, mystery, picture books, young adult. "Familiarize yourself with our list. We look for original, unique stories. Do something that hasn't been done." *Agented submissions only.* No unsolicited manuscripts.

Recent Title(s): *The Best Place to Read*, by Debbie Bertram & Susan Bloom; *Top-Secret, Personal Beeswax: A Journal by Junie B. (and Me)*, by Barbara Park; *The Pup Speaks Up*, by Anna Jane Hays.

N **RAVENHAWK™ BOOKS**, The 6DOF Group, 7739 Broadway Blvd., #95, Tucson AZ 85710. E-mail: ravenhawk6dof@yahoo.com. Website: www.ravenhawk.biz. Estab. 1998. Publishes hardcover and paperback originals. **Pays 45-60% royalty.** Publishes book 18 months after acceptance of ms. Accepts simultaneous submissions. Ms guidelines for SASE; book catalog on website only. Fantasy (space fantasy, sword and sorcery), horror (dark fantasy, futuristic, psychological, supernatural), humor, literary, mainstream/contemporary, mystery (amateur sleuth, cozy, police procedural, private eye/hardboiled), religious (religious mystery/suspense, religious thriller), romance (contemporary, romantic suspense), science fiction (hard science/technological, soft/sociological), short story collections, young adult (adventure, easy-to-read, fantasy/science fiction, horror, mystery/suspense, problem novels, series). Query with SASE.

N **RED DRESS INK**, Harlequin Enterprises, Ltd., 233 Broadway, New York NY 10279. Website: www.eharlequin.com. ; www.reddressink.com. **Acquisitions:** Margaret O'Neill Marbury, senior editor; Farrin Jacobs, associate editor. Publishes hardcover and trade paperback originals. **Publishes 24-36 titles/year. Receives 250 queries and 300 mss/year. 30-35% of books from first-time authors; 40% from unagented writers. Pays 7½% royalty. Offers advance.** Accepts simultaneous submissions. Book catalog online; ms guidelines online.

Fiction: Adventure, confession, humor, literary, mainstream/contemporary, multicultural, regional, romance, short story collections, contemporary women's fiction. Red Dress Ink publishes "stories that reflect the lifestyles of today's urban, single women. They show life as it is, with a strong touch of humor, hipness and energy." Word length: 90,000-110,000 words. Point of view: first person/third person, as well as multiple viewpoints, if needed. Settings: urban locales in North America or well-known international settings, such as London or Paris. Tone: fun, up-to-the-minute, clever, appealing, realistic. Submit proposal package including 3 sample chapter(s), synopsis, cover letter or submit complete ms.

Recent Title(s): *Fashionistas*, by Lynn Messina; *The Thin Pink Line*, by Lauren Baratz-Logsted; *Engaging Men*, by Lynda Curnyn.

Tips: Audience is women 18-55. "These books are *Ally McBeal* meets *Sex and the City*, *Bridget Jones's Diary* meets *The Girls' Guide to Hunting and Fishing*. The style of writing is light, highly accessible, clever, funny and full of witty observations. The dialogue is sharp and true-to-life. These are characters you can immediately identify with in a story you just can't put down!"

RED HEN PRESS, P.O. Box 3537, Granada Hills CA 91394. (818)831-0649. Fax: (818)831-6659. E-mail: editor@redhen.org. Website: www.redhen.org. **Acquisitions:** Mark E. Cull, publisher/editor (fiction); Katherine Gale, poetry editor (poetry, literary fiction). Estab. 1993. Publishes trade paperback originals. **Publishes 10 titles/year. Receives 2,000 queries and 500 mss/year. 10% of books from first-time authors; 90% from unagented writers.** Publishes book 1 year after acceptance of ms. Accepts simultaneous submissions. Responds in 1 month to queries; 2 months to proposals; 3 months to mss. Book catalog and ms guidelines available via website or free; ms guidelines online.

- Red Hen Press is a nonproft organization specializing in literary fiction and nonfiction. Currently de-emphasizing poetry.

Nonfiction: Biography, children's/juvenile, cookbook. Subjects include anthropology/archeology, cooking/foods/nutrition, ethnic, gay/lesbian, language/literature, memoirs, travel, women's issues/studies, political/social interest. Query with SASE. Reviews artwork/photos as part of ms package. Send photocopies.

Fiction: "We prefer high-quality literary fiction." Ethnic, experimental, feminist, gay/lesbian, historical, literary, mainstream/contemporary, poetry, poetry in translation, short story collections. "We prefer high-quality literary fiction." Query with SASE.

Poetry: Query or submit 5 sample poems.

Recent Title(s): *Letters from the Underground*, by Abbie and Anita Hoffman; *Tisch*, by Stephen Dixon.

Tips: "Audience reads poetry, literary fiction, intelligent nonfiction. If you have an agent, we may be too small since we don't pay advances. Write well. Send queries first. Be willing to help promote your own book."

[N] **RED WHEEL/WEISER**, 368 Congress St., Boston MA 02210. (617)542-1324. Fax: (617)482-9676. Website: www.redwheelweiser.com. **Acquisitions:** Pat Bryce, acquisitions editor. Estab. 1956. Publishes hardcover and trade paperback originals and reprints. **Publishes 60-75 titles/year; imprint publishes 20-25 titles/year. Receives 2,000 queries and 2,000 mss/year. 20% of books from first-time authors; 50% from unagented writers. Pays royalty.** Publishes book 1 year after acceptance of ms. Accepts simultaneous submissions. Responds in 2 months to queries; 3 months to proposals; 3 months to mss. Book catalog free; ms guidelines online.

Imprints: Red Wheel, Conari Press, Weiser.

Nonfiction: Gift book, self-help, inspirational, esoteric subjects including magic, Wicca, astrology, tarot. Subjects include child guidance/parenting, New Age, spirituality, women's issues/studies. Query with SASE or submit proposal package including outline, 2 sample chapter(s), TOC. Reviews artwork/photos as part of ms package. Send photocopies.

Recent Title(s): *Snap Out of It*, by Ilene Segalove; *The Odd Girls' Book of Spells*, by Cal Garrison; *How to Live in the World and Still Be Happy*, by Hugh Prather.

REFERENCE PRESS INTERNATIONAL, P.O. Box 4126, Greenwich CT 06831. (203)622-6860. Fax: (707)929-0282. **Acquisitions:** Cheryl Lacoff, senior editor. Publishes hardcover and trade paperback originals. **Publishes 6 titles/year. Receives 50 queries and 20 mss/year. 75% of books from first-time authors; 90% from unagented writers. Pays royalty or makes outright purchase. Offers determined by project advance.** Publishes book 6 months after acceptance of ms. Accepts simultaneous submissions. Responds in 3 months to queries.

O- Reference Press specializes in gift books, instructional, reference and how-to titles.

Nonfiction: Gift book, how-to, illustrated book, multimedia (audio, video, CD-ROM), reference, technical, instructional. Subjects include Americana, art/architecture, business/economics, education, gardening, hobbies, money/finance, photography, anything related to the arts or crafts field. "Follow the guidelines as stated concerning subjects and types of books we're looking for." Query with SASE or submit outline, 1-3 sample chapter(s). Reviews artwork/photos as part of ms package. Send photocopies.

Recent Title(s): *Who's Who in the Peace Corps* (alumni directory).

REFERENCE SERVICE PRESS, 5000 Windplay Dr., Suite 4, El Dorado Hills CA 95762. (916)939-9620. Fax: (916)939-9626. E-mail: findaid@aol.com. Website: www.rspfunding.com. **Acquisitions:** Stuart Hauser, acquisitions editor. Estab. 1977. Publishes hardcover originals. **Publishes 10-20 titles/year. 100% from unagented writers. Pays 10% royalty. Offers advance.** Publishes book 6 months after acceptance of ms. Accepts simultaneous submissions. Responds in 2 months to queries. Book catalog for #10 SASE.

O- Reference Service Press focuses on the development and publication of financial aid resources in any format (print, electronic, e-book, etc.). We are interested in financial aid publications aimed at specific groups (e.g., minorities, women, veterans, the disabled, undergraduates majoring in specific subject areas, specific types of financial aid, etc.).

Nonfiction: Specializes in financial aid opportunities for students in or having these characteristics: women, minorities, veterans, the disabled, etc. Reference. Subjects include agriculture/horticulture, art/architecture, business/economics, education, ethnic, health/medicine, history, religion, science, sociology, women's issues/studies, disabled. Submit outline, sample chapter(s).

Recent Title(s): *Financial Aids for Women, 2003-2005*.

Tips: "Our audience consists of librarians, counselors, researchers, students, re-entry women, scholars and other fundseekers."

[A] **REGAN BOOKS**, HarperCollins, 10 E. 53rd St., New York NY 10022. (212)207-7400. Fax: (212)207-6951. Website: www.reganbooks.com. **Acquisitions:** Judith Regan, president/publisher; Cal Morgan, editorial director. Estab. 1994. Publishes hardcover and trade paperback originals. **Publishes 75 titles/year. Receives 7,500 queries and 5,000 mss/year. Pays royalty on retail price. Offers variable advance.** Publishes book 1 year after acceptance of ms. Accepts simultaneous submissions. Responds in 3 months to proposals.

O- Regan Books publishes general fiction and nonfiction: biography, self-help, style and gardening books, and is known for contemporary topics and controversial authors and titles.

Nonfiction: Subjects include agriculture/horticulture, alternative lifestyles, Americana, animals, anthropology/archeology, art/architecture, business/economics, child guidance/parenting, community, computers/electronic, contemporary culture, cooking/foods/nutrition, creative nonfiction, education, ethnic, fashion/beauty, film/cinema/stage, gardening, gay/lesbian, government/politics, health/medicine, history, hobbies, humanities, language/literature, memoirs, military/war, money/finance, multicultural, music/dance, nature/environment, New Age, philosophy, photography, psychology, recreation, regional, religion, science, sex, social sciences, sociology, software, spirituality, sports, translation, travel, true crime, women's issues/studies, world affairs. No unsolicited mss. *Agented submissions only.* Reviews artwork/photos as part of ms package. Send photocopies.

Fiction: Adventure, comic books, confession, erotica, ethnic, experimental, fantasy, feminist, gay/lesbian, gothic, hi-lo, historical, horror, humor, juvenile, literary, mainstream/contemporary, military/war, multicultural, multimedia, mystery, occult, picture books, plays, poetry, poetry in translation, regional, religious, romance, science fiction, short story collections, spiritual, sports, suspense, translation, western, young adult. No unsolicited mss. *Agented submissions only.*

Recent Title(s): *Stupid White Men*, by Michael Moore; *Let Freedom Ring*, by Sean Haninty; *Maybe You Never Cry Again*, by Bernie Mac.

REGNERY PUBLISHING, INC., Eagle Publishing, One Massachusetts Ave., NW, Washington DC 20001. (202)216-0600. Website: www.regnery.com. Publisher: Marji Ross. **Acquisitions:** Harry Crocker, executive editor (bestsellers); Bernadette Malone, editor; Jed Donahue, editor (biography, American history). Estab. 1947. Publishes hardcover and paperback originals and reprints. **Publishes 30 titles/year. 0% from unagented writers. Pays 8-15% royalty on retail price. Offers $0-50,000 advance.** Publishes book 1 year after acceptance of ms. Does not accept simultaneous submissions. Responds in 3 months to queries; 3 months to proposals; 3 months to mss.

Imprints: Gateway Editions, LifeLine Press, Capital Press.

Regnery publishes conservative, well-written, well-produced, sometimes controversial books. Currently emphasizing health and business books.

Nonfiction: Biography, current affairs. Subjects include business/economics, government/politics, health/medicine, history, money/finance. *Agented submissions only. No unsolicited mss.*

Recent Title(s): *Bias: A CBS Insider Exposés How the Media Distort the News*; *Shakedown: Exposing the Real Jesse Jackson*; *The Final Days: The Last, Desparate Abuses of Power by the Clinton White House*, by Barbara Olson.

Tips: "We seek high-impact, headline-making, bestseller treatments of pressing current issues by established experts in the field."

REPUBLIC OF TEXAS PRESS, Rowman & Littlefield Publishing Group, 3164 Harbinger Lane, Dallas TX 75287. Phone/Fax: (972)672-4965. E-mail: dundeeh@aol.com. **Acquisitions:** Janet Harris, acquisitions editor. Publishes trade and mass market paperback originals. **Publishes 28-32 titles/year. Receives 400 queries and 300 mss/year. 95% from unagented writers. Pays 8% royalty on net receipts. Offers small advance.** Publishes book 1 year after acceptance of ms. Accepts simultaneous submissions. Responds in 2 months to queries. Book catalog for #10 SASE.

Republic of Texas Press specializes in Texas history and general Texana.

Nonfiction: Biography, humor. Subjects include ethnic, general nonfiction, history, nature/environment, regional, sports, travel, women's issues/studies, Old West, Texas military, ghost and mystery stories, trivia. Submit table of contents, 2 sample chapters, target audience, author bio and SASE.

Recent Title(s): *The Alamo Story: From Early History to Current Conflicts*, by J.R. Edmondson; *Exploring Houston with Children*, by Elaine Galit and Vikk Simmons; *A Yankee Chicks Guide to Survival in Texas*, by Sophia Dembling.

Tips: "We are interested in anything relating to Texas. From the wacky to the most informative, any nonfiction concept will be considered. Our market is adult."

RESOURCE PUBLICATIONS, INC., 160 E. Virginia St., Suite #290, San Jose CA 95112-5876. (408)286-8505. Fax: (408)287-8748. E-mail: info@rpinet.com. Website: www.rpinet.com/ml/. **Acquisitions:** Acquisition Director. Estab. 1973. Publishes paperback originals. **Publishes 12-18 titles/year. 30% of books from first-time authors; 99% from unagented writers. Pays 8% royalty (for a first project). Offers $250-1,000 advance.** Responds in 10 weeks to queries. Book catalog online; ms guidelines online.

Resource Publications publishes books to help liturgists and ministers make the imaginative connection between liturgy and life.

Nonfiction: How-to, reference, self-help. Subjects include child guidance/parenting, education, music/dance, religion. Professional ministry resources for worship, education, clergy and other leaders, for use in Roman Catholic and mainline Protestant churches. Submit proposal package including résumé. Reviews artwork/photos as part of ms package.

Fiction: Fables; Anecdotes; Faith Sharing Stories; Stories useful in preaching or teaching. Query with SASE.

Recent Title(s): *Adult Children of Divorced Parents*; *Performing Parables*; *The Catholic Wedding Answer Book.*

Tips: "We are publishers and secondarily we are book packagers. Pitch your project to us for publication first. If we can't take it on on that basis, we may be able to take it on as a packaging and production project."

RESURRECTION PRESS, Catholic Book Publishing, Co., 77 W. End Rd., Totowa NJ 07512-1405. Fax: (973)890-2410. **Acquisitions:** Emilie Cerar, editor. Publishes trade paperback originals and reprints. **Publishes 8-10 titles/year. Receives 100 queries and 100 mss/year. 25% of books from first-time authors; 100% from unagented writers. Pays 5-10% royalty. Offers $250-2,000 advance.** Publishes book 1 year after acceptance of ms. Accepts simultaneous submissions. Responds in 1 month to queries; 1 month to proposals; 2 months to mss. Book catalog and ms guidelines free.

Resurrection Press publishes religious, devotional and inspirational titles.

Nonfiction: Self-help. Subjects include religion. Query with SASE or submit outline, 2 sample chapter(s). Reviews artwork/photos as part of ms package. Send photocopies.

Recent Title(s): *Grace Notes*, by Lorraine Murray; *Feasts of Life*, by Fr. Jim Vlaun.

FLEMING H. REVELL PUBLISHING, Baker Book House, P.O. Box 6287, Grand Rapids MI 49516. Fax: (616)676-2315. Website: www.bakerbooks.com. **Acquisitions:** Lonnie Hull DuPont, interim editorial director; Bill Petersen, senior acquisitions editor; Jane Campbell, senior editor (Chosen Books); Jennifer Leep, acquisitions editor. Estab. 1870. Publishes hardcover, trade paperback and mass market paperback originals and reprints. **Publishes 50 titles/year; imprint publishes**

10 titles/year. Pays 14-18% royalty on wholesale price. Offers advance. Publishes book 1 year after acceptance of ms.
Imprints: Chosen Books, Spire Books.

- "We no longer accept unsolicited mss."

O→ Revell publishes to the heart (rather than to the head). For 125 years, Revell has been publishing evangelical books for the personal enrichment and spiritual growth of general Christian readers.

Nonfiction: Biography, coffee table book, how-to, self-help. Subjects include child guidance/parenting, religion, Christian living.

Fiction: Religious.

Recent Title(s): *Making Children Mind Without Losing Yours*, by Dr. Kevin Leman (nonfiction); *Woman of Grace*, by Kathleen Morgan (fiction).

MORGAN REYNOLDS PUBLISHING, 620 S. Elm St., Suite 223, Greensboro NC 27406. Fax: (336)275-1152. E-mail: info@morganreynolds.com. Website: www.morganreynolds.com. **Acquisitions:** Laura Shoemaker, editor. Publishes hardcover originals. **Publishes 20-24 titles/year. Receives 250-300 queries and 100-150 mss/year. 50% of books from first-time authors; 100% from unagented writers.** Publishes book 8 months after acceptance of ms. Accepts simultaneous submissions. Responds in 3 months to queries.

O→ Morgan Reynolds publishes nonfiction books for juvenile and young adult readers. "We prefer lively, well-written biographies of interesting contemporary and historical figures for our biography series. Books for our Great Events series should be insightful and exciting looks at critical periods. We are interested in more well-known subjects rather than the esoteric." Currently emphasizing great scientists, composers, philosophers, world writers. De-emphasizing sports figures.

Nonfiction: "We do not always publish the obvious subjects. Don't shy away from less popular subjects. We also publish nonfiction related to great events." Biography. Subjects include Americana (young adult/juvenile oriented), business/economics, government/politics, history, language/literature, military/war, money/finance, women's issues/studies. No children's books, picture books or fiction. Query with SASE.

Recent Title(s): *MS: The Story of Gloria Steinem*, by Elizabeth Wheaton; *Great Society: The Story of Lyndon Baines Johnson*, by Nancy Colbert.

Tips: "Request our writer's guidelines and visit our website. We will be happy to send a catalog if provided with 80 cents postage."

N **RFF PRESS**, Resources for the Future, 1616 P St., NW, Washington DC 20036. (202)328-5086. Fax: (202)328-5137. E-mail: rffpress@rff.org. Website: www.rffpress.org. **Acquisitions:** Don Reisman, publisher. Publishes hardcover, trade paperback and electronic originals. **Publishes 20 titles/year. Pays royalty on wholesale price.** Publishes book 6 months after acceptance of ms. Accepts simultaneous submissions. Responds in 1 month to queries; 1 month to proposals; 2 months to mss. Book catalog online; ms guidelines free.

Nonfiction: "We focus on social science approaches to environmental and natural resource issues." Reference, technical, textbook. Subjects include agriculture/horticulture, business/economics, government/politics, history, nature/environment, science. "We do not publish works that are purely opinion driven. Inquire via e-mail or letter; no phone calls." Submit proposal package including outline. Reviews artwork/photos as part of ms package. Send photocopies.

Recent Title(s): *Battling Resistance to Antibiotics and Pesticides: An Economic Approach*, edited by Ramanan Laxminarayan; *On Borrowed Time? Assessing the Threat of Mineral Depletion*, by John E. Tilton; *The Contextual Determinants of Malaria*, edited by Elizabeth A. Casman and Hadi Dowlatabadi.

Tips: Audience is scholars, policy makes, activists, businesses, the general public.

RICHBORO PRESS, P.O. Box 6, Southampton PA 18966. (215)355-6084. Fax: (215)364-2212. **Acquisitions:** George Moore, editor. Estab. 1979. Publishes hardcover, trade paperback originals and software. **Publishes 4 titles/year. Receives 500 submissions/year. 90% from unagented writers. Pays 15% royalty on retail price. Offers advance.** Publishes book 1 year after acceptance of ms. Does not accept simultaneous submissions. Responds in 2 months to queries. Book catalog free; Writer's guidelines for $1 and #10 SASE.

Nonfiction: Cookbook, how-to. Subjects include cooking/foods/nutrition, gardening, software. Query with SASE. Prefers complete ms via electronic media.

RISING MOON, Northland Publishing, LLC, P.O. Box 1389, Flagstaff AZ 86002-1389. (928)774-5251. Fax: (928)774-0592. E-mail: editorial@northlandpub.com. Website: www.northlandpub.com. **Acquisitions:** Theresa Howell, kids editor. Estab. 1988. Publishes hardcover and trade paperback originals. **Publishes 8-10 titles/year. Receives 1,000 submissions/year. 20% of books from first-time authors; 20% from unagented writers. Pays royalty. Sometimes pays flat fee. Offers advance.** Publishes book 1-2 years after acceptance of ms. Accepts simultaneous submissions. Responds in 3 months to queries. Call for book catalog; ms guidelines online.

O→ Rising Moon's objective is to provide children with entertaining and informative books that follow the heart and tickle the funny bone. Rising Moon is no longer publishing middle-grade children's fiction.

Fiction: Picture books (broad subjects with wide appeal and universal themes). "We are also looking for exceptional bilingual stories (Spanish/English), activity books, fractured fairy tales, and original stories with a Southwest flavor." Submit complete ms with SASE of adequate size and postage. No e-mail submissions.

Recent Title(s): *Kissing Coyotes*, by Monica Vaughan and Ken Spengler.

Tips: "Our audience is composed of regional southwest interest readers."

RISING TIDE PRESS, 526 E. 16th St., Tucson AZ 85701. (800)311-3565. Fax: (520)798-1530. Website: www.risingtidepress.com. **Acquisitions:** Jean Reehl, partner (mystery, adventure, nonfiction); Judy Wood, partner (science fiction, young adult fiction). Estab. 1988. Publishes trade paperback originals. **Publishes 10-15 titles/year. Receives 1,000 queries and 600 mss/year. 75% of books from first-time authors; 100% from unagented writers. Pays on wholesale price.** Publishes book 6-18 months after acceptance of ms. Does not accept simultaneous submissions. Responds in 2 months to queries; 2 months to proposals; 3 months to mss. Book catalog for $1; ms guidelines for #10 SASE and on the website.

"We are committed to publishing books by, for and about strong women and their lives."

Nonfiction: Subjects include women's issues/studies, lesbian nonfiction. Query with outline, entire ms and large SASE. Reviews artwork/photos as part of ms package. Send photocopies.

Fiction: Women's fiction only. Adventure, erotica, fantasy, feminist, historical, horror, humor, literary, mainstream/contemporary, mystery, occult, romance, science fiction, suspense, western, mixed genres. "Major characters must be women and stories must depict strong women characters." Looking for romance and mystery. Query with SASE or submit synopsis, 1 page outline/synopsis or submit complete ms.

Recent Title(s): *Taking Risks*, by Judith McDaniel; *Undercurrents*, by Laurel Mills.

Tips: "We welcome unpublished authors. 2 cash prizes awarded annually. Any material submitted should be proofed. No multiple submissions."

RIVER CITY PUBLISHING, River City Publishing, LLC, 1719 Mulberry St., Montgomery AL 36106. (334)265-6753. Fax: (334)265-8880. E-mail: agordon@rivercitypublishing.com. Website: www.rivercitypublishing.com. **Acquisitions:** Ashley Gordon, editor. Publishes hardcover and trade paperback originals and reprints. **Publishes 12 titles/year; imprint publishes 5 titles/year. Receives 100 queries and 400 mss/year. 20% of books from first-time authors; 75% from unagented writers. Pays 10-15% royalty on retail price. Offers $500-5,000 advance.** Publishes book 1 year after acceptance of ms. Accepts simultaneous submissions. Responds in 3 months to queries; 4 months to proposals; 1 year to mss. Ms guidelines free.

Imprints: Starrhill Press, Black Belt Press.

Nonfiction: Biography, coffee table book, illustrated book. Subjects include art/architecture, creative nonfiction, ethnic, gardening, government/politics, health/medicine, history, language/literature, memoirs, multicultural, music/dance, photography, regional, sports, travel. Submit proposal package including outline, 2 sample chapter(s). Reviews artwork/photos as part of ms package. Send photocopies.

Fiction: Ethnic, historical, literary, multicultural, poetry, regional, short story collections. Submit proposal package including 2 sample chapter(s), synopsis.

Poetry: Query.

Recent Title(s): *Speaks the Nightbird*, by Robert McCammon (historical fiction); *Southern Scenes*, by Starr Smith (travel); *It's Christmas*, by Kathryn Tucker Windham (memoir).

N **RIVER OAK PUBLISHING**, Cook Communications Ministries, 9412 S. Darlington Ave., Tulsa OK 74137. E-mail: info@riveroakpublishing.com. Website: www.riveroakpublishing.com. **Acquisitions:** Jeff Dunn, acquisitions editor. Publishes hardcover, trade paperback and mass market paperback originals and reprints. **Publishes 15-20 titles/year. Receives 1,000 queries and 500 mss/year. 5% of books from first-time authors; 25% from unagented writers. Pays royalty on wholesale price. Offers negotiable advance.** Publishes book 18 months after acceptance of ms. Accepts simultaneous submissions. Responds in 1 month to queries; 6 months to proposals; 6 months to mss. Ms guidelines for #10 on at the website.

Fiction: "We are looking for the best in various genres of Christian fiction." Adventure, fantasy, historical, humor, mystery, religious, romance, spiritual, sports, western. Query with SASE.

Recent Title(s): *Mutiny's Curse*, by Dan L. Thrapp; *Q*, by Paul Nigro; *A Place Called Wiregrass*, by Michael Morris.

Tips: "Our books are written for Christian readers desiring to strengthen their walk with God. We look for what you believe, not what you are against. We like creative ways to present biblically-correct inspirational stories."

A **ROC BOOKS**, New American Library, A Division of Penguin Putnam, Inc., 375 Hudson St., New York NY 10014. (212)366-2000. Website: www.penguinputnam.com. **Acquisitions:** Laura Anne Gilman, executive editor; Jennifer Heddle, editor. Publishes mass market, trade and hardcover originals. **Publishes 36 titles/year. Receives 500 queries/year. Pays royalty. Offers negotiable advance.** Accepts simultaneous submissions. Responds in 2-3 months to queries.

"We're looking for books that are a good read, that people will want to pick up time and time again."

Fiction: Fantasy, horror, science fiction. "Roc tries to strike a balance between fantasy and science fiction. We strongly discourage unsolicited submissions." Query with SASE or submit 1-2 sample chapter(s), synopsis.

Recent Title(s): *Shadows and Light*, by Anne Bishop; *The Peshawer Lancers*, by S.M. Stirling.

N **ROCK SPRING PRESS**, 6015 Morrow St. E., Suite 106, Jacksonville FL 32217. E-mail: submissions@rockspringpress.com. Submissions E-mail: submissions@rockspringpress.com. Website: www.rockspringpress.com. Publisher: Alice Platt. Estab. 2002. Publishes hardcover originals. **Pays 12-15% royalty on wholesale price.** Publishes book 8-12 months after acceptance of ms. Accepts simultaneous submissions. Responds in 3 months to queries; 3 months to proposals; 3 months to mss. Ms guidelines for #10 SASE.

Nonfiction: Subjects include general nonfiction, nature/environment, travel. "We are looking for descriptive travel writing that informs the reader about the experience of being in, or traveling to, a place. We are also interested in books that make nature and the environment accessible to the average reader." No travel guides. Submit proposal package including outline, 3 sample chapter(s), marketing ideas for the book or submit complete ms. Reviews artwork/photos as part of ms package. e-mail low resolution scans.

Tips: "Our audience is reasonably well-educated (bachelor's degree) adults interested in travel and their natural environment. Proofread, proofread, proofread. What you send should be as good as you envision the final product. Please make sure submissions are typed and double-spaced."

ROSE PUBLISHING, 4455 Torrance Blvd., #259, Torrance CA 90503. (310)370-8962. Fax: (310)370-7492. E-mail: rosepubl@aol.com. Website: www.rose-publishing.com. **Acquisitions:** Carol R. Witte, editor. **Publishes 5-10 titles/year. 5% of books from first-time authors; 100% from unagented writers. Makes outright purchase.** Publishes book 18 months after acceptance of ms. Accepts simultaneous submissions. Responds in 3 months to proposals; 2 months to mss. Book catalog free.

O→ "We publish Bible reference materials in chart, poster or pamphlet form, easy-to-understand and appealing to children, teens or adults on Bible study, prayer, basic beliefs, Scripture memory, salvation, sharing the gospel, worship, abstinence, creation."

Nonfiction: Reference, pamphlets, group study books. Subjects include religion, science, sex, spirituality, Bible studies, Christian history, counseling aids, cults/occult, curriculum, Christian discipleship, evangelism/witnessing, Christian living, marriage, prayer, creation, singles issues. No fiction or poetry. Submit proposal package including outline, photocopies of chart contents or poster artwork. Reviews artwork/photos as part of ms package. Send photocopies.

Recent Title(s): *Charts on the Denominations Comparisons*; *Feasts and Holidays of Israel*; *100 Things to Know About the Person You Might Marry.*

Tips: Audience includes both church (Bible study leaders, Sunday school teachers [all ages], pastors, youth leaders) and home (parents, home schoolers, children, youth, high school and college). Open to topics that supplement Sunday School curriculum or Bible study, junior high creation materials, Tabernacle worksheets, Bible study, reasons to believe, books of the Bible.

THE ROSEN PUBLISHING GROUP, 29 E. 21st St., New York NY 10010. Estab. 1950. Publishes nonfiction hardcover originals. **50% of books from first-time authors; 95% from unagented writers. Makes outright purchase of $200-3,000 for sale to school and public libraries.** Publishes book approximately 9 months after acceptance of ms. Does not accept simultaneous submissions. Responds in 2 months to proposals. Book catalog and ms guidelines free.

Imprints: PowerKids Press (nonfiction books for grades K-4 that are supplementary to the curriculum). Topics include conflict resolution, character building, history, science, social studies and multicultural titles. Contact: Joanne Randolph, editorial director. Rosen Central (nonfiction for grades 5-8 on a wide range of topics) and Rosen Young Adult. Topics include social issues, health, sports, self-esteem, history and science. Contact: Iris Rosoff, editorial director.

Nonfiction: Children's/juvenile, reference, self-help, textbook, young adult. Subjects include ethnic, health/medicine, history, multicultural (ethnographic studies), religion, science. Areas of particular interest include American history; science; health; sports; careers; coping with social, medical and personal problems; social studies; high interest subjects. Submit outline, 1 sample chapter(s).

Recent Title(s): *Primary Sources of E American History*; *When Disaster Strikes!*; *Terrorist Attacks.*

Tips: "The writer has the best chance of selling our firm a book on vocational guidance, personal social adjustment, a topic corellated directly to the 5-12 grade social studies or science curriculum, or high-interest, low reading-level material for teens."

[N] **ROUTLEDGE, INC.**, 29 W. 35th St., New York NY 10001-2299. (212)216-7800. Fax: (212)563-2269. Website: routledge-ny.com. **Acquisitions:** Linda Hollick, vice president/publisher. Estab. 1836. in New York. **Publishes 175 titles/year. 10% of books from first-time authors; 95% from unagented writers. Pays royalty. Offers advance.** Publishes book 1 year after acceptance of ms. Accepts simultaneous submissions. Responds in 3 months to queries. Ms guidelines online.

Imprints: Theatre Arts Books, Routledge Falmer, Brunner-Routledge.

O→ The Routledge list includes humanities, social sciences, reference. Monographs, reference works, hardback and paperback upper-level texts, academic general interest.

Nonfiction: Reference, textbook. Subjects include education, ethnic, gay/lesbian, government/politics, history, music/dance, psychology, women's issues/studies, literary criticism, social sciences, geography, cultural studies. Query with proposal package, including toc, intro, sample chapter, overall prospectus, cv and SASE.

[N] **ROWMAN & LITTLEFIELD PUBLISHING GROUP**, 4501 Forbes Blvd., Suite 200, Lanham MD 20706. (301)459-3366. Website: www.rowmanlittlefield.com. Publishes hardcover and trade paperback originals and reprints. **Publishes 1,000 titles/year. Offers advance.** Does not accept simultaneous submissions. Ms guidelines online.

Imprints: AltaMira Press, Ivan R. Dee, Derrydale Press, Lexington Books, New Amsterdam Books, Rowman & Littlefield Publishers, Madison Books, Scarecrow Press, University Press of America, Vestal Press, Taylor Trade Publishing.

ROXBURY PUBLISHING CO., P.O. Box 491044, Los Angeles CA 90049. (310)473-3312. **Acquisitions:** Claude Teweles, publisher. Estab. 1981. Publishes hardcover and paperback originals and reprints. **Publishes 15-20 titles/year. Pays royalty.** Accepts simultaneous submissions. Responds in 2 months to queries.

O→ Roxbury publishes college textbooks in the humanities and social sciences only.

Nonfiction: Textbook (college-level textbooks and supplements only). Subjects include humanities, social sciences, sociology, political science, family studies, criminology, criminal justice. Query with SASE or submit outline, sample chapter(s), synopsis or submit complete ms.

ROYAL FIREWORKS PUBLISHING, 1 First Ave., P.O. Box 399, Unionville NY 10988. (845)726-4444. Fax: (845)726-3824. E-mail: rfpress@frontiernet.net. Website: www.rfpress.com. **Acquisitions:** William Neumann, editor (young adult); Myrna Kemnitz, editor (education). Estab. 1977. Publishes library binding and trade paperback originals, reprints and textbooks. **Publishes 75-140 titles/year. Receives 1,000 queries and 400 mss/year. 30-50% of books from first-time**

authors; 98% from unagented writers. Pays 5-10% royalty on wholesale price. Publishes book 9 months after acceptance of ms. Does not accept simultaneous submissions. Responds in 3 months to mss. Book catalog for $3.85; ms guidelines for #10 SASE.

Nonfiction: Textbook. Subjects include child guidance/parenting, education. "We do books for gifted children, their parents and teachers." Submit complete ms. Reviews artwork/photos as part of ms package. Send photocopies.

Fiction: Young adult. "We do novels for children from 8-16. We do a lot of historical fiction, science fiction, adventure, mystery, sports, etc. We are concerned about the values." No drugs, sex, swearing. Submit complete ms.

Recent Title(s): *Grammar Voyage*, by Michael Thompson; *Double Vision*, by Jerry Chris; *A Few Screws Loose*, by Maryann Easley.

Tips: Audience is comprised of gifted children, their parents and teachers, and children (8-18) who read.

RUMINATOR BOOKS, 1648 Grand Ave., St. Paul MN 55105. (651)699-7038. Fax: (651)699-7190. E-mail: books@ruminator.com. Website: www.ruminator.com. **Acquisitions:** Pearl Kilbride. Publishes hardcover originals, trade paperback originals and reprints. **Publishes 8-10 titles/year. Receives 1,200 queries and 1,000 mss/year. 60% from unagented writers. Royalty varies. Offers varying advance.** Publishes book 12-18 months after acceptance of ms. Accepts simultaneous submissions. Responds in 4 months to proposals. Book catalog for 9×12 SAE with 2 first-class stamps; ms guidelines for #10 SASE and on website.

O→ Ruminator Books is an independent press dedicated to publishing literary works from diverse voices and bringing political, social and cultural ideas to a wide and varied readership. Currently emphasizing culture studies, political, travel, memoirs, nature, history, world views. De-emphasizing spirituality, cooking, romance, mysteries, how-to, business, poetry.

Nonfiction: Subjects include government/politics, history, language/literature, memoirs, nature/environment, travel, world-views, culture studies. No how-to, self-help/instructional, children's or poetry mss. Submit proposal package, including letter, outline and at least one sample chapter with SASE.

Fiction: Literary, adult fiction. Query with SASE or submit proposal package including outline, sample chapter(s), SASE.

Recent Title(s): *Facing the Congo*, by Jeffrey Tayler; *The Last Summer of Reason*, by Tahar Djarat; *An Algerian Childhood* (anthology).

RUTGERS UNIVERSITY PRESS, 100 Joyce Kilmer Ave., Piscataway NJ 08854-8099. (732)445-7762. Fax: (732)445-7039. Website: rutgerspress.rutgers.edu. **Acquisitions:** Leslie Mitchner, editor-in-chief/associate director (humanities); Kristi Long, senior editor (social sciences); Audra Wolfe, editor (science, health & medicine). Estab. 1936. Publishes hardcover originals and trade paperback originals and reprints. **Publishes 90 titles/year. Receives 1,500 queries and 300 mss/year. 30% of books from first-time authors; 70% from unagented writers. Pays 7½-15% royalty. Offers $1,000-10,000 advance.** Publishes book 1 year after acceptance of ms. Responds in 1 month to proposals. Book catalog and ms guidelines available via website or with SASE; ms guidelines online.

O→ "Our press aims to reach audiences beyond the academic community with accessible scholarly and regional books."

Nonfiction: Reference. Subjects include art/architecture (art history), ethnic, film/cinema/stage, gay/lesbian, government/politics, health/medicine, history, multicultural, nature/environment, regional, religion, sociology, women's issues/studies, African-American studies, Asian-American studies, history of science and technology, literature, literary criticism, human evolution, ecology, media studies. Books for use in undergraduate courses. Submit outline, 2-3 sample chapter(s). Reviews artwork/photos as part of ms package. Send photocopies.

Recent Title(s): *The Great Communication Gap: Why Americans Feel So Alone*, by Laura Pappano.

Tips: Both academic and general audiences. "Many of our books have potential for undergraduate course use. We are more trade-oriented than most university presses. We are looking for intelligent, well-written and accessible books. Avoid overly narrow topics."

RUTLEDGE HILL PRESS, Thomas Nelson, P.O. Box 141000, Nashville TN 37214-1000. (615)902-2333. Fax: (615)902-2340. Website: www.rutledgehillpress.com. **Acquisitions:** Lawrence Stone, publisher. Estab. 1982. Publishes hardcover and trade paperback originals and reprints. **Publishes 40-50 titles/year. Receives 1,000 submissions/year. 40% of books from first-time authors; 80% from unagented writers. Pays royalty. Offers advance.** Publishes book 10 months after acceptance of ms. Responds in 2 months to queries. Book catalog for 9×12 SASE; ms guidelines for #10 SASE.

O→ "We are a publisher of market-specific books, focusing on particular genres or regions."

Nonfiction: Biography, cookbook, humor. Subjects include cooking/foods/nutrition, travel (regional), women's issues/studies, Civil War history. "The book should have a unique marketing hook. Books built on new ideas and targeted to a specific U.S. region are welcome. Please, no fiction, children's, academic, poetry or religious works, and we won't even look at *Life's Little Instruction Book* spinoffs or copycats." Submit cover letter that includes brief marketing strategy and author bio, outline and sample chapters. Reviews artwork/photos as part of ms package.

Recent Title(s): *A Gentleman Entertains*, by John Bridges and Bryan Curtis; *101 Secrets a Good Dad Knows*, by Walter Browder and Sue Ellen Browder; *I Hope You Dance*, by Tia Sillers and Mark Sanders.

SAE INTERNATIONAL, Society of Automotive Engineers, 400 Commonwealth Dr., Warrendale PA 15096. (724)776-4841. E-mail: writeabook@sae.org. Website: www.sae.org. **Acquisitions:** Jeff Worsinger, product developer; Martha Swiss, product developer; Kris Hattman, product developer; Erin Moore, product developer; Matt Milles, product developer; Theresa Wertz, product developer. Estab. 1905. Publishes hardcover and trade paperback originals, Web and CD-ROM based electronic product. **Publishes 30-40 titles/year. Receives 250 queries and 75 mss/year. 30-40% of books from first-time authors; 100% from unagented writers. Pays royalty. Offers possible advance.** Publishes book 9-10 months after acceptance of ms. Accepts simultaneous submissions. Responds in 2 months to queries. Book catalog free; ms guidelines online.

O→ "Automotive means anything self-propelled. We are a professional society serving this area, which includes aircraft, spacecraft, marine, rail, automobiles, trucks and off-highway vehicles." Currently emphasizing engineering.

Nonfiction: Biography, multimedia (CD-ROM, Web-based), reference, technical, textbook. Query with SASE. Reviews artwork/photos as part of ms package. Send photocopies.

Recent Title(s): *Formula 1 Technology*; *Ford: The Dust and the Glory.*

Tips: "Audience is automotive engineers, technicians, car buffs, aerospace engineers, technicians and historians."

SAFARI PRESS, INC., 15621 Chemical Lane, Building B, Huntington Beach CA 92649-1506. (714)894-9080. Fax: (714)894-4949. E-mail: info@safaripress.com. Website: www.safaripress.com. **Acquisitions:** Jacqueline Neufeld, editor. Estab. 1985. Publishes hardcover originals and reprints and trade paperback reprints. **Publishes 25-30 titles/year. 50% of books from first-time authors; 99% from unagented writers. Pays 8-15% royalty on wholesale price.** Does not accept simultaneous submissions. Book catalog for $1; ms guidelines online.

- The editor notes that she receives many mss outside the areas of big-game hunting, wingshooting, and sporting firearms, and these are always rejected.

O→ Safari Press publishes books **only** on big-game hunting, sporting, firearms, and wingshooting; this includes African, North American, European, Asian, and South American hunting and wingshooting. Does not want books on 'outdoors' topics (hiking, camping, canoeing, etc.).

Nonfiction: Biography (of hunters), how-to (hunting and wingshooting stories), hunting adventure stories. Subjects include hunting, firearms, wingshooting, "We discourage autobiographies, unless the life of the hunter or firearms maker has been exceptional. We routinely reject manuscripts along the lines of 'Me and my buddies went hunting for... and a good time was had by all!" No outdoors topics (hiking, camping, canoeing, fishing, etc.). Query with SASE or submit outline.

Recent Title(s): *Royal Quest: The Hunting Saga of H.I.H. Prince Abdorreza of Iran*; *The Best of Holland & Holland: England's Premier Gunmaker*; *Cannibals and Big Game: True Tales of Cannibals, Big-Game Hunting, and Exploration in Portuguese West Africa, 1917-1921.*

SAGAMORE PUBLISHING, (formerly Sport Publishing LLC), 804 N. Neil St., Suite 100, Champaign IL 61820. (217)363-2072. Fax: (217)363-2073. **Acquisitions:** Joseph Bannor, Sr., CEO (parks, recreation, leisure). Estab. 1974. Publishes hardcover and trade paperback originals. **Publishes 10 titles/year. Receives 1,000 queries and 35 mss/year. 40% of books from first-time authors; 100% from unagented writers. Pays 7-15% royalty.** Publishes book 6 months after acceptance of ms. Accepts simultaneous submissions. Responds in 1 month to queries. Book catalog and ms guidelines free or online.

O→ "Sagamore Publishing has been a leader in the parks and recreation field for over 20 years. We are now expanding into the areas of tourism and recreation for special populations such as people with autism or ADD/ADHD, and outdoor adventure and wildlife."

Nonfiction: Reference, textbook. Subjects include education, health/medicine, nature/environment, recreation, outdoor adventure, tourism. Submit proposal package, including outline, 1 sample chapter and market projections. Reviews artwork/photos as part of ms package. Send photocopies.

Recent Title(s): *Outdoor Recreation in American Life*, by Ken Cordell (textbook/reference).

Tips: "We strongly encourage potential authors to submit a marketing prospective with any manuscript they submit."

SALEM PRESS, INC., Magill's Choice, 131 N. El Molino, Suite 350, Pasadena CA 91101. (626)584-0106. Fax: (626)584-1525. Website: www.salempress.com. **Acquisitions:** Dawn P. Dawson. **Publishes 20-22 titles/year. Receives 15 queries/year. Work-for-hire pays 5-15¢/word.** Responds in 1 month to queries; 1 month to proposals. Book catalog online.

Nonfiction: Reference. Subjects include business/economics, ethnic, government/politics, health/medicine, history, language/literature, military/war, music/dance, nature/environment, philosophy, psychology, science, sociology, women's issues/studies. "We accept vitas for writers interested in supplying articles/entries for encyclopedia-type entries in library reference books. Will also accept multi-volume book ideas from people interested in being a general editor." Query with SASE.

SANTA MONICA PRESS, LLC, P.O. Box 1076, Santa Monica CA 90406. Website: www.santamonicapress.com. **Acquisitions:** Acquistions Editor. Estab. 1991. Publishes trade paperback originals. **Publishes 6-10 titles/year. Receives 500+ submissions/year. 25% of books from first-time authors; 75% from unagented writers. Pays 4-10% royalty on wholesale price. Offers $500-2,500 advance.** Publishes book 6-18 months after acceptance of ms. Accepts simultaneous submissions. Responds in 1-2 months to proposals. Book catalog for 9×12 SASE with 83¢ postage; ms guidelines online.

O→ "At Santa Monica Press, we're not afraid to cast a wide editorial net. Our vision extends from lively and modern how-to books to offbeat looks at popular culture, from film history to literature."

Nonfiction: Biography, gift book, how-to, humor, illustrated book, reference. Subjects include Americana, creative nonfiction, film/cinema/stage, health/medicine, language/literature, memoirs, music/dance, spirituality, sports, travel, contemporary culture, film/cinema/stage, general nonfiction. **All unsolicited mss returned unopened.** Submit proposal package, including outline, 2-3 sample chapters, biography, marketing and publicity plans, analysis of competitive titles, SASE with appropriate postage. Reviews artwork/photos as part of ms package. Send photocopies.

Recent Title(s): *James Dean Died Here: The Locations of America's Pop Culture Landmarks*, by Chris Epting; *Redneck Haiku*, by Mary K. Witte; *Jackson Pollock: Memories Arrested in Space*, by Martin Gray.

Tips: "Visit our website before submitting to get a clear idea of the types of books we publish. Carefully analyze your book's competition and tell us what makes your book different—and what makes it better. Also let us know what promotional and marketing opportunities you, as the author, bring to the project."

SARABANDE BOOKS, INC., 2234 Dundee Rd., Suite 200, Louisville KY 40205. (502)458-4028. Fax: (502)458-4065. E-mail: sarabandeb@aol.com. Website: www.sarabandebooks.org. **Acquisitions:** Sarah Gorham, editor-in-chief. Estab. 1994. Publishes hardcover and trade paperback originals. **Publishes 10 titles/year. Receives 500 queries and 2,000 mss/year. 35% of books from first-time authors; 75% from unagented writers. Pays royalty. 10% on actual income received. Also pays in author's copies. Offers $500-1,000 advance.** Publishes book 18 months after acceptance of ms. Accepts simultaneous submissions. Responds in 3 months to queries; 6 months to mss. Book catalog free; ms guidelines for (contest only) for #10 SASE or on website.

O→ "Sarabande Books was founded to publish poetry and short fiction, as well as the occasional literary essay collection. We look for works of lasting literary value. We are actively seeking creative nonfiction."

Fiction: Literary, short story collections, novellas. Short story collections, 250 pages maximum, 150 pages minimum. Queries in September only. "We do publish short novels (less than 250 pages). Sarabade does not publish genre fiction." Query with SASE. Query with 1 sample story. Include 1 page bio and listing of publishing credits.

Poetry: "Poetry of superior artistic quality. Otherwise no restraints or specifications." Submissions in September only. Query or submit 10 sample poems.

Recent Title(s): *Portrait of My Mother, Who Posed Nude in Wartime*, by Marjorie Sandor (fiction); *The Day Before*, by Dick Allen (poetry).

Tips: Sarabande publishes for a general literary audience. "Know your market. Read—and buy—books of literature." Sponsors contests.

SAS PUBLISHING, SAS Campus Dr., Cary NC 27513-2414. (919)677-8000. Fax: (919)677-4444. E-mail: sasbbu@sas.com. Website: www.sas.com/pubs. **Acquisitions:** Julie M. Platt, editor-in-chief. Estab. 1976. Publishes hardcover and trade paperback originals. **Publishes 40 titles/year. Receives 30 submissions/year. 50% of books from first-time authors; 100% from unagented writers. Payment negotiable. Offers negotiable advance.** Does not accept simultaneous submissions. Responds in 2 weeks to queries. Book catalog and ms guidelines via website or with SASE; ms guidelines online.

O→ SAS publishes books for SAS software users, "both new and experienced."

Nonfiction: Technical, textbook. Subjects include software, statistics. "SAS Publishing develops and writes books inhouse. Through Books by Users Press, we also publish books by SAS users on a variety of topics relating to SAS software. Books by Users Press titles enhance users' abilities to use SAS effectively. We're interested in publishing manuscripts that describe or illustrate using any of SAS products, including JMP software. Books must be aimed at SAS or JMP users, either new or experienced. Tutorials are particularly attractive, as are descriptions of user-written applications for solving real-life business, industry or academic problems. Books on programming techniques using SAS are also desirable. Manuscripts must reflect current or upcoming software releases, and the author's writing should indicate an understanding of SAS and the technical aspects covered in the manuscript." Query with SASE or submit outline, sample chapter(s). Reviews artwork/photos as part of ms package.

Recent Title(s): *The Little SAS Book: A Primer, Second Edition*, by Lora D. Delwiche and Susan J. Slaughter.

Tips: "If I were a writer trying to market a book today, I would concentrate on developing a manuscript that teaches or illustrates a specific concept or application that SAS users will find beneficial in their own environments or can adapt to their own needs."

SASQUATCH BOOKS, 119 S. Main, Suite 400, Seattle WA 98104. (206)467-4300. Fax: (206)467-4301. E-mail: custserve@sasquatchbooks.com. Website: www.sasquatchbooks.com. President: Chad Haight. **Acquisitions:** Gary Luke, editorial director. Estab. 1986. Publishes regional hardcover and trade paperback originals. **Publishes 30 titles/year. 20% of books from first-time authors; 75% from unagented writers. Pays royalty on cover price. Offers wide range advance.** Publishes book 6 months after acceptance of ms. Does not accept simultaneous submissions. Responds in 3 months to queries. Book catalog for 9×12 SAE with 2 first-class stamps; ms guidelines online.

O→ Sasquatch Books publishes books for a West Coast regional audience-Alaska to California. Currently emphasizing outdoor recreation, cookbooks and history.

Nonfiction: "We are seeking quality nonfiction works about the Pacific Northwest and West Coast regions (including Alaska to California). The literature of place includes how-to and where-to as well as history and narrative nonfiction." Reference. Subjects include animals, art/architecture, business/economics, cooking/foods/nutrition, gardening, history, nature/environment, recreation, regional, sports, travel, women's issues/studies, outdoors. Query first, then submit outline and sample chapters with SASE.

Recent Title(s): *One Hundred Demons*, by Lynda Barry; *Best Places: Northwest*; *The Northern Lights*, by Calvin Hall and Daryl Pederson.

Tips: "We sell books through a range of channels in addition to the book trade. Our primary audience consists of active, literate residents of the West Coast."

SCHERF BOOKS, Subsidiary of Scherf Inc., P.O. Box 80180, Las Vegas NV 89180-0180. (702)243-4895. Fax: (702)243-7460. Website: www.scherf.com. Estab. 1990. Publishes hardcover and paperback originals. **Pays 5-10% royalty. Offers negotiable advance.** Publishes book 12-18 months after acceptance of ms. Accepts simultaneous submissions. Responds in 1 month to queries; up to 4 months to mss.

Fiction: Adventure, ethnic (general), horror (dark fantasy, futuristic, psychological, supernatural), literary, mainstream/contemporary, multicultural, mystery, religious (inspirational, religious mystery/suspense, religious thriller), young adult (adventure, easy-to-read, mystery/suspense, series). Query with SASE.

SCHOCKEN BOOKS, Knopf Publishing Group, Random House, Inc., 1745 Broadway, New York NY 10019. (212)572-2838. Fax: (212)572-6030. Website: www.schocken.com. **Acquisitions:** Altie Karper, editorial director. Estab. 1945. Publishes hardcover and trade paperback originals and reprints. **Publishes 9-12 titles/year. Small% of books from first-time authors; small% from unagented writers. Offers varied advance.** Accepts simultaneous submissions.

"Schocken publishes quality Judaica in all areas—fiction, history, biography, current affairs, spirituality and religious practices, popular culture and cultural studies."

Recent Title(s): *One People Two Worlds*, by Ammiel Hirsch and Yosef Reinman; *The Rebbe's Army*, by Sue Fishkoff; *Reading the Women of the Bible*, by Tikva Frymer-Kensky.

SCHOLASTIC LIBRARY PUBLISHING, (formerly Grolier Publishing Co., Inc.), division of Scholastic Inc., 90 Sherman Turnpike, Danbury CT 06816. (203)797-3500. Fax: (203)797-3197. Website: www.scholasticlibrary.com. Estab. 1895. Publishes hardcover and trade paperback originals. Does not accept simultaneous submissions.

Imprints: Children's Press, Grolier Online, Franklin Watts.

- This publisher accepts agented submissions only.

"Grolier Publishing is a leading publisher of reference, educational and children's books. We provide parents, teachers and librarians with the tools they need to enlighten children to the pleasure of learning and prepare them for the road ahead."

SCHOLASTIC PRESS, Scholastic Inc., 557 Broadway, New York NY 10012. (212)343-6100. Fax: (212)343-4713. Website: www.scholastic.com. **Acquisitions:** Elizabeth Szabla, editorial director. Publishes hardcover originals. **Publishes 50 titles/year. Receives 2,500 queries/year. 5% of books from first-time authors. Pays royalty on retail price. Offers variable advance.** Publishes book 18-24 months after acceptance of ms. Does not accept simultaneous submissions. Responds in 2 months to queries; 6-8 months to mss.

Scholastic Press publishes "fresh, literary picture book fiction and nonfiction; fresh, literary non-series or non-genre-oriented middle grade and young adult fiction." Currently emphasizing "subtly handled treatments of key relationships in children's lives; unusual approaches to commonly dry subjects, such as biography, math, history or science." De-emphasizing fairy tales (or retellings), board books, genre or series fiction (mystery, fantasy, etc.).

Nonfiction: Children's/juvenile, general interest. *Agented submissions only.*

Fiction: Juvenile, picture books, novels. Wants "fresh, exciting picture books and novels—inspiring, new talent." *Agented submissions only.*

Recent Title(s): *The Three Questions*, by Jon J. Muth; *Dear Mrs. LaRue*, by Mark Teague; *When Mariam Sang*, by Pam Muñoz Ryan, illustrated by Brian Selznick.

SCHREIBER PUBLISHING, INC., 51 Monroe St., Suite 101, Rockville MD 20850. (301)424-7737 ext. 28. Fax: (301)424-2336. E-mail: spbooks@aol.com. Website: www.schreiberpublishing.com. President: Morry Schreiber. **Acquisitions:** Linguistics Editor; Judaica Editor. Publishes hardcover and trade paperback originals and reprints. **Publishes 8 titles/year. Receives 40 queries and 12 mss/year. 80% of books from first-time authors; 95% from unagented writers. Pays negotiable royalty on retail price.** Publishes book 6 months after acceptance of ms. Accepts simultaneous submissions. Responds in 1 month to queries; 1 month to proposals; 1 month to mss. Book catalog free or on website; ms guidelines free.

Schreiber publishes reference books and dictionaries for better language and translation work, as well as Judaica books emphasizing Jewish culture and religion. Currently emphasizing multicultural dictionaries and parochial books.

Nonfiction: Biography, children's/juvenile, coffee table book, gift book, humor, multimedia (CD-ROM), reference, textbook. Subjects include history, language/literature, memoirs, money/finance, multicultural, religion, science, translation. Query with SASE; or submit proposal package, including: outline, 1 sample chapter and table of contents. Reviews artwork/photos as part of ms package. Send photocopies.

Recent Title(s): *Questioning the Bible*, by Morry Soffer; *Spanish Business Dictionary.*

SCHROEDER PUBLISHING CO., INC., P.O. Box 3009, Paducah KY 42002-3009. (270)898-6211. Fax: (270)898-8890. E-mail: editor@collectorbooks.com. Website: www.collectorbooks.com. Estab. 1973. Publishes hardcover and trade paperback orginals. **Publishes 95 titles/year; imprint publishes 65 (Collector Books); 30 (American Quilter's Society) titles/year. Receives 150 queries and 100 mss/year. 60% of books from first-time authors; 100% from unagented writers. Pays 5% royalty on retail price.** Publishes book 6 months after acceptance of ms. Accepts simultaneous submissions. Responds in 1 month to queries; 1 month to proposals; 1 month to mss. Book catalog online; ms guidelines online.

Imprints: Collector Books; American Quilter's Society.

Nonfiction: Coffee table book, gift book, how-to, illustrated book, reference, self-help, textbook. Subjects include general nonfiction, hobbies, antiques and collectibles. Submit proposal package including outline, 2 sample chapter(s). Reviews artwork/photos as part of ms package. Send transparencies or prints.

Recent Title(s): *Schroeder's Antiques Price Guide*, by Sharon Huxford (reference); *Vintage Golf Club Collectibles*, by Ronald John (reference); *Collector's Encyclopedia of Depression Glass*, by Gene Florence (reference).

Tips: Audience consists of collectors, garage sale and flea market shoppers, antique dealers, E-bay shoppers, and quilters.

SCIENCE & HUMANITIES PRESS, P.O. Box 7151, Chesterfield MO 63006-7151. (636)394-4950. Fax: (636)394-1381. E-mail: pub@sciencehumanitiespress.com. Website: www.sciencehumanitiespress.com. **Acquisitions:** Dr. Bud Banis, publisher. Publishes trade paperback originals and reprints, and electronic originals and reprints. **Publishes 20-30 titles/year. Receives 200 queries and 50 mss/year. 25% of books from first-time authors; 100% from unagented writers. Pays 8% royalty on retail price.** Publishes book 6-12 after acceptance of ms. Accepts simultaneous submissions. Responds

in 3 months to queries; 3 months to proposals; 6 months to mss. Book catalog online; ms guidelines online.
Imprints: Science & Humanities Press, BeachHouse Books, MacroPrintBooks (large print editions), Heuristic Books, Early Editions Books.
Nonfiction: Biography, cookbook, gift book, how-to, humor, reference, self-help, technical, textbook, medical, disabilities adaptation. Subjects include Americana, business/economics, child guidance/parenting, computers/electronic, cooking/foods/nutrition, creative nonfiction, education, government/politics, health/medicine, history, hobbies, language/literature, memoirs, military/war, money/finance, philosophy, psychology, recreation, regional, science, sex, sociology, software, spirituality, sports, travel, women's issues/studies, math/statistics, management science. "Submissions are best as brief descriptions by e-mail, including some description of the author's background/credentials, and thoughts on approach to nontraditional or specialized markets. Why is the book important and who would buy it. Prefer description by e-mail. Need not be a large format proposal."
Fiction: *Does not accept unsolicited mss.* Adventure, fantasy, historical, humor, literary, mainstream/contemporary, military/war, mystery, plays, poetry, regional, religious, romance, science fiction, short story collections, spiritual, sports, suspense, western, young adult. "We prefer books with a theme that gives a market focus. Brief description by e-mail."
Poetry: Prefers structured poetry with a theme. "Send a brief description by e-mail with a few samples."
Recent Title(s): *To Norma Jeane with Love, Jimmie*, by Jim Dougherty/LC Van Savage (biography); *Growing Up on Route 66*, by Michael Lund (coming of age); *Avoiding Attendants from Hell: A Practical Guide to Finding, Hiring, and Keeping Personal Care Attendants*, by June Price.
Tips: Sales are primarily through the Internet, special orders, reviews in specialized media, direct sales to libraries, special organizations and use as textbooks. "Our expertise is electronic publishing for continuous short-run in-house production rather than mass distribution to retail outlets. This allows us to commit to books that might not be financially successful in conventional book store environments and to keep books in print and available for extended periods of time. Books should be of types that would sell steadily over a long period of time, rather than those that require rapid rollout and bookstore shelf exposure for a short time. We consider the nurture of new talent part of our mission but enjoy experienced authors as well. We are proud that many of our books are second, third and fourth books from authors who were once our first-time authors. A good book is not a one-time accident."

N SCORPIO STUDIOS PRESS, Scorpio Studios Multimedia, 4570 Van Nuys Blvd., #185, Sherman Oaks CA 91403. Website: www.scorpiostudios.org/publishing/main.html. **Acquisitions:** Jude Chao, president/director of acquisitions (fiction). Estab. 2002. Publishes trade paperback, mass market paperback and electronic originals. **Publishes 8 titles/year. 100% of books from first-time authors. Pays 20-35% royalty on retail price. Negotiable advance, when offered.** Publishes book 8 months after acceptance of ms. Does not accept simultaneous submissions. Responds in 1 week to queries; 1 month to proposals; 3 months to mss. Ms guidelines online.
Nonfiction: All unsolicited mss returned unopened.
Fiction: Adventure, comic books, experimental, fantasy, horror, literary, mainstream/contemporary, multimedia, occult, science fiction, genre-bending. "We are looking for talented new writers with unique views and unique ways of expressing their views. Scorpio Studios and Scorpio Studios Press are all about creativity, innovation and thinking outside the box. We do not publish formulaic and/or clichéd fiction." Query with SASE or submit proposal package including 1 sample chapter(s), synopsis, author bio.
Tips: Scorpio Studios Press caters to intelligent, open-minded readers whose reading tastes extend beyond the traditional formulae and who enjoy discovering the work of gifted, new writers. "Although our submission guidelines are relatively loose, we do ask that you be professional. As with any market, first do your homework. Check out our website to learn more about who we are, what we do and what we are like. When you submit to us, tell us why you think your work would be particularly suitable for us. A little research goes a long way—and so does good, polished writing."

A SCRIBNER, Simon & Schuster, 1230 Avenue of the Americas, New York NY 10020. (212)698-7000. Website: www.simonsays.com. **Acquisitions:** Nan Graham (literary fiction, nonfiction); Sarah McGrath (fiction, nonfiction); Susanne Kirk (fiction); Lisa Drew (nonfiction); Rachel Sussman (fiction, nonfiction); Brant Rumble (fiction, nonfiction); Colin Harrison (fiction, nonfiction). Publishes hardcover originals. **Publishes 70-75 titles/year. Receives thousands queries/year. 20% of books from first-time authors; 0% from unagented writers. Pays 7½-15% royalty. Offers variable advance.** Publishes book 9 months after acceptance of ms. Accepts simultaneous submissions. Responds in 3 months to queries.
Imprints: Rawson Associates; Lisa Drew Books; Scribner Classics (reprints only); Scribner Poetry (by invitation only); Simple Abundance Press.
Nonfiction: Biography. Subjects include education, ethnic, gay/lesbian, health/medicine, history, language/literature, nature/environment, philosophy, psychology, religion, science, criticism. *Agented submissions only.*
Fiction: Literary, mystery, suspense. *Agented submissions only.*
Recent Title(s): *That Old Ace in the Hole*, by Annie Proulx; *Cosmopolis*, by Don DeLillo; *Grave Secrets*, by Kathy Reichs.

N SEAL PRESS, 300 Queen Anne Ave. N., #375, Seattle WA 98109. (206)722-1838. Fax: (206)285-9410. Website: www.sealpress.com. **Acquisitions:** Attn: Seal Press. Estab. 1976. Publishes trade paperback originals. **Publishes 20 titles/year. Receives 1,000 queries and 750 mss/year. 25% of books from first-time authors; 70% from unagented writers. Pays variable royalty on retail price. Pays variable advance.** Publishes book 18 months after acceptance of ms. Accepts simultaneous submissions. Responds in 2 months to queries. Book catalog and ms guidelines for SASE or online; ms guidelines online.
Imprints: Adventura Books (travel/outdoors), Live Girls (Third-Wave, young feminist).

O-→ "Seal Press is an imprint of Avalon Publishing Group, feminist book publisher interested in original, lively, radical, empowering and culturally diverse nonfiction by women addressing contemporary issues from a feminist perspective or speak positively to the experience of being female." Currently emphasizing women outdoor adventurists, young feminists. De-emphasizing fiction.

Nonfiction: Biography (women only), literary nonfiction essays. Subjects include Americana, child guidance/parenting, contemporary culture, creative nonfiction, ethnic, gay/lesbian, memoirs, multicultural, nature/environment, sex, travel, women's issues/studies, popular culture. No unsolicited mss. Query with SASE. Reviews artwork/photos as part of ms package. Send photocopies.

Fiction: Ethnic, feminist, gay/lesbian, literary, multicultural. Must fall within Adventura or Live Girls imprints. "We are interested in alternative voices." No unsolicited mss. Query with SASE or submit outline, 2 sample chapter(s), synopsis.

Recent Title(s): *The Big Rumpus*, by Ayun Halliday; *Atlas of the Heart*, by Ariel Gore.

Tips: "Our audience is generally composed of women interested in reading about contemporary issues addressed from a feminist perspective."

SEAWORTHY PUBLICATIONS, INC., 215 S. Park St., Suite #1, Port Washington WI 53074. (262)268-9250. Fax: (262)268-9208. E-mail: publisher@seaworthy.com. Website: www.seaworthy.com. **Acquisitions:** Joseph F. Janson, publisher. Publishes trade paperback originals, hardcover originals and reprints. **Publishes 8 titles/year. Receives 150 queries and 40 mss/year. 60% of books from first-time authors; 100% from unagented writers. Pays 15% royalty on wholesale price. Offers $1,000 advance.** Publishes book 6 months after acceptance of ms. Does not accept simultaneous submissions. Responds in 1 month to queries. Book catalog and ms guidelines on website or for #10 SASE; ms guidelines online.

O-→ Seaworthy Publications is a nautical book publisher that primarily publishes books of interest to recreational boaters and serious bluewater cruisers, including cruising guides, how-to books about boating. Currently emphasizing how-to.

Nonfiction: Illustrated book, reference, technical. Subjects include hobbies (sailing, boating), regional (boating guide books). Regional guide books, first-person adventure, reference, technical—all dealing with boating. Query with SASE or submit 3 sample chapter(s), table of contents. Prefers electronic query via e-mail. Reviews artwork/photos as part of ms package. Send photocopies or color prints.

Recent Title(s): *Financial Freedom Afloat*, by Charles Tuller.

Tips: "Our audience consists of sailors, boaters, and those interested in the sea, sailing or long distance cruising."

SEEDLING PUBLICATIONS, INC., 4522 Indianola Ave., Columbus OH 43214-2246. (614)267-7333. Fax: (614)267-4205. E-mail: lsalem@jinl.com. Website: www.seedlingpub.com. **Acquisitions:** Josie Stewart, vice president. Estab. 1992. Publishes in an 8-, 12-, or 16-page format for beginning readers. **Publishes 10-20 titles/year. Receives 450 mss/year. 50% of books from first-time authors; 100% from unagented writers. Pays royalty or makes outright purchase. Offers advance.** Publishes book 1 year after acceptance of ms. Accepts simultaneous submissions. Responds in 6 months to queries. Ms guidelines for #10 SASE.

O-→ "We are an education niche publisher, producing books for beginning readers. Stories must include language that is natural to young children and story lines that are interesting to 5-7-year-olds and written at their beginning reading level."

Nonfiction: Children's/juvenile. Science, math or social studies concepts are considered. Does not accept mss or queries via fax. Reviews artwork/photos as part of ms package. Send photocopies.

Fiction: Juvenile. Submit complete ms.

Recent Title(s): *Molly Makes a Graph*, by Lynn Salem, Josie Stewart; *Dragonflies Are Super Bugs*, by Clare Mischica.

Tips: "Follow our guidelines. Do not submit full-length picture books or chapter books. We are an education niche publisher. Our books are for children, ages 5-7, who are just beginning to read independently. We do not accept stories that rhyme or poetry at this time. Try your manuscript with young readers. Listen for text that doesn't flow when the child reads the story. Rewrite until the text sounds natural to beginning readers. Visit our website to be sure your manuscript fits our market." Does not accept manuscripts via fax. Does not accept queries at all.

SELF-COUNSEL PRESS, 1704 N. State St., Bellingham WA 92225. (360)676-4530. Website: www.self-counsel.com. **Acquisitions:** Richard Day, managing editor. Estab. 1971. Publishes trade paperback originals. **Publishes 30 titles/year. Receives 1,500 queries/year. 30% of books from first-time authors; 90% from unagented writers. Pays 10% royalty on net receipts. Offers rarely advance.** Publishes book 8 months after acceptance of ms. Accepts simultaneous submissions. Responds in 2 months to queries. Book catalog via website or upon request; ms guidelines online.

O-→ Self-Counsel Press publishes a range of quality self-help books written in practical, non-technical style by recognized experts in the fields of business, financial or legal guidance for people who want to help themselves.

Nonfiction: How-to, reference, self-help. Subjects include business/economics, computers/electronic, money/finance, Legal issues for lay people. Submit proposal package including outline, 2 sample chapter(s), résumé.

Recent Title(s): *What Your Lawyer Doesn't Want You to Know*, by Douglas R. Eikermann; *Rightfully Yours: How to Get Past-Due Child Support, Alimony, & Your Ex's Pension*, by Gary Shulman.

SERGEANT KIRKLAND'S PRESS, 101 Mount Rock Rd., Newville PA 17241. (717)776-6585. E-mail: seagraver@kirklands.org. Website: www.kirklands.org. **Acquisitions:** Pia S. Seagrave, Ph.D., editor-in-chief. Publishes hardcover and trade paperback originals, hardcover reprints. **Publishes 28 titles/year. Receives 200 queries and 150 mss/year. 70% of books from first-time authors; 90% from unagented writers. Pays 10% royalty.** Publishes book 6 months after acceptance of ms. Does not accept simultaneous submissions. Responds in 3 months to queries; 3 months to proposals; 4 months to mss. Book catalog and ms guidelines online; ms guidelines online.

O— Currently emphasizing American history of academic and regional interest—colonial, African-American, Civil War, WWII and Vietnam periods.

Nonfiction: Biography, reference. Subjects include Americana, anthropology/archeology, government/politics, history, military/war, Jewish-Holocaust, slavery. Query with SASE or submit complete ms. Reviews artwork/photos as part of ms package. Send photocopies.

Recent Title(s): *Sara's Children: The Destruction of the Chmielnik*, by Suzan Hagstrom (Holocaust).

Tips: "Have your work professionally edited and be sure it meets the general standards of the *Chicago Manual of Style*."

SEVEN STORIES PRESS, 140 Watts St., New York NY 10013. (212)226-8760. Fax: (212)226-1411. E-mail: info@sevenstories.com. Website: www.sevenstories.com. **Acquisitions:** Daniel Simon; Greg Ruggiero; Tom McCarthy. Estab. 1995. Publishes hardcover and trade paperback originals. **Publishes 40-50 titles/year. 15% of books from first-time authors; 5% from unagented writers. Pays 7-15% royalty on retail price. Offers advance.** Publishes book 1-3 years after acceptance of ms. Accepts simultaneous submissions. Book catalog and ms guidelines free; ms guidelines online.

O— Seven Stories Press publishes literary/activist fiction and nonfiction "on the premise that both are works of the imagination and that there is no contradiction in publishing the two side by side." Currently emphasizing politics, social justice, biographies, foreign writings.

Nonfiction: Biography. Subjects include general nonfiction. Responds only if interested. No unsolicited mss. Query with SASE. **All unsolicited mss returned unopened.**

Fiction: Literary. No unsolicited mss. Query with SASE. **All unsolicited mss returned unopened.**

Recent Title(s): *Power and Terror*, by Noam Chomsky; *First Loves*, by Ted Solotaroff; *A History of Color*, by Stanley Moss.

[N] **SHAMBHALA PUBLICATIONS, INC.**, 300 Massachusetts Ave., Boston MA 02115. (617)424-0030. Fax: (617)236-1563. E-mail: editors@shambhala.com. Website: www.shambhala.com. **Acquisitions:** Eden Steinberg, editor; Emily Bower, editor; David O'Neal, managing editor; Peter Turner, president; Beth Frankl, editor. Estab. 1969. Publishes hardcover and trade paperback originals and reprints. **Publishes 90-100 titles/year. Receives 2,000 queries and 500-700 mss/year. 30% of books from first-time authors; 80% from unagented writers. Pays 8% royalty on retail price.** Publishes book 1 year after acceptance of ms. Accepts simultaneous submissions. Responds in 1 month to queries; 2 months to proposals; 2 months to mss. Book catalog free; ms guidelines free.

Nonfiction: Autobiography, biography, reference, self-help. Subjects include alternative lifestyles, anthropology/archeology, art/architecture, creative nonfiction, general nonfiction, health/medicine, humanities, language/literature, memoirs, philosophy, religion, spirituality, women's issues/studies. Query with SASE or submit proposal package including outline, 2 sample chapter(s), résumé, synopsis, TOC or submit complete ms. Reviews artwork/photos as part of ms package.

⊘ **SHAW BOOKS**, WaterBrook Press, 2375 Telstar Dr. #160, Colorado Springs CO 80920-1029. (719)590-4999. Fax: (719)590-8977. **Acquisitions:** Elisa Fryling Stanford, editor. Estab. 1967. Publishes mostly trade paperback originals. **Publishes 25 titles/year. Receives 1,000 submissions/year. 10-20% of books from first-time authors. Offers advance.** Publishes book 18 months after acceptance of ms. Responds in 6 months to queries.

O— "We are looking for unique mss from a Christian perspective on the topics below. Queries accepted but not unsolicited mss."

Nonfiction: Subjects include creative nonfiction, education, general nonfiction, language/literature, parenting, health and wellness, literary topics all from a Christian perspective. "We are looking for adult nonfiction with different twists—self-help manuscripts with fresh insight and colorful, vibrant writing style." *No fiction, poetry or unsolicited mss.* Query with SASE.

Recent Title(s): *The Creative Call*, by Janice Elsheimer; *Penguins and Golden Calves*, by Madeleine L'Engle; *Real Love for Real Life*, by Andi Ashworth.

SHEEP MEADOW PRESS, P.O. Box 1345, Riverdale NY 10471. (718)548-5547. Fax: (718)884-0406. E-mail: sheepmdwpr@aol.com. **Acquisitions:** Stanley Moss, publisher. Publishes hardcover and trade paperback originals and reprints. **Publishes 10-12 titles/year. Pays 7-10% royalty on retail price.** Book catalog free.

Poetry: Submit complete ms.

SIERRA CLUB BOOKS, 85 Second St., San Francisco CA 94105. (415)977-5500. Fax: (415)977-5792. E-mail: danny.moses@sierraclub.org. Website: www.sierraclub.org/books. **Acquisitions:** Danny Moses, editor-in-chief. Estab. 1962. Publishes hardcover and paperback originals and reprints. **Publishes approximately 15 titles/year. Receives 1,000 submissions/year. 50% from unagented writers. Pays royalty. Offers $5,000-15,000 average advance.** Publishes book 1 year after acceptance of ms. Accepts simultaneous submissions. Responds in 1 month to queries; 2 months to proposals; 3 months to mss. Book catalog online; ms guidelines online.

Imprints: Sierra Club Books for Children.

O— The Sierra Club was founded to help people to explore, enjoy and preserve the nation's forests, waters, wildlife and wilderness. The books program publishes quality trade books about the outdoors and the protection of the natural world.

Nonfiction: Subjects include general nonfiction, nature/environment. A broad range of environmental subjects: outdoor adventure, women in the outdoors; literature, including travel and works on the spiritual aspects of the natural world; natural history and current environmental issues. Does *not* want "proposals for large color photographic books without substantial text; how-to books on building things outdoors; books on motorized travel; or any but the most professional studies of animals." No fiction or poetry. Query with SASE. Reviews artwork/photos as part of ms package. Send photocopies.

Recent Title(s): *Downhill Slide: Why the Corporate Ski Industry is Bad for Skiing, Ski Towns, and the Environment*, by Hal Clifford; *Breaking Gridlock: Moving Towards Transportation That Works*, by Jim Motavalli; *My Story as Told by Water*, by David James Duncan.

SILHOUETTE BOOKS, 233 Broadway, New York NY 10279. (212)553-4200. Fax: (212)227-8969. Website: www.eharlequin.com. Editorial Director, Silhouette Books: Tara Gavin. **Acquisitions:** Mavis Allen, associate senior editor (Silhouette Romance); Karen Taylor Richman, senior editor (Silhouette Special Editions); Melissa Jeglinski, senior editor (Silhouette Desire); Leslie Wainger, executive editor (Silhouette Intimate Moments). Estab. 1979. Publishes mass market paperback originals. **Publishes over 350 titles/year. Receives approximately 4,000 submissions/year. Pays royalty. Offers advance.** Publishes book 1-3 years after acceptance of ms. Does not accept simultaneous submissions. Ms guidelines online.

Imprints: *Silhouette Romance* (contemporary adult romances, 53,000-58,000 words); *Silhouette Desire* (contemporary adult romances, 55,000-60,000 words); *Silhouette Intimate Moments* (contemporary adult romances, 80,000 words); *Harlequin Historicals* (adult historical romances, 95,000-105,000 words); *Silhouette Special Edition* (contemporary adult romances, 75,000-80,000 words).

O→ Silhouette publishes contemporary adult romances.

Fiction: Romance (contemporary and historical romance for adults). "We are interested in seeing submissions for all our lines. No manuscripts other than the types outlined. Manuscript should follow our general format, yet have an individuality and life of its own that will make it stand out in the readers' minds." *No unsolicited mss.* Send query letter, 2 page synopsis and SASE to head of imprint.

Recent Title(s): *Cordina's Crown Jewel*, by Nora Roberts; *Letters to Kelly*, by Suzanne Brockman.

Tips: "The romance market is constantly changing, so when you read for research, read the latest books and those that have been recommended to you by people knowledgeable in the genre. We are actively seeking new authors for all our lines, contemporary and historical."

SILMAN-JAMES PRESS, 3624 Shannon Rd., Los Angeles CA 90027. (323)661-9922. E-mail: silmanjamespress@earthlink.net. **Acquisitions:** Gwen Feldman, Jim Fox, publishers. Publishes trade paperback originals and reprints. **Publishes 6-10 titles/year. Receives 75 queries and 50 mss/year. 50% of books from first-time authors; 80% from unagented writers. Pays variable royalty on retail price.** Responds in 1 month to queries; 2 months to proposals; 3 months to mss. Book catalog free.

Imprints: Siles Press (publishes chess books and other nonfiction subjects).

Nonfiction: Pertaining to film, theatre, music, peforming arts. Biography, how-to, reference, technical, textbook. Submit proposal package including outline, 1+ sample chapter(s) or submit complete ms. Reviews artwork/photos as part of ms package. Send photocopies.

Recent Title(s): *Book on Acting: Improvisation Technique for the Professional Actor in Film, Theatre, and Television*, by Stephen Book; *Dealmaking in the Film and Television, 2nd Ed*, by Mark Litwak.

Tips: "Our audience ranges from people with a general interest in film (fans, etc.) to students of film and performing arts to industry professionals. We will accept 'query' phone calls."

SILVER DAGGER MYSTERIES, The Overmountain Press, P.O. Box 1261, Johnson City TN 37605. (423)926-2691. Fax: (423)232-1252. Website: www.silverdaggermysteries.com. **Acquisitions:** Alex Foster, acquisitions editor. Estab. 1999. Publishes hardcover and trade paperback originals and reprints. **Publishes 30 titles/year; imprint publishes 15 titles/year. Receives 200 queries and 50 mss/year. 50% of books from first-time authors; 50% from unagented writers. Pays 15% royalty. on realized price.** Publishes book 2 years after acceptance of ms. Accepts simultaneous submissions. Responds in 1 month to queries; 3 months to proposals; 6 months to mss. Book catalog and ms guidelines online; ms guidelines online.

O→ Silver Dagger publishes mysteries that take place in the American South. Emphasizing cozies, police procedurals, hard-boiled detectives.

Fiction: Mystery (amateur sleuth, cozy, police procedural, private eye/hardboiled), young adult (mystery). "We look for average-length books of 60-80,000 words." No horror or science fiction. Query with SASE or submit proposal package including outline, 3 sample chapter(s), synopsis, author bio. **All unsolicited mss returned unopened.**

Recent Title(s): *Killer Looks*, by Laura Young; *Justice Betrayed*, by Daniel Bailey.

Tips: "We publish cozies, hard-boiled and police procedural mysteries. Check the website for specific guidelines and submission dates. Due to a large number of submissions, we only review at certain times of the year."

SILVER LAKE PUBLISHING, 2025 Hyperion Ave., Los Angeles CA 90027. (323)663-3082. Fax: (323)663-3084. E-mail: publicity@silverlakepub.com. Submissions E-mail: jwalsh@silverlakepub.com. Website: www.silverlakepub.com. Estab. 1998. Publishes hardcover and trade paperback originals and reprints. **Publishes 8-10 titles/year. Pays royalty.** Publishes book 1 year after acceptance of ms. Accepts simultaneous submissions. Book catalog free; ms guidelines free.

Nonfiction: How-to, reference. Subjects include business/economics, money/finance. Submit outline, 1 sample chapter(s), résumé, cover letter.

Recent Title(s): *True Odds*, by James Walsh; *Business Plans to Game Plans*, by Jan B. King.

SILVER MOON PRESS, 160 Fifth Ave., New York NY 10010. (212)242-6499. Fax: (212)242-6799. **Acquisitions:** Hope Killcoyne, managing editor. Publishes hardcover originals. **Publishes 5-8 titles/year. Receives 600 queries and 400 mss/year. 60% of books from first-time authors; 70% from unagented writers. Pays 7-10% royalty. Offers 500-1,000 advance.** Publishes book 18 months after acceptance of ms. Accepts simultaneous submissions. Responds in 2 months to queries; 2 months to proposals; 3-6 months to mss. Book catalog for 9×12 SASE; ms guidelines for #10 SASE.

O→ Publishes educational material for grades 3-8.

Nonfiction: Biography, test prep material. Subjects include education, history, language/literature, multicultural. Query with SASE or submit proposal package including outline, 1-3 sample chapter(s).

Fiction: Historical, multicultural, biographical. Query with SASE or submit proposal package including 1-3 sample chapter(s), synopsis.

Recent Title(s): *Thunder on the Sierra*, by Kathy Balmes (social studies, historical fiction); *Raid at Red Mill*, by Mary McGahan (historical fiction); *A Silent Witness in Harlem*, by Eve Creary (historical fiction).

N **SKINNER HOUSE BOOKS**, The Unitarian Universalist Association, 25 Beacon St., Boston MA 02108. (617)742-2100 ext. 601. Fax: (617)742-7025. Website: www.uua.org/skinner. **Acquisitions:** Ari McCarthy, marketing coordinator. Estab. 1975. Publishes trade paperback originals and reprints. **Publishes 8-10 titles/year. 50% of books from first-time authors; 100% from unagented writers. Pays 5-10% royalty on net receipts.** Publishes book 1 year after acceptance of ms. Does not accept simultaneous submissions. Responds in 3 months to queries. Book catalog for 6×9 SAE with 3 first-class stamps; ms guidelines online.

"We publish titles in Unitarian Universalist faith, liberal religion, history, biography, worship, and issues of social justice. We also publish a selected number of inspirational titles of poetic prose and meditations. Writers should know that Unitarian Universalism is a liberal religious denomination committed to progressive ideals." Currently emphasizing spiritual memoir. De-emphasizing juvenile.

Nonfiction: Biography, self-help. Subjects include gay/lesbian, religion, women's issues/studies, inspirational, church leadership. Query with SASE. Reviews artwork/photos as part of ms package. Send photocopies. Query with SASE.

Recent Title(s): *Get a God! More Conversations with Coyote*, by Webster Kitchell; *Swingin on the Garden Gate: A Spiritual Memoir*, by Elizabeth Andrew; *Standing Before Us: Unitarian Universalist Women and Social Reform, 1776-1936*, ed. by Dorothy May Emerson.

Tips: "From outside our denomination, we are interested in manuscripts that will be of help or interest to liberal churches, Sunday School classes, parents, ministers and volunteers. Inspirational/spiritual and children's titles must reflect liberal Unitarian Universalist values. Fiction for youth is being considered."

SLACK, INC., 6900 Grove Rd., Thorofare NJ 08086. (856)848-1000. Fax: (856)853-5991. E-mail: amcshane@slackinc.com. Website: www.slackbooks.com. **Acquisitions:** Amy E. McShane, editorial director. Estab. 1960. Publishes hardcover and softcover originals. **Publishes 45 titles/year. Receives 80 queries and 23 mss/year. 75% of books from first-time authors; 100% from unagented writers. Pays 10% royalty. Offers advance.** Publishes book 8 months after acceptance of ms. Accepts simultaneous submissions. Responds in 1 month to queries; 1 month to proposals; 3 months to mss. Book catalog and ms guidelines free; ms guidelines online.

SLACK, INC. publishes academic textbooks and professional reference books on various medical topics in an expedient manner.

Nonfiction: Multimedia (CD-ROMs), textbook (medical). Subjects include health/medicine, ophthalmology, athletic training, physical therapy, occupational therapy, orthopedics, gastroenterology. Submit proposal package including outline, 2 sample chapter(s), market profile and cv. Reviews artwork/photos as part of ms package. Send photocopies.

Recent Title(s): *Developmental and Functional Hand Grasps*, by Sandra Edwards, et. al.; *Phacoemulsification: Principles and Techniques, 2nd ed*, by Lucio Buratto, et. al.

GIBBS SMITH, PUBLISHER, P.O. Box 667, Layton UT 84041. (801)544-9800. Fax: (801)544-5582. E-mail: info@gibbs-smith.com. Website: www.gibbs-smith.com. **Acquisitions:** Suzanne Taylor, editorial director, humor. Estab. 1969. Publishes hardcover and trade paperback originals. **Publishes 50 titles/year. Receives 1,500-2,000 submissions/year. 8-10% of books from first-time authors; 50% from unagented writers. Pays 8-14% royalty on gross receipts. Offers $2,000-3,000 advance.** Publishes book 1-2 years after acceptance of ms. Accepts simultaneous submissions. Responds in 1 month to queries; 10 weeks to proposals; 10 weeks to mss. Book catalog for 9×12 SAE and $2.13 in postage; ms guidelines online.

"We publish books that enrich and inspire humankind." Currently emphasizing interior decorating and design, home reference. De-emphasizing novels and short stories.

Nonfiction: Humor, illustrated book, textbook, children's. Subjects include art/architecture, humor, nature/environment, regional, interior design. Query with SASE or submit outline, several completed sample chapter(s), author's cv. Reviews artwork/photos as part of ms package. Send sample illustrations if applicable.

Fiction: Only short works oriented to gift market. No novels or short stories. Submit synopsis with sample illustration, if applicable. Send query letter or short gift book ms directly to the editorial director.

Recent Title(s): *French Influences*, by Betty Lou Phillips (nonfiction); *101 Things to Do with a Cake Mix*, by Stephanie Ashcraft (cookbook).

SOCIETY OF MANUFACTURING ENGINEERS, One SME Dr., P.O. Box 930, Dearborn MI 48121. (313)425-3280. Fax: (313)425-3417. E-mail: bking@sme.org. Website: www.sme.org. **Acquisitions:** Robert King, manager. Publishes hardcover and trade paperback originals. **Publishes 6 titles/year. Receives 20 queries and 10 mss/year. 90% of books from first-time authors; 100% from unagented writers. Pays 5-15% royalty on wholesale price or retail price.** Publishes book 8 months after acceptance of ms. Responds in 1 month to queries; 1 month to proposals; 1 month to mss. Book catalog and ms guidelines free or online; ms guidelines online.

Nonfiction: "Seeking manuscripts that would assist manufacturing practitioners in increasing their productivity, quality and/or efficiency." Technical, textbook. Subjects include engineering, industry. Query with SASE. Reviews artwork/photos as part of ms package. Send photocopies.

Recent Title(s): *Lean Manufacturing for Small Business*; *Electrical Discharge Machining*.

Tips: Audience is "manufacturing practitioners and management, indiviuduals wishing to advance their careers in the industry or to enhance productivity, quality, and efficiency within a manufacturing operation."

SOHO PRESS, INC., 853 Broadway, New York NY 10003. (212)260-1900. Fax: (212)260-1902. Website: www.sohopress.com. **Acquisitions:** Juris Jurjevics, publisher/editor-in-chief; Laura Hruska, associate publisher. Estab. 1986. Publishes hardcover and trade paperback originals. **Publishes 40 titles/year. Receives 7,000 submissions/year. 75% of books from first-time authors; 40% from unagented writers. Pays 10-15% royalty on retail price. Offers advance.** Publishes book within 1 year after acceptance of ms. Accepts simultaneous submissions. Responds in 2 months to queries; 2 months to mss. Book catalog for 6×9 SAE with 2 first-class stamps; ms guidelines online.

O→ Soho Press publishes literate fiction and nonfiction. Currently emphasizing mystery, literary fiction, thrillers. De-emphasizing cooking, how-to.

Nonfiction: Autobiography, biography, autobiography; literary. Subjects include contemporary culture, history, memoirs, military/war, translation, travel. No self-help, how-to or cookbooks. Submit outline, sample chapter(s).

Fiction: Adventure, ethnic, feminist, historical, literary, mainstream/contemporary, mystery (police procedural), suspense, translation. Query with SASE or submit complete ms.

Recent Title(s): *Since the Layoffs*, by Iain Levison; *Maisie Doggs*, by Jacqueline Winspear.

Tips: "Soho Press publishes discerning authors for discriminating readers, finding the strongest possible writers and publishing them." Soho Press also publishes series: Hera (historical fiction reprints with accurate and strong female lead characters) and Soho Crime (mysteries set overseas, noir, procedurals).

SOMA PUBLISHING, INC., 4441 DeHaro St., Suite 1130, San Francisco CA 94107. (415)252-4350. Fax: (415)252-4352. E-mail: info@baybooks.com. **Acquisitions:** James Connolly, editorial director (james.connolly@baybooks.com). Publishes hardcover originals, trade paperback originals and reprints. **Publishes 10 titles/year. Receives 30 queries/year. 50% of books from first-time authors. Royalties vary substantially. Offers $0-25,000 advance.** Publishes book 6 months after acceptance of ms. Accepts simultaneous submissions. Responds in 3 months to queries. Book catalog for 9×12 SAE with 3 first-class stamps.

Nonfiction: Coffee table book, cookbook, gift book, how-to, illustrated book. Subjects include Americana, cooking/foods/nutrition, health/medicine. "We also publish titles related to public and cable television series" Query with SASE.

Recent Title(s): *Savor the Southwest*, by Barbara Fenzl (cooking); *Low Carb Meals in Minutes*, by Linda Gassenheimer; *Designs for a Healthy Home*, by Dan Phillips.

SOUNDPRINTS, The Trudy Corp., 353 Main Ave., Norwalk CT 06851. (203)846-2274. Fax: (203)846-1776. E-mail: soundprints@soundprints.com. Website: www.soundprints.com. **Acquisitions:** Chelsea Shriver, assistant editor. Estab. 1988. Publishes hardcover originals. **Publishes 15-30 titles/year. Receives 200 queries/year. 90% from unagented writers. Makes outright purchase.** Publishes book 2 years after acceptance of ms. Accepts simultaneous submissions. Responds in 1 month to queries. Book catalog via website or on request; ms guidelines for #10 SASE.

- As a small publisher with very specific guidelines for well-defined series, Soundprints is not able to accept unsolicited manuscripts for publication. All of Soundprints' authors are contracted to create manuscripts to our specifications, depending on our needs. Soundprints is interested in reviewing the work of new potential authors. Please submit only published writing samples.

O→ Soundprints publishes picture books that portray a particular animal and its habitat. All books are reviewed for accuracy by curators from the Smithsonian Institution and other wildlife experts.

Nonfiction: Children's/juvenile, illustrated book. Subjects include animals, nature/environment. "We focus on worldwide wildlife and habitats. Subject animals must be portrayed realistically and must not be anthropomorphic. Meticulous research is required. All books are illustrated in full color." Query with SASE.

Fiction: Juvenile. "Most of our books are under license from the Smithsonian Institution and are closely curated fictional stories based on fact. We never do stories of anthropomorphic animals. When we publish juvenile fiction, it will be about wildlife or history and all information in the book *must* be accurate." Query with SASE.

Recent Title(s): *Bumblebee at Apple Tree Lane*, by Laura Gates Galvin; *Sockeye's Journey Home: The Story of a Pacific Salmon*, by Barbara Gaines Winkelman.

Tips: "Our books are written for children from ages four through eight. Our most successful authors can craft a wonderful story which is derived from authentic wildlife or historic facts. First inquiry to us should ask about our interest in publishing a book about a specific animal or habitat."

SOURCEBOOKS, INC., P.O. Box 4410, Naperville IL 60567. (630)961-3900. Fax: (630)961-2168. Website: www.sourcebooks.com. Publisher: Dominique Raccah. **Acquisitions:** Todd Stocke, editorial director (nonfiction trade); Deborah Werksman (Sourcebooks Hysteria, Sourcebooks Casablanca). Estab. 1987. Publishes hardcover and trade paperback originals. **Publishes 120 titles/year. 30% of books from first-time authors; 25% from unagented writers. Pays royalty on wholesale price. Offers advance.** Publishes book 1 year after acceptance of ms. Accepts simultaneous submissions. Responds in 3 months to queries. Book catalog online; ms guidelines online.

Imprints: Sourcebooks Casablanca (love/relationships); Sourcebooks Hysteria (women's humor/gift book); Sourcebooks Landmark; Sourcebooks MediaFusion (multimedia); Sphinx Publishing (self-help legal).

O→ Sourcebooks publishes many forms of nonfiction titles, generally in the how-to and reference areas, including books on parenting, self-help/psychology, business and health. Focus is on practical, useful information and skills. It also continues to publish in the reference, New Age, history, current affairs and travel categories. Currently emphasizing gift, women's interest, history, reference.

Nonfiction: "We seek unique books on traditional subjects and authors who are smart and aggressive." Biography, gift book, how-to, illustrated book, multimedia, reference, self-help, technical, textbook. Subjects include art/architecture, business/economics, child guidance/parenting, history, military/war, money/finance, psychology, science, sports, women's issues/studies, contemporary culture. Books for small business owners, entrepreneurs and students. "A key to submitting books to us is to explain how your book helps the reader, why it is different from the books already out there (please do your homework) and the author's credentials for writing this book. Books likely to succeed with us are self-help, parenting and childcare, psychology, women's issues, how-to, history, reference, biography, humor, gift books or books with strong artwork." Query with SASE. 2-3 sample chapters (not the first). No complete mss. Reviews artwork/photos as part of ms package.

Recent Title(s): *Poetry Speaks*, edited by Elise Paschen and Rebekah Presson Mosby.

Tips: "Our market is a decidedly trade-oriented bookstore audience. We also have very strong penetration into the gift store market. Books which cross over between these two very different markets do extremely well with us. Our list is a solid mix of unique and general audience titles and series-oriented projects. In other words, we are looking for products that break new ground either in their own areas or within the framework of our series of imprints. We love to develop books in new areas or develop strong titles in areas that are already well developed."

SOUTH END PRESS, 7 Brookline St., Cambridge MA 02139. (617)547-4002. Fax: (617)547-1333. E-mail: southend@southendpress.org. Website: www.southendpress.org. Estab. 1977. Publishes library and trade paperback originals and reprints. **Publishes 10 titles/year. Receives 400 queries and 100 mss/year. 30% of books from first-time authors; 95% from unagented writers. Pays 11% royalty on wholesale price. Offers occasionally $500-2,500 advance.** Publishes book 9 months after acceptance of ms. Accepts simultaneous submissions. Responds in up to 3 months to queries; up to 3 months to proposals. Book catalog and ms guidelines free; ms guidelines online.

O→ South End Press publishes nonfiction political books with a left/feminist/antiracist perspective.

Nonfiction: Subjects include ethnic, gay/lesbian, government/politics, health/medicine, history, nature/environment (environment), philosophy, science, sociology, women's issues/studies, economics, world affairs. Query with SASE or submit 2 sample chapter(s), intro or conclusion and annotated toc. Reviews artwork/photos as part of ms package. Send photocopies.

Recent Title(s): *War Talk*, by Arundhati Roy; *Culture and Resistance*, by Edward Said.

SOUTHERN ILLINOIS UNIVERSITY PRESS, P.O. Box 3697, Carbondale IL 62902-3697. (618)453-2281. Fax: (618)453-1221. Website: www.siu.edu/-siupress. **Acquisitions:** Rick Stetter, director (Civil War history, trade nonfiction); Karl Kageff, senior sponsoring editor (composition, film/theater, rhetoric, sports); Susan Wilson, associate director (American history). Estab. 1956. Publishes hardcover and trade paperback originals and reprints. **Publishes 50-60 titles/year; imprint publishes 4-6 titles/year. Receives 800 queries and 300 mss/year. 45% of books from first-time authors; 99% from unagented writers. Pays 5-10% royalty on wholesale price. Offers rarely advance.** Publishes book 1 year after acceptance of ms. Does not accept simultaneous submissions. Responds in 3 months to queries. Book catalog and ms guidelines free.

Imprints: Shawnee Books, Shawnee Classics (regional reprint series), Writing Baseball, Crab Orchard Award Series in Poetry, Theater in the Americas.

O→ "Scholarly press specializes in film and theater studies, rhetoric and composition studies, American history, aviation studies, regional and nonfiction trade, women's studies. No fiction." Currently emphasizing theater, film, American history. De-emphasizing literary criticism.

Nonfiction: Biography, reference (scholarly). Subjects include Americana, military/war, film/cinema/stage, true crime. Query with SASE or submit proposal package including including synopsis, table of contents, author's vita.

Recent Title(s): *Chicago Death Trip: The Iroquois Fire of 1903*, by Nat Brandt (Illinois history); *The Terministic Screen: Rhetorical Perspective on Film*, edited by David Blakesley (film); *Women in Turmoil: Six Plays by Mercedes de Acosta*, edited by Robert A. Schanke (theater).

SOUTHERN METHODIST UNIVERSITY PRESS, P.O. Box 750415, Dallas TX 75275-0415. (214)768-1433. Fax: (214)768-1428. Website: www.tamu.edu/upress. **Acquisitions:** Kathryn Lang, senior editor. Estab. 1937. Publishes hardcover and trade paperback originals and reprints. **Publishes 10-12 titles/year. Receives 500 queries and 500 mss/year. 75% of books from first-time authors; 95% from unagented writers. Pays up to 10% royalty on wholesale price, 10 author's copies. Offers $500 advance.** Publishes book 1 year after acceptance of ms. Does not accept simultaneous submissions. Responds in 1 week to queries; 1 month to proposals; up to 1 year to mss. Book catalog free; ms guidelines online.

O→ Southern Methodist University publishes for the general, educated audience in the fields of literary fiction, ethics and human values, film and theater, regional studies. Currently emphasizing literary fiction. De-emphasizing scholarly, narrowly focused academic studies.

Nonfiction: Subjects include creative nonfiction, medical, ethics/human values, film/theater, regional history. Query with SASE or submit outline, 3 sample chapter(s), author bio, table of contents. Reviews artwork/photos as part of ms package. Send photocopies.

Fiction: Literary, short story collections, novels. "We are willing to look at 'serious' or 'literary' fiction." No "mass market, science fiction, formula, thriller, romance." Query with SASE.

Recent Title(s): *How the Water Feels: Stories*, by Paul Eggers; *Requiem for a Summer Cottage: A Novel*, by Barbara Lockhart.

SPECTRA BOOKS, Subsidiary of Random House, Inc., 1745 Broadway, New York NY 10019. (212)782-8632. Fax: (212)782-9174. Website: www.bantamdell.com. Estab. 1985. Publishes hardcover originals, paperback originals and trade paperbacks. **Pays royalty. Offers negotiable advance.** Accepts simultaneous submissions. Responds in 6 months to mss. Ms guidelines for #10 SASE.

Fiction: Fantasy, literary, science fiction. Needs include novels that attempt to broaden the traditional range of science fiction and fantasy. Strong emphasis on characterization. Especially well written traditional science fiction and fantasy will be considered. No fiction that doesn't have as least some element of speculation or the fantastic. Query with 3 sample chapters and a short (no more that 3 double-spaced) synopsis.

THE SPEECH BIN, INC., 1965 25th Ave., Vero Beach FL 32960-3062. (561)770-0007. **Acquisitions:** Jan J. Binney, senior editor. Estab. 1984. Publishes trade paperback originals. **Publishes 10-20 titles/year. Receives 500 mss/year. 50% of books from first-time authors; 90% from unagented writers. Pays negotiable royalty on wholesale price. Offers advance.** Publishes book 1 year after acceptance of ms. Does not accept simultaneous submissions. Responds in 3 months to queries. Book catalog for 9×12 SASE.

O→ Publishes professional materials for specialists in rehabilitation, particularly speech-language pathologists and audiologists, special educators, occupational and physical therapists, and parents and caregivers of children and adults with developmental and post-trauma disabilities."

Nonfiction: Booklets, children's/juvenile (preschool-teen), how-to, illustrated book, reference, textbook, games for children and adults. Subjects include education, health/medicine, communication disorders, education for handicapped persons. Query with SASE or submit outline, sample chapter(s). Reviews artwork/photos as part of ms package. Send photocopies.

Fiction: "Booklets or books for children and adults about handicapped persons, especially with communication disorders. This is a potentially new market for The Speech Bin." Query with SASE or submit outline, sample chapter(s), synopsis.

Recent Title(s): *I Can Say S*; *I Can Say R*.

Tips: "Books and materials must be clearly presented, well written and competently illustrated. We have added books and materials for use by other allied health professionals. We are also looking for more materials for use in treating adults and very young children with communication disorders. Please do not fax or e-mail manuscripts to us." The Speech Bin is increasing their number of books published per year and is especially interested in reviewing treatment materials for adults and adolescents.

SPENCE PUBLISHING CO., 111 Cole St., Dallas TX 75207. (214)939-1700. Fax: (214)939-1800. E-mail: muncy@spencepublishing.com. Website: www.spencepublishing.com. **Acquisitions:** Mitchell Muncy, editor-in-chief. Estab. 1995. Publishes hardcover and trade paperback originals. **Publishes 8-10 titles/year. Pays 12% royalty on net receipts.** Accepts simultaneous submissions. Responds in 1 month to queries; 2 months to proposals. Book catalog free or on website; ms guidelines online.

O→ "We look for original works of commentary and analysis on culture and society. Originality, uniqueness and historical perspective are especially desired." Currently de-emphasizing narratives, very broad "world view" books, exposés of "political corretness" in universities.

Nonfiction: Subjects include education, government/politics, philosophy, religion, sociology, women's issues/studies, contemporary culture, film/cinema/stage. No proposal accepted without prior request for guidelines. Under no circumstances send ms before query.

Recent Title(s): *All Shook Up: Music, Passion and Politics*, by Carson Holloway.

Tips: "We publish books on culture and society from a generally (though not exclusively) conservative point of view. We seek books with a fresh approach to serious questions of public and private life that propose constructive alternatives to the status quo."

SPI BOOKS, 99 Spring St., 3rd Floor, New York NY 10012. (212)431-5011. Fax: (212)431-8646. E-mail: publicity@spibooks.com. Website: www.spibooks.com. **Acquisitions:** Ian Shapolsky, acquisitions editor (pop culture, how-to, exposé, entertainment, Judaica, business, conspiracy, children's); Jill Olofsson, acquisitions editor (how-to, self-help, health). Estab. 1991. Publishes hardcover originals and reprints, trade paperback originals and reprints. **Publishes 20-30 titles/year. 5% of books from first-time authors; 50% from unagented writers. Pays 6-15% royalty on retail price. Offers $1,000-10,000 advance.** Publishes book 3-6 months after acceptance of ms. Accepts simultaneous submissions. Responds in 2 months to queries; 2 months to proposals; 2 months to mss. Book catalog online; ms guidelines free.

Nonfiction: Autobiography, biography, children's/juvenile, coffee table book, cookbook, gift book, how-to, humor, illustrated book, reference, scholarly, self-help, textbook. Subjects include Americana, animals, business/economics, child guidance/parenting, community, contemporary culture, cooking/foods/nutrition, creative nonfiction, education, ethnic, general nonfiction, government/politics, health/medicine, history, hobbies, humanities, language/literature, memoirs, military/war, money/finance, multicultural, music/dance, nature/environment, New Age, philosophy, psychology, regional, religion, sex, social sciences, sociology, spirituality, sports, translation, travel, women's issues/studies, world affairs, exposé, conspiracy. "Aside from a quality editorial product, we request a marketing plan, suggested by the author, to supplement our own ideas for successfully marketing/promoting their book." Query with SASE or submit proposal package including outline, sample chapter(s). Reviews artwork/photos as part of ms package. Send photocopies.

Recent Title(s): *Don't Be a Slave to What You Crave*, by Dr. Daisy Merey (health); *Princess Diana: The Hidden Evidence*, by King & Beveridge (conspiracy); *Steve Martin: The Magic Years*, by Morris Walker (biography).

Tips: "Advise us how to reach the market for the legions of interested buyers of your book. Be specific if you can help us target marketing opportunities and promotional possibilities, particularly those that are not obvious. Also, let us know if there are any friends/contacts/connections you can draw upon to assist us in getting the message out about the significance of your book."

SPINSTERS INK, P.O. Box 22005, Denver CO 80222. (303)761-5552. Fax: (303)761-5284. E-mail: spinster@spinsters-ink.com. Website: www.spinsters-ink.com. Publisher: Kathy Hovis. **Acquisitions:** Sharon Silvas, editor. Estab. 1978. Publishes trade paperback originals and reprints. **Publishes 6 titles/year. Receives 400 submissions/year. 50% of books from first-time authors; 95% from unagented writers. Pays 7-11% royalty on retail price.** Publishes book 18 months after acceptance of ms. Does not accept simultaneous submissions. Responds in 3 months to queries; 3 months to mss. Book catalog free; ms guidelines for SASE or on website; ms guidelines online.

- Spinsters Ink was sold to Hovis Publishing, publisher of the monthly newspaper *Colorado Woman News*.

O→ "Spinsters Ink publishes novels and nonfiction works that deal with significant issues in women's lives from a feminist perspective: Books that not only name these crucial issues, but—more important—encourage change and growth. We are committed to publishing works by women writing from the periphery, fat women, Jewish women, lesbians, old women, poor women, rural women, women examining classism, women of color, women with disabilities, women who are writing books that help make the best in our lives more possible."

Nonfiction: Feminist analysis for positive change. Subjects include women's issues/studies. "We do not want to see work by men or anything that is not specific to women's lives (humor, children's books, etc.)." Query with SASE. Reviews artwork/photos as part of ms package.

Fiction: Ethnic, feminist, gay/lesbian, mystery (amateur sleuth, private eye/hardboiled), science fiction (soft/sociological), short story collections, women's. "We do not publish poetry or short fiction. We are interested in fiction that challenges, women's language that is feminist, stories that treat lifestyles with the diversity and complexity they deserve. We are also interested in genre fiction, especially mysteries." Wants "full-length quality fiction—thoroughly edited novels which display deep characterization, theme and style. We *only* consider books by women. No books by men, or books by men, or books with sexist, racist or ageist content." Submit outline, sample chapter(s), synopsis. No faced or e-mailed queries.

Recent Title(s): *Angel*, by Anita Mason; *Perfection*, by Anita Mason; *Night Driving*, by Michelene Esposito.

SQUARE ONE PUBLISHERS, INC., 115 Herricks Rd., Garden City Park NY 11040. (516)535-2010. Fax: (516)535-2014. Website: www.squareonepublishers.com. Publisher: Rudy Shur. **Acquisitions:** Acquisitions Editor. Publishes trade paperback originals. **Publishes 20 titles/year. Receives 500 queries and 100 mss/year. 95% of books from first-time authors; 95% from unagented writers. Pays 10-15% royalty on wholesale price. Offers variable advance.** Publishes book 10 months after acceptance of ms. Accepts simultaneous submissions. Responds in 1 month to queries; 1 month to proposals; 1 month to mss. Book catalog and ms guidelines free or on website; ms guidelines online.

Nonfiction: Cookbook, how-to, reference, self-help. Subjects include animals, art/architecture, business/economics, child guidance/parenting, health/medicine, hobbies, money/finance, nature/environment, psychology, regional, religion, spirituality, sports, travel, writers' guides, cooking/foods, gaming/gambling. Query with SASE or submit proposal package including outline, author bio, introduction, synopsis, SASE. Reviews artwork/photos as part of ms package. Send photocopies.

Recent Title(s): *Kids Who Laugh*, by Louis R. Franzini, Ph.D. (parenting/psychology); *Retiring Right 2002*, by Lawrence Kaplan (personal finance); *How to Publish Your Articles*, by Shirley Kawa-Jump (reference/writing).

Tips: "We focus on making our books accessible, accurate, and interesting. They are written for people who are looking for the best place to start, and who don't appreciate the terms 'dummy,' 'idiot,' or 'fool' on the cover of their books. We look for smartly written, informative books that have a strong point of view, and that are authored by people who know their subjects well."

ST. ANTHONY MESSENGER PRESS, 28 W. Liberty St., Cincinnati OH 45202-6498. (513)241-5615. Fax: (513)241-0399. E-mail: books@americancatholic.org. Website: www.americancatholic.org. Publisher: The Rev. Jeremy Harrington, O.F.M. **Acquisitions:** Lisa Biedenbach, managing editor; Katie Carroll, book editor (children's). Estab. 1970. Publishes trade paperback originals. **Publishes 15-25 titles/year. Receives 200 queries and 50 mss/year. 5% of books from first-time authors; 99% from unagented writers. Pays 10-12% royalty on net receipts. Offers $1,000 average advance.** Publishes book 18 months after acceptance of ms. Responds in 1 month to queries; 2 months to proposals; 2 months to mss. Book catalog for 9×12 SAE with 4 first-class stamps; ms guidelines online.

O→ "St. Anthony Messenger Press/Franciscan Communications seeks to communicate the word that is Jesus Christ in the styles of Saints Francis and Anthony. Through print and electronic media marketed in North America and worldwide, we endeavor to evangelize, inspire and inform those who search for God and seek a richer Catholic, Christian, human life. Our efforts help support the life, ministry and charities of the Franciscan Friars of St. John the Baptist Province, who sponsor our work." Currently emphasizing prayer/spirituality. De-emphasizing children's.

Nonfiction: Family-based religious education programs. Subjects include education, history, religion, sex, Catholic identity and teaching, prayer and spirituality resources, Scripture study. Query with SASE or submit outline, attn: Katie Carroll. Reviews artwork/photos as part of ms package.

Recent Title(s): *Lessons from the School of Suffering: A Young Priest with Cancer Teaches Us How to Live*, by Rev. Jim Willig and Tammy Bundy; *Praying the Gospels Through Poetry: Lent to Easter*, by Peggy Rosenthal; *Can You Find Followers?: Introducing Your Child to Disciples*, by Phil Gallery and Janet Harlow.

Tips: "Our readers are ordinary 'folks in the pews' and those who minister to and educate these folks. Writers need to know the audience and the kind of books we publish. Manuscripts should reflect best and current Catholic theology and doctrine." St. Anthony Messenger Press especially seeks books which will sell in bulk quantities to parishes, teachers, pastoral ministers, etc. They expect to sell at least 5,000 to 7,000 copies of a book.

ST. MARY'S PRESS, 702 Terrace Heights, Winona MN 55987-1318. (800)533-8095. Fax: (800)344-9225. Website: www.smp.org. Ms guidelines online.

Nonfiction: Subjects include religion (prayers), spirituality. Titles for Catholic youth and their parents, teachers and youth

ministers. Query with SASE or submit proposal package including outline, 1 sample chapter(s). Brief author biography.
Recent Title(s): *Catholic Youth Bible*, edited by Brian Singer-Towns.
Tips: "Do research online of Saint Mary Press book lists before submitting proposal."

STACKPOLE BOOKS, 5067 Ritter Rd., Mechanicsburg PA 17055. Fax: (717)796-0412. E-mail: jschnell@stackpolebooks.com. Website: www.stackpolebooks.com. **Acquisitions:** Judith Schnell, editorial director (fly fishing, sports); Chris Evans, editor (history); Mark Allison, editor (nature); Ed Skender, editor (military guides); Kyle Weaver, editor (Pennsylvania). Estab. 1935. Publishes hardcover and paperback originals and reprints. **Publishes 80 titles/year. Offers industry standard advance.** Publishes book 1 year after acceptance of ms. Does not accept simultaneous submissions. Responds in 1 month to queries.

O→ "Stackpole maintains a growing and vital publishing program by featuring authors who are experts in their fields, from outdoor activities to Civil War history."

Nonfiction: Subjects include history (especially Civil War), military/war, nature/environment, recreation, sports, wildlife, outdoor skills, fly fishing, paddling, climbing. Query with SASE. Does not return unsolicited mss. Reviews artwork/photos as part of ms package.
Recent Title(s): *Trout from Small Streams*; *Lincoln's Spymaster*; *The Book of Field and Roadside*.
Tips: "Stackpole seeks well-written, authoritative manuscripts for specialized and general trade markets. Proposals should include chapter outline, sample chapter and illustrations and author's credentials."

STANDARD PUBLICATIONS, INC., P.O. Box 2226, Champaign IL 61825-2226. (217)898-7825. E-mail: spi@standardpublications.com. **Acquisitions:** Borislav Dzodo. Estab. 2001. publishes trade paperback originals and reprints. **Publishes 4 titles/year. Receives 20 queries and 8 mss/year. 50% of books from first-time authors; 100% from unagented writers. Pays 5-10% royalty on wholesale price or makes outright purchase of $200-10,000.** Publishes book 8 months after acceptance of ms. Accepts simultaneous submissions. Responds in 1 month to queries; 2 months to proposals; 2 months to mss.

O→ Publishes books for women at home, and for males interested in how-to information or technical content that is hard to find.

Nonfiction: Biography, booklets, how-to, illustrated book, reference, technical, textbook. Subjects include business/economics, child guidance/parenting, ethnic, gardening, general nonfiction, hobbies, money/finance, recreation, sex, translation. "We have three primary focuses for the next two years. In order of priority: 1. Content of a technical nature that is difficult to find. Usually associated with trades that often restrict their knowledge or the popular public perception of legal restrictions. Examples are locksmithing, gun maintenance, magic, legal, survival. 2. How-to books in areas such as home theater, telescopes, specialized trades, etc. 3. Expanding our line of books on astrology, the occult, palm reading, horoscope, etc." Query with SASE or submit proposal package including outline, 3 sample chapter(s) or submit complete ms. Reviews artwork/photos as part of ms package. Send photocopies.
Recent Title(s): *Visual Guide to Lock Picking*, by Mark McCloud (how-to); *Nostradamus, His Works and Prophecies*, by Theodore Garencieres.
Tips: "Use Amazon.com sales rankings as a free and easy form of market research to determine the suitability of your topic matter."

STANDARD PUBLISHING, Standex International Corp., 8121 Hamilton Ave., Cincinnati OH 45231. (513)931-4050. Website: www.standardpub.com. Vice President, Church Resources: Mark Taylor. Managing Director, Church Resources: Paul Learned. Managing Director, Children's Publishing: Diane Stortz. **Acquisitions:** Ruth Frederick (children's ministry resources), Dale Reeves (Empowered Youth Products). Estab. 1866. Publishes hardcover and paperback originals and reprints. **Pays royalty.** Publishes book 18 months after acceptance of ms. Does not accept simultaneous submissions. Responds in 3 months to queries. Ms guidelines online.

O→ Standard specializes in religious books for children and religious education. De-emphasizing board books.

Nonfiction: Children's/juvenile, illustrated book, reference. Subjects include education, religion, picture books, Christian education (teacher training, working with volunteers), quiz, puzzle, crafts (to be used in Christian education). Query with SASE.
Recent Title(s): *My Good Night Bible*, by Susan Lingo (nonfiction); *Can God See Me?*, by JoDee McConnaughhay (fiction); *Edible Object Talks*, by Susan Lingo.

STANFORD UNIVERSITY PRESS, 1450 Page Mill Rd., Palo Alto CA 94304-1124. (650)723-9434. Fax: (650)725-3457. Website: www.sup.org. Estab. 1925. **Publishes 120 titles/year. Receives 1,500 submissions/year. 40% of books from first-time authors; 95% from unagented writers. Pays variable royalty (sometimes none). Offers occasional advance.** Publishes book 1 year after acceptance of ms. Does not accept simultaneous submissions. Responds in 6 weeks to queries. Ms guidelines online.

O→ Stanford University Press publishes scholarly books in the humanities and social sciences, along with professional books in business, economics and management science; also high-level textbooks and some books for a more general audience.

Nonfiction: Scholarly, textbook, professional books. Subjects include anthropology/archeology, business/economics, ethnic (studies), gay/lesbian, government/politics, history, humanities, language/literature, nature/environment, philosophy, psychology, religion, science, social sciences, sociology, history and culture of China, Japan and Latin America; European history; linguistics; geology; medieval and classical studies. Query with prospectus and an outline. Reviews artwork/photos as part of ms package.
Recent Title(s): *The Selected Poetry of Robinson Jeffers*.

Tips: "The writer's best chance is a work of original scholarship with an argument of some importance."

STARBURST PUBLISHERS, P.O. Box 4123, Lancaster PA 17604. (717)293-0939. Fax: (717)293-1945. E-mail: editorial @starburstpublishers.com. Website: www.starburstpublishers.com. **Acquisitions:** Editorial Department. Estab. 1982. Publishes hardcover and trade paperback originals. **Publishes 15-20 titles/year. Receives 1,000 submissions/year. 50% of books from first-time authors; 75% from unagented writers. Pays 6-16% royalty on wholesale price. "Individual arrangement with writer depending on the ms as well as writer's experience as a published author." Offers varies advance.** Publishes book 1 year after acceptance of ms. Accepts simultaneous submissions. Responds in 1 month to queries; 2 months to mss. Book catalog for 9×12 SAE with 4 first-class stamps; ms guidelines online.

O→ Starburst publishes quality self-help, health and inspirational titles for the trade and religious markets. Currently emphasizing inspirational gift, Bible study and Bible reference, how-to and health books. De-emphasizing fiction.

Nonfiction: "We are looking for books that inspire, teach and help today's average American." Cookbook, gift book, how-to, self-help, Christian; general nonfiction. Subjects include business/economics, child guidance/parenting, cooking/foods/nutrition, education, gardening, general nonfiction, health/medicine, money/finance, nature/environment, psychology, recreation, religion, counseling/career guidance, home, real estate. Submit proposal package including outline, 3 sample chapter(s), author bio, competitive analysis. "All unsolicited queries or proposals with attached files are simply deleted, often unanswered." Reviews artwork/photos as part of ms package. Send photocopies.

Fiction: Adventure, fantasy, historical, horror, military/war, religious, romance (contemporary, historical), suspense, western, Inspirational, spiritual. "We are only looking for good wholesome fiction that inspires or fiction that teaches self-help principles. We are also looking for successfully self-published fiction." Query with SASE or submit outline, 3 sample chapter(s), synopsis, author bio.

Recent Title(s): *Learn the Word: The Bible for Teens* (nonfiction); *Stories for the Spirit-Filled Believer*, by Christine Bolley (nonfiction).

Tips: "Fifty percent of our line goes into the Christian marketplace, fifty percent into the general marketplace. We have direct sales representatives in both the Christian and general (bookstore, catalog, price club, mass merchandiser, library, health and gift) marketplace. Write on an issue that slots you on talk shows and thus establishes your name as an expert and writer."

STEEPLE HILL, Harlequin Enterprises, 233 Broadway, New York NY 10279. Website: www.eharlequin.com. **Acquisitions:** Tara Gavin, editorial director; Joan Marlow Golan, senior editor; Diane Grecco, assistant editor. Estab. 1997. Publishes mass market paperback originals. **Pays royalty. Offers advance.** Does not accept simultaneous submissions. Ms guidelines online.

Imprints: Love Inspired.

O→ "This series of contemporary, inspirational love stories portrays Christian characters facing the many challenges of life, faith and love in today's world."

Fiction: Romance (Christian, 70,000 words), Inspirational romance. Query with SASE or submit 3 sample chapter(s), synopsis.

Recent Title(s): *Loving Hearts*, by Gail Gayner Martin.

Tips: "Drama, humor and even a touch of mystery all have a place in this series. Subplots are welcome and should further the story's main focus or intertwine in a meaningful way. Secondary characters (children, family, friends, neighbors, fellow church members, etc.) may all contribute to a substantial and satisfying story. These wholesome tales of romance include strong family values and high moral standards. While there is no premarital sex between characters, a vivid, exciting romance that is presented with a mature perspective, is essential. Although the element of faith must clearly be present, it should be well integrated into the characterizations and plot. The conflict between the main characters should be an emotional one, arising naturally from the well-developed personalities you've created. Suitable stories should also impart an important lesson about the powers of trust and faith."

STENHOUSE PUBLISHERS, 477 Congress St., Suite 4B, Portland ME 04101-3451. (207)253-1600. Fax: (207)253-5121. E-mail: wvarner@stenhouse.com. Website: www.stenhouse.com. **Acquisitions:** William Varner, senior editor. Estab. 1993. Publishes paperback originals. **Publishes 15 titles/year. Receives 300 queries/year. 30% of books from first-time authors; 99% from unagented writers. Pays royalty on wholesale price. Offers very modest advance.** Accepts simultaneous submissions. Responds in 1 month to queries; 3 months to mss. Book catalog and ms guidelines free or online; ms guidelines online.

O→ Stenhouse publishes exclusively professional books for teachers, K-12.

Nonfiction: Subjects include education (specializing in literacy). "All our books are a combination of theory and practice." No children's books or student texts. Query with SASE or submit outline. Reviews artwork/photos as part of ms package. Send photocopies.

Recent Title(s): *Reconsidering Read-Aloud*, by Mary Lee Hahn; *Writing for Real*, by Ross M. Burkhardt; *Knowing How*, by Mary C. McMackin and Barbara Seigel.

[N] **STILLWATER PUBLISHING CO.**, P.O. Box 606, Stillwater MN 55082. E-mail: publisher@stillwater-publishing.com. Submissions E-mail: submissions@stillwater-publishing.com. Website: www.stillwater-publishing.com. **Acquisitions:** Wm. Schmaltz, publisher; Jane Esbensen Moore, editor. Estab. 2001. Publishes harcover originals, trade paperback originals and reprints, mass market paperback originals and reprints. **Publishes 6 titles/year. Receives 50 queries and 25 mss/year. 90% of books from first-time authors; 100% from unagented writers. Pays 8-15% royalty on wholesale price. Offers $250-2,500 advance.** Publishes book 9 months after acceptance of ms. Accepts simultaneous submissions. Responds in 1 month to queries; 1 month to proposals; 3 months to mss. Book catalog online; ms guidelines online.

Nonfiction: Autobiography, biography, children's/juvenile, coffee table book, how-to, humor, illustrated book, reference, scholarly, technical. Subjects include Americana, anthropology/archeology, art/architecture, creative nonfiction, ethnic, general nonfiction, history, hobbies, humanities, language/literature, memoirs, military/war, translation. Submit complete ms. Reviews artwork/photos as part of ms package. Send photocopies.
Fiction: Adventure, comic books, historical, horror, humor, juvenile, literary, mainstream/contemporary, military/war, mystery, short story collections, suspense, translation, western, young adult. Submit complete ms.
Recent Title(s): *Trail of a Tramp*, by Leon Livingston (biography); *Ways of a Hobo*, by Leon Livingston (biography).
Tips: Audience is people who are interested in specialized topics or subjects that are not easily found in mainstream publishers. "We are willing to consider anything that's well written. We like helping authors who have been rejected by the mainstream publishers."

STONEYDALE PRESS, 523 Main St., Stevensville MT 59870. (406)777-2729. Fax: (406)777-2521. E-mail: daleburk@montana.com. **Acquisitions:** Dale A. Burk, publisher. Estab. 1976. Publishes hardcover and trade paperback originals. **Publishes 4-6 titles/year. Receives 40-50 queries and 6-8 mss/year. 90% from unagented writers. Pays 12-15% royalty. Offers advance.** Publishes book 18 months after acceptance of ms. Does not accept simultaneous submissions. Responds in 2 months to queries. Book catalog available.

O-- "We seek to publish the best available source books on big game hunting, historical reminiscence and outdoor recreation in the Northern Rocky Mountain region."

Nonfiction: How-to (hunting books). Subjects include regional, sports, historical reminiscences. Query with SASE.
Recent Title(s): *Lewis & Clark on the Upper Missouri*, by Jeanne O'Neil; *Montana's Bitterroot Valley*, by Russ Lawrence.

STYLUS PUBLISHING, LLC, 22883 Quicksilver Dr., Sterling VA 20166. Website: styluspub.com. **Acquisitions:** John von Knorring, publisher. Estab. 1996. Publishes hardcover and trade paperback originals. **Publishes 6-10 titles/year. Receives 50 queries and 6 mss/year. 50% of books from first-time authors; 100% from unagented writers. Pays 5-10% royalty on wholesale price. Offers advance.** Publishes book 6 months after acceptance of ms. Does not accept simultaneous submissions. Responds in 1 month to queries. Book catalog free; ms guidelines online.

O-- "We publish in higher education (diversity, professional development, distance education, teaching, administration) and training (training and development for corporate, nonprofit and government organizations)."

Nonfiction: Scholarly. Subjects include business/economics, education, training. Query or submit outline, 1 sample chapter with SASE. Reviews artwork/photos as part of ms package. Send photocopies.
Recent Title(s): *Working Virtually*; *Making It on Broken Promises*; *The Art of Changing the Brain.*

SUCCESS PUBLISHING, 3419 Dunham Rd., Warsaw NY 14569-9735. (716)786-5663. **Acquisitions:** Allan H. Smith, president (home-based business); Ginger Smith (business); Dana Herbison (home/craft); Robin Garretson (fiction). Estab. 1982. Publishes mass market paperback originals. **Publishes 6 titles/year. Receives 175 submissions and 10 mss/year. 90% of books from first-time authors; 100% from unagented writers. Pays 7-12% royalty. Offers $500-1,000 advance.** Publishes book 10 months after acceptance of ms. Accepts simultaneous submissions. Responds in 2 months to queries. Book catalog and ms guidelines for #10 SAE with 2 first-class stamps.

O-- Success publishes guides that focus on the needs of the home entrepreneur to succeed as a viable business. Currently emphasizing starting a new business. De-emphasizing self-help/motivation books. Success Publishing notes that it is looking for ghostwriters.

Nonfiction: Children's/juvenile, how-to, self-help. Subjects include business/economics, child guidance/parenting, hobbies, money/finance, craft/home-based business. "We are looking for books on how-to subjects such as home business and sewing." Query with SASE.
Recent Title(s): *How to Find a Date/Mate*, by Dana Herbison.
Tips: "Our audience is made up of housewives, hobbyists and owners of home-based businesses."

SUN BOOKS/SUN PUBLISHING, P.O. Box 5588, Santa Fe NM 87502-5588. (505)471-5177. E-mail: info@sunbooks.com. Website: www.sunbooks.com. **Acquisitions:** Skip Whitson, director. Publishes trade paperback originals and reprints. **Publishes 10-15 titles/year. Receives hundreds submissions/year. 5% of books from first-time authors; 90% from unagented writers. Pays 5% royalty on retail price or makes outright purchase.** Publishes book 16 months after acceptance of ms. Responds in 2 months to queries; 2 months to proposals; 6 months to mss. Book catalog online.
Nonfiction: Biography, cookbook, how-to, humor, illustrated book, reference, self-help, technical. Subjects include Americana, anthropology/archeology, business/economics, cooking/foods/nutrition, creative nonfiction, education, government/politics, health/medicine, history, language/literature, memoirs, money/finance, multicultural, nature/environment, philosophy, psychology, regional, religion, sociology, travel, women's issues/studies, metaphysics, motivational, inspirational, Oriental studes. Query with SASE. Preferably via e-mail. Reviews artwork/photos as part of ms package. Send photocopies.
Recent Title(s): *Eight Pillars of Prosperity*, by James Allen; *Ambition and Success*, by Orson Swett Marden; *Cheerfulness as a Life Power*, by Orson Swett Marden.

SUNBELT PUBLICATIONS, 1250 Fayette St., El Cajon CA 92020. (619)258-4911. Fax: (619)258-4916. E-mail: mail@sunbeltpub.com. Website: www.sunbeltpub.com. **Acquisitions:** Jennifer Redmond, publications coordinator; Lowell Lindsay, publisher (natural history). Publishes hardcover and trade paperback originals and reprints. **Publishes 6-10 titles/year. Receives 30 queries and 20 mss/year. 80% of books from first-time authors; 100% from unagented writers. Pays 10-14% royalty.** Accepts simultaneous submissions. Responds in 1 month to queries; 1 month to proposals; 3 months to mss. Book catalog and ms guidelines free or online; ms guidelines online.

O-- "We are interested in the cultural and natural history of the 'The Californias' in the U.S. and Mexico."

Nonfiction: "We publish multi-language pictorials, natural science and outdoor guidebooks, regional references and stories that celebrate the land and its people." Coffee table book, how-to, reference, guidebooks. Subjects include anthropology/archeology, history (regional), nature/environment (natural history), recreation, regional, travel. Query with SASE or submit proposal package including outline, 1-2 sample chapter(s) or submit complete ms. Reviews artwork/photos as part of ms package. Send photocopies.

Recent Title(s): *Baja Legends*, by Greg Niemann (history/travel); *More Adventures with Kids in San Diego*, by Judy Botello and Kt Paxton (regional guidebook).

Tips: "Our audience is interested in natural science or the cultural history of California and Baja California, Mexico. They want specific information that is accurate and up-to-date. Our books are written for an adult audience that is primarily interested in adventure and the outdoors. Our guidebooks lead to both personal and armchair adventure and travel. Authors must be willing to actively promote their book through book signings, the media, and lectures/slide shows for intended audiences."

N **SWEDENBORG FOUNDATION PUBLISHERS**, 320 N. Church St., West Chester PA 19380. (610)430-3222. Fax: (610)430-7982. E-mail: editor@swedenborg.com. Website: www.swedenborg.com. **Acquisitions:** Mary Lou Bertucci, senior editor. Estab. 1849. Publishes trade paperback originals and reprints. **Publishes 5 titles/year.** Does not accept simultaneous submissions. Responds in 1 month to queries; 3 months to proposals; 3 months to mss. Book catalog and ms guidelines free; ms guidelines online.

Imprints: Chrysalis Books, Swedenborg Foundation Press.

"The Swedenborg Foundation publishes books by and about Emanuel Swedenborg (1688-1772), his ideas, how his ideas have influenced others, and related topics. A Chrysalis book is a spiritually focused book presented with a nonsectarian perspective that appeals to open-minded, well-educated seekers of all traditions. Appropriate topics include—but are not limited to—science, mysticism, spiritual growth and development, wisdom traditions, healing and spirituality, as well as subjects that explore Swedenborgian concepts, such as: near-death experience, angels, biblical interpretation, mysteries of good and evil, etc. Although Chrysalis Books explore topics of general spirituality, a work must actively engage the thought of Emanuel Swedenborg and show an understanding of his philosophy in order to be accepted for publication."

Nonfiction: Self-help, spiritual growth and development. Subjects include philosophy, psychology, religion, science. Query with SASE or submit proposal package including outline, sample chapter(s), synopsis. "I personally prefer e-mail." Reviews artwork/photos as part of ms package. Send photocopies.

Recent Title(s): *Healing as a Sacred Path: A Story of Personal, Medical, and Spiritual Transformation*, by L. Robert Keck; *Emanuel Swedenborg: Visionary Savant in the Age of Reason*, by Ernst Benz; *Kant on Swedenborg*, edited and translated by Gregory Johnson.

A **NAN A. TALESE**, Random House, Inc., 1745 Broadway, New York NY 10019. (212)782-8918. Fax: (212)782-9261. Website: www.nantalese.com. **Acquisitions:** Nan A. Talese, editorial director. Publishes hardcover originals. **Publishes 15 titles/year. Receives 400 queries and 400 mss/year. Pays variable royalty on retail price. Offers varying advance.** Publishes book 1 year after acceptance of ms. Accepts simultaneous submissions. Responds in 1 week to queries; 2 weeks to proposals; 2 weeks to mss. Agented submissions only.

Nan A. Talese publishes nonfiction with a powerful guiding narrative and relevance to larger cultural interests, and literary fiction of the highest quality.

Nonfiction: Biography. Subjects include contemporary culture, history, philosophy, sociology. *Agented submissions only.*

Fiction: Literary. Well written narratives with a compelling story line, good characterization and use of language. We like stories with an edge. *Agented submissions only.*

Recent Title(s): *You Are Not a Stranger Here*, by Adam Haslett; *Oryx and Crake*, by Margaret Atwood; *My Losing Season*, by Pat Conroy.

Tips: "Audience is highly literate people interested in story, information and insight. We want well-written material. See our website."

JEREMY P. TARCHER, INC., Penguin Group USA, 375 Hudson St., New York NY 10014. (212)366-2000. Website: www.penguinputnam.com. Publisher: Joel Fotinos. **Acquisitions:** Mitch Horowitz, senior editor; Wendy Hubbert, senior editor; Sara Carder, editor. Estab. 1972. Publishes hardcover and trade paperback originals and reprints. **Publishes 40-50 titles/year. Receives 750 queries and 750 mss/year. 10% of books from first-time authors; 5% from unagented writers. Pays royalty. Offers advance.** Accepts simultaneous submissions. Book catalog free.

Tarcher's vision is to publish ideas and works about human consciousness that were large enough to include all aspects of human experience.

Nonfiction: How-to, self-help. Subjects include business/economics, child guidance/parenting, gay/lesbian, health/medicine, nature/environment, philosophy, psychology, religion, women's issues/studies. Query with SASE.

Recent Title(s): *The Hard Question*, by Susan Piver; *The Hydrogen Economy*, by Jeremy Rifkin.

Tips: "Our audience seeks personal growth through books. Understand the imprint's focus and categories. We stick with the tried and true."

TCU PRESS, P.O. Box 298300, TCU, Fort Worth TX 76129. (817)257-7822. Fax: (817)257-5075. **Acquisitions:** Judy Alter, director; James Ward Lee, acquisitions editor; Susan Petty, editor. Estab. 1966. Publishes hardcover originals, some reprints. **Publishes 6-10 titles/year. Receives 100 submissions/year. 10% of books from first-time authors; 75% from unagented writers. Pays 10% royalty on net receipts.** Publishes book 16 months after acceptance of ms. Does not accept simultaneous submissions. Responds in 3 months to queries.

O-╖ TCU publishes "scholarly works and regional titles of significance focusing on the history and literature of the American West." Currently emphasizing women's studies.

Nonfiction: Biography, children's/juvenile, coffee table book, scholarly. Subjects include Americana, art/architecture, contemporary culture, ethnic, history, language/literature, multicultural, regional, women's issues/studies, American studies, criticism. Query with SASE. Reviews artwork/photos as part of ms package.

Fiction: Historical, young adult.

Recent Title(s): *Paul Baker and the Integration of Abilities*, edited by Robert Flynn and Eugene McKinney; *Texas Autobiographies*, by Bert Almon.

Tips: "Regional and/or Texana nonfiction has best chance of breaking into our firm. Our list focuses on the history of literature of the American West, although recently we have branched out into literary criticism, women's studies and Mexican-American studies."

TEACHERS COLLEGE PRESS, 1234 Amsterdam Ave., New York NY 10027. (212)678-3929. Fax: (212)678-4149. Website: www.teacherscollegepress.com. Director: Carole P. Saltz. **Acquisitions:** Brian Ellerbeck, executive acquisitions editor. Estab. 1904. Publishes hardcover and paperback originals and reprints. **Publishes 60 titles/year. Pays industry standard royalty. Offers advance.** Publishes book 1 year after acceptance of ms. Does not accept simultaneous submissions. Responds in 2 months to queries. Book catalog free; ms guidelines online.

O-╖ Teachers College Press publishes a wide range of educational titles for all levels of students: early childhood to higher education. "Publishing books that respond to, examine and confront issues pertaining to education, teacher training and school reform."

Nonfiction: Subjects include computers/electronic, education, film/cinema/stage, government/politics, history, philosophy, sociology, women's issues/studies. "This university press concentrates on books in the field of education in the broadest sense, from early childhood to higher education: good classroom practices, teacher training, special education, innovative trends and issues, administration and supervision, film, continuing and adult education, all areas of the curriculum, computers, guidance and counseling and the politics, economics, philosophy, sociology and history of education. We have recently added women's studies to our list. The Press also issues classroom materials for students at all levels, with a strong emphasis on reading and writing and social studies." Submit outline, sample chapter(s).

Recent Title(s): *Cultural Miseducation: In Search of a Democratic Solution*, by Jane Roland Martin.

TEACHING & LEARNING CO., 1204 Buchanan St., P.O. Box 10, Carthage IL 62321-0010. (217)357-2591. Fax: (217)357-6789. E-mail: customerservice@teachinglearning.com. Website: www.teachinglearning.com. **Acquisitions:** Jill Day, vice president of production. Estab. 1994. **Publishes 60 titles/year. Receives 25 queries and 200 mss/year. 25% of books from first-time authors; 98% from unagented writers. Pays royalty.** Accepts simultaneous submissions. Responds in 3 months to queries; 9 months to proposals; 9 months to mss. Book catalog and ms guidelines free.

O-╖ Teaching & Learning Company publishes teacher resources (supplementary activity/idea books) for grades pre K-8. Currently emphasizing "more math for all grade levels, more primary science material."

Nonfiction: Children's/juvenile. Subjects include art/architecture, education, language/literature, science, teacher resources in language arts, reading, math, science, social studies, arts and crafts, responsibility education. No picture books or storybooks. Submit table of contents, introduction, 3 sample chapters with SASE. Reviews artwork/photos as part of ms package. Send photocopies.

Recent Title(s): *Group Project Student Role Sheets*, by Christine Boardman Moen (nonfiction); *Poetry Writing Handbook*, by Greta Barclay Lipson, Ed.D. (poetry); *Four Square Writing Methods (3 books)*, by Evan and Judith Gould.

Tips: "Our books are for teachers and parents of pre K-8th grade children."

TEMPLE UNIVERSITY PRESS, 1601 N. Broad St., USB 305, Philadelphia PA 19122-6099. (215)204-8787. Fax: (215)204-4719. E-mail: tempress@tempa.edu. Website: www.temple.edu/tempress/. **Acquisitions:** Janet Francendese, editor-in-chief; Peter Wissoker, senior acquisitions editor (communications, urban studies, geography, law); Micah Kleit, senior acquisitions editor. Estab. 1969. **Publishes 60 titles/year. Offers advance.** Publishes book 10 months after acceptance of ms. Does not accept simultaneous submissions. Responds in 2 months to queries. Book catalog free; ms guidelines online.

O-╖ "Temple University Press has been publishing useful books on Asian-Americans, law, gender issues, film, women's studies and other interesting areas for nearly 30 years for the goal of social change."

Nonfiction: Subjects include ethnic, government/politics, health/medicine, history (American), photography, regional (Philadelphia), sociology, women's issues/studies, labor studies, urban studies, Latin American, Asian American, African American, public policy. "No memoirs, fiction or poetry." Query with SASE. Reviews artwork/photos as part of ms package.

Recent Title(s): *Fireweed: A Political Autobiography*, by Gerda Lerner.

TEN SPEED PRESS, P.O. Box 7123, Berkeley CA 94707. (510)559-1600. Fax: (510)524-1052. E-mail: info@tenspeed.com. Website: www.tenspeed.com. **Acquisitions:** Kirsty Melville, Ten Speed Press publisher; Lorena Jones, Ten Speed Press editorial director; Jo Ann Deck, Celestial Arts/Crossing Press publisher. Estab. 1971. Publishes trade paperback originals and reprints. **Publishes 120 titles/year; imprint publishes 70 titles/year. 40% of books from first-time authors; 40% from unagented writers. Pays 15-20% royalty on net receipts. Offers $2,500 average advance.** Publishes book 1 year after acceptance of ms. Accepts simultaneous submissions. Responds in 3 months to queries. Book catalog for 9×12 SAE with 6 first-class stamps; ms guidelines online.

Imprints: Celestial Arts; Crossing Press; Tricycle Press.

O-╖ Ten Speed Press publishes authoritative books for an audience interested in innovative ideas. Currently emphasizing cookbooks, career, business, alternative education, and offbeat general nonfiction gift books.

Nonfiction: Subjects include business/economics, child guidance/parenting, cooking/foods/nutrition, gardening, health/medicine, money/finance, nature/environment, New Age (mind/body/spirit), recreation, science. "No fiction." Query with SASE or submit proposal package including sample chapter(s).

Recent Title(s): *How to Be Happy, Dammit*, by Karen Salmansohn; *The Bread Baker's Apprentice*, by Peter Reinhart.

Tips: "We like books from people who really know their subject, rather than people who think they've spotted a trend to capitalize on. We like books that will sell for a long time, rather than nine-day wonders. Our audience consists of a well-educated, slightly weird group of people who like food, the outdoors and take a light but serious approach to business and careers. Study the backlist of each publisher you're submitting to and tailor your proposal to what you perceive as their needs. Nothing gets a publisher's attention like someone who knows what he or she is talking about, and nothing falls flat like someone who obviously has no idea who he or she is submitting to."

TEXAS A&M UNIVERSITY PRESS, College Station TX 77843-4354. (979)845-1436. Fax: (979)847-8752. E-mail: fdl@tampress.tamu.edu. Website: www.tamu.edu/upress. **Acquisitions:** Mary Lenn Dixon, editor-in-chief (presidential studies, anthropology, borderlands, western history); Shannon Davies, senior editor (natural history, agriculture); Jim Sadkovich, editor (military, eastern Europe, nautical archeaology). Estab. 1974. **Publishes 50 titles/year. Pays royalty. Offers advance.** Publishes book 1 year after acceptance of ms. Does not accept simultaneous submissions. Responds in 1 month to queries. Book catalog free; ms guidelines online.

O‑ Texas A&M University Press publishes a wide range of nonfiction, scholarly trade and crossover books of regional and national interest, "reflecting the interests of the university, the broader scholarly community, and the people of our state and region."

Nonfiction: Subjects include agriculture/horticulture, anthropology/archeology, art/architecture, business/economics, government/politics, history (American and Western), language/literature (Texas and western), military/war, nature/environment, photography, regional (Texas and the Southwest), Mexican-US borderlands studies, nautical archaeology, ethnic studies, natural history, presidential studies, business history. Query with SASE.

Recent Title(s): *The White House World*, edited by Martha Joynt Kumas and Terry Sullivan.

Tips: Proposal requirements are posted on the website.

[N] **TEXAS STATE HISTORICAL ASSOCIATION**, 2.306 Richardson Hall, University Station, Austin TX 78712. (512)471-1525. Fax: (512)471-1551. Website: www.tsha.utexas.edu. **Acquisitions:** George B. Ward, assistant director. Estab. 1897. Publishes hardcover and trade paperback originals and reprints. **Publishes 8 titles/year. Receives 50 queries and 50 mss/year. 10% of books from first-time authors; 95% from unagented writers. Pays 10% royalty on net cash proceeds.** Publishes book 1 year after acceptance of ms. Does not accept simultaneous submissions. Responds in 2-3 months to mss. Book catalog and ms guidelines free; ms guidelines online.

O‑ "We are interested in scholarly historical articles and books on any aspect of Texas history and culture."

Nonfiction: Biography, coffee table book, illustrated book, reference, scholarly. Subjects include history. Query with SASE. Reviews artwork/photos as part of ms package. Send photocopies.

Recent Title(s): *El Llano Estacado: Exploration and Imagination on the High Plains of Texas and New Mexico, 1536-1860*, by John Miller Morris (history); *I Would Rather Sleep in Texas: A History of the Lower Rio Grande Valley and the People of the Santa Anita Land Grant*, by Mary Margaret McAllen Amberson.

TEXAS WESTERN PRESS, The University of Texas at El Paso, 500 W. University Ave., El Paso TX 79968-0633. (915)747-5688. Fax: (915)747-7515. E-mail: bobbi@utep.edu. Website: www.utep.edu/twp/. Director: Dr. Jon Amastae. **Acquisitions:** Bobbi McConaughey Gonzales. Estab. 1952. Publishes hardcover and paperback originals. **Publishes 7-8 titles/year. Pays standard 10% royalty. Offers advance.** Does not accept simultaneous submissions. Responds in 2 months to queries. Book catalog and ms guidelines free; ms guidelines online.

Imprints: Southwestern Studies.

O‑ Texas Western Press publishes books on the history and cultures of the American Southwest, especially historical and biographical works about West Texas, New Mexico, northern Mexico and the US-Mexico borderlands. Currently emphasizing developing border issues, economic issues of the border. De-emphasizing coffee table books.

Nonfiction: Scholarly, technical. Subjects include education, health/medicine, history, language/literature, nature/environment, regional, science, social sciences. Historic and cultural accounts of the Southwest (West Texas, New Mexico, northern Mexico). Also art, photographic books, Native American and limited regional ficiton reprints. Occasional technical titles. "Our *Southwestern Studies* use manuscripts of up to 30,000 words. Our hardback books range from 30,000 words up. The writer should use good exposition in his work. Most of our work requires documentation. We favor a scholarly, but not overly pedantic, style. We specialize in superior book design." Query with SASE or submit outline. Follow *Chicago Manual of Style*.

Recent Title(s): *Frontier Cavalryman*, by Marcos Kinevan; *James Wiley Magoffin*, by W.H. Timmons.

Tips: Texas Western Press is interested in books relating to the history of Hispanics in the US, will experiment with photo-documentary books, and is interested in seeing more 'popular' history and books on Southwestern culture/life. "We try to treat our authors professionally, produce handsome, long-lived books and aim for quality, rather than quantity of titles carrying our imprint."

THIRD WORLD PRESS, P.O. Box 19730, Chicago IL 60619. (773)651-0700. Fax: (773)651-7286. E-mail: twpress3@aol.com. Publisher: Haki R. Madhubuti. **Acquisitions:** Gwendolyn Mitchell, editor. Estab. 1967. Publishes hardcover and trade paperback originals and reprints. **Publishes 20 titles/year. Receives 200-300 queries and 200 mss/year. 20% of books from first-time authors; 80% from unagented writers. Pays royalty on retail price. Individual arrangement with author depending on the book, etc. Offers advance.** Publishes book 18 months after acceptance of ms. Accepts simultaneous submissions. Responds in 6 weeks to queries; 5 months to mss. Book catalog free; ms guidelines for #10 SASE.

• Third World Press is open to submissions in July only.

Nonfiction: Children's/juvenile, illustrated book, reference, self-help, textbook, African-centered; African-American materials. Subjects include anthropology/archeology, education, ethnic, government/politics, health/medicine, history, language/literature, philosophy, psychology, regional, religion, sociology, women's issues/studies, Black studies, literary criticism. Query with SASE or submit outline, 5 sample chapter(s). Reviews artwork/photos as part of ms package. Send photocopies.

Fiction: Ethnic, feminist, historical, juvenile (animal, easy-to-read, fantasy, historical, contemporary), literary, mainstream/contemporary, picture books, plays, short story collections, young adult (easy-to-read/teen, folktales, historical), African-centered; African-American materials, preschool/picture book. "We primarily publish nonfiction, but will consider fiction by and about blacks." Query with SASE or submit outline, 5 sample chapter(s), synopsis.

Poetry: African-centered and African-American materials. Submit complete ms.

Recent Title(s): *Special Internet*, by Chris Benson; *Tough Notes: A Healing Call for Creating Exceptional Black Men*, by Haki R. Madhubuti; *The Paradox of Loyalty*, edited by Julianne Malveaux and Reginna A. Green.

THORNDIKE PRESS, The Gale Group, 295 Kenney Memorial Dr., Waterville ME 04901. (207)859-1000. Fax: (207)859-1006. E-mail: hazel.rumney@gale.com. **Acquisitions:** Hazel Rumney, editor (romance, western, women's fiction); Jamie Knobloch, editorial director. Estab. 1979. Publishes hardcover originals, reprints and large print reprints. **Publishes 112 titles/year. Receives 1,000 queries and 1,000 mss/year. 60% of books from first-time authors; 75% from unagented writers. Pays royalty on wholesale price. Offers $1,000-2,000 advance.** Publishes book 8 months after acceptance of ms. Accepts simultaneous submissions. Responds in 3 months to queries; 3 months to proposals; 4-6 months to mss. Book catalog free; ms guidelines for #10 SASE.

Imprints: Five Star (contact: Hazel Rumney).

Fiction: Romance, western, women's. "We want highly original material that contains believable motivation, with little repetitive introspection. Show us how a character feels, rather that tell us. Humor is good; clichés are not." Submit proposal package including 3 sample chapter(s), synopsis.

Recent Title(s): *Friends and Enemies*, by Susan Oleksiw (mystery); *Desparate Acts*, by Jane Candia Coleman (romance).

Tips: Audience is intelligent readers looking for something different and satisfying. "We want highly original material that contains believable motivation, with little repetitive introspection. Show us how a character feels, rather than tell us. Humor is good; cliches are not."

THREE FORKS BOOKS, The Globe Pequot Press, 825 Great Northern Blvd., Suites 327 & 328, Helena MT 59601. (406)442-6597. Fax: (406)457-5461. Website: www.globepequot.com. **Acquisitions:** Erin Turner, executive editor. Publishes hardcover and trade paperback originals. **Publishes 4 titles/year. 80% of books from first-time authors; 80% from unagented writers. Pays variable royalty.** Does not accept simultaneous submissions. Responds in 2 months to queries. Book catalog and ms guidelines free; ms guidelines online.

Three Forks specializes in regional cookbooks *or* cookbooks with a unique, non-food theme. We do not publish single-food themed cookbooks.

Nonfiction: Cookbook. Subjects include regional. Query with SASE or submit proposal package. Reviews artwork/photos as part of ms package. Send photocopies, no originals.

Recent Title(s): *Whistleberries, Stirabout, & Depression Cake* (food history); *Chocolate Snowball* (cookbook).

THUNDER'S MOUTH PRESS, Avalon Publishing Group, 161 William St., New York NY 10038. (646)375-2570. Fax: (646)375-2571. Website: www.avalonpub.com. Publisher: Neil Ortenberg. **Acquisitions:** Gayle Watkins, acquisitions editor. Estab. 1982. Publishes hardcover and trade paperback originals and reprints, almost exclusively nonfiction. **Publishes 70-80 titles/year. Receives 1,000 submissions/year. 15% from unagented writers. Pays 7-10% royalty on retail price. Offers $1,500 average advance.** Publishes book 8 months after acceptance of ms. Does not accept simultaneous submissions. Responds in 2 months to queries.

Nonfiction: Biography. Subjects include government/politics, Popular Culture. *No unsolicited mss.*

Recent Title(s): *Hindsight*, Boris Vallejo.

TIARE PUBLICATIONS, P.O. Box 493, Lake Geneva WI 53147-0493. Fax: (262)249-0299. E-mail: info@tiare.com. Website: www.tiare.com. **Acquisitions:** Gerry L. Dexter, president. Estab. 1986. Publishes trade paperback originals. **Publishes 6-12 titles/year. Receives 25 queries and 10 mss/year. 40% of books from first-time authors; 100% from unagented writers. Pays 15% royalty on wholesale price or retail price.** Publishes book 3 months after acceptance of ms. Does not accept simultaneous submissions. Responds in 1 month to queries.

Imprints: LimeLight Books, Balboa Books.

Tiare offers a wide selection of books for the radio communications enthusiast. LimeLight publishes general nonfiction on subjects ranging from crime to root beer. Balboa offers big band and jazz titles.

Nonfiction: How-to, technical, general. Subjects include computers/electronic, general nonfiction, music/dance, jazz/big bands. Query with SASE.

Recent Title(s): *Air-Ways—The Insider's Guide to Air Travel.*

TIDEWATER PUBLISHERS, Cornell Maritime Press, Inc., P.O. Box 456, Centreville MD 21617-0456. (410)758-1075. Fax: (410)758-6849. **Acquisitions:** Charlotte Kurst, managing editor. Estab. 1938. Publishes hardcover and paperback originals. **Publishes 7-9 titles/year. Receives 150 submissions/year. 41% of books from first-time authors; 99% from unagented writers. Pays 7½-15% royalty on retail price.** Publishes book 1 year after acceptance of ms. Does not accept simultaneous submissions. Responds in 2 months to queries. Book catalog for 10×13 SAE with 5 first-class stamps.

O→ Tidewater Publishers issues adult nonfiction works related to the Chesapeake Bay area, Delmarva or Maryland in general. "The only fiction we handle is juvenile and must have a regional focus."

Nonfiction: Regional subjects only. Children's/juvenile, cookbook, illustrated book, reference. Subjects include art/architecture, history, regional, natural history, folklore, Chesapeake watercraft. Query with SASE or submit outline, sample chapter(s). Reviews artwork/photos as part of ms package.

Fiction: Regional juvenile fiction only. Query with SASE or submit outline, sample chapter(s), synopsis.

Recent Title(s): *Chesapeake 123*, by Priscilla Cummings, illustrated by David Aiken; *Chesapeake Wildlife*, by Pat Vojtech.

Tips: "Our audience is made up of readers interested in works that are specific to the Chesapeake Bay and Delmarva Peninsula area. We do not publish personal narratives, adult fiction or poetry."

TILBURY HOUSE, PUBLISHERS, imprint of Harpswell Press, Inc., 2 Mechanic St., Gardiner ME 04345. (207)582-1899. Fax: (207)582-8227. E-mail: tilbury@tilburyhouse.com. Website: www.tilburyhouse.com. Publisher: Jennifer Bunting (New England, maritime, children's). **Acquisitions:** Audrey Maynard, children's book editor. Estab. 1990. Publishes hardcover originals, trade paperback originals. **Publishes 10 titles/year. Pays royalty.** Book catalog free; ms guidelines online.

Nonfiction: Biography, children's/juvenile, coffee table book. Subjects include animals, art/architecture, education, ethnic (children's), general nonfiction, history, memoirs, multicultural (children's), regional (New England). Submit complete ms. Reviews artwork/photos as part of ms package. Send photocopies.

Fiction: Regional (New England adult).

Recent Title(s): *Travels with Tarra*, by Carol Buckley (children's nonfiction); *Saving Birds*, by Pete Salmansohn & Stephen Kress (children's nonfiction); *Carpet Boys' Guest*, by Pegi Deitz Shea (children's fiction).

TIMBERWOLF PRESS, INC., 202 N. Allen Dr., Suite A, Allen TX 75013. (972)359-0911. Fax: (972)359-0525. E-mail: submissions@timberwolfpress.com. Website: www.timberwolfpress.com. **Acquisitions:** Carol Woods, senior editor. Publishes trade paperback originals. **Publishes 24-30 titles/year. Receives 700+ queries and 400+ mss/year. 57% of books from first-time authors; 86% from unagented writers. Pays royalty on wholesale price. Offers industry standard advance or better.** Publishes book 1 year after acceptance of ms. Accepts simultaneous submissions. Responds in 1 month to queries; 3 months to mss. Book catalog and ms guidelines on website; ms guidelines online.

Fiction: Fantasy, military/war, mystery, science fiction, suspense. "In addition to the p-book, we present each title in next generation fully-cast, dramatized, unabridged audio theatre, available in the usual formats; and downloadable in all formats from our website. So our stories must maintain tension and pace. Think exciting. Think breathless. Think terrific story, terrific characters, terrific writing." Query via e-mail only. Fiction only.

Recent Title(s): *Soldier of the Legion*, by Marshall Thomas (military science fiction); *Book Two of Bronwyn Tetralogy: Silk & Steel*, by Ron Miller (fantasy).

Tips: "We accept e-queries and e-submissions only: *submissions@timberwolfpress.com*. And polish that query. Grammar, punctuation, and spelling are as important in e-queries and e-submissions as they are in p-queries."

MEGAN TINGLEY BOOKS, imprint of Little, Brown & Co., 1271 Avenue of the Americas, New York NY 10020. (212)522-8700. Fax: (212)522-7997. Website: www.lb-kids.com. **Acquisitions:** Megan Tingley, editor-in-chief (picture books); Sara Morling, editorial assistant (YA novels). Publishes hardcover and trade paperback originals and reprints. **Publishes 80-100 titles/year; imprint publishes 10-20 titles/year. Receives 500-1,000 queries and 500-1,000 mss/year. 2% of books from first-time authors; 5% from unagented writers. Pays 0-15% royalty on retail price or makes outright purchase.** Publishes book 2 years after acceptance of ms. Accepts simultaneous submissions. Responds in 1 month to queries; 2-3 months to proposals; 2-3 months to mss.

O→ Megan Tingley Books is an imprint of the children's book department of Little, Brown and Company. Currently emphasizing picture books for the very young. Does not want genre novels (mystery, science fiction, romance).

Nonfiction: Children's/juvenile. Subjects include animals, art/architecture, cooking/foods/nutrition, creative nonfiction, ethnic, gay/lesbian, history, hobbies, language/literature, memoirs, multicultural, music/dance, nature/environment, photography, science, sports, all juvenile interests. *Agented submissions and queries only.* Ideally, books should be about a subject that hasn't been dealt with for children before. Reviews artwork/photos as part of ms package. Send photocopies. No original pieces.

Fiction: Juvenile, picture books, young adult. *Agented submissions only.* Strong, contemporary female characters preferred. No genre novels (romance, mystery, science fiction, etc.).

Recent Title(s): *Otto Goes to the Beach*, by Todd Parr; *O'Baby!*, by Leo Landry; *Keeping You a Secret*, by Julie Ann Peters.

Tips: "Do your research. Know our submission policy. Do not fax or call."

THE TOBY PRESS, LTD., P.O. Box 8531, New Milford CT 06776-8531. Fax: (203)830-8512. Website: www.tobypress.com. **Acquisitions:** Editorial Director (fiction, biography). Publishes hardcover originals and paperbacks. **Publishes 20-25 titles/year. Receives 300 queries/year. 50% of books from first-time authors; 10% from unagented writers. Offers advance.** Publishes book up to 2 year after acceptance of ms. Accepts simultaneous submissions.

O→ The Toby Press publishes literary fiction.

Nonfiction: Biography.

Fiction: Literary.

Recent Title(s): *Failing Paris*, by Samantha Dunn (fiction); *Before Hiroshima*, by Joshua Barkan (fiction).

TORCHDOG PRESS, 1032 Irving St. #514, San Francisco CA 94122-2200. (415)753-3778. E-mail: torchdog@torchdog.com. Website: www.torchdog.com. Kevin Rush, publisher. **Acquisitions:** Connor McLean, managing editor. Publishes trade paperback originals. **100% of books from first-time authors; 100% from unagented writers. Pays 6-8% royalty on retail price or makes outright purchase of $100-400.** Publishes book 6 months after acceptance of ms. Accepts simultaneous submissions. Responds in 1 month to queries; 3 months to mss. Book catalog online; ms guidelines for #10 SASE.

Fiction: Comic books (graphic novels), young adult. "Torchdog Press is dedicated to providing realistic, relevant and faith-filled fiction for Catholic teens aged 13-16." Prefers stories with an edge, a contemporary voice, and gently interwoven spirituality. Humor a plus. Will consider historical fiction and science fiction. Nothing heavy-handed or didactic. Submit complete ms.

Recent Title(s): *Earthquake Weather*, by Kevin Rush (young adult); *Sift the Gnat and Swallow the Camel: The Comedy Stylings of Jesus Christ.*

Tips: "Our audience is Catholic teens in Catholic junior high and high school. They are trying to integrate their faith into their daily lives in the real world. They face all the trials and temptations of contemporary teens. Please, no sanitized saints leading perfect lives and making all the right decisions. Torchdog books are not for ivory tower separatists who think religion can insulate kids from the real world. Our books are for kids living in the real world, trying to figure out where their faith fits in."

TOWER PUBLISHING, 588 Saco Rd., Standish ME 04084. (207)642-5400. Fax: (207)642-5463. E-mail: info@towerpub.com. Website: www.towerpub.com. **Acquisitions:** Michael Lyons, president. Estab. 1772. Publishes hardcover originals and reprints, trade paperback originals. **Publishes 22 titles/year. Receives 60 queries and 30 mss/year. 10% of books from first-time authors; 90% from unagented writers. Pays royalty on net receipts.** Publishes book 6 months after acceptance of ms. Accepts simultaneous submissions. Responds in 1 month to queries; 2 months to proposals; 2 months to mss. Book catalog and ms guidelines on website.

O-π Tower Publishing specializes in business and professional directories and legal books.

Nonfiction: Reference. Subjects include business/economics. Looking for legal books of a national stature. Query with SASE or submit outline.

TOWLEHOUSE PUBLISHING CO., 1312 Bell Grimes Lane, Nashville TN 37207. (615)366-9120. Fax: (615)366-9161. E-mail: vermonte@aol.com. Website: www.towlehouse.com. **Acquisitions:** Mike Towle, president/publisher (nonfiction, sports, gift books, pop culture, cookbooks, Christianity). Publishes hardcover, trade paperback and mass market paperback originals, hardcover and trade paperback reprints. **Publishes 10-12 titles/year. Receives 100-250 mss/year. 75% of books from first-time authors; 80% from unagented writers. Pays 8-20% royalty on wholesale price. Offers $500-2,000 advance.** Publishes book 9 months after acceptance of ms. Accepts simultaneous submissions. Responds in 4-6 months to queries.

O-π "We publish nonfiction books about America that are informative and entertaining." Currently emphasizing 'potent quotables' and Good Golf! series of books. Rare exceptions. De-emphasizing cookbooks and poetry.

Nonfiction: Subjects include Americana, creative nonfiction, government/politics, history, religion, sports, insta-books dictated by headlines and milestone anniversaries of significant events. "I don't solicit children's books, poetry or non-Christian religious titles. Authors using profanity, obscenities or other vulgar or immoral language in their books need not contact me." Query with SASE or submit proposal package including outline, 2 sample chapter(s), author bio, letter containing marketing plan. Reviews artwork/photos as part of ms package. Send photocopies.

Recent Title(s): *Quotable Rudy*, by Monte Carpenter ("Potent Quotables"); *Gentlemen Only*, by Robbie Williams and Lee Heffernan (Good Golf!).

Tips: "Send one proposal for one book at a time. If you send me a query listing three, four or more 'ideas' for books, I will immediately know that you lack the commitment needed to author a book. Send a SASE for anything you send me. I don't accept fiction unless you're a bestselling fiction author."

⊘ **TOY BOX PRODUCTIONS**, 7532 Hickory Hills Court, Whites Creek TN 37189. (615)299-0822. Fax: (615)876-3931. E-mail: leeann@crttoybox.com. Website: www.crttoybox.com. Estab. 1995. Publishes mass market paperback originals. **Publishes 4 titles/year. 100% of books from first-time authors; 100% from unagented writers. Pays 10-15% royalty on wholesale price.** Does not accept simultaneous submissions. Book catalog online.

• "We are not accepting new submissions at this time."

Nonfiction: Audiocassettes, biography, children's/juvenile. Subjects include Americana, education, religion. **All unsolicited mss returned unopened.**

Recent Title(s): *Holy Moses*, by Joe Loesch.

TRAFALGAR SQUARE PUBLISHING, P.O. Box 257, N. Pomfret VT 05053-0257. (802)457-1911. Fax: (802)457-1913. E-mail: tsquare@sover.net. Website: www.horseandriderbooks.com. Publisher: Caroline Robbins. **Acquisitions:** Martha Cook, managing editor. Estab. 1987. Publishes hardcover and trade paperback originals and reprints. **Publishes 10 titles/year. Pays royalty. Offers advance.** Responds in 2 months to queries.

O-π "We publish high quality instructional books for horsemen and horsewomen, always with the horse's welfare in mind."

Nonfiction: "We publish books for intermediate to advanced riders and horsemen." Subjects include animals (horses). "No stories, children's books or horse biographies." Query with SASE or submit proposal package including outline, 1-2 sample chapter(s), Letter of writer's qualifications and audience for book's subject.

Recent Title(s): *Horse Housing*, by Richard Klimesh and Cherry Hill; *Yoga for Equestrians*, by Linda Benedik; *Dressage Principles Illuminated*, by Charles de Kunffy.

TRAILS MEDIA GROUP, INC., (formerly Prairie Oak Press), P.O. Box 317, Black Earth WI 53515. (608)767-8000. Fax: (608)767-5444. E-mail: books@wistrails.com. Website: www.trailsbooks.com. Director: Anne McKenna. **Acquisitions:** Stan Stoga, acquisitions editor. Publishes hardcover originals, trade paperback originals and reprints. **Publishes 12 titles/year. Pays royalty. Offers advance.** Does not accept simultaneous submissions. Responds in 3 months to proposals.

Imprints: Prairie Classics, Acorn Guides, Trails Books, Prairie Oak Press.

O- Trails Media Group publishes exclusively Midwest regional nonfiction. Currently emphasizing travel, sports, recreation.

Nonfiction: "Any work considered must have a strong tie to Wisconsin and/or the Midwest region." Subjects include art/architecture, gardening, general nonfiction, history, regional, sports, travel, folklore, general trade subjects. No poetry or fiction. Query with SASE or submit outline, 1 sample chapter(s).

Tips: "When we say we publish regional works only, we mean Wisconsin, Minnesota, Michigan, Illinois, Iowa, Indiana. Please do not submit books of national interest. We cannot consider them."

TRANSNATIONAL PUBLISHERS, INC., 410 Saw Mill River Rd., Ardsley NY 10502. (914)693-5100. Fax: (914)693-4430. E-mail: info@transnationalpubs.com. Website: www.transnationalpubs.com. Publisher: Heike Fenton. **Acquisitions:** John Berger, VP/publishing director. Estab. 1980. **Publishes 45-50 titles/year. Receives 40-50 queries and 30 mss/year. 60% of books from first-time authors; 95% from unagented writers. Pays royalty.** Publishes book 6-9 months after acceptance of ms. Accepts simultaneous submissions. Responds in 1 month to queries. Book catalog and ms guidelines free.

O- "We provide specialized international law publications for the teaching of law and law-related subjects in law school classroom, clinic and continuing legal education settings." Currently emphasizing any area of international law that is considered a current issue/event.

Nonfiction: Reference, technical, textbook. Subjects include business/economics, government/politics, women's issues/studies, international law. Query with SASE or submit proposal package including sample chapter(s), table of contents and introduction.

Recent Title(s): *Media and Conflict*, by Etyan Gilboa; *Human Rights Protection for Refugees*, by Joan M. Fitzpatrick; *Reconciling Environment and Trade*, by Edith Brown Weiss and John Jackson.

TRAVELERS' TALES, 330 Townsend St., Suite 208, San Francisco CA 94107. (415)227-8600. Fax: (415)227-8600. E-mail: submit@travelerstales.com (submissions) or ttales@. Website: www.travelerstales.com. **Acquisitions:** James O'Reilly and Larry Habegger, series editors. Publishes anthologies, single author narratives, and consumer books. **Publishes 8-10 titles/year. Pays $100 honorarium for anthology pieces.** Accepts simultaneous submissions. Book catalog for SASE; ms guidelines online.

Imprints: Travelers' Tales Guides, Footsteps, Travelers' Tales Classics.

Nonfiction: Subjects include travel, personal nonfiction travel stories and consumer books.

Recent Title(s): *Travelers' Tales Tibet LC*, edited by James O'Reilly and Larry Habegger; *Sand in My Bra and Other Misadventures*, edited by Jennifer Leo.

Tips: "We publish personal, nonfiction stories and anecdotes—funny, illuminating, adventurous, frightening or grim. Stories should reflect that unique alchemy that occurs when you enter unfamiliar territory and begin to see the world differently as a result. Stories that have already been published, including book excerpts, are welcome as long as the authors retain the copyright or can obtain permission from the copyright holder to reprint the material. We do not publish fiction."

N **TREBLE HEART BOOKS**, 1284 Overlook Dr., Sierra Vista AZ 85635. (520)458-5602. Fax: (520)458-5618.Submissions E-mail: submissions@trebleheartbooks.com. Website: www.trebleheartbooks.com. **Acquisitions:** Lee Emory, owner/publisher (fiction, nonfiction, romance, mystery, suspense, paranormal, metaphysical, historical, Westerns, thrillers—no children's books). Estab. 2001. Publishes trade paperback originals and reprints (limited), and electronic originals. **Publishes 48 titles/year. Receives 500 queries and 1,000 mss/year. 50% of books from first-time authors; 90% from unagented writers. Pays 15-35% royalty on wholesale price or retail price.** Publishes book 6-8 months after acceptance of ms. Does not accept simultaneous submissions. Responds in 3 weeks to queries; 2 months to proposals; 3-4 months to mss. Ms guidelines online.

Imprints: MountainView (inspirational fiction and nonfiction, most faiths); Sundowners (Westerns).

Nonfiction: How-to, humor, self-help. Subjects include creative nonfiction, general nonfiction, health/medicine, New Age, psychology, religion, spirituality, women's issues/studies. "Writing skills must be top notch to make it here. We have 12 editors to serve. Study the guidelines and write in the lively, active voice with a fresh slant." Submit complete ms. Query by e-mail. Reviews artwork/photos as part of ms package. tiff or PDF files on CD or via e-mail.

Fiction: Adventure, fantasy, historical, horror, humor, mainstream/contemporary, mystery, occult, religious, romance, science fiction, short story collections, spiritual, suspense, western. "Follow our guidelines. Authors are encouraged to write outside of the box here, but traditional stories and plots are also accepted if handled with a fresh twist or approach." Submit proposal package including 3 sample chapter(s), synopsis or submit complete ms. Query by e-mail.

Recent Title(s): *Simple and Effective Career Management*, by Kathleen Wells, Ph.D. (career aid); *Heart Block*, by Soo Kim Abboud, M.D. (medical thriller).

Tips: "We love book lovers who want to be entertained or are interested in religion, spirituality (metaphysical) fiction and nonfiction. Ages from 13-100." "We accept unagented submissions, but do not accept hard copy manuscripts. All submissions must come to us via e-mail or attachment. We now require a 90-day exclusive to have time to move the manuscript through our reading staff before you submit elsewhere. Study and follow our guidelines and style sheets."

TRICYCLE PRESS, Ten Speed Press, P.O. Box 7123, Berkeley CA 94707. (510)559-1600. Website: www.tenspeed.com. **Acquisitions:** Nicole Geiger, publisher; Abigail Samoun, assistant editor. Estab. 1993. Publishes hardcover and trade paperback originals. **Publishes 18-20 titles/year. 20% of books from first-time authors; 60% from unagented writers. Pays 15-20% royalty on net receipts. Offers $0-9,000 advance.** Publishes book 1-2 years after acceptance of ms. Accepts simultaneous submissions. Responds in 2-4 weeks to queries; 4-6 months to mss. Book catalog and ms guidelines for 9×12 SAE with 3 first-class stamps.

O→ "Tricycle Press looks for something outside the mainstream; books that encourage children to look at the world from a possibly alternative angle. We have been trying to expand into the educational market and middle grade fiction."

Nonfiction: Biography, children's/juvenile, gift book, how-to, humor, illustrated book, self-help, picture books; activity books. Subjects include animals, art/architecture, creative nonfiction, film/cinema/stage, gardening, health/medicine, multicultural, music/dance, nature/environment, photography, science, travel, geography, math. Submit complete ms for activity books; 2-3 chapters or 20 pages for others. Reviews artwork/photos as part of ms package. Send photocopies.

Fiction: Young adult (middle grade novels). "One-off middle grade novels (no series)—quality fiction, 'tween fiction." Query with SASE. Board books and picture books: Submit complete ms. Middle grade books: Send complete outline and 2-3 sample chapters (ages 9-14). Query with synopsis and SASE for all others.

Recent Title(s): *Hey, Little Ant*, by Phillip and Hannah Hoose, illustrated by Debbie Tilley; *The Young Adventurer's Guide to Everest: From Avalanche to Zopkio*, by Jonathan Chester; *Don't Laugh at Me*, by Steve Seskin and Allen Shamblin, illustrated by Glin Dibley.

THE TRINITY FOUNDATION, PO Box 68, Unicoi TN 37692. (423)743-0199. Fax: (423)743-2005. E-mail: jrob1517@aol.com. Website: www.trinityfoundation.org. **Acquisitions:** John Robbins. Publishes hardcover and paperback originals and reprints. **Publishes 5 titles/year. Makes outright purchase of $1-1,500.** Publishes book 9 months after acceptance of ms. Responds in 1 month to queries; 1 month to proposals; 3 months to mss. Book catalog online.

Nonfiction: "Only books that confirm to the philosophy and theology of the Westminster Confession of Faith." Textbook. Subjects include business/economics, education, government/politics, history, philosophy, religion, science. Query with SASE. Very few unsolicited mss meet our requirements. Read at least 1 of our books before sending a query.

TRINITY PRESS INTERNATIONAL, 4775 Linglestown Rd., Harrisburg PA 17112. **Acquisitions:** Henry Carrigan, editorial director. Estab. 1989. Publishes trade paperback originals and reprints. **Publishes 40 titles/year. Pays 10% royalty on wholesale price. Offers advance.** Publishes book 9 months after acceptance of ms. Accepts simultaneous submissions. Book catalog free.

O→ Trinity Press International is an ecumenical publisher of serious books on theology and the Bible for the religious academic community, religious professionals, and serious book readers. Currently emphasizing religion and science, ethics, Biblical studies, film and religion, and religion and culture books.

Nonfiction: Textbook. Subjects include history (as relates to the Bible), religion, Christian/theological studies. Submit outline, 1 sample chapter(s).

Recent Title(s): *Dancing with the Sacred*, by Karl Peters.

TRIUMPH BOOKS, 601 S. LaSalle St., Suite 500, Chicago IL 60605. (312)939-3330. Fax: (312)663-3557. Website: www.triumphbooks.com. **Acquisitions:** Thomas Bast, editorial director (sports). Publishes hardcover originals and trade paperback originals and reprints. **Publishes 24-30 titles/year. Receives 300 queries and 150 mss/year. 25% of books from first-time authors; 40% from unagented writers. Pays 10-20% royalty on wholesale price. Offers $3,000-50,000 advance.** Publishes book 1 year after acceptance of ms. Accepts simultaneous submissions. Responds in 1 month to queries; 2 months to proposals; 2 months to mss. Book catalog free.

Nonfiction: Biography, coffee table book, gift book, humor, illustrated book. Subjects include recreation, sports, health, sports business/motivation. Query with SASE or submit proposal package including outline, 1-2 sample chapter(s). Reviews artwork/photos as part of ms package. Send photocopies.

Recent Title(s): *Competitive Leadership*, by Brian Billick with James A. Peterson, Ph.D.; *Few and Chosen*, by Whitey Ford with Phil Pope.

TRUMAN STATE UNIVERSITY PRESS, 100 E. Normal St., Kirksville MO 63501-4221. (660)785-7336. Fax: (660)785-4480. E-mail: tsup@truman.edu. Website: tsup.truman.edu. **Acquisitions:** Paula Presley, director/editor-in-chief (nonfiction); Nancy Rediger (contemporary narrative poetry); Raymond Mentzer (early modern history). **Publishes 8-10 titles/year. Pays 7% royalty on net receipts.** Ms guidelines online.

Nonfiction: Biography, illustrated book, textbook, monographs; early modern. Subjects include Americana, history (early modern), art history, literature.

Recent Title(s): *Surely as Birds Fly*, by H.L. Hix; *Werewolves, Witches, and Wandering Spirits*, edited by Kathryn A. Edwards; *Victorian America*, by Margaret Baker Graham.

TURTLE BOOKS, 866 United Nations Plaza, Suite #525, New York NY 10017. (212)644-2020. Fax: (212)223-4387. Website: www.turtlebooks.com. **Acquisitions:** John Whitman, publisher (children's picture books). Publishes hardcover and trade paperback originals. **Publishes 6-8 titles/year. Receives 1,000 mss/year. 25% of books from first-time authors; 50% from unagented writers. Pays royalty on retail price. Offers advance.** Publishes book 12 months after acceptance of ms. Accepts simultaneous submissions.

O→ Turtle Books publishes children's picture books.

Nonfiction: Children's/juvenile, illustrated book. Subjects include animals, education, history, language/literature, multicultural, nature/environment, regional, Any subject suitable for a children's picture book. Submit complete ms. Reviews artwork/photos as part of ms package. Send photocopies, no original art.

Fiction: Adventure, ethnic, fantasy, historical, multicultural, regional, sports, western. Subjects suitable for children's picture books. "We are looking for good stories which can be illustrated as children's picture books." Submit complete ms.

Poetry: Must be suitable for an illustrated children's book format. Submit complete ms.

Recent Title(s): *Keeper of the Swamp*, by Ann Garrett; *The Crab Man*, by Patricia Van West; *Alphabet Fiesta*, by Anne Miranda (children's picture books).

Tips: "Our preference is for stories rather than concept books. We will consider only children's picture book manuscripts."

TURTLE PRESS, S.K. Productions, P.O. Box 290206, Wethersfield CT 06129-0206. (860)721-1198. Fax: (860)529-7775. E-mail: editorial@turtlepress.com. Website: www.turtlepress.com. **Acquisitions:** Cynthia Kim, editor. Publishes hardcover originals, trade paperback originals and reprints. **Publishes 4-8 titles/year. Pays 8-10% royalty. Offers $500-1,500 advance.** Accepts simultaneous submissions. Responds in 1 month to queries. Ms guidelines online.

O→ Turtle Press publishes sports and martial arts nonfiction for a specialty niche audience. Currently emphasizing martial arts, eastern philosophy. De-emphasizing self-help.

Nonfiction: How-to, self-help. Subjects include philosophy, sports, martial arts. "We prefer tightly targeted topics on which there is little or no information available in the market, particularly for our sports and martial arts titles." Query with SASE. Query with SASE.

Recent Title(s): *Warrior Speed*, by Ted Weimann; *The Art of Harmony*, by Sang H. Kim; *Fighting Science*, by Martina Sprague.

TUTTLE PUBLISHING, 153 Milk St., 4th Floor, Boston MA 02109. Publishing Director: Ed Walters. **Acquisitions:** Editorial Acquisitions. Estab. 1832. Publishes hardcover and trade paperback originals and reprints. **Publishes 125 titles/year. Receives 1,000 queries/year. 20% of books from first-time authors; 40% from unagented writers. Pays 5-10% royalty on net or retail price, depending on format and kind of book. Offers advance.** Publishes book 18 months after acceptance of ms. Accepts simultaneous submissions. Responds in 4 months to proposals.

O→ "Tuttle is America's leading publisher of books on Japan and Asia."

Nonfiction: Self-help. Subjects include ethnic, health/medicine, philosophy (Eastern), religion (Eastern), Taoist. Query with SASE or submit outline. Cannot guarantee return of ms.

Recent Title(s): *Zen Master Raven*, by Robert Aitken; *Bruce Lee: The Celebrated Life of the Golden Dragon*, by John Little; *Haiku: Poetry Ancient and Modern*, by Jackie Hardy.

[A] **TWENTY-FIRST CENTURY BOOKS**, Millbrook Press, 2 Old New Milford Rd., Brookfield CT 06804. (203)740-2220. Executive Vice President/Publisher: Jean Reynolds. Editor in Chief: Amy Shields. Senior Editor: Kristen Bettcher. **Acquisitions:** Ben Tomek, manuscript coordinator. Publishes hardcover originals. **Publishes 40 titles/year. Receives 200 queries and 50 mss/year. 20% of books from first-time authors. Pays 5-8% royalty. Offers advance.** Publishes book 18 months after acceptance of ms. Does not accept simultaneous submissions.

O→ Twenty-First Century Books publishes nonfiction science, technology and social issues titles for children and young adults. "We no longer accept unsolicited manuscripts. Agented submissions only, please."

Nonfiction: Children's/juvenile, young adult. Subjects include government/politics, health/medicine, history, military/war, nature/environment, science, current events, social issues. "We publish primarily in series of four or more titles, for ages 12 and up, and single titles for grades 7 and up. No picture books, fiction or adult books." *Agented submissions only.*

Recent Title(s): *Global Warming*; *The War on Hunger.*

TWO DOT, imprint of The Globe Pequot Press., 825 Great Northern Blvd., Suites 327 & 328, Helena MT 59601. (406)442-6597. Fax: (406)457-5461. Website: www.globepequot.com. **Acquisitions:** Erin Turner, executive editor. Publishes hardcover and trade paperback originals. **Publishes 20 titles/year. 30% of books from first-time authors; 80% from unagented writers. Pays royalty on net price.** Accepts simultaneous submissions. Responds in 3 months to queries. Book catalog online; ms guidelines online.

O→ "Two Dot looks for lively writing for a popular audience, well-researched, on regional themes." Currently emphasizing popular history, western history, regional history, biography collections, western Americana. De-emphasizing scholarly writings, children's books, memoirs fiction, poetry.

Nonfiction: Subjects include Americana (western), history, regional. Three state-by-state series of interest: *More than Petticoats* (notable women); *It Happened In ...* (state histories); and *Outlaw Tales* (by state). Submit outline, 1-2 sample chapter(s), SASE. Reviews artwork/photos as part of ms package. Send photocopies.

Recent Title(s): *Love Untamed: Romances of the Old West*, by Chris Enss and Jo Ann Chartier; *Sacagawea Speaks*, by Joyce Badgley Hunsaker; *It Happened in the Civil War*, by Michael R. Bradley.

⊘ **TYNDALE HOUSE PUBLISHERS, INC.**, 351 Executive Dr., Carol Stream IL 60188. (630)668-8300. Website: www.tyndale.com. **Acquisitions:** Manuscript Review Committee. Estab. 1962. Publishes hardcover and trade paperback originals and mass paperback reprints. **Publishes 225-250 titles/year. 5% of books from first-time authors. Pays negotiable royalty. Offers negotiable advance.** Publishes book 9 months after acceptance of ms. Accepts simultaneous submissions. Responds in 3 months to queries; 6 months to mss. Ms guidelines for 9X12 SAE and $2.40 for postage or visit website.

O→ Tyndale House publishes "practical, user-friendly Christian books for the home and family."

Nonfiction: Children's/juvenile, self-help (Christian growth). Subjects include child guidance/parenting, religion, devotional/inspirational, theology/Bible doctrine, contemporary/critical issues. Prefers agented submissions. Query with SASE or submit outline. *No unsolicited mss.*

Fiction: Romance, Christian (children's, general, inspirational, mystery/suspense, thriller, romance). Prefers agented submissions. Should read romance (historical, contemporary), suspense, historical and contemporary. Christian truths must be woven into the story organically. No short story collections. Youth books: character building stories with Christian perspective. Especially interested in ages 10-14. "We primarily publish Christian historical romances, with occasional contemporary, suspense or standalones." No short story collections. Query with SASE or submit outline, 3 sample chapter(s), synopsis. *No unsolicited mss.*

Recent Title(s): *The Absolutes*, by James Robison; *Apocalypse Dawn*, by Mel Odom; *Into the Nevernight*, by Anne DeGraof.

[N] TZIPORA PUBLICATIONS, INC., 175 E. 96 St., #10-O, New York NY 10128. (212)427-5399. Fax: (413)638-9158. E-mail: tziporapub@msn.com. **Acquisitions:** Dina Grossman, publisher (success stories of immigrants in the U.S.). Estab. 2002. Publishes hardcover, trade paperback, mass market paperback, and electronic originals. **Publishes 7 titles/year. Receives 30 queries and 2 mss/year. 90% of books from first-time authors; 100% from unagented writers. Pays 10-15% royalty. Offers $1,000 advance.** Publishes book 6 months after acceptance of ms. Accepts simultaneous submissions. Responds in 1 month to queries; 1 month to proposals; 2 months to mss. Book catalog for #10 SASE; ms guidelines for #10 SASE.

Nonfiction: Subjects include community, contemporary culture, creative nonfiction, general nonfiction, government/politics, humanities, memoirs, multicultural, philosophy, psychology, religion, social sciences, translation, women's issues/studies, world affairs, fundamentalism. "We will be concentrating on books about successes and universal opportunities immigrants find in America. Please see *Kane & Abel* by J. Archer as an example." Query with SASE or submit proposal package including outline, 1-3 sample chapter(s), author bio. Reviews artwork/photos as part of ms package. Send photocopies or color copies, e-mail attachments.

Fiction: Fiction-based or real stories. "We will be concentrating on books about successes and universal opportunities immigrants find in America. Please see *Kane & Abel* by J. Archer as an example." Query with SASE or submit proposal package including 1-3 sample chapter(s), synopsis, author bio.

Recent Title(s): *How We Returned To Egypt*, by Dina Grossman.

Tips: "Our audience is anyone who needs inspiration in order to move ahead in life. The hero of the stories will be introduced to the public in numerous ways." "Just do it!"

[N] UAHC PRESS, 633 Third Ave., New York NY 10017-6778. (212)650-4120. Fax: (212)650-4119. E-mail: press@uahc.org. Website: www.uahcpress.com. **Acquisitions:** Rabbi Hara Person, editor (subjects related to Judaism). Publishes hardcover and trade paperback originals. **Publishes 22 titles/year. Receives 500 queries and 400 mss/year. 70% of books from first-time authors; 90% from unagented writers. Pays 3-5% royalty on retail price or makes outright purchase of $500-2,000. Offers $500-2,000 advance.** Publishes book 9 months after acceptance of ms. Does not accept simultaneous submissions. Responds in 2 months to queries; 6 months to proposals; 6 months to mss. Book catalog and ms guidelines free or on website.

O→ UAHC Press publishes books related to Judaism.

Nonfiction: Biography, children's/juvenile, coffee table book, cookbook, gift book, how-to, illustrated book, multimedia (CD), reference, textbook. Subjects include art/architecture (synagogue), child guidance/parenting (Jewish), cooking/foods/nutrition (Jewish), education (Jewish), ethnic (Judaism), government/politics, history (Jewish), language/literature (Hebrew), military/war (as relates to Judaism), music/dance, nature/environment, philosophy (Jewish), religion (Judaism only), sex (as it relates to Judaism), spirituality (Jewish). Submit proposal package including outline, 1-2 sample chapter(s), author bio.

Fiction: Jewish, liberal content. Picture book length only. Juvenile, children's picture books. Submit complete ms with author bio.

Recent Title(s): *Talmud for Everyday Living: Employer-Employee Relations*, by Hillel Gamoran (nonfiction); *The Gift of Wisdom*, by Steven E. Steinbock (textbook for grades 5-7); *Solomon and the Trees*, by Matt Biers-Ariel (picture book).

Tips: "Look at some of our books. Have an understanding of the Reform Judaism community. In addition to bookstores, we sell to Jewish congregations and Hebrew day schools."

UCLA AMERICAN INDIAN STUDIES CENTER, 3220 Campbell Hall, Box 951548, UCLA, Los Angeles CA 90095-1548. (310)825-7315. Fax: (310)206-7060. E-mail: aiscpubs@ucla.edu. Website: www.sscnet.ucla.edu/indian. **Acquisitions:** Hanay Geiogamah, interim director. Estab. 1979. Publishes hardcover and trade paperback originals. **Publishes 4 titles/year. Receives 10 queries and 8 mss/year. 60% of books from first-time authors; 100% from unagented writers. Pays 8% royalty on retail price.** Publishes book 8-12 months after acceptance of ms. Accepts simultaneous submissions. Responds in 2 months to queries; 3 months to mss. Book catalog and ms guidelines free and on website.

O→ "We publish nonfiction, fiction and poetry by and about Native Americans. We publish the *American Indian Culture and Research Journal*, which accepts poetry submissions.

Nonfiction: Reference, scholarly. Subjects include Americana, anthropology/archeology, ethnic, government/politics, health/medicine, history, language/literature, multicultural, religion, sociology, contemporary culture. Submit proposal package including outline, 2 sample chapter(s). Reviews artwork/photos as part of ms package. Send photocopies.

Fiction: Ethnic, literary, plays, poetry, religious, short story collections, American Indian. Submit proposal package including synopsis or submit complete ms. cover letter.

Poetry: Query or submit complete ms.

Recent Title(s): *Songs from an Outcast*; *Indian Gaming: Who Wins?*; *A Sacred Path: The Way of the Muscogee Creeks.*

N **UNION SQUARE PUBLISHING**, Cardoza Publishing, 857 Broadway, 3rd Floor, New York NY 10003. E-mail: carissa@cardozapub.com. **Acquisitions:** Carissa Alden, acquisitions editor (biographies, word books, cultural studies); Michelle Knoetgen, acquisitions editor (sports, athletics, general nonfiction). Estab. 2002. Publishes hardcover originals, trade paperback originals and reprints, mass market paperback originals. **Publishes 5-10 titles/year. Receives 10 queries and 5 mss/year. 80% of books from first-time authors; 95% from unagented writers. Pays 5-6% royalty on retail price. Offers $1,000-10,000 advance.** Publishes book 7 months after acceptance of ms. Accepts simultaneous submissions. Responds in 1-2 months to queries; 1-2 months to proposals; 2-3 months to mss. Ms guidelines by email.

Nonfiction: Autobiography, biography, cookbook, how-to, self-help. Subjects include anthropology/archeology, community, contemporary culture, cooking/foods/nutrition, education, ethnic, general nonfiction, government/politics, history, hobbies, humanities, language/literature, memoirs, multicultural, music/dance, nature/environment, philosophy, recreation, religion, social sciences, sociology, spirituality, sports, translation. "Union Square Publishing is a new imprint of a long-established company, and we have yet to determine the exact role it will fill in the publishing world. We began by publishing books on writing, words, and language. We are looking to do more similar projects, but we would be happy to consider any interesting nonfiction proposals we receive." Query with SASE or submit complete ms. Reviews artwork/photos as part of ms package. Send photocopies.

Fiction: Fantasy, feminist, literary, mainstream/contemporary, military/war, multicultural, mystery, religious, science fiction, short story collections, spiritual, sports, translation, western. "As our budget for fiction proposals is limited, we would prefer not to receive particularly experimental or unusual manuscripts—we simply don't have the resources to handle them." Query with SASE or submit proposal package including 1-2 sample chapter(s), credentials.

Recent Title(s): *The Complete Guide to Successful Publishing*, by Avery Cardoza (how-to); *Word Master*, by J.G. Barton (language).

Tips: "Audience is word lovers, aspiring publishers, bibliophiles. Potentially the general market, depending on what other titles we publish in the future."

UNITY HOUSE, Unity School of Christianity, 1901 NW Blue Parkway, Unity Village MO 64065-0001. (816)524-3550 ext. 3190. Fax: (816)251-3552. Website: www.unityworldhq.org. **Acquisitions:** Michael Maday, editor. Estab. 1903. Publishes hardcover and trade paperback originals and reprints. **Publishes 16 titles/year. Receives 500 submissions/year. 30% of books from first-time authors; 95% from unagented writers. Pays 10-15% royalty on net receipts. Offers advance.** Publishes book 13 months after acceptance of ms. Does not accept simultaneous submissions. Responds in 2 weeks to queries; 2 weeks to proposals; 1 month to mss. Book catalog free; ms guidelines online.

O→ "Unity House publishes metaphysical Christian books based on Unity principles, as well as inspirational books on metaphysics and practical spirituality. All manuscripts must reflect a spiritual foundation and express the Unity philosophy, practical Christianity, universal principles, and/or metaphysics."

Nonfiction: "Writers should be familiar with principles of metaphysical Christianity but not feel bound by them. We are interested in works in the related fields of holistic health, spiritual psychology and the philosophy of other world religions." Reference (spiritual/metaphysical), self-help, inspirational. Subjects include health/medicine (holistic), philosophy (perennial/New Thought), psychology (transpersonal), religion (spiritual/metaphysical Bible interpretation/modern Biblical studies). Query with book proposal, including cover letter, summarizing unique features and suggested sales and marketing strategies, toc or project outline and 1-3 sample chapters with SASE. Reviews artwork/photos as part of ms package. Send photocopies.

Fiction: Juvenile, picture books, spiritual, young adult, visionary fiction, inspirtational, metaphysical. Query with SASE.

Recent Title(s): *Looking In For Number One*, by Alan Cohen; *The Vortex Shift*, by Mario DeFerrari.

THE UNIVERSITY OF AKRON PRESS, 374B Bierce Library, Akron OH 44325-1703. (330)972-5342. Fax: (330)972-8364. E-mail: uapress@uakron.edu. Website: www.uakron.edu/uapress. **Acquisitions:** Michael Carley, director. Estab. 1988. Publishes hardcover and trade paperback originals. **Publishes 8-12 titles/year. Receives 400-500 queries and 100 mss/year. 40% of books from first-time authors; 100% from unagented writers. Pays 5-10% royalty. Offers (possible) advance.** Publishes book 10-12 months after acceptance of ms. Responds in 2 months to queries; 2 months to proposals; 3 months to mss. Book catalog free; ms guidelines online.

O→ "The University of Akron Press strives to be the University's ambassador for scholarship and creative writing at the national and international levels." Currently emphasizing technology and the environment, Ohio history and culture, poetry, history of law, political science, and international, political, and economic history. De-emphasizing fiction.

Nonfiction: Scholarly. Subjects include history, regional, science, environment, technology, law, political science. "We publish mostly in our four nonfiction series: Technology and the Environment; Ohio History and Culture; Law, Politics and Society, and International, Political, and Economic History." Query with SASE. Reviews artwork/photos as part of ms package. Send photocopies.

Poetry: Follow the guidelines and submit manuscripts only for the contest. www.uakron.edu/uapress/poetry.html.

Recent Title(s): *The Holden Arboretum*, by Steve Love and Ian Adams; *The Good Kiss*, by George Bilgere.

Tips: "We have mostly an audience of general educated readers, with a more specialized audience of public historians, sociologists and political scientists for the scholarly series."

UNIVERSITY OF ALABAMA PRESS, P.O. Box 870380, Tuscaloosa AL 35487-0380. (205)348-5180. Fax: (205)348-9201. Website: www.uapress.ua.edu. **Acquisitions:** Daniel J.J. Ross, director (American history, southern history and culture, American military history, American religious history, Latin American history, Jewish studies); Daniel Waterman, acquisitions editor for humanities (American literature and criticism, rhetoric and communication, literary journalism, African-American studies, women's studies, public administration, theater, natural history and environmental studies, regional studies, including regional trade titles); Judith Knight, acquisition editor (American archaeology, southeastern archaeology, Caribbean archaeology, historical archaeology, ethnohistory, anthropology). Estab. 1945. Publishes nonfiction hardcover and paperbound originals and fiction paperback reprints. **Publishes 55-60 titles/year. Receives 400 submissions/year. 70% of books from first-time authors; 95% from unagented writers. Offers advance.** Publishes book 1 year after acceptance of ms. Responds in 2 weeks to queries. Book catalog free; ms guidelines for #10 SASE.

Nonfiction: Biography, scholarly. Subjects include anthropology/archeology, community, government/politics, history, language/literature, religion, translation. Considers upon merit almost any subject of scholarly interest, but specializes in communications, military history, political science and public administration, literary criticism and biography, history, Jewish studies and archaeology of the Southeastern US. Accepts nonfiction translations. Query with SASE. Reviews artwork/photos as part of ms package.

Fiction: Reprints of works by contemporary Southern writers.

Tips: Please direct inquiry to appropriate acquisitions editor. University of Alabama Press responds to an author within 2 weeks upon receiving the manuscript. If they think it is unsuitable for Alabama's program, they tell the author at once. If the manuscript warrants it, they begin the peer-review process, which may take two to four months to complete. During that process, they keep the author fully informed.

[N] **UNIVERSITY OF ALASKA PRESS**, P.O. Box 756240, UAF, Fairbanks AK 99775-6240. (907)474-5831 or (888)252-6657 toll free in US. Fax: (907)474-5502. E-mail: fypress@uaf.edu. Website: www.uaf.edu/uapress. Estab. 1967. Publishes hardcover originals, trade paperback originals and reprints. **Publishes 5-10 titles/year. Receives 100 submissions/year. Pays 7½-10% royalty on net receipts.** Publishes book within 2 years after acceptance of ms. Does not accept simultaneous submissions. Responds in 2 months to queries. Book catalog free; ms guidelines online.

Imprints: Classic Reprints, LanternLight Library, Oral Biographies, Rasmuson Library Historical Translation Series.

O→ "The mission of the University of Alaska Press is to encourage, publish and disseminate works of scholarship that will enhance the store of knowledge about Alaska and the North Pacific Rim, with a special emphasis on the circumpolar regions."

Nonfiction: Biography, reference, technical, textbook, Scholarly nonfiction relating to Alaska-circumpolar regions. Subjects include agriculture/horticulture, Americana (Alaskana), animals, anthropology/archeology, art/architecture, education, ethnic, government/politics, health/medicine, history, language/literature, military/war, nature/environment, regional, science, translation, women's issues/studies. Nothing that isn't northern or circumpolar. Query with SASE or submit outline. Reviews artwork/photos as part of ms package.

Recent Title(s): *Alaska Natives & American Laws, 2nd Ed*, by David Case and David Voluck; *Yukon Relief Expedition*, by V.L. Rausch and D.L. Baldwin; *Ice Window: Letters from a Bering Strait Village*, by Kathleen Lopp Smith and Verbeck Smith.

Tips: "Writers have the best chance with scholarly nonfiction relating to Alaska, the circumpolar regions and North Pacific Rim. Our audience is made up of scholars, historians, students, libraries, universities, individuals and the general Alaskan public."

[N] **UNIVERSITY OF ARIZONA PRESS**, 355 S. Euclid Ave., Suite 103, Tucson AZ 85719-6654. (520)621-1441. Fax: (520)621-8899. E-mail: uapress@uapress.arizona.edu. Website: www.uapress.arizona.edu. **Acquisitions:** Christine Szuter, director; Patti Hartmann, senior editor. Estab. 1959. Publishes hardcover and paperback originals and reprints. **Publishes 50 titles/year. Receives 300-400 submissions/year. 30% of books from first-time authors; 95% from unagented writers. Royalty terms vary; usual starting point for scholarly monography is after sale of first 1,000 copies. Offers advance.** Publishes book 1 year after acceptance of ms. Does not accept simultaneous submissions. Responds in 3 months to queries. Book catalog available via website or upon request; ms guidelines online.

- *Blue Horses Rush In*, by Luci Tapahonso was the winner of the 1998 MPBA Regional Poetry Award.

O→ "University of Arizona is a publisher of scholarly books and books of the Southwest."

Nonfiction: Subjects include Americana, anthropology/archeology, ethnic, nature/environment, regional, science, women's issues/studies, western and environmental history. Scholarly books about anthropology, Arizona, American West, archaeology, Native American studies, Latino studies, environmental science, global change, Latin America, Native Americans, natural history, space sciences and women's studies. Query with SASE or submit sample chapter(s), résumé. Current Curriculum Vitae. Reviews artwork/photos as part of ms package.

Recent Title(s): *Speaking for the Generations*, Simon Ortiz (Native American studies).

Tips: "Perhaps the most common mistake a writer might make is to offer a book manuscript or proposal to a house whose list he or she has not studied carefully. Editors rejoice in receiving material that is clearly targeted to the house's list, 'I have approached your firm because my books complement your past publications in—... ,' presented in a straightforward, businesslike manner."

THE UNIVERSITY OF ARKANSAS PRESS, 201 Ozark Ave., Fayetteville AR 72701-1201. (479)575-3246. Fax: (479)575-6044. E-mail: uaprinfo@cavern.uark.edu. Website: www.uapress.com. **Acquisitions:** Lawrence J. Malley, director and editor-in-chief. Estab. 1980. Publishes hardcover and trade paperback originals and reprints. **Publishes 30 titles/year. Receives 1,000 submissions/year. 30% of books from first-time authors; 95% from unagented writers. Pays royalty on net receipts.** Publishes book 1 year after acceptance of ms. Responds in 3 months to proposals. Book catalog and ms guidelines on website or on request.

O→ The University of Arkansas Press publishes series on Ozark studies, the Civil War in the West, poetry and poetics, and sport and society.

Nonfiction: Subjects include government/politics, history (Southern), humanities, nature/environment, regional, Arkansas,

African-American studies, Middle Eastern studies, poetry/poetics. Accepted mss must be submitted on disk. Query with SASE or submit outline, sample chapter(s), résumé.

Recent Title(s): *Breach of Faith*; *Architects of Globalism.*

[N] **UNIVERSITY OF CALIFORNIA PRESS**, 2120 Berkeley Way, Berkeley CA 94720. (510)642-4247. Website: www.ucpress.edu. Director: Lynne E. Withey. **Acquisitions:** Reed Malcolm, editor (religion and Asian studies); Doris Kretschmer, executive editor (natural history, biology); Deborah Kirshman, editor (art); Sheila Levine, editorial director; Monica McCormick, editor (African studies, history); Naomi Schneider, executive editor (sociology, politics, gender studies); Blake Edgar, editor (science); Linda Norton, editor (poetry); Stephanie Fay, editor (art); Stan Holwitz, editor (anthropology, sociology); Laura Cerruti, editor (poetry); Mary Francis, editor (music, film). Estab. 1893. Publishes hardcover and paperback originals and reprints. **Publishes 180 titles/year. Offers advance.** Response time varies, depending on the subject. Enclose return postage to queries. Ms guidelines online.

- University of California Press publishes mostly hardcover nonfiction written by scholars.

Nonfiction: Scholarly. Subjects include history, language/literature, nature/environment, social sciences, translation, art, studies, social sciences, natural sciences, some high-level popularizations. No length preference. Query with SASE.

Fiction: Publishes fiction only in translation.

Recent Title(s): *The Commercialization of Intimate Life*, by Arlie Hochschild; *Pathologies of Power*, by Paul Farmer; *Late Beethoven*, by Maynard Solomon.

[N] **UNIVERSITY OF GEORGIA PRESS**, 330 Research Dr., Athens GA 30602-4901. (706)369-6130. Fax: (706)369-6131. E-mail: books@ugapress.uga.edu. Website: www.ugapress.org. Estab. 1938. Publishes hardcover originals, trade paperback originals and reprints. **Publishes 85 titles/year. Receives 600 queries/year. 33% of books from first-time authors; 66% from unagented writers. Pays 7-10% royalty on net receipts. Offers rare, varying advance.** Publishes book 1 year after acceptance of ms. Does not accept simultaneous submissions. Responds in 2 months to queries. Book catalog and ms guidelines for #10 SASE; ms guidelines online.

Nonfiction: Biography. Subjects include government/politics, history (American), nature/environment, regional, environmental studies, literary nonfiction. Query with SASE or submit 1 sample chapter(s), author bio, Reviews artwork/photos as part of ms package. Send if essential to book.

Fiction: Short story collections published in Flannery O'Connor Award Competition. Query #10 SASE for guidelines and submission periods. Charges $20 submission fee. "No phone calls accepted."

Poetry: Published only through contemporary poetry series competition. Query first for guidelines and submission periods. Charges $20 submission fee. #10 SASE for guidelines.

Recent Title(s): *Deep in Our Hearts: Nine White Women in the Freedom Movement*, by Connie Curry et al; *As Eve Said to the Serpent: On Landscape, Gender and Art*, by Rebecca Solnit; *Big Bend*, by Bill Roorbach.

UNIVERSITY OF IDAHO PRESS, P.O. Box 444416, Moscow ID 83844-4416. (208)885-3300. Fax: (208)885-3301. E-mail: uipress@uidaho.edu. Website: www.uidaho.edu/uipress. **Acquisitions:** Ivar Nelson, director. Estab. 1972. Publishes hardcover and trade paperback originals and reprints. **Publishes 8-10 titles/year. Receives 150-250 queries and 25-50 mss/year. 100% from unagented writers. Pays 10% royalty on net receipts. Offers occasional advance.** Publishes book 1 year after acceptance of ms. Accepts simultaneous submissions. Responds in 6 months to queries. Book catalog and ms guidelines free; ms guidelines online.

- Major genre published by the Press include the history of Idaho, the northern Rocky Mountains and the region; the natural history of the same area; Native American culture and history; mining history; Hemingway studies; Idaho human rights series; ecological literary criticism, resource and policy studies; and literature of the region and the West.

Nonfiction: Biography, reference, technical, textbook. Subjects include Americana, anthropology/archeology, ethnic, history, language/literature, nature/environment, recreation, regional, women's issues/studies, folklore. "Writers should contact us to discuss projects in advance. Be aware of the constraints of scholarly publishing, and avoid submitting queries and manuscripts in areas in which the press doesn't publish." Query with SASE or submit proposal package including sample chapter(s), contents and vita. Reviews artwork/photos as part of ms package. Send photocopies.

Recent Title(s): *Lewis and Clark's Mountain Wilds*, by Sharon A. Ritter; *Rediscovering Vardis Fisher*, by Joseph M. Flora.

UNIVERSITY OF ILLINOIS PRESS, 1325 S. Oak St., Champaign IL 61820-6903. (217)333-0950. Fax: (217)244-8082. E-mail: sears@uillinois.edu. Website: www.press.uillinois.edu. **Acquisitions:** Willis Regier, director (literature, classics, music, military history); Joan Catapano, associate director and editor-in-chief (women's studies, film, African American studies); Elizabeth Dulany (American religion, anthropology, western history, Native American studies); Laurie Matheson (American history, labor history, American studies); Richard Wentworth (sport history). Estab. 1918. Publishes hardcover and trade paperback originals and reprints. **Publishes 150 titles/year. 50% of books from first-time authors; 95% from unagented writers. Pays 0-10% royalty on net receipts. Offers $1,000-1,500 (rarely) advance.** Publishes book 1 year after acceptance of ms. Responds in 1 month to queries. Book catalog for 9 × 12 SAE with 2 first-class stamps; ms guidelines online.

- University of Illinois Press publishes "scholarly books and serious nonfiction" with a wide range of study interests. Currently emphasizing American history, especially immigration, labor, African American, and military; American religion, music, women's studies, and film.

Nonfiction: Biography, reference, scholarly, scholarly. Subjects include Americana, animals, cooking/foods/nutrition, government/politics, history (especially American history), language/literature, military/war, music/dance (especially American music), philosophy, regional, sociology, sports, translation, film/cinema/stage. Always looking for "solid, scholarly books in American history, especially social history; books on American popular music, and books in the broad area of American studies." Query with SASE or submit outline.

Recent Title(s): *Thermin: Ether Music and Espionage*, by Albert Glinsky (nonfiction); *Fanny Herself*, by Edna Ferber (fiction); *Songs from Michael Tree*, by Michael Harper (poetry).

Tips: "Serious scholarly books that are broad enough and well-written enough to appeal to nonspecialists are doing well for us in today's market."

UNIVERSITY OF IOWA PRESS, 119 W. Park Rd., Iowa City IA 52242-1000. (319)335-2000. Fax: (319)335-2055. Website: www.uiowa.edu/uiowapress. **Acquisitions:** Holly Carver, director; Prasenjit Gupta, acquisitions editor. Estab. 1969. Publishes hardcover and paperback originals. **Publishes 35 titles/year. Receives 300-400 submissions/year. 30% of books from first-time authors; 95% from unagented writers. Pays 7-10% royalty on net receipts.** Publishes book 1 year after acceptance of ms. Responds in within 6 months to queries. Book catalog free; ms guidelines online.

O⇁ "We publish authoritative, original nonfiction that we market mostly by direct mail to groups with special interests in our titles and by advertising in trade and scholarly publications."

Nonfiction: Subjects include anthropology/archeology, creative nonfiction, history (regional), language/literature, nature/environment, American literary studies. Looks for evidence of original research; reliable sources; clarity of organization; complete development of theme with documentation, supportive footnotes and/or bibliography; and a substantive contribution to knowledge in the field treated. Use *Chicago Manual of Style*. Query with SASE or submit outline. Reviews artwork/photos as part of ms package.

Fiction: Currently publishes the Iowa Short Fiction Award selections. Competition guidelines available on website. See Competition and Awards section for further information.

Poetry: Currently publishes winners of the Iowa Poetry Prize Competition, Kuhl House Poets, poetry anthologies. Competition guidelines available on website.

Recent Title(s): *Embalming Mom: Essays in Life*, by Janet Burroway.

Tips: "Developing a series in creative nonfiction."

UNIVERSITY OF MAINE PRESS, 126A College Ave., Orono ME 04473. (207)866-0573. Fax: (207)866-2084. E-mail: umpress@umit.maine.edu. Website: www.umaine.edu/umpress. **Acquisitions:** Editorial Director. Publishes hardcover and trade paperback originals and reprints. **Publishes 4 titles/year. Receives 50 queries and 25 mss/year. 50% of books from first-time authors; 90% from unagented writers.** Publishes book 1 year after acceptance of ms.

Nonfiction: Scholarly. Subjects include history, regional, science. "We are an academic book publisher, interested in scholarly works on regional history, regional life sciences, Franco-American studies. Authors should be able to articulate their ideas on the potential market for their work." Query with SASE.

Recent Title(s): *Maine Amphibians and Reptiles*, by Hunter, Calhoun, et al; *Finding Katahdin, An Exploration of Maine's Past*, by Amy Hassinger.

UNIVERSITY OF MISSOURI PRESS, 2910 LeMone Blvd., Columbia MO 65201. (573)882-7641. Fax: (573)884-4498. Website: www.system.missouri.edu/upress. **Acquisitions:** (Mr.) Clair Willcox, acquisitions editor; Beverly Jarrett, editor-in-chief (American history, political philosophy, intellectual history, women's studies, African-American studies). Estab. 1958. Publishes hardcover and paperback originals and paperback reprints. **Publishes 60 titles/year. Receives 500 submissions/year. 40-50% of books from first-time authors; 90% from unagented writers. Pays up to 10% royalty on net receipts.** Publishes book within 1 year after acceptance of ms. immediately to queries; 3 months to mss. Book catalog free; ms guidelines online.

O⇁ University of Missouri Press publishes primarily scholarly nonfiction in the humanities and social sciences. Currently emphasizing American history, political philosophy, literary criticism, African-American studies, women's studies.

Nonfiction: Scholarly. Subjects include history (American), regional (studies of Missouri and the Midwest), social sciences, women's issues/studies, political philosophy, African American studies. Consult *Chicago Manual of Style*. No mathematics or hard sciences. Query with SASE or submit outline, sample chapter(s).

Recent Title(s): *Seasons in the Sun: The Story of Big League Baseball in Missouri*, by Roger D. Launius; *Du Bois and His Rivals*, by Raymond Wolters.

N **UNIVERSITY OF NEBRASKA PRESS**, 233 N. 8th St., Lincoln NE 68588-0225. (402)472-3581. Fax: (402)472-0308. E-mail: pressmail@unl.edu. Website: nebraskapress.unl.edu. **Acquisitions:** Gary Dunham, editor-in-chief (Native American studies); Ladette Randolph, acquisitions editor (creative nonfiction). Publishes hardcover and trade paperback originals and trade paperback reprints. **Publishes 140 titles/year. Receives 1,000 queries and 100 mss/year. 60% of books from first-time authors; 95% from unagented writers. Pays 5-10% royalty on wholesale price. Offers 500-1,000 advance.** Publishes book 1 year after acceptance of ms. Responds in 1 month to queries; 1 month to proposals; 2 months to mss. Book catalog and ms guidelines free; ms guidelines online.

Imprints: Bison Books

Nonfiction: Biography, cookbook, reference, textbook. Subjects include agriculture/horticulture, animals, anthropology/archeology, creative nonfiction, history, memoirs, military/war, multicultural, nature/environment, religion, sports, translation, women's issues/studies, Native American studies. Query with SASE.

Recent Title(s): *Quilting Lessons*, by Janet Berlo (creative nonfiction); *The Midsummer Classic*, by David Vincent (sports); *Sarah Winnemucca*, by Sally Zanjani (Native American memoir).

UNIVERSITY OF NEVADA PRESS, MS 166, Reno NV 89557. (775)784-6573. Fax: (775)784-6200. E-mail: johare@unr.edu. **Acquisitions:** Joanne O'Hare, editor-in-chief (environmental arts and humanities series, western literature series, gambling series, Shepperson series in history and humanities); Sara Velez Mallea, editor (Basque studies). Estab. 1961. Publishes hardcover and paperback originals and reprints. **Publishes 35 titles/year. 20% of books from first-time authors; 99% from unagented writers. Pays 10% royalty on net receipts.** Publishes book 18 months after acceptance of ms. Does not accept simultaneous submissions. Responds in 2 months to queries. Book catalog and ms guidelines free.

O⊸ "We are the first university press to sustain a sound series on Basque studies—New World and Old World."

Nonfiction: Biography. Subjects include anthropology/archeology, community, ethnic (studies), history (regional and natural), language/literature, nature/environment (history), regional (history and geography), current affairs, ethno-nationalism, gambling and gaming, Basque studies. No juvenile books. Submit complete ms. *Writer's Market* recommends a query with SASE first. Reviews artwork/photos as part of ms package. Send photocopies.

Recent Title(s): *Futures at Stake: Youth, Gambling and Society*, edited by Howard J. Shaffer, Matthew N. Hall, Joni Vander Bilt, and Elizabeth M. George; *Looking for Steinbeck's Ghost*, by Jackson J. Benson; *Greening the Lyre: Environmental Poetics and Ethics*, by David W. Gilcrest.

UNIVERSITY OF NEW MEXICO PRESS, 1720 Lomas Blvd. NE, Albuquerque NM 87131-1591. (505)277-2346. E-mail: unmpress@unm.edu. Website: www.unmpress.com. **Acquisitions:** Evelyn Schlatter, managing editor (anthropology, archelogy, multicultural); David Holtby, acquisitions editor (history, Latin America). Estab. 1929. Publishes hardcover originals and trade paperback originals and reprints. **Publishes 70 titles/year. Receives 600 submissions/year. 12% of books from first-time authors; 90% from unagented writers. Pays variable royalty. Offers advance.** Does not accept simultaneous submissions. *Writer's Market* recommends allowing 2 months for reply to queries. Book catalog free.

O⊸ "The Press is well known as a publisher in the fields of anthropology, archeology, Latin American studies, photography, architecture and the history and culture of the American West, fiction, some poetry, Chicano/a studies and works by and about American Indians. We focus on American West, Southwest and Latin American regions."

Nonfiction: Biography, children's/juvenile, illustrated book, multimedia, scholarly. Subjects include Americana, anthropology/archeology, art/architecture, creative nonfiction, ethnic, gardening, gay/lesbian, government/politics, history, language/literature, memoirs, military/war, multicultural, music/dance, nature/environment, photography, regional, religion, science, translation, travel, women's issues/studies, contemporary culture, cinema/stage, true crime, general nonfiction. "No how-to, humor, juvenile, self-help, software, technical or textbooks." Query with SASE. Reviews artwork/photos as part of ms package. Send photocopies.

Recent Title(s): *Creek Indian Medicine Ways*, by David Lewis, Jr. and Ann T. Jordan; *Adventures with Ed: A Portrait of Abbey*, by Jack Loeffler.

THE UNIVERSITY OF NORTH CAROLINA PRESS, P.O. Box 2288, Chapel Hill NC 27515-2288. (919)966-3561. Fax: (919)966-3829. E-mail: uncpress@unc.edu. Website: www.uncpress.unc.edu. **Acquisitions:** David Perry, editor-in-chief (regional trade, Civil War); Charles Grench, senior editor (American history, European history, law and legal studies, business and economic history, classics, political or social science); Elaine Maisner, editor (Latin American studies, religious studies, anthropology, regional trade, folklore); Sian Hunter, editor (literary studies, women's studies, American studies, African American studies, social medicine, Appalachian studies, media studies); Mark Simpson-Vos, associate editor (publishing projects). Publishes hardcover originals, trade paperback originals and reprints. **Publishes 90 titles/year. Receives 300 queries and 200 mss/year. 50% of books from first-time authors; 98% from unagented writers. Pays variable royalty on wholesale price. Offers variable advance.** Publishes book 1 year after acceptance of ms. Responds in 3-4 weeks to queries; 3-4 weeks to proposals; 2 weeks to mss. Book catalog and ms guidelines free or on website; ms guidelines online.

O⊸ "UNC Press publishes nonfiction books for academic and general audiences. We have a special interest in trade and scholarly titles about our region. We do not, however, publish original fiction, drama, or poetry, memoirs of living persons, or festshriften."

Nonfiction: Biography, cookbook, multimedia (CD-ROM). Subjects include Americana, anthropology/archeology, art/architecture, cooking/foods/nutrition, gardening, government/politics, health/medicine, history, language/literature, military/war, multicultural, music/dance, nature/environment, philosophy, photography, regional, religion, translation, women's issues/studies, African American studies, American studies, cultural studies, Latin American studies, media studies, gender studies, social medicine, Appalachian studies. Submit proposal package including outline, c.v., cover letter, abstract, and table of contents. Reviews artwork/photos as part of ms package. Send photocopies.

UNIVERSITY OF NORTH TEXAS PRESS, P.O. Box 311336, Denton TX 76203-1336. Fax: (940)565-4590. E-mail: rchrisman@unt.edu or kdevinney@unt.edu. Website: www.unt.edu/untpress. Director: Ronald Chrisman. **Acquisitions:** Karen DeVinney, managing editor. Estab. 1987. Publishes hardcover and trade paperback originals and reprints. **Publishes 14-16 titles/year. Receives 500 queries/year. 95% from unagented writers. Pays 7-10% royalty on net receipts.** Publishes book 1-2 years after acceptance of ms. Does not accept simultaneous submissions. Responds in 3 months to queries. Book catalog for 8½×11 SASE; ms guidelines online.

O⊸ We are dedicated to producing the highest quality scholarly, academic and general interest books. We are committed to serving all peoples by publishing stories of their cultures and experiences that have been overlooked. Currently emphasizing military history, Texas history and Texas literature, Mexican-American studies.

Nonfiction: Subjects include agriculture/horticulture, Americana, ethnic, government/politics, history, language/literature, military/war, nature/environment, regional, women's issues/studies. Query with SASE. Reviews artwork/photos as part of ms package. Send photocopies.

Poetry: The only poetry we publish is the winner of the Vassar Miller Prize in Poetry, an annual, national competition with a $1,000 prize and publication of the winning manuscript each fall. Query.

Recent Title(s): *Capt. John H. Rogers, Texas Ranger*; *The Light Crust Doughboys Are on the Air!*.

Tips: "We publish series called War and the Southwest; Texas Folklore Society Publications; the Western Life Series; Literary Biographies of Texas Writers; practical guide series; Al-Filo: Mexican-American studies; North Texas crime and criminal justice; Katherine Anne Porter Prize in Short Fiction."

N **UNIVERSITY OF OKLAHOMA PRESS**, 1005 Asp Ave., Norman OK 73019-6051. E-mail: cerankin@ou.edu. Website: www.oupress.com. **Acquisitions:** Charles E. Rankin, editor-in-chief (U.S. West, military history, Oklahoma history); Jean Hurtado, acquisitions editor (U.S. West, natural history, political science, women's studies); JoAnn Reece, acquisitions editor (American Indian studies, Latin American studies, Mesoamerican studies); Karen Wieder (literary studies); Greta Mohon (paperbacks). Estab. 1928. Publishes hardcover and paperback originals and reprints. **Publishes 100 titles/year. Standard royalty for comparable books. Offers advance.** Publishes book 18 months after acceptance of ms. Does not accept simultaneous submissions. Responds in 3 months to queries. Book catalog for $1 and 9×12 SAE with 6 first-class stamps.

Imprints: Red River Books (paperbacks), Plains Reprints.

O→ University of Oklahoma Press publishes books for both a scholarly and general audience.

Nonfiction: Subjects include Americana, ethnic, government/politics, history (natural, military), language/literature, military/war (history), regional (Western U.S. history), science (natural), women's issues/studies, American Indian studies, literary theory, classical studies, Mesoamerican studies. No unsolicited poetry or fiction. Query with SASE or submit outline, 1-2 sample chapter(s), résumé. Use *Chicago Manual of Style* for ms guidelines. Reviews artwork/photos as part of ms package.

Recent Title(s): *Sam Houston*, by James L. Haley (American history); *Blood of the Prophets: Brigham Young and the Massacre at Mountain Meadows* (U.S. Western history); *Diminished Democracy: From Membership to Management in American Civic Life*, by Theda Skocpol (political science).

UNIVERSITY OF PENNSYLVANIA PRESS, 4200 Pine St., Philadelphia PA 19104-4011. (215)898-6261. Fax: (215)898-0404. Website: www.upenn.edu/pennpress. Director: Eric Halpern. **Acquisitions:** Jerome Singerman, humanities editor; Peter Agree, social sciences editor; Jo Joslyn, art and architecture editor; Robert Lockhart, history editor. Estab. 1890. Publishes hardcover and paperback originals and reprints. **Publishes 75 titles/year. Receives 1,000 submissions/year. 20-30% of books from first-time authors; 95% from unagented writers. Royalty determined on book-by-book basis. Offers advance.** Publishes book 10 months after delivery of ms after acceptance of ms. Does not accept simultaneous submissions. Responds in 3 months to queries. Book catalog online; ms guidelines online.

Nonfiction: "Serious books that serve the scholar and the professional, student and general reader." Scholarly. Subjects include Americana, anthropology/archeology, art/architecture, business/economics, history (American, art), sociology, literary criticism, cultural studies, ancient studies, medieval studies. Follow the *Chicago Manual of Style*. No unsolicited mss. Query with SASE or submit outline, résumé. Reviews artwork/photos as part of ms package. Send photocopies.

UNIVERSITY OF SCRANTON PRESS, University of Scranton, Linden and Monroe, Scranton PA 18510. (570)941-4228. Fax: (570)941-4309. E-mail: scrantonpress@scranton.edu. Website: www.scrantonpress.com. **Acquisitions:** Patty Mecadon, director. Estab. 1981. Publishes paperback originals. **Publishes 5 titles/year. Receives 200 queries and 45 mss/year. 60% of books from first-time authors; 100% from unagented writers. Pays 10% royalty.** Publishes book within 1 year after acceptance of ms. Does not accept simultaneous submissions. Book catalog and ms guidelines free.

Imprints: Ridge Row Press

O→ The University of Scranton Press, a member of the Association of Jesuit University Presses, publishes primarily scholarly monographs in theology, philosophy, and the culture and history of northeast Pennsylvania.

Nonfiction: Looking for clear editorial focus: theology/religious studies; philosophy/philosophy of religion; scholarly treatments; the culture of northeast Pennsylvania. Scholarly monographs. Subjects include art/architecture, language/literature, philosophy, regional, religion, sociology. Query with SASE or submit outline, 2 sample chapter(s).

Poetry: Only poetry related to northeast Pennsylvania.

Recent Title(s): *The Illustrated Spiritual Exercises*, edited by Jerome Nadal; *The Rise and Fall of Seranton Municipal Airport*, by William Hallstead, III; *One in a Million*, by Mary G. Clark, RN, PA-C.

UNIVERSITY OF SOUTH CAROLINA PRESS, 937 Assembly St., Carolina Plaza, 8th Floor, Columbia SC 29208. (803)777-5243. Fax: (803)777-0160. Website: www.sc.edu/uscpress. **Acquisitions:** Curtis Clark, director (trade books); Barry Blose, acquisitions editor (literature, religious studies, rhetoric, communication, social work); Alexander Moore, acquisitions editor (history, regional studies). Estab. 1944. Publishes hardcover originals, trade paperback originals and reprints. **Publishes 50-55 titles/year. Receives 1,000 queries and 250 mss/year. 30% of books from first-time authors; 95% from unagented writers.** Publishes book 1 year after acceptance of ms. Accepts simultaneous submissions. Responds in 3 months to mss. Book catalog and ms guidelines free; ms guidelines online.

O→ "We focus on scholarly monographs and regional trade books of lasting merit."

Nonfiction: Biography, illustrated book, monograph. Subjects include art/architecture, history (American, Civil War, culinary, maritime, women's), language/literature, regional, religion, rhetoric, communication. "Do not submit entire unsolicited manuscripts or projects with limited scholarly value." Query with SASE or submit proposal package and outline and 1 sample chapter and résumé with SASE. Reviews artwork/photos as part of ms package. Send photocopies.

Recent Title(s): *South Carolina and the American Revolution: A Battlefield History*, by John W. Gordon; *Against the Stream: Growing Up Where Hitler Used to Live*, by Anna Elisabeth Rosmus; *The Last Romantic: A Poet among Publishers:*

An Oral Autobiography by John Hall Wheelock, edited by Matthew J. Bruccoli with Judith S. Baughman.

THE UNIVERSITY OF TENNESSEE PRESS, 110 Conference Center, Knoxville TN 37996-4108. (865)974-3321. Fax: (865)974-3724. E-mail: custserv@utpress.org. Website: www.utpress.org. **Acquisitions:** Joyce Harrison, acquisitions editor (scholarly books); Jennifer Siler, director (regional trades, fiction). Estab. 1940. **Publishes 30 titles/year. Receives 450 submissions/year. 35% of books from first-time authors; 99% from unagented writers. Pays negotiable royalty on net receipts.** Does not accept simultaneous submissions. Book catalog for 12x16 SAE with 2 first-class stamps; ms guidelines online.

O→ "Our mission is to stimulate scientific and scholarly research in all fields; to channel such studies, either in scholarly or popular form, to a larger number of people; and to extend the regional leadership of the University of Tennessee by stimulating research projects within the South and by non-university authors."

Nonfiction: Scholarly, American studies only. Subjects include Americana, anthropology/archeology (historical), art/architecture (vernacular), ethnic, history, language/literature, regional, religion (history sociology, anthropology, biography only), women's issues/studies, African-American studies, Appalachian studies, folklore/folklife, material culture. Prefers "scholarly treatment and a readable style. Authors usually have Ph.D.s." Submissions in other fields, and submissions of poetry, textbooks, plays and translations are not invited. Submit outline, 2 sample chapter(s), author bio. Reviews artwork/photos as part of ms package.

Fiction: Query with SASE or submit synopsis, author bio.

Recent Title(s): *The Marriage of Anna Maye Potts*, by DeWitt Henry (fiction).

Tips: "Our market is in several groups: scholars; educated readers with special interests in given scholarly subjects; and the general educated public interested in Tennessee, Appalachia and the South. Not all our books appeal to all these groups, of course, but any given book must appeal to at least one of them."

UNIVERSITY OF TEXAS PRESS, P.O. Box 7819, Austin TX 78713-7819. (512)471-7233. Fax: (512)232-7178. E-mail: utpress@uts.cc.utexas.edu. Website: www.utexas.edu/utpress/. **Acquisitions:** Theresa May, assistant director/editor-in-chief (social sciences, Latin American studies); James Burr, sponsorings editor (humanities, classics); William Bishel (sciences; Texas history). Estab. 1952. **Publishes 90 titles/year. Receives 1,000 submissions/year. 50% of books from first-time authors; 99% from unagented writers. Pays royalty on net receipts. Offers occasional advance.** Publishes book 18-24 months after acceptance of ms. Does not accept simultaneous submissions. Responds in 3 months to queries. Book catalog and ms guidelines free; ms guidelines online.

O→ "In addition to publishing the results of advanced research for scholars worldwide, UT Press has a special obligation to the people of its state to publish authoritative books on Texas. We do not publish fiction or poetry, except for some Latin American and Middle Eastern literature in translation."

Nonfiction: Biography, scholarly. Subjects include anthropology/archeology, art/architecture, ethnic, film/cinema/stage, history, language/literature, nature/environment, regional, science, translation, women's issues/studies, natural history; American, Latin American, Native American, Latino and Middle Eastern studies; classics and the ancient world, film, contemporary regional architecture, geography, ornithology, biology. Also uses specialty titles related to Texas and the Southwest, national trade titles and regional trade titles. Query with SASE or submit outline, 2 sample chapter(s). Reviews artwork/photos as part of ms package.

Fiction: Latin American and Middle Eastern translation. Latin American and Middle Eastern fiction only in translations. No poetry. Query with SASE or submit outline, 2 sample chapter(s).

Recent Title(s): *Remembering Childhood in the Middle East*, by Fernea; *Andean Entrepreneurs*, by Meisch; *Generation Multiplex*, by Shary.

Tips: "It's difficult to make a manuscript over 400 double-spaced pages into a feasible book. Authors should take special care to edit out extraneous material. We look for sharply focused, in-depth treatments of important topics."

[N] **UNIVERSITY PRESS OF AMERICA**, 4501 Forbes Ave., Suite 200, Lanham MD 20706. (301)459-3366. Fax: (301)429-5749. E-mail: jrothman@rowman.com. Website: www.univpress.com. **Acquisitions:** Acquisitions Department. Estab. 1975. Publishes hardcover and paperback originals. **Publishes 500 titles/year. 100% from unagented writers. Pays royalty.** Publishes book ASAP after acceptance of ms. quickly to queries. Book catalog online; ms guidelines online.

UNIVERSITY PRESS OF COLORADO, 5589 Arapahoe, Suite 206C, Boulder CO 80303. (720)406-8849. Fax: (720)406-3443. Director: Darrin Pratt. **Acquisitions:** Sandy Crooms, editor. Estab. 1965. Publishes hardcover and paperback originals. **Publishes 30-40 titles/year. Receives 1,000 submissions/year. 50% of books from first-time authors; 95% from unagented writers. Pays 5-15% royalty on net receipts. Offers advance.** Publishes book within 2 years after acceptance of ms. Accepts simultaneous submissions. Responds in 6 months to queries. Book catalog free.

O→ "We are a university press that publishes scholarly nonfiction in the disciplines of the American West, Native American studies, archeology, environmental studies and regional interest titles." Currently de-emphasizing fiction, poetry, biography.

Nonfiction: Scholarly. Subjects include nature/environment, regional. Length: 250-500 pages. Query with SASE. Reviews artwork/photos as part of ms package.

Recent Title(s): *Reversing the Lens: Ethnicity Race, Gender, and Sexuality Through Film*, by Jun Xing and Lane Ryo Hirabayashi; *International Environmental Cooperation: Politics and Diplomacy in Pacific Asia*, by Paul G. Harris.

Tips: "We have series on mining history and on Mesoamerican worlds."

UNIVERSITY PRESS OF KANSAS, 2501 W. 15th St., Lawrence KS 66049-3905. (785)864-4154. Fax: (785)864-4586. E-mail: upress@ku.edu. Website: www.kansaspress.ku.edu. **Acquisitions:** Michael J. Briggs, editor-in-chief (military history, political science, law); Nancy Scott Jackson, acquisitions editor (western history, American studies, environmental studies, women's studies); Fred M. Woodward, director, (political science, presidency, regional). Estab. 1946. Publishes hardcover originals, trade paperback originals and reprints. **Publishes 55 titles/year. Receives 600 queries/year. 20% of books from first-time authors; 98% from unagented writers. Pays 5-15% royalty on net receipts. Offers selective advance.** Publishes book 10 months after acceptance of ms. Does not accept simultaneous submissions. Responds in 1 month to proposals. Book catalog and ms guidelines free.

O┳ The University Press of Kansas publishes scholarly books that advance knowledge and regional books that contribute to the understanding of Kansas, the Great Plains and the Midwest.

Nonfiction: Biography, scholarly. Subjects include Americana, anthropology/archeology, government/politics, history, military/war, nature/environment, philosophy, regional, sociology, women's issues/studies. "We are looking for books on topics of wide interest based on solid scholarship and written for both specialists and informed general readers. Do not send unsolicited complete manuscripts." Submit outline, sample chapter(s), cover letter, cv, prospectus. Reviews artwork/photos as part of ms package. Send photocopies.

Recent Title(s): *Spies in Vietnam: Espionage and Intrigue from Napoleon to the Holocaust*, by David Alvarez; *The Modern American Presidency*, by Lewis L. Gould.

UNIVERSITY PRESS OF KENTUCKY, 663 S. Limestone, Lexington KY 40508-4008. (859)257-2951. Fax: (859)323-1873. Website: www.kentuckypress.com. **Acquisitions:** Stephen Wrinn, director and editor. Estab. 1943. Publishes hardcover and paperback originals and reprints. **Publishes 60 titles/year. Royalty varies.** Publishes book 1 year after acceptance of ms. Responds in 2 months to queries. Book catalog free; ms guidelines online.

O┳ "We are a scholarly publisher, publishing chiefly for an academic and professional audience, as well as books about Kentucky, the upper South, Appalachia, and the Ohio Valley."

Nonfiction: Biography, reference, scholarly (monographs). Subjects include history, military/war (history), regional, women's issues/studies, political science, film studies, American and African-American studies, folklore, Kentuckiana and regional books, Appalachian studies. "No textbooks, genealogical material, lightweight popular treatments, how-to books or books unrelated to our major areas of interest. The Press does not consider original works of fiction or poetry." Query with SASE.

UNIVERSITY PRESS OF MISSISSIPPI, 3825 Ridgewood Rd., Jackson MS 39211-6492. (601)432-6205. Fax: (601)432-6217. E-mail: press@ihl.state.ms.us. **Acquisitions:** Craig Gill, editor-in-chief (regional studies, art, folklore, fiction, memoirs); Seetha Srinivasan, director (African-American studies, popular culture, literature). Estab. 1970. Publishes hardcover and paperback originals and reprints. **Publishes 60 titles/year. Receives 750 submissions/year. 20% of books from first-time authors; 90% from unagented writers. Competitive royalties and terms. Offers advance.** Publishes book 1 year after acceptance of ms. Does not accept simultaneous submissions. Responds in 3 months to queries. Book catalog for 9×12 SAE with 3 first-class stamps.

Imprints: Muscadine Books (regional trade), Banner Books (literary reprints).

O┳ "University Press of Mississippi publishes scholarly and trade titles, as well as special series, including: American Made Music; Conversations with Public Intellectuals; Interviews with filmmakers; Faulkner and Yoknapatawpha; Folklife in the South; Literary Conversations; Studies in Popular Culture; Understanding Health and Sickness; Writers and Their Work."

Nonfiction: Biography, scholarly. Subjects include Americana, art/architecture, ethnic (minority studies), government/politics, health/medicine, history, language/literature, music/dance, photography, regional (Southern), folklife, literary criticism, popular culture with scholarly emphasis, literary studies. "We prefer a proposal that describes the significance of the work and a chapter outline." Submit outline, sample chapter(s), cv.

Fiction: Commissioned trade editions by prominent writers.

Recent Title(s): *The War of Our Childhood: Memories of World War II*, by Wolfgang W.E. Samuel; *Red Midnight*, by Thomas Hal Phillips.

N **UNIVERSITY PRESS OF NEW ENGLAND**, 1 Court St., Suite 250, Lebanon NH 03766. Website: www.upne.com. Director: Richard Abel. **Acquisitions:** John Landrigan, editor (American/northeastern studies, fiction, biography, cultural studies); Phyllis Deutsch, executive editor (Jewish studies, art, biography, American studies, religion); Ellen Wicklum, editor (nature, American/regional studies). Estab. 1970. Publishes hardcover and trade paperback originals, trade paperback reprints. **Publishes 80 titles/year. Pays standard royalty. Offers occasional advance.** Responds in 2 months to queries. Book catalog and ms guidelines for 9×12 SASE and 5 first-class stamps; ms guidelines online.

O┳ "University Press of New England is a consortium of universities: Dartmouth, Brandeis, Tufts, University of New Hampshire and Middlebury College. We publish academic studies for an academic audience as well as nonfiction aimed at the educated reader/intellectual. We also encourage regional (New England) work (academic, fiction, art or otherwise)." Currently emphasizing American studies, cultural studies.

Nonfiction: Biography. Subjects include Americana (New England material culture), art/architecture, music/dance, nature/environment, regional (New England), American studies, Jewish studies. Submit outline, 1-2 sample chapter(s). No electronic submissions.

Fiction: Only New England novels, literary fiction and reprints.

Recent Title(s): *Erasure*, by Percival Everett (fiction); *The Dickinsons of Amherst*, by Jerome Liebling (photography, biography); *The Ice Chronicles: The Quest to Understand Global Climate Change*, by Paul Mayewski and Frank White (nonfiction, science).

N **UNPUBLISHEDNOVELS.COM**, 414 S. Cloverdale, Suite 208, Los Angeles CA 90036-3444. (323)932-0698. E-mail: editor@unpublishednovels.com. Website: www.unpublishednovels.com. **Acquisitions:** Marge McLeon, editor (novels). Estab. 2002. Publishes electronic originals. **Publishes 50 titles/year. Receives 100 queries and 50 mss/year. 100% of books from first-time authors; 100% from unagented writers.** Publishes book 1-2 months after acceptance of ms. Accepts simultaneous submissions. Responds in 1-2 weeks to queries; 1-2 months to mss. Book catalog online; ms guidelines online.

Fiction: Gothic, historical, horror, humor, juvenile, mainstream/contemporary, mystery, romance, science fiction, suspense, western, young adult. "We want only writers who have never been published and are tired of the costs of self-publishing and fee-oriented agents. We expect quality writing. We want you to receive money for your work. Marketing of your manuscript will involve helping yourself and UnpublishedNovels.com by telling your friends where they can buy your work and passing the word." Submit Proposal package including synopsis and personal information online.

Recent Title(s): *Precious Cargo*, by Marge McLeon (historical romance).

Tips: "Our audience is readers who are tired of reading the books those publishers 'think' everyone wants to read." "We want quality books. We believe that having to pay 'any amount of money' to have your book published or read should no longer be an acceptable way to get your manuscript published. The writer can still promote their work by telling agents and publishers where to find it if they are interested. Our company only requests the Internet rights are given to UnpublishedNovels.com. All other rights are retained by the writer."

UPSTART BOOKS, Highsmith Press, P.O. Box 800, Fort Atkinson WI 53538-0800. (920)563-9571. Fax: (920)563-4801. E-mail: mmulder@highsmith.com. Website: www.highsmith.com. **Acquisitions:** Matt Mulder, director of publications. Estab. 1990. Publishes hardcover and paperback originals. **Publishes 20 titles/year. Receives 500-600 queries and 400-500 mss/year. 30% of books from first-time authors; 100% from unagented writers. Pays 10-12% royalty on net receipts. Offers $250-1,000 advance.** Publishes book 6 months after acceptance of ms. Accepts simultaneous submissions. Responds in 1 month to queries; 2 months to proposals. Book catalog online; ms guidelines online.

Imprints: Alleyside Press, Upstart Books (creative supplemental reading, library and critical thinking skills materials designed to expand the learning environment).

- Upstart Books publishes educational resources to meet the practical needs of librarians, educators, readers, library users, media specialists, schools and related institutions, and to help them fulfill their valuable functions.

Nonfiction: Children's/juvenile, reference. Subjects include education, language/literature, multicultural. "We are primarily interested in manuscripts that stimulate or strengthen reading, library and information-seeking skills and foster critical thinking." Query with outline and 1-2 sample chapters. Reviews artwork/photos as part of ms package. Send transparencies.

Fiction: "Our current emphasis is on storytelling collections for preschool-grade 6. We prefer stories that can be easily used by teachers and children's librarians, multicultural topics, and manuscripts that feature fold and cut, flannelboard, tangram, or similar simple patterns that can be reproduced. No longer accepting children's picture book mss.

Recent Title(s): *Finger Tales*, by Joan Hilyer Phelps; *Characters with Character*, by Diane Findlay.

THE URBAN LAND INSTITUTE, 1025 Thomas Jefferson St. NW, Washington DC 20007-5201. (202)624-7000. Fax: (202)624-7140. Website: www.uli.org. **Acquisitions:** Rachelle Levitt, senior vice president/publisher. Estab. 1936. Publishes hardcover and trade paperback originals. **Publishes 15-20 titles/year. Receives 20 submissions/year. 2% of books from first-time authors; 100% from unagented writers. Pays 10% royalty on gross sales. Offers $1,500-2,000 advance.** Publishes book 6 months after acceptance of ms. Does not accept simultaneous submissions. Book catalog and ms. guidelines via website or 9×12 SAE.

- The Urban Land Institute publishes technical books on real estate development and land planning.

Nonfiction: Technical. Subjects include money/finance, design and development. "The majority of manuscripts are created inhouse by research staff. We acquire two or three outside authors to fill schedule and subject areas where our list has gaps. We are not interested in real estate sales, brokerages, appraisal, making money in real estate, opinion, personal point of view, or mauscripts negative toward growth and development." Query with SASE. Reviews artwork/photos as part of ms package.

Recent Title(s): *Place Making: Developing Town Centers, Main Streets, and Urban Villages*; *Transforming Suburban Business Districts*.

UTAH STATE UNIVERSITY PRESS, 7800 Old Main Hill, Logan UT 84322-7800. (435)797-1362. Fax: (435)797-0313. Website: www.usu.edu/usupress. **Acquisitions:** Michael Spooner, director (composition, poetry); John Alley, editor (history, folklore, fiction). Estab. 1972. Publishes hardcover and trade paperback originals and reprints. **Publishes 18 titles/year. Receives 250 submissions/year. 8% of books from first-time authors. Pays royalty on net receipts.** Publishes book 18 months after acceptance of ms. Does not accept simultaneous submissions. Responds in 1 month to queries. Book catalog free; ms guidelines online.

- Utah State University Press publishes scholarly works in the academic areas noted below. Currently interested in book-length scholarly manuscripts dealing with folklore studies, composition studies, Native American studies and history.

Nonfiction: Biography, reference, scholarly, textbook. Subjects include history (of the West), regional, folklore, the West, Native American studies, studies in composition and rhetoric. Query with SASE. Reviews artwork/photos as part of ms package. Send photocopies.

Recent Title(s): *The Anguish of Snails*, by Barre Toelken; *Uranium Frenzy*, by Raye Ringholz; *The Owl Question*, by Faith Shearin.

Tips: Utah State University Press also sponsors the annual May Swenson Poetry Award.

VANDAMERE PRESS, P.O. Box 17446, Clearwater FL 33762. (727)556-0950. Fax: (727)556-2560. **Acquisitions:** Jerry Frank, senior acquistions editor. Estab. 1984. Publishes hardcover and trade paperback originals and reprints. **Publishes 8-**

15 titles/year. Receives 750 queries and 2,000 mss/year. 25% of books from first-time authors; 90% from unagented writers. Pays royalty. on revenues generated. Offers advance. Publishes book 1-3 years after acceptance of ms. Accepts simultaneous submissions. Responds in 6 months to queries.

O¬ Vandamere publishes high-quality work with solid, well-documented research and minimum author/political bias.

Nonfiction: Biography, illustrated book, reference. Subjects include Americana, education, health/medicine, history, military/war, photography, regional (Washington D.C./Mid-Atlantic), women's issues/studies, disability/healthcare issues. No New Age. Submit outline, 2-3 sample chapter(s). Send photocopies.

Fiction: Adventure, erotica, humor, mystery, suspense. Submit 5-10 sample chapter(s), synopsis.

Recent Title(s): *Ask What You Can Do for Your Country*, by Dan Fleming (nonfiction); *Cry Me a River*, by Patricia Hagan (fiction).

Tips: "Authors who can provide endorsements from significant published writers, celebrities, etc., will *always* be given serious consideration. Clean, easy-to-read, *dark* copy is essential. Patience in waiting for replies is essential. All unsolicited work is looked at, but at certain times of the year our review schedule will stop. No response without SASE. No electronic submissions or queries."

VANDERBILT UNIVERSITY PRESS, VU Station B 351813, Nashville TN 37235. (615)322-3585. Fax: (615)343-8823. E-mail: vupress@vanderbilt.edu. Website: www.vanderbilt.edu/vupress. **Acquisitions:** Michael Ames, director. Publishes hardcover originals and trade paperback originals and reprints. **Publishes 20-25 titles/year. Receives 500 queries/year. 25% of books from first-time authors; 90% from unagented writers. Pays 8% royalty on net receipts. Offers rare advance.** Publishes book 10 months after acceptance of ms. Accepts simultaneous submissions. Responds in 2 weeks to proposals. Book catalog free; ms guidelines online.

- Also distributes for and co-publishes with Country Music Foundation.

O¬ "Vanderbilt University Press publishes books on health care, social sciences, education and regional studies, for both academic and general audiences that are intellectually significant, socially relevant and of practical importance."

Nonfiction: Biography, scholarly, textbook. Subjects include Americana, anthropology/archeology, education, ethnic, government/politics, health/medicine, history, language/literature, multicultural, music/dance, nature/environment, philosophy, women's issues/studies. Submit prospectus, sample chapter, cv. Reviews artwork/photos as part of ms package. Send photocopies.

Recent Title(s): *A Good-Natured Riot: The Birth of the Grand Ole Opry*, by Charles K. Wolfe; *Invisible Work: Borges and Translation*, by Efrain Kristal; *Smoke in Their Eyes: Lessons Learned in Movement Leadership from the Tobacco Wars*, by Michael Pertschuk.

Tips: "Our audience consists of scholars and educated general readers."

VENTURE PUBLISHING, INC., 1999 Cato Ave., State College PA 16801. (814)234-4561. Fax: (814)234-1561. E-mail: vpublish@venturepublish.com. Website: www.venturepublish.com. **Acquisitions:** Geof Godbey, editor. Estab. 1978. Publishes hardcover and paperback originals and reprints. **Publishes 10-12 titles/year. Receives 50 queries and 20 mss/year. 40% of books from first-time authors; 100% from unagented writers. Pays royalty on wholesale price. Offers advance.** Publishes book 9 months after acceptance of ms. Does not accept simultaneous submissions. Responds in 1 month to queries; 2 months to proposals; 2 months to mss. Book catalog and ms guidelines for SASE or online; ms guidelines online.

O¬ Venture Publishing produces quality educational publications, also workbooks for professionals, educators, and students in the fields of recreation, parks, leisure studies, therapeutic recreation and long term care.

Nonfiction: Scholarly (college academic), textbook, professional. Subjects include nature/environment (outdoor recreation management and leadership texts), recreation, sociology (leisure studies), long-term care nursing homes, therapeutic recreation. "Textbooks and books for recreation activity leaders high priority." Submit outline, 1 sample chapter(s).

Recent Title(s): *Interpretation of Cultural and Natural Resources, 2nd ed*, by Kanudson, Cable & Beck; *Leisure in Your Life, 6th ed*, by Geof Godbey; *Dementia Care Programming: An Identity Focused Approach*, by Dunne.

[N] **VERSO**, 180 Varick St., 10th Floor, New York NY 10014. (212)807-9680. Fax: (212)807-9152. E-mail: versony@versobooks.com. Website: www.versobooks.com. **Acquisitions:** Niels Hooper, general manager. Estab. 1970. Publishes hardcover and trade paperback originals. **Publishes 40-60 titles/year. Receives 300 queries and 150 mss/year. 10% of books from first-time authors; 95% from unagented writers. Pays royalty. Offers advance.** Publishes book 1 year after acceptance of ms. Accepts simultaneous submissions. Responds in 5 months to queries. Book catalog free; ms guidelines online.

O¬ "Our books cover economics, politics, cinema studies, and history (among other topics), but all come from a critical, Leftist viewpoint, on the border between trade and academic."

Nonfiction: Illustrated book. Subjects include business/economics, government/politics, history, philosophy, sociology, women's issues/studies. "We are loosely affiliated with *New Left Review* (London). We are not interested in academic monographs." Submit proposal package including 1 sample chapter(s).

Recent Title(s): *Late Victorian Holocausts*, by Mike Davis.

[A] **VIKING**, Penguin Putnam Inc., 375 Hudson St., New York NY 10014. (212)366-2000. Publisher: Clare Ferraro. Publishes hardcover and trade paperback originals. **Pays 10-15% royalty on retail price. Offers negotiable advance.** Publishes book 12-18 months after acceptance of ms. Accepts simultaneous submissions. Responds in 6 months to queries.

O¬ Viking publishes a mix of academic and popular fiction and nonfiction.

Nonfiction: Biography. Subjects include business/economics, child guidance/parenting, cooking/foods/nutrition, health/

medicine, history, language/literature, music/dance, philosophy, women's issues/studies. *Agented submissions only.*
Fiction: Literary, mainstream/contemporary, mystery, suspense. *Agented submissions only.*
Recent Title(s): *A Common life*, by Jan Karon (novel); *A Day Late and a Dollar Short*, by Terry McMillan (novel); *In the Heart of the Sea*, by Nathaniel Philbrick (National Book Award winner).

VIKING CHILDREN'S BOOKS, Children's Division of Penguin Putnam Inc., 345 Hudson St., New York NY 10014. (212)366-2000. Website: www.penguinputnam.com. President/Publisher: Regina Hayes. **Acquisitions:** Catherine Frank. Publishes hardcover originals. **Publishes 60 titles/year. Receives 7,500 queries/year. 25% of books from first-time authors; 50% from unagented writers. Pays 5-10% royalty on retail price. Offers negotiable advance.** Publishes book 1 year after acceptance of ms. Responds in 4 months to queries. *Does not accept unsolicited submissions.*

Viking Children's Books publishes high-quality trade books for children including fiction, nonfiction, picture books and novelty books for pre-schoolers through young adults.

Nonfiction: Children's/juvenile. Query with SASE or submit outline, 3 sample chapter(s), SASE.
Fiction: Juvenile, picture books, young adult. Submit complete ms. for novels, picture books, chapter books with SASE.
Recent Title(s): *Ten*, by Vladimir Rodunsky; *Keeper of the Doves*, by Betsy Byars; *Catalyst*, by Laurie Halse Anderson.

VINTAGE BOOKS & ANCHOR BOOKS, Knopf Publishing Group, Random House Inc., 1745 Broadway Ave., New York NY 10019. Website: www.randomhouse.com. Vice President: LuAnn Walther. Editor-in-Chief: Martin Asher. **Acquisitions:** Submissions Department. Publishes trade paperback originals and reprints. **Publishes 200 titles/year. Receives 700 queries/year. 5% of books from first-time authors; less than 1% from unagented writers. Pays 4-8% royalty on retail price. Offers $2,500 and up advance.** Publishes book 1 year after acceptance of ms. Accepts simultaneous submissions. Responds in 6 months to queries.
Nonfiction: Biography. Subjects include anthropology/archeology, business/economics, child guidance/parenting, education, ethnic, gay/lesbian, government/politics, health/medicine, history, language/literature, military/war, nature/environment, philosophy, psychology, regional, science, sociology, translation, travel, women's issues/studies. *Agented submissions only.*
Fiction: Literary, mainstream/contemporary, short story collections. *Agented submissions only.*
Recent Title(s): *A Heartbreaking Work of Staggering Genius*, by Dave Eggers.

VINTAGE IMAGES, P.O. Box 160, Spencerville MD 20868. (301)879-6522. Fax: (301)879-6524. E-mail: vimages@erols.com. Website: www.vintageimages.com. **Acquisitions:** Brian Smolens, president. Publishes trade paperback originals. **Publishes 8 titles/year. Pays 4-8% royalty on wholesale price.** Publishes book 5 months after acceptance of ms. Does not accept simultaneous submissions. Ms guidelines online.

"We publish photographic poster books and need writers who are exceptionally creative. This is truly a creative writing exercise."

Nonfiction: Gift book, humor, illustrated book, poster books. Subjects include Americana, photography.
Recent Title(s): *Fishing Tales: A Vintage Images Poster Book.*
Tips: "We are interested in creative writers who can weave a humorous/dramatic theme around 36 vintage photos (early 1900s)."

VISIONS COMMUNICATIONS, 200 E. 10th St., #714, New York NY 10003. (212)529-4029. Fax: (212)529-4029. E-mail: bayeun@aol.com. **Acquisitions:** Beth Bay. Estab. 1994. Visions specializes in trade and reference books. Publishes hardcover originals and paperback originals and reprints. **Publishes 5 titles/year. Pays 5-20% royalty on retail price.** Publishes book 6 months after acceptance of ms. Responds in 1 month to queries; 3 months to mss. Ms guidelines free.
Nonfiction: Children's/juvenile, how-to, reference, self-help, technical, textbook. Subjects include art/architecture, business/economics, health/medicine, psychology, religion, science, women's issues/studies, scholarly, engineering. Submit proposal package including outline, 3 sample chapter(s).
Recent Title(s): *Illuminating Engineering*, by Joseph Murdoch; *Restructuring Electricity Markets*, by Charles Cichetti.

VITAL HEALTH PUBLISHING, P.O. Box 152, Ridgefield CT 06877. (203)894-1882. Fax: (203)894-1866. E-mail: info@vitalhealth.net. Website: www.vitalhealth.net. **Acquisitions:** David Richard, publishing director (health, nutrition, ecology, creativity). Estab. 1997. Publishes trade paperback originals and reprints. **Publishes 10 titles/year; imprint publishes 5-6 titles/year. Receives 50 queries and 20 mss/year. 25% of books from first-time authors; 90% from unagented writers. Pays 15-20% royalty on wholesale price for top authors; pays in copies 30-40% of the time. Offers $1,000-5,000 advance.** Publishes book 6-8 months after acceptance of ms. Does not accept simultaneous submissions. Responds in 2 months to queries; 1-3 months to proposals; 2-4 months to mss. Book catalog online; Discuss with editor.
Imprints: Vital Health Publishing, Enhancement Books.

Nonfiction books for a health-conscious, well-educated, creative audience.

Nonfiction: Audiocassettes, children's/juvenile, cookbook, self-help. Subjects include health/medicine, music/dance, New Age, philosophy, spirituality. "All titles must be related to health. Because we have a holistic philosophy, this includes nutrition, ecology, creativity and spirituality. Submit proposal package including outline, 1 sample chapter(s), cover letter describing the project. Reviews artwork/photos as part of ms package. Send photocopies or color prints.
Poetry: "Minimal poetry published and strictly related to health." Query.
Recent Title(s): *Trace Your Genes to Health*, by Chris Reading, M.D. (nonfiction); *Our Children's Health*, by Bonnie Minsky, L.C.N. and Lisa Holk, N.D. (nonfiction); *On Wings of Spirit: The American Physician's Poetry Association Anthology*, by John Graham-Pole (poetry).
Tips: "View our website to compare our titles to your manuscript."

VIVISPHERE PUBLISHING, Net Pub Corporation, 2 Neptune Rd., Poughkeepsie NY 12601. (845)463-1100. Fax: (845)463-0018. Website: www.vivisphere.com. Estab. 1995. Publishes paperback originals and paperback reprints. **Pays 10-15% royalty, and 25 author's copies.** Publishes book 3-12 months after acceptance of ms. Accepts simultaneous submissions. Responds in 3 months to queries. Book catalog free; ms guidelines for free or on website.

Fiction: Adventure, ethnic, fantasy, feminist, gay/lesbian, historical, horror, literary, mainstream/contemporary, military/war, mystery, religious, romance, science fiction, suspense, western. Query with SASE.

VOLCANO PRESS, INC., P.O. Box 270, Volcano CA 95689-0270. (209)296-4991. Fax: (209)296-4995. E-mail: ruth@volcanopress.com. Website: www.volcanopress.com. **Acquisitions:** Ruth Gottstein, publisher. Estab. 1969. Publishes trade paperback originals. **Publishes 4-6 titles/year. Pays royalty on net receipts. Offers $500-1,000 advance.** Does not accept simultaneous submissions. Responds in 1 month to queries. Book catalog free.

O→ "We believe that the books we are producing today are of even greater value than the gold of yesteryear and that the sybolism of the term 'Mother Lode' is still relevant to our work."

Nonfiction: Self-help. Subjects include health/medicine, multicultural, women's issues/studies. "We publish women's health and social issues, particularly in the field of domestic violence." Query with SASE or submit outline. No e-mail or fax submissions.

Recent Title(s): *Ghost Towns of Amador*, by Andrews; *Journal and Letters from the Mines*, John Doble.

Tips: "Look at our titles on the Web or in our catalog, and submit materials consistent with what we already publish."

VOYAGEUR PRESS, 123 N. Second St., Stillwater MN 55082. (651)430-2210. Fax: (651)430-2211. E-mail: mdregni@voyageurpress.com. **Acquisitions:** Michael Dregni, editorial director. Estab. 1972. Publishes hardcover and trade paperback originals. **Publishes 50 titles/year. Receives 1,200 queries and 500 mss/year. 10% of books from first-time authors; 90% from unagented writers. Pays royalty. Offers advance.** Publishes book 1 year after acceptance of ms. Accepts simultaneous submissions. Responds in 3 months to queries.

O→ "Voyageur Press is internationally known as a leading publisher of quality natural history, wildlife and regional books."

Nonfiction: Coffee table book (smaller format photographic essay books), cookbook. Subjects include Americana, cooking/foods/nutrition, history (natural), hobbies, nature/environment, regional, collectibles, outdoor recreation. Query with SASE or submit outline. Reviews artwork/photos as part of ms package. Send transparencies (duplicates and tearsheets only).

Recent Title(s): *This Old Tractor* (stories and photos about farm tractors); *Last Standing Woman* (Native American novel).

Tips: "We publish books for a sophisticated audience interested in natural history and cultural history of a variety of subjects. Please present as focused an idea as possible in a brief submission (one page cover letter; two page outline or proposal). Note your credentials for writing the book. Tell all you know about the market niche and marketing possibilities for proposed book."

WADSWORTH PUBLISHING CO., 10 Davis Dr., Belmont CA 94002. (650)595-2350. Fax: (650)637-7544. Website: www.wadsworth.com. **Acquisitions:** Sean Wakely, editorial director; Steve Wainwright, editor (philosophy/religion); Holly Allen, editor (communications, radio/TV/film/theater); David Patom, editor (political science); Clark Baxter, publisher (history/music); Annie Mitchell, editor (communications and speech); Lin Marshall, editor (sociology/anthropology [upper level]); Lisa Gebo, senior editor (psychology and helping professions); Sabra Horne, senior editor (criminal justice, sociology); Dan Alpert, editor (education/special education); Vicki Knight, executive editor (psychology); Peter Marshall, publisher (health/nutrition); Edith Brady, editor (psychology); Marianne Tafliner, senior editor (psychology). Estab. 1956. Publishes hardcover and paperback originals and software. **Publishes 300 titles/year. 35% of books from first-time authors; 99% from unagented writers. Pays 5-15% royalty on net receipts. Offers Not automatic policy advance.** Publishes book 1 year after acceptance of ms. Accepts simultaneous submissions. Book catalog via website or with SASE; Ms guidelines via website or with SASE.

O→ Wadsworth publishes college-level textbooks in social sciences, humanities, education and college success.

Nonfiction: Multimedia, textbook, multimedia products: higher education only. Subjects include anthropology/archeology, cooking/foods/nutrition, education, health/medicine, language/literature, music/dance, nature/environment, philosophy, psychology, religion (studies), science, sociology, software, counseling, criminal justice, speech and mass communications, Broadcasting, TV and film productions, college success. Query with SASE or submit outline, sample chapter(s). Synopsis.

Recent Title(s): *Production and Operations Management*, 7th edition, Norman Gaither.

J. WESTON WALCH, PUBLISHER, P.O. Box 658, Portland ME 04104-0658. (207)772-3105. Fax: (207)774-7167. Website: www.walch.com. **Acquisitions:** Susan Blair, editor-in-chief. Estab. 1927. **Publishes 100 titles/year. Receives 300 submissions/year. 10% of books from first-time authors; 95% from unagented writers. Pays 5-8% royalty on flat rate.** Publishes book 6 months after acceptance of ms. Accepts simultaneous submissions. Responds in 2 months to queries. Book catalog for 9×12 SAE with 5 first-class stamps; ms guidelines for #10 SASE.

O→ "We focus on English/language arts, math, social studies and science teaching resources for middle school through adult assessment titles."

Nonfiction: Formats include teacher resources, reproducibles. Subjects include education (mathematics, middle school, social studies, remedial and special education), government/politics, history, language/literature, science, social sciences, technology. Most titles are assigned by us, though we occasionally accept an author's unsolicited submission. We have a great need for author/artist teams and for authors who can write at third- to seventh-grade levels. Looks for sense of organization, writing ability, knowledge of subject, skill of communicating with intended audience. We do *not* want textbooks or anthologies. All authors should have educational writing experience. *Query first.* Query with SASE. Reviews artwork/photos as part of ms package.

WALKER AND CO., Walker Publishing Co., 435 Hudson St., New York NY 10014. Fax: (212)727-0984. Publisher: George Gibson. Adult Nonfiction Editor: Jacqueline Johnson. Juvenile Publisher: Emily Easton. Juvenile Editor: Timothy Travaglini. **Acquisitions:** Submissions to Adult Nonfiction Editor limited to agents, published authors and writers wtih professional credentials in their field of expertise. Children's books to "Submissions Editor-Juvenile." Estab. 1959. Publishes hardcover and trade paperback originals. **Publishes 70 titles/year. Receives 3,500 submissions/year. Pays 7½-12% on paperback, 10-15% on hardcover. Offers competitive advance.** Publishes book 1 year after acceptance of ms. Accepts simultaneous submissions. Responds in 3 months to queries. Book catalog for 9×12 SAE with 3 first-class stamps.

Imprints: Walker & Co. Books for Young Readers.

O→ Walker publishes general nonfiction on a variety of subjects as well as children's books.

Nonfiction: Adult. Subjects include health/medicine, history (science and technology), nature/environment, science (popular), sports (baseball). Query with SASE. No phone calls.

Fiction: Juvenile (fiction, nonfiction), picture books (juvenile). Query with SASE.

Recent Title(s): *Salt*, by Mark Kurlansky (history); *IQ Goes to School* (juvenile); *Lusitania*, by Diana Preston (history).

WALSWORTH PUBLISHING CO., Donning Co. Publishers, 306 N. Kansas Ave., Marceline MO 64658. (800)369-2646, ext. 3269. Fax: (660)258-7798. E-mail: steve.mull@walsworth.com. Website: www.donning.com. **Acquisitions:** Steve Mull, general manager. Publishes hardcover originals and reprints. **Publishes 40-50 titles/year. Receives 25 queries and 50 mss/year. 70% of books from first-time authors; 99% from unagented writers. Pays 5-15% royalty on wholesale price. Offers advance.** Does not accept simultaneous submissions. Ms guidelines free.

O→ Publishes coffee table books.

Nonfiction: Coffee table book. Subjects include agriculture/horticulture, business/economics, ethnic, history (community, college, agricultural, business/economic), military/war, sports. Query with SASE.

WALTSAN PUBLISHING, LLC, 5000 Barnett St., Fort Worth TX 76103-2006. (817)429-2512. E-mail: sandra@waltsan.com. Website: www.waltsan.com. **Publishes 40-60 titles/year. Receives 1,500 queries and 1,000 mss/year. 95% of books from first-time authors; 95% from unagented writers. Pays 20% royalty on wholesale price.** Publishes book 9-18 months after acceptance of ms. Accepts simultaneous submissions. Responds in 2 months to queries; 2 months to proposals; 4-6 months to mss. Book catalog online; ms guidelines online.

Nonfiction: Subjects include general nonfiction. "We look at any nonfiction subject." Query with SASE or via website or submit proposal package, including outline and 3 sample chapters or submit complete ms. Reviews artwork/photos as part of ms package. Send photocopies.

Fiction: "We look at all fiction." Full-length or collections equal to full-length only. Query with SASE or submit proposal package including 3 sample chapter(s), synopsis or submit complete ms.

Recent Title(s): *Shadows and Stones*, by Bernita Stark (dark fiction of shape changers and vampires); *Kite Paper, Papel de Barrilete*, by Sue Littleton (love poem with Spanish and English texts); *Jules Verne Classics*, edited by Walter Wellborn.

Tips: Audience is computer literate, generally higher income and intelligent. "When possible, authors record their manuscript to include audio on the CD. Check our website for guidelines and sample contract." Initial queries and proposals may be submitted on paper. Mss accepted for publication must be submitted electronically—no exceptions. Only publishes on CDs and other removable media.

[A] **WARNER ASPECT**, imprint of Warner Books, 1271 Avenue of the Americas, New York NY 10020. (212)522-7200. Website: twbookmark.com. Editor: Jaime Levine. Publishes hardcover, trade paperback, mass market paperback originals and mass market paperback reprints. **Publishes 30 titles/year. Receives 500 queries and 350 mss/year. 5-10% of books from first-time authors; 1% from unagented writers. Pays royalty on retail price. Offers $5,000-up advance.** Publishes book 14 months after acceptance of ms. Responds in 3 months to mss.

O→ "We're looking for 'epic' stories in both fantasy and science fiction. Also seeking writers of color to add to what we've already published by Octavia E. Butler, Nalo Hopkinson, Walter Mosley, etc."

Fiction: Fantasy, science fiction. "Mistake writers often make is "hoping against hope that being unagented won't make a difference. We simply don't have the staff to look at unagented projects." *Agented submissions only.*

Recent Title(s): *Hidden Empire*, by Kevin J. Anderson; *The Elder Gods*, by David & Leigh Eddings.

[A] **WARNER BOOKS**, Time & Life Building, 1271 Avenue of the Americas, New York NY 10020. (212)522-7200. Website: www.twbookmark.com. President/Time Warner Book Group: Maureen Egen. **Acquisitions:** (Ms.) Jamie Raab, senior vice president/publisher (general nonfiction and fiction); Les Pockell, associate publisher (general nonfiction); Rick Horgan, vice president/executive editor (general nonfiction and fiction, thrillers); Amy Einhorn, editorial director, trade paperback (popular culture, business, fitness, self-help); Beth de Guzman, editorial director, mass market (fiction, romance, nonfiction); Rick Wolff, vice president/executive editor (business, humor, sports); Sara Ann Freed, editor-in-chief, Mysterious Press (mysteries, suspense); Caryn Karmatz Rudy, senior editor (fiction, general nonfiction, popular culture); Diana Baroni, executive editor (health, fitness, general nonfiction and fiction); John Aherne, editor (popular culture, men's health, New Age, movie tie-ins, general fiction); Rolf Zettersten, vice president/Warner Faith (books for the CBA market); (Ms.) Jaime Levine, editor/Aspect (science fiction); Karen Koszto Inyik, senior editor (women's fiction). Estab. 1960. Publishes hardcover, trade paperback and mass market paperback originals and reprints and e-books. **Publishes 250 titles/year. Pays variable royalty. Offers variable advance.** Publishes book 2 years after acceptance of ms. Accepts no unsolicited mss to queries.

Imprints: Mysterious Press (mystery/suspense), Warner Aspect (science fiction and fantasy), Warner Vision, Warner

Forever, Warner Business, Walk Worthy Press, Warner Faith (Christian fiction and nonfiction).

O→ Warner publishes general interest fiction and nonfiction.

Nonfiction: Biography, humor, reference, self-help. Subjects include business/economics, contemporary culture, cooking/foods/nutrition, health/medicine, history, psychology, spirituality, sports, current affairs, human potential. *No unsolicited mss.*

Fiction: Fantasy, horror, mainstream/contemporary, mystery, romance, science fiction, suspense, thrillers. *Agented submissions only. No unsolicited mss.*

Recent Title(s): *Up Country*, by Nelson DeMille; *Nights in Rodanthe*, by Nicholas Sparks; *Rich Dad Poor Dad*, by Robert T. Kiyosaki with Sharon L. Lechter.

WASHINGTON STATE UNIVERSITY PRESS, Pullman WA 99164-5910. (800)354-7360. Fax: (509)335-8568. E-mail: wsupress@wsu.edu. Website: www.wsupress.wsu.edu. **Acquisitions:** Glen Lindeman, editor. Estab. 1928. Publishes hardcover originals, trade paperback originals and reprints. **Publishes 8-10 titles/year. Receives 200-250 submissions/year. 40% of books from first-time authors. Most books from unagented writers. Pays 5% royalty graduated according to sales.** Publishes book 18 months after acceptance of ms. Responds in 2 months to queries. Ms guidelines online.

O→ WSU Press publishes books on the history, pre-history, culture, and politics of the West, particularly the Pacific Northwest.

Nonfiction: Biography. Subjects include cooking/foods/nutrition (history), government/politics, history, nature/environment, regional, essays. "We seek manuscripts that focus on the Pacific Northwest as a region. No poetry, novels, literary criticism, how-to books. We welcome innovative and thought-provoking titles in a wide diversity of genres, from essays and memoirs to history, archaeology and political science." Submit outline, sample chapter(s). Reviews artwork/photos as part of ms package.

Recent Title(s): *The Cayton Legacy: An African American Family*; *Washington Territory*; *The Restless Northwest: A Geographical Story.*

Tips: "We have developed our marketing in the direction of regional and local history and have attempted to use this as the base upon which to expand our publishing program. In regional history, the secret is to write a good narrative—a good story—that is substantiated factually. It should be told in an imaginative, clever way. Have visuals (photos, maps, etc.) available to help the reader envision what has happened. Tell the regional history story in a way that ties it to larger, national, and even international events. Weave it into the large pattern of history."

N A **WATERBROOK PRESS**, Subsidiary of Random House, 2375 Telstar Dr., Suite 160, Colorado Springs CO 80920. (719)590-4999. Fax: (719)590-8977. Website: www.waterbrookpress.com. **Acquisitions:** Laura Barker, editorial director (nonfiction); Dudley Delffs, editor (fiction). Estab. 1996. Publishes hardcover and trade paperback originals. **Publishes 70 titles/year; imprint publishes 20-55 titles/year. Receives 1,500 queries/year. 15-25% of books from first-time authors; 25% from unagented writers. Pays royalty.** Publishes book 11 months after acceptance of ms. Accepts simultaneous submissions. Responds in 1-2 months to queries; 1-2 months to proposals; 1-2 months to mss. Book catalog online.

Imprints: Shaw Books (Elisa Stanford, editor).

Nonfiction: Autobiography, biography, children's/juvenile, self-help. Subjects include child guidance/parenting, general nonfiction, health/medicine, money/finance, religion, spirituality. "We publish books on unique topics with a Christian perspective." *Agented submissions only.*

Fiction: Adventure, historical, literary, mainstream/contemporary, mystery, religious, romance, science fiction, spiritual, suspense. *Agented submissions only.*

Recent Title(s): *Every Man's Battle*, by Steve Arterburn & Fred Stoeker (Christian living); *Get Over It and On With It*, by Michelle McKinney Hammono (Christian living); *A Name of Her Own*, by Jane Kirkpatrick (historical fiction).

WATSON-GUPTILL PUBLICATIONS, Billboard Publications, Inc., 770 Broadway, New York NY 10003. (646)654-5000. Fax: (646)654-5486. Website: www.watsonguptill.com. **Acquisitions:** Candace Raney, executive editor (fine art, art technique, pop culture); Bob Nirkind, executive editor (Billboard-music, popular culture); Joy Acquilino, senior editor (crafts); Victoria Craven, senior editor (Amphoto-photography, lifestyle); Alison Hagge (graphic design, architecture); Julie Mazur (children's books). Publishes hardcover and trade paperback originals and reprints. **Receives 150 queries and 50 mss/year. 50% of books from first-time authors; 75% from unagented writers. Pays royalty on wholesale price.** Publishes book 9 months after acceptance of ms. Responds in 2 months to queries; 3 months to proposals. Book catalog free; ms guidelines online.

Imprints: Watson-Guptill, Amphoto, Whitney Library of Design, Billboard Books, Back Stage Books.

O→ Watson-Guptill is an arts book publisher.

Nonfiction: How-to (instructionals). Subjects include art/architecture, music/dance, photography, Lifestyle, Pop culture, Theater. "Writers should be aware of the kinds of books (arts, crafts, graphic designs, instructional) Watson-Guptill publishes before submitting. Although we are growing and will consider new ideas and approaches, we will not consider a book if it is clearly outside of our publishing program." Query with SASE or submit proposal package including outline, 1-2 sample chapter(s). Reviews artwork/photos as part of ms package. Send photocopies or transparencies.

Recent Title(s): *The Tao of Watercolor*, by Jeanne Carbonetti; *American Impressionism*, by Elizabeth Prelinger; *Manga Mania*, by Christopher Hart.

Tips: "We are an art book publisher."

WEATHERHILL, INC., 41 Monroe Turnpike, Trumbull CT 06611. (203)459-5090. Fax: (203)459-5095. E-mail: weatherhill@weatherhill.com. Website: www.weatherhill.com. **Acquisitions:** Raymond Furse, editorial director. Estab. 1962. Publishes hardcover and trade paperback originals and reprints. **Publishes 36 titles/year. Receives 250 queries and 100 mss/year. 20% of books from first-time authors; 95% from unagented writers. Pays 12-18% royalty on wholesale price. Offers up to $10,000 advance.** Publishes book 8 months after acceptance of ms. Accepts simultaneous submissions. Responds in 1 month to proposals. Book catalog and ms guidelines free.

O‑ Weatherhill publishes exclusively Asia-related nonfiction and Asian fiction and poetry in translation.

Nonfiction: Asia related topics only. Biography, coffee table book, cookbook, gift book, how-to, humor, illustrated book, reference, self-help. Subjects include anthropology/archeology, art/architecture, cooking/foods/nutrition, gardening, history, humor, language/literature, music/dance, nature/environment, photography, regional, religion, sociology, translation, travel, martial arts. Submit outline, 2 sample chapter(s), and sample illustrations (if applicable). Reviews artwork/photos as part of ms package. Send photocopies.

Fiction: "We publish only important Asian writers in translation. Asian fiction is a hard sell. Authors should check funding possibilities from appropriate sources: Japan Foundation, Korea Foundation, etc." Submit synopsis.

Poetry: Only Asian poetry in translation. Query.

Recent Title(s): *Buddha and Christ*, by Robert Elinor; *Hapkido*, by Marc Tedeschi.

WEIDNER & SONS PUBLISHING, P.O. Box 2178, Riverton NJ 08077. (856)486-1755. E-mail: weidner@waterw.com. Website: www.weidnerpublishing.com. **Acquisitions:** James H. Weidner, president. Estab. 1967. Publishes hardcover and trade paperback originals and reprints. **Publishes 10-20 titles/year; imprint publishes 10 titles/year. Receives hundreds queries and 50 mss/year. 100% of books from first-time authors; 90% from unagented writers. Pays 10% royalty on wholesale price. Offers advance.** Accepts simultaneous submissions. Responds in 1 month to queries. Ms guidelines online.

Imprints: Bird Sci Books, Delaware Estuary Press, Hazlaw Books, Medlaw Books, Pulse Publications, Tycooly Publishing USA.

O‑ Weidner & Sons publishes primarily science, text and reference books for scholars, college students and researchers.

Nonfiction: Reference, technical, textbook. Subjects include agriculture/horticulture, animals, business/economics, child guidance/parenting, computers/electronic, education, gardening, health/medicine, hobbies (electronic), language/literature, nature/environment, psychology, science, ecology/environment. "At present, our needs are rather specific, and it will save authors time and money to ensure the topic is within our needs. We do not publish fiction; never poetry. No topics in the 'pseudosciences': occult, astrology, New Age and metaphysics, etc. Suggest 2 copies of ms, double spaced, along with PC disk in Word or PageMaker." Submit outline, sample chapter(s), include e-mail address for faster response, SASE. Reviews artwork/photos as part of ms package. Send photocopies.

Recent Title(s): *The Huntington Sexual Behavior Scale*, by Vince Huntington (Perspectives in Psychology series).

N **WELCOME ENTERPRISES, INC.**, 6 W. 18th St., New York NY 10011. (212)989-3200. Fax: (212)989-3205. E-mail: info@welcomebooks.biz. Website: www.welcomebooks.biz. **Acquisitions:** Leah Tabori, publisher/editor; Natasha Tabori Fried, editor; Katrina Fried, editor; Alice Wong, editor. Estab. 1980. **Publishes 8 titles/year. Pays 7½% royalty on net receipts.**

Nonfiction: Children's/juvenile, illustrated book. Subjects include art/architecture, language/literature. Query with SASE.

Recent Title(s): *Flight: A Celebration of 100 years in Art and Literature*; *Searchings*; *The Little Big Book for Boys*.

WESCOTT COVE PUBLISHING CO., P.O. Box 130, Stamford CT 06904. (203)322-0998. Fax: (203)322-1388. **Acquisitions:** Julius M. Wilensky, president. Estab. 1968. Publishes trade paperback originals and reprints. **Publishes 4 titles/year. Receives 15 queries and 10 mss/year. 25% of books from first-time authors; 95% from unagented writers. Pays 5-10% royalty on retail price. Offers $1,000-1,500 advance.** Publishes book 1 year after acceptance of ms. Accepts simultaneous submissions. Responds in 1 week to queries. Book catalog free.

O‑ "We publish the most complete cruising guides, each one an authentic reference for the area covered."

Nonfiction: "All titles are nautical books; half of them are cruising guides. Mostly we seek out authors knowledgeable in sailing, navigation, cartography and the area we want covered. Then we commission them to write the book." How-to, humor, illustrated book, reference. Subjects include history, hobbies, regional, sports, travel, nautical. Query with SASE or submit outline, 1-2 sample chapter(s), SASE.

Recent Title(s): *Chesapeake Bay Cruising Guide Volume I, Upper Bay*, by Tom Neale.

Tips: "We publish cruising guides and nautical books."

WESLEYAN UNIVERSITY PRESS, 110 Mount Vernon St., Middletown CT 06459. (860)685-2420. Website: www.wesleyan.edu/wespress. Director: Tom Radko. **Acquisitions:** Suzanna Tamminen, editor-in-chief. Estab. 1959. Publishes hardcover originals and paperbacks. **Publishes 40 titles/year. Receives 1,500 queries and 1,000 mss/year. 10% of books from first-time authors; 80% from unagented writers. Pays 0-8% royalty. Offers up to $3,000 advance.** Publishes book 1-3 years after acceptance of ms. Accepts simultaneous submissions. Responds in 1 month to queries; 2 months to proposals; 3 months to mss. Book catalog free; Manuscript guidelines online for free with #10 SASE.

O‑ Wesleyan University Press is a scholarly press with a focus on poetry, music, dance and cultural studies.

Nonfiction: Biography, scholarly, textbook. Subjects include ethnic (studies), film/cinema/stage, gay/lesbian (studies), history, language/literature, music/dance, philosophy, psychology. Submit proposal package including outline, introductory letter, curriculum vitae, table of contents. Reviews artwork/photos as part of ms package. Send photocopies.

Fiction: Science fiction. "We publish very little fiction, less than 3% of our entire list."

Poetry: "Writers should request a catalog and guidelines." Submit 5-10 sample poems.

Recent Title(s): *The Grand Permission: New Writings on Poetics and Motherhood*, edited by Patricia Dienstfrey &

Brenda Hillman (poetry); *Global Noise: Rap and Hip Hop Outside the USA*, edited by Tony Mitchell (music); *Mysterious Island*, by Jules Verne.

WESTCLIFFE PUBLISHERS, P.O. Box 1261, Englewood CO 80150. (303)935-0900. Fax: (303)935-0903. E-mail: editor@westcliffepublishers.com. Website: www.westcliffepublishers.com. Linda Doyle, associate publisher. **Acquisitions:** Jenna Samelson, managing editor. Estab. 1981. Publishes hardcover originals, trade paperback originals and reprints. **Publishes 18 titles/year. Receives 100 queries and 60 mss/year. 50% of books from first-time authors; 100% from unagented writers. Pays royalty on retail price. Offers advance.** Publishes book 18 months after acceptance of ms. Accepts simultaneous submissions. Responds in 1 month to queries. Book catalog free; ms guidelines online.

O→ "Westcliffe Publishers produces the highest quality in regional photography and essays for our outdoor guidebooks, coffee table-style books, and calendars. As an eco-publisher our mission is to foster environmental awareness by showing the beauty of the natural world." Strong concentration on color guide books, outdoor sports, history.

Nonfiction: Coffee table book, gift book, illustrated book, reference. Subjects include Americana, animals, gardening, history, nature/environment, photography, regional, sports (outdoor), travel. "Writers need to do their market research to justify a need in the marketplace." Submit proposal package including outline. Westcliffe will contact you for photos, writing samples.

Recent Title(s): *Colorado: 1870-2000*, by John Fielder; *Haunted Texas Vacations*, by Lisa Farwell.

Tips: Audience are nature and outdoors enthusiasts and photographers. "Just call us!"

WESTERN PSYCHOLOGICAL SERVICES, Manson Western Corp., 12031 Wilshire Blvd., Los Angeles CA 90025. (310)478-2061. Fax: (310)478-2061. E-mail: smanson@wpspublish.com. Website: www.wpspublish.com. **Acquisitions:** Susan Madden, director of marketing. Estab. 1948. Publishes trade paperback originals. **Publishes 6 titles/year. Receives 6 queries and 12 mss/year. 75% of books from first-time authors; 80% from unagented writers. Pays 5-10% royalty on wholesale price.** Publishes book 1 year after acceptance of ms. Accepts simultaneous submissions. Responds in 1 month to queries. Book catalog free; ms guidelines online.

O→ Western Psychological Services publishes practical books used by therapists, counselors, social workers and others in the helping field working with children and adults.

Nonfiction: Self-help. Subjects include child guidance/parenting, education, multicultural, psychology. Submit complete ms. *Writer's Market* recommends a query first. Reviews artwork/photos as part of ms package. Send photocopies.

Fiction: Expressing feelings, understanding and dealing with emotional problems. Submit complete ms. *Writer's Market* recommends query first.

Recent Title(s): *Psychodiagnostics and Personality Assessment: Third Edition*, by Donald P. Ogden.

WESTERNLORE PRESS, P.O. Box 35305, Tucson AZ 85740. (520)297-5491. Fax: (520)297-1722. **Acquisitions:** Lynn R. Bailey, editor. Estab. 1941. **Publishes 6-12 titles/year. Pays standard royalty on retail price.** Does not accept simultaneous submissions. Responds in 2 months to queries.

O→ Westernlore publishes Western Americana of a scholarly and semischolarly nature.

Nonfiction: Biography, scholarly. Subjects include Americana, anthropology/archeology, history, regional, historic sights, restoration, ethnohistory pertaining to the American West. Re-publication of rare and out-of-print books. Length: 25,000-100,000 words. Query with SASE.

Recent Title(s): *The Apache Kid*, by de la Gaza (Western history); *Cochise County Stalwarts, vol. I & II.*

WESTWINDS PRESS, Graphic Arts Center Publishing, P.O. Box 10306, Portland OR 97296-0306. (503)226-2402. Fax: (503)223-1410. Website: www.gacpc.com. **Acquisitions:** Tricia Brown, acquisitions editor. Estab. 1999. Publishes hardcover and trade paperback originals and reprints. **Publishes 5-7 titles/year. Receives hundreds of submissions/year. 10% of books from first-time authors; 90% from unagented writers. Pays 10-14% royalty on net receipts or makes outright purchase. Offers advance.** Publishes book an average of 2 years after acceptance of ms. Accepts simultaneous submissions. Responds in 6 months to queries. Book catalog and ms guidelines for 9×12 SAE with 6 first-class stamps; ms guidelines online.

Nonfiction: Children's/juvenile, cookbook. Subjects include history, memoirs, regional (Western regional states—nature, travel, cookbooks, Native American culture, adventure, outdoor recreation, sports, the arts and children's books), guidebooks.

Recent Title(s): *Sharkabet: A Sea of Sharks from A to Z* (children's book); *The Colorado Almanac: Facts About Colorado* (reference).

Tips: "Book proposals that are professionally written and polished with a clear market receive our most careful consideration. We are looking for originality. We publish a wide range of books for a wide audience. Some of our books are clearly for travelers, others for those interested in outdoor recreation or various regional subjects. If I were a writer trying to market a book today, I would research the competition (existing books) for what I have in mind, and clearly (and concisely) express why my idea is different and better. I would describe the book buyers (and readers)—where they are, how many of them are there, how they can be reached (organizations, publications), why they would want or need my book."

WHITE CLIFFS MEDIA, INC., Editorial Dept., P.O. Box 6083, Incline Village NV 89450. Website: www.wc-media.com. **Acquisitions:** Lawrence Aynesmith. Estab. 1985. Publishes hardcover and trade paperback originals. **Publishes 5-10 titles/year. 50% of books from first-time authors; 50% from unagented writers. Pays 5-12% royalty or makes outright purchase.** Publishes book 1 year after acceptance of ms. Does not accept simultaneous submissions. Responds in 2 months to queries; 4 months to proposals; 6 months to mss. Book catalog online.

O→ Publishes music titles for an academic and general audience.

Nonfiction: Biography, textbook. Subjects include anthropology/archeology, ethnic, music/dance. Query. Reviews artwork/photos as part of ms package. Send photocopies.

Recent Title(s): *The Healing Power of the Drum*, by Robert Lawrence Friedman.

Tips: "Distribution is more difficult due to the large number of publishers. Writers should send proposals that have potential for mass markets as well as college texts, and that will be submitted and completed on schedule. Our audience reads college texts, general interest trade publications. If I were a writer trying to market a book today, I would send a book on music comparable in quality and mass appeal to a book like Stephen Hawking's *A Brief History of Time*."

WHITE MANE BOOKS, White Mane Publishing Co. Inc., 63 W. Burd St., P.O. Box 708, Shippensburg PA 17257. (717)532-2237. Fax: (717)532-6110. E-mail: editorial@whitemane.com. Website: www.whitemane.com. **Acquisitions:** Harold Collier, vice president/acquisitions editor. Estab. 1987. Publishes hardcover, and trade paperback originals and reprints. **Publishes 60 titles/year; imprint publishes 12-18 titles/year. Receives 300 queries and 50 mss/year. 50% of books from first-time authors; 75% from unagented writers. Pays royalty on monies received. Offers advance.** Publishes book 18 months after acceptance of ms. Accepts simultaneous submissions. Responds in 1 month to queries; 1 month to proposals; 3 months to mss. Book catalog and ms guidelines free for SASE.

Imprints: White Mane Books; Burd Street Press (military history, emphasis on American Civil War); Ragged Edge Press (religious); White Mane Kids (historically based children's fiction).

O→ "White Mane Publishing Company, Inc., continues its tradition of publishing the finest military history, regional, religious and children's historical fiction books." Currently emphasizing American Civil War, World War II, children's historical fiction. Does not want picture books.

Nonfiction: Children's/juvenile, reference (adult), scholarly. Subjects include history, military/war, women's issues/studies. Query with SASE. Reviews artwork/photos as part of ms package. Send photocopies.

Fiction: Historical, juvenile (middle grade), young adult. Query with SASE.

Recent Title(s): *Gettysburg's Bloody Wheatfield*, by Jay Jorgensen (adult nonfiction); *Slaves Who Dared: The Stories of Ten African American Heroes*, by Mary Garrison (White Mane Kids).

WHITEHORSE PRESS, P.O. Box 60, North Conway NH 03860-0060. (603)356-6556. Fax: (603)356-6590. **Acquisitions:** Dan Kennedy, publisher. Estab. 1988. Publishes trade paperback originals. **Publishes 10-20 titles/year. Pays 10% royalty on wholesale price.** Does not accept simultaneous submissions. Responds in 1 month to queries.

Nonfiction: "We are actively seeking nonfiction books to aid motorcyclists in topics such as motorcycle safety, restoration, repair and touring. We are especially interested in technical subjects related to motorcycling." How-to, reference. Subjects include travel. Query with SASE.

Recent Title(s): *How to Set Up Your Motorcycle Workshop*, by Charlie Masi (trade paperback).

Tips: "We like to discuss project ideas at an early stage and work with authors to develop those ideas to fit our market."

ALBERT WHITMAN AND CO., 6340 Oakton St., Morton Grove IL 60053-2723. (847)581-0033. Website: www.awhitmanco.com. **Acquisitions:** Kathleen Tucker, editor-in-chief. Estab. 1919. Publishes hardcover originals and paperback reprints. **Publishes 30 titles/year. Receives 5,000 submissions/year. 20% of books from first-time authors; 70% from unagented writers. Pays 10% royalty for novels; 5% for picture books. Offers advance.** Publishes book an average of 18 months after acceptance of ms. Accepts simultaneous submissions. Responds in 6 weeks to queries; 3-4 months to mss. Book catalog for 8×10 SAE with 3 first-class stamps; ms guidelines for #10 SASE.

O→ Albert Whitman publishes good books for children on a variety of topics: holidays (i.e., Halloween), special needs (such as diabetes) and problems like divorce. The majority of our titles are picture books with less than 1,500 words." De-emphasizing bedtime stories.

Nonfiction: All books are for ages 2-12. Children's/juvenile, illustrated book. Subjects include animals, anthropology/archeology, art/architecture, computers/electronic, cooking/foods/nutrition, ethnic, gardening, health/medicine, history, hobbies, language/literature, music/dance, nature/environment, photography, recreation, religion, science, sports, travel, social studies, math. Submit complete ms. if it is picture book length; otherwise query with SASE.

Fiction: "All books are for ages 2-12." Adventure, ethnic, fantasy, historical, humor, mystery, holiday, concept books (to help children deal with problems), family. Currently emphasizing picture books; de-emphasizine folf tales and bedtime stories. No young adult and adult books. Submit complete ms. for picture books; for longer works submit query with outline and sample chapters.

Recent Title(s): *Pumpkin Jack*, by Will Hubbell.

Tips: "We sell mostly to libraries, but our bookstore sales are growing. We recommend you study our catalog or visit our website before submitting your work."

WHITSTON PUBLISHING CO., INC., 1717 Central Ave., Suite 201, Albany NY 12205. (518)452-1900. Fax: (518)452-1777. E-mail: whitston@capital.net. Website: www.whitston.com. **Acquisitions:** Michael Laddin, publisher. Estab. 1969. Publishes hardcover and trade paperback originals. **Publishes 15-25 titles/year. Receives 200 submissions/year. 20% of books from first-time authors; 100% from unagented writers. Pays royalities after sale of 500 copies.** Publishes book 1 year after acceptance of ms. Does not accept simultaneous submissions. Responds in 6 months to queries.

O→ Whitston focuses on literature, politics, history, business and the sciences.

Nonfiction: "We publish nonfiction books in the humanities. We also publish reference bibliographies and indexes." Subjects include art/architecture, business/economics, government/politics, health/medicine, history, language/literature, social sciences. Query with SASE. Reviews artwork/photos as part of ms package.

Recent Title(s): *Mark Twain Among the Scholars*; *Hustlers, Heroes & Hooligans: Reporting on the New York Experience*; *Life after Layoff*.

MARKUS WIENER PUBLISHERS, INC., 231 Nassau St., Princeton NJ 08542. (609)921-1141. **Acquisitions:** Shelley Frisch, editor-in-chief. Estab. 1981. Publishes hardcover originals and trade paperback originals and reprints. **Publishes 15 titles/year; imprint publishes 5 titles/year. Receives 50-150 queries and 50 mss/year. Pays 10% royalty on net receipts.** Publishes book 1 year after acceptance of ms. Does not accept simultaneous submissions. Responds in 2 months to queries; 2 months to proposals. Book catalog free.

Imprints: Princeton Series on the Middle East, Topics in World History.

O→ Markus Wiener publishes textbooks in history subjects and regional world history.

Nonfiction: Textbook. Subjects include history, world affairs, Caribbean studies, Middle East, Africa.

Recent Title(s): *Afro-Cuban Music*, by Maya Roy (Middle East studies); *Cuban Legends*, by Salvador Bueno, illustrations by Sigi Kaolen; *The Levant*, by William Harris.

MICHAEL WIESE PRODUCTIONS, 11288 Ventura Blvd., Suite 621, Studio City CA 91604. (818)379-8799. E-mail: kenlee@mwp.com. Website: www.mwp.com. **Acquisitions:** Ken Lee, vice president. Estab. 1981. Publishes trade paperback originals. **Publishes 12-14 titles/year. Receives 30-50 queries/year. 90% of books from first-time authors. Pays 10% royalty on retail price. Offers $1,000-15,000 advance.** Publishes book 10 months after acceptance of ms. Accepts simultaneous submissions. Responds in 1 week to queries; 1 week to proposals; 2 months to mss. Book catalog online.

O→ Michael Wiese publishes how-to books for professional film or video makers, film schools and bookstores.

Nonfiction: How-to. Subjects include professional film and videomaking. Submit outline, 3 sample chapter(s). Call before submitting.

Recent Title(s): *Script Partners*, by Claudia Johnson and Matt Stevens; *Digital Moviemaking, 2nd Ed*, by Scott Billups.

Tips: Audience is professional filmmakers, writers, producers, directors, actors and university film students.

WILDCAT CANYON PRESS, Council Oak Books, 2105 E. 15th St., Suite B, Tulsa OK 74105. E-mail: order@wildcatcanyon.com. Website: www.wildcatcanyon.com; www.counciloakbooks.com. **Acquisitions:** Acquisitions Editor. **Publishes 10-12 titles/year. Receives 500 queries and 300 mss/year. Pays 12-16% royalty on wholesale price. Offers $1,000-3,000 advance.** Publishes book 9 months after acceptance of ms. Accepts simultaneous submissions. Responds in 6 months to queries. Book catalog and ms guidelines free; ms guidelines online.

O→ Wildcat Canyon Press publishes quality books on self-care, relationships, parenting, fashion and food.

Nonfiction: Gift book, self-help, lifestyle (fashion and food). Query with SASE or submit proposal package including outline, SASE. E-queries are accepted. Reviews artwork/photos as part of ms package. Send photocopies.

Recent Title(s): *The Hip Girl's Handbook to Home, Car and Money Stuff*; *Straight Women, Gay Men*; *Absolutely Fabulous Relationships*.

Tips: "We are looking for fun and practical book projects that work well in both the traditional bookstore and gift markets."

WILDER PUBLISHING CENTER, 919 Lafond Ave., St. Paul MN 55104. (651)659-6013. Fax: (651)642-2061. E-mail: vlh@wilder.org. Website: www.wilder.org. **Acquisitions:** Vincent Hyman, director. Publishes trade paperback originals. **Publishes 6 titles/year. Receives 30 queries and 15 mss/year. 75% of books from first-time authors; 100% from unagented writers. Pays 10% royalty on net receipts. Books are sold through direct mail; average discount is 20%. Offers $1,000-3,000 advance.** Publishes book 18 months after acceptance of ms. Does not accept simultaneous submissions. Responds in 1 month to queries; 1 month to proposals; 3 months to mss. Book catalog and ms guidelines free or online; ms guidelines online.

O→ Wilder Publishing Center emphasizes community and nonprofit organization management and development.

Nonfiction: Subjects include nonprofit management, organizational development, community building. "We are seeking mss that report 'best practice' methods using handbook or workbook formats for nonprofit and community development managers." Submit 3 sample chapter(s). Phone query OK before submitting proposal with detailed chapter outline, SASE, statement of unique selling points, identification of audience.

Recent Title(s): *The Lobbying and Advocacy Handbook for Nonprofit Organizations*; *The Wilder Nonprofit Guide to Crafting Effective Mission and Vision Statements*; *The Five Life Stages of Nonprofit Organizations*.

Tips: "Writers must be practitioners with a passion for their work in nonprofit management or community building and experience presenting their techniques at conferences. We seek practical, not academic books. Our books identify professional challenges faced by our audiences and offer practical, step-by-step solutions."

WILDERNESS PRESS, 1200 Fifth St., Berkley CA 94710. (510)558-1666. Fax: (510)558-1696. E-mail: mail@wildernesspress.com. Website: www.wildernesspress.com. **Acquisitions:** Jannie Dresser, managing editor. Estab. 1967. Publishes paperback originals. **Publishes 12 titles/year. Receives 75 submissions/year. 20% of books from first-time authors; 95% from unagented writers. Pays 5-8% royalty on retail price. Offers $1,000 average advance.** Publishes book 8-12 months after acceptance of ms. Does not accept simultaneous submissions. Responds in 2 months to queries. Book catalog and ms guidelines online.

O→ "We publish books and maps that focus on activities in nature, including titles that describe outdoor sporting and recreational activities, and topics related to the environment and nature. We do not publish journals, essays, poetry, or memoirs."

Nonfiction: How-to (outdoors). Subjects include nature/environment, recreation, trail guides for hikers and backpackers. "We publish books about the outdoors. Most are trail guides for hikers and backpackers, but we also publish how-to books about the outdoors. The manuscript must be accurate. The author must research an area in person. If writing a trail guide, you must walk all the trails in the area your book is about. Outlook must be strongly conservationist. Style must be appropriate for a highly literate audience." Download proposal guidelines from website.

Recent Title(s): *Traditional Lead Climbing*; *Washington's Highest Mountains*; *Wild Soundscapes*.

JOHN WILEY & SONS, INC., 111 River St., Hoboken NJ 07030. Website: www.wiley.com. General Interest Publisher: K. Allan. **Acquisitions:** Editorial Department. Estab. 1807. Publishes hardcover originals, trade paperback originals and reprints. **Pays competitive rates. Offers advance.** Accepts simultaneous submissions. Book catalog online; ms guidelines online.

O→ "The General Interest group publishes nonfiction books for the consumer market."

Nonfiction: Biography, children's/juvenile, reference, narrative nonfiction. Subjects include history, memoirs, psychology, science (popular), African American interest, health/self-improvement. Query with SASE.

Recent Title(s): *A Word a Day*, by Ann Garg; *Jackie Robinson and the Integration of Baseball*, by Scott Simon; *The 30-Day Low-Carb Diet Solution*, by Michael and Mary Dan Eades.

WILLIAMSON PUBLISHING CO., P.O. Box 185, Church Hill Rd., Charlotte VT 05445. Website: www.williamsonbooks.com. **Acquisitions:** Susan Williamson, editorial director. Estab. 1983. Publishes trade paperback originals. **Publishes 15-17 titles/year. Receives 1,000 queries/year. 75% of books from first-time authors; 90% from unagented writers. Pays royalty on net receipts or makes outright purchase. Offers standard advance.** Publishes book 18 months after acceptance of ms. Does not accept simultaneous submissions. Responds in 4 months to queries. Book catalog for 8½×11 SAE with 4 first-class stamps; ms guidelines online.

- Williamson's success is based on its reputation for excellence. Its books win top awards year in and year out, including Parents Choice (3 in Fall 2001), Oppenheim, and Children's Book Council.

O→ "Our mission is to help every child fulfull his/her potential and experience personal growth through active learning. We want 'our kids' to be able to work toward a culturally rich, ethnically diverse, peaceful nation and global community." Currently emphasizing creative approaches to specific areas of science, history, cultural experiences, diversity.

Nonfiction: Biography, how-to, self-help. Subjects include animals, anthropology/archeology, art/architecture, business/economics, cooking/foods/nutrition, ethnic, government/politics, health/medicine, history, hobbies, language/literature, memoirs, money/finance, multicultural, music/dance, nature/environment, photography, psychology, science, women's issues/studies, world affairs, geography, early learning skills, careers, arts, crafts. "Williamson has five very successful children's book series: *Little Hands* (ages 2-6), *Kids Can* (ages 6-12), *Quick Starts for Kids* (64 pages, ages 8 and up), *Tales Alive* (folktales plus activities, ages 4-10) and *Kaleidoscope Kids* (96 pages, single subject, ages 8-14). They must incorporate learning through doing. *No picture books, story books, or fiction please!* Please don't call concerning your submission. It never helps your review, and it takes too much of our time. With an SASE, you'll hear from us." Query with SASE or submit 1-2 sample chapter(s), toc, SASE.

Recent Title(s): *Awesome Ocean Science*, by Cindy A. Littlefield; *The Lewis & Clark Expedition*, by Carol A. Johmann; *The Kids' Guide to First Aid*, by Karen Buhler Gale, R.N. (Parents' Choice Recommended, Children's Health Digest Education Award).

Tips: "Our children's books are used by kids, their parents, and educators. They encourage self-discovery, creativity and personal growth. Our books are based on the philosophy that children learn best by doing, by being involved. Our authors need to be excited about their subject area and equally important, excited about kids. Please, please, please no storybooks of any kind."

WILLOW CREEK PRESS, P.O. Box 147, 9931 Highway 70 W., Minocqua WI 54548. (715)358-7010. Fax: (715)358-2807. E-mail: andread@willowcreekpress.com. Website: www.willowcreekpress.com. **Acquisitions:** Andrea Donner, managing editor. Estab. 1986. Publishes hardcover and trade paperback originals and reprints. **Publishes 25 titles/year. Receives 400 queries and 150 mss/year. 15% of books from first-time authors; 50% from unagented writers. Pays 6-15% royalty on wholesale price. Offers $2,000-5,000 advance.** Publishes book within 18 months after acceptance of ms. Accepts simultaneous submissions. Responds in 2 months to queries. Ms guidelines online.

O→ "We specialize in nature, outdoor, and sporting topics, including gardening, wildlife and animal books. Pets, cookbooks, and a few humor books and essays round out our titles." Currently emphasizing pets (mainly dogs and cats), wildlife, outdoor sports (hunting, fishing). De-emphasizing essays, fiction.

Nonfiction: Coffee table book, cookbook, how-to, humor, illustrated book, reference. Subjects include animals, cooking/foods/nutrition, gardening, humor, nature/environment, recreation, sports, travel, wildlife, pets. Submit outline, 1 sample chapter(s), SASE. Reviews artwork/photos as part of ms package.

Recent Title(s): *101 Uses for a Dog*; *Castwork: Reflections of Fly-Fishing Guides & the American West*; *Lab Rules: Virtues of Canine Character.*

WILSHIRE BOOK CO., 12015 Sherman Rd., North Hollywood CA 91605-3781. (818)765-8579. Fax: (818)765-2922. E-mail: mpowers@mpowers.com. Website: www.mpowers.com. Publisher: Melvin Powers. **Acquisitions:** Rights Department. Estab. 1947. Publishes trade paperback originals and reprints. **Publishes 25 titles/year. Receives 2,000 submissions/year. 80% of books from first-time authors; 75% from unagented writers. Pays standard royalty. Offers advance.** Publishes book 6 months after acceptance of ms. Accepts simultaneous submissions. Responds in 2 months to queries. Ms guidelines online.

Nonfiction: How-to, self-help, motivational/inspiration, recovery. Subjects include psychology, personal success, entrepreneurship, humor, Internet marketing, mail order, horsmanship, trick training for horses. Minimum 50,000 words. Query with SASE or submit outline, 3 sample chapter(s), author bio, analysis of book's competition or submit complete ms. Reviews artwork/photos as part of ms package. Send photocopies.

Fiction: Adult allegories that teach principles of psychological growth or offer guidance in living. Minimum 25,000 words. Allegories only. No standard novels or short stories. Query with SASE or submit 3 sample chapter(s), synopsis or submit complete ms.

Recent Title(s): *The Princess Who Believed in Fairy Tales*, by Marcia Grad; *The Knight in Rusty Armor*, by Robert Fisher; *Think & Grow Rich*, by Napoleon Hill.

Tips: "We are vitally interested in all new material we receive. Just as you hopefully submit your manuscript for publication, we hopefully read every one submitted, searching for those that we believe will be successful in the marketplace. Writing and publishing must be a team effort. We need you to write what we can sell. We suggest that you read the successful books that are similar to the manuscript you want to write. Analyze them to discover what elements make them winners. Duplicate those elements in your own style, using a creative new approach and fresh material, and you will have written a book we can catapult onto the bestseller list."

WINDRIVER PUBLISHING, INC., P.O. Box 911540, St. George UT 84791-1540. (435)634-8037. Fax: (435)688-0138. E-mail: info@windriverpublishing.com. Website: www.windriverpublishing.com. **Acquisitions:** E. Keith Howick, Jr., president; Gail Howick, vice president. Estab. 2003. Publishes hardcover originals and reprints, trade paperback originals, mass market originals. **Publishes 24 titles/year. Receives 500 queries and 300 mss/year. 95% of books from first-time authors; 90% from unagented writers. Pays 5-10% royalty on retail price.** Publishes book 7 months after acceptance of ms. Accepts simultaneous submissions. Responds in 1 month to queries; 1 month to proposals; 2 months to mss. Book catalog online; ms guidelines online.

Nonfiction: Autobiography, biography, children's/juvenile, cookbook, humor, self-help. Subjects include cooking/foods/nutrition, gardening, general nonfiction, government/politics, history, hobbies, New Age, religion, science, spirituality. Submit proposal package including 3 sample chapter(s), view online for complete specs or submit complete ms. Reviews artwork/photos as part of ms package. Send transparencies.

Fiction: Adventure, fantasy, historical, humor, juvenile, literary, military/war, mystery, religious, science fiction, spiritual, suspense, young adult. Submit proposal package including 3 sample chapter(s), synopsis, view online for complete specs or submit complete ms.

Recent Title(s): *The Second Coming of Jesus the Messiah*, by E. Keith Howick (religious); *The Miracles of Jesus the Messiah*, by E. Keith Howick (religious).

Tips: "We do not accept manuscripts containing graphic or gratuitous profanity, sex or violence."

WINDSOR BOOKS, Windsor Marketing Corp., P.O. Box 280, Brightwaters NY 11718-0280. (631)321-7830. Website: www.windsorpublishing.com. **Acquisitions:** Jeff Schmidt, managing editor. Estab. 1968. Publishes hardcover and trade paperback originals, reprints, and very specific software. **Publishes 6 titles/year. Receives approximately 40 submissions/year. 60% of books from first-time authors; 90% from unagented writers. Pays 10% royalty on retail price; 5% on wholesale price (50% of total cost). Offers variable advance.** Publishes book an average of 6 months after acceptance of ms. Accepts simultaneous submissions. Responds in 2 weeks to queries. Book catalog and ms guidelines free.

"Our books are for serious investors."

Nonfiction: Interested in books on strategies, methods for investing in the stock market, options market and commodities markets. How-to, technical. Subjects include business/economics (investing in stocks and commodities), money/finance, software. Query with SASE or submit outline, sample chapter(s). Reviews artwork/photos as part of ms package.

Tips: "We sell through direct mail to our mailing list and other financial lists. Writers must keep their work original; this market tends to have a great deal of information overlap among publications."

WINDSTORM CREATIVE, LTD, 7419 Ebbert Dr. SE, Port Orchard WA 98367. Website: www.windstormcreative.com. **Acquisitions:** (Ms.) Cris Newport, senior editor. Estab. 1989. Publishes trade paperback originals and reprints. **Publishes 50 titles/year. Receives 5,200 queries and 15,000 mss/year. Pays 10-15% royalty on wholesale price.** Publishes book 1-2 years after acceptance of ms. Accepts simultaneous submissions. Responds in 6 months to mss. Ms guidelines online.

Publisher of fiction, poetry, Internet guides, episode guides, nonfiction.

Fiction: Adventure, erotica, experimental, fantasy, gay/lesbian, gothic, historical, humor, literary, science fiction, young adult, contemporary, bisexual. No horror, children's books, "bestseller" fiction, spy or espionage novels, "thrillers," any work which describes childhood sexual abuse or in which this theme figures prominently. "You must download a submission label and form from the website. If submissions arrive without label, they will be destroyed."

Recent Title(s): *The Sitka Incident*, by Walt Larson (fiction); *The New Breed: Bad Boys, Gents and Barbarians 2*, edited by Rudy Kikel (gay poetry); *The Babylon 5: Crusade Episode Guide: An Unofficial, Independent Guide with Critiques*, by Sandy Van Densen and Loriann De Giacomo.

Tips: "Visit website for detailed submission instructions."

WINDWARD PUBLISHING, INC., 3943 Meadowbrook Road, Minneapolis MN 55426. (952)938-9330. Fax: (952)938-7353. E-mail: feedback@finney-hobar.com. Website: www.finney-hobar.com. **Acquisitions:** Alan E. Krysan, president. Estab. 1973. Publishes trade paperback originals. **Publishes 6-10 titles/year. Receives 80 queries and 20 mss/year. 35% of books from first-time authors; 100% from unagented writers. Pays 10% royalty on wholesale price. Offers advance.** Publishes book 6-12 months after acceptance of ms. Accepts simultaneous submissions. Responds in 6 weeks to queries.

Windward publishes illustrated natural history and recreation books.

Nonfiction: Illustrated book, handbooks, field guides. Subjects include agriculture/horticulture, animals, gardening, nature/environment, recreation, science, sports, natural history. Query with SASE. Reviews artwork/photos as part of ms package.

Recent Title(s): *Birds of the Water, Sea, and Shore*, by Romashko; *Sea Turtles Hatching*, by Orr.

WISDOM PUBLICATIONS, 199 Elm St., Somerville MA 02144. (617)776-7416 ext. 28. Fax: (617)776-7841. E-mail: editorial@wisdompubs.org. Website: www.widsompubs.org. Publisher: Timothy McNeill. **Acquisitions:** David Kittlestrom, senior editor. Estab. 1976. Publishes hardcover originals, trade paperback originals and reprints. **Publishes 20-25 titles/**

year. Receives 300 queries/year. 50% of books from first-time authors; 95% from unagented writers. Pays 4-8% royalty on wholesale price. Offers advance. Publishes book within 2 years after acceptance of ms. Does not accept simultaneous submissions. Book catalog and ms guidelines online.

O→ Wisdom Publications is dedicated to making available authentic Buddhist works for the benefit of all. "We publish translations, commentaries and teachings of past and contemporary Buddhist masters and original works by leading Buddhist scholars." Currently emphasizing popular applied Buddhism, scholarly titles.

Nonfiction: Reference, self-help, textbook (Buddhist). Subjects include philosophy (Buddhist or comparative Buddhist/Western), psychology, religion, Buddhism, Tibet. Query with SASE. Reviews artwork/photos as part of ms package. Send photocopies.

Poetry: Buddhist. Query.

Recent Title(s): *Essence of the Heart Sutra*, by The Dalai Lama.

Tips: "We are basically a publisher of Buddhist books—all schools and traditions of Buddhism. Please see our catalog or our website *before* you send anything to us to get a sense of what we publish."

WISH PUBLISHING, P.O. Box 10337, Terre Haute IN 47801. (812)478-3529. Fax: (812)447-1836. E-mail: holly@wishpublishing.com. Website: www.wishpublishing.com. **Acquisitions:** Holly Kondras, president. Publishes hardcover and trade paperback originals. **Publishes 5-10 titles/year. Pays 10-18% royalty on wholesale price.** Accepts simultaneous submissions. Responds in 2 months to queries; 2 months to proposals; 2 months to mss. Book catalog and ms guidelines free or online; ms guidelines online.

Nonfiction: Biography, children's/juvenile, reference. Subjects include health/medicine, sports, women's issues/studies. Query with SASE or submit proposal package including outline, 2 sample chapter(s), author bio. Reviews artwork/photos as part of ms package. Send photocopies.

Recent Title(s): *Hard Fought Victories: Women Coaches Making a Difference* (sports); *Total Fitness for Women* (fitness); *Girls' Basketball: Building a Winning Team* (sports).

Tips: Audience is women and girls who play sports and their coaches, parents and supporters.

WIZARDS OF THE COAST, P.O. Box 707, Renton WA 98057-0707. (425)226-6500. Website: www.wizards.com. Executive Editor: Mary Kirchoff. **Acquisitions:** Peter Archer, editorial director. Publishes hardcover and trade paperback originals and trade paperback reprints. Wizard of the Coast publishes games as well, including Dungeons & Dragons® role-playing game. **Publishes 50-60 titles/year. Receives 600 queries and 300 mss/year. 25% of books from first-time authors; 35% from unagented writers. Pays 4-8% royalty on retail price. Offers $4,000-6,000 average advance.** Publishes book 1 year after acceptance of ms. Accepts simultaneous submissions. Responds in 4 months to queries. Ms guidelines for #10 SASE.

Imprints: Dragonlance Books; Forgotten Realms Books; Magic: The Gathering Books; Legend of the Five Rings Books; Dungeons & Dragons Books.

O→ Wizards of the Coast publishes science fiction and fantasy shared world titles. Currently emphasizing solid fantasy writers. De-emphasizing gothic fiction.

Nonfiction: "All of our nonfiction books are generated inhouse."

Fiction: Fantasy, gothic, science fiction, short story collections. "We currently publish only work-for-hire novels set in our trademarked worlds. No violent or gory fantasy or science fiction." Request guidelines, then query with outline/synopsis and 3 sample chapters.

Recent Title(s): *The Thousand Orcs*, by R.A. Salvatore.

Tips: "Our audience largely is comprised of highly imaginative 12-30 year-old males."

WOODBINE HOUSE, 6510 Bells Mill Rd., Bethesda MD 20817. (301)897-3570. Fax: (301)897-5838. E-mail: ngpaul@woodbinehouse.com. Website: www.woodbinehouse.com. **Acquisitions:** Nancy Gray Paul, acquisitions editor. Estab. 1985. Publishes hardcover and trade paperback originals. **Publishes 8 titles/year. 90% from unagented writers. Pays 10-12% royalty.** Publishes book 18 months after acceptance of ms. Accepts simultaneous submissions. Responds in 8 months to queries. Book catalog and ms guidelines for 6×9 SAE with 3 first-class stamps; ms guidelines online.

O→ Woodbine House publishes books for or about individuals with disabilities to help those individuals and their families live fulfilling and satisfying lives in their homes, schools and communities.

Nonfiction: Publishes books for and about children with disabilities. Reference. Subjects include health/medicine. "I more carefully consider opening envelopes that are wrapped with excessive tape, are bulky, have return addresses that do not match the postal stamp, or display unusual handwriting. In cases such as this, I would consider returning envelopes to sender. I recommend authors send only envelopes that are clear and free of that which is described above. In addition, I would suggest authors send a SASE that is self-adhesive." No personal accounts or general parenting guides. Submit outline, 3 sample chapter(s). Reviews artwork/photos as part of ms package.

Fiction: Picture books (children's). Submit complete ms. with SASE.

Recent Title(s): *Activity Schedules for Children with Autism: Teaching Independent Behavior*, by Lynn McClannahan and Patricia Krantz; *Children with Fragile X Syndrome: A Parents' Guide*, by Jayne Dixon Weber, Ed.

Tips: "Do not send us a proposal on the basis of this description. Examine our catalog or website and a couple of our books to make sure you are on the right track. Put some thought into how your book could be marketed (aside from in bookstores). Keep cover letters concise and to the point; if it's a subject that interests us, we'll ask to see more."

[N] **WOODLAND PUBLISHING, INC.**, 448 E. 800 North, Orem UT 84097. (801)434-8113. Fax: (801)334-1913. Website: www.woodlandpublishing.com. Publisher: Calvin Harper. **Acquisitions:** Cord Udall, editor. Estab. 1974. Publishes perfect bound and trade paperback originals. **Publishes 20 titles/year. Receives 100 queries and 60 mss/year. 50% of**

books from first-time authors; 100% from unagented writers. Offers advance. Publishes book 6 months after acceptance of ms. Accepts simultaneous submissions. Responds in 1 month. *Writers Market* recommends allowing 2 months for reply to proposals. Book catalog and ms guidelines for #10 SASE or online.

O→ "Our readers are interested in herbs and other natural health topics. Most of our books are sold through health food stores."

Nonfiction: Subjects include health/medicine (alternative). Query with SASE.

Recent Title(s): *Soy Smart Health*, by Neil Soloman, M.D.

Tips: "Our readers are interested in herbs and other natural health topics. Most of our books are sold through health food stores."

WORDWARE PUBLISHING, INC., 2320 Los Rios Blvd., Suite 200, Plano TX 75074. (972)423-0090. Fax: (972)881-9147. E-mail: jhill@wordware.com. Website: www.wordware.com. President: Russell A. Stultz. **Acquisitions:** Jim Hill, publisher. Estab. 1983. Publishes trade paperback and mass market paperback originals. **Publishes 50-60 titles/year. Receives 100-150 queries and 50-75 mss/year. 40% of books from first-time authors; 95% from unagented writers. Pays 8% royalty on wholesale price. Offers advance.** Publishes book 6 months after acceptance of ms. Accepts simultaneous submissions. Responds in 2 weeks to queries. Book catalog free; ms guidelines online.

O→ Wordware publishes computer/electronics books covering a broad range of technologies for professional programmers and developers with special emphasis in game development, animation and modeling.

Nonfiction: Reference, technical, textbook. Subjects include computers/electronic. "Wordware publishes advanced titles for developers and professional programmers." Submit proposal package including 2 sample chapter(s), table of contents, target audience summation, competing books.

Recent Title(s): *Game Design Theory and Practice*, by Richard Rouse; *Light Wave 3D 7.0 Character Animation*, by Timothy Albee.

WORKMAN PUBLISHING CO., 708 Broadway, New York NY 10003. (212)254-5900. Fax: (212)254-8098. Website: www.workman.com. Editor-in-chief: Susan Bolotin. **Acquisitions:** Suzanne Rafer, executive editor (cookbook, child care, parenting, teen interest); Ruth Sullivan, Jennifer Griffin, Margot Herrera, Richard Rosen, senior editors. David Allender, senior editor, juvenile. Estab. 1967. Publishes hardcover and trade paperback originals. **Publishes 40 titles/year. Receives thousands of queries/year. Open to first-time authors. Pays variable royalty on retail price. Offers variable advance.** Publishes book 1 year after acceptance of ms. Accepts simultaneous submissions. Responds in 5 months to queries. Book catalog free; ms guidelines online.

Imprints: Artisan; Greenwich Workshop Press.

O→ "We are a trade paperback house specializing in a wide range of popular nonfiction. We publish no adult fiction and very little children's fiction. We also publish a full range of full color wall and Page-A-Day calendars."

Nonfiction: Cookbook, gift book, how-to, humor. Subjects include child guidance/parenting, cooking/foods/nutrition, gardening, health/medicine, humor, sports, travel. Query with SASE first for guidelines. Reviews artwork/photos as part of ms package.

Recent Title(s): *The Wine Bible*, by Karen MacNeil; *Heal Your Headache*, by David Buchholz, M.D.

Tips: "No phone calls please. We do not accept submissions via fax or e-mail."

WRITER'S DIGEST BOOKS, F&W Publications, 4700 E. Galbraith Rd., Cincinnati OH 45236. (513)531-2690. Website: www.writersdigest.com. Estab. 1920. Publishes primarily hardcover originals. **Publishes 14 titles/year. Receives 500 queries and 100 mss/year. 20% from unagented writers. Pays 10-20% royalty on net receipts. Offers average $5,000 and up advance.** Publishes book 18 months after acceptance of ms. Accepts simultaneous submissions. Responds in 2 months to queries. Book catalog for 9×12 SAE with 6 first-class stamps.

O→ Writer's Digest Books is the premiere source for books about writing, publishing instructional and reference books for writers. Typical mss are 60,000-80,000 words.

Nonfiction: How-to, reference, instructional books for writers. "Our instruction books stress results and how specifically to achieve them. Should be well-researched, yet lively and readable. We do *not* want to see books telling readers how to crack specific nonfiction markets: *Writing for the Computer Market* or *Writing for Trade Publications*, for instance. We are most in need of fiction technique books written by published authors. Be prepared to explain how the proposed book differs from existing books on the subject." No fiction or poetry. Query with SASE or submit outline, sample chapter(s), SASE.

Recent Title(s): *Pocket Muse*, by Monica Wood; *Writing the Breakout Novel*, by Donald Maass.

Tips: Writer's Digest Books also publishes instructional books for photographers. They must instruct about the creative craft, as opposed to instructing about marketing. Contact is Jerry Jackson.

N **WRITINGCAREER.COM**, P.O. Box 14061, Surfside Beach SC 29575. Website: www.writingcareer.com. **Acquisitions:** Brian Konradt, publisher (how-to). Estab. 2003. Publishes electronic originals and reprints. **Publishes 12 titles/year. 100% from unagented writers. Pays 50% royalty on retail price.** Publishes book 1 month after acceptance of ms. Accepts simultaneous submissions. Responds in 1 month to queries. Book catalog online; ms guidelines online.

Nonfiction: Subjects include writing, freelancing, screenwriting, editing, marketing, copywriting, style guides, etc. "We are a niche market with specific needs. We only publish nonfiction how-to books on the creative and business aspects of writing." Query at www.writingcareer.com/epublishing.shtml.

Recent Title(s): *Writing Industry Reports*, by Jennie S. Bev; *Freelance Writing for Vet Hospitals*, by Stanley Burkhardt.

Tips: WritingCareer.com targets writers—freelancers, staff writers, hobbyists—who want to master their writing, marketing, and business skills. "Browse our book titles at WritingCareer.com to better understand what we publish and sell."

YAHBOOKS PUBLISHING, 30799 Pinetree Rd., #356, Cleveland OH 44124. (216)233-5961. Fax: (440)247-1581. E-mail: eric@yahbooks.com. Website: www.yahbooks.com. Estab. 2001. publishes trade paperback originals. **Publishes 5 titles/year. Pays 10-30% royalty on wholesale price or makes outright purchase of $0-50,000.** Publishes book 0-6 months after acceptance of ms. Accepts simultaneous submissions. Responds in 1 month to queries; 1 month to proposals; 1-2 months to mss.

Nonfiction: Children's/juvenile, gift book, how-to. Subjects include computers/electronic. Submit outline, sample chapter(s) or submit complete ms. Reviews artwork/photos as part of ms package. Send photocopies.

Recent Title(s): *You Are Here College Internet Guide*, by Eric Leebow (Internet/college); *You Are Here High School Internet Guide*, by Eric Leebow (Internet/teen/high school); *You Are Here Kids & Family Internet Guide*, by Eric Leebow (Internet/family).

Tips: "We publish a book series of Internet guides. Variety of audiences."

YMAA PUBLICATION CENTER, 4354 Washington St., Roslindale MA 02131. (617)323-7215. Fax: (617)323-7417. E-mail: ymaa@aol.com. Website: www.ymaa.com. **Acquisitions:** David Ripianzi, director. Estab. 1982. Publishes hardcover and trade paperback originals and reprints. **Publishes 10 titles/year. Receives 50 queries and 20 mss/year. 25% of books from first-time authors; 100% from unagented writers. Pays 7-10% royalty on net receipts.** Publishes book 18 months after acceptance of ms. Accepts simultaneous submissions. Responds in 3 months to proposals. Book catalog online; ms guidelines free.

O→ "YMAA publishes books on Chinese Chi Kung (Qigong), Taijiquan, (Tai Chi) and Asian martial arts. We are expanding our focus to include books on healing, wellness, meditation and subjects related to Asian culture and Asian medicine." De-emphasizing fitness books.

Nonfiction: "We are most interested in Asian martial arts, Chinese medicine and Chinese Qigong. We publish Eastern thought, health, meditation, massage and East/West synthesis." How-to, multimedia, self-help. Subjects include ethnic, health/medicine (Chinese), history, philosophy, spirituality, sports, Asian martial arts, Chinese Qigong. "We no longer publish or solicit books for children. We also produce instructional videos to accompany our books on traditional Chinese martial arts, meditation, massage and Chi Kung." Submit proposal package including outline, 1 sample chapter(s), author bio, SASE. Reviews artwork/photos as part of ms package. Send photocopies and 1-2 originals to determine quality of photo/line art.

Recent Title(s): *A Woman's Qigong Guide*, by Yanling Johnson; *Exploring Tai Chi*, by John Loupos.

Tips: "If you are submitting health-related material, please refer to an Asian tradition. Learn about author publicity options as your participation is mandatory."

ZEBRA BOOKS, Kensington, 850 Third Ave., 16th Floor, New York NY 10022. (212)407-1500. Website: www.kensingtonbooks.com. **Acquisitions:** Michaela Hamilton, editor-in-chief; Ann La Farge, executive editor; Kate Duffy, editorial director (romance); John Scognamiglio, editorial director; Karen Thomas, editorial director Dafina; Elaine Sparber, senior editor (health); Bruce Bender, managing director(Citadel); Margaret Wolf, editor; Richard Ember, editor; Bob Shuman, senior editor; Jeremie Ruby-Strauss, senior editor; Miles Lott, editor. Publishes hardcover originals, trade paperback and mass market paperback originals and reprints. **Publishes 600 titles/year.** Publishes book 12-18 months after acceptance of ms. Accepts simultaneous submissions. Book catalog online; Please no queries. Send synopsis and sample chapters with SASE.

Imprints: Kensington, Zebra, Pinnacle, Dafina, Brava, Twin Streams, Strapless, Citadel.

O→ Zebra Books is dedicated to women's fiction, which includes, but is not limited to romance.

Fiction: Zebra books is dedicated to women's fiction, which includes, but is not limited to romance. Submit sample chapter(s), synopsis, SASE. Please no queries.

ZONDERVAN, HarperCollins Publishers, 5300 Patterson Ave. SE, Grand Rapids MI 49530-0002. (616)698-6900. Fax: (616)698-3454. E-mail: zpub@zondervan.com. Website: www.zondervan.com. Executive VP: Scott Bolinder. **Acquisitions:** Manuscript Review Editor. Estab. 1931. Publishes hardcover and trade paperback originals and reprints. **Publishes 120 titles/year. Receives 3,000 submissions/year. 10% of books from first-time authors; 60% from unagented writers. Pays 14% royalty on net amount received on sales of cloth and softcover trade editions; 12% royalty on net amount received on sales of mass market paperbacks. Offers variable advance.** Responds in 2 months to queries; 3 months to proposals; 4 months to mss. Ms guidelines online.

Imprints: Zonderkidz, Inspirio (includes Bible covers, devotional calendars).

O→ "Our mission is to be the leading Christian communications company meeting the needs of people with resources that glorify Jesus Christ and promote biblical principles."

Nonfiction: All religious perspective (evangelical). Autobiography, biography, children's/juvenile, reference, self-help, textbook. Subjects include history, humanities, memoirs, religion, Christian living, devotional, Bible study resources, preaching, counseling, college and seminary textbooks, discipleship, worship, and church renewal for pastors, professionals and lay leaders in ministry, theological and biblical reference books. Submit outline, 1 sample chapter(s). "We only accept faxed mss."

Fiction: Some adult fiction (mainstream, biblical). Refer to nonfiction. "Inklings-style" fiction of high literary quality. Christian relevance in all cases. Will *not* consider collections of short stories. Query with SASE or submit outline, 1 sample chapter(s), synopsis.

Recent Title(s): *Purpose Driven Life*, by Rick Warren (Christian living); *Cape Refuge*, by Terri Blackstock (fiction).

Canadian & International Book Publishers

Canadian and international book publishers share the same mission as their U.S. counterparts—publishing timely books on subjects of concern and interest to a targetable audience. Most of the publishers listed in this section, however, differ from U.S. publishers in that their needs tend toward subjects that are specific to their country or intended for a Canadian or international audience. Some are interested in submissions from writers outside of the U.S. only. There are many regional publishers that concentrate on region-specific subjects.

U.S. writers hoping to do business with Canadian or international publishers should follow specific paths of research to find out as much about their intended markets as possible. The listings will inform you about what kinds of books the Canadian and international companies publish and tell you whether they are open to receiving submissions from writers outside the U.S. To further target your markets and see very specific examples of the books these houses are publishing, send for catalogs from publishers, or check their websites.

Once you have determined which publishers will accept your work, it is important to understand the differences that exist between U.S. mail and international mail. U.S. postage stamps are useless on mailings originating outside of the U.S. When enclosing a SASE for return of your query or manuscript from a publisher outside the U.S. (including Canada), you must include International Reply Coupons (IRCs) or postage stamps from that country. For more information on international mail process and purchasing Canadian postage stamps, see Mailing Submissions in the Getting Published section.

There has always been more government subsidy of publishing in Canada than in the U.S. However, with continued cuts in such subsidies, government support is on the decline. There are a few author-subsidy publishers in Canada and, as with author-subsidy publishers in the U.S., writers should proceed with caution when they are presented with this option.

Publishers offering author-subsidy arrangements (sometimes referred to as "joint venture," "co-publishing," or "cooperative publishing") are not listed in *Writer's Market*. If one of the publishers in this section offers you an author-subsidy contract, asks you to pay for all, or part, of the cost of any aspect of publishing (printing, marketing, etc.), or asks you to guarantee the purchase of a number of books yourself, please let us know about that company immediately.

Canadian publishers are indicated by the 🍁 symbol, and markets located outside of the U.S. and Canada are indicated by the 🌐 symbol. Writer's interested in additional Canadian and international book publishing markets should consult *Literary Market Place* (R.R. Bowker & Co.), and *The Canadian Writer's Market* (McClelland & Stewart).

For a list of publishers according to their subjects of interest, see the nonfiction and fiction sections of the Book Publishers' Subject Index. Information on book publishers listed in the previous edition of *Writer's Market* but not included in this edition can be found in the General Index.

🌐 **A&C BLACK PUBLISHERS, LTD.**, Bloomsbury plc, 37 Soho Square, London W1D 3QZ England. (020)7758-0200. Fax: (020)7758-0222. **Acquisitions:** Sarah Fecher, editor (children's nonfiction); Jon Appleton, editor (children's fiction); Janet Murphy, editor (nautical); Charlotte Jenkins (sport); Linda Lambert, editor (arts and crafts); Jessica Hodge, editor (theater, writing, reference); Nigel Redman, editor (ornithology). Publishes hardcover and trade paperback originals, trade paperback reprints. **Publishes 170 titles/year; imprint publishes 10-20 titles/year. Receives 3,000 queries and 650 mss/year. 5% of books from first-time authors; 70% from unagented writers. Pays royalty on retail price or net**

receipts; makes outright purchase very occasionally on short children's books. Offers £1,500-6,000 advance. Publishes book 9 months after acceptance of ms. Accepts simultaneous submissions. Responds in 1 month to queries; 2 months to proposals; 2 months to mss. Book catalog free.

Imprints: Adlard Coles Nautical (Janet Murphy, editor), Christopher Helm/Pica Press (Nigel Redman, editor), Herbert Press (Linda Lambert, editor).

Nonfiction: Children's/juvenile, how-to, illustrated book, reference. Subjects include art/architecture, creative nonfiction, education, multicultural, music/dance, nature/environment, recreation, sports, travel, nutrition. Query with SASE or submit proposal package including outline, 2 sample chapter(s) or submit complete ms. Reviews artwork/photos as part of ms package. Send transparencies.

Fiction: Juvenile. Submit 2 sample chapter(s), synopsis or submit complete ms.

Recent Title(s): *Raptors of the World*, by James Ferguson-Lees, et al; *Printmaking for Beginners*, by Jane Stobart; *A Cartoon History of the Earth*.

ADVENTURE BOOK PUBLISHERS, Durksen Enterprises Ltd., #712-3545-32 Ave. NE, Calgary AB T1Y 6M6 Canada. (403)285-6844. E-mail: adventure@puzzlesbyshar.com. Website: www.puzzlesbyshar.com/adventurebooks. Publishes electronic and print books. **Publishes 30-50 titles/year. Receives 1,000 queries and 200 mss/year. 100% of books from first-time authors; 100% from unagented writers. Pays 20% royalty.** Publishes book approximately 7 months after acceptance of ms. Accepts simultaneous submissions. Responds in 1 month to queries; 1 month to proposals; 5 months to mss. Book catalog and ms guidelines online.

Nonfiction: Biography, children's/juvenile, cookbook, how-to, humor, self-help. Subjects include Americana, animals, cooking/foods/nutrition, creative nonfiction, history, military/war, nature/environment. Query with synopsis via e-mail only. Reviews artwork/photos as part of ms package. GIF or JPEG images via e-mail.

Fiction: Adventure, fantasy (space fantasy, sword and sorcery), historical (general), humor, military/war, mystery (amateur sleuth, cozy, police procedural, private eye/hardboiled), romance (contemporary, historical, romantic suspense), science fiction (hard science/technological, soft/sociological), western (frontier saga, traditional), young adult (adventure, fantasy/science fiction, mystery/suspense, problem novels, romance, series, sports, western). Query with 1-2 page synopsis via e-mail only. Accepts ms submissions "only by invitation and in accordance with guidelines given to those invited."

Recent Title(s): *The Twisted Mile*, by Jeffrey Waller (action/adventure); *Beyond the Cliffs of Kerry*, by Amanda Hughes (romance/historical).

Tips: "We specialize in unpublished writers since they are the ones who need the most help and encouragement. As such, we do not encourage agency submissions. Manuscripts by invitation only. Do not send materials/manuscripts/queries via regular mail unless specifically requested."

IAN ALLAN PUBLISHING, LTD., Riverdene Business Park, Molesey Rd., Hersham, Surrey KT12 4RG United Kingdom. (+44)1932 266600. Fax: (+44)1932 266601. E-mail: info@ianallanpub.co.uk. Website: www.ianallanpub.co.uk. **Acquisitions:** Peter Waller, publishing manager. Publishes hardcover, trade paperback and mass market paperback originals and reprints. **Publishes 120 titles/year. Receives 300 queries and 50 mss/year. 5% of books from first-time authors; 95% from unagented writers. Payment is subject to contract and type of publication.** Publishes book 6 months after acceptance of ms. Accepts simultaneous submissions. Book catalog free.

Imprints: OPC, Dial House, Midland Publishing, Ian Allan Publishing.

Nonfiction: Illustrated book. Subjects include history, hobbies, military/war, sports, travel. Query with SASE. Reviews artwork/photos as part of ms package.

Recent Title(s): *War Without Garlands*, by Kershaw (military history); *Enigma U-Boats*, by Showell (naval history); *Without Enigma*, by Macksey (military history).

Tips: Audience is enthusiasts and historians. "We don't publish books with a strong autobiographical bias—e.g., military reminiscences—and no fiction/children's/poetry."

ALLISON & BUSBY/LONDON HOUSE, Bon Marche Centre, 241 Ferndale Rd., London SW9 8BJ England. 44(0)20 7738 7888. Fax: 44(0)20 7733 4244. E-mail: all@allisonbusby.co.uk. Website: www.allisonandbusby.ltd.uk. Roderick Dymott, publishing director (nonfiction: biography, history, crime/criminology, topical issues); David Shelley, editor (literary fiction, crime fiction). Publishes hardcover, trade paperback, mass market paperback originals and reprints. **Publishes 72 titles/year. Receives 1,000 queries and 600 mss/year. 15% of books from first-time authors; 20% from unagented writers. Pays 7½-10% royalty. Offers $1,750 minimum advance.** Publishes book 8 months after acceptance of ms. Accepts simultaneous submissions. Responds in 2 weeks to queries; 2 weeks to proposals; 1 month to mss. Book catalog free or on website; ms guidelines online.

Nonfiction: Biography. Subjects include history, biography, topical issues, the paranormal, crime/criminology, mind/body/spirit, current affairs. Submit proposal package including outline, 2 sample chapter(s). Reviews artwork/photos as part of ms package. Send photocopies.

Fiction: Experimental. "We are looking for young, literary writers to move into the future with us on our literary fiction and mystery lines." Submit proposal package including outline, 2 sample chapter(s).

Recent Title(s): *Sensual Woman*, Sarah Bartlett (topical issues); *Candleland*, Marlyn Waites (mystery/crime fiction).

Tips: "Write a snappy, interesting covering letter. If you have been published before (in magazines or by another publisher) state when and where."

THE ALTHOUSE PRESS, University of Western Ontario, Faculty of Education, 1137 Western Rd., London ON N6G 1G7 Canada. (519)661-2096. Fax: (519)661-3833. E-mail: press@uwo.ca. Website: www.edu.uwo.ca/althousepress. Director: Dr. Greg Dickinson. **Acquisitions:** Katherine Butson, editorial assistant. Publishes trade paperback originals and reprints. **Publishes 1-5 titles/year. Receives 30 queries and 19 mss/year. 50% of books from first-time authors; 100% from unagented writers. Pays 10% royalty. Offers $300 advance.** Publishes book 6 months after acceptance of ms. Accepts simultaneous submissions. Responds in 1 month to queries; 4 months to mss. Book catalog and ms guidelines free; ms guidelines online.

O→ "The Althouse Press publishes both scholarly research monographs in education, and professional books and materials for educators in elementary schools, secondary schools, and faculties of education." De-emphasizing curricular or instructional materials intended for use by elementary or secondary school students.

Nonfiction: Subjects include education (scholarly). "Do not send incomplete manuscripts that are only marginally appropriate to our market and limited mandate." Reviews artwork/photos as part of ms package. Send photocopies.

Recent Title(s): *Writing in the Dark*, by Max Van Manen; *The Fifty Fatal Flaws of Essay Writing*, by Glen Downey.

Tips: Audience is practicing teachers and graduate education students.

AMBER LANE PRESS, LTD., Church St., Charlbury 0X7 3PR United Kingdom. 01608 810024. Fax: 01608 810024. E-mail: jamberlane@aol.com. **Acquisitions:** Judith Scott, managing editor (drama/theater/music). Publishes hardcover and trade paperback originals, trade paperback reprints. **Publishes 5 titles/year. Receives 10 queries and 6 mss/year. 20% of books from first-time authors; 10% from unagented writers. Pays 7½-12% royalty. Offers £250-1,000 (sterling pounds) advance.** Publishes book 18 months after acceptance of ms. Accepts simultaneous submissions. Responds in 1 month to queries. Book catalog free.

O→ Amber Lane Press aims "to help promote British theatre and modern drama in general."

Nonfiction: Biography, how-to, reference. Subjects include music/dance. Submit proposal package including outline, 2 sample chapter(s).

Fiction: Plays. "All plays need to be staged professionally by a major theater/theater company." Submit complete ms.

Recent Title(s): *Theatre in a Cool Climate*, Vera Gottlieb and Colin Chambers, eds.; *Oroonoko*, Aphra Behn, adapted by Biyi Bandele (play); *Strindberg and Love*, by Eivor Martinus (biography).

Tips: "Explain why the book would be different from anything else already published on the subject."

ANNICK PRESS, LTD., 15 Patricia Ave., Toronto ON M2M 1H9 Canada. (416)221-4802. Fax: (416)221-8400. E-mail: annick@annickpress.com. Website: www.annickpress.com. **Acquisitions:** Rick Wilks, director (picture books, nonfiction, young adult fiction); Colleen MacMillan, associate publisher (YA, juvenile nonfiction). Publishes hardcover and trade paperback originals and mass market paperback reprints. **Publishes 25 titles/year. Receives 5,000 queries and 3,000 mss/year. 20% of books from first-time authors; 80-85% from unagented writers. Pays 8% royalty. Offers $2,000-4,000 advance.** Publishes book 2 years after acceptance of ms. Does not accept simultaneous submissions. Responds in 1 month to queries; 2 months to proposals; 3 months to mss. Book catalog free; ms guidelines online.

O→ Annick Press maintains "a commitment to high quality books that entertain and challenge. Our publications share fantasy and stimulate imagination, while encouraging children to trust their judgment and abilities." *Does not accept unsolicited mss.*

Nonfiction: Children's/juvenile. Query with SASE. Reviews artwork/photos as part of ms package. Send photocopies.

Fiction: Juvenile, young adult. Query with SASE.

Recent Title(s): *The Mole Sisters and the Cool Breeze*, by Roslyn Schwartz; *Rocksy*, by Loris Lesynski; *The Losers' Club*, by John Lekich.

ANVIL PRESS, 6 W. 17th Ave., Vancouver BC V5Y 1Z4 Canada. (604)876-8710. Fax: (604)879-2667. E-mail: anvil@anvilpress.com. Website: www.anvilpress.com. **Acquisitions:** Brian Kaufman. Estab. 1988. Publishes trade paperback originals. **Publishes 8-10 titles/year. Receives 300 queries/year. 80% of books from first-time authors; 70% from unagented writers. Pays 15% royalty on net receipts. Offers Average advance $400 advance.** Publishes book 8 months after acceptance of ms. Accepts simultaneous submissions. Responds in 2 months to queries; 2 months to proposals; 6 months to mss. Book catalog for 9×12 SAE with 2 first-class stamps; ms guidelines online.

O→ "Anvil Press publishes contemporary adult fiction, poetry and drama, giving voice to up-and-coming Canadian writers, exploring all literary genres, discovering, nurturing, and promoting new Canadian literary talent." Currently emphasizing urban/suburban themed fiction and poetry; de-emphasizing historical novels

Fiction: Experimental, literary, short story collections. Contemporary, modern literature—no formulaic or genre. Query with SASE.

Poetry: "Get our catalog, look at our poetry. We do very little poetry—maybe 1-2 titles per year." Query or submit 12 sample poems.

Recent Title(s): *Snatch*, by Judy MacInnes Jr. (poetry); *Touched*, by Jodi Lundgren (fiction).

Tips: Audience is young, informed, educated, aware, with an opinion, culturally active (films, books, the performing arts). "No U.S. authors, unless selected as the winner of our 3-Day Novel Contest. Research the appropriate publisher for your work."

ARCTURUS PUBLISHING, Unit 26, 151-153 Bermondsey St., London SE1 3HA England. (44)(0)2074079600. Fax: (44)(0)2074079444. E-mail: info@stopwatch.co.uk. Publishes hardcover, trade paperback, and mass market paperback originals and reprints. **Publishes 30-40 titles/year. 40% of books from first-time authors; 90% from unagented writers. Pays 5-10% royalty on wholesale price.** Publishes book 6 months after acceptance of ms. Accepts simultaneous submissions. Responds in 2 months to queries; 2 months to proposals; 2 months to mss. Book catalog free; ms guidelines free.

Nonfiction: Autobiography, biography, booklets, children's/juvenile, humor, reference, self-help, textbook. Subjects include creative nonfiction, education, general nonfiction, health/medicine, history, hobbies, military/war, New Age, philosophy, recreation, religion, sports. "We are primarily interested in developing the history and military lists." Query with

SASE or submit proposal package including outline, 1 sample chapter(s) or submit complete ms. Reviews artwork/photos as part of ms package. Send photocopies.

Fiction: Erotica, horror, humor, Crime. "Plans are afoot for a fiction list beginning 2003." Query with SASE or submit proposal package including 1 sample chapter(s), synopsis or submit complete ms.

Recent Title(s): *Fighting Them On the Beaches*, by Nigel Cawthorne (military nonfiction); *Over the Top*, by Martin Marix Evans (military nonfiction); *Tales of the Supernatural*, by Robin Brockman (horror).

Tips: "Our audience is intelligent, general readers of all ages and interests."

ARSENAL PULP PRESS, Suite 103, 1014 Homer St., Vancouver BC V6B 2W9 Canada. (604)687-4233. Fax: (604)687-4283. E-mail: contact@arsenalpulp.com. Website: www.arsenalpulp.com. **Acquisitions:** Blaine Kyllo, managing editor. Estab. 1980. Publishes hardcover and trade paperback originals, and trade paperback reprints. **Publishes 20 titles/year. Receives 400 queries and 200 mss/year. 40% of books from first-time authors; 100% from unagented writers.** Publishes book 1 year after acceptance of ms. Accepts simultaneous submissions. Responds in 2 months to queries; 4 months to proposals; 4 months to mss. Book catalog for 9×12 SAE with 2 first-class stamps or online; ms guidelines online.

Nonfiction: Cookbook, illustrated book, literary, cultural studies. Subjects include art/architecture, cooking/foods/nutrition, creative nonfiction, ethnic (Canadian, aboriginal issues), gay/lesbian, history (cultural), language/literature, multicultural, music/dance (popular), regional (British Columbia), sex, sociology, travel, women's issues/studies, film. Submit proposal package including outline, 2-3 sample chapter(s). Reviews artwork/photos as part of ms package.

Fiction: Erotica, ethnic (general), experimental, feminist, gay/lesbian, literary, multicultural, short story collections. No children's books or genre fiction, i.e., westerns, romance, horror, mystery, etc. Submit proposal package including outline, 2-3 sample chapter(s), synopsis.

Recent Title(s): *The Garden of Vegan: How It All Vegan Again!*, by Barnard & Kramer (nonfiction cookbook); *One Man's Trash*, by Ivan E. Coyote (short stories).

BEACH HOLME PUBLISHERS, LTD., 226-2040 W. 12th Ave., Vancouver BC V6J 2G2 Canada. (604)733-4868. Fax: (604)733-4860. E-mail: bhp@beachholme.bc.ca. Website: www.beachholme.bc.ca. **Acquisitions:** Michael Carroll, publisher (adult and young adult fiction, poetry, creative nonfiction); Jen Hamilton, production manager; Trisha Telep, publicity and marketing coordinator. Estab. 1971. Publishes trade paperback originals. **Publishes 14 titles/year. Receives 1,000 submissions/year. 40% of books from first-time authors; 75% from unagented writers. Pays 10% royalty on retail price. Offers $500 average advance.** Publishes book 1 year after acceptance of ms. Does not accept simultaneous submissions. Responds in 4 months to queries. Ms guidelines online.

Imprints: Porcepic Books (literary); Sandcastle Books (children's/YA); Prospect Books (nonfiction).

Beach Holme seeks "to publish excellent, emerging Canadian fiction, nonfiction, and poetry, and to contribute to Canadian materials for children with quality young adult historical novels."

Nonfiction: Subjects include creative nonfiction. Query with SASE or submit outline, 2 sample chapter(s).

Fiction: Experimental, literary, poetry, young adult (Canada historical/regional), Adult literary fiction from authors published in Canadian literary magazines. Interested in excellent quality, imaginative writing from writers published in Canadian literary magazines. Query with SASE or submit outline, 2 sample chapter(s).

Recent Title(s): *Hail Mary Corner*, by Brian Payton; *Tiger in Trouble*, by Eric Walters.

Tips: "Make sure the manuscript is well written. We see so many that only the unique and excellent can't be put down. Prior publication is a must. This doesn't necessarily mean book-length manuscripts, but a writer should try to publish his or her short fiction or poetry."

BERG PUBLISHERS, Oxford International Publishers, 1st Floor, Angel Court, 81 St. Clements St., Oxford, Oxfordshire 0X4 1AW United Kingdom. (44)1865-245104. Fax: (44)1865-791165. E-mail: enquiry@bergpublishers.com. Website: www.bergpublishers.com. **Acquisitions:** Kathryn Earle, editorial and managing director (anthropology, fashion, material culture); Kathleen May, senior commissioning editor (history & politics); Anne Hobbs, publishing assistant. Publishes hardcover and trade paperback originals. **Publishes 50 titles/year. Receives 700 queries and 100 mss/year. 98% from unagented writers. Pays royalty on wholesale price.** Publishes book 9 months after acceptance of ms. Does not accept simultaneous submissions. Responds in 2 months to queries; 2 months to proposals; 4 months to mss. Book catalog free; ms guidelines online.

Berg Publishers publishes "academic books aimed at an undergraduate and postgraduate readership only." Currently emphasizing fashion, sport, material culture, leisure studies, consumption, cultural history. De-emphasizing literary studies.

Nonfiction: Textbook. Subjects include anthropology/archeology, history, sociology, sports, fashion. Submit proposal package including outline.

Recent Title(s): *'Don We Now Our Gay Apparel': Gay Men's Dress in the 20th Century*, by Shaun Cole; *The Internet: An Ethnographic Approach*, by Daniel Miller & Don Slater; *Filming Women in the Third Reich*, by Jo Fox.

BETWEEN THE LINES, 720 Bathurst St., Suite #404, Toronto ON M5S 2R4 Canada. (416)535-9914. Fax: (416)535-1484. E-mail: btlbooks@web.ca. Website: www.btlbooks.com. **Acquisitions:** Paul Eprile, editorial coordinator. Publishes trade paperback originals. **Publishes 8 titles/year. Receives 350 queries and 50 mss/year. 80% of books from first-time authors; 95% from unagented writers. Pays 8% royalty.** Publishes book 1 year after acceptance of ms. Accepts simultaneous submissions. Responds in 2 months to queries; 2 months to proposals; 4 months to mss. Book catalog and ms guidelines for 8½×11 SAE and IRCs; ms guidelines online.

"We are a small independent house concentrating on politics and public policy issues, social issues, gender issues, international development, education, and the environment. We publish mainly Canadian authors."

Nonfiction: Subjects include education, gay/lesbian, government/politics, health/medicine, history, memoirs, social sciences, sociology, women's issues/studies. Submit proposal package including outline, 2-3 sample chapter(s). Reviews artwork/photos as part of ms package.

Recent Title(s): *Wealth By Stealth: Corporate Crime, Corporate Law, and the Perversion of Democracy; AIDS Activist: Michael Lynch and the Politics of Community.*

BIRLINN, LTD., West Newington House, 10 Newington Rd., Edinburgh EH9 1QS Scotland United Kingdom. E-mail: info@birlinn.co.uk. Website: www.birlinn.co.uk. **Acquisitions:** Hugh Andrew, managing director. Publishes hardcover, trade and mass market originals; trade and mass market reprints. **Publishes 80 titles/year; imprint publishes 5 titles/year. Receives 50 queries and 25 mss/year. 10% of books from first-time authors; 90% from unagented writers. Pays 8% royalty on net receipts. Offers ”0-2,000 advance.** Publishes book 1 year after acceptance of ms. Accepts simultaneous submissions. Responds in 1 month to queries; 1 month to proposals; 1 month to mss. Book catalog free.

Imprints: John Donald, Ltd. (Hugh Andrew, managing director).

Nonfiction: Biography, gift book, humor, reference, textbook, academic. Subjects include anthropology/archeology, creative nonfiction, education, history, language/literature, memoirs, military/war, nature/environment, religion, sports, travel. Query with SASE, or submit proposal package including outline. Reviews artwork/photos as part of ms package. Send photocopies.

Fiction: Historical, military/war, regional, sports. Query with SASE or submit proposal package including 2 sample chapter(s), synopsis.

Recent Title(s): *Mull*, Jo Currie; *Shackleton's Boat Journey*, Frank Worsley; *Queen's Country*, Robert Smith.

Tips: A wide and varied national and international audience.

THE BOOKS COLLECTIVE, 214-21, 10405 Jasper Ave., Edmonton AB T5J 3S2 Canada. (780)448-0590. Fax: (780)448-0640. Website: www.bookscollective.com. Estab. 1992. Publishes hardcover and trade paperback originals. **Publishes 10-12 titles/year; imprint publishes 2-5 titles/year. 30-60% of books from first-time authors; 90% from unagented writers. Pays 6-12% royalty on retail price. Offers $250-500 (Canadian) advance.** Publishes book 1 year after acceptance of ms. Does not accept simultaneous submissions. Responds in 1 month to queries; 1 month to proposals; 6 months to mss. Book catalog for 9×12 SAE with 4 first-class Canadian stamps or on website; ms guidelines online.

Imprints: Tesseract Books, River Books, Slipstream Books.

"All nonfiction projects are developed from query letters or are developed in-house. Always query first." Canadian authors only (expats or living abroad, landed immigrants OK). All non-Canadian submissions returned unread."

Nonfiction: Biography, multimedia. Subjects include creative nonfiction, language/literature, memoirs, multicultural. Query with SASE or submit proposal package including outline, 1-3 sample chapter(s), résumé. Reviews artwork/photos as part of ms package. Send photocopies.

Fiction: Experimental, fantasy, feminist, gay/lesbian, horror, literary, mainstream/contemporary, multicultural, multimedia, plays, poetry, regional, science fiction, short story collections, translation. Tesseract Books publishes an annual anthology of Canadian speculative short fiction and poetry. Query with SASE or submit proposal package including 1-3 sample chapter(s), résumé, synopsis, or submit complete ms.

Poetry: Query or submit 5-10 sample poems or submit complete ms.

Recent Title(s): *Tinka's New Dress*, by Ronnie Burkett (contemporary drama); *Gypsy Messenger*, by Marijan Megla (poetry); *The Healer* (speculative fiction).

Tips: "Our books are geared for literate, intelligent readers of literary mainstream, cutting edge, and speculative writing. If you do not know our titles, query first or write for guidelines. Look up our titles and study suitability of your manuscript. We are a writers' co-op—expect long timelines. Unless your manuscript is of surpassing excellence it will not survive omission of an SASE."

BOREALIS PRESS, LTD., 110 Bloomingdale St., Ottawa ON K2C 4A4 Canada. (613)798-9299. Fax: (613)798-9747. E-mail: borealis@istar.ca. Website: www.borealispress.com. Frank Tierney, president. **Acquisitions:** Glenn Clever, senior editor. Estab. 1972. Publishes hardcover and paperback originals and reprints. **Publishes 10-20 titles/year. Receives 400-500 submissions/year. 80% of books from first-time authors; 95% from unagented writers. Pays 10% royalty on net receipts. 3 free author's copies.** Publishes book 18 months after acceptance of ms. Does not accept simultaneous submissions. Responds in 2 months to queries; 4 months to mss. Book catalog and ms guidelines online.

Imprints: Tecumseh Press.

"Our mission is to publish work which will be of lasting interest in the Canadian book market." Currently emphasizing Canadian fiction, nonfiction, drama, poetry. De-emphasizing children's books.

Nonfiction: Biography, children's/juvenile, reference. Subjects include government/politics, history, language/literature, regional. "Only material Canadian in content." Looks for "style in tone and language, reader interest and maturity of outlook." Query with SASE or submit outline, 2 sample chapter(s). *No unsolicited mss.* Reviews artwork/photos as part of ms package.

Fiction: Adventure, ethnic, historical, juvenile, literary, mainstream/contemporary, romance, short story collections, young adult. "Only material Canadian in content and dealing with significant aspects of the human situation." Query with SASE, or submit 1-2 sample chapter(s), synopsis. *No unsolicited mss.*

Recent Title(s): *Canada's Governors General At Play*, by James Noonan; *James McGill of Montreal*, by John Cooper; *Musk Oxen of Gango*, by Mary Burpee.

THE BOSTON MILLS PRESS, 132 Main St., Erin ON N0B 1T0 Canada. (519)833-2407. Fax: (519)833-2195. E-mail: books@bostonmillspress.com. Website: www.bostonmillspress.com. President: John Denison. **Acquisitions:** Noel Hudson, managing editor. Estab. 1974. Publishes hardcover and trade paperback originals. **Publishes 20 titles/year. Receives 100 submissions/year. 40% of books from first-time authors; 95% from unagented writers. Pays 8-15% royalty on retail price. Offers advance.** Publishes book 2 years after acceptance of ms. Accepts simultaneous submissions. Responds in 2 months to queries. Book catalog free.

Boston Mills Press publishes specific market titles of Canadian and American interest including history, transportation, and regional guidebooks. "We like very focused books aimed at the North American market."

Nonfiction: Coffee table book, gift book, illustrated book. Subjects include Americana, art/architecture, cooking/foods/nutrition, creative nonfiction, gardening, history, military/war, nature/environment, photography, recreation, regional, sports, travel, Canadiana. "We're interested in anything to do with Canadian or American history—especially transportation." No autobiographies. Query with SASE. Reviews artwork/photos as part of ms package. Send photocopies.

BOULEVARD BOOKS UK, Babel Guides to World Fiction in Translation, 71 Lytton Rd., Oxford OX4 3NY United Kingdom. Phone/fax: 01865 712 931. E-mail: raybabel@dircon.co.uk. Website: www.babelguides.com. **Acquisitions:** Ray Keenoy, senior editor (literary critiques of world fiction, contemporary world fiction in translation). Publishes trade paperback originals. **Publishes 5 titles/year. Receives 50 queries and 50 mss/year. 25% of books from first-time authors; 25% from unagented writers. Pays 6-15% royalty or makes outright purchase.** Publishes book 2 years after acceptance of ms. Does not accept simultaneous submissions. Responds in 1 month to queries; 3 months to proposals; 3 months to mss. Book catalog and ms guidelines online.

Nonfiction: Reference. Subjects include language/literature, translation. Query with IRCs.

Fiction: "The only fiction we publish are translations from non-English languages." Query with IRCs.

Recent Title(s): *Babel Guide to Jewish Fiction*, various (literary reference, nonfiction); *Hotel Atlantico*, J.G. Noll (literary fiction from Brazil and Italy).

Tips: "We are narrowly focused, check out our books first."

BRICK BOOKS, Box 20081, 431 Boler Rd., London ON N6K 4G6 Canada. (519)657-8579. E-mail: brick.books@sympatico.ca. Website: www.brickbooks.ca. **Acquisitions:** Don McKay, editor (poetry), Stan Dragland, editor (poetry). Publishes trade paperback originals. **Publishes 6 titles/year. Receives 60 queries and 120 mss/year. 30% of books from first-time authors; 100% from unagented writers. Pays 10% royalty in books.** Publishes book 2 years after acceptance of ms. Responds in 1 month to queries; 3 months to proposals; 5 months to mss. Book catalog and ms guidelines free or online; ms guidelines online.

- Brick Books has a reading period of January 1-April 30. Manuscripts received outside that reading period will be returned.

Poetry: Writers must be Canadian citizens or landed immigrants. Query or submit 8-10 sample poems.

Recent Title(s): *Songs for Relinquishing the Earth*, Jan Zwicky; *Short Talks*, Anne Carson; *Rest on the Flight into Egypt*, A.F. Moritz.

Tips: "Writers without previous publications in literary journals or magazines are rarely considered by Brick Books for publication."

BROADVIEW PRESS, LTD., P.O. Box 1243, Peterborough ON K9J 7H5 Canada. (705)743-8990. Fax: (705)743-8353. E-mail: customerservice@broadviewpress.com. Website: www.broadviewpress.com. **Acquisitions:** Julia Gaunce, humanities editor (humanities—English, philosophy); Mical Moser, history editor; Michael Harrison, vice president (social sciences—political science, sociology, anthropology). Estab. 1985. **Publishes 50-60 titles/year. Receives 500 queries and 200 mss/year. 10% of books from first-time authors; 99% from unagented writers. Pays royalty.** Publishes book 1 year after acceptance of ms. Accepts simultaneous submissions. Responds in 1 month to queries; 2 months to proposals; 4 months to mss. Book catalog free; ms guidelines online.

"We publish in a broad variety of subject areas in the arts and social sciences. We are open to a broad range of political and philosophical viewpoints, from liberal and conservative to libertarian and Marxist, and including a wide range of feminist viewpoints."

Nonfiction: Biography, reference, textbook. Subjects include anthropology/archeology, gay/lesbian, history, language/literature, philosophy, religion, sociology, women's issues/studies. "All titles must have some potential for university or college-level course use. Crossover titles are acceptable." Query with SASE or submit proposal package. Reviews artwork/photos as part of ms package. Send photocopies.

Recent Title(s): *A Short History of the Middle Ages*, by Barbara Rosenwein.

Tips: "Our titles often appeal to a broad readership; we have many books that are as much of interest to the general reader as they are to academics and students."

BROKEN JAW PRESS, Box 596, Station A, Fredericton NB E3B 5A6 Canada. (506)454-5127. Fax: (506)454-5127. E-mail: jblades@nbnet.nb.ca. Website: www.brokenjaw.com. Publisher: Joe Blades. **Acquisitions:** R.M. Vaughan, editor (Canadian drama); Rob McLennan, editor (Canadian poetry, critical essays). Publishes Canadian-authored trade paperback originals and reprints. **Publishes 8-12 titles/year. 50% of books from first-time authors; 100% from unagented writers. Pays 10% royalty on retail price. Offers $0-100 advance.** Publishes book 18 months after acceptance of ms. Does not accept simultaneous submissions. Responds in 1 year to mss. Book catalog for 9×12 SAE with 2 first-class Canadian stamps in Canada; ms guidelines online.

Imprints: Book Rat, SpareTime Editions, Dead Sea Physh Products, Maritimes Arts Projects Productions.

"We are a small, mostly literary Canadian publishing house."

Nonfiction: Illustrated book, self-help. Subjects include creative nonfiction, gay/lesbian, history, language/literature, regional, women's issues/studies, contemporary culture. Reviews artwork/photos as part of ms package.
Fiction: Literary.
Recent Title(s): *What Was Always Hers*, by Uma Parameswaran (fiction); *Bagne, or, Criteria for Heaven*, by Rob McLennan (poetry).
Tips: "We don't want unsolicited manuscripts or queries, except in the context of the New Muse Award and the Poet's Corner Award. Please see the award guidelines on our website."

THE BRUCEDALE PRESS, P.O. Box 2259, Port Elgin ON N0H 2C0 Canada. (519)832-6025. Website: www.bmts.com/~brucedale. **Acquisitions:** Anne Duke Judd, editor-in-chief. Publishes hardcover and trade paperback originals. **Publishes 3 titles/year. Receives 50 queries and 30 mss/year. 75% of books from first-time authors; 100% from unagented writers. Pays royalty.** Publishes book 1 year after acceptance of ms. Accepts simultaneous submissions. Book catalog and ms guidelines for #10 SASE (Canadian postage or IRC) or online; ms guidelines online.

The Brucedale Press publishes books and other materials of regional interest and merit as well as literary, historical, and/or pictorial works.

Nonfiction: Biography, children's/juvenile, humor, illustrated book, reference. Subjects include history, humor, language/literature, memoirs, military/war, nature/environment, photography. "Invitations to submit are sent to writers and writers' groups on The Brucedale Press mailing list when projects are in progress. Send a #10 SASE to have your name added to the list. Unless responding to an invitation to submit, query first, with outline and sample chapter for book-length submissions. Submit full manuscript of work intended for children. A brief résumé of your writing efforts and successes is always of interest, and may bring future invitations, even if the present submission is not accepted for publication." Reviews artwork/photos as part of ms package.
Fiction: Fantasy, feminist, historical, humor, juvenile, literary, mainstream/contemporary, mystery, plays, poetry, romance, short story collections, young adult.
Recent Title(s): *Barns of the Queen's Bush*, by Jon Radojkovic; *Thirty Years on Call: A Country Doctor's Family Life*, by Doris Pennington; *The Quilted Grapevine*, by Nancy-Lou Patterson.
Tips: "Our focus is very regional. In reading submissions, I look for quality writing with a strong connection to the Queen's Bush area of Ontario. Suggest all authors visit our website, get a catalog, and read our books before submitting."

CANADIAN LIBRARY ASSOCIATION, 328 Frank St., Ottawa ON K2P 0X8 Canada. (613)232-9625, ext. 322. Fax: (613)563-9895. E-mail: publishing@cla.ca. Website: www.cla.ca. Publishes trade paperback originals. **Publishes 4 titles/year. Receives 10 queries and 5 mss/year. 50% of books from first-time authors; 100% from unagented writers. Pays 10% royalty on wholesale price.** Publishes book 6 months after acceptance of ms. Does not accept simultaneous submissions. Responds in 1 month to queries; 3 months to proposals; 3 months to mss. Book catalog and ms guidelines free.

"CLA publishes practical/professional/academic materials with a Canadian focus or direct Canadian application as a service to CLA members and to contribute to the professional development of library staff."

Nonfiction: Reference, textbook. Subjects include history, language/literature, library science. Query with SASE, or submit outline. Reviews artwork/photos as part of ms package. Send photocopies.
Recent Title(s): *The B2B Canadian Research Sourcebook: Your Essential Guide*; *Demystifying Copyright: A Researcher's Guide to Copyright in Canadian Libraries and Archives.*
Tips: Audience is library and information scientists.

CANADIAN PLAINS RESEARCH CENTER, University of Regina, Regina SK S4S 0A2 Canada. (306)585-4795. Fax: (306)585-4699. E-mail: brian.mlazgar@uregina.ca. Website: www.cprc.uregina.ca. **Acquisitions:** Brian Mlazgar, coordinator. Estab. 1973. Publishes scholarly paperback originals and some casebound originals. **Publishes 8-10 titles/year. Receives 15-20 submissions/year. 35% of books from first-time authors.** Publishes book 2 years after acceptance of ms. Does not accept simultaneous submissions. Responds in 6 months to queries. Book catalog and ms guidelines free.

Canadian Plains Research Center publishes scholarly research on the Canadian plains.

Nonfiction: Biography, illustrated book, technical, textbook. Subjects include business/economics, government/politics, history, nature/environment, regional, sociology. "The Canadian Plains Research Center publishes the results of research on topics relating to the Canadian Plains region, although manuscripts relating to the Great Plains region will be considered. Material *must* be scholarly. Do not submit health, self-help, hobbies, music, sports, psychology, recreation or cookbooks unless they have a scholarly approach." Query with SASE or submit complete ms. Reviews artwork/photos as part of ms package.
Recent Title(s): *Discover Saskatchewan*, by Nilson (guide to historic sites and markers).
Tips: "Pay attention to manuscript preparation and accurate footnoting, according to *Chicago Manual of Style*."

CAPALL BANN PUBLISHING, Auton Farm, Milverton, Somerset, TA4 1NE United Kingdom. (0044)1823 401528. Fax: (0044)1823 401529. E-mail: enquiries@capallbann.co.uk. Website: www.capallbann.co.uk. **Acquisitions:** Julia Day (MBS, healing, animals); Jon Day (MBS, religion). Publishes trade and mass market paperback originals and trade paperback and mass market paperback reprints. **Publishes 46 titles/year. Receives 800 queries and 450 mss/year. 50% of books from first-time authors; 100% from unagented writers. Pays 10% royalty on net sales.** Publishes book 8 months after acceptance of ms. Accepts simultaneous submissions. Responds in 2-6 weeks to queries; 2 months to proposals; 2 months to mss. Book catalog free; ms guidelines online.

"Our mission is to publish books of real value to enhance and improve readers' lives."

Nonfiction: Illustrated book, reference, self-help. Subjects include animals, anthropology/archeology, gardening, health/

medicine, music/dance, nature/environment, philosophy, religion, spirituality, women's issues/studies, new age. Submit outline. Reviews artwork/photos as part of ms package. Send photocopies.

Recent Title(s): *Everything You Wanted to Know About Your Body, But So Far Nobody's Been Able to Tell You*; *Real Fairies*, by David Tame.

CARSWELL THOMSON, (formerly Carswell Thomson Professional Publishing), One Corporate Plaza 2075 Kennedy Rd., Scarborough ON M1T 3V4 Canada. (416)298-5024. Fax: (416)298-5094. E-mail: robert.freeman@carswell.com. Website: www.carswell.com. **Acquisitions:** Robert Freeman, vice president, legal, accounting and finance, and corporate groups. Publishes hardcover originals. **Publishes 150-200 titles/year. 30-50% of books from first-time authors. Pays 5-15% royalty on wholesale price. Offers $1,000-5,000 advance.** Publishes book 6 months after acceptance of ms. Accepts simultaneous submissions. Responds in 3 months to queries. Book catalog and ms guidelines free.

- Carswell Thomson is Canada's national resource of information and legal interpretations for law, accounting, tax and business professionals.

Nonfiction: Reference (legal, tax). "Canadian information of a regulatory nature is our mandate." Submit proposal package including outline, résumé.

Tips: Audience is Canada and persons interested in Canadian information; professionals in law, tax, accounting fields; business people interested in regulatory material.

CHA PRESS, 17 York St., Ottawa ON K1N 9J6 Canada. (613)241-8005, ext. 264. Fax: (613)241-5055. E-mail: chapress@cha.ca. Website: www.cha.ca. **Acquisitions:** Eleanor Sawyer, director of publishing. **Publishes 6-8 titles/year. Receives 5 queries and 3 mss/year. 40% of books from first-time authors; 90% from unagented writers. Pays 10-17% royalty on retail price, or makes outright purchase of $250-1,000. Offers $500-1,500 advance.** Responds in 3 months to queries. Book catalog and ms guidelines free.

- CHA Press strives to be Canada's health administration textbook publisher. "We serve readers in our broad continuum of care in regional health authorities, hospitals, and health care facilities and agencies, which are governed by trustees." Currently emphasizing history of regionalization; accountability of boards/executives; executives and leadership. De-emphasizing hospital-based issues of any type.

Nonfiction: How-to, textbook, guides. Subjects include health/medicine, history. Query with SASE or submit outline.

Recent Title(s): *The Anthology of Readings in Long-Term Care, 3rd Ed*, edited by Eleanor Sawyer, Marion Stephens and Cynthia Rorak; *Caring, the Human Mode of Being*, by Sr. M. Simone Roach, CSM; *What Good is Health Care?*, by Dr. Nuala P. Kenny.

Tips: Audience is healthcare facility managers (senior/middle); policy analysts/researchers; nurse practitioners and other healthcare professionals; trustees. "CHA Press is looking to expand its frontlist in 2003 to include governance, risk management, security and safety, health system reform, and quality assessment. Don't underestimate amount of time it will take to write or mistake generic 'how-to' health for mass media as appropriate for CHA's specialty press."

CHARLTON PRESS, P.O. Box 820, Station Willowdale B, North York ON M2K 2R1 Canada. Fax: (416)488-4656. E-mail: chpress@charltonpress.com. Website: www.charltonpress.com. **Acquisitions:** Jean Dale, managing editor. Publishes trade paperback originals and reprints. **Publishes 15 titles/year. Receives 30 queries and 5 mss/year. 10% of books from first-time authors; 100% from unagented writers. Pays 10% royalty on wholesale price, or makes variable outright purchase.** Publishes book 6 months after acceptance of ms. Accepts simultaneous submissions. Responds in 1 month to queries; 1 month to proposals; 2 months to mss. Book catalog free.

Nonfiction: Reference (price guides on collectibles). Subjects include hobbies (numismatics, toys, military badges, ceramic collectibles, sports cards). Submit outline. Reviews artwork/photos as part of ms package. Send photocopies.

Recent Title(s): *Royal Doulton Figurines*, by J. Dale (reference guide).

CHEMTEC PUBLISHING, 38 Earswick Dr., Toronto-Scarborough ON M1E 1C6 Canada. (416)265-2603. Fax: (416)265-1399. E-mail: info@chemtec.org. Website: www.chemtec.org. **Acquisitions:** Anna Wypych, president. Publishes hardcover originals. **Publishes 5 titles/year. Receives 10 queries and 7 mss/year. 20% of books from first-time authors. Pays 5-15% royalty on retail price.** Publishes book 6 months after acceptance of ms. Accepts simultaneous submissions. Responds in 2 months to queries; 4 months to mss. Book catalog and ms guidelines free.

- Chemtec publishes books on polymer chemistry, physics, and technology. "Special emphasis is given to process additives and books which treat subject in comprehensive manner."

Nonfiction: Technical, textbook. Subjects include science, environment, chemistry, polymers. Submit outline, sample chapter(s).

Recent Title(s): *Handbook of Fillers*, by George Wypych; *Handbook of Solvents*, by multiple authors.

Tips: Audience is industrial research and universities.

CICERONE PRESS, 2 Police Square, Milnthorpe, Cumbria LA7 7PY United Kingdom. 015395 62069. Fax: 015395 63417. E-mail: info@cicerone.co.uk. Website: www.cicerone.co.uk. **Acquisitions:** Jonathan Williams, acquisitions editor. Publishes hardcover and trade paperback originals and reprints. **Publishes 24 titles/year. Receives 50-100 queries and 50 mss/year. 35% of books from first-time authors; 100% from unagented writers.** Publishes book 1 year after acceptance of ms. Does not accept simultaneous submissions. Responds in 2 months to mss. Book catalog online.

- Cicerone specializes in guides to the great outdoors—hiking, climbing, cycling, mountaineering, etc. No fiction or poetry.

Nonfiction: Reference. Subjects include sports, travel. Query with SASE, or submit outline, 2 sample chapter(s).

Recent Title(s): *Walking in the Alps*, by Kev Reynolds (topography nonfiction).

COACH HOUSE BOOKS, 401 Huron St. on bpNichol Lane, Toronto ON M5S 2G5 Canada. (416)979-2217. Fax: (416)977-1158. E-mail: mail@chbooks.com. Website: www.chbooks.com. **Acquisitions:** Alana Wilcox, editor. Publishes trade paperback originals. **Publishes 16 titles/year. 80% of books from first-time authors; 100% from unagented writers. Pays 10% royalty on retail price.** Publishes book 1 year after acceptance of ms. Does not accept simultaneous submissions. Responds in 6 months to queries. Ms guidelines online.

Nonfiction: Artists' books. Query with SASE. *All unsolicited mss returned unopened.*

Fiction: Experimental, literary, plays. "Consult website for submissions policy." *All unsolicited mss returned unopened.*

Poetry: Consult website for guidelines. Query.

Recent Title(s): *Fidget*, by K. Goldsmith (poetry); *Eunoia*, by Christian Bök (poetry); *Lenny Bruce Is Dead*, by Jonathan Goldstein (fiction).

COMPENDIUM PUBLISHING, LTD., 43 Frith St., 1st Floor, London W1V 5TE United Kingdom. (0207)287-4570. Fax: (0207)494-0583. E-mail: compendiumpub@aol.com. Website: www.compendiumpublishing.com. **Acquisitions:** Simon Forty, editorial director. Publishes hardcover originals and reprints, trade paperback originals, and reprints. **Publishes 40 titles/year. Receives 500 mss/year. 70% of books from first-time authors; 80% from unagented writers. Pays 5-12½% royalty on net receipts or makes outright purchase of $3,000-10,000.** Publishes book 18 months after acceptance of ms. Accepts simultaneous submissions. Responds in 1 month to queries; 3 months to proposals; 3 months to mss.

Nonfiction: Coffee table book, cookbook, gift book, illustrated book, reference, self-help, technical. Subjects include anthropology/archeology, art/architecture, cooking/foods/nutrition, gardening, gay/lesbian, history, hobbies, military/war, nature/environment, photography, recreation, sex, sports, travel, women's issues/studies, transport. Submit outline, sample chapter(s), or submit complete ms.

Recent Title(s): *Native Tribes of North America*, by M. Johnson; *War Films*, by A. Evans.

CONSTABLE & ROBINSON, LTD., (formerly Constable Publishers), Constable & Robinson, 3 The Lanchesters, 162 Fulham Palace Rd., London WG 9ER United Kingdom. 0208-741-3663. Fax: 0208-748-7562. **Acquisitions:** (Ms.) Carol O'Brien (biography: historical and literary, Celtic interest, pre-WWII military history, travel literature); Krystyna Green (crime fiction); Dan Hind (politics, current affairs, nonfiction); Pete Duncan (health, popular science, psychology, photographic, true crime, nonfiction); Nicola Chalton (history, survival & endurance, nonfiction). Publishes hardcover and trade paperback originals. **Publishes 160 titles/year. Receives 3,000 queries and 1,000 mss/year. Offers advance.** Publishes book 1 year after acceptance of ms. Accepts simultaneous submissions. Responds in 1 month to queries; 1 month to proposals; 3 months to mss. Book catalog free.

Imprints: Constable Hardback, Robinson Paperback.

Nonfiction: Biography. Subjects include health/medicine, history, military/war, psychology, science (popular), travel, politics, current affairs. Query with SASE, or submit 3 sample chapter(s), list of chapter titles. Reviews artwork/photos as part of ms package. Send photocopies.

Fiction: Crime/whodunnit. *Agented submissions only.*

Recent Title(s): *Hunted*, by David Fletcher (biography/travel); *Panzerkrieg*, by Mike Syron and Peter McCarthy (military history); *Shanghai Baby*, by Wei Hui (fiction).

CORMORANT BOOKS, INC., 895 Don Mills Rd., 400-2 Park Centre, Toronto ON M3C 1W3 Canada. (416)445-3333. Fax: (416)445-5967. Website: www.cormorantbooks.com. **Acquisitions:** Marc Côté, publisher. Publishes hardcover, trade paperback originals and reprints. **Publishes 16-20 titles/year. Receives 500 queries and 300 mss/year. 50% of books from first-time authors; 50% from unagented writers. Pays 8-15% royalty on retail price. Offers $500-15,000 advance.** Publishes book 1-2 years after acceptance of ms. Accepts simultaneous submissions. Responds in 1 months to queries; 1 month to proposals; 3 months to mss. Book catalog and ms guidelines free or online.

Cormorant publishes Canadian fiction and essay collections, occasional nonfiction titles, usually on literary themes. Currently emphasizing novels. De-emphasizing short stories.

Nonfiction: Biography. Subjects include creative nonfiction, history, memoirs, philosophy. Query with SASE.

Fiction: Cormorant is a highly literary company with hundreds of awards for literary excellence. Adventure, confession, ethnic, experimental, feminist, gay/lesbian, historical, humor, literary, mainstream/contemporary, multicultural, mystery, plays, poetry, regional, short story collections, translation. Query with SASE, or submit 3 sample chapter(s), synopsis or submit complete ms.

Recent Title(s): *Doing the Heart Good*, by Neil Bissoondath (novel); *Cumberland*, by Michael V. Smith (novel); *Thinking and Singing: Poetry and the Practice of Philosophy*, edited by Tim Lilburn (essay collection).

Tips: "Writers should determine, from a study of our list, whether their fiction or essay collection would be appropriate. *Canadian authors only.*"

COTEAU BOOKS, Thunder Creek Publishing Co-operative, Ltd., 401-2206 Dewdney Ave., Suite 401, Regina SK S4R 1H3 Canada. (306)777-0170. Fax: (306)522-5152. E-mail: coteau@coteaubooks.com. Website: www.coteaubooks.com. **Acquisitions:** Geoffrey Ursell, publisher. Estab. 1975. Publishes trade paperback originals and reprints. **Publishes 20 titles/year. Receives 200 queries and 200 mss/year. 50% of books from first-time authors; 100% from unagented writers. Pays 10% royalty on retail price.** Publishes book 1 year after acceptance of ms. Does not accept simultaneous submissions. Responds in 2 months to queries; 6 months to mss. Book catalog free; ms guidelines online.

"Our mission is to publish the finest in Canadian fiction, nonfiction, poetry, drama, and children's literature, with an emphasis on Saskatchewan and prairie writers." De-emphasizing science fiction, picture books.

Nonfiction: Coffee table book, reference. Subjects include creative nonfiction, ethnic, history, language/literature, memoirs, regional, sports, travel. Canadian authors only. Submit 3-4 sample chapter(s), author bio, SASE.

Fiction: Ethnic, fantasy, feminist, gay/lesbian, historical, humor, juvenile, literary, mainstream/contemporary, multicultural, multimedia, mystery, plays, poetry, regional, short story collections, spiritual, sports, young adult, Novels, short fiction, middle years. Canadian authors only. No science fiction. No children's picture books. Submit 3-4 sample chapter(s), author bio, SASE.
Poetry: Submit 20-25 sample poems, or submit complete ms.
Recent Title(s): *In the Same Boat*, juvenile fiction series for ages 8 and up (promotes familiarity with other cultures); *Penelope's Way*, by Blanche Howard (novel); *Out of Her Backpack*, by Laura Cutler (short stories).
Tips: "Look at past publications to get an idea of our editorial program. We do not publish romance, horror, or picture books, but are interested in juvenile and teen fiction from Canadian authors. Submissions may be made by e-mail (maximum 20 pages) with attachments."

CRESCENT MOON PUBLISHING, P.O. Box 393, Maidstone Kent ME14 5XU United Kingdom. E-mail: jrobinson@crescentmoon.org.uk. Website: www.crescentmoon.org.uk. **Acquisitions:** Jeremy Robinson, director (arts, media, cinema, literature); Cassidy Hushes (visual arts). Estab. 1988. Publishes hardcover and trade paperback originals. **Publishes 25 titles/year. Receives 300 queries and 400 mss/year. 1% of books from first-time authors; 1% from unagented writers. Pays royalty. Offers negotiable advance.** Publishes book 18 months after acceptance of ms. Accepts simultaneous submissions. Responds in 2 months to queries; 4 months to proposals; 4 months to mss. Book catalog free; ms guidelines free.
Imprints: Joe's Press, Pagan America Magazine, Passion Magazine.
"Our mission is to publish the best in contemporary work, in poetry, fiction, and critical studies, and selections from the great writers." Currently emphasizing nonfiction (media, film, music, painting). De-emphasizing children's books.
Nonfiction: Biography, children's/juvenile, illustrated book, reference, scholarly (academic), textbook. Subjects include Americana, art/architecture, gardening, language/literature, music/dance, philosophy, religion, travel, women's issues/studies. Query with SASE, or submit outline, 2 sample chapter(s). Reviews artwork/photos as part of ms package. Send photocopies.
Fiction: Erotica, experimental, feminist, gay/lesbian, literary, short story collections, translation. "Does not publish fiction at present, but will consider high quality new work." Query with SASE, or submit outline, 2 sample chapter(s), synopsis.
Poetry: "We prefer a small selection of the poet's very best work at first. We prefer free or nonrhyming poetry. Do not send too much material." Query, or submit 6 sample poems.
Recent Title(s): *Nuclear War in the UK* (nonfiction); *Andy Goldworthy in Close-UP* (nonfiction).
Tips: "Our audience is interested in new contemporary writing."

CRESSRELLES PUBLISHING CO., LTD., 10 Station Rd., Industrial Estate, Colwall, Malvern Worcestershire WR13 6RN United Kingdom. Phone/fax: 01684 540154. E-mail: simonsmith@cressrelles4drama.fsbusiness.co.uk. Publishes hardcover and trade paperback originals. **Publishes 10-20 titles/year. Pays royalty on retail price.** Book catalog free.
Imprints: Kenyon-Deane, J. Garnet Miller, New Playwright's Network, Actinic Press.
Nonfiction: Subjects include drama (plays), theater. Submit complete ms.

THE C.W. DANIEL CO., LTD., 1 Church Path, Saffron, Walden Essex CB10 1JP United Kingdom. (011)44 1799 526216. Fax: (011)44 1799 513462. E-mail: cwdaniel@dial.pipex.com. Website: www.cwdaniel.com. **Acquisitions:** Ian Miller, publisher. Publishes trade paperback originals. **Publishes 15 titles/year. Receives 500 queries and 300 mss/year. 40% of books from first-time authors; 90% from unagented writers. Pays 8-15% royalty.** Publishes book 9 months after acceptance of ms. Accepts simultaneous submissions. Responds in 1 month to queries; 1 month to proposals; 1 month to mss. Book catalog free.
Nonfiction: Self-help (mind, body, spirit). Subjects include health/medicine, spirituality. "We do not have either staff nor time to accept half-finished work." Submit proposal package including outline, 2 sample chapter(s). Reviews artwork/photos as part of ms package. Send photocopies.
Recent Title(s): *Seeing the Wider Picture*, by Charlotte Parnell (meditation); *Children Who Have Lived Before*, by Trutz Hardo (reincarnation); *Five Feel-Good Factors*, by Jan Sadler (self-help).
Tips: Audience is comprised of intelligent, middle-class women on the whole. "We are only interested in books written by authors who have a heart-felt need or obsession with their subject."

N **DAY BOOKS**, Orchard Piece, Crawborough, Charlbury Oxfordshire OX7 3TX United Kingdom. E-mail: diaries@day-books.com. Submissions E-mail: ef@day-books.com. Website: www.day-books.com. **Acquisitions:** James Sanderson, managing editor (diaries and biographies). Estab. 1997. Publishes hardcover originals and trade paperback reprints. **Publishes 4 titles/year. Receives 30 queries and 30 mss/year. 10% of books from first-time authors; 80% from unagented writers. Pays 10% royalty on wholesale price. Offers $1,000-2,500 advance.** Publishes book 1 year after acceptance of ms. Accepts simultaneous submissions. Responds in 1 month to queries; 1 month to proposals; 1 month to mss. Book catalog online; ms guidelines free.
Nonfiction: Autobiography, biography, scholarly. Subjects include general nonfiction, history, memoirs, regional. Query with SASE or submit proposal package or submit complete ms. Reviews artwork/photos as part of ms package. Send photocopies.
Recent Title(s): *Inside Stalin's Russia: The Diaries of Reader Bullard, 1930-1934*, by Julian and Margaret Bullard (history/biography); *Lifting the Latch: A Life on the Land*, by Sheila Stewart (social history/biography).

N **DRAGON MOON PRESS**, Box 64312, 5512 Fourth St. NW, Calgary AB T2K 6J0 Canada. E-mail: publisher@dragonmoon.ab.ca. Website: www.dragonmoonpress.com. **Acquisitions:** Christine Mains, submissions editor (fantasy, science fiction). Estab. 1992. Publishes hardcover, trade paperback, mass market paperback, and electronic originals. **Publishes 1-2 titles/year. 100% of books from first-time authors. Pays 8-15% royalty on retail price.** Publishes book 2 years after acceptance of ms. Accepts simultaneous submissions. Responds in 4 months to queries; 4 months to proposals; 8 months to mss. Book catalog and ms guidelines on website.

Fiction: Fantasy, horror (dark fantasy, futuristic, supernatural, vampires), science fiction (hard science/technological, soft/sociological), "strong, traditional fantasy featuring dragons, high adventure and great magic!" "Publishing is becoming more accessible to the general public through the use of technology. With the interest in self-publishing, the market is becoming flooded with both gems and trash. This makes the need for publishers important, as gateways and as filters to the public. At Dragon Moon Press, we continue to improve how we do business and continue to seek out quality manuscripts and authors. We are publishing more trade paperbacks because we can print short runs as needed and not invest so heavily in traditional offset printing. We are also receiving many high quality manuscripts that we feel deserve to be published." No talking animals, no vampires. Query with SASE or submit proposal package including outline, 3 sample chapter(s), synopsis.

Recent Title(s): *The Chronicles of Rafe and Askana*, by Lisa Lee and Tee Morris (fantasy); *The Dragon Reborn*, by Kathleen H. Nelson (fantasy).

Tips: "First, be patient. Read our guidelines at dragonmoonpress.com. Not following our submission guidelines can be grounds for automatic rejection. Second, we view publishing as a family affair. Be ready to participate in the process, and show some enthusiasm and understanding in what we do. Remember also, this is a business and not about egos, so keep yours on a leash! Finally, educate yourself about the industry and the truths surrounding it. The first book will not make you rich. Neither will your second. The reward with Dragon Moon Press is not so much in money as it is in the experience and the satisfaction in the final work. Show us a great story with well-developed characters and plot lines, show us that you are interested in the industry, and show us your desire to create a great book, and you may just find yourself published by Dragon Moon Press."

DUNDURN PRESS, LTD., 8 Market St., Suite 200, Toronto ON M5E 1M6 Canada. (416)214-5544. Website: www.dundurn.com. **Acquisitions:** Acquisitions Editor. Estab. 1972. Publishes hardcover and trade paperback originals and reprints. **Publishes 50-60 titles/year. Receives 600 submissions/year. 50% of books from first-time authors; 85% from unagented writers. Pays 10% royalty on net receipts.** Publishes book an average of 1 year after acceptance of ms. Accepts simultaneous submissions. Responds in 3-4 months to queries. Ms guidelines online.

Dundurn publishes books by Canadian authors.

Nonfiction: Subjects include art/architecture, history (Canadian and military), music/dance (drama), regional, art history, theater, serious and popular nonfiction.

Fiction: Literary, mystery, young adult. "No romance, science fiction or experimental." Query with SASE, and submit sample chapter(s), synopsis, author bio.

Recent Title(s): *Exile*, by Ann Ireland (novel); *One Soldier's Story* (military history); *Colossal Canadian Failures* (popular nonfiction).

ECCENOVA EDITIONS, P.O. Box 50001, 15-1594 Fairfield Rd., Victoria BC V8V 1B6 Canada. Fax: (250)595-8401. E-mail: acquisitions@eccenova.com. Website: www.eccenova.com. Estab. 2003. Publishes hardcover and trade paperback originals. **Publishes 6 titles/year. Receives 40-50 queries and 15 mss/year. 90% of books from first-time authors; 90% from unagented writers. Pays 15% royalty on wholesale price.** Publishes book 9 months after acceptance of ms. Does not accept simultaneous submissions. Responds in 1 week to e-mail queries; 1 month to proposals; 3 months to mss. Book catalog and ms guidelines online.

Nonfiction: Scholarly. Subjects include anthropology/archeology, art/architecture, astrology/psychic, creative nonfiction, education, history, humanities, language/literature, literary criticism, New Age, philosophy, religion, science, social sciences, sociology, spirituality, women's issues/studies, magic/occult, theater. "We like to see solid argument construction and good research. Scholarly works should be 'toned down' for a more lay-audience, but must be credible and well supported, no matter how outlandish the premise! We have a preference for maverick thinkers who dare to challenge the status quo, but, in order to have credibility, the author should make the most of his/her credentials and training/experience in the field. We have strong interests in religion, philosophy, and science, but are open to all humanities subjects. We can accept only greyscale/b&w images (if any) for the text-block." Query via e-mail or with SASE. Reviews artwork/photos as part of ms package. Send photocopies.

Recent Title(s): *Goddess in the Grass: Serpentine Mythology and the Great Goddess*, by Linda Foubister; *Aleph Through the Looking Glass: Three Steps to Writing in Hebrew*, by Jonathan Lavie; *Black Magick Woman: The Sinister Side of the Song of Solomon*, by Janet Tyson.

Tips: "Our audience is well educated and open-minded. They appreciate a challenge to their ideas and like a good 'story' behind the research. Many are mature university students looking for support material for humanities/science courses, or instructors looking for unique 'readers.' Because this company is founded on the idea of creating a unique library of human knowledge, emulating the Library at Alexandria, we are more interested in quality than quantity. We look for works that open new avenues of investigation, or shed new light on old ones. We value original thought, so try not to create a book that rests, solely, on other people's work. Query first, explaining why you wrote the book, what your credentials are, and how you think it meets the criterium of originality."

ECRITS DES FORGES, C.P. 335, 1497 Laviolette, Trois-Rivieres QC G9A 5G4 Canada. (819)379-9813. Fax: (819)376-0774. E-mail: ecrits.desforges@tr.cgocable.ca. **Acquisitions:** Gaston Bellemare, president. Publishes hardcover originals. **Publishes 40 titles/year. Receives 30 queries and 1,000 mss/year. 10% of books from first-time authors; 90% from unagented writers. Pays 10-30% royalty. Offers 50% advance.** Publishes book 9 months after acceptance of ms. Accepts simultaneous submissions. Responds in 9 months to queries. Book catalog free.

Ecrits des Forges publishes only poetry written in French.

Poetry: Submit 20 sample poems.

Recent Title(s): *Ode au St-Laurent*, by Gatien Lapointe (poetry).

ECW PRESS, 2120 Queen St. E., Suite 200, Toronto ON M4E 1E2 Canada. (416)694-3348. Fax: (416)698-9906. E-mail: info@ecwpress.com. Website: www.ecwpress.com. **Acquisitions:** Jack David, president (nonfiction); Michael Holmes, literary editor (fiction, poetry); Jennifer Hale, associate editor (pop culture, entertainment). Estab. 1979. Publishes hardcover and trade paperback originals. **Publishes 40 titles/year; imprint publishes 8 titles/year. Receives 500 queries and 300 mss/year. 30% of books from first-time authors. Pays 8-12% royalty on net receipts. Offers $300-5,000 advance.** Publishes book 18 months after acceptance of ms. Accepts simultaneous submissions. Responds in 1 month to queries; 2 months to proposals; 4 months to mss. Book catalog and ms guidelines free; ms guidelines online.

ECW publishes nonfiction about people or subjects that have a substantial fan base. Currently emphasizing books about music, Wicca, gambling, TV and movie stars.

Nonfiction: Biography (popular), humor. Subjects include business/economics, creative nonfiction, gay/lesbian, general nonfiction, government/politics, health/medicine, history, memoirs, money/finance, regional, sex, sports, women's issues/studies, contemporary culture, Wicca, gambling, TV and movie stars. Submit proposal package including outline, 4-5 sample chapter(s), IRC, SASE. Reviews artwork/photos as part of ms package. Send photocopies.

Fiction: "We publish literary fiction and poetry from Canadian authors exclusively. Literary, mystery, poetry, short story collections, suspense. Submit proposal package including 1-2 sample chapter(s), synopsis, IRC, SASE.

Poetry: "We publish Canadian poetry exclusively." Query or submit 4-5 sample poems.

Recent Title(s): *Too Close to the Falls*, by Catherine Gildiner; *Blakwidow: My First Year as a Professional Wrestler*, by Amanda Storm; *Burn*, by Paul Vermeersch (poetry).

Tips: "Visit our website *and* read a selection of our books."

EDGE SCIENCE FICTION AND FANTASY PUBLISHING, Box 1714, Calgary AB T2P 2L7 Canada. (403)254-0160. Fax: (403)254-0456. E-mail: editor@edgewebsite.com. Website: www.edgewebsite.com. **Acquisitions:** Brian Hades. Estab. 1996. Publishes hardcover and trade paperback originals. **Publishes 2-4 titles/year. Receives 480 queries and 400 mss/year. 70% of books from first-time authors; 75% from unagented writers. Pays 10% royalty on wholesale price. Offers negotiable advance.** Publishes book 18 months after acceptance of ms. Does not accept simultaneous submissions. Responds in 1 month to queries; 1 month to proposals; 4-5 months to mss. Ms guidelines online.

"We want to encourage, produce, and promote thought-provoking and well-written science fiction and fantasy literature."

Fiction: Fantasy (space fantasy, sword and sorcery), science fiction (hard science/technological, soft/sociological). "We are looking for all types of fantasy and science fiction, except juvenile/young adult, horror, erotica, religious fiction, short stories, dark/gruesome fantasy, or poetry." Query with SASE, or submit outline, 3 sample chapter(s), synopsis, Check website for guidelines or send SAE & IRCS for same.

Recent Title(s): *The Black Chalice*, by Marie Jakober (historical fantasy); *Lyskarion: The Song of the Wind*, by Janice Cullum (fantasy); *Throne Price*, Lynda Williams and Allison Sinclair (science fantasy).

Tips: "Send us your best, polished, completed manuscript. Use proper manuscript format. Take the time before you submit to get a critique from someone who can offer you useful advice. When in doubt, visit our website for helpful resources, FAQs, and other tips."

AIDAN ELLIS PUBLISHING, Whinfield, Herbert Road, Salcombe Devon TQ8 8HN United Kingdom. (pl44)1548 842755. Fax: (pl44)1548 844356. E-mail: aidan@aepub.demon.co.uk. Website: www.aepub.demon.co.uk. **Acquisitions:** Aidan Ellis (nonfiction). Publishes hardcover and trade paperback originals. **Publishes 6 titles/year. Receives 300 mss/year. 1% of books from first-time authors; 90% from unagented writers. Pays 10% royalty. Offers advance.** Does not accept simultaneous submissions. Responds in 2 months to queries. Book catalog for free or on website.

Nonfiction: Biography, coffee table book, cookbook, gift book. Subjects include art/architecture, cooking/foods/nutrition, gardening, history, nature/environment, translation, travel. Query with SASE, or submit outline, 2 sample chapter(s).

EMPYREAL PRESS, P.O. Box 1746, Place Du Parc, Montreal QC HZW 2R7 Canada. Website: www.skarwood.com. Publishes trade paperback originals. **Publishes 1-2 titles/year. 50% of books from first-time authors; 90% from unagented writers.** Book catalog for #10 SASE.

"Our mission is the publishing of unique Canadian literature—writing grounded in discipline and in imagination."

Fiction: Experimental, feminist, gay/lesbian, literary, short story collections. *Absolutely no unsolicited mss* due to our being an extremely small and backlogged operation.

Recent Title(s): *Winter Spring Summer Fall*, by Robert Sandiford; *The Surface of Time*, by Louis Dudek; *Saint Francis of Esplanade*, by Sonja A. Skarstedt (drama).

FERNHURST BOOKS, Duke's Path, High St., Arundel, West Sussex United Kingdom. 01903-882277. Fax: 01903-882715. E-mail: sales@fernhurstbooks.co.uk. Website: www.fernhurstbooks.co.uk. **Acquisitions:** Tim Davison, publisher. Publishes mass market paperback originals. **Publishes 12 titles/year. Receives 2-4 queries/year. 50% of books from first-time authors; 90% from unagented writers. Pays 10% royalty. Offers advance.** Publishes book up to 1 year after acceptance of ms. Does not accept simultaneous submissions. Book catalog free.

Fernhurst publishes books on watersports, producing practical, highly-illustrated handbooks on sailing and watersports. Currently emphasizing sailing and maintenance

Nonfiction: Gift book, how-to, humor. Subjects include sports. Submit proposal package including outline. *No unsolicited mss.* Reviews artwork/photos as part of ms package.

FERNWOOD PUBLISHING, LTD., 8422 St. Margarets Bay Rd., Site 2A, Box 5, Black Pointe NS B0J 1B0 Canada. (902)857-1388. E-mail: info@fernwoodbooks.ca. Website: www.fernwoodbooks.ca. **Acquisitions:** Errol Sharpe, publisher (social science); Wayne Antony, editor (social science). Publishes trade paperback originals. **Publishes 12-15 titles/year. Receives 80 queries and 30 mss/year. 40% of books from first-time authors; 100% from unagented writers. Pays 7-10% royalty on wholesale price. Offers advance.** Publishes book 1 year after acceptance of ms. Accepts simultaneous submissions. Responds in 6 weeks to proposals. Ms guidelines online.

"Fernwood's objective is to publish critical works which challenge existing scholarship."

Nonfiction: Reference, textbook, scholarly. Subjects include agriculture/horticulture, anthropology/archeology, business/economics, education, ethnic, gay/lesbian, government/politics, health/medicine, history, language/literature, multicultural, nature/environment, philosophy, regional, sex, sociology, sports, translation, women's issues/studies, contemporary culture, world affairs. "Our main focus is in the social sciences and humanities, emphasizing labor studies, women's studies, gender studies, critical theory and research, political economy, cultural studies, and social work—for use in college and university courses." Submit proposal package including outline, sample chapter(s). Reviews artwork/photos as part of ms package. Send photocopies.

Recent Title(s): *Social Torment: Globalization in Atlantic Canada*, by Thom Workman; *Accounting for Genocide: Canada's Bureaucratic Assault on Aboriginal People*, by Dean Neu and Richard Therrien; *Black Canadians: History, Experience, Social Conditioning*, by Joseph Mensah.

FINDHORN PRESS, 305A The Park, Findhorn, Forres Scotland IV36 3TE United Kingdom. 01309-690582. Fax: 01309-690036. E-mail: info@findhornpress.com. Website: www.findhornpress.com. **Acquisitions:** Thierry Bogliolo, publisher. Publishes trade paperback originals. **Publishes 12 titles/year. Receives 1,000 queries/year. 50% of books from first-time authors. Pays 10-15% royalty on wholesale price.** Publishes book 1 year after acceptance of ms. Book catalog and ms guidelines online.

Nonfiction: Self-help. Subjects include health/medicine, nature/environment, spirituality. Submit proposal package including outline, 1 sample chapter(s), marketing plan.

FLARESTACK PUBLISHING, 41 Buckley's Green, Alvechurch, Birmingham B48 7NG United Kingdom. (0121)445-2110. Fax: (01527)68571. E-mail: flare.stack@virgin.net. **Acquisitions:** Charles Johnson, editor. Estab. 1995. Publishes original trade paperbacks. **Publishes 12 titles/year. Pays 25% royalties, plus 6 complimentary copies.** Responds in 6 weeks to queries; 2 months to mss.

Flarestack Publishing aims to "find an audience for new poets, so beginners are welcome, but the work has to be strong and clear."

Poetry: "Normally we expect a few previous magazine acceptances, but no previous collection publication." Query first with a maximum of 6 sample poems, SASE, and cover letter with brief bio and publication credits.

Tips: "Most beginning poets show little evidence of reading poetry before writing it! Join a poetry workshop. For chapbook publishing, we are looking for coherent first collections that take risks, make leaps, and come clean."

FLY LEAF PRESS, 4 Spencer Villas, Glenageary, County Dublin Ireland. (353)1-2845906. Fax: (353)1-2806231. E-mail: Flyleaf@indigo.ie. Website: www.flyleaf.ie. **Acquisitions:** James Ryan, managing editor (family history). Publishes hardcover originals. **Publishes 3 titles/year. Receives 15 queries and 10 mss/year. 60% of books from first-time authors; 100% from unagented writers. Pays 7-10% royalty on wholesale price.** Publishes book 6 months after acceptance of ms. Does not accept simultaneous submissions. Responds in 1 month to mss. Book catalog available free by request or online at website.

Nonfiction: Subjects include history, hobbies, family history. Submit proposal package including outline, 1 sample chapter(s).

Recent Title(s): *Sources for Irish Family History*, by James G. Ryan; *Longford & Its People*, by David Leahy.

Tips: Audience is family history hobbyists, history students, local historians.

GOOSE LANE EDITIONS, 469 King St., Fredericton NB E3B 1E5 Canada. (506)450-4251. Fax: (506)459-4991. Website: www.gooselane.com. **Acquisitions:** Laurel Boone, editorial director. Estab. 1954. Publishes hardcover and paperback originals and occasional reprints. **Publishes 12-14 titles/year. Receives 500 submissions/year. 20% of books from first-time authors; 75% from unagented writers. Pays 8-12% royalty on retail price. Offers $100-200, negotiable advance.** Does not accept simultaneous submissions. Responds in 6 months to queries. with IRC or Canadian stamps first-class stamps.

Goose Lane publishes literary fiction and nonfiction from well-read and highly skilled Canadian authors.

Nonfiction: Biography, illustrated book. Subjects include art/architecture, history, language/literature, nature/environment, regional, women's issues/studies. Query with SASE.

Fiction: Historical, literary (novels), mainstream/contemporary, short story collections. "Our needs in fiction never change: Substantial, character-centered literary fiction. No children's, YA, mainstream, mass market, genre, mystery, thriller, confessional or science fiction. Not suitable for mainstream or mass market submissions. No genres, confessional works (fiction or autobiographical), thrillers, or other mystery books." Query with SASE. Send SASE "with Canadian stamps, International Reply Coupons, cash, check, or money order. No U.S. stamps please."

Recent Title(s): *Tent of Blue*, by Rachael Preston (fiction); *Coasts of Canada: A History*, by Lesley Choyce (nonfiction).

Tips: "Writers should send us outlines and samples of books that show a very well-read author who, in either fiction or nonfiction, has highly developed literary skills. Our books are almost all by Canadians living in Canada; we seldom consider submissions from outside Canada. If I were a writer trying to market a book today, I would contact the targeted publisher with a query letter and synopsis, and request manuscript guidelines. Purchase a recent book from the publisher in a relevant area, if possible. Always send an SASE with IRCs or suffient return postage in Canadian stamps for reply to your query and for any material you'd like returned should it not suit our needs."

GUERNICA EDITIONS, Box 117, Station P, Toronto ON M5S 2S6 Canada. (416)658-9888. Fax: (416)657-8885. E-mail: guernicaeditions@cs.com. Website: www.guernicaeditions.com. **Acquisitions:** Antonio D'Alfonso, editor/publisher (poetry, nonfiction, novels); Ken Scambray, editor (US reprints). Estab. 1978. Publishes trade paperback originals, reprints and software. **Publishes 25 titles/year. Receives 1,000 submissions and 750 mss/year. 20% of books from first-time authors; 99% from unagented writers. Pays 8-10% royalty on retail price, or makes outright purchase of $200-5,000. Offers $200-2,000 advance.** Publishes book 10 months after acceptance of ms. Does not accept simultaneous submissions. Responds in 1 month to queries; 6 months to proposals; 1 year to mss. Book catalog online.

Guernica Editions is an independent press dedicated to the bridging of cultures. "We do original and translations of fine works. We are seeking essays on authors and translations with less emphasis on poetry."

Nonfiction: Biography. Subjects include art/architecture, creative nonfiction, ethnic, film/cinema/stage, gay/lesbian, government/politics, history, language/literature, memoirs, multicultural, music/dance, philosophy, psychology, regional, religion, sex, translation, women's issues/studies. Query with SASE. **All unsolicited mss returned unopened.** Reviews artwork/photos as part of ms package. Send photocopies.

Fiction: Erotica, feminist, gay/lesbian, literary, multicultural, plays, poetry, poetry in translation, translation. "We wish to open up into the fiction world and focus less on poetry. We specialize in European, especially Italian, translations." Query with SASE. **All unsolicited mss returned unopened.**

Poetry: Feminist, gay/lesbian, literary, multicultural, poetry in translation. "We wish to have writers in translation. Any writer who has translated Italian poetry is welcomed. Full books only. Not single poems by different authors, unless modern, and used as an anthology. First books will have no place in the next couple of years." Query.

Recent Title(s): *Reel Canadians*, by Angela Baldassarre; *Italian Women in Black Dresses*, by Maria Mazziotti Gillan; *Song for My Father*, by Miriam Packer.

HAMBLEDON AND LONDON, 102 Gloucester Ave., London NW1 8HX United Kingdom. 0044 207 586 0817. Fax: 0044 207 586 9970. E-mail: ajm@hambledon.co.uk. Website: www.hambledon.co.uk. **Acquisitions:** Tony Morris, commissioning director (all history). Publishes hardcover and trade paperback originals. **Publishes 20 titles/year; imprint publishes 20 titles/year. Receives 750 queries and 150 mss/year. 10% of books from first-time authors; 90% from unagented writers. Pays 0-10% royalty on retail price.** Publishes book 6 months after acceptance of ms. Accepts simultaneous submissions. Responds in 1 week to queries; 2 weeks to proposals; 1 month to mss. Book catalog online; ms guidelines free.

"We publish high quality history at an affordable price for the general reader as well as the specialist."

Nonfiction: Biography (historical). Subjects include history, language/literature. Submit outline. Reviews artwork/photos as part of ms package. Send photocopies.

Recent Title(s): *Churchill: A Study in Greatness*, by Geoffrey Best; *Pilgrimage in Medieval England*, by Diana Webb.

HARLEQUIN ENTERPRISES, LTD., 225 Duncan Mill Rd., Don Mills ON M3B 3K9 Canada. (416)445-5860. Website: www.eharlequin.com. **Acquisitions:** Randall Toye, editorial director Toronto (Gold Eagle, Worldwide Library); Tara Gavin, editorial director New York (Silhouette, Harlequin, Steeple Hill, Red Dress Ink); Karin Stoecker, editorial director UK; Diane Moggy, editorial director Toronto (MIRA, Red Dress Ink). U.S.: 233 Broadway, 10th Floor, New York NY 10279. (212)553-4200. UK: Eton House, 18-24 Paradise Lane, Richmond, Surrey, TW9 1SR, United Kingdom. Estab. 1949. Publishes mass market paperback originals and reprints. **Publishes 700+ titles/year. Pays royalty. Offers advance.** Publishes book 1-3 years after acceptance of ms. Does not accept simultaneous submissions. Responds in 6 weeks to queries; 3 months to mss. Ms guidelines online.

Imprints: Harlequin, Silhouette, MIRA, Gold Eagle, Worldwide Mysteries, Steeple Hill, Red Dress Ink.

Fiction: Adventure (heroic), mystery, romance, suspense (romantic suspense only). Query with SASE.

Tips: "The quickest route to success is to follow directions for submissions: Query first. We encourage first novelists. Before sending a manuscript, read as many current Harlequin titles as you can. It's very important to know the genre, what readers are looking for and the series most appropriate for your submission."

HARLEQUIN MILLS & BOON, LTD., Harlequin Enterprises, Ltd., Eton House, 18-24 Paradise Rd., Richmond Surrey TW9 1SR United Kingdom. (44)0208-288-2800. Website: www.millsandboon.co.uk. Editorial Director: K. Stoecker. **Acquisitions:** Tessa Shapcott, senior editor (Harlequin Presents); Samantha Bell, senior editor (Harlequin Romance); Linda Fildew, editor (Mills & Boon Historicals); and Sheila Hodgson, editor (Mills & Boon Medicals). Estab. 1908-1909. Publishes mass market paperback originals. **Pays advance against royalty.** Publishes book 2 years after acceptance of ms. Does not accept simultaneous submissions. Responds in 5 months to mss. Ms guidelines online.

Imprints: Harlequin, Silhouette, MIRA, Mills & Boon.

"World's largest publisher of brand name category romance; books are available for translation into more than 20 languages and distributed in more than 100 international markets."

Fiction: Romance (contemporary, historical, regency period, medical). Query with SASE or submit 3 sample chapter(s), synopsis.

Recent Title(s): *A Cowboy's Secret*, by Anne McAllister; *Blood Brothers*, by Anne McAllister and Lucy Gordon.

Tips: "Study a wide selection of our current paperbacks to gain an understanding of our requirements, then write from the heart."

HARPERCOLLINS PUBLISHERS (NEW ZEALAND), LTD., 31 View Rd., Glenfield, Auckland New Zealand. Website: www.harpercollins.co.nz. **Acquisitions:** Ian Watt, publisher. **Publishes 8-10 titles/year. Pays royalty.** Ms guidelines online.

Imprints: Flamingo, HarperCollins, Voyager.

Fiction: Adult fiction: Flamingo and HarperCollins imprints (40,000+ words); Junior fiction: 8-11 years (15-20,000 words). Submit outline, synopsis or submit complete ms.

Tips: "It helps if the author and story have New Zealand connections/content."

HELTER SKELTER PUBLISHING, 4 Denmark St., London WC2H 8LL United Kingdom. (44)171 836 1151. Fax: (44)171 240 9880. E-mail: helter@skelter.demon.co.uk. **Acquisitions:** Sean Body, editor (music, film). Publishes hardcover and trade paperback originals and trade paperback reprints. **Publishes 10 titles/year. Receives 50 queries and 30 mss/year. 50% of books from first-time authors; 60% from unagented writers. Pays 8-12½% royalty on retail price. Offers $1,000-6,000 advance.** Publishes book 6 months after acceptance of ms. Accepts simultaneous submissions. Responds in 1 month to queries. Book catalog free.

Imprints: Firefly.

"Our mission is to publish high quality books about music and cinema subjects of enduring appeal."

Nonfiction: Biography. Subjects include music/dance. Submit outline, 2 sample chapter(s). Reviews artwork/photos as part of ms package. Send photocopies.

Recent Title(s): *Waiting for the Man*, Harry Shapiro.

Tips: "The subject artist should have a career spanning at least five years."

HERITAGE HOUSE PUBLISHING CO., LTD., 301-3555 Outrigger Rd., Nanoose Bay BC V9P 9K1 Canada. (250)468-5328. Fax: (250)468-5318. E-mail: publisher@heritagehouse.ca. Website: www.heritagehouse.ca. **Acquisitions:** Rodger Touchie, publisher/president. Publishes trade paperback originals. **Publishes 10-12 titles/year. Receives 200 queries and 60 mss/year. 50% of books from first-time authors; 100% from unagented writers. Pays 9% royalty. Offers advance.** Publishes book 1 year after acceptance of ms. Does not accept simultaneous submissions. Responds in 2 months to queries. Book catalog for #10 SASE; ms guidelines online.

Heritage House is primarily a regional publisher of Western Canadiana and the Pacific Northwest. "We aim to publish and distribute good books that entertain and educate our readership regarding both historic and contemporary Western Canada and Pacific Northwest."

Nonfiction: Biography, how-to, illustrated book. Subjects include animals, anthropology/archeology, cooking/foods/nutrition, history, nature/environment, recreation, regional, sports. "Writers should include a sample of their writing, an overview sample of photos or illustrations to support the text and a brief letter describing who they are writing for." Query with SASE or submit outline, 2-3 sample chapter(s). Reviews artwork/photos as part of ms package. Send photocopies.

Fiction: Very limited. Only author/illustrator collaboration.

Recent Title(s): *Daggers Unsheathed: The Political Assassination of Glen Clark*, by Judi Tyabji Wilson (political history); *Ordinary People, Extraordinary Lives: Recipients of the Order of British Columbia*, by Goody Niosi (people); *War on Our Doorstep: The Unknown Campaign on North America's West Coast*, by Brendan Coyle (war history).

Tips: "Our books appeal to residents and visitors to the northwest quadrant of the continent. Present your material only after you have done your best."

HIPPOPOTAMUS PRESS, 22 Whitewell Rd., Frome, Somerset BA11 4EL United Kingdom. 0173-466653. Fax: 01373-466653. **Acquisitions:** R. John, editor; M. Pargitter (poetry); Anna Martin (translation). Publishes hardcover and trade paperback originals. **Publishes 6-12 titles/year. 90% of books from first-time authors; 90% from unagented writers. Pays 7½-10% royalty on retail price. Offers advance.** Publishes book 10 months after acceptance of ms. Accepts simultaneous submissions. Responds in 1 month to queries. Book catalog free.

Imprints: Hippopotamus Press, *Outposts* Poetry Quarterly; distributor for University of Salzburg Press.

Hippopotamus Press publishes first full collections of verse by those well represented in the mainstream poetry magazines of the English speaking world.

Nonfiction: Subjects include language/literature, translation. Query with SASE, or submit complete ms.

Poetry: "Read one of our authors! Poets often make the mistake of submitting poetry not knowing the type of verse we publish." Query or submit complete ms.

Recent Title(s): *Mystic Bridge*, Edward Lowbury.

Tips: "We publish books for a literate audience. We have a strong link to the Modernist tradition. Read what we publish."

HOUSE OF ANANSI PRESS, 110 Spadina Ave., Suite 801, Toronto ON M5V 2K4 Canada. (416)445-3333. Fax: (416)445-5967. E-mail: info@anansi.ca. Website: www.anansi.ca. **Acquisitions:** Martha Sharpe, publisher. Estab. 1967. Publishes hardcover and trade paperback originals and paperback reprints. **Publishes 10-15 titles/year. Receives 750 queries/year. 5% of books from first-time authors; 99% from unagented writers. Pays 8-15% royalty on retail price. Offers $500-2,000 advance.** Publishes book 9 months after acceptance of ms. Accepts simultaneous submissions. Responds in 2 months to queries; 3 months to proposals; 4 months to mss. Book catalog free; ms guidelines online.

"Our mission is to publish the best new literary writers in Canada and to continue to grow and adapt along with the Canadian literary community, while maintaining Anansi's rich history."

Nonfiction: Biography. Subjects include anthropology/archeology, gay/lesbian, government/politics, history, language/literature, philosophy, science, sociology, women's issues/studies. "Our nonfiction list is literary, but not overly academic. Some writers submit academic work better suited for university presses or pop-psychology books, which we do not publish." Query with SASE or submit outline, 2 sample chapter(s). Reviews artwork/photos as part of ms package. Send photocopies.

Fiction: Ethnic (general), experimental, feminist, gay/lesbian, literary, short story collections, translation. "We publish literary fiction by Canadian authors. Authors must have been published in established literary magazines and/or journals. We only want to consider sample chapters." Query with SASE, or submit outline, 2 sample chapter(s), synopsis.

Poetry: "We only publish book-length works by Canadian authors. Poets must have a substantial résumé of published poems in literary magazines or journals. We only want samples from a manuscript." Submit 10-15 sample poems.

Recent Title(s): *The Rights Revolution*, by Michael Ignatieff (nonfiction); *This All Happened*, by Michael Winter (fiction); *A Pair of Scissors*, by Sharon Thesen (poetry).

Tips: "Submit often to magazines and journals. Read and buy other writers' work. Know and be a part of your writing community."

HOW TO BOOKS, LTD., 3 Newtec Place, Magdalen Rd., Oxford OX4 1RE Great Britain. (00144)1865 793806. Fax: (00144)1865 248780. E-mail: info@howtobooks.co.uk. Website: www.howtobooks.co.uk. **Acquisitions:** Nikki Read, commissioning editor (self-help, business, careers, home & family, living & working abroad). Publishes trade paperback originals and reprints. **Publishes 70 titles/year. Receives 200 queries and 100 mss/year. 80% of books from first-time authors; 90% from unagented writers.** Accepts simultaneous submissions. Responds in 1 month to queries; 1 month to proposals; 2 months to mss. Book catalog free or on website; ms guidelines free.

Imprints: Essentials (6 titles/year), Herbal Health (8 titles/year), How-To Books (100 titles/year), How To Reference (6 titles/year), Small Business Starters (4 titles/year).

Nonfiction: How-to, reference, self-help. Subjects include business/economics, child guidance/parenting, creative nonfiction, money/finance. "Submit a proposal you feel strongly about and can write knowledgably. Have a look at our catalog/website to see what we publish. We ask authors to send a synopsis before steering them toward a specific imprint." Submit proposal package including outline, 1 sample chapter(s).

Recent Title(s): *Be a Successful Consultant*, by Susan Nash; *Buying a Property in France*, by Clive Kristen; *365 Steps to Self-Confidence*, by David Lawrence-Preston.

Tips: "Our books are aimed at people who want to improve their lives, their careers, their general skills. Our authors have to have a passion and extensive knowledge about their subject area. Send us a proposal first; because we are a series publisher, submitted books have to fit into our format."

N **HUMANITAS**, 990 Picard, Brossard QC J4W 1S5 Canada. (650)466-9737. Fax: (650)466-9737. **Acquisitions:** Constantin Stoiciu, president. Publishes hardcover originals. **Publishes 14 titles/year. Receives 200 queries and 200 mss/year. 20% of books from first-time authors. Pays 10-12% royalty on wholesale price.** Publishes book 2 months after acceptance of ms. Accepts simultaneous submissions. Book catalog free; ms guidelines free.

Humanitas is interested only in mss written in French.

Nonfiction: Biography. Subjects include history, language/literature, philosophy, photography, science. Query. Reviews artwork/photos as part of ms package. Send photocopies.

Fiction: Fantasy, romance, short story collections. Query with SASE.

Poetry: Query.

Recent Title(s): *L'avenir du Francais dans le Monde*, by Axel Maugey; *Ruptures et Permanences*, by Paul-Emile Roy; *Le Fuyard*, by Constantin Stoiciu.

INSOMNIAC PRESS, 192 Spadina Ave., Suite 403, Toronto ON M5T 2C2 Canada. (416)504-6270. Fax: (416)504-9313. E-mail: mike@insomniacpress.com. Website: www.insomniacpress.com. Estab. 1992. Publishes trade paperback originals and reprints, mass market paperback originals, and electronic originals and reprints. **Publishes 20 titles/year. Receives 250 queries and 1,000 mss/year. 50% of books from first-time authors; 80% from unagented writers. Pays 10-15% royalty on retail price. Offers $500-1,000 advance.** Publishes book 6 months after acceptance of ms. Accepts simultaneous submissions. Responds in 1 week to queries; 2 months to proposals; 2 months to mss. Ms guidelines online.

Nonfiction: Gift book, humor, self-help. Subjects include business/economics, creative nonfiction, gay/lesbian, government/politics, health/medicine, language/literature, money/finance, multicultural, religion, true crime. Very interested in areas such as true crime and generally in well-written and well-researched nonfiction on topics of wide interest. Query via e-mail, submit proposal package including outline, 2 sample chapters, or submit complete ms. Reviews artwork/photos as part of ms package. Send photocopies.

Fiction: Comic books, ethnic, experimental, gay/lesbian, humor, literary, mainstream/contemporary, multicultural, mystery, poetry, suspense. We publish a mix of commercial (mysteries) and literary fiction. Query via e-mail, submit proposal package including synopsis or submit complete ms.

Poetry: "Our poetry publishing is limited to 2-4 books per year and we are often booked up a year or two in advance." Submit complete ms.

Recent Title(s): *Landscape with Shipwreck: First Person Cinema and the Films of Phillip Hoffman*, edited by Karyn Sandlos and Mike Hoolboom (film studies); *Pedigree Girls*, by Sherwin Tija (humor/cartoon); *Ashes Are Bone and Dust*, by Jill Battson (poetry).

Tips: "We envision a mixed readership that appreciates up-and-coming literary fiction and poetry as well as solidly researched and provocative nonfiction. Peruse our website and familiarize yourself with what we've published in the past."

INSTITUTE OF PSYCHOLOGICAL RESEARCH, INC., 34 Fleury St. W., Montréal QC H3L 1S9 Canada. (514)382-3000. Fax: (514)382-3007. **Acquisitions:** Robert Chevrier, advisor; Dr. Nicholas Chevrier, vice president, scientific affairs. Estab. 1958. Publishes hardcover and trade paperback originals and reprints. **Publishes 12 titles/year. Receives 15 submissions/year. 10% of books from first-time authors; 100% from unagented writers. Pays 10-12% royalty.** Publishes book 6 months after acceptance of ms. Responds in 2 months to queries.

O-r Institute of Psychological Research publishes psychological tests and science textbooks for a varied professional audience.

Nonfiction: Textbook. Subjects include philosophy, psychology, science, translation. "We are looking for psychological tests in French or English." Query with SASE, or submit complete ms.

Recent Title(s): *épreuve individuelle d'habileté mentale*, by Jean-Marc Chevrier (intelligence test).

Tips: "Psychologists, guidance counselors, professionals, schools, school boards, hospitals, teachers, government agencies and industries comprise our audience."

ISER BOOKS, Faculty of Arts Publications, Memorial University of Newfoundland, FM 2006, St. John's NF A1S 5S7 Canada. (709)737-8343. Fax: (709)737-7560. Website: www.mun.ca/iser/. **Acquisitions:** Al Potter, manager. Publishes trade paperback originals. **Publishes 3-4 titles/year. Receives 10-20 queries and 10 mss/year. 45% of books from first-time authors; 85% from unagented writers. Pays 6-10% royalty on wholesale price.** Publishes book 6 months after acceptance of ms. Does not accept simultaneous submissions. Responds in 1 month to queries; 2 months to proposals; 4 months to mss. Book catalog and ms guidelines free.

O-r Iser Books publishes research within such disciplines and in such parts of the world as are deemed of relevance to Newfoundland and Labrador.

Nonfiction: Biography, reference. Subjects include anthropology/archeology, ethnic, government/politics, history, multicultural, recreation, regional, sociology, translation, women's issues/studies. Query with SASE, or submit proposal package including outline, 2-3 sample chapter(s).

Recent Title(s): *Cows Don't Know It's Sunday: Agricultural Life in St. John's*, by Hilda Chaulk Murray; *Enclosing the Commons: Individual Transferable Quotas in the Nova Scotia Fishery*, by Richard Apostle, Bonnie McCay, and Knut M. Mikalsen.

N **KEY PORTER BOOKS**, 70 The Esplanade, 3rd Floor, Toronto ON L5R 3Z5 Canada. (416)862-7777. Fax: (416)862-2304. E-mail: info@keyporter.com. Website: www.keyporter.com. **Acquisitions:** Anna Porter, publisher/CEO (personality books, international packages); Clare McKeon, editor-in-chief/vice president (fiction, health, business, general trade). Estab. 1979. Publishes hardcover and trade paperback originals and reprints. **Publishes 100 titles/year; imprint publishes 6-12 titles/year. Receives 1,000 queries and 500 mss/year. 40% of books from first-time authors; 50% from unagented writers. Pays royalty.** Accepts simultaneous submissions. Responds in 4 months to queries; 6 months to proposals; 6 months to mss. Book catalog free.

Imprints: Key Porter Kids, Sarasota, L&OD.

Nonfiction: Autobiography, biography, children's/juvenile, coffee table book, cookbook, gift book, how-to, humor, illustrated book, self-help. Subjects include agriculture/horticulture, alternative lifestyles, animals, art/architecture, business/economics, child guidance/parenting, community, contemporary culture, cooking/foods/nutrition, creative nonfiction, ethnic, gardening, general nonfiction, government/politics, health/medicine, history, house & home, humanities, marine subjects, memoirs, military/war, money/finance, nature/environment, photography, psychology, science, sex, social sciences, sociology, spirituality, sports, translation, travel, women's issues/studies, world affairs, young adult. Query with SASE. Reviews artwork/photos as part of ms package. Send photocopies.

Fiction: Adventure, comic books, confession, erotica, ethnic, experimental, fantasy, feminist, gay/lesbian, gothic, hi-lo, historical, humor, juvenile, literary, mainstream/contemporary, military/war, multicultural, multimedia, occult, picture books, regional, religious, short story collections, spiritual, sports, translation, western, young adult. Query with SASE.

KINDRED PRODUCTIONS, 4-169 Riverton Ave., Winnipeg MB R2L 2E5 Canada. (204)669-6575. Fax: (204)654-1865. E-mail: kindred@mbconf.ca. Website: www.kindredproductions.com. **Acquisitions:** Marilyn Hudson, manager. Publishes trade paperback originals and reprints. **Publishes 3 titles/year. 1% of books from first-time authors; 100% from unagented writers. Pays 10-15% royalty on net receipts.** Publishes book 18 months after acceptance of ms. Accepts simultaneous submissions. Responds in 3 months to queries; 5 months to mss. Ms guidelines online.

O-r "Kindred Productions publishes, promotes, and markets print and nonprint resources that will shape our Christian faith and discipleship from a Mennonite Brethren perspective." Currently emphasizing inspirational with crossover potential. De-emphasizing personal experience, biographical. No children's books or fiction.

Nonfiction: Subjects include religion, inspirational. "Our books cater primarily to our Mennonite Brethren denomination readers." Query with SASE, or submit outline, 2-3 sample chapter(s).

Recent Title(s): *Liberty in Confinement*, by Johannes Reimer; *God's Orchard: Fruit of the Spirit in Action*, by Helen Lepp Friesen.

Tips: "Most of our books are sold to churches, religious bookstores, and schools. We are concentrating on inspirational books. We do not accept children's manuscripts."

N **JESSICA KINGSLEY PUBLISHERS, LTD.**, 116 Pentonville Rd., London N1 9JB United Kingdom. (44)171-833-2307. Fax: (44)171-837-2917. E-mail: post@jkp.com. Website: www.jkp.com. **Acquisitions:** Jessica Kingsley, managing director (autism, pastoral thealogy, arts therapy/psychiatry). Publishes hardcover and trade paperback originals and trade paperback reprints. **Publishes 100 titles/year. Receives 500 queries and 30 mss/year. 20% of books from first-time authors; 99% from unagented writers. Pays royalty on wholesale price. Offers advance.** Publishes book 5 months after acceptance of ms. Does not accept simultaneous submissions. Responds in 1 month to queries; 1 month to proposals; 3 months to mss. Book catalog for free or on website; ms guidelines free.

O-r "We publish titles that present a combination of theory and practice." Currently emphasizing autism spectrum.

Nonfiction: Reference, self-help, technical, textbook, scholarly. Subjects include child guidance/parenting, health/medicine, psychology, religion, sex, spirituality. Submit proposal package including outline, 1 sample chapter(s), résumé. Reviews artwork/photos as part of ms package. Send photocopies.

Recent Title(s): *Asperger's Syndrome: A Guide for Parents & Professionals*, Tony Attwood (professional self-help).

Tips: "Do not go through an agent. Proposals must be for books within the subject areas we publish. No fiction or poetry."

LAMBRECHT PUBLICATIONS, 1763 Maple Bay Rd., Duncan BC V9L 5N6 Canada. (250)748-8722 or toll free at (866)774-4372. Fax: (250)748-8723. E-mail: helgal@cowichan.com. Website: www.lamb.herbalnetworks.com. **Acquisitions:** Helga Lambrecht, publisher. Publishes hardcover, trade paperback originals and reprints. **Publishes 2 titles/year. Receives 6 queries/year. 50% of books from first-time authors. Pays 10% royalty on retail price. Offers advance.** Does not accept simultaneous submissions. Book catalog free.

O‒ Lambrecht publishes local history books and cookbooks.

Nonfiction: Subjects include cooking/foods/nutrition, history, regional. *All unsolicited mss returned unopened.*

LES ÉDITIONS DU VERMILLON, 305 St. Patrick St., Ottawa ON K1N 5K4 Canada. (613)241-4032. Fax: (613)241-3109. E-mail: editver@ca.inter.net. **Acquisitions:** Jacques Flamand, editorial director. Publishes trade paperback originals. **Publishes 15-20 titles/year. Pays 10% royalty.** Publishes book 18 months after acceptance of ms. Responds in 6 months to mss. Book catalog free.

Fiction: Juvenile, literary, religious, short story collections, young adult. Query with SASE.

Recent Title(s): *Parrot Fever*, by Joe Rosenblatt, translated by Andrée Christensen and Jacques Flamand (bilingual poetry); *Lettres Urgentes au Vingt et Uniēme Siēcle*, by Yvette Granier-Barkun; *Cigale d'Avant-Poēme*, by Andrée Christensen (poetry).

LEXISNEXIS CANADA, INC., (formerly LexisNexis Butterworths), 75 Clegg Rd., Markham ON L6G 1A1 Canada. (905)479-2665. Fax: (905)479-2826. E-mail: info@lexisnexis.ca. Website: www.lexisnexis.ca. **Acquisitions:** Product Development Director. **Publishes 100 titles/year. 50% of books from first-time authors; 100% from unagented writers. Pays 5-15% royalty on wholesale price.** Publishes book 4 months after acceptance of ms. Accepts simultaneous submissions. Responds in 1 month to queries. Book catalog free; ms guidelines online.

O‒ LexisNexis Canada, Inc., publishes professional reference material for the legal, business, and accounting markets under the Butterworths imprint and operates the Quicklaw and LexisNexis online services.

Nonfiction: Multimedia (CD-ROM, Quicklaw, and LexisNexis online services), reference (legal and law for business), legal and accounting newspapers.

Recent Title(s): *Police Guide to Search & Seizure*, by Fontana & Keeshan; *Copyright Law in Canada*, by Handa; *Introduction to Canadian Insurance Law*, by Brown.

Tips: Audience is legal community, business, medical, accounting professions.

LOBSTER PRESS, 1620 Sherbrooke St. W, Suites C & D, Montreal QC H3H 1C9 Canada. (514)904-1100. Fax: (514)904-1101. Website: www.lobsterpress.com. **Acquisitions:** Gabriella Mancini, editorial manager. Publishes hardcover, trade paperback and mass market paperback originals. **Publishes 25 titles/year. Receives 200 queries and 1,500 mss/year. 90% of books from first-time authors; 75% from unagented writers. Pays 5-10% royalty on retail price. Offers $1,000-6,000 (Canadian) advance.** Publishes book 2 years after acceptance of ms. Does not accept simultaneous submissions. Responds in 3 months to queries; 10 months to proposals; 1 year to mss.

- Lobster Press is presently not accepting submissions.

Nonfiction: Children's/juvenile, illustrated book, self-help. Subjects include child guidance/parenting, creative nonfiction, history, sex, travel. Query with SASE (IRC or Canadian postage only), or submit complete ms. Reviews artwork/photos as part of ms package. Send photocopies.

Fiction: Adventure (for children), historical (for children), juvenile, picture books, young adult. Submit complete ms.

Recent Title(s): *The Hockey Card*, by Jack Sieniatycki and Avi Slodovnick, illustrated by Doris Barrette (picture book).

LONE PINE PUBLISHING, 10145 81st Ave., Edmonton AB T6E 1W9 Canada. (403)433-9333. Fax: (403)433-9646. Website: www.lonepinepublishing.com. **Acquisitions:** Nancy Foulds, editorial director. Estab. 1980. Publishes trade paperback originals and reprints. **Publishes 12-40 titles/year. Receives 800 submissions/year. 75% of books from first-time authors; 95% from unagented writers. Pays royalty.** Does not accept simultaneous submissions. Responds in 3 months to queries. Book catalog free.

Imprints: Lone Pine, Home World, Pine Candle, and Pine Cone.

O‒ Lone Pine publishes natural history and outdoor recreation—including gardening—titles, and some popular history and ghost story collections by region. " 'The World Outside Your Door' is our motto—helping people appreciate nature and their own special place." Currently emphasizing ghost stories by region, popular history.

Nonfiction: Subjects include animals, gardening, nature/environment, recreation, regional. The list is set for the next year and a half, but we are interested in seeing new material. Query with SASE, or submit outline, sample chapter(s). Reviews artwork/photos as part of ms package.

Recent Title(s): *Perennials for Michigan*, by Alison Beck and Nancy Szerlag; *Ghost Stories for Christmas*, by Jo-Anne Christensen; *Bugs of Washington & Oregon*, by John Acorn and Ian Sheldon.

Tips: "Writers have their best chance with recreational or nature guidebooks. Most of our books are strongly regional in nature."

N LTDBOOKS, 200 N. Service Rd. W., Unit 1, Suite 301, Oakville ON L6M 2Y1 Canada. (905)847-6060. Fax: (905)847-6060. E-mail: publisher@ltdbooks.com. Website: www.ltdbooks.com. **Acquisitions:** Dee Lloyd, editor; Terry Shiels, editor. Estab. 1999. Publishes electronic originals on disk or by download as well as selected trade paperback titles. **Publishes 15 titles/year. Pays 30% royalty on electronic titles and flat rate on trade paperbacks.** Publishes book more than 1 year after acceptance of ms. Accepts simultaneous submissions. Responds in 1 month to queries; 2-3 months to mss. Ms guidelines online.

- This publisher is now closed to submissions until further notice; check website for updates.

"LTDBooks, an energetic presence in the rapidly expanding e-book market, is a multi-genre, royalty-paying fiction publisher specializing in high quality stories with strong characters and great ideas."

Fiction: Adventure, fantasy (space fantasy, sword and sorcery), historical (general), horror (dark fantasy, futuristic, psychological, supernatural), literary, mainstream/contemporary, mystery (amateur sleuth, cozy, police procedural, private eye/hardboiled), romance (contemporary, futuristic/time travel, gothic, historical, regency period, romantic suspense), science fiction (hard science/technological, soft/sociological), suspense (amateur sleuth, cozy, police procedural, private eye/hardboiled), western, young adult (adventure, fantasy/science fiction, historical, horror, mystery/suspense, problem novels, romance, series, sports, western), thriller/espionage. Prefers queries by e-mail. "Our new trade paperback program started June 2001." Query with SASE. Follow guidelines on website.

Recent Title(s): *Shadow Dweller Series*, by J.C. Wilder; *The Accidental Goddess*, by Linnea Sinclair writing as Megan Sybil Baker.

Tips: "We publish only fiction. All of our books are electronic (as download or on disk) with ongoing additions to our new trade paperback program."

LYNX IMAGES, INC., P.O. Box 5961, Station A, Toronto ON M5W 1P4 Canada. (416)925-8422. Fax: (925)952-8352. E-mail: info@lynximages.com. Website: www.lynximages.com. **Acquisitions:** Russell Floren, president; Andrea Gutsche, director; Barbara Chisholm, producer. Publishes hardcover and trade paperback originals. **Publishes 6 titles/year. Receives 100 queries and 50 mss/year. 80% of books from first-time authors; 80% from unagented writers. Offers 40% advance.** Publishes book 1 year after acceptance of ms. Accepts simultaneous submissions. Ms guidelines online.

Lynx publishes historical tourism, travel, Canadian history, Great Lakes history. Currently emphasizing travel, history, nature. De-emphasizing boating, guides.

Nonfiction: Coffee table book, gift book, multimedia. Subjects include history, nature/environment, travel. Reviews artwork/photos as part of ms package.

Recent Title(s): *General Stores of Canada*, by R.B. Fleming; *Ghosts of the Great Lakes*, by Megan Long; *Places Lost*, by Scott Walden.

MANOR HOUSE PUBLISHING, INC., 452 Cottingham Crescent, Ancaster ON L9G 3V6 Canada. (905)648-2193. Fax: (905)648-8369. E-mail: mdavie@thestar.ca. Website: www.manor-house.biz. **Acquisitions:** Mike Davie, president (novels, poetry, and nonfiction). Estab. 1998. Publishes hardcover, trade paperback, and mass market paperback originals, and mass market paperback reprints. **Publishes 5-6 titles/year. Receives 30 queries and 20 mss/year. 90% of books from first-time authors; 90% from unagented writers. Pays 10-15% royalty on retail price.** Publishes book 12-14 months after acceptance of ms. Accepts simultaneous submissions. Responds in 1 month to queries; 1 month to proposals; 1 month to mss. Book catalog online; ms guidelines by email.

Nonfiction: Biography, coffee table book, how-to, humor, illustrated book, self-help. Subjects include alternative lifestyles, anthropology/archeology, business/economics, community, general nonfiction, history, sex, social sciences, sociology, spirituality. "We are a Canadian publisher, so manuscripts should be Canadian in content and aimed as much as possible at a wide, general audience." Query with SASE or submit proposal package including outline, 3 sample chapter(s), author bio or submit complete ms. Reviews artwork/photos as part of ms package. Send photocopies.

Fiction: Adventure, experimental, gothic, historical, horror, humor, juvenile, literary, mainstream/contemporary, mystery, occult, poetry, regional, romance, short story collections, young adult. "Stories should have Canadian settings and characters should be Canadian, but content should have universal appeal to wide audience." Query with SASE or submit proposal package including 3 sample chapter(s), synopsis, author bio or submit complete ms.

Poetry: "Poetry should engage, provoke, involve the reader. (I don't like yawning when I read.)" Query or submit 12-20 sample poems or submit complete ms.

Recent Title(s): *Political Losers*, by Michael B. Davie (politics/science); *Broken Dreams*, by Amanda Hyde (young adult novel); *Mystical Poetry*, by Deborah Morrison (poetry).

Tips: "Our audience includes everyone—the general public/mass audience." "Self-edit your work first, make sure it is well written with strong Canadian content."

MARCUS BOOKS, P.O. Box 327, Queensville ON L0G 1R0 Canada. (905)967-0219. Fax: (905)967-0216. **Acquisitions:** Tom Rieder, president. Publishes trade paperback originals and reprints. **Receives 12 queries and 6 mss/year. 90% of books from first-time authors; 100% from unagented writers. Pays 10% royalty on retail price.** Publishes book 6 months after acceptance of ms. Does not accept simultaneous submissions. Responds in 4 months to mss. Book catalog for $1.

Nonfiction: Subjects include health/medicine. "Interested in alternative health and esoteric topics." Submit outline, 3 sample chapter(s).

MERCAT PRESS, 10 Coates Crescent, Edinburgh EH3 7AL Scotland. E-mail: mercat@btopenworld.com. Website: www.mercatpress.com. **Acquisitions:** Sean Costello, editorial manager; Tom Johnstone, editorial manager. Publishes hardcover and trade paperback originals and hardcover and trade paperback reprints. **Publishes 30 titles/year. Receives 200 queries and 100 mss/year. 10% of books from first-time authors; 85% from unagented writers. Pays 7½-10% royalty on retail price.** Publishes book 6 months after acceptance of ms. Accepts simultaneous submissions. Responds in 1 month to queries. Book catalog free or on website.

Nonfiction: Biography, children's/juvenile, cookbook, reference, textbook. Subjects include agriculture/horticulture, art/

architecture, cooking/foods/nutrition, gardening, government/politics, history, language/literature, memoirs, music/dance, nature/environment, regional, sociology. Scottish interest only. Query with IRCs, or submit proposal package, including outline and 2 sample chapters.

Recent Title(s): *Scottish Cookery*, by Catherine Brown (cookbook); *Hell of a Journey: On Foot Through the Scottish Highlands in Winter*, by Mike Cawthorne (travel).

Tips: "Consult our website for an idea of the type of books we publish."

MIRA BOOKS, an imprint of Harlequin, 225 Duncan Mill Rd., Don Mills ON M3B3K9 Canada. Website: www.eharlequin.com. **Acquisitions:** Dianne Moggy, editorial director. Publishes paperback orginals. **Pays royalty. Offers advance.** not available.

Fiction: Historical (romance), mainstream/contemporary, suspense (romance), relationship novels.

MONARCH BOOKS, Monarch Concorde House, Grenville Place, London NW7 3SA Great Britain. (44)020 8959 3668. Fax: (44)020 8959 3678. E-mail: tonyc@angushudson.com. **Acquisitions:** Tony Collins, editorial director (Christian literature). Publishes hardcover, trade paperback and mass market paperback originals and reprints. **Publishes 33 titles/year. Receives 600-800 queries and 400 mss/year. 10% of books from first-time authors; 90% from unagented writers. Pays 10-15% royalty. Offers $1,000-4,000 advance.** Publishes book 8 months after acceptance of ms. Accepts simultaneous submissions. Responds in 2 weeks to queries. Book catalog and ms guidelines free.

Imprints: Monarch

"We publish primarily for the evangelical Christian market, providing tools and resources for Christian leaders." Monarch Books has recently started publishing and distributing in the US and Canada through an arrangement with Kregel Books.

Nonfiction: Biography, humor, reference, self-help. Subjects include child guidance/parenting, creative nonfiction, philosophy, psychology, religion, science, sex, sociology. Query with SASE, or submit proposal package including outline, 2 sample chapter(s).

Recent Title(s): *Clash of the Worlds: What Christians Can Do in a World of Cultures in Conflict*, by David Burnett (nonfiction).

Tips: "Think about who you are writing for. What will a reader get as benefit from reading your book?"

MOOSE ENTERPRISE BOOK & THEATRE PLAY PUBLISHING, 684 Walls Side Rd., Sault Ste. Marie ON P6A 5K6 Canada. (705)779-3331. Fax: (705)779-3331. **Acquisitions:** Richard Mousseau, owner/editor (fiction, history, general); Edmond Alcid, editor (poetry, children's, general). Publishes trade and mass market paperback originals. **Publishes 7-10 titles/year. Receives 10-15 queries and 10 mss/year. 60% of books from first-time authors; 100% from unagented writers. Pays 20-40% royalty on retail price.** Publishes book 6 months after acceptance of ms. Responds in 1 month to queries; 2 months to proposals; 2 months to mss. Book catalog and ms guidelines for #10 SASE.

Nonfiction: Biography, children's/juvenile. Subjects include history, memoirs, military/war. Query with SASE, or submit proposal package including outline, 2 sample chapter(s), author bio. Reviews artwork/photos as part of ms package. Send photocopies.

Fiction: Adventure, historical, horror, humor, juvenile, military/war, mystery, picture books, plays, poetry, regional, science fiction, short story collections, western, young adult. Query with SASE, or submit proposal package including 2 sample chapter(s), synopsis, author bio.

Poetry: Send author's bio and summary of project, typed, double-spaced, one-sided. Query or submit 5 sample poems.

Recent Title(s): *A Long Exciting Trip to Peace*, by Angus Harnden (military/history); *Executor of Mercy*, by Edmond Alcid (adventure/novel); *Poems From My Heart*, by Gordon Hysen (poetry).

Tips: "Send only material that is of moral quality. Send bio of author."

NAPOLEON PUBLISHING, Transmedia Enterprises, Inc., 3266 Yonge St., #1005, Toronto ON M4N 3P6 Canada. (416)730-9052. Fax: (416)226-9975. E-mail: transmedia@sympatico.ca. Website: www.napoleonpublishing.com. **Acquisitions:** A. Thompson, editor. Estab. 1990. Publishes hardcover and trade paperback originals and reprints. **Publishes 8 titles/year; imprint publishes 4 titles/year. Receives 200 queries and 100 mss/year. 50% of books from first-time authors; 80% from unagented writers.** Publishes book 18 months after acceptance of ms. Accepts simultaneous submissions. Responds in 1 month to queries; 3 months to proposals; 6 months to mss. Book catalog online; ms guidelines online.

Nonfiction: Biography (children's), children's/juvenile. Query with SASE or submit outline, 1 sample chapter(s).

Fiction: Adventure (children's), historical, juvenile, mainstream/contemporary, mystery, picture books, suspense, young adult. Query with SASE or submit complete ms.

Tips: "We want Canadian resident authors only."

NATURAL HERITAGE/NATURAL HISTORY, INC., P.O. Box 95, Station O, Toronto ON M4A 2M8 Canada. (416)694-7907. Fax: (416)690-0819. E-mail: info@naturalheritagebooks.com. Website: www.naturalheritagebooks.com. **Acquisitions:** Barry Penhale, publisher. Publishes hardcover and trade paperback originals. **Publishes 12-15 titles/year. 50% of books from first-time authors; 85% from unagented writers. Pays 8-10% royalty on retail price. Offers advance.** Publishes book 2 years after acceptance of ms. Does not accept simultaneous submissions. Responds in 4 months to queries; 6 months to proposals; 6 months to mss. Book catalog free; ms guidelines for #10 SASE.

Imprints: Natural Heritage.

Currently emphasizing heritage, history, nature.

Nonfiction: Subjects include anthropology/archeology, art/architecture, ethnic, history, nature/environment, photography, recreation, regional, women's issues/studies. Submit outline.

Fiction: Historical, short story collections. Query with SASE.

Recent Title(s): *Canoeing a Continent: On the Trail of Alexander Mackenzie*, by Max Finkelstein (nonfiction); *Algonquin Wildlife: Lessons in Survival*, by Norm Quinn (fiction); *The Underground Railroad: Next Stop, Toronto!*, by Adrienne Shadd, Afua Cooper, and Karolyn Smardz Frost (young adult nonfiction).

Tips: "We are a Canadian publisher in the natural heritage and history fields."

NEW SOCIETY PUBLISHERS, P.O. Box 189, Gabriola BC V0R 1X0 Canada. (250)247-9737. Fax: (250)247-7471. E-mail: info@newsociety.com. Website: www.newsociety.com. **Acquisitions:** Chris Plant, editor. Publishes trade paperback originals and reprints and electronic originals. **Publishes 20 titles/year. Receives 300 queries and 200 mss/year. 50% of books from first-time authors; 80% from unagented writers. Pays 10-12% royalty on wholesale price. Offers $0-5,000 advance.** Publishes book 6 months after acceptance of ms. Accepts simultaneous submissions. Responds in 1 month to queries; 2 months to proposals. Book catalog and ms guidelines free or online.

Nonfiction: Biography, how-to, illustrated book, self-help. Subjects include business/economics, child guidance/parenting, creative nonfiction, education, government/politics, memoirs, nature/environment, philosophy, regional. Query with SASE or submit proposal package including outline, 2 sample chapter(s). Reviews artwork/photos as part of ms package. Send photocopies.

Recent Title(s): *Be the Difference: A Beginner's Guide to Changing the World*, by Danny Seo (activism).

Tips: Audience is activists, academics, progressive business people, managers. "Don't get an agent!"

NEWEST PUBLISHERS, LTD., 201, 8540-109 St., Edmonton AB T6G 1E6 Canada. (780)432-9427. Fax: (780)433-3179. E-mail: info@newestpress.com. Website: www.newestpress.com. **Acquisitions:** Ruth Linka, general manager. Estab. 1977. Publishes trade paperback originals. **Publishes 13-16 titles/year. Receives 200 submissions/year. 40% of books from first-time authors; 90% from unagented writers. Pays 10% royalty.** Publishes book 18 months after acceptance of ms. Accepts simultaneous submissions. Responds in 6 months to queries. Book catalog for 9×12 SASE; ms guidelines online.

NeWest publishes Western Canadian fiction, nonfiction, poetry and drama.

Nonfiction: Literary/essays (Western Canadian authors, Western Canadian and Northern themes). Subjects include ethnic, government/politics, history (Western Canada), nature/environment (northern), Canadiana. Query.

Fiction: Literary. "Our press is interested in Western Canadian writing." Submit complete ms.

Recent Title(s): *Big Rig*, by Don McTavish (nonfiction).

NORBRY PUBLISHING, LTD., 73 Leeming St., Hamilton ON L8L 5T4 Canada. (905)308-9877. Fax: (905)308-9869. E-mail: beckyp@norbry.com. Website: www.norbry.com. **Acquisitions:** Rebecca Pembry, president. Publishes mass market paperback originals. **Publishes 9 titles/year. 100% from unagented writers. Pays 10-20% royalty on retail price.** Publishes book 6 months after acceptance of ms. Accepts simultaneous submissions. Book catalog free; ms guidelines free.

Nonfiction: Multimedia (CD-ROM and network), textbook, online courseware, testing systems, assessment tools, and course management systems. Subjects include business/economics, computers/electronic, education, software, accounting. Query with SASE. Submit also by e-mail. Reviews artwork/photos as part of ms package. Send photocopies.

Recent Title(s): *Learning Simply Accounting 2003 for Windows*, by Harvey Freedman and Carl Smith; *ACCPAC 5.0 Advantage*, by John Stammers; *Principles of Financial Accounting*, by Hans Eckart, et. al.

NOVALIS, Bayard Presse Canada, 49 Front St. E, Toronto ON M5E 1B3 Canada. (416)363-3303. Fax: (416)363-9409. E-mail: cservice@novalis.ca. Website: www.novalis.ca. **Acquisitions:** Kevin Burns, commissioning editor; Michael O'Hearn, publisher; Anne Louise Mahoney, managing editor. Editorial offices: Novalis, St. Paul University, 223 Main St., Ottawa ON K1S 1C4, Canada. Phone: (613)782-3039. Fax: (613)751-4020. E-mail: kburns@ustpaul.ca. Publishes hardcover and trade paperback originals and trade paperback reprints. **Publishes 40 titles/year. 20% of books from first-time authors; 50% from unagented writers. Pays 10-15% royalty on wholesale price. Offers $300-2,000 advance.** Publishes book 9 months after acceptance of ms. Responds in 2 months to queries; 1 month to proposals; 2 months to mss. Book catalog for free or online; ms guidelines free.

"Novalis publishes books about faith, religion, and spirituality in their broadest sense. Based in the Catholic tradition, our interest is strongly ecumenical. Regardless of their denominational perspective, our books speak to the heart, mind, and spirit of people seeking to deepen their faith and understanding."

Nonfiction: Biography, children's/juvenile, gift book, humor, illustrated book, reference, self-help. Subjects include child guidance/parenting, education (Christian or Catholic), memoirs, multicultural, nature/environment, philosophy, religion, spirituality. Query with SASE.

Recent Title(s): *The Art of Soul—An Artists Guide to Spirituality*, by Regina Coupar (spirituality/creativity); *The Doctor Will Not See You Now—The Autobiography of a Blind Physician*, by Jane Poulson (autobiography/spirituality); *Who Knows the Shape of God—Homilies and Reflections*, by Corbin Eddy (theology/bible study).

ONEWORLD PUBLICATIONS, 185 Banbury Rd., Oxford OX2 7AR United Kingdom. (44)1865-310597. Fax: (44)1865-310598. E-mail: submissions@oneworld-publications.com. Website: www.oneworld-publications.com. **Acquisitions:** Juliet Mabey, editorial director (psychology, philosophy, social issues); Novin Doostdar, commissioning editor (religion, history); Victoria Warner, editor (unsolicited mss). Publishes hardcover and trade paperback originals and trade paperback reprints. **Publishes 40 titles/year. Receives 250 queries and 50 mss/year. 95% from unagented writers. Pays 8-10% royalty on wholesale price. Offers $500-4,000 advance.** Publishes book 18 months after acceptance of ms. Does not accept simultaneous submissions. Responds in 1 month to queries. Book catalog and ms guidelines for free or on website.

O-r "We publish authoritative books by academics for a general readership and cross-over student market. Authors must be well qualified." Currently emphasizing religion, history, philosophy. De-emphasizing self-help.

Nonfiction: Gift book, reference, self-help, textbook. Subjects include government/politics, history, multicultural, philosophy, psychology, religion, science, sociology, women's issues/studies. Query with SASE, or submit proposal package including outline, 1-3 sample chapter(s).

Recent Title(s): *The Fifth Dimension*, John Hick.

Tips: "We don't require agents—just good proposals with enough hard information."

OOLICHAN BOOKS, P.O. Box 10, Lantzville BC V0R 2H0 Canada. E-mail: oolichan@island.net. Website: www.oolichan.com. **Acquisitions:** Ron Smith, publisher (poetry, literary fiction, literary nonfiction); Hiro Boga, editor (literary fiction, poetry, creative nonfiction). Estab. 1974. Publishes hardcover and trade paperback originals and reprints. **Publishes 8 titles/year. Receives 2,500 queries and 2,000 mss/year. 30% of books from first-time authors. Pays royalty on retail price.** Publishes book 6-12 months after acceptance of ms. Accepts simultaneous submissions. Responds in 1 month to queries; 1 month to proposals; 1-3 months to mss. Book catalog and ms guidelines online.

Nonfiction: Biography, literary nonfiction. Subjects include creative nonfiction, history (regional, community), multicultural, regional, travel. "We try to publish creative nonfiction titles each year which are of regional, national, and international interest." Query with SASE, or submit proposal package including outline, 3 sample chapter(s), publishing history, author bio, SASE.

Fiction: Literary, multicultural, poetry, short story collections. "We try to publish at least 2 literary fiction titles each year. We receive many more deserving submissions than we are able to publish, so we publish only outstanding work. We try to balance our list between emerging and established writers, and have published many first-time writers who have gone on to win or be shortlisted for major literary awards, both nationally and internationally." Query with SASE, or submit proposal package including 3 sample chapter(s), publishing history, synopsis, author bio, SASE.

Poetry: "We are one of the few small literary presses in Canada that still publishes poetry. We try to include 2 or 3 poetry titles each year. We attempt to balance our list between emerging and established poets. Our poetry titles have won or been shortlisted for major national awards, including the Governor General's Award, the BC Book Prizes, and the Alberta Awards. Query, or submit 10 sample poems.

Recent Title(s): *Here In Hope: A Natural History*, by J.M. Bridgeman (community history); *The Last We Heard of Leonard*, by Rachel Wyatt (linked short stories); *The Book of Contradictions*, by George McWhirter (poetry).

Tips: "Our audience is adult readers who love good books and good literature. Our audience is regional and national, as well as international. Follow our submission guidelines. Check out some of our titles at your local library or bookstore to get an idea of what we publish. Don't send us the only copy of your manuscript. Let us know if your submission is simultaneous, and inform us if it is accepted elsewhere. Above all, keep writing!"

ORCA BOOK PUBLISHERS, P.O. Box 5626, Victoria BC V8R 6S4 Canada. (250)380-1229. Fax: (250)380-1892. E-mail: orca@orcabook.com. Website: www.orcabook.com. **Acquisitions:** Maggie DeVries, editor (picture books, young readers); Andrew Wooldridge, editor (juvenile fiction, teen fiction); Bob Tyrrell, publisher (YA, teen). Estab. 1984. Publishes hardcover and trade paperback originals, and mass market paperback originals and reprints. **Publishes 30 titles/year. Receives 2,500 queries and 1,000 mss/year. 20% of books from first-time authors; 75% from unagented writers. Pays 10% royalty.** Publishes book 12-18 months after acceptance of ms. Does not accept simultaneous submissions. Responds in 1 month to queries; 1 month to proposals; 1-2 months to mss. Book catalog for 8 1/2X11 SASE; ms guidelines online.

- "Only publishes Canadian authors."

Nonfiction: Subjects include multicultural, picture books. Query with SASE.

Fiction: Hi-lo, juvenile (5-9 years), literary, mainstream/contemporary, young adult (10-18 years). "Ask for guidelines, find out what we publish." Looking for "contemporary fiction." "No romance, science fiction." Query with SASE, or submit proposal package including outline, 2-5 sample chapter(s), synopsis, SASE.

Recent Title(s): *Before Wings*, by Beth Goobie (teen fiction); *No Two Snowflakes*, by Sheree Fitch (picture book).

Tips: "Our audience is for students in grades K-12. Know our books, and know the market."

ORIENT PAPERBACKS, A Division of Vision Books Pvt Ltd., Madarsa Rd., Kashmere Gate Delhi 110 006 India. +911-11-386-2267. Fax: +911-11=386-2935. Website: www.orientpaperbacks.com. **Pays royalty on copies sold.**

Fiction: Length: 40,000 words minimum. Send cover letter, brief summary, 1 sample chapter and author's bio data. "We send writers' guidelines on accepting a proposal."

PETER OWEN PUBLISHERS, 73 Kenway Rd., London SW5 ORE United Kingdom. 020-8373 5628. Fax: 020-8373 6760. E-mail: admin@peterowen.com. Website: www.peterowen.com. **Acquisitions:** Antonia Owen. Publishes hardcover originals and trade paperback originals and reprints. **Publishes 20-30 titles/year. Receives 3,000 queries and 800 mss/year. 70% from unagented writers. Pays 7½-10% royalty. Offers negotiable advance.** Publishes book 1 year after acceptance of ms. Accepts simultaneous submissions. Responds in 2 months to queries; 3 months to proposals; 3 months to mss. Book catalog for SASE, SAE with IRC or on website.

O-r "We are far more interested in proposals for nonfiction than fiction at the moment." No poetry or short stories.

Nonfiction: Biography. Subjects include art/architecture, history, language/literature, memoirs, translation, travel, women's issues/studies. Query with SASE, or submit outline, 1-3 sample chapter(s). Submit complete ms with return postage.

Fiction: Literary, translation. "No first novels and authors should be aware that we publish very little new fiction these days." Does not accept short stories, only excerpts from novels of normal length. Submit sample chapter(s), synopsis. Query with SASE or by e-mail. Submissions by agent preferred.

Recent Title(s): *Almodóvar: Labrynths of Passion*, by Gwynne Edwards (nonfiction); *Doubting Thomas*, by Atle Naess (translation, novel).

PACIFIC EDUCATIONAL PRESS, Faculty of Education, University of British Columbia, Vancouver BC V6T 1Z4 Canada. Fax: (604)822-6603. E-mail: pep@interchange.ubc.ca. **Acquisitions:** Catherine Edwards, director. Publishes trade paperback originals and cloth reference books. **Publishes 2-4 titles/year. Receives 60 submissions/year. 15% of books from first-time authors; 100% from unagented writers.** Accepts simultaneous submissions. Responds in 6 months to mss. Book catalog and ms guidelines for 9×12 SAE with IRCs.

O→ Pacific Educational Press publishes books on the subject of education for an adult audience of teachers, scholars, librarians, and parents. Currently emphasizing literature, education, social studies education, international issues, mathematics, science.

Recent Title(s): *Teaching to Wonder: Responding to Poetry in the Secondary Classroom*, by Carl Leggo; *The Canadian Anthology of Social Studies*, by Roland Case and Penney Clark; *Teaching Shakespeare on Screen*, by Neil Bechervaise.

PEDLAR PRESS, P.O. Box 26, Station P, Toronto ON M5S 2S6 Canada. (416)534-2011. Fax: (416)535-9677. E-mail: feralgrl@interlog.com. **Acquisitions:** Beth Follett, editor (fiction, poetry). Publishes hardcover and trade paperback originals. **Publishes 4-6 titles/year. Receives 50-60 mss/year. 50% of books from first-time authors; 100% from unagented writers. Pays 10% royalty on retail price. Offers $200-400 advance.** Publishes book 1 year after acceptance of ms. Accepts simultaneous submissions. Responds in 1 month to queries; 6 months to mss. Book catalog and ms guidelines for #10 SASE.

O→ Niche is outsider voices, experimental style, and form. Please note: Pedlar will not consider USA authors until 2004. Currently emphasizing experimental fiction.

Nonfiction: Illustrated book. Subjects include creative nonfiction, gay/lesbian, language/literature, sex, women's issues/studies. Submit proposal package including outline, 5 sample chapter(s). Reviews artwork/photos as part of ms package. Send photocopies.

Fiction: Erotica, experimental, feminist, gay/lesbian, humor, literary, picture books, poetry, short story collections, translation. Query with SASE or submit proposal package including 5 sample chapter(s), synopsis.

Recent Title(s): *Mouthing the Words*, by Camilla Gibb (fiction); *Chez 100*, by Fiona Smyth (art book).

Tips: "We select manuscripts according to our taste. Be familiar with some if not most of our recent titles."

PENGUIN BOOKS CANADA, LTD., The Penguin Group, 10 Alcorn Ave., Suite 300, Toronto ON M4V 3B2 Canada. (416)925-0068. **Acquisitions:** Diane Turbide, editorial director (literary nonfiction, biography, social issue; history/current events); Barbara Berson, senior editor (literary fiction and nonfiction; children's and young adult fiction); Cynthia Good, president/publisher. **Offers advance.** Does not accept simultaneous submissions.

Nonfiction: Any Canadian subject by any Canadian authors. Query with SASE. *No unsolicited mss.*

Recent Title(s): *Titans*, by Peter C. Newman (business); *Home From the Vinyl Café*, by Stuart McLean (fiction); *Happiness*, by Will Ferguson.

PIPERS' ASH, LTD., Pipers' Ash, Church Rd., Christian Malford, Chippenham, Wiltshire SN15 4BW United Kingdom. +44(01249)720-563. Fax: 0870 0568916. E-mail: pipersash@supamasu.com. Website: www.supamasu.com. **Acquisitions:** Manuscript Evaluation Desk. Estab. 1976. Publishes hardcover and electronic originals. **Publishes 12 titles/year. Receives 1,000 queries and 400 mss/year. 90% of books from first-time authors; 100% from unagented writers. Pays 10% royalty on wholesale price, and 5 author copies.** Publishes book 6 months after acceptance of ms. Does not accept simultaneous submissions. Responds in 1 month to queries; 1 month to proposals; 3 months to mss. Book catalog for A5 SASE and on website; ms guidelines online.

Imprints: Salisbury, Canterbury, Lincoln, Gloucester, Durhm, Ely.

Nonfiction: Autobiography, biography, booklets, children's/juvenile, coffee table book, how-to, self-help. Subjects include creative nonfiction, ethnic, history, humanities, language/literature, military/war, philosophy, recreation, religion, translation. "Visit website." Query with SASE.

Fiction: Adventure, confession, feminist, historical, juvenile, literary, mainstream/contemporary, military/war, plays, poetry, poetry in translation, regional, religious, romance (contemporary, romantic suspense), science fiction (hard science/technological, soft/sociological), short story collections, sports, suspense, translation, western (frontier saga, traditional), young adult (adventure, fantasy/science fiction). Currently emphasizing stage plays. "We publish 30,000-word novels and short story collections. Visit our website." Query with SASE or submit sample chapter(s), 25-word synopsis (that sorts out the writers from the wafflers).

Poetry: Submit 60 sample poems.

Recent Title(s): *A Web of Cries*, by Dr. Pamela Bakker (poetry); *The Wirksworth Saga*, by Frank Priestley (local history); *Stay? No way!*, by Vivienne Coranger (teenage novel).

Tips: "Visit website."

PLAYWRIGHTS CANADA PRESS, 54 Wolseley St., 2nd Floor, Toronto ON M5T 1A5 Canada. (416)703-0013. Fax: (416)703-0059. E-mail: angela@puc.ca. Website: www.playwrightscanada.com. **Acquisitions:** Angela Rebeiro, publisher. Estab. 1972. Publishes paperback originals and reprints of plays. **Receives 40 submissions/year. 50% of books from first-time authors; 50% from unagented writers. Pays 10% royalty on retail price.** Publishes book 6 months-1 year after acceptance of ms. Responds in 2-3 months to queries. Ms guidelines online.

O→ Playwrights Canada Press publishes only drama by Canadian citizens or landed immigrants, which has received professional production

Recent Title(s): *The Gwendolyn Poems*, by Claudia Dey; *Voices from Canada: Focus on 30 Plays*, by Albert Reiner-

Glaap; *Between the Lines: The Process of Dramaturgy*, by Judith Rudakoff and Lynn Thompson.

DAVID PORTEOUS EDITIONS, P.O. Box 5, Chudleigh, Newton Abbot, Devon TQ13 0YZ United Kingdom. E-mail: editorial@davidporteous.com. Website: www.davidporteous.com. **Acquisitions:** David Porteous, publisher (arts, crafts, hobbies). Estab. 1992. Publishes hardcover originals and trade paperback originals and reprints. **Publishes 3-5 titles/year. 90% of books from first-time authors; 99% from unagented writers. Pays 5% royalty on wholesale price.** Does not accept simultaneous submissions. Responds in 1 month to queries; 2 months to proposals; 2 months to mss. Book catalog online.

Nonfiction: How-to, illustrated book. Subjects include art/architecture, hobbies. "We publish practical, illustrated books showing step-by-step instructions." Query with SASE. Reviews artwork/photos as part of ms package. Send photocopies or digital images.

Recent Title(s): *Create Greeting Cards with Glass Painting Techniques*, by Joan Dale (craft); *Paul Riley's Watercolour Workshop*, by Paul Riley (art instruction); *Knitting for Teddies*, by Catherine Bouquevel (craft).

Tips: "We publish for an International market. So the content must be suitable for the U.S.A., U.K., South Africa, Australia and New Zealand."

PRESSES DE L'UNIVERSITÉ DE MONTREAL, Case postale 6128, Succursale Centre-ville, Montreal QC M3C 3S7 Canada. (514)343-6933. Fax: (514)343-2232. E-mail: pum@umontreal.ca. Website: www.pum.umontreal.ca. **Acquisitions:** Rene Bonenfant, editor-in-chief. Street address: 3535 Queen-Mary, Suite 206, Montreal QC M3V 1H8 Canada. Publishes hardcover and trade paperback originals. **Publishes 40 titles/year. Pays 8-12% royalty on net receipts.** Publishes book 6 months after acceptance of ms. Responds in 1 month to queries; 1 month to proposals; 3 months to mss. Book catalog and ms guidelines free.

Nonfiction: Reference, textbook. Subjects include education, health/medicine, history, language/literature, philosophy, psychology, sociology, translation. Submit outline, 2 sample chapter(s).

PRODUCTIVE PUBLICATIONS, P.O. Box 7200 Station A, Toronto ON M5W 1X8 Canada. (416)483-0634. Fax: (416)322-7434. **Acquisitions:** Iain Williamson, owner. Estab. 1985. Publishes trade paperback originals. **Publishes 24 titles/year. Receives 160 queries and 40 mss/year. 80% of books from first-time authors; 100% from unagented writers. Pays 10-15% royalty on wholesale price.** Publishes book 6 months after acceptance of ms. Accepts simultaneous submissions. Responds in 1 month to queries; 1 month to proposals; 3 months to mss. Book catalog free.

O→ "Productive Publications publishes books to help readers succeed and to help them meet the challenges of the new information age and global marketplace." Interested in books on business, computer software, the Internet for business purposes, investment, stock market and mutual funds, etc. Currently emphasizing computers, software, small business, business management, entrepreneurship. De-emphasizing jobs, how to get employment.

Nonfiction: How-to, reference, self-help, technical. Subjects include business/economics (small business and management), computers/electronic, money/finance, software (business). "We are interested in small business/entrepreneurship/self-help (business)—100 to 300 pages." Submit outline. Reviews artwork/photos as part of ms package. Send photocopies.

Recent Title(s): *How to Deliver Excellent Customer Service: A Step-by-Step Guide for Every Business*, by Julie Olley; *Market Your Professional Service*, by Jerome Shure.

Tips: "We are looking for books written by knowledgable, experienced experts who can express their ideas clearly and simply."

PURICH PUBLISHING, Box 23032, Market Mall Post Office, Saskatoon SK S7J 5H3 Canada. (306)373-5311. Fax: (306)373-5315. E-mail: purich@sasktel.net. Website: www.purichpublishing.com. **Acquisitions:** Donald Purich, publisher (law, Aboriginal issues); Karen Bolstad, publisher (history, education). Publishes trade paperback originals. **Publishes 3-5 titles/year. 20% of books from first-time authors. Pays 8-12% royalty on retail price. Offers negotiable advance.** Publishes book within 4 months of completion of editorial work, after acceptance of ms. Accepts simultaneous submissions. Responds in 1 month to queries; 3 months to mss. Book catalog free.

O→ Purich pubishes books on law, Aboriginal/Native American issues, and Western Canadian history and education for the academic and professional trade reference market.

Nonfiction: Reference, technical, textbook. Subjects include education, government/politics, history, Aboriginal issues. "We are a specialized publisher and only consider work in our subject areas." Query with SASE.

Recent Title(s): *Aboriginal and Treaty Rights in the Maritimes*, by Thomas Isaac.

RENDEZVOUS PRESS, Transmedia Enterprises, Inc., 3266 Yonge St., #1005, Toronto ON M4N 3P6 Canada. (416)730-9052. Fax: (416)226-9975. E-mail: transmedia@sympatico.ca. Website: www.rendezvouspress.com. **Acquisitions:** A. Thompson, editor. Estab. 1990. Publishes hardcover and trade paperback originals and reprints. **Publishes 8 titles/year; imprint publishes 4 titles/year. Receives 200 queries and 100 mss/year. 50% of books from first-time authors; 80% from unagented writers.** Publishes book 18 months after acceptance of ms. Accepts simultaneous submissions. Responds in 1 month to queries; 3 months to proposals; 6 months to mss. Book catalog online; ms guidelines online.

Nonfiction: Biography (children's), children's/juvenile. Query with SASE or submit outline, 1 sample chapter(s).

Fiction: Adventure (children's), historical, juvenile, mainstream/contemporary, mystery, picture books, suspense, young adult. Query with SASE or submit complete ms.

Recent Title(s): *Little Boy Blues*, by Mary Jane Maffini; *Dead Cow in Aisle Three*, by H. Mel Malton; *Death Goes Shopping*, by Jessica Burton.

Tips: "Canadian resident authors only."

ROCKY MOUNTAIN BOOKS, #4 Spruce Centre SW, Calgary AB T3C 3B3 Canada. (403)249-9490. Fax: (403)249-2968. E-mail: tonyd@rmbooks.com. Website: www.rmbooks.com. **Acquisitions:** Tony Daffern, publisher. Publishes trade paperback originals. **Publishes 5 titles/year. Receives 30 queries/year. 75% of books from first-time authors; 100% from unagented writers. Pays 12% royalty on net receipts.** Rarely offers advance. Publishes book 1 year after acceptance of ms. Does not accept simultaneous submissions. Responds in 1 month to queries. Book catalog and ms guidelines free.

O‑ Rocky Mountain Books publishes on outdoor recreation, mountains, and mountaineering in Western Canada.

Nonfiction: Biography, how-to. Subjects include nature/environment, recreation, regional, travel. "Our main area of publishing is outdoor recreation guides to Western and Northern Canada." Query with SASE.

Recent Title(s): *Pushing the Limits: The Story of Canadian Mountaineering*, by Chic Scott.

RONSDALE PRESS, 3350 W. 21st Ave., Vancouver BC V6S 1G7 Canada. (604)738-4688. Fax: (604)731-4548. Website: www.ronsdalepress.com. **Acquisitions:** Ronald B. Hatch, director (fiction, poetry, social commentary); Veronica Hatch, managing director (children's literature). Estab. 1988. Publishes trade paperback originals. **Publishes 10 titles/year. Receives 300 queries and 800 mss/year. 60% of books from first-time authors; 95% from unagented writers. Pays 10% royalty on retail price.** Publishes book 6 months after acceptance of ms. Accepts simultaneous submissions. Responds in 2 weeks to queries; 2 months to proposals; 3 months to mss. Book catalog for #10 SASE; ms guidelines online.

O‑ Ronsdale publishes fiction, poetry, regional history, biography and autobiography, books of ideas about Canada, as well as children's books. Currently emphasizing YA historical fiction.

Nonfiction: Biography, children's/juvenile. Subjects include history (Canadian), language/literature, nature/environment, regional.

Fiction: Literary, short story collections, novels. *Canadian authors only.* Query with at least the first 80 pages. Short story collections must have some previous magazine publication.

Poetry: "Poets should have published some poems in magazines/journals and should be well-read in contemporary masters." Submit complete ms.

Recent Title(s): *Eyewitness*, by Margaret Thompson (YA historical fiction); *When Eagles Call*, by Susan Dobbie (novel).

Tips: "Ronsdale Press is a literary publishing house, based in Vancouver, and dedicated to publishing books from across Canada, books that give Canadians new insights into themselves and their country. We aim to publish the best Canadian writers."

SAXON HOUSE CANADA, P.O. Box 6947, Station A, Toronto ON M5W 1X6 Canada. (416)488-7171. Fax: (416)488-2989. **Acquisitions:** Dietrich Hummell, editor-in-chief; W.H. Wallace, general manager (history, philosophy); Carla Saxon, CEO (printed music). Publishes hardcover originals and trade paperback reprints. **Publishes 4 titles/year. Receives 6 queries and 20 mss/year. 20% of books from first-time authors; 80% from unagented writers. Pays royalty on wholesale price or makes outright purchase. Offers advance.** Publishes book 15 months after acceptance of ms. Accepts simultaneous submissions. Responds in 4 months to mss.

Nonfiction: Illustrated book. Subjects include history, music (printed music), philosophy, religion. Submit proposal package including 3 sample chapter(s), résumé. Reviews artwork/photos as part of ms package. Send photocopies.

Fiction: Historical, literary. Submit proposal package including 3 sample chapter(s), résumé.

Recent Title(s): *The Journey to Canada*, by David Mills (history); *Voices From the Lake*, by E.M. Watts (illustrated ancient American Indian legend); *The Wine of Babylon*, by David Mills (epic poem).

Tips: "We want books with literary integrity. Historical accuracy and fresh narrative skills."

SCHOLASTIC CANADA, LTD., 175 Hillmount Rd., Markham ON L6C 1Z7 Canada. (905)887-7323. Fax: (905)887-3643. Website: www.scholastic.ca. Publishes hardcover and trade paperback originals. **Publishes 40 titles/year; imprint publishes 4 titles/year. 3% of books from first-time authors; 50% from unagented writers. Pays 5-10% royalty on retail price. Offers $1,000-5,000 (Canadian) advance.** Publishes book 1 year after acceptance of ms. Does not accept simultaneous submissions. Responds in 3 months to queries; 6 months to proposals. Book catalog for 8½×11 SAE with 2 first-class stamps (IRC or Canadian stamps only).

Imprints: North Winds Press, Les editions Scholastic.

O‑ Scholastic publishes books by Canadians and/or about Canada. Currently emphasizing Canadian interest, middle-grade fiction.

Nonfiction: Biography, children's/juvenile. Subjects include history, hobbies, nature/environment, recreation, science, sports. *Agented submissions only. No unsolicited mss.*

Fiction: Juvenile (middle grade), young adult. *No unsolicited mss. Agented submissions only.*

Recent Title(s): *Zoom*, by Robert Munch and Michael Martchenko; *Alone in an Untamed Land*, by Maxine Trollier; *Made in Canada—101 Amazing Achievements*, by Bev Spencer.

SEVERN HOUSE PUBLISHERS, 9-15 High St., Sutton, Surrey SM1 1DF United Kingdom. (0208)770-3930. Fax: (0208)770-3850. **Acquisitions:** Amanda Stewart, editorial director. Publishes hardcover and trade paperback originals and reprints. **Publishes 150 titles/year. Receives 400-500 queries and 50 mss/year. Pays 7½-15% royalty on retail price. Offers $750-5,000 advance.** Accepts simultaneous submissions. Responds in 3 months to proposals. Book catalog free.

O‑ Severn House is currently emphasizing suspense, romance, mystery. Large print imprint from existing authors.

Fiction: Adventure, fantasy, historical, horror, mainstream/contemporary, mystery, romance, short story collections, suspense. *Agented submissions only.*

Recent Title(s): *The Streets of Town*, by John Gardner; *The Networks*, by Ted Albeury; *Weekend Warriors*, by Fern Michaels.

SNOWAPPLE PRESS, Box 66024, Heritage Postal Outlet, Edmonton AB T6J 6T4 Canada. (780)437-0191. **Acquisitions:** Vanna Tessier, editor. Estab. 1991. Publishes hardcover originals, trade paperback originals and reprints, mass market paperback originals and reprints. **Publishes 3-4 titles/year. Receives 300 queries/year. 50% of books from first-time authors; 100% from unagented writers. Pays 10-50% royalty on retail price or makes outright purchase. or pays in contributor copies. Pays honorarium. Offers $100-200 advance.** Publishes book 12-18 months after acceptance of ms. Responds in 1 month to queries; 3 months to proposals; 3 months to mss.

"We focus on topics that are interesting, unusual and controversial." *No unsolicited mss.*

Fiction: Adventure, ethnic, experimental, fantasy, feminist, historical, literary, mainstream/contemporary, mystery, short story collections, translation, young adult (adventure, mystery/suspense). Query with SASE. Send 1-page cover letter.

Poetry: Query with IRC.

Recent Title(s): *Thistle Creek*, by Vanna Tessier (fiction); *The Last Waltz of Chopin*, by Gilberto Finzi (fiction).

Tips: "We are a small press that will publish original, interesting, and entertaining fiction and poetry."

SOUND AND VISION PUBLISHING, LTD., 359 Riverdale Ave., Toronto ON M4J 1A4 Canada. (416)465-2828. Fax: (416)465-0755. E-mail: musicbooks@soundandvision.com. Website: www.soundandvision.com. **Acquisitions:** Geoff Savage. Publishes trade paperback originals. **Publishes 3-5 titles/year. Receives 25 queries/year. 85% of books from first-time authors; 100% from unagented writers. Pays royalty on wholesale price. Offers $500-2,000 advance.** Does not accept simultaneous submissions. Responds in 1 month to queries.

Sound and Vision specializes in books on musical humor and quotation books.

Nonfiction: Humor. Subjects include humor, music/dance. Query with SASE.

Recent Title(s): *The Thing I've Played with the Most*, by David E. Walden; *Opera Antics and Anecdotes*, by Stephen Tanner, cartoons by Umberto Taccola.

STELLER PRESS, LTD., 13-4335 W. 10th Ave., Vancouver BC V6R 2H6 Canada. (604)222-2955. Fax: (604)222-2965. E-mail: harful@telus.net. **Acquisitions:** Guy Chadsey, publisher (outdoors/gardening). Publishes trade paperback originals. **Publishes 4 titles/year. 75% of books from first-time authors; 100% from unagented writers. Pays royalty on retail price. Offers $500-2,000 advance.** Accepts simultaneous submissions. Responds in 6 months to queries.

"All titles are specific to the Pacific Northwest." Currently emphasizing gardening, history, outdoors. De-emphasizing fiction, poetry.

Nonfiction: Subjects include gardening, history, nature/environment, regional, travel.

Recent Title(s): *Roses For the Pacific Northwest*, by Christine Allen; *Herbs For the Pacific Northwest*, by Moira Carlson.

SUMAIYAH DISTRIBUTORS PVT, LTD., 4228/1 Ansari Rd., Daryaganj, 2nd Floor, New Delhi Delhi 110002 India. (011)23244148. Fax: (011)23244133. E-mail: sumaiyah@vsnl.net. **Acquisitions:** Mohd. Aslam Khan, managing director (medical and allied health sciences); Mrs. Feroza Khanam, acquisitions editor (marketing sales, customer service and development). Estab. 2000. **Publishes 10 titles/year. Receives 8 queries and 5 mss/year. 90% of books from first-time authors. Pays 10-12% royalty. Offers $400-800 advance.** Publishes book 3 months after acceptance of ms. Accepts simultaneous submissions. Responds in 1 month to mss. Book catalog and ms guidelines free.

Nonfiction: Illustrated book, technical, textbook, medical and allied health sciences management, quick reference manual and self-guide book. Subjects include health/medicine. Submit complete ms. Reviews artwork/photos as part of ms package.

Recent Title(s): *Understanding Human Histology*, by Dr. Abrar Khan (textbook for undergraduate medical and allied health).

Tips: "We place strong emphasis on materials that teach quick grasp of the subject for the busy student, practitioners and researchers. And the writers should clearly indicate what book is about and audience."

TESSERACT BOOKS, The Books Collective, 214-21 10405 Jasper Ave., Edmonton AB T5J 3S2 Canada. (780)448-0590. Fax: (780)448-0640. E-mail: promo@bookscollective.com. Website: www.bookscollective.com. **Acquisitions:** Candas Jame Dorsey, editor. Publishes hardcover and trade paperback originals. **Publishes 6 titles/year. Receives 50 queries and 350 mss/year. 80% of books from first-time authors; 90% from unagented writers. Pays 8% royalty on retail price.** Publishes book 18 months after acceptance of ms. Accepts simultaneous submissions. Responds in 2 months to queries; 4 months to proposals; 6 months to mss. Book catalog for 9×12 SAE with 2 first-class stamps; ms guidelines online.

Imprints: River Books, Slipstream Books (Timothy J. Anderson, editor).

Nonfiction: Biography. Subjects include memoirs. "Our only nonfiction titles are striking, powerful memoirs." Query with SASE, or submit outline, 3 sample chapter(s), SASE.

Fiction: Experimental, fantasy, poetry, science fiction, short story collections. Submit 3 sample chapter(s), synopsis, SASE.

Poetry: Query.

Tips: "Audience is people interested in unusual stories, academics, people outside the mainstream. We only publish Canadian authors."

THOMPSON EDUCATIONAL PUBLISHING, INC., 6 Ripley Ave., Suite 200, Toronto ON M6S 3N9 Canada. (416)766-2763. Fax: (416)766-0398. E-mail: publisher@thompsonbooks.com. Website: www.thompsonbooks.com. **Acquisitions:** Keith Thompson, president. **Publishes 10 titles/year. Receives 15 queries and 10 mss/year. 80% of books from first-time authors; 100% from unagented writers. Pays 10% royalty on net receipts.** Publishes book 1 year after acceptance of ms. Does not accept simultaneous submissions. Responds in 1 month to queries. Book catalog free; ms guidelines online.

Thompson Educational specializes in high-quality educational texts in the social sciences and humanities.

Nonfiction: Textbook. Subjects include business/economics, education, ethnic, government/politics, multicultural, sociology, sports, women's issues/studies. Submit outline, 1 sample chapter(s), résumé.

Recent Title(s): *Juvenile Justice Systems*, edited by N. Bala, J. Hornick, H.N. Snyder, and J.J. Paetsch.

TITAN BOOKS, LTD., 144 Southwark St., London SE1 OUP England. Fax: (0207)620-0032. E-mail: editorial@titanemail.com. **Acquisitions:** D. Barraclough, editorial manager. Publishes trade and mass market paperback originals and reprints. **Publishes about 100 titles/year. Receives 1,000 queries and 500 mss/year. 1% of books from first-time authors; 50% from unagented writers. Pays 6-8% royalty on retail price. Offers variable advance.** Accepts simultaneous submissions. Responds in 1 month to queries; 3 months to proposals; 6 months to mss. Ms guidelines for #10 SASE.

Titan Books publishes film and TV titles.

Nonfiction: Biography, how-to, illustrated books. Subjects include film/cinema/stage, film and TV. Submit outline, sample chapter(s), SASE.

Recent Title(s): *Spielberg, Truffaut & Me: Close Encounters of the Third Kind, An Actor's Diary*, by Bob Balaban; *You Can Be a Movie Extra*, by Rob Martin.

TOUCHWOOD EDITIONS, (formerly Horsdal & Schubart Publishers, Ltd.), #6-356 Simcoe St., Victoria BC V8V 1L1 Canada. (250)360-0829. Fax: (250)385-0829. **Acquisitions:** Vivian Sinclair, managing editor. Publishes trade paperback originals and reprints. **Publishes 8-10 titles/year. 50% of books from first-time authors; 100% from unagented writers. Pays 15% royalty on wholesale price.** Publishes book 6 months after acceptance of ms. Accepts simultaneous submissions. Responds in 1 month to queries. Book catalog free.

Nonfiction: Biography. Subjects include anthropology/archeology, art/architecture, creative nonfiction, government/politics, history, nature/environment, recreation, regional. Query with SASE, or submit outline, 2-3 sample chapter(s), synopsis. Reviews artwork/photos as part of ms package. Send photocopies.

Recent Title(s): *The Journey*, by Bill Gallaher; *Old Stones*, by Anthea Penne; *Voyages of Hope*, by Peter Johnson.

Tips: "Our area of interest is Western and Northern Canada. We would like more creative nonfiction and history as stories."

TRADEWIND BOOKS, 1809 Maritime Mews, Granville Island, Vancouver BC V6H 3W7 Canada. (604)662-4405. Fax: (604)730-0153. E-mail: tradewindbooks@eudoramail.com. Website: www.tradewindbooks.com. **Acquisitions:** Michael Katz, publisher (picturebooks, young adult); Carol Frank, art director (picturebooks); Tiffany Stone (acquisitions editor). Publishes hardcover and trade paperback originals. **Publishes 5 titles/year. Receives 1,000 submissions/year. 10% of books from first-time authors; 50% from unagented writers. Pays 7% royalty on retail price. Offers variable advance.** Publishes book 3 years after acceptance of ms. Accepts simultaneous submissions. Responds in 2 months to mss. Book catalog and ms guidelines online.

Tradewind Books publishes juvenile picture books and young adult novels. Requires that submissions include evidence that author has read at least 3 titles published by Tradewind Books.

Fiction: Juvenile. Query with SASE, or submit proposal package including 2 sample chapter(s), synopsis.

Recent Title(s): *The Sea King*; *My Animal Friends*; *Pigmalion*.

TRENTHAM BOOKS, LTD., Westview House, 734 London Rd., Stoke on Trent ST4 5NP United Kingdom. (0044)1782 745567. Fax: (0044)745553. E-mail: tb@trentham-books.co.uk. Website: www.trentham-books.co.uk. **Acquisitions:** Gillian Klein, commissioning editor (education, race). Publishes hardcover and trade paperback originals. **Publishes 32 titles/year. Receives 1,000 queries and 600 mss/year. 60% of books from first-time authors; 70% from unagented writers. Pays 7½% royalty on wholesale price.** Publishes book 4 months after acceptance of ms. Does not accept simultaneous submissions. Responds in 1 month to queries. Book catalog for #10 SASE; ms guidelines online.

Imprints: Trentham.

"Our mission is to enhance the work of professionals in education, law, and social work." Currently emphasizing curriculum, professional behavior. De-emphasizing theoretical issues.

Nonfiction: Technical, textbook. Subjects include education, ethnic, multicultural, psychology, women's issues/studies, language/literacy. Query with SASE.

Recent Title(s): *Children's Literature and National Identity*, by Margaret Meek, ed.; *Lifelong Learning and the New Educational Order*, by John Field.

TURNSTONE PRESS, 607-100 Arthur St., Winnipeg MB R3B 1H3 Canada. (204)947-1555. Fax: (204)942-1555. E-mail: info@turnstonepress.com. Website: www.ravenstonebooks.com. **Acquisitions:** Todd Besant, managing editor; Sharon Caseburg, acquisitions editor. Estab. 1976. Publishes trade paperback originals, mass market for literary mystery imprint. **Publishes 10-12 titles/year. Receives 1,000 mss/year. 25% of books from first-time authors; 75% from unagented writers. Pays 10% royalty on retail price and 10 author's copies. Offers advance.** Publishes book 1 year after acceptance of ms. Does not accept simultaneous submissions. Responds in 4 months to queries. Book catalog for #10 SASE; ms guidelines online.

Imprints: Ravenstone (literary mystery fiction).

Turnstone Press is a literary press that publishes Canadian writers with an emphasis on writers from, and writing on, the Canadian West. Currently emphasizing novels, nonfiction travel, adventure travel, poetry. Does not consider formula or mainstream work.

Nonfiction: Subjects include travel, adventure travel, cultural/social issues, Canadian literary criticism. Query with SASE, literary curriculum vitae, and 50-page sample.

Fiction: Literary, regional (Western Canada), short story collections, contemporary, novels. *Canadian authors only.* Query with SASE, literary curriculum vitae, and 50-page sample.

Poetry: Submit complete ms.

Recent Title(s): *Macaws of Death*, by Karen Dudley (mystery); *The Girl With the Full Figure Is Your Daughter*, by Oscar Martens (fiction); *Alarum Within*, by Kimmy Beach (poetry).

Tips: "Writers are encouraged to view our list and check if submissions are appropriate. Although we publish new authors, we prefer if first-time authors have publishing credits in literary magazines. Would like to see more adventure travel as well as eclectic novels. Would like to see 'nonformula' writing for the Ravenstone imprint, especially literary thrillers, urban mystery, and noir."

THE UNIVERSITY OF ALBERTA PRESS, Ring House 2, Edmonton AB T6G 2E1 Canada. (780)492-3662. Fax: (780)492-0719. E-mail: u.a.p@ualberta.ca. Website: www.uap.ualberta.ca. Estab. 1969. Publishes paperback orginals and reprints. **Publishes 18-25 titles/year. Receives 400 submissions/year. 60% of books from first-time authors. Pays maximum 10% royalty on net price. Offers varies advance.** Publishes book within 2 years after acceptance of ms. Does not accept simultaneous submissions. Responds in 3 months to queries. Ms guidelines online.

"Award-winning publisher The University of Alberta Press has published excellent scholarly works and fine books for general audiences. Our program is particularly strong in the areas of biography, history, language, literature, natural history and books of regional interest. Within each of those broad subject areas we have published in a variety of specific fields. We are pursuing manuscripts in our areas of strength and expertise, as listed above, and inviting submissions in several new areas including travel/adventure writing, business, health and social policy. We do not accept unsolicited novels or poetry. Please see our website for details."

Fiction: Ethnic, experimental, feminist, literary, short story collections, translation. Query with SASE.

UNIVERSITY OF CALGARY PRESS, 2500 University Dr. NW, Calgary AB T2N 1N4 Canada. (403)220-7578. Fax: (403)282-0085. E-mail: ucpress@ucalgary.ca. Website: www.uofcpress.com. **Acquisitions:** Walter Hildebrandt, director. Publishes hardcover and trade paperback originals and reprints. **Publishes 25-30 titles/year.** Publishes book 20 months after acceptance of ms. Does not accept simultaneous submissions. Responds in 1 month to queries; 2 months to proposals; 2 months to mss. Book catalog free; ms guidelines online.

"University of Calgary Press is committed to the advancement of scholarship through the publication of first-rate monographs, and academic and scientific journals."

Nonfiction: Scholarly. Subjects include art/architecture, philosophy, travel, women's issues/studies, world affairs. Canadian studies, post-modern studies, native studies, history, and heritage of the Canadian and American heartland, 3 new series (Latin American & Caribbean, African, and Northern Lights), international relations. Submit outline, 2 sample chapter(s), SASE. Reviews artwork/photos as part of ms package. Send photocopies.

Recent Title(s): *Dialogues on Cultural Studies: Interviews with Contemporary Critics*, edited by Shaobo Xie and Fengzhen Wang; *Grassroots Governance: Chiefs in Africa and the Afro-Caribbean*, edited by Donald I. Ray and P.S. Reddy.

UNIVERSITY OF MANITOBA PRESS, 301 St. John's College, University of Manitoba, Winnipeg MB R3T 2M5 Canada. (204)474-9495. Fax: (204)474-7566. Website: www.umanitoba.ca/uofmpress. **Acquisitions:** David Carr, director. Estab. 1967. Publishes nonfiction hardcover and trade paperback originals. **Publishes 4-6 titles/year. Pays 5-15% royalty on wholesale price. Offers advance.** Does not accept simultaneous submissions. Responds in 3 months to queries.

Nonfiction: Scholarly. Subjects include ethnic, history, regional, women's issues/studies. Western Canadian history. Query with SASE.

Recent Title(s): *A National Crime*, John Milloy (native/history).

Tips: "Western Canadian focus or content is important."

UNIVERSITY OF OTTAWA PRESS, 542 King Edward, Ottawa ON K1N 6N5 Canada. (613)562-5246. Fax: (613)562-5247. E-mail: press@uottawa.ca. Website: www.uopress.uottawa.ca. **Acquisitions:** Vicki Bennett, director. Estab. 1936. **Publishes 22 titles/year. Receives 250 submissions/year. 20% of books from first-time authors; 95% from unagented writers. Pays 5-10% royalty on net receipts.** Publishes book 6-12 months after acceptance of ms. Does not accept simultaneous submissions. Responds in 1 month to queries; 6 months to mss. Book catalog free; ms guidelines free.

The University Press publishes books for the scholarly and serious nonfiction audiences. They were "the first *officially* bilingual university publishing house in Canada. Our goal is to help the publication of cutting edge research—books written to be useful to active researchers but accessible to an interested public." Currently emphasizing French in North America, language rights, social sciences, translation, Canadian studies. De-emphasizing medieval studies, criminology.

Nonfiction: Reference, textbook. Subjects include education, government/politics, history, language/literature, nature/environment, philosophy, regional, religion, sociology, translation, women's issues/studies. Submit outline, sample chapter(s).

Recent Title(s): *Finding a Way: Legacy of the Past, Recipe for the Future*, by Ken Dryden; *Computer-Aided Translation Technology a Practical Introduction*, by Lynne Bowker.

Tips: "No unrevised theses! Envision audience of academic specialists and readers of serious nonfiction."

VANWELL PUBLISHING, LTD., 1 Northrup Crescent, P.O. Box 2131, St. Catharines ON L2R 7S2 Canada. (905)937-3100. Fax: (905)937-1760. **Acquisitions:** Angela Dobler, general editor; Simon Kooter, military editor (collections, equipment, vehicles, uniforms, artifacts); Ben Kooter, publisher (general military). Estab. 1983. Publishes trade originals and reprints. **Publishes 7-9 titles/year. Receives 100 submissions/year. 85% of books from first-time authors; 100% from unagented writers. Pays 10% royalty on retail price.** Publishes book 1 year after acceptance of ms. Does not accept simultaneous submissions. Responds in 6 months to queries. Book catalog free.

Vanwell is considered Canada's leading naval heritage publisher. Currently emphasizing military aviation, biography, WWI and WWII histories.

Nonfiction: Biography, reference, scholarly. Subjects include history, military/war, regional. Query with SASE. Reviews artwork/photos as part of ms package.

Recent Title(s): *The Ships of Canada's Naval Services*, by Ken Macpherson and Ron Barrie; *The Heritage of Canadian Military Music*, by Jack Kopstein and Ian Pearson.

Tips: "The writer has the best chance of selling a manuscript to our firm which is in keeping with our publishing program, well written and organized. Our audience: older male, history buff, war veteran; regional tourist; students. *Canadian only* military/aviation, naval, military/history have the best chance with us. We see more interest in collective or cataloguing forms of history, also in modeling and recreating military historical artifacts."

VÉHICULE PRESS, Box 125, Place du Parc Station, Montreal QC H2X 4A3 Canada. (514)844-6073. Fax: (514)844-7543. Website: www.vehiculepress.com. **Acquisitions:** Simon Dardick, president/publisher. Estab. 1973. Publishes trade paperback originals by *Canadian authors only.* **Publishes 15 titles/year. Receives 250 submissions/year. 20% of books from first-time authors; 95% from unagented writers. Pays 10-15% royalty on retail price. Offers $200-500 advance.** Publishes book 1 year after acceptance of ms. Responds in 4 months to queries. Book catalog for 9×12 SAE with IRCs.
Imprints: Signal Editions (poetry), Dossier Quebec (history, memoirs).

"Montreal's Véhicule Press has published the best of Canadian and Quebec literature—fiction, poetry, essays, translations, and social history."

Nonfiction: Autobiography, biography. Subjects include government/politics, history, language/literature, memoirs, regional, sociology. Especially looking for Canadian social history. Query with SASE. Reviews artwork/photos as part of ms package.
Fiction: Feminist, literary, regional, short story collections, translation. No romance, formula writing. Query with SASE.
Poetry: Contact: Carmine Starnino.
Recent Title(s): *Doug: The Doug Harvey Story*, by William Brown (nonfiction); *Helix: New & Selected Poems*, by John Steffler; *Telling Stories: New English Fiction from Quebec*, edited by Claude Lalumière.
Tips: "We are interested only in Canadian authors."

WALL & EMERSON, INC., 6 O'Connor Dr., Toronto ON M4K 2K1 Canada. (416)467-8685. Fax: (416)352-5368. E-mail: wall@wallbooks.com. Website: www.wallbooks.com. **Acquisitions:** Byron E. Wall, president (history of science, mathematics). Estab. 1987. Publishes hardcover originals and reprints. **Publishes 3 titles/year. Receives 10 queries and 8 mss/year. 50% of books from first-time authors; 100% from unagented writers. Pays 5-12% royalty on wholesale price.** Publishes book 1 year after acceptance of ms. Accepts simultaneous submissions. Responds in 1 month to queries; 1 month to proposals; 3 months to mss. Book catalog and ms guidelines free or online.

"We are most interested in textbooks for college courses that meet well-defined needs and are targeted to their audiences." Currently emphasizing adult education, engineering. De-emphasizing social work.

Nonfiction: Reference, textbook. Subjects include education, health/medicine, philosophy, science. "We are looking for any undergraduate text that meets the needs of a well-defined course in colleges in the U.S. and Canada." Submit proposal package including outline, 2 sample chapter(s).
Recent Title(s): *Princinples of Engineering Economic Analysis*; *Voices Past and Present.*
Tips: "Our audience consists of college undergraduate students and college libraries. Our ideal writer is a college professor writing a text for a course he or she teaches regularly. If I were a writer trying to market a book today, I would identify the audience for the book, and write directly to the audience throughout the book. I would then approach a publisher that publishes books specifically for that audience."

WEIGL EDUCATIONAL PUBLISHERS, LTD., 6325 10th St. SE, Calgary AB T2H 2Z9 Canada. (403)233-7747. Fax: (403)233-7769. E-mail: info@weigl.com. Website: www.weigl.com. **Acquisitions:** Linda Weigl, president. Publishes hardcover originals and reprints, school library softcover. **Publishes 104 titles/year. 100% from unagented writers. Makes outright purchase.** Accepts simultaneous submissions. Responds ASAP to queries. Book catalog and ms guidelines free.

Textbook publisher catering to juvenile and young adult audience (K-12).

Nonfiction: Children's/juvenile, textbook, library series. Subjects include animals, education, government/politics, history, nature/environment, science. Query with SASE.
Recent Title(s): *Understanding Global Issues*; *Celebrating Cultures*; *Folk Heroes.*

WHICH?, LTD., 2 Marylebone Rd., London NW1 4DF United Kingdom. 020 7770 7000. Fax: 020 7770 7600. E-mail: books@which.net. Website: www.which.net. **Publishes 25-30 titles/year. Receives 30 queries/year. 95% from unagented writers. Pays royalty on retail price.** Publishes book 6 months after acceptance of ms. Responds in 1 month to queries. Book catalog free or online at website.
Nonfiction: How-to, reference, self-help. Subjects include business/economics, computers/electronic, gardening, health/medicine, hobbies, money/finance, software, travel. Query with SASE.
Recent Title(s): *The Which? Book of Wiring and Lighting*, by Mike Lawrence (manual for amateur electricians).
Tips: "We rarely take on proposals from authors, and when we do we expect to have a lot of influence on the content, tone, etc., of the text. But occasionally a relevant submission comes in that fulfills our requirements of independence, reliability, where a successful commission and publication, has resulted."

WHITECAP BOOKS, LTD., 351 Lynn Ave., North Vancouver BC V7J 2C4 Canada. (604)980-9852. Fax: (604)980-8197. E-mail: whitecap@whitecap.ca. Website: www.whitecap.ca. **Acquisitions:** Leanne McDonald, rights and aquisitions associate. Publishes hardcover and trade paperback originals. **Publishes 24 titles/year. Receives 500 queries and 1,000 mss/year. 20% of books from first-time authors; 90% from unagented writers. Pays royalty. Offers negotiated advance.** Publishes book 18 months after acceptance of ms. Accepts simultaneous submissions. Responds in 2 months to proposals.

O‑ Whitecap Books publishes a wide range of nonfiction with a Canadian and international focus. Currently emphasizing children's nonfiction, natural history. De-emphasizing children's fiction.

Nonfiction: Children's/juvenile, coffee table book, cookbook. Subjects include animals, cooking/foods/nutrition, gardening, history, nature/environment, recreation, regional, travel. "We require an annotated outline. Writers should take the time to research our list. This is especially important for children's writers." Submit outline, 1 sample chapter(s), SASE. Reviews artwork/photos as part of ms package. Send photocopies.

Recent Title(s): *Seasons In the Rockies*, by Darwin Wiggett, Tom Till, Rebecca Gambo (nonfiction); *The Queen, The Bear and The Bumblebee*, by Dini Petty (fiction).

Tips: "We want well-written, well-researched material that presents a fresh approach to a particular topic."

WOODHEAD PUBLISHING, LTD., Abington Hall, Abington, Cambridge CB1 6AH United Kingdom. (pl44)1223-891358. Fax: (pl44)1223-893694. E-mail: wp@woodhead-publishing.com. Website: www.woodhead-publishing.com. **Acquisitions:** Francis Dodds (food science, technology, and nutrition); Patricia Morrison (materials engineering, textile technology, welding and joining); Neil Wenborn (finance, investment). Publishes hardcover originals. **Publishes 40 titles/year. 75% of books from first-time authors; 99% from unagented writers. Pays 10% royalty on wholesale price.** Publishes book 6 months after acceptance of ms. Does not accept simultaneous submissions. Book catalog for free or on website; ms guidelines online.

Imprints: Woodhead Publishing, Abington Publishing, Gresham Books.

Nonfiction: Technical. Subjects include money/finance (investments), food science, materials engineering, textile technology, welding and joining. Submit proposal package including outline. Reviews artwork/photos as part of ms package. Send photocopies.

Recent Title(s): *Yoghurt: Science and Technology*; *Oil Trading Manual*; *The Welding Workplace*.

YORK PRESS, LTD., 152 Boardwalk Dr., Toronto ON M4L 3X4 Canada. (416)690-3788. Fax: (416)690-3797. E-mail: yorkpress@sympatico.ca. Website: www3.sympatico.ca/yorkpress. **Acquisitions:** Dr. S. Elkhadem, general manager/editor. Estab. 1975. Publishes trade paperback originals. **Publishes 10 titles/year. Receives 50 submissions/year. 10% of books from first-time authors; 100% from unagented writers. Pays 10-20% royalty on wholesale price. Offers advance.** Publishes book 6 months after acceptance of ms. Does not accept simultaneous submissions. Responds in 2 weeks to queries.

O‑ "We publish scholarly books and creative writing of an experimental nature."

Nonfiction: Reference, scholarly, textbook. Subjects include language/literature. Query with SASE.

Fiction: Experimental. "Fiction of an experimental nature by well-established writers." Query with SASE.

Recent Title(s): *Herman Melville: Romantic & Prophet*, by C.S. Durer (scholarly literary criticism); *The Moonhare*, by Kirk Hampton (experimental novel).

Tips: "If I were a writer trying to market a book today, I would spend a considerable amount of time examining the needs of a publisher *before* sending my manuscript to him. The writer must adhere to our style manual and follow our guidelines exactly."

ZED BOOKS, 7 Cynthia St., London N1 9JF United Kingdom. 44-71-837-4014. Fax: 44-71-833-3960. E-mail: zedbooks@zedbooks.demon.co.uk. Website: www.zedbooks.demon.co.uk. **Acquisitions:** Robert Molten (international affairs, politics, development, environment, Third World, gender studies, cultural studies, social sciences). Publishes hardcover and trade paperback originals. **Publishes 40-45 titles/year. Receives 300 queries and 150 mss/year. 25% of books from first-time authors; 95-100% from unagented writers. Pays 7½-10% royalty on retail price or net receipts. Offers $1,000 advance.** Publishes book 9 months after acceptance of ms. Accepts simultaneous submissions. Responds in 1 week to queries; 1 month to proposals; 3 months to mss. Book catalog free; ms guidelines online.

Nonfiction: Textbook. Subjects include agriculture/horticulture, anthropology/archeology, business/economics, education, government/politics, health/medicine, history, money/finance, multicultural, nature/environment, sociology, women's issues/studies. Submit proposal package including outline, 2 sample chapter(s), or submit complete ms.

Consumer Magazines

Selling your writing to consumer magazines is as much an exercise of your marketing skills as it is of your writing abilities. Editors of consumer magazines are looking not only for good writing, but for good writing which communicates pertinent information to a specific audience—their readers. Why are editors so particular about the readers to which they appeal? Because it's only by establishing a core of faithful readers with identifiable and quantifiable traits that magazines attract advertisers. And with many magazines earning up to half their income from advertising, it is in their own best interest to know their readers' tastes and provide them with articles and features that will keep their readers coming back.

APPROACHING THE CONSUMER MAGAZINE MARKET

Marketing skills will help you successfully discern a magazine's editorial slant, and write queries and articles that prove your knowledge of the magazine's readership. The one complaint we hear from magazine editors more than any other is that many writers don't take the time to become familiar with their magazine before sending a query or manuscript. As a result, editors' desks become cluttered with inappropriate submissions.

You can gather clues about a magazine's readership—and thus establish your credibility with the magazine's editor—in a number of ways:

- Start with a careful reading of the magazine's listing in this section of *Writer's Market*. Most listings offer very straightforward information about the magazine's slant and audience.
- Study a magazine's writer's guidelines, if available. These are written by each particular magazine's editors and are usually quite specific about the magazine's needs and readership.
- Check a magazine's website. Often, writer's guidelines and a selection of articles are included on a publication's website. A quick check of archived articles lets you know if ideas you want to propose have already been covered.
- Perhaps most important, read several current issues of the target magazine.
- If possible, talk to an editor by phone. Many will not take phone queries, particularly those at the higher-profile magazines, but many editors of smaller publications will spend the time to help a writer over the phone.

Writers who can correctly and consistently discern a publication's audience and deliver stories that speak to that target readership will win out every time over writers who simply write what they write and send it where they will.

WHAT EDITORS WANT

In nonfiction, editors continue to look for short feature articles covering specialized topics. Editors want crisp writing and expertise. If you are not an expert in the area about which you are writing, make yourself one through research.

Always query before sending your manuscript. Don't e-mail or fax a query unless an editor specifically mentions openness to this in the listing. Publishing, despite all the electronic advancements, is still a very paper-oriented industry. Once a piece has been accepted, however, many publishers prefer to receive your submission via disk or e-mail so they can avoid re-keying the manuscript.

Fiction editors prefer to receive complete short story manuscripts. Writers must keep in mind that marketing fiction is competitive and editors receive far more material than they can publish. For this reason, they often do not respond to submissions unless they are interested in using the story. Before submitting material, check the market's listing for fiction requirements to ensure your story is appropriate for that market. More comprehensive information on fiction markets can be found in *Novel & Short Story Writer's Market* (Writer's Digest Books).

Many writers make their articles do double duty, selling first or one-time rights to one publisher and second serial or reprint rights to another noncompeting market. The heading, **Reprints**, offers details when a market indicates whether they accept previously published submissions, with submission format and payment information if available.

Regardless of the type of writing you do, keep current on trends and changes in the industry. Trade magazines such as *Writer's Digest*, *Folio: The Magazine for Magazine Management*, and *Advertising Age* will keep you abreast of start-ups and shutdowns and other writing/business trends.

PAYMENT

Writers make their living by developing a good eye for detail. When it comes to marketing material, the one detail of interest to almost every writer is the question of payment. Most magazines listed here have indicated pay rates; some give very specific payment-per-word rates, while others state a range. Any agreement you come to with a magazine, whether verbal or written, should specify the payment you are to receive and when you are to receive it. Some magazines pay writers only after the piece in question has been published (on publication). Others pay as soon as they have accepted a piece and are sure they are going to use it (on acceptance).

In *Writer's Market*, those magazines that pay on acceptance have been highlighted with the phrase **pays on acceptance** set in bold type. Payment from these markets should reach you faster than from markets that pay on publication. There is, however, some variance in the industry as to what constitutes payment "on acceptance"—some writers have told us of two- and three-month waits for checks from markets that supposedly pay on acceptance. It is never out of line to ask an editor when you might expect to receive payment for an accepted article.

So what is a good pay rate? There are no standards; the principle of supply and demand operates at full throttle in the business of writing and publishing. As long as there are more writers than opportunities for publication, wages for freelancers will never skyrocket. Rates vary widely from one market to the next. Smaller circulation magazines and some departments of the larger magazines will pay a lower rate.

Editors know that the listings in *Writer's Market* are read and used by writers with a wide range of experience, from those as-yet unpublished writers just starting out, to those with a successful, profitable freelance career. As a result, many magazines publicly report pay rates in the lower end of their actual pay ranges. Experienced writers will be able to successfully negotiate higher pay rates for their material. Newer writers should be encouraged that as their reputation grows (along with their clip file), they will be able to command higher rates. The article "How Much Should I Charge?" on page 71, gives you an idea of pay ranges for different freelance jobs, including those directly associated with magazines.

INFORMATION AT-A-GLANCE

In the Consumer Magazine section, symbols identify comparative payment rates (**$–$$$$**); new listings (**N**); and magazines that do not accept unsolicited manuscripts (⊘). Different sections of *Writer's Market* include other symbols; check the front and back inside covers for an explanation of all the symbols used throughout the book.

Important information is highlighted in boldface—the "quick facts" you won't find in any other market book, but should know before you submit your work. To clearly identify the editorial "point person" at each magazine, the word "**Contact:**" identifies the appropriate person to query at each magazine. We also highlight what percentage of the magazine is freelance written, how many manuscripts a magazine buys per year of nonfiction, fiction, poetry, and fillers, and respective pay rates in each category.

Information on publications listed in the previous edition of *Writer's Market* but not included in this edition may be found in the General Index.

ANIMAL

The publications in this section deal with pets, racing and show horses, and other domestic animals and wildlife. Magazines about animals bred and raised for the market are classified in the Farm category of Trade, Technical & Professional Journals. Publications about horse racing can be found in the Sports section.

$ $ THE AMERICAN QUARTER HORSE JOURNAL, P.O. Box 32470, Amarillo TX 79120. (806)376-4811. Fax: (806)349-6400. E-mail: aqhajrnl@aqha.org. Website: www.aqha.com. Editor-in-Chief: Jim Jennings. **Contact:** Jim Bret Campbell, editor. **30% freelance written.** Prefers to work with published/established writers. Monthly official publication of the American Quarter Horse Association. Estab. 1948. Circ. 70,000. **Pays on acceptance.** Publishes ms an average of 3 months after acceptance. Byline given. Buys first North American serial rights. Submit seasonal material 6 months in advance. Accepts queries by mail, e-mail, fax. Responds in 2 weeks to queries.

O‑‑ Break in by "writing about topics tightly concentrated on the Quarter Horse industry while maintaining strong journalistic skills."

Nonfiction: Book excerpts, essays, how-to (fitting, grooming, showing, or anything that relates to owning, showing, or breeding), interview/profile (feature-type stories—must be about established horses or people who have made a contribution to the business), new product, opinion, personal experience, photo feature, technical (equine updates, new surgery procedures, etc.), travel, informational (educational clinics, current news). **Buys 40 mss/year.** Length: 800-2,000 words. **Pays $150-600.**

Photos: Reviews 2¼×2¼, 4×5, or 35mm transparencies, 4×5 glossy prints.

▣ The online magazine carries original content not found in the print edition. Contact: Jim Bret Campbell.

Tips: "Writers must have a knowledge of the horse business."

$ $ APPALOOSA JOURNAL, Appaloosa Horse Club, 2720 West Pullman Rd., Moscow ID 83843-0903. (208)882-5578. Fax: (208)882-8150. E-mail: journal@appaloosa.com. Website: www.appaloosajournal.com. **Contact:** Robin Hendrickson, editor. **20-40% freelance written.** Monthly magazine covering Appaloosa horses. Estab. 1946. Circ. 25,000. Pays on publication. Publishes ms an average of 3 months after acceptance. Byline given. Buys first North American serial rights. Responds in 1 month to queries; 2 months to mss. Sample copy for free. Writer's guidelines online.

• *Appaloosa Journal* no longer accepts material for columns.

Nonfiction: Historical/nostalgic, interview/profile, photo feature. **Buys 15-20 mss/year.** Query with or without published clips or send complete ms. Length: 800-2,000 words. **Pays $150-400.**

Photos: Send photos with submission. Payment varies. Captions, identification of subjects required.

▣ The online magazine carries original content not found in the print edition. Contact: Michelle Anderson, online editor.

Tips: "Articles by writers with horse knowledge, news sense, and photography skills are in great demand. If it's a strong article about an Appaloosa, the writer has a pretty good chance of publication. A good understanding of the breed and the industry, breeders, and owners is helpful. Make sure there's some substance and a unique twist."

$ $ $ ASPCA ANIMAL WATCH, The American Society for the Prevention of Cruelty to Animals, 345 Park Ave. S., 9th Floor, New York NY 10010. (212)876-7700. Fax: (212)410-0087. E-mail: editor@aspca.org. Website: www.aspca.org. **Contact:** Marion Lane, editor. **60% freelance written.** Quarterly magazine covering animal welfare: companion animals, endangered species, farm animals, wildlife, animals in entertainment (rodeo, circus, roadside zoos), laboratory animals and humane consumerism, i.e., fur, ivory, etc. "The ASPCA's mission is to alleviate pain, fear, and suffering in all animals. As the voice of the ASPCA, *Animal Watch* is our primary means of communicating with and informing our membership. In addition to in-depth, timely coverage and original reporting on important humane issues, *Animal Watch* provides practical advice on companion animal care and the human/companion animal bond. The ASPCA promotes the adoption and responsible care of companion animals, and through the magazine we encourage stewardship in areas such as training, behavior, exercise, and veterinary care." Estab. 1980. Circ. 330,000. **Pays on acceptance.** Publishes ms an average of 4 months after acceptance. Byline given. Buys first North American serial rights and the right to post stories on website for 6 months. Editorial lead time 6 months. Submit seasonal material 6 months in advance. Accepts simultaneous submissions. Responds in 3 months to queries. Sample copy for 10×13 SAE and 4 first-class stamps.

• Accepts queries by mail and e-mail, but e-mail preferred.

O‑‑ Break in with a submission to the Animals Abroad, Animal Watchers, or Light Watch columns.

Nonfiction: Essays, exposé, historical/nostalgic, how-to, humor (respectful), interview/profile, photo feature, investigative, news, advocacy. No stories told from animals' point of view, religious stories, fiction or poetry, articles with strident animal rights messages or articles with graphic details. **Buys 70-80 mss/year.** Length: 350-3,000 words. **Pays $100-900.**

Photos: State availability with submission. Reviews transparencies, prints, digital images (300 PSI). Negotiates payment individually. Captions, identification of subjects, model releases required.

Columns/Departments: Animal Watchers (profile of celebrity, ordinary person or group doing something unique to help animals), 150-900 words; Light Watch (humor and light news), 150-300 words; Animals Abroad (first person by someone abroad), 1,000 words; Animals & the Law (balanced report on a legal or legislative subject), 650-700 words; Viewpoint (personal essay on humane subjects), 650-700 words. **Buys 10 mss/year.** Query with or without published clips. **Pays $75-225.**

Tips: "The most important assets for an *Animal Watch* contributor are familiarity with the animal welfare movement in the U.S. and the ability to write lively, well-researched articles. We are always looking for ingenious problem-solving tips as well as positive stories about people and groups and businesses who are helping to protect animals in some way and may inspire others to do the same. We know the problems—share with us some solutions, some approaches that are working. Everything we publish includes 'How you can help....' We are as likely to assign a feature as a short piece for one of the departments."

N $ CANTER MAGAZINE, The Literary Journal for Horse People, P.O. Box 720522, San Jose CA 95172. E-mail: editors@cantermagazine.com. Website: www.cantermagazine.com. **Contact:** Becki Bell, editor. **60% freelance written.** Quarterly magazine covering horses. "We focus primarily on the horse's role in world history, culture, art, and literature." Estab. 2001. Circ. 2,000. Pays on publication. Publishes ms an average of 6 months after acceptance. Byline given. Offers 25% kill fee. Buys first North American serial, second serial (reprint), electronic rights. Editorial lead time 1 month. Submit seasonal material 6 months in advance. Accepts queries by e-mail. Accepts previously published material. Responds in 4-6 weeks to queries. Sample copy for $4.95 and 9×12 SAE with 4 first-class stamps. Writer's guidelines online.

Nonfiction: Essays, general interest, historical/nostalgic, interview/profile, photo feature, travel. No how-to, veterinary information, or practical horse ownership material. **Buys 16 mss/year.** Query. Length: 800-2,000 words. **Pays $10-25 for assigned articles.**

Photos: State availability with submission. Reviews 3×5 prints. Buys one-time rights. Offers no additional payment for photos accepted with ms. Captions, identification of subjects required.

Columns/Departments: Tales Retold (horse-related myths and legends), 500 words; Hoofnotes (personal experience), 500 words; The Hobby Horse (horse-related collectibles/hobbies), 1,000 words. **Buys 12 mss/year.** Query. **Pays $10-25.**

Fiction: Historical, humorous, mainstream. No fantasy, science fiction, etc. **Buys 4 mss/year.** Send complete ms. Length: 200-1,000 words. **Pays $10-25.**

Fillers: Newsbreaks. **Buys 8/year.** Length: 200-300 words. **Pays $5.**

Tips: "Always remember the horseless. We are geared toward both horse owners and nonowners, so avoid subjects and language that might only be meaningful to people who have horses of their own."

$ $ CAT FANCY, Cat Care for the Responsible Owner, Fancy Publications, Inc., P.O. Box 6050, Mission Viejo CA 92690. (949)855-8822. Website: www.catfancy.com. **Contact:** Bridget Johnson, editor. **90% freelance written.** Monthly magazine covering all aspects of responsible cat ownership. Estab. 1965. Pays on publication. Buys first North American serial rights. Editorial lead time 6 months. Responds in 3 months to queries. Writer's guidelines online.

- *Cat Fancy* does not accept unsolicited mss.

Nonfiction: Engaging presentation of expert, up-to-date information. Must be cat oriented. No unsolicited mss. Writing should not be gender specific. How-to, humor, photo feature, travel, behavior, health, lifestyle, cat culture, entertainment. **Buys 70 mss/year.** Query with published clips. Length: 1,000-2,000 words. **Pays $50-450.**

Photos: Seeking photos of happy, healthy, well-groomed cats and kittens in studio or indoor settings. Buys one-time rights. Negotiates payment individually. Captions, identification of subjects, model releases required.

Columns/Departments: Most of our columns are written by regular contributors who are recognized experts in their fields.

Tips: "No fiction or poetry. Please read recent issues to become acquainted with our style and content. Show us in your query how you can contribute something new and unique. No phone queries."

$ $ CATS USA, Guide to Buying and Caring for Purebred Kittens, Fancy Publications, P.O. Box 6050, Mission Viejo CA 92690. (949)855-8822. **Contact:** Bridget Johnson, editor. **90% freelance written.** Annual publication for purebred kitten buyers. Estab. 1993. Pays on publication. Buys first North American serial rights. Editorial lead time 6 months. Responds in 3 months to queries. Sample copy not available. Writer's guidelines for #10 SASE.

Nonfiction: Healthcare, training, breed information. **Buys 20 mss/year.** Query with published clips. Length: 1,000-2,000 words. **Pays $50-450.**

Photos: Looking for happy, healthy, well-groomed purebred cats and kittens in studio or indoor settings. Guidelines for #10 SASE. Buys one-time rights. Negotiates payment individually. Captions, identification of subjects, model releases required.

Tips: "No fiction or poetry. Please read a recent issue to become acquainted with our style and content. Show us in your query how you can contribute something new and unique. No phone queries."

$ $ THE CHRONICLE OF THE HORSE, P.O. Box 46, Middleburg VA 20118-0046. (540)687-6341. Fax: (540)687-3937. Website: www.chronofhorse.com. Editor: John Strassburger. Managing Editor: Trisha Booker. **Contact:** Beth Rasin, assistant editor. **80% freelance written.** Weekly magazine covering horses. "We cover English riding sports, including horse showing, grand prix jumping competitions, steeplechase racing, foxhunting, dressage, endurance riding, handicapped riding and combined training. We are the official publication for the national governing bodies of many of the above sports. We feature news, how-to articles on equitation and horse care and interviews with leaders in the various fields." Estab. 1937. Circ. 22,000. Pays for features on acceptance; news and other items on publication. Publishes ms an average of 4 months after acceptance. Byline given. Buys first North American serial rights, makes work-for-hire assignments. Submit seasonal material 3 months in advance. Accepts queries by mail, e-mail. Responds in 5-6 weeks to queries. Sample copy for \$2 and 9×12 SAE. Writer's guidelines online.

O‑ Break in by "clearing a small news assignment in your area ahead of time."

Nonfiction: General interest, historical/nostalgic (history of breeds, use of horses in other countries and times, art, etc.), how-to (trailer, train, design a course, save money, etc.), humor (centered on living with horses or horse people), interview/profile (of nationally known horsemen or the very unusual), technical (horse care, articles on feeding, injuries, care of foals, shoeing, etc.). Special issues: Steeplechase Racing (January); American Horse in Sport and Grand Prix Jumping (February); Horse Show (March); Intercollegiate (April); Kentucky 4-Star Preview (April); Junior and Pony (April); Dressage (June); Horse Care (July); Combined Training (August); Hunt Roster (September); Amateur (November); Stallion (December). No Q&A interviews, clinic reports, Western riding articles, personal experience or wild horses. **Buys 300 mss/year.** Query with or without published clips or send complete ms. Length: 6-7 pages. **Pays \$150-250.**

Photos: State availability with submission. Reviews prints or color slides; accepts color for b&w reproduction. Buys one-time rights. Pays \$25-30. Identification of subjects required.

Columns/Departments: Dressage, Combined Training, Horse Show, Horse Care, Racing over Fences, Young Entry (about young riders, geared for youth), Horses and Humanities, Hunting, Vaulting, Handicapped Riding, Trail Riding, 1,000-1,225 words; News of major competitions ("clear assignment with us first"), 1,500 words. Query with or without published clips or send complete ms. **Pays \$25-200.**

The online magazine carries original content not found in the print edition and includes writer's guidelines. Contact: Melinda Goslin, online editor.

Tips: "Get our guidelines. Our readers are sophisticated, competitive horsemen. Articles need to go beyond common knowledge. Freelancers often attempt too broad or too basic a subject. We welcome well-written news stories on major events, but clear the assignment with us."

\$ \$ DOG FANCY, Fancy Publications, Inc., P.O. Box 6050, Mission Viejo CA 92690-6050. Fax: (949)855-3045. E-mail: dogfancy@fancypubs.com. Website: www.dogfancy.com. **Contact:** Allan Reznik, editor. **95% freelance written.** Monthly magazine for men and women of all ages interested in all phases of dog ownership. Estab. 1970. Circ. 286,000. Pays on publication. Publishes ms an average of 6 months after acceptance. Byline given. Offers negotiable kill fee. Buys first North American serial, nonexclusive electronic and other rights. Submit seasonal material 6 months in advance. Accepts queries by mail. Responds in 2 months to queries. Sample copy for \$5.50. Writer's guidelines online.

Nonfiction: Book excerpts, general interest, how-to, humor, inspirational, interview/profile, personal experience, photo feature, travel. "No stories written from a dog's point of view." **Buys 100 mss/year.** Query. Length: 850-1,500 words. **Pays \$200-500.**

Photos: State availability with submission. Reviews contact sheets, transparencies, prints. Buys electronic rights. Offers no additional payment for photos accepted with ms.

Columns/Departments: Health and Medicine, 600-700 words; Training and Behavior, 800 words. **Buys 24 mss/year.** Query by mail only. **Pays \$300-400.**

The online magazine contains original content not found in the print version. Contact: Mary McHale.

Tips: "We're looking for the unique experience that enhances the dog/owner relationship—with the dog as the focus of the story, not the owner. Medical articles are assigned to veterinarians. Note that we write for a lay audience (nontechnical), but we do assume a certain level of intelligence. Read the magazine before making a pitch. Make sure your query is clear, concise, and relevant."

N \$ DOG SPORTS MAGAZINE, 5325 W. Mount Hope Rd., Lansing MI 48917. (517)322-2221. Fax: (517)322-9509. E-mail: chercar@asd.net. Website: www.dogsports.com. Editor: Cheryl Carlson. **5% freelance written.** Monthly tabloid covering working dogs. Estab. 1979. Circ. 2,000. Pays on publication. Publishes ms an average of 1 month after acceptance. Byline given. Buys first North American serial, second serial (reprint) rights. Editorial lead time 1 month. Submit seasonal material 1 month in advance. Accepts queries by mail, e-mail. Accepts previously published material. Accepts simultaneous submissions. Sample copy free or online.

Nonfiction: Essays, general interest, how-to (working dogs), humor, interview/profile, technical. **Buys 5 mss/year.** Send complete ms. **Pays \$50.**

Photos: State availability with submission. Reviews prints. Buys all rights. Offers no additional payment for photos accepted with ms. Captions, identification of subjects required.

N \$ DOG WORLD, 3 Burroughs, Irvine CA 92618. Website: www.dogworldmag.com. **Contact:** Maureen Kochan, editor. **95% freelance written.** Monthly magazine covering dogs. "We write for the serious dog enthusiast and participant, including breeders, veterinarians, exhibitors, groomers, agility competitors, etc., as well as a general audience interested in in-depth information about dogs." Estab. 1915. Circ. 58,000. Pays on publication. Byline given. Buys exclusive worldwide print rights for six months and nonexclusive electronic rights. Editorial lead time 6 months. Submit seasonal material 6 months in advance. Accepts queries by mail. Responds in 3 months to queries. Writer's guidelines for #10 SASE.

Nonfiction: General interest (on dogs including health care, veterinary medicine, grooming, legislation, responsible ownership, obedience training, kennel operations, dog sports, breed spotlights and histories), historical/nostalgic, new product, technical, canine art. Special issues: July (breed standards); March (puppy). No fluffy poems or pieces about dogs. **Buys approximately 50 mss/year.** Query by mail only with SASE. Query should include a list of points the story will cover and a list of experts the writer plans to interview. Length: 2,000-2,500 words. **Pays negotiable rate.** Sometimes pays expenses of writers on assignment.

Photos: State availability with submission. Buys one-time rights. Offers no additional payment for photos accepted with ms; negotiates payment individually for professional photos. Current rate for cover photo is $500; inside color photo $50-175; b&w $25-50, depending on size used. Payment on publication.

Tips: "Get a copy of the magazine and our writer's guidelines. Stories should cover a very narrowly focused topic in great depth. Be able to translate technical and medical articles into language the average reader can understand. Be ready to quote experts through live interviews."

N $ $ EQUESTRIAN MAGAZINE, The Official Magazine of Equestrian Sport Since 1937, American Horse Shows Association, 4047 Iron Works Parkway, Lexington KY 40511. (859)225-6923. Fax: (859)231-6662. E-mail: editor@equestrian.org. Website: www.equestrian.org. **Contact:** Christine E. Stafford, editor-in-chief. **10-30% freelance written.** Magazine published 10 times/year covering the equestrian sport. Estab. 1937. Circ. 75,000. Pays on publication. Byline given. Offers 50% kill fee. Buys first North American serial, first rights. Editorial lead time 1-5 months. Accepts queries by mail, e-mail, fax, phone. Sample copy and writer's guidelines free.

Nonfiction: Interview/profile, technical, all equestrian-related. **Buys 20-30 mss/year.** Query with published clips. Length: 500-3,500 words. **Pays $200-500.** Sometimes pays expenses of writers on assignment.

Photos: State availability with submission. Reviews contact sheets. Buys one-time rights. Offers $50-200/photo. Captions, identification of subjects, model releases required.

Columns/Departments: Horses of the Past (famous equines); Horse People (famous horsemen/women), both 500-1,000 words. **Buys 20-30 mss/year.** Query with published clips. **Pays $100.**

Tips: "Write via e-mail in first instance with samples, résumé, then mail original clips."

$ EQUINE JOURNAL, 103 Roxbury St., Keene NH 03431-8801. (603)357-4271. Fax: (603)357-7851. E-mail: editorial@equinejournal.com. Website: www.equinejournal.com. **Contact:** Kathleen Labonville, managing editor. **90% freelance written.** Monthly tabloid covering horses—all breeds, all disciplines. "To educate, entertain, and enable amateurs and professionals alike to stay on top of new developments in the field. Covers horse-related activities from all corners of New England, New York, New Jersey, Pennsylvania, and the Midwest." Estab. 1988. Circ. 26,000. Pays on publication. Byline given. Buys first North American serial, electronic rights. Editorial lead time 3 months. Submit seasonal material 4 months in advance. Accepts queries by mail, e-mail, fax, phone. Responds in 2 months to queries. Writer's guidelines online.

Nonfiction: General interest, how-to, interview/profile. **Buys 100 mss/year.** Query with published clips or send complete ms. Length: 1,500-3,000 words.

Photos: Send photos with submission. Reviews prints. Pays $10.

Columns/Departments: Horse Health (health-related topics), 1,200-1,500 words. **Buys 12 mss/year.** Query.

Fillers: Short humor. Length: 500-1,000 words. **Pays $40-75.**

N EQUUS, PRIMEDIA Enthusiast Group, 656 Quince Orchard Rd., Suite 600, Gaithersburg MD 20878-1409. (301)977-3900. Fax: (301)990-9015. E-mail: equuslts@aol.com. Website: www.equisearch.com. Editor: Laurie Prinz. Monthly magazine covering equine behavior. Provides the latest information from the world's top veterinarians, equine researchers, riders and trainers. Circ. 148,465. Sample copy not available.

$ $ FIELD TRIAL MAGAZINE, Androscoggin Publishing, Inc., P.O. Box 98, Milan NH 03588-0098. (617)449-6767. Fax: (603)449-2462. E-mail: birddog@ncia.net. Website: www.fielddog.com/ftm. **Contact:** Craig Doherty, editor. **75% freelance written.** Quarterly magazine covering field trials for pointing dogs. "Our readers are knowledgeable sports men and women who want interesting and informative articles about their sport." Estab. 1997. Circ. 6,000. Pays on publication. Publishes ms an average of 6 months after acceptance. Byline given. Buys first North American serial rights. Editorial lead time 3 months. Submit seasonal material 6 months in advance. Accepts queries by mail, e-mail, fax. Accepts simultaneous submissions. Responds in 2 weeks to queries; 2 months to mss. Sample copy free or online. Writer's guidelines online.

Nonfiction: Book excerpts, essays, general interest, historical/nostalgic, how-to, interview/profile, opinion, personal experience. No hunting articles. **Buys 12-16 mss/year.** Query. Length: 1,000-3,000 words. **Pays $100-300.**

Photos: Send photos with submission. Buys one-time rights. Offers no additional payment for photos accepted with ms. Captions, identification of subjects required.

Fiction: Fiction that deals with bird dogs and field trials. **Buys 4 mss/year.** Send complete ms. Length: 1,000-2,500 words. **Pays $100-250.**

Tips: "Make sure you have correct and accurate information—we'll work with a writer who has good solid info even if the writing needs work."

N $ $ THE GAITED HORSE, The One Magazine for all Gaited Horses, P.O. Box 3070, Deer Park WA 99006-3070. (509)276-4930. Fax: (877)320-2233. E-mail: tgheditor@thegaitedhorse.com. Website: www.thegaitedhorse.com. **Contact:** Rhonda Hart Poe, editor. Quarterly magazine. "Subject matter must relate in some way to gaited horses." Estab. 1998. Circ. 12,000. Pays on publication. Publishes ms an average of 2 months after acceptance. Byline given. Buys first North American serial rights, makes work-for-hire assignments. Editorial lead time 4 months. Submit seasonal material 4 months in advance. Accepts queries by mail, e-mail. Accepts simultaneous submissions. Responds in 6 weeks to queries; 1 month to mss. Sample copy for $3. Writer's guidelines online.

Nonfiction: Wants anything related to gaited horses, lifestyles, art, etc. Book excerpts, essays, exposé, general interest (gaited horses), historical/nostalgic, how-to, humor, interview/profile, new product, personal experience, photo feature, travel. "No 'My first horse' stories." **Buys 25 mss/year.** Query or send complete ms. Length: 1,000-2,500 words. **Pays $50-300.**

Photos: State availability of or send photos with submission. Reviews prints (3×5 or larger). Buys one-time rights. Negotiates payment individually. Captions, identification of subjects, model releases required.

Columns/Departments: Through the Legal Paces (equine owners rights & responsibilities); Horse Cents (financial advice for horse owners); Health Check (vet advice); Smoother Trails (trail riding), all 500-1,000 words. **Buys 24 mss/year.** Query. **Pays $100.**

Fillers: Anecdotes, newsbreaks, short humor. **Buys 20/year.** Length: 5-300 words. **Pays $10-50.**

Tips: "We are actively seeking to develop writers from within the various gaited breeds and equine disciplines. If you have a unique perspective on these horses, we would love to hear from you. Submit a query that targets any aspect of gaited horses and you'll have my attention."

$ THE GREYHOUND REVIEW, P.O. Box 543, Abilene KS 67410-0543. (785)263-4660. Fax: (785)263-4689. E-mail: nga@jc.net. Website: www.ngagreyhounds.com. Editor: Gary Guccione. **Contact:** Tim Horan, managing editor. **20% freelance written.** Monthly magazine covering greyhound breeding, training and racing. Estab. 1911. Circ. 4,000. **Pays on acceptance.** Byline given. Buys first rights. Submit seasonal material 2 months in advance. Responds in 2 weeks to queries; 1 month to mss. Sample copy for $3. Writer's guidelines free.

Nonfiction: "Articles must be targeted at the greyhound industry: from hard news, special events at racetracks to the latest medical discoveries." How-to, interview/profile, personal experience. Do not submit gambling systems. **Buys 24 mss/year.** Query. Length: 1,000-10,000 words. **Pays $85-150.**

Reprints: Send photocopy. Pays 100% of amount paid for original article.

Photos: State availability with submission. Reviews 35mm transparencies, 8×10 prints. Buys one-time rights. Pays $10-50 photo. Identification of subjects required.

$ HORSE & COUNTRY CANADA, Equine Publications, Inc., 422 Kitley Line 3, Toledo ON K0E 1Y0, Canada. (613)275-1684. Fax: (613)275-1807. **Contact:** Judith H. McCartney, editor. **40% freelance written.** Bimonthly magazine covering equestrian issues. "A celebration of equestrian sport and the country way of life." Estab. 1994. Circ. 14,000. Pays on publication. Publishes ms an average of 3 months after acceptance. Byline sometimes given. Buys one-time rights. Accepts queries by mail.

Nonfiction: Book excerpts, historical/nostalgic, how-to, inspirational, new product, travel. Query with published clips. Length: 1,200-1,700 words. **Pays $25-150.** Sometimes pays expenses of writers on assignment.

Photos: Send photos with submission. Reviews prints. Buys one-time rights. Pays $15-125/photo or negotiates payment individually. Captions required.

Columns/Departments: Back to Basics (care for horses); Ask the Experts (how-to with horses); Nutrition (for horses), all 800 words. Query with published clips. **Pays $25-150.**

$ $ $ HORSE & RIDER, The Magazine of Western Riding, Primedia, P.O. Box 4101, 741 Corporate Circle, Suite A, Golden CO 80401. (720)836-1257. Fax: (720)836-1245. E-mail: horse&rider@primediamags.com. Website: www.horseandrider.com. **Contact:** Darrell Dodds, editor/associate publisher. **10% freelance written.** Monthly magazine covering Western horse industry, competition, recreation. "*Horse & Rider*'s mission is to educate, inform, and entertain both competitive and recreational riders with tightly focused training articles, practical stable management techniques, hands-on healthcare tips, safe trail-riding practices, well-researched consumer advice, and a behind-the-scenes, you-are-there approach to major equine events." Estab. 1961. Circ. 164,000. **Pays on acceptance.** Publishes ms an average of 1 year after acceptance. Byline given. Offers $75 kill fee. Buys first North American serial rights. Editorial lead time 2 months. Submit seasonal material 6 months in advance. Accepts queries by mail. Responds in 3 months to queries; 3 months to mss. Sample copy and writer's guidelines online.

- Does *not accept* e-mail submissions.

Nonfiction: Book excerpts, general interest, how-to (horse training, horsemanship), humor, interview/profile, new product, personal experience, photo feature, travel, horse health care, trail riding. **Buys 5-10 mss/year.** Send complete ms. Length: 1,000-3,000 words. **Pays $150-1,000.**

Photos: State availability of or send photos with submission. Buys rights on assignment or stock. Negotiates payment individually. Captions, identification of subjects, model releases required.

The online magazine carries original content not found in the print edition. Contact: Darrell Dodds.

Tips: Writers should have "patience, ability to accept critical editing, and extensive knowledge of the Western horse industry and our publication."

$ $ HORSE ILLUSTRATED, The Magazine for Responsible Horse Owners, Fancy Publications, Inc., P.O. Box 6050, Mission Viejo CA 92690-6050. (949)855-8822. Fax: (949)855-3045. E-mail: horseillustrated@fancypubs.com. Website: www.horseillustratedmagazine.com. Managing Editor: Elizabeth Moyer. **Contact:** Moira Harris, editor. **90% freelance written.** Prefers to work with published/established writers but will work with new/unpublished writers. Monthly magazine covering all aspects of horse ownership. "Our readers are adults, mostly women, between the ages of 18 and 40; stories should be geared to that age group and reflect responsible horse care." Estab. 1976. Circ. 216,930. Pays on publication. Publishes ms an average of 8 months after acceptance. Byline given. Buys one-time rights, requires first North American rights among equine publications. Submit seasonal material 6 months in advance. Accepts queries by mail. Responds in 3 months to queries. Writer's guidelines for #10 SASE.

Nonfiction: "We are looking for authoritative, in-depth features on trends and issues in the horse industry. Such articles must be queried first with a detailed outline of the article and clips. We rarely have a need for fiction." General interest, historical/nostalgic, how-to (horse care, training, veterinary care), inspirational, photo feature. No "little girl" horse stories, "cowboy and Indian" stories or anything not *directly* relating to horses. **Buys 20 mss/year.** Query or send complete ms. Length: 1,000-2,000 words. **Pays $100-400.**

Photos: Send photos with submission. Reviews 35mm and medium format transparencies, 4×6 prints.

Tips: "Freelancers can break in at this publication with feature articles on Western and English training methods; veterinary and general care how-to articles; and horse sports articles. We rarely use personal experience articles. Submit photos with training and how-to articles whenever possible. We have a very good record of developing new freelancers into regular contributors/columnists. We are always looking for fresh talent, but certainly enjoy working with established writers who 'know the ropes' as well. We are accepting less unsolicited freelance work—much is now assigned and contracted."

$ $ THE HORSE, Your Guide to Equine Health Care, P.O. Box 4680, Lexington KY 40544-4680. (859)276-6771. Fax: (859)276-4450. E-mail: kherbert@thehorse.com. Website: www.thehorse.com. Managing Editor: Christy West. **Contact:** Kimberly S. Herbert, editor. **75% freelance written.** Monthly magazine covering equine health and care. *The Horse* is an educational/news magazine geared toward the hands-on horse owner. Estab. 1983. Circ. 40,000. **Pays on acceptance.** Publishes ms an average of 3 months after acceptance. Byline given. Buys first world and electronic rights Accepts queries by mail, e-mail. Responds in 3 months to queries. Sample copy for $2.95 or online. Writer's guidelines online.

O‑ Break in with short horse health news items.

Nonfiction: How-to, technical, topical interviews. "No first-person experiences not from professionals; this is a technical magazine to inform horse owners." **Buys 90 mss/year.** Query with published clips. Length: 250-4,000 words. **Pays $50-710 for assigned articles.**

Photos: Send photos with submission. Reviews transparencies. $35-350. Captions, identification of subjects required.

Columns/Departments: News Front (news on horse health), 100-500 words; Equinomics (economics of horse ownership); Step by Step (feet and leg care); Nutrition; Reproduction; Back to Basics, all 1,500-2,200 words. **Buys 50 mss/year.** Query with published clips. **Pays $50-400.**

The online magazine carries original content not found in the print edition, mostly news items.

Tips: "We publish reliable horse health care and management information from top industry professionals and researchers around the world. Manuscript must be submitted electronically or on disk."

N $ HORSEPOWER, Magazine for Young Horse Lovers, Horse Publications Group, P.O. Box 670, Aurora ON L4G 4J9, Canada. Fax: (905)841-1530. E-mail: info@horse-canada.com. Website: www.horse-canada.com. **Contact:** Susan Stafford, editor. **50% freelance written.** Bimonthly magazine covering horse care and training for teens and preteens (ages 8-16). "Safety when dealing with horses is our first priority. Also, explaining techniques, etc., in terms kids can understand without over-simplifying." Estab. 1988. Circ. 10,000. Pays on publication. Publishes ms an average of 6 months after acceptance. Byline given. Buys one-time rights. Editorial lead time 2 months. Submit seasonal material 4 months in advance. Accepts queries by mail, e-mail, fax. Accepts simultaneous submissions. Responds in 3 weeks to queries; 6 months to mss. Sample copy for $2.95. Writer's guidelines for #10 SASE.

Nonfiction: How-to (horse care, grooming, training, etc.), humor, interview/profile (famouse riders). **Buys 6 mss/year.** Query or send complete ms. Length: 500-1,200 words. **Pays $50-75.** Pays in contributor copies upon request.

Reprints: Accepts previously published submissions.

Photos: Send photos with submission. Reviews 4×6 prints, GIF/JPEG files. Buys one-time rights. Offers $10-15/photo. Captions required.

Columns/Departments: How To ... (step-by-step), 1,000 words. **Buys 3 mss/year.** Query or send complete ms. **Pays $50-75.**

Fiction: Adventure, humorous, slice-of-life vignettes. Nothing too young for the readership or stories about "How I Won the Big Race," etc. **Buys 2 mss/year.** Length: 500-1,200 words. **Pays $50-75.**

Tips: "Writers must have a firm grasp on all aspects of horse ownership, training, health care, etc. Most of our readers are quite intelligent and do not want to be talked down to. Articles must not be too simplistic."

$ I LOVE CATS, I Love Cats Publishing, 16 Meadow Hill Lane, Armonk NY 10504. (908)222-0990. Fax: (908)222-8228. E-mail: yankee@izzy.net. Website: www.iluvcats.com. **Contact:** Lisa Allmendinger, editor. **100% freelance written.** Bimonthly magazine. "*I Love Cats* is a general interest cat magazine for the entire family. It caters to cat lovers of all ages. The stories in the magazine include fiction, nonfiction, how-to, humorous, and columns for the cat lover." Estab. 1989. Circ. 50,000. Pays on publication. Publishes ms an average of 2 years after acceptance. Byline given. Must sign copyright consent form. Buys all rights. Editorial lead time 6 months. Submit seasonal material 9 months in advance. Accepts queries by mail, e-mail. Responds in 3 months to queries. Sample copy for $6. Writer's guidelines online.

Nonfiction: Essays, general interest, how-to, humor, inspirational, interview/profile, new product, opinion, personal experience, photo feature. No poetry. **Buys 100 mss/year.** Send complete ms. Length: 500-1,000 words. **Pays $50-125, contributor copies or other premiums if requested.** Sometimes pays expenses of writers on assignment.

Photos: Please send copies; art will no longer be returned. Send photos with submission. Buys all rights. Offers no additional payment for photos accepted with ms. Identification of subjects required.

Fiction: Adventure, fantasy, historical, humorous, mainstream, mystery, novel excerpts, slice-of-life vignettes, suspense. "This is a family magazine. No graphic violence, pornography or other inappropriate material. *I Love Cats* is strictly 'G-rated.'" **Buys 100 mss/year.** Send complete ms. Length: 500-1,000 words. **Pays $25-125.**

Fillers: Anecdotes, facts, short humor. **Buys 25/year. Pays $25.**

Tips: "Please keep stories short and concise. Send complete manuscript with photos, if possible. I buy lots of first-time authors. Nonfiction pieces with color photos are always in short supply. With the exception of the standing columns, the rest of the magazine is open to freelancers. Be witty, humorous, or take a different approach to writing."

$ $ KITTENS USA, Adopting and Caring for Your Kitten, Fancy Publications, P.O. Box 6050, Mission Viejo CA 92690. (949)855-8822. **Contact:** Bridget Johnson, editor. **90% freelance written.** Annual publication for kitten buyers. Estab. 1997. Pays on publication. Buys first North American serial rights. Editorial lead time 6 months. Responds in 3 months to queries. Sample copy not available. Writer's guidelines for #10 SASE.

Nonfiction: Healthcare, training, adoption. **Buys 20 mss/year.** Query with published clips. Length: 1,000-2,000 words. **Pays $50-450.**

Photos: Looking for happy, healthy, well-groomed kittens in studio or indoor settings. Guidelines for #10 SASE. Buys one-time rights. Negotiates payment individually. Captions, identification of subjects, model releases required.

Tips: "No fiction or poetry. Please read recent issues to become acquainted with our style and content. Show us in your query how you can contribute something new and unique. No phone queries."

$ MINIATURE DONKEY TALK, Miniature Donkey Talk, Inc., 1338 Hughes Shop Rd., Westminster MD 21158-2911. (410)875-0118. Fax: (410)857-9145. E-mail: minidonk@qis.net. Website: www.qis.net/~minidonk/mdt.htm. Bonnie Gross, editor. **65% freelance written.** Bimonthly magazine covering miniature donkeys or donkeys, with articles on healthcare, promotion, and management of donkeys for owners, breeders, or donkey lovers. Estab. 1987. Circ. 4,925. **Pays on acceptance.** Publishes ms an average of 4 months after acceptance. Byline given. Buys first, second serial (reprint) rights. Editorial lead time 2 months. Submit seasonal material 3 months in advance. Accepts queries by mail, e-mail, fax. Accepts previously published material. Responds in 2 weeks to queries; 1 month to mss. Sample copy for $5. Writer's guidelines free.

Nonfiction: Book excerpts, humor, interview/profile, personal experience. **Buys 6 mss/year.** Query with published clips. Length: 700-7,000 words. **Pays $25-150.**

Photos: State availability with submission. Reviews 3×5 prints. Buys one-time rights. Offers no additional payment for photos accepted with ms. Identification of subjects required.

Columns/Departments: Humor, 2,000 words; Healthcare, 2,000-5,000 words; Management, 2,000 words. **Buys 50 mss/year.** Query. **Pays $25-100.**

Fiction: Humorous. **Buys 6 mss/year.** Query. Length: 3,000-7,000 words. **Pays $25-100.**

Fillers: Anecdotes, facts, gags to be illustrated by cartoonist, short humor. **Buys 12/year.** Length: 200-2,000 words. **Pays $15-35.**

Tips: "Simply send your manuscript. If on topic and appropriate, good possibility it will be published. We accept the following types of material: breeder profiles—either of yourself or another breeder. The full address and/or telephone number of the breeder will not appear in the article as this would constitute advertising; coverage of nonshow events such as fairs, donkey gatherings, holiday events, etc. We do not pay for coverage of an event that you were involved in organizing; detailed or specific instructional or training material. We're always interested in people's training methods; relevant, informative equine health pieces. We much prefer they deal specifically with donkeys; however, we will consider articles specifically geared toward horses. If at all possible, substitute the word 'horse' for donkey. We reserve the right to edit, change, delete, or add to health articles as we deem appropriate. Please be very careful in the accuracy of advice or treatment and review the material with a veterinarian; farm management articles; and fictional stories on donkeys."

$ $ MUSHING, Stellar Communications, Inc., P.O. Box 149, Ester AK 99725-0149. (907)479-0454. Fax: (907)479-3137. E-mail: editor@mushing.com. Website: www.mushing.com. Publisher: Todd Hoener. **Contact:** Deirdre Alida Helfferich, managing editor. Bimonthly magazine covering all aspects of the growing sports of dogsledding, skijoring, carting, dog packing, and weight pulling. "*Mushing* promotes responsible dog care through feature articles and updates on working animal health care, safety, nutrition, and training." Estab. 1987. Circ. 6,000. Pays within 3 months of publication. Publishes ms an average of 4 months after acceptance. Byline given. Buys first, second serial (reprint) rights. Submit seasonal material 4 months in advance. Accepts queries by mail, e-mail, fax, phone. Responds in 8 months to queries. Sample copy for $5 ($6 US to Canada). Writer's guidelines online.

Nonfiction: "We consider articles on canine health and nutrition, sled dog behavior and training, musher profiles and interviews, equipment how-to's, trail tips, expedition and race accounts, innovations, sled dog history, current issues, personal experiences, and humor." Historical/nostalgic, how-to. Special issues: Iditarod and Long-Distance Racing (January/February); Expeditions/Peak of Race Season (March/April); Health and Nutrition (May/June); Musher and Dog Profiles, Summer Activities (July/August); Equipment, Fall Training (September/October); Races and Places (November/December). Query with or without published clips. Considers complete ms with SASE. Length: 1,000-2,500 words. **Pays $50-250.** Sometimes pays expenses of writers on assignment.

Photos: "We look for good b&w and quality color for covers and specials." Send photos with submission. Reviews contact sheets, negatives, transparencies, prints. Buys one time and second reprint rights. Pays $20-165/photo. Captions, identification of subjects, model releases required.

Columns/Departments: Length: 500-1,000 words. Query with or without published clips or send complete ms.

Fiction: Considers short, well-written and relevant or timely fiction. Query with or without published clips or send complete ms. **Payment varies.**

Fillers: Anecdotes, facts, newsbreaks, short humor, cartoons, puzzles. Length: 100-250 words. **Pays $20-35.**

Tips: "Read our magazine. Know something about dog-driven, dog-powered sports."

N $ $ PAINT HORSE JOURNAL, American Paint Horse Association, P.O. Box 961023, Fort Worth TX 76161-0023. (817)834-2742. Fax: (817)222-8466. E-mail: jnice@apha.com. Website: www.apha.com. **Contact:** Jennifer Nice, editor. **10% freelance written.** Works with a small number of new/unpublished writers/year. Monthly magazine for people who raise, breed and show Paint horses. Estab. 1966. Circ. 30,000. **Pays on acceptance.** Byline given. Offers negotiable kill fee. Buys first North American serial rights. first North American serial, reprint Submit seasonal material 3 months in advance. Accepts queries by mail, e-mail, fax. Sample copy for $4.50. Writer's guidelines online.

Nonfiction: General interest (personality pieces on well-known owners of Paints), historical/nostalgic (Paint horses in the past—particular horses and the breed in general), how-to (train and show horses), photo feature (Paint horses). **Buys 4-5 mss/year.** Query. Length: 1,000-2,000 words. **Pays $35-450.**

Reprints: Send ms with rights for sale noted by e-mail preferrably. Pays 30-50% of amount paid for an original article.

Photos: Photos must illustrate article and must include registered Paint horses. Send photos with submission. Reviews 35mm or larger transparencies, 3×5 or larger color glossy prints. Offers no additional payment for photos accepted with accompanying ms. Captions required.

Tips: "Well-written first person articles are welcomed. Submit items that show a definite understanding of the horse business. Be sure you understand precisely what a Paint horse is as defined by the American Paint Horse Association. Use proper equine terminology. Photos with copy are almost always essential."

$ ROCKY MOUNTAIN RIDER MAGAZINE, Regional All-Breed Horse Monthly, P.O. Box 1011, Hamilton MT 59840. (406)363-4085. Fax: (406)363-1056. Website: www.rockymountainrider.com. **Contact:** Natalie Riehl, editor. **90% freelance written.** Monthly magazine for horse owners and enthusiasts. Estab. 1993. Circ. 14,500. Pays on publication. Publishes ms an average of 6 months after acceptance. Byline given. Buys one-time rights. Submit seasonal material 6 months in advance. Accepts simultaneous submissions. Responds in 1 month to queries; 2 months to mss. Sample copy for free. Writer's guidelines for #10 SASE.

Nonfiction: Book excerpts, essays, general interest, historical/nostalgic, humor, interview/profile, new product, personal experience, photo feature, travel, cowboy poetry. **Buys 100 mss/year.** Send complete ms. Length: 500-2,000 words. **Pays $15-90.**

Photos: Send photos with submission. Reviews 3×5 prints. Buys one-time rights. Pays $5/photo. Captions, identification of subjects required.

Poetry: Light verse, traditional. **Buys 25 poems/year.** Submit maximum 10 poems. Length: 6-36 lines. **Pays $10.**

Fillers: Anecdotes, facts, gags to be illustrated by cartoonist, short humor. Length: 200-750 words. **Pays $15.**

Tips: "*RMR* is looking for positive, human interest stories that appeal to an audience of horsepeople. We accept profiles of unusual people or animals, history, humor, anecdotes, cowboy poetry, coverage of regional events, and new products. We aren't looking for many 'how-to' or training articles, and are not currently looking at any fiction."

$ $ TROPICAL FISH HOBBYIST MAGAZINE, The World's Most Widely Read Aquarium Monthly, TFH Publications, Inc., One TFH Plaza, Neptune City NJ 07753. (732)988-8400. Fax: (732)988-9635. E-mail: editor@tfh.com. **Contact:** David Borchowitz, editor. **90% freelance written.** Monthly magazine covering tropical fish. Estab. 1952. Circ. 35,000. **Pays on acceptance.** Byline given. Buys all rights. Editorial lead time 3 months. Submit seasonal material 6 months in advance. Accepts queries by e-mail. Responds immediately on electronic queries to queries. Writer's guidelines by e-mail.

Nonfiction: "We cover any aspect of aquarium science, aquaculture, and the tropical fish hobby. Our readership is diverse—from neophytes to mini reef specialists. We require well-researched, well-written, and factually accurate copy, preferably with photos." **Buys 100-150 mss/year. Pays $100-250.**

Photos: State availability with submission. Reviews 2×2 transparencies. Buys multiple nonexclusive rights. Negotiates payment individually. Identification of subjects, model releases required.

Tips: "With few exceptions, all communication and submission must be electronic. We want factual, interesting, and relevant articles about the aquarium hobby written by people who are obviously knowledgeable. We publish an enormous variety of article types. Review several past issues to get an idea of the scope."

ART & ARCHITECTURE

Listed here are publications about art, art history, specific art forms and architecture written for art patrons, architects, artists, and art enthusiasts. Publications addressing the business and management side of the art industry are listed in the Art, Design & Collectibles category of the Trade section. Trade publications for architecture can be found in Building Interiors, and Construction & Contracting sections.

$ $ THE AMERICAN ART JOURNAL, Kennedy Galleries, Inc., 730 Fifth Ave., New York NY 10019. (212)541-9600. Fax: (212)977-3833. **Contact:** Jayne A. Kuchna, editor-in-chief. Prefers to work with published/established writers; works with a small number of new/unpublished writers each year. Annual magazine covering American art history of the 17th, 18th, 19th and 20th centuries, including painting, sculpture, architecture, photography, cultural history, etc., for people with a serious interest in American art, and who are already knowledgeable about the subject. Readers are scholars, curators, collectors, students of American art, or persons with a strong interest in Americana. Circ. 2,000. **Pays on acceptance.** Publishes ms an average of 6 months after acceptance. Byline given. all rights, but will reassign rights to writers. Responds in 2 months to queries. Sample copy for $18.

Nonfiction: "All articles are about some phase or aspect of American art history. No how-to articles written in a casual or 'folksy' style. Writing style must be formal and serious." Historical. **Buys 10-15 mss/year.** Length: 2,500-8,000 words. **Pays $400-600.**

Photos: Reviews b&w only. Purchased with accompanying ms. Offers no additional payment for photos. Captions required.

Tips: "Articles must be scholarly, thoroughly documented, well-researched, well-written and illustrated. Whenever possible, all manuscripts must be accompanied by b&w photographs which have been integrated into the text by the use of numbers."

N $ $ AMERICAN ARTIST, VNU Business Media, 770 Broadway, New York NY 10003-9595. (646)654-5220. Fax: (646)654-5514. E-mail: mail@myamericanartist.com. Website: www.myamericanartist.com. **Contact:** M. Stephen Doherty, editor-in-chief. Monthly magazine covering art. Written to provide information on outstanding representational artists living in the U.S. Estab. 1937. Circ. 116,526. Editorial lead time 18 weeks. Accepts queries by mail. Responds in 6-8 weeks to queries. Sample copy for $3.95. Writer's guidelines by e-mail.

Nonfiction: Essays, exposé, interview/profile, personal experience, technical. Query with published clips and résumé. Length: 1,500-2,000 words. **Pays $500.**

$ $ $ AMERICANSTYLE MAGAZINE, The Rosen Group, 3000 Chestnut Ave., Suite 304, Baltimore MD 21211. (410)889-3093. Fax: (410)243-7089. E-mail: hoped@rosengrp.com. Website: www.americanstyle.com. **Contact:** Hope Daniels, editor. **80% freelance written.** Quarterly magazine covering arts, crafts, travel, and interior design. "*AmericanStyle* is a full-color lifestyle publication for people who love art. Our mandate is to nurture collectors with information that will increase their passion for contemporary art and craft and the artists who create it. *AmericanStyle*'s primary audience is contemporary craft collectors and enthusiasts. Readers are college-educated, age 35+, high-income earners with the financial means to collect art and craft, and to travel to national art and craft events in pursuit of their passions." Estab. 1994. Circ. 60,000. Pays on publication. Publishes ms an average of 6 months after acceptance. Buys first North American serial rights. Editorial lead time 9 months. Submit seasonal material 1 year in advance. Accepts queries by mail, e-mail, fax. Sample copy for $3. Writer's guidelines online.

- *AmericanStyle* is especially interested in freelance ideas about arts travel, profiles of contemporary craft collectors, and established studio artists.

Nonfiction: Specialized arts/crafts interests. Length: 300-2,500 words. **Pays $500-800.** Sometimes pays expenses of writers on assignment.

Photos: Send photos with submission. Reviews oversized transparencies, 35mm slides. Negotiates payment individually. Captions required.

Columns/Departments: Portfolio (profiles of emerging artists); Arts Walk; Origins; One on One, all 800-1,200 words. Query with published clips. **Pays $500-700.**

Tips: "This is not a hobby-crafter magazine. Country crafts or home crafting is not our market. We focus on contemporary American craft art, such as ceramics, wood, fiber, glass, metal."

N $ ARCHITECTURAL DIGEST, The International Magazine of Interior Design, Conde Nast Publications, Inc., 6300 Wilshire Blvd., Suite 1100, Los Angeles CA 90048. (323)965-3700. Fax: (323)937-1458. E-mail: letters@achdigest.com. Website: www.archdigest.com. Editor: Paige Rense. **Contact:** Submissions Editor. Monthly magazine covering architecture. A global magazine that offers a look at the homes of the rich and famous. Other topics include travel, shopping, automobiles, and technology. Estab. 1920. Circ. 821,992. Accepts queries by mail. Sample copy for $5 on newstands. Writer's guidelines by e-mail.

Nonfiction: Send 3 samples of your work with a brief cover letter. Include a paragraph on who else you've written for and paragraph on any ideas you have on stories for *Architectural Digest.* Query with published clips.

$ $ $ ART & ANTIQUES, TransWorld Publishing, Inc., 2100 Powers Ferry Rd., Suite 300, Atlanta GA 30339. (770)955-5656. Fax: (770)952-0669. Editor: Barbara S. Tapp. **Contact:** Patti Verbanas, managing editor. **90% freelance written.** Magazine published 11 times/year covering fine art and antique collectibles and the people who collect them and/or create them. "*Art & Antiques* is the authoritative source for elegant, sophisticated coverage of the treasures collectors love, the places to discover them, and the unique ways collectors use them to enrich their environments." Circ. 170,000. **Pays on acceptance.** Byline given. Offers 25% kill fee or $250. Buys all rights. Editorial lead time 8 months. Submit seasonal material 8 months in advance. Accepts queries by mail. Responds in 6 weeks to queries; 2 months to mss. Sample copy and writer's guidelines free.

Nonfiction: "We publish 1 'interior design with art and antiques' focus feature a month." Essays, interview/profile (especially interested in profiles featuring collectors outside the Northwest and Northern California areas). Special issues: Designing with art & antiques (September and April); Asian art & antiques (February); Contemporary art (January and December). **Buys 200 mss/year.** Query with or without published clips. Length: 200-1,200 words. **Pays $200-1,200 for assigned articles.** Pays $50 toward expenses of writers on assignment.

Photos: Scouting shots. Send photos with submission. Reviews contact sheets, transparencies, prints. Captions, identification of subjects required.

Columns/Departments: Art & Antiques Update (trend coverage and timely news of issues and personalities), 100-350 words; Review (thoughts and criticisms on a variety of worldwide art exhibitions throughout the year), 600-800 words; Value Judgements (experts highlight popular to undiscovered areas of collecting), 600-800 words; Emerging Artists (an artist on the cusp of discovery), 600-800 words; Discoveries (collections in lesser-known museums and homes open to the public), 800-900 words; Studio Session (peek into the studio of an artist who is currently hot or is a revered veteran allowing the reader to watch the artist in action), 800-900 words; Then & Now (the best reproductions being created today and the craftspeople behind the work), 800-900 words; World View (major art and antiques news worldwide; visuals preferred but not necessary), 600-800 words; Travelling Collector (hottest art and antiques destinations, dictated by those on editorial calendar; visuals preferred but not necessary), 800-900 words; Essay (first-person piece tackling a topic in a nonacademic way; visuals preferred but not necessary); Profile (profiles those who are noteworthy and describes their interests and passions; very character-driven and should reveal their personalities), 600-800 words. **Buys 200 mss/year.** Query by mail only with or without published clips. **Pays $150-900.**

Fillers: Facts, newsbreaks. **Buys 22/year.** Length: 150-300 words. **Pays $150-300.**

The online magazine carries original content not found in the print edition, though there is no payment. Contact: Joel Groover (jgroover@billian.com).

Tips: "Send scouting shots with your queries. We are a visual magazine and no idea will be considered without visuals. We are good about responding to writers in a timely fashion—excessive phone calls are not appreciated, but do check in if you haven't heard from us in 2 months. We like colorful, lively and creative writing."

N $ ART CALENDAR MAGAZINE, The Business Magazine for Visual Artists, P.O. Box 2675, Salisbury MD 21802. Fax: (410)749-9626. E-mail: info@artcalendar.com. Website: www.artcalendar.com. **Contact:** Carolyn Proeber, publisher. **100% freelance written.** Monthly magazine. Estab. 1986. Circ. 7,700. Pays on publication. Accepts previously published material. Sample copy for $5 prepaid. Writer's guidelines online.

- "We welcome nuts-and-bolts, practical articles of interest to serious visual artists, emerging or professional." Examples: marketing how-to's, first-person stories on how an artist has built his career or an aspect of it, interviews with artists (business/career-building emphasis), and pieces on business practices and other topics of use to artists. The tone of our magazine is practical, can-do, and uplifting. Writers may use as many or as few words as necessary to tell the whole story.

Nonfiction: Essays (the psychology of creativity), how-to, interview/profile (successful artists with a focus on what made them successful — not necessarily rich and famous artists, but the guy-next-door who paints all day and makes a decent living doing it.), personal experience (artists making a difference (art teachers working with disabled students, bringing a community together, etc.), technical (new equipment, new media, computer software, Internet sites that are way cool that no one has heard of yet), Cartoons, art law, including pending legislation that affects artists (copyright law, Internet regulations, etc.). "We like nuts-and-bolts information about making a living as an artist. We do not run reviews or art historical pieces, nor do we like writing characterized by "critic-speak," philosophical hyperbole, psychological arrogance, politics, or New Age religion. Also, we do not condone a get-rich-quick attitude." Send complete ms. **Pays $100.** We can make other arrangements in lieu of pay, i.e. a subscription or copies of the magazine in which your article appears.

Reprints: Send photocopy or typed ms and information about when and where the material previously appeared. Pays $50.

Photos: Reviews b&w glossy or color prints. Pays $25.

Columns/Departments: "If an artist or freelancer sends us good articles regularly, and based on results we feel that s/he is able to produce a column at least three times per year, we will invite him to be a Contributing Writer. If a gifted artist-writer can commit to producing an article on a monthly basis, we will offer him a regular column and the title Contributing Editor." Send complete ms.

$ $ ART SPIRIT!, Art Spirit! Inc., P.O. Box 460669, Fort Lauderdale FL 33346. (954)763-3338. Fax: (954)763-4481. E-mail: sherryf@achildismissing.org. **Contact:** Sherry Friedlander, editor. **90% freelance written.** Magazine published 3 times/year. "Art Spirit! covers music, art, drama, dance, special events." Estab. 1998. Circ. 20,000. Pays on publication. Publishes ms an average of 10 weeks after acceptance. Byline given. Buys first North American serial rights. Editorial lead time 3 months. Accepts queries by mail, e-mail, fax, phone. Accepts previously published material. Responds in 2 weeks to queries. Sample copy by e-mail. Writer's guidelines free.

Nonfiction: "Must be about arts." Interview/profile, photo feature. Length: 650-1,500 words. **Pays $100-200.**

Photos: State availability of or send photos with submission.

Tips: "Information should interest the arts group."

$ ARTICHOKE, Writings About the Visual Arts, Artichoke Publishing, 208-901 Jervis St., Vancouver BC V6E 2B6, Canada. Fax: (604)683-1941. E-mail: editor@artichoke.ca. Website: www.artichoke.ca. **Contact:** Paula Gustafson, editor. **90% freelance written.** Triannual magazine. "*Artichoke* is Western Canada's visual arts magazine. Writers must be familiar with Canadian art and artists." Estab. 1989. Circ. 1,500. **Pays on acceptance.** Publishes ms an average of 6 months after acceptance. Byline given. Offers 50% kill fee. Buys one-time rights. Editorial lead time 6 months. Accepts queries by mail, e-mail, fax. Accepts simultaneous submissions. Responds in 1 week to queries; 2 weeks to mss. Sample copy for free. Writer's guidelines online.

Nonfiction: Essays, interview/profile, opinion, critical reviews about Canadian visual art. "*Artichoke* does not publish fiction, poetry, or academic jargon." **Buys 100 mss/year.** Query with or without published clips or send complete ms. Length: 1,000-2,500 words. **Pays $125.**

Photos: State availability of or send photos with submission. Reviews transparencies, prints. Buys one-time rights. Offers no additional payment for photos accepted with ms. Captions, identification of subjects required.

$ $ THE ARTIST'S MAGAZINE, F&W Publications, Inc., 4700 E. Galbraith Rd., Cincinnati OH 45236. (513)531-2690, ext. 1467. Fax: (513)531-2902. E-mail: tamedit@fwpubs.com. Website: www.artistsmagazine.com. Editor: Sandra Carpenter. **Contact:** Senior Editor. **60% freelance written.** Works with a large number of new/unpublished writers each year. Monthly magazine covering primarily two-dimensional art instruction for working artists. "Ours is a highly visual approach to teaching the serious amateur artist techniques that will help him improve his skills and market his work. The style should be crisp and immediately engaging." Circ. 200,000. Pays on publication. Publishes ms an average of 6 months after acceptance. Bionote given for feature material. Offers 25% kill fee. Buys first North American serial, second serial (reprint) rights. Responds in 3 months to queries. Sample copy for $4.50. Writer's guidelines online.

- Writers must have working knowledge of art techniques. This magazine's most consistent need is for instructional feature articles written in the artist's voice.

Nonfiction: "The emphasis must be on how the reader can learn some method of improving his artwork; or the marketing of it." Instructional only—how an artist uses a particular technique, how he handles a particular subject or medium, or how he markets his work. No unillustrated articles; no seasonal material; no travel articles; no profiles. **Buys 60 mss/year.** Length: 1,200-1,800 words. **Pays $200-350 and up.** Sometimes pays expenses of writers on assignment.

Photos: "Transparencies—in 4×5 or 35mm slide format—are required with every accepted article since these are essential for our instructional format. Full captions must accompany these." Buys one-time rights.

Tips: "Look at several current issues and read the author's guidelines carefully. Submissions must include artwork. Remember that our readers are fine artists."

$ ARTNEWS, ABC, 48 W. 38th St., New York NY 10018. (212)398-1690. Fax: (212)768-4002. E-mail: mgronlunde@artnews.com. Website: www.artnewsonline.com. **Contact:** Melissa Gronlunde, executive editor. Monthly "*Artnews* reports on art, personalities, issues, trends and events that shape the international art world. Investigative features focus on art ranging from old masters to contemporary, including painting, sculpture, prints and photography. Regular columns offer exhibition and book reviews, travel destinations, investment and appreciation advice, design insights and updates on major art world figures." Estab. 1902. Circ. 82,911. Accepts queries by mail, e-mail, fax, phone. Sample copy not available.

$ AZURE DESIGN, ARCHITECTURE AND ART, 460 Richmond St. W., Suite 601, Toronto ON M5V 1Y1, Canada. (416)203-9674. Fax: (416)203-9842. E-mail: azure@azureonline.com. Website: www.azureonline.com. **Contact:** Nelda Rodger, editor. **50% freelance written.** Magazine covering design and architecture. Estab. 1985. Circ. 20,000. Pays on publication. Publishes ms an average of 1 month after acceptance. Offers variable kill fee. Buys first rights. Editorial lead time up to 45 days. Responds in 6 weeks to queries. Sample copy not available.

Nonfiction: Buys 25-30 mss/year. Length: 350-2,000 words. **Payment varies.**

Columns/Departments: Trailer (essay/photo on something from the built environment); and Forms & Functions (coming exhibitions, happenings in world of design), both 300-350 words. **Buys 30 mss/year.** Query. **Payment varies.**

Tips: "Try to understand what the magazine is about. Writers must be well versed in the field of architecture and design. It's very unusual to get something from someone I haven't worked quite closely with and gotten a sense of who the writer is. The best way to introduce yourself is by sending clips or writing samples and describing what your background is in the field."

N $ BOMB MAGAZINE, New Arts Publications, 594 Broadway, Suite 905, New York NY 10012-3289. (212)4313943. Fax: (212)4315880. E-mail: info@bombsite.com. Website: www.bombsite.com. Editor: Betsy Sussler. Managing Editor: Nell McClister. Quarterly magazine providing interviews between artists, writers, musicians, directors and actors. Written, edited and produced by industry professionals and funded by those interested in the arts. Publishes "work which is unconventional and contains an edge, whether it be in style or subject matter." Estab. 1981. Circ. 36,000. Pays on publication. Publishes ms an average of 3-6 months after acceptance. Buys first, one-time rights. Editorial lead time 3-4 months. Accepts queries by mail. Responds in 3-5 months to mss. Sample copy for $7, plus $1.42 postage and handling. Writer's guidelines by e-mail.

Fiction: Send completed ms with SASE. Experimental, novel excerpts, contemporary. No genre: romance, science fiction, horror, western. Length: 10-12 pages average. **Pays $100, and contributor's copies.**

Poetry: Send completed ms with SASE. Submit no more than 25 pages. Length: No more than 25 pages in length.

Tips: Mss should be typed, double-spaced, proofread adn should be final drafts.

$ $ DIRECT ART MAGAZINE, Slow Art Productions, 870 Sixth Ave., New York NY 10001. (212)725-0999. E-mail: slowart@aol.com. Website: www.slowart.com. **Contact:** Paul Winslow, editor. **75% freelance written.** Semiannual fine art magazine covering alternative, anti-establishment, left-leaning fine art. Estab. 1998. Circ. 10,000. **Pays on acceptance.** Byline sometimes given. Buys one-time, electronic rights. Editorial lead time 2 months. Submit seasonal material 3 months in advance. Accepts queries by mail, e-mail. Accepts simultaneous submissions. Responds in 2 weeks to queries; 1 month to mss. Sample copy for 9×12 SAE and 10 first-class stamps. Writer's guidelines for #10 SASE.

Nonfiction: T.P. Lowens, managing editor. Essays, exposé, historical/nostalgic, how-to, humor, inspirational, interview/profile, opinion, personal experience, photo feature, technical. **Buys 4-6 mss/year.** Query with published clips. Length: 1,000-3,000 words. **Pays $100-500.**

Reprints: Accepts previously published submissions.

Photos: State availability of or send photos with submission. Reviews 35mm slide transparencies, digital files on CD (TIF format). Buys one-time rights. Negotiates payment individually.

Columns/Departments: Query with published clips. **Pays $100-500.**

N $ ESPACE, Sculpture, Centre de Diffusion 3D, 4888 St. Denis, Montreal QC H2J 2L6, Canada. (514)844-9858. Fax: (514)844-3661. E-mail: espace@espace-sculpture.com. Website: www.espace-sculpture.com. **Contact:** S. Fisette, editor. **95% freelance written.** Quarterly magazine covering sculpture events. "Canada's only sculpture publication, *Espace* represents a critical tool for the understanding of contemporary sculpture. Published 4 times a year, in English and French, *Espace* features interviews, in-depth articles, and special issues related to various aspects of three dimensionality. Foreign contributors guarantee an international perspective and diffusion." Estab. 1987. Circ. 1,400. Pays on publication. Publishes ms an average of 3 months after acceptance. Byline given. Buys all rights. Editorial lead time 5 months. Submit seasonal material 3 months in advance. Accepts queries by mail. Accepts simultaneous submissions. Sample copy for free.

Nonfiction: Essays, exposé. **Buys 60 mss/year.** Query. Length: 1,000-1,400 words. **Pays $50/page.**

Reprints: Accepts previously published submissions.

Photos: Send photos with submission. Reviews transparencies, prints. Offers no additional payment for photos accepted with ms.

$ L.A. ARCHITECT, The Magazine of Design in Southern California, Balcony Press, 512 E. Wilson, Glendale CA 91206. (818)956-5313. Fax: (818)956-5904. E-mail: laura@balconypress.com. Website: www.laarch.com. **Contact:** Laura Hull, editor. **80% freelance written.** Bimonthly magazine covering architecture, interiors, landscape, and other design disciplines. "*L.A. Architect* is interested in architecture, interiors, product, graphics, and landscape design as well as news about the arts. We encourage designers to keep us informed on projects, techniques, and products that are innovative, new, or nationally newsworthy. We are especially interested in new and renovated projects that illustrate a high degree of design integrity and unique answers to typical problems in the urban cultural and physical environment." Estab. 1999. Circ. 20,000. Pays on publication. Publishes ms an average of 3 months after acceptance. Byline given. Makes work-for-hire assignments. Editorial lead time 4 months. Submit seasonal material 4 months in advance. Accepts queries by mail, e-mail, fax. Responds in 1 month to queries; 1 month to mss. Sample copy for $3. Writer's guidelines online.

Nonfiction: Book excerpts, essays, historical/nostalgic, interview/profile, new product. "No technical, foo-foo interiors, or non-Southern California subjects." **Buys 20 mss/year.** Length: 500-2,000 words. **Payment negotiable.**

Photos: State availability with submission. Buys one-time rights. Offers no additional payment for photos accepted with ms. Captions, identification of subjects, model releases required.

Tips: "Our magazine focuses on contemporary and cutting-edge work either happening in Southern California or designed by a Southern California designer. We like to find little-known talent which has not been widely published. We are not like *Architectural Digest* in flavor so avoid highly decorative subjects. Each project, product, or event should be accompanied by a story proposal or brief description and select images. Do not send original art without our written request; we make every effort to return materials we are unable to use, but this is sometimes difficult and we must make advance arrangements for original art."

N $ LOLA, P.O. Box 265, Station C, Toronto ON M6J 3P4, Canada. (416)532-5258. E-mail: catherine@lolamagazine.com. Website: www.lolamagazine.com. Executive Editor: Sally McKay. **Contact:** Catherine Osborne, editor. **90% freelance written.** Quarterly magazine covering contemporary visual arts. "*Lola* is a contemporary visual arts magazine published 4 times a year. *Lola* offers readers profiles on contemporary artists, spotlights on art trends, and opinionated and critical views that are written in a compelling and intelligent journalistic manner." Estab. 1997. Circ. 27,000. Pays on publication. Publishes ms an average of 3-6 months after acceptance. Byline given. Offers 30% kill fee. Buys first, electronic rights. Editorial lead time 2-4 months. Submit seasonal material 6 months in advance. Accepts queries by mail, e-mail. Responds in 6 weeks to queries; 3 months to mss. Sample copy for $5 (Canadian). Writer's guidelines online.

Nonfiction: Essays, historical/nostalgic, humor, interview/profile, opinion, contemporary visual art. No fiction, poetry, illustration, graphic design, or academic writing that is not written in a journalistic manner. Query with published clips. Length: 600-2,000 words. **Pays 50¢/word.** Sometimes pays expenses of writers on assignment.

Photos: Sally McKay, executive editor/art director. State availability with submission. Reviews GIF/JPEG files. Buys one-time rights. Negotiates payment individually.

Tips: "Familiarize yourself with our magazine before sending queries and story ideas. Our focus is on Canadian contemporary art, and in particular, Toronto. Our main interest is in articles that relate to Canadian readers."

$ $ THE MAGAZINE ANTIQUES, Brant Publications, 575 Broadway, New York NY 10012. (212)941-2800. Fax: (212)941-2819. **Contact:** Allison Ledes, editor. **75% freelance written.** Monthly magazine. "Articles should present new information in a scholarly format (with footnotes) on the fine and decorative arts, architecture, historic preservation, and landscape architecture." Estab. 1922. Circ. 61,556. Pays on publication. Publishes ms an average of 6 months after acceptance. Byline given. Buys all rights. Editorial lead time 6 months. Submit seasonal material 6 months in advance. Responds in 3 weeks to queries; 6 months to mss. Sample copy for $10.50.

Nonfiction: Historical/nostalgic, scholarly. **Buys 50 mss/year.** Length: 2,850-3,000 words. **Pays $250-500.** Sometimes pays expenses of writers on assignment.

Photos: State availability with submission. Reviews contact sheets, negatives, transparencies, prints. Buys one-time rights. Captions, identification of subjects required.

$ $ $ $ METROPOLIS, The Magazine of Architecture and Design, Bellerophon Publications, 61 W. 23rd St., 4th Floor, New York NY 10010. (212)627-9977. Fax: (212)627-9988. E-mail: edit@metropolismag.com. Website: www.metropolismag.com. Executive Editor: Martin Pedersen. **Contact:** Julien Devereux, managing editor. **80% freelance written.** Monthly magazine (combined issues February/March and August/September) for consumers interested in architecture and design. Estab. 1981. Circ. 45,000. Pays 60-90 days after acceptance. Publishes ms an average of 3 months after acceptance. Byline given. Makes work-for-hire assignments. Submit seasonal material 3 months in advance. Accepts queries by mail, e-mail, fax. Responds in 8 months to queries. Sample copy for $7. Writer's guidelines online.

Nonfiction: Martin Pedersen, executive editor. Essays (design, architecture, urban planning issues and ideas), interview/profile (of multi-disciplinary designers/architects). No profiles on individual architectural practices, information from public relations firms, or fine arts. **Buys 30 mss/year.** Length: 1,500-4,000 words. **Pays $1,500-4,000.**

Photos: Reviews contact sheets, 35mm or 4×5 transparencies, 8×10 b&w prints. Buys one-time rights. Payment offered for certain photos. Captions required.

Columns/Departments: The Metropolis Observed (architecture, design, and city planning news features), 100-1,200 words, **pays $100-1,200**; Perspective (opinion or personal observation of architecture and design), 1,200 words, **pays $1,200**; Enterprise (the business/development of architecture and design), 1,500 words, **pays $1,500**; In Review (architecture and book review essays), 1,500 words, **pays $1,500**. Direct queries to Julien Devereux, managing editor. **Buys 40 mss/year.** Query with published clips.

Tips: "Metropolis strives to tell the story of design to a lay person with an interest in the built environment, while keeping the professional designer engaged. The magazine examines the various design disciplines (architecture, interior design, product design, graphic design, planning, and preservation) and their social/cultural context. We're looking for the new, the obscure, or the wonderful. Also, be patient and don't expect an immediate answer after submission of query."

N $ $ MIX, independent art and culture magazine, Parallelogramme Artist-Run Culture and Publishing, Inc., 401 Richmond St. #446, Toronto ON M5V 3A8, Canada. (416)506-1012. Fax: (416)506-0141. E-mail: info@mixmagazine.com. Website: www.mixmagazine.com. **Contact:** Claudia McKay, editor. **95% freelance written.** Quarterly magazine covering Artist-Run gallery activities. "Mix represents and investigates contemporary artistic practices and issues, especially in the progressive Canadian artist-run scene." Estab. 1975. Circ. 3,500. Pays on publication. Publishes ms an average of 6 months after acceptance. Byline given. Offers 40% kill fee. Buys first North American serial rights. Editorial lead time 6 months. Submit seasonal material 4 months in advance. Accepts queries by mail, e-mail, fax. Responds in 2 months to queries; 3 months to mss. Sample copy for $6.95, 8½ × 10¼ SAE and 6 first-class stamps. Writer's guidelines online.

Nonfiction: Essays, interview/profile. **Buys 12-20 mss/year.** Query with published clips. Length: 750-3,500 words. **Pays $100-450.**

Reprints: Send photocopy of article and information about when and where the article previously appeared.

Photos: State availability with submission. Buys one-time rights. Captions, identification of subjects required.

Columns/Departments: Features, 1,000-3,000 words; Art Reviews, 500 words. Query with published clips. **Pays $100-450.**

The online magazine carries original content not found in the print edition and includes writer's guidelines.

Tips: "Read the magazine and other contemporary art magazines. Understand the idea 'artist-run.' We're not interested in 'artsy-phartsy' editorial but rather pieces that are critical, dynamic and would be of interest to nonartists too."

$ $ MODERNISM MAGAZINE, 333 N. Main St., Lambertville NJ 08530. (609)397-4104. Fax: (609)397-9377. E-mail: cara@modernismmagazine.com. Website: www.modernismmagazine.com. Publisher: David Rago. **Contact:** Cara Greenberg, editor-in-chief. **70% freelance written.** Quarterly magazine covering 20th century art and design. "We are interested in objects and the people who created them. Our coverage begins in the 1920s with Art Deco and related movements, and ends with 1980s Post-Modernism, leaving contemporary design to other magazines. Our emphasis is on the decorative arts—furniture, pottery, glass, textiles, metalwork, and so on—but we're moving toward more coverage of painting and sculpture." Estab. 1998. Circ. 20,000. Pays on publication. Publishes ms an average of 4 months after acceptance. Byline given. Offers 25% kill fee. Buys all rights. Editorial lead time 6 months. Submit seasonal material 6 months in advance. Accepts queries by mail, e-mail, fax. Accepts previously published material. Accepts simultaneous submissions. Responds in 1 month to queries. Sample copy for $6.95. Writer's guidelines free.

Nonfiction: Book excerpts, essays, historical/nostalgic, interview/profile, new product, photo feature. "No first-person." **Buys 20 mss/year.** Query with published clips. Length: 2,000-2,500 words. **Pays $400 for assigned articles.**

Reprints: Accepts previously published submissions.

Photos: State availability of or send photos with submission. Reviews contact sheets, transparencies, prints. Buys one-time rights. Negotiates payment individually. Captions, identification of subjects required.

Tips: "Articles should be well-researched, carefully reported, and directed at a popular audience with a special interest in the Modernist movement. Please don't assume readers have prior familiarity with your subject; be sure to tell us the who, what, why, when, and how of whatever you're discussing."

$ $ SOUTHWEST ART, Sabot Publishing, 5444 Westheimer Rd., Suite 1440, Houston TX 77056. (713)296-7900. Fax: (713)850-1314. E-mail: southwestart@southwestart.com. Website: www.southwestart.com. **Contact:** Editors. **60% freelance written.** Monthly magazine "directed to art collectors interested in artists, market trends, and art history of the American West." Estab. 1971. Circ. 60,000. **Pays on acceptance.** Publishes ms an average of 1 year after acceptance. Byline given. Offers $125 kill fee. Not copyrighted. Submit seasonal material 8 months in advance. Accepts queries by mail, e-mail, fax. Responds in 6 months to mss.

Nonfiction: Book excerpts, interview/profile. No fiction or poetry. **Buys 70 mss/year.** Query with published clips. Length: 1,400-1,600 words. **Pays $600 for assigned articles.**

Photos: "Photographs, color print-outs, and videotapes will not be considered." Reviews 35mm, 2¼, 4×5 transparencies. Negotiates rights. Captions, identification of subjects required.

Tips: "Research the Southwest art market, send slides or transparencies with queries, send writing samples demonstrating knowledge of the art world."

N $ WATERCOLOR, VNU Business Media, 770 Broadway, New York NY 10003. (646)654-5600. Fax: (646)654-5514. E-mail: mail@americanartist.com. Website: www.myamericanartist.com. Editor: E. Lynne Moss. Quarterly magazine. Devoted to watermedia artists. Circ. 80,000. Editorial lead time 4 months. Sample copy not available.

$ $ $ WILDLIFE ART, The Art Journal of the Natural World, Pothole Publications, Inc., 1428 E. Cliff Rd., Burnsville MN 55337. Fax: (952)736-1030. E-mail: publisher@winternet.com. Website: www.wildlifeartmag.com. Editor-in-Chief: Robert Koenke. **Contact:** Beth Mischek, editor. **80% freelance written.** Bimonthly magazine. "*Wildlife Art* is the world's largest wildlife art magazine. Features cover interviews on living artists as well as wildlife art masters, illustrators and conservation organizations. Special emphasis on landscape and plein-air paintings. Audience is publishers, collectors, galleries, museums, show promoters worldwide." Estab. 1982. Circ. 50,000. **Pays on acceptance.** Publishes ms an average of 6 months after acceptance. Byline given. Offers negotiable kill fee. Buys second serial (reprint) rights. Accepts queries by mail, phone. Responds in 6 months to queries. Sample copy for 9×12 SAE and 10 first-class stamps. Writer's guidelines online.

Nonfiction: General interest, historical/nostalgic, interview/profile. **Buys 40 mss/year.** Query with published clips, include artwork samples. Length: 800-5,000 words. **Pays $150-900.**

Columns/Departments: Buys 6 mss/year. Pays $100-300.

Tips: "Best way to break in is to offer concrete story ideas; new talent; a new unique twist of artistic excellence."

ASSOCIATIONS

Association publications allow writers to write for national audiences while covering local stories. If your town has a Kiwanis, Lions, or Rotary Club chapter, one of its projects might merit a story in the club's magazine. If you are a member of the organization, find out before you write an article if the publication pays members for stories; some associations do not. In addition, some association publications gather their own club information and rely on freelancers solely for outside features. Be sure to find out what these policies are before you submit a manuscript. Club-financed magazines that carry material not directly related to the group's activities are classified by their subject matter in the Consumer and Trade sections.

N $ $ $ $ AAUW OUTLOOK, American Association of University Women, 1111 16th St. NW, Washington DC 20036. (202)785-7737. E-mail: editor@aauw.org. Website: www.aauw.org. **Contact:** Jodi Lipson, editor. **10% freelance written.** Published 2-4 times/year. Magazine covering women, equity, and education. Circ. 150,000. **Pays on acceptance.** Publishes ms an average of 1 month after acceptance. Byline given. Buys first North American serial rights. Editorial lead time 3 months. Accepts queries by e-mail, phone.

Nonfiction: Interview/profile, photo feature, book reviews and features. **Buys 3 mss/year.** Query with published clips. Length: 1,500-2,000 words. **Pays $1,200-1,600 for assigned articles.**

Photos: State availability with submission. Buys one-time rights. Offers $25-50 per photo.

Columns/Departments: Book Review (women, education, equity), 500 words. **Buys 2-3 mss/year.** Query. **Pays $200-500.**

Tips: "Contact us first. We plan our editorial calendar, identify topics, then hire a writer to write that specific article. Tell us where you got our name and send clips."

$ AMERICA@WORK, AFL-CIO, 815 16th St. NW, Washington DC 20006. Fax: (202)508-6908. Website: www.aflcio.org. **Contact:** Tula A. Connell, editor. **10% freelance written.** Monthly magazine covering issues of interest to working families/union members. Estab. 1996. Circ. 160,000. Pays on publication. Publishes ms an average of 3 months after acceptance. Byline given. Buys first North American serial rights. Editorial lead time 2 months. Submit seasonal material 3 months in advance. Accepts queries by mail, fax. Sample copy for $2.50. Writer's guidelines not available.

Nonfiction: Essays, how-to, interview/profile, historical. **Buys 5-6 mss/year.** Query. Length: 600-2,000 words. **Payment varies depending on length.**

Photos: State availability with submission. Buys one-time rights. Identification of subjects, model releases required.

N $ $ $ $ AMERICAN EDUCATOR, American Federation of Teachers, 555 New Jersey Ave., Washington DC 20001. (202)879-4420. Fax: (202)879-4534. E-mail: amered@aft.org. Website: www.aft.org/american_educator/index.html. Editor: Ruth Wattenberg. **Contact:** Lisa Hansel, assistant editor. **50% freelance written.** Quarterly magazine covering education, condition of children, and labor issues. "*American Educator*, the quaterly magazine of the American Federation of Teachers, reaches over 800,000 public school teachers, higher education faculty, and education researchers and policymakers. The magazine concentrates on significant ideas and practices in education, civics, and the condition of children in America and around the world." Estab. 1977. Circ. 850,000. Pays on publication. Publishes ms an average of 2-6 months after acceptance. Byline given. Offers 50% kill fee. Buys one-time, electronic rights. Editorial lead time 1 year. Submit seasonal material 6 months in advance. Accepts queries by mail, e-mail, fax. Accepts previously published material. Accepts simultaneous submissions. Responds in 2 months to queries; 6 months to mss. Sample copy online. Writer's guidelines online.

Nonfiction: Book excerpts, essays, historical/nostalgic, interview/profile, discussions of educational research. No pieces that are not supportive of the public schools. **Buys 8 mss/year.** Query with published clips. Length: 1,000-7,000 words. **Pays $750-3,000 for assigned articles; $300-1,000 for unsolicited articles.** Pays expenses of writers on assignment.

Photos: State availability with submission. Reviews contact sheets, negatives, transparencies, 8×10 prints, GIF/JPEG files. Buys one-time rights. Negotiates payment individually. Captions, identification of subjects, model releases required.

N $ $ CANADIAN ESCAPES, August Communications, 225-530 Century St., Winnipeg MB R3H 0Y3, Canada. Fax: (866)957-0217. E-mail: r.naud@august.ca. Managing Editor: Sean Thiessen. **Contact:** Rachel Naud, editor. **60% freelance written.** Bimonthly magazine covering Canadian travel. "*Canadian Escapes* is a bimonthly association magazine written for the Tourism Industry Association of Canada. It promotes Canadian travel." Estab. 2002. Circ. 2,500. Pays 1 month after publication. Publishes ms an average of 1-2 months after acceptance. Byline given. Buys all rights. Editorial lead time 4 months. Submit seasonal material 6 months in advance. Accepts queries by mail, e-mail, fax. Sample copy for free.

Nonfiction: "All articles are written for general travelers. The magazine is targeted to industry tourism professionals."

General interest, historical/nostalgic, interview/profile, travel. **Buys 30 mss/year.** Query with published clips. Length: 1,000-2,500 words. **Pays 15-30¢/word.**

Photos: State availability with submission. Reviews GIF/JPEG files. Buys all rights. Negotiates payment individually. Captions required.

Tips: "Review the Tourism Industry Association of Canada's website, www.tiac-aitc.ca."

$ $ DAC NEWS, Official Publication of the Detroit Athletic Club, Detroit Athletic Club, 241 Madison Ave., Detroit MI 48226. (313)442-1034. Fax: (313)442-1047. E-mail: kenv@thedac.com. **Contact:** Kenneth Voyles, editor/publisher. **20% freelance written.** Magazine published 10 times/year. "*DAC News* is the magazine for Detroit Athletic Club members. It covers club news and events, plus general interest features." Estab. 1916. Circ. 4,700. Pays on publication. Publishes ms an average of 3 months after acceptance. Byline given. Buys one-time rights, makes work-for-hire assignments. Editorial lead time 3 months. Submit seasonal material 3 months in advance. Accepts queries by mail, phone. Accepts previously published material. Responds in 1 month to queries. Sample copy for free.

Nonfiction: General interest, historical/nostalgic, photo feature. "No politics or social issues—this is an entertainment magazine. We do not acccept unsolicited manuscripts or queries for travel articles." **Buys 2-3 mss/year.** Length: 1,000-2,000 words. **Pays $100-500.** Sometimes pays expenses of writers on assignment.

Photos: Illustrations only. State availability with submission. Reviews transparencies, 4×6 prints. Buys one-time rights. Negotiates payment individually. Captions, identification of subjects, model releases required.

Tips: "Review our editorial calendar. It tends to repeat from year to year, so a freelancer with a fresh approach to one of these topics will get our attention quickly. It helps if articles have some connection with the DAC, but this is not absolutely necessary. We also welcome articles on Detroit history, Michigan history, or automotive history."

N $ $ DCM, Data Center Management: Bringing Insight and Ideas to the Data Center Community, Atwood Publishing, LLC, 11600 College Blvd., Suite 100, Overland Park KS 66210. Fax: (913)469-0806. E-mail: dstack@atwood.com. Website: www.afcom.com. Executive Editor: Len Eckhaus. **Contact:** Debi Stack, managing editor. **50% freelance written.** Bimonthly magazine covering data center management. "*DCM* is the slick, 4-color, bimonthly publication for members of AFCOM, the leading association for data center management." Estab. 1988. Circ. 4,000 worldwide. Pays on acceptance for assigned articles and on publication for unsolicited articles. Publishes ms an average of 3 months after acceptance. Byline given. Offers 0-10% kill fee. Buys all rights. Editorial lead time 6-12 months. Submit seasonal material 6 months in advance. Responds in 1-3 weeks to queries; 1-3 months to mss. Writer's guidelines online.

- Prefers queries by e-mail.

Nonfiction: How-to, technical, management as it relates to and includes examples of data centers and data center managers. Special issues: "The January/February issue is the annual 'Emerging Technologies' issue. Articles for this issue are visionary and product neutral." No product reviews, interviews/profiles, reprints of any kind, or general tech or management articles. **Buys 15+ mss/year.** Query with published clips. Length: 2,000 word maximum. **Pays 30¢/word and up, based on writer's expertise.**

Photos: "We rarely consider freelance photos." State availability with submission. Reviews GIF/JPEG files. Buys one-time rights. Offers no additional payment for photos accepted with ms. Identification of subjects, model releases required.

Tips: "See Top 10 Reasons for Rejection online."

$ $ THE ELKS MAGAZINE, 425 W. Diversey P, Chicago IL 60614-6196. (773)755-4740. E-mail: elksmag@elks.org. Website: www.elks.org/elksmag. Editor: Fred D. Oakes. **Contact:** Anna L. Idol, managing editor. **25% freelance written.** Magazine published 10 times/year with basic mission of being the "voice of the Elks." All material concerning the news of the Elks is written in-house. Estab. 1922. Circ. 1,120,000. **Pays on acceptance.** Buys first North American serial rights. Responds in 1 week to queries Responds in 1 month with a yes/no on ms purchase to mss. Sample copy for 9×12 SAE with 4 first-class stamps or online. Writer's guidelines online.

- Accepts queries by mail, but purchase decision is based on final mss only.

Nonfiction: "We're really interested in seeing manuscripts on business, technology, history, or just intriguing topics, ranging from sports to science." No fiction, politics, religion, controversial issues, travel, first-person, fillers, or verse. **Buys 20-30 mss/year.** Send complete ms. Length: 1,500-2,500 words. **Pays 20¢/word.**

Photos: If possible, please advise where photographs may be found. Photographs taken and submitted by the writer are paid for separately at $25 each. Vertical scenics-send transparencies, slides. $475 for one-time cover rights.

Tips: "Please try us first. We'll get back to you soon."

N $ $ FRANCHISE CANADA MAGAZINE, August Communications, 225-530 Century St., Winnipeg MB R3H 0Y4, Canada. Fax: (866)957-0217. E-mail: d.johnson@august.ca. Website: www.august.ca. Managing Editor: Sean Thiessen. **Contact:** Denyse Johnson, editor. **70% freelance written.** Bimonthly magazine covering the franchising industry in Canada. "*Franchise Canada Magazine* is written for the Canadian Franchise Association. It is written for potential franchise owners to promote franchising and educate them about the industry." Estab. 1999. Circ. 4,500. **Pays on acceptance.** Publishes ms an average of 2 months after acceptance. Byline given. Buys all rights. Accepts queries by mail, e-mail, fax. Sample copy online.

Nonfiction: How-to (investigate a franchise system—research methods), interview/profile (CFA franchise members/businesses), technical (aspects of franchising). **Buys 30 mss/year.** Query with published clips. Length: 1,000-2,500 words. **Pays 15-30¢/word.**

Photos: State availability with submission. Reviews GIF/JPEG files. Buys all rights. Negotiates payment individually. Captions required.

Columns/Departments: At Your Service (profiles on CFA member-support services), 1,500 words; Franchisor Profiles

(profiles on CFA members), 1,500-2,500 words. **Buys 12 mss/year.** Query with published clips. **Pays 15-30¢/word.**
Tips: "Research the Canadian Franchise Association website."

$ $ THE KEEPER'S LOG, U.S. Lighthouse Society, 244 Kearny St., San Francisco CA 94108. (415)362-7255. **Contact:** Wayne Wheeler, editor. **10% freelance written.** Quarterly magazine covering lighthouses, lightships, and human interest relating to them. "Our audience is national (some foreign members). The magazine carries historical and contemporary information (articles) relating to technical, human interest, history, etc." Estab. 1984. Circ. 11,000. Pays on publication. Publishes ms an average of 6 months after acceptance. Byline given. Buys first rights. Editorial lead time 6 months. Accepts queries by mail. Responds in 1 week to queries. Sample copy for $5. Writer's guidelines for #10 SASE.
Nonfiction: Historical/nostalgic, personal experience, photo feature, technical. Ghost stories need not apply. **Buys 1 mss/year.** Query. Length: 2,500-5,000 words. **Pays $200-400.**
Photos: State availability with submission. Reviews 5×7 prints. Offers no additional payment for photos accepted with ms. Identification of subjects required.

$ $ $ $ KIWANIS, 3636 Woodview Trace, Indianapolis IN 46268-3196. (317)875-8755. Fax: (317)879-0204. E-mail: jbrockley@kiwanis.org. Website: www.kiwanis.org. **Contact:** Jack Brockley, managing editor. **10% freelance written.** Magazine published 10 times/year for business and professional persons and their families. Estab. 1917. Circ. 240,000. **Pays on acceptance.** Publishes ms an average of 6 months after acceptance. Byline given. Offers 40% kill fee. Buys first rights. Accepts queries by mail, e-mail, fax. Responds in 1 month to queries. Sample copy and writer's guidelines for 9×12 SAE with 5 first class stamps. Writer's guidelines online.

- No unsolicited mss.

Nonfiction: Articles about social and civic betterment, small-business concerns, children, science, education, religion, family, health, recreation, etc. Emphasis on objectivity, intelligent analysis, and thorough research of contemporary issues. Positive tone preferred. Concise, lively writing, absence of clichés, and impartial presentation of controversy required. Articles must include information and quotations from international sources. "We have a continuing need for articles that concern helping youth, particularly prenatal through age 5: day care, developmentally appropriate education, early intervention for at-risk children, parent education, safety and health. No fiction, personal essays, profiles, travel pieces, fillers, or verse of any kind. A light or humorous approach is welcomed where the subject is appropriate and all other requirements are observed." **Buys 20 mss/year.** Length: 1,500-2,500 words. **Pays $400-1,500.** Sometimes pays expenses of writers on assignment.
Photos: "We accept photos submitted with manuscripts. Our rate for a manuscript with good photos is higher than for one without." Buys one-time rights. Identification of subjects, model releases required.
Tips: "We will work with any writer who presents a strong feature article idea applicable to our magazine's audience and who will prove he or she knows the craft of writing. First, obtain writer's guidelines and a sample copy. Study for general style and content. When querying, present detailed outline of proposed manuscript's focus and editorial intent. Indicate expert sources to be used, as well as possible Kiwanis sources for quotations and anecdotes. Present a well-researched, smoothly written manuscript that contains a 'human quality' with the use of anecdotes, practical examples, quotations, etc."

$ $ THE LION, 300 W. 22nd St., Oak Brook IL 60523-8815. (630)571-5466. Fax: (630)571-8890. E-mail: rkleinfe@lionsclubs.org. Website: www.lionsclubs.org. **Contact:** Robert Kleinfelder, senior editor. **35% freelance written.** Works with a small number of new/unpublished writers each year. Monthly magazine covering service club organization for Lions Club members and their families. Estab. 1918. Circ. 490,000. **Pays on acceptance.** Publishes ms an average of 5 months after acceptance. Byline given. Buys all rights. Accepts queries by mail, e-mail, fax, phone. Responds in 1 month to queries. Sample copy and writer's guidelines free.
Nonfiction: Welcomes humor, if sophisticated but clean; no sensationalism. Prefers anecdotes in articles. Photo feature (must be of a Lions Club service project), informational (issues of interest to civic-minded individuals). No travel, biography, or personal experiences. **Buys 40 mss/year.** Length: 500-1,500 words. **Pays $100-750.** Sometimes pays expenses of writers on assignment.
Photos: Purchased with accompanying ms. "Photos should be at least 5×7 glossies; color prints or slides are preferred. Be sure photos are clear and as candid as possible." Total purchase price for ms includes payment for photos accepted with ms. Captions required.
Tips: "Send detailed description of proposed article. Query first and request writer's guidelines and sample copy. Incomplete details on how the Lions involved actually carried out a project and poor quality photos are the most frequent mistakes made by writers in completing an article assignment for us. No gags, fillers, quizzes, or poems are accepted. We are geared increasingly to an international audience. Writers who travel internationally could query for possible assignments, although only locally related expenses could be paid."

N $ $ $ THE MEETING PROFESSIONAL, Meeting Professionals International, 4455 LBJ Freeway, Suite 1200, Dallas TX 75244-5903. Fax: (972)702-3096. E-mail: publications@mpiweb.org. Website: www.mpiweb.org/news. Associate Publisher: Bruce MacMillan. Managing Editor: John Delavan. **Contact:** Angela Chiarello, editorial assistant. **60% freelance written.** Monthly magazine covering the global meeting idustry. "*The Meeting Professional* delivers strategic editorial content on meeting industry trends, opportunities and items of importance in the hope of fostering professional development and career enhancement. The magazine is mailed monthly to 19,000 MPI members and 11,500 qualified nonmember subscribers and meeting industry planners. It is also distributed at major industry shows, such as IT&ME and EIBTM, at MPI conferences, and upon individual request." Circ. 32,000. **Pays on acceptance.** Publishes ms an average of 2-3 months after acceptance. Byline given. Offers a negotiable kill fee. Buys all rights. Editorial lead time 2 months.

Submit seasonal material 3 months in advance. Accepts queries by mail, e-mail, fax. Accepts simultaneous submissions. Sample copy for free. Writer's guidelines by e-mail.

Nonfiction: General interest, how-to, interview/profile, travel, industry-related. No duplications from other industry publications. **Buys 60 mss/year.** Query with published clips. Length: 1,000-2,500 words. **Pays 50-75¢/word for assigned articles.**

Tips: "Understand and have experience within the industry. Writers who are familiar with our magazine and our competitors are better able to get our attention, send better queries, and get assignments."

$ PERSPECTIVE, Pioneer Clubs, P.O. Box 788, Wheaton IL 60189-0788. (630)876-5735. Fax: (630)293-3053. E-mail: ballenpowell@pioneerclubs.org. Website: www.pioneerclubs.org. **Contact:** Rebecca Allen-Powell, editor. **15% freelance written.** Triannual magazine for "volunteer leaders of clubs for girls and boys age 2-grade 12. Clubs are sponsored by local churches throughout North America." Estab. 1967. Circ. 24,000. **Pays on acceptance.** Publishes ms an average of 6 months after acceptance. Byline given. Buys first North American serial, second serial (reprint), all rights. Submit seasonal material 9 months in advance. Accepts queries by mail, e-mail, fax, phone. Accepts previously published material. Responds in 2 weeks to queries. Sample copy and writer's guidelines for $2.25 and 9 × 12 SAE with 6 first-class stamps.

O- Break in by having "access to a Pioneer Clubs program in a local church and being willing to work on assignment. Almost all our articles are assigned to freelancers or to someone in a local church who runs Pioneer Clubs."

Nonfiction: How-to (relationship skills, leadership skills), inspirational, interview/profile (Christian education leaders, club leaders), personal experience (of club leaders). **Buys 0-2 mss/year.** Length: 800-1,200 words. **Pays $50-120.**

Reprints: Send photocopy of article or typed ms with rights for sale noted and information about when and where the material previously appeared.

Columns/Departments: Storehouse (game, activity, outdoor activity, service project suggestions—all related to club projects for age 2-grade 12). **Buys 0-2 mss/year.** Send complete ms. **Pays $8-15.**

Tips: "Submit articles directly related to club work, practical in nature, i.e., ideas for leader training in communication, discipline, teaching skills. However, most of our articles are assigned. Writers who have contact with a Pioneer Clubs program in their area and who are interested in working on assignment are welcome to contact us."

$ $ PERSPECTIVES IN HEALTH, Pan American Health Organization, 525 23rd St. NW, Washington DC 20037-2895. (202)974-3122. Fax: (202)974-3143. E-mail: eberwind@paho.org. Website: www.paho.org. **Contact:** Donna Eberwine, editor. **80% freelance written.** Magazine published 3 times/year covering international public health with a focus on the Americas. "*Perspectives in Health*, the popular magazine of the Pan American Health Organization (PAHO), was created in 1996 to serve as a forum on current issues in the area of international public health and human development. PAHO works with the international community, government institutions, nongovernmental organizations, universities, community groups, and others to strengthen national and local public health systems and to improve the health and well-being of the peoples of the Americas." Estab. 1996. Circ. 10,000. **Pays on acceptance.** Publishes ms an average of 6 months after acceptance. Byline given. Buys first North American serials rights and electronic rights to post articles on the PAHO website. Editorial lead time 2 months. Accepts queries by mail, e-mail, fax, phone. Responds in 3 weeks to queries; 1 month to mss. Sample copy and writer's guidelines free.

- Each issue of *Perspectives in Health* is published in English and Spanish.

Nonfiction: Subject matter: Culturally insightful and scientifically sound articles related to international public health and human development issues and programs affecting North America, Latin America, and the Caribbean. The story angle should have wide relevancy—i.e., capturing national and particularly international concerns, even if the setting is local—and should be high in human interest content: "international public health with a human face." General topics may include (but are not limited to) AIDS and other sexually transmitted diseases, maternal and child health, the environment, food and nutrition, cardiovascular diseases, cancer, mental health, oral health, violence, veterinary health, disaster preparedness, health education and promotion, substance abuse, water and sanitation, and issues related to the health and well-being of women, adolescents, workers, the elderly, and minority groups in the countries of the Americas. Historical pieces on the region's public health "trail blazers" and innovators are also welcome. General interest, historical/nostalgic, interview/profile, opinion, personal experience, photo feature. No highly technical, highly bureaucratic articles. **Buys 12 mss/year.** Query with or without published clips or send complete ms. Length: 1,500-3,000 words. **Pays $250.** Sometimes pays expenses of writers on assignment.

Photos: State availability with submission. Reviews contact sheets, negatives, transparencies, prints. Buys one-time rights. Negotiates payment individually. Captions, identification of subjects, model releases required.

Columns/Departments: Last Word, 750 words. **Buys 2 mss/year.** Query with or without published clips or send complete ms. **Pays $100.**

Tips: "*Perspectives* puts the human face on international public health issues and programs. All facts must be documented. Quote people involved with the programs described. Get on-site information—not simply an Internet-research story."

$ $ RECREATION NEWS, Official Publication of the ESM Association of the Capital Region, 7339 D Hanover Pkwy., Greenbelt MD 20770. (301)474-4600. Fax: (301)474-6283. E-mail: editor@recreationnews.com. Website: www.recreationnews.com. **Contact:** Francis X. Orphe, editor. **85% freelance written.** Monthly guide to leisure-time activities for federal and private industry workers covering outdoor recreation, travel, fitness and indoor pasttimes. Estab. 1979. Circ. 110,000. Pays on publication. Publishes ms an average of 8 months after acceptance. Byline given. Buys first, second serial (reprint) rights. Submit seasonal material 10 months in advance. Accepts queries by mail, e-mail, fax, phone. Accepts previously published material. Accepts simultaneous submissions. Responds in 2 months to queries. Sample copy and writer's guidelines for 9 × 12 SAE with $1.05 in postage.

Nonfiction: Articles Editor. Historical/nostalgic (Washington-related), personal experience (with recreation, life in Washington), travel (mid-Atlantic travel only), sports; hobbies. Special issues: skiing (December). **Buys 45 mss/year.** Query with published clips. Length: 800-2,000 words. **Pays $50-300.**

Reprints: Send tearsheet or typed ms with rights for sale noted and information about when and where the material previously appeared. Pays $50.

Photos: Photo Editor. Call for details.

Tips: "Our writers generally have a few years of professional writing experience and their work runs to the lively and conversational. We like more manuscripts in a wide range of recreational topics, including the off-beat. The areas of our publication most open to freelancers are general articles on travel and sports, both participational and spectator, also historic in the DC area. In general, stories on sites visited need to include info on nearby places of interest and places to stop for lunch, to shop, etc."

$ $ $ SCOUTING, Boy Scouts of America, 1325 W. Walnut Hill Lane, P.O. Box 152079, Irving TX 75015-2079. (972)580-2367. Fax: (972)580-2367. E-mail: 103064.3363@compuserve.com. Website: www.scoutingmagazine.org. Executive Editor: Scott Daniels. **Contact:** Jon C. Halter, editor. **80% freelance written.** Magazine published 6 times/year covering Scouting activities for adult leaders of the Boy Scouts, Cub Scouts, and Venturing. Estab. 1913. Circ. 1,000,000. **Pays on acceptance.** Publishes ms an average of 18 months after acceptance. Byline given. Offers 25% kill fee. Buys first North American serial rights. Editorial lead time 1 year. Submit seasonal material 1 year in advance. Accepts queries by mail, fax. Accepts previously published material. Accepts simultaneous submissions. Responds in 1 month to queries; 2 months to mss. Sample copy for $2.50 and 9×12 SAE with 4 first-class stamps or online. Writer's guidelines online.

- Break in with "a profile of an outstanding Scout leader who has useful advice for new volunteer leaders (especially good if the situation involves urban Scouting or Scouts with disabilities or other extraordinary roles)."

Nonfiction: Program activities, leadership techniques and styles, profiles, inspirational, occasional general interest for adults (humor, historical, nature, social issues, trends). Inspirational, interview/profile. **Buys 20-30 mss/year.** Query with published clips and SASE. Length: 600-1,200 words. **Pays $750-1,000 for major articles, $300-500 for shorter features.** Pays expenses of writers on assignment.

Reprints: Send photocopy of article and information about when and where the article previously appeared. "First-person accounts of meaningful Scouting experiences (previously published in local newspapers, etc.) are a popular subject."

Photos: State availability with submission. Reviews transparencies, prints. Buys one-time rights. Identification of subjects required.

Columns/Departments: Way It Was (Scouting history), 600-750 words; Family Talk (family—raising kids, etc.), 600-750 words. **Buys 8-12 mss/year.** Query. **Pays $300-500.**

Fillers: "Limited to personal accounts of humorous or inspirational Scouting experiences." Anecdotes, short humor. **Buys 15-25/year.** Length: 50-150 words. **Pays $25 on publication.**

- The online version carries original content not found in the print edition and includes writer's guidelines. Contact: Scott Daniels.

Tips: "*Scouting* magazine articles are mainly about successful program activities conducted by or for Cub Scout packs, Boy Scout troops, and Venturing crews. We also include features on winning leadership techniques and styles, profiles of outstanding individual leaders, and inspirational accounts (usually first person) or *Scouting*'s impact on an individual, either as a youth or while serving as a volunteer adult leader. Because most volunteer Scout leaders are also parents of children of Scout age, *Scouting* is also considered a family magazine. We publish material we feel will help parents in strengthening their families (because they often deal with communicating and interacting with young people, many of these features are useful to a reader in both roles as parent and Scout leader)."

N **$ $ SOUTH AMERICAN EXPLORER**, South American Explorers, 126 Indian Creek Rd., Ithaca NY 14850. (607)277-0488. Fax: (607)277-6122. E-mail: don@saexplorers.org. Website: www.saexplorers.org. **Contact:** Don Montague, editor-in-chief. **80% freelance written.** Quarterly travel/scientific/educational journal covering exploration, conservation, anthropology, ethnography, field sports, natural history, history, archeology, linguistics, and just about anything relating to South America. "The *South American Explorer* goes primarily (but not exclusively) to members of the South American Explorers. Readers are interested in all the above subjects as well as endangered peoples, wildlife protection, volunteer opportunities, etc." Estab. 1977. Circ. 10,000. Pays on publication. Publishes ms an average of 2-3 months after acceptance. Byline given. Buys first rights. Editorial lead time 3 months. Accepts queries by mail, e-mail, fax, phone. Accepts previously published material. Accepts simultaneous submissions. Responds in 1 week to queries; 2 months to mss. Sample copy online. Writer's guidelines free.

Nonfiction: All content must relate to South America in some way. Book excerpts, essays, exposé, general interest, historical/nostalgic, how-to, humor, inspirational, interview/profile, new product, opinion, personal experience, photo feature, religious, technical, travel. No "My South American Vacation," "The Extraterrestrial Origins of Machu Picchu," "Encounters with the Amazon Yeti," "My Journal of Traveling Through South America." **Buys 20 mss/year.** Query with or without published clips or send complete ms. Length: 1,000-4,500 words. **Pays $50-400 for assigned articles; $50-300 for unsolicited articles.**

Photos: Send photos with submission. Reviews contact sheets, negatives, transparencies, prints, GIF/JPEG files. Buys one-time rights. Negotiates payment individually. Captions required.

Columns/Departments: Ask the Doctor; South American Explorers; Book Reviews; Movie Reviews; News Shorts; Tips and Notes; Cyber Page. **Buys 6 mss/year.** Send complete ms. **Pays $50-250.**

Fillers: Length: 500-1,500 words.

$ $ THE TOASTMASTER, Toastmasters International, 23182 Arroyo Vista, Rancho Santa Margarita CA 92688. (949)858-8255. Fax: (949)858-1207. E-mail: pubs@toastmasters.org. Website: www.toastmasters.org. **Contact:** Suzanne

Frey, editor; KellyAnn LaCascia, associate editor. **50% freelance written.** Monthly magazine on public speaking, leadership, and club concerns. "This magazine is sent to members of Toastmasters International, a nonprofit educational association of men and women throughout the world who are interested in developing their communication and leadership skills. Members range from novice to professional speakers and from a wide variety of ethnic and cultural backgrounds, as Toastmasters is an international organization." Estab. 1933. Circ. 185,000. **Pays on acceptance.** Publishes ms an average of 1 year after acceptance. Byline given. Buys first, second serial (reprint), all rights. Submit seasonal material 3-4 months in advance. Accepts previously published material. Accepts simultaneous submissions. Responds in 2-3 months to queries; 2-3 months to mss. Sample copy for 9×12 SASE with 4 first-class stamps. Writer's guidelines for #10 SASE, online or by e-mail.

Nonfiction: "Toastmasters members are requested to view their submissions as contributions to the organization. Sometimes asks for book excerpts and reprints without payment, but original contribution from individuals outside Toastmasters will be paid for at stated rates." How-to, humor, interview/profile (well-known speakers and leaders), communications, leadership, language use. **Buys 50 mss/year.** Query by mail or e-mail (e-mail preferred). Length: 1,000-2,500 words. **Pays $250-350.** Sometimes pays expenses of writers on assignment.

Reprints: Send ms with rights for sale noted and information about when and where the material previously appeared. Pays 50-70% of amount paid for an original article.

Tips: "We are looking primarily for 'how-to' articles on subjects from the broad fields of communications and leadership which can be directly applied by our readers in their self-improvement and club programming efforts. Concrete examples are useful. *Avoid sexist or nationalist language and 'Americanisms' such as football examples, etc.*"

$ TRAIL & TIMBERLINE, The Colorado Mountain Club, 710 10th St., Suite 200, Golden CO 80401. (303)279-3080, ext. 105. Fax: (303)279-9690. E-mail: beckwt@cmc.org. Website: www.cmc.org. **Contact:** Tom Beckwith, editor. **80% freelance written.** Bimonthly official publication of the Colorado Mountain Club. "Articles in *Trail & Timberline* conform to the mission statement of the Colorado Mountain Club to unite the energy, interest, and knowledge of lovers of the Colorado mountains, to collect and disseminate information, to stimulate public interest, and to encourage preservation of the mountains of Colorado and the Rocky Mountain region." Estab. 1918. Circ. 10,500. Pays on publication. Publishes ms an average of 2 months after acceptance. Byline given. Buys all rights. Editorial lead time 6 months. Submit seasonal material 6 months in advance. Accepts queries by mail, e-mail. Accepts previously published material. Responds in 1 week to queries; 1 month to mss. Sample copy for $5. Writer's guidelines online.

Nonfiction: Essays, humor, personal experience, photo feature, travel. **Buys 10-15 mss/year.** Query. Length: 500-2,000 words. **Pays $50.**

Photos: Send photos with submission. Reviews contact sheets, 35mm transparencies, 3×5 or larger prints, GIF/JPEG files. Buys one-time rights. Offers no additional payment for photos accepted with ms. Captions, identification of subjects, model releases required.

Columns/Departments: Wild Colorado (conservation/public lands issues), 1,000 words; Education (mountain education/natural history), 500-1,000 words. **Buys 6-12 mss/year.** Query. **Pays $50.**

Poetry: Jared Smith, associate editor, poetry. Avant-garde, free verse, traditional. **Buys 6-12 poems/year.**

Tips: "Writers should be familiar with the purposes and ethos of the Colorado Mountain Club before querying. Writer's guidelines are available and should be consulted—particularly for poetry submissions. All submissions must conform to the mission statement of the Colorado Mountain Club."

$ $ VFW MAGAZINE, Veterans of Foreign Wars of the United States, 406 W. 34th St., Kansas City MO 64111. (816)756-3390. Fax: (816)968-1169. E-mail: pbrown@vfw.org. Website: www.vfw.org. **Contact:** Rich Kolb, editor-in-chief. **40% freelance written.** Monthly magazine on veterans' affairs, military history, patriotism, defense, and current events. "*VFW Magazine* goes to its members worldwide, all having served honorably in the armed forces overseas from World War II through the war on terrorism." Circ. 1,800,000. **Pays on acceptance.** Byline given. Offers 50% kill fee. Buys first rights. Submit seasonal material 6 months in advance. Accepts queries by mail, e-mail, fax. Responds in 2 months to queries. Sample copy for 9×12 SAE with 5 first-class stamps.

- Break in with "fresh and innovative angles on veterans' rights; stories on little-known exploits in U.S. military history. Will be particularly in the market for Korean War battle accounts during 2001-2003. Upbeat articles about severely disabled veterans who have overcome their disabilities; feel-good patriotism pieces; current events as they relate to defense policy; health and retirement pieces are always welcome."

Nonfiction: Veterans' and defense affairs, recognition of veterans and military service, current foreign policy, American armed forces abroad and international events affecting US national security are in demand. **Buys 25-30 mss/year.** Query with 1-page outline, résumé, and published clips. Length: 1,000 words. **Pays up to $500 maximum unless otherwise negotiated.**

Photos: Send photos with submission. Reviews contact sheets, negatives, color (2¼×2¼) preferred transparencies, 5×7 or 8×10 b&w prints. Buys first North American rights. Captions, identification of subjects required.

Tips: "Absolute accuracy and quotes from relevant individuals are a must. Bibliographies useful if subject required extensive research and/or is open to dispute. Counsult *The Associated Press Stylebook* for correct grammar and punctuation. Please enclose a 3-sentence biography describing your military service and your military experience in the field in which you are writing. No phone queries."

N $ $ VINTAGE SNOWMOBILE MAGAZINE, Vintage Snowmobile Club of America, P.O. Box 508, Luverne MN 56156. (507)283-1860. Fax: (507)449-0004. E-mail: snowmobiles@iw.net. Website: www.vsca.com. **Contact:** Terry Hoffman, editor. **75% freelance written.** Quarterly magazine covering vintage snowmobiles and collectors. *Vintage Snowmobile Magazine* deals with vintage snowmobiles and is sent to members of the Vintage Snowmobile Club of America.

Estab. 1987. Circ. 2,400. **Pays on acceptance.** Publishes ms an average of 3 months after acceptance. Byline sometimes given. Buys first North American serial rights. Editorial lead time 2 months. Submit seasonal material 3 months in advance. Accepts queries by mail, e-mail, fax, phone. Responds in 1 month to queries; 2 months to mss.

Nonfiction: General interest, historical/nostalgic, humor, photo feature, coverage of shows. Query with published clips. Length: 200-2,000 words. **Pays 10-12¢/word for assigned articles; 3-5¢/word for unsolicited articles.** Sometimes pays expenses of writers on assignment.

Photos: Send photos with submission. Reviews 3×5 prints, GIF/JPEG files. Buys all rights. Negotiates payment individually.

Columns/Departments: Featured Sleds Stories, 500 words. Query with published clips. **Pays 10-12¢/word.**

Fillers: Gags to be illustrated by cartoonist. **Buys 3/year.**

ASTROLOGY, METAPHYSICAL & NEW AGE

Magazines in this section carry articles ranging from shamanism to extraterrestrial phenomena. The following publications regard astrology, psychic phenomena, metaphysical experiences, and related subjects as sciences or as objects of serious study. Each has an individual personality and approach to these phenomena. If you want to write for these publications, be sure to read them carefully before submitting.

$ $ $ BODY & SOUL, Balanced Living in a Busy World, New Age Publishing, Inc., 42 Pleasant St., Watertown MA 02472. (617)926-0200. Website: www.bodyandsoulmag.com. Editor-in-Chief: Seth Bauer. Managing Editor: Elizabeth Phillips. **Contact:** Editorial Department. **90% freelance written.** Works with a small number of new/unpublished writers each year. Bimonthly magazine emphasizing "personal fulfillment and social change. The audience we reach is college-educated, social-service/hi-tech oriented, 25-55 years of age, concerned about social values, humanitarianism and balance in personal life." Estab. 1974. Circ. 225,000. **Pays on acceptance.** Publishes ms an average of 4 months after acceptance. Byline sometimes given. Offers 25% kill fee. Buys first North American serial, electronic rights. Editorial lead time 6 months. Submit seasonal material 6 months in advance. Accepts queries by mail. Accepts simultaneous submissions. Responds in 2 months to queries; 2 months to mss. Sample copy for $5 and 9×12 SAE. Writer's guidelines online.

O→ No phone calls. The process of decision making takes time and involves more than one editor. An answer cannot be given over the phone.

Nonfiction: Book excerpts, essays, how-to (travel on business, select a computer, reclaim land, plant a garden), inspirational, interview/profile, new product, personal experience, religious, travel. **Buys 100+ mss/year.** Query with published clips. Length: 100-2,500 words. **Pays 75¢-$1/word.** Pays expenses of writers on assignment.

Reprints: Send tearsheet or photocopy.

Photos: Send photos with submission. Reviews transparencies. Buys one-time rights. Negotiates payment individually. Captions, model releases required.

Columns/Departments: Manuscript Editor. Holistic Health, Food/Nutrition, Spirit, Home, Community, Travel, Life Lessons. 600-1,300 words. **Buys 50 mss/year.** Query with published clips. **Pays 75¢-$1/word.**

Tips: "Submit short, specific news items to the Upfront department. Query first with clips. A query is one to two paragraphs—if you need more space than that to *present* the idea, then you don't have a clear grip on it. The next open area is columns: Reflections often takes first-time contributors. Read the magazine and get a sense of type of writing run in column. In particular we are interested in seeing inspirational, first-person pieces that highlight an engaging idea, experience or issue. We are also looking for new cutting-edge thinking. No e-mail or phone queries, please. Begin with a query, résumé and published clips — we will contact you for the manuscript."

$ $ FATE MAGAZINE, P.O. Box 460, Lakeville MN 55044. (952)431-2050. E-mail: fate@fatemag.com. Website: www.fatemag.com. **Contact:** Editor. **70% freelance written.** Estab. 1948. Circ. 20,000. Pays on publication. Byline given. Buys all rights. Responds in 3 months to queries.

Nonfiction: Personal psychic and mystical experiences, 350-500 words. **Pays $25.** Articles on parapsychology, Fortean phenomena, cryptozoology, spiritual healing, flying saucers, new frontiers of science, and mystical aspects of ancient civilizations, 500-3,000 words. Must include complete authenticating details. Prefers interesting accounts of single events rather than roundups. "We very frequently accept manuscripts from new writers; the majority are individual's first-person accounts of their own psychic/mystical/spiritual experiences. We do need to have all details, where, when, why, who and what, included for complete documentation. We ask for a notarized statement attesting to truth of the article." Query. **Pays 10¢/word.**

Photos: Buys slides, prints, or digital photos/illustrations with ms. Pays $10.

Fillers: Fillers are especially welcomed and must be be fully authenticated also, and on similar topics. Length: 50-300 words.

Tips: "We would like more stories about *current* paranormal or unusual events."

$ MAGICAL BLEND MAGAZINE, A Primer for the 21st Century, P.O. Box 600, Chico CA 95927. (530)893-9037. Fax: (530)893-9076. E-mail: info@magicalblend.com. Website: www.magicalblend.com. **Contact:** Michael Peter Langevin, editor. **50% freelance written.** Bimonthly magazine covering social and mystical transformation. "*Magical Blend* endorses no one pathway to spiritual growth, but attempts to explore many alternative possibilities to help transform the planet." Estab. 1980. Circ. 100,000. Pays on publication. Publishes ms an average of 2 months after acceptance. Byline given. Responds in 6 months to mss. Sample copy for free. Writer's guidelines for #10 SASE.

O⁻ Break in by "writing a great article that gives our readers something they can use in their daily lives or obtain 'name' interviews."

Nonfiction: "Articles must reflect our standards; see our magazine." Book excerpts, essays, general interest, inspirational, interview/profile, religious, travel. No poetry or fiction. **Buys 24 mss/year.** Send complete ms. Length: 1,000-2,000 words. **Pays $35-100.**

Photos: State availability with submission. Reviews transparencies. Buys all rights. Negotiates payment individually. Identification of subjects, model releases required.

Fillers: Newsbreaks. **Buys 12-20/year.** Length: 300-450 words. **Pays variable rate.**

$ NEW YORK SPIRIT MAGAZINE, 107 Sterling Place, Brooklyn NY 11217. (800)634-0989. Fax: (718)230-3459. E-mail: office@nyspirit.com. Website: www.nyspirit.com. **Contact:** Paul English, editor. Bimonthly tabloid covering spirituality and personal growth and transformation. "We are a magazine that caters to the holistic health community in New York City." Circ. 50,000. **Pays on acceptance.** Publishes ms an average of 3 months after acceptance. Byline given. Buys first rights. Editorial lead time 1 month. Accepts previously published material. Accepts simultaneous submissions. Responds in 1 month to queries. Sample copy for 8×10 SAE and 10 first-class stamps. Writer's guidelines online.

Nonfiction: Essays, how-to, humor, inspirational, interview/profile, photo feature. **Buys 30 mss/year.** Query with or without published clips. Length: 1,000-3,500 words. **Pays $150 maximum.**

Photos: State availability with submission. Model releases required.

Columns/Departments: Fitness (new ideas in staying fit), 1,500 words. **Pays $150.**

Fiction: Humorous, mainstream, inspirational. **Buys 5 mss/year.** Query with published clips. Length: 1,000-3,500 words. **Pays $150.**

Tips: "Be vivid and descriptive. We are *very* interested in hearing from new writers."

$ PANGAIA, Earthwise Spirituality, Blessed Bee, Inc., P.O. Box 641, Point Arena CA 95468. Fax: (707)882-2793. E-mail: info@pangaia.com. Website: www.pangaia.com. Editor: Anne Newkirk Niven. Managing Editor: Elizabeth Barrette. **50% freelance written.** Quarterly magazine of Earth spirituality covering Earth-based religions. "We publish articles pertinent to an Earth-loving readership. Mysticism, science, humor, tools all are described." Estab. 1994. Circ. 8,500. Pays on publication. Publishes ms an average of 6 months after acceptance. Byline given. Offers $10 kill fee. Buys first North American serial, electronic rights. Editorial lead time 6 months. Submit seasonal material 6 months in advance. Accepts queries by mail, e-mail. Responds in 2 months to queries. Sample copy for $5. Writer's guidelines online.

Nonfiction: Book excerpts, essays, how-to, humor, inspirational, interview/profile, photo feature, religious, Reviews. Special issues: "Land Before Time" (Winter 2003-2004); "Arts & Culture" (Spring 2004); "Animal Magic" (Summer 2004); "Science and Magic" (Autumn 2004). No material on unrelated topics. **Buys 30 mss/year.** Query. Length: 500-5,000 words. **Pays $10-3¢/word.** Sometimes pays with contributor copies or other premiums rather than a cash payment if negotiated/requested by writer. Sometimes pays expenses of writers on assignment.

Photos: State availability with submission. Reviews 5×7 prints, GIF/JPEG files. Buys one-time rights. Negotiates payment individually. Model releases required.

Fiction: Ethnic, fantasy, religious, science fiction, Pagan/Gaian. No grim or abstract stories. **Buys 5 mss/year.** Send complete ms. Length: 500-5,000 words. **Pays $10-3¢/word.**

Poetry: Will consider most forms. Free verse, traditional. "Avoid clichés like the burning times. Do not send forms with rhyme/meter unless those features are executed perfectly." **Buys 12 poems/year.** Submit maximum 5 poems. Length: 3-100 lines. **Pays $10.**

Tips: "Share a spiritual insight that can enlighten others. Back up your facts with citations where relevant, and make those facts sound like the neatest thing since self-lighting charcoal. Explain how to solve a problem; offer a new way to make the world a better place. We would also like to see serious scholarship on nature religion topics, material of interest to intermediate or advanced practicioners, which is both accurate and engaging."

$ SHAMAN'S DRUM, A Journal of Experiential Shamanism, Cross-Cultural Shamanism Network, P.O. Box 270, Williams OR 97544. (541)846-1313. Fax: (541)846-1204. **Contact:** Timothy White, editor. **75% freelance written.** Quarterly educational magazine of cross-cultural shamanism. "*Shaman's Drum* seeks contributions directed toward a general but well-informed audience. Our intent is to expand, challenge, and refine our readers' and our understanding of shamanism in practice. Topics include indigenous medicineway practices, contemporary shamanic healing practices, ecstatic spiritual practices, and contemporary shamanic psychotherapies. Our overall focus is cross-cultural, but our editorial approach is culture-specific—we prefer that authors focus on specific ethnic traditions or personal practices about which they have significant firsthand experience. We are looking for examples of not only how shamanism has transformed individual lives but also practical ways it can help ensure survival of life on the planet. We want material that captures the heart and feeling of shamanism and that can inspire people to direct action and participation, and to explore shamanism in greater depth." Estab. 1985. Circ. 14,000. Publishes ms an average of 6 months after acceptance. Byline given. Buys first North American serial, first rights. Editorial lead time 1 year. Accepts previously published material. Responds in 3 months to queries. Sample copy for $7. Writer's guidelines for #10 SASE.

Nonfiction: Book excerpts, essays, interview/profile (please query), opinion, personal experience, photo feature. No fiction, poetry, or fillers. **Buys 16 mss/year.** Send complete ms. Length: 5,000-8,000 words. **Pays 5-8¢/word, "depending on how much we have to edit."**

Reprints: Send ms with rights for sale noted and information about when and where the material previously appeared. Pays 50% of amount paid for an original article.

Photos: Send photos with submission. Reviews contact sheets, transparencies, All size prints. Buys one-time rights. Offers $40-50/photo. Identification of subjects required.

Columns/Departments: Judy Wells, Earth Circles. Timothy White, Reviews. Earth Circles (news format, concerned with issues, events, organizations related to shamanism, indigenous peoples, and caretaking Earth. Relevant clippings also sought. Reviews (in-depth reviews of books about shamanism or closely related subjects such as indigenous lifestyles, ethnobotany, transpersonal healing, and ecstatic spirituality), 500-1,500 words. **Buys 8 mss/year.** Query. **Pays 5¢/word.**

Tips: "All articles must have a clear relationship to shamanism, but may be on topics which have not traditionally been defined as shamanic. We prefer original material that is based on, or illustrated with, first-hand knowledge and personal experience. Articles should be well documented with descriptive examples and pertinent background information. Photographs and illustrations of high quality are always welcome and can help sell articles."

$WHOLE LIFE TIMES, P.O. Box 1187, Malibu CA 90265. (310)317-4200. E-mail: editor@wholelifetimes.com. Website: www.wholelifetimes.com. **Contact:** Kerri Hikida, associate editor. Monthly tabloid for cultural creatives. Estab. 1979. Circ. 58,000. Pays within 1-2 months after publication. Byline given. Buys first North American serial rights. Accepts queries by mail, e-mail. Sample copy for $3. Writer's guidelines for #10 SASE.

Nonfiction: Social justice, food health, alternative healing, eco-travel, political issues, spiritual, conscious business, leading-edge information, relevant celebrity profiles. Special issues: Healing Arts, Food & Nutrition, Spirituality, New Beginnings, Relationships, Longevity, Arts/Cultures Travel, Vitamins and Supplements, Women's Issues, Sexuality, Science & Metaphysics, Environment/Simple Living. **Buys 60 mss/year.** Query with published clips or send complete ms. **Payment varies.**

Reprints: Send ms with rights for sale noted and information about when and where the material previously appeared. Pays 50% of amount paid for an original article.

Columns/Departments: Healing; Parenting; Finance; Food; Personal Growth; Relationships; Humor; Travel; Politics; Sexuality; Spirituality; and Psychology. Length: 750-1,200 words.

Tips: "Queries should be professionally written and show an awareness of current topics of interest in our subject area. We welcome investigative reporting and are happy to see queries that address topics in a political context. We are especially looking for articles on health and nutrition. No monthly columns sought."

AUTOMOTIVE & MOTORCYCLE

Publications in this section detail the maintenance, operation, performance, racing, and judging of automobiles and recreational vehicles. Publications that treat vehicles as means of shelter instead of as a hobby or sport are classified in the Travel, Camping & Trailer category. Journals for service station operators and auto and motorcycle dealers are located in the Trade Auto & Truck section.

$ $AMERICAN IRON MAGAZINE, TAM Communications, Inc., 1010 Summer St., Stamford CT 06905. (203)425-8777. Fax: (203)425-8775. **Contact:** Chris Maida, editor. **60% freelance written.** Family-oriented magazine publishing 13 issues/year covering Harley-Davidson and other US brands with a definite emphasis on Harleys. Circ. 110,000. Pays on publication. Publishes ms an average of 6 months after acceptance. Byline given. Not copyrighted. Responds in 6 months to queries. Sample copy for $10.

Nonfiction: "Clean and nonoffensive. Stories include bike features, touring stories, how-to tech stories with step-by-step photos, historical pieces, events, opinion, and various topics of interest to the people who ride Harley-Davidsons." No fiction. **Buys 60 mss/year. Pays $250 for touring articles with slides to first-time writers.**

Photos: Send SASE for return of photos. Reviews color slides for tour stories.

Tips: "We're not looking for stories about the top 10 biker bars or do-it-yourself tattoos. We're looking for articles about motorcycling, the people, and the machines. If you understand the Harley mystique and can write well, you have a good chance of being published."

$AMERICAN MOTORCYCLIST, American Motorcyclist Association, 13515 Yarmouth Dr., Pickerington OH 43147. (614)856-1900. Fax: (614)856-1920. E-mail: bwood@ama-cycle.org. Website: www.ama-cycle.org. **Contact:** Bill Wood, managing editor. **10% freelance written.** Monthly magazine for "enthusiastic motorcyclists, investing considerable time and money in the sport. We emphasize the motorcyclist, not the vehicle." Estab. 1947. Circ. 260,000. Pays on publication. Byline given. Buys first North American serial rights. Editorial lead time 3 months. Submit seasonal material 4 months in advance. Accepts queries by mail, e-mail. Responds in 5 weeks to queries; 6 weeks to mss. Sample copy for $1.25. Writer's guidelines free.

Nonfiction: Interview/profile (with interesting personalities in the world of motorcycling), personal experience, travel. **Buys 8 mss/year.** Query with or without published clips or send complete ms. Length: 1,000-2,500 words. **Pays minimum $8/published column inch.**

Photos: Send photos with submission. Reviews transparencies, prints. Buys one-time rights. Pays $50/photo minimum. Captions, identification of subjects required.

Tips: "Our major category of freelance stories concerns motorcycling trips to interesting North American destinations. Prefers stories of a timeless nature."

N $ $ $ $AUTOWEEK, Crain Communications, Inc., 1155 Gratiot Ave., Detroit MI 48207. (313)446-6041. Fax: (313)446-0347. E-mail: bgritzinger@crain.com. Website: www.autoweek.com. Editor: Dutch Mandell. Managing Editor:

Roger Hart. **Contact:** Bob Gritzinger, news editor. **33% freelance written.** Weekly magazine. "*AutoWeek* is the country's only weekly magazine for the auto enthusiast." Estab. 1958. Circ. 300,000. Pays on publication. Publishes ms an average of 1 month after acceptance. Byline given. Buys first North American serial rights. Accepts queries by mail, e-mail, fax, phone.

Nonfiction: Historical/nostalgic, interview/profile, new product, travel. **Buys 100 mss/year.** Query. Length: 700-3,000 words. **Pays $1/word.** Sometimes pays expenses of writers on assignment.

Mike Floyd, editor.

$ $ BACKROADS, Motorcycles, Travel & Adventure, Backroads, Inc., P.O. Box 317, Branchville NJ 07826. (973)948-4176. Fax: (973)948-0823. E-mail: editor@backroadsusa.com. Website: www.backroadsusa.com. Managing Editor: Shira Kamil. **Contact:** Brian Rathjen, editor/publisher. **80% freelance written.** Monthly tabloid covering motorcycle touring. "*Backroads* is a motorcycle tour magazine geared toward getting motorcyclists on the road and traveling. We provide interesting destinations, unique roadside attractions and eateries, plus Rip & Ride Route Sheets. We cater to all brands. If you really ride, you need *Backroads*." Estab. 1995. Circ. 40,000. Pays on publication. Publishes ms an average of 3 months after acceptance. Byline given. Buys one-time rights. Editorial lead time 1 month. Submit seasonal material 3 months in advance. Accepts queries by mail, e-mail, fax. Accepts previously published material. Responds in 3 weeks to queries. Sample copy for $2. Writer's guidelines free.

Nonfiction: Shira Kamil, editor/publisher. Essays (motorcycle/touring), how-to, humor, new product, opinion, personal experience, technical, travel. "No long diatribes on 'How I got into motorcycles.'" **Buys 2-4 mss/year.** Query. Length: 500-2,500 words. **Pays 10¢/word minimum for assigned articles; 5¢/word minimum for unsolicited articles.** Pays writers contributor copies or other premiums for short pieces.

Photos: Send photos with submission. Reviews contact sheets. Offers no additional payment for photos accepted with ms.

Columns/Departments: We're Outta Here (weekend destinations), 500-750 words; Great All-American Diner Run (good eateries with great location), 300-800 words; Thoughts from the Road (personal opinion/insights), 250-500 words; Mysterious America (unique and obscure sights), 300-800 words; Big City Getaway (day trips), 500-750 words. **Buys 20-24 mss/year.** Query. **Pays 2¢/word-$50/article.**

Fiction: Adventure, humorous. **Buys 2-4 mss/year.** Query. Length: 500-1,500 words. **Pays 2-4¢/word.**

Fillers: Facts, newsbreaks. Length: 100-250 words.

Tips: "We prefer destination-oriented articles in a light, layman's format, with photos (negatives or transparencies preferred). Stay away from any name-dropping and first-person references."

N $ $ CANADIAN BIKER MAGAZINE, P.O. Box 4122, Victoria BC V8X 3X4, Canada. (250)384-0333. Fax: (250)384-1832. E-mail: edit@canadianbiker.com. Website: canadianbiker.com. **Contact:** John Campbell, editor. **65% freelance written.** Magazine covering motorcycling. "A family-oriented motorcycle magazine whose purpose is to unite Canadian motorcyclists from coast to coast through the dissemination of information in a non-biased, open forum. The magazine reports on new product, events, touring, racing, vintage and custom motorcycling as well as new industry information." Estab. 1980. Circ. 20,000. Publishes ms an average of 1 year after acceptance. Byline given. Buys first rights. Editorial lead time 3 months. Accepts queries by mail, e-mail, fax, phone. Responds in 6 weeks to queries; 6 months to mss. Sample copy for $5 or online. Writer's guidelines free.

Nonfiction: All nonfiction must include photos and/or illustrations. General interest, historical/nostalgic, how-to, interview/profile (Canadian personalities preferred), new product, technical, travel. **Buys 12 mss/year.** Query with or without published clips or send complete ms. Length: 500-1,500 words. **Pays $100-200 for assigned articles; $80-150 for unsolicited articles.**

Photos: State availability of or send photos with submission. Reviews 4×4 transparencies, 3×5 prints. Buys one-time rights. Negotiates payment individually. Captions, identification of subjects, model releases required.

Tips: "We're looking for more racing features, rider profiles, custom sport bikes, quality touring stories, 'extreme' riding articles. Contact editor first before writing anything. Have original ideas, an ability to write from an authoritative point of view, and an ability to supply quality photos to accompany text. Writers should be involved in the motorcycle industry and be intimately familiar with some aspect of the industry which would be of interest to readers. Observations of the industry should be current, timely and informative."

N $ $ $ $ CAR AND DRIVER, Hachette Filipacchi Magazines, Inc., 2002 Hogback Rd., Ann Arbor MI 48105-9795. (734)971-3600. Fax: (734)971-9188. E-mail: spence1cd@aol.com. Website: www.caranddriver.com. **Contact:** Steve Spence, managing editor. Monthly magazine for auto enthusiasts; college-educated, professional, median 24-35 years of age. Estab. 1956. Circ. 1,300,000. **Pays on acceptance.** Byline given. Offers 25% kill fee. Buys first North American serial rights. Accepts queries by mail, e-mail, fax. Responds in 2 months to queries.

Nonfiction: Articles about automobiles, new and old. All road tests are staff-written. "Unsolicited manuscripts are not accepted. Query letters must be addressed to the Managing Editor. Rates are generous, but few manuscripts are purchased from outside." **Buys 1 mss/year. Pays max $3,000/feature; $750-1,500/short piece.** Pays expenses of writers on assignment.

Photos: Color slides and b&w photos sometimes purchased with accompanying ms.

The online magazine carries original content not found in the print edition. Contact: Brad Nevin, online editor.

Tips: "It is best to start off with an interesting query and to stay away from nuts-and-bolts ideas because that will be handled in-house or by an acknowledged expert. Our goal is to be absolutely without flaw in our presentation of automotive facts, but we strive to be every bit as entertaining as we are informative. We do not print this sort of story: 'My Dad's Wacky, Lovable Beetle.' "

N $ CAR CRAFT, PRIMEDIA Enthusiast Group, 6420 Wilshire Blvd., Los Angeles CA 90048-5502. (323)782-2000. Fax: (323)782-2223. E-mail: carcraft@primediacmmg.com. Website: www.carcraft.com. Editor-in-Chief: Matt King. Monthly magazine. Created to appeal to drag racing and high performance auto owners. Circ. 383,334. Editorial lead time 3 months. Sample copy not available.

N $ $ CLASSIC TRUCKS, Primedia/McMullen Argus Publishing, 2400 E. Katella Ave., Suite 1100, Anaheim CA 92806. (714)939-2400. E-mail: webmaster@mcmullenargus.com. Website: www.mcmullenargus.com. **Contact:** James Rizzo, editor. Monthly magazine covering classic trucks from the 1930s to 1973. Estab. 1994. Circ. 60,000. Pays on publication. Byline given. Buys first North American serial rights. Editorial lead time 4 months. Submit seasonal material 4 months in advance. Writer's guidelines free.

Nonfiction: How-to, interview/profile, new product, technical, travel. Query. Length: 1,500-5,000 words. **Pays $75-200/page; $100/page maximum for unsolicited articles.**

Photos: Send photos with submission. Reviews transparencies, 5×7 prints. Buys one-time rights. Negotiates payment individually. Captions, identification of subjects, model releases required.

Columns/Departments: Buys 24 mss/year. Query.

$ CRUISING RIDER MAGAZINE, Running in Style, P.O. Box 1943, Sedona AZ 86336. (928)282-9293. E-mail: joshua@verdenet.com. **Contact:** Joshua Placa, editor. **10% freelance written.** Pays on publication. Buys all rights.

N $ $ $ FOUR WHEELER MAGAZINE, P.O. Box 420235, Palm Coast FL 32142. E-mail: fourwheeler@primediacmmg.com. Website: www.fourwheeler.com. **Contact:** Jon Thompson, editor. **20% freelance written.** Works with a small number of new/unpublished writers each year. Monthly magazine covering four-wheel-drive vehicles, back-country driving, competition and travel adventure. Estab. 1963. Circ. 355,466. Pays on publication. Publishes ms an average of 4 months after acceptance. Buys all rights. Submit seasonal material 4 months in advance. Accepts queries by mail. Sample copy not available.

Nonfiction: 4WD competition and travel/adventure articles, technical, how-tos, and vehicle features about unique four-wheel drives. "We like the adventure stories that bring four wheeling to life in word and photo: mud-running deserted logging roads, exploring remote, isolated trails or hunting/fishing where the 4x4 is a necessity for success." Query with photos. Length: 1,200-2,000 words; average 4-5 pages when published. **Pays $200-300/feature vehicles; $350-600/travel and adventure; $100-800/technical articles.**

Photos: Requires professional quality color slides and b&w prints for every article. Prefers Kodachrome 64 or Fujichrome 50 in 35mm or 2¼ formats. "Action shots a must for all vehicle features and travel articles." Captions required.

Tips: "Show us you know how to use a camera as well as the written word. The easiest way for a new writer/photographer to break into our magazine is to read several issues of the magazine, then query with a short vehicle feature that will show his or her potential as a creative writer/photographer."

$ $ FRICTION ZONE, Your Motorcycle Lifestyle Magazine, P.O. Box 530, Idyllwild CA 92549-0530. (909)659-9500. Fax: (909)659-8182. E-mail: editor@friction-zone.com. Website: www.friction-zone.com. **Contact:** Amy Holland, editor/publisher. **60% freelance written.** Monthly magazine covering motorcycles. Estab. 1999. Circ. 20,000. Pays on publication. Publishes ms an average of 1 month after acceptance. Byline given. Buys first North American serial rights. Editorial lead time 6 weeks. Submit seasonal material 2 months in advance. Accepts queries by mail, e-mail, fax. Responds in 2 weeks to queries; 1 month to mss. Sample copy for $4.50 or on website. Writer's guidelines online.

Nonfiction: General interest, historical/nostalgic, how-to, humor, inspirational, interview/profile, new product, opinion, photo feature, technical, travel, medical (relating to motorcyclists), book reviews (relating to motorcyclists). Does not accept first-person writing. **Buys 1 mss/year.** Query. Length: 1,000-3,000 words. **Pays 20¢/word.** Sometimes pays expenses of writers on assignment.

Photos: Send photos with submission. Reviews negatives, slides. Buys one-time rights. Offers $15/published photo. Captions, identification of subjects, model releases required.

Columns/Departments: Health Zone (health issues relating to motorcyclists); Motorcycle Engines 101 (basic motorcycle mechanics); Road Trip (California destination review including hotel, road, restaurant), all 2,000 words. **Buys 60 mss/year.** Query. **Pays 20¢/word.**

Fiction: Motorcycle related. Query. Length: 2,000-3,000 words. **Pays 20¢/word.**

Fillers: Anecdotes, facts, gags to be illustrated by cartoonist, newsbreaks, short humor. Length: 2,000-3,000 words. **Pays 20¢/word.**

Tips: "Query via e-mail with sample writing."

N $ HOT ROD MAGAZINE, PRIMEDIA Enthusiast Group, 6420 Wilshire Bvld. 10th Fl, Los Angeles CA 90048-5502. (323)782-2000. Fax: (323)782-2223. E-mail: hotrod@primedia.com. Website: www.hotrod.com. Editor: David Freiburger. Monthly magazine covering hot rods. Focuses on 50's and 60's cars outfitted with current drive trains and the nostalgia associated with them. Circ. 805,035. Editorial lead time 3 months. Sample copy not available.

N $ LATINOS ON WHEELS, On Wheels, Inc., 585 E. Larned St., Suite 100, Detroit MI 48226-4369. (313)963-2209. Fax: (313)963-7778. E-mail: latinos@onwheelsinc.com. Website: www.onwheelsinc.com/lowmagazine. Editor-in-Chief: Andres Tobar. Quarterly magazine. Supplement to leading Latino newspapers in the U.S. Provides Latino car buyers and car enthusiasts with the most relevant automotive trends. Circ. 500,000. Sample copy not available.

N $ LOWRIDER MAGAZINE, PRIMEDIA Enthusiast Group, 2400 E. Katella Ave., Suite 1100, Anaheim CA 92806-5945. (714)939-2400. E-mail: webmaster@mcmullenargus.com. Website: www.lowridermagazine.com; www.mcmullenargus.com. Editor: Ralph Fuentes. Monthly magazine. Covers the national and international lowriding scene with high impact, full-color vehicle and event features. Circ. 212,500. Editorial lead time 3 months. Sample copy not available.

$ $ $ $ MOBILE ENTERTAINMENT, Technology In Motion, (formerly *Car Stereo Review's Mobile Entertainment*), Hachette Filipacchi Magazines, 1633 Broadway, 45th Floor, New York NY 10019. (212)767-6000. Fax: (212)333-2434. E-mail: mobileentertainment@hfmus.com. **Contact:** Mike Mettler, editor-in-chief. **25% freelance written.** Published 6 times/year. "*Mobile Entertainment* is geared toward the mobile-electronics enthusiast, encompassing such things as mobile video, product test reports, installation techniques, new technologies such as MP3 and navigation, and music." Estab. 1987. Circ. 140,000. **Pays on acceptance.** Publishes ms an average of 3 months after acceptance. Byline given. Offers 25% kill fee. Buys first North American serial rights. Editorial lead time 4 months. Accepts queries by mail, e-mail, fax. Responds in 6 weeks to queries; 2 months to mss. Sample copy and writers guidelines free.

Nonfiction: "As we are a highly specialized publication, we won't look at anything nonspecific to our audience's needs." How-to (installation techniques), interview/profile, new product, technical. **Buys 10-20 mss/year.** Query with published clips. Length: 200-3,000 words. **Pays $40-5,000 for assigned articles; $40-2,000 for unsolicited articles.** Sometimes pays expenses of writers on assignment.

Photos: State availability with submission. Reviews contact sheets, negatives, transparencies. Buys one-time rights. Negotiates payment individually. Identification of subjects, model releases required.

Tips: "As we are experts in our field, and looked to as being the 'authority,' writers must have some knowledge of electronics, car stereo applications, and theory, especially in relation to the car environment. Our readers are not greenhorns, and expect expert opinions. Be aware of the differences between mobile and portable electronics technology versus home entertainment."

$ MOMENTUM, Hachette Filipacchi Media U.S., Inc., 460 W 34th Street, New York NY 10001. (212)767-6000. Fax: (212)560-2190. Editor: Donald Klein. Magazine published 3 times/year. Published excluvively for the Mercedes-Benz owner who appreciates quality, elegance, adventure and style. Circ. 575,000. Sample copy not available.

$ MOTOR AGE, Advanstar Communications, Inc., 150 Strafford Ave., Suite 210, Wayne PA 19087-3114. (610)687-2587. Fax: (610)687-1419. E-mail: motorage@advanstar.com. Website: www.motorage.com. Editor: Bill Cannon. Monthly magazine. Edited as a technical journal for automotive service dealers and technicians in the U.S. Circ. 143,147. Sample copy not available.

$ $ $ MOTOR TREND, Primedia, 6420 Wilshire Blvd., Los Angeles CA 90048. (323)782-2220. E-mail: motortrend@primedia.com. Website: www.motortrend.com. **Contact:** Kevin Smith, editorial director. **5-10% freelance written.** Only works with published/established writers. Monthly magazine for automotive enthusiasts and general interest consumers. Circ. 1,250,000. Publishes ms an average of 3 months after acceptance. Buys all rights. Accepts queries by mail. Responds in 1 month to queries. Sample copy not available.

Nonfiction: "Automotive and related subjects that have national appeal. Emphasis on domestic and imported cars, road tests, driving impressions, auto classics, auto, travel, racing, and high-performance features for the enthusiast. Packed with facts. Freelancers should confine queries to photo-illustrated exotic drives and other feature material; road tests and related activity are handled inhouse. Fact-filled query suggested for all freelancers."

Photos: Buys photos of prototype cars and assorted automotive matter. Pays $25-500 for transparencies.

Columns/Departments: Car care (query Matt Stone, senior editor).

$ OUTLAW BIKER, Outlaw Biker Enterprises, Inc., 5 Marine View Plaza, Suite 207, Hoboken NJ 07030. (201)653-2700. Fax: (201)653-7892. E-mail: editor@outlawbiker.com. Website: www.outlawbiker.com. **Contact:** Chris Miller, editor. **50% freelance written.** Magazine published 6 times/year covering bikers and their lifestyle. "All writers must be insiders of biker lifestyle. Features include coverage of biker events, profiles, and humor." Estab. 1983. Circ. 150,000. Pays on publication. Publishes ms an average of 3 months after acceptance. Byline given. Buys first rights. Editorial lead time 3 months. Submit seasonal material 5 months in advance. Accepts queries by mail, e-mail, fax. Accepts previously published material. Accepts simultaneous submissions. Responds in 2 weeks to queries; 2 months to mss. Sample copy for $5.98. Writer's guidelines for #10 SASE.

Nonfiction: Historical/nostalgic, humor, new product, personal experience, photo feature, travel. Special issues: Daytona Special, Sturgis Special (annual bike runs). "No first time experiences—our readers already know." **Buys 10-12 mss/year.** Send complete ms. Length: 100-1,000 words.

Photos: Send photos with submission. Reviews transparencies, prints. Buys one-time rights. Offers $0-10/photo. Captions, identification of subjects, model releases required.

Columns/Departments: Buys 10-12 mss/year. Send complete ms.

Fiction: Adventure, erotica, fantasy, historical, humorous, romance, science fiction, slice-of-life vignettes, suspense. No racism. **Buys 10-12 mss/year.** Send complete ms. Length: 500-2,500 words.

Poetry: Avant-garde, free verse, haiku, light verse, traditional. **Buys 10-12 poems/year.** Submit maximum 12 poems. Length: 2-1,000 lines.

Fillers: Anecdotes, facts, gags to be illustrated by cartoonist, newsbreaks, short humor. **Buys 10-12/year.** Length: 500-2,000 words.

The online version of *Outlaw Biker* carries original content not found in the print edition. Contact: Chris Miller.

Tips: "Writers must be insiders of the biker lifestyle. Manuscripts with accompanying photographs as art are given higher priority."

$ PETERSEN'S CUSTOM CLASSIC TRUCKS, PRIMEDIA Enthusiast Group, P.O. Box 57456, Boulder CO 80322. E-mail: customclassic@primedia.com. Website: www.customclassictrucks.com. Editor-in-Chief: Rich Boyd. Managing Editor: J. David Jones. Bimonthly magazine. Contains a compilation of technical articles, historical reviews, coverage of top vintage truck events and features dedicated to the fast growing segment of the truck market that includes vintage pickups and sedan deliveries. Circ. 104,376. Sample copy not available.

N $ POPULAR HOT RODDING, PRIMEDIA Enthusiast Group, 2400 E. Katella Ave., Suite 1100, Anaheim CA 92806. (714)939-2400. E-mail: phr@primedia.com. Website: www.popularhotrodding.com. Editor: Cameron Evans. Monthly magazine. Written for the automotive enthusiast by highlighting features that emphasize performance, bolt-on accessories, replacement parts, safety and the sport of drag racing. Circ. 182,000. Sample copy not available.

$ $ RIDER MAGAZINE, Ehlert Publishing Group, 2575 Vista Del Mar Dr., Ventura CA 93001. E-mail: editor@ridermagazine.com. Website: www.ridermagazine.com. **Contact:** Mark Tuttle, editor. **60% freelance written.** Monthly magazine covering motorcycling. "*Rider* serves the all-brand motorcycle lifestyle/enthusiast with a slant toward travel and touring." Estab. 1974. Circ. 107,000. Pays on publication. Publishes ms an average of 6-12 months after acceptance. Byline given. Offers 25% kill fee. Buys first North American serial, electronic rights. Editorial lead time 4 months. Submit seasonal material 6 months in advance. Accepts queries by mail. Responds in 2 months to queries. Sample copy for $2.95. Writer's guidelines for #10 SASE.

- "The articles we do buy often share the following characteristics: 1. The writer queried us in advance by regular mail (not by telephone or e-mail) to see if we needed or wanted the story. 2. The story was well written and of proper length. 3. The story had sharp, uncluttered photos taken with the proper film—*Rider* does not buy stories without photos."

Nonfiction: General interest, historical/nostalgic, how-to (re: motorcycling), humor, interview/profile, personal experience, travel. Does not want to see "fiction or articles on 'How I Began Motorcycling.'" **Buys 40-50 mss/year.** Query. Length: 750-2,000 words. **Pays $150-750.**

Photos: Send photos with submission. Reviews contact sheets, transparencies, 5×7 (b&w only) prints. Buys one-time and electronic rights. Offers no additional payment for photos accepted with ms. Captions required.

Columns/Departments: Favorite Rides (short trip), 850-1,100 words. **Buys 12 mss/year.** Query. **Pays $150-750.**

Tips: "We rarely accept manuscripts without photos (slides or b&w prints). Query first. Follow guidelines available on request. We are most open to feature stories (must include excellent photography) and material for 'Rides, Rallies and Clubs.' Include information on routes, local attractions, restaurants, and scenery in favorite ride submissions."

$ $ ROAD BIKE, TAM Communications, 1010 Summer St., Stamford CT 06905. (203)425-8777. Fax: (203)425-8775. E-mail: laurab@roadbikemag.com. **Contact:** Laura Brengelman, editor. **70% freelance written.** Monthly magazine covering motorcycling—tour, travel, project and custom bikes, products, and tech. Estab. 1993. Circ. 50,000. Pays on publication. Publishes ms an average of 6 months after acceptance. Byline given. Editorial lead time 4 months. Submit seasonal material 6 months in advance. Accepts queries by mail, fax. Writer's guidelines free.

Nonfiction: How-to (motorcycle, travel, camping), interview/profile (motorcycle related), new product, photo feature (motorcycle events or gathering places with minimum of 1,000 words text), travel. No fiction. **Buys 100 mss/year.** Query with or without published clips or send complete ms. Length: 1,000-3,500 words. **Pays $15-400.**

Photos: Send photos with submission (slides preferred, prints accepted, b&w contact sheets for how-to). Buys one-time rights. Offers no additional payment for photos accepted with ms. Captions required.

Columns/Departments: Reviews (products, media, all motorcycle related), 300-750 words, plus 1 or more photos. Query with published clips or send complete ms. **Pays $15-400.**

Fillers: Facts.

N $ $ ROAD KING, Parthenon Publishing, 28 White Bridge Rd., Suite 209, Nashville TN 37205. Fax: (615)627-2197. Website: www.roadking.com. **Contact:** Lisa Waddle, editor. **25% freelance written.** Bimonthly magazine covering the trucking industry. **Pays on acceptance.** Publishes ms an average of 3 months after acceptance. Byline given. Offers 30% kill fee. Buys first North American serial, electronic rights. Editorial lead time 3-4 months. Submit seasonal material 4 months in advance. Accepts queries by mail, fax. Accepts previously published material. Accepts simultaneous submissions. Responds in 3-4 weeks to queries. Sample copy for #10 SASE. Writer's guidelines free.

Nonfiction: Book excerpts, general interest, historical/nostalgic, how-to, humor, new product. **Buys 12 mss/year.** Query with published clips. Length: 100-800 words. **Pays $50-700.** Pays expenses of writers on assignment.

Photos: Michael Nott, art director. Send photos with submission. Negotiates payment individually.

N $ SPORT COMPACT CAR, PRIMEDIA Enthusiast Group, 2400 E. Katella Ave., Anaheim CA 92806. (714)939-2400. E-mail: sportcompactcar@primedia.com. Website: www.sportcompactcarweb.com. Editor: Scott Oldham. Monthly magazine. Targeted to owners and potential buyers of new compacts who seek inside information regarding performance, personalization and cosmetic enhancement of the vehicles. Circ. 117,000. Editorial lead time 4 months. Sample copy not available.

N $ SPORT RIDER, PRIMEDIA Enthusiast Group, 6420 Wilshire Blvd. 17th Fl, Los Angeles CA 90048. (323)782-2000. Fax: (323)782-2372. E-mail: srmail@primedia.com. Website: www.primedia.com. Editor-in-Chief: Kent Kunitsugu. Bimonthly magazine. Written for enthusiast of sport/street motercycles and emphasizes performance, both in the motorcycle and the rider. Circ. 108,365. Sample copy not available.

N $ SPORT TRUCK, PRIMEDIA Enthusiast Group, P.O. Box 51607, Boulder CO 80322. E-mail: sporttruck@primedia.com. Website: www.sporttruck.com. Editor-in-Chief: Dan Sanchez. Monthly magazine. Covers the entire range of light duty trucks and sport utility vehicles with an emphasis on performance and personalization. Circ. 200,357. Sample copy not available.

N $ SUPER CHEVY, PRIMEDIA Enthusiast Group, 2400 Katella Ave., 11th Floor, Anaheim CA 92806-5945. (714)939-2400. Fax: (714)572-1864. E-mail: webmaster@mcmullenargus.com. Website: www.superchevy-web.com. Editor: Terry Cole. Monthly magazine. Reports on various forms of motorsports where Cheverolet cars and engines are in competition. Circ. 198,995. Sample copy not available.

N $ TRAINS, Kalmbach Publishing Company, PO Box 1612, Waukesha WI 53187-1612. (262)796-8776. Fax: (262)796-1142. E-mail: editor@trainsmag.com. Website: www.trainsmag.com. Editor: Mark Hemphill. Monthly magazine. Appeals to consumers interested in learning about the function and history of the train industry. Circ. 130,385. Editorial lead time 2 months. Sample copy not available.

$ $ TRUCK TREND, The SUV & Pickup Authority, P.O. Box 53525, Boulder CO 80322. E-mail: trucktrend@primediacmmg.com. Website: www.trucktrend.com. **Contact:** David E. Davis, editor-in-chief. **60% freelance written.** Bimonthly magazine covering trucks, SUVs, minivans, vans, and travel. "*Truck Trend* readers want to know about what's new in the world of sport-utilities, pickups, and vans. What to buy, how to fix up, and where to go." Estab. 1998. Circ. 125,000. Pays on publication. Publishes ms an average of 3 months after acceptance. Byline given. Buys all rights. Editorial lead time 5 months. Submit seasonal material 6 months in advance. Accepts queries by mail. Sample copy for #10 SASE. Writer's guidelines not available.

Nonfiction: How-to, travel. Special issues: Towing; Hot Rod Truck; ½ Ton Pickup; Diesel. No personal experience, humor, or religious. **Buys 12 mss/year.** Query. Length: 500-1,800 words. **Pays $150-300/page.** Sometimes pays expenses of writers on assignment.

Photos: Send photos with submission. Reviews transparencies. Buys all rights. Offers no additional payment for photos accepted with ms. Captions, identification of subjects, model releases required.

The online magazine carries original content not found in the print edition.

Tips: "Know the subject/audience. Start by using a previous story as a template. Call editor for advice after flushing story out. Understand the editor is looking to freelancers to make life easier."

N $ TRUCKIN', PRIMEDIA Enthusiast Group, 2400 E. Katella Ave., Suite 1100, Anaheim CA 92806. (714)939-2400. E-mail: webmaster@mcmullenargus.com. Website: www.truckinweb.com. Editor: Steve Warner. Monthly magazine. Written for pickup drivers and enthusiasts. Circ. 186,606. Editorial lead time 3 months. Sample copy not available.

AVIATION

Professional and private pilots and aviation enthusiasts read the publications in this section. Editors want material for audiences knowledgeable about commercial aviation. Magazines for passengers of commercial airlines are grouped in the Inflight category. Technical aviation and space journals, and publications for airport operators, aircraft dealers, and others in aviation businesses are listed under Aviation & Space in the Trade section.

$ $ $ $ AIR & SPACE MAGAZINE, Smithsonian Institution, P.O. Box 37012, Victor Bldg. 7100, MRC 951, Washington DC 20013-7012. (202)275-1230. Fax: (202)275-1886. E-mail: editors@airspacemag.com. Website: www.airspacemag.com. Editor: George Larson. **Contact:** Linda Shiner, executive editor (features); Pat Trenner, senior editor (departments). **80% freelance written.** Bimonthly magazine covering aviation and aerospace for a nontechnical audience. "The emphasis is on the human rather than the technological, on the ideas behind the events. Features are slanted to a technically curious, but not necessarily technically knowledgeable audience. We are looking for unique angles to aviation/aerospace stories, history, events, personalities, current and future technologies, that emphasize the human-interest aspect." Estab. 1985. Circ. 225,000. **Pays on acceptance.** Byline given. Offers kill fee. Buys first North American serial rights. Accepts queries by mail, e-mail, fax. Responds in 3 months to queries. Sample copy for $5. Writer's guidelines online.

"We're looking for 'reader service' articles—a collection of helpful hints and interviews with experts that would help our readers enjoy their interest in aviation. An example: An article telling readers how they could learn more about the space shuttle, where to visit, how to invite an astronaut to speak to their schools, what books are most informative, etc. A good place to break in is our 'Soundings' department."

Nonfiction: The editors are actively seeking stories covering space and general or business aviation. Book excerpts, essays, general interest (on aviation/aerospace), historical/nostalgic, humor, photo feature, technical. **Buys 50 mss/year.** Query with published clips. Length: 1,500-3,000 words. **Pays $1,500-3,000.** Pays expenses of writers on assignment.

Photos: Refuses unsolicited material. State availability with submission. Reviews 35 mm transparencies, digital files.

Columns/Departments: Above and Beyond (first person), 1,500-2,000 words; Flights and Fancy (whimsy), approximately 800 words. Soundings (brief items, timely but not breaking news), 500-700 words. **Buys 25 mss/year.** Query with published clips. **Pays $150-300.**

The online version carries original content not found in the print edition. Contact: Linda Shiner, Pat Trenner.

Tips: "We continue to be interested in stories about space exploration. Also, writing should be clear, accurate, and engaging. It should be free of technical and insider jargon, and generous with explanation and background. The first step every aspiring contributor should take is to study recent issues of the magazine."

$ $ AIR LINE PILOT, The Magazine of Professional Flight Deck Crews, Air Line Pilots Association, 535 Herndon Pkwy., P.O. Box 1169, Herndon VA 20172. (703)481-4460. Fax: (703)689-4370. E-mail: magazine@alpa.org. Website: www.alpa.org. **Contact:** Gary DiNunno, editor. **10% freelance written.** Prefers to work with published/established writers; works with a small number of new/unpublished writers each year. Magazine published 10 times/year for airline pilots covering commercial aviation industry information—economics, avionics, equipment, systems, safety—that affects a pilot's life in a professional sense. Also includes information about management/labor relations trends, contract negotiations, etc. Estab. 1931. Circ. 95,000. **Pays on acceptance.** Publishes ms an average of 6 months after acceptance. Offers 50% kill fee. all rights except book rights Submit seasonal material 6 months in advance. Responds in 2 months to queries. Sample copy for $2. Writer's guidelines online.

Nonfiction: Humor, inspirational, photo feature, technical. **Buys 20 mss/year.** Query with or without published clips or send complete ms and SASE. Length: 700-3,000 words. **Pays $100-600 for assigned articles; $50-600 for unsolicited articles.**

Reprints: Send photocopy of article or typed ms with rights for sale noted and information about when and where the material previously appeared. Payment varies.

Photos: "Our greatest need is for strikingly original cover photographs featuring ALPA flight deck crew members and their airlines in their operating environment." Send photos with submission. Reviews contact sheets, 35mm transparencies, 8×10 prints. Buys all rights for cover photos, one-time rights for inside color. Offers $10-35/b&w photo, $20-50 for color used inside and $400 for color used as cover. For cover photography, shoot vertical rather than horizontal. Identification of subjects required.

Tips: "For our feature section, we seek aviation industry information that affects the life of a professional pilot's career standpoint. We also seek material that affects a pilot's life from a job security and work environment standpoint. Any airline pilot featured in an article must be an Air Line Pilot Association member in good standing. Our readers are very experienced and require a high level of technical accuracy in both written material and photographs."

$ BALLOON LIFE, Balloon Life Magazine, Inc., 2336 47th Ave. SW, Seattle WA 98116-2331. (206)935-3649. Fax: (206)935-3326. E-mail: tom@balloonlife.com. Website: www.balloonlife.com. **Contact:** Tom Hamilton, editor-in-chief. **75% freelance written.** Monthly magazine covering sport of hot air ballooning. Publishes material "about the sport of hot air ballooning. Readers participate as pilots, crew, official observers at events and spectators." Estab. 1986. Circ. 4,000. Pays on publication. Publishes ms an average of 3-4 months after acceptance. Byline given. Offers 50-100% kill fee. Buys first North American serial, one-time rights. Buys nonexclusive, all rights. Submit seasonal material 4 months in advance. Accepts queries by e-mail, fax. Accepts previously published material. Accepts simultaneous submissions. Responds in 3 weeks to queries; 1 month to mss. Sample copy for 9×12 SAE with $2 postage. Writer's guidelines for #10 SASE.

Nonfiction: Book excerpts, general interest, how-to (flying hot air balloons, equipment techniques), interview/profile, new product, technical, events/rallies, safety seminars, balloon clubs/organizations, letters to the editor. **Buys 150 mss/year.** Query with or without published clips or send complete ms. Length: 1,000-1,500 words. **Pays $50-75 for assigned articles; $25-50 for unsolicited articles.** Pays expenses of writers on assignment.

Reprints: Send tearsheet, photocopy or typed ms with rights for sale noted and information about when and where the material previously appeared. Pays 100% of amount paid for an original article or story.

Photos: Send photos with submission. Reviews transparencies, prints. Buys nonexclusive, all rights. Offers $15/inside photos, $50/cover. Identification of subjects required.

Columns/Departments: Hangar Flying (real-life flying experience that others can learn from), 800-1,500 words; Crew Quarters (devoted to some aspect of crewing), 900 words; Preflight (a news and information column), 100-500 words; **pays $50**. Logbook (recent balloon events—events that have taken place in last 3-4 months), 300-500 words; **pays $20. Buys 60 mss/year.** Send complete ms. **Pays $20-50.**

Fiction: Tom Hamilton, editor. Humorous, related to hot air ballooning. **Buys 3-5 mss/year.** Send complete ms. Length: 800-1,500 words. **Pays $25-75, and contributor's copies.**

Tips: "This magazine slants toward the technical side of ballooning. We are interested in articles that help to educate and provide safety information. Also stories with manufacturers, important individuals, and/or of historic events and technological advances important to ballooning. The magazine attempts to present articles that show 'how-to' (fly, business opportunities, weather, equipment). Both our Feature Stories section and Logbook section are where most manuscripts are purchased."

$ $ CESSNA OWNER MAGAZINE, Jones Publishing, Inc., N7450 Aanstad Rd., P.O. Box 5000, Iola WI 54945. (715)445-5000. Fax: (715)445-4053. E-mail: jenniferj@cessnaowner.org. Website: www.cessnaowner.org. **Contact:** Jennifer Julin, publisher. **50% freelance written.** Monthly magazine covering Cessna single and twin-engine aircraft. "*Cessna Owner Magazine* is the official publication of the Cessna Owner Organization (C.O.O.). Therefore, our readers are Cessna aircraft owners, renters, pilots, and enthusiasts. Articles should deal with buying/selling, flying, maintaining, or modifying Cessnas. The purpose of our magazine is to promote safe, fun, and affordable flying." Estab. 1975. Circ. 6,000. Pays on publication. Publishes ms an average of 3 months after acceptance. Byline given. Buys first, one-time, second serial (reprint) rights, makes work-for-hire assignments. Editorial lead time 1 month. Submit seasonal material 3 months in advance. Accepts queries by mail, e-mail, fax, phone. Accepts previously published material. Responds in 2 weeks to queries; 1 month to mss. Sample copy and writer's guidelines free or on website.

Nonfiction: "We are always looking for articles about Cessna aircraft modifications. We also need articles on Cessna twin-engine aircraft. April, July, and October are always big issues for us, because we attend various airshows during these months and distribute free magazines. Feature articles on unusual, highly modified, or vintage Cessnas are especially welcome during these months. Good photos are also a must." Historical/nostalgic (of specific Cessna models), how-to (aircraft repairs and maintenance), new product, personal experience, photo feature, technical (aircraft engines and airframes). Special issues: Engines (maintenance, upgrades); Avionics (purchasing, new products). **Buys 48 mss/year.** Query. Length: 1,500-3,500 words. **Pays 7-11¢/word.**

Reprints: Send mss via e-mail with rights for sale noted and information about when and where the material previously appeared.

Photos: Send photos with submission. Reviews 3×5 and larger prints. Captions, identification of subjects required.

N **$ FLYING MAGAZINE**, Hachette Filipacchi Media U.S., Inc., 500 W Putnam Ave., Greenwich CT 06830. (203)622-2706. Fax: (203)622-2725. E-mail: flyedit@hfmus.com. Website: www.flyingmag.com. Editor: J. Mac McClellan Managing Editor: Elizabeth Murray. Monthly magazine covering aviation. Edited for active pilots through coverage of new product development and application in the general aviation market. Estab. 1927. Circ. 306,000. Editorial lead time 3 months. Accepts queries by mail, e-mail, fax. Sample copy for $3.99.

- *Flying* is almost entirely staff written, use of freelance material is limited.

Nonfiction: "We are looking for the most unusual and best-written material that suits *Flying*. Most subjects in aviation have already been done so fresher ideas and approaches to stories are particularly valued. We buy 'I Learned About Flying From That' articles, as well as an occasional feature with and without photographs supplied." Send complete ms.

$ GENERAL AVIATION NEWS, N.W. Flyer, Inc., P.O. Box 39099, Lakewood WA 98439-0099. (888)333-5937. Fax: (253)471-9911. E-mail: janice@generalaviationnews.com. Website: www.generalaviationnews.com. **Contact:** Janice Wood, editor. **30% freelance written.** Prefers to work with published/established writers. Biweekly tabloid covering general, regional, national, and international aviation stories of interest to pilots, aircraft owners, and aviation enthusiasts. Estab. 1949. Circ. 35,000. Pays 1 month after publication. Publishes ms an average of 3 months after acceptance. Byline given. Buys first North American serial, second serial (reprint) rights. Submit seasonal material 6 months in advance. Accepts queries by mail, e-mail, fax, phone. Responds in 2 months to queries. Sample copy for $3.50. Writer's guidelines for #10 SASE.

Break in by having "an aviation background, being up to date on current events, and being able to write. A 1,000-word story with good photos is the best way to see your name in print.

Nonfiction: "We stress news. A controversy over an airport, a first flight of a new design, storm or flood damage to an airport, a new business opening at your local airport—those are the sort of projects that may get a new writer onto our pages, if they arrive here soon after they happen. We are especially interested in reviews of aircraft." Personality pieces involving someone who is using his or her airplane in an unusual way, and stories about aviation safety are of interest. Query first on historical, nostalgic features, and profiles/interviews. **Buys 100 mss/year.** Query with or without published clips or send complete ms. Length: 500-2,000 words. **Pays up to $10/printed column inch.** Sometimes pays expenses of writers on assignment.

Photos: Shoot clear, up-close photos, preferably color prints or slides. Send photos with submission. Pays $10/b&w photo and $50/cover photo 1 month after publication. Captions, identification of subjects required.

Tips: "The longer the story, the less likely it is to be accepted. If you are covering controversy, send us both sides of the story. Most of our features and news stories are assigned in response to a query."

$ $ PIPERS MAGAZINE, Jones Publishing, Inc., N7450 Aanstad Rd., P.O. Box 5000, Iola WI 54945. (715)445-5000. Fax: (715)445-4053. E-mail: jenniferj@piperowner.org. Website: www.piperowner.org. **Contact:** Jennifer Julin. **50% freelance written.** Monthly magazine covering Piper single and twin engine aircraft. "*Pipers Magazine* is the official publication of the Piper Owner Society (P.O.S). Therefore, our readers are Piper aircraft owners, renters, pilots, mechanics and enthusiasts. Articles should deal with buying/selling, flying, maintaining or modifying Pipers. The purpose of our magazine is to promote safe, fun and affordable flying." Estab. 1988. Circ. 5,000. Pays on publication. Publishes ms an average of 3 months after acceptance. Buys first, one-time, second serial (reprint) rights, makes work-for-hire assignments. Editorial lead time 1 month. Submit seasonal material 3 months in advance. Accepts queries by mail, e-mail, fax, phone. Accepts previously published material. Responds in 2 weeks to queries; 1 month to mss. Sample copy for free. Writer's guidelines free.

Nonfiction: "We are always looking for articles about Piper aircraft modifications. We also are in need of articles on Piper twin engine aircraft, and late-model Pipers. April, July, and October are always big issues for us, because we attend airshows during these months and distribute free magazines." Feature articles on unusual, highly-modified, vintage, late-model, or ski/float equipped Pipers are especially welcome. Good photos are a must. Historical/nostalgic (of specific models of Pipers), how-to (aircraft repairs & maintenance), new product, personal experience, photo feature, technical (aircraft engines and airframes). **Buys 48 mss/year.** Query. Length: 1,500-3,500 words. **Pays 7-11¢/word.**

Reprints: Send mss by e-mail with rights for sale noted and information about when and where the material previously appeared.

Photos: Send photos with submission. Reviews transparencies, 3×5 and larger prints. Offers no additional payment for photos accepted. Captions, identification of subjects required.

$ $ PLANE AND PILOT, Werner Publishing Corp., 12121 Wilshire Blvd., Suite 1200, Los Angeles CA 90025. (310)820-1500. Fax: (310)826-5008. E-mail: editors@planeandpilot.com. Website: www.planeandpilotmag.com. Editor: Lyn Freeman. **Contact:** Jenny Shearer, managing editor. **100% freelance written.** Monthly magazine covering general aviation. "We think a spirited, conversational writing style is most entertaining for our readers. We are read by private and corporate pilots, instructors, students, mechanics and technicians—everyone involved or interested in general aviation." Estab. 1964. Circ. 130,000. Pays on publication. Publishes ms an average of 3 months after acceptance. Byline given. Offers kill fee. Buys all rights. Submit seasonal material 4 months in advance. Accepts previously published material. Responds in 2 months to queries. Sample copy for $5.50. Writer's guidelines online.

Nonfiction: How-to, new product, personal experience, technical, travel, pilot efficiency, pilot reports on aircraft. **Buys 75 mss/year.** Query. Length: 1,000-1,800 words. **Pays $200-500.** Pays expenses of writers on assignment.

Reprints: Send tearsheet, photocopy or typed ms with rights for sale noted and information about when and where the material previously appeared. Pays 50% of amount paid for original article.

Photos: Submit suggested heads, decks and captions for all photos with each story. Submit b&w photos in proof sheet form with negatives or 8×10 prints with glossy finish. Submit color photos in the form of 2¼×2¼ or 4×5 or 35mm transparencies in plastic sleeves. Buys all rights. Offers $50-300/photo.
Columns/Departments: Readback (any newsworthy items on aircraft and/or people in aviation), 100-300 words; Jobs & Schools (a feature or an interesting school or program in aviation), 1,000-1,500 words; and Travel (any traveling done in piston-engine aircraft), 1,000-2,500 words. **Buys 30 mss/year.** Send complete ms. **Pays $200-500.**
Tips: "Pilot proficiency articles are our bread and butter. Manuscripts should be kept under 1,800 words."

$ $ PRIVATE PILOT, Y-Visionary, Inc., 265 S. Anita Dr., #120, Orange CA 92868. (714)939-9991, ext. 234. Fax: (714)939-9909. E-mail: bfedorko@earthlink.net. Website: www.privatepilotmag.com. **Contact:** Bill Fedorko, editoral director. **40% freelance written.** Monthly magazine covering general aviation. "*Private Pilot* is edited for owners and pilots of single and multi-engine aircraft." Estab. 1965. Circ. 85,000. Pays on publication. Publishes ms an average of 4 months after acceptance. Byline given. Offers 15% or $75 kill fee. Buys first North American serial rights. Editorial lead time 3 months. Submit seasonal material 6 months in advance. Accepts queries by mail, fax. Responds in 2 months to queries. Writer's guidelines for #10 SASE.
Nonfiction: General interest, historical/nostalgic, how-to, humor, inspirational, interview/profile, new product, opinion, personal experience, technical, travel, aircraft types. **Buys 12-15 mss/year.** Query. Length: 800-3,000 words. **Pays $350-650.** Sometimes pays expenses of writers on assignment.
Photos: State availability with submission. Reviews 35mm transparencies. Buys one-time rights. Negotiates payment individually. Captions, identification of subjects, model releases required.
Fiction: Adventure, historical, humorous, slice-of-life vignettes, all aviation related. **Buys 12-15 mss/year.** Query. Length: 800-3,500 words. **Pays $300-600.**
The online version carries original content not found in the print edition. Contact: Bill Fedorko, online editor.
Tips: "Send good queries. Readers are pilots who want to read about aircraft, places to go, and ways to save money."

$ WOMAN PILOT, Aviatrix Publishing, Inc., P.O. Box 485, Arlington Heights IL 60006-0485. (847)797-0170. Fax: (847)797-0161. E-mail: womanpilot@womanpilot.com. Website: www.womanpilot.com. **Contact:** Editor. **80% freelance written.** Bimonthly magazine covering women who fly all types of aircraft and careers in all areas of aviation. Personal profiles, historical articles and current aviation events. Estab. 1993. Circ. 6,000. Pays on publication. Publishes ms an average of 5 months after acceptance. Byline given. Buys first North American serial rights. Accepts queries by mail, e-mail, phone. Accepts previously published material. Sample copy for $3. Writer's guidelines for #10 SASE or online.
Break in with "interesting stories about women in aerospace with great photos."
Nonfiction: Book excerpts, historical/nostalgic, humor, interview/profile, new product, personal experience, photo feature. **Buys 35 mss/year.** Query with published clips or send complete ms. Length: 500-4,000 words. **Pays $20-55 for assigned articles; $20-40 for unsolicited articles.**
Reprints: Send tearsheet or typed ms with rights for sale noted and information about when and where the material previously appeared.
Photos: State availability of or send photos with submission. Buys one-time rights. Negotiates payment individually. Captions, identification of subjects, model releases required.
Fiction: Adventure, historical, humorous, slice-of-life vignettes. **Buys 4 mss/year.** Query with or without published clips. Length: 500-2,000 words. **Pays $20-35.**
Fillers: Cartoons. **Buys 6/year. Pays $10-20.**
The online version carries original content not found in the print edition and contains articles from back issues. Contact: Editor.
Tips: "If a writer is interested in writing articles from our leads, she/he should send writing samples and explanation of any aviation background. Include any writing background."

BUSINESS & FINANCE

Business publications give executives and consumers a range of information from local business news and trends to national overviews and laws that affect them. National and regional publications are listed below in separate categories. Magazines that have a technical slant are in the Trade section under Business Management, Finance, or Management & Supervision categories.

National

N $ $ THE BUSINESS JOURNAL, Serving San Jose and Silicon Valley, American City Business Journals Inc., 96 N. Third St., Suite 100, San Jose CA 95112. (408)295-3800. Fax: (408)295-5028. E-mail: sanjose@bizjournals.com. Website: www.amcity.com/sanjose. Editor: Gregg Parker. **Contact:** Robert Celaschi, managing editor. **2-5% freelance written.** Weekly tabloid covering a wide cross-section of industries. "Our stories are written for business people. Our audience is primarily upper-level management." Estab. 1983. Circ. 13,200. Pays on publication. Byline given. Offers $75 kill fee. Buys all rights. Editorial lead time 1 month. Accepts queries by e-mail. Responds in 2 weeks to queries. Sample copy for free. Writer's guidelines free.
Nonfiction: News/feature articles specifically assigned. **Buys 300 mss/year.** Query. Length: 700-2,500 words. **Pays $175-400.**

Photos: State availability with submission. Reviews 5×7 prints. Offers $25/photo used.

Tips: "Just call or e-mail (preferable) and say you are interested. We give almost everyone a chance."

$ $ $ $ BUSINESS 2.0 MAGAZINE, Time Inc., 5 Thomas Mellon Circle, Suite 305, San Francisco CA 94134. Fax: (415)656-8660. E-mail: freelancers@business2.com. Website: www.business2.com. Managing Editor: Judy Lewenthal. **Contact:** James Daly, editor-in-chief. Monthly magazine covering business in the Internet economy. Estab. 1998. Circ. 350,000. Pays on publication. Publishes ms an average of 3 months after acceptance. Byline given. Offers 20% kill fee. Buys all rights. Editorial lead time 2 months. Submit seasonal material 4 months in advance. Accepts queries by e-mail. Accepts simultaneous submissions. Sample copy for free. Writer's guidelines online.

Break in with fresh ideas on web-enabled business transformation—from the way companies are conceived and financed to how they develop markets and retain customers.

Nonfiction: Essays, exposé, new product, opinion, travel, new business ideas for the Internet. **Buys 40-50 mss/year.** Query with published clips. Length: 150-3,000 words. **Pays $1/word.** Pays expenses of writers on assignment.

The online magazine carries original content not found in the print edition. Contact: Ed Homicit, online editor.

$ $ DOLLARS AND SENSE: THE MAGAZINE OF ECONOMIC JUSTICE, Economic Affairs Bureau, 740 Cambridge St., Cambridge MA 02141-1401. (617)876-2434. Fax: (617)876-0008. E-mail: dollars@dollarsandsense.org. Website: www.dollarsandsense.org. **Contact:** Amy Gluckman or Adria Scharf, co-editors. **10% freelance written.** Bimonthly magazine covering economic, environmental, and social justice. "We explain the workings of the U.S. and international economics, and provide left perspectives on current economic affairs. Our audience is a mix of activists, organizers, academics, unionists, and other socially concerned people." Estab. 1974. Circ. 8,000. Pays on publication. Publishes ms an average of 4 months after acceptance. Byline given. Editorial lead time 3 months. Submit seasonal material 2 months in advance. Accepts queries by mail, e-mail, fax, phone. Sample copy for $5 or on website. Writer's guidelines online.

Nonfiction: Exposé, political economics. **Buys 6 mss/year.** Query with published clips. Length: 700-2,500 words. **Pays $0-200.** Sometimes pays expenses of writers on assignment.

Photos: State availability with submission. Buys one-time rights. Negotiates payment individually. Captions, identification of subjects required.

Tips: "Be familiar with our magazine and the types of communities interested in reading us. *Dollars and Sense* is a progressive economics magazine that explains in a popular way both the workings of the economy and struggles to change it. Articles may be on the environment, the World Bank, community organizing, urban conflict, inflation, unemployment, union reform, welfare, changes in government regulation-a broad range of topics that have an economic theme. Find samples of our latest issue on our homepage."

$ FORBES, Forbes, Inc., 60 5th Ave., New York NY 10011. (212)660-2200. Fax: (212)620-2273. E-mail: readers@forbes.com. Website: www.forbes.com. Editor-in-Chief: Steve Forbes. Editor: William Baldwin. Biweekly magazine. Edited for top business management professionals and for those aspiring to positions of corporate leadership. Circ. 921,410. Editorial lead time 2 months. Sample copy not available.

$ $ $ $ HISPANIC BUSINESS, Hispanic Business, Inc., 425 Pine Ave., Santa Barbara CA 93117. Fax: (805)964-5539. E-mail: Leslie.Dinaberg@hbinc.com. Website: www.hispanicbusiness.com. Editor: Jesus Chavarria. **Contact:** Leslie Dinaberg, managing editor; Tim Dougherty, senior editor. **50-60% freelance written.** Monthly magazine covering Hispanic business. "For more than 2 decades, *Hispanic Business* magazine has documented the growing affluence and power of the Hispanic community. Our magazine reaches the most educated, affluent Hispanic business and community leaders. Stories should have relevance for the Hispanic business community." Estab. 1979. Circ. 220,000 (rate base); 990,000 (readership base). Pays on publication. Publishes ms an average of 1 month after acceptance. Byline given. Offers 50% kill fee. Buys all rights. Editorial lead time 1-3 months. Submit seasonal material 2 months in advance. Accepts queries by mail, e-mail. Accepts simultaneous submissions. Responds in 3 weeks to queries; 1 month to mss. Sample copy for free.

Nonfiction: Leslie Dinaberg, managing editor. Interview/profile, travel. **Buys 120 mss/year.** Query with published clips. Length: 650-2,000 words. **Pays $50-1,500.** Pays in contributor copies upon request. Sometimes pays expenses of writers on assignment.

Photos: State availability with submission. Reviews GIF/JPEG files. Buys all rights. Negotiates payment individually. Captions required.

Columns/Departments: Tim Dougherty, senior editor. Tech Pulse (technology); The Traveler (travel); Money Matters (financial); LegalEase (legal), all 650 words. **Buys 40 mss/year.** Query with published clips. **Pays $50-450.**

Tips: "E-mail or snail mail queries with published clips are the most effective."

$ $ $ $ INDUSTRYWEEK, Leadership in Manufacturing, Penton Media, Inc., Penton Media Bldg., 1300 E. 9th St., Cleveland OH 44114. (216)696-7000. Fax: (216)696-7670. E-mail: tvinas@industryweek.com. Website: www.industryweek.com. Editor-in-Chief: Patricia Panchak. **Contact:** Tonya Vinas, managing editor. **30% freelance written.** Magazine published 12 times/year. "*IndustryWeek* connects marketers and manufacturers and provides information that helps manufacturers drive continuous improvement throughout the enterprise. Every issue of *IndustryWeek* is edited for the management teams of today's most competitive manufacturing companies, as well as decision-makers in the service industries that support manufacturing growth and productivity." Estab. 1970. Circ. 233,000. **Pays on acceptance.** Publishes ms an average of 2 months after acceptance. Byline given. Buys all rights. Accepts queries by e-mail. Responds in 1 month to queries. Sample copy and writer's guidelines online.

Nonfiction: Book excerpts, exposé, interview/profile. "No first-person articles." **Buys 25 mss/year.** Query with published clips. Length: 1,800-3,000 words. **Pays average of $1/word for all articles; reserves right to negotiate.** Sometimes pays expenses of writers on assignment.

Photos: Reviews contact sheets, negatives, transparencies, prints. Buys one-time rights. Negotiates payment individually. Captions, identification of subjects required.

Tips: "Pitch wonderful ideas targeted precisely at our audience. Read, re-read, and understand the writer's guidelines. *IndustryWeek* readers are primarily senior executives—people with the title of vice president, executive vice president, senior vice president, chief executive officer, chief financial officer, chief information officer, chairman, managing director, and president. *IW*'s executive readers oversee global corporations. While *IW*'s primary target audience is a senior executive in a U.S. firm, your story should provide information that any executive anywhere in the world can use. *IW*'s audience is primarily in companies in manufacturing and manufacturing-related industries."

$ $ $ LATIN TRADE, Your Business Source for Latin America, 95 Merrick Way, Suite 600, Coral Gables FL 33134. (305)358-8373. Fax: (305)358-9166. Website: www.latintrade.com. **Contact:** Mike Zellner, editor. **55% freelance written.** Monthly magazine covering Latin American business. "*Latin Trade* covers cross-border business in Latin America for top executives doing business with the region." Estab. 1993. Circ. 105,000. Pays on publication. Publishes ms an average of 3 months after acceptance. Byline given. Offers 25% kill fee. Buys all rights, makes work-for-hire assignments. Editorial lead time 3 months. Submit seasonal material 6 months in advance. Accepts queries by mail, e-mail. Responds in 2 weeks to queries. Sample copy and writer's guidelines free.

Nonfiction: Exposé, historical/nostalgic, humor, interview/profile, travel, business news. No one-source stories or unsolicited stories. **Buys 50 mss/year.** Query with published clips. Length: 800-2,000 words. **Pays $200-1,000.** Sometimes pays expenses of writers on assignment.

Photos: State availability with submission. Reviews contact sheets. Buys one-time rights. Negotiates payment individually. Identification of subjects required.

N ⊘ $ MONEY, Time, Inc., 1271 Avenue of the Americas, 32nd Floor, New York NY 10020. (212)522-1212. Fax: (212)522-0189. E-mail: money_letters@moneymail.com. Website: money.cnn.com. Editor: Norman Pearlstine. Managing Editor: Robert Safian. Monthly magazine covering finance. "*Money* magazine offers sophisticated coverage in all aspects of personal finance for individuals, business executives, and personal investors." Estab. 1972. Circ. 1,945,265. Editorial lead time 2 months. Sample copy for $3.95.

- "*Money* magazine does not accept unsolicited manuscripts and almost never uses freelance writers."

$ $ $ MYBUSINESS MAGAZINE, Hammock Publishing, 3322 W. End Ave., Suite 700, Nashville TN 37203. Fax: (615)690-3401. E-mail: sscully@hammock.com. Website: www.mybusinessmag.com. **Contact:** Shannon Scully, managing editor. **75% freelance written.** Bimonthly magazine for small businesses. "We are a guide to small business success, however that is defined in the new small business economy. We explore the methods and minds behind the trends and celebrate the men and women leading the creation of the new small business economy." Estab. 1999. Circ. 600,000. **Pays on acceptance.** Publishes ms an average of 4 months after acceptance. Byline given. Offers 30% kill fee. Buys first North American serial, electronic rights. Editorial lead time 4 months. Submit seasonal material 5 months in advance. Accepts queries by mail, fax. Accepts simultaneous submissions. Responds in 3 weeks to queries. Sample copy free. Writer's guidelines online.

Nonfiction: Book excerpts, how-to (small business topics), humor, new product. **Buys 8 mss/year.** Query with published clips. Length: 200-1,800 words. **Pays $75-1,000.** Pays expenses of writers on assignment.

Tips: *MyBusiness* is sent bimonthly to the 600,000 members of the National Federation of Independent Business. "We're here to help small business owners by giving them a range of how-to pieces that evaluate, analyze, and lead to solutions."

$ $ THE NETWORK JOURNAL, Black Professional and Small Business News, The Network Journal Communication, 29 John St., Suite 1402, New York, NY 10038. (212)962-3791. Fax: (212)962-3537. E-mail: editors@tnj.com. Website: www.tnj.com. Editor: Rosalind McLymont. **Contact:** Aziz Adetimirn, publisher. **25% freelance written.** Monthly magazine covering business and career articles. *The Network Journal* caters to Black professionals and small-business owners, providing quality coverage on business, financial, technology and career news germane to the Black community. Estab. 1993. Circ. 15,000. Pays on publication. Byline given. Buys all rights. Editorial lead time 2 months. Submit seasonal material 3 months in advance. Accepts queries by mail, e-mail, fax, phone. Accepts previously published material. Accepts simultaneous submissions. Sample copy for $1 or online. Writer's guidelines for SASE or online.

Nonfiction: How-to, interview/profile. Send complete ms. Length: 1,200-1,500 words. **Pays $150-200.** Sometimes pays expenses of writers on assignment.

Photos: Send photos with submission. Buys one-time rights. Offers $25/photo. Identification of subjects required.

Columns/Departments: Book reviews, 700-800 words; career management and small business development, 800 words. **Pays $100.**

The online magazine carries original content not found in the print version and includes writer's guidelines.

Tips: "We are looking for vigorous writing and reporting for our cover stories and feature articles. Pieces should have gripping leads, quotes that actually say something and that come from several sources. Unless it is a column, please do not submit a 1-source story. Always remember that your article must contain a nutgraph—that's usually the third paragraph telling the reader what the story is about and why you are telling it now. Editorializing should be kept to a minimum. If you're writing a column, make sure your opinions are well-supported."

$ PERDIDO, Leadership with a Conscience, High Tide Press, 3650 W. 183rd St., Homewood IL 60430-2603. (708)206-2054. Fax: (708)206-2044. E-mail: editor1@hightidepress.com. Website: www.perdidomagazine.com. **Contact:** Monica Regan, editor. **60% freelance written.** Quarterly magazine covering leadership and management as they relate to mission-oriented organizations. "We are concerned with what's happening in organizations that are mission-oriented—as opposed to merely profit-oriented. *Perdido* is focused on helping conscientious leaders put innovative ideas into practice. We seek pragmatic articles on management techniques as well as esoteric essays on social issues. The readership of *Perdido* is comprised mainly of CEOs, executive directors, vice presidents, and program directors of nonprofit and for-profit organizations. We try to make the content of *Perdido* accessible to all decision-makers, whether in the nonprofit or for-profit world, government, or academia. *Perdido* actively pursues diverse opinions and authors from many different fields." Estab. 1994. Circ. 6,000. Pays on publication. Publishes ms an average of 3 months after acceptance. Byline given. Buys first North American serial, second serial (reprint) rights. Editorial lead time 4 months. Submit seasonal material 6 months in advance. Accepts queries by mail, e-mail, fax, phone. Accepts previously published material. Accepts simultaneous submissions. Responds in 2 months to queries. Sample copy for 6×9 SASE with 2 first-class stamps or online. Writer's guidelines for #10 SASE or by e-mail.

Nonfiction: Book excerpts, essays, humor, inspirational, interview/profile. **Buys 4-8 mss/year.** Query with published clips. Length: 1,000-5,000 words.

Photos: State availability with submission. Reviews 5×7 prints. Buys one-time rights. Negotiates payment individually. Captions, identification of subjects, model releases required.

Columns/Departments: Book Review (new books on management/leadership), 800 words.

Tips: "Potential writers for *Perdido* should rely on the magazine's motto—Leadership with a Conscience—as a starting point for ideas. We're looking for thoughtful reflections or management that help people succeed. We're not asking for step-by-step recipes—'do this, do that.' In *Perdido*, we want readers to find thought-provoking, open-minded explorations of the moral dimensions of leadership from a socially aware, progressive perspective."

N $ **PROFESSIONAL BUILDER**, Reed Business Information, 2000 Clearwater Drive, Oak Brook IL 60523. (630)320-7000. Fax: (630)288-8145. E-mail: editor@housingzone.com. Website: www.housingzone.com/pb. **Contact:** Heather McCune, editor. Magazine published 17 times/year covering the business of building. Designed as a resource to help builders run succesful and profitable businesses. Circ. 127,277. Editorial lead time 1 month. Accepts queries by mail, e-mail. Sample copy not available.

Nonfiction: Query.

$ $ $ $ **PROFIT, Your Guide to Business Success**, 1 Mt. Pleasant Rd., 11th Floor, Toronto ON M4Y 2Y5, Canada. (416)764-1402. Fax: (416)764-1404. E-mail: profit@profitmag.ca. Website: www.profitguide.com. Publisher: Kerry Mitchell. **Contact:** Ian Portsmouth, managing editor. **80% freelance written.** Magazine published 8 times/year covering small and medium businesses. "We specialize in specific, useful information that helps our readers manage their businesses better. We want Canadian stories only." Estab. 1982. Circ. 110,000. **Pays on acceptance.** Publishes ms an average of 2 months after acceptance. Byline given. Offers variable kill fee. Buys first North American serial, electronic rights. Submit seasonal material 6 months in advance. Accepts queries by mail, e-mail, fax, phone. Responds in 1 month to queries; 6 weeks to mss. Sample copy for 9×12 SAE with 84¢ postage. Writer's guidelines free.

Nonfiction: How-to (business management tips), strategies and Canadian business profiles. **Buys 50 mss/year.** Query with published clips. Length: 800-2,000 words. **Pays $500-2,000.** Pays expenses of writers on assignment.

Columns/Departments: Finance (info on raising capital in Canada), 700 words; Marketing (marketing strategies for independent business), 700 words. **Buys 80 mss/year.** Query with published clips. **Pays $150-600.**

The online magazine carries original content not found in the print edition. Contact: Andrea Szego, online editor.

Tips: "We're wide open to freelancers with good ideas and some knowledge of business. Read the magazine and understand it before submitting your ideas—which should have a Canadian focus."

$ $ $ $ **REPORT ON BUSINESS MAGAZINE**, Globe and Mail, 444 Front St. W., Toronto ON M5V 2S9, Canada. (416)585-5000. E-mail: rob@globeandmail.ca. Website: www.robmagazine.com. **Contact:** Edward Greenspon, editor-in-chief. **50% freelance written.** Monthly business magazine "covering business like *Forbes* or *Fortune* which tries to capture major trends and personalities." Circ. 300,000. **Pays on acceptance.** Publishes ms an average of 4 months after acceptance. Byline given. Offers 50% kill fee. Buys first North American serial rights. Responds in 3 weeks to queries. Sample copy for free.

Nonfiction: Book excerpts, exposé, interview/profile, new product, photo feature. Special issues: Quarterly technology report. **Buys 30 mss/year.** Query with published clips. Length: 2,000-4,000 words. **Pays $200-3,000.** Pays expenses of writers on assignment.

Tips: "For features send a one-page story proposal. We prefer to write about personalities involved in corporate events."

N $ **SMARTMONEY MAGAZINE**, 250 W. 55th St., 10th Floor, New York NY 10019. E-mail: editors@smartmoney.com. Website: www.smartmoney.com. Executive Editor: Mike Oneal. Deputy Editor: Mark Vamos. **Contact:** Igor Greenwald, senior editor; Stephanie AuWerter, associate editor; Stacey L. Bradford, associate editor; Cintra Scott, associate editor.

$ $ **TECHNICAL ANALYSIS OF STOCKS & COMMODITIES, The Traders' Magazine**, Technical Analysis, Inc., 4757 California Ave. SW, Seattle WA 98116-4499. (206)938-0570. Fax: (206)938-1307. E-mail: editor@traders.com. Website: www.traders.com. Publisher: Jack K. Hutson. **Contact:** Jayanthi Gopalakrishnan, editor. **85% freelance written.** Magazine covers methods of investing and trading stocks, bonds and commodities (futures), options, mutual funds, and precious metals using technical analysis. Estab. 1982. Circ. 65,000. Pays on publication. Publishes ms an average of 6 months after acceptance. Byline given. Buys all rights. Accepts previously published material. Responds in 1 month to queries. Sample copy for $5. Writer's guidelines online.

- Eager to work with new/unpublished writers.

Nonfiction: How-to (trade), humor (cartoons), technical (trading and software aids to trading), reviews, utilities, real world trading (actual case studies of trades and their results). "No newsletter-type, buy-sell recommendations. The article subject must relate to trading psychology, technical analysis, charting or a numerical technique used to trade securities or futures. Almost universally requires graphics with every article." **Buys 150 mss/year.** Query with published clips or send complete ms. Length: 1,000-4,000 words. **Pays $100-500.**

Reprints: Send tearsheet with rights for sale noted and information about when and where the material previously appeared.

Photos: Christine M. Morrison, art director. State availability with submission. Buys one time and reprint rights. Pays $60-350 for b&w or color negatives with prints or positive slides. Captions, identification of subjects, model releases required.

Columns/Departments: Length: 800-1,600 words. **Buys 100 mss/year.** Query. **Pays $50-300.**

Fillers: Karen Wasserman, fillers editor. Must relate to trading stocks, bonds, options, mutual funds, commodities, or precious metals. Cartoons on investment humor. **Buys 20/year.** Length: 500 words. **Pays $20-50.**

Tips: "Describe how to use technical analysis, charting, or computer work in day-to-day trading of stocks, bonds, commodities, options, mutual funds, or precious metals. A blow-by-blow account of how a trade was made, including the trader's thought processes, is the very best-received story by our subscribers. One of our primary considerations is to instruct in a manner that the layperson can comprehend. We are not hypercritical of writing style."

N $ $ $ $ **TELETALK COMMUNICATOR**, Televerage, Inc., P.O. Box 1745, Cape Girardeau MO 63702. (888)637-2412. Fax: (888)632-2547. E-mail: jennifer@herman.net. Website: www.televerage.com. Editor: Dale Nabors. **Contact:** Jennifer Herman, managing editor. **80% freelance written.** Monthly magazine covering the telemarketing industry. "This is a national business magazine for the teleservices industry. Substancial, practical insights into the industry are encouraged. This publication deals less with technology than other magazines in the industry." Estab. 2002. Circ. more than 30,000. Pays on publication. Publishes ms an average of 2 months after acceptance. Byline sometimes given. Not copyrighted. Buys all rights. Editorial lead time 2 months. Submit seasonal material 2 months in advance. Accepts queries by mail, e-mail. Accepts simultaneous submissions. Responds in 6 weeks to queries; 2 months to mss. Sample copy online. Writer's guidelines online.

Nonfiction: "We are open to new types of freelance submissions, and we hope to establish long-term relationships with several new writers." General interest, historical/nostalgic, how-to, humor, inspirational, interview/profile, new product, opinion, photo feature, technical. No product pitches or self-promoting articles. Send complete ms. Length: 250-3,000 words. **Pays $75-1,500.** Some writers receive 3 complimentary copies in addition to payment.

Photos: Reviews prints, GIF/JPEGS (depending on quality), 35 mm, 2¼x2¼, or 4×5 slide formats; send 2 copies. Send photos with submission. Buys all rights. Negotiates payment individually. Identification of subjects, model releases required.

Columns/Departments: Buys variable number of mss/year. Send complete ms. **Pays $75-1,500.**

Fillers: Anecdotes, facts, newsbreaks, short humor. **Buys variable number of/year.** Length: 150-500 words. **Pays payment varies.**

Tips: "It is helpful to contact the managing editor directly. We are especially interested in stories about innovative ideas, interviews, news, and events related to the industry, and other original pieces."

Regional

$ $ **ALASKA BUSINESS MONTHLY**, Alaska Business Publishing, 501 W. Northern Lights Blvd., Suite 100, Anchorage AK 99503-2577. (907)276-4373. Fax: (907)279-2900. E-mail: editor@akbizmag.com. Website: www.akbizmag.com. **Contact:** Debbie Cutler, editor. **80% freelance written.** Magazine covering Alaska-oriented business and industry. "Our audience is Alaska businessmen and women who rely on us for timely features and up-to-date information about doing business in Alaska." Estab. 1985. Circ. 10,000. Pays on publication. Publishes ms an average of 4 months after acceptance. Byline given. Offers $50 kill fee. Buys all rights. Editorial lead time 5 months. Submit seasonal material 5 months in advance. Accepts queries by mail, e-mail, fax. Accepts previously published material. Responds in 1 month to queries. Sample copy for 9×12 SAE and 4 first-class stamps. Writer's guidelines free.

Nonfiction: General interest, how-to, interview/profile, new product (Alaska), opinion. No fiction, poetry, or anything not pertinent to Alaska. **Buys approximately 130 mss/year.** Send complete ms. Length: 500-2,000 words. **Pays $150-300.** Sometimes pays expenses of writers on assignment.

Photos: State availability with submission.

Columns/Departments: Required Reading (business book reviews); Right Moves; Alaska this Month; Monthly Calendars (all Alaska related), all 500-1,200 words. **Buys 12 mss/year.** Send complete ms. **Pays $50-75.**

Tips: "Send a well-written manuscript on a subject of importance to Alaska businesses. We seek informative, entertaining articles on everything from entrepreneurs to heavy industry. We cover all Alaska industry to include mining, tourism, timber, transportation, oil and gas, fisheries, finance, insurance, real estate, communications, medical services, technology, and construction. We also cover Native and environmental issues, and occasionally feature Seattle and other communities in the Pacific Northwest."

N $ $ **ATLANTIC BUSINESS MAGAZINE**, Communications Ten Ltd., 197 Water St., St. John's NF A1C 6E7, Canada. (709)726-9300. Fax: (709)726-3013. E-mail: dchafe@atlanticbusinessmagazine.com. Website: www.atlanticbusinessmagazine.com. Managing Editor: Edwina Hutton. **Contact:** Dawn Chafe, editor. **60% freelance written.** Bimonthly magazine covering business in Atlantic Canada. "We discuss positive business developments, emphasizing that the 4 Atlantic provinces are a great place to do business." Estab. 1989. Circ. 30,000. Pays on publication. Publishes ms an average of 1 month after acceptance. Byline given. Buys one-time rights. Editorial lead time 2 months. Accepts queries by mail, e-mail, fax, phone. Sample copy and writer's guidelines free.

Nonfiction: Exposé, general interest, interview/profile, new product. "We don't want religious, technical, or scholarly material. We are not an academic magazine." **Buys 36 mss/year.** Query with published clips. Length: 1,500-2,400 words. **Pays $300-750.** Sometimes pays expenses of writers on assignment.

Photos: Send photos with submission. Reviews contact sheets, transparencies, prints. Buys one-time rights. Negotiates payment individually. Captions, identification of subjects required.

Columns/Departments: Query with published clips.

Tips: "Writers should submit their areas of interest as well as samples of their work and, if possible, suggested story ideas."

N $ **BLUE RIDGE BUSINESS JOURNAL**, Landmark, Inc., 347 W. Campbell Ave., Roanoke VA 24016. (540)777-6462. Fax: (540)777-6471. E-mail: dan@bizjournal.com. Website: www.roanokebiz.com. **Contact:** Dan Smith, editor. **75% freelance written.** Monthly. "We take a regional slant on national business trends, products, methods, etc. Interested in localized features and news stories highlighting business activity." Estab. 1989. Circ. 15,000. **Pays on acceptance.** Publishes ms an average of 1 month after acceptance. Byline given. Buys all rights. Editorial lead time 10 days. Accepts queries by mail, e-mail, fax. Accepts previously published material. Responds immediately to queries. Call the editor for sample copies and/or writer's guidelines.

Nonfiction: Regional business. Special issues: Health Care and Hospitals; Telecommunications; Building and Construction; Investments; Personal Finance and Retirement Planning; Guide to Architectural; Engineering and Construction Services; and Manufacturing and Industry. No columns or stories that are not pre-approved. **Buys 120-150 mss/year.** Query. Length: 500-2,000 words.

Photos: State availability with submission. Buys all rights. Offers $10/photo. Captions, identification of subjects required.

Tips: "Talk to the editor. Offer knowledgeable ideas (if accepted they will be assigned to that writer). We need fast turnaround, accurate reporting, neat dress, non-smokers. More interested in writing samples than educational background."

$ $ **BUSINESS LONDON**, Bowes Publishers, 1147 Gainsburough Rd., London ON N5Y 4X3, Canada. (519)472-7601. Fax: (519)473-7859. **Contact:** Gord Delamont, editor. **70% freelance written.** Monthly magazine covering London business. "Our audience is primarily small and medium businesses and entrepreneurs. Focus is on success stories and how to better operate your business." Estab. 1987. Circ. 14,000. Pays on publication. Publishes ms an average of 3 months after acceptance. Byline given. Offers 50% kill fee. Buys first rights. Editorial lead time 3 months. Responds in 3 months to mss. Sample copy for #10 SASE. Writer's guidelines free.

Nonfiction: How-to (business topics), humor, interview/profile, new product (local only), personal experience (must have a London connection). **Buys 30 mss/year.** Query with published clips. Length: 250-1,500 words. **Pays $125-500.**

Photos: Send photos with submission. Reviews contact sheets, transparencies. Buys one-time rights. Negotiates payment individually. Identification of subjects required.

Tips: "Phone with a great idea. The most valuable thing a writer owns is ideas. We'll take a chance on an unknown if the idea is good enough."

$ $ **BUSINESS NEW HAVEN**, Second Wind Media, Ltd., 1221 Chapel St., New Haven CT 06511. Fax: (203)781-3482. E-mail: news@businessnewhaven.com. Website: www.businessnewhaven.com. **Contact:** Michael C. Bingham, editor. **33% freelance written.** Biweekly regional business publication covering the Connecticut business community. "*Business New Haven* is a business-to-business vehicle targeted to business owners and managers." Estab. 1993. Circ. 14,000. Pays on publication. Byline given. Buys one-time, all rights. Editorial lead time 1 month. Accepts queries by mail, e-mail, fax. Sample copy online. Writer's guidelines by e-mail. Editorial calendar online.

Nonfiction: How-to, interview/profile, new product, technical. **Buys 40 mss/year.** Query with published clips. Length: 500-2,500 words. **Pays $25-200.** Sometimes pays expenses of writers on assignment.

Photos: State availability with submission. Buys all rights. Negotiates payment individually. Identification of subjects required.

Tips: "We publish only stories specific to Connecticut business."

$ **BUSINESS NH MAGAZINE**, 404 Chestnut St., Suite 201, Manchester NH 03101-1831. (603)626-6354. Fax: (603)626-6359. E-mail: edit@businessnhmagazine.com. **Contact:** Stephanie McLaughlin, editor. **25% freelance written.** Monthly magazine covering business, politics and people of New Hampshire. "Our audience consists of the owners and top managers of New Hampshire businesses." Estab. 1983. Circ. 15,000. Pays on publication. Publishes ms an average of 2 months after acceptance. Byline given. Accepts queries by e-mail, fax.

Nonfiction: How-to, interview/profile. "No unsolicited manuscripts; interested in New Hampshire writers only." **Buys 24 mss/year.** Query with published clips and résumé. Length: 750-2,500 words. **Payment varies.**

Photos: Both b&w and color photos used. Buys one-time rights. Payment varies.

Tips: "I *always* want clips and résumé with queries. Freelance stories are almost always assigned. Stories *must* be local to New Hampshire."

N $ **CANADIAN MONEYSAVER**, Canadian MoneySaver, Inc., Box 370, Bath ON K0H 1G0, Canada. (613)352-7448. Fax: (613)352-7700. E-mail: moneyinfo@canadianmoneysaver.ca. Website: www.canadianmoneysaver.ca. **Contact:** Dale Ennis, editor. **80% freelance written.** Monthly magazine covering personal finance. "*Canadian MoneySaver* contains practical money articles on tax, investment, retirement, and financial planning for everyday use." Estab. 1981. Circ. 76,300. Pays on publication. Publishes ms an average of 1 month after acceptance. Byline given. Offers 100% kill fee. Buys first rights. Editorial lead time 1 month. Submit seasonal material 1 month in advance. Accepts queries by mail, e-mail, fax, phone. Responds in 2 weeks to queries; 1 month to mss. Sample copy online. Writer's guidelines free.

Nonfiction: How-to (personal finance), personal experience. Query with published clips. Length: 800-2,000 words. **Pays $150 minimum; maximum negotiable for assigned articles.**

$ CRAIN'S DETROIT BUSINESS, Crain Communications, Inc., 1155 Gratiot, Detroit MI 48207-2997. (313)446-0419. Fax: (313)446-1687. E-mail: jmelton@crain.com. Website: www.crainsdetroit.com. Editor: Mary Kramer. Executive Editor: Cindy Goodaker. **Contact:** James Melton, special sections editor. **15% freelance written.** Weekly tabloid covering business in the Detroit metropolitan area—specifically Wayne, Oakland, Macomb, Washtenaw, and Livingston counties. Estab. 1985. Circ. 150,000. Pays on publication. Publishes ms an average of 1 month after acceptance. Byline given. Buys all rights. Accepts queries by mail, e-mail. Sample copy for $1.50. Writer's guidelines online.

- *Crain's Detroit Business* uses only area writers and local topics.

Nonfiction: New product, technical, business. **Buys 50 mss/year.** Query with published clips. Length: 30-40 words/column inch. **Pays $10-15/column inch.** Pays expenses of writers on assignment.

Photos: State availability with submission.

Tips: "Contact special sections editor in writing with background and, if possible, specific story ideas relating to our type of coverage and coverage area. We only use *local* writers."

$ IN BUSINESS WINDSOR, Cornerstone Publications, Inc., 1775 Sprucewood Ave., Unit 1, LaSalle ON N9J 1X7, Canada. (519)250-2880. Fax: (519)250-2881. E-mail: inbiz2@mnsi.net. Website: www.inbizwin.com. **Contact:** Gary Baxter, general manager; Kelly O'Sullivan, associate editor. **70% freelance written.** Monthly magazine covering business. "We focus on issues/ideas which are of interest to businesses in and around Windsor and Essex County (Ontario). Most stories deal with business and finance; occasionally we will cover health and sports issues that affect our readers." Estab. 1988. Circ. 10,000. **Pays on acceptance.** Byline given. Buys first rights. Editorial lead time 3 months. Submit seasonal material 3 months in advance. Accepts queries by mail, e-mail, fax. Responds in 2 weeks to queries; 1 month to mss. Sample copy for $3.50.

Nonfiction: General interest, how-to, interview/profile. **Buys 25 mss/year.** Query with published clips. Length: 800-1,500 words. **Pays $70-150.** Sometimes pays expenses of writers on assignment.

$ $ INGRAM'S, Show-Me Publishing, Inc., 306 E. 12th St., Suite 1014, Kansas City MO 64106. (816)842-9994. Fax: (816)474-1111. E-mail: editorial@ingramsonline.com. **Contact:** Editor. **50% freelance written.** Monthly magazine covering Kansas City business/executive lifestyle for "upscale, affluent business executives and professionals. Looking for sophisticated writing with style and humor when appropriate." Estab. 1975. Circ. 26,000. Pays 1 month after publication. Publishes ms an average of 2 months after acceptance. Byline given. Buys first, electronic rights. Editorial lead time 2 months. Submit seasonal material 3 months in advance. Accepts queries by mail, fax. Responds in 6 weeks to queries. Sample copy for $3.

Nonfiction: "All articles must have a Kansas City angle. We don't accept unsolicited manuscripts except for opinion column." General interest, how-to (business and personal finance related), interview/profile (Kansas City execs, politicians, celebrities), opinion, technical. **Buys 30 mss/year.** Query with published clips. Length: 500-3,000 words. **Pays $175-350.** Sometimes pays expenses of writers on assignment.

Columns/Departments: Say So (opinion), 1,500 words. **Buys 12 mss/year. Pays $100 max.**

Tips: "Writers must understand the publication and the audience—knowing what appeals to a business executive, entrepreneur, or professional in Kansas City."

$ ROCHESTER BUSINESS JOURNAL, Rochester Business Journal, Inc., 55 St. Paul St., Rochester NY 14604. (585)546-8303. Fax: (585)546-3398. E-mail: rackley@rbj.net. Website: www.rbjdaily.com. Editor: Paul Ericson. Managing Editor: Mike Dickinson. **Contact:** Reid Ackley, associate editor. **10% freelance written.** Weekly tabloid covering local business. "The *Rochester Business Journal* is geared toward corporate executives and owners of small businesses, bringing them leading-edge business coverage and analysis first in the market." Estab. 1984. Circ. 10,000. Pays on publication. Publishes ms an average of 1 month after acceptance. Byline given. Buys first, second serial (reprint), electronic rights. Editorial lead time 6 weeks. Accepts queries by mail, e-mail, fax. Responds in 1 week to queries. Sample copy for free or by e-mail. Writer's guidelines online.

Nonfiction: How-to (business topics), news features, trend stories with local examples. Do not query about any topics that do not include several local examples—local companies, organizations, universities, etc. **Buys 110 mss/year.** Query with published clips. Length: 1,000-2,000 words. **Pays $150.**

Tips: "The *Rochester Business Journal* prefers queries from local published writers who can demonstrate the ability to write for a sophisticated audience of business readers. Story ideas should be about business trends illustrated with numerous examples of local companies participating in the change or movement."

$ $ TEXAS TECHNOLOGY, Dallas, Austin, Houston and San Antonio editions, (also publishes *California Technology, Colorado Technology*, and *Illinois Technology* with the same requirements and procedures), Power Media Group, 13490 TI Blvd., Suite 100, Dallas TX 75243. (972)690-6222, ext. 16. Fax: (972)690-6333. E-mail: afriedrichs@thetechmag.com. Website: www.thetechmag.com. **Contact:** Alan Friedrichs, editor. **95% freelance written.** Monthly magazine covering technology, business, and lifestyle. "*Texas Technology* (and sibling magazines *California Technology, Colorado Technology*, and *Illinois Technology*) are high-tech lifestyle magazines. We publish articles that discuss how technology affects our lives and work. Our audience is a mix of techies and mainstream consumers." Estab. 1997. Circ. 689,000 (total for all 4 publications). Pays on publication. Byline given. Offers $20 kill fee. Buys first North American serial, second serial (reprint), electronic rights, makes work-for-hire assignments. Editorial lead time 3 months. Submit seasonal material 1 month in advance. Accepts queries by mail, e-mail. Accepts simultaneous submissions. Responds in 3 weeks to queries; 1 month to mss. Sample copy and writer's guidelines free.

Nonfiction: Essays, exposé, general interest, historical/nostalgic, humor, interview/profile, new product, technical. "No computer hardware articles." **Buys 50 mss/year.** Query with published clips. Length: 1,200-3,500 words. **Pays $100-350.**
Photos: State availability with submission. Reviews contact sheets. Buys all rights. Negotiates payment individually. Captions, identification of subjects, model releases required.

$ $ VERMONT BUSINESS MAGAZINE, 2 Church St., Burlington VT 05401-4445. (802)863-8038. Fax: (802)863-8069. E-mail: info@vermontbiz.com. Website: www.vermontbiz.com. **Contact:** Timothy McQuiston, editor. **80% freelance written.** Monthly tabloid covering business in Vermont. Circ. 8,000. Pays on publication. Publishes ms an average of 1 month after acceptance. Byline given. Buys one-time rights. Responds in 2 months to queries. Sample copy for 11 × 14 SAE and 7 first-class stamps.
Nonfiction: Business trends and issues. **Buys 200 mss/year.** Query with published clips. Length: 800-1,800 words. **Pays $100-200.**
Reprints: Send tearsheet and information about when and where the material previously appeared.
Photos: Send photos with submission. Reviews contact sheets. Offers $10-35/photo. Identification of subjects required.
Tips: "Read daily papers and look for business angles for a follow-up article. We look for issue and trend articles rather than company or businessman profiles. Note: Magazine accepts Vermont-specific material only. The articles must be about Vermont."

CAREER, COLLEGE & ALUMNI

Three types of magazines are listed in this section: University publications written for students, alumni, and friends of a specific institution; publications about college life for students; and publications on career and job opportunities. Literary magazines published by colleges and universities are listed in the Literary & "Little" section.

$ $ AMERICAN CAREERS, Career Communications, Inc., 6701 W. 64th St., Overland Park KS 66202. (800)669-7795. Fax: (913)362-7788. Website: www.carcom.com. **Contact:** Mary Pitchford, editor. **50% freelance written.** High school and technical school student publication covering careers, career statistics, skills needed to get jobs. "*American Careers* provides career, salary, and education information to middle school and high school students. Self-tests help them relate their interests and abilities to future careers. Articles on résumés, interviews, etc., help them develop employability skills." Estab. 1989. Circ. 500,000. Pays 1 month after acceptance. Byline given. Buys all rights, makes work-for-hire assignments. Accepts queries by mail. Accepts simultaneous submissions. Sample copy for $3. Writer's guidelines for #10 SASE.

O→ Break in by "sending us query letters with samples and résumés. We want to 'meet' the writer before making an assignment."

Nonfiction: Career and education features related to career paths, including arts and communication, business, law, government, finance, construction, technology, health services, human services, manufacturing, engineering, and natural resources and agriculture. "No preachy advice to teens or articles that talk down to students." **Buys 20 mss/year.** Query by mail only with published clips. Length: 300-1,000 words. **Pays $100-450.** Pays expenses of writers on assignment.
Photos: State availability with submission. Buys all rights. Negotiates payment individually. Captions, identification of subjects, model releases required.
Tips: "Letters of introduction or query letters with samples and résumés are ways we get to know writers. Samples should include how-to articles and career-related articles. Articles written for teenagers also would make good samples. Short feature articles on careers, career-related how-to articles, and self-assessment tools (10-20 point quizzes with scoring information) are primarily what we publish."

$ $ THE BLACK COLLEGIAN, The Career & Self Development Magazine for African-American Students, IMDiversity, Inc., 909 Poydras St., 36th Floor, New Orleans LA 70112. (504)523-0154. Fax: (504)523-0271. E-mail: robert@black-collegiate.com. Website: www.black-collegian.com. **Contact:** Robert Miller, vice president/editor. **25% freelance written.** Semiannual magazine for African-American college students and recent graduates with an interest in career and job information, African-American cultural awareness, personalities, history, trends, and current events. Estab. 1970. Circ. 122,000. Pays 1 month after publication. Byline given. Buys one-time rights. Submit seasonal material 2 months in advance. Accepts queries by mail, e-mail, fax. Responds in 6 months to queries. Sample copy for $5 (includes postage) and 9 × 12 SAE. Writer's guidelines for #10 SASE.
Nonfiction: Material on careers, sports, black history, news analysis. Articles on problems and opportunities confronting African-American college students and recent graduates. Book excerpts, exposé, general interest, historical/nostalgic, how-to (develop employability), inspirational, interview/profile, opinion, personal experience. Query. Length: 900-1,900 words. **Pays $100-500 for assigned articles.**
Photos: State availability of or send photos with submission. Reviews 8 × 10 prints. Captions, identification of subjects, model releases required.

The online magazine carries original content in addition to what's included in the print edition. Contact: Robert Miller, online editor.

Tips: Articles are published under primarily 5 broad categories: job hunting information, overviews of career opportunities and industry reports, self-development information, analyses and investigations of conditions and problems that affect African-Americans, and celebrations of African-American success.

$ $ $ $ BROWN ALUMNI MAGAZINE, Brown University, Box 1854, Providence RI 02912-1854. (401)863-2873. Fax: (401)863-9599. E-mail: alumni_magazine@brown.edu. Website: www.brownalumnimagazine.com. Editor: Norman Boucher. **Contact:** Elizabeth Smith, office manager. Bimonthly magazine covering the world of Brown University and its alumni. "We are an editorially independent, general interest magazine covering the on-campus world of Brown University and the off-campus world of its alumni." Estab. 1900. Circ. 80,000. **Pays on acceptance.** Publishes ms an average of 3 months after acceptance. Byline given. Offers 25-30% kill fee. Buys North American serial and Web rights. Editorial lead time 3 months. Submit seasonal material 4 months in advance. Accepts queries by mail, e-mail, fax. Responds in 1 month to queries; 2 months to mss. Sample copy for free. Writer's guidelines not available.

Nonfiction: Book excerpts, essays, exposé, general interest, historical/nostalgic, humor, interview/profile, opinion, personal experience, photo feature, travel, profiles. No articles unconnected to Brown or its alumni. **Buys 50 mss/year.** Query with published clips. Length: 150-4,000 words. **Pays $200-2,000 for assigned articles; $100-1,500 for unsolicited articles.** Pays expenses of writers on assignment.

Photos: State availability with submission. Reviews contact sheets, transparencies, prints. Buys one-time rights. Negotiates payment individually. Captions, identification of subjects required.

Columns/Departments: Under the Elms (news items about campus), 100-400 words; Arts & Culture (reviews of Brown-authored works), 200-500 words; Alumni P.O.V. (essays by Brown alumni), 750 words; Sports (reports on Brown sports teams and athletes), 200-500 words. **Buys 10-20 mss/year.** Query with published clips. **Pays $100-500.**

Tips: "Be imaginative and be specific. A Brown connection is required for all stories in the magazine, but a Brown connection alone does not guarantee our interest. Ask yourself: Why should readers care about your proposed story? Also, we look for depth and objective reporting, not boosterism."

$ $ CIRCLE K MAGAZINE, 3636 Woodview Trace, Indianapolis IN 46268-3196. (317)875-8755. Fax: (317)879-0204. E-mail: ckimagazine@kiwanis.org. Website: www.circlek.org. **Contact:** Shanna Mooney, executive editor. **60% freelance written.** Magazine published 5 times/year. "Our readership consists almost entirely of above-average college students interested in voluntary community service and leadership development. They are politically and socially aware and have a wide range of interests." Circ. 15,000. **Pays on acceptance.** Byline given. Buys first North American serial rights. Accepts queries by mail, e-mail, fax. Responds in 2 months to queries. Sample copy for large SAE with 3 first-class stamps or on website. Writer's guidelines online.

- Break in by offering "fresh ideas for stories dealing with college students who are not only concerned with themselves. Our readers are concerned with making their communities better."

Nonfiction: Articles published in *Circle K* are of 2 types—serious and light nonfiction. "We are interested in general interest articles on topics concerning college students and their lifestyles, as well as articles dealing with careers, community concerns, and leadership development." "No first-person confessions, family histories, or travel pieces." Query. Length: 1,500-2,000 words. **Pays $150-400.**

Photos: Purchased with accompanying ms; total price includes both photos and ms. Captions required.

Tips: "Query should indicate author's familiarity with the field and sources. Subject treatment must be objective and in-depth, and articles should include illustrative examples and quotes from persons involved in the subject or qualified to speak on it. We are open to working with new writers who present a good article idea and demonstrate that they've done their homework concerning the article subject itself, as well as concerning our magazine's style. We're interested in college-oriented trends, for example: entrepreneur schooling, high-tech classrooms, music, leisure, and health issues."

$ $ $ $ EXPERIENCE MAGAZINE, The Magazine for Building Your Career, 1 Faneuil Hall Marketplace, 3rd Floor, Boston MA 02109. Fax: (617)305-7901. Website: www.experience.com. Editor: Danyel Barnard. **Contact:** Christopher Bordeau, associate editor. **50% freelance written.** Quarterly magazine on career development for young professionals. Estab. 1999. Circ. 1 million. Pays 45 days after acceptance. Publishes ms an average of 3 months after acceptance. Byline given. Offers 25% kill fee. Buys all rights. Editorial lead time 5 months. Accepts queries by mail, fax. Sample copy for free. Writer's guidelines for free or online.

Nonfiction: How-to, interview/profile, career-related. **Buys 20-30 mss/year.** Query with published clips. Length: 1,000-2,500 words. **Pays $500-2,500.** Sometimes pays expenses of writers on assignment.

$ FLORIDA LEADER, (for college students), P.O. Box 14081, Gainesville FL 32604-2081. (352)373-6907. Fax: (352)373-8120. E-mail: info@studentleader.com. Website: www.floridaleader.com. Publisher: W.H. Oxendine, Jr. **Contact:** Stephanie Reck, associate editor. **10% freelance written.** Triannual magazine. College magazine, feature-oriented, especially activities, events, interests and issues pertaining to college students. Estab. 1983. Circ. 50,000. Pays on publication. Publishes ms an average of 2 months after acceptance. Byline given. Submit seasonal material 6 months in advance. Accepts queries by mail, e-mail, fax. Responds in 2 months to queries. Sample copy for $3.50, 9×12 SAE with 5 first-class stamps. Writer's guidelines online.

Nonfiction: Practical tips for going to college, student life and leadership development. How-to, humor, interview/profile, Feature (All multi-sourced and Florida college related). "No lengthy individual profiles or articles without primary and secondary sources of attribution." Length: 900 words. **Pays $35-75.** Sometimes pays expenses of writers on assignment.

Photos: State availability with submission. Reviews negatives, transparencies. Captions, identification of subjects, model releases required.

Columns/Departments: College Life, The Lead Role, In Every Issue (quizzes, tips), Florida Forum (features Florida high school students), 250-1,000 words. **Buys 2 mss/year.** Query.

- The online magazine carries original content not found in the print edition. Contact: Stephanie Reck and Butch Oxendine, online editors.

Tips: "Read other high school and college publications for current issues, interests. Send manuscripts or outlines for review. All sections open to freelance work. Always looking for lighter, humorous articles as well as features on Florida colleges and universities, careers, jobs. Multi-sourced (5-10) articles are best."

$ $ $ $ HARVARD MAGAZINE, Harvard Magazine, Inc., 7 Ware St., Cambridge MA 02138. (617)495-5746. Fax: (617)495-0324. Website: www.harvardmagazine.com. **Contact:** John S. Rosenberg, editor. **35-50% freelance written.** Bimonthly magazine for Harvard University faculty, alumni, and students. Estab. 1898. Circ. 225,000. Pays on publication. Publishes ms an average of 4 months after acceptance. Byline given. Buys one-time print and website rights. Editorial lead time 1 year. Accepts queries by mail, fax. Responds in 1 month to queries; 1 month to mss. Sample copy online. Writer's guidelines not available.

Nonfiction: Book excerpts, essays, interview/profile, journalism on Harvard-related intellectual subjects. **Buys 20-30 mss/year.** Query with published clips. Length: 800-10,000 words. **Pays $250-2,000.** Pays expenses of writers on assignment.

$ $ $ $ NOTRE DAME MAGAZINE, University of Notre Dame, 538 Grace Hall, Notre Dame IN 46556-5612. (574)631-5335. Fax: (574)631-6767. E-mail: ndmag@nd.edu. Website: www.nd.edu/~ndmag. Managing Editor: Carol Schaal. **Contact:** Kerry Temple, editor. **75% freelance written.** Quarterly magazine covering news of Notre Dame and education and issues affecting contemporary society. "We are a university magazine with a scope as broad as that found at a university, but we place our discussion in a moral, ethical, spiritual context reflecting our Catholic heritage." Estab. 1972. Circ. 142,000. **Pays on acceptance.** Publishes ms an average of 1 year after acceptance. Byline given. Buys first, electronic rights. Accepts queries by mail, e-mail, fax. Responds in 2 months to queries. Sample copy online. Writer's guidelines online.

Nonfiction: Opinion, personal experience, religious. **Buys 35 mss/year.** Query with published clips. Length: 600-3,000 words. **Pays $250-1,500.** Sometimes pays expenses of writers on assignment.

Photos: State availability with submission. Reviews transparencies, 8×10 prints, b&w contact sheets. Buys one-time and electronic rights. Identification of subjects, model releases required.

Columns/Departments: Perspectives (essays, often written in first person, deal with a wide array of issues—some topical, some personal, some serious, some light). Query with or without published clips or send complete ms.

The online version carries original content not found in the print edition and includes writer's guidelines. Contact: Carol Schaal.

Tips: "The editors are always looking for new writers and fresh ideas. However, the caliber of the magazine and frequency of its publication dictate that the writing meet very high standards. The editors value articles strong in storytelling quality, journalistic technique, and substance. They do not encourage promotional or nostalgia pieces, stories on sports, or essays which are sentimentally religious."

$ $ OREGON QUARTERLY, The Magazine of the University of Oregon, 5228 University of Oregon Chapman Hall, Eugene OR 97403-5228. (541)346-5048. Fax: (541)346-5571. E-mail: quarterly@oregon.uoregon.edu. Website: www.uoregon.edu/~oq. Assistant Editor: Brett Campbell. **Contact:** Guy Maynard. **50% freelance written.** Quarterly magazine covering people and ideas at the University of Oregon and the Northwest. Estab. 1919. Circ. 100,000. **Pays on acceptance.** Publishes ms an average of 3 months after acceptance. Byline given. Buys first North American serial rights. Accepts queries by mail, e-mail. Accepts previously published material. Responds in 2 months to queries. Sample copy for 9×12 SAE with 4 first-class stamps or on website. Writer's guidelines online.

Break in to the magazine with a profile (400 or 800 words) of a University of Oregon alumnus. Best to query first.

Nonfiction: Northwest issues and culture from the perspective of UO alumni and faculty. **Buys 30 mss/year.** Query with published clips. Length: 250-2,500 words. **Pays $100-750.** Sometimes pays expenses of writers on assignment.

Reprints: Send photocopy and information about when and where the material previously appeared. Pays 50% of amount paid for an original article.

Photos: State availability with submission. Reviews 8×10 prints. Buys one-time rights. Offers $10-25/photo. Identification of subjects required.

Fiction: Publishes novel excerpts.

Tips: "Query with strong, colorful lead; clips."

$ THE PENN STATER, Penn State Alumni Association, Hintz Family Alumni Center, University Park PA 16802. (814)865-2709. Fax: (814)863-5690. E-mail: pennstater@psu.edu. Website: www.alumni.psu.edu. **Contact:** Tina Hay, editor. **75% freelance written.** Bimonthly magazine covering Penn State and Penn Staters. Estab. 1910. Circ. 123,000. **Pays on acceptance.** Publishes ms an average of 4 months after acceptance. Byline given. Offers 50% kill fee. Buys first North American serial, second serial (reprint) rights. Editorial lead time 3 months. Submit seasonal material 8 months in advance. Accepts queries by mail, e-mail, fax. Accepts previously published material. Accepts simultaneous submissions. Responds in 3 months to queries. Sample copy and writer's guidelines free.

Nonfiction: Stories must have Penn State connection. Book excerpts (by Penn Staters), general interest, historical/nostalgic, interview/profile, personal experience, photo feature, book reviews, science/research. No unsolicited mss. **Buys 20 mss/year.** Query with published clips. Length: 200-3,000 words. **Pays competitive rates.** Pays expenses of writers on assignment.

Reprints: Send photocopy and information about when and where the material previously appeared. Payment varies.

Photos: Send photos with submission. Reviews transparencies, prints. Buys one-time rights. Negotiates payment individually. Captions required.

Tips: "We are especially interested in attracting writers who are savvy in creative nonfiction/literary journalism. Most stories must have a Penn State tie-in. No phone calls."

$ $ THE PURDUE ALUMNUS, Purdue Alumni Association, Purdue Memorial Union 160, 101 N. Grant St., West Lafayette IN 47906-6212. (765)494-5182. Fax: (765)494-9179. E-mail: slmartin@purdue.edu. Website: www.purdue.edu/PAA. **Contact:** Sharon Martin, editor. **50% freelance written.** Prefers to work with published/established writers; works with small number of new/unpublished writers each year. Bimonthly magazine covering subjects of interest to Purdue University alumni. Estab. 1912. Circ. 65,000. Pays on publication. Publishes ms an average of 2 months after acceptance. Byline given. Buys first rights, makes work-for-hire assignments. Submit seasonal material 6 months in advance. Accepts queries by mail. Accepts previously published material. Accepts simultaneous submissions. Responds in 3 weeks to queries. Sample copy for 9×12 SAE with 2 first-class stamps. Writer's guidelines online.

Nonfiction: Focus is on alumni, campus news, issues, and opinions of interest to 65,000 members of the Alumni Association. Feature style, primarily university-oriented. Issues relevant to education. General interest, historical/nostalgic, humor, interview/profile, personal experience. **Buys 12-20 mss/year.** Length: 1,500-2,500 words. **Pays $250-500 for assigned articles.** Pays expenses of writers on assignment.

Photos: State availability with submission. Reviews 5×7 prints, b&w contact sheets.

Tips: "We have more than 300,000 living, breathing Purdue alumni. If you can find a good story about one of them, we're interested. We use local freelancers to do campus pieces."

$ $ RIPON COLLEGE MAGAZINE, P.O. Box 248, Ripon WI 54971-0248. (920)748-8364. Fax: (920)748-9262. E-mail: boonel@ripon.edu. Website: www.ripon.edu. **Contact:** Loren J. Boone, editor. **15% freelance written.** Quarterly magazine that "contains information relating to Ripon College and is mailed to alumni and friends of the college." Estab. 1851. Circ. 14,000. Pays on publication. Publishes ms an average of 3 months after acceptance. Byline given. Makes work-for-hire assignments. Accepts queries by mail, e-mail, fax, phone. Responds in 2 weeks to queries.

Nonfiction: Historical/nostalgic, interview/profile. **Buys 4 mss/year.** Query with or without published clips or send complete ms. Length: 250-1,000 words. **Pays $25-350.**

Photos: State availability with submission. Reviews contact sheets. Buys one-time rights. Offers additional payment for photos accepted with ms. Captions, model releases required.

Tips: "Story ideas must have a direct connection to Ripon College."

$ $ $ $ RUTGERS MAGAZINE, Rutgers University, Alexander Johnston Hall, 101 Somerset St., New Brunswick NJ 08901. (732)932-7084, ext. 618. Fax: (732)932-6950. E-mail: rutgersmagazine@ur.rutgers.edu. **Contact:** Renee Olson, editor. **30% freelance written.** University magazine published 3 times/year of "general interest, but articles must have a Rutgers University or alumni tie-in." Circ. 70,000. **Pays on acceptance.** Publishes ms an average of 4 months after acceptance. Byline given. Offers kill fee. Buys first North American serial rights. Submit seasonal material 8 months in advance. Accepts queries by mail, e-mail, fax. Responds in 1 month to queries. Sample copy for $3 and 9×12 SAE with 5 first-class stamps.

Nonfiction: Essays, general interest, historical/nostalgic, interview/profile, photo feature, science/research; art/humanities. No articles without a Rutgers connection. **Buys 10-15 mss/year.** Query with published clips. Length: 1,200-3,500 words. **Pays $1,200-2,200.** Pays expenses of writers on assignment.

Photos: State availability with submission. Buys one-time rights. Payment varies. Identification of subjects required.

Columns/Departments: Sports; Alumni Profiles (related to Rutgers), all 1,200-1,800 words. **Buys 4-6 mss/year.** Query with published clips. **Pays competitively.**

Tips: "Send an intriguing query backed by solid clips. We'll evaluate clips and topic for most appropriate use."

N $ SCHOLASTIC ADMINISTR@TOR MAGAZINE, Scholastic, Inc., 557 Broadway, New York NY 10012. (212)343-6205. Fax: (212)343-4808. E-mail: lrenwick@scholastic.com. Website: www.scholastic.com/administrator. Executive Editor: Lucile Renwick. Quarterly magazine. Focuses on helping today's school administrators and education technology leaders in their efforts to improve the management of schools. Circ. 100,000. Editorial lead time 1 month. Sample copy not available.

$ SUCCEED, The Magazine for Continuing Education, Ramholtz Publishing, Inc., 1200 South Ave., Suite 202, Staten Island NY 10314. (718)761-4800. Fax: (718)761-3300. E-mail: editorial@collegebound.net. **Contact:** Gina LaGuardia, editor-in-chief. **85% freelance written.** Quarterly magazine. "*SUCCEED*'s readers are interested in continuing education, whether it be for changing careers or enhancing their current career." Estab. 1994. Circ. 155,000. Pays on publication. Publishes ms an average of 4 months after acceptance. Byline given. Buys first, second serial (reprint) rights. Editorial lead time 4 months. Submit seasonal material 4 months in advance. Accepts queries by mail, e-mail. Accepts previously published material. Accepts simultaneous submissions. Responds in 5 weeks to queries. Sample copy for $1.87. Writer's guidelines for 9×12 SASE.

- Break in with "an up-to-date, expert-driven article of interest to our audience with personal, real-life anecdotes as support—not basis—for exploration."

Nonfiction: Essays, exposé, general interest, how-to (change careers), interview/profile (interesting careers), new product, opinion, personal experience. **Buys 25 mss/year.** Query with published clips. Length: 1,000-1,500 words. **Pays $75-150.** Sometimes pays expenses of writers on assignment.

Reprints: Send photocopy.

Photos: Send photos with submission. Reviews negatives, prints. Buys one-time rights. Offers no additional payment for photos accepted with ms. Captions, identification of subjects required.

Columns/Departments: Tech Zone (new media/technology), 300-700 words; To Be... (personality/career profile), 600-800 words; Financial Fitness (finance, money management), 100-300 words; Memo Pad (short, newsworthy items that relate to today's changing job market and continuing education); Solo Success (how readers can "do it on their own," with recommended resources, books, and software). **Buys 10 mss/year.** Query with published clips. **Pays $50-75.**

Fillers: Facts, newsbreaks. **Buys 5/year.** Length: 50-200 words.

Tips: "Stay current and address issues of importance to our readers—lifelong learners and those in career transition. They're ambitious, hands-on, and open to advice, new areas of opportunity, etc."

N $ TRANSFORMATIONS, A Journal of People and Change, (formerly *WPI Journal*), Worcester Polytechnic Institute, 100 Institute Rd., Worcester MA 01609-2280. Fax: (508)831-5820. E-mail: transformations@wpi.edu. Website: www.wpi.edu/news/transformations/. **Contact:** Carol Cambo, editor. **50% freelance written.** Quarterly alumni magazine covering science and engineering/education/business personalities and related technologies and issues for 25,000 alumni, primarily engineers, scientists, managers, media. Estab. 1897. Circ. 28,000. Pays on publication. Publishes ms an average of 6 months after acceptance. Byline given. Buys one-time rights. Accepts queries by mail, e-mail. Accepts previously published material. Accepts simultaneous submissions. Responds in 1 month to queries. Sample copy online.

Nonfiction: Interview/profile (alumni in engineering, science, etc.), photo feature, features on people and programs at WPI. Query with published clips. Length: 300-3,000 words. **Pays negotiable rate.** Sometimes pays expenses of writers on assignment.

Photos: State availability with submission. Reviews contact sheets. Pays negotiable rate. Captions required.

The online magazine carries original content not found in the print edition.

Tips: "Submit outline of story, story idea or published work. Features are most open to freelancers with excellent narrative skills, and an ability to understand and convey complex technologies in an engaging way. Keep in mind that this is an alumni magazine, so most articles focus on the college and its graduates."

CHILD CARE & PARENTAL GUIDANCE

Magazines in this section address the needs and interests of families with children. Some publications are national in scope, others are geographically specific. Some offer general advice for parents, while magazines such as *Catholic Parent* answer the concerns of smaller groups. Other markets that buy articles about child care and the family are included in the Religious and Women's sections and in the Trade Education and Counseling section. Publications for children can be found in the Juvenile and Teen & Young Adult sections.

$ $ ALL ABOUT KIDS MAGAZINE, Midwest Parenting Publications, 1077 Celestial St., #101, Cincinnati OH 45202. (513)684-0501. Fax: (513)684-0507. E-mail: editor@aak.com. Website: www.aak.com. **Contact:** Tom Wynne, editor. **100% freelance written.** Monthly magazine *All About Kids* covers a myriad of parenting topics and pieces of information relative to families and children in greater Cincinnati. Estab. 1985. Circ. 60,000. Pays on publication. Publishes ms an average of 6 months after acceptance. Byline given. Buys first, electronic rights. Editorial lead time 3 months. Submit seasonal material 6 months in advance. Accepts queries by mail. Writer's guidelines online.

Nonfiction: Exposé, general interest, historical/nostalgic, how-to (family projects, crafts), humor, inspirational, interview/profile, opinion, photo feature, travel. Special issues: Maternity (January); Special Needs Children (May). No product or book reviews. **Buys 50 mss/year.** Send complete ms. Length: 750-3,000 words. **Pays $50-250 for assigned articles; $50-100 for unsolicited articles.**

Photos: State availability with submission.

Fillers: Anecdotes, facts, gags to be illustrated by cartoonist, short humor. **Buys 20/year.** Length: 350-800 words. **Pays $50-100.**

Tips: "Submit full-text articles with query letter. Keep in mind the location of the magazine and try to include relevant sidebars, sources, etc."

$ ATLANTA PARENT/ATLANTA BABY, 2346 Perimeter Park Dr., Suite 101, Atlanta GA 30341. (770)454-7599. Fax: (770)454-7699. E-mail: atlantaparent@atlantaparent.com. Website: www.atlantaparent.com. Publisher: Liz White. **Contact:** Amy Dusek, managing editor. **50% freelance written.** Pays on publication. Publishes ms an average of 3 months after acceptance. Byline given. Buys one-time rights. Submit seasonal material 6 months in advance. Accepts queries by mail, e-mail. Accepts previously published material. Responds in 4 months to queries. Sample copy for $3.

Nonfiction: General interest, how-to, humor, interview/profile, travel. Special issues: Private School (January); Camp (February); Birthday Parties (March and September); Maternity and Mothering (May and October); Childcare (July); Back-to-School (August); Teens (September); Holidays (November/December). No religious or philosophical discussions. **Buys 60 mss/year.** Query with or without published clips or send complete ms. Length: 800-1,500 words. **Pays $5-50.** Sometimes pays expenses of writers on assignment.

Reprints: Send tearsheet or photocopy with rights for sale noted and information about when and where the material previously appeared. **Pays $30-50.**

Photos: State availability of or send photos with submission. Reviews 3×5 photos. Buys one-time rights. Offers $10/photo.

Tips: "Articles should be geared to problems or situations of families and parents. Should include down-to-earth tips and be clearly written. No philosophical discussions. We're also looking for well-written humor."

$ BIG APPLE PARENT/QUEENS PARENT/WESTCHESTER PARENT, Family Communications, Inc., 9 E. 38th St., 4th Floor, New York NY 10016. (212)889-6400. Fax: (212)689-4958. E-mail: hellonwheels@parentsknow.com. Website: www.parentsknow.com. **Contact:** Helen Freedman, executive editor. **90% freelance written.** Monthly tabloid covering

New York City family life. "*BAP* readers live in high-rise Manhattan apartments; it is an educated, upscale audience. Often both parents are working full time in professional occupations. Child-care help tends to be one on one, in the home. Kids attend private schools for the most part. While not quite a suburban approach, some of our *QP* readers do have backyards (though most live in high-rise apartments). It is a more middle-class audience in Queens. More kids are in day care centers; majority of kids are in public schools. Our Westchester county edition is for suburban parents." Estab. 1985. Circ. 80,000, *Big Apple*; 70,000, *Queens Parent*; 70,000, *Westchester Parent*. Pays 2 months after publication. Byline given. Offers 50% kill fee. Buys first New York area rights. Submit seasonal material 3 months in advance. Accepts queries by mail, e-mail, fax. Accepts simultaneous submissions. Responds immediately to queries. Sample copy and writer's guidelines free.

Break in with "Commentary (op ed); newsy angles—but everything should be targeted to parents. We love journalistic pieces (as opposed to essays, which is what we mostly get.)"

Nonfiction: Book excerpts, exposé, general interest, how-to, inspirational, interview/profile, opinion, personal experience, family health, education. "We're always looking for news and coverage of controversial issues." **Buys 150 mss/year.** Query with or without published clips or send complete ms. Length: 600-1,000 words. **Pays $35-50.** Sometimes pays expenses of writers on assignment.

Reprints: Send tearsheet or typed ms with rights for sale noted and information about when and where the material previously appeared. Pays same as article rate.

Columns/Departments: Dads; Education; Family Finance. **Buys 50-60 mss/year.** Send complete ms.

Tips: "We have a very local focus; our aim is to present articles our readers cannot find in national publications. To that end, news stories and human interest pieces must focus on New York and New Yorkers. We are always looking for news and newsy pieces; we keep on top of current events, frequently giving issues that may relate to parenting a local focus so that the idea will work for us as well. We are not currently looking for essays, humor, or travel."

N $ $ **BIRMINGHAM FAMILY TIMES**, United Parenting Publications, Inc., 2821 2nd Ave. S., Suite F, Birmingham AL 35233. (205)326-0846. Fax: (205)326-0139. E-mail: birminghamfamily@unitedad.com. Website: www.parenthood.com. Regional Editor: Deirdre Wilson. **Contact:** Carol Muse Evans, associate editor. **80% freelance written.** Monthly magazine covering family issues/parenting—local angle for Birmingham and Alabama. "We are primarily interested in both serious and fun issues of interest to Alabama and Birmingham-area families. We primarily buy stories with a local slant. If you're writing about a general family issue, you need to contact our parent company in Boston. However, if you have an Alabama/Birmingham connection with your piece, we're very interested in hearing from you." Circ. 60,000. Pays on publication. Publishes ms an average of 2-4 months after acceptance. Byline given. Buys first North American serial, electronic rights. Editorial lead time 2 or more months. Submit seasonal material 6 or more months in advance. Accepts queries by mail, e-mail. Accepts simultaneous submissions. Sample copy online. Writer's guidelines for #10 SASE.

Nonfiction: General interest, interview/profile, photo feature, travel, parenting, baby, teen features. "No first-person, 'How I taught my kids to...,' no essays. We are generally a magazine offering information to parents on parenting and childhood issues. We don't do a lot of fluff." **Buys 24 or more mss/year.** Query with or without published clips. Length: 500-1,500 words. **Pays $50-300 for assigned articles.** Sometimes pays expenses of writers on assignment.

Photos: State availability with submission. Buys first North American serial and electronic rights. Negotiates payment individually. Identification of subjects required.

Tips: "It would be difficult for someone not familiar with Birmingham/Alabama to do our features with a local angle. However, it can be done if a person is willing to search out local contacts for such stories. We do accept some family travel features, but they must be within a day's drive from our area. Stories of a more national/generic audience should be submitted to our parent publication found at www.parenthood.com."

$ **BOISE FAMILY MAGAZINE, Magazine for Treasure Valley Parents**, 13191 W. Scotfield St., Boise ID 83713-0899. (208)938-2119. Fax: (208)938-2117. E-mail: boisefamily@cs.com. Website: www.boisefamily.com. **Contact:** Liz Buckingham, editor. **90% freelance written.** Monthly magazine covering parenting, education, child development. "Geared to parents with children 14 years and younger. Focus on education, interest, activities for children. Positive parenting and healthy families." Estab. 1993. Circ. 19,000. Pays on publication. Publishes ms an average of 3 months after acceptance. Byline given. Offers 50% kill fee. Buys first North American serial rights. Editorial lead time 3 months. Submit seasonal material 3 months in advance. Accepts queries by mail, e-mail. Accepts simultaneous submissions. Responds in 2 months to queries. Sample copy for $1.50. Writer's guidelines online.

Nonfiction: Essays, how-to, interview/profile, new product. Special issues: Women's Health and Maternity (January); Birthday Party Fun; Family Choice Awards (February); Education; Home & Garden (March); Summer Camps (April); Kids' Sports Guide (May); Summer, Family Travel; Fairs & Festivals (June/July); Back-to-School; the Arts (August/September); Fall Fun; Children's Health (October); Winter Family Travel; Holiday Ideas (November); Holiday Crafts and Traditions (December). No political or religious affiliation-oriented articles. **Buys 10 mss/year.** Query with published clips. Length: 900-1,300 words. **Pays $50-100.** Sometimes pays expenses of writers on assignment.

Reprints: Accepts previously published submissions.

Photos: State availability with submission. Reviews 3×5 prints. Buys one-time rights. Negotiates payment individually. Captions required.

Columns/Departments: Crafts, travel, finance, parenting. Length: 700-900 words. Query with published clips. **Pays $50-100.**

$ **CATHOLIC PARENT**, Our Sunday Visitor, 200 Noll Plaza, Huntington IN 46750-4310. (260)356-8400. Fax: (260)356-8472. E-mail: cparent@osv.com. Website: www.osv.com. **Contact:** Woodeene Koenig-Bricker, editor. **95% freelance written.** Bimonthly magazine. "We look for practical, realistic parenting articles written for a primarily Roman Catholic audience. The key is practical, not pious." Estab. 1993. Circ. 36,000. **Pays on acceptance.** Publishes ms an average of 6 months after acceptance. Byline given. Offers variable kill fee. Buys first North American serial rights. Editorial lead time 6 months. Submit seasonal material 6 months in advance. Accepts simultaneous submissions. Responds in 2 months to queries. Sample copy for $3.

• *Catholic Parent* is extremely receptive to first-person accounts of personal experiences dealing with parenting issues that are moving, emotionally engaging and uplifting for the reader. Bear in mind the magazine's mission to provide practical information for parents.

Nonfiction: Essays, how-to, humor, inspirational, personal experience, religious. **Buys 50 mss/year.** Send complete ms. Length: 850-1,200 words. **Payment varies.** Sometimes pays expenses of writers on assignment.

Photos: State availability with submission.

Columns/Departments: This Works (parenting tips), 200 words. **Buys 50 mss/year.** Send complete ms. **Pays $15-25.**

Tips: No poetry or fiction.

$ $ CHICAGO PARENT, Wednesday Journal, Inc., 141 S. Oak Park Ave., Oak Park IL 60302-2972. (708)386-5555. Fax: (708)524-8360. E-mail: sschultz@chicagoparent.com. Website: www.chicagoparent.com. **Contact:** Susy Schultz, editor. **60% freelance written.** Monthly tabloid. "*Chicago Parent* has a distinctly local approach. We offer information, inspiration, perspective and empathy to Chicago-area parents. Our lively editorial mix has a 'we're all in this together' spirit, and articles are thoroughly researched and well written." Estab. 1988. Circ. 125,000 in three zones covering the 6-county Chicago metropolitan area. Pays on publication. Publishes ms an average of 2 months after acceptance. Byline given. Offers 10-50% kill fee. Buys first, electronic rights. Editorial lead time 4 months. Submit seasonal material 4 months in advance. Accepts queries by mail. Responds in 6 weeks to queries. Sample copy for $3.95 and 11×17 SAE with $1.65 postage. Writer's guidelines for #10 SASE.

O→ Break in by "writing 'short stuff' items (front-of-the-book short items on local people, places and things of interest to families)."

Nonfiction: Essays, exposé, how-to (parent-related), humor, interview/profile, travel, local interest; investigative features. Special issues: include Chicago Baby and Healthy Child. "No pot-boiler parenting pieces, simultaneous submissions, previously published pieces or non-local writers (from outside the 6-county Chicago metropolitan area)." **Buys 40-50 mss/year.** Query with published clips. Length: 200-2,500 words. **Pays $25-300 for assigned articles; $25-100 for unsolicited articles.** Pays expenses of writers on assignment.

Photos: State availability with submission. Reviews contact sheets, negatives, prints. Buys one-time rights. Offers $0-40/photo; negotiates payment individually. Captions, identification of subjects required.

Columns/Departments: Healthy Child (kids' health issues), 850 words; Getaway (travel pieces), up to 1,200 words; other columns not open to freelancers. **Buys 30 mss/year.** Query with published clips or send complete ms. **Pays $100.**

Tips: "We don't like pot-boiler parenting topics and don't accept many personal essays unless they are truly compelling."

$ $ $ $ CHILD, Gruner + Jahr, 375 Lexington Ave., New York NY 10017-5514. (212)499-2000. Fax: (212)499-2038. Website: www.child.com. Editor-in-Chief: Miriam Arond. Managing Editor: Polly Chevalier. **Contact:** Submissions. **95% freelance written.** Monthly magazine covering parenting. Estab. 1986. Circ. 1,020,000. **Pays on acceptance.** Byline given. Offers 25% kill fee. Buys all rights. Editorial lead time 5 months. Submit seasonal material 6 months in advance. Accepts queries by mail. Responds in 2 months to queries. Sample copy for $3.95. Writer's guidelines for #10 SASE.

Nonfiction: Book excerpts, essays, interview/profile, personal experience, travel, health, timely trend stories on topics that affect today's parents. No poetry or fiction. **Buys 50 feature, 20-30 short mss/year.** Query with published clips. Length: 650-2,500 words. **Pays $1/word and up for assigned articles.** Sometimes pays expenses of writers on assignment.

Photos: State availability with submission. Reviews transparencies. Buys one-time rights. Negotiates payment individually.

Columns/Departments: What I Wish Every Parent Knew (personal essay); How They Do It (highlighting the experience of real parents in unique situations, explaining how they keep their lives in balance). **Buys 10 mss/year.** Query with published clips. **Pays $1/word and up.**

The online magazine carries original content not found in the print edition. Contact: Kathleen Tripp, online editor.

Tips: "Stories should include opinions from experts as well as anecdotes from parents to illustrate the points being made. Lifestyle is key. Send a well-written query that meets our editorial needs. *Child* receives too many inappropriate submissions. Please consider your work carefully before submitting."

$ COUNTY KIDS, Journal Register Co., 877 Post Rd., Westport CT 06880. (203)226-8877. Fax: (203)221-7540. E-mail: countykids@ctcentral.com. Website: www.countykids.com. **Contact:** Linda Greco, managing editor. **70% freelance written.** Monthly tabloid for Connecticut parents. "We publish articles that are well researched and informative, yet written in a casual tone." Estab. 1988. Circ. 44,000. Pays on publication. Byline given. Buys first North American serial, second serial (reprint), electronic rights. Editorial lead time 2 months. Submit seasonal material 3 months in advance. Accepts queries by mail, e-mail, fax. Accepts simultaneous submissions. Responds in 2 months to queries. Sample copy free. Writer's guidelines online.

Nonfiction: Essays, exposé, general interest, how-to, humor, interview/profile, new product, opinion, personal experience, photo feature. Special issues: Camp; Daycare Options; Back-to-School; Divorce/Single Parenting. No fiction, poetry, or cute kids stories. **Buys 40 mss/year.** Query with or without published clips or send complete ms. Length: 800-2,000 words. **Pays $35-100 for assigned articles; $25-75 for unsolicited articles.**

Reprints: Accepts previously published submissions.

Photos: Send photos with submission. Reviews contact sheets, prints. Buys one-time rights. Offers no additional payment for photos accepted with ms. Identification of subjects required.

Columns/Departments: Mom's View/Dad's View (personal experience/humor), 800 words; Double Digits (tips on parenting teens), 800 words; Museum Moments (reviews of Connecticut museums), 800 words; Parentphernalia (fast facts, local news, parenting tips), 400 words. **Buys 25 mss/year.** Send complete ms. **Pays $25-35.**

Tips: "*County Kids* is looking for strong features with a Connecticut slant. We give preferences to local writers. Mom's View and Dad's View columns are a great way to get published in *County Kids*, as long as they're humorous and casual. Features sent with photos will be given priority, as will those with sidebars."

$ $ EXPECTING, Family Communications, 37 Hanna Ave., Suite 1, Toronto ON M6K 1W9, Canada. (416)537-2604. Fax: (416)538-1794. **Contact:** Tracy Cooper, editor. **100% freelance written.** Semiannual digest-sized magazine. Writers must be Canadian health professionals. Articles address all topics relevant to expectant parents. Estab. 1995. Circ. 100,000. **Pays on acceptance.** Publishes ms an average of 6 months after acceptance. Byline given. Buys all rights. Editorial lead time 6 months. Accepts queries by mail, fax. Responds in 2 months to queries.

Nonfiction: Medical. **Buys 6 mss/year.** Query with published clips. Length: 1,000-2,000 words. **Pays $300 (more for some articles).** Sometimes pays expenses of writers on assignment.

Photos: State availability with submission. Buys all rights. Negotiates payment individually. Identification of subjects required.

$ $ FAMILY DIGEST, The Black Mom's Best Friend!, Family Digest Association, 696 San Ramon Valley Blvd., #349, Danville CA 94526. Fax: (925)838-4948. E-mail: editor@familydigest.com. **Contact:** John Starch, associate editor. **90% freelance written.** Quarterly magazine. "Our mission: Help black moms/female heads-of-household get more out of their roles as wife, mother, homemaker. Editorial coverage includes parenting, health, love and marriage, travel, family finances, and beauty and style. All designed to appeal to black moms." Estab. 1997. Circ. 400,000. Pays on publication. Publishes ms an average of 6 months after acceptance. Buys first North American serial, all rights. Editorial lead time 2 months. Submit seasonal material 3 months in advance. Accepts queries by e-mail. Accepts previously published material. Accepts simultaneous submissions. Responds in 1 month to queries. Writer's guidelines by e-mail.

Nonfiction: "We are not political. We do not want articles that blame others. We do want articles that improve the lives of our readers." Book excerpts, general interest (dealing with relationships), historical/nostalgic, how-to, humor, inspirational, interview/profile, personal experience. Query with published clips. Length: up to 3,000 words. **Pays $100-500.** Sometimes pays expenses of writers on assignment.

Photos: Reviews negatives, transparencies, prints. Offers no additional payment for photos accepted with ms. Captions, identification of subjects, model releases required.

Columns/Departments: Food; Travel; Family; Parenting; Love and Marriage; Health; Family Finances; Beauty and Style. **Buys 100 mss/year.** Query with published clips. **Pays $100-500.**

Fiction: Erotica, ethnic, historical, humorous, novel excerpts, romance. Query with published clips.

Fillers: Anecdotes, facts, gags to be illustrated by cartoonist, short humor. **Buys 100 mss/year.** Length: 50-250 words.

$ THE FAMILY DIGEST, P.O. Box 40137, Fort Wayne IN 46804. **Contact:** Corine B. Erlandson, manuscript editor. **95% freelance written.** Bimonthly magazine. "*The Family Digest* is dedicated to the joy and fulfillment of the Catholic family and its relationship to the Catholic parish." Estab. 1945. Circ. 150,000. Pays within 1-2 months of acceptance. Byline given. Buys first North American serial rights. Submit seasonal material 7 months in advance. Accepts queries by mail. Accepts previously published material. Responds in 1-2 months to queries. Sample copy and writer's guidelines for 6×9 SAE with 2 first-class stamps.

Nonfiction: Family life, parish life, prayer life, Catholic traditions. How-to, inspirational, religious. **Buys 60 unsolicited mss/year.** Send complete ms. Length: 750-1,200 words. **Pays $40-60 for accepted articles.**

Reprints: Send ms with rights for sale noted and information about when and where the material previously appeared.

Fillers: Anecdotes, tasteful humor based on personal experience. **Buys 18/year.** Length: 25-100 words. **Pays $25.**

Tips: "Prospective freelance contributors should be familiar with the publication and the types of articles we accept and publish. We are especially looking for upbeat articles which affirm the simple ways in which the Catholic faith is expressed in daily life. Articles on family and parish life, including seasonal articles, how-to pieces, inspirational, prayer, spiritual life, and Church traditions, will be gladly reviewed for possible acceptance and publication."

$ $ $ $ FAMILYFUN, Disney Magazine Publishing, Inc., 244 Main St., Northampton MA 01060-3107. (413)585-0444. Fax: (413)586-5724. Website: www.familyfun.com. **Contact:** Jean Graham, editorial assistant. Magazine covering activities for families with kids ages 3-12. "*Family Fun* is about all the great things families can do together. Our writers are either parents or authorities in a covered field." Estab. 1991. Circ. 1,500,000. **Pays on acceptance.** Byline sometimes given. Offers 25% kill fee. Buys simultaneous rights, makes work-for-hire assignments. Editorial lead time 6 months. Submit seasonal material 6 months in advance. Accepts simultaneous submissions. Responds in 3 months to queries. Sample copy for $3. Writer's guidelines online.

Nonfiction: Book excerpts, essays, general interest, how-to (crafts, cooking, educational activities), humor, interview/profile, personal experience, photo feature, travel. Special issues: Crafts and Holidays. **Buys dozens of mss/year.** Query with published clips. Length: 850-3,000 words. **Pays $1.25/word.** Pays expenses of writers on assignment.

Photos: State availability with submission. Reviews contact sheets, negatives, transparencies. Buys all rights. Offers $75-500/photo. Identification of subjects, model releases required.

Columns/Departments: Family Almanac, Nicole Blasenak, assistant editor (simple, quick, practical, inexpensive ideas and projects—outings, crafts, games, nature activities, learning projects, and cooking with children), 200-400 words; query or send ms; **pays $100-$200/article or $150 for ideas.** Family Traveler, Adrienne Stolarz, (brief, newsy items about family travel, what's new, what's great, and especially, what's a good deal), 100-125 words; send ms; **pays $100, also pays $50 for ideas.** Family Ties, Kathy Whittemore, senior editor (first-person column that spotlights some aspect of family life that is humorous, inspirational, or interesting); 1,300 words; send ms; **pays $1,625.** My Great Idea, Dawn Chipman, senior editor (explains fun and inventive ideas that have worked for writer's own family); 800-1,000 words; query or send ms; **pays $1,250 on acceptance;** also publishes best letters from writers and readers following column, send to My Great Ideas Editor, 100-150 words, **pays $50 on publication. Buys 20-25 mss/year.**

Tips: "Many of our writers break into *FF* by writing for Family Almanac or Family Traveler (front-of-the-book departments)."

N $ HEALTHY BEGINNINGS, HEALTHY GROWING, HEALTHY CHOICES, Bridge Communications, Inc., 1450 Pilgrim Rd., Birmingham MI 48009-1006. (248)646-1020. E-mail: bridgcomm@aol.com. Website: www.bridge-comm.com. Editor: Alice R. McCarthy, Ph.D. Semiannual (March and October publication dates) 4-page, 4-color newsletters written for parents of children in grades preK-3, 4-5, and 6-8. Mental and physical health topics, plus strong support for school health programs including student health education. No advertising except books related to children's health. Circ. 600,000-1,000,000 yearly. Editorial lead time 4 months. Sample copies available.

$ HOME EDUCATION MAGAZINE, P.O. Box 1083, Tonasket WA 98855. (509)486-1351. E-mail: hem-editor@home-ed-magazine.com. Website: www.home-ed-magazine.com. **Contact:** Helen E. Hegener, managing editor. **80% freelance written.** Bimonthly magazine covering home-based education. We feature articles which address the concerns of parents who want to take a direct involvement in the education of their children—concerns such as socialization, how to find curriculums and materials, testing and evaluation, how to tell when your child is ready to begin reading, what to do when homeschooling is difficult, teaching advanced subjects, etc. Estab. 1983. Circ. 32,000. **Pays on acceptance.** Publishes ms an average of 4 months after acceptance. Byline given. Buys first North American serial, first, one-time, electronic rights. Submit seasonal material 6 months in advance. Accepts queries by mail, e-mail. Responds in 2 months to queries. Sample copy for $6.50. Writer's guidelines for #10 SASE or via e-mail.

Break in by "reading our magazine, understanding how we communicate with our readers, having an understanding of homeschooling, and being able to communicate that understanding clearly."

Nonfiction: Essays, how-to (related to home schooling), humor, interview/profile, personal experience, photo feature, technical. **Buys 40-50 mss/year.** Query with or without published clips or send complete ms. Length: 750-2,500 words. **Pays $50-100.** Sometimes pays expenses of writers on assignment.

Photos: Send photos with submission. Reviews enlargements, 35mm prints, b&w, CD-ROMs. Buys one-time rights. Pays $100/cover; $12/inside b&w photos. Identification of subjects required.

Tips: "We would like to see how-to articles (that don't preach, just present options); articles on testing, accountability, working with the public schools, socialization, learning disabilities, resources, support groups, legislation, and humor. We need answers to the questions that homeschoolers ask. Please, no teachers telling parents how to teach. Personal experience with homeschooling is most preferred approach."

$ HOMESCHOOLING TODAY, P.O. Box 468, Barker TX 77413. Fax: (832)201-7620. E-mail: publisher@homeschooltoday.com. Website: www.homeschooltoday.com. **Contact:** Stacy McDonald, editor. **75% freelance written.** Bimonthly magazine covering homeschooling. "We are a practical magazine for homeschoolers with a broadly Christian perspective." Estab. 1992. Circ. 25,000. Pays on publication. Publishes ms an average of 1 year after acceptance. Byline given. Offers 25% kill fee. Buys first rights. Editorial lead time 6 months. Submit seasonal material 1 year in advance. Accepts queries by mail, e-mail, fax. Accepts simultaneous submissions. Responds in 1 month to queries; 2 months to mss. Sample copy and writer's guidelines free.

Nonfiction: Book excerpts, how-to, inspirational, interview/profile, new product. No fiction or poetry. **Buys 30 mss/year.** Query. Length: 500-2,500 words. **Pays 8¢/word.**

Photos: State availability with submission. Buys one-time rights. Offers no additional payment for photos accepted with ms. Captions, identification of subjects required.

N $ INSTRUCTOR MAGAZINE, For Teachers of Grades K-8, Scholastic, Inc., 524 Broadway, New York NY 10012. (212)343-6100. Fax: (212)965-7497. E-mail: instructor@scholastic.com. Website: www.scholastic.com/instructor. Editor: Terry Cooper. Managing Editor: Jennifer Prescott. 8 times/ year Geared toward teachers, curriculum coordinators, principals and supervisors of kindergarten through 8th grade classes. Circ. 200,391. Editorial lead time 2 months. Submit seasonal material 6 months in advance. Accepts queries by mail. Responds in 3 months to queries; 3 months to mss. Sample copy for $3.00. Writer's guidelines by e-mail.

Nonfiction: Features Department. (Classroom management and practice; education trends and issues; professional development; lesson plans). Query with or without published clips or send complete ms. Length: 800-1,200 words.

Columns/Departments: Departments Editor. Activities and Tips (activities and tips for teachers), 250 words; Lesson Units (lesson- planning units on a specific curriculum area or theme) 400-800 words; Cyber Hunt Activities (tech-based activities in the classroom)250 words; End of the Day (personal essays about a teacher's experience with kids) 400-500 words. Query with or without published clips or send complete ms.

Tips: "As you write, think: How can I make this article most useful for teachers? Write in your natural voice. We shy away from wordy, academic prose. Let us know what grade/subject you teach and name and location of your school."

$ $ METRO PARENT MAGAZINE, Metro Parent Publishing Group, 24567 Northwestern Hwy., Suite 150, Southfield MI 48075. (248)352-0990. Fax: (248)352-5066. E-mail: sdemaggio@metroparent.com. Website: www.metroparent.com. **Contact:** Susan DeMaggio, editor. **75% freelance written.** Monthly magazine covering parenting, women's health, education. "We are a local magazine on parenting topics and issues of interest to Detroit-area parents. Related issues: *Ann Arbor Parent; African/American Parent; Metro Baby Magazine.*" Circ. 85,000. Pays on publication. Publishes ms an average of 3 months after acceptance. Byline given. Buys first rights. Editorial lead time 3 months. Submit seasonal material 3 months in advance. Accepts queries by mail, e-mail. Accepts previously published material. Accepts simultaneous submissions. Responds in 2 weeks to queries; 3 months to mss. Sample copy for $2.50.

Nonfiction: Essays, humor, inspirational, personal experience. **Buys 100 mss/year.** Send complete ms. Length: 1,500-2,500 words. **Pays $50-300 for assigned articles.**

Photos: State availability with submission. Buys one-time rights. Offers $100-200/photo or negotiates payment individually. Captions required.

Columns/Departments: Women's Health (latest issues of 20-40 year olds), 750-900 words; Solo Parenting (advice for single parents); Family Finance (making sense of money and legal issues); Tweens 'N Teens (handling teen "issues"), 750-800 words. **Buys 50 mss/year.** Send complete ms. **Pays $75-150.**

$ METROKIDS MAGAZINE, The Resource for Delaware Valley Families, Kidstuff Publications, Inc., 1080 N. Delaware Ave., #702, Philadelphia PA 19125-4330. (215)291-5560. Fax: (215)291-5563. E-mail: info@metrokids.com; editor@metrokids.com. Website: www.metrokids.com. **Contact:** Tom Livingston, executive editor. **25% freelance written.** Monthly tabloid providing information for parents and kids in Philadelphia, South Jersey, and surrounding counties. Estab. 1990. Circ. 125,000. Pays on publication. Byline given. Buys one-time rights. Submit seasonal material 4 months in advance. Accepts queries by e-mail. Accepts previously published material. Writer's guidelines by e-mail.

- Responds only if interested.

Nonfiction: General interest, how-to, new product, travel, parenting, health. Special issues: Educator's Edition (March & September; field trips, school enrichment, teacher, professional development); Camps (December-June); Special Kids (August; children with special needs); Vacations and Theme Parks (May, June); What's Happening (January; guide to events and activities); Kids 'N Care (July; guide to childcare). **Buys 40 mss/year.** Query with published clips. Length: 800-1,500 words. **Pays $1-50.** Sometimes pays expenses of writers on assignment.

Reprints: Send photocopy and information about when and where the material previously appeared. Pays $20-40.

Photos: State availability with submission. Buys one-time rights. Captions required.

Columns/Departments: Techno Family (CD-ROM and website reviews); Body Wise (health); Style File (fashion and trends); Woman First (motherhood); Practical Parenting (financial parenting advice); all 800-1,000 words. **Buys 25 mss/year.** Query. **Pays $1-50.**

Tips: "We prefer e-mail queries or submissions. Because they're so numerous, we don't reply unless interested. We are interested in feature articles (on specified topics) or material for our regular departments (with a regional/seasonal base). Articles should cite expert sources and the most up-to-date theories and facts. We are looking for a journalistic-style of writing. Editorial calendar available on request. We are also interested in finding local writers for assignments."

$ NORTHWEST FAMILY MAGAZINE, Best Solution Co., 7907 212th St. SW, Suite 201, Edmonds WA 98026. (425)775-6546. Fax: (425)775-6951. E-mail: nwfamilysubmissions@earthlink.net. Website: www.nwfamily.com. **Contact:** Chris Hopf, editor. **50% freelance written.** Monthly magazine providing information on parenting issues and helping local families to be in touch with resources, events, and places in the Northwest and Western Washington State. Estab. 1995. Circ. 50,000. Pays on publication. Publishes ms an average of 6 months after acceptance. Byline sometimes given. Buys one-time rights. Editorial lead time 3 months. Submit seasonal material 6 months in advance. Accepts queries by mail, e-mail. Accepts previously published material. Accepts simultaneous submissions. Responds in 3 weeks to queries; 3 months to mss. Sample copy for $1.25. Writer's guidelines for #10 SASE.

Nonfiction: Essays, general interest, how-to (relating to children), humor, inspirational, interview/profile, new product, personal experience, photo feature, travel. **Buys 40-50 mss/year.** Send complete ms. Length: 300-1,400 words. **Pays $25-45.** Sometimes pays expenses of writers on assignment.

Reprints: Accepts previously published submissions.

Photos: State availability with submission. Reviews negatives, prints (any size). Buys one-time rights. Negotiates payment individually. Model releases required.

Columns/Departments: School News (information about schools, especially local), 100-300 words; Community News (quick information for families in Western Washington), 100-300 words; Reviews (videos/books/products for families), 100-300 words; Teen News (information of interest to parents of teens), 50-300 words. **Buys 8-10 mss/year.** Send complete ms. **Pays $10-20.**

Poetry: Avant-garde, free verse, haiku, light verse, traditional. "No heavy or negative content." **Buys 6 poems/year.** Submit maximum 5 poems. Length: 6-25 lines. **Pays $5-20.**

Tips: "Send entire article with word count. Topic should apply to parents (regional focus increases our need for your article) and be addressed in a positive manner—'How-to' not 'How not to.'"

$$$$ PARENTING MAGAZINE, 530 Fifth Ave., 4th Floor, New York NY 10036. (212)522-8989. Fax: (212)522-8699. Editor-in-Chief: Janet Chan. Executive Editor: Lisa Bain. **Contact:** Articles Editor. Magazine published 10 times/year "for mothers of children from birth to 12, and covering both the emotional and practical aspects of parenting." Estab. 1987. **Pays on acceptance.** Byline given. Offers 25% kill fee. Buys a variety of rights, including electronic rights. Sample copy for $2.95 and 9×12 SAE with 5 first-class stamps. Writer's guidelines for #10 SASE.

Nonfiction: Book excerpts, personal experience, child development/behavior/health; investigative reports. **Buys 20-30 mss/year.** Query with or without published clips. Length: 1,000-2,500 words. **Pays $1,000-3,000.** Pays expenses of writers on assignment.

Columns/Departments: Query to the specific departmental editor. Ages and Stages (child development and behavior), 100-400 words; Children's Health, 100-350 words. **Buys 50-60 mss/year.** Query. **Pays $50-400.**

Tips: "The best guide for writers is the magazine itself. Please familiarize yourself with it before submitting a query."

$ PEDIATRICS FOR PARENTS, Pediatrics for Parents, Inc., P.O. Box 63716, Philadelphia PA 19147-3321. Fax: (419)858-7221. E-mail: rich.sagall@pobox.com. **Contact:** Richard J. Sagall, editor. **10% freelance written.** Monthly newsletter covering children's health. "*Pediatrics For Parents* emphasizes an informed, common-sense approach to childhood health care. We stress preventative action, accident prevention, when to call the doctor and when and how to handle a situation at home. We are also looking for articles that describe general, medical and pediatric problems, advances, new treatments, etc. All articles must be medically accurate and useful to parents with children—prenatal to adolescence." Estab. 1981. Circ. 500. Pays on publication. Publishes ms an average of 4 months after acceptance. Byline given. Buys first North American serial, electronic rights. Accepts queries by mail, e-mail, fax. Accepts previously published material. Accepts simultaneous submissions. Responds in 1 month to queries. Sample copy online. Writer's guidelines online.

Nonfiction: Medical. No first person or experience. **Buys 10 mss/year.** Query with or without published clips or send complete ms. Length: 500-1,000 words. **Pays $10-50.**

Reprints: Accepts previously published submissions.

$ SAN DIEGO FAMILY MAGAZINE, San Diego County's Leading Resource for Parents & Educators Who Care!, P.O. Box 23960, San Diego CA 92193-3960. (619)685-6970. Fax: (619)685-6978. Website: www.sandiegofamily.com. **Contact:** Claire Yezbak Fadden, editor. **75% freelance written.** Monthly magazine for parenting and family issues. "*SDFM* strives to provide informative, educational articles emphasizing positive parenting for our typical readership of educated mothers, ages 25-45, with an upper-level income. Most articles are factual and practical, a few are humor and personal experience. Editorial emphasis is uplifting and positive." Estab. 1982. Circ. 120,000. Pays on publication. Byline given. Buys first, one-time, second serial (reprint) rights. Editorial lead time 2 months. Submit seasonal material 3 months in advance. Accepts previously published material. Responds in 2 months to queries; 3 months to mss. Sample copy for $4.50 with 9×12 SAE. Writer's guidelines online.

- No e-mail queries.

Nonfiction: How-to, interview/profile (influential or noted persons or experts included in parenting or the welfare of children), parenting, new baby help, enhancing education, family activities, articles of specific interest to San Diego. "No rambling, personal experience pieces." **Buys 75 mss/year.** Send complete ms. Length: 800 words maximum. **Pays $1.25/column inch.**

Reprints: Send ms with rights for sale noted and information about when and where the material previously appeared.

Photos: State availability with submission. Reviews contact sheets, 3½×5 or 5×7 prints. Buys one-time rights. Negotiates payment individually. Identification of subjects required.

Columns/Departments: Kids' Books (topical book reviews—women's interest, grandparenting, fitness, health, cooking, home and garden), 800 words. **Buys 12 mss/year.** Query. **Pays $1.25/column inch.**

Fillers: Facts, newsbreaks (specific to family market). **Buys 10/year.** Length: 50-200 words. **Pays $1.25/column inch minimum.**

N $ SCHOLASTIC PARENT AND CHILD, Scholastic, Inc., 557 Broadway, New York NY 10012. (212)343-6100. Fax: (212)343-4801. E-mail: parentand child@scholastic.com. Website: parentandchildonline.com. Editor-in-Chief: Pam Abrams. Bimonthly magazine. Published to keep active parents up-to-date on children's learning and development while in pre-school or child-care enviroment. Circ. 1,224,098. Editorial lead time 6 weeks. Sample copy not available.

$ $ SOUTH FLORIDA PARENTING, 200 E. Las Olas Blvd., Fort Lauderdale FL 33301. (954)747-3050. Fax: (954)747-3055. E-mail: vmccash@sfparenting.com. Website: www.sfparenting.com. **Contact:** Vicki McCash Brennan, managing editor. **90% freelance written.** Monthly magazine covering parenting, family. "*South Florida Parenting* provides news, information, and a calendar of events for readers in Southeast Florida. The focus is on positive parenting and things to do or information about raising children in South Florida." Estab. 1990. Circ. 110,000. Pays on publication. Byline given. Buys one-time, second serial (reprint) rights, makes work-for-hire assignments. Editorial lead time 4 months. Submit seasonal material 5 months in advance. Accepts queries by mail, e-mail, fax. Accepts previously published material. Accepts simultaneous submissions. Responds in 2 months to queries; 6 months to mss. Sample copy for 9×12 SAE with $2.95 postage. Writer's guidelines for #10 SASE.

- Preference given to writers based in South Florida.

O→ Best bet to break in: "Be a local South Florida resident (particular need for writers from the Miami-Dade area) and address contemporary parenting topics and concerns."

Nonfiction: How-to (parenting issues), humor (preferably not first-person humor about kids and parents), interview/profile, personal experience, family and children's issues. Special issues: Education/Women's Health (January); Birthday Party (February); Summer Camp (March); Maternity (April); Florida/Vacation Guide (May); Kid Crown Awards (July); Back to School (August); Education (September); Holiday (December). **Buys 60+ mss/year.** Query with published clips or send complete ms. Length: 500-2,000 words. **Pays $40-300.**

Reprints: Send photocopy or e-mail on spec. **Pays $25-50.**

Photos: State availability with submission. Reviews negatives, transparencies, prints. Buys one-time rights. Sometimes offers additional payment for photos accepted with ms.

Columns/Departments: Baby Basics (for parents of infants); Family Health (child health); Preteen Power (for parents of preteens); Family Money (family finances), all 500-750 words.

Tips: "We want information targeted to the South Florida market. Multicultural and well-sourced is preferred. A unique approach to a universal parenting concern will be considered for publication. Profiles or interviews of courageous parents. Opinion pieces on child rearing should be supported by experts and research should be listed. First-person stories should be fresh and insightful. All writing should be clear and concise. Submissions can be typewritten, double-spaced, but the preferred format is on diskette or by e-mail attachment."

N $ $ TIDEWATER PARENT, Portfolio Publishing, 1300 Diamond Springs Rd., Suite 102, Virginia Beach VA 23455. (757)222-3100. Fax: (757)363-1767. E-mail: jodonnel@pilotonline.com. **Contact:** Jennifer O'Donnell, editor. **85% freelance written.** Monthly tabloid. "All our readers are parents of children age 0-11. Our readers demand stories that will help them tackle the challenges and demands they face daily as parents." Estab. 1980. Circ. 40,000. Pays on publication. Byline given. Offers 10% kill fee. Buys first North American serial rights. Editorial lead time 2 months. Submit seasonal material 3 months in advance. Accepts queries by mail, e-mail, fax. Accepts previously published material. Accepts simultaneous submissions. Responds in 1 month to queries; 4 months to mss. Sample copy for free. Writer's guidelines free.

Nonfiction: Essays, general interest, historical/nostalgic, how-to, humor, interview/profile, personal experience, religious, travel. No poetry or fiction. **Buys 60 mss/year.** Query with or without published clips or send complete ms. Length: 500-3,000 words. **Pays $35-200.**

Photos: State availability of or send photos with submission. Buys one-time rights. Negotiates payment individually. Captions required.

Columns/Departments: Music and Video Software (reviews), both 600-800 words; also Where to Go, What to Do, Calendar Spotlight and Voices. **Buys 36 mss/year.** Send complete ms. **Pays $35-50.**

Tips: "Articles for *Tidewater Parent* should be informative and relative to parenting. An informal, familiar tone is preferable to a more formal style. Avoid difficult vocabulary and complicated sentence structure. A conversational tone works best. Gain your reader's interest by using real-life situations, people or examples to support what you're saying."

N $ TODAY'S PARENT, Today's Parent Group, 269 Richmond St. W., Toronto ON M5V 1X1, Canada. (416)596-8680. Fax: (416)596-1991. Website: www.todaysparent.com. Editor: Linda Lewis. Monthly magazine. Edited for parents with children up to the age of twelve. Circ. 175,000. Editorial lead time 5 months. Sample copy not available.

$ $ $ $ TODAY'S PARENT PREGNANCY & BIRTH, 269 Richmond St. W, Toronto ON M5V 1X1, Canada. (416)596-8680. Fax: (416)596-1991. Website: www.todaysparent.com. **Contact:** Editor. **100% freelance written.** Magazine published 3 times/year. "*P&B* helps, supports and encourages expectant and new parents with news and features related to pregnancy, birth, human sexuality and parenting." Estab. 1973. Circ. 200,000. **Pays on acceptance.** Publishes ms an average of 8 months after acceptance. Buys first North American serial rights. Editorial lead time 6 months. Responds in 6 weeks to queries. Sample copy and writer's guidelines for #10 SASE.

Nonfiction: Features about pregnancy, labor and delivery, post-partum issues. **Buys 12 mss/year.** Query with published clips. Length: 600-2,500 words. **Pays $350-2,000.** Sometimes pays expenses of writers on assignment.

Photos: State availability with submission. Rights negotiated individually. Pay negotiated individually.

Tips: "Our writers are professional freelance writers with specific knowledge in the childbirth field. *P&B* is written for a Canadian audience using Canadian research and sources."

$ $ TWINS, The Magazine for Parents of Multiples, The Business Word, Inc., 11211 E. Arapahoe Rd., Suite 100, Centennial CO 80112-3851. (303)290-8500 or (888)55TWINS. Fax: (303)290-9025. E-mail: twins.editor@businessword.com. Website: www.twinsmagazine.com. Editor-in-Chief: Susan J. Alt. **Contact:** Sharon Withers, managing editor. **80% freelance written.** Bimonthly magazine covering parenting multiples. "*TWINS* is an international publication that provides informational and educational articles regarding the parenting of twins, triplets, and more. All articles must be multiple specific and have an upbeat, hopeful, and/or positive ending." Estab. 1984. Circ. 55,000. Pays on publication. Byline given. Buys first North American serial rights. Editorial lead time 4 months. Submit seasonal material 6 months in advance. Accepts queries by mail, e-mail, fax. Accepts simultaneous submissions. Response time varies to queries. Sample copy for $5 or on website. Writer's guidelines online.

Nonfiction: Interested in seeing twin-specific discipline articles. Personal experience (first-person parenting experience), professional experience as it relates to multiples. Nothing on cloning, pregnancy reduction or fertility issues. **Buys 12 mss/year.** Query with or without published clips or send complete ms. Length: 1,300 words. **Pays $25-250 for assigned articles; $25-100 for unsolicited articles.**

Photos: State availability with submission. Offers no additional payment for photos accepted with ms. Identification of subjects required.

Columns/Departments: Special Miracles (miraculous stories about multiples with a happy ending), 800-850 words. **Buys 12-20 mss/year.** Query with or without published clips or send complete ms. **Pays $40-75.**

Tips: "All department articles must have a happy ending, as well as teach a lesson helpful to parents of multiples."

$ WESTERN NEW YORK FAMILY, Western New York Family, Inc., 3147 Delaware Ave., Buffalo NY 14217. (716)836-3486. Fax: (716)836-3680. E-mail: wnyfamily@aol.com. Website: www.wnyfamilymagazine.com. **Contact:** Michele Miller, editor/publisher. **90% freelance written.** Monthly magazine covering parenting in Western New York. "Readership is largely composed of families with children ages newborn to 14 years. Although most subscriptions are in the name of the mother, 91% of fathers also read the publication. Strong emphasis is placed on how and where to find family-oriented events, as well as goods and services for children, in Western New York." Estab. 1984. Circ. 22,500. Pays on publication. Publishes ms an average of 3 months after acceptance. Byline given. Buys one-time, second serial (reprint), simultaneous rights. Editorial lead time 3 months. Submit seasonal material 3 months in advance. Accepts previously published material. Accepts simultaneous submissions. Responds only if interested to queries. Sample copy for $2.50 and 9×12 SAE with $1.06 postage. Writer's guidelines online.

O→ Break in with either a "cutting edge" topic that is new and different in its relevance to current parenting challenges and trends or a "timeless" topic which is "evergreen" and can be kept on file to fill last minute holes.

Nonfiction: How-to (craft projects for kids, holiday, costume, etc.), humor (as related to parenting), personal experience (parenting related), travel (family destinations). Special issues: Birthday Celebrations (January); Cabin Fever (February); Seeking Spring (March); Having a Baby (April); Mother's Day (May); Father's Day (June); Summer Fun (July and August); Back to School (September); Halloween Happenings (October); Family Issues (November); and Holiday Happenings (December). **Buys 100 mss/year.** Send complete ms by mail or e-mail. Unsolicited e-mail attachments are not accepted; paste text of article into body of e-mail. Length: 750-3,000 words. **Pays $50-150 for assigned articles; $25-50 for unsolicited articles.** Sometimes pays expenses of writers on assignment.

Reprints: Accepts previously published submissions.

Photos: State availability with submission. Reviews 3×5 prints, JPEG files via e-mail. Buys one-time rights. Offers no additional payment for photos accepted with ms. Captions, identification of subjects, model releases required.

Fillers: Facts. **Buys 10/year.** Length: 450 words. **Pays $20.**

Tips: "We are interested in well-researched, nonfiction articles on surviving the newborn, preschool, school age, and adolescent years. Our readers want practical information on places to go and things to do in the Buffalo area and nearby Canada. They enjoy humorous articles about the trials and tribulations of parenthood as well as 'how-to' articles (i.e., tips for finding a sitter, keeping your sanity while shopping with preschoolers, ideas for holidays and birthdays, etc.). Articles on making a working parent's life easier are of great interest as are articles written by fathers. We also need more material on preteen and young teen (13-15) issues. More material on multicultural families and their related experiences, traditions, etc., would be of interest in 2003. We prefer a warm, conversational style of writing."

N $ $ WHAT'S UP KIDS? FAMILY MAGAZINE, 496 Metler Rd., Ridgeville ON L0S 1M0, Canada. E-mail: editor@whatsupkids.com. Website: www.whatsupkids.com. **Contact:** Jennifer McKenzie-Pellegrini, editor. **95% freelance written.** Bimonthly magazine covering topics of interest to young families. "Editorial is aimed at parents of kids brith-age 10 (approximately). Kids Fun Section offers a section just for kids. We're committed to providing top-notch content." Estab. 1997. Circ. 200,000. **Pays on acceptance.** Publishes ms an average of 4 months after acceptance. Byline given. Buys all rights. Editorial lead time 6 months. Submit seasonal material 6 months in advance. Accepts queries by mail, e-mail. Accepts previously published material. Responds in 2-4 weeks to queries. Sample copy for free. Writer's guidelines online at website or by e-mail.

Nonfiction: General interest, humor, inspirational, interview/profile, new product, personal experience, travel. No religious (one sided) or op-ed. **Buys 50 mss/year.** Query with published clips. Length: 1,000-3,500 words. **Pays $100-350 for assigned articles.** Sometimes pays expenses of writers on assignment.

Photos: State availability with submission. Reviews GIF/JPEG files. Buys all rights. Offers $50/photo. Captions, identification of subjects, model releases required.

Columns/Departments: What's Up in Health (general family health), 800-1,000 words; What's Up in Finance (family finance advice), 800-1,000 words; What's Up in Crafts (craft ideas), 800-1,000 words; Parent to Parent (personal experience), 1,000-1,500 words. **Buys variable number of mss/year.** Query with published clips. **Pays $150.**

Tips: "Currently, we only accept submissions from Canadian writers. Writers should send résumé, clips, and query. Be patient! I will respond as quickly as possible. We're growing and as we grow, payment will grow too!"

$ WORKING MOTHER MAGAZINE, 260 Madison Ave., 3rd Floor, New York NY 10016. (212)351-6400. Fax: (212)351-6487. E-mail: editors@workingmother.com. Website: www.workingmother.com. **Contact:** Articles Department. **90% freelance written.** Prefers to work with published/established writers; works with a small number of new/unpublished writers each year. Monthly magazine for women who balance a career with the concerns of parenting. Circ. 925,000. Publishes ms an average of 4 months after acceptance. Byline given. Offers kill fee. Buys all rights. Submit seasonal material 6 months in advance. Accepts queries by mail. Sample copy for $5; available by calling (800)925-0788. Writer's guidelines online.

Nonfiction: Service, humor, child development, material pertinent to the working mother's predicament. Humor, service; child development; material perinent to the working mother's predicament. **Buys 9-10 mss/year.** Query. Length: 1,500-2,000 words. Pays expenses of writers on assignment.

Tips: "We are looking for pieces that help the reader. In other words, we don't simply report on a trend without discussing how it specifically affects our readers' lives and how they can handle the effects. Where can they look for help if necessary?"

COMIC BOOKS

N $ THE COMICS JOURNAL, Fantagraphics Books, 7563 Lake City Way NE, Seattle WA 98115. (206)524-1967. Fax: (206)524-2104. E-mail: milo@tcj.com. Website: www.tcj.com. **Contact:** Milo George, managing editor. Monthly magazine covering the comics medium from an arts-first perspective. *The Comics Journal* is one of the nation's most respected single-arts magazines, providing its readers with an eclectic mix of industry news, professional interviews, and reviews of current work. Due to its reputation as the American magazine with an interest in comics as an art form, the *Journal* has subscribers worldwide, and in this country serves as an important window into the world of comics for several general arts and news magazines. Byline given. Buys exclusive rights to articles that run in print or online versions for 6 months after initial publication. Rights then revert back to the writer. Accepts queries by mail, e-mail. Writer's guidelines online.

- In 2002, *The Journal* won the Utne Independent Press Award for arts and literature coverage.

Nonfiction: "We're obviously not the magazine for the discussion of comic 'universes,' character re-boots, and Spider-Man's new costume—beyond, perhaps, the business or cultural implications of such events." Essays, general interest, how-to, humor, interview/profile, opinion. Send complete ms. Length: 2,000-3,000 words. **Pays 4¢/word, and 1 contributor's copy.**

Columns/Departments: On Theory, Art and Craft (2,000-3,000 words); Firing Line bullets (600-1,000 words); Hit List (100 words); Comics Library (up to 5,000 words). Send complete ms. **Pays 4¢/word, and 1 contributor's copy.**

Contact: Dirk Deppey, webmaster (dirk@fantagraphics.com).

Tips: "Like most magazines, the best writers guideline is to look at the material within the magazine and give something that approximates that material in terms of approach and sophistication. Anything else is a waste of time."

$ $ WIZARD: THE COMICS MAGAZINE, Wizard Entertainment, 151 Wells Ave., Congers NY 10920-2036. (845)268-2000. Fax: (845)268-0053. E-mail: andyserwin@hotmail.com. Website: www.wizardworld.com. Editor: Brian Cunningham. Senior Editor: Joe Yanarella. **Contact:** Andy Serwin, managing editor. **25% freelance written.** Monthly magazine covering the comic book industry and related entertainment fields, including TV, movies, and home video. Estab. 1991. Circ. 209,000. Pays on publication. Publishes ms an average of 3 months after acceptance. Byline given. Offers 50% kill fee. Buys all rights. Editorial lead time 4 months. Accepts queries by mail, e-mail, fax. Responds in 6 weeks to queries. Sample copy and writer's guidelines free.

Nonfiction: Historical/nostalgic, how-to, humor, interview/profile, new product, personal experience, photo feature, first-person diary. No columns or opinion pieces. **Buys 50 mss/year.** Query with or without published clips. Length: 250-4,000 words. **Pays 15-20¢/word.** Sometimes pays expenses of writers on assignment.

Photos: State availability with submission. Buys all rights. Negotiates payment individually. Identification of subjects required.

Columns/Departments: Video Stuff (comic book, science fiction, and top-selling video games); Manga Mania (the latest news, anime, manga, toys, etc., from Japan); Coming Attractions (comic book-related movies and TV shows), 150-500 words. Query with published clips. **Pays $75-500.**

Tips: "Send plenty of samples showing the range of your writing styles. Have a good knowledge of comic books. Read a few issues to get the feel of the conversational 'Wizard Style.'"

CONSUMER SERVICE & BUSINESS OPPORTUNITY

Some of these magazines are geared to investing earnings or starting a new business; others show how to make economical purchases. Publications for business executives and consumers interested in business topics are listed under Business & Finance. Those on how to run specific businesses are classified by category in the Trade section.

N $ CONSUMER REPORTS, Consumers Union of US, Inc., 101 Truman Ave., Yonkers NY 10703-1057. (914)378-2000. Fax: (914)378-2904. Website: www.consumerreports.org. Managing Editor: David Heim. **Contact:** Margot Slade, editor. **5% freelance written.** Monthly magazine. "*Consumer Reports* is the leading product-testing and consumer-service magazine in the U.S. We buy very little freelance material, mostly from proven writers we have used before for finance and health columns." Estab. 1936. Circ. 14,000,000. **Pays on acceptance.** Publishes ms an average of 2 months after acceptance. Offers negotiable kill fee. Buys all rights. Editorial lead time 4 months. Submit seasonal material 6 months in advance. Accepts queries by mail.

Nonfiction: Technical, personal finance, personal health. **Buys 12 mss/year.** Query. Length: 1,000 words. **Pays variable rate.**

$ $ HOME BUSINESS MAGAZINE, United Marketing & Research Company, Inc., 9582 Hamilton Ave. PMB 368, Huntington Beach CA 92646. Fax: (714)962-7722. E-mail: admin@homebusinessmag.com. Website: www.homebusinessmag.com. **Contact:** Stacy Henderson, online editor. **75% freelance written.** "*Home Business Magazine* covers every angle of the home-based business market including: cutting edge editorial by well-known authorities on sales and marketing, business operations, the home office, franchising, business opportunities, network marketing, mail order and other subjects to help readers choose, manage and prosper in a home-based business; display advertising, classified ads and a directory of home-based businesses; technology, the Internet, computers and the future of home-based business; home-office editorial including management advice, office set-up, and product descriptions; business opportunities, franchising and work-from-home success stories." Estab. 1993. Circ. 80,000. Pays on publication. Publishes ms an average of 6 months after acceptance. Byline given. Makes work-for-hire assignments. Editorial lead time 4 months. Submit seasonal material 6 months in advance. Accepts queries by mail, e-mail, fax. Accepts previously published material. Accepts simultaneous submissions. Sample copy for 9×12 SAE and 8 first-class stamps. Writer's guidelines for #10 SASE.

Nonfiction: Book excerpts, general interest, how-to (home business), inspirational, interview/profile, new product, personal experience, photo feature, technical, mail order; franchise; business management; internet; finance network marketing. No non-home business related topics. **Buys 40 mss/year.** Send complete ms. Length: 200-1,000 words. **Pays 20¢/word for assigned articles; $0-65 for unsolicited articles.**

Photos: Send photos with submission. Buys one-time rights. Offers no additional payment for photos accepted with ms. Identification of subjects required.

Columns/Departments: Marketing & Sales; Money Corner; Home Office; Management; Technology; Working Smarter; Franchising; Network Marketing, all 650 words. Send complete ms.

The online magazine carries original content not found in the print edition. Contact: Herb Wetenkamp, online editor.

Tips: "Send complete information by mail as per our writer's guidelines and e-mail if possible. We encourage writers to submit Feature Articles (2-3 pages) and Departmental Articles (1 page). Please submit polished, well-written, organized material. It helps to provide subheadings within the article. Boxes, lists and bullets are encouraged because they make your article easier to read, use and reference by the reader. A primary problem in the past is that articles do not stick to the subject of the title. Please pay attention to the focus of your article and to your title. Please don't call to get the status of your submission. We will call if we're interested in publishing the submission."

$ KIPLINGER'S PERSONAL FINANCE, 1729 H St. NW, Washington DC 20006. (202)887-6400. Fax: (202)331-1206. Website: www.kiplinger.com. Editor: Fred W. Frailey. **Contact:** Dayl Sanders, office manager. **10% freelance written.** Prefers to work with published/established writers. Monthly magazine for general, adult audience intersted in personal finance and consumer information. "*Kiplinger's* is a highly trustworthy source of information on saving and investing, taxes, credit, home ownership, paying for college, retirement planning, automobile buying, and many other personal finance topics." Estab. 1947. Circ. 1,300,000. **Pays on acceptance.** Publishes ms an average of 2 months after acceptance. Buys all rights. Responds in 1 month to queries.

Nonfiction: "Most material is staff-written, but we accept some freelance. Thorough documentation is required for fact-checking." Query with published clips. Pays expenses of writers on assignment.

Tips: "We are looking for a heavy emphasis on personal finance topics. Currently all work is provided by in-house writers."

$ $ LIVING SAFETY, A Canada Safety Council Publication for Safety in the Home, Traffic and Recreational Environments, 1020 Thomas Spratt Place, Ottawa ON K1G 5L5, Canada. (613)739-1535. Fax: (613)739-1566. E-mail: jsmith@safety-council.org. Website: www.safety-council.org. **Contact:** Jack Smith, editor-in-chief. **65% freelance written.** Quarterly magazine covering off-the-job safety. "Off-the-job health and safety magazine covering topics in the home, traffic, and recreational environments. Audience is the Canadian employee and his/her family." Estab. 1983. Circ. 100,000. **Pays on acceptance.** Publishes ms an average of 2 months after acceptance. Byline given. Buys all rights. Editorial lead time 4 months. Submit seasonal material 6 months in advance. Accepts queries by mail. Accepts previously published material. Accepts simultaneous submissions. Responds in 1 month to queries. Sample copy and writer's guidelines free.

Nonfiction: General interest, how-to (safety tips, health tips), personal experience. **Buys 24 mss/year.** Query with published clips. Length: 1,000-2,500 words. **Pays $500 maximum.** Sometimes pays expenses of writers on assignment.

Reprints: Send tearsheet.

Photos: State availability with submission. Reviews contact sheets, negatives, transparencies, prints. Offers no additional payment for photos accepted with ms. Identification of subjects required.

CONTEMPORARY CULTURE

These magazines often combine politics, current events, and cultural elements such as art, literature, film and music, to examine contemporary society. Their approach to institutions is typically irreverent and investigative. Some, like *Generation X Journal*, report on alternative culture and appeal to a young adult "Generation X" audience. Others treat mainstream culture for a baby boomer generation audience.

$ $ $ $ A&U, America's AIDS Magazine, Art & Understanding, Inc., 25 Monroe St., Suite 205, Albany NY 12210-2729. (518)426-9010. Fax: (518)436-5354. E-mail: mailbox@aumag.org. Website: www.aumag.org. **Contact:** David Waggoner, editor-in-chief. **50% freelance written.** Monthly magazine covering cultural, political, and medical responses to AIDS/HIV. Estab. 1991. Circ. 205,000. Pays 30-60 days after publication. Publishes ms an average of 3 months after acceptance. Byline given. Offers 20% kill fee. Buys first North American serial rights. Editorial lead time 6 months. Accepts queries by mail, fax, phone. Accepts simultaneous submissions. Responds in 1 month to queries; 2 months to mss. Sample copy for $5. Writer's guidelines online.

Nonfiction: Book excerpts, essays, general interest, how-to, humor, interview/profile, new product, opinion, personal experience, photo feature, travel, reviews (film, theater, art exhibits, video, music, other media), medical news. **Buys 120 mss/year.** Query with published clips. Length: 800-4,800 words. **Pays $250-2,500 for assigned articles.** Sometimes pays expenses of writers on assignment.

Photos: State availability with submission. Reviews contact sheets, up to 4×5 transparencies, 4×5 to 8×10 prints. Buys one-time rights. Offers $50-500/photo. Captions, identification of subjects, model releases required.

Columns/Departments: The Culture of AIDS (reviews of books, music, film), 800 words; Viewpoint (personal opinion), 900-1,500 words. **Buys 100 mss/year.** Send complete ms. **Pays $100-250.**

Fiction: Chael Needle, managing editor. Unpublished work only; accepts prose, poetry, and drama. Send complete ms. Length: less than 1,500 words. **Pays $50-150.**

Poetry: Any length/style (shorter works preferred). **Pays $50.**

The online magazine carries original content not found in the print edition. Contact: David Waggoner.

Tips: "We're looking for more articles on youth and HIV/AIDS; more international coverage; more small-town America coverage."

$ $ $ ADBUSTERS, Journal of the Mental Environment, The Media Foundation, 1243 W. 7th Ave., Vancouver BC V6H 1B7, Canada. (604)736-9401. Fax: (604)737-6021. Website: www.adbusters.org. Managing Editor: Aiden Enns. **Contact:** Kalle Lasn, editor. **50% freelance written.** Bimonthly magazine. "We are an activist journal of the mental environment." Estab. 1989. Circ. 90,000. Pays 1 month after publication. Byline given. Buys first rights. Accepts queries by mail, e-mail, fax. Accepts simultaneous submissions. Writer's guidelines online.

Nonfiction: Essays, exposé, interview/profile, opinion. **Buys variable mss/year.** Query. Length: 250-3,000 words. **Pays $100/page for unsolicited articles; 50¢/word for solicited articles.**

Fiction: Inquire about themes.

Poetry: Inquire about themes.

$ $ THE AMERICAN SCHOLAR, Phi Beta Kappa, 1606 New Hampshire Ave. NW, Washington DC 20009. (202)265-3808. Fax: (202)265-0083. E-mail: scholar@pbk.org. Editor: Anne Fadiman. **Contact:** Jean Stipicevic, managing editor. **100% freelance written.** Quarterly journal. "Our intent is to have articles written by scholars and experts but written in nontechnical language for an intelligent audience. Material covers a wide range in the arts, sciences, current affairs, history, and literature." Estab. 1932. Circ. 25,000. Pays on publication. Publishes ms an average of 1 year after acceptance. Byline given. Offers 50% kill fee. Buys first rights. Editorial lead time 6 months. Submit seasonal material 6 months in advance. Accepts queries by mail, e-mail, fax. Responds in 2 weeks to queries; 2 months to mss. Sample copy for $9. Writer's guidelines for #10 SASE.

Nonfiction: Essays, historical/nostalgic, humor. **Buys 40 mss/year.** Query. Length: 3,000-5,000 words. **Pays $500 maximum.**

Poetry: "We have no special requirements of length, form, or content for original poetry." Rob Farnsworth, poetry editor. **Buys 25 poems/year.** Submit maximum 3-4 poems. **Pays $50.**

N $ BACK STAGE, VNU Business Media, 770 Broadway, New York NY 10003. (646)654-5500. Fax: (646)654-5743. E-mail: backstage@backstage.com. Website: www.backstage.com. Editor: Shelly Eaker. Managing Editor: David Sheward. Weekly magazine covering performing arts. "*Back Stage* was created for actors, singers, dancers, and associated performing arts professionals." Circ. 33,000. Accepts queries by mail. Sample copy for $3.25.

N $ $ BIG BROTHER, LFP, Inc., 8484 Wilshire Blvd., Suite 900, Beverly Hills CA 90211. (323)651-5400. Fax: (323)951-0384. E-mail: bigbrothers@lfp.com. Website: www.bigbrothermagazine.com. Managing Editor: Chris Nieratko. **Contact:** Dave Carnie, editor. Monthly magazine covering skateboard culture. A lifestyle publication that features interviews, music reviews and photographic coverage of skateboards. Geared toward the "core skateboarder." Estab. 1992. Circ. 103,627. Editorial lead time 3 weeks. Accepts queries by mail, e-mail. Sample copy for $ 3.99 at newstands. Writer's guidelines by e-mail.

Nonfiction: Interview/profile, photo feature, technical. Query or send completed ms. **Pays 25¢/word. Interviews: $50 for 1 page; $100 for 2-4 pages; $200 for 5+ pages.**

Photos: Rick Kosick, photo editor. Send photos with submission. Reviews contact sheets, negatives, transparencies, prints. Cover: $400; 2-page spread: $300; full page: 150; ½ page: $100; ¼ page: $75; spot photo $30. Captions, identification of subjects required.

Tips: "If you have an idea for an article, the best thing to do is just do it, send it to us, and then call and tell us it's coming. Then we'll decide if we like your idea. Your article's chances of being accepted, however, will be greatly increased if it is accompanied by photos."

$ $ $ $ BOOK, The Magazine for the Reading Life, West Egg Communications LLC, 252 W. 37th St., 5th Floor, New York NY 10018. (212)659-7070. Fax: (212)736-4455. E-mail: alanger@bookmagazine.com. Website: www.bookmagazine.com. Editor-in-Chief: Jerome Kramer. **Contact:** Adam Langer, senior editor. **50% freelance written.** Bimonthly magazine covering books and reading. Estab. 1998. Circ. 750,000. Pays 30 days after publication. Byline sometimes given. Offers kill fee. Buys first, electronic rights, makes work-for-hire assignments. Editorial lead time 4 months. Submit seasonal material 4 months in advance. Accepts queries by mail, e-mail, fax. Sample copy online. Writer's guidelines online.

Nonfiction: Book excerpts, essays, interview/profile. Query with published clips. Length: 1,000-4,000 words. **Pays 50¢-$1.50/word.**

Photos: Send photos with submission. Buys one-time rights. Identification of subjects required.

Columns/Departments: Shop Watch (bookstore profiles); Locations (literary travel); Group Dynamics (book-group tips, stories); Web Catches (related to books online), all 1,500 words. **Buys 36 mss/year.** Query with published clips. **Pays $500-750.**

Fiction: Literary short stories. **Buys 6 mss/year.** Send complete ms. Length: 1,000-6,000 words. **Pays $500-3,000.**

$ BOOKPAGE, Promotion, Inc., 2143 Belcourt Ave., Nashville TN 37212. (615)292-8926. Fax: (615)292-8249. E-mail: lynn@bookpage.com. Website: www.bookpage.com. **Contact:** Ms. Lynn L. Green, editor. **90% freelance written**. Monthly newspaper covering new book releases. "*BookPage is a general interest consumer publication which covers a broad range of books. Bookstores and libraries buy BookPage* in quantity to use as a way to communicate with their regular customers/patrons and keep them up to date on new releases. *BookPage* reviews almost every category of new books including popular and literary fiction, biography, memoir, history, science and travel. Many specialty genres (mystery, science fiction, business and finance, romance, cooking and audio books) are covered by regular columnists and are rarely assigned to other reviewers. We carry few, if any, reviews of backlist books, poetry, short story collections or scholarly books. *BookPage* editors assign all books to be reviewed, choosing from the hundreds of advance review copies we receive each month. We do not publish unsolicited reviews." Estab. 1988. Circ. 500,000. Byline given. Editorial lead time 3 months. Accepts queries by mail, e-mail, fax. Sample copy online. Writer's guidelines free.

Columns/Departments: Romance: Love, Exciting and New, 1,000 words; Business, 1,500 words; New and Good, 800 words; Mystery/Audio, 800-1,000 words. Query with published clips. **Pays $20/400-word review.**

Tips: "If you are interested in being added to our large roster of freelance reviewers, send an e-mail to the editor with a brief bio, a description of your reading interests, and samples of your writing particularly any book reviews you have written. We prefer experienced writers who can effectively communicate, with imagination and originality, what they liked about a particular book."

$ BOSTON REVIEW, E53-407, M.I.T., Cambridge MA 02139. (617)253-3642. Fax: (617)252-1549. E-mail: bostonreview@mit.edu. Website: bostonreview.mit.edu. Editors: Deb Chasman and Josh Cohen. **Contact:** Dan Ochsner, managing editor. **90% freelance written.** Bimonthly magazine of cultural and political analysis, reviews, fiction, and poetry. "The editors are committed to a society and culture that foster human diversity and a democracy in which we seek common grounds of principle amidst our many differences. In the hope of advancing these ideals, the *Review* acts as a forum that seeks to enrich the language of public debate." Estab. 1975. Circ. 20,000. Publishes ms an average of 4 months after acceptance. Byline given. Buys first North American serial, first rights. Accepts simultaneous submissions. Responds in 4 months to queries. Sample copy for $5 or online. Writer's guidelines online.

- The *Boston Review* also offers a poetry contest. See Contests & Awards/Poetry section.

Nonfiction: Critical essays and reviews. "We do not accept unsolicited book reviews. If you would like to be considered for review assignments, please send your résumé along with several published clips." **Buys 50 mss/year.** Query with published clips.

Fiction: Jodi Daynard, fiction editor. "I'm looking for stories that are emotionally and intellectually substantive and also interesting on the level of language. Things that are shocking, dark, lewd, comic, or even insane are fine so long as the fiction is *controlled* and purposeful in a masterly way. Subtlety, delicacy, and lyricism are attractive too." Ethnic, experimental, contemporary, prose poem. "No romance, erotica, genre fiction." **Buys 5 mss/year.** Send complete ms. Length: 1,200-5,000 words. **Pays $50-100, and 5 contributor's copies.**

Poetry: Mary Jo Bang and Timothy Donnelly, poetry editors.

N $ CANADIAN DIMENSION, Dimension Publications Inc., 91 Albert St., Room 2-B, Winnipeg MB, R3B 1G5, Canada. (204)957-1519. E-mail: info@canadiandimension.mb.ca. Website: www.canadiandimension.mb.ca. **Contact:** Ed Janzen. **80% freelance written.** Bimonthly magazine covering socialist perspective. "We bring a socialist perspective to bear on events across Canada and around the world. Our contributors provide in-depth coverage on popular movements, peace, labour, women, aboriginal justice, environment, third world and eastern Europe." Estab. 1963. Circ. 2,000. Pays on publication. Publishes ms an average of 6 months after acceptance. Accepts previously published material. Accepts simultaneous submissions. Responds in 6 weeks to queries. Sample copy for $2. Writer's guidelines online.

Nonfiction: Interview/profile, opinion, reviews; political commentary and analysis; journalistic style. **Buys 8 mss/year.** Length: 500-2,000 words. **Pays $25-100.**

Reprints: Send ms with rights for sale noted and information about when and where the material previously appeared.

N $$$ COMMENTARY, American Jewish Committee, 165 E. 56th St., New York NY 10022. (212)891-1400. Fax: (212)891-6700. E-mail: editorial@commentarymagazine.com. Website: www.commentarymagazine.com. Editor: Neal Kozodoy. Managing Editor: Gary Rosen. **Contact:** Benjamin Balint, assistant editor. Monthly magazine. Pays on publication. Publishes ms an average of 2 months after acceptance. Byline given. Buys all rights. Accepts queries by mail, e-mail. Writer's guidelines not available.

Nonfiction: Essays, opinion. **Buys 4 mss/year.** Query. Length: 2,000-8,000 words. **Pays $400-1,200.**

Tips: "Unsolicited manuscripts must be accompanied by a self-addressed, stamped envelope."

$$ COMMON GROUND, Common Ground Publishing, 201-3091 W. Broadway, Vancouver BC V6K 2G9, Canada. (604)733-2215. Fax: (604)733-4415. E-mail: editor@commongroundmagazine.com. Website: www.commongroundmagazine.com. Senior Editor: Joseph Roberts. **Contact:** Robert Scheer, associate editor. **90% freelance written.** Monthly tabloid covering health, environment, spirit, creativity, and wellness. "We serve the cultural creative community." Estab. 1984. Circ. 70,000. Pays on publication. Publishes ms an average of 1 month after acceptance. Byline given. Buys one-time, second serial (reprint) rights. Editorial lead time 3 months. Submit seasonal material 3 months in advance. Accepts queries by e-mail. Accepts simultaneous submissions. Responds in 6 weeks to queries; 3 months to mss. Sample copy for $5. Writer's guidelines online.

Nonfiction: All topics must fit into "Body, Mind, Spirit" or environment themes. Book excerpts, how-to, inspirational, interview/profile, opinion, personal experience, religious, travel, call to action. **Buys 12 mss/year.** Send complete ms. Length: 500-2,500 words. **Pays 10¢/word (Canadian).**

Reprints: Accepts previously published submissions.

Photos: State availability with submission. Buys one-time rights. Offers no additional payment for photos accepted with ms. Captions required.

$$$ FIRST THINGS, Institute on Religion & Public Life, 156 Fifth Ave., Suite 400, New York NY 10010. (212)627-1985. Fax: (212)627-2184. E-mail: ft@firstthings.com. Website: www.firstthings.com. Editor-in-Chief: Richard John Neuhaus. Managing Editor: Alicia Moiser. Associate Editor: Damon Linker. **Contact:** James Nuechterlein, editor. **70% freelance written.** "Intellectual journal published 10 times/year containing social and ethical commentary in broad sense, religious and ethical perspectives on society, culture, law, medicine, church and state, morality and mores." Estab. 1990. Circ. 32,000. Pays on publication. Publishes ms an average of 4 months after acceptance. Byline given. Buys all rights. Editorial lead time 2 months. Submit seasonal material 5 months in advance. Responds in 3 weeks to mss. Sample copy and writer's guidelines for #10 SASE.

Nonfiction: Essays, opinion. **Buys 60 mss/year.** Send complete ms. Length: 1,500-6,000 words. **Pays $400-1,000.** Sometimes pays expenses of writers on assignment.

Poetry: Traditional. **Buys 25-30 poems/year.** Length: 4-40 lines. **Pays $50.**

Tips: "We prefer complete manuscripts (hard copy, double-spaced) to queries, but will reply if unsure."

$ $ FRANCE TODAY, FrancePress Inc., 1 Hallidie Plaza, Suite 505, San Francisco CA 94102. (415)981-9088. Fax: (415)981-9177. E-mail: info@francetoday.com. Website: www.francentral.com. **Contact:** Lisel Fay, editor. **90% freelance written.** Tabloid published 10 times/year covering contemporary France. "*France Today* is a feature publication on contemporary France including sociocultural analysis, business, trends, current events and travel." Estab. 1989. Circ. 25,000. Pays on publication. Publishes ms an average of 5 months after acceptance. Byline given. Buys first North American serial, second serial (reprint) rights. Submit seasonal material 4 months in advance. Accepts queries by mail, e-mail, fax. Accepts previously published material. Responds in 3 months to queries. Sample copy for 10×13 SAE with 5 first-class stamps.

Nonfiction: Essays, exposé, general interest, historical/nostalgic, humor, interview/profile, personal experience, travel. Special issues: Paris, France on the Move, France On a Budget, Summer Travel, The French Palate, French Around the World, France Adventure. "No travel pieces about well-known tourist attractions." **Buys 50 mss/year.** Query with or without published clips or send complete ms. Length: 500-2,000 words. **Pays $150-300.**

Reprints: Send ms with rights for sale noted and information about when and where the material previously appeared. Pay varies.

Photos: Buys one-time rights. Offers $25/photo. Identification of subjects required.

N $ $ $ FW MAGAZINE, FW Omni Media Corp., 460 Richmond St. W., Toronto ON M5V 1Y1, Canada. (416)591-6537. Fax: (416)591-2390. E-mail: angela@myfw.com. Website: www.myfw.com. Managing Editor: Angela Ryan. **Contact:** P.J. Tarasuk, editorial director. **80% freelance written.** Bimonthly magazine. "We are a lifestyle magazine that is geared to both males and females. Our readership is between 18-34 years old. We focus on the hottest new trends for our readers. We profile people in their 20s doing exciting ventures." Estab. 1993. Circ. 500,000. Pays on publication. Byline given. Offers 50% kill fee. Buys first, electronic rights. Editorial lead time 2 months. Submit seasonal material 3 months in advance. Accepts queries by fax, phone. Accepts simultaneous submissions. Responds to queries in 1 month if interested to queries; 2 months to mss. Sample copy for free. Writer's guidelines online.

Nonfiction: Angela Ryan, senior editor. Exposé, general interest, how-to, interview/profile, new product, personal experience, photo feature, travel. **Buys 83 mss/year.** Query with published clips. Length: 500-3,000 words. **Pays $300-1,000.** Sometimes pays expenses of writers on assignment.

Photos: State availability with submission. Reviews contact sheets, negatives. Buys one-time rights. Negotiates payment individually. Captions, identification of subjects, model releases required.

Columns/Departments: Body (the newest trends in fitness); Travel (the new "hotspots" on a budget); Work (interesting jobs for people in their 20s); Fashion (profile new designers and trends); all 1,000 words. **Buys 50 mss/year.** Query. **Pays $300-1,000.**

The online version carries original content not found in the print edition. Contact: Angela Ryan, online editor.

Tips: "It is best to simply call P.J. Tarasuk at (416)591-6537 or Rose Cefalu at our L.A. office (323)931-3433."

N $ GENERATION X JOURNAL, Speaking for Our Generation, 411 W. Front, Wayland IA 52654. (319)601-9128. E-mail: lstoops01@sprintpcs.com. Editor: Les Stoops. **Contact:** Kathy Stoops, managing editor. **95% freelance written.** Newsletter published every 4 months covering the generation who came of age in the late '80s and early '90s. Estab. 2003. **Pays on acceptance.** Publishes ms an average of 3 months after acceptance. Buys one-time rights. Editorial lead time 4 months. Submit seasonal material 4 months in advance. Accepts queries by mail, e-mail. Accepts simultaneous submissions. Responds in 1 month to queries; 5 months to mss. Sample copy for #10 SASE. Writer's guidelines for #10 SASE.

Nonfiction: Book excerpts, essays, exposé, general interest, historical/nostalgic, how-to, humor, inspirational, interview/profile, opinion, personal experience, religious (but practical), travel. No sexually explicit material; religious pieces are fine, but cannot be preachy. Send complete ms. Length: 500-2,000 words. **Pays $5-15.**

Columns/Departments: Politicrat Corner (any political views), 500-2,000 words; Ethnic View (views life as a minority), 500-2,000 words; Gen-X Poetry (realistic, humorous poetry), 5-15 lines; Success Stories (a Gen-xer who is successful, how they did it, etc.), 500-2,000 words. Send complete ms. **Pays $5-15.**

Fiction: Adventure, confessions, ethnic, experimental, fantasy, historical, humorous, mainstream, mystery, religious, romance, slice-of-life vignettes, political pieces, success stories. No erotica or horror. Send complete ms. Length: 500-2,500 words. **Pays $5-15.**

Poetry: Avant-garde, free verse, haiku, light verse, traditional. Submit maximum 5 poems. Length: 5-25 lines.

Fillers: Anecdotes, short humor. Length: 10-100 words. **Pays $5-15.**

Tips: "Be thought provoking in your ideas. Gen-X cab spot half-baked thinking and are ruthlessly realistic."

N $ $ HEADS MAGAZINE, Worldwide Heads, P.O. Box 1319, Hudson QC J0P 1H0, Canada. (450)458-1934. Fax: (450)458-2977. E-mail: stuff@headsmagazine.com. Website: www.headsmagazine.com. **Contact:** Editor. **100% freelance written.** Magazine published every 6 weeks covering the marijuana lifestyle. "*Heads Magazine* is a counter-culture publication concerning the lifestyle surrounding marijuana use and propogation." Estab. 2000. Circ. 75,000. Pays 3 months after publication. Publishes ms an average of 3 months after acceptance. Byline given. Buys all rights. Editorial lead time 3 months. Submit seasonal material 4 months in advance. Accepts queries by mail, e-mail, fax. Accepts simultaneous submissions. Sample copy for $5 (US) or online at website. Writer's guidelines for $5 (US) or by e-mail.

- The editor will contact the writer only if query/ms is usable.

Nonfiction: Book excerpts, exposé, general interest, how-to (grow info), humor, interview/profile, new product, opinion, personal experience, photo feature, travel. **Buys 150 mss/year.** Query with published clips or send complete ms. Length: 600-1,500 words. **Pays $50-200.**

Photos: Send photos with submission. Reviews contact sheets, prints, GIF/JPEG files. Buys all rights. Negotiates payment individually. Captions, model releases required.

Columns/Departments: Marijuana Notes & News (news items about marijuana), 80-150 words; Heads Destination (travel stories), 1,000-2,000 words; Heads Musician (feature story about a musician—pot oriented), 1,000-2,000 words; Ahead of Their Times (groundbreaking member of the counter-culture), 600-1,000 words. **Buys 64 mss/year.** Send complete ms. **Pays $50-200.**

Fillers: Facts, newsbreaks. Length: 50-150 words. **Pays $5-15.**

N $ THE LIST, The List Ltd., 14 High St., Edinburgh EH1 1TE, Scotland. (0131) 558 1191. Fax: (0131) 557 8500. E-mail: editor@list.co.uk. Website: www.list.co.uk. Managing Editor: Robin Hodge. **Contact:** Mark Fisher, editor. **25% freelance written.** Biweekly magazine covering Glasgow and Edinburgh arts, events, listings, and lifestyle. "*The List* is pitched at educated 18-35 year olds." Estab. 1985. Circ. 15,000. Pays on publication. Publishes ms an average of 2 weeks after acceptance. Byline given. Offers 100% kill fee. Buys first, second serial (reprint) rights. Editorial lead time 1 month. Submit seasonal material 1 month in advance. Accepts queries by mail, e-mail. Accepts simultaneous submissions. Sample copy not available.

Nonfiction: Interview/profile, opinion, travel. Query with published clips. Length: Word Length: 300 words. **Pays £60-80.** Sometimes pays expenses of writers on assignment.

Columns/Departments: Reviews, 50-650 words, **pays £16-35/word**; Book Reviews, 150 words, **pays £14/word**; Comic Reviews, 100 words, **pays £10/word**; TV/Video Reviews, 100 words, **pays £10/word**; Record Reviews, 100 words, **pays £10/word**. Query with published clips.

N $ $ $ $ MARCH MAGAZINE, A Magazine of Culture, Art and Politics, March Publications, 1720 NW Lovejoy St., Suite 208, Portland OR 97209-2338. (503)226-2795. E-mail: editors@marchmagazine.com. Website: www.marchmagazine.com. **Contact:** Adam Van Loon, editor. **95% freelance written.** Quarterly magazine. "*March* features writing that exemplifies the experience of contemporary culture. We strike a balance between the mainstream and the microcosm, the political and the personal, the literary and the popular. We publish compelling, gripping writing of high quality and original thought but without pretense or stuffiness." Estab. 2002. Circ. 40,000. Pays on publication. Publishes ms an average of 3-4 months after acceptance. Byline given. Buys first North American serial, electronic rights. Editorial lead time 2-3 months. Accepts queries by mail, e-mail. Responds in 1-2 months to queries; 1-2 months to mss. Sample copy not available. Writer's guidelines online.

Nonfiction: Book excerpts, essays, exposé, general interest, historical/nostalgic, interview/profile, personal experience. **Buys 80 mss/year.** Query with or without published clips or send complete ms. Length: 2,000-6,000 words. **Pays 50¢-$1/word.** Sometimes pays expenses of writers on assignment.

Fiction: Experimental, mainstream, western.

Poetry: Avant-garde, free verse, traditional. Submit maximum 6 poems. Length: 100-200 lines.

$ $ $ $ MOTHER JONES, Foundation for National Progress, 731 Market St., Suite 600, San Francisco CA 94103. (415)665-6637. Fax: (415)665-6696. E-mail: query@motherjones.com. Website: www.motherjones.com. Editor: Roger Cohn. **Contact:** Clara Jeffery, deputy editor; Alastair Paulin, managing editor; Eric Bates, investigative editor; Roger Cohn, editor-in-chief; Monika Bauerlein, features editor; Tim Dickinson, associate editor. **80% freelance written.** Bimonthly magazine covering politics, investigative reporting, social issues, and pop culture. "*Mother Jones* is a 'progressive' magazine—but the core of its editorial well is reporting (i.e., fact-based). No slant required. MotherJones.com is an online sister publication." Estab. 1976. Circ. 175,000. Pays on publication. Publishes ms an average of 4 months after acceptance. Byline given. Offers 33% kill fee. Buys first North American serial, first, one-time, electronic rights. Editorial lead time 4 months. Submit seasonal material 6 months in advance. Responds in 2 months to queries. Sample copy for $6 and 9×12 SAE. Writer's guidelines online.

Nonfiction: Exposé, interview/profile, photo feature, current issues; policy; investigative reporting. **Buys 70-100 mss/year.** Query with published clips. Length: 2,000-5,000 words. **Pays $1/word.** Sometimes pays expenses of writers on assignment.

Columns/Departments: Outfront (short, newsy and/or outrageous and/or humorous items), 200-800 words; Profiles of "Hellraisers," 500 words. **Pays $1/word.**

Tips: "We're looking for hard-hitting, investigative reports exposing government cover-ups, corporate malfeasance, scientific myopia, institutional fraud or hypocrisy; thoughtful, provocative articles which challenge the conventional wisdom (on the right or the left) concerning issues of national importance; and timely, people-oriented stories on issues such as the environment, labor, the media, health care, consumer protection, and cultural trends. Send a great, short query and establish your credibility as a reporter. Explain what you plan to cover and how you will proceed with the reporting. The query should convey your approach, tone and style, and should answer the following: What are your specific qualifications to write on this topic? What 'ins' do you have with your sources? Can you provide full documentation so that your story can be fact-checked?"

$ NEW HAVEN ADVOCATE, News & Arts Weekly, New Mass Media Inc., 900 Chapel St., Suite 1100, New Haven CT 06510. (203)789-0010. Fax: (203)787-1418. E-mail: editor@newhavenadvocate.com. Website: www.newhavenadvocate.com. **Contact:** Joshua Mamis, editor. **10% freelance written.** Weekly tabloid. "Alternative, investigative, cultural reporting with a strong voice. We like to shake things up." Estab. 1975. Circ. 55,000. Pays on publication. Byline given. Buys one-time rights. Buys on speculation Editorial lead time 1 month. Submit seasonal material 2 months in advance. Accepts simultaneous submissions. Responds in 1 month to queries. Sample copy not available.

Nonfiction: Book excerpts, essays, exposé, general interest, humor, interview/profile. **Buys 15-20 mss/year.** Query with published clips. Length: 750-2,000 words. **Pays $50-150.** Sometimes pays expenses of writers on assignment.

Photos: State availability with submission. Buys one-time rights. Captions, identification of subjects, model releases required.

Tips: "Strong local focus; strong literary voice, controversial, easy-reading, contemporary, etc."

$ OUTRÉ, The World of UltraMedia, Filmfax, Inc., P.O. Box 1900, Evanston IL 60204. (847)866-7155. E-mail: filmfax@xsite.net. Website: www.filmfax.com. **Contact:** James J.J. Wilson, managing editor/story editor. **100% freelance written.** Quarterly magazine covering popular culture of the mid-20th century through the present, with an emphasis on the '50s and '60s. Main areas of focus are music, TV, science fiction, illustrative art, comic books, movies, books, and other pop culture icons such as drive-in movies, Route 66, etc. "Most of our features are interviews with musicians, artists, writers, actors, and the other people involved in the various areas of 20th century pop culture, although we do publish historical essays if the material is comprehensive and beyond common knowledge. We also publish reviews of current releases in video/DVD, books, and CDs relating to our general subject areas." Estab. 1994. Circ. 25,000. Pays on publication. Publishes ms an average of 6-12 months after acceptance. Byline given. Buys first North American serial rights. Editorial lead time 6-12 months. Accepts queries by mail, e-mail. Accepts previously published material. Responds in 1-2 weeks to queries; 1 month to mss. Sample copy for free. Writer's guidelines online.

Nonfiction: Book excerpts, essays, historical/nostalgic, interview/profile, new product, opinion, personal experience, photo feature. No general criticism or pieces which do not contain information not commonly known to genre film fans. **Buys 60 mss/year.** Query. Length: 300-15,000 words. **Pays 3¢/word.**

Photos: State availability with submission. Buys one-time rights. Offers no additional payment for photos accepted with ms. Identification of subjects required.

Columns/Departments: Accepts reviews of books, CDs, and video/DVDs. **Buys 50 mss/year.** Query. **Pays 3¢/word.**

Fiction: "We publish fiction very seldom, less than 1 story/year. Inquire in advance."

Tips: "Send us an e-mail or letter describing what ideas you have that may fit our format. As a specialty publication, reading the magazine is the best way to get a feel for what we like to publish."

N $ READERS & WRITERS MAGAZINE, The Source for San Diego's Literary Arts Culture, P.O. Box 2310519, Encinitas CA 92023-0519. (760)632-9268. E-mail: editor@rwmag.com. Website: www.rwmag.com. **Contact:** Charles McStravick, editorial director. **50% freelance written.** Monthly magazine. "*Readers & Writers* is a monthly periodical for San Diego area residents that focuses on the pleasure of reading and the joys of writing. Besides book reviews, *Readers & Writers* contains a monthly feature article and several special sections, as well as an extensive local resources segment, a services directory, and an event calendar containing all local reading- and writing-related events." Estab. 2000. Circ. 50,000. **Pays on acceptance.** Publishes ms an average of 2 months after acceptance. Byline given. Buys first North American serial, first, second serial (reprint), electronic rights. Editorial lead time 2 months. Submit seasonal material 3 months in advance. Accepts queries by mail, e-mail. Accepts simultaneous submissions. Responds in 2 months to queries. Sample copy for $2. Writer's guidelines for #10 SASE or by e-mail to copy@rwmag.com.

Nonfiction: Essays, interview/profile, personal experience, photo feature (with reading- or writing-related themes), book reviews. "We do not print fiction or poetry." **Buys 24-48 mss/year.** Query with published clips or send complete ms. Length: 450-800 words/book reviews; 1,400-3,300 words/features. **Pays $20/book review; $35-75/article.**

Photos: Send color copies or JPEGS. State availability of or send photos with submission. Buys one-time rights. Negotiates payment individually. Identification of subjects required.

Tips: "When putting together our editorial calendar, we look for articles that will appeal to either readers, writers, or both. We strongly encourage queries for articles that have a local flavor or otherwise incorporate local, San Diego events."

$ $ SHEPHERD EXPRESS, Alternative Publications, Inc., 413 N. Second St., Milwaukee WI 53203. (414)276-2222. Fax: (414)276-3312. E-mail: editor@shepherd-express.com. Website: www.shepherd-express.com. **Contact:** Doug Hissou, metro editor or Dave Luhrssen, art and entertainment editor. **50% freelance written.** Weekly tabloid covering "news and arts with a progressive news edge and a hip entertainment perspective." Estab. 1982. Circ. 58,000. Pays on publication. Publishes ms an average of 2 weeks after acceptance. Submit seasonal material 1 month in advance. Accepts simultaneous submissions. Sample copy for $3.

Nonfiction: Book excerpts, essays, exposé, opinion. **Buys 200 mss/year.** Query with published clips or send complete ms. Length: 900-2,500 words. **Pays $35-300 for assigned articles; $10-200 for unsolicited articles.** Sometimes pays expenses of writers on assignment.

Photos: State availability with submission. Reviews prints. Buys one-time rights. Negotiates payment individually. Captions, identification of subjects, model releases required.

Columns/Departments: Opinions (social trends, politics, from progressive slant), 800-1,200 words; Books Reviewed (new books only: Social trends, environment, politics), 600-1,200 words. **Buys 10 mss/year.** Send complete ms.

Tips: "Include solid analysis with point of view in tight but lively writing. Nothing cute. Do not tell us that something is important, tell us why."

N $ SKYLINE MAGAZINE, Skyline Publications, P.O. Box 295, Stormville NY 12582-5417. (845)227-5171. Fax: (845)226-8392. E-mail: skylineeditor@aol.com. Website: www.skylinepublications.com. Managing Editor: H. Thomas Beck. **Contact:** Victoria Valentine, publisher/editor. **80% freelance written.** Bimonthly magazine covering fiction/nonfiction stories, articles, essays, interviews, poetry, fine art, photography, and special, unique features including human interest. "*Skyline Magazine* publishes the excellent work of both established and new authors. Our readers and authors range in age from 17-100. We hope to bring the world together by presenting all forms of the arts through individual expression. We seek fiction and nonfiction stories, human-interest articles/essays, interviews about unique and/or accomplished everyday individuals, as well as celebrities. We feel everyone has something to say that would be of interest to others. Life holds many stories and we are open to all. We normally do not publish politics or religious material. In each issue we publish at least one student author and one student artist." Estab. 2001. Circ. 1,650. Publishes ms an average of 1-3 months after acceptance. Byline given. Buys first North American serial rights. Editorial lead time 3 months. Submit seasonal material 4 months in advance. Accepts queries by mail, e-mail. Responds in 6-8 weeks to queries; 2-3 months to mss. Sample copy for $2.50, plus $1.50 postage. Writer's guidelines online or by e-mail.

- Electronic submissions are preferred via website submission form.

Nonfiction: Book excerpts, essays, general interest, historical/nostalgic, humor, inspirational, interview/profile, personal experience, photo feature, travel. Nothing political, religious, or gay/lesbian. No erotica. **Buys 18-36 mss/year.** Send complete ms, include synopsis and bio. **Pays $25-100. Pays in contributor copies.**

Photos: State availability with submission. Reviews 4×6 prints, GIF/JPEG files. Buys one-time rights. Offers no additional payment for photos accepted with ms. Captions, model releases required.

Columns/Departments: Special Features (human-interest profiles that are unique, motivational, inspirational, and informative), 2,500 words; Interview/Profiles, 2,500-3,500 words; Student Author Spotlight (high school juniors/seniors submit stories and art), 2,500 words. **Buys 12 mss/year.** Send complete ms, synopsis, and bio. **Pays negotiable rate for celebrity/well-known interviews/profiles; others in contributor copies.**

Fiction: Adventure, ethnic, experimental, fantasy, historical, horror, humorous, mainstream, mystery, novel excerpts, romance, science fiction, slice-of-life vignettes, suspense, western. No erotica. Nothing political or religious. **Buys 24-30 mss/year.** Length: 1,500-3,500 words. **Pays in contributor copies.**

Poetry: "We're looking for good, original poetry. The particular 'school' is unimportant; however, no 'greeting card' adolescent poems. The poetry should have the craft and imagery, and communicate a message on several levels. Robert Frost's 'Mending Wall' or 'Death of the Hired Man' are good examples. William Stafford's 'Traveling Through the Dark' is another example of classic, modern poetry that moves the reader. If the poem rhymes, then make the rhyme sublime. Any subject matter is acceptable except hate diatribes. Always proof your work before submitting." Avant-garde, free verse, haiku, light verse, traditional. Nothing political or religious. **Buys 200 poems/year.** Submit maximum 6 poems.

Fillers: Anecdotes, facts, gags to be illustrated by cartoonist, newsbreaks, short humor. **Buys 12/year.** Length: 150-350 words. **Pays in contributor copies.**

Tips: "Submit your best, edited work. We look for intelligent, unique subjects and bold characterizations, and of utmost importance, surprise and/or impactful conclusions. We seek powerful authors who possess excellent grammar, punctuation, and writing skills. We will give you your first publishing credit, but please send us your most professional work. For beginngers: If writing classes are not an option, there are many fine 'how to write' books that will help you achieve a professional, marketable manuscript. Regardless of your interesting theme, if your manuscript is poorly written, we will not consider it."

N $UTNE READER, 1624 Harmon Place, Suite 330, Minneapolis MN 55403. (612)338-5040. Fax: (612)338-6043. E-mail: editor@utne.com. Website: www.utne.com. **Contact:** Craig Cox, executive editor. Accepts queries by mail, e-mail, fax. Writer's guidelines online.

- The *Utne Reader* has been a finalist three times for the National Magazine Award for general excellence.
- Break in with submissions for 'View.'

Reprints: Send tearsheet or photocopy with rights for sale noted and information about when and where the material previously appeared.

Tips: "State the theme(s) clearly, let the narrative flow, and build the story around strong characters and a vivid sense of place. Give us rounded episodes, logically arranged."

N $ $THE WOMEN'S REVIEW OF BOOKS, Wellesley College, 106 Central St., Wellesley MA 02481. E-mail: lgardiner@wellesley.edu. Website: www.wellesley.edu/womensreview. **Contact:** Linda Gardiner, editor. **100% freelance written.** Monthly tabloid covering books by and about women. Offers "feminist review of recent books on the lives of women past and present." Estab. 1983. Circ. 11,000. Pays on publication. Publishes ms an average of 1 month after acceptance. Byline given. Buys first North American serial rights. Accepts queries by mail, phone. Responds in 2 months to queries. Sample copy for free. Writer's guidelines online.

Nonfiction: Book reviews. "We do not consider any unsolicited submissions. Queries only." **Buys 250 mss/year.** Query with published clips. **Pays $75-300.** Sometimes pays expenses of writers on assignment.

Tips: "We work only with experienced book reviewers."

$YES!, A Journal of Positive Futures, Positive Futures Network, P.O. Box 10818, Bainbridge Island WA 98110. (206)842-0216. Fax: (206)842-5208. E-mail: editors@futurenet.org. Website: www.futurenet.org. Executive Editor: Sarah Ruth van Gelder. Quarterly magazine covering sustainability and community. "Interested in stories on building a positive future: sustainability, overcoming divisiveness, ethical business practices, etc." Estab. 1996. Circ. 14,000. Pays on publication. Byline given. Editorial lead time 4 months. Accepts queries by mail. Accepts previously published material. Accepts simultaneous submissions. Responds in 1 month to queries; 6 months to mss. Sample copy and writer's guidelines online.

- Break in with book reviews.

Nonfiction: "Please check website for a detailed call for submission before each issue." Book excerpts, essays, humor, interview/profile, personal experience, photo feature, technical, environmental. Query with published clips. Length: 200-3,500 words. **Pays $20-50 for assigned articles.** Pays writers with 1-year subsciption and 2 contributor copies.

Reprints: Send photocopy or typed ms with rights for sale noted and information about when and where the material previously appeared. Pays 100% of amount paid for an original article.

Photos: State availability with submission. Reviews contact sheets, negatives, transparencies, prints. Buys one-time rights. Offers $20-75/photo. Identification of subjects required.

Columns/Departments: Query with published clips. **Pays $20-60.**
Tips: "Read and become familiar with the publication's purpose, tone and quality. We are about facilitating the creation of a better world. We are looking for writers who want to participate in that process. *Yes!* is less interested in bemoaning the state of our problems than in highlighting promising solutions. We are highly unlikely to accept submissions that simply state the author's opinion on what needs to be fixed and why. Our readers know *why* we need to move towards sustainability; they are interested in *how* to do so."

DETECTIVE & CRIME

Fans of detective stories want to read accounts of actual criminal cases, detective work, and espionage. Markets specializing in crime fiction are listed under Mystery publications.

$ P I MAGAZINE, Journal of Professional Investigators, Eastern Publishing Co., 870 Pompton Ave., Suite B2, P.O. Box 360, Cedar Grove NJ 07009. (973)571-0400. Fax: (973)571-0505. E-mail: editor@pi.org. Website: www.pimagazine.com. Publisher/Editor-in-Chief: Jimmie Mesis. **Contact:** Grace Elting Castle, editor. **90% freelance written.** Magazine published 6 times/year. "Audience includes U.S., Canada, and professional investigators in 20-plus countries, law enforcement, attorneys, process servers, paralegals, and other legal professionals." Estab. 1988. Pays on publication. Accepts queries by mail, e-mail. Sample copy for $6.95. Writer's guidelines online.

- New publisher and editor, 2002. No payment for unsolicited materials.

Nonfiction: "Manuscripts must include educational material for professional investigators. Profiles are accepted if they offer information on how other professionals can use the knowledge or expertise utilized by the person profiled. Accounts of real cases are used only as part of an educational piece. Investigators with special expertise should query for educational articles to exceed 1,000 words." **Buys up to 75 mss/year.** Query. Length: 1,000-2,000 words. **Pays $50-150 for articles up to 1,000 words; $10-50 for articles of 500 words or less.**
Photos: State availability with submission. May offer additional payment for photos accepted with ms. Identification of subjects, model releases required.
Tips: "*PI Magazine* has a new publisher and editor-in-chief, a new editor, and a new focus! Please review the August 2002 issue (or later) to understand the magazine before submitting a query. Avoid clichés and television inspired concepts of PIs. Great way to get the editor's attention: There are numerous special sections that need shorts of 500 words or less. $10-50." E-mail attachments will not be opened.

DISABILITIES

These magazines are geared toward disabled persons and those who care for or teach them. A knowledge of disabilities and lifestyles is important for writers trying to break in to this field; editors regularly discard material that does not have a realistic focus. Some of these magazines will accept manuscripts only from disabled persons or those with a background in caring for disabled persons.

$ $ ABILITIES, Canada's Lifestyle Magazine for People with Disabilities, Canadian Abilities Foundation, #501-489 College St., Toronto ON M6G 1A5, Canada. (416)923-1885. Fax: (416)923-9829. E-mail: able@abilities.ca. Website: www.abilities.ca. Editor: Raymond Cohen. **Contact:** Lisa Bendall, managing editor. **50% freelance written.** Quarterly magazine covering disability issues. "*Abilities* provides information, inspiration, and opportunity to its readers with articles and resources covering health, travel, sports, products, technology, profiles, employment, recreation, and more." Estab. 1987. Circ. 45,000. Pays on publication. Publishes ms an average of 3 months after acceptance. Byline given. Offers 50% kill fee. Buys first rights. Editorial lead time 3 months. Submit seasonal material 4 months in advance. Accepts queries by mail, e-mail, fax. Responds in 3 months to queries. Sample copy for free. Writer's guidelines for #10 SASE, online, or by e-mail.
Nonfiction: Book excerpts, general interest, how-to, humor, inspirational, interview/profile, new product, opinion, personal experience, photo feature, travel. Does not want "articles that 'preach to the converted'—contain info that people with disabilities likely already know, such as what it's like to have a disability." **Buys 30-40 mss/year.** Query or send complete ms. Length: 500-2,500 words. **Pays $50-400 (Canadian) for assigned articles; $50-300 (Canadian) for unsolicited articles.**
Reprints: Sometimes accepts previously published submissions (if stated as such).
Photos: State availability with submission.
Columns/Departments: The Lighter Side (humor), 600 words; Profile, 1,200 words.
Tips: "Do not contact by phone—send something in writing. Send a great idea that we haven't done before, and make a case for why you'd be able to do a good job with it. Be sure to include a relevant writing sample."

$ $ $ $ ARTHRITIS TODAY, Arthritis Foundation, 1330 W. Peachtree St., Atlanta GA 30309. (404)872-7100. Fax: (404)872-9559. E-mail: atmail@arthritis.org. Website: www.arthritis.org. Editor: Marcy O'Koon Moss. Managing Editor: Lissa Poirot. **50% freelance written.** Bimonthly magazine covering living with arthritis; latest in research/treatment. "*Arthritis Today* is a consumer health magazine and is written for the more than 70 million Americans who have arthritis and for the millions of others whose lives are touched by an arthritis-related disease. The editorial content is designed to help the person with arthritis live a more productive, independent, and pain-free life. The articles are upbeat and provide practical advice, information and inspiration." Estab. 1987. Circ. 650,000. **Pays on acceptance.** Byline given. Offers kill fee. Buys first North American serial, second serial (reprint), electronic rights. Editorial lead time 6 months. Submit seasonal material 6 months in advance. Accepts queries by mail, e-mail, fax. Accepts simultaneous submissions. Responds in 2 months to queries. Sample copy for 9×11 SAE with 4 first-class stamps. Writer's guidelines online.

Nonfiction: General interest, how-to (tips on any aspect of living with arthiritis), inspirational, new product (arthritis related), opinion, personal experience, photo feature, technical, travel (tips, news), service, nutrition, general health, lifestyle. **Buys 12 unsolicited mss/year.** Query with or without published clips or send complete ms. Length: 150-2,000 words. **Pays $100-2,000.** Pays expenses of writers on assignment.

Photos: Send photos with submission. Reviews prints. Buys one-time rights. Negotiates payment individually. Identification of subjects required.

Columns/Departments: Research Spotlight (research news about arthritis); LifeStyle (travel, leisure), 100-300 words; Well Being (arthritis-specific medical news), 100-300 words; Hero (personal profile of people with arthritis), 100-300 words. **Buys 10 mss/year.** Query with published clips. **Pays $150-300.**

Fillers: Facts, gags to be illustrated by cartoonist, short humor. **Buys 10/year.** Length: 40-100 words. **Pays $80-150.**

Tips: "Our readers are already well informed. We need ideas and writers that give in-depth, fresh, interesting information that truly adds to their understanding of their condition and their quality of life. Quality writers are more important than good ideas. The staff generates many of our ideas but needs experienced, talented writers who are good reporters to execute them. Please provide published clips. In addition to articles specifically about living with arthritis, we look for articles to appeal to an older audience on subjects such as hobbies, general health, lifestyle, etc."

N $ $ CAREERS & the disABLED, Equal Opportunity Publications, 445 Broad Hollow Rd., Suite 425, Melville NY 11747. (631)421-9421. Fax: (631)421-0359. E-mail: jschneider@eop.com. Website: www.eop.com. **Contact:** James Schneider, editor. **60% freelance written.** Quarterly magazine offering "role-model profiles and career guidance articles geared toward disabled college students and professionals, and promotes personal and professional growth." Estab. 1967. Circ. 10,000. Pays on publication. Publishes ms an average of 6 months after acceptance. Byline given. Buys first North American serial rights. Editorial lead time 6 months. Submit seasonal material 6 months in advance. Accepts queries by mail, e-mail, fax, phone. Accepts previously published material. Accepts simultaneous submissions. Responds in 3 weeks to queries. Sample copy for 9×12 SAE with 5 first-class stamps.

Nonfiction: Essays, general interest, how-to, interview/profile, new product, opinion, personal experience. **Buys 30 mss/year.** Query. Length: 1,000-2,500 words. **Pays 10¢/word, $350 maximum.** Sometimes pays expenses of writers on assignment.

Reprints: Accepts previously published submissions and information about when and where the material previously appeared.

Photos: Reviews transparencies, prints. Buys one-time rights. Offers $15-50/photo. Captions, identification of subjects, model releases required.

Tips: "Be as targeted as possible. Role-model profiles and specific career guidance strategies that offer advice to disabled college students are most needed."

$ $ DIABETES INTERVIEW, Kings Publishing, 3715 Balboa St., San Francisco CA 94121. (415)258-2828. Fax: (415)387-3604. E-mail: daniel@diabetesinterview.com. Website: www.diabetesinterview.com. **Contact:** Daniel Trecroci, managing editor. **40% freelance written.** Monthly tabloid covering diabetes care. "*Diabetes Interview* covers the latest in diabetes care, medications, and patient advocacy. Personal accounts are welcome as well as medical-oriented articles by MDs, RNs, and CDEs (certified diabetes educators)." Estab. 1991. Circ. 40,000. Pays on publication. Publishes ms an average of 2 months after acceptance. Byline given. Buys all rights. Editorial lead time 2 months. Submit seasonal material 2 months in advance. Accepts queries by mail, e-mail, fax, phone. Sample copy online. Writer's guidelines free.

Nonfiction: Essays, how-to, humor, inspirational, interview/profile, new product, opinion, personal experience. **Buys 25 mss/year.** Query. **Pays 20¢/word.**

Reprints: Accepts previously published submissions.

Photos: State availability of or send photos with submission. Negotiates payment individually.

Tips: "Be actively involved in the diabetes community or have diabetes. However, writers need not have diabetes to write an article, but it must be diabetes-related."

$ $ DIABETES SELF-MANAGEMENT, R.A. Rapaport Publishing, Inc., 150 W. 22nd St., Suite 800, New York NY 10011-2421. (212)989-0200. Fax: (212)989-4786. E-mail: editor@diabetes-self-mgmt.com. Website: www.diabetesselfmanagement.com. **Contact:** Ingrid Strauch, managing editor. **20% freelance written.** Bimonthly magazine. "We publish how-to health care articles for motivated, intelligent readers who have diabetes and who are actively involved in their own health care management. All articles must have immediate application to their daily living." Estab. 1983. Circ. 480,000. Pays on publication. Byline given. Offers 20% kill fee. Buys all rights. Submit seasonal material 6 months in advance. Accepts queries by mail, e-mail, fax. Responds in 6 weeks to queries. Sample copy for $4 and 9×12 SAE with 6 first-class stamps or online. Writer's guidelines for #10 SASE.

- "We are extremely generous regarding permission to republish."

O-→ Break in by having extensive knowledge of diabetes.

Nonfiction: How-to (exercise, nutrition, diabetes self-care, product surveys), technical (reviews of products available, foods sold by brand name, pharmacology), travel (considerations and prep for people with diabetes). No personal experiences, personality profiles, exposés, or research breakthroughs. **Buys 10-12 mss/year.** Query with published clips. Length: 2,000-2,500 words. **Pays $400-700 for assigned articles; $200-700 for unsolicited articles.**

Tips: "The rule of thumb for any article we publish is that it must be clear, concise, useful, and instructive, and it must have immediate application to the lives of our readers. If your query is accepted, expect heavy editorial supervision."

$ DIALOGUE, Blindskills, Inc., P.O. Box 5181, Salem OR 97304-0181. (800)860-4224; (503)581-4224. Fax: (503)581-0178. E-mail: blindskl@teleport.com. Website: www.blindskills.com. **Contact:** Carol M. McCarl, editor. **60% freelance written.** Quarterly journal covering the visually impaired. Estab. 1961. Circ. 1,100. Pays on publication. Publishes ms an average of 8 months after acceptance. Byline given. Buys first rights. Editorial lead time 3 months. Accepts queries by mail, e-mail, fax. One free sample on request. Available in Braille, 4-track audio cassette, large print, and disk (for compatible IBM computer). Writer's guidelines online.

O-π Break in by "using accurate punctuation, grammar, and structure, and writing about pertinent subject matter."

Nonfiction: Features material by visually impaired writers. Essays, general interest, historical/nostalgic, how-to (life skills methods used by visually impaired people), humor, interview/profile, personal experience, sports, recreation, hobbies. No controversial, explicit sex, religious, or political topics. **Buys 80 mss/year.** Send complete ms. Length: 500-1,200 words. **Pays $10-35 for assigned articles; $10-25 for unsolicited articles.**

Columns/Departments: All material should be relative to blind and visually impaired readers. Careers, 1,000 words; What Do You Do When? (dealing with sight loss), 1,000 words. **Buys 80 mss/year.** Send complete ms. **Pays $10-25.**

Fiction: Publishes material by visually impaired writers. Adventure, humorous, slice-of-life vignettes, first-person experiences. No controversial, explicit sex, religious, or political topics. **Buys 6-8 mss/year.** Send complete ms. Length: 800-1,200 words. **Pays $15-25.**

N $ $ HEARING HEALTH, Voice International Publications, Inc., 1050 17th St. NW, #701, Washington DC 20036. (202)289-5850. Fax: (202)293-1805. E-mail: info@hearinghealthmag.com. Website: www.hearinghealthmag.com. **Contact:** Lorraine Short, editor. **20% freelance written.** Quarterly magazine covering issues and concerns pertaining to hearing and hearing loss. Estab. 1984. Circ. 20,000. Pays on publication. Byline given. Buys one-time rights. Editorial lead time 2 months. Submit seasonal material 4 months in advance. Accepts queries by mail, fax. Accepts previously published material. Accepts simultaneous submissions. Responds in 6 weeks to queries; 2 months to mss. Sample copy for $2 or online. Writer's guidelines for #10 SASE or online.

O-π "Break in with a fresh approach—positive, a splash of humor—or well-researched biographical or historical pieces about people with hearing loss."

Nonfiction: Book excerpts, essays, exposé, general interest, historical/nostalgic, humor, inspirational, interview/profile, new product, opinion, personal experience, photo feature, technical, travel. No self-pitying over loss of hearing. Query with published clips. Length: 500-2,000 words. **Pays $75-200.** Sometimes pays expenses of writers on assignment.

Reprints: Accepts previously published submissions.

Photos: State availability with submission. Reviews contact sheets. Buys one-time rights. Negotiates payment individually. Captions, identification of subjects, model releases required.

Columns/Departments: Kidink (written by kids with hearing loss), 300 words; People (shares stories of successful, everyday people who have loss of hearing), 300-400 words. **Buys 2 mss/year.** Query with published clips.

Fiction: Fantasy, historical, humorous, novel excerpts, science fiction. **Buys 2 mss/year.** Query with published clips. Length: 400-1,500 words.

Poetry: Avant-garde, free verse, light verse, traditional. **Buys 2 poems/year.** Submit maximum 2 poems. Length: 4-50 lines.

Fillers: Anecdotes, facts, gags to be illustrated by cartoonist, newsbreaks, short humor. **Buys 6/year.** Length: 25-1,500 words.

Tips: "We look for fresh stories, usually factual but occasionally fictitious, about coping with hearing loss. A positive attitude is a must for *Hearing Health*. Unless one has some experience with deafness or hearing loss—whether their own or a loved one's—it's very difficult to 'break in' to our publication. Experience brings about the empathy and understanding—the sensitivity—and the freedom to write humorously about any handicap or disability."

$ KALEIDOSCOPE, Exploring the Experience of Disability Through Literature and the Fine Arts, Kaleidoscope Press, 701 S. Main St., Akron OH 44311-1019. (330)762-9755. Fax: (330)762-0912. E-mail: mshiplett@udsakron.org. Website: www.udsakron.org. **Contact:** Gail Willmott, senior editor. **75% freelance written.** Eager to work with new/unpublished writers. Semiannual magazine. Subscribers include individuals, agencies, and organizations that assist people with disabilities and many university and public libraries. Appreciates work by established writers as well. Especially interested in work by writers with a disability, but features writers both with and without disabilities. "Writers without a disability must limit themselves to our focus, while those with a disability may explore any topic (although we prefer original perspectives about experiences with disability)." Estab. 1979. Circ. 1,000. Pays on publication. Byline given. Buys first, reprints permitted with credit given to original publication rights. Rights return to author upon publication. Accepts queries by mail, fax. Accepts previously published material. Accepts simultaneous submissions. Responds in 3 weeks to queries; 6 months to mss. Sample copy for $5 prepaid. Writer's guidelines online.

O-π Submit photocopies with SASE for return of work. Please type submissions (double spaced). All submissions should be accompanied by an autobiographical sketch. May include art or photos that enhance works, prefer b&w with high contrast.

Nonfiction: Articles related to disability. Book excerpts, essays, humor, interview/profile, personal experience, book reviews, articles related to disability. Special issues: Mental Illness (July 2004, deadline March 2004); Parents and Children (January 2005, deadline August 2004). **Buys 8-15 mss/year.** Length: 5,000 words maximum. **Pays $25-125, plus 2 copies.**

Reprints: Send ms with rights for sale noted and information about when and where the material previously appeared.

Photos: Send photos with submission.

Fiction: Fiction Editor. Short stories, novel excerpts. Traditional and experimental styles. Works should explore experiences with disability. Use people-first language. "We look for well-developed plots, engaging characters and realistic dialogue. We lean toward fiction that emphasizes character and emotions rather than action-oriented narratives." "No fiction that is stereotypical, patronizing, sentimental, erotic, or maudlin. No romance, religious or dogmatic fiction; no children's literature." Length: 5,000 words maximum. **Pays $10-125, and 2 contributor's copies; additional copies $6.**

Poetry: "Do not get caught up in rhyme scheme. High quality with strong imagery and evocative language." Reviews any style. **Buys 12-20 poems/year.** Submit maximum 5 poems.

Tips: "Articles and personal experiences should be creative rather than journalistic and with some depth. Writers should use more than just the simple facts and chronology of an experience with disability. Inquire about future themes of upcoming issues. Sample copy very helpful. Works should not use stereotyping, patronizing, or offending language about disability. We seek fresh imagery and thought-provoking language."

ENTERTAINMENT

This category's publications cover live, filmed, or videotaped entertainment, including home video, TV, dance, theater, and adult entertainment. In addition to celebrity interviews, most publications want solid reporting on trends and upcoming productions. Magazines in the Contemporary Culture and General Interest sections also use articles on entertainment. For those publications with an emphasis on music and musicians, see the Music section.

$ CINEASTE, America's Leading Magazine on the Art and Politics of the Cinema, Cineaste Publishers, Inc., 304 Hudson St., 6th Floor, New York NY 10013-1015. (212)366-5720. Fax: (212)366-5724. E-mail: cineaste@cineaste.com. **Contact:** Gary Crowdus, editor-in-chief. **30% freelance written.** Quarterly magazine covering motion pictures with an emphasis on social and political perspective on cinema. Estab. 1967. Circ. 11,000. Pays on publication. Publishes ms an average of 4 months after acceptance. Byline given. Offers 50% kill fee. Buys first North American serial rights. Editorial lead time 3 months. Submit seasonal material 4 months in advance. Accepts queries by mail, e-mail, fax. Responds in 1 month to queries. Sample copy for $5. Writer's guidelines for #10 SASE.

O⁻ Break in by "being familiar with our unique editorial orientation—we are not just another film magazine."

Nonfiction: Book excerpts, essays, exposé, historical/nostalgic, humor, interview/profile, opinion. **Buys 20-30 mss/year.** Query with published clips. Length: 2,000-5,000 words. **Pays $30-100.**

Photos: State availability with submission. Reviews transparencies, 8×10 prints. Buys one-time rights. Offers no additional payment for photos accepted with ms. Identification of subjects required.

Columns/Departments: Homevideo (topics of general interest or a related group of films); A Second Look (new interpretation of a film classic or a reevaluation of an unjustly neglected release of more recent vintage); Lost and Found (film that may or may not be released or otherwise seen in the US but which is important enough to be brought to the attention of our readers), all 1,000-1,500 words. Query with published clips. **Pays $50 minimum.**

Tips: "We dislike academic jargon, obtuse Marxist terminology, film buff trivia, trendy 'buzz' phrases, and show biz references. We do not want our writers to speak of how they have 'read' or 'decoded' a film, but to view, analyze, and interpret. The author's processes and quirks should be secondary to the interests of the reader. Warning the reader of problems with specific films is more important to us than artificially 'puffing' a film because its producers or politics are agreeable. One article format we encourage is an omnibus review of several current films, preferably those not reviewed in a previous issue. Such an article would focus on films that perhaps share a certain political perspective, subject matter, or generic concerns (e.g., films on suburban life, or urban violence, or revisionist Westerns). Like individual film reviews, these articles should incorporate a very brief synopsis of plots for those who haven't seen the films. The main focus, however, should be on the social issues manifested in each film, and how it may reflect something about the current political/social/esthetic climate."

$ DANCE INTERNATIONAL, Scotiabanti Dance Centre, 677 Davie St., Vancouver BC V6B 2G6, Canada. (604)681-1525. Fax: (604)681-7732. E-mail: danceint@direct.ca. Website: www.danceinternational.org. **Contact:** Maureen Riches, editor. **100% freelance written.** Quarterly magazine covering dance arts. "Articles and reviews on current activities in world dance, with occasional historical essays; reviews of dance films, video, and books." Estab. 1973. Circ. 4,500. Pays on publication. Publishes ms an average of 3 months after acceptance. Byline given. Offers 50% kill fee. Buys one-time rights. Editorial lead time 3 months. Submit seasonal material 6 weeks in advance. Accepts queries by mail, e-mail, fax, phone. Responds in 2 weeks to queries; 1 month to mss. Sample copy for $7. Writer's guidelines for #10 SASE.

Nonfiction: Book excerpts, essays, historical/nostalgic, interview/profile, personal experience, photo feature. **Buys 100 mss/year.** Query. Length: 1,200-2,200 words. **Pays $40-150.**

Photos: Send photos with submission. Reviews prints. Offers no additional payment for photos accepted with ms. Identification of subjects required.

Columns/Departments: Dance Bookshelf (recent books reviewed), 1,200 words; Regional Reports (events in each region), 1,200-2,000 words. **Buys 100 mss/year.** Query. **Pays $60-70.**

Tips: "Send résumé and samples of recent writings."

$ DANCE SPIRIT, Lifestyle Ventures, LLC, 250 W. 57th St., Suite 420, New York NY 10107. (212)265-8890. Fax: (212)265-8908. E-mail: editor@dancespirit.com. Website: www.dancespirit.com. **Contact:** Sara Jarrett, features editor. **50% freelance written.** Monthly magazine covering all dance disciplines. "*Dance Spirit* is a special interest teen magazine for girls and guys who study and perform either through a studio or a school dance performance group." Estab. 1997. Circ.

130,000. Pays on publication. Publishes ms an average of 4 months after acceptance. Byline given. Offers 25% kill fee. Buys all rights. Editorial lead time 3 months. Submit seasonal material 8 months in advance. Accepts queries by mail, e-mail, fax. Responds in 3 months to queries; 4 months to mss. Sample copy for $4.95.

Nonfiction: Personal experience, photo feature, dance-related articles only. **Buys 100 mss/year.** Query with published clips. Length: 600-1,200 words. **Pays $100.** Sometimes pays expenses of writers on assignment.

Photos: Reviews transparencies. Buys all rights. Negotiates payment individually. Captions, identification of subjects, model releases required.

Columns/Departments: Ballet; Jazz; Tap; Swing; Hip Hop; Lyrical; Pom; Body; Beauty; City Focus; Choreography; Stars; Nutrition.

The online magazine carries original content not found in the print edition. Contact: Sara Jarrett.

Tips: "Reading the magazine can't be stressed enough. We look for writers with a dance background and experienced dancers/choreographers to contribute; succinct writing style, hip outlook."

N $ DESIGN NEWS, Reed Business Information, 275 Washington St., Newton MA 02458-1646. (617)558-4660. Fax: (617)558-4402. E-mail: dnonline@reedbusiness.com. Website: www.designnews.com. Editor: Karen Auguston Field. Semi-monthly magazine dedicated to reporting on the latest technology that OEM design engineers can use in their jobs. Circ. 180,070. Editorial lead time 4-6 months. Sample copy not available.

$ $ DIRECTED BY, The Cinema Quarterly, Visionary Media, P.O. Box 1722, Glendora CA 91740-1722. Fax: (626)963-0235. E-mail: visionarycinema@yahoo.com. Website: www.directed-by.com. **Contact:** Carsten Dau, editor. **25% freelance written.** Quarterly magazine covering the craft of directing a motion picture. "Our articles are for readers particularly knowledgeable about the art and history of movies from the director's point of view. Our purpose is to communicate our enthusiasm and interest in all levels of serious filmmaking." Estab. 1998. Circ. 42,000. Pays on publication. Publishes ms an average of 3 months after acceptance. Byline given. Offers 50% kill fee. Buys all rights. Editorial lead time 3 months. Submit seasonal material 3 months in advance. Accepts queries by mail, e-mail. Accepts simultaneous submissions. Responds in 6 weeks to queries. Sample copy for $5. Writer's guidelines free or by e-mail.

Nonfiction: Essays, historical/nostalgic, interview/profile, photo feature, on-set reports. No gossip, celebrity-oriented material, or movie reviews. **Buys 12 mss/year.** Query. Length: 500-7,500 words. **Pays $50-750.** Sometimes pays expenses of writers on assignment.

Photos: State availability with submission. Reviews contact sheets. Buys all rights. Offers no additional payment for photos accepted with ms. Captions, identification of subjects required.

Columns/Departments: Trends (overview/analysis of specific moviemaking movements/genres/subjects), 1,500-2,000 words; Focus (innovative take on the vision of a contemporary director), 1,500-2,000 words; Appreciation (overview of deceased/foreign director), 1,000-1,500 words; Final Cut (spotlight interview with contemporary director), 3,000 words; Perspectives (interviews/articles about film craftspeople other than directors), 1,500-2,000 words. **Buys 12 mss/year.** Query. **Pays $50-750.**

Tips: "We have been inundated with 'shelf-life' article queries and cannot publish even a fraction of them. Please note: We are only interested in writers who have direct access to a notable director of a current film which has not been significantly covered in previous issues of magazines; said director must be willing to grant an exclusive peronal interview to *DIRECTED BY.*"

$ $ EAST END LIGHTS, The Quarterly magazine for Elton John Fans, P.O. Box 621, Joplin MO 64802-0621. Phone/fax: (417)776-4120. E-mail: eel@accessthemusic.com. **Contact:** Mark Norris, publisher. **90% freelance written.** Quarterly magazine covering Elton John. "In one way or another, a story must relate to Elton John, his activities or associates (past and present). We appeal to discriminating Elton fans. No gushing fanzine material. No current concert reviews." Estab. 1990. Circ. 1,700. Pays 3 weeks after publication. Publishes ms an average of 3 months after acceptance. Byline given. Offers 100% kill fee. Buys first, second serial (reprint) rights. Submit seasonal material 6 months in advance. Accepts queries by mail, e-mail, fax. Accepts previously published material. Responds in 2 months to queries. Sample copy for $5.

Nonfiction: Book excerpts, essays, exposé, general interest, historical/nostalgic, humor, interview/profile. **Buys 20 mss/year.** Query with or without published clips or send complete ms. Length: 400-1,000 words. **Pays $20-250 for assigned articles; $20-150 for unsolicited articles.** Pays in contributor copies only when author requests it.

Reprints: Send tearsheet or photocopy with rights for sale noted and information about when and where the material previously appeared. Pays 50%.

Photos: State availability with submission. Reviews negatives, 5×7 prints, high-resolution digital files. Buys one-time and all rights. Offers $20-200/photo.

Columns/Departments: Clippings (nonwire references to Elton John in other publications), maximum 200 words. **Buys 12 mss/year.** Send complete ms. **Pays $20-50.**

Tips: "Approach us with a well-thought-out story idea. We prefer interviews with Elton-related personalities—past or present; try to land an interview we haven't done. We are particularly interested in music/memorabilia collecting of Elton material."

$ $ FANGORIA, Horror in Entertainment, Starlog Communications, Inc., 475 Park Ave. S., 7th Floor, New York NY 10016. (212)689-2830. Fax: (212)889-7933. Website: www.fangoria.com. **Contact:** Anthony Timpone, editor. **95% freelance written.** Works with a small number of new/unpublished writers each year. Magazine published 10 times/year covering horror films, TV projects, comics, videos, and literature, and those who create them. "We provide an assignment sheet (deadlines, info) to writers, thus authorizing queried stories that we're buying." Estab. 1979. Pays on publication.

Publishes ms an average of 3 months after acceptance. Byline given. Buys all rights. Submit seasonal material 4 months in advance. Accepts queries by mail. Responds in 6 weeks to queries. Sample copy for $8 and 10×13 SAE with 4 first-class stamps. Writer's guidelines for #10 SASE.

O→ Break in by "reading the magazine regularly and exhibiting a professional view of the genre."

Nonfiction: Book excerpts, interview/profile of movie directors, makeup FX artists, screenwriters, producers, actors, noted horror/thriller novelists and others—with genre credits; special FX and special makeup FX how-it-was-dones (on filmmaking only). Occasional "think" pieces, opinion pieces, reviews, or sub-theme overviews by industry professionals. Avoids most articles on science-fiction films—see listing for sister magazine *Starlog* in *Writer's Market* science fiction consumer magazine section. **Buys 120 mss/year.** Query with published clips. Length: 1,000-3,500 words. **Pays $100-250.** Sometimes pays expenses of writers on assignment.

Photos: State availability with submission. Reviews transparencies, prints (b&w, color) electronically. Captions, identification of subjects required.

Columns/Departments: Monster Invasion (exclusive, early information about new film productions; also mini-interviews with filmmakers and novelists). Query with published clips. **Pays $45-75.**

The online magazine carries original content not found in the print edition.

Tips: "Other than recommending that you study one or several copies of *Fangoria*, we can only describe it as a horror film magazine consisting primarily of interviews with technicians and filmmakers in the field. Be sure to stress the interview subjects' words—not your own opinions as much. We're very interested in small, independent filmmakers working outside of Hollywood. These people are usually more accessible to writers, and more cooperative. *Fangoria* is also sort of a *de facto* bible for youngsters interested in movie makeup careers and for young filmmakers. We are devoted only to *reel* horrors—the fakery of films, the imagery of the horror fiction of a Stephen King or a Clive Barker—*we do not* want nor would we *ever* publish articles on real-life horrors, murders, etc. A writer must *like* and *enjoy* horror films and horror fiction to work for us. If the photos in *Fangoria* disgust you, if the sight of (*stage*) blood repels you, if you feel 'superior' to horror (and its fans), you aren't a writer for us and we certainly aren't the market for you. We love giving new writers their *first* chance to break into print in a national magazine. We are currently looking for Arizona- and Las Vegas-based correspondents."

$ FILMFAX, The Magazine of Film and Unusual Television, Filmfax, Inc., P.O. Box 1900, Evanston IL 60204. (847)866-7155. E-mail: Filmfax@xsite.net. Website: www.filmfax.com. **Contact:** James J.J. Wilson, managing editor/story editor. **100% freelance written.** Bimonthly magazine covering films and television for the silent era through the 1970s, focusing mainly on horror, science fiction, westerns, and comedy. "Most of our features are interviews with actors, directors, writers, and the other people involved in making classic genre films, although we do publish articles on films and people if the material is comprehensive and beyond common knowledge. We also publish reviews of current releases in video/DVD, books, and CDs related to our general subject." Estab. 1986. Circ. 30,000. Pays on publication. Publishes ms an average of 6-12 months after acceptance. Byline given. Buys first North American serial rights. Editorial lead time 6-12 months. Accepts queries by mail, e-mail. Accepts previously published material. Responds in 1-2 weeks to queries; 1 month to mss. Sample copy for free. Writer's guidelines online.

Nonfiction: Book excerpts, essays, historical/nostalgic, interview/profile, new product, opinion, personal experience, photo feature. No general criticism or pieces which do not contain information not commonly known to genre film fans. **Buys 60 mss/year.** Query. Length: 300-15,000 words. **Pays 3¢/word.**

Photos: State availability with submission. Buys one-time rights. Offers no additional payment for photos accepted with ms. Identification of subjects required.

Columns/Departments: Accepts reviews of books, CDs, and videos/DVDs. **Buys 50 mss/year.** Query. **Pays 3¢/word.**

Fiction: "We publish fiction very seldom, less than 1 story/year. Inquire in advance."

Tips: "Send us an e-mail or letter describing what ideas you have that may fit our format. As a specialty publication, reading the magazine is the best way to get a feel for what we like to publish."

$ 5678 MAGAZINE, Champion Media, P.O. Box 8886, Gaithersburg MD 20898. (301)871-7160. Fax: (301)519-1019. E-mail: durand5678@aol.com. Website: www.5678magazine.com. **Contact:** Barry Durand, editor. **50% freelance written.** Monthly magazine covering dance: Couples, line, country, swing. "All articles with a dance or dance music slant. Interviews, reviews, features—today's social dance." Estab. 1999. Circ. 10,000. Pays on publication. Publishes ms an average of 2 months after acceptance. Byline given. Buys first rights. Editorial lead time 2 months. Accepts queries by e-mail. Sample copy for free. Writer's guidelines by e-mail.

Nonfiction: Historical/nostalgic, how-to, humor, interview/profile, photo feature. **Buys 60 mss/year.** Query. Length: 600-2,000 words. **Pays $35-100.** Sometimes pays expenses of writers on assignment.

Photos: Send photos with submission. Buys one-time rights. Negotiates payment individually. Captions, identification of subjects required.

Fiction: Humorous, slice-of-life vignettes. **Buys 10 mss/year.** Query. Length: 600-1,500 words. **Pays $35-100.**

N $ HOME THEATER, PRIMEDIA Enthusiast Group, 6420 Wilshire Blvd., Loa Angeles CA 90048-5502. (323)782-2000. Fax: (323)782-2080. E-mail: htletters@primedia.com. Website: www.hometheatermag.com. Managing Editor: Adrienne Maxwell. **Contact:** Maureen Jenson, editor. Monthly magazine covering audio, video, high-end components,and movies and music. Covers the home theater lifestyle. Estab. 1995. Circ. 109,422. Accepts queries by e-mail. Sample copy for $4.95.

Nonfiction: Send résumé.

Columns/Departments: Query with published clips.

$ $ MOVIEMAKER MAGAZINE, MovieMaker Publishing Co., 2265 Westwood Blvd., #479, Los Angeles CA 90064. (310)234-9234. Fax: (310)234-9293. E-mail: jwood@moviemaker.com. Website: www.moviemaker.com. Editor: Timothy Rhys. **Contact:** Jennifer Wood, managing editor. **95% freelance written.** Quarterly magazine covering film, independent cinema, and Hollywood. "*MovieMaker*'s editorial is a progressive mix of in-depth interviews and criticism, combined with practical techniques and advice on financing, distribution, and production strategies. Behind-the-scenes discussions with Hollywood's top moviemakers, as well as independents from around the globe, are routinely found in *MovieMaker*'s pages." Estab. 1993. Circ. 50,000. Pays within 1 month upon publication. Publishes ms an average of 2 months after acceptance. Byline given. Offers variable kill fee. Buys all rights. Editorial lead time 3 months. Submit seasonal material 4 months in advance. Accepts queries by mail, e-mail, fax. Accepts simultaneous submissions. Responds in 2 months to queries; 2 months to mss. Sample copy online. Writer's guidelines by e-mail.

- E-mail queries preferred.

Nonfiction: Exposé, general interest, historical/nostalgic, how-to, interview/profile, new product, technical. **Buys 10 mss/year.** Query with published clips. Length: 800-3,000 words. **Pays $75-500 for assigned articles.**

Photos: State availability with submission. Rights purchased negotiable. Payment varies for photos accepted with ms. Identification of subjects required.

Columns/Departments: Documentary; Home Cinema (home video/DVD reviews); How They Did It (first-person filmmaking experiences); Festival Beat (film festival reviews); World Cinema (current state of cinema from a particular country). Query with published clips. **Pays $75-300.**

Tips: "The best way to begin working with *MovieMaker* is to send a list of 'pitches' along with your résumé and clips. As we receive a number of résumés each week, we want to get an early sense of not just your style of writing, but the kinds of subjects that interest you most as they relate to film. E-mail is the preferred method of correspondence, and please allow 2-4 weeks before following up on a query or résumé. Queries should be submitted in writing, rather than phone calls."

$ $ $ REQUEST MAGAZINE, Request Media, Inc., 10400 Yellow Circle Dr., Minnetonka MN 55343. (952)931-8740. Fax: (952)931-8490. E-mail: editors@requestmagazine.com. Website: www.requestmagazine.com. **Contact:** Heidi Raschke, editor. **70% freelance written.** Bimonthly magazine. "*Request* offers sharp, enthusiastic coverage of the latest and best in music, movies, home video and all manner of entertainment." Membership magazine for Musicland Group. Estab. 1989. Circ. 1.3 million. Pays as files go to press. Publishes ms an average of 2 months after acceptance. Byline given. Offers 50% kill fee. Buys first, electronic rights. Editorial lead time 4 months. Submit seasonal material 4 months in advance. Accepts queries by e-mail. Accepts simultaneous submissions. Sample copy for $2.95. Writer's guidelines by e-mail.

Nonfiction: Essays, general interest, humor, interview/profile, photo feature, reviews. **Buys 10-20 mss/year.** Query with published clips. Length: 150-2,500 words. **Pays $50-1,000.** Sometimes pays expenses of writers on assignment.

Photos: Send photos with submission. Reviews contact sheets. Photo rights negotiable. Negotiates payment individually. Identification of subjects required.

Columns/Departments: Reviews (short, efficient CD and video reviews), 100-200 words. Query with published clips. **Pays $50-100.**

Tips: "We prefer enthusiastic pitches on noteworthy artists or releases, ideally with a pre-determined level of interview access or research. Our core audience consists of avid music and movie lovers aged 21 to 35."

$ $ RUE MORGUE, Horror in Culture & Entertainment, Marrs Media, Inc., 700 Queen St. E., Toronto ON M4M 1G9, Canada. E-mail: info@rue-morgue.com. Website: www.rue-morgue.com. Associate Editor: Mary Beth Hollyer. **Contact:** Rod Gudino, editor. **50% freelance written.** Bimonthly magazine covering horror entertainment. "A knowledge of horror entertainment (films, books, games, toys, etc.)." Estab. 1997. Pays on publication. Publishes ms an average of 4 months after acceptance. Byline given. Buys all rights. Editorial lead time 2 months. Submit seasonal material 4 months in advance. Accepts queries by e-mail. Responds in 6 weeks to queries; 2 months to mss. Sample copy not available. Writer's guidelines by e-mail.

Nonfiction: Essays, exposé, historical/nostalgic, interview/profile, new product, travel. No fiction. Reviews done by staff writers. **Buys 10 mss/year.** Query with published clips or send complete ms. Length: 500-2,000 words. **Pays $50-200.**

Columns/Departments: Classic Cut (historical essays on classic horror films, books, games, comic books, music), 500-700 words. **Buys 1-2 mss/year.** Query with published clips. **Pays $40.**

Tips: "The editor is most responsive to hard-to-get interviews with famous horror personalities corresponding with related releases. We also are always looking out for analytical/historical essays on historical topics. Published examples: Leon Theremin, Soren Kierkegaard, horror subgenres."

$ $ $ $ SOUND & VISION, Hachette Filipacchi Magazines, Inc., 1633 Broadway, New York NY 10019. (212)767-6000. Fax: (212)767-5615. E-mail: soundandvisionmag@hfmus.com. Website: www.soundandvisionmag.com. Editor-in-Chief: Bob Ankosko. Entertainment Editor: Ken Richardson. **Contact:** Michael Gaughn, features editor. **50% freelance written.** Published 10 times/year. Provides readers with authoriative information on the entertainment technologies and products that will impact their lives. Estab. 1958. Circ. 450,000. **Pays on acceptance.** Publishes ms an average of 4 months after acceptance. Byline given. Buys first North American serial, electronic rights. Accepts queries by mail, e-mail, fax. Sample copy for 9×12 SAE and 11 first-class stamps.

Nonfiction: Home theater, audio, video and multimedia equipment plus movie and music reviews, how-to-buy and how-to-use A/V gear, interview/profile. **Buys 25 mss/year.** Query with published clips. Length: 1,500-3,000 words. **Pays $1,000-1,500.**

Tips: "Send proposals or outlines, rather than complete articles, along with published clips to establish writing ability.

Publisher assumes no responsibility for return or safety of unsolicited art, photos or manuscripts."

N $STAR MAGAZINE, American Media, Inc., 5401 NW Broken Sound Blvd., Boca Raton FL 33487. E-mail: letters@starmagazine.com. Website: www.starmagazine.com..

N $ $ TAKE ONE, Film & Television in Canada, Canadian Independent Film & Television Publishing Association, 252-128 Danforth Ave., Toronto ON M4K 1N1, Canada. (416)944-1096. Fax: (416)465-4356. E-mail: takeone@interlog.com. Website: www.takeonemagazine.ca. **Contact:** Wyndham Wise, editor-in-chief. **100% freelance written.** Quarterly magazine covering Canadian film and television. "*Take One* is a special interest magazine that focuses exclusively on Canadian cinema, filmmakers, and Canadian television." Estab. 1992. Circ. 5,000/issue. Pays on publication. Publishes ms an average of 2 months after acceptance. Byline given. Offers 50% kill fee. Buys one-time, electronic rights. Editorial lead time 3 months. Submit seasonal material 3 months in advance. Accepts queries by mail, e-mail, fax, phone. Sample copy online.

Nonfiction: Essays, historical/nostalgic, interview/profile, opinion. Query. Length: 2,000-4,000 words. **Pays 12¢/word.** Sometimes pays expenses of writers on assignment.

$TELE REVISTA, Su Mejor Amiga, Teve Latino Publishing, Inc., P.O. Box 145179, Coral Gables FL 33114-5179. (305)445-1755. Fax: (305)445-3907. E-mail: telerevista@aol.com. Website: www.telerevista.com. **Contact:** Ana Pereiro, editor. **100% freelance written.** Monthly magazine covering Hispanic entertainment (US and Puerto Rico). "We feature interviews, gossip, breaking stories, behind-the-scenes happenings, etc." Estab. 1986. Pays on publication. Publishes ms an average of 3 months after acceptance. Byline sometimes given. Buys all rights. Editorial lead time 2 months. Submit seasonal material 3 months in advance. Accepts queries by mail, e-mail, fax. Sample copy for free.

Nonfiction: Exposé, interview/profile, opinion, photo feature. **Buys 200 mss/year.** Query. **Pays $25-75.**

Photos: State availability of or send photos with submission. Buys all rights. Negotiates payment individually. Captions required.

Columns/Departments: Buys 60 mss/year. Query. **Pays $25-75.**

Fillers: Anecdotes, facts, gags to be illustrated by cartoonist, newsbreaks, short humor.

N $ $ $ $XXL MAGAZINE, Harris Publications, 1115 Broadway, 8th Floor, New York NY 10010. (212)462-9500. E-mail: zenat@harris-pub.com. **Contact:** Zena Tsarfin, managing editor. **50% freelance written.** Bimonthly magazine "*XXL* is hip-hop on a higher level, an upscale urban lifestyle magazine." Estab. 1997. Circ. 250,000. Pays on publication. Byline given. Offers 25% kill fee. Buys all rights. Editorial lead time 2 months. Submit seasonal material 3 months in advance. Accepts queries by mail, e-mail. Sample copy not available.

Nonfiction: Interview/profile, music; entertainment; luxury materialism. Query with published clips. Length: 200-5,000 words. **Pays $1/word.** Pays expenses of writers on assignment.

Photos: State availability with submission. Reviews contact sheets, transparencies, prints. Buys 3 month "no-see" rights. Captions, model releases required.

Tips: Please send clips, query and cover letter by mail or e-mail.

ETHNIC & MINORITY

Ideas and concerns of interest to specific nationalities and religions are covered by publications in this category. General interest lifestyle magazines for these groups are also included. Many ethnic publications are locally oriented or highly specialized and do not wish to be listed in a national publication such as *Writer's Market*. Query the editor of an ethnic publication with which you're familiar before submitting a manuscript, but do not consider these markets closed because they are not listed in this section. Additional markets for writing with an ethnic orientation are located in the following sections: Career, College & Alumni; Juvenile; Literary & "Little"; Men's; Women's; and Teen & Young Adult.

$AFRICAN VOICES, African Voices Communications, Inc., 270 W. 96th St., New York NY 10025. (212)865-2982. Fax: (212)316-3335. E-mail: africanvoices@aol.com. Website: www.africanvoices.com. Managing Editor: Layding Kaliba. **Contact:** Carolyn A. Butts, publisher/editor; Debbie Officer, book review editor. **85% freelance written.** Quarterly magazine covering art, film, culture. "*African Voices* is dedicated to highlighting the art, literature, and history of people of color." Estab. 1992. Circ. 20,000. Pays on publication. Publishes ms an average of 3-6 months after acceptance. Byline given. Buys first North American serial rights. Editorial lead time 3 months. Submit seasonal material 3 months in advance. Accepts queries by mail. Accepts previously published material. Accepts simultaneous submissions. Responds in 3 months to queries. Sample copy for $5 or online. Writer's guidelines online.

Nonfiction: Book excerpts, essays, historical/nostalgic, humor, inspirational, interview/profile, photo feature, travel. Query with published clips. Length: 1,200-2,500 words. **Pays $25-100.**

Reprints: Accepts previously published submissions.

Photos: State availability with submission. Buys one-time rights. Negotiates payment individually.

Fiction: Kim Horne, fiction editor. Adventure, condensed novels, erotica, ethnic, experimental, fantasy, historical, horror, humorous, mainstream, mystery, novel excerpts, religious, romance, science fiction, serialized novels, slice-of-life vignettes, suspense, African-American. **Buys 4 mss/year.** Send complete ms. Length: 500-2,500 words. **Pays $25-50.**

Poetry: Layding Kaliba, managing editor/poetry editor. Avant-garde, free verse, haiku, traditional. **Buys 10 poems/year.** Submit maximum 5 poems. Length: 5-100 lines. **Pays $10-20.**

$ AIM MAGAZINE, AIM Publishing Company, P.O. Box 1174, Maywood IL 60153. (708)344-4414. Fax: (206)543-2746. E-mail: ruthone@earthlink.net. Website: aimmagazine.org. **Contact:** Dr. Myron Apilado, editor. **75% freelance written.** Works with a small number of new/unpublished writers each year. Quarterly magazine on social betterment that promotes racial harmony and peace for high school, college and general audience. Publishes material "to purge racism from the human bloodstream through the written word—that is the purpose of *Aim Magazine*. Estab. 1975. Circ. 10,000. Pays on publication. Publishes ms an average of 3 months after acceptance. Byline given. Offers 60% kill fee. Buys first, one-time rights. Submit seasonal material 6 months in advance. Accepts queries by mail, e-mail. Accepts simultaneous submissions. Responds in 2 months to queries; 1 month to mss. Sample copy and writer's guidelines for $4 and 9×12 SAE with $1.70 postage or online.

Nonfiction: Exposé (education), general interest (social significance), historical/nostalgic (Black or Indian), how-to (create a more equitable society), interview/profile (one who is making social contributions to community), book reviews; reviews of plays. No religious material. **Buys 16 mss/year.** Send complete ms. Length: 500-800 words. **Pays $25-35.**

Photos: Reviews b&w prints. Captions, identification of subjects required.

Fiction: Ruth Apilado, associate editor. "Fiction that teaches the brotherhood of man." Ethnic, historical, mainstream, suspense. Open. No "religious" mss. **Buys 20 mss/year.** Send complete ms. Length: 1,000-1,500 words. **Pays $25-35.**

Poetry: Avant-garde, free verse, light verse. No "preachy" poetry. **Buys 20 poems/year.** Submit maximum 5 poems. Length: 15-30 lines. **Pays $3-5.**

Fillers: Anecdotes, newsbreaks, short humor. **Buys 30/year.** Length: 50-100 words. **Pays $5.**

Tips: "Interview anyone of any age who unselfishly is making an unusual contribution to the lives of less fortunate individuals. Include photo and background of person. We look at the nations of the world as part of one family. Short stories and historical pieces about Blacks and Indians are the areas most open to freelancers. Subject matter of submission is of paramount concern for us rather than writing style. Articles and stories showing the similarity in the lives of people with different racial backgrounds are desired."

$ $ AMBASSADOR MAGAZINE, National Italian American Foundation, 1860-19 St. NW, Washington DC 20009. (202)387-0600. Fax: (202)387-0800. E-mail: kevin@niaf.org. Website: www.niaf.org. **Contact:** Kevin Heitz. **50% freelance written.** Magazine for Italian-Americans covering Italian-American history and culture. "We publish nonfiction articles on little-known events in Italian-American history and articles on Italian-American culture, traditions, and personalities living and dead." Estab. 1989. Circ. 20,000. Pays on approval of final draft. Byline given. Offers 50% or $100 kill fee. Buys second serial (reprint) rights. Editorial lead time 3 months. Accepts queries by mail, e-mail, fax. Accepts previously published material. Accepts simultaneous submissions. Responds in 1 month to queries. Sample copy and writer's guidelines free.

Nonfiction: Historical/nostalgic, interview/profile, personal experience, photo feature. **Buys 12 mss/year.** Send complete ms. Length: 1,500-2,500 words. **Pays $200.**

Photos: Send photos with submission. Reviews contact sheets, prints. Buys one-time rights. Offers no additional payment for photos accepted with ms. Captions, identification of subjects required.

Tips: "Good photos, clear prose, and a good storytelling ability are all prerequisites."

$ $ THE B'NAI B'RITH IJM, (formerly *The B'Nai B'Rith International Jewish Monthly*), B'nai B'rith International, 2020 K St. NW, Washington DC 20006. (202)857-2708. Fax: (202)857-2781. E-mail: ijm@bnaibrith.org. Website: bbinet.org. **Contact:** Elana Harris, managing editor. **90% freelance written.** Quarterly magazine "specializing in social, political, historical, religious, cultural, 'lifestyle,' and service articles relating chiefly to the Jewish communities of North America and Israel. Write for the American Jewish audience, i.e., write about topics from a Jewish perspective." Estab. 1886. Circ. 110,000. Pays on publication. Publishes ms an average of 6 months after acceptance. Byline given. Offers 25% kill fee. Buys first rights. Editorial lead time 3 months. Submit seasonal material 5 months in advance. Accepts queries by mail, e-mail, fax. Accepts simultaneous submissions. Responds in 1 month to queries; 6 weeks to mss. Sample copy for $2. Writer's guidelines for #10 SASE or by e-mail.

Nonfiction: General interest pieces of relevance to the Jewish community of US and abroad. Interview/profile, photo feature, religious, travel. "No Holocaust memoirs, first-person essays/memoirs, fiction, or poetry." **Buys 14-20 mss/year.** Query with published clips. Length: 1,000-2,500 words. **Pays $300-750 for assigned articles; $300-700 for unsolicited articles.** Sometimes pays expenses of writers on assignment.

Photos: "Rarely assigned." Buys one-time rights.

Columns/Departments: Carla Lancit, assistant editor. Up Front (book, CD reviews, small/short items with Jewish interest), 150-200 words. **Buys 3 mss/year.** Query. **Pays $50.**

Tips: "Know what's going on in the Jewish world. Look at other Jewish publications also. Writers should submit clips with their queries. Read our guidelines carefully and present a good idea expressed well. Proofread your query letter."

N $ CELTIC HERITAGE, Clansman Publishing Ltd., P.O. Box 8805, Station A, Halifax NS B3K 5M4, Canada. (902)835-6244. Fax: (902)835-0080. E-mail: celtic@hfx.eastlink.ca. Website: www.celticheritage.ns.ca. **Contact:** Alexa Thompson, managing editor. **95% freelance written.** Bimonthly magazine covering culture of North Americans of Celtic descent. "The magazine chronicles the stories of Celtish people who have settled in North America, with a focus on the stories of those who are not mentioned in history books. We also feature Gaelic language articles, history of Celtic people, traditions, music, and folklore. We profile Celtic musicians and include reviews of Celtic books, music, and videos." Estab. 1987. Circ. 8,000 (per issue). Pays on publication. Publishes ms an average of 2 months after acceptance. Byline given.

Buys all rights. Editorial lead time 2 months. Submit seasonal material 3 months in advance. Accepts queries by mail, e-mail, fax, phone. Accepts previously published material. Responds in 1 week to queries; 1 month to mss. Sample copy for free. Writer's guidelines online.

Nonfiction: Essays, general interest, historical/nostalgic, interview/profile, opinion, personal experience, travel, Gaelic language, Celtic music reviews, profiles of Celtic musicians, Celtic history, traditions, and folklore. No fiction, poetry, historical stories already well publicized. **Buys 100 mss/year.** Query or send complete ms. Length: 800-2,500 words. **Pays $50-75 (Canadian). All writers receive a complimentary subscription.** "We have, on rare occasion, run an advertisement for a writer in lieu of payment."

Photos: State availability with submission. Reviews 35mm transparencies, 5×7 prints, GIF/JPEG files (200 dpi). Buys one-time rights. Negotiates payment individually. Captions, identification of subjects, model releases required.

Columns/Departments: "We do not have specific columns/departments. Suggest writers send query first if interested in developing a column." Length: 800-2,500 words. Query. **Pays $50-75 (Canadian).**

Fillers: Anecdotes, facts. **Buys 2-3/year.** Length: 300-500 words. **Pays $30-50 (Canadian).**

Tips: "The easiest way to get my attention is to submit a query by e-mail. We are so short staffed that we do not have much time to start a correspondence by regular post."

$ CONGRESS MONTHLY, American Jewish Congress, 15 E. 84th St., New York NY 10028. (212)879-4500. **Contact:** Rochelle Mancini, managing editor. **90% freelance written.** Bimonthly magazine. "*Congress Monthly*'s readership is popular, but well-informed; the magazine covers political, social, economic, and cultural issues of concern to the Jewish community in general and to the American Jewish Congress in particular." Estab. 1933. Circ. 35,000. Pays on publication. Publishes ms an average of 3 months after acceptance. Byline given. Buys one-time rights. Submit seasonal material 2 months in advance. Responds in 2 months to queries.

Nonfiction: General interest ("current topical issues geared toward our audience"). Travel, book, film, and theater reviews. No technical material. Query. Length: 1,000-2,500 words. **Pays amount determined by article length and author experience.**

Photos: State availability with submission. Reviews b&w prints.

$ FILIPINAS, A Magazine for All Filipinos, Filipinas Publishing, Inc., 1468 Huntington Ave., Suite 300, South San Francisco CA 94080. (650)872-8650. Fax: (650)872-8651. E-mail: mail@filipinasmag.com. Website: www.filipinasmag.com. **Contact:** Mona Lisa Yuchengco, editor/publisher. Monthly magazine focused on Filipino-American affairs. "*Filipinas* answers the lack of mainstream media coverage of Filipinos in America. It targets both Filipino immigrants and American-born Filipinos, gives in-depth coverage of political, social, cultural events in the Philippines and in the Filipino-American community. Features role models, history, travel, food and leisure, issues, and controversies." Estab. 1992. Circ. 40,000. Pays on publication. Publishes ms an average of 5 months after acceptance. Byline given. Offers $10 kill fee. Buys first, all rights. Editorial lead time 2 months. Submit seasonal material 4 months in advance. Accepts queries by mail, e-mail, fax. Responds in 3 weeks to queries; 5 months to mss. Writer's guidelines for 9½×4 SASE or on website.

O┳ Break in with "a good idea outlined well in the query letter. Also, tenacity is key. If one idea is shot down, come up with another."

Nonfiction: Interested in seeing "more issue-oriented pieces, unusual topics regarding Filipino-Americans and stories from the Midwest and other parts of the country other than the coasts." Exposé, general interest, historical/nostalgic, inspirational, interview/profile, opinion, personal experience, travel. No academic papers. **Buys 80-100 mss/year.** Query with published clips. Length: 800-1,500 words. **Pays $50-75.**

Photos: State availability with submission. Reviews 2¼×2¼ and 4×5 transparencies. Buys one-time rights. Offers $15-35/photo. Captions, identification of subjects required.

Columns/Departments: Cultural Currents (Filipino traditions, beliefs), 1,500 words. Query with published clips. **Pays $50-75.**

$ $ GERMAN LIFE, Zeitgeist Publishing, Inc., 1068 National Hwy., LaVale MD 21502. (301)729-6190. Fax: (301)729-1720. E-mail: ccook@germanlife.com. Website: www.germanlife.com. **Contact:** Carolyn Cook, editor. **50% freelance written.** Bimonthly magazine covering German-speaking Europe. "*German Life* is for all interested in the diversity of German-speaking culture, past and present, and in the various ways that the United States (and North America in general) has been shaped by its German immigrants. The magazine is dedicated to solid reporting on cultural, historical, social, and political events." Estab. 1994. Circ. 40,000. Pays on publication. Byline given. Buys first North American serial rights. Editorial lead time 4 months. Submit seasonal material 6 months in advance. Accepts queries by mail, e-mail. Responds in 2 months to queries; 3 months to mss. Sample copy for $4.95 and SAE with 4 first-class stamps. Writer's guidelines online.

Nonfiction: General interest, historical/nostalgic, interview/profile, photo feature, travel. Special issues: Oktoberfest-related (October); Seasonal Relative to Germany, Switzerland, or Austria (December); Travel to German-speaking Europe (April). **Buys 50 mss/year.** Query with published clips. Length: 800-1,500 words. **Pays $200-500 for assigned articles; $200-350 for unsolicited articles.**

Photos: State availability with submission. Reviews color transparencies, 5×7 color or b&w prints. Buys one-time rights. Offers no additional payment for photos accepted with ms. Identification of subjects required.

Columns/Departments: German-Americana (regards specific German-American communities, organizations, and/or events past or present), 1,200 words; Profile (portrays prominent Germans, Americans, or German-Americans), 1,000 words; At Home (cuisine, etc. relating to German-speaking Europe), 800 words; Library (reviews of books, videos, CDs, etc.), 300 words. **Buys 30 mss/year.** Query with published clips. **Pays $50-150.**

Fillers: Facts, newsbreaks. Length: 100-300 words. **Pays $50-150.**

Tips: "The best queries include several informative proposals. Writers should avoid overemphasizing autobiographical experiences/stories."

N $ HERITAGE FLORIDA JEWISH NEWS, P.O. Box 300742, Fern Park FL 32730-0742. (407)834-8787. E-mail: heritagefl@aol.com. Website: www.heritagefl.com. Publisher/Editor: Jeffrey Gaeser. **Contact:** Kim Fischer, assistant editor. **20% freelance written.** Weekly tabloid on Jewish subjects of local, national and international scope, except for special issues. "Covers news of local, national and international scope of interest to Jewish readers and not likely to be found in other publications." Estab. 1976. Circ. 3,500. Pays on publication. Byline given. Buys first North American serial, first, one-time, second serial (reprint), simultaneous rights. Submit seasonal material 3 months in advance. Accepts queries by mail, e-mail. Accepts previously published material. Responds in 1 month to queries. Sample copy for $1 and 9×12 SASE.

Nonfiction: "Especially needs articles for these annual issues: Rosh Hashanah, Financial, Chanukah, Celebration (wedding and bar mitzvah), Passover, Health and Fitness, Education, Travel and Savvy Seniors. No ficion, poems, first-person experiences." General interest, interview/profile, opinion, photo feature, religious, travel. **Buys 50 mss/year.** Send complete ms. Length: 500-1,000 words. **Pays 50¢/column inch.**

Reprints: Send ms with rights for sale noted.

Photos: State availability with submission. Reviews prints, up to 8×10. Buys one-time rights. Offers $5/photo. Captions, identification of subjects required.

$ HORIZONS, The Jewish Family Journal, Targum Press, 22700 W. Eleven Mile Rd., Southfield MI 48034. Fax: (888)298-9992. E-mail: horizons@netvision.net.il. Website: www.targum.com. Managing Editor: Moshe Dombey. **Contact:** Miriam Zakon, chief editor. **100% freelance written.** Quarterly magazine covering the Orthodox Jewish family. "We include fiction and nonfiction, memoirs, essays, historical, and informational articles, all of interest to the Orthodox Jew." Estab. 1994. Circ. 5,000. Pays 4-6 weeks after publication. Publishes ms an average of 6 months after acceptance. Byline given. Buys one-time rights. Editorial lead time 6 months. Submit seasonal material 8 months in advance. Accepts queries by mail, e-mail, fax. Accepts simultaneous submissions. Responds in 1 week to queries; 2 months to mss. Writer's guidelines available.

Nonfiction: Essays, historical/nostalgic, humor, inspirational, interview/profile, opinion, personal experience, photo feature, travel. **Buys 150 mss/year.** Send complete ms. Length: 350-3,000 words. **Pays $5-150.**

Photos: State availability with submission. Buys one-time rights. Offers no additional payment for photos accepted with ms.

Fiction: Historical, humorous, mainstream, slice-of-life vignettes. Nothing not suitable to Orthodox Jewish values. **Buys 10-15 mss/year.** Send complete ms. Length: 800-3,000 words. **Pays $20-100.**

Poetry: Free verse, haiku, light verse, traditional. **Buys 30-35 poems/year.** Submit maximum 4 poems. Length: 3-28 lines. **Pays $5-10.**

Fillers: Anecdotes, short humor. **Buys 20/year.** Length: 50-120 words. **Pays $5.**

Tips: "*Horizons* publishes for the Orthodox Jewish market and therefore only accepts articles that are of interest to this market. We do not accept submissions dealing with political issues or Jewish legal issues. The tone is light and friendly and we therefore do not accept submissions that are of a scholarly nature. Our writers must be very familiar with our market. Anything that is not suitable for our readership doesn't stand a chance, no matter how high its literary merit."

N $ INTERNATIONAL EXAMINER, 622 S. Washington, Seattle WA 98104. (206)624-3925. Fax: (206)624-3046. E-mail: editor@iexaminer.org. Website: www.iexaminer.org. **Contact:** Nhien Nguyen, managing editor. **75% freelance written.** Biweekly journal of Asian-American news, politics, and arts. "We write about Asian-American issues and things of interest to Asian-Americans. We do not want stuff about Asian things (stories on your trip to China, Japanese Tea Ceremony, etc. will be rejected). Yes, we are in English." Estab. 1974. Circ. 12,000. Pays on publication. Publishes ms an average of 1 month after acceptance. Buys one-time rights. Editorial lead time 1 month. Submit seasonal material 2 months in advance. Accepts simultaneous submissions. Writer's guidelines for #10 SASE.

Nonfiction: Essays, exposé, general interest, historical/nostalgic, humor, interview/profile, opinion, personal experience, photo feature. **Buys 100 mss/year.** Query by mail, fax, or e-mail with published clips. Length: 750-5,000 words depending on subject. **Pays $25-100.** Sometimes pays expenses of writers on assignment.

Reprints: Accepts previously published submissions (as long as not published in same area). Send typed ms with rights for sale noted and information about when and where the material previously appeared. Payment negotiable.

Photos: State availability with submission. Reviews contact sheets. Buys one-time rights. Negotiates payment individually. Captions, identification of subjects required.

Fiction: Asian-American authored fiction by or about Asian-Americans. Novel excerpts. **Buys 1-2 mss/year.** Query.

Tips: "Write decent, suitable material on a subject of interest to Asian-American community. All submissions are reviewed; all good ones are contacted. It helps to call and run idea by editor before or after sending submissions."

$ $ ITALIAN AMERICA, Official Publication of the Order Sons of Italy in America, Order Sons of Italy in America, 219 E St. NE, Washington DC 20002. (202)547-2900. Fax: (202)546-8168. E-mail: nationaloffice@osia.org. Website: www.osia.org. **Contact:** Dr. Dona De Sanctis, editor/deputy executive director. **20% freelance written.** Quarterly magazine. "*Italian America* strives to provide timely information about OSIA, while reporting on individuals, institutions, issues, and events of current or historical significance in the Italian-American community." Estab. 1996. Circ. 65,000. Pays on publication. Publishes ms an average of 3 months after acceptance. Byline given. Offers 50% kill fee. Buys worldwide nonexclusive rights. Editorial lead time 3 months. Accepts queries by mail, e-mail, fax. Accepts simultaneous submissions. Sample copy for free. Writer's guidelines online.

Nonfiction: Essays, exposé, historical/nostalgic, interview/profile, opinion, personal experience, travel, current events.

Buys 10 mss/year. Query with published clips. Length: 1,000-1,200 words. **Pays $50-250.**

Tips: "Stories should be unique, not standard."

$ $ $ JEWISH ACTION, Union of Orthodox Jewish Congregations of America, 11 Broadway, 14th Floor, New York NY 10004-1302. (212)613-8146. Fax: (212)613-0646. E-mail: zeideld@ou.org. Website: www.ou.org. Editor: Nechama Carmel. **Contact:** Dassi Zeidel, assistant editor. **80% freelance written.** Quarterly magazine covering a vibrant approach to Jewish issues, Orthodox lifestyle, and values. Circ. 40,000. Pays 2 months after publication. Byline given. Not copyrighted. Submit seasonal material 4 months in advance. Responds in 3 months to queries. Sample copy online. Writer's guidelines for #10 SASE or by e-mail.

- Prefers queries by e-mail. Mail and fax OK.

O→ Break in with a query for "Just Between Us" column.

Nonfiction: Current Jewish issues, history, biography, art, inspirational, humor, music, book reviews. "We are not looking for Holocaust accounts. We welcome essays about responses to personal or societal challenges." **Buys 30-40 mss/year.** Query with published clips. Length: 1,000-3,000 words. **Pays $100-400 for assigned articles; $75-150 for unsolicited articles.**

Photos: Send photos with submission. Identification of subjects required.

Columns/Departments: Just Between Us (personal opinion on current Jewish life and issues), 1,000 words. **Buys 4 mss/year.**

Fiction: Must have relevance to Orthodox reader. Length: 1,000-2,000 words.

Poetry: Buys limited number poems/year. Pays $25-75.

Tips: "Remember that your reader is well educated and has a strong commitment to Orthodox Judaism. Articles on the holidays, Israel, and other common topics should offer a fresh insight. Because the magazine is a quarterly, we do not generally publish articles which concern specific timely events."

N $ KHABAR, The Community Magazine, Khabar Inc., 2376 Shallowford Terrace, Atlanta GA 30341. (770)451-3067. Fax: (770)986-9113. E-mail: parthiv@khabar.com. Website: www.khabar.com. **Contact:** Parthiv N. Parekh, editor. **50% freelance written.** Monthly magazine covering the Asian and Indian community in Georgia. "Content relating to Indian-American and/or immigrant experience." Estab. 1992. Circ. 14,000. Pays on publication. Publishes ms an average of 2 months after acceptance. Offers 35% kill fee. Buys one-time, second serial (reprint), simultaneous, electronic rights. Editorial lead time 2 months. Submit seasonal material 2 months in advance. Accepts queries by mail, e-mail. Accepts previously published material. Accepts simultaneous submissions. Sample copy for free. Writer's guidelines free or by e-mail.

Nonfiction: Essays, interview/profile, opinion, personal experience, travel. **Buys 5 mss/year.** Query with or without published clips or send complete ms. Length: 750-4,000 words. **Pays $50-125 for assigned articles; $25-100 for unsolicited articles.**

Reprints: Accepts previously published submissions.

Photos: State availability of or send photos with submission. Negotiates payment individually. Captions, identification of subjects required.

Columns/Departments: Book Review, 1,200 words; Music Review, 800 words; Spotlight (profiles), 1,200-3,000 words. All columns must feature Indian or Asian Americans. **Buys 5 mss/year.** Query with or without published clips or send complete ms. **Pays $25-100.**

Fiction: Ethnic. **Buys 5 mss/year.** Query with or without published clips or send complete ms. **Pays $25-100.**

Tips: "Ask for our 'content guidelines' document by e-mail or otherwise by writing to us."

N $ $ $ $ LATINA MAGAZINE, Latina Media Ventures, 1500 Broadway, 7th Floor, New York NY 10036. (212)642-0200. E-mail: editor@latina.com. Website: www.latina.com. Editorial Director: Betty Cortina. Editor-in-Chief: Sylvia Martinez. **40-50% freelance written.** Monthly magazine covering Latina lifestyle. "*Latina Magazine* is the leading bilingual lifestyle publication for Hispanic women in the United States today. Covering the best of Latino fashion, beauty, culture, and food, the magazine also features celebrity profiles and interviews." Estab. 1996. Circ. 250,000. Pays on publication. Publishes ms an average of 2-3 months after acceptance. Byline given. Offers 25% kill fee. Buys first, second serial (reprint), electronic rights. Editorial lead time 3 months. Submit seasonal material 4-5 months in advance. Accepts queries by e-mail. Responds in 1 month to queries; 1-2 months to mss. Sample copy online.

- Editors are in charge of their individual sections and pitches should be made directly to them. Do not make pitches directly to the editor-in-chief or the editorial director as they will only be routed to the relevant section editor. E-mail addresses for specific editors are listed next to the contact names in each section.

Nonfiction: Specific sections, editors, and e-mail addresses are: Entertainment Calendar, Elizabeth Carroll (ecarroll@latina.com); Becoming Latina; Chronicles, Dolores Prida (dprida@latina.com); Issues and News, Della De LaFuente (ddelafuente@latina.com); Real People, Love & Sex, Nancy Gavilanes, assistant editor (ngavilanes@latina.com); Health and Wellness, Ana Pelayo (apelayo@latina.com); Fashion, Victoria Sanchez, fashion director (vsanchez@latino.com); Beauty, Yesenia Almonte, beauty editor (valmonte@latina.com). Essays, how-to, humor, inspirational, interview/profile, new product, personal experience. Special issues: The 10 Latinas Who Changed the World (December). "We do not feature an extensive amount of celebrity content or entertainment content, and freelancers should be sensitive to this. The magazine does not contain book or album reviews, and we do not write stories covering an artist's new project. We do not attend press junkets and do not cover press conferences. Please note that we are a lifestyle magazine, not an entertainment magazine." **Buys 15-20 mss/year.** Query with published clips. Length: 300-2,200 words. **Pays $1/word.** Pays expenses of writers on assignment.

Photos: Adrienne Aurichio, photo director. State availability with submission. Reviews contact sheets, transparencies, GIF/JPEG files. Buys one-time rights. Negotiates payment individually. Identification of subjects required.

Columns/Departments: Becoming Latina; Chronicles, Dolores Prida (dprida@latina.com), 300-600 words; Social Issues and News, Della De LaFuente (ddelafuente@latina.com), 400-2,000 words; Real Women Stories, Love & Sex, Nancy Gavilanes, assistant editor (ngavilanes@latina.com), 400-800 words; Health and Wellness, Ana Pelayo (apelayo@latina.com), 400-800 words; Fashion, Victoria Sanchez, fashion director (vsanchez@latina.com); Beauty, Yesenia Almonte, beauty editor (valmonte@latina.com). **Buys 25-40 mss/year.** Query with published clips. **Pays $1/word.**

Tips: "*Latina*'s features cover a wide gamut of topics, including fashion, beauty, wellness, and personal essays. The magazine runs a wide variety of features on news and service topics (from the issues affecting Latina adolescents to stories dealin with anger). If you are going to make a pitch, please keep the following things in mind.All pitches should include statistics or some background reporting that demonstrates why a developing trend is important. Also, provide examples of women who can provide a personal perspective. Profiles and essays need to have a strong personal journey angle. We will not cover someone just because they are Hispanic. When pitching stories about a particular person, please let us know the following: timeliness (Is this someone who is somehow tied to breaking news events? Has their story been heard?); the 'wow' factor (Why is this person remarkable? What elements make this story a standout? What sets your subject apart from other women?); target our audience (please note that the magazine targets acculturated, English-dominant Latina women between the ages of 18-39)."

$ $ NA'AMAT WOMAN, Magazine of NA'AMAT USA, the Women's Labor Zionist Organization of America, NA'AMAT USA, 350 Fifth Ave., Suite 4700, New York NY 10118. (212)563-5222. Fax: (212)563-5710. **Contact:** Judith A. Sokoloff, editor. **80% freelance written.** Magazine published 4 times/year covering Jewish themes and issues, Israel, women's issues, and social and political issues. "Magazine covering a wide variety of subjects of interest to the Jewish community—including political and social issues, arts, profiles; many articles about Israel; and women's issues. Fiction must have a Jewish theme. Readers are the American Jewish community." Estab. 1926. Circ. 20,000. Pays on publication. Byline given. Buys first North American serial, first, one-time, second serial (reprint) rights, makes work-for-hire assignments. Accepts queries by mail, fax. Responds in 3 months to queries; 3 months to mss. Sample copy for 9X11½ SAE and $1.20 postage. Writer's guidelines for #10 SASE.

Nonfiction: "All articles must be of particular interest to the Jewish community." Exposé, general interest (Jewish), historical/nostalgic, interview/profile, opinion, personal experience, photo feature, travel, art, music, social, and political issues, Israel. **Buys 20 mss/year.** Query with or without published clips or send complete ms. **Pays 10-15¢/word.**

Photos: State availability with submission. Buys one-time rights. Pays $25-55 for 4×5 or 5×7 prints. Captions, identification of subjects required.

Columns/Departments: Film and book reviews with Jewish themes. **Buys 20 mss/year.** Query with published clips or send complete ms. **Pays 10¢/word.**

Fiction: "Intelligent fiction with Jewish slant. No maudlin nostalgia or trite humor." Ethnic, historical, humorous, novel excerpts, women-oriented. **Buys 3 mss/year.** Query with published clips or send complete ms. Length: 2,000-3,000 words. **Pays 10¢/word and 2 contributor's copies.**

$ $ NATIVE PEOPLES MAGAZINE, The Arts and Lifeways, 5333 N. 7th St., Suite 224, Phoenix AZ 85012. (602)265-4855. Fax: (602)265-3113. E-mail: dgibson@nativepeoples.com. Website: www.nativepeoples.com. **Contact:** Daniel Gibson, editor. Bimonthly magazine covering Native Americans. "High-quality reproduction with full color throughout. The primary purpose of this magazine is to offer a sensitive portrayal of the arts and lifeways of Native peoples of the Americas." Estab. 1987. Circ. 50,000. Pays on publication. Byline given. Buys one-time rights. Accepts queries by mail, e-mail, fax. Responds in 2 months to queries. Writer's guidelines online.

Nonfiction: Pathways (travel section) department most open to freelancers. Looking for articles on educational, economic and political development; occasional historic pieces; Native events. Interview/profile (of interesting and leading Natives from all walks of life, with an emphasis on arts), personal experience. **Buys 35 mss/year.** Query with published clips. Length: 1,000-2,500 words. **Pays 25¢/word.**

Photos: State availability with submission. Reviews transparencies, prefers 35mm slides. Also accepts electronic photo images, inquire for details. Buys one-time rights. Offers $45-150/page rates, $250/cover photos. Identification of subjects required.

Tips: "We are focused upon authenticity and a positive portrayal of present-day Native American life and cultural practices. Our stories portray role models of Native people, young and old, with a sense of pride in their heritage and culture. Therefore, it is important that the Native American point of view be incorporated in each story."

N $ $ RUSSIAN LIFE, RIS Publications, P.O. Box 567, Montpelier VT 05601. (802)223-4955. E-mail: ruslife@rispubs.com. Website: www.rispubs.com. Editor: Mikhail Ivanov. **Contact:** Paul Richardson, publisher. **40% freelance written.** Bimonthly magazine covering Russian culture, history, travel and business. "Our readers are informed Russophiles with an avid interest in all things Russian. But we do not publish personal travel journals or the like." Estab. 1956. Circ. 15,000. Pays on publication. Publishes ms an average of 2 months after acceptance. Byline given. Offers $25 kill fee. Buys first rights. Editorial lead time 2 months. Submit seasonal material 3 months in advance. Accepts queries by mail. Accepts previously published material. Responds in 1 month to queries. Sample copy for 9×12 SAE and 6 first-class stamps. Writer's guidelines online.

Break in with a "good travel essay piece covering remote regions of Russia."

Nonfiction: General interest, photo feature, travel. No personal stories, i.e., "How I came to love Russia." **Buys 15-20 mss/year.** Query. Length: 1,000-6,000 words. **Pays $100-300.**

Reprints: Accepts previously published submissions

Photos: Send photos with submission. Reviews contact sheets. Buys one-time rights. Negotiates payment individually. Captions required.

The online magazine carries original content not found in the print editions.

Tips: "A straightforward query letter with writing sample or manuscript (not returnable) enclosed."

$ $ SCANDINAVIAN REVIEW, The American-Scandinavian Foundation, 58 Park Ave., New York NY 10016. (212)879-9779. Fax: (212)686-1157. Website: www.amscan.org. **Contact:** Richard J. Litell, editor. **75% freelance written.** Triannual magazine for contemporary Scandinavia. Audience: Members, embassies, consulates, libraries. Slant: Popular coverage of contemporary affairs in Scandinavia. Estab. 1913. Circ. 4,000. Pays on publication. Publishes ms an average of 2 months after acceptance. Byline given. Buys first North American serial, second serial (reprint) rights. Editorial lead time 3 months. Submit seasonal material 3 months in advance. Accepts previously published material. Responds in 6 weeks to queries. Sample copy online. Writer's guidelines free.

Nonfiction: General interest, interview/profile, photo feature, travel (must have Scandinavia as topic focus). Special issues: Scandinavian travel. No pornography. **Buys 30 mss/year.** Query with published clips. Length: 1,500-2,000 words. **Pays $300 maximum.**

Photos: Reviews 3×5 transparencies, prints. Buys one-time rights. Pays $25-50/photo; negotiates payment individually. Captions required.

$ UPSCALE MAGAZINE, Bronner Brothers, 600 Bronner Brothers Way, Atlanta GA 30310. (404)758-7467. Fax: (404)755-9892. Website: www.upscalemagazine.com. **Contact:** Joyce E. Davis, senior editor. Monthly magazine covering topics for "upscale African-American/black interests. *Upscale* offers to take the reader to the 'next level' of life's experience. Written for the black reader and consumer, *Upscale* provides information in the realms of business, news, lifestyle, fashion and beauty, and arts and entertainment." Estab. 1989. Circ. 250,000. Pays on publication. Publishes ms an average of 4 months after acceptance. Byline given. Offers 25% kill fee. Buys first North American serial rights. Editorial lead time 3-4 months. Accepts queries by mail. Accepts simultaneous submissions. Responds in 1 month to queries; 2 months to mss. Sample copy online. Writer's guidelines online.

Photos: State availability with submission. Negotiates payment individually. Captions, identification of subjects, model releases required.

Columns/Departments: Constance Clemons, office manager. News & Business (factual, current); Lifestyle (travel, home, wellness, etc.); Beauty & Fashion (tips, trends, upscale fashion, hair); and Arts & Entertainment (artwork, black celebrities, entertainment). **Buys 6-10 mss/year.** Query with published clips. **Payment different for each department.**

Tips: "Make queries informative and exciting. Include entertaining clips. Be familiar with issues affecting black readers. Be able to write about them with ease and intelligence."

FOOD & DRINK

Magazines appealing to gourmets, health-conscious consumers, and vegetarians are classified here. Some publications emphasize "the art and craft" of cooking for food enthusiasts who enjoy developing these skills as a leisure activity. Another popular trend stresses healthy eating and food choices. Many magazines in the Health & Fitness category present a holistic approach to well-being through nutrition and fitness for healthful living. Magazines in General Interest and Women's categories also buy articles on food topics. Journals aimed at food processing, manufacturing, and retailing are in the Trade section.

$ $ $ $ BON APPETIT, America's Food and Entertaining Magazine, Conde Nast Publications, Inc., 6300 Wilshire Blvd., Los Angeles CA 90048. (323)965-3600. Fax: (323)937-1206. Website: epicurious.com. Editor-in-Chief: Barbara Fairchild. Senior Editor: Hugh Garvey. **Contact:** Victoria von Biel, executive editor. **50% freelance written.** Monthly magazine covering fine food, restaurants, and home entertaining. "*Bon Appetit* readers are upscale food enthusiasts and sophisticated travelers. They eat out often and entertain 4-6 times a month." Estab. 1975. Circ. 1,331,853. **Pays on acceptance.** Byline given. Buys all rights. Submit seasonal material 1 year in advance. Accepts queries by mail. Responds in 6 weeks to queries. Writer's guidelines for #10 SASE.

Nonfiction: Travel (food-related), food feature, personal essays. "No cartoons, quizzes, poetry, historic food features, or obscure food subjects." **Buys 50 mss/year.** Query with published clips. No phone calls or e-mails. Length: 150-2,000 words. **Pays $100-2,000.** Pays expenses of writers on assignment.

Photos: Never send photos.

Tips: "We are not generally interested in receiving specific queries, but we do look for new good writers. They must have a good knowledge of *Bon Appetit* and the related topics of food and entertaining (as shown in accompanying clips). A light, lively style is a plus. Nothing long and pedantic, please."

$ GOURMET, The Magazine of Good Living, Conde Nast Publications, Inc., 4 Times Square, New York NY 10036. (212)286-2860. Fax: (212)286-2672. Website: www.gourmet.com. Editor-in-Chief: Ruth Reichl. **Contact:** John Willoughby, executive editor. Monthly magazine for sophisticated readers who have a passion for food and travel. Byline given. Offers 25% kill fee. Accepts queries by mail. Responds in 2 months to queries. Sample copy for free.

Nonfiction: Looking for "articles on reminiscence, single foods, and ethnic cuisines." **Buys 25-30 mss/year.** Query with published clips. Length: 200-3,000 words. Pays expenses of writers on assignment.

$ $ KASHRUS MAGAZINE, The Bimonthly for the Kosher Consumer and the Trade, The Kashrus Institute, P.O. Box 204, Parkville Station, Brooklyn NY 11204. (718)336-8544. **Contact:** Rabbi Yosef Wikler, editor. **25% freelance**

written. Prefers to work with published/established writers, but will work with new/unpublished writers. Bimonthly magazine covering the kosher food industry and food production. Estab. 1980. Circ. 10,000. Pays on publication. Publishes ms an average of 2 months after acceptance. Byline given. Offers 50% kill fee. Buys first, second serial (reprint) rights. Submit seasonal material 2 months in advance. Accepts queries by mail, phone. Accepts previously published material. Accepts simultaneous submissions. Responds in 1 week to queries; 2 weeks to mss. Sample copy for $3.

Nonfiction: General interest, interview/profile, new product, personal experience, photo feature, religious, technical, travel. Special issues: International Kosher Travel (October); Passover (March). **Buys 8-12 mss/year.** Query with published clips. Length: 1,000-1,500 words. **Pays $100-250 for assigned articles; up to $100 for unsolicited articles.** Sometimes pays expenses of writers on assignment.

Reprints: Send tearsheet or photocopy and information about when and where the material previously appeared. Pays 25-50% of amount paid for an original article.

Photos: No guidelines; send samples or call. State availability with submission. Buys one-time rights. Offers no additional payment for photos accepted with ms.

Columns/Departments: Book Review (cookbooks, food technology, kosher food), 250-500 words; People In the News (interviews with kosher personalities), 1,000-1,500 words; Regional Kosher Supervision (report on kosher supervision in a city or community), 1,000-1,500 words; Food Technology (new technology or current technology with accompanying pictures), 1,000-1,500 words; Travel (international, national), must include Kosher information and Jewish communities, 1,000-1,500 words; Regional Kosher Cooking, 1,000-1,500 words. **Buys 8-12 mss/year.** Query with published clips. **Pays $50-250.**

Tips: "*Kashrus Magazine* will do more writing on general food technology, production, and merchandising as well as human interest travelogs and regional writing in 2003 than we have done in the past. Areas most open to freelancers are interviews, food technology, cooking and food preparation, dining, regional reporting, and travel, but we also feature healthy eating and lifestyles, redecorating, catering, and hospitals and health care. We welcome stories on the availability and quality of kosher foods and services in communities across the U.S. and throughout the world. Some of our best stories have been by non-Jewish writers about kosher observance in their region. We also enjoy humorous articles. Just send a query with clips and we'll try to find a storyline that's right for you, or better yet, call us to discuss a storyline."

$ $ PRIMO RISTORANTE, (formerly *Ristorante*), Foley Publishing, P.O. Box 73, Liberty Corner NJ 07938. (908)766-6006. Fax: (908)766-6607. E-mail: barmag@aol.com. Website: www.bartender.com. **Contact:** Raymond Foley, publisher or Jaclyn Foley, editor. **75% freelance written.** Bimonthly magazine covering "Italian anything!" "*Primo Ristorante—The magazine for the Italian Connoisseur.* For Italian restaurants and those who love Italian food, travel, wine and all things Italian!" Estab. 1994. Circ. 40,000. Pays on publication. Publishes ms an average of 3 months after acceptance. Byline sometimes given. Buys first North American serial, one-time rights. Editorial lead time 3 months. Submit seasonal material 3 months in advance. Accepts previously published material. Responds in 1 month to queries; 2 months to mss. Sample copy and writer's guidelines for 9×12 SAE and 4 first-class stamps.

Nonfiction: Book excerpts, general interest, historical/nostalgic, how-to (prepare Italian foods), humor, new product, opinion, personal experience, travel. **Buys 25 mss/year.** Send complete ms. Length: 100-1,000 words. **Pays $100-350 for assigned articles; $75-300 for unsolicited articles.** Sometimes pays expenses of writers on assignment.

Reprints: Send tearsheet or photocopy and information about when and where the material previously appeared. Pays 25% of amount paid for an original article.

Photos: Send photos with submission. Reviews 3×5 prints. Buys one-time rights. Negotiates payment individually. Captions, model releases required.

Columns/Departments: Send complete ms. **Pays $50-200.**

Fillers: Anecdotes, facts, short humor. **Buys 10/year. Pays $10-50.**

N $ SAVEUR, World Publications, Inc., 304 Park Avenue S 8th Fl, New York NY 10010. (212)219-7400. Fax: (212)219-4696. E-mail: saveur@worldpub.net. Website: www.saveur.com. Editor: Coleman Andrews. Managing Editor: Ann McCarthy. **Contact:** Kathleen Brennan, senior editor. Magazine published 8 times/year covering exotic foods. Written for sophisticated, upscale lovers of food, wine, travel and adventure. Estab. 1994. Circ. 390,589. Accepts queries by mail. Sample copy for $5 at newsstands. Writer's guidelines by e-mail.

Nonfiction: Query with published clips.

Columns/Departments: Query with published clips.

Tips: "Queries and stories should be detailed and specific, and personal ties to the subject matter are important—let us know why you should be the one to write the story. Familiarize yourself with our departments, and the magazine style as a whole, and pitch your stories accordingly. Also, we rarely assign restaurant-based pieces, and the selections "Classis" and "Source" are almost always staff-written."

$ $ WINE PRESS NORTHWEST, Tri-City Herald, 107 N. Cascade St., Kennewick WA 99336. (509)582-1564. Fax: (509)582-1510. E-mail: editor@winepressnw.com. Website: www.winepressnw.com. Managing Editor: Eric Degerman. **Contact:** Andy Perdue, editor. **50% freelance written.** Quarterly magazine covering Pacific Northwest wine (Washington, Oregon, British Columbia, Idaho). "We focus narrowly on Pacific Northwest wine. If we write about travel, it's where to go to drink NW wine. If we write about food, it's what goes with NW wine. No beer, no spirits." Estab. 1998. Circ. 12,000. Pays on publication. Publishes ms an average of 3 months after acceptance. Byline given. Offers 20% kill fee. Buys first North American serial, electronic rights. Editorial lead time 3 months. Submit seasonal material 3 months in advance. Accepts queries by mail, e-mail, fax. Accepts simultaneous submissions. Responds in 1 month to queries. Sample copy free or online. Writer's guidelines free.

Nonfiction: General interest, historical/nostalgic, interview/profile, new product, photo feature, travel. No "beer, spirits, non-NW (California wine, etc.)" **Buys 30 mss/year.** Query with published clips. Length: 1,500-2,500 words. **Pays $300.** Sometimes pays expenses of writers on assignment.

Photos: State availability with submission. Reviews contact sheets. Buys one-time rights. Negotiates payment individually. Identification of subjects required.

The online magazine carries original content not found in the print edition. Contact: Andy Perdue, online editor.

Tips: "Writers must be familiar with *Wine Press Northwest* and should have a passion for the region, its wines, and cuisine."

$ $ $ WINE SPECTATOR, M. Shanken Communications, Inc., 387 Park Ave. S., New York NY 10016. (212)684-4224. Fax: (212)684-5424. E-mail: winespec@mshanken.com. Website: www.winespectator.com. **Contact:** Thomas Matthews, executive editor. **20% freelance written.** Prefers to work with published/established writers. Biweekly news magazine. Estab. 1976. Circ. 323,000. Pays within 30 days of publication. Publishes ms an average of 2 months after acceptance. Byline given. Buys all rights, makes work-for-hire assignments. Submit seasonal material 4 months in advance. Accepts queries by mail, fax. Responds in 3 months to queries. Sample copy for $5. Writer's guidelines for #10 SASE.

Nonfiction: General interest (news about wine or wine events), interview/profile (of wine, vintners, wineries), opinion, photo feature, travel, dining and other lifestyle pieces. No "winery promotional pieces or articles by writers who lack sufficient knowledge to write below just surface data." Query. Length: 100-2,000 words. **Pays $100-1,000.**

Photos: Send photos with submission. Buys all rights. Pays $75 minimum for color transparencies. Captions, identification of subjects, model releases required.

The online magazine carries original content not found in the print edition. Contact: Dana Nigro, news editor.

Tips: "A solid knowledge of wine is a must. Query letters essential, detailing the story idea. New, refreshing ideas which have not been covered before stand a good chance of acceptance. *Wine Spectator* is a consumer-oriented news magazine, but we are interested in some trade stories; brevity is essential."

$ $ WINE X MAGAZINE, Wine, Food and an Intelligent Slice of Vice, X Publishing, Inc., 880 Second St., Santa Rosa CA 95404-4611. (707)545-0992. E-mail: winexus@winexmagazine.com. Website: www.winexmagazine.com. **Contact:** Darryl Roberts, editor/publisher. **100% freelance written.** Bimonthly magazine covering wine and other beverages. "*Wine X* is a lifestyle magazine for young adults featuring wine, beer, spirits, music, movies, fashion, food, coffee, celebrity interviews, health/fitness." Estab. 1997. Circ. 35,000. Pays on publication. Publishes ms an average of 3 months after acceptance. Byline given. Not copyrighted. Buys first North American and international serial, electronic rights for 3 years. Editorial lead time 3 months. Submit seasonal material 4 months in advance. Accepts queries by e-mail. Responds in 3 weeks to queries. Sample copy for $7. Writer's guidelines online.

Nonfiction: Essays, new product, personal experience, photo feature, travel. No restaurant reviews, wine collector profiles. **Buys 6 mss/year.** Query. Length: 500-1,500 words. **Pays $50-250 for assigned articles; $50-150 for unsolicited articles.** Sometimes pays expenses of writers on assignment.

Photos: Reviews transparencies. Buys one-time rights. Offers no additional payment for photos accepted with ms. Identification of subjects, model releases required.

Columns/Departments: Wine; Other Beverages; Lifestyle, all 1,000 words. **Buys 72 mss/year.** Query.

Fiction: Buys 6 mss/year. Query. Length: 1,000-1,500 words. **No payment for fiction.**

Poetry: Avant-garde, free verse, haiku, light verse, traditional. **Buys 2 poems/year.** Submit maximum 3 poems. Length: 10-1,500 lines.

Fillers: Short humor. **Buys 6/year.** Length: 100-500 words. **Pays $0-50.**

GAMES & PUZZLES

These publications are written by and for game enthusiasts interested in both traditional games and word puzzles, and newer role-playing adventure, computer, and video games. Other puzzle markets may be found in the Juvenile section.

$ THE BRIDGE BULLETIN, American Contract Bridge League, 2990 Airways Blvd., Memphis TN 38116-3847. (901)332-5586, ext. 291. Fax: (901)398-7754. E-mail: editor@acbl.org. Website: www.acbl.org. Managing Editor: Paul Linxwiler. **Contact:** Brent Manley, editor. **20% freelance written.** Monthly magazine covering duplicate (tournament) bridge. Estab. 1938. Circ. 155,000. Pays on publication. Publishes ms an average of 3 months after acceptance. Byline given. Buys first, second serial (reprint) rights. Editorial lead time 2 months. Accepts queries by mail, e-mail. Accepts previously published material. Accepts simultaneous submissions.

Break in with a "humorous piece about bridge."

Nonfiction: Book excerpts, essays, how-to (play better bridge), humor, interview/profile, new product, personal experience, photo feature, technical, travel. **Buys 6 mss/year.** Query. Length: 500-2,000 words. **Pays $50/page.**

Photos: State availability with submission. Buys all rights. Negotiates payment individually. Identification of subjects required.

Tips: "Articles must relate to contract bridge in some way. Cartoons on bridge welcome."

$ $ CHESS LIFE, United States Chess Federation, 3054 US Route 9W, New Windsor NY 12553-7698. (845)562-8350, ext. 153. Fax: (845)236-4852. E-mail: magazines@uschess.org. Website: www.uschess.org. **Contact:** Peter Kurzdorfer, editor. **15% freelance written.** Works with a small number of new/unpublished writers/year. Monthly magazine. "*Chess Life* is the official publication of the United States Chess Federation, covering news of most major chess events, both here and abroad, with special emphasis on the triumphs and exploits of American players." Estab. 1939. Circ. 70,000. Publishes ms an average of 8 months after acceptance. Byline given. Buys first rights. Submit seasonal material 8 months in advance. Accepts queries by mail, e-mail, fax, phone. Accepts simultaneous submissions. Responds in 3 months to mss. Sample copy and writer's guidelines for 9×11 SAE with 5 first-class stamps.

Nonfiction: All must have some relation to chess. General interest, historical/nostalgic, humor, interview/profile (of a famous chess player or organizer), photo feature (chess centered), technical. No "stories about personal experiences with chess." **Buys 30-40 mss/year.** Query with samples if new to publication. Length: 3,000 words maximum. **Pays $100/page (800-1,000 words).** Sometimes pays expenses of writers on assignment.

Reprints: Send tearsheet, photocopy or typed ms with rights for sale noted and information about when and where the material previously appeared.

Photos: Reviews b&w contact sheets and prints, and color prints and slides. Buys all or negotiable rights. Pays $25-35 inside; $100-300 for covers. Captions, identification of subjects, model releases required.

Columns/Departments: Chess Review (brief articles on unknown chess personalities) and "Chess in Everyday Life."

Fillers: Submit with samples and clips. Buys first or negotiable rights to cartoons and puzzles. **Pays $25 upon acceptance.**

Tips: "Articles must be written from an informed point of view—not from view of the curious amateur. Most of our writers are specialized in that they have sound credentials as chess players. Freelancers in major population areas (except New York and Los Angeles, which we already have covered) who are interested in short personality profiles and perhaps news reporting have the best opportunities. We're looking for more personality pieces on chess players around the country; not just the stars, but local masters, talented youths, and dedicated volunteers. Freelancers interested in such pieces might let us know of their interest and their range. Could be we know of an interesting story in their territory that needs covering. Examples of published articles include a locally produced chess television program, a meeting of chess set collectors from around the world, chess in our prisons, and chess in the works of several famous writers."

GAY & LESBIAN INTEREST

The magazines listed here cover a wide range of politics, culture, news, art, literature, and issues of general interest to gay and lesbian communities. Magazines of a strictly sexual content are listed in the Sex section.

$ $ CURVE MAGAZINE, Outspoken Enterprises, Inc., 1550 Bryant St., Suite 510, San Francisco CA 94103. Fax: (415)863-1609. E-mail: editor@curvemag.com. Website: www.curvemag.com. Editor-in-Chief: Frances Stevens. **Contact:** Gretchen Lee, managing editor. **40% freelance written.** Magazine published 8 times/year covering lesbian general interest categories. "We want dynamic and provocative articles written by, about, and for lesbians." Estab. 1991. Circ. 68,000. Pays on publication. Byline given. Offers 25% kill fee. Buys first North American serial rights. Editorial lead time 4 months. Submit seasonal material 6 months in advance. Accepts queries by mail, e-mail, fax. Sample copy for $3.95 with $2 postage. Writer's guidelines online.

Nonfiction: General interest, photo feature, travel, celebrity interview/profile. Special issues: Pride issue (June); Music issue (July/August). No essays, fiction, or poetry. **Buys 25 mss/year.** Query. Length: 200-2,500 words. **Pays $30-375.**

Photos: Send photos with submission. Buys one-time rights. Offers $50-100/photo; negotiates payment individually. Captions, identification of subjects, model releases required.

Tips: "Feature articles generally fit into 1 of the following categories: Celebrity profiles (lesbian, bisexual, or straight women who are icons for the lesbian community or actively involved in coalition-building with the lesbian community); community segment profiles—e.g., lesbian firefighters, drag kings, sports teams (multiple interviews with a variety of women in different parts of the country representing a diversity of backgrounds); noncelebrity profiles (activities of unknown or low-profile lesbian and bisexual activists/political leaders, athletes, filmmakers, dancers, writers, musicians, etc.); controversial issues (spark a dialogue about issues that divide us as a community, and the ways in which lesbians of different backgrounds fail to understand and support one another. We are not interested in inflammatory articles that incite or enrage readers without offering a channel for action); trends (community trends in a variety of areas, including sports, fashion, image, health, music, spirituality, and identity); and visual essays (most of our fashion pieces are developed and produced in-house. However, we welcome input from freelancers and from time to time publish outside work)."

N $ ECHO MAGAZINE, ACE Publishing, Inc., P.O. Box 16630, Phoenix AZ 85011-6630. (602)266-0550. Fax: (602)266-0773. E-mail: editor@echomag.com. Website: www.echomag.com. **Contact:** Buddy Early, acting editor. **30-40% freelance written.** Biweekly magazine covering gay and lesbian issues. "*Echo Magazine* is a newsmagazine for gay, lesbian, bisexual, and transgendered persons in the Phoenix metro area and throughout the state of Arizona. Editorial content needs to be pro-gay, that is, supportive of GLBT equality in all areas of American life." Estab. 1989. Circ. 15,000-18,000. Pays on publication. Publishes ms an average of less than 1 month after acceptance. Byline given. Buys all rights. Editorial lead time 1-2 months. Submit seasonal material 1-2 months in advance. Accepts queries by e-mail. Responds in 2 weeks to queries; 1 month to mss. Sample copy online. Writer's guidelines by e-mail.

Nonfiction: Book excerpts, essays, historical/nostalgic, humor, interview/profile, opinion, personal experience, photo feature, travel. Special issues: Pride Festival (April); Arts issue (August); Holiday Gift/Decor (December). No "articles on topics unrelated to our GLBT readers, or anything that is not pro-gay." **Buys 10-20 mss/year.** Query. Length: 500-2,000 words. **Pays $30-40.**

Photos: State availability with submission. Reviews contact sheets, GIF/JPEG files. Buys all rights. Negotiates payment individually. Captions, identification of subjects, model releases required.

Columns/Departments: Guest Commentary (opinion on GLBT issues), 500-1,000 words; Arts/Entertainment (profiles

of GLBT or relevant celebrities, or arts issues), 800-1,500 words. **Buys 5-10 mss/year.** Query. **Pays $30-40.**
Tips: "Know Phoenix (or other areas of Arizona) and its GLBT community. Please don't send nongay-related or nonpro-gay material. Research your topics thoroughly and write professionally. Our print content and online contenty are very similar."

$ $ $ $ GENRE, Genre Publishing, 7080 Hollywood Blvd., #818, Hollywood CA 90028. (323)467-8300. Fax: (323)467-8365. E-mail: genre@genremagazine.com. Website: www.genremagazine.com. Editor: Morris Weissinger. **Contact:** John Mok, assistant editor. **60% freelance written.** Monthly magazine. "*Genre*, America's best-selling gay men's lifestyle magazine, covers entertainment, fashion, travel and relationships in a hip, upbeat, upscale voice." Estab. 1991. Circ. 50,000. Pays on publication. Publishes ms an average of 3 months after acceptance. Byline given. Offers 25% kill fee. Buys first North American serial, electronic rights. Editorial lead time 10 weeks. Submit seasonal material 10 weeks in advance. Accepts queries by mail, e-mail, fax. Sample copy for $6.95 ($5 plus $1.95 postage). Writer's guidelines for #10 SASE.
Nonfiction: Essays, exposé, general interest, historical/nostalgic, how-to, humor, inspirational, interview/profile, new product, opinion, personal experience, photo feature, religious, travel, relationships, fashion. Not interested in articles on 2 males negotiating a sexual situation or coming out stories. **Buys variable number mss/year.** Query with published clips. Length: 500-1,500 words. **Pays $150-1,600.**
Photos: State availability with submission. Reviews contact sheets, prints (3×5 or 5×7). Buys one-time rights. Negotiates payment individually. Model releases required.
Columns/Departments: Body (how to better the body); Mind (how to better the mind); Spirit (how to better the spirit), all 700 words; Reviews (books, movies, music, travel, etc.), 500 words. **Buys variable number of mss/year.** Query with published clips or send complete ms. **Pays $200 maximum.**
Fiction: Adventure, experimental, horror, humorous, mainstream, mystery, novel excerpts, religious, romance, science fiction, slice-of-life vignettes, suspense. **Buys 10 mss/year.** Send complete ms. Length: 2,000-4,000 words.
Tips: "Like you, we take our journalistic responsibilities and ethics very seriously, and we subscribe to the highest standards of the profession. We expect our writers to represent original work that is not libelous and does not infringe upon the copyright or violate the right of privacy of any other person, firm or corporation."

$ $ GIRLFRIENDS MAGAZINE, Lesbian culture, politics, and entertainment, 3415 Cèsar Chàvez, Suite 101, San Francisco CA 94110. (415)648-9464. Fax: (415)648-4705. E-mail: jen@girlfriendsmag.com. Website: www.girlfriendsmag.com. **Contact:** Jen Phillips, assistant editor. Monthly lesbian magazine. "*Girlfriends* provides its readers with intelligent, entertaining and visually pleasing coverage of culture, politics, and entertainment—all from an informed and critical lesbian perspective." Estab. 1994. Circ. 75,000. Pays on publication. Publishes ms an average of 6 months after acceptance. Byline given. Offers 50% kill fee. Buys first rights. use for advertising/promoting *Girlfriends* Editorial lead time 3 months. Submit seasonal material 6 months in advance. Accepts queries by mail, e-mail. Accepts simultaneous submissions. Responds in 3 weeks to queries; 2 months to mss. Sample copy for $4.95 plus $1.50 s/h or online. Writer's guidelines online.

- *Girlfriends* is not accepting fiction, poetry or fillers.

O╤ Break in by sending a letter detailing interests and story ideas, plus résumé and published samples.

Nonfiction: Book excerpts, essays, exposé, historical/nostalgic, humor, interview/profile, new product, opinion, personal experience, photo feature, religious, technical, travel, investigative features. Special issues: Sex, music, bridal, sports and Hollywood issues, breast cancer issue. Special features: Best lesbian restaurants in the US; best places to live. **Buys 20-25 mss/year.** Query with published clips. Length: 1,000-3,500 words. **Pays 10-25¢/word.**
Reprints: Send photocopy or typed ms with rights for sale noted and information about when and where the material previously appeared. Negotiable payment.
Photos: Send photos with submission. Reviews contact sheets, 4×5 or 2¼ × 2¼ transparencies, prints. Buys one-time rights. Offers $30-250/photo. Captions, identification of subjects, model releases required.
Columns/Departments: Book reviews, 900 words; Music reviews, 600 words; Travel, 600 words; Opinion pieces, 1,000 words; Humor, 600 words. Query with published clips. **Pays 15¢/word.**
Tips: "Be unafraid of controversy—articles should focus on problems and debates raised in lesbian culture, politics, and sexuality. Avoid being 'politically correct.' We don't just want to know what's happening in the lesbian world, we want to know how what's happening in the world affects lesbians."

$ $ THE GUIDE, To Gay Travel, Entertainment, Politics, and Sex, Fidelity Publishing, P.O. Box 990593, Boston MA 02199-0593. (617)266-8557. Fax: (617)266-1125. E-mail: theguide@guidemag.com. Website: www.guidemag.com. **Contact:** French Wall, editor. **25% freelance written.** Monthly magazine on the gay and lesbian community. Estab. 1981. Circ. 30,000. **Pays on acceptance.** Publishes ms an average of 2 months after acceptance. Offers negotiable kill fee. Buys first rights. Submit seasonal material 2 months in advance. Accepts queries by mail, e-mail. Accepts previously published material. Accepts simultaneous submissions. Responds in 3 months to queries. Sample copy for 9×12 SAE and 8 first-class stamps. Writer's guidelines for #10 SASE.
Nonfiction: Book excerpts (if yet unpublished), essays, exposé, general interest, historical/nostalgic, humor, interview/profile, opinion, personal experience, photo feature, religious. **Buys 24 mss/year.** Query with or without published clips or send complete ms. Length: 500-5,000 words. **Pays $85-240.**
Reprints: Occasionally buys previously published submissions. Pays 100% of amount paid for an original article.
Photos: Send photos with submission. Reviews contact sheets. Buys one-time rights. Pays $15/image used. Captions, identification of subjects, model releases required.
Tips: "Brevity, humor, and militancy appreciated. Writing on sex, political analysis, and humor are particularly appreciated. We purchase very few freelance travel pieces; those that we do buy are usually on less commercial destinations."

N $ HX MAGAZINE, Two Queens, Inc., 230 W. 17th St., 8th Floor, New York NY 10011. (212)352-3535. Fax: (212)352-3596. E-mail: editor@hx.com. Website: www.hx.com. **Contact:** Trent Straube, editor. **25% freelance written.** Weekly magazine covering gay New York City nightlife and entertainment. "We publish a magazine for gay men who are interested in New York City nightlife and entertainment." Estab. 1991. Circ. 39,000. Pays on publication. Publishes ms an average of 1 month after acceptance. Byline given. Buys first North American serial, second serial (reprint), electronic rights. Editorial lead time 2 months. Submit seasonal material 2 months in advance. We must be exclusive East Coast publisher to accept. Only responds if interested to queries. Sample copy not available.
Nonfiction: General interest, arts and entertainment; celebrity profiles; reviews. **Buys 50 mss/year.** Query with published clips. Length: 500-2,000 words. **Pays $50-150; $25-100 for unsolicited articles.**
Reprints: Send tearsheet or photocopy with rights for sale noted and information about when and where the material previously appeared. Pays 50% of amount paid for an original article.
Photos: State availability with submission. Reviews contact sheets, negatives, 8×10 prints. Buys one-time, reprint and electronic reprint rights. Captions, identification of subjects, model releases required.
Columns/Departments: Buys 200 mss/year. Query with published clips. **Pays $25-125.**

$ IN THE FAMILY, The Magazine for Queer People and Their Loved Ones, Family Magazine, Inc., 7850 N. Silverbell Rd., Suite 114-188, Tucson AZ 85743. (520)579-8043. E-mail: lmarkowitz@aol.com. Website: www.inthefamily.com. **Contact:** Laura Markowitz, editor. **20% freelance written.** Quarterly magazine covering lesbian, gay, transgender, and bisexual family relationships. "Using the lens of psychotherapy, our magazine looks at the complexities of L/G/B/T family relationships as well as professional issues for L/G/B/T therapists." Estab. 1995. Circ. 3,000. Pays on publication. Publishes ms an average of 3 months after acceptance. Byline given. Offers 25% kill fee. Buys first rights. Editorial lead time 6 months. Submit seasonal material 4 months in advance. Responds in 1 month to queries; 3 months to mss. Sample copy for $6. Writer's guidelines online.
Nonfiction: Essays, exposé, humor, opinion, personal experience, photo feature. "No autobiography or erotica." **Buys 4 mss/year.** Length: 2,500-4,000 words. **Pays $100-300 for assigned articles; $35-150 for unsolicited articles.** Sometimes pays expenses of writers on assignment.
Photos: State availability with submission. Reviews contact sheets. Buys one-time rights. Negotiates payment individually. Captions, identification of subjects, model releases required.
Columns/Departments: Ellen Elgart, senior editor. Family Album (aspects of queer family life), 1,500 words; A Look at Research (relevant social science findings), 1,500 words; The Last Word (gentle humor), 800 words. **Buys 4 mss/year.** Send complete ms. **Pays $35-150.**
Fiction: Helena Lipstadt, fiction editor. Confessions, ethnic, slice-of-life vignettes, family life theme for G/L/B/Ts. No erotica, science fiction, horror, romance, serialized novels, or westerns. **Buys 4 mss/year.** Send complete ms. Length: 1,000-2,500 words. **Pays $35-100.**
Poetry: Helena Lipstadt, fiction editor. Avant-garde, free verse, haiku, light verse, traditional. **Buys 4 poems/year.** Submit maximum 6 poems. Length: 10-35 lines. **Pays $35.**
Tips: "*In the Family* takes an in-depth look at the complexities of lesbian, gay, transgender, and bisexual family relationships, including couples and intimacy, money, sex, extended family, parenting, and more. Readers include therapists of all sexual orientations as well as family members of lesbian, gay, and bisexuals, and also queer people who are interested in what therapists have to say about such themes as how to recover from a gay bashing; how to navigate single life; how to have a good divorce; how to understand bisexuality; how to come out to children; how to understand fringe sexual practices; how to reconcile homosexuality and religion. Therapists read it to learn the latest research about working with queer families, to learn from the regular case studies and clinical advice columns. Family members appreciate the multiple viewpoints in the magazine. We look for writers who know something about these issues and who have an engaging, intelligent, narrative style. We are allergic to therapy jargon and political rhetoric."

N $ $ INSTINCT MAGAZINE, Instinct Publishing, 15335 Morrison St., Suite 325, Sherman Oaks CA 91403. (818)205-9033. Fax: (818)205-9093. E-mail: editor@instinctmag.com. Website: www.instinctmag.com. Editor: Ben R. Rogers. **Contact:** Alexander Cho, associate editor. **60% freelance written.** Monthly magazine covering gay men's life and style issues. "*Instinct* is a blend of *Cosmo* and *Maxim* for gay men. We're smart, sexy, irreverent, and more than a bit un-PC, a unique style that has made us the No. 1 gay men's magazine in the U.S." Estab. 1997. Circ. 60,000+. Pays on publication. Byline given. Offers 20% kill fee. Buys all rights. Editorial lead time 2 months. Accepts queries by mail, e-mail, phone. Accepts simultaneous submissions. Sample copy online. Writer's guidelines free.
Nonfiction: "Be inventive and specific—an article on 'dating' isn't saying much and will need a twist, for example." Exposé, general interest, humor, interview/profile, personal experience, travel. **Buys 10 mss/year.** Query with or without published clips. Length: 800-2,400 words. **Pays $150-300.** Sometimes pays expenses of writers on assignment.
Photos: Buys all rights. Negotiates payment individually. Captions, identification of subjects, model releases required.
Columns/Departments: Health (gay, off-kilter), 800 words; Fitness (irreverent), 500 words; Movies, Books (edgy, sardonic), 800 words; Music, Video Games (indie, underground), 800 words. **Pays $150-250.**
Tips: "While *Instinct* publishes a wide variety of features and columns having to do with gay men's issues, we maintain our signature irreverent, edgy, un-PC tone throughout. When pitching stories (e-mail is preferred), be as specific as possible, and try to think beyond the normal scope of 'gay relationship' features. An article on 'Dating Tips,' for example, will not be considered, while an article on 'Tips on Dating Two Guys At Once' is more our slant."

$ $ $ METROSOURCE, MetroSource Publishing, Inc., 180 Varick St., 5th Floor, New York NY 10014. (212)691-5127. Fax: (212)741-2978. E-mail: rwalsh@metrosource.com; eandersson@metrosource.com; letters@metrosource.com. Website: www.metrosource.com. **Contact:** Richard Walsh, editor-in-chief; Paul Hagen, assistant editor; Nick Steele, creative director. **70% freelance written.** Magazine published 5 times/year. "*MetroSource* is an upscale, glossy, 4-color lifestyle magazine targeted to an urban, professional gay and lesbian readership." Estab. 1990. Circ. 85,000. Pays on publication. Publishes ms an average of 2 months after acceptance. Byline given. Editorial lead time 3 months. Submit seasonal material 4 months in advance. Accepts queries by mail, e-mail, fax, phone. Accepts simultaneous submissions. Sample copy for $5.

Nonfiction: Exposé, interview/profile, opinion, photo feature, travel. **Buys 20 mss/year.** Query with published clips. Length: 1,000-2,500 words. **Pays $100-900.**

Photos: State availability with submission. Negotiates payment individually. Captions, model releases required.

Columns/Departments: Book, film, television, and stage reviews; health columns; and personal diary and opinion pieces. Word lengths vary. Query with published clips. **Pays $200.**

$ OUT, 80 8th Ave., Suite 315, New York NY 10011. (212)242-8100. Fax: (212)242-8338. Website: www.out.com. Editor-in-Chief: Brendan Lemon. **Contact:** Department Editor. **80% freelance written.** Monthly national magazine covering gay and lesbian general-interest topics. "Our subjects range from current affairs to culture, from fitness to finance." Estab. 1992. Circ. 120,000. Pays on publication. Publishes ms an average of 3 months after acceptance. Byline given. Offers 25% kill fee. Buys first North American serial rights. second serial (reprint) rights for anthologies (additional fee paid) and 30-day reprint rights (additional fee paid if applicable) Editorial lead time 3 months. Submit seasonal material 5 months in advance. Accepts queries by mail. Accepts simultaneous submissions. Responds in 6 weeks to queries; 2 months to mss. Sample copy for $6. Writer's guidelines for #10 SASE.

Nonfiction: Book excerpts, essays, exposé, general interest, historical/nostalgic, humor, interview/profile, new product, opinion, personal experience, photo feature, travel, fashion/lifestyle. **Buys 200 mss/year.** Query with published clips and SASE. Length: 50-1,500 words. **Pays variable rate.** Sometimes pays expenses of writers on assignment.

Photos: State availability with submission. Reviews contact sheets, transparencies, prints. Buys one-time rights. Negotiates payment individually. Captions, identification of subjects, model releases required.

Tips: "*Out*'s contributors include editors and writers from the country's top consumer titles: Skilled reporters, columnists, and writers with distinctive voices and specific expertise in the fields they cover. But while published clips and relevant experience are a must, the magazine also seeks out fresh, young voices. The best guide to the kind of stories we publish is to review our recent issues—is there a place for the story you have in mind? Be aware of our long lead time. No phone queries, please."

$ OUTSMART, Up & Out Communications, 3406 Audubon Place, Houston TX 77006. (713)520-7237. Fax: (713)522-3275. E-mail: tim@outsmartmagazine.com. Website: www.outsmartmagazine.com. **Contact:** Tim Brookovev, editor. **70% freelance written.** Monthly magazine concerned with gay, lesbian, bisexual, and transgender issues. "*OutSmart* offers vibrant and thoughtful coverage of the stories that appeal most to an educated gay audience." Estab. 1994. Circ. 60,000. Pays on publication. Byline given. Buys one-time, simultaneous rights. Permission to publish on website. Editorial lead time 3 months. Submit seasonal material 4 months in advance. Accepts queries by mail, e-mail, fax. Accepts previously published material. Accepts simultaneous submissions. Responds in 6 weeks to queries; 2 months to mss. Sample copy and writer's guidelines online.

Nonfiction: Historical/nostalgic, interview/profile, opinion, personal experience, photo feature, travel, health/wellness; local/national news. **Buys 24 mss/year.** Send complete ms. Length: 450-2,000 words. **Negotiates payment individually.**

Reprints: Send photocopy.

Photos: State availability with submission. Reviews 4×6 prints. Buys one-time rights. Negotiates payment individually. Identification of subjects required.

The online magazine carries original content not found in the print edition and includes writer's guidelines.

Tips: "*OutSmart* is a mainstream publication that covers culture, politics, personalities, entertainment, and health/wellness as well as local and national news and events. It is our goal to address the diversity of the lesbian, gay, bisexual, and transgender community, fostering understanding among all Houston's citizens."

$ WISCONSIN IN STEP, In Step, Inc., 1661 N. Water St., #411, Milwaukee WI 53202. (414)278-7840. Fax: (414)278-5868. E-mail: editor@instepnews.com. Website: www.instepnews.com. Managing Editor: Jorge Cabal. **Contact:** William Attewell, editor. **30% freelance written.** Biweekly consumer tabloid for gay and lesbian readers. Estab. 1984. Circ. 15,000. Buys first North American serial, second serial (reprint) rights. Submit seasonal material 2 months in advance. Accepts queries by mail, e-mail. Accepts simultaneous submissions. Responds in 3 weeks to queries; 1 month to mss. Sample copy for $3. Writer's guidelines for #10 SASE.

Nonfiction: Book excerpts, exposé, historical/nostalgic, interview/profile, new product, opinion, religious, travel. Query. Length: 500-2,000 words. **Pays $15-100.**

Photos: State availability with submission. Reviews 5×7 prints. Buys one-time rights. Negotiates payment individually. Captions, identification of subjects, model releases required.

The online magazine carries original content not found in the print edition. Contact: William Attewell, online editor.

Tips: "E-mail flawless copy samples to get my attention. Be patient."

GENERAL INTEREST

General interest magazines need writers who can appeal to a broad audience—teens and senior citizens, wealthy readers, and the unemployed. Each magazine still has a personality that suits

its audience—one that a writer should study before sending material to an editor. Other markets for general interest material are in these Consumer sections: Contemporary Culture; Ethnic/Minority; Inflight; Men's; Regional; and Women's.

$ AMERICAN PROFILE, Publishing Group of America, 341 Cool Springs Blvd., Suite 400, Franklin TN 37067. (615)468-6000. Fax: (615)468-6100. E-mail: editorial@americanprofile.com. Website: www.americanprofile.com. **Contact:** Peter Fossel, editor. **95% freelance written.** Weekly magazine with national and regional editorial celebrating the people, places, and experiences of hometowns across America. The 4-color magazine is distributed through small to medium-size community newspapers. Estab. 2000. Circ. 4,600,000. **Pays on acceptance.** Byline given. Buys first, electronic, 6-month exclusive rights rights. Editorial lead time 3 months. Submit seasonal material 6 months in advance. Accepts queries by mail. Responds in 1 month to queries; 1 month to mss. Writer's guidelines online.

• In addition to a query, first-time writers should include 2-3 published clips.

Nonfiction: General interest, how-to, interview/profile. No fiction, nostalgia, poetry, essays. **Buys 250 mss/year.** Query with published clips. Length: 450-1,200 words. Pays expenses of writers on assignment.

Photos: State availability with submission. Reviews transparencies. Buys one-time rights, nonexclusive after 6 months. Negotiates payment individually. Captions, identification of subjects, model releases required.

Columns/Departments: Health; Family; Finances; Home; Gardening.

Tips: "We appreciate hard-copy submissions and 1-paragraph queries for short manuscripts (fewer than 500 words) on food, gardening, nature, profiles, health, and home projects for small-town audiences. Must be out of the ordinary. Please visit the website to see our writing style."

$ $ $ $ THE ATLANTIC MONTHLY, 77 N. Washington St., Boston MA 02114. (617)854-7749. Fax: (617)854-7877. Website: www.theatlantic.com. Editor: Michael Kelly. Managing Editor: Cullen Murphy. **Contact:** C. Michael Curtis, senior editor. Monthly magazine of arts and public affairs. General magazine for an educated readership with broad cultural interests. Estab. 1857. Circ. 500,000. **Pays on acceptance.** Byline given. Buys first North American serial rights. Accepts queries by mail. Response time varies to queries Responds in 2 months or less to mss to mss. Writer's guidelines online.

Nonfiction: Reportage preferred. Book excerpts, essays, general interest, humor, personal experience, religious, travel. Query with or without published clips or send complete ms. All unsolicited mss must be accompanied by SASE. Length: 1,000-6,000 words. **Payment varies**. Sometimes pays expenses of writers on assignment.

Fiction: C. Michael Curtis, senior editor. "Seeks fiction that is clear, tightly written with strong sense of 'story' and well-defined characters." Literary and contemporary fiction. "Seeks fiction that is clear, tightly written with strong sense of 'story' and well-defined characters." **Buys 10-12 mss/year.** Send complete ms. Length: 2,000-6,000 words. **Pays $3,000.**

Poetry: Peter Davison, poetry editor. **Buys 40-60 poems/year.**

The online magazine carries original content not found in the print edition. Contact: Kate Bacon, online editor.

Tips: Writers should be aware that this is not a market for beginner's work (nonfiction and fiction), nor is it truly for intermediate work. Study this magazine before sending only your best, most professional work. When making first contact, "cover letters are sometimes helpful, particularly if they cite prior publications or involvement in writing programs. Common mistakes: melodrama, inconclusiveness, lack of development, unpersuasive characters and/or dialogue."

$ BIBLIOPHILOS, A Journal of History, Literature, and the Liberal Arts, The Bibliophile Publishing Co., Inc., 200 Security Building, Fairmont WV 26554. (304)366-8107. **Contact:** Dr. Gerald J. Bobango, editor. **65-70% freelance written.** Quarterly literary magazine concentrating on 19th century American and European history and literature. "We see ourself as a forum for new and unpublished writers, historians, philosophers, literary critics and reviewers, and those who love animals. Audience is academic-oriented, college graduate, who believes in traditional Aristotelian-Thomistic thought and education, and has a fair streak of the Luddite in him/her. Our ideal reader owns no television, has never sent nor received e-mail, and avoids shopping malls at any cost. He loves books." Estab. 1981. Circ. 400. Pays on publication. Publishes ms an average of 9 months after acceptance. Byline given. Buys first North American serial rights. Editorial lead time 6 months. Submit seasonal material 6 months in advance. Accepts queries by mail. Accepts simultaneous submissions. Responds in 2 weeks to queries; 1 month to mss. Sample copy for $5.25., Writer's guidelines for 9½×4 SAE with 2 first-class Stamps.

Break in with "either prose or poetry which is illustrative of man triumphing over and doing without technology, pure Ludditism, if need be. Send material critical of the socialist welfare state, constantly expanding federal government (or government at all levels), or exposing the inequities of affirmative action, political correctness, and the mass media packaging of political candidates. We want to see a pre-1960 worldview."

Nonfiction: Book excerpts, essays, general interest, historical/nostalgic, humor, interview/profile, opinion, personal experience, photo feature, travel, book review-essay, literary criticism. Special issues: Upcoming theme issues include an annual all book-review issue, containing 10-15 reviews and review-essays, or poetry about books and reading. Does not want to see "anything that Oprah would recommend, or that Erma Bombeck or Ann Landers would think humorous or interesting. No 'I found Jesus and it changed my life' material." **Buys 25-30 mss/year.** Query by mail only. Length: 1,500-3,000 words. **Pays $5-35.**

Photos: State availability with submission. Reviews b&w 4×6 prints. Buys one-time rights. Negotiates payment individually. Identification of subjects required.

Columns/Departments: Features (fiction and nonfiction, short stories), 1,500-3,000 words; Poetry (batches of 5, preferably thematically related), 3-150 lines; Reviews (book reviews or review essays on new books or individual authors, current and past), 1,000-1,500 words; Opinion (man triumphing over technology and technocrats, the facade of modern education, computer fetishism), 1,000-1,500 words. **Buys 20 mss/year.** Query by mail only. **Pays $25-40.**

Fiction: Adventure, ethnic, historical, horror, humorous, mainstream, mystery, novel excerpts, romance, slice-of-life vignettes, suspense, western, utopian, Orwellian. "No 'I found Jesus and it turned my life around'; no 'I remember Mama, who was a saint and I miss her terribly'; no gay or lesbian topics; no drug culture material; nothing harping on political correctness; nothing to do with healthy living, HMOs, medical programs, or the welfare state, unless it is against statism in these areas." **Buys 25-30 mss/year.** Length: 1,500-3,000 words. **Pays $25-40.**

Poetry: "Formal and rhymed verse gets read first." Free verse, light verse, traditional, political satire, doggerel.

N $ $ CIA—CITIZEN IN AMERICA, CIA—Citizen in America, Inc., 30 Ford St., Glen Cove, Long Island NY 11542. (516)671-4047. E-mail: ciamc@webtv.net. **Contact:** John J. Maddox, magazine coordinator. **100% freelance written.** Magazine published 9 times/year covering first amendment responsibilities. "*CIA—Citizen in America* trys to strengthen democracy here and abroad by allowing the freedom of expression in all forms possible through the press. *CIA* does not shy away from controversy." Estab. 1998. Pays on publication. Publishes ms an average of 3 months after acceptance. Byline sometimes given. Offers $100 kill fee. Buys first North American serial, first, one-time, simultaneous rights, makes work-for-hire assignments. Accepts queries by mail, e-mail, phone. Accepts simultaneous submissions. Responds in 2 weeks to queries; 1-2 months to mss. Sample copy for $10. Writer's guidelines for #10 SASE.

Nonfiction: Essays, exposé, general interest, historical/nostalgic, humor, inspirational, opinion, personal experience, religious, travel. Does not want "any manuscript that deliberately exploits or promotes racial, religious, or gender bigotry." **Buys 175+ mss/year.** Send complete ms. Length: 2,200 words maximum. **Pays $100-600, plus 1 copy for assigned articles; $42-100, plus 1 copy for unsolicited articles.**

Photos: State availability with submission. Reviews 4×6 prints. Offers no additional payment for photos accepted with ms. Identification of subjects required.

Columns/Departments: Say It (freedom of speech on any subject), 100 words; A Choice of Humor (humor, made up or heard), 250 words; Second Time Around (those who had 2+ marriages, with comments), 50 words; Academe (photos of individuals who are in college, with brief bio), 50 words. **Buys 90+ mss/year.** Send complete ms. **Pays $10.**

Fiction: Adventure, erotica, ethnic, experimental, historical, humorous, mainstream, religious, romance, science fiction, slice-of-life vignettes, western, war stories. No screen or plays. **Buys 100+ mss/year.** Send complete ms. Length: 250-2,500 words. **Pays $42-100.**

Poetry: Avant-garde, free verse, light verse, traditional. No poems "with no meaning intended." **Buys 45+ poems/year.** Submit maximum 5 poems. Length: 50 lines maximum.

Fillers: Anecdotes, facts, short humor. **Buys 25+/year.** Length: 200 words maximum. **Pays $10.**

Tips: "Writers should consciously shy away from getting an 'ego' or 'celebrity' boost in this publication. Therefore, writers should have a fervent desire to publish work for others to read. Rule of thumb is: If the writer feels good writing it, *CIA* will feel the same reading and, hopefully, publishing it."

$ $ $ DIVERSION, 1790 Broadway, New York NY 10019. (212)969-7500. Fax: (212)969-7557. Website: www.diversion.com. **Contact:** Ed Wetschler, editor-in-chief. Monthly magazine covering travel and lifestyle, edited for physicians. "*Diversion* offers an eclectic mix of interests beyond medicine. Regular features include stories on domestic and foreign travel destinations, food and wine, sports cars, gardening, photography, books, electronic gear, and the arts. Although *Diversion* doesn't cover health subjects, it does feature profiles of doctors who excel at nonmedical pursuits or who engage in medical volunteer work." Estab. 1973. Circ. 176,000. Pays 3 months after acceptance. Byline given. Offers 25% kill fee. Editorial lead time 4 months. Responds in 1 month to queries. Sample copy for $4.50. Guidelines available.

- Break in by "querying with a brief proposal describing the focus of the story and why it would interest our readers. Include credentials and published clips."

Nonfiction: "We get so many travel and food queries that we're hard pressed to even read them all. Far better to query us on culture, the arts, sports, technology, etc." **Buys 70 mss/year.** Query with proposal, published clips, and author's credentials. Length: 1,800-2,000 words. **Pays $50-1,200.**

Columns/Departments: Travel, food & wine, photography, gardening, cars, technology. Length: 1,200 words.

N $ EBONY, Johnson Publishing Company, Inc., 820 S. Michigan Ave., Chicago IL 60605. (312)322-9200. Fax: (312)322-9375. Website: www.ebony.com. Editor: Lerone Bennett Jr. Monthly magazine covering topics ranging from education and history to entertainment, art, government, health, travel, sports and social events. African-American oriented consumer interest magazine. Circ. 1,728,986. Editorial lead time 3 months. Sample copy not available.

$ EDUCATION IN FOCUS, Books for All Times, Inc., P.O. Box 202, Warrenton VA 20188. (540)428-3175. E-mail: staff@bfat.com. Website: www.bfat.com. **Contact:** Joe David, editor. **80% freelance written.** Semiannual newsletter for public interested in education issues at all levels. "We are always looking for intelligent articles that provide educationally sound ideas that enhance the understanding of what is happening or what should be happening in our schools today. We are not looking for material that might be published by the Department of Education. Instead we want material from liberated and mature thinkers and writers, tamed by reason and humanitarianism." Estab. 1989. Circ. 1,000. **Pays on acceptance.** Publishes ms an average of 2 months after acceptance. Byline given. Buys first, one-time, second serial (reprint), book, newsletter and internet rights rights. Editorial lead time 2 months. Accepts queries by mail, e-mail. Accepts simultaneous submissions. Responds in 1 month to queries. Sample copy for #10 SASE.

Nonfiction: "We prefer documented, intelligent articles that deeply inform. The best way to be quickly rejected is to send articles that defend the public school system as it is today, or was!" Book excerpts, exposé, general interest. **Buys 4-6 mss/year.** Query with published clips or send complete ms. Length: 3,000 words. Some longer articles can be broken into 2 articles—1 for each issue. **Pays $25-75.**

Tips: "Maintain an honest voice and a clear focus on the subject."

$ $ GRIT, American Life and Traditions, Ogden Publications, 1503 SW 42nd St., Topeka KS 66609-1265. (785)274-4300. Fax: (785)274-4305. E-mail: grit@grit.com. Website: www.grit.com. **Contact:** Ann Crahan, editor-in-chief. **90% freelance written.** Open to new writers. Biweekly. "*Grit* is good news. As a wholesome, family-oriented magazine published for more than a century and distributed nationally, *Grit* features articles about family lifestyles, traditions, values, and pastimes. *Grit* accents the best of American life and traditions—past and present. Our readers are ordinary people doing extraordinary things, with courage, heart, determination, and imagination. Many of them live in small towns and rural areas across the country; others live in cities but share many of the values typical of small-town America." Estab. 1882. Circ. 90,000. Pays on publication. Byline given. Buys first North American serial, first, one-time rights. Submit seasonal material 6 months in advance. Accepts queries by mail. Sample copy and writer's guidelines for $4 and 11 × 14 SASE with 4 first-class stamps. Sample articles on website.

O→ Break in through Departments such as Pet Tales, Looking Back, Poetry.

Nonfiction: The best way to sell work is by reading each issue cover to cover. Humor, interview/profile, features (timely, newsworthy, touching but with a *Grit* angle), readers' true stories, outdoor hobbies, collectibles, gardening, crafts, hobbies, leisure pastimes. Special issues: Gardening (January-October); Health (twice a year); Travel (spring and fall); Collectibles; Pet issue; Christmas. Query by mail only. Prefers full ms with photos. Length: Main features run 1,200-1,500 words. Department features average 800-1,000 words. **Pays 15¢/word for features; plays flat rate for departments.**

Photos: Professional quality photos (b&w prints or color slides/prints) increase acceptability of articles. Send photos with submission. Pays up to $25 each in features according to quality, placement, and color/b&w. Payment for department photos included in flat rate.

Fiction: Fiction Department. Short stories, 1,500-2,000 words; may also purchase accompanying art if of high quality and appropriate. Need serials (romance, westerns, mysteries), 3,500-10,000 words. Send ms with SASE to Fiction Dept. Adventure, condensed novels, mainstream, mystery, religious, romance, science fiction, western, nostalgia. "No sex, violence, drugs, obscene words, abuse, alcohol, or negative diatribes." Send complete ms. Length: 1,200-4,000-6,000 words.

Tips: "Articles should be directed to a national audience, mostly 40 years and older. Sources identified fully. Our readers are warm and loving. They want to read about others with heart. Tell us stories about someone unusual, an unsung hero, an artist of the backroads, an interesting trip with an emotional twist, a memory with a message, an ordinary person accomplishing extraordinary things. Tell us stories that will make us cry with joy." Send complete ms with photos for consideration.

$ $ $ $ HARPER'S MAGAZINE, 666 Broadway, 11th Floor, New York NY 10012. (212)420-5720. Fax: (212)228-5889. Website: www.harpers.org. Editor: Lewis H. Lapham. **Contact:** Ann Gollin, editor's assistant. **90% freelance written.** Monthly magazine for well-educated, socially concerned, widely read men and women who value ideas and good writing. "*Harper's Magazine* encourages national discussion on current and significant issues in a format that offers arresting facts and intelligent opinions. By means of its several shorter journalistic forms—Harper's Index, Readings, Forum, and Annotation—as well as with its acclaimed essays, fiction, and reporting, *Harper's* continues the tradition begun with its first issue in 1850: to inform readers across the whole spectrum of political, literary, cultural, and scientific affairs." Estab. 1850. Circ. 216,000. **Pays on acceptance.** Publishes ms an average of 3 months after acceptance. Offers negotiable kill fee. Vary with author and material. Accepts previously published material. Responds in 6 weeks to queries. Sample copy for $3.95.

Nonfiction: "For writers working with agents or who will query first only, our requirements are: public affairs, literary, international and local reporting, and humor." Publishes 1 major report/issue. Length: 4,000-6,000 words. Publishes 1 major essay/issue. Length: 4,000-6,000 words. "These should be construed as topical essays on all manner of subjects (politics, the arts, crime, business, etc.) to which the author can bring the force of passionate and informed statement." Humor. No interviews; no profiles. No unsolicited poems will be accepted. **Buys 2 mss/year.** Complete ms and query must include SASE. Length: 4,000-6,000 words.

Reprints: Accepted for Readings section. Send typed ms with rights for sale noted and information about when and where the article previously appeared.

Photos: Occasionally purchased with ms; others by assignment. Stacey Clarkson, art director. State availability with submission. Pays $50-500.

Fiction: Publishes 1 short story/month. Humorous. Query. Length: 3,000-5,000 words. **Generally pays 50¢-$1/word.**

Tips: "Some readers expect their magazines to clothe them with opinions in the way that Bloomingdale's dresses them for the opera. The readers of *Harper's Magazine* belong to a different crowd. They strike me as the kind of people who would rather think in their own voices and come to their own conclusions."

$ $ $ $ HOPE MAGAZINE, How to be Part of the Solution, Hope Publishing, Inc., P.O. Box 160, Brooklin ME 04616. (207)359-4651. Fax: (207)359-8920. E-mail: info@hopemag.com. Website: www.hopemag.com. Editor-in-chief/Publisher: Jon Wilson. Editor: Kimberly Ridley. Associate Editor: Lane Fisher. Assistant Editor: Todd Nelson. **Contact:** Sarah T. Bray, editorial assistant. **90% freelance written.** Bimonthly magazine covering humanity at its best and worst. "*Hope* is a solutions-oriented journal focused on people addressing personal and societal challenges with uncommon courage and integrity. A magazine free of religious, political, or New Age affiliation, *Hope* awakens the impulse we all have—however hidden or distant—to make our world more liveable, humane, and genuinely loving. We strive to evoke empathy among readers." Estab. 1996. Circ. 22,000. Pays on publication. Publishes ms an average of 6 months after acceptance. Byline given. Offers 20% kill fee. Buys first, one-time, second serial (reprint) rights. Editorial lead time 4 months. Submit seasonal material 6 months in advance. Accepts queries by mail. Accepts simultaneous submissions. Responds in 6 months to queries. Sample copy for $5. Writer's guidelines online.

Nonfiction: Book excerpts, essays, general interest, interview/profile, personal experience, photo feature, features. Nothing explicitly religious, political or New Age. **Buys 50-75 mss/year.** Query with published clips or writing samples and SASE. Length: 250-3,000 words. **Pays $50-1,500.** Sometimes pays expenses of writers on assignment.

Photos: "We are very interested in and committed to the photo essay form, and enthusiastically encourage photographers and photojournalists to query us with ideas, or to submit images for thematic photo essays." State availability of or send photos with submission. Reviews contact sheets, 5×7 prints. Buys one-time rights. Negotiates payment individually. Captions, identification of subjects required.

Columns/Departments: Departments Editor. Signs of Hope (inspiring dispatches/news), 250-500 words; Arts of Hope (reviews and discussions of music, art, and literature related to hope), 1,000-2,000 words; Book Reviews (devoted primarily to nonfiction works in widely diverse subject areas related to struggle and triumph), 500-800 words. **Buys 50-60 mss/year.** Query with published clips or send complete ms and SASE. **Pays $50-150.**

Tips: "Write very personally, and very deeply. We're not looking for shallow 'feel-good' pieces. Approach uncommon subjects. Cover the ordinary in extraordinary ways. Go to the heart. Surprise us. Many stories we receive are too 'soft.' Absolutely no phone queries."

N $ INTERNET WORLD, Penton Media, 16 Thorndal Circle, Darien CT 06820-5421. (203)559-2919. Fax: (203)559-2910. E-mail: editors@iw.com. Website: www.internetworld.com. Executive Editor: John Zipperer. Managing Editor: Jennifer Hawthorne. Monthly magazine. Edited for internet professionals - today's experts in, Internet business strategy, technical implementation, programing and design. Circ. 225,000. Editorial lead time 6 weeks. Sample copy not available.

$ MESSENGER MAGAZINE, Everyone Learns by Reading, Topaz Marketing & Distributing, 1014 Franklin SE, Grand Rapids MI 49507-1327. (616)243-4114, ext. 20. E-mail: wmathis@orimessenger.org. Website: www.themessengermagazine.com. President & CEO: Patricia E. Mathis. **Contact:** Walter L. Mathis, Sr., executive director. Semimonthly magazine covering African Americans and other ethnic groups that promotes education and economic empowerment for all people. "We are guided by the principles of fine press and are open to everyone regardless of their race, gender or religion." Estab. 1998. Circ. 10,000/issue. Pays on publication. Byline given. Buys unlimited rights and makes work-for-hire assignments. Editorial lead time 1 month. Submit seasonal material 1 month in advance. Accepts queries by mail, e-mail. Responds in 2 weeks to queries. Sample copy online. Writer's guidelines online.

Nonfiction: Topics must pertain to the following categories: education, economics/finance, business, technology, health, arts/culture, politics, family/society, history, or seasonal pieces. Length: 250-1,000 words. **Pays up to $25. All paid articles must be requested and approved by the president/CEO.**

Photos: Every article must included photograph(s); exceptioins within discretion of editor. Negotiates payment individually. Identification of subjects, model releases required.

Tips: "We do not pay for stories sent in to us that are not requested by us. If you send us an article, and we publish it, there will be no fees."

N $ NEW YORK TIMES UPFRONT, Scholastic, Inc., 557 Broadway, New York NY 10012-3999. (212)343-6239. Fax: (212)343-6659. E-mail: pyoung@scholastic.com. Website: www.upfrontmagazine.com. Editor: Peter Young. Biweekly magazine. Collaboration between The New York Times and Scholastic, Inc. designed as a news magazine specifically for teenagers. Circ. 200,000. Editorial lead time 1-2 months. Sample copy not available.

$ THE NEW YORKER, The New Yorker, Inc., 4 Times Square, New York NY 10036. (212) 286-5900. Website: www.newyorker.com. Editor: David Remnick. Weekly magazine. A quality magazine of interesting, well-written stories, articles, essays and poems for a literate audience. Estab. 1925. Circ. 750,000. **Pays on acceptance.** Responds in 3 months to mss. Writer's guidelines online.

- *The New Yorker* receives approximately 4,000 submissions per month.
- For e-mail submissions: fiction@newyorker.com (fiction); talkofthetown@newyorker.com (Talk of the Town); shouts@newyorker.com (Shouts & Murmurs); poetry@newyorker.com (poetry).

Fiction: Deborah Treisman, fiction editor. Publishes 1 ms/issue. Send complete ms. **Payment varies.**

Poetry: Send poetry to "Poetry Department."

Tips: "Be lively, original, not overly literary. Write what you want to write, not what you think the editor would like."

$ $ $ THE OLD FARMER'S ALMANAC, Yankee Publishing, Inc., Main St., Dublin NH 03444. (603)563-8111. Fax: (603)563-8252. Website: www.almanac.com. **Contact:** Janice Stillman, editor. **95% freelance written.** Annual magazine covering weather, gardening, history, oddities, lore. "*The Old Farmer's Almanac* is the oldest continuously published periodical in North America. Since 1792, it has provided useful information for people in all walks of life: tide tables for those who live near the ocean; sunrise tables and planting charts for those who live on the farm or simply enjoy gardening; recipes for those who like to cook; and forecasts for those who don't like the question of weather left up in the air. The words of the *Almanac*'s founder, Robert B. Thomas, guide us still. 'Our main endeavor is to be useful, but with a pleasant degree of humour.'" Estab. 1792. Circ. 3,750,000. **Pays on acceptance.** Publishes ms an average of 9 months after acceptance. Byline given. Offers 33% kill fee. Buys first North American serial, electronic, all rights. Editorial lead time 6 months. Submit seasonal material 1 year in advance. Accepts queries by mail. Responds in 3 weeks to queries; 2 months to mss. Sample copy for $5 at bookstores or online. Writer's guidelines online.

Nonfiction: General interest, historical/nostalgic, how-to (garden, cook, save money), humor, weather, natural remedies, obscure facts, history, popular culture. No personal weather recollections/accounts, personal/family histories. Query with published clips. Length: 800-2,500 words. **Pays 65¢/word.** Sometimes pays expenses of writers on assignment.

Fillers: Anecdotes, short humor. **Buys 1-2/year.** Length: 100-200 words. **Pays 50¢/word.**

The online magazine carries original content not found in the print edition.

Tips: "Read it. Think differently. Read writer's guidelines online."

$ OPEN SPACES, Open Spaces Publications, Inc., PMB 134, 6327-C SW Capitol Hwy., Portland OR 97239-1937. (503)227-5764. Fax: (503)227-3401. E-mail: info@open-spaces.com. Website: www.open-spaces.com. President: Penny Harrison. Managing Editor: James Bradley. **Contact:** Elizabeth Arthur, editor. **95% freelance written.** Quarterly general interest magazine. "*Open Spaces* is a forum for informed writing and intelligent thought. Articles are written by experts in various fields. Audience is varied (CEOs and rock climbers, politicos and university presidents, etc.) but is highly educated and loves to read good writing." Estab. 1997. Pays on publication. Publishes ms an average of 6 months after acceptance. Byline given. Offers 20% kill fee. Rights purchased vary with author and material. Editorial lead time 9 months. Accepts queries by mail, fax. Accepts simultaneous submissions. Sample copy for $10 or online. Writer's guidelines online.

Nonfiction: Essays, general interest, historical/nostalgic, how-to (if clever), humor, interview/profile, personal experience, travel. **Buys 35 mss/year.** Query with published clips. Length: 1,500-2,500 words; major articles: 2,500-6,000 words. **Pays variable amount.**

Photos: State availability with submission. Buys one-time rights. Captions, identification of subjects required.

Columns/Departments: David Williams, departments editor. Books (substantial topics such as the Booker Prize, The Newbery, etc.); Travel (must reveal insight); Sports (past subjects include rowing, swing dancing, and ultimate); Unintended Consequences, 1,500-2,500 words. **Buys 20-25 mss/year.** Query with published clips or send complete ms. **Payment varies.**

Fiction: Ellen Teicher, fiction editor. "Quality is far more important than type. Read the magazine." "Excellence is the issue - not subject matter." **Buys 8 mss/year.** Length: 2,000-6,000 words. **Pay varies.**

Poetry: "Again, quality is far more important than type." Susan Juve-Hu Bucharest, poetry editor. Submit maximum 3 poems with SASE.

Fillers: Anecdotes, short humor, cartoons; interesting or amusing Northwest facts; expressions, etc.

Tips: "*Open Spaces* reviews all manuscripts submitted in hopes of finding writing of the highest quality. We present a Northwest perspective as well as a national and international one. Best advice is read the magazine."

$ THE OXFORD AMERICAN, The Southern Magazine of Good Writing, The Oxford American, Inc., 303 President Clinton Ave., Little Rock AR 72201. (501)907-6418. Fax: (501)907-6419. E-mail: smirnoff@oxfordamericanmag.com. Website: www.oxfordamericanmag.com. Editor: Marc Smirnoff. **Contact:** Editorial Staff. **50-65% freelance written.** Bimonthly magazine covering the South. "*The Oxford American* is a general-interest literary magazine about the South." Estab. 1992. Circ. 30,000. Pays on publication. Publishes ms an average of 6 months after acceptance. Byline given. Offers 25% kill fee. Buys first North American serial, first, one-time rights. Editorial lead time 2 months. Submit seasonal material 4 months in advance. Accepts queries by mail. Responds in 3 weeks to queries; 3 months to mss. Sample copy for $6.50. Writer's guidelines online.

- Break in with "a brief, focused query highlighting the unusual, fresh aspects to your pitch, and clips. All pitches must have some Southern connection."

Nonfiction: Essays, general interest, humor, interview/profile, personal experience, reporting, memoirs concerning the South. **Buys 6 mss/year.** Query with published clips or send complete ms. **Payment varies.** Sometimes pays expenses of writers on assignment.

Photos: Buys one-time rights. Negotiates payment individually. Captions required.

Columns/Departments: Send complete ms. **Payment varies.**

Fiction: Marc Smirnoff, editor. Novel excerpts, short stories. **Buys 10 mss/year.** Send complete ms. **Payment varies.**

Tips: "Like other editors, I stress the importance of being familiar with the magazine. Those submitters who know the magazine always send in better work because they know what we're looking for. To those who don't bother to at least flip through the magazine, let me point out we only publish articles with some sort of Southern connection."

$$$$ PARADE, The Sunday Magazine, Parade Publications, Inc., 711 Third Ave., New York NY 10017. (212)450-7000. Fax: (212)450-7284. E-mail: steven_florio@parade.com. Website: www.parade.com. Editor: Lee Kravitz. Managing Editor: Lamar Graham. **Contact:** Steven Florio, assistant editor. **95% freelance written.** Weekly magazine for a general interest audience. Estab. 1941. Circ. 81,000,000. **Pays on acceptance.** Publishes ms an average of 5 months after acceptance. Kill fee varies in amount. Buys one-time, all rights. Editorial lead time 1 month. Accepts queries by mail, fax. Accepts simultaneous submissions. Sample copy online. Writer's guidelines online.

Nonfiction: Publishes general interest (on health, trends, social issues or anything of interest to a broad general audience), interview/profile (of news figures, celebrities and people of national significance), and "provocative topical pieces of news value." Spot news events are not accepted, as *Parade* has a 2-month lead time. No fiction, fashion, travel, poetry, cartoons, nostalgia, regular columns, personal essays, quizzes, or fillers. Unsolicited queries concerning celebrities, politicians, sports figures, or technical are rarely assigned. **Buys 150 mss/year.** Query with published clips. Length: 1,000-1,200 words. **Pays $2,500 minimum.** Pays expenses of writers on assignment.

Tips: "If the writer has a specific expertise in the proposed topic, it increases a writer's chances for breaking in. Send a well-researched, well-written 1-page proposal and enclose a SASE. Do not submit completed manuscripts."

N $ PEOPLE, Time, Inc., 1271 Avenue of The Americas, New York NY 10020. (212)522-1212. Fax: (212)522-1359. E-mail: editor@people.com. Website: www.people.com. Editor-in-Chief: Noman Pearlstine. Weekly magazine. Designed as a forumn for personality journalism through the of short articles on contemporary news events and people. Circ. 3,617,127. Editorial lead time 3 months. Sample copy not available.

$$$$ READER'S DIGEST, Reader's Digest Rd., Pleasantville NY 10570-7000. Website: www.readersdigest.com. **Contact:** Editorial Correspondence. Monthly general interest magazine. "We are looking for contemporary stories of lasting interest that give the magazine variety, freshness and originality." Estab. 1922. Circ. 13,000,000. **Pays on acceptance.** Byline given. Buys exclusive world periodical and electronic rights, among others. Editorial lead time 3 months. Submit seasonal material 6 months in advance. Accepts queries by mail. Accepts previously published material.

Nonfiction: Address article queries and tearsheets of published articles to the editors. Book excerpts, essays, exposé, general interest, historical/nostalgic, humor, inspirational, interview/profile, opinion, personal experience. Does not read or return unsolicited mss. **Buys 100 mss/year.** Query with published clips. Length: 1,000-2,500 words. **Original article rates generally begin at $5,000.**

Reprints: Send tearsheet or photocopy with rights for sale noted and information about when and where the material previously appeared. **Pays $1,200/*Reader's Digest* page** for World Digest rights (usually split 50/50 between original publisher and writer).

Columns/Departments: "Life's Like That contributions must be true, unpublished stories from one's own experience, revealing adult human nature, and providing appealing or humorous sidelights on the American scene. Length: 100 words maximum. **Pays $400 on publication.** True, unpublished stories are also solicited for Humor in Uniform, Campus Comedy, Virtual Hilarity and All in a Day's Work. Length: 100 words maximum. **Pays $400 on publication.** Towards More Picturesque Speech—the *first* contributor of each item used in this department is paid **$50 for original material, $35 for reprints**. For items used in Laughter, the Best Medicine, Personal Glimpses, Quotable Quotes, Notes From All Over, Points to Ponder and elsewhere in the magazine payment is as follows; to the *first* contributor of each from a published source, **$35 for original material, $30/*Reader's Digest* two-column line.**" Original contributions become the property of *Reader's Digest* upon acceptance and payment. Previously published material must have source's name, date and page number. Contributions cannot be acknowledged or returned. Send complete anecdotes to *Reader's Digest*, Box 100, Pleasantville NY 10572-0100, fax to (914)238-6390 or e-mail laughlines@readersdigest.com.

Tips: "Roughly half the 20-odd articles we publish every month are reprinted from magazines, newspapers, books and other sources. The remaining 10 or so articles are original—most of them assigned, some submitted on speculation. While many of these are written by regular contributors, we're always looking for new talent and for offbeat subjects that help give our magazine variety, freshness and originality. Above all, in the writing we publish, *The Digest* demands accuracy—down to the smallest detail. Our worldwide team of 60 researchers scrutinizes every line of type, checking every fact and examining every opinion. For an average issue, they will check some 3500 facts with 1300 sources. So watch your accuracy. There's nothing worse than having an article fall apart in our research checking because an author was a little careless with his reporting. We make this commitment routinely, as it guarantees that the millions of readers who believe something simply because they saw it in *Reader's Digest* have not misplaced their trust."

N $ $ $ $ READER'S DIGEST (CANADA), 1125 Stanley St., Montreal QC H3B 5H5, Canada. (514)940-0751. E-mail: editor@readersdigest.ca. Website: www.readersdigest.ca. Editor-in-Chief: Murray Lewis. **Contact:** Ron Starr, senior associate editor. **10-25% freelance written.** Monthly magazine of general interest articles and subjects. Estab. 1948. Circ. 1,300,000. **Pays on acceptance for original works.** Pays on publication for "pickups." Byline given. Offers $500 (Canadian) kill fee. one-time rights (for reprints), all rights (for original articles). Submit seasonal material 5 months in advance. Accepts queries by mail, e-mail. Accepts previously published material. Responds in 5 weeks to queries. Writer's guidelines for #10 SASE with Canadian postage or #10 SAE with 1 IRC.

Nonfiction: Senior Associate Editor: Ron Starr. "We're looking for true stories that depend on emotion and reveal the power of our relationships to help us overcome adversity; also for true first-person accounts of an event that changed a life for the better or led to new insight. No fiction, poetry or articles too specialized, technical or esoteric—read *Reader's Digest* to see what kind of articles we want." General interest, how-to (general interest), inspirational, personal experience. Query with published clips. Length: 3,000-5,000 words. **Pays minimum of $2,700.** Pays expenses of writers on assignment.

Reprints: Send previously published material to Peter Des Lauriers, senior associate editor. Payment is negotiable.

Photos: State availability with submission.

The online magazine carries original content not found in the print edition. Contact: Peter Des Lauriers.

Tips: "*Reader's Digest* usually finds its freelance writers through other well-known publications in which they have previously been published. There are guidelines available and writers should read *Reader's Digest* to see what kind of stories we look for and how they are written. We do not accept unsolicited manuscripts."

$ REUNIONS MAGAZINE, P.O. Box 11727, Milwaukee WI 53211-0727. (414)263-4567. Fax: (414)263-6331. E-mail: reunions@execpc.com. Website: www.reunionsmag.com. **Contact:** Edith Wagner, editor. **75% freelance written.** Bimonthly magazine covering reunions—all aspects and types. "*Reunions Magazine* is primarily for people actively planning family, class, military, and other reunions. We want easy, practical ideas about organizing, planning, researching/searching, attending, or promoting reunions." Estab. 1990. Circ. 18,000. Pays on publication. Publishes ms an average of 1 year after acceptance. Byline given. Buys one-time rights. Editorial lead time 6 months. Submit seasonal material 1 year in advance. Accepts queries by mail, e-mail, fax. Accepts previously published material. Responds in about 1 year to queries. Sample copy and writer's guidelines for #10 SASE or online.

Nonfiction: "We can't get enough about reunion activities, particularly family reunions with multigenerational activities. We would also like more reunion food-related material." Needs reviewers for books, videos, software (include your requirements). Special features: Ethnic/African-American family reunions; food, kids stuff, theme parks, small venues (bed & breakfasts, dormitories, condos); golf, travel and gaming features; themes, cruises, ranch reunions and reunions in various US locations. Historical/nostalgic, how-to, humor, interview/profile, new product, personal experience, photo feature, travel. **Buys 50 mss/year.** Query with published clips. Length: 500-2,500 (prefers work on the short side). **Pays $25-50.** Often rewards with generous copies.

Reprints: Send tearsheet, photocopy or typed ms with rights for sale noted and information about when and where the material previously appeared. Usually pays $10.

Photos: Always looking for vertical cover photos screaming: "Reunion!" Prefer print pictures; e-mail pictures (TIFF or JPG). State availability with submission. Reviews contact sheets, negatives, 35mm transparencies, prints. Offers no additional payment for photos accepted with ms. Captions, identification of subjects, model releases required.

Fillers: Must be reunion-related. Anecdotes, facts, short humor. **Buys 20-40/year.** Length: 50-250 words. **Pays $5.**

The online magazine carries original content and includes writer's guidelines and articles. Contact: Edith Wagner, online editor.

Tips: "All copy must be reunion-related with strong, real reunion examples and experiences. Write a lively account of an interesting or unusual reunion, either upcoming or soon after while it's hot. Tell readers why the reunion is special, what went into planning it, and how attendees reacted. Our "Masterplan" section, about family reunion planning, is a great place for a freelancer to start by telling her/his own reunion. Send us how-tos or tips about any of the many aspects of reunion organizing. Open your minds to different types of reunions—they're all around!"

$ $ $ $ ROBB REPORT, The Magazine for the Luxury Lifestyle, Curtco Media Labs, 1 Acton Place, Acton MA 01720. (978)264-7500. Fax: (978)264-7505. E-mail: miken@robbreport.com. Website: www.robbreport.com. **Contact:** Mike Nolan, editor. **60% freelance written.** Monthly magazine. "We are a lifestyle magazine geared toward active, affluent readers. Addresses upscale autos, luxury travel, boating, technology, lifestyles, watches, fashion, sports, investments, collectibles." Estab. 1976. Circ. 111,000. Pays on publication. Byline given. Offers 25% kill fee. Buys first North American serial, all rights. Submit seasonal material 5 months in advance. Accepts queries by mail, fax. Responds in 2 months to queries; 1 month to mss. Sample copy for $10.95, plus shipping and handling. Writer's guidelines for #10 SASE.

Nonfiction: General interest (autos, lifestyle, etc), interview/profile (prominent personalities/entrepreneurs), new product (autos, boats, consumer electronics), travel (international and domestic). Special issues: Home issue (October); Recreation (March). **Buys 60 mss/year.** Query with published clips. Length: 500-3,500 words. **Pays $150-2,000.** Sometimes pays expenses of writers on assignment.

Photos: State availability with submission. Buys one-time rights. Payment depends on article.

The online magazine carries original content not found in the print edition. Contact: Mike Nolan.

Tips: "Show zest in your writing, immaculate research, and strong thematic structure, and you can handle most any assignment. We want to put the reader there, whether the article is about test driving a car, fishing for marlin, touring a luxury home, or profiling a celebrity. The best articles will be those that tell compelling stories. Anecdotes should be used liberally, especially for leads, and the fun should show in your writing."

$ SALON, 22 4th St., 16th Floor, San Francisco CA 94103. (415)645-9200. Fax: (415)645-9204. E-mail: ruth@salon.com. Website: www.salon.com. Vice President of Content/Executive Editor: Gary Kamiya. **Contact:** Ruth Henrich, associate managing editor. Monthly magazine. Accepts queries by e-mail. Responds in 3 weeks to queries. Writer's guidelines online.

Nonfiction: *Salon* does not solicit fiction or poetry submissions and will not be able to respond to such submissions. Spend some time familiarizing yourself with various sites and features. Query with published clips or send complete ms.

Tips: "We ask that you please send the text of your query or submission in plain text in the body of your e-mail, rather than as an attached file, as we may not be able to read the format of your file. Please put the words "EDITORIAL SUBMISSIONS" in the subject line of the e-mail. You can find the editor's name on our Salon Staff page. And please tell us a little about yourself—your experience and background as a writer and qualifications for writing a particular story. If you have clips you can send us via e-mail, or Web addresses of pages that contain your work, please send us a representative sampling (no more than 3 or 4, please)."

$ $ THE SATURDAY EVENING POST, The Saturday Evening Post Society, 1100 Waterway Blvd., Indianapolis IN 46202. (317)634-1100. Fax: (317)637-0126. E-mail: letters@satevepost.org. Website: www.satevepost.org. Travel Editor: Holly Miller. **Contact:** Patrick Perry, managing editor. **30% freelance written.** Bimonthly general interest, family-oriented magazine focusing on physical fitness, preventive medicine. "Ask almost any American if he or she has heard of *The Saturday Evening Post*, and you will find that many have fond recollections of the magazine from their childhood days. Many readers recall sitting with their families on Saturdays awaiting delivery of their *Post* subscription in the mail. *The Saturday Evening Post* has forged a tradition of 'forefront journalism.' *The Saturday Evening Post* continues to stand at the journalistic forefront with its coverage of health, nutrition, and preventive medicine." Estab. 1728. Circ. 400,000. Pays on publication. Publishes ms an average of 3 months after acceptance. Byline given. Buys second serial (reprint), all rights. Submit seasonal material 4 months in advance. Accepts queries by mail, fax. Accepts simultaneous submissions. Responds in 1 month to queries; 6 weeks to mss. Writer's guidelines online.

Nonfiction: Book excerpts, how-to (gardening, home improvement), humor, interview/profile, travel, medical; health; fitness. "No political articles or articles containing sexual innuendo or hypersophistication." **Buys 25 mss/year.** Query with or without published clips or send complete ms. Length: 750-2,500 words. **Pays $150 minumum, negotiable maximum.** Sometimes pays expenses of writers on assignment.

Photos: State availability with submission. Reviews negatives, transparencies. Buys one-time or all rights. Offers $50 minimum, negotiable maximum per photo. Identification of subjects, model releases required.

Columns/Departments: Travel (destinations); Post Scripts (well-known humorists); Post People (activities of celebrities). Length 750-1,500. **Buys 16 mss/year.** Query with published clips or send complete ms. **Pays $150 minimum, negotiable maximum.**

Poetry: Light verse.

Fillers: Post Scripts Editor: Steve Pettinga. Anecdotes, short humor. **Buys 200/year.** Length: 300 words. **Pays $15.**

Tips: "Areas most open to freelancers are Health, Fitness, Research Breakthroughs, Nutrition, Post Scripts and Travel.

For travel we like text-photo packages, pragmatic tips, side bars and safe rather than exotic destinations. Query by mail, not phone. Send clips."

$ $ $ $ SMITHSONIAN MAGAZINE, MRC 951, P.O. Box 37012, Washington DC 20013-7012. (202)275-2000. E-mail: articles@simag.si.edu. Website: www.smithsonianmag.si.edu. Editor-in-chief: Carey Winfrey. **Contact:** Marlane A. Liddell, articles editor. **90% freelance written.** Monthly magazine for associate members of the Smithsonian Institution; 85% with college education. "*Smithsonian Magazine's* mission is to inspire fascination with all the world has to offer by featuring unexpected and entertaining editorial that explores different lifestyles, cultures and peoples, the arts, the wonders of nature and technology and much more. The highly educated, innovative readers of *Smithsonian* share a unique desire to celebrate life, seeking out the timely as well as timeless, the artistic as well as the academic and the thought-provoking as well as the humorous." Circ. 2,300,000. **Pays on acceptance.** Publishes ms an average of 6 months after acceptance. Offers 33% kill fee. Buys first North American serial rights. Editorial lead time 2 months. Submit seasonal material 3 months in advance. Accepts queries by e-mail. Responds in 2 months to queries. Sample copy for $5, c/o Judy Smith. Writer's guidelines online.

O→ "We consider focused subjects that fall within the general range of Smithsonian Institution interests, such as: cultural history, physical science, art and natural history. We are always looking for offbeat subjects and profiles. We do not consider fiction, poetry, political and news events, or previously published articles. We publish only twelve issues a year, so it is difficult to place an article in *Smithsonian*, but please be assured that all proposals are considered."

Nonfiction: "Our mandate from the Smithsonian Institution says we are to be interested in the same things which now interest or should interest the Institution: Cultural and fine arts, history, natural sciences, hard sciences, etc." **Buys 120-130 feature (up to 5,000 words) and 12 short (500-650 words) mss/year.** Query with published clips. **Pays various rates per feature, $1,500 per short piece.** Pays expenses of writers on assignment.

Photos: Purchased with or without ms and on assignment. "Illustrations are not the responsibility of authors, but if you do have photographs or illustration materials, please include a selection of them with your submission. In general, 35mm color transparencies or black-and-white prints are perfectly acceptable. Photographs published in the magazine are usually obtained through assignment, stock agencies, or specialized sources. No photo library is maintained and photographs should be submitted only to accompany a specific article proposal." Send photos with submission. Pays $400/full color page. Captions required.

Columns/Departments: Last Page humor, 550-700 words. **Buys 12-15 department articles/year.** Length: 1,000-2,000 words. Send complete ms. **Pays $1,000-1,500.**

Tips: "We prefer a written proposal of one or two pages as a preliminary query. The proposal should convince us that we should cover the subject, offer descriptive information on how you, the writer, would treat the subject and offer us an opportunity to judge your writing ability. Background information and writing credentials and samples are helpful. All unsolicited proposals are sent to us on speculation and you should receive a reply within eight weeks. Please include a self-addressed stamped envelope. We also accept proposals via electronic mail at articles@simag.si.edu. If we decide to commission an article, the writer receives full payment on acceptance of the manuscript. If the article is found unsuitable, one-third of the payment serves as a kill fee."

$ $ $ THE SUN, A Magazine of Ideas, The Sun Publishing Co., 107 N. Roberson St., Chapel Hill NC 27516. (919)942-5282. Fax: (919)932-3101. Website: www.thesunmagazine.org. **Contact:** Sy Safransky, editor. **90% freelance written.** Monthly magazine. "We are open to all kinds of writing, though we favor work of a personal nature." Estab. 1974. Circ. 50,000. Pays on publication. Publishes ms an average of 6-12 months after acceptance. Byline given. Buys first, one-time rights. Accepts previously published material. Responds in 3 months to queries. Sample copy for $5. Writer's guidelines online.

- Responds in 3-6 months.

Nonfiction: Book excerpts, essays, general interest, interview/profile, opinion, personal experience, spiritual. **Buys 50 mss/year.** Send complete ms. Length: 7,000 words maximum. **Pays $300-1,250.** Complimentary subscription is given in addition to payment (applies to payment for *all* works, not just nonfiction).

Reprints: Send photocopy and information about when and where the material previously appeared. Pays 50% of amount paid for original article or story.

Photos: Send photos with submission. Reviews b&w prints. Buys one-time rights. Offers $50-200/photo. Model releases required.

Fiction: "We avoid stereotypical genre pieces like science fiction, romance, western, and horror. Read an issue before submitting." Literary. **Buys 20 mss/year.** Send complete ms. Length: 7,000 words maximum. **Pays $300-750.**

Poetry: Free verse, prose poems, short and long poems. **Buys 24 poems/year.** Submit maximum 6 poems. **Pays $50-250.**

$ $ $ $ TOWN & COUNTRY, The Hearst Corp., 1700 Broadway, New York NY 10019. (212)903-5000. Fax: (212)262-7107. Website: www.townandcountrymag.com. **Contact:** John Cantrell, deputy editor. **40% freelance written.** Monthly lifestyle magazine. "*Town & Country* is a lifestyle magazine for the affluent market. Features focus on fashion, beauty, travel, interior design, and the arts, as well as individuals' accomplishments and contributions to society." Estab. 1846. Circ. 488,000. **Pays on acceptance.** Byline given. Offers 25% kill fee. Buys first North American serial, electronic rights. Accepts queries by mail. Responds in 2 months to queries.

Nonfiction: "We're looking for engaging service articles for a high income, well-educated audience, in numerous categories: travel, personalities, interior design, fashion, beauty, jewelry, health, city news, the arts, philanthropy." General interest, interview/profile, travel. Rarely publishes work not commissioned by the magazine. Does not publish poetry, short stories, or fiction. **Buys 25 mss/year.** Query by mail only with relevant clips before submitting. Length: Column items, 100-300 words; feature stories, 800-2,000 words. **Pays $2/word.**

Tips: "We have served the affluent market for over 150 years, and our writers need to be expert in the needs and interests of that market. Most of our freelance writers start by doing short pieces for our front-of-book columns, then progress from there."

$ $ $ TROIKA, Wit, Wisdom & Wherewithal, Lone Tout Publications, Inc., P.O. Box 1006, Weston CT 06883. (203)319-0873. E-mail: submit@troikamagazine.com. Website: www.troikamagazine.com. **Contact:** Celia Meadow, editor. **95% freelance written.** Quarterly magazine covering general interest, lifestyle. "A magazine for men and women seeking a balanced, three-dimensional lifestyle: Personal achievement, family commitment, community involvement. Readers are upscale, educated, 30-50 age bracket. The *Troika* generation is a mix of what is called the X generation and the baby boomers. We are that generation. We grew up with sex, drugs and rock 'n roll, but now it really is our turn to make a difference, if we so choose." Estab. 1993. Circ. 120,000. Pays 90 days from publication. Publishes ms an average of 6 months after acceptance. Byline given. Buys first North American serial, internet rights rights. Editorial lead time 3 months. Submit seasonal material 6 months in advance. Accepts queries by mail, e-mail. Accepts previously published material. Accepts simultaneous submissions. Responds in 4 months to mss. Sample copy for $5 or online. Writer's guidelines for #10 SASE or online.

Nonfiction: Essays, exposé, general interest, how-to (leisure activities, pro bono finance), humor, inspirational, interview/profile (music related), personal experience, international affairs; environment; parenting; cultural. **Buys 1,000 mss/year.** Query with or without published clips or send complete ms. Length: 800-3,000 words. **Pays $200-1,000 for assigned articles.**

Reprints: Send photocopy and information about when and where the material previously appeared.

Photos: State availability with submission. Reviews negatives, transparencies. Offers no additional payment for photos accepted with ms. Captions, identification of subjects, model releases required.

Columns/Departments: Literati; Pub Performances (literary, theater, arts, culture); Blueprints (architecture, interior design, fashion); Body of Facts (science); Hippocratic Horizons (health); Home Technology; Capital Commitments (personal finance); Athletics; Leisure; Mondiale (international affairs); all 750-1,200 words. **Buys 100 mss/year.** Query with or without published clips or send complete ms. **Pays $200 maximum.**

Fiction: Adventure, confessions, historical, mainstream, mystery, novel excerpts, slice-of-life vignettes, suspense, contemporary. **Buys 100 mss/year.** Send complete ms. Length: 3,000 words maximum. **Pays $200 maximum.**

The online magazine carries original content not found in the print edition and includes writer's guidelines.

$ THE WORLD & I, The Magazine for Lifelong Learners, News World Communications, Inc., 3600 New York Ave. NE, Washington DC 20002. (202)635-4000. Fax: (202)269-9353. E-mail: editor@worldandimag.com. Website: www.worldandi.com. Editor: Morton A. Kaplan. Executive Editor: Michael Marshall. **Contact:** Gary Rowe, editorial office manager. **90% freelance written.** Monthly magazine. "A broad interest magazine for the thinking, educated person." Estab. 1986. Circ. 30,000. Pays on publication. Publishes ms an average of 6 months after acceptance. Byline given. Offers 20% kill fee. Submit seasonal material 5 months in advance. Accepts queries by mail. Accepts previously published material. Responds in 6 weeks to queries; 10 weeks to mss. Sample copy for $5 and 9×12 SASE. Writer's guidelines online.

Nonfiction: "Description of Sections: Current Issues: Politics, economics and strategic trends covered in a variety of approaches, including special report, analysis, commentary and photo essay. The Arts: International coverage of music, dance, theater, film, television, craft, design, architecture, photography, poetry, painting and sculpture—through reviews, features, essays, opinion pieces and a 6-page Gallery of full-color reproductions. Life: Surveys all aspects of life in 22 rotating subsections which include: Travel and Adventure (first person reflections, preference given to authors who provide photographic images), Profile (people or organizations that are 'making a difference'), Food and Garden (must be accompanied by photos), Education, Humor, Hobby, Family, Consumer, Trends, and Health. Send SASE for complete list of subsections. Natural Science: Covers the latest in science and technology, relating it to the social and historical context, under these headings: At the Edge, Impacts, Nature Walk, Science and Spirit, Science and Values, Scientists: Past and Present, Crucibles of Science and Science Essay. Book World: Excerpts from important, timely books (followed by commentaries) and 10-12 scholarly reviews of significant new books each month, including untranslated works from abroad. Covers current affairs, intellectual issues, contemporary fiction, history, moral/religious issues and the social sciences. Currents in Modern Thought: Examines scholarly research and theoretical debate across the wide range of disciplines in the humanities and social sciences. Featured themes are explored by several contributors. Investigates theoretical issues raised by certain current events, and offers contemporary reflection on issues drawn from the whole history of human thought. Culture: Surveys the world's people in these subsections: Peoples (their unique characteristics and cultural symbols), Crossroads (changes brought by the meeting of cultures), Patterns (photo essay depicting the daily life of a distinct culture), Folk Wisdom (folklore and practical wisdom and their present forms), and Heritage (multicultural backgrounds of the American people and how they are bound to the world). Photo Essay: Patterns, a 6- or 8-page photo essay, appears monthly in the Culture section. Emphasis is placed on comprehensive photographic coverage of a people or group, their private or public lifestyle, in a given situation or context. Accompanying word count: 300-500 words. Photos must be from existing stock, no travel subsidy. Life & Ideals, a 6- or 8-page photo essay, occasionally appears in the Life section. First priority is given to those focused on individuals or organizations that are 'making a difference.' Accompanying word count: 700-1,000 words." No *National Enquirer*-type articles. **Buys 1,200 mss/year.** Query with published clips. Length: 1,000-5,000 words. **Pays per article basis for assigned articles.** Seldom pays expenses of writers on assignment.

Reprints: Send ms with rights for sale noted and information about when and where the material previously appeared.

Photos: State availability with submission. Reviews contact sheets, transparencies, prints. Buys one-time rights. Payment negotiable. Identification of subjects, model releases required.

Fiction: Novel excerpts.

Poetry: Arts Editor. Avant-garde, free verse, haiku, light verse, traditional. **Buys 4-6 poems/year.** Submit maximum 5 poems. **Pays $30-75.**

Tips: "We accept articles from journalists, but also place special emphasis on scholarly contributions. It is our hope that the magazine will enable the best of contemporary thought, presented in accessible language, to reach a wider audience than would normally be possible through the academic journals appropriate to any given discipline."

HEALTH & FITNESS

The magazines listed here specialize in covering health and fitness topics for a general audience. Health and fitness magazines have experienced a real boom lately. Most emphasize developing healthy lifestyle choices in exercise, nutrition, and general fitness. Many magazines offer alternative healing and therapies that are becoming more mainstream, such as medicinal herbs, health foods, and a holistic mind/body approach to well-being. As wellness is a concern to all demographic groups, publishers have developed editorial geared to specific audiences: African-American women, older readers, men, women. Also see the Sports/Miscellaneous section where publications dealing with health and particular sports may be listed. For magazines that cover healthy eating, refer to the Food & Drink section. Many general interest publications are also potential markets for health or fitness articles. Health topics from a medical perspective are listed in the Medical category of Trade, Technical & Professional Journals.

$ $ AMERICAN FITNESS, 15250 Ventura Blvd., Suite 200, Sherman Oaks CA 91403. (818)905-0040. Fax: (818)990-5468. Website: www.afaa.com. Publisher: Roscoe Fawcett. **Contact:** Dr. Meg Jordan, editor. **75% freelance written.** Bimonthly magazine covering exercise and fitness, health, and nutrition. "We need timely, in-depth, informative articles on health, fitness, aerobic exercise, sports nutrition, age-specific fitness, and outdoor activity." Absolutely no first-person accounts. Need well-reserched articles for professional readers. Circ. 42,000. Pays 6 weeks after publication. Publishes ms an average of 6 months after acceptance. Byline given. Submit seasonal material 4 months in advance. Accepts queries by mail, fax. Accepts previously published material. Accepts simultaneous submissions. Responds in 6 weeks to queries. Sample copy for $3 and SAE with 6 first-class stamps.

Nonfiction: Needs include health and fitness, including women's issues (pregnancy, family, pre- and post-natal, menopause, and eating disorders); new research findings on exercise techniques and equipment; aerobic exercise; sports nutrition; sports medicine; innovations and trends in aerobic sports; tips on teaching exercise and humorous accounts of fitness motivation; physiology; youth and senior fitness. Historical/nostalgic (history of various athletic events), inspirational, interview/profile (fitness figures), new product (plus equipment review), personal experience (successful fitness story), photo feature (on exercise, fitness, new sport), travel (activity adventures). No articles on unsound nutritional practices, popular trends, or unsafe exercise gimmicks. **Buys 18-25 mss/year.** Query with published clips or send complete ms. Length: 800-1,200 words. **Pays $200 for features, $80 for news.** Sometimes pays expenses of writers on assignment.

Photos: Sports, action, fitness, aquatic aerobics competitions, and exercise class. "We are especially interested in photos of high-adrenalin sports like rock climbing and mountain biking." Reviews transparencies, prints. Usually buys all rights; other rights purchased depend on use of photo. Pays $35 for transparencies. Captions, identification of subjects, model releases required.

Columns/Departments: Research (latest exercise and fitness findings); Alternative paths (nonmainstream approaches to health, wellness, and fitness); Strength (latest breakthroughs in weight training); Clubscene (profiles and highlights of fitness club industry); Adventure (treks, trails, and global challenges); Food (low-fat/nonfat, high-flavor dishes); Homescene (home-workout alternatives); Clip 'n' Post (concise exercise research to post in health clubs, offices or on refrigerators). Length: 800-1,000 words. Query with published clips or send complete ms. **Pays $100-140.**

Tips: "Make sure to quote scientific literature or good research studies and several experts with good credentials to validate exercise trend, technique, or issue. Cover a unique aerobics or fitness angle, provide accurate and interesting findings, and write in a lively, intelligent manner. Please, no first-person accouts of 'how I lost weight or discovered running.' *AF* is a good place for first-time authors or regularly published authors who want to sell spin-offs or reprints."

$ $ $ $ AMERICAN HEALTH & FITNESS, CANUSA Publishing, 5775 McLaughlin Rd., Mississauga ON L5R 3P7, Canada. Fax: (905)507-2372. E-mail: editorial@ahfmag.com. Website: www.ahfmag.com. Publisher: Robert Kennedy. **Contact:** Kerrie-Lee Brown, editor-in-chief. **85% freelance written.** Bimonthly magazine. "*American Health & Fitness* is designed to help male fitness buffs (18-39) to keep fit, strong, virile, and healthy through sensible diet and exercise." Estab. 2000. Circ. 350,000. **Pays on acceptance.** Publishes ms an average of 4 months after acceptance. Byline given. Buys all rights. Editorial lead time 4 months. Submit seasonal material 5 months in advance. Accepts queries by mail, fax. Responds in 1 month to queries; 6 months to mss. Sample copy for $5.

Nonfiction: Exposé, general interest, how-to, humor, inspirational, interview/profile, new product, personal experience, photo feature, travel, bodybuilding and weight training, health & fitness tips, diet, medical advice, profiles, workouts, nutrition. **Buys 80-100 mss/year.** Send complete ms. Length: 1,400-2,000 words. **Pays $350-1,500 for assigned articles;**

$350-1,000 for unsolicited articles. Sometimes pays expenses of writers on assignment.

Photos: Send photos with submission. Reviews 35mm transparencies, 8×10 prints. Buys all rights. Offers $50-1,000/photo. Captions, identification of subjects required.

Columns/Departments: Chiropractic; Personal Training; Strength & Conditioning; Dental; Longevity; Natural Health. **Buys 40 mss/year.** Send complete ms. **Pays $100-1,000.**

Fillers: Anecdotes, facts, gags to be illustrated by cartoonist, newsbreaks, short humor. **Buys 50-100/year.** Length: 100-200 words. **Pays $50-100.**

The online magazine carries original content not found in the print edition. Contact: Kerrie-Lee Brown.

$ $ ASCENT MAGAZINE, Expanding the Mind of Yoga, Timeless Books, 837 Rue Gilford, Montreal QC H2J 1P1, Canada. (514)499-3999. Fax: (514)499-3904. E-mail: info@ascentmagazine.com. Website: www.ascentmagazine.com. Editor: Clea McDougall. **Contact:** Lesley Marian Neilson, managing editor. **75% freelance written.** Quarterly magazine covering yoga and spiritual living. "*Ascent* publishes unique and personal perspectives on yoga and spirituality. Our goal is to explore what it means to be truly human, to think deeply, and live a meaningful life in today's world." Estab. 1999. Circ. 6,000. Pays on publication. Publishes ms an average of 3 months after acceptance. Byline given. Offers 20% kill fee. Buys all rights. Editorial lead time 4 months. Submit seasonal material 6 months in advance. Accepts queries by e-mail. Responds in 1 month to queries; 1 month to mss. Sample copy for $5. Writer's guidelines online.

Nonfiction: Essays, interview/profile, personal experience, photo feature, religious. Special issues: Women in Spiritual Life (Summer 2003); Myth and Storytelling (Fall 2003); Renunciation (Winter 2003). No academic articles or promotional articles for specific yoga school or retreats. **Buys 30 mss/year.** Query with published clips. Length: 800-3,500 words. **Pays 20¢/word (Canadian).** Sometimes pays expenses of writers on assignment.

Photos: Joe Ollmann, designer. Reviews GIF/JPEG files. Buys one-time rights. Negotiates payment individually.

Columns/Departments: Personal Reflection (personal story of change/revelation), 800 words; Reviews (books and CDs), 500 words. **Buys 10 mss/year.** Query with published clips. **Pays $50-150 (Canadian).**

Tips: "*Ascent* publishes mainly personal, reflective nonfiction. Make sure to tell us how you will bring a personal, intimate tone to your article. Send a detailed query with writing samples. Give us a good idea of your potential as a writer."

$ $ $ BETTER NUTRITION, SABOT Publishing, 301 Concourse Blvd., Richmond VA 23059. (804)346-0990. Fax: (804)346-2281. E-mail: editorial@betternutrition.com. Website: www.betternutrition.com. **Contact:** Jerry Shaver, managing editor. **57% freelance written.** Monthly magazine covering nutritional news and approaches to optimal health. "The new *Better Nutrition* helps people (men, women, families, old and young) integrate nutritious food, the latest and most effective dietary supplements, and exercise/personal care into healthy lifestyles." Estab. 1938. Circ. 480,000. Pays on publication. Publishes ms an average of 2 months after acceptance. Byline given. Buys varies according to article rights. Editorial lead time 3 months. Accepts queries by mail, e-mail. Sample copy for free.

Nonfiction: Each issue has multiple features, clinical research crystallized into accessible articles on nutrition, health, alternative medicine, disease prevention. **Buys 120-180 mss/year.** Query. Length: 400-1,200 words. **Pays $400-1,000.**

Photos: State availability with submission. Reviews 4×5 transparencies, 3×5 prints. Buys one time rights or non-exclusive reprint rights. Negotiates payment individually. Captions, identification of subjects, model releases required.

Columns/Departments: Health Watch; Nutrition News; Women's Health; Earth Medicine; Healing Herbs; Better Hair, Skin & Nails; Herb Update; Health in Balance; Book Zone; Supplement Update; Natural Energy; Children's Health; Sports Nutrition; Earth Watch; Homeopathy; Botanical Medicine; Meatless Meals; Trim Time; Healthier Pets; Ayurvedic Medicine; Longevity; Healing Herbs; Frontiers of Science.

Tips: "Be on top of what's newsbreaking in nutrition and supplementation. Interview experts. Fact-check, fact-check, fact-check. Send in a résumé (including Social Security/IRS number), a couple of clips and a list of article possibilities."

$ $ CLIMBING, PRIMEDIA Enthusiast Group, 0326 Highway 133, Suite 190, Carbondale CO 81623. (970)963-9449. Fax: (970)9639442. E-mail: climbing@climbing.com. Website: www.climbing.com. Editor: Jonathon Thesenga. Magazine published 9 times/year covering climbing and mountaineering. Provides features on rock climbing and mountaneering worldwide. Estab. 1970. Circ. 51,000. Pays on publication. Editorial lead time 6 weeks. Accepts queries by e-mail. Sample copy for $ 4.99. Writer's guidelines online.

Nonfiction: SASE returns. Interview/profile (Interesting climbers), personal experience (Climbing adventures), Surveys of different areas. Query. Length: 2,000-5,000 words. **Pays 35¢/word.**

Photos: State availability with submission. Reviews negatives, 35mm transparencies, prints. Pays $75 minimum / $700 maximum.

Columns/Departments: Roadworthy (destination mini-features), 500-1,500 words; High and Wild (well-known and obscure mountain destinations), 1,000-2,000 words; Training, 1,000-1,500 words; Medicine, 1,000-1,500 words; Equipment, (reviews technical climbing gear) 1,000-2,000 words; Just Out, (review of one piece of equipment), 500-600 words; Tech Tip, (how-to description of techniques), 250-500 words; Players (profiles of climbers), 750 words; Reviews (reviews books, guidebooks, films, CD-Roms and videos), 200-300 words; Perspective (personal opinion or experience), 200-300 words. Query. **Payment varies.**

$ $ DELICIOUS LIVING!, Feel Good/Live Well, New Hope Natural Media, 1401 Pearl St., Suite 200, Boulder CO 80302. E-mail: delicious@newhope.com. Website: www.healthwell.com. Editorial Director: Karen Raterman. **Contact:** Lara Evans, managing editor. **85% freelance written.** Monthly magazine covering natural products, nutrition, alternative medicines, herbal medicines. "*Delicious Living!* magazine empowers natural foods store shoppers to make health-conscious choices in their lives. Our goal is to improve consumers' perception of the value of natural methods in achieving health. To do this, we educate consumers on nutrition, disease prevention, botanical medicines and natural personal care products."

Estab. 1985. Circ. 420,000. **Pays on acceptance.** Publishes ms an average of 6 months after acceptance. Byline given. Offers 20% kill fee. Editorial lead time 6 months. Submit seasonal material 8 months in advance. Accepts simultaneous submissions. Responds in 3 months to queries. Sample copy and writer's guidelines free.

Nonfiction: Book excerpts, how-to, interview/profile, personal experience (regarding natural or alternative health), health nutrition; herbal medicines; alternative medicine; environmental. **Buys 150 mss/year.** Query with published clips. Length: 500-2,000 words. **Pays $100-700 for assigned articles; $50-300 for unsolicited articles.**

Photos: State availability with submission. Reviews 3×5 prints. Buys one-time rights. Offers no additional payment for photos accepted with ms. Identification of subjects required.

Columns/Departments: Herbs (scientific evidence supporting herbal medicines), 1,500 words; Nutrition (new research on diet for good health), 1,200 words; Dietary Supplements (new research on vitamins/minerals, etc.), 1,200 words. Query with published clips. **Pays $100-500.**

The online magazine carries original content not found in the print edition. Contact: Kim Stewart, online editor.

Tips: "Highlight any previous health/nutrition/medical writing experience. Demonstrate a knowledge of natural medicine, nutrition, or natural products. Health practitioners who demonstrate writing ability are ideal freelancers."

$ $ HEALING LIFESTYLES & SPAS, (formerly *Healing Retreats & Spas*), 5036 Carpinteria Ave., Carpinteria CA 93013. (805)745-5413. Fax: (805)745-5643. E-mail: editorial@healinglifestyles.com. Website: www.healinglifestyles.com. Editor: Melissa Scott. **90% freelance written.** "*Healing Lifestyles & Spas* is a bimonthly magazine committed to healing, health, and living a well-rounded, more natural life. In each issue we cover retreats, spas, organic living, natural food, herbs, beauty, alternative medicine, bodywork, spirituality, and features on the alternative lifestyle." Estab. 1996. Circ. 45,000. Pays on publication. Publishes ms an average of 2-10 months after acceptance. Editorial lead time 6 months. Submit seasonal material 6-9 months in advance. Accepts queries by mail, e-mail. Responds in 6 weeks to queries.

Nonfiction: "We will consider all in-depth features relating to spas, retreats, lifestyle issues, mind/body well being, yoga, enlightening profiles, and women's health issues." Travel (domestic and international). No fiction or poetry. Query. Length: 1,000-2,000 words. **Pays $150-500, depending on length, research, experience, and availability and quality of images.**

Photos: "If you are doing your own photography, you must use slide film or provide a Mac formatted CD with image resolution of at least 300 dpi." Send photos with submission. Captions required.

Columns/Departments: All Things New & Natural (short pieces outlining new health trends, alternative medicine updates, and other interesting tidbits of information), 50-200 words; Guinea Pig (first-hand information on new modalities, fitness classes, etc.), 100-200 words; Media Reviews, 100 words; Urban Retreats (focuses on a single city and explores its natural side), 1,200-1,600 words; Getting Started (101 on the spa lifestyle), 900-1,200 words; Sex, 1,000-1,600 words; Good For You (organic natural food articles and recipes), 1,000-1,200 words; Day Spa (unique day spas around the country), 400-500 words; Spa à la carte (explores a new treatment or modality on the spa menu), 600-1,000 words. Query.

$ $ $ $ HEALTH, Time, Inc., Southern Progress Corp., 2100 Lakeshore Dr., Birmingham AL 35209. Fax: (205)445-5123. Website: www.health.com. Vice President/Editor: Doug Crichton. **Contact:** Stephanie Wolford, office manager. Magazine published 10 times/year covering health, fitness, and nutrition. "Our readers are predominantly college-educated women in their 30s, 40s, and 50s. Edited to focus not on illness, but on wellness events, ideas, and people." Estab. 1987. Circ. 1,350,000. **Pays on acceptance.** Byline given. Offers 33% kill fee. Buys first publication and online rights rights. Accepts queries by mail, fax. Accepts simultaneous submissions. Responds in 2 months to queries to mss. Sample copy for $5 to Back Issues. Writer's guidelines for #10 SASE.

- *Health* has joined other Time, Inc. Southern Progress magazines such as *Cooking Light*, *Southern Accents*, and *Coastal Living*.

Nonfiction: No unsolicited mss. **Buys 25 mss/year.** Query with published clips and SASE. Length: 1,200 words. **Pays $1-1.50/word.** Pays expenses of writers on assignment.

Columns/Departments: Food, Mind, Healthy Looks, Fitness, Relationships.

Tips: "We look for well-articulated ideas with a narrow focus and broad appeal. A query that starts with an unusual local event and hooks it legitimately to some national trend or concern is bound to get our attention. Use quotes, examples and statistics to show why the topic is important and why the approach is workable. We need to see clear evidence of credible research findings pointing to meaningful options for our readers. Stories should offer practical advice and give clear explanations."

$ $ HEPATITIS, Management and Treatment—A Practical Guide for Patients, Families, and Friends, Quality Publishing, Inc., 523 N. Sam Houston Tollway E., Suite 300, Houston TX 77060. (281)272-2744. E-mail: editor@hepatitismag.com. Website: www.hepatitismag.com. **Contact:** Managing Editor. **70-80% freelance written.** Quarterly magazine covering Hepatitis health news. Estab. 1999. Circ. 25,000. Pays on publication. Publishes ms an average of 2 months after acceptance. Byline given. Buys first North American serial, electronic rights. Editorial lead time 6 months. Submit seasonal material 4 months in advance. Accepts queries by mail, e-mail. Accepts simultaneous submissions. Responds in 6 weeks to queries. Sample copy and writer's guidelines free.

Nonfiction: Inspirational, interview/profile, new product, personal experience. "We do not want any one-source or no-source articles." **Buys 42-48 mss/year.** Query with or without published clips. Length: 1,500-2,500 words. Sometimes pays expenses of writers on assignment.

Photos: Send photos with submission. Reviews transparencies, prints, GIF/JPEG files. Rights negotiated, usually purchases one-time rights. Offers no additional payment for photos accepted with ms. Identification of subjects required.

Columns/Departments: General news or advice on Hepatitis written by a doctor or healthcare professional, 1,500-2,000 words. **Buys 12-18 mss/year.** Query. **Pays $375-500.**

Tips: "Be specific in your query. Show me that you know the topic you want to write about. And show me that you can write a solid, well-rounded story."

N $ **HERE'S HEALTH**, Emap, Greater London House, Hampstead Rd., London NW1 7EJ, England. (020) 7347 1893. Fax: (020) 7347 1897. Editor: Colette Harris. **Contact:** Lisa Howells, features editor. **80% freelance written.** Monthly magazine covering complementary and alternative health. "*Here's Health* focuses on holistic health and well being." Estab. 1950. Circ. 25,000. **Pays on acceptance.** Publishes ms an average of 3 months after acceptance. Byline given. Buys all rights. Editorial lead time 3-4 months. Submit seasonal material 3-4 months in advance. Accepts queries by mail, fax. Accepts simultaneous submissions. Sample copy for 1 SAE and 2 first-class stamps.

Photos: Adam Blarde, art editor. State availability with submission. Reviews contact sheets, transparencies, prints. Buys all rights. Negotiates payment individiually. Captions, identification of subjects, model releases required.

$ $ $ **MAMM MAGAZINE, Courage, Respect & Survival**, MAMM L.L.C., 54 W. 22nd St., 4th Floor, New York NY 10010. (646)365-1350. Fax: (646)365-1369. E-mail: editorial@mamm.com. Website: www.mamm.com. Managing Editor: Craig Moskowitz. **Contact:** Gwen Darien, editor-in-chief. **80% freelance written.** Magazine published 10 times/year covering cancer prevention, treatment, and survival for women. "*MAMM* gives its readers the essential tools and emotional support they need before, during and after diagnosis of breast, ovarian and other female reproductive cancers. We offer a mix of survivor profiles, conventional and alternative treatment information, investigative features, essays, and cutting-edge news." Estab. 1997. Circ. 100,000. Pays within 45 days of publication. Publishes ms an average of 3 months after acceptance. Byline given. Offers 20% kill fee. Buys exclusive rights up to 3 months after publishing, first rights after that. Editorial lead time 4 months. Submit seasonal material 4 months in advance. Accepts simultaneous submissions. Sample copy and writer's guidelines free.

Nonfiction: Book excerpts, essays, exposé, historical/nostalgic, how-to, humor, inspirational, interview/profile, opinion, personal experience, photo feature. **Buys 90 mss/year.** Query with published clips. Length: 200-3,000 words. **Pays $50-1,000.** Sometimes pays expenses of writers on assignment.

Photos: Send photos with submission. Reviews contact sheets, negatives. Buys first rights. Negotiates payment individually. Identification of subjects required.

Columns/Departments: Cancer Girl (humor/experience); Opinion (cultural/political); International Dispatch (experience), all 600 words. **Buys 30 mss/year.** Query with published clips. **Pays $250-300. Buys 6 mss/year.** Query with published clips.

$ $ $ $ **MEN'S HEALTH**, Rodale, 33 E. Minor St., Emmaus PA 18098. (610)967-5171. Fax: (610)967-7725. E-mail: bill.stieg@rodale.com. Website: www.menshealth.com. Editor-in-Chief: David Zinczenko. Executive Editor: Peter Moore. **Contact:** Bill Stieg, senior editor. **50% freelance written.** Magazine published 10 times/year covering men's health and fitness. "*Men's Health* is a lifestyle magazine showing men the practical and positive actions that make their lives better, with articles covering fitness, nutrition, relationships, travel, careers, grooming, and health issues." Estab. 1986. Circ. 1,600,000. **Pays on acceptance.** Offers 25% kill fee. Buys all rights. Accepts queries by mail, fax. Responds in 3 weeks to queries. Writer's guidelines for #10 SASE.

Freelancers have the best chance with the front-of-the-book piece, Malegrams.

Nonfiction: "Authoritative information on all aspects of men's physical and emotional health. We rely on writers to seek out the right experts and to either tell a story from a first-person vantage or get good anecdotes." **Buys 30 features/year; 360 short mss/year.** Query with published clips. Length: 1,200-4,000 words for features, 100-300 words for short pieces. **Pays $1,000-5,000 for features; $100-500 for short pieces.**

Columns/Departments: Length: 750-1,500 words. **Buys 80 mss/year. Pays $750- 2,000.**

The online magazine carries original content not included in the print edition. Contact: Fred Zahradnick, online associate.

Tips: "We have a wide definition of health. We believe that being successful in every area of your life is being healthy. The magazine focuses on all aspects of health, from stress issues to nutrition to exercise to sex. It is 50% staff written, 50% from freelancers. The best way to break in is not by covering a particular subject, but by covering it within the magazine's style. There is a very particular tone and voice to the magazine. A writer has to be a good humor writer as well as a good service writer. Prefers mail queries. No phone calls, please."

$ $ $ **MUSCLE & FITNESS, The Science of Living Super-Fit**, Weider Health & Fitness, 21100 Erwin St., Woodland Hills, CA 91367. (818)884-6800. Fax: (818)595-0463. Website: www.muscle-fitness.com. **Contact:** Jo Ellen Krumm, managing editor. **50% freelance written.** Monthly magazine covering bodybuilding and fitness for healthy, active men and women. It contains a wide range of features and monthly departments devoted to all areas of bodybuilding, health, fitness, injury prevention and treatment, and nutrition. Editorial fulfills 2 functions: information and entertainment. Special attention is devoted to how-to advice and accuracy. Estab. 1950. Circ. 500,000. Pays on publication. Publishes ms an average of 2 months after acceptance. Editorial lead time 5 months. Submit seasonal material 6 months in advance. Accepts queries by mail. Accepts previously published material. Responds in 1 month to queries.

Nonfiction: "All features and departments are written on assignment." Book excerpts, how-to (training), humor, interview/profile, photo feature. **Buys 120 mss/year.** Does not accept unsolicited mss. Length: 800-1,800 words. **Pays $400-1,000 for assigned articles.** Pays expenses of writers on assignment.

Reprints: Send photocopy with rights for sale noted and information about when and where the material previously appeared. Payment varies.

Photos: State availability with submission.

Tips: "Know bodybuilders and bodybuilding. Read our magazine regularly (or at least several issues), come up with new information or a new angle on our subject matter (bodybuilding training, psychology, nutrition, diets, fitness, etc.), then pitch us in terms of providing useful, unique, how-to information for our readers. Send a 1-page query letter (as described in *Writer's Market*) to sell us on your idea and on you as the best writer for that article. Send a sample of your published work."

N $ $ **MUSCLE MAG INTERNATIONAL**, 6465 Airport Rd., Mississauga ON L4V 1E4, Canada. (905)678-7311. Fax: (905)678-9236. **Contact:** Johnny Fitness, editor. **80% freelance written.** Monthly magazine for 16- to 60-year-old men and women interested in physical fitness and overall body improvement. "We do not care if a writer is known or unknown; published or unpublished. We simply want good instructional articles on bodybuilding." Submit complete mss with IRCs. Estab. 1972. Circ. 300,000. **Pays on acceptance.** Publishes ms an average of 4 months after acceptance. Byline given. Buys all rights. Accepts queries by mail, fax, phone. Responds in 2 months to mss.

Nonfiction: Articles on ideal physical proportions and importance of supplements in the diet, training for muscle size. Should be helpful and instructional and appeal to young men and women who want to live life in a vigorous and healthy style. "We would like to see articles for the physical culturist on new muscle-building techniques or an article on fitness testing. Also now actively looking for good instructional articles on hardcore fitness." **Buys 200 mss/year.** Length: 1,200-1,600 words. **Pays 20¢/word.** Sometimes pays expenses of writers on assignment.

Photos: Color and b&w photos are purchased with or without ms. Pays $50 for 8×10 glossy exercise photos; $50 for 8×10 b&w posing shots. Pays $1,000 for color cover and $50 for color used inside magazine (transparencies). More for.

Columns/Departments: Nutrition Talk (eating for top results); Shaping Up (improving fitness and stamina).

Fillers: Newsbreaks, puzzles, quotes of the champs. Length: Open length. **Pays $50 minimum.**

Tips: "The best way to break in is to seek out the muscle-building 'stars' and do in-depth interviews with biography in mind. Color training picture support essential. Writers have to make their articles informative in that readers can apply them to help gain bodybuilding success. Specific fitness articles should quote experts and/or use scientific studies to strengthen their theories. Write strong articles full of 'how-to' information. We want to genuinely help our readers build better, fitter, stronger bodies."

N $ **NATURAL BEAUTY & HEALTH MAGAZINE, A Primer for Holistic Health and Natural Living**, P.O. Box 600, Chico CA 95927. (530)893-9076. E-mail: info@magicalblend.com. Website: www.nbhonline.com. **Contact:** Michael Peter Langevin, editor. **50% freelance written.** Bimonthly magazine covering alternative healing practices, bodywork, self-help, and spiritual perspectives on wellness. "*Natural Beauty & Health Magazine* exists to aid individuals in achieving better lives, both physically and spiritually. We hold that health is as much a state of the mind as a condition of the body." Estab. 2001. Circ. 100,000. Pays on publication. Publishes ms an average of 2 months after acceptance. Byline given. Responds in 2-6 months to mss. Sample copy for free. Writer's guidelines for #10 SASE.

- Break in by "writing an engaging article about some unique perspective on healthy or balanced living or some form of healing trasnformation with practical advice for readers on how to achieve it or interview a recognizable celebrity with a natural lifestyle."

Nonfiction: "Articles must reflect our standards; see our magazine." Book excerpts, essays, general interest, inspirational, interview/profile, travel, spiritual. No poetry or fiction. **Buys 24 mss/year.** Send complete ms. Length: 500-2,000 words. **Pays $35-100.**

Photos: State availability with submission. Reviews transparencies. Buys all rights. Negotiates payment individually. Identification of subjects, model releases required.

Fillers: Alternative health news. **Buys 12-20/year.** Length: 200-500 words. **Pays variable rate.**

N $ $ $ $ **PHYSICAL**, Franklin Publications/Basic Mediagroup, Inc., 11050 Santa Monica Blvd., Los Angeles CA 90025. (310)445-7505. Fax: (310)445-7587. E-mail: bbush@physicalmag.com. Managing Editor: Susan Leh. **Contact:** Bill Bush, editor-in-chief. **90% freelance written.** Monthly magazine covering physical fitness, sports nutrition, and body building. Custom publication for General Nutrition Center gold card club members. Directed at a very active, mostly male reader with emphasis on "the physical lifestyle" of good nutrition, regular exercise, and dietary supplementation of sports nutrition. Estab. 1998. Circ. 600,000-700,000. **Pays on acceptance.** Publishes ms an average of 4-5 months after acceptance. Byline given. Offers 25% kill fee. Buys first North American serial, electronic rights. Editorial lead time 6 months. Submit seasonal material 6 months in advance. Accepts queries by mail, e-mail, fax. Accepts simultaneous submissions. Responds in 1 month to queries; 4 months to mss. Sample copy for free. Writer's guidelines by e-mail.

Nonfiction: General interest, how-to (exercise, build muscle, lose weight, etc.), inspirational, personal experience, technical, sports training, nutrition, workouts. No "soft girlie topics, gear or boy toys, automobiles, or electronics." **Buys 100-120 mss/year.** Query with or without published clips. Length: 800-1,800 words. **Pays $500-1,500 for assigned articles; $0-1,000 for unsolicited articles.** Sometimes pays expenses of writers on assignment.

Photos: Buys one-time rights. Negotiates payment individually. Captions, identification of subjects, model releases required.

Tips: "Keep our reader in mind—buyer of sports nutrition and health food, vitamins, and herbal products at General Nutrition Centers—articles should promote 'the physical lifestyle' of nutrition and exercise."

N $ **PREVENTION**, Rodale, Inc., 33 E. Minor St., Emmaus PA 18098-0099. Website: www.prevention.com. Senior Associates Editor: Shelley Drozd. Monthly magazine covering health and fitness. Written to motivate, inspire and enable male and female readers ages 35 and over to take charge of their health, to become healthier and happier, and to improve the lives of family and friends. Estab. 1950. Circ. 3,200,000.

- *Prevention* does not accept, nor do they acknowledge, unsolicited submissions.

$ $ $ $ SHAPE MAGAZINE, Weider Publications Inc., 21100 Erwin St., Woodland Hills CA 91367. (818)595-0593. Fax: (818)704-7620. Website: www.shapemag.com. Editor-in-Chief: Anne Russell. **Contact:** Lynn Perkin, EIC assistant. **70% freelance written.** Prefers to work with published/established writers. Monthly magazine covering women's health and fitness. "*Shape* reaches women who are committed to healthful, active lifestyles. Our readers are participating in a variety of fitness-related activities, in the gym, at home and outdoors, and they are also proactive about their health and are nutrition conscious." Estab. 1981. Circ. 1,600,000. **Pays on acceptance.** Offers 33% kill fee. Buys second serial (reprint), all rights. Submit seasonal material 8 months in advance. Responds in 2 months to queries. Sample copy for 9×12 SAE and 4 first-class stamps.

Nonfiction: "We use some health and fitness articles written by professionals in their specific fields." Book excerpts, exposé (health, fitness, nutrition related), how-to (get fit), health/fitness, recipes. "No articles that haven't been queried first." **Buys 27 features/year and 36-54 short mss/year.** Query by mail only with published clips. Length: 2,500 words for features, 1,000 words for shorter pieces. **Pays $1/word, on average.**

Tips: "Review a recent issue of the magazine. Not responsible for unsolicited material. We reserve the right to edit any article."

$ $ VIBRANT LIFE, A Magazine for Healthful Living, Review and Herald Publishing Association, 55 W. Oak Ridge Dr., Hagerstown MD 21740-7390. (301)393-4019. Fax: (301)393-4055. E-mail: vibrantlife@rhpa.org. Website: www.vibrantlife.com. **Contact:** Larry Becker, editor. **80% freelance written.** Enjoys working with published/established writers; works with a small number of new/unpublished writers each year. Bimonthly magazine covering health articles (especially from a prevention angle and with a Christian slant). "The average length of time between acceptance of a freelance-written manuscript and publication of the material depends upon the topics: some immediately used; others up to 2 years." Estab. 1885. Circ. 50,000. **Pays on acceptance.** Byline given. Offers 50% kill fee. Buys first serial, first world serial, or sometimes second serial (reprint) rights. Submit seasonal material 9 months in advance. Accepts queries by mail, e-mail, fax. Accepts previously published material. Responds in 1 month to queries. Sample copy for $1. Writer's guidelines online.

Nonfiction: "We seek practical articles promoting better health and a more fulfilled life. We especially like features on breakthroughs in medicine, and most aspects of health. We need articles on how to integrate a person's spiritual life with their health. We'd like more in the areas of exercise, nutrition, water, avoiding addictions of all types, and rest—all done from a wellness perspective." Interview/profile (with personalities on health). **Buys 50-60 feature articles/year and 6-12 short mss/year.** Send complete ms. Length: 500-1,500 words for features, 25-250 words for short pieces. **Pays $75-300 for features, $50-75 for short pieces.**

Reprints: Send tearsheet and information about when and where the material previously appeared. Pays 50% of amount paid for an original article.

Photos: Not interested in b&w photos. Send photos with submission. Reviews 35mm transparencies.

Columns/Departments: Buys 12-18 department articles/year. Length: 500-650 words. **Pays $75-175.**

Tips: "*Vibrant Life* is published for baby boomers, particularly young professionals, age 40-55. Articles must be written in an interesting, easy-to-read style. Information must be reliable; no faddism. We are more conservative than other magazines in our field. Request a sample copy, and study the magazine and writer's guidelines."

$ $ $ $ VIM & VIGOR, America's Family Health Magazine, 1010 E. Missouri Ave., Phoenix AZ 85014-2601. (602)395-5850. Fax: (602)395-5853. E-mail: careyj@mcmurry.com. Website: www.vigormagazine.com. **Contact:** Carey Jones, associate publisher/editor. **75% freelance written.** Quarterly magazine covering health and healthcare. Estab. 1985. Circ. 1,100,000. **Pays on acceptance.** Publishes ms an average of 3 months after acceptance. Byline given. Buys all rights. Sample copy for 9×12 SAE with 8 first-class stamps or online. Writer's guidelines for #10 SASE.

Nonfiction: "Absolutely no complete manuscripts will be accepted/returned. All articles are assigned. Send published samples for assignment consideration. Any queries regarding story ideas will be placed on the following year's conference agenda and will be addressed on a topic-by-topic basis." Health, disease, medical breakthroughs, exercise/fitness trends, wellness, healthcare. **Buys 12 mss/year.** Send published clips by mail or e-mail. Length: 500-1,500 words. **Pays 75¢-$1.20/word.** Pays expenses of writers on assignment.

Tips: "Writers must have consumer healthcare experience."

$ WEIGHT WATCHERS MAGAZINE, W/W Publishing Group, 747 3rd Ave., 24th Floor, New York NY 10017. (212)207-8800. Fax: (212)588-1733. Editor-in-Chief: Nancy Gagliardi. Executive Editor: Geri Anne Fennessey. Associate Editor: Lisa Harris. Assistant Editor: Nicole DeCowsy. **70% freelance written.** Bimonthly magazine mostly for women interested in weight loss, including healthy lifestyle/behavior information/advice, news on health, nutrition, fitness, beauty, fashion, psychology and food/recipes. Estab. 1968. Circ. 1,000,000. **Pays on acceptance.** Offers 25% kill fee. Buys first North American serial rights. Editorial lead time 3-12 months. Accepts queries by mail.

Nonfiction: Covers diet, nutrition, motivation/psychology, food, spas, beauty, fashion, and products for both the kitchen and an active lifestyle. Articles have an authoritative, yet friendly tone. How-to and service information crucial for all stories. Query with published clips. Length: 700-1,500 words.

Columns/Departments: Accepts editorial in health, fitness, diet, inspiration, nutrition.

Tips: "Well-developed, tightly written queries always a plus, as are trend pieces. We're always on the lookout for a fresh angle on an old topic. Sources must be reputable; we prefer subjects to be medical professionals with university affiliations who are published in their field of expertise. Lead times require stories to be seasonal, long-range, and forward-looking. We're looking for fresh, innovative stories that yield worthwhile information for women interested in losing weight—the latest exercise alternatives, a suggestion of how they can reduce stress, nutritional information that may not be common knowledge, reassurance about their lifestyle or health concerns, etc. Familiarity with the Weight Watchers philosophy/program is a plus."

$ $ $ $ YOGA JOURNAL, 2054 University Ave., Suite 600, Berkeley CA 94704. (510)841-9200. Fax: (510)644-3101. E-mail: editorial@yogajournal.com. Website: www.yogajournal.com. **Contact:** Kathryn Arnold, editor-in-chief. **75% freelance written.** Bimonthly magazine covering the practice and philosophy of yoga. Estab. 1975. Circ. 130,000. Pays within 90 days of acceptance. Publishes ms an average of 10 months after acceptance. Byline given. Offers kill fee on assigned articles. Buys first North American serial rights. Submit seasonal material 4 months in advance. Accepts queries by mail. Accepts previously published material. Responds in 3 months to queries. Sample copy for $4.99. Writer's guidelines online.

Nonfiction: "Yoga is a main concern, but we also highlight other conscious living/New Age personalities and endeavors (nothing too 'woo-woo'). In particular we welcome articles on the following themes: 1. Leaders, spokepersons, and visionaries in the yoga community; 2. The practice of hatha yoga; 3. Applications of yoga to everyday life; 4. Hatha yoga anatomy and kinesiology, and therapeutic yoga; 5. Nutrition and diet, cooking, and natural skin and body care." Book excerpts, how-to (yoga, exercise, etc.), inspirational, interview/profile, opinion, photo feature, travel (yoga-related). Does not want unsolicited poetry or cartoons. "Please avoid New Age jargon and in-house buzz words as much as possible." **Buys 50-60 mss/year.** Query with SASE. Length: 2,500-6,000 words. **Pays $800-2,000.**

Reprints: Send tearsheet or photocopy with rights for sale noted and information about when and where the material previously appeared.

Columns/Departments: Health (self-care; well-being); Body-Mind (hatha Yoga; other body-mind modalities; meditation; yoga philosophy; Western mysticism); Community (service; profiles; organizations; events), Length: 1,500-2,000 words. **Pays $400-800.** Living (books; video; arts; music), 800 words. **Pays $200-250.** World of Yoga, Spectrum (brief yoga and healthy living news/events/fillers), 150-600 words. **Pays $50-150.** "We encourage a well-written query letter outlining your subject and describing its appeal."

Tips: "Please read our writer's guidelines before submission. Do not e-mail or fax unsolicited manuscripts."

$ YOUR HEALTH & FITNESS, General Learning Communications, 900 Skokie Blvd., Northbrook IL 60062-1574. (847)205-3000. Fax: (847)564-8197. Website: www.glcomm.com. **Contact:** Debb Bastian, editorial director. **90% freelance written.** Prefers to work with published/established writers. Quarterly magazine. Needs "general, educational material on health, fitness, and safety that can be read and understood easily by the lay person. We also have a need for more technical health-related material written for a general audience, such as information on specific procedures and diseases." Estab. 1969. Circ. 1,000,000. Pays after publication. Publishes ms an average of 6 months after acceptance. Buys all rights.

O→ "All article topics assigned. No queries; if you're interested in writing for the magazine, send a cover letter, résumé/curriculum vitae, and writing samples. Topics are determined approximately 1 year in advance of publication by editors. No unsolicited manuscripts."

Nonfiction: All article topics are assigned. General interest (health-related). **Buys approximately 65 mss/year.** Send a résumé and cover letter accompanied by several published writing samples on health and/or health-related topics. Length: 300-1,000 words. **Payment varies, commensurate with experience and appropriate assignment.**

Tips: "Write to a general audience with only a surface knowledge of health and fitness topics. Possible subjects include exercise and fitness, psychology, nutrition, safety, disease, drug data, and health concerns. No phone queries."

HISTORY

Listed here are magazines and other periodicals written for historical collectors, genealogy enthusiasts, historic preservationists and researchers. Editors of history magazines look for fresh accounts of past events in a readable style. Some publications cover an era, while others may cover a region or subject area, such as aviation history.

$ $ AMERICA'S CIVIL WAR, Primedia History Group, 741 Miller Dr., SE, Suite D-2, Leesburg VA 20175-8920. (703)779-8318. Fax: (703)779-8310. E-mail: americascivilwar@thehistorynet.com. Website: www.thehistorynet.com. Managing Editor: Carl von Wodtke. **Contact:** Dana Shoaf, editor. **95% freelance written.** Bimonthly magazine covering "popular history and straight historical narrative for both the general reader and the Civil War buff covering strategy, tactics, personalities, arms and equipment." Estab. 1988. Circ. 78,000. Pays on publication. Publishes ms an average of 2 years after acceptance. Byline given. Buys all rights. Accepts queries by mail, e-mail, fax. Responds in 3 months to queries; 6 months to mss. Sample copy for $5. Writer's guidelines for #10 SASE or online.

Nonfiction: Historical/nostalgic, book notices; preservation news. No fiction or poetry. **Buys 24 mss/year.** Query. Length: 3,500-4,000 words and should include a 500-word sidebar. **Pays $300 and up.**

Photos: Send photos with submission or cite sources. "We'll order." Captions, identification of subjects required.

Columns/Departments: Personality (profiles of Civil War personalities); Men & Material (about weapons used); Commands (about units); Eyewitness to War (historical letters and diary excerpts). Length: 2,000 words. **Buys 24 mss/year.** Query. **Pays $150 and up.**

The online magazine carries original content not found in the print edition and includes writer's guidelines. Contact: Roger Vance.

Tips: "All stories must be true. We do not publish fiction or poetry. Write an entertaining, well-researched, informative and unusual story that grabs the reader's attention and holds it. Include suggested readings in a standard format at the end of your piece. Manuscript must be typed, double-spaced on one side of standard white 8½×11, 16 to 30 pound paper—no onion skin paper or dot matrix printouts. All submissions are on speculation. Prefer subjects to be on disk (IBM- or Macintosh-compatible floppy disk) as well as a hard copy. Choose stories with strong art possibilities."

$ AMERICAN HERITAGE, 28 W. 23rd St., New York NY 10010. (212)367-3100. E-mail: mail@americanheritage.com. Website: www.americanheritage.com. **Contact:** Richard Snow, editor. **70% freelance written.** Magazine published 6 times/year. "*American Heritage* writes from a historical point of view on politics, business, art, current and international affairs, and our changing lifestyles. The articles are written with the intent to enrich the reader's appreciation of the sometimes nostalgic, sometimes funny, always stirring panorama of the American experience." Circ. 350,000. **Pays on acceptance.** Publishes ms an average of 6-12 months after acceptance. Byline given. Buys first North American serial, all rights. Submit seasonal material 1 year in advance. Responds in 2 months to queries. Writer's guidelines for #10 SASE.

- Before submitting material, "check our index to see whether we have already treated the subject."

Nonfiction: Wants "historical articles by scholars or journalists intended for intelligent lay readers rather than for professional historians." Emphasis is on authenticity, accuracy, and verve. "Interesting documents, photographs, and drawings are always welcome. Style should stress readability and accuracy." Historical/nostalgic. **Buys 30 unsolicited mss/year.** Query. Length: 1,500-6,000 words. **Payment varies.** Sometimes pays expenses of writers on assignment.

Tips: "We have over the years published quite a few 'firsts' from young writers whose historical knowledge, research methods, and writing skills met our standards. The scope and ambition of a new writer tell us a lot about his or her future usefulness to us. A major article gives us a better idea of the writer's value. Everything depends on the quality of the material. We don't really care whether the author is 20 and unknown, or 80 and famous, or vice versa. No phone calls, please."

$ $ AMERICAN HISTORY, 741 Miller Dr., Suite D2 SE, Leesburg VA 20175. (717)657-9555. Website: www.thehistorynet.com. **Contact:** Philip George, editor. **60% freelance written.** Bimonthly magazine of cultural, social, military, and political history published for a general audience. Estab. 1966. Circ. 95,000. **Pays on acceptance.** Byline given. Buys first rights. Responds in 10 weeks to queries. Sample copy and guidelines for $5 (includes 3rd class postage) or $4 and 9×12 SAE with 4 first-class stamps. Writer's guidelines for #10 SASE or online.

Nonfiction: Features events in the lives of noteworthy historical figures and accounts of important events in American history. Also includes pictorial features on artists, photographers, and graphic subjects. "Material is presented on a popular rather than a scholarly level." **Buys 20 mss/year.** Query by mail only with published clips and SASE. Length: 2,000-4,000 words depending on type of article. **Pays $500-600.**

Photos: Welcomes suggestions for illustrations.

The online magazine occasionally carries some original content not included in the print edition. Contact: Christine Techky, managing editor.

Tips: "Key prerequisites for publication are thorough research and accurate presentation, precise English usage, and sound organization, a lively style, and a high level of human interest. Unsolicited manuscripts not considered. Inappropriate materials include: fiction, book reviews, travelogues, personal/family narratives not of national significance, articles about collectibles/antiques, living artists, local/individual historic buildings/landmarks, and articles of a current editorial nature. Currently seeking articles on significant Civil War subjects. No phone, fax, or e-mail queries, please."

$ THE ARTILLERYMAN, Historical Publications, Inc., 234 Monarch Hill Rd., Tunbridge VT 05077. (802)889-3500. Fax: (802)889-5627. E-mail: mail@civilwarnews.com. **Contact:** Kathryn Jorgensen, editor. **60% freelance written.** Quarterly magazine covering antique artillery, fortifications, and crew-served weapons 1750-1900 for competition shooters, collectors, and living history reenactors using artillery. "Emphasis on Revolutionary War and Civil War but includes everyone interested in pre-1900 artillery and fortifications, preservation, construction of replicas, etc." Estab. 1979. Circ. 2,000. Pays on publication. Publishes ms an average of 6 months after acceptance. Byline given. Not copyrighted. Buys one-time rights. Accepts queries by mail, e-mail, fax. Accepts previously published material. Accepts simultaneous submissions. Responds in 3 weeks to queries. Sample copy and writer's guidelines for 9×12 SAE with 4 first-class stamps.

Break in with a historical or travel piece featuring artillery—the types and history of guns and their use.

Nonfiction: Interested in "artillery *only*, for sophisticated readers. Not interested in other weapons, battles in general." Historical/nostalgic, how-to (reproduce ordnance equipment/sights/implements/tools/accessories, etc.), interview/profile, new product, opinion (must be accompanied by detailed background of writer and include references), personal experience, photo feature, technical (must have footnotes), travel (where to find interesting antique cannon). **Buys 24-30 mss/year.** Send complete ms. Length: 300 words minimum. **Pays $20-60.** Sometimes pays expenses of writers on assignment.

Reprints: Send tearsheet or photocopy and information about when and where the material previously appeared. Pays 100% of amount paid for an original article.

Photos: Send photos with submission. Pays $5 for 5×7 and larger b&w prints. Captions, identification of subjects required.

Tips: "We regularly use freelance contributions for Places-to-Visit, Cannon Safety, The Workshop, and Unit Profiles departments. Also need pieces on unusual cannon or cannon with a known and unique history. To judge whether writing style and/or expertise will suit our needs, writers should ask themselves if they could knowledgeably talk *artillery* with an expert. Subject matter is of more concern than writer's background."

$ $ AVIATION HISTORY, Primedia History Group, 741 Miller Dr., SE, Suite D-2, Leesburg VA 20175-8920. (703)771-9400. Fax: (703)779-8345. E-mail: AviationHistory@thehistorynet.com. Website: www.thehistorynet.com. Managing Editor: Carl von Wodtke. **Contact:** Arthur Sanfelici, editor. **95% freelance written.** Bimonthly magazine covering military and civilian aviation from first flight to the jet age. It aims to make aeronautical history not only factually accurate and complete, but also enjoyable to a varied subscriber and newsstand audience. Estab. 1990. Circ. 60,000. Pays on publication. Publishes ms an average of 2 years after acceptance. Byline given. Buys all rights. Editorial lead time 6 months.

Submit seasonal material 1 year in advance. Accepts queries by mail, e-mail, fax. Accepts simultaneous submissions. Responds in 3 months to queries; 6 months to mss. Sample copy for $5. Writer's guidelines for #10 SASE or online.

Nonfiction: Historical/nostalgic, interview/profile, personal experience. **Buys 24 mss/year.** Query. Length: Feature articles should be 3,500-4,000 words, each with a 500-word sidebar, author's biography, and book suggestions for further reading. **Pays $300.**

Photos: State availability of art and photos with submissions, cite sources. "We'll order." Reviews contact sheets, negatives, transparencies. Buys one-time rights. Identification of subjects required.

Columns/Departments: People and Planes; Enduring Heritage; Aerial Oddities; Art of Flight, all 2,000 words. **Pays $150**. Book reviews, 300-750 words, **pays minimum $40**.

The online magazine carries original content not found in the print edition and includes writer's guidelines. Contact: Roger Vance.

Tips: "Choose stories with strong art possibilities. Include a hard copy as well as an IBM- or Macintosh-compatible floppy disk. Write an entertaining, informative, and unusual story that grabs the reader's attention and holds it. All stories must be true. We do not publish fiction or poetry."

N $ BRITISH HERITAGE, PRIMEDIA Enthusiast Group, 6405 Flank Dr., Harrisburg PA 17112. (717)657-9555. Fax: (717)657-9552. E-mail: britishheritage_magazine@primediamags.com. Website: www.britishheritage.com. Managing Editor: Bruce Heydt. Bimonthly magazine covering British heritage. Presents comprehensive information and background of British culture for admirers and those interested in learning about life (past and present) in England, Scotland, and Wales. Circ. 77,485. **Pays on acceptance.** Buys all rights. Editorial lead time 6 months. Accepts queries by mail, e-mail. Sample copy not available. Writer's guidelines by e-mail.

Nonfiction: Historical/nostalgic (British History), interview/profile, travel. **Buys 30 mss/year.** Send complete ms.

Columns/Departments: In History's Court (two writers take up opposing sides in a historical debate), 1,500 words; Great Britons (biographical sketches of interesting British personalities), 2,000 words; Rendezvous with Destiny (highlight a specific historical personality focusing on a historic turning point) 1,500 words; It Happened Here (describe a historic home, castle, cathedral, etc.) 2,000 words; Wayfaring (travel oriented features) 2,000 words; Historymakers (interviews with eyewitnesses to historic events) 2,000 words. . British Heritage does not accept unsolicited manuscripts in "In History's Court" The following departments are generally written by the editorial staff or by a regularly commissioned contributing editor; The Game's Afoot, Hindsight, Timeline, The Private Side, Keepsakes, and Reviews.

N $ $ CIVIL WAR TIMES, 6405 Flank Dr., Harrisburg PA 17112. (717)657-9555. Fax: (717)657-9552. E-mail: CivilWarTimes.magazine@Primedia.com. Website: www.thehistorynet.com. Editor: Jim Kushlan. **Contact:** Carl Zebrowski, managing editor (book and product reviews contact). **90% freelance written.** Works with a small number of new/unpublished writers each year. Magazine published 6 times/year. "*Civil War Times* is the full-spectrum magazine of the Civil War. Specifically, we look for nonpartisan coverage of battles, prominent military and civilian figures, the home front, politics, military technology, common soldier life, prisoners and escapes, period art and photography, the naval war, blockade-running, specific regiments, and much more." Estab. 1962. Circ. 108,000. **Pays on acceptance.** Publishes ms an average of 18 months after acceptance. Buys unlimited usage rights. Submit seasonal material 1 year in advance. Responds in 3-6 months to queries. Sample copy for $5.50. Writer's guidelines for #10 SASE.

Nonfiction: Interview/profile, photo feature, Civil War historical material. "Don't send us a comprehensive article on a well-known major battle. Instead, focus on some part or aspect of such a battle, or some group of soldiers in the battle. Similar advice applies to major historical figures like Lincoln and Lee. Positively no fiction or poetry." **Buys 20 freelance mss/year.** Query with clips and SASE. **Pays $75-750.**

Photos: Jeff King, art director.

Tips: "We're very open to new submissions. Send query after examining writer's guidelines and several recent issues. Include photocopies of photos that could feasibly accompany the article. Confederate soldiers' diaries and letters are welcome."

$ $ GATEWAY HERITAGE, Missouri Historical Society, P.O. Box 11940, St. Louis MO 63112-0040. (314)746-4558. Fax: (314)746-4548. E-mail: vwmonks@mohistory.org. Website: www.mohistory.org. **Contact:** Vicky Monks, editor. **75% freelance written.** Quarterly magazine covering Missouri history. "*Gateway Heritage* is a popular history magazine which is sent to members of the Missouri Historical Society. Thus, we have a general audience with an interest in history." Estab. 1980. Circ. 9,000. Pays on publication. Publishes ms an average of 6 months after acceptance. Byline given. Offers $75 kill fee. Buys first North American serial rights. Editorial lead time 6 months. Submit seasonal material 1 year in advance. Accepts queries by mail, e-mail, fax. Responds in 2 weeks to queries; 2 months to mss. Sample copy for 9×12 SAE and 7 first-class stamps. Writer's guidelines for #10 SASE.

Nonfiction: Book excerpts, interview/profile, photo feature, historical, scholarly essays, Missouri biographies, viewpoints on events, first-hand historical accounts, regional architectural history, literary history. No genealogies. **Buys 12-15 mss/year.** Query with published clips. Length: 3,500-5,000 words. **Pays $200 (average).**

Photos: State availability with submission.

Columns/Departments: Literary Landmarks (biographical sketches and interviews of famous Missouri literary figures), 1,500-2,500 words; Missouri Biographies (biographical sketches of famous and interesting Missourians), 1,500-2,500 words; Gateway Album (excerpts from diaries and journals), 1,500-2,500 words. **Buys 6-8 mss/year.** Query with published clips. **Pays $250-500.**

Tips: "Ideas for our departments are a good way to break in to *Gateway Heritage*."

$ GOOD OLD DAYS, America's Premier Nostalgia Magazine, House of White Birches, 306 E. Parr Rd., Berne IN 46711. (219)589-4000. E-mail: editor@goodolddaysonline.com. Website: www.goodolddays-magazine.com. **Contact:** Ken Tate, editor. **75% freelance written.** Monthly magazine of first person nostalgia, 1935-1960. "We look for strong narratives showing life as it was in the first half of the 20th century. Our readership is comprised of nostalgia buffs, history enthusiasts, and the people who actually lived and grew up in this era." Pays on contract. Publishes ms an average of 8 months after acceptance. Byline given. Prefers all rights, but will negotiate for First North American serial and one-time rights. Submit seasonal material 10 months in advance. Responds in 2 months to queries. Sample copy for $2. Writer's guidelines online.

- Queries accepted, but are not necessary.

Nonfiction: Regular features: Good Old Days on Wheels (transportation auto, plane, horse-drawn, tram, bicycle, trolley, etc.); Good Old Days In the Kitchen (favorite foods, appliances, ways of cooking, recipes); Home Remedies (herbs and poultices, hometown doctors, harrowing kitchen table operations). Historical/nostalgic, humor, personal experience, photo feature, favorite food/recipes, year-round seasonal material, biography, memorable events, fads, fashion, sports, music, literature, entertainment. No fiction accepted. **Buys 350 mss/year.** Query or send complete ms. Length: 500-1,500 words. **Pays $20-100, depending on quality and photos.**

Photos: "Send original or professionally copied photographs. Do not submit laser-copied prints." Send photos with submission. Identification of subjects required.

Tips: "Most of our writers are not professionals. We prefer the author's individual voice, warmth, humor, and honesty over technical ability."

N **$ LIGHTHOUSE DIGEST**, Lighthouse Digest, P.O. Box 1690, Wells ME 04090. (207)646-0515. Fax: (207)646-0516. E-mail: timh@lhdigest.com. Website: www.lighthousedigest.com. **Contact:** Tim Harrison, editor. **15% freelance written.** Monthly magazine covering historical, fiction and news events about lighthouses and similar maritime stories. Estab. 1989. Circ. 24,000. Pays on publication. Publishes ms an average of 4 months after acceptance. Byline given. Buys one-time, electronic rights. Editorial lead time 3 months. Submit seasonal material 3 months in advance. Accepts queries by e-mail. Accepts simultaneous submissions. Responds in 6 weeks to queries. Sample copy for free. Writer's guidelines not available.

Nonfiction: Exposé, general interest, historical/nostalgic, humor, inspirational, personal experience, photo feature, religious, technical, travel. No historical data taken from books. **Buys 30 mss/year.** Send complete ms. Length: 2,500 words maximum. **Pays $75.**

Photos: Send photos with submission. Reviews prints. Buys all rights. Offers no additional payment for photos accepted with ms. Captions, identification of subjects required.

Fiction: Adventure, historical, humorous, mystery, religious, romance, suspense. **Buys 2 mss/year.** Send complete ms. Length: 2,500 words maximum. **Pays $75-150.**

Tips: "Read our publication and visit the website."

$ $ MILITARY HISTORY, Primedia History Group, 741 Miller Dr., SE, Suite D-2, Leesburg VA 20175-8920. (703)771-9400. Fax: (703)779-8345. E-mail: militaryhistory@thehistorynet.com. Website: www.thehistorynet.com. Managing Editor: Carl von Wodtke. **Contact:** Jon Guttman, editor. **95% freelance written.** "We'll work with anyone, established or not, who can provide the goods and convince us of its accuracy." Bimonthly magazine covering all military history of the world. "We strive to give the general reader accurate, highly readable, often narrative popular history, richly accompanied by period art." Circ. 112,000. 30 days after publication. Publishes ms an average of 2 years after acceptance. Byline given. Buys all rights. Submit seasonal material 1 year in advance. Accepts queries by mail, e-mail, fax. Responds in 3 months to queries; 6 months to mss. Sample copy for $5. Writer's guidelines for #10 SASE or online.

Nonfiction: "The best way to break into our magazine is to write an entertaining, informative and unusual story that grabs the readers attention and holds it." Historical/nostalgic, interview/profile (military figures of commanding interest), personal experience (only occasionally). **Buys 30 mss/year.** Query with published clips. "Submit a short, self-explanatory query summarizing the story proposed, its highlights, and/or significance. State also your own expertise, access to sources or proposed means of developing the pertinent information." Length: 4,000 words with a 500-word sidebar. **Pays $400.**

Columns/Departments: Intrigue; Weaponry; Perspectives; Personality; Reviews (books, video, CD-ROMs, software—all relating to military history). Length: 2,000 words. **Buys 24 mss/year.** Query with published clips. **Pays $200.**

The online magazine contains content not found in the print edition and includes writer's guidelines. Contact: Roger Vance.

Tips: "We would like journalistically 'pure' submissions that adhere to basics, such as full name at first reference, same with rank, and definition of prior or related events, issues cited as context or obscure military 'hardware.' Read the magazine, discover our style, and avoid subjects already covered. Pick stories with strong art possibilities (real art and photos), send photocopies, tell us where to order the art. Avoid historical overview; focus upon an event with appropriate and accurate context. Provide bibliography. Tell the story in popular but elegant style. Include a hard copy as well as an IBM- or Macintosh-compatible floppy disk."

$ $ PERSIMMON HILL, National Cowboy and Western Heritage Museum, 1700 NE 63rd St., Oklahoma City OK 73111. (405)478-6404. Fax: (405)478-4714. E-mail: editor@nationalcowboymuseum.org. Website: www.nationalcowboymuseum.org. **Contact:** M.J. Van Deventer, editor. **70% freelance written.** Prefers to work with published/established writers; works with a small number of new/unpublished writers each year. Quarterly magazine for an audience interested in Western art, Western history, ranching, and rodeo, including historians, artists, ranchers, art galleries, schools, and libraries. Estab. 1970. Circ. 15,000. Pays on publication. Publishes ms an average of 2 years after acceptance. Byline given. Buys first rights. Responds in 3 months to queries. Sample copy for $10.50, including postage. Writer's guidelines for #10 SASE or on website.

- The editor of *Persimmon Hill* reports: "We need more material on rodeo, both contemporary and historical. And we need more profiles on contemporary working ranches in the West."

Nonfiction: Historical and contemporary articles on famous Western figures connected with pioneering the American West, Western art, rodeo, cowboys, etc. (or biographies of such people), stories of Western flora and animal life and environmental subjects. "We want thoroughly researched and historically authentic material written in a popular style. May have a humorous approach to subject." "No broad, sweeping, superficial pieces; i.e., the California Gold Rush or rehashed pieces on Billy the Kid, etc." **Buys 35-50 mss/year.** Query by mail only with clips. Length: 1,500 words. **Pays $150-250.**
Photos: Purchased with ms or on assignment. Reviews color transparencies, glossy b&w prints. Pays according to quality and importance for b&w and color photos. Captions required.
Tips: "Send us a story that captures the spirit of adventure and indvidualism that typifies the Old West or reveals a facet of the Western lifestyle in comtemporary society. Excellent illustrations for articles are essential! We lean towards scholarly, historical, well-researched articles. We're less focused on Western celebrities than some of the other contemporary Western magazines."

$ PRESERVATION MAGAZINE, National Trust for Historic Preservation, 1785 Massachusetts Ave. NW, Washington DC 20036. (202)588-6388. Fax: (202)588-6266. E-mail: preservation@nthp.org. Website: preservationonline.org. **Contact:** James Conaway, editor-in-chief. **75% freelance written.** Prefers to work with published/established writers. Bimonthly magazine covering preservation of historic buildings in the US. "We cover subjects related in some way to place. Most entries are features, department, or opinion pieces." Circ. 250,000. Pays on publication. Publishes ms an average of 1 month after acceptance. Byline given. Offers variable kill fee. Buys one-time rights. Accepts queries by mail, e-mail, fax. Responds in 2 months to queries. Writer's guidelines online.
Nonfiction: Book excerpts, essays, historical/nostalgic, humor, interview/profile, new product, opinion, photo feature, travel, features, news. **Buys 30 mss/year.** Query with published clips. Length: 500-3,500 words. Sometimes pays expenses of writers on assignment, but not long-distance travel.

The online magazine carries original content not found in the print edition. Contact: Margaret Foster.

Tips: "Do not send or propose histories of buildings, descriptive accounts of cities or towns or long-winded treatises. Best bet for breaking in is via Preservation Online, Preservation News (news features, 500-1,000 words), Bricks & Mortar (brief profile or article, 250-500 words)."

$ $ $ TIMELINE, Ohio Historical Society, 1982 Velma Ave., Columbus OH 43211-2497. (614)297-2360. Fax: (614)297-2367. E-mail: timeline@ohiohistory.org. **Contact:** Christopher S. Duckworth, editor. **90% freelance written.** Works with a small number of new/unpublished writers each year. Bimonthly magazine covering history, prehistory, and the natural sciences, directed toward readers in the Midwest. Estab. 1984. Circ. 19,000. **Pays on acceptance.** Publishes ms an average of 1 year after acceptance. Byline given. Offers $75 minimum kill fee. Buys first North American serial, all rights. Submit seasonal material 6 months in advance. Accepts queries by mail, e-mail, fax. Responds in 3 weeks to queries; 6 weeks to mss. Sample copy for $6 and 9×12 SAE. Writer's guidelines for #10 SASE.
Nonfiction: Topics include the traditional fields of political, economic, military, and social history; biography; the history of science and technology; archaeology and anthropology; architecture; the fine and decorative arts; and the natural sciences including botany, geology, zoology, ecology, and paleontology. Book excerpts, essays, historical/nostalgic, interview/profile (of individuals), photo feature. **Buys 22 mss/year.** Query. Length: 1,500-6,000 words. Also vignettes of 500-1,000 words. **Pays $100-900.**
Photos: Submissions should include ideas for illustration. Send photos with submission. Reviews contact sheets, transparencies, 8×10 prints. Buys one-time rights. Captions, identification of subjects, model releases required.
Tips: "We want crisply written, authoritative narratives for the intelligent lay reader. An Ohio slant may strengthen a submission, but it is not indispensable. Contributors must know enough about their subject to explain it clearly and in an interesting fashion. We use high-quality illustration with all features. If appropriate illustration is unavailable, we can't use the feature. The writer who sends illustration ideas with a manuscript has an advantage, but an often-published illustration won't attract us."

$ $ TRACES OF INDIANA AND MIDWESTERN HISTORY, Indiana Historical Society, 450 W. Ohio St., Indianapolis IN 46202-3269. (317)232-1877. Fax: (317)233-0857. E-mail: rboomhower@indianahistory.org. Website: www.indianahistory.org/traces.htm. Executive Editor: Thomas A. Mason. **Contact:** Ray E. Boomhower, managing editor. **80% freelance written.** Quarterly magazine on Indiana and Midwestern history. "Conceived as a vehicle to bring to the public good narrative and analytical history about Indiana in its broader contexts of region and nation, *Traces* explores the lives of artists, writers, performers, soldiers, politicians, entrepreneurs, homemakers, reformers, and naturalists. It has traced the impact of Hoosiers on the nation and the world. In this vein, the editors seek nonfiction articles that are solidly researched, attractively written, and amenable to illustration, and they encourage scholars, journalists, and freelance writers to contribute to the magazine." Estab. 1989. Circ. 11,000. **Pays on acceptance.** Publishes ms an average of 6 months after acceptance. Byline given. Buys one-time rights. Submit seasonal material 1 year in advance. Responds in 3 months to mss. Sample copy and writer's guidelines for $5.25 (make checks payable to Indiana Historical Society) and 9×12 SAE with 7 first-class stamps or on website. Writer's guidelines for #10 SASE.
Nonfiction: Book excerpts, historical essays, historical photographic features on topics of biography, literature, folklore, music, visual arts, politics, economics, industry, transportation, and sports. **Buys 20 mss/year.** Send complete ms. Length: 2,000-4,000 words. **Pays $100-500.**
Photos: Send photos with submission. Reviews contact sheets, transparencies, photocopies, prints. Buys one-time rights.

Pays "reasonable photographic expenses." Captions, identification of subjects, permissions required.

Tips: "Freelancers should be aware of prerequisites for writing history for a broad audience. Should have some awareness of this magazine and other magazines of this type published by Midwestern historical societies. Preference is given to subjects with an Indiana connection and authors who are familiar with *Traces*. Quality of potential illustration is also important."

$ $ $ TRUE WEST, True West Publishing, Inc., P.O. Box 8008, Cave Creek AZ 85327. (888)587-1881. Fax: (480)575-1903. E-mail: editor@truewestmagazine.com. Website: www.truewestmagazine.com. Executive Editor: Bob Boze Bell. **Contact:** R.G. Robertson, managing editor. **70% freelance written.** Works with a small number of new/unpublished writers each year. Magazine published 10 times/year. covering Western American history from prehistory 1800 to 1930. "We want reliable research on significant historical topics written in lively prose for an informed general audience. More recent topics may be used if they have a historical angle or retain the Old West flavor of trail dust and saddle leather." Estab. 1953. Circ. 90,000. Pays on publication. Byline given. Buys first North American serial rights. Editorial lead time 3 months. Accepts queries by mail, e-mail. Sample copy for $3 and 9 × 12 SASE. Writer's guidelines online. Editorial calendar online.

● No unsolicited mss.

O-π "We are looking for historically accurate stories on the Old West that make you wonder 'What happens next?'"

Nonfiction: No fiction, poetry, or unsupported, undocumented tales. **Buys 30 mss/year.** Query. Length: 1,000-3,000 words. **Pays $50-800.**

Photos: State availability with submission. Reviews contact sheets, negatives, 4 × 5 transparencies, 4 × 5 prints. Buys one-time rights. Offers $10-75/photo. Captions, identification of subjects, model releases required.

Columns/Departments: Book Reviews, 50-60 words (no unsolicited reviews). **Pays $25.**

Fillers: Anecdotes, facts, gags to be illustrated by cartoonist, newsbreaks, short humor. **Buys 30/year.** Length: 50-600 words.

Tips: "Read our magazines and follow our guidelines. A freelancer is most likely to break in with us by submitting thoroughly researched, lively prose on relatively obscure topics or by being assigned to write for 1 of our departments. First-person accounts rarely fill our needs. Historical accuracy and strict adherence to the facts are essential. We much prefer material based on primary sources (archives, court records, documents, contemporary newspapers and first-person accounts) to those that rely mainly on secondary sources (published books, magazines, and journals)."

$ $ VIETNAM, Primedia History Group, 741 Miller Dr., SE, #D-2, Leesburg VA 20175-8920. (703)771-9400. Fax: (703)779-8345. E-mail: Vietnam@thehistorynet.com. Website: www.thehistorynet.com. Managing Editor: Carl von Wodtke. **Contact:** David T. Zabecki, editor. **90% freelance written.** Bimonthly magazine providing in-depth and authoritative accounts of the many complexities that made the war in Vietnam unique, including the people, battles, strategies, perspectives, analysis, and weaponry. Estab. 1988. Circ. 48,000. Pays on publication. Publishes ms an average of 2 years after acceptance. Byline given. Buys all rights. Accepts queries by mail, e-mail, fax. Responds in 3 months to queries; 6 months to mss. Sample copy for $5. Writer's guidelines for #10 SASE.

Nonfiction: Historical/nostalgic (military), interview/profile, personal experience. "Absolutely no fiction or poetry; we want straight history, as much personal narrative as possible, but not the gung-ho, shoot-'em-up variety, either." **Buys 24 mss/year.** Query. Length: 4,000 words maximum; sidebars 500 words. **Pays $300 for features.**

Photos: Send photos with submission or state availability and cite sources. Identification of subjects required.

Columns/Departments: Arsenal (about weapons used, all sides); Personality (profiles of the players, all sides); Fighting Forces (various units or types of units: air, sea, rescue); Perspectives. Length: 2,000 words. Query. **Pays $150.**

The online magazine contains content not found in the print edition and includes writer's guidelines. Contact: Roger Vance.

Tips: "Choose stories with strong art possibilities. Send hard copy plus an IBM- or Macintosh-compatible floppy disk. All stories must be true. We do not publish fiction or poetry. All stories should be carefully researched, third-person articles or firsthand accounts that give the reader a sense of experiencing historical events."

$ $ WILD WEST, Primedia History Group, 741 Miller Dr., SE, Suite D-2, Leesburg VA 20175-8920. (703)771-9400. Fax: (703)779-8345. E-mail: wildwest@thehistorynet.com. Website: www.thehistorynet.com. Managing Editor: Carl von Wodtke. **Contact:** Gregory Lalire, editor. **95% freelance written.** Bimonthly magazine covering the history of the American frontier, from its eastern beginnings to its western terminus. "*Wild West* covers the popular (narrative) history of the American West—events, trends, personalities, anything of general interest." Estab. 1988. Circ. 83,500. Pays on publication. Publishes ms an average of 2 years after acceptance. Byline given. Not copyrighted. Buys all rights. Editorial lead time 6 months. Submit seasonal material 1 year in advance. Accepts queries by mail, e-mail. Accepts simultaneous submissions. Responds in 3 months to queries; 6 months to mss. Sample copy for $5. Writer's guidelines for #10 SASE or online.

Nonfiction: Historical/nostalgic (Old West). No excerpts, travel, etc. Articles can be "adapted from" book. No fiction or poetry—nothing current. **Buys 36 mss/year.** Query. Length: 3,500 words with a 500-word sidebar. **Pays $300.**

Photos: State availability with submission. Reviews negatives, transparencies. Buys one-time rights. Offers no additional payment for photos accepted with ms. Captions, identification of subjects required.

Columns/Departments: Gunfighters & Lawmen, 2,000 words; Westerners, 2,000 words; Warriors & Chiefs, 2,000 words; Western Lore, 2,000 words; Guns of the West, 1,500 words; Artists West, 1,500 words; Books Reviews, 250 words. **Buys 36 mss/year.** Query. **Pays $150 for departments; book reviews paid by the word, minimum $40.**

The online magazine carries original content not found in the print edition. Contact: Roger Vance, online editor.

Tips: "Always query the editor with your story idea. Successful queries include a description of sources of information and suggestions for color and b&w photography or artwork. The best way to break into our magazine is to write an entertaining, informative and unusual story that grabs the reader's attention and holds it. We favor carefully researched, third-person articles that give the reader a sense of experiencing historical events. Include a hard copy as well as an IBM- or Macintosh-compatible floppy disk."

$ $ WORLD WAR II, Primedia History Group, 741 Miller Dr., SE, Suite D-2, Leesburg VA 20175-8920. (703)771-9400. Fax: (703)779-8345. E-mail: worldwarii@thehistorynet.com. Website: www.thehistorynet.com. Managing Editor: Carl von Wodtke. **Contact:** Christopher Anderson, editor. **95% freelance written.** Prefers to work with published/established writers. Bimonthly magazine covering "military operations in World War II—events, personalities, strategy, national policy, etc." Estab. 1986. Circ. 146,000. Pays on publication. Publishes ms an average of 2 years after acceptance. Byline given. Buys all rights. Accepts queries by mail, e-mail, fax. Responds in 3 months to queries; 6 months to mss. Sample copy for $5. Writer's guidelines for #10 SASE or online.

Nonfiction: World War II military history. Submit anniversary-related material 1 year in advance. No fiction. **Buys 24 mss/year.** Query. Length: 4,000 words with a 500-word sidebar. **Pays $300 and up.**

Photos: For photos and other art, send photocopies and cite sources. "We'll order." State availability with submission. Captions, identification of subjects required.

Columns/Departments: Undercover (espionage, resistance, sabotage, intelligence gathering, behind the lines, etc.); Personality (WWII personalities of interest); Armament (weapons, their use and development); Commands (unit histories); One Man's War (personal profiles), all 2,000 words. Book reviews, 300-750 words. **Buys 30 (plus book reviews) mss/year.** Query. **Pays $150 and up.**

The online magazine contains content not found in the print edition and includes writer's guidelines. Contact: Roger Vance.

Tips: "List your sources and suggest further readings in standard format at the end of your piece—as a bibliography for our files in case of factual challenge or dispute. All submissions are on speculation. Include a hard copy as well as an IBM- or Macintosh-compatible floppy disk. All stories must be true. We do not publish fiction or poetry. Stories should be carefully researched."

HOBBY & CRAFT

Magazines in this category range from home video to cross-stitch. Craftspeople and hobbyists who read these magazines want new ideas while collectors need to know what is most valuable and why. Collectors, do-it-yourselfers, and craftspeople look to these magazines for inspiration and information. Publications covering antiques and miniatures are also listed here. Publications covering the business side of antiques and collectibles are listed in the Trade Art, Design & Collectibles section.

$ ANTIQUE & COLLECTIBLES NEWSMAGAZINE, Krause Publications, P.O. Box 12589, El Cajon CA 92022. (619)593-2926. Fax: (619)447-7187. E-mail: editorialnow@aol.com. Website: www.collect.com. **Contact:** Manny Cruz, managing editor. **45% freelance written.** Monthly magazine covering antiques and collectibles. *Antique & Collectibles* reaches antique collectors situated in Southern California, Nevada, and Arizona. Estab. 1979. Circ. 27,500. Pays on publication. Publishes ms an average of 2 months after acceptance. Byline given. Buys first, electronic rights. Editorial lead time 1 month. Accepts queries by mail, e-mail. Accepts simultaneous submissions. Sample copy for free. Writer's guidelines free.

Nonfiction: General interest, how-to, interview/profile, photo feature. Query. Length: 500-1,200 words. **Pays $25-60.**

Photos: Send photos with submission. Reviews contact sheets. Buys all rights. Negotiates payment individually. Captions required.

Tips: "Be knowledgable in antiques and collecting and have good photos."

N $ $ ANTIQUE REVIEW, PO Box 1050, Dubuque IA 52004-1050. (800)480-0131. E-mail: kunkell@krause.com. Website: www.collect.com. **Contact:** Linda Kunkel, editor. **60% freelance written.** Eager to work with new/unpublished writers. Monthly tabloid for an antique-oriented readership, "generally well-educated, interested in Early American furniture and decorative arts, as well as folk art." Estab. 1975. Circ. 6,000. Pays on publication. Publishes ms an average of 3 months after acceptance. Byline given. Buys first North American serial, second serial (reprint) rights. Accepts queries by mail, e-mail, phone. Accepts previously published material. Responds in 3 months to queries. Sample copy for #10 SASE.

Nonfiction: "The articles we desire concern history and production of furniture, pottery, china, and other quality Americana. In some cases, contemporary folk art items are acceptable. We are also interested in reporting on antiques shows and auctions with statements on conditions and prices." Query should show "author's familiarity with antiques, an interest in the historical development of artifacts relating to early America, and an awareness of antiques market." **Buys 60-90 mss/year.** Query with published clips. Length: 200-2,000 words. **Pays $100-200.** Sometimes pays expenses of writers on assignment.

Reprints: Send tearsheet, photocopy or typed ms with rights for sale noted and information about when and where the material previously appeared. Pays 100% of amount paid for an original article.

Photos: Articles with photographs receive preference. Send photos with submission. Reviews 3×5 or larger glossy b&w or color prints. Payment included in ms price. Captions required.

Tips: "Give us a call and let us know of specific interests. We are more concerned with the background in antiques than in writing abilities. The writing can be edited, but the knowledge imparted is of primary interest. A frequent mistake is being too general, not becoming deeply involved in the topic and its research. We are interested in primary research into America's historic material culture."

$ $ ANTIQUES & COLLECTING MAGAZINE, 1006 S. Michigan Ave., Chicago IL 60605. (312)939-4767. Fax: (312)939-0053. E-mail: acmeditor@interaccess.com. **Contact:** Therese Nolan, editor. **80% freelance written.** Monthly magazine covering antiques and collectibles. Estab. 1931. Circ. 20,000. Pays on publication. Publishes ms an average of 3 months after acceptance. Byline given. Buys first rights. Editorial lead time 2 months. Submit seasonal material 3 months in advance. Accepts queries by mail, e-mail, fax, phone. Responds in 3 weeks to queries; 2 months to mss. Sample copy for free. Writer's guidelines for free or by e-mail.

Nonfiction: Book excerpts, general interest, historical/nostalgic, how-to, interview/profile, opinion, personal experience, photo feature, features about antiques and collectibles made before 1970. **Buys 40-50 mss/year.** Query. Length: 1,000-1,600 words. **Pays $150-250, plus 4 copies.**

Photos: Send photos with submission. Reviews transparencies, prints. Buys one-time rights. Offers no additional payment for photos accepted with ms. Captions, identification of subjects required.

Fillers: Anecdotes, facts.

$ AUTOGRAPH COLLECTOR, Odyssey Publications, 510-A South Corona Mall, Corona CA 91719. (909)371-7137. Fax: (909)371-7139. E-mail: dbtogi@aol.com. Website: www.autographcollector.com. **Contact:** Ev Phillips, editor. **80% freelance written.** Monthly magazine covering the autograph collecting hobby. "The focus of *Autograph Collector* is on documents, photographs or any collectible item that has been signed by a famous person, whether a current celebrity or historical figure. Articles stress how and where to locate celebrities and autograph material, authenticity of signatures and what they are worth." Byline given. Offers negotiable kill fee. Buys all rights. Editorial lead time 2 months. Submit seasonal material 3 months in advance. Accepts queries by mail, e-mail, fax, phone. Responds in 2 weeks to queries. Sample copy and writer's guidelines free.

Nonfiction: "Articles must address subjects that appeal to autograph collectors and should answer six basic questions: Who is this celebrity/famous person? How do I go about collecting this person's autograph? Where can I find it? How scarce or available is it? How can I tell if it's real? What is it worth?" Historical/nostalgic, how-to, interview/profile, personal experience. **Buys 25-35 mss/year.** Query. Length: 1,600-2,000 words. **Pays 5¢/word.** Sometimes pays expenses of writers on assignment.

Photos: State availability with submission. Reviews transparencies, prints. Buys one-time rights. Offers $3/photo. Captions, identification of subjects required.

Columns/Departments: "*Autograph Collector* buys 8-10 columns per month written by regular contributors." **Buys 90-100 mss/year.** Query. **Pays $50 or as determined on a per case basis.**

Fillers: Anecdotes, facts. **Buys 20-25/year.** Length: 200-300 words. **Pays $15.**

Tips: "Ideally writers should be autograph collectors themselves and know their topics thoroughly. Articles must be well-researched and clearly written. Writers should remember that *Autograph Collector* is a celebrity-driven magazine and name recognition of the subject is important."

$ BEAD & BUTTON, Kalmbach Publishing, 21027 Crossroads Circle, Waukesha WI 53186. (262)796-8776. E-mail: akorach@beadandbutton.com. Website: www.beadandbutton.com. Editor: Alice Korach. **Contact:** Lora Groszkiewicz, editorial assistant. **50% freelance written.** "*Bead & Button* is a bimonthly magazine devoted to techniques, projects, designs and materials relating to beads, buttons, and accessories. Our readership includes both professional and amateur bead and button makers, hobbyists, and enthusiasts who find satisfaction in making beautiful things." Estab. 1994. Circ. 80,000. **Pays on acceptance.** Publishes ms an average of 4 months after acceptance. Byline given. Offers $75 kill fee. Buys all rights. Accepts queries by mail, e-mail, fax. Writer's guidelines online.

Nonfiction: Historical/nostalgic (on beaded jewelry history), how-to (make beaded jewelry and accessories), humor (or inspirational -1 endpiece for each issue), interview/profile. **Buys 24-30 mss/year.** Send complete ms. Length: 750-3,000 words. **Pays $75-300.**

Photos: Send photos with submission. Offers no additional payment for photos accepted with ms. Identification of subjects required.

Columns/Departments: Chic & Easy (fashionable jewelry how-to); Beginner (easy-to-make jewelry how-to); Simply Earrings (fashionable earring how-to); Fun Fashion (trendy jewelry how-to), all 1,500 words. **Buys 12 mss/year.** Send complete ms. **Pays $75-150.**

Tips: "*Bead & Button* magazine primarily publishes how-to articles by the artists who have designed the piece. We publish one profile and one historical piece per issue. These would be the only applicable articles for non-artisan writers. Also our humorous and inspirational endpiece might apply."

$ $ BLADE MAGAZINE®, The World's #1 Knife Publication, Krause Publications, 700 E. State St., Iola WI 54990. (715)445-2214. Fax: (715)445-4087. E-mail: blademagazine@krause.com. Website: www.blademag.com. Editor: Steve Shackleford. **Contact:** Joe Kertzman, managing editor. **60% freelance written.** Monthly magazine for knife enthusiasts who want to know as much as possible about quality knives and edged tools, handmade and factory knife industries, antique knife collecting, etc. *Blade* is designed to highlight the romance and history of man's oldest tool, the knife. Our readers are into any and all knives used as tools/collectibles. Estab. 1973. Circ. 75,000. Pays on publication. Publishes ms an average of 1 year after acceptance. Byline given. Offers $20 kill fee. Buys all rights. Editorial lead time 4 months. Submit seasonal material 4 months in advance. Accepts queries by mail, e-mail, fax, phone. Responds in 3 months to queries. Sample copy for #10 SASE.

Nonfiction: "We would like to see articles on knives in adventuresome lifesaving situations." Book excerpts, exposé, general interest, historical/nostalgic (on knives), how-to, humor, new product, personal experience, photo feature, technical, travel, adventure (on a knife theme), celebrities who own knives, knives featured in movies with shots from the movie, etc. No articles on how to use knives as weapons. No poetry. **Buys 50 mss/year.** Query. Length: 1,000-1,500 words. **Pays $125-300. "We will pay top dollar in the knife market."** Sometimes pays expenses of writers on assignment.

Photos: State availability of or send photos with submission. Offers no additional payment for photos accepted with ms. Captions, identification of subjects required.

Columns/Departments: Buys 60 mss/year. Query. **Pays $150-250.**

Fillers: Anecdotes, facts, newsbreaks. **Buys 1-2/year.** Length: 50-200 words. **Pays $25-50.**

Tips: "We are always willing to read submissions from anyone who has read a few copies and studied the market. The ideal article for us is a piece bringing out the romance, legend, and love of man's oldest tool—the knife. We like articles that place knives in peoples' hands—in life saving situations, adventure modes, etc. (Nothing gory or with the knife as the villain.) People and knives are good copy. We are getting more and better written articles from writers who are reading the publication beforehand. That makes for a harder sell for the quickie writer not willing to do his homework. Go to knife shows and talk to the makers and collectors. Visit knifemakers' shops and knife factories. Read anything and everything you can find on knives and knifemaking."

$ BREW YOUR OWN, The How-to Homebrew Beer Magazine, Battenkill Communications, 5053 Main St., Suite A, Manchester Center VT 05255. (802)362-3981. Fax: (802)362-2377. E-mail: edit@byo.com. Website: www.byo.com. **Contact:** Kathleen Ring, editor. **85% freelance written.** Monthly magazine covering home brewing. "Our mission is to provide practical information in an entertaining format. We try to capture the spirit and challenge of brewing while helping our readers brew the best beer they can." Estab. 1995. Circ. 42,000. **Pays on acceptance.** Publishes ms an average of 4 months after acceptance. Byline given. Offers 25% kill fee. Buys all rights. Editorial lead time 3 months. Submit seasonal material 3 months in advance. Accepts queries by mail, e-mail, fax. Responds in 2 months to queries. Writer's guidelines online.

Break in by "sending a detailed query in 1 of 2 key areas: how to brew a specific, interesting style of beer (with step-by-step recipes) or how to build your own specific piece of brewing equipment."

Nonfiction: Informational pieces on equipment, ingredients, and brewing methods. Historical/nostalgic, how-to (home brewing), humor (related to home brewing), interview/profile (of professional brewers who can offer useful tips to home hobbyists), personal experience, trends. **Buys 75 mss/year.** Query with published clips or description of brewing expertise. Length: 800-3,000 words. **Pays $50-150, depending on length, complexity of article and experience of writer.** Sometimes pays expenses of writers on assignment.

Photos: State availability with submission. Reviews contact sheets, transparencies, 5×7 prints, slides, and electronic images. Buys all rights. Negotiates payment individually. Captions required.

Columns/Departments: News (humorous, unusual news about homebrewing), 50-250 words; Last Call (humorous stories about homebrewing), 700 words. **Buys 12 mss/year.** Query with or without published clips. **Pays $50.**

Tips: "*Brew Your Own* is for anyone who is interested in brewing beer, from beginners to advanced all-grain brewers. We seek articles that are straightforward and factual, not full of esoteric theories or complex calculations. Our readers tend to be intelligent, upscale, and literate."

$ $ CERAMICS MONTHLY, 735 Ceramic Place, Westerville OH 43081. (614)895-4213. Fax: (614)891-8960. E-mail: editorial@ceramicsmonthly.org. Website: www.ceramicsmonthly.org. **Contact:** Renée Fairchild, assistant editor. **70% freelance written.** Monthly magazine (except July and August) covering the ceramic art and craft field. "Technical and business information for potters and ceramic artists." Estab. 1953. Circ. 39,000. Pays on publication. Byline given. Editorial lead time 3 months. Submit seasonal material 6 months in advance. Accepts queries by mail, e-mail, fax, phone. Responds in 6 weeks to queries; 2 months to mss. Writer's guidelines online.

Nonfiction: Essays, how-to, interview/profile, opinion, personal experience, technical. **Buys 100 mss/year.** Send complete ms. Length: 500-3,000 words. **Pays 10¢/word.**

Photos: Send photos with submission. Reviews original slides or 2¼ or 4×5 transparencies. Offers $25 for photos. Captions required.

Columns/Departments: Upfront (workshop/exhibition review), 500-1,000 words. **Buys 20 mss/year.** Send complete ms.

$ $ CLASSIC TOY TRAINS, Kalmbach Publishing Co., 21027 Crossroads Circle, Waukesha WI 53187. (262)796-8776. Fax: (262)796-1142. E-mail: editor@classictoytrains.com. Website: www.classictoytrains.com. **Contact:** Neil Besougloff, editor. **80% freelance written.** Magazine published 9 times/year covering collectible toy trains (O, S, Standard, G scale, etc.) like Lionel, American Flyer, Marx, Dorfan, etc. "For the collector and operator of toy trains, *CTT* offers full-color photos of layouts and collections of toy trains, restoration tips, operating information, new product reviews and information, and insights into the history of toy trains." Estab. 1987. Circ. 65,000. **Pays on acceptance.** Publishes ms an average of 1 year after acceptance. Byline given. Buys all rights. Editorial lead time 3 months. Submit seasonal material 6 months in advance. Accepts queries by mail, e-mail. Responds in 3 weeks to queries; 1 month to mss. Sample copy for $5.50, plus s&h. Writer's guidelines online.

Nonfiction: General interest, historical/nostalgic, how-to (restore toy trains; design a layout; build accessories; fix broken toy trains), interview/profile, personal experience, photo feature, technical. **Buys 90 mss/year.** Query. Length: 500-5,000 words. **Pays $75-500.** Sometimes pays expenses of writers on assignment.

Photos: Send photos with submission. Reviews 4×5 transparencies, 5×7 prints or 35mm slides preferred. Buys all rights. Offers no additional payment for photos accepted with ms or $15-75/photo. Captions required.

Fillers: Uses cartoons. **Buys 6/year. Pays $30.**

Tips: "It's important to have a thorough understanding of the toy train hobby; most of our freelancers are hobbyists themselves. One-half to two-thirds of *CTT*'s editorial space is devoted to photographs; superior photography is critical."

$ COLLECTIBLES CANADA, Canada's Guide to Contemporary Collectible Art, Trajan Publishing, 103 Lakeshore Rd., Suite 202, St. Catharines ON L2N 2T6, Canada. (905)646-7744, ext. 229. Fax: (905)646-0995. E-mail: susanpennell@look.ca. Website: www.collectiblescanada.ca. Editor: Susan Pennell. Executive Editor: Mary Lynn McCauley. **90% freelance written.** Quarterly magazine covering contemporary collectible art and gifts. "We provide news and profiles of limited edition collectible art from a positive perspective. We are an informational tool for collectors who want to read about the products they love." Circ. 12,000. Pays 1 month after publication. Publishes ms an average of 3 months after acceptance. Byline given. Buys first North American serial rights. Editorial lead time 3 months. Submit seasonal material 3 months in advance. Accepts queries by mail, e-mail, fax. Responds in 1 month to queries. Sample copy for $3.95 (Canadian) and $2.50 IRC. Writer's guidelines for #10 SASE.

Nonfiction: Historical/nostalgic (collectibles), interview/profile, new product, technical, collectible art such as figurines, dolls, bears, prints, etc. No articles on antique-related subjects ("we cover contemporary collectibles"). No articles about stamp, coin, or sports collecting. **Buys 16 mss/year.** Query with published clips. Length: 500-1,200 words. **Pays $75-120 (Canadian).** Sometimes pays expenses of writers on assignment.

Photos: State availability with submission. Reviews negatives, transparencies, prints. Buys one-time rights. Negotiates payment individually. Identification of subjects required.

Columns/Departments: Book reviews (positive slant, primarily informational). Length: 500-800 words.

Tips: "Read the magazine first. Writers who can offer an article with a unique angle based on collectibles. Examples of past article ideas: 'The History of Fabergé,' 'Crossing the Lines: How Collectibles Go From Art Print To Figurine, To Plate To Doll.' Send an e-mail with your idea and I'll evaluate it promptly."

$ $ COLLECTOR'S MART, Contemporary Collectibles, Gifts & Home Decor, Krause Publications, 700 E. State St., Iola WI 54990. (715)445-2214. Fax: (715)445-4087. E-mail: collectorsmart@krause.com. Website: www.collectorsmart.net. **Contact:** Mary L. Sieber, editor. **50% freelance written.** Quarterly magazine covering contemporary collectibles, gifts, and home decor for collectors of all types. Estab. 1976. Circ. 36,000. Pays on publication. Publishes ms an average of 6 months after acceptance. Byline given. Buys perpetual nonexclusive rights. Editorial lead time 2 months. Submit seasonal material 4 months in advance. Accepts queries by mail, e-mail, fax. Responds in 1 month to mss. Writer's guidelines available.

Break in with "exciting, interesting theme topics for collections, i.e., seaside, fun and functional, patio decor, etc."

Nonfiction: Inspirational, interview/profile (artists of collectibles), new product. **Buys 10-15 mss/year.** Send complete ms. Length: 750-1,000 words. **Pays $50-300.**

Photos: Send only color photos with submission. Reviews transparencies, prints, electronic images. Buys one-time rights. Offers no additional payment for photos accepted with ms. Captions required.

The online magazine carries original content not found in the print edition. Contact: Mary L. Sieber.

Tips: "We're looking for more pieces on unique Christmas theme collectibles, i.e., tree toppers. Also includes giftware and home decor."

$ $ COLLECTORS NEWS, P.O. Box 306, Grundy Center IA 50638. (319)824-6981. Fax: (319)824-3414. E-mail: collectors@collectors-news.com. Website: collectors-news.com. **Contact:** Linda Kruger, managing editor. **20% freelance written.** Works with a small number of new/unpublished writers each year. Monthly magazine-size publication on offset, glossy cover, covering antiques, collectibles, and nostalgic memorabilia. Estab. 1959. Circ. 9,000. Pays on publication. Publishes ms an average of 1 year after acceptance. Byline given. Buys first rights, makes work-for-hire assignments. Submit seasonal material 3 months in advance. Accepts queries by mail, e-mail, fax, phone. Responds in 2 weeks to queries; 6 weeks to mss. Sample copy for $4 and 9×12 SAE. Writer's guidelines free.

Break in with articles on collecting online; history and values of collectibles and antiques; collectors with unique and/or extensive collections; using collectibles in the home decor; and any 20th century and timely subjects.

Nonfiction: General interest (any subject re: collectibles, antique to modern), historical/nostalgic (relating to collections or collectors), how-to (display your collection, care for, restore, appraise, locate, add to, etc.), interview/profile (covering individual collectors and their hobbies, unique or extensive; celebrity collectors, and limited edition artists), technical (in-depth analysis of a particular antique, collectible, or collecting field), travel ("hot" antiquing places in the US). Special issues: 12-month listing of antique and collectible shows, flea markets, and conventions (January includes events January-December; June includes events June-May); Care & Display of Collectibles (September); holidays (October-December). **Buys 36 mss/year.** Query with sample of writing. Length: 800-1,000 words. **Pays $1.10/column inch.**

Photos: "Articles must be accompanied by photographs for illustration." A selection of 2-8 images is suggested. "Articles are eligible for full-color front page consideration when accompanied by quality color prints, high resolution electronic images and/or color transparencies. Only 1 article is highlighted on the cover/month. Any article providing a color photo selected for front page use receives an additional $25." Reviews color or b&w images. Buys first rights. Payment for photos included in payment for ms. Captions required.

Tips: "Present a professionally written article with quality illustrations—well-researched and documented information."

N $ COUNTRY ALMANAC, Harris Publications, Inc., 1115 Broadway, New York NY 10010. (212)807-7100. Fax: (212)463-9958. E-mail: countryletters@yahoo.com. Website: www.countryalmanacmag.com. Editor: James Baaggett. Quarterly magazine. Written as a home service magazine containing articles ranging from country crafts, home-spun decorating and making heirlooms, to the best in affordable mail-order collectibles. Circ. 302,111. Editorial lead time 2 months. Sample copy not available.

N $ CQ AMATEUR RADIO, The Radio Amateur's Journal, CQ Communications, Inc., 25 Newbridge Rd., Hicksville NY 11801. Fax: (516)681-2926. E-mail: cq@cq-amateur-radio.com. Website: www.cq-amateur-radio.com. Managing Editor: Gail Schieber. **Contact:** Richard Moseson, editor. **40% freelance written.** Monthly magazine covering amateur (ham) radio. "*CQ* is published for active ham radio operators and is read by radio amateurs in over 100 countries. All articles must deal with amateur radio. Our focus is on operating and on practical projects. A thorough knowledge of amateur radio is required." Estab. 1945. Circ. 60,000. Pays on publication. Publishes ms an average of 6 months after acceptance. Byline given. Buys first North American serial rights. Editorial lead time 4 months. Submit seasonal material 4 months in advance. Accepts queries by mail, e-mail, fax. Responds in 3 weeks to queries; 3 months to mss. Sample copy for free. Writer's guidelines online.

Nonfiction: Historical/nostalgic, how-to, interview/profile, personal experience, technical, all related to amateur radio. **Buys 50-60 mss/year.** Query. Length: 2,000-4,000 words. **Pays $40/published page.**

Photos: State availability with submission. Reviews contact sheets, 4×6 prints, electronic photos also OK, tiff or JPEG files with 300 dpi resolution. Buys one-time rights. Offers no additional payment for photos accepted with ms. Captions, identification of subjects, model releases required.

Tips: "You must know and understand ham radio and ham radio operators. Most of our writers (95%) are licensed hams. Because our readers span a wide area of interests within amateur radio, don't assume they are already familiar with your topic. Explain. At the same time, don't write down to the readers. They are intelligent, well-educated people who will understand what you're saying when written and explained in plain English."

N $ $ THE CRAFT FACTOR, Saskatchewan Craft Council, 813 Broadway Ave., Saskatoon SK S7N 1B5, Canada. (306)653-3616. E-mail: scc.editor@shaw.ca. **Contact:** Gale Alaie, editor. **100% freelance written.** Semiannual magazine covering craft and related subjects. Estab. 1975. Circ. 1,500. Pays on publication. Byline sometimes given. Offers $50 kill fee. Buys first rights. Editorial lead time 2 months. Accepts queries by mail, e-mail, phone. Sample copy for free. Writer's guidelines free.

Nonfiction: Historical/nostalgic, interview/profile, technical. Length: 500-1,500 words. **Pays $75-250.** Sometimes pays expenses of writers on assignment.

Photos: Reviews transparencies, slides.

N $ $ CREATING KEEPSAKES, Scrapbook Magazine, PRIMEDIA Enthusiast Group, 14901 Heritage Crest Way, Bluffdale UT 84065. (801)984-2070. Fax: (801)984-2080. E-mail: editorial@creatingkeepsakes.com. Website: www.creatingkeepsakes.com. Editor: Jana Lillie. Monthly magazine covering scrapbooks. Written for scrapbook lovers and those with a box of photos high in the closet. Circ. 100,000. Editorial lead time 6 weeks. Accepts queries by mail. Sample copy not available.

Nonfiction: Accepts articles on a variety of scrapbook and keepsake topics. Query. Length: 800-1,200 words.

Columns/Departments: Scrapbook Basics (introduces basic how-tos for beginning scrapbookers), 800-1,200 words; Journaling Ideas (Shares ideas on how to use words most effectivvely to communicate important details and stories behind your photos), 800-1,200 words. Query. **Pays $200-400.**

Tips: "Should we opt to pursue the article you've proposed, we will ask you to supply the complete article on disk in WordPerfect, Word or ASCII format. Please supply a paper copy as well. The article should be lively and easy to read, contain solid content, and be broken up with subheads or sidebars as appropriate. We will provide addidtional guidelines to follow upon acceptance of your query."

$ $ CROCHET WORLD, House of White Birches, P.O. Box 776, Henniker NH 03242. Fax: (219)589-8093. Website: www.whitebirches.com. **Contact:** Susan Hankins, editor. **100% freelance written.** Bimonthly magazine covering crochet patterns. "*Crochet World* is a pattern magazine devoted to the art of crochet. We also feature a Q&A column, letters (swap shop) column, and occasionally nonpattern manuscripts, but it must be devoted to crochet." Estab. 1978. Circ. 75,000. Pays on publication. Byline given. Buys all rights. Editorial lead time 4 months. Submit seasonal material 6 months in advance. Responds in 1 month to queries. Sample copy for $2. Writer's guidelines free.

Nonfiction: How-to (crochet). **Buys 0-2 mss/year.** Send complete ms. Length: 500-1,500 words. **Pays $50.**

Columns/Departments: Touch of Style (crocheted clothing); It's a Snap! (quick 1-night simple patterns); Pattern of the Month, each issue. **Buys dozens of mss/year.** Send complete pattern. **Pays $40-300.**

Poetry: Strictly crochet-related. **Buys 0-5 poems/year.** Submit maximum 2 poems. Length: 6-10 lines. **Pays $10-20.**

Fillers: Anecdotes, facts, short humor. **Buys 0-10/year.** Length: 25-200 words. **Pays $5-30.**

Tips: "Be aware that this is a pattern-generated magazine for crochet designs. I prefer the actual item sent along with complete directions/graphs etc., over queries. In some cases a photo submission or good sketch will do. Crocheted designs must be well-made and original and directions must be complete. Write for designer's guidelines which detail how to submit designs. Noncrochet items, such as fillers, poetry *must* be crochet-related, not knit, not sewing, etc."

$ DANCING USA, The Art of Ballroom Dance, Dancing USA LLC, 200 N. York Rd., Elmhurst IL 60126-2750. (630)782-1260. Fax: (630)617-9950. E-mail: editor@dancingusa.com. Website: www.dancingusa.com. **Contact:** Michael Fitzmaurice, editor. **60% freelance written.** Works with new writers. Bimonthly magazine covering ballroom, swing and Latin dance: how-tos, technique, floor craft; source for dance videos, CDs, shoes, where to dance. Estab. 1983. Circ. 20,000. Pays on publication. Publishes ms an average of 6 months after acceptance. Byline given. Buys first North American serial rights. Editorial lead time 3 months. Submit seasonal material 4 months in advance. Accepts queries by mail, e-mail, fax. Responds in 2 months to queries; 2 months to mss. Sample copy for free. Writer's guidelines online.

Nonfiction: Book excerpts, exposé, historical/nostalgic, how-to, humor, inspirational, interview/profile, new product, personal experience, photo feature, travel, commentary, all dance related. **Buys 30-40 mss/year.** Send complete ms. Length: 1,000-2,000 words. **Pays $25-75 for assigned articles; $10-50 for unsolicited articles.**

Photos: Send photos with submission. No additional payment.

Fiction: Looking for any type of fiction that includes a style of ballroom, Latin, or swing dance, or the industry or enjoyment of ballroom dance as a main theme.

Tips: "Works with new writers. Hot Stuff department features new dance-related products, books, and music. Four to 8 features/issue from freelancers include dancer profiles, history of dancers, entertainers, expert dance advice, promoting dance. Each issue tries to include a city dance guide, a style of dance, dance functions, a major dance competition, and a celebrity profile. Example: Denver, Tango, Weddings, U.S. Championships, and Rita Moreno."

$ $ DECORATIVE ARTIST'S WORKBOOK, F&W Publications, Inc., 4700 E. Galbraith Rd., Cincinnati OH 45236. (513)531-2690, ext. 1461. E-mail: dawedit@fwpubs.com. Website: www.decorativeartist.com. **Contact:** Anne Hevener, editor. **75% freelance written.** Bimonthly magazine covering decorative painting projects and products of all sorts. Offers "straightforward, personal instruction in the techniques of decorative painting." Estab. 1987. Circ. 90,000. **Pays on acceptance.** Byline given. Offers 25% kill fee. Buys first North American serial rights. Submit seasonal material 8 months in advance. Accepts queries by mail, e-mail. Responds in 2 weeks to queries. Sample copy for $8 and 9×12 SAE with 5 first-class stamps. Writer's guidelines online.

Nonfiction: How-to (related to decorative painting projects), new product, technique. **Buys 30 mss/year.** Query with slides or photos. Length: 1,200-1,800 words. **Pays 15-25¢/word.**

The online magazine carries original content not found in the print edition. Contact: Anne Hevener, online editor.

Tips: "Create a design, surface, or technique that is fresh and new to decorative painting. I'm looking for experts in the field who, through their own experience, can artfully describe the techniques involved. How-to articles are most open to freelancers skilled in decorative painting. Be sure to query with photo/slides, and show that you understand the extensive graphic requirements for these pieces and can provide painted progressives—painted illustrations that show works in progress."

$ $ DOLLHOUSE MINIATURES, Kalmbach Publishing Co., 21027 Crossroads Circle, Waukesha WI 53187-1612. (262)796-8776. Fax: (262)796-1383. E-mail: cstjacques@dhminiatures.com. Website: www.dhminiatures.com. Editor: Candice St. Jacques. **50% freelance written.** Monthly magazine covering dollhouse scale miniatures. "*Dollhouse Miniatures* is America's best-selling miniatures magazine and the definitive resource for artisans, collectors, and hobbyists. It promotes and supports the large national and international community of miniaturists through club columns, short reports, and by featuring reader projects and ideas." Estab. 1971. Circ. 35,000. **Pays on acceptance.** Byline given. Offers 10% kill fee. Buys all rights. Editorial lead time 6 months. Submit seasonal material 6 months in advance. Accepts queries by mail, e-mail. Responds in 1 month to queries; 2 months to mss. Sample copy free (1 copy). Contact: Customer Service (800)533-6644 or customerservice@kalmbach.com. Writer's guidelines online.

Nonfiction: How-to (miniature projects of various scales in variety of media), interview/profile (artisans, collectors), photo feature (dollhouses, collections, museums). No articles on miniature shops or essays. **Buys 50-60 mss/year.** Query with or without published clips or send complete ms. Length: 500-1,500 words. **Pays $50-350 for assigned articles; $0-200 for unsolicited articles.** Pays expenses of writers on assignment.

Photos: Send photos with submission. Reviews 35mm slides and larger, 3×5 prints. Buys all rights. Photos are paid for with ms. Seldom buys individual photos. Captions, identification of subjects required.

Tips: "Familiarity with the miniatures hobby is very helpful. Accuracy to scale is extremely important to our readers. A complete package (manuscripts/photos) has a better chance of publication."

$ DOLLMAKING, Your Resource for Creating & Costuming Modern Porcelain Dolls, Jones Publishing, N7450 Aanstad Rd., P.O. Box 5000, Iola WI 54945. Fax: (715)445-4053. E-mail: dolledit@pressenter.com. Website: www.dollmakingartisan.com. **Contact:** Stacy D. Carlson, editor. **50% freelance written.** Bimonthly magazine covering porcelain dollmaking. "*Dollmaking*'s intent is to entertain and inform porcelain and sculpted modern doll artists and costumers with the newest projects and techniques. It is meant to be a resource for hobby enthusiasts." Estab. 1985. Circ. 15,000. Pays on publication. Byline sometimes given. Buys all rights. Editorial lead time 4 months. Submit seasonal material 4 months in advance. Accepts queries by mail, e-mail, fax, phone. Sample copy online. Writer's guidelines free.

Nonfiction: Inspirational, interview/profile, personal experience. **Buys 12 mss/year.** Query. Length: 800 words. **Pays $75-150 for assigned articles.**

Photos: State availability with submission. Reviews 2½ x 2½ transparencies. Buys all rights. Negotiates payment individually.

Columns/Departments: Sewing Q&A (readers write in with sewing questions), 1,600 words. **Buys 2-3 mss/year.** Query. **Pays $75.**

Fillers: Anecdotes. **Buys 6/year.** Length: 500-800 words. **Pays $55-75.**

Tips: "The best way to break in is to send a manuscript of something the author has written concerning porcelain dollmaking and costuming. The article may be a personal story, a special technique used when making a doll, a successful doll fundraiser, sewing tips for dolls, or anything that would be of interest to a serious doll artisan. If no manuscript is available, at least send a letter of interest."

$ $ $ FAMILY TREE MAGAZINE, Discover, Preserve & Celebrate Your Family's History, F&W Publications, 4700 E. Galbraith Rd., Cincinnati OH 45236. (513)531-2690. Fax: (513)891-7153. E-mail: ftmedit@fwpubs.com. Website:

www.familytreemagazine.com. **Contact:** Allison Stacy, editor. **75% freelance written.** Bimonthly magazine covering family history, heritage, and genealogy research. "*Family Tree Magazine* is a general-interest consumer magazine that helps readers discover, preserve, and celebrate their family's history. We cover genealogy, ethnic heritage, personal history, genealogy websites and software, scrapbooking, photography and photo preservation, and other ways that families connect with their past." Estab. 1999. Circ. 85,000. **Pays on acceptance.** Publishes ms an average of 6 months after acceptance. Byline given. Offers 25% kill fee. Buys first, electronic rights. Editorial lead time 8 months. Submit seasonal material 8 months in advance. Accepts queries by mail, e-mail. Responds in 1 month to queries. Sample copy for $7 or on website. Writer's guidelines online.

O⊸ Break in by suggesting a "useful, timely idea for our Toolkit section on a resource that our readers would love to discover."

Nonfiction: "Articles are geared to beginners but never talk down to the audience. We emphasize sidebars, tips, and other reader-friendly 'packaging,' and each article aims to give the reader the resources necessary to take the next step in his or her quest for their personal past." Book excerpts, historical/nostalgic, how-to (genealogy), new product (photography, computer), technical (genealogy software, photography equipment), travel (with ethnic heritage slant). **Buys 60 mss/year.** Query with published clips. Length: 500-3,500 words. **Pays $75-800.** Sometimes pays expenses of writers on assignment.

Photos: State availability with submission. Reviews color transparencies. Buys one-time rights. Negotiates payment individually. Captions required.

The online magazine carries original content not found in the print edition and includes writer's guidelines. Contact: Allison Stacy, editor.

Tips: "We see too many broad, general stories on genealogy or records, and personal accounts of 'How I found great-aunt Sally' without how-to value."

$ $ FIBERARTS, The Magazine of Textiles, Altamont Press, 67 Broadway, Asheville NC 28801. (828)253-0467. Fax: (828)236-2869. E-mail: assteditor@fiberartsmagazine.com. Website: www.fiberartsmagazine.com. **Contact:** Sunita Patterson, editor. **90% freelance written.** Magazine published 5 times/year covering textiles as art and craft (contemporary trends in fiber sculpture, weaving, quilting, surface design, stitchery, papermaking, basketry, felting, wearable art, knitting, fashion, crochet, mixed textile techniques, ethnic dying, eccentric tidbits, etc.) for textile artists, craftspeople, collectors, teachers, museum and gallery staffs, and enthusiasts. Estab. 1975. Circ. 23,745. Pays on publication. Publishes ms an average of 4 months after acceptance. Byline given. Buys first rights. Accepts queries by mail. Sample copy for $5. Writer's guidelines online.

Nonfiction: "Please be very specific about your proposal. Also, an important consideration in accepting an article is the kind of photos that you can provide as illustration. We like to see photos in advance." Essays, interview/profile (artist), opinion, personal experience, photo feature, technical, education, trends, exhibition reviews, textile news, book reviews, ethnic. Query with brief outline, prose synopsis, SASE, and visuals. No phone or e-mail queries. Length: 250-2,000 words. **Pays $70-550.**

Photos: Color slides or large format transparencies must accompany every query. The more photos to choose from, the better. Please include caption information. The names and addresses of those mentioned in the article or to whom the visuals are to be returned are necessary. Captions required.

Columns/Departments: Commentary (thoughtful opinion on a topic of interest to our readers), 400 words; Notable Events; Worldwide Connections; The Creative Process; Fiber Hot Spots; Collections; Practical Matters, 450 words and 2-4 photos; Profile (focuses on one artist), 450 words and 1 photo; Reviews (exhibits and shows; summarize quality, significance, focus and atmosphere, then evaluate selected pieces for aesthetic quality, content and technique—because we have an international readership, brief biographical notes or quotes might be pertinent for locally or regionally known artists), 500 words and 3-5 photos. (Do not cite works for which visuals are unavailable; you are not eligible to review a show in which you have participated as an artist, organizer, curator or juror.). **Pays $100-150.**

Tips: "Our writers are very familiar with the textile field, and this is what we look for in a new writer. Familiarity with textile techniques, history or events determines clarity of an article more than a particular style of writing. The writer should also be familiar with *Fiberarts* magazine. The professional is essential to the editorial depth of *Fiberarts* and must find timely information in the pages of the magazine. Our editorial philosophy is that the magazine must provide the non-professional textile enthusiast with the inspiration, support, useful information and direction to keep him or her excited, interested and committed. Although we address serious issues relating to the fiber arts as well as light, we're looking for an accessible rather than overly scholarly tone."

$ FIBRE FOCUS, Magazine of the Ontario Handweavers and Spinners, 217 Maki Ave., Sudburyon ON P3E 2P3, Canada. E-mail: karend@vianet.on.ca. Website: www.ohs.on.ca. **Contact:** Karen Danielson, editor. **90% freelance written.** Quarterly magazine covering handweaving, spinning, basketry, beading, and other fibre arts. "Our readers are weavers and spinners who also do dyeing, knitting, basketry, feltmaking, papermaking, sheep raising, and craft supply. All articles deal with some aspect of these crafts." Estab. 1957. Circ. 1,000. Pays within 30 days after publication. Byline given. Buys one-time rights. Editorial lead time 6 months. Submit seasonal material 6 months in advance. Accepts previously published material. Responds in 1 month to queries. Sample copy for $5 Canadian. Writer's guidelines online.

Nonfiction: How-to, interview/profile, new product, opinion, personal experience, technical, travel, book reviews. **Buys 40-60 mss/year.** Length: Varies. **Pays $30 Canadian/published page.**

Photos: Send photos with submission. Reviews 4×6 color prints. Buys one-time rights. Offers additional payment for photos accepted with ms. Captions, identification of subjects required.

Fiction: Humorous, slice-of-life vignettes. **Pays $30 Canadian/published page.**

Tips: "Visit the OHS website for current information."

$ $ FINE TOOL JOURNAL, Antique & Collectible Tools, Inc., 27 Fickett Rd., Pownal ME 04069. (207)688-4962. Fax: (207)688-4831. E-mail: ceb@finetoolj.com. Website: www.finetoolj.com. **Contact:** Clarence Blanchard, president. **90% freelance written.** Quarterly magazine specializing in older or antique hand tools from all traditional trades. Readers are primarily interested in woodworking tools, but some subscribers have interests in such areas as leatherworking, wrenches, kitchen, and machinist tools. Readers range from beginners just getting into the hobby to advanced collectors and organizations. Estab. 1970. Circ. 2,500. Pays on publication. Publishes ms an average of 6 months after acceptance. Byline given. Offers $50 kill fee. Buys first, second serial (reprint) rights. Editorial lead time 9 months. Submit seasonal material 6 months in advance. Accepts queries by mail. Accepts previously published material. Responds in 2 months to queries; 3 months to mss. Sample copy for $5. Writer's guidelines for #10 SASE.

Nonfiction: "We're looking for articles about tools from all trades. Interests include collecting, preservation, history, values and price trends, traditional methods and uses, interviews with collectors/users/makers, etc. Most articles published will deal with vintage, pre-1950, hand tools. Also seeking articles on how to use specific tools or how a specific trade was carried out. However, how-to articles must be detailed and not just of general interest. We do on occasion run articles on modern toolmakers who produce traditional hand tools." General interest, historical/nostalgic, how-to (make, use, fix and tune tools), interview/profile, personal experience, photo feature, technical. **Buys 24 mss/year.** Send complete ms. Length: 400-2,000 words. **Pays $50-200.** Pays expenses of writers on assignment.

Photos: Send photos with submission. Reviews 4×5 prints. Buys all rights. Negotiates payment individually. Identification of subjects, model releases required.

Columns/Departments: Stanley Tools (new finds and odd types), 300-400 words; Tips of the Trade (how to use tools), 100-200 words. **Buys 12 mss/year.** Send complete ms. **Pays $30-60.**

Tips: "The easiest way to get published in the *Journal* is to have personal experience or know someone who can supply the detailed information. We are seeking articles that go deeper than general interest and that knowledge requires experience and/or research. Short of personal experience, find a subject that fits our needs and that interests you. Spend some time learning the ins and outs of the subject and with hard work and a little luck you will earn the right to write about it."

$ FINESCALE MODELER, Kalmbach Publishing Co., 21027 Crossroads Circle, P.O. Box 1612, Waukesha WI 53187. (414)796-8776. Fax: (414)796-1383. E-mail: tthompson@finescale.com. Website: www.finescale.com. **Contact:** Paul Boyer. **80% freelance written.** Eager to work with new/unpublished writers. Magazine published 10 times/year "devoted to how-to-do-it modeling information for scale model builders who build non-operating aircraft, tanks, boats, automobiles, figures, dioramas, and science fiction and fantasy models." Circ. 60,000. **Pays on acceptance.** Publishes ms an average of 14 months after acceptance. Byline given. Buys all rights. Responds in 6 weeks to queries; 3 months to mss. Sample copy for 9×12 SAE and 3 first-class stamps.

- *Finescale Modeler* is especially looking for how-to articles for car modelers.

Nonfiction: How-to (build scale models), technical (research information for building models). Query or send complete ms. Length: 750-3,000 words. **Pays $55 published page minimum.**

Photos: Send photos with submission. Reviews transparencies, color prints. Buys one-time rights. Pays $7.50 minimum for transparencies and $5 minimum for color prints. Captions, identification of subjects required.

Columns/Departments: *FSM* Showcase (photos plus description of model); *FSM* Tips and Techniques (model building hints and tips). **Buys 25-50 mss/year.** Send complete ms. **Pays $25-50.**

Tips: "A freelancer can best break in first through hints and tips, then through feature articles. Most people who write for *FSM* are modelers first, writers second. This is a specialty magazine for a special, quite expert audience. Essentially, 99% of our writers will come from that audience."

$ $ KITPLANES, For designers, builders, and pilots of experimental aircraft, A Primedia Publication, 8745 Aero Dr., Suite 105, San Diego CA 92123. (858)694-0491. Fax: (858)694-8147. E-mail: dave@kitplanes.com. Website: www.kitplanes.com. Managing Editor: Brian Clark. **Contact:** Dave Martin, editor. **80% freelance written.** Eager to work with new/unpublished writers. Monthly magazine covering self-construction of private aircraft for pilots and builders. Estab. 1984. Circ. 72,000. Pays on publication. Publishes ms an average of 3 months after acceptance. Byline given. Buys complete rights, except book rights. Submit seasonal material 6 months in advance. Accepts queries by mail, e-mail. Responds in 2 weeks to queries; 6 weeks to mss. Sample copy for $6. Writer's guidelines online.

Nonfiction: "We are looking for articles on specific construction techniques, the use of tools, both hand and power, in aircraft building, the relative merits of various materials, conversions of engines from automobiles for aviation use, installation of instruments and electronics." General interest, how-to, interview/profile, new product, personal experience, photo feature, technical. No general-interest aviation articles, or "My First Solo" type of articles. **Buys 80 mss/year.** Query. Length: 500-3,000 words. **Pays $70-600 including story photos for assigned articles.**

Photos: State availability of or send photos with submission. Buys one-time rights. Pays $300 for cover photos. Captions, identification of subjects required.

Tips: "*Kitplanes* contains very specific information—a writer must be extremely knowledgeable in the field. Major features are entrusted only to known writers. I cannot emphasize enough that articles must be directed at the individual aircraft builder. We need more 'how-to' photo features in all areas of homebuilt aircraft."

$ KNITTING DIGEST, House of White Birches, 306 E. Parr Rd., Berne IN 46711. (260)589-4000. Fax: (260)589-8093. E-mail: knitting_digest@whitebirches.com. Website: www.whitebirches.com. **Contact:** Carol Alexander, editor. **100% freelance written.** Bimonthly magazine covering knitting designs and patterns. "We print only occasional articles, but are always open to knitting designs and proposals." Estab. 1993. Circ. 50,000. Pays within 6 months. Publishes ms an average of 11 months after acceptance. Byline given. Offers 100% kill fee. Buys all rights. Accepts queries by mail, e-mail. Responds in 2 months to queries; 6 months to mss. Sample copy not available. Writer's guidelines for #10 SASE.

Nonfiction: How-to (knitting skills), technical (knitting field). **Buys 4-6 mss/year.** Send complete ms. Length: 500 words maximum. **Pays variable amount. Also pays in contributor copies.**

Tips: "Clear concise writing. Humor is appreciated in this field, as much as technical tips. The magazine is a digest, so space is limited. All submissions must be typed and double-spaced."

$ $ KNIVES ILLUSTRATED, The Premier Cutlery Magazine, 265 S. Anita Dr., Suite 120, Orange CA 92868-3310. (423)894-8319. Fax: (423)892-7254. E-mail: editorial@knivesillustrated.com. Website: www.knivesillustrated.com. **Contact:** Bruce Voyles, editor. **40-50% freelance written.** Bimonthly magazine covering high-quality factory and custom knives. "We publish articles on different types of factory and custom knives, how-to make knives, technical articles, shop tours, articles on knife makers and artists. Must have knowledge about knives and the people who use and make them. We feature the full range of custom and high tech production knives, from miniatures to swords, leaving nothing untouched. We're also known for our outstanding how-to articles and technical features on equipment, materials and knife making supplies. We do not feature knife maker profiles as such, although we do spotlight some makers by featuring a variety of their knives and insight into their background and philosophy." Estab. 1987. Circ. 35,000. Pays on publication. Byline given. Editorial lead time 3 months. Accepts queries by mail, e-mail, fax. Responds in 2 weeks to queries. Sample copy available. Writer's guidelines for #10 SASE.

Nonfiction: General interest, historical/nostalgic, how-to, interview/profile, new product, photo feature, technical. **Buys 35-40 mss/year.** Query. Length: 400-2,000 words. **Pays $100-500.**

Photos: Send photos with submission. Reviews 35mm, 2¼ × 2¼ , 4×5 transparencies, 5×7 prints, electronic images in TIF, GIP or JPEG Mac format. Negotiates payment individually. Captions, identification of subjects, model releases required.

Tips: "Most of our contributors are involved with knives, either as collectors, makers, engravers, etc. To write about this subject requires knowledge. A 'good' writer can do OK if they study some recent issues. If you are interested in submitting work to *Knives Illustrated* magazine, it is suggested you analyze at least two or three different editions to get a feel for the magazine. It is also recommended that you call or mail in your query to determine if we are interested in the topic you have in mind. While verbal or written approval may be given, all articles are still received on a speculation basis. We cannot approve any article until we have it in hand, whereupon we will make a final decision as to its suitability for our use. Bear in mind we do not suggest you go to the trouble to write an article if there is doubt we can use it promptly."

$ LAPIDARY JOURNAL, 60 Chestnut Ave., Suite 201, Devon PA 19333-1312. (610)964-6300. Fax: (610)293-0977. E-mail: lj_editorial@primediasi.com. Website: www.lapidaryjournal.com. Editor: Merle White. **Contact:** Hazel Wheaton, managing editor. **70% freelance written.** Monthly magazine covering gem, bead and jewelry arts. "Our audience is hobbyists who usually have some knowledge of and proficiency in the subject before they start reading. Our style is conversational and informative. There are how-to projects and profiles of artists and materials." Estab. 1947. Circ. 53,000. **Pays on acceptance.** Publishes ms an average of 4 months after acceptance. Byline given. one-time and worldwide rights. Editorial lead time 3 months. Accepts queries by mail, e-mail. Sample copy online.

Nonfiction: Looks for conversational and lively narratives with quotes and anecdotes; Q&A's; interviews. How-to (jewelry/craft), interview/profile, new product, personal experience, technical, travel. Special issues: Bead Annual, Gemstone Annual, Jewelry Design issue. **Buys 100 mss/year.** Query. Length: 1,500-2,500 words preferred; 1,000-3,500 words acceptable; longer works occasionally published serially. Pays some expenses of writers on assignment.

Reprints: Send photocopy.

Tips: "Some knowledge of jewelry, gemstones and/or minerals is a definite asset. *Jewelry Journal* is a section within *Lapidary Journal* that offers illustrated, step-by-step instruction in gem cutting, jewelry making, and beading. Please request a copy of the *Jewelry Journal* guidelines for greater detail."

$ $ THE LEATHER CRAFTERS & SADDLERS JOURNAL, 331 Annette Court, Rhinelander WI 54501-2902. (715)362-5393. Fax: (715)362-5391. E-mail: journal@newnorth.net. Managing Editor: Dorothea Reis. **Contact:** William R. Reis, publisher. **100% freelance written.** Bimonthly magazine. "A leather-working publication with how-to, step-by-step instructional articles using full-size patterns for leathercraft, leather art, custom saddle, boot and harness making, etc. A complete resource for leather, tools, machinery, and allied materials, plus leather industry news." Estab. 1990. Circ. 9,000. Pays on publication. Publishes ms an average of 2 months after acceptance. Byline given. Buys first North American serial, second serial (reprint) rights. Submit seasonal material 6 months in advance. Accepts queries by mail, e-mail, fax, phone. Accepts previously published material. Accepts simultaneous submissions. Responds in 1 month to mss. Sample copy for $5. Writer's guidelines for #10 SASE.

O→ Break in with a how-to, step-by-step leather item article from beginner through masters and saddlemaking.

Nonfiction: "I want only articles that include hands-on, step-by-step, how-to information." How-to (crafts and arts, and any other projects using leather). **Buys 75 mss/year.** Send complete ms. Length: 500-2,500 words. **Pays $20-250 for assigned articles; $20-150 for unsolicited articles.**

Reprints: Send tearsheet or photocopy. Pays 50% of amount paid for an original article.

Photos: Send good contrast color print photos and full-size patterns and/or full-size photo-carve patterns with submission. Lack of these reduces payment amount. Captions required.

Columns/Departments: Beginners; Intermediate; Artists; Western Design; Saddlemakers; International Design; and Letters (the open exchange of information between all peoples). Length: 500-2,500 words on all. **Buys 75 mss/year.** Send complete ms. **Pays 5¢/word.**

Fillers: Anecdotes, facts, gags to be illustrated by cartoonist, newsbreaks. Length: 25-200 words. **Pays $5-20.**

Tips: "We want to work with people who understand and know leathercraft and are interested in passing on their knowledge to others. We would prefer to interview people who have achieved a high level in leathercraft skill."

$ LINN'S STAMP NEWS, Amos Press, 911 Vandemark Rd., P.O. Box 29, Sidney OH 45365. (937)498-0801. Fax: (800)340-9501. E-mail: linns@linns.com. Website: www.linns.com. Editorial Director: Michael Laurence. **Contact:** Michael Schreiber, editor. **50% freelance written.** Weekly tabloid on the stamp collecting hobby. All articles must be about philatelic collectibles. Our goal at *Linn's* is to create a weekly publication that is indispensable to stamp collectors. Estab. 1928. Circ. 46,000. Pays within one month of publication. Publishes ms an average of 3 months after acceptance. Byline given. Buys first print and electronic rights. Submit seasonal material 2 months in advance. Responds in 6 weeks to queries. Sample copy for free. Writer's guidelines online.

Nonfiction: General interest, historical/nostalgic, how-to, interview/profile, technical, club and show news, current issues, auction realization and recent discoveries. "No articles merely giving information on background of stamp subject. Must have philatelic information included." **Buys 50 mss/year.** Send complete ms. Length: 500 words maximum. **Pays $50.** Sometimes pays expenses of writers on assignment.

Photos: Good illustrations a must. Provide captions on a separate sheet of paper. Send scans with submission. Reviews digital color at twice actual size (300 dpi). Buys all rights. Offers no additional payment for photos accepted with ms. Captions required.

Tips: "Check and double check all facts. Footnotes and bibliographies are not appropriate to newspaper style. Work citation into the text. Even though your subject might be specialized, write understandably. Explain terms. *Linn's* features are aimed at a broad audience of relatively novice collectors. Keep this audience in mind. Provide information in such a way to make stamp collecting more interesting to more people."

$ LOST TREASURE, INC., P.O. Box 451589, Grove OK 74345. (918)786-2182. Fax: (918)786-2192. E-mail: managingeditor@losttreasure.com. Website: www.losttreasure.com. **Contact:** Patsy Beyerl, managing editor. **75% freelance written.** Monthly and annual magazines covering lost treasure. Estab. 1966. Circ. 55,000. Pays on publication. Byline given. Buys all rights. Accepts queries by mail, e-mail, fax. Responds in 1 month to queries; 2 months to mss. Sample copy for #10 SASE. Writer's guidelines for 10×13 SAE with $1.47 postage or online.

Nonfiction: *Lost Treasure*, a monthly, is composed of lost treasure stories, legends, folklore, how-to articles, treasure hunting club news, who's who in treasure hunting, tips. Length: 500-1,500 words. *Treasure Cache*, an annual, contains stories about documented treasure caches with a sidebar from the author telling the reader how to search for the cache highlighted in the story. **Buys 225 mss/year.** Query on *Treasure Cache* only. Length: 1,000-2,000 words. **Pays 4¢/word.**

Photos: Black & white or color prints, hand-drawn or copied maps, art with source credit with mss will help sell your story. We are always looking for cover photos with or without accompanying ms. Pays $100/published cover photo. Must be 35mm color slides, vertical. Pays $5/published photo. Captions required.

Tips: "We are only interested in treasures that can be found with metal detectors. Queries welcome but not required. If you write about famous treasures and lost mines, be sure we haven't used your selected topic recently and story must have a new slant or new information. Source documentation required. How-tos should cover some aspect of treasure hunting and how-to steps should be clearly defined. If you have a *Treasure Cache* story we will, if necessary, help the author with the sidebar telling how to search for the cache in the story. *Lost Treasure* articles should coordinate with theme issues when possible."

N $ MCCALL'S QUILTING, PRIMEDIA Enthusiast Group, 741Corporate Circle, Suite A, Golden CO 80401. (303)278-1010. Fax: (303)277-0307. E-mail: mcq@primediasi.com. Website: www.mccallsquilting.com. Editor: Beth Hayes. **Contact:** Editor. Bimonthly magazine covering quiltmaking. Attracts quilters of all skill levels with a variety of complete, how-to quilting projects, including bed size quilts, wall hangings, wearables and small projects. Estab. 1993. Circ. 162,000. Buys limited exclusive copyright license rights. Editorial lead time 6-9 months. Submit seasonal material 6-9 months in advance. Accepts queries by mail. Responds in 6 weeks to queries. Sample copy for $5.95. Writer's guidelines by e-mail.

Tips: "For any design or article, include a detailed description of the project to help us make an informed decision."

$ $ MEMORY MAKERS, The First Source for Scrapbooking Ideas, Satellite Press, 12365 Huron St., Suite 500, Denver CO 80234. (303)452-1968. Fax: (303)452-2164. E-mail: editorial@memorymakersmagazine.com. Website: www.memorymakersmagazine.com. **Contact:** Deborah Mock, editor. **50% freelance written.** Magazine published 8 times/year covering creative scrapbook ideas and craft techniques. "*Memory Makers* is an international magazine that showcases ideas and stories of scrapbookers. It includes articles with information, instructions, and products that apply to men and women who make creative scrapbooks." Estab. 1996. Circ. 285,000. Pays on project completion. Publishes ms an average of 6 months after acceptance. Byline given. Buys first rights. Editorial lead time 6 months. Submit seasonal material 6 months in advance. Accepts queries by mail, e-mail. Accepts simultaneous submissions. Writer's guidelines online.

- Break in with articles on "unique craft techniques that can apply to scrapbooking, and personal stories of how scrapbooking has impacted someone's life."

Nonfiction: Historical/nostalgic, how-to (scrapbooking), inspirational, interview/profile, new product, personal experience, photography. No "all-encompassing how-to scrapbook" articles. **Buys 6-10 mss/year.** Query with published clips. Length: 1,000-1,500 words. **Pays $500-750.**

Columns/Departments: Keeping It Safe (issues surrounding the safe preservation of scrapbooks); Scrapbooking 101 (how-to scrapbooking techniques for beginners); Photojournaling (new and useful ideas for improving scrapbook journaling); Modern Memories (computer and modern technology scrapbooking issues), all 600-800 words. Query with published clips. **Pays $200-350.**

$ MINIATURE QUILTS, Chitra Publications, 2 Public Ave., Montrose PA 18801. (570)278-1984. Fax: (570)278-2223. E-mail: chitraed@epix.net. Website: www.quilttownusa.com. **Contact:** Phyllis Montange, production coordinator. **40%**

freelance written. Bimonthly magazine on miniature quilts. "We seek articles of an instructional nature (all techniques), profiles of talented quiltmakers, and informational articles on all aspects of miniature quilts. Miniature is defined as quilts made up of blocks smaller than 5 inches." Estab. 1990. Circ. 70,000. Pays on publication. Publishes ms an average of 6 months after acceptance. Byline given. Buys second serial (reprint) rights. Submit seasonal material 8 months in advance. Accepts queries by mail, fax. Responds in 2 months to queries. Writer's guidelines online.

O→ "Best bet—a quilter writing about a new or unusual quilting technique."

Nonfiction: How-to, interview/profile (quilters who make small quilts), photo feature (about noteworthy miniature quilts or exhibits). Query. Length: 1,500 words maximum. **Pays $75/published page of text.**

Photos: Send photos with submission. Reviews 35mm slides and larger transparencies. Offers $20/photo. Captions, identification of subjects, model releases required.

$ MODEL RAILROADER, P.O. Box 1612, Waukesha WI 53187. Fax: (262)796-1142. E-mail: mrmag@mrmag.com. Website: www.trains.com. **Contact:** Russ Larson, publisher or Terry Thompson, editor. Monthly magazine for hobbyists interested in scale model railroading. "We publish articles on all aspects of model-railroading and on prototype (real) railroading as a subject for modeling." Byline given. Buys exclusive rights. Accepts queries by mail, e-mail, fax. Responds in 2 months to queries.

O→ "Study publication before submitting material." First-hand knowledge of subject almost always necessary for acceptable slant.

Nonfiction: Wants construction articles on specific model railroad projects (structures, cars, locomotives, scenery, benchwork, etc.). Also photo stories showing model railroads. Query. **Pays base rate of $90/page.**

Photos: Buys photos with detailed descriptive captions only. Pays $15 and up, depending on size and use. Full color cover earns $200.

Tips: "Before you prepare and submit any article, you should write us a short letter of inquiry describing what you want to do. We can then tell you if it fits our needs and save you from working on something we don't want."

$ MONITORING TIMES, Grove Enterprises, Inc., 7540 Hwy. 64 W., Brasstown NC 28902-0098. (828)837-9200. Fax: (828)837-2216. E-mail: editor@monitoringtimes.com. Website: www.monitoringtimes.com. Publisher: Robert Grove. **Contact:** Rachel Baughn, editor. **15% freelance written.** Monthly magazine for radio hobbyists. Estab. 1982. Circ. 20,000. Pays on publication. Publishes ms an average of 4 months after acceptance. Byline given. Buys first North American serial, second serial (reprint) rights. Submit seasonal material 4 months in advance. Accepts queries by mail, e-mail. Accepts previously published material. Responds in 1 month to queries. Sample copy for 9×12 SAE and 9 first-class stamps. Writer's guidelines online.

O→ Break in with a shortwave station profile or topic, or scanning topics of broad interest.

Nonfiction: General interest, how-to, humor, interview/profile, personal experience, photo feature, technical. **Buys 50 mss/year.** Query. Length: 1,500-3,000 words. **Pays average of $50/published page.**

Reprints: Send photocopy and information about when and where the material previously appeared. Pays 25% of amount paid for an original article.

Photos: Send photos with submission. Buys one-time rights. Captions required.

Columns/Departments: "Query managing editor."

Tips: "Need articles on radio communications systems and shortwave broadcasters. We are accepting more technical projects."

$ NUMISMATIST MAGAZINE, (formerly *The Numismatist*), American Numismatic Association, 818 N. Cascade Ave., Colorado Springs CO 80903-3279. (719)632-2646. Fax: (719)634-4085. E-mail: magazine@money.org. **Contact:** Barbara Gregory, editor/publisher. Monthly magazine covering numismatics (study of coins, tokens, medals, and paper money). Estab. 1888. Circ. 28,500. Pays on publication. Publishes ms an average of 1 year after acceptance. Byline given. Buys perpetual, but nonexclusive rights. Editorial lead time 2 months. Sample copy for free.

Nonfiction: "Submitted material should present new information and/or constitute a contribution to numismatic education for the experienced collector and beginner alike." Book excerpts, essays, historical/nostalgic, opinion, technical. Special issues: First Strike, a supplement for young or new collectors, is published twice yearly, in December and June. **Buys 60 mss/year.** Query or send complete ms. Length: 2,500 words maximum. **Pays $3/column inch.** Sometimes pays expenses of writers on assignment.

Photos: Send photos with submission. Negotiates payment individually. Captions, identification of subjects required.

Columns/Departments: Send complete ms. **Pays $25-100.**

$ PACK-O-FUN, Projects For Kids & Families, Clapper Communications, 2400 Devon Ave., Des Plaines IL 60018-4618. (847)635-5800. Fax: (847)635-6311. Website: www.craftideas.com. Editor: Billie Ciancio. **Contact:** Irene Mueller, managing editor. **85% freelance written.** Bimonthly magazine covering crafts and activities for kids and those working with kids. Estab. 1951. Circ. 102,000. Pays 45 days after signed contract. Byline given. Buys all rights. Editorial lead time 6 months. Submit seasonal material 8 months in advance. Accepts queries by mail, fax. Accepts previously published material. Accepts simultaneous submissions. Responds in 2 months to queries. Sample copy for $3.50 or online.

Nonfiction: "We request quick and easy, inexpensive crafts and activities. Projects must be original, and complete instructions are required upon acceptance." **Payment negotiable.**

Reprints: Send tearsheet and information about when and where the material previously appeared.

Photos: Photos of project may be submitted in place of project at query stage.

Tips: "*Pack-O-Fun* is looking for original how-to projects for kids and those working with kids. Write simple instructions for crafts to be done by children ages 5-13 years. We're looking for recyclable ideas for throwaways. We accept fiction if accompanied by a craft or in skit form (appropriate for classrooms, scouts or Bible school groups). It would be helpful to check out our magazine before submitting."

$ PIECEWORK MAGAZINE, Interweave Press, Inc., 201 E. Fourth St., Loveland CO 80537-5655. (970)669-7672. Fax: (970)667-8317. E-mail: piecework@interweave.com. Website: www.interweave.com. Editor: Jeane Hutchins. **Contact:** Jake Rexus, assistant editor. **90% freelance written.** Bimonthly magazine covering needlework history. "*PieceWork* celebrates the rich tradition of needlework and the history of the people behind it. Stories and projects on embroidery, cross-stitch, knitting, crocheting, and quilting, along with other textile arts, are featured in each issue." Estab. 1993. Circ. 60,000. Pays on publication. Byline given. Offers 30% kill fee. Buys first North American serial rights. Editorial lead time 6 months. Submit seasonal material 6 months in advance. Accepts queries by mail, e-mail, fax, phone. Responds in 6 months to queries. Sample copy and writer's guidelines free.

Nonfiction: Book excerpts, historical/nostalgic, how-to, interview/profile, new product. No contemporary needlework articles. **Buys 25-30 mss/year.** Send complete ms. Length: 1,000-2,000 words. **Pays $100/printed page.**

Photos: State availability of or send photos with submission. Reviews transparencies, prints. Buys one-time rights. Captions, identification of subjects, model releases required.

Tips: "Submit a well-researched article on a historical aspect of needlework complete with information on visuals and suggestion for accompanying project."

$ POPULAR COMMUNICATIONS, CQ Communications, Inc., 25 Newbridge Rd., Hicksville NY 11801. (516)681-2922. Fax: (516)681-2926. E-mail: popularcom@aol.com. Website: www.popular-communications.com. **Contact:** Harold Ort, editor. **25% freelance written.** Monthly magazine covering the radio communications hobby. Estab. 1982. Circ. 40,000. Pays on publication. Publishes ms an average of 6 months after acceptance. Byline given. Buys first North American serial rights. Editorial lead time 3 months. Submit seasonal material 6 months in advance. Accepts queries by mail, e-mail. Responds in 1 month to queries; 2 months to mss. Sample copy for free. Writer's guidelines for #10 SASE.

Nonfiction: General interest, how-to (antenna construction), humor, new product, photo feature, technical. **Buys 6-10 mss/year.** Query. Length: 1,800-3,000 words. **Pays $35/printed page.**

Photos: State availability with submission. Negotiates payment individually. Captions, identification of subjects, model releases required.

Tips: "Either be a radio enthusiast or know one who can help you before sending us an article."

$ $ POPULAR WOODWORKING, F&W Publications, 4700 E. Galbraith Rd., Cincinnati OH 45236. (513)531-2690, ext 1407. E-mail: popwood@fwpubs.com. Website: www.popularwoodworking.com. Editor: Steve Shanesy. **Contact:** Christopher Schwarz, senior editor. **45% freelance written.** Bimonthly magazine. "*Popular Woodworking* invites woodworkers of all levels into a community of professionals who share their hard-won shop experience through in-depth projects and technique articles, which help the readers hone their existing skills and develop new ones. Related stories increase the readers' understanding and enjoyment of their craft. Any project submitted must be aesthetically pleasing, of sound construction and offer a challenge to readers. On the average, we use four freelance features per issue. Our primary needs are 'how-to' articles on woodworking. Our secondary need is for articles that will inspire discussion concerning woodworking. Tone of articles should be conversational and informal, as if the writer is speaking directly to the reader. Our readers are the woodworking hobbyist and small woodshop owner. Writers should have an extensive knowledge of woodworking, or be able to communicate information gained from woodworkers." Estab. 1981. Circ. 200,000. **Pays on acceptance.** Publishes ms an average of 10 months after acceptance. Byline given. Buys first world rights rights. Submit seasonal material 6 months in advance. Accepts queries by mail, e-mail, fax, phone. Accepts previously published material. Responds in 2 months to queries. Sample copy for $4.50 and 9×12 SAE with 6 first-class stamps or online. Writer's guidelines online.

- "The project must be well designed, well constructed, well built and well finished. Technique pieces must have practical application."

Nonfiction: How-to (on woodworking projects, with plans), humor (woodworking anecdotes), technical (woodworking techniques). Special issues: Workshop issue, tool buying guide. No tool reviews. **Buys 40 mss/year.** Query with or without published clips or send complete ms. **Pay starts at $150/published page.**

Reprints: Send photocopy with rights for sale noted and information about when and where the material previously appeared. Pays 25% of amount paid for an original article.

Photos: Photographic quality affects acceptance. Need sharp close-up color photos of step-by-step construction process. Send photos with submission. Reviews color only, slides and transparencies, 3×5 glossies acceptable. Captions, identification of subjects required.

Columns/Departments: Tricks of the Trade (helpful techniques), Out of the Woodwork (thoughts on woodworking as a profession or hobby, can be humorous or serious), 500-1,500 words. **Buys 20 mss/year.** Query.

- The online version of this publication contains material not found in the print edition. Contact: Christopher Schwarz.

Tips: "Write an 'Out of the Woodwork' column for us and then follow up with photos of your projects. Submissions should include materials list, complete diagrams (blueprints not necessary), and discussion of the step-by-step process. We have become more selective on accepting only practical, attractive projects with quality construction. We are also looking for more original topics for our other articles."

$ THE PYSANKA, Starwind Press, P.O. Box 98, Ripley OH 45167. (937)392-4549. E-mail: susannah@techgallery.com. **Contact:** Susannah West, editor. **90% freelance written.** Quarterly newsletter covering wax-resist egg decoration. "*The Pysanka* examines the art of wax-resist egg decoration (pysanky). Its audience is artists and hobbyists who create this style egg." Estab. 2000. Circ. 100. **Pays on acceptance.** Publishes ms an average of 3 months after acceptance. Byline given.

Offers 100% kill fee. Buys first North American serial rights. Editorial lead time 3 months. Submit seasonal material 3 months in advance. Accepts queries by mail, e-mail. Accepts previously published material. Responds in 2 months to queries; 2 months to mss. Sample copy for $3. Writer's guidelines for #10 SASE.

Nonfiction: Historical/nostalgic, how-to, interview/profile, new product, opinion, personal experience, photo feature, travel. **Buys 16-20 mss/year.** Query or send complete ms. Length: 500-900 words. **Pays $10.**

Reprints: Accepts previously published submissions.

Photos: State availability with submission. Negotiates payment individually. Identification of subjects required.

Columns/Departments: Around and About (reviews of interesting places to visit related to the craft), 300-500 words; Passing the Torch (workshop experiences), 200-500 words; On the Pysanky Bookshelf (book reviews), 100-200 words. **Buys 8-12 mss/year.** Query. **Pays $5-10.**

Fiction: Ethnic. **Buys 4 mss/year.** Send complete ms. Length: 2,000-5,000 words. **Pays 1¢/word.**

Tips: "The writer should be familiar with the wax-resist style of egg decoration, ideally an artist or hobbyist who makes this style of egg."

N $ QUILTER'S NEWSLETTER MAGAZINE, PRIMEDIA Enthusiast Group, 741 Corporate Circle, Suite A, Golden CO 80401. (303)278-1010. Fax: (303)277-0307. E-mail: questions@qnm.com. Website: www.quiltersnewsletter.com. Editor: Mary Leman Austin. Published 10 times/year covering quilt making. Written for quilt enthusiasts. Estab. 1969. Circ. 185,000. Pays on publication. Publishes ms an average of 1 year after acceptance. Accepts queries by mail. Responds in 6-8 weeks to mss. Sample copy online. Writer's guidelines online.

Nonfiction: SASE Returns. Historical/nostalgic, how-to (design techniques, presentation of a single technique or concept with step-by-step approach), interview/profile, new product, reviews- quilt books and videos. Send complete ms.

Photos: Color only, no b&w. Reviews 2×2, 4×5 or larger transparencies, 35mm slides. Negotiates payment individually. Captions required.

Tips: "Our decision will be based on the freshness of the material, the interest of the material to our readers, whether we have recently published similar material or already have something similar in our inventory, how well it fits into the balance of the material we have on hand, how much rewriting or editing we think it will require, and the quality of the slides, photos or illustrations you include."

N $ $ THE QUILTER, All American Crafts, Inc., 243 Newton-Sparta Rd., Newton NJ 07860. (973)383-8080. Fax: (973)383-8133. E-mail: editors@thequiltermag.com. Website: www.thequiltermag.com. **Contact:** Laurette Koserowski, editor. **45% freelance written.** Bimonthly magazine on quilting. Estab. 1988. Pays on publication. Publishes ms an average of 6 months after acceptance. Byline given. Submit seasonal material 6 months in advance. Accepts queries by mail, phone. Responds in 2 months to queries. Sample copy for 9×12 SAE and 4 first-class stamps. Writer's guidelines online.

Nonfiction: Quilts and quilt patterns with instructions, quilt-related projects, interview/profile, photo feature—all quilt related. Query with published clips. Length: 350-1,000 words. **Pays 10-12¢/word.**

Photos: Send photos with submission. Reviews transparencies, prints. Buys one-time or all rights. Offers $10-15/photo. Captions, identification of subjects required.

Columns/Departments: Feature Teacher (qualified quilt teachers with teaching involved—with slides); Profile (award-winning and interesting quilters). Length: 1,000 words maximum. **Pays 10¢/word, $15/photo.**

N $ QUILTWORKS TODAY, (formerly *Traditional Quiltworks* and *Quilting Today*), Chitra Publications, 2 Public Ave., Montrose PA 18801. (570)278-1984. Fax: (570)278-2223. E-mail: chitraed@epix.net. Website: www.quilttownusa.com. **Contact:** Connie Ellsworth, production manager. **40% freelance written.** Bimonthly magazine covering quilting, traditional and contemporary. "We seek articles with 1 or 2 magazine pages of text, and quilts that illustrate the content. (Each page of text is approximately 750 words, 6,500 characters, or 3 double-spaced typewritten pages.) Please submit double-spaced manuscripts with wide margins. Submit your article in both hard copy and on a MacIntosh formatted disk, or if using a PC, save as MS-DOS text." Estab. 2002. Circ. 70,000. Pays on publication. Publishes ms an average of 6 months after acceptance. Byline given. Buys second serial (reprint) rights. Submit seasonal material 8 months in advance. Accepts queries by mail, e-mail, fax. Responds in 1 month to queries; 2 months to mss. Writer's guidelines online.

Nonfiction: How-to (for various quilting techniques), interview/profile, new product, personal experience, photo feature, instructional, quilting education. **Buys 12-18 mss/year.** Query or send complete ms. **Pays $75/full page of published text.**

Reprints: Send photocopy and information about when and where the material previously appeared.

Photos: Send photos with submission. Reviews 35mm slides and larger transparenices (color). Offers $20/photo. Captions, identification of subjects required.

Tips: "Our publication appeals to new and experienced traditional quilters."

$ RENAISSANCE MAGAZINE, division of Queue, Inc., 1450 Barnum Ave., Suite 207, Bridgeport CT 06610. (800)232-2224. Fax: (800)775-2729. E-mail: editor@renaissancemagazine.com. Website: www.renaissancemagazine.com. **Contact:** Kim Guarnaccia, managing editor. **90% freelance written.** Bimonthly magazine covering the history of the Middle Ages and the Renaissance. "Our readers include historians, reenactors, roleplayers, medievalists, and Renaissance Faire enthusiasts." Estab. 1996. Circ. 33,000. Pays on publication. Publishes ms an average of 1 year after acceptance. Byline given. Buys first North American serial rights. Editorial lead time 6 months. Submit seasonal material 4 months in advance. Accepts queries by mail, e-mail, fax, phone. Accepts previously published material. Responds in 3 weeks to queries; 2 months to mss. Sample copy for $9. Writer's guidelines online.

- The editor reports an interest in seeing costuming "how-to" articles; and Renaissance Festival "insider" articles.

O— Break in by submitting short (500-1,000 word) articles as fillers or querying on upcoming theme issues.

Nonfiction: Essays, exposé, historical/nostalgic, how-to, interview/profile, new product, opinion, photo feature, religious, travel. **Buys 25 mss/year.** Query or send ms. Length: 1,000-5,000 words. **Pays 7¢/word.**

Photos: State availability with submission. Reviews contact sheets, negatives, transparencies, prints. Buys all rights. Offers no additional payment for photos accepted with ms or negotiates payment separately. Captions, identification of subjects, model releases required.

Columns/Departments: Book reviews, 500 words. Include original or good copy of book cover. "For interested reviewers, books can be supplied for review; query first." **Pays 7¢/word.**

Tips: "Send in all articles in the standard manuscript format with photos/slides or illustrations for suggested use. Writers *must* be open to critique, and all historical articles should also include a recommended reading list. A SASE must be included to receive a response to any submission."

$ $ ROCK & GEM, The Earth's Treasures, Minerals and Jewelry, Miller Magazines, Inc., 4880 Market St., Ventura CA 93003-7783. (805)644-3824, ext. 29. Fax: (805)644-3875. E-mail: editor@rockngem.com. Website: www.rockngem.com. **Contact:** Lynn Varon, managing editor. **99% freelance written.** Monthly magazine covering rockhounding field trips, how-to lapidiary projects, minerals, fossils, gold prospecting, mining, etc. "This is not a scientific journal. Its articles appeal to amateurs, beginners, and experts, but its tone is conversational and casual, not stuffy. It's for hobbyists." Estab. 1971. Circ. 55,000. Pays on publication. Byline given. Buys first North American serial rights. Editorial lead time 4 months. Submit seasonal material 6 months in advance. Accepts queries by mail. Writer's guidelines online.

Nonfiction: General interest, how-to, personal experience, photo feature, travel. Does not want to see "The 25th Anniversary of the Pet Rock," or anything so scientific that it could be a thesis. **Buys 156-200 mss/year.** Send complete ms. Length: 2,000-4,000 words. **Pays $100-250.**

Photos: Accepts prints, slides or digital art on disk or CD only (provide thumbnails). Send photos with submission. Offers no additional payment for photos accepted with ms. Captions required.

Tips: "We're looking for more how-to articles and field trips with maps. Read writers guidelines very carefully and follow all instructions in them. Then be patient. Your manuscript may be published within a month or even a year from date of submission."

$ $ RUG HOOKING MAGAZINE, Stackpole Magazines, 1300 Market St., Suite 202, Lemoyne PA 17043-1420. (717)234-5091. Fax: (717)234-1359. E-mail: rughook@paonline.com. Website: www.rughookingonline.com. Editor: Wyatt Myers. **Contact:** Lisa McMullen, editorial assistant. **75% freelance written.** Magazine published 5 times/year covering the craft of rug hooking. "This is the only magazine in the world devoted exclusively to rug hooking. Our readers are both novices and experts. They seek how-to pieces, features on fellow artisans and stories on beautiful rugs, new and old." Estab. 1989. Circ. 11,000. **Pays on acceptance.** Publishes ms an average of 1 year after acceptance. Byline given. Buys all rights. Editorial lead time 6 months. Submit seasonal material 6 months in advance. Accepts queries by mail, e-mail, fax. Responds in 2 months to queries. Sample copy for $5.

Nonfiction: Also buys 2, 100-page books/year. How-to (hook a rug or a specific aspect of hooking), personal experience. **Buys 30 mss/year.** Query with published clips. Length: 825-2,475 words. **Pays $72-283.50.** Sometimes pays expenses of writers on assignment.

Reprints: Send photocopy and information about when and where the material previously appeared.

Photos: Send photos with submission. Reviews 2×2 transparencies, 3×5 prints. Buys all rights. Negotiates payment individually. Identification of subjects required.

$ SCALE AUTO ENTHUSIAST, Kalmbach Publishing Co., 21027 Crossroads Circle, P.O. Box 1612, Waukesha WI 53187-1612. (262)796-8776. Fax: (262)796-1383. E-mail: jhaught@kalmbach.com. Website: www.scaleautomag.com. **Contact:** Jim Haught, managing editor. **70% freelance written.** Magazine published 8 times/year covering model car building. "We are looking for model builders, collectors, and enthusiasts who feel their models and/or modeling techniques and experiences would be of interest and benefit to our readership." Estab. 1979. Circ. 35,000. Pays on publication. Publishes ms an average of 1 year after acceptance. Byline given. Buys all rights. Editorial lead time 4 months. Submit seasonal material 4 months in advance. Accepts queries by mail, e-mail, fax, phone. Responds in 3 months to queries; 3 months to mss. Sample copy and writer's guidelines free or on website.

Nonfiction: Book excerpts, historical/nostalgic, how-to (build models, do different techniques), interview/profile, personal experience, photo feature, technical. Query or send complete ms. Length: 750-3,000 words. **Pays $60/published page.**

Photos: When writing how-to articles be sure to take photos *during* the project. Send photos with submission. Reviews negatives, 35mm color transparencies, color glossy. Buys all rights. Negotiates payment individually. Captions, identification of subjects, model releases required.

Columns/Departments: Buys 50 mss/year. Query. **Pays $60.**

Tips: "First and foremost, our readers like how-to material: how-to paint, how-to scratchbuild, how-to chop a roof, etc. Basically, our readers want to know how to make their own models better. Therefore, any help or advice you can offer is what modelers want to read. Also, the more photos you send, taken from a variety of views, the better choice we have in putting together an outstanding article layout. Send us more photos than you would ever possibly imagine we could use. This permits us to pick and choose the best of the bunch."

$ $ SEW NEWS, The Fashion Magazine for People Who Sew, Primedia Enthusiast Group, 741 Corporate Circle, Suite A, Golden CO 80401. (303)278-1010. Fax: (303)277-0370. E-mail: sewnews@sewnews.com. Website: www.sewnews.com. **Contact:** Linda Turner Griepentrog, editor. **90% freelance written.** Works with a small number of new/unpublished writers each year. Monthly magazine covering fashion-sewing. "Our magazine is for the beginning home sewer to the professional dressmaker. It expresses the fun, creativity, and excitement of sewing." Estab. 1980. Circ. 175,000. **Pays on acceptance.** Publishes ms an average of 6 months after acceptance. Byline given. Buys all rights. Submit seasonal material

6 months in advance. Accepts queries by mail, e-mail, fax. Responds in 2 months to mss. Sample copy for $5.99. Writer's guidelines for #10 SAE with 2 first-class stamps or online.

- All stories submitted to *Sew News* must be on disk or by e-mail.

Nonfiction: How-to (sewing techniques), interview/profile (interesting personalities in home-sewing field). **Buys 200-240 mss/year.** Query with published clips if available. Length: 500-2,000 words. **Pays $25-500 for assigned articles.**

Photos: Prefers color photos or slides, or e-mail submission. Send photos with submission. Buys all rights. Payment included in ms price. Identification of subjects required.

The online magazine carries some original content not found in the print edition and includes writer's guidelines. *Sew News* has a free online newsletter.

Tips: "Query first with writing sample and outline of proposed story. Areas most open to freelancers are how-to and sewing techniques; give explicit, step-by-step instructions, plus rough art. We're using more home decorating and soft craft content."

N $ SHUTTLE SPINDLE & DYEPOT, Handweavers Guild of America, Inc., 3327 Duluth Highway, Two Executive Concourse, Suite 201, Duluth GA 30096. (770)495-7702. Fax: (770)495-7703. E-mail: weavespindye@compuserve.com. Website: www.weavespindye.org. Publications Manager: Pat King. **Contact:** Sandra Bowles, editor-in-chief. **60% freelance written.** Quarterly magazine. "Quarterly membership publication of the Handweavers Guild of America, Inc., *Shuttle Spindle & Dyepot* magazine seeks to encourage excellence in contemporary fiber arts and to support the preservation of techniques and traditions in fiber arts. It also provides inspiration for fiber artists of all levels and develops public awareness and appreciation of the fiber arts. *Shuttle Spindle & Dyepot* appeals to a highly educated, creative and very knowledgeable audience of fiber artists and craftsmen—weavers, spinners, dyers and basket makers." Estab. 1969. Circ. 30,000. Pays on publication. Publishes ms an average of 6 months after acceptance. Byline given. Buys first North American serial, second serial (reprint), electronic rights. Editorial lead time 8 months. Submit seasonal material 8 months in advance. Accepts queries by mail, e-mail, fax, phone. Sample copy for $7.50 plus shipping. Writer's guidelines online.

Articles featuring up-and-coming artists, new techniques, cutting-edge ideas and designs, fascinating children's activities, and comprehensive fiber collections are a few examples of "best bet" topics.

Nonfiction: Inspirational, interview/profile, new product, personal experience, photo feature, technical, travel. "No self-promotional and no articles from those without knowledge of area/art/artists." **Buys 40 mss/year.** Query with published clips. Length: 1,000-2,000 words. **Pays $75-150.**

Photos: State availability with submission. Offers no additional payment for photos accepted with ms. Captions, identification of subjects, model releases required.

Columns/Departments: Books and Videos, News and Information, Calendar and Conference, Travel and Workshop, Guildview (all fiber/art related).

Tips: "Become knowledgeable about the fiber arts and artists. The writer should provide an article of importance to the weaving, spinning, dyeing and basket making community. Query by telephone (once familiar with publication) by appointment helps editor and writer."

$ SPORTS COLLECTORS DIGEST, Krause Publications, 700 E. State St., Iola WI 54990. (715)445-2214. Fax: (715)445-4087. E-mail: kpsports@aol.com. Website: www.krause.com. **Contact:** T.S. O'Connell, editor. **25% freelance written.** Works with a small number of new/unpublished writers each year. Weekly magazine covering sports memorabilia. "We serve collectors of sports memorabilia—baseball cards, yearbooks, programs, autographs, jerseys, bats, balls, books, magazines, ticket stubs, etc." Estab. 1952. Circ. 38,000. Pays after publication. Publishes ms an average of 3 months after acceptance. Byline given. Buys first North American serial rights. Submit seasonal material 3 months in advance. Responds in 5 weeks to queries; 2 months to mss. Sample copy for free.

Nonfiction: General interest (new card issues, research older sets), historical/nostalgic (old staduims, old collectibles, etc.), how-to (buy cards, sell cards and other collectibles, display collectibles, ways to get autographs, jerseys and other memorabilia), interview/profile (well-known collectors, ball players—but must focus on collectibles), new product (new card sets), personal experience (what I collect and why-type stories). No sports stories. "We are not competing with *The Sporting News*, *Sports Illustrated* or your daily paper. Sports collectibles only." **Buys 50-75 mss/year.** Query. Length: 300-3,000 words. **Pays $100-150.**

Reprints: Send tearsheet. Pays 100% of amount paid for an original article.

Photos: Unusual collectibles. Send photos with submission. Buys all rights. Pays $25-150 for b&w prints. Identification of subjects required.

Columns/Departments: Length: 500-1,500 words. "We have all the columnists we need but welcome ideas for new columns." **Buys 100-150 mss/year.** Query. **Pays $90-150.**

Tips: "If you are a collector, you know what collectors are interested in. Write about it. No shallow, puff pieces; our readers are too smart for that. Only well-researched articles about sports memorabilia and collecting. Some sports nostalgia pieces are OK. Write only about the areas you know about."

$ $ TATTOO REVUE, Art & Ink Enterprises, Inc., 5 Marine View Plaza, Suite 207, Hoboken NJ 07030. (201)653-2700. Fax: (201)653-7892. E-mail: inked@skinartmag.com. Website: www.skinart.com. Editor: Jean Chris Miller. **Contact:** Glen Gubernat, managing editor. **25% freelance written.** Interview and profile magazine published 10 times/year covering tattoo artists, their art and lifestyle. "All writers must have knowledge of tattoos. Features include interviews with tattoo artists and collectors." Estab. 1990. Circ. 100,000. Pays on publication. Publishes ms an average of 3 months after acceptance. Byline given. Buys one-time rights. Editorial lead time 3 months. Submit seasonal material 5 months in advance. Accepts queries by mail, e-mail, fax. Accepts previously published material. Accepts simultaneous submissions. Responds in 2 weeks to queries. Sample copy for $5.98. Writer's guidelines for #10 SASE.

Nonfiction: Book excerpts, historical/nostalgic, humor, interview/profile, photo feature. Special issues: Publishes special convention issues—dates and locations provided upon request. "No first-time experiences—our readers already know." **Buys 10-30 mss/year.** Query with published clips or send complete ms. Length: 500-2,500 words. **Pays $50-200.**

Photos: Send photos with submission. Reviews transparencies, prints. Buys one-time rights. Offers $0-10/photo. Captions, identification of subjects, model releases required.

Columns/Departments: Buys 10-30 mss/year. Query with or without published clips or send complete ms. **Pays $25-50.**

Fiction: Adventure, erotica, fantasy, historical, humorous, science fiction, suspense. "No stories featuring someone's tattoo coming to life!" **Buys 10-30 mss/year.** Query with published clips or send complete ms. Length: 500-2,500 words. **Pays $50-100.**

Poetry: Avant-garde, free verse, haiku, light verse, traditional. **Buys 10-30 poems/year.** Submit maximum 12 poems. Length: 2-1,000 lines. **Pays $10-25.**

Fillers: Anecdotes, facts, gags to be illustrated by cartoonist, newsbreaks, short humor. **Buys 10-20/year.** Length: 50-2,000 words.

The online magazine carries original content not found in the print edition. Contact: Chris Miller.

Tips: "All writers must have knowledge of tattoos! Either giving or receiving."

$ $ THREADS, Taunton Press, 63 S. Main St., P.O. Box 5506, Newtown CT 06470. (203)426-8171. E-mail: threads@taunton.com. Website: www.threadsmagazine.com. **Contact:** Carol Spier, editor. Bimonthly magazine covering sewing, garment construction, home decor and embellishments (quilting and embroidery). "We're seeking proposals from hands-on authors who first and foremost have a skill. Being an experienced writer is of secondary consideration." Estab. 1985. Circ. 165,000. Byline given. Offers $150 kill fee. Buys one-time, second serial (reprint) rights. Editorial lead time 4 months. Responds in 1-2 months to queries. Writer's guidelines for free or online.

Nonfiction: "We prefer first-person experience." **Pays $150/page.**

Columns/Departments: Product reviews; Book reviews; Tips; Closures (stories of a humorous nature). Query. **Pays $150/page.**

Tips: "Send us a proposal (outline) with photos of your own work (garments, samplers, etc.)."

$ $ TOY FARMER, Toy Farmer Publications, 7496 106 Ave. SE, LaMoure ND 58458-9404. (701)883-5206. Fax: (701)883-5209. E-mail: zekesez@aol.com. Website: www.toyfarmer.com. President/Publisher: Cathy Scheibe. **Contact:** Cheryl Hegvik, editorial assistant. **65% freelance written.** Monthly magazine covering farm toys. Estab. 1978. Circ. 27,000. Pays on publication. Byline given. Buys first North American serial rights. Editorial lead time 3 months. Submit seasonal material 3 months in advance. Accepts queries by mail, e-mail, fax, phone. Accepts previously published material. Responds in 1 month to queries; 2 months to mss. Sample copy for $4. Writer's guidelines available upon request.

- Youth involvement is strongly encouraged.

Nonfiction: General interest, historical/nostalgic, humor, interview/profile, new product, personal experience, technical, book introductions. **Buys 100 mss/year.** Query with published clips. Length: 800-1,500 words. **Pays 10¢/word.** Sometimes pays expenses of writers on assignment.

Photos: Must be 35mm originals. State availability with submission. Reviews transparencies. Buys one-time rights. Offers no additional payment for photos accepted with ms.

Columns/Departments: "We have regular monthly columns; so freelance work should not duplicate column subjects."

$ $ TOY SHOP, Krause Publications, 700 E. State St., Iola WI 54990. (715)445-2214. Fax: (715)445-4087. E-mail: korbecks@krause.com. Website: www.toyshopmag.com. **Contact:** Sharon Korbeck, editorial director. **85-90% freelance written.** Biweekly tabloid covering toy collecting. "We cover primarily vintage collectible toys from the 1930s-present. Stories focus on historical toy companies, the collectibility of toys, and features on prominent collections." Estab. 1988. Circ. 40,000. Pays on publication. Publishes ms an average of 8-30 months after acceptance. Byline given. Buys perpetual nonexclusive rights. Editorial lead time 6 months. Submit seasonal material 1 year in advance. Accepts queries by mail, e-mail. Accepts simultaneous submissions. Responds in 2 months to queries. Sample copy for $4.50 (plus first-class postage). Writer's guidelines online.

Nonfiction: Historical/nostalgic (toys, toy companies), interview/profile (toy collectors), new product (toys), photo feature, features on old toys. No opinion, broad topics, or poorly researched pieces. **Buys 100 mss/year.** Query. Length: 500-1,500 words. **Pays $50-200.** Contributor's copies included in payment. Sometimes pays expenses of writers on assignment.

Reprints: Send photocopy and information about when and where the material previously appeared.

Photos: State availability of or send photos with submission. Reviews negatives, transparencies, 3×5 prints, and electronic photos. Rights purchased with ms rights. Negotiates payment individually. Captions, identification of subjects, model releases required.

Columns/Departments: Collector Profile (profile of toy collectors), 700-1,000 words. **Buys 25 mss/year.** Query. **Pays $50-150.**

Tips: "Articles must be specific. Include historical info, quotes, values of toys, and photos with story. Talk with toy dealers and get to know the market."

$ $ TOY TRUCKER & CONTRACTOR, Toy Farmer Publications, 7496 106th Ave. SE, LaMoure ND 58458-9404. (701)883-5206. Fax: (701)883-5209. E-mail: zekesez@aol.com. Website: www.toytrucker.com. President/Publisher: Cathy Scheibe. **Contact:** Cheryl Hegvik, editorial assistant. **75% freelance written.** Monthly magazine covering collectible toys. "We are a magazine on hobby and collectible toy trucks and construction pieces." Estab. 1990. Circ. 6,500. Pays on publication. Byline given. Buys first North American serial rights. Editorial lead time 3 months. Submit seasonal material

3 months in advance. Accepts queries by mail, e-mail, fax, phone. Accepts previously published material. Responds in 1 month to queries; 2 months to mss. Sample copy for $4. Writer's guidelines available on request.

Nonfiction: Historical/nostalgic, interview/profile, new product, personal experience, technical. **Buys 35 mss/year.** Query. Length: 800-2,400 words. **Pays 10¢/word.** Sometimes pays expenses of writers on assignment.

Photos: Must be 35mm originals. Send photos with submission. Offers no additional payment for photos accepted with ms. Captions, identification of subjects, model releases required.

Tips: "Send sample work that would apply to our magazine. Also, we need more articles on collectors or builders. We have regular columns, so a feature should not repeat what our columns do."

$ $ WEEKEND WOODCRAFTS, EGW Publishing Inc., 1041 Shary Circle, Concord CA 94518. (925)671-9852. Fax: (925)671-0692. E-mail: editor@weekendwoodcrafts.com. Website: www.weekendwoodcrafts.com. **Contact:** Robert Joseph, editor. Bimonthly magazine covering woodworking/crafts. "Projects that can be completed in one weekend." Estab. 1992. Circ. 91,000. Pays half on acceptance and half on publication. Publishes ms an average of 3 months after acceptance. Byline given. Buys first rights. Editorial lead time 2 months. Submit seasonal material 2 months in advance. Accepts queries by mail, e-mail. Accepts simultaneous submissions. Responds in 2 months to mss. Sample copy online. Writer's guidelines free.

Nonfiction: How-to (tips and tech), woodworking projects. **Buys 10 mss/year.** Send complete ms. Length: 400-1,500 words. **Pays $100-500.**

Photos: Send photos with submission. Reviews contact sheets, 4×6 prints. Buys all rights. Offers no additional payment for photos accepted with ms.

Tips: "Build simple and easy weekend projects, build one- to two-hour projects."

N $ WESTERN & EASTERN TREASURES, People's Publishing Co., Inc., P.O. Box 219, San Anselmo CA 94979. E-mail: treasurenet@prodigy.net. Website: www.treasurenet.com. **Contact:** Rosemary Anderson, managing editor. **100% freelance written.** Monthly magazine covering hobby/sport of metal detecting/treasure hunting. "*Western & Eastern Treasures* provides concise, yet comprehensive coverage of every aspect of the sport/hobby of metal detecting and treasure hunting with a strong emphasis on current, accurate information; innovative, field-proven advice and instruction; and entertaining, effective presentation." Estab. 1966. Circ. 50,000. Pays on publication. Publishes ms an average of 3 months after acceptance. Byline given. Buys all rights. Editorial lead time 4 months. Submit seasonal material 3-4 months in advance. Responds in 3 months to mss. Sample copy for 9×12 SAE and 5 first-class stamps. Writer's guidelines for #10 SASE.

Nonfiction: How-to (tips and finds for metal detectorists), interview/profile (only people in metal detecting), personal experience (positive metal detector experiences), technical (only metal detecting hobby-related), helping in local community with metal detecting skills (i.e., helping local police locate evidence at crime scenes—all volunteer basis). Special issues: Silver & Gold Annual (editorial deadline February each year)—looking for articles 1,500+ words, plus photos on the subject of locating silver and/or gold using a metal detector. No fiction, poetry, or puzzles. **Buys 150+ mss/year.** Send complete ms. Length: 600-1,500 words. **Pays 2¢/word for assigned articles.** Sometimes pays in contributor copies as trade for advertising space.

Photos: Steve Anderson, vice president. Send photos with submission. Reviews 35mm transparencies, prints. Buys all rights. Offers $5 minimum/photo. Captions, identification of subjects required.

$ $ WOODSHOP NEWS, Soundings Publications, Inc., 10 Bokum Rd., Essex CT 06426-1185. (860)767-8227. Fax: (860)767-0645. E-mail: editorial@woodshopnews.com. Website: www.woodshopnews.com. **Contact:** A.J. Hamler, editor. **20% freelance written.** Monthly tabloid "covering woodworking for professionals and hobbyists. Solid business news and features about woodworking companies. Feature stories about interesting professional and amateur woodworkers. Some how-to articles." Estab. 1986. Circ. 85,000. Pays on publication. Publishes ms an average of 3 months after acceptance. Byline given. Offers 25% kill fee. Buys first North American serial rights. Submit seasonal material 4 months in advance. Accepts queries by mail, e-mail, fax. Responds in 1 month to queries. Sample copy online. Writer's guidelines free.

- *Woodshop News* needs writers in major cities in all regions except the Northeast. Also looking for more editorial opinion pieces.

Nonfiction: How-to (query first), interview/profile, new product, opinion, personal experience, photo feature. Key word is "newsworthy." No general interest profiles of "folksy" woodworkers. **Buys 15-25 mss/year.** Query with published clips or send complete ms. Length: 100-1,200 words. **Pays $50-500 for assigned articles; $40-250 for unsolicited articles.** Pays expenses of writers on assignment.

Photos: Send photos with submission. Reviews contact sheets, prints. Buys one-time rights. Offers $20-35/color photo; $250/color cover, usually with story. Captions, identification of subjects required.

Columns/Departments: Pro Shop (business advice, marketing, employee relations, taxes, etc., for the professional written by an established professional in the field); Finishing (how-to and techniques, materials, spraybooths, staining; written by experienced finishers), both 1,200-1,500 words. **Buys 18 mss/year.** Query. **Pays $200-300.**

Fillers: Small filler items, briefs, or news tips that are followed up by staff reporters. **Pays $10.**

Tips: "The best way to start is a profile of a professional woodworker in your area. Find a unique angle about the person or business and stress this as the theme of your article. Avoid a broad, general-interest theme that would be more appropriate to a daily newspaper. Our readers are woodworkers who want more depth and more specifics than would a general readership. If you are profiling a business, we need standard business information such as gross annual earnings/sales, customer base, product line and prices, marketing strategy, etc. Color 35 mm photos are a must. We need more freelance writers from the Mid-Atlantic, Midwest, and West Coast."

$ $ WOODWORK, A Magazine For All Woodworkers, Ross Periodicals, 42 Digital Dr., #5, Novato CA 94949. (415)382-0580. Fax: (415)382-0587. E-mail: woodwork@rossperiodicals.com. Publisher: Tom Toldrian. **Contact:** John Lavine, editor. **90% freelance written.** Bimonthly magazine covering woodworking. "We are aiming at a broad audience of woodworkers, from the enthusiast to professional. Articles run the range from intermediate to complex. We cover such subjects as carving, turning, furniture, tools old and new, design, techniques, projects, and more. We also feature profiles of woodworkers, with the emphasis being always on communicating woodworking methods, practices, theories, and techniques. Suggestions for articles are always welcome." Estab. 1986. Circ. 50,000. Pays on publication. Byline given. Buys first North American serial, second serial (reprint) rights. Accepts queries by mail, e-mail, fax. Sample copy for $5 and 9×12 SAE with 6 first-class stamps. Writer's guidelines for #10 SASE.

Nonfiction: How-to (simple or complex, making attractive furniture), interview/profile (of established woodworkers that make attractive furniture), photo feature (of interest to woodworkers), technical (tools, techniques). "Do not send a how-to unless you are a woodworker." Query. Length: 1,500-2,000 words. **Pays $150/published page.**

Photos: Send photos with submission. Reviews 35mm slides. Buys one-time rights. Pays higher page rate for photos accepted with ms. Captions, identification of subjects required.

Columns/Departments: Tips and Techniques column, **pays $35-75.** Interview/profiles of established woodworkers (bring out woodworker's philosophy about the craft, opinions about what is happening currently). Good photos of attractive furniture a must. Section on how-to desirable. Query with published clips.

Tips: "Our main requirement is that each article must directly concern woodworking. If you are not a woodworker, the interview/profile is your best, really only chance. Good writing is essential as are good photos. The interview must be entertaining, but informative and pertinent to woodworkers' interests. Include sidebar written by the profile subject."

HOME & GARDEN

The baby boomers' turn inward, or "cocooning," has caused an explosion of publications in this category. Gardening magazines in particular have blossomed, as more people are developing leisure interests at home. Some magazines here concentrate on gardens; others on the how-to of interior design. Still others focus on homes and gardens in specific regions of the country. Be sure to read the publication to determine its focus before submitting a manuscript or query.

$ THE ALMANAC FOR FARMERS & CITY FOLK, Greentree Publishing, Inc., #319, 840 S. Rancho Dr., Suite 4, Las Vegas NV 89106. (702)387-6777. Website: www.thealmanac.com. **Contact:** Lucas McFadden, editor. **30-40% freelance written.** Annual almanac of "down-home, folksy material pertaining to farming, gardening, homemaking, animals, etc." Deadline: March 31. Estab. 1983. Circ. 500,000. Pays on publication. Publishes ms an average of 6 months after acceptance. Byline given. Buys first North American serial rights. Sample copy for $4.99. Writer's guidelines not available.

O→ Break in with short, humorous, gardening, or how-to pieces.

Nonfiction: Essays, general interest, historical/nostalgic, how-to (any home or garden project), humor. No fiction or controversial topics. "Please, no first-person pieces!" **Buys 30 mss/year.** No queries please. Editorial decisions made from ms only. Send complete ms by mail. Length: 350-1,400 words. **Pays $45/page.**

Poetry: Buys 1-4 poems/year. Pays $45 for full pages, otherwise proportionate share thereof.

Fillers: Uses 60/year. Anecdotes, facts, short humor, gardening hints. Length: 125 words maximum. **Pays $10-45.**

Tips: "Typed submissions essential as we scan in manuscript. Short, succinct material is preferred. Material should appeal to a wide range of people and should be on the 'folksy' side, preferably with a thread of humor woven in. No first-person pieces."

$ $ THE AMERICAN GARDENER, A Publication of the American Horticultural Society, 7931 E. Boulevard Dr., Alexandria VA 22308-1300. (703)768-5700. Fax: (703)768-7533. E-mail: editor@ahs.org. Website: www.ahs.org. Managing Editor: Mary Yee. **Contact:** David J. Ellis, editor. **70% freelance written.** Bimonthly magazine covering gardening and horticulture. "*The American Gardener* is the official publication of the American Horticultural Society (AHS), a national, nonprofit, membership organization for gardeners, founded in 1922. The AHS mission is 'to open the eyes of all Americans to become responsible caretakers of the earth, to celebrate America's diversity through the arts and sciences of horticulture, and to lead this effort by sharing the Society's unique national resources with all Americans." All articles in *The American Gardener* are also published on members-only website. Estab. 1922. Circ. 28,000. Pays on publication. Publishes ms an average of 6 months after acceptance. Byline given. Offers 25% kill fee. Buys first North American serial rights. Editorial lead time 4 months. Submit seasonal material at least 1 year in advance. Accepts queries by mail. Responds in 3 months to queries. Sample copy for $5. Writer's guidelines for #10 SASE.

Nonfiction: "Feature-length articles include in-depth profiles of individual plant groups; profiles of prominent American horticulturists and gardeners (living and dead); profiles of unusual public or private gardens; descriptions of historical developments in American gardening; descriptions of innovative landscape design projects (especially relating to use of regionally native plants or naturalistic gardening); and descriptions of important plant breeding and research programs tailored to a lay audience. We run a few how-to articles; these should address relatively complex or unusual topics that most other gardening magazines won't tackle—photography needs to be provided." **Buys 30 mss/year.** Query with published clips. Length: 1,500-2,500 words. **Pays $300-500, depending on complexity and author's experience.**

Reprints: Rarely purchases second rights. Send photocopy of article with information about when and where the material previously appeared. Payment varies.

Photos: Must be accompanied by postage-paid return mailer. State availability with submission. Reviews transparencies.

Buys one-time rights, plus limited rights to run article on members-only website. Offers $40-300/photo. Identification of subjects required.

Columns/Departments: Conservationist's Notebook (addresses issues in plant conservation that are relevant or of interest to gardeners); Natural Connections (explains a natural phenomenon—plant and pollinator relationships, plant and fungus relationships, parasites—that may be observed in nature or in the garden), 750-1,200 words. **Buys 10 mss/year.** Query with published clips. **Pays $50-250.**

Tips: "The majority of our readers are advanced, passionate amateur gardeners; about 20 percent are horticultural professionals. Most prefer not to use synthetic chemical pesticides. Our articles are intended to bring this knowledgeable group new information, ranging from the latest scientific findings that affect plants to in-depth profiles of specific plant groups, and the history of gardening and gardens in America."

$ $ ATLANTA HOMES AND LIFESTYLES, Weisner Publishing LLC, 1100 Johnson Ferry Rd., Suite 595, Atlanta GA 30342. (404)252-6670. Fax: (404)252-6673. Website: www.atlantahomesmag.com. Editor-in-Chief: Oma Blaise. **Contact:** Clint Rossman, editor. **65% freelance written.** Magazine published 8 times/year. "*Atlanta Homes and Lifestyles* is designed for the action-oriented, well-educated reader who enjoys his/her shelter, its design and construction, its environment, and living and entertaining in it." Estab. 1983. Circ. 33,091. Pays on publication. Publishes ms an average of 6 months after acceptance. Byline given. Buys all rights. Accepts queries by mail, fax. Responds in 3 months to queries. Sample copy for $3.95. Writer's guidelines online.

Nonfiction: Interview/profile, new product, photo feature, well-designed homes, gardens, local art, remodeling, food, preservation, entertaining. "We do not want articles outside respective market area, not written for magazine format, or that are excessively controversial, investigative or that cannot be appropriately illustrated with attractive photography." **Buys 35 mss/year.** Query with published clips. Length: 500-1,200 words. **Pays $400.** Sometimes pays expenses of writer on assignment.

Photos: Most photography is assigned. State availability with submission. Reviews transparencies. Buys one-time rights. Pays $40-50/photo. Captions, identification of subjects, model releases required.

Columns/Departments: Short Takes (newsy items on home and garden topics); Quick Fix (simple remodeling ideas); Cheap Chic (stylish decorating that is easy on the wallet); Digging In (outdoor solutions from Atlanta's gardeners); Big Fix (more extensive remodeling projects); Real Estate News. Length: 350-500 words. Query with published clips. **Pays $50-200.**

Tips: "Query with specific new story ideas rather than previously published material."

$ $ AUSTIN HOME & LIVING, Publications & Communications, Inc., 11675 Jollyville Rd., Suite 201, Austin TX 78759. (512)381-0576. Fax: (512)331-3950. E-mail: bronas@pcinews.com. Website: www.austinhomeandliving.com. Editor: Carrie Watson. **Contact:** Brona Stockton, associate publisher. **75% freelance written.** Bimonthly magazine. "*Austin Home & Living* showcases the homes found in Austin and provides tips on food, gardening, and decorating." Estab. 1994. Circ. 20,000. Pays on publication. Publishes ms an average of 4 months after acceptance. Byline given. Offers 100% kill fee. Buys all rights. Editorial lead time 4 months. Submit seasonal material 6 months in advance. Accepts queries by mail, e-mail, fax. Responds in 1 month to queries; 2 months to mss. Sample copy for free. Writer's guidelines online.

Nonfiction: How-to, interview/profile, new product, travel. **Buys 18 mss/year.** Query with published clips. Length: 500-2,000 words. **Pays $200 for assigned articles.** Pays expenses of writers on assignment.

Photos: State availability of or send photos with submission. Reviews negatives, transparencies, prints. Buys all rights. Offers no additional payment for photos accepted with ms. Captions required.

$ BACKHOME, Your Hands-On Guide to Sustainable Living, Wordsworth Communications, Inc., P.O. Box 70, Hendersonville NC 28793. (828)696-3838. Fax: (828)696-0700. E-mail: backhome@ioa.com. Website: www.backhomemagazine.com. **Contact:** Lorna K. Loveless, editor. **80% freelance written.** Bimonthly magazine. *BackHome* encourages readers to take more control over their lives by doing more for themselves: productive organic gardening; building and repairing their homes; utilizing alternative energy systems; raising crops and livestock; building furniture; toys and games and other projects; creative cooking. *BackHome* promotes respect for family activities, community programs, and the environment. Estab. 1990. Circ. 26,000. Pays on publication. Publishes ms an average of 1 year after acceptance. Byline given. Offers $25 kill fee at publisher's discretion. Buys first North American serial rights. Editorial lead time 3 months. Submit seasonal material 6 months in advance. Accepts queries by mail, e-mail, fax, phone. Accepts previously published material. Responds in 6 weeks to queries; 2 months to mss. Sample copy $5 or online. Writer's guidelines online.

- The editor reports an interest in seeing "more alternative energy experiences, *good* small houses, workshop projects (for handy persons, not experts), and community action others can copy."

O→ Break in by writing about personal experience (especially in overcoming challenges) in fields in which *BackHome* focuses.

Nonfiction: How-to (gardening, construction, energy, homebusiness), interview/profile, personal experience, technical, self-sufficiency. No essays or old-timey reminiscences. **Buys 80 mss/year.** Query. Length: 750-5,000 words. **Pays $35 (approximately)/printed page.**

Reprints: Send photocopy and information about when and where the material previously appeared. Pays $35/printed page.

Photos: Send photos with submission. Reviews 35mm slides, color prints, and JPEG photo attachments of 300 dpi. Buys one-time rights. Offers additional payment for photos published. Identification of subjects required.

Tips: "Very specific in relating personal experiences in the areas of gardening, energy, and homebuilding how-to. Third-person approaches to others' experiences are also acceptable but somewhat less desirable. Clear color photo prints, especially those in which people are prominent, help immensely when deciding upon what is accepted."

N $ BIRDS & BLOOMS, Reiman Publications, 5400 S. 60th St., Greendale WI 53129. E-mail: editors@birdsandblooms.com. Website: www.birdsandblooms.com. **Contact:** Jeff Nowak, editor. **15% freelance written.** Bimonthly magazine focusing on the "beauty in your own backyard. *Birds & Blooms* is a sharing magazine that lets backyard enthusiasts chat with each other by exchanging personal experiences. This makes *Birds & Blooms* more like a conversation than a magazine, as readers share tips and tricks on producing beautiful blooms and attracting feathered friends to their backyards." Estab. 1995. Circ. 1,900,000. Pays on publication. Publishes ms an average of 7 months after acceptance. Byline given. Buys all rights. Editorial lead time 2 months. Submit seasonal material 4 months in advance. Accepts queries by mail, e-mail. Accepts simultaneous submissions. Responds in 2 months to queries; 2 months to mss. Sample copy for $2, 9×12 SAE and $1.95 postage. Writer's guidelines for #10 SASE.

Nonfiction: Essays, how-to, humor, inspirational, personal experience, photo feature, natural crafting and plan items for building backyard accents. No bird rescue or captive bird pieces. **Buys 12-20 mss/year.** Send complete ms. Length: 250-1,000 words. **Pays $100-400.**

Photos: Trudi Bellin, photo coordinator. Send photos with submission. Reviews transparencies, prints. Buys one-time rights. Identification of subjects required.

Columns/Departments: Backyard Banter (odds, ends and unique things); Bird Tales (backyard bird stories); Local Lookouts (community backyard happenings), all 200 words. **Buys 12-20 mss/year.** Send complete ms. **Pays $50-75.**

Fillers: Anecdotes, facts, gags to be illustrated by cartoonist. **Buys 25/year.** Length: 10-250 words. **Pays $10-75.**

Tips: "Focus on conversational writing—like you're chatting with a neighbor over your fence. Manuscripts full of tips and ideas that people can use in backyards across the country have the best chance of being used. Photos that illustrate these points also increase chances of being used."

$ $ CALIFORNIA HOMES, The Magazine of Architecture, the Arts and Distinctive Design, McFadden-Bray Publishing Corp., P.O. Box 8655, Newport Beach CA 92658. (949)640-1484. Fax: (949)640-1665. E-mail: edit@calhomesmagazine.com. **Contact:** Susan McFadden, editor. **80% freelance written.** Bimonthly magazine covering California interiors, architecture, some food, travel, history, current events in the field. Estab. 1997. Circ. 60,000. Pays on publication. Publishes ms an average of 3 months after acceptance. Byline given. Offers 50% kill fee. Buys first North American serial rights. Editorial lead time 3 months. Submit seasonal material 6 months in advance. Accepts queries by mail, e-mail, fax. Responds in 1 month to queries; 2 months to mss. Sample copy for $7.50. Writer's guidelines for #10 SASE.

Nonfiction: Query. Length: 500-1,000 words. **Pays $250-500.** Sometimes pays expenses of writers on assignment.

Photos: State availability with submission. Buys one-time rights. Negotiates payment individually. Captions required.

$ $ $ $ CANADIAN GARDENING MAGAZINE, Avid Media, Inc., 340 Ferrier St., Suite 210, Markham ON L3R 2Z5, Canada. (905)475-8440. Fax: (905)475-9246. E-mail: satterthwaite@canadiangardening.com. Website: www.canadiangardening.com. Managing Editor: Christina Selby. **Contact:** Aldona Satterthwaite, editor. Mostly freelance written. Magazine published 8 times/year covering Canadian gardening. "*Canadian Gardening* is a national magazine aimed at the avid home gardener. Our readers are city gardeners with tiny lots, country gardeners with rolling acreage, indoor gardeners, rooftop gardeners, and enthusiastic beginners and experienced veterans. Estab. 1990. Circ. 152,000. **Pays on acceptance.** Byline given. Offers 25-50% kill fee. Buys electronic rights. Editorial lead time 3 months. Submit seasonal material 3 months in advance. Accepts queries by mail, e-mail, fax. Accepts simultaneous submissions. Responds in 3 months to queries. Writer's guidelines online.

Nonfiction: How-to (planting and gardening projects), humor, personal experience, technical, plant and garden profiles, practical advice. **Buys 100 mss/year.** Query. Length: 200-2,000 words. **Pays $50-1,500 (Canadian).** Sometimes pays expenses of writers on assignment.

Photos: Send photos with submission. Reviews color transparencies. Negotiates payment individually.

$ $ $ $ CANADIAN HOME WORKSHOP, The Do-It-Yourself Magazine, Avid Media, Inc., 340 Ferrier St., Suite 210, Markham ON L3R 2Z5, Canada. (905)475-8440. Fax: (905)475-9246. E-mail: letters@canadianhomeworkshop.com. Website: www.canadianhomeworkshop.com. **Contact:** Douglas Thomson, editor. **90% freelance written**, half of these are assigned. Magazine published 10 times/year covering the "do-it-yourself" market including woodworking projects, renovation, restoration, and maintenance. Circ. 120,000. Pays 1 month after receipt. Byline given. Offers 50% kill fee. Rights are negotiated with author. Submit seasonal material 6 months in advance. Responds in 6 weeks to queries. Sample copy for 9×12 SAE. Writer's guidelines for #10 SASE.

Nonfiction: How-to (home maintenance, renovation, woodworking projects, and features). **Buys 40-60 mss/year.** Query with published clips. Length: 1,500-2,500 words. **Pays $800-2,000.** Pays expenses of writers on assignment.

Photos: Send photos with submission. Payment for photos, transparencies negotiated with the author. Captions, identification of subjects, model releases required.

Tips: "Freelancers must be aware of our magazine format. Products used in how-to articles must be readily available across Canada. Deadlines for articles are four months in advance of cover date. How-tos should be detailed enough for the amateur but appealing to the experienced. Articles must have Canadian content: sources, locations, etc."

$ $ CANADIAN HOMES & COTTAGES, The In-Home Show Ltd., 2650 Meadowvale Blvd., Unit 4, Mississauga ON L5N 6M5, Canada. (905)567-1440. Fax: (905)567-1442. E-mail: jnaisby@homesandcottages.com. Website: www.homesandcottages.com. Assistant Editor: Steven Chester. **Contact:** Janice Naisby, editor-in-chief. **75% freelance written.** Magazine published 6 times/year covering building and renovating; "technically comprehensive articles." Estab. 1987. Circ. 65,000. Pays on publication. Publishes ms an average of 2 months after acceptance. Byline given. Offers 10% kill fee. Buys first North American serial rights. Editorial lead time 3 months. Submit seasonal material 3 months in advance. Accepts queries by mail. Sample copy for SAE. Writer's guidelines for #10 SASE.

Nonfiction: Looking for how-to projects and simple home improvement ideas. Humor (building and renovation related), new product, technical. **Buys 32 mss/year.** Query. Length: 1,000-2,000 words. **Pays $300-750.** Sometimes pays expenses of writers on assignment.

Photos: Send photos with submission. Reviews transparencies, prints. Buys one-time rights. Negotiates payment individually. Captions, identification of subjects required.

Tips: "Read our magazine before sending in a query. Remember that you are writing to a Canadian audience."

N $ CANADIAN LIVING, Transcontinental Media, Inc., 25 Sheppard Ave W, Suite 100, Toronto ON M2N 6S7, Canada. E-mail: letters@canadianliving.com. Website: www.canadianliving.com. Editor: Charlotte Empey. Managing Editor: Susan Antonacci. **Contact:** Submissions Editor. Monthly magazine covering Canadian lifestyles. Written as a family lifestyle magazine with emphasis on practical information for women at home and in business. Circ. 542,815. Editorial lead time 3 months. Accepts queries by mail, e-mail. Sample copy not available. Writer's guidelines by e-mail.

Nonfiction: General interest, how-to, interview/profile. Travel articles or features dealing with career or workplace issues. Query. Length: 750-2,500 words.

$ $ COLORADO HOMES & LIFESTYLES, Wiesner Publishing, LLC, 7009 S. Potomac St., Centennial CO 80112-4029. (303)662-5204. Fax: (303)662-5307. E-mail: submissions@coloradohomesmag.com. Website: www.coloradohomesmag.com. **75% freelance written.** Upscale shelter magazine published 9 times/year containing beautiful homes, landscapes, art and artists, food and wine, architecture, calendar, antiques, etc. All of Colorado is included. Geared toward home-related and lifestyle areas, personality profiles, etc. Estab. 1981. Circ. 35,000. **Pays on acceptance.** Publishes ms an average of 3 months after acceptance. Byline given. Offers 15% kill fee. Buys first North American serial rights. Editorial lead time 3 months. Submit seasonal material 1 year in advance. Accepts queries by mail, e-mail. Accepts simultaneous submissions. Responds in 2 months to queries. Sample copy for #10 SASE. Writer's guidelines online.

- The editor reports that *Colorado Homes & Lifestyles* is doing many more lifestyle articles and needs more unusual and interesting worldwide travel stories.

Nonfiction: Fine homes and furnishings, regional interior design trends, interesting personalities and lifestyles—all with a Colorado slant. Book excerpts, general interest, historical/nostalgic, new product, photo feature. No personal essays, religious, humor, technical. **Buys 50-75 mss/year.** Query with published clips. Length: 1,200-1,500 words. **Pays $200-300.** Sometimes pays expenses of writers on assignment.

Photos: Send photos with submission. Reviews transparencies, b&w glossy prints, CDs, digital images, slides. Identification of subjects, title and caption suggestions appreciated. photographic credits required.

Tips: "Send query, lead paragraph, clips. Send ideas for story or stories. Include some photos, if applicable. The more interesting and unique the subject the better. A frequent mistake made by writers is failure to provide material with a style and slant appropriate for the magazine, due to poor understanding of the focus of the magazine."

$ $ CONCRETE HOMES, Publications and Communications, Inc. (PCI), 11675 Jollyville Rd., Suite 201, Austin TX 78759. Fax: (512)331-3950. E-mail: homes@pcinews.com. Website: concretehomesmagazine.com. Editor: Eugene Morgan. **Contact:** Brona Stockton, associate publisher. **85% freelance written.** Bimonthly magazine covering homes built with concrete. "*Concrete Homes* is a publication designed to be informative to consumers, builders, contractors, architects, etc., who are interested in concrete homes. The magazine profiles concrete home projects (they musy be complete) and offers how-to and industry news articles." Estab. 1999. Circ. 25,000. Pays on publication. Publishes ms an average of 2 months after acceptance. Byline given. Offers 100% kill fee. Buys all rights. Editorial lead time 2 months. Submit seasonal material 3-4 months in advance. Accepts queries by mail, e-mail. Accepts simultaneous submissions. Responds in 1 month to queries; 1 month to mss. Sample copy and writer's guidelines online.

Nonfiction: How-to, interview/profile, new product, technical. **Buys 30-40 mss/year.** Query or query with published clips. Length: 800-2,000 words. **Pays $200-250.** Sometimes pays expenses of writers on assignment.

Photos: State availability with submission. Reviews 8×10 transparencies, prints, GIF/JPEG files. Buys all rights. Offers no additional payment for photos accepted with ms. Captions required.

Tips: "Demonstrate awareness of concrete homes and some knowledge of the construction/building industry."

$ $ $ $ COTTAGE LIFE, Quarto Communications, 54 St. Patrick St., Toronto ON M5T 1V1, Canada. (416)599-2000. Fax: (416)599-0800. E-mail: editorial@cottagelife.com. Website: www.cottagelife.com. Managing Editor: Catherine Collins. **Contact:** Penny Caldwell, editor. **80% freelance written.** Bimonthly magazine. "*Cottage Life* is written and designed for the people who own and spend time at waterfront cottages throughout Canada and bordering U.S. states, with a strong focus on Ontario. The magazine has a strong service slant, combining useful 'how-to' journalism with coverage of the people, trends, and issues in cottage country. Regular columns are devoted to boating, fishing, watersports, projects, real estate, cooking, nature, personal cottage experience, and environmental, political, and financial issues of concern to cottagers." Estab. 1988. Circ. 70,000. **Pays on acceptance.** Publishes ms an average of 2 months after acceptance. Byline given. Offers 50-100% kill fee. Buys first North American serial rights. Sample copy not available. Writer's guidelines free.

Nonfiction: Book excerpts, exposé, historical/nostalgic, how-to, humor, interview/profile, personal experience, photo feature, technical. **Buys 90 mss/year.** Query with published clips and SAE with Canadian postage or IRCs. Length: 1,500-3,500 words. **Pays $100-2,200 for assigned articles; $50-1,000 for unsolicited articles.** Sometimes pays expenses of writers on assignment.

Columns/Departments: On the Waterfront (front department featuring short news, humor, human interest, and service items). Length: 400 words maximum. Pays $100. Cooking, Real Estate, Fishing, Nature, Watersports, Personal Experience and Issues. Length: 150-1,200 words. Query with published clips and SAE with Canadian postage or IRCs. **Pays $100-750.**

Tips: "If you have not previously written for the magazine, the 'On the Waterfront' section is an excellent place to break in."

N $ COUNTRY DECORATING IDEAS, Harris Publications, Inc., 1115 Broadway, New York NY 10010. (212)807-7100. Fax: (212)627-4678. E-mail: countryletters@yahoo.com. Website: www.countrydecoratingideas.com. Editor: James Baggett. Quarterly magazine. Offers features on do-it-yourself ideas and affordable advice on country decorating for the home. Circ. 360,183. Editorial lead time 2 months. Sample copy not available.

N $ COUNTRY GARDENS, Meredith Corporation, 1716 Locust St., Des Moines IA 50309-3023. (515)284-3000. Fax: (515)284-2773. E-mail: cgardens@mdp.com. Website: www.countryhomemagazine.com. Editor: Carol Sama Sheehan. **Contact:** Marsha Jahns; managing editor. Quarterly magazine covering gardening. Devoted to presenting readers with illustrated examples of outstanding gardening concepts, ideas and designs. Estab. 1992. Circ. 350,000. Editorial lead time 7 months. Accepts queries by mail. Sample copy for $3.95.

Nonfiction: Query.

Columns/Departments: Query.

$ COUNTRY LIVING, The Hearst Corp., 224 W. 57th St., New York NY 10019. (212)649-3509. E-mail: countryliving@hearst.com. **Contact:** Marjorie Gage, senior editor. Monthly magazine covering home design and interior decorating with an emphasis on country style. "A lifestyle magazine for readers who appreciate the warmth and traditions associated with American home and family life. Each monthly issue embraces American country decorating and includes features on furniture, antiques, gardening, home building, real estate, cooking, entertaining and travel." Estab. 1978. Circ. 1,600,000. Sample copy not available. Writer's guidelines not available.

Nonfiction: Most open to freelancers: Antiques articles from authorities. **Buys 20-30 mss/year.** Send complete ms and SASE. **Payment varies.**

Columns/Departments: Query first.

Tips: "Know the magazine, know the market and know how to write a good story that will interest *our* readers."

$ COUNTRY SAMPLER, Country Sampler, Inc., 707 Kautz Rd., St. Charles IL 60174. (630)377-8000. Fax: (630)377-8194. Website: www.sampler.com. Publisher: Margaret Borst. **Contact:** Paddy Kalahar Buratto, editor. Bimonthly magazine. "*Country Sampler* is a country decorating, antiques, and collectibles magazine and a country product catalog." Estab. 1984. Circ. 426,771. Accepts queries by mail, fax. Sample copy not available.

Nonfiction: "Furniture, accessories, and decorative accents created by artisans throughout the country are displayed and offered for purchase directly from the maker. Fully decorated room settings show the readers how to use the items in their homes to achieve the warmth and charm of the country look."

Tips: "Send photos and story idea for a country-style house tour. Story should be regarding decorating tips and techniques."

$ $ COUNTRY SAMPLER DECORATING IDEAS, Emmis Communications, 707 Kautz Rd., St. Charles IL 60174. Fax: (630)377-8194. E-mail: decideas@sampler.emmis.com. Website: www.decoratingideas.com. Managing Editor: Rita M. Woker. **Contact:** Mike Morris, editor. **60% freelance written.** Bimonthly magazine on home decor and home improvement. "This magazine is devoted to providing do-it-yourself decorating solutions for the average homeowner, through step-by-step projects, topical articles, and real-life feature stories that inspire readers to create the country home of their dreams." **Pays on acceptance.** Publishes ms an average of 6 months after acceptance. Byline given. Makes work-for-hire assignments. Editorial lead time 4 months. Submit seasonal material 6 months in advance. Accepts queries by mail, e-mail, fax. Responds in 1 month to queries; 3 months to mss. Sample copy not available. Writer's guidelines free.

Nonfiction: Book excerpts, how-to (decorating projects), interview/profile, photo feature, house tours. Special issues: Decorate With Paint (March, May, July, September, and November). No opinion or fiction. **Buys 50 mss/year.** Query with published clips. Length: 500-1,500 words. **Pays $250-375.**

Photos: State availability with submission. Reviews transparencies, 3×5 prints. Buys negotiable rights. Negotiates payment individually. Captions, identification of subjects, model releases required.

Tips: "Query letters accompanied by published clips are your best bet. We do not accept unsolicited articles, but pay on acceptance for assigned articles. So it is best to sell us on an article concept and support that concept with similar published articles."

$ DECORATING IDEAS, Woman's Day Special Interest Publications, Hachette-Filipacchi Media, U.S., 1633 Broadway, New York NY 10019. (212)767-6000. Fax: (212)767-5618. Website: www.womansday.com/specials. Editors: Jean Nayar, Jane Chesnutt, Olivia Monjo, Kitty Cox. **Contact:** Amanda Rock, assistant managing editor. Magazine published 4 times/year covering home decorating. "This magazine aims to inspire and teach readers how to create a beautiful home." **Pays on acceptance.** Publishes ms an average of 3 months after acceptance. Byline given. Offers up to 25% kill fee. Buys all rights. Editorial lead time 6 months. Submit seasonal material 10 months in advance. Accepts queries by mail, fax. Responds in 2 months to mss. Sample copy not available. Writer's guidelines for #10 SASE.

Nonfiction: Book excerpts, general interest, how-to (home decor projects for beginner/intermediate skill levels—sewing, woodworking, painting, etc.), interview/profile, new product, photo feature, technical, collectibles, hard-to-find services, unique stores. Query with published clips. Length: 250-1,000 words. **Payment varies based on length, writer, importance**. Sometimes pays expenses of writers on assignment.

Photos: Send representative photos with query. Buys one-time rights. Model releases required.

Columns/Departments: Step by Step (how-to instructions for 1 or 2 relevant projects that can be completed in a day or 2), 400-800 words; Collecting; Furniture Finds; Spotlight On...; Style Notes; Swatches; Where to Find It; Let's Go

Shopping; Finishing Touches. **Payment varies based on length, writer, and level/amount of research required.**

Tips: "Send a brief, clear query letter with recent, relevant (published) clips, and be patient. Before and after photos are very helpful, as are photos of ideas for Step by Step column. In addition to specific ideas and projects (for which how-to information is provided), we look at decorating trends, provide advice on how to get the most design for your money (with and without help from a professional), and highlight noteworthy new products and services." No phone queries, please. Part of *Woman's Day* Special Interest Publications.

$ $ EARLY AMERICAN LIFE, Celtic Moon Publishing, Inc., 207 House Ave., Suite 103, Camp Hill PA 17011. (717)730-6263. Fax: (717)730-7385. E-mail: ginnys@celticmooninc.com. Website: www.earlyamericanlife.com. **Contact:** Virginia Stimmel, editor. **20% freelance written.** Bimonthly magazine for "people who are interested in capturing the warmth and beauty of the 1600-1840 period and using it in their homes and lives today. They are interested in antiques, traditional crafts, architecture, restoration, and collecting." Estab. 1970. Circ. 130,000. Pays on publication. Publishes ms an average of 1 year after acceptance. Byline given. Buys worldwide rights. Accepts queries by mail, e-mail, fax. Responds in 3 months to queries. Sample copy and writer's guidelines for 9×12 SAE with 4 first-class stamps.

O━ Break in "by offering highly descriptive, entertaining, yet informational articles on social culture, decorative arts, antiques, or well-restored and appropriately furnished homes that reflect middle-class American life prior to 1850."

Nonfiction: "Social history (the story of the people, not epic heroes and battles), travel to historic sites, antiques and reproductions, restoration, architecture, and decorating. We try to entertain as we inform. We're always on the lookout for good pieces on any of our subjects. Would like to see more on how real people did something great to their homes." **Buys 40 mss/year.** Query with or without published clips or send complete ms. Length: 750-3,000 words. **Pays $100-600.**

Tips: "Our readers are eager for ideas on how to bring early America into their lives. Conceive a new approach to satisfy their related interests in arts, crafts, travel to historic sites, and especially in houses decorated in the Early American style. Write to entertain and inform at the same time. Be prepared to help us with sources for illustrations."

$ $ $ FINE GARDENING, Taunton Press, 63 S. Main St., P.O. Box 5506, Newtown CT 06470-5506. (203)426-8171. Fax: (203)426-3434. E-mail: fg@taunton.com. Website: www.finegardening.com. **Contact:** Todd Meier, executive editor. Bimonthly magazine. "High-value magazine on landscape and ornamental gardening. Articles written by avid gardeners—first person, hands-on gardening experiences." Estab. 1988. Circ. 200,000. **Pays on acceptance.** Publishes ms an average of 6 months after acceptance. Byline given. Buys all rights. Editorial lead time 1 year. Submit seasonal material 1 year in advance. Accepts queries by mail, e-mail, fax. Sample copy not available. Writer's guidelines free.

Nonfiction: How-to, personal experience, photo feature, Book review. **Buys 60 mss/year.** Query. Length: 1,000-3,000 words. **Pays $300-1,200.**

Photos: Send photos with submission. Reviews digital. Serial rights.

Columns/Departments: Book, video and software reviews (on gardening); Last Word (essays/serious, humorous, fact or fiction). Length: 250-500 words. **Buys 30 mss/year.** Query. **Pays $50- 200.**

Tips: "It's most important to have solid first-hand experience as a gardener. Tell us what you've done with your own landscape and plants."

$ $ FINE HOMEBUILDING, The Taunton Press, 63 S. Main St., P.O. Box 5506, Newtown CT 06470-5506. (800)309-8919. Fax: (203)426-3434. E-mail: fh@taunton.com. Website: www.taunton.com. **Contact:** Kevin Ireton, editor-in-chief. Bimonthly magazine for builders, architects, contractors, owner/builders and others who are seriously involved in building new houses or reviving old ones. Estab. 1981. Circ. 300,000. Pays half on acceptance, half on publication. Publishes ms an average of 1 year after acceptance. Byline given. Offers on acceptance payment as kill fee. Buys first rights. Reprint rights Responds in 1 month to queries. Sample copy not available. Writer's guidelines for SASE and on website.

Nonfiction: "We're interested in almost all aspects of home building, from laying out foundations to capping cupolas." Query with outline, description, photographs, sketches and SASE. **Pays $150/published page.**

Photos: "Take lots of work-in-progress photos. Color print film, ASA 400, from either Kodak or Fuji works best. If you prefer to use slide film, use ASA 100. Keep track of the negatives; we will need them for publication. If you're not sure what to use or how to go about it, feel free to call for advice."

Columns/Departments: Tools & Materials, Reviews, Questions & Answers, Tips & Techniques, Cross Section, What's the Difference?, Finishing Touches, Great Moments, Breaktime, Drawing Board (design column). Query with outline, description, photographs, sketches and SASE. **Payment varies.**

Tips: "Our chief contributors are home builders, architects and other professionals. We're more interested in your point of view and technical expertise than your prose style. Adopt an easy, conversational style and define any obscure terms for non-specialists. We try to visit all our contributors and rarely publish building projects we haven't seen, or authors we haven't met."

N $ GARDEN COMPASS, Streamopolis, 1450 Front St., San Diego CA 92101. (619)239-2202. Fax: (619)239-4621. E-mail: editor@gardencompass.com. Website: www.gardencompass.com. **Contact:** Siri Jostad, editor. **70% freelance written.** Bimonthly magazine covering gardening. *Garden Compass* is "entertaining and offers sound practical advice for West Coast gardeners." Estab. 1992. Circ. 112,000. Pays on publication. Publishes ms an average of 10 weeks after acceptance. Byline given. Offers $50 kill fee. Not copyrighted. Buys first North American serial rights. Editorial lead time 6 months. Submit seasonal material 6 months in advance. Accepts queries by mail, e-mail. Accepts simultaneous submissions. Responds in 1 month to queries. Sample copy for free.

Photos: Siri Jostad, editor; Laurie Miller, art director. State availability of or send photos with submission. Reviews contact sheets, transparencies, GIF/JPEG files. Buys one-time rights. Negotiates payment individually. Identification of subjects required.

Columns/Departments: Pest Patrol (plant posts/diseases), 400-800 words; e-Gardening (garden info on the Web), 400-800 words; Book Review (gardening books), 400-600 words; Fruit Trees, 800-1,200 words. Query with published clips. **Payment varies.**

Fillers: Anecdotes, facts, newsbreaks. Length: 30-150 words. **Pays $25.**

$ $ $ GARDENING HOW-TO, North American Media Group, 12301 Whitewater Dr., Minnetonka MN 55343. (952)988-7474. Fax: (952)936-9333. E-mail: mpestel@namginc.com. Website: www.gardeningclub.com. **Contact:** Mary Pestel, associate editor. **40% freelance written.** Bimonthly magazine covering gardening/horticulture. "*Gardening How-To* is the bimonthly publication of the National Home Gardening Club, headquartered in Minnetonka, Minnesota. As the primary benefit of membership in the Club, the magazine's aim is to provide timely, interesting, and inspiring editorial that will appeal to our audience of intermediate- to advanced-level home gardeners." Estab. 1996. Circ. 600,000. **Pays on acceptance.** Publishes ms an average of 4 months after acceptance. Byline given. Offers 25% kill fee. Buys one-time rights. Editorial lead time 6 months. Submit seasonal material 6 months in advance. Accepts queries by mail, e-mail, fax. Sample copy for $3. Writer's guidelines for free or by e-mail.

Nonfiction: Buys 36 mss/year. Query with published clips. Length: 1,000-2,000 words. **Pays $200-1,000.** Sometimes pays expenses of writers on assignment.

Photos: State availability with submission. Buys one-time rights. Negotiates payment individually.

$ THE HERB COMPANION, Ogden Publications, Inc., 1503 SW 42nd St., Topeka KS 66609. (785)274-4300. Fax: (785)274-4305. E-mail: herbcompanion@realhealthmedia.com. Website: www.discoverherbs.com. **Contact:** Dawna Edwards, editor. **80% freelance written.** Bimonthly magazine about herbs: culture, history, culinary, crafts and some medicinal use for both experienced and novice herb enthusiasts. Pays on publication. Byline given. Buys all rights. Editorial lead time 4 months. Accepts queries by mail, e-mail, fax. Responds in 2 months to queries. Sample copy for $6. Writer's guidelines online.

Nonfiction: Practical horticultural, original recipes, historical, herbal crafts, helpful hints, and book reviews. How-to, interview/profile. Submit by mail only detailed query or ms. Length: 4 pages or 1,000 words. **Pays according to length, story type, and experience.**

Photos: Returns photos and artwork. Send photos with submission. Reviews transparencies.

Tips: "New approaches to familiar topics are especially welcome. If you aren't already familiar with the content, style and tone of the magazine. Technical accuracy is essential. Please use scientific as well as popular names for plants and cover the subject in depth while avoiding overly academic presentation. Information should be made accessible to the reader, and we find this is best accomplished by writing from direct personal experience where possible and always in an informal style."

N $ $ THE HERB QUARTERLY, EGW Publishing Co., 1041 Shary Circle, Concord CA 94518. (925)671-9852. E-mail: jenniferbarrett@earthlink.net. Website: www.herbquarterly.com. **Contact:** Jennifer Barrett, editor. **95% freelance written.** Quarterly magazine covering herbs and their uses. "Now in its 25th year, *The Herb Quarterly* brings readers the joy of herbs and the herb garden each season, with recipes, remedies, and growing advice." Estab. 1978. Circ. 45,000. Pays on publication. Publishes ms an average of 3 months after acceptance. Byline given. Offers 25% kill fee. Buys first North American serial rights. Editorial lead time 6 months. Submit seasonal material 6-12 months in advance. Accepts queries by mail, e-mail. Responds in 1 month to queries; 2 months to mss. Sample copy for free. Writer's guidelines free.

Nonfiction: Book excerpts, historical/nostalgic, how-to (cooking, crafts, gardening), interview/profile (herbalist), new product, opinion, personal experience, photo feature, technical (gardening), travel (gardeners around the world). **Buys 21+ mss/year.** Query with or without published clips or send complete ms. Length: 250-2,500 words. **Pays $50-350.** Provides contributor copies in addition to payment. Sometimes pays expenses of writers on assignment.

Tips: "Please read the magazine before submitting. We prefer specific information (whether natural health approaches or gardening advice) rather than general."

$ HOME DIGEST, Your Guide to Home and Life Improvement, Home Digest International, Inc., 268 Lakeshore Rd. E., Unit 604, Oakville ON L6J 7S4, Canada. (905)844-3361. Fax: (905)849-4618. E-mail: homedigesteditor@sympatico.ca. Website: www.home-digest.com. **Contact:** William Roebuck, editor. **25% freelance written.** Quarterly magazine covering home and life management for families in the greater Toronto region. "*Home Digest* has a strong service slant, combining useful how-to journalism with coverage of the trends and issues of home ownership and family life. In essence, our focus is on the concerns of families living in their own homes." Estab. 1995. Circ. 550,000. Pays on publication. Publishes ms an average of 3 months after acceptance. Byline given. Buys first North American serial rights and the rights to archive articles on the magazine's website. Editorial lead time 3 months. Submit seasonal material 5 months in advance. Accepts queries by mail, e-mail, fax. Accepts previously published material. Accepts simultaneous submissions. Responds in 1 month to queries. Sample copy for 9×6 SAE and 2 Canadian first-class stamps. Writer's guidelines online.

Nonfiction: General interest, how-to (household hints, basic home renovation, decorating), humor (living in Toronto). No opinion, fashion, or beauty. **Buys 8 mss/year.** Query. Length: 350-700 words. **Pays $35-100 (Canadian).**

Photos: Send photos with submission. Reviews prints. Buys one-time rights. Pays $10-20/photo. Captions, identification of subjects, model releases required.

Columns/Departments: Household Hints (tested tips that work); Health & Fitness News (significant health/body/fitness news); Home Renovation Tips; all 300-350 words. **Buys 4-6 mss/year.** Query. **Pays $40-50 (Canadian).**

Tips: "Base your ideas on practical experiences. We're looking for 'uncommon' advice that works."

N $ HOME MAGAZINE, Hachette Filipacchi Media U.S., Inc., 1633 Broadway, New York NY 10019. (212)767-6000. Fax: (212)489-4576. E-mail: ltriantafillou@hfmmag.com. Website: www.homemag.com. Editor: Peter Lemos. Monthly magazine. Written for the American home owner and home enthusiast. Circ. 1,020,938. Sample copy not available.

$ $ $ $ HORTICULTURE, Gardening at Its Best, 98 N. Washington St., Boston MA 02114. (617)742-5600. Fax: (617)367-6364. E-mail: edit@hortmag.com. Website: www.hortmag.com. **Contact:** Thomas Fischer, executive editor. Magazine published 8 times/year. "*Horticulture*, the country's oldest gardening magazine, is designed for active amateur gardeners. Our goal is to offer a blend of text, photographs and illustrations that will both instruct and inspire readers." Circ. 250,000. Byline given. Offers kill fee. Buys first North American serial, one-time rights. Submit seasonal material 10 months in advance. Accepts queries by mail, e-mail, fax. Responds in 3 months to queries. Sample copy not available. Writer's guidelines for SASE or by e-mail.

Nonfiction: "We look for an encouraging personal experience, anecdote and opinion. At the same time, a thorough article should to some degree place its subject in the broader context of horticulture." Include disk where posisble. **Buys 15 mss/year.** Query with published clips, subject background material and SASE. Length: 1,000-2,000 words. **Pays $600-1,500.** Pays expenses of writers on assignment if previously arranged with editor.

Columns/Departments: Length: 100-1,500 words. Query with published clips, subject background material and SASE. Include disk where possible. **Pays $50-750.**

Tips: "We believe every article must offer ideas or illustrate principles that our readers might apply on their own gardens. No matter what the subject, we want our readers to become better, more creative gardeners."

N $ HOUSE & GARDEN, Condé Nast Publications, Inc., 4 Times Square, New York NY 10036. (212)286-4580. Fax: (212)286-8533. E-mail: letters@house-and-garden.com. Website: www.house-and-garden.com. Editor: Dominique Browning. Written as the definitive voice of design and style for the home and garden, *House & Garden* provides access to top home design projects from the best architects, decorators, and landscape designers from around the world. Circ. 753,186. Editorial lead time 4 months. Sample copy not available.

$ $ LAKESTYLE, Celebrating life on the water, Bayside Publications, Inc., P.O. Box 170, Excelsior MN 55331. (952)470-1380. Fax: (952)470-1389. E-mail: editor@lakestyle.com. Website: www.lakestyle.com. **Contact:** Nancy Jahnke, editor. **50% freelance written.** Quarterly magazine. "*Lakestyle* is committed to celebrating the lifestyle chosen by lake home and cabin owners." Estab. 2000. Circ. 40,000. Pays on publication. Publishes ms an average of 3 months after acceptance. Byline given. Offers 10% kill fee. Buys all rights. Editorial lead time 2 months. Submit seasonal material 3 months in advance. Accepts queries by mail, e-mail, fax, phone. Accepts previously published material. Responds in 3 weeks to queries; 1 month to mss. Sample copy for $5. Writer's guidelines online.

Nonfiction: Essays, historical/nostalgic, how-to, humor, inspirational, interview/profile, new product, photo feature. No direct promotion of product. **Buys 15 mss/year.** Query with or without published clips or send complete ms. Length: 500-2,500 words. **Pays 25-50¢/word for assigned articles; 10-25¢/word for unsolicited articles.** Sometimes pays expenses of writers on assignment.

Photos: State availability of or send photos with submission. Rights purchased vary. Offers no additional payment for photos accepted with ms. Captions, identification of subjects, model releases required.

Columns/Departments: Lakestyle Entertaining (entertaining ideas); Lakestyle Gardening (gardening ideas); On the Water (boating/playing on the lake); Hidden Treasures (little known events); At the Cabin (cabin owner's information); all approximately 1,000 words. **Buys 10 mss/year.** Query with or without published clips or send complete ms. **Pays 10-25¢/word.**

Tips: "*Lakestyle* is interested in enhancing the lifestyle chosen by our readers, a thorough knowledge of cabin/lake home issues helps writers fulfill this goal."

$ $ LOG HOME LIVING, Home Buyer Publications, Inc., 4125-T Lafayette Center Dr., Suite 100, Chantilly VA 20151. (703)222-9411. Fax: (703)222-3209. E-mail: plobred@homebuyerpubs.com. Website: www.loghomeliving.com. **Contact:** Kevin Ireland, editor. **90% freelance written.** Monthly magazine for enthusiasts who are dreaming of, planning for, or actively building a log home. Estab. 1989. Circ. 132,000. **Pays on acceptance.** Publishes ms an average of 6 months after acceptance. Byline given. Offers $100 kill fee. Buys first, second serial (reprint) rights. Editorial lead time 6 months. Submit seasonal material 6 months in advance. Accepts queries by mail. Accepts previously published material. Responds in 6 weeks to queries. Sample copy for $4. Writer's guidelines for #10 SASE.

Nonfiction: Book excerpts, how-to (build or maintain log home), interview/profile (log-home owners), personal experience, photo feature (log homes), technical (design/decor topics), travel. "We do not want historical/nostalgic material." **Buys 6 mss/year.** Query. Length: 1,000-2,000 words. **Pays $250-500.** Pays expenses of writers on assignment.

Reprints: Send tearsheet or photocopy and information about when and where the material previously appeared. Pays $100-200 for reprint rights.

Photos: State availability with submission. Reviews contact sheets, 4×5 transparencies, 4×6 prints. Buys one-time rights. Negotiates payment individually.

Tips: "*Log Home Living* is devoted almost exclusively to modern manufactured and handcrafted kit log homes. Our interest in historical or nostalgic stories of very old log cabins, reconstructed log homes, or one-of-a-kind owner-built homes is secondary and should be queried first."

N $ MIDWEST HOME AND GARDEN, U.S. Trust Bldg., 730 S. Second Ave., Minneapolis MN 55402. Fax: (612)371-5801. E-mail: editor@mnmo.com. Website: www.mnmo.com. **Contact:** Pamela Hill Nettleton, editor. **50% freelance written.** "*Midwest Home and Garden* is an upscale shelter magazine showcasing innovative architecture, interesting interior design, and beautiful gardens of the Midwest." Estab. 1997. Circ. 80,000. **Pays on acceptance.** Byline given. Accepts queries by mail, e-mail, fax. Writer's guidelines online.

Nonfiction: Profiles of regional designers, architects, craftspeople related to home and garden. Photo-driven articles on home decor and design, and gardens. Book excerpts, essays, how-to (garden and design), interview/profile (brief), new product, photo feature. Query with résumé, published clips, and SASE. Length: 300-1,000 words. **Payment negotiable.**

Columns/Departments: Back Home (essay on home/garden topics), 800 words; Design Directions (people and trends in home and garden), 300 words.

Tips: "We are always looking for great new interior design, architecture, and gardens—in Minnesota and in the Midwest."

$ $ MOUNTAIN LIVING, Wiesner Publishing, 7009 S. Potomac St., Englewood CO 80112. (303)397-7600. Fax: (303)397-7619. E-mail: irawlings@mountainliving.com. Website: www.mountainliving.com. **Contact:** Irene Rawlings, editor. **50% freelance written.** Bimonthly magazine covering "shelter and lifestyle issues for people who live in, visit, or hope to live in the mountains." Estab. 1994. Circ. 35,000. **Pays on acceptance.** Publishes ms an average of 4 months after acceptance. Byline given. Offers 15% kill fee. Buys all rights. Editorial lead time 6 months. Submit seasonal material 6 months in advance. Accepts queries by mail, e-mail, phone. Accepts simultaneous submissions. Responds in 6 weeks to queries; 2 months to mss. Sample copy for $5 or on website.

Nonfiction: Photo feature, travel, home features. **Buys 30 mss/year.** Query with published clips. Length: 1,200-2,000 words. **Pays $250-500.** Sometimes pays expenses of writers on assignment.

Photos: Provide photos (slides, transparencies, or on disk, saved as TIFF and at least 300 dpi). State availability with submission. Buys one-time rights. Negotiates payment individually.

Columns/Departments: Art; Travel. Length: 300-1,500 words. **Buys 35 mss/year.** Query with published clips. **Pays $50-500.**

Tips: "A deep understanding of and respect for the mountain environment is essential. Think out of the box. We love to be surprised. Write a brilliant, short query, and always send clips."

$ $ $ $ ORGANIC GARDENING, Rodale, 33 E. Minor, Emmaus PA 18098. (610)967-8363. Fax: (610)967-7722. E-mail: og@rodale.com. Website: www.organicgardening.com. **Contact:** Willi Evans, editorial assistant. **75% freelance written.** Bimonthly magazine. "*Organic Gardening* is for gardeners who garden, who enjoy gardening as an integral part of a healthy lifestyle. Editorial shows readers how to grow anything they choose without chemicals. Editorial details how to grow flowers, edibles and herbs, as well as information on ecological landscaping. Also organic topics including soil building and pest control." Circ. 300,000. Pays between acceptance and publication. Byline given. Buys all rights. Accepts queries by mail, fax. Responds in 3 months to queries. Sample copy not available.

Nonfiction: "The natural approach to the whole home landscape." Query with published clips and outline. **Pays up to $1/word for experienced writers.**

■ The online magazine carries original content not found in the print edition. Contact: Scott Meyer, online editor.

Tips: "If you have devised a specific technique that's worked in your garden, have insight into the needs and uses of a particular plant or small group of plants, or have designed whole gardens that integrate well with their environment, and, if you have the capacity to clearly describe what you've learned to other gardeners in a simple but engaging manner, please send us your article ideas. Read a recent issue of the magazine thoroughly before you submit your ideas. The scope and tone of our content has changed dramatically in the last year—be sure your ideas and your approach to presenting them jibe with the magazine as it is now. If you have an idea that you believe fits with our content, send us a one-page description of it that will grab our attention in the same manner you intend to entice readers into your article. Be sure to briefly explain why your idea is uniquely suited to our magazine. (We will not publish an article that has already appeared elsewhere. Also, please tell us if you are simultaneously submitting your idea to another magazine.) Tell us about the visual content of your idea—that is, what photographs or illustrations would you suggest be included with your article to get the ideas and information across to readers? If you have photographs, let us know. If you have never been published before, consider whether your idea fits into our Gardener to Gardener department. The shorter, narrowly focused articles in the department and its conversational tone make for a more accessible avenue into the magazine for inexperienced writers."

$ $ PEOPLE, PLACES & PLANTS, 512 Memorial Hwy., N. Yarmouth ME 04097. (207)827-4783. Fax: (207)829-6814. E-mail: paul@ppplants.com. Website: newenglandgardening.com. Paul Tukey, editor-in-chief. **50% freelance written.** Gardening magazine published 6 times/year focusing on New England. "We now publish 2 editions: One focuses on New England and New York state, the other focuses on the Mid-Atlantic states (metro New York to Virginia)." Circ. 52,000. **Pays on acceptance.** Publishes ms an average of 3 months after acceptance. Buys first rights. Responds in 1 month to queries. Sample copy by e-mail. Writer's guidelines by e-mail.

Nonfiction: Know the subject at hand; anecdotes help get readers interested in stories. Query. **Pays $50-500.**

Photos: Reviews Slides. $50-500.

$ $ ROMANTIC HOMES, Y-Visionary Publishing, 265 Anita Dr., Suite 120, Orange CA 92868. (714)939-9991. Fax: (714)939-9909. Website: www.romantichomesmag.com. Editor: Eileen Paulin. **Contact:** Catherine Yarnovich, executive managing editor. **70% freelance written.** Monthly magazine covering home decor. "*Romantic Homes* is the magazine for women who want to create a warm, intimate, and casually elegant home—a haven that is both a gathering place for family and friends and a private refuge from the pressures of the outside world. The *Romantic Homes* reader is personally involved in the decor of her home. Features offer unique ideas and how-to advice on decorating, home furnishings, and gardening. Departments focus on floor and wall coverings, paint, textiles, refinishing, architectural elements, artwork, travel, and entertaining. Every article responds to the reader's need to create a beautiful, attainable environment, providing her with the style ideas and resources to achieve her own romantic home." Estab. 1994. Circ. 140,000. **Pays on acceptance.** Publishes ms an average of 2 months after acceptance. Byline given. Buys all rights. Editorial lead time 5 months. Submit seasonal material 6 months in advance. Accepts queries by mail, fax. Accepts simultaneous submissions. Responds in 2 weeks to queries; 2 months to mss. Writer's guidelines for #10 SASE.

Nonfiction: "Not just for dreaming, *Romantic Homes* combines unique ideas and inspirations with practical how-to advice on decorating, home furnishings, remodeling, and gardening for readers who are actively involved in improving their homes. Every article responds to the reader's need to know how to do it and where to find it." Essays, how-to, new product, personal experience, travel. **Buys 150 mss/year.** Query with published clips. Length: 1,000-1,200 words. **Pays $500.**

Photos: State availability of or send photos with submission. Reviews transparencies. Buys all rights. Captions, identification of subjects, model releases required.

Columns/Departments: Departments cover antiques, collectibles, artwork, shopping, travel, refinishing, architectural elements, flower arranging, entertaining, and decorating. Length: 400-600 words. **Pays $250.**

Tips: "Submit great ideas with photos."

N $ $ SAN DIEGO HOME/GARDEN LIFESTYLES, McKinnon Enterprises, Box 719001, San Diego CA 92171-9001. (858)571-1818. Fax: (858)571-6379. E-mail: sdhg@san.rr.com. Senior Editor: Phyllis Van Doren. **Contact:** Eva Ditler, managing editor. **50% freelance written.** Monthly magazine covering homes, gardens, food, intriguing people, real estate, art, culture, and local travel for residents of San Diego city and county. Estab. 1979. Circ. 50,000. Pays on publication. Publishes ms an average of 3 months after acceptance. Byline given. Buys first North American serial rights. Submit seasonal material 3 months in advance. Accepts queries by mail, e-mail, fax, phone. Responds in 3 months to queries. Sample copy for $4.

Nonfiction: Residential architecture and interior design (San Diego-area homes only), remodeling (must be well-designed-little do-it-yourself), residential landscape design, furniture, other features oriented toward upscale readers interested in living the cultured good life in San Diego. Articles must have a local angle. Query with published clips. Length: 700-2,000 words. **Pays $50-350 for assigned articles.**

Tips: "No out-of-town, out-of-state subject material. Most freelance work is accepted from local writers. Gear stories to the unique quality of San Diego. We try to offer only information unique to San Diego—people, places, shops, resources, etc. We plan more food and entertaining-at-home articles and more articles on garden products. We also need more in-depth reports on major architecture, environmental, and social aspects of life in San Diego and the border area."

$ $ SEATTLE HOMES AND LIFESTYLES, Wiesner Publishing LLC, 1221 East Pike St., Suite 305, Seattle WA 98122-3930. (206)322-6699. Fax: (206)322-2799. E-mail: falbert@seattlehomesmag.com. Website: www.seattlehomesmag.com. **Contact:** Fred Albert, editor. **60% freelance written.** Magazine published 8 times/year covering home design and lifestyles. "*Seattle Homes and Lifestyles* showcases the finest homes and gardens in the Northwest, and the personalities and lifestyles that make this region special. We try to help our readers take full advantage of the resources the region has to offer with in-depth coverage of events, travel, entertaining, shopping, food, and wine. And we write about it with a warm, personal approach that underscores our local perspective." Estab. 1996. Circ. 30,000. **Pays on acceptance.** Publishes ms an average of 2 months after acceptance. Byline given. Offers 25% kill fee. Buys first, electronic rights. Editorial lead time 3 months. Submit seasonal material 4 months in advance. Accepts previously published material. Accepts simultaneous submissions. Responds in 4 months to queries.

Nonfiction: General interest, how-to (decorating, cooking), interview/profile, photo feature, travel. "No essays, journal entries, sports coverage." **Buys 95 mss/year.** Query with published clips via mail. Length: 300-1,500 words. **Pays $125-375.**

Photos: State availability with submission. Reviews contact sheets, transparencies, prints. Buys one-time rights. Negotiates payment individually. Captions, identification of subjects, model releases required.

Columns/Departments: Profiles (human interest/people making contribution to community), 300 words; Design Watch (service pieces related to home design), 1,200 words; Taking Off (travel to a Northwest region, not 1 sole destination), 1,500 words; Artisan's Touch (craftperson producing work for the home), 400 words.

Tips: "We're always looking for experienced journalists with clips that demonstrate a knack for writing engaging, informative features. We're also looking for writers knowledgeable about architecture and decorating who can communicate a home's flavor and spirit through the written word. Since all stories are assigned by the editor, please do not submit manuscripts. Send a résumé and 3 published samples of your work. Story pitches are not encouraged. Please mail all submissions—do not e-mail or fax. Please don't call—we'll call you if we have an assignment. Writers from the Seattle area only (except travel)."

$ SOUTHERN ACCENTS, Southern Progress Corp., 2100 Lakeshore Dr., Birmingham AL 35209. (205)445-6000. Fax: (205)445-6990. Website: www.southernaccents.com. **Contact:** Frances MacDougall, executive editor. "*Southern Accents* celebrates the finest of the South." Estab. 1977. Circ. 370,000. Accepts queries by mail. Responds in 2 months to queries.

Nonfiction: "Each issue features the finest homes and gardens along with a balance of features that reflect the affluent lifestyles of its readers, including architecture, antiques, entertaining, collecting, and travel." Query by mail with SASE, bio, clips, and photos.

The online magazine carries original content not found in the print edition. Contact: Christina Bennett, assistant online editor.

Tips: "Query us only with specific ideas targeted to our current columns."

N $ MARTHA STEWART LIVING, Time Publishing, Inc., 20 W. 43rd St., 25th Floor, New York NY 10036. E-mail: mstewart@marthastewart.com. Website: www.marthastewart.com. **Contact:** Editorial. Monthly magazine offering readers a unique combination of inspiration and how-to information focusing on our 8 core areas: Home, Cooking & Entertaining, Gardening, Crafts, Holidays, Keeping, Weddings, and Baby.

$ $ $ STYLE AT HOME, Transcontinental Media, Inc., 25 Sheppard Ave. W., Suite 100, Toronto ON M2N 6S7, Canada. (416)733-7600. Fax: (416)218-3632. E-mail: letters@styleathome.com. Managing Editor: Laurie Grassi. **Contact:** Gail Johnston Habs, editor. **85% freelance written.** Magazine published 9 times/year. "The number one magazine choice of Canadian women aged 25 to 54 who have a serious interest in decorating. Provides an authoritative, stylish collection of inspiring and accessible interiors, decor projects; reports on style design trends." Estab. 1997. Circ. 195,000. **Pays on acceptance.** Byline given. Offers 50% kill fee. Buys first, electronic rights. Editorial lead time 4 months. Submit seasonal material 6 months in advance. Accepts queries by mail, e-mail. Responds in 1 month to queries; 2 weeks to mss. Writer's guidelines by e-mail.

- Break in by "familiarizing yourself with the type of interiors we show. Be very up to date with the design and home decor market in Canada. Provide a lead to a fabulous home or garden."

Nonfiction: Interview/profile, new product. "No how-to; these are planned in-house." **Buys 80 mss/year.** Query with published clips; include scouting shots with interior story queries. Length: 300-700 words. **Pays $300-1,000.** Sometimes pays expenses of writers on assignment.

Columns/Departments: Humor (fun home decor/renovating experiences), 500 words. Query with published clips. **Pays $250-500.**

N $ $ TEXAS GARDENER, The Magazine for Texas Gardeners, by Texas Gardeners, Suntex Communications, Inc., P.O. Box 9005, Waco TX 76714-9005. (254)848-9393. Fax: (254)848-9779. E-mail: suntex@calpha.com. **Contact:** Chris Corby, editor. **80% freelance written.** Works with a small number of new/unpublished writers each year. Bimonthly magazine covering vegetable and fruit production, ornamentals, and home landscape information for home gardeners in Texas. Estab. 1981. Circ. 30,000. Pays on publication. Publishes ms an average of 4 months after acceptance. Byline given. Buys first North American serial, all rights. Submit seasonal material 6 months in advance. Accepts queries by mail, e-mail, fax. Responds in 2 months to queries. Sample copy for $2.95 and SAE with 5 first-class stamps. Writer's guidelines for #10 SASE.

Nonfiction: "We use articles that relate to Texas gardeners. We also like personality profiles on hobby gardeners and professional horticulturists who are doing somehting unique." How-to, humor, interview/profile, photo feature. **Buys 50-60 mss/year.** Query with published clips. Length: 800-2,400 words. **Pays $50-200.**

Photos: "We prefer superb color and b&w photos; 90% of photos used are color." Send photos with submission. Reviews contact sheets, 2¼×2¼ or 35mm color transparencies, 8×10 b&w prints. Pays negotiable rates. Identification of subjects, model releases required.

Columns/Departments: Between Neighbors. **Pays $25.**

Tips: "First, be a Texan. Then come up with a good idea of interest to home gardeners in this state. Be specific. Stick to feature topics like 'How Alley Gardening Became a Texas Tradition.' Leave topics like 'How to Control Fire Blight' to the experts. High quality photos could make the difference. We would like to add several writers to our group of regular contributors and would make assignments on a regular basis. Fillers are easy to come up with in-house. We want good writers who can produce accurate and interesting copy. Frequent mistakes made by writers in completing an article assignment for us are that articles are not slanted toward Texas gardening, show inaccurate or too little gardening information, or lack good writing style."

$ $ TIMBER FRAME HOMES, Home Buyer Publications, 4125 Lafayette Center Dr., Suite 100, Chantilly VA 20151. Fax: (703)222-3209. E-mail: editor@timberframehomes.com. Website: www.timberframehomes.com. **Contact:** Tracy M. Ruff, editor. **50% freelance written.** Quarterly magazine for people who own or are planning to build contemporary timber frame homes. It is devoted exclusively to timber frame homes that have a freestanding frame and wooden joinery. Our interest in historical, reconstructed timber frames and one-of-a-kind owner-built homes is secondary and should be queried first. Estab. 1991. Circ. 92,500. **Pays on acceptance.** Publishes ms an average of 3 months after acceptance. Byline given. Offers $100 kill fee. Buys first rights. Accepts queries by mail, e-mail. Sample copy for $4. Writer's guidelines for #10 SASE.

Nonfiction: Book excerpts, general interest, how-to, interview/profile, new product, photo feature, technical. No historical articles. **Buys 15 mss/year.** Query with published clips. Length: 1,200-1,400 words. **Pays $300-500.** Sometimes pays expenses of writers on assignment.

Photos: State availability with submission. Reviews contact sheets, transparencies, prints. Buys one-time rights. Negotiates payment individually.

Columns/Departments: Constructive Advice (timber frame construction); Interior Elements (decorating); Drawing Board (design), all 1,200-1,400 words. **Buys 6 mss/year.** Query with published clips. **Pays $300-500.**

$ $ UNIQUE HOMES, Network Communications, 327 Wall St., Princeton NJ 08540. (609)688-1110. Fax: (609)688-0201. E-mail: lkim@uniquehomes.com. Website: www.uniquehomes.com. Editor: Kathleen Carlin-Russell. **Contact:** Lauren Baier Kim, managing editor. **30% freelance written.** Bimonthly magazine covering luxury real estate for consumers and the high-end real estate industry. "Our focus is the luxury real estate market, i.e., trends and luxury homes (including luxury home architecture, interior design, and landscaping)." Pays on publication. Publishes ms an average of 3 months after acceptance. Byline given. Buys all rights. Editorial lead time 4 months. Submit seasonal material 4 months in advance. Accepts queries by mail, e-mail, fax. Responds in 1 month to queries; 4 months to mss. Sample copy online. Writer's guidelines not available.

Nonfiction: Looking for luxury interiors, architecture and landscaping, high-end luxury real estate profiles on cities and geographical regions. Luxury real estate, interior design, landscaping, home features. Special issues: Golf Course Living; Resort Living; Ski Real Estate; Farms, Ranches and Country Estates; Waterfront Homes; International Homes. **Buys 36 mss/year.** Query with published clips and résumé. Length: 500-1,500 words. **Pays $150-500.**

Photos: State availability with submission. Reviews transparencies, prints. Buys one-time rights. Offers no additional payment for photos accepted with ms. Captions required.

Columns/Departments: News and Reviews (timely shorts on real estate news and trends), 100 words; Creating Your Unique Home, 1,500 words. **Buys 18 mss/year.** Query with published clips and résumé. **Pays $150-550.**

Tips: "Always looking for creative and interesting story ideas on interior decorating, architecture, and landscaping for the luxury home. For profiles on specific geographical areas, seeking writers with an in-depth personal knowledge of the luxury real estate trends in those locations."

HUMOR

Publications listed here specialize in gaglines or prose humor, some for readers and others for performers or speakers. Other publications that use humor can be found in nearly every category in this book. Some have special needs for major humor pieces; some use humor as fillers; many others are interested in material that meets their ordinary fiction or nonfiction requirements but also has a humorous slant. The majority of humor articles must be submitted as complete manuscripts or on speculation because editors usually can't know from a query whether or not the piece will be right for them.

$ COMEDY WRITERS ASSOCIATION NEWSLETTER, P.O. Box 605, Times Plaza Station, 542 Atlantic Ave., Brooklyn NY 11217-0605. (718)855-5057. E-mail: makinsonrobert@hotmail.com. **Contact:** Robert Makinson, editor. **10% freelance written.** Semiannual newsletter on comedy writing for association members. Estab. 1989. **Pays on acceptance.** Publishes ms an average of 3 months after acceptance. Byline given. Buys all rights. Accepts queries by mail, e-mail. Responds in 2 weeks to queries; 1 month to mss. Sample copy for $5. Writer's guidelines for #10 SASE.

Nonfiction: "You may submit articles and byline will be given if used, but at present payment is only made for jokes. Emphasis should be on marketing, not general humor articles." How-to (articles about marketing, directories, Internet, new trends). Query. Length: 250-500 words.

Tips: "The easiest way to be mentioned in the publication is to submit short jokes. (Payment is $2-4/joke). Jokes for professional speakers preferred. Include SASE when submitting jokes."

$ FUNNY TIMES, A Monthly Humor Review, Funny Times, Inc., P.O. Box 18530, Cleveland Heights OH 44118. (216)371-8600. Fax: (216)371-8696. E-mail: ft@funnytimes.com. Website: www.funnytimes.com. **Contact:** Raymond Lesser, Susan Wolpert, editors. **10% freelance written.** Monthly tabloid for humor. "*Funny Times* is a monthly review of America's funniest cartoonists and writers. We are the *Reader's Digest* of modern American humor with a progressive/peace-oriented/environmental/politically activist slant." Estab. 1985. Circ. 63,000. Pays on publication. Publishes ms an average of 3 months after acceptance. Byline given. Buys one-time, second serial (reprint) rights. Editorial lead time 2 months. Accepts previously published material. Accepts simultaneous submissions. Responds in 3 months to mss. Sample copy for $3 or 9×12 SAE with 4 first-class stamps. Writer's guidelines online.

Nonfiction: "We only publish humor or interviews with funny people (comedians, comic actors, cartoonists, etc.). Everything we publish is very funny. If your piece isn't extremely funny then don't bother to send it. Don't send us anything that's not outrageously funny. Don't send anything that other people haven't already read and told you they laughed so hard they peed their pants." Essays (funny), humor, interview/profile, opinion (humorous), personal experience (absolutely funny). **Buys 36 mss/year.** Send complete ms. Length: 500-700 words. **Pays $50 minimum.**

Reprints: Accepts previously published submissions.

Columns/Departments: Query with published clips.

Fiction: Ray Lesser and Susan Wolpert, editors. Humorous. "Anything funny." **Buys 6 mss/year.** Query with published clips. Length: 500-700 words. **Pays $50-150.**

Fillers: Short humor. **Buys 6/year. Pays $20.**

Tips: "Send us a small packet (1-3 items) of only your very funniest stuff. If this makes us laugh we'll be glad to ask for more. We particularly welcome previously published material that has been well-received elsewhere."

N $ SLIPSHOD MAGAZINE, 6500 25th Ave. NE, Seattle WA 98115. E-mail: slipshodmagazine@yahoo.com. Website: www.slipshodmagazine.com. **Contact:** Tristan Devin, editor. **50% freelance written.** Monthly magazine. "*Slipshod* is a literate humor magazine. We publish anything that makes us laugh (fiction, personal essays, cartoons, etc.)." Estab. 2001. Circ. 200. **Pays on acceptance.** Publishes ms an average of 2 months after acceptance. Byline given. Offers 100% kill fee. Not copyrighted. Buys one-time rights. Editorial lead time 1 month. Submit seasonal material 2 months in advance. Accepts queries by e-mail. Responds in 2 weeks to queries; 1 month to mss. Sample copy online. Writer's guidelines online.

Nonfiction: Humor. No news satires, verse. **Buys 12 mss/year.** Send complete ms. Length: 500-2,000 words. **Pays $5-50.** A sample copy is included upon publication.

Fiction: Humorous. "We do not want anything too obscure or heady; neither do we want anything profane or simpleminded. Also, we see far too many stories in the sttle of Donald Bartheleme." **Buys 12 mss/year.** Send complete ms. Length: 2,000 words maximum. **Pays $5-50.**

Fillers: Gags to be illustrated by cartoonist, short humor. **Buys 30/year.** Length: 2,000 words maximum. **Pays $0-20.**

Tips: "Don't be cute or jokey. Respect the intelligence and sense of humor of your audience. Make us laugh out loud."

INFLIGHT

Most major inflight magazines cater to business travelers and vacationers who will be reading during the flight, about the airline's destinations and other items of general interest.

$ $ $ $ ATTACHÉ MAGAZINE, Pace Communications, 1301 Carolina St., Greensboro NC 27401. (336)378-6065. Fax: (336)378-8278. E-mail: attacheedit@attachemag.com. Website: www.attachemag.com. Editor: Lance Elko. **Contact:** Submissions Editor. **75% freelance written.** Monthly magazine for travelers on U.S. Airways. "We focus on 'the best of the world' and use a humorous view." Estab. 1997. Circ. 441,000. **Pays on acceptance.** Publishes ms an average of 4 months after acceptance. Byline given. Offers kill fee. Buys first global serial rights. Editorial lead time 3 months. Accepts queries by mail, e-mail. Responds in 6 weeks to queries; 1 month to mss. Sample copy for $7.50 or online. Writer's guidelines online.

Nonfiction: Features are highly visual, focusing on some unusual or unique angle of travel, food, business, or other topic approved by an *Attaché* editor." Book excerpts, essays, general interest, personal experience, travel, food; lifestyle; sports. **Buys 50-75 mss/year.** Query with published clips. Length: 350-2,500 words. **Pays $350-2,500.** Sometimes pays expenses of writers on assignment.

Photos: State availability with submission. Reviews contact sheets, negatives, transparencies. Buys one-time rights. Negotiates payment individually. Identification of subjects, model releases required.

Columns/Departments: Passions includes several topics such as "Vices," "Food," "Golf," "Sporting," "Shelf Life," and "Things That Go"; Paragons features short lists of the best in a particular field or category, as well as 400-word pieces describing the best of something—for example, the best home tool, the best ice cream in Paris, and the best reading library. Each piece should lend itself to highly visual art. Informed Sources are departments of expertise and first-person accounts; they include "How It Works," "Home Front," "Improvement," and "Genius at Work." **Buys 50-75 mss/year.** Query. **Pays $500-2,000.**

Tips: "We look for cleverly written, entertaining articles with a unique angle, particularly pieces that focus on 'the best of' something. Study the magazine for content, style and tone. Queries for story ideas should be to the point and presented clearly. Any correspondence should include SASE."

$ $ $ HEMISPHERES, Pace Communications for United Airlines, 1301 Carolina St., Greensboro NC 27401. (336)383-5800. E-mail: hemiedit@aol.com. Website: www.hemispheresmagazine.com. **Contact:** Mr. Randy Johnson, editor; Mr. Selby Bateman, senior editor. **95% freelance written.** Monthly magazine for the educated, sophisticated business and recreational frequent traveler on an airline that spans the globe. "*Hemispheres* is an inflight magazine that interprets 'inflight' to be a mode of delivery rather than an editorial genre. As such, Hemispheres' task is to engage, intrigue and entertain its primary readers—an international, culturally diverse group of affluent, educated professionals and executives who frequently travel for business and pleasure on United Airlines. The magazine offers a global perspective and a focus on topics that cross borders as often as the people reading the magazine. That places our emphasis on ideas, concepts, and culture rather than products. We present that perspective in a fresh, artful and sophisticated graphic enviroment." Estab. 1992. Circ. 500,000. **Pays on acceptance.** Publishes ms an average of 4-6 months after acceptance. Byline given. Offers 20% kill fee. first worldwide rights Editorial lead time 8 months. Submit seasonal material 8 months in advance. Accepts queries by mail. Responds in 2 months to queries; 4 months to mss. Sample copy for $7.50. Writer's guidelines for #10 SASE.

Nonfiction: "Keeping 'global' in mind, we look for topics that reflect a modern appreciation of the world's cultures and environment. No 'What I did (or am going to do) on a trip to....'" General interest, humor, personal experience. Query with published clips. Length: 500-3,000 words. **Pays 50¢/word and up.**

Photos: Reviews photos "only when we request them." State availability with submission. Buys one-time rights. Negotiates payment individually. Captions, identification of subjects, model releases required.

Columns/Departments: Making a Difference (Q&A format interview with world leaders, movers, and shakers. A 500-600 word introduction anchors the interview. "We want to profile an international mix of men and women representing a variety of topics or issues, but all must truly be making a difference. No puffy celebrity profiles."); 15 Fascinating Facts (a snappy selection of 1- or 2-sentence obscure, intriguing, or travel-service-oriented items that the reader never knew about a city, state, country, or destination.); Executive Secrets (things that top executives know); Case Study (Business strategies of international companies or organizations. No lionizations of CEOs. Strategies should be the emphasis. "We want international candidates."); Weekend Breakway (Takes us just outside a major city after a week of business for several activities for a physically active, action-packed weekend. This isn't a sedentary "getaway" at a "property."); Roving Gourmet (Insider's guide to interesting eating in major city, resort area, or region. The slant can be anything from ethnic to expensive; not just "best." The 4 featured eateries span a spectrum from "hole in the wall," to "expense account lunch," and on to "big deal dining."); Collecting (occasional 800-word story on collections and collecting that can emphasize travel); Eye on Sports (global look at anything of interest in sports); Vintage Traveler (options for mature, experienced travelers); Savvy Shopper (Insider's tour of best places in the world to shop. Savvy Shopper steps beyond all those stories that just mention the great shopping at a particular destination. A shop-by-shop, gallery-by-gallery tour of the best places in the world.); Science and Technology (Substantive, insightful stories on how technology is changing our lives and the business world. Not just another column on audio components or software. No gift guides!); Aviation Journal (For those fascinated with aviation. Topics range widely.); Terminal Bliss (a great airports guide series); Grape And Grain (wine and spirits with emphasis on education, not one-upmanship); Show Business (films, music, and entertainment); Musings (humor or just curious musings); Quick Quiz (tests to amuse and educate); Travel Trends (brief, practical, invaluable, global, trend-oriented); Book Beat (Tackles topics like the Wodehouse Society, the birth of a book, the competition between local bookshops and national chains. Please, no review proposals.); What the World's Reading (residents explore how current bestsellers tell us what their country is thinking). Length: 1,400 words. Query with published clips. **Pays 50¢/word and up.**

Fiction: Lisa Fann, fiction editor and Shelby Bateman, senior editor. Adventure, ethnic, historical, humorous, mainstream, mystery, explorations of those issues common to all people but within the context of a particular culture. **Buys 14 mss/year.** Send complete ms. Length: 1,000-4,000 words. **Pays 50¢/word and up.**

Tips: "We increasingly require writers of 'destination' pieces or departments to 'live whereof they write.' Increasingly want to hear from U.S., U.K., or other English-speaking/writing journalists (business & travel) who reside outside the U.S. in Europe, South America, Central America, and the Pacific Rim—all areas that United flies. We're not looking for writers who aim at the inflight market. *Hemispheres* broke the fluffy mold of that tired domestic genre. Our monthly readers are a global mix on the cutting edge of the global economy and culture. They don't need to have the world filtered by U.S. writers. We want a Hong Kong restaurant writer to speak for that city's eateries, so we need English-speaking writers around the globe. That's the 'insider' story our readers respect. We use resident writers for departments such as Roving Gourmet, Savvy Shopper, On Location, 3 Perfect Days, and Weekend Breakaway, but authoritative writers can roam in features. Sure we cover the U.S., but with a global view: No 'in this country' phraseology. 'Too American' is a frequent complaint for queries. We use U.K. English spellings in articles that speak from that tradition and we specify costs in local currency first before U.S. dollars. Basically, all of above serves the realization that today, 'global' begins with respect for 'local.' That approach permits a wealth of ways to present culture, travel, and business for a wide readership. We anchor that with a reader-service mission that grounds everything in 'how to do it.'"

$ MIDWEST AIRLINES MAGAZINE, (formerly *Midwest Express Magazine*), Paradigm Communications Group, 2701 First Ave., Suite 250, Seattle WA 98121. **Contact:** Eric Lucas, managing editor. **90% freelance written.** Bimonthly magazine for Midwest Airlines. "Positive depiction of the changing economy and culture of the U.S., plus travel and leisure features." Estab. 1993. Circ. 35,000. Pays on publication. Byline given. Buys first North American serial rights. Editorial lead time 9 months. Accepts queries by mail. Responds in 6 weeks to queries. Sample copy for 9×12 SASE. Writer's guidelines free.

- *Midwest Express* continues to look for *sophisticated* travel and golf writing.

Nonfiction: Travel, business, sports and leisure. Special issues: "Need good ideas for golf articles in spring." No humor, how-to, or fiction. **Buys 20-25 mss/year.** Query by mail only with published clips and résumé. Length: 250-3,000 words. **Pays $100 minimum.** Sometimes pays expenses of writers on assignment.

Columns/Departments: Preview (arts and events), 200-400 words; Portfolio (business), 200-500 words. **Buys 12-15 mss/year.** Query with published clips. **Pays $100-150.**

Tips: "Article ideas *must* encompass areas within the airline's route system. We buy quality writing from reliable writers. Editorial philosophy emphasizes innovation and positive outlook. Do not send manuscripts unless you have no clips."

$ $ $ $ SOUTHWEST AIRLINES SPIRIT, 4255 Amon Carter Blvd., Fort Worth TX 76155. (817)967-1804. Fax: (817)967-1571. E-mail: john@spiritmag.com. Website: www.spiritmag.com. **Contact:** John Clark, editor. Monthly magazine for passengers on Southwest Airlines. Estab. 1992. Circ. 357,521. **Pays on acceptance.** Byline given. Buys first North American serial, electronic rights. Responds in 1 month to queries.

Nonfiction: "Seeking lively, accessible, entertaining, relevant, and trendy travel, business, lifestyle, sports, celebrity, food, tech-product stories on newsworthy/noteworthy topics in destinations served by Southwest Airlines; well-researched and reported; multiple source only. Experienced magazine professionals only." **Buys about 40 mss/year.** Query by mail only with published clips. Length: 1,500 words (features). **Pays $1/word.** Pays expenses of writers on assignment.

Columns/Departments: Length: 800-900 words. **Buys about 21 mss/year.** Query by mail only with published clips.

Fillers: Buys 12/year. Length: 250 words. **Pays variable amount.**

Tips: "*Southwest Airlines Spirit* magazine reaches more than 2.5 million readers every month aboard Southwest Airlines. Our median reader is a college-educated, 38-40-year-old traveler with a household income around $90,000. Writers must have proven magazine capabilities, a sense of fun, excellent reporting skills, a smart, hip style, and the ability to provide take-away value to the reader in sidebars, charts, and/or lists."

$ $ SPIRIT OF ALOHA, The Inflight Magazine of Aloha Airlines and Island Air, Honolulu Publishing Co., Ltd., 707 Richards St., Suite 525, Honolulu HI 96813. (808)524-7400. Fax: (808)531-2306. E-mail: jotaguro@honpub.com. Website: www.spiritofaloha.com. **Contact:** Janice Otaguro, editor. **80% freelance written.** Bimonthly magazine covering visitor activities/destinations and Hawaii culture and history. "Although we are an inflight magazine for an inter-island airline, we try to keep our editorial as fresh and lively for residents as much as for visitors." Estab. 1978. Circ. 100,000. **Pays on acceptance.** Publishes ms an average of 2 months after acceptance. Byline given. Buys first rights. Editorial lead time 2 months. Submit seasonal material 2 months in advance. Accepts queries by mail, e-mail. Responds in 2 months to queries. Sample copy and writer's guidelines free.

Nonfiction: All must be related to Hawaii. Book excerpts, general interest, historical/nostalgic, interview/profile, photo feature, travel. No poetry or "How I spent my vacation in Hawaii" type pieces. **Buys 24 mss/year.** Query with published clips. Length: 1,500-2,000 words. **Pays $500.** Sometimes pays expenses of writers on assignment.

Photos: State availability with submission. Reviews transparencies. Buys one-time rights. Negotiates payment individually. Captions, identification of subjects, model releases required.

$ $ $ WASHINGTON FLYER MAGAZINE, 1707 L St., NW, Suite 800, Washington DC 20036. Fax: (202)331-2043. E-mail: readers@themagazinegroup.com. Website: www.fly2dc.com. **Contact:** Michael McCarthy, editor-in-chief. **60% freelance written.** Bimonthly magazine for business and pleasure travelers at Washington National and Washington

Dulles International airports INSI. "Primarily affluent, well-educated audience that flies frequently in and out of Washington, DC." Estab. 1989. Circ. 182,000. **Pays on acceptance.** Byline given. Offers 25% kill fee. Buys first North American serial rights. Submit seasonal material 4 months in advance. Accepts queries by mail, e-mail, fax. Responds in 10 weeks to queries. Sample copy and writer's guidelines for 9×12 SAE with $2 postage. Writer's guidelines online. Editorial calendar online.

O-π "First understand the magazine—from the nuances of its content to its tone. Best departments to get your foot in the door are 'Washington Insider' and 'Mini Escapes.' The former deals with new business, the arts, sports, etc. in Washington. The latter: getaways that are within four hours of Washington by car. Regarding travel, we're less apt to run stories on sedentary pursuits (e.g., inns, B&Bs, spas). Our readers want to get out and discover an area, whether it's DC or Barcelona. Action-oriented activities work best. Also, the best way to pitch is via e-mail. Our mail is sorted by interns, and sometimes I never get queries. E-mail is so immediate, and I can give a more personal response."

Nonfiction: One international destination feature per issue, determined 6 months in advance. One feature per issue on aspect of life in Washington. General interest, interview/profile, travel, business. No personal experiences, poetry, opinion or inspirational. **Buys 20-30 mss/year.** Query with published clips. Length: 800-1,200 words. **Pays $500-900.**

Photos: State availability with submission. Reviews negatives, almost always color transparencies. Buys one-time rights. Considers additional payment for top-quality photos accepted with ms. Identification of subjects required.

Columns/Departments: Washington Insider, Travel, Hospitality, Airports and Airlines, Restaurants, Shopping, all 800-1,200 words. Query. **Pays $500-900.**

Tips: "Know the Washington market and issues relating to frequent business/pleasure travelers as we move toward a global economy. With a bimonthly publication schedule it's important that stories remain viable as possible during the magazine's two-month 'shelf life.' No telephone calls, please and understand that most assignments are made several months in advance. Queries are best sent via e-mail."

JUVENILE

Just as children change and grow, so do juvenile magazines. Children's magazine editors stress that writers must read recent issues. A wide variety of issues are addressed in the numerous magazines for the baby boom echo. Respecting nature, developing girls' self-esteem, and establishing good healthy habits all find an editorial niche. This section lists publications for children up to age 12. Magazines for young people 13-19 appear in the Teen and Young Adult category. Many of the following publications are produced by religious groups and, where possible, the specific denomination is given. For additional juvenile/young adult markets, see our sister publication *Children's Writer's & Illustrator's Market* (Writer's Digest Books).

N $ $ **AMERICAN GIRL**, Pleasant Company Publications, 8400 Fairway Place, Middleton WI 53562. (608)836-4848. E-mail: im_agmag_editor@pleasantco.com. Website: www.americangirl.com. Executive Editor: Kristi Thom. Managing Editor: Barbara Stretchberry. **Contact:** Magazine Department Assistant. **5% freelance written.** Bimonthly 4-color magazine covering hobbies, crafts, profiles, and history of interest to girls ages 8-12. "Four-color bimonthly magazine for girls age 8-12. We want thoughtfully developed children's literature with good characters and plots." Estab. 1992. Circ. 750,000. **Pays on acceptance.** Byline given for larger features, not departments. Offers 50% kill fee. Buys first North American serial, all rights. Editorial lead time 6 months. Submit seasonal material 6 months in advance. Accepts queries by mail. Accepts previously published material. Accepts simultaneous submissions. Responds in 3 months to queries. Sample copy for $3.95 (check made out to *American Girl*) and 9×12 SAE with $1.94 postage. Writer's guidelines online.

O-π Best opportunity for freelancers is the Girls Express section. "We're looking for short profiles of girls who are into sports, the arts, interesting hobbies, cultural activities, and other areas. A key: The girl must be the 'star' and the story must be from her point of view. Be sure to include the age of the girls you're pitching to us. If you have any photo leads, please send those, too. We also welcome how-to stories—how to send away for free things, hot ideas for a cool day, how to write the President and get a response. In addition, we're looking for easy crafts that can be explained in a few simple steps. Stories in Girls Express have to be told in no more than 175 words. We prefer to receive ideas in query form rather than finished manuscripts."

Nonfiction: Pays $300 minimum for feature articles. Pays expenses of writers on assignment.

Photos: "We prefer to shoot." State availability with submission. Buys all rights.

Columns/Departments: Girls Express (short profiles of girls with unusual and interesting hobbies that other girls want to read about), 175 words; Giggle Gang (puzzles, games, etc.—especially looking for seasonal). Query.

Fiction: Magazine Department Assistant. Adventure, condensed novels, ethnic, historical, humorous, slice-of-life vignettes. No romance, science fiction, fantasy. **Buys 6 mss/year.** Query with published clips. Length: 2,300 words maximum. **Pays $500 minimum.**

$ $ **ARCHAEOLOGY'S DIG MAGAZINE**, Cobblestone Publishing, 30 Grove St., Suite C, Peterborough NH 03458-1454. (603)924-7209. Fax: (603)924-7380. E-mail: cfbakeriii@meganet.net. Website: www.digonsite.com. **Contact:** Rosalie Baker, editor. **75% freelance written.** Bimonthly magazine covering archaeology for kids ages 9-14. Estab. 1999. Circ. 20,000. Pays on publication. Publishes ms an average of 4 months after acceptance. Byline given. Buys all rights. Editorial lead time 6 months. Submit seasonal material 3 months in advance. Accepts queries by mail. Responds in several months to queries; 1 month to mss. Sample copy for $4.95 with 8x11 SASE or $9 without SASE. Writer's guidelines online.

- Does *not* accept unsolicited material.

Nonfiction: Personal experience, photo feature, travel, archaeological excavation reports. No fiction. Occasional paleontology stories accepted. **Buys 30-40 mss/year.** Query with published clips. Length: 100-1,000 words. **Pays 20-25¢/word.**

Photos: State availability with submission. Buys one-time rights. Negotiates payment individually. Identification of subjects required.

Tips: "Please remember that this is a children's magazine for kids ages 9-14 so the tone is as kid-friendly as possible given the scholarship involved in researching and describing a site or a find."

$ BABYBUG, Carus Publishing Co., P.O. Box 300, Peru IL 61354. (815)224-6656. Editor-in-Chief: Marianne Carus. **Contact:** Paula Morrow, executive editor. **50% freelance written.** Board-book magazine published monthly except for combined May/June and July/August issues. "*Babybug* is 'the listening and looking magazine for infants and toddlers,' intended to be read aloud by a loving adult to foster a love of books and reading in young children ages 6 months-2 years." Estab. 1994. Circ. 45,000. Pays on publication. Publishes ms an average of 18 months after acceptance. Byline given. Buys variable rights. Editorial lead time 10 months. Submit seasonal material 1 year in advance. Accepts simultaneous submissions. Sample copy for $5. Writer's guidelines online.

Nonfiction: General interest. **Buys 10-20 mss/year.** Send complete ms. Length: 1-10 words. **Pays $25.**

Fiction: Anything for infants and toddlers. Adventure, humorous. **Buys 10-20 mss/year.** Send complete ms. Length: 2-8 short sentences. **Pays $25 and up.**

Poetry: Buys 30 poems/year. Submit maximum 5 poems. Length: 2-8 lines. **Pays $25.**

Tips: "Imagine having to read your story or poem—out loud—50 times or more! That's what parents will have to do. Babies and toddlers demand, 'Read it again'—your material must hold up under repetition."

$ $ $ $ BOYS' LIFE, Boy Scouts of America, P.O. Box 152079, Irving TX 75015-2079. (972)580-2355. Fax: (972)580-2079. Website: www.boyslife.org. **Contact:** Michael Goldman, senior editor. **75% freelance written.** Prefers to work with published/established writers; works with small number of new/unpublished writers each year. Monthly magazine covering activities of interest to all boys ages 6-18. Most readers are Boy Scouts or Cub Scouts. "*Boys' Life* covers Boy Scout activities and general interest subjects for ages 8 to 18, Boy Scouts, Cub Scouts and others of that age group." Estab. 1911. Circ. 1,300,000. **Pays on acceptance.** Publishes ms an average of 1 year after acceptance. Buys one-time rights. Accepts queries by mail, fax. Responds in 2 months to queries. Sample copy for $3 and 9×12 SAE. Writer's guidelines for #10 SASE or online.

Nonfiction: Subject matter is broad, everything from professional sports to American history to how to pack a canoe. Look at a current list of the BSA's more than 100 merit badge pamphlets for an idea of the wide range of subjects possible. Uses strong photo features with about 500 words of text. Separate payment or assignment for photos. How-to, photo feature, hobby and craft ideas. **Buys 60 mss/year.** Query with SASE. No phone queries. Length: Major articles run 500-1,500 words; preferred length is about 1,000 words, including sidebars and boxes. **Pays $400-1,500.** Pays expenses of writers on assignment.

Columns/Departments: Darrin Scheid, associate editor. "Science, nature, earth, health, sports, space and aviation, cars, computers, entertainment, pets, history, music are some of the columns for which we use 300-750 words of text. This is a good place to show us what you can do." **Buys 75-80 mss/year.** Query. **Pays $250-300.**

Fiction: Rich Haddaway, associate editor. Include SASE. Adventure, humorous, mystery, science fiction, western, sports. **Buys 12-15 mss/year.** Send complete ms. Length: 1,000-1,500 words. **Pays $750 minimum.**

Fillers: Freelance comics pages and scripts.

Tips: "We strongly recommend reading at least 12 issues of the magazine before you submit queries. We are a good market for any writer willing to do the necessary homework."

$ BREAD FOR GOD'S CHILDREN, Bread Ministries, Inc., P.O. Box 1017, Arcadia FL 34265. (863)494-6214. Fax: (863)993-0154. E-mail: bread@sunline.net. Editor: Judith M. Gibbs. **Contact:** Donna Wade, editorial secretary. **10% freelance written.** Published 8 times/year. "An interdenominational Christian teaching publication published 8 times/year written to aid children and youth in leading a Christian life." Estab. 1972. Circ. 10,000. Pays on publication. Publishes ms an average of 6 months after acceptance. Byline given. Buys first rights. Accepts queries by mail. Accepts simultaneous submissions. Responds in 6 months to mss. Three sample copies for 9×12 SAE and 5 first-class stamps. Writer's guidelines for #10 SASE.

- Break in with a good story about a 6-10 year old gaining insight into a spiritual principle—without an adult preaching the message to him.

Reprints: Send tearsheet and information about when and where the material previously appeared.

Columns/Departments: Let's Chat (children's Christian values), 500-700 words; Teen Page (youth Christian values), 600-800 words; Idea Page (games, crafts, Bible drills). **Buys 5-8 mss/year.** Send complete ms. **Pays $30.**

Fiction: "We are looking for writers who have a solid knowledge of Biblical principles and are concerned for the youth of today living by those principles. Our stories must be well written, with the story itself getting the message across—no preaching, moralizing, or tag endings." No fantasy, science fiction, or nonChristian themes. **Buys 15-20 mss/year.** Send complete ms. Length: 600-800 words (young children), 900-1,500 words (older children). **Pays $40-50.**

Tips: "We're looking for more submissions on healing miracles and reconciliation/restoration. Follow usual guidelines for careful writing, editing, and proofreading. We get many manuscripts with misspellings, poor grammar, careless typing. Know your subject—writer should know the Lord to write about the Christian life. Study the publication and our guidelines."

$ $ CALLIOPE, Exploring World History, Cobblestone Publishing Co., 30 Grove St., Suite C, Peterborough NH 03458-1454. (603)924-7209. Fax: (603)924-7380. Website: www.cobblestonepub.com. Editors: Rosalie and Charles Baker. **Contact:** Rosalie F. Baker, editor. **More than 50% freelance written**. Magazine published 9 times/year covering world history (East and West) through 1800 AD for 8 to 14 year olds. Articles must relate to the issue's theme. "*Calliope* covers world history (east/west) and lively, original approaches to the subject are the primary concerns of the editors in choosing material. For 8-14 year olds." Estab. 1990. Circ. 11,000. Pays on publication. Byline given. Buys all rights. Responds in several monts (if interested, response 5 months before publication date to mss. Sample copy for $4.50 and 7½×10½ SASE with 4 first-class stamps or online. Writer's guidelines for #10 SAE and 1 first-class stamp or on website.

O→ Break in with a "well-written query on a topic that relates directly to an upcoming issue's theme, a writing sample that is well-researched and concise and a bibliography that includes new research."

Nonfiction: Articles must relate to the theme. Essays, general interest, historical/nostalgic, how-to (activities), humor, interview/profile, personal experience, photo feature, technical, travel, recipes. No religious, pornographic, biased, or sophisticated submissions. **Buys 30-40 mss/year.** Query by mail only with published clips. Length: 700-800 words for feature articles; 300-600 words for supplemental nonfiction. **Pays 20-25¢/printed word.**

Photos: State availability with submission. Reviews contact sheets, color slides and b&w prints. Buys one-time rights. Pays $15-100 (color cover negotiated).

Columns/Departments: Activities (crafts, recipes, projects), up to 700 words. Query by mail only with published clips. **Pays on individual basis.**

Fiction: Rosalie Baker, editor. All fiction must be theme-related. **Buys 10 mss/year.** Query with or without published clips. Length: 1,000 words maximum. **Pays 20-25¢/word.**

Fillers: Puzzles and games (no word finds); crossword and other word puzzles using the vocabulary of the issue's theme; mazes and picture puzzles that relate to the theme. **Pays on individual basis.**

Tips: "A query must consist of all of the following to be considered (please use nonerasable paper): a brief cover letter stating the subject and word length of the proposed article; a detailed 1-page outline explaining the information to be presented in the article; an extensive bibliography of materials the author intends to use in preparing the article; a self-addressed stamped envelope. (Authors are urged to use primary resources and up-to-date scholarly resources in their bibliography.) Writers new to *Calliope* should send a writing sample with the query. In all correspondence, please include your complete address as well as a telephone number where you can be reached."

N $ $ CHILDREN'S MAGIC WINDOW MAGAZINE, ProMark Publishing, P.O. Box 390, Perham MN 56573. Website: www.childrensmagicwindow.com. Editor: Joan Foster. Managing Editor: George Rowel. **Contact:** Mike Hoffman, production director. **70% freelance written.** Bimonthly magazine covering children's stories. "*Children's Magic Window* is a bimonthly, full-color magazine for all 6-12 year olds. Features 96 colorful pages of educational and entertaining stories, games, puzzles, magic, jokes, riddles, mazes, and fun facts. Challenging, yet lots of fun. Features sports and celebrity profiles, articles on health, history, nutrition, animals, and more." Estab. 1999. Circ. 10,000. Pays on publication. Publishes ms an average of 5 months after acceptance. Byline given. Offers 25% kill fee. Buys all rights. Editorial lead time 5 months. Submit seasonal material 8 months in advance. Accepts queries by mail. Responds in 6 weeks to queries; 5 months to mss. Sample copy for $5. Writer's guidelines for #10 SASE.

Nonfiction: General interest, historical/nostalgic, humor, photo feature. "We avoid all topics involving sex, drugs, alcohol, or violence." **Buys 20 mss/year.** Query with published clips or send complete ms. Length: 400-1,000 words. **Pays $0-400.** Pays in contributor copies upon author request.

Photos: Send photos with submission. Reviews contact sheets, up to 8×10 prints. Buys all rights. Negotiates payment individually. Model releases required.

Columns/Departments: Fun Facts (short explanation of any topic), up to 70 words; Science Fun (2-page spread involving interesting science projects); Make It Yourself (2-page spread of a craft or skill); Magic (2-page spread of a unique trick and how to perfom it). **Buys 1 or 2 for each department for each issue**. Send complete ms. **Pays up to $80.**

Fiction: Joan Foster, editor. "Fiction should be written for the 9-12 age group. Must challenge the reader and yet be easily understood. Look for pieces that are exciting and fresh." Experimental, fantasy, historical, humorous, mystery, suspense. "We avoid all topics involving sex, drugs, alcohol, or violence." **Buys 28 mss/year.** Send complete ms. Length: Up to 1,000. **Pays up to $400.**

Poetry: Joan Foster, editor. Light verse. **Buys 20 poems/year.** Submit maximum 2 poems. Length: Up to 10 lines maximum.

Fillers: Anecdotes, facts, gags to be illustrated by cartoonist, short humor. **Buys 50/year.** Length: Up to 80 words maximum. **Pays up to $20.**

Tips: "We are mostly concerned about finding entertaining, yet educational; fun, yet challenging material. We are looking for pieces that are entertaining for kids and at the same time can be interesting for adults. We want the contents of our magazine to make reading fun for the young reader."

N $ CLUB CONNECTION, A Missionettes Magazine for Girls, The General Council of the Assemblies of God, 1445 N. Boonville Ave., Springfield MO 65802. (417)862-2781. Fax: (417)862-0503. E-mail: clubconnection@ag.org. Website: www.clubconnection.ag.org. Editor: Debby Seler. Managing Editor: Lori VanVeen. **Contact:** Ranee Carter, assistant editor. **25% freelance written.** Quarterly magazine covering Christian discipleship. "*Club Connection* is a Christian-based magazine for girls ages 6-12." Estab. 1997. Circ. 12,000. Pays on publication. Publishes ms an average of 6-12 months after acceptance. Buys first, one-time rights. Editorial lead time 6 months. Submit seasonal material 9-12 months in advance. Accepts queries by mail, e-mail, fax. Responds in 1 month to queries; 1-2 months to mss. Sample copy for free. Writer's guidelines online.

Nonfiction: Historical/nostalgic, how-to (fun activities for girls), humor, inspirational, interview/profile, personal experience, religious. Special issues: A Look At Nature: trees, flowers, insects, butterflies, etc. (Spring 2003); A View of the World: geography, mountains, oceans and seas, summer vacation (Summer 2003); The Bigger Picture: science, the universe, astronauts, back to school (Fall 2003); The Perfect Plan: God's unique design in all creation, Jesus, salvation, Christmas (Winter 2003). No songs or poetry. **Buys 8 mss/year.** Send complete ms. Length: 250-800 words. **Pays $35-50 for assigned articles; $25-40 for unsolicited articles.**

Photos: Send photos with submission. Reviews 3½x5 prints. Buys one-time rights. Offers $10/photo. Captions, identification of subjects required.

Fiction: Adventure, confessions, ethnic, historical, humorous, mainstream, mystery, religious. No songs or poetry. **Buys 8 mss/year.** Send complete ms. Length: 250-800 words. **Pays $25-50.**

Tips: "Our goal is to offer a Christ-centered, fun magazine for girls. We look for word count, age appropriateness, and relevancy to today's girls when selecting articles. Writing to theme's is also helpful. They can be found on our website."

N $ CLUBHOUSE JR., Focus on the Family, 8605 Explorer Dr., Colorado Springs CO 80920. Editor: Annette Bourland. **Contact:** Suzanne Hadley, associate editor. Monthly magazine for 4-8 year olds. Estab. 1988. Circ. 96,000. Publishes ms an average of 1 year after acceptance. Byline given. Buys first rights. Accepts queries by mail. Accepts simultaneous submissions. Responds in 2 months to queries. Sample copy for $1.25 and 8×10 SASE. Writer's guidelines for #10 SASE.

Poetry: "Poetry should have a strong message that supports traditional values. No cute but pointless work." Submit maximum 5 poems. **Pays $50-100.**

$ $ CLUBHOUSE MAGAZINE, Focus on the Family, 8605 Explorer Dr., Colorado Springs CO 80920. (719)531-3400. Fax: (719)531-3499. Website: www.clubhousemagazine.org. Editor: Jesse Florea. **Contact:** Suzanne Hadley, associate editor. **25% freelance written.** Monthly magazine. "*Clubhouse* readers are 8-12 year old boys and girls who desire to know more about God and the Bible. Their parents (who typically pay for the membership) want wholesome, educational material with Scriptural or moral insight. The kids want excitement, adventure, action, humor, or mystery. Your job as a writer is to please both the parent and child with each article." Estab. 1987. Circ. 114,000. **Pays on acceptance.** Publishes ms an average of 6-12 months after acceptance. Byline given. Buys first North American serial, first, one-time, electronic rights. Editorial lead time 5 months. Submit seasonal material 7 months in advance. Responds in 2 months to mss. Sample copy for $1.50 with 9×12 SASE. Writer's guidelines for #10 SASE.

Nonfiction: Jesse Florea, editor. Essays, how-to, humor, inspirational, interview/profile, personal experience, photo feature, religious. "Avoid Bible stories without a unique format or overt visual appeal. Avoid informational-only, science, or educational articles. Avoid biographies told encyclopedia or textbook style." **Buys 3 mss/year.** Send complete ms. Length: 800-1,200 words. **Pays $25-450 for assigned articles; 10-25¢/word for unsolicited articles.**

Photos: Send photos with submission. Reviews 4×6 prints. Buys one-time rights. Negotiates payment individually. Identification of subjects required.

Columns/Departments: Lookout (news/kids in community), 50 words. **Buys 2 mss/year.** Send complete ms. **Pays $75.**

Fiction: Jesse Florea, editor. Adventure, humorous, mystery, religious, suspense, western, holiday. Avoid contemporary, middle-class family settings (existing authors meet this need), poems (rarely printed), stories dealing with boy-girl relationships. "No science fiction." **Buys 10 mss/year.** Send complete ms. Length: 400-1,500 words. **Pays $200 and up for first time contributor, and 5 contributor's copies; additional copies available.**

Fillers: Facts, newsbreaks. **Buys 2/year.** Length: 40-100 words.

$ $ COBBLESTONE, Discover American History, Cobblestone Publishing, 30 Grove St., Suite C, Peterborough NH 03458-1457. (603)924-7209. Fax: (603)924-7380. Website: www.cobblestonepub.com. **Contact:** Meg Chorlian, editor. Monthly magazine (September-May) covering American history for children ages 8-14. **100% freelance written (except letters and departments); approximately 1 issue/year is by assignment.** Prefers to work with published/established writers "Each issue presents a particular theme, making it exciting as well as informative. Half of all subscriptions are for schools." All material must relate to monthly theme. Estab. 1979. Circ. 30,000. Pays on publication. Publishes ms an average of 4 months after acceptance. Byline given. Offers 50% kill fee. Buys all rights. Editorial lead time 8 months. Accepts queries by mail, fax. Accepts simultaneous submissions. Responds in 4 months to queries. Sample copy for $4.95 and 7½×10½ SAE with 4 first-class stamps. Writer's guidelines for #10 SASE and 1 first-class stamp or on website.

Nonfiction: "Request a copy of the writer's guidelines to find out specific issue themes in upcoming months." Historical/nostalgic, interview/profile, personal experience, plays, biography, recipes, activities. No material that editorializes rather than reports. **Buys 80 mss/year.** Query by mail with published clips, outline, and bibliography. Length: Feature articles 600-800 words; supplemental nonfiction 300-500 words. **Pays 20-25¢/printed word.**

Photos: Photos must relate to theme. State availability with submission. Reviews contact sheets, transparencies, prints. Buys one-time rights. Offers $15-50 for nonprofessional quality, up to $100 for professional quality. Captions, identification of subjects required.

Columns/Departments: Puzzles and Games (no word finds); crosswords and other word puzzles using the vocabulary of the issue's theme.

Fiction: Adventure, ethnic, historical, biographical fiction relating to theme. Has to be very strong and accurate. **Buys 5 mss/year.** Query with published clips. Length: 500-800 words. **Pays 20-25¢/word.**

Poetry: Must relate to theme. Free verse, light verse, traditional. **Buys 3 poems/year.** Length: Up to 50 lines.

Tips: "Review theme lists and past issues of magazine to see what we look for."

$ $ CRICKET, Carus Publishing Co., P.O. Box 300, Peru IL 61354-0300. (815)224-6656. **Contact:** Marianne Carus, editor-in-chief. Monthly magazine for children ages 9-14. Magazine for children, ages 9-12. Estab. 1973. Circ. 73,000. Pays on publication. Publishes ms an average of 6-24 months after acceptance. Byline given. Rights vary. Submit seasonal material 1 year in advance. Accepts previously published material. Responds in 3 months to mss. Sample copy for $5 and 9×12 SAE. Writer's guidelines for SASE and on website.

- *Cricket* is looking for more fiction and nonfiction for the older end of its 9-14 age range. It also seeks humorous stories and mysteries (*not* detective spoofs), fantasy and original fairy tales, stand-alone excerpts from unpublished novels, and well-written/researched science articles.

Nonfiction: A short bibliography is required for all nonfiction articles. Travel, adventure, biography, foreign culture, geography, history, natural science, science, social science, sports, technology. Send complete ms. Length: 200-1,500 words. **Pays 25¢/word maximum.**

Reprints: send ms with rights for sale noted and information about when and where the material previously appeared. Pays 50% of amount paid for an original article.

Fiction: Adventure, ethnic, fantasy, historical, humorous, mystery, novel excerpts, science fiction, suspense, western, folk and fairy tales. No didactic, sex, religious, or horror stories. **Buys 75-100 mss/year.** Send complete ms. Length: 200-2,000 words. **Pays 25¢/word maximum, and 2 contributor's copies; $2 charge for extras.**

Poetry: Buys 20-30 poems/year. Length: 25 lines maximum. **Pays $3/line maximum.**

$ CRUSADER MAGAZINE, P.O. Box 7259, Grand Rapids MI 49510-7259. (616)241-5616. Fax: (616)241-5558. Website: www.calvinistcadets.org. **Contact:** G. Richard Broene, editor. **40% freelance written.** Works with a small number of new/unpublished writers each year. Magazine published 7 times/year. "*Crusader Magazine* shows boys 9-14 how God is at work in their lives and in the world around them." Estab. 1958. Circ. 10,000. **Pays on acceptance.** Publishes ms an average of 4-11 months after acceptance. Byline given. Buys first North American serial, one-time, second serial (reprint), simultaneous rights. Rights purchased vary with author and material. Accepts previously published material. Accepts simultaneous submissions. Responds in 2 months to queries. Sample copy for 9×12 SASE. Writer's guidelines for #10 SASE.

- Accepts queries and submissions by mail.

Nonfiction: Articles about young boys' interests: sports (articles about athletes and developing Christian character through sports; photos appreciated), outdoor activities (camping skills, nature study, survival exercises; practical 'how to do it' approach works best. 'God in nature' themes also appreciated if done without preachiness), science, crafts (made with easily accessible materials; must provide clear, accurate instructions), and problems. Emphasis is on a Christian perspective, but no simplistic moralisms. How-to, humor, inspirational, interview/profile, personal experience, informational. Special issues: Write for new themes list in February. **Buys 20-25 mss/year.** Send complete ms. Length: 500-1,500 words. **Pays 2-5¢/word.**

Reprints: Send ms with rights for sale noted. Payment varies.

Photos: Pays $4-25 for photos purchased with ms.

Columns/Departments: Project Page (uses simple projects boys 9-14 can do on their own).

Fiction: "Considerable fiction is used. Fast-moving stories that appeal to a boy's sense of adventure or sense of humor are welcome. Adventure, religious, spiritual, sports. "Avoid preachiness. Avoid simplistic answers to complicated problems. Avoid long dialogue and little action." No fantasy, science fiction, fashion, horror or erotica. Send complete ms. Length: 900-1,500 words. **Pays 4-6¢/word, and 1 contributor's copy.**

Fillers: Short humor, any type of puzzles.

Tips: "Best time to submit stories/articles is early in calendar year—in March or April. Also remember readers are boys ages 9-14. Stories must reflect or add to the theme of the issue."

$ $ CURRENT HEALTH 1, The Beginning Guide to Health Education, General Learning Communications, 900 Skokie Blvd., Suite 200, Northbrook IL 60062-4028. (847)205-3141. Fax: (847)564-8197. E-mail: crubenstein@glcomm.com. **Contact:** Carole Rubenstein, senior editor. **95% freelance written.** An educational health periodical published monthly, September-April/May. "Our audience is 4th-7th grade health education students. Articles should be written at a 5th grade reading level. The information must be accurate, timely, accessible, and highly readable." Estab. 1976. Circ. 152,000. Pays on publication. Publishes ms an average of 4 months after acceptance. Buys all rights. Sample copy available with 85¢ postage.

Nonfiction: Health curriculum. **Buys 64 mss/year.** Query with introductory letter, résumé, and clips. *No unsolicited mss. Articles are on assignment only.* Length: 950-2,000 words. **Pays $150-450.**

Tips: "We are looking for good writers with preferably an education and/or health background, who can write for the age group in a scientifically accurate and engaging way. Ideally, the writer should be an expert in the area in which he or she is writing. All topics are open to freelancers: disease, drugs, fitness and exercise, psychology, nutrition, first aid and safety, relationships, and personal health."

$ DISCOVERIES, Word Action Publishing Co., 6401 The Paseo, Kansas City MO 64131. (816)333-7000, ext. 2728. Fax: (816)333-4439. E-mail: jjsmith@nazarene.org. Editor: Virginia Folsom. **Contact:** Julie Smith, editorial assistant. **80% freelance written.** Weekly Sunday school take-home paper. "Our audience is third and fourth graders. We require that the stories relate to the Sunday school lesson for that week." Circ. 18,000. **Pays on acceptance.** Publishes ms an average of 1-2 year after acceptance. Byline given. Buys multi-use rights. Accepts queries by mail, e-mail, fax. Accepts previously published material. Accepts simultaneous submissions. Responds in 6 weeks to queries. Sample copy for SASE. Writer's guidelines for SASE.

O-ᵤ "Query before sending submissions. Make sure content is Biblically correct and relevant where necessary."

Fiction: Kathy Hendrixson, editorial assistant. Submit contemporary, true-to-life portrayals of 8-10 year olds, written for a third- to fourth-grade reading level. Religious themes. Must relate to our theme list. No fantasy, science fiction, abnormally mature or precocious children, personification of animals. Nothing preachy. No unrealistic dialogue. **Buys 50 mss/year.** Send complete ms. **Pays $25.**

Fillers: Gags to be illustrated by cartoonist, puzzles, trivia (any miscellaneous area of interest to 8-10 year olds, including hobbies, fun activities, weird information, etc.). We accept spot cartoons *only*. **Buys 130/year.** Length: 50-100 words. **Pays $10 for trivia and puzzles, and $15 for cartoons.**

Tips: "Follow our theme list, read the Bible verses that relate to the theme."

$ $ DISCOVERY TRAILS, Gospel Publishing House, 1445 N. Boonville Ave., Springfield MO 65802-1894. (417)831-8000. Fax: (417)862-6059. E-mail: rl-discoverytrails@gph.org. Website: www.radiantlife.org. **Contact:** Sinda S. Zinn, editor. **98% freelance written.** Weekly 4-page Sunday school take-home paper. *Discovery Trails* is written for boys and girls 10-12 (slanted toward older group). Fiction, adventure stories showing children applying Christian principles in everyday living are used in the paper. Estab. 1954. Circ. 20,000. **Pays on acceptance.** Publishes ms an average of 18 months after acceptance. Byline given. Buys one-time, second serial (reprint), simultaneous rights. Editorial lead time 18 months. Submit seasonal material 18 months in advance. Accepts simultaneous submissions. Responds in 1 month to queries. Sample copy for #10 SASE. Writer's guidelines online.

Nonfiction: Wants articles with reader appeal, emphasizing some phase of Christian living or historical, scientific, or natural material which includes a spiritual lesson. Submissions should include a bibliography of facts. **Buys 15-20 mss/year.** Send complete ms. Length: 500 words maximum. **Pays 7-10¢/word.**

Reprints: Send ms with rights for sale noted and information about when and where the material previously appeared. Pays 7¢/word.

Fiction: Wants fiction that presents realistic characters working out their problems according to Bible principles, presenting Christianity in action without being preachy. Serial stories acceptable. Adventure, historical, humorous, mystery, religious, spiritual, sports. No Bible fiction, "Halloween," "Easter bunny", "Santa Claus" or science fiction stories. **Buys 80-90 mss/year.** Send complete ms. Length: 800-1,00 words. **Pays 7-10¢/word, and 3 contributor's copies.**

Poetry: Light verse, traditional. **Buys 10 poems/year.** Submit maximum 2-3 poems. **Pays $5-15.**

Fillers: Bits & Bytes of quirky facts, puzzles, interactive activities, quizzes, word games, and fun activities that address social skills on a focused topic with accurate research, vivid writing, and spiritual emphasis. Crafts, how-to articles, recipes should be age appropriate, safe and cheap, express newness/originality and accuracy, a clear focus, and an opening that makes kids want to read and do it. **Buys 8-10/year.** Length: 300 words maximum.

Tips: "Follow the guidelines, remember the story should be interesting—carried by dialogue and action rather than narration—and appropriate for a Sunday school take-home paper. Don't send groups of stories in 1 submission."

$ $ THE FRIEND, 50 E. North Temple, Salt Lake City UT 84150-3226. Fax: (801)240-2270. **Contact:** Vivian Paulsen, managing editor. **50% freelance written.** Eager to work with new/unpublished writers as well as established writers. Monthly publication of The Church of Jesus Christ of Latter-Day Saints for children ages 3-11. Circ. 275,000. **Pays on acceptance.** Buys all rights. Submit seasonal material 10 months in advance. Responds in 2 months to mss. Sample copy and writer's guidelines for $1.50 and 9×12 SAE with 4 first-class stamps.

Nonfiction: "*The Friend* is particularly interested in stories based on true experiences." Special issues: Christmas, Easter. Submit complete ms with SASE. No queries, please. Length: 1,000 words maximum. **Pays 10¢/word minimum.**

Poetry: Serious, humorous, holiday. Any form with child appeal. **Pays $25 minimum.**

Tips: "Do you remember how it feels to be a child? Can you write stories that appeal to children ages 3-11 in today's world? We're interested in stories with an international flavor and those that focus on present-day problems. Send material of high literary quality slanted to our editorial requirements. Let the child solve the problem—not some helpful, all-wise adult. No overt moralizing. Nonfiction should be creatively presented—not an array of facts strung together. Beware of being cutesy."

$ $ GIRLS' LIFE, Monarch Publishing, 4517 Harford Rd., Baltimore MD 21214. Fax: (410)254-0991. Website: www.girlslife.com. Editor: Karen Bokram. **Contact:** Kelly A. White, executive editor. Bimonthly magazine covering girls ages 9-15. Estab. 1994. Circ. 2,000,000. Pays on publication. Publishes ms an average of 3 months after acceptance. Byline given. Buys all rights. Editorial lead time 4 months. Submit seasonal material 5 months in advance. Accepts queries by mail. Responds in 1 month to queries. Sample copy for $5 or online. Writer's guidelines online.

Nonfiction: Book excerpts, essays, general interest, how-to, humor, inspirational, interview/profile, new product, travel, beauty, relationship, sports. Special issues: Back to School (August/September); Fall, Halloween (October/November); Holidays, Winter (December/January); Valentine's Day, Crushes (February/March); Spring, Mother's Day (April/May); and Summer, Father's Day (June/July). **Buys 40 mss/year.** Query by mail with published clips. Submit complete mss on spec only. Length: 700-2,000 words. **Pays $350/regular column; $500/feature.**

Photos: State availability with submission. Reviews contact sheets, negatives, transparencies. Negotiates payment individually. Captions, identification of subjects, model releases required.

Columns/Departments: Buys 20 mss/year. Query with published clips. **Pays $150-450.**

Tips: Send queries with published writing samples and detailed résumé. "Have new ideas, a voice that speaks to our audience—not *down* to our audience—and supply artwork source."

$ GUIDE, True Stories Pointing to Jesus, Review and Herald Publishing Association, 55 W. Oak Ridge Dr., Hagerstown MD 21740. (301)393-4038. Fax: (301)393-4055. E-mail: guide@rhpa.org. Website: www.guidemagazine.org. **Contact:** Randy Fishell, editor, or Rachel Whitaker, assistant editor. **90% freelance written.** Weekly magazine featuring all-true stories showing God's involvement in 10- to 14-year-olds' lives. Estab. 1953. Circ. 33,000. **Pays on acceptance.** Publishes ms an average of 6 months after acceptance. Byline given. Buys first North American serial rights. Editorial lead time 8 months. Submit seasonal material 8 months in advance. Accepts queries by mail, e-mail, fax. Responds in 1 month to queries. Sample copy for SAE and 2 first-class stamps. Writer's guidelines online.

Break in with "a true story that shows in a clear way that God is involved in a 10- to 14-year-old's life."

Nonfiction: Religious. "No fiction. Nonfiction should set forth a clearly evident spiritual application." **Buys 300 mss/year.** Send complete ms. Length: 750-1,500 words. **Pays $25-125.**

Reprints: Send photocopy. Pays 50% of usual rates.

Fillers: Games, puzzles, religious. **Buys 75/year. Pays $25-40.**

Tips: "The majority of 'misses' are due to the lack of a clearly evident (not 'preachy') spiritual application."

N $ HIGH ADVENTURE, General Council of the Assemblies of God/Royal Rangers, 1445 N. Boonville Ave., Springfield MO 65802-1894. (417)862-2781, ext. 4177. Fax: (417)831-8230. E-mail: royalrangers@ag.org. Website: www.royalrangers.ag.org. **Contact:** Jerry Parks, editor. **60-70% freelance written.** Quarterly magazine. "*High Adventure* is a quarterly Royal Rangers magazine for boys. This 16-page, 4-color periodical is designed to provide boys with worthwhile leisure reading to challenge them to higher ideals and greater spiritual dedication; and to perpetuate the spirit of Royal Rangers ministry through stories, crafts, ideas, and illustrations." Estab. 1971. Circ. 87,000. Pays on publication. Publishes ms an average of 6-12 months after acceptance. Buys one-time, electronic rights. Buys first or all rights. Editorial lead time 3 months. Submit seasonal material 3 months in advance. Accepts queries by mail, e-mail, fax. Accepts previously published material. Accepts simultaneous submissions. Responds in 1 month to queries; 3-6 months to mss. Sample copy and writer's guidelines for 9×12 SAE and 2 first-class stamps. Writer's guidelines for SASE, by e-mail or fax. Editorial calendar for #10 SASE.

Nonfiction: General interest, historical/nostalgic, humor, inspirational, personal experience, religious. No objectionable language, innuendo, immoral, or non-Christian materials. **Buys 10-12 mss/year.** Send complete ms. Length: 200-1,000 words. **Pays 6¢/word for assigned articles.**

Fiction: Adventure, historical, humorous, religious, camping. No objectionable language, innuendo, immoral, or non-Christian materials. **Buys 30 mss/year.** Send complete ms. Length: 200-1,000 words. **Pays 6¢/word, plus 3 contributor's copies.**

Fillers: Anecdotes, facts, short humor. **Buys 25-30/year.** Length: 25-100 words. **Pays 6¢/word.**

Tips: "Consider the (middle/upper elementary) average age of readership when making a submission."

$ HIGHLIGHTS FOR CHILDREN, 803 Church St., Honesdale PA 18431-1824. (570)253-1080. Fax: (570)251-7847. Website: www.highlights.com. Editor: Christine French Clark. **Contact:** Manuscript Submissions. **80% freelance written.** Monthly magazine for children ages 2-12. "This book of whholesome fun is dedicated to helping children grow in basic skills and knowledge, in creativeness, in ability to think and reason, in sensitivity to others, in high ideals, and worthy ways of living—for children are the world's most important people. We publish stories for beginning and advanced readers. Up to 400 words for beginners (ages 3-7), up to 800 words for advanced (ages 8-12)." Estab. 1946. Circ. 2,500,000. **Pays on acceptance.** Buys all rights. Accepts queries by mail. Responds in 2 months to queries. Sample copy for free. Writer's guidelines for SASE or on website.

Nonfiction: "We need articles on science, technology, and nature written by persons with strong backgrounds in those fields. Contributions always welcomed from new writers, especially engineers, scientists, historians, teachers, etc., who can make useful, interesting facts accessible to children. Also writers who have lived abroad and can interpret the ways of life, especially of children, in other countries in ways that will foster world brotherhood. Sports material, arts features, biographies, and articles of general interest to children. Direct, original approach, simple style, interesting content, not rewritten from encyclopedias. State background and qualifications for writing factual articles submitted. Include references or sources of information. Articles geared toward our younger readers (3-7) especially welcome, up to 400 words. Also buys original party plans for children ages 4-12, clearly described in 300-600 words, including drawings or samples of items to be illustrated. Also, novel but tested ideas in crafts, with clear directions. Include samples. Projects must require only free or inexpensive, easy-to-obtain materials. Especially desirable if easy enough for early primary grades. Also, fingerplays with lots of action, easy for very young children to grasp and to dramatize. Avoid wordiness. We need creative-thinking puzzles that can be illustrated, optical illusions, brain teasers, games of physical agility, and other 'fun' activities." Query. Length: 800 words maximum. **Pays $50 for party plans; $25 for craft ideas; $25 for fingerplays.**

Photos: Reviews color 35mm slides, photos, or art reference materials that are helpful and sometimes crucial in evaluating mss.

Fiction: Marileta Robinson, senior editor. Unusual, meaningful stories appealing to both girls and boys, ages 2-12. "Vivid, full of action. Engaging plot, strong characterization, lively language." Prefers stories in which a child protagonist solves a dilemma through his or her own resources. Seeks stories that the child ages 8-12 will eagerly read, and the child ages 2-7 will begin to read and/or will like to hear when read aloud (400-800 words). "We publish stories in the suspense/adventure/mystery, fantasy and humor categories, all requiring interesting plots and a number of illustration possiblities. Also need rebuses (picture stories 125 words or under), stories with urban settings, stories for beginning readers (100-400 words), sports and humorous stories and mysteries. We also would like to see more material of 1-page length (300-400 words), both fiction and factual. War, crime, and violence are taboo." Adventure, fantasy, historical, humorous, animal, contemporary, folktales, multi-cultural, problem-solving, sports. "No war, crime or violence." Send complete ms. **Pays $100 minimum.**

The online magazine carries original content not found in the print edition.

Tips: "We are pleased that many authors of children's literature report that their first published work was in the pages of *Highlights*. It is not our policy to consider fiction on the strength of the reputation of the author. We judge each submission on its own merits. With factual material, however, we do prefer that writers be authorities in their field or people with first-hand experience. In this manner we can avoid the encyclopedic article that merely restates information readily available elsewhere. We don't make assignments. Query with simple letter to establish whether the nonfiction subject is likely to be of interest. A beginning writer should first become familiar with the type of material that *Highlights* publishes. Include special qualifications, if any, of author. Write for the child, not the editor. Write in a voice that children understand and relate to. Speak to today's kids, avoiding didactic, overt messages. Even though our general principles haven't changed over the years, we are contemporary in our approach to issues. Avoid worn themes."

$ $ ⊘ HUMPTY DUMPTY'S MAGAZINE, Children's Better Health Institute, P.O. Box 567, Indianapolis IN 46206-0567. (317)636-8881. Fax: (317)684-8094. E-mail: cbhiseif@tcon.net. Website: www.humptydumptymag.org. **Contact:** Nancy S. Axelrad, editor. **25% freelance written.** Magazine published 8 times/year covering health, nutrition, hygiene, fitness, and safety for children ages 4-6. "Our publication is designed to entertain and to educate young readers in healthy lifestyle habits. Fiction, poetry, pencil activities should have an element of good nutrition or fitness." Estab. 1948. Circ. 350,000. Pays on publication. Publishes ms an average of 8 months after acceptance. Byline given. Buys all rights. Editorial lead time 8 months. Submit seasonal material 10 months in advance. Accepts simultaneous submissions. Responds in 3 months to queries. Sample copy for $1.75. Writer's guidelines for SASE or on website.

- All work is on speculation only; queries are not accepted nor are stories assigned.

Nonfiction: "Material must have a health theme—nutrition, safety, exercise, hygiene. We're looking for articles that encourage readers to develop better health habits without preaching. Very simple factual articles that creatively teach readers about their bodies. We use several puzzles and activities in each issue—dot-to-dot, hidden pictures, and other activities that promote following instructions, developing finger dexterity, and working with numbers and letters." Include word count. **Buys 3-4 mss/year.** Send complete ms. Length: 300 words maximum. **Pays 22¢/word.**

Photos: Send photos with submission. Buys all rights. Offers no additonal payment for photos accepted with ms.

Columns/Departments: Mix & Fix (no-cook recipes), 100 words. All ingredients must be nutritious—low fat, no sugar, etc.—and tasty. **Buys 8 mss/year.** Send complete ms. **Payment varies.**

Fiction: Nancy Axelrad, editor. "We use some stories in rhyme and a few easy-to-read stories for the beginning reader. All stories should work well as read-alouds. Currently we need health/sports/fitness stories. We try to present our health material in a positive light, incorporating humor and a light approach wherever possible. Avoid stereotyping. Characters in contemporary stories should be realistic and reflect good, wholesome values." Include word count. Juvenile health-related material. "No inanimate talking objects, animal stories and science fiction." **Buys 4-6 mss/year.** Send complete ms. Length: 350 words maximum. **Pays 22¢/word for stories, plus 10 contributor's copies.**

Tips: "We would like to see more holiday stories, articles and activities. Please send seasonal material at least eight months in advance."

$ $ JACK AND JILL, Children's Better Health Institute, P.O. Box 567, Indianapolis IN 46206-0567. (317)636-8881. Fax: (317)684-8094. E-mail: cbhiseif@tcon.net. Website: jackandjillmag.org. **Contact:** Daniel Lee, editor. **50% freelance written.** Magazine published 8 times/year for children ages 7-10. "Material will not be returned unless accompanied by SASE with sufficient postage." No queries. May hold material being seriously considered for up to 1 year. Estab. 1938. Circ. 200,000. Pays on publication. Publishes ms an average of 8 months after acceptance. Byline given. Buys all rights. Submit seasonal material 8 months in advance. Responds in 10 weeks to mss. Sample copy for $1.75. Writer's guidelines online.

O‑━ Break in with nonfiction about ordinary kids with a news hook—something that ties in with current events, matters the kids are seeing on television and in mainstream news—i.e., space exploration, scientific advances, sports, etc.

Nonfiction: "Because we want to encourage youngsters to read for pleasure and for information, we are interested in material that will challenge a young child's intelligence *and* be enjoyable reading. Our emphasis is on good health, and we are in particular need of articles, stories, and activities with health, safety, exercise, and nutrition themes. We try to present our health material in a positive light—incorporating humor and a light approach wherever possible without minimizing the seriousness of what we are saying. Straight factual articles are OK if they are short and interestingly written. We would rather see, however, more creative alternatives to the straight factual article. Items with a news hook will get extra attention. We'd like to see articles about interesting kids involved in out-of-the-ordinary activities. We're also interested in articles about people with unusual hobbies for our Hobby Shop department." **Buys 10-15 mss/year.** Send complete ms. Length: 500-800 words. **Pays 17¢/word minimum.**

Photos: When appropriate, photos should accompany ms. Reviews sharp, contrasting b&w glossy prints. Sometimes uses color slides, transparencies, or good color prints. Buys one-time rights. Pays $15/photo.

Fiction: May include, but is not limited to, realistic stories, fantasy, adventure-set in past, present, or future. "All stories need a well-developed plot, action, and incident. Humor is highly desirable. Stories that deal with a health theme need not have health as the primary subject." **Buys 20-25 mss/year.** Send complete ms. Length: 500-800 words. **Pays 15¢/word minimum.**

Fillers: Puzzles (including various kinds of word and crossword puzzles), poems, games, science projects, and creative craft projects. "We get a lot of these. To be selected, an item needs a little extra spark and originality. Instructions for activities should be clearly and simply written and accompanied by models or diagram sketches. We also have a need for recipes. Ingredients should be healthful; avoid sugar, salt, chocolate, red meat, and fats as much as possible. In all material, avoid references to eating sugary foods, such as candy, cakes, cookies, and soft drinks."

Tips: "We are constantly looking for new writers who can tell good stories with interesting slants—stories that are not full of out-dated and time-worn expressions. We like to see stories about kids who are smart and capable, but not sarcastic or smug. Problem-solving skills, personal responsibility, and integrity are good topics for us. Obtain *current* issues of the magazine and *study* them to determine our present needs and editorial style."

N $JUST WEIRD ENOUGH, Science Fiction, Fantasy & Fable, Meadowdance Community Group, LLP, P.O. Box 247, Plainfield VT 05667-0247. E-mail: editor@justweirdenough.com. Website: www.justweirdenough.com. **Contact:** Luc Reid, editor. **100% freelance written.** Quarterly magazine covering juvenile science fiction and fantasy. "We publish original fiction, poetry, and art with imaginative or impossible elements, including science fiction, fantasy, and alternate history. Submissions should be engaging, meaningful, and fun for our 9- to 14-year-old readers, and written material should be at an appropriate reading level." Estab. 2003. **Pays on acceptance.** Publishes ms an average of 3-6 months after acceptance. Byline given. Buys first North American serial rights. Editorial lead time 3-6 months. Submit seasonal material 6 months in advance. Accepts queries by mail, e-mail. Accepts previously published material. Responds in 3 weeks to queries; 2 months to mss. Writer's guidelines for #10 SASE, online at website, or by e-mail (proguidelines@justweirdenough.com).

Fiction: E-mail queries accepted at: fiction@justweirdenough.com. Fantasy, science fiction, juvenile only, any speculative genre. "No nonfiction, games, puzzles, activities, horror, occult, vampire stories, religious material (it's fine for stories to be religious, but stories should not promote or deprecate any religion), gore, gratuitous violence, material that is demeaning or dismissive of women or any other group of people, or didactic or condescending stories." **Buys 14 mss/year.** Send complete ms. Length: 2,500 words maximum. **Pays $10-75.**

Poetry: Poetry queries accepted at: poetry@justweirdenough.com. Free verse, haiku, light verse, traditional. "Please do not send us poetry that does not have a science fiction, fantasy, or other speculative theme." **Buys 12 poems/year.** Submit maximum 5 poems. Length: 30 line maximum.

Tips: "We're particularly interested in material that promotes egalitarianism, real-world nonviolence, ecological sensibility, diversity, and other positive, cooperative themes—without preaching. A good example of this approach is *Huckleberry Finn*, in which no character, including the escaped slave, and the boy who's helping him, ever considers that slavery itself might be wrong."

$ $LADYBUG, The Magazine for Young Children, Carus Publishing Co., P.O. Box 300, Peru IL 61354-0300. (815)224-6656. Editor-in-Chief: Marianne Carus. **Contact:** Paula Morrow, executive editor. Monthly magazine for children ages 2-6. "We look for quality writing—quality literature, no matter the subject. For young children, ages 2-6." Estab. 1990. Circ. 134,000. Pays on publication. Byline given. For recurring features, pays flat fee and copyright becomes property of Cricket Magazine Group. Buys second serial (reprint), all rights. Rights purchased vary. Submit seasonal material 1 year in advance. Accepts previously published material. Responds in 3 months to mss. Sample copy for $5 and 9×12 SAE. Guidelines only for #10 SASE. Writer's guidelines for #10 SASE or on website.

- *Ladybug* needs imaginative activities based on concepts and interesting, appropriate nonfiction. See sample issues. Also needs articles and parent-child activities for its online parent's companion.

Nonfiction: Can You Do This?, 1-2 pages; The World Around You, 2-4 pages; activities based on concepts (size, color, sequence, comparison, etc.), 1-2 pages. "Most *Ladybug* nonfiction is in the form of illustration. We'd like more simple science, how-things-work, and behind the scenes on a preschool level." **Buys 35 mss/year.** Send complete ms; no queries. Length: 250-300 words. **Pays 25¢/word.**

Fiction: Marianne Carus, editor-in-chief. Adventure, ethnic, fantasy, humorous, mainstream, mystery, folklore, pre-school, read-out-loud stories and realistic fiction. **Buys 30 mss/year.** Send complete ms. Length: 850 words maximum. **Pays 25¢/word (less for reprints).**

Poetry: Light verse, traditional, humorous. **Buys 40 poems/year.** Submit maximum 5 poems. Length: 20 lines maximum. **Pays $3/line, with $25 minimum.**

Fillers: "We welcome interactive activities: rebuses, up to 100 words; *original* fingerplays and action rhymes (up to 8 lines)." Anecdotes, facts, short humor. **Buys 10/year.** Length: 250 words maximum. **Pays 25¢/word.**

Tips: "Reread manuscript *before* sending in. Keep within specified word limits. Study back issues before submitting to learn about the types of material we're looking for. Writing style is paramount. We look for rich, evocative language and a sense of joy or wonder. Remember that you're writing for preschoolers—be age-appropriate but not condescending. A story must hold enjoyment for both parent and child through repeated read-aloud sessions. Remember that people come in all colors, sizes, physical conditions, and have special needs. Be inclusive!"

$MY FRIEND, The Catholic Magazine for Kids, Pauline Books & Media/Daughters of St. Paul, 50 St. Pauls Ave., Jamaica Plain, Boston MA 02130-3495. (617)522-8911. Fax: (617)541-9805. E-mail: myfriend@pauline.org. Website: www.myfriendmagazine.org. Editor-in-Chief: Sister Donna William Giaimo. **Contact:** Sister Maria Grace Dateno, editor. **25% freelance written.** Magazine published 10 times/year for children ages 6-12. "*My Friend* is a 32-page monthly Catholic magazine for boys and girls. Its goal is to communicate religious truths and positive values in an enjoyable and attractive way." Theme list available. Send a SASE to the above address. Estab. 1979. Circ. 8,000. **Pays on acceptance.** Publishes ms an average of 1 year after acceptance. Buys worldwide publication rights. Responds in 2 months to mss. Sample copy for $2 and 9×12 SASE ($1.29). Writer's guidelines and theme list for #10 SASE.

Fiction: Sister Kathryn James Hermes, editor. "We are looking for stories that immediately grab the imagination of the reader. Good dialogue, realistic character development, current lingo are necessary. A child protagonist must resolve a dilemma through his or her own resources. Not all the stories of each issue have to be directly related to the theme. We continue to need stories that are simply fun and humorous. We also appreciate an underlying awareness of current events and current global tensions. Ever since September 11, kids are very sensitive to such realities." Religious, sports. Send complete ms. Length: 600-1,200 words. **Pays $75-150.**

Tips: "For fiction, we prefer the submission of manuscripts to query letters. If you are not sure whether a story would be appropriate for *My Friend*, please request our complete guidelines, theme list, and a sample issue (see above). For nonfiction articles, you may query by e-mail, but most are written by staff and contributing authors."

$ NATURE FRIEND, Carlisle Press, 2673 TR 421, Sugarcreek OH 44681. (330)852-1900. Fax: (330)852-3285. Managing Editor: Elaine Miller. **Contact:** Marvin Wengerd, editor. **80% freelance written.** Monthly magazine covering nature. "*Nature Friend* includes stories, puzzles, science experiments, nature experiments—all submissions need to honor God as creator." Estab. 1983. Circ. 10,000. Pays on publication. Publishes ms an average of 10 months after acceptance. Byline given. Buys first, one-time rights. Editorial lead time 4 months. Submit seasonal material 3 months in advance. Accepts simultaneous submissions. Responds in 4 months to mss. Sample copy for $2.50 postage paid. Writer's guidelines for $4 postage paid.

O-π Break in with a "conversational story about a nature subject that imparts knowledge and instills Christian values."

Nonfiction: How-to (nature, science experiments), photo feature, articles about interesting/unusual animals. No poetry, evolution, animals depicted in captivity. **Buys 50 mss/year.** Send complete ms. Length: 250-900 words. **Pays 5¢/word.**

Photos: Send photos with submission. Reviews prints. Buys one-time rights. Offers $35-50/photo. Captions, identification of subjects required.

Columns/Departments: Learning By Doing, 500-900 words. "I need more hands-on, how-to articles." **Buys 20 mss/year.** Send complete ms.

Fillers: Facts, puzzles, short essays on something current in nature. **Buys 35/year.** Length: 150-250 words. **Pays 5¢/word.**

Tips: "We want to bring joy and knowledge to children by opening the world of God's creation to them. We endeavor to create a sense of awe about nature's creator and a respect for His creation. I'd like to see more submissions on hands-on things to do with a nature theme (not collecting rocks or leaves—real stuff). Also looking for good stories that are accompanied by good photography."

$ $ NEW MOON, The Magazine for Girls & Their Dreams, New Moon Publishing, Inc., 34 E. Superior St., #200, Duluth MN 55802. (218)728-5507. Fax: (218)728-0314. E-mail: girl@newmoon.org. Website: www.newmoon.org. **Contact:** Deb Mylin, managing editor. **25% freelance written.** Bimonthly magazine covering girls ages 8-14, edited by girls aged 8-14. "In general, all material should be pro-girl and feature girls and women as the primary focus. *New Moon* is for every girl who wants her voice heard and her dreams taken seriously. *New Moon* celebrates girls, explores the passage from girl to woman, and builds healthy resistance to gender inequities. The *New Moon* girl is true to herself and *New Moon* helps her as she pursues her unique path in life, moving confidently into the world." Estab. 1992. Circ. 30,000. Pays on publication. Publishes ms an average of 6 months after acceptance. Byline given. Buys all rights. Editorial lead time 6 months. Submit seasonal material 8 months in advance. Accepts queries by mail, e-mail, fax. Accepts simultaneous submissions. Responds in 2 months to mss. Sample copy for $6.75 or online. Writer's guidelines for SASE or online.

O-π Adult writers can break in with "Herstory articles about less well-known women from all over the world, especially if it relates to one of our themes. Same with Women's Work articles. Girls can break in with essays and articles (nonfiction) that relate to a theme."

Nonfiction: Essays, general interest, humor, inspirational, interview/profile, opinion, personal experience (written by girls), photo feature, religious, travel, multicultural/girls from other countries. No fashion, beauty, or dating. **Buys 20 mss/year.** Query with or without published clips or send complete ms. Length: 600 words. **Pays 6-12¢/word.**

Photos: State availability with submission. Buys one-time rights. Negotiates payment individually. Captions, identification of subjects required.

Columns/Departments: Women's Work (profile of a woman and her job(s) relating the the theme), 600 words; Herstory (historical woman relating to theme), 600 words. **Buys 10 mss/year.** Query. **Pays 6-12¢/word.**

Fiction: Prefers girl-written material. All girl-centered. Adventure, fantasy, historical, humorous, slice-of-life vignettes. **Buys 6 mss/year.** Send complete ms. Length: 900-1,200 words. **Pays 6-12¢/word.**

Poetry: No poetry by adults.

Tips: "We'd like to see more girl-written feature articles that relate to a theme. These can be about anything the girl has done personally, or she can write about something she's studied. Please read *New Moon* before submitting to get a sense of our style. Writers and artists who comprehend our goals have the best chance of publication. We love creative articles—both nonfiction and fiction—that are not condescending to our readers. Keep articles to suggested word lengths; avoid stereotypes. Refer to our guidelines and upcoming themes."

$ ON THE LINE, Mennonite Publishing House, 616 Walnut Ave., Scottdale PA 15683-1999. (724)887-8500. Fax: (724)887-3111. E-mail: mary@mph.org. Website: www.mph.org. **Contact:** Mary Clemens Meyer, editor. **90% freelance written.** Works with a small number of new/unpublished writers each year. Monthly Christian magazine for children ages 9-14. "*On the Line* helps upper elementary and junior high children understand and appreciate God, the created world, themselves, and others." Estab. 1908. Circ. 5,500. **Pays on acceptance.** Publishes ms an average of 1 year after acceptance. Byline given. Buys one-time rights. Submit seasonal material 6 months in advance. Accepts previously published material. Accepts simultaneous submissions. Responds in 1 month to mss. Sample copy for 9×12 SAE and 2 first-class stamps. Writer's guidelines free.

Nonfiction: How-to (things to make with easy-to-get materials including food recipes), informational (300-500 word articles on wonders of nature, people who have made outstanding contributions). **Buys 95 mss/year.** Send complete ms. **Pays $15-35.**

Reprints: Send ms with rights for sale noted and information about when and where the material previously appeared. Pays 75% of amount paid for an original article.

Photos: Limited number of photos purchased with or without ms. Total purchase price for ms includes payment for photos. Pays $25-50 for 8×10 b&w or color photos.

Fiction: Adventure, humorous, religious, everyday problems. No fantasy or fictionalized Bible stories. Wants more mystery and humorous. **Buys 50 mss/year.** Send complete ms. Length: 1,000-1,800 words. **Pays 3-5¢/word.**

Poetry: Light verse, religious. Length: 3-12 lines. **Pays $10-25.**
Fillers: Appropriate puzzles, cartoons, and quizzes.
Tips: "Study the publication first. We need short, well-written how-to and craft articles; also more puzzles. Don't send query; we prefer to see the complete manuscript."

$ $ OWL MAGAZINE, The Discovery Magazine for Children, Owl Group (owned by Bayard Press), 49 Front St. E., 2nd Floor, Toronto ON M5E 1B3, Canada. (416)340-2700. Fax: (416)340-9769. E-mail: owl@owl.on.ca. Website: www.owlkids.com. **Contact:** Mary Beth Leatherdale, editor. **25% freelance written.** Works with small number of new writers each year. Magazine published 10 times/year covering general interest topics. Aims to interest 9-13 year olds in their world through accurate, factual information presented in an easy, lively style. Estab. 1976. Circ. 75,000. Pays on publication. Byline given. Buys all rights. Submit seasonal material 1 year in advance. Accepts queries by mail, e-mail, fax. Responds in 3 months to queries. Sample copy for $4.28. Writer's guidelines for SAE (large envelope if requesting sample copy), and money order for $1 postage (no stamps, please).
Nonfiction: Book excerpts, general interest, how-to, humor, personal experience (real life children in real situations), photo feature (natural science, international wildlife and outdoor features), science, nature and environmental features, puzzles, activities. No problem stories with drugs, sex or moralistic views, or talking animal stories. **Buys 6 mss/year.** Query with published clips. Length: 500-1,500 words. **Pays $200-700 (Canadian).**
Photos: Send for photo package before submitting material. State availability with submission. Identification of subjects required.
Tips: "Write for editorial guidelines first. Review back issues of the magazine for content and style. Know your topic and approach it from an unusual perspective. Our magazine never talks down to children. Our articles have a very light conversational tone and this must be reflected in any writing that we accept. We would like to see more articles about science and technology that aren't too academic."

$ $ POCKETS, The Upper Room, 1908 Grand Ave., P.O. Box 340004, Nashville TN 37203-0004. (615)340-7333. Fax: (615)340-7267. E-mail: pockets@upperroom.org. Website: www.pockets.org; www.upperroom.org/pockets. Editor: Janet R. Knight. **Contact:** Lynn Gilliam, associate editor. **60% freelance written.** Monthly (except February) magazine covering children's and families' spiritual formation. "We are a Christian, inter-denominational publication for children 6-11 years of age. Each issue reflects a specific theme." Estab. 1981. Circ. 94,000. **Pays on acceptance.** Publishes ms an average of 1 year to 18 months after acceptance. Byline given. Buys first North American serial rights. Submit seasonal material 1 year in advance. Accepts previously published material. Responds in 6 weeks to mss. Sample copy for 9×12 SAE and 4 first-class stamps. Writer's guidelines, themes, and due dates avaialble online.

- *Pockets* publishes fiction and poetry, as well as short-short stories (no more than 600 words) for children 5-7. They publish 1 of these stories/issue. Eager to work with new/unpublished writers.

Nonfiction: Each issue reflects a specific theme; themes available online or send #10 SASE. Interview/profile, personal experience, religious (retold scripture stories). No violence or romance. **Buys 5 mss/year.** Length: 400-1,000 words. **Pays 14¢/word.**
Reprints: Accepts one-time previously published submissions. Send typed ms with rights for sale noted and information about when and where the material previously appeared.
Photos: No photos unless they accompany an article. Send photos with submission. Reviews contact sheets, transparencies, prints. Buys one-time rights. Pays $25/photo.
Columns/Departments: Poetry and Prayer (related to themes), maximum 24 lines; Pocketsful of Love (family communications activities), 300 words; Peacemakers at Work (profiles of children working for peace, justice, and ecological concerns), 300-800 words. **Pays 14¢/word**. Activities/Games (related to themes). **Pays $25 and up**. Kids Cook (simple recipes children can make alone or with minimal help from an adult). **Pays $25. Buys 20 mss/year.**
Fiction: Lynn W. Gilliam, associate editor; Amy Bremers, assistant editor; Patricia P. McIntyre, editorial assistant. "Submissions do not need to be overtly religious. They should reflect daily living, lifestyle, and problem-solving based on living as faithful disciples. They should help children experience the Christian life that is not always a neatly wrapped moral package but is open to the continuing revelation of God's will for their lives." Adventure, ethnic, historical, religious, slice-of-life vignettes. No fantasy, science fiction, talking animals. **Buys 44 mss/year.** Send complete ms. Length: 600-1,400 words. **Pays 14¢/word, plus 2-5 contributor's copies.**
Poetry: **Buys 22 poems/year.** Length: 4-24 lines. **Pays $2/line, $25 minimum.**

The online magazine carries original content not found in the print edition and includes writer's guidelines, themes, and fiction-writing contest guidelines. Contact: Lynn Gilliam, associate editor.

Tips: "Theme stories, role models, and retold scripture stories are most open to freelancers. Poetry is also open. It is very helpful if writers read our writer's guidelines and themes on our website. We have an annual fiction writing contest. Contest guidelines available with #10 SASE or on our website."

N $ SCIENCE WORLD, Scholastic, Inc., 557 Broadway, New York NY 10012-3902. (212)343-6100. Fax: (212)343-6945. E-mail: scienceworld@scholastic.com. Website: www.scholastic.com. Editor: Mark Bregman. Biweekly magazine. Science publication for students grades 7-10. Circ. 404,597. Editorial lead time 3 weeks. Sample copy not available.

$ $ SPIDER, The Magazine for Children, Cricket Magazine Group, P.O. Box 300, Peru IL 61354. (815)224-6656. Fax: (815)224-6615. Website: www.spidermag.com. Editor: Heather Delabre. **Contact:** Submissions Editor. **80% freelance written.** Monthly magazine covering literary, general interest. "*Spider* introduces 6- to 9-year-old children to the highest quality stories, poems, illustrations, articles, and activities. It was created to foster in beginning readers a love of reading and discovery that will last a lifetime. We're looking for writers who respect children's intelligence." Estab. 1994. Circ.

87,000. Pays on publication. Publishes ms an average of 2-3 years after acceptance. Byline given. Rights vary. Editorial lead time 9 months. Accepts previously published material. Accepts simultaneous submissions. Responds in 4 months to mss. Sample copy for $5. Writer's guidelines for #10 SASE or on website.

Nonfiction: A bibliography is required with all nonfiction submissions. Nature, animals, science & technology, environment, foreign culture, history. **Buys 6-8 mss/year.** Send complete ms. Length: 300-800 words. **Pays 25¢/word.**

Reprints: Send photocopy with rights for sale noted and information about when and where the material previously appeared.

Photos: Send photos with submission. Reviews contact sheets, 35mm to 4×4 transparencies, 8×10 prints. Buys one-time rights. Offers $35-50/photo. Captions, identification of subjects, model releases required.

Fiction: Marianne Carus, editor-in-chief-. Adventure, ethnic, fantasy, historical, humorous, mystery, science fiction, suspense, realistic fiction, folk tales, fairy tales. No romance, horror, religious. **Buys 15-20 mss/year.** Send complete ms. Length: 300-1,000 words. **Pays 25¢/word and 2 contributor's copies; additional copies $2.**

Poetry: Free verse, traditional, nonsense, humorous, serious. No forced rhymes, didactic. **Buys 10-20 poems/year.** Submit maximum 5 poems. Length: 20 lines maximum. **Pays $3/line maximum.**

Fillers: Puzzles, crafts, recipes, mazes, games, brainteasers, engaging math and word activities. **Buys 15-20/year. Pays payment depends on type of filler.**

Tips: "We'd like to see more of the following: engaging nonfiction, fillers, and 'takeout page' activities; folktales, fairy tales, science fiction, and humorous stories. Most importantly, do not write down to children."

$ STONE SOUP, The Magazine by Young Writers and Artists, Children's Art Foundation, P.O. Box 83, Santa Cruz CA 95063-0083. (831)426-5557. Fax: (831)426-1161. E-mail: editor@stonesoup.com. Website: www.stonesoup.com. **Contact:** Ms. Gerry Mandel, editor. **100% freelance written.** Bimonthly magazine of writing and art by children, including fiction, poetry, book reviews, and art by children through age 13. Audience is children, teachers, parents, writers, artists. "We have a preference for writing and art based on real-life experiences; no formula stories or poems." Estab. 1973. Circ. 20,000. Pays on publication. Publishes ms an average of 3 months after acceptance. Buys all rights. Submit seasonal material 6 months in advance. Responds in 1 month to mss. Sample copy for $5 or online. Writer's guidelines online.

- Don't send queries, just submissions. No e-mail submissions. "We only respond to submissions accompanied by a SASE."

Nonfiction: Historical/nostalgic, personal experience, book reviews. **Buys 12 mss/year. Pays $40.**

Fiction: Adventure, ethnic, experimental, fantasy, historical, humorous, mystery, science fiction, slice-of-life vignettes, suspense. "We do not like assignments or formula stories of any kind." **Buys 60 mss/year.** Send complete ms. Length: 150-2,500 words. **Pays $40 for stories. Authors also receive 2 copies and discounts on additional copies and on subscriptions.**

Poetry: Avant-garde, free verse. **Buys 12 poems/year. Pays $40/poem.**

The online magazine carries original content not found in the print edition and includes writer's guidelines. Contact: Ms. Gerry Mandel, online editor.

Tips: "All writing we publish is by young people ages 13 and under. We do not publish any writing by adults. We can't emphasize enough how important it is to read a couple of issues of the magazine. We have a strong preference for writing on subjects that mean a lot to the author. If you feel strongly about something that happened to you or something you observed, use that feeling as the basis for your story or poem. Stories should have good descriptions, realistic dialogue, and a point to make. In a poem, each word must be chosen carefully. Your poem should present a view of your subject, and a way of using words that are special and all your own."

$ STORY FRIENDS, Mennonite Publishing House, 616 Walnut Ave., Scottdale PA 15683-1999. (724)887-8500. Fax: (724)887-3111. **Contact:** Susan R. Swan, editor. **80% freelance written.** Monthly magazine for children ages 4-9. "*Story Friends* is planned to nurture faith development in 4-9 year olds." Estab. 1905. Circ. 7,000. **Pays on acceptance.** Publishes ms an average of 1 year after acceptance. Byline given. Buys one-time, second serial (reprint) rights. Submit seasonal material 6 months in advance. Accepts simultaneous submissions. Responds in 2 months to queries. Sample copy for 9×12 SAE and 2 first-class stamps. Writer's guidelines for #10 SASE.

Nonfiction: How-to (craft ideas for young children), photo feature. **Buys 20 mss/year.** Length: 300-500 words. **Pays 3-5¢/word.**

Reprints: Send photocopy with rights for sale noted and information about when and where the material previously appeared. Pays 100% of amount paid for an original article.

Photos: Send photos with submission. Reviews 8½×11 b&w prints. Buys one-time rights. Offers $20-25/photo. Model releases required.

Fiction: Buys 50 mss/year. Send complete ms. Length: 300-800 words. **Pays 3-5¢/word.**

Poetry: Traditional. **Buys 20 poems/year.** Length: 4-16 lines. **Pays $10/poem.**

Tips: "Send stories that children from a variety of ethnic backgrounds can relate to; stories that deal with experiences similar to all children. Send stories with a humorous twist. We're also looking for well-planned puzzles that challenge and promote reading readiness."

$ $ TURTLE MAGAZINE FOR PRESCHOOL KIDS, Children's Better Health Institute, P.O. Box 567, Indianapolis IN 46206-0567. (317)636-8881. Fax: (317)684-8094. E-mail: cbhiseif@tcon.net. Website: www.turtlemag.org. **Contact:** (Ms.) Terry Harshman, editor. Bimonthly magazine. General interest, interactive magazine with the purpose of helping preschoolers develop healthy minds and bodies. Magazine of picture stories and articles for preschool children 2-5 years old. Estab. 1978. Circ. 300,000. Pays on publication. Byline given. Buys all rights. Submit seasonal material 8 months in advance. Responds in 3 months to queries. Sample copy for $1.75. Writer's guidelines for #10 SASE.

• May hold mss for up to 1 year before acceptance/publication.

Nonfiction: "We use very simple science experiments. These should be pretested. We also publish simple, healthful recipes." Length: 100-300 words. **Pays up to 22¢/word.**

Fiction: "Not buying much fiction right now except for rebus stories. All material should have a health or fitness slant. We no longer buy stories about 'generic' turtles because we now have PokeyToes, our own trade-marked turtle character. All should 'move along' and lend themselves well to illustration. Writing should be energetic, enthusiastic, and creative—like preschoolers themselves. No queries, please." No queries. Send complete ms. Length: 150-300 words. **Pays up to 22¢/word, and 10 contributor's copies.** "We use short verse on our inside front cover and back cover."

Tips: "We are looking for more short rebus stories, easy science experiments, and simple, nonfiction health articles. We are trying to include more material for our youngest readers. Material must be entertaining and written from a healthy lifestyle perspective."

$ $ U.S. KIDS, A Weekly Reader Magazine, Children's Better Health Institute, P.O. Box 567, Indianapolis IN 46206-0567. (317)636-8881. Fax: (317)684-8094. E-mail: cbhiseif@tcon.net. Website: www.uskids.org. **Contact:** Daniel Lee, editor. **50% freelance written.** Magazine published 8 times/year featuring "kids doing extraordinary things, especially activities related to health, sports, the arts, interesting hobbies, the environment, computers, etc." Estab. 1987. Circ. 230,000. Pays on publication. Publishes ms an average of 4 months after acceptance. Byline given. Buys all rights. Editorial lead time 6 months. Submit seasonal material 6 months in advance. Responds in 4 months to mss. Sample copy for $2.95 or online. Writer's guidelines for #10 SASE.

• *U.S. Kids* is being retargeted to a younger audience.

Nonfiction: Especially interested in articles with a health/fitness angle. General interest, how-to, interview/profile, science, kids using computers, multicultural. **Buys 16-24 mss/year.** Send complete ms. Length: 400 words maximum. **Pays up to 25¢/word.**

Photos: State availability with submission. Reviews contact sheets, negatives, transparencies, color photocopies, or prints. Buys one-time rights. Negotiates payment individually. Captions, identification of subjects, model releases required.

Columns/Departments: Real Kids (kids doing interesting things); Fit Kids (sports, healthy activities); Computer Zone. Length: 300-400 words. Send complete ms. **Pays up to 25¢/word.**

Fiction: Buys very little fictional material. **Buys 1-2 mss/year.** Send complete ms. Length: 400 words. **Pays up to 25¢/word.**

Poetry: Light verse, traditional, kid's humorous, health/fitness angle. **Buys 6-8 poems/year.** Submit maximum 6 poems. Length: 8-24 lines. **Pays $25-50.**

Fillers: Facts, newsbreaks, short humor, puzzles, games, activities. Length: 200-500 words. **Pays 25¢/word.**

Tips: "We are retargeting the magazine for first-, second-, and third-graders, and looking for fun and informative articles on activities and hobbies of interest to younger kids. Special emphasis on fitness, sports, and health. Availability of good photos a plus."

$ $ WILD OUTDOOR WORLD (W.O.W.) (r), Joy Publications, LLC, P.O. Box 1329, Helena MT 59624. (406)449-1335. Fax: (406)449-9197. E-mail: wowgirl@qwest.net. **Contact:** Carolyn Zieg Underwood, editorial director. **75% freelance written.** Magazine published 5 times/year covering North American wildlife and recycling for children ages 8-12. "*W.O.W.* emphasizes the conservation of North American wildlife and habitat and the importance of recycling to conserve our natural resources. Articles reflect sound principles of ecology and environmental education. It stresses the 'web of life,' nature's balance and the importance of habitat." Estab. 1993. Circ. 150,000. **Pays on acceptance.** Publishes ms an average of 18 months after acceptance. Byline given. Buys first North American serial, electronic rights. Editorial lead time 4 months. Submit seasonal material 8 months in advance. Accepts queries by mail, e-mail, fax. Accepts simultaneous submissions. Responds in 2 months to queries. Sample copy for 9×12 SAE and 3 first-class stamps. Writer's guidelines for #10 SASE.

O→ Break in with scientific accuracy, strong habitat focus; both educational and fun to read.

Nonfiction: Mainly looking for recycling stories. Has plenty of wildlife material for time being. **Buys 24-30 mss/year.** Query. Length: 600-850 words. **Pays $100-200 maximum.**

Photos: *No unsolicited photos.* State availability with submission. Reviews 35mm transparencies. Buys one-time rights. Offers $50-250/photo. Captions, identification of subjects, model releases required.

Columns/Departments: Making a Difference (kids' projects that improve their environment and surrounding habitat), 500 words; Short Stuff (short items, puzzles, games, interesting facts about nature and recycling), 300 words. **Buys 25-30 mss/year.** Query. **Pays $50-100.**

Fillers: Facts. **Buys 15-20/year.** Length: 300 words maximum. **Pays $50-100.**

LITERARY & "LITTLE"

Fiction, poetry, essays, book reviews, and scholarly criticism comprise the content of the magazines listed in this section. Some are published by colleges and universities, and many are regional in focus.

Everything about "little" literary magazines is different than other consumer magazines. Most carry few or no ads, and many do not seek them. Circulations under 1,000 are common. Sales often come more from the purchase of sample copies than from the newsstand.

The magazines listed in this section cannot compete with the pay rates and exposure of the high-circulation general interest magazines also publishing fiction and poetry. But most "little" literary magazines don't try. They are more apt to specialize in publishing certain kinds of fiction or poetry: traditional, experimental, works with a regional sensibility, or the fiction and poetry of new and younger writers. For that reason, and because fiction and poetry vary so widely in style, writers should *always* invest in the most recent copies of the magazines they aspire to publish in.

Many "little" literary magazines pay contributors only in copies of the issues in which their works appear. *Writer's Market* lists only those that pay their contributors in cash. However, *Novel & Short Story Writer's Market* includes nonpaying fiction markets, and has in-depth information about fiction techniques and markets. The same is true of *Poet's Market* for nonpaying poetry markets (both books are published by Writer's Digest Books). Many literary agents and book editors regularly read these magazines in search of literary voices not found in mainstream writing. There are also more literary opportunities listed in the Contests & Awards section.

$ACM (ANOTHER CHICAGO MAGAZINE), Left Field Press, 3709 N. Kenmore, Chicago IL 60613. E-mail: editors@anotherchicagomag.com. Website: www.anotherchicagomag.com. **Contact:** Barry Silesky, poetry editor. Biannual magazine with an emphasis on quality, experimental, politically aware prose, fiction, poetry, reviews, cross-genre work, and essays. Estab. 1977. Circ. 2,000. Publishes ms an average of 6-12 months after acceptance. Buys first North American serial rights. Accepts simultaneous submissions. Responds in 3 months to queries; 6 months to mss. Sample copy for $8 ppd. Writer's guidelines online.

Nonfiction: Essays.

Fiction: Sharon Solwitz, fiction editor. Ethnic, experimental, contemporary, prose poem. No religious, strictly genre or editorial. **Pays small honorarium when possible, contributor's copies and 1 year subscription.**

Poetry: Appreciates traditional to experimental verse with an emphasis on message, especially poems with strong voices articulating social or political concerns. Barry Silesky. No religious verse. Submit 3-4 typed poems at a time.

Tips: "Buy a copy—subscribe and support your own work."

$ACORN, A Journal of Contemporary Haiku, redfox press, P.O. Box 186, Philadelphia PA 19105. E-mail: missias@earthlink.net. Website: home.earthlink.net/~missias/acorn.html. **Contact:** A.C. Missias, editor. Biannual magazine dedicated to publishing "the best of contemporary English language haiku, and in particular to showcasing individual poems that reveal the extraordinary moments found in everyday life." Estab. 1998. Publishes ms an average of 1-6 months after acceptance. Buys first, one-time rights. Accepts queries by mail, e-mail. Responds in 3 weeks to mss. Writer's guidelines online.

Poetry: Decisions made by editor on a rolling basis. Poems judged purely on their own merits, not dependent on other work taken. Sometimes acceptance conditional on minor edits. Often comments on rejected poems. Accepts poetry written by children. Haiku. Does not want epigrams, musings, and overt emotion poured into 17 syllables; surreal, science fiction, or political commentary 'ku;' strong puns or raunchy humor. Syllable counting generally discouraged. Submit 5-25 poems at a time. Length: 1-5 lines.

Tips: "This is primarily a journal for those with a focused interest in haiku, rather than an outlet for the occasional short jottings of longer-form poets. It is a much richer genre than one might surmise from many of the recreational websites that claim to promote 'haiku' and bound to appeal to many readers and writers, especially those attuned to the world around them."

$AFRICAN AMERICAN REVIEW, Saint Louis University, Shannon Hall 119, 220 N. Grand Blvd., St. Louis MO 63103-2007. (314)977-3703. Fax: (314)977-3649. E-mail: keenanam@slu.edu. Website: aar.slu.edu. Editor: Joe Weixlmann. **Contact:** Aileen Keenan, managing editor. **65% freelance written.** Quarterly magazine covering African-American literature and culture. "Essays on African-American literature, theater, film, art and culture generally; interviews; poetry and fiction by African-American authors; book reviews." Estab. 1967. Circ. 2,067. Pays on publication. Publishes ms an average of 1 year after acceptance. Byline given. Buys first North American serial rights. Editorial lead time 1 year. Responds in 1 month to queries; 3 months to mss. Sample copy for $8. Writer's guidelines online.

Nonfiction: Essays, interview/profile. **Buys 30 mss/year.** Query. Length: 3,500-6,000 words. **Pays $50-150.** Pays in contributors copies upon request.

Photos: State availability with submission. Pays $100 for covers. Captions required.

Fiction: Ethnic, experimental, mainstream. "No children's/juvenile/young adult/teen." **Buys 4 mss/year.** Length: 2,500-5,000 words. **Pays $25-100, and 10 contributor's copies.**

$AGNI, Creative Writing Program, Boston University, 236 Bay State Rd., Boston MA 02215. (617)353-7135. Fax: (617)353-7134. E-mail: agni@bu.edu. Website: www.bu.edu/agni. **Contact:** Eric Grunwald, managing editor. Biannual magazine. "Eclectic literary magazine publishing first-rate poems and stories." Estab. 1972. Circ. 4,000. Pays on publication. Publishes ms an average of 6 months after acceptance. Byline given. Buys first North American serial rights. Rights to reprint in *AGNI* anthology (with author's consent). Editorial lead time 1 year. Accepts queries by mail. Accepts simultaneous submissions. Responds in 2 weeks to queries; 4 months to mss. Sample copy for $10 or online. Writer's guidelines for #10 SASE.

• Reading period September 1-May 31 only.

Fiction: Sven Birkerts, editor. Stories, prose poems. "No science fiction or romance." **Buys 6-12 mss/year. Pays $10/page up to $150, 2 contributor's copies, 1-year subscription, and 4 gift copies.**

Poetry: Buys more than 140 poems/year. Submit maximum 5 poems. with SASE **Pays $20-150.**

The online magazine carries original content not found inthe print edition. Contact: Sven Birkerts, editor.

Tips: "We're looking for extraordinary translations from little-translated languages. It is important to look at a copy of *AGNI* before submitting, to see if your work might be compatible. Please write for guidelines or a sample."

$ $ ALASKA QUARTERLY REVIEW, ESB 208, University of Alaska-Anchorage, 3211 Providence Dr., Anchorage AK 99508. (907)786-6916. E-mail: ayaqr@uaa.alaska.edu. Website: www.uaa.alaska.edu/aqr. **Contact:** Ronald Spatz, executive editor. **95% freelance written.** Semiannual magazine publishing fiction, poetry, literary nonfiction, and short plays in traditional and experimental styles. *AQR* "publishes fiction, poetry, literary nonfiction and short plays in traditional and experimental styles." Estab. 1982. Circ. 2,500. Honorariums on publication when funding permits. Publishes ms an average of 6 months after acceptance. Byline given. Buys first North American serial rights. Upon request, rights will be transferred back to author after publication. Accepts queries by mail, e-mail. Responds in 4 months to queries; 4 months to mss. Sample copy for $6. Writer's guidelines online.

• *Alaska Quarterly* reports they are always looking for freelance material and new writers.

Nonfiction: Literary nonfiction: essays and memoirs. **Buys 0-5 mss/year.** Query. Length: 1,000-20,000 words. **Pays $50-200 subject to funding.** Pays in contributor's copies and subscription when funding is limited.

Fiction: Experimental and traditional literary forms. No romance, children's, or inspirational/religious. Publishes novel excerpts. **Buys 20-26 mss/year**. Also publishes drama: experimental and traditional one-act plays. **Buys 0-2 mss/year.** Experimental, contemporary, prose poem. "If the works in *Alaska Quarterly Review* have certain characteristics, they are these: freshness, honesty, and a compelling subject. What makes a piece stand out from the multitude of other submissions? The voice of the piece must be strong—idiosyncratic enough to create a unique persona. We look for the demonstration of craft, making the situation palpable and putting it in a form where it becomes emotionally and intellectually complex. One could look through our pages over time and see that many of the pieces published in the *Alaska Quarterly Review* concern everyday life. We're not asking our writers to go outside themselves and their experiences to the absolute exotic to catch our interest. We look for the experiential and revelatory qualities of the work. We will, without hesitation, champion a piece that may be less polished or stylistically sophisticated, if it engages me, surprises me, and resonates for me. The joy in reading such a work is in discovering something true. Moreover, in keeping with our mission to publish new writers, we are looking for voices our readers do not know, voices that may not always be reflected in the dominant culture and that, in all instances, have something important to convey." Length: not exceeding 100 pages. **Pays $50-200 subject to funding; pays in contributor's copies and subscriptions when funding is limited.**

Poetry: Avant-garde, free verse, traditional. No light verse. **Buys 10-30 poems/year.** Submit maximum 10 poems. **Pays $10-50 subject to availability of funds; pays in contributor's copies and subscriptions when funding is limited.**

The online magazine carries original content not found in the print edition and includes writer's guidelines.

Tips: "All sections are open to freelancers. We rely almost exclusively on unsolicited manuscripts. *AQR* is a nonprofit literary magazine and does not always have funds to pay authors."

$ THE AMERICAN DISSIDENT, ContraOstrich Press, 1837 Main St., Concord MA 01742. E-mail: enmarge@aol.com. Website: www.geocities.com/enmarge. **Contact:** G. Tod Slone, editor. **100% freelance written.** Semiannual magazine "offering hardcore criticism of all American icons and institutions in English, French, or Spanish. Writers must be free of dogma, clear in mind, critical in outlook, and courageous in behavior." Estab. 1998. Circ. 200. Pays on publication. Publishes ms an average of 9 months after acceptance. Byline given. Buys first North American serial, one-time rights. Editorial lead time 6 months. Accepts queries by mail. Responds in 3 weeks to queries; 3 months to mss. Sample copy for $7. Writer's guidelines online.

Nonfiction: Essays, interview/profile, opinion, personal experience. **Buys 2-4 mss/year.** Query. Length: 250-750 words. **Pays $5 for assigned articles.** Pays in contributor's copies for poetry submissions and book reviews.

Photos: State availability with submission. Reviews prints. Buys one-time rights. Negotiates payment individually. Identification of subjects required.

Poetry: Free verse. Poetry with a message, not poetry for the sake of poetry, as in *l'art pour l'art*. Submit maximum 3-5 poems.

Tips: "*The American Dissident* publishes well-written dissident work (in English, French, or Spanish) that expresses some sort of visceral indignation regarding the nation, preferably on a personal-experience level. Writers are not on the edge where they ought to be. They've become too gregarious, comfortable, inbred, self-congratulating, and incapable of acting or speaking as individuals. It's time writers force themselves to stand alone against the herd and permit courage and action to prevail over fear and inaction. They need to harness the wondrous energy produced when courage triumphs over fear. Writers must speak out against corruption and the suppression of the First Amendement, especially in their immediate surroundings. Do not send general critique, but rather personal-experience prose. *The American Dissident* seeks that rare essay of truth that risks, be it ostracism from other writers, loss of reading invitations, book contracts, literary prizes, money, or even job. No pain, no gain; no fear, no risk."

N $ ANCIENT PATHS, A Journal of Christian Art and Literature, P.O. Box 7505, Fairfax Station VA 22039. E-mail: skylar.burris@gte.net. Website: www.literatureclassics.com/ancientpaths/magazine/table.html. **Contact:** Skylar Hamilton Burris, editor. **99% freelance written.** Semiannual magazine covering Christianity/religion. "*Ancient Paths* publishes quality fiction and creative nonfiction for a literate Christian audience. Religious themes are usually subtle, and the magazine has non-Christian readers as well as some content by non-Christian authors. However, writers should be comfortable appearing in a Christian magazine." Estab. 1998. Circ. 175-200. Pays on publication. Publishes ms an average of 2 months after acceptance. Byline given. Not copyrighted. Buys one-time, electronic rights. Submit seasonal material 3 months in advance. Accepts queries by mail, e-mail. Accepts previously published material. Accepts simultaneous submissions. Responds in 1 week to queries; 4-5 weeks to mss. Sample copy for $3.50. Writer's guidelines online. Editorial calendar online.

Nonfiction: Book excerpts, historical/nostalgic, religious, Book reviews of poetry chapbooks. No devotions, sermons, or lessons. **Buys 1-10 mss/year.** Send complete ms. Length: 250-2,500 words. **Pays $2, and 1 copy.** Pays in contributor copies if the author chooses to credit $3 toward additional copy instead of $2 payment.

Fiction: Fantasy, historical, humorous, mainstream, mystery, novel excerpts, religious, science fiction, slice-of-life vignettes, western. No retelling of Bible stories. **Buys 4-10 mss/year.** Send complete ms. Length: 250-2,500 words. **Pays $2, and 1 copy.**

Poetry: Free verse, traditional. No avant-garde, prose poetry, or poor meter. **Buys 25-60 poems/year.** Submit maximum 5 poems. Length: 4-60 lines. **Pays $1/poem, plus contributor's copy.**

Tips: "Make the reader think as well as feel. Do not simply state a moral message; no preaching, nothing didactic. You should have something meaningful to say, but be subtle. Show, don't tell."

$ THE ANTIGONISH REVIEW, St. Francis Xavier University, P.O. Box 5000, Antigonish NS B2G 2W5, Canada. (902)867-3962. Fax: (902)867-5563. E-mail: tar@stfx.ca. Website: www.antigonishreview.com. Managing Editor: Josephine Mensch. **Contact:** B. Allan Quigley, editor. **100% freelance written.** Quarterly magazine. Literary magazine for educated and creative readers. Estab. 1970. Circ. 850. Pays on publication. Publishes ms an average of 4 months after acceptance. Byline given. Offers variable kill fee. Rights retained by author. Editorial lead time 4 months. Submit seasonal material 4 months in advance. Accepts queries by mail, fax. Responds in 1 month to queries; 4 months to mss. Sample copy for $4 or online. Writer's guidelines for #10 SASE or online.

Nonfiction: Essays, interview/profile, book reviews/articles. No academic pieces. **Buys 15-20 mss/year.** Query. Length: 1,500-5,000 words. **Pays $50-150.**

Fiction: Allan Quigley, editor. Literary. Contemporary, prose poem. No erotica. **Buys 35-40 mss/year.** Send complete ms. Length: 500-5,000 words. **Pays $50 for stories.**

Poetry: Buys 100-125 poems/year. Submit maximum 5 poems. **Pays in copies.**

Tips: "Send for guidelines and/or sample copy. Send ms with cover letter and SASE with submission."

$ ANTIOCH REVIEW, P.O. Box 148, Yellow Springs OH 45387-0148. Website: www.antioch.edu/review. **Contact:** Robert S. Fogarty, editor. Quarterly magazine for general, literary, and academic audience. "Literary and cultural review of contemporary issues, and literature for general readership." Estab. 1941. Circ. 5,100. Pays on publication. Publishes ms an average of 10 months after acceptance. Byline given. Buys first, one-time rights. Rights revert to author upon publication. Accepts queries by mail. Responds in 2 months to mss. Sample copy for $6. Writer's guidelines online.

- Responds in 3 months.

Nonfiction: "Contemporary articles in the humanities and social sciences, politics, economics, literature, and all areas of broad intellectual concern. Somewhat scholarly, but never pedantic in style, eschewing all professional jargon. Lively, distinctive prose insisted upon. We *do not* read simultaneous submissions." Length: 2,000-8,000 words. **Pays $10/printed page.**

Fiction: Fiction editor. "Quality fiction only, distinctive in style with fresh insights into the human condition." Experimental, contemporary. No science fiction, fantasy, or confessions. Length: generally under 8,000. **Pays $10/printed page.**

Poetry: "No light or inspirational verse."

N $ ANTIPODES, 8 Big Island, Warwick NY 10990. E-mail: kane@vassar.edu. Biannual magazine of Australian poetry, fiction, criticism, and reviews of Australian writing. Estab. 1987. Circ. 500. Buys first North American serial rights. Accepts queries by mail. Responds in 2 months to queries. Sample copy for $17.

- Prints works from Australian writers only.

Nonfiction: Staff reviews books of poetry in 500-1,500 words. Essays, opinion.

Fiction: Prints Australian fiction only.

Poetry: Prints work from Australian poets only. Has published poetry by Les Murray, Jan Owen, and John Kinsella. No restrictions as to form, length, subject matter, or style. Paul Kane, poetry editor. **Buys 24 poems/year.** Submit maximum 3-5 poems.

$ ARC, Canada's National Poetry Magazine, Arc Poetry Society, Box 7219, Ottawa ON K1L 8E4, Canada. E-mail: arc.poetry@cyberus.ca. Website: www.cyberus.ca/~arc.poetry. **Contact:** John Barton, Rita Donovan, co-editors. Semiannual magazine featuring poetry, poetry-related articles, and criticism. "Our focus is poetry, and Canadian poetry in general, although we do publish writers from elsewhere. We are looking for the best poetry from new and established writers. We often have special issues. Send a SASE for upcoming special issues and contests." Estab. 1978. Circ. 1,500. Pays on publication. Publishes ms an average of 6 months after acceptance. Byline given. Buys one-time rights. Responds in 4 months to queries. Writer's guidelines for #10 SASE.

Nonfiction: Essays, interview/profile, book reviews. Query first. Length: 500-4,000 words. **Pays $30/printed page (Canadian), and 2 copies.**

Photos: Query first. Buys one-time rights. Pays $300 for 10 photos.

Poetry: Avant-garde, free verse. **Buys 60 poems/year.** Submit maximum 6 poems. **Pays $30/printed page (Canadian).**

Tips: "Please include brief biographical note with submission."

N $ ARTFUL DODGE, Dept. of English, College of Wooster, Wooster OH 44691. (330)263-2332. Website: www.wooster.edu/artfuldodge. **Contact:** Daniel Bourne, poetry editor. Annual magazine that "takes a strong interest in poets who are continually testing what they can get away with successfully in regard to subject, perspective, language, etc., but who also show mastery of the current American poetic techniques—its varied textures and its achievement in the illumination of the particular." "There is no theme in this magazine, except literary power. We also have an ongoing interest in translations from Central/Eastern Europe and elsewhere." Estab. 1979. Circ. 1,000. Buys first North American serial rights. Accepts queries by mail. Accepts simultaneous submissions. Responds in 1 year to mss. Sample copy for $7. Writer's guidelines for #10 SASE.

Fiction: Ron Antonucci, fiction editor. Experimental, prose poem. "We judge by literary quality, not by genre. We are especially interested in fine English translations of significant prose writers. Translations should be submitted with original texts." **Pays 2 contributor's copies and honorarium of $5/page, "thanks to funding from the Ohio Arts Council."**

Poetry: "We are interested in poems that utilize stylistic persuasions both old and new to good effect. We are not afraid of poems which try to deal with large social, political, historical, and even philosophical questions—especially if the poem emerges from one's own life experience and is not the result of armchair pontificating." "We don't want cute, rococo surrealism, someone's warmed-up, left-over notion of an avant-garde that existed 10-100 years ago, or any last bastions of rhymed verse in the civilized world." **Buys 20 poems/year.** Submit maximum 6 poems.

Tips: "Poets may send books for review consideration; however, there is no guarantee we can review them."

N $ ARTS & LETTERS, Journal of Contemporary Culture, Georgia College & State University, Campus Box 89, Milledgeville GA 31061. E-mail: al@gcsu.edu. Website: al.gcsu.edu. **Contact:** Martin Lammon, editor. Semiannual magazine covering poetry, fiction, creative nonfiction, and commentary on contemporary culture. "The journal features the mentors interview series, the world poetry translation series, and color reproductions of original artistic prints. Also, it is the only journal nationwide to feature authors and artists that represent such an eclectic range of creative work." Estab. 1999. Circ. 1,500. Pays on publication. Publishes ms an average of 6-12 months after acceptance. Rights revert to author after publication. Responds in 2 months to mss. Sample copy for $5, plus $1 for postage. Writer's guidelines online.

Fiction: Ruth Knafo Setton, fiction editor. No genre fiction. **Buys 6 mss/year.** Length: 3,000-7,500 words. **Pays $10 minimum or $50/published page.**

Poetry: Susan Atefat-Peckham, poetry editor.

Tips: "An obvious, but not gimmicky, attention to fresh usage of language. A solid grasp of the craft of story writing. Fully realized work."

$ BELLINGHAM REVIEW, Mail Stop 9053, Western Washington University, Bellingham WA 98225. (360)650-4863. E-mail: bhreview@cc.wwu.edu. Website: www.wwu.edu/~bhreview. Editor: Brenda Miller. **Contact:** Poetry, Fiction, or Creative Nonfiction Editor. **100% freelance written.** Semiannual nonprofit magazine. *Bellingham Review* seeks literature of palpable quality; stories, essays, and poems that nudge the limits of form or execute traditional forms exquisitely. Estab. 1977. Circ. 1,600. Pays on publication when funding allows. Publishes ms an average of 6 months after acceptance. Byline given. Buys first North American serial rights. Editorial lead time 6 months. Accepts simultaneous submissions. Responds in 3 months to mss. Sample copy for $7. Writer's guidelines online.

Nonfiction: Nonfiction Editor. Essays, personal experience. Does not want anything nonliterary. **Buys 4-6 mss/year.** Send complete ms. Length: 9,000 words maximum. **Pays as funds allow, plus contributor copies.**

Fiction: Fiction Editor. Literary short fiction. Does not want anything nonliterary. **Buys 4-6 mss/year.** Send complete ms. Length: 9,000 words maximum. **Pays as funds allow.**

Poetry: Poetry Editor. Avant-garde, free verse, traditional. Will not use light verse. **Buys 10-30 poems/year.** Submit maximum 3 poems. **Pays as funds allow.**

Tips: "Open submission period is from October 1-February 1. Manuscripts arriving between February 2 and September 30 will be returned unread." The *Bellingham Review* holds 3 annual contests: the 49th Parallel Poetry Award, the Annie Dillard Award in Nonfiction, and the Tobias Wolff Award in Fiction. Submissions December 1-March 15. See the individual listings for these contests under Contests & Awards for full details.

$ BLACK WARRIOR REVIEW, P.O. Box 862936, Tuscaloosa AL 35486-0027. (205)348-4518. Website: www.webdelsol.com/bwr. **90% freelance written.** Semiannual magazine of fiction, poetry, essays, art, and reviews. "We publish contemporary fiction, poetry, reviews, essays, photography and interviews for a literary audience. We strive to publish the most compelling, best written work that we can find." Estab. 1974. Circ. 2,000. Pays on publication. Publishes ms an average of 6 months after acceptance. Byline given. Buys first rights. Accepts simultaneous submissions. Responds in 4 months to mss. Sample copy for $8. Writer's guidelines online.

- Stories and poems in recent *Best American Short Stories*, *Best American Poetry* and *Pushcart Prize* anthologies. Responds in 3 months.

Nonfiction: Dan Kaplan, editor. Interview/profile, book reviews, literary/personal essays. **Buys 5 mss/year.** No queries; send complete ms. **Pays up to $100, copies, and a 1-year subscription.**

Fiction: Jennifer Gravley, fiction editor. Publishes novel excerpts if under contract to be published. One story/chapter per envelope, please. Contemporary, short and short-short fiction. Want "work that is conscious of form, good experimental writing, short-short fiction, writing that is more than competent - that sings. No genre fiction please." **Buys 10 mss/year.** Length:7,500 words. **Pays up to $150, copies, and a 1-year subscription.**

Poetry: Braden Welborn, poetry editor. **Buys 35 poems/year.** Submit 3-6 poems. **Pays up to $75, copies, and a 1-year subscription.**

Tips: "Read *BWR* before submitting. Send us only your best work. Address all submissions to the appropriate genre editor."

N $ BOOKLIST, American Library Association, 50 E. Huron St., Chicago IL 60611. (312)280-5715. Fax: (312)337-6787. E-mail: booklist@ala.org. Website: www.ala.org/booklist. **Contact:** Bill Ott, editor. **30% freelance written.** Biweekly magazine covering library selection, book publishing. Estab. 1905. Circ. 26,000. Pays on publication. Publishes ms an average of 6 weeks after acceptance. Byline given. Buys all rights. Editorial lead time 3 months. Submit seasonal material 6 months in advance. Accepts queries by mail, fax. Sample copy for free. Writer's guidelines online.

- *Booklist* does not accept unsolicited mss.

Nonfiction: No unsolicited mss. Reviews must be assigned by editors. Query with published clips. Length: 140-200 words. **Payment varies for assigned articles.**

Columns/Departments: Writers & Readers (established writers talk about writing for the library audience), 1,000 words. **Buys 4 mss/year.** Query with published clips. **Payment varies.**

Tips: "Already-published reviewers are the best prospects. Must demonstrate an understanding of the subject matter and of the public and/or school library markets. Unsolicited reviews or articles are not welcome."

$ $ BOULEVARD, Opojaz, Inc., 6614 Clayton Rd., PMB 325, Richmond Heights MO 63117. (314)862-2643. Fax: (314)781-7250. Website: www.richardburgin.com. **Contact:** Richard Burgin, editor. **100% freelance written.** Triannual magazine covering fiction, poetry, and essays. "*Boulevard* is a diverse literary magazine presenting original creative work by well-known authors, as well as by writers of exciting promise." Estab. 1985. Circ. 11,000. Pays on publication. Publishes ms an average of 9 months after acceptance. Byline given. Offers no kill fee. Buys first North American serial rights. Accepts queries by mail, phone. Accepts simultaneous submissions. Responds in 2 weeks to queries; 3 months to mss. Sample copy for $8. Writer's guidelines online.

O→ Break in with "a touching, intelligent, and original story, poem or essay."

Nonfiction: Book excerpts, essays, interview/profile, opinion, photo feature. "No pornography, science fiction, children's stories, or westerns." **Buys 10 mss/year.** Send complete ms. Length: 8,000 words maximum. **Pays $50-350 (sometimes higher).**

Fiction: Confessions, experimental, mainstream, novel excerpts. "We do not want erotica, science fiction, romance, western, or children's stories." **Buys 20 mss/year.** Send complete ms. Length: 8,000 words maximum. **Pays $150-350.**

Poetry: Avant-garde, free verse, haiku, traditional. "Do not send us light verse." **Buys 80 poems/year.** Submit maximum 5 poems. Length: 200 lines. **$25-250 (sometimes higher).**

Tips: "Read the magazine first. The work *Boulevard* publishes is generally recognized as among the finest in the country. We continue to seek more good literary or cultural essays. Send only your best work."

N $ BRAIN, CHILD, The Magazine for Thinking Mothers, March Press, P.O. Box 1161, Harrisonburg VA 22803. E-mail: editor@brainchildmag.com. Website: www.brainchildmag.com. Co-Editors: Jennifer Niesslein and Stephanie Wilkinson. **90% freelance written.** Quarterly magazine covering the experience of motherhood. "*Brain, Child* reflects modern motherhood—the way it really is. We like to think of *Brain, Child* as a community, for and by mothers who like to think about what raising kids does for (and to) the mind and soul. *Brain, Child* isn't your typical parenting magazine. We couldn't cupcake-decorate our way out of a paper bag. We are more 'literary' than 'how-to,' more *New Yorker* than *Parents*. We shy away from expert advice on childrearing in favor of first-hand reflections by great writers (Jane Smiley, Barbara Ehrenreich, Anne Tyler) on life as a mother. Each quarterly issue is full of essays, features, humor, reviews, fiction, art, cartoons, abd our readers' own stories. Our philosophy is pretty simple: Motherhood is worthy of literature. And there are a lot of ways to mother, all of them interesting. We're proud to be publishing articles and essays that are smart, down to earth, sometimes funny, and sometimes poignant." Estab. 2000. Circ. 12,000. Pays on publication. Publishes ms an average of 6 months after acceptance. Byline given. Buys first North American serial, electronic, *Brain, Child* anthology rights rights. Editorial lead time 3 months. Submit seasonal material 6 months in advance. Accepts queries by mail, e-mail. Accepts previously published material. Accepts simultaneous submissions. Responds in 1 month to queries; 1-3 months to mss. Sample copy online. Writer's guidelines online.

Nonfiction: Essays (including debate), humor, in-depth features. No how-to articles, advice, or tips. **Buys 40-50 mss/year.** Query with published clips for features and debate essays; send complete ms for essays. Length: 800-5,000 words. **Payment varies.** Sometimes pays expenses of writers on assignment.

Photos: State availability with submission. Reviews contact sheets, prints, GIF/JPEG files. Model releases required.

Fiction: "We publish fiction that has a strong motherhood theme." Mainstream, literary. No genre fiction. **Buys 4 mss/year.** Send complete ms. Length: 800-5,000 words. **Payment varies.**

$ $ BRICK, A Literary Journal, Brick, Box 537, Station Q, Toronto ON M4T 2M5, Canada. E-mail: info@brickmag.com. Website: www.brickmag.com. Editor: Michael Redhill. **Contact:** Vivien Leong, managing/contributing editor. **90% freelance written.** Semiannual magazine covering literature and the arts. "We publish literary nonfiction of a very high quality on a range of arts and culture subjects." Estab. 1975. Circ. 3,000. Pays on publication. Publishes ms an average of 3 months after acceptance. Byline given. Buys first world, first serial, one-time rights. Editorial lead time 5 months. Accepts queries by mail, e-mail. Responds in 6 weeks to queries; 4 months to mss. Sample copy for $12, plus $3 shipping. Writer's guidelines online.

Nonfiction: Essays, historical/nostalgic, interview/profile, opinion, travel. No fiction, poetry, personal real-life experience, or book reviews. **Buys 30-40 mss/year.** Send complete ms. Length: 250-2,500 words. **Pays $75-500 (Canadian).**

Photos: State availability with submission. Reviews transparencies, prints, GIF/JPEG files. Buys one-time rights. Offers $25-50/photo.

Tips: "*Brick* is interested in polished work by writers who are widely read and in touch with contemporary culture. The magazine is serious, but not fusty. We like to feel the writer's personality in the piece, too."

$ $ THE CAPILANO REVIEW, 2055 Purcell Way, North Vancouver BC V7J 3H5, Canada. E-mail: tcr@capcollege.bc.ca. Website: www.capcollege.bc.ca/dept/TCR/tcr. **Contact:** Sharon Thesen, editor. **100% freelance written.** "Triannual visual and literary arts magazine that publishes only what the editors consider to be the very best fiction, poetry, drama, or visual art being produced. *TCR* editors are interested in fresh, original work that stimulates and challenges readers. Over the years, the magazine has developed a reputation for pushing beyond the boundaries of traditional art and writing. We are interested in work that is new in concept and in execution." Estab. 1972. Circ. 900. Pays on publication. Publishes ms an average of 2-4 months after acceptance. Byline given. Buys first North American serial rights. Accepts queries by mail. Responds in 1 month to queries; 4 months to mss. Sample copy for $9. Writer's guidelines for #10 SASE with IRC or Canadian stamps or online.

Fiction: Query by mail or send complete ms with SASE and Canadian postage or IRCs. Experimental, novel excerpts, literary. "No traditional, conventional fiction. Want to see more innovative, genre-blurring work." **Buys 10-15 mss/year.** Length: 6,000 words. **Pays $50-200.**

Poetry: Submit maximum 5-10 poems (with SASE and Canadian postage or IRCs). Avant-garde, free verse. **Buys 40 poems/year. Pays $50-200.**

$ THE CHARITON REVIEW, Truman State University, Kirksville MO 63501-9915. (660)785-4499. Fax: (660)785-7486. **Contact:** Jim Barnes, editor. **100% freelance written.** Semiannual (fall and spring) magazine covering contemporary fiction, poetry, translation, and book reviews. "We demand only excellence in fiction and fiction translation for a general and college readership." Estab. 1975. Circ. 600. Pays on publication. Publishes ms an average of 6 months after acceptance. Byline given. Buys first North American serial rights. Accepts queries by mail. Responds in 1 week to queries; 1 month to mss. Sample copy for $5 and 7x10 SAE with 4 first-class stamps.

Nonfiction: Essays (essay reviews of books). **Buys 2-5 mss/year.** Send complete ms. Length: 1,000-5,000 words. **Pays $15.**

Fiction: Ethnic, experimental, mainstream, novel excerpts, traditional. "We are not interested in slick or sick material." **Buys 6-10 mss/year.** Send complete ms. Length: 1,000-6,000 words. **Pays $5/page (up to $50).**

Poetry: Avant-garde, traditional. **Buys 50-55 poems/year.** Submit maximum 5 poems. Length: Open. **Pays $5/page.**

Tips: "Read *Chariton*. Know the difference between good literature and bad. Know what magazine might be interested in your work. We are not a trendy magazine. We publish only the best. All sections are open to freelancers. Know your market or you are wasting your time—and mine. Do *not* write for guidelines; the only guideline is excellence."

$ THE CHATTAHOOCHEE REVIEW, Georgia Perimeter College, 2101 Womack Rd., Dunwoody GA 30338-4497. (770)551-3019. Website: www.chattahoochee-review.org. **Contact:** Lawrence Hetrick, editor. Quarterly magazine. "We publish a number of Southern writers, but *Chattahoochee Review* is not by design a regional magazine. All themes, forms, and styles are considered as long as they impact the whole person: heart, mind, intuition, and imagination." Estab. 1980. Circ. 1,350. Pays on publication. Publishes ms an average of 3 months after acceptance. Byline given. Buys first rights. Accepts queries by mail. Accepts simultaneous submissions. Responds in 2 weeks to queries; 4 months to mss. Sample copy for $6. Writer's guidelines online.

Nonfiction: "We look for distinctive, honest personal essays and creative nonfiction of any kind, including the currently popular memoiristic narrative. We publish interviews with writers of all kinds: literary, academic, journalistic, and popular. We also review selected current offerings in fiction, poetry, and nonfiction, including works on photography and the visual arts, with an emphasis on important southern writers and artisits. We do not often, if ever, publish technical, critical, theoretical, or scholarly work about literature although we are interested in essays written for general readers about writers, their careers, and their work." Essays (interviews with authors, reviews). **Buys 10 mss/year.** Send complete ms. Length: 5,000 words maximum.

Photos: State availability with submission. Buys one-time rights. Negotiates payment individually. Identification of subjects required.

Fiction: Accepts all subject matter except science fiction and romance. "No juvenile, romance, science fiction." **Buys 12 mss/year.** Send complete ms. Length: 6,000 words maximum. **Pays $20/page.**

Poetry: Avant-garde, free verse, haiku, light verse, traditional. **Buys 60 poems/year.** Submit maximum 5 poems. **Pays $30/poem.**

Tips: "Become familiar with our journal and the type of work we regularly publish."

$ CHELSEA, Chelsea Associates, P.O. Box 773 Cooper Station, New York NY 10276-0773. **Contact:** Alfredo de Palchi, editor. **70% freelance written.** Semiannual magazine. "We stress style, variety, originality. No special biases or requirements. Flexible attitudes, eclectic material. We take an active interest, as always, in cross-cultural exchanges, superior translations, and are leaning toward cosmopolitan, interdisciplinary techniques, but maintain no strictures against traditional modes." Estab. 1958. Circ. 1,800. Pays on publication. Publishes ms an average of 6 months after acceptance. Byline given. Buys first North American serial rights. Accepts queries by mail. Responds in 3-5 months to mss. Sample copy for $6. Writer's guidelines and contest guidelines available for #10 SASE.

- *Chelsea* also sponsors fiction and poetry contests. Poetry Deadline: December 15; Fiction Deadline: June 15. Send SASE for guidelines.

Nonfiction: Essays, book reviews (query first with sample). **Buys 6 mss/year.** Send complete ms with SASE. Length: 6,000 words. **Pays $15/page.**

Fiction: Mainstream, novel excerpts, literary. **Buys 12 mss/year.** Send complete ms. Length: 5,000-6,000 words. **Pays $15/page.**

Poetry: Avant-garde, free verse, traditional. **Buys 60-75 poems/year. Pays $15/page.**

Tips: "We only accept written correspondence. We are looking for more super translations, first-rate fiction, and work by writers of color. No need to query; submit complete manuscript. We suggest writers look at a recent issue of *Chelsea*."

$ $ CHICKEN SOUP FOR THE SOUL, 101 Stories to Open the Heart and Rekindle the Spirit, Chicken Soup for the Soul Enterprises, Inc., P.O, Box 30880, Santa Barbara CA 93130. (805)682-6311. Fax: (805)563-2945. E-mail: nautio@chickensoup.com. Website: www.chickensoup.com. Managing Editor: Heather McNamara. **Contact:** Nancy Mitchell-Autio, acquisitions editor. **95% freelance written.** Paperback with 8-12 publications/year featuring inspirational, heartwarming, uplifting short stories. Estab. 1993. Circ. Over 40 titles; 60 million books in print. Pays on publication. Publishes ms an average of 8 months after acceptance. Byline given. Buys all rights. Accepts queries by mail, e-mail, fax. Accepts previously published material. Accepts simultaneous submissions. Responds upon consideration to queries. Sample copy not available. Writer's guidelines online.

Nonfiction: Humor, inspirational, personal experience, religious. Special issues: Traveling sisterhood, Mother-Daughter stories, Christian teen, Christmas stories, stories by and/or about men, on love, kindness, parenting, family, Nascar racing, athletes, teachers, fishing, adoption, volunteers. No sermon, essay, eulogy, term paper, journal entry, political, or controversial issues. **Buys 1,000 mss/year.** Send complete ms. Length: 300-1,200 words. **Pays $300.**

Poetry: Traditional. No controversial poetry. **Buys 50 poems/year.** Submit maximum 5 poems. **Pays $300.**

Fillers: Anecdotes, facts, gags to be illustrated by cartoonist, short humor. **Buys 50/year. Pays $300.**

Tips: "We prefer submissions to be sent via our website at www.chickensoup.com. Print submissions should be on 8½×11 paper in 12 point Times New Roman font. Type authors contact information appears on the first page of story. Stories are to be nonfiction. No anonymous or author unknown submissions are accepted. We do not return submissions."

N $ $ CICADA MAGAZINE, Cricket Magazine Group, P.O. Box 300, Peru IL 61354. (815)224-6656. Fax: (815)224-6615. Website: www.cricketmag.com.; www.cicadamag.com. Editor-in-Chief: Marianne Carus. Executive Editor: Deborah-Vetter. Associate Editor: Tracy C. Schoenle. Senior Art Director: Ron McCutchan. **Contact:** Submissions Editor. **100% freelance written.** Bimonthly magazine for teenagers and young adults. "*Cicada*, for ages 14 and up, publishes original short stories, poems, and first-person essays written for teens and young adults." Estab. 1998. Circ. 15,000. Pays on publication. Publishes ms an average of 1 year after acceptance. Byline given. Rights vary. Accepts queries by mail. Accepts previously published material. Accepts simultaneous submissions. Responds in 3 months to mss. Sample copy for $8.50. Writer's guidelines for SASE and on website.

Nonfiction: Looking for first-person experiences that are relevant and interesting to teenagers. Essays, personal experience. Send complete ms. Length: up to 5,000 words. **Pays 25¢/word.**

Reprints: Send ms. Payment varies.

Fiction: Deborah Vetter, executive editor. Looking for realistic, contemporary, historical fiction, adventure, humor, fantasy, science fiction. Main protagonist should be age 14 or older. Stories should have a genuine teen sensibility and be aimed at readers in high school or college. Adventure, fantasy, historical, humorous, mainstream, mystery, romance, science fiction, western, sports. Send complete ms. Length: 3,000-15,000 words. **Pays 25¢/word, and 2 contributor's copies.**

Poetry: Looking for serious or humorous; rhymed or free verse. Free verse, light verse, traditional. Length: Up to 25 lines. **Pays up to $3/line.**

Tips: "An exact word count should be noted on each manuscript submitted. For poetry, indicate number of lines instead. Word count includes every word, but does not include the title of the manuscript or the author's name."

N $ CITY SLAB, Urban Tales of the Grotesque, City Slab Publications, 1705 Summit Ave., #211, Seattle WA 98122. (206)568-4343. E-mail: dave@cityslab.com. Website: www.cityslab.com. **Contact:** Dave Lindschmior, editor. **90% freelance written.** Quarterly magazine covering horror and horror/crime mix. "*City Slab* magazine is hard-edged, adult fiction." Estab. 2002. Pays on publication. Publishes ms an average of 3 months after acceptance. Byline given. Offers 50% kill fee. Buys first North American serial rights. Accepts queries by mail, e-mail. Responds in 3 weeks to queries; 2 months to mss. Sample copy for $6. Writer's guidelines online.

Nonfiction: Essays, interview/profile, photo feature. **Buys 4 mss/year.** Send complete ms. Length: 2,000-3,000 words. **Pays $50-100, plus contributor copies.**

Photos: State availability of or send photos with submission. Reviews JPEG files. Buys one-time rights. Offers no additional payment for photos accepted with ms. Model releases required.

Fiction: "*City Slab* wants to publish well-thought-out, literary-quality horror." Erotica, experimental, horror. Does not want to see children/youth in sexually oriented stories. **Buys 24 mss/year.** Send complete ms. Length: 5,000 words maximum. **Pays 1-10¢/word.**

Tips: "Read not only the horror greats—Barker, King, Campbell, Lovecraft, etc., but also the classics—Dickens, Hemingway, Oates, Steinbeck to see how a great tale is woven."

$ COLORADO REVIEW, Center for Literary Publishing, Department of English, Colorado State University, Fort Collins CO 80523. (970)491-5449. E-mail: creview@colostate.edu. Website: www.coloradoreview.com. **Contact:** Stephanie G'Schwind, editor. Literary magazine published 3 times/year. Estab. 1972. Circ. 1,300. Pays on publication. Publishes ms an average of 1 year after acceptance. Byline given. Buys first North American serial, "we assign copyright to author on request." rights. Editorial lead time 1 year. Responds in 2 months to mss. Sample copy for $10. Writer's guidelines online.

Nonfiction: Personal essays, creative nonfiction. **Buys 3-5 mss/year.** Send complete ms. **Pays $5/page.**

Fiction: Short fiction. No genre fiction. Ethnic, experimental, mainstream, contemporary. "No genre fiction." **Buys 15-20 mss/year.** Send complete ms. Length: under 6,000. **Pays $5/page.**

Poetry: Considers poetry of any style. Don Revell or Jorie Graham, poetry editors. **Buys 60-100 poems/year. Pays $5/page.**

Tips: Manuscripts are read from September 1 to April 30. Manuscripts recieved between May 1 and August 30 will be returned unread.

$ $ CONFRONTATION, A Literary Journal, Long Island University, Brookville NY 11548. (516)299-2720. Fax: (516)299-2735. E-mail: mtucker@liu.edu. Assistant to Editor: Michael Hartnett. **Contact:** Martin Tucker, editor-in-chief. **75% freelance written.** Semiannual magazine. "We are eclectic in our taste. Excellence of style is our dominant concern." Estab. 1968. Circ. 2,000. Pays on publication. Publishes ms an average of 1 year after acceptance. Byline given. Offers kill fee. Buys first North American serial, first, one-time, all rights. Accepts queries by mail, e-mail, phone. Accepts simultaneous submissions. Responds in 3 weeks to queries; 2 months to mss. Sample copy for $3. Writer's guidelines not available.

Nonfiction: Essays, personal experience. **Buys 15 mss/year.** Send complete ms. Length: 1,500-5,000 words. **Pays $100-300 for assigned articles; $15-300 for unsolicited articles.**

Photos: State availability with submission. Buys one-time rights. Offers no additional payment for photos accepted with ms.

Fiction: Jonna Semeiks. "We judge on quality, so genre is open." Experimental, mainstream, novel excerpts, slice-of-life vignettes, contemporary, prose poem. "No 'proselytizing' literature or genre fiction." **Buys 60-75 mss/year.** Send complete ms. Length: 6,000 words. **Pays $25-250.**

Poetry: Michael Hartnett. Avant-garde, free verse, haiku, light verse, traditional. **Buys 60-75 poems/year.** Submit maximum 6 poems. Length: Open. **Pays $10-100.**

Tips: "Most open to fiction and poetry. Study our magazine."

$ THE CONNECTICUT POETRY REVIEW, The Connecticut Poetry Review Press, P.O. Box 818, Stonington CT 06378. Managing Editor: Harley More. **Contact:** J. Claire White. **60% freelance written.** Annual magazine covering poetry/literature. Estab. 1981. Circ. 500. **Pays on acceptance.** Byline sometimes given. Buys first rights. Editorial lead time 4 months. Submit seasonal material 4 months in advance. Accepts queries by mail. Responds in 1 month to queries; 3 months to mss. Sample copy for $3.50 and #10 SASE. Writer's guidelines for #10 SASE.

Nonfiction: Book excerpts, essays. **Buys 18 mss/year.**

Fiction: Experimental.

Poetry: Avant-garde, free verse, haiku, traditional. No light verse. **Buys 20-30 poems/year.** Submit maximum 4 poems. Length: 3-25 lines. **Pays $5-10.**

N $ CONTEMPORARY VERSE 2, The Canadian Journal of Poetry and Critical Writing, Contemporary Verse 2, Inc., 207-100 Arthur St., Winnipeg MB R3B 1H3, Canada. (204)949-1365. Fax: (204)942-5754. E-mail: cv2@mb.sympatico.ca. Website: www.contemporaryverse2.ca. **Contact:** Clarise Foster, managing editor. **75% freelance written.** Quarterly magazine covering poetry and critical writing about poetry. "*CV2* publishes poetry of demonstrable quality as well as critical writing in the form of interviews, essays, articles, and reviews. With the critical writing we tend to focus on intelligent but accessible to create a discussion of poetry which will interest a broad range of readers, including those who might be skeptical about the value of poetry." Estab. 1975. Circ. 600. Pays on publication. Byline given. Offers 50% kill fee. Not copyrighted. Buys first North American serial, second serial (reprint) rights. Editorial lead time 3-6 months. Submit seasonal material 3-6 months in advance. Accepts queries by mail, e-mail, phone. Responds in 2-3 weeks to queries; 3-8 months to mss. Sample copy for $8. Writer's guidelines online.

Nonfiction: Essays, interview/profile, book reviews. No content that is not about poetry. **Buys 10-30 mss/year.** Query. Length: 800-3,000 words. **Pays $40-130 for assigned articles.** Pays in contributor copies only if requested by the author.

Poetry: Avant-garde, free verse. No rhyming verse, traditionally inspirational. **Buys 110-120 poems/year.** Submit maximum 6 poems.

N $ CRABGRASS ARIA, 1124 Columbia NE, Albuquerque NM 87106. E-mail: art_coop@yahoo.com. Website: www.geocities.com/art_coop. **Contact:** Charli Valdes, editor. **100% freelance written.** Annual magazine. Estab. 1996. Pays on publication. Buys first North American serial, one-time, electronic, one-time anthology rights. Accepts queries by mail. Accepts simultaneous submissions. Sample copy not available. Writer's guidelines for #10 SASE.

Nonfiction: Needs memoir that is original and has an edge to it. Art, travel, environmental with global appeal, profiles and news that elicits personality, local perspectives from around the globe. Strange, fresh ideas and style. Global perspective, international and comparative content. Scholarly articles with zip. Also needs translations. Buys 1-5 translation mss/year. Must have permission of the author. Submit with original and with translator's preface. **Pays $25, plus contributor copies for translations**. Special issues: Themes include Ekphrasis, immigration, Spain, dogs. The magazine is not strictly a theme-oriented magazine. "Please submit your work regardless of upcoming themes." **Buys 2-7 mss/year.** Send complete ms with cover sheet, bio, and publications list. Length: 1,000-10,000 words. **Pays $50 minimum, plus contributor copies.**

Photos: Buys one-time rights. Negotiates payment individually. Identification of subjects, model releases required.

Fiction: Needs fiction with strong characters, enticing plots, strange and fresh ideas and style. Global perspective, international and comparative content. Code switching, play with language (and languages). No science fiction, horror, fantasy, juvenile, etc. **Buys 2-7 mss/year.** Length: 1,000-10,000 words. **Pays $50, plus contributor copies.**

Poetry: No science fiction, horror, fantasy, juvenile, etc. **Buys 6-20 poems/year.**

$ DESCANT, Descant Arts & Letters Foundation, P.O. Box 314, Station P, Toronto ON M5S 2S8, Canada. (416)593-2557. Fax: (416)593-9362. E-mail: descant@web.net. Website: www.descant.on.ca. Editor: Karen Mulhallen. **Contact:** Mary Newberry, managing editor. Quarterly journal. Estab. 1970. Circ. 1,200. Pays on publication. Publishes ms an average of 16 months after acceptance. Editorial lead time 4 months. Accepts queries by mail, e-mail, phone. Sample copy for $8. Writer's guidelines online.

- Pays $100 honorarium, plus 1-year's subscription for accepted submissions of any kind.

Nonfiction: Book excerpts, essays, interview/profile, personal experience, historical.

Photos: State availability with submission. Reviews contact sheets, prints. Buys one-time rights. Offers no additional payment for photos accepted with ms.

Fiction: Short stories or book excerpts. Maximum length 6,000 words; 3,000 words or less preferred. Ethnic, experimental, historical, humorous. No gothic, religious, beat. Send complete ms. **Pays $100 (Canadian); additional copies $8.**

Poetry: Free verse, light verse, traditional. Submit maximum 6 poems.

Tips: "Familiarize yourself with our magazine before submitting."

N $ DOWNSTATE STORY, 1825 Maple Ridge, Peoria IL 61614. (309)688-1409. E-mail: ehopkins@prairienet.org. Website: www.wiu.edu/users/mfgeh/dss. **Contact:** Elaine Hopkins, editor. Annual magazine covering short fiction with some connection with Illinois or the Midwest. "Short fiction—some connection with Illinois or the Midwest." Estab. 1992. Circ. 500. **Pays on acceptance.** Publishes ms an average of 1 year after acceptance. Buys first rights. Accepts simultaneous submissions. "ASAP" to mss. Sample copy for $8. Writer's guidelines online.

Fiction: Adventure, ethnic, experimental, historical, horror, humorous, mainstream, mystery, romance, science fiction, suspense, western. No porn. **Buys 10 mss/year.** Length: 300-2,000 words. **Pays $50.**

Tips: Wants more political fiction. Publishes short shorts and literary essays.

$ DREAMS & VISIONS, New Frontiers in Christian Fiction, Skysong Press, 35 Peter St. S., Orillia ON L3V 5A8, Canada. (705)329-1770. Fax: (705)329-1770. E-mail: skysong@bconnex.net. Website: www.bconnex.net/~skysong. **Contact:** Steve Stanton, editor. **100% freelance written.** Semiannual magazine. "Innovative literary fiction for adult Christian readers." Estab. 1988. Circ. 200. Pays on publication. Publishes ms an average of 1 year after acceptance. Byline given. Buys first North American serial, second serial (reprint) rights. Editorial lead time 1 year. Accepts queries by mail, e-mail. Accepts simultaneous submissions. Responds in 6 weeks to queries; 6 months to mss. Sample copy for $4.95. Writer's guidelines online.

Fiction: Experimental, fantasy, humorous, mainstream, mystery, novel excerpts, religious, science fiction, slice-of-life vignettes. "We do not publish stories that glorify violence or perversity." **Buys 10 mss/year.** Send complete ms. Length: 2,000-6,000 words. **Pays ½¢/word.**

$ DREAMS OF DECADENCE, Vampire Poetry and Fiction, DNA Publications, P.O. Box 2988, Radford VA 24143-2988. (540)763-2925. Fax: (540)763-2924. E-mail: dreamsofdecadence@dnapublications.com. Website: www.dnapublications.com/dreams. **Contact:** Angela Kessler, editor. Quarterly magazine featuring vampire fiction and poetry. Specializes in "vampire fiction and poetry for vampire fans." Estab. 1995. Circ. 7,500. Pays on publication. Publishes ms an average of 6 months after acceptance. Buys first North American serial rights. Accepts simultaneous submissions. Responds in 1 month to queries; 1 month to mss. Sample copy for $5. Writer's guidelines online.

Fiction: "I like elegant prose with a Gothic feel. The emphasis is on dark fantasy rather than horror. No vampire feeds, vampire has sex, someone becomes a vampire pieces." Vampires. "I am not interested in seeing the clichés redone." **Buys 30-40 mss/year.** Send complete ms. Length: 1,000-15,000 words. **Pays 1-5¢/word.**

Poetry: "Looking for all forms; however, the less horrific and the more explicitly vampiric a poem is, the more likely it is to be accepted." **Pays $3/short poem; $5/long poem; $20/featured poet.**

Tips: "We look for atmospheric, well-written stories with original ideas, not rehashes."

$ $ EVENT, Douglas College, P.O. Box 2503, New Westminster BC V3L 5B2, Canada. (604)527-5293. Fax: (604)527-5095. E-mail: event@douglas.bc.ca. Website: event.douglas.bc.ca. **Contact:** Ian Cockfield, managing editor. **100% freelance written.** Magazine published 3 times/year containing fiction, poetry, creative nonfiction, notes on writing, and reviews. "We are eclectic and always open to content that invites involvement. Generally, we like strong narrative." Estab. 1971. Circ. 1,250. Pays on publication. Publishes ms an average of 8 months after acceptance. Byline given. Buys first North American serial rights. Accepts queries by mail, e-mail, fax, phone. Accepts simultaneous submissions. Responds in 1 month to queries; 6 months to mss. Sample copy for $5. Writer's guidelines online.

- *Event* does not read mss in July, August, December, and January. No e-mail submissions. All submissions must include SASE (Canadian postage or IRCs only).

Fiction: Christine Dewar, fiction editor. "We look for readability, style, and writing that invites involvement." Submit maximum 2 stories. Humorous, contemporary. "No technically poor or unoriginal pieces." **Buys 12-15 mss/year.** Send complete ms. Length: 5,000 words maximum. **Pays $22/page to $500.**

Poetry: "We tend to appreciate the narrative and sometimes the confessional modes." Gillian Harding-Russell, poetry editor. Free verse, prose. No light verse. **Buys 30-40 poems/year.** Submit maximum 10 poems. **Pays $25-500.**

Tips: "Write well and read some past issues of *Event*."

N $ FICTION, c/o Department of English, City College, 138th St. & Covenant Ave., New York NY 10031. (212)650-6319. E-mail: fiction@fictioninc.com. Website: www.fictioninc.com. **Contact:** Mark J. Mirsky, editor; Kathy Fowler, managing editor. Semiannual magazine. "As the name implies, we publish only fiction; we are looking for the best new writing available, leaning toward the unconventional. *Fiction* has traditionally attempted to make accessible the unaccessible, to bring the experimental to a broader audience." Estab. 1972. Circ. 4,000. Publishes ms an average of 1 year after acceptance. Buys first rights. Accepts simultaneous submissions. Responds in 3 months to mss. Sample copy for $5. Writer's guidelines online.

Fiction: Experimental, humorous, contemporary, literary, translations. No romance, science fiction, etc. **Buys 24-40 mss/year.** Length: 5,000 words. **Pays $114.**

Tips: "The guiding principle of *Fiction* has always been to go to terra incognita in the writing of the imagination and to ask that modern fiction set itself serious questions, if often in absurd and comedic voices, interrogating the nature of the real and the fantastic. It represents no particular school of fiction, except the innovative. Its pages have often been a harbor for writers at odds with each other. As a result of its willingness to publish the difficult, experimental, unusual, while not excluding the well known, *Fiction* has a unique reputation in the U.S. and abroad as a journal of future directions."

$ FIELD, Contemporary Poetry & Poetics, Oberlin College Press, 10 N. Professor St., Oberlin OH 44074-1095. (440)775-8408. Fax: (440)775-8124. E-mail: oc.press@oberlin.edu. Website: www.oberlin.edu/~ocpress. **Contact:** Linda Slocum, managing editor. **60% freelance written.** Semiannual magazine of poetry, poetry in translation, and essays on contemporary poetry by poets. No electronic submissions. Estab. 1969. Circ. 1,500. Pays on publication. Byline given. Buys first rights. Editorial lead time 4 months. Accepts queries by mail, e-mail, fax, phone. Responds in 6 weeks to mss. Sample copy for $7. Writer's guidelines online.

Poetry: Buys 100 poems/year. Submit maximum 5 with SASE poems. **Pays $15/page.**

Tips: "Submit 3-5 of your best poems with a cover letter. No simultaneous submissions and include a SASE. Keep trying! Submissions are read year-round."

$ THE FIRST LINE, K Street Ink, P.O. Box 0382, Plano TX 75025-0382. E-mail: info@thefirstline.com. Website: www.thefirstline.com. Co-editors: David LaBounty and Jeff Adams. **Contact:** Robin LaBounty, ms coordinator. **95% freelance written.** Quarterly magazine. *The First Line* is a magazine that explores the different directions writers can take when they start from the same place. All stories must be written with the first line provided by the magazine. Estab. 1999. Circ. 250. Pays on publication. Publishes ms an average of 1 month after acceptance. Byline given. Buys first North American serial, electronic rights. Editorial lead time 2 months. Accepts queries by mail, e-mail. Responds in 1 week to queries; 2 months to mss. Sample copy for $3. Writer's guidelines online.

Nonfiction: David LaBounty, editor. Essays, interview/profile, Book Reviews. **Buys 4-8 mss/year.** Query. Length: 300-1,000 words. **Pays $5 for assigned articles; $5 for unsolicited articles.**

Fiction: Adventure, ethnic, experimental, fantasy, historical, horror, humorous, mainstream, mystery, romance, science fiction, suspense, western. No stories that do not start with the issue's first sentence. **Buys 40-60 mss/year.** Send complete ms. Length: 300-1,500 words. **Pays $5.**

$ FRANK, An International Journal of Contemporary Writing & Art, Association Frank, 32 rue Edouard Vaillant, Montreuil, France. (33)(1)48596658. Fax: (33)(1)48596668. E-mail: submissions@readfrank.com. Website: www.readfrank.com or www.frank.ly. **Contact:** David Applefield, editor. **80% freelance written.** Magazine covering contemporary writing of all genres. Bilingual. "Writing that takes risks and isn't ethnocentric is looked upon favorably." Estab. 1983. Circ. 4,000. Pays on publication. Publishes ms an average of 1 year after acceptance. Byline given. Buys one-time rights. Editorial lead time 6 months. Responds in 1 month to queries; 2 months to mss. Sample copy for $10. Writer's guidelines online.

Nonfiction: Interview/profile, travel. **Buys 2 mss/year.** Query. **Pays $100 for assigned articles.**

Photos: State availability with submission. Buys one-time rights. Negotiates payment individually.

Fiction: Experimental, novel excerpts, international. "At *Frank*, we publish fiction, poetry, literary and art interviews, and translations. We like work that falls between existing genres and has social or political consciousness." **Buys 8 mss/year.** Send complete ms. Length: 1,000-3,000 words. **Pays $10/printed page.**

Poetry: Avant-garde, translations. **Buys 20 poems/year.** Submit maximum 10 poems. **Pays $20.**

Tips: "Suggest what you do or know best. Avoid query form letters—we won't read the manuscript. Looking for excellent literary/cultural interviews with leading American writers or cultural figures. Very receptive to new Foreign Dossiers of writing from a particular country."

N $ FUTURES MYSTERIOUS ANTHOLOGY MAGAZINE, 3039 38th Ave., Minneapolis MN 55406-2140. (612)724-4023. E-mail: babs@fmam.biz. Website: www.futuresforstorylovers.com. Editor: Barbara (Babs) Lakey. **Contact:** Babs Lakey, publisher. **98% freelance written.** Bimonthly print and online magazine. "We nourish writers and artists; attempt to throw out the net so they can fly without fear! The futures in commodities is a good analog for writers and artists. Their work, in many cases, is greatly undervalued. Their future market value will be higher than can be imagined. In the writing community there is a tremendous amount of energy; a rolling boil. It takes the form of many people with talent and motivation anxious to unleash their creative juices." Estab. 1998. Circ. 2,000. Pays on publication. Publishes ms an average of 8 months after acceptance. Byline given. Buys first rights. Editorial lead time 8 months. Submit seasonal material 6 months in advance. Accepts queries by e-mail. Accepts simultaneous submissions. Responds in 1 week to queries; 2 months to mss. Sample copy for $5 includes shipping. Writer's guidelines online.

- The publisher reports that the print magazine now publishes fiction only.

O-π "Break in through the Starting Line column for new writers. tell us you're view!"

Nonfiction: Sally Carson, editor. Essays, exposé, general interest, historical/nostalgic, how-to, humor, inspirational, new product, opinion, personal experience, photo feature, technical, success stories with a point. "No political ranting or sappy memoirs." **Buys 50 mss/year.** Query. Length: 250-2,000 words. **No pay online yet; ad space given.**

Columns/Departments: Sally Carson, editor. Starting Line (fiction from first time publications, 1,000-4,000 words;

Writer's Share (comments on life of a writer), 100 words. **Buys 60 mss/year.** Send complete ms. **No pay online yet; ad space given.**

Fiction: Brian Lawrence, editor. "We do serialized fiction too and love artists who are writers/writers who are artists. Illustrate your own work if you like." Adventure, ethnic, experimental, fantasy, historical, horror, humorous, mainstream, mystery, romance, science fiction, suspense, western, Cartoons. "We would like to see more thrillers, more mystery and suspense, also family mainstream. No erotica or pornography." **Buys 120-150 mss/year.** Send complete ms. Length: 500-12,000 words. **Pays $5-25.**

Poetry: Scott Robison, editor. Avant-garde, free verse, light verse, traditional, narrative. **Buys 40-80 poems/year.** Submit maximum 5 poems. **Pays $2-5.**

Fillers: Illustrations with humor. **Pays $5-25.**

The online magazine contains nonfiction, poetry, reviews and columns (the print version contains fiction only). Contact: Sally Carson (ealake1@aol.com) for nonfiction and columns, George Scott (futuresreviews@aol.com) for book and short story reviews, Scott Robison (poemfutures@hotmail.com) for poetry.

Tips: "Reading what we have published is still the best but we do love to see excitement and enthusiasm for the craft, and those who care enough to self-edit. Send SASE for anything you want returned and do not send mail that requires a signature on arrival. Give us a try. We want to see you succeed."

$THE GEORGIA REVIEW, The University of Georgia, 012 Gilbert Hall, University of Georgia, Athens GA 30602-9009. (706)542-3481. Fax: (706)542-0047. E-mail: garev@uga.edu. Website: www.uga.edu/garev. Managing Editor: Annette Hatton. **Contact:** T.R. Hummer, editor. **99% freelance written.** Quarterly journal. "Our readers are educated, inquisitive people who read a lot of work in the areas we feature, so they expect only the best in our pages. All work submitted should show evidence that the writer is at least as well-educated and well-read as our readers. Essays should be authoritative but accessible to a range of readers." Estab. 1947. Circ. 5,000. Pays on publication. Publishes ms an average of 6 months after acceptance. Byline given. Buys first North American serial rights. Accepts queries by mail. Responds in 2 weeks to queries; 3 months to mss. Sample copy for $7. Writer's guidelines online.

- No simultaneous or electronic submissions.

Nonfiction: Essays. "For the most part we are not interested in scholarly articles that are narrow in focus and/or overly burdened with footnotes. The ideal essay for *The Georgia Review* is a provocative, thesis-oriented work that can engage both the intelligent general reader and the specialist." **Buys 12-20 mss/year.** Send complete ms. **Pays $40/published page.**

Photos: Send photos with submission. Reviews 5×7 prints or larger. Buys one-time rights. Offers no additional payment for photos accepted with ms.

Fiction: "We seek original, excellent writing not bound by type. Experimental. Ordinarily we do not publish novel excerpts or works translated into English, and we strongly discourage authors from submitting these." **Buys 12-20 mss/year.** Send complete ms. Length: Open. **Pays $40/published page.**

Poetry: "We seek original, excellent poetry." **Buys 60-75 poems/year.** Submit maximum 5 poems. **Pays $3/line.**

Tips: "Unsolicited manuscripts will not be considered from May 15-August 15 (annually); all such submissions received during that period will be returned unread."

$THE GETTYSBURG REVIEW, Gettysburg College, Gettysburg PA 17325. (717)337-6770. Fax: (717)337-6775. Website: www.gettysburgreview.com. **Contact:** Peter Stitt, editor. Quarterly magazine. "Our concern is quality. Manuscripts submitted here should be extremely well written." Reading period September-May. Estab. 1988. Circ. 4,000. Pays on publication. Publishes ms an average of within 1 year after acceptance. Byline given. Buys first North American serial rights. Editorial lead time 1 year. Submit seasonal material 9 months in advance. Accepts queries by mail, fax. Accepts simultaneous submissions. Responds in 1 month to queries; 3-6 months to mss. Sample copy for $7. Writer's guidelines online.

Nonfiction: Essays. **Buys 20 mss/year.** Send complete ms. Length: 3,000-7,000 words. **Pays $25/page.**

Fiction: Mark Drew, assisant editor. High quality, literary. Experimental, historical, humorous, mainstream, novel excerpts, serialized novels, contemporary. "We require that fiction be intelligent, and esthetically written." **Buys 20 mss/year.** Send complete ms. Length: 2,000-7,000 words. **Pays $25/page.**

Poetry: Buys 50 poems/year. Submit maximum 3 poems. **Pays $2/line.**

$$GLIMMER TRAIN STORIES, Glimmer Train Press, Inc., 710 SW Madison St., Suite 504, Portland OR 97205. (503)221-0836. Fax: (503)221-0837. E-mail: linda@glimmertrain.com. Website: www.glimmertrain.com. **Contact:** Linda Swanson-Davies, co-editor. **90% freelance written.** Quarterly magazine of literary short fiction. "We are interested in well-written, emotionally-moving short stories published by unknown, as well as known, writers." Estab. 1991. Circ. 16,000. **Pays on acceptance.** Publishes ms an average of up to 2 years after acceptance. Byline given. Buys first rights. Accepts queries by e-mail. Responds in 3 months to mss. Sample copy for $9.95 or on website. Writer's guidelines online.

Fiction: Susan Burmeister-Brown and Linda Swanson-Davies. "Open to stories of all themes, all subjects." **Buys 32 mss/year.** Length: up to 12,000. **Pays $500.**

Tips: To submit a story, use the form on the website. All stories should be submitted via this electronic format. See *Glimmer Train*'s contest listings in Contest and Awards section.

$$ GRAIN LITERARY MAGAZINE, Saskatchewan Writers Guild, P.O. Box 67, Saskatoon SK S7K 3K1, Canada. (306)244-2828. Fax: (306)244-0255. E-mail: grain@sasktel.net. Website: www.grainmagazine.ca. Buisiness Administrator: Jennifer Still. **Contact:** Elizabeth Philips, editor. **100% freelance written.** Quarterly magazine covering poetry, fiction, creative nonfiction, drama. "*Grain* publishes writing of the highest quality, both traditional and innovative in nature. The *Grain* editors' aim: To publish work that challenges readers; to encourage promising new writers; and to produce a well-designed, visually interesting magazine." Estab. 1973. Circ. 1,600. Pays on publication. Publishes ms an average of 11 months after acceptance. Byline given. Buys first, "we expect acknowledgment if the piece is republished elsewhere." rights. Canadian, serial Editorial lead time 6 months. Accepts queries by mail, e-mail, fax, phone. Responds in 1 month to queries; 4 months to mss. Sample copy online. Writer's guidelines for #10 SASE or online.

Nonfiction: Interested in creative nonfiction.

Photos: Submit 12-20 slides and b&w prints, short statement (200 words), and brief résumé. Reviews transparencies, prints. Pays $100 for front cover art, $30/photo.

Fiction: Marlis Wesseler, fiction editor. Literary fiction of all types. Experimental, mainstream, Contemporary, prose poem. "No romance, confession, science fiction, vignettes, mystery." **Buys 40 mss/year.** Length: "No more than 30 pages." **Pays $40-175.**

Poetry: "High quality, imaginative, well-crafted poetry. Submit maximum 10 poems and SASE with postage or IRC's. Avant-garde, free verse, haiku, traditional. No sentimental, end-line rhyme, mundane." **Buys 78 poems/year. Pays $40-175.**

Tips: "Sweat the small stuff. Pay attention to detail, credibility. Make sure you have researched your piece and that the literal and metaphorical support one another."

$ GRANTA, The Magazine of New Writing, Granta Publications, 2⅓ Hanover Yard, Noel Rd., London NI 8BE, England. (44)(0)20 7704 9776. E-mail: editorial@granta.com. Website: www.granta.com. Editor: Ian Jack. **Contact:** Helen Gordon, editorial assistant. **100% freelance written.** Quarterly 256-page paperback book. "*Granta* magazine publishes fiction, reportage, biography and autobiography, history, travel and documentary photography. It rarely publishes 'writing about writing.' The realistic narrative - the story - is its primary form." Estab. 1979. Circ. 80,000. Pays on publication. Byline given. Offers kill fee, amount determined by arrangement. Buys world English language rights, first serial rights (minimum). "We hold more rights in pieces we commission." Editorial lead time 3 months. Accepts simultaneous submissions. Responds in 3 months to mss. Sample copy for $12.95. Writer's guidelines online.

- Queries not necessary.

Nonfiction: Ian Jack, editor. No articles or reporting whose relevancy will not last the life span of the magazine. The pieces we publish should last for several years (as the issues themselves do).

Fiction: Ian Jack, editor. **Buys no more than 2 short stories or synopsis and first chapter of a novel.** "Please do not send more than 2 stories at a time." Novel excerpts, literary. No genre fiction. Length: No limits on length. **Payment varies.**

Tips: "You must be familiar with the magazine and ask yourself honestly if you feel your piece meets our criteria. We receive many submissions every day, many of which are completely unsuitable for *Granta* (however well written).

N $ HADROSAUR TALES, Hadrosaur Productions, P.O. Box 8468, Las Cruces NM 88006-8468. E-mail: hadrosaur.productions@verizon.net. Website: www.zianet.com/hadrosaur. **Contact:** David Lee Summers, editor. **95% freelance written.** Triannual magazine published 3 times/year covering science fiction and fantasy. "*Hadrosaur Tales* is a literary science fiction and fantasy magazine published 3 times a year. We publish short stories, poetry, and articles with themes related to science fiction and fantasy. Above all, we are looking for thought-provoking ideas and good writing. Speculative fiction set in the past, present, and future is welcome. Likewise, contemporary or historical fiction is welcome as long as it has a mythic or science fictional element. Our target audience includes adult fans of the science fiction and fantasy genres along with anyone else who enjoys thought-provoking and entertaining writing." Estab. 1995. Circ. 150. **Pays on acceptance.** Publishes ms an average of 9 months after acceptance. Byline given. Offers 100% kill fee. Buys one-time rights. Editorial lead time 9-12 months. Submit seasonal material 1 year in advance. Accepts queries by mail, e-mail. Accepts previously published material. Responds in 1 week to queries; 1 month to mss. Sample copy for $6.95. Writer's guidelines online.

Nonfiction: Interview/profile, technical, articles on the craft of writing. "We do not want to see unsolicited articles—please query first if you have an idea that you think would be suitable for *Hadrosaur Tales'* audience. We do not want to see negative or derogatory articles." **Buys 1-3 mss/year.** Query. Length: 1,000-3,000 words. **Pays $4-6 for assigned articles.**

Fiction: David L. Summers, editor. Erotica, fantasy, horror, science fiction. "We do not want to see stories with graphic violence. Do not send 'mainstream' fiction with no science fictional or fantastic elements. Do not send stories with copyrighted characters, unless you're the copyright holder." **Buys 25-30 mss/year.** Send complete ms. Length: 1,000-6,000 words. **Pays $6-10.**

Poetry: Avant-garde, free verse, haiku, light verse, traditional. "Do not send 'mainstream' poetry with no science fictional or fantastic elements. Do not send poems featuring copyrighted characters, unless you're the copyright holder." **Buys 24-30 poems/year.** Submit maximum 5 poems. Length: 3-50 lines.

Tips: "Let your imagination soar to its greatest heights and write down the results. Above all, we are looking for thought-provoking ideas and good writing. Our emphasis is on character-oriented science fiction and fantasy. If we don't believe in the people living the story, we generally won't believe in the story itself. Queries are accepted year-round. Please submit complete manuscripts only during our annual reading periods: May 1-June 15 and November 1-December 15."

$ HAPPY, 240 E. 35th St., Suite 11A, New York NY 10016. E-mail: bayardx@aol.com. **Contact:** Bayard, editor. Quarterly. Estab. 1995. Circ. 500. Pays on publication. Publishes ms an average of 6-12 months after acceptance. Byline given. Buys one-time rights. Accepts queries by mail. Accepts simultaneous submissions. Responds in 1 month to queries. Sample copy for $15. Writer's guidelines for #10 SASE.

Fiction: "We accept anything that's beautifully written. Genre isn't important. It just has to be incredible writing." Erotica, ethnic, experimental, fantasy, horror, humorous, novel excerpts, science fiction, short stories. No "television rehash or religious nonsense." Want more work that is "strong, angry, empowering, intelligent, God-like, expressive." **Buys 100-130 mss/year.** Send complete ms. Length: 6,000 words maximum. **Pays 1-5¢/word.**

Tips: "Don't bore us with the mundane—blast us out of the water with the extreme!"

$ HARPUR PALATE, a literary journal at Binghamton University, English Department, P.O. Box 6000, Binghamton University, Binghamton NY 13902-6000. E-mail: lmoffit0@binghamton.edu. Website: harpurpalate.binghamton.edu. **Contact:** Letitia Moffitt, fiction editor; Anne Rashid and Thomas Rechtin, poetry editors. **100% freelance written.** Semiannual literary magazine. "We believe writers should explore different genres to tell their stories. *Harpur Palate* accepts pieces regardless of genre, as long as the works pay attention to craft, structure, language, and the story well told." Estab. 2000. Circ. 500. Pays on publication. Publishes ms an average of 1-2 months after acceptance. Byline given. Buys first North American serial, electronic rights. Editorial lead time 3 months. Accepts queries by mail, e-mail. Accepts simultaneous submissions. Responds in 1 week to queries; 3 months to mss. Sample copy for $7.50, plus $1.18 shipping and handling, or on website. Writer's guidelines online.

Fiction: Toiya Kristen Finley, fiction editor. "We believe that journals published by creative writing programs should reflect the work of the students in the programs. Creative writing students at Binghamton express themselves in a spectrum of styles and genres, and *Harpur Palate* believes that writers who explore the boundaries of genre should have the opportunity to place their work in a literary journal. We're open to pieces that may have a hard time fitting in other venues." Adventure, ethnic, experimental, fantasy, historical, horror, humorous, mainstream, mystery, novel excerpts, science fiction, suspense, literary, fabulism, magical realism, metafiction, slipstream (genre blending). "No solipsistic or self-centered fiction or autobiography pretending to be fiction. No pornography, excessive profanity, or shock value for shock value's sake." **Buys 20-30 mss/year.** Length: 250-8,000 words. **Pays $5-20.**

Poetry: "We are open to speculative as well as realistic themes in poetry." Avant-garde, free verse, haiku, traditional, experimental, blank verse, long poems, lyrical, narrative, prose poems, sonnets, tanka, villanelles. No poems longer than 10 pages. No pornography, excessive profanity, or shock value for shock value's sake. No response without SASE. **Buys 40-50 poems/year.** Submit maximum 3-5 poems. **Pays $5-10.**

Tips: "Send a cover letter and short bio along with your manuscript. If you have an e-mail address, please include with your cover letter. Reading period for Winter issue: August 1-October 15; reading period for Summer issue: January 1-March 15. Submissions sent between reading periods will not be read. *Harpur Palate* sponsors a fiction contest during the spring and a poetry contest during the fall. The Winter issue also contains a Writing By Degrees Conference supplement. The editorial boards choose manuscripts during final selection committees after the deadline. If we would like to hold your fiction or poetry manuscript for final selection, we will inform you. Wherever you submit, always send a professional cover letter and mansucript. First impressions are of the utmost importance."

$ HAYDEN'S FERRY REVIEW, Arizona State University, Box 871502, Arizona State University, Tempe AZ 85287-1502. (480)965-1243. Fax: (480)965-2229. E-mail: hfr@asu.edu. Website: www.haydensferryreview.org. **Contact:** Fiction, Poetry, or Art Editor. **85% freelance written.** Semiannual magazine. "*Hayden's Ferry Review* publishes best quality fiction, poetry, and creative nonfiction from new, emerging, and established writers." Estab. 1986. Circ. 1,300. Pays on publication. Publishes ms an average of 6 months after acceptance. Byline given. Buys first North American serial rights. Editorial lead time 3 months. Accepts queries by mail. Accepts simultaneous submissions. Responds in 2 weeks to queries; 3 months to mss. Sample copy for $6. Writer's guidelines online.

- No electronic submissions.

Nonfiction: Essays, interview/profile, personal experience. **Buys 2 mss/year.** Send complete ms. Length: Open. **Pays $25-100.**

Photos: Send photos with submission. Reviews slides. Buys one-time rights. Offers $25/photo.

Fiction: Fiction editor. Editors change every 1-2 years. Ethnic, experimental, humorous, slice-of-life vignettes, contemporary, prose poem. **Buys 10 mss/year.** Send complete ms. Length: Open. **Pays $25-100.**

Poetry: Avant-garde, free verse, haiku, light verse, traditional. **Buys 60 poems/year.** Submit maximum 6 poems. Length: Open. **Pays $25-100.**

$ THE HOLLINS CRITIC, P.O. Box 9538, Hollins University, Roanoke VA 24020-1538. E-mail: acockrell@hollins.edu. Website: www.hollins.edu/academics/critic. Editor: R.H.W. Dillard. Managing Editor: Amanda Cockrell. **Contact:** Cathryn Hankla, poetry editor. **100% freelance written.** Magazine published 5 times/year. Estab. 1964. Circ. 400. Pays on publication. Publishes ms an average of 2 years after acceptance. Byline given. Buys first North American serial rights. Accepts queries by mail. Accepts simultaneous submissions. Responds in 2 months to mss. Sample copy for $1.50. Writer's guidelines for #10 SASE.

- No e-mail submissions. Send complete ms.

Poetry: "We read poetry only from September to May." Avant-garde, free verse, traditional. **Buys 16-20 poems/year.** Submit maximum 5 poems. **Pays $25.**

Tips: "We accept unsolicited poetry submissions; all other content is by prearrangement."

$ HUNGER MOUNTAIN, The Vermont College Journal of Arts & Letters, Vermont College/Union Institute & University, 36 College St., Montpelier VT 05602. Fax: (802)828-8649. E-mail: hungermtn@tui.edu. Website: www.hungermtn.org. **Contact:** Caroline Mercurio, managing editor. **30% freelance written.** Semiannual perfect-bound journal covering high quality fiction, poetry, creative nonfiction, interviews, photography, and artwork reproductions. Accepts high quality work from unknown, emerging, or successful writers and artists. No genre fiction, drama, children's writing, or academic articles, please. Estab. 2002. Pays on publication. Publishes ms an average of 1 year after acceptance. Byline given. Buys first North American serial rights. Submit seasonal material 6 months in advance. Accepts queries by mail. Responds in 1

month to queries; 3 months to mss. Sample copy for $10. Writer's guidelines for free, online at website, or by e-mail.
Nonfiction: Creative nonfiction only. All book reviews and interviews will be solicited. Book excerpts, essays, opinion, personal experience, photo feature, religious, travel. Special issues: "We will publish special issues, hopefully yearly, but we do not know yet the themes of these issues." No informative or instructive articles, please. Query with published clips. **Pays $5/page (minimum $30).** Sometimes pays expenses of writers on assignment.
Photos: Send photos with submission. Reviews contact sheets, transparencies, prints, GIF/JPEG files. Slides preferred. Buys one-time rights. Negotiates payment individually. Query with published clips. **Pays $25-100.**
Poetry: Avant-garde, free verse, haiku, traditional, nature, narrative, experimental, etc. No light verse, humor/quirky/catchy verse, greeting card verse. **Buys 10 poems/year.**
Tips: "We want high quality work! Submit in duplicate. Manuscripts must be typed, prose double-spaced. Poets submit at least 3 poems. No multiple genre submissions. We need more b&w photography and short shorts. Fresh viewpoints and human interest are very important, as is originality. We are committed to publishing an outstanding journal of arts & letters. Do not send entire novels, manuscripts, or short story collections. Do not send previously published work."

$ THE ICONOCLAST, 1675 Amazon Rd., Mohegan Lake NY 10547-1804. **Contact:** Phil Wagner, editor. **90% freelance written.** Bimonthly literary magazine. "Aimed for a literate general audience with interests in fine (but accessible) fiction and poetry." Estab. 1992. Circ. 600. **Pays on acceptance.** Publishes ms an average of 9-12 months after acceptance. Byline given. Buys first North American serial rights. Editorial lead time 1-2 months. Accepts queries by mail. Responds in 2 weeks to queries; 1 month to mss. Sample copy for $2.50. Writer's guidelines for #10 SASE.
Nonfiction: Essays, humor, reviews, literary/cultural matters. Does not want "anything that would be found in the magazines on the racks of supermarkets or convenience stores." **Buys 6-10 mss/year.** Query. Length: 250-2,500 words. **Pays 1¢/word.** Pays in contributor copies for previously published articles.
Photos: Line drawings preferred. State availability with submission. Reviews 4×6, b&w only prints. Buys one-time rights. Negotiates payment individually.
Columns/Departments: Book reviews (fiction/poetry), 250-500 words. **Buys 6 mss/year.** Query. **Pays 1¢/word.**
Fiction: Buys more fiction and poetry than anything else. Adventure, ethnic, experimental, fantasy, humorous, mainstream, novel excerpts, science fiction, literary. No character studies, slice-of-life, pieces strong on attitude/weak on plot. **Buys 25 mss/year.** Send complete ms. Length: 250-3,000 words. **Pays 1¢/word.**
Poetry: Avant-garde, free verse, haiku, light verse, traditional. No religious, greeting card, beginner rhyming. **Buys 75 poems/year.** Submit maximum 4 poems. Length: 2-50 lines. **Pays $2-5.**
Tips: "Professional conduct and sincerity help. Know it's the best you can do on a work before sending it out. Skill is the luck of the prepared. Everything counts. We love what we do, and are serious about it—and expect you to share that attitude. Remember: You're writing for paying subscribers. Ask Yourself: Would I pay money to read what I'm sending? We don't reply to submissions without a SASE, nor do we e-mail replies."

$ INDIANA REVIEW, Indiana University, Ballantine Hall 465, 1020 E. Kirkwood, Bloomington IN 47405-7103. (812)855-3439. Website: www.indiana.edu/~inreview. **Contact:** Danit Brown, editor. **100% freelance written.** Semiannual Biannual magazine. "*Indiana Review*, a nonprofit organization run by IU graduate students, is a journal of previously unpublished poetry and fiction. Literary interviews and essays also considered. We publish innovative fiction and poetry. We're interested in energy, originality, and careful attention to craft. While we publish many well-known writers, we also welcome new and emerging poets and fiction writers." Estab. 1976. Circ. 2,000. Pays on publication. Publishes ms an average of an average of 3-6 months after acceptance. Byline given. Buys first North American serial rights. Accepts queries by mail, e-mail, phone. Accepts simultaneous submissions. Responds in 2 weeks to queries; 3 months to mss. Sample copy for $8. Writer's guidelines online.

O→ Break in with 500-1,000 word book reviews of fiction, poetry, nonfiction, and literary criticism published within the last 2 years, "since this is the area in which there's the least amount of competition."

Nonfiction: Essays, interview/profile, creative nonfiction, reviews. No "coming of age/slice of life pieces." **Buys 5-7 mss/year.** Send complete ms. Length: 9,000 words maximum. **Pays $5/page, plus 2 contributor's copies.**
Fiction: Danit Brown, fiction editor. "We look for daring stories which integrate theme, language, character, and form. We like polished writing, humor, and fiction which has consequence beyond the world of its narrator." Ethnic, experimental, mainstream, novel excerpts, literary, short fictions, translations. No genre fiction. **Buys 14-18 mss/year.** Send complete ms. Length: 250-15,000 words. **Pays $5/page, plus 2 contributor's copies.**
Poetry: Looks for inventive and skillful writing. Avant-garde, free verse. **Buys 80 poems/year.** Submit maximum 6 poems. Length: 5 lines minimum. **Pays $5/page, plus 2 contributor's copies.**
Tips: "We're always looking for non-fiction essays that go beyond merely autobiographical revelation and utilize sophisticated organization and slightly radical narrative strategies. We want essays that are both lyrical and analytical where confession does not mean nostalgia. Read us before you submit. Often reading is slower in summer and holiday months. Only submit work to journals you would proudly subscribe to, then subscribe to a few. Take care to read the latest 2 issues and specifically mention work you identify with and why. Submit work that 'stacks up' with the work we've published." Offers annual poetry, fiction, short-short/prose-poem prizes. See website for details.

$ THE IOWA REVIEW, 308 EPB, The University of Iowa, Iowa City IA 52242. (319)335-0462. Fax: (319)335-2535. E-mail: iareview@blue.weeg.uiowa.edu. Website: www.uiowa.edu/~iareview/. **Contact:** David Hamilton, editor. Triannual magazine. "Stories, essays, poems for a general readership interested in contemporary literature." Estab. 1970. Circ. 2,000. Pays on publication. Publishes ms an average of an average of 12-18 months after acceptance. Buys first North American serial, nonexclusive anthology, classroom, and online serial rights rights. Responds in 3 months to queries; 3 months to mss. Sample copy for $7 and online. Writer's guidelines online.

• This magazine uses the help of colleagues and graduate assistants. Its reading period is September 1-March 1. **Pays $10/page, and 2 contributor's copies; additional copies 30% off cover price.**

Tips: "We publish essays, reviews, novel excerpts, stories, and poems, and would like for our essays not always to be works of academic criticism. We have no set guidelines as to content or length, but strongly recommend that writers read a sample issue before submitting." **Buys 65-80 unsolicited ms/year.** Submit complete ms with SASE. **Pays $20 for the first page and $15 for each subsequent page of poetry or prose.**

N $IRREANTUM, Exploring Mormon Literature, The Association for Mormon Letters, P.O. Box 51364, Provo UT 84605. (801)373-9730. E-mail: irreantum2@cs.com. Website: www.aml-online.org. **Contact:** Tory Anderson. Quarterly magazine. "While focused on Mormonism, *Irreantum* is a cultural, humanities-oriented magazine, not a religious magazine. Our guiding principle is that Mormonism is grounded in a sufficiently unusual, cohesive, and extended historical and cultural experience that it has become like a nation, an ethnic culture. We can speak of Mormon literature at least as surely as we can of a Jewish or Southern literature. *Irreantum* publishes stories, one-act dramas, stand-alone novel and drama excerpts, and poetry by, for, or about Mormons (as well as author interviews, essays, and reviews). The magazine's audience includes readers of any or no religious faith who are interested in literary exploration of the Mormon culture, mindset, and worldview through Mormon themes and characters. *Irreantum* is currently the only magazine devoted to Mormon literature." Estab. 1999. Circ. 400. Pays on publication. Publishes ms an average of 3-12 months after acceptance. Buys one-time, electronic rights. Accepts queries by e-mail. Accepts previously published material. Accepts simultaneous submissions. Responds in 2 weeks to queries; 2 months to mss. Sample copy for $5. Writer's guidelines by e-mail. Editorial calendar available via e-mail.

• Also publishes short shorts, literary essays, literary criticism, and poetry.

Fiction: Adventure, ethnic, experimental, fantasy, historical, horror, humorous, mainstream, mystery, religious, romance, science fiction, suspense. **Buys 12 mss/year.** Length: 1,000-7,000 words. **Pays $0-100.**

Tips: "*Irreantum* is not interested in didactic or polemnical fiction that primarily attempts to prove or disprove Mormon doctrine, history, or corporate policy. We encourage beginning writers to focus on human elements first, with Mormon elements introduced only as natural and organic to the story. Readers can tell if you are honestly trying to explore human experience or if you are writing with a propagandistic agenda either for or against Mormonism. For conservative, orthodox Mormon writers, beware of sentimentalism, simplistic resolutions, and foregone conclusions."

$THE JOURNAL, The Ohio State University, 164 W. 17th Ave., Columbus OH 43210. (614)292-4076. Fax: (614)292-7816. E-mail: thejournal@osu.edu. Website: www.cohums.ohio-state.edu/english/journals/the_journal/. **Contact:** Fiction Editor, Poetry Editor, Nonfiction Editor, Poetry Review Editor. **100% freelance written.** Semiannual magazine. "We're open to all forms; we tend to favor work that gives evidence of a mature and sophisticated sense of the language." Estab. 1972. Circ. 1,500. Pays on publication. Publishes ms an average of 1 year after acceptance. Byline given. Buys first North American serial rights. Accepts queries by mail. Accepts simultaneous submissions. Responds in 2 weeks to queries; 2 months to mss. Sample copy for $7 or online. Writer's guidelines online.

Nonfiction: Essays, interview/profile. **Buys 2 mss/year.** Query. Length: 2,000-4,000 words. **Pays $30 maximum.**

Columns/Departments: Reviews of contemporary poetry, 2,000-4,000 words. **Buys 2 mss/year.** Query. **Pays $30.**

Fiction: Kathy Fagan (poetry); Michelle Herman (fiction). Novel excerpts, literary short stories. No romance, science fiction or religious/devotional. Length: Open. **Pays $30.**

Poetry: Avant-garde, free verse, traditional. **Buys 100 poems/year.** Submit maximum 5 poems. **Pays $30.**

$KALLIOPE, a journal of women's literature & art, Florida Community College at Jacksonville, 11901 Beach Blvd., Jacksonville FL 32246. (904)646-2081. Website: www.fccj.org/kalliope. **Contact:** Mary Sue Koeppel, editor. **100% freelance written.** Biannual magazine. "*Kalliope* publishes poetry, short fiction, reviews, and b&w art, usually by women artists. We look for artistic excellence." Estab. 1978. Circ. 1,600. Pays on publication. Publishes ms an average of 3 months after acceptance. Byline given. Buys first rights. "We accept only unpublished work. Copyright returned to author upon request." Accepts queries by mail. Responds in 1 week to queries; 3 months to mss. Sample copy for $9 (recent issue) or $4 (back copy), or see sample issues on website. Writer's guidelines online.

• *Kalliope's* reading period is September-April.

O→ Break in with a "finely crafted poem or short story or a Q&A with an established, well-published woman poet or literary novelist."

Nonfiction: Interview/profile (Q&A), reviews of new works of poetry and fiction. **Buys 6 mss/year.** Send complete ms. Length: 500-2,000 words. **Pays $10 honorarium if funds are available, otherwise 2 copies or subscription.**

Photos: "Visual art should be sent in groups of 4-10 works. We require b&w professional quality, glossy prints made from negatives. Please supply photo credits, model releases, date of work, title, medium, and size on the back of each photo submitted. Include artist's résumé where applicable. We welcome an artist's statement of 50-75 words."

Fiction: Fiction Editor. Ethnic, experimental, novel excerpts, literary. "Quality short fiction by women writers. No science fiction or fantasy. Would like to see more experimental fiction." **Buys 12 mss/year.** Send complete ms. Length: 100-2,000 words. **Pays $10 honorarium if funds are available, otherwise 2 copies or subscription.**

Poetry: Avant-garde, free verse, haiku, traditional. **Buys 75 poems/year.** Submit maximum 3-5 poems. Length: 2-120 lines. **Pays $10 honorarium if funds are available, otherwise 2 copies or subscription.**

Tips: "We publish the best of the material submitted to us each issue. (We don't build a huge backlog and then publish from that backlog for years.) Although we look for new writers and usually publish several with each issue alongside already established writers, we love it when established writers send us their work. We've recently published Tess Gallagher, Marge Piercy, Maxine Kumin, and 1 of the last poems by Denise Levertov. Send a bio with all submissions."

$ THE KENYON REVIEW, Kenyon College, Gambier OH 43022. (740)427-5208. Fax: (740)427-5417. E-mail: kenyonreview@kenyon.edu. Website: www.kenyonreview.org. **Contact:** David H. Lynn, editor. **100% freelance written.** Triannual magazine covering contemporary literature and criticism. An international journal of literature, culture, and the arts dedicated to an inclusive representation of the best in new writing (fiction, poetry, essays, interviews, criticism) from established and emerging writers. Estab. 1939. Circ. 5,000. Pays on publication. Publishes ms an average of 1 year after acceptance. Byline given. Buys first rights. Editorial lead time 1 year. Submit seasonal material 1 year in advance. Accepts queries by mail. Responds in 3-4 months to queries; 4 months to mss. Sample copy $10 single issue, $13 double issue (Summer/Fall), includes postage and handling. Writer's guidelines online.

- Because of editor's sabbatical, unsolicited mss received after March 31, 2003, will not be read until September 1, 2004. Length: 3-15 typeset pages preferred. **Pays $10-15/page.**

N $ KIRKUS REVIEWS, VNU Business Media, 770 Broadway, 6th Floor, New York NY 10003. (646)654-5000. Fax: (646)654-4706. E-mail: kirkusrev@kirkus reviews.com. Website: www.kirkusreviews.com. Editor: Anne Larsen. Managing Editor: Chuck Shelton. Semimonthly magazine. Publication reviews of fiction, nonfiction, juvenile and young adult books for libraries, booksellers, publishers, producers and agents. Sample copy not available.

$ THE KIT-CAT REVIEW, 244 Halstead Ave., Harrison NY 10528. (914)835-4833. **Contact:** Claudia Fletcher, editor. **100% freelance written.** Quarterly magazine. "*The Kit-Cat Review* is named after the 18th Century Kit-Cat Club, whose members included Addison, Steele, Congreve, Vanbrugh, and Garth. Its purpose is to promote/discover excellence and originality. Some issues are part anthology." The Spring issue includes the winner of the annual Gavin Fletcher Memorial Prize for Poetry of $1,000. The winning poem is published shortly thereafter in a *Kit-Cat Review* ad in the *American Poetry Review*. Estab. 1998. Circ. 500. **Pays on acceptance.** Byline given. Buys one-time rights. Accepts queries by mail, phone. Responds in 1 week to queries; 1 month to mss. Sample copy for $7 (payable to Claudia Fletcher).

Nonfiction: "Shorter pieces stand a better chance of publication." Book excerpts, essays, general interest, historical/nostalgic, humor, interview/profile, personal experience, travel. **Buys 4 mss/year.** Send complete ms with brief bio and SASE. Length: 5,000 words maximum. **Pays $25-100.**

Fiction: Experimental, novel excerpts, slice-of-life vignettes. No stories with "O. Henry-type formula endings. Shorter pieces stand a better chance of publication." **Buys 20 mss/year.** Send complete ms. Length: 5,000 words maximum. **Pays $25-100.**

Poetry: Free verse, traditional. No excessively obscure poetry. **Buys 100 poems/year. Pays $10-100.**

Tips: "Obtaining a sample copy is strongly suggested. Include a short bio, SASE, and word count for fiction and nonfiction submissions."

N $ LYNX EYE, ScribbleFest Literary Group, 542 Mitchell Dr., Los Osos CA 93402. (805)528-8146. Fax: (805)528-7676. E-mail: pamccully@aol.com. Co-Editors Pam McCully, Kathryn Morrison. **Contact:** Pam McCully. **100% freelance written.** Quarterly journal. "Each issue of *Lynx Eye* offers thoughtful and thought-provoking reading." Estab. 1994. Circ. 500. **Pays on acceptance.** Publishes ms an average of 6 months after acceptance. Byline given. Offers 100% kill fee. Buys first North American serial rights. Editorial lead time 6 months. Submit seasonal material 6 months in advance. Accepts queries by mail. Accepts simultaneous submissions. Responds in 3 weeks to queries; 4 months to mss. Sample copy for $7.95. Writer's guidelines for #10 SASE.

Nonfiction: Essays. No memoirs. **Buys 6 mss/year.** Send complete ms. Length: 500-5,000 words. **Pays $10 for unsolicited articles.**

Fiction: Adventure, condensed novels, erotica, ethnic, experimental, fantasy, historical, horror, humorous, mainstream, mystery, novel excerpts, romance, science fiction, serialized novels, western. "No horror with gratuitous violence or YA stories." **Buys 50 mss/year.** Send complete ms. Length: 500-5,000 words. **Pays $10.**

Poetry: Avant-garde, free verse, haiku, light verse, traditional. **Buys 50 poems/year.** Submit maximum 6 poems. Length:30 lines. **Pays $10.**

Tips: "Know your craft, including grammar, usage, active verbs, well-constructed sentences and paragraphs, and fully developed characters. We accept never-before-published work only"

$ THE MALAHAT REVIEW, The University of Victoria, P.O. Box 1700, STN CSC, Victoria BC V8W 2Y2, Canada. (250)721-8524. E-mail: malahat@uvic.ca (for queries only). Website: www.malahatreview.com. **Contact:** Marlene Cookshaw, editor. **100% freelance written.** Eager to work with new/unpublished writers. Quarterly magazine covering poetry, fiction, and reviews. Estab. 1967. Circ. 1,000. **Pays on acceptance.** Publishes ms an average of 6 months after acceptance. Byline given. Offers 100% kill fee. Buys second serial (reprint) rights. first world rights Accepts queries by mail, e-mail. Responds in 2 weeks to queries; 3 months to mss. Sample copy for $10 (US). Writer's guidelines online.

Nonfiction: "Query first about review articles, critical essays, interviews, and visual art, which we generally solicit." Include SASE with Canadian postage or IRCs. **Pays $30/magazine page.**

Fiction: "General ficton and poetry." **Buys 20 mss/year.** Send complete ms. Length: 20 pages maximum. **Pays $30/magazine page.**

Poetry: Avant-garde, free verse, traditional. **Buys 100 poems/year.** Length: 5-10 pages. **Pays $30/magazine page.**

Tips: "Please do not send more than 1 manuscript (the one you consider your best) at a time. See *The Malahat Review's* long poem and novella contests in Contest & Awards section."

N $ $ MANOA, A Pacific Journal of International Writing, English Dept., University of Hawaii, Honolulu HI 96822. (808)956-3070. Fax: (808)956-7808. E-mail: fstewart@hawaii.edu. Website: www2.hawaii.edu/mjournal. **Contact:** Frank Stewart, editor. Semiannual magazine. "High quality literary fiction, poetry, essays, personal narrative, reviews. About half of each issue devoted to U.S. writing, and half new work from Pacific and Asian nations. Our audience is primarily in the U.S., although expanding in Pacific countries. U.S. writing need not be confined to Pacific settings or subjects." Estab. 1989. Circ. 2,500. Pays on publication. Byline given. Buys first North American serial rights. Non-exclusive, one-time print Editorial lead time 6 months. Submit seasonal material 8 months in advance. Accepts simultaneous submissions. Responds in 3 weeks to queries 2 months to poetry mss; 4 months to fiction to mss. Sample copy for $10 (US). Writer's guidelines online.

Nonfiction: Book excerpts, essays, interview/profile, creative nonfiction or personal narrative related to literature or nature; book reviews on recent books in arts, humanities and natural sciences, usually related to Asia, the Pacific or Hawaii or published in these places. No Pacific exotica. **Buys 3-4, excluding reviews mss/year.** Send complete ms. Length: 1,000-5,000 words. **Pays $25/printed page.**

Fiction: Ian MacMillan, fiction editor. "We're potentially open to anything of literary quality, though usually not genre fiction as such." Mainstream, contemporary, excerpted novel. No Pacific exotica. **Buys 12-18 in the US (excluding translation) mss/year.** Send complete ms. Length: 1,000-7,500 words. **Pays $100-500 normally ($25/printed page).**

Poetry: No light verse. **Buys 40-50 poems/year.** Submit maximum 5-6 poems poems. **Pays $25.**

Tips: "Although we are a Pacific journal, we are a general interest U.S. literary journal, not limited to Pacific settings or subjects."

$THE MASSACHUSETTS REVIEW, South College, University of Massachusetts, Amherst MA 01003-9934. (413)545-2689. Fax: (413)577-0740. E-mail: massrev@external.umass.edu. Website: www.massreview.org. **Contact:** Corwin Ericson, managing editor; Mary Heath, Paul Jenkins, David Lenson, editors. Quarterly magazine. Estab. 1959. Circ. 1,200. Pays on publication. Publishes ms an average of 18 months after acceptance. Buys first North American serial rights. Accepts queries by mail, e-mail, fax. Accepts simultaneous submissions. Responds in 3 months to queries; 3 months to mss. Sample copy for $7. Writer's guidelines online.

- Does not respond to mss without SASE.

Nonfiction: Articles on all subjects. No reviews of single books. Send complete ms or query with SASE. Length: 6,500 words maximum. **Pays $50.**

Fiction: Short stories. Wants more prose less than 30 pages. "No mystery of science fiction." **Buys 10 mss/year.** Send complete ms. Length: 25-30 pages maximum. **Pays $50.**

Poetry: Submit maximum 6 poems. **Pays 35¢/line to $10 maximum.**

Tips: "No manuscripts are considered June-October. No fax or e-mail submissions. No simultaneous submissions."

$MICHIGAN QUARTERLY REVIEW, 3574 Rackham Bldg., 915 E. Washington, University of Michigan, Ann Arbor MI 48109-1070. (734)764-9265. E-mail: dorisk@umich.edu. Website: www.umich.edu/~mqr. **Contact:** Laurence Goldstein, editor. **75% freelance written.** Quarterly magazine. "An interdisciplinary journal which publishes mainly essays and reviews, with some high-quality fiction and poetry, for an intellectual, widely read audience." Estab. 1962. Circ. 1,500. Pays on publication. Publishes ms an average of 1 year after acceptance. Byline given. Buys first serial rights. Accepts queries by mail. Responds in 2 months to queries; 2 months to mss. Sample copy for $4. Writer's guidelines online.

- The Laurence Goldstein Award is a $1,000 annual award to the best poem published in the *Michigan Quarterly Review* during the previous year. Prefers to work with published/established writers.

Nonfiction: "*MQR* is open to general articles directed at an intellectual audience. Essays ought to have a personal voice and engage a significant subject. Scholarship must be present as a foundation, but we are not interested in specialized essays directed only at professionals in the field. We prefer ruminative essays, written in a fresh style and which reach interesting conclusions. We also like memoirs and interviews with significant historical or cultural resonance." **Buys 35 mss/year.** Query. Length: 2,000-5,000 words. **Pays $100-150.**

Fiction: Fiction Editor. No restrictions on subject matter or language. "We are very selective. We like stories which are unusual in tone and structure, and innovative in language." "No genre fiction written for a market. Would like to see more fiction about social, political, cultural matters, not just centered on a love relationship or dysfunctional family." **Buys 10 mss/year.** Send complete ms. Length: 1,500-7,000 words. **Pays $10/published page.**

Poetry: Buys 10 poems/year. Pays $10/published page.

Tips: "Read the journal and assess the range of contents and the level of writing. We have no guidelines to offer or set expectations; every manuscript is judged on its unique qualities. On essays—query with a very thorough description of the argument and a copy of the first page. Watch for announcements of special issues which are usually expanded issues and draw upon a lot of freelance writing. Be aware that this is a university quarterly that publishes a limited amount of fiction and poetry that it is directed at an educated audience, one that has done a great deal of reading in all types of literature."

$MID-AMERICAN REVIEW, Department of English, Bowling Green State University, Bowling Green OH 43403. (419)372-2725. Fax: (419)372-6805. Website: www.bgsu.edu/midamericanreview. **Contact:** Michael Czyzniejewski, editor-in-chief. Willing to work with new/unpublished writers. Semiannual magazine of "the highest quality fiction, poetry, and translations of contemporary poetry and fiction." Also publishes critical articles and book reviews of contemporary literature. "We try to put the best possible work in front of the biggest possible audience. We publish serious fiction and poetry, as well as critical studies in contemporary literature, translations and book reviews." Estab. 1981. Pays on publication when funding is available. Publishes ms an average of 6 months after acceptance. Byline given. Buys first North American serial, one-time rights. Accepts queries by mail, phone. Responds in 4 months to mss. Sample copy for $7 (current issue), $5 (back issue); rare back issues $10. Writer's guidelines online.

O‐╖ "Grab our attention with something original—even experimental—but most of all, well-written."

Nonfiction: Essays (articles focusing on contemporary authors and topics of current literary interest), short book reviews (500-1,000 words). **Pays $10/page up to $50, pending funding.**

Fiction: Character-oriented, literary, experimental, short short. Experimental, Memoir, prose poem, traditional. "No genre fiction. Would like to see more short shorts." **Buys 12 mss/year.** Length: 25 pages words. **Pays $10/page up to $50, pending funding.**

Poetry: Karen Craigo, poetry editor. Strong imagery and sense of visio. **Buys 60 poems/year. Pays $10/page up to $50, pending funding.**

Tips: "We are seeking translations of contemporary authors from all languages into English; submissions must include the original. We would also like to see more creative nonfiction."

N $ **miller's pond**, H&H Press, RR 2, Box 239, Middlebury Center PA 16935. (570)376-3361. E-mail: cjhoughtaling@usa.net. Website: www.millerspondpoetry.com. **Contact:** David Cazden, editor. **100% freelance written.** Annual magazine featuring poetry with poetry book/chapbook reviews and interviews of poets. E-mail submissions must be on the form from the website. Estab. 1998. Circ. 200. Pays on publication. Publishes ms an average of 1 year after acceptance. Byline given. Buys one-time rights. Editorial lead time 1 year. Accepts queries by mail, e-mail. Accepts simultaneous submissions. Responds in 10 months to queries; 10 months to mss. Sample copy for $7, plus $3 p&h. Writer's guidelines online.

Nonfiction: Interview/profile (2,000 words), poetry chapbook reviews (500 words). **Buys 1-2 mss/year.** Query or send complete ms. **Pays $5.**

Poetry: Free verse. No religious, horror, vulgar, rhymed, preachy, lofty, trite, overly sentimental. **Buys 30-35 poems/year.** Submit maximum 3-5 poems. Length: 40 lines maximum. **Pays $2.**

The online magazine carries original content not found in the print edition and includes writer's guidelines. Contact: Julie Damerell, online editor.

Tips: "View our website to see what we like. Study the contemporary masters: Billy Collins, Maxine Kumin, Colette Inez, Vivian Shipley. Always enclose SASE."

$ $ **THE MISSOURI REVIEW**, 1507 Hillcrest Hall, University of Missouri, Columbia MO 65211. (573)882-4474. Fax: (573)884-4671. E-mail: missouri_@missouri.edu. Website: www.missourireview.org. Associate Editor: Evelyn Somers. Poetry Editor: Marta Ferguson. **Contact:** Speer Morgan, editor. **90% freelance written.** Triannual magazine. "We publish contemporary fiction, poetry, interviews, personal essays, cartoons, special features—such as 'History as Literature' series and 'Found Text' series—for the literary and the general reader interested in a wide range of subjects." Estab. 1978. Circ. 5,500. Offers signed contract. Byline given. Editorial lead time 6 months. Accepts queries by mail, e-mail, phone. Responds in 2 weeks to queries; 3 months to mss. Sample copy for $8 or online. Writer's guidelines online.

Nonfiction: Evelyn Somers, associate editor. Book excerpts, essays. No literary criticism. **Buys 10 mss/year.** Send complete ms. **Pays $30/printed page, up to $750.**

Fiction: Condensed novels, ethnic, humorous, mainstream, novel excerpts, literary. No genre fiction. **Buys 25 mss/year.** Send complete ms. Length: No preferred length. **Pays $30/printed page up to $750.**

Poetry: Publishes 3-5 poetry features of 6-12 pages per issue. "Please familiarize yourself with the magazine before submitting poetry." Marta Ferguson, poetry editor. **Buys 50 poems/year. Pays $125-250.**

The online magazine carries original content not found in the print edition and includes writer's guidelines. Contact: Hoa Ngo, online editor.

Tips: "Send your best work."

$ **MODERN HAIKU, An Independent Journal of Haiku and Haiku Studies**, P.O. Box 68, Lincoln IL 62656. Website: www.family-net.net/~brooksbooks/modernhaiku. **Contact:** Lee Gurga, editor. **85% freelance written.** Magazine published 3 times/year. "*Modern Haiku* publishes high quality material only. Haiku and related genres, articles on haiku, haiku book reviews, and translations compose its contents. It has an international circulation and is widely subscribed to by university, school, and public libraries. Estab. 1969. Circ. 625. Pays on acceptance for poetry; on publication for prose. Publishes ms an average of 3 months after acceptance. Byline given. Buys first North American serial rights. Editorial lead time 4 months. Accepts queries by mail, phone. Responds in 1 week to queries; 2 weeks to mss. Sample copy for $6.65. Writer's guidelines online.

Nonfiction: Essays (anything related to haiku). **Buys 40 mss/year.** Send complete ms. **Pays $5/page.**

Columns/Departments: Haiku & Senryu; Haibun; Articles (on haiku and related genres); book reviews (books of haiku or related genres), 4 pages maximum. **Buys 15 mss/year.** Send complete ms. **Pays $5/page.**

Poetry: Haiku, senryu. Does not want "general poetry, sentimental, and pretty-pretty haiku or overtly pornographic." **Buys 800 poems/year.** Submit maximum 24 poems. **Pays $1.**

Tips: "Study the history of haiku, read books about haiku, learn the aesthetics of haiku and methods of composition. Write about your sense perceptions of the suchness of entities, avoid ego-centered interpretations."

$ **NEW ENGLAND REVIEW**, Middlebury College, Middlebury VT 05753. (802)443-5075. E-mail: nereview@middlebury.edu. Website: www.middlebury.edu/~nereview/. Editor: Stephen Donadio. Managing Editor: Jodee Stanley Rubins. **Contact:** On envelope: Poetry, Fiction, or Nonfiction Editor; on letter: Stephen Donadio. Quarterly magazine. Serious literary only. Reads September 1 to May 31 (postmarked dates). Estab. 1978. Circ. 2,000. Pays on publication. Publishes ms an average of 6 months after acceptance. Byline given. Buys first North American serial, first, second serial (reprint) rights. Accepts simultaneous submissions. Responds in 2 weeks to queries; 3 months to mss. Sample copy for $7. Writer's guidelines online.

Nonfiction: Serious literary only. Rarely accepts previously published submissions (out of print or previously published abroad only.) **Buys 20-25 mss/year.** Send complete ms. Length: 7,500 words maximum, though exceptions may be made. **Pays $10/page ($20 minimum), and 2 copies.**

Fiction: Stephen Donadio, editor. Send 1 story at a time. Serious literary only, novel excerpts. **Buys 25 mss/year.** Send complete ms. Length: Prose length: 10,000 words maximum, double spaced. Novellas: 30,000 words maximum. **Pays $10/page ($20 minimum), and 2 copies.**

Poetry: Buys 75-90 poems/year. Submit maximum 6 poems. **Pays $10/page ($20 minimum), and 2 copies.**

Tips: "We consider short fiction, including shorts, short-shorts, novellas, and self-contained extracts from novels. We consider a variety of general and literary, but not narrowly scholarly nonfiction; long and short poems; speculative, interpretive, and personal essays; book reviews; screenplays; graphics; translations; critical reassessments; statements by artists working in various media; interviews; testimonies; and letters from abroad. We are committed to exploration of all forms of contemporary cultural expression in the United States and abroad. With few exceptions, we print only work not published previously elsewhere."

$ NEW LETTERS, University of Missouri-Kansas City, University House, 5101 Rockhill Rd., Kansas City MO 64110-2499. (816)235-1168. Fax: (816)235-2611. E-mail: newletters@umkc.edu. Website: umkc.edu/newletters. Editor: Robert Stewart. **100% freelance written.** Quarterly magazine. "*New Letters* is intended for the general literate reader. We publish literary fiction, nonfiction, essays, poetry. We also publish art." Estab. 1934. Circ. 2,500. Pays on publication. Publishes ms an average of 5 months after acceptance. Byline given. Buys first North American serial rights. Editorial lead time 6 months. Submit seasonal material 6 months in advance. Accepts queries by mail, e-mail. Responds in 1 month to queries; 3 months to mss. Sample copy for $7 or sample articles on website. Writer's guidelines online.

- Submissions are not read between May 15 and October 15.

Nonfiction: Essays. No self-help, how-to, or nonliterary work. **Buys 8-10 mss/year.** Send complete ms. Length: 5,000 words maximum. **Pays $40-100.**

Photos: Send photos with submission. Reviews contact sheets, 2×4 transparencies, prints. Buys one-time rights. Pays $10-40/photo.

Fiction: Ethnic, experimental, humorous, mainstream, Contemporary. No genre fiction. **Buys 15-20 mss/year.** Send complete ms. Length: 5,000 words maximum. **Pays $30-75.**

Poetry: Avant-garde, free verse, haiku, traditional. No light verse. **Buys 40-50 poems/year.** Submit maximum 6 poems. Length: Open. **Pays $10-25.**

Tips: "We aren't interested in essays that are footnoted, essays usually described as scholarly or critical. Our preference is for creative nonfiction or personal essays. We prefer shorter stories and essays to longer ones (an average length is 3,500-4,000 words). We have no rigid preferences as to subject, style, or genre, although commercial efforts tend to put us off. Even so, our only fixed requirement is on *good* writing."

$ THE NEW QUARTERLY, new directions in Canadian writing, St. Jerome's University, 200 University Ave. W., Waterloo ON N2L 3G3, Canada. (519)884-8111, ext. 290. E-mail: newquart@watarts.uwaterloo.ca. Website: www.newquarterly.uwaterloo.ca. Editor: Kim Jernigan. **95% freelance written.** Quarterly book covering Canadian fiction and poetry. "Emphasis on emerging writers and genres, but we publish more traditional work as well if the language and narrative structure are fresh." Estab. 1981. Circ. 800. Pays on publication. Publishes ms an average of 4 months after acceptance. Byline given. Buys first Canadian rights. Editorial lead time 6 months. Accepts queries by mail, e-mail. Accepts simultaneous submissions. Responds in 2 weeks to queries; 4 months to mss. Sample copy for $12 (cover price, plus mailing). Writer's guidelines for #10 SASE or online.

- Open to Canadian writers only.

Fiction: Kim Jernigan, Rae Crossman, Mark Spielmacher, Rosalynn Worth, fiction editors. *Canadian work only.* "We are not interested in genre fiction. We are looking for innovative, beautifully crafted, deeply felt literary fiction." **Buys 20-25 mss/year.** Send complete ms. Length: 20 pages maximum. **Pays $150/story.**

Poetry: *Canadian work only.* Lesley Elliott, Randi Patterson, John Vardon, Andrew Stubbs, poetry editors. Avant-garde, free verse, traditional. **Buys 60-80 poems/year.** Submit maximum 5 poems. Length: 4½ inches typeset.

Tips: "Reading us is the best way to get our measure. We don't have preconceived ideas about what we're looking for other than that it must be Canadian work (Canadian writers, not necessarily Canadian content). We want something that's fresh, something that will repay a second reading, something in which the language soars and the feeling is complexly rendered."

N $ A NEW SONG, New Song Press, P.O. Box 629, WBB, Dayton OH 45409-0629. E-mail: nsongpress@aol.com. Website: www.newsongpress.com. **Contact:** Susan Jelus, editor. **2% freelance written.** Semiannual poetry magazine. "*A New Song* publishes contemporary, spiritually based free verse. We choose poems that deal with nature, love, beauty, real life, people, mystery, grief, death, personal growth, God, ideas, fresh insights into Bible characters, and justice. We try to address the way faith interfaces with real life." Estab. 1995. Circ. 350. Pays on publication. Publishes ms an average of 6 months after acceptance. Byline given. Buys first North American serial rights. Editorial lead time 8 months. Submit seasonal material 1 year in advance. Accepts queries by mail, e-mail. Accepts simultaneous submissions. Sample copy for $5. Writer's guidelines online.

Nonfiction: Interview/profile (contemporary poets), poetry book reviews (of books published in the last 3 years; prefer a spiritual slant). **Buys 2 mss/year.** Query or send complete ms. Length: 500-2,000 words. **Pays $35-50.**

Poetry: Avant-garde, free verse. No rhyming poetry. **Buys 75-100 poems/year. Pays in copies only for poems.**

$ $ NEW YORK STORIES, LaGuardia/CUNY, 31-10 Thomson Ave., Long Island City NY 11101. (718)482-5673. E-mail: nystories@lagcc.cuny.edu. Website: www.newyorkstories.org. **Contact:** Daniel Caplice Lynch, editor-in-chief. **100% freelance written.** Magazine published 3 times/year. "Our purpose is to publish quality short fiction and New York-centered nonfiction. We look for fresh approaches, artistic daring, and story telling talent. We are especially interested in work that explores NYC's diversity—ethnic, social, sexual, psychological, economic, and geographical." Estab. 1998. Circ.

1,500. Pays on publication. Publishes ms an average of 6 months after acceptance. Byline given. Buys first North American serial rights. Editorial lead time 6 months. Submit seasonal material 6 months in advance. Accepts queries by mail, e-mail. Accepts previously published material. Accepts simultaneous submissions. Responds in 2 weeks to queries; 6 months to mss. Sample copy for $4. Writer's guidelines online.
Nonfiction: Essays, personal experience, all must be related to New York City. **Buys 25-30 mss/year.** Send complete ms. Length: 300-6,000 words. **Pays $100-750.**
Photos: Send photos with submission. Buys one-time rights. Negotiates payment individually. Model releases required.
Fiction: Seeks quality above all; also minority writers, New York City themes. Ethnic, experimental, humorous, mainstream. **Buys 25 mss/year.** Send complete ms. Length: 300-6,000 words. **Pays $100-750.**
Tips: "Send your best work. Try briefer pieces, cultivate a fresh approach. For the NYC nonfiction pieces, look on your doorstep. Fresh angles of vision and psychological complexity are the hallmarks of our short stories."

$ $ NORTH CAROLINA LITERARY REVIEW, A Magazine of North Carolina Literature, Culture, and History, English Dept., East Carolina University, Greenville NC 27858-4353. (252)328-1537. Fax: (252)328-4889. E-mail: bauerm@mail.ecu.edu. Website: www.ecu.edu/nclr. **Contact:** Margaret Bauer, editor. Annual magazine published in fall covering North Carolina writers, literature, culture, history. "Articles should have a North Carolina slant. First consideration is always for quality of work. Although we treat academic and scholarly subjects, we do not wish to see jargon-laden prose; our readers, we hope, are found as often in bookstores and libraries as in academia. We seek to combine the best elements of magazine for serious readers with best of scholarly journal." Estab. 1992. Circ. 750. Pays on publication. Publishes ms an average of 1 year after acceptance. Byline given. Buys first North American serial rights. Rights returned to writer on request. Editorial lead time 6 months. Accepts queries by mail, e-mail. Responds in 1 month to queries; 6 months to mss. Sample copy for $10-15. Writer's guidelines online.

O→ Break in with an article related to the special feature topic. Check the website for upcoming topics and deadlines.
Nonfiction: North Carolina-related material only. Book excerpts, essays, exposé, general interest, historical/nostalgic, humor, interview/profile, opinion, personal experience, photo feature, travel, reviews, short narratives, surveys of archives. "No jargon-laden academic articles." **Buys 25-35 mss/year.** Query with published clips. Length: 500-5,000 words. **Pays $50-300.**
Photos: State availability with submission. Reviews 5×7 or 8×10 prints; snapshot size or photocopy OK. Buys one-time rights. Pays $25-250. Captions and identification of subjects required; releases (when appropriate) required.
Columns/Departments: NC Writers (interviews, biographical/bibliographic essays); Reviews (essay reviews of North Carolina-related (fiction, creative nonfiction, poetry). Query with published clips. **Pays $50-300.**
Fiction: Must be North Carolina related—either by a North Carolina-connected writer or set in North Carolina. **Buys 3-4 mss/year.** Query. Length: 5,000 words maximum. **Pays $50-300.**
Poetry: *North Carolina poets only.* **Buys 8-10 poems/year.** Length: 30-150 lines. **Pays $25-50.**
Fillers: Buys 2-10/year. Length: 50-300 words. **Pays $25-50.**
Tips: "By far the easiest way to break in is with special issue sections. We are especially interested in reports on conferences, readings, meetings that involve North Carolina writers, and personal essays or short narratives with a strong sense of place. See back issues for other departments. Interviews are probably the other easiest place to break in; no discussions of poetics/theory, etc., except in reader-friendly (accessible) language; interviews should be personal, more like conversations, that explore connections between a writer's life and his/her work."

$ NORTHWEST FLORIDA REVIEW, Okaloosa Island Press-The Gavis Corp., P.O. Box 734, Mary Esther FL 32569. E-mail: nwfreview@cs.com. Editor: Mario A. Petaccia. **Contact:** Marie Liberty, fiction. **100% freelance written.** Semiannual magazine. "No special slant or philosophy, just good writing in fiction, poetry, and articles." Estab. 2001. Circ. 1,500. Pays on publication. Byline given. Buys first North American serial rights. Editorial lead time 3 months. Submit seasonal material 9 months in advance. Accepts queries by mail, e-mail. Accepts simultaneous submissions. Responds in 1 month to queries; 3 months to mss. Sample copy for $5. Writer's guidelines for #10 SASE.
Nonfiction: Book excerpts, essays, humor, interview/profile. No religious, technical, travel, or how-to. **Buys 2 mss/year.** Send complete ms. Length: 1,000-3,000 words. **Pays $20.**
Photos: Buys one-time rights. Offers no additional payment for photos accepted with ms. Identification of subjects required.
Fiction: Experimental, humorous, mainstream, novel excerpts. **Buys 8 mss/year.** Send complete ms. Length: 1,500-5,000 words. **Pays $20.**
Poetry: Free verse. No haiku or light verse. **Buys 40-50 poems/year.** Submit maximum 3-5 poems. Length: 10-50 lines. **Pays $5.**
Tips: "Read the best magazine or subscribe to *NWFR* to see what we like."

N $ NOTRE DAME REVIEW, University of Notre Dame, English Department, Creative Writing, Notre Dame IN 46556. (574)631-6952. Fax: (574)631-8209. E-mail: english.ndreview.1@nd.edu. Website: www.nd.edu/~ndr/review.htm. Senior Editor: Steve Tomasula. Editor: John Matthias. **Contact:** William O'Rourke, fiction editor. Semiannual magazine. "The *Notre Dame Review* is an indepenent, noncommercial magazine of contemporary American and international fiction, poetry, criticism, and art. We are especially interested in work that takes on big issues by making the invisible seen, that gives voice to the voiceless. In addition to showcasing celebrated authors like Seamus Heaney and Czelaw Milosz, the *Notre Dame Review* introduces readers to authors they may have never encountered before, but who are doing innovative and important work. In conjunction with the *Notre Dame Review*, the online companion to the printed magazine, the *Notre Dame Re-view* engages readers as a community centered in literary rather than commercial concerns, a community we reach out to through critique and commentary as well as aesthetic experience." Estab. 1995. Circ. 2,000. Pays on publication. Publishes ms an average of 6 months after acceptance. Buys first North American serial rights. Accepts simultaneous submissions. Responds in 4 months to mss. Sample copy for $6. Writer's guidelines online. **Buys 10 mss/year.** Length: 3,000-3,000 words. **Pays $5-25.**

Tips: "We're looking for high quality work that takes on big issues in a literary way. Please read our back issues before submitting."

N $ $ ON SPEC MAGAZINE, Copper Pig Writers Society, Box 4727, Edmonton AB T6E 5G6, Canada. (780)413-0215. Fax: (780)413-1538. E-mail: onspec@canada.com. Website: www.onspec.ca. **Contact:** Jena Snyder, production editor. **100% freelance written.** Quarterly magazine. "*On Spec Magazine* was launched in 1989 by the nonprofit Copper Pig Writers' Society to provide a voice and a paying market for Canadian writers working in the speculative genre. Aside from the then-biannual *Tesseracts* anthology, there were almost no speculative fiction markets in Canada for Canadian writers. *On Spec* was created to provide this market. *On Spec* is published quarterly by the Copper Pig Writers Society, a collective whose members all writers themselves donate their professional services and their time. Our readers have told us what they want is fiction, fiction and more fiction, and that's what we give them: each 112-page issue of the digest-size magazine typically contains one or two poems and nonfiction pieces, some illustrations, and at least ten short stories, all in the speculative genre." Estab. 1989. **Pays on acceptance.** Byline given. Buys first rights. Accepts queries by mail. Sample copy not available. Writer's guidelines free.

Fiction: Fantasy, horror, science fiction. **Buys 40-50 mss/year.** Send complete ms. Length: 1,000-6,000 words. **Pays $50-180 (Canadian).**

Tips: "The *On Spec* editors are looking for original, unpublished science fiction—fantasy, horror, ghost stories, fairy stories, magic realism, or any other speculative material. Since our mandate is to provide a market for the Canadian viewpoint, strong preference is given to submissions by Canadians."

$ ONE-STORY, One-Story LLC, P.O. Box 1326, New York NY 10156. Website: www.one-story.com. Publisher: Maribeth Batcha. Editor: Hannah Tinti. **Contact:** Maribeth Batcha and Hannah Tinti. **100% freelance written.** Literary magazine covering one short story. "*One-Story* is a literary magazine that contains, simply, **one story**. It is a subscription-only magazine. Every 3 weeks subscribers are sent *One Story* in the mail. *One Story* is artfully designed, lightweight, easy to carry, and ready to entertain on buses, in bed, in subways, in cars, in the park, in the bath, in the waiting rooms of doctor's, on the couch, or in line at the supermarket. Subscribers also have access to a website, www.one-story.com, where they can learn more about *One-Story* authors, and hear about *One-Story* readings and events. There is always time to read One Story." Estab. 2002. Circ. 2,000. Pays on publication. Publishes ms an average of 3-6 months after acceptance. Byline given. Buys first North American serial rights. Buys the rights to publish excerpts on website and in promotional materials. Editorial lead time 3-4 months. Accepts queries by e-mail. Accepts simultaneous submissions. Responds in 2-3 months to mss. Sample copy for $5. Writer's guidelines online.

- Accepts submissions via website only.

Fiction: Literary short stories. *One-Story* only accepts short stories. Do not send excerpts. Do not send more than 1 story at a time. **Buys 18 mss/year.** Send complete ms. Length: 3,000-10,000 words. **Pays $100.**

Tips: "*One-Story* is looking for stories that are strong enough to stand alone. Therefore they must be very good. We want the best you can give. We want our socks knocked off."

$ THE PARIS REVIEW, 541 E. 72nd St., New York NY 10021. (212)861-0016. Fax: (212)861-4504. Website: www.theparisreview.com. **Contact:** George A. Plimpton, editor. Quarterly magazine. "Fiction and poetry of superlative quality, whatever the genre, style or mode. Our contributors include prominent, as well as less well-known and previously unpublished writers. Writers at Work interview series includes important contemporary writers discussing their own work and the craft of writing." Pays on publication. Buys all, first english-language rights. Accepts queries by mail. Accepts simultaneous submissions. Responds in 4 months to mss. Sample copy for $15 (includes postage). Writer's guidelines online.

- Address submissions to proper department.

Fiction: Study the publication. Annual Aga Khan Fiction Contest award of $1,000. Query. Length: No length limit. **Payment varies depending on length.**

Poetry: Study the publication. Richard Howard, poetry editor.

N $ $ PARTISAN REVIEW, Partisan Review, 236 Bay State Rd., Boston MA 02215. (617)353-4260. Website: www.partisanreview.org. **Contact:** Edith Kurzweil, editor. **100% freelance written.** Quarterly journal covering literature, politics, art, culture, and film. "*Partisan Review* is an independent quarterly whose editorial focus is on world literature and contemporary culture. The journal publishes fiction, essays, and poetry with an emphasis on the arts, and political and social commentary. Our primary audience is the general intellectual and public scholars." Estab. 1934. Circ. 8,000. Pays on publication. Publishes ms an average of 6 months after acceptance. Byline given. Buys first North American serial, first rights. Editorial lead time 3 months. Accepts queries by mail. Responds in 2 weeks to queries; 2 months to mss. Sample copy for $8.50. Writer's guidelines free.

Nonfiction: Book excerpts, essays, exposé, general interest, historical/nostalgic, interview/profile, personal experience, religious, travel. Query. Length: 5,000 words maximum. **Pays $100-300.**

Photos: State availability with submission. Reviews GIF/JPEG files. Buys one-time rights. Offers no additional payment for photos accepted with ms. Captions required.

Fiction: Fiction Editor. Ethnic, experimental, historical, mainstream, novel excerpts, religious, slice-of-life vignettes, contemporary, prose poem. **Buys 6 mss/year.** Send complete ms. Length: 5,000 words maximum. **Pays $100-300.**

Poetry: Don Shane, editor. Avant-garde, free verse, haiku, light verse, traditional. **Buys 40 poems/year.** Submit maximum 6 poems.

$ PEEKS & VALLEYS, A New England Fiction Journal, Davis Publications, P.O. Box 708, Newport NH 03773-0708. (603)863-5896. Fax: (603)863-8198. E-mail: hotdog@nhvt.net. Website: www.peeksandvalleys.com. **Contact:** Cindy Davis, editor. **100% freelance written.** Quarterly magazine covering short stories. "We especially would like to see submissions by children." Estab. 1999. **Pays on acceptance.** Publishes ms an average of 8 months after acceptance. Byline given. Not copyrighted. Buys one-time, second serial (reprint) rights. Editorial lead time 4 months. Submit seasonal material 6 months in advance. Accepts queries by mail, e-mail, fax. Accepts previously published material. Accepts simultaneous submissions. Responds in 1 month to queries; 2 months to mss. Sample copy for $4. Writer's guidelines online.

Fiction: Adventure, ethnic, fantasy, historical, horror, humorous, mainstream, mystery, religious, romance, science fiction, slice-of-life vignettes, suspense, western. No talking animals, sex, or obscenity. **Buys 30 mss/year.** Send complete ms. Length: 3,000 words. **Pays $5 and up.**

Poetry: Light verse, traditional. **Buys 5 poems/year.** Submit maximum 2 poems. Length: 30 lines.

N $ PENINSULAR, Literary Magazine, Cherrybite Publications, Linden Cottage, 45 Burton Rd., Neston Cheshire CH64 4AE, England. 0151 353 0967. Fax: 0870 165 6282. E-mail: helicon@globalnet.co.uk. Website: www.cherrybite.co.uk. **Contact:** Shelagh Nugent, editor. Quarterly magazine. "We're looking for brilliant short fiction to make the reader think/laugh/cry. A lively, up-and-coming quality magazine." Estab. 1985. Circ. 400. Pays on publication. Publishes ms an average of 3-6 months after acceptance. Buys one-time rights. Accepts previously published material. Accepts simultaneous submissions. Responds in 1 week to queries; 2 weeks to mss. Sample copy for $5 (cannot accept checks, only dollar bills). Writer's guidelines online.

Fiction: Adventure, ethnic, fantasy, historical, horror, humorous, science fiction, gay/lesbian, literary, New Age, psychic/supernatural/occult. No animals telling stories, cliches, pornography, children's fiction, or purple prose. **Buys 40 mss/year.** Length: 1,000-4,000 words. **Pays £5 sterling/1,000 words, or can pay in copies and subscriptions.**

Tips: "We look for impeccable presentation and grammar, outstanding prose, original story line and the element of difference that forbids me to put the story down. A good opening paragraph usually grabs me. Read 1 or 2 copies and study the guidelines. A beginning writer should read as much as possible. The trend seems to be for stories written in first person/present tense and for stories without end leaving the reader thinking, 'So what?' Stories not following this trend stand more chance of being published by me!"

N $ PLANET-THE WELSH INTERNATIONALIST, P.O. Box 44, Aberystwyth Ceredigion SY23 3ZZ, Cymru/Wales UK. 01970-611255. Fax: 01970-611197. E-mail: planet.enquiries@planetmagazine.org.uk. Website: www.planetmagazine.org.uk. **Contact:** John Barnie, fiction editor. Bimonthly journal. "A literary/cultural/political journal centered on Welsh affairs but with a strong interest in minority cultures in Europe and elsewhere." Circ. 1,400. Sample copy for £4. Writer's guidelines online.

Fiction: Would like to see more "inventive, imaginative fiction that pays attention to language and experiments with form." No magical realism, horror, science fiction. Length: 1,500-4,000 words. **Pays £40/1,000 words.**

Tips: "We do not look for fiction which necessarily has a 'Welsh' connection, which some writers assume from our title. We try to publish a broad range of fiction and our main criterion is quality. Try to read copies of any magazine you submit to. Don't write out of the blue to a magazine which might be completely inappropriate to your work. Recognize that you are likely to have a high rejection rate, as magazines tend to favor writers from their own countries."

$ PLEIADES, Pleiades Press, Department of English & Philosophy, Central Missouri State University, Martin 336, Warrensburg MO 64093. (660)543-4425. Fax: (660)543-8544. E-mail: kdp8106@cmsu2.cmsu.edu. Website: www.cmsu.edu/englphil/pleiades.html. **Contact:** Kevin Prufer, editor. **100% freelance written.** Semiannual journal. "We publish contemporary fiction, poetry, interviews, literary essays, special-interest personal essays, reviews for a general and literary audience." (5½×8½ perfect bound). Estab. 1991. Circ. 3,000. Pays on publication. Publishes ms an average of 9 months after acceptance. Byline given. Buys first North American serial, second serial (reprint) rights. Occasionally requests rights for TV, radio reading, website. Editorial lead time 9 months. Accepts queries by mail, e-mail, phone. Accepts simultaneous submissions. Responds in 2 months to queries; 2 months to mss. Sample copy for $5 (back issue), $6 (current issue). Writer's guidelines for #10 SASE.

- "We also sponsor the Lena-Miles Wever Todd Poetry Series competition, a contest for the best book manuscript by an American poet. The winner receives $1,000, publication by Pleiades Press, and distribution by Louisiana State University Press. Deadline September 30. Send SASE for guidelines."

Nonfiction: Book excerpts, essays, interview/profile, reviews. "Nothing pedantic, slick, or shallow." **Buys 4-6 mss/year.** Send complete ms. Length: 2,000-4,000 words. **Pays $10.**

Fiction: Ethnic, experimental, humorous, mainstream, novel excerpts, magic realism. No science fiction, fantasy, confession, erotica. **Buys 16-20 mss/year.** Send complete ms. Length: 2,000-6,000 words. **Pays $10.**

Poetry: Avant-garde, free verse, haiku, light verse, traditional. "Nothing didactic, pretentious, or overly sentimental." **Buys 40-50 poems/year.** Submit maximum 6 poems. **Pays $3/poem, and contributor copies.**

Tips: "Show care for your material and your readers—submit quality work in a professional format. Include cover letter with brief bio and list of publications. Include SASE."

$ $ PLOUGHSHARES, Emerson College, Department M, 120 Boylston St., Boston MA 02116. Website: www.pshares.org. **Contact:** Don Lee, editor. Triquarterly magazine for "readers of serious contemporary literature." "Our mission is to present dynamic, contrasting views on what is valid and important in contemporary literature, and to discover and advance significant literary talent. Each issue is guest-edited by a different writer. We no longer structure issues around preconceived themes." Estab. 1971. Circ. 6,000. Pays on publication. Publishes ms an average of 6 months after acceptance. Offers Offers 50% kill fee for assigned ms not published. kill fee. Buys first North American serial rights. Accepts simultaneous submissions. Responds in 5 months to mss. Sample copy for $9 (back issue). Writer's guidelines online.

- A competitive and highly prestigious market. Rotating and guest editors make cracking the line-up even tougher, since it's difficult to know what is appropriate to send. The reading period is August 1-March 31.

Nonfiction: Essays (personal and literary; accepted only occasionally). Length: 6,000 words maximum. **Pays $25/printed page, $50-250.**

Fiction: Mainstream, literary. "No genre (science fiction, detective, gothic, adventure, etc.), popular formula or commerical fiction whose purpose is to entertain rather than to illuminate." **Buys 25-35 mss/year.** Length: 300-6,000 words. **Pays $25/printed page, $50-250.**

Poetry: Avant-garde, free verse, traditional, blank verse. Length: Open. **Pays $25/printed page, $50-250.**

Tips: "We no longer structure issues around preconceived themes. If you believe your work is in keeping with our general standards of literary quality and value, submit at any time during our reading period."

$ POETRY, Modern Poetry Association, 60 W. Walton St., Chicago IL 60610. Fax: (312)255-3702. E-mail: poetry@poetrymagazine.org. Website: www.poetrymagazine.org. Editor: Joseph Parisi. Managing Editor: Helen Klaviter. **Contact:** Stephen Young, senior editor. **100% freelance written.** Monthly magazine. Estab. 1912. Circ. 10,000. Pays on publication. Publishes ms an average of 9 months after acceptance. Byline given. Buys all rights. Copyright returned to author on request. Accepts queries by mail. Responds in 1 month to queries; 4 months to mss. Sample copy for $5.50 or online at website. Writer's guidelines online.

Nonfiction: Reviews (most are solicited). **Buys 14 mss/year.** Query. Length: 1,000-2,000 words. **Pays $50/page.**

Poetry: All styles and subject matter. **Buys 180-250 poems/year.** Submit maximum 4 poems. Length: Open. **Pays $2/line.**

N $ POTTERSFIELD PORTFOLIO, Stork and Press, P.O. Box 40, Station A, Sydney NS B1P 6G9, Canada. Website: www.magomania.com. Managing Editor: Douglas Arthur Brown. Biannual magazine. "*Pottersfield Portfolio* is always looking for poetry and fiction that provides fresh insights and delivers the unexpected. The stories and poems that capture our attention will be the ones that most effectively blend an intriguing voice with imaginative language. Our readers expect to be challenged, enlightened and entertained." Estab. 1979. Circ. 2,000. Pays on publication. Publishes ms an average of 6 months after acceptance. Byline given. Buys first North American serial, first canadian serial rights rights. Editorial lead time 3 months. Accepts simultaneous submissions. Responds in 6 months to mss. Sample copy for $9 (US). Writer's guidelines online.

- Non-Canadian submissions by invitation only.

Nonfiction: Book excerpts, essays, interview/profile, photo feature. **Buys 6 mss/year.** Query. Length: 500-5,000 words.

Fiction: Fiction editor. Experimental, novel excerpts, short fiction. No fantasy, horror, mystery, religious, romance, science fiction, western. **Buys 12-15 mss/year.** Send complete ms. Length: 500-5,000 words. **Pays contributor's copy and $10 Canadian/printed page to a maximum of $50.**

Poetry: Poetry editor. Avant-garde, free verse, traditional. **Buys 20-30 poems/year.** Submit maximum 4 poems.

Tips: Looking for creative nonfiction, essays.

N $ THE PRAIRIE JOURNAL, Journal of Canadian Literature, Prairie Journal Trust, P.O. Box 61203, Brentwood P.O., Calgary AB T2L 2K6, Canada. E-mail: prairiejournal@yahoo.com. Website: www.geocities.com/prairiejournal. **Contact:** A. Burke, editor. **100% freelance written.** Semiannual magazine publishing quality poetry, short fiction, drama, literary criticism, reviews, bibliography, interviews, profiles, and artwork. "The audience is literary, university, library, scholarly, and creative readers/writers." Estab. 1983. Circ. 600. Pays on publication. Publishes ms an average of 4-6 months after acceptance. Byline given. Buys first North American serial, electronic, in canada author retains copyright with acknowledgement appreciated rights. Editorial lead time 4-6 months. Accepts queries by mail, e-mail. Responds in 2 weeks to queries; 6 months to mss. Sample copy for $5. Writer's guidelines online.

Nonfiction: Essays, humor, interview/profile, literary. No inspirational, news, religious, or travel. **Buys 25-40 mss/year.** Query with published clips. Length: 100-3,000 words. **Pays $100, plus copy.**

Photos: State availability with submission. Rights purchased is negotiable. Offers additional payment for photos accepted with ms.

Columns/Departments: Reviews (books from small presses publishing poetry, short fiction, essays, and criticism), 200-1,000 words. **Buys 5 mss/year.** Query with published clips. **Pays $10-50.**

Fiction: A.E. Burke, editor. Literary. No genre (romance, horror, western—sagebrush or cowboys), erotic, science fiction, or mystery. **Buys 6 mss/year.** Send complete ms. Length: 100-3,000 words. **Pays $10-75.**

Poetry: Avant-garde, free verse, haiku. No heroic couplets or greeting card verse. **Buys 25-35 poems/year.** Submit maximum 6-8 poems. Length: 3-50 lines. **Pays $5-50.**

Tips: "We publish many, many new writers and are always open to unsolicited submissions because we are 100% freelance." Do not send U.S. stamps, always use IRCs.

$ PRISM INTERNATIONAL, Department of Creative Writing, Buch E462-1866 Main Mall, University of British Columbia, Vancouver BC V6T 1Z1, Canada. (604)822-2514. Fax: (604)822-3616. E-mail: prism@interchange.ubc.ca. Website: prism.arts.ubc.ca. Executive Editor: Mark Mallet. **Contact:** Billeh Nickerson, editor. **100% freelance written.** Eager to work with new/unpublished writers. Quarterly magazine emphasizing contemporary literature, including translations, for university and public libraries, and private subscribers. "An international journal of contemporary writing - fiction, poetry, drama, creative nonfiction and translation." Readership: "public and university libraries, individual subscriptions, bookstores - a world-wide audience concerned with the contemporary in literature." Estab. 1959. Circ. 1,200. Pays on publication. Publishes ms an average of 4 months after acceptance. Buys first North American serial, selected authors are paid an additional $10/page for digital rights rights. Accepts queries by mail, fax, phone. Responds in 4 months to queries; 4 months to mss. Sample copy for $7 or on website. Writer's guidelines online.

Break in by "sending unusual or experimental work (we get mostly traditional submissions) and playing with forms (e.g., nonfiction, prose poetry, etc.)."

Nonfiction: "Creative nonfiction that reads like fiction. Nonfiction pieces should be creative, exploratory, or experimental in tone rather than rhetorical, academic, or journalistic." No reviews, tracts, or scholarly essays. **Pays $20/printed page.**

Fiction: For Drama: one-acts preferred. Also interested in seeing dramatic monologues. **Buys 3-5 mss/year**. Send complete ms. Length: 25 pages maximum. **Pays $20/printed page**. Experimental, novel excerpts, traditional. New writing that is contemporary and literary. Short stories and self-contained novel excerpts. Works of translation are eagerly sought and should be accompanied by a copy of the original. Would like to see more translations. "No gothic, confession, religious, romance, pornography, or sci-fi." Also looking for creative nonfiction that is literary, not journalistic, in scope and tone. **Buys 12-16 mss/year.** Send complete ms. Length: 25 pages maximum. **Pays $20/printed page, and 1-year subscription.**

Poetry: Buys 10 poems/issue. Avant-garde, traditional. Submit maximum 6 poems. **Pays $40/printed page, and 1-year subscription.**

Tips: "We are looking for new and exciting fiction. Excellence is still our No. 1 criterion. As well as poetry, imaginative nonfiction and fiction, we are especially open to translations of all kinds, very short fiction pieces and drama which work well on the page. Translations must come with a copy of the original language work. We pay an additional $10/printed page to selected authors whose work we place on our online version of *Prism*."

$ QUARTERLY WEST, University of Utah, 200 S. Central Campus Dr., Room 317, Salt Lake City UT 84112-9109. (801)581-3938. E-mail: dhawk@earthlink.net. Website: www.utah.edu/quarterlywest. **Contact:** David Hawkins, editor-in-chief. Semiannual magazine. "We publish fiction, poetry, and nonfiction in long and short formats, and will consider experimental as well as traditional works." Estab. 1976. Circ. 1,900. Pays on publication. Publishes ms an average of 6 months after acceptance. Buys first North American serial, all rights. Accepts queries by mail. Accepts simultaneous submissions. Responds in 6 months to mss. Sample copy for $7.50 or online. Writer's guidelines online.

Nonfiction: Essays, interview/profile, personal experience, travel, book reviews. **Buys 2-3 mss/year.** Send complete ms. Length: 10,000 words maximum. **Pays $25.**

Fiction: Jeff Chapman. No preferred lengths; interested in longer, fuller short stories and short shorts. Ethnic, experimental, humorous, mainstream, novel excerpts, slice-of-life vignettes, short shorts, translations. No detective, science fiction or romance. **Buys 6-10 mss/year.** Send complete ms. Length: No preferred length; interested in longer, "fuller" short stories, as well as short shorts. **Pays $15-50, and 2 contributor's copies.**

Poetry: Nicole Walker. Avant-garde, free verse, traditional. **Buys 40-50 poems/year.** Submit maximum 5 poems. **Pays $15-100.**

Tips: "We publish a special section of short shorts every issue, and we also sponsor a biennial novella contest. We are open to experimental work—potential contributors should read the magazine! Don't send more than 1 story/submission. Biennial novella competition guidelines available upon request with SASE. We prefer work with interesting language and detail—plot or narrative are less important. We don't do Western themes, or religious work."

$ $ QUEEN'S QUARTERLY, A Canadian Review, Queen's University, Kingston ON K7L 3N6, Canada. (613)533-2667. Fax: (613)533-6822. E-mail: qquarter@post.queensu.ca. Website: info.queensu.ca/quarterly. **Contact:** Joan Harcourt, literary editor. **95% freelance written.** Quarterly magazine covering a wide variety of subjects, including science, humanities, arts and letters, politics, and history for the educated reader. "A general interest intellectual review, featuring articles on science, politics, humanities, arts and letters. Book reviews, poetry and fiction." Estab. 1893. Circ. 3,000. Pays on publication. Publishes ms an average of 6-12 months after acceptance. Byline given. Buys first North American serial rights. Responds in 2-3 months to queries. Sample copy for $6.50. Writer's guidelines online.

Submissions can be sent as e-mail attachment or on hard copy with a SASE (Canadian postage).

Fiction: Historical, mainstream, novel excerpts, short stories, women's. Length: 2,500-3,000 words. **Pays $100-300 for fiction, 2 contributor's copies and 1-year subscription; additional copies $5.**

Poetry: Buys 25 poems/year. Submit maximum 6 poems.

N $ QWF (QUALITY WOMEN'S FICTION), Breaking the Boundaries of Women's Fiction, 18 Warwick Crescent, Harrogate N. Yorks HG2 8JA, United Kingdom. 01788 334302. Fax: 01788 334702. E-mail: jo@qwfmagazine.co.uk. Editor: Jo Good. **Contact:** Sally Zigmond, assistant editor. Bimonthly magazine. "*QWF* gets under the skin of the female experience and exposés emotional truth." Estab. 1994. Circ. 2,000. Pays on publication. Publishes ms an average of 18 months after acceptance. Buys first British serial rights. Accepts queries by mail, e-mail. Accepts previously published material. Responds in 2 weeks to queries; 3 months to mss. Writer's guidelines by e-mail.

Fiction: Does not read mss June-August. Erotica, ethnic, experimental, fantasy, horror, humorous, science fiction, feminist, gay, lesbian, literary, new age, psychic/supernatural/occult, translations. **Buys 72 mss/year.** Length: 1,000-4,500 words. **Pays £10 sterling maximum.**

Tips: "Take risks with subject matter. Study at least 1 copy of *QWF*. Ensure story is technically sound."

$ RARITAN, A Quarterly Review, 31 Mine St., New Brunswick NJ 08903. (732)932-7887. Fax: (732)932-7855. Editor: Jackson Lears. **Contact:** Stephanie Volmer, managing editor. Quarterly magazine covering literature, history, fiction, and general culture. Estab. 1981. Circ. 3,500. Pays on publication. Publishes ms an average of 1 year after acceptance. Byline given. Buys first North American serial rights. Editorial lead time 5 months. Accepts queries by mail. Sample copy not available. Writer's guidelines not available.

- *Raritan* no longer accepts previously published or simultaneous submissions.

Nonfiction: Book excerpts, essays. **Buys 50 mss/year.** Send complete ms. Length: 15-30 pages.

$RIVER STYX, Big River Association, 634 N. Grand Blvd., 12th Floor, St. Louis MO 63103. (314)533-4541. Fax: (314)533-3345. Website: www.riverstyx.org. Senior Editors: Quincy Troupe and Michael Castro. **Contact:** Richard Newman, editor. Triannual magazine. "*River Styx* publishes the highest quality fiction, poetry, interviews, essays, and visual art. We are an internationally distributed multicultural literary magazine." Mss read May-November. Estab. 1975. Pays on publication. Publishes ms an average of 1 year after acceptance. Byline given. Buys first North American serial, one-time rights. Accepts queries by mail. Accepts simultaneous submissions. Responds in 4 months to mss. Sample copy for $7. Writer's guidelines online.

- *River Styx* has won several prizes, including Best American Poetry 1998; Pushcart Prize; and Stanley Hanks Prizes.

Nonfiction: Essays, interview/profile. **Buys 2-5 mss/year.** Send complete ms. **Pays 2 contributor copies, plus 1 year subscription; pays $8/page, if funds are available.**

Photos: Send photos with submission. Reviews 5×7 or 8×10 b&w and color prints and slides. Buys one-time rights. Pays 2 contributor copies, plus 1-year subscription; $8/page if funds are available.

Fiction: Ethnic, experimental, mainstream, novel excerpts, short stories, literary. "No genre fiction, less thinly veiled autobiography." **Buys 6-9 mss/year.** Send complete ms. Length: no more than 23-30 manuscript pages. **Pays 2 contributor copies, plus 1-year subscription; $8/page if funds are available.**

Poetry: Avant-garde, free verse, formal. No religious. **Buys 40-50 poems/year.** Submit maximum 3-5 poems. **Pays 2 contributor copies, plus a 1-year subscription; $8/page if funds are available.**

N $ ROOM OF ONE'S OWN, A Canadian Quarterly of Women's Literature and Criticism, West Coast Feminist Literary Magazine Society, P.O. Box 46160, Station D, Vancouver BC V6J 5G5, Canada. Website: www.roommagazine.com. **Contact:** Growing Room Collective. **100% freelance written.** Quarterly journal of feminist literature. "*Room of One's Own* is Canada's oldest feminist literary journal. Since 1975, *Room* has been a forum in which women can share their unique perspectives on the world, each other and themselves." Estab. 1975. Circ. 1,000. Pays on publication. Publishes ms an average of 1 year after acceptance. Byline given. Buys first North American serial rights. Editorial lead time 9 months. Responds in 3 months to queries; 6 months to mss. Sample copy for $7 or online. Writer's guidelines online.

Nonfiction: Reviews. **Buys 1-2 mss/year.** Send complete ms. Length: 1,000-2,500 words. **Pays $35 (Canadian), and a 1-year subscription.**

Fiction: Feminist literature—short stories, creative nonfiction, essays by, for, and about women. "No humor, science fiction, romance." **Buys 40 mss/year.** Length: 2,000-5,000 words. **Pays $35 (Canadian), and a 1-year subscription.**

Poetry: Avant-garde, free verse. "Nothing light, undeveloped." **Buys 40 poems/year.** Submit maximum 6 poems. Length: 3-80 lines. **Pays $35 (Canadian), and a 1-year subscription.**

$ROSEBUD, The Magazine For People Who Enjoy Good Writing, Rosebud, Inc., P.O. Box 459, Cambridge WI 53523. (608)423-4750. Fax: (608)423-9609. Website: www.rsbd.net; www.hyperionstudio.com/rosebud. **Contact:** Rod Clark, editor. **85% freelance written.** Quarterly magazine "for people who love to read and write. Our readers like good storytelling, real emotion, a sense of place and authentic voice." Estab. 1993. Circ. 9,000. Pays on publication. Publishes ms an average of 1-3 months after acceptance. Byline given. Buys first, one-time, second serial (reprint) rights. Editorial lead time 3 months. Submit seasonal material 3 months in advance. Accepts previously published material. Accepts simultaneous submissions. to queries; 3 months to mss. Sample copy for $6.95 or sample articles online. Writer's guidelines for SASE or on website.

- Charges $1.00 reading fee. Responds in approximately 40 days.

Nonfiction: Essays, general interest, humor, personal experience, travel, memoirs that have a literary sensibility. "No editorializing." Send complete ms. Length: 1,200-1,800 words. **Pays $30.**

Reprints: Send tearsheet or photocopy. Pays 100% of amount paid for an original article.

Photos: State availability with submission. Buys one-time rights. Offers no additional payment for photos accepted with ms. Captions, identification of subjects, model releases required.

Fiction: Adventure, condensed novels, ethnic, experimental, historical, humorous, mainstream, novel excerpts, romance, science fiction, serialized novels, slice-of-life vignettes, suspense. "No formula pieces." **Buys 80 mss/year.** Send complete ms. Length: 1,200-1,800 words. **Pays $15, and 3 contributor's copies; additional copies $4.40.**

Poetry: Avant-garde, free verse, traditional. No inspirational poetry. **Buys 36 poems/year.** Submit maximum 5 poems. Length: Open. **Pays 3 contributor copies.**

Tips: "Something has to 'happen' in the pieces we choose, but what happens inside characters is much more interesting to us than plot manipulation. We prefer to respond with an individualized letter (send SASE for this) and recycle submitted manuscripts. We will return your manuscript only if you send sufficient postage. Only manuscripts accompanied by a $1 fee will be read."

$THE SAINT ANN'S REVIEW, A Journal of Contemporary Arts and Letters, Saint Ann's School, 129 Pierrepont St., Brooklyn NY 11201. E-mail: sareview@saintanns.k12.ny.us. Website: www.saintannsreview.com. **Contact:** Beth Bosworth, Editor. **100% freelance written.** Semiannual literary magazine. "We seek fully realized work, distinguished by power and craft." Estab. 2000. Circ. 2,000. Pays on publication. Publishes ms an average of 4 months after acceptance. Byline given. Buys first North American serial rights. Submit seasonal material 4 months in advance. Accepts queries by mail. Responds in 1 month to queries; 4 months to mss. Sample copy for $10. Writer's guidelines online.

Nonfiction: Book excerpts (occasionally), essays, humor, interview/profile, personal experience, photo feature. **Buys 6 mss/year.** Query with or without published clips or send complete ms. Length: 7,500 words maximum. **Pays $40/published page.**

Photos: Send photos with submission. Reviews transparencies, prints, GIF/JPEG files; black and white art. Buys one-time rights. Offers $75/photo page or art page.

Columns/Departments: Book reviews, 1,500 words. **Buys 4 mss/year.** Send complete ms by mail only. **Pays $40/published page.**

Fiction: Ethnic, experimental, fantasy, historical, humorous, mainstream, slice-of-life vignettes, translations. **Buys 15 mss/year.** Length: 7,500 words maximum. **Pays $40/published page.**

Poetry: Avant-garde, free verse, haiku, light verse, traditional, translations. **Buys 30 poems/year.** Submit maximum 5 poems. **Pays $75/page.**

N $ SAN DIEGO WRITERS' MONTHLY, 3910 Chapman St., San Diego CA 92101. (619)266-0896. E-mail: macarthy@sandiegomag.com. Website: www.sandiego-online.com/entertainment/sdwm. **Contact:** Michael T. MacCarthy, editor. Monthly magazine. "*San Diego Writers' Monthly* publishes excellent fiction from around the country with an emphasis on the writing community of San Diego county." Estab. 1991. Circ. 500. Pays on publication. Buys one-time rights. Accepts queries by mail. Accepts previously published material. Sample copy for $4. Writer's guidelines for #10 SASE.

Fiction: Adventure, ethnic, fantasy, historical, horror, humorous, mainstream, mystery, religious, romance, science fiction, suspense, western, family saga, literary, new age/mystic/spiritual, regional (southwest US), thriller/espionage. No children's/juvenile, erotica, occult, translations. **Buys 24 mss/year.** Length: 2,500-4,000 words. **Pays $15-25.**

Tips: Reviews novels, short story collections or nonfiction books of interest to writers. Looks for "good, tight, entertaining writing. Follow the guidelines."

N $ THE SEATTLE REVIEW, Box 354330, University of Washington, Seattle WA 98195. (206)543-2302. E-mail: seaview@english.washington.edu. Website: depts.washington.edu/engl/seaview1.html. **Contact:** Colleen J. McElroy, editor. Semiannual magazine. "Includes general fiction, poetry, craft essays on writing, and one interview per issue with a Northwest writer." Estab. 1978. Circ. 1,000. Pays on publication. Buys first North American serial rights. Responds in 8 months to mss. Sample copy for $6. Writer's guidelines online.

Fiction: Wants more creative nonfiction. "We also publish a series called Writers and their Craft, which deals with aspects of writing fiction (also poetry)—point of view, characterization, etc, rather than literary criticism, each issue." Does not read mss June-September. Ethnic, experimental, fantasy, historical, horror, humorous, mainstream, mystery, novel excerpts, science fiction, suspense, western, Contemporary; Feminist; Gay; Lesbian; Literary; Psychic/Supernatural/Occult; Regional; Translations. Nothing in "bad taste (porn, racist, etc.)." **Buys 4-10 mss/year.** Send complete ms. Length: 500-10,000 words. **Pays $0-100.**

Poetry: Pros.

Tips: "Beginners do well in our magazine if they send clean, well-written manuscripts. We've published a lot of 'first stories' from all over the country and take pleasure in discovery."

N $ THE SEWANEE REVIEW, University of the South, 735 University Ave., Sewanee TN 37383-1000. (931)598-1246. E-mail: rjones@sewanee.edu. Website: www.sewanee.edu/sreview/home.html. Editor: George Core. **Contact:** Fiction Editor. Quarterly magazine. "A literary quarterly, publishing original fiction, poetry, essays on literary and related subjects, and book reviews for well-educated readers who appreciate good American and English literature." Estab. 1892. Circ. 3,500. Pays on publication. Buys first North American serial, second serial (reprint) rights. Responds in 6 weeks to mss. Sample copy for $8.50. Writer's guidelines online.

Fiction: Does not read mss June 1-August 31. Literary, contemporary. No erotica, science fiction, fantasy or excessively violent or profane material. **Buys 10-15 mss/year.** Length: 6,000-7,500 words. **Pays $10-12/printed page; 2 contributor copies.**

Tips: "Send only 1 story at a time with a serious and sensible cover letter. We think fiction is of greater general interest than any other literary mode."

N $ SHENANDOAH, The Washington and Lee University Review, Washington and Lee University, Troubadour Theater, 2nd Floor, Lexington VA 24450-0303. (540)458-8765. Website: shenandoah.wlu.edu. Managing Editor: Lynn Leech. **Contact:** R.T. Smith, editor. Quarterly magazine. Estab. 1950. Circ. 2,000. Pays on publication. Publishes ms an average of 10 months after acceptance. Byline given. Buys first North American serial, one-time rights. Responds in 2 months to mss. Sample copy for $8. Writer's guidelines online.

Nonfiction: Book excerpts, essays. **Buys 6 mss/year.** Send complete ms. **Pays $25/page.**

Fiction: Mainstream, novel excerpts. No sloppy, hasty, slight fiction. **Buys 15 mss/year.** Send complete ms. **Pays $25/page.**

Poetry: No inspirational, confessional poetry. **Buys 70 poems/year.** Submit maximum 6 poems. Length: Open. **Pays $2.50/line.**

$ SHORT STUFF, for Grown-ups, Bowman Publications, 712 W. 10th St., Loveland CO 80537. (970)669-9139. E-mail: shortstf89@aol.com. **Contact:** Donnalee Bowman, editor. **98% freelance written.** Bimonthly magazine. "We are perhaps an enigma in that we publish only clean stories in any genre. We'll tackle any subject, but don't allow obscene language or pornographic description. Our magazine is for grown-ups, *not* X-rated 'adult' fare." Estab. 1989. Circ. 10,400. Payment and contract upon publication. Byline given. Buys first North American serial rights. Editorial lead time 3 months. Submit seasonal material 3 months in advance. Responds in 6 months to mss. Sample copy for $1.50 and 9×12 SAE with 5 first-class stamps. Writer's guidelines for #10 SASE.

Break in with "a good, tight story. Cover letters stating what a great story is enclosed really turn me off, just a personal bit about the author is sufficient."

Nonfiction: Most nonfiction is staff written. Humor. Special issues: "We are holiday oriented and each issue reflects the appropriate holidays. **Buys 30 mss/year.** Send complete ms. Length: 500-1,500 words. **Payment varies.**

Photos: Send photos with submission. Buys one-time rights. Offers no additional payment for photos accepted with ms. Identification of subjects required.

Fiction: Adventure, historical, humorous, mainstream, mystery, romance, science fiction, suspense, western. **Buys 144 mss/year.** Send complete ms. Length: 500-1,500 words. **Payment varies.**

Fillers: Anecdotes, short humor. **Buys 200/year.** Length: 20-500 words. **Payment varies.**

Tips: "Don't send floppy disks or cartridges. Do include cover letter about the author, not a synopsis of the story. We are holiday oriented; mark on *outside* of envelope if story is for Easter, Mother's Day, etc. We receive 500 manuscripts each month. This is up about 200%. Because of this, I implore writers to send one manuscript at a time. I would not use stories from the same author more than once an issue and this means I might keep the others too long. Please don't e-mail your stories! If you have an e-mail address, please include that with cover letter so we can contact you. If no SASE, we destroy ms."

$ THE SOUTHERN REVIEW, 43 Allen Hall, Louisiana State University, Baton Rouge LA 70803-5001. (225)578-5108. Fax: (225)578-5098. E-mail: bmacon@lsu.edu. Website: www.lsu.edu/thesouthernreview. **Contact:** John Easterly, associate editor. **100% freelance written.** Works with a moderate number of new/unpublished writers each year. Quarterly magazine "with emphasis on contemporary literature in the United States and abroad, and with special interest in Southern culture and history." No queries. Reading period: September-May. Estab. 1935. Circ. 3,100. Pays on publication. Publishes ms an average of 6 months after acceptance. Byline given. Buys first North American serial rights. Accepts queries by mail. Responds in 2 months to mss. Sample copy for $8. Writer's guidelines online.

Nonfiction: Essays with careful attention to craftsmanship, technique, and seriousness of subject matter. "Willing to publish experimental writing if it has a valid artistic purpose. Avoid extremism and sensationalism. Essays should exhibit thoughtful and sometimes severe awareness of the necessity of literary standards in our time." Emphasis on contemporary literature, especially southern culture and history. No footnotes. **Buys 25 mss/year.** Length: 4,000-10,000 words. **Pays $12/page.**

Fiction: Short stories of lasting literary merit, with emphasis on style and technique; novel excerpts. "We emphasize style and substantial content. No mystery, fantasy or religious mss." Length: 4,000-8,000 words. **Pays $12/page.**

Poetry: Length: 1-4 pages. **Pays $20/page.**

$ STAND MAGAZINE, Department of English, VCU, Richmond VA 23284-2005. (804)828-1331. E-mail: dlatane@vcu.edu. Website: www.people.vcu.edu. Managing Editor: Jon Glover. **Contact:** David Latané, U.S. editor. **75% freelance written.** Quarterly magazine covering short fiction, poetry, criticism, and reviews. "*Stand Magazine* is concerned with what happens when cultures and literatures meet, with translation in its many guises, with the mechanics of language, with the processes by which the policy receives or disables its cultural makers. *Stand* promotes debate of issues that are of radical concern to the intellectual community worldwide." Estab. 1952. Circ. 3,000 worldwide. Pays on publication. Publishes ms an average of 10 months after acceptance. Byline given. first world rights Editorial lead time 2 months. Accepts queries by mail. Responds in 6 weeks to queries; 3 months to mss. Sample copy for $12. Writer's guidelines for #10 SASE with sufficient number of IRCs or online.

Nonfiction: "Reviews are commissioned from known freelancers." Reviews of poetry/fiction. **Buys 8 mss/year.** Query. Length: 200-5,000 words. **Pays $30/1,000 words.**

Fiction: Adventure, ethnic, experimental, historical, mainstream. "No genre fiction." **Buys 12-14 mss/year.** Send complete ms. Length: 8,000 words maximum. **Payment varies.**

Poetry: Avant-garde, free verse, traditional. **Buys 100-120 poems/year.** Submit maximum 6 poems. **Pays $37.50/poem.**

Tips: "Poetry/fiction areas are most open to freelancers. *Stand* is published in England and reaches an international audience. North American writers should submit work to the U.S. address. While the topic or nature of submissions does not have to be 'international,' writers may do well to keep in mind the range of *Stand*'s audience."

$ THE STRAIN, Interactive Arts Magazine, 11702 Webercrest, Houston TX 77048. **Contact:** Norman Clark Stewart, Jr., editor. **80% freelance written.** Monthly magazine. Estab. 1987. Pays on publication. Publishes ms an average of 4 years after acceptance. Byline given. Buys first, one-time, second serial (reprint) rights, makes work-for-hire assignments. Accepts previously published material. Responds in 2 years to queries; 2 years to mss.

Nonfiction: Alicia Alder, articles editor. Essays, exposé, how-to, humor, photo feature, technical. **Buys 2-20 mss/year.** Send complete ms. **Pays $5 minimum.**

Reprints: Send ms with rights for sale noted and information about when and where the material previously appeared.

Photos: Send photos with submission. Reviews transparencies, prints. Buys one-time rights. Identification of subjects, model releases required.

Columns/Departments: Charlie Mainze, editor. Multimedia performance art. Send complete ms. **Pays $5 minimum.**

Fiction: Michael Bond, editor. **Buys 1-35 mss/year.** Send complete ms. **Pays $5 minimum.**

Poetry: Annas Kinder, editor. Avant-garde, free verse, light verse, traditional. **Buys 100 poems/year.** Submit maximum 5 poems. **Pays $5 minimum.**

N $ SUNDRY: A JOURNAL OF THE ARTS, Sundry Publications, 109 Jepson Ave., St. Clairsville OH 43950. (740)526-0215. E-mail: sundrysubmissions@yahoo.com. **Contact:** Peter L. Riesbeck, editor-in-chief. **100% freelance written.** Monthly magazine. "*Sundry* is a journal of the arts publishing high quality short fiction of nearly any genre. We pride ourselves on our eclectic theme and are eager to work with new, unpublished writers looking to polish their styles. We're especially seeking short fiction from any genre that has a strong narrative quality and that takes the reader somewhere else. Any 'slice-of-life' style stories should be character driven and well-developed." Estab. 2002. Circ. 500. **Pays on**

acceptance. Byline given. Buys one-time rights. Editorial lead time 3 months. Submit seasonal material 3 months in advance. Accepts queries by mail, e-mail. Accepts previously published material. Accepts simultaneous submissions. Responds in 2 weeks to queries; 3 months to mss. Sample copy for #10 SASE. Writer's guidelines by e-mail.

Nonfiction: Essays, general interest, historical/nostalgic, humor. **Buys 10 mss/year.** Query. Length: 7,500 words maximum. **$10-40 for unsolicited articles.**

Photos: Send photos with submission. Reviews GIF/JPEG files. Buys one-time rights. Offers $5-15/photo.

Fiction: Ethnic, experimental, historical, humorous, mystery, science fiction, serialized novels, suspense. No erotica, romance, or confessions. **Buys 50 mss/year.** Send complete ms. Length: 7,500 words. **Pays $10-50.**

Poetry: Avant-garde, free verse, haiku, light verse, traditional. No sonnets. **Buys 75 poems/year.** Submit maximum 15 poems. Length: 50 lines maximum.

$ TAMPA REVIEW, University of Tampa Press, 401 W. Kennedy Blvd., Tampa FL 33606. (813)253-6266. Fax: (813)258-7593. Website: tampareview.ut.edu. **Contact:** Richard B. Mathews, editor. Semiannual magazine published in hardback format. An international literary journal publishing art and literature from Florida and Tampa Bay as well as new work and translations from throughout the world. Estab. 1988. Circ. 500. Pays on publication. Publishes ms an average of 10 months after acceptance. Byline given. Buys first North American serial rights. Editorial lead time 18 months. Accepts queries by mail. Responds in 5 months to mss. Sample copy for $7. Writer's guidelines online.

Nonfiction: Elizabeth Winston, nonfiction editor. General interest, interview/profile, personal experience, creative nonfiction. No "how-to" articles, fads, journalistic reprise, etc. **Buys 6 mss/year.** Send complete ms. Length: 250-7,500 words. **Pays $10/printed page.**

Photos: State availability with submission. Reviews contact sheets, negatives, transparencies, prints, digital files. Buys one-time rights. Offers $10/photo. Captions, identification of subjects required.

Fiction: Lisa Birnbaum and Kathleen Ochshorn, fiction editors. Ethnic, experimental, fantasy, historical, mainstream, Literary. "We are far more interested in quality than in genre. Nothing sentimental as opposed to genuinely moving, nor self-conscious style at the expense of human truth." **Buys 6 mss/year.** Send complete ms. Length: 200-5,000 words. **Pays $10/printed page.**

Poetry: Don Morrill and Martha Serpas, poetry editors. Avant-garde, free verse, haiku, light verse, traditional, visual/experimental. No greeting card verse, hackneyed, sing-song, rhyme-for-the-sake-of-rhyme. **Buys 45 poems/year.** Submit maximum 10 poems. Length: 2-225 lines.

Tips: "Send a clear cover letter stating previous experience or background. Our editorial staff considers submissions between September and December for publication in the following year."

$ THEMA, Box 8747, Metairie LA 70011-8747. (504)887-1263. E-mail: thema@cox.net. **Contact:** Virginia Howard, editor. **100% freelance written.** Triannual magazine covering a different theme for each issue. Upcoming themes for SASE. "*Thema* is designed to stimulate creative thinking by challenging writers with unusual themes, such as 'safety in numbers' and 'the power of whim.' Appeals to writers, teachers of creative writing, and general reading audience." Estab. 1988. Circ. 350. **Pays on acceptance.** Publishes ms an average of within 6 months after acceptance. Byline given. Buys one-time rights. Accepts queries by mail, e-mail. Accepts previously published material. Accepts simultaneous submissions. Responds in 1 week to queries; 5 months to mss. Sample copy for $8. Writer's guidelines for #10 SASE.

Reprints: Send ms with rights for sale noted and information about when and where the material previously appeared. Pays the same amount paid for original.

Fiction: Special Issues: Stone, Paper, Scissors (November 1, 2003); While You Were Out (March 1, 2004); Hey, Watch This! (July 1, 2004). Adventure, ethnic, experimental, fantasy, historical, humorous, mainstream, mystery, novel excerpts, religious, science fiction, slice-of-life vignettes, suspense, western, contemporary, sports, prose poem. "No erotica." **Buys 30 mss/year.** Length: fewer than 6,000 words preferred. **Pays $10-25.**

Poetry: Avant-garde, free verse, haiku, light verse, traditional. "No erotica." **Buys 27 poems/year.** Submit maximum 3 poems. Length: 4-50 lines. **Pays $10.**

Tips: "Be familiar with the themes. *Don't submit* unless you have an upcoming theme in mind. Specify the target theme on the first page of your manuscript or in a cover letter. Put your name on *first* page of manuscript only. (All submissions are judged in blind review after the deadline for a specified issue.) Most open to fiction and poetry. Don't be hasty when you consider a theme—mull it over and let it ferment in your mind. We appreciate interpretations that are carefully constructed, clever, subtle, well thought out."

$ $ THE THREEPENNY REVIEW, P.O. Box 9131, Berkeley CA 94709. (510)849-4545. Website: www.threepennyreview.com. **Contact:** Wendy Lesser, editor. **100% freelance written.** Works with small number of new/unpublished writers each year. Quarterly tabloid. "We are a general interest, national literary magazine with coverage of politics, the visual arts, and the performing arts as well." Estab. 1980. Circ. 9,000. **Pays on acceptance.** Publishes ms an average of 1 year after acceptance. Byline given. Buys first North American serial rights. Accepts simultaneous submissions. Responds in 1 month to queries; 2 months to mss. Sample copy for $12 or online. Writer's guidelines online.

- Does not read mss in summer months.

Nonfiction: Essays, exposé, historical/nostalgic, personal experience, book, film, theater, dance, music, and art reviews. **Buys 40 mss/year.** Query with or without published clips or send complete ms. Length: 1,500-4,000 words. **Pays $200.**

Fiction: No fragmentary, sentimental fiction. **Buys 10 mss/year.** Send complete ms. Length: 800-4,000 words. **Pays $200.**

Poetry: Free verse, traditional. No poems "without capital letters or poems without a discernible subject." **Buys 30 poems/year.** Submit maximum 5 poems. **Pays $100.**

Tips: "Nonfiction (political articles, memoirs, reviews) is most open to freelancers."

$ $ $ TIN HOUSE, McCormack Communications, Box 10500, Portland OR 97296. (503)274-4393. Fax: (503)222-1154. Website: www.tinhouse.com. Editor-in-Chief: Win McCormack. Managing Editor: Holly Macarthur. Editors: Rob Spillman, Elissa Schappell. **Contact:** Lee Montgomery. **90% freelance written.** Quarterly magazine. "We are a general interest literary quarterly. Our watchword is quality. Our audience is people interested in literature in all its aspects, from the mundane to the exalted." Estab. 1998. Circ. 5,000. Pays on publication. Publishes ms an average of 6 months after acceptance. Byline given. Buys first North American serial rights. anthology rights Editorial lead time 6 months. Submit seasonal material 6 months in advance. Accepts queries by mail. Accepts simultaneous submissions. Responds in 6 weeks to queries; 3 months to mss. Sample copy for $15. Writer's guidelines online.

Nonfiction: Book excerpts, essays, interview/profile, personal experience. Send complete ms. Length: 5,000 words maximum. **Pays $50-800 for assigned articles; $50-500 for unsolicited articles.** Sometimes pays expenses of writers on assignment.

Columns/Departments: Lost and Found (mini-reviews of forgotten or under appreciated books), up to 500 words; Readable Feasts (fiction or nonfiction literature with recipes), 2,000-3,000 words; Pilgrimage (journey to a personally significant place, especially literary), 2,000-3,000 words. **Buys 15-20 mss/year.** Send complete ms. **Pays $50-500.**

Fiction: Experimental, mainstream, novel excerpts, literary. **Buys 15-20 mss/year.** Send complete ms. Length: 5,000 words maximum. **Pays $200-800.**

Poetry: Amy Bartlett, poetry editor. Avant-garde, free verse, traditional. No prose masquerading as poetry. **Buys 40 poems/year.** Submit maximum 5 poems. **Pays $50-150.**

Tips: "Remember to send a SASE with your submission."

N $ TWENTY-FOUR HOURS, 3456 N. Hills Dr., #135, Austin TX 78731. (512)342-2327. E-mail: increasethegrease@elvis.com. Website: www.23skidoo.org/~hours. **Contact:** Josh Medsker, publisher/editor. **80% freelance written.** Quarterly magazine. "*Twenty-Four Hours* is a literary magazine that loves new writers. We want to promote the kind of people who would travel around the country via Greyhound, then come back and publish a zine about it. The only thing we as of our readers is that they put everything they have into their work." Estab. 2001. Circ. 100. Pays on publication. Publishes ms an average of 3 months after acceptance. Byline given. Buys first North American serial, electronic, anthology rights. Editorial lead time 1 month. Accepts queries by mail, e-mail. Responds in 1 month to queries. Sample copy for $3 and an SAE with 3 First-Class stamps. Writer's guidelines online.

Nonfiction: Book excerpts, essays, historical/nostalgic, how-to (start a literary zine, start a series of slam poetry events, bind books by hand), interview/profile, personal experience, travel. **Buys 16 mss/year.** Query. **Pays $10, plus 1 contributor copy.** Pays in contributor copies for book reviews, zine reviews, and literary news.

Photos: State availability with submission. Reviews GIF/JPEG files. Buys one-time rights and anthology rights. Negotiates payment individually. Captions, identification of subjects required.

Columns/Departments: Book Reviews (novels and autobiographies), 500-700 words; Zine Reviews (travel zines and personal zines), 200-300 words; Literary News (local to wherever you are), 100-500 words. **Buys 30 mss/year. Pays in contributor copies.**

Fiction: Ethnic, experimental, historical, mainstream, science fiction, slice-of-life vignettes, crime/pulp. **Buys 16 mss/year.** Query with published clips. Length: 3,000 words maximum. **Pays $10.**

Poetry: Avant-garde, free verse, haiku, slam poetry. **Buys 10 poems/year.** Submit maximum 2 poems.

Tips: "We love literature in all its forms. We cover traditional literary magazine territory such as short fiction nd poetry, but also feature interviews with writers and others in the literary world—that's one half. The other half of *Twenty-Four Hours*' mission is to feature zine excerpts, interviews, with zine editors, and to generally promote the zine world to the literary world at large. We highly recommend buying an issue before submitting or querying."

N $ ⊕ UTOPIA DEL SUR, The Latin American Literary Journal, Utopia del Sur Foundation, Pedro de Mendoza 155, 14 "A", Buenos Aires, Argentina 1156. E-mail: editor@utopiadelsur.org. Website: www.utopiadelsur.org. **Contact:** Kevin Carrel Footer, editor. **90% freelance written.** Semiannual magazine. "*Utopia del Sur: The Latin American Literary Journal* publishes the finest writing from or about Latin America. All writers who draw their inspiration from Latin America may submit their work for consideration. We publish both established writers and new voices in creative nonfiction, fiction, and poetry. *Utopia del Sur* tells the stories of Latin America through fine writing and photography. We look forward to receiving your submissions." Estab. 2000. Circ. 500. Pays on publication. Publishes ms an average of 6 months after acceptance. Byline given. Not copyrighted. Buys first, second serial (reprint), electronic rights. Rights purchased varies. Editorial lead time 3 months. Accepts queries by e-mail. Accepts previously published material. Accepts simultaneous submissions. Responds in 1 month to queries; 3 months to mss. Sample copy online. Writer's guidelines online.

Nonfiction: "Send your best work and we will gladly review it." Book excerpts, essays, interview/profile, literary essays, literary travel, literary journalism, book reviews and excerpts. **Buys 10 mss/year.** Length: Varies. **Pays $25 maximum.**

Photos: State availability with submission. Reviews GIF/JPEG files. Buys one-time rights. Negotiates payment individually.

Fiction: John Fernandes, fiction editor. "Send your best work and we will be glad to review it." Literary fiction in all its forms. **Buys 10 mss/year.** Send complete ms. Length: Varies. **Pays $25 maximum.**

Poetry: Maria Volonté, poetry editor. **Buys 10 poems/year.** Submit maximum 5 poems. Length: Varies.

Tips: "*Utopia del Sur* looks for the best writing and photography from or about Latin America. New writers have as good a chance as established writers in breaking in to our publication if their work is well-crafted and true. Quality matters to us above all, so submit your finest work. We accept manuscripts in English, Spanish, and Portuguese, though we publish in English whenever possible. We prefer electronic submissions."

$ VIRGINIA QUARTERLY REVIEW, University of Virginia, One West Range, P.O. Box 400223, Charlottesville VA 22904-4223. (434)924-3124. Fax: (434)924-1397. Website: www.virginia.edu/vqr. **Contact:** Staige D. Blackford, editor. Quarterly magazine. "A national journal of literature and thought. A lay, intellectual audience; people who are not out-and-out scholars but who are interested in ideas and literature." Estab. 1925. Circ. 4,000. Pays on publication. Publishes ms an average of 1 year after acceptance. Byline given. Buys first, "will transfer upon request." rights. Editorial lead time 6 months. Submit seasonal material 6 months in advance. Responds in 2 weeks to queries; 2 months to mss. Sample copy for $5. Writer's guidelines online.

Nonfiction: Book excerpts, essays, general interest, historical/nostalgic, humor, inspirational, personal experience, travel. Send complete ms. Length: 2,000-4,000 words. **Pays $10/page maximum.**

Fiction: Adventure, ethnic, historical, humorous, mainstream, mystery, novel excerpts, romance, serialized novels. "No pornography." Send complete ms. Length: 3,000-7,000 words. **Pays $10/page maximum.**

Poetry: Gregory Orr, poetry editor. All type. Submit maximum 5 poems. **Pays $1/line.**

$ WEST BRANCH, Bucknell Hall, Bucknell University, Lewisburg PA 17837-2029. (570)577-1853. Fax: (570)577-1885. E-mail: westbranch@bucknell.edu. Website: www.bucknell.edu/westbranch. Managing Editor: Andrew Ciotola. **Contact:** Paula Closson Buck, editor. Semiannual literary magazine. "*West Branch* is an aesthetic conversation between the traditional and the innovative in poetry, fiction and nonfiction. It brings writers, new and established, to the rooms where they will be heard, and where they will, no doubt, rearrange the furniture." Pays on publication. Byline given. Buys first North American serial rights. Accepts queries by mail. Accepts simultaneous submissions. Sample copy for $3. Writer's guidelines online.

Nonfiction: Book excerpts, essays, general interest, historical/nostalgic, opinion, personal experience, travel, literary. **Buys 4-5 mss/year.** Send complete ms. **Pays $20-100 ($10/page).**

Fiction: Experimental, historical, humorous, novel excerpts, serialized novels, slice-of-life vignettes, literary. No genre fiction. **Buys 10-12 mss/year.** Send complete ms. **Pays $20-100 ($10/page).**

Poetry: Avant-garde, free verse, haiku, traditional, formal, experimental. **Buys 30-40 poems/year.** Submit maximum 6 poems. **Pays $20-100 ($10/page).**

Tips: "Please send only one submission at a time and do not send another work until you have heard about the first. Send no more than 6 poems or 30 pages of prose at once. We accept simultaneous submissions if they are clearly marked as such, and if we are notified immediately upon acceptance elsewhere. Manuscripts must be accompanied by the customary return materials; we cannot respond by e-mail or postcard. All manuscripts should be typed, with the author's name on each page; prose must be double-spaced. We recommend that you acquaint yourself with the magazine before submitting."

$ 🍁 WEST COAST LINE, A Journal of Contemporary Writing & Criticism, West Coast Review Publishing Society, 2027 E. Annex, 8888 University Dr., Simon Fraser University, Burnaby BC V5A 1S6, Canada. (604)291-4287. Fax: (604)291-4622. E-mail: wcl@sfu.ca. Website: www.sfu.ca/west-coast-line. **Contact:** Roger Farr, managing editor. Triannual magazine of contemporary literature and criticism. Estab. 1990. Circ. 500. Pays on publication. Buys one-time rights. Editorial lead time 4 months. Accepts queries by mail, e-mail. Responds in up to 6 months to queries; up to 6 months to mss. Sample copy for $10. Writer's guidelines for SASE (US must include IRC).

Nonfiction: Essays (literary/scholarly/critical), experimental prose. "No journalistic articles or articles dealing with nonliterary material." **Buys 8-10 mss/year.** Send complete ms. Length: 1,000-5,000 words. **Pays $8/page, 2 contributor's copies and a year's free subscription.**

Fiction: Experimental, novel excerpts. **Buys 3-6 mss/year.** Send complete ms. Length: 1,000-7,000 words. **Pays $8/page.**

Poetry: Avant-garde. "No light verse, traditional." **Buys 10-15 poems/year.** Submit maximum maximum 5-6 poems.

Tips: "Submissions must be either scholarly or formally innovative. Contributors should be familiar with current literary trends in Canada and the U.S. Scholars should be aware of current schools of theory. All submissions should be accompanied by a brief cover letter; essays should be formatted according to the MLA guide. The publication is not divided into departments. We accept innovative poetry, fiction, experimental prose and scholarly essays."

$ WESTERN HUMANITIES REVIEW, University of Utah, English Department, 255 S. Central Campus Dr., Room 3500, Salt Lake City UT 84112-0494. (801)581-6070. Fax: (801)585-5167. E-mail: whr@mail.hum.utah.edu. Website: www.hum.utah.edu/whr. **Contact:** Paul Ketzle, managing editor. Biannual magazine for educated readers. Estab. 1947. Circ. 1,000. Pays on publication. Publishes ms an average of 1 year after acceptance. Buys all rights. Accepts simultaneous submissions. Sample copy for $10. Writer's guidelines online.

- "We read manuscripts between September 1 and May 1. Manuscripts sent outside of these dates will be returned unread."

Nonfiction: Barry Weller, editor-in-chief. Authoritative, readable articles on literature, art, philosophy, current events, history, religion, and anything in the humanities. Interdisciplinary articles encouraged. Departments on films and books. **Buys 4-5 unsolicited mss/year.** Send complete ms. **Pays $5/published page.**

Fiction: Karen Brennan and Robin Hemley, fiction editors. Experimental. **Buys 8-12 mss/year.** Send complete ms. **Pays $5/published page (when funds available).**

Poetry: Richard Howard, poetry editor.

Tips: "Because of changes in our editorial staff, we urge familiarity with *recent* issues of the magazine. Inappropriate material will be returned without comment. We do not publish writer's guidelines because we think that the magazine itself conveys an accurate picture of our requirements. Please, *no* e-mail submissions."

$ WHETSTONE, Barrington Area Arts Council, Box 1266, Barrington IL 60011. (847)382-5626. Fax: (847)382-3685. **Contact:** Dale Griffith, editor-in-chief; Lanny Ori, Charles White, associate editors; Anna Husain, managing editor. **100%**

freelance written. Annual magazine featuring fiction, creative nonfiction, and poetry. "We publish work by emerging and established authors for readers hungry for poetry and prose of substance." Estab. 1982. Circ. 800. Pays on publication. Publishes ms an average of 14 months after acceptance. Byline given. Not copyrighted. Buys first North American serial rights. Accepts queries by mail. Accepts simultaneous submissions. Responds in 6 months to mss. Sample copy and writer's guidelines for $5.

O→ To break in, "send us your best work after it has rested long enough for you to forget it and therefore can look at it objectively to fine-tune before submitting."

Nonfiction: Essays (creative). "No articles." **Buys 0-3 mss/year.** Send complete ms. Length: 500-5,000 words. **Pays 2 copies, and variable cash payment.**

Fiction: Novel excerpts, short stories. **Buys 10-12 mss/year.** Send complete ms. Length: 500-5,000 words. **Pays 2 copies, and variable cash payment.**

Poetry: Free verse, traditional. "No light verse, for children, political poems." **Buys 10-20 poems/year.** Submit maximum 6 poems. **Pays 2 copies, and variable cash payment.**

Tips: "We look for fresh approaches to material. We appreciate careful work. Send us your best. We welcome unpublished authors. Though we pay in copies and small monetary amounts that depend on the generosity of our patrons and subscribers, we offer prizes for work published in *Whetstone*. These prizes total $1,000, and are given to 3 or more writers. The editors make their decisions at the time of publication. *This is not a contest.* In addition, we nominate authors for *Pushcart*; *Best American Short Stories*; *Poetry and Essays*; *O. Henry Awards*; *Best of the South*; Illinois Arts Council Awards; and other prizes and anthologies as they come to our attention. Though our press run is moderate, we work for our authors and offer a prestigious vehicle for their work."

N $ WINDSOR REVIEW, A Journal of the Arts, Dept. of English, University of Windsor, Windsor ON N9B 3P4, Canada. (519)253-4232, ext. 2290. Fax: (519)973-7050. E-mail: uwrevu@windsor.ca. Website: venus.uwindsor.ca/english/review.htm. Editor: Katherine Quinsey. **Contact:** Alistair MacLeod, fiction editor. Semiannual magazine. "We try to offer a balance of fiction and poetry distinguished by excellence." Estab. 1965. Circ. 250. Pays on publication. Publishes ms an average of 6 months after acceptance. Buys one-time rights. Accepts queries by e-mail. Responds in 1 month to queries; 6 weeks to mss. Sample copy for $7 (US). Writer's guidelines online.

Fiction: Literary. No genre fiction (science fiction, romance), "but would consider if writing is good enough." Length: 1,000-5,000 words. **Pays $50.**

Tips: "Good writing, strong characters, experimental fiction is appreciated."

$ WORLD WIDE WRITERS, P.O. Box 3229, Bournemouth BH1 1ZS, England. E-mail: writintl@globalnet.co.uk. Website: www.worldwidewriters.net. **Contact:** Frederick E. Smith, editor. Sample copy not available. Writer's guidelines online.

$ $ THE YALE REVIEW, Yale University, P.O. Box 208243, New Haven CT 06520-8243. (203)432-0499. Website: www.yale.edu. Associate Editor: Susan Bianconi. **Contact:** J.D. McClatchy, editor. **20% freelance written.** Quarterly magazine. Estab. 1911. Circ. 7,000. Pays prior to publication. Publishes ms an average of 6 months after acceptance. Buys one-time rights. Responds in 2 months to queries; 2 months to mss. Sample copy for $9, plus postage. Writer's guidelines online.

• *The Yale Review* has published work chosen for the Pushcart anthology, *The Best American Poetry*, and the O. Henry Award.

Nonfiction: Authoritative discussions of politics, literature and the arts. No previously published submissions. Send complete ms with cover letter and SASE. Length: 3,000-5,000 words. **Pays $400-500.**

Fiction: Buys quality fiction. Length: 3,000-5,000 words. **Pays $400-500.**

Poetry: Pays $100-250.

$ $ $ ZOETROPE: ALL STORY, AZX Publications, The Sentinel Bldg., 916 Kearny St., San Francisco CA 94133. (415)788-7500. E-mail: info@all-story.com. Website: www.all-story.com. **Contact:** Francis Ford Coppola, publisher; Tamara Straus, editor. Quarterly magazine specializing in the best of contemporary short fiction. "*Zoetrope: All Story* presents a new generation of classic stories. Estab. 1997. Circ. 20,000. Publishes ms an average of 5 months after acceptance. Byline given. Buys first North American serial rights. Accepts queries by mail. Accepts simultaneous submissions. Responds in 5 months (if SASE included) to mss. Sample copy for $5.95. Writer's guidelines online.

Fiction: Literary short stories, one-act plays. **Buys 32-40 mss/year.** Send complete ms. **Pays $1,000.**

Current and select back issues can be found online. "The website features current news, events, contests, workshops, writer's guidelines, and more. In addition, the site links to Francis Ford Coppola's virtual studio, which is host to an online workshop for short story writers."

$ ZUZU'S PETALS QUARTERLY, P.O. Box 4853, Ithaca NY 14852. (607)539-1141. E-mail: fiction@zuzu.com. Website: www.zuzu.com. **Contact:** Doug DuCap, fiction editor. "Arouse the senses; stimulate the mind." Estab. 1992. Publishes ms an average of 4-6 months after acceptance. Accepts simultaneous submissions. Responds in 2 weeks to queries 2 weeks to 2 months to mss. Back issue for $5.

Fiction: Length: 1,000-6,000 words.

$ ZYZZYVA, The Last Word: West Coast Writers & Artists, P.O. Box 590069, San Francisco CA 94159-0069. (415)752-4393. Fax: (415)752-4391. E-mail: editor@zyzzyva.org. Website: www.zyzzyva.org. **Contact:** Howard Junker, editor. **100% freelance written.** Works with a small number of new/unpublished writers each year. Magazine published in March, August, and November. "We feature work by West Coast writers only. We are essentially a literary magazine, but of wide-ranging interests and a strong commitment to nonfiction." Estab. 1985. Circ. 4,000. **Pays on acceptance.**

Publishes ms an average of 3 months after acceptance. Byline given. First North American serial and one-time anthology rights Accepts queries by mail, e-mail, fax, phone. Responds in 1 week to queries; 1 month to mss. Sample copy for $7 or online. Writer's guidelines online.

Nonfiction: Book excerpts, general interest, historical/nostalgic, humor, personal experience. **Buys 50 mss/year.** Query by mail or e-mail. Length: Open. **Pays $50.**

Photos: Reviews copies or slides only.

Fiction: Ethnic, experimental, humorous, mainstream. **Buys 20 mss/year.** Send complete ms. Length: Open. **Pays $50.**

Poetry: Buys 20 poems/year. Submit maximum 5 poems. Length: 3-200 lines. **Pays $50.**

Tips: "West Coast writers means those currently living in California, Alaska, Washington, Oregon, or Hawaii."

MEN'S

Magazines in this section offer features on topics of general interest primarily to men. Magazines that also use material slanted toward men can be found in Business & Finance, Child Care & Parental Guidance, Ethnic/Minority, Gay & Lesbian Interest, General Interest, Health & Fitness, Military, Relationships, and Sports sections. Magazines featuring pictorial layouts accompanied by stories and articles of a sexual nature, both gay and straight, appear in the Sex section.

$ CIGAR AFICIONADO, M. Shanken Communications, Inc., 387 Park Ave. S., New York NY 10016. (212)684-4224. Fax: (212)684-5424. Website: www.cigaraficionado.com. Editor: Marvin Shanken. **Contact:** Gordon Mott, executive editor. **75% freelance written.** Bimonthly magazine covering cigars and men's lifestyle. Estab. 1992. Circ. 300,000. **Pays on acceptance.** Publishes ms an average of 9 months after acceptance. Byline given. Offers 25% kill fee. Buys all rights. Editorial lead time 3 months. Submit seasonal material 3 months in advance. Accepts queries by mail, fax. Responds in 2 months to queries. Sample copy and writer's guidelines for SASE.

Nonfiction: Buys 80-100 mss/year. Query. Length: 2,000 words. **Payment varies.** Sometimes pays expenses of writers on assignment.

Columns/Departments: Length: 1,000 words. **Buys 20 mss/year. Payment varies.**

The online magazine carries original content not found in the print edition. Contact: Dave Savona, online editor.

$ GC MAGAZINE, LPI Publishing, P.O. Box 331775, Fort Worth TX 76163. (817)640-1306. Fax: (817)633-9045. E-mail: cabaret@flash.net. Managing Editor: Thomas Foss. **Contact:** Rosa Atwood, editor. **80% freelance written.** Monthly magazine. "*GC Magazine* is a general entertainment magazine for men. We include entertainment celebrity interviews (movies, music, books) along with general interest articles for adult males." Estab. 1994. Circ. 53,000. Pays on publication. Publishes ms an average of 3 months after acceptance. Buys one-time rights. Editorial lead time 3 months. Submit seasonal material 6 months in advance. Accepts queries by mail, e-mail, fax. Accepts previously published material. Accepts simultaneous submissions. Responds in 1 month to queries. Sample copy for $1.50. Writer's guidelines for #10 SASE.

Nonfiction: Book excerpts, essays, exposé, general interest, historical/nostalgic, how-to, humor, interview/profile, opinion, personal experience, technical, travel, dating tips. No religious or "feel good" articles. **Buys 100 mss/year.** Query. Length: 1,000-2,000 words. **Pays 2¢/word.** Sometimes pays expenses of writers on assignment.

Reprints: Accepts previously published submissions.

Photos: State availability with submission. Reviews 3×5 prints, GIF/JPEG files. Buys one-time rights. Offers no additional payment for photos accepted with ms. Model releases required.

Columns/Departments: Actress feature (film actress interviews), 2,500 words; Author feature (book author interviews), 1,500 words; Music feature (singer or band interviews), 1,500 words. **Buys 50 mss/year.** Query. **Pays 2¢/word.**

Fiction: Adventure, erotica, experimental, fantasy, historical, horror, humorous, mainstream, mystery, science fiction, suspense, western. No romance. **Buys 12 mss/year.** Send complete ms. Length: 1,000-3,000 words. **Pays 1¢/word, plus contributor copies.**

Tips: "Submit material typed and free of errors. Writers should think of magazines like *Maxim* and *Details* when determining article ideas for our magazine. Our primary readership is adult males and we are seeking original and unique articles."

$ $ $ $ HEARTLAND USA, UST Publishing, 100 W. Putnam Ave., Greenwich CT 06830-5316. (203)622-3456. Fax: (203)863-7296. E-mail: husaedit@att.net. **Contact:** Brad Pearson, editor. **95% freelance written.** Bimonthly magazine for working men. "*HUSA* is a general interest lifestyle magazine for adult males—active outdoorsmen. The editorial mix includes hunting, fishing, sports, automotive, how-to, country music, human interest, and wildlife." Estab. 1991. Circ. 1,200,000. **Pays on acceptance.** Byline given. Offers 20% kill fee. Buys first North American serial, second serial (reprint) rights. Submit seasonal material 1 year in advance. Accepts queries by mail, e-mail, fax. Accepts previously published material. Accepts simultaneous submissions. Responds in 1 month to queries. Sample copy for free. Writer's guidelines for #10 SASE.

Nonfiction: Book excerpts, general interest, historical/nostalgic, how-to, humor, inspirational, interview/profile, new product, personal experience, photo feature, technical, travel. "No fiction or dry expository pieces." **Buys 30 mss/year.** Query with or without published clips or send complete ms. Length: 350-1,200 words. **Pays 50¢-$1/word for assigned articles; 25-80¢/word for unsolicited articles.** Sometimes pays expenses of writers on assignment.

Reprints: Send photocopy and information about when and where the material previously appeared. Pays 25% of amount paid for an original article.

Photos: Send photos with submission. Reviews transparencies. Buys one-time rights. Identification of subjects required.

Tips: "Features with the possibility of strong photographic support are open to freelancers, as are our departments. We look for a relaxed, jocular, easy-to-read style, and look favorably on the liberal use of anecdote or interesting quotations. Our average reader sees himself as hardworking, traditional, rugged, confident, uncompromising, and daring."

N $ $ $ INDY MEN'S MAGAZINE, The Guy's Guide to the Good Life, Table Moose Media, 5114 Brookstone Lane, Indianapolis IN 46240. (317)255-3850. E-mail: lou@indymensmagazine.com. Website: www.indymensmagazine.com. **Contact:** Lou Harry, editor-in-chief. **50% freelance written.** Monthly magazine. Estab. 2002. Circ. 50,000. Pays on publication. Byline given. Offers 10% kill fee. Buys first North American serial rights. Editorial lead time 3 months. Submit seasonal material 1 year in advance. Accepts queries by e-mail. Accepts simultaneous submissions. Responds in 2 weeks to queries; 1 month to mss. Sample copy for $5. Writer's guidelines by e-mail.

Nonfiction: Essays, travel. No generic pieces that could run anywhere. No advocacy pieces. **Buys 50 mss/year.** Query. Length: 100-2,000 words. **Pays $75-800 for assigned articles; $50-400 for unsolicited articles.** Sometimes pays expenses of writers on assignment.

Photos: State availability with submission. Reviews contact sheets, transparencies, prints, GIF/JPEG files. Buys one-time rights. Negotiates payment individually. Identification of subjects required.

Columns/Departments: Balls (opinionated sports pieces), 1,400 words; Dad Files (introspective parenting essays), 1,400 words; Men At Work (Indianapolis men and their jobs), 400 words; Trippin' (experiential travel), 1,500 words. **Buys 30 mss/year.** Query with published clips. **Pays $75-400.**

Fiction: "The piece needs to hold our attention from the first paragraph." Adventure, fantasy, historical, horror, humorous, mainstream, mystery, science fiction, suspense. **Buys 12 mss/year.** Send complete ms. Length: 1,000-6,000 words. **Pays $100-400.**

Tips: "We don't believe in wasting our reader's time, whether it's in a 50-word item or a 6,000-word Q&A. Our readers are smart, and they appreciate our sense of humor. Write to entertain and engage."

$ $ $ $ THE INTERNATIONAL, The Magazine of Adventure and Pleasure for Men, Tomorrow Enterprises, 2228 E. 20th St., Oakland CA 94606. (510)532-6501. Fax: (510)536-5886. E-mail: tonyattomr@aol.com. **Contact:** Mr. Anthony L. Williams, managing editor. **70% freelance written.** Monthly magazine covering "bush and seaplane flying, seafaring, pleasure touring, etc., with adventure stories from all men who travel on sexual tours to Asia, Latin America, The Caribbean, and the Pacific." Estab. 1997. Circ. 5,000. Pays on publication. Publishes ms an average of 2 months after acceptance. Buys first rights. Editorial lead time 2 months. Submit seasonal material 3 months in advance. Accepts queries by mail, e-mail. Accepts simultaneous submissions. Responds in 2 weeks to queries; 2 months to mss. Writer's guidelines free.

Nonfiction: Seafaring storis of all types published with photos. Military and veteran stories also sought as well as ex-pats living abroad. Especially interested in airplane flying stories with photos. Exposé, general interest, historical/nostalgic, humor, interview/profile, opinion, personal experience, photo feature, travel. No pornography, family, or "honeymoon" type travel. **Buys 40-50 mss/year.** Send complete ms. Length: 700 words maximum. **Pays $100-2,000 for assigned articles; $25-1,000 for unsolicited articles.** Sometimes pays expenses of writers on assignment.

Photos: Send photos with submission. Reviews negatives, 3×5 prints. Buys one-time or all rights. Offers no additional payment for photos accepted with ms. Identification of subjects required.

Columns/Departments: Asia/Pacific Beat; Latin America/Caribbean Beat (nightlife, adventure, air & sea), 450 words; Lifestyles Abroad (expatriate men's doings overseas), 600-1,000 words. **Buys 25 mss/year.** Send complete ms. **Pays $25-1,000.**

Fillers: Anecdotes, facts, gags to be illustrated by cartoonist, newsbreaks, short humor. **Buys 25/year.** Length: 200-600 words. **Pays $25-100.**

Tips: "If a single male lives in those parts of the world covered, and is either a pleasure tourist, pilot, or seafarer, we are interested in his submissions. He can visit our upcoming website or contact us directly. Stories from female escorts or party girls are also welcomed."

N $ KING, Harris Publications, Inc., 1115 Broadway, New York NY 10010. (212)807-7100. Fax: (212)807-0216. E-mail: kingmag@harris-pub.com. Website: www.king-mag.com. Editor: Datwon Thomas. Bimonthly magazine. Edited for today's urban male. Circ. 150,000. Editorial lead time 8 months. Sample copy not available.

N $ MACHINE DESIGN, Penton Media, Penton Media Bldg., 1300 E. 9th Street., Cleveland OH 49114-1503. (216)931-9412. Fax: (216)621-8469. E-mail: mdeditor@penton.com. Website: www.machinedesign.com. Editor: Ronald Kohl. **Contact:** Kenneth Korane, managing editor. Semimonthly magazine covering machine design. Covers the design engineering of manufactured products, across the entire spectrum of the idustry for people who perform design engineering functions. Circ. 185,163. Editorial lead time 3 weeks. Accepts queries by mail, e-mail. Sample copy not available.

Nonfiction: How-to, new product, technical. Query with or without published clips or send complete ms.

Columns/Departments: Query with or without published clips or send complete ms.

N $ MAXIM, Dennis Publishing, 1040 Avenue of The Americas, 16th Floor, New York NY 10018-3703. (212)302-2626. Fax: (212)302-2635. E-mail: editors@maximmag.com. Website: www.maximonline.com. Editor: Keith Blanchard. Monthly magazine relationships, sex, women, careers and sports. Written for young, professional men interested in fun and informative articles. Circ. 2,569,172. Editorial lead time 5 months. Sample copy for $3.99 at newstands.

$ MEN'S JOURNAL, Wenner Media, Inc., 1290 Avenue of the Americas, New York NY 10104-0298. (212)484-1616. Fax: (212)484-3434. Website: www.mensjournal.com. Editor: Bob Wallace. Executive Editor: Mark Horowitz. Senior Editor: Claire Martin. **Contact:** Tyler Graham, assistant editor. Monthly magazine covering general lifestyle for men, ages 25-49. "*Men's Journal* is for active men with an interest in participatory sports, travel, fitness, and adventure. It provides practical, informative articles on how to spend quality leisure time." Estab. 1992. Circ. 650,000. Accepts queries by mail, fax.

• *Men's Journal* won the National Magazine Award for Personal Service.

Nonfiction: Features and profiles 2,000-7,000 words; shorter features of 400-1,200 words; equipment and fitness stories, 400-1,800 words. Book excerpts, essays, exposé, general interest, historical/nostalgic, how-to, humor, new product, personal experience, photo feature, travel. Query with SASE. **Payment varies.**

$$$$ SMOKE MAGAZINE, Life's Burning Desires, Lockwood Publications, 26 Broadway, Floor 9M, New York NY 10004. (212)391-2060. Fax: (212)827-0945. E-mail: editor@smokemag.com. Website: www.smokemag.com. Senior Editor: Mark Bernardo. **Contact:** Alyson Boxman Levine, editor-in-chief. **75% freelance written.** Quarterly magazine covering cigars and men's lifestyle issues. "A large majority of *Smoke's* readers are affluent men, ages 28-50; active, educated and adventurous." Estab. 1995. Circ. 175,000. Pays 2 months after publication. Publishes ms an average of 3 months after acceptance. Byline given. Offers 25% kill fee. Buys first rights. Editorial lead time 2 months. Submit seasonal material 6 months in advance. Accepts queries by mail, e-mail. Accepts simultaneous submissions. Responds in 6 weeks to queries; 3 months to mss. Sample copy for $4.99.

O─ Break in with "good nonfiction that interests guys—beer, cuisine, true-crime, sports, cigars, of course. Be original."

Nonfiction: Essays, exposé, general interest, historical/nostalgic, how-to, humor, interview/profile, opinion, personal experience, photo feature, technical, travel, true crime. **Buys 25 mss/year.** Query with published clips. Length: 1,500-3,000 words. **Pays $500-1,500.** Sometimes pays expenses of writers on assignment.

Photos: State availability with submission. Reviews 2¼×2¼ transparencies. Negotiates payment individually. Identification of subjects required.

Columns/Departments: Smoke Undercover, Smoke Slant (humor); What Lew Says (cigar industry news); Workin' Stiffs (world's best jobs), all 1,500 words. **Buys 20 mss/year.** Query with published clips. **Pays $500-1,500.**

Fillers: Anecdotes, facts, gags to be illustrated by cartoonist, newsbreaks, short humor. **Buys 12 fillers/year.** Length: 200-500 words. **Pays $200-500.**

The online magazine carries original content not found in the print edition.

Tips: "Send a short, clear query with clips. Go with your field of expertise: Cigars, sports, music, true crime, etc."

$$ UMM (URBAN MALE MAGAZINE), Canada's Only Lifestyle and Fashion Magazine for Men, UMM Publishing Inc., 70 George St., Suite 200, Ottawa ON K1N 5V9, Canada. (613)723-6216. Fax: (613)723-1702. E-mail: editor@umm.ca. Website: www.umm.ca. Editor: Abbis Mahmoud. **Contact:** David Sachs, senior editor. **100% freelance written.** Bimonthly magazine covering men's interests. "Our audience is young men, aged 18-24. We focus on Canadian activities, interests, and lifestyle issues. Our magazine is fresh and energetic and we look for original ideas carried out with a spark of intelligence and/or humour (and you'd better spell humour with a 'u')." Estab. 1998. Circ. 90,000. Pays 1 month after publication. Publishes ms an average of 3 months after acceptance. Byline given. Buys first North American serial rights. Editorial lead time 3 months. Submit seasonal material 4 months in advance. Accepts queries by e-mail. Accepts simultaneous submissions. Responds in 6 weeks to queries; 6 weeks to mss.

Nonfiction: Book excerpts, exposé, general interest, historical/nostalgic, how-to, humor, interview/profile, new product, personal experience, travel, adventure, cultural, sports, music. **Buys 80 mss/year.** Query with published clips. Length: 1,200-3,500 words. **Pays $100-400.** Sometimes pays expenses of writers on assignment.

Photos: State availability with submission. Reviews contact sheets, prints. Buys one-time rights. Negotiates payment individually.

Fillers: Anecdotes, facts, short humor. **Buys 35/year.** Length: 100-500 words. **Pays $50-150.**

Tips: "Be familiar with our magazine before querying. We deal with all subjects of interest to young men, especially those with Canadian themes. We are very open-minded. Original ideas and catchy writing are key."

MILITARY

These publications emphasize military or paramilitary subjects or other aspects of military life. Technical and semitechnical publications for military commanders, personnel, and planners, as well as those for military families and civilians interested in Armed Forces activities are listed here. Publications covering military history can be found in the History section.

$$ AIR FORCE TIMES, Army Times Publishing Co., 6883 Commercial Dr., Springfield VA 22159. (703)750-8646. Fax: (703)750-8601. Website: www.airforcetimes.com. **Contact:** Lance Bacon, managing editor. Weeklies edited separately for Army, Navy, Marine Corps, and Air Force military personnel and their families. They contain career information such as pay raises, promotions, news of legislation affecting the military, housing, base activities and features of interest to military people. Estab. 1940. **Pays on acceptance.** Byline given. Offers kill fee. Buys first rights. Accepts queries by mail, e-mail, phone. Accepts simultaneous submissions. Responds in 1 month to queries. Sample copy for #10 SASE. Writer's guidelines for #10 SASE.

Nonfiction: Features of interest to career military personnel and their families. No advice pieces. **Buys 150-175 mss/year.** Query. Length: 750-2,000 words. **Pays $100-500.**

Columns/Departments: Length: 500-900. **Buys 75 mss/year. Pays $75-125.**

The online magazines carry original content not found in the print editions. Websites: www.armytimes.com; www.navytimes.com; www.airforcetimes.com; www.marinecorpstimes.com. Contact: Neff Hudson, online editor.

Tips: Looking for "stories on active duty, reserve and retired military personnel; stories on military matters and localized military issues; stories on successful civilian careers after military service."

$ $ ARMY MAGAZINE, 2425 Wilson Blvd., Arlington VA 22201-3385. (703)841-4300. Fax: (703)841-3505. E-mail: armymag@ausa.org. Website: www.ausa.org. **Contact:** Mary Blake French, editor-in-chief. **70% freelance written.** Prefers to work with published/established writers. Monthly magazine emphasizing military interests. Estab. 1904. Circ. 90,000. Pays on publication. Publishes ms an average of 5 months after acceptance. Byline given. Buys all rights. Submit seasonal material 3 months in advance. Accepts queries by mail. Sample copy for 9×12 SAE with $1 postage or online. Writer's guidelines for 9×12 SAE with $1 postage or online.

• *Army Magazine* looks for shorter articles.

Nonfiction: "We would like to see more pieces about little-known episodes involving interesting military personalities. We especially want material lending itself to heavy, contributor-supplied photographic treatment. The first thing a contributor should recognize is that our readership is very savvy militarily. 'Gee-whiz' personal reminiscences get short shrift, unless they hold their own in a company in which long military service, heroism and unusual experiences are commonplace. At the same time, *Army* readers like a well-written story with a fresh slant, whether it is about an experience in a foxhole or the fortunes of a corps in battle." Historical/nostalgic (military and original), humor (military feature-length articles and anecdotes), interview/profile, photo feature. No rehashed history. No unsolicited book reviews. **Buys 40 mss/year.** Submit complete ms (hard copy and disk). Length: 1,000-1,500 words. **Pays 12-18¢/word.**

Photos: Send photos with submission. Reviews transparencies, prints, slides, high-resolution digital photos. Buys all rights. Pays $50-100 for 8×10 b&w glossy prints; $50-350 for 8×10 color glossy prints or 2¼×2¼ transparencies; 35mm and high resolution digital photos. Captions required.

$ $ ARMY TIMES, Times News Group, Inc., 6883 Commercial Dr., Springfield VA 22159. (703)750-9000. Fax: (703)750-8622. E-mail: features@atpco.com. Website: www.armytimes.com. **Contact:** Chuck Vinch, managing editor. Weekly for Army military personnel and their families containing career information such as pay raises, promotions, news of legislation affecting the military, housing, base activities and features of interest to military people. Estab. 1940. Circ. 230,000. **Pays on acceptance.** Byline given. Offers kill fee. Makes work-for-hire assignments. Accepts queries by mail, e-mail. Accepts simultaneous submissions. Responds in 1 month to queries. Sample copy and writer's guidelines for #10 SASE.

O━ Break in by "proposing specific feature stories that only you can write-things we wouldn't be able to get from 'generic' syndicated or wire material. The story must contain an element of mystery and/or surprise, and be entertaining as well as informative. Above all, your story must have a direct connection to military people's needs and interests."

Nonfiction: Features of interest to career military personnel and their families: food, relationships, parenting, education, retirement, shelter, health, and fitness, sports, personal appearance, community, recreation, personal finance, entertainment. No advice please. **Buys 150-175 mss/year.** Query. Length: 750-2,000 words. **Pays $100-500.**

Columns/Departments: Length: 500-900 words. **Buys 75 mss/year. Pays $75-125.**

▣ The online magazines carry original content not found in the print editions. Contact: Kent Miller, online editor.

Tips: Looking for "stories on active duty, reserve and retired military personnel; stories on military matters and localized military issues; stories on successful civilian careers after military service."

N $ COMBAT HANDGUNS, Harris Publication, Inc., 1115 Broadway, New York NY 10010-3450. (212)807-7100. Fax: (212)807-1479. E-mail: combat@harris-custsvc.com. Website: www.combathandguns.com. Editor: Harry Kane. Magazine published 8 times/year covering combat handguns. Written for handgun owners and collectors. Circ. 126,498. Editorial lead time 2 months. Accepts queries by mail, e-mail. Sample copy not available.

Nonfiction: Query.

Photos: Send photos with submission. Reviews GIF/JPEG files. Captions required.

$ $ MARINE CORPS TIMES, Army Times Publishing Co., 6883 Commercial Dr., Springfield VA 22159. (703)750-9000. Fax: (703)750-8767. E-mail: marinelet@atpco.com. Website: www.marinecorpstimes.com. **Contact:** Chris Lawson, managing editor, *Army Times*; Alex Neil, managing editor, *Navy Times*; Julie Bird, managing editor, *Air Force Times*; Rob Colenso, managing editor, *Marine Corps Times*. Weeklies edited separately for Army, Navy, Marine Corps, and Air Force military personnel and their families. They contain career information such as pay raises, promotions, news of legislation affecting the military, housing, base activities and features of interest to military people. Estab. 1940. Circ. 230,000 (combined). Pays on publication. Byline given. Offers kill fee. Buys first rights. Accepts queries by mail, e-mail, phone. Accepts simultaneous submissions. Responds in 1 month to queries. Sample copy for #10 SASE. Writer's guidelines for #10 SASE.

Nonfiction: Features of interest to career military personnel and their families, including stories on current military operations and exercises. No advice pieces. **Buys 150-175 mss/year.** Query. Length: 750-2,000 words. **Pays $100-500.**

Columns/Departments: Length: 500-900 words. **Buys 75 mss/year. Pays $75-125.**

▣ The online magazines carry original content not found in the print editions. Websites: www.armytimes.com; www.navytimes.com; www.airforcetimes.com. Contact: Kent Miller, online editor.

Tips: Looking for "stories on active duty, reserve and retired military personnel; stories on military matters and localized military issues; stories on successful civilian careers after military service."

$ $ $ $ MILITARY OFFICER, (formerly *The Retired Officer Magazine*), 201 N. Washington St., Alexandria VA 22314-2539. (800)234-6622. Fax: (703)838-8179. E-mail: editor@troa.org. Website: www.troa.org. Editor: Col. Warren S. Lacy, USA-Ret. Managing Editor: Molly Wyman. **Contact:** Molly Wyman. **60% freelance written.** Prefers to work with published/established writers. Monthly magazine for officers of the 7 uniformed services and their families. "*Military Officer* covers topics such as current military/political affairs, military history, travel, finance, hobbies, health and fitness, and military family and retirement lifestyles." Estab. 1945. Circ. 389,000. **Pays on acceptance.** Publishes ms an average of 1 year after acceptance. Byline given. Buys first North American serial rights. Accepts queries by mail, e-mail, fax. Responds in 3 months to queries. Sample copy and writer's guidelines for 9×12 SAE with 6 first-class stamps or online.

Nonfiction: Current military/political affairs, health and wellness, recent military history, travel, military family life-style. Emphasis now on current military and defense issues. "We rarely accept unsolicited manuscripts." **Buys 48 mss/year.** Query with résumé, sample clips and SASE. Length: 800-2,500 words. **Pays up to $1,800.**

Photos: Query with list of stock photo subjects. Original slides and transparencies must be suitable for color separation. Reviews transparencies. Pays $20 for each 8×10 b&w photo (normal halftone) used. Pays $75-250 for inside color; $300 for cover.

The online magazine carries original content not found in the print edition and includes writer's guidelines. Contact: Ronda Reid, online editor.

$ $ MILITARY TIMES, Times News Group, Inc. (subsidiary of Gannett Corp.), 6883 Commercial Dr., Springfield VA 22159. Fax: (703)750-8781. E-mail: features@atpco.com. Website: www.militarycity.com. Managing Editor: David Craig. **Contact:** Phillip Thompson, Lifeline editor. **25% freelance written.** Weekly tabloid covering lifestyle topics for active, retired, and reserve military members and their families. "Features need to have real military people in them, and appeal to readers in all the armed services. Our target audience is 90% male, young, fit and adventurous, mostly married and often with young children. They move frequently. Writer queries should approach ideas with those demographics and facts firmly in mind." Circ. 300,000. **Pays on acceptance.** Publishes ms an average of 2 months after acceptance. Byline given. Buys first, electronic rights. Editorial lead time 2 months. Submit seasonal material 3 months in advance. Accepts queries by mail, e-mail, fax. Accepts simultaneous submissions. Responds in 6 weeks to queries. Sample copy for $2.25 or online. Writer's guidelines for SAE with 1 first-class stamp or by e-mail.

"Greatest need is in the adventure categories of sports, recreation, outdoor, personal fitness, and running. Personal finance features are especially needed, but they must be specifically tailored to our military audience's needs and interests."

Nonfiction: Book excerpts, how-to, interview/profile, new product, photo feature, technical, travel, sports, recreation, entertainment, health, personal fitness, self-image (fashion, trends), relationships, personal finance, food. "No poems, war memoirs or nostalgia, fiction, travel pieces that are too upscale (luxury cruises) or too focused on military monuments/museums." **Buys 110 mss/year.** Query with published clips. Length: 300-1,500 words. **Pays $100-500.** Sometimes pays expenses of writers on assignment.

Photos: State availability with submission. Reviews transparencies. Offers work-for-hire. Offers $75/photo. Captions, identification of subjects required.

Columns/Departments: Running (how-to for experienced runners, tips, techniques, problem-solving), 500 words; Personal Fitness (how-to, tips, techniques for working out, improving fitness), 500 words. **Buys 40 mss/year.** Query. **Pays $100-200.**

Tips: "Our Lifelines section appears every week with a variety of services, information, and entertainment articles on topics that relate to readers' off-duty lives; or to personal dimensions of their on-duty lives. Topics include food, relationships, parenting, education, retirement, shelter, health and fitness, sports, personal appearances, community, recreation, personal finance, and entertainment. We are looking for articles about military life, its problems and how to handle them, as well as interesting things people are doing, on the job and in their leisure. Keep in mind that our readers come from all of the military services. For instance, a story can focus on an Army family, but may need to include families or sources from other services as well. The editorial 'voice' of the section is familiar and conversational; good-humored without being flippant; sincere without being sentimental; savvy about military life but in a relevant and subtle way, never forgetting that our readers are individuals first, spouses or parents or children second, and service members third."

$ $ NAVAL HISTORY, U.S. Naval Institute, 291 Wood Rd., Annapolis MD 21402-5034. (410)295-1079. Fax: (410)295-1049. E-mail: fschultz@usni.org. Website: www.navalinstitute.org. Associate Editors: Colin Babb and Giles Roblyer. **Contact:** Fred L. Schultz, editor-in-chief. **90% freelance written.** Bimonthly magazine covering naval and maritime history, worldwide. "We are committed, as a publication of the 127-year-old U.S. Naval Institute, to presenting the best and most accurate short works in international naval and maritime history. We do find a place for academicians, but they should be advised that a good story generally wins against a dull topic, no matter how well researched." Estab. 1988. Circ. 40,000. **Pays on acceptance.** Publishes ms an average of 2 years after acceptance. Byline given. Buys all rights. Editorial lead time 6 months. Submit seasonal material 6 months in advance. Accepts queries by mail, e-mail, fax, phone. Responds in 1 month to queries; 2 months to mss. Sample copy for $3.95 and SASE, or on website. Writer's guidelines online.

Nonfiction: Book excerpts, essays, historical/nostalgic, humor, inspirational, interview/profile, personal experience, photo feature, technical. **Buys 50 mss/year.** Query. Length: 1,000-3,000 words. **Pays $300-500 for assigned articles; $75-400 for unsolicited articles.**

Photos: State availability with submission. Reviews contact sheets, transparencies, 4×6 or larger prints, and digital submissions or CD-ROM. Buys one-time rights. Offers $10 minimum. Captions, identification of subjects, model releases required.

Fillers: Anecdotes, newsbreaks (naval-related), short humor. **Buys 40-50/year.** Length: 50-1,000 words. **Pays $10-50.**

Tips: "A good way to break in is to write a good, concise, exciting story supported by primary sources and substantial illustrations. Naval history-related news items (ship decommissionings, underwater archaeology, etc.) are also welcome.

Because our story bank is substantial, competition is severe. Tying a topic to an anniversary many times is an advantage. We still are in need of Korean and Vietnam War-era material."

$ PARAMETERS, U.S. Army War College Quarterly, U.S. Army War College, 122 Forbes Ave., Carlisle PA 17013-5238. (717)245-4943. E-mail: parameters@carlisle.army.mil. Website: www.carlisle.army.mil/usawc/parameters. **Contact:** Col. Robert H. Taylor, USA Ret., editor. **100% freelance written.** Prefers to work with published/established writers or experts in the field. Readership consists of senior leaders of US defense establishment, both uniformed and civilian, plus members of the media, government, industry and academia. Subjects include national and international security affairs, military strategy, military leadership and management, art and science of warfare, and military history with contemporary relevance. Estab. 1971. Circ. 13,500. Pays on publication. Publishes ms an average of 6 months after acceptance. Byline given. Buys first North American serial rights. Accepts queries by mail, e-mail, phone. Responds in 6 weeks to queries. Sample copy free or online. Writer's guidelines online.

Nonfiction: Prefers articles that deal with current security issues, employ critical analysis, and provide solutions or recommendations. Liveliness and verve, consistent with scholarly integrity, appreciated. Theses, studies, and academic course papers should be adapted to article form prior to submission. Documentation in complete endnotes. Send complete ms. Length: 4,500 words average. **Pays $150 average.**

Tips: "Make it short; keep it interesting; get criticism and revise accordingly. Write on a contemporary topic. Tackle a subject only if you are an authority. No fax submissions." Encourage e-mail submissions.

$ $ PROCEEDINGS, U.S. Naval Institute, 291 Wood Rd., Annapolis MD 21402-5034. (410)268-6110. Fax: (410)295-7940. E-mail: frainbow@usni.org. Website: www.usni.org. Editor: Fred H. Rainbow. **Contact:** Gordon Keiser, senior editor. **80% freelance written.** Monthly magazine covering Navy, Marine Corps, Coast Guard issues. Estab. 1873. Circ. 100,000. **Pays on acceptance.** Publishes ms an average of 9 months after acceptance. Byline given. Buys all rights. Editorial lead time 3 months. Responds in 2 months to queries. Sample copy for $3.95. Writer's guidelines online.

Nonfiction: Essays, historical/nostalgic, interview/profile, photo feature, technical. **Buys 100-125 mss/year.** Query with or without published clips or send complete ms. Length: 3,000 words. **Pays $60-150/printed page for unsolicited articles.**

Photos: State availability of or send photos with submission. Reviews transparencies, prints. Buys one-time rights. Offers $25/photo maximum.

Columns/Departments: Comment & Discussion (letters to editor), 750 words; Commentary (opinion), 900 words; Nobody Asked Me, But... (opinion), less than 1,000 words. **Buys 150-200 mss/year.** Query or send complete ms. **Pays $34-150.**

Fillers: Anecdotes. **Buys 20/year.** Length: 100 words. **Pays $25.**

$ $ $ $ SOLDIER OF FORTUNE, The Journal of Professional Adventurers, 5735 Arapahoe Ave., Suite A-5, Boulder CO 80303-1340. (303)449-3750. Fax: (303)444-5617. E-mail: editor@sofmag.com. Website: www.sofmag.com. Editor: Robert Brown. Deputy Editor: Tom Reisinger. **50% freelance written.** Monthly magazine covering military, paramilitary, police, combat subjects, and action/adventure. "We are an action-oriented magazine; we cover combat hot spots around the world. We also provide timely features on state-of-the-art weapons and equipment; elite military and police units; and historical military operations. Readership is primarily active-duty military, veterans, and law enforcement." Estab. 1975. Circ. 60,000. Byline given. Offers 25% kill fee. Buys first rights. Responds in 3 weeks to queries; 1 month to mss. Sample copy for $5. Writer's guidelines for #10 SASE.

Nonfiction: Exposé, general interest, historical/nostalgic, how-to (on weapons and their skilled use), humor, interview/profile, new product, personal experience, photo feature (No. 1 on our list), technical, travel, combat reports, military unit reports, and solid Vietnam and Operation Iraqi Freedom articles. "No 'How I won the war' pieces; no op-ed pieces unless they are fully and factually backgrounded; no knife articles (staff assignments only). All submitted articles should have good art; art will sell us on an article." **Buys 75 mss/year.** Query with or without published clips or send complete ms. Send mss to articles editor; queries to managing editor. Length: 2,000-3,000 words. **Pays $150-250/page.**

Reprints: Send disk copy, photocopy of article and information about when and where the material previously appeared. Pays 25% of amount paid for an original article.

Photos: Send photos with submission. Reviews contact sheets, transparencies. Buys one-time rights. Pays $500 for cover photo. Captions, identification of subjects required.

Fillers: Bulletin Board editor. Newsbreaks (military/paramilitary related has to be documented). Length: 100-250 words. **Pays $50.**

Tips: "Submit a professionally prepared, complete package. All artwork with cutlines, double-spaced typed manuscript with 5.25 or 3.5 IBM-compatible disk, if available, cover letter including synopsis of article, supporting documentation where applicable, etc. Manuscript must be factual; writers have to do their homework and get all their facts straight. One error means rejection. Vietnam features, if carefully researched and art heavy, will always get a careful look. Combat reports, again, with good art, are number one in our book and stand the best chance of being accepted. Military unit reports from around the world are well received as are law-enforcement articles (units, police in action). If you write for us, be complete and factual; pros read *Soldier of Fortune*, and are very quick to let us know if we (and the author) err."

MUSIC

Music fans follow the latest industry news in these publications that range from opera to hip hop. Types of music and musicians or specific instruments are the sole focus of some magazines. Publications geared to the music industry and professionals can be found in the Trade Music section. Additional music and dance markets are found in the Contemporary Culture and Entertainment sections.

N $ AMERICAN COUNTRY, Music Monthly, Publishing Services Inc., 1336 Edna SE, Suite 6, Grand Rapids MI 49507. (616)458-1011. Fax: (616)458-2285. E-mail: brucep@gogrand.com. **Contact:** Bruce L. Parrott, editor. **50% freelance written.** Monthly tabloid covering country music. "*American Country* is a country music publication syndicated to radio stations around the country and featuring articles on country artists, album reviews, recipes, etc." Estab. 1992. Circ. 300,000. Pays on publication. Publishes ms an average of 2 months after acceptance. Byline given. Buys one-time rights, makes work-for-hire assignments. Editorial lead time 2 months. Accepts queries by e-mail, fax. Accepts simultaneous submissions. Responds in 1 week to queries.

Nonfiction: Interview/profile, new product (all pertaining to country music). No country music news. **Buys 40-50 mss/year.** Query with published clips. Length: 1,000-2,000 words. **Pays $10-50.**

Columns/Departments: CD Jukebox (album reviews), 50-100 words. **Buys 35-50 mss/year.** Query with published clips. **Pays $10.**

Tips: "Call and tell me the kind of stuff you're doing and send some copies. Have existing contacts within the Nashville music scene."

$ $ AMERICAN RECORD GUIDE, Record Guide Productions, 4412 Braddock St., Cincinnati OH 45204. (513)941-1116. E-mail: rightstar@aol.com. **Contact:** Donald Vroon, editor. **90% freelance written.** Bimonthly 6×9 book covering classical music for music lovers and record collectors. Estab. 1935. Circ. 8,000. Pays on publication. Publishes ms an average of 2 months after acceptance. Byline given. Buys all rights. Editorial lead time 2 months. Accepts queries by mail, e-mail. Accepts previously published material. Accepts simultaneous submissions. Sample copy for $7. Writer's guidelines free.

Nonfiction: Essays. **Buys 30-45 full-length mss and hundreds of reviews mss/year.** Query. **Pays $50-350 for assigned articles; $50-150 for unsolicited articles.**

$ AMERICAN SONGWRITER MAGAZINE, 50 Music Square W., Suite 604, Nashville TN 37203-3227. (615)321-6096. Fax: (615)321-6097. E-mail: info@americansongwriter.com. Website: www.americansongwriter.com. Managing Editor: Lou Heffernan. **Contact:** Vernell Hackett, editor. **30% freelance written.** Bimonthly magazine about songwriters and the craft of songwriting for many types of music, including pop, country, rock, metal, jazz, gospel, and r&b. Estab. 1984. Circ. 5,000. Pays on publication. Publishes ms an average of 2 months after acceptance. Offers 25% kill fee. Buys first North American serial rights. Accepts previously published material. Responds in 2 months to queries. Sample copy for $4. Writer's guidelines for #10 SASE.

Nonfiction: General interest, interview/profile, new product, technical, home demo studios, movie and TV scores, performance rights organizations. **Buys 20 mss/year.** Query with published clips. Length: 300-1,200 words. **Pays $25-60.**

Reprints: send tearsheet or photocopy and information about when and where the material previously appeared. Pays same amount as paid for an original article.

Photos: Send photos with submission. Reviews 3×5 prints. Buys one-time rights. Offers no additional payment for photos accepeted with ms. Identification of subjects required.

Tips: "*American Songwriter* strives to present articles which can be read a year or 2 after they were written and still be pertinent to the songwriter reading them."

$ $ BLUEGRASS UNLIMITED, Bluegrass Unlimited, Inc., P.O. Box 771, Warrenton VA 20188-0771. (540)349-8181 or (800)BLU-GRAS. Fax: (540)341-0011. E-mail: editor@bluegrassmusic.com. Website: www.bluegrassmusic.com. Editor: Peter V. Kuykendall. **Contact:** Sharon Watts, managing editor. **60% freelance written.** Prefers to work with published/established writers. Monthly magazine covering bluegrass, acoustic, and old-time country music. Estab. 1966. Circ. 27,000. Pays on publication. Publishes ms an average of 4 months after acceptance. Byline given. Offers negotiated kill fee. Buys first North American serial, one-time, second serial (reprint), all rights. Submit seasonal material 4 months in advance. Accepts queries by mail, e-mail, fax. Responds in 2 weeks to queries; 2 months to mss. Sample copy for free. Writer's guidelines for #10 SASE.

Nonfiction: General interest, historical/nostalgic, how-to, interview/profile, personal experience, photo feature, travel. No "fan"-style articles. **Buys 60-70 mss/year.** Query with or without published clips. Length: Open. **Pays 8-10¢/word.**

Reprints: Send photocopy with rights for sale noted and information about when and where the material previously appeared. Payment is negotiable.

Photos: State availability of or send photos with submission. Reviews 35mm transparencies and 3×5, 5×7 and 8×10 b&w and color prints. Buys all rights. Pays $50-175 for transparencies; $25-60 for b&w prints; $50-250 for color prints. Identification of subjects required.

Fiction: Ethnic, humorous. **Buys 3-5 mss/year.** Query. Length: Negotiable. **Pays 8-10¢/word.**

Tips: "We would prefer that articles be informational, based on personal experience or an interview with lots of quotes from subject, profile, humor, etc."

$ $ CHAMBER MUSIC, Chamber Music America, 305 Seventh Ave., New York NY 10001-6008. (212)242-2022. Fax: (212)242-7955. E-mail: kkrenz@chamber-music.org. Website: www.chamber-music.org/magazine. **Contact:** Karissa Krenz, editor. Bimonthly magazine covering chamber music. Estab. 1977. Circ. 13,000. Pays on publication. Publishes ms an average of 5 months after acceptance. Byline given. Offers kill fee. Buys first rights. Editorial lead time 4 months. Accepts queries by mail, phone.

Nonfiction: Book excerpts, essays, humor, opinion, personal experience, issue-oriented stories of relevance to the chamber music fields written by top music journalists and critics, or music practitioners. No artist profiles, no stories about opera or symphonic work. **Buys 35 mss/year.** Query with published clips. Length: 2,500-3,500 words. **Pays $500 minimum.** Sometimes pays expenses of writers on assignment.

Photos: State availability with submission. Offers no payment for photos accepted with ms.

N $ CHART MAGAZINE, Canada's Music Magazine, Chart Communications, Inc., 41 Britain St., Suite 200, Toronto ON M5A 1R7, Canada. (416)363-3101. Fax: (416)363-3109. E-mail: chart@chartattack.com. Website: www.chartattack.com. Editor: Nada Laskovski. **Contact:** Aaron Brophy, managing editor. **90% freelance written.** Monthly magazine. *Chart Magazine* has a "cutting edge attitude toward music and pop culture to fit with youth readership." Estab. 1990. Circ. 40,000 (paid). Pays on publication. Publishes ms an average of 3-6 months after acceptance. Byline given. Buys first North American serial, electronic rights. Editorial lead time 2 months. Submit seasonal material 3 months in advance. Accepts queries by mail, e-mail, fax, phone. Responds in 4-6 weeks to queries; 2-3 months to mss. Sample copy for $6 U.S. (via mail order). Writer's guidelines free.

Nonfiction: All articles must relate to popular music and/or pop culture. Book excerpts, essays, exposé, humor, interview/profile, personal experience, photo feature. Nothing that isn't related to popular music and pop culture (i.e., film, books, video games, fashion, etc., that would appeal to a hip youth demographic). Query with published clips and send complete ms. Length: Word length varies. **Payment varies.**

Photos: Claman Chu, art director. Send photos with submission. Buys all rights. Negotiates payment individually.

N $ GIG MAGAZINE, United Entertainment Media, Inc., 2800 Campus Drive, San Mateo CA 94403. (415)386-2435. Fax: (650)513-4642. E-mail: jleslie@musicplayer.com. Website: www.gigmag.com. Editor: Jimmy Leslie. Monthly magazine targeted to professional musicians, DJ's, and members of bands from all genres. Circ. 50,000. Editorial lead time 4 months. Sample copy not available.

$ $ $ GUITAR ONE, The Magazine You Can Play, 6 E. 32nd St., 11th Floor, New York NY 10016. Fax: (212)251-0840. E-mail: guitarone@cherrylane.com. Website: www.guitaronemag.com. **Contact:** Troy Nelson, editor-in-chief. **75% freelance written.** Monthly magazine covering guitar news, artists, music, gear. Estab. 1996. Circ. 140,000. Pays on publication. Publishes ms an average of 1 month after acceptance. Byline given. Offers 50% kill fee. Buys one-time rights. Editorial lead time 3 months. Accepts queries by mail, e-mail, fax. Accepts simultaneous submissions. Sample copy online.

Nonfiction: Interview/profile (with guitarists). **Buys 15 mss/year.** Query with published clips. Length: 2,000-5,000 words. **Pays $300-1,200 for assigned articles; $150-800 for unsolicited articles.** Sometimes pays expenses of writers on assignment.

Photos: State availability with submission. Reviews negatives, transparencies, prints. Buys one-time rights. Negotiates payment individually.

Columns/Departments: Opening Axe (newsy items on artists), 450 words; Soundcheck (records review), 200 words; Gear Box (equipment reviews), 800 words.

Tips: "Find an interesting feature with a nice angle that pertains to guitar enthusiasts. Submit a well-written draft or samples of work."

$ $ MODERN DRUMMER, 12 Old Bridge Rd., Cedar Grove NJ 07009. (201)239-4140. Fax: (201)239-7139. Editorial Director: William F. Miller. Senior Editor: Rick Van Horn. **Contact:** Ronald Spagnardi, editor-in-chief. **60% freelance written.** Monthly magazine for "student, semipro, and professional drummers at all ages and levels of playing ability, with varied specialized interests within the field." Circ. 102,000. Pays on publication. Publishes ms an average of 3 months after acceptance. Buys all rights. Accepts previously published material. Responds in 2 weeks to queries. Sample copy for $4.99. Writer's guidelines for #10 SASE.

Nonfiction: "All submissions must appeal to the specialized interests of drummers." How-to, interview/profile, new product, personal experience, technical, informational. **Buys 40-50 mss/year.** Query with published clips or send complete ms. Length: 5,000-8,000 words. **Pays $200-500.**

Reprints: Send photocopy with rights for sale noted and information about when and where the material previously appeared.

Photos: Reviews color transparencies, 8×10 b&w prints. Purchased with accompanying ms.

Columns/Departments: Jazz Drummers Workshop; Rock Perspectives; Rock 'N' Jazz Clinic; Driver's Seat (Big Band); In The Studio; Show Drummers Seminar; Teachers Forum; Drum Soloist; The Jobbing Drummer; Strictly Technique; Shop Talk; Latin Symposium; Book Reviews; Record Reviews; Video Reviews. Profile columns: Portraits; Up & Coming; From the Past. Length: 500-1,000 words. "Technical knowledge of area required for most columns." **Buys 40-50 mss/year.** Send complete ms. **Pays $50-150.**

Tips: "*MD* is looking for music journalists rather than music critics. Our aim is to provide information, not to make value judgments. Therefore, keep all articles as objective as possible. We are interested in how and why a drummer plays a certain way; the readers can make their own decisions about whether or not they like it."

$ MUSIC FOR THE LOVE OF IT, 67 Parkside Dr., Berkeley CA 94705. (510)654-9134. Fax: (510)654-4656. E-mail: tedrust@musicfortheloveofit.com. Website: www.musicfortheloveofit.com. **Contact:** Ted Rust, editor. **20% freelance written.** Bimonthly newsletter covering amateur musicianship. "A lively, intelligent source of ideas and enthusiasm for a musically literate audience of adult amateur musicians." Estab. 1988. Circ. 600. Pays on publication. Publishes ms an average of 2 months after acceptance. Byline given. Buys one-time rights. Editorial lead time 1 month. Submit seasonal material 1 month in advance. Accepts queries by mail, e-mail, fax, phone. Responds in 1 week to queries; 1 month to mss. Sample copy for $6. Writer's guidelines online.

Break in with "a good article, written from a musician's point of view, with at least 1 photo."

Nonfiction: Essays, historical/nostalgic, how-to, personal experience, photo feature. No concert reviews, star interviews, CD reviews. **Buys 6 mss/year.** Query. Length: 500-1,500 words. **Pays $50, or gift subscriptions.**

Photos: State availability with submission. Reviews 4×6 prints or larger. Buys one-time rights. Offers no additional payment for photos accepted with ms. Identification of subjects required.

Tips: "We're looking for more good how-to articles on musical styles. Love making music. Know something about it."

$ RELIX MAGAZINE, Music for the Mind, 180 Varick St., 4th Floor, New York NY 10014. (646)230-0100. Website: www.relix.com. **Contact:** Aeve Baldwin, editor-in-chief. **40% freelance written.** Bimonthly magazine focusing on new and independent bands, classic rock, lifestyles, and music alternatives such as roots, improvisational music, psychedelia, and jambands. Estab. 1974. Circ. 100,000. Pays on publication. Publishes ms an average of 4 months after acceptance. Byline given. Buys all rights. Accepts queries by mail, e-mail. Accepts previously published material. Responds in 6 months to queries. Sample copy for $5. Writer's guidelines online.

Nonfiction: Feature topics include jambands, reggae, Grateful Dead, bluegrass, jazz, country, rock, experimental, electronic, and world music; also deals with environmental, cultural, and lifestyle issues. Historical/nostalgic, humor, interview/profile, new product, photo feature, technical, live reviews, new artists, hippy lifestyles, food, mixed media, books. Query by mail with published clips if available or send complete ms. Length: 300-1,500 words. **Pays variable rates.**

Photos: "Whenever possible, submit complete artwork with articles."

Columns/Departments: Query with published clips or send complete ms. **Pays variable rates.**

Tips: "The best part of working with freelance writers is discovering new music we might never have stumbled across."

N $ ROLLING STONE, Warner Media, 1290 Avenue of The Americas, New York NY 10104. (212)484-1616. Fax: (212)484-1664. E-mail: letters@rollingstone.com. Website: www.rollingstone.com. Editor: Jann S. Wenner. Biweekly magazine. Geared towards young adults interested in news of popular music, entertainment and the arts, current news events, politics and American culture. Circ. 1,254,200. Editorial lead time 1 month. Sample copy not available.

$ SPIN, 205 Lexington Ave., 3rd Floor, New York NY 10016. (212)231-7400. Fax: (212)231-7312. E-mail: feedback@spin.com. Website: www.spin.com. Publisher: Jon Chalon. **Contact:** Sia Michel, editor-in-chief. Monthly magazine covering music and popular culture. "*Spin* covers progressive rock as well as investigative reporting on issues from politics, to pop culture. Editorial includes reviews, essays, profiles and interviews on a wide range of music from rock to jazz. It also covers sports, movies, politics, humor, fashion and issues—from AIDS research to the environment. The editorial focuses on the progressive new music scene and young adult culture more from an 'alternative' perspective as opposed to mainstream pop music. The magazine discovers new bands as well as angles for the familiar stars." Estab. 1985. Circ. 540,000.

Nonfiction: Features are not assigned to writers who have not established a prior relationship with *Spin.* Cultural, political or social issues. New writers: submit complete ms with SASE. Established writers: query specific editor with published clips.

Columns/Departments: Most open to freelancers: Exposure (short articles on popular culture, TV, movies, books), 200-500 words, query Maureen Callahan, associate editor; Reviews (record reviews), 100 words, queries/mss to Alex Pappademas, senior editor; Noise (music and new artists), query Tracey Pepper, senior associate editor. Query before submitting.

Tips: "The best way to break into the magazine is the Exposure and Reviews sections. We primarily work with seasoned, professional writers who have extensive national magazine experience and very rarely make assignments based on unsolicited queries."

$ $ $ SYMPHONY, American Symphony Orchestra League, 33 W. 60th St., Fifth Floor, New York NY 10023-7905. (212)262-5161, ext. 247. Fax: (212)262-5198. E-mail: editor@symphony.org. Website: www.symphony.org. **Contact:** Melinda Whiting, editor-in-chief. **50% freelance written.** Bimonthly magazine for the orchestra industry and classical music enthusiasts covering classical music, orchestra industry, musicians. Writers should be knowledgeable about classical music and have critical or journalistic/repertorial approach. Circ. 18,500. **Pays on acceptance.** Publishes ms an average of 2 months after acceptance. Byline given. Buys first, one-time rights. Editorial lead time 6 months. Submit seasonal material 8 months in advance. Accepts queries by mail, e-mail, phone. Accepts simultaneous submissions. Writer's guidelines online.

Nonfiction: Book excerpts, essays, inspirational, interview/profile, opinion, personal experience (rare), photo feature (rare), issue features, trend pieces (by assignment only; pitches welcome). Does not want to see reviews, interviews. **Buys 30 mss/year.** Query with published clips. Length: 900-3,500 words. **Pays $300-800.** Sometimes pays expenses of writers on assignment.

Photos: State availability of or send photos with submission. Reviews contact sheets, negatives, prints, electronic photos (preferred). Buys one-time rights. Offers no additional payment for photos accepted with ms. Captions, identification of subjects required.

Columns/Departments: Repertoire (orchestral music—essays); Comment (personal views and opinions); Currents (electronic media developments); In Print (books); On Record (CD, DVD, video), all 1,000 words. **Buys 12 mss/year.** Query with published clips.

Tips: "We need writing samples before assigning pieces. We prefer to craft the angle with the writer, rather than adapt an existing piece. Pitches and queries should demonstrate a clear relevance to the American orchestra industry and should be timely."

N $ TRADITION, Nat. Trad. C.M.A., P.O. Box 492, Anita IA 50020. (712)762-4363. Fax: (712)762-4363. Editor: Bob Everhart. **20% freelance written.** Bimonthly magazine covering pioneer and old-time music. "Our 2,500 members are devoted fans of old-time, traditional mountain, country, bluegrass and folk music. Everything we print must be directed toward that audience." Estab. 1976. Circ. 2,500. Pays on publication. Publishes ms an average of 3 months after acceptance. Byline sometimes given. Buys one-time rights. Editorial lead time 3 months. Submit seasonal material 3 months in advance.

Accepts previously published material. Accepts simultaneous submissions. Responds in 3 months to queries. Sample copy and writer's guidelines for $4 and SASE.

Nonfiction: Book excerpts, essays, general interest, historical/nostalgic, personal experience, travel. **Buys 6-8 mss/year.** Query. **Pays $5-25.**

Photos: State availability with submission. Buys one-time rights. Offers no additional payment for photos accepted with ms. Identification of subjects required.

Poetry: Traditional.

Fillers: Anecdotes, facts, short humor.

$$$$ VIBE, 215 Lexington Ave., 6th Floor, New York NY 10016. (212)448-7300. Fax: (212)448-7400. E-mail: vibe@vibe.com. Website: www.vibe.com. Managing Editor: Jacklyn Monk. Managing Editor: Andrea Rosengarten. **Contact:** Individual editors as noted. Monthly magazine covering urban music and culture. "*Vibe* chronicles and celebrates urban music and the youth culture that inspires and consumes it." Estab. 1993. Circ. 800,000. Pays on publication. Buys first North American serial rights. Editorial lead time 4 months. Responds in 2 months to queries. Sample copy available on newsstands. Writer's guidelines for #10 SASE.

Nonfiction: Robert Simpson, deputy editor; Shani Saxon, music editor. Cultural, political or social issues. Query with published clips, résumé and SASE. Length: 800-3,000 words. **Pays $1/word.**

Columns/Departments: Start (introductory news-based section), 350-740 words, send queries to Brett Johnson, senior editor. Revolutions (music reviews), 100-800 words, send queries to Craig Seymour, associate music editor. Book reviews, send queries Robert Morales, senior editor. Query with published clips, résumé and SASE. **Pays $1/word.**

Tips: "A writer's best chance to be published in *Vibe* is through the Start or Revolutions Sections. Keep in mind that *Vibe* is a national magazine, so ideas should have a national scope. People in Cali should care as much about the story as people in NYC. Also, *Vibe* has a four-month lead time. What we work on today will appear in the magazine four or more months later. Stories must be timely with respect to this fact."

MYSTERY

These magazines buy fictional accounts of crime, detective work, mystery, and suspense. Skim through other sections to identify markets for fiction; some will consider mysteries. Markets for true crime accounts are listed under Detective & Crime.

$ HARDBOILED, Gryphon Publications, P.O. Box 209, Brooklyn NY 11228. Website: www.gryphonbooks.com. **Contact:** Gary Lovisi, editor. **100% freelance written.** Semiannual book covering crime/mystery fiction and nonfiction. "Hard-hitting crime fiction and private-eye stories—the newest and most cutting-edge work and classic reprints." Estab. 1988. Circ. 1,000. Pays on publication. Publishes ms an average of 18 months after acceptance. Byline given. Offers 100% kill fee. Buys first North American serial, one-time rights. Editorial lead time 1 year. Submit seasonal material 9 months in advance. Accepts queries by mail, fax. Accepts previously published material. Accepts simultaneous submissions. Responds in 2 weeks to queries; 1 month to mss. Sample copy for $8 or double issue for $20 (add $1.50 book postage). Writer's guidelines for #10 SASE.

Nonfiction: Book excerpts, essays, exposé. **Buys 4-6 mss/year.** Query. Length: 500-3,000 words. **Pays 1 copy.**

Reprints: Query first.

Photos: State availability with submission.

Columns/Departments: Occasional review columns/articles on hardboiled writers. **Buys 2-4 mss/year.** Query.

Fiction: Mystery, hardboiled crime, and private-eye stories, all on the cutting edge. No "pastches, violence for the sake of violence." **Buys 40 mss/year.** Query with or without published clips or send complete ms. Length: 500-3,000 words. **Pays $5-50.**

Tips: Best bet for breaking in is short hard crime fiction filled with authenticity and brevity.

$ ALFRED HITCHCOCK'S MYSTERY MAGAZINE, Dell Magazines, 475 Park Ave. S., 11th Floor, New York NY 10016. (212)686-7188. Website: www.themysteryplace.com. Editor: Linda Landrigan. **100% freelance written.** Monthly magazine featuring new mystery short stories. Estab. 1956. Circ. 615,000. Pays on publication. Byline given. Buys first, foreign rights rights. Submit seasonal material 7 months in advance. Responds in 3 months to mss. Sample copy for $5. Writer's guidelines for SASE or on website.

Fiction: Original and well-written mystery and crime fiction. "Because this is a mystery magazine, the stories we buy must fall into that genre in some sense or another. We are interested in nearly every kind of mystery, however: stories of detection of the classic kind, police procedurals, private eye tales, suspense, courtroom dramas, stories of espionage, and so on. We ask only that the story be about crime (or the threat or fear of one). We sometimes accept ghost stories or supernatural tales, but those also should involve a crime." Mystery. No sensationalism. Send complete ms. Length: Up to 14,000 words. **Pays 8¢/word.**

Tips: "No simultaneous submissions, please. Submissions sent to *Alfred Hitchcock's Mystery Magazine* are not considered for or read by *Ellery Queen's Mystery Magazine*, and vice versa."

$ ✪ THE MYSTERY REVIEW, A Quarterly Publication for Mystery Readers, C. von Hessert & Associates, P.O. Box 233, Colborne ON K0K 1S0, Canada. E-mail: mystrev@reach.net. Website: www.themysteryreview.com. **Contact:** Barbara Davey, editor. **80% freelance written.** Quarterly magazine covering mystery and suspense. "Our readers are interested in mystery and suspense books, films. All topics related to mystery—including real life unsolved mysteries." Estab. 1992. Circ. 8,500 (80% of distribution is in US). Pays on publication. Publishes ms an average of 6 months after acceptance. Byline given. Buys first North American serial rights. Editorial lead time 6 months. Submit seasonal material 6 months in advance. Accepts queries by mail, e-mail, fax. Responds in 6 weeks to queries; 1 month to mss. Sample copy for $7.50. Writer's guidelines online.

Nonfiction: Interview/profile, true-life mysteries. Query. Length: 2,000-5,000 words. **Pays $30 maximum.**

Photos: Send photos with submission. Buys all rights. Offers no additional payment for photos accepted with ms. Identification of subjects, model releases required.

Columns/Departments: Book reviews (mystery/suspense titles only), 500 words; Truly Mysterious ("unsolved," less-generally-known, historical, or contemporary cases; photos/illustrations required), 2,000-5,000 words; Book Shop Beat (bookstore profiles; questionnaire covering required information available from editor), 500 words. **Buys 50 mss/year.** Query with published clips. **Pays $10-30.**

Fillers: Puzzles, trivia, shorts (items related to mystery/suspense). **Buys 4/year.** Length: 100-500 words. **Pays $10-20.**

$ ELLERY QUEEN'S MYSTERY MAGAZINE, Dell Magazines Fiction Group, 475 Park Ave. S., 11th Floor, New York NY 10016. (212)686-7188. Fax: (212)686-7414. E-mail: elleryqueen@dellmagazines.com. Website: www.themysteryplace.com. **Contact:** Janet Hutchings, editor. **100% freelance written.** Magazine published 11 times/year featuring mystery fiction. "*Ellery Queen's Mystery Magazine* welcomes submissions from both new and established writers. We publish every kind of mystery short story: the psychological suspense tale, the deductive puzzle, the private eye case—the gamut of crime and detection from the realistic (including the policeman's lot and stories of police procedure) to more imaginative (including "locked rooms" and "impossible crimes"). *EQMM* has been in continuous publication since 1941. From the beginning three general criteria have been employed in evaluating submissions: We look for strong writing, an original and exciting plot, and professional craftmanship. We encourage writers whose work meets these general criteria to read an issue of *EQMM* before making a submission." Magazine for lovers of mystery fiction. Estab. 1941. Circ. 300,000 readers. **Pays on acceptance.** Publishes ms an average of 6-12 months after acceptance. Byline given. Buys first North American serial rights. Accepts previously published material. Accepts simultaneous submissions. Responds in 3 months to mss. Sample copy for $5. Writer's guidelines for online or for SASE.

Fiction: "We publish every type of mystery: the suspense story, the psychological study, the private-eye story, the deductive puzzle—the gamut of crime and detection from the realistic (including stories of police procedure) to the more imaginative (including 'locked rooms' and 'impossible crimes'). We always need detective stories. Special consideration given to anything timely and original." No sex, sadism, or sensationalism-for-the-sake-of-sensationalism, no gore or horror. Seldom publishes parodies or pastiches. **Buys up to 120 mss/year.** Send complete ms. Length: Most stories 2,500-10,000 words. Accepts longer and shorter submissions—including minute mysteries of 250 words, and novellas of up to 20,000 words from established authors. **Pays 5-8¢/word, occasionally higher for established authors.**

Poetry: Short mystery verses, limericks. Length: 1 page, double spaced maximum.

Tips: "We have a Department of First Stories to encourage writers whose fiction has never before been in print. We publish an average of 11 first stories every year."

NATURE, CONSERVATION & ECOLOGY

These publications promote reader awareness of the natural environment, wildlife, nature preserves, and ecosystems. Many of these "green magazines" also concentrate on recycling and related issues, and a few focus on environmentally-conscious sustainable living. They do not publish recreation or travel articles except as they relate to conservation or nature. Other markets for this kind of material can be found in the Regional, Sports (Hiking & Backpacking in particular), and Travel, Camping & Trailer categories, although magazines listed there require that nature or conservation articles be slanted to their specialized subject matter and audience.

$ ALTERNATIVES JOURNAL, Canadian Environmental Ideas and Action, Alternatives, Inc., Faculty of Environmental Studies, University of Waterloo, Waterloo ON N2L 3GL, Canada. (519)888-4442. Fax: (519)746-0292. E-mail: editor@alternativesjournal.ca. Website: www.alternativesjournal.ca. Editor: Robert Gibson. **Contact:** Cheryl Lousley, executive editor. **90% freelance written.** Quarterly magazine covering environmental issues with Canadian relevance. Estab. 1971. Circ. 4,800. Pays on publication. Publishes ms an average of 5 months after acceptance. Byline given. Offers 50% kill fee. Buys first rights. Editorial lead time 7 months. Submit seasonal material 5 months in advance. Accepts queries by mail, e-mail, fax. Accepts simultaneous submissions. Sample copy free for Canadian writers only. Writer's guidelines online.

Nonfiction: Book excerpts, essays, exposé, humor, interview/profile, opinion. **Buys 50 mss/year.** Query with published clips. Length: 800-3,000 words. **Pays $50-150 (Canadian).** All contributors receive a free subscription in addition to payment. Sometimes pays expenses of writers on assignment.

Photos: State availability with submission. Buys one-time rights. Offers $35-75/photo. Identification of subjects required.

$$$ AMERICAN FORESTS, American Forests, P.O. Box 2000, Washington DC 20013. (202)955-4500. Fax: (202)887-1075. E-mail: mrobbins@amfor.org. Website: www.americanforests.org. **Contact:** Michelle Robbins, editor. **75% freelance written.** Quarterly magazine "of trees and forests published by a nonprofit citizens' organization that strives to help people plant and care for trees for ecosystem restoration and healthier communities." Estab. 1895. Circ. 25,000. **Pays on acceptance.** Publishes ms an average of 8 months after acceptance. Byline given. Buys one-time rights. Submit seasonal material 5 months in advance. Accepts queries by mail, e-mail. Accepts previously published material. Responds in 2 months to queries. Sample copy for $2. Writer's guidelines online.

O→ Break in with "stories that resonate with city dwellers who love trees, or small, forestland owners (private). This magazine is looking for more urban and suburban-oriented pieces.

Nonfiction: All articles should emphasize trees, forests, forestry and related issues. General interest, historical/nostalgic, how-to, humor, inspirational. **Buys 8-12 mss/year.** Query. Length: 1,200-2,000 words. **Pays $250-1,000.**

Reprints: Send tearsheet or typed ms with rights for sale noted and information about when and where the material previously appeared. Pays 50% of amount paid for original article.

Photos: Originals only. Send photos with submission. Reviews 35mm or larger transparencies, glossy color prints. Buys one-time rights. Offers no additional payment for photos accompanying ms. Captions required.

Tips: "We're looking for more good urban forestry stories, and stories that show cooperation among disparate elements to protect/restore an ecosystem. Query should have honesty and information on photo support. We *do not* accept fiction or poetry at this time."

N $ $ THE ATLANTIC SALMON JOURNAL, The Atlantic Salmon Federation, P.O. Box 5200, St. Andrews NB E5B 3S8, Canada. Fax: (506)529-4985. E-mail: asfpub@nbnet.nb.ca. Website: www.asf.ca. **Contact:** Jim Gourlay, editor. **50-68% freelance written.** Quarterly magazine covering conservation efforts for the Atlantic salmon, catering to "affluent and responsive audience—the dedicated angler and conservationist." Circ. 10,000. Pays on publication. Publishes ms an average of 6 months after acceptance. Byline given. Buys first North American serial rights. One-time rights to photos Submit seasonal material 3 months in advance. Accepts simultaneous submissions. Responds in 2 months to queries. Sample copy for 9×12 SAE with $1 (Canadian), or IRC. Writer's guidelines free.

Nonfiction: "We are seeking articles that are pertinent to the focus and purpose of our magazine, which is to inform and entertain our membership on all aspects of the Atlantic salmon and its environment, preservation and conservation." Exposé, historical/nostalgic, how-to, humor, interview/profile, new product, opinion, personal experience, photo feature, technical, travel, conservation; science; research and management. **Buys 15-20 mss/year.** Query with published clips. Length: 1,500-2,500 words. **Pays $200-400.** Sometimes pays expenses of writers on assignment.

Photos: State availability with submission. Pays $50 for 3×5 or 5×7 b&w prints; $50-100 for 2¼ × 3¼ or 35mm color slides. Captions, identification of subjects required.

Columns/Departments: Conservation issues and salmon research; the design, construction and success of specific flies (*Fit To Be Tied*); interesting characters in the sport; opinion pieces by knowledgeable writers, 900 words; *Casting Around* (short, informative, entertaining reports, book reviews and quotes from the world of Atlantic salmon angling and conservation). Query. **Pays $50-250.**

Tips: "Articles must reflect informed and up-to-date knowledge of Atlantic salmon. Writers need not be authorities, but research must be impeccable. Clear, concise writing is essential, and submissions must be typed. The odds are that a writer without a background in outdoor writing and wildlife reporting will not have the 'informed' angle I'm looking for. Our readership is well read and critical of simplification and generalization."

$ THE BEAR DELUXE MAGAZINE, Orlo, P.O. Box 10342, Portland OR 97296. (503)242-1047. E-mail: bear@orlo.org. Website: www.orlo.org. **Contact:** Tom Webb, editor. **80% freelance written.** Semiannual magazine. "*The Bear Deluxe Magazine* provides a fresh voice amid often strident and polarized environmental discourse. Street level, solution-oriented, and nondogmatic, *The Bear Deluxe* presents lively creative discussion to a diverse readership." Estab. 1993. Circ. 19,000. Pays on publication. Publishes ms an average of 2 months after acceptance. Byline given. Offers 25% kill fee. Buys first, one-time rights. Editorial lead time 3 months. Submit seasonal material 4 months in advance. Accepts queries by mail, e-mail. Accepts previously published material. Accepts simultaneous submissions. Responds in 3 months to queries; 6 months to mss. Sample copy for $3. Writer's guidelines for #10 SASE or on website.

Nonfiction: Book excerpts, essays, exposé, general interest, interview/profile, new product, opinion, personal experience, photo feature, travel, artist profiles. Special issues: Publishes 1 theme/2 years. **Buys 40 mss/year.** Query with published clips. Length: 250-4,500 words. **Pays 5¢/word.** Sometimes pays expenses of writers on assignment.

Photos: State availability with submission. Reviews contact sheets, transparencies, 8×10 prints. Buys one-time rights. Offers $30/photo. Identification of subjects, model releases required.

Columns/Departments: Reviews (almost anything), 300 words; Talking Heads (creative first person), 500 words; News Bites (quirk of eco-news), 300 words; Portrait of an Artist (artist profiles), 1,200 words. **Buys 16 mss/year.** Query with published clips. **Pays 5¢/word, subscription, and copies.**

Fiction: "Stories must have some environmental context." Adventure, condensed novels, historical, horror, humorous, mystery, novel excerpts, science fiction, western. "No detective, children's or horror." **Buys 8 mss/year.** Query with or without published clips or send complete ms. Length: 750-4,500 words. **Pays free subscription to the magazine, conttributot's copies and 5¢/word; additional copies for postage.**

Poetry: Avant-garde, free verse, haiku, light verse, traditional. **Buys 16-20 poems/year.** Submit maximum 5 poems. Length: 50 lines maximum. **Pays $10, subscription, and copies.**

Fillers: Facts, newsbreaks, short humor. **Buys 10/year.** Length: 100-750 words. **Pays 5¢/word, subscription, and copies.**

Tips: "Offer to be a stringer for future ideas. Get a copy of the magazine and guidelines, and query us with specific nonfiction ideas and clips. We're looking for original, magazine-style stories, not fluff or PR. Fiction, essay, and poetry writers should know we have an open and blind review policy and should keep sending their best work even if rejected once. Be as specific as possible in queries."

$ BIRD WATCHER'S DIGEST, Pardson Corp., P.O. Box 110, Marietta OH 45750. (740)373-5285. E-mail: editor@birdwatchersdigest.com. Website: www.birdwatchersdigest.com. **Contact:** William H. Thompson III, editor. **60% freelance**

written. Works with a small number of new/unpublished writers each year. Bimonthly magazine covering natural history—birds and bird watching. "*BWD* is a nontechnical magazine interpreting ornithological material for amateur observers, including the knowledgeable birder, the serious novice and the backyard bird watcher; we strive to provide good reading and good ornithology." Estab. 1978. Circ. 90,000. Pays on publication. Publishes ms an average of 2 years after acceptance. Byline given. Buys one-time, second serial (reprint) rights. Submit seasonal material 6 months in advance. Accepts previously published material. Responds in 2 months to queries. Sample copy for $3.99 or online. Writer's guidelines online.

Nonfiction: "We are especially interested in fresh, lively accounts of closely observed bird behavior and displays and of bird-watching experiences and expeditions. We often need material on backyard subjects such as bird feeding, housing, gardenening on less common species or on unusual or previously unreported behavior of common species." Book excerpts, how-to (relating to birds, feeding and attracting, etc.), humor, personal experience, travel (limited, we get many). No articles on pet or caged birds; none on raising a baby bird. **Buys 45-60 mss/year.** Send complete ms. Length: 600-3,500 words. **Pays from $100.**

Photos: Send photos with submission. Reviews transparencies, prints. Buys one-time rights. Pays $75 minimum for transparencies.

The online magazine carries content not found in the print edition and includes writer's guidelines.

Tips: "We are aimed at an audience ranging from the backyard bird watcher to the very knowledgeable birder; we include in each issue material that will appeal at various levels. We always strive for a good geographical spread, with material from every section of the country. We leave very technical matters to others, but we want facts and accuracy, depth and quality, directed at the veteran bird watcher and at the enthusiastic novice. We stress the joys and pleasures of bird watching, its environmental contribution, and its value for the individual and society."

$ $ BIRDER'S WORLD, Enjoying Birds at Home and Beyond, Kalmbach Publishing Co., P.O. Box 1612, Waukesha WI 53187-1612. Fax: (262)798-6468. E-mail: mail@birdersworld.com. Website: www.birdersworld.com. Editor: Charles J. Hagner. Managing Editor: Diane Jolie. Associate Editor: Matt Schlag-Mendenhall. **Contact:** Rosemary Nowak, editorial assistant. Bimonthly magazine covering wild birds and birdwatching. "*Birder's World* is a magazine designed for people with a broad interest in wild birds and birdwatching. Our readers are curious and generally well-educated with varying degrees of experience in the world of birds. No poetry, fiction, or puzzles please." Estab. 1987. Circ. 70,000. **Pays on acceptance.** Byline given. Offers $100 kill fee. Buys one-time rights. Accepts queries by mail. Writer's guidelines for #10 SASE or by e-mail.

Nonfiction: Essays, how-to (attracting birds), interview/profile, personal experience, photo feature (bird photography), travel (birding trips in North America), book reviews, product reviews/comparisons, bird biology, endangered or threatened birds. No poetry, fiction, or puzzles. **Buys 60 mss/year.** Query with published clips or send complete ms. Length: 500-2,400 words. **Pays $200-450.** Sometimes pays expenses of writers on assignment.

Photos: State availability with submission. Buys one-time rights. Identification of subjects required.

$ $ $ CALIFORNIA WILD, Natural Science for Thinking Animals, California Academy of Sciences, Golden Gate Park, San Francisco CA 94118. (415)750-7117. Fax: (415)221-4853. E-mail: kkhowell@calacademy.org. Website: www.calacademy.org/calwild. **Contact:** Keith Howell, editor. **75% freelance written.** Quarterly magazine covering natural sciences and the environment. "Our readers' interests range widely from ecology to geology, from endangered species to anthropology, from field identification of plants and birds to armchair understanding of complex scientific issues." Estab. 1948. Circ. 32,000. Pays prior to publication. Publishes ms an average of 3 months after acceptance. Byline given. Offers 50% kill fee; maximum $200. Buys first North American serial, one-time rights. Editorial lead time 3 months. Submit seasonal material 6 months in advance. Accepts queries by mail, fax. Responds in 6 weeks to queries; 6 months to mss. Sample copy for 9×12 SASE or on website. Writer's guidelines online.

Nonfiction: Personal experience, photo feature, biological, and earth sciences. Special issues: Mostly California pieces, but also from Pacific Ocean countries. No travel pieces. **Buys 20 mss/year.** Query with published clips. Length: 1,000-3,000 words. **Pays $250-1,000 for assigned articles; $200-800 for unsolicited articles.** Sometimes pays expenses of writers on assignment.

Photos: State availability with submission. Reviews transparencies. Buys one-time rights. Offers $75-150/photo. Identification of subjects, model releases required.

Columns/Departments: A Closer Look (unusual places); Wild Lives (description of unusual plant or animal); In Pursuit of Science (innovative student, teacher, young scientist), all 1,000-1,500 words; Skywatcher (research in astronomy), 2,000-3,000 words. **Buys 12 mss/year.** Query with published clips. **Pays $200-400.**

Fillers: Facts. **Pays $25-50.**

Tips: "We are looking for unusual and/or timely stories about California environment or biodiversity."

$ $ $ CANADIAN WILDLIFE, Tribute Publishing, 71 Barber Greene Rd., Don Mills ON M3C 2A2, Canada. (416)445-0544. Fax: (416)445-2894. E-mail: wild@tribute.ca. Editor: Kendra Toby. **Contact:** Katherine Balpataky, assistant editor. **90% freelance written.** Magazine published 5 times/year covering wildlife conservation. Includes topics pertaining to wildlife, endangered species, conservation, and natural history. When possible, it is beneficial if articles have a Canadian slant or the topic has global appeal. Estab. 1995. Circ. 25,000. **Pays on acceptance.** Publishes ms an average of 3 months after acceptance. Byline given. Offers 15% kill fee. Buys first North American serial rights. Editorial lead time 3 months. Submit seasonal material 4 months in advance. Accepts queries by mail, e-mail, fax. Responds in 3 weeks to queries; 2 months to mss. Sample copy for $3.25 (Canadian). Writer's guidelines free.

Nonfiction: Book excerpts, interview/profile, photo feature, science/nature. Special issues: Oceans issue (every June). No standard travel stories. **Buys 20 mss/year.** Query with published clips. Length: 800-2,500 words. **Pays $500-1,200 for assigned articles; $300-1,000 for unsolicited articles.** Sometimes pays expenses of writers on assignment.

Photos: Send photos with submission. Reviews transparencies. Buys one-time rights. Negotiates payment individually. Captions, identification of subjects, model releases required.

Columns/Departments: Vistas (science news), 200-500 words; Book Reviews, 100-150 words. **Buys 15 mss/year.** Query with published clips. **Pays $50-250.**

Tips: "*Canadian Wildlife* is a benefit of membership in the Canadian Wildlife Federation. Nearly 25,000 people currently receive the magazine. The majority of these men and women are already well versed in topics concerning the environment and natural science; writers, however, should not make assumptions about the extent of a reader's knowledge of topics."

$$$ CONSCIOUS CHOICE, The Journal of Ecology & Natural Living, Dragonfly Chicago LLC, 920 N. Franklin, Suite 202, Chicago IL 60610-3179. Fax: (312)751-3973. E-mail: rebecca@consciouschoice.com. Website: www.consciouschoice.com. **Contact:** Rebecca Ephraim, editor. **95% freelance written.** Monthly tabloid covering the environment, natural health, and natural foods. Estab. 1988. Circ. 100,000. Pays on publication. Publishes ms an average of 6 months after acceptance. Byline given. Offers 50% kill fee. Buys first North American serial, electronic rights. Editorial lead time 6 months. Submit seasonal material 6 months in advance. Accepts queries by mail, e-mail. Accepts simultaneous submissions. Responds in 6 weeks to queries; 1 month to mss. Sample copy online. Writer's guidelines free, online, or by e-mail.

Nonfiction: General interest (to cultural creatives), interview/profile, new product, personal experience, technical, inspirational/self-development, environment. **Buys 5 mss/year.** Query with published clips. Length: 1,500 words. **Pays $150-1,000.** Sometimes pays expenses of writers on assignment.

$$ E THE ENVIRONMENTAL MAGAZINE, Earth Action Network, P.O. Box 5098, Westport CT 06881-5098. (203)854-5559. Fax: (203)866-0602. E-mail: info@emagazine.com. Website: www.emagazine.com. **Contact:** Jim Motavalli, editor. **60% freelance written.** Bimonthly magazine. "*E Magazine* was formed for the purpose of acting as a clearinghouse of information, news, and commentary on environmental issues." Estab. 1990. Circ. 50,000. Pays on publication. Byline given. Buys first North American serial rights. Editorial lead time 3 months. Submit seasonal material 6 months in advance. Accepts queries by mail, e-mail, fax. Accepts simultaneous submissions. Sample copy for $5 or online. Writer's guidelines online.

- The editor reports an interest in seeing more investigative reporting.

Nonfiction: On spec or free contributions welcome. Exposé (environmental), how-to, new product, book review, feature (in-depth articles on key natural environmental issues). **Buys 100 mss/year.** Query with published clips. Length: 100-4,000 words. **Pays 30¢/word.**

Photos: State availability with submission. Reviews printed samples, e.g., magazine tearsheets, postcards, etc., to be kept on file. Buys one-time rights. Negotiates payment individually. Identification of subjects required.

Columns/Departments: In Brief/Currents (environmental news stories/trends), 400-1,000 words; Conversations (Q&As with environmental "movers and shakers"), 2,000 words; Tools for Green Living; Your Health; Eco-Travel; Eco-Home; Eating Right; Green Business; Consumer News (each 700-1,200 words). On spec or free contributions welcome. Query with published clips.

Contact: Jim Motavalli, online editor.

Tips: "Contact us to obtain writer's guidelines and back issues of our magazine. Tailor your query according to the department/section you feel it would be best suited for. Articles must be lively, well researched, balanced, and relevant to a mainstream, national readership." On spec or free contributions welcome.

N $ THE FRUGAL ENVIRONMENTALIST, The Frugal Environmentalist, P.O. Box 1654, Brattleboro VT 05302-1654. E-mail: info@frugalgreen.com. Website: www.frugalgreen.com. **Contact:** Editor. **10-20% freelance written.** Quarterly magazine covering frugal environmental living. "*The Frugal Environmentalist* is dedicated to showing readers how to make affordable, eco-friendly lifestyle choices. Our audience is concerned about the environment but lacks the money to make expensive lifestyle choices like buying solar panels and taking eco-tourist vacations." Estab. 2003. Pays on publication. Publishes ms an average of 3-6 months after acceptance. Buys first rights; also reserves the right to publish on website and in any anthology of back issues that may be published. Accepts queries by mail. Accepts simultaneous submissions. Responds in 1 month to queries; 2 months to mss. Sample copy for $5. Writer's guidelines for #10 SASE or by e-mail.

Nonfiction: How-to (practical advice for affordable ways to make eco-friendly lifestyle choices), personal experience (stories of frugal environmental living). "We do not want any articles that talk at length about environmental problems without talking about solutions individuals can implement in their everyday lives. We are not interested in anything that requires spending a lot of money. If you believe you must own an electric car, go on expensive eco-tourism vacations, and buy overpriced organic TV dinners to be an environmentalist, don't even bother submitting to us." Query or send complete ms. Length: 500-1,500 words. **Pays $25-50, plus a 1-year subscription to the magazine for unsolicited articles.**

Tips: "We are actively seeking freelance writers to work with but are not a traditional environmental magazine. If you understand our style and angle, you'll have a much better chance of getting published with us. Writers should think about the practical aspects of environmentalism—i.e., what can ordinary people do in their everyday lives to affect positive change. We are not a political magazine, nor are we focused on 'saving the whales' environmentalism, not unless you can show how a simple, affordable everyday action can help save the whales. For personal experience stories, show us how you've made affordable, eco-friendly lifestyle changes in your own life. While it's good to include the factors that motivated you, focus mostly on what you did, how you did it, and any obstacles you encountered along the way; we want readers to be inspired by your story, and also feel empowered to make changes in their lives based on what you've done. If possible, back up your article with data that illustrates the problem and/or show the readers what good can come of making certain changes. Our overall goal is to empower our readers to make positive changes in their everyday lives, and to prove that you don't have to be rich to be an environmentalist."

N $ $ HIGH COUNTRY NEWS, High Country Foundation, P.O. Box 1090, Paonia CO 81428-1090. (970)527-4898. E-mail: betsym@hcn.org. Website: www.hcn.org. **Contact:** Greg Hanscom, editor. **80% freelance written.** Weekly tabloid covering Rocky Mountain West, the Great Basin, and Pacific Northwest environment, rural communities, and natural resource issues in 10 western states for environmentalists, politicians, companies, college classes, government agencies, grass roots activists, public land managers, etc. Estab. 1970. Circ. 23,000. Pays on publication. Publishes ms an average of 2 months after acceptance. Byline given. Buys one-time rights. Accepts queries by mail. Responds in 1 month to queries. Sample copy for SAE or online. Writer's guidelines online.

Nonfiction: Exposé (government, corporate), interview/profile, personal experience, photo feature (centerspread), reporting (local issues with regional importance). **Buys 100 mss/year.** Query. Length: up to 3,000 words. **Pays 20¢/word minimum.** Sometimes pays expenses of writers on assignment.

Reprints: Send tearsheet and information about when and where the material previously appeared. Pays 15¢/word.

Photos: Send photos with submission. Reviews b&w prints. Captions, identification of subjects required.

Columns/Departments: Roundups (topical stories), 800 words; opinion pieces, 1,000 words.

Tips: "We use a lot of freelance material, though very little from outside the Rockies. Familiarity with the newspaper is a must. Start by writing a query letter. We define 'resources' broadly to include people, culture, and aesthetic values, not just coal, oil, and timber."

$ $ $ ⊘ HOOKED ON THE OUTDOORS, 2040 30th St., Suite A, Boulder CO 80301. (303)449-5119. Fax: (303)449-5126. E-mail: query@ruhooked.com. Website: www.ruhooked.com. **Contact:** Nancy Coulter-Parker, editor-in-chief. **60% freelance written.** "*Hooked on the Outdoors* magazine is a bimonthly travel and gear guide for outdoorsy folk of all ages, shapes, sizes, religions, and mantras. No matter the background, all have the North American backyard in common. *Hooked* is the outdoor guide for readers who are multi-sport oriented and, just the same, people new to the outdoors, providing affordable, close to home destinations and gear alternative." Estab. 1998. Circ. 150,000. Pays within 30 days of publication. Publishes ms an average of 4 months after acceptance. Byline given. Offers 15% kill fee. Buys first North American serial, electronic rights. Editorial lead time 3 months. Submit seasonal material 1 year in advance. Accepts queries by mail, e-mail. Accepts simultaneous submissions. Responds in 6 weeks to queries. Sample copy for $5 and SAE with $1.75 postage. Writer's guidelines online.

Nonfiction: Book excerpts, essays, exposé, general interest, humor, interview/profile, new product, opinion, personal experience, photo feature, travel. Special issues: Travel Special (April 2003); Grassroots (conservation, clubs, outdoor schools, events; April 2002). **Buys 4 mss/year.** Query with published clips. Length: 350-2,500 words. **Pays 35-50¢/word.** Sometimes pays expenses of writers on assignment.

Photos: State availability with submission. Reviews contact sheets. Buys one-time rights. Offers $25-290. Captions, model releases required.

Columns/Departments: Buys 30 mss/year. Query with published clips. **Pays 35-50¢/word.**

Tips: "Send well thought out, complete queries reflective of research. Writers ought not query on topics already covered."

$ $ $ NATIONAL PARKS, 1300 19th St. NW, Suite 300, Washington DC 20036. (202)223-6722. Fax: (202)659-0650. E-mail: npmag@npca.org. Website: www.npca.org/. Editor-in-chief: Linda Rancourt. **Contact:** Jenell Talley, publications coordinator. **60% freelance written.** Prefers to work with published/established writers. Bimonthly magazine for a largely unscientific but highly educated audience interested in preservation of National Park System units, natural areas, and protection of wildlife habitat. Estab. 1919. Circ. 300,000. **Pays on acceptance.** Publishes ms an average of 2 months after acceptance. Offers 33% kill fee. Responds in 5 months to queries. Sample copy for $3 and 9×12 SASE or online. Writer's guidelines online.

Nonfiction: All material must relate to US national parks. Exposé (on threats, wildlife problems in national parks), descriptive articles about new or proposed national parks and wilderness parks; natural history pieces describing park geology, wildlife or plants; new trends in park use; legislative issues. No poetry, philosophical essays, or first-person narratives. No unsolicited mss. Length: 1,500 words. **Pays $1,300 for full-length features; $750 for service articles.**

Photos: No color prints or negatives. Send for guidelines. Not responsible for unsolicited photos. Send photos with submission. Reviews color slides. Pays $150-350 inside; $525 for covers. Captions required.

Tips: "Articles should have an original slant or news hook and cover a limited subject, rather than attempt to treat a broad subject superficially. Specific examples, descriptive details, and quotes are always preferable to generalized information. The writer must be able to document factual claims, and statements should be clearly substantiated with evidence within the article. *National Parks* does not publish fiction, poetry, personal essays, or 'My trip to...' stories."

$ $ $ $ NATIONAL WILDLIFE, National Wildlife Federation, 11100 Wildlife Center Dr., Reston VA 20190. (703)438-6510. Fax: (703)438-6544. E-mail: pubs@nwf.org. Website: www.nwf.org/nationalwildlife. **Contact:** Mark Wexler, editor. **75% freelance written.** Assigns almost all material based on staff ideas. Assigns few unsolicited queries. Bimonthly magazine. "Our purpose is to promote wise use of the nation's natural resources and to conserve and protect wildlife and its habitat. We reach a broad audience that is largely interested in wildlife conservation and nature photography." Estab. 1963. Circ. 500,000. **Pays on acceptance.** Publishes ms an average of 1 year after acceptance. Offers 25% kill fee. Buys all rights. Submit seasonal material 8 months in advance. Accepts queries by mail, e-mail, fax. Responds in 6 weeks to queries. Writer's guidelines for #10 SASE.

Nonfiction: General interest (2,500 word features on wildlife, new discoveries, behavior, or the environment), how-to (an outdoor or nature related activity), interview/profile (people who have gone beyond the call of duty to protect wildlife and its habitat, or to prevent environmental contamination and people who have been involved in the environment or conservation in interesting ways), personal experience (outdoor adventure), photo feature (wildlife), short 700-word features on an unusual individual or new scientific discovery relating to nature. "Avoid too much scientific detail. We prefer anecdotal, natural history material." **Buys 50 mss/year.** Query with or without published clips. Length: 750-2,500 words. **Pays $800-3,000.** Sometimes pays expenses of writers on assignment.

Photos: John Nuhn, photo editor. Send photos with submission. Reviews Kodachrome or Fujichrome transparencies. Buys one-time rights.

Tips: "Writers can break in with us more readily by proposing subjects (initially) that will take only 1 or 2 pages in the magazine (short features)."

N $ $ $ NATURE CANADA, Canadian Nature Federation, 1 Nicholas St., Suite 606, Ottawa ON K1N 7B7, Canada. Fax: (613)562-3371. E-mail: naturecanada@cnf.ca. Website: www.cnf.ca. **Contact:** Pamela Feeny, editor. Magazine published 3 times/year covering conservation, natural history and environmental/naturalist community. "Editorial content reflects the goals and priorities of the Canadian Nature Federation as a conservation organization with a focus on our program areas. *Nature Canada* is written for an audience interested in nature. Its content supports the Canadian Nature Federation's philosophy that all species have a right to exist regardless of their usefulness to humans. We promote the awareness, understanding and enjoyment of nature." Estab. 1971. Circ. 19,000. Pays on publication. Publishes ms an average of 3 months after acceptance. Byline given. Offers $100 kill fee. Buys all CNF rights (including electronic). Author retains resale rights elsewhere. Editorial lead time 3 months. Submit seasonal material 6 months in advance. Responds in 3 months to mss. Sample copy for $5. Writer's guidelines online.

Nonfiction: Canadian environmental issues and natural history. **Buys 8 mss/year.** Query with published clips. Length: 1,500-2,000 words. **Pays 50¢/word (Canadian).**

Photos: State availability with submission. Buys one-time rights. Offers $50-200/photo (Canadian). Identification of subjects required.

Columns/Departments: Connections (Canadians making a difference for the environment), 700 words; Pathways (national parks to visit); Terra Firma (grassroots conservation initiatives of our affiliates), 700 words; Trailhead (Canadian environmental news and events), 200-400 words. **Buys 10 mss/year.** Query with published clips. **Pays 50¢/word (Canadian).**

Tips: "Our readers are knowledgeable about nature and the environment so contributors should have a good understanding of the subject. We also deal exclusively with Canadian issues and species. E-mail queries preferred."

$ NORTHERN WOODLANDS MAGAZINE, Vermont Woodlands Magazine, Inc., 1776 Center Rd., P.O. Box 471, Corinth VT 05039-0471. (802)439-6292. Fax: (802)439-6296. E-mail: anne@northernwoodlands.com. Website: www.northernwoodlands.com. **Contact:** Anne Margolis. **40-60% freelance written.** Quarterly magazine covering natural history, conservation, and forest management in the Northeast. "*Northern Woodlands* strives to inspire landowners' sense of stewardship by increasing their awareness of the natural history and the principles of conservation and forestry that are directly related to their land. We also hope to increase the public's awareness of the social, economic, and environmental benefits of a working forest." Estab. 1994. Circ. 12,000. **Pays on acceptance.** Publishes ms an average of 6 months after acceptance. Byline given. Buys one-time rights. Editorial lead time 6 months. Submit seasonal material 6 months in advance. Accepts queries by mail, e-mail. Accepts previously published material. Accepts simultaneous submissions. Responds in 2 weeks to queries; 1½ months to mss. Sample copy online. Writer's guidelines online.

Nonfiction: Book excerpts, essays, how-to (related to woodland management), interview/profile. No product reviews, first-person travelogues, cute animal stories, opinion, or advocacy pieces. **Buys 15-20 mss/year.** Query with published clips. Length: 500-3,000 words. **Pays 10¢/word.** Sometimes pays expenses of writers on assignment.

Photos: State availability with submission. Reviews transparencies, prints. Buys one-time rights. Offers $25-75/photo. Identification of subjects required.

Columns/Departments: A Place in Mind (essays on places of personal significance), 600-800 words. **Pays $100.** Knots and Bolts (seasonal natural history items or forest-related news items), 300-600 words. **Pays 10¢/word.** Wood Lit (book reviews), 600 words. **Pays $25.** Field Work (profiles of people who work in the woods, the wood-product industry, or conservation field), 1,500 words. **Pays 10¢/word. Buys 30 mss/year.** Query with published clips.

Poetry: Free verse, light verse, traditional. **Buys 4 poems/year.** Submit maximum 5 poems. **Pays $25.**

Tips: "We will work with subject-matter experts to make their work suitable for our audience."

$ $ $ ONEARTH, The Natural Resources Defense Council, 40 W. 20th St., New York NY 10011. Fax: (212)727-1773. E-mail: amicus@nrdc.org. Website: www.nrdc.org. **Contact:** Kathrin Day Lassila, editor. **75% freelance written.** Quarterly magazine covering national and international environmental issues. "*The Amicus Journal* is intended to provide the general public with a journal of thought and opinion on environmental affairs, particularly those relating to policies of national and international significance." Estab. 1979. Circ. 250,000. Pays on publication. Publishes ms an average of 6 months after acceptance. Byline given. Offers variable kill fee. Buys first North American serial, simultaneous, electronic rights. Submit seasonal material 6 months in advance. Accepts queries by mail, e-mail. Responds in 3 months to queries. Sample copy for $5. Writer's guidelines for #10 SASE.

Nonfiction: Environmental features. **Buys 12 mss/year.** Query with published clips. Length: 3,000. **Pays 50¢/word.** Sometimes pays expenses of writers on assignment.

Photos: State availability with submission. Reviews contact sheets, color transparencies, 8×10 b&w prints. Buys one-time rights. Negotiates payment individually. Captions, identification of subjects, model releases required.

Columns/Departments: News & Comment (summary reporting of environmental issues, tied to topical items), 700-2,000 words; International Notebook (new or unusual international environmental stories), 700-2,000 words; People, 2,000 words; Reviews (in-depth reporting on issues and personalities, well-informed essays on books of general interest to environmentalists interested in policy and history), 500-1,000 words. Query with published clips. **Payment negotiable.**

Poetry: All poetry should be rooted in nature. Brian Swann, poetry editor. Avant-garde, free verse, haiku. **Buys 12 poems/year.** Length: 1 ms page. **Pays $75.**

Tips: "Please stay up to date on environmental issues, and review *OnEarth* before submitting queries. Except for editorials all departments are open to freelance writers. Queries should precede manuscripts, and manuscripts should conform to the *Chicago Manual of Style*. *Amicus* needs interesting environmental stories—of local, regional or national import—from writers who can offer an on-the-ground perspective. Accuracy, high-quality writing, and thorough knowledge of the environmental subject are vital."

$ $ ORION, The Orion Society, 187 Main St., Great Barrington MA 01230. E-mail: orion@orionsociety.org. Website: www.oriononline.org. Executive Editor: H. Emerson Blake. **Contact:** Aina Barten, features editor. **30% freelance written.** Quarterly magazine covering the environment. "*Orion* is a quarterly magazine that explores the relationship between people and nature, examines human communities and how they fit into the larger natural community, and strives to renew our spiritual connection to the world. It is a forum of many voices that, collectively, seek to create a philosophy that guides our relationships with nature. *Orion* publishes literary nonfiction, short stories, interviews, poetry, reviews, and visual images related to this exploration. *Orion* is meant as a lively, personal, informative, and provocative dialogue. We look for compelling, reflective writing that connects readers to important issues by heightening awareness of the interconnections between humans and nature. We generally do not select material that is academic or theoretical, nor do we select material that is overly journalistic or overly topical. Literary journalism is welcome." Estab. 1982. Circ. 20,000. Pays on publication. Publishes ms an average of 8 months after acceptance. Byline given. Buys first North American serial rights. Editorial lead time 4 months. Submit seasonal material 6 months in advance. Accepts queries by mail, e-mail. Accepts simultaneous submissions. Responds in 4-8 weeks to queries; 4-6 months to mss. Sample copy online. Writer's guidelines online.

Nonfiction: Essays, exposé, historical/nostalgic, humor, personal experience, photo feature, travel. No "What I learned during my walk in the woods"; personal hiking adventure/travel anecdotes; writing that deals with the natural world in only superficial ways. **Buys 8-20 mss/year.** Send complete ms. Length: 600-5,000 words. **Pays 10-20¢/word.** Pays in contributor copies if requested.

Photos: State availability with submission. Reviews contact sheets, prints. Buys one-time rights. Negotiates payment individually.

Columns/Departments: Features (any subject or slant), 2,500-5,000 words; Arts and the Earth (ways in which the arts are expressing and changing our thinking about nature), 1,200-2,500 words; Profile (stories of individuals working for a healthy world), 1,200-2,500 words; Natural Excursions (encounters with the natural world), 1,200-2,500 words; Deep Green (our spiritual relationship with nature and how it is being re-established), 1,200-2,500 words; Book Reviews (dealing with the context as well as content of environmental texts), 600-800 words; Coda (our endpaper), 600 words. **Buys 5-10 mss/year.** Send complete ms. **Pays 10-20¢/word; $100/book review.**

Fiction: Adventure, ethnic, historical, humorous, mainstream, slice-of-life vignettes. No manuscripts that don't carry an environmental message or involve the landscape/nature as a major character. **Buys 0-1 mss/year.** Send complete ms. Length: 1,200-4,000 words. **Pays 10-20¢/word.**

Poetry: Avant-garde, free verse, haiku, light verse, traditional. No cliché nature poetry. **Buys 20-30 poems/year.** Submit maximum 8 poems.

Tips: "It is absolutely essential that potential submitters read at least one issue of *Orion* before sending work. We are not your typical environmental magazine, and we approach things rather differently than, say, *Sierra* or *Audobon*. We are most impressed by and most likely to work with writers whose submissions show that they know our magazine."

$ $ $ OUTDOOR AMERICA, Izaak Walton League of America, 707 Conservation Lane, Gaithersburg MD 20878. (301)548-0150. Fax: (301)548-9409. E-mail: oa@iwla.org. Website: www.iwla.org. **Contact:** Jason McGarvey, editor. Quarterly magazine covering national conservation efforts/issues related to and involving members of the Izaak Walton League. "A 4-color publication, *Outdoor America* is received by League members, as well as representatives of Congress and the media. Our audience, located predominantly in the midwestern and mid-Atlantic states, enjoys traditional recreational pursuits, such as fishing, hiking, hunting, and boating. All have a keen interest in protecting the future of our natural resources and outdoor recreation heritage." Estab. 1922. Circ. 40,000. **Pays on acceptance.** Publishes ms an average of 2 months after acceptance. Accepts queries by mail, e-mail. Sample copy for $2.50. Writer's guidelines online.

Nonfiction: Conservation and natural resources issue stories with a direct connection to the work and members of the Izaak Walton League. Essays on outdoor ethics and conservation. Query or send ms for short items (500 words or less). Features are planned 6-12 months in advance. Length: 350-3,000 words. **Pays $150-1,000.**

$ $ $ $ SIERRA, 85 Second St., 2nd Floor, San Francisco CA 94105-3441. (415)977-5656. Fax: (415)977-5794. E-mail: sierra.letters@sierraclub.org. Website: www.sierraclub.org. Editor-in-chief: Joan Hamilton. Senior Editors: Reed McManus, Paul Rauber. **Contact:** Robert Schildgen, managing editor. Works with a small number of new/unpublished writers each year. Bimonthly magazine emphasizing conservation and environmental politics for people who are well educated, activist, outdoor-oriented, and politically well informed with a dedication to conservation. Estab. 1893. Circ. 695,000. **Pays on acceptance.** Publishes ms an average of 4 months after acceptance. Byline given. Offers negotiable kill fee. Buys first North American serial rights. Accepts queries by mail, fax. Accepts previously published material. Responds in 2 months to queries. Sample copy for $3 and SASE, or online. Writer's guidelines online.

- The editor reports an interest in seeing pieces on environmental "heroes," thoughtful features on new developments in solving environmental problems, and outdoor adventure stories with a strong environmental element.

Nonfiction: Exposé (well-documented articles on environmental issues of national importance such as energy, wilderness, forests, etc.), general interest (well-researched nontechnical pieces on areas of particular environmental concern), interview/profile, photo feature (photo essays on threatened or scenic areas), journalistic treatments of semitechnical topic (energy sources, wildlife management, land use, waste management, etc.). No "My trip to ..." or "Why we must save wildlife/nature" articles; no poetry or general superficial essays on environmentalism; no reporting on purely local environmental issues. **Buys 30-36 mss/year.** Query with published clips. Length: 800-3,000 words. **Pays $450-4,000.**

Reprints: Send photocopy with rights for sale noted and information about when and where the material previously appeared. Payment negotiable.

Photos: Tanuja Mehrotra, art and production manager. Send photos with submission. Buys one-time rights. Pays maximum $300 for transparencies; more for cover photos.

Columns/Departments: Food for Thought (food's connection to environment); Good Going (adventure journey); Hearth & Home (advice for environmentally sound living); Body Politics (health and the environment); Profiles (biographical look at environmentalists); Hidden Life (exposure of hidden environmental problems in everyday objects); Lay of the Land (national/international concerns), 500-700 words; Mixed Media (essays on environment in the media; book reviews), 200-300 words. **Pays $50-500.**

The online magazine carries original content not found in the print edition and includes writer's guidelines.

Tips: "Queries should include an outline of how the topic would be covered and a mention of the political appropriateness and timeliness of the article. Statements of the writer's qualifications should be included."

$ SNOWY EGRET, The Fair Press, P.O. Box 29, Terre Haute IN 47808. (812)829-1910. Editor: Philip C. Repp. Managing Editor: Ruth C. Acker. **Contact:** Editors. **95% freelance written.** Semiannual literary magazine featuring nature writing. "We publish works which celebrate the abundance and beauty of nature, and examine the variety of ways in which human beings interact with landscapes and living things. Nature writing from literary, artistic, psychological, philosophical, and historical perspectives." Estab. 1922. Circ. 400. Pays on publication. Publishes ms an average of 6 months after acceptance. Byline given. Buys first North American serial, second serial (reprint), one-time anthology rights, or reprints rights. Editorial lead time 2 months. Accepts queries by mail. Accepts simultaneous submissions. Responds in 1 month to queries; 2 months to mss. Sample copy for 9×12 SASE and $8. Writer's guidelines for #10 SASE.

Break in with "an essay, story, or short description based on a closely observed first-hand encounter with some aspect of the natural world."

Nonfiction: Essays, general interest, interview/profile, personal experience, travel. **Buys 10 mss/year.** Send complete ms. Length: 500-10,000 words. **Pays $2/page.**

Columns/Departments: Jane Robertson, Woodnotes editor. Woodnotes (short descriptions of personal encounters with wildlife or natural settings), 200-2,000 words. **Buys 12 mss/year. Pays $2/page.**

Fiction: Fiction Editor. Nature-oriented works (in which natural settings, wildlife, or other organisms and/or characters who identify with the natural world are significant components. "No genre fiction, e.g., horror, western romance, etc." **Buys 4 mss/year.** Send complete ms. Length: 500-10,000 words. **Pays $2/page.**

Poetry: Avant-garde, free verse, traditional. **Buys 30 poems/year.** Submit maximum 5 poems. **Pays $4/poem or page.**

Tips: "The writers we publish invariably have a strong personal identification with the natural world, have examined their subjects thoroughly, and write about them sincerely. They know what they're talking about and show their subjects in detail, using, where appropriate, detailed description and dialogue."

$ $ $ $ WILDLIFE CONSERVATION, 2300 Southern Blvd., Bronx NY 10460. E-mail: nsimmons@wcs.org. Website: www.wcs.org. **Contact:** Nancy Simmons, senior editor. Bimonthly magazine for environmentally aware readers. Offers 25% kill fee. Buys first North American serial rights. Accepts simultaneous submissions. Responds in 1 month to queries. Sample copy for $5.95 (includes postage). Writer's guidelines available for SASE or via e-mail.

Nonfiction: "We want well-reported articles on conservation issues, conservation successes, and straight natural history based in author's research." **Buys 30 mss/year.** Query with published clips. Length: 300-2,000 words. **Pays $1/word for features and department articles, and $150/short piece.**

PERSONAL COMPUTERS

Personal computer magazines continue to evolve. The most successful have a strong focus on a particular family of computers or widely-used applications and carefully target a specific type of computer use. Although as technology evolves, some computers and applications fall by the wayside. Be sure you see the most recent issue of a magazine before submitting material.

N Ø $ BASELINE, Ziff Davis Media, Inc., 28 E. 28th St., New York NY 10016. (212)503-5435. Fax: (212)503-5454. E-mail: baseline@ziffdavis.com. Website: www.baselinemag.com. Editor-in-Chief: Tom Steinert-Threlkeld. Managing Editor: Anna Maria Virzi. **Contact:** Joshua Weinberger, assistant editor. Magazine published 11 times/year covering "pricing, planning, and managing the implementation of next generation IT solutions." "*Baseline* is edited for senior IT and coroporate management business leaders." Circ. 125,000. Editorial lead time 6 weeks.

- Managing Editor Maria Virzi says, "Most of the reporting and writing is done by staff writers and editors."

$ $ COMPUTOREDGE, San Diego, Denver and Albuquerque's Computer Magazine, The Byte Buyer, Inc., P.O. Box 83086, San Diego CA 92138. (858)573-0315. Fax: (858)573-0205. E-mail: submissions@computoredge.com. Website: www.computoredge.com. Executive Editor: Leah Steward. **Contact:** Patricia Smith, senior editor. **90% freelance written.** "We are the nation's largest regional computer weekly, providing San Diego, Denver, and Albuquerque with entertaining articles on all aspects of computers. We cater to the novice/beginner/first-time computer buyer. Humor is welcome." Published as *Computer Edge* in San Diego and Denver; published as *Computer Scene* in Albuquerque. Estab. 1983. Circ. 175,000. Pays 1 month after publication. Byline given. Offers $15 kill fee. Buys first North American serial, electronic rights. Submit seasonal material 2 months in advance. Accepts queries by e-mail. Responds in 2 months to queries. Sample copy for SAE with 7 first-class stamps or on website. Writer's guidelines online.

• Accepts electronic submissions only. Put the issue number for which you wish to write in the subject line of your e-mail message. No attachments.

Nonfiction: Pays $100 for publication in 1 of the magazines; $150 for publication in 2 of the magazines; $200 if published in all 3 magazines. General interest (computer), how-to, humor, personal experience. **Buys 150 mss/year.** Send complete ms. Length: 1,000-1,200 words.

Columns/Departments: Beyond Personal Computing (BPC)(a reader's personal experience, humor, and sometimes fiction), 800-1,000 words. **Pays $50 for publication in 1 of the magazines; $75 for publication in 2 of the magazines; $100 if published in all 3 magazines.** Mac Madness (Macintosh-related), 800-900 words; I Don't Do Windows (alternative operating systems), 800-900 words. **Buys 80 mss/year.** Send complete ms. **Pays $75 for publication in 1 of the magazines; $110 for publication in 2 of the magazines; $145 if published in all 3 magazines.**

Tips: "Be relentless. Convey technical information in an understandable, interesting way. We like light material, but not fluff. Write as if you're speaking with a friend. Avoid the typical 'Love at First Byte' and the 'How My Grandmother Loves Her New Computer' article. We do not accept poetry. Avoid sexual innuendoes/metaphors. Reading a sample issue is advised."

$ $ $ LAPTOP, Bedford Communications, 1410 Broadway, 21st Floor, New York NY 10018. (212)807-8220. E-mail: jmckenna@bedfordmags.com. Website: www.bedfordmags.com. Editor-in-Chief: David. A. Finck. **Contact:** Jessica McKenna, managing editor. **60% freelance written.** Monthly magazine covering mobile computing, such as laptop computers, PDAs, software, and peripherals; industry trends. "Publication is geared toward the mobile technology laptop computer buyer, with an emphasis on the small office." Estab. 1991. Pays on publication. Publishes ms an average of 3 months after acceptance. Byline given. Offers 20% kill fee. Buys all rights. Editorial lead time 4 months. Accepts queries by e-mail. Responds in 4 months to queries. Sample copy online. Writer's guidelines not available.

Nonfiction: How-to (e.g., how to install a CD-ROM drive), technical, hands-on reviews, features. **Buys 80-100 mss/year.** Length: 300-3,500 words. **Pays $150-1,250.** Sometimes pays expenses of writers on assignment.

Tips: "Send résumé with feature-length clips (technology-related, if possible) to editorial offices. Unsolicited manuscripts are not accepted or returned."

$ $ $ $ MACADDICT, Imagine Media, 150 North Hill Dr., Brisbane CA 94005. (415)468-4684. Fax: (415)468-4686. E-mail: editor@macaddict.com. Website: www.macaddict.com. Managing Editor: Jennifer Morgan. **Contact:** Rik Myslewski, editor-in-chief. **35% freelance written.** Monthly magazine covering Macintosh computers. "*MacAddict* is a magazine for Macintosh computer enthusiasts of all levels. Writers must know, love and own Macintosh computers." Estab. 1996. Circ. 180,000. Pays on publication. Publishes ms an average of 3 months after acceptance. Byline given. Buys all rights. Editorial lead time 3 months. Submit seasonal material 2 months in advance. Accepts queries by mail, e-mail. Responds in 1 month to queries.

Nonfiction: How-to, new product, technical. No humor, case studies, personal experience, essays. **Buys 30 mss/year.** Query with or without published clips. Length: 250-7,500 words. **Pays $50-2,500.**

Columns/Departments: Reviews (always assigned), 300-750 words; How-to's (detailed, step-by-step), 500-2,500 words; features, 1,000-2,500 words. **Buys 20 mss/year.** Query with or without published clips. **Pays $50-2,500.**

Fillers: Narasu Rebbapragada, editor. Get Info. **Buys 20/year.** Length: 50-500 words. **Pays $25-200.**

The online magazine carries original content not found in the print edition. Contact: Niko Coucouvanis, online editor.

Tips: "Send us an idea for a short one to two page how-to and/or send us a letter outlining your publishing experience and areas of Mac expertise so we can assign a review to you (reviews editor is Niko Coulo). Your submission should have great practical hands-on benefit to a reader, be fun to read in the author's natural voice, and include lots of screenshot graphics. We require electronic submissions. Impress our reviews editor with well-written reviews of Mac products and then move up to bigger articles from there."

N $ PC MAGAZINE, Ziff-Davis Media, Inc., 28 E. 28th St., New York NY 10016. (212)503-3500. Fax: (212)503-5799. E-mail: pcmag@ziffdavis.com. Website: www.pcmag.com. Editor: Michael Miller. Managing Editor: Paul Ross. Monthly magazine. "We haven't received needs information for this listing. However, we have provided their general contact information until we receive a response to our queries for more information." Circ. 1,228,658. Editorial lead time 4 months. Sample copy not available.

N $ PC WORLD, PC World Communications, Inc., 501 2nd St., Suite 600, San Francisco CA 94107. (415)243-0500. Fax: (415)442-1891. E-mail: letters@pcworld.com. Website: www.pcworld.com. Editor: Harry McCracken. Managing Editor: Kimberly Brinson. Senior Associate Editor: Grace Aquino. Senior Associate Editor: Sean Captain. Senior Editor: Anush Yegyazarian. **Contact:** Article Proposals. Monthly magazine covering personal computers. "*PC World* was created to cover developments in the world of personal computers for PC proficient business managers." Circ. 1,251,390. Editorial lead time 3 months. Accepts queries by mail. Sample copy not available. Writer's guidelines by e-mail.

• "We have very few opportunities for writers who are not already contributing to the magazine."

"One way we discover new talent is by assigning short tips and how-to pieces."

Nonfiction: How-to, reviews, news items, features. Query. **Payment varies.**

Tips: "Once you're familiar with *PC World*, you can write us a query letter. Your letter should answer the following questions as specifically and consisely as possible. What is the problem, technique, or product you want to discuss? Why will *PC World* readers be interested in it? Which section of the magazine do you think it best fits? What is the specific audience for the piece (e.g., database or LAN users, desktop publishers, and so on)?"

$ $ $ SMART COMPUTING, Sandhills Publishing, 131 W. Grand Dr., Lincoln NE 68521. (800)544-1264. Fax: (402)479-2104. E-mail: editor@smartcomputing.com. Website: www.smartcomputing.com. Managing Editor: Chris Trumble. **Contact:** Ron Kobler, editor-in-chief. **45% freelance written.** Monthly magazine. "We focus on plain-English computing articles with an emphasis on tutorials that improve productivity without the purchase of new hardware." Estab. 1990. Circ. 300,000. **Pays on acceptance.** Publishes ms an average of 2 months after acceptance. Byline given. Offers 25% kill fee. Buys all rights. Editorial lead time 4 months. Submit seasonal material 4 months in advance. Accepts queries by mail, e-mail. Accepts simultaneous submissions. Responds in 1 month to queries. Sample copy for $7.99. Writer's guidelines for #10 SASE.

Break in with "any article containing little-known tips for improving software and hardware performance and Web use. We're also seeking clear reporting on key trends changing personal technology."

Nonfiction: How-to, new product, technical. No humor, opinion, personal experience. **Buys 250 mss/year.** Query with published clips. Length: 800-3,200 words. **Pays $240-960.** Pays expenses of writers on assignment up to $75.

Photos: Send photos with submission. Buys all rights. Offers no additional payment for photos accepeted with ms. Captions required.

The online magazine carries original content not found in the print edition. Contact: Corey Russmand, online editor.

Tips: "Focus on practical, how-to computing articles. Our readers are intensely productivity-driven. Carefully review recent issues. We receive many ideas for stories printed in the last 6 months."

$ WIRED MAGAZINE, Condé Nast Publications, 520 Third St., 3rd Floor, San Francisco CA 94107-1815. (415)276-5000. Fax: (415)276-5150. E-mail: submit@wiredmag.com. Website: www.wired.com/wired. Publisher: Dean Shutte. Editor-in-chief: Chris Anderson. Managing Editor: Rebecca Smith Hurd. Editor: Blaise Zerega. **Contact:** Chris Baker, editorial assistant. **95% freelance written.** Monthly magazine covering technology and digital culture. "We cover the digital revolution and related advances in computers, communications and lifestyles." Estab. 1993. Circ. 500,000. Pays on publication. Publishes ms an average of 3 months after acceptance. Byline given. Offers 25% kill fee. Buys all rights for items less than 1,000 words, first North American serial rights for pieces over 1,000 words. Editorial lead time 3 months. Responds in 3 weeks to queries. Sample copy for $4.95. Writer's guidelines by e-mail.

Nonfiction: Essays, interview/profile, opinion. "No poetry or trade articles." **Buys 85 features, 130 short pieces, 200 reviews, 36 essays, and 50 other mss/year.** Query. Pays expenses of writers on assignment.

Tips: "Send query letter with clips to Chris Baker. Read the magazine. We get too many inappropriate queries. We need quality writers who understand our audience, and who understand how to query."

PHOTOGRAPHY

Readers of these magazines use their cameras as a hobby and for weekend assignments. To write for these publications, you should have expertise in photography. Magazines geared to the professional photographer can be found in the Trade Professional Photography section.

$ $ PC PHOTO, Werner Publishing Corp., 12121 Wilshire Blvd., 12th Floor, Los Angeles CA 90025. Fax: (310)826-5008. E-mail: pceditors@wernerpublishing.com. Website: www.pcphotomag.com. Managing Editor: Chris Robinson. **Contact:** Rob Sheppard, editor. **60% freelance written.** Bimonthly magazine covering digital photography. "Our magazine is designed to help photographers better use digital technologies to improve their photography." Estab. 1997. Circ. 175,000. Pays on publication. Publishes ms an average of 4 months after acceptance. Byline given. Buys one-time rights. Editorial lead time 6 months. Submit seasonal material 6 months in advance. Accepts queries by mail. Responds in 1 month to queries. Sample copy for #10 SASE or online. Writer's guidelines online.

Nonfiction: How-to, personal experience, photo feature. **Buys 30 mss/year.** Query. Length: 1,200 words. **Pays $500 for assigned articles; approximately $400 for unsolicited articles.**

Photos: Send photos with submission. Reviews contact sheets, inkjet prints. Do not send original transparencies or negatives. Buys one-time rights. Offers $100-200/photo.

Tips: "Since *PCPHOTO* is a photography magazine, we must see photos before any decision can be made on an article, so phone queries are not appropriate. Ultimately, whether we can use a particular piece or not will depend greatly on the photographs and how they fit in with material already in our files. We take a fresh look at the modern photographic world by encouraging photography and the use of new technologies. Editorial is intended to demystify the use of modern equipment by emphasizing practical use of the camera and the computer, highlighting the technique rather than the technical."

N $ PETERSEN'S PHOTOGRAPHIC MAGAZINE, PRIMEDIA Enthusiast Group, 6420 Wilshire Blvd., Los Angeles CA 90048-5502. (323)782-2000. Fax: (323)782-2465. E-mail: photographic@primedia.com. Website: www.photographic.com. Editor: Ron Leach. Managing Editor: Gregg Doty. Monthly magazine. Written as a how-to magazine for amateur through professional photographers. Circ. 204,537. Editorial lead time 3 months. Sample copy not available.

$ $ PHOTO LIFE, Canada's Photography Magazine, Apex Publications, Inc., One Dundas St. W., Suite 2500, P.O. Box 84, Toronto ON M5G 1Z3, Canada. (800)905-7468. Fax: (800)664-2739. E-mail: editor@photolife.com. Website:

www.photolife.com. **Contact:** Anita Dammer and Darwin Wiggett, editors-in-chief. **15% freelance written.** Bimonthly magazine. "*Photo Life* is geared to an audience of advanced amateur photographers. *Photo Life* is not a technical magazine per se, but techniques should be explained in enough depth to make them clear." Estab. 1976. Circ. 45,000. Pays on publication. Publishes ms an average of 1 year after acceptance. Byline given. Buys one-time rights. Editorial lead time 4 months. Submit seasonal material 6 months in advance. Accepts queries by mail, e-mail. Accepts simultaneous submissions. Responds in 3 months to queries. Sample copy for $5.50. Writer's guidelines online.

Nonfiction: How-to (photo tips, technique), inspirational, photo feature, technical, travel. **Buys 10 mss/year.** Query with published clips or send complete ms. **Pays $100-600 (Canadian).**

Photos: Reviews transparencies, prints. Buys one-time rights. Negotiates payment individually. Captions, model releases required.

Tips: "We will review any relevant submissions that include a full text or a detailed outline of an article proposal. Accompanying photographs are necessary, as the first decision of acceptance will be based upon images. Most of the space available in the magazine is devoted to our regular contributors. Therefore, we cannot guarantee publication of other articles within any particular period of time. Currently, we are overflowing with travel articles. You are still welcome to submit to this category, but the waiting period may be longer than expected (up to 1½ years). You may, however, use your travel photography to explain photo techniques. A short biography is optional."

$ $ PHOTO TECHNIQUES, Preston Publications, Inc., 6600 W. Touhy Ave., Niles IL 60714. (847)647-2900. Fax: (847)647-1155. E-mail: jwhite@phototechmag.com. Website: www.phototechmag.com. Publisher: S. Tinsley Preston III. Editor: Joe White. **50% freelance written.** Prefers to work with experienced photographer-writers; happy to work with excellent photographers whose writing skills are lacking. Bimonthly publication covering photochemistry, lighting, optics, processing, and printing, Zone System, digital imaging/scanning/printing, special effects, sensitometry, etc. Aimed at serious amateurs. Article conclusions should be able to be duplicated by readers. Estab. 1979. Circ. 35,000. Pays within 3 weeks of publication. Publishes ms an average of 8 months after acceptance. Byline given. Buys one-time rights. Sample copy for $5. Writer's guidelines online.

Nonfiction: How-to, photo feature, technical (product review), special interest articles within the above listed topics. Query or send complete ms. Length: Open, but most features run approximately 2,500 words or 3-4 magazine pages. **Pays $125-450 for well-researched technical articles.**

Photos: Photographers have a much better chance of having their photos published if the photos accompany a written article. Prefers JPEGs scanned at 300 dpi and sent via e-mail or CD-ROM, or prints, slides, and transparencies. Buys one-time rights. Manuscript payment includes payment for photos. Captions, technical information required.

Tips: "Study the magazine! Virtually all writers we publish are readers of the magazine. We are now more receptive than ever to articles about photographers, history, aesthetics, and informative backgrounders about specific areas of the photo industry or specific techniques. Successful writers for our magazine are doing what they write about."

N $ POPULAR PHOTOGRAPHY & IMAGING, Hachette Filipacchi Media U.S., Inc., 1633 Broadway Fl 43, New York NY 10019. (212)767-6000. Fax: (212)767-5602. E-mail: popeditor@aol.com. Website: www.popphoto.com. Editor: Jason Schneider. Monthly magazine edited for amateur to professional photographers. Provides incisive instructional articles, authoritative tests of photographic equipment; covers still and digital imaging; travel, color, nature, and large-format columns, plus up-to-date industry information. Circ. 453,944. Editorial lead time 2 months. Sample copy not available.

$ TODAY'S PHOTOGRAPHER INTERNATIONAL, The Make Money With Your Camera Magazine, P.O. Box 777, Lewisville NC 27023. (336)945-9867. Fax: (336)945-3711. Website: www.aipress.com. Editor: Vonda H. Blackburn. **Contact:** Sarah Hinshaw, associate editor. **100% freelance written.** Bimonthly magazine addressing "how to make money—no matter where you live—with the equipment that you currently own." Editor's sweepstakes pays $500 for the best story in each issue. Estab. 1986. Circ. 78,000. Publishes ms an average of 6 months after acceptance. Byline given. Buys one-time rights. Editorial lead time 6 months. Submit seasonal material 6 months in advance. Accepts simultaneous submissions. Responds in 3 weeks to queries; 3 months to mss. Sample copy for $2, 9×12 SAE and 4 first-class stamps or for $3. Writer's guidelines online.

Nonfiction: How-to, new product, opinion, personal experience, photo feature, technical, travel. No "What I did on my summer vacation" stories.

Photos: State availability with submission. Reviews transparencies, prints. Buys one-time rights. Offers no additional payment for photos accepted with ms. Captions, identification of subjects, model releases required.

Columns/Departments: Vonda Blackburn, editor. Books (how-to photography), 200-400 words; Sports (how-to photograph sports), 1,000 words. **Buys 40 mss/year.** Query. **Payment negotiable.**

Tips: Present a complete submission package containing: your manuscript, photos (with captions, model releases and technical data) and an inventory list of the submission package.

POLITICS & WORLD AFFAIRS

These publications cover politics for the reader interested in current events. Other publications that will consider articles about politics and world affairs are listed under the Business & Finance, Contemporary Culture, Regional, and General Interest sections. For listings of publications geared toward the professional, see Government & Public Service in the Trade section.

$ $ $ $ CALIFORNIA JOURNAL, 2101 K St., Sacramento CA 95816. (916)444-2840. Fax: (916)444-2339. E-mail: edit@statenet.com. Editor: David Lesher. **Contact:** Jim Evans, managing editor. **70% freelance written.** Monthly magazine "with nonpartisan coverage aimed at a literate, well-informed, well-educated readership with strong involvement in California issues, politics, or government." Estab. 1970. Circ. 12,000. Pays on publication. Publishes ms an average of 3 months after acceptance. Byline given. Buys all rights. Accepts queries by mail, fax. Responds in 2 weeks to queries; 2 months to mss.

Nonfiction: Political analysis. Interview/profile (of state and local government officials), opinion (on politics and state government in California). No outright advocacy pieces, fiction, poetry, product pieces. **Buys 10 unsolicited mss/year.** Query. Length: 800-2,000 words. **Pays $300-2,000.** Sometimes pays expenses of writers on assignment.

Photos: State availability with submission. Reviews contact sheets. Buys all rights. Negotiates payment individually. Identification of subjects required.

Columns/Departments: Soapbox (opinion on current affairs), 800 words. **Does not pay.**

Tips: "Be well-versed in political and environmental affairs as they relate to California."

$ $ CHURCH & STATE, Americans United for Separation of Church and State, 518 C St. NE, Washington DC 20002. (202)466-3234. Fax: (202)466-3353. E-mail: americansunited@au.org. Website: www.au.org. **Contact:** Joseph Conn, editor. **10% freelance written.** Monthly magazine emphasizing religious liberty and church/state relations matters. Strongly advocates separation of church and state. Readership is well-educated. Estab. 1947. Circ. 40,000. **Pays on acceptance.** Publishes ms an average of 2 months after acceptance. Buys all rights. Accepts queries by mail. Accepts simultaneous submissions. Responds in 2 months to queries. Sample copy and writer's guidelines for 9×12 SAE with 3 first-class stamps.

Nonfiction: Exposé, general interest, historical/nostalgic, interview/profile. **Buys 11 mss/year.** Query. Length: 800-1,600 words. **Pays $150-300 for assigned articles.** Sometimes pays expenses of writers on assignment.

Reprints: Send tearsheet, photocopy or typed ms with rights for sale noted and information about when and where the material previously appeared.

Photos: Send photos with submission. Buys one-time rights. Pays negotiable fee for b&w prints. Captions required.

Tips: "We're looking for feature articles on underreported local church-state controversies. We also consider 'viewpoint' essays that offer a unique or personal take on church-state issues. We are not a religious magazine. You need to see our magazine before you try to write for it."

$ COMMONWEAL, A Review of Public Affairs, Religion, Literature and the Arts, Commonweal Foundation, 475 Riverside Dr., Room 405, New York NY 10115. (212)662-4200. Fax: (212)662-4183. E-mail: editors@commonwealmagazine.org. Website: www.commonwealmagazine.org. Editor: Paul Baumann. **Contact:** Patrick Jordan, managing editor. Biweekly journal of opinion edited by Catholic lay people, dealing with topical issues of the day on public affairs, religion, literature, and the arts. Estab. 1924. Circ. 20,000. Pays on publication. Byline given. Buys all rights. Submit seasonal material 2 months in advance. Responds in 2 months to queries. Sample copy for free. Writer's guidelines online.

Nonfiction: Essays, general interest, interview/profile, personal experience, religious. **Buys 30 mss/year.** Query with published clips. Length: 2,000-2,500 words. **Pays $75-100.**

Columns/Departments: Upfronts (brief, newsy reportorials, giving facts, information and some interpretation behind the headlines of the day), 750-1,000 words; Last Word (usually of a personal nature, on some aspect of the human condition: spiritual, individual, political, or social), 800 words.

Poetry: Rosemary Deen and Daria Donnelly, editors. Free verse, traditional. **Buys 20 poems/year. Pays 75¢/line.**

Tips: "Articles should be written for a general but well-educated audience. While religious articles are always topical, we are less interested in devotional and churchy pieces than in articles which examine the links between 'worldly' concerns and religious beliefs."

N $ THE ECONOMIST, Economist Group of London, 25 St. James St., London England SW1A-1HG, United Kingdom. (44207)830-7000. Fax: (44207)839-2968. Website: www.economist.com. Editor: Bill Emmott. Weekly magazine. Edited for senior manegement and policy makers in business, government and finance throughout the world. Estab. 1843. Circ. 403,131. Sample copy not available.

$ $ EMPIRE STATE REPORT, The Independent Magazine of Politics, Policy, and the Business of Government, P.O. Box 9001, Mount Vernon NY 10552-9001. (914)699-2020. Fax: (914)699-2025. E-mail: sacunto@cinn.com. Website: www.empirestatereport.com. **Contact:** Stephen Acunto, Jr., associate publisher/executive editor. Monthly magazine with "timely and independent information on politics, policy, and governance for local and state officials throughout New York State." Estab. 1974. Circ. 16,000. Pays up to 2 months after publication. Byline given. Buys first North American serial rights. Accepts queries by mail, e-mail, fax, phone. Responds in 1 month to queries; 2 months to mss. Sample copy for $4.50 with 9×12 SASE or online. Writer's guidelines online.

Specifically looking for journalists with a working knowledge of legislative issues in New York State and how they affect businesses, municipalities, and all levels of government.

Nonfiction: Essays, exposé, interview/profile, opinion, analysis. **Buys 48 mss/year.** Query with published clips. Length: 500-4,500 words. **Pays $100-700.** Sometimes pays expenses of writers on assignment.

Photos: Send photos with submission. Reviews any size prints. Identification of subjects required.

Columns/Departments: Empire State Notebook (short news stories about state politics), 300-900 words; Perspective (opinion pieces), 800-850 words. Perspectives does not carry remuneration.

The online magazine carries original content not found in the print edition and includes writer's guidelines. Contact: Stephen Acunto Jr.

Tips: "We are seeking journalists and nonjournalists from throughout New York State who can bring a new perspective and/or forecast on politics, policy, and the business of government. Query first for columns."

$ $ IDEAS ON LIBERTY, 30 S. Broadway, Irvington-on-Hudson NY 10533. (914)591-7230. Fax: (914)591-8910. E-mail: srichman@cfee.org. Website: www.fee.org. Publisher: Foundation for Economic Education. **Contact:** Sheldon Richman, editor. **85% freelance written.** Monthly publication for "the layman and fairly advanced students of liberty." Estab. 1946. Pays on publication. Publishes ms an average of 5 months after acceptance. Byline given. all rights, including reprint rights. Sample copy for 7½×10½ SASE with 4 first-class stamps.

- Eager to work with new/unpublished writers.

Nonfiction: "We want nonfiction clearly analyzing and explaining various aspects of the free market, private property, limited-government philosophy. Though a necessary part of the literature of freedom is the exposure of collectivistic cliches and fallacies, our aim is to emphasize and explain the positive case for individual responsibility and choice in a free-market economy. We avoid name-calling and personality clashes. Ours is an intelligent analysis of the principles underlying a free-market economy. No political strategies or tactics." **Buys 100 mss/year.** Query with SASE. Length:3,500 words. **Pays 10¢/word.** Sometimes pays expenses of writers on assignment.

Tips: "It's most rewarding to find freelancers with new insights, fresh points of view. Facts, figures and quotations cited should be fully documented, to their original source, if possible."

$ THE LABOR PAPER, Serving Southern Wisconsin, Union-Cooperative Publishing, 3030 39th Ave., Suite 110, Kenosha WI 53144. (262)657-6116. Fax: (262)657-6153. **Contact:** Mark T. Onosko, publisher. **30% freelance written.** Weekly tabloid covering union/labor news. Estab. 1935. Circ. 12,000. Pays on publication. Publishes ms an average of 2 months after acceptance. Byline given. Buys all rights. Editorial lead time 1 month. Submit seasonal material 1 month in advance. Accepts queries by mail, fax. Accepts simultaneous submissions. Sample copy and writer's guidelines free.

Nonfiction: Exposé, general interest, historical/nostalgic, humor, inspirational. **Buys 4 mss/year.** Query with published clips. Length: 300-1,000 words. Sometimes pays expenses of writers on assignment.

Photos: State availability with submission. Negotiates payment individually. Captions required.

$ $ THE NATION, 33 Irving Place, 8th Floor, New York NY 10003. (212)209-5400. Fax: (212)982-9000. E-mail: submissions@thenation.com. Website: www.thenation.com. **Contact:** Peggy Suttle, assistant to editor. **75% freelance written.** Works with a small number of new/unpublished writers each year. Weekly magazine "firmly committed to reporting on the issues of labor, national politics, business, consumer affairs, environmental politics, civil liberties, foreign affairs and the role and future of the Democratic Party." Estab. 1865. Pays on other. Buys first rights. Accepts queries by mail, e-mail, fax. Sample copy for free. Writer's guidelines online.

- See the Contests & Awards section for the Discovery-*The Nation* poetry contest.

Nonfiction: "We welcome all articles dealing with the social scene, from an independent perspective." Queries encouraged. **Buys 100 mss/year. Pays $225-300.** Sometimes pays expenses of writers on assignment.

Columns/Departments: Editorial, 500-700 words. **Pays $100.**

Poetry: *The Nation* publishes poetry of outstanding aesthetic quality. Send poems with SASE. See the Contests & Awards section for the Discovery—*The Nation* poetry contest. Grace Shulman, poetry editor. **Payment negotiable.**

The online magazine carries original content not found in the print edition and includes writer's guidelines. Contact: Katrina Vanden Heuvel, editor.

Tips: "We are a journal of left/liberal political opinion covering national and international affairs. We are looking both for reporting and for fresh analysis. On the domestic front, we are particularly interested in civil liberties; civil rights; labor, economics, environmental and feminist issues and the role and future of the Democratic Party. Because we have readers all over the country, it's important that stories with a local focus have real national significance. In our foreign affairs coverage we prefer pieces on international political, economic and social developments. As the magazine which published Ralph Nader's first piece (and there is a long list of *Nation* "firsts"), we are seeking new writers."

$ THE NATIONAL VOTER, League of Women Voters, 1730 M St. NW, #1000, Washington DC 20036. (202)429-1965. Fax: (202)429-0854. E-mail: nationalvoter@lwv.org. Website: www.lwv.org. **Contact:** Shirley Tabata Ponomareff, editor. Magazine published 3 times/year. "*The National Voter* provides background, perspective and commentary on public policy issues confronting citizens and their leaders at all levels of government. And it empowers people to make a difference in their communities by offering guidance, maturation and models for action." Estab. 1951. Circ. 100,000. Pays on publication. Byline given. Makes work-for-hire assignments. Editorial lead time 2 months. Accepts queries by mail, e-mail. Sample copy for free.

Nonfiction: Exposé, general interest, interview/profile. No essays, personal experience, religious,opinion. **Buys 2-3 mss/year.** Query with published clips. Length: 200-4,000 words. **Payment always negotiated.** Pays expenses of writers on assignment.

Photos: State availability with submission. Reviews contact sheets. Buys one-time rights. Offers no additional payment for photos accepted with ms. Captions, identification of subjects required.

$ THE NEW REPUBLIC, 1331 H St. NW, Suite 700, Washington DC 20005. (202)508-4444. Fax: (202)628-9383. E-mail: tnr@aol.com. Website: www.thenewrepublic.com. Editor-in-Chief, Chairman: Martin Peretz. Executive Editor: Christopher Orr. **Contact:** Leon Wieseltier, literary editor. Magazine.

Contact: Christiane Culhane, assistant editor; Jonathan Cohn, editor.

$ PROGRESSIVE POPULIST, Journal from America's Heartland, P.O. Box 150517, Austin TX 78715-0517. (512)447-0455. Fax: (603)649-7871. E-mail: editor@populist.com. Website: www.populist.com. Managing Editor: Art Cullen. **Contact:** Jim Cullen, editor. **90% freelance written.** Biweekly tabloid covering politics and economics. "We cover issues of interest to workers, small businesses, and family farmers and ranchers." Estab. 1995. Circ. 7,000. Pays quarterly. Publishes ms an average of 1 month after acceptance. Byline given. Buys first North American serial, second serial (reprint) rights. Editorial lead time 3 weeks. Submit seasonal material 1 month in advance. Accepts queries by mail, e-mail, fax, phone. Accepts previously published material. Accepts simultaneous submissions. Sample copy and writer's guidelines free.

Nonfiction: "We cover politics and economics. We are interested not so much in the dry reporting of campaigns and elections, or the stock markets and GNP, but in how big business is exerting more control over both the government and ordinary people's lives, and what people can do about it." Essays, exposé, general interest, historical/nostalgic, humor, interview/profile, opinion. "We are not much interested in 'sound-off' articles about state or national politics, although we accept letters to the editor. We prefer to see more 'journalistic' pieces, in which the writer does enough footwork to advance a story beyond the easy realm of opinion." **Buys 400 mss/year.** Query. Length: 600-1,000 words. **Pays $15-50.** Pays writers with contributor copies or other premiums if preferred by writer.

Reprints: Send photocopy with rights for sale noted and information about when and where the material previously appeared.

Photos: State availability with submission. Buys one-time rights. Negotiates payment individually. Identification of subjects required.

Tips: "We do prefer submissions by e-mail. I find it's easier to work with e-mail and for the writer it probably increases the chances of getting a response."

$ $ THE PROGRESSIVE, 409 E. Main St., Madison WI 53703-2899. (608)257-4626. Fax: (608)257-3373. E-mail: editorial@progressive.org. Website: www.progressive.org. **Contact:** Matthew Rothschild, editor. **75% freelance written.** Monthly. Estab. 1909. Pays on publication. Publishes ms an average of 6 weeks after acceptance. Byline given. Accepts queries by mail. Responds in 1 month to queries. Sample copy for 9×12 SAE with 4 first-class stamps or sample articles online. Writer's guidelines online.

Nonfiction: Investigative reporting (exposé of corporate malfeasance and governmental wrongdoing); electoral coverage (a current electoral development that has national implications); social movement pieces (important or interesting event or trend in the labor movement, or the GLBT movement, or in the area of racial justice, disability rights, the environment, women's liberation); foreign policy pieces (a development of huge moral importance where the US role may not be paramount); interviews (a long Q&A with a writer, activist, political figure, or musician who is widely known or doing especially worthwhile work); activism (highlights the work of activists and activist groups; increasingly, we are looking for good photographs of a dynamic or creative action, and we accompany the photos with a caption); book reviews (cover two or three current titles on a major issue of concern). Primarily interested in articles that interpret, from a progressive point of view, domestic and world affairs. Occasional lighter features. "*The Progressive* is a *political* publication. General interest is inappropriate." "We do not want editorials, satire, historical pieces, philosophical peices or columns." Query. Length: 500-4,000 words. **Pays $250-500.**

Poetry: publishes one original poem a month. "We prefer poems that connect up-in one fashion or another, however obliquely-with political concerns. **Pays $150.**

Tips: "Sought-after topics include electoral coverage, social movement, foreign policy, activism and book reviews."

$ $ $ $ REASON, Free Minds and Free Markets, Reason Foundation, 3415 S. Sepulveda Blvd., Suite 400, Los Angeles CA 90034. (310)391-2245. Fax: (310)390-8986. E-mail: gillespie@reason.com. Website: www.reason.com. **Contact:** Nick Gillespie, editor-in-chief. **30% freelance written.** Monthly magazine covering politics, current events, culture, ideas. "*Reason* covers politics, culture and ideas from a dynamic libertarian perspective. It features reported works, opinion pieces, and book reviews." Estab. 1968. Circ. 55,000. **Pays on acceptance.** Byline given. Offers kill fee. Buys first North American serial, first, all rights. Editorial lead time 2 months. Submit seasonal material 3 months in advance. Accepts queries by mail, e-mail. Responds in 6 weeks to queries; 2 months to mss. Sample copy for $4. Writer's guidelines online.

Nonfiction: Book excerpts, essays, exposé, general interest, humor, interview/profile, opinion. No products, personal experience, how-to, travel. **Buys 50-60 mss/year.** Query with published clips. Length: 1,000-5,000 words. **Pays $300-2,000.** Sometimes pays expenses of writers on assignment.

The online magazine carries original content not found in the print edition and includes writer's guidelines. Contact: Nick Gillespie.

Tips: "We prefer queries of no more than one or two pages with specifically developed ideas about a given topic rather than more general areas of interest. Enclosing a few published clips also helps."

$ TOWARD FREEDOM, A Progressive Perspective on World Events, Toward Freedom, Inc., P.O. Box 468, Burlington VT 05402-0468. (802)654-8024. E-mail: editor@towardfreedom.com. Website: www.towardfreedom.com. **Contact:** Greg Guma, editor. **75% freelance written.** Magazine published 8 times/year covering politics/culture, focus on Third World, Europe, and global trends. "*Toward Freedom* is an internationalist journal with a progressive perspective on political, cultural, human rights, and environmental issues around the world. Also covers the United Nations, the post-nationalist movements and U.S. foreign policy." Estab. 1952. Circ. 3,500. Pays on publication. Byline given. Buys first North American serial, one-time rights. Editorial lead time 1 month. Accepts queries by mail, e-mail. Responds in 3 months to queries. Sample copy for $3. Writer's guidelines online.

Break in with "a clear, knowledgeable, and brief query, either by e-mail or U.S. mail, along with the basis of your knowledge about the subject. We're also looking for a new hook for covering subjects we follow, as well as comparisons between the U.S. and other places. We're also eager to break stories that are being 'censored' in mainstream media."

Nonfiction: Essays, interview/profile, opinion, personal experience, travel, features, book reviews, foreign, political analysis. Special issues: Women's Visions (March); Global Media (December/January). **Buys 50-75 mss/year.** Query. Length: 700-2,500 words.

Photos: Send photos with submission. Reviews prints. Buys one-time rights. Offers $35 maximum/photo. Identification of subjects required.

Columns/Departments: *TF* Reports (from foreign correspondents); UN; Beyond Nationalism; Art and Book Reviews; 800-1,200 words. **Buys 10-20 mss/year.** Query. **Pays up to 10¢/word.** Last Word (creative commentary), 900 words. **Buys 8 mss/year.** Query. **Pays $100.**

The online magazine carries original content not found in the print edition and includes guidelines. Contact: Greg Guma.

Tips: "We're looking for articles linking politics and culture; effective first-person storytelling; proposals for global solutions with realistic basis and solid background; provocative viewpoints within the progressive tradition; political humor. We receive too many horror stories about human rights violations, lacking constructive suggestions and solutions; knee-jerk attacks on imperialism."

N $ **U.S. NEWS & WORLD REPORT**, U.S. News & World Report, Inc., 1050 Thomas Jefferson Street NW., Washington DC 20007. (202)955-2000. Fax: (202)955-2685. E-mail: letters@usnews.com. Website: www.usnews.com. Editor: Mortimer B. Zuckerman. Weekly magazine. A weekly national magazine devoted largely to reporting and analyzing national and international affairs, politics, business, health, science, technology and social trends. Circ. 2,018,621. Editorial lead time 10 days. Sample copy not available.

$ $ **WASHINGTON MONTHLY**, The Washington Monthly Co., 733 15th St. NW, Suite 520, Washington DC 20005. (202)393-5155. Fax: (202)393-2444. E-mail: editors@washingtonmonthly.com. Website: www.washingtonmonthly.com. Editor: Paul Glastris. **Contact:** Stephanie Mencimer, editor, or Nicholas Thompson, editor. **50% freelance written.** Monthly magazine covering politics, policy, media. "We are a neo-liberal publication with a long history and specific views—please read our magazine before submitting." Estab. 1969. Circ. 20,000. Pays on publication. Publishes ms an average of 2 months after acceptance. Byline given. Buys all rights. Editorial lead time 2 months. Submit seasonal material 4 months in advance. Accepts queries by mail, e-mail, fax, phone. Responds in 3 weeks to queries; 2 months to mss. Sample copy for 11×17 SAE with 5 first-class stamps or by e-mail. Writer's guidelines online.

Nonfiction: Book excerpts, essays, exposé, general interest, historical/nostalgic, interview/profile, opinion, personal experience, technical, first-person political. "No humor, how-to, or generalized articles." **Buys 20 mss/year.** Query with or without published clips or send complete ms. Length: 1,500-5,000 words. **Pays 10¢/word.**

Photos: State availability with submission. Reviews contact sheets, prints. Buys one-time rights. Negotiates payment individually.

Columns/Departments: Memo of the Month (memos); On Political Books, Booknotes (both reviews of current political books), 1,500-3,000 words. **Buys 10 mss/year.** Query with published clips or send complete ms. **Pays 10¢/word.**

Tips: "Call our editors to talk about ideas. Always pitch articles showing background research. We're particularly looking for first-hand accounts of working in government. We also like original work showing that the government is or is not doing something important. We have writer's guidelines, but do your research first."

N $ **THE WEEKLY STANDARD**, News America Incorporated, 1150 17th St., NW, Suite 505, Washington DC 20036. E-mail: editor@weeklystandard.com. Website: www.weeklystandard.com. Publisher: Terry Eastland. **Contact:** William Kristol, editor; Fred Barnes, executive editor. Weekly magazine.

$ **WORLD POLICY JOURNAL**, World Policy Institute, 66 Fifth Ave., 9th Floor, New York NY 10011. (212)229-5808. Fax: (212)807-1294. E-mail: wrigleyl@newschool.edu. Website: www.worldpolicy.org. Editor: Karl E. Mayer. **Contact:** Linda Wrigley, managing editor. **10% freelance written.** Quarterly journal covering international politics, economics, and security isssues, as well as historical and cultural essays, book reviews, profiles, and first-person reporting from regions not covered in the general media. "We hope to bring principle and proportion, as well as a sense of reality and direction to America's discussion of its role in the world." Circ. 8,000. Pays on publication. Publishes ms an average of 3 months after acceptance. Byline given. Buys all rights. Accepts queries by mail. Responds in 3 months to queries. Sample copy for $7.95 and 9×12 SASE with 10 first-class stamps. Writer's guidelines online.

Nonfiction: Articles that "define policies that reflect the shared needs and interests of all nations of the world." Query. Length: 2,500-4,500 words. **Pays variable commission rate.**

PSYCHOLOGY & SELF-IMPROVEMENT

These publications focus on psychological topics, how and why readers can improve their own outlooks, and how to understand people in general. Many General Interest, Men's, and Women's publications also publish articles in these areas. Magazines treating spiritual development appear in the Astrology, Metaphysical & New Age section, as well as in Religion, while markets for holistic mind/body healing strategies are listed in the Health & Fitness section.

$ $ $ $ **PSYCHOLOGY TODAY**, Sussex Publishers, Inc., 49 E. 21st St., 11th Floor, New York NY 10010. (212)260-7210. Fax: (212)260-7445. E-mail: psychtoday@aol.com. Website: www.psychologytoday.com. **Contact:** Carin Gorrell, senior editor. Bimonthly magazine. "*Psychology Today* explores every aspect of human behavior, from the cultural trends that shape the way we think and feel to the intricacies of modern neuroscience. We're sort of a hybrid of a science magazine, a health magazine and a self-help magazine. While we're read by many psychologists, therapists and social workers, most of our readers are simply intelligent and curious people interested in the psyche and the self." Estab. 1967. Circ. 331,400. Pays on publication. Publishes ms an average of 3 months after acceptance. Byline given. Buys first North American serial rights. Editorial lead time 5 months. Accepts queries by mail. Responds in 1 month to queries. Sample copy for $3.50. Writer's guidelines for #10 SASE.

Nonfiction: "Nearly any subject related to psychology is fair game. We value originality, insight and good reporting; we're not interested in stories or topics that have already been covered *ad nauseum* by other magazines unless you can provide a fresh new twist and much more depth. We're not interested in simple-minded 'pop psychology.'" No fiction, poetry or first-person essays on "How I Conquered Mental Disorder X." **Buys 20-25 mss/year.** Query with published clips. Length: 1,500-4,000 words. **Pays $1,000-2,500.**

Columns/Departments: News Editor. News & Trends, 150-300 words. Query with published clips. **Pays $150-300.**

$ ROSICRUCIAN DIGEST, Rosicrucian Order, AMORC, 1342 Naglee Ave., San Jose CA 95191-0001. (408)947-3600. Website: www.rosicrucian.org. **Contact:** Robin M. Thompson, editor-in-chief. Quarterly magazine (international) emphasizing mysticism, science, philosophy, and the arts for educated men and women of all ages seeking alternative answers to life's questions. **Pays on acceptance.** Publishes ms an average of 6 months after acceptance. Byline given. Buys first, second serial (reprint) rights. Accepts queries by mail, phone. Responds in 3 months to queries. Sample copy for free. Writer's guidelines for #10 SASE.

Nonfiction: How to deal with life—and all it brings us—in a positive and constructive way. Informational articles—new ideas and developments in science, the arts, philosophy, and thought. Historical sketches, biographies, human interest, psychology, philosophical, and inspirational articles. "We are always looking for good articles on the contributions of ancient civilizations to today's civilizations, the environment, ecology, inspirational (nonreligious) subjects. Know your subject well and be able to capture the reader's interest in the first paragraph. Be willing to work with the editor to make changes in the manuscript." No religious, astrological, or political material, or articles promoting a particular group or system of thought. Most articles are written by members or donated, but we're always open to freelance submissions. No book-length mss. Query. Length: 1,500-2,000 words. **Pays 6¢/word.**

Reprints: Prefers typed ms with rights for sale noted and information about when and where the article previously appeared, but tearsheet or photcopy acceptable. Pays 50% of amount paid for an original article.

Tips: "We're looking for more pieces on these subjects: our connection with the past—the important contributions of ancient civilizations to today's world and culture and the relevance of this wisdom to now; how to channel teenage energy/angst into positive, creative, constructive results (preferably written by teachers or others who work with young people—written for frustrated parents); and the vital necessity of raising our environmental consciousness if we are going to survive the coming millennium or even century."

$ SCIENCE OF MIND MAGAZINE, 3251 W. Sixth St., P.O. Box 75127, Los Angeles CA 90075-0127. (213)388-2181. Fax: (213)388-1926. E-mail: edit@scienceofmind.com. Website: www.scienceofmind.com. Publisher and Editor-in-Chief: Randall Friesen. Assistant Editor: Jan Suzukawa. **30% freelance written.** Monthly magazine featuring articles on spirituality, self-help, and inspiration. "Our publication centers on oneness of all life and spiritual empowerment through the application of Science of Mind principles." **Pays on acceptance.** Publishes ms an average of 5 months after acceptance. Byline given. Buys first North American serial rights. Submit seasonal material 6 months in advance. Writer's guidelines online.

Nonfiction: Book excerpts, essays, inspirational, interview/profile, personal experience (of Science of Mind), spiritual. **Buys 35-45 mss/year.** Length: 750-2,000 words. **Payment varies. Pays in copies for some features written by readers.**

The online version contains material not found in the print edition.

Tips: "We are interested in how to use spiritual principles in worldly situations or other experiences of a spiritual nature having to do with Science of Mind principles."

N $ SHARED VISION, Improving the Quality of Your Life, Morphic Media, 873 Beatty St., Suite 203, Vancouver BC V6K 1Y4, Canada. (604)733-5062. Fax: (604)731-1050. E-mail: editor@shared-vision.com. Website: www.shared-vision.com. Managing Editor: Rex Weyler. **Contact:** Sonya Weir, editor. **50% freelance written.** Monthly magazine covering health and wellness, environment, personal growth, spirituality, and global issues. Estab. 1988. Circ. 40,000 monthly. Pays on publication. Byline given. Buys first North American serial rights. Editorial lead time 3 months. Submit seasonal material 3 months in advance. Accepts queries by mail, e-mail, fax. Accepts previously published material. Sample copy for free. Writer's guidelines by e-mail.

Nonfiction: Book excerpts, general interest, inspirational, personal experience, travel, health, environment. Query with published clips.

Photos: Offers no additional payment for photos accepted with ms. Identification of subjects required.

Columns/Departments: Health Focus (health issues, topical); Footnotes (first-person inspirational). Query with published clips.

Tips: "Reading the magazine is the optimum method. E-mail the editor for writer's guidelines."

REGIONAL

Many regional publications rely on staff-written material, but others accept work from freelance writers who live in or know the region. The best regional publication to target with your submissions is usually the one in your hometown, whether it's a city or state magazine or a Sunday supplement in a newspaper. Since you are familiar with the region, it is easier to propose suitable story ideas.

Listed first are general interest magazines slanted toward residents of, and visitors to, a particular region. Next, regional publications are categorized alphabetically by state, followed by Canada and international countries. Publications that report on the business climate of a region are grouped in the regional division of the Business & Finance category. Recreation and travel publications specific to a geographical area are listed in the Travel, Camping & Trailer section. Keep in mind also that many regional publications specialize in specific areas and are listed according to those sections. Regional publications are not listed if they only accept material from a select group of freelancers in their area or if they did not want to receive the number of queries and manuscripts a national listing would attract. If you know of a regional magazine that is not listed, approach it by asking for writer's guidelines before you send unsolicited material.

General

$ $ BLUE RIDGE COUNTRY, Leisure Publishing, 3424 Brambleton Ave., Roanoke VA 24018. (540)989-6138. Fax: (540)989-7603. E-mail: info@leisurepublishing.com. Website: www.blueridgecountry.com. **Contact:** Kurt Rheinheimer, editor-in-chief. **75% freelance written.** Bimonthly magazine. "The magazine is designed to celebrate the history, heritage and beauty of the Blue Ridge region. It is aimed at adult, upscale readers who enjoy living or traveling in the mountain regions of Virginia, North Carolina, West Virginia, Maryland, Kentucky, Tennessee, South Carolina and Georgia." Estab. 1988. Circ. 80,000. Pays on publication. Publishes ms an average of 8 months after acceptance. Byline given. Offers $50 kill fee for commissioned pieces only. Buys first, second serial (reprint) rights. Submit seasonal material 6 months in advance. Accepts queries by mail, e-mail, fax. Responds in 2 months to queries; 2 months to mss. Sample copy for 9×12 SAE with 6 first-class stamps or online. Writer's guidelines online.

Nonfiction: "Looking for more backroads travel, history and legend/lore pieces." General interest, historical/nostalgic, personal experience, photo feature, travel. **Buys 25-30 mss/year.** Query with or without published clips or send complete ms. Length: 750-2,000 words. **Pays $50-250 for assigned articles; $25-250 for unsolicited articles.**

Photos: Send photos with submission. Reviews transparencies. Buys one-time rights. Pays $25-50/photo. Identification of subjects required.

Columns/Departments: Country Roads (shorts on people, events, travel, ecology, history, antiques, books); Mountain Inns (reviews of inns); Mountain Delicacies (cookbooks and recipes). **Buys 30-42 mss/year.** Query. **Pays $10-40.**

Tips: "Would like to see more pieces dealing with contemporary history (1940s-70s). Freelancers needed for regional departmental shorts and 'macro' issues affecting whole region. Need field reporters from all areas of Blue Ridge region. Also, we need updates on the Blue Ridge Parkway, Appalachian Trail, national forests, ecological issues, preservation movements."

$ CHRONOGRAM, Luminary Publishing, P.O. Box 459, New Paltz NY 12561. Fax: (914)256-0349. E-mail: info@chronogram.com. Website: www.chronogram.com. **Contact:** Brian K. Mahoney, editor. **50% freelance written.** Monthly magazine covering regional arts and culture. "*Chronogram* features accomplished, literary writing on issues of cultural, spiritual, and idea-oriented interest." Estab. 1994. Circ. 20,000. Pays on publication. Publishes ms an average of 3 months after acceptance. Byline given. Buys one-time rights. Editorial lead time 2 months. Submit seasonal material 3 months in advance. Accepts queries by mail, e-mail. Accepts simultaneous submissions. Responds in 2 weeks to queries; 6-8 weeks to mss. Sample copy online. Writer's guidelines online.

Nonfiction: Book excerpts, essays, exposé, general interest, historical/nostalgic, humor, interview/profile, opinion, personal experience, photo feature, religious, travel. "No health practitioners writing about their own healing modality." **Buys 24 mss/year.** Query with published clips. Length: 1,000-3,500 words. **Pays $75-150.**

Photos: State availability with submission. Reviews contact sheets. Buys one-time rights. Negotiates payment individually. Captions required.

Poetry: Franci Levine Grater, poetry editor. Avant-garde, free verse, haiku, traditional.

Tips: "The editor's ears are always open for new voices and all story ideas are invited for pitching. *Chronogram* welcomes all voices and viewpoints as long as they are expressed well. We discriminate solely based on the quality of the writing, nothing else. Clear, thoughtful writing on any subject will be considered for publication in *Chronogram*. We publish a good deal of introspective first-person narratives and find that in the absence of objectivity, subjectivity at least is a quantifiable middle ground between ranting opinion and useless facts."

$ $ $ $ COWBOYS & INDIANS MAGAZINE, The Premier Magazine of the West, USFR Media Group, 6688 N. Central Expressway, Suite 650, Dallas TX 75206. (214)750-8222. Fax: (214)750-4522. E-mail: queries@cowboysindians.com. Website: www.cowboysindians.com. Editor: Margaret Pickworth. **Contact:** Queries. **60% freelance written.** Magazine published 8 times/year covering people and places of the American West. "The Premier Magazine of the West, *Cowboys & Indians* captures the romance, drama, and grandeur of the American frontier—both past and present—like no other publication. Undeniably exclusive, the magazine covers a broad range of lifestyle topics: art, home interiors, travel, fashion, Western film, and Southwestern cuisine." Estab. 1993. Circ. 101,000. Pays on publication. Publishes ms an average of 2 months after acceptance. Byline given. Offers 20% kill fee. Buys first North American serial, electronic rights. Editorial lead time 4 months. Submit seasonal material 6 months in advance. Accepts queries by mail, e-mail, fax. Sample copy for $5. Writer's guidelines by e-mail.

Nonfiction: Book excerpts, exposé, general interest, historical/nostalgic, interview/profile, photo feature, travel, art. No essays, humor, poetry, or opinion. **Buys 40-50 mss/year.** Query. Length: 500-3,000 words. **Pays $250-5,000 for assigned articles; $250-1,000 for unsolicited articles.**

Photos: State availability with submission. Reviews contact sheets, 2¼×2¼ transparencies. Buys one-time rights. Negotiates payment individually. Captions, identification of subjects required.

Columns/Departments: Art; Travel; Music; Home Interiors; all 200-1,000 words. **Buys 50 mss/year.** Query. **Pays $200-1,500.**

Tips: "Our readers are educated, intelligent, and well-read Western enthusiasts, many of whom collect Western Americana, read other Western publications, attend shows and have discerning tastes. Therefore, articles should assume a certain level of prior knowledge of Western subjects on the part of the reader. Articles should be readable and interesting to the novice and general interest reader as well. Please keep your style lively, above all things, and fast-moving, with snappy beginnings and endings. Wit and humor are always welcome."

$ $ NOW AND THEN, The Appalachian Magazine, Center for Appalachian Studies and Services, P.O. Box 70556-ETSU, Johnson City TN 37614-0556. (423)439-5348. Fax: (423)439-6340. E-mail: woodsidj@mail.etsu.edu. Website: cass.etsu.edu/n&t/. Managing Editor: Nancy Fischman. **Contact:** Jane Harris Woodside, editor-in-chief. **80% freelance written.** Triannual magazine covering Appalachian region from Southern New York to Northern Mississippi. "*Now & Then* accepts a variety of writing genres: fiction, poetry, nonfiction, essays, interviews, memoirs, and book reviews. All submissions must relate to Appalachia and to the issue's specific theme. Our readership is educated and interested in the region." Estab. 1984. Circ. 1,000. Pays on publication. Publishes ms an average of 4 months after acceptance. Byline given. Buys all, holds copyright rights. Editorial lead time 6 months. Accepts queries by mail, e-mail, fax. Accepts simultaneous submissions. Responds in 5 months to queries; 5 months to mss. Sample copy for $5. Writer's guidelines online.

Nonfiction: Book excerpts, essays, general interest, historical/nostalgic, humor, interview/profile, opinion, personal experience, photo feature, book reviews from and about Appalachia. "We don't consider articles which have nothing to do with Appalachia; articles which blindly accept and employ regional stereotypes (dumb hillbillies, poor and downtrodden hillfolk, and miners)." Query with published clips. Length: 1,000-2,500 words. **Pays $30-250 for assigned articles; $30-100 for unsolicited articles.** Sometimes pays expenses of writers on assignment.

Reprints: Send ms with rights for sale noted and information about when and where the material previously appeared. Pays 100% of amount paid for original article (typically $15-60).

Photos: State availability with submission. Buys one-time rights. Offers no additional payment for photos accepted with ms. Captions, identification of subjects required.

Fiction: "Fiction has to relate to Appalachia and to the issue's theme in some way." Adventure, ethnic, experimental, fantasy, historical, humorous, mainstream, slice-of-life vignettes, excerpted novel, prose poem. "Absolutely has to relate to Appalachian theme. Can be about adjustment to new environment, themes of leaving and returning, for instance. Nothing unrelated to region." **Buys 3-4 mss/year.** Send complete ms. Length: 750-2,500 words. **Pays $30-100.**

Poetry: Free verse, haiku, light verse, traditional. "No stereotypical work about the region. I want to be surprised and embraced by the language, the ideas, even the form." **Buys 25-30 poems/year.** Submit maximum 5 poems. **Pays $10.**

Tips: "Get a copy of the magazine and read it. Then make sure your submission has a connection to Appalachia (check out http://cass.etsu.edu/cass/apregion.htm) and fits in with an upcoming theme."

$ $ $ $ SUNSET MAGAZINE, Sunset Publishing Corp., 80 Willow Rd., Menlo Park CA 94025-3691. (650)321-3600. Fax: (650)327-7537. E-mail: editservices@sunset.com. Website: www.sunset.com. Editor-in-Chief: Katie Tamony. **Contact:** Peter Fish, senior travel editor; Kathleen Brenzel, senior garden editor. Monthly magazine covering the lifestyle of the Western states. "*Sunset* is a Western lifestyle publication for educated, active consumers. Editorial provides localized information on gardening and travel, food and entertainment, home building and remodeling." Freelance articles should be timely and only about the 13 Western states. Garden section accepts queries by mail. Travel section prefers queries by e-mail. **Pays on acceptance.** Byline given. Sample copy not available. Guidelines for freelance travel items for #10 SASE addressed to Editorial Services.

Nonfiction: "Travel items account for the vast majority of *Sunset's* freelance assignments, although we also contract out some short garden items. However *Sunset* is largely staff-written." Travel (in the West). **Buys 50-75 mss/year.** Query. Length: 550-750 words. **Pays $1/word.**

Columns/Departments: Building & Crafts, Food, Garden, Travel. Travel Guide length: 300-350 words. Direct queries to specific editorial department.

Tips: "Here are some subjects regularly treated in *Sunset*'s stories and Travel Guide items: Outdoor recreation (i.e., bike tours, bird-watching spots, walking or driving tours of historic districts); indoor adventures (i.e., new museums and displays, hands-on science programs at aquariums or planetariums, specialty shopping); special events (i.e., festivals that celebrate a region's unique social, cultural, or agricultural heritage). Also looking for great weekend getaways, backroad drives, urban adventures and culinary discoveries such as ethnic dining enclaves. Planning and assigning begins a year before publication date."

$ $ VILLAGE PROFILE, Community Maps, Guides and Directories, Progressive Publishing, Inc., 33 N. Geneva, Elgin IL 60120. (800)600-0134, ext. 215. E-mail: peted@villageprofilemail.com. Website: www.villageprofile.com. **Contact:** Pete Densmore, production editor. **50% freelance written.** Annual local community guides covering 40 states. "We publish community guides and maps for (primarily) chambers of commerce across the U.S. Editorial takes on a factual, yet upbeat, positive view of communities. Writers need to be able to make facts and figures 'friendly,' to present information to be used by residents as well as businesses, as guides are used for economic development." Publishes 350 projects/year. Estab. 1988. **Pays on acceptance.** Publishes ms an average of 4 months after acceptance. Byline given. Buys electronic, all rights, makes work-for-hire assignments. Editorial lead time 2 months. Accepts queries by mail, e-mail. Sample copy for 9×12 SASE. Writer's guidelines free.

Nonfiction: Buys 100 mss/year. Query with published clips and geographic availability. Length: 1,000-4,000 words. **Pays $200-500 for assigned articles.** Sometimes pays expenses of writers on assignment.

Photos: State availability with submission. Negotiates payment individually. Identification of subjects required.

Tips: "Writers must meet deadlines, know how to present a positive image of a community without going overboard with adjectives and adverbs! Know how to find the info you need if our contact (typically a busy chamber executive) needs your help doing so. Availability to 'cover' a region/area is a plus."

$ YANKEE, Yankee Publishing, Inc., P.O. Box 520, Dublin NH 03444-0520. (603)563-8111. Fax: (603)563-8252. E-mail: queries@yankeepub.com. Website: www.yankeemagazine.com. Editor: Michael Carlton. **Contact:** (Ms.) Sam Darley, editorial assistant. **60% freelance written.** Monthly magazine covering New England. "Our mission is to express and perhaps, indirectly, preserve the New England culture—and to do so in an entertaining way. Our audience is national and has one thing in common—it loves New England." Estab. 1935. Circ. 500,000. Pays within 30 days of acceptance. Publishes ms an average of 10 months after acceptance. Byline given. Offers kill fee. Buys all rights. Submit seasonal material 1 year in advance. Accepts queries by mail. Accepts simultaneous submissions. Responds in 2 months to queries. Writer's guidelines for #10 SASE.

- Include SASE for a response. Does not respond to e-mail queries, except if interested.

Nonfiction: Essays, general interest, humor, interview/profile. "No 'good old days' pieces, no dialect, humor and nothing outside New England!" **Buys 30 mss/year.** Query with published clips and SASE. Length: Not to exceed 2,500 words. **Pays as per assignment.** Pays expenses of writers on assignment when appropriate.

Photos: Call Leonard Loria, art director. Reviews contact sheets, transparencies. Buys one-time rights. Identification of subjects required.

Columns/Departments: Food; Home; Travel.

Tips: "Submit lots of ideas. Don't censor yourself—let *us* decide whether an idea is good or bad. We might surprise you. Remember we've been publishing for 65 years, so chances are we've already done every 'classic' New England subject. Try to surprise us—it isn't easy. Study the ones we publish—the format should be apparent. It is to your advantage to read several issues of the magazine before sending us a query or a manuscript. *Yankee* does not publish fiction, poetry, or cartoons as a routine format, nor do we solicit submissions."

Alabama

$ $ ALABAMA HERITAGE, University of Alabama, Box 870342, Tuscaloosa AL 35487-0342. (205)348-7467. Fax: (205)348-7473. Website: www.alabamaheritage.com. **Contact:** Donna L. Cox, editor. **75% freelance written.** "*Alabama Heritage* is a nonprofit historical quarterly published by the University of Alabama and the Alabama Department of Archives and History for the intelligent lay reader. We are interested in lively, well-written, and thoroughly researched articles on Alabama/Southern history and culture. Readability and accuracy are essential." Estab. 1986. Pays on publication. Byline given. Buys first, second serial (reprint) rights. Accepts queries by mail. Responds in 1 month to queries; 1 month to mss. Sample copy for $6, plus $2.50 for shipping. Writer's guidelines for #10 SASE.

Nonfiction: Buys 12-16 feature mss/year and 10-14 short pieces. Historical. "We do not publish fiction, poetry, book reviews, articles on current events or living artists, and personal/family reminiscences." Query. Length: 750-4,000 words. **Pays $50-250.** Sends 10 copies to each author.

Photos: Reviews contact sheets. Buys one-time rights. Identification of subjects required.

Tips: "Authors need to remember that we regard history as a fascinating subject, not as a dry recounting of dates and facts. Articles that are lively and engaging, in addition to being well researched, will find interested readers among our editors. No term papers, please. All areas are open to freelance writers. Best approach is a written query."

$ $ ALABAMA LIVING, Alabama Rural Electric Assn., P.O. Box 244014, Montgomery AL 36124. (334)215-2732. Fax: (334)215-2733. E-mail: dgates@areapower.com. Website: alabamaliving.com. Darryl Gates, editor. **80% freelance written.** Monthly magazine covering topics of interest to rural and suburban Alabamians. "Our magazine is an editorially balanced, informational and educational service to members of rural electric cooperatives. Our mix regularly includes Alabama history, Alabama features, gardening, outdoor, and consumer pieces." Estab. 1948. Circ. 365,000. **Pays on acceptance.** Byline given. Not copyrighted. Editorial lead time 4 months. Submit seasonal material 4 months in advance. Accepts queries by mail, e-mail. Accepts simultaneous submissions. Responds in 1 month to queries. Sample copy for free.

- Break in with a bit of history or nostalgia about Alabama or the Southeast and pieces about "little-known" events in Alabama history or "little-known" sites.

Nonfiction: Historical/nostalgic (rural-oriented), inspirational, personal experience (Alabama). Special issues: Gardening (March); Travel (April); Home Improvement (May); Holiday Recipes (December). **Buys 20 mss/year.** Send complete ms. Length: 500-750 words. **Pays $250 minimum for assigned articles; $75 minimum for unsolicited articles.**

Reprints: Send ms with rights for sale noted. Pays $75.

$ $ MOBILE BAY MONTHLY, PMT Publishing, P.O. Box 66200, Mobile AL 36660. (251)473-6269. Fax: (251)479-8822. E-mail: deblina@pmtpublishing.com. **Contact:** Deblina Chakraborty, assistant editor. **25% freelance written.** "*Mo-*

bile Bay Monthly is a monthly lifestyle magazine for the South Alabama/Gulf Coast region focusing on the people, ideas, issues, arts, homes, food, culture, and businesses that make Mobile Bay an interesting place." Estab. 1990. Circ. 10,000. Pays on publication. Publishes ms an average of 4 months after acceptance. Byline given. Buys first rights. Editorial lead time 4 months. Submit seasonal material 6 months in advance. Accepts queries by mail, e-mail, fax. Sample copy for $2. Writer's guidelines not available.

Nonfiction: General interest, historical/nostalgic, how-to (home renovations, etc.), interview/profile, personal experience, photo feature, travel (must be along the Gulf Coast). **Buys 10 mss/year.** Query with published clips. Length: 1,200-3,000 words. **Pays $100-300.**

Photos: State availability with submission. Buys one-time rights. Negotiates payment individually. Identification of subjects required.

Tips: "We use mostly local writers. Strong familiarity with the Mobile area is a must. No phone calls; please send query letters with writing samples."

N $ **SOUTHERN LIVING**, Southern Progress Corp., 2100 Lakeshore Drive, Birmingham AL 35209. (205)445-6000. Fax: (205)445-6700. E-mail: southernliving@spc.com. Website: www.southernliving.com. Editor: Derrick Belden. Managing Editor: Clay Norden. **Contact:** Sara Askew Orr. Monthly magazine covering the southern lifestyle. Publication addressing the tastes and interest of contemporary southerners. Estab. 1966. Circ. 2,526,799. Buys all rights. Editorial lead time 3 months. Accepts queries by mail. Sample copy for $4.99 at newsstands. Writer's guidelines by e-mail.

Columns/Departments: Southern Journal: "Above all, it must be Southern. We need comments on life in this region—written from the standpoint of a person who is intimately familiar with this part of the world. It's personal, almost always involving something that happened to the writer or someone he or she knows very well. Most of the articles submitted are reminiscences, but we take special note of stories that are contemporary in their point of view." Length: 500 words.

Alaska

$ $ $ **ALASKA, Exploring Life on the Last Frontier**, 301 Arctic Slope Ave., Suite 300, Anchorage AK 99518. (907)272-6070. Website: www.alaskamagazine.com. **Contact:** Donna Rae Thompson, editorial assistant. **70% freelance written.** Eager to work with new/unpublished writers. Magazine published 10 times/year covering topics "uniquely Alaskan." Estab. 1935. Circ. 180,000. Pays on publication. Publishes ms an average of 6 months after acceptance. Byline given. Buys first, one-time rights. Submit seasonal material 1 year in advance. Accepts queries by mail. Responds in 2 months to queries; 2 months to mss. Sample copy for $3 and 9×12 SAE with 7 first-class stamps. Writer's guidelines online.

- Break in by "doing your homework. Make sure a similar story has not appeared in the magazine within the last 5 years. It must be about Alaska."

Nonfiction: Historical/nostalgic, humor, interview/profile, personal experience, photo feature, travel, adventure, outdoor recreation (including hunting, fishing), Alaska destination stories. No fiction or poetry. **Buys 40 mss/year.** Query. Length: 100-2,500 words. **Pays $100-1,250.**

Photos: Send photos with submission. Reviews 35mm or larger transparencies, slides labeled with your name. Captions, identification of subjects required.

Tips: "We're looking for top-notch writing—original, well researched, lively. Subjects must be distinctly Alaskan. A story on a mall in Alaska, for example, won't work for us; every state has malls. If you've got a story about a Juneau mall run by someone who is also a bush pilot and part-time trapper, maybe we'd be interested. The point is *Alaska* stories need to be vivid, focused and unique. Alaska is like nowhere else—we need our stories to be the same way."

Arizona

$ $ $ $ **ARIZONA HIGHWAYS**, 2039 W. Lewis Ave., Phoenix AZ 85009-9988. (602)712-2024. Fax: (602)254-4505. E-mail: queryeditor@azhighways.com. Website: www.arizonahighways.com. **Contact:** Beth Deveny, senior editor. **100% freelance written.** Magazine that is state-owned, designed to help attract tourists into and through Arizona. Estab. 1925. Circ. 425,000. **Pays on acceptance.** Buys first North American serial rights. Accepts queries by mail, e-mail, fax. Responds in 1 month to queries; 1 month to mss. Sample copy not available. Writer's guidelines online.

- Break in with "a concise query written with flair, backed by impressive clips that reflect the kind of writing that appears in *Arizona Highways*. The easiest way to break into the magazine for writers new to us is to propose short items for the Off-Ramp section, contribute short humor anecdotes for the Humor page, or submit 650-word pieces for the Along the Way column."

Nonfiction: Feature subjects include narratives and exposition dealing with history, anthropology, nature, wildlife, armchair travel, out of the way places, small towns, Old West history, Indian arts and crafts, travel, etc. Travel articles are experience-based. All must be oriented toward Arizona. "We deal with professionals only, so include a list of current credits." **Buys 50 mss/year.** Query with a lead paragraph and brief outline of story. Length: 600-1,800 words. **Pays $1/word.** Pays expenses of writers on assignment.

Photos: "We use transparencies of medium format, 4×5, and 35mm when appropriate to the subject matter, or they display exceptional quality or content. We prefer 35mm at 100 ISO or slower. Each transparency must be accompanied by information attached to each photograph: where, when, what. No photography will be reviewed by the editors unless the photographer's name appears on each and every transparency." Peter Ensenberger, photo editor. Buys one-time rights. Pays $100-600.

Columns/Departments: Focus on Nature (short feature in first or third person dealing with the unique aspects of a single species of wildlife), 800 words; Along the Way (short essay dealing with life in Arizona, or a personal experience keyed to Arizona), 800 words; Back Road Adventure (personal back-road trips, preferably off the beaten path and outside major metro areas), 1,000 words; Hike of the Month (personal experiences on trails anywhere in Arizona), 500 words; Arizona Humor (amusing short anecdotes about Arizona), 200 words maximum. **Pays $50-1,000, depending on department.**

The online magazine carries original content not found in the print edition. Contact: Robert J. Early, editor.

Tips: "Writing must be of professional quality, warm, sincere, in-depth, well peopled, and accurate. Avoid themes that describe first trips to Arizona, the Grand Canyon, the desert, Colorado River running, etc. Emphasis is to be on Arizona adventure and romance as well as flora and fauna, when appropriate, and themes that can be photographed. Double check your manuscript for accuracy. Our typical reader is a 50-something person with the time, the inclination, and the means to travel."

$ $ DESERT LIVING, (formerly *City AZ*), 342 E. Thomas, Phoenix AZ 85012. (602)667-9798. Fax: (602)508-9454. E-mail: dawson@desertlivingmag.com. Website: www.desertlivingmag.com. **Contact:** Dawson Fearnow, editor. **75% freelance written.** Bimonthly lifestyle and culture magazine "with an emphasis on modern design, culinary trends, cultural trends, fashion, great thinkers of our time and entertainment." Estab. 1997. Circ. 40,000. Pays 1 month after publication. Byline given. Offers 50% kill fee. Buys first, electronic rights. Editorial lead time 3 months. Submit seasonal material 3 months in advance. Accepts queries by mail, e-mail, fax, phone. Responds in 3 weeks to queries; 2 months to mss. Sample copy for e-mail request. Writer's guidelines not available.

Nonfiction: General interest, interview/profile, new product, photo feature, travel, architecture. Query with published clips. Length: 300-2,000 words. **Pays $25-400.**

Photos: State availability with submission. Reviews contact sheets, negatives, transparencies, prints. Buys one-time or electronic rights. Negotiates payment individually. Identification of subjects, model releases required.

Columns/Departments: Design (articles on industrial/product design and firms, 2,000 words. **Buys 100 mss/year.** Query with published clips.

$ PHOENIX MAGAZINE, Cities West Publishing, Inc., 4041 N. Central Ave., Suite 530, Phoenix AZ 85012. (602)234-0840. Fax: (602)604-0169. E-mail: phxmag@citieswestpub.com. **Contact:** Kathy Montgomery, managing editor. **70% freelance written.** Monthly magazine covering regional issues, personalities, events, neighborhoods, customs, and history of metro Phoenix. Estab. 1966. Circ. 60,000. Pays on publication. Publishes ms an average of 3 months after acceptance. Byline given. Buys first North American serial rights. Submit seasonal material 1 year in advance. Accepts queries by mail, e-mail. Responds in 2 months to queries; 2 months to mss. Sample copy for $3.95 and 9×12 SASE with 5 first-class stamps. Writer's guidelines for #10 SASE.

- Break in with "short pieces of 150-600 words for the Phoenix-files highlighting local trends, architecture, and personalities, or with other short features of 750-1,000 words on same topics. Avoid the obvious. Look for the little-known, the funky, and the offbeat."

Nonfiction: General interest, interview/profile, investigative, historical, service pieces (where to go and what to do around town). "No material dealing with travel outside the region or other subjects that don't have an effect on the area. No fiction or personal essays, please." **Buys 50 mss/year.** Query with published clips. Length: 150-2,000 words.

Tips: "Our audience consists of well-educated, affluent Phoenicians. Articles must have strong local connection, vivid, lively writing, and present new information or a new way of looking at things."

$ $ TUCSON LIFESTYLE, Conley Publishing Group, Ltd., Suite 12, 7000 E. Tanque Verde Rd., Tucson AZ 85715-5318. (520)721-2929. Fax: (520)721-8665. E-mail: tucsonlife@aol.com. **Contact:** Scott Barker, executive editor. **90% freelance written.** Prefers to work with published/established writers. Monthly magazine covering Tucson-related events and topics. Estab. 1982. Circ. 32,000. **Pays on acceptance.** Publishes ms an average of 6 months after acceptance. Byline given. Buys first North American serial rights. Submit seasonal material 1 year in advance. Accepts queries by mail, e-mail, fax. Responds in 2 months to queries; 3 months to mss. Sample copy for $2.95, plus $3 postage. Writer's guidelines free.

- Features are not open to freelancers.

Nonfiction: All stories need a Tucson angle. "Avoid obvious tourist attractions and information that most residents of the Southwest are likely to know. No anecdotes masquerading as articles. Not interested in fish-out-of-water, Easterner-visiting-the-Old-West pieces." **Buys 20 mss/year. Pays $50-500.**

Photos: Query about electronic formats. Reviews contact sheets, 2¼×2¼ transparencies, 5×7 prints. Buys one-time rights. Pays $25-100/photo. Identification of subjects required.

Columns/Departments: Lifestylers (profiles of interesting Tucsonans). Query. **Pays $100-200.**

Tips: "Style is not of paramount importance; good, clean copy with an interesting lead is a must."

California

$ $ BRENTWOOD MAGAZINE, (formerly *BRNTWD Magazine*), PTL Productions, 2118 Wilshire Blvd., #1060, Santa Monica CA 90403. (310)390-0251. Fax: (310)390-0261. E-mail: dylan@brntwdmagazine.com. Website: www.brntwdmagazine.com. **Contact:** Dylan Nugent, editor-in-chief. **100% freelance written.** Bimonthly magazine covering entertainment, business, lifestyles, reviews. "Wanting in-depth interviews with top entertainers, politicians, and similar individuals. Also travel, sports, adventure." Estab. 1995. Circ. 70,000. Pays on publication. Byline given. Editorial lead time 3 months.

Submit seasonal material 3 months in advance. Accepts queries by mail, e-mail, phone. Accepts simultaneous submissions. Sample copy for $5. Writer's guidelines available.

O→ Break in with "strong editorial pitches on unique personalities, trends, or travel destinations."

Nonfiction: Book excerpts, exposé, general interest, historical/nostalgic, humor, interview/profile, new product, opinion, personal experience, photo feature, travel. **Buys 80 mss/year.** Query with published clips. Length: 1,000-2,500 words. **Pays 10-15¢/word.**

Photos: State availability with submission. Reviews contact sheets, negatives, prints. Offers no additional payment for photos accepted with ms. Captions, identification of subjects required.

Columns/Departments: Reviews (film/books/theater/museum), 100-500 words; Sports (Southern California angle), 200-600 words. **Buys 20 mss/year.** Query with or without published clips or send complete ms. **Pays 15¢/word.**

Tips: "Los Angeles-based writers preferred for most articles."

$ $ $ $ DIABLO MAGAZINE, The Magazine of the East Bay, Diablo Publications, 2520 Camino Diablo, Walnut Creek CA 94597. (925)943-1111. Fax: (925)943-1045. E-mail: d-mail@diablopubs.com. Website: www.diablomag.com. Editor: Susan Safipour. **Contact:** Scott Adler, managing editor. **50% freelance written.** Monthly magazine covering regional travel, food, homestyle, and profiles in Contra Costa and southern Alameda counties and selected areas of Oakland and Berkeley. Estab. 1979. Circ. 45,000. **Pays on acceptance.** Publishes ms an average of 3 months after acceptance. Byline given. Offers 25% kill fee. Buys first rights. Editorial lead time 3 months. Submit seasonal material 5 months in advance. Accepts queries by mail, e-mail, fax. Sample copy online. Writer's guidelines online.

Nonfiction: General interest, interview/profile, new product, photo feature, technical, travel. No restaurant profiles, out of country travel, nonlocal topics. **Buys 60 mss/year.** Query with published clips. Length: 600-3,000 words. **Pays $300-2,000.** Sometimes pays expenses of writers on assignment.

Photos: State availability with submission. Buys one-time rights. Negotiates payment individually.

Columns/Departments: Tech; Parenting; Homestyle; Food; Books; Health; Profiles; Local Politics, all 1,000 words. Query with published clips.

Tips: "We prefer San Francisco Bay area writers who are familiar with the area."

$ $ THE EAST BAY MONTHLY, The Berkeley Monthly, Inc., 1301 59th St., Emeryville CA 94608. (510)658-9811. Fax: (510)658-9902. E-mail: editorial@themonthly.com. **Contact:** Kira Halpern, editor. **95% freelance written.** Monthly tabloid. "We feature distinctive, intelligent articles of interest to *East Bay* readers." Estab. 1970. Circ. 80,000. Pays on publication. Byline given. Buys first, second serial (reprint) rights. Editorial lead time 2+ months. Submit seasonal material 3 months in advance. Accepts queries by mail, e-mail. Accepts simultaneous submissions. Responds in 1 month to queries; 1 month to mss. Sample copy for $1. Writer's guidelines for #10 SASE or by e-mail.

Nonfiction: All articles must have a local angle. Topics include essays (first person), exposés, general interest, humor, interview/profile, personal experience, arts, culture, lifestyles. Essays (first-person), exposé, general interest, humor, interview/profile, personal experience, photo feature, arts, culture, lifestyles. No fiction or poetry. Query with published clips. Length: 1,500-3,000 words. **Pays $250-700.**

Reprints: Send tearsheet and information about when and where the material previously appeared.

Photos: State availability with submission. Negotiates payment individually. Identification of subjects required.

Columns/Departments: Shopping Around (local retail news), 2,000 words; First Person, 2,000 words. Query with published clips.

$ LOS ANGELES TIMES MAGAZINE, Los Angeles Times, 202 W. First St., Los Angeles CA 90012. (213)237-7811. Fax: (213)237-7386. **Contact:** Alice Short, editor. **50% freelance written.** Weekly magazine of regional general interest. Circ. 1,384,688. Payment schedule varies. Publishes ms an average of 2 months after acceptance. Byline given. Buys first North American serial rights. Submit seasonal material 3 months in advance. Accepts simultaneous submissions. Responds in 2 months to queries; 2 months to mss. Sample copy and writer's guidelines free.

Nonfiction: Covers California, the West, the nation, and the world. Essays (reported), general interest, interview/profile, investigative and narrative journalism. Query with published clips. Length: 2,500-4,500 words.

Photos: Query first; prefers to assign photos. Reviews color transparencies, b&w prints. Buys one-time rights. Payment varies. Captions, identification of subjects, model releases required.

Tips: "Prospective contributors should know their subject well and be able to explain why a story merits publication. Previous national magazine writing experience preferred."

$ $ ORANGE COAST MAGAZINE, The Magazine of Orange County, Orange Coast Kommunications, Inc., 3701 Birch St., Suite 100, Newport Beach CA 92660. (949)862-1133. Fax: (949)862-0133. E-mail: tborgatta@orangecoastmagazine.com. Website: www.orangecoastmagazine.com. **Contact:** Tina Borgatta, editor. **90% freelance written.** Monthly magazine "designed to inform and enlighten the educated, upscale residents of Orange County, California; highly graphic and well researched." Estab. 1974. Circ. 52,000. Pays on publication. Publishes ms an average of 3-4 months after acceptance. Byline given. Offers 20% kill fee. Buys first North American serial rights. Editorial lead time 3-4 months. Submit seasonal material 6 months in advance. Accepts queries by mail. Accepts simultaneous submissions. Responds in 1-2 months to queries; 1-2 months to mss. Sample copy for #10 SASE and 6 first-class stamps. Writer's guidelines for #10 SASE.

O→ Break in with Short Cuts (topical briefs of about 250 words), **pays $75**; Escape (Pacific Time Zone travel pieces of about 600 words), **pays $250.**

Nonfiction: Absolutely no phone queries. General interest (with Orange County focus), inspirational, interview/profile (prominent Orange County citizens), personal experience, religious, travel, guides to activities and services. Special issues:

Health, Beauty, and Fitness (January); Dining (March); International Travel (April); Home Design (June); Family/Education (August); Arts (September); Local Travel (October). "We do not accept stories that do not have specific Orange County angles. We want profiles on local people, stories on issues going on in our community, informational stories using Orange County-based sources. We cannot emphasize the local angle enough." **Buys up to 65 mss/year.** Query with published clips. Length: 1,000-3,000 words. **Pays $250-700 for assigned articles.**

Photos: State availability with submission. Buys one-time rights. Negotiates payment individually. Captions, identification of subjects required.

Columns/Departments: Escape (travel destinations within the Pacific Time Zone), 600 words; Short Cuts (stories for the front of the book that focus on Orange County issues, people, and places), 250 words. **Buys up to 25 mss/year.** Query with published clips. **Pays $50 minimum; $75 (Short Cuts); $250 (Escapes).**

Tips: "We're looking for more local personality profiles, analysis of current local issues, local takes on national issues. Most features are assigned to writers we've worked with before. Don't try to sell us 'generic' journalism. *Orange Coast* prefers articles with specific and unusual angles focused on Orange County. A lot of freelance writers ignore our Orange County focus. We get far too many generalized manuscripts."

$ $ PALM SPRINGS LIFE, The California Prestige Magazine, Desert Publications, Inc., 303 N. Indian Canyon, Palm Springs CA 92262. (760)325-2333. Fax: (760)325-7008. E-mail: steve@palmspringslife.com. **Contact:** Steven R. Biller, editor. **80% freelance written.** Monthly magazine covering "affluent resort/southern California/Palm Springs desert resorts. *Palm Springs Life* celebrates the good life." Estab. 1958. Circ. 20,000. Pays on publication. Publishes ms an average of 3 months after acceptance. Byline given. Offers 20% kill fee. Buys all rights. Negotiable Submit seasonal material 6 months in advance. Responds in 4-6 weeks to queries. Sample copy for $3.95. Writer's guidelines not available.

- Increased focus on desert region and business writing opportunities.

Nonfiction: Book excerpts, essays, interview/profile. Query with published clips. Length: 500-2,500 words. **Pays $80-500.**

Photos: State availability with submission. Reviews contact sheets. Buys all rights. Pays $50-200/photo. Captions, identification of subjects, model releases required.

Columns/Departments: Desert Metropolis (local news), 50-250 words; Applause! (fine arts and entertainment), 100-500 words. **Buys 12 mss/year.** Query with or without published clips. **Pays $50-250.**

$ PALO ALTO WEEKLY, Embarcadero Publishing Co., 703 High St., P.O. Box 1610, Palo Alto CA 94301. (650)326-8210. Fax: (650)326-3928. Website: www.paloaltoonline.com. **Contact:** Tyler Hanley, editorial assistant. **5% freelance written.** Semiweekly tabloid focusing on local issues and local sources. Estab. 1979. Circ. 48,000. Pays on publication. Publishes ms an average of 1 month after acceptance. Byline given. Offers 50% kill fee. Buys first rights. Submit seasonal material 2 months in advance. Accepts queries by mail. Responds in 2 weeks to queries. Sample copy for 9×12 SAE and 2 first-class stamps. Writer's guidelines not available.

- *Palo Alto Weekly* covers sports and has expanded its arts and entertainment coverage. It is still looking for stories in Palo Alto/Stanford area or features on people from the area.

Nonfiction: General interest, historical/nostalgic, interview/profile, photo feature. Special issues: Together (weddings—mid-February); Interiors (May, October). Nothing that is not local; no travel. **Buys 25 mss/year.** Query with published clips. Length: 700-1,000 words. **Pays $35-60.** Payment is negotiable.

Photos: Send photos with submission. Reviews contact sheets, 5×7 prints. Buys one-time rights. Pays $10 minimum/photo. Captions, identification of subjects, model releases required.

Tips: "Writers have the best chance if they live within circulation area and know publication and area well. DON'T send generic, broad-based pieces. The most open sections are food, interiors, and sports. Longer 'cover story' submissions may be accepted. Keep it LOCAL."

$ $ SACRAMENTO MAGAZINE, Sacramento Magazines Corp., 706 56th St., Suite 210, Sacramento CA 95819. (916)452-6200. Fax: (916)452-6061. E-mail: krista@sacmag.com. Website: www.sacmag.com. Managing Editor: Darlena Belushin McKay. **Contact:** Krista Minard, editor. **100% freelance written.** Works with a small number of new/unpublished writers each year. Monthly magazine with a strong local angle on local issues, human interest and consumer items for readers in the middle to high income brackets. Estab. 1975. Circ. 29,000. Pays on publication. Publishes ms an average of 3 months after acceptance. Generally buys first North American serial rights and electronic rights, rarely second serial (reprint) rights. Accepts queries by mail. Responds in 2 months to queries; 2 months to mss. Sample copy for $4.50. Writer's guidelines for #10 SASE.

O→ Break in with submissions to City Lights.

Nonfiction: Local isues vital to Sacramento quality of life. "No e-mail, fax or phone queries will be answered." **Buys 5 unsolicited feature mss/year.** Query. Length: 1,500-3,000 words, depending on author, subject matter and treatment. **Pays $250 and up.** Sometimes pays expenses of writers on assignment.

Photos: Send photos with submission. Buys one-time rights. Payment varies depending on photographer, subject matter and treatment. Captions, identification of subjects, location and date required.

Columns/Departments: Business, home and garden, first person essays, regional travel, gourmet, profile, sports, city arts (1,000-1,800 words); City Lights (250-300 words). **Pays $50-400.**

$ $ SACRAMENTO NEWS & REVIEW, Chico Community Publishing, 1015 20th St., Sacramento CA 95814. (916)498-1234. Fax: (916)498-7920. E-mail: billf@newsreview.com or jacksong@newsreview.com. Website: www.newsreview.com. **Contact:** Bill Forman, editor; Jackson Griffith, arts and lifestyle editor. **25% freelance written.** Magazine. "We are an alternative news and entertainment weekly. We maintain a high literary standard for submissions; unique or alternative slant. Publication aimed at a young, intellectual audience; submissions should have an edge and strong voice." Estab. 1989. Circ. 95,000. Pays on publication. Publishes ms an average of 2 months after acceptance. Byline given. Offers 10% kill fee. Buys first, electronic rights. Editorial lead time 2 months. Submit seasonal material 2 months in advance. Accepts queries by mail, e-mail, fax, phone. Accepts simultaneous submissions. Responds in 1 month to queries; 2 months to mss. Sample copy for 50¢.

Nonfiction: Essays, exposé, general interest, humor, interview/profile, personal experience. Does not want to see travel, product stories, business profile. **Buys 20-30 mss/year.** Query with published clips. Length: 750-5,000 words. **Pays $40-500.** Sometimes pays expenses of writers on assignment.

Photos: State availability with submission. Reviews 8×10 prints. Buys one-time rights. Negotiates payment individually. Identification of subjects required.

Columns/Departments: In the Mix (CD/TV/book reviews), 150-750 words. **Buys 10-15 mss/year.** Query with published clips. **Pays $10-200.**

$ $ $ $ SAN FRANCISCO, Focus on the Bay Area, 243 Vallejo St., San Francisco CA 94111. (415)398-2800. Fax: (415)398-6777. E-mail: ltrottier@sanfran.com. Website: www.sanfran.com. **Contact:** Lisa Trottier, managing editor. **50% freelance written.** Prefers to work with published/established writers. Monthly city/regional magazine. Estab. 1968. Circ. 180,000. Pays on publication. Publishes ms an average of 2 months after acceptance. Byline given. Offers 25% kill fee. Submit seasonal material 5 months in advance. Responds in 2 months to queries; 2 months to mss. Sample copy for $3.95.

Nonfiction: All stories should relate in some way to the San Francisco Bay Area (travel excepted). Exposé, interview/profile, travel, arts; politics; public issues; sports; consumer affairs. Query with published clips. Length: 200-4,000 words. **Pays $100-2,000 and some expenses.**

$ VENTURA COUNTY REPORTER, 1567 Spinnaker Dr., Suite 202, Ventura CA 93001. (805)658-2244. Fax: (805)658-7803. E-mail: editor@vcreporter.com. Website: vcreporter.com. **Contact:** Sharon McKenna, editor. **35% freelance written.** Weekly tabloid covering local news. Circ. 35,000. Pays on publication. Publishes ms an average of 2 weeks after acceptance. Byline given. Buys first North American serial rights. Accepts queries by mail, e-mail, fax. Responds in 3 weeks to queries. Sample copy not available. Writer's guidelines not available.

- Works with a small number of new/unpublished writers each year.

Nonfiction: Ventura County slant predominates. General interest (local slant), humor, interview/profile, travel (local-within 500 miles). Length: 2,000-3,000 words. **Payment varies.**

Photos: Send photos with submission. Reviews b&w contact sheet.

Columns/Departments: Entertainment; Dining News; News; Feature; Culture. Send complete ms. **Payment varies.**

Tips: "As long as topics are up-beat with a local slant, we'll consider them."

Colorado

$ $ $ ASPEN MAGAZINE, Ridge Publications, 720 E. Durant Ave., Suite E-8, Aspen CO 81611. (970)920-4040, ext. 25. Fax: (970)920-4044. E-mail: edit@aspenmagazine.com. Website: www.aspenmagazine.com. Editor: Janet C. O'Grady. **Contact:** Dana R. Butler, managing editor. **30% freelance written.** Bimonthly magazine covering Aspen and the Roaring Fork Valley. "All things Aspen, written in a sophisticated, insider-oriented tone." Estab. 1974. Circ. 20,000. Pays within 3 months of publication. Byline sometimes given. Offers 10% kill fee. Buys first North American serial, electronic rights. Editorial lead time 2 months. Accepts queries by mail, e-mail, fax. Accepts simultaneous submissions. Responds in 2 months to queries; 6 months to mss. Sample copy for 9×12 SAE and 10 first-class stamps. Writer's guidelines for #10 SASE.

- Responds only to submissions including a SASE.

Nonfiction: Essays, new product, photo feature, historical, environmental and local issues, architecture and design, sports and outdoors, arts. "We do not publish general interest articles without a strong Aspen hook. We do not publish 'theme' (skiing in Aspen) or anniversary (40th year of Aspen Music Festival) articles, fiction, poetry, or prewritten manuscripts." **Buys 30-60 mss/year.** Query with published clips. Length: 50-4,000 words. **Pays $50-1,000.** Sometimes pays expenses of writers on assignment.

Photos: State availability with submission. Reviews contact sheets, negatives, transparencies, prints. Identification of subjects, model releases required.

$ $ STEAMBOAT MAGAZINE, Sundance Plaza, 1250 S. Lincoln Ave., P.O. Box 881659, Steamboat Springs CO 80488. (970)871-9413. Fax: (970)871-1922. E-mail: info@steamboatmagazine.com. Website: www.allaboutsteamboat.com. **Contact:** Deborah Olsen, editor. **80% freelance written.** Semiannual magazine "showcasing the history, people, lifestyles, and interests of Northwest Colorado. Our readers are generally well-educated, well-traveled, upscale, active people visiting our region to ski in winter and recreate in summer. They come from all 50 states and many foreign countries. Writing should be fresh, entertaining, and informative." Estab. 1978. Circ. 30,000. Pays 50% on acceptance, 50% on publication. Publishes ms an average of 6 months after acceptance. Byline given. Buys exclusive rights. Submit seasonal material 1 year in advance. Accepts queries by mail, e-mail, fax, phone. Responds in 3 months to queries. Sample copy for $3.95 and SAE with 10 first-class stamps. Writer's guidelines free.

Nonfiction: Book excerpts, essays, general interest, historical/nostalgic, humor, interview/profile, photo feature, travel. **Buys 10-15 mss/year.** Query with published clips. Length: 150-1,500 words. **Pays $50-300 for assigned articles.** Sometimes pays expenses of writers on assignment.

Photos: "Prefers to review lightboxes, JPEGs, and dupes. Will request original transparencies when needed." State availability with submission. Buys one-time rights. Pays $50-250/photo. Captions, identification of subjects required.
Tips: "Stories must be about Steamboat Springs and the Tampa Valley to be considered. We're looking for new angles on ski/snowboard stories and activity-related stories. Please query first with ideas to make sure subjects are fresh and appropriate. We try to make subjects and treatments 'timeless' in nature because our magazine is a 'keeper' with a multi-year shelf life."

Connecticut

$ $ $ CONNECTICUT MAGAZINE, Journal Register Company, 35 Nutmeg Dr., Trumbull CT 06611. (203)380-6600. Fax: (203)380-6610. E-mail: dsalm@connecticutmag.com. Website: www.connecticutmag.com. Editor: Charles Monagan. **Contact:** Dale Salm, managing editor. **75% freelance written.** Prefers to work with published/established writers who know the state and live/have lived here. Monthly magazine "for an affluent, sophisticated, suburban audience. We want only articles that pertain to living in Connecticut." Estab. 1971. Circ. 93,000. Pays on publication. Publishes ms an average of 4 months after acceptance. Byline given. Offers 20% kill fee. Buys first North American serial rights. Submit seasonal material 4 months in advance. Accepts queries by mail, e-mail, fax. Responds in 6 weeks to queries. Sample copy not available. Writer's guidelines for #10 SASE.

Freelancers can best break in with "First" (short, trendy pieces with a strong Connecticut angle); find a story that is offbeat and write it in a lively, interesting manner.

Nonfiction: Interested in seeing hard-hitting investigative pieces and strong business pieces (not advertorial). Book excerpts, exposé, general interest, interview/profile, topics of service to Connecticut readers. Special issues: Dining/entertainment, northeast/travel, home/garden and Connecticut bride twice/year. Also, business (January) and healthcare once/year. No personal essays. **Buys 50 mss/year.** Query with published clips. Length: 3,000 words maximum. **Pays $600-1,200.** Sometimes pays expenses of writers on assignment.
Photos: Send photos with submission. Reviews contact sheets, transparencies. Buys one-time rights. Pays $50 minimum/photo. Identification of subjects, model releases required.
Columns/Departments: Business, Health, Politics, Connecticut Calendar, Arts, Dining Out, Gardening, Environment, Education, People, Sports, Media, From the Field (quirky, interesting regional stories with broad appeal). Length: 1,500-2,500 words. **Buys 50 mss/year.** Query with published clips. **Pays $400-700.**
Fillers: Short pieces about Connecticut trends, curiosities, interesting short subjects, etc. Length: 150-400 words. **Pays $75-150.**

The online magazine carries original content not found in the print edition. Contact: Charles Monagan, online editor.

Tips: "Make certain your idea has not been covered to death by the local press and can withstand a time lag of a few months. Again, we don't want something that has already received a lot of press."

N $ $ $ $ NORTHEAST MAGAZINE, The Hartford Courant, 285 Broad St., Hartford CT 06115-2510. (860)241-3700. Fax: (860)241-3853. E-mail: northeast@courant.com. Website: www.ctnow.com. Editor: Larry Bloom. **Contact:** Jane Bronfman, editorial assistant. **5% freelance written.** Weekly magazine for a Connecticut audience. Estab. 1982. Circ. 316,000. **Pays on acceptance.** Publishes ms an average of 5 months after acceptance. Byline given. Accepts queries by mail. Responds in 3 months to queries. Sample copy and writer's guidelines available.
Nonfiction: "We are primarily interested in hard-hitting nonfiction articles spun off the news and compelling personal stories, as well as humor, fashion, style and home. We have a strong emphasis on Connecticut subject matter." General interest (has to have a strong Connecticut tie-in), historical/nostalgic, In-depth investigations of stories behind the news (has to have strong Connecticut tie-in); Personal Essays (humorous or anecdotal). No poetry. **Buys 10 mss/year.** Query. Length: 750-2,500 words. **Pays $200-1,500.**
Photos: Most are assigned. "Do not send originals." State availability with submission.
Fiction: Confined to yearly fiction issue and "Word For Word" column (excerpts of soon-to-be published books by Connecticut authors or with Connecticut tie-ins). Length: 750-1,500 words.
Tips: "Less space available for all types of writing means our standards for acceptance will be much higher. It is to your advantage to read several issues of the magazine before submitting a manuscript or query. Virtually all our pieces are solicited and assigned by us, with about two percent of what we publish coming in 'over the transom.'"

Delaware

$ $ DELAWARE TODAY, 3301 Lancaster Pike, Suite 5C, Wilmington DE 19805. (302)656-1809. Fax: (302)656-5843. E-mail: editors@delawaretoday.com. Website: www.delawaretoday.com. **Contact:** Marsha Mah, editor. **50% freelance written.** Monthly magazine geared toward Delaware people, places and issues. "All stories must have Delaware slant. No pitches such as Delawareans will be interested in a national topic." Estab. 1962. Circ. 25,000. Pays on publication. Publishes ms an average of 4 months after acceptance. Byline given. Offers 50% kill fee. all rights for 1 year. Editorial lead time 3 months. Submit seasonal material 6 months in advance. Responds in 2 months to queries. Sample copy for $2.95.
Nonfiction: Historical/nostalgic, interview/profile, photo feature, lifestyles, issues. Special issues: Newcomer's Guide to Delaware. **Buys 40 mss/year.** Query with published clips. Length: 100-3,000 words. **Pays $50-750 for assigned articles.** Sometimes pays expenses of writers on assignment.

Photos: State availability with submission. Buys one-time rights. Negotiates payment individually. Identification of subjects required.
Columns/Departments: Business, Health, History, People, all 1,500 words. **Buys 24 mss/year.** Query with published clips. **Pays $150-250.**
Fillers: Anecdotes, newsbreaks, short humor. **Buys 10/year.** Length: 100-200 words. **Pays $50-75.**
Tips: "No story ideas that we would know about, i.e., a profile of the governor. Best bets are profiles of quirky/unique Delawareans that we'd never know about or think of."

District of Columbia

$ $ WASHINGTON CITY PAPER, 2390 Champlain St. NW, Washington DC 20009. (202)332-2100. Fax: (202)332-8500. E-mail: mail@washcp.com. Website: www.washingtoncitypaper.com. **Contact:** Tom Scocca. **50% freelance written.** "Relentlessly local alternative weekly in nation's capital covering city and regional politics, media and arts. No national stories." Estab. 1981. Circ. 93,000. Pays on publication. Publishes ms an average of 6 weeks after acceptance. Byline given. Offers 10% kill fee for assigned stories. Buys first rights. Editorial lead time 7-10 days. Responds in 1 month to queries. Writer's guidelines online.
Nonfiction: Tom Scocca (district line); Erik Wemple. "Our biggest need for freelancers is in the District Line section of the newspaper: short, well-reported and local stories. These range from carefully-drawn profiles to sharp, hooky approaches to reporting on local institutions. We don't want op-ed articles, fiction, poetry, service journalism or play by play accounts of news conferences or events. We also purchase, but more infrequently, longer 'cover-length' stories that fit the criteria stated above. Full guide to freelance submissions can be found on website." **Buys 100 mss/year.** Query with published clips or send complete ms. Length: District Line: 800-2,500 words; Covers: 4,000-10,000 words. **Pays 10-40¢/word.** Sometimes pays expenses of writers on assignment.
Photos: Make appointment to show portfolio to Jandos Rothstein, art director. Pays minimum of $75.
Columns/Departments: Leonard Roberge, arts editor. Music Writing (eclectic). **Buys 100 mss/year.** Query with published clips or send complete ms. **Pays 10-40¢/word.**
Tips: "Think local. Great ideas are a plus. We are willing to work with anyone who has a strong idea, regardless of vita."

N $ $ $ THE WASHINGTONIAN, 1828 L St. NW, #200, Washington DC 20036. (202)296-3600. Fax: (202)862-3526. E-mail: editorial@washingtonian.com. Website: www.washingtonian.com. **Contact:** Cindy Rich, assistant editor. **20-25% freelance written.** Monthly magazine. "Writers should keep in mind that we are a general interest city-and-regional magazine. Nearly all our articles have a hard Washington connection. And, please, no political satire." Estab. 1965. Circ. 160,000. Pays on publication. Publishes ms an average of 3 months after acceptance. Byline given. Buys first North American serial, limited, nonexclusive electronic rights. Editorial lead time 10 weeks. Accepts queries by mail, fax. Writer's guidelines online.
Nonfiction: Book excerpts, exposé, general interest, historical/nostalgic (with specific Washington, D.C. focus), interview/profile, personal experience, photo feature, travel. **Buys 15-30 mss/year.** Query with published clips. **Pays 50¢/word.** Sometimes pays expenses of writers on assignment.
Columns/Departments: Bill O'Sullivan. First Person (personal experience that somehow illuminates life in Washington area), 650-700 words. **Buys 9-12 mss/year.** Query. **Pays $325.**
The online magazine carries original content not found in the print edition. Contact: Cheryl Haser, online editor.
Tips: "The types of articles we publish include service pieces; profiles of people; investigative articles; rating pieces; institutional profiles; first-person articles; stories that cut across the grain of conventional thinking; articles that tell the reader how Washington got to be the way it is; light or satirical pieces (send the complete manuscript, not the idea, because in this case execution is everything). Subjects of articles include the federal government, local government, dining out, sports, business, education, medicine, fashion, environment, how to make money, how to spend money, real estate, performing arts, visual arts, travel, health, nightlife, home and garden, self-improvement, places to go, things to do, and more. Again, we are interested in almost anything as long as it relates to the Washington area. We don't like puff pieces or what we call 'isn't-it-interesting' pieces. In general, we try to help our readers understand Washington better, to help our readers live better, and to make Washington a better place to live. Also, remember—a magazine article is different from a newspaper story. Newspaper stories start with the most important facts, are written in short paragraphs with a lot of transitions, and usually can be cut from the bottom up. A magazine article usually is divided into sections that are like 400-word chapters of a very short book. The introductory section is very important—it captures the reader's interest and sets the tone for the article. Scenes or anecdotes often are used to draw the reader into the subject matter. The next section then might foreshadow what the article is about without trying to summarize it—you want to make the reader curious. Each succeeding section develops the subject. Any evaluations or conclusions come in the closing section."

Florida

$ $ $ $ BOCA RATON MAGAZINE, JES Publishing, 6413 Congress Ave., Suite 100, Boca Raton FL 33487. (561)997-8683. Fax: (561)997-8909. E-mail: lisao@bocamag.com. Website: www.bocamag.com. **Contact:** Lisa Ocker, editor. **70% freelance written.** Bimonthly lifestyle magazine "devoted to the residents of South Florida, featuring fashion, interior design, food, people, places, and issues that shape the affluent South Florida market." Estab. 1981. Circ. 20,000. **Pays on acceptance.** Publishes ms an average of 3 months after acceptance. Byline given. Buys second serial (reprint) rights. Submit seasonal material 7 months in advance. Accepts simultaneous submissions. Responds in 1 month to queries. Sample copy for $4.95 and 10×13 SAE with 10 first-class stamps. Writer's guidelines for #10 SASE.

Nonfiction: General interest, historical/nostalgic, humor, interview/profile, photo feature, travel. Special issues: Interior Design (September-October); Real Estate (March-April); Best of Boca (July-August). Query with published clips or send complete ms. Length: 800-2,500 words. **Pays $350-1,500.**

Reprints: Send tearsheet. Payment varies.

Photos: Send photos with submission.

Columns/Departments: Body & Soul (health, fitness and beauty column, general interest); Hitting Home (family and social interactions); History or Arts (relevant to South Florida), all 1,000 words. Query with published clips or send complete ms. **Pays $350-400.**

Tips: "We prefer shorter manuscripts, highly localized articles, excellent art/photography."

N $ $ EMERALD COAST MAGAZINE, Rowland Publishing, Inc., P.O. Box 1837, Tallahassee FL 32302. E-mail: editorial@rowlandinc.com. Website: www.rowlandinc.com. **Contact:** Julie Strauss Bettinger, editor. **50% freelance written.** Quarterly magazine. Lifestyle publication celebrating life on Florida's Emerald Coast. "All content has an Emerald Coast (Northwest Florida) connection. This includes Panama City, Seaside, Sandestin, Destin, Fort Walton Beach, and Pensacola. We encourage our writers to use creative nonfiction techniques." Estab. 2000. Circ. 17,800. **Pays on acceptance.** Publishes ms an average of 3 months after acceptance. Byline given. Buys first North American serial rights. Editorial lead time 4-6 months. Submit seasonal material 6 months in advance. Accepts queries by mail, e-mail. Accepts previously published material. Accepts simultaneous submissions. Responds in 3 months to queries; 3 months to mss. Sample copy for $4. Writer's guidelines by e-mail.

Nonfiction: All must have an Emerald Coast slant. Book excerpts, essays, historical/nostalgic, inspirational, interview/profile, new product, personal experience, photo feature. No fiction, poetry, or travel. No general interest—"we are Northwest Florida specific." **Buys 4-6 mss/year.** Query with published clips. Length: 2,000-3,500 words. **Pays $100-300.** Pays in contributor copies as special arrangements through publisher. Sometimes pays expenses of writers on assignment.

Photos: Send photos with submission. Reviews prints, GIF/JPEG files. Buys one-time rights. Negotiates payment individually. Captions, identification of subjects, model releases required.

Columns/Departments: The Sporting Life (sports topics related to the Emerald Coast), 750-1,500 words; Chef's Choice (profile of chef in Northwest Florida), approximately 700 words, plus recipe. **Buys 4 mss/year.** Query with published clips. **Pays $100-300.**

Tips: "We're looking for fresh ideas and new slants that are related to Florida's Emerald Coast. Because we work so far in advance, it is difficult to be timely, so be sure to give us ideas that aren't too time specific."

$ $ FLORIDA MONTHLY MAGAZINE, Florida Media, Inc., 102 Drennen Rd., Suite C-5, Orlando FL 32806. (407)816-9596. Fax: (407)816-9373. E-mail: editor@floridamagazine.com. Website: www.floridamagazine.com. Publisher: E. Douglas Cifers. **Contact:** Kristen Cifers. Monthly lifestyle magazine covering Florida travel, food and dining, heritage, homes and gardens, and all aspects of Florida lifestyle. Full calendar of events each month. Estab. 1981. Circ. 225,235. Pays on publication. Publishes ms an average of 5 months after acceptance. Byline given. Buys first rights. Editorial lead time 3 months. Submit seasonal material 6 months in advance. Accepts queries by mail, e-mail, fax. Responds in 2 months to queries. Sample copy for $5. Writer's guidelines for #10 SASE.

- Interested in material on areas outside of the larger cities.
- Break in with stories specific to Florida showcasing the people, places, events, and things that are examples of Florida's rich history and culture.

Nonfiction: Historical/nostalgic, interview/profile, travel, general Florida interest, out-of-the-way Florida places, dining, attractions, festivals, shopping, resorts, bed & breakfast reviews, retirement, real estate, business, finance, health, recreation, sports. **Buys 50-60 mss/year.** Query with published clips. Length: 500-2,500 words. **Pays $100-400 for assigned articles; $50-250 for unsolicited articles.**

Photos: Send photos with submission. Reviews 3×5 color prints and slides. Offers $6/photo. Captions required.

Columns/Departments: Golf; Homes & Gardenings; Heritage (all Florida-related); 750 words. **Buys 24 mss/year.** Query with published clips. **Pays $75-250.**

$ FT. MYERS MAGAZINE, And Pat, LLC, 15880 Summerlin Rd., Suite 189, Fort Myers FL 33908. Fax: (516)771-4482. E-mail: ftmyers@optonline.net. Managing Editor: Andrew Elias. **Contact:** Pat Simms-Elias, editor. **90% freelance written.** Bimonthly magazine covering media, arts, recreation, lifestyles in Fort Myers and southwest Florida. Audience: 25- to 55-year-old educated, active, successful males and females. Content: Arts, media, design, technology, sports, health, travel, home and garden. Estab. 2001. Circ. 20,000. Pays on publication. Publishes ms an average of 3 months after acceptance. Byline given. Offers 50% kill fee. Buys one-time, second serial (reprint) rights. Editorial lead time 3 months. Submit seasonal material 3 months in advance. Accepts queries by mail, e-mail, fax. Accepts previously published material. Accepts simultaneous submissions. Responds in 3 months to queries; 3 months to mss. Writer's guidelines for #10 SASE or by e-mail.

Nonfiction: Book excerpts, essays, exposé, general interest, historical/nostalgic, how-to, humor, interview/profile, new product, opinion, personal experience, technical, travel. **Buys 60-75 mss/year.** Query with or without published clips or send complete ms. Length: 300-1,500 words. **Pays $40-150.** Will pay in copies or in ad barter at writer's request. Sometimes pays expenses of writers on assignment.

Reprints: Accepts previously published submissions.

Photos: State availability of or send photos with submission. Reviews 4×5 to 8×10 prints. Buys one-time rights. Negotiates payment individually; generally offers $10-50/photo. Captions, identification of subjects required.

Columns/Departments: Media: books, music, video, film, theater, Internet, software (news, previews, reviews, interviews, profiles), 300-1,500 words. Lifestyles: art & design, science & technology, house & garden, health & nutrition, sports & recreation, travel & leisure, food & drink (news, interviews, previews, reviews, profiles, advice), 300-1,500 words. **Buys 60 mss/year.** Query with or without published clips or send complete ms. **Pays $40-150.**

Fiction: Humorous, slice-of-life vignettes. **Buys 5 mss/year.** Query with or without published clips or send complete ms. Length: 300-1,500 words. **Pays $40-150.**

$ $ $ GULFSHORE LIFE, 9051 N. Tamiami Trail, Suite 202, Naples FL 34108. (239)594-9980. Fax: (239)594-9986. E-mail: info@gulfshorelifemag.com. Website: www.gulfshorelifemag.com. **Contact:** Daniel Lindley, senior editor. **75% freelance written.** Magazine published 10 times/year for "southwest Florida, the workings of its natural systems, its history, personalities, culture and lifestyle." Estab. 1970. Circ. 35,000. Pays on publication. Publishes ms an average of 4 months after acceptance. Byline given. Buys first North American serial rights. Submit seasonal material 8 months in advance. Accepts queries by mail, e-mail, fax. Accepts simultaneous submissions. Sample copy for 9×12 SAE and 10 first-class stamps.

Nonfiction: All articles must be related to southwest Florida. Historical/nostalgic, interview/profile, issue/trend. **Buys 100 mss/year.** Query with published clips. Length: 500-3,000 words. **Pays $100-1,000.**

Photos: Send photos with submission. Reviews 35mm transparencies, 5×7 prints. Buys one-time rights. Pays $50-100. Identification of subjects, model releases required.

Tips: "We buy superbly written stories that illuminate southwest Florida personalities, places and issues. Surprise us!"

$ $ TALLAHASSEE MAGAZINE, Rowland Publishing Inc., P.O. Box 1837, Tallahassee FL 32302. E-mail: editorial@rowlandinc.com. Website: www.rowlandinc.com. **Contact:** Julie Strauss Bettinger, editor. **50% freelance written.** Bimonthly magazine covering life in Florida's Capital Region. "All content has a Tallahassee, Florida connection. We encourage our writers to use creative nonfiction techniques." Estab. 1978. Circ. 17,000. **Pays on acceptance.** Publishes ms an average of 3 months after acceptance. Byline given. Buys first North American serial rights. Editorial lead time 4-6 months. Submit seasonal material 6 months in advance. Accepts queries by mail, e-mail. Accepts simultaneous submissions. Responds in 3 months to queries; 3 months to mss. Sample copy for $4. Writer's guidelines by e-mail.

Nonfiction: All must have a Tallahassee slant. Book excerpts, essays, historical/nostalgic, inspirational, interview/profile, new product, personal experience, photo feature, travel, sports, business, Calendar items. No fiction, poetry, or travel. No general interest—"we are Tallahassee, Florida specific." **Buys 6 mss/year.** Query with published clips. Length: 2,000-3,500 words. **Pays $100-300.**

Photos: Send photos with submission. Reviews prints, GIF/JPEG files. Buys one-time rights. Negotiates payment individually. Captions, identification of subjects, model releases required.

Columns/Departments: The Sporting Life (sports topics related to Tallahassee), 750-1,500 words; Faces In the Crowd (people profiles related to Tallahassee), 1,500-3,000 words; Workday (profiles of people in business at work, related to Tallahassee), 1,500-3,500 words. **Buys 3-6 mss/year.** Query with published clips. **Pays $100-300.**

Tips: "We're looking for fresh ideas and new slants that are related to Florida's Capital Region. Because we work so far in advance, it is difficult to be timely, so be sure to give us ideas that aren't too time specific."

Georgia

$ $ $ $ ATLANTA, 1330 W. Peachtree St. NE, Suite 450, Atlanta GA 30309. (404)872-3100. Fax: (404)870-6219. E-mail: sfreeman@atlantamag.emmis.com. Website: www.atlantamagazine.com. **Contact:** Scott Freeman, executive editor or Betsy Riley, senior editor. Monthly magazine that explores people, pleasures, useful information, regional happenings, restaurants, shopping, etc., for a general adult audience in Atlanta, including subjects in government, sports, pop culture, urban affairs, arts, and entertainment. "*Atlanta* magazine articulates the special nature of Atlanta and appeals to an audience that wants to understand and celebrate the uniqueness of the region. The magazine's mission is to serve as a tastemaker by virtue of in-depth information and authoritative, provocative explorations of issues, personalities, and lifestyles." Circ. 69,000. **Pays on acceptance.** Byline given. Offers 25% kill fee. Buys first North American serial rights. Accepts queries by mail, e-mail, phone. Responds in 2 months to queries. Sample copy online.

Nonfiction: "*Atlanta* magazine articulates the special nature of Atlanta and appeals to an audience that wants to understand and celebrate the uniqueness of the region. The magazine's mission is to serve as a tastemaker by virtue of in-depth information and authoritative, provocative explorations of issues, personalities, and lifestyles." General interest, interview/profile, travel. **Buys 36-40 mss/year.** Query with published clips. Length: 1,500-5,000 words. **Pays $300-2,000.** Pays expenses of writers on assignment.

Columns/Departments: Essay, travel. **Length:** 1,000-1,500 words. **Buys 30 mss/year.** Query with published clips. **Pays $500.**

Fiction: Novel excerpts.

Fillers: Buys 80/year. Length: 75-175 words. **Pays $50-100.**

Tips: "Writers must know what makes their piece a story rather than just a subject."

N $ $ ATLANTA TRIBUNE: THE MAGAZINE, Black Atlanta's Business & Politics, L&L Communications, 875 Old Roswell Rd, Suite C-100, Roswell GA 30076. Fax: (770)642-6501. E-mail: rsherrell@atlantatribune.com. Website: www.atlantatribune.com. **Contact:** Fred Robinson, editor. **30% freelance written.** Monthly magazine covering African-American business, careers, technology, wealth-building, politics, and education. "The *Atlanta Tribune* is written for Atlanta's black executives, professionals and entrepreneurs with a primary focus of business, careers, technology, wealth-building, politics, and education. Our publication serves as an advisor that offers helpful information and direction to the black entrepreneur." Estab. 1987. Circ. 30,000. Pays on publication. Byline given. Offers 10% kill fee. Buys electronic, all rights. Editorial lead time 3 months. Submit seasonal material 4 months in advance. Accepts queries by e-mail. Responds in 6 weeks to queries. Sample copy online or mail a request. Writer's guidelines online.

- Break in with "the ability to write feature stories that give insight into Black Atlanta's business community, technology, businesses, and career and wealth-building opportunities. Also, stories with real social, political or economic impact."

Nonfiction: "Our special sections include Black History; Real Estate; Scholarship Roundup." Book excerpts, how-to (business, careers, technology), interview/profile, new product, opinion, technical. **Buys 100 mss/year.** Query with published clips. Length: 1,400-2,500 words. **Pays $250-600.** Sometimes pays expenses of writers on assignment.
Photos: State availability with submission. Reviews 2¼ x 2¼ transparencies. Buys one-time rights. Negotiates payment individually. Identification of subjects, model releases required.
Columns/Departments: Business; Careers; Technology; Wealth-Building; Politics and Education; all 400-600 words. **Buys 100 mss/year.** Query with published clips. **Pays $100-200.**

- The online version contains material not found in the print edition and includes writer's guidelines. Contact: Monét Cooper, associate managing editor.

Tips: "Send a well-written, convincing query by e-mail that demonstrates that you have thoroughly read previous issues and reviewed our online writer's guidelines."

$ FLAGPOLE MAGAZINE, Flagpole, P.O. Box 1027, Athens GA 30603. (706)549-9523. Fax: (706)548-8981. E-mail: editor@flagpole.com. Website: www.flagpole.com. **Contact:** Pete McCommons, editor. **75% freelance written.** Local "alternative" weekly with a special emphasis on popular (and unpopular) music. "Will consider stories on national, international musicians, authors, politicians, etc., even if they don't have a local or regional news peg. However, those stories should be original, irreverent enough to justify inclusion. Of course, local/Southern news/feature stories are best. We like reporting, storytelling more than opinion pieces." Estab. 1987. Circ. 16,000. Pays on publication. Publishes ms an average of 1 month after acceptance. Byline given. Makes work-for-hire assignments. Editorial lead time 2 months. Submit seasonal material 2 months in advance. Responds in 2 weeks to queries; 1 month to mss. Sample copy online.
Nonfiction: Book excerpts, essays, exposé, interview/profile, new product, personal experience. **Buys 50 mss/year.** Query by e-mail. Length: 600-2,000 words.
Reprints: Send tearsheet, photocopy or typed ms with rights for sale noted and information about when and where the material previously appeared.
Photos: State availability with submission. Reviews prints. Buys one-time rights. Negotiates payment individually. Captions required.
Columns/Departments: Lit. (book reviews), 800 words. **Buys 30 mss/year.** Send complete ms. **Pays 7¢/word.**
Tips: "Read our publication online before querying, but don't feel limited by what you see. We can't afford to pay much, so we're open to young/inexperienced writer-journalists looking for clips. Fresh, funny/insightful voices make us happiest, as does reportage over opinion. If you've ever succumbed to the temptation to call a pop record 'ethereal' we probably won't bother with your music journalism. No faxed submissions, please."

$ $ GEORGIA MAGAZINE, Georgia Electric Membership Corp., P.O. Box 1707, Tucker GA 30085. (770)270-6950. Fax: (770)270-6995. E-mail: ann.orowski@georgiaemc.com. Website: www.georgiamagazine.org. **Contact:** Ann Orowski, editor. **50% freelance written.** "We are a monthly magazine for and about Georgians, with a friendly, conversational tone and human interest topics." Estab. 1945. Circ. 444,000. Pays on publication. Publishes ms an average of 4 months after acceptance. Byline given. Buys first North American serial, electronic rights. Editorial lead time 2 months. Submit seasonal material 6 months in advance. Accepts simultaneous submissions. Responds in 1 month to subjects of interest to queries. Sample copy for $2. Writer's guidelines for #10 SASE.
Nonfiction: General interest (Georgia-focused), historical/nostalgic, how-to (in the home and garden), humor, inspirational, interview/profile, photo feature, travel. **Buys 24 mss/year.** Query with published clips. Length: 800-1,000 words; 500 words for smaller features and departments. **Pays $50-300.**
Photos: State availability with submission. Reviews contact sheets, transparencies, prints. Buys one-time rights. Negotiates payment individually. Identification of subjects, model releases required.

$ $ KNOW ATLANTA MAGAZINE, New South Publishing, 1303 Hightower Trail, Suite 101, Atlanta GA 30350. (770)650-1102. Fax: (770)650-2848. E-mail: editor1@knowatlanta.com. Website: www.knowatlanta.com. **Contact:** Geoff Kohl, editor. **80% freelance written.** Quarterly magazine covering the Atlanta area. "Our articles offer information on Atlanta that would be useful to newcomers—homes, schools, hospitals, fun things to do, anything that makes their move more comfortable." Estab. 1986. Circ. 192,000. Pays on publication. Byline given. Offers 100% kill fee. Buys first North American serial rights. Editorial lead time 2 months. Submit seasonal material 2 months in advance. Accepts queries by mail, e-mail, fax. Accepts previously published material. Sample copy for free.

- "Know the metro Atlanta area, especially hot trends in real estate. Writers who know about international relocation trends and commercial real estate topics are hot."

Nonfiction: General interest, how-to (relocate), interview/profile, personal experience, photo feature. No fiction. **Buys 20 mss/year.** Query with clips. Length: 1,000-2,000 words. **Pays $100-500 for assigned articles; $100-300 for unsolicited articles.** Sometimes pays expenses of writers on assignment.
Reprints: Accepts previously published submissions.
Photos: Send photos with submission, if available. Reviews contact sheets. Buys one-time rights. Negotiates payment individually. Captions, identification of subjects required.

$ $ POINTS NORTH MAGAZINE, Serving Atlanta's Stylish Northside, All Points Interactive Media Corp., 568 Peachtree Pkwy., Suite 116, Cumming GA 30041-6820. (770)844-0969. Fax: (770)844-0968. E-mail: managingeditor@ptsnorth.com. Website: www.ptsnorth.com. Managing Editor: Carolyn Williams. **Contact:** Managing Editor. **85% freelance written.** Monthly magazine covering lifestyle (regional). "*Points North* is a first-class lifestyle magazine for affluent residents of suburban communities in north metro Atlanta." Estab. 2000. Circ. 50,000. **Pays on acceptance.** Publishes ms an average of 1 month after acceptance. Byline given. Offers negotiable (for assigned articles only) kill fee. Buys electronic, first serial (in the southeast with a 6 month moratorium) rights. Editorial lead time 2 months. Submit seasonal material 5 months in advance. Accepts queries by mail, e-mail, fax. Accepts previously published material. Responds in 6-8 weeks to queries; 6-8 months to mss. Sample copy for $3.

Nonfiction: General interest, historical/nostalgic, interview/profile, travel, area-specific topics. No political, controversial, advertorial, new age, health and fitness, sports (particularly golf). **Buys 50-60 mss/year.** Query with published clips. Length: 1,200-2,500 words. **Pays $350-500.**

Photos: "We do not accept photos until article acceptance. Do not send photos with query." State availability with submission. Reviews slide transparencies, 4×6 prints, GIF/JPEG files. Offers no additional payment for photos accepted with ms. Captions, identification of subjects, model releases required.

Tips: "The best way for a freelancer, who is interested in being published, is to get a sense of the types of articles we're looking for by reading the magazine."

Idaho

$ $ SUN VALLEY MAGAZINE, Valley Publishing LLC, 12 E. Bullion, Suite B, Hailey ID 83333. (208)788-0770. Fax: (208)788-3881. E-mail: info@sunvalleymag.com. Website: www.sunvalleymag.com. **Contact:** Laurie C. Sammis, editor. **95% freelance written.** Quarterly magazine covering the lifestyle of the Sun Valley area. *Sun Valley Magazine* "presents the lifestyle of the Sun Valley area and the Wood River Valley, including recreation, culture, profiles, history and the arts." Estab. 1973. Circ. 17,000. Pays on publication. Publishes ms an average of 5 months after acceptance. Byline given. Buys first North American serial, electronic rights. Editorial lead time 1 year. Submit seasonal material 14 months in advance. Accepts queries by mail. Accepts previously published material. Accepts simultaneous submissions. Responds in 5 weeks to queries; 2 months to mss. Sample copy for $4.95 and $3 postage. Writer's guidelines for #10 SASE.

Nonfiction: "All articles are focused specifically on Sun Valley, the Wood River Valley and immediate surrounding areas." Historical/nostalgic, interview/profile, photo feature, travel. Special issues: Sun Valley home design and architecture, Spring; Sun Valley weddings/wedding planner, summer. Query with published clips. **Pays $40-500.** Sometimes pays expenses of writers on assignment.

Reprints: Only occasionally purchases reprints.

Photos: State availability with submission. Reviews transparencies. Buys one-time rights and some electronic rights. Offers $60-275/photo. Identification of subjects, model releases required.

Columns/Departments: Conservation issues, winter/summer sports, health & wellness, mountain-related activities and subjects, home (interior design), garden. All columns must have a local slant. Query with published clips. **Pays $40-300.**

Tips: "Most of our writers are locally based. Also, we rarely take submissions that are not specifically assigned, with the exception of fiction. However, we always appreciate queries."

Illinois

$ $ $ $ CHICAGO MAGAZINE, 500 N. Dearborn, Suite 1200, Chicago IL 60610-4901. Fax: (312)222-0699. E-mail: tritsch@chicagomag.com. Website: www.chicagomag.com. **Contact:** Shane Tritsch, managing editor. **50% freelance written.** Prefers to work with published/established writers. Monthly magazine for an audience which is "95% from Chicago area; 90% college educated; upper income, overriding interests in the arts, politics, dining, good life in the city and suburbs. Most are in 25-50 age bracket, well-read and articulate." Estab. 1968. Circ. 175,000. **Pays on acceptance.** Publishes ms an average of 3 months after acceptance. Buys first rights. Submit seasonal material 4 months in advance. Accepts queries by mail, e-mail. Responds in 1 month to queries. For sample copy, send $3 to Circulation Dept. Writer's guidelines for #10 SASE.

Nonfiction: "On themes relating to the quality of life in Chicago: Past, present, and future." Writers should have "a general awareness that the readers will be concerned, influential, longtime Chicagoans. We generally publish material too comprehensive for daily newspapers." Exposé, humor, personal experience, think pieces, profiles, spot news, historical articles. **Buys 100 mss/year.** Query; indicate specifics, knowledge of city and market, and demonstrable access to sources. Length: 200-6,000 words. **Pays $100-3,000 and up.** Pays expenses of writers on assignment.

Photos: Usually assigned separately, not acquired from writers. Reviews 35mm transparencies, color and b&w glossy prints.

The online editor is Deborah Wilk.

Tips: "Submit detailed queries, be business-like and avoid clichéd ideas."

$ $ $ $ CHICAGO READER, Chicago's Free Weekly, Chicago Reader, Inc., 11 E. Illinois St., Chicago IL 60611. (312)828-0350. Fax: (312)828-9926. E-mail: mail@chicagoreader.com. Website: www.chicagoreader.com. Editor: Alison True. **Contact:** Kiki Yablon, managing editor. **50% freelance written.** Weekly alternative tabloid for Chicago. Estab. 1971. Circ. 136,000. Pays on publication. Publishes ms an average of 3 months after acceptance. Byline given. No kill fee. Buys one-time rights. Editorial lead time up to 6 months. Accepts queries by mail, e-mail, fax. Accepts previously published material. Accepts simultaneous submissions. Responds if interested to queries. Sample copy for free. Writer's guidelines free or online.

Nonfiction: Book excerpts, essays, exposé, general interest, historical/nostalgic, humor, interview/profile, opinion, personal experience, photo feature. No celebrity interviews, national news or issues. **Buys 500 mss/year.** Send complete ms. Length: 4,000-50,000 words. **Pays $100-3,000.** Sometimes pays expenses of writers on assignment.

Reprints: Accepts previously published submissions.

Columns/Departments: Reading, First Person, Cityscape, Neighborhood News, all 1,500-2,500 words; arts and entertainment reviews, up to 1,200 words; calendar items, 400-1,000 words.

Tips: "Our greatest need is for full-length magazine-style feature stories on Chicago topics. We're *not* looking for: hard news (What the Mayor Said About the Schools Yesterday); commentary and opinion (What I Think About What the Mayor Said About the Schools Yesterday); poetry. We are not particularly interested in stories of national (as opposed to local) scope, or in celebrity for celebrity's sake (â la *Rolling Stone*, *Interview*, etc.). More than half the articles published in the *Reader* each week come from freelancers, and once or twice a month we publish one that's come in 'over the transom'—from a writer we've never heard of and may never hear from again. We think that keeping the *Reader* open to the greatest possible number of contributors makes a fresher, less predictable, more interesting paper. We not only publish unsolicited freelance writing, we depend on it. Our last issue in December is dedicated to original fiction."

Indiana

$ $ EVANSVILLE LIVING, Tucker Publishing Group, 100 NW Second St., Suite 220, Evansville IN 47715-5725. (812)426-2115. Fax: (812)426-2134. E-mail: ktucker@evansvilleliving.com. Website: www.evansvilleliving.com. **Contact:** Kristen Tucker, editor/publisher; Shellie Benson, managing editor (sbenson@evansvillelivingmagazine.com). **80-100% freelance written.** Bimonthly magazine covering Evansville, Indiana, and the greater area. "*Evansville Living* is the only full-color, glossy, 100+ page city magazine for the Evansville, Indiana, area. Regular departments include: Home Style, Garden Style, Day Tripping, Sporting Life, and Local Flavor (menus)." Estab. 2000. Circ. 50,000. **Pays on acceptance.** Publishes ms an average of 3 months after acceptance. Byline given. Buys all rights. Editorial lead time 6 months. Submit seasonal material 6 months in advance. Accepts queries by mail, e-mail, fax. Accepts previously published material. Sample copy for $5 or online. Writer's guidelines for free or by e-mail.

Nonfiction: Essays, general interest, historical/nostalgic, photo feature, travel. **Buys 60-80 mss/year.** Query with published clips. Length: 200-600 words. **Pays $100-300.** Sometimes pays expenses of writers on assignment.

Reprints: Accepts previously published submissions.

Photos: State availability with submission. Reviews contact sheets, negatives, transparencies, prints. Buys all rights. Negotiates payment individually. Captions, identification of subjects required.

Columns/Departments: Home Style (home); Garden Style (garden); Sporting Life (sports); Local Flavor (menus), all 1,500 words. Query with published clips. **Pays $100-300.**

$ $ $ INDIANAPOLIS MONTHLY, Emmis Publishing Corp., 40 Monument Circle, Suite 100, Indianapolis IN 46204. (317)237-9288. Fax: (317)684-2080. Website: www.indianapolismonthly.com. **Contact:** Deborah Way, editor. **30% freelance written.** Prefers to work with published/established writers. "*Indianapolis Monthly* attracts and enlightens its upscale, well-educated readership with bright, lively editorial on subjects ranging from personalities to social issues, fashion to food. Its diverse content and attention to service make it the ultimate source by which the Indianapolis area lives." Estab. 1977. Circ. 45,000. **Pays on acceptance.** Publishes ms an average of 2 months after acceptance. Byline given. Offers negotiable kill fee. Buys first North American serial, one-time rights. Editorial lead time 3 months. Submit seasonal material 3 months in advance. Accepts queries by mail, e-mail. Accepts simultaneous submissions. Responds in 3 weeks to queries. Sample copy for $6.10.

- This magazine is using more first-person essays, but they must have a strong Indianapolis or Indiana tie. It will consider nonfiction book excerpts of material relevant to its readers.

Nonfiction: Must have a strong Indianapolis or Indiana angle. Book excerpts (by Indiana authors or with strong Indiana ties), essays, exposé, general interest, interview/profile, photo feature. No poetry, fiction, or domestic humor; no "How Indy Has Changed Since I Left Town," "An Outsider's View of the 500," or generic material with no or little tie to Indianapolis/Indiana. **Buys 35 mss/year.** Query by mail with published clips. Length: 200-3,000 words. **Pays $50-1,000.**

Reprints: Send ms with rights for sale noted and information about when and where the material previously appeared *Accepts reprints only from noncompeting markets.*

Photos: State availability with submission. Buys one-time rights. Negotiates payment individually. Captions, identification of subjects, model releases required.

Tips: "Our standards are simultaneously broad and narrow: Broad in that we're a general interest magazine spanning a wide spectrum of topics, narrow in that we buy only stories with a heavy emphasis on Indianapolis (and, to a lesser extent, Indiana). Simply inserting an Indy-oriented paragraph into a generic national article won't get it: All stories must pertain primarily to things Hoosier. Once you've cleared that hurdle, however, it's a wide-open field. We've done features on national celebrities—Indianapolis native David Letterman and *Mir* astronaut David Wolf of Indianapolis, to name 2—and we've published 2-paragraph items on such quirky topics as an Indiana gardening supply house that sells insects by mail. Query with clips showing lively writing and solid reporting. No phone queries, please."

Iowa

N **$ MIDWEST LIVING**, Meredith Corporation, 1716 Locust Street, Des Moines IA 50309-3038. (515)284-3000. Fax: (515)284-3836. E-mail: mwl@mdp.com. Website: www.midwestliving.com. Editor: Dan Kaercher. Bimonthly magazine covering Midwestern families. Regional service magazine that celebrates the interest, values, and lifestyles of Midwestern families. Estab. 1986. Circ. 822,148. **Pays on acceptance.** Buys all rights. Editorial lead time 6 months. Accepts queries by mail, e-mail. Sample copy for $3.95. Writer's guidelines by e-mail.

Nonfiction: General interest (good eating, festivals and fairs), historical/nostalgic (interesting slices of Midwestern history, customs, traditions and the people who preserve them), interview/profile (towns, neighborhoods, families,people whose stories exemplify the Midwest spirit an values), travel (Midwestern destinations with emphasis on the fun and affordable). Query.

Photos: State availability with submission.

Tips: "As general rule of thumb, we're looking for stories that are useful to the reader with information of ideas they can act on in their own lives. Most important, we want stories that have direct relevance to our Midwest audience."

Kansas

$ $ KANSAS!, Kansas Department of Commerce and Housing, 1000 SW Jackson St., Suite 100, Topeka KS 66612-1354. (785)296-3479. Fax: (785)296-6988. E-mail: ksmagazine@kansascommerce.com. **90% freelance written.** Quarterly magazine emphasizing Kansas travel attractions and events. Estab. 1945. Circ. 52,000. **Pays on acceptance.** Publishes ms an average of 1 year after acceptance. Byline given. Buys one-time rights. Submit seasonal material 8 months in advance. Accepts queries by mail. Responds in 2 months to queries. Sample copy and writer's guidelines available.

Nonfiction: "Material must be Kansas-oriented and have good potential for color photographs. The focus is on travel with articles about places and events that can be enjoyed by the general public. In other words, events must be open to the public, places also. Query letter should clearly outline story. We are especially interested in Kansas freelancers who can supply their own quality photos." General interest, photo feature, travel. Query by mail. Length: 750-1,250 words. **Pays $200-400.** Pays mileage and lodging of writers on assignment.

Photos: "We are a full-color photo/manuscript publication." Send photos (original transparencies only) with query. Pays $50-75 (generally included in ms rate) for 35mm or larger format transparencies. Captions required.

Tips: "History and nostalgia stories do not fit into our format because they can't be illustrated well with color photos. Submit a query letter describing 1 appropriate idea with outline for possible article and suggestions for photos."

$ $ RELOCATING IN KANSAS CITY, Showcase Publishing, Inc., P.O. Box 8680, Prairie Village KS 66208. (913)648-5757. Fax: (913)648-5783. Editor: Dave Leathers. **Contact:** Andrea Darr, associate editor. Annual relocation guides, free for people moving to the area. Estab. 1986. Pays on publication. Byline given. Buys one-time rights. Editorial lead time 4 months. Submit seasonal material 4 months in advance. Accepts queries by mail, fax. Accepts previously published material. Accepts simultaneous submissions. Responds in 1 month to queries; 1 month to mss. Sample copy for $5.

Nonfiction: Historical/nostalgic, travel, local issues. **Buys 8 mss/year.** Query with published clips. Length: 600-1,000 words. **Pays $60-350.** Sometimes pays expenses of writers on assignment.

Reprints: Accepts previously published submissions.

Photos: Reviews transparencies. Buys one-time rights. Offers no additional payment for photos accepted with ms. Identification of subjects required.

Tips: "Really read and understand our audience."

Kentucky

$ BACK HOME IN KENTUCKY, Back Home in Kentucky, Inc., P.O. Box 710, Clay City KY 40312-0710. (606)663-1011. Fax: (606)663-1808. E-mail: info@backhomeinky.com. **Contact:** Jerlene Rose, editor/publisher. **50% freelance written.** Magazine published 6 times/year "covering Kentucky heritage, people, places, events. We reach Kentuckians and 'displaced' Kentuckians living outside the state." Estab. 1977. Circ. 8,000. Pays on publication. Publishes ms an average of 6 months after acceptance. Byline given. Buys first North American serial rights. Submit seasonal material 6 months in advance. Responds in 2 months to queries. Sample copy for $3 and 9×12 SAE with $1.23 postage affixed. Writer's guidelines for #10 SASE.

- Interested in profiles of Kentucky gardeners, cooks, craftspeople.

Nonfiction: Historical/nostalgic (Kentucky-related eras or profiles), photo feature (Kentucky places and events), travel (unusual/little-known Kentucky places), profiles (Kentucky cooks, gardeners, and craftspersons), memories (Kentucky related). No inspirational or religion. **Buys 20-25 mss/year.** Query with or without published clips or send complete ms. Length: 500-2,000 words. **Pays $50-150 for assigned articles; $25-75 for unsolicited articles.** "In addition to normal payment, writers receive 2 copies of issue containing their article."

Photos: Looking for color transparencies for covers (inquire for specific topics). Vertical format. Pays $50-150. Photo credits given. For inside photos, send photos with submission. Reviews transparencies, 4×6 prints. Rights purchased depends on situation. Occasionally offers additional payment for photos accepted with ms. Identification of subjects, model releases required.

Columns/Departments: Travel, crafts, gardeners, and cooks (all Kentucky related), 500-750 words. **Buys 10-12 mss/year.** Query with published clips. **Pays $15-40.**

Tips: "We work mostly with unpublished or emerging writers who have a feel for Kentucky's people, places, and events. Areas most open are little known places in Kentucky, unusual history, and profiles of interesting Kentuckians, and Kentuckians with unusual hobbies or crafts."

$ $ KENTUCKY MONTHLY, Vested Interest Publications, 213 St. Clair St., Frankfort KY 40601. (502)227-0053. Fax: (502)227-5009. E-mail: membry@kentuckymonthly.com or smvest@kentuckymonthly.com. Website: www.kentuckymonthly.com. Publisher: Stephen M. Vest. **Contact:** Michael Embry, editor. **75% freelance written.** Monthly magazine. "We publish stories about Kentucky and Kentuckians, including those who live elsewhere." Estab. 1998. Circ. 40,000. Pays within 3 months of publication. Publishes ms an average of 3 months after acceptance. Byline given. Buys first North American serial rights. Editorial lead time 3 months. Submit seasonal material 4 months in advance. Accepts queries by mail, e-mail, fax. Accepts simultaneous submissions. Responds in 2 weeks to queries; 1 month to mss. Sample copy online. Writer's guidelines online.

Nonfiction: Book excerpts, general interest, historical/nostalgic, how-to, humor, interview/profile, photo feature, religious, travel, all with a Kentucky angle. **Buys 60 mss/year.** Query with or without published clips. Length: 300-2,000 words. **Pays $25-350 for assigned articles; $20-100 for unsolicited articles.**

Photos: State availability with submission. Reviews negatives. Buys all rights. Captions required.

Fiction: Adventure, historical, mainstream, novel excerpts. **Buys 10 mss/year.** Query with published clips. Length: 1,000-5,000 words. **Pays $50-100.**

Tips: "We're looking for more fashion, home, and garden, first-person experience, mystery. Please read the magazine to get the flavor of what we're publishing each month. We accept articles via e-mail, fax, and mail."

$ $ LOUISVILLE MAGAZINE, 137 W. Muhammad Ali Blvd., Suite 101, Louisville KY 40202-1438. (502)625-0100. Fax: (502)625-0109. E-mail: loumag@loumag.com. Website: www.louisville.com/loumag. **Contact:** Bruce Allar, editor. **60% freelance written.** Monthly magazine "for and generally about people of the Louisville Metro area. Routinely covers arts, entertainment, business, sports, dining, and fashion. Features range from news analysis/exposé to humorous commentary. We like lean, clean prose, crisp leads." Estab. 1950. Circ. 26,500. Publishes ms an average of 3 months after acceptance. Byline given. Offers 20% kill fee. Buys first North American serial rights. Editorial lead time 6 weeks. Submit seasonal material 6 months in advance. Accepts queries by mail, e-mail, fax. Responds in 3 months to queries. Sample copy online.

Nonfiction: Essays, exposé, general interest, historical/nostalgic, interview/profile, photo feature. Special issues: Kentucky Derby (April); Pocket Guide to Louisville (May); Dining & Entertaining Guide (September); Louisville Bride (December). **Buys 75 mss/year.** Query. Length: 500-3,500 words. **Pays $50-600 for assigned articles.**

Photos: State availability with submission. Buys one-time rights. Offers $25-50/photo. Identification of subjects required.

Columns/Departments: End Insight (essays), 750 words. **Buys 10 mss/year.** Send complete ms. **Pays $100-150.**

Louisiana

$ $ SUNDAY ADVOCATE MAGAZINE, P.O. Box 588, Baton Rouge LA 70821-0588. (225)383-1111 ext. 0199. Fax: (225)388-0351. E-mail: glangley@theadvocate.com. Website: www.theadvocate.com. **Contact:** Tim Belehrad, news/features editor. **5% freelance written.** "Freelance features are put on our website." Estab. 1925. Pays on publication. Publishes ms an average of 3 months after acceptance. Byline given. Buys one-time rights.

O→ Break in with travel articles.

Nonfiction: Well-illustrated, short articles; must have local, area, or Louisiana angle, in that order of preference. **Buys 24 mss/year. Pays $100-200.**

Reprints: Send tearsheet or typed ms with rights for sale noted and information about when and where the material previously appeared. Pays $100-200.

Photos: Photos purchased with ms. Pays $30/published color photo.

Tips: "Style and subject matter vary. Local interest is most important. No more than 4 to 5 typed, double-spaced pages."

Maine

$ $ $ $ MAINE TIMES, Maine Times Publishing Co., P.O. Box 2129, Bangor ME 04402. (207)947-4410. Fax: (207)947-4458. E-mail: bketchum@mainetimes.com. Website: www.mainetimes.com. **Contact:** Brad Ketchum Jr., editor. **50% freelance written.** Monthly lifestyle magazine covering the state of Maine. "*Maine Times* is a publication with long and short items on Maine lifestyle, people, arts, adventures, environment, and events. Seeks good writing. For assigned stories we buy the material but follow a liberal reprint policy. For submitted pieces we pay for one-time rights." Estab. 1968 as a weekly tabloid, relaunched in May 2003 as a monthly 9x11 magazine. Circ. 100,000. **Pays on acceptance.** Byline given. Offers kill fee. Editorial lead time 2 months. Accepts queries by mail, e-mail, fax.

Nonfiction: Essays (750-1,000 words), opinion (400-600 words), personal experience (750-1,000 words), reviews (400-600 words). **Buys 75 mss/year.** Length: 1,800-3,500 words (features). **Pays 50¢-$1.50/word.**

Columns/Departments: Short items of 150-350 words. **Buys 100 mss/year.**

Tips: "*Maine Times* is a lively, upbeat, and well-written magazine that focuses solely on Maine in its many forms. Its editorial objective is to inform, inspire, educate, and entertain those who are, have been, or want to be residents of the state, as well as those who visit it regularly."

Maryland

$ $ BALTIMORE MAGAZINE, Inner Harbor East 1000 Lancaster St., Suite 400, Baltimore MD 21202. (410)752-4200. Fax: (410)625-0280. E-mail: iken@baltimoremag.com. Website: www.baltimoremagazine.net. **Contact:** Ken Iglehart, managing editor. **50-60% freelance written.** Monthly. "Pieces must address an educated, active, affluent reader and must have a very strong Baltimore angle." Estab. 1907. Circ. 70,000. Pays within 1 month of publication. Byline given. first rights in all media Submit seasonal material 4 months in advance. Accepts queries by mail, e-mail. Sample copy for $4.45. Writer's guidelines online.

O→ Break in through "Baltimore Inc. and B-Side-these are our shortest, newsiest sections and we depend heavily on tips and reporting from strangers. Please note that we are exclusively local. Submissions without a Baltimore angle may be ignored."

Nonfiction: Book excerpts (Baltimore subject or author), essays, exposé, general interest, historical/nostalgic, humor, interview/profile (with a Baltimorean), new product, personal experience, photo feature, travel (local and regional to Maryland *only*). "Nothing that lacks a strong Baltimore focus or angle." Query by mail with published clips or send complete ms. Length: 1,000-3,000 words. **Pays 30-40¢/word.** Sometimes pays expenses of writers on assignment.

Columns/Departments: Hot Shot, Health, Education, Sports, Parenting, Politics. Length: 1,000-2,500 words. "The shorter pieces are the best places to break into the magazine." Query with published clips.

The online magazine carries original content not found in the print edition. Contact: Mary-Rose Nelson, online editor.

Tips: "Writers who live in the Baltimore area can send résumé and published clips to be considered for first assignment. Must show an understanding of writing that is suitable to an educated magazine reader and show ability to write with authority, describe scenes, help reader experience the subject. Too many writers send us newspaper-style articles. We are seeking: 1) *Human interest features*—strong, even dramatic profiles of Baltimoreans of interest to our readers. 2) *First-person accounts* of experience in Baltimore, or experiences of a Baltimore resident. 3) *Consumer*—according to our editorial needs, and with Baltimore sources. Writers should read/familiarize themselves with style of *Baltimore Magazine* before submitting."

$ CHESAPEAKE LIFE MAGAZINE, Alter Communications, 1040 Park Ave., Suite 200, Baltimore MD 21201. (443)451-6023. Fax: (443)451-6027. E-mail: editor@chesapeakelifemag.com. Website: www.chesapeakelifemag.com. **Contact:** Kessler Burnett, editor. **80% freelance written.** Bimonthly magazine covering restaurant reviews, personalities, home design, travel, regional calendar of events, feature articles, gardening. "*Chesapeake Life* is a regional magazine covering the Chesapeake areas of Maryland, Virginia, and Southern Delaware." Estab. 1995. Circ. 85,000. Pays on publication. Byline given. Buys first North American serial rights. Editorial lead time 2 months. Accepts queries by mail, e-mail, fax, phone. Writer's guidelines free.

Nonfiction: Book excerpts, general interest, historical/nostalgic, interview/profile, photo feature, travel. Query with published clips. Length: Open.

Photos: Send photos with submission. Buys one-time rights. Negotiates payment individually.

Massachusetts

$ BOSTON MAGAZINE, 300 Massachusetts Ave., Boston MA 02115. (617)262-9700. Fax: (617)267-1774. Website: www.bostonmagazine.com. **Contact:** Jon Marcus, editor. **10% freelance written.** Monthly magazine covering the city of Boston. Estab. 1962. Circ. 125,000. Pays on publication. Publishes ms an average of 3 months after acceptance. Byline given. Offers 20% kill fee. Buys first North American serial rights. Editorial lead time 2 months. Submit seasonal material 4 months in advance. Accepts queries by mail, fax. Responds in 2 weeks to queries.

Nonfiction: Book excerpts, exposé, general interest, interview/profile, politics; crime; trends; fashion. **Buys 20 mss/year.** Query. *No unsolicited mss.* Length: 1,200-12,000 words. Pays expenses of writers on assignment.

Photos: State availability with submission. Buys one-time rights. Negotiates payment individually.

Columns/Departments: Dining, Finance, City Life, Personal Style, Politics, Ivory Tower, Media, Wine, Boston Inc., Books, Theater, Music. Query.

Tips: "Read *Boston*, and pay attention to the types of stories we use. Suggest which column/department your story might best fit, and keep your focus on the city and its environs. We like a strong narrative style, with a slightly 'edgy' feel—we rarely do 'remember when' stories. Think *city* magazine."

$ $ CAPE COD LIFE, including Martha's Vineyard and Nantucket, Cape Cod Life, Inc., P.O. Box 1385, Pocasset MA 02559-1385. (508)564-4466. Fax: (508)564-4470. Website: www.capecodlife.com. Editor: Brian F. Shortsleeve. **Contact:** Janice Rohlf, managing editor. **80% freelance written.** Magazine published 7 times/year focusing on "area lifestyle, history and culture, people and places, business and industry, and issues and answers for year-round and summer residents of Cape Cod, Nantucket, and Martha's Vineyard as well as nonresidents who spend their leisure time here." Circ. 45,000. Pays 1 month after publication. Byline given. Offers 20% kill fee. Buys first North American serial rights, makes work-for-hire assignments. Submit seasonal material 6 months in advance. Accepts queries by mail. Responds in 3 months to queries; 3 months to mss. Sample copy for $5. Writer's guidelines for #10 SASE.

Nonfiction: Book excerpts, general interest, historical/nostalgic, interview/profile, new product, photo feature, travel, gardening, marine, nautical, nature, arts, antiques. **Buys 20 mss/year.** Query with or without published clips. Length: 1,000-3,000 words. **Pays $100-500.**

Photos: Photo guidelines for #10 SASE. Buys first rights with right to reprint. Pays $25-225. Captions, identification of subjects required.

The online magazine carries original material not found in the print edition.

Tips: "Freelancers submitting *quality* spec articles with a Cape Cod and Islands angle have a good chance at publication. We like to see a wide selection of writer's clips before giving assignments. We also publish *Cape Cod Home: Living and Gardening on the Cape and Islands* covering architecture, landscape design, and interior design with a Cape and Islands focus."

$ $ PROVINCETOWN ARTS, Provincetown Arts, Inc., 650 Commercial St., P.O. Box 35, Provincetown MA 02657. (508)487-3167. Fax: (508)487-8634. Website: www.capecodaccess.com. **Contact:** Christopher Busa, editor. **90% freelance written.** Annual magazine covering contemporary art and writing. "*Provincetown Arts* focuses broadly on the artists and writers who inhabit or visit the Lower Cape, and seeks to stimulate creative activity and enhance public awareness of the cultural life of the nation's oldest continuous art colony. Drawing upon a 75-year tradition rich in visual art, literature, and theater, *Provincetown Arts* offers a unique blend of interviews, fiction, visual features, reviews, reporting, and poetry." Estab. 1985. Circ. 8,000. Pays on publication. Publishes ms an average of 4 months after acceptance. Offers 50% kill fee. Buys first, one-time, second serial (reprint) rights. Editorial lead time 6 months. Submit seasonal material 6 months in advance. Responds in 3 weeks to queries; 2 months to mss. Sample copy for $10. Writer's guidelines for #10 SASE.

Nonfiction: Book excerpts, essays, humor, interview/profile. **Buys 40 mss/year.** Send complete ms. Length: 1,500-4,000 words. **Pays $150 minimum for assigned articles; $125 minimum for unsolicited articles.**

Photos: Send photos with submission. Reviews 8×10 prints. Buys one-time rights. Offers $20-$100/photo. Identification of subjects required.

Fiction: Mainstream, novel excerpts. Plans special fiction issue. **Buys 7 mss/year.** Send complete ms. Length: 500-5,000 words. **Pays $75-300.**

Poetry: Buys 25 poems/year. Submit maximum 3 poems. **Pays $25-150.**

$ $ WORCESTER MAGAZINE, 172 Shrewsbury St., Worcester MA 01604-4636. (508)755-8004. Fax: (508)755-4734. E-mail: editorial@worcestermag.com. Website: www.worcestermag.com. **Contact:** Michael Warshaw, editor. **10% freelance written.** Weekly tabloid emphasizing the central Massachusetts region, especially the city of Worcester. Estab. 1976. Circ. 40,000. Pays on publication. Publishes ms an average of 3 weeks after acceptance. Byline given. Buys all rights. Submit seasonal material 2 months in advance. Accepts queries by mail, e-mail, fax.

- Does not respond to unsolicited material.

O→ Break in with "back of the book arts and entertainment articles."

Nonfiction: "We are interested in any piece with a local angle." Essays, exposé (area government, corporate), general interest, historical/nostalgic, humor, opinion (local), personal experience, photo feature, religious, interview (local). **Buys less than 75 mss/year.** Length: 500-1,500 words. **Pays 10¢/ word.**

Michigan

$ $ $ ANN ARBOR OBSERVER, Ann Arbor Observer Co., 201 E. Catherine, Ann Arbor MI 48104. Fax: (734)769-3375. E-mail: hilton@aaobserver.com. Website: www.arborweb.com. **Contact:** John Hilton, editor. **50% freelance written.** Monthly magazine. "We depend heavily on freelancers and we're always glad to talk to new ones. We look for the intelligence and judgment to fully explore complex people and situations, and the ability to convey what makes them interesting. We've found that professional writing experience is not a good predictor of success in writing for the *Observer*. So don't let lack of experience deter you. Writing for the *Observer* is, however, a demanding job. Our readers range from U-M faculty members to hourly workers at Eaton. That means articles have to be both accurate and accessible." Estab. 1976. Circ. 63,000. Pays on publication. Publishes ms an average of 2 months after acceptance. Byline given. Accepts queries by mail, e-mail, fax, phone. Responds in 3 weeks to queries; several months to mss. Sample copy for 12½×15 SAE with $3 postage. Writer's guidelines for #10 SASE.

Nonfiction: Historical, investigative features, profiles, brief vignettes. Must pertain to Ann Arbor. **Buys 75 mss/year.** Length: 100-7,000 words. **Pays up to $1,000.** Sometimes pays expenses of writers on assignment.

Columns/Departments: Inside Ann Arbor (short, interesting tidbits), 300-500 words. **Pays $150.** Around Town (unusual, compelling ancedotes), 750-1,500 words. **Pays $150-200.**

Tips: "If you have an idea for a story, write a 100-200-word description telling us why the story is interesting. We are open most to intelligent, insightful features of up to 5,000 words about interesting aspects of life in Ann Arbor."

$ HOUR DETROIT, Hour Media LLC, 117 W. Third St., Royal Oak MI 48067. (248)691-1800. Fax: (248)691-4531. E-mail: editorial@hourdetroit.com. Website: www.hourdetroit.com. Managing Editor: George Bulanda. Senior Editor: Rebecca Powers. **Contact:** Ric Bohy, editor. **50% freelance written.** Monthly magazine. "General interest/lifestyle magazine aimed at a middle- to upper-income readership aged 17-70." Estab. 1996. Circ. 45,000. **Pays on acceptance.** Publishes ms an average of 2 months after acceptance. Byline given. Offers 30% kill fee. Buys first North American serial rights. Editorial lead time 1½ months. Submit seasonal material 12 months in advance. Accepts queries by mail, e-mail, fax. Sample copy for $6.

Nonfiction: Book excerpts, exposé, general interest, historical/nostalgic, interview/profile, new product, photo feature, technical, travel. **Buys 150 mss/year.** Query with published clips. Length: 300-2,500 words. Sometimes pays expenses of writers on assignment.

Photos: State availability with submission.

$ $ TRAVERSE, Northern Michigan's Magazine, Prism Publications, 148 E. Front St., Traverse City MI 49684. Fax: (231)941-8391. E-mail: traverse@traversemagazine.com. Website: www.traversemagazine.com. **Contact:** Jeff Smith, editor. **20% freelance written.** Monthly magazine covering northern Michigan life. "*Traverse* is a celebration of the life and environment of northern Michigan." Estab. 1981. Circ. 30,000. **Pays on acceptance.** Byline given. Offers 10% kill fee. Buys first North American serial rights. Editorial lead time 1 year. Submit seasonal material 1 year in advance. Accepts queries by mail, e-mail, fax, phone. Accepts simultaneous submissions. Responds in 2 months to queries. Sample copy for $3. Writer's guidelines for #10 SASE.

Nonfiction: Book excerpts, essays, general interest, historical/nostalgic, humor, interview/profile, personal experience, photo feature, travel. No fiction or poetry. **Buys 24 mss/year.** Query with published clips or send complete ms. Length: 1,000-3,200 words. **Pays $150-500.** Sometimes pays expenses of writers on assignment.

Photos: State availability with submission. Buys one-time rights. Negotiates payment individually.

Columns/Departments: Up in Michigan Reflection (essays about northern Michigan); Reflection on Home (essays about northern homes), both 700 words. **Buys 18 mss/year.** Query with published clips or send complete ms. **Pays $100-200.**

Tips: "When shaping an article for us, consider first that it must be strongly rooted in our region. The lack of this foundation element is one of the biggest reasons for our rejecting material. If you send us a piece about peaches, even if it does an admirable job of relaying the history of peaches, their medicinal qualities, their nutritional magnificence, and so on, we are likely to reject if it doesn't include local farms as a reference point. We want sidebars and extended captions designed to bring in a reader not enticed by the main subject. We cover the northern portion of the Lower Peninsula and to a lesser degree the Upper Peninsula. General categories of interest include nature and the environment, regional culture, personalities, the arts (visual, performing, literary), crafts, food & dining, homes, history, and outdoor activities (e.g., fishing, golf, skiing, boating, biking, hiking, birding, gardening). We are keenly interested in environmental and land-use issues but seldom use material dealing with such issues as health care, education, social services, criminal justice, and local politics. We use service pieces and a small number of how-to pieces, mostly focused on small projects for the home or yard. Also, we value research. We need articles built with information. Many of the pieces we reject use writing style to fill in for information voids. Style and voice are strongest when used as vehicles for sound research."

Minnesota

$ $ LAKE COUNTRY JOURNAL MAGAZINE, Evergreen Press of Brainerd, P.O. Box 465, Brainerd MN 56401. Fax: (218)825-7816. E-mail: jodi@lakecountryjournal.com. Website: www.lakecountryjournal.com. **Contact:** Jodi Schwen, editor or Beth Hautala, assistant editor. **90% freelance written.** Bimonthly magazine covering central Minnesota's lake country. "We target a specific geographical niche in central Minnesota. The writer must be familiar with our area. We promote positive family values, foster a sense of community, increase appreciation for our natural and cultural environments, and provide ideas for enhancing the quality of our lives." Estab. 1996. Circ. 14,500. Pays on publication. Publishes ms an average of 6 months after acceptance. Byline given. Offers 25% kill fee. Buys first North American serial, second serial (reprint), electronic rights. Submit seasonal material 1 year in advance. Accepts queries by mail, e-mail. Responds in 2 months to queries; 3 months to mss. Sample copy for $6. Writer's guidelines online.

O→ Break in by "submitting department length first—they are not scheduled as far in advance as features. Always in need of original fillers."

Nonfiction: Essays, general interest, how-to, humor, interview/profile, personal experience, photo feature. "No articles that come from writers who are not familiar with our target geographical location." **Buys 30 mss/year.** Query with or without published clips. Length: 1,000-1,500 words. **Pays $100-175.** Sometimes pays expenses of writers on assignment.

Reprints: Accepts previously published submissions.

Photos: State availability with submission. Reviews transparencies. Buys one-time rights. Negotiates payment individually. Identification of subjects, model releases required.

Columns/Departments: Profile-People from Lake Country, 800 words; Essay, 800 words; Health (topics pertinent to central Minnesota living), 500 words; Family Fun, 500 words. **Buys 40 mss/year.** Query with published clips. **Pays $50-75.**

Fiction: Adventure, humorous, mainstream, slice-of-life vignettes, literary, also family fiction appropriate to Lake Country and seasonal fiction. **Buys 6 mss/year.** Length:1,500 words. **Pays $100-175.**

Poetry: Free verse. "Never use rhyming verse, avant-garde, experimental, etc." **Buys 20 poems/year.** Submit maximum 4 poems. Length: 8-32 lines. **Pays $25.**

Fillers: Anecdotes, short humor. **Buys 20/year.** Length: 100-500 words. **Pays $25.**

Tips: "Most of the people who will read your articles live in the north central Minnesota lakes area. All have some significant attachment to the area. We have readers of various ages, backgrounds, and lifestyles. After reading your article, we hope to have a deeper understanding of some aspect of our community, our environment, ourselves, or humanity in general. Tell us something new. Show us something we didn't see before. Help us grasp the significance of your topic. Use analogies, allusions, and other literary techniques to add color to your writing. Add breadth by making the subject relevant to all readers—especially those who aren't already interested in your subject. Add depth by connecting your subject with timeless insights. If you can do this without getting sappy or didactic or wordy or dull, we're looking for you."

$ $ LAKE SUPERIOR MAGAZINE, Lake Superior Port Cities, Inc., P.O. Box 16417, Duluth MN 55816-0417. (218)722-5002. Fax: (218)722-4096. E-mail: edit@lakesuperior.com. Website: www.lakesuperior.com. **Contact:** Konnie LeMay, editor. **60% freelance written.** Works with a small number of new/unpublished writers each year. Please include phone number and address with e-mail queries. Bimonthly magazine covering contemporary and historic people, places and current events around Lake Superior. Estab. 1979. Circ. 20,000. Pays on publication. Publishes ms an average of 10 months after acceptance. Byline given. Buys first North American serial, second serial (reprint) rights. Submit seasonal material 1 year in advance. Accepts queries by mail, e-mail. Responds in 3 months to queries. Sample copy for $3.95 and 5 first-class stamps. Writer's guidelines for #10 SASE.

Nonfiction: Book excerpts, general interest, historical/nostalgic, humor, interview/profile (local), personal experience, photo feature (local), travel (local), city profiles, regional business, some investigative. **Buys 45 mss/year.** Query with published clips. Length: 300-2,200 words. **Pays $60-600.** Sometimes pays expenses of writers on assignment.

Photos: "Quality photography is our hallmark." Send photos with submission. Reviews contact sheets, 2×2 and larger transparencies, 4×5 prints. Offers $40/image; $125 for covers. Captions, identification of subjects, model releases required.

Columns/Departments: Current events and things to do (for Events Calendar section), less than 300 words; Around The Circle (media reviews; short pieces on Lake Superior; Great Lakes environmental issues; themes, letters and short pieces on events and highlights of the Lake Superior Region); I Remember (nostalgic lake-specific pieces), up to 1,100 words; Life Lines (single personality profile with photography), up to 900 words. Other headings include Destinations, Nature, Wilderness Living, Heritage, Shipwreck, Chronicle, Lake Superior's Own, House for Sale. **Buys 20 mss/year.** Query with published clips. **Pays $60-90.**

Fiction: Ethnic, historic, humorous, mainstream, novel excerpts, slice-of-life vignettes, ghost stories. Must be targeted regionally. **Buys 2-3 mss/year.** Query with published clips. Length: 300-2,500 words. **Pays $1-125.**

The online magazine carries original content not found in the print edition. Contact: Konnie Lemay, online editor.

Tips: "Well-researched queries are attended to. We actively seek queries from writers in Lake Superior communities. We prefer manuscripts to queries. Provide enough information on why the subject is important to the region and our readers, or why and how something is unique. We want details. The writer must have a thorough knowledge of the subject and how it relates to our region. We prefer a fresh, unused approach to the subject which provides the reader with an emotional involvement. Almost all of our articles feature quality photography, color or black and white. It is a prerequisite of all nonfiction. All submissions should include a *short* biography of author/photographer; mug shot sometimes used. Blanket submissions need not apply."

$ MINNESOTA MONTHLY, U.S. Trust Bldg., 730 S. Second Ave., Minneapolis MN 55402. Fax: (612)371-5801. E-mail: phnettleton@mnmo.com. Website: www.mnmo.com. **Contact:** Pamela Hill Nettleton, editor. **50% freelance written.** "*Minnesota Monthly* is a regional lifestyle publication written for a sophisticated, well-educated audience living in the Twin Cities area and in greater Minnesota." Estab. 1967. Circ. 80,000. **Pays on acceptance.** Accepts queries by mail, e-mail. Writer's guidelines online.

"The Journey column/department (2,000 words) is probably the best break-in spot for freelancers. Submit, in its entirety, a diary or journal of a trip, event, or experience that changed your life. Past journeys: being an actress on a cruise ship, a parent's death, making a movie."

Nonfiction: Regional issues, arts, services, places, people, essays, exposé, general interest, historical/nostalgia, interview/profile, new product, photo feature, travel in Minnesota. "We want exciting, excellent, compelling writing with a strong Minnesota angle." Query with résumé, published clips, and SASE. Length: 1,000-4,000 words. **Payment negotiable.**

Columns/Departments: Portrait (photo-driven profile), 360 words; Just Asking (sassy interview with a Minnesota character or celebrity), 900 words; Midwest Traveler, 950-2,000 words; Postcards (chatty notes from Midwest towns), 300 words; Journey (diary/journal of a life-changing experience), 2,000 words. Query with résumé, published clips, and SASE. **Payment negotiable.**

Fiction: Fiction in the June issue, and a November fiction contest, The Tamarack Awards.

Tips: "Our readers are bright, artsy, and involved in their communities. Writing should reflect that. Stories must all have a strong Minnesota angle. If you can write well, try us! Familiarize yourself with a few recent issues before you query."

N $ $ $ MPLS. ST. PAUL MAGAZINE, MSP Communications, 220 S. 6th St., Suite 500, Minneapolis MN 55402-4507. (612)339-7571. Fax: (612)339-5806. E-mail: edit@mspcommunications.com. Website: www.mspmag.com. Editor: Brian Anderson. Managing Editor: Jean Marie Hamilton. Monthly magazine. "*Mpls. St. Paul Magazine* is a city magazine serving upscale readers in the Minneapolis-St. Paul metro area." Pays on publication. Buys all rights. Editorial lead time 3 months. Accepts queries by mail, e-mail, fax. Sample copy for $8. Writer's guidelines online.

Nonfiction: Book excerpts, essays, exposé, general interest, historical/nostalgic, interview/profile, personal experience, photo feature, travel. **Buys 150 mss/year.** Query with published clips. Length: 750-2,500 words. **Pays 50¢/word for assigned articles.**

Photos: Jim Nelson, art director.

Mississippi

$ $ MISSISSIPPI MAGAZINE, Downhome Publications, 5 Lakeland Circle, Jackson MS 39216. (601)982-8418. Fax: (601)982-8447. **Contact:** Kelli Bozeman, editor. **90% freelance written.** Bimonthly magazine covering Mississippi—the state and its lifestyles. "We are interested in positive stories reflecting Mississippi's rich traditions and heritage, and focusing on the contributions the state and its natives have made to the arts, literature, and culture. In each issue we showcase homes and gardens, lifestyle issues, food, design, art, and more." Estab. 1982. Circ. 39,000. Pays on publication. Publishes ms an average of 6 months after acceptance. Byline given. Offers 50% kill fee. Buys first North American serial rights. Editorial lead time 6 months. Submit seasonal material 1 year in advance. Accepts queries by mail, fax. Accepts simultaneous submissions. Responds in 3 months to queries. Writer's guidelines for #10 SASE.

Nonfiction: General interest, historical/nostalgic, how-to (home decor), interview/profile, personal experience, travel. "No opinion, political, essay, book reviews, exposé." **Buys 15 mss/year.** Query. Length: 900-1,500 words. **Pays $150-350 for assigned articles; $75-200 for unsolicited articles.**

Photos: Send photos with query. Reviews transparencies, prints. Buys one-time rights. Negotiates payment individually. Captions, identification of subjects, model releases required.

Columns/Departments: Gardening (short informative article on a specific plant or gardening technique), 750-1,000 words; Culture Center (story about an event or person relating to Mississippi's art, music, theatre, or literature), 750-1,000 words; On Being Southern (Personal essay about life in Mississippi. Only ms submissions accepted.), 750 words. **Buys 6 mss/year.** Query. **Pays $150-225.**

Missouri

N $KANSAS CITY MAGAZINE, 118 Southwest Blvd., 3rd Floor, Kansas City MO 64108. (816)421-4111. Fax: (816)221-8350. Website: www.kcmag.com. **Contact:** Leigh Elmore, editor. **75% freelance written.** Magazine published 10 times a year. "Our mission is to celebrate living in Kansas City. We are a consumer lifestyle/general interest magazine focused on Kansas City, its people and places." Estab. 1994. Circ. 31,000. **Pays on acceptance.** Publishes ms an average of 3 months after acceptance. Byline given. Offers 10% kill fee. Buys first North American serial rights. Editorial lead time 4 months. Submit seasonal material 6 months in advance. Accepts queries by mail, e-mail, fax. Accepts simultaneous submissions. Sample copy for 8½×11 SAE or online.

Nonfiction: Exposé, general interest, interview/profile, photo feature. **Buys 15-20 mss/year.** Query with published clips. Length: 250-3,000 words.

Photos: Buys one-time rights. Negotiates payment individually.

Columns/Departments: Entertainment (Kansas City only), 1,000 words; Food (Kansas City food and restaurants only), 1,000 words. **Buys 10 mss/year.** Query with published clips.

$ $MISSOURI LIFE, Missouri Life, Inc., P.O. Box 421, Fayette MO 65248-0421. (660)248-3489. Fax: (660)248-2310. E-mail: info@missourilife.com. Website: www.missourilife.com. Editor-in-Chief: Danita Allen Wood. **Contact:** Sona Pai, managing editor. **70% freelance written.** Bimonthly magazine covering the state of Missouri. "*Missouri Life*'s readers are mostly college-educated people with a wide range of travel and lifestyle interests. Our magazine discovers the people, places, and events—both past and present—that make Missouri a good place to live and/or visit." Estab. 1999. Circ. 50,000. **Pays on acceptance.** Byline given. Offers negotiable kill fee. Buys all, nonexclusive rights. Editorial lead time 3 months. Submit seasonal material 6 months in advance. Accepts queries by mail, fax. Responds in 1 month to queries; 2 months to mss. Sample copy online. Writer's guidelines online.

Nonfiction: General interest, historical/nostalgic, interview/profile, travel, all Missouri related. **Buys 18 feature length mss/year.** Query. Length: 300-2,000 words. **Pays $50-600; 20¢/word.**

Photos: State availability with submission. Reviews transparencies. Buys all rights nonexclusive. Offers $50-150/photo. Captions, identification of subjects, model releases required.

Columns/Departments: Best of Missouri (people and places, past and present, written in an almanac style), 300 words maximum; Missouri Artist (features a Missouri artist), 500 words; Made in Missouri (products and businesses native to Missouri), 500 words; Missouri Memory (a personal memory of Missouri gone by), 500 words; Missouri Hands (crafts and other items by Missouri artists that don't fall into 'fine art' category), 500 words; Day Trip (on museum event, etc., accompanied by sidebar listing specialty restaurants and other areas of interest close to featured spot), 300-500 words; Missouri Homes (on home of particular historic or other interest—preferably open to public), 500-600 words. **Pays $50-200.**

$ $RELOCATING TO THE LAKE OF THE OZARKS, Showcase Publishing Inc, P.O. Box 8680, Prairie Village KS 66208. (913)648-5757. Fax: (913)648-5783. Editor: Dave Leathers. **Contact:** Andrea Darr, associate editor. Annual relocation guides, free for people moving to the area. Pays on publication. Publishes ms an average of 6 months after acceptance. Byline given. Buys one-time rights. Editorial lead time 4 months. Submit seasonal material 4 months in advance. Accepts queries by mail, fax. Accepts previously published material. Accepts simultaneous submissions. Responds in 1 month to queries; 1 month to mss. Sample copy for $5.

Nonfiction: Historical/nostalgic, travel, local issues. **Buys 8 mss/year.** Query with published clips. Length: 600-1,000 words. **Pays $60-350.** Sometimes pays expenses of writers on assignment.

Reprints: Accepts previously published submissions.

Photos: State availability of or send photos with submission. Reviews transparencies. Buys one-time rights. Offers no additional payment for photos accepted with ms. Identification of subjects required.

Tips: "Really read and understand our audience."

$RIVER HILLS TRAVELER, Todd Publishing, Route 4, Box 4396, Piedmont MO 63957. (573)223-7143. Fax: (573)223-2117. E-mail: btodd@semo.net. Website: www.deepozarks.com. **Contact:** Bob Todd, online editor. **50% freelance written.** Monthly tabloid covering "outdoor sports and nature in the southeast quarter of Missouri, the east and central Ozarks. Topics like those in *Field & Stream* and *National Geographic*." Estab. 1973. Circ. 7,500. Pays on publication. Publishes ms an average of 2 months after acceptance. Byline given. Buys one-time rights. Editorial lead time 2 months. Submit seasonal material 1 year in advance. Accepts queries by e-mail. Accepts simultaneous submissions. Responds in 2 months to queries. Sample copy for SAE or online. Writer's guidelines online.

Nonfiction: Historical/nostalgic, how-to, humor, opinion, personal experience, photo feature, technical, travel. "No stories about other geographic areas." **Buys 80 mss/year.** Query with writing samples. Length: 1,500 word maximum. **Pays $15-50.** Sometimes pays expenses of writers on assignment.

Reprints: Send ms with rights for sale noted and information about when and where the material previously appeared.

Photos: Send photos with submission. Buys one-time rights. Negotiates payment individually. Pays $25 for covers.

The online magazine carries original content not found in the print edition and includes writer's guidelines. Contact: Bob Todd, online editor.

Tips: "We are a 'poor man's' *Field & Stream* and *National Geographic*—about the eastern Missouri Ozarks. We prefer stories that relate an adventure that causes a reader to relive an adventure of his own or consider embarking on a similar adventure. Think of an adventure in camping or cooking, not just fishing and hunting. How-to is great, but not simple instructions. We encourage good first-person reporting."

N $ $ **SPRINGFIELD! MAGAZINE**, Springfield Communications, Inc., P.O. Box 4749, Springfield MO 65808-4749. (417)882-4917. **Contact:** Robert Glazier, editor. **85% freelance written.** Eager to work with a small number of new/unpublished writers each year. "This is an extremely local and provincial monthly magazine. No *general* interest articles." Estab. 1979. Circ. 10,000. Pays on publication. Publishes ms an average of 3-24 months after acceptance. Byline given. First serial rights. Submit seasonal material 1 year in advance. Responds in 3 months to queries; 6 months to mss. Sample copy for $5.30 and 9½×12½ SAE.

Nonfiction: Local interest *only*; no material that could appeal to other magazines elsewhere. Book excerpts (Springfield authors only), exposé (local topics only), historical/nostalgic (top priority, but must be local history), how-to, humor, interview/profile (needs more on females than males), personal experience, photo feature, travel (1 page/month). **Buys 150 mss/year.** Query with published clips by mail only or send complete ms with SASE. Length: 500-3,000 words. **Pays $35-250 for assigned articles.**

Photos: Send photos with query or ms. "Needs more photo features of a nostalgic bent." Reviews contact sheets, 4×6 color, 5×7 b&w glossy prints. Buys one-time rights. Pays $5-$35 for b&w, $10-50 for color. Captions, identification of subjects, model releases required.

Columns/Departments: Length varies, usually 500-2,500 words. **Buys 150 mss/year.** Query by mail or send complete ms.

Tips: "We prefer writers read 8 or 10 copies of our magazine prior to submitting any material for our consideration. The magazine's greatest need is for features which comment on these times in Springfield. We are overstocked with nostalgic pieces right now. We also need profiles about young women and men of distinction."

Montana

$ $ **MONTANA MAGAZINE**, Lee Enterprises, P.O. Box 5630, Helena MT 59604-5630. (406)443-2842. Fax: (406)443-5480. E-mail: editor@montanamagazine.com. Website: www.montanamagazine.com. **Contact:** Beverly R. Magley, editor. **90% freelance written.** Bimonthly magazine. "Strictly Montana-oriented magazine that features community profiles, contemporary issues, wildlife and natural history, travel pieces." Estab. 1970. Circ. 40,000. Publishes ms an average of 1 year after acceptance. Byline given. Buys one-time rights. Submit seasonal material 1 year in advance. Accepts simultaneous submissions. Responds in 6 months to queries. Sample copy for $5 or online. Writer's guidelines online.

- Accepts queries by e-mail. No phone calls.

Nonfiction: Query by September for summer material; March for winter material. Essays, general interest, interview/profile, photo feature, travel. Special issues: Special features on summer and winter destination points. No 'me and Joe' hiking and hunting tales; no blood-and-guts hunting stories; no poetry; no fiction; no sentimental essays. **Buys 30 mss/year.** Query with samples and SASE. Length: 300-3,000 words. **Pays 15¢/word.** Sometimes pays expenses of writers on assignment.

Reprints: Send photocopy of article with rights for sale noted and information about when and where the material previously appeared. Pays 50% of amount paid for an original article.

Photos: Send photos with submission. Reviews contact sheets, 35mm or larger format transparencies, 5×7 prints. Buys one-time rights. Offers additional payment for photos accepted with ms. Captions, identification of subjects, model releases required.

Columns/Departments: Memories (reminisces of early-day Montana life), 800-1,000 words; Outdoor Recreation, 1,500-2,000 words; Community Festivals, 500 words, plus b&w or color photo; Montana-Specific Humor, 800-1,000 words. Query with samples and SASE.

Tips: "We avoid commonly known topics so Montanans won't ho-hum through more of what they already know. If it's time to revisit a topic, we look for a unique slant."

Nevada

$ $ **NEVADA MAGAZINE**, 401 N. Carson St., Carson City NV 89701-4291. (775)687-5416. Fax: (775)687-6159. E-mail: editor@nevadamagazine.com. Website: www.nevadamagazine.com. Editor: David Moore. **Contact:** Joyce Hollister, associate editor. **50% freelance written.** Works with a small number of new/unpublished writers each year. Bimonthly magazine published by the state of Nevada to promote tourism. Estab. 1936. Circ. 80,000. Pays on publication. Publishes ms an average of 8 months after acceptance. Byline given. Buys first North American serial rights. Submit seasonal material 6 months in advance. Accepts queries by mail, e-mail. Responds in 1 month to queries. Sample copy for $1. Writer's guidelines for #10 SASE.

O‑ Break in with shorter departments, rather than trying to tackle a big feature. Good bets are Dining Out, Recreation, Casinoland, Side Trips, and Roadside Attractions.

Nonfiction: "We welcome stories and photos on speculation." Nevada topics only. Historical/nostalgic, humor, interview/profile, personal experience, photo feature, travel, recreational, think pieces. **Buys 40 unsolicited mss/year.** Send complete ms or query. Length: 500-1,800 words. **Pays $50-500.**

Photos: Send photo material with accompanying ms. Name, address, and caption should appear on each photo or slide. Denise Barr, art director. Buys one-time rights. Pays $20-100 for color transparencies and glossy prints.

Tips: "Keep in mind the magazine's purpose is to promote Nevada tourism. Keys to higher payments are quality and editing effort (more than length). Send cover letter; no photocopies. We look for a light, enthusiastic tone of voice without being too cute; articles bolstered by facts and thorough research; and unique angles on Nevada subjects."

$ $ RELOCATING TO LAS VEGAS, Showcase Publishing, Inc., P.O. Box 8680, Prairie Village KS 66208. (913)648-5757. Fax: (913)648-5783. Editor: Dave Leathers. **Contact:** Andrea Darr, associate editor. Annual relocation guides, free for people moving to the area. Pays on publication. Publishes ms an average of 6 months after acceptance. Byline given. Buys one-time rights. Editorial lead time 4 months. Submit seasonal material 4 months in advance. Accepts queries by mail, e-mail. Responds in 1 month to queries; 1 month to mss. Sample copy for $5.

Nonfiction: Historical/nostalgic, travel, local issues. **Buys 8 mss/year.** Query with published clips. Length: 650-1,000 words. **Pays $60-350.** Sometimes pays expenses of writers on assignment.

Reprints: Accepts previously published submissions.

Photos: State availability with submission. Reviews transparencies. Buys one-time rights. Offers no additional payment for photos accepted with ms. Identification of subjects required.

Tips: "Really read and understand our audience."

New Hampshire

$ $ NEW HAMPSHIRE MAGAZINE, McLean Communications, Inc., 150 Dow St., Manchester NH 03101. (603)624-1442. E-mail: editor@nhmagazine.com. Website: www.nhmagazine.com. **Contact:** Rick Broussard, editor. **50% freelance written.** Monthly magazine devoted to New Hampshire. "We want stories written for, by, and about the people of New Hampshire with emphasis on qualities that set us apart from other states. We feature lifestyle, adventure, and home-related stories with a unique local angle." Estab. 1986. Circ. 24,000. Pays on publication. Byline given. Offers 25% kill fee. Buys all rights. Editorial lead time 3 months. Submit seasonal material 3 months in advance. Accepts queries by mail, e-mail, fax. Accepts simultaneous submissions. Responds in 2 months to queries; 3 months to mss. Writer's guidelines online. Editorial calendar online.

Nonfiction: Essays, general interest, historical/nostalgic, photo feature, business. **Buys 30 mss/year.** Query with published clips. Length: 800-2,000 words. **Pays $50-300.** Sometimes pays expenses of writers on assignment.

Photos: State availability with submission. Rights purchased vary. Possible additional payment for photos accepted with ms. Captions, identification of subjects, model releases required.

The online magazine carries original content not found in the print edition. Contact: Rick Broussard, online editor.

Tips: Network Publications publishes 1 monthly magazine entitled *New Hampshire Magazine* and a "specialty" publication called *Destination New Hampshire*. "In general, our articles deal with the people of New Hampshire—their lifestyles and interests. We also present localized stories about national and international issues, ideas, and trends. We will only use stories that show our readers how these issues have an impact on their daily lives. We cover a wide range of topics, including healthcare, politics, law, real-life dramas, regional history, medical issues, business, careers, environmental issues, the arts, the outdoors, education, food, recreation, etc. Many of our readers are what we call 'The New Traditionalists'—aging Baby Boomers who have embraced solid American values and contemporary New Hampshire lifestyles."

New Jersey

$ $ $ $ NEW JERSEY MONTHLY, The Magazine of the Garden State, New Jersey Monthly LLC, 55 Park Place, P.O. Box 920, Morristown NJ 07963-0920. (973)539-8230. Fax: (973)538-2953. E-mail: editor@njmonthly.com. Website: www.njmonthly.com. **Contact:** Christopher Hann, senior editor. **75-80% freelance written.** Monthly magazine covering "just about anything to do with New Jersey, from news, politics, and sports to decorating trends and lifestyle issues. Our readership is well-educated, affluent, and on average our readers have lived in New Jersey 20 years or more." Estab. 1976. Circ. 95,000. Pays on completion of fact-checking. Publishes ms an average of 3 months after acceptance. Byline given. Offers 20% kill fee. Buys first North American serial rights. Editorial lead time 3 months. Submit seasonal material 6 months in advance. Accepts queries by mail, e-mail, fax, phone. Accepts simultaneous submissions. Responds in 2 months to queries. Writer's guidelines for $2.95.

- This magazine continues to look for strong investigative reporters with novelistic style and solid knowledge of New Jersey issues.

Nonfiction: Book excerpts, essays, exposé, general interest, historical/nostalgic, humor, interview/profile, personal experience, photo feature, travel (within New Jersey), arts, sports, politics. "No experience pieces from people who used to live in New Jersey or general pieces that have no New Jersey angle." **Buys 90-100 mss/year.** Query with published magazine clips and SASE. Length: 1,200-3,500 words. **Pays $750-2,500.** Pays reasonable expenses of writers on assignment with prior approval.

Photos: Joe Broda, art director. State availability with submission. Reviews transparencies, prints. Buys one-time rights. Payment negotiated. Identification of subjects, model releases required.

Columns/Departments: Exit Ramp (back page essay usually originating from personal experience but written in a way that tells a broader story of statewide interest), 1,200 words. **Buys 12 mss/year.** Query with published clips. **Pays $400.**

Fillers: Anecdotes (for front-of-book "Garden Variety" section; typically lighter, sassier, more offbeat fare). **Buys 12-15/year.** Length: 200-250 words. **Pays $100.**

Tips: "The best approach: Do your homework! Read the past year's issues to get an understanding of our well-written, well-researched articles that tell a tale from a well-established point of view."

$ $ NEW JERSEY SAVVY LIVING, CTB, LLC, P.O. Box 607, Short Hills NJ 07078-0607. (973)379-7749. Fax: (973)379-4116. Website: www.njsavvyliving.com. **Contact:** Lee Lusardi, editor. **90% freelance written.** Magazine published 5 times/year covering New Jersey residents with affluent lifestyles. "*Savvy* is a regional magazine for an upscale audience, ages 35-65. We focus on lifestyle topics such as decorating, fashion, people, travel, and gardening." Estab. 1997. Circ. 60,000. Pays on publication. Publishes ms an average of 3 months after acceptance. Byline given. Offers $50 kill fee. variable rights. Editorial lead time 3 months. Accepts queries by mail. Accepts previously published material. Accepts simultaneous submissions. Response time varies to queries. Sample copy for 9×12 SAE.

Nonfiction: General interest, historical/nostalgic, how-to, humor, inspirational, interview/profile, photo feature, travel, home/decorating. Special issues: Home (April). No investigative, fiction, personal experience, and non-New Jersey topics (excluding travel). **Buys 50 mss/year.** Query with published clips. Length: 900-2,000 words. **Pays $250-500.**

Reprints: Accepts previously published submissions (nonconflicting markets only)

Photos: State availability with submission. Reviews contact sheets, negatives, transparencies, prints. Buys one-time rights. Offers no additional payment for photos accepted with ms. Captions, identification of subjects, model releases required.

Columns/Departments: Wine & Spirits (wine trends); Savvy Shoppers (inside scoop on buying); Intrepid Diner (restaurant review); Home Gourmet (from food to hostess gifts at home), all 900-1,000 words. **Buys 25 mss/year.** Query with published clips. **Pays $250.**

Fillers: Sandra Lowich, associate editor. Facts, newsbreaks. Length: 125-250 words. **Pays $25-50.**

Tips: "Offer ideas of interest to an upscale New Jersey readership. We love articles that utilize local sources and are well focused. Trends are always a good bit, so come up with a hot idea and make us believe you can deliver."

$ $ THE SANDPAPER, Newsmagazine of the Jersey Shore, The SandPaper, Inc., 1816 Long Beach Blvd., Surf City NJ 08008-5461. (609)494-5900. Fax: (609)494-1437. E-mail: letters@thesandpaper.net. **Contact:** Jay Mann, managing editor (jaymann@thesandpaper.net). **10% freelance written.** Weekly tabloid covering subjects of interest to Jersey shore residents and visitors. "*The SandPaper* publishes 2 editions covering many of the Jersey Shore's finest resort communities including Long Beach Island and Ocean City, New Jersey. Each issue includes a mix of news, human interest features, opinion columns, and entertainment/calendar listings." Estab. 1976. Circ. 60,000. Pays on publication. Publishes ms an average of 1 month after acceptance. Byline given. Offers 100% kill fee. Buys first, all rights. Submit seasonal material 3 months in advance. Accepts queries by mail, e-mail, fax, phone. Accepts simultaneous submissions. Responds in 1 month to queries. Sample copy for 9×12 SAE with 8 first-class stamps.

O-→ "The opinion page and columns are most open to freelancers." Send SASE for return of ms.

Nonfiction: Must pertain to New Jersey shore locale. Essays, general interest, historical/nostalgic, humor, opinion, arts, entertaining news, reviews; also environmental submissons relating to the ocean, wetlands, and pinelands. **Buys 10 mss/year.** Send complete ms. Length: 200-2,000 words. **Pays $25-200.** Sometimes pays expenses of writers on assignment.

Reprints: Send photocopy and information about when and where the material previously appeared. Pays 25-50% of amount paid for an original article.

Photos: Send photos with submission. Buys one-time or all rights. Offers $8-25/photo.

Columns/Departments: Speakeasy (opinion and slice-of-life, often humorous); Commentary (forum for social science perspectives); both 1,000-1,500 words, preferably with local or Jersey Shore angle. **Buys 50 mss/year.** Send complete ms. **Pays $30.**

Tips: "Anything of interest to sun worshippers, beach walkers, nature watchers, and water sports lovers is of potential interest to us. There is an increasing coverage of environmental issues. We are steadily increasing the amount of entertainment-related material in our publication. Articles on history of the shore area are always in demand."

New Mexico

[N] **$ $ NEW MEXICO MAGAZINE**, Lew Wallace Bldg., 495 Old Santa Fe Trail, Santa Fe NM 87501. (505)827-7447. Website: www.nmmagazine.com. Editor-in-Chief: Emily Drabanski. Associate Publisher: Jon Bowman. Senior Editor: Walter K. Lopez. Associate Editor/Photo Editor: Steve Larese. **Contact:** Any editor. Monthly magazine emphasizing New Mexico for a college-educated readership with above-average income and interest in the Southwest. Estab. 1923. Circ. 120,000. **Pays on acceptance.** Publishes ms an average of 8 months after acceptance. Buys first North American serial rights. Submit seasonal material 1 year in advance. Accepts queries by mail. Accepts previously published material. Responds in 2 months to queries. Sample copy for $3.95. Writer's guidelines for SASE.

Nonfiction: New Mexico subjects of interest to travelers. Historical, cultural, informational articles. "We are looking for more short, light and bright stories for the 'Asi Es Nuevo Mexico' section. Also, we are buying 12 mss per year for our Makin Tracks series." **Buys 7-10 mss/issue**. General interest, historical/nostalgic, interview/profile, travel. "No columns, cartoons, poetry or non-New Mexico subjects." Query by mail with 3 published writing samples. No phone or fax queries. Length: 250-1,500 words. **Pays $100-600.**

Reprints: Rarely publishes reprints but sometimes publishes excerpts from novels and nonfiction books.

Photos: Purchased as portfolio or on assignment. "Photographers interested in photo assignments should send tearsheets to photo editor Steve Larese; slides or transparencies with complete caption information are accepted. Photographers name and telephone number should be affixed to the image mount." Buys one-time rights. Captions, model releases required.

Tips: "Your best bet is to write a fun, lively short feature (200-350 words) for our Asi Es Nuevo Mexico section that is a superb short manuscript on a little-known person, aspect of history or place to see in New Mexico. Faulty research will ruin a writer's chances for the future. Good style, good grammar. No generalized odes to the state or the Southwest. No sentimentalized, paternalistic views of Indians or Hispanics. No glib, gimmicky 'travel brochure' writing. No first-person vacation stories. We're always looking for well-researched pieces on unusual aspects of New Mexico and lively writing."

New York

$ $ ADIRONDACK LIFE, P.O. Box 410, Jay NY 12941-0410. (518)946-2191. Fax: (518)946-7461. E-mail: aledit@adirondacklife.com. Website: www.adirondacklife.com. **Contact:** Mary Thill and Galen Crane, co-editors. **70% freelance written.** Prefers to work with published/established writers. Magazine published 8 issues/year, including special Annual Outdoor Guide, emphasizes the Adirondack region and the North Country of New York State in articles covering outdoor activities, history, and natural history directly related to the Adirondacks. Estab. 1970. Circ. 50,000. Pays 2-3 months after acceptance. Publishes ms an average of 6 months after acceptance. Byline given. Buys first North American serial, web rights. Submit seasonal material 1 year in advance. Accepts queries by mail, e-mail. Sample copy for $3 and 9×12 SAE. Writer's guidelines online. Editorial calendar online.

O→ "For new writers, the best way to break in to the magazine is through departments."

Nonfiction: "*Adirondack Life* attempts to capture the unique flavor and ethos of the Adirondack mountains and North Country region through feature articles directly pertaining to the qualities of the area." Special issues: Outdoors (May); Single-topic Collector's issue (September). **Buys 20-25 unsolicited mss/year.** Query with published clips. Length: 2,500-5,000 words. **Pays 25¢/word.** Sometimes pays expenses of writers on assignment.

Photos: All photos must have been taken in the Adirondacks. Each issue contains a photo feature. Purchased with or without ms on assignment. All photos must be individually identified as to the subject or locale and must bear the photographer's name. Send photos with submission. Reviews color transparencies, prints (b&w). Pays $125 for full page, b&w, or color; $300 for cover (color only,vertical in format). Credit line given.

Columns/Departments: Special Places (unique spots in the Adirondack Park); Watercraft; Barkeater (personal to political essays); Wilderness (environmental issues); Working (careers in the Adirondacks); Home; Yesteryears; Kitchen; Profile; Historic Preservation; Sporting Scene. Length: 1,200-2,400 words. Query with published clips. **Pays 25¢/word.**

Fiction: Considers first-serial novel excerpts in its subject matter and region.

Tips: "Do not send a personal essay about your meaningful moment in the mountains. We need factual pieces about regional history, sports, culture, and business. We are looking for clear, concise, well-organized manuscripts that are strictly Adirondack in subject. Check back issues to be sure we haven't already covered your topic. Please do not send unsolicited manuscripts via e-mail. Check out our guidelines online."

$ BEYOND THE BADGE, 47-01 Greenpoint Ave., #114, Sunnyside NY 11104-1709. (347)723-6287. Fax: (718)389-7312. E-mail: beyondthebadge@hotmail.com. **Contact:** Liz Martinez DeFranco, editor. Quarterly magazine. *Beyond the Badge* is distributed to police officers, peace officers, federal agents, corrections officers, auxiliary police officers, probation and parole officers, civilian employees of law enforcement agencies, etc., in the New York metropolitan area. Estab. 2001. Buys one-time rights. Accepts queries by e-mail. Accepts previously published material. Accepts simultaneous submissions. Sample copy for $5, plus a 9×12 SASE. Writer's guidelines by e-mail.

Nonfiction: "We are seeking stories on travel; law enforcement product/news; books with a LE hook; movies and other entertainment that our readers would enjoy knowing about; worthy LE-related Internet sites; the latest developments in forensics and technology; health articles with a LE spin; investigation techniques; innovative international, national, regional, or local (inside and outside of the New York area) approaches to LE or crime prevention issues; other topics of interest to our reader population. General interest. "We see too many pieces that are dry and not enjoyable to read. Even if the topic is serious or scientific, present the material as though you were telling a friend about it." Query. Length: 1,000-1,500 words. **Pays $100.**

Photos: Photos are very helpful and much appreciated; however, there is no additional pay for photos. Inclusion of photos does increase chances of publication.

Columns/Departments: Book'Em (book reviews/excerpts/author interviews); Internet Guide; Screening Room (movie reviews); Your Finances; Management in Focus; Health Department; Forensics Lab; Technology. Query. **Pays $75.**

Tips: "Writers should keep in mind that this is a lifestyle magazine whose readers happen to be cops, not a cop magazine with some lifestyle topics in it."

$ $ BUFFALO SPREE MAGAZINE, David Laurence Publications, Inc., 5678 Main St., Buffalo NY 14221. (716)634-0820. Fax: (716)810-0075. E-mail: info@buffalospree.com. Website: www.buffalospree.com. **Contact:** Elizabeth Licata, editor. **90% freelance written.** Bimonthly city regional magazine. Estab. 1967. Circ. 25,000. Pays on publication. Publishes ms an average of 1 month after acceptance. Byline given. Buys first North American serial rights. Accepts queries by mail, e-mail, fax. Responds in 6 months to queries. Sample copy for $3.95 and 9×12 SAE with 9 first-class stamps.

Nonfiction: "Most articles are assigned not unsolicited." Interview/profile, travel, issue-oriented features, arts, living, food, regional. **Buys 5-10 mss/year.** Query with résumé and published clips. Length: 1,000-2,000 words. **Pays $125-250.**

Tips: "Send a well-written, compelling query or an interesting topic, and *great* clips. We no longer regularly publish fiction or poetry. Prefers material that is Western New York related."

N $ $ $ CITY LIMITS, New York's Urban Affairs News Magazine, City Limits Community Information Service, 120 Wall St., 20th Floor, New York NY 10005. (212)479-3344. Fax: (212)344-6457. E-mail: citylimits@citylimits.org. Website: www.citylimits.org. **Contact:** Alyssa Katz, editor. **50% freelance written.** Monthly magazine covering urban politics and policy. "*City Limits* is a 25-year-old nonprofit magazine focusing on issues facing New York City and its neighborhoods, particularly low-income communities. The magazine is strongly committed to investigative journalism, in-depth policy analysis and hard-hitting profiles." Estab. 1976. Circ. 4,000. Pays on publication. Publishes ms an average of 3 months after acceptance. Byline given. Offers 50% kill fee. Buys first North American serial, second serial (reprint) rights. Editorial lead time 2 months. Accepts queries by mail, e-mail, fax. Accepts simultaneous submissions. Sample copy for $2.95. Writer's guidelines free.

Nonfiction: Book excerpts, exposé, humor, interview/profile, opinion, photo feature. No essays, polemics. **Buys 25 mss/year.** Query with published clips. Length: 400-3,500 words. **Pays $100-1,200 for assigned articles; $100-800 for unsolicited articles.** Pays expenses of writers on assignment.

Photos: State availability with submission. Reviews contact sheets, negatives, transparencies. Offers $50-100/photo.

Columns/Departments: Making Change (nonprofit business); Big Idea (policy news); Book Review, all 800 words; Urban Legend (profile); First Hand (Q&A), both 350 words. **Buys 15 mss/year.** Query with published clips. **Pays $100-200.**

Tips: "*City Limits'* specialty is covering low-income communities. We want to know how the news of the day is going to affect neighborhoods—at the grassroots. Among the issues we're looking for stories about housing, health care, criminal justice, child welfare, education, economic development, welfare reform, politics and government."

N $ $ $ $ NEW YORK MAGAZINE, Primedia Magazines, 444 Madison Ave., New York NY 10022. (212)508-0700. Website: www.newyorkmetro.com. **Contact:** Kelly Maloni, editor-in-chief. **25% freelance written.** Weekly magazine focusing on current events in the New York metropolitan area. Circ. 433,813. **Pays on acceptance.** Offers 25% kill fee. Buys electronic rights. First World Serial Submit seasonal material 2 months in advance. Responds in 1 month to queries. Sample copy for $3.50 or on website. Writer's guidelines not available.

Nonfiction: New York-related journalism that covers lifestyle, politics and business. Query by mail. **Pays $1/word.** Pays expenses of writers on assignment.

The online magazine carries original content not found in the print edition.

Tips: "Submit a detailed query to John Homans, *New York*'s executive editor. If there is sufficient interest in the proposed piece, the article will be assigned."

$ $ SYRACUSE NEW TIMES, A. Zimmer, Ltd., 1415 W. Genesee St., Syracuse NY 13204. Fax: (315)422-1721. E-mail: editorial@syracusenewtimes.com. Website: newtimes.rway.com. **Contact:** Molly English, editor. **50% freelance written.** Weekly tabloid covering news, sports, arts, and entertainment. "*Syracuse New Times* is an alternative weekly that can be topical, provocative, irreverent, and intensely local." Estab. 1969. Circ. 46,000. Pays on publication. Publishes ms an average of 1 month after acceptance. Byline given. Buys one-time rights. Editorial lead time 3 months. Submit seasonal material 3 months in advance. Accepts simultaneous submissions. Responds in 2 weeks to queries; 1 month to mss. Sample copy for 9×12 SAE and 2 first-class stamps. Writer's guidelines online.

Nonfiction: Essays, general interest. **Buys 200 mss/year.** Query by mail with published clips. Length: 250-2,500 words. **Pays $25-200.**

Photos: State availability of or send photos with submission. Reviews 8×10 prints, color slides. Buys one-time rights. Offers $10-25/photo or negotiates payment individually. Identification of subjects required.

Tips: "Move to Syracuse and query with strong idea."

$ TIME OUT NEW YORK, Time Out New York Partners, LP, 627 Broadway, 7th Floor, New York NY 10012. (212)539-4444. Fax: (212)253-1174. E-mail: letters@timeoutny.com. Website: www.timeoutny.com. Editor-in-Chief: Cyndi Stivers. **Contact:** Annie Bell, editorial assistant. **20% freelance written.** Weekly magazine covering entertainment in New York City. "Those who want to contribute to *Time Out New York* must be intimate with New York City and its environs." Estab. 1995. Circ. 120,000. Pays on publication. Publishes ms an average of 1 month after acceptance. Byline sometimes given. Offers 25% kill fee. Makes work-for-hire assignments. Accepts queries by mail, fax, phone. Responds in 2 months to queries.

Pitch ideas to the editor of the section to which you would like to contribute (i.e., film, music, dance, etc.). Be sure to include clips or writing samples with your query letter. No unsolicited mss.

Nonfiction: Essays, general interest, how-to, humor, interview/profile, new product, travel (primarily within NYC area), reviews of various entertainment topics. No essays, articles about trends, unpegged articles. Query with published clips. Length: 250-1,500 words.

Columns/Departments: Around Town (Billie Cohen); Art (Tim Griffin); Books & Poetry (Maureen Shelly); Technology (Adam Wisnieski); Cabaret (H. Scott Jolley); Check Out (Zoe Wolff); Clubs (Bruce Tantum); Comedy (Joe Grossman); Dance (Gia Kourlas); Eat Out (Salma Abdelnour); Film; Gay & Lesbian (Les Simpson); Kids (Barbara Aria); Music: Classical & Opera (Steve Smith); Music: Rock, Jazz, etc. (Elisabeth Vincentelli); Radio (Ian Landau); Sports (Brett Martin); Television (Michael Freidson); Theater (Jason Zinoman); Video (Michael Freidson).

The online magazine carries original content not found in the print edition. Contact: Amy Brill, online editor.
Tips: "We're always looking for quirky, less-known news about what's going on in New York City."

North Carolina

$ $ AAA CAROLINAS GO MAGAZINE, 6600 AAA Dr., Charlotte NC 28212. Fax: (704)569-7815. Website: www.aaacarolinas.com. Managing Editor: Sarah Bembry. **Contact:** Tom Crosby, editor. **20% freelance written.** Member publication for the American Automobile Association covering travel, auto-related issues. "We prefer stories that focus on travel and auto safety in North and South Carolina and surrounding states." Estab. 1922. Circ. 750,000. Pays on publication. Byline given. Buys all rights. Editorial lead time 2 months. Accepts queries by mail. Sample copy and writer's guidelines for #10 SASE.

Nonfiction: Travel, auto safety. Length:750 words. **Pays 15¢/word.**

Photos: Send photos with submission. Reviews slides. Buys all rights. Offers no additional payment for photos accepted with ms. Identification of subjects required.

The online magazine carries original content not found in the print edition. Contact: Sarah Bembry.

Tips: "Submit regional stories relating to Carolinas travel."

$ $ CHARLOTTE MAGAZINE, Abarta Media, 127 W. Worthington Ave., Suite 208, Charlotte NC 28203. (704)335-7181. Fax: (704)335-3739. E-mail: editor@charlottemag.com. Website: www.charlottemagazine.com. **Contact:** Richard H. Thurmond, editorial director. **75% freelance written.** Monthly magazine covering Charlotte life. "This magazine tells its readers things they didn't know about Charlotte, in an interesting, entertaining, and sometimes provocative style." Circ. 30,000. Pays within 30 days of acceptance. Publishes ms an average of 3 months after acceptance. Byline given. Offers 25% kill fee. Buys first North American serial rights. Editorial lead time 3 months. Submit seasonal material 6 months in advance. Accepts queries by mail, e-mail. Accepts simultaneous submissions. Responds in 6 months to mss. Sample copy for 8 1/2×11 SAE and $2.09.

Nonfiction: Book excerpts, exposé, general interest, historical/nostalgic, interview/profile, photo feature, travel. **Buys 90-100 mss/year.** Query with published clips. Length: 200-3,000 words. **Pays 20-40¢/word.** Sometimes pays expenses of writers on assignment.

Photos: State availability with submission. Buys one-time rights. Negotiates payment individually. Identification of subjects required.

Columns/Departments: Buys 35-50 mss/year. Pays 20-40¢/word.

Tips: "A story for *Charlotte* magazine could only appear in *Charlotte* magazine. That is, the story and its treatment are particularly germane to this area."

N $ $ CHARLOTTE PLACE MAGAZINE, Sandbar Communications, Inc., P.O. Box 22555, Charleston SC 29401. Fax: (843)856-7444. E-mail: rlmaggy@aol.com. **Contact:** Robin Maggy, editor-in-chief. Semiannual magazine covering Charlotte, North Carolina. Articles include interior design, art, profiles, opinions, gardening, money. Estab. 1995. Pays on publication. Publishes ms an average of 3 months after acceptance. Byline given. Buys first rights. Editorial lead time 6 months. Submit seasonal material 6 months in advance. Accepts queries by mail, e-mail, fax. Responds in 2 weeks to queries. Writer's guidelines by e-mail.

Nonfiction: How-to, interview/profile. **Buys 30 mss/year.** Query with published clips. Length: 1,200-3,500 words. **Pays 20¢/published word.** Sometimes pays expenses of writers on assignment.

Photos: State availability with submission. Reviews transparencies. Buys one-time rights. Negotiates payment individually. Captions, identification of subjects required.

Columns/Departments: Health & Wellness; In the Spotlight; Money Matters; Object Lesson; Past & Present; Talkback; Visual Arts; Weekend Gardener; all 1,200-3,500 words. **Pays 20¢/published word.**

Tips: "We are looking for articles that deviate from the traditional. As the writer, it is important to captivate the reader and make the reader feel, smell, and taste the subject matter at hand."

$ $ OUR STATE, Down Home in North Carolina, Mann Media, P.O. Box 4552, Greensboro NC 27404. (336)286-0600. Fax: (336)286-0100. E-mail: editorial@ourstate.com. Website: www.ourstate.com. **Contact:** Vicky Jarrett, editor-in-chief. **95% freelance written.** Monthly magazine covering North Carolina. "*Our State* is dedicated to providing editorial about the history, destinations, out-of-the-way places, and culture of North Carolina." Estab. 1933. Circ. 97,000. Pays on publication. Publishes ms an average of 6-24 months after acceptance. Byline given. Buys first North American serial rights. Editorial lead time 4 months. Submit seasonal material 4 months in advance. Accepts queries by mail, fax. Responds in 6 weeks to queries; 2 months to mss. Sample copy for $6. Writer's guidelines for #10 SASE.

Nonfiction: Book excerpts, historical/nostalgic, how-to, humor, personal experience, photo feature, travel. **Buys 60 mss/year.** Send complete ms. Length: 1,200-1,500 words. **Pays $300-500 for assigned articles; $50-125 for unsolicited articles.**

Photos: State availability with submission. Reviews 35mm or 4×6 transparencies. Buys one-time rights. Negotiates payment individually. Pays $15-350/photo, depending on size; $125-50 for photos assigned to accompany specific story; $500 maximum for cover photos. Identification of subjects required.

Columns/Departments: Tar Heel Memories (remembering something specific about North Carolina), 1,200 words; Tar Heel Profile (profile of interesting North Carolinian), 1,500 words; Tar Heel Literature (review of books by North Carolina writers and about North Carolina), 300 words. **Buys 40 mss/year.** Send complete ms. **Pays $50-300.**

Tips: "We are developing a style for travel stories that is distinctly *Our State*. That style starts with outstanding photographs, which not only depict an area, but interpret it and thus become an integral part of the presentation. Our stories need not dwell on listings of what can be seen. Concentrate instead on the experience of being there, whether the destination is a hiking trail, a bed and breakfast, a forest, or an urban area. What thoughts and feelings did the experience evoke? We want to know why you went there, what you experienced, and what impressions you came away with. With at least 1 travel story an issue, we run a short sidebar called, "If You're Going." It explains how to get to the destination; rates or admission costs if there are any; a schedule of when the attraction is open or list of relevant dates; and an address and phone number for readers to write or call for more information. This sidebar eliminates the need for general-service information in the story."

North Dakota

N $ $ **NORTH DAKOTA LIVING MAGAZINE**, North Dakota Association of Rural Electric Cooperatives, 3201 Nygren Dr. NW, P.O. Box 727, Mandan ND 58554-0727. (701)663-6501. Fax: (701)663-3745. E-mail: kbrick@ndarec.com. Website: www.ndarec.com. **Contact:** Kent Brick, editor. **20% freelance written.** Monthly magazine covering information of interest to memberships of electric cooperatives and telephone cooperatives. "We publish a general interest magazine for North Dakotans. We treat subjects pertaining to living and working in the northern Great Plains. We provide progress reporting on electric cooperatives and telephone cooperatives." Estab. 1954. Circ. 70,000. **Pays on acceptance.** Publishes ms an average of 6 months after acceptance. Byline given. Buys one-time rights, makes work-for-hire assignments. Editorial lead time 6 months. Submit seasonal material 6 months in advance. Accepts queries by mail, e-mail. Accepts previously published material. Accepts simultaneous submissions. Sample copy not available. Writer's guidelines not available.

Nonfiction: General interest, historical/nostalgic, how-to, humor, interview/profile, new product, travel. **Buys 20 mss/year.** Query with published clips. Length: 1,500-2,000 words. **Pays $100-500 minimum for assigned articles; $300-600 for unsolicited articles.** Sometimes pays expenses of writers on assignment.

Photos: State availability with submission. Reviews contact sheets. Buys one-time rights. Negotiates payment individually. Identification of subjects required.

Columns/Departments: Energy use and financial planning, both 750 words. **Buys 6 mss/year.** Query with published clips. **Pays $100-300.**

Fiction: Historical, humorous, slice-of-life vignettes, western. **Buys 1 mss/year.** Query with published clips. Length: 1,000-2,500 words. **Pays $100-400.**

Tips: "Deal with what's real: real data, real people, real experiences, real history, etc."

Ohio

$ **BEND OF THE RIVER MAGAZINE**, P.O. Box 859, Maumee OH 43537. (419)893-0022. **Contact:** R. Lee Raizk, publisher. **90% freelance written.** This magazine reports that it is eager to work with new/unpublished writers. "We buy material that we like whether it is by an experienced writer or not." Monthly magazine for readers interested in northwestern Ohio history and nostalgia. Estab. 1972. Circ. 7,500. Pays on publication. Publishes ms an average of 6 months after acceptance. Byline given. Buys one-time rights. Submit seasonal material 2 months in advance. Responds in 1 month to queries. Sample copy for $1.25. Writer's guidelines not available.

Nonfiction: "We deal heavily with Northwestern Ohio history and nostalgia. We are looking for old snapshots of the Toledo area to accompany articles, personal reflection, etc." Historical/nostalgic. Special issues: Deadline for holiday issue is November 1. **Buys 75 unsolicited mss/year.** Query with or without published clips or send complete ms. Length: 1,500 words. **Pays $25 on up.**

Reprints: Send tearsheet and information about when and where the material previously appeared. Pays 100% of the amount paid for the original article.

Photos: Purchases b&w or color photos with accompanying ms. Pays $5 minimum. Captions required.

Tips: "Any Toledo area, well-researched nostalgia, local history will be put on top of the heap. If you send a picture with a manuscript, it gets an A+! We pay a small amount but usually use our writers often and through the years. We're loyal."

$ $ $ **CINCINNATI MAGAZINE**, Emmis Publishing Corporation, One Centennial Plaza, 705 Central Ave., Suite 175, Cincinnati OH 45202. (513)421-4300. Fax: (513)562-2746. E-mail: editor@cintimag.emmis.com. **Contact:** Linda Vaccariello, senior editor. Monthly magazine emphasising Cincinnati living. Circ. 30,000. Pays on publication. Byline given. Buys first rights. Sample copy not available. Writer's guidelines not available.

Nonfiction: Articles on personalities, business, sports, lifestyle, history relating to Cincinnati and Northern Kentucky. **Buys 12 mss/year.** Query. Length: 2,500-3,500 words. **Pays $500-1,000.**

Columns/Departments: Cincinnati dining, media, arts and entertainment, people, homes, politics, sports. Length: 1,000-1,500 words. **Buys 10-15 mss/year.** Query. **Pays $300-400.**

Tips: "Freelancers may find a market in Home section (10 times/year), special advertising sections on varying topics from golf to cardiac care (query Special Projects Managing Editor Mary Beth Crocker). Always query in writing, with clips. All articles have a local focus. No generics, please. Also: No movie, book, theater reviews, poetry, or fiction."

$ $ $ **CLEVELAND MAGAZINE**, City Magazines, Inc., 1422 Euclid Ave., #730Q, Cleveland OH 44115. (216)771-2833. Fax: (216)781-6318. E-mail: editorial@clevelandmagazine.com. Website: www.clevelandmagazine.com. **Contact:** Steve Gleydura, editorial director. **60% freelance written.** Mostly by assignment. Monthly magazine with a strong Cleveland/Northeast Ohio angle. Estab. 1972. Circ. 50,000. Pays on publication. Publishes ms an average of 3 months after acceptance. Byline given. Buys first, second serial (reprint), electronic rights. Editorial lead time 6 months. Submit seasonal material 8 months in advance. Accepts queries by mail, e-mail, fax. Accepts simultaneous submissions. Responds in 2 months to queries. Sample copy not available.

Nonfiction: General interest, historical/nostalgic, humor, interview/profile, travel, home and garden. Query with published clips. Length: 800-4,000 words. **Pays $250-1,200.**

Columns/Departments: My Town (Cleveland first-person stories), 1,500 words. Query with published clips. **Pays $300.**

$ DARKE COUNTY PROFILE, 4952 Bishop Rd., Greenville OH 45331. (937)547-0048. Fax: (937)547-9503. E-mail: profile@woh.rr.com. **Contact:** Diana J. Linder, editor. **15% freelance written.** Monthly magazine covering people and places in the Darke County area. Estab. 1994. Circ. 500. Pays on publication. Publishes ms an average of 3-6 months after acceptance. Byline given. Buys one-time rights. Editorial lead time 3 months. Submit seasonal material 3 months in advance. Accepts previously published material. Responds in 3-6 months to mss. Sample copy for $2. Writer's guidelines by e-mail.

Nonfiction: Diana J. Linder. General interest, how-to (crafts), humor, inspirational, personal experience, travel. No foul language, graphic violence, or pornography. **Buys 10-12 mss/year.** Send complete ms. Length: 500-1,500 words. **Pays $15-20.** Pays 1-year subscription for work published for the first time in the *Profile*.

Photos: Send photos with submission. Buys one-time rights. Pays $3.50/photo. Captions required.

Fiction: Diana J. Linder. Adventure, condensed novels, humorous, mainstream, mystery, romance, suspense, western. No violence, foul language, or sexually explicit material. **Buys 12-14 mss/year.** Send complete ms. Length: 500-1,500 words. **Pays $15-20.**

Fillers: Diana J. Linder. Anecdotes, facts, short humor. **Buys 6-12/year.** Length: 250-500 words. **Pays $5-10.**

Tips: Write tight and send neatly typed mss with a SASE.

$ $ $ NORTHERN OHIO LIVE, LIVE Publishing Co.11320 Juniper Rd., Cleveland OH 44106. (216)721-1800. Fax: (216)721-2525. E-mail: ssphar@livepub.com. **Contact:** Sarah R. Sphar, managing editor. **70% freelance written.** Monthly magazine covering Northern Ohio politics, arts, entertainment, education, and dining. "Reader demographic is mid-30s to 50s, though we're working to bring in the late 20s. Our readers are well educated, many with advanced degrees. They're interested in Northern Ohio's cultural scene and support it." Estab. 1980. Circ. 35,000. Pays on 20th of publication month. Publishes ms an average of 1 month after acceptance. Byline given. Offers 33% kill fee. Buys first North American serial rights. Editorial lead time 3 months. Submit seasonal material 4 months in advance. Responds in 3 weeks to queries; 2 months to mss. Sample copy for $3. Writer's guidelines not available.

Nonfiction: All should have a Northern Ohio slant. Essays, exposé, general interest, humor, interview/profile, photo feature, travel. Special issues: Gourmet Guide (restaurants) (May). **Buys 100 mss/year.** Query with published clips. Length: 1,000-3,500 words. **Pays $100-1,000.** Sometimes pays expenses of writers on assignment.

Reprints: Send photocopy and information about when and where the material previously appeared.

Photos: State availability with submission. Reviews contact sheets, 4×5 transparencies, 3×5 prints. Buys one-time rights. Negotiates payment individually. Identification of subjects required.

Columns/Departments: News & Reviews (arts previews, personality profiles, general interest), 800-1,800 words. **Pays $200-300.** Time & Place (personal essay), 400-450 words. **Pays $100.** Must be local authors. **Buys 60-70 mss/year.** Query with published clips.

Fiction: Novel excerpts.

Tips: "Don't send submissions not having anything to do with Northern Ohio. Must have some tie to the Northeast Quadrant of Ohio. We are not interested in stories appearing in every other outlet in town. What is the new angle?"

$ $ $ $ OHIO MAGAZINE, Great Lakes Publishing Co., 1422 Euclid Ave., Suite 730, Cleveland OH 44115. (216)771-2833. E-mail: editorial@ohiomagazine.com. Website: www.ohiomagazine.com. **Contact:** Richard Osborne, editorial director. **50% freelance written.** Monthly magazine emphasizing Ohio-based travel, news and feature material that highlights what's special and unique about the state. Estab. 1978. Circ. 95,000. Pays on publication. Publishes ms an average of 6 months after acceptance. Byline given. Buys first North American serial, one-time, second serial (reprint), all rights. First serial rights Submit seasonal material 6 months in advance. Accepts queries by mail, e-mail, fax. Responds in 3 months to queries; 3 months to mss. Sample copy for $3 and 9×12 SAE or online. Writer's guidelines online.

- Break in by "knowing the magazine—read it thoroughly for several issues. Send good clips—that show your ability to write on topics we cover. We're looking for thoughtful stories on topics that are more contextual and less shallow. I want queries that show the writer has some passion for the subject."

Nonfiction: Length: 1,000-3,000 words. **Pays $600-1,800.** Sometimes pays expenses of writers on assignment.

Reprints: Send tearsheet or photocopy and information about when and where the material previously appeared. Pays 50% of amount paid for an original article.

Photos: Rob McGarr, art director. Rate negotiable.

Columns/Departments: Length: 100-1,500 words. **Buys minimum 20 unsolicited mss/year. Pays $50-500.**

Tips: "Freelancers should send all queries in writing, not by telephone. Successful queries demonstrate an intimate knowledge of the publication. We are looking to increase our circle of writers who can write about the state in an informative and upbeat style. Strong reporting skills are highly valued."

$ $ OVER THE BACK FENCE, Southern Ohio's Own Magazine, Panther Publishing LLC, P.O. Box 756, Chillicothe OH 45601. (740)772-2165. Fax: (740)773-7626. E-mail: backfenc@bright.net. Website: www.backfence.com. Sarah Williamson, managing editor. Quarterly magazine. "We are a regional magazine serving 30 counties in Southern Ohio. *Over The Back Fence* has a wholesome, neighborly style. It appeals to readers from young adults to seniors, showcasing art and travel opportunities in the area." Estab. 1994. Circ. 15,000. Pays on publication. Publishes ms an average of 1 year after acceptance. Byline given. Buys one-time North American serial rights, makes work-for-hire assignments. Editorial lead time 1 year. Submit seasonal material 1 year in advance. Accepts queries by mail. Accepts simultaneous submissions. Responds in 3 months to queries. Sample copy for $4 or on website. Writer's guidelines online.

O-π Break in with personality profiles (1,000 words), short features, columns (600 words), and features (1,000 words).

Nonfiction: General interest, historical/nostalgic, humor, inspirational, interview/profile, personal experience, photo feature, travel. **Buys 9-12 mss/year.** Query with or without published clips or send complete ms. Length: 750-1,000 words. **Pays 10¢/word minimum, negotiable depending on experience.**

Reprints: Send photocopy of article or short story and typed ms with rights for sale noted, and information about when and where the material previously appeared. Payment negotiable.

Photos: "If sending photos as part of a text/photo package, please request our photo guidelines and submit color transparencies." Reviews color, 35mm or larger transparencies, prints. Buys one-time rights. $25-100/photo. Captions, identification of subjects, model releases required.

Columns/Departments: The Arts, 750-1,000 words; History (relevant to a designated county), 750-1,000 words; Inspirational (poetry or short story), 600-850 words; Profiles From Our Past, 300-600 words; Sport & Hobby, 750-1,000 words; Our Neighbors (i.e., people helping others), 750-1,000 words. All must be relevant to Southern Ohio. **Buys 24 mss/year.** Query with or without published clips or send complete ms. **Pays 10¢/word minimum, negotiable depending on experience.**

Fiction: Humorous. **Buys 4 mss/year.** Query with published clips. Length: 300-850 words. **Pays 10¢/word minimum, negotiable depending on experience.**

Poetry: Wholesome, traditional free verse, light verse, and rhyming. **Buys 4 poems/year.** Submit maximum 4 poems. Length: 4-32 lines. **Pays 10¢/word or $25 minimum.**

Tips: "Our approach can be equated to a friendly and informative conversation with a neighbor about interesting people, places, and events in Southern Ohio (counties: Adams, Athens, Brown, Clark, Clinton, Coshocton, Fayette, Fairfield, Gallia, Greene, Highland, Hocking, Jackson, Lawrence, Meigs, Morgan, Muskingum, Noble, Perry, Pickaway, Pike, Ross, Scioto, Vinton, Warren, and Washington)."

$ $ THE PLAIN DEALER SUNDAY MAGAZINE, Plain Dealer Publishing Co., Plain Dealer Plaza, 1801 Superior Ave., Cleveland OH 44114. (216)999-4546. Fax: (216)515-2039. E-mail: eburbach@plaind.com. **Contact:** Ellen Stein Burbach, editor. **50% freelance written.** Weekly magazine focusing on Cleveland and Northeastern Ohio. Circ. 500,000. Pays on publication. Publishes ms an average of 2 months after acceptance. Byline given. Buys first, one-time, all web rights. Submit seasonal material 3 months in advance. Accepts queries by mail, e-mail, fax. Responds in 1 month to queries; 2 months to mss. Sample copy for $1.

O-π "Start small, with 'North by Northeast' pieces."

Nonfiction: Must include focus on northeast Ohio people, places, and issues. Book excerpts, essays, exposé, general interest, historical/nostalgic, humor, inspirational, interview/profile, new product, personal experience, photo feature, travel (only personal essays or local ties). **Buys 50-100 (feature) mss/year.** Query with published clips or send complete ms. Length: 800-4,000 words. **Pays $150-650 for assigned articles.**

Reprints: Send ms with rights for sale noted and information about when and where the material previously appeared.

Columns/Departments: North by Northeast (short upfront pieces), **pays $20-70**; Essays (personal perspective, memoir OK), **pays $150-200**, 900 words maximum; The Back Burner (food essays with recipe), **pays $200**.

Tips: "We're always looking for superior writers and great stories."

Oklahoma

$ $ OKLAHOMA TODAY, Colcord Bldg., 15 N. Robinson, Suite 100, Oklahoma City OK 73102-5403. (405)521-2496. Fax: (405)522-4588. E-mail: mccune@oklahomatoday.com. Website: www.oklahomatoday.com. **Contact:** Louisa McCune, editor-in-chief. **80% freelance written.** Works with approximately 25 new/unpublished writers each year. Bimonthly magazine covering people, places, and things Oklahoman. "We are interested in showing off the best Oklahoma has to offer; we're pretty serious about our travel slant but regularly run history, nature, and personality profiles." Estab. 1956. Circ. 45,000. Pays on publication. Publishes ms an average of 6 months after acceptance. Byline given. Buys first worldwide serial rights. Submit seasonal material 1 year in advance. Accepts queries by mail, e-mail. Responds in 4 months to queries. Sample copy for $3.95 and 9×12 SASE or online. Writer's guidelines online.

- *Oklahoma Today* has won Magazine of the Year, awarded by the International Regional Magazine Association, 4 out of the last 10 years, and in 1999 won *Folio* magazine's Editorial Excellence Award for Best Regional Magazine.

O-π "Start small. Look for possibilities for 'The Range.' Even letters to the editor are good ways to 'get some ink.' "

Nonfiction: Book excerpts (on Oklahoma topics), historical/nostalgic (Oklahoma only), interview/profile (Oklahomans only), photo feature (in Oklahoma), travel (in Oklahoma). No phone queries. **Buys 20-40 mss/year.** Query with published clips. Length: 250-3,000 words. **Pays $25-750.**

Photos: "We are especially interested in developing contacts with photographers who live in Oklahoma or have shot here. Send samples." Photo guidelines for SASE. Reviews 4×5, 2¼×2¼, and 35mm color transparencies, high-quality transparencies, slides, and b&w prints. Buys one-time rights to use photos for promotional purposes. Pays $50-750 for color. Captions, identification of subjects required.

Fiction: Novel excerpts, occasionally short fiction.

Tips: "The best way to become a regular contributor to *Oklahoma Today* is to query us with 1 or more story ideas, each developed to give us an idea of your proposed slant. We're looking for lively, concise, well-researched and reported stories, stories that don't need to be heavily edited and are not newspaper style. We have a 3-person full-time editorial staff, and freelancers who can write and have done their homework get called again and again."

Oregon

$ $ OREGON COAST, 4969 Highway 101 N. #2, Florence OR 97439-0130. (541)997-8401, ext. 123 or (800)348-8401, ext. 123. E-mail: theresa@ohwy.com. Website: www.ohwy.com. **Contact:** Theresa Baer, managing editor. **65% freelance written.** Bimonthly magazine covering the Oregon Coast. Estab. 1982. Circ. 50,000. Pays after publication. Publishes ms an average of up to 1 year after acceptance. Byline given. Offers 33% (on assigned stories only, not on stories accepted on spec) kill fee. Buys first North American serial rights. Submit seasonal material 6 months in advance. Accepts queries by mail, e-mail. Responds in 3 months to queries. Sample copy for $4.50. Writer's guidelines for #10 SASE.

- This company also publishes *Northwest Travel.*

O→ Break in with "great photos with a story that has a great lead and no problems during fact-checking. Like stories that have a slightly different take on 'same-old' subjects and have good anecdotes and quotes. Stories should have satisfying endings."

Nonfiction: "A true regional with general interest, historical/nostalgic, humor, interview/profile, personal experience, photo feature, travel, and nature as pertains to Oregon Coast." **Buys 55 mss/year.** Query with published clips. Length: 500-1,500 words. **Pays $75-250, plus 2-5 contributor copies.**

Reprints: Send tearsheet or photocopy and information about when and where the material previously appeared. Pays an average of 60% of the amount paid for an original article.

Photos: Photo submissions with no ms or stand alone or cover photos. Barb Grano, photo editor. Send photos with submission. Reviews 35mm or larger transparencies. Buys one-time rights. Captions, identification of subjects, model releases (for cover), photo credits required.

Fillers: Newsbreaks (no-fee basis).

Tips: "Slant article for readers who do not live at the Oregon Coast. At least 1 historical article is used in each issue. Manuscript/photo packages are preferred over manuscripts with no photos. List photo credits and captions for each historic print or color slide. Check all facts, proper names, and numbers carefully in photo/manuscript packages. Must pertain to Oregon Coast somehow."

Pennsylvania

$ $ BERKS COUNTY LIVING, West Lawn Graphic Communications, P.O. Box 642, Shillington PA 19607. (610)775-0640. Fax: (610)775-7412. E-mail: prohland@berkscountyliving.com. Website: www.berkscountyliving.com. **Contact:** Pam Rohland, editor. **90% freelance written.** Bimonthly magazine covering topics of interest to people living in Berks County, Pennsylvania. Estab. 2000. Circ. 36,000. Pays on publication. Publishes ms an average of 4 months after acceptance. Byline given. Offers 25% kill fee. Buys first North American serial rights. Editorial lead time 6 months. Submit seasonal material 4 months in advance. Accepts queries by mail, e-mail, fax. Accepts previously published material. Accepts simultaneous submissions. Responds in 1 week to queries; 1 month to mss. Sample copy for 9×12 SAE and 2 first-class stamps. Writer's guidelines for #10 SASE. Editorial calendar online.

Nonfiction: Articles must be associated with Berks County, Pennsylvania. Exposé, general interest, historical/nostalgic, how-to, humor, inspirational, interview/profile, new product, photo feature, travel, food, health. **Buys 25 mss/year.** Query. Length: 750-2,000 words. **Pays $150-400.** Sometimes pays expenses of writers on assignment.

Reprints: Accepts previously published submissions.

Photos: State availability with submission. Reviews 35mm or greater transparencies, any size prints. Buys one-time rights. Negotiates payment individually. Captions, identification of subjects, model releases required.

$ $ CENTRAL PA, WITF, Inc., 1982 Locust Lane, Harrisburg PA 17109. (717)221-2800. Fax: (717)221-2630. E-mail: centralpa@centralpa.org. Website: www.centralpa.org. **Contact:** Steve Kennedy, senior editor. **90% freelance written.** Monthly magazine covering life in Central Pennsylvania. Estab. 1982. Circ. 42,000. Pays on publication. Publishes ms an average of 4 months after acceptance. Offers 20% kill fee. Buys first North American serial rights. Editorial lead time 3 months. Submit seasonal material 6 months in advance. Accepts queries by mail, e-mail, fax. Accepts simultaneous submissions. Responds in 6 weeks to queries. Sample copy for $3.50 and SASE. Writer's guidelines online.

O→ Break in through Central Stories, Thinking Aloud, blurbs, and accompanying events calendar.

Nonfiction: Essays, general interest, historical/nostalgic, how-to, humor, interview/profile, opinion, personal experience, photo feature, travel. Special issues: Dining/Food (January); Regional Insider's Guide (July); Best of Central PA (December). **Buys 50 mss/year.** Query with published clips or send complete ms. Length: 800-3,000 words. **Pays $200-750 for assigned articles; $50-500 for unsolicited articles.** Sometimes pays expenses of writers on assignment.

Photos: State availability with submission. Reviews contact sheets, transparencies, prints. Buys one-time rights. Negotiates payment individually. Identification of subjects required.

Columns/Departments: Central Stories (quirky, newsy, regional), 300 words; Thinking Aloud (essay), 1,200 words; Cameo (interview), 800 words. **Buys 90 mss/year.** Query with published clips or send complete ms. **Pays $50-100.**

Tips: "Wow us with something you wrote, either a clip or a manuscript on spec. If it's off target but shows you can write well and know the region, we'll ask for more. We're looking for creative nonfiction, with an emphasis on conveying valuable information through near literary-quality narrative."

$ $ PENNSYLVANIA, Pennsylvania Magazine Co., P.O. Box 755, Camp Hill PA 17001-0755. (717)697-4660. E-mail: pamag@aol.com. Publisher: Albert E. Holliday. **Contact:** Matt Holliday, editor. **90% freelance written.** Bimonthly magazine covering people, places, events, and history in Pennsylvania. Estab. 1981. Circ. 33,000. Pays on acceptance except for articles (by authors unknown to us) sent on speculation. Publishes ms an average of 9 months after acceptance. Byline given. 25% kill fee for assigned articles. Buys first North American serial, one-time rights. Submit seasonal material 9 months in advance. Accepts queries by mail, e-mail. Responds in 4-6 weeks to queries. Sample copy for $2.95. Writer's guidelines for #10 SASE.

O→ Break in with "a text/photo package—learn to take photos or hook up with a photographer who will shoot for our rates."

Nonfiction: Features include general interest, historical, photo feature, vacations and travel, people/family success stories—all dealing with or related to Pennsylvania. Will not consider without illustrations; send photocopies of possible illustrations with query or ms. Include SASE. Nothing on Amish topics, hunting, or skiing. **Buys 75-120 mss/year.** Query. Length: 750-2,500 words. **Pays 10-15¢/word.**

Reprints: Send photocopy with rights for sale noted and information about when and where the material previously appeared. Pays 5¢/word.

Photos: No original slides or transparencies. Americana Photo Journal (includes 1-4 interesting photos and a 250-word caption); Photography Essay (highlights annual photo essay contest entries). Reviews 35mm 2¼×2¼ color transparencies, 5×7 to 8×10 color and b&w prints. Buys one-time rights. Pays $15-25 for inside photos; up to $100 for covers. Captions required.

Columns/Departments: Panorama (short items about people, unusual events, family and individually owned consumer-related businesses), 250-900 words; Almanac (short historical items), 1,000-2,500 words; Museums, 400-500 words. All must be illustrated. Include SASE. Query. **Pays 10-15¢/word.**

Tips: "Our publication depends upon freelance work—send queries."

$ $ PENNSYLVANIA HERITAGE, Pennsylvania Historical and Museum Commission and the Pennsylvania Heritage Society, Commonwealth Keystone Bldg., Plaza Level, 400 North St., Harrisburg PA 17120-0053. (717)787-7522. Fax: (717)787-8312. E-mail: miomalley@state.pa.us. Website: www.paheritage.org. **Contact:** Michael J. O'Malley III, editor. **90% freelance written.** Prefers to work with published/established writers. Quarterly magazine. "*Pennsylvania Heritage* introduces readers to Pennsylvania's rich culture and historic legacy, educates and sensitizes them to the value of preserving that heritage and entertains and involves them in such a way as to ensure that Pennsylvania's past has a future. The magazine is intended for intelligent lay readers." Estab. 1974. Circ. 10,000. Pays on publication. Publishes ms an average of 1 year after acceptance. Byline given. Buys all rights. Accepts queries by mail, e-mail. Responds in 10 weeks to queries; 8 months to mss. Sample copy for $5 and 9×12 SAE or online. Writer's guidelines for #10 SASE or online.

• *Pennsylvania Heritage* is now considering freelance submissions that are shorter in length (2,000-3,000 words), pictorial/photographic essays, biographies of famous (and not-so-famous) Pennsylvanians and interviews with individuals who have helped shape, make, preserve the Keystone State's history and heritage.

Nonfiction: "Our format requires feature-length articles. Manuscripts with illustrations are especially sought for publication. We are now looking for shorter (2,000 words) manuscripts that are heavily illustrated with publication-quality photographs or artwork. We are eager to work with experienced travel writers for destination pieces on historical sites and museums that make up 'The Pennsylvania Trail of History.'" Art, science, biographies, industry, business, politics, transportation, military, historic preservation, archaeology, photography, etc. No articles which in no way relate to Pennsylvania history or culture. **Buys 20-24 mss/year.** Prefers to see mss with suggested illustrations. Length: 2,000-3,500 words. **Pays $100-500.**

Photos: State availability of or send photos with submission. Buys one-time rights. $25-200 for transparencies; $5-75 for b&w photos. Captions, identification of subjects required.

Tips: "We are looking for well-written, interesting material that pertains to any aspect of Pennsylvania history or culture. Potential contributors should realize that, although our articles are popularly styled, they are not light, puffy, or breezy; in fact they demand strident documentation and substantiation (sans footnotes). The most frequent mistake made by writers in completing articles for us is making them either too scholarly or too sentimental or nostalgic. We want material which educates, but also entertains. Authors should make history readable and enjoyable. Our goal is to make the Keystone State's history come to life in a meaningful, memorable way."

$ PHILADELPHIA MAGAZINE, 1818 Market St., 36th Floor, Philadelphia PA 19103. (215)564-7700. Fax: (215)656-3502. Website: www.phillymag.com. President/Publisher: David R. Lipson. **Contact:** Larry Platt, editor. Monthly magazine. "*Philadelphia* is edited for the area's community leaders and their families. It provides in-depth reports on crucial and controversial issues confronting the region—business trends, political analysis, metropolitan planning, sociological trends—plus critical reviews of the cultural, sports and entertainment scene." Estab. 1908. Circ. 133,083. **Pays on acceptance.** Accepts queries by mail. Sample copy not available. Writer's guidelines not available. Editorial calendar online.

O→ Break in by sending queries along with clips. "Remember that we are a general interest magazine that focuses exclusively on topics of interest in the Delaware Valley."

Nonfiction: "Articles range from law enforcement to fashion, voting trends to travel, transportation to theater, also includes the background studies of the area newsmakers." Query with clips and SASE.

Tips: "*Philadelphia Magazine* readers are an affluent, interested and influential group who can afford the best the region has to offer. They're the greater Philadelphia area residents who care about the city and its politics, lifestyles, business and culture."

N **$ $ PHILADELPHIA STYLE, Philadelphia's Premier Magazine for Lifestyle & Fashion**, Philadelphia Style Magazine, LLC, 141 League St., Philadelphia PA 19147. Fax: (215)468-6530. E-mail: info@phillystylemag.com. Website: www.phillystylemag.com. Editor: John M. Colabelli. **Contact:** Jennifer Goldstein, articles editor. **90% freelance written.** Bimonthly magazine covering upscale living in the Philadelphia region. Topics include: fashion (men's and women's), home and design, real estate, dining, beauty, travel, arts and entertainment, and more. "Our magazine is a positive look at the best ways to live and play in the Philadelphia region. Submitted articles should speak to an upscale, educated audience of professionals that live in the Delaware Valley." Estab. 1999. Circ. 45,000. Pays on publication. Publishes ms an average of 2 months after acceptance. Byline given. Offers 25% kill fee. Buys first rights. Editorial lead time 2-4 months. Submit seasonal material 6 months in advance. Accepts queries by mail, e-mail, fax. Sample copy not available.

- Break in "with ideas for our real estate section (reviews/stories of area neighborhoods, home and design, architecture, and other new ideas you may have)."

Nonfiction: General interest, interview/profile, travel, region-specific articles. "We are not looking for articles that do not have a regional spin." **Buys 100+ mss/year.** Query with published clips or send complete ms. Length: 300-2,500 words. **Pays $50-500.**

Columns/Departments: Life in the City (fresh, quirky, regional reporting on books, real estate, art, retail, dining, events, and little-known stories/facts about the region), 100-500 words; Vanguard (people on the forefront of Philadelphia's arts, media, fashion, business, and social scene), 500-700 words; In the Neighborhood (reader-friendly reporting on up-and-coming areas of the region including dining, shopping, attractions, and recreation), 2,000-2,500 words; Debuts (pitch articles about new regional retail operations that would be of interest to readers), 700-1,000 words; Company We Keep (compelling profiles of regional businesses that are nationally known and/or growing), 1,000-1,500 words. Query with published clips or send complete ms. **Pays $50-500.**

Tips: "Mail queries with clips or manuscripts. Articles should speak to a stylish, educated audience."

$ $ $ $ PITTSBURGH MAGAZINE, WQED Pittsburgh, 4802 Fifth Ave., Pittsburgh PA 15213. (412)622-1360. Website: www.pittsburghmag.com. **Contact:** Michelle Pilecki, executive editor. **70% freelance written.** Monthly magazine. "*Pittsburgh* presents issues, analyzes problems, and strives to encourage a better understanding of the community. Our region is Western Pennsylvania, Eastern Ohio, Northern West Virginia, and Western Maryland." Estab. 1970. Circ. 75,000. Pays on publication. Publishes ms an average of 2 months after acceptance. Byline given. Offers kill fee. Buys first North American serial, second serial (reprint) rights. Submit seasonal material 6 months in advance. Accepts queries by mail. Responds in 2 months to queries. Sample copy for $2 (old back issues). Writer's guidelines online or via SASE.

- The editor reports a need for more hard news and stories targeting readers in their 30s and 40s, especially those with young families. Prefers to work with published/established writers. The monthly magazine is purchased on newsstands and by subscription, and is given to those who contribute $40 or more/year to public TV in western Pennsylvania.

Nonfiction: "Without exception—whether the topic is business, travel, the arts, or lifestyle—each story is clearly oriented to Pittsburghers of today and to the greater Pittsburgh region of today." Must have greater Pittsburgh angle. No fax, phone, or e-mail queries. No complete mss. Exposé, lifestyle, sports, informational, service, business, medical, profile. "We have minimal interest in historical articles and we do not publish fiction, poetry, advocacy, or personal reminiscence pieces." Query in writing with outline and clips. Length: 3,500 words maximum. **Pays $300-1,500+.**

Photos: Query. Pays prenegotiated expenses of writer on assignment. Model releases required.

Columns/Departments: The Front (short, front-of-the-book items). Length: 300 words maximum. **Pays $50-150.**

- The online magazine carries original content not found in the print edition. Contact: Michelle Pilecki, executive editor.

Tips: "Best bet to break in is through hard news with a region-wide impact or service pieces or profiles with a regional interest. The point is that we want more stories that reflect our region, not just a tiny part. And we *never* consider any story without a strong regional focus. We do not respond to fax and e-mail queries."

$ $ WESTSYLVANIA, Westylvania Heritage Corp., P.O. Box 565, 105 Zee Plaza, Hollidaysburg PA 16648-0565. (814)696-9380. Fax: (814)696-9569. E-mail: jschumacher@westsylvania.org. Website: www.westsylvania.com. **Contact:** Jerilynn "Jerry" Schumacher, editor. **90% freelance written.** Quarterly magazine in south-central and southwestern Pennsylvania, plus parts of Ohio, Maryland, West Virginia, Virginia, and Kentucky. "*Westsylvania* magazine celebrates the heritage and lifestyles of south-central and southwestern Pennsylvania. Articles must reflect the region's natural, industrial, transportational, and/or cultural heritage in some fashion. This is not a history magazine. Stories should show how the region's history still influences contemporary life." Estab. 1997. Circ. 10,000-14,000. Pays on publication. Publishes ms an average of 4 months after acceptance. Byline given. Offers $50 kill fee. Buys first North American serial, web rights. Editorial lead time 6-12 months. Submit seasonal material 2 months in advance. Accepts queries by mail, e-mail, fax. Accepts simultaneous submissions. Sample copy online. Writer's guidelines online.

- Break in with "a well-written query that spotlights a little-known person, place, or event in the Westsylvania region. We particularly seek stories on what people are doing to preserve their own heritage, such as cleaning up a trout stream or restoring a theater. How-to articles welcome. First-person accounts accepted only for assigned columns."

Nonfiction: Book excerpts, historical/nostalgic, interview/profile, religious, travel, business, wildlife, outdoors, photography. *No unsolicited mss.* **Buys 30 mss/year.** Query with published clips. Length: 750-2,500 words. **Pays $75-300 for assigned articles.**

Photos: State photo ideas or availability with submission. Use of high-quality digital images encouraged. Buys one-time rights for magazine or Website. Negotiates payments individually. Captions, identification of subjects, model releases required.

Columns/Departments: First Person (assigned columns only), 500-700 words; Book Reviews (informational), 500 words; Vintage Ventures (business stories), 750 words; Spirit of Westsylvania (inspirational), 750 words. **Buys 15 mss/year.** Query with published clips. **Pays with free subscription or check up to $125, depending.**

Fillers: Anecdotes, facts, short humor. Length: 50-500 words. **Pays $25-100.**

Tips: Poorly written queries will receive no response. "Striving for people oriented stories with lively active verbs."

$ $ WHERE & WHEN, Pennsylvania's Travel Guide, Engle Publishing, 1425 W. Main St., P.O. Box 500, Mount Joy PA 17552. (800)800-1833, ext. 2544. Fax: (717)492-2570. E-mail: wsroyal@engleonline.com. Website: www.whereandwhen.com. **Contact:** Wendy Royal, editor. Quarterly magazine covering travel and tourism in Pennsylvania. "*Where & When* presents things to see and do in Pennsylvania." Circ. 100,000. Pays on publication. Byline given. Offers 50% kill fee. Buys first North American serial rights. Editorial lead time 6 months. Submit seasonal material 6 months in advance. Responds in 1 month to queries. Sample copy and writer's guidelines free.

- This publication is now using mainly staff writers, though this may change in the future.

Nonfiction: Travel. **Buys 20-30 mss/year.** Query. Length: 800-2,500 words. **Pays $150-400.**

Photos: State availability with submission. Reviews transparencies, prints, slides. Buys one-time rights. Negotiates payment individually. Captions, identification of subjects required.

Columns/Departments: Bring the Kids (children's attractions); Heritage Traveler (state heritage parks); Small Town PA (villages and hamlets in Pennsylvania); On the Road Again (attractions along a particular road), all 800-1,200 words. **Buys 10 mss/year.** Query. **Pays $100-250.**

Rhode Island

$ $ $ RHODE ISLAND MONTHLY, The Providence Journal Co., 280 Kinsley Ave., Providence RI 02903. (401)421-8200. Fax: (401)277-8080. E-mail: paula_bodah@rimonthly.com. Website: www.rimonthly.com. Editor: Paula M. Bodah. **Contact:** Sarah Francis, managing editor. **50% freelance written.** Monthly magazine. "*Rhode Island Monthly* is a general interest consumer magazine with a strict Rhode Island focus." Estab. 1988. Circ. 41,000. **Pays on acceptance.** Publishes ms an average of 3 months after acceptance. Byline given. Offers 25% kill fee. Buys all rights for 90 days from date of publication. Editorial lead time 3 months. Submit seasonal material 6 months in advance. Accepts queries by mail, e-mail, fax. Responds in 6 weeks to queries. Sample copy online. Writer's guidelines not available.

Nonfiction: Exposé, general interest, interview/profile, photo feature. **Buys 40 mss/year.** Query with published clips. Length: 1,800-3,000 words. **Pays $600-1,200.** Sometimes pays expenses of writers on assignment.

South Carolina

$ CHARLESTON MAGAZINE, P.O. Box 1794, Mt. Pleasant SC 29465-1794. (843)971-9811. Fax: (843)971-0121. E-mail: dshankland@charlestonmag.com. Website: charlestonmag.com. **Contact:** Darcy Shankland, editor. **80% freelance written.** Bimonthly magazine covering current issues, events, arts and culture, leisure pursuits, travel, and personalities, as they pertain to the city of Charleston and surrounding areas. "A Lowcountry institution for more than 30 years, *Charleston Magazine* captures the essence of Charleston and her surrounding areas—her people, arts and architecture, culture and events, and natural beauty." Estab. 1972. Circ. 25,000. Pays 1 month after publication. Byline given. Buys one-time rights. Submit seasonal material 4 months in advance. Accepts queries by mail, e-mail, fax. Sample copies may be ordered at cover price from office. Writer's guidelines for #10 SASE.

Nonfiction: "Must pertain to the Charleston area and its present culture." General interest, humor, interview/profile, opinion, photo feature, travel, food, architecture, sports, current events/issues, art. "Not interested in 'Southern nostalgia' articles or gratuitous history pieces." **Buys 40 mss/year.** Query with published clips and SASE. Length: 150-1,500 words. **Payment negotiated.** Sometimes pays expenses of writers on assignment.

Reprints: Send photocopy and information about when and where the material previously appeared. Payment negotiable.

Photos: Send photos with submission. Reviews contact sheets, transparencies, slides. Buys one-time rights. Identification of subjects required.

Columns/Departments: Channel Markers (general local interest), 50-400 words; Local Seen (profile of local interest), 500 words; In Good Taste (restaurants and culinary trends in the city), 1,000-1,200 words, plus recipes; Chef at Home (profile of local chefs), 1,200 words, plus recipes; On the Road (travel opportunities near Charleston), 1,000-1,200 words; Southern View (personal experience about Charleston life), 750 words; Doing Business (profiles of exceptional local businesses and entrepreneurs), 1,000-1,200 words; Native Talent (local profiles), 1,000-1,200 words; Top of the Shelf (reviews of books with Southern content or by a Southern author), 750 words.

Tips: "Charleston, although a city with a 300-year history, is a vibrant, modern community with a tremendous dedication to the arts and no shortage of newsworthy subjects. We're looking for the freshest stories about Charleston—and those don't always come from insiders, but also outsiders who are keenly observant."

$ $ HILTON HEAD MONTHLY, Frey Media, Inc., 2 Park Lane, Hilton Head Island SC 29928. Fax: (843)842-5743. E-mail: hhmeditor@hargray.com. **Contact:** Rob Kaufman, editor. **75% freelance written.** Monthly magazine covering the business, people, and lifestyle of Hilton Head, South Carolina. "Our mission is to provide fresh, upbeat reading about the residents, lifestyle and community affairs of Hilton Head Island, an upscale, intensely pro-active resort community on the Eastern seaboard. We are not even remotely 'trendy,' but we like to see how national trends/issues play out on a local level. Especially interested in: home design and maintenance, entrepreneurship, nature, area history, golf/tennis/boating, volunteerism." Circ. 28,000. **Pays on acceptance.** Publishes ms an average of 6 months after acceptance. Byline given. Offers 50% kill fee. Buys first North American serial rights, makes work-for-hire assignments. Editorial lead time 3 months. Submit seasonal material 4 months in advance. Accepts queries by mail, e-mail, fax. Accepts previously published material. Accepts simultaneous submissions. Responds in 1 week to queries; 4 months to mss. Sample copy for $3.

Nonfiction: Essays (short, personal), general interest, historical/nostalgic (history only), how-to (home related), humor, interview/profile (Hilton Head residents only), opinion (general humor or Hilton Head Island community affairs), personal experience, travel. No "exposé interviews with people who are not Hilton Head residents; profiles of people, events, or businesses in Beaufort, South Carolina; Savannah, Georgia; Charleston; or other surrounding cities, unless it's within a travel piece." **Buys 225-250 mss/year.** Query with published clips. Length: 800-2,000 words. **Pays 10¢/word.**

Photos: State availability with submission. Reviews contact sheets, prints, slides; any size. Buys one-time rights. Negotiates payment individually.

Columns/Departments: Wellness (any general healthcare topic, especially for an older audience), 800-1,100 words; Focus (profile of Hilton Head Island personality/community leader), 1,000-1,300 words; Community (profile of Hilton Head Island volunteer organization), 800-1,100 words. Query with published clips. **Pays 15¢/word minimum.**

Tips: "Give us concise, bullet-style descriptions of what the article covers (in the query letter); choose upbeat, pro-active topics; delight us with your fresh (not trendy) description and word choice."

$ SANDLAPPER, The Magazine of South Carolina, The Sandlapper Society, Inc., P.O. Box 1108, Lexington SC 29071-1108. (803)359-9941. Fax: (803)359-0629. E-mail: aida@sandlapper.org. Website: www.sandlapper.org. Editor: Robert P. Wilkins. **Contact:** Aida Rogers, managing editor. **60% freelance written.** Quarterly magazine focusing on the positive aspects of South Carolina. "*Sandlapper* is intended to be read at those times when people want to relax with an attractive, high-quality magazine that entertains and informs them about their state." Estab. 1989. Circ. 18,000 with a readership of 60,000. Pays during the dateline period. Publishes ms an average of 1 year after acceptance. Byline given. Buys first North American serial rights and the right to reprint. Submit seasonal material 6 months in advance. Accepts queries by mail, e-mail, fax. Sample copy online. Writer's guidelines for #10 SASE.

Nonfiction: Feature articles and photo essays about South Carolina's interesting people, places, cuisine, things to do. Occasional history articles. Essays, general interest, humor, interview/profile, photo feature. Query with clips and SASE. Length: 500-2,500 words. **Pays $100/published page.** Sometimes pays expenses of writers on assignment.

Photos: "*Sandlapper* buys b&w prints, color transparencies, and art. Photographers should submit working cutlines for each photograph. While prints and slides are preferred, we do accept digital images in the following format only: JPEGs at 300 dpi (minimum), at 8½×11-inch size. Please provide digital images on CD or IBM-compatible disk, accompanied by a proof or laser print." Pays $25-75, $100 for cover or centerspread photo.

The online version contains material not found in the print edition. Contact: Dan Harmon.

Tips: "We're not interested in articles about topical issues, politics, crime, or commercial ventures. Avoid first-person nostalgia and remembrances of places that no longer exist. We look for top-quality literature. Humor is encouraged. Good taste is a standard. Unique angles are critical for acceptance. Dare to be bold, but not too bold."

South Dakota

$ DAKOTA OUTDOORS, South Dakota,, Hipple Publishing Co., P.O. Box 669 333 W. Dakota Ave., Pierre SD 57501-0669. (605)224-7301. Fax: (605)224-9210. E-mail: office@capjournal.com. Editor: Kevin Hipple. **Contact:** Rachel Engbrecht, managing editor. **85% freelance written.** Monthly magazine on Dakota outdoor life, focusing on hunting and fishing. Estab. 1974. Circ. 7,000. Pays on publication. Publishes ms an average of 2 months after acceptance. Byline given. Submit seasonal material 3 months in advance. Accepts queries by mail, e-mail. Accepts simultaneous submissions. Responds in 3 months to queries. Sample copy for 9×12 SAE and 3 first-class stamps. Writer's guidelines by e-mail.

Nonfiction: "Topics should center on fishing and hunting experiences and advice. Other topics such as boating, camping, hiking, environmental concerns and general nature will be considered as well." General interest, how-to, humor, interview/profile, personal experience, technical (all on outdoor topics-prefer in the Dakotas). **Buys 120 mss/year.** Send complete ms. Length: 500-2,000 words. **Pays $5-50. Sometimes pays in contributor's copies or other premiums (inquire).**

Reprints: Send ms with rights for sale noted and information about when and where the material previously appeared. 50% of amount paid for an original article.

Photos: Send photos with submission. Reviews 3×5 or 5×7 prints. Buys one-time rights. Offers no additonal payment for photos accepted with ms or negotiates payment individually. Identification of subjects required.

Columns/Departments: Kids Korner (outdoors column addressing kids 12-16 years of age). Length: 50-500 words. **Pays $5-15.**

Fiction: Adventure, humorous. **Buys 15 mss/year.** Send complete ms.

Fillers: Anecdotes, facts, gags to be illustrated by cartoonist, newsbreaks, short humor, line drawings of fish and game.

Tips: "Submit samples of manuscript or previous works for consideration; photos or illustrations with manuscript are helpful."

Tennessee

N $ $ MEMPHIS, Contemporary Media, 460 Tennessee St., Suite 200, Memphis TN 38103. (901)521-9000. Fax: (901)521-0129. E-mail: memmag@memphismagazine.com. Website: www.memphismagazine.com. Editor: James Roper. Managing Editor: Frank Murtaugh. **Contact:** Michael Finger, senior editor. **30% freelance written.** Works with a small number of new/unpublished writers. Monthly magazine covering Memphis and the local region. "Our mission is to provide Memphis with a colorful and informative look at the people, places, lifestyles and businesses that make the Bluff City unique." Estab. 1976. Circ. 24,000. Pays on publication. Publishes ms an average of 2 months after acceptance. Byline given. Offers 25% kill fee. Buys first North American serial rights. Editorial lead time 2 months. Submit seasonal material 3 months in advance. Accepts queries by mail, e-mail, fax. Accepts simultaneous submissions. Responds in 2 months to queries. Sample copy for free or online. Writer's guidelines free.

Nonfiction: "Virtually all of our material has strong Memphis area connections." Essays, general interest, historical/nostalgic, interview/profile, photo feature, travel, Interiors/exteriors. Special issues: Restaurant Guide and City Guide. **Buys 20 mss/year.** Query with published clips. Length: 500-3,000 words. **Pays 10-30¢/word.** Sometimes pays expenses of writers on assignment.

Photos: State availability with submission. Reviews contact sheets, transparencies. Buys one-time rights.

Columns/Departments: IntroSpective (personal experiences/relationships), 1,000-1,500 words; CityScape (local events/issues), 1,500-2,000 words; City Beat (peaople, places and things-some quirky), 200-400 words. **Buys 10 mss/year.** Query. **Pays 10-20¢/word.**

Fiction: Marilyn Sadler, associate editor. One story published annually as part of contest. Send complete ms. Length: 1,500-3,000 words.

Tips: "Send a query letter with specific ideas that apply to our short columns and departments. Good ideas that apply specifically to these sections will often get published."

Texas

N **$ $ $ HOUSTON PRESS**, New Times, Inc., 1621 Milam, Suite 100, Houston TX 77002. (713)280-2400. Fax: (713)280-2444. Website: www.houstonpress.com. Editor: Margaret Downing. Managing Editor: George Flynn. Associate Editor: Lauren Kern. **Contact:** Melissa Sonzala, editorial administrator. **40% freelance written.** Weekly tabloid covering "news and arts stories of interest to a Houston audience. If the same story could run in Seattle, then it's not for us." Estab. 1989. Pays on publication. Publishes ms an average of 2 weeks after acceptance. Byline given. Buys first North American serial, website rights. Editorial lead time 2 months. Submit seasonal material 3 months in advance. Sample copy for $3.

Nonfiction: Exposé, general interest, interview/profile, arts reviews; music. Query with published clips. Length: 300-4,500 words. **Pays $10-1,000.** Sometimes pays expenses of writers on assignment.

Photos: State availability with submission. Buys all rights. Negotiates payment individually. Identification of subjects required.

$ $ $ PAPERCITY, Dallas Edition, Urban Publishers, 3303 Lee Parkway, #340, Dallas TX 75219. (214)521-3439. Fax: (214)521-3178. E-mail: trish@papercitymag.com. **Contact:** Trish Donnally, managing editor; Holly Moore, Houston editor. **10% freelance written.** Monthly magazine. "*Papercity* covers fashion, food, entertainment, home design and decoratives for urban Dallas, Houston, and San Francisco. Our writing is lively, brash, sexy—it's where to read about the hottest restaurants, great chefs, where to shop, what's cool to buy, where to go and the chicest places to stay—from sexy, small hotels in New York, Los Angeles, London and Morocco, to where to buy the newest trends in Europe. We cover local parties with big photo spreads, and a hip nightlife column." Estab. 1994 (Houston); 1998 (Dallas); 2002 (San Francisco). Circ. 85,000 (Dallas). Pays on publication. Publishes ms an average of 1 month after acceptance. Byline given. Offers 10% kill fee. Buys first North American serial rights. Editorial lead time 2 months. Submit seasonal material 4 months in advance. Accepts queries by mail, e-mail, fax. Accepts simultaneous submissions. Responds in 3 weeks to queries; 1 month to mss. Sample copy for 9×12 SAE with $1.50 in first-class stamps. Writer's guidelines for #10 SASE or by e-mail.

Nonfiction: General interest, interview/profile, new product, travel, home decor, food. Special issues: Bridal (February); Travel (April); Restaurants (August). No straight profiles on anyone, especially celebrities. **Buys 10-12 mss/year.** Query with published clips. Length: 150-3,000 words. **Pays 35-50¢/word.**

Photos: State availability with submission. Reviews contact sheets, transparencies, prints. Buys one-time rights. Negotiates payment individually.

Tips: "Read similar publications such as *W*, *Tattler*, *Wallpaper*, *Martha Stewart Living* for new trends, style of writing, hip new restaurants. We try to be very 'of the moment' so give us something in Dallas, Houston, New York, Los Angeles, London, etc., that we haven't heard yet. Chances are if other hip magazines are writing about it so will we."

$ $ $ TEXAS HIGHWAYS, The Travel Magazine of Texas, Box 141009, Austin TX 78714-1009. (512)486-5858. Fax: (512)486-5879. E-mail: editors@texashighways.com. Website: www.texashighways.com. **Contact:** Jill Lawless, managing editor. **80% freelance written.** Monthly magazine "encourages travel within the state and tells the Texas story to readers around the world." Estab. 1974. Circ. 300,000. **Pays on acceptance.** Publishes ms an average of 1 year after acceptance. Buys first North American serial, electronic rights. Accepts queries by mail. Responds in 2 months to queries. Writer's guidelines online.

Nonfiction: "Subjects should focus on things to do or places to see in Texas. Include historical, cultural, and geographical aspects if appropriate. Text should be meticulously researched. Include anecdotes, historical references, quotations and, where relevant, geologic, botanical, and zoological information." Query with description, published clips, additional background materials (charts, maps, etc.) and SASE. Length: 1,200-1,500 words. **Pays 40-50¢/word.**

Tips: "We like strong leads that draw in the reader immediately and clear, concise writing. Be specific and avoid superlatives. Avoid overused words. Don't forget the basics—who, what, where, why, and how."

$ TEXAS PARKS & WILDLIFE, 3000 South I.H. 35, Suite 120, Austin TX 78704. (512)912-7000. Fax: (512)707-1913. E-mail: magazine@tpwd.state.tx.us. Website: www.tpwmagazine.com. Managing Editor: Mary-Love Bigony. **Contact:** Michael Berryhill, editorial director. **80% freelance written.** Monthly magazine featuring articles about Texas hunting, fishing, birding, outdoor recreation, game and nongame wildlife, state parks, environmental issues. All articles must be about Texas. Estab. 1942. Circ. 150,000. **Pays on acceptance.** Publishes ms an average of 6 months after acceptance. Byline given. Kill fee determined by contract, usually $200-250. Buys first rights. Submit seasonal material 6 months in advance. Accepts queries by mail. Responds in 1 month to queries; 3 months to mss. Sample copy online. Writer's guidelines online.

• *Texas Parks & Wildlife* needs more hunting and fishing material.

Nonfiction: General interest (Texas only), how-to (outdoor activities), photo feature, travel (state parks). **Buys 60 mss/year.** Query with published clips. Length: 500-2,500 words.

Photos: Send photos to photo editor. Reviews transparencies. Buys one-time rights. Offers $65-350/photo. Captions, identification of subjects required.

Tips: "Read outdoor pages of statewide newspapers to keep abreast of news items that can lead to story ideas. Feel free to include more than one story idea in one query letter. All areas are open to freelancers. All articles must have a Texas focus."

$ $ WHERE DALLAS MAGAZINE, Abarta Media, 4809 Cole Ave., Suite 165, Dallas TX 75205. (214)522-0050. Fax: (214)522-0504. E-mail: pfelps@abartapub.com. **Contact:** Paula Felps, editor. **75% freelance written.** Monthly magazine. "*WHERE Dallas* is part of the *WHERE Magazine International* network, the world's largest publisher of travel magazines. Published in more than 46 cities around the world, travelers trust *WHERE* to guide them to the best in shopping, dining, nightlife, and entertainment." Estab. 1996. Circ. 45,000. Pays on publication. Publishes ms an average of 2 months after acceptance. Byline given. Buys all rights. Editorial lead time 2 months. Submit seasonal material 2 months in advance. Accepts queries by mail, e-mail. Accepts simultaneous submissions. Sample copy for $3.

Break in with "a solid idea—solid meaning the local Dallas angle is *everything*. We're looking for advice and tips that would/could only come from those living in the area."

Nonfiction: General interest, historical/nostalgic, photo feature, travel, special events. **Buys 20 mss/year.** Query with published clips. Length: 650-1,000 words. **Pays $200-300.** Sometimes pays expenses of writers on assignment.

Photos: Send photos with submission. Reviews transparencies. Buys one time rights, all rights on cover photos. Captions, identification of subjects, model releases required.

Columns/Departments: Pays $100-450.

Tips: "To get our attention, send clips with clever, punchy writing, like you might find in a society or insider column in the newspaper. We're also looking for writers with an expertise in shopping, with knowledge of fashion/art/antiques/collectibles."

Vermont

$ $ VERMONT LIFE MAGAZINE, 6 Baldwin St., Montpelier VT 05602-2109. (802)828-3241. Fax: (802)828-3366. E-mail: tom.slayton@state.vt.us. Website: www.vtlife.com. **Contact:** Thomas K. Slayton, editor-in-chief. **90% freelance written.** Prefers to work with published/established writers. Quarterly magazine. "*Vermont Life* is interested in any article, query, story idea, photograph or photo essay that has to do with Vermont. As the state magazine, we are most favorably impressed with pieces that present positive aspects of life within the state's borders." Estab. 1946. Circ. 80,000. Publishes ms an average of 9 months after acceptance. Byline given. Offers kill fee. Buys first North American serial rights. Submit seasonal material 1 year in advance. Accepts queries by mail, e-mail, fax. Responds in 1 month to queries. Writer's guidelines online.

Break in with "short humorous Vermont anecdotes for our 'Postboy' column."

Nonfiction: Wants articles on today's Vermont, those which portray a typical or, if possible, unique aspect of the state or its people. Style should be literate, clear, and concise. Subtle humor favored. No "Vermont clichés," and please do not send first-person accounts of your vacation trip to Vermont. **Buys 60 mss/year.** Query by letter essential. Length: 1,500 words average. **Pays 25¢/word.**

Photos: Buys photos with mss; buys seasonal photographs alone. Prefers b&w contact sheets to look at first on assigned material. Color submissions must be 4×5 or 35mm transparencies. Gives assignments but only with experienced photographers. Query in writing. Buys one-time rights. Pays $75-200 inside color; $500 for cover. Captions, identification of subjects, model releases required.

The online version contains material not found in the print edition. Contact: Andrew Jackson.

Tips: "Writers who read our magazine are given more consideration because they understand that we want authentic articles about Vermont. If a writer has a genuine working knowledge of Vermont, his or her work usually shows it. Vermont is changing and there is much concern here about what this state will be like in years ahead. It is a beautiful, environmentally sound place now and the vast majority of residents want to keep it so. Articles reflecting such concerns in an intelligent, authoritative, non-hysterical way will be given very careful consideration. The growth of tourism makes us interested in intelligent articles about specific places in Vermont, their history and attractions to the traveling public."

Virginia

N **$ $ VIRGINIA LIVING**, Cape Fear Publishing, 109 E. Cary St., Richmond VA 23219. (804)343-7539. E-mail: gpollard@pilotonline.com. Website: www.virginialiving.com. **Contact:** Garland Pollard, editor. **95% freelance written.**

Bimonthly magazine covering life and lifestyle in Virginia. "We are a large-format (10×13) glossy magazine covering life in Virginia, from food, architecture, and gardening, to issues, profiles, and travel. Estab. 2002. Circ. 50,000. Pays on publication. Publishes ms an average of 4 months after acceptance. Byline given. Offers 50% kill fee. Not copyrighted. Buys first North American serial rights. Editorial lead time 6 months. Submit seasonal material 6 months in advance. Accepts queries by mail. Accepts simultaneous submissions. Responds in 5 weeks to queries; 1 month to mss. Sample copy for $5. Writer's guidelines online.

Nonfiction: Book excerpts, essays, exposé, general interest, historical/nostalgic, interview/profile, new product, personal experience, photo feature, travel. No fiction, poetry, previously published articles, and stories with a firm grasp of the obvious. **Buys 180 mss/year.** Query with published clips or send complete ms. Length: 300-3,000 words. **Pays $60-700.** Sometimes pays expenses of writers on assignment.

Photos: Tyler Darden, art director. Reviews contact sheets, 6×7 transparencies, 8×10 prints, GIF/JPEG files. Buys one-time rights. Negotiates payment individually. Captions, identification of subjects, model releases required.

Columns/Departments: Beauty; Travel; Books; Events; Sports (all with a unique Virginia slant), all 1,000-1,500 words. **Buys 50 mss/year.** Send complete ms. **Pays $120-200.**

Tips: "A freelancer would get the best reception if they send clips via mail before they query. I can then sit down with them and read them. In addition, queries should be about fresh subjects in Virginia. Stories about Williamsburg, Chincoteague ponies, Monticello, the Civil War, and other press release-type stories. We prefer to introduce new subjects, faces, and ideas, and get beyond the many clichés of Virginia. Freelancers would also do well to think about what time of the year they are pitching stories for, as well as art possibilities. We are a large-format magazine close to the size of the old-look magazine, so photography is a key component to our stories."

Washington

$ $ NSPIRIT CULTURAL NEWS MAGAZINE, NW Writers' Corp., P.O. Box 24873, Federal Way WA 98093. Fax: (253)839-3207. E-mail: nwwriterscorp@aol.com. Website: www.nwwriters.com. Managing Editor: Orisade Awodola. **Contact:** Editorial Review Committee. **80% freelance written.** Monthly magazine covering cultural issues. "*NSpirit Cultural NewsMAGAZINE* is a family-oriented, 32-page, color glossy consumer magazine. Its focus is to provide empowering articles, which include women's issues, cultural issues, civil rights and social justice, ethnic issues, psychology, and recovery; essays; literary works; and visual art, for purposes of education and economic development in the King County, Greater Puget Sound, and parts of Pierce County areas." Estab. 1998. Circ. 50,000. Pays on publication. Publishes ms an average of 1 month after acceptance. Byline given. Buys first North American serial rights. Editorial lead time 2 months. Submit seasonal material 3 months in advance. Accepts queries by mail, e-mail, fax. Accepts simultaneous submissions. Responds in 1 month to queries; 2 months to mss. Sample copy for #10 SASE. Writer's guidelines for #10 SASE.

Nonfiction: Della Westerfield, senior editor. Book excerpts, general interest, inspirational, interview/profile, personal experience. Special issues: Christmas/Hanukkah (December); Martin Luther King, Jr. Birthday (January); Festival Sundiata, Giraffe Project (February); Bill & Melinda Gates, Millennium Scholarship Fund (March); Earth Day/Environmental (April); Mother's Day/Mental Health Month (May); Father's Day/Graduations (June); Independence Day/America (July); Salvation Army/US Peace Corps (September); Cancer Awareness Month (October); Thanksgiving (November). No politics, violence, racial/discrimination. **Buys 6-8 mss/year.** Query with published clips. Length: 750 words. **Pays $50-250 for assigned articles.** Sometimes pays expenses of writers on assignment.

Photos: State availability of or send photos with submission. Reviews contact sheets, GIF/JPEG files. Buys one-time rights. Offers no additional payment for photos accepted with ms. Identification of subjects required.

$ $ SEATTLE MAGAZINE, Tiger Oak Publications Inc., 423 Third Ave. W., Seattle WA 98119. (206)284-1750. Fax: (206)284-2550. E-mail: rachel@seattlemag.com. Website: www.seattlemag.com. **Contact:** Rachel Hart, editor. Monthly magazine "serving the Seattle metropolitan area. Articles should be written with our readers in mind. They are interested in social issues, the arts, politics, homes and gardens, travel and maintaining the region's high quality of life." Estab. 1992. Circ. 45,000. Pays on or about 30 days after publication. Publishes ms an average of 3 months after acceptance. Byline given. Offers 25% kill fee. Buys first rights. Editorial lead time 6 months. Submit seasonal material 6 months in advance. Accepts queries by mail, e-mail, fax. Responds in 2 months to queries. Sample copy for #10 SASE. Writer's guidelines online.

Break in by "suggesting short, newsier stories with a strong Seattle focus."

Nonfiction: Book excerpts (local), essays, exposé, general interest, humor, interview/profile, photo feature, travel, local/regional interest. No longer accepting queries by mail. Query with published clips. Length: 100-2,000 words. **Pays $50 minimum.** Sometimes pays expenses of writers on assignment.

Photos: State availability with submission. Buys one-time rights. Negotiates payment individually.

Columns/Departments: Scoop, Urban Safari, Voice, Trips, People, Environment, Hot Button, Fitness, Fashion, Eat and Drink. Query with published clips. **Pays $100-300.**

Tips: "The best queries include some idea of a lead and sources of information, plus compelling reasons why the article belongs specifically in *Seattle Magazine*. In addition, queries should demonstrate the writer's familiarity with the magazine. New writers are often assigned front- or back-of-the-book contents, rather than features. However, the editors do not discourage writers from querying for longer articles and are especially interested in receiving trend pieces, in-depth stories with a news hook and cultural criticism with a local angle."

$ $ $ SEATTLE WEEKLY, Village Voice, 1008 Western Ave., Suite 300, Seattle WA 98104. (206)623-0500. Fax: (206)467-4377. E-mail: editorial@seattleweekly.com. Website: seattleweekly.com. **Contact:** Audrey van Buskirk. **20%**

freelance written. Weekly tabloid covering arts, politics, food, business and books with local and regional emphasis. Estab. 1976. Circ. 105,000. Pays on publication. Publishes ms an average of 1 month after acceptance. Byline given. Offers variable kill fee. Buys first North American serial rights. Submit seasonal material 2 months in advance. Responds in 1 month to queries. Sample copy for $3.

Nonfiction: Book excerpts, exposé, general interest, historical/nostalgic (Northwest), humor, interview/profile, opinion. **Buys 6-8 mss/year.** Query with cover letter, résumé, published clips and SASE. Length: 500-3,000 words. **Pays $50-800.** Sometimes pays expenses of writers on assignment.

Reprints: Send tearsheet. Payment varies.

Tips: "The *Seattle Weekly* publishes stories on Northwest politics and art, usually written by regional and local writers, for a mostly upscale, urban audience; writing is high-quality magazine style."

Wisconsin

$ $ $ MILWAUKEE MAGAZINE, 417 E. Chicago St., Milwaukee WI 53202. (414)273-1101. Fax: (414)273-0016. E-mail: john.fennell@qg.com. Website: www.milwaukeemagazine.com. **Contact:** John Fennell, editor. **40% freelance written.** Monthly magazine. "We publish stories about Milwaukee, of service to Milwaukee-area residents and exploring the area's changing lifestyle, business, arts, politics, and dining." Circ. 40,000. Pays on publication. Publishes ms an average of 2 months after acceptance. Byline given. Offers 20% kill fee. Buys first rights. Submit seasonal material 6 months in advance. Accepts queries by mail, e-mail. Responds in 6 weeks to queries. Sample copy for $4.

Nonfiction: Essays, exposé, general interest, historical/nostalgic, interview/profile, photo feature, travel, food and dining, and other services. "No articles without a strong Milwaukee or Wisconsin angle." Length: 2,500-6,000 words for full-length features; 800 words for 2-page "breaker" features (short on copy, long on visuals). **Buys 30-50 mss/year.** Query with published clips. **Pays $400-1,000 for full-length, $150-400 for breaker.** Sometimes pays expenses of writers on assignment.

Columns/Departments: Insider (inside information on Milwaukee, exposé, slice-of-life, unconventional angles on current scene), up to 500 words; Mini Reviews for Insider, 125 words. Query with published clips.

Tips: "Pitch something for the Insider, or suggest a compelling profile we haven't already done. Submit clips that prove you can do the job. The department most open is Insider. Think short, lively, offbeat, fresh, people-oriented. We are actively seeking freelance writers who can deliver lively, readable copy that helps our readers make the most out of the Milwaukee area. Because we're only human, we'd like writers who can deliver copy on deadline that fits the specifications of our assignment. If you fit this description, we'd love to work with you."

$ $ WISCONSIN TRAILS, P.O. Box 317, Black Earth WI 53515-0317. (608)767-8000. Fax: (608)767-5444. E-mail: lkearney@wistrails.com. Website: www.wistrails.com. **Contact:** Laura Kearney, assistant editor. **40% freelance written.** Bimonthly magazine for readers interested in Wisconsin and its contemporary issues, personalities, recreation, history, natural beauty, and arts. Estab. 1960. Circ. 55,000. Pays 1 month from publication. Publishes ms an average of 6 months after acceptance. Byline given. Buys first North American serial, one-time rights. Submit seasonal material 1 year in advance. Accepts queries by mail, e-mail, fax. Responds in 4 months to queries. Sample copy for $4.95. Writer's guidelines for #10 SASE.

O-- "We're looking for active articles about people, places, events, and outdoor adventures in Wisconsin. We want to publish 1 in-depth article of statewide interest or concern/issue, and several short (600-1,500 words) articles about short trips, recreational opportunities, personalities, restaurants, inns, history, and cultural activities. We're looking for more articles about out-of-the-way Wisconsin places that are exceptional in some way and engaging pieces on Wisconsin's little-known and unique aspects."

Nonfiction: "Our articles focus on some aspect of Wisconsin life: an interesting town or event, a person or industry, history or the arts, and especially outdoor recreation. We do not use first-person essays or biographies about people who were born in Wisconsin but made their fortunes elsewhere. No poetry or fiction. No articles that are too local for our regional audience, or articles about obvious places to visit in Wisconsin. We need more articles about the new and little-known." **Buys 3 unsolicited mss/year.** Query or send outline. Length: 1,000-3,000 words. **Pays 25¢/word for assigned articles.** Sometimes pays expenses of writers on assignment.

Photos: Photographs purchased with or without mss, or on assignment. Color photos usually illustrate an activity, event, region, or striking scenery. Prefer photos with people in scenery. Reviews 35mm or larger transparencies. Pays $65-125 for inside color; $250 for covers. Captions, labels with photographer's name required.

Tips: "When querying, submit well-thought-out ideas about stories specific to people, places, events, arts, outdoor adventures, etc., in Wisconsin. Include published clips with queries. Do some research—many queries we receive are pitching ideas for stories we recently have published. Know the tone, content, and audience of the magazine. Refer to our writer's guidelines, or request them, if necessary."

Wyoming

$ WYOMING RURAL ELECTRIC NEWS (WREN), 340 W. B St., Suite 101, Casper WY 82601. (307)682-7527. Fax: (307)682-7528. E-mail: wren@coffey.com. **Contact:** Kris Wendtland, editor. **20% freelance written.** Monthly magazine for audience of small town residents, vacation-home owners, farmers, and ranchers. Estab. 1955. Circ. 35,000. Pays on publication. Publishes ms an average of 1 month after acceptance. Byline given. Buys one-time rights. Submit seasonal material 2 months in advance. Accepts queries by mail, e-mail, fax, phone. Responds in 3 months to queries. Sample copy for $2.50 and 9×12 SASE. Writer's guidelines for #10 SASE.

O→ "You have just learned something. It is so amazing you just have to find out more. You call around. You search on the Web. You go to the library. Everything you learn about it makes you want to know more. In a matter of days, all your friends are aware that you are into something. You don't stop talking about it. You're totally confident that they find it interesting too. Now, write it down and send it to us. We are excited just wondering what you find so amazing! Come on, tell us! Tell us!"

Nonfiction: "We print science, ag, how-to, and human interest but not fiction. Topics of interest in general include: hunting, cooking, gardening, commodities, sugar beets, wheat, oil, coal, hard rock mining, beef cattle, electric technologies such as lawn mowers, car heaters, air cleaners and assorted gadgets, surge protectors, pesticators, etc." Wants science articles with question/answer quiz at end—test your knowledge. Buys electrical appliance articles. Articles welcome that put present and/or future in positive light. No nostalgia. No sad stories. **Buys 4-10 mss/year.** Send complete ms. Length: 500-800 words. **Pays up to $140, plus 4 copies.**

Reprints: Send tearsheet or photocopy and information about when and where the material previously appeared.

Photos: Color only.

Tips: "Always looking for fresh, new writers, original perspectives. Submit entire manuscript. Don't submit a regionally set story from some other part of the country. Photos and illustrations (if appropriate) are always welcomed. We don't care if you misspell words. We don't care if your grammar is poor. We want factual articles that are blunt, to the point, accurate."

Canadian/International

$ $ ABACO LIFE, Caribe Communications, P.O. Box 37487, Raleigh NC 27627. (919)859-6782. Fax: (919)859-6769. E-mail: jimkerr@mindspring.com. Website: www.abacolife.com. Managing Editor: Cathy Kerr. **Contact:** Jim Kerr, editor/publisher. **50% freelance written.** Quarterly magazine covering Abaco, an island group in the Northeast Bahamas. "*Abaco Life* editorial focuses entirely on activities, history, wildlife, resorts, people and other subjects pertaining to the Abacos. Readers include locals, vacationers, second-home owners, and other visitors whose interests range from real estate and resorts to scuba, sailing, fishing, and beaches. The tone is upbeat, adventurous, humorous. No fluff writing for an audience already familiar with the area." Estab. 1979. Circ. 10,000. Pays on publication. Publishes ms an average of 2 months after acceptance. Byline given. Offers 40% kill fee. Buys one-time rights. Editorial lead time 2 months. Submit seasonal material 4 months in advance. Accepts queries by mail, e-mail. Accepts simultaneous submissions. Responds in 2 weeks to queries; 2 months to mss. Sample copy for $2. Writer's guidelines free.

Nonfiction: General interest, historical/nostalgic, how-to, interview/profile, personal experience, photo feature, travel. "No general first-time impressions. Articles must be specific, show knowledge and research of the subject and area—'Abaco's Sponge Industry'; 'Diving Abaco's Wrecks'; 'The Hurricane of '36.'" **Buys 8-10 mss/year.** Query or send complete ms. Length: 400-2,000 words. **Pays $150-350.**

Photos: State availability of or send photos with submission. Reviews transparencies, prints. Buys one-time rights. Offers $25-100/photo. Negotiates payment individually. Captions, identification of subjects, model releases required.

▣ The online magazine carries original content not found in the print edition. Contact: Jim Kerr, online editor.

Tips: "Travel writers must look deeper than a usual destination piece, and the only real way to do that is spend time in Abaco. Beyond good writing, which is a must, we like submissions on Microsoft Word or Works, but that's optional. Color slides are also preferred over prints, and good ones go a long way in selling the story. Read the magazine to learn its style."

$ $ $ $ ✚ ALBERTAVIEWS, The Magazine About Alberta for Albertans, Local Perspectives Publishing, Inc., Suite 208-320 23rd Ave. SW, Calgary AB T2S 0J2, Canada. (403)243-5334. Fax: (403)243-8599. E-mail: editor@albertaviews.ab.ca. Website: www.albertaviews.ab.ca. Publisher/Editor: Jackie Flanagan. **Contact:** Michael Hall, assistant editor. **50% freelance written.** Bimonthly magazine covering Alberta culture: politics, economy, social issues, and art. "We are a regional magazine providing thoughtful commentary and background information on issues of concern to Albertans. Most of our writers are Albertans." Estab. 1997. Circ. 30,000. Pays on publication. Publishes ms an average of 3 months after acceptance. Byline given. Offers 50% kill fee. Buys first North American serial, electronic rights. Editorial lead time 3 months. Submit seasonal material 3 months in advance. Accepts queries by e-mail. Responds in 6 weeks to queries; 2 months to mss. Sample copy for free. Writer's guidelines online.

Nonfiction: Does not want anything not directly related to Alberta. Essays. **Buys 18 mss/year.** Query with published clips. Length: 3,000-5,000 words. **Pays $1,000-1,500 for assigned articles; $350-750 for unsolicited articles.** Sometimes pays expenses of writers on assignment.

Photos: State availability with submission. Buys one-time rights, Web rights. Negotiates payment individually.

Fiction: Only fiction by Alberta writers. **Buys 6 mss/year.** Send complete ms. Length: 2,500-4,000 words. **Pays $1,000 maximum.**

$ $ $ ✚ THE BEAVER, Canada's History Magazine, Canada's National History Society, 478-167 Lombard Ave., Winnipeg MB R3B 0T6, Canada. (204)988-9300. Fax: (204)988-9309. E-mail: cnhs@historysociety.ca. Website: www.historysociety.ca. Associate Editor: Doug Whiteway. **Contact:** Annalee Greenberg, editor. **65% freelance written.** Bimonthly magazine covering Canadian history. Estab. 1920. Circ. 41,000. **Pays on acceptance.** Byline given. Offers $200 kill fee. Buys first North American serial, electronic rights. Editorial lead time 4 months. Submit seasonal material 8 months in advance. Accepts queries by mail. Accepts simultaneous submissions. Responds in 6 weeks to queries; 2 months to mss. Sample copy for 9×12 SAE and 2 first-class stamps. Writer's guidelines online.

O-π Break in with a "new interpretation based on solid new research; entertaining magazine style."
Nonfiction: Photo feature (historical), historical (Canadian focus). Does not want anything unrelated to Canadian history. **Buys 30 mss/year.** Query with published clips. Length: 600-3,500 words. **Pays $400-1,000 for assigned articles; $300-600 for unsolicited articles.** Sometimes pays expenses of writers on assignment.
Photos: State availability with submission. Buys one-time rights. Offers no additional payment for photos accepted with ms. Identification of subjects, model releases required.
Columns/Departments: Book and other media reviews and Canadian history subjects, 600 words ("These are assigned to freelancers with particular areas of expertise, i.e., women's history, labour history, French regime, etc."). **Buys 15 mss/year. Pays $125.**
Tips: "*The Beaver* is directed toward a general audience of educated readers, as well as to historians and scholars. We are in the market for lively, well-written, well-researched, and informative articles about Canadian history that focus on all parts of the country and all areas of human activity. Subject matter covers the whole range of Canadian history, with particular emphasis on social history, politics, exploration, discovery and settlement, aboriginal peoples, business and trade, war, culture and sport. Articles are obtained through direct commission and by submission. Queries should be accompanied by a stamped, self-addressed envelope. *The Beaver* publishes articles of various lengths, including long features (from 1,500-3,500 words) that provide an in-depth look at an event, person or era; short, more narrowly focused features (from 600-1,500 words). Longer articles may be considered if their importance warrants publication. Articles should be written in an expository or interpretive style and present the principal themes of Canadian history in an original, interesting and informative way."

$ BRAZZIL, Brazzil, P.O. Box 50536, Los Angeles CA 90050. (323)255-8062. Fax: (323)257-3487. E-mail: brazzil@brazzil.com. Website: www.brazzil.com. **Contact:** Rodney Mello, editor. **60% freelance written.** Monthly magazine covering Brazilian culture. Estab. 1989. Circ. 12,000. Pays on publication. Publishes ms an average of 2 months after acceptance. Byline given. Offers 10% kill fee. Buys one-time rights. Editorial lead time 2 months. Submit seasonal material 2 months in advance. Accepts queries by mail, e-mail, fax, phone. Accepts simultaneous submissions. Responds in 2 weeks to queries. Sample copy free or online. Writer's guidelines online.
Nonfiction: "All subjects have to deal in some way with Brazil and its culture. We assume our readers know very little or nothing about Brazil, so we explain everything." Book excerpts, essays, exposé, general interest, historical/nostalgic, humor, interview/profile, opinion, personal experience, travel. **Buys 15 mss/year.** Query. Length: 800-5,000 words. **Pays $20-50.** Pays writers with contributor copies or other premiums by mutual agreement.
Photos: State availability with submission. Reviews prints. Buys one-time rights. Offers no additional payment for photos accepted with ms. Identification of subjects required.
The online version of *Brazzil* contains content not included in the print edition. Contact: Rodney Mello, online editor.
Tips: "We are interested in anything related to Brazil: politics, economy, music, behavior, profiles. Please document material with interviews and statistical data if applicable. Controversial pieces are welcome."

$ $ $ CANADIAN GEOGRAPHIC, 39 McArthur Ave., Ottawa ON K1L 8L7, Canada. (613)745-4629. Fax: (613)744-0947. E-mail: editorial@canadiangeographic.ca. Website: www.canadiangeographic.ca. **Contact:** Rick Boychuk, editor. **90% freelance written.** Works with a small number of new/unpublished writers each year. Bimonthly magazine. "*Canadian Geographic*'s colorful portraits of our ever-changing population show readers just how important the relationship between the people and the land really is." Estab. 1930. Circ. 240,000. **Pays on acceptance.** Publishes ms an average of 3 months after acceptance. Buys first Canadian rights. Accepts queries by mail, e-mail, fax. Responds in 1 month to queries. Sample copy for $5.95 (Canadian) and 9×12 SAE or online.
• *Canadian Geographic* reports a need for more articles on earth sciences. Canadian writers only.
Nonfiction: Buys authoritative geographical articles, in the broad geographical sense, written for the average person, not for a scientific audience. Predominantly Canadian subjects by Canadian authors. **Buys 30-45 mss/year.** Query. Length: 1,500-3,000 words. **Pays 80¢/word minimum.** Sometimes pays expenses of writers on assignment.
Photos: Pays $75-400 for color photos, depending on published size.

$ $ OUTDOOR CANADA MAGAZINE, 340 Ferrier St., Suite 210, Markham ON L3R 2Z5, Canada. (905)475-8440. Fax: (905)475-9246. E-mail: editorial@outdoorcanada.ca. Website: www.outdoorcanada.ca. **Contact:** Patrick Walsh, editor-in-chief. **90% freelance written.** Works with a small number of new/unpublished writers each year. Magazine published 8 times/year emphasizing hunting, fishing, and related pursuits in Canada *only*. Estab. 1972. Circ. 80,000. Pays on publication. Publishes ms an average of 8 months after acceptance. Byline given. Buys first rights. Submit seasonal material 1 year in advance. Accepts queries by mail, e-mail. Responds in 1 month to queries. Writer's guidelines online.
Nonfiction: How-to, fishing, hunting, outdoor issues, outdoor destinations in Canada. **Buys 35-40 mss/year.** Query. Length: 2,500 words. **Pays $500 and up for assigned articles.**
Reprints: Send information about when and where the article previously appeared. Payment varies.
Photos: Emphasize people in the Canadian outdoors. Pays $100-250 for 35mm transparencies and $400/cover. Captions, model releases required.
Fillers: Short news pieces. **Buys 30-40/year.** Length: 100-500 words. **Pays $50 and up.**
The online magazine carries original content not found in the print edition. Contact: Aaron Kylie, online editor.

$ $ $ $ TORONTO LIFE, 59 Front St. E., Toronto ON M5E 1B3, Canada. (416)364-3333. Fax: (416)955-4982. E-mail: editorial@torontolife.com. Website: www.torontolife.com. **Contact:** John Macfarlane, editor. **95% freelance written.** Prefers to work with published/established writers. Monthly magazine emphasizing local issues and social trends, short humor/satire, and service features for upper income, well-educated and, for the most part, young Torontonians. Circ. 92,574. **Pays on acceptance.** Publishes ms an average of 4 months after acceptance. Byline given. Pays 50% kill fee for commissioned articles only. Buys first North American serial rights. Responds in 3 weeks to queries. Sample copy for $4.50 with SAE and IRCs.

Nonfiction: Uses most types of articles. **Buys 17 mss/issue**. Query with published clips and SASE. Length: 1,000-6,000 words. **Pays $500-5,000.**

Columns/Departments: "We run about 5 columns an issue. They are all freelanced, though most are from regular contributors. They are mostly local in concern and cover politics, business, performing arts, media, design, and food." Length: 2,000 words. Query with published clips and SASE. **Pays $2,000.**

Tips: "Submissions should have strong Toronto orientation."

$ UP HERE, Explore Canada's Far North, OUTCROP: The Northern Publishers, P.O. Box 1350, Yellowknife NT X1A 2N9, Canada. (867)920-4367. Fax: (867)873-2844. E-mail: cooper@uphere.ca. Website: www.uphere.ca. **Contact:** Cooper Langford, editor. **50% freelance written.** Magazine published 8 times/year covering general interest about Canada's Far North. "We publish features, columns, and shorts about people, wildlife, native cultures, travel, and adventure in Yukon, Northwest Territories, and Nunavut. Be informative, but entertaining." Estab. 1984. Circ. 35,000. Pays on publication. Byline given. Offers 50% kill fee. Buys first North American serial rights. Editorial lead time 6 months. Accepts queries by mail, e-mail, fax. Sample copy for $3.50 (Canadian) and 9×12 SASE with $1.45 Canadian postage.

Break in with "precise queries with well-developed focuses for the proposed story."

Nonfiction: Essays, general interest, how-to, humor, interview/profile, new product, personal experience, photo feature, technical, travel, lifestyle/culture, historical. **Buys 25-30 mss/year.** Query. Length: 1,500-3,000 words. **Fees are negotiable.**

Photos: "*Please* do not send unsolicited original photos, slides." Send photos with submission. Reviews transparencies, prints. Buys one-time rights. Captions, identification of subjects required.

Columns/Departments: Write for updated guidelines, visit website, or e-mail. **Buys 25-30 mss/year.** Query with published clips.

The online magazine carries original content not found in the print edition. Contact: Cooper Langford or Mifi Purvis, online editors.

Tips: "We like well-researched, concrete adventure pieces, insights about Northern people and lifestyles, readable natural history. Features are most open to freelancers—travel, adventure, and so on. We don't want a comprehensive 'How I spent my summer vacation' hour-by-hour account. We want stories with angles, articles that look at the North through a different set of glasses. Photos are important; you greatly increase your chances with top-notch images."

$ $ $ VANCOUVER MAGAZINE, Transcontinental Publications, Inc., Suite 500, 2608 Granville St., Vancouver BC V6H 3V3, Canada. (604)877-7732. Fax: (604)877-4823. E-mail: mmallan@vancouvermagazine.com. Website: www.vancouvermagazine.com. **Contact:** Matthew Mallon, editor. **70% freelance written.** Monthly magazine covering the city of Vancouver. Estab. 1967. Circ. 65,000. **Pays on acceptance.** Byline given. Offers negotiable kill fee. Buys first North American serial rights. Editorial lead time 2 months. Submit seasonal material 6 months in advance. Accepts queries by mail, e-mail, fax, phone. Accepts simultaneous submissions. Responds in 2 weeks to queries; 1 month to mss. Sample copy for $5. Writer's guidelines for #10 SASE or by e-mail.

Nonfiction: "We prefer to work with writers from a conceptual stage and have a 6-week lead time. Most stories are under 1,500 words. Please be aware that we don't publish poetry and rarely publish fiction." Book excerpts, essays, historical/nostalgic, humor, interview/profile, new product, personal experience, photo feature, travel. **Buys 200 mss/year.** Query. Length: 200-3,000 words. **Pays 50¢/word.** Sometimes pays expenses of writers on assignment.

Photos: State availability with submission. Reviews contact sheets, negatives, transparencies, prints, GIF/JPEG files. Buys negotiable rights. Negotiates payment individually. Captions, identification of subjects, model releases required.

Columns/Departments: Sport; Media; Business; City Issues, all 1,500 words. Query. **Pays 50¢/word.**

Tips: "Read back issues of the magazine, or visit our website. Almost all of our stories have a strong Vancouver angle. Submit queries by e-mail. Do not send complete stories."

$ $ $ $ WESTWORLD MAGAZINE, Canada Wide Magazines and Communications, 4180 Lougheed Hwy., 4th Floor, Burnaby BC V5C 6A7, Canada. Fax: (604)299-9188. E-mail: arose@canadawide.com. **Contact:** Anne Rose, editor. **80% freelance written.** Quarterly magazine distributed to members of B.C. Automobile Association, with a focus on local (British Columbia), regional, and international travel. Estab. 1983. Circ. 500,000. Pays on acceptance and publication. Byline given. Offers 50% kill fee. Buys first North American serial, second serial (reprint) rights. Editorial lead time at least 6 months. Submit seasonal material 1 year in advance. Accepts simultaneous submissions. Writer's guidelines currently under revision.

- Editorial lineup for following year determined in June; queries held for consideration at that time. No phone calls.

Nonfiction: Travel (domestic and international). "No purple prose." Query with published clips and lead paragraph of proposed article. Length: 1,500-2,000 words (features). **Pays 50¢-$1/word.**

Reprints: Send photocopy and information about when and where the material previously appeared. Pays approximately 50% of amount paid for an original article.

Photos: State availability of photos with submission, do not send photos until requested. Buys one-time rights. Offers writers $35-75/photo. Captions, identification of subjects, model releases required.

Columns/Departments: Query with published clips and sample lead paragraph of proposed article. **Pays 50-80¢/word.**

Tips: "Please don't send gushy, travelogue articles filled with glowing adjectives about pristine lakes and snowtipped mountains. We prefer experiential, fact-filled travel stories (emphasis on story) and adventures from professional writers that are a good read, as well as informative and extremely well researched with practical tips and sidebars. Approach an old topic/destination in a fresh/original way."

RELATIONSHIPS

These publications focus on lifestyles and relationships of single adults. Other markets for this type of material can be found in the Women's category. Magazines of a primarily sexual nature, gay or straight, are listed under the Sex category. The Gay & Lesbian Interest section contains general interest editorial targeted to that audience.

$ $ MARRIAGE PARTNERSHIP, Christianity Today International, 465 Gundersen Dr., Carol Stream IL 60188. Fax: (630)260-0114. E-mail: mp@marriagepartnership.com. Website: www.marriagepartnership.com. Executive Editor: Marshall Shelley. Managing Editor: Ginger E. Kolbaba. **Contact:** Raelynn Eickhoff, editorial coordinator. **50% freelance written.** Quarterly magazine covering Christian marriages. "Our readers are married Christians. Writers must understand our readers." Estab. 1988. Circ. 55,000. **Pays on acceptance.** Publishes ms an average of 9 months after acceptance. Byline given. Offers 50% kill fee. Buys first North American serial rights. Editorial lead time 6 months. Submit seasonal material 1 year in advance. Accepts queries by mail, e-mail, fax. Responds in 10 weeks to queries; 2 months to mss. Sample copy for $5 or online. Writer's guidelines online.

Nonfiction: Book excerpts, essays, how-to, humor, inspirational, interview/profile, opinion, personal experience, religious. **Buys 20 mss/year.** Query with or without published clips. Length: 1,200-2,300 words. **Pays 15-30¢/word for assigned articles; 15¢/word for unsolicited articles.**

Columns/Departments: Starting Out (opinion by/for newlyweds), 1,000 words; Soul to Soul (inspirational), 1,500 words; Work It Out (problem-solving), 1,000 words; Back from the Bruik (marriage in recovery), 1,800 words. **Buys 10 mss/year.** Query with or without published clips. **Pays 15-30¢/word.**

Tips: "Think of topics with a fresh slant. Be ever mindful of our readers. Writers who can communicate with freshness, clarity, and insight will receive serious consideration. We are looking for writers who are willing to candidly speak about their own marriages. We strongly urge writers who are interested in contributing to *Marriage Partnership* to read several issues to become thoroughly acquainted with our tone and slant."

RELIGIOUS

Religious magazines focus on a variety of subjects, styles, and beliefs. Most are sectarian, but a number approach topics such as public policy, international affairs, and contemporary society from a nondenominational perspective. Fewer religious publications are considering poems and personal experience articles, but many emphasize special ministries to singles, seniors, or other special interest groups. Such diversity makes reading each magazine essential for the writer hoping to break in. Educational and inspirational material of interest to church members, workers and leaders within a denomination or religion is needed by the publications in this category. Religious magazines for children and teenagers can be found in the Juvenile and Teen & Young Adult sections. Other religious publications can be found in the Contemporary Culture and Ethnic/Minority sections as well. Spiritual topics are also addressed in the Astrology, Metaphysical & New Age section as well as in the Health & Fitness section. Publications intended to assist professional religious workers in teaching and managing church affairs are classified in Church Administration & Ministry in the Trade section.

$ ALIVE NOW, 1908 Grand Ave., P.O. Box 340004, Nashville TN 37203-0004. E-mail: alivenow@upperroom.org. Website: www.alivenow.org. **Contact:** Melissa Tidwell. Bimonthly thematic magazine for a general Christian audience interested in reflection and meditation. Circ. 70,000. Writer's guidelines online.

Poetry: Avant-garde, free verse. Length: 10-45 lines.

$ $ AMERICA, 106 W. 56th St., New York NY 10019. (212)581-4640. Fax: (212)399-3596. E-mail: articles@americamagazine.org. Website: www.americamagazine.org. **Contact:** The Rev. Thomas J. Reese, editor. Published weekly for adult, educated, largely Roman Catholic audience. Estab. 1909. **Pays on acceptance.** Byline given. Buys all rights. Responds in 3 weeks to queries. Writer's guidelines online.

Nonfiction: "We publish a wide variety of material on religion, politics, economics, ecology, and so forth. We are not a parochial publication, but almost all pieces make some moral or religious point." Articles on theology, spirituality, current political, social issues. "We are not interested in purely informational pieces or personal narratives which are self-contained and have no larger moral interest." Length: 1,500-2,000 words. **Pays $50-300.**

Poetry: Only 10-12 poems published a year, thousands turned down. Paul Mariani, poetry editor. **Buys 10-12 poems/year.** Length: 15-30 lines.

$ THE ANNALS OF SAINT ANNE DE BEAUPRÉ, Redemptorist Fathers, P.O. Box 1000, St. Anne De Beaupré QC G0A 3C0, Canada. (418)827-4538. Fax: (418)827-4530. Editor: Father Bernard Mercier, CSs.R. **Contact:** Father Roch

Achard, managing editor. **20% freelance written.** Monthly religious magazine. "Our mission statement includes dedication to Christian family values and devotion to St. Anne." Estab. 1885. Circ. 32,000. **Pays on acceptance.** Buys first North American serial, first, please state "rights" for sale rights. Editorial lead time 6 months. Submit seasonal material 6 months in advance. Responds in 1 month to queries. Sample copy and writer's guidelines for 8½×11 SAE and IRCs.

Nonfiction: Inspirational, religious. **Buys 150 mss/year.** Send complete ms. Length: 500-1,500 words. **Pays 3-4¢/word, plus 3 copies.**

Fiction: Religious, inspirational. "No senseless, mockery." **Buys 100 mss/year.** Send complete ms. Length: 500-1,500 words. **Pays 3-4¢/word.**

Tips: "Write something inspirational with spiritual thrust. Reporting rather than analysis is simply not remarkable. Each article must have a spiritual theme. Please only submit first North American rights manuscripts with the rights clearly stated. We maintain an article bank and pick from it for each month's needs which loosely follows the religious themes for each month. Right now, our needs lean toward nonfiction of approximately 1,100 words."

$ THE ASSOCIATE REFORMED PRESBYTERIAN, Associate Reformed Presbyterian General Synod, 1 Cleveland St., Suite 110, Greenville SC 29601-3696. (864)232-8297, ext. 237. Fax: (864)271-3729. E-mail: arpmaged@arpsynod.org. Website: www.arpsynod.org. **Contact:** Ben Johnston, editor. **5% freelance written.** Works with a small number of new/unpublished writers each year. Monthly Christian magazine serving a conservative, evangelical, and Reformed denomination. "We are the official magazine of our denomination. Articles generally relate to activities within the denomination - conferences, department work, etc., with a few special articles that would be of general interest to readers." Estab. 1976. Circ. 6,000. **Pays on acceptance.** Publishes ms an average of 4 months after acceptance. Byline given. Not copyrighted. Buys first, one-time, second serial (reprint) rights. Submit seasonal material 4 months in advance. Accepts queries by mail, e-mail, fax. Accepts simultaneous submissions. Responds in 1 month to queries. Sample copy for $1.50. Writer's guidelines for #10 SASE.

Nonfiction: Book excerpts, essays, inspirational, opinion, personal experience, religious. **Buys 10-15 mss/year.** Query. Length: 400-2,000 words. **Pays $25-75.**

Reprints: Send information about when and where the article previously appeared. Pays 100% of amount paid for an original article.

Photos: State availability with submission. Buys one-time rights. Offers $25 maximum/photo. Captions, identification of subjects required.

Fiction: "Currently overstocked." Religious, children's. "Stories should portray Christian values. No retelling of Bible stories or 'talking animal' stories. Stories for youth should deal with resolving real issues for young people." Length: 300-750 words (children); 1,250 maximum (youth). **Pays $50 maximum.**

Tips: "Feature articles are the area of our publication most open to freelancers. Focus on a contemporary problem and offer Bible-based solutions to it. Provide information that would help a Christian struggling in his daily walk. Writers should understand that we are denominational, conservative, evangelical, Reformed, and Presbyterian. A writer who appreciates these nuances would stand a much better chance of being published here than one who does not."

N $ $ BEACON, EFCA Today, Evangelical Free Church of America, 418 Fourth St., NE, Charlottesville VA 22902. Fax: (434)961-2507. E-mail: dianemc@journeygroup.com. Website: www.efca.org/beacon/beacon.html. **Contact:** Diane McDougall, editor. **1% freelance written.** Bimonthly magazine. "*Beacon* informs readers of the vision and activities of the Evangelical Free Church of America. Its readers are EFCA leaders—pastors, elders, deacons, Sunday-school teachers, ministry volunteers." Circ. 35,000. **Pays on acceptance.** Publishes ms an average of 3 months after acceptance. Byline given. Offers 50% kill fee. Buys first North American serial, electronic, efca-related church use (if free) rights. Editorial lead time 6 months. Submit seasonal material 6-8 months in advance. Accepts queries by mail, e-mail, fax. Accepts previously published material. Accepts simultaneous submissions. Sample copy for $1 with SAE and 5 first-class stamps. Writer's guidelines free.

Nonfiction: How-to, inspirational, religious. No poetry or pieces longer than 1,000 words. **Buys 12-18 mss/year.** Query with published clips. Length: 550-1,000 words. **Pays $126.50-260.** Sometimes pays expenses of writers on assignment.

Photos: State availability with submission. Offers no additional payment for photos accepted with ms. Captions, identification of subjects required.

Tips: "Be familiar with the Evangelical Free Church of America—its vision and mission—and then look for local church stories that highlight that vision/mission. Keep in mind that *Beacon* is geared to church leaders rather than everyone in the pews."

$ $ BEC-WORLD, (formerly *The Standard*), Baptist General Conference, 2002 S. Arlington Heights Rd., Arlington Heights IL 60005. Fax: (847)228-5376. E-mail: bputman@baptistgeneral.org. Website: www.bgcworld.org. **Contact:** Bob Putman, editor. **35% freelance written.** Nonprofit, religious, evangelical Christian magazine published 10 times/year covering the Baptist General Conference. "*BEC-WORLD* is the official magazine of the Baptist General Conference (BGC). Articles related to the BGC, our churches, or by/about BGC people receive preference." Circ. 20,000. Pays on publication. Byline given. Offers 50% kill fee. Buys first rights. Editorial lead time 6 months. Submit seasonal material 6 months in advance. Accepts queries by e-mail. Responds in 1 month to queries; 2 months to mss. Sample copy for #10 SASE. Writer's guidelines free.

Nonfiction: General interest, how-to, inspirational, photo feature, religious, profile, infographics, sidebars related to theme. No sappy religious pieces, articles not intended for our audience. Ask for a sample instead of sending anything first. **Buys 20-30 mss/year.** Query with published clips. Length: 300-1,200 words. **Pays $60-280.** Sometimes pays expenses of writers on assignment.

Photos: State availability with submission. Reviews prints, some high-resolution digital. Buys one-time rights. Offers $15/photo. Captions, identification of subjects, model releases required.
Columns/Departments: Around the BGC (blurbs of news happening in the BGC), 50-150 words. Send complete ms. **Pays $15-20.**
Tips: "Please study the magazine and the denomination. We will send sample copies to interested freelancers and give further information about our publication needs upon request. Freelancers who are interested in working an assignment are welcome to express their interest."

$ BIBLE ADVOCATE, Bible Advocate Press, Church of God (Seventh Day), P.O. Box 33677, Denver CO 80233. (303)452-7973. E-mail: bibleadvocate@cog7.org/ba/. Website: www.cog7.org/ba/. Editor: Calvin Burrell. **Contact:** Sherri Langton, associate editor. **25% freelance written.** Religious magazine published 10 times/year. "Our purpose is to advocate the Bible and represent the Church of God (Seventh Day) to a Christian audience." Estab. 1863. Circ. 13,500. Pays on publication. Publishes ms an average of 9 months after acceptance. Byline given. Offers 50% kill fee. Buys first, second serial (reprint), electronic rights. Editorial lead time 3 months. Submit seasonal material 6 months in advance. Accepts queries by mail, e-mail. Accepts simultaneous submissions. Responds in 2 months to queries. Sample copy for 9×12 SAE and 3 first-class stamps. Writer's guidelines online.
Nonfiction: Inspirational, opinion, personal experience, religious, Biblical studies. No articles on Christmas or Easter. **Buys 20-25 mss/year.** Send complete ms and SASE. Length: 1,500 words. **Pays $25-55.**
Reprints: Send ms with rights for sale noted.
Photos: Send photos with submission. Reviews prints. Offers payment for photos accepted with ms. Identification of subjects required.
Columns/Departments: Viewpoint (opinion), 600-700 words. **Buys 3 mss/year.** Send complete ms and SASE. **No payment for opinion pieces.**
Poetry: Free verse, traditional. No avant-garde. **Buys 10-12 poems/year.** Submit maximum 5 poems. Length: 5-20 lines. **Pays $20.**
Fillers: Anecdotes, facts. **Buys 5/year.** Length: 50-400 words. **Pays $10-20.**
Tips: "Be fresh, not preachy! We're trying to reach a younger audience now, so think how you can cover contemporary and biblical topics with this audience in mind. Articles must be in keeping with the doctrinal understanding of the Church of God (Seventh Day). Therefore, the writer should become familiar with what the Church generally accepts as truth as set forth in its doctrinal beliefs. We reserve the right to edit manuscripts to fit our space requirements, doctrinal stands and church terminology. Significant changes are referred to writers for approval. No fax or handwritten submissions, please."

N $ $ CATHOLIC DIGEST, 185 Willow St., P.O. Box 6001, Mystic CT 06355. (860)536-2611. Fax: (860)536-5600. E-mail: cdsubmissions@bayardpubs.com. Website: www.CatholicDigest.org. Editor: Richard J. Reece. **Contact:** Articles Editor. **15% freelance written.** Monthly magazine. "Publishes features and advice on topics ranging from health, psychology, humor, adventure, and family, to ethics, spirituality, and Catholics, from modern-day heroes to saints through the ages. Helpful and relevant reading culled from secular and religious periodicals." Estab. 1936. Circ. 509,385. Pays on acceptance for articles. Publishes ms an average of 4 months after acceptance. Byline given. Buys first, one-time, second serial (reprint) rights. Editorial lead time 4 months. Submit seasonal material 5 months in advance. Accepts queries by mail, e-mail, fax. Responds in 2 months to mss. Sample copy free. Writer's guidelines online.
Nonfiction: "Most articles we use are reprinted." Book excerpts, essays, general interest, historical/nostalgic, how-to, humor, inspirational, interview/profile, personal experience, religious, travel. **Buys 60 mss/year.** Send complete ms. Length: 1,000-3,000 words. **Pays $200-400.**
Reprints: Send tearsheet or typed ms with rights for sale noted and information about when and where the material previously appeared. Pays $100.
Photos: State availability with submission. Reviews contact sheets, transparencies, prints. Negotiates payment individually. Captions, identification of subjects, model releases required.
Columns/Departments: Buys 75 mss/year. Send complete ms. **Pays $4-50.**
Fillers: Filler Editor. Open Door (statements of true incidents through which people are brought into the Catholic faith, or recover the Catholic faith they had lost), 200-500 words; People Are Like That (original accounts of true incidents that illustrate the instinctive goodness of human nature), 200-500 words; Perfect Assist (original accounts of gracious or tactful remarks or actions), 200-500 words; also publishes jokes, short anecdotes, quizzes, and informational paragraphs. **Buys 200/year.** Length: 1 line minimum, 500 words maximum. **Pays $2/per published line upon publication.**

The online magazine carries original content not found in the print edition and includes writer's guidelines. Contact: Kathleen Stauffer, managing editor.

Tips: "We're a lot more aggressive with inspirational/pop psychology/how-to articles these days. Spiritual and all other wellness self-help is a good bet for us. We would also like to see material with an innovative approach to traditional religion, articles that show new ways of looking at old ideas, problems."

$ $ CATHOLIC FORESTER, Catholic Order of Foresters, 355 Shuman Blvd., P.O. Box 3012, Naperville IL 60566-7012. Fax: (630)983-3384. E-mail: cofpr@aol.com. Website: www.catholicforester.com. Editor: Mary Ann File. **Contact:** Patricia Baron, associate editor. **20% freelance written.** Quarterly magazine for members of the Catholic Order of Foresters, a fraternal insurance benefit society. *Catholic Forester* articles cover varied topics to create a balanced issue for the purpose of informing, educating, and entertaining our readers. Circ. 100,000. **Pays on acceptance.** Buys first North American serial rights. Editorial lead time 6 months. Submit seasonal material 6 months in advance. Responds in 3 months to mss. Sample copy for 9×12 SAE and 4 first-class stamps. Writer's guidelines online.
Nonfiction: Inspirational, religious, travel, health, parenting, financial, money management, humor. **Buys 12-16 mss/**

year. Send complete ms by mail, fax, or e-mail. Rejected material will not be returned without accompanying SASE. Length: 500-1,500 words. **Pays 30¢/word.**

Photos: State availability with submission. Buys one-time rights. Negotiates payment individually.

Fiction: Humorous, religious. **Buys 12-16 mss/year.** Length: 500-1,500 words. **Pays 30¢/word.**

Poetry: Light verse, traditional. **Buys 3 poems/year.** Length: 15 lines maximum. **Pays 30¢/word.**

Tips: "Our audience includes a broad age spectrum, ranging from youth to seniors. Nonfiction topics that appeal to our members include health and wellness, money management and budgeting, parenting and family life, interesting travels, insurance, nostalgia, and humor. A good children's story with a positive lesson or message would rate high on our list."

N $ $ CATHOLIC WORLD REPORT, Ignatius Press, P.O. Box 1608, South Lancaster MA 01561-1608. Website: www.cwnews.com. Editor: Philip F. Lawler. Managing Editor: Domenico Bettinelli. **Contact:** Editor. **65% freelance written.** Monthly magazine covering Catholicism. "*Catholic World Report* covers world news from the Orthodox Catholic perspective." Estab. 1990. Circ. 20,000. Pays on publication. Publishes ms an average of 1-2 months after acceptance. Buys first rights. Editorial lead time 1 month. Submit seasonal material 1-2 months in advance. Accepts queries by mail. Responds in 1-2 weeks to queries; 1-2 months to mss. Sample copy online.

Nonfiction: Interview/profile, religious, news coverage. No opinion or inspiration. **Buys 25 mss/year.** Query. **Pays $50-600 for unsolicited articles.**

N $ $ $ CHARISMA & CHRISTIAN LIFE, The Magazine About Spirit-Led Living, Strang Communications Co., 600 Rinehart Rd., Lake Mary FL 32746. (407)333-0600. Fax: (407)333-7100. E-mail: charisma@strang.com. Website: www.charismamag.com. Editor: J. Lee Grady. Managing Editor: Jimmy Stewart. **Contact:** Adrienne Gaines, associate editor. **80% freelance written.** Monthly magazine covering items of interest to the Pentecostal or independent charismatic reader. "More than half of our readers are Christians who belong to Pentecostal or independent charismatic churches, and numerous others participate in the charismatic renewal in mainline denominations." Estab. 1975. Circ. 250,000. Pays on publication. Publishes ms an average of 3 months after acceptance. Byline given. Offers $50 kill fee. Buys all rights. Editorial lead time 4 months. Submit seasonal material 5 months in advance. Accepts queries by mail, e-mail. Sample copy for free. Writer's guidelines by e-mail.

Nonfiction: Andy Butcher, senior writer. Book excerpts, exposé, general interest, interview/profile, religious. No fiction, poetry, columns/departments, or sermons. **Buys 40 mss/year.** Query. Length: 2,000-3,000 words. **Pays $800 (maximum) for assigned articles.** Pays expenses of writers on assignment.

Photos: Brenda Haun. State availability with submission. Reviews contact sheets, $2\frac{1}{4} \times 2\frac{1}{4}$ transparencies, 3×5 or larger prints, GIF/JPEG files. Buys one-time rights. Negotiates payment individually. Model releases required.

Tips: "Be especially on the lookout for news stories, trend articles, or interesting personality profiles that relate specifically to the Christian reader."

$ $ THE CHRISTIAN CENTURY, Christian Century Foundation, 104 S. Michigan Ave., Suite 700, Chicago IL 60605-1150. (312)263-7510. Fax: (312)263-7540. E-mail: main@christiancentury.org. Website: www.christiancentury.org. **Contact:** David Heim, executive editor. **90% freelance written.** Eager to work with new/unpublished writers. Biweekly magazine for ecumenically-minded, progressive Protestant church people, both clergy and lay. "Authors must have a critical and analytical perspective on the church and be familiar with contemporary theological discussion." Estab. 1884. Circ. 30,000. Pays on publication. Publishes ms an average of 3 months after acceptance. Byline given. Buys all rights. Editorial lead time 1 month. Submit seasonal material 4 months in advance. Accepts queries by mail. Accepts simultaneous submissions. Responds in 1 week to queries; 2 months to mss. Sample copy for $3. Writer's guidelines online.

Nonfiction: "We use articles dealing with social problems, ethical dilemmas, political issues, international affairs, and the arts, as well as with theological and ecclesiastical matters. We focus on issues of church and society, and church and culture." Essays, humor, interview/profile, opinion, religious. No inspirational. **Buys 150 mss/year.** Send complete ms; query appreciated, but not essential. Length: 1,000-3,000 words. **Pays $75-200 for assigned articles; $75-150 for unsolicited articles.**

Photos: State availability with submission. Reviews any size prints. Buys one-time rights. Offers $25-100/photo.

Fiction: Humorous, religious, slice-of-life vignettes. No moralistic, unrealistic fiction. **Buys 4 mss/year.** Send complete ms. Length: 1,000-3,000 words. **Pays $75-200.**

Poetry: Jill Pelaez Baumgaertner, poetry editor. Avant-garde, free verse, haiku, traditional. No sentimental or didactic poetry. **Buys 50 poems/year.** Length: 20 lines. **Pays $50.**

Tips: "We seek manuscripts that articulate the public meaning of faith, bringing the resources of religious tradition to bear on such topics as poverty, human rights, economic justice, international relations, national priorities, and popular culture. We are equally interested in articles that probe classical theological themes. We welcome articles that find fresh meaning in old traditions and which adapt or apply religious traditions to new circumstances. Authors should assume that readers are familiar with main themes in Christian history and theology; are unthreatened by the historical-critical study of the Bible; and are already engaged in relating faith to social and political issues. Many of our readers are ministers or teachers of religion at the college level."

$ $ CHRISTIAN HOME & SCHOOL, Christian Schools International, 3350 E. Paris Ave. SE, Grand Rapids MI 49512. (616)957-1070, ext. 239. Fax: (616)957-5022. E-mail: rogers@csionline.org. Website: www.csionline.org/chs. Executive Editor: Gordon L. Bordewyk. **Contact:** Roger Schmurr, senior editor. **30% freelance written.** Works with a small number of new/unpublished writers each year. Bimonthly magazine covering family life and Christian education. "*Christian Home & School* is designed for parents in the United States and Canada who send their children to Christian schools and are concerned about the challenges facing Christian families today. These readers expect a mature, Biblical perspective in the articles, not just a Bible verse tacked onto the end." Estab. 1922. Circ. 70,000. Pays on publication. Publishes ms an average of 4 months after acceptance. Byline given. Buys first North American serial rights. Submit seasonal material 4 months in advance. Accepts queries by mail, e-mail. Responds in 1 month to queries. Sample copy and writer's guidelines for 9×12 SAE with 4 first-class stamps. Writer's guidelines only for #10 SASE or online.

- The editor reports an interest in seeing articles on how to experience and express forgiveness in your home, raise polite kids in a rude world, combat procrastination, let kids maintin a relationship with your former spouse, and promote good educational practices in Christian schools.

O→ Break in by picking a contemporary parenting situation/problem and writing to Christian parents.

Nonfiction: "We publish features on issues that affect the home and school and profiles on interesting individuals, providing that the profile appeals to our readers and is not a tribute or eulogy of that person." Book excerpts, interview/profile, opinion, personal experience, articles on parenting and school life. **Buys 40 mss/year.** Send complete ms. Length: 1,000-2,000 words. **Pays $175-250.**

Photos: "If you have any color photos appropriate for your article, send them along."

Tips: "Features are the area most open to freelancers. We are publishing articles that deal with contemporary issues that affect parents. Use an informal easy-to-read style rather than a philosophical, academic tone. Try to incorporate vivid imagery and concrete, practical examples from real life. We look for manuscripts with a mature Christian perspective."

N $ $ CHRISTIAN LEADER, U.S. Conference of Mennonite Brethren Churches, Box 220, Hillsboro KS 67063. (620)947-5543. Fax: (620)947-3266. E-mail: christianleader@usmb.org. **Contact:** Connie Faber, interim editor. **20% freelance written.** Monthly magazine covering news and issues related to the Mennonite Brethren denomination. Estab. 1936. Circ. 10,000. Pays on publication. Publishes ms an average of 5 months after acceptance. Byline given. Buys first rights. Editorial lead time 3 months. Submit seasonal material 5 months in advance. Accepts queries by mail, e-mail, fax. Accepts previously published material. Accepts simultaneous submissions. Sample copy for $1.60. Writer's guidelines free.

Nonfiction: Book excerpts, essays, how-to, humor, inspirational, interview/profile, opinion, personal experience, religious. **Buys 30 mss/year.** Query or send complete ms. Length: 1,000-2,500 words. **Pays 10¢/word.** Sometimes pays expenses of writers on assignment.

Photos: State availability with submission. Buys one-time rights.

Fiction: Religious. **Buys 2 mss/year.** Length: 1,000-2,500 words. **Pays 10¢/word.**

Poetry: Avant-garde, free verse, haiku, light verse, traditional. **Buys 2 poems/year.**

Tips: "We ask that writers contact the editor if they are interested in writing an article or have one they've already written. The *Leader* operates on the 'theme' approach, laying out topics we will tackle each month, so we tend to look for articles on those specific topics. However, we have up to 4 issues a year that do not have 'themes'; we publish a variety of articles on different topics in those issues. Most articles published are between 1,200 and 1,700 words; and we operate on a 'first-rights' basis. We also ask writers to submit articles by e-mail via an attachment in Microsoft Word."

$ $ CHRISTIAN READER, Stories of Faith, Hope and God's Love, Christianity Today, 465 Gundersen Dr., Carol Stream IL 60188. (630)260-6200. Fax: (630)260-0114. E-mail: creditor@christianreader.net. Website: www.christianreader.net. Managing Editor: Edward Gilbreath. **Contact:** Cynthia Thomas, editorial coordinator. **25% freelance written.** Bimonthly magazine for adult evangelical Christian audience. Estab. 1963. Circ. 185,000. Pays on acceptance; on publication for humor pieces. Byline given. Editorial lead time 5 months. Submit seasonal material 8 months in advance. Accepts queries by mail. Accepts simultaneous submissions. Responds in 1 month to queries. Sample copy for 5×8 SAE and 4 first-class stamps. Writer's guidelines online.

Nonfiction: Book excerpts, general interest, historical/nostalgic, humor, inspirational, interview/profile, personal experience, photo feature, religious. **Buys 100-125 mss/year.** Query with or without published clips or send complete ms. Length: 250-1,500 words. **Pays $125-600 depending on length.** Pays expenses of writers on assignment.

Reprints: Send tearsheet, photocopy or typed ms with rights for sale noted and information about when and where the material previously appeared. Pays 35-50% of amount paid for an original article.

Photos: Send photos with submission. Reviews transparencies, prints. Buys one-time rights. Negotiates payment individually. Identification of subjects required.

Columns/Departments: Humor Us (adult church humor, kids say and do funny things, and humorous wedding tales), 50-200 words. **Pays $35.**

Fillers: Anecdotes, short fillers. **Buys 10-20/year.** Length: 100-250 words. **Pays $35.**

Tips: "Most of our articles are reprints or staff written. Freelance competition is keen, so tailor submissions to meet our needs by observing the following: The *Christian Reader* audience is truly a general interest one, including men and women, urban professionals and rural homemakers, adults of every age and marital status, and Christians of every church affiliation. We seek to publish a magazine that people from the variety of ethnic groups in North America will find interesting and relevant."

N $ $ CHRISTIAN RESEARCH JOURNAL, 30162 Tomas, Rancho Santa Margarita CA 92688-2124. (949)858-6100. Fax: (949)858-6111. E-mail: elliot.miller@equip.org. Website: www.equip.org. Managing Editor: Melanie Cogdill. **Contact:** Elliot Miller, editor-in-chief. **75% freelance written.** Quarterly magazine. "The *Journal* is an apologetics magazine probing today's religious movements, promoting doctrinal discernment and critical thinking, and providing reasons for Christian faith and ethics." Pays on publication. Publishes ms an average of 3 months after acceptance. Byline sometimes given. Offers 50% kill fee. Buys first rights. Submit seasonal material 4 months in advance. Accepts queries by mail, e-mail, fax. Accepts simultaneous submissions. Responds in 4 months to queries; 4 months to mss. Sample copy for $6. Writer's guidelines by e-mail.

Nonfiction: Essays, opinion (rekigious viewpoint), religious, ethics, book reviews, features on cults, witnessing tips. No fiction or general Christian living topics. **Buys 30 mss/year.** Query or send complete ms (if e-mail ms, must mail disk with ms as well). Length: 4,000-6,000 words. **Pays 16¢/word.**

Columns/Departments: Features, 4,500 words; Effective Evangelism, 1,700 words; Viewpoint, 875 words; News Watch, 2,500 words. Query or send complete ms. **Pays 16¢/word.**

Tips: "We are most open to features on cults, apologetics, Christian discernment, ethics, book reviews, opinion pieces, and witnessing tips. Be familiar with the *Journal* in order to know what we are looking for."

$ THE CHRISTIAN RESPONSE, A Newsletter for Concerned Christians, HAPCO Industries, P.O. Box 125, Staples MN 56479-0125. (218)894-1165. E-mail: hapco@brainerd.net. Website: www.brainerd.net/~hapco/. **Contact:** Hap Corbett, editor. **10% freelance written.** Bimonthly newsletter "responding to anti-Christian bias from a Christian perspective." Estab. 1993. Circ. 300. **Pays on acceptance.** Publishes ms an average of 2 months after acceptance. Byline given. Buys one-time rights. Editorial lead time 2 months. Submit seasonal material 6 months in advance. Accepts queries by mail, e-mail, phone. Responds in 2 weeks to queries. Sample copy for $1 (or 3 first-class stamps). Writer's guidelines for #10 SASE.

Nonfiction: Examples of anti-Christian bias in America. **Buys 4-6 mss/year.** Send complete ms. Length: 200-750 words. **Pays $5-20.**

Fillers: Anecdotes, facts, newsbreaks. **Buys 2-4/year.** Length: 150 words. **Pays $5-20.**

Tips: "We want exposés of anti-Christian bias or denial of civil rights to people because of religious beliefs."

$ $ CHRISTIAN SOCIAL ACTION, 100 Maryland Ave. NE, Washington DC 20002. (202)488-5631. Fax: (202)488-1617. E-mail: ghackola@umc-gbcs.org. **Contact:** Gretchen Hakola, editor. **10% freelance written.** Works with a small number of new/unpublished writers each year. Bimonthly magazine for "United Methodist clergy and lay people interested in in-depth analysis of social issues, with emphasis on the church's role or involvement in these issues." Circ. 50,000. Pays on publication. Publishes ms an average of 2 months after acceptance. Rights purchased vary with author and material. Accepts queries by mail, e-mail. Responds in 2 months to queries. Writer's guidelines online.

Nonfiction: "This is the social action publication of The United Methodist Church published by the denomination's General Board of Church and Society. Our publication tries to relate social issues to the church—what the church can do, is doing; why the church should be involved. We only accept articles relating to social issues, e.g., war, draft, peace, race relations, welfare, police/community relations, labor, population problems, drug and alcohol problems. No devotional, 'religious,' superficial material, highly technical articles, personal experience or poetry." **Buys 10-15 mss/year.** Query to show that you have expertise on a particular social issue, give credentials, and reflect a readable writing style. Length: 2,000 words maximum. **Pays $200-250.** Sometimes pays expenses of writers on assignment.

Reprints: Send tearsheet and information about when and where the material previously appeared. Payment negotiable.

Tips: "Write on social issues, but not superficially; we're more interested in finding an expert who can write (e.g., on human rights, alcohol problems, peace issues) than a writer who attempts to research a complex issue. Be clear, be brief, be understandable. No poetry."

$ $ CHRISTIANITY TODAY, 465 Gundersen Dr., Carol Stream IL 60188-2498. (630)260-6200. Fax: (630)260-8428. E-mail: cteditor@christianitytoday.com. Website: www.christianitytoday.com. **Contact:** Mark Galli, managing editor. **80% freelance written, but mostly assigned**. Works with a small number of new/unpublished writers each year. Monthly magazine. "*Christianity Today* believes that the vitality of the American church depends on its adhering to and applying the Biblical teaching as it meets today's challenges. It attempts to Biblically assess people, events, and ideas that shape evangelical life, thought, and mission. It employs analytical reporting, commentary, doctrinal essays, interviews, cultural reviews, and the occasional realistic narrative." Estab. 1956. Circ. 154,000. Publishes ms an average of 6 months after acceptance. Buys first rights. Submit seasonal material at least 8 months in advance. Accepts queries by mail, e-mail, fax. Responds in 3 months to queries. Sample copy and writer's guidelines for 9×12 SAE with 3 first-class stamps.

Nonfiction: Buys 6 unsolicited mss/year. Query. Length: 1,200-5,200 words. **Pays 25-35¢/word.** Sometimes pays expenses of writers on assignment.

Reprints: Rarely accepts previously published submissions. Pays 25% of amount paid for an original article.

Columns/Departments: The CT Review (books, the arts, and popular culture). Length: 700-1,500 words. **Buys 6 mss/year.** *Query only.*

The online magazine carries original content not found in the print edition. Contact: Ted Olsen, online editor.

Tips: "We are developing more of our own manuscripts and requiring a much more professional quality from others. Queries without SASE will not be answered and manuscripts not containing SASE will not be returned."

$ $ CHRYSALIS READER, R.R. 1, Box 4510, Dillwyn VA 23936. (804)983-3021. E-mail: chrysalis@hovac.com. Website: www.swedenborg.com. Managing Editor: Susanna van Rensselaer. **Contact:** Richard Butterworth, editorial associate. **90% freelance written.** Annual literary magazine on spiritually related topics. "It is very important to send for writer's guidelines and sample copies before submitting. Content of fiction, articles, reviews, poetry, etc., should be directly focused on that issue's theme and directed to the educated, intellectually curious reader." Estab. 1985. Circ. 3,000. Pays at page-proof stage. Publishes ms an average of 9 months after acceptance. Byline given. Buys first rights, makes work-for-hire assignments. Accepts queries by mail, e-mail. Responds in 1 month to queries; 4 months to mss. Sample copy for $10 and 8½×11 SAE. Writer's guidelines online.

- E-mail for themes and guidelines (no mss will be accepted by e-mail).

Nonfiction: Spiritual Well-Being (2003); Letting Go (2004); Partners (2005). Essays, interview/profile. **Buys 20 mss/year.** Query. Length: 2,500-3,500 words. **Pays $50-250 for assigned articles; $50-150 for unsolicited articles.**

Photos: Send suggestions for illustrations with submission. Buys original artwork for cover and inside copy; b&w illustrations related to theme; **pays $25-150**. Buys one-time rights. Offers no additional payment for photos accepted with ms. Captions, identification of subjects required.

Fiction: Robert Tucker, fiction editor. Short fiction more likely to be published. Adventure, experimental, historical, mainstream, mystery, science fiction, Fiction (leading to insight), contemporary, spiritual, sports. No religious, juvenile, preschool. **Buys 10 mss/year.** Query. Length: 2,500-3,500 words. **Pays $50-150.**

Poetry: Rob Lawson, senior editor. Avant-garde and traditional, but not overly religiou. **Buys 15 poems/year.** Submit maximum 6 poems. **Pays $25.**

$ $ COLUMBIA, 1 Columbus Plaza, New Haven CT 06510. (203)772-2130. Fax: (203)752-4109. E-mail: tim.hickey@kofc-supreme.com. Website: www.kofc.org. **Contact:** Tim S. Hickey, editor. Monthly magazine for Catholic families. Caters primarily to members of the Knights of Columbus. Estab. 1921. Circ. 1,500,000. **Pays on acceptance.** Buys first North American serial rights. Accepts queries by mail, e-mail, fax. Sample copy and writer's guidelines free.

Nonfiction: Fact articles directed to the Catholic layman and his family dealing with current events, social problems, Catholic apostolic activities, education, ecumenism, rearing a family, literature, science, arts, sports and leisure. No reprints, poetry, or cartoons. **Buys 20 mss/year.** Query with SASE. Length: 1,000-1,500 words. **Pays $300-600.**

The online magazine carries original content not found in the print edition. Contact: Tim S. Hickey, online editor.

Tips: "Few unsolicited manuscripts are accepted."

$ $ CONSCIENCE, A Newsjournal of Catholic Opinion, Catholics for a Free Choice, 1436 U St. NW, Suite 301, Washington DC 20009-3997. (202)986-6093. E-mail: conscience@catholicsforchoice.org. Website: www.catholicsforchoice.org. **Contact:** Editor. **60% freelance written.** Sometimes works with new/unpublished writers. Quarterly newsjournal covering reproductive health and rights including, but not limited to, abortion rights in the church, and church-state issues in US and worldwide. "A feminist, pro-choice perspective is a must, and knowledge of Christianity and specifically Catholicism is helpful." Estab. 1980. Circ. 12,000. Pays on publication. Publishes ms an average of 2 months after acceptance. Byline given. Buys first North American serial rights, makes work-for-hire assignments. Accepts queries by mail, e-mail. Responds in 4 months to queries. Sample copy for 9×12 SAE and 4 first-class stamps. Writer's guidelines for #10 SASE.

Nonfiction: Especially needs material that recognizes the complexity of reproductive issues and decisions, and offers original, honest insight. "Writers should be aware that we are a nonprofit organization." Book excerpts, interview/profile, opinion, personal experience (a small amount), issue analysis. **Buys 4-8 mss/year.** Query with published clips or send complete ms. Length: 1,500-3,500 words. **Pays $150-200.**

Reprints: Send ms with rights for sale noted and information about when and where the material previously appeared. Pays 20-30% of amount paid for an original article.

Photos: Prefers b&w prints. State availability with submission. Identification of subjects required.

Columns/Departments: Book Reviews, 600-1,200 words. **Buys 4-8 mss/year. Pays $75.**

Tips: "Say something new on the issue of abortion, or sexuality, or the role of religion or the Catholic church, or women's status in the church. Thoughtful, well-researched, and well-argued articles needed. The most frequent mistakes made by writers in submitting an article to us are lack of originality and wordiness."

$ CORNERSTONE, Cornerstone Communications, Inc., 939 W. Wilson, Chicago IL 60640-5718. (773)561-2450 ext. 2080. Fax: (773)989-2076. E-mail: poetry@cornerstonemag.com. Website: www.cornerstonemag.com. Editor: Jon Trott. **Contact:** Submissions Editor. **10% freelance written.** Eager to work with new/unpublished writers. Irregularly published magazine covering contemporary issues in the light of Evangelical Christianity. Estab. 1972. Pays after publication. Byline given. Buys first North American serial rights. Submit seasonal material 6 months in advance. Accepts simultaneous submissions. Does not return mss. Sample copy and writer's guidelines for 8½ × 11 SAE with 5 first-class stamps.

- "We will contact you *only* if your work is accepted for possible publication. We *encourage* simultaneous submissions because we take so long to get back to people! E-mail all poetry submissions to poetry@cornerstonemag.com (if e-mail is unavailable to you, we accept hard copies). Send no queries."

Poetry: "No limits *except* for epic poetry ("We've not the room!"). Avant-garde, free verse, haiku, light verse, traditional. **Buys 5-10 poems/year.** Submit maximum 5 poems. **Payment negotiated. 1-15 lines: $10; over 15 lines: $25.**

The online version carries original content not found in the print edition. Contact: Jon Trott, online editor.

Tips: "A display of creativity which expresses a biblical world view without clichés or cheap shots at non-Christians is the ideal. We are known as one of the most avant-garde magazines in the Christian market, yet attempt to express orthodox beliefs in today's language. *Any* writer who does this well may be published by *Cornerstone*."

$ THE COVENANT COMPANION, Covenant Publications of the Evangelical Covenant Church, 5101 N. Francisco Ave., Chicago IL 60625. (773)784-3000. Fax: (773)784-4366. E-mail: communication@covchurch.org. Website: www.covchurch.org. **Contact:** Donald L. Meyer, editor or Jane K. Swanson-Nystrom, managing editor. **10-15% freelance written.** "As the official monthly periodical of the Evangelical Covenant Church, we seek to inform the denomination we serve and encourage dialogue on issues within the church and in our society." Circ. 16,000. Publishes ms an average of 2 months after acceptance. Byline given. Submit seasonal material 4 months in advance. Accepts queries by mail, e-mail. Accepts simultaneous submissions. Writer's guidelines online.

Nonfiction: Inspirational, religious, contemporary issues. **Buys 40 mss/year.** Send complete ms. Unused mss returned only if accompanied by SASE. Length: 500-2,000 words. **Pays $50-100 for assigned articles.**

Reprints: Send tearsheet, photocopy or typed ms with rights for sale noted and information about when and where the material previously appeared.

Photos: Send photos with submission. Reviews prints. Buys one-time rights. Offers no additional payment for photos accepted with ms. Identification of subjects required.

$ $ $ DECISION, Billy Graham Evangelistic Association, 2 Parkway Plaza, 4828 Parkway Plaza Blvd., Suite 200, Charlotte NC 28217. (704)401-2432. Fax: (704)401-3009. E-mail: submissions@bgea.org. Website: www.decisionmag.org. Editor: Kersten Beckstrom. **Contact:** Bob Paulson, managing editor. **10% freelance written.** Works each year with small number of new/unpublished writers, as well as a solid stable of experienced writers. Monthly magazine with a mission "to set forth to every reader the Good News of salvation in Jesus Christ with such vividness and clarity that he or she will be drawn to make a commitment to Christ; to encourage, teach, and strengthen Christians." Estab. 1960. Circ. 1,200,000. Pays on publication. Publishes ms an average of up to 18 months after acceptance. Byline given. Offers 50% kill fee. Buys first rights. Assigns work-for-hire mss, articles, projects. Editorial lead time 8 months. Submit seasonal material 10 months in advance. Responds in 3 months to mss. Sample copy for 9×12 SAE and 4 first-class stamps. Writer's guidelines online.

- Include telephone number with submission.

O→ "The best way to break in to our publication is to submit an article that has some connection to the Billy Graham Evangelistic Association or Samaritan's Purse, but also has strong takeaway for the personal lives of the readers."

Nonfiction: How-to, inspirational, personal experience, religious, motivational. **Buys approximately 20 mss/year.** Send complete ms. Length: 400-1,500 words. **Pays $30-260.** Pays expenses of writers on assignment.

Photos: State availability with submission. Reviews prints. Buys one-time rights. Captions, identification of subjects, model releases required.

Columns/Departments: Where Are They Now? (people who have become Christians through Billy Graham Ministries), 500-600 words. **Buys 12 mss/year.** Send complete ms. **Pays $85.**

Poetry: Amanda Knoke, assistant editor. Free verse, light verse, traditional. **Buys 6 poems/year.** Submit maximum 7 poems. Length: 4-16 lines. **Pays 60¢/word.**

Fillers: Anecdotes. **Buys 50/year.** Length: 300-500 words. **Pays $25-75.**

Tips: "Articles should have some connection to the ministry of Billy Graham or Franklin Graham. For example, you may have volunteered in one of these ministries or been touched by them. The article does not need to be entirely about that connection, but it should at least mention the connection. Testimonies and personal experience articles should show how God intervened in your life, and how you have been transformed by God. SASE required with submissions."

N $ DEVO'ZINE, Just for Teens, 1908 Grand Ave., P.O. Box 340004, Nashville TN 37203-0004. Website: www.devozine.org. Bimonthly magazine for youth ages 12-18. Offers meditations, scripture, prayers, poems, stories, songs, and feature articles to "aid youth in their prayer life, introduce them to spiritual disciplines, help them shape their concept of God, and encourage them in the life of discipleship." Sample copy not available. Writer's guidelines online.

Nonfiction: General interest, inspirational, personal experience, religious, devotional.

Poetry: Length: 20 lines.

$ $ DISCIPLESHIP JOURNAL, NavPress, a division of The Navigators, P.O. Box 35004, Colorado Springs CO 80935-0004. (719)531-3514. Fax: (719)598-7128. E-mail: sue.kline@navpress.com. Website: www.disciple shipjournal.com. **Contact:** Sue Kline, editor. **90% freelance written.** Works with a small number of new/unpublished writers each year. Bimonthly magazine. "The mission of *Discipleship Journal* is to help believers develop a deeper relationship with Jesus Christ, and to provide practical help in understanding the scriptures and applying them to daily life and ministry. We prefer those who have not written for us before begin with nontheme articles about almost any aspect of Christian living. We'd like more articles that explain a Bible passage and show how to apply it to everyday life, as well as articles about developing a relationship with Jesus; reaching the world; growing in some aspect of Christian character; or specific issues related to leadership and helping other believers grow." Estab. 1981. Circ. 130,000. **Pays on acceptance.** Publishes ms an average of 6 months after acceptance. Byline given. Buys first North American serial, second serial (reprint), electronic rights. Submit seasonal material 6 months in advance. Accepts queries by mail, e-mail, fax. Responds in 6-8 weeks to queries. Sample copy for $2.56 and 9×12 SAE or online. Writer's guidelines online.

O→ Break in through departments (On the Home Front, Getting into God's Word, DJ Plus) and with nontheme feature articles.

Nonfiction: "We'd like to see more articles that encourage involvement in world missions; help readers in personal evangelism, follow-up, and Christian leadership; or show how to develop a real relationship with Jesus." Book excerpts (rarely), how-to (grow in Christian faith and disciplines; help others grow as Christians; serve people in need; understand and apply the Bible), inspirational, interpretation/application of the Bible. No personal testimony; humor; poetry; anything not directly related to Christian life and faith; politically partisan articles. **Buys 80 mss/year.** Query with published clips and SASE only. Length: 500-2,500 words. **Pays 25¢/word for first rights.** Sometimes pays expenses of writers on assignment.

Reprints: Send tearsheet and information about when and where the material previously appeared. Pays 5¢/word for reprints.

Tips: "Our articles are meaty, not fluffy. Study writer's guidelines and back issues and try to use similar approaches. Don't preach. Polish before submitting. About half of the articles in each issue are related to one theme. We are looking for more practical articles on ministering to others and more articles on growing in Christian character. Be vulnerable. Show the reader that you have wrestled with the subject matter in your own life. Use personal illustrations. We can no longer accept unsolicited manuscripts. Query first."

$ $ THE DOOR, P.O. Box 1444, Waco TX 76703-1444. (214)827-2625. Fax: (254)752-4915. E-mail: robert_darden@baylor.edu. Website: www.thedoormagazine.com. **Contact:** Robert Darden, senior editor. **90% freelance written.** Works with a large number of new/unpublished writers each year. Bimonthly magazine. "*The Door* is the world's only oldest and largest religious humor and satire magazine." Estab. 1969. Circ. 7,500. Pays on publication. Publishes ms an average of 1 year after acceptance. Buys first rights. Accepts queries by mail. Responds in 3 months to mss. Sample copy for $5.95. Writer's guidelines online.

O→ Read several issues of the magazine first! Get the writer's guidelines.

Nonfiction: Looking for humorous/satirical articles on church renewal, Christianity and organized religion. Exposé, humor, interview/profile, religious. No book reviews or poetry. **Buys 45-50 mss/year.** Send complete ms. Length: 1,500 words maximum; 750-1,000 preferred. **Pays $50-250.** Sometimes pays expenses of writers on assignment.

Reprints: Send ms with rights for sale noted and information about when and where the material previously appeared.

The online magazine carries original content not found in the print edition. Contact: Robert Darden.

Tips: "We look for someone who is clever, on our wave length, and has some savvy about the evangelical church. We are very picky and highly selective. The writer has a better chance of breaking in with our publication with short articles since we are a bimonthly publication with numerous regular features and the magazine is only 52 pages. The most frequent mistake made by writers is that they do not understand satire. They see we are a humor magazine and consequently come off funny/cute (like *Reader's Digest*) rather than funny/satirical (like *National Lampoon*)."

$ DOVETAIL, A Journal By and For Jewish/Christian Families, Dovetail Institute for Interfaith Family Resources, 775 Simon Greenwell Lane, Boston KY 40107. (502)549-5499. Fax: (502)549-3543. E-mail: di-ifr@bardstown.com. Website: www.dovetailinstitute.org. **Contact:** Mary Helene Rosenbaum, editor. **75% freelance written.** Bimonthly newsletter for interfaith families. "All articles must pertain to life in an interfaith (primarily Jewish/Christian) family. We are broadening our scope to include other sorts of interfaith mixes. We accept all kinds of opinions related to this topic." Estab. 1992. Circ. 1,500. Pays on publication. Publishes ms an average of 9 months after acceptance. Byline given. Buys first, one-time, second serial (reprint) rights. Editorial lead time 6 months. Submit seasonal material 6 months in advance. Accepts queries by mail, e-mail, fax, phone. Accepts previously published material. Accepts simultaneous submissions. Responds in 3 months to queries. Sample copy for 9×12 SAE and 3 first-class stamps. Writer's guidelines free.

O→ Break in with "a fresh approach to standard interfaith marriage situations."

Nonfiction: Book reviews, 500 words. **Pays $15, plus 2 copies**. Book excerpts, interview/profile, opinion, personal experience. No fiction. **Buys 5-8 mss/year.** Send complete ms. Length: 800-1,000 words. **Pays $25, plus 2 copies.**

Photos: Send photos with submission. Reviews 5×7 prints. Buys one-time rights. Offers no additional payment for photos accepted with ms. Identification of subjects, model releases required.

Fillers: Anecdotes, short humor. **Buys 1-2/year.** Length: 25-100 words. **Pays $10.**

Tips: "Write on concrete, specific topics related to Jewish/Christian or other dual-faith intermarriage: no proselytizing, sermonizing, or general religious commentary. Successful freelancers are part of an interfaith family themselves, or have done solid research/interviews with members of interfaith families. We look for honest, reflective personal experience. We're looking for more on alternative or nontraditional families, e.g., interfaith gay/lesbian, single parent raising child in departed partner's faith."

$ THE EVANGELICAL BAPTIST, Fellowship of Evangelical Baptist Churches in Canada, 18 Louvigny, Lorraine QC J6Z 1T7, Canada. (450)621-3248. Fax: (450)621-0253. E-mail: eb@fellowship.ca. Website: www.fellowship.ca. **Contact:** Ginette Cotnoir, managing editor. **30% freelance written.** Magazine published 5 times/year covering religious, spiritual, Christian living, denominational, and missionary news. "We exist to enhance the life and ministry of the church leaders of our association of churches—including pastors, elders, deacons, and all the men and women doing the work of the ministry in local churches." Estab. 1953. Circ. 3,000. Pays on publication. Publishes ms an average of 6 months after acceptance. Byline given. Buys one-time, second serial (reprint) rights. Editorial lead time 4 months. Accepts queries by mail, e-mail. Accepts previously published material. Accepts simultaneous submissions. Sample copy for 9×12 SAE with $1.50 in Canadian first-class stamps. Writer's guidelines for #10 SASE (Canadian stamps only).

O→ Break in with items for "Church Life (how-to and how-we articles about church ministries, e.g., small groups, worship, missions) or columns (Joy in the Journey, View from the Pew)."

Nonfiction: Religious. No poetry, fiction, puzzles. **Buys 12-15 mss/year.** Send complete ms. Length: 500-2,400 words. **Pays $25-50.**

Photos: State availability with submission. Reviews prints. Buys one-time rights. Offers no additional payment for photos accepted with ms. Captions required.

Columns/Departments: Church Life (practical articles about various church ministries, e.g., worship, Sunday school, missions, seniors, youth, discipleship); Joy in the Journey (devotional article regarding a lesson learned from God in everyday life); View from the Pew (light, humorous piece with spiritual value on some aspect of Christian living), all 600-800 words. **Buys 10 mss/year.** Send complete ms. **Pays $25-50.**

Tips: "Columns and departments are the best places for freelancers. Especially looking for practical articles for Church Life from writers who are themselves involved in a church ministry. Looking for 'how-to' and 'how-we' approach."

N **$ EVANGELICAL MISSIONS QUARTERLY, A Professional Journal Serving the Missions Community**, Billy Graham Center/Wheaton College, P.O. Box 794, Wheaton IL 60189. (630)752-7158. Fax: (630)752-7155. E-mail: emqjournal@aol.com. Website: www.billygrahamcenter.org/emis. Editor: A. Scott Moreau. **Contact:** Managing Editor. **67% freelance written.** Quarterly magazine covering evangelical missions. "This is a professional journal for evangelical missionaries, agency executives, and church members who support global missions ministries." Estab. 1964. Circ. 7,000. Pays on publication. Publishes ms an average of 18 months after acceptance. Byline given. Offers negotiable kill fee. Buys electronic, all rights. Editorial lead time 1 year. Accepts queries by mail, e-mail, fax, phone. Accepts previously published material. Responds in 2 weeks to queries. Sample copy free. Writer's guidelines online.

Nonfiction: Essays, interview/profile, opinion, personal experience, religious. No sermons, poetry, straight news. **Buys 24 mss/year.** Query. Length: 800-3,000 words. **Pays $50-100.**

Photos: Send photos with submission. Buys first rights. Offers no additional payment for photos accepted with ms. Identification of subjects required.

Columns/Departments: In the Workshop (practical how to's), 800-2,000 words; Perspectives (opinion), 800 words. **Buys 8 mss/year.** Query. **Pays $50-100.**

$ $ EVANGELIZING TODAY'S CHILD, Child Evangelism Fellowship, Inc., Box 348, Warrenton MO 63383-0348. (636)456-4321. Fax: (636)456-4321. E-mail: etceditor@cefonline.com. Website: www.cefonline.com/etcmag. **Contact:** Elsie Lippy, editor. **50% freelance written.** Bimonthly magazine. "Our purpose is to equip Christians to win the world's children to Christ and disciple them. Our readership is Sunday school teachers, Christian education leaders, and children's workers in every phase of Christian ministry to children 4-12 years old." Estab. 1942. Circ. 17,000. Pays within 3 months of acceptance. Publishes ms an average of 6 months after acceptance. Byline given. Offers kills fee if assigned. Buys first North American serial, electronic rights. Submit seasonal material 6 months in advance. Accepts queries by mail, e-mail. Responds in 2 months to queries. Sample copy for $2. Writer's guidelines online.

Nonfiction: Unsolicited articles welcomed from writers with Christian education training or current experience in working with children. **Buys 35 mss/year.** Query. Length: 900 words. **Pays 10-14¢/word.**

Reprints: Send photocopy and information about when and where the material previously appeared. Pays 35% of amount paid for an original article.

N $ $ FAITH TODAY, Seeking to Inform, Equip, and Inspire Christians Across Canada, Evangelical Fellowship of Canada, MIP Box 3745, Markham ON L3R 0Y4, Canada. (905)479-5885. Fax: (905)479-4742. E-mail: ft@efc-canada.com. Website: www.faithtoday.ca. Managing Editor: Gail Reid. **Contact:** Bill Fledderus, senior editor. Bimonthly magazine. "*FT* is an interdenominational, evangelical magazine that informs Canadian Christians on issues facing church and society, and on events within the church community. It focuses on the communal life of local congregations and corporate faith interacting with society more than on personal spiritual life. Writers should have a thorough understanding of the Canadian evangelical community." Estab. 1983. Circ. 18,000. Pays on publication. Publishes ms an average of 4 months after acceptance. Byline given. Offers 30-50% kill fee. Buys first rights. Editorial lead time 4 months. Accepts queries by mail, e-mail, fax. Responds in 6 weeks to queries. Sample copy for SASE in Canadian postage. Writer's guidelines online.

O-- Break in by "researching the Canadian field and including in your query a list of the Canadian contacts (Christian or not) that you intend to interview."

Nonfiction: Book excerpts (Canadian authors only), essays (Canadian authors only), interview/profile (Canadian subjects only), opinion, religious, news feature. **Buys 75 mss/year.** Query. Length: 400-2,000 words. **Pays $100-500 Canadian, more for cover topic material.** Sometimes pays expenses of writers on assignment.

Reprints: Send photocopy. Rarely used. Pays 50% of amount paid for an original article.

Photos: State availability with submission. Reviews contact sheets. Buys one-time rights. Identification of subjects required.

Tips: "Query should include brief outline and names of the sources you plan to interview in your research. Use Canadian postage on SASE."

$ THE FIVE STONES, Newsletter for Small Churches, The American Baptist Churches—USA, 69 Weymouth St., Providence RI 02906. (401)861-9405. Fax: (401)861-9405. E-mail: pappas@tabcom.org. **Contact:** Anthony G. Pappas, editor. **50% freelance written.** Quarterly magazine covering congregational dynamics in smaller churches. "*The Five Stones* is a resource for leaders in smaller congregations. Target audience: pastors, lay leaders, denominational officers." Estab. 1980. Circ. 500. Pays on publication. Publishes ms an average of 1 year after acceptance. Byline given. Not copyrighted. Buys one-time rights. Editorial lead time 6 months. Submit seasonal material 6 months in advance. Accepts queries by mail, e-mail, fax, phone. Accepts previously published material. Accepts simultaneous submissions. Responds in 6 weeks to queries; 6 months to mss. Sample copy for SASE. Writer's guidelines for SASE or by fax.

Nonfiction: "Articles must be specific to small church-related issues." Book excerpts, essays, historical/nostalgic, how-to, humor, inspirational, interview/profile, personal experience, religious. **Buys 8-12 mss/year.** Send complete ms. Length: 500-3,000 words. **Pays $10.**

Reprints: Accepts previously published submissions.

Photos: State availability with submission. Reviews GIF/JPEG files. Buys one-time rights. Offers no additional payment for photos accepted with ms. Identification of subjects required.

Columns/Departments: Small Town; Urban; Stewardship; Evangelism; Mission; Church Life; Reources; Humor (all first-person), all 500-2,500 words. **Buys 20 mss/year.** Send complete ms. **Pays $10.**

Fiction: Tim Pappas, editor. Ethnic, historical, humorous, religious, slice-of-life vignettes. **Buys 4 mss/year.** Send complete ms. Length: 300-3,000 words. **Pays $5 (maximum), and 2 contributor's copies.**

Tips: "First-person experiences. Focus on current issues of congregational life. Submit stories of positive events or learnings from negative ones."

$ FORWARD IN CHRIST, The Word from the WELS, WELS, 2929 N. Mayfair Rd., Milwaukee WI 53222-4398. (414)256-3210. Fax: (414)256-3862. E-mail: fic@sab.wels.net. Website: www.wels.net. **Contact:** Gary P. Baumler, editor. **5% freelance written.** Monthly magazine covering WELS news, topics, issues. The material usually must be written by or about WELS members. Estab. 1913. Circ. 56,000. Pays on publication. Publishes ms an average of 6 months after acceptance. Byline given. Buys one-time rights. Editorial lead time 3 months. Submit seasonal material 4 months in advance.

Accepts queries by mail, e-mail, fax. Responds in 2 months to queries. Sample copy and writer's guidelines free.
Nonfiction: Julie Tessmer, senior communications assistant. Personal experience, religious. Query. Length: 550-1,200 words. **Pays $75/page, $125/2 pages.** Sometimes pays expenses of writers on assignment.
Photos: State availability with submission. Reviews contact sheets. Buys one-time rights, plus 1 month on Web. Negotiates payment individually. Captions, identification of subjects, model releases required.
Fillers: Gary Baumler, editor.
Tips: "Topics should be of interest to the majority of the members of the synod—the people in the pews. Articles should have a Christian viewpoint, but we don't want sermons. We suggest you carefully read at least 5 or 6 issues with close attention to the length, content, and style of the features."

$ GOD ALLOWS U-TURNS, True Stories of Hope and Healing. An ongoing book series project, The God Allows U-Turns Project, P.O. Box 717, Faribault MN 55021-0717. Fax: (507)334-6464. E-mail: editor@godallowsuturns.com. Website: www.godallowsuturns.com. **Contact:** Allison Gappa Bottke, editor. **100% freelance written.** Christian inspirational book series. "Each anthology contains approximately 100 uplifting, encouraging, and inspirational true stories written by contributors from all over the world. Multiple volumes are planned." Published by Barbour Publishing in association with Alive Communications, Inc. Estab. 2000. Pays on publication. Byline given. Accepts previously published material. Accepts simultaneous submissions. Writer's guidelines online.

- Accepts stories by mail, e-mail, fax. Prefers submissions via website or e-mail, but *does not accept stories as e-mail attachments*. Responds *only* when a story is selected for publication. For a list of current *God Allows U-Turns* books open to submissions, as well as related opportunities, go to www.godallowsuturns.com. Timelines vary, so send stories any time as they may fit another volume. You may submit the same story to more than 1 volume, but you must send a separate copy to each. When submitting, indicate which volume it is for.

Nonfiction: "Open to well-written personal inspirational pieces showing how faith in God can inspire, encourage, and heal. True stories that must touch our emotions." Essays, historical/nostalgic, humor, inspirational, interview/profile, personal experience, religious. **Buys 100+ mss/year. Pays $50, plus 1 copy of anthology.**
Tips: "Read a current volume. See the website for a sample story. Keep it real. Ordinary people doing extraordinary things with God's help. These true stories must touch our emotions. Our contributors are a diverse group with no limits on age or denomination."

$ $ GROUP MAGAZINE, Group Publishing Inc., P.O. Box 481, Loveland CO 80539. (970)669-3836. Fax: (970)669-3269. E-mail: kdieterich@youthministry.com. Website: www.groupmag.com. Publisher: Tim Gilmour. **Contact:** Kathy Dietrich. **60% freelance written.** Bimonthly magazine covering youth ministry. "Writers must be actively involved in youth ministry. Articles we accept are practical, not theoretical, and focused for local church youth workers." Estab. 1974. Circ. 57,000. **Pays on acceptance.** Publishes ms an average of 6 months after acceptance. Byline given. Offers $20 kill fee. Buys all rights. Submit seasonal material 7 months in advance. Responds in 2 months to queries. Sample copy for $2 and 9×12 SAE. Writer's guidelines online.
Nonfiction: How-to (youth ministry issues). No personal testimony, theological or lecture-style articles. **Buys 50-60 mss/year.** Query. Length: 250-2,200 words. **Pays $40-250.** Sometimes pays expenses of writers on assignment.
Tips: "Submit a youth ministry idea to one of our mini-article sections—we look for tried-and-true ideas youth ministers have used with kids."

$ JEWISH FRONTIER, Labor Zionist Letters, P.O. Box 4013, Amity Station, New Haven CT 06525. (203)675-1441. Fax: (203)397-4903. E-mail: jewish-frontier@yahoo.com. Website: www.jewishfrontier.org/frontier. **Contact:** Bennett Lovett-Graff, managing editor. **100% freelance written.** Bimonthly intellectual journal covering progressive Jewish issues. "Reportage, essays, reviews, and occasional fiction and poetry, with a progressive Jewish perspective, and a particular interest in Israeli and Jewish-American affairs." Estab. 1934. Circ. 2,600. **Pays on acceptance.** Publishes ms an average of 4 months after acceptance. Byline given. Buys first, second serial (reprint), electronic rights. Editorial lead time 4 months. Submit seasonal material 2 months in advance. Accepts queries by mail, e-mail. Accepts previously published material. Accepts simultaneous submissions. Responds in 1 month to queries; 2 months to mss. Sample copy for 9×12 SASE and 3 first-class stamps, and online at website. Writer's guidelines online.
Nonfiction: Must have progressive Jewish focus, or will not be considered. Book excerpts, essays, exposé, historical/nostalgic, interview/profile, opinion, personal experience. **Buys 20 mss/year.** Query. Length: 1,000-2,500 words. **Pays 5¢/word.**
Photos: State availability with submission. Buys all rights. Offers no additional payment for photos accepted with ms. Captions, identification of subjects required.
Columns/Departments: Essays (progressive Jewish opinion), 1,000-2,500 words; Articles (progressive Jewish reportage), 1,000-2,500 words); Reviews, 500-1,000 words. **Buys 12 mss/year.** Query. **Pays $5¢/word.**
Poetry: Avant-garde, free verse, haiku, traditional. **Buys 12 poems/year.** Submit maximum 3 poems. Length: 7-25 lines. **Pays $5¢/word.**
Tips: "Send queries with strong ideas first. *Jewish Frontier* particularly appreciates original thinking on its topics related to progressive Jewish matters."

$ $ LEADERS IN ACTION, CSB Ministries, P.O. Box 150, Wheaton IL 60189. (630)582-0630. Fax: (630)582-0623. E-mail: dchristensen@csbministries.org. Website: csbministries.org. **Contact:** Deborah Christensen, editor. Magazine published 3 times/year covering leadership issues for CSB Ministries leaders. "*Leaders in Action* is distributed to leaders with CSB Ministries across North America. CSB is a nonprofit, nondenominational agency dedicated to winning and training boys and girls to serve Jesus Christ. Hundreds of churches throughout the U.S. and Canada make use of our wide range of services." Estab. 1960. Circ. 6,000. **Pays on acceptance.** Publishes ms an average of 3 months after acceptance. Byline given. Offers $35 kill fee. Buys first, second serial (reprint) rights. Editorial lead time 3 months. Responds in 1 week to queries. Sample copy for $1.50 and 10×13 SAE with 4 first-class stamps. Writer's guidelines for #10 SASE.

Nonfiction: Religious leadership. **Buys 8 mss/year.** Query. Length: 500-1,500 words. **Pays 5-10¢/word.** Sometimes pays expenses of writers on assignment.

Reprints: Send ms with rights for sale noted. Pays 50% of amount paid for an original article.

Tips: "We're looking for writers who can encourage and inspire leaders of children and youth, and work within a tight deadline. We work by assignment only. Send writing samples so we can determine how you might fit with our editorial goals."

$ LIFEGLOW, Christian Record Services, P.O. Box 6097, Lincoln NE 68506. Website: www.christianrecord.org. **Contact:** Gaylena Gibson, editor. **95% freelance written.** Large print Christian publication for sight-impaired over age 25 covering health, handicapped people, uplifting articles. Estab. 1984. Circ. 35,000. **Pays on acceptance.** Publishes ms an average of 3 years after acceptance. Byline given. Buys one-time rights. Accepts previously published material. Accepts simultaneous submissions. Responds in 1 year to mss. Sample copy for 7×10 SAE and 5 first-class stamps. Writer's guidelines for #10 SASE.

O→ "Write for an interdenominational Christian audience."

Nonfiction: Essays, general interest, historical/nostalgic, humor, inspirational, interview/profile, personal experience, travel, adventure, biography, careers, handicapped, health, hobbies, marriage, nature. **Buys 40 mss/year.** Send complete ms. Length: 200-1,400 words. **Pays 4-5¢/word, and complimentary copies.**

Photos: Send photos with submission. Buys one-time rights. Negotiates payment individually.

Columns/Departments: Baffle U! (puzzle), 150 words, **pays $15-25/puzzle**; Vitality Plus (current health topics), length varies, **pays 4¢/word. Buys 10 mss/year.** Send complete ms.

Fillers: Anecdotes, facts, short humor. **Buys very few/year.** Length: 300 words maximum. **Pays 4¢/word.**

Tips: "Make sure manuscript has a strong ending that ties everything together and doesn't leave us dangling. Pretend someone else wrote it—would it hold your interest? Draw your readers into the story by being specific rather than abstract or general."

$ $ LIGHT AND LIFE MAGAZINE, Free Methodist Church of North America, P.O. Box 535002, Indianapolis IN 46253-5002. (317)244-3660. Fax: (317)248-9055. E-mail: llmauthors@fmcna.org. **Contact:** Doug Newton, editor. Works with a small number of new/unpublished writers each year. Bimonthly magazine emphasizing evangelical Christianity with Wesleyan slant for a cross section of adults. Also includes discipleship guidebook and national/international and denominational religion news. Estab. 1868. Circ. 19,000. Pays on publication. Byline given. Buys first North American serial rights. Accepts queries by mail. Sample copy for $4. Writer's guidelines for #10 SASE.

Nonfiction: Send complete ms. Length: varies. **Pays 9¢/word, 10¢/word if submitted on disk.**

$ $ LIGUORIAN, One Liguori Dr., Liguori MO 63057-9999. (636)464-2500. Fax: (636)464-8449. E-mail: liguorianeditor@liguori.org. Website: www.liguorian.org. Managing Editor: Cheryl Plass. **Contact:** Fr. William Parker, CSSR, editor-in-chief. **25% freelance written.** Prefers to work with published/established writers. Magazine published 10 times/year for Catholics. "Our purpose is to lead our readers to a fuller Christian life by helping them better understand the teachings of the gospel and the church and by illustrating how these teachings apply to life and the problems confronting them as members of families, the church, and society." Estab. 1913. Circ. 220,000. **Pays on acceptance.** Offers 50% kill fee. Buys all rights. Buys all rights but will reassign rights to author after publication upon written request. Submit seasonal material 8 months in advance. Accepts queries by mail, e-mail, fax, phone. Responds in 3 months to mss. Sample copy for 9×12 SAE with 3 first-class stamps or online. Writer's guidelines for #10 SASE and on website.

Nonfiction: Pastoral, practical, and personal approach to the problems and challenges of people today. "No travelogue approach or unresearched ventures into controversial areas. Also, no material found in secular publications—fad subjects that already get enough press, pop psychology, negative or put-down articles." **Buys 40-50 unsolicited mss/year.** Length: 400-2,000 words. **Pays 10-12¢/word.** Sometimes pays expenses of writers on assignment.

Photos: Photographs on assignment only unless submitted with and specific to article.

Fiction: Fr. Allan Weinert, CSSR, editor-in-chief. Religious, senior citizen/retirement. Send complete ms. Length: 1,500-2,000 words preferred. **Pays 10-12¢/word and 5 contributor's copies.**

$ THE LIVING CHURCH, Living Church Foundation, 816 E. Juneau Ave., P.O. Box 514036, Milwaukee WI 53203. (414)276-5420. Fax: (414)276-7483. E-mail: tlc@livingchurch.org. Managing Editor: John Schuessler. **Contact:** David Kalvelage, editor. **50% freelance written.** Weekly magazine on the Episcopal Church. News or articles of interest to members of the Episcopal Church. Estab. 1878. Circ. 9,000. Does not pay unless article is requested. Publishes ms an average of 3 months after acceptance. Byline given. Buys one-time rights. Editorial lead time 3 weeks. Submit seasonal material 1 month in advance. Accepts queries by mail, e-mail, fax. Responds in 2 weeks to queries; 1 month to mss. Sample copy for free. Writer's guidelines online.

Nonfiction: Opinion, personal experience, photo feature, religious. **Buys 10 mss/year.** Send complete ms. Length: 1,000 words. **Pays $25-100.** Sometimes pays expenses of writers on assignment.

Photos: Send photos with submission. Reviews any size prints. Buys one-time rights. Offers $15-50/photo.

Columns/Departments: Benediction (devotional), 250 words; Viewpoint (opinion), under 1,000 words. Send complete ms. **Pays $50 maximum.**

Poetry: Light verse, traditional.

$ $ THE LOOKOUT, For Today's Growing Christian, Standard Publishing, 8121 Hamilton Ave., Cincinnati OH 45231-9981. (513)931-4050. Fax: (513)931-0950. E-mail: lookout@standardpub.com. Website: www.standardpub.com. Administrative Assistant: Sheryl Overstreet. **Contact:** Shawn McMullen, editor. **50% freelance written.** Weekly magazine for Christian adults, with emphasis on spiritual growth, family life, and topical issues. "Our purpose is to provide Christian adults with practical, Biblical teaching and current information that will help them mature as believers." Estab. 1894. Circ. 100,000. **Pays on acceptance.** Publishes ms an average of 1 year after acceptance. Byline given. Offers 33% kill fee. Buys first, one-time rights. Editorial lead time 6 months. Submit seasonal material 9 months in advance. Accepts previously published material. Accepts simultaneous submissions. Responds in 1 month to queries; 10 weeks to mss. Sample copy for $1. Writer's guidelines by e-mail.

- Audience is mainly conservative Christians. Manuscripts only accepted by mail.

Nonfiction: "Writers need to send for current theme list. We also use inspirational short pieces." Inspirational, interview/profile, opinion, personal experience, religious. No fiction or poetry. **Buys 100 mss/year.** Query with or without published clips or send complete ms. Length: Check guidelines. **Pays 5-12¢/word.** Sometimes pays expenses of writers on assignment.

Reprints: Accepts previously published submissions. Pays 60% of amount paid for an original article.

Photos: State availability with submission. Buys one-time rights. Offers no additional payment for photos accepted with ms. Identification of subjects required.

Tips: "*The Lookout* publishes from a theologically conservative, nondenominational, and noncharismatic perspective. It is a member of the Evangelical Press Association. We have readers in every adult age group, but we aim primarily for those aged 30-55. Most readers are married and have elementary to young adult children. But a large number come from other home situations as well. Our emphasis is on the needs of ordinary Christians who want to grow in their faith, rather than on trained theologians or church leaders. As a Christian general-interest magazine, we cover a wide variety of topics—from individual discipleship to family concerns to social involvement. We value well-informed articles that offer lively and clear writing as well as strong application. We often address tough issues and seek to explore fresh ideas or recent developments affecting today's Christians."

N $ $ THE LUTHERAN, Magazine of the Evangelical Lutheran Church in America, 8765 W. Higgins Rd., Chicago IL 60631-4183. (773)380-2540. Fax: (773)380-2751. E-mail: lutheran@elca.org. Website: www.thelutheran.org. Managing Editor: Sonia Solomonson. **Contact:** David L. Miller, editor. **15% freelance written.** Monthly magazine for "lay people in church. News and activities of the Evangelical Lutheran Church in America, news of the world of religion, ethical reflections on issues in society, personal Christian experience." Estab. 1988. Circ. 600,000. **Pays on acceptance.** Publishes ms an average of 6 months after acceptance. Byline given. Offers 50% kill fee. Buys first rights. Submit seasonal material 4 months in advance. Accepts queries by mail, e-mail. Responds in 6 weeks to queries. Sample copy free. Writer's guidelines online.

Break in by checking out the theme list on the website and querying with ideas related to these themes.

Nonfiction: Inspirational, interview/profile, personal experience, photo feature, religious. "No articles unrelated to the world of religion." **Buys 40 mss/year.** Query with published clips. Length: 500-1,500 words. **Pays $400-700 for assigned articles; $100-500 for unsolicited articles.** Pays expenses of writers on assignment.

Photos: Send photos with submission. Reviews contact sheets, transparencies, prints. Buys one-time rights. Offers $50-175/photo. Captions, identification of subjects required.

Columns/Departments: Lite Side (humor—church, religious), In Focus, Living the Faith, Values & Society, In Our Churches, Our Church at Work, 25-100 words. Send complete ms. **Pays $10.**

The online magazine carries original content not found in the print edition. Contact: Lorel Fox, online editor.

Tips: "Writers have the best chance selling us feature articles."

$ THE LUTHERAN DIGEST, The Lutheran Digest, Inc., P.O. Box 4250, Hopkins MN 55343. (952)933-2820. Fax: (952)933-5708. E-mail: tldi@lutherandigest.com. Website: www.lutherandigest.com. **Contact:** David L. Tank, editor. **95% freelance written.** Quarterly magazine covering Christianity from a Lutheran perspective. "Articles frequently reflect a Lutheran Christian perspective, but are not intended to be sermonettes. Popular stories show how God has intervened in a person's life to help solve a problem." Estab. 1953. Circ. 110,000. **Pays on acceptance.** Publishes ms an average of 6 months after acceptance. Byline given. Buys first, second serial (reprint) rights. Editorial lead time 9 months. Submit seasonal material 9 months in advance. Accepts queries by mail. Accepts previously published material. Accepts simultaneous submissions. Responds in 1 month to queries; 4 months to mss. Sample copy for $3.50. Writer's guidelines online.

Break in with "reprints from other publications that will fill less than three pages of *TLD*. Articles of 1 or 2 pages are even better. As a digest, we primarily look for previously published articles to reprint, however, we do publish about twenty to thirty percent original material. Articles from new writers are always welcomed and seriously considered."

Nonfiction: General interest, historical/nostalgic, how-to (personal or spiritual growth), humor, inspirational, personal experience, religious, nature, God's unique creatures. Does not want to see "personal tributes to deceased relatives or friends. They are seldom used unless the subject of the article is well known. We also avoid articles about the moment a person finds Christ as his or her personal savior." **Buys 50-60 mss/year.** Send complete ms. Length: 1,500 words. **Pays $25-50.**

Reprints: Accepts previously published submissions. "We prefer this as we are a digest and 70-80% of our articles are reprints."

Photos: "We seldom print photos from outside sources." State availability with submission. Buys one-time rights.

Tips: "An article that tugs on the 'heart strings' just a little and closes leaving the reader with a sense of hope is a writer's best bet to breaking into *The Lutheran Digest*."

$ THE LUTHERAN JOURNAL, P.O. Box 28158, Oakdale MN 55128. (651)702-0086. Fax: (651)702-0074. Publisher: Vance Lichty. **Contact:** Editorial Assistant. Magazine published 2 times/year for Lutheran Church members, middle age and older. Estab. 1938. Circ. 130,000. Pays on publication. Byline given. Buys one-time rights. Accepts simultaneous submissions. Responds in 4 months to queries. Sample copy for 9×12 SAE with 80¢ postage.

Nonfiction: Historical/nostalgic, how-to, humor, inspirational, interview/profile, personal experience, religious, interesting or unusual church projects, think articles. **Buys 25-30 mss/year.** Send complete ms. Length: 1,500 words maximum; occasionally 2,000 words. **Pays 1-4¢/word.**

Reprints: Send tearsheet, photocopy or typed ms with rights for sale noted and information about when and where the material previously appeared. Pays up to 50% of amount paid for an original article.

Photos: Send photocopies of b&w and color photos with accompanying ms. Please do not send original photos.

Poetry: Buys 2-3 poems/issue, as space allows. Pays $5-30.

Tips: "We strongly prefer a warm, personal style of writing that speaks directly to the reader. In general, writers should seek to convey information rather than express personal opinion, though the writer's own personality should be reflected in the article's style. Send submissions with SASE so we may respond."

$ LUTHERAN PARTNERS, Augsburg Fortress, Publishers, ELCA (DM), 8765 W. Higgins Rd., Chicago IL 60631-4195. (773)380-2884. Fax: (773)380-2829. E-mail: lpartmag@elca.org. Website: www.elca.org/lp. **Contact:** William A. Decker, managing editor. **15-20% freelance written.** Bimonthly magazine covering issues of religious leadership. "We are a leadership magazine for the ordained and rostered lay ministers of the Evangelical Lutheran Church in America (ELCA), fostering an exchange of opinions on matters involving theology, leadership, mission, and service to Jesus Christ. Know your audience: ELCA congregations and the various kinds of leaders who make up this church and their prevalent issues of leadership." Estab. 1979. Circ. 20,000. Pays on publication. Publishes ms an average of 6 months after acceptance. Byline given. Buys first, one-time, second serial (reprint), electronic rights. Editorial lead time 6 months. Submit seasonal material 6 months in advance. Accepts queries by mail, e-mail, fax, phone. Accepts previously published material. Accepts simultaneous submissions. Responds in 1 month to queries; 6 months to mss. Sample copy for $2. Writer's guidelines online.

- The editor reports an interest in seeing articles on various facets of ministry from the perspectives of ethnic authors (Hispanic, African-American, Asian, Native American, Arab-American).

O‒ Break in through "Jottings" (practical how-to articles involving congregational ministry ideas, 500 words maximum)."

Nonfiction: Historical/nostalgic, how-to (leadership in faith communities), humor (religious cartoon), inspirational, opinion (religious leadership issues), religious, book reviews (query book review editor). "No exposés, articles primarily promoting products/services, or anti-religion." **Buys 15-20 mss/year.** Query with published clips or send complete ms. Length: 500-2,000 words. **Pays $25-170.** Pays in copies for book reviews.

Photos: State availability with submission. Buys one-time rights. Generally offers no additional payment for photos accepted with ms. Captions, identification of subjects required.

Columns/Departments: Review Editor. Partners Review (book reviews), 700 words. Query or submit ms. **Pays in copies.**

Fiction: Rarely accepts religious fiction. Query.

Poetry: Free verse, haiku, light verse, traditional, hymns. **Buys 6-10 poems/year.** Submit maximum 10 poems. **Pays $50-75.**

Fillers: Practical ministry (education, music, youth, social service, administration, worship, etc.) in congregation. **Buys 3-6/year.** Length: 500 words. **Pays $25.**

Tips: "Know congregational life, especially from the perspective of leadership, including both ordained pastor and lay staff. Think current and future leadership needs. It would be good to be familiar with ELCA rostered pastors, lay ministers, and congregations."

$ MENNONITE BRETHREN HERALD, 3-169 Riverton Ave., Winnipeg MB R2L 2E5, Canada. (204)669-6575. Fax: (204)654-1865. E-mail: mbherald@mbconf.ca. Website: www.mbherald.com. **Contact:** Jim Coggins, editor; Susan Brandt, managing editor. **25% freelance written.** Triweekly family publication "read mainly by people of the Mennonite Brethren faith, reaching a wide cross section of professional and occupational groups, including many homemakers. Readership includes people from both urban and rural communities. It is intended to inform members of events in the church and the world, serve personal and corporate spiritual needs, serve as a vehicle of communication within the church, serve conference agencies and reflect the history and theology of the Mennonite Brethren Church." Estab. 1962. Circ. 16,500. Pays on publication. Publishes ms an average of 6 months after acceptance. Byline given. Not copyrighted. Buys one-time rights. Accepts queries by e-mail, fax. Responds in 6 months to queries. Sample copy for $1 and 9×12 SAE with 2 IRCs. Writer's guidelines online.

- "Articles and manuscripts not accepted for publication will be returned if a SASE (Canadian stamps or IRCs) is provided by the writers."

Nonfiction: Articles with a Christian family orientation; youth directed, Christian faith and life, and current issues. Wants articles critiquing the values of a secular society, attempting to relate Christian living to the practical situations of daily living; showing how people have related their faith to their vocations. Send complete ms. Length: 250-1,500 words. **Pays $30-40.** Pays expenses of writers on assignment.

Reprints: Send tearsheet, photocopy or typed ms with rights for sale noted and information about when and where the material previously appeared. Pays 70% of amount paid for an original article.

Photos: Photos purchased with ms.

Columns/Departments: Viewpoint (Christian opinion on current topics), 850 words. Crosscurrent (Christian opinion on music, books, art, TV, movies), 350 words.

Poetry: Length: 25 lines maximum.

Tips: "We like simple style, contemporary language and fresh ideas. Writers should take care to avoid religious cliches."

$ $ MESSAGE MAGAZINE, Review and Herald Publishing Association, 55 West Oak Ridge Dr., Hagerstown MD 21740. (301)393-4099. Fax: (301)393-4103. E-mail: message@rhpa.org. Website: www.messagemagazine.org. Editor: Ron C. Smith. **Contact:** Pat Sparks Harris, administrative secretary. **10-20% freelance written.** Bimonthly magazine. "*Message* is the oldest religious journal addressing ethnic issues in the country. Our audience is predominantly black and Seventh-day Adventist; however, *Message* is an outreach magazine geared to the unchurched." Estab. 1898. Circ. 120,000. **Pays on acceptance.** Publishes ms an average of 12 months after acceptance. Byline given. first North American serial rights Editorial lead time 6 months. Submit seasonal material 6 months in advance. Responds in 9 months to queries. Sample copy by e-mail. Writer's guidelines by e-mail.

Nonfiction: General interest (to a Christian audience), how-to (overcome depression; overcome defeat; get closer to God; learn from failure, etc.), inspirational, interview/profile (profiles of famous African Americans), personal experience (testimonies), religious. **Buys 10 mss/year.** Send complete ms. Length: 800-1,200 words. **Payment varies.**

Photos: State availability with submission. Buys one-time rights. Identification of subjects required.

Columns/Departments: Voices in the Wind (community involvement/service/events/health info); Message, Jr. (stories for children with a moral, explain a biblical or moral principle); Recipes (no meat or dairy products—12-15 recipes and an intro); Healthspan (health issues); all 500 words. Send complete ms. for Message, Jr. and Healthspan. Query editorial assistant with published clips for Voices in the Wind and Recipes. **Pays $50-300.**

The online version contains material not found in the print edition.

Tips: "Please look at the magazine before submitting manuscripts. *Message* publishes a variety of writing styles as long as the writing style is easy to read and flows—please avoid highly technical writing styles."

$ THE MESSENGER OF THE SACRED HEART, Apostleship of Prayer, 661 Greenwood Ave., Toronto ON M4J 4B3, Canada. (416)466-1195. **Contact:** Rev. F.J. Power, S.J., editor. **20% freelance written.** Monthly magazine for "Canadian and U.S. Catholics interested in developing a life of prayer and spirituality; stresses the great value of our ordinary actions and lives." Estab. 1891. Circ. 15,000. **Pays on acceptance.** Byline given. Buys first North American serial, first rights. Submit seasonal material 5 months in advance. Responds in 1 month to queries. Sample copy for $1 and 7½×10½ SAE. Writer's guidelines for #10 SASE.

Fiction: Religious/inspirational, stories about people, adventure, heroism, humor, drama. No poetry. **Buys 12 mss/year.** Send complete ms. Length: 750-1,500 words. **Pays 6¢/word, and 3 contributor's copies.**

Tips: "Develop a story that sustains interest to the end. Do not preach, but use plot and characters to convey the message or theme. Aim to move the heart as well as the mind. Before sending, cut out unnecessary or unrelated words or sentences. If you can, add a light touch or a sense of humor to the story. Your ending should have impact, leaving a moral or faith message for the reader."

$ MOODY MAGAZINE, Moody Bible Institute, 820 N. LaSalle Blvd., Chicago IL 60610. (312)329-2164. Fax: (312)329-2149. E-mail: moodyedit@moody.edu. Website: www.moodymagazine.com. **Contact:** Elizabeth Cody Newenhuyse, managing editor. Bimonthly magazine for evangelical Christians. "Our readers are evangelical Christians active in their churches, concerned about applying their faith in daily living, and engaged in the world." Estab. 1900. Circ. 100,000. **Pays on acceptance.** Byline given. Buys first North American serial rights. Accepts queries by e-mail. Responds in 2 months to queries. Sample copy for 9×12 SAE with $2 first-class postage. Writer's guidelines online.

Tips: "We strongly prefer experienced professionals with a solid track record to write for us—and we like building relationships with writers. Read 2 recent issues of the magazine before you query us. We are revamping our editorial approach and are moving toward being more assignment-based and are less open to queries than in the past, but will encourage writers who catch our editorial vision. Read guidelines for a detailed description of our needs."

$ NORTH AMERICAN VOICE OF FATIMA, Barnabite Fathers-North American Province, National Shrine Basilica of Our Lady of Fatima, 1023 Swann Rd., P.O. Box 167, Youngstown NY 14174-0167. (716)754-7489. Fax: (716)754-9130. E-mail: voice@fatimashrine.com. Website: www.fatimashrine.com. **Contact:** Rev. Peter M. Calabrese, CRSP, editor. **90% freelance written.** Quarterly magazine covering Catholic spirituality. "The Barnabite Fathers wish to share the joy and challenge of the Gospel and to foster devotion to Our Lady, Mary, the Mother of the Redeemer and Mother of the Church who said at Cana: 'Do whatever He tells you.'" Estab. 1961. Circ. 1,200. Pays on publication. Publishes ms an average of 3 months after acceptance. Byline given. Buys first North American serial, one-time, second serial (reprint) rights, makes work-for-hire assignments. Editorial lead time 2 months. Submit seasonal material 2 months in advance. Accepts queries by mail, e-mail. Accepts simultaneous submissions. Responds in 3 weeks to queries Does not return unsolicited mss to mss. Sample copy for free. Writer's guidelines online.

Nonfiction: Inspirational, personal experience, religious. **Buys 32 mss/year.** Send complete ms. Length: 500-1,250 words. **Pays 5¢/word.**

Photos: Send photos with submission. Buys one-time rights. Offers no additional payment for photos accepted with ms. Identification of subjects required.

Columns/Departments: Book Reviews (religious), 500 words or less. Send complete ms. **Pays 5¢/word.**

Poetry: Free verse, traditional. **Buys 16-20 poems/year.** Length: 4 lines minimum. **Pays $10-25.**

Tips: "We are a Catholic spirituality magazine that publishes articles on faith-based themes—also inspirational or uplifting stories. While Catholic we also publish articles by non-Catholic Christians."

$THE PENTECOSTAL MESSENGER, Messenger Publishing House, P.O. Box 850, Joplin MO 64802-0850. (417)624-7050. Fax: (417)624-7102. E-mail: pm@pcg.org. Website: www.pcg.org. **Contact:** John Mallinak, editor. Will accept freelance material occasionally. Monthly magazine dedicated to encourgaing and informing ministers and lay leaders. "*The Pentecostal Messenger* is the official organ of the Pentecostal Church of God. It goes to ministers and church members." Estab. 1919. Circ. 5,000. Pays on publication. Byline given. Buys second serial (reprint), simultaneous rights. Accepts queries by mail, e-mail, phone. Accepts simultaneous submissions. Sample copy for 9×12 SAE and 2 first-class stamps. Writer's guidelines free.

Nonfiction: Interested in articles that deal with leadership issues, church growth, and how-to articles in regard to church programs and outreach, etc. Send complete ms. Length: 400-1,200 words. **Pays 2¢/word.**

Reprints: Send tearsheet, photocopy or typed ms with rights for sale noted and information about when and where the material previously appeared.

$PIME WORLD, PIME Missionaries, 17330 Quincy St., Detroit MI 48221-2765. (313)342-4066. Fax: (313)342-6816. E-mail: pimeworld@pimeusa.org. Website: www.pimeusa.org. **Contact:** Cari Hartman, publications manager. **10% freelance written.** Bimonthly magazine supplemented with a newsletter, *Pime World's North America*. "Our focus is on educating North American Catholics on the missionary nature of the Church and inviting them to realize their call to be missionaries. The magazine and newsletter also serve the purpose of introducing the missionaries by emphasizing the IR activities throughout the world. Our audience is largely high school educated, conservative in both religion and politics." Estab. 1954. Circ. 16,000. Pays on publication. Publishes ms an average of 5 months after acceptance. Byline given. Buys one-time rights. Editorial lead time 2 months. Submit seasonal material 2 months in advance. Accepts queries by mail, e-mail, fax, phone. Accepts simultaneous submissions. Responds in 2 weeks to queries; 2 months to mss. Sample copy for free. Writer's guidelines for #10 SASE.

Nonfiction: Missionary activities of the Catholic church in the world, especially in Bangladesh, Brazil, Myanmar, Cameroon, Guinea Bissau, Hong Kong, India, Ivory Coast, Japan, Papua New Guinea, the Philippines, and Thailand. Query or send complete ms. Length: 200-500 words. **Pays $15 flat rate upon publication; 501-1,000 words pays $25 flat rate upon publication.**

Reprints: Accepts previously published submissions.

Photos: State availability of or send photos with submission. Buys one-time rights. Pays $10/color photo. Identification of subjects required.

Tips: "Articles produced from a faith standpoint dealing with current issues of social justice, evangelization, witness, proclamation, pastoral work in the foreign missions, etc. Interviews of missionaries, both religious and lay, welcome. Good quality color photos greatly appreciated."

$ $THE PLAIN TRUTH, Renewing Faith & Values, Plain Truth Ministries, 300 W. Green St., Pasadena CA 91129. Fax: (626)304-8172. E-mail: phyllis_duke@ptm.org. Website: www.ptm.org. Editor: Greg Albrecht. **Contact:** Phyllis Duke, assistant editor. **90% freelance written.** Bimonthly magazine. "We seek to reignite the flame of shattered lives by illustrating the joy of a new life in Christ." Estab. 1935. Circ. 70,000. Pays on publication. Publishes ms an average of 8 months after acceptance. Byline given. Offers $50 kill fee. Buys all-language rights for *The Plain Truth* and its affiliated publications. Editorial lead time 6 months. Submit seasonal material 6 months in advance. Accepts queries by mail, e-mail. Accepts simultaneous submissions. Sample copy for 9×12 SAE and 5 first-class stamps. Writer's guidelines online.

Nonfiction: Inspirational, interview/profile, personal experience, religious. **Buys 48-50 mss/year.** Query with published clips and SASE. *No unsolicited mss.* Length: 750-2,500 words. **Pays 25¢/word.**

Reprints: Send tearsheet or photocopy of article or typed ms with rights for sale noted and information about when and where the article previously appeared with SASE for response. Pays 15¢/word.

Photos: State availability with submission. Reviews transparencies, prints. Buys one-time rights. Negotiates payment individually. Captions required.

The online magazine carries original content not found in the print edition and includes writer's guidelines.

Tips: "Material should offer Biblical solutions to real-life problems. Both first-person and third-person illustrations are encouraged. Articles should take a unique twist on a subject. Material must be insightful and practical for the Christain reader. All articles must be well researched and Biblically accurate without becoming overly scholastic. Use convincing arguments to support your Christian platform. Use vivid word pictures, simple and compelling language, and avoid stuffy academic jargon. Captivating anecdotes are vital."

$ PRAIRIE MESSENGER, Catholic Journal, Benedictine Monks of St. Peter's Abbey, P.O. Box 190, Muenster SK S0K 2Y0, Canada. (306)682-1772. Fax: (306)682-5285. E-mail: pm.canadian@stpeters.sk.ca. Website: www.stpeters.sk.ca/prairie_messenger. Editor: Rev. Andrew Britz, OSB. **Contact:** Maureen Weber, associate editor. **10% freelance written.** Weekly Catholic journal with strong emphasis on social justice, Third World, and ecumenism. Estab. 1904. Circ. 7,300. Pays on publication. Publishes ms an average of 4 months after acceptance. Byline given. Not copyrighted. Buys first North American serial, first, one-time, second serial (reprint), simultaneous rights. Submit seasonal material 3 months in advance. Accepts queries by mail, e-mail, fax, phone. Responds in 2 months to queries. Sample copy for 9×12 SAE with $1 Canadian postage or IRCs. Writer's guidelines online.

Nonfiction: Interview/profile, opinion, religious. "No articles on abortion." **Buys 15 mss/year.** Send complete ms. Length: 250-600 words. **Pays $40-60.** Sometimes pays expenses of writers on assignment.

Photos: Send photos with submission. Reviews 3×5 prints. Buys all rights. Offers $15/photo. Captions required.

$ PRESBYTERIAN RECORD, 50 Wynford Dr., Toronto ON M3C 1J7, Canada. (416)444-1111. Fax: (416)441-2825. E-mail: dharris@presbyterian.ca. Website: www.presbyterian.ca/record. **Contact:** David Harris, editor. **30% free-**

lance written. Eager to work with new/unpublished writers. Monthly magazine for a church-oriented, family audience. Circ. 47,500. Pays on publication. Publishes ms an average of 4 months after acceptance. Buys first North American serial, one-time, simultaneous rights. Submit seasonal material 3 months in advance. Accepts queries by e-mail. Sample copy for 9×12 SAE with $1 Canadian postage or IRCs or online.

• Responds in 2 months on accepted ms.

Nonfiction: Check a copy of the magazine for style. Inspirational, interview/profile, personal experience, religious. Special issues: Evangelism; Spirituality; Education. No material solely or mainly US in context. No sermons, accounts of ordinations, inductions, baptisms, receptions, church anniversaries, or term papers. **Buys 5-10 unsolicited mss/year.** Query. Length: 600-1,500 words. **Pays other rates for assigned articles. Pays $150 (Canadian) for unsolicited articles.** Sometimes pays expenses of writers on assignment.

Reprints: Send tearsheet, photocopy or typed ms with rights for sale noted and information about when and where the material previously appeared.

Photos: When possible, photos should accompany ms; e.g., current events, historical events, and biographies. Pays $50 (Canadian) for glossy photos.

Columns/Departments: Vox Populi (items of contemporary and often controversial nature), 700 words; Mission Knocks (new ideas for congregational mission and service), 700 words.

Tips: "There is a trend away from maudlin, first-person pieces redolent with tragedy and dripping with simplistic, pietistic conclusions. Writers often leave out those parts which would likely attract readers, such as anecdotes and direct quotes. Using active rather than passive verbs also helps most manuscripts."

$ $ PRESBYTERIANS TODAY, Presbyterian Church (U.S.A.), 100 Witherspoon St., Louisville KY 40202-1396. (502)569-5637. Fax: (502)569-8632. E-mail: today@pcusa.org. Website: www.pcusa.org/today. **Contact:** Eva Stimson, editor. **45% freelance written.** Prefers to work with published/established writers. Denominational magazine published 10 times/year covering religion, denominational activities, and public issues for members of the Presbyterian Church (U.S.A.). "The magazine's purpose is to increase understanding and appreciation of what the church and its members are doing to live out their Christian faith." Estab. 1867. Circ. 63,000. **Pays on acceptance.** Publishes ms an average of 6 months after acceptance. Byline given. Offers 50% kill fee. Buys first North American serial rights. Editorial lead time 3 months. Submit seasonal material 3 months in advance. Accepts queries by mail, e-mail, fax, phone. Responds in 2 weeks to queries; 1 month to mss. Sample copy free. Writer's guidelines online.

O→ Break in with a "short feature for our 'Spotlight' department (300 words)."

Nonfiction: "Most articles have some direct relevance to a Presbyterian audience; however, *Presbyterians Today* also seeks well-informed articles written for a general audience that help readers deal with the stresses of daily living from a Christian perspective." How-to (everyday Christian living), inspirational, Presbyterian programs, issues, people. **Buys 20 mss/year.** Send complete ms. Length: 1,000-1,800 words. **Pays $300 maximum for assigned articles; $75-300 for unsolicited articles.**

Photos: State availability with submission. Reviews contact sheets, transparencies, color prints, digital images. Buys one-time rights. Negotiates payment individually. Identification of subjects required.

$ $ PRISM MAGAZINE, America's Alternative Evangelical Voice, Evangelicals for Social Action, 10 E. Lancaster Ave., Wynnewood PA 19096. (610)645-9391. Fax: (610)649-8090. E-mail: kristyn@esa-online.org. Website: www.esa-online.org. **Contact:** Kristyn Komarnicki, editor. **50% freelance written.** Bimonthly magazine covering Christianity and social justice. For holistic, Biblical, socially-concerned, progressive Christians. Estab. 1993. Circ. 5,000. Pays on publication. Publishes ms an average of 4-6 months after acceptance. Byline given. Buys first North American serial rights. Editorial lead time 4 months. Submit seasonal material 4 months in advance. Accepts queries by mail, e-mail. Responds in 1 month to queries; 3 months to mss. Sample copy for $3. Writer's guidelines free.

• "We're a nonprofit, some writers are pro bono." Occasionally accepts previously published material.

Nonfiction: Book excerpts (to coincide with book release date), essays, interview/profile (ministry). **Buys 10-12 mss/year.** Send complete ms. Length: 500-3,000 words. **Pays $75-300 for assigned articles; $25-200 for unsolicited articles.**

Photos: Send photos with submission. Reviews prints, JPEG files. Buys one-time rights. Pays $25/photo published; $150 if photo used on cover.

Tips: "We look closely at stories of holistic ministry. It's best to request a sample copy to get to know *PRISM*'s focus/style before submitting—we receive so many submissions that are not appropriate."

$ PURPOSE, 616 Walnut Ave., Scottdale PA 15683-1999. (724)887-8500. Fax: (724)887-3111. E-mail: horsch@mph.org. Website: www.mph.org. **Contact:** James E. Horsch, editor. **95% freelance written.** Weekly magazine "for adults, young and old, general audience with varied interests. My readership is interested in seeing how Christianity works in difficult situations. Magazine focuses on Christian discipleship—how to be a faithful Christian in the midst of everday life situations. Uses personal story form to present models and examples to encourage Christians in living a life of faithful discipleship." Estab. 1968. Circ. 11,000. **Pays on acceptance.** Publishes ms an average of 8 months after acceptance. Buys one-time rights. Submit seasonal material 6 months in advance. Accepts previously published material. Accepts simultaneous submissions. Responds in 3 months to queries. Sample copy and writer's guidelines for 6×9 SAE and 2 first-class stamps. Writer's guidelines free.

Nonfiction: Inspirational stories from a Christian perspective. "I want upbeat stories that deal with issues faced by believers in family, business, politics, religion, gender, and any other areas—and show how the Christian faith resolves them. *Purpose* conveys truth through quality fiction or true life stories. Our magazine accents Christian discipleship. Christianity affects all of life, and we expect our material to demonstrate this. I would like story-type articles about individuals, groups, and organizations who are intelligently and effectively working at such problems as hunger, poverty, international understanding, peace, justice, etc., because of their faith. Essays and how-to-do-it pieces must include a lot of anecdotal, life exposure examples." **Buys 130 mss/year.** Send complete ms. Length: 750 words. **Pays 5¢/word maximum. Buys one-time rights only.**

Reprints: Send tearsheet, photocopy or typed ms with rights for sale noted and information about when and where the material previously appeared.

Photos: Photos purchased with ms must be sharp enough for reproduction; requires prints in all cases. Pays $20. Captions required.

Fiction: "Produce the story with specificity so that it appears to take place somewhere and with real people." Historical, humorous, religious. No militaristic/narrow patriotism or racism. Send complete ms. Length:750 words. **Pays up to 5¢ for stories, and 2 contributor's copies.**

Poetry: Free verse, light verse, traditional, blank verse. **Buys 130 poems/year.** Length: 12 lines. **Pays $7.50-20/poem depending on length and quality. Buys one-time rights only.**

Fillers: Anecdotal items up to 599 words. **Pays 4¢/word maximum.**

Tips: "We are looking for articles which show the Christian faith working at issues where people hurt. Stories need to be told and presented professionally. Good photographs help place material with us."

$ QUEEN OF ALL HEARTS, Montfort Missionaries, 26 S. Saxon Ave., Bay Shore NY 11706-8993. (631)665-0726. Fax: (631)665-4349. E-mail: montfort@optonline.net. Website: www.montfortmissionaries.com. **Contact:** Roger Charest, S.M.M., managing editor. **50% freelance written.** Bimonthly magazine covering "Mary, Mother of Jesus, as seen in the sacred scriptures, tradition, history of the church, the early Christian writers, lives of the saints, poetry, art, music, spiritual writers, apparitions, shrines, ecumenism, etc." Magazine of "stories, articles and features on the Mother of God by explaining the Scriptural basis and traditional teaching of the Catholic Church concerning the Mother of Jesus, her influence in fields of history, literature, art, music, poetry, etc." Estab. 1950. Circ. 2,000. **Pays on acceptance.** Publishes ms an average of 6-12 months after acceptance. Byline given. Not copyrighted. Submit seasonal material 6 months in advance. Accepts queries by mail, e-mail, fax, phone. Responds in 2 months to queries. Sample copy for $2.50 with 9X12 SAE.

Nonfiction: Essays, inspirational, interview/profile, personal experience, religious (Marialogical and devotional). **Buys 25 mss/year.** Send complete ms. Length: 750-2,500 words. **Pays $40-60.**

Photos: Send photos with submission. Reviews transparencies. Buys one-time rights. Pay varies.

Fiction: Religious. "No mss not about Our Lady, the Mother of God, the Mother of Jesus." **Buys 6 mss/year.** Send complete ms. Length: 1,500-2,500 words. **Pays $40-60.**

Poetry: Joseph Tusiani, poetry editor. Free verse. **Buys approximately 10 poems/year.** Submit maximum 2 poems. **Pays in contributor copies.**

$ $ REFORM JUDAISM, Union of American Hebrew Congregations, 633 Third Ave., New York NY 10017-6778. (212)650-4240. Website: www.uahc.org/rjmag/. Editor: Aron Hirt-Manheimer. **Contact:** Joy Weinberg, managing editor. **30% freelance written.** Quarterly magazine of Reform Jewish issues. "*Reform Judaism* is the official voice of the Union of American Hebrew Congregations, linking the institutions and affiliates of Reform Judaism with every Reform Jew. *RJ* covers developments within the Movement while interpreting events and Jewish tradition from a Reform perspective." Pays on publication. Publishes ms an average of 3 months after acceptance. Byline given. Offers kill fee for commissioned articles. Buys first North American serial rights. Submit seasonal material 6 months in advance. Accepts previously published material. Responds in 2 months to queries; 2 months to mss. Sample copy for $3.50. Writer's guidelines online.

Nonfiction: Book excerpts, exposé, general interest, historical/nostalgic, inspirational, interview/profile, opinion, personal experience, photo feature, travel. **Buys 30 mss/year.** Submit complete ms with SASE. Length: Cover stories: 2,500-3,500 words; major feature: 1,800-2,500 words; secondary feature: 1,200-1,500 words; department (e.g., Travel): 1,200 words; letters: 200 words maximum; opinion: 525 words maximum. **Pays 30¢/word.** Sometimes pays expenses of writers on assignment.

Reprints: Send tearsheet, photocopy or typed ms with rights for sale noted and information about when and where the material previously appeared. Usually does not publish reprints.

Photos: Send photos with submission. Reviews 8×10/color or slides and b&w prints. Buys one-time rights. Pays $25-75. Identification of subjects required.

Fiction: Sophisticated, cutting-edge, superb writing. **Buys 4 mss/year.** Send complete ms. Length: 600-2,500 words. **Pays 30¢/word.**

The online magazine carries original content not found in the print edition and includes writer's guidelines.

Tips: "We prefer a stamped postcard including the following information/checklist: __Yes, we are interested in publishing; __No, unfortunately the submission doesn't meet our needs; __Maybe, we'd like to hold on to the article for now. Submissions sent this way will receive a faster response."

$ REVIEW FOR RELIGIOUS, 3601 Lindell Blvd., Room 428, St. Louis MO 63108-3393. (314)977-7363. Fax: (314)977-7362. E-mail: review@slu.edu. Website: www.reviewforreligious.org. **Contact:** David L. Fleming, S.J., editor. **100% freelance written.** Quarterly magazine for Roman Catholic priests, brothers, and sisters. Estab. 1942. Pays on publication. Publishes ms an average of 9 months after acceptance. Byline given. Buys first North American serial rights. Rarely buys second serial (reprint) rights. Accepts queries by mail, fax. Responds in 2 months to queries. Writer's guidelines online.

Nonfiction: Spiritual, liturgical, canonical matters only. Not for general audience. Length: 1,500-5,000 words. **Pays $6/page.**

Tips: "The writer must know about religious life in the Catholic Church and be familiar with prayer, vows, community life, and ministry."

$SCP JOURNAL and SCP NEWSLETTER, Spiritual Counterfeits Project, P.O. Box 4308, Berkeley CA 94704-4308. (510)540-0300. Fax: (510)540-1107. E-mail: scp@scp-inc.org. Website: www.scp-inc.org/. **Contact:** Tal Brooke, editor. **5-10% freelance written.** Prefers to work with published/established writers. "The *SCP Journal* and *SCP Newsletter* are quarterly publications geared to reach demanding nonbelievers while giving Christians authentic insight into the very latest spiritual and cultural trends." Targeted audience is the educated lay reader. Estab. 1975. Circ. 18,000. Pays on publication. Publishes ms an average of 6 months after acceptance. Byline given. Buys negotiable rights. Accepts simultaneous submissions. Responds in 3 months to queries. Sample copy for $8.75. Writer's guidelines online.

- Less emphasis on book reviews and more focus on specialized "single issue" topics.

Nonfiction: Book excerpts, essays, exposé, interview/profile, opinion, personal experience, religious. Query by telephone. Length: 2,500-3,500 words. **Payment negotiated by phone.**

Reprints: Call for telephone inquiry first. Payment is negotiated.

Photos: State availability with submission. Reviews contact sheets, prints, slides. Buys one-time rights. Offers no additional payment for photos accepted with ms. Captions, identification of subjects, model releases required.

Tips: "The area of our publication most open to freelancers is specialized topics covered by *SCP.* Do not send unsolicited samples of your work until you have checked with us by phone to see if it fits *SCP*'s area of interest and publication schedule. The usual profile of contributors is that they are published within the field, have advanced degrees from top ranked universities, as well as experience that makes their work uniquely credible."

N $THE SECRET PLACE, Educational Ministries, ABC/USA, P.O. Box 851, Valley Forge PA 19482-0851. (610)768-2240. **Contact:** Kathleen Hayes, senior editor. **100% freelance written.** Quarterly devotional covering Christian daily devotions. Estab. 1938. Circ. 150,000. **Pays on acceptance.** Byline given. Buys first rights. Editorial lead time 1 year. Submit seasonal material 9 months in advance. Sample copy for free. Writer's guidelines for #10 SASE.

Nonfiction: Inspirational. **Buys about 400 mss/year.** Send complete ms. Length: 100-200 words. **Pays $15 for assigned articles.**

Poetry: Avant-garde, free verse, light verse, traditional. **Buys 12-15/year poems/year.** Submit maximum 6 poems. Length: 4-30 lines. **Pays $15.**

$ $SHARING THE VICTORY, Fellowship of Christian Athletes, 8701 Leeds Rd., Kansas City MO 64129. (816)921-0909. Fax: (816)921-8755. E-mail: stv@fca.org. Website: www.fca.org. Editor: David Smale. **50% freelance written.** Prefers to work with published/established writers, but works with a growing number of new/unpublished writers each year. Published 9 times/year. "We seek to encourage and enable athletes and coaches at all levels to take their faith seriously on and off the 'field.'" Estab. 1959. Circ. 90,000. Pays on publication. Publishes ms an average of 4 months after acceptance. Byline given. Buys first rights. Submit seasonal material 6 months in advance. Responds in 3 months to queries; 3 months to mss. Sample copy for $1 and 9×12 SAE with 3 first-class stamps. Writer's guidelines online.

Nonfiction: Inspirational, interview/profile (with name athletes and coaches solid in their faith), personal experience, photo feature. No "sappy articles on 'I became a Christian and now I'm a winner.'" **Buys 5-20 mss/year.** Query. Length: 500-1,000 words. **Pays $100-200 for unsolicited articles.**

Photos: State availability with submission. Reviews contact sheets. Buys one-time rights. Pay based on size of photo.

Tips: "Profiles and interviews of particular interest to coed athlete, primarily high school and college age. Our graphics and editorial content appeal to youth. The area most open to freelancers is profiles on or interviews with well-known athletes or coaches (male, female, minorities) and offbeat but interscholastic team sports."

$ $SIGNS OF THE TIMES, Pacific Press Publishing Association, P.O. Box 5353, Nampa ID 83653-5353. (208)465-2579. Fax: (208)465-2531. E-mail: mmoore@pacificpress.com. **Contact:** Marvin Moore, editor. **40% freelance written.** Works with a small number of new/unpublished writers each year. Monthly magazine. "We are a monthly Seventh-day Adventist magazine encouraging the general public to practice the principles of the Bible." Estab. 1874. Circ. 200,000. **Pays on acceptance.** Publishes ms an average of 6-18 months after acceptance. Byline given. Offers kill fee. Buys first North American serial, one-time, second serial (reprint) rights. Editorial lead time 1 year. Submit seasonal material 1 year in advance. Responds in 1 month to queries; 2-3 months to mss. Sample copy and writer's guidelines for 9×12 SAE with 3 first-class stamps. Writer's guidelines online.

Nonfiction: "We want writers with a desire to share the good news of reconciliation with God. Articles should be people-oriented, well-researched, and should have a sharp focus. Gospel articles deal with salvation and how to experience it. While most of our gospel articles are assigned or picked up from reprints, we do occasionally accept unsolicited manuscripts in this area. Gospel articles should be 1,250 words. Christian lifestyle articles deal with the practical problems of everyday life from a Biblical and Christian perspective. These are typically 1,000-1,200 words. We request that authors include sidebars that give additional information on the topic whenever possible. First-person stories must illuminate a spiritual or moral truth that the individual in the story learned. We especially like stories that hold the reader in suspense or that have an unusual twist at the end. First-person stories are typically 1,000 words long." General interest, how-to, humor, inspirational, interview/profile, personal experience, religious. **Buys 75 mss/year.** Query by mail only with or without published clips or send complete ms. Length: 500-1,500 words. **Pays 10-20¢/word.**

Reprints: Send tearsheet, photocopy or typed ms with rights for sale noted and information about when and where the material previously appeared. Pays 50% of amount paid for an original article.

Photos: Merwin Stewart, photo editor. Reviews b&w contact sheets, 35mm color transparencies, 5×7 or 8×10 b&w prints. Buys one-time rights. Pays $35-300 for transparencies; $20-50 for prints. Captions, identification of subjects, model releases required.

Fillers: "Short fillers can be inspirational/devotional, Christian lifestyle, stories, comments that illuminate a Biblical text—in short, anything that might fit in a general Christian magazine." Length: 500-600 words.

Tips: "The audience for *Signs of the Times* includes both Christians and non-Christians of all ages. However, we recommend that our authors write with the non-Christian in mind, since most Christians can easily relate to articles that are written from a non-Christian perspective, whereas many non-Christians will have no interest in an article that is written from a Christian perspective. While *Signs* is published by Seventh-day Adventists, we mention even our own denominational name in the magazine rather infrequently. The purpose is not to hide who we are but to make the magazine as attractive to non-Christian readers as possible. We are especially interested in articles that respond to the questions of everyday life that people are asking and the problems they are facing. Since these questions and problems nearly always have a spiritual component, articles that provide a Biblical and spiritual response are especially welcome. Any time you can provide us with 1 or more sidebars that add information to the topic of your article, you enhance your chance of getting our attention. Two kinds of sidebars seem to be especially popular with readers: those that give information in lists, with each item in the list consisting of only a few words or at the most a sentence, or those that give technical information or long explanations that in the main article might get the reader too bogged down in detail. Whatever their length, sidebars need to be part of the total word count of the article. We like the articles in *Signs of the Times* to have interest-grabbing introductions. One of the best ways to do this is with anecdotes, particularly those that have a bit of suspense or conflict."

$ SOCIAL JUSTICE REVIEW, 3835 Westminster Place, St. Louis MO 63108-3472. (314)371-1653. Fax: (314)371-0889. E-mail: centbur@juno.com. Website: www.socialjusticereview.org. **Contact:** The Rev. John H. Miller, C.S.C., editor. **25% freelance written.** Works with a small number of new/unpublished writers each year. Bimonthly magazine. Estab. 1908. Publishes ms an average of 1 year after acceptance. Not copyrighted, however special articles within the magazine may be copyrighted, or an occasional special issue has been copyrighted due to author's request. Buys first North American serial rights. Accepts queries by mail. Sample copy for 9×12 SAE and 3 first-class stamps.

Nonfiction: Scholarly articles on society's economic, religious, social, intellectual, political problems with the aim of bringing Catholic social thinking to bear upon these problems. Query by mail only with SASE. Length: 2,500-3,000 words. **Pays about 2¢/word.**

Reprints: Send ms with rights for sale noted and information about when and where the material previously appeared. Pays about 2¢/word.

Tips: "Write moderate essays completely compatible with papal teaching and readable to the average person."

$ SPIRITUAL LIFE, 2131 Lincoln Rd. NE, Washington DC 20002-1199. (202)832-8489. Fax: (202)832-8967. E-mail: edodonnell@aol.com. Website: www.spiritual-life.org. **Contact:** Br. Edward O'Donnell, O.C.D., editor. **80% freelance written.** Prefers to work with published/established writers. Quarterly magazine for "largely Christian, well-educated, serious readers." Circ. 12,000. **Pays on acceptance.** Publishes ms an average of 1 year after acceptance. Buys first North American serial rights. Responds in 2 months to queries. Sample copy and writer's guidelines for 7x10 or larger SAE with 5 first-class stamps.

Nonfiction: Serious articles of contemporary spirituality and its pastoral application to everday life. High quality articles about our encounter with God in the present day world. Language of articles should be college level. Technical terminology, if used, should be clearly explained. Material should be presented in a postive manner. Buys inspirational and think pieces. "Brief autobiographical information (present occupation, past occupations, books and articles published, etc.) should accompany article." Sentimental articles or those dealing with specific devotional practices not accepted. No fiction or poetry. **Buys 20 mss/year.** Length: 3,000-5,000 words. **Pays $50 minimum, and 2 contributor's copies.**

$ $ ST. ANTHONY MESSENGER, 28 W. Liberty St., Cincinnati OH 45202-6498. (513)241-5615. Fax: (513)241-0399. E-mail: stanthony@americancatholic.org. Website: www.americancatholic.org. **Contact:** Father Pat McCloskey, O.F.M., editor. **55% freelance written.** Monthly general interest magazine for a national readership of Catholic families, most of which have children or grandchildren in grade school, high school, or college. "*St. Anthony Messenger* is a Catholic family magazine which aims to help its readers lead more fully human and Christian lives. We publish articles which report on a changing church and world, opinion pieces written from the perspective of Christian faith and values, personality profiles, and fiction which entertains and informs." Estab. 1893. Circ. 324,000. **Pays on acceptance.** Publishes ms an average of 1 year after acceptance. Byline given. Buys first North American serial, electronic rights. Buys electronic, first worldwide serial rights. Submit seasonal material 6 months in advance. Accepts queries by mail, e-mail, fax. Accepts simultaneous submissions. Responds in 3 weeks to queries; 2 months to mss. Sample copy for 9×12 SAE with 4 first-class stamps. Writer's guidelines online.

Nonfiction: How-to (on psychological and spiritual growth, problems of parenting/better parenting, marriage problems/marriage enrichment), humor, inspirational, interview/profile, opinion (limited use; writer must have special qualifications for topic), personal experience (if pertinent to our purpose), photo feature, informational, social issues. **Buys 35-50 mss/year.** Query with published clips. Length: 1,500-2,500 words. **Pays 16¢/word.** Sometimes pays expenses of writers on assignment.

Fiction: Mainstream, religious, senior citizen/retirement. "We do not want mawkishly sentimental or preachy fiction. Stories are most often rejected for poor plotting and characterization; bad dialogue—listen to how people talk; inadequate motivation. Many stories say nothing, are 'happenings' rather than stories." No fetal journals, no rewritten Bible stories. **Buys 12 mss/year.** Send complete ms. Length: 2,000-3,000 words. **Pays 16¢/word maximum and 2 contributor's coopies; $1 charge for extras.**

Poetry: "Our poetry needs are very limited." Submit maximum 4-5 poems. Length: Up to 20-25 lines; the shorter, the better. **Pays $2/line; $20 minimum.**

Tips: "The freelancer should consider why his or her proposed article would be appropriate for us, rather than for *Redbook* or *Saturday Review.* We treat human problems of all kinds, but from a religious perspective. Articles should reflect Catholic theology, spirituality, and employ a Catholic terminology and vocabulary. We need more articles on prayer, scripture,

Catholic worship. Get authoritative information (not merely library research); we want interviews with experts. Write in popular style; use lots of examples, stories, and personal quotes. Word length is an important consideration."

$ STANDARD, Nazarene International Headquarters, 6401 The Paseo, Kansas City MO 64131. (816)333-7000. Fax: (816)333-4439. E-mail: evlead@nazarene.org. Website: www.nazarene.org. **Contact:** Dr. Everett Leadingham, editor. **100% freelance written.** Works with a small number of new/unpublished writers each year. Weekly inspirational paper with Christian reading for adults. Inspirational reading for adults. "In *Standard* we want to show Christianity in action, and we prefer to do that through stories that hold the reader's attention." Estab. 1936. Circ. 130,000. **Pays on acceptance.** Publishes ms an average of 14-18 months after acceptance. Byline given. Buys Buys one-time rights, whether first or reprint rights. Submit seasonal material 6 months in advance. Accepts simultaneous submissions. Writer's guidelines and sample copy for SAE with 2 first-class stamps.

- Accepts submissions by mail, e-mail. No queries needed.

Fiction: Prefers fiction-type stories *showing* Christianity in action. Send complete ms. Length: 600-1,800 words. **Pays 3½¢/word for first rights; 2¢/word for reprint rights, and contributor's copies.**

Poetry: Free verse, haiku, light verse, traditional. **Buys 50 poems/year.** Submit maximum 5 poems. Length: 30 lines. **Pays 25¢/line.**

Tips: "Stories should express Christian principles without being preachy. Setting, plot, and characterization must be realistic."

$ TODAY'S PENTECOSTAL EVANGEL, (formerly *Pentecostal Evangel*), The General Council of the Assemblies of God, 1445 N. Boonville, Springfield MO 65802-1894. (417)862-2781. Fax: (417)862-0416. E-mail: pe@ag.org. Website: www.pe.ag.org. Editor: Hal Donaldson. **5% freelance written.** Works with a small number of new/unpublished writers each year. Weekly magazine emphasizing news of the Assemblies of God for members of the Assemblies and other Pentecostal and charismatic Christians. Estab. 1913. Circ. 250,000. **Pays on acceptance.** Publishes ms an average of 6 months after acceptance. Byline given. Buys first North American serial, second serial (reprint), electronic rights. Submit seasonal material 6 months in advance. Accepts queries by mail, e-mail, fax, phone. Responds in 3 months to queries. Sample copy for $1 or online. Writer's guidelines online.

Nonfiction: Inspirational, personal experience, informational (articles on homelife that convey Christian teaching), news, human interest, evangelical, current issues, seasonal. Send complete ms. Length: 500-1,200 words. **Pays up to $150.**

Photos: Photos purchased without accompanying ms. Pays $30 for 8×10 b&w glossy prints; $50 for 35mm or larger color transparencies Total purchase price for ms includes payment for photos.

Tips: "We publish first-person articles concerning spiritual experiences; that is, answers to prayer for help in a particular situation, of unusual conversions or healings through faith in Christ. All articles submitted to us should be related to religious life. We are Protestant, evangelical, Pentecostal, and any doctrines or practices portrayed should be in harmony with the official position of our denomination (Assemblies of God)."

$ TRICYCLE, THE BUDDHIST REVIEW, The Buddhist Ray, Inc, 92 Vandam St., New York NY 10013. (212)645-1143. Fax: (212)645-1493. E-mail: editorial@tricycle.com. Website: www.tricycle.com. Editor-in-Chief: James Shaheen. **Contact:** Caitlin Van Dusen, associate editor. **80% freelance written.** Quarterly magazine covering the impact of Buddhism on Western culture. "*Tricycle* readers tend to be well educated and open minded." Estab. 1991. Circ. 60,000. Pays on publication. Byline given. Offers 25% kill fee. Buys one-time rights. Editorial lead time 3 months. Accepts queries by mail, e-mail, fax. Accepts simultaneous submissions. Responds in 3 months to queries; 3 months to mss. Sample copy for $7.50 or online at website. Writer's guidelines online.

Nonfiction: Book excerpts, essays, general interest, historical/nostalgic, humor, inspirational, interview/profile, personal experience, photo feature, religious, travel. **Buys 4-6 mss/year.** Length: 1,000-5,000 words.

Photos: State availability with submission. Reviews contact sheets. Buys one-time rights. Negotiates payment individually. Captions, identification of subjects required.

Columns/Departments: Reviews (film, books, tapes), 600 words; Science and Gen Next, both 700 words. **Buys 6-8 mss/year.** Query.

Poetry: *Tricycle* reports that they publish "very little poetry" and do not encourage unsolicited submissions.

Tips: "*Tricycle* is a Buddhist magazine, and we can only consider Buddhist-related submissions."

$ $ U.S. CATHOLIC, Claretian Publications, 205 W. Monroe St., Chicago IL 60606. (312)236-7782. Fax: (312)236-8207. E-mail: editors@uscatholic.org. Website: www.uscatholic.org. Editor: Fr. John Molyneux, CMF. Editorial Director: Anne Spencer Ellis. Executive Editor: Meinrad Scherer-Emunds. **Contact:** Fran Hurst, editorial assistant. **100% freelance written.** Monthly magazine covering Roman Catholic spirituality. "*U.S. Catholic* is dedicated to the belief that it makes a difference whether you're Catholic. We invite and help our readers explore the wisdom of their faith tradition and apply their faith to the challenges of the 21st century." Estab. 1935. Circ. 50,000. **Pays on acceptance.** Publishes ms an average of 2-3 months after acceptance. Byline given. Buys first North American serial rights. Editorial lead time 8 months. Submit seasonal material 6 months in advance. Accepts queries by mail, e-mail, fax, phone. Responds in 1 month to queries; 2 months to mss. Sample copy for large SASE. Guidelines by e-mail or on website.

Nonfiction: Essays, inspirational, opinion, personal experience, religious. **Buys 100 mss/year.** Send complete ms. Length: 2,500-3,500 words. **Pays $250-600.** Sometimes pays expenses of writers on assignment.

Photos: State availability with submission.

Columns/Departments: Pays $250-600.

Fiction: Maureen Abood, literary editor. Ethnic, mainstream, religious, slice-of-life vignettes. **Buys 4-6 mss/year.** Send complete ms. Length: 2,500-3,000 words. **Pays $300.**

Poetry: Maureen Abood, literary editor. Free verse. "No light verse." **Buys 12 poems/year.** Submit maximum 5 poems. Length: 50 lines. **Pays $75.**

$ THE UNITED CHURCH OBSERVER, 478 Huron St., Toronto ON M5R 2R3, Canada. (416)960-8500. Fax: (416)960-8477. E-mail: general@ucobserver.org. Website: www.ucobserver.org. **Contact:** Muriel Duncan, editor. **20% freelance written.** Prefers to work with published/established writers. Monthly newsmagazine for people associated with The United Church of Canada. Deals primarily with events, trends, and policies having religious significance. Most coverage is Canadian, but reports on international or world concerns will be considered. Pays on publication. Publishes ms an average of 4 months after acceptance. Byline usually given. first serial rights and occasionally all rights. Accepts queries by mail, e-mail, fax.

Nonfiction: Occasional opinion features only. Extended coverage of major issues is usually assigned to known writers. Submissions should be written as news, no more than 1,200 words length, accurate, and well-researched. No opinion pieces or poetry. Queries preferred. **Rates depend on subject, author, and work involved.** Pays expenses of writers on assignment as negotiated.

Reprints: Send tearsheet or photocopy and information about when and where the material previously appeared. Payment negotiated.

Photos: Buys photographs with mss. Color or b&w, electronic mail. Payment varies.

Tips: "The writer has a better chance of breaking in at our publication with short articles; this also allows us to try more freelancers. Include samples of previous *news* writing with query. Indicate ability and willingness to do research, and to evaluate that research. The most frequent mistakes made by writers in completing an article for us are organizational problems, lack of polished style, short on research, and a lack of inclusive language."

$ THE UPPER ROOM, Daily Devotional Guide, P.O. Box 340004, Nashville TN 37203-0004. (615)340-7252. Fax: (615)340-7267. E-mail: theupperroommagazine@upperroom.org. Website: www.upperroom.org. Editor and Publisher: Stephen D. Bryant. **Contact:** Marilyn Beaty, editorial assistant. **95% freelance written.** Eager to work with new/unpublished writers. Bimonthly magazine "offering a daily inspirational message which includes a Bible reading, text, prayer, 'Thought for the Day,' and suggestion for further prayer. Each day's meditation is written by a different person and is usually a personal witness about discovering meaning and power for Christian living through scripture study which illuminates daily life." Circ. 2.2 million (U.S.); 385,000 outside U.S. Pays on publication. Publishes ms an average of 1 year after acceptance. Byline given. Buys first North American serial, translation rights rights. Submit seasonal material 14 months in advance. Sample copy and writer's guidelines with a 4×6 SAE and 2 first-class stamps. Guidelines only for #10 SASE or online.

- "Manuscripts are not returned. If writers include a stamped, self-addressed postcard, we will notify them that their writing has reached us. This does not imply acceptance or interest in purchase. Does not respond unless material is accepted for publication."

Nonfiction: Inspirational, personal experience, Bible-study insights. Special issues: Lent and Easter; Advent. No poetry, lengthy "spiritual journey" stories. **Buys 365 unsolicited mss/year.** Send complete ms by mail or e-mail. Length:300 words. **Pays $25/meditation.**

Tips: "The best way to break in to our magazine is to send a well-written manuscript that looks at the Christian faith in a fresh way. Standard stories and sermon illustrations are immediately rejected. We very much want to find new writers and welcome good material. We are particularly interested in meditations based on Old Testament characters and stories. Good repeat meditations can lead to work on longer assignments for our other publications, which pay more. A writer who can deal concretely with everyday situations, relate them to the Bible and spiritual truths, and write clear, direct prose should be able to write for *The Upper Room*. We want material that provides for more interaction on the part of the reader—meditation suggestions, journaling suggestions, space to reflect and link personal experience with the meditation for the day. Meditations that are personal, authentic, exploratory, and full of sensory detail make good devotional writing."

$ $ THE UU WORLD, Unitarian Universalist Association, 25 Beacon St., Boston MA 02108-2800. (617)742-2100. Fax: (617)742-7025. E-mail: world@uua.org. Website: www.uuworld.org. Editor: Tom Stites. **Contact:** Teresa Schwartz. **50% freelance written.** Bimonthly magazine "to promote and inspire denominational self-reflection; to inform readers about the wide range of Unitarian Universalist values, purposes, activities, aesthetics, and spiritual attitudes, and to educate readers about the history, personalities, and congregations that comprise UUism; to enhance its dual role of leadership and service to member congregations." Estab. 1987. Circ. 120,000. **Pays on acceptance.** Publishes ms an average of 1 year after acceptance. Byline given. Buys one-time rights. Editorial lead time 3 months. Submit seasonal material 3 months in advance. Accepts queries by mail, e-mail, fax. Responds in 3 months to queries; 3 months to mss. Sample copy for 9×12 SAE or online. Writer's guidelines online.

Nonfiction: All articles must have a clear UU angle. Essays, historical/nostalgic (Unitarian or Universalist focus), inspirational, interview/profile (with UU individual or congregation), photo feature (of UU congregation or project), religious. Special issues: "We are planning issues on family, spirituality, and welfare reform." No unsolicited poetry or fiction. **Buys 5 mss/year.** Query with published clips. Length: 1,500-3,500 words. **Pays $400 minimum for assigned articles.** Sometimes pays expenses of writers on assignment.

Photos: State availability with submission. Reviews contact sheets. Buys one-time rights. Offers no additional payment for photos accepted with ms. Captions, identification of subjects, model releases required.

Columns/Departments: Living the Faith (profiles of UUs and UU congregations). **Pays $250-500 for assigned articles.**

$ $ THE WAR CRY, The Salvation Army, 615 Slaters Lane, Alexandria VA 22313. (703)684-5500. Fax: (703)684-5539. E-mail: war_cry@usn.salvationarmy.org. Website: www.thewarcry.com. Managing Editor: Jeff McDonald. **Contact:** Lt. Colonel Marlene Chase, editor-in-chief. **10% freelance written.** Biweekly magazine covering army news and Christian devotional writing. Estab. 1881. Circ. 400,000. **Pays on acceptance.** Publishes ms an average of 2 months-1 year after acceptance. Byline given. Buys first, one-time rights. Editorial lead time 6 weeks. Submit seasonal material 1 year in advance. Accepts previously published material. Accepts simultaneous submissions. Responds in 2 months to mss. Sample copy, theme list, and writer's guidelines free for #10 SASEor online.

- Responds in 4-6 weeks to articles submitted on speculation.

"A best bet would be a well-written profile of an exemplary Christian or a recounting of a person's experiences that deepened the subject's faith and showed God in action. Most popular profiles are of Salvation Army programs and personnel."

Nonfiction: Humor, inspirational, interview/profile, personal experience, religious. No missionary stories, confessions. **Buys 40 mss/year.** Send complete ms. **Pays up to 20¢/word for assigned articles; 15-20¢/word for unsolicited articles.** Sometimes pays expenses of writers on assignment.

Reprints: Send ms with rights for sale noted and information about when and where the material previously appeared. Pays 12¢/word.

Photos: Buys one-time rights. Offers $35-200/photo. Identification of subjects required.

Fiction: Religious, for college age youth. "No fantasy, science fiction or New Age." **Buys 5-10 mss/year.** Send complete ms. Length: 1,200-1,500 words. **Pays up to 10-20¢/word; 12¢ for reprints, and 2 contributor's copies.**

Poetry: Free verse. **Buys 10-20/year poems/year.** Submit maximum 5 poems. Length: 16 lines. **Pays $20-50.**

Fillers: Anecdotes (inspirational). **Buys 10-20/year.** Length: 200-500 words. **Pays 15-20¢/word.**

Tips: "We are soliciting more short fiction, inspirational articles and poetry, interviews with Christian athletes, evangelical leaders and celebrities, and theme-focused articles."

$ THE WESLEYAN ADVOCATE, The Wesleyan Publishing House, P.O. Box 50434, Indianapolis IN 46250-0434. (317)570-5204. Fax: (317)570-5260. E-mail: communications@wesleyan.org. Executive Editor: Dr. Norman G. Wilson. **Contact:** Jerry Brecheisen, managing editor. Monthly magazine of The Wesleyan Church. Estab. 1842. Circ. 20,000. Pays on publication. Byline given. Buys first rights or simultaneous rights (prefers first rights). Submit seasonal material 6 months in advance. Accepts simultaneous submissions. Responds in 2 weeks to queries. Sample copy for $2. Writer's guidelines for #10 SASE.

Nonfiction: Humor, inspirational, religious. No poetry accepted. Send complete ms. Length: 500-700 words. **Pays $25-150.**

Reprints: Send photocopy of article and typed ms with rights for sale noted and information about when and where the material previously appeared.

Tips: "Write for a guide."

$ $ WHISPERS FROM HEAVEN, Publications International, Ltd., 7373 N. Cicero, Lincolnwood IL 60712. Fax: (847)329-5387. E-mail: vsmith@pubint.com. Editor: Julie Greene. Managing Editor: Becky Bell. **Contact:** Vicki Smith, acquisitions editor. **100% freelance written.** Bimonthly magazine covering inspirational human-interest. "We're looking for real-life experiences (personal and otherwise) that lift the human spirit and illuminate positive human traits and values: Though many stories may deal with (the overcoming of) tragedy and/or difficult times, descriptions shouldn't be too visceral and the emphasis should be on adversity overcome with a positive result. *Whispers*, though inspiring, is not overtly religious." Estab. 1999. Circ. 50,000. **Pays on acceptance.** Publishes ms an average of 5 months after acceptance. Byline given. Buys all rights. Editorial lead time 5 months. Submit seasonal material 5 months in advance. Accepts queries by mail, e-mail, fax. Writer's guidelines free.

Nonfiction: Essays, general interest, inspirational, personal experience, religious. "Nothing overtly religious or anything that explores negative human characteristics." **Buys 150 mss/year.** Query with or without published clips. Length: 800-1,200 words. **Pays $100-225.** Pays expenses of writers on assignment.

Tips: "We are particularly fond of stories (when warranted) that have a 'twist' at the end—an extra bit of surprising information that adds meaning and provides an emotional connecting point to the story itself."

$ WOMAN'S TOUCH, Assemblies of God Women's Ministries Department (GPH), 1445 N. Boonville Ave., Springfield MO 65802-1894. (417)862-2781. Fax: (417)862-0503. E-mail: womanstouch@ag.org. Website: www.ag.org/womanstouch. **Contact:** Darla Knoth, managing editor. **50% freelance written.** Willing to work with new/unpublished writers. Bimonthly inspirational magazine for women. "Articles and contents of the magazine should be compatible with Christian teachings as well as human interests. The audience is women of all walks of life." Estab. 1977. Circ. 15,000. Pays on publication. Publishes ms an average of 10 months after acceptance. Byline given. Buys first, second, or one-time and electronic rights. Editorial lead time 10 months. Submit seasonal material 10 months in advance. Accepts queries by mail, e-mail, fax. Responds in 3 months to queries. Sample copy for 9½×11 SAE with 3 first-class stamps or online. Writer's guidelines online.

Nonfiction: Book excerpts, general interest, inspirational, personal experience, religious, health. No fiction, poetry. **Buys 30 mss/year.** Send complete ms. Length: 200-600 words. **Pays $10-50 for assigned articles; $10-35 for unsolicited articles.**

Reprints: Send photocopy and information about when and where the material previously appeared. Pays 50-75% of amount paid for an original article.

Columns/Departments: A Final Touch (inspirational/human interest), 400 words; A Better You (health/wellness), 400 words; A Lighter Touch (true, unpublished anecdotes), 100 words.

The online magazine carries original content not found in the print edition and includes writer's guidelines. Contact: Darla Knoth, online editor.

Tips: "Submit manuscripts on current issues of interest to women. Familiarize yourself with *Woman's Touch* by reading 2 issues before submitting an article."

N **$ WORLD PULSE**, Billy Graham Center at Wheaton College, P.O. Box 794, Wheaton IL 60189. (630)752-7158. Fax: (630)752-7155. E-mail: pulsenews@aol.com. Website: www.worldpulseonline.com. **Contact:** Editor. **50% freelance written.** Biweekly newsletter covering evangelical missions. "News and features on world evangelization written from an evangelical position." Estab. 1965. Circ. 4,000. Pays on publication. Byline given. Offers negotiable kill fee. Buys first North American serial, electronic rights. Accepts queries by mail, e-mail, fax. Sample copy and writer's guidelines free.

Nonfiction: Interview/profile, personal experience, photo feature, religious. No poetry, sermons, or humor. **Buys 50 mss/year.** Query. Length: 500-1,000 words. **Pays $30-100.**

Photos: State availability with submission. Reviews prints. Buys one-time rights. Offers $25 for photos/article. Identification of subjects required.

Columns/Departments: InterView (Q&A with newsmakers), 300-500 words.

Tips: "*Pulse* is not a daily newspaper. Don't write a vanilla news story (with just the 5 Ws and an H). Sprinkle human interest and memorable facts throughout the story. Try to inform and entertain."

RETIREMENT

On January 1, 1996, the first baby boomer turned 50. With peak earning power and increased leisure time, this generation is able to pursue varied interests while maintaining active lives. More people are retiring in their 50s, while others are starting a business or traveling and pursuing hobbies. These publications give readers specialized information on health and fitness, medical research, finances, and other topics of interest, as well as general articles on travel destinations and recreational activities.

$ $ $ $ AARP THE MAGAZINE, (formerly *Modern Maturity*), AARP, 601 E St. NW, Washington DC 20049. (202)434-6880. Website: www.aarp.org. **Contact:** Hugh Delehanty, editor. **50% freelance written.** Prefers to work with published/established writers. Bimonthly magazine. "*AARP The Magazine* is devoted to the varied needs and active life interests of AARP members, age 50 and over, covering such topics as financial planning, travel, health, careers, retirement, relationships, and social and cultural change. Its editorial content serves the mission of AARP seeking through education, advocacy and service to enhance the quality of life for all by promoting independence, dignity, and purpose." Circ. 21,500,000. **Pays on acceptance.** Publishes ms an average of 6 months after acceptance. Byline given. Buys exclusive first worldwide publication rights. Submit seasonal material 6 months in advance. Responds in 3 months to queries. Sample copy and writer's guidelines free.

Nonfiction: Careers, workplace, practical information in living, financial and legal matters, personal relationships, consumerism. Query first by mail only. *No unsolicited mss.* Length: Up to 2,000 words. **Pays up to $3,000.** Sometimes pays expenses of writers on assignment.

Photos: Photos purchased with or without accompanying mss. Pays $250 and up for color; $150 and up for b&w.

Fiction: Very occasional short fiction.

Tips: "The most frequent mistake made by writers in completing an article for us is poor follow-through with basic research. The outline is often more interesting than the finished piece. We do not accept unsolicited manuscripts."

$ ALIVE!, A Magazine for Christian Senior Adults, Christian Seniors Fellowship, P.O. Box 46464, Cincinnati OH 45246-0464. (513)825-3681. Editor: J. David Lang. **Contact:** A. June Lang, office editor. **60% freelance written.** Bimonthly magazine for senior adults 50 and older. "We need timely articles about Christian seniors in vital, productive lifestyles, travel or ministries." Estab. 1988. Pays on publication. Byline given. Buys first, second serial (reprint) rights. Submit seasonal material 6 months in advance. Responds in 2 months to mss. Sample copy for 9×12 SAE with 3 first-class stamps. Writer's guidelines for #10 SASE.

- Membership $18/year. Organization membership may be deducted from payment at writer's request.

Nonfiction: General interest, humor, inspirational, interview/profile, photo feature, religious, travel. **Buys 25-50 mss/year.** Send complete ms and SASE. Length: 600-1,200 words. **Pays $18-75.**

Reprints: Send tearsheet, photocopy or typed ms with rights for sale noted and information about when and where the material previously appeared. Pays 60-75% of amount paid for an original article.

Photos: State availability with submission. Buys one-time rights. Offers $10-25. Identification of subjects, model releases required.

Columns/Departments: Heart Medicine (humorous personal anecdotes; prefer grandparent/granchild stories or anecdotes re: over-55 persons), 10-100 words. **Buys 50 mss/year.** Send complete ms and SASE. **Pays $2-25.**

Fiction: Adventure, humorous, religious, romance, slice-of-life vignettes, motivational, inspirational. **Buys 12 mss/year.** Send complete ms. Length: 600-1,200 words. **Pays $20-60.**

Fillers: Anecdotes, facts, gags to be illustrated by cartoonist, short humor. **Buys 15/year.** Length: 50-500 words. **Pays $2-15.**

Tips: "Include SASE and information regarding whether manuscript is to be returned or tossed."

$ FIFTY SOMETHING MAGAZINE, Jet Media, 7533-C Tyler Blvd., Mentor OH 44060. (440)953-2200. Fax: (440)953-2202. E-mail: linde@apk.net. **Contact:** Linda Lindeman DeCarlo, publisher. **80% freelance written.** Quarterly magazine covering nostalgia. "We are focusing on the 50-and-better reader." Estab. 1990. Circ. 10,000. Pays on publication.

Publishes ms an average of 6 months after acceptance. Byline given. Offers 5% kill fee. Buys one-time, second serial (reprint), simultaneous rights. Editorial lead time 6 months. Submit seasonal material 6 months in advance. Accepts queries by mail, e-mail. Accepts previously published material. Accepts simultaneous submissions. Responds in 3 months to queries; 3 months to mss. Sample copy for 9×12 SAE and 4 first-class stamps. Writer's guidelines for #10 SASE.

Nonfiction: Book excerpts, essays, exposé, general interest, historical/nostalgic, how-to, humor, inspirational, interview/profile, new product, opinion, personal experience, photo feature, travel. **Buys 10 mss/year.** Length: 500-1,500 words. **Pays $10-100.** Sometimes pays expenses of writers on assignment.

Photos: Send photos with submission. Reviews 4×6 prints, GIF/JPEG files. Buys one-time rights. Negotiates payment individually. Captions, identification of subjects, model releases required.

Columns/Departments: Health & Fitness (good news/tips), 500 words; Travel (unique trips), 1,000 words; Humor (aging issues), 500 words; Finance (tips), 500 words. **Buys 10 mss/year.** Send complete ms. **Pays $10-100.**

Fiction: Adventure, confessions, ethnic, experimental, fantasy, historical, humorous, mainstream, mystery, novel excerpts, romance, slice-of-life vignettes, suspense, western. No erotica or horror. **Buys 10 mss/year.** Send complete ms. Length: 500-1,500 words. **Pays $10-100.**

Poetry: Avant-garde, free verse, light verse, traditional. **Buys 10 poems/year.** Submit maximum 5 poems. Length: 10-25 lines.

Fillers: Anecdotes, facts, gags to be illustrated by cartoonist, newsbreaks, short humor. **Buys 10/year.** Length: 50-150 words. **Pays $10-100.**

$ MATURE YEARS, The United Methodist Publishing House, 201 Eighth Ave. S., Nashville TN 37202-0801. (615)749-6292. Fax: (615)749-6512. E-mail: matureyears@umpublishing.org. **Contact:** Marvin W. Cropsey, editor. **50% freelance written.** Prefers to work with published/established writers. Quarterly magazine "designed to help persons in and nearing the retirement years understand and appropriate the resources of the Christian faith in dealing with specific problems and opportunities related to aging." Magazine "helps persons in and nearing retirement to appropriate the resources of the Christian faith as they seek to face the problems and opportunities related to aging." Estab. 1954. Circ. 55,000. **Pays on acceptance.** Publishes ms an average of 1 year after acceptance. Buys first North American serial rights. Submit seasonal material 14 months in advance. Responds in 2 weeks to queries; 2 months to mss. Sample copy for $5 and 9×12 SAE. Writer's guidelines for #10 SASE or by e-mail.

Nonfiction: Especially important are opportunities for older adults to read about service, adventure, fulfillment, and fun. How-to (hobbies), inspirational, religious, travel (special guidelines), older adult health, finance issues. **Buys 75-80 mss/year.** Send complete ms; e-mail submissions preferred. Length: 900-2,000 words. **Pays $45-125.** Sometimes pays expenses of writers on assignment.

Reprints: Send tearsheet, photocopy or typed ms with rights for sale noted and information about when and where the material previously appeared. Pays at same rate as for previously unpublished material.

Photos: Send photos with submission. Typically buys one-time rights. Negotiates pay individually. Captions, model releases required.

Columns/Departments: Health Hints (retirement, health), 900-1,500 words; Going Places (travel, pilgrimage), 1,000-1,500 words; Fragments of Life (personal inspiration), 250-600 words; Modern Revelations (religious/inspirational), 900-1,500 words; Money Matters (personal finance), 1,200-1,800 words; Merry-Go-Round (cartoons, jokes, 4-6 line humorous verse); Puzzle Time (religious puzzles, crosswords). **Buys 4 mss/year.** Send complete ms. **Pays $25-45.**

Fiction: Marvin Cropsey, editor. Humorous, religious, slice-of-life vignettes, retirement years nostalgia, intergenerational relationships. "We don't want anything poking fun at old age, saccharine stories or anything not for older adults. Must show older adults (age 55 plus) in a positive manner." **Buys 4 mss/year.** Send complete ms. Length: 1,000-2,000 words. **Pays $60-125.**

Poetry: Free verse, haiku, light verse, traditional. **Buys 24 poems/year poems/year.** Submit maximum 6 poems. Length: 3-16 lines. **Pays $5-20.**

$ PLUS, 823 Via Esteban, San Luis Obispo CA 93401. (805)544-8711. Fax: (805)544-4450. E-mail: gbrand@plusmagazine.net. Publisher: Rick Goyt. **Contact:** George Brand, editor. **60% freelance written.** Monthly magazine covering seniors to inform and entertain the "over-50" but young-at-heart audience. Estab. 1981. Circ. 60,000. Pays on publication. Publishes ms an average of 2 months after acceptance. Byline given. Buys one-time rights. Editorial lead time 2 months. Submit seasonal material 2 months in advance. Accepts queries by mail. Accepts simultaneous submissions. Responds in 2 weeks to queries; 1 month to mss. Sample copy for 9×12 SAE with $2 postage.

Nonfiction: Historical/nostalgic, humor, interview/profile, personal experience, travel, book reviews, entertainment, health. Special issues: Going Back to School; Christmas (December); Travel (October, April). No finance, automotive, heavy humor, poetry, or fiction. **Buys 60-70 mss/year.** Query with SASE or send complete ms. Length: 900-1,200 words. **Pays $1.50/inch.**

Photos: Send photos with submission. Reviews transparencies, 5×7 prints. Offers $5-15/photo.

Tips: "Request and read a sample copy before submitting."

ROMANCE & CONFESSION

Listed here are publications that need stories of romance ranging from ethnic and adventure to romantic intrigue and confession. Each magazine has a particular slant; some are written for young adults, others to family-oriented women. Some magazines also are interested in general interest nonfiction on related subjects.

N **$ BLACK ROMANCE**, Sterling/ MacFadden Partnership, 333 7th Ave., 11th Floor, New York NY 10001. (212)780-3500. Fax: (212)979-4825. Editor: Lisa Finn. Bimonthly magazine. "*Black Romance* publishes romantic stories told from a black woman's viewpoint. All stories should be 16 typed pages or slightly shorter. Stories are written from the first person and must contain 2 romantic, sensual scenes." **Pays $100** 1 month after publication. Sample copy for free. Writer's guidelines for #10 SASE.

N **$ JIVE**, Sterling/MacFadden Partnership, 333 7th Ave., 11th Floor, New York NY 10001. (212)780-3500. Fax: (212)979-4825. E-mail: blackromancemag@hotmail.com. Website: www.sterlingmacfadden.com. Editor: Marcia Mahan. Monthly magazine. "*Jive* contains first-person romance stories written from a black woman's viewpoint. Two romantic scenes are strongly advised. Stories should be no longer than 16 pages." **Pays $100/story**, 1 month after publication. Sample copy for free. Writer's guidelines by e-mail or for #10 SASE.

$ TRUE CONFESSIONS, Macfadden Women's Group, 333 Seventh Ave., New York NY 10001. (212)979-4898. Fax: (212)979-4825. E-mail: trueconfessionstales@yahoo.com. **Contact:** Pat Byrdsong, editorial director. **98% freelance written.** Monthly magazine for high-school-educated, working class women, teens through maturity. "*True Confessions* is a women's magazine featuring true-to-life stories about working class women and their families. Circ. 200,000. Pays 1 month after publication. Publishes ms an average of 4 months after acceptance. Buys all rights. Submit seasonal material 8 months in advance. Accepts queries by e-mail. Responds in 3 months to queries; 15 months to mss. Sample copy for $2.99.

- Eager to work with new/unpublished writers. Prefers writers to query via e-mail before submitting stories.

O─ "If you have a strong story to tell, tell it simply and convincingly. We always have a need for 4,000-word stories with dramatic impact about dramatic events." Asian-, Latina-, Native- and African-American stories are encouraged.

Nonfiction: Timely, exciting, true, emotional first-person stories on the problems that face today's women. The narrators should be sympathetic, and the situations they find themselves in should be intriguing, yet realistic. Many stories may have a strong romantic interest and a high moral tone; however, personal accounts or "confessions," no matter how controversial the topic, are encouraged and accepted. Careful study of current issue is suggested. Send complete ms. No simultaneous submissions. SASE required. Length: 4,000-7,000 words, and mini stories 1,000-1,500 words. **Pays 3¢/word.**

Columns/Departments: Family Zoo (pet feature), 50 words or less, **pays $50 for pet photo and story.** All other features are 200-300 words: My Moment With God (a short prayer); Incredible But True (an incredible/mystical/spiritual experience); My Man (a man who has been special in your life); Woman to Woman (a point of view about a contemporary subject matter or a woman overcoming odds). **Pays $65** for all features; **$75** for My Moment With God. Send complete ms and SASE.

Fiction: Pat Byrdson, editorial director. Query. Length: 3,000-7,500 words. **Pays 3¢/word or a flat $100 rate for mini-stories, and 1 contributor's copy.**

Poetry: Poetry should rhyme. Length: 4-20 lines. **Pays $10 minimum.**

Tips: "Our magazine is almost 100% freelance. We purchase all stories that appear in our magazine. Read 3-4 issues before sending submissions. Do not talk down to our readers. We prefer manuscripts on disk (saved asRTF files) as well as hard copy."

$ TRUE ROMANCE, Sterling/MacFadden Partnership, 333 Seventh Ave., New York NY 10001. (212)979-4898. E-mail: pvitucci@sterlingmacfadden.com. Website: www.truestorymail.com. **Contact:** Pat Vitucci, editor. **100% freelance written.** Monthly magazine for women, teens through retired, offering compelling confession stories based on true happenings, with reader identification and strong emotional tone. No third-person material. Estab. 1923. Circ. 225,000. Pays 1 month after publication. Buys all rights. Submit seasonal material 6 months in advance. Accepts queries by mail, e-mail, fax. Responds in 8 months to queries.

Nonfiction: Confessions, true love stories, mini-adventures; problems and solutions; dating and marital and child-rearing difficulties. Realistic, yet unique stories dealing with current problems, everyday events; strong emotional appeal. **Buys 180 mss/year.** Submit ms. Length: 6,000-9,000 words. **Pays 3¢/word; slightly higher rates for short-shorts.**

Columns/Departments: That's My Child (photo and 50 words); Loving Pets (photo and 50 words), **both pay $50;** Cupid's Corner (photo and 500 words about you and spouse), **pays $100;** Passages(2,000-4,000 words about a unique experience), **pays 3¢/word**; As I Lived It (3,000-5,000 words for literary short stories in first and third person), **pays 3¢/word.**

Poetry: Light romantic poetry. Length: 24 lines maximum. **Pays $10-30.**

Tips: "A timely, well-written story that is told by a sympathetic narrator who sees the central problem through to a satisfying resolution is *all* important to break into *True Romance*. We are always looking for interesting, emotional, identifiable stories."

$ TRUE STORY, Sterling/Macfadden Partnership, 333 Seventh Ave., 11th Floor, New York NY 10001. (212)979-4825. Fax: (212)979-7342. E-mail: hdalton@sterlingmacfadden.com. Website: www.truestorymail.com. **Contact:** Tina Pappalardo or Heather Dalton, editors. **80% freelance written.** Monthly magazine for young married, blue-collar women, 20-35; high school education; increasingly broad interests; home-oriented, but looking beyond the home for personal fulfillment. Circ. 580,000. Pays 1 month after publication. Byline given. Buys all rights. Submit seasonal material 1 year in advance. Responds in 1 year to queries. Writer's guidelines online.

O→ Subject matter can range from light romances to sizzling passion, from all-out tearjerkers to happily-ever-after endings, and everything in between.

Nonfiction: "First-person stories covering all aspects of women's interest: love, marriage, family life, careers, social problems, etc. The best direction a new writer can be given is to carefully study several issues of the magazine; then submit a fresh, exciting, well-written true story. We have no taboos. It's the handling and believability that make the difference between a rejection and an acceptance." **Buys about 125 full-length mss/year.** Submit only complete mss and disk for stories. Length: 2,000-8,000 words. **Pays 5¢/word; $100 minimum. Pays a flat rate for columns or departments, as announced in the magazine.**

Tips: "*True Story* is unique because all of our stories are written from the hearts of real people, and deal with all of the issues that affect us today—parenthood, relationships, careers, family affairs, and social concerns. All of our stories are written in first person, and should be no less than 2,000 words and no more than 10,000. If you have access to a computer, we require you to send your submission on a disk, along with a clean hard copy of the story. Please keep in mind, all files must be saved as rich text format (RTF)."

RURAL

These publications draw readers interested in rural lifestyles. Surprisingly, many readers are from urban centers who dream of or plan to build a house in the country. Magazines featuring design, construction, log homes, and "country" style interior decorating appear in Home & Garden.

$ $ THE COUNTRY CONNECTION, Ontario's Green Magazine, Pinecone Publishing, P.O. Box 100, Boulter ON K0L 1G0, Canada. (613)332-3651. E-mail: magazine@pinecone.on.ca. Website: www.pinecone.on.ca. **Contact:** Gus Zylstra, editor. **100% freelance written.** Magazine published 3 times/year covering nature, environment, history and nostalgia, "the arts," and "green travel." "*The Country Connection* is a magazine for true nature lovers and the rural adventurer. Building on our commitment to heritage, cultural, artistic, and environmental themes, we continually add new topics to illuminate the country experience of people living within nature. Our goal is to chronicle rural life in its many aspects, giving 'voice' to the countryside." Estab. 1989. Circ. 10,000. Pays on publication. Publishes ms an average of 4 months after acceptance. Byline given. Buys first rights. Editorial lead time 4 months. Accepts queries by mail, e-mail, phone. Sample copy for $4.55. Writer's guidelines online.

Nonfiction: General interest, historical/nostalgic, humor, opinion, personal experience, travel, lifestyle, leisure, art and culture, vegan recipes. No hunting, fishing, animal husbandry, or pet articles. **Buys 50 mss/year.** Send complete ms. Length: 500-2,000 words. **Pays 7-10¢/word.**

Photos: Send photos with submission. Reviews transparencies, prints. Buys one-time rights. Offers $10-50/photo. Captions required.

Columns/Departments: Pays 7-10¢/word.

Fiction: Adventure, fantasy, historical, humorous, slice-of-life vignettes, country living. **Buys 4 mss/year.** Send complete ms. Length: 500-1,500 words. **Pays 7-10¢/word.**

The online magazine carries original content not found in the print edition. Contact: Gus Zylstra.

Tips: "Canadian content only. Send manuscript with appropriate support material such as photos, illustrations, maps, etc. Do not send U.S. stamps."

$ COUNTRY FOLK, Salaki Publishing & Design, HC77, Box 608, Pittsburg MO 65724. (417)993-5944. Fax: (417)993-5944. E-mail: salaki@countryfolkmag.com. Website: www.countryfolkmag.com. **Contact:** Susan Salaki, editor. **100% freelance written.** Bimonthly magazine. "*Country Folk* publishes true stories and history of the Ozarks." Estab. 1994. Circ. 10,000. Pays on publication. Publishes ms an average of 3 months after acceptance. Byline given. Buys first rights. Editorial lead time 2 months. Submit seasonal material 3 months in advance. Accepts queries by mail, e-mail, fax, phone. Responds in 1 month to queries; 2 months to mss. Sample copy for $4.75. Writer's guidelines online.

- *Country Folk* has increased from quarterly to bimonthly and doubled its circulation.

Nonfiction: Historical/nostalgic (true pieces with family names and real places), how-to, humor, inspirational, personal experience, photo feature, true ghost stories of the Ozarks. **Buys 10 mss/year.** Prefers e-mail submissions. Length: 750-1,000 words. **Pays $5-20.** "Pays writers with contributor copies or other premiums if we must do considerable editing to the work."

Photos: Send photos with submission. Buys one-time rights.

Fiction: Historical, humorous, mystery, novel excerpts. **Buys 10 mss/year.** Send complete ms. Length: 750-1,000 words. **Pays $5-50.**

Poetry: Haiku, light verse, traditional. **Buys 25 poems/year.** Submit maximum 3 poems. **Pays $1-5.**

Fillers: Anecdotes, facts, gags to be illustrated by cartoonist, newsbreaks, short humor. **Buys 25/year. Pays $1-5.**

Tips: "We want material from people who are born and raised in the country, especially the Ozark region. We accept submissions in any form, handwritten or typed. Many of the writers and poets whose work we publish are first-time submissions. Most of the work we publish is written by older men and women who have heard stories from their parents and grandparents about how the Ozark region was settled in the 1800s. Almost any writer who writes from the heart about a true experience from his or her youth will get published. Our staff edits for grammar and spelling errors. All the writer has to be concerned about is conveying the story."

$ $ FARM & RANCH LIVING, Reiman Media Group, 5925 Country Lane, Greendale WI 53129. (414)423-0100. Fax: (414)423-8463. E-mail: editors@farmandranchliving.com. Website: www.farmandranchliving.com. **Contact:** Nick Pabst, editor. **30% freelance written.** Eager to work with new/unpublished writers. Bimonthly magazine aimed at families that farm or ranch full time. "*F&RL* is *not* a 'how-to' magazine—it focuses on people rather than products and profits." Estab. 1978. Circ. 400,000. Pays on publication. Publishes ms an average of 6 months after acceptance. Byline given. Buys first, one-time rights. Submit seasonal material 6 months in advance. Accepts queries by mail, e-mail, fax. Responds in 6 weeks to queries. Sample copy for $2. Writer's guidelines for #10 SASE.

O→ Break in with "photo-illustrated stories about present-day farmers and ranchers."

Nonfiction: Humor (rural only), inspirational, interview/profile, personal experience (farm/ranch related), photo feature, nostalgia, prettiest place in the country (photo/text tour of ranch or farm). No how-to articles or stories about "hobby farmers" (doctors or lawyers with weekend farms); no issue-oriented stories (pollution, animal rights, etc.). **Buys 30 mss/year.** Query with or without published clips or send complete ms. Length: 600-1,200 words. **Pays up to $200 for text/photo package. Payment for Prettiest Place negotiable.**

Reprints: Send photocopy with rights for sale noted. Payment negotiable.

Photos: Scenic. State availability with submission. Buys one-time rights. Pays $75-200 for 35mm color slides.

Fillers: Anecdotes, short humor (with farm or ranch slant), jokes. **Buys 10/year.** Length: 50-150 words. **Pays $10-25.**

Tips: "Our readers enjoy stories and features that are upbeat and positive. A freelancer must see *F&RL* to fully appreciate how different it is from other farm publications—ordering a sample is strongly advised (not available on newsstands). Photo features (about interesting farm or ranch families) and personality profiles are most open to freelancers."

$ FARM TIMES, 504 Sixth St., Rupert ID 83350. (208)436-1111. Fax: (208)436-9455. E-mail: farmtimeseditor@safelink.net. **Contact:** Terri McAffee, managing editor. **50% freelance written.** Monthly tabloid for agriculture-farming/ranching. "*Farm Times* is dedicated to rural living in the Intermountain and Pacific Northwest. Stories related to farming and ranching in the states of Idaho, Montana, Nevada, Oregon, Utah, Washington, and Wyoming are our mainstay, but farmers and ranchers do more than just work. Human interest articles that appeal to rural readers are used on occasion." Estab. 1987. Pays on publication. Byline given. Editorial lead time 1 month. Submit seasonal material 3 months in advance. Accepts queries by mail, e-mail. Responds in 2 months to queries. Sample copy for $2.50 or online. Writer's guidelines for #10 SASE.

• The editor reports an interest in seeing articles about global agriculture issues and trends that affect the Pacific Northwest and Intermountain West agriculture producer, rural health care, and Western water issues.

O→ Break in by writing tight, and including photos, charts, or graphs, if possible.

Nonfiction: Always runs 1 feature article of interest to women. Exposé, general interest, how-to, interview/profile, new product (few), opinion, farm or ranch issues, late breaking news. Special issues: Irrigation; Chemical/Fertilizer; Potato Production. No humor, essay, first person, personal experience, or book excerpts. **Buys 200 mss/year.** Query with published clips or send complete ms. Length: 500-800 words. **Pays $1.50/column inch.**

Reprints: Send ms with rights for sale noted and information about when and where the material previously appeared. Pays 100% of amount paid for an original article.

Photos: Send photos with submission. Reviews 3×5 or larger prints, contact sheets with negatives, 300 dpi TIFF files. Buys one-time rights. Offers $7/b&w or color photos inside, $35/color front page A Section cover. Captions, identification of subjects, model releases required.

Columns/Departments: Horse (horse care/technical), 500-600 words; Rural Religion (interesting churches/missions/religious activities), 600-800 words; Dairy (articles of interest to dairy farmers), 600-800 words. **Buys 12 mss/year.** Query. **Pays $1.50/column inch.**

Tips: "Ag industry-related articles should have a Pacific Northwest and Intermountain West slant (crops, production techniques, etc.), or how they pertain to the global market. Write tight, observe desired word counts. Feature articles can vary between agriculture and rural living. Good quality photos included with manuscript increase publication chances. Articles should have farm/ranch/rural slant on various topics: health, travel (farmers vacation, too), financial, gardening/landscape, etc."

$ $ MOTHER EARTH NEWS, Ogden Publications, 1503 SW 42nd St., Topeka KS 66609-1265. (785)274-4300. E-mail: letters@motherearthnews.com. Website: www.motherearthnews.com. Managing Editor: K.C. Compton. **Contact:** Cheryl Long, editor. Mostly written by staff and team of established freelancers. Bimonthly magazine emphasizing country living, country skills, natural health and sustainable technologies for both long-time and would-be ruralists. "*Mother Earth News* is dedicated to presenting information that helps readers be more self-sufficient, financially independent, and environmentally aware." Circ. 350,000. Pays on publication. Byline given. Submit seasonal material 5 months in advance. Responds in 6 months to mss. Sample copy for $5. Writer's guidelines for #10 SASE.

• *Mother Earth News* was recently purchased by Ogden Publications, publishers of *Grit* and *Capper's*.

Nonfiction: How-to, alternative energy systems; organic gardening; home building; home retrofit and maintenance; energy-efficient structures; seasonal cooking; home business. No fiction, please. **Buys 35-50 mss/year.** Query. "Sending us a short, to-the-point paragraph is often enough. If it's a subject we don't need at all, we can answer it immediately. If it tickles our imagination, we'll ask to take a look at the whole piece." Length: 300-3,000 words. **Payment negotiated.**

Columns/Departments: Country Lore (down-home solutions to everyday problems); Herbs & Remedies (home healing, natural medicine); Energy & Environment (ways to conserve energy while saving money; also alternative energy).

Tips: "Probably the best way to break in is to study our magazine, digest our writer's guidelines, and send us a concise article illustrated with color transparencies that we can't resist. When folks query and we give a go-ahead on speculation, we often offer some suggestions. Failure to follow those suggestions can lose the sale for the author. We want articles that tell what real people are doing to take charge of their own lives. Articles should be well-documented and tightly written treatments of topics we haven't already covered."

N $ RANGE MAGAZINE, The Cowboy Spirit on American Outback, Purple Coyote, 106 E. Adams, Carson City NV 89706. (775)884-2200. Fax: (775)884-2213. Website: www.rangemagazine.com. Editor: C.J. Hadley. **Contact:** Barbara Wies, associate publisher. **70% freelance written.** Quarterly magazine. "*RANGE Magazine* covers ranching and farming as available resources." Estab. 1991. Pays on publication. Publishes ms an average of 6 months after acceptance. Buys first North American serial rights, makes work-for-hire assignments. Accepts queries by mail. Responds in 6-8 weeks to queries; 3-6 months to mss. Sample copy for free. Writer's guidelines for #10 SASE.

Nonfiction: Book excerpts, humor, interview/profile, personal experience, photo feature. No rodeos or anything by a writer not familiar with *RANGE*. Query. Length: 1,000-1,500 words. **Pays $100.** Sometimes pays expenses of writers on assignment.

Photos: C.J. Hadley, editor/publisher. State availability with submission. Reviews 35mm transparencies, 4×6 prints. Buys one-time rights. Negotiates payment individually. Captions, identification of subjects, model releases required.

$ RURAL HERITAGE, 281 Dean Ridge Lane, Gainesboro TN 38562-5039. (931)268-0655. E-mail: editor@ruralheritage.com. Website: www.ruralheritage.com. Publisher: Allan Damerow. **Contact:** Gail Damerow, editor. **98% freelance written.** Willing to work with a small number of new/unpublished writers. Bimonthly magazine devoted to the training and care of draft animals. Estab. 1976. Circ. 6,500. Pays on publication. Publishes ms an average of 6 months after acceptance. Byline given. Buys first English language rights. Submit seasonal material 6 months in advance. Accepts queries by mail, e-mail. Responds in 3 months to queries. Sample copy for $8. Writer's guidelines online.

Nonfiction: How-to (farming with draft animals), interview/profile (people using draft animals), photo feature. No articles on *mechanized* farming. **Buys 100 mss/year.** Query or send complete ms. Length: 1,200-1,500 words. **Pays 5¢/word.**

Photos: Six covers/year (color transparency or 5×7 horizontal print), animals in harness $100. Photo guidelines for #10 SASE or on website. Send photos with submission. Buys one-time rights. Pays $10. Captions, identification of subjects required.

Poetry: Traditional. **Pays $5-25.**

Tips: "Thoroughly understand our subject: working draft animals in harness. We'd like more pieces on plans and instructions for constructing various horse-drawn implements and vehicles. Always welcome are: 1.) Detailed descriptions and photos of horse-drawn implements, 2.) Prices and other details of draft animal and implement auctions and sales."

$ $ RURALITE, P.O. Box 558, Forest Grove OR 97116-0558. (503)357-2105. Fax: (503)357-8615. E-mail: ruralite@ruralite.org. Website: www.ruralite.org. **Contact:** Curtis Condon, editor-in-chief. **80% freelance written.** Works with new, unpublished writers. Monthly magazine aimed at members of consumer-owned electric utilities throughout 10 western states, including Alaska. Publishes 48 regional editions. Estab. 1954. Circ. 325,000. **Pays on acceptance.** Byline given. Buys first, sometimes reprint rights. Accepts queries by mail. Responds in 1 month to queries. Sample copy for 10×13 SAE with 4 first-class stamps; guidelines also online. Writer's guidelines online.

Nonfiction: Looking for well-written nonfiction, dealing primarily with human interest topics. Must have strong Northwest perspective and be sensitive to Northwest issues and attitudes. Wide range of topics possible, from energy-related subjects to little-known travel destinations to interesting people living in areas served by consumer-owned electric utilities. Family-related issues, Northwest history (no encyclopedia rewrites), people and events, unusual tidbits that tell the Northwest experience are best chances for a sale. **Buys 50-60 mss/year.** Query first; unsolicited mss submitted without request rarely read by editors. Length: 300-2,000 words. **Pays $50-450.**

Reprints: Send ms with rights for sale noted and information about when and where the material previously appeared. Pays 50% of amount paid for an original article.

Photos: "Illustrated stories are the key to a sale. Stories without art rarely make it. Black-and-white prints, color slides, all formats accepted."

Tips: "Study recent issues. Follow directions when given an assignment. Be able to deliver a complete package (story and photos). We're looking for regular contributors to whom we can assign topics from our story list after they've proven their ability to deliver quality mss."

SCIENCE

These publications are published for laymen interested in technical and scientific developments and discoveries, applied science, and technical or scientific hobbies. Publications of interest to the personal computer owner/user are listed in the Personal Computers section. Journals for scientists and engineers are listed in Trade in various sections.

$ $ $ $ AMERICAN ARCHAEOLOGY, The Archaeological Conservancy, 5301 Central Ave. NE, #902, Albuquerque NM 87108-1517. (505)266-9668. Fax: (505)266-0311. E-mail: tacmag@nm.net. Website: www.americanarchaeology.org. Assistant Editor: Tamara Stewart. **Contact:** Michael Bawaya, editor. **60% freelance written.** Quarterly magazine. "We're a popular archaeology magazine. Our readers are very interested in this science. Our features cover important digs, prominent archaeologists, and most any aspect of the science. We only cover North America." Estab. 1997. Circ. 35,000. **Pays on acceptance.** Publishes ms an average of 3 months after acceptance. Byline given. Offers 20% kill fee. Buys one-time, electronic rights. Editorial lead time 3 months. Accepts queries by mail, e-mail, fax. Responds in 3 weeks to queries; 1 month to mss.

Nonfiction: Archaeology. No fiction, poetry, humor. **Buys 15 mss/year.** Query with published clips. Length: 1,500-3,000 words. **Pays $700-1,500.** Sometimes pays expenses of writers on assignment.
Photos: State availability with submission. Reviews transparencies, prints. Buys one-time rights. Offers $300-1,000/photo shoot. Negotiates payment individually. Identification of subjects required.
Tips: "Read the magazine. Features must have a considerable amount of archaeological detail."

$ $ $ $ ARCHAEOLOGY, Archaeological Institute of America, 36-36 33rd St., Long Island NY 11106. (718)472-3050. Fax: (718)472-3051. E-mail: peter@archaeology.org. Website: www.archaeology.org. **Contact:** Peter A. Young, editor-in-chief. **35% freelance written.** Magazine. "*Archaeology* combines worldwide archaeological findings with photography, specially rendered maps, drawings, and charts. Articles cover current excavations, recent discoveries, and special studies of ancient cultures. Regular features: newsbriefs, film and book reviews, current museum exhibits. The only magazine of its kind to bring worldwide archaeology to the attention of the general public." Estab. 1948. Circ. 220,000. Pays on publication. Byline given. Offers 25% kill fee. Buys world rights. Submit seasonal material 6 months in advance. Accepts queries by mail, e-mail, fax. Accepts simultaneous submissions. Sample copy and writer's guidelines free.
Nonfiction: Essays, general interest. **Buys 6 mss/year.** Query preferred. Length: 1,000-3,000 words. **Pays $1,500 maximum.** Sometimes pays expenses of writers on assignment.
Photos: Send photos with submission. Reviews 4×5 color transparencies, 35mm color slides. Identification of subjects, credits required.

■ The online magazine carries original content not found in the print edition. Contact: Mark Rose, online editor.
Tips: "We reach nonspecialist readers interested in art, science, history, and culture. Our reports, regional commentaries, and feature-length articles introduce readers to recent developments in archaeology worldwide."

$ $ ASTRONOMY, Kalmbach Publishing, 21027 Crossroads Circle, P.O. Box 1612, Waukesha WI 53187-1612. (262)796-8776. Fax: (262)798-6468. E-mail: astro@astronomy.com. Editor: David J. Eicher. Managing Editor: Patricia Lantier. **50% of articles submitted and written by science writers; includes commissioned and unsolicited**. Monthly magazine covering the science and hobby of astronomy. "Half of our magazine is for hobbyists (who may have little interest in the heavens in a scientific way); the other half is directed toward armchair astronomers who may be intrigued by the science." Estab. 1973. Circ. 160,000. **Pays on acceptance.** Byline given. Buys first North American serial, one-time, all rights. Responds in 1 month to queries to queries Responds in 3 months (unsolicited mss) to mss. Writer's guidelines for #10 SASE or online.

- "We are governed by what is happening in astronomical research and space exploration. It can be up to a year before we publish a manuscript." Query for electronic submissions.

Nonfiction: Book excerpts, new product (announcements), photo feature, technical, space, astronomy. **Buys 25 mss/year.** Query. Length: 500-3,000 words. **Pays $50-500.**
Photos: Send photos with submission. Pays $25/photo. Captions, identification of subjects, model releases required.
Tips: "Submitting to *Astronomy* could be tough. (Take a look at how technical astronomy is.) But if someone is a physics teacher or an amateur astronomer, he or she might want to study the magazine for a year to see the sorts of subjects and approaches we use, and then submit a proposal."

$ POPULAR SCIENCE, The What's New Magazine, Time4Media, 2 Park Ave., New York NY 10016. (212)779-5000. Fax: (212)779-5103. E-mail: bill.phillips@time4.com. Website: www.popsci.com. Editor-in-Chief: Scott Mowbray. **Contact:** William G. Phillips, executive editor. **50% freelance written.** Monthly magazine for the well-educated adult, interested in science, technology, new products. "*Popular Science* is devoted to exploring (and explaining) to a nontechnical, but knowledgeable, readership the technical world around us. We cover all of the sciences, engineering, and technology, and above all, products. We are largely a 'thing'-oriented publication: things that fly or travel down a turnpike, or go on or under the sea, or cut wood, or reproduce music, or build buildings, or make pictures. We are especially focused on the new, the ingenious, and the useful. Contributors should be as alert to the possibility of selling us pictures and short features as they are to major articles. Freelancers should study the magazine to see what we want and avoid irrelevant submissions." Estab. 1872. Circ. 1,450,000. **Pays on acceptance.** Byline given. Offers 25% kill fee. Buys first North American serial, second serial (reprint) rights. Editorial lead time 3 months. Accepts queries by mail, e-mail, fax. Responds in 1 month to queries. Writer's guidelines online.
Tips: "Probably the easiest way to break in here is by covering a news story in science and technology that we haven't heard about yet. We need people to be acting as scouts for us out there, and we are willing to give the most leeway on these performances. We are interested in good, sharply focused ideas in all areas we cover. We prefer a vivid, journalistic style of writing, with the writer taking the reader along with him, showing the reader what he saw, through words."

$ $ $ $ SCIENTIFIC AMERICAN, 415 Madison Ave., New York NY 10017. (212)754-0550. Fax: (212)755-1976. E-mail: editors@sciam.com. Website: www.sciam.com. **Contact:** Philip Yam, news editor. Monthly magazine covering developments and topics of interest in the world of science. Query before submitting. "*Scientific American* brings its readers directly to the wellspring of exploration and technological innovation. The magazine specializes in first-hand accounts by the people who actually do the work. Their personal experience provides an authoritative perspective on future growth. Over 100 of our authors have won Nobel Prizes. Complementing those articles are regular departments written by *Scientific American*'s staff of professional journalists, all specialists in their fields. *Scientific American* is the authoritative source of advance information. Authors are the first to report on important breakthroughs, because they're the people who make them. It all goes back to *Scientific American*'s corporate mission: to link those who use knowledge with those who create it." Estab. 1845. Circ. 710,000.

Nonfiction: Freelance opportunities mostly in the news scan section; limited opportunity in feature well. **Pays $1/word average.** Pays expenses of writers on assignment.

$ $ SKY & TELESCOPE, The Essential Magazine of Astronomy, Sky Publishing Corp., 49 Bay State Rd., Cambridge MA 02138. (617)864-7360. Fax: (617)576-0336. E-mail: editors@skyandtelescope.com. Website: skyandtelescope.coom. Editor: Richard Tresch Fienberg. **Contact:** Bud Sadler, managing editor. **15% freelance written.** Monthly magazine covering astronomy. "*Sky & Telescope* is the magazine of record for astronomy. We cover amateur activities, research news, equipment, book, and software reviews. Our audience is the amateur astronomer who wants to learn more about the night sky." Estab. 1941. Circ. 125,000. Pays on publication. Publishes ms an average of 6 months after acceptance. Byline given. Buys first rights. Editorial lead time 4 months. Submit seasonal material 1 year in advance. Accepts queries by mail, e-mail, fax. Responds in 3 weeks to queries; 1 month to mss. Sample copy for $4.99. Writer's guidelines online.

Nonfiction: Essays, historical/nostalgic, how-to, opinion, personal experience, photo feature, technical. No poetry, crosswords, New Age, or alternative cosmologies. **Buys 10 mss/year.** Query. Length: 1,500-4,000 words. **Pays at least 25¢/word.** Sometimes pays expenses of writers on assignment.

Photos: Send photos with submission. Reviews contact sheets. Buys one-time rights. Negotiates payment individually. Identification of subjects required.

Columns/Departments: Focal Point (opinion), 800 words; Books & Beyond (reviews), 800 words; Amateur Astronomers (profiles), 1,500 words. **Buys 20 mss/year.** Query. **Pays 25¢/word.**

Tips: "Good artwork is key. Keep the text lively and provide captions."

N $ $ $ $ STARDATE, University of Texas, 1 University Station, AZ100, Austin TX 78712. Fax: (512)471-5060. E-mail: rjohnson@stardate.org. Website: stardate.org. **Contact:** Rebecca Johnson, editor. **80% freelance written.** Bimonthly magazine covering astronomy. "*StarDate* is written for people with an interest in astronomy and what they see in the night sky, but no special astronomy training or background." Estab. 1975. Circ. 10,000. **Pays on acceptance.** Publishes ms an average of 4 months after acceptance. Byline given. Offers 25% kill fee. Buys first North American serial, electronic rights. Editorial lead time 6 months. Submit seasonal material 6 months in advance. Accepts queries by mail, e-mail, fax. Responds in 6 weeks to queries. Sample copy and writer's guidelines free.

- No unsolicited mss.
- "*StarDate* magazine covers a wide range of topics related to the science of astronomy, space exploration, skylore, and skywatching. Many of our readers rely on the magazine for most of their astronomy information, so articles may cover recent discoveries or serve as a primer on basic astronomy or astrophysics. We also introduce our readers to historical people and events in astronomy and space exploration, as well as look forward to what will make history next year or 50 years from now. *StarDate* topics should appeal to a wide audience, not just professional or amateur astronomers. Topics are not limited to hard-core science. When considering topics, look for undercovered subjects, or give a familiar topic a unique spin. Research findings don't have to make the front page of every newspaper in the country to be interesting. Also, if you'd like to write an historical piece, look for offbeat items and events; we've already covered Copernicus, Kepler, Tycho, Newton and the like pretty well."

Nonfiction: General interest, historical/nostalgic, interview/profile, photo feature, technical, travel, research in astronomy. "No first-person; first stargazing experiences; paranormal." **Buys 8 mss/year.** Query with published clips. Length: 1,500-3,000 words. **Pays $500-1,500.** Sometimes pays expenses of writers on assignment.

Photos: Send photos with submission. Reviews transparencies, prints. Buys one-time rights. Negotiates payment individually. Identification of subjects required.

Columns/Departments: Astro News (short astronomy news item), 250 words. **Buys 6 mss/year.** Query with published clips. **Pays $100-200.**

Tips: "Keep up to date with current astronomy news and space missions. No technical jargon."

N $ SUPER SCIENCE, Scholastic, Inc., 557 Broadway, New York NY 10012-3999. (212)343-6470. Fax: (212)343-4459. E-mail: www.superscience@scholastic.com. Website: www.scholasticnews.com. **Contact:** Patricia Jones, senior managing editor. Magazine published 8 times/year. Designed has a hands on science magazine to turn kids on to science through experiments and science news that touches their lives. Circ. 200,000. Sample copy not available.

Nonfiction: Send résumé and several published clips.

$ $ WEATHERWISE, The Magazine About the Weather, Heldref Publications, 1319 18th St. NW, Washington DC 20036. (202)296-6267. Fax: (202)296-5149. E-mail: ww@heldref.org. Website: www.weatherwise.org. Associate Editor: Kimbra Cutlip. Assistant Editor: Ellen Fast. **Contact:** Doyle Rice, managing editor. **75% freelance written.** Bimonthly magazine covering weather and meteorology. "*Weatherwise* is America's only magazine about the weather. Our readers range from professional weathercasters and scientists to basement-bound hobbyists, but all share a common craving for information about weather as it relates to the atmospheric sciences, technology, history, culture, society, art, etc." Estab. 1948. Circ. 32,000. Pays on publication. Publishes ms an average of 6 months after acceptance. Byline given. Buys all rights. Editorial lead time 6-9 months. Submit seasonal material 9 months in advance. Accepts queries by mail, e-mail, fax, phone. Responds in 2 months to queries. Sample copy for $4 and 9×12 SAE with 10 first-class stamps. Writer's guidelines online.

- "First, familiarize yourself with the magazine by taking a close look at the most recent 6 issues. (You can also visit our website, which features the full text of many recent articles.) This will give you an idea of the style of writing we prefer in *Weatherwise*. Then, read through our writer's guidelines (available from our office or on our website) which detail the process for submitting a query letter. As for the subject matter, keep your eyes and ears open for the latest research and/or current trends in meteorology and climatology that may be appropriate for the general readership of *Weatherwise*. And always keep in mind weather's awesome power and beauty—its 'fun, fury, and fascination' that so many of our readers enjoy."

Nonfiction: Book excerpts, essays, general interest, historical/nostalgic, how-to, interview/profile, new product, opinion, personal experience, photo feature, technical, travel. Special issues: Photo Contest (September/October deadline June 1). "No blow-by-blow accounts of the biggest storm to ever hit your backyard." **Buys 15-18 mss/year.** Query with published clips. Length: 1,500-2,500 words. **Pays $200-500 for assigned articles; $0-300 for unsolicited articles.** Sometimes pays expenses of writers on assignment.

Photos: Reviews contact sheets, negatives, prints, electronic files. Buys one-time rights. Negotiates payment individually. Captions, identification of subjects required.

Columns/Departments: Front & Center (news, trends, opinion), 300-400 words; Weather Talk (folklore and humor), 1,000 words. **Buys 12-15 mss/year.** Query with published clips. **Pays $0-200.**

Tips: "Don't query us wanting to write about broad types like the Greenhouse Effect, the Ozone Hole, El Niño, etc. Although these are valid topics, you can bet you won't be able to cover it all in 2,000 words. With these topics and all others, find the story within the story. And whether you're writing about a historical storm or new technology, be sure to focus on the human element—the struggles, triumphs, and other anecdotes of individuals."

SCIENCE FICTION, FANTASY & HORROR

These publications often publish experimental fiction and many are open to new writers. More information on these markets can be found in the Contests & Awards section under the Fiction heading.

$ $ ABSOLUTE MAGNITUDE, Science Fiction Adventures, DNA Publications, P.O. Box 2988, Radford VA 24143-2988. E-mail: absolutemagnitude@dnapublications.com. Website: www.dnapublications.com/. **Contact:** Warren Lapine, editor-in-chief. **95% freelance written.** Quarterly magazine featuring science fiction short stories. "We specialize in action/adventure science fiction with an emphasis on hard science fiction short stories." Estab. 1993. Circ. 8,000. **Pays on acceptance.** Publishes ms an average of 6 months after acceptance. Byline given. Buys first, first english language serial rights. Editorial lead time 6 months. Accepts simultaneous submissions. Responds in 1 month to mss. Sample copy for $5. Writer's guidelines online.

- This editor is still looking for tightly plotted stories that are character driven. He is now purchasing more short stories than before. "Do not query—send complete manuscript."

Fiction: Science fiction. No fantasy, horror, funny science fiction. **Buys 40 mss/year.** Send complete ms. Length: 1,000-20,000 words. **Pays 7-10¢/word.**

Poetry: Any form. Best chance with light verse. **Buys 4 poems/issue**. Submit maximum 5 poems. Length: Up to 25,000 words. **Pays $10/poem.**

Tips: "We are very interested in working with new writers, but we are not interested in 'drawer-cleaning' exercises. There is no point in sending less than your best effort if you are interested in a career in writing. We do not use fantasy, horror, satire, or funny science fiction. We're looking for character-driven, action/adventure-based technical science fiction. We want tightly plotted stories with memorable characters. Characters should be the driving force behind the action of the story; they should not be thrown in as an afterthought. We need to see both plot development and character growth. Stories which are resolved without action on the protagonist's part do not work for us; characters should not be spectators in situations completely beyond their control or immune to their influence. Some of our favorite writers are Roger Zelazny, Frank Herbert, Robert Silverberg, and Fred Saberhagen."

$ $ ANALOG SCIENCE FICTION & FACT, Dell Magazine Fiction Group, 475 Park Ave. S., 11th Floor, New York NY 10016. (212)686-7188. Fax: (212)686-7414. E-mail: analog@dellmagazines.com. Website: www.analogsf.com. **Contact:** Dr. Stanley Schmidt, editor. **100% freelance written.** Eager to work with new/unpublished writers. Monthly magazine for general future-minded audience. Accepts queries for serials and fact articles only; query by mail. Estab. 1930. Circ. 50,000. **Pays on acceptance.** Publishes ms an average of 10 months after acceptance. Byline given. Not copyrighted. Buys first North American serial, nonexclusive foreign serial rights. Responds in 1 month to queries (send queries for serials and fact articles only) to queries. Sample copy for $5. Writer's guidelines online.

O→ Break in by telling an "unforgettable story in which an original, thought-provoking, plausible idea plays an indispensible role."

Nonfiction: Looking for illustrated technical articles dealing with subjects of not only current but future interest, i.e., topics at the present frontiers of research whose likely future developments have implications of wide interest. **Buys 11 mss/year.** Query by mail only. Length: 5,000 words. **Pays 6¢/word.**

Fiction: "Basically, we publish science fiction stories. That is, stories in which some aspect of future science or technology is so integral to the plot that, if that aspect were removed, the story would collapse. The science can be physical, sociological, or psychological. The technology can be anything from electronic engineering to biogenetic engineering. But the stories must be strong and realistic, with believable people doing believable things—no matter how fantastic the background might be." Science fiction. "No fantasy or stories in which the scientific background is implausible or plays no essential role." **Buys 60-100 unsolicited mss/year.** Length: 2,000-80,000 words. **Pays 4¢/word for novels; 5-6¢/word for novelettes; 6-8¢/word for shorts under 7,500 words; $450-600 for intermediate lengths.**

Tips: "In query give clear indication of central ideas and themes and general nature of story line—and what is distinctive or unusual about it. We have no hard-and-fast editorial guidelines, because science fiction is such a broad field that I don't want to inhibit a new writer's thinking by imposing 'Thou Shalt Not's.' Besides, a really good story can make an editor swallow his preconceived taboos. I want the best work I can get, regardless of who wrote it—and I need new writers. So I work closely with new writers who show definite promise, but of course it's impossible to do this with every new writer. No occult or fantasy."

N $ ARTEMIS MAGAZINE, Science and Fiction for a Space-Faring Age, LRC Publications, Inc., 1380 E. 17th St., Suite 201, Brooklyn NY 11230-6011. E-mail: magazine@lrcpubs.com. Website: www.lrcpublications.com. **Contact:** Ian Randal Strock, editor. **90% freelance written.** Quarterly magazine covering the Artemis Project and manned space flight/colonization in general. "As part of the Artemis Project, we present lunar and space development in a positive light. The magazine is an even mix of science and fiction. We are a proud sponsor of the Artemis Project, which is constructing a commercial, manned moon base. We publish science articles for the intelligent layman, and near-term, near-Earth hard science fiction stories." Estab. 1999. **Pays on acceptance.** Publishes ms an average of 3-12 months after acceptance. Byline given. Buys first world English serial rights. Editorial lead time 3 months. Accepts queries by mail. Responds in 2 months to queries. Sample copy for $5 and a 9×12 SAE with 4 first-class stamps. Writer's guidelines for SASE or on website.

Nonfiction: Essays, general interest, how-to (get to, build, or live in a lunar colony), humor, interview/profile, new product, opinion, technical, travel. **Buys 12-16 mss/year.** Send complete ms. Length: 5,000 words maximum. **Pays 3-5¢/word.**

Photos: State availability of or send photos with submission. Reviews transparencies, prints. Buys one-time rights. Negotiates payment individually. Captions, identification of subjects, model releases required.

Columns/Departments: News Notes (news of interest regarding the moon and manned space flight), under 300 words. **Buys 15-20 mss/year.** Send complete ms. **Pays 3-5¢/word.**

Fiction: Science fiction. "We publish near-term, near-Earth, hard science fiction. We don't want to see non-that." Adventure, science fiction. No fantasy, inspirational. **Buys 12-16 mss/year.** Send complete ms. Length: 15,000 words maximum (shorter is better). **Pays 3-5¢/word, and 3 contributor's copies.**

Fillers: Newsbreaks, short humor, cartoons. **Buys 4-12/year.** Length: 100 words maximum. **Pays 3-5¢/word.**

Tips: "Know your material, and write me the best possible article/story you can. You want us to read your manuscript, so show us the courtesy of reading our magazine. Also, the Artemis Project website (www.asi.org) may be a good source of inspiration."

$ ASIMOV'S SCIENCE FICTION, Dell Magazine Fiction Group, 475 Park Avenue S., 11th Floor, New York NY 10016. (212)686-7188. Fax: (212)686-7414. E-mail: asimovs@dellmagazines.com. Website: www.asimovs.com. Executive Editor: Sheila Williams. **Contact:** Gardner Dozois, editor. **98% freelance written.** Works with a small number of new/unpublished writers each year. Magazine published 11 times/year, including 1 double issue. Magazine consists of science fiction and fantasy stories for adults and young adults. Publishes "the best short science fiction available." Estab. 1977. Circ. 50,000. **Pays on acceptance.** Publishes ms an average of 6-12 months after acceptance. Buys first North American serial, nonexclusive foreign serial rights; reprint rights occasionally. Accepts queries by mail. Accepts previously published material. Responds in 2 months to queries; 3 months to mss. Sample copy for $5. Writer's guidelines for #10 SASE or online.

Fiction: Science fiction primarily. Some fantasy and humor but no "sword and sorcery." No explicit sex or violence that isn't integral to the story. "It is best to read a great deal of material in the genre to avoid the use of some very old ideas." **Buys 10mss/issue.** Send complete ms and SASE with *all* submissions. Fantasy, science fiction. No horror or psychic/supernatural. Would like to see more hard science fiction. Length: 750-15,000 words. **Pays 5-8¢/word.**

Poetry: Length: 40 lines maximum. **Pays $1/line.**

Tips: "In general, we're looking for 'character-oriented' stories, those in which the characters, rather than the science, provide the main focus for the reader's interest. Serious, thoughtful, yet accessible fiction will constitute the majority of our purchases, but there's always room for the humorous as well. Borderline fantasy is fine, but no Sword & Sorcery, please. A good overview would be to consider that all fiction is written to examine or illuminate some aspect of human existence, but that in science fiction the backdrop you work against is the size of the universe. Please do not send us submissions on disk or via e-mail. We've bought some of our best stories from people who have never sold a story before."

$ CHALLENGING DESTINY, New Fantasy & Science Fiction, Crystalline Sphere Publishing, RR #6, St. Marys ON N4X 1C8, Canada. (519)885-6012. E-mail: csp@golden.net. Website: home.golden.net/~csp/. **Contact:** Dave Switzer, editor. **80% freelance written.** Quarterly magazine covering science fiction and fantasy. "We publish all kinds of science fiction and fantasy short stories." Estab. 1997. Circ. 200. Pays on publication. Publishes ms an average of 5 months after acceptance. Byline given. Buys first North American serial rights. Accepts queries by mail, e-mail. Accepts simultaneous submissions. Responds in 1 week to queries; 1 month to mss. Sample copy for $7.50 (Canadian), $6.50 (US). Writer's guidelines for #10 SASE, 1 IRC, or online.

Fiction: Fantasy, science fiction. No horror, short short stories. **Buys 24 mss/year.** Send complete ms. Length: 2,000-10,000 words. **Pays 1¢/word (Canadian), plus 2 contributors copies.**

Tips: "We're interested in stories where violence is rejected as a means for solving problems. We're also interested in stories with philosophical, political, or religious themes. We're not interested in stories where the good guys kill the bad guys and then live happily ever after. Read an issue to see what kind of stories we publish. Many of the stories we publish are between 4,000 and 8,000 words and have interesting characters, ideas, and plot."

$ FLESH AND BLOOD, Quiet Tales of Horror & Dark Fantasy, Flesh & Blood Press, 121 Joseph St., Bayville NJ 08721. E-mail: horrorjack@aol.com. Website: www.fleshandbloodpress.com. **Contact:** Jack Fisher, editor-in-chief. **99% freelance written.** Quarterly magazine covering horror/dark fantasy. "We publish fiction with heavy emphasis on the supernatural, fantastic, and/or bizarre." Estab. 1997. Circ. 500. Pays within 3 months of acceptance. Publishes ms an average of 10 months after acceptance. Editorial lead time 2 months. Accepts queries by mail, e-mail. Responds in 2 weeks to queries; 2 months to mss. Sample copy for $6 (check payable to Jack Fisher). Writer's guidelines online.

- The editor reports an interest in seeing powerful vignettes/stories with surrealism-avante-garde(ism) to them and original, unique ghost stories. The magazine recently won Best Magazine of the Year Award in the Jobs in Hell newsletter contest.

Fiction: Fantasy, horror, slice-of-life vignettes, dark fantasy. "Nothing that isn't dark, strange, odd, and/or offbeat." **Buys 32-36 mss/year.** Length: 100-4,500 words. **4-5¢/word.**

Poetry: Avant-garde, free verse, horror/dark fantasy surreal, bizarre. "No rhyming poetry." **Buys 24-36 poems/year.** Submit maximum 5 poems. **Pays $10-20.**

Tips: "We like subtle horror over gore. Don't let the title of the magazine deceive you; we don't want 'flesh' and 'blood'—we want just the opposite: subtle horror, dark fantasy, stories and poems that are strange, unclassifiable, fantastic, bizzare, quirky, and/or downright weird, but always dark in theme, style, plot, and tone."

$ THE MAGAZINE OF FANTASY & SCIENCE FICTION, Spilogale, Inc., P.O. Box 3447, Hoboken NJ 07030. (201)876-2551. Fax: (201)876-2551. E-mail: fandsf@aol.com. Website: www.fsfmag.com.; www.sfsmag.com. **Contact:** Gordon Van Gelder, editor. **100% freelance written.** Monthly magazine covering fantasy fiction and science fiction. "*The Magazine of Fantasy and Science Fiction* publishes various types of science fiction and fantasy short stories and novellas, making up about 80% of each issue. The balance of each issue is devoted to articles about science fiction, a science column, book and film reviews, cartoons, and competitions." Estab. 1949. Circ. 70,000. **Pays on acceptance.** Publishes ms an average of 9-12 months after acceptance. Byline given. Buys first North American serial, foreign serial rights. Submit seasonal material 8 months in advance. Accepts previously published material. Responds in 2 months to queries. Sample copy for $5. Writer's guidelines for SASE, by e-mail or on website.

Columns/Departments: Curiosities (forgotten books), 250 words. **Buys 11 mss/year. Pays $50.**

Fiction: Prefers character-oriented stories. Adventure, fantasy, horror, science fiction. No electronic submissions. **Buys 70-100 mss/year.** Send complete ms. Length: Up to 25,000 words. **Pays 5-8¢/word; additional copies $2.10.**

Tips: "We need more hard science fiction and humor."

N $ ON SPEC, P.O. Box 4727, Station South, Edmonton AB T6E 5G6, Canada. (780)413-0215. Fax: (780)413-1538. E-mail: onspec@earthling.net. Website: www.icomm.ca/onspec/. General Editor: Jena Snyder; Fiction Editors: Barry Hammond, Susan MacGregor, Hazel Sangster, Jena Snyder, Diane L. Walton. **Contact:** Editorial Collective. **95% freelance written.** Quarterly magazine covering Canadian science fiction, fantasy and horror. "We publish speculative fiction by new and established writers, with a strong preference for Canadian authored works." Estab. 1989. Circ. 2,000. **Pays on acceptance.** Publishes ms an average of 6-18 months after acceptance. Byline given. Buys first North American serial rights. Editorial lead time 6 months. Accepts queries by mail, phone. Accepts simultaneous submissions. Responds in 2 weeks to queries 2 months after deadline to mss to mss. Sample copy for $7. Writer's guidelines for #10 SASE or on website.

Nonfiction: Commissioned only.

Fiction: Fantasy, horror, science fiction, magic realism. No media tie-in or shaggy-alien stories. No condensed or excerpted novels, religious/inspirational stories, fairy tales. **Buys 50 mss/year.** Send complete ms. Length: 1,000-6,000 words.

Poetry: "We rarely buy rhyming or religious material." Barry Hammond, poetry editor. Avant-garde, free verse. **Buys 6 poems/year.** Submit maximum 10 poems. Length: 4-100 lines. **Pays $20.**

Tips: "We want to see stories with plausible characters, a well-constructed, consistent, and vividly described setting, a strong plot and believable emotions; characters must show us (not tell us) their emotional responses to each other and to the situation and/or challenge they face. Also: don't send us stories written for television. We don't like media tie-ins, so don't watch TV for inspiration! Read, instead! Absolutely no e-mailed or faxed submissions. Strong preference given to submissions by Canadians."

$ $ STARLOG MAGAZINE, The Science Fiction Universe, Starlog Group, 475 Park Ave. S., 7th Floor, New York NY 10016-1689. Fax: (212)889-7933. E-mail: allan.dart@starloggroup.com. Website: www.starlog.com. **Contact:** David McDonnell, editor. **90% freelance written.** Monthly magazine covering "the science fiction/fantasy genre: its films, TV, books, art, and personalities. We often provide writers with a list of additional questions for them to ask interviewees. Manuscripts *must* be submitted on computer disk or by e-mail." Estab. 1976. Pays on publication. Publishes ms an average of 3 months after acceptance. Byline given. Offers kill fee only to mss. Buys all rights. Accepts queries by mail, e-mail, fax. Responds in 1 month to queries. Sample copy for $7. Writer's guidelines for #10 SASE.

- "We are somewhat hesitant to work with unpublished writers. We concentrate on interviews with actors, directors, writers, producers, special effects technicians, and others. Be aware that 'science fiction' and 'Trekkie' are seen as derogatory terms by our readers and by us."

- Break in by "doing something fresh, imaginative or innovative—or all three. Or by getting an interview we can't get or didn't think of. The writers who sell to us try *hard* and manage to meet one or more challenges."

Nonfiction: "We also sometimes cover science fiction/fantasy animation. We prefer article format as opposed to Q&A interviews." Book excerpts (having directly to do with science fiction films, TV, or literature), interview/profile (actors, directors, screenwriters—who've done science fiction films—and science fiction novelists), movie/TV set visits. No personal opinion think pieces/essays. *No* first person. Avoid articles on horror films/creators. Query first with published clips. Length: 500-3,000 words. **Pays $35 (500 words or less); $50-75 (sidebars); $150-275 (1,000-4,000 words).**

Reprints: Pays $50 for *each* reprint in each foreign edition or such.

Photos: "No separate payment for photos provided by film studios or TV networks." State availability with submission.

Buys all rights. Photo credit given. Pays $10-25 for color slide transparencies depending on quality. Captions, identification of subjects, credit line required.

Columns/Departments: Booklog (book reviews by assignment only). **Buys 150 reviews/year.** Book review, 125 words maximum. No kill fee. Query with published clips. **Pays $15 each.**

This online magazine carries original content not found in the print edition. Contact: David McDonnell, online editor.

Tips: "Absolutely *no fiction*. We do *not* publish it and we throw away fiction manuscripts from writers who *can't* be bothered to include SASE. Nonfiction only please! We are always looking for *fresh* angles on the various *Star Trek* shows and *Star Wars*. Read the magazine more than once and don't just rely on this listing. Know something about science fiction films, TV, and literature. Most full-length major assignments go to freelancers with whom we're already dealing. But if we like your clips and ideas, it's possible we'll give *you* a chance. No phone calls for *any* reason please—we *mean* that!"

N $ **STARSHIP EARTH**, Black Moon Publishing, P.O. Box 484, Bellaire OH 43906. (740)676-5659. E-mail: starshipearth@hotmail.com. Managing Editor: Kirin Lee. **Contact:** Silver Shadowhorse, fiction editor. **15% freelance nonfiction; 100% freelance fiction written.** Magazine published 8 times/year featuring science fiction. "*Starship Earth* is geared toward science fiction fans of all ages. We do mostly nonfiction, but do print short stories. Our nonfiction focus: profiles of actors and industry people, conventions, behind the scenes articles on films and TV shows. We do cover action/adventure films and TV as well. Heavy *Star Trek* focus. We cover classic science fiction, too." Estab. 1996. Circ. 30,000. Pays on publication. Publishes ms an average of 18 months after acceptance. Byline sometimes given. Buys first, one-time rights. Editorial lead time 1 year. Submit seasonal material 6 months in advance. Accepts queries by mail. Responds in 3 weeks to queries; 4 months to mss. Writer's guidelines for #10 SASE.

- *Starship Earth* is planning an anthology of short stories of up to 4,000 words. Stories submitted to *Starship Earth* will automatically be considered.

Nonfiction: General interest, how-to (relating to science fiction, writing, model building, crafts, etc.), interview/profile, new product (relating to sciece of science fiction), personal experience, photo feature, travel (relating to attending conventions), Behind the scenes of film/TV science fiction; Book reviews. **Buys variable number of mss/year.** Query. Length: up to 3,000 words. Please query for longer pieces. **Pays ½-3¢/word.** Pays in copies for book or film reviews. Sometimes pays expenses of writers on assignment.

Photos: State availability with submission. Reviews transparencies, Prints. Buys one-time rights. Negotiates payment individually. Captions, identification of subjects, model releases required.

Columns/Departments: Jenna Dawson, assistant editor. Costumes, conventions/events, science fiction music, upcoming book, film, TV releases, film reviews, book reviews, new products, all up to 700 words. Query. **Does not pay for columns/departments pieces.**

Fiction: Ms. Silver Shadowhorse, editor. Fantasy, historical, science fiction. No erotic content, horror, "Sword & Sorcery," explicit violence, explicit language or religious material. "Short story needs are filled for the next year." **Buys variable number of mss/year.** Query. Length: 500-3,000 words. **Pays ½-3¢/word.**

Fillers: Jenna Dawson, assistant editor. Anecdotes, facts, newsbreaks, short humor. Length: 50-250 words. **Pays does not pay for fillers.**

Tips: "Follow guidelines and present a professional package. We are willing to work with new and unpublished writers in most areas. All manuscripts must be in standard format. We are always looking for new or unusual angles on old science fiction shows/films, conventions, costumes, fx and people in the business. Articles from interviews must have sparkle and be interesting to a variety of readers. Absolutely no gossip or fluff. Anyone sending a disposable manuscript can simply include their e-mail address instead of a SASE for reply. No religious content or sword and sorcery. No violence that doesn't further the plot."

SEX

Magazines featuring pictorial layouts accompanied by stories and articles of a sexual nature, both gay and straight, are listed in this section. Dating and single lifestyle magazines appear in the Relationships section. Other markets for articles relating to sex can be found in the Men's and Women's sections.

N $ **BUTTIME STORIES**, Hounds of Hell Publishing, P.O. Box 1319, Hudson QC J0P 1H0, Canada. (450)458-1934. Fax: (450)458-2977. **Contact:** Editor. **100% freelance written.** Monthly men's magazine covering anal adventure. "All Hounds of Hell Publishing titles deal with hardcore sex." Estab. 1996. Circ. 40,000. Pays on 3-month terms. Publishes ms an average of 3 months after acceptance. Byline sometimes given. Buys all rights. Editorial lead time 3 months. Accepts queries by mail, e-mail, fax, phone. Accepts simultaneous submissions. Sample copy for $5 (US)/issue. Writer's guidelines for #10 SASE or by e-mail.

Fiction: "We will not accept anything to do with violence, children, nonconsenting sex, or degradation." **Buys 64 mss/year.** Send complete ms. Length: 1,300-2,000 words. **Pays $10-15/1,000 words.**

Tips: "Story length should not exceed 2,000 words. Cut the introduction—get straight to the sex. Stories of 800-1,200 words are needed. Open with a bang—is it interesting? Does it excite the reader? Be very descriptive and very graphic, but not violent. Be explicitly descriptive. We want to smell leather, taste the skin, and feel the action as it takes place. But the sex must be enjoyable for all participants; nobody does anything in these stories against their will."

$ CHEATERS CLUB, Hounds of Hell Publishing, P.O. Box 1319, Hudson QC J0P 1H0, Canada. (450)458-1934. Fax: (450)458-2977. **Contact:** Editor. **100% freelance written.** Monthly men's magazine covering "swingers, lesbians, couples who invite others to join them; threesomes, foursomes, and moresomes. All Hounds of Hell Publishing titles deal with hardcore sex." Estab. 1996. Circ. 40,000. Pays on 3-month terms. Publishes ms an average of 3 months after acceptance. Byline sometimes given. Buys all rights. Editorial lead time 3 months. Accepts queries by mail, e-mail, fax, phone. Accepts simultaneous submissions. Sample copy for $5 (US)/issue. Writer's guidelines for #10 SASE or by e-mail.

Fiction: "We will not accept anything to do with violence, children, nonconsenting sex, or degradation." **Buys 64 mss/year.** Send complete ms. Length: 1,300-2,000 words. **Pays $10-15/1,000 words.**

Tips: "Story length should not exceed 2,000 words. Cut the introduction—get straight to the sex. Stories of 800-1,200 words are needed. Open with a bang—is it interesting? Does it excite the reader? Be very descriptive and very graphic, but not violent. Be explicitly descriptive. We want to smell leather, taste the skin, and feel the action as it takes place. But the sex must be enjoyable for all participants; nobody does anything in these stories against their will."

N $ $ EXOTIC MAGAZINE, X Publishing, 818 SW 3rd Ave. #1324, Portland OR 97204. Fax: (503)241-7239. Website: www.xmag.com. **Contact:** Gary Aker, editor. Monthly magazine covering adult entertainment, sexuality. "*Exotic* is pro-sex, informative, amusing, mature, intelligent. Our readers rent and/or buy adult videos, visit strip clubs and are interested in topics related to the adult entertainment industry and sexuality/culture. Don't talk down to them or fire too far over their heads. Many readers are computer literate and well-traveled. We're also interested in insightful fetish material. We are not a 'hard core' publication." Estab. 1993. Circ. 120,000. Pays 30 days after publication. Byline given. Buys first North American serial rights; and online rights; may negotiate second serial (reprint) rights. Accepts queries by fax. Accepts simultaneous submissions. Responds in 2 weeks to queries; 2 months to mss. Sample copy for 9×12 SAE and 5 first-class stamps. Writer's guidelines for #10 SASE.

Nonfiction: Interested in seeing articles about Viagra, auto racing, gambling, insider porn industry and real sex worker stories. Exposé, general interest, historical/nostalgic, how-to, humor, interview/profile, travel, News. No "men writing as women, articles about being a horny guy, opinion pieces pretending to be fact pieces." **Buys 36 mss/year.** Send complete ms. Length: 1,000-1,800 words. **Pays 10¢/word up to $150.**

Reprints: Send ms with rights for sale noted and information about when and where the material previously appeared. Pays 100% of amount paid for an original article.

Photos: Rarely buys photos. Most provided by staff. Reviews prints. Negotiates payment individually. Model releases required.

Fiction: "We are currently overwhelmed with fiction submissions. Please only send fiction if it's really amazing." Erotica, slice-of-life vignettes. Send complete ms. Length: 1,000-1,800 words. **Pays 10¢/word up to $150.**

Tips: "Read adult publications, spend time in the clubs doing more than just tipping and drinking. Look for new insights in adult topics. For the industry to continue to improve, those who cover it must also be educated consumers and affiliates. Please type, spell-check and be realistic about how much time the editor can take 'fixing' your manuscript."

$ FIRST HAND, Experiences For Loving Men, Firsthand, Ltd., 310 Cedar Lane, Teaneck NJ 07666. (201)836-9177. Fax: (201)836-5055. E-mail: firsthand3@aol.com. Publisher: Sal Nolan. **Contact:** Don Dooley, editor. **75% freelance written.** Eager to work with new/unpublished writers. Magazine published 12 times/year covering homosexual erotica. Estab. 1980. Circ. 70,000. Pays on publication. Publishes ms an average of 8 months after acceptance. Byline given. all rights (exceptions made) and second serial (reprint) rights Submit seasonal material 10 months in advance. Responds in 4 months to mss. Sample copy for $5.99. Writer's guidelines for #10 SASE.

Reprints: Send photocopy. Pays 50% of amount paid for original articles.

Fiction: "We prefer fiction in the first person which is believable—stories based on the writer's actual experience have the best chance. We're not interested in stories which involve underage characters in sexual situations. Other taboos include bestiality, rape—except in prison stories, as rape is an unavoidable reality in prison—and heavy drug use. Writers with questions about what we can and cannot depict should write for our guidelines, which go into this in more detail. We print mostly self-contained stories; we will look at novel excerpts, but only if they stand on their own." Erotica. Length: Up to 5,000 words; average 2,000-3,000 words.

Tips: "*First Hand* is a very reader-oriented publication for gay men. Half of each issue is made up of letters from our readers describing their personal experiences, fantasies, and feelings. Our readers are from all walks of life, all races and ethnic backgrounds, all classes, all religious and political affiliations, and so on. They are very diverse, and many live in far-flung rural areas or small towns; for some of them, our magazines are the primary source of contact with gay life, in some cases the only support for their gay identity. Our readers are very loyal and save every issue. We return that loyalty by trying to reflect their interests—for instance, by striving to avoid the exclusively big-city bias so common to national gay publications. So bear in mind the diversity of the audience when you write."

N $ $ GENESIS, Magna Publications, 210 Route 4 E., Suite 211, Paramus NJ 07652. (201)843-4004. Fax: (201)843-8636. E-mail: genesis@magnapublishing.com. Website: www.genesismagazine.com. Editor: Paul Gambino. **Contact:** Dan Davis, executive editor. **85% freelance written.** Monthly magazine. "Monthly men's sophisticate with explicit pictorials of women in sexual situations, celebrity interviews, erotic and non-erotic fiction, exposé, product and media reviews, lifestyle pieces." Estab. 1974. Circ. 450,000. Pays on publication. Publishes ms an average of 3 months after acceptance. Byline given. Offers 50% kill fee. Buys first, second serial (reprint) rights. Editorial lead time 4 months. Submit seasonal material 6 months in advance. Accepts previously published material. Accepts simultaneous submissions. Responds in 1 month to queries; 2 months to mss. Sample copy for $6.99. Writer's guidelines for #10 SASE.

- Submissions not returned.

Nonfiction: Exposé, general interest, how-to, humor, interview/profile, new product, personal experience, photo feature,

Film, music, book, etc., reviews; Lifestyle pieces. "No investigative articles not backed up by facts." **Buys 24 mss/year.** Send complete ms. Length: 150-2,500 words. **Pays 22¢/word.** Sometimes pays expenses of writers on assignment.

Reprints: Send tearsheet, photocopy or typed ms with rights for sale noted and information about when and where the material previously appeared. Pays 50% of amount paid for an original article.

Photos: State availability with submission. Reviews 4×5 transparencies, 8×10 prints, slides. Buys first/exclusive rights. Negotiates payment individually. Captions, identification of subjects, model releases required.

Fiction: Confessions, erotica, humorous, romance. **Buys 24 mss/year.** Query with or without published clips or send complete ms. Length: 2,500-3,500 words. **Pays $500.**

Fillers: Anecdotes, facts, newsbreaks, short humor. **Buys 24/year.** Length: 25-500 words. **Pays 22¢/word, $50 minimum.**

Tips: "Be patient, original and detail-oriented."

N $ $ $ $ HUSTLER, HG Inc., 8484 Wilshire Blvd., Suite 900, Beverly Hills CA 90211. Fax: (323)651-2741. E-mail: dkapelovitz@lfp.com. Website: www.hustler.com. Editor: Bruce David. **Contact:** Dan Kapelovitz, features editor. **60% freelance written.** Magazine published 13 times/year. "*Hustler* is the no-nonsense men's magazine, one that is willing to speak frankly about society's sacred cows and exposé its hypocrites. The *Hustler* reader expects honest, unflinching looks at hard topics—sexual, social, political, personality profile, true crime." Estab. 1974. Circ. 750,000. Pays as boards ship to printer. Publishes ms an average of 3 months after acceptance. Byline given. Offers 20% kill fee. Buys all rights. Editorial lead time 4 months. Submit seasonal material 6 months in advance. Accepts queries by mail, e-mail, fax. Responds in 2 weeks to queries; 1 month to mss. Writer's guidelines for #10 SASE.

- *Hustler* is most interested in well-researched nonfiction reportage focused on sexual practices and subcultures.

Nonfiction: Book excerpts, exposé, general interest, how-to, interview/profile, personal experience, trends. **Buys 30 mss/year.** Query. Length: 3,500-4,000 words. **Pays $1,500.** Sometimes pays expenses of writers on assignment.

Columns/Departments: Sex play (some aspect of sex that can be encapsulated in a limited space), 2,500 words. **Buys 13 mss/year.** Send complete ms. **Pays $750.**

Fiction: "Difficult fiction market. While sex is a required element in *Hustler* fiction, we are not a market for traditional erotica-do not write a 'Hot Letter.' A successful fiction submission will both arouse the reader and take him into a world he may not be able to visit on his own. What an author is able to dream up in front of a computer is rarely as compelling as the product of first-hand experience and keen observation." **Buys 2 mss/year.** Send complete ms. Length: 3,000-3,500 words. **Pays $1,000.**

Fillers: Jokes and "Graffilthy," bathroom wall humor. **Pays $50-100.**

Tips: "Don't try and mimic the *Hustler* style. If a writer needs to be molded into our voice, we'll do a better job of it than he or she will. Avoid first- and second-person voice. The ideal manuscript is quote-rich, visual and is narratively driven by events and viewpoints that push one another forward."

$ KEY CLUB, Hounds of Hell Publishing, P.O. Box 1319, Hudson QC J0P 1H0, Canada. (450)458-1934. Fax: (450)458-2977. **Contact:** Editor. **100% freelance written.** Monthly men's magazine covering "first time anal virgins, new partners, new toys, new experiences. All Hounds of Hell Publishing titles deal with hardcore sex." Estab. 1996. Circ. 40,000. Pays on 3-month terms. Publishes ms an average of 3 months after acceptance. Byline sometimes given. Buys all rights. Editorial lead time 3 months. Accepts queries by mail, e-mail, fax, phone. Accepts simultaneous submissions. Sample copy for $5 (US)/issue. Writer's guidelines for #10 SASE.

Fiction: Erotica. "We will not accept anything to do with violence, children, nonconsenting sex, or degradation." **Buys 64 mss/year.** Send complete ms. Length: 1,300-2,000 words. **Pays $10-15/1,000 words.**

Tips: "Story length should not exceed 2,000 words. Cut the introduction—get straight to the sex. Stories of 800-1,200 words are needed. Open with a bang—is it interesting? Does it excite the reader? Be very descriptive and very graphic, but not violent. Be explicitly descriptive. We want to smell leather, taste the skin, and feel the action as it takes place. But the sex must be enjoyable for all participants; nobody does anything in these stories against their will."

$ OPTIONS, The *Bi*-Monthly, AJA Publishing, P.O. Box 392, White Plains NY 10602. (914)591-2011. E-mail: Dianaed t@bellsouth.net. Website: www.youngandtight.com/men. Editor: Don Stone. **Contact:** Diana Sheridan, associate editor. **Mostly freelance written**. Sexually explicit magazine published 10 times/year for and about bisexuals and to a lesser extent homosexuals. "Stories and letters about bisexuality. Positive approach. Safe-sex encounters unless the story clearly pre-dates the AIDS situation." Estab. 1977. Circ. 100,000. Pays on publication. Publishes ms an average of 10 months after acceptance. Byline given, usually pseudonymous. Buys all rights. Accepts queries by mail, e-mail. Sample copy for $2.95 and 6×9 SAE with 5 first-class stamps. Writer's guidelines for #10 SASE or by e-mail.

- Buys almost no seasonal material. Accepts queries, but prefers to receive complete ms. Generally responds to postal mail queries in 3 weeks, and usually replies overnight to e-mail submissions.

Fiction: "We don't usually get enough true first-person stories and need to buy some from writers. They must be bisexual, mostly man/man, hot, and believable. They must not read like fiction." Erotica, bisexual. **Buys 80 mss/year.** Send complete ms. Length: 2,000-3,000 words. **Pays $100.**

Tips: "We use many more male/male pieces than female/female. No longer buying 'letters'. We get enough real ones."

$ $ PENTHOUSE VARIATIONS, General Media Communications, Inc., 11 Penn Plaza, 12th Floor, New York NY 10001. (212)702-6000. E-mail: variations@generalmedia.com. **Contact:** Barbara Pizio, executive editor. **100% freelance written.** Monthly category-oriented, erotica magazine. Estab. 1978. Circ. 200,000. **Pays on acceptance.** Publishes ms an average of 14 months after acceptance. Buys all rights. Editorial lead time 7 months. Submit seasonal material 10 months in advance. Responds in 1 month to queries; 2 months to mss. Sample copy from (888)312-BACK. Writer's guidelines for #10 SASE or by e-mail.

Nonfiction: Book excerpts, interview/profile, personal experience. "No previously published fiction, no humor, no poetry, no children, no one under 21, no relatives, no pets, no coercion." **Buys 50 mss/year.** Query by mail only or send complete ms. Do not submit unsolicited mss via e-mail. Length: 3,000-3,500 words. **Pays $400 maximum.**

Fiction: "*Variations* publishes couple-oriented narratives in which a person fully describes his or her favorite sex scenes squarely focused within 1 of the magazine's usual categories, in highly explicit erotic detail, using the best possible language." Erotica. Length: 3,000-3,500 words. **Pays $400 maximum.**

Tips: "Read the magazine to familiarize yourself with our voice, style, and categories. Write about what you're familiar with and the most comfortable discussing. We're looking for focused manuscripts which are carefully crafted by excellent writers. We are always glad to work with new writers who choose to go the distance to write successful stories for us."

$ STICKY BUNS, Hounds of Hell Publishing, P.O. Box 1319, Hudson QC J0P 1H0, Canada. (450)458-1934. Fax: (450)458-2977. **Contact:** Editor. **100% freelance written.** Monthly men's magazine covering "the anal fetish as well as S&M and bondage. All Hounds of Hell Publishing titles deal with hardcore sex." Estab. 1996. Circ. 40,000. Pays on 3-month terms. Publishes ms an average of 3 months after acceptance. Byline sometimes given. Buys all rights. Editorial lead time 3 months. Accepts queries by mail, e-mail, fax, phone. Accepts simultaneous submissions. Sample copy for $5 (US)/issue. Writer's guidelines for #10 SASE.

Fiction: Looking for "anal adventures; very sticky, lots of wet descriptions, oils, etc. We will not accept anything to do with violence, children, nonconsenting sex, or degradation." **Buys 64 mss/year.** Send complete ms. Length: 1,300-2,000 words. **Pays $10-15/1,000 words.**

Tips: "Story length should not exceed 2,000 words. Cut the introduction—get straight to the sex. Stories of 800-1,200 words are needed. Open with a bang—is it interesting? Does it excite the reader? Be very descriptive and very graphic, but not violent. Be explicitly descriptive. We want to smell leather, taste the skin, and feel the action as it takes place. But the sex must be enjoyable for all participants; nobody does anything in these stories against their will."

N $ $ SWANK, Swank Publications, 210 Route 4 E., Suite 211, Paramus NJ 07652. (201)843-4004. Fax: (201)843-8636. E-mail: genesismag@aol.com. Website: www.swankmag.com. Editor: Paul Gambino. **Contact:** D.J., associate editor. **75% freelance written.** Works with new/unpublished writers. Monthly magazine on "sex and sensationalism, lurid. High quality adult erotic entertainment." Audience of men ages 18-38, high school and some college education, medium income, skilled blue-collar professionals, union men, some white-collar. Estab. 1954. Circ. 400,000. Pays on publication. Publishes ms an average of 4 months after acceptance. Byline given, pseudonym if wanted. Buys first North American serial rights. Submit seasonal material 6 months in advance. Accepts queries by mail. Accepts previously published material. Responds in 3 weeks to queries; 1 month to mss. Sample copy for $6.95. Writer's guidelines for #10 SASE.

- *Swank* reports a need for more nonfiction, non-sex-related articles.

Nonfiction: Exposé (researched), adventure must be accompanied by color photographs. "We buy articles on sex-related topics, which don't need to be accompanied by photos." Interested in unusual lifestyle pieces. How-to, interviews with entertainment, sports and sex industry celebrities. Buys photo pieces on autos, action, adventure. "It is strongly recommended that a sample copy is reviewed before submitting material." **Buys 34 mss/year.** Query with or without published clips. **Pays $350-500.** Sometimes pays expenses of writers on assignment.

Reprints: Send tearsheet, photocopy or typed ms with rights for sale noted and information about when and where the material previously appeared. Pays 50% of amount paid for an original article.

Photos: "Articles have a much better chance of being purchased if you have accompanying photos." Alex Suarez, art director. Model releases required.

Fiction: "All of the fiction used by *Swank* is erotic in some sense—that is, both theme and content are sexual. New angles are always welcome. We will consider stories that are not strictly sexual in theme (humor, adventure, detective stories, etc.). However, these types of stories are much more likely to be considered if they portray some sexual element, or scene, within their context."

Tips: "All erotic fiction currently being used by *Swank* must follow certain legal guidelines."

$ WICKED FETISHES, Hounds of Hell Publishing, P.O. Box 1319, Hudson QC J0P 1H0, Canada. (450)458-1934. Fax: (450)458-2977. **Contact:** Editor. **100% freelance written.** Monthly "men's sophisticate" digest covering "fetish, domination/submission, feet, etc.—within the law. All Hounds of Hell Publishing titles deal with hardcore sex." Estab. 1996. Circ. 40,000. Pays on 3-month terms. Publishes ms an average of 3 months after acceptance. Byline sometimes given. Buys all rights. Editorial lead time 3 months. Accepts queries by mail, e-mail, fax, phone. Accepts simultaneous submissions. Sample copy for $5 (US)/issue. Writer's guidelines for #10 SASE.

Fiction: "We will not accept anything to do with violence, children, nonconsenting sex, or degradation." **Buys 64 mss/year.** Send complete ms. Length: 1,300-2,000 words. **Pays $10-15/1,000 words.**

Tips: "Story length should not exceed 2,000 words. Cut the introduction—get straight to the sex. Stories of 800-1,200 words are needed. Open with a bang—is it interesting? Does it excite the reader? Be very descriptive and very graphic, but not violent. Be explicitly descriptive. We want to smell leather, taste the skin, and feel the action as it takes place. But the sex must be enjoyable for all participants; nobody does anything in these stories against their will."

SPORTS

A variety of sports magazines, from general interest to sports medicine, are covered in this section. For the convenience of writers who specialize in one or two areas of sport and outdoor writing, the publications are subcategorized by the sport or subject matter they emphasize. Publications in related categories (for example, Hunting & Fishing; Archery & Bowhunting) often buy similar material. Writers should read through this entire section to become familiar with the subcategories. Publications on horse breeding and hunting dogs are classified in the Animal section, while horse racing is listed here. Publications dealing with automobile or motorcycle racing can be found in the Automotive & Motorcycle category. Markets interested in articles on exercise and fitness are listed in the Health & Fitness section. Outdoor publications that promote the preservation of nature, placing only secondary emphasis on nature as a setting for sport, are in the Nature, Conservation & Ecology category. Regional magazines are frequently interested in sports material with a local angle. Camping publications are classified in the Travel, Camping & Trailer category.

Archery & Bowhunting

$ $ BOW & ARROW HUNTING, Y-Visionary Publishing, LP, 265 S. Anita Dr., Suite 120, Orange CA 92868-3310. (714)939-9991. Fax: (714)939-9909. E-mail: editorial@bowandarrowhunting.com. Website: www.bowandarrowhunting.com. **Contact:** Joe Bell, editor. **70% freelance written.** Magazine published 9 times/year covering bowhunting. "Dedicated to serve the serious bowhunting enthusiast. Writers must be willing to share their secrets so our readers can become better bowhunters." Estab. 1962. Circ. 90,000. Pays on publication. Publishes ms an average of 2 months after acceptance. Byline given. Buys all rights. Submit seasonal material 6 months in advance. Accepts queries by mail. Accepts simultaneous submissions. Responds in 1 month to queries; 6 weeks to mss. Sample copy and writer's guidelines free.

Nonfiction: How-to, humor, interview/profile, opinion, personal experience, technical. **Buys 60 mss/year.** Send complete ms. Length: 1,700-3,000 words. **Pays $200-450.**

Photos: Send photos with submission. Reviews contact sheets, 35mm and 2¼×2¼ transparencies, 5×7 prints. Buys one-time or all rights. Offers no additional payment for photos accepted with ms. Captions required.

Fillers: Facts, newsbreaks. **Buys 12/year.** Length: 500 words. **Pays $20-100.**

Tips: "Inform readers how they can become better at the sport, but don't forget to keep it fun! Sidebars are recommended with every submission."

$ $ BOWHUNTER, The Number One Bowhunting Magazine, Primedia Enthusiast Publications, 6405 Flank Dr., Harrisburg PA 17112. (717)657-9555. Fax: (717)657-9552. E-mail: bowhunter_magazine@primediamags.com. Website: www.bowhunter.com. Founder/Editor Emeritus: M.R. James. **Contact:** Jeff Waring, associate publisher/managing editor. **50% freelance written.** Bimonthly magazine covering hunting big and small game with bow and arrow. "We are a special-interest publication, produced by bowhunters for bowhunters, covering all aspects of the sport. Material included in each issue is designed to entertain and inform readers, making them better bowhunters." Estab. 1971. Circ. 181,426. **Pays on acceptance.** Publishes ms an average of 3 months to 2 years after acceptance. Byline given. Buys exclusive first, worldwide publication rights. Submit seasonal material 8 months in advance. Accepts queries by mail, e-mail, fax. Responds in 2 weeks to queries; 1 month to mss. Sample copy for $2 and 8½×11 SAE with appropriate postage. Writer's guidelines for #10 SASE or on website.

Nonfiction: "We publish a special 'Big Game' issue each Fall (September) but need all material by mid-March. Another annual publication, Whitetail Bowhunter, is staff written or by assignment only. Our latest special issue is the Gear Specia, which highlights the latest in equipment. We don't want articles that graphically deal with an animal's death. And, please, no articles written from the animal's viewpoint." General interest, how-to, interview/profile, opinion, personal experience, photo feature. **Buys 60 plus mss/year.** Query. Length: 250-2,000 words. **Pays $500 maximum for assigned articles; $100-400 for unsolicited articles.** Sometimes pays expenses of writers on assignment.

Photos: Send photos with submission. Reviews 35mm and 2¼×2¼ transparencies, 5×7 and 8×10 prints. Buys one-time rights. Offers $75-250/photo. Captions required.

Fiction: Dwight Schuh, editor. Bowhunting, outdoor adventure. Send complete ms. Length: 500-2,000 words. **Pays $100-$350.**

Tips: "A writer must know bowhunting and be willing to share that knowledge. Writers should anticipate *all* questions a reader might ask, then answer them in the article itself or in an appropriate sidebar. Articles should be written with the reader foremost in mind; we won't be impressed by writers seeking to prove how good they are—either as writers or bowhunters. We care about the reader and don't need writers with 'I' trouble. Features are a good bet because most of our material comes from freelancers. The best advice is: Be yourself. Tell your story the same as if sharing the experience around a campfire. Don't try to write like you think a writer writes."

Baseball

N $ $ BASEBALL AMERICA, Baseball America Inc., P.O. Box 2089, Durham NC 27702. (919)682-9635. Fax: (919)682-2880. E-mail: willlingo@baseballamerica.com. Website: www.baseballamerica.com. Editor: Allan Simpson. **Contact:** Will Lingo, managing editor. **10% freelance written.** Biweekly tabloid covering baseball. "*Baseball America* is read by industry insiders and passionate, knowledgeable fans. Writing should go beyond routine baseball stories to include more depth or a unique angle." Estab. 1981. Circ. 80,000. Pays on publication. Publishes ms an average of 2 months after acceptance. Byline given. Buys one-time rights. Editorial lead time 1 month. Submit seasonal material 2 months in advance. Accepts previously published material. Accepts simultaneous submissions. Sample copy for $3.25.

Nonfiction: Historical/nostalgic, interview/profile, theme or issue-oriented baseball features. "No major league player features that don't cover new ground; superficial treatments of baseball subjects." **Buys 10 mss/year.** Send complete ms. Length: 100-2,000 words. **Pays $10-500 for assigned articles; $10-250 for unsolicited articles.**

Photos: State availability with submission. Buys one-time rights. Negotiates payment individually. Identification of subjects required.

Tips: "We use little freelance material, in part because we have a large roster of excellent correspondents and because much of what we receive is too basic or superficial for our readership. Sometimes writers stray too far the other way and get too arcane. But we're always interested in great stories that baseball fans haven't heard yet."

N $FANTASY BASEBALL, Krause Publications, Inc., 700 E. State Street, Iola WI 54990-0001. (715)445-2214. Fax: (715)445-4087. E-mail: info@krause.com. Website: www.collect.com. Editor: Greg Ambrosius. Quarterly magazine. Published for fantasy baseball league players. Circ. 130,000. Editorial lead time 6 weeks.

N $JUNIOR BASEBALL, America's Youth Baseball Magazine, 2D Publishing, P.O. Box 9099, Canoga Park CA 91309. (818)710-1234. E-mail: dave@juniorbaseball.com. Website: www.juniorbaseball.com. **Contact:** Dave Destler, editor/publisher. **25% freelance written.** Bimonthly magazine covering youth baseball. "Focused on youth baseball players ages 7-17 (including high school) and their parents/coaches. Edited to various reading levels, depending upon age/skill level of feature." Estab. 1996. Circ. 50,000. Pays on publication. Publishes ms an average of 4 months after acceptance. Byline given. Buys all rights. Editorial lead time 3 months. Submit seasonal material 4 months in advance. Accepts simultaneous submissions. Responds in 2 weeks to queries; 1 month to mss. Sample copy for $5 and online.

Nonfiction: How-to (skills, tips, features, how to play better baseball, etc.), interview/profile (with major league players; only on assignment), personal experience (from coaches' or parents' perspective). "No trite first-person articles about your kid." No fiction or poetry. **Buys 8-12 mss/year.** Query. Length: 500-1,000 words. **Pays $50-100.**

Photos: Photos can be e-mailed in 300 dpi JPEGs. State availability with submission. Reviews 35mm transparencies, 3×5 prints. Offers $10-100/photo; negotiates payment individually. Captions, identification of subjects required.

Columns/Departments: When I Was a Kid (a current Major League Baseball player profile); Parents Feature (topics of interest to parents of youth ball players); all 1,000-1,500 words. In the Spotlight (news, events, new products), 50-100 words; Hot Prospect (written for the 14 and older competitive player. High school baseball is included, and the focus is on improving the finer points of the game to make the high school team, earn a college scholarship, or attract scouts, written to an adult level), 500-1,000 words. **Buys 8-12 mss/year. Pays $50-100.**

Tips: "Must be well-versed in baseball! Having a child who is very involved in the sport, or have extensive hands-on experience in coaching baseball, at the youth, high school or higher level. We can always use accurate, authoritative skills information and good photos to accompany is a big advantage! This magazine is read by experts."

N $USA TODAY SPORTS WEEKLY, Gannet Co., Inc., 7950 Jones Branch Drive, McLean VA 22108-0001. (703)854-3400. Fax: (703)854-2034. E-mail: sportsweekly@usatoday.com. Website: www.usatoday.com. Publisher/Executive Editor: Lee Ivory. Weekly magazine. Provides complete coverage of baseball and football combined into a year-round publication. Circ. 266,526. Editorial lead time 2 months. Sample copy not available.

Basketball

$ $ $SLAM, Harris Publications, 1115 Broadway, 8th Floor, New York NY 10010. E-mail: susan@harris-pub.com. Website: www.slamonline.com. **Contact:** Susan Price, managing editor. **70% freelance written.** Magazine published 10 times/year covering basketball; sports journalism with a hip-hop sensibility targeting ages 13-24. Estab. 1994. Circ. 200,000. Pays on publication. Publishes ms an average of 3 months after acceptance. Byline given. Offers 25% kill fee. Buys all rights. Accepts queries by mail, e-mail, fax. Writer's guidelines free.

Nonfiction: Interview/profile, team story. **Buys 150 mss/year.** Query with published clips. Length: 200-3,000 words. **Pays $100-1,000 for assigned articles.** Sometimes pays expenses of writers on assignment.

Photos: State availability with submission. Buys one-time rights. Negotiates payment individually.

The online magazine carries original content not found in the print edition. Contact: Lang Whitaker, online editor.

Tips: "Pitch profiles of unknown players; send queries, not manuscripts; do not try to fake a hip-hop sensibility. Never contact the editor-in-chief. Story meetings are held every 6-7 weeks at which time all submissions are considered."

Bicycling

$BICYCLING, Rodale Press, Inc., 135 N. Sixth St., Emmaus PA 18098. (610)967-5171. Fax: (610)967-8960. E-mail: bicycling@rodale.com. Website: www.bicycling.com. Publisher: Nicholas Freedman. **Contact:** Doug Donaldson, associate editor. **50% freelance written.** Magazine published 11 times/year. "*Bicycling* features articles about fitness, training, nutrition, touring, racing, equipment, clothing, maintenance, new technology, industry developments, and other topics of interest to committed bicycle riders. Editorially, we advocate for the sport, industry, and the cycling consumer." Estab. 1961. Circ. 280,000. **Pays on acceptance.** Byline given. Buys all rights. Submit seasonal material 6 months in advance. Accepts previously published material. Responds in 2 months to queries. Sample copy for $3.50. Writer's guidelines for #10 SASE.

0→ "There are 2 great break-in opportunities for writers: 1.) 'Noblest Invention' (750-word column) offers writers a chance to tell us why the bicycle is the greatest bit of machinery ever created. 2.) 'Ask the Wrench' maintenance feature showcases a local bike mechanic's know-how. If you know a great mechanic, this is a chance to get in the magazine."

Nonfiction: "We are a cycling lifestyle magazine. We seek readable, clear, well-informed pieces that show how cycling is part of our readers' lives. We sometimes run articles that are inspirational, and inspiration might flavor even our most technical pieces. No fiction or poetry." How-to (on all phases of bicycle touring, repair, maintenance, commuting, new products, clothing, riding technique, nutrition for cyclists, conditioning), photo feature (on cycling events), technical (opinions about technology), travel (bicycling must be central here), fitness. **Buys 10 unsolicited mss/year.** Query. **Payment varies.** Sometimes pays expenses of writers on assignment.

Reprints: Send tearsheet or photocopy and information about when and where the material previously appeared.

Photos: State availability of or send photos with submission. Pays $15-250/photo. Captions, model releases required.

Tips: "Don't send us travel pieces about where you went on summer vacation. Travel/adventure stories have to be about something larger than just visiting someplace on your bike and meeting quirky locals."

N $ BIKE MIDWEST, Columbus Sports Publications, 1350 W. Fifth Ave., #30, Columbus OH 43212. (614)486-2202. Fax: (614)486-3650. E-mail: bsb@buckeyesports.com. **Contact:** Nicole Weis, editor. **35% freelance written.** Monthly (April-October) tabloid covering bicycling. "We like articles to be in a more casual voice so our readers feel more like a friend than just a customer." Estab. 1986. Circ. 35,000. Pays on publication. Publishes ms an average of 1 month after acceptance. Byline given. Offers 100% or $75 kill fee. Buys all rights. Editorial lead time 1 month. Submit seasonal material 1 month in advance. Accepts queries by mail, e-mail, fax. Accepts simultaneous submissions. Responds in 2 months to queries; 2 months to mss. Sample copy and writer's guidelines free.

Nonfiction: Essays, general interest, historical/nostalgic, how-to (bicycle mechanics, i.e., how to change a flat tire, etc.), humor, inspirational, interview/profile, new product, opinion, personal experience, technical, travel. Special issues: April and October issues cover travel and tourism by bicycle. Nothing nonbike related. **Buys 14 mss/year.** Send complete ms. Length: 1,000-2,000 words. **Pays $35-75.**

Reprints: Accepts previously published submissions.

Photos: Send photos with submission. Reviews negatives, 3½×5 prints. Buys all rights. Offers $25-50/photo. Captions, identification of subjects, model releases required.

Columns/Departments: Metal Cowboy (experiences on a bicycle), 1,800 words; Bicycling News (experiences in bicycling), 1,200 words. **Buys 14 mss/year.** Send complete ms. **Pays $35-75.**

Tips: "Articles must be informative and/or engaging. Our readers like to be entertained. They also look for lots of information when articles are technical (product reviews, etc.)"

$ CRANKMAIL, Cycling in Northeastern Ohio, P.O. Box 33249, Cleveland OH 44133-0249. E-mail: editor@crankmail.com. Website: www.crankmail.com. **Contact:** James Guilford, editor/publisher. Monthly magazine covering bicycling in all aspects. "Our publication serves the interests of bicycle enthusiasts established, accomplished adult cyclists. These individuals are interested in reading about the sport of cycling, bicycles as transportation, ecological tie-ins, sports nutrition, the history and future of bicycles and bicycling." Estab. 1977. Circ. 1,000. Pays on publication. Byline given. Buys one-time, second serial (reprint) rights. Editorial lead time 1 month. Submit seasonal material 3 months in advance. Sample copy for $1. Writer's guidelines for #10 SASE.

Nonfiction: Essays, historical/nostalgic, how-to, humor, interview/profile, personal experience, technical, travel. "No articles encouraging folks to start bicycling—our readers are already cyclists." Send complete ms. Length: 600-1,800 words. **Pays $10 minimum for unsolicited articles.**

Reprints: Send ms with rights for sale noted and information about when and where the material previously appeared.

Fiction: Publishes very short novel excerpts.

Fillers: Cartoons. **Pays $5-10.**

The online magazine carries original content, and content not found in the print edition. Contact: James Guilford, online editor.

N $ $ CYCLE CALIFORNIA! MAGAZINE, P.O. Box 189, Mountain View CA 94042. (650)961-2663. Fax: (650)968-9030. E-mail: tcorral@cyclecalifornia.com. Website: www.cyclecalifornia.com. **Contact:** Tracy L. Corral, editor/publisher. **75% freelance written.** Magazine published 11 times/year "covering Northern California bicycling events, races, people. Issues (topics) covered include bicycle commuting, bicycle politics, touring, racing, nostalgia, history, anything at all to do with riding a bike." Estab. 1995. Circ. 26,000. Pays on publication. Publishes ms an average of 3 months after acceptance. Byline given. Buys first North American serial rights. Editorial lead time 6 weeks. Submit seasonal material 6 weeks in advance. Accepts queries by mail, e-mail, phone. Accepts simultaneous submissions. Responds in 1 month to queries. Sample copy for 10×13 SAE with 3 first-class stamps. Writer's guidelines for #10 SASE.

Nonfiction: Historical/nostalgic, how-to, interview/profile, opinion, personal experience, technical, travel. Special issues: Bicycle Tour & Travel (January/February). No articles about any sport that doesn't relate to bicycling, no product reviews. **Buys 36 mss/year.** Query with or without published clips. Length: 500-1,500 words. **Pays 3-10¢/word.**

Photos: Send photos with submission. Reviews 3×5 prints. Buys one-time rights. Negotiates payment individually. Identification of subjects required.

Columns/Departments: Buys 2-3 mss/year. Query with published clips. **Pays 3-10¢/word.**

Tips: "E-mail or call editor with good ideas. While we don't exclude writers from other parts of the country, articles really should reflect a Northern California slant, or be of general interest to bicyclists. We prefer stories written by people who like and use their bikes."

$ CYCLE WORLD, Hachette Filipacchi Media U.S., Inc., 1499 Monrovia Ave., Newport Beach CA 92663. (949)720-5300. Fax: (949)631-0651. E-mail: cycleworld@hfmus.com. Website: www.cycleworld.com. Editor: David Edwards. Monthly magazine. Geared towards motorcycle owners and buyers, accesory buyers, potential buyers and enthusiasts of the overall sport of motorcycling. Circ. 319,489. Sample copy not available.

N **$ MX RACER**, PRIMEDIA Enthusiast Group, 6420 Wilshire Blvd., Los Angeles CA 90048-5502. (323)782-2000. Fax: (323)782-2372. E-mail: mxrmail@primedia.com. Website: www.primedia.com. Editor: Corey Neuer. Magazine published 6 times/year. Dedicated to give fans and newcomers to motorcross racing a unique perspective on the sport. Circ. 58,000. Sample copy not available.

Boating

$ $ CANOE & KAYAK MAGAZINE, Canoe America Associates, 10526 NE 68th St., Suite 3, Kirkland WA 98033. (425)827-6363. Fax: (425)827-1893. E-mail: editor@canoekayak.com. Website: www.canoekayak.com. Editor: Ross Prather. **Contact:** Robin Stanton, managing editor. **75% freelance written.** Bimonthly magazine. "*Canoe & Kayak Magazine* is North America's No. 1 paddlesports resource. Our readers include flatwater and whitewater canoeists and kayakers of all skill levels. We provide comprehensive information on destinations, technique and equipment. Beyond that, we cover canoe and kayak camping, safety, the environment, and the history of boats and sport." Estab. 1972. Circ. 70,000. Pays on publication. Publishes ms an average of 6 months after acceptance. Byline given. first international rights, which includes electronic and anthology rights Editorial lead time 6 months. Submit seasonal material 8 months in advance. Accepts queries by mail, e-mail. Responds in 2 months to queries. Sample copy and writer's guidelines for 9×12 SAE with 7 first-class stamps.

O→ Break in with good out-of-the-way destination or Put-In (news) pieces with excellent photos. "Take a good look at the types of articles we publish before sending us any sort of query."

Nonfiction: Historical/nostalgic, how-to (canoe, kayak camp, load boats, paddle whitewater, etc.), personal experience, photo feature, technical, travel. Special issues: Whitewater Paddling; Beginner's Guide; Kayak Touring; Canoe Journal. "No cartoons, poems, stories in which bad judgement is portrayed or 'Me and Molly' articles." **Buys 25 mss/year.** Query with or without published clips or send complete ms. Length: 400-2,500 words. **Pays $100-800 for assigned articles; $100-500 for unsolicited articles.**

Photos: "Some activities we cover are canoeing, kayaking, canoe fishing, camping, canoe sailing or poling, backpacking (when compatible with the main activity) and occasionally inflatable boats. We are not interested in groups of people in rafts, photos showing disregard for the environment or personal safety, gasoline-powered engines unless appropriate to the discussion, or unskilled persons taking extraordinary risks." State availability with submission. Reviews 35mm transparencies, 4×6 prints. Buys one-time rights. Offers $75-500/photo. Captions, identification of subjects, model releases required.

Columns/Departments: Put In (environment, conservation, events), 500 words; Destinations (canoe and kayak destinations in US, Canada), 1,500 words; Essays, 750 words. **Buys 40 mss/year.** Send complete ms. **Pays $100-350.**

Fillers: Anecdotes, facts, newsbreaks. **Buys 20/year.** Length: 200-500 words. **Pays $25-50.**

Tips: "Start with Put-In articles (short featurettes) or short, unique equipment reviews. Or give us the best, most exciting article we've ever seen—with great photos. Read the magazine before submitting."

$ $ $ CHESAPEAKE BAY MAGAZINE, Boating at Its Best, Chesapeake Bay Communications, 1819 Bay Ridge Ave., Annapolis MD 21403. (410)263-2662. Fax: (410)267-6924. E-mail: editor@cbmmag.net. Managing Editor: Jane Meneely. **Contact:** Wendy Mitman Clarke, executive editor. **60% freelance written.** Monthly magazine covering boating and the Chesapeake Bay. "Our readers are boaters. Our writers should know boats and boating. Read the magazine before submitting." Estab. 1972. Circ. 46,000. Pays within 2 months after acceptance. Publishes ms an average of 1 year after acceptance. Byline given. Buys first North American serial rights. Editorial lead time 1 year. Submit seasonal material 1 year in advance. Accepts queries by mail, e-mail, fax, phone. Accepts simultaneous submissions. Responds in 2 months to queries; 3 months to mss. Sample copy for $5.19 prepaid.

O→ "Read our Channel 9 column and give us some new ideas. These are short news items, profiles, and updates (200-800 words)."

Nonfiction: Destinations, boating adventures, how-to, marina reviews, history, nature, environment, lifestyles, personal and institutional profiles, boat-type profiles, boatbuilding, boat restoration, boating anecdotes, boating news. **Buys 30 mss/year.** Query with published clips. Length: 300-3,000 words. **Pays $100-1,000.** Pays expenses of writers on assignment.

Photos: Buys one-time rights. Offers $75-250/photo, $400/day rate for assignment photography. Captions, identification of subjects required.

Tips: "Send us unedited writing samples (not clips) that show the writer can write, not just string words together. We look for well-organized, lucid, lively, intelligent writing."

$ $ $ $ CRUISING WORLD, The Sailing Co., 5 John Clarke Rd., Newport RI 02840-0992. (401)845-5100. Fax: (401)845-5180. Website: www.cruisingworld.com. Editor: Herb McCormick. Managing Editor: Elaine Lembo. **Contact:** Tim Murphy, executive editor. **60% freelance written.** Monthly magazine covering sailing, cruising/adventuring, do-it-yourself boat improvements. "*Cruising World* is a publication by and for sailboat owners who spend time in home waters as well as voyaging the world. Its readership is extremely loyal, savvy, and driven by independent thinking." Estab. 1974. Circ. 155,000. **Pays on acceptance for articles;** on publication for photography. Publishes ms an average of 18 months after acceptance. Byline given. Buys 6-month, all-world, first time rights (amendable). Editorial lead time 3 months. Submit seasonal material 1 year in advance. Accepts queries by mail. Responds in 1 month to queries; 4 months to mss. Sample copy for free. Writer's guidelines online.

Nonfiction: Book excerpts, essays, exposé, general interest, historical/nostalgic, how-to, humor, interview/profile, new product, opinion, personal experience, photo feature, technical, travel. No travel articles that have nothing to do with cruising aboard sailboats from 20-50 feet in length. **Buys dozens of mss/year.** Send complete ms. **Pays $50-1,500 for assigned articles; $50-1,000 for unsolicited articles.** Sometimes pays expenses of writers on assignment.

Photos: Send photos with submission. Reviews negatives, transparencies, color slides preferred. Buys one-time rights. Negotiates payment individually. Also buys stand-alone photos. Captions required.

Columns/Departments: Shoreline (sailing news, people, and short features; contact Nim Marsh), 500 words maximum; Hands-on Sailor (refit, voyaging, seamanship, how-to; contact Darrell Nicholson), 1,000-1,500 words. **Buys dozens of mss/year.** Query with or without published clips or send complete ms. **Pays $100-700.**

Tips: "*Cruising World's* readers know exactly what they want to read, so our best advice to freelancers is to carefully read the magazine and envision which exact section or department would be the appropriate place for proposed submissions."

N $ GOOD OLD BOAT, The Sailing Magazine for the Rest of Us, Partnership for Excellence, Inc., 7340 Niagra Lane N., Maple Grove MN 55311. (763)420-8923. Fax: (763)420-8921. E-mail: karen@goodoldboat.com. Website: www.goodoldboat.com. **Contact:** Karen Larson, editor. **90% freelance written.** Bimonthly magazine covering sailing. "*Good Old Boat* magazine focuses on maintaining, upgrading, and loving cruising sailboats that are 10 years old and older. Readers see themselves as part of a community of sailors who share similar maintenance and replacement concerns which are not generally addressed in the other sailing publications. Our readers do much of the writing about projects they have done on their boats and the joy they receive from sailing them." Estab. 1998. Circ. 20,000. Pays 2 months in advance of publication. Publishes ms an average of 12-18 months after acceptance. Buys first North American serial rights. Editorial lead time 4 months. Submit seasonal material 12-15 months in advance. Accepts queries by mail, e-mail, fax. Accepts previously published material. Accepts simultaneous submissions. Responds in 1-2 weeks to queries; 2-6 months to mss. Sample copy for free. Writer's guidelines online.

Nonfiction: General interest, historical/nostalgic, how-to, interview/profile, personal experience, photo feature, technical. "Articles which are written by nonsailors serve no purpose for us." **Buys 150 mss/year.** Query or send complete ms. **Payment varies, refer to published rates on website.**

Photos: State availability of or send photos with submission. "We do not pay additional fees for photos except when they run as covers, center spread photo features, or are specifically requested to support an article."

Tips: "Our shorter pieces are the best way to break into our magazine. We publish many Simple Solutions and Quick & Easy pieces. These are how-to tips that have worked for sailors on their boats. In addition, our readers send lists of projects which they've done on their boats and which they could write for publication. We respond to these queries with a thumbs up or down by project. Articles are submitted on speculation, but they have a better chance of being accepted once we have approved of the suggested topic."

$ $ HEARTLAND BOATING, The Waterways Journal, Inc., 319 N. Fourth St., Suite 650, St. Louis MO 63102. (314)241-4310. Fax: (314)241-4207. E-mail: info@heartlandboating.com. Website: www.heartlandboating.com. **Contact:** Krista Grueninger, editor. **70% freelance written.** Magazine published 9 times/year covering recreational boating on the inland waterways of mid-America, from the Great Lakes south to the Gulf of Mexico and over to the east. "Our writers must have experience with, and a great interest in, boating, particularly in the area described above. *Heartland Boating*'s content is both informative and humorous—describing boating life as the heartland boater knows it. We are boaters and enjoy the outdoor, water-oriented way of life. The content reflects the challenge, joy, and excitement of our way of life afloat. We are devoted to both power and sailboating enthusiasts throughout middle America; houseboats are included. The focus is on the freshwater inland rivers and lakes of the heartland, primarily the waters of the Tennessee, Cumberland, Ohio, Missouri, Illinois, and Mississippi rivers, the Tennessee-Tombigbee Waterway, The Gulf Intracoastal Waterway, and the lakes along these waterways." Estab. 1989. Circ. 12,000. Pays on publication. Byline given. Buys first North American serial, first, electronic rights. Editorial lead time 3 months. Submit seasonal material 6 months in advance. Accepts queries by mail, e-mail, fax, phone. Accepts previously published material. Responds in 2 months to queries. Sample copy for $5. Writer's guidelines online.

Nonfiction: How-to (articles about navigation information and making time spent aboard easier and more comfortable), humor, personal experience (sharing expericenes aboard and on cruises in our coverage area), technical (boat upkeep and maintenance), travel (along the rivers and on the lakes in our coverage area and on-land stops along the way). Special issues: Annual Boat Show/New Products issue in December looks at what is coming out on the market for the coming year. **Buys 110 mss/year.** Query with published clips or send complete ms. Length: 850-1,500 words. **Pays $100-300.**

Reprints: Send tearsheet, photocopy or typed ms and information about when and where the material previously appeared.

Photos: Send photos with submission. Reviews transparencies, prints. Buys one-time rights. Offers no additional payment for photos accepted with ms.

Columns/Departments: Food Afloat (recipes easy to make when aboard), Books Aboard (book reviews), Handy Hints (small boat improvement projects), Waterways History (on-water history tidbits), all 850 words. **Buys 45 mss/year.** Query with published clips or send complete ms. **Pays $75-150.**

Tips: "We usually plan an editorial schedule for the coming year in August. Submitting material between May and July will be most helpful for the planning process, although we accept submissions year-round."

$ $ HOUSEBOAT MAGAZINE, The Family Magazine for the American Houseboater, Harris Publishing, Inc., 360 B St., Idaho Falls ID 83402. Fax: (208)522-5241. E-mail: hbeditor@houseboatmagazine.com. Website: www.houseboatmagazine.com. **Contact:** Steve Smede, editor. **40% freelance written.** Monthly magazine for houseboaters, who enjoy reading everything that reflects the unique houseboating lifestyle. If it is not a houseboat-specific article, please do not query. Estab. 1990. Circ. 25,000. Pays on publication. Publishes ms an average of 3 months after acceptance. Byline given. Offers 25% kill fee. Buys first North American serial, electronic rights. Editorial lead time 6 months. Submit seasonal material 6 months in advance. Accepts simultaneous submissions. Responds in 1 month to queries; 2 months to mss. Sample copy for $5. Writer's guidelines online.

- No unsolicited mss. Accepts queries by mail and fax, but e-mail strongly preferred.

Nonfiction: How-to, interview/profile, new product, personal experience, travel. **Buys 36 mss/year.** Query. Length: 1,000-1,200 words. **Pays $150-300.**

Photos: Often required as part of submission package. Color prints discouraged. Digital prints are unacceptable. Seldom purchases photos without ms, but occasionally buys cover photos. Reviews transparencies, high-resolution electronic images. Buys one-time rights. Offers no additional payment for photos accepted with ms. Captions, model releases required.

Columns/Departments: Pays $100-200.

Tips: "As a general rule, how-to articles are always in demand. So are stories on unique houseboats or houseboaters. You are less likely to break in with a travel piece that does not revolve around specific people or groups. Personality profile pieces with excellent supporting photography are your best bet."

N $LIVING ABOARD, Acres, U.S.A., P.O. Box 91299, Austin TX 78709-1299. (512)892-4446. Fax: (512)892-4448. E-mail: editor@livingaboard.com. Website: www.livingaboard.com. Managing Editor: Sam Bruce. **Contact:** Linda Ridihalgh, editor. **95% freelance written.** Bimonthly magazine covering living on boats/cruising. Estab. 1973. Circ. 7,500. Pays on publication. Publishes ms an average of 3-6 months after acceptance. Byline given. Buys first North American serial, first, one-time, second serial (reprint) rights. Accepts queries by mail, e-mail, fax. Responds in 1-2 weeks to queries; 1-2 months to mss. Sample copy online. Writer's guidelines free.

Nonfiction: How-to (buy, furnish, maintain, provision a boat), interview/profile, personal experience, technical (as relates to boats), travel (on the water), Cooking Aboard with Recipes. Send complete ms. **Pays 5¢/word.**

Columns/Departments: Cooking Aboard (how to prepare healthy and nutritious meals in the confines of a galley; how to entertain aboard a boat), 1,000-1,500 words. **Buys 6 mss/year.** Send complete ms. **Pays 5¢/word.**

Tips: "Articles should have a positive tone and promote the liveaboard lifestyle."

$NORTHERN BREEZES, SAILING MAGAZINE, Northern Breezes, Inc., 3949 Winnetka Ave. N, Minneapolis MN 55427. (763)542-9707. Fax: (763)542-8998. E-mail: info@sailingbreezes.com. Website: www.sailingbreezes.com. Managing Editor: Thom Burns. **Contact:** Zach Luse, editor. **70% freelance written.** Magazine published 8 times/year. for the Great Lakes and Midwest sailing community. Focusing on regional cruising, racing, and day sailing. Estab. 1989. Circ. 22,300. Pays on publication. Byline given. Buys first North American serial rights. Editorial lead time 1 months. Submit seasonal material 3 months in advance. Accepts queries by mail, e-mail, fax, phone. Accepts previously published material. Responds in 1 month to queries; 2 months to mss. Sample copy for free. Writer's guidelines online.

Nonfiction: Book excerpts, how-to (sailing topics), humor, inspirational, interview/profile, new product, personal experience, photo feature, technical, travel. No boating reviews. **Buys 24 mss/year.** Query with published clips. Length: 300-3,500 words.

Reprints: Accepts previously published submissions.

Photos: Send photos with submission. Reviews negatives, 35mm slides, 3×5 or 4×6 prints. Buys one-time rights. Offers no additional payment for photos accepted with ms. Captions required.

Columns/Departments: This Old Boat (sailboat), 500-1,000 words; Surveyor's Notebook, 500-800 words. **Buys 8 mss/year.** Query with published clips. **Pays $50-150.**

The online magazine carries original content not found in the print edition and includes writer's guidelines. Contact: Zach Luse, online editor.

Tips: "Query with a regional connection already in mind."

$ $OFFSHORE, Northeast Boating at its Best, Offshore Communications, Inc., 500 Victory Rd., Marina Bay, North Quincy MA 02171. (617)221-1400. Fax: (617)847-1871. E-mail: editors@offshoremag.net. Website: www.offshoremag.net. **Contact:** Editorial Department. **80% freelance written.** Monthly magazine covering power and sailboating on the coast from Maine to New Jersey. Estab. 1976. Circ. 35,000. **Pays on acceptance.** Publishes ms an average of 5 months after acceptance. Byline given. Offers 50% kill fee. Buys first North American serial rights. Submit seasonal material 6 months in advance. Accepts queries by mail. Accepts simultaneous submissions. Writer's guidelines for #10 SASE.

Nonfiction: Articles on boats, boating, New York, New Jersey, and New England coastal places and people, Northeast coastal history. **Buys 90 mss/year.** Query with or without published clips or send complete ms. Length: 1,200-2,500 words. **Pays $350-500 for features, depending on length.**

Photos: Reviews 35mm slides. Buys one-time rights. Pays $150-300. Identification of subjects required.

Tips: "Writers must demonstrate a familiarity with boats and with the Northeast coast. Specifically we are looking for articles on boating destinations, boating events (such as races, rendezvous, and boat parades), on-the-water boating adventures, boating culture, maritime museums, maritime history, boating issues (such as safety and the environment), seamanship, fishing, how-to stories, and essays. Note: Since *Offshore* is a regional magazine, all stories must focus on the area from New Jersey to Maine. We are always open to new people, the best of whom may gradually work their way into regular writing assignments. Important to ask for (and follow) our writer's guidelines if you're not familiar with our magazine."

$ $ PACIFIC YACHTING, Western Canada's Premier Boating Magazine, OP Publishing Ltd., 1080 Howe St., Suite 900, Vancouver BC V6Z 2T1, Canada. (604)606-4644. Fax: (604)687-1925. E-mail: editor@pacificyachting.com. Website: www.pacificyachting.com. **90% freelance written.** Monthly magazine covering all aspects of recreational boating on British Columbia's coast. "The bulk of our writers and photographers not only come from the local boating community, many of them were long-time *PY* readers before coming aboard as a contributor. The *PY* reader buys the magazine to read about new destinations or changes to old haunts on the British Columbia coast and to learn the latest about boats and gear." Circ. 19,000. Pays on publication. Publishes ms an average of 6 months after acceptance. Byline given. Buys first North American serial, simultaneous rights. Editorial lead time 4 months. Submit seasonal material 6 months in advance. Accepts queries by mail, e-mail, fax. Sample copy for $4.95, plus postage charged to credit card. Writer's guidelines free.

Nonfiction: Historical/nostalgic (British Columbia coast only), how-to, humor, interview/profile, personal experience, technical (boating related), travel, cruising, and destination on the British Columbia coast. "No articles from writers who are obviously not boaters!" Query. Length: 1,500-2,000 words. **Pays $150-500.** Pays expenses of writers on assignment.

Photos: Send photos with submission. Reviews transparencies, 4×6 prints, and slides. Buys one-time rights. Offers no additional payment for photos accepted with ms. Offers $25-300 for photos accepted alone. Identification of subjects required.

Columns/Departments: Currents (current events, trade and people news, boat gatherings, and festivities), 50-250 words. Reflections; Cruising, both 800-1,000 words. Query. **Payment varies.**

Tips: "We strongly encourage queries before submission (written with SAE and IRCs, or by phone or e-mail). Our reader wants you to balance important navigation details with first-person observations, blending the practical with the romantic. Write tight, write short, write with the reader in mind, write to inform, write to entertain. Be specific, accurate, and historic."

$ $ PONTOON & DECK BOAT, Harris Publishing, Inc., 360 B. St., Idaho Falls ID 83402. (208)524-7000. Fax: (208)522-5241. E-mail: brady@pdbmagazine.com. Website: www.pdbmagazine.com. **Contact:** Brady L. Kay, editor. **15% freelance written.** Magazine published 10 times/year. "We are a boating niche publication geared toward the pontoon and deck boating lifestyle and consumer market. Our audience is comprised of people who utilize these boats for varied family activities and fishing. Our magazine is promotional of the PDB industry and its major players. We seek to give the reader a twofold reason to read our publication: to celebrate the lifestyle, and to do it aboard a first-class craft." Estab. 1995. Circ. 84,000. Pays on publication. Byline given. Buys one-time rights. Editorial lead time 2 months. Submit seasonal material 3 months in advance. Accepts simultaneous submissions. Responds in 6 weeks to queries; 3 months to mss. Sample copy and writer's guidelines free.

Nonfiction: How-to, personal experience, technical, remodeling, rebuilding. "We are saturated with travel pieces, no general boating, humor, fiction, or poetry." **Buys 15 mss/year.** Query with or without published clips or send complete ms. Length: 600-2,000 words. **Pays $50-300.** Sometimes pays expenses of writers on assignment.

Photos: State availability with submission. Reviews transparencies. Rights negotiable. Captions, model releases required.

Columns/Departments: No Wake Zone (short, fun quips); Better Boater (how-to). **Buys 6-12 mss/year.** Query with published clips. **Pays $50-150.**

Tips: "Be specific to pontoon and deck boats. Any general boating material goes to the slush pile. The more you can tie together the lifestyle, attitudes, and the PDB industry, the more interest we'll take in what you send us."

$ $ $ POWER & MOTORYACHT, Primedia, Inc., 260 Madison Ave., 8th Floor, New York NY 10016. (917)256-2200. Fax: (917)256-2282. E-mail: diane_byrne@primediamags.com. Website: www.powerandmotoryacht.com. Editor: Richard Thiel. Managing Editor: Eileen Mansfield. **Contact:** Diane M. Byrne, executive editor. **25% freelance written.** Monthly magazine covering powerboats 24 feet and larger with special emphasis on the 35-foot-plus market. "Readers have an average of 32 years experience boating, and we give them accurate advice on how to choose, operate, and maintain their boats as well as what electronics and gear will help them pursue their favorite pastime. In addition, since powerboating is truly a lifestyle and not just a hobby for them, *Power & Motoryacht* reports on a host of other topics that affect their enjoyment of the water: chartering, sportfishing, and the environment, among others. Articles must therefore be clear, concise, and authoritative; knowledge of the marine industry is mandatory. Include personal experience and information for marine industry experts where appropriate." Estab. 1985. Circ. 157,000. **Pays on acceptance.** Publishes ms an average of 4-6 months after acceptance. Byline given. Offers 33% kill fee. Buys all rights. Editorial lead time 4-6 months. Submit seasonal material 4-6 months in advance. Accepts queries by mail, e-mail, fax. Accepts simultaneous submissions. Responds in 1 month to queries. Sample copy for 10×12 SASE. Writer's guidelines for #10 SASE.

Nonfiction: How-to, interview/profile, personal experience, photo feature, travel. No unsolicited mss or articles about sailboats and/or sailing yachts (including motorsailers). **Buys 20-25 mss/year.** Query with published clips. Length: 800-1,500 words. **Pays $500-1,000 for assigned articles.** Sometimes pays expenses of writers on assignment.

Photos: Aimee Colon, art director. State availability with submission. Reviews 8×10 transparencies, GIF/JPEG files (minimum 300 dpi). Buys one-time rights. Offers no additional payment for photos accepted with ms. Captions, identification of subjects required.

Tips: "Take a clever or even unique approach to a subject, particularly if the topic is dry/technical. Pitch us on yacht cruises you've taken, particularly if they're in off-the-beaten-path locations."

$ $ POWER BOATING CANADA, 1020 Brevik Place, Suites 4 & 5, Mississauga ON L4W 4N7, Canada. (905)624-8218. Fax: (905)624-6764. E-mail: editor@powerboating.com. Website: www.powerboating.com. **Contact:** Steve Fennell, editor. **70% freelance written.** Bimonthly magazine covering recreational power boating. "*Power Boating Canada* offers boating destinations, how-to features, boat tests (usually staff written), lifestyle pieces—with a Canadian slant—and appeal to recreational power boaters across the country." Estab. 1984. Circ. 42,000. Pays on publication. Publishes ms an average of 3 months after acceptance. Byline given. Buys first North American serial rights. Editorial lead time 2 months. Submit seasonal material 3 months in advance. Accepts previously published material. Responds in 1 month to queries; 2 months to mss. Sample copy for free.

Nonfiction: "Any articles related to the sport of power boating, especially boat tests." Historical/nostalgic, how-to, interview/profile, personal experience, travel (boating destinations). No general boating articles or personal anectdotes. **Buys 40-50 mss/year.** Query. Length: 1,200-2,500 words. **Pays $150-300 (Canadian).** Sometimes pays expenses of writers on assignment.

Reprints: Send photocopy with rights for sale noted and information about when and where the material previously appeared.

Photos: Send photos with submission. Reviews contact sheets, negatives, transparencies, prints. Buys one-time rights. Payment varies; no additional payment for photos accepted with ms. Captions, identification of subjects required.

$ $ $ SAIL, 98 N. Washington St., 2nd Floor, Boston MA 02114. (617)720-8600. Fax: (617)723-0912. E-mail: sailmail@primediasi.com. Website: www.sailmagazine.com or www.sailbuyersguide.com. Editor: Peter Nielsen. **Contact:** Amy Ullrich, managing editor. **30% freelance written.** Monthly magazine "written and edited for everyone who sails—aboard a coastal or bluewater cruiser, trailerable, one-design or offshore racer, or daysailer. How-to and technical articles concentrate on techniques of sailing and aspects of design and construction, boat systems, and gear; the feature section emphasizes the fun and rewards of sailing in a practical and instructive way." Estab. 1970. Circ. 180,000. **Pays on acceptance.** Publishes ms an average of 1 year after acceptance. Byline given. Buys first North American and other rights. Accepts queries by mail, e-mail, fax. Responds in 3 months to queries. Writer's guidelines for SASE or online (download).

Nonfiction: How-to, personal experience, technical, distance cruising, destinations. Special issues: "Cruising, chartering, commissioning, fitting-out, special race (e.g., America's Cup), Top 10 Boats." **Buys 50 mss/year.** Query. Length: 1,500-3,000 words. **Pays $200-800.** Sometimes pays expenses of writers on assignment.

Photos: Prefers transparencies. Payment varies, up to $700 if photo used on cover. Captions, identification of subjects, credits required.

Columns/Departments: Sailing Memories (short essay); Sailing News (cruising, racing, legal, political, environmental); Under Sail (human interest). Query. **Pays $25-400.**

The online magazine carries original content not found in the print edition and includes writer's guidelines. Contact: Kimball Livingston, online editor.

Tips: "Request an articles' specification sheet. We look for unique ways of viewing sailing. Skim old issues of *Sail* for ideas about the types of articles we publish. Always remember that *Sail* is a sailing magazine. Stay away from gloomy articles detailing all the things that went wrong on your boat. Think constructively and write about how to avoid certain problems. You should focus on a theme or choose some aspect of sailing and discuss a personal attitude or new philosophical approach to the subject. Notice that we have certain issues devoted to special themes—for example, chartering, electronics, commissioning, and the like. Stay away from pieces that chronicle your journey in the day-by-day style of a logbook. These are generally dull and uninteresting. Select specific actions or events (preferably sailing events, not shorebound activities), and build your articles around them. Emphasize the sailing."

$ $ SEA KAYAKER, Sea Kayaker, Inc., P.O. Box 17029, Seattle WA 98107-0729. (206)789-1326. Fax: (206)781-1141. E-mail: editorial@seakayakermag.com. Website: www.seakayakermag.com. Editor: Christopher Cunningham. **Contact:** Karin Redmond, executive editor. **95% freelance written.** Bimonthly publication. "*Sea Kayaker* is a bimonthly publication with a worldwide readership that covers all aspects of kayak touring. It is well known as an important source of continuing education by the most experienced paddlers." Estab. 1984. Circ. 30,000. Pays on publication. Publishes ms an average of 6 months after acceptance. Byline given. Offers 10% kill fee. Buys first North American serial rights. Editorial lead time 4 months. Submit seasonal material 4 months in advance. Accepts queries by mail, e-mail, fax, phone. Responds in 2 months to queries. Sample copy for $7.30 (US), samples to other countries extra. Writer's guidelines online.

Nonfiction: Essays, historical/nostalgic, how-to (on making equipment), humor, new product, personal experience, technical, travel. Unsolicited gear reviews are not accepted. **Buys 50 mss/year.** Query with or without published clips or send complete ms. Length: 1,500-5,000 words. **Pays 18-20¢/word for assigned articles; 15-17¢/word for unsolicited articles.**

Photos: Send photos with submission. Reviews transparencies, prints. Buys one-time rights. Offers $15-400. Captions, identification of subjects required.

Columns/Departments: Technique; Equipment; Do-It-Yourself; Food; Safety; Health; Environment; Book Reviews; all 1,000-2,500 words. **Buys 40-45 mss/year.** Query. **Pays 15-20¢/word.**

Tips: "We consider unsolicited manuscripts that include a SASE, but we give greater priority to brief descriptions (several paragraphs) of proposed articles accompanied by at least 2 samples—published or unpublished—of your writing. Enclose a statement as to why you're qualified to write the piece and indicate whether photographs or illustrations are available to accompany the piece."

N $ SEA MAGAZINE, America's Western Boating Magazine, Duncan McIntosh Co., 17782 Cowan, Irvine CA 92614. (949)660-6150. Fax: (949)660-6172. Website: www.goboatingamerica.com. **Contact:** Eston Ellis, managing editor. Monthly magazine covering West Coast power boating. Estab. 1908. Circ. 50,000. Pays on publication. Publishes ms an average of 3 months after acceptance. Byline given. Buys first North American serial rights. Editorial lead time 3 months. Submit seasonal material 6 months in advance. Accepts simultaneous submissions. Responds in 3 months to queries. Writer's guidelines online.

Nonfiction: "News you can use" is kind of our motto. All articles should aim to help boat owners make the most of their boating experience. How-to, new product, personal experience, technical, travel. **Buys 36 mss/year.** Query with or without published clips or send complete ms. Length: 1,000-1,500 words. **Payment varies.** Sometimes pays expenses of writers on assignment.

Photos: State availability with submission. Reviews transparencies. Buys one-time rights. Offers $50-250/photo. Captions, identification of subjects, model releases required.

N $ $ SOUTHERN BOATING MAGAZINE, The South's Largest Boating Magazine, Southern Boating & Yachting, Inc., 330 N. Andrews Ave., Ft. Lauderdale FL 33301. (954)522-5515. Fax: (954)522-2260. E-mail: sboating@southernboating.com. Website: southernboating.com. Editor: Skip Allen. **Contact:** David Strickland, executive editor. **50% freelance written.** Monthly magazine. "Upscale monthly yachting magazine focusing on SE U.S., Bahamas, Caribbean, and Gulf of Mexico." Estab. 1972. Circ. 40,000. Pays on publication. Publishes ms an average of 2 months after acceptance. Byline given. Buys one-time rights. Editorial lead time 6 weeks. Submit seasonal material 2 months in advance. Accepts queries by mail, e-mail, fax, phone. Accepts previously published material. Sample copy for free. Editorial calendar online.

O→ Break in with destination, how-to, and technical articles.

Nonfiction: How-to (boat maintenance), travel (boating related, destination pieces). **Buys 100 mss/year.** Query. Length: 600-3,000 words. **Pays $200.**

Photos: State availability of or send photos with submission. Reviews transparencies, prints. Buys one-time rights. Offers $50/photo maximum. Captions, identification of subjects, model releases required.

Columns/Departments: Weekend Workshop (how-to/maintenance), 600 words; What's New in Electronics (electronics), 1,000 words; Engine Room (new developments), 1,000 words. **Buys 24 mss/year.** Query. **Pays $150.**

$ $ $ TRAILER BOATS MAGAZINE, Poole Publications, Inc., 20700 Belshaw Ave., Carson CA 90746-3510. (310)537-6322. Fax: (310)537-8735. E-mail: editors@trailerboats.com. Website: www.trailerboats.com. Executive Editor: Ron Eldridge. **Contact:** Jim Henricks, editor. **50% freelance written.** Monthly magazine covering legally trailerable power boats and related powerboating activities. Estab. 1971. Circ. 100,000. **Pays on acceptance.** Publishes ms an average of 3 months after acceptance. Byline given. Buys all rights. Editorial lead time 4 months. Submit seasonal material 5 months in advance. Responds in 1 month to queries. Sample copy for 9×12 SAE with 7 first-class stamps.

Nonfiction: General interest (trailer boating activities), historical/nostalgic (places, events, boats), how-to (repair boats, installation, etc.), humor (almost any power boating-related subject), interview/profile, personal experience, photo feature, technical, travel (boating travel on water or highways), product evaluations. Special issues: Annual new boat review. No "How I Spent My Summer Vacation" stories, or stories not directly connected to trailerable boats and related activities. **Buys 70-80 unsolicited mss/year.** Query. Length: 1,000-2,500 words. **Pays $150-1,000.** Sometimes pays expenses of writers on assignment.

Photos: Send photos with submission. Reviews 2¼×2¼ and 35mm slides transparencies. Buys all rights. Captions, identification of subjects, model releases required.

Columns/Departments: Over the Transom (funny or strange boating photos); Watersports (boat-related); Marine Electronics (what and how to use); Boating Basics (elementary boating tips), all 1,000-1,500 words. **Buys 60-70 mss/year.** Query. **Pays $250-450.**

Tips: "Query should contain short general outline of the intended material; what kind of photos; how the photos illustrate the piece. Write with authority, covering the subject with quotes from experts. Frequent mistakes are not knowing the subject matter or the audience. The writer may have a better chance of breaking in at our publication with short articles and fillers if they are typically hard-to-find articles. We do most major features inhouse, but try how-to stories dealing with smaller boats, installation and towing tips, boat trailer repair. Good color photos will win our hearts every time."

$ $ WOODENBOAT MAGAZINE, The Magazine for Wooden Boat Owners, Builders, and Designers, WoodenBoat Publications, Inc., P.O. Box 78, Brooklin ME 04616. (207)359-4651. Fax: (207)359-8920. Website: www.woodenboat.com. Editor-in-Chief: Jonathan A. Wilson. Senior Editor: Mike O'Brien. Associate Editor: Tom Jackson. **Contact:** Matthew P. Murphy, editor. **50% freelance written.** Bimonthly magazine for wooden boat owners, builders, and designers. "We are devoted exclusively to the design, building, care, preservation, and use of wooden boats, both commercial and pleasure, old and new, sail and power. We work to convey quality, integrity, and involvement in the creation and care of these craft, to entertain, inform, inspire, and to provide our varied readers with access to individuals who are deeply experienced in the world of wooden boats." Estab. 1974. Circ. 106,000. Pays on publication. Publishes ms an average of 1 year after acceptance. Byline given. Offers variable kill fee. Buys first North American serial rights. Accepts previously published material. Accepts simultaneous submissions. Responds in 2 months to queries; 2 months to mss. Sample copy for $4.50. Writer's guidelines for #10 SASE.

Nonfiction: Technical (repair, restoration, maintenance, use, design, and building wooden boats). No poetry, fiction. **Buys 50 mss/year.** Query with published clips. Length: 1,500-5,000 words. **Pays $300/1,000 words.** Sometimes pays expenses of writers on assignment.

Reprints: Send tearsheet or typed ms with rights for sale noted and information about when and where the material previously appeared.

Photos: Send photos with submission. Reviews negatives. Buys one-time rights. Pays $15-75 b&w, $25-350 color. Identification of subjects required.

Columns/Departments: Currents pays for information on wooden boat-related events, projects, boatshop activities, etc. Uses same columnists for each issue. Length: 250-1,000 words. Send complete information. **Pays $5-50.**

Tips: "We appreciate a detailed, articulate query letter, accompanied by photos, that will give us a clear idea of what the author is proposing. We appreciate samples of previously published work. It is important for a prospective author to become familiar with our magazine. Most work is submitted on speculation. The most common failure is not exploring the subject material in enough depth."

Gambling

$ $ PLAYERS' GUIDE TO SPORTS BOOKS, Players Guide, 11000 S. Eastern Ave., #1618, Henderson NV 89052-2965. (702)361-4602. Fax: (702)361-4605. E-mail: buzzdaly@aol.com. Website: www.buzzdaly.com. **Contact:** Buzz Daly, editor. **20-50% freelance written.** Annual magazine, weekly tabloid, and website covering sports wagering and online gaming. "We address the needs and interests of people who bet on sports. We focus on legal activities in Las Vegas and off shore, and do features on bookmakers, oddsmakers, professional bettors, etc. Although many readers are casual/recreationally, we do not 'dumb down' our coverage. Our readers are regular bettors who do not apologize for this activity." Estab. 1994. Circ. 75,000. **Pays on acceptance.** Byline given. Offers 10% or 100% kill fee. Buys first, electronic rights. Editorial lead time 2 months. Accepts queries by mail, e-mail. Responds in 2 weeks to queries; 1 week to mss. Sample copy for $3.95.

Nonfiction: "Our magazine is an annual. Our period for obtaining stories is from mid-March to early June. But our website uses material all year long." Book excerpts, interview/profile, new product. No exposés, handicapping tips, stories about losing, getting stiffed, etc. We have no interest in stories based on trite material or clichés." **Buys variable number of mss/year.** Query with published clips. Length: 300-1,500 words. **Pays $50-400.** Sometimes pays expenses of writers on assignment.

Photos: Send photos with submission. Reviews contact sheets, prints. Buys one-time rights. Offers no additional payment for photos accepted with ms. Identification of subjects, model releases required.

Tips: "A writer must be a bettor to be considered as a contributor. He does not need to state it, we can tell by the material. We look for fresh insight and original story ideas. However, an old idea presented imaginatively and with sophistication will be considered. For instance, the ups and downs of being or dealing with a local bookmaker, with revealing anecdotes, falls within our parameters. We have no interest in hard luck stories, bad beats, etc."

General Interest

N **$ $ METROSPORTS, New York**, MetroSports Publishing, Inc., 259 W. 30th St., 3rd Floor, New York NY 10001. (212)563-7329. Fax: (212)563-7573. E-mail: jshweder@metrosports.com. Website: www.metrosportsny.com. **Contact:** Jeremy Shweder, editor. **50% freelance written.** Monthly magazine covering amateur sports and fitness. "We focus on participatory sports (not team sports) for an active, young audience that likes to exercise." Estab. 1987. Circ. 100,000. Pays on publication. Byline given. Offers 50% kill fee. Buys first, electronic rights. Editorial lead time 3 months. Submit seasonal material 6 months in advance. Accepts queries by mail, e-mail, fax. Accepts previously published material. Accepts simultaneous submissions. Responds in 3-4 weeks to queries; 1-2 months to mss. Sample copy online. Writer's guidelines by e-mail.

Nonfiction: Essays, general interest, historical/nostalgic, how-to (train for a triathlon, set a new 5K P.R., train for an adventure race, etc.), humor, inspirational, interview/profile, new product, opinion, personal experience, technical, travel. Special issues: Holiday Gift Guide (December). "We don't publish anything related to team sports (basketball, baseball, football, etc.), golf, tennis." **Buys 24 mss/year.** Query with published clips. Length: 800-3,000 words. **Pays $100-300.** Sometimes pays expenses of writers on assignment.

Photos: State availability with submission. Reviews slides transparencies, 3×5 prints, GIF/JPEG files (300 dpi). Buys one-time rights. Negotiates payment individually. Captions, identification of subjects required.

Columns/Departments: Running (training, nutrition, profiles), 800 words; Cycling (training, nutrition, profiles), 800 words; Cool Down (first-person essay), 800-1,000 words. **Buys 15 mss/year.** Query with published clips. **Pays $100-250.**

Tips: "Read the magazine, know what we cover. E-mail queries or mail with published clips. No phone calls, please."

$ $ ROCKY MOUNTAIN SPORTS MAGAZINE, Rocky Mountain Sports, Inc., 2525 15th St., #1A, Denver CO 80211. (303)477-9770. Fax: (303)477-9747. E-mail: rheaton@rockymountainsports.com. Website: www.rockymountainsports.com. Publisher: Mary Thorne. **Contact:** Rebecca Heaton, editor. **50% freelance written.** Monthly magazine covering nonteam-related sports in Colorado. "*Rocky* is a magazine for sports-related lifestyles and activities. Our mission is to reflect and inspire the active lifestyle of Rocky Mountain residents." Estab. 1986. Circ. 80,000. Pays on publication. Publishes ms an average of 2 months after acceptance. Byline given. Buys second serial (reprint) rights. Editorial lead time 3 months. Submit seasonal material 5 months in advance. Accepts queries by mail, e-mail, fax. Accepts previously published material. Responds in 3 weeks to queries; 2 months to mss. Sample copy and writer's guidelines for #10 SASE.

- The editor says she wants to see mountain outdoor sports writing *only*. No ball sports, hunting, or fishing.
- Break in with "Rocky Mountain angle—off-the-beaten-path."

Nonfiction: How-to, humor, inspirational, interview/profile, new product, opinion, personal experience, photo feature, travel. Special issues: Skiing & Snowboarding (November); Nordic (December) Snowshoeing (January); Running (March); Adventure Travel (April); Triathlon (May); Paddling and Climbing (June); Road Cycling & Camping (July); Mountain Biking & Hiking (August); Women's Sports & Marathon (September); Health Club (October). No articles on football, baseball, basketball, or other sports covered in depth by newspapers. **Buys 24 mss/year.** Query with published clips. Length: 1,500 words maximum. **Pays $150 minimum.**

Reprints: Send photocopy and information about when and where the material previously appeared. Pays 20-25% of amount paid for original article.

Photos: State availability with submission. Reviews transparencies, prints. Buys one-time rights. Captions, identification of subjects required.

Columns/Departments: Starting Lines (short newsy items); Running; Cycling; Climbing; Triathalon; Fitness, Nutrition; Sports Medicine; Off the Beaten Path (sports we don't usually cover). **Buys 20 mss/year.** Query. **Pays $25-300.**

Tips: "Have a Colorado angle to the story, a catchy cover letter, good clips, and demonstrate that you've read and understand our magazine and its readers."

$ SILENT SPORTS, Waupaca Publishing Co., P.O. Box 152, Waupaca WI 54981-9990. (715)258-5546. Fax: (715)258-8162. E-mail: info@silentsports.net. Website: www.silentsports.net. **Contact:** Greg Marr, editor. **75% freelance written.** Monthly magazine covering running, cycling, cross-country skiing, canoeing, kayaking, snowshoeing, in-line skating, camping, backpacking, and hiking aimed at people in Wisconsin, Minnesota, northern Illinois, and portions of Michigan and Iowa. "Not a coffee table magazine. Our readers are participants from rank amateur weekend athletes to highly competitive racers." Estab. 1984. Circ. 10,000. Pays on publication. Publishes ms an average of 3 months after acceptance. Byline given. Offers 20% kill fee. Buys one-time rights. Submit seasonal material 4 months in advance. Accepts queries by mail, e-mail, fax. Accepts previously published material. Responds in 3 months to queries. Sample copy and writer's guidelines for 10×13 SAE with 7 first-class stamps.

- The editor needs local angles on in-line skating, recreation bicycling, and snowshoeing.

Nonfiction: All stories/articles must focus on the Upper Midwest. General interest, how-to, interview/profile, opinion, technical, travel. **Buys 25 mss/year.** Query. Length: 2,500 words maximum. **Pays $15-100.** Sometimes pays expenses of writers on assignment.

Reprints: Send ms with rights for sale noted and information about when and where the material previously appeared. Pays 50% of amount paid for an original article.

Photos: State availability with submission. Reviews transparencies. Buys one-time rights. Pays $5-15 for b&w story photos; $50-100 for color covers.

Tips: "Where-to-go and personality profiles are areas most open to freelancers. Writers should keep in mind that this is a regional, Midwest-based publication. We want only stories/articles with a focus on our region."

$ SPORTS ETC, The Northwest's Outdoor Magazine, Sports Etc, 11715 Greenwood Ave. N., Seattle WA 98133. (206)418-0747. Fax: (206)418-0746. E-mail: staff@sportsetc.com. Website: www.sportsetc.com. **Contact:** Carolyn Price, editor. **80% freelance written.** Monthly magazine covering outdoor recreation in the Pacific Northwest. "Writers must have a solid knowledge of the sport they are writing about. They must be doers." Estab. 1988. Circ. 40,000. Pays on publication. Publishes ms an average of 3 months after acceptance. Byline given. Buys first rights. Editorial lead time 2 months. Submit seasonal material 4 months in advance. Accepts queries by mail, e-mail, fax. Accepts previously published material. Accepts simultaneous submissions. Sample copy and writer's guidelines for $3.

Nonfiction: Interview/profile, new product, travel. Query with published clips. Length: 750-1,500 words. **Pays $10-50.** Sometimes pays expenses of writers on assignment.

Photos: Send photos with submission. Reviews negatives, transparencies. Buys all rights. Captions, identification of subjects, model releases required.

Columns/Departments: Your Health (health and wellness), 750 words. **Buys 10-12 mss/year.** Query with published clips. **Pays $40-50.**

Tips: "*Sports Etc* is written for the serious Pacific Northwest outdoor recreationalist. The magazine's look, style and editorial content actively engage the reader, delivering insightful perspectives on the sports it has come to be known for—alpine skiing, bicycling, hiking, in-line skating, kayaking, marathons, mountain climbing, Nordic skiing, running, and snowboarding. *Sports Etc* magazine wants vivid writing, telling images, and original perspectives to produce its smart, entertaining monthly."

$ SPORTS ILLUSTRATED, Time Inc. Magazine Co., Sports Illustrated Bldg., 135 W. 50th St., New York NY 10020. (212)522-1212. E-mail: story_queries@simail.com. Associate Publishers: Sheila Buckley and John Rodenburg. **Contact:** Chris Hunt, articles editor; Mark Marvic, senior editor. Weekly magazine. "*Sports Illustrated* reports and interprets the world of sport, recreation, and active leisure. It previews, analyzes, and comments upon major games and events, as well as those noteworthy for character and spirit alone. It features individuals connected to sport and evaluates trends concerning the part sport plays in contemporary life. In addition, the magazine has articles on such subjects as sports gear and swim suits. Special departments deal with sports equipment, books, and statistics." Estab. 1954. Circ. 3,339,000. Accepts queries by mail. Responds in 4-6 weeks to queries.

- Do not send photos or graphics. Please include a SASE for return of materials.

N $ $ TWIN CITIES SPORTS, Twin Cities Sports Publishing, Inc., 3009 Holmes Ave. S., Minneapolis MN 55408. (612)825-1034. Fax: (612)825-6452. E-mail: kryan@twincitiessports.com. Website: www.twincitiessports.com. Editor: Jeff Banowetz. **Contact:** Kyle Ryan, managing editor. **75% freelance written.** Monthly magazine covering amateur sports and fitness. "We focus on participatory sports (not team sports) for an active, young audience that likes to exercise." Estab. 1987. Circ. 50,000. Pays on publication. Publishes ms an average of 2 months after acceptance. Byline given. Offers 50% kill fee. Buys first, electronic rights. Editorial lead time 3 months. Submit seasonal material 6 months in advance. Accepts queries by mail, e-mail, fax. Accepts previously published material. Accepts simultaneous submissions. Responds in 3-4 weeks to queries; 1-2 months to mss. Sample copy online. Writer's guidelines by e-mail.

Nonfiction: Essays, general interest, historical/nostalgic, how-to (train for a triathlon, set a new 5K P.R., train for an adventure race), humor, inspirational, interview/profile, new product, opinion, personal experience, technical, travel. Special issues: Holiday Gift Guide (December). "We don't publish anything related to team sports (basketball, baseball, football, etc.), golf, tennis. **Buys 24 mss/year.** Query with published clips. Length: 800-3,000 words. **Pays $100-300.** Sometimes pays expenses of writers on assignment.

Photos: State availability with submission. Reviews slides transparencies, 3×5 prints, GIF/JPEG files (300 dpi). Buys one-time rights. Negotiates payment individually. Captions, identification of subjects required.

Columns/Departments: Running (training, nutrition, profiles), 800 words; Cycling (training, nutrition, profiles), 800 words; Cool Down (first-person essay), 800-1,000 words. **Buys 15 mss/year.** Query with published clips. **Pays $100-250.**

Tips: "Read the magazine, know what we cover. E-mail queries or mail with published clips. No phone calls, please."

Golf

$ $ ARIZONA, THE STATE OF GOLF, Arizona Golf Association, 7226 N. 16th St., Suite 200, Phoenix AZ 85020. (602)944-3035. Fax: (602)944-3228. E-mail: rchrist@azgolf.org. Website: www.azgolf.org. **Contact:** Russ Christ, editor. **50% freelance written.** Quarterly magazine covering golf in Arizona, the official publication of the Arizona Golf Association. Estab. 1999. Circ. 45,000. **Pays on acceptance.** Byline given. Buys all rights. Editorial lead time 6 months. Submit seasonal material 3 months in advance. Accepts queries by mail. Accepts previously published material. Accepts simultaneous submissions. Sample copy and writer's guidelines free.

Nonfiction: Book excerpts, essays, historical/nostalgic, how-to (golf), humor, inspirational, interview/profile, new product, opinion, personal experience, photo feature, travel (destinations). **Buys 5-10 mss/year.** Query with or without published clips. Length: 500-2,000 words. **Pays $50-500.** Sometimes pays expenses of writers on assignment.

Reprints: Accepts previously published submissions.

Photos: State availability with submission. Reviews contact sheets. Rights purchased varies. Negotiates payment individually. Captions, identification of subjects required.

Columns/Departments: Short Strokes (golf news and notes), Improving Your Game (golf tips), Out of Bounds (guest editorial, 800 words). Query.

$ $ CHICAGO DISTRICT GOLFER, TPG Sports, Inc., 11855 Archer Ave., LaMont IL 60439. (630)257-2005. Fax: (630)257-2088. Website: www.tpgsports.com or www.cdga.org. **Contact:** Kathy Raulston, editor. **90% freelance written.** Bimonthly magazine covering golf in Illinois, the official publication of the Chicago District Golf Association and Golf Association of Illinois. Estab. 1922. Circ. 71,000. Pays on acceptance or publication. Byline given. Buys all rights. Editorial lead time 2 months. Submit seasonal material 3 months in advance. Accepts queries by mail, e-mail. Accepts previously published material. Accepts simultaneous submissions. Sample copy and writer's guidelines free.

Nonfiction: General interest, historical/nostalgic, how-to (golf), humor, interview/profile, opinion, personal experience, travel. **Buys 25-35 mss/year.** Query with or without published clips. Length: 500-5,000 words. **Pays $50-500.** Sometimes pays expenses of writers on assignment.

Reprints: Accepts previously published submissions.

Photos: State availability with submission. Reviews contact sheets. Negotiates payment individually. Captions, identification of subjects required.

Columns/Departments: CDGA/GAI Update (news and notes); Club Profile; Friends of the Game; Chicago District Lesson. Query.

$ $ $ GOLF CANADA, Official Magazine of the Royal Canadian Golf Association, RCGA/Relevant Communications, Golf House Suite 1, 1333 Dorval Dr., Oakville ON L6M 4X7, Canada. (905)849-9700. Fax: (905)845-7040. E-mail: golfcanada@rcga.org. Website: www.rcga.org. **Contact:** John Tenpenny, editor. **80% freelance written.** Magazine published 4 times/year covering Canadian golf. "*Golf Canada* is the official magazine of the Royal Canadian Golf Association, published to entertain and enlighten members about RCGA-related activities and to generally support and promote amateur golf in Canada." Estab. 1994. Circ. 159,000. **Pays on acceptance.** Byline given. Offers 100% kill fee. Buys first translation, electronic rights. Editorial lead time 3 months. Submit seasonal material 6 months in advance. Accepts queries by mail, e-mail, fax, phone. Accepts previously published material. Sample copy for free.

Nonfiction: Historical/nostalgic, interview/profile, new product, opinion, photo feature, travel. No professional golf-related articles. **Buys 42 mss/year.** Query with published clips. Length: 750-3,000 words. **Pays 60¢/word including electronic rights.** Sometimes pays expenses of writers on assignment.

Photos: State availability with submission. Reviews contact sheets, negatives, transparencies, prints. Buys all rights. Negotiates payment individually. Captions required.

Columns/Departments: Guest Column (focus on issues surrounding the Canadian golf community), 700 words. Query. **Pays 60¢/word including electronic rights.**

Tips: "Keep story ideas focused on Canadian competitive golf."

N $ GOLF DIGEST, The Golf Digest Companies, 5520 Park Ave., Box 395, Trumbull CT 06611. (203)373-7000. Fax: (203)371-2162. E-mail: editor@golfdigest.com. Website: www.golfdigest.com. Editor: Jerry Tarde. Managing Editor: Roger Schiffman. **Contact:** Craig Bestrom; features editor. Monthly magazine covering the sport of golf. Written for all golf enthusiasts, whether recreational, amateur, or professional player. Estab. 1950. Circ. 1,550,000. Editorial lead time 6 months. Accepts queries by mail. Sample copy for $3.95.

- Golf Digest does not accept any unsolicited materials.

Nonfiction: Query.

Columns/Departments: Query.

N $ GOLF FOR WOMEN, Condé Nast Company Magazine, 4 Times Square, 7th Floor, New York NY 10036. (212)286-2888. Fax: (212)286-5340. E-mail: editors@golfforwomen.com. Website: www.golfdigest.com/gfw. Managing Editor: Mary Novitsky. **Contact:** Joe Bargmann, executive editor. **50% freelance written.** Bimonthly magazine covering golf instruction, travel, lifestyle. "Our magazine is the leading authority on the game for women. We celebrate the traditions and lifestyle of golf, explore issues surrounding the game with incisive features, and we present traditional women's and fashion magazine fare—fashion, beauty, relationship stories—all with a strong golf angle. Travel is also a big component of our coverage. We package everything in a modern, sophisticated way that suits our affluent, educated readers." Circ. 500,000. **Pays on acceptance.** Byline given. Offers variable kill fee (25% standard)... Buys all rights, including online. Accepts queries by mail, e-mail, fax.

Nonfiction: Book excerpts, essays, general interest, historical/nostalgic, how-to (golf related), humor, inspirational, interview/profile, new product, personal experience, photo feature, travel. **Buys 50 mss/year.** Query. Length: 250-2,500 words. **Payment negotiated.** Sometimes pays expenses of writers on assignment.

Photos: State availability with submission. Buys one-time rights and online usage rights. Negotiates payment individually. Model releases required.

Columns/Departments: Fitness; Beauty; Get There (travel); Fashion; First Person; Health. **Pays per piece or per word; fees negotiated.**

$ $ GOLF TRAVELER, Official Publication of Golf Card International, Affinity Group, Inc., 2575 Vista del Mar, Ventura CA 93001. Fax: (805)667-4217. E-mail: golf@golfcard.com. Website: www.golfcard.com. **Contact:** Valerie Law, editorial director. **20% freelance written.** Quarterly magazine and monthly e-newsletter "are the membership publications for the Golf Card, an organization that offers its members reduced or waived greens fees at 3,500 affiliated golf courses in North America." Estab. 1976. Circ. 100,000. **Pays on acceptance.** Byline given. Offers 33% kill fee. Buys first North American serial, electronic rights. Editorial lead time 3 months. Submit seasonal material 3 months in advance. Accepts queries by mail, e-mail, fax. Accepts previously published material. Accepts simultaneous submissions. Responds in 1 month to queries. Sample copy for $3, plus 9×12 SASE.

Nonfiction: Book excerpts, essays, how-to, interview/profile, new product, personal experience, photo feature, technical. No poetry or cartoons. **Buys 8 mss/year.** Query with published clips or send complete ms. Length: 500-1,500 words. **Pays $75-500.**

Reprints: Accepts previously published submissions.

Photos: Send photos with submission. Reviews transparencies, digital images. Buys one-time rights. Negotiates payment individually. Identification of subjects required.

The online magazine carries original content not found in the print edition. Contact: Ken Cohen.

N **$ $ THE GOLFER**, 551 5th Ave., New York NY 10176. (212)867-7070. Fax: (212)867-8550. E-mail: thegolfer@walrus.com. Editor: H.K. Pickens. **Contact:** Colin Sheehan, senior editor. **40% freelance written.** Bimonthly magazine covering golf. "A sophisticated, controversational tone for a lifestyle-oriented magazine." Estab. 1994. Circ. 253,000. Pays on publication. Publishes ms an average of 2 months after acceptance. Byline given. Offers negotiable kill fee. Buys all rights. Editorial lead time 2 months. Submit seasonal material 4 months in advance. Accepts queries by mail, e-mail, fax. Accepts previously published material. Accepts simultaneous submissions. Sample copy for free.

Nonfiction: Book excerpts, essays, general interest, historical/nostalgic, how-to, humor, inspirational, interview/profile, new product, opinion, personal experience, photo feature, technical, travel. Send complete ms. Length: 300-2,000 words. **Pays $150-600.**

Reprints: Accepts previously published submissions.

Photos: Send photos with submission. Reviews any size transparencies. Buys one-time rights.

$ $ MINNESOTA GOLFER, 6550 York Ave. S., Suite 211, Edina MN 55435. (952)927-4643. Fax: (952)927-9642. E-mail: editor@mngolf.org. Website: www.mngolf.org. **Contact:** W.P. Ryan, editor. **25-50% freelance written.** Bimonthly magazine covering golf in Minnesota, the official publication of the Minnesota Golf Association. Estab. 1975. Circ. 72,500. Pays on acceptance or publication. Byline given. Buys all rights. Editorial lead time 3 months. Accepts queries by mail, fax.

- Do not send queries by e-mail.

Nonfiction: Book excerpts, essays, historical/nostalgic, how-to (golf), humor, inspirational, interview/profile, new product, opinion, personal experience, photo feature. **Buys 6-12 mss/year.** Query with published clips. Length: 500-2,500 words. **Pays $50-500.** Sometimes pays expenses of writers on assignment.

Photos: State availability with submission. Reviews contact sheets, transparencies, digital images. Rights purchased varies. Negotiates payment individually. Captions, identification of subjects required.

Columns/Departments: Punch shots (golf news and notes); Q Notes (news and information targeted to beginners, junior golfers); Great Drives (featured hole in Minnesota). Query.

$ $ $ PACIFIC/ALBERTA GOLF, (formerly *Pacific Golf*), Canada Wide Magazines & Communications Ltd., 4180 Lougheed Hwy., 4th Floor, Burnaby BC V5C 6A7, Canada. (604)299-7311. Fax: (604)299-9188. E-mail: acollette@canadawide.com. **Contact:** Ann Collette, editor. **80% freelance written.** Quarterly magazine. "*Pacific Golf* appeals to Western Canada's golfers and reflects the West Coast golf experience. We concentrate on the new, the influential, Canadian golfers, and subject matter based in British Columbia." Circ. 30,000. Pays on publication. Publishes ms an average of 2 months after acceptance. Byline given. Offers variable kill fee. first Canadian rights. Editorial lead time 4 months. Submit seasonal material 4 months in advance. Responds in 6 weeks to mss. Sample copy not available.

Nonfiction: Query with published clips. Length: 500-1,800 words. **Pays 40-50¢/word.** Sometimes pays expenses of writers on assignment.

Photos: State availability with submission.

N **$ $ TEXAS GOLFER MAGAZINE**, Golfer Magazines, Inc., 5 Briardale, Houston TX 77027. (713)680-1680. Fax: (713)680-0138. Editor: Bob Gray. **Contact:** Mike Haines, Publisher. **10% freelance written.** Monthly tabloid covering golf in Texas. Estab. 1984. Circ. 50,000. Pays on publication. Publishes ms an average of 2 months after acceptance. Byline given. Buys first, one-time, second serial (reprint) rights. Editorial lead time 2 months. Submit seasonal material 3 months in advance. Responds in 2 weeks to queries; 1 month to mss. Sample copy for free. Prefers direct phone discussion for writer's guidelines.

- *Texas Golfer Magazine* was created by the merger of two publications: *Goulf Coast Golfer* and *North Texas Golfer.*

Nonfiction: Book excerpts, humor, personal experience, all golf-related. No stories about golf outside of Texas. **Buys 20 mss/year.** Query. **Pays 10-40¢/word.**
Photos: State availability with submission. Reviews contact sheets, prints. Buys one-time rights. No additional payment for photos accepted with ms, but pays $125 for cover photo. Captions, identification of subjects required.
Tips: "Most of our purchases are in how-to area, so writers must know golf quite well and play the game."

Guns

$ $ THE ACCURATE RIFLE, Precision Shooting, Inc., 222 McKee St., Manchester CT 06040-4800. (860)645-8776. Fax: (860)643-8215. Website: www.theaccuraterifle.com. **Contact:** Dave Brennan, editor. **30-35% freelance written.** Monthly magazine covering "the specialized field of 'extreme rifle accuracy' excluding rifle competition disciplines." Estab. 2000. Circ. 8,000. Pays on publication. Publishes ms an average of 3 months after acceptance. Byline given. Buys first North American serial rights. Editorial lead time 2 months. Submit seasonal material 3 months in advance. Accepts queries by mail, fax. Responds in 2 weeks to queries; 1 month to mss. Sample copy for free. Writer's guidelines not available.
Nonfiction: General interest, historical/nostalgic, how-to, humor, interview/profile, personal experience. "Nothing common to newsstand firearms publications. This has a very sophisticated and knowledgable readership." **Buys 36 mss/year.** Query. Length: 1,800-3,000 words. **Pays $200-500.**
Photos: Send photos with submission. Reviews 4×6 prints. Buys one-time rights. Offers no additional payment for photos accepted with ms. Captions required.
Tips: "Call the editor first and tell him what topic you propose to write about. Could save time and effort."

$ $ GUN DIGEST, DBI Books, Inc., Division of Krause Publications, 700 E. State St., Iola WI 54990. (888)457-2873. Fax: (715)445-4087. **Contact:** Ken Ramage, editor-in-chief. **50% freelance written.** Prefers to work with published/established writers, but works with a small number of new/unpublished writers each year. Annual journal covering guns and shooting. Estab. 1944. **Pays on acceptance.** Publishes ms an average of 20 months after acceptance. Byline given. Buys all rights. Accepts queries by mail. Responds as time allows to queries.
Nonfiction: Buys 25 mss/year. Query. Length: 500-5,000 words. **Pays $100-600 for text/art package.**
Photos: Prefers 8×10 b&w prints. Slides, transparencies OK. No digital. State availability with submission. Payment for photos included in payment for ms. Captions required.
Tips: Award of $1,000 to author of best article (juried) in each issue.

$ $ MUZZLE BLASTS, National Muzzle Loading Rifle Association, P.O. Box 67, Friendship IN 47021. (812)667-5131. Fax: (812)667-5137. E-mail: mblastdop@seidata.com. Website: www.nmlra.org. Editor: Eric A. Bye. **Contact:** Terri Trowbridge, director of publications. **65% freelance written.** Monthly magazine. "Articles must relate to muzzleloading or the muzzleloading era of American history." Estab. 1939. Circ. 23,000. Pays on publication. Publishes ms an average of 6 months after acceptance. Byline given. Offers $50 kill fee. Buys first North American serial, one-time, second serial (reprint) rights. Editorial lead time 4 months. Submit seasonal material 6 months in advance. Responds in 1 month to mss. Sample copy and writer's guidelines free.
Nonfiction: Book excerpts, general interest, historical/nostalgic, how-to, humor, interview/profile, new product, personal experience, photo feature, technical, travel. "No subjects that do not pertain to muzzleloading." **Buys 80 mss/year.** Query. Length: 2,500 words. **Pays $150 minimum for assigned articles; $50 minimum for unsolicited articles.**
Photos: Send photos with submission. Reviews 5×7 prints. Buys one-time rights. Negotiates payment individually. Captions, model releases required.
Columns/Departments: Buys 96 mss/year. Query. **Pays $50-200.**
Fiction: Must pertain to muzzleloading. Adventure, historical, humorous. **Buys 6 mss/year.** Query. Length: 2,500 words. **Pays $50-300.**
Fillers: Facts. **Pays $50.**

$ $ PRECISION SHOOTING, Precision Shooting, Inc., 222 McKee St., Manchester CT 06040-4800. (860)645-8776. Fax: (860)643-8215. Website: www.precisionshooting.com. **Contact:** Dave Brennan, editor. **30-35% freelance written.** Monthly magazine covering "the specialized field of 'extreme rifle accuracy' including rifle competition disciplines." Estab. 1956. Circ. 17,500. Pays on publication. Publishes ms an average of 3 months after acceptance. Byline given. Buys first North American serial rights. Editorial lead time 2 months. Submit seasonal material 3 months in advance. Accepts queries by mail, fax. Responds in 2 weeks to queries; 1 month to mss. Sample copy for free. Writer's guidelines not available.
Nonfiction: General interest, historical/nostalgic, how-to, humor, interview/profile, personal experience. "Nothing common to newsstand firearms publications. This has a very sophisticated and knowledgeable readership." **Buys 36 mss/year.** Query. Length: 1,800-3,000 words. **Pays $200-500.**
Photos: Send photos with submission. Reviews 4×6 prints. Buys one-time rights. Offers no additional payment for photos accepted with ms. Captions required.
Tips: "Call the editor first and tell him what topic you propose to write about. Could save time and effort."

$ $ SHOTGUN NEWS, Primedia, Box 1790, Peoria IL 61656. (309)679-5408. Fax: (309)679-5476. E-mail: sgnews@primediasi.com. Website: www.shotgunnews.com. **Contact:** Robert W. Hunnicutt, general manager/editor. **95% freelance written.** Tabloid published every 10 days covering firearms, accessories, ammunition and militaria. "The nation's oldest and largest gun sales publication. Provides up-to-date market information for gun trade and consumers." Estab. 1946. Circ.

100,000. **Pays on acceptance.** Publishes ms an average of 3 months after acceptance. Byline given. Buys first North American serial rights. Editorial lead time 1 month. Submit seasonal material 3 months in advance. Responds in 1 month to queries. Sample copy for free.

Nonfiction: Historical/nostalgic, how-to, technical. No political pieces, fiction or poetry. **Buys 50 mss/year.** Query. Length: 1,000-3,000 words. **Pays $200-500 for assigned articles.** Sometimes pays expenses of writers on assignment.

Photos: Send photos with submission. Reviews prints. Buys one-time rights. Offers no additional payment for photos accepted with ms. Captions required.

Hiking & Backpacking

$ $ $ $ BACKPACKER, Rodale, 33 E. Minor St., Emmaus PA 18098-0099. (610)967-8296. Fax: (610)967-8181. E-mail: pflax@backpacker.com. Website: www.backpacker.com. **Contact:** Peter Flax, features editor. **50% freelance written.** Magazine published 9 times/year covering wilderness travel for backpackers. Estab. 1973. Circ. 295,000. **Pays on acceptance.** Byline given. Buys one-time, all rights. Accepts queries by mail, e-mail, fax. Responds in 6 weeks to queries. Writer's guidelines online.

Nonfiction: "What we want are features that let us and the readers 'feel' the place, and experience your wonderment, excitement, disappointment, or other emotions encountered 'out there.' If we feel like we've been there after reading your story, you've succeeded." Essays, exposé, historical/nostalgic, how-to, humor, inspirational, interview/profile, new product, personal experience, technical, travel. No step-by-step accounts of what you did on your summer vacation—stories that chronicle every rest stop and gulp of water. Query with published clips. Length: 750-4,000 words. **Pays $250-5,000.**

Photos: State availability with submission. Buys one-time rights. Payment varies.

Columns/Departments: Signpost, "News From All Over" (adventure, environment, wildelife, trails, techniques, organizations, special interests—well-written, entertaining, short, newsy item), 50-500 words; Getaways (great hiking destinations, primarily North America), includes weekend, 250-500 words, weeklong, 250-1000, multi-destination guides, 500-1500 words, and dayhikes, 50-200 words, plus travel news and other items; Fitness (in-the-field health column), 750-1,200 words; Food (food-related aspects of wilderness: nutrition, cooking techniques, recipes, products and gear), 500-750 words; Know How (ranging from beginner to expert focus, written by people with solid expertise, details ways to improve performance, how-to-do-it instructions, information on equipment manufacturers, and places readers can go), 300-1,000 words; Senses (capturing a moment in backcountry through sight, sound, smell, and other senses, paired with an outstanding photo), 150-200 words. **Buys 50-75 mss/year.**

The online magazine carries original content not found in the print edition.

Tips: "Our best advice is to read the publication—most freelancers don't know the magazine at all. The best way to break in is with an article for the Weekend Wilderness, Know How, or Signpost Department."

$ OUTSIDE, Mariah Media, Inc., Outside Plaza, 400 Market St., Santa Fe NM 87501. (505)989-7100. Website: www.outsidemag.com. Editor: Hal Espen. **Contact:** Assistant to the Editor. **90% freelance written.** Monthly magazine. "*Outside* is a monthly national magazine for active, educated, upscale adults who love the outdoors and are concerned about its preservation." Estab. 1977. Circ. 550,000. Pays after acceptance. Publishes ms an average of 3 months after acceptance. Byline given. Offers 25% kill fee. Buys first North American serial rights. Submit seasonal material 5 months in advance. Writer's guidelines online. Editorial calendar online.

Nonfiction: Book excerpts, essays, general interest, how-to, interview/profile (major figures associated with sports, travel, environment, outdoor), photo feature (outdoor photography), technical (reviews of equipment, how-to), travel (adventure, sports-oriented travel). Do not want to see articles about sports that we don't cover (basketball, tennis, golf, etc.). **Buys 40 mss/year.** Query with published clips. Length: 1,500-4,000 words. Pays expenses of writers on assignment.

Photos: "Do not send photos; if we decide to use a story, we may ask to see the writer's photos." Reviews transparencies. Buys one-time rights. Captions, identification of subjects required.

Columns/Departments: Dispatches (news, events, short profiles relevant to outdoors), 200-1,000 words; Destinations (places to explore, news, and tips for adventure travelers), 250-400 words; Review (evaluations of products), 200-1,500 words. **Buys 180 mss/year.** Query with published clips.

The online magazine carries original content not found in the print edition. Contact: Mike Roberts, online editor.

Tips: "Prospective writers should study the magazine before querying. Look at the magazine for our style, subject matter, and standards." The departments are the best areas for freelancers to break in.

Hockey

$ $ MINNESOTA HOCKEY JOURNAL, Official Publication of Minnesota Hockey, Inc., c/o TPG Sports, Inc., 6160 Summit Dr., Suite 375, Minneapolis MN 55430. (763)595-0808. Fax: (763)595-0016. E-mail: greg@tpgsports.com. Website: www.tpgsports.com. Editor: Greg Anzlec. **50% freelance written.** Journal published 4 times/year. Estab. 2000. Circ. 40,000. Pays on publication. Byline given. Buys all rights. Editorial lead time 6 months. Submit seasonal material 4 months in advance. Accepts previously published material. Accepts simultaneous submissions. Sample copy and writer's guidelines free.

Nonfiction: Essays, general interest, historical/nostalgic, how-to (play hockey), humor, inspirational, interview/profile, new product, opinion, personal experience, photo feature, travel, hockey camps, pro hockey, juniors, college, Olympics, youth, etc. **Buys 5-10 mss/year.** Query. Length: 500-5,000 words. **Pays $100-500.** Sometimes pays expenses of writers on assignment.

Reprints: Accepts previously published submissions.
Photos: State availability with submission. Reviews contact sheets. Rights purchased vary. Negotiates payment individually. Captions, identification of subjects required.
Columns/Departments: Hot Shots (news and notes); Open Ice (opinion). **Pays $50-250.**
Fillers: Anecdotes, facts, gags to be illustrated by cartoonist, newsbreaks, short humor, game page with puzzles. **Buys 5-10 mss/year.** Length: 10-100 words. **Pays $25-250.**

Horse Racing

N $ $ **THE AMERICAN QUARTER HORSE RACING JOURNAL**, American Quarter Horse Association, P.O. Box 32470, Amarillo TX 79120. (806)376-4888. Fax: (806)349-6400. E-mail: richc@aqha.org. Website: www.aqha.com/racing. Executive Editor: Jim Jennings. **Contact:** Richard Chamberlain, editor. **10% freelance written.** Monthly magazine. "The official racing publication of the American Quarter Horse Association. We promote American Quarter Horse racing. Articles include training, breeding, nutrition, sports medicine, health, history, etc." Estab. 1988. Circ. 9,000. **Pays on acceptance.** Publishes ms an average of 3 months after acceptance. Buys first North American serial rights. Submit seasonal material 3 months in advance. Accepts queries by mail, e-mail. Accepts previously published material. Responds in 1 month to queries. Sample copy and writer's guidelines free.
Nonfiction: Historical/nostalgic (must be on Quarter Horses or people associated with them), how-to (training), opinion, nutrition, health, breeding. Special issues: Yearlings (August), All-American Futurity (September), Stallions (December). Query. Length: 700-1,500 words. **Pays $150-300.**
Reprints: Send photocopy and information about when and where the material previously appeared.
Photos: Send photos with submission. Additional payment for photos accepted with ms might be offered. Captions, identification of subjects required.
Fiction: Novel excerpts.
The online magazine carries original content not found in the print edition. Contact: Richard Chamberlain, online editor.
Tips: "Query first—must be familiar with Quarter Horse racing and be knowledgeable of the sport. The *Journal* directs its articles to those who own, train, and breed racing Quarter Horses, as well as fans and handicappers. Most open to features covering breeding, raising, training, nutrition, and health care utilizing knowledgeable sources with credentials."

$ $ **AMERICAN TURF MONTHLY**, Star Sports Corp., 115 S. Corona Ave., Suite 1A, Valley Stream NY 11580. (516)599-2121. Fax: (516)599-0451. E-mail: editor@americanturf.com. Website: www.americanturf.com. **Contact:** James Corbett, editor-in-chief. **90% freelance written.** Monthly magazine covering Thoroughbred racing, handicapping, and wagering. "Squarely focused on Thoroughbred handicapping and wagering. *ATM* is a magazine for horseplayers, not owners, breeders, or 12-year-old girls enthralled with ponies." Estab. 1946. Circ. 28,000. Pays on publication. Publishes ms an average of 4 months after acceptance. Byline given. Makes work-for-hire assignments. Editorial lead time 2 months. Submit seasonal material 2 months in advance. Accepts queries by mail, e-mail. Responds in 1 month to queries. Sample copy and writer's guidelines free.
Nonfiction: Handicapping and wagering features. Special issues: Triple Crown/Kentucky Derby (May); Saratoga/Del Mar (August); Breeder's Cup (November). No historical essays, bilious 'guest editorials,' saccharine poetry, fiction. **Buys 50 mss/year.** Query. Length: 800-2,000 words. **Pays $75-300 for assigned articles; $100-500 for unsolicited articles.**
Photos: Send photos with submission. Reviews 3×5 transparencies, prints. Buys one-time rights. Offers $25 interior; $150 for cover. Identification of subjects required.
Fillers: Newsbreaks, short humor. **Buys 5/year.** Length: 400 words. **Pays $25.**
The online magazine carries original content not found in the print version. Contact: Dana Romick, online editor.
Tips: "Send a good query letter specifically targeted at explaining how this contribution will help our readers to cash a bet at the track!"

$ $ **HOOF BEATS**, United States Trotting Association, 750 Michigan Ave., Columbus OH 43215. (614)224-2291. Fax: (614)222-6791. **Contact:** Dean A. Hoffman, editor; Nicole Kraft, associate editor. **50% freelance written.** Monthly magazine covering harness racing for the participants of the sport of harness racing. "We cover all aspects of the sport—racing, breeding, selling, etc." Estab. 1933. Circ. 13,500. Pays on publication. Publishes ms an average of 3 months after acceptance. Byline given. Buys negotiable rights. Submit seasonal material 4 months in advance. Responds in 1 months to mss. Free sample copy postpaid.
Nonfiction: General interest, historical/nostalgic, humor, inspirational, interview/profile, new product, personal experience, photo feature, horse care. **Buys 15-20 mss/year.** Length: open. **Pays $100-400.** Negotiable.
Photos: State availability with submission. Reviews prints, electronic images. Buys one-time rights. Negotiates payment individually. Identification of subjects required.

Hunting & Fishing

N $ $ $ **AMERICAN HUNTER**, 11250 Waples Mill Rd., Fairfax VA 22030-9400. (703)267-1335. Fax: (703)267-3971. E-mail: publications@nrahq.org. Website: www.nra.org. Editor-in-Chief: John Zent. **Contact:** Scott Olmsted, associate editor. Monthly magazine for hunters who are members of the National Rifle Association. "*American Hunter* contains articles dealing with various sport hunting and related activities both at home and abroad. With the encouragment of the sport as a prime game management tool, emphasis is on technique, sportsmanship and safety. In each issue hunting equipment and firearms are evaluated, legislative happenings affecting the sport are reported, lore and legend are retold and the business of the Association is recorded in the Official Journal section." Circ. 1,000,000. **Pays on acceptance.** Byline given. Buys first North American serial, second serial (reprint) rights. Accepts queries by mail, e-mail. Responds in 3 months to queries. Writer's guidelines for #10 SASE.

Nonfiction: Factual material on all phases of hunting: Expository how-to, where-to, and general interest pieces; humor: personal narratives; and semi-technical articles on firearms, wildlife management or hunting. Features fall into five categories: Deer, upland birds, waterfowl, big game and varmints/small game. Special issues: Pheasants, whitetail tactics, black bear feed areas, mule deer, duck hunters' transport by land and sea, tech topics to be decided; rut strategies, muzzleloader moose and elk, fall turkeys, staying warm, goose talk, long-range muzzleloading. Not interested in material on fishing, camping, or firearms knowledge. Query. Length: 1,800-2,000 words. **Pays up to $800.**

Reprints: Send ms with rights for sale noted and information about when and where the material previously appeared.

Photos: No additional payment made for photos used with ms; others offered from $75-600.

Columns/Departments: Hunting Guns, Hunting Loads and Public Hunting Grounds. Study back issues for appropriate subject matter and style. Length: 1,200-1,500 words. **Pays $300-450.**

Tips: "Although unsolicited manuscripts are welcomed, detailed query letters outlining the proposed topic and approach are appreciated and will save both writers and editors a considerable amount of time. If we like your story idea, you will be contacted by mail or phone and given direction on how we'd like the topic covered. NRA Publications accept all manuscripts and photographs for consideration on a specualtion basis only. Story angles should be narrow, but coverage must have depth. How-to articles are popular with readers and might range from methods for hunting to techniques on making gear used on successful hunts. Where-to articles should contain contacts and information needed to arrange a similar hunt. All submissions are judged on three criteria: Story angle (it should be fresh, interesting, and informative); quality of writing (clear and lively—capable of holding the readers' attention throughout); and quality and quantity of accompanying photos (sharpness, reproduceability, and connection to text are most important.)"

$ $ ARKANSAS SPORTSMAN, Game & Fish, P.O. Box 741, Marietta GA 30061. (770)953-9222. Fax: (770)933-9510. E-mail: ken_duke@primediamags.com. Website: arkansassportsmanmag.com. **Contact:** Ken Duke, editor. See *Game & Fish*. Accepts queries by mail, e-mail.

$ $ BASSMASTER MAGAZINE, B.A.S.S. Publications, 5845 Carmichael Pkwy., Montgomery AL 36117. (334)272-9530. Fax: (334)396-8230. E-mail: editorial@bassmaster.com. Website: www.bassmaster.com. **Contact:** James Hall, editor. **80% freelance written.** Magazine published 11 times/year about largemouth, smallmouth, and spotted bass, offering "how-to" articles for dedicated beginning and advanced bass fishermen, including destinations and new product reviews. Estab. 1968. Circ. 600,000. **Pays on acceptance.** Publishes ms an average of less than 1 year after acceptance. Byline given. Buys electronic rights. Editorial lead time 2 months. Submit seasonal material 6 months in advance. Accepts queries by mail, e-mail. Responds in 2 months to queries. Sample copy for $2. Writer's guidelines for #10 SASE.

- Needs destination stories (how to fish a certain area) for the Northwest and Northeast.

Nonfiction: Historical/nostalgic, how-to (patterns, lures, etc.), interview/profile (of knowledgeable people in the sport), new product (reels, rods, and bass boats), travel (where to go fish for bass), conservation related to bass fishing. "No first-person, personal experience-type articles." **Buys 100 mss/year.** Query. Length: 500-1,500 words. **Pays $100-600.**

Photos: Send photos with submission. Reviews transparencies. Buys all rights. Offers no additional payment for photos accepted with ms, but pays $700 for color cover transparencies. Captions, model releases required.

Columns/Departments: Short Cast/News/Views/Notes/Briefs (upfront regular feature covering news-related events such as new state bass records, unusual bass fishing happenings, conservation, new products, and editorial viewpoints). Length: 250-400 words. **Pays $100-300.**

Fillers: Anecdotes, newsbreaks. **Buys 4-5/year.** Length: 250-500 words. **Pays $50-100.**

Tips: "Editorial direction continues in the short, more direct how-to article. Compact, easy-to-read information is our objective. Shorter articles with good graphics, such as how-to diagrams, step-by-step instruction, etc., will enhance a writer's articles submitted to *Bassmaster Magazine*. The most frequent mistakes made by writers in completing an article for us are poor grammar, poor writing, poor organization, and superficial research. Send in detailed queries outlining specific objectives of article, obtain writer's guidelines. Be as concise as possible."

N $ $ BC OUTDOORS HUNTING & SHOOTING, OP Publishing, 1080 Howe, Suite 99, Vancouver BC V6Z 2T1, Canada. (604)606-4644. Fax: (604)687-1925. E-mail: bcoutdoors@oppublishing.com. Website: www.oppublishing.com. **Contact:** Tracey Ellis, coordinating editor. **80% freelance written.** Biannual magazine covering hunting, shooting, camping, and backroads. Pays on publication. Publishes ms an average of 3 months after acceptance. Byline given. Offers kill fee. Buys first North American serial rights. Sample copy and writer's guidelines for 8×10 SAE with 7 Canadian first-class stamps or IRC.

Nonfiction: "We would like to receive how-to, where-to features dealing with hunting in British Columbia." How-to (new or innovative articles on hunting subjects), personal experience (outdoor adventure), outdoor topics specific to British Columbia. **Buys 50 mss/year.** Query. Length: 1,700-2,000 words. **Pays $300-500.**

Photos: State availability with submission. Buys one-time rights. Captions, identification of subjects required.

Tips: "Wants in-depth information, professional writing only. Emphasis on environmental issues. Those pieces with a conservation component have a better chance of being published. Subject must be specific to British Columbia. We receive many manuscripts written by people who obviously do not know the magazine or market. The writer has a better chance of breaking in with short, lesser-paying articles and fillers, because we have a stable of regular writers who produce most main features."

$ BC OUTDOORS SPORT FISHING AND OUTDOOR ADVENTURE, (formely *BC Outdoors Sport Fishing*), OP Publishing, 1080 Howe St., Suite 900, Vancouver BC V6Z 2T1, Canada. (604)606-4644. Fax: (604)687-1925. E-mail: bcoutdoors@oppublishing.com. Website: www.bcsportfishing.com. **Contact:** Tracey Ellis, coordinating editor. **80% freelance written.** Magazine published 6 times/year covering fresh and saltwater fishing, camping, and backroads. Pays on publication. Publishes ms an average of 3 months after acceptance. Byline given. Offers kill fee. Buys first North American serial rights. Sample copy and writer's guidelines for 8×10 SAE with 7 Canadian first-class stamps or IRC.

Nonfiction: "We would like to receive how-to, where-to features dealing with fishing in British Columbia." How-to (new or innovative articles on fishing subjects), personal experience (outdoor adventure), outdoor topics specific to British Columbia. Query. Length: 1,700-2,000 words.

Photos: State availability with submission. Buys one-time rights. Captions, identification of subjects required.

Tips: "Wants in-depth information, professional writing only. Emphasis on environmental issues. Those pieces with a conservation component have a better chance of being published. Subject must be specific to British Columbia. We receive many manuscripts written by people who obviously do not know the magazine or market. The writer has a better chance of breaking in with short, lesser-paying articles and fillers, because we have a stable of regular writers who produce most main features."

$ $ BUGLE, Elk Country and the Hunt, Rocky Mountain Elk Foundation, 2291 W. Broadway, Missoula MT 59808. (406)523-4570. Fax: (406)543-7710. E-mail: bugle@rmef.org. Website: www.elkfoundation.org. Editor: Dan Crockett. **Contact:** Lee Cromrich, assistant editor. **50% freelance written.** Bimonthly magazine covering elk conservation and elk hunting. "*Bugle* is the membership publication of the Rocky Mountain Elk Foundation, a nonprofit wildlife conservation group. Our readers are predominantly hunters, many of them conservationists who care deeply about protecting wildlife habitat. Hunting stories and essays should celebrate the hunting experience, demonstrating respect for wildlife, the land, and the hunt. Articles on elk behavior or elk habitat should include personal observations and entertain as well as educate." Estab. 1984. Circ. 132,000. **Pays on acceptance.** Publishes ms an average of 9 months after acceptance. Byline given. Offers variable kill fee. Buys one-time rights. Editorial lead time 6 months. Submit seasonal material 6 months in advance. Accepts queries by mail, e-mail, fax, phone. Accepts previously published material. Responds in 1 month to queries; 3 months to mss. Sample copy for $5. Writer's guidelines online.

> Preparation: "Read as many issues of *Bugle* as possible to know what the Elk Foundation and magazine are about. Then write a strong query with those things in mind. Send it with clips of other published or unpublished pieces representative of story being proposed."

Nonfiction: Book excerpts, essays, general interest (elk related), historical/nostalgic, humor, interview/profile, opinion, personal experience, photo feature. No how-to, where-to. **Buys 20 mss/year.** Query with or without published clips or send complete ms. Length: 1,500-4,500 words. **Pays 20¢/word, and 3 contributor copies; more issues at cost.**

Reprints: Send ms with rights for sale noted and information about when and where the material previously appeared. Pays 75% of amount paid for original article.

Columns/Departments: Situation Ethics, 1,000-2,000 words; Thoughts & Theories, 1,500-4,000 words; Women in the Outdoors, 1,000-2,500 words. **Buys 13 mss/year.** Query with or without published clips or send complete ms. **Pays 20¢/word.**

Fiction: Adventure, historical, humorous, novel excerpts, slice-of-life vignettes, western, human interest, natural history, conservation. No fiction that doesn't pertain to elk or elk hunting. No formula outdoor or how-to writing. No stories of disrespect to wildlife. **Buys 4 mss/year.** Query with or without published clips or send complete ms. Length: 1,500-4,500 words. **Pays 20¢/word.**

Poetry: Free verse. **Buys 6 poems/year.** Submit maximum 6 poems.

Tips: "Creative queries (250-500 words) that showcase your concept and your style remain the most effective approach. We're hungry for submissions for 3 specific columns: Situation Ethics, Thoughts & Theories, and Women in the Outdoors. Send a SASE for guidelines. We also welcome strong, well-reasoned opinion pieces on topics pertinent to hunting and wildlife conservation, and humorous pieces about elk behavior or encounters with elk (hunting or otherwise). We'd also like to see more humor; more natural history pertaining to elk and elk country; more good, thoughtful writing from women."

$ $ CALIFORNIA GAME & FISH, Game & Fish, Box 741, Marietta GA 30061. **Contact:** Burt Carey, editor. See *Game & Fish*.

$ $ DEER & DEER HUNTING, Krause Publications, 700 E. State St., Iola WI 54990-0001. (715)445-2214. Fax: (715)445-4087. Website: www.deeranddeerhunting.com. **Contact:** Dan Schmidt, editor. **95% freelance written.** Magazine published 9 times/year covering white-tailed deer and deer hunting. "Readers include a cross section of the deer hunting population—individuals who hunt with bow, gun, or camera. The editorial content of the magazine focuses on white-tailed deer biology and behavior, management principle and practices, habitat requirements, natural history of deer, hunting techniques, and hunting ethics. We also publish a wide range of 'how-to' articles designed to help hunters locate and get close to deer at all times of the year. The majority of our readership consists of 2-season hunters (bow and gun) and approximately one-third camera hunt." Estab. 1977. Circ. 140,000. **Pays on acceptance.** Byline given. Editorial lead time 6 months. Submit seasonal material 6 months in advance. Accepts queries by mail. Responds in 3 months to queries. Sample copy for 9×12 SASE. Writer's guidelines free.

Nonfiction: General interest, historical/nostalgic, how-to, inspirational, photo feature. No "Joe and me" articles. **Buys**

30-50 mss/year. Query. Length: 750-3,000 words. **Pays $150-450 for assigned articles; $150-325 for unsolicited articles.** Sometimes pays expenses of writers on assignment.

Photos: Send photos with submission. Reviews transparencies. Negotiates payment individually. Captions, identification of subjects, model releases required.

Fiction: "Mood" deer hunting pieces. **Buys 9 mss/year.** Send complete ms.

Fillers: Facts, newsbreaks. **Buys 40-50/year.** Length: 100-500 words. **Pays $15-150.**

Tips: "Feature articles dealing with deer biology or behavior should be documented by scientific research (the author's or that of others) as opposed to a limited number of personal observations."

N $ $ **THE DRAKE MAGAZINE, For People Who Fish**, Paddlesport Publishing, P.O. Box 5450, Steamboat Springs CO 80477-5450. (970)879-1450. Fax: (970)870-1404. E-mail: bieline@aol.com. Website: www.drakemag.com. **Contact:** Tom Bie, managing editor. **70% freelance written.** Annual magazine for people who love fishing. Pays 30 days after publication. Publishes ms an average of 1 year after acceptance. Byline given. Buys first North American serial rights. Editorial lead time 1 year. Submit seasonal material 1 year in advance. Accepts queries by mail. Responds in 6 months to mss.

To break in "Tippets is the best bet: Short, 200-600 word essays on any aspect of the fishing world. Rodholders is another good area (profiles of people who fish)."

Nonfiction: Book excerpts, essays, general interest, historical/nostalgic, humor, interview/profile, opinion, personal experience, photo feature, travel (fishing related). **Buys 8 mss/year.** Query. Length: 250-3,000 words. **Pays 10-20¢/word "depending on the amount of work we have to put into the piece."**

Photos: State availability with submission. Reviews contact sheets, negatives, transparencies. Buys one-time rights. Offers $25-250/photo.

The online magazine carries original content not found in the print version. Contact: Tom Bie, online editor.

$ $ $ **FIELD & STREAM**, 2 Park Ave., Time 4 Media, New York NY 10016-5695. (212)779-5000. Fax: (212)779-5114. E-mail: fsmagazine@aol.com. Website: fieldandstream.com. Editor: Sid Evans. **Contact:** David E. Petzal, deputy editor. **50% freelance written.** Monthly magazine. "Broad-based service magazine for the hunter and fisherman. Editorial content consists of articles of penetrating depth about national hunting, fishing, and related activities. Also humor and personal essays, nostalgia, fiction, and 'mood pieces' on the hunting or fishing experience and profiles on outdoor people." Estab. 1895. Circ. 1,500,000. **Pays on acceptance.** Byline given. Buys first rights. Accepts queries by mail, e-mail. Responds in 2 weeks to queries. Sample copy not available. Writer's guidelines for #10 SASE.

Nonfiction: Length: 1,500 words for features. Payment varies depending on the quality of work, importance of the article. **Pays $800 and up to $1,000 and more on a sliding scale for major features. Query by mail or e-mail (fsmagazine@aol.com).**

Photos: Send photos with submission. Reviews slides (prefers color). Buys first rights. When purchased separately, pays $450 minimum for color.

Online version of magazine carries original content not contained in the print edition. Contact: Elizabeth Burnham.

Tips: "Writers are encouraged to submit queries on article ideas. These should be no more than a paragraph or 2, and should include a summary of the idea, including the angle you will hang the story on, and a sense of what makes this piece different from all others on the same or a similar subject. Many queries are turned down because we have no idea what the writer is getting at. Be sure that your letter is absolutely clear. We've found that if you can't sum up the point of the article in a sentence or 2, the article doesn't have a point. Pieces that depend on writing style, such as humor, mood, and nostalgia or essays often can't be queried and may be submitted in manuscript form. The same is true of short tips. All submissions to *Field & Stream* are on an on-spec basis. Before submitting anything, however, we encourage you to *study*, not simply read, the magazine. Many pieces are rejected because they do not fit the tone or style of the magazine, or fail to match the subject of the article with the overall subject matter of *Field & Stream*. Above all, study the magazine before submitting anything."

$ **THE FISHERMAN**, LIF Publishing Corp., 14 Ramsey Rd., Shirley NY 11967-4704. (631)345-5200. Fax: (631)345-5304. E-mail: melfish@aol.com. Publisher: Fred Golofaro. Associate Publisher: Pete Barrett. **Contact:** Tom Melton, managing editor. **75% freelance written.** Weekly magazine covering fishing with an emphasis on saltwater. Circ. 110,000. Pays on publication. Byline given. Offers variable kill fee. Submit seasonal material 2 months in advance. Accepts queries by mail, e-mail. Responds in 6 weeks to queries. Sample copy and writer's guidelines free.

Nonfiction: General interest, historical/nostalgic, how-to, interview/profile, personal experience, photo feature, technical, travel. Special issues: Boat & Motor Buyer's Guide and Winter Workbench (January); Inshore Fishing (April); Saltwater Fly, Party Boat, Black Bass (May); Offshore Fishing (June); Surf Fishing (August); Striped Bass (October). "No 'Me and Joe' tales. We stress how, when, where and why." **Buys 300 mss/year.** Length: 1,000-1,500 words. **Pays $110-150.**

Photos: Send photos with submission. Offers no additional payment for photos accepted with ms, but offers $50-100 for single color cover photos. Identification of subjects required.

Tips: "Focus on specific how-to and where-to subjects within each region."

$ **FISHING & HUNTING NEWS**, Outdoor Empire Publishing, 424 N. 130th St., Seattle WA 98133. (206)624-3845. Fax: (206)695-8512. E-mail: staff@fishingandhuntingnews.com. Website: www.fhnews.com/. **Contact:** John Marsh, managing editor. **95% freelance written.** Bimonthly magazine covering fishing and hunting. "We focus on upcoming fishing and hunting opportunities in your area—where to go and what to do once you get there." Estab. 1954. Circ. 85,000. Pays on publication. Publishes ms an average of 1 month after acceptance. Byline given. Buys first North American serial, second serial (reprint), electronic rights. Editorial lead time 1 month. Submit seasonal material 2 months in advance. Accepts queries by mail, e-mail. Sample copy and writer's guidelines free.

Nonfiction: How-to (local fishing and hunting), where-to. **Buys 5,000 mss/year.** Query with published clips. Length: 350-2,000 words. **Pays $25-125 and up.** Seldom pays expenses of writers on assignment.

Photos: State availability with submission. Buys all rights. Captions required.

Tips: "*F&H News* is published in 7 local editions across the western U.S., Great Lakes, and mid-Atlantic states. We look for reports of current fishing and hunting opportunity, plus technique- or strategy-related articles that can be used by anglers and hunters in these areas."

$ $ FLORIDA GAME & FISH, Game & Fish, Box 741, Marietta GA 30061. (770)953-9222. **Contact:** Jimmy Jacobs, editor. See *Game & Fish*.

$ $ FLORIDA SPORTSMAN, Wickstrom Communications Division of PRIMEDIA Special Interest Publications, 2700 S. Kanner Hwy., Stuart FL 34994. (772)219-7400. Fax: (772)219-6900. E-mail: editor@floridasportsman.com. Website: www.floridasportsman.com. **Contact:** Jeff Weakley, editor. **30% freelance written.** Monthly magazine covering fishing, boating, and related sports—Florida and Caribbean only. "*Florida Sportsman* is edited for the boatowner and offshore, coastal, and fresh water fisherman. It provides a how, when, and where approach in its articles, which also includes occasional camping, diving, and hunting stories—plus ecology; in-depth articles and editorials attempting to protect Florida's wilderness, wetlands, and natural beauty." Circ. 115,000. **Pays on acceptance.** Publishes ms an average of 6 months after acceptance. Byline given. Buys nonexclusive additional rights. Submit seasonal material 6 months in advance. Accepts queries by mail. Responds in 2 months to queries; 1 month to mss. Sample copy for free. Writer's guidelines for #10 SASE.

Nonfiction: "We use reader service pieces almost entirely—how-to, where-to, etc. One or 2 environmental pieces/issue as well. Writers must be Florida based, or have lengthy experience in Florida outdoors. All articles must have strong Florida emphasis. We do not want to see general how-to-fish-or-boat pieces which might well appear in a national or wide-regional magazine." Essays (environment or nature), how-to (fishing, hunting, boating), humor (outdoors angle), personal experience (in fishing, etc.), technical (boats, tackle, etc., as particularly suitable for Florida specialities). **Buys 40-60 mss/year.** Query. Length: 1,500-2,500 words. **Pays $475.**

Photos: Send photos with submission. Reviews 35mm transparencies, 4×5 and larger prints. Buys all rights. Offers no additional payment for photos accepted with ms. Pays up to $750 for cover photos.

Tips: "Feature articles are most open to freelancers; however there is little chance of acceptance unless contributor is an accomplished and avid outdoorsman *and* a competent writer-photographer with considerable experience in Florida."

N $ FLY FISHERMAN MAGAZINE, PRIMEDIA Enthusiast Group, 6405 Flank Drive, Harrisburg PA 17112-2750. (717)657-9555. Fax: (717)657-9552. Website: www.flyshop.com. Editor: John Randolph. Published 6 times/year covering fly fishing. Written for anglers who fish primarily with a fly rod and for other anglers who would like to learn more about fly fishing. Circ. 122,560. Sample copy not available.

$ $ FLYFISHING & TYING JOURNAL, A Compendium for the Complete Fly Fisher, Frank Amato Publications, P.O. Box 82112, Portland OR 97282. (503)653-8108. Fax: (503)653-2766. E-mail: kim@amatobooks.com. Website: www.amatobooks.com. **Contact:** Kim Koch, editor. **100% freelance written.** Quarterly magazine covering flyfishing and fly tying for both new and veteran anglers. Every issue is seasonally focused: Spring, summer, fall and winter. Estab. 1980. Circ. 60,000. Pays on publication. Byline given. Buys first rights. Editorial lead time up to 1 year. Submit seasonal material up to 1 year in advance. Accepts queries by mail, e-mail. Responds in 2 months to queries; 2 months to mss. Writer's guidelines for #10 SASE. Attn: Kim Koch.

Nonfiction: How-to. **Buys 55-60 mss/year.** Query. Length: 1,000-2,000 words. **Pays $200-600.**

Photos: State availability with submission. Reviews transparencies. Buys one-time rights. Offers no additional payment for photos accepted with ms. Captions, identification of subjects, model releases required.

$ FUR-FISH-GAME, 2878 E. Main, Columbus OH 43209-9947. **Contact:** Mitch Cox, editor. **65% freelance written.** Monthly magazine for outdoorsmen of all ages who are interested in hunting, fishing, trapping, dogs, camping, conservation, and related topics. Estab. 1900. Circ. 111,000. **Pays on acceptance.** Publishes ms an average of 7 months after acceptance. Byline given. Buys first, all rights. Responds in 2 months to queries. Sample copy for $1 and 9×12 SAE. Writer's guidelines for #10 SASE.

Nonfiction: "We are looking for informative, down-to-earth stories about hunting, fishing, trapping, dogs, camping, boating, conservation, and related subjects. Nostalgic articles are also used. Many of our stories are 'how-to' and should appeal to small-town and rural readers who are true outdoorsmen. Some recents articles have told how to train a gun dog, catch big-water catfish, outfit a bowhunter, and trap late-season muskrat. We also use personal experience stories and an occasional profile, such as an article about an old-time trapper. 'Where-to' stories are used occasionally if they have broad appeal." Query. Length: 500-3,000 words. **Pays $50-150 or more for features depending upon quality, photo support, and importance to magazine.**

Photos: Send photos with submission. Reviews transparencies, color prints (5×7 or 8×10). Pays $25 for separate freelance photos. Captions, credits required.

Tips: "We are always looking for quality how-to articles about fish, game animals, or birds that are popular with everyday outdoorsmen but often overlooked in other publications, such as catfish, bluegill, crappie, squirrel, rabbit, crows, etc. We also use articles on standard seasonal subjects such as deer and pheasant, but like to see a fresh approach or new technique. Instructional trapping articles are useful all year. Articles on gun dogs, ginseng, and do-it-yourself projects are also popular with our readers. An assortment of photos and/or sketches greatly enhances any manuscript, and sidebars, where applicable, can also help. No phone queries, please."

$ $ GAME & FISH, 2250 Newmarket Pkwy., Suite 110, Marietta GA 30067. (770)953-9222. Fax: (770)933-9510. Website: gameandfish.about.com. **Contact:** Ken Dunwoody, editorial director. **90% freelance written.** Publishes 30 different monthly outdoor magazines, each one covering the fishing and hunting opportunities in a particular state or region (see individual titles and editors). Estab. 1975. Circ. 575,000. Pays 3 months prior to cover date of issue. Publishes ms an average of 7 months after acceptance. Byline given. Offers negotiable kill fee. Buys first North American serial rights. Submit seasonal material 8 months in advance. Accepts queries by mail, fax. Responds in 3 months to queries. Sample copy for $3.50 and 9×12 SASE. Writer's guidelines for #10 SASE.

Nonfiction: Prefers queries over unsolicited mss. Length: 1,500-2,400 words. **Pays $125-300; additional payment made for electronic rights.**

Photos: Reviews transparencies, b&w prints. Buys one-time rights. Cover photos $250, inside color $75, and b&w $25. Captions, identification of subjects required.

Fiction: Humorous, nostalgia pertaining to hunting and fishing. Length: 1,100-2,500 words. **Pays $125-250; additional payment made for electronic rights.**

Online magazine occasionally carries original content not found in the print edition. Contact: Dave Schaefer.

Tips: "Our readers are experienced anglers and hunters, and we try to provide them with useful, specific articles about where, when, and how to enjoy the best hunting and fishing in their state or region. We also cover topics concerning game and fish management. Most articles should be tightly focused and aimed at outdoorsmen in 1 particular state. After familiarizing themselves with our magazine(s), writers should query the appropriate state editor (see individual listings) or send to Ken Dunwoody."

$ $ GEORGIA SPORTSMAN, Game & Fish, Box 741, Marietta GA 30061. (770)953-9222. **Contact:** Jimmy Jacobs, editor. See *Game & Fish*.

$ $ GREAT PLAINS GAME & FISH, Game & Fish, Box 741, Marietta GA 30061. (770)953-9222. **Contact:** Nick Gilmore, editor. See *Game & Fish*.

$ $ ILLINOIS GAME & FISH, Game & Fish, Box 741, Marietta GA 30061. (770)953-9222. **Contact:** Dennis Schmidt, editor. See *Game & Fish*.

N **$ IN-FISHERMAN**, PRIMEDIA Enthusiast Group, 2 In Fisherman Drive, Brainerd MN 56425-8098. (218)829-1648. Fax: (218)829-2371. Website: www.in-fisherman.com. Editor: Doug Stange. Magazine published 8 times/year. Written for freshwaters anglers from beginners to professionals. Circ. 301,258. Editorial lead time 2 months. Sample copy not available.

$ $ INDIANA GAME & FISH, Game & Fish, Box 741, Marietta GA 30061. (770)953-9222. **Contact:** Ken Freel, editor. See *Game & Fish*.

$ $ IOWA GAME & FISH, Game & Fish, Box 741, Marietta GA 30061. (770)953-9222. **Contact:** Ken Duke, editor. See *Game & Fish*.

$ $ KENTUCKY GAME & FISH, Game & Fish, Box 741, Marietta GA 30061. (770)953-9222. **Contact:** Ken Freel, editor. See *Game & Fish*.

$ $ LOUISIANA GAME & FISH, Game & Fish, Box 741, Marietta GA 30061. (770)953-9222. Fax: (770)933-9510. E-mail: ken_duke@primediamags.com. Website: LAgameandfish.com. **Contact:** Ken Duke, editor. See listing for *Game & Fish*. Accepts queries by e-mail.

$ $ MARLIN, The International Sportfishing Magazine, World Publications, Inc., P.O. Box 8500, Winter Park FL 32790. (407)628-4802. Fax: (407)628-7061. E-mail: editor@marlinmag.com. Website: www.marlinmag.com. **Contact:** Dave Ferrell, editor. **90% freelance written.** Bimonthly magazine. "*Marlin* covers the sport of big game fishing (billfish, tuna, dorado and wahoo). Our readers are sophisticated, affluent, and serious about their sport—they expect a high-class, well-written magazine that provides information and practical advice." Estab. 1982. Circ. 50,000. **Pays on acceptance.** Publishes ms an average of 3 months after acceptance. Byline given. Buys first North American serial rights. Submit seasonal material 3 months in advance. Accepts previously published material. Sample copy free with SASE. Writer's guidelines online.

Nonfiction: General interest, how-to (bait-rigging, tackle maintenance, etc.), new product, personal experience, photo feature, technical, travel. "No freshwater fishing stories. No 'Me & Joe went fishing' stories." **Buys 30-50 mss/year.** Query with published clips. Length: 800-3,000 words. **Pays $250-500.**

Reprints: Send photocopy and information about when and where the material previously appeared. Pays 50-75% of amount paid for original article.

Photos: State availability with submission. Reviews original slides. Buys one-time rights. Offers $50-300 for inside use, $1,000 for a cover.

Columns/Departments: Tournament Reports (reports on winners of major big game fishing tournaments), 200-400 words; Blue Water Currents (news features), 100-400 words. **Buys 25 mss/year.** Query. **Pays $75-250.**

Tips: "Tournament reports are a good way to break in to *Marlin*. Make them short but accurate, and provide photos of fishing action or winners' award shots (*not* dead fish hanging up at the docks). We always need how-tos and news items. Our destination pieces (travel stories) emphasize where and when to fish, but include information on where to stay also. For features: Crisp, high action stories with emphasis on exotic nature, adventure, personality, etc.—nothing flowery or academic. Technical/how-to: concise and informational—specific details. News: Again, concise with good details—watch for legislation affecting big game fishing, outstanding catches, new clubs and organizations, new trends, and conservation issues."

$ MICHIGAN OUT-OF-DOORS, P.O. Box 30235, Lansing MI 48909. (517)371-1041. Fax: (517)371-1505. E-mail: dknick@mucc.org. Website: www.mucc.org. **Contact:** Dennis C. Knickerbocker, editor. **75% freelance written.** Monthly magazine emphasizing Michigan outdoor recreation, especially hunting and fishing, conservation, nature, and environmental affairs. Estab. 1947. Circ. 90,000. **Pays on acceptance.** Publishes ms an average of 6 months after acceptance. Byline given. Buys first North American serial rights. Submit seasonal material 6 months in advance. Accepts queries by mail, phone. Responds in 1 month to queries. Sample copy for $3.50. Writer's guidelines for free or on website.

O→ Break in by "writing interestingly about an *unusual* aspect of Michigan natural resources and/or outdoor recreation.

Nonfiction: "Stories must have a Michigan slant unless they treat a subject of universal interest to our readers." Exposé, historical/nostalgic, how-to, interview/profile, opinion, personal experience, photo feature. Special issues: Archery Deer and Small Game Hunting (October); Firearm Deer Hunting (November); Cross-country Skiing and Early-ice Lake Fishing (December or January); Camping/Hiking (May); Family Fishing (June). No humor or poetry. **Buys 96 mss/year.** Send complete ms. Length: 1,000-2,000 words. **Pays $90 minimum for feature stories.**

Photos: Buys one-time rights. Offers no additional payment for photos accepted with ms; others $20-175. Captions required.

Tips: "Top priority is placed on true accounts of personal adventures in the out-of-doors—well-written tales of very unusual incidents encountered while hunting, fishing, camping, hiking, etc."

$ $ MICHIGAN SPORTSMAN, Game & Fish, Box 741, Marietta GA 30061. (770)953-9222. **Contact:** Dennis Schmidt, editor. See *Game & Fish.*

$ $ MID-ATLANTIC GAME & FISH, Game & Fish, Box 741, Marietta GA 30061. (770)953-9222. **Contact:** Ken Freel, editor. See *Game & Fish.*

$ MIDWEST OUTDOORS, MidWest Outdoors, Ltd., 111 Shore Dr., Burr Ridge IL 60527-5885. (630)887-7722. Fax: (630)887-1958. E-mail: glaulunen@midwestoutdoors.com. Website: www.MidWestOutdoors.com. **Contact:** Gene Laulunen, editor. **100% freelance written.** Monthly tabloid emphasizing fishing, hunting, camping, and boating. Estab. 1967. Circ. 45,000. Pays on publication. Publishes ms an average of 3 months after acceptance. Byline given. Buys simultaneous rights. Submit seasonal material 2 months in advance. Accepts previously published material. Accepts simultaneous submissions. Responds in 3 weeks to queries. Sample copy for $1 or online. Writer's guidelines for #10 SASE or online.

- Submissions may be e-mailed to info@midwestoutdoors.com (Microsoft Word format preferred).

Nonfiction: How-to (fishing, hunting, camping in the Midwest), where-to-go (fishing, hunting, camping within 500 miles of Chicago). "We do not want to see any articles on 'my first fishing, hunting, or camping experiences,' 'cleaning my tackle box,' 'tackle tune-up,' 'making fishing fun for kids,' or 'catch and release.'" **Buys 1,800 unsolicited mss/year.** Send complete ms. Length: 1,000-1,500 words. **Pays $15-30.**

Reprints: Send tearsheet.

Photos: Reviews slides and b&w prints. Buys all rights. Offers no additional payment for photos accompanying ms. Captions required.

Columns/Departments: Fishing; Hunting. Send complete ms. **Pays $30.**

Tips: "Break in with a great unknown fishing hole or new technique within 500 miles of Chicago. Where, how, when, and why. Know the type of publication you are sending material to."

$ $ MINNESOTA SPORTSMAN, Game & Fish, Box 741, Marietta GA 30061. (770)953-9222. **Contact:** Dennis Schmidt, editor. See *Game & Fish.*

$ $ MISSISSIPPI GAME & FISH, Game & Fish, Box 741, Marietta GA 30061. (770)953-9222. **Contact:** Jimmy Jacobs, editor. See listing for *Game & Fish.*

Nonfiction: How-to (hunting and fishing).

$ $ MISSOURI GAME & FISH, Game & Fish, Box 741, Marietta GA 30061. (770)953-9222. Fax: (770)933-9510. E-mail: ken_duke@primediamags.com. Website: missourigameandfish.com. **Contact:** Ken Duke, editor. See listing for *Game & Fish.*

$ $ MUSKY HUNTER MAGAZINE, P.O. Box 340, St. Germain WI 54558. (715)477-2178. Fax: (715)477-8858. Editor: Jim Saric. **Contact:** Steve Heiting. **90% freelance written.** Bimonthly magazine on musky fishing. "Serves the vertical market of musky fishing enthusiasts. We're interested in how-to where-to articles." Estab. 1988. Circ. 34,000. Pays on publication. Publishes ms an average of 4 months after acceptance. Byline given. Buys first, one-time rights. Submit seasonal material 4 months in advance. Responds in 2 months to queries. Sample copy for 9×12 SAE with $1.93 postage. Writer's guidelines for #10 SASE.

Nonfiction: Historical/nostalgic (related only to musky fishing), how-to (modify lures, boats, and tackle for musky fishing), personal experience (must be musky fishing experience), technical (fishing equipment), travel (to lakes and areas for musky fishing). **Buys 50 mss/year.** Send complete ms. Length: 1,000-2,500 words. **Pays $100-300 for assigned articles; $50-300 for unsolicited articles.** Payment of contributor copies or other premiums negotiable.

Photos: Send photos with submission. Reviews 35mm transparencies, 3×5 prints. Buys one-time rights. Offers no additional payment for photos accepted with ms. Identification of subjects required.

$ $ NEW ENGLAND GAME & FISH, Game & Fish, Box 741, Marietta GA 30061. (770)953-9222. **Contact:** Steve Carpenteri, editor. See *Game & Fish.*

N $ $ NEW JERSEY LAKE SURVEY FISHING MAPS GUIDE, New Jersey Sportsmen's Guides, P.O. Box 100, Somerdale NJ 08083. (856)783-1271. Fax: (856)783-1271. **Contact:** Steve Perrone, editor. **40% freelance written.** Biannual magazine covering freshwater lake fishing. "*New Jersey Lake Survey Fishing Maps Guide* is edited for freshwater fishing for trout, bass, perch, catfish, and other species. It contains 140 pages and approximately 100 full-page maps of the surveyed lakes that illustrate contours, depths, bottom characteristics, shorelines, and vegetation present at each location. The guide includes a 10-page chart which describes over 250 fishing lakes in New Jersey. It also includes more than 125 fishing tips and 'Bass'n Notes.'" Estab. 1989. Circ. 3,500. **Pays on acceptance.** Publishes ms an average of 6 months after acceptance. Byline given. Buys first rights, makes work-for-hire assignments. Editorial lead time 6 months. Accepts queries by mail, fax. Sample copy for $14.50 postage paid.

Nonfiction: How-to fishing, freshwater fishing. Length: 500-2,000 words. **Pays $75-250.**

Photos: State availability with submission. Reviews transparencies, 4×5 slides, or 4×6 prints. Buys one-time rights. Captions, identification of subjects, model releases required.

Tips: "We want queries with published clips of articles describing fishing experiences on New Jersey lakes and ponds."

$ $ NEW YORK GAME & FISH, Game & Fish, Box 741, Marietta GA 30061. (770)953-9222. **Contact:** Steve Carpenteri, editor. See *Game & Fish*.

$ $ NORTH AMERICAN WHITETAIL, The Magazine Devoted to the Serious Trophy Deer Hunter, Game & Fish, 2250 Newmarket Pkwy., Suite 110, Marietta GA 30067. (770)953-9222. Fax: (770)933-9510. **Contact:** Gordon Whittington, editor. **70% freelance written.** Magazine published 8 times/year about hunting trophy-class white-tailed deer in North America, primarily the US. "We provide the serious hunter with highly sophisticated information about trophy-class whitetails and how, when, and where to hunt them. We are not a general hunting magazine or a magazine for the very occasional deer hunter." Estab. 1982. Circ. 130,000. Pays 65 days prior to cover date of issue. Publishes ms an average of 6 months after acceptance. Byline given. Offers negotiable kill fee. Buys first North American serial rights. Submit seasonal material 10 months in advance. Accepts queries by mail, fax, phone. Responds in 3 months to mss. Sample copy for $3.50 and 9×12 SAE with 7 first-class stamps. Writer's guidelines for #10 SASE.

Nonfiction: How-to, interview/profile. **Buys 50 mss/year.** Query. Length: 1,000-3,000 words. **Pays $150-400.**

Photos: Send photos with submission. Reviews 35mm transparencies, 8×10 prints. Buys one-time rights. Offers no additional payment for photos accepted with ms. Captions, identification of subjects required.

Columns/Departments: Trails and Tails (nostalgic, humorous, or other entertaining styles of deer-hunting material, fictional or nonfictional), 1,200 words. **Buys 8 mss/year.** Send complete ms. **Pays $150.**

Tips: "Our articles are written by persons who are deer hunters first, writers second. Our hard-core hunting audience can see through material produced by nonhunters or those with only marginal deer-hunting expertise. We have a continual need for expert profiles/interviews. Study the magazine to see what type of hunting expert it takes to qualify for our use, and look at how those articles have been directed by the writers. Good photography of the interviewee and his hunting results must accompany such pieces."

$ $ NORTH CAROLINA GAME & FISH, Game & Fish, Box 741, Marietta GA 30061. (770)953-9222. Fax: (770)933-9510. **Contact:** David Johnson, editor. See *Game & Fish*.

$ $ OHIO GAME & FISH, Game & Fish, Box 741, Marietta GA 30061. (770)953-9222. **Contact:** Steve Carpenteri, editor. See *Game & Fish*.

$ $ OKLAHOMA GAME & FISH, Game & Fish, Box 741, Marietta GA 30061. (770)953-9222. Fax: (770)933-9510. **Contact:** Nick Gilmore, editor. See *Game & Fish*.

$ $ $ $ OUTDOOR LIFE, The Sportsman's Authority Since 1898, Time 4 Media, Inc., 2 Park Ave., New York NY 10016. (212)779-5000. Fax: (212)779-5366. E-mail: olmagazine@aol.com. Website: www.outdoorlife.com. Editor-in-Chief: Todd W. Smith. Senior Managing Editor: Camille Cozzone Rankin. **Contact:** Colin Moore, executive editor. **60% freelance written.** Magazine published 9 times/year covering hunting and fishing in North America. "*Outdoor Life* is a major national source of information for American and Canadian hunters and anglers. It offers news, regional reports, adventure stories, how-to, regular advice from experts, profiles, and equipment tests." Estab. 1898. Circ. 900,000. **Pays on acceptance.** Publishes ms an average of 6 months after acceptance. Byline given. Buys all rights. Editorial lead time 4 months. Submit seasonal material 5 months in advance. Accepts queries by mail, e-mail, fax. Responds in 1 month to queries; 2 months to mss. Sample copy for 9×12 SAE plus proper postage. Writer's guidelines for #10 SASE.

Nonfiction: All articles must pertain to hunting and fishing pursuits. How-to, personal experience, interesting/wild news stories, adventure stories. Query with published clips. Length: 100-2,000 words. **Pays $500-3,000.**

Photos: Do not send photos until requested.

Columns/Departments: Frank Miniter, senior editor (gear); Colin Moore, executive editor (hunting/fishing, bonus sections); John Snow (Regionals; Snap Shots). Regionals, 150-300 words; Snap Shots, 150 words; Private Lessons, 500-700 words. **Buys 200 mss/year.** Query with published clips. **Pays $75-500.**

Fillers: John Snow, articles editor for Snap Shots section. Facts, newsbreaks. **Buys 40-50/year.** Length: 150 words. **Pays $50-350.**

Tips: "If someone catches a record fish or takes a record game animal, or has a great adventure/survival story, they may try to submit a full-length feature, but the story must be exceptional."

$ $ PENNSYLVANIA ANGLER & BOATER, Pennsylvania Fish and Boat Commission, P.O. Box 67000, Harrisburg PA 17106-7000. (717)705-7844. E-mail: amichaels@state.pa.us. Website: www.fish.state.pa.us. **Contact:** Art Michaels, editor. **80% freelance written.** Bimonthly magazine covering fishing, boating, and related conservation topics in Pennsylvania. Circ. 30,000. Pays 2 months after acceptance. Publishes ms an average of 8 months after acceptance. Byline given. Buys varying rights. Submit seasonal material 8 months in advance. Responds in 1 month to queries; 2 months to mss.

Sample copy for 9×12 SAE with 9 first-class stamps. Writer's guidelines for #10 SASE.

Nonfiction: How-to (and where-to), technical. No saltwater or hunting material. **Buys 100 mss/year.** Query. Length: 500-2,500 words. **Pays $25-300.**

Photos: Send photos with submission. Reviews 35mm and larger transparencies. Rights purchased vary. Offers no additional payment for photos accompanying mss. Captions, identification of subjects, model releases required.

$ $ PENNSYLVANIA GAME & FISH, Game & Fish, Box 741, Marietta GA 30061. (770)953-9222. **Contact:** Steve Carpenteri, editor. See *Game & Fish*.

$ $ RACK MAGAZINE, Adventures in Trophy Hunting, Buckmasters Ltd., P.O. Box 244022, Montgomery AL 36124-4022. (800)240-3337. Fax: (334)215-3535. E-mail: mhandley@buckmasters.com. Website: www.rackmag.com. **Contact:** Mike Handley, editor. **10-15% freelance written.** Hunting magazine published monthly (August-January). "*Rack Magazine* caters to deer hunters and chasers of other big game animals who prefer short stories detailing the harvests of exceptional specimens. There are no how-to, destination, or human interest stories; only pieces describing particular hunts." Estab. 1999. Circ. 125,000. Pays on publication. Publishes ms an average of 11 months after acceptance. Byline given. Buys first North American serial, second serial (reprint) rights. Editorial lead time 9 months. Accepts queries by e-mail, phone. Accepts previously published material. Accepts simultaneous submissions. Responds in 1 month to queries. Sample copy for free. Writer's guidelines by e-mail.

Nonfiction: Interview/profile, personal experience. *Rack Magazine* does not use how-to, destination, humor, general interest, or hunter profiles. **Buys 35-40 mss/year.** Query. Length: 500-1,500 words. **Pays $250.**

Reprints: Accepts previously published submissions.

Photos: Send photos with submission. Reviews transparencies. Captions, identification of subjects required.

Tips: "We're only interested in stories about record book animals (those scoring high enough to qualify for BTR, B&C, P&Y, SCI, or Longhunter). Whitetails must be scored by a certified BTR/Buckmasters measurer and their antlers must register at least 160-inches on the BTR system. Deer scoring 190 or better on the B&C or P&Y scales would be candidates, but the hunter would have to have his or her buck scored by a BTR measurer."

$ $ ROCKY MOUNTAIN GAME & FISH, Game & Fish, Box 741, Marietta GA 30061. Fax: (770)933-9510. **Contact:** Burt Carey, editor. See *Game & Fish*.

$ $ SALT WATER SPORTSMAN MAGAZINE, 263 Summer St., Boston MA 02210. (617)303-3660. Fax: (617)303-3661. E-mail: editor@saltwatersportsman.com. Website: www.saltwatersportsman.com. **Contact:** Barry Gibson, editor. **85% freelance written.** Monthly magazine. "*Salt Water Sportsman* is edited for serious marine sport fishermen whose lifestyle includes the pursuit of game fish in US waters and around the world. It provides information on fishing trends, techniques, and destinations, both local and international. Each issue reviews offshore and inshore fishing boats, high-tech electronics, innovative tackle, engines, and other new products. Coverage also focuses on sound fisheries management and conservation." Circ. 165,000. **Pays on acceptance.** Publishes ms an average of 5 months after acceptance. Byline given. Offers 100% kill fee. Buys first North American serial rights. Submit seasonal material 8 months in advance. Accepts queries by mail, e-mail, fax. Accepts previously published material. Responds in 1 month to queries. Sample copy for #10 SASE. Writer's guidelines online.

Nonfiction: "Readers want solid how-to, where-to information written in an enjoyable, easy-to-read style. Personal anecdotes help the reader identify with the writer." How-to, personal experience, technical, travel (to fishing areas). **Buys 100 mss/year.** Query. Length: 1,200-2,000 words. **Pays $300-750.**

Reprints: Send tearsheet. Pays up to 50% of amount paid for original article.

Photos: Reviews color slides. Pays $1,500 minimum for 35mm, 2¼×2¼ or 8×10 transparencies for cover. Offers additional payment for photos accepted with ms. Captions required.

Columns/Departments: Sportsman's Tips (short, how-to tips and techniques on salt water fishing, emphasis is on building, repairing, or reconditioning specific items or gear). Send complete ms.

Tips: "There are a lot of knowledgeable fishermen/budding writers out there who could be valuable to us with a little coaching. Many don't think they can write a story for us, but they'd be surprised. We work with writers. Shorter articles that get to the point which are accompanied by good, sharp photos are hard for us to turn down. Having to delete unnecessary wordage—conversation, clichés, etc.—that writers feel is mandatory is annoying. Often they don't devote enough attention to specific fishing information."

$ $ SHOTGUN SPORTS MAGAZINE, P.O. Box 6810, Auburn CA 95604. (530)889-2220. Fax: (530)889-9106. E-mail: shotgun@shotgunsportsmagazine.com. **Contact:** Linda Martin, production coordinator. **50% freelance written.** Welcomes new writers. Magazine published 11 times/year. "We cover all the shotgun sports and shotgun hunting—sporting clays, trap, skeet, hunting, gunsmithing, shotshell patterning, shotsell reloading, mental training for the shotgun sports, shotgun tests, anything 'shotgun.'" Pays on publication. Publishes ms an average of 1-6 months after acceptance. Buys all rights. Sample copy and writer's guidelines available by contacting Linda Martin, production coordinator.

- Responds within 3 weeks. Subscription: $31 (US); $38 (Canada); $66 (foreign).

Nonfiction: Current needs: "Anything with a 'shotgun' subject. Tests, think pieces, roundups, historical, interviews, etc. No articles promoting a specific club or sponsored hunting trip, etc." Submit complete ms with photos by mail with SASE. Can submit by e-mail. Length: 1,000-5,000 words. **Pays $50-200.**

Photos: "5×7 or 8×10 b&w or 4-color with appropriate captions. On disk or e-mailed at least 5-inches and 300 dpi (contact Graphics Artist for details)." Reviews transparencies (35 mm or larger), b&w, or 4-color. Send photos with submission.

Tips: "Do not fax manuscript. Send good photos. Take a fresh approach. Create a professional, yet friendly article. Send diagrams, maps, and photos of unique details, if needed. For interviews, more interested in 'words of wisdom' than a list of accomplishments. Reloading articles must include source information and backup data. Check your facts and data! If you can't think of a fresh approach, don't bother. If it's not about shotguns or shotgunners, don't send it. Never say, 'You don't need to check my data; I never make mistakes.'"

$ $ SOUTH CAROLINA GAME & FISH, Game & Fish, Box 741, Marietta GA 30061. (770)953-9222. **Contact:** David Johnson, editor. See *Game & Fish*.

$ $ SOUTH CAROLINA WILDLIFE, P.O. Box 167, Rembert Dennis Bldg., Columbia SC 29202-0167. (803)734-3972. E-mail: scwmed@scdnr.state.sc.us. Editor: Linda Renshaw. **Contact:** Caroline Foster, managing editor. **75% freelance written.** Bimonthly magazine for South Carolinans interested in wildlife and outdoor activities. Estab. 1954. Circ. 50,000. **Pays on acceptance.** Publishes ms an average of 6 months after acceptance. Byline given. Buys first rights. Responds in 2 months to queries. Sample copy for free.

Nonfiction: "Realize that the topic must be of interest to South Carolinans and that we must be able to justify using it in a publication published by the state department of natural resources—so if it isn't directly about outdoor recreation, a certain plant or animal, it must be somehow related to the environment and conservation. Readers prefer a broad mix of outdoor related topics (articles that illustrate the beauty of South Carolina's outdoors and those that help the reader get more for his/her time, effort, and money spent in outdoor recreation). These 2 general areas are the ones we most need. Subjects vary a great deal in topic, area and style, but must all have a common ground in the outdoor resources and heritage of South Carolina. Review back issues and query with a 1-page outline citing sources, giving ideas for photographs, explaining justification, and giving an example of the first 2 paragraphs." Does not need any column material. Generally does not seek photographs. The publisher assumes no responsibility for unsolicited material. **Buys 25-30 mss/year.** Query. Length: 1,000-3,000 words. **Pays up to $500.**

Tips: "We need more writers in the outdoor field who take pride in the craft of writing and put a real effort toward originality and preciseness in their work. Query on a topic we haven't recently done. Frequent mistakes made by writers in completing an article are failure to check details and go in-depth on a subject."

$ $ SPORT FISHING, The Magazine of Saltwater Fishing, 460 N. Orlando Ave., Suite 200, Winter Park FL 32789-7061. (407)571-4576. Fax: (407)571-4577. E-mail: doug.olander@worldpub.net. **Contact:** Doug Olander, editor-in-chief. **50% freelance written.** Magazine covering saltwater sports fishing. Estab. 1986. Circ. 150,000. Pays within 6 weeks of acceptance. Byline given. Offers $100 kill fee. Buys first North American serial, one-time rights. Submit seasonal material 5 months in advance. Accepts queries by mail, e-mail, fax. Responds in 2 weeks to queries. Sample copy for #10 SASE. Writer's guidelines for #10 SASE or by e-mail.

O→ Break in with freelance pieces for the "Tips & Techniques News" and "Fish Tales" departments.

Nonfiction: How-to (rigging & techniques tips), technical, conservation, where-to (all on sport fishing). **Buys 32-40 mss/year.** Query. Length: 2,000-3,000 words. **Pays $500-600.**

Photos: Send photos with submission. Reviews transparencies and returns within 1 week. Buys one-time rights. Pays $75-300 inside; $1,000 cover.

Columns/Departments: Fish Tales (humorous sport fishing anecdotes); Rigging (how-to rigging for sport fishing); Technique (how-to technique for sport fishing), 800-1,200 words. **Buys 8-24 mss/year.** Send complete ms. **Pays $250.**

Tips: "Don't query unless you are familiar with the magazine; note—*saltwater only.* Find a fresh idea or angle to an old idea. We welcome the chance to work with new/unestablished writers who know their stuff—and how to say it."

$ $ TENNESSEE SPORTSMAN, Game & Fish, Box 741, Marietta GA 30061. (770)953-9222. **Contact:** David Johnson, editor. See *Game & Fish*.

$ $ TEXAS SPORTSMAN, Game & Fish, Box 741, Marietta GA 30061. (770)953-9222. **Contact:** Nick Gilmore, editor. See *Game & Fish*.

$ $ TIDE MAGAZINE, Coastal Conservation Association, 6919 Portwest Dr., Suite 100, Houston TX 77024. (713)626-4222. Fax: (713)626-5852. E-mail: tide@joincca.org. **Contact:** Doug Pike, editor. Bimonthly magazine on saltwater fishing and conservation of marine resources. Estab. 1977. Circ. 60,000. Pays on publication. Byline given. Buys one-time rights. Submit seasonal material 6 months in advance. Responds in 1 month to queries.

Nonfiction: Essays, exposé, general interest, historical/nostalgic, humor, opinion, personal experience, travel, Related to saltwater fishing and Gulf/Atlantic coastal habitats. **Buys 40 mss/year.** Query with published clips. Length: 1,200-1,500 words. **Pays $300-400 for ms/photo package.**

Photos: Reviews negatives, 35mm transparencies, color prints. Buys one-time rights. Pays $50-200. Captions required.

$ $ TURKEY CALL, Wild Turkey Center, P.O. Box 530, Edgefield SC 29824-0530. (803)637-3106. Fax: (803)637-0034. E-mail: bmccreery@nwtf.net or dhowlett@nwtf.net. Editor: Doug Howlett. **Contact:** Beth McCreery, publishing assistant; Jason Gilbertson, managing editor. **50-60% freelance written.** Eager to work with new/unpublished writers and photographers. Bimonthly educational magazine for members of the National Wild Turkey Federation. Estab. 1973. Circ. 150,000. Pays on acceptance for assigned articles, on publication for unsolicited articles. Publishes ms an average of 6 months after acceptance. Byline given. Buys one-time rights. Accepts queries by mail, e-mail. Accepts previously published material. Responds in 6 weeks to queries. Sample copy for $3 and 9×12 SAE. Writer's guidelines for #10 SASE or online.

- Queries required. Submit complete package if article is assigned. Wants original mss only.

O→ Break in with a knowledgeable, fresh point of view. Articles must be tightly written.

Nonfiction: Feature articles dealing with the hunting and management of the American wild turkey. Must be accurate information and must appeal to national readership of turkey hunters and wildlife management experts. May use some fiction that educates or entertains in a special way. Length: Up to 2,500 words. **Pays $100 for short fillers of 600-700 words, $200-500 for features.**

Reprints: Send photocopy and information about when and where the material previously appeared. Pays 50% of amount paid for the original article.

Photos: "We want quality photos submitted with features." Art illustrations also acceptable. "We are using more and more inside color illustrations." No typical hunter-holding-dead-turkey photos or setups using mounted birds or domestic turkeys. Photos with how-to stories must make the techniques clear (example: how to make a turkey call; how to sculpt or carve a bird in wood). Reviews transparencies. Buys one-time rights. Pays $35 minimum for b&w photos and simple art illustrations; up to $175 for inside color, reproduced any size; $200-400 for covers.

Tips: "The writer should simply keep in mind that the audience is 'expert' on wild turkey management, hunting, life history, and restoration/conservation history. He/she must know the subject. We are buying more third person, more fiction, more humor—in an attempt to avoid the 'predictability trap' of a single subject magazine."

$ $ VIRGINIA GAME & FISH, Game & Fish, Box 741, Marietta GA 30061. (770)953-9222. **Contact:** David Johnson, editor. See *Game & Fish*.

$ $ WASHINGTON-OREGON GAME & FISH, Game & Fish, Box 741, Marietta GA 30061. **Contact:** Burt Carey, editor. See *Game & Fish*.

$ $ WEST VIRGINIA GAME & FISH, Game & Fish, Box 741, Marietta GA 30061. (770)953-9222. **Contact:** Ken Freel, editor. See *Game & Fish*.

N $ $ WESTERN OUTDOORS, 185 Avenida La Pata, San Clemente CA 92673. (949)366-0030. Fax: (949)366-0804. E-mail: woutdoors@aol.com. **Contact:** Lew Carpenter, editor. **60% freelance written.** Magazine emphasizing fishing, boating for California, Oregon, Washington, Baja California, and Alaska. "We are the West's leading authority on fishing techniques, tackle and destinations, and all reports present the latest and most reliable information." Estab. 1961. Circ. 100,000. **Pays on acceptance.** Publishes ms an average of 6 months after acceptance. Buys first North American serial rights. Submit seasonal material 6 months in advance. Accepts queries by mail, e-mail, fax. Responds in 6 weeks to queries. Sample copy for free. Writer's guidelines for #10 SASE.

Nonfiction: Where-to (catch more fish, improve equipment, etc.), how-to informational, photo feature. "We do not accept poetry or fiction." **Buys 36-40 assigned mss/year.** Query. Length: 1,500-2,000 words. **Pays $450-600.**

Photos: Reviews 35mm slides. Offers no additional payment for photos accepted with ms; pays $350-500 for covers. Captions required.

Tips: "Provide a complete package of photos, map, trip facts and manuscript written according to our news feature format. Excellence of color photo selections make a sale more likely. Include sketches of fishing patterns and techniques to guide our illustrators. Graphics are important. The most frequent mistake made by writers in completing an article for us is that they don't follow our style. Our guidelines are quite clear. One query at a time via mail, e-mail, fax. No phone calls. You can become a regular *Western Outdoors* byliner by submitting professional quality packages of fine writing accompanied by excellent photography. Pros anticipate what is needed, and immediately provide whatever else we request. Furthermore, they meet deadlines!"

$ $ WISCONSIN SPORTSMAN, Game & Fish, Box 741, Marietta GA 30061. (770)953-9222. **Contact:** Dennis Schmidt, editor. See *Game & Fish*.

Martial Arts

N $ $ BLACK BELT, Black Belt Communications, Inc., 24900 Anza Dr., Unit E, Valencia CA 91355. (661)257-4066. Fax: (661)257-3028. E-mail: byoung@sabot.net. Website: www.blackbeltmag.com. **Contact:** Robert Young, executive editor. **80% freelance written.** Works with a small number of new/unpublished writers each year. Monthly magazine emphasizing martial arts for both experienced practitioner and layman. Estab. 1961. Circ. 100,000. Pays on publication. Publishes ms an average of 1 year after acceptance. Buys all rights. Submit seasonal material 6 months in advance. Accepts queries by mail, e-mail, fax, phone. Accepts simultaneous submissions. Responds in 3 weeks to queries. Writer's guidelines online.

Nonfiction: Exposé, how-to, interview/profile, new product, personal experience, technical, travel, Informational; Health/fitness; Training. "We never use personality profiles." **Buys 40-50 mss/year.** Query with outline. Length: 1,200 words minimum. **Pays $100-300.**

Photos: Very seldom buys photographs without accompanying ms. Total purchase price for ms includes payment for photos. Captions, model releases required.

$ $ INSIDE KUNG-FU, The Ultimate In Martial Arts Coverage!, CFW Enterprises, 4201 Vanowen Place, Burbank CA 91505. (818)845-2656. Fax: (818)845-7761. E-mail: davecater@cfwenterprises.com. **Contact:** Dave Cater, editor. **90% freelance written.** Monthly magazine for those with "traditional, modern, athletic, and intellectual tastes. The magazine slants toward little-known martial arts and little-known aspects of established martial arts." Estab. 1973. Circ. 125,000. Pays on publication date on magazine cover. Publishes ms an average of 6 months after acceptance. Byline given. Buys first North American serial rights. Editorial lead time 6 months. Submit seasonal material 6 months in advance. Accepts simultaneous submissions. Responds in 1 month to queries; 2 months to mss. Sample copy for $5.95 and 9×12 SAE with 5 first class stamps. Writer's guidelines for #10 SASE.

Nonfiction: "Articles must be technically or historically accurate." *Inside Kung-Fu* is looking for external type articles (fighting, weapons, multiple hackers). Book excerpts, essays, exposé (topics relating to martial arts), general interest, historical/nostalgic, how-to (primarily technical materials), inspirational, interview/profile, new product, personal experience, photo feature, technical, travel, cultural/philosophical. No "sports coverage, first-person articles, or articles which constitute personal aggrandizement." **Buys 120 mss/year.** Query or send complete ms. Length: 1,500-3,000 words (8-10 pages, typewritten and double-spaced). **Pays $125-175.**

Reprints: Send tearsheet or typed ms with rights for sale noted and information about when and where the material previously appeared. No payment.

Photos: State availability of or send photos with submission. Reviews contact sheets, negatives, 5×7 or 8×10 color prints. Buys all rights. No additional payment for photos. Captions, identification of subjects, model releases required.

Fiction: "Fiction must be short (1,000-2,000 words) and relate to the martial arts. We buy very few fiction pieces." Adventure, historical, humorous, mystery, novel excerpts, suspense. **Buys 2-3 mss/year.**

Tips: "See what interests the writer. May have a better chance of breaking in at our publication with short articles and fillers since smaller pieces allow us to gauge individual ability, but we're flexible—quality writers get published, period. The most frequent mistakes made by writers in completing an article for us are ignoring photo requirements and model releases (always No. 1—and who knows why? All requirements are spelled out in writer's guidelines)."

$ $ JOURNAL OF ASIAN MARTIAL ARTS, Via Media Publishing Co., 821 W. 24th St., Erie PA 16502-2523. (814)455-9517. E-mail: info@goviamedia.com. Website: www.goviamedia.com. **Contact:** Michael A. DeMarco, editor. **90% freelance written.** Quarterly magazine covering "all historical and cultural aspects related to Asian martial arts, offering a mature, well-rounded view of this uniquely fascinating subject. Although the journal treats the subject with academic accuracy (references at end), writing need not lose the reader!" Estab. 1991. Pays on publication. Publishes ms an average of 1 year after acceptance. Byline given. Buys first, second serial (reprint) rights. Submit seasonal material 6 months in advance. Responds in 1 month to queries; 2 months to mss. Sample copy for $10. Writer's guidelines for #10 SASE.

Nonfiction: "All articles should be backed with solid, reliable reference material." Essays, exposé, historical/nostalgic, how-to (martial art techniques and materials, e.g., weapons), interview/profile, personal experience, photo feature (place or person), religious, technical, travel. "No articles overburdened with technical/foreign/scholarly vocabulary, or material slanted as indirect advertising or for personal aggrandizement." **Buys 30 mss/year.** Query with short background and martial arts experience. Length: 2,000-10,000 words. **Pays $150-500.**

Photos: State availability with submission. Reviews contact sheets, negatives, transparencies, prints. Buys one-time and reprint rights. Offers no additional payment for photos accepted with ms. Identification of subjects, model releases required.

Columns/Departments: Location (city, area, specific site, Asian or non-Asian, showing value for martial arts, researchers, history); Media Review (film, book, video, museum for aspects of academic and artistic interest).**Length:** 1,000-2,500 words. **Buys 16 mss/year.** Query. **Pays $50-200.**

Fiction: Adventure, historical, humorous, slice-of-life vignettes, translation. No material that does not focus on martial arts culture. **Buys 1 mss/year.** Query. Length: 1,000-10,000 words. **Pays $50-500, or copies.**

Poetry: Avant-garde, free verse, haiku, light verse, traditional, translation. "No poetry that does not focus on martial arts culture." **Buys 2 poems/year.** Submit maximum 10 poems. **Pays $10-100, or copies.**

Fillers: Anecdotes, facts, gags to be illustrated by cartoonist, newsbreaks, short humor. **Buys 2/year.** Length: 25-500 words. **Pays $1-50, or copies.**

Tips: "Always query before sending a manuscript. We are open to varied types of articles; most however require a strong academic grasp of Asian culture. For those not having this background, we suggest trying a museum review, or interview, where authorities can be questioned, quoted, and provide supportive illustrations. We especially desire articles/reports from Asia, with photo illustrations, particularly of a martial art style, so readers can visually understand the unique attributes of that style, its applications, evolution, etc. 'Location' and media reports are special areas that writers may consider, especially if they live in a location of martial art significance."

$ KUNGFU QIGONG, Wisdom for Body and Mind, Pacific Rim Publishing, 40748 Encyclopedia Circle, Fremont CA 94538. (510)656-5100. Fax: (510)656-8844. E-mail: editor@kungfumagazine.com. Website: www.kungfumagazine.com. **Contact:** Article Submissions. **70% freelance written.** Bimonthly magazine covering Chinese martial arts and culture. "*Kungfu Qigong* covers the full range of Kungfu culture, including healing, philosophy, meditation, yoga, Fengshui, Buddhism, Taoism, history, and the latest events in art and culture, plus insightful features on the martial arts." Circ. 50,000. Pays on publication. Byline given. Buys first North American serial, electronic rights. Editorial lead time 4 months. Submit seasonal material 4 months in advance. Accepts queries by mail, e-mail, fax, phone. Responds in 2 months to queries; 3 months to mss. Sample copy for $3.99 or online. Writer's guidelines online.

Nonfiction: Book excerpts, exposé, general interest, historical/nostalgic, how-to, interview/profile, personal experience, photo feature, religious, technical, travel, cultural perspectives. No poetry or fiction. **Buys 100 mss/year.** Query. Length: 500-2,500 words. **Pays $35-125.**

Photos: Send photos with submission. Reviews 5×7 prints, GIF/JPEG files. Buys one-time rights. Offers no additional payment for photos accepted with ms. Captions, identification of subjects required.

Tips: "Check out our website and get an idea of past articles."

$ $ T'AI CHI, Leading International Magazine of T'ai Chi Ch'uan, Wayfarer Publications, P.O. Box 39938, Los Angeles CA 90039. (323)665-7773. Fax: (323)665-1627. E-mail: taichi@tai-chi.com. Website: www.tai-chi.com/magazine.htm. **Contact:** Marvin Smalheiser, editor. **90% freelance written.** Bimonthly magazine covering T'ai Chi Ch'uan as a martial art and for health and fitness. "Covers T'ai Chi Ch'uan and other internal martial arts, plus qigong and Chinese health, nutrition, and philosophical disciplines. Readers are practitioners or laymen interested in developing skills and insight for self-defense, health, and self-improvement." Estab. 1977. Circ. 30,000. Pays on publication. Publishes ms an average of 3 months after acceptance. Byline given. Buys first North American serial rights. Editorial lead time 3 months. Submit seasonal material 6 months in advance. Accepts queries by mail, e-mail, fax. Responds in 3 weeks to queries; 3 months to mss. Sample copy for $3.95. Writer's guidelines online.

O→ Break in by "understanding the problems our readers have to deal with learning and practicing T'ai Chi, and developing an article that deals with 1 or more of those problems.

Nonfiction: Book excerpts, essays, how-to (on T'ai Chi Ch'uan, qigong, and related Chinese disciplines), interview/profile, personal experience. "Do not want articles promoting an individual, system, or school." **Buys 100-120 mss/year.** Query with or without published clips or send complete ms. Length: 1,200-4,500 words. **Pays $75-500.** Sometimes pays expenses of writers on assignment.

Photos: Send photos with submission. Reviews color transparencies, color or b&w 4×6 or 5×7 prints. Buys one-time and reprint rights. Offers no additional payment for photos accepted with ms, but overall payment takes into consideration the number and quality of photos. Captions, identification of subjects, model releases required.

Tips: "Think and write for practitioners and laymen who want information and insight, and who are trying to work through problems to improve skills and their health. No promotional material."

Miscellaneous

$ACTION PURSUIT GAMES, CFW Enterprises, Inc., 4201 Vanowen Place, Burbank CA 91505. (818)845-2656. Fax: (818)845-7761. E-mail: editor@actionpursuitgames.com. Website: www.actionpursuitgames.com. **Contact:** Daniel Reeves, editor. **60% freelance written.** Monthly magazine covering paintball. Estab. 1987. Circ. 85,000. Pays on publication. Publishes ms an average of 2 months after acceptance. Byline given. Buys electronic rights. print rights Editorial lead time 3 months. Submit seasonal material 6 months in advance. Accepts queries by e-mail. Sample copy for 9×12 SAE and 5 first-class stamps. Writer's guidelines online.

Nonfiction: Essays, exposé, general interest, historical/nostalgic, how-to, humor, interview/profile, new product, opinion, personal experience, technical, travel, all paintball-related. No sexually oriented material. **Buys 100+ mss/year.** Length: 500-1,000 words. **Pays 100.** Sometimes pays expenses of writers on assignment.

Photos: Send photos with submission. Reviews transparencies, prints. Buys all rights, web and print. Negotiates payment individually. Captions, identification of subjects, model releases required.

Columns/Departments: Guest Commentary, 400 words; TNT (tournament news), 500-800 words; Young Guns, 300 words; Scenario Game Reporting, 300-500 words. **Buys 24 mss/year. Pays $100.**

Fiction: Adventure, historical, must be paintball related. **Buys 1-2 mss/year.** Send complete ms. Length: 500 words. **Pays $100.**

Poetry: Avant-garde, free verse, haiku, light verse, traditional, must be paintball related. **Buys 1-2 poems/year.** Submit maximum 1 poems. Length: 20 lines.

Fillers: Anecdotes, gags to be illustrated by cartoonist. **Buys 2-4/year.** Length: 20-50 words. **Pays $25.**

Tips: "Good graphic support is critical. Read writer's guidelines at website; read website, www.actionpursuitgames.com, and magazine."

$ $AMERICAN CHEERLEADER, Lifestyle Ventures, LLC, 250 W. 57th St., Suite 420, New York NY 10107. (212)265-8890. Fax: (212)265-8908. E-mail: snoone@lifestyleventures.com. Website: www.americancheerleader.com. Managing Editor: Marisa Walker. Senior Editor: Jennifer Smith. **Contact:** Sheila Noone, editor-in-chief. **30% freelance written.** Bimonthly magazine covering high school and college cheerleading. "We try to keep a young, informative voice for all articles—'for cheerleaders, by cheerleaders.'" Estab. 1995. Circ. 200,000. Pays on publication. Publishes ms an average of 4 months after acceptance. Byline given. Offers 25% kill fee. Buys all rights. Editorial lead time 3 months. Submit seasonal material 4 months in advance. Accepts queries by mail, e-mail. Responds in 3 weeks to queries; 2 months to mss. Sample copy for $2.95. Writer's guidelines free.

Nonfiction: How-to (cheering techniques, routines, pep songs, etc.), interview/profile (celebrities and media personalities who cheered). Special issues: Tryouts (April); Camp Basics (June); College (October); Competition (December). No professional cheerleading stories, i.e., no Dallas Cowboy cheerleaders. **Buys 12-16 mss/year.** Query with published clips. Length: 400-1,500 words. **Pays $100-250 for assigned articles; $100 maximum for unsolicited articles.** Sometimes pays expenses of writers on assignment.

Photos: State availability with submission. Reviews transparencies, 5×7 prints. Rights purchased varies. Offers $50/photo. Model releases required.

Columns/Departments: Gameday Beauty (skin care, celeb how-tos), 600 words; Health & Fitness (teen athletes), 1,000 words; Profiles (winning squads), 1,000 words. **Buys 12 mss/year.** Query with published clips. **Pays $100-250.**

The online magazine carries original content not found in the print edition.

Tips: "We invite proposals from freelance writers who are involved in or have been involved in cheerleading—i.e., coaches, sponsors, or cheerleaders. Our writing style is upbeat and 'sporty' to catch and hold the attention of our teenaged readers. Articles should be broken down into lots of sidebars, bulleted lists, Q&As, etc."

N $ $ $ATV MAGAZINE/ATV SPORT, Ehlert Publishing, 6420 Sycamore Lane, Maple Grove MN 55369. Fax: (763)383-4499. E-mail: ghansen@affinitygroup.com. Website: www.atvnews.com. Managing Editor: Jerrod Kelley. **Contact:** Glenn Hausen, editor. **20% freelance written.** Bimonthly magazine covering all-terrain vehicles. "Devoted to covering all the things ATV owners enjoy, from hunting to racing, farming to trail riding." Pays on magazine shipment to printer.

Byline given. Buys all rights. Editorial lead time 6 months. Accepts queries by mail, e-mail, fax. Responds in 3 weeks to queries. Sample copy and writer's guidelines for #10 SASE.

Nonfiction: How-to, interview/profile, new product, personal experience, photo feature, technical, travel. **Buys 15-20 mss/year.** Query with published clips. Length: 200-2,000 words. **Pays $100-1,000.** Sometimes pays expenses of writers on assignment.

Photos: State availability with submission. Rights purchased vary. Negotiates payment individually. Captions, identification of subjects required.

Tips: "Writers must have experience with ATVs, and should own one or have regular access to at least one ATV."

$ CANADIAN RODEO NEWS, Canadian Rodeo News, Ltd., #223, 2116 27th Ave. NE, Calgary AB T2E 7A6, Canada. (403)250-7292. Fax: (403)250-6926. E-mail: crn@rodeocanada.com. Website: www.rodeocanada.com. **Contact:** Jennifer Jones, editor. **60% freelance written.** Monthly tabloid covering "Canada's professional rodeo (CPRA) personalities and livestock. Read by rodeo participants and fans." Estab. 1964. Circ. 4,000. Pays on publication. Publishes ms an average of 1 month after acceptance. Byline given. Buys first, second serial (reprint) rights. Editorial lead time 1 month. Submit seasonal material 1 month in advance. Accepts queries by mail, e-mail, fax. Accepts simultaneous submissions. Responds in 1 month to queries; 2 months to mss. Sample copy and writer's guidelines free with SASE.

Nonfiction: General interest, historical/nostalgic, interview/profile. **Buys 70-80 mss/year.** Query. Length: 500-1,200 words. **Pays $30-60.**

Reprints: Send photocopy of article or typed ms with rights for sale noted and information about when and where the material previously appeared. Pays 100% of amount paid for an original article.

Photos: Send photos with submission. Reviews 4×6 prints. Buys one-time rights. Offers $15-25/cover photo.

Tips: "Best to call first with the story idea to inquire if it is suitable for publication. Readers are very knowledgeable of the sport, so writers need to be as well."

N $ FANTASY SPORTS, Krause Publications, Inc., 700 E. State Street, Iola WI 54990-0001. (715)445-2214. Fax: (715)445-4087. Website: fanatasysportsmag.com. Editor: Greg Ambrosius. Managing Editor: Tom Kessenich. Quarterly magazine. Devoted to rotisserie and fantasy sports leagues. Circ. 120,000. Sample copy not available.

$ $ FENCERS QUARTERLY MAGAZINE, 848 S. Kimbrough, Springfield MO 65806. (417)866-4370. E-mail: editor@fencersquarterly.com. Editor-in-Chief: Nick Evangelista. **Contact:** Anita Evangelista, managing editor. **60% freelance written.** Quarterly magazine covering fencing, fencers, history of sword/fencing/dueling, modern techniques and systems, controversies, personalities of fencing, personal experience. "This is a publication for all fencers and those interested in fencing; we favor the grassroots level rather than the highly-promoted elite. Readers will have a grasp of terminology of the sword and refined fencing skills—writers must be familiar with fencing and current changes and controversies. We are happy to air any point of view on any fencing subject, but the material must be well-researched and logically presented." Estab. 1996. Circ. 5,000. Pays prior to or at publication. Publishes ms an average of 6 months after acceptance. Byline given. Offers 25% kill fee. Buys first North American serial, second serial (reprint), electronic rights, makes work-for-hire assignments. Editorial lead time 3 months. Submit seasonal material 6 months in advance. Accepts queries by mail, e-mail. Accepts simultaneous submissions. Sample copy by request. Writer's guidelines by request.

- Responds in 1 week or less for e-mail; 1 month for snail mail if SASE; no reply if no SASE and material not usable.

Nonfiction: "All article types acceptable—however, we have seldom used fiction or poetry (though will consider if has special relationship to fencing)." How-to should reflect some aspect of fencing or gear. Personal experience welcome. No articles "that lack logical progression of thought, articles that rant, 'my weapon is better than your weapon' emotionalism, puff pieces, or public relations stuff." **Buys 100 mss/year.** Query with or without published clips or send complete ms. Length: 100-4,000 words. **Pays $100-200 (rarely) for assigned articles; $10-60 for unsolicited articles.**

Photos: Send photos by mail or as e-mail attachment. Prefers prints, all sizes. Buys all rights. Negotiates payment individually. Captions, identification of subjects, model releases required.

Columns/Departments: Cutting-edge news (sword or fencing related), 100 words; Reviews (books/films), 300 words; Fencing Generations (profile), 200-300 words; Tournament Results (veteran events only, please), 200 words. **Buys 40 mss/year.** Send complete ms. **Pays $10-20.**

Fiction: Will consider all as long as strong fencing/sword slant is major element. No erotica. Query with or without published clips or send complete ms. Length: 1,500 words maximum. **Pays $25-100.**

Poetry: Will consider all which have distinct fencing/sword element as central. No erotica. Submit maximum 10 poems. Length: Up to 100 lines. **Pays $10.**

Fillers: Anecdotes, facts, gags to be illustrated by cartoonist, newsbreaks. **Buys 30/year.** Length: 100 words maximum. **Pays $5.**

Tips: "We love new writers! Professionally presented work impresses us. We prefer complete submissions, and e-mail or disk (in rich text format) are our favorites. Ask for our writer's guidelines. Always aim your writing to knowledgeable fencers who are fascinated by this subject, take their fencing seriously, and want to know more about its history, current events, and controversies. Action photos should show proper form—no flailing or tangled-up images, please. We want to know what the 'real' fencer is up to these days, not just what the Olympic contenders are doing. If we don't use your piece, we'll tell you why not."

$ $ POLO PLAYERS' EDITION, Rizzo Management Corp., 3500 Fairlane Farms Rd., Suite 9, Wellington FL 33414. (561)793-9524. Fax: (561)793-9576. E-mail: info@poloplayersedition.com. Website: www.poloplayersedition.com. **Contact:** Gwen Rizzo, editor. Monthly magazine on polo-the sport and lifestyle. "Our readers are affluent, well educated, well read, and highly sophisticated." Circ. 6,150. **Pays on acceptance.** Publishes ms an average of 2 months after acceptance.

Kill fee varies. Buys first North American serial rights, makes work-for-hire assignments. Submit seasonal material 3 months in advance. Accepts queries by mail, e-mail, fax. Accepts simultaneous submissions. Responds in 3 months to queries. Writer's guidelines for #10 SAE with 2 stamps.

Nonfiction: Historical/nostalgic, interview/profile, personal experience, photo feature, technical, travel. Special issues: Annual Art Issue/Gift Buying Guide; Winter Preview/Florida Supplement. **Buys 20 mss/year.** Query with published clips or send complete ms. Length: 800-3,000 words. **Pays $150-400 for assigned articles; $100-300 for unsolicited articles.** Sometimes pays expenses of writers on assignment.

Reprints: Send tearsheet or typed ms with rights for sale noted and information about when and where the material previously appeared. Pays 50% of amount paid for an original article.

Photos: State availability of or send photos with submission. Reviews contact sheets, transparencies, prints. Buys one-time rights. Offers $20-150/photo. Captions required.

Columns/Departments: Yesteryears (historical pieces), 500 words; Profiles (clubs and players), 800-1,000 words. **Buys 15 mss/year.** Query with published clips. **Pays $100-300.**

Tips: "Query us on a personality or club profile or historic piece or, if you know the game, state availability to cover a tournament. Keep in mind that ours is a sophisticated, well-educated audience."

$ $ PRIME TIME SPORTS & FITNESS, GND Prime Time Publishing, P.O. Box 6097, Evanston IL 60204. (847)784-1194. Fax: (847)784-1194. E-mail: dadorner@aol.com. Website: www.bowldtalk.com. Managing Editor: Steven Ury. **Contact:** Dennis A. Dorner, editor. **80% freelance written.** Monthly magazine covering seasonal pro sports, health club sports and fitness. Estab. 1974. Circ. 35,000. Pays on publication. Publishes ms an average of 6 months after acceptance. Byline given. all rights; will assign back to author in 85% of cases. Submit seasonal material 6 months in advance. Accepts queries by mail, e-mail. Accepts simultaneous submissions. Responds in 6 months to queries. Sample copy on request. Writer's guidelines online.

Break in with a 400-600-word fiction piece, or a 400-word instructional article.

Nonfiction: "We love short articles that get to the point. Nationally oriented big events and national championships." Book excerpts (fitness and health), exposé (in tennis, fitness, racquetball, health clubs, diets), general interest, historical/nostalgic, how-to (expert instructional pieces on any area of coverage), humor (large market for funny pieces on health clubs and fitness), inspirational, interview/profile, new product, opinion (only from recognized sources who know what they are talking about), personal experience (definitely humor), photo feature (on related subjects), technical (on exercise and sport), travel (related to fitness, tennis camps, etc.), adult (slightly risque and racy fitness); news reports (on racquetball, handball, tennis, running events). Special issues: Swimwear (March); Baseball Preview (April); Summer Fashion (July); Pro Football Preview (August); Aerobic Wear (September); Fall Fashion (October); Ski Issue (November); Workout and Diet Routines (December/January). "No articles on local only tennis and racquetball tournaments without national appeal." **Buys 150 mss/year.** Length: 2,000 words maximum. **Pays $50-200.** Sometimes pays expenses of writers on assignment.

Reprints: Send tearsheet, photocopy or typed ms with rights for sale noted and information about when and where the material previously appeared. Pays 20% of amount paid for an original article or story.

Photos: Specifically looking for fashion photo features. Nancy Thomas, photo editor. Send photos with submission. Buys all rights. Pays $20-75 for b&w prints. Captions, identification of subjects, model releases required.

Columns/Departments: George Thomas, column/department editor. New Products; Fitness Newsletter; Handball Newsletter; Racquetball Newsletter; Tennis Newsletter; News & Capsule Summaries; Fashion Spot (photos of new fitness and bathing suits and ski equipment). **Length:** 50-250 words ("more if author has good handle to cover complete columns"). "We want more articles with photos and we are searching for 1 woman columnist, Diet and Nutrition." **Buys 100 mss/year.** Send complete ms. **Pays $25-50.**

Fiction: Judy Johnson, fiction editor. "Upbeat stories are needed." Erotica, fantasy, humorous, novel excerpts, religious, romance. **Buys 20 mss/year.** Send complete ms. Length: 500-2,500 words maximum. **Pays $100-250.**

Poetry: Free verse, haiku, light verse, traditional, *on related subjects only.* Length: Up to 150 words. **Pays $25-50.**

The online magazine carries original content not found in the print edition and includes writer's guidelines. Contact: Bob Eres, online editor.

Tips: "Send us articles dealing with court club sports, exercise, and nutrition that exemplify an upbeat 'you can do it' attitude. Pro sports previews 3-4 months ahead of their seasons are also needed. Good short fiction or humorous articles can break in. Expert knowledge of any related subject can bring assignments; any area is open. We consider everything as a potential article, but are turned off by credits, past work, and degrees. We have a constant demand for well-written articles on instruction, health and trends in both. Other articles needed are professional sports training techniques, fad diets, tennis and fitness resorts, photo features with aerobic routines. A frequent mistake made by writers is in length—articles are too long. When we assign an article, we want it newsy if it's news and opinion if opinion."

N $ $ RACQUETBALL MAGAZINE, United States Racquetball Association, 1685 W. Uintah, Colorado Springs CO 80904. (719)635-5396. Fax: (719)635-0685. E-mail: lmojer@racqmag.com. Website: www.racqmag.com. **Contact:** Linda Mojer, director of communications. **20-30% freelance written.** Bimonthly magazine "geared toward a readership of informed, active enthusiasts who seek entertainment, instruction, and accurate reporting of events." Estab. 1990. Circ. 45,000. Pays on publication. Publishes ms an average of 2 months after acceptance. Buys one-time rights. Editorial lead time 3 months. Submit seasonal material 3 months in advance. Accepts simultaneous submissions. Responds in 2 months to queries. Sample copy for $4. Writer's guidelines online.

Nonfiction: How-to (instructional racquetball tips), humor, interview/profile (personalities who play racquetball). **Buys 2-3 mss/year.** Send complete ms. Length: 1,500-3,000 words. **Pays $100.** Sometimes pays expenses of writers on assignment.

Reprints: Send ms with rights for sale noted and information about when and where the material previously appeared.

Photos: Send photos with submission. Reviews 3×5 prints. Buys one-time rights. Negotiates payment individually. Identification of subjects, model releases required.
Fiction: Humorous. **Buys 1-2 mss/year.** Send complete ms. Length: 1,500-3,000 words. **Pays $100-250.**

$ RUGBY MAGAZINE, Rugby Press, Ltd., 2350 Broadway, New York NY 10024. (212)787-1160. Fax: (212)595-0934. E-mail: rugbymag@aol.com. Website: www.rugbymag.com. Editor: Ed Hagerty. **Contact:** Ed Hagerty. **75% freelance written.** Monthly tabloid. "*Rugby Magazine* is the journal of record for the sport of rugby in the U.S. Our demographics are among the best in the country." Estab. 1975. Circ. 10,000. Pays on publication. Publishes ms an average of 2 months after acceptance. Byline given. Buys all rights. Editorial lead time 1 month. Submit seasonal material 2 months in advance. Accepts queries by mail, e-mail, fax, phone. Accepts simultaneous submissions. Responds in 2 weeks to queries; 1 month to mss. Sample copy for $4. Writer's guidelines free.
Nonfiction: Book excerpts, essays, general interest, historical/nostalgic, how-to, humor, interview/profile, new product, opinion, personal experience, photo feature, technical, travel. **Buys 15 mss/year.** Send complete ms. Length: 600-2,000 words. **Pays $50 minimum.** Pays expenses of writers on assignment.
Reprints: Send tearsheet or typed ms with rights for sale noted and information about when and where the material previously appeared. Payment varies.
Photos: Send photos with submission. Reviews negatives, transparencies, prints. Buys all rights. Offers no additional payment for photos accepted with ms.
Columns/Departments: Nutrition (athletic nutrition), 900 words; Referees' Corner, 1,200 words. **Buys 2-3 mss/year.** Query with published clips. **Pays $50 maximum.**
Fiction: Condensed novels, humorous, novel excerpts, slice-of-life vignettes. **Buys 1-3 mss/year.** Query with published clips. Length: 1,000-2,500 words. **Pays $100.**
Tips: "Give us a call. Send along your stories or photos; we're happy to take a look. Tournament stories are a good way to get yourself published in *Rugby Magazine*."

N $ SURFING, PRIMEDIA Enthusiast Group, 950 Calle Amanecer, Suite C, San Clemente CA 93673-4203. (949)492-7873. Fax: (949)498-6485. E-mail: surfing@primedia.com. Website: www.surfingthemag.com. Editor: Evan Slater. **Contact:** Matt Walker, senior editor. Monthly magazine covering surfing. Edited for the active surfing enthusiast who enjoys the beach lifestyle. Estab. 1964. Circ. 108,035. Sample copy for $3.99.

$ $ TENNIS WEEK, Tennis News, Inc., 15 Elm Place, Rye NY 10580. (914)967-4890. Fax: (914)967-8178. **Contact:** Andre Christopher, managing editor. **10% freelance written.** Monthly magazine covering tennis. "For readers who are either tennis fanatics or involved in the business of tennis." Estab. 1974. Circ. 97,000. Pays on publication. Byline given. Buys all rights. Editorial lead time 1 month. Submit seasonal material 1 month in advance. Responds in 1 month to queries. Sample copy for $4.
Nonfiction: Buys 15 mss/year. Query with or without published clips. Length: 1,000-2,000 words. **Pays $300.**

N $ TIGER INSIDER, Upstate Publishing, Inc., PMB 125, 1027 S. Pendleton St., Suite B, Easley SC 29673. Fax: (305)675-0365. E-mail: thetigerinsider@thetigernet.com. Website: www.Thetigernet.com. **Contact:** Tommy Hood, managing editor. **100% freelance written.** Bimonthly magazine covering Clemson football. "*Tiger Insider* covers Clemson football and everything that surrounds it—the players, coaches, recruits. Anything remotely associated with Clemson football is considered for publication in the magazine. National issues that are relevant to Clemson football are also considered for inclusion in the magazine." Estab. 1999. Circ. 1,000. Pays on publication. Byline given. Offers 50% kill fee. Buys one-time rights. Editorial lead time 2 months. Submit seasonal material 2 months in advance. Accepts queries by mail, e-mail, fax. Accepts simultaneous submissions. Sample copy online. Writer's guidelines by e-mail.
Nonfiction: Book excerpts, interview/profile, college football. **Buys 30 mss/year.** Query with published clips. Length: 800-2,500 words. **Pays $50-100.**
Reprints: Accepts previously published submissions.
Photos: State availability with submission. Reviews GIF/JPEG files. Buys one-time rights. Negotiates payment individually. Identification of subjects required.
Tips: "E-mail with query and clips. Our readers are diehard Clemson football fans and consider anything remotely associated with Clemson football important: Where are they now? Features on recruits. Features on the schools that Clemson recruits against are all appropriate as well as features on current Clemson players and coaches."

Motor Sports

N $ $ AUTO RACING DIGEST, Century Publishing, 990 Grove St., Evanston IL 60201. (847)491-6440. Fax: (847)491-6203. Editor: William Wagner. **Contact:** Scott Plagenhoef, managing editor. **100% freelance written.** Bimonthly digest. "focusing on NASCAR, cart, F1, and the IRL." Estab. 1974. Circ. 50,000. Pays on publication. Publishes ms an average of 1 month after acceptance. Byline given. Offers 50% kill fee. Buys all rights. Editorial lead time 6 weeks. Submit seasonal material 6 weeks in advance. Accepts simultaneous submissions. Responds in 1 month to queries. Sample copy for $5.
Nonfiction: Essays, exposé, general interest, opinion, technical. No "remember when" pieces. No personal experience unless extraordinary. **Buys 70 mss/year.** Query. Length: 1,200-2,000 words. **Pays $100-300.**
Photos: State availability with submission. Reviews negatives, 35mm, 4×6 transparencies, 8×10 prints, digital photos. Buys one-time rights. Offers $15-60/photo; $100 for cover. Identification of subjects required.
Tips: "Query by mail. Clips should reflect subject matter you're trying to sell me."

N $DIRT RIDER, PRIMEDIA Enthusiast Group, 6420 Wilshire Blvd., 17th Floor, Los Angeles CA 90048-5502. (323)782-2390. Fax: (323)782-2372. E-mail: drmail@primedia.com. Website: www.primedia.com. Editor: Ken Faught. Managing Editor: Terry Masaoka. Monthly magazine devoted to the sport of off-road motorcycle riding that showcases the many ways enthusiast can enjoy dirt bikes. Circ. 201,342. Sample copy not available.

N $THE HOOK MAGAZINE, The Magazine for Antique & Classic Tractor Pullers, Greer Town, Inc., 209 S. Marshall, Box 16, Marshfield MO 65706. (417)468-7000. Fax: (417)859-6075. E-mail: thehook@pcis.net. Website: pcis.net/thehook. Managing Editor: Sherry Linville. **Contact:** Dana Greer Marlin, owner/president. **80% freelance written.** Bimonthly magazine covering tractor pulling. Estab. 1992. Circ. 6,000. Pays on publication. Byline given. Buys one-time, electronic rights. Editorial lead time 6 months. Submit seasonal material 6 months in advance. Accepts queries by mail, e-mail, fax. Accepts previously published material. Accepts simultaneous submissions. Responds in 3 weeks to queries; 2 months to mss. Sample copy for 8½×11 SAE with 4 first-class stamps or online. Writer's guidelines for #10 SASE.

O→ "Our magazine is easy to break into. Puller profiles are your best bet. Features on individuals and their tractors, how they got into the sport, what they want from competing."

Nonfiction: How-to, interview/profile, new product, personal experience, photo feature, technical, event coverage. **Buys 25 mss/year.** Send complete ms. Length: 500-1,500 words. **Pays $70 for technical articles; $35 for others.**

Photos: Send photos with submission. Reviews 3×5 prints. Buys one-time and online rights. Negotiates payment individually. Captions, identification of subjects, model releases required.

Fillers: Anecdotes, short humor. **Buys 6/year.** Length: 100 words.

Tips: "Write real. Our readers don't respond well to scholarly tomes. Use your everyday voice in all submissions and your chances will go up radically."

$ $SAND SPORTS MAGAZINE, Wright Publishing Co., Inc., P.O. Box 2260, Costa Mesa CA 92628. (714)979-2560, ext. 107. Fax: (714)979-3998. Website: www.sandsports.net. **Contact:** Michael Sommer, editor. **20% freelance written.** Bimonthly magazine covering vehicles for off-road and sand dunes. Estab. 1995. Circ. 25,000. Pays on publication. Byline given. Buys first, one-time rights. Editorial lead time 3 months. Submit seasonal material 6 months in advance. Accepts queries by mail. Sample copy and writer's guidelines free.

Nonfiction: How-to (technical-mechanical), photo feature, technical. **Buys 20 mss/year.** Query. Length: 1,500 words minimum. **Pays $125-175/page.** Sometimes pays expenses of writers on assignment.

Photos: Send photos with submission. Reviews contact sheets, transparencies, 5×7 prints. Buys one-time rights. Negotiates payment individually. Captions, identification of subjects, model releases required.

Olympics

$USA GYMNASTICS, 201 S. Capitol Ave., Suite 300, Pan American Plaza, Indianapolis IN 46225. (317)237-5050. Fax: (317)237-5069. E-mail: lpeszek@usa-gymnastics.org. Website: www.usa-gymnastics.org. **Contact:** Luan Peszek, editor. **5% freelance written.** Bimonthly magazine covering gymnastics—national and international competitions. Designed to educate readers on fitness, health, safety, technique, current topics, trends, and personalities related to the gymnastics/fitness field. Readers are gymnasts ages 7-18, parents, and coaches. Estab. 1981. Circ. 95,000. Pays on publication. Publishes ms an average of 4 months after acceptance. Byline given. Buys all rights. Submit seasonal material 4 months in advance. Accepts queries by e-mail, fax. Accepts simultaneous submissions. Responds in 2 months to queries. Sample copy for $5.

Nonfiction: General interest, how-to (related to fitness, health, gymnastics), inspirational, interview/profile, opinion (Open Floor section), photo feature. **Buys 3 mss/year.** Query. Length: 1,500 words maximum. **Payment negotiable.**

Reprints: Send photocopy.

Photos: Send photos with submission. Buys all rights. Offers no additional payment for photos accepted with ms. Identification of subjects required.

Tips: "Any articles of interest to gymnasts (men, women, rhythmic gymnastics, trampoline, and tumbling), coaches, judges, and parents, are what we're looking for. This includes nutrition, toning, health, safety, trends, techniques, timing, etc."

Running

N $INSIDE TEXAS RUNNING, 14201 Memorial Dr., Suite 204, Houston TX 77079. (281)759-0555. Fax: (281)759-7766. E-mail: rfnews@ix.netcom.com. Website: www.insidetexasrunning.com. **Contact:** Lance Phegley, editor. **70% freelance written.** Monthly (except June and August) tabloid covering running and running-related events. "Our audience is made up of Texas runners who may also be interested in cross training." Estab. 1977. Circ. 10,000. **Pays on acceptance.** Publishes ms an average of 2 months after acceptance. Byline given. Buys one-time, exclusive Texas rights. Submit seasonal material 2 months in advance. Responds in 1 month to mss. Sample copy for $1.50. Writer's guidelines for #10 SASE.

O→ "The best way to break in to our publication is to submit brief (2 or 3 paragraphs) fillers for our 'Texas Roundup' section."

Nonfiction: Various topics of interest to runners: Profiles of newsworthy Texas runners of all abilities; unusual events; training interviews. Special issues: Fall Race Review (September); Marathon Focus (October); Shoe Review (March); Resource Guide (December). **Buys 20 mss/year.** Send complete ms. Length: 500-1,500 words. **Pays $100 maximum for assigned articles; $50 maximum for unsolicited articles.**

Reprints: Send tearsheet, photocopy or typed ms with rights for sale noted and information about when and where the material previously appeared.

Photos: Send photos with submission. Buys one-time rights. Offers $25 maximum/photo. Captions required.

The online magazine carries original content not found in the print edition.

Tips: "Writers should be familiar with the sport and the publication."

N $ $ NEW YORK RUNNER, New York Road Runners, 9 E. 89th St., New York NY 10128. (212)423-2260. Fax: (212)423-0879. E-mail: newyorkrun@nyrrc.org. Website: www.nyrrc.org. **Contact:** Gordon Bakoulis, editor. Bimonthly regional sports magazine covering running, walking, nutrition, and fitness. Estab. 1958. Circ. 45,000. **Pays on acceptance.** Byline given. Offers 33% kill fee. Buys first North American serial rights. Submit seasonal material 4 months in advance. Accepts queries by mail, e-mail, fax. Responds in 2 months to queries. Sample copy for $3. Writer's guidelines for #10 SASE.

- Material should be of interest to members of the New York Road Runners.

Nonfiction: Running and marathon articles. Interview/profile (of runners). **Buys 15 mss/year.** Query. Length: 750-1,000 words. **Pays $50-350.**

Columns/Departments: Running Briefs (anything noteworthy in the running world, such as new products and volunteer opportunities), 250-500 words. Query.

Tips: "Be knowledgeable about the sport of running."

$ $ $ $ RUNNER'S WORLD, Rodale, 135 N. 6th St., Emmaus PA 18098. (610)967-5171. Fax: (610)967-8883. E-mail: rwedit@rodale.com. Website: www.runnersworld.com. Deputy Editor: Bob Wischnia. **Contact:** Adam Bean, managing editor. **5% freelance written.** Monthly magazine on running, mainly long-distance running. "The magazine for and about distance running, training, health and fitness, nutrition, motivation, injury prevention, race coverage, personalities of the sport." Estab. 1966. Circ. 500,000. Pays on publication. Publishes ms an average of 6 months after acceptance. Byline given. Buys all rights. Submit seasonal material 6 months in advance. Accepts queries by mail. Responds in 2 months to queries. Writer's guidelines online.

Break in through columns 'Women's Running,' 'Human Race,' and 'Finish Line.' Also 'Warmups,' which mixes international running news with human interest stories. If you can send us a unique human interest story from your region, we will give it serious consideration.

Nonfiction: How-to (train, prevent injuries), interview/profile, personal experience. No "my first marathon" stories. No poetry. **Buys 5-7 mss/year.** Query. **Pays $1,500-2,000.** Pays expenses of writers on assignment.

Photos: State availability with submission. Buys one-time rights. Identification of subjects required.

Columns/Departments: Finish Line (back-of-the-magazine essay, personal experience-humor); Women's Running (essay page written by and for women). **Buys 24 mss/year.** Send complete ms. **Pays $300.**

The online magazine carries original content not found in the print edition. Contact: Marty Post.

Tips: "We are always looking for 'Adventure Runs' from readers—runs in wild, remote, beautiful, and interesting places. These are rarely race stories but more like backtracking/running adventures. Great color slides are crucial, 2,000 words maximum."

$ $ RUNNING TIMES, The Runner's Best Resource, Fitness Publishing, Inc., 213 Danbury Rd., Wilton CT 06897. (203)761-1113. Fax: (203)761-9933. E-mail: editor@runningtimes.com. Website: www.runningtimes.com. Managing Editor: Marc Chalufour. **Contact:** Jonathan Beverly, editor. **40% freelance written.** Magazine published 10 times/year covering distance running and racing. "*Running Times* is the national magazine for the experienced running participant and fan. Our audience is knowledgeable about the sport and active in running and racing. All editorial relates specifically to running: improving performance, enhancing enjoyment, or exploring events, places, and people in the sport." Estab. 1977. Circ. 75,000. Pays on publication. Publishes ms an average of 3 months after acceptance. Byline given. Buys first North American serial, second serial (reprint), electronic rights. Editorial lead time 4 months. Submit seasonal material 6 months in advance. Accepts queries by mail, e-mail. Responds in 1 month to queries; 2 months to mss. Sample copy for $5. Writer's guidelines online.

Nonfiction: Book excerpts, essays, historical/nostalgic, how-to (training), humor, inspirational, interview/profile, new product, opinion, personal experience (with theme, purpose, evidence of additional research and/or special expertise), photo feature, travel, news, reports. No basic, beginner how-to, generic fitness/nutrition, or generic first-person accounts. **Buys 25 mss/year.** Query. Length: 1,500-3,000 words. **Pays $200-500 for assigned articles; $100-300 for unsolicited articles.** Sometimes pays expenses of writers on assignment.

Photos: State availability with submission. Buys one-time rights. Negotiates payment individually. Identification of subjects required.

Columns/Departments: Training (short topics related to enhancing performance), 1,000 words; Sports-Med (application of medical knowledge to running), 1,000 words; Nutrition (application of nutritional principles to running performance), 1,000 words. **Buys 15 mss/year.** Query. **Pays $50-200.**

Fiction: Any genre, with running-related theme or characters. **Buys 1-2 mss/year.** Send complete ms. Length: 1,500-3,000 words. **Pays $100-500.**

Tips: "Thoroughly get to know runners and the running culture, both at the participant level and the professional, elite level."

$ $ TRAIL RUNNER, The Magazine of Running Adventure, Big Stone Publishing, 1101 Village Rd. UL-4D, Carbondale CO 81623. (970)704-1442. Fax: (970)963-4965. E-mail: mbenge@bigstonepub.com. Website: www.trailrunnermag.com. **Contact:** Michael Benge, editor. **65% freelance written.** Bimonthly magazine covering all aspects of off-road running. "The only nationally circulated 4-color glossy magazine dedicated to covering trail running." Estab. 1999. Circ. 40,000. Pays on publication. Publishes ms an average of 2 months after acceptance. Byline given. Offers $50 kill fee. Buys first North American serial, electronic rights. Editorial lead time 3 months. Submit seasonal material 5 months in advance. Accepts queries by mail, e-mail. Accepts simultaneous submissions. Responds in 3 weeks to queries; 2 months to mss. Sample copy for $3. Writer's guidelines online.

Nonfiction: Essays, exposé, general interest, historical/nostalgic, how-to, humor, inspirational, interview/profile, new product, opinion, personal experience, photo feature, technical, travel, racing. No gear reviews, race results. **Buys 30-40 mss/year.** Query with published clips. Length: 800-2,000 words. **Pays 30-40¢/word.** Sometimes pays expenses of writers on assignment.

Photos: Send photos with submission. Reviews 35mm transparencies, prints. Buys one-time rights. Offers $50-250/photo. Identification of subjects, model releases required.

Columns/Departments: Monique Cole, senior editor. Training (race training, altitude training, etc.), 800 words; Adventure (off-beat aspects of trail running), 600-800 words; Wanderings (personal essay on any topic related to trail running), 600 words; Urban Escapes (urban trails accessible in and around major US sites), 800 words; Personalities (profile of a trail running personality), 1,000 words. **Buys 5-10 mss/year.** Query with published clips. **Pays 30-40¢/word.**

Fiction: Adventure, fantasy, slice-of-life vignettes. **Buys 1-2 mss/year.** Query with published clips. Length: 1,000-1,500 words. **Pays 25-35¢/word.**

Fillers: Anecdotes, facts, gags to be illustrated by cartoonist, newsbreaks, short humor. **Buys 50-60/year.** Length: 75-400 words. **Pays 25-35¢/word.**

The online version contains material not found in the print edition. Contact: Phil Mislinski.

Tips: "Best way to break in is with interesting and unique trail running news, notes, and nonsense from around the world. Also, check the website for more info."

$ $ TRIATHLETE MAGAZINE, The World's Largest Triathlon Magazine, Triathlon Group of North America, 2037 San Elijo, Cardiff CA 92007. (760)634-4100. Fax: (760)634-4110. E-mail: cgandolfo@triathletemag.com. Website: www.triathletemag.com. **Contact:** Christina Gandolfo, editor. **50% freelance written.** Monthly magazine. "In general, articles should appeal to seasoned triathletes, as well as eager newcomers to the sport. Our audience includes everyone from competitive athletes to people considering their first event." Estab. 1983. Circ. 50,000. Pays on publication. Byline given. Buys second serial (reprint), all rights. Editorial lead time 3 months. Submit seasonal material 6 months in advance. Accepts queries by mail, e-mail. Accepts simultaneous submissions. Sample copy for $5.

Nonfiction: How-to, interview/profile, new product, photo feature, technical. "No first-person pieces about your experience in triathlon or my-first-triathlon stories." **Buys 36 mss/year.** Query with published clips. Length: 1,000-3,000 words. **Pays $200-600.** Sometimes pays expenses of writers on assignment.

Photos: State availability with submission. Reviews transparencies. Buys first North American rights. Offers $50-300/photo.

Tips: "Writers should know the sport and be familiar with the nuances and history. Training-specific articles that focus on new, but scientifically based, methods are good, as are seasonal training pieces."

Skiing & Snow Sports

$ SKATING, United States Figure Skating Association, 20 First St., Colorado Springs CO 80906-3697. (719)635-5200. Fax: (719)635-9548. E-mail: skatingmagazine@usfsa.org. **Contact:** Laura Fawcett, editor. Official publication of the USFSA published 10 times/year. "*Skating* magazine is the official publication of U.S. Figure Skating, and thus we cover skating at both the championship and grass roots level." Estab. 1923. Circ. 45,000. Pays on publication. Publishes ms an average of 3 months after acceptance. Byline given. Buys first rights. Accepts queries by mail, e-mail, fax.

- The best way for a writer to break in is through the "Ice Time with—..." department, which features USFSA members (skaters, volunteers, etc.) who have unique or interesting stories to tell. This is a feature that highlights members and their accomplishments and stories on and off the ice (800-1,500 words).

Nonfiction: General interest, historical/nostalgic, how-to, interview/profile (background and interests of skaters, volunteers, or other USFSA members), photo feature, technical and competition reports, figure skating issues and trends, sports medicine. **Buys 10 mss/year.** Query. Length: 500-2,500 words. **Payment varies.**

Photos: Photos purchased with or without accompanying ms. Query. Pays $15 for 8×10 or 5×7 b&w glossy prints, and $35 for color prints or transparencies.

Columns/Departments: Ice Breaker (news briefs); Foreign Competition Reports; Ice Time With... (features on USFSA members); Health and Fitness; In Synch (synchronized skating news); Takeoff (up-and-coming athletes). Length: 500-2,000 words.

Tips: "We want writing by experienced persons knowledgeable in the technical and artistic aspects of figure skating with a new outlook on the development of the sport. Knowledge and background in technical aspects of figure skating is helpful, but not necessary to the quality of writing expected. We would like to see articles and short features on USFSA volunteers, skaters, and other USFSA members who normally wouldn't get recognized, as opposed to features on championship-level athletes, which are usually assigned to regular contributors. Good quality color photos are a must with submissions. Also would be interested in seeing figure skating 'issues and trends' articles, instead of just profiles. No professional skater material. Synchronized skating and adult skating are the 2 fastest growing aspects of the USFSA. We would like to see more stories dealing with these unique athletes."

$ $ $ SKI MAGAZINE, Times Mirror Magazines, 929 Pearl St., Suite 200, Boulder CO 80302. (303)448-7600. Fax: (303)448-7638. E-mail: mdrummey@skimag.com. Website: www.skimag.com. Editor-in-Chief: Kendall Hamilton. **Contact:** Maureen Drummey, associate editor. **60% freelance written.** Magazine published 8 times/year. "*Ski* is a ski-lifestyle publication written and edited for recreational skiers. Its content is intended to help them ski better (technique), buy better (equipment and skiwear), and introduce them to new experiences, people, and adventures." Estab. 1936. Circ. 430,000. **Pays on acceptance.** Publishes ms an average of 3 months after acceptance. Byline given. Offers 15% kill fee. Buys first North American serial rights. Submit seasonal material 8 months in advance. Accepts queries by mail, e-mail. Sample copy for 9 × 12 SAE and 5 first-class stamps.

- Does not accept unsolicited mss, and assumes no responsibility for their return.

Nonfiction: Essays, historical/nostalgic, how-to, humor, interview/profile, personal experience. **Buys 5-10 mss/year.** Send complete ms. Length: 1,000-3,500 words. **Pays $500-1,000 for assigned articles; $300-700 for unsolicited articles.** Pays expenses of writers on assignment.

Photos: Send photos with submission. Buys one-time rights. Offers $75-300/photo. Captions, identification of subjects, model releases required.

Columns/Departments: See magazine.

Fillers: Facts, short humor. **Buys 10/year.** Length: 60-75 words. **Pays $50-75.**

Online magazine carries original content not found in the print edition. Contact: Doug Sabanosh (dsabanosh@skimag.com).

Tips: "Writers must have an extensive familiarity with the sport and know what concerns, interests, and amuses skiers. Start with short pieces ('hometown hills,' 'dining out,' 'sleeping in'). Columns are most open to freelancers."

$ $ $ $ SKIING, Time 4 Media, Inc., 929 Pearl St., Suite 200, Boulder CO 80302. (303)448-7600. Fax: (303)448-7676. E-mail: editors@skiingmag.com. Website: www.skiingmag.com. Editor-in-Chief: Perkins Miller. **Contact:** Helen Olsson, executive editor. Magazine published 7 times/year for skiers who deeply love winter, who live for travel, adventure, instruction, gear, and news. "*Skiing* is the user's guide to winter adventure. It is equal parts jaw-dropping inspiration and practical information, action and utility, attitude and advice. It relates the lifestyles of dedicated skiers and captures their spirit of daring and exploration. Dramatic photography transports readers to spine-tingling mountains with breathtaking immediacy. Reading *Skiing* is almost as much fun as being there." Estab. 1948. Circ. 400,000. Byline given. Offers 40% kill fee.

Nonfiction: Buys 10-15 feature (1,500-2,000 words) and 12-24 short (100-500 words) mss/year. Query. **Pays $1,000-2,500/feature; $100-500/short piece.**

Columns/Departments: Length: 200-1,000 words. **Buys 2-3 mss/year.** Query. **Pays $150-1,000.**

The online magazine carries original content not found in the print edition. Contact: Kari Keller, online coordinator.

Tips: "Consider less obvious subjects: smaller ski areas, specific local ski cultures, unknown aspects of popular resorts. Be expressive, not merely descriptive! We want readers to feel the adventure in your writing—to tingle with the excitement of skiing steep powder, of meeting intriguing people, of reaching new goals or achieving dramatic new insights. We want readers to have fun, to see the humor in and the lighter side of skiing and their fellow skiers."

$ $ SNOW GOER, Ehlert Publishing Group, 6420 Sycamore Ln., Maple Grove MN 55369. Fax: (763)383-4499. E-mail: eskogman@affinitygroup.com. Website: www.snowmobilenews.com. **Contact:** Eric Skogman, editor. **5% freelance written.** Magazine published 6 times/year covering snowmobiling. "*Snow Goer* is a hard-hitting, tell-it-like-it-is magazine designed for the ultra-active snowmobile enthusiast. It is fun, exciting, innovative and on the cutting edge of technology and trends." Estab. 1967. Circ. 76,000. Pays on publication. Publishes ms an average of 5 months after acceptance. Byline given. Buys first, one-time rights. Editorial lead time 5 months. Submit seasonal material 6 months in advance. Accepts queries by mail, e-mail, fax. Accepts simultaneous submissions. Responds in 3 months to queries. Sample copy for 8 × 10 SAE and 4 first-class stamps.

Nonfiction: General interest, how-to, interview/profile, new product, personal experience, photo feature, technical, travel. **Buys 6 mss/year.** Query. Length: 500-4,000 words. **Pays $50-500.** Sometimes pays expenses of writers on assignment.

Photos: State availability with submission. Reviews contact sheets, prints. Buys one-time rights or all rights. Negotiates payment individually. Captions, identification of subjects required.

$ $ SNOWEST MAGAZINE, Harris Publishing, 360 B St., Idaho Falls ID 83402. (208)524-7000. Fax: (208)522-5241. E-mail: lindstrm@snowest.com. Website: snowest.com. Publisher: Steve Janes. **Contact:** Lane Lindstrom, editor. **10-25% freelance written.** Monthly magazine. "*SnoWest* covers the sport of snowmobiling, products, and personalities in the western states. This includes mountain riding, deep powder, and trail riding, as well as destination pieces, tech tips, and new model reviews." Estab. 1972. Circ. 160,000. Pays on publication. Publishes ms an average of 2 months after acceptance. Byline given. Buys first North American serial rights. Editorial lead time 6 months. Submit seasonal material 3 months in advance. Sample copy and writer's guidelines free.

Nonfiction: How-to (fix a snowmobile, make it high performance), new product, technical, travel. **Buys 3-5 mss/year.** Query with published clips. Length: 500-1,500 words. **Pays $150-300.**

Photos: Send photos with submission. Buys one-time rights. Negotiates payment individually. Captions, identification of subjects required.

$ $ $ TRANSWORLD STANCE, Transworld Media, 353 Airport Rd., Oceanside CA 92054. (760)722-7777. Fax: (760)722-0653. Website: www.stancemag.com. **Contact:** Kevin Imamura, editor; Ted Newsome, editor-in-chief; Chandra Conway, managing editor; Nolan Woodrell, associate editor. **50-75% freelance written.** Bimonthly consumer magazine geared toward teen males. "*Stance* is a lifestyle magazine written from the perspective of skateboarders and snowboarders. The main focus is celebrities (from our world as well as everywhere else), products, music, and fashion." Estab. 2000. Circ. 100,000. Pays on publication. Publishes ms an average of 4 months after acceptance. Byline given. Offers 50% kill

fee. Makes work-for-hire assignments. Editorial lead time 4 months. Submit seasonal material 6 months in advance. Accepts queries by mail, e-mail, fax. Sample copy for 8x11 SAE and 4 first-class stamps.
Nonfiction: Historical/nostalgic, how-to (customize cars, buy a car), humor, interview/profile, new product, technical, travel (how to travel cross country and through Europe for cheap). Length: 25-1,500 words. **Pays 60¢/word minimum.** Sometimes pays expenses of writers on assignment.
Photos: Send photos with submission. Reviews contact sheets. Buys one-time rights. Negotiates payment individually. Identification of subjects, model releases required.
Columns/Departments: Nolan Woodrell, associate editor. Product Fix (product reviews); Cover Girl (cover feature), 300-500 words; Now Playing (video game reviews), 100-150 words; Media Injection (book/video/magazine reviews), 100 words. Query. **Pays 60¢/word.**
Fillers: Facts, gags to be illustrated by cartoonist.
Tips: "We like to include as many how-to's and service-oriented pieces as possible."

Soccer

N $ $ SOCCER DIGEST, Century Publishing, 990 Grove St., Evanston IL 60201. (847)491-6440. Fax: (847)491-6203. **Contact:** Scott Plagenhoef, managing editor. **80% freelance written.** "Bimonthly digest featuring investigative reportage on national and international soccer. Writers must be well-established and previously published." Estab. 1977. Circ. 45,000. Pays on publication. Publishes ms an average of 1 month after acceptance. Byline given. Offers 50% kill fee. Buys all rights. Editorial lead time 6 weeks. Submit seasonal material 2 months in advance. Accepts queries by mail, e-mail. Accepts simultaneous submissions. Responds in 1 month to queries. Sample copy for $5. Writer's guidelines free.
Nonfiction: Essays, exposé, general interest, interview/profile, opinion. No how-to, nostalgic, humor, personal experience. **Buys 40 mss/year.** Query. Length: 1,200-2,000 words. **Pays $100-300.**
Photos: State availability with submission. Reviews negatives, 35mm transparencies, 8×10 prints, digital photos, JPEG or TIFF files. Buys one-time rights. Offers $15-60/photo, $100 for cover. Captions required.
Tips: "Send query by mail or e-mail. Include related clips—do not deluge us with cooking clips (for example) if you're trying to sell me a sports story!"

$ $ SOCCER NOW, Official Publication of the American Youth Soccer Organization, American Youth Soccer Organization, 12501 S. Isis Ave., Hawthorne CA 90250. (800)USA-AYSO or (310)643-6455. Fax: (310)643-5310. E-mail: soccernow@ayso.org. Website: www.soccer.org. **Contact:** Melissa Bean Sterzick, editor. Quarterly magazine covering soccer (AYSO and professional). "For AYSO members, both players (age 5-18) and their parents. Human interest about AYSO players and adult volunteers, or professional players (especially if they played in AYSO as kids)." Estab. 1976. Circ. 470,000. Pays on publication. Publishes ms an average of 3 months after acceptance. Byline given. Makes work-for-hire assignments. Editorial lead time 3 months. Accepts queries by mail, e-mail, fax. Responds in 1 month to queries. Sample copy free on request.
Nonfiction: General interest (soccer), historical/nostalgic, how-to (playing tips subject to approval by Director of Coaching), interview/profile, personal experience, photo feature. Query. Length: 400-1,000 words. **Pays $50-200.** Sometimes pays expenses of writers on assignment.
Photos: Send photos with submission. Reviews contact sheets, transparencies, prints. Buys one-time rights. Offers $0-50/photo. Identification of subjects required.
Columns/Departments: Headlines (news); Team Tips (instructional); Game Zone (games for kids—e.g., soccer-related word puzzles). Query. **Pays $0-50.**

Water Sports

$ $ IMMERSED MAGAZINE, The International Technical Diving Magazine, Immersed LLC, FDR Station, P.O. Box 947, New York NY 10150-0947. (845)469-1003. Fax: (845)469-1005. E-mail: bernie@immersed.com. Website: www.immersed.com. **Contact:** Bernie Chowdhury. **60% freelance written.** Quarterly magazine covering scuba diving. "Advances on the frontier of scuba diving are covered in theme-oriented issues that examine archeology, biology, history, gear, and sciences related to diving. We emphasize training, education, and safety." Estab. 1996. Circ. 25,000. Pays on publication. Byline given. Offers kill fee. Buys one-time, electronic rights. Editorial lead time 6 months. Accepts queries by mail, e-mail, fax, phone. Sample copy online. Writer's guidelines for #10 SASE.

O→ Break in with "how-to equipment rigging stories or travel stories on unusual but accessible destinations."

Nonfiction: Historical/nostalgic, how-to, interview/profile, new product, personal experience, photo feature, technical, travel. No poetry, opinion diatribes, axe-grinding exposés. **Buys 30 mss/year.** Query. Length: 500-2,000 words. **Pays $150-250.** Sometimes pays expenses of writers on assignment.
Photos: Send photos with submission. Reviews transparencies, prints. Buys one-time and promotional website rights. Offers no additional payment for photos accepted with ms. Captions required.
Columns/Departments: Technically Destined (travel), 1,200 words; Rigging For Success (how-to, few words/heavily illustrated); Explorer (personality profile), 2,000 words; Tech Spec (product descriptions), 1,000 words; New Products (product press releases), 200 words; Book Review (book review), 800 words. **Buys 12 mss/year.** Query. **Pays $150-250.**
Fillers: Newsbreaks. **Pays 35¢/word.**
Tips: "Query first with a short, punchy paragraph that describes your story and why it would be of interest to our readers. There's bonus points for citing which feature or department would be most appropriate for your story."

$ $ PADDLER MAGAZINE, World's No. 1 Canoeing, Kayaking and Rafting Magazine, Paddlesport Publishing, P.O. Box 775450, Steamboat Springs CO 80477-5450. (970)879-1450. Fax: (970)870-1404. E-mail: rico@paddlermagazine.com. Website: www.paddlermagazine.com. Editor: Eugene Buchanan. **Contact:** Tom Bie, managing editor. **70% freelance written.** Bimonthly magazine covering paddle sports. "*Paddler* magazine is written by and for those knowledgeable about river running, flatwater canoeing and sea kayaking. Our core audience is the intermediate to advanced paddler, yet we strive to cover the entire range from beginners to experts. Our editorial coverage is divided between whitewater rafting, whitewater kayaking, canoeing and sea kayaking. We strive for balance between the Eastern and Western U.S. paddling scenes and regularly cover international expeditions. We also try to integrate the Canadian paddling community into each publication." Estab. 1991. Circ. 80,000. Pays on publication. Publishes ms an average of 6 months after acceptance. Byline given. Buys first North American serial rights. One-time electronic rights Editorial lead time 3 months. Submit seasonal material 6 months in advance. Accepts queries by mail, e-mail. Responds in 6 months to queries. Sample copy for $3 with 8æ×11 SASE. Writer's guidelines online.

O━ Break in through "The Hotline section at the front of the magazine."

Nonfiction: Book excerpts, essays, general interest, historical/nostalgic, how-to, humor, inspirational, interview/profile, new product, opinion, personal experience, photo feature, technical, travel (must be paddlesport related). **Buys 75 mss/year.** Query. Length: 100-3,000 words. **Pays 10-25¢/word (more for established writers) for assigned articles; 10-20¢/word for unsolicited articles.** Sometimes pays expenses of writers on assignment.

Photos: Submissions should include photos or other art. State availability with submission. Reviews contact sheets, negatives, transparencies. Buys one-time rights. Offers $25-200/photo.

Columns/Departments: Hotline (timely news and exciting developments relating to the paddling community. Stories should be lively and newsworthy), 150-750 words; Paddle People (unique people involved in the sport and industry leaders), 600-800 words; Destinations (informs paddlers of unique places to paddle—we often follow regional themes and cover all paddling disciplines); submissions should include map and photo, 800 words. Marketplace (gear reviews, gadgets and new products, and is about equipment paddlers use, from boats and paddles to collapsible chairs, bivy sacks and other accessories), 250-800 words. Paddle Tales (short, humorous anecdotes), 75-300 words. Skills (a "How-to" forum for experts to share tricks of the trade, from playboating techniques to cooking in the backcountry), 250-1,000 words. Query. **Pays 20-25¢/word.**

Tips: "We prefer queries, but will look at manuscripts on speculation. No phone queries please. Be familiar with the magazine and offer us unique, exciting ideas. Most positive responses to queries are on spec, but we will occasionally make assignments."

N $ RODALE'S SCUBA DIVING, Rodale, Inc., 6600 Abercorn Street, Suite 208, Savannah GA 31405. (912)351-6234. Fax: (912)351-0735. E-mail: edit@scubadiving.com. Website: www.scubadiving.com. Managing Editor: Buck Butler. **Contact:** Keith Phillips. Monthly magazine covering scuba diving. Edited for scuba divers of all skill levels. Estab. 1992. Circ. 146,826. Buys all rights. Editorial lead time 10 weeks. Accepts queries by mail, e-mail, fax, phone. Sample copy for $3.50. Writer's guidelines by e-mail.

Nonfiction: "No first person essays or puff pieces on dive destinations and operators." Query.

Columns/Departments: Seaviews (lively and engaging stories that are heavy on news and/or how-to information), 500 words or less; North American Travel (great diving/scuba adventures that are close to home and can be done in a long weekend) 750 words, including Dive In sidebar; Exotic Travel (off-the-beaten path destinations) 1,00 words. Query.

$ $ SPORT DIVER, World Publications, 460 N. Orlando Ave., Suite 200, Winter Park FL 32789-2988. (407)571-4584. Fax: (407)571-4585. E-mail: annlouise.tuke@worldpub.net. Website: www.sportdiver.com. Kirk Brown, managing editor. **75% freelance written.** Magazine published 10 times/year covering scuba diving. "We portray the adventure and fun of diving—the reasons we all started diving in the first place." Estab. 1993. Circ. 250,000. Pays on publication. Byline given. Offers 25% kill fee. Buys first North American serial rights. Editorial lead time 3 months. Submit seasonal material 4 months in advance. Accepts queries by e-mail. Responds in 2 weeks to queries; 3 months to mss. Writer's guidelines online.

Nonfiction: Personal experience, travel, diving. No nondiving related articles. **Buys 150 mss/year.** Query with SASE. Length: 500-2,000 words. **Pays $300-500.**

Photos: State availability with submission. Reviews transparencies. Buys one-time rights. Offers $50-200/photo; $1,000 for covers. Captions required.

Columns/Departments: Divebriefs (shorts), 150-450 words. Query. **Pays $50-250.**

The online magazine carries original content not included in the print edition. Contact: Martin Kuss, online editor.

Tips: "Know diving, and even more importantly, know how to write. It's getting much more difficult to break into the market due to a recent series of takeovers."

N $ SURFER MAGAZINE, PRIMEDIA Enthusiast Group, PO Box 1028, Dana Point CA 92629-5028. (949)496-5922. Fax: (949)496-7849. E-mail: surferedit@primedia.com. Website: www.surfermag.com. Editor: Sam George. Monthly magazine edited for the avid surfers and those who follow the beach, wave riding scene. Circ. 118,570. Editorial lead time 10 weeks. Sample copy not available.

N $ TRANSWORLD SURF, Time 4 Media, 353 Airport Road, Oceanside CA 92054. (760)722-7777. Fax: (760)722-0653. Website: www.transworldsurf.com. Editor-in-Chief: Joel Patterson. Magazine published 11 times/year. Publication designed to promote the growth of the sport of surfing. Circ. 103,600.

$ THE WATER SKIER, USA Water Ski, 1251 Holy Cow Rd., Polk City FL 33868-8200. (863)324-4341. Fax: (863)325-8259. E-mail: satkinson@usawaterski.org. Website: www.usawaterski.org. Scott Atkinson, editor. **10-20% freelance writ-**

ten. Magazine published 9 times/year. "*The Water Skier* is the membership magazine of USA Water Ski, the national governing body for organized water skiing in the United States. The magazine has a controlled circulation and is available only to USA Water Ski's membership, which is made up of 20,000 active competitive water skiers and 10,000 members who are supporting the sport. These supporting members may participate in the sport but they don't compete. The editorial content of the magazine features distinctive and informative writing about the sport of water skiing only." Estab. 1951. Circ. 30,000. Byline given. Offers 30% kill fee. Editorial lead time 4 months. Submit seasonal material 6 months in advance. Responds in 2 weeks to queries. Sample copy for $3.50. Writer's guidelines for #10 SASE.

O→ Most open to material for feature articles (query editor with your idea).

Nonfiction: Historical/nostalgic (has to pertain to water skiing), interview/profile (call for assignment), new product (boating and water ski equipment), travel (water ski vacation destinations). **Buys 10-15 mss/year.** Query. Length: 1,500-3,000 words. **Pays $100-150.**

Reprints: Send photocopy. Payment negotiable.

Photos: State availability with submission. Reviews contact sheets. Buys all rights. Negotiates payment individually. Captions, identification of subjects required.

Columns/Departments: The Water Skier News (small news items about people and events in the sport), 400-500 words. Other topics include safety, training (3-event, barefoot, disabled, show ski, ski race, kneeboard, and wakeboard); champions on their way; new products. Query. **Pays $50-100.**

The online magazine carries original content not found in the print edition. Contact: Scott Atkinson, online editor.

Tips: "Contact the editor through a query letter (please, no phone calls) with an idea. Avoid instruction, these articles are written by professionals. Concentrate on articles about the people of the sport. We are always looking for interesting stories about people in the sport. Also, short news features which will make a reader say to himself, 'Hey, I didn't know that.' Keep in mind that the publication is highly specialized about the sport of water skiing."

TEEN & YOUNG ADULT

Publications in this category are for teens (13-19). Publications for college students are in the Career, College & Alumni section. Those for younger children are in the Juvenile section.

N $ **ALLOYGIRL**, 151 W. 26th Street, New York NY 10001-6810. (212)244-4307. Fax: (212)244-4311. Website: www.alloygirl.com. Editor: Fiona Gibb. Quarterly magazine covering teen fashion and beauty trends, and entertainment. Written for girls 14-21. Circ. 500,000. Editorial lead time 4 months. Sample copy not available.

N $ $ **BREAKAWAY MAGAZINE**, Focus on the Family, 8605 Explorer Dr., Colorado Springs CO 80920. (719)531-3400. Fax: (719)531-3499. Website: www.breakawaymag.com. Associate Editor: Jeremy V. Jones. **Contact:** Michael Ross, editor. **25% freelance written.** Monthly magazine covering extreme sports, Christian music artists, and new technology relevant to teen boys. "This fast-paced, 4-color publication is designed to creatively teach, entertain, inspire, and challenge the emerging teenager. It also seeks to strengthen a boy's self-esteem, provide role models, guide a healthy awakening to girls, make the Bible relevant, and deepen their love for family, friends, church, and Jesus Christ." Estab. 1990. Circ. 96,000. **Pays on acceptance.** Publishes ms an average of 5-12 months after acceptance. Byline given. Offers $25 kill fee. Buys first North American serial, first, one-time, electronic rights. Editorial lead time 3 months. Submit seasonal material 6 months in advance. Accepts queries by mail. Responds in 2-3 months to queries; 2-3 months to mss. Sample copy for $1.50 and 9×12 SASE with 3 First-class stamps. Writer's guidelines for #10 SASE.

Nonfiction: Inspirational, interview/profile, personal experience. **Buys up to 6 mss/year.** Send complete ms. Length: 700-2,000 words. **Pays 12-15¢/word.**

Columns/Departments: Truth Encounter (spiritual/Biblical application devotional for teen guys), 600 words. **Buys 2-3 mss/year.** Send complete ms. **Pays 12-15¢/word.**

Fiction: Adventure, humorous, religious, suspense. "Avoid Christian jargon, clichés, preaching, and other dialogue that isn't realistic or that interrupts the flow of the story." **Buys 3-4 mss/year.** Send complete ms. Length: 600-2,000 words. **Pays 12-15¢/word.**

Tips: "Some of our readers get spiritual nurture at home and at church; many don't. To reach both groups, the articles must be written in ways that are compelling, bright, out of the ordinary. Nearly every adult in a boy's life is an authority figure. We would like you, through the magazine, to be seen as a friend! We also want *Breakaway* to be a magazine any pre-Christian teen could pick up and understand without first learning 'Christianese.' Stories should spiritually challenge, yet be spiritually inviting."

$ $ **CAMPUS LIFE**, Christianity Today, Inc., 465 Gundersen Dr., Carol Stream IL 60188. (630)260-6200. Fax: (630)260-0114. E-mail: clmag@campuslife.net. Website: www.campuslife.net. **Contact:** Chris Lutes, editor. **35% freelance written.** Magazine published 9 times/year for the Christian life as it relates to today's teen. "*Campus Life* is a magazine for high-school and early college-age teenagers. Our editorial slant is not overtly religious. The indirect style is intended to create a safety zone with our readers and to reflect our philosophy that God is interested in all of life. Therefore, we publish 'message stories' side by side with general interest, humor, etc. We are also looking for stories that help high school students consider a Christian college education." Estab. 1942. Circ. 100,000. **Pays on acceptance.** Publishes ms an average of 5 months after acceptance. Byline given. Offers 50% kill fee. Buys first, one-time rights. Editorial lead time 4 months. Accepts queries by mail, e-mail, fax. Responds in 6 weeks to queries. Sample copy for $3 and 9½×11 SAE with 3 first-class stamps. Writer's guidelines online.

• No unsolicited mss.

Nonfiction: Humor, personal experience, photo feature. **Buys 15-20 mss/year.** Query with published clips. Length: 750-1,500 words. **Pays 15-20¢/word minimum.**

Reprints: Send tearsheet, photocopy or typed ms with rights for sale noted and information about when and where the material previously appeared. Pays $50.

Fiction: Buys 1-5 mss/year. Query with or without published clips. Length: 1,000-2,000 words. **Pays 15-20¢/word, and 2 contributor's copies.**

Tips: "The best way to break in to *Campus Life* is through writing first-person or as-told-to first-person stories. We want stories that capture a teen's everyday 'life lesson' experience. A first-person story must be highly descriptive and incorporate fictional technique. While avoiding simplistic religious answers, the story should demonstrate that Christian values or beliefs brought about a change in the young person's life. But query first with theme information telling the way this story would work for our audience."

$ COLLEGE BOUND MAGAZINE, The College Bound Network, 1200 South Ave., Suite 202, Staten Island NY 10314. (718)761-4800. Fax: (718)761-3300. E-mail: editorial@collegebound.net. Website: www.collegeboundmag.com. Editor-in-Chief: Gina LaGuardia. **Contact:** Dawn Kessler, senior editor. **70% freelance written.** Monthly magazine. "*College Bound Magazine* is designed to provide high school students with an inside look at all aspects of college life. College students from around the country (and those young at heart!) are welcome to serve as correspondents to provide our teen readership with real-life accounts and cutting-edge, expert advice on the college admissions process and beyond." Estab. 1987. Circ. 100,000 (regional issues). Pays 1 month upon publication. Publishes ms an average of 3-4 months after acceptance. Byline given. Buys first North American serial, first, electronic rights. Editorial lead time 4 months. Submit seasonal material 4 months in advance. Accepts queries by mail, e-mail. Accepts previously published material. Responds in 6 weeks to queries; 2 months to mss. Sample copy for 9×12 SAE and $2.27 postage. Writer's guidelines online.

Nonfiction: How-to (apply for college, prepare for the interview, etc.), personal experience (college experiences). No fillers, poetry, or fiction. **Buys 250+ mss/year.** Query with published clips. Length: 650-1,500 words. **Pays $50-100, plus 2 or 3 issues of magazine.**

Photos: Gina LaGuardia, editor-in-chief. State availability with submission. Buys one-time rights. Offers no additional payment for photos accepted with ms. Captions, identification of subjects required.

Columns/Departments: "Most departments are written in-house." **Buys 25 mss/year.** Query with published clips. **Pays $40-70.**

Fillers: Pays $15-25.

The online magazine carries original content not found in the print edition.

Tips: "College correspondents from around the country (and those young at heart) are welcome to serve as correspondents to provide our teen readership with both personal accounts and cutting-edge, expert advice on the college admissions process and beyond. We're looking for well-researched articles packed with real-life student anecdotes and expert insight on everything from dealing with dorm life, choosing the right college, and joining a fraternity or sorority, to college dating, cool campus happenings, scholarship scoring strategies, and other college issues."

N $ THE CONQUEROR, United Pentecostal Church International, 8855 Dunn Rd., Hazelwood MO 63042-2299. (314)837-7300. Fax: (314)837-4503. E-mail: youth@upci.org. Website: www.upci.org/youth. **Contact:** Travis Miller, editor. **80% freelance written.** Bimonthly magazine covering Christian youth. "*The Conqueror* addresses the social, intellectual, and spiritual concerns of youth aged 12-21 years from a Christian viewpoint." Estab. 1957. Circ. 6,000. Pays on publication. Publishes ms an average of 4 months after acceptance. Buys one-time rights. Editorial lead time 4 months. Submit seasonal material 4 months in advance. Accepts queries by mail, e-mail, fax. Accepts simultaneous submissions. Responds in 2 months to mss. Sample copy for 9×12 SAE with 3 first-class stamps. Writer's guidelines online.

Nonfiction: Essays, general interest, historical/nostalgic, inspirational, personal experience, religious. **Buys 18 mss/year.** Send complete ms. Length: 250-1,250 words. **Pays 6.5¢/word.**

Reprints: Accepts previously published submissions.

Photos: State availability with submission. Offers no additional payment for photos accepted with ms.

Columns/Departments: Time Out for Truth (applying Biblical truth to everyday living), 750 words. **Buys 6-10 mss/year.** Send complete ms. **Pays 6.5¢/word.**

Fiction: Adventure, ethnic, historical, humorous, mainstream, religious, slice-of-life vignettes. Send complete ms. Length: 250-1,250 words. **Pays 6.5¢/word.**

Poetry: Traditional. **Buys 2-4 poems/year.** Submit maximum 5 poems. **Pays $15.**

Fillers: Anecdotes, gags to be illustrated by cartoonist, short humor. **Buys 4/year.** Length: 100 words. **Pays $15.**

Tips: "Choose subjects relevant to single youth. Most subjects *are* relevant if properly handled. Today's youth are interested in more than clothes, fashion, careers and dating. Remember our primary objective: Inspiration—to portray happy, victorious living through faith in God."

N $ $ $ $ COSMOGIRL!, A Cool New Magazine for Teens, The Hearst Corporation, 224 W. 57th St., 3rd Floor, New York NY 10019. (212)649-3000. Fax: (212)489-9664. E-mail: inbox@cosmogirl.com. Website: www.cosmogirl.com. Editor: Atoosa Rubenstein. **Contact:** Kim St. Clair Bodden, managing editor. Monthly magazine covering fashion, beauty, photos and profiles of young celebs, advice, health and fitness, dating, relationships and finance. "CosmoGIRL! has the voice of a cool older sister. The magazine is conversational, funny, down-to-earth, and honest. We never talk down to our readers, who are 12- to 17-year-old girls." Estab. 1999. Circ. 1,054,638. Byline given. Offers 25% of orginal fee kill fee. Buys all rights. Editorial lead time 2 months. Accepts queries by mail. Responds in 2 months to queries. Sample copy for $2.99. Writer's guidelines by e-mail.

Nonfiction: Look at the masthead of a current issue for the appropriate editor. Looking for features with a news bent that pertains to teenagers' lives; quizzes; relationship stories; dynamic first-person stories. Interview/profile, opinion, personal experience. **Pays $1/ word.** Pays expenses of writers on assignment.

Photos: Put name, phone # and address on back of all photos. Send photos with submission.

Tips: "We expect writers to use industry experts for the piece; teen psychologists, people who have written books on whatever subject you're writing on. We prefer to consult with experts that are on the cutting edge of their field; the more specific the area of expertise, the better."

$ENCOUNTER, meeting God Face-to-Face, Standard Publishing, 8121 Hamilton Ave., Cincinnati OH 45231-2323. (513)931-4050. Fax: (513)931-0950. E-mail: kcarr@standardpub.com. Website: www.standardpub.com. **Contact:** Kelly Carr, editor. **90% freelance written.** Weekly magazine for "teens, age 13-19, from Christian backgrounds who generally receive this publication in their Sunday School classes or through subscriptions. We use freelance material in every issue. Our theme list is available on a quarterly basis. E-mail us to join." Estab. 1951. Circ. 35,000. **Pays on acceptance.** Publishes ms an average of 1 year after acceptance. Byline given. Buys first, second serial (reprint) rights. Submit seasonal material 1 year in advance. Accepts queries by mail, e-mail. Accepts previously published material. Accepts simultaneous submissions. Responds in 2 months to queries. Sample copy and writer's guidelines for 9×12 SAE with 2 first-class stamps.

Nonfiction: "We use articles on current issues from a christian point of view. Articles should speak directly to teens without being preachy. We are also interested in quizzes, interviews, and teen profiles." General interest (school, church, family, dating, sports, part-time jobs, music), humor, inspirational, interview/profile, personal experience, religious. No puzzles. Submit complete ms. Include Social Security umber on ms. Length: 800-1,100 words. **Pays 6-8¢/word.**

Reprints: Send ms with rights for sale noted. Pays 6¢/word.

Fiction: "Stories must appeal to younger and older teenagers and have well-constructed, interesting plots. The main characters should be contemporary teens who cope with modern-day problems using christian principles. Stories should be authentic and realistic." Adventure, humorous, religious, suspense. Short stories that have Christian principles. "No non-religious fiction." Send complete ms. Length: 800-1,100 words. **Pays 6-8¢/word.**

Tips: "Get to know teens before you begin to write for them. Evaluate their ideas, language, thoughts, and trends in order to effectively reach the teen market. Many manuscripts are rejected simply because the plot or vocabulary is outdated. Teens look for authenticity—all types of manuscripts should speak directly to teens using dialogue, situations, and illustrations that relate to them. The bottom line: Be real."

$FLORIDA LEADER, (for high school students), Oxendine Publishing, Inc., P.O. Box 14081, Gainesville FL 32604-2081. (352)373-6907. Fax: (352)373-8120. E-mail: info@studentleader.com. Website: www.floridaleader.com. Editor: W. H. Oxendine, Jr. **Contact:** Stephanie Reck, associate editor. Triannual magazine covering high school and pre-college youth. Estab. 1983. Circ. 50,000. Pays on publication. Publishes ms an average of 3 months after acceptance. Buys all rights. Submit seasonal material 4 months in advance. Accepts queries by mail, e-mail, fax. Accepts simultaneous submissions. Responds in 2 months to queries. Sample copy for $3.50 and 8×11 SAE, with 3 first-class stamps. Writer's guidelines online.

Nonfiction: Practical tips for going to college, student life, and leadership development. "No lengthy individual profiles or articles without primary and secondary sources of attribution." How-to, new product. Length: 250-1,000 words. **Payment varies. Pays students or first-time writers with contributor's copies.**

Photos: Send photos with submission. Reviews contact sheets, negatives, transparencies. Buys all rights. Offers $50/photo maximum. Captions, identification of subjects, model releases required.

Columns/Departments: College Life, The Lead Role, In Every Issue (quizzes, tips), Florida Forum (features Florida high school students), 250-1,000 words. **Buys 2 mss/year.** Query. **Pays $35-75.**

Fillers: Facts, newsbreaks, tips, book reviews. Length: 100-300 words. **Pays no payment.**

Tips: "Read other high school and college publications for current issues, interests. Send manuscripts or outlines for review. All sections open to freelance work. Always looking for lighter, humorous articles as well as features on Florida colleges and universities, careers, jobs. Multi-sourced (5-10) articles are best."

$ $GUIDEPOSTS FOR TEENS, Guideposts, 1050 Broadway, Suite 6, Chesterton IN 46304. (219)929-4429. Fax: (219)926-3839. E-mail: gp4t@guideposts.org. Website: www.gp4teens.com. Editor-in-Chief: Mary Lou Carney. **Contact:** Betsy Kohn, editor. **90% freelance written.** Bimonthly magazine serving as an inspiration for teens. "*Guideposts for Teens* is a 4-color, value-centered magazine that offers teens ages 12-18 true, first-person stories packed with adventure and inspiration. Our mission is to empower teens through lively, positive, thought-provoking content: music reviews, how-tos, advice, volunteer opportunities, news, quizzes, profiles of positive role models—both celebrity and ordinary teens. *Guideposts for Teens* helps our readers discover sound values that will enable them to lead successful, hope-filled lives." Estab. 1998. Circ. 250,000. **Pays on acceptance.** Byline sometimes given. Offers 25% kill fee. Buys all rights. Editorial lead time 6 months. Submit seasonal material 6 months in advance. Accepts queries by mail, e-mail. Accepts simultaneous submissions. Responds in 1 month to queries; 2 months to mss. Sample copy for $4.50. Writer's guidelines online.

Nonfiction: Nothing written from an adult point of view. How-to, humor, inspirational, interview/profile, personal experience, religious. **Buys 80 mss/year.** Query. Length: 700-2,000 words. **Pays $175-500 for assigned articles; $150-400 for unsolicited articles.** Pays expenses of writers on assignment.

Photos: State availability with submission. Buys one-time rights. Negotiates payment individually. Identification of subjects required.

Columns/Departments: Quiz (teen-relevant topics, teen language), 1,000 words; How-to (strong teen voice/quotes, teen topics), 750-1,000 words; Profiles (teens who initiate change/develop service projects), 300-500 words. **Buys 40 mss/year.** Query with published clips. **Pays $175-400.**

The online magazine carries original content not found in the print edition. Contact: Chris Lyon, managing editor.

Tips: "We are eagerly looking for a number of things: teen how-to pieces, quizzes, humor. Most of all, though, we are about TRUE STORIES in the *Guideposts* tradition. Teens in dangerous, inspiring, miraculous situations. These first-person (ghostwritten) true narratives are the backbone of *GP4T*—and what sets us apart from other publications."

N $ INSIGHT, A Spiritual Lift for Teens, The Review and Herald Publishing Association, 55 W. Oak Ridge Dr., Hagerstown MD 21740. E-mail: insight@rhpa.org. Website: www.insightmagazine.org. **Contact:** Dwain Neilson Esmond, editor. **80% freelance written.** Weekly magazine covering spiritual life of teenagers. "*Insight* publishes true dramatic stories, interviews, and community and mission service features that relate directly to the lives of Christian teenagers, particularly those with a Seventh-day Adventist background." Estab. 1970. Circ. 20,000. Pays on publication. Publishes ms an average of 4 months after acceptance. Byline given. Buys first, second serial (reprint) rights. Editorial lead time 6 months. Submit seasonal material 6 months in advance. Accepts queries by mail, e-mail, fax. Responds in 1 month to mss. Sample copy for $2 and #10 SASE. Writer's guidelines online.

- "'Big Deal' appears in *Insight* often, covering a topic of importance to teens. Each feature contains: An opening story involving real teens (can be written in first-person), "Scripture Picture" (a sidebar that discusses what the Bible says about the topic) and another sidebar (optional) that adds more perspective and help.

Nonfiction: How-to (teen relationships and experiences), humor, interview/profile, personal experience, photo feature, religious. **Buys 120 mss/year.** Send complete ms. Length: 500-2,000 words. **Pays $25-150 for assigned articles; $25-125 for unsolicited articles.**

Reprints: Send ms with rights for sale noted and information about when and where the material previously appeared. Pays $50.

Photos: State availability with submission. Reviews contact sheets, negatives, transparencies, prints. Buys one-time rights. Negotiates payment individually. Model releases required.

Columns/Departments: Big Deal (topic of importance to teens) 1,200-1,700 words; Interviews (Christian culture figures, especially musicians), 2,000 words; It Happened to Me (first-person teen experiences containing spiritual insights), 1,000 words; On the Edge (dramatic true stories about Christians), 2,000 words; So I Said...(true short stories in the first person of common, everyday events and experiences that taught the writer something), 300-500 words. Send complete ms. **Pays $25-125.**

Tips: "Skim 2 months of *Insight*. Write about your teen experiences. Use informed, contemporary style and vocabulary. Become a Christian if you haven't already."

$ $ LISTEN MAGAZINE, Celebrating Positive Choices, The Health Connection, 55 W. Oak Ridge Dr., Hagerstown MD 21740. (301)393-3294. Fax: (301)393-4055. E-mail: listen@healthconnection.org. Website: www.listenmagazine.org. Editor: Anita Jacobs. **Contact:** Anita Jacobs, editor. **50% freelance written.** Monthly magazine specializing in tobacco, drug, and alcohol prevention, presenting positive alternatives to various tobacco, drug, and alcohol dependencies. "*Listen* is used in many high school classes and by professionals: medical personnel, counselors, law enforcement officers, educators, youth workers, etc. *Listen publishes fiction about giving teens choices about real-life situations and moral issues in a secular way." Circ. 40,000.* **Pays on acceptance.** Publishes ms an average of 6 months after acceptance. Byline given. Buys first rights. first rights for use in *Listen*, reprints, and associated material. Accepts queries by mail, e-mail, fax. Accepts previously published material. Accepts simultaneous submissions. Responds in 2 months to queries. Sample copy for $2 and 9×12 SASE. Writer's guidelines for SASE, by e-mail, fax or on website.

Break in with "a fresh approach with a surprise ending."

Nonfiction: Seeks articles that deal with causes of drug use such as poor self-concept, family relations, social skills, peer pressure. Especially interested in youth-slanted articles or personality interviews encouraging nonalcoholic and nondrug ways of life and showing positive alternatives. Also interested in good activity articles of interest to teens; an activity that teens would want to do instead of taking abusive substances because they're bored. Teenage point of view is essential. Also seeks narratives which portray teens dealing with youth conflicts, especially those related to the use of or temptation to use harmful substances. Growth of the main character should be shown. "Submit an article with an ending that catches you by surprise. We don't want typical alcoholic story/skid-row bum, or AA stories. We are also being inundated with drunk-driving accident stories. Unless yours is unique, consider another topic." **Buys 30-50 unsolicited mss/year.** Query. Length: 1,000-1,200 words. **Pays 5-10¢/word.** Sometimes pays expenses of writers on assignment.

Reprints: Send photocopy of article or typed ms with rights for sale noted and information about when and where the material previously appeared. Pays their regular rates.

Photos: Color photos preferred, but b&w acceptable. Purchased with accompanying ms. Captions required.

Fiction: Anti-drug, alcohol, tobacco, positive role models. Query with published clips or send complete ms. Length: 1,000-1,200. **Pays $50-250, and 3 contributor's copies; additional copies $2.**

Fillers: Word square/general puzzles are also considered. **Pays $15.**

Tips: "True stories are good, especially if they have a unique angle. Other authoritative articles need a fresh approach. In query, briefly summarize article idea and logic of why you feel it's good. Make sure you've read the magazine to understand our approach."

$ $ LIVE, A Weekly Journal of Practical Christian Living, Gospel Publishing House, 1445 N. Boonville Ave., Springfield MO 65802-1894. (417)862-2781. Fax: (417)862-6059. E-mail: rl-live@gph.org. Website: www.radiantlife.org. **Contact:** Paul W. Smith, senior editor, adult resources. **100% freelance written.** Weekly magazine for weekly distribution covering practical Christian living. "*LIVE* is a take-home paper distributed weekly in young adult and adult Sunday school classes. We seek to encourage Christians in living for God through fiction and true stories which apply Biblical principles to everyday problems." Estab. 1928. Circ. 115,000. **Pays on acceptance.** Publishes ms an average of 18 months after acceptance. Byline given. Buys first, second serial (reprint) rights. Editorial lead time 12 months. Submit seasonal material 18 months in advance. Accepts queries by mail, e-mail, fax, phone. Accepts simultaneous submissions. Responds in 2 weeks to queries; 2 months to mss. Sample copy for SASE. Writer's guidelines for SASE or on website.

O→ Break in with "true stories that demonstrate how the principles in the Bible work in everyday circumstances as well as crises."

Nonfiction: Inspirational, religious. No preachy articles or stories that refer to religious myths (e.g., Santa Claus, Easter Bunny, etc.). **Buys 50-100 mss/year.** Send complete ms. Length: 400-1,500 words. **Pays 7-10¢/word.**

Reprints: Send tearsheet, photocopy or typed ms with rights for sale noted and information about when and where the material previously appeared. Pays 7¢/word.

Photos: Send photos with submission. Reviews 35mm transparencies and 3×4 prints or larger. Buys one-time rights. Offers $35-60/photo. Identification of subjects required.

Fiction: Paul W. Smith, editor. Religious, inspirational, prose poem. No preachy fiction, fiction about Bible characters, or stories that refer to religious myths (e.g., Santa Claus, Easter Bunny, etc.). No science or Bible fiction. No controversial stories about such subjects as feminism, war or capital punishment. **Buys 50 mss/year.** Send complete ms. Length: 800-1,600 words. **Pays 7-10¢/word.**

Poetry: Free verse, haiku, light verse, traditional. **Buys 15-24 poems/year.** Submit maximum 3 poems. Length: 12-25 lines. **Pays $35-60.**

Fillers: Anecdotes, short humor. **Buys 12-36/year.** Length: 300-600 words. **Pays 7-10¢/word.**

Tips: "Don't moralize or be preachy. Provide human interest articles with Biblical life application. Stories should consist of action, not just thought-life; interaction, not just insight. Heroes and heroines should rise above failures, take risks for God, prove that scriptural principles meet their needs. Conflict and suspense should increase to a climax! Avoid pious conclusions. Characters should be interesting, believable, and realistic. Avoid stereotypes. Characters should be active, not just pawns to move the plot along. They should confront conflict and change in believable ways. Describe the character's looks and reveal his personality through his actions to such an extent that the reader feels he has met that person. Readers should care about the character enough to finish the story. Feature racial, ethnic, and regional characters in rural and urban settings."

N $ $ THE NEW ERA, 50 E. North Temple, Salt Lake City UT 84150. (801)240-2951. Fax: (801)240-2270. E-mail: cur-editorial-newera@ldschurch.org. **Contact:** Richard Romney, managing editor. **20% freelance written.** Monthly magazine for young people (ages 12-18) of the Church of Jesus Christ of Latter-day Saints (Mormon), their church leaders and teachers. Estab. 1971. Circ. 230,000. **Pays on acceptance.** Publishes ms an average of 1 year after acceptance. Byline given. Buys all rights. Submit seasonal material 1 year in advance. Accepts queries by mail, e-mail, fax. Responds in 2 months to queries. Sample copy for $1.50 and 9×12 SAE with 2 first-class stamps. Writer's guidelines for SASE.

Nonfiction: Material that shows how the Church of Jesus Christ of Latter-day Saints is relevant in the lives of young people today. Must capture the excitement of being a young Latter-day Saint. Special interest in the experiences of young Mormons in other countries. No general library research or formula pieces without the *New Era* slant and feel. How-to, humor, inspirational, interview/profile, personal experience, informational. Query. Length: 150-1,200 words. **Pays 3-12¢/word.** Pays expenses of writers on assignment.

Photos: Uses b&w photos and transparencies with manuscripts. Individual photos used for *Photo of the Month*. Payment depends on use, $10-125 per photo.

Columns/Departments: Of All Things (news of young Mormons around the world); How I Know; Scripture Lifeline. **Pays 3-12¢/word.**

Poetry: Must relate to editorial viewpoint. Free verse, light verse, traditional, blank verse, all other forms. **Pays 25¢/line minimum.**

Tips: "The writer must be able to write from a Mormon point of view. We're especially looking for stories about successful family relationships and personal growth. We anticipate using more staff-produced material. This means freelance quality will have to improve. Try breaking in with a department piece for 'How I Know' or 'Scripture Lifeline.' Well-written, personal experiences are always in demand."

N $ ONE WORLD MAGAZINE, The Hearst Corp., 648 Broadway, Suite 201, New York NY 10012-2301. (212)375-9500. Fax: (212)375-9095. E-mail: letters@oneworldmag.com. Website: www.oneworldmag.com. Editor-in-Chief: Raquel Cepeda. Bimonthly magazine. "*One World Magazine* is an urban lifestyle magazine focusing on the hip-hop scene in the States and abroad for the 18-34 multicultural set of men and women." Circ. 225,000. Editorial lead time 1 month. Sample copy not available.

Tips: "We're always looking for pitches related to the international hip-hop scene."

$ $ SPIRIT, Lectionary-based Weekly for Catholic Teens, Good Ground Press, 1884 Randolph Ave., St. Paul MN 55105-1700. (651)690-7010. Fax: (651)690-7039. E-mail: jmcsj9@aol.com. Managing Editor: Therese Sherlock, CSJ. **Contact:** Joan Mitchell, CSJ, editor. **50% freelance written.** Weekly newsletter for religious education of Catholic high schoolers. "We want realistic fiction and nonfiction that raises current ethical and religious questions and that deals with conflicts that teens face in multi-racial contexts. The fact we are a religious publication does *not* mean we want pious, moralistic fiction." Estab. 1981. Circ. 26,000. Pays on publication. Publishes ms an average of 6 months after acceptance. Byline given. Buys all rights. Editorial lead time 6 months. Submit seasonal material 6 months in advance. Accepts queries by mail, e-mail, fax. Accepts simultaneous submissions. Responds in 1 month to queries. Sample copy and writer's guidelines free.

Nonfiction: "No Christian confessional, born-again pieces." Interview/profile, personal experience, religious, Roman Catholic leaders, human interest features, social justice leaders, projects, humanitarians. **Buys 4 mss/year.** Query with published clips or send complete ms. Length: 1,000-1,200 words. **Pays $200-225 for assigned articles; $150 for unsolicited articles.**

Photos: State availability with submission. Reviews 8×10 prints. Buys one-time rights. Offers $85-125/photo. Identification of subjects required.

Fiction: "We want realistic pieces for and about teens—nonpedantic, nonpious. We need good Christmas stories that show spirit of the season, and stories about teen relationship conflicts (boy/girl, parent/teen)." Conflict vignettes. **Buys 10 mss/year.** Query with published clips or send complete ms. Length: 1,000-1,200 words. **Pays $150-200.**

Tips: "Writers must be able to write from and for teen point of view rather than adult or moralistic point of view. In nonfiction, interviewed teens must speak for themselves. Query to receive call for stories, spec sheet, sample issues."

N $ TEEN BEAT, Laufer Media, 6430 Sunset Blvd., Hollywood CA 90028. (323)462-4267. Fax: (323)462-4341. Editor: Leesa Coble. Bimonthly magazine. Written for today's teenage girls featuring popular personalities from T.V., movies and music. Circ. 154,743. Sample copy not available.

N $ TIGER BEAT, Laufer Media, 6430 Sunset Blvd., Suite 700, Hollywood CA 90028. (323)462-4267. Fax: (323)462-4341. Editor: Leesa Coble. Bimonthly magazine. Dedicated to serve the young female fans of musical acts, T.V., and movie stars. Circ. 300,000. Editorial lead time 3 months. Sample copy not available.

$ TWIST, Bauer Publishing, 270 Sylvan Ave., Englewood Cliffs NJ 07632. Fax: (201)569-4458. E-mail: twistmail@aol.com. Website: www.twistmagazine.com. Editor: Liz Nice. **Contact:** Kristin McKeon Nieto, deputy editor. **5% freelance written.** Monthly entertainment magazine targeting 14- to 19-year-old girls. Estab. 1997. Circ. 700,000. **Pays on acceptance.** Publishes ms an average of 3 months after acceptance. Offers 20% kill fee. Buys first North American serial rights. Editorial lead time 3 months. Submit seasonal material 4 months in advance. Accepts queries by mail. Accepts simultaneous submissions. Responds in 1 month to queries. Writer's guidelines online.

Nonfiction: "No articles written from an adult point of view about teens—i.e., a mother's or teacher's personal account." Personal experience (real teens' experiences, preferably in first person). **Payment varies according to assignment.** Pays expenses of writers on assignment.

Photos: State availability with submission. Negotiates payment individually. Identification of subjects, model releases required.

The online magazine carries original content not found in the print edition. Contact: Hicran Kuday.

Tips: "Tone must be conversational, neither condescending to teens nor trying to be too slangy. If possible, send clips that show an ability to write for the teen market. We are in search of real-life stories, and writers who can find teens with compelling real-life experiences (who are willing to use their full names and photographs in the magazine). Please refer to a current issue to see examples of tone and content. No e-mail queries or submissions, please."

$ $ WHAT MAGAZINE, What! Publishers Inc., 108-93 Lombard Ave., Winnipeg MB R3B 3B1, Canada. (204)985-8160. Fax: (204)957-5638. E-mail: what@whatmagazine.ca. **Contact:** Barbara Chabai, editor/publisher. **40% freelance written.** Magazine published 5 times during the school year covering teen issues and pop culture. "*What Magazine* is distributed to high school students across Canada. We produce a mag that is empowering, interactive and entertaining. We respect the reader—today's teens are smart and creative (and critical)." Estab. 1987. Circ. 250,000. Pays 1 month after publication. Publishes ms an average of 3 months after acceptance. Byline given. Offers negotiable kill fee. Buys first North American serial rights. Editorial lead time 5 months. Submit seasonal material 5 months in advance. Accepts queries by mail, e-mail, fax. Responds in 2 months to queries; 1 month to mss. Sample copy for 9×12 SAE with Canadian postage. Writer's guidelines for #10 SAE with Canadian postage.

Nonfiction: General interest, interview/profile, issue-oriented features. No cliché teen material. **Buys 6-10 mss/year.** Query with published clips. Length: 700-1,900 words. **Pays $175-400 (Canadian).** Sometimes pays expenses of writers on assignment.

Photos: Send photos with submission. Reviews transparencies, 4×6 prints. Negotiates payment individually. Identification of subjects required.

Tips: "We have an immediate need for savvy freelancers to contribute features, short articles, interviews, and reviews that speak to our intelligent teen audience. Looking for fresh talent and new ideas in the areas of entertainment, pop culture, teen issues, international events as they relate to readers, celebs and 'real people' profiles, lifestyle articles, extreme sports and any other stories of relevance to today's Canadian teen."

N $ WINNER, Saying No To Drugs and Yes To Life, The Health Connection, 55 W. Oak Ridge Dr., Hagerstown MD 21740. (301)393-3294. Fax: (301)393-4055. E-mail: winner@healthconnection.org. Website: www.winnermagazine.org. **Contact:** Anita Jacobs, editor. **30% freelance written.** Monthly magazine covering positive lifestyle choices for students in grades 4-6. "*Winner* is a teaching tool to help students learn the dangers in abusive substances, such as tobacco, alcohol, and other drugs, as well as at-rish behaviors. It also focuses on everyday problems such as dealing with divorce, sibling rivalry, coping with grief, and healthy diet, to mention just a few." Estab. 1956. Circ. 12,000. **Pays on acceptance.** Publishes ms an average of 6-9 months after acceptance. Byline sometimes given. Offers 50% kill fee. Buys first North American serial, first rights. Editorial lead time 5 months. Submit seasonal material 6-8 months in advance. Accepts queries by mail, e-mail, fax, phone. Accepts simultaneous submissions. Responds in 4-6 weeks to queries; 2-3 months to mss. Sample copy for $2 and 9×12 SAE with 2 First-Class stamps. Writer's guidelines for SASE, by e-mail, fax or on website.

Nonfiction: General interest, humor, drug/alcohol/tobacco activities, personalities, family relationships, friends. No occult, mysteries. "I prefer true-to-life stories." Query or send complete ms. Length: 600-650 words. **Pays $50-80.** Sometimes pays expenses of writers on assignment.
Photos: Doug Bendall, designer. State availability of or send photos with submission. Reviews GIF/JPEG files. Buys one-time rights. Negotiates payment individually. Model releases required.
Columns/Departments: Personality (kids making a difference in their community), 600 words; Fun & Games (dangers of tobacco, alcohol, and other drugs), 400 words. **Buys 9 mss/year.** Query. **Pays $50-80.**
Fiction: Humorous, true-to-life stories dealing with problems preteens face. No suspense or mystery. **Buys 18 mss/year.** Send complete ms. Length: 600-650 words. **Pays $50-80.**

$WITH, The Magazine for Radical Christian Youth, Faith and Life Press, 722 Main St., P.O. Box 347, Newton KS 67114-0347. (316)283-5100. Fax: (316)283-0454. E-mail: carold@mennoniteusa.org. Website: www.withonline.org. **Contact:** Carol Duerksen, editor. **60% freelance written.** Magazine published 6 times/year for teenagers. "We are a Christian youth magazine that strives to help youth be radically commited to a personal relationship with Jesus Christ, to peace and justice, and to sharing God's good news through word and action." Estab. 1968. Circ. 4,000. **Pays on acceptance.** Publishes ms an average of 1 year after acceptance. Byline given. Buys one-time rights. Submit seasonal material 6 months in advance. Accepts queries by mail, fax. Accepts previously published material. Accepts simultaneous submissions. Responds in 1 month to queries; 2 months to mss. Sample copy for 9×12 SAE with 4 first-class stamps. Writer's guidelines and theme list for #10 SASE. Additional detailed guidelines for first-person stories, how-to articles, and/or fiction available for #10 SASE.

O→ Break in with "well-written true stories from teen's standpoint."

Nonfiction: How-to, humor, personal experience, religious, youth. **Buys 15 mss/year.** Send complete ms. Length: 400-1,800 words. **Pays 5¢/word for simultaneous rights, higher rates for articles written on assignment; 3¢/word for reprint rights and for unsolicited articles.** Sometimes pays expenses of writers on assignment.
Reprints: Send ms with rights for sale noted and information about when and where the material previously appeared. Pays 60% of amount paid for an original article.
Photos: Send photos with submission. Reviews 8×10 color prints. Buys one-time rights. Offers $10-50/photo. Identification of subjects required.
Fiction: Ethnic, humorous, mainstream, religious, youth, parables. **Buys 15 mss/year.** Send complete ms. Length: 500-2,000 words. **Pays 5¢/word for simultaneous rights, higher rates for articles written on assignment; 3¢/word for reprint rights and for unsolicited articles.**
Poetry: Avant-garde, free verse, haiku, light verse, traditional. **Buys 0-2 poems/year. Pays $10-25.**
Tips: "We're looking for more wholesome humor, not necessarily religious—fiction, nonfiction, cartoons, light verse. Christmas and Easter material has a good chance with us because we receive so little of it."

N $YM, Gruner & Jahr, 15 E. 26th St., New York NY 10010. Website: www.ym.com. Editor-in-Chief: Christina Kelly. Publisher: Laura McEwen. **Contact:** Jana Siegal Banin, senior features editor. **75% freelance written.** Magazine published 11 times/year. Magazine covering teenage girls/dating. "We are a national magazine for young women ages 13-24. They're bright, enthusiastic, and inquisitive. Our goal is to guide them—in effect, to be a 'best friend' and help them through the many exciting, yet often challenging, experiences of young adulthood." Estab. 1940s. Circ. 2,200,000. **Pays on acceptance.** Byline given. Offers 25% kill fee. Buys all rights. Editorial lead time 4 months. Submit seasonal material 5 months in advance. Accepts simultaneous submissions. Responds in 1 month to queries. Writer's guidelines free.
Nonfiction: How-to, interview/profile, personal experience, first-person stories. Special issues: "*YM* publishes 1 special prom issue a year." Query with published clips. Length: 2,000 words maximum. Pays expenses of writers on assignment.
Fiction: "We also accept fiction submissions."
Tips: "Our relationship articles are loaded with advice from psychologists and real teenagers. Areas most open to freelancers are: 2,000-word stories covering a personal triumph over adversity—incorporating a topical social/political problem; 2,000-word relationship stories; 1,200-word relationship articles; and 800-word quizzes. All articles should be lively and informative, but not academic in tone, and any 'expert' opinions (psychologists, authors, and teachers) should be included as a supplement to the feelings and experiences of young women. Do not call our offices."

$YOUNG & ALIVE, Christian Record Services, P.O. Box 6097, Lincoln NE 68506. Website: www.christianrecord.org. **Contact:** Gaylena Gibson, editor. **95% freelance written.** Large-print Christian material for sight-impaired people age 12-25 (also in braille), covering health, handicapped people, uplifting articles. "Write for an interdenominational Christian audience—we also like to portray handicapped individuals living normal lives or their positive impact on those around them." Submit seasonal material anytime. Estab. 1976. Circ. 25,000 large print; 3,000 braille. **Pays on acceptance.** Publishes ms an average of 3 years after acceptance. Byline given. Buys one-time rights. Accepts simultaneous submissions. Responds in 1 year to mss. Sample copy for 7×10 SAE with 5 first-class stamps. Writer's guidelines for #10 SASE or included with sample copy.
Nonfiction: Essays, general interest, historical/nostalgic, humor, inspirational, personal experience, travel, adventure (true), biography, camping, careers, handicapped, health, hobbies, holidays, nature, sports. **Buys 40 mss/year.** Send complete ms. Length: 200-1,400 words. **Pays 4-5¢/word, and complimentary copies.**
Photos: Send photos with submission. Reviews 3×5 to 10×12 prints. Buys one-time rights. Negotiates payment individually. Model releases required.
Fillers: Anecdotes, facts, short humor. Length: 300 words maximum. **Pays 4¢/word.**
Tips: "Make sure article has a strong ending that ties everything together. Pretend someone else wrote it—would it hold your interest? Draw your readers into the story by being specific rather than abstract or general."

$ $ YOUNG SALVATIONIST, The Salvation Army, P.O. Box 269, Alexandria VA 22313-0269. (703)684-5500. Fax: (703)684-5539. E-mail: ys@usn.salvationarmy.org. Website: www.thewarcry.com. **Contact:** Laura Ezzell, managing editor. **80% freelance written.** Monthly magazine for high school teens. "Only material with Christian perspective with practical real-life application will be considered." Circ. 48,000. **Pays on acceptance.** Publishes ms an average of 6 months after acceptance. Byline given. Buys first North American serial, first, one-time, second serial (reprint) rights. Submit seasonal material 6 months in advance. Responds in 2 months to mss. Sample copy for 9×12 SAE with 3 first-class stamps or on website. Writer's guidelines and theme list for #10 SASE or on website.

- Works with a small number of new/unpublished writers each year. Accepts complete mss by mail and e-mail.

O→ "Our greatest need is for nonfiction pieces based in real life rather than theory or theology. Practical living articles are especially needed. We receive many fiction submissions but few good nonfiction."

Nonfiction: "Articles should deal with issues of relevance to teens (high school students) today; avoid 'preachiness' or moralizing." How-to, humor, inspirational, interview/profile, personal experience, photo feature, religious. **Buys 60 mss/year.** Send complete ms. Length: 1,000-1,500 words. **Pays 15¢/word for first rights.**

Reprints: Send tearsheet, photocopy or typed ms with rights for sale noted and information about when and where the material previously appeared. Pays 10¢/word for reprints.

Fiction: Only a small amount is used. Adventure, fantasy, humorous, religious, romance, science fiction, (all from a Christian perspective). **Buys few mss/year.** Length: 500-1,200 words. **Pays 15¢/word.**

Tips: "Study magazine, familiarize yourself with the unique 'Salvationist' perspective of *Young Salvationist*; learn a little about the Salvation Army; media, sports, sex, and dating are strongest appeal."

$ $ YOUTH UPDATE, St. Anthony Messenger Press, 28 W. Liberty St., Cincinnati OH 45202-6498. (513)241-5615. Fax: (513)241-0399. E-mail: carolann@americancatholic.org. Website: www.americancatholic.org. **Contact:** Carol Ann Morrow, editor. **90% freelance written.** Monthly newsletter of faith life for teenagers. *Youth Update* is "designed to attract, instruct, guide, and challenge Catholics of high school age by applying the Gospel to modern problems/situations." Circ. 20,000. **Pays on acceptance.** Publishes ms an average of 6 months after acceptance. Byline given. Responds in 3 months to queries. Sample copy for #10 SASE. Writer's guidelines by e-mail.

Nonfiction: Inspirational, practical self help, spiritual. No fiction. **Buys 12 mss/year.** Query or send outline. "Identify yourself on the envelope; don't use lots of stamps, but have your envelope weighed and postage neatly affixed." **Pays $400-475.**

The online magazine mirrors the print edition. Contact: Carol Ann Morrow.

Tips: "Write for a 15 year old with a C+ average."

TRAVEL, CAMPING & TRAILER

Travel magazines give travelers in-depth information about destinations, detailing the best places to go, attractions in the area, and sites to see—but they also keep them up to date about potential negative aspects of these destinations. Publications in this category tell tourists and campers the where-tos and how-tos of travel. This category is extremely competitive, demanding quality writing, background information, and professional photography. Each publication has its own slant. Sample copies should be studied carefully before sending submissions.

$ AAA GOING PLACES, Magazine for Today's Traveler, AAA Auto Club South, 1515 N. Westshore Blvd., Tampa FL 33607. (813)289-5923. Fax: (813)289-6245. Editor-In-Chief: Sandy Klim. **50% freelance written.** Bimonthly magazine on auto tips, cruise travel, tours. Estab. 1982. Circ. 2,500,000. Pays on publication. Publishes ms an average of 6 months after acceptance. Byline given. Buys one-time rights. Submit seasonal material 9 months in advance. Accepts simultaneous submissions. Responds in 2 months to queries; 2 months to mss. Sample copy not available. Writer's guidelines for SAE.

Nonfiction: Travel stories feature domestic and international destinations with practical information and where to stay, dine, and shop, as well as personal anecdotes and historical background; they generally relate to tours currently offered by AAA Travel Agency. Historical/nostalgic, how-to, humor, interview/profile, personal experience, photo feature, travel. Special issues: Cruise Guide and Europe Issue. **Buys 15 mss/year.** Send complete ms. Length: 500-1,500 words. **Pays $50/printed page.**

Photos: State availability with submission. Reviews 2×2 transparencies. Offers no additional payment for photos accepted with ms. Captions required.

Columns/Departments: AAAway We Go (local attractions in Florida, Georgia, or Tennessee).

Tips: "We prefer lively, upbeat stories that appeal to a well-traveled, sophisticated audience, bearing in mind that AAA is a conservative company."

$ $ ARUBA NIGHTS, Nights Publications, Inc., 1831 Rene Levesque Blvd. W., Montreal QC H3H 1R4, Canada. (514)931-1987. Fax: (514)931-6273. E-mail: editor@nightspublications.com. Website: www.nightspublications.com. **Contact:** Sonya Plowman, editor. **90% freelance written.** Annual magazine covering the Aruban vacation lifestyle experience with an upscale, upbeat touch. Estab. 1988. Circ. 225,000. **Pays on acceptance.** Publishes ms an average of 9 months after acceptance. Byline given for feature articles. Buys first North American serial, first caribbean rights. Editorial lead time 1 month. Accepts queries by mail, e-mail, fax. Responds in 2 weeks to queries; 1 month to mss. Writer's guidelines by e-mail.

O→ *Aruba Nights* is looking for more articles on nightlife experiences.

Nonfiction: General interest, historical/nostalgic, how-to (relative to Aruba vacationers), humor, inspirational, interview/profile, opinion, personal experience, photo feature, travel, ecotourism, Aruban culture, art, activities, entertainment, topics relative to vacationers in Aruba. "No negative pieces." **Buys 5-10 mss/year.** Send complete ms, include SAE with Canadian postage or IRC. Length: 250-750 words. **Pays $100-250.**

Photos: State availability with submission. Reviews transparencies. Buys one-time rights. Pays $50/photo. Captions, identification of subjects, model releases required.

Tips: "Be descriptive and entertaining and make sure stories are factually correct. Stories should immerse the reader in a sensory adventure. Focus on specific, individual aspects of the Aruban lifestyle and vacation experience (e.g., art, music, culture, a colorful local character, a personal experience, etc.), rather than generalized overviews. Provide an angle that will be entertaining to vacationers who are already there. E-mail submissions preferred."

$ $ ASU TRAVEL GUIDE, ASU Travel Guide, Inc., 1525 Francisco Blvd. E., San Rafael CA 94901. (415)459-0300. Fax: (415)459-0494. E-mail: christopher_gil@asutravelguide.com. Website: www.asutravelguide.com. **Contact:** Christopher Gil, managing editor. **80% freelance written.** Quarterly guidebook covering international travel features and travel discounts for well-traveled airline employees. Estab. 1970. Circ. 40,000. **Pays on acceptance.** Publishes ms an average of 4 months after acceptance. Byline given. Buys first North American serial, first, second serial (reprint) rights. Submit seasonal material 6 months in advance. Accepts previously published material. Accepts simultaneous submissions. Responds in 1 year to queries; 1 year to mss. Sample copy for 6×9 SAE and 5 first-class stamps. Writer's guidelines for #10 SASE.

Nonfiction: International travel articles "similar to those run in consumer magazines. Not interested in amateur efforts from inexperienced travelers or personal experience articles that don't give useful information to other travelers." Destination pieces only; no "Tips on Luggage" articles. Unsolicited mss or queries without SASE will not be acknowledged. No telephone queries. Travel (international). **Buys 16 mss/year.** Length: 1,800 words. **Pays $200.**

Reprints: Send tearsheet and information about when and where the material previously appeared. Pays 100% of amount paid for an original article.

Photos: "Interested in clear, high-contrast photos." Reviews 5×7 and 8×10 b&w or color prints, JPEGs (300 dpi). Payment for photos is included in article price; photos from tourist offices are acceptable.

Tips: "Query with samples of travel writing and a list of places you've recently visited. We appreciate clean and simple style. Keep verbs in the active tense and involve the reader in what you write. Avoid 'cute' writing, coined words, and stale clichés. The most frequent mistakes made by writers in completing an article for us are: 1) Lazy writing—using words to describe a place that could describe any destination such as 'there is so much to do in (fill in destination) that whole guidebooks have been written about it'; 2) Including fare and tour package information—our readers make arrangements through their own airline."

$ $ BONAIRE NIGHTS, Nights Publications, Inc., 1831 René Levesque Blvd. W., Montreal QC H3H 1R4, Canada. (514)931-1987. Fax: (514)931-6273. E-mail: editor@nightspublications.com. **Contact:** Sonya Plowman, editor. **90% freelance written.** Annual magazine covering Bonaire vacation experience. Estab. 1993. Circ. 65,000. Byline given for features. Buys first North American serial, first caribbean rights. Editorial lead time 1 month. Accepts queries by mail, e-mail, fax. Responds in 2 weeks to queries; 1 month to mss. Writer's guidelines by e-mail.

Nonfiction: General interest, historical/nostalgic, how-to, humor, interview/profile, opinion, personal experience, photo feature, travel, lifestyle, local culture, art, architecture, activities, scuba diving, snorkeling, ecotourism. **Buys 6-9 mss/year.** E-mail submissions preferred. Mailed mss must include an e-mail address for correspondence. Length: 250-750 words. **Pays $100-250.**

Photos: State availability with submission. Pays $50/published photo. Captions, identification of subjects, model releases required.

Tips: "Focus on the Bonaire lifestyle, what sets it apart from other islands. We want personal experience on specific attractions and culture, not generalized overviews. Be positive and provide an angle that will appeal to vacationers who are already there. Our style is upbeat, friendly, fluid, and descriptive."

$ CAMPERWAYS, MIDWEST RV TRAVELER, FLORIDA RV TRAVELER, NORTHEAST OUTDOORS, SOUTHERN RV & SOUTHWEST RV TRAVELER, (formerly *Camperways*, *Camp-Orama*, *Carolina RV Traveler*, *Florida RV Traveler*, *Northeast Outdoors*, *Southern RV* & *Texas RV*), Woodall Publications Corp., 2575 Vista Del Mar Dr., Ventura CA 93001. (800)323-9076. Fax: (805)667-4122. E-mail: editor@woodallpub.com. Website: www.woodalls.com. **Contact:** Jennifer Detweiler, senior managing editor. **75% freelance written.** Monthly tabloids covering RV lifestyle. "We're looking for articles of interest to RVers. Lifestyle articles, destinations, technical tips, interesting events and the like make up the bulk of our publications. We also look for region-specific travel and special interest articles." Circ. 30,000. **Pays on acceptance.** Byline given. Offers 50% kill fee. Buys first North American serial rights. Accepts queries by mail, e-mail. Sample copy for free. Writer's guidelines for #10 SASE.

- Accepts queries in June, July, and August for upcoming year.

Nonfiction: How-to, humor, personal experience, technical, travel. No "Camping From Hell" articles. **Buys approximately 500 mss/year.** Length: 500-2,000 words. **Payment varies.**

Photos: Prefers slides. State availability with submission. Reviews negatives, 4×5 transparencies, 4×5 prints. Buys first North American serial rights. Captions, identification of subjects required.

Columns/Departments: On annual contract with regular writers. Submit ideas via e-mail or mail, with several sample columns.

Tips: "Be an expert in RVing. Make your work readable to a wide variety of readers, from novices to full-timers."

$ CAMPING CANADA'S RV LIFESTYLE MAGAZINE, (formerly *Camping Canada's RV Lifestyles*), 1020 Brevik Place, Mississauga ON L4W 4N7, Canada. (905)624-8218. Fax: (905)624-6764. Website: www.rvlifemag.com. **Contact:** Norm Rosen, vp special projects. **50% freelance written.** Magazine published 7 times/year (monthly January-June and November). "*Camping Canada's RV Lifestyle Magazine* is geared to readers who enjoy travel/camping. Upbeat pieces only. Readers vary from owners of towable trailers or motorhomes to young families and entry-level campers (no tenting)." Estab. 1971. Circ. 51,000. Pays on publication. Byline given. Buys first North American serial rights. Editorial lead time 2 months. Responds in 1 month to queries; 2 months to mss. Sample copy for free. Writer's guidelines not available.

Nonfiction: How-to, personal experience, technical, travel. No inexperienced, unresearched, or too general pieces. **Buys 20-30 mss/year.** Query. Length: 1,200-2,000 words. **Payment varies.**

Photos: Send photos with submission. Buys one-time rights. Offers no additional payment for photos accepted with ms.

Tips: "Pieces should be slanted toward RV living. All articles must have an RV slant. Canadian content regulations require 95% Canadian writers."

$ CAMPING TODAY, Official Publication of the Family Campers & RVers, 126 Hermitage Rd., Butler PA 16001-8509. (724)283-7401. **Contact:** DeWayne Johnston, June Johnston, editors. **30% freelance written.** Monthly official membership publication of the FCRV. *Camping Today* is "the largest nonprofit family camping and RV organization in the United States and Canada. Members are heavily oriented toward RV travel, both weekend and extended vacations. Concentration is on member activities in chapters. Group is also interested in conservation and wildlife. The majority of members are retired." Estab. 1983. Circ. 25,000. Pays on publication. Publishes ms an average of 6 months after acceptance. Byline given. Buys one-time rights. Submit seasonal material 3 months in advance. Accepts simultaneous submissions. Responds in 2 months to queries; 2 months to mss. Sample copy and guidelines for 4 first-class stamps. Writer's guidelines for #10 SASE.

Nonfiction: Humor (camping or travel related), interview/profile (interesting campers), new product, technical (RVs related), travel (interesting places to visit by RV, camping). **Buys 10-15 mss/year.** Query by mail only or send complete ms with photos. Length: 750-2,000 words. **Pays $50-150.**

Reprints: Send ms with rights for sale noted and information about when and where the material previously appeared. Pays 35-50% of amount paid for original article.

Photos: "Need b&w or sharp color prints inside (we can make prints from slides) and vertical transparencies for cover." Send photos with submission. Captions required.

Tips: "Freelance material on RV travel, RV maintenance/safety, and items of general camping interest throughout the United States and Canada will receive special attention. Good photos increase your chances."

$ $ $ COAST TO COAST MAGAZINE, Affinity Group, Inc., 2575 Vista Del Mar Dr., Ventura CA 93001. (805)667-4100. Fax: (805)667-4217. E-mail: vlaw@affinitygroup.com. Website: www.coastresorts.com. **Contact:** Valerie Law, editorial director. **80% freelance written.** Magazine published 8 times/year for members of Coast to Coast Resorts. "*Coast to Coast* focuses on travel, recreation, and good times, with most stories targeted to recreational vehicle owners." Estab. 1983. Circ. 200,000. **Pays on acceptance.** Publishes ms an average of 4 months after acceptance. Byline given. Offers 33% kill fee. Buys first North American serial rights. Editorial lead time 5 months. Submit seasonal material 5 months in advance. Accepts queries by mail, e-mail, fax. Accepts previously published material. Accepts simultaneous submissions. Responds in 6-8 weeks to queries; 1-2 months to mss. Sample copy for $4 and 9×12 SASE. Writer's guidelines for #10 SASE.

Nonfiction: Book excerpts, essays, general interest, how-to, interview/profile, new product, personal experience, photo feature, technical, travel. No poetry, cartoons. **Buys 70 mss/year.** Query with published clips or send complete ms. Length: 800-2,500 words. **Pays $75-1,000.**

Reprints: Send photocopy and information about when and where the material previously appeared. Pays approximately 50% of amount paid for original article.

Columns/Departments: Pays $150-400.

Tips: "Send clips or other writing samples with queries, or story ideas will not be considered."

$ $ CURACAO NIGHTS, Nights Publications, Inc., 1831 Rene Levesque Blvd. W., Montreal QC H3H 1R4, Canada. (514)931-1987. Fax: (514)931-6273. E-mail: editor@nightspublications.com. **Contact:** Sonya Plowman, editor. **90% freelance written.** Annual magazine covering the Curacao vacation experience. "We are seeking upbeat, entertaining lifestyle articles; colorful profiles of locals; lively features on culture, activities, nightlife, ecotourism, special events, gambling, how-to features, humor. Our audience is North American vacationers." Estab. 1989. Circ. 155,000. Byline given. Buys first North American serial, first caribbean rights. Editorial lead time 1 month. Accepts queries by mail, e-mail, fax. Responds in 2 weeks to queries; 1 month to mss. Writer's guidelines by e-mail.

Nonfiction: General interest, historical/nostalgic, how-to (help a vacationer get the most from their vacation), humor, interview/profile, opinion, personal experience, photo feature, travel, ecotourism, lifestyle, local culture, art, activities, nightlife, topics relative to vacationers in Curacao. "No negative pieces, generic copy, or stale rewrites." **Buys 5-10 mss/year.** Query with published clips, include SASE and either Canadian postage or IRC, though e-mail submissions are preferred. Length: 250-750 words. **Pays $100-300.**

Photos: State availability with submission. Reviews transparencies. Buys one-time rights. Pays $50/photo. Captions, identification of subjects, model releases required.

Tips: "Demonstrate your voice in your query letter. Focus on individual aspects of the island lifestyle and vacation experience (e.g., art, music, culture, a colorful local character, a personal experience, etc.), rather than a generalized overview. Provide an angle that will be entertaining to vacationers who are already on the island. Our style is upbeat, friendly, and fluid."

$ $ $ ENDLESS VACATION MAGAZINE, Endless Vacation, 9998 N. Michigan Rd., Carmel IN 46032-9640. (317)805-8120. Fax: (317)805-9507. Website: www.rci.com; www.evmediakit.com. **Contact:** Julie Woodard, senior editor. Prefers to work with published/established writers. Bimonthly magazine. "*Endless Vacation* is the vacation-idea magazine edited for people who love to travel. Each issue offers articles for America's dedicated and frequent leisure travelers—time-share owners. Articles and features explore the world through a variety of vacation opportunities and options for travelers who average 4 weeks of leisure travel each year." Estab. 1974. Circ. 1,541,107. **Pays on acceptance.** Publishes ms an average of 6 months after acceptance. Byline given. Buys first North American serial rights. Accepts queries by mail, fax. Accepts simultaneous submissions. Responds in 2 months to queries. Sample copy for $5 and 9×12 SAE with 5 first-class stamps. Writer's guidelines for #10 SASE.

Nonfiction: Senior Editor. Most articles are from established writers already published in *Endless Vacation. Accepts very few unsolicited pieces.* **Buys 24 mss/year.** Query with published clips via mail (no phone calls). Length: 1,500-2,000 words. **Pays $500-1,200 for assigned articles; $250-800 for unsolicited articles.** Sometimes pays expenses of writers on assignment.

Photos: Reviews transparencies, 35mm slides. Buys one-time rights. Pays $300-1,300/photo. Identification of subjects required.

Columns/Departments: Weekender (on domestic weekend vacation travel); Healthy Traveler; Family Vacationing; Destinations, 800-1,000 words. Also Taste (on food-related travel topics) and news items for Facts, Fads and Fun Stuff column on travel news, products, and the useful and unique in travel, 100-200 words. Query with published clips via mail (no phone calls). **Pays $100-800.**

Tips: "Study the magazine and the writer's guidelines before you query us. Also check out www.evmediakit.com, which includes a reader profile and the magazine's current editorial calendar. The best way to break in to writing for *Endless Vacation* is through departments (Weekender, for example) and smaller pieces (Facts, Fads & Fun Stuff and Taste). Queries should be well developed."

$ $ FAMILY MOTOR COACHING, Official Publication of the Family Motor Coach Association, 8291 Clough Pike, Cincinnati OH 45244-2796. (513)474-3622. Fax: (513)388-5286. E-mail: magazine@fmca.com. Website: www.fmca.com. Director of Communications: Pamela Wisby Kay. **Contact:** Robbin Gould, editor. **80% freelance written.** "We prefer that writers be experienced RVers." Monthly magazine emphasizing travel by motorhome, motorhome mechanics, maintenance, and other technical information. "*Family Motor Coaching* magazine is edited for the members and prospective members of the Family Motor Coach Association who own or are about to purchase self-contained, motorized recreational vehicles known as motorhomes. Featured are articles on travel and recreation, association news and activities, plus articles on new products and motorhome maintenance and repair. Approximately ⅓ of editorial content is devoted to travel and entertainment, ⅓ to association news, and ⅓ to new products, industry news, and motorhome maintenance." Estab. 1963. Circ. 140,000. **Pays on acceptance.** Publishes ms an average of 8 months after acceptance. Byline given. Buys first North American serial rights. Submit seasonal material 4 months in advance. Accepts queries by mail, e-mail, fax. Responds in 3 months to queries. Sample copy for $3.99. Writer's guidelines for #10 SASE.

Nonfiction: How-to (do-it-yourself motor home projects and modifications), humor, interview/profile, new product, technical, motorhome travel (various areas of North America accessible by motorhome), bus conversions, nostalgia. **Buys 90-100 mss/year.** Query with published clips. Length: 1,000-2,000 words. **Pays $100-500.**

Photos: State availability with submission. Prefers North American serial rights but will consider one-time rights on photos only. Offers no additional payment for b&w contact sheets, 35mm 2¼×2¼ color transparencies, or high-resolution electronic images (300 dpi and at least 4×5 in size). Captions, model releases, photo credits required.

Tips: "The greatest number of contributions we receive are travel; therefore, that area is the most competitive. However, it also represents the easiest way to break in to our publication. Articles should be written for those traveling by self-contained motorhome. The destinations must be accessible to motorhome travelers and any peculiar road conditions should be mentioned."

$ $ $ FRONTIER MAGAZINE, Adventure Media, 3983 S. McCarran Blvd., No. 434, Reno NV 89502. (775)856-3532. E-mail: frontier@adventuremedia.com. Website: www.frontiermag.com. **Contact:** Laura Hengstler, editor. **60% freelance written.** Monthly magazine covering travel, with special emphasis on the Rocky Mountain states. "*Frontier Magazine* is a sophisticated yet fun-to-read magazine that celebrates the Rocky Mountain lifestyle. It celebrates those attitudes, traditions, and issues that define the modern west." Estab. 1998. Circ. 250,000. Pays on publication. Publishes ms an average of 4 months after acceptance. Byline given. Offers 25% kill fee. Buys first North American serial rights. Editorial lead time 4 months. Submit seasonal material 4 months in advance. Accepts queries by mail, e-mail. Responds in 2 months to queries; 2 months to mss. Sample copy for $2 (shipping and handling). Writer's guidelines online. Editorial calendar online.

Nonfiction: Essays, general interest, historical/nostalgic, humor (essays), interview/profile, photo feature, travel. Special issues: Golf guide (October); Ski guide (November). "We do not accept fiction, religious, or how-to articles." **Buys 15 mss/year.** Query with published clips. Length: 350-1,500 words. **Pays 25-50¢/word.**

Photos: State availability with submission. Reviews duplicate slides only. Buys one-time rights. Negotiates payment individually. Identification of subjects required.

Columns/Departments: Nancy Alton, senior editor. Local Color (tourist-oriented events around the route system), 50-500 words; Creature Comforts (hotel/restaurant reviews), 700 words; Local Flavor (restaurants, chefs, or specialty cuisine along the Frontier Airline route system). **Buys 30 mss/year.** Query with published clips. **Pays $50-150.**

Tips: "Know the airline's route system—we accept stories only from/about these areas. Submit clips with all queries."

$ $ INTERNATIONAL LIVING, Agora Ireland Ltd., 5 Catherine St., Waterford Ireland. 353-51-304-557. Fax: 353-51-304-561. E-mail: kforster@internationalliving.com. Website: www.internationalliving.com. Managing Editor: Laura Sheridan. **Contact:** Kerry Forster, assistant editor. **50% freelance written.** Monthly newsletter covering retirement, travel, investment, and real estate overseas. "We do not want descriptions of how beautiful places are. We want specifics, recommendations, contacts, prices, names, addresses, phone numbers, etc. We want offbeat locations and off-the-beaten-track spots." Estab. 1981. Circ. 500,000. Pays on publication. Publishes ms an average of 3 months after acceptance. Byline given. Offers 25-50% kill fee. Buys all rights. Editorial lead time 2 months. Submit seasonal material 3 months in advance. Accepts queries by mail, e-mail, fax. Accepts simultaneous submissions. Responds in 2 months to mss. Sample copy for #10 SASE. Writer's guidelines online.

Break in by writing about something real. If you find it a chore to write the piece you're sending us, then chances are, we don't want it.

Nonfiction: How-to (get a job, buy real estate, get cheap airfares overseas, start a business, etc.), interview/profile (entrepreneur abroad), new product (travel), personal experience, travel, shopping, cruises. Special issues: "We produce special issues each year focusing on Asia, Eastern Europe, and Latin America." No descriptive, run-of-the-mill travel articles. **Buys 100 mss/year.** Send complete ms. Length: 500-2,000 words. **Pays $200-500 for assigned articles; $100-400 for unsolicited articles.**

Photos: State availability with submission. Reviews contact sheets, negatives, transparencies, prints. Buys all rights. Offers $50/photo. Identification of subjects required.

Fillers: Facts. **Buys 20/year.** Length: 50-250 words. **Pays $25-50.**

The online magazine carries original content not found in the print version. Contact: Len Galvin, online editor (lgalvin@internationalliving.com).

Tips: "Make recommendations in your articles. We want first-hand accounts. Tell us how to do things: how to catch a cab, order a meal, buy a souvenir, buy property, start a business, etc. *International Living*'s philosophy is that the world is full of opportunities to do whatever you want, whenever you want. We will show you how."

N $ THE INTERNATIONAL RAILWAY TRAVELER, Hardy Publishing Co., Inc., P.O. Box 3747, San Diego CA 92163. (619)260-1332. Fax: (619)296-4220. E-mail: irteditor@aol.com. Website: www.irtsociety.com. **Contact:** Gena Holle, editor. **100% freelance written.** Monthly newsletter covering rail travel. Estab. 1983. Circ. 3,500. Pays within 1 month of the publication date. Byline given. Offers 25% kill fee. Buys first North American serial, electronic rights. Editorial lead time 4 months. Submit seasonal material 6 months in advance. Responds in 1 month to queries; 2 months to mss. Sample copy for $6. Writer's guidelines for #10 SASE.

Nonfiction: General interest, how-to, interview/profile, new product, opinion, personal experience, travel, book reviews. **Buys 48-60 mss/year.** Query with published clips or send complete ms. Length: 800-1,200 words. **Pays 3¢/word.**

Photos: Include SASE for return of photos. Send photos with submission. Reviews contact sheets, negatives, transparencies, 8×10 (preferred) and 5×7 prints. Buys first North American serial rights, Electronic rights. Offers $10 b&w; $20 cover photo. Costs of converting slides and negatives to prints are deducted from payment. Captions, identification of subjects required.

Tips: "We want factual articles concerning world rail travel which would not appear in the mass-market travel magazines. *IRT* readers and editors love stories and photos on off-beat train trips as well as more conventional train trips covered in unconventional ways. With *IRT,* the focus is on the train travel experience, not a blow-by-blow description of the view from the train window. Be sure to include details (prices, passes, schedule info, etc.) for readers who might want to take the trip. E-mail queries, submissions encouraged. Digital photo submissions (at least 300 dpi) also encouraged."

$ $ INTERVAL WORLD, 6262 Sunset Dr., Miami FL 33243. E-mail: intervaleditors@interval-intl.com. Website: www.intervalworld.com. Editor: Elizabeth Willard. **Contact:** Amy Drew Teitler, managing editor. **34% freelance written.** Quarterly magazine covering travel. *Interval World* magazine is distributed to Interval International members in the US, Canada, and Caribbean. Estab. 1980. Circ. 800,000. **Pays on acceptance.** Publishes ms an average of 3 months after acceptance. Byline given. Editorial lead time 6 months. Accepts queries by mail, e-mail. Sample copy and writer's guidelines not available.

Nonfiction: How-to, new product, photo feature, travel, health, pastimes, adventure travel. **Buys 20-25 mss/year. Pays 25¢/word.**

Photos: State availability with submission. Reviews transparencies. Buys print and electronic rights. Negotiates payment individually. Captions, identification of subjects, model releases required.

Tips: "Send résumé, cover letter, and several clips (preferably travel). Do not send unsolicited submissions/articles."

$ $ $ $ ISLANDS, Islands Media Corp., P.O. Box 4728, Santa Barbara CA 93140-4728. (805)745-7100. Fax: (805)745-7102. E-mail: editorial@islands.com. Website: www.islands.com. **Contact:** James Badham, editor. **95% freelance written.** Magazine published 8 times/year covering "accessible and once-in-a-lifetime islands from many different perspectives: travel, culture, lifestyle. We ask our authors to give us the essence of the island and do it with literary flair." Estab. 1981. Circ. 220,000. **Pays on acceptance.** Publishes ms an average of 8 months after acceptance. Byline given. Offers 25% kill fee. Buys all rights. Accepts queries by mail, e-mail, fax. Responds in 2 months to queries; 6 weeks to mss. Sample copy for $6. Writer's guidelines for #10 SASE or online.

Nonfiction: "Each issue contains 3-4 feature articles and numerous departments. Any authors who wish to be commissioned should send a detailed proposal for an article, an estimate of costs (if applicable), and samples of previously published work. The majority of our feature manuscripts are commissioned." Book excerpts, essays, general interest, interview/profile, personal experience, photo feature, travel, island-related material. No service stories. **Buys 25 feature mss/year.**

Query with published clips or send complete ms. Length: 2,000-4,000 words. **Pays $750-3,500.** Sometimes pays expenses of writers on assignment.

Photos: "Fine color photography is a special attraction of *Islands*, and we look for superb composition, technical quality, and editorial applicability." Label slides with name and address, include captions, and submit in protective plastic sleeves. Reviews 35mm transparencies. Buys one-time rights. Pays $75-300 for 35mm transparencies. Identification of subjects required.

Columns/Departments: Horizons section and ArtBeat (all island related), 200-600 words; Crossroads (columns and experiences that highlight island life), 500-1,500 words; IslandWise (travel experiences, classic island hotel, classic island eatery, great enrichment experience), 700-1,000 words; Insiders (list 10 things to do in well-visited islands), 800 words. **Buys 50 mss/year.** Query with published clips. **Pays $25-1,000.**

Tips: "A freelancer can best break in to our publication with front- or back-of-the-book stories. Stay away from general, sweeping articles. We will be using big name writers for major features; will continue to use newcomers and regulars for columns and departments."

$ $ ⊘ MICHIGAN LIVING, AAA Michigan, 2865 Waterloo, Troy MI 48084. (248)816-9265. Fax: (248)816-2251. E-mail: michliving@aol.com. **Contact:** Ron Garbinski, editor. **50% freelance written.** Magazine published 6 times/year. "*Michigan Living* is edited for the residents of Michigan and contains information about travel and lifestyle activities in Michigan, the U.S., and around the world. Regular features include a calendar of coming events, restaurant, and overnight accomodations reviews and news of special interest to Auto Club members." Estab. 1922. Circ. 1,099,000. Pays on publication. Publishes ms an average of 6 months after acceptance. Byline given. Offers 20% kill fee. Buys first North American serial rights. Submit seasonal material 9 months in advance. Accepts queries by e-mail. Responds in 6 weeks to queries.

Nonfiction: Travel articles on US and Canadian topics. **Buys 0 unsolicited mss/year.** Query. Length: 200-1,000 words. **Pays $75-600 for assigned articles.**

Photos: Photos purchased for editorial calendar stories only. Reviews transparencies. Pays $450 for cover photos; $50-400 for color transparencies.

Tips: "In addition to descriptions of things to see and do, articles should contain accurate, current information on costs the traveler would encounter on his trip. Items such as lodging, meal and entertainment expenses should be included, not in the form of a balance sheet but as an integral part of the piece. We want the sounds, sights, tastes, smells of a place or experience so one will feel he has been there and knows if he wants to go back. Requires travel-related queries via e-mail only."

$ $ MOTORHOME, TL Enterprises, 2575 Vista Del Mar Dr., Ventura CA 93001. (805)667-4100. Fax: (805)667-4484. Website: www.motorhomemagazine.com. Editorial Director: Barbara Leonard. **Contact:** Sherry McBride, senior managing editor. **60% freelance written.** Monthly magazine. "*MotorHome* is a magazine for owners and prospective buyers of self-propelled recreational vehicles who are active outdoorsmen and wide-ranging travelers. We cover all aspects of the RV lifestyle; editorial material is both technical and nontechnical in nature. Regular features include tests and descriptions of various models of motorhomes, travel adventures, and hobbies pursued in such vehicles, objective analysis of equipment and supplies for such vehicles, and do-it-yourself articles. Guides within the magazine provide listings of manufacturers, rentals, and other sources of equipment and accessories of interest to enthusiasts. Articles must have an RV slant and excellent transparencies accompanying text." Estab. 1968. Circ. 144,000. **Pays on acceptance.** Publishes ms an average of within 1 year after acceptance. Byline given. Offers 30% kill fee. Buys first North American serial, electronic rights. Editorial lead time 4 months. Submit seasonal material 6 months in advance. Accepts queries by mail, fax. Responds in 1 month to queries; 2 months to mss. Sample copy for free. Writer's guidelines for #10 SASE.

Break in with *Crossroads* items.

Nonfiction: General interest, historical/nostalgic, how-to, humor, interview/profile, new product, personal experience, photo feature, technical, travel, celebrity profiles, recreation, lifestyle, legislation, all RV related. No diaries of RV trips or negative RV experiences. **Buys 120 mss/year.** Query with or without published clips. Length: 250-2,500 words. **Pays $300-600.**

Photos: Send photos with submission. Reviews 35mm slides. Buys one-time rights. Offers no additional payment for art accepted with ms. Pays $500+ for covers. Captions, identification of subjects, model releases required.

Columns/Departments: Crossroads (offbeat briefs of people, places, and events of interest to travelers), 100-200 words; Keepers (tips, resources). Query with or without published clips or send complete ms. **Pays $100.**

The online magazine carries original content not found in the print version. Contact: Barbara Leonard, editorial director.

Tips: "If a freelancer has an idea for a good article, it's best to send a query and include possible photo locations to illustrate the article. We prefer to assign articles and work with the author in developing a piece suitable to our audience. We are in a specialized field with very enthusiastic readers who appreciate articles by authors who actually enjoy motorhomes. The following areas are most open: Crossroads—brief descriptions of places to see or special events, with 1 photo/slide, 100-200 words; travel—places to go with a motorhome, where to stay, what to see and do, etc.; and how-to—personal projects on author's motorhomes to make travel easier, unique projects, accessories. Also articles on motorhome-owning celebrities, humorous experiences. Be sure to submit appropriate photography (35mm slides) with at least 1 good motorhome shot to illustrate travel articles. No phone queries, please."

$ $ $ PORTHOLE CRUISE MAGAZINE, Panoff Publishing, 4517 NW 31st Ave., Wingate Commons, Ft. Lauderdale FL 33309-3403. (954)377-7777. Fax: (954)377-7000. E-mail: rgrizzle@ppigroup.com. Website: www.porthole.com. Editorial Director: Dale Rim. **Contact:** Ralph Grizzle, editor. **90% freelance written.** Bimonthly magazine covering the cruise industry. "*Porthole Cruise Magazine* entices its readers into taking a cruise vacation by delivering information that is timely, accurate, colorful, and entertaining." Estab. 1992. Circ. 35,000. Pays on publication. Publishes ms an average of 6 months after acceptance. Byline given. Offers 35% kill fee. Buys second serial (reprint), electronic, first international serial rights. Editorial lead time 8 months. Submit seasonal material 5 months in advance. Accepts queries by mail, e-mail, fax. Accepts simultaneous submissions. Sample copy for 8×11 SAE and $3 postage. Writer's guidelines by e-mail.

Nonfiction: General interest (cruise related), historical/nostalgic, how-to (pick a cruise, not get seasick, travel tips), humor, interview/profile (crew on board or industry executives), new product, personal experience, photo feature, travel (off-the-beaten-path, adventure, ports, destinations, cruises), onboard fashion, spa articles, duty-free shopping, port shopping, ship reviews. No articles on destinations that can't be reached by ship. "Please, please do not send us accounts of your lovely, spectacular, or breathtaking family cruise vacations from the point of embarkation to debarkation. Concentrate on vivid details (must include dialogue), personal experiences, and go beyond the normal. Include out-of-the-ordinary subject matter. Try to transport the reader from the pages to the places you traveled rather than simply giving a laundry list of what you saw. Please don't write asking for a cruise so that you can do an article! You must be an experienced cruise writer to do a ship review." **Buys 75 mss/year.** Query with published clips or send complete ms. Length: 1,000-3,000 words. **Pays $400-1,200 for assigned articles; $250-1,000 for unsolicited articles.** Pays expenses of writers on assignment.

Reprints: Send photocopy of article or typed ms with rights for sale noted and information about when and where the material previously appeared. Negotiates payment.

Photos: Linda Douthat, creative director. State availability with submission. Reviews transparencies, prints. Buys one-time rights. Negotiates payment individually. Captions, identification of subjects, model releases required.

$ $ THE SOUTHERN TRAVELER, AAA Auto Club of Missouri, 12901 N. Forty Dr., St. Louis MO 63141. (314)523-7350. Fax: (314)523-6982. Website: www.aaatravelermags.com. Editor: Michael J. Right. **Contact:** Deborah Klein, managing editor. **80% freelance written.** Bimonthly magazine. Estab. 1997. Circ. 130,000. **Pays on acceptance.** Byline given. Not copyrighted. Buys first North American serial, second serial (reprint) rights. Accepts simultaneous submissions. Responds in 1 month to queries; 1 month to mss. Sample copy for 12½×9½ SAE and 3 first-class stamps. Writer's guidelines for #10 SASE.

O→ Query, with best chance for good reception January-March for inclusion in following year's editorial calendar.

Nonfiction: "We feature articles on regional and world travel, area history, auto safety, highway and transportation news." **Buys 30 mss/year.** Query. Length: 2,000 words maximum. **Pays $250 maximum.**

Reprints: Send ms with rights for sale noted and information about when and where the material previously appeared. Pays $125-150.

Photos: State availability with submission. Reviews transparencies. One-time photo reprint rights. Offers no additional payment for photos accepted with ms. Captions required.

Tips: "Editorial schedule is set 18 months in advance (available online). Some stories available throughout the year, but most are assigned early. Travel destinations and tips are most open to freelancers; auto-related topics handled by staff. Make story bright and quick to read. We see too many 'Here's what I did on my vacation' manuscripts. Go easy on first-person accounts."

$ $ ST. MAARTEN NIGHTS, Nights Publications, Inc., 1831 Rene Levesque Blvd. W., Montreal QC H3H 1R4, Canada. (514)931-1987. Fax: (514)931-6273. E-mail: editor@nightspublications.com. Website: www.nightspublications.com. **Contact:** Sonya Plowman, editor. **90% freelance written.** Annual magazine covering the St. Maarten/St. Martin vacation experience seeking "upbeat, entertaining, lifestyle articles." "Our audience is the North American vacationer." Estab. 1981. Circ. 225,000. **Pays on acceptance.** Publishes ms an average of 9 months after acceptance. Byline given. Buys first North American serial, first caribbean rights rights. Editorial lead time 1 month. Accepts queries by mail, e-mail, fax. Responds in 2 weeks to queries; 1 month to mss. Writer's guidelines by e-mail.

- E-mail queries preferred. All submissions must include an e-mail address for correspondence.

O→ "Let the reader experience the story; utilize the senses; be descriptive."

Nonfiction: Lifestyle with a lively, upscale touch. Include SASE with Canadian postage or IRC. General interest, historical/nostalgic, how-to (gamble), humor, interview/profile, opinion, personal experience, photo feature, travel, colorful profiles of islanders, sailing, ecological, ecotourism, local culture, art, activities, entertainment, nightlife, special events, topics relative to vacationers in St. Maarten/St. Martin. **Buys 8-10 mss/year.** Query with published clips. Length: 250-750 words. **Pays $100-300.**

Photos: State availability with submission. Reviews transparencies. Buys one-time rights. Pays $50/photo. Captions, identification of subjects, model releases required.

Tips: "Our style is upbeat, friendly, fluid, and descriptive. Our magazines cater to tourists who are already at the destination, so ensure your story is of interest to this particular audience. We welcome stories that offer fresh angles to familiar tourist-related topics."

$ $ TIMES OF THE ISLANDS, The International Magazine of the Turks & Caicos Islands, Times Publications Ltd., P.O. Box 234, Caribbean Place, Providenciales Turks & Caicos Islands, British West Indies. (649)946-4788. Fax: (649)946-4788. E-mail: timespub@tciway.tc. Website: www.timespub.tc. **Contact:** Kathy Borsuk, editor. **60% freelance written.** Quarterly magazine covering the Turks & Caicos Islands. "*Times of the Islands* is used by the public and private sector to inform visitors and potential investors/developers about the Islands. It goes beyond a superficial overview of tourist attractions with in-depth articles about natural history, island heritage, local personalities, new development, offshore finance, sporting activities, visitors' experiences, and Caribbean fiction." Estab. 1988. Circ. 6,000-9,000. Pays on publication. Publishes ms an average of 6 months after acceptance. Byline given. Buys second serial (reprint) rights. Publication rights for 6 months with respect to other publications distributed in Caribbean. Editorial lead time 4 months. Submit seasonal material at least 4 months in advance. Accepts queries by mail, fax. Accepts simultaneous submissions. Responds in 6 weeks to queries; 2 months to mss. Sample copy for $6. Writer's guidelines online.

Nonfiction: Book excerpts, essays, general interest (Caribbean art, culture, cooking, crafts), historical/nostalgic, humor, interview/profile (locals), personal experience (trips to the Islands), photo feature, technical (island businesses), travel, book reviews, nature, ecology, business (offshore finance), watersports. **Buys 20 mss/year.** Query. Length: 500-3,000 words. **Pays $200-600.**

Reprints: Send photocopy and information about when and where the material previously appeared. Payment varies.

Photos: Send photos with submission. Reviews slides, prints, digital photos. Pays $15-100/photo. Identification of subjects required.

Columns/Departments: On Holiday (unique experiences of visitors to Turks & Caicos), 500-1,500 words. **Buys 4 mss/year.** Query. **Pays $200.**

Fiction: Adventure, ethnic, historical, humorous, mystery, novel excerpts. **Buys 2-3 mss/year.** Query. Length: 1,000-3,000 words. **Pays $250-400.**

Tips: "Make sure that the query/article specifically relates to the Turks and Caicos Islands. The theme can be general (ecotourism, for instance), but the manuscript should contain specific and current references to the Islands. We're a high-quality magazine, with a small budget and staff, and are very open-minded to ideas (and manuscripts). Writers who have visited the Islands at least once would probably have a better perspective from which to write."

$ TRANSITIONS ABROAD, P.O. Box 1300, Amherst MA 01004-1300. (413)256-3414. Fax: (413)256-0373. E-mail: editor@transitionsabroad.com. Website: www.transitionsabroad.com. **Contact:** Clay Hubbs, editor. **80-90% freelance written.** Bimonthly magazine resource for low-budget international travel, often with an educational or work component. Focus is on the alternatives to mass tourism. Estab. 1977. Circ. 20,000. Pays on publication. Byline given. Buys first, second serial (reprint) rights. Accepts queries by e-mail. Responds in 1 month to queries; 1 month to mss. Sample copy for $6.45. Writer's guidelines online.

O→ Break in by sending "a concisely written fact-filled article—or even a letter to Info Exchange—of no more than 1,000 words with up-to-date practical information, based on your own experience, on how readers can combine travel and learning or travel and work."

Nonfiction: Lead articles (up to 1,500 words) provide first-hand practical information on independent travel to featured country or region (see topics schedule). **Pays $50-100.** Also, how to find educational and specialty travel opportunities, practical information (evaluation of courses, special interest and study tours, economy travel), travel (new learning and cultural travel ideas). Foreign travel only. Few destination ("tourist") pieces or first-person narratives. *Transitions Abroad* is a resource magazine for independent, educated, and adventurous travelers, not for armchair travelers or those addicted to packaged tours or cruises. Emphasis on information—which must be usable by readers—and on interaction with people in host country. **Buys 20 unsolicited mss/year.** Prefer e-mail queries that indicate familiarity with the magazine. Query with credentials and SASE. Include author's bio and e-mail with submissions. Length: 500-1,500 words. **Pays $25-100.**

Photos: Photos increase likelihood of acceptance. Send photos with submission. Buys one-time rights. Pays $10-45 for color prints or color slides, $150 for covers (color slides only). Captions, identification of subjects required.

Columns/Departments: Worldwide Travel Bargains (destinations, activities, and accomodations for budget travelers—featured in every issue); Tour and Program Notes (new courses or travel programs); Travel Resources (new information and ideas for independent travel); Working Traveler (how to find jobs and what to expect); Activity Vacations (travel opportunities that involve action and learning, usually by direct involvement in host culture); Responsible Travel (information on community-organized tours). Length: 1,000 words maximum. **Buys 60 mss/year.** Send complete ms. **Pays $20-50.**

Fillers: Info Exchange (information, preferably first hand—having to do with travel, particularly offbeat educational travel and work or study abroad). **Buys 10/year.** Length: 750 words maximum. **Pays complimentary 1-year subscription.**

The online magazine carries original content not found in the print edition and includes writer's guidelines.

Tips: "We like nuts and bolts stuff, practical information, especially on how to work, live, and cut costs abroad. Our readers want usable information on planning a travel itinerary. Be specific: names, addresses, current costs. We are very interested in educational and long-stay travel and study abroad for adults and senior citizens. *Overseas Travel Planner* published each year in July provides best information sources on work, study, and independent travel abroad. Each bimonthly issue contains a worldwide directory of educational and specialty travel programs."

$ $ $ $ TRAVEL + LEISURE, American Express Publishing Corp., 1120 Avenue of the Americas, New York NY 10036. (212)382-5600. E-mail: tlquery@aexpub.com. Website: www.travelandleisure.com. Editor-in-Chief: Nancy Novogrod. Executive Editor: Barbara Peck. Managing Editor: Mark Orwoll. **Contact:** Editor. **80% freelance written.** "*Travel + Leisure* is a monthly magazine edited for affluent travelers. It explores the latest resorts, hotels, fashions, foods, and drinks." Circ. 925,000. **Pays on acceptance.** Byline given. Offers 25% kill fee. Buys first world rights. Accepts queries by mail, e-mail. Responds in 6 weeks to queries; 6 weeks to mss. Sample copy for $5.50 from (800)888-8728 or P.O. Box 2094, Harlan IA 51537-4094. Writer's guidelines online.

O→ There is no single editorial contact for *Travel + Leisure*. It is best to find the name of the editor of each section, as appropriate for your submission.

Nonfiction: Travel. **Buys 40-50 feature (3,000-5,000 words) and 200 short (125-500 words) mss/year.** Query (e-mail preferred). **Pays $4,000-6,000/feature; $100-500/short piece.** Pays expenses of writers on assignment.

Photos: Discourages submission of unsolicited transparencies. Buys one-time rights. Payment varies. Captions required.

Columns/Departments: Length: 1,200-2,500 words. **Buys 125-150 mss/year. Pays $1,000-2,500.**

Tips: "Queries should not be generic, but suggest ideas for specific departments in the magazine."

$ $ TRAVEL AMERICA, The U.S. Vacation Magazine, World Publishing Co., 990 Grove St., Evanston IL 60201-4370. (847)491-6440. **Contact:** Randy Mink, managing editor. **80% freelance written.** Bimonthly magazine covering US vacation travel. Estab. 1985. Circ. 240,000. Byline given. Buys first North American serial rights. Submit seasonal material 6 months in advance. Accepts queries by mail. Responds in 1 month to queries; 6 weeks to mss. Sample copy for $5 and 9×12 SASE with $1.75 postage.

Nonfiction: Primarily destination-oriented travel articles and resort/hotel profiles and roundups, but will consider essays, how-to, humor, nostalgia, Americana. "U.S. destination travel features must have personality and strong sense of place, developed through personal experiences, quotes, humor, human interest, local color. We prefer people-oriented writing, not dry guidebook accounts and brochure-style fluff. Always in the market for nationwide roundup stories—past roundups have included U.S. Gambling Meccas and Top 10 Amusement Parks. Also short slices of Americana focusing on nostalgia, collectibles and crafts, ethnic communities and celebrations, special events. It is best to study current contents and query by mail only first." **Buys 60 mss/year.** Length: 1,000 words. **Pays $150-300.**

Reprints: Send ms with rights for sale noted. Payment varies.

Photos: Top-quality original color slides preferred. Prefers photo feature package (ms, plus slides), but will purchase slides only to support a work-in-progress. Buys one-time rights. Captions required.

Tips: "Because we are heavily photo-oriented, superb slides are our foremost concern. The most successful approach is to send 2-3 sheets of slides with the query or complete manuscript. Include a list of other subjects you can provide as a photo feature package."

$ TRAVEL NATURALLY, Nude Recreation, (formerly *Naturally*), Internaturally, Inc. Publishing Co., P.O. Box 317, Newfoundland NJ 07435-0317. (973)697-3552. Fax: (973)697-8313. Website: www.internaturally.com. **Contact:** Bernard Loibl, editor. **90% freelance written.** Quarterly magazine covering wholesome family nude recreation and travel locations. "*Travel Naturally* nude recreation looks at why millions of people believe that removing clothes in public is a good idea, and at places specifically created for that purpose—with good humor, but also in earnest. *Travel Naturally* nude recreation takes you to places where your personal freedom is the only agenda, and to places where textile-free living is a serious commitment." Estab. 1981. Circ. 35,000. Pays on publication. Byline given. Buys first, one-time rights. Editorial lead time 4 months. Submit seasonal material 4 months in advance. Accepts queries by mail, e-mail, fax. Accepts simultaneous submissions. Sample copy for $9. Writer's guidelines free.

Nonfiction: Frequent contributors and regular columnists, who develop a following through *Travel Naturally*, are paid from the Frequent Contributors Budget. Payments increase on the basis of frequency of participation. General interest, interview/profile, personal experience, photo feature, travel. **Buys 12 mss/year.** Send complete ms. Length: 2 pages. **Pays $70/published page, including photos.**

Reprints: Accepts previously published submissions.

Photos: Send photos with submission. Reviews contact sheets, negatives, transparencies, prints. Buys one-time rights. Payment for photos included in payment forms.

Fillers: Cheryl Hanenberg, associate editor. Anecdotes, facts, gags to be illustrated by cartoonist, newsbreaks, short humor.

Tips: "*Travel Naturally* nude recreation invokes the philosophies of naturism and nudism, but also activities and beliefs in the mainstream that express themselves, barely: spiritual awareness, New Age customs, pagan and religious rites, alternative and fringe lifestyle beliefs, artistic expressions, and many individual nude interests. Our higher purpose is simply to help restore our sense of self. Although the term 'nude recreation' may, for some, conjure up visions of sexual frivolities inappropriate for youngsters—because that can also be technically true—these topics are outside the scope of *Travel Naturally* magazine. Here the emphasis is on the many varieties of human beings, of all ages and backgrounds, recreating in their most natural state, at extraordinary places, their reasons for doing so, and the benefits they derive."

$ $ VOYAGEUR, The Magazine of Carlson Hospitality Worldwide, Pace Communications, 1301 Carolina St., Greensboro NC 27401. (336)378-6065. Fax: (336)378-8272. Editor: Jaci H. Ponzoni. **Contact:** Sarah Lindsay, senior editor. **90% freelance written.** Quarterly in-room magazine for Radisson hotels and affiliates. "*Voyageur* is an international magazine published quarterly for Carlson Hospitality Worldwide and distributed in the rooms of Radisson Hotels & Resorts, Park Plaza and Park Inn hotels, and Country Inns & Suites By Carlson throughout North and South America, Europe, Australia, Africa, Asia, and the Middle East. All travel-related stories must be in destinations where Radisson, Country Inns & Suites, or Park have hotels." Estab. 1992. Circ. 160,000. Pays on publication. Publishes ms an average of 2 months after acceptance. Offers 25% kill fee. Buys first North American serial rights. Editorial lead time 4 months. Submit seasonal material 6 months in advance. Accepts queries by mail. Responds in 2 months to queries; 2 months to mss. Sample copy for $5. Writer's guidelines for #10 SASE.

O→ Break in with a "well-thought-out, well-written, well-researched query on a city or area the writer lives in or knows well—one where Carlson has a presence (Radisson, Country Inns, or Park)."

Nonfiction: The cover story is "a multi-destination feature with an overall theme, such as romantic weekend getaways. We like these articles to capture the distinctive atmosphere of a destination, while at the same time providing readers with a possible itinerary for a visit. All destinations are locations where Carlson has a major presence. We have a strong preference for writers who live in the city/region covered by the story. Typically, we use 4 different writers for 4 separate destinations in a single issue." Length: 425 words, plus sidebar of contact information for travelers. Adventures are first-person articles (with an "in-the-moment" feel) that "focus on active travel opportunities that reflect the unique aspects of a destination. They usually describe adventures that can be accomplished in a weekend or less (i.e., traditional outdoor sports, visits to historic sites, a 1-day cooking class at a local cooking school). Activities must be near destinations with Carlson properties." Length: 475 words. Travel. Query with published clips. **Pays $500-525/piece.** Sometimes pays expenses of writers on assignment.

Photos: State availability with submission. Reviews contact sheets, transparencies, prints. Buys one-time rights. Negotiates payment individually. Identification of subjects, model releases required.

Columns/Departments: A place-specific shopping story with cultural context and upscale attitude, 300 words and 50-word mini-sidebar; Agenda (insights into conducting business and traveling for business internationally), 350 words; Port of Call (an evocative first-person look back at an appealing destination visited by Radisson Seven Seas Cruises), 350 words. **Buys 28-32 mss/year.** Query with published clips. **Pays $375.**

Tips: "We look for authoritative, energetic, and vivid writing to inform and entertain business and leisure travelers, and we are actively seeking writers with an authentic European, Asian, Latin American, African, or Australian perspective. Travel stories should be authoritative yet personal."

N $ WESTERN RV NEWS, P.O. Box 847, Redmond OR 97756. (541)548-2255. Fax: (541)548-2288. E-mail: editor@westernrvnews.com. Website: www.westernrvnews.com. **Contact:** Terie Snyder, editor. **50% freelance written.** Monthly magazine for owners of recreational vehicles and those interested in the RV lifestyle. Estab. 1966. Pays on publication. Publishes ms an average of 6 months after acceptance. Byline given. Buys first, second serial (reprint) rights. Accepts queries by mail, e-mail, fax. Accepts simultaneous submissions. Responds in 2 months to queries; 2 months to mss. Sample copy for 9×12 SAE and 5 first-class stamps. Writer's guidelines for #10 SASE.

Nonfiction: How-to (RV oriented, purchasing considerations, maintenance), humor (RV experiences), new product (with ancillary interest to RV lifestyle), personal experience (varying or unique RV lifestyles), technical (RV systems or hardware), travel. "No articles without an RV slant." **Buys 100 mss/year.** Submit complete ms on paper, disk, or by e-mail. Length: 250-1,400 words. **Pays 8¢/word for first rights.**

Reprints: Photocopy of article or typed ms with rights for sale noted and information about when and where the material previously appeared. Pays 5¢/word.

Photos: Color slides and prints are accepted with article at a rate of $5/photo used. Digital photos are also accepted through e-mail or on disk (CD, Zip, etc.), but must be at a minimum resolution of 300 dpi at published size (generally, 5×7 inches is adequate). Captions, identification of subjects, model releases required.

Fillers: Encourage anecdotes, RV-related tips, and short humor. Length: 50-250 words. **Pays $5-25.**

Tips: "Highlight the RV lifestyle! Western travel articles should include information about the availability of RV sites, dump stations, RV parking, and accessibility. Thorough research and a pleasant, informative writing style are paramount. Technical, how-to, and new product writing is also of great interest. Photos enhance the possibility of article acceptance."

$ $ WOODALL'S REGIONALS, 2575 Vista Del Mar Dr., Ventura CA 93001. E-mail: editor@woodallpub.com. Website: www.woodalls.com. **Contact:** Dee Reed, assistant editor. Monthly magazine for RV and camping enthusiasts. Woodall's Regionals include *Camper Ways*, *Midwest RV Traveler*, *Northeast Outdoors*, *Florida RV Traveler*, *Southern RV*, *Texas RV*, and *Southwest RV Traveler*. Byline given. Buys first rights. Accepts queries by mail, e-mail. Responds in 1-2 months to queries. Sample copy for free. Writer's guidelines free.

Nonfiction: "We need interesting and tightly focused feature stories on RV travel and lifestyle, campground spotlights and technical articles that speak to both novices and experienced RVers." **Buys 500 mss/year.** Query with published clips. Length: 500-1,700 words. **Pays $250-400/feature; $75-150/department article and short piece.**

WOMEN'S

Women have an incredible variety of publications available to them. A number of titles in this area have been redesigned to compete in the crowded marketplace. Many have stopped publishing fiction and are focusing more on short, human interest nonfiction articles. Magazines that also use material slanted to women's interests can also be found in the following categories: Business & Finance; Child Care & Parental Guidance; Contemporary Culture; Food & Drink; Gay & Lesbian Interest; Health & Fitness; Hobby & Craft; Home & Garden; Relationships; Religious; Romance & Confession; and Sports.

$ $ BBW, Real Women, Real Beauty, Aeon Publishing Group, Inc., P.O. Box 1297, Elk Grove CA 95759-1297. Fax: (916)684-7628. E-mail: sesmith@bbwmagazine.com. Website: www.bbwmagazine.com. **Contact:** Sally E. Smith, editor-in-chief. **50% freelance written.** Bimonthly magazine covering fashion and lifestyle for women size 16+. "*BBW* strives to inspire women of all sizes of large to celebrate their beauty and enrich their lives by providing them with affirming information and resources in the areas of fashion and beauty, health and well-being, entertainment and romance, and work and leisure." Estab. 1979. Circ. 100,000. Pays on publication. Publishes ms an average of 2 months after acceptance. Byline given. Offers 20% kill fee. Buys all rights. Editorial lead time 4 months. Accepts queries by mail, e-mail, fax. Responds in 3 months to queries; 3 months to mss. Sample copy for $5. Writer's guidelines for #10 SASE, online, or by e-mail.

Nonfiction: Book excerpts, essays, exposé, general interest, how-to (beauty/style), humor, new product, opinion, photo feature, travel. "No first-person narratives, poetry, fiction." **Buys 18 mss/year.** Query with published clips. Length: 800-2,500 words. **Pays $125-500.**

Photos: State availability with submission. Reviews contact sheets, negatives, 2¼×2¼ transparencies, slides. Buys all rights. Offers no additional payment for photos accepted with ms. Captions, model releases required.

Columns/Departments: Personal Best (improve well-being), 1,200 words; Careers (tools to manage/enhance careers), 1,500 words; Finance (increase financial security), 1,200 words; Perspectives (male perspective), 800 words; Last Word (humorous end page), 700 words; Destinations (travel within US), 1,200 words; Entertaining, 1,000 words. **Buys 30 mss/year.** Query with published clips. **Pays $125-250.**

Fillers: Anecdotes, facts (products, trends, style, fashion, reviews). **Buys 12/year.** Length: 100-200 words. **Pays $25.**

Tips: "Pitch specific articles/topics—2-3 sentences summarizing your proposed topic, and communicating how the piece will be written, i.e., interviews, sidebars, etc."

$ $ $ BRIDAL GUIDE, R.F.P., LLC, 3 E. 54th St., 15th Floor, New York NY 10022. (212)838-7733. Fax: (212)308-7165. Website: www.bridalguide.com. Editor-in-Chief: Diane Forden. **Contact:** Cybele Eidenschenk, executive editor; Laurie Bain Wilson, travel editor for travel features. **20% freelance written.** Bimonthly magazine covering relationships, sexuality, fitness, wedding planning, psychology, finance, travel. Only works with experienced/published writers. **Pays on acceptance.** Accepts queries by mail. Responds in 3 months to queries; 3 months to mss. Sample copy for $5 and SAE with 4 first-class stamps. Writer's guidelines available.

Nonfiction: "Please do not send queries concerning beauty, fashion, or home design stories since we produce them in-house. We do not accept personal wedding essays, fiction, or poetry. Address travel queries to travel editor." All correspondence accompanied by an SASE will be answered. **Buys 100 mss/year.** Query with published clips from national consumer magazines. Length: 1,000-2,000 words. **Pays 50¢/word.**

Photos: Photography and illustration submissions should be sent to the art department. Robin Zachary, art director; Kelly Roberts, associate art director.

Columns/Departments: The only columns written by freelancers cover wedding-planning issues.

Tips: "We are looking for service-oriented, well-researched pieces that are journalistically written. Writers we work with use at least 3 top expert sources, such as physicians, book authors, and business people in the appropriate field. Our tone is conversational, yet authoritative. Features are also generally filled with real-life anecdotes. We also do features that are completely real-person based—such as roundtables of bridesmaids discussing their experiences, or grooms-to-be talking about their feelings about getting married. In queries, we are looking for a well-thought-out idea, the specific angle of focus the writer intends to take, and the sources he or she intends to use. Queries should be brief and snappy—and titles should be supplied to give the editor an even better idea of the direction the writer is going in."

$ $ $ $ 🍁 CHATELAINE, One Mount Pleasant Rd., Toronto ON M4Y 2Y5, Canada. (416)764-1888. Fax: (416)764-2431. E-mail: editors@chatelaine.com. Website: www.chatelaine.com. **Contact:** Kim Pittaway, managing editor. Monthly magazine. "*Chatelaine* is edited for Canadian women ages 25-49, their changing attitudes and lifestyles. Key editorial ingredients include health, finance, social issues and trends, as well as fashion, beauty, food and home decor. Regular departments include Health pages, Entertainment, Humour, How-to." **Pays on acceptance.** Byline given. Offers 25-50% kill fee. Buys first, electronic rights. Accepts queries by mail. Sample copy not available. Writer's guidelines for #10 SASE with postage.

Nonfiction: Seeks "agenda-setting reports on Canadian national issues and trends as well as pieces on health, careers, personal finance and other facts of Canadian life." **Buys 50 mss/year.** Query with published clips and SASE. Length: 1,000-2,500 words. **Pays $1,000-2,500.** Pays expenses of writers on assignment.

Columns/Departments: Length: 500-1,000 words. Query with published clips and SASE. **Pays $500-750.**

The online magazine carries original content not found in the print edition. Contact: Denise Foote, online editor.

$ $ COMPLETE WOMAN, For All The Women You Are, Associated Publications, Inc., 875 N. Michigan Ave., Suite 3434, Chicago IL 60611-1901. (312)266-8680. Editor: Bonnie L. Krueger. **Contact:** Lora Wintz, executive editor. **90% freelance written.** Bimonthly magazine. "Manuscripts should be written for today's busy women, in a concise, clear format with useful information. Our readers want to know about the important things: sex, love, relationships, career, and self-discovery. Examples of true-life anecdotes incorporated into articles work well for our readers, who are always interested in how other women are dealing with life's ups and downs." Estab. 1980. Circ. 350,000. Pays 45 days after acceptance. Publishes ms an average of 6 months after acceptance. Byline given. Buys first North American serial, second serial (reprint), simultaneous rights. Editorial lead time 6 months. Submit seasonal material 5 months in advance. Accepts queries by mail. Accepts simultaneous submissions. Responds in 2 months to queries; 2 months to mss. Sample copy not available. Writer's guidelines for #10 SASE.

"Break in with writing samples that relate to the magazine. Also, the editor reports a need for more relationship stories."

Nonfiction: "We want self-help articles written for today's woman. Articles that address dating, romance, sexuality, and relationships are an integral part of our editorial mix, as well as inspirational and motivational pieces." Book excerpts, exposé (of interest to women), general interest, how-to (beauty/diet-related), humor, inspirational, interview/profile (celebrities), new product, personal experience, photo feature, sex, love, relationship advice. **Buys 60-100 mss/year.** Query with published clips or send complete ms. Length: 800-2,000 words. **Pays $160-400.** Sometimes pays expenses of writers on assignment.

Reprints: Send tearsheet, photocopy or typed ms with rights for sale noted and information about when and where the material previously appeared.

Photos: Photo features with little or no copy should be sent to Mary Munro. Send photos with submission. Reviews 2.25 or 35mm transparencies, 5×7 prints. Buys one-time rights. Pays $35-100/photo. Captions, identification of subjects, model releases required.

Tips: "Freelance writers should review publication, review writer's guidelines, then submit their articles for review. We're looking for new ways to explore the usual topics, written in a format that will be easy for our readers (24-40+ women) to understand. We also like sidebar information that readers can review quickly before or after reading the article. Our focus is relationship-driven, with an editorial blend of beauty, health, and career."

$ $ $ $ CONDÉ NAST BRIDE'S, Condé Nast, 4 Times Square, 6th Floor, New York NY 10036. Fax: (212)286-8331. Website: www.brides.com. Editor-in-Chief: Millie Bratten. **Contact:** Sally Kilbridge, managing editor. **75% freelance written.** Bimonthly magazine covering all things related to the bride—engagement, the wedding, and marriage. All articles are written for the engaged woman planning her wedding. Estab. 1934. Circ. 500,000. **Pays on acceptance.** Publishes ms an average of 6 months after acceptance. Byline given. Offers 15% kill fee. Buys all rights. Editorial lead time 6 months. Submit seasonal material 1 year in advance. Accepts queries by mail. Responds in 3 months to queries. Sample copy not available. Writer's guidelines for #10 SASE.

Nonfiction: Topic (1) Personal essays on wedding planning, aspects of weddings or marriage. Length: 800 words. Written by brides, grooms, attendants, family members, friends in the first person. The writer's unique experience qualifies them to tell this story. (2) Articles on specific relationship and lifestyle issues. Length: 800 words. Select a specialized topic in the areas of relationships, religion, in-laws, second marriage, finances, careers, health, fitness, nutrition, sex, decorating, or entertaining. Written either by experts (attorneys, doctors, financial planners, marriage counselors, etc) or freelancers who interview and quote experts and real couples. (3) In-depth explorations of relationship and lifestyle issues. Length: 2,000-3,000 words. Well-researched articles on finances, health, sex, wedding, and marriage trends. Should include statistics, quotes from experts and real couples, a resolution of the issues raised by each couple. Book excerpts, essays, how-to, personal experience. No humor. **Buys 36 mss/year.** Query with published clips. Length: 800-2,000 words. **Pays $1/word for assigned articles.** Pays expenses of writers on assignment.

Photos: State availability with submission. Negotiates payment individually.

Columns/Departments: Length: 750 words. Query with published clips. **Pays $1/word.**

Tips: "We look for relationship pieces that will help a newlywed couple adjust to marriage. Wedding planning articles are usually written by experts or depend on a lot of interviews with experts. Writers should have a good idea of what we would and would not do: Read the 3 or 4 most recent issues. What separates us from the competition is quality-writing, photographs, amount of information. All articles are assigned with some consumer slant, with the exception of personal essays."

[N] [⊘] $ COSMOPOLITAN, The Hearst Corp., 224 W. 57th St., New York NY 10019. (212)649-2000. **Contact:** Michele Promaulayko, executive editor. **25% freelance written.** Monthly magazine for 18- to 35-year-old single, married, divorced women. "*Cosmopolitan* is edited for young women for whom beauty, fashion, fitness, career, relationships, and personal growth are top priorities. Nutrition, home/lifestyle and celebrities are other interests reflected in the editorial lineup." Estab. 1886. Circ. 2,300,100. **Pays on acceptance.** Byline given. Offers 10-15% kill fee. Buys all magazine rights and occasionally negotiates first North American rights Submit seasonal material 6 months in advance. Sample copy for $2.95. Writer's guidelines for #10 SASE.

- "We do not accept unsolicited manuscripts and rarely accept queries."

Nonfiction: Book excerpts, how-to, humor, opinion, personal experience, anything of interest to young women.

Tips: "Combine information with entertainment value, humor and relatability." Needs "information- and emotion- and fun-packed relationship and sex service stories; first-person stories that display triumph over tragedy."

$ $ $ $ FAMILY CIRCLE MAGAZINE, Gruner & Jahr, 375 Lexington Ave., New York NY 10017-5514. (212)499-2000. Fax: (212)499-1987. E-mail: nclark@familycircle.com. Website: www.familycircle.com. Editor-in-Chief: Susan Ungaro. **Contact:** Nancy Clark, deputy editor. **80% freelance written.** Magazine published every 3 weeks. "We are a national women's service magazine which covers many stages of a woman's life, along with her everyday concerns about social, family, and health issues." Estab. 1932. Circ. 5,000,000. Byline given. Offers 20% kill fee. Buys one-time, all rights. Editorial lead time 4 months. Submit seasonal material 4 months in advance. Responds in 2 months to queries; 2 months to mss. Sample copy not available. Writer's guidelines for #10 SASE. Editorial calendar online.

O-ᴿ Break in with "Women Who Make A Difference." Send queries to Marilyn Balamaci, senior editor.

Nonfiction: "We look for well-written, well-reported stories told through interesting anecdotes and insightful writing. We want well-researched service journalism on all subjects." Essays, humor, opinion, personal experience, women's interest subjects such as family and personal relationships, children, physical and mental health, nutrition and self-improvement. No fiction or poetry. **Buys 200 mss/year.** Query with SASE. Length: 1,000-2,500 words. **Pays $1/word.** Pays expenses of writers on assignment.

Columns/Departments: Women Who Make a Difference (profiles of volunteers who have made a significant impact on their community), 1,500 words; Profiles in Courage/Love (dramatic narratives about women and families overcoming adversity), 2,000 words; Full Circle (opinion/point of view on current issue/topic of general interest to our readers), 750 words; Humor, 750 words. **Buys 200 mss/year.** Query with published clips and SASE. **Pays $1/word.**

Tips: "Query letters should be concise and to the point. Also, writers should keep close tabs on *Family Circle* and other women's magazines to avoid submitting recently run subject matter."

$ $ $ $ [Canada] FLARE MAGAZINE, 777 Bay St., 7th Floor, Toronto ON M5W 1A7, Canada. Fax: (416)596-5184. E-mail: editors@flare.com. Website: www.flare.com. **Contact:** Kim Izzo, features editor. Monthly magazine for women ages 17-34. Byline given. Offers 50% kill fee. Buys first North American serial, electronic rights. Accepts queries by e-mail. Response time varies to queries. Sample copy for #10 SASE. Writer's guidelines online.

Nonfiction: Looking for "women's fashion, beauty, health, sociological trends and celebrities." **Buys 24 mss/year.** Query. Length: 200-1,200 words. **Pays $1/word.** Pays expenses of writers on assignment.

[N] $ [International] FOR WOMEN, P.O. Box 381, 4 Selsdon Way, London E14 9GL, England. 020 7308 5363. E-mail: ecoldwell@nasnet.co.uk. Editor: Liz Beresford. Managing Editor: Ric Porter. **Contact:** Elizabeth Coldwell, fiction editor. **50% freelance written.** Magazine published every 6 weeks covering women's sexuality and relationships. Estab. 1992. Circ. 60,000.

Pays at the end of the month of publication. Publishes ms an average of 3-4 months after acceptance. Byline given. Buys all rights. Sample copy not available. Writer's guidelines by e-mail.

Fiction: "We are allowed to be explicit in the language we use, but the erotic content should be sensual, rather than crude. Stories with a gay/lesbian theme or those which deal with mild bondage/SM are acceptable as long as it is made clear that both partners are willing participants. Some attempt should be made to incorporate a plot. Detailed descriptions of sexual encounters are often very erotic, but our readers also like believable characters and an imaginative setting for the action." Erotica. "We are not allowed to print stories which deal with anything illegal, including underage sex, anal sex (unless those taking part are over 18 and in private—i.e. no threesomes!), incest, beastiality, and anything which features extreme violence or appears to glorify rape or the use of force in a sexual encounter." No stories where a character's motivation is to extract revenge for a previous sexual wrong or in which a character is punished in some way for expressing his/her sexuality. **Buys 18 mss/year.** Send complete ms. Length: 2,000-3,000 words. **Pays £150.**

Tips: "Please try to avoid the following plot twists, which we receive more frequently than any other, and which have become increasingly hard to render in an original or surprising way: woman has sexual encounter with a 'stranger' who turns out to be her husband/regular partner; woman has sexual encounter with a 'stranger' who turns out to be a ghost/vampire; or man has sexual encounter with a 'woman' who turns out to be a man."

$ $ THE LINK & VISITOR, Baptist Women's Missionary Society of Ontario and Quebec, 30 Arlington Ave., Toronto ON M6G 3K8, Canada. (416)651-7192. Fax: (416)651-0438. E-mail: linkvis@baptistwomen.com. **Contact:** Editor. **50% freelance written.** Magazine published 6 times/ year "designed to help Baptist women grow their world, faith, relationships, creativity, and mission vision-evangelical, egalitarian, Canadian." Estab. 1878. Circ. 4,000. Pays on publication. Publishes ms an average of 6 months after acceptance. Byline given. Buys one-time, second serial (reprint), simultaneous rights, makes work-for-hire assignments. Editorial lead time 2 months. Submit seasonal material 4 months in advance. Accepts simultaneous submissions. Sample copy for 9×12 SAE with 2 first-class Canadian stamps. Writer's guidelines free.

Nonfiction: "Articles must be Biblically literate. No easy answers, American mindset or U.S. focus, retelling of Bible stories, sermons." Inspirational, interview/profile, religious. **Buys 30-35 mss/year.** Send complete ms. Length: 750-2,000 words. **Pays 5-10¢/word (Canadian).** Sometimes pays expenses of writers on assignment.

Photos: State availability with submission. Reviews prints. Buys one-time rights. Offers no additional payment for photos accepted with ms. Captions required.

Tips: "We cannot use unsolicited manuscripts from non-Canadian writers. When submitting by e-mail, please send stories as messages, not as attachments."

$ LONG ISLAND WOMAN, Maraj, Inc., P.O. Box 176, Malverne NY 11565. E-mail: editor@liwomanonline.com. Website: www.liwomanonline.com. **Contact:** A. Nadboy, managing editor. **40% freelance written.** Monthly magazine covering issues of importance to women—health, family, finance, arts, entertainment, fitness, travel, home. Estab. 2001. Circ. 37,000. Pays within 1 month of publication. Publishes ms an average of 3 months after acceptance. Byline given. Offers 33% kill fee. Buys one-time rights for print and online use. Editorial lead time 3 months. Submit seasonal material 3 months in advance. Accepts queries by mail, e-mail. Accepts previously published material. Accepts simultaneous submissions. Responds in 8 weeks to queries; 3 months to mss. Sample copy for $5. Writer's guidelines online. Editorial calendar online.

Nonfiction: Book excerpts, general interest, how-to, humor, interview/profile, new product, travel, reviews. **Buys 30-40 mss/year.** Query with published clips or send complete ms. Length: 300-1,500 words. **Pays $50-150 for assigned articles; $35-120 for unsolicited articles.**

Reprints: Accepts previously published submissions.

Photos: State availability of or send photos with submission. Reviews 5×7 prints. Captions, identification of subjects, model releases required.

Columns/Departments: Humor; Health Issues; Family Issues; Financial and Business Issues; Book Reviews and Books; Arts and Entertainment; Travel and Leisure; Home and Garden; Fitness; all 500-1,000 words. **Buys 30-40 mss/year.** Query with published clips or send complete ms. **Pays $35-150.**

$ $ MORE MAGAZINE, Meredith Corp., 125 Park Ave., New York NY 10017. Fax: (212)455-1433. Editor-in-Chief: Susan Crandell. **Contact:** Stephanie Woodard, articles editor. **90% freelance written.** Magazine published 10 times/year covering smart, sophisticated women in their mid-40s to mid-60s. Estab. 1998. Circ. 850,000. **Pays on acceptance.** Publishes ms an average of 3 months after acceptance. Byline given. Offers 25% kill fee. Buys first North American serial, first, all rights. Editorial lead time 4 months. Submit seasonal material 6 months in advance. Accepts queries by mail, fax. Responds in 3 months to queries; 3 months to mss. Sample copy not available. Writer's guidelines for #10 SASE.

Nonfiction: Essays, exposé, general interest, interview/profile, personal experience, travel, crime; food. **Buys 50 mss/year.** Query with published clips. Length: 300-2,500 words. **Pays variable rate depending on writer/story length.** Pays expenses of writers on assignment.

Photos: State availability with submission. Negotiates payment individually. Captions, identification of subjects, model releases required.

Columns/Departments: Buys 20 mss/year. Query with published clips. **Pays $300.**

$ $ $ $ MS. MAGAZINE, 1600 Wilson Blvd., #801, Arlington VA 22209. (703)522-4201. Fax: (703)522-2219. E-mail: info@msmagazine.com. Website: www.msmagazine.com. Editor-in-Chief: Elaine Lafferty. **Contact:** Manuscripts Editor. **30% freelance written.** Bimonthly magazine on women's issues and news. Estab. 1972. Circ. 150,000. Byline given. Offers 30% kill fee. Buys first North American serial rights. Responds in 2 months to queries; 2 months to mss. Sample copy for $9. Writer's guidelines online.

- No unsolicited fiction or poetry.

Nonfiction: International and national (US) news, the arts, books, popular culture, feminist theory and scholarship, ecofeminism, women's health, spirituality, political and economic affairs, photo essays. **Buys 4-5 feature (3,500 words) and 4-5 short (500 words) mss/year.** Query with published clips. Length: 300-3,500 words. **Pays $1/word.** Pays expenses of writers on assignment.

Reprints: Send tearsheet or typed ms with rights for sale noted and information about when and where the material previously appeared. Pays 50% of amount paid for original article.

Photos: State availability with submission. Buys one-time rights. Identification of subjects, model releases required.

Columns/Departments: Length: 3,000 words maximum. **Buys 4-5 mss/year. Pays $1/word.**

Tips: Needs "international and national women's news, investigative reporting, personal narratives, humor, world-class fiction and poetry, and prize-winning journalists and feminist thinkers."

N $ ORGANIC STYLE, Rodale, 733 3rd Ave., 15th Floor, New York NY 10017-3293. (212)697-2042. Fax: (212)573-0291. E-mail: organicstyle@rodale.com. Website: www.organicstyle.com. Editor: Peggy Northrop. Beauty and Fashion Editor: Lee Golden. Bimonthly magazine. Written for women searching for natural and organic alternatives and dedicated to exploring the art of living in balance. Estab. 2001. Circ. 500,000. Editorial lead time 3 months. Accepts queries by mail. Sample copy for $3.50.

$ $ GRACE ORMONDE WEDDING STYLE, Elegant Publishing, Inc., P.O. Box 89, Barrington RI 02806. (401)245-9726. Fax: (401)245-5371. E-mail: yanni@weddingstylemagazine.com. Website: www.weddingstylemagazine.com. Editor: Grace Ormonde. **Contact:** Yannis Tzoumas, editorial director/publisher. Annual magazine covering wedding and special event planning resource. "*Grace Ormonde Wedding Style* is a wedding and special event planning magazine with editorial covering home and home decorating, women's health issues, cooking, beauty, and travel." Estab. 1997. Circ. 225,000. Pays on publication. Publishes ms an average of 4 months after acceptance. Accepts queries by mail, e-mail, fax. Sample copy not available. Writer's guidelines not available.

Nonfiction: General interest, how-to, interview/profile, personal experience, travel. **Buys 35 mss/year.** Query. Length: 300-3,500 words. **Pays $100-300.** Sometimes pays expenses of writers on assignment.

Photos: State availability with submission. Reviews transparencies. Negotiates payment individually.

Columns/Departments: Wedding related (flowers, beauty, etc.), 450 words, buys 25 mss/year; Women's Health, 3,000 words, buys 1 ms/year; Home Decorating/Cooking, 400 words, buys 5 mss/year; Travel, 350 words, buys 3 mss/year. Query. **Pays $100-300.**

$ ⊘ REDBOOK MAGAZINE, 224 W. 57th St., New York NY 10019. (212)649-2000. Website: www.redbookmag.com. Editor-in-chief: Ellen Kunes. Market/Sittings Editor: Allegra Colletti. Assistant Articles Editor: Nicole Grippo. Features Director: Andrea Bauman. Deputy Editor: Lisa Lombardi. Monthly magazine. "*Redbook* addresses young married women between the ages of 28 and 42. Most of our readers are married with children 10 and under; over 60 percent work outside the home. The articles entertain, educate and inspire our readers to confront challenging issues. Each article must be timely and relevant to *Redbook* readers' lives." Estab. 1903. Circ. 3,200,000. **Pays on acceptance.** Publishes ms an average of 6 months after acceptance. Rights purchased vary with author and material. Responds in 3 months to queries; 3 months to mss. Sample copy not available. Writer's guidelines online.

O— "Please review at least the past six issues of *Redbook* to better understand subject matter and treatment."

Nonfiction: Articles Department. Subjects of interest: Social issues, parenting, sex, marriage, news profiles, true crime, dramatic narratives, health. Query with published clips and SASE. Length: Articles: 2,500-3,000 words; short articles, 1,000-1,500 words.

Tips: "Most *Redbook* articles require solid research, well-developed anecdotes from on-the-record sources, and fresh, insightful quotes from established experts in a field that pass our 'reality check' test. Articles must apply to women in our demographics."

$ $ ⊘ TODAY'S CHRISTIAN WOMAN, 465 Gundersen Dr., Carol Stream IL 60188-2498. (630)260-6200. Fax: (630)260-0114. E-mail: tcwedit@christianitytoday.com. Website: www.todayschristianwoman.net. Editor: Jane Johnson Struck. Senior Associate Editor: Camerin Courtney. **Contact:** Corrie Cutrer, assistant editor. **50% freelance written.** Bimonthly magazine for Christian women of all ages, single and married, homemakers, and career women. "*Today's Christian Woman* seeks to help women deal with the contemporary issues and hot topics that impact their lives, as well as provide depth, balance, and a Biblical perspective to the relationships they grapple with daily in the following arenas: family, friendship, faith, marriage, single life, self, work, and health." Estab. 1978. Circ. 260,000. **Pays on acceptance.** Publishes ms an average of 6-12 months after acceptance. Byline given. Buys first rights. Submit seasonal material 9 months in advance. Accepts queries by mail, e-mail, fax. Responds in 2 months to queries; 2 months to mss. Sample copy for $5. Writer's guidelines for #10 SASE or online.

Nonfiction: How-to, narrative, inspirational. *Practical* spiritual living articles, 1,500-1,800 words. Humor (light, first-person pieces that include some spiritual distinctive), 1,000-1,500 words. Issues (third-person, anecdotal articles that report on scope of trends or hot topics, and provide perspective and practical take away on issues, plus sidebars), 1,800 words. How-to, inspirational. Query. No unsolicited mss. "The query should include article summary, purpose, and reader value, author's qualifications, suggested length, date to send, and SASE for reply." **Pays 20-25¢/word.**

Columns/Departments: Faith @ Work (recent true story of how you shared your faith with someone on the job), 100-200 words; **pays $25.** Readers' Picks (a short review of your current favorite CD or book, and why), 200 words; **pays $25.**

My Story (first-person, true-life dramatic story of how you solved a problem or overcame a difficult situation), 1,500-1,800 words; **pays $300.** Small Talk (true humorous or inspirational anecdotes about children), 50-100 words; **pays $25.** Does not return or acknowledge submissions to these departments.

Tips: "Articles should be practical and contain a distinct evangelical Christian perspective. While *TCW* adheres strictly to this underlying perspective in all its editorial content, articles should refrain from using language that assumes a reader's familiarity with Christian or church-oriented terminology. Bible quotes and references should be used selectively. All Bible quotes should be taken from the New International Version if possible. All articles should be highly anecdotal, personal in tone, and universal in appeal."

N $ W, Fairchild Publications, Inc., 7 W. 34th St., New York NY 10001. (212)630-4000. Fax: (212)630-3566. Website: www.fairchildpub.com. Editor: Etta Froio. Monthly magazine. Written for today's contemporary woman whose fashion sensibility and sense of style define her own look, in her own way. Circ. 471,265. Editorial lead time 2 weeks. Sample copy not available.

$ WEDDINGBELLS, (U.S.), WEDDINGBELLS, Inc., 34 King St. E., Suite 1200, Toronto ON M5C 2X8, Canada. (416)363-1574. Fax: (416)363-6004. E-mail: info@weddingbells.com. Website: www.weddingbells.com. Editor: Crys Stewart. **Contact:** Michael Killingsworth, managing editor. **10% freelance written.** Semiannual magazine covering bridal, wedding, setting up home. Estab. 2000. Circ. 350,000. Pays on completion of assignment. Publishes ms an average of 6 months after acceptance. Byline sometimes given. Offers 25% kill fee. Buys first North American serial, second serial (reprint), electronic rights. Accepts queries by mail, fax. Responds in 2 months to queries.

Nonfiction: Book excerpts, bridal service pieces. **Buys 22 mss/year.** Query with published clips. **Pays variable rates for assigned articles.** Sometimes pays expenses of writers on assignment.

$ WOMEN ALIVE, Encouraging Excellence in Holy Living, Women Alive, Inc., P.O. Box 480052, Kansas City MO 64145. Phone/fax: (913)402-1369. E-mail: ahinthorn@kc.rr.com. Website: www.womenalivemagazine.org. Managing Editor: Jeanette Littleton. **Contact:** Aletha Hinthorn, editor. **50% freelance written.** Bimonthly magazine covering Christian living. "*Women Alive* encourages and equips women to live holy lives through teaching them to live out Scripture." Estab. 1984. Circ. 4,000. Pays on publication. Publishes ms an average of 6 months after acceptance. Byline given. Buys first North American serial, first, one-time, second serial (reprint), simultaneous rights. Editorial lead time 4 months. Submit seasonal material 4 months in advance. Accepts queries by mail, e-mail. Accepts simultaneous submissions. Responds in 6 weeks to mss. Sample copy for 9×12 SAE and 3 first-class stamps. Writer's guidelines not available.

Nonfiction: Inspirational, opinion, personal experience, religious. **Buys 30 mss/year.** Send complete ms. Length: 500-1,500 words.

Photos: State availability with submission. Offers no additional payment for photos accepted with ms.

$ WOMEN IN BUSINESS, American Business Women's Association (The ABWA Company, Inc.), 9100 Ward Pkwy., P.O. Box 8728, Kansas City MO 64114-0728. (816)361-6621. Fax: (816)361-4991. E-mail: abwa@abwahq.org. Website: www.abwa.org. **Contact:** Kathleen Isaacson, editor. **30% freelance written.** Bimonthly magazine covering issues affecting working women. "How-to features for career women on business trends, small-business ownership, self-improvement, and retirement issues. Profiles business women." Estab. 1949. Circ. 47,000. **Pays on acceptance.** Publishes ms an average of 3 months after acceptance. Byline given. Buys first North American serial rights. Editorial lead time 3 months. Accepts queries by mail, e-mail, fax. Accepts simultaneous submissions. Responds in 3 weeks to queries; 2 months to mss. Sample copy for 9×12 SAE and 4 first-class stamps. Writer's guidelines for #10 SASE.

O-w Break in by "having knowledge of the business world and how women fit into it."

Nonfiction: How-to, interview/profile, computer/Internet. No fiction or poetry. **Buys 3% of submitted mss/year.** Query. Length: 500-1,000 words. **Pays variable rates.**

Photos: State availability with submission. Reviews prints. Buys all rights. Offers no additional payment for photos accepted with ms. Identification of subjects required.

Columns/Departments: Life After Business (concerns of retired business women); It's Your Business (entrepreneurial advice for business owners); Health Spot (health issues that affect women in the work place). Length: 315-700 words. Query. **Payment varies.**

Trade, Technical & Professional Journals

Many writers who pick up *Writer's Market* for the first time do so with the hope of selling an article or story to one of the popular, high-profile consumer magazines found on newsstands and in bookstores. Many of those writers are surprised to find an entire world of magazine publishing that exists outside the realm of commercial magazines and that they may have never known about—trade journals. Writers who *have* discovered trade journals have found a market that offers the chance to publish regularly in subject areas they find interesting, editors who are typically more accessible than their commercial counterparts, and pay rates that rival those of the big-name magazines. *(Editor's note: For more information on writing for trade publications, see Writing for Trade and Business Publications on page 57).*

Trade journal is the general term for any publication focusing on a particular occupation or industry. Other terms used to describe the different types of trade publications are business, technical, and professional journals. They are read by truck drivers, bricklayers, farmers, fishermen, heart surgeons, and just about everyone else working in a trade or profession. Trade periodicals are sharply angled to the specifics of the professions on which they report. They offer business-related news, features, and service articles that will foster their readers' professional development.

Trade magazine editors tell us their readers are a knowledgeable and highly interested audience. Writers for trade magazines have to either possess knowledge about the field in question or be able to report it accurately from interviews with those who do. Writers who have or can develop a good grasp of a specialized body of knowledge will find trade magazine editors who are eager to hear from them. And since good writers with specialized knowledge are a somewhat rare commodity, trade editors tend, more than typical consumer magazine editors, to cultivate ongoing relationships with writers. If you can prove yourself as a writer who "delivers," you will be paid back with frequent assignments and regular paychecks.

An ideal way to begin your foray into trade journals is to write for those that report on your present profession. Whether you've been teaching dance, farming, or working as a paralegal, begin by familiarizing yourself with the magazines that serve your occupation. After you've read enough issues to have a feel for the kinds of pieces the magazines run, approach the editors with your own article ideas. If you don't have experience in a profession but can demonstrate an ability to understand (and write about) the intricacies and issues of a particular trade that interests you, editors will still be willing to hear from you.

Photographs help increase the value of most stories for trade journals. If you can provide photos, mention that in your query. Since selling photos with a story usually means a bigger paycheck, it's worth any freelancer's time to develop basic camera skills.

Query a trade journal as you would a consumer magazine. Most trade editors like to discuss an article with a writer first and will sometimes offer names of helpful sources. Mention any direct experience you may have in the industry in your query letter. Send a résumé and clips if they show you have some background or related experience in the subject area. Read each listing carefully for additional submission guidelines.

To stay abreast of new trade magazines starting up, watch for news in *Folio: The Magazine for Magazine Management* and *Advertising Age* magazines. Another source for information about trade publications is the *Business Publication Advertising Source*, published by Standard

Rate and Data Service (SRDS) which is available in most libraries. Designed primarily for people who buy ad space, the volume provides names and addresses of thousands of trade journals, listed by subject matter.

Information on trade publications listed in the previous edition of *Writer's Market* but not included in this edition can be found in the General Index.

ADVERTISING, MARKETING & PR

Trade journals for advertising executives, copywriters, and marketing and public relations professionals are listed in this category. Those whose main focus is the advertising and marketing of specific products, such as home furnishings, are classified under individual product categories. Journals for sales personnel and general merchandisers can be found in the Selling & Merchandising category.

$ $ BIG IDEA, Detroit's Connection to the Communication Arts, Big Idea, 2145 Crooks Rd., Suite 208, Troy MI 48084. (248)458-5500. Fax: (248)458-7099. E-mail: info@bigideaweb.com. Website: www.bigideaweb.com. **Contact:** Conny Coon, managing editor (send e-mail queries to ccoon@bigideaweb.com). **75% freelance written.** Monthly magazine covering creative and communication arts in Southeastern Michigan. "We are a trade magazine specifically for creative professionals in the advertising, marketing and communication arts industry in Southeastern Michigan. Detroit is the third largest advertising market in the U.S. We are the resource for anyone in the agency, film and video, printing, post production, interactive, art and design, illustration, or photography." Estab. 1994. Circ. 10,000. **Pays on acceptance.** Publishes ms an average of 2 months after acceptance. Byline sometimes given. Offers 100% kill fee. Editorial lead time 2 months. Accepts queries by mail, e-mail, fax. Accepts previously published material. Responds in 6 weeks to queries. and 4 first-class stamps.

Nonfiction: Conny Coon, VP Editorial. **Buys 10-12 mss/year.** Query with published clips. Length: 1,500-2,500 words. **Pays $100-350 for assigned articles.** Sometimes pays expenses of writers on assignment.

Photos: State availability with submission. Reviews GIF/JPEG files. Offers no additional payment for photos accepted with ms. Captions, identification of subjects, model releases required.

$ $ $ BRAND PACKAGING, Stagnito Communications, 210 S. Fifth St., St. Charles IL 60174. (630)377-0100. Fax: (630)377-1688. E-mail: bswientek@stagnito.com. Website: www.brandpackaging.com. Senior Editor: Jim George. **Contact:** Bob Swientek, editor. **15% freelance written.** Magazine published 10 times/year covering how packaging can be a marketing tool. "We publish strategies and tactics to make products stand out on the shelf. Our market is brand managers who are marketers but need to know something about packaging." Estab. 1997. Circ. 33,000. **Pays on acceptance.** Publishes ms an average of 2 months after acceptance. Byline given. Makes work-for-hire assignments. Editorial lead time 3 months. Submit seasonal material 3 months in advance. Accepts queries by mail, fax. Sample copy for free.

Nonfiction: How-to, interview/profile, new product. **Buys 10 mss/year.** Send complete ms. Length: 600-2,400 words. **Pays 40-50¢/word.**

Photos: State availability with submission. Reviews contact sheets, 35mm transparencies, 4×5 prints. Buys one-time rights. Negotiates payment individually. Identification of subjects required.

Columns/Departments: Emerging Technology (new packaging technology), 600 words. **Buys 10 mss/year.** Query. **Pays $150-300.**

Tips: "Be knowledgeable on marketing techniques and be able to grasp packaging techniques. Be sure you focus on packaging as a marketing tool. Use concrete examples. We are not seeking case histories at this time."

$ DECA DIMENSIONS, 1908 Association Dr., Reston VA 20191. (703)860-5000. Fax: (703)860-4013. E-mail: deca_dimensions@deca.org. Website: www.deca.org. **Contact:** Cindy Sweeney, editor. **30% freelance written.** Quarterly magazine covering marketing, professional development, business, career training during school year (no issues published May-August). "*DECA Dimensions* is the membership magazine for DECA—The Association of Marketing Students—primarily ages 15-19 in all 50 states, the U.S. territories, Germany, and Canada. The magazine is delivered through the classroom. Students are interested in developing professional, leadership, and career skills." Estab. 1947. Circ. 160,000. Pays on publication. Byline given. Buys first, second serial (reprint) rights. Editorial lead time 3 months. Submit seasonal material 4 months in advance. Accepts queries by mail, e-mail, fax, phone. Accepts simultaneous submissions. Sample copy for free.

Nonfiction: "Interested in seeing trends/forecast information of interest to audience (How do you forecast? Why? What are the trends for the next 5 years in fashion or retail?)." Essays, general interest, how-to (get jobs, start business, plan for college, etc.), interview/profile (business leads), personal experience (working), leadership development. **Buys 10 mss/year.** Send complete ms. Length: 800-1,000 words. **Pays $125 for assigned articles; $100 for unsolicited articles.**

Reprints: Send ms and information about when and where the material previously appeared. Pays 85% of amount paid for an original article.

Columns/Departments: Professional Development; Leadership, 350-500 words. **Buys 6 mss/year.** Send complete ms. **Pays $75-100.**

$ MEDIA INC., Pacific Northwest Media, Marketing and Creative Services News, P.O. Box 24365, Seattle WA 98124-0365. (206)382-9220. Fax: (206)382-9437. E-mail: media@media-inc.com. Website: www.media-inc.com. Publisher: James Baker. **Contact:** Hilary Smith, editor. **30% freelance written.** Quarterly magazine covering Northwest U.S. media, advertising, marketing, and creative-service industries. Audience is Northwest ad agencies, marketing professionals, media and creative-service professionals. Estab. 1987. Circ. 10,000. Byline given. Responds in 1 month to queries. Sample copy for 9×12 SAE and 6 first-class stamps.

Tips: "It is best if writers live in the Pacific Northwest and can report on local news and events in Media Inc.'s areas of business coverage."

$ $ $ PROMO MAGAZINE, Insights and Ideas for Building Brands, Primedia, 11 Riverbend Dr., Stamford CT 06907. (203)358-9900. Fax: (203)358-9900. E-mail: kjoyce@primediabusiness.com. Website: www.promomagazine.com. **Contact:** Kathleen Joyce, editor. **5% freelance written.** Monthly magazine covering promotion marketing. "*Promo* serves marketers, and stories must be informative, well written, and familiar with the subject matter." Estab. 1987. Circ. 25,000. Pays on publication. Publishes ms an average of 2 months after acceptance. Byline given. Offers 25% kill fee. Buys first North American serial rights. Editorial lead time 3 months. Submit seasonal material 3 months in advance. Responds in 1 month to queries. Sample copy for $5.

Nonfiction: Exposé, general interest, how-to (marketing programs), interview/profile, new product (promotion). "No general marketing stories not heavily involved in promotions." Generally does not accept unsolicited mss, query first. **Buys 6-10 mss/year.** Query with published clips. Length: Variable. **Pays $1,000 maximum for assigned articles; $500 maximum for unsolicited articles.** Sometimes pays expenses of writers on assignment.

Photos: State availability with submission. Reviews contact sheets, negatives. Negotiates payment individually. Captions, identification of subjects, model releases required.

Tips: "Understand that our stories aim to teach marketing professionals about successful promotion strategies. Case studies or new promos have the best chance."

$ $ SIGN BUILDER ILLUSTRATED, America's How-To Sign Magazine, Simmons-Boardman Publishing Corp., 345 Hudson St., 12th Floor, New York NY 10014. (252)355-5806. Fax: (252)355-5690. E-mail: jwooten@sbpub.com. Website: www.signshop.com. **Contact:** Jeff Wooten, editor. **40% freelance written.** Monthly magazine covering sign and graphic industry. "*Sign Builder Illustrated* targets sign professionals where they work: on the shop floor. Our topics cover the broadest spectrum of the sign industry, from design to fabrication, installation, maintenance and repair. Our readers own a similarly wide range of shops, including commercial, vinyl, sign erection and maintenance, electrical and neon, architectural, and awnings." Estab. 1987. Circ. 14,500. **Pays on acceptance.** Publishes ms an average of 3 months after acceptance. Byline given. Offers 10% kill fee. Buys all rights. Editorial lead time 3 months. Submit seasonal material 4 months in advance. Accepts queries by mail, e-mail, fax, phone. Accepts simultaneous submissions. Responds in 1 month to queries. Sample copy for free. Writer's guidelines free.

Nonfiction: Historical/nostalgic, how-to, humor, interview/profile, photo feature, technical. **Buys 50-60 mss/year.** Query. Length: 1,000-1,500 words. **Pays $250-550 for assigned articles.**

Photos: Send photos with submission. Reviews 3×5 prints. Buys all rights. Negotiates payment individually. Captions, identification of subjects required.

Tips: "Be very knowledgeable about a portion of the sign industry you are covering. We want our readers to come away from each article with at least one good idea, one new technique, or one more 'trick of the trade.' At the same time, we don't want a purely textbook listing of 'do this, do that.' Our readers enjoy *Sign Builder Illustrated* because the publication speaks to them in a clear and lively fashion, from one sign professional to another. We want to engage the reader who has been in the business for some time. While there might be a place for basic instruction in new techniques, our average paid subscriber has been in business over twenty years, employs over seven people, and averages of $800,000 in annual sales. These people aren't neophytes content with retread articles they can find anywhere. It's important for our writers to use anecdotes and examples drawn from the daily sign business."

$ $ SIGNS OF THE TIMES, The Industry Journal Since 1906, ST Publications, Dept. WM, 407 Gilbert Ave., Cincinnati OH 45202-2285. (513)421-2050. Fax: (513)421-5144. E-mail: sconner@stpubs.com. Website: www.signweb.com. **Contact:** Susan Conner, senior editor. **15-30% freelance written.** Monthly magazine covering the sign and outdoor advertising industries. Estab. 1906. Circ. 17,000. Pays on publication. Publishes ms an average of 3 months after acceptance. Byline given. Buys variable rights. Accepts queries by mail, e-mail, fax, phone. Responds in 3 months to queries. Sample copy and writer's guidelines for 9×12 SAE with 10 first-class stamps.

Nonfiction: Historical/nostalgic (regarding the sign industry), how-to (carved signs, goldleaf, etc.), interview/profile (focusing on either a signshop or a specific project), photo feature (query first), technical (sign engineering, etc.). Nothing "nonspecific on signs, an example being a photo essay on 'signs I've seen.' We are a trade journal with specific audience interests." **Buys 15-20 mss/year.** Query with published clips. **Pays $150-500.**

Reprints: Send tearsheet or typed ms with rights for sale noted and information about when and where the material previously appeared. Payment is negotiated.

Photos: "Sign industry-related photos only. We sometimes accept photos with funny twists or misspellings." Send photos with submission.

Fillers: Open to queries; request rates.

The online version contains material not found in the print edition.

Tips: "Be thoroughly familiar with the sign industry, especially in the CAS-related area. Have an insider's knowledge plus an insider's contacts."

ART, DESIGN & COLLECTIBLES

The businesses of art, art administration, architecture, environmental/package design, and antiques/collectibles are covered in these listings. Art-related topics for the general public are located in the Consumer Art & Architecture category. Antiques and collectibles magazines for enthusiasts are listed in Consumer Hobby & Craft. (Listings of markets looking for freelance artists to do artwork can be found in *Artist's and Graphic Designer's Market*, Writer's Digest Books.)

$ $ AIRBRUSH ACTION MAGAZINE, Action, Inc., 3209 Atlantic Ave., P.O. Box 438, Allenwood NJ 08720. (732)223-7078. Fax: (732)223-2855. E-mail: cstieglitz@monmouth.com. Website: www.airbrushaction.com. **Contact:** Cliff Stieglitz, editor. **80% freelance written.** Bimonthly magazine covering the spectrum of airbrush applications: Illustration, T-shirt airbrushing, fine art, automotive and sign painting, hobby/craft applications, wall murals, fingernails, temporary tattoos, artist profiles, reviews and more. Estab. 1985. Circ. 35,000. Pays 1 month after publication. Publishes ms an average of 6 months after acceptance. Byline given. Buys all rights. Editorial lead time 6 months. Submit seasonal material 6 months in advance. Accepts queries by mail, e-mail, fax, phone. Accepts simultaneous submissions.

Nonfiction: Current primary focus on automotive, motorcycle, and helmet kustom kulture arts. How-to, humor, inspirational, interview/profile, new product, personal experience, technical. Nothing unrelated to airbrush. Query with published clips. **Pays 15¢/word.** Sometimes pays expenses of writers on assignment.

Photos: Send photos with submission. Buys all rights. Negotiates payment individually. Captions, identification of subjects, model releases required.

Columns/Departments: Query with published clips.

The online version contains material not found in the print edition. Contact: Cliff Stieglitz.

Tips: "Send bio and writing samples. Send well-written technical information pertaining to airbrush art. We publish a lot of artist profiles—they all sound the same. Looking for new pizzazz!"

$ $ ANTIQUEWEEK, DMG World Media (USA), P.O. Box 90, Knightstown IN 46148-0090. (765)345-5133, ext. 189. Fax: (800)695-8153. E-mail: connie@antiqueweek.com. Website: www.antiqueweek.com. Managing Editor: Connie Swaim. **80% freelance written.** Weekly tabloid covering antiques and collectibles with 2 editions: Eastern and Central, plus monthly *AntiqueWest*. "*AntiqueWeek* has a wide range of readership from dealers and auctioneers to collectors, both advanced and novice. Our readers demand accurate information presented in an entertaining style." Estab. 1968. Circ. 50,000. Pays on publication. Byline given. Offers 10% kill fee or $25. Buys first, second serial (reprint) rights. Submit seasonal material 1 month in advance. Accepts queries by mail, e-mail, fax. Sample copy for free. Writer's guidelines for #10 SASE.

Nonfiction: Historical/nostalgic, how-to, interview/profile, opinion, personal experience, antique show and auction reports, feature articles on particular types of antiques and collectibles. **Buys 400-500 mss/year.** Query. Length: 1,000-2,000 words. **Pays $50-250.**

Reprints: Send tearsheet or typed ms with rights for sale noted and information about when and where the material previously appeared.

Photos: Send photos with submission. Identification of subjects required.

Tips: "Writers should know their topics thoroughly. Feature articles must be well researched and clearly written. An interview and profile article with a knowledgeable collector might be the break for a first-time contributor. We seek a balanced mix of information on traditional antiques and 20th century collectibles."

$ THE APPRAISERS STANDARD, New England Appraisers Association, 5 Gill Terrace, Ludlow VT 05149-1003. (802)228-7444. Fax: (802)228-7444. E-mail: llt44@ludl.tds.net. Website: www.newenglandappraisers.net. **Contact:** Linda L. Tucker, publisher/editor. **50% freelance written.** Works with a small number of new/unpublished writers each year. Quarterly publication covering the appraisals of antiques, art, collectibles, jewelry, coins, stamps, and real estate. "The writer should be knowledgeable on the subject, and the article should be written with appraisers in mind, with prices quoted for objects, good pictures and descriptions of articles being written about.'. Estab. 1980. Circ. 1,300. Pays on publication. Publishes ms an average of 1 year after acceptance. Short bio and byline given. first and simultaneous rights. Submit seasonal material 2 months in advance. Accepts queries by mail, e-mail. Accepts simultaneous submissions. Responds in 1 month to queries; 2 months to mss. Sample copy for 9×12 SAE with 78¢ postage. Writer's guidelines for #10 SASE.

Nonfiction: "All geared toward professional appraisers." Interview/profile, personal experience, technical, travel. Query with or without published clips or send complete ms. Length: 700 words. **Pays $50.**

Reprints: Send ms with rights for sale noted and information about when and where the material previously appeared.

Photos: Send photos with submission. Reviews negatives, prints. Buys one-time rights. Offers no additional payment for photos accepted with ms. Identification of subjects required.

Tips: "Interviewing members of the association for articles, reviewing, shows, and large auctions are all ways for writers who are not in the field to write articles for us. Articles should be geared to provide information which will help the appraisers with ascertaining value, detecting forgeries or reproductions, or simply providing advice on appraising the articles.

$ ARCHITECTURAL RECORD, McGraw-Hill, 2 Penn Plaza, 9th Floor, New York NY 10121. (212)904-2594. Fax: (212)904-4256. Website: www.architecturalrecord.com. Editor: Robert Ivy, FAIA; Managing Editor: Ingrid Whitehead. **Contact:** Linda Ransey. **50% freelance written.** Monthly magazine covering architecture and design. "Our readers are architects, designers, and related professionals." Estab. 1891. Circ. 110,000. Pays on publication. Publishes ms an average of 2 months after acceptance. Byline given. Offers 25% kill fee. Buys all rights. Editorial lead time 2 months. Submit seasonal material 2 months in advance. Accepts queries by mail. Responds in 2 weeks to queries; 2 months to mss. Sample copy and writer's guidelines online.

$ $ ART MATERIALS RETAILER, Fahy-Williams Publishing, 171 Reed St., P.O. Box 1080, Geneva NY 14456-8080. (315)789-0458. Fax: (315)789-4263. E-mail: tmanzer@fwpi.com. Website: www.artmaterialsretailer.com. **Contact:** Tina Manzer, editor. **10% freelance written.** Quarterly magazine. Estab. 1998. Pays on publication. Byline given. Buys one-time rights. Editorial lead time 2 months. Submit seasonal material 3 months in advance. Accepts simultaneous submissions. Responds in 3 weeks to queries; 3 months to mss. Sample copy for free. Writer's guidelines free.

Nonfiction: Book excerpts, how-to, interview/profile, personal experience. **Buys 2 mss/year.** Send complete ms. Length: 1,500-3,000 words. **Pays $50-250.** Sometimes pays expenses of writers on assignment.

Photos: State availability with submission. Reviews transparencies. Buys one-time rights. Offers no additional payment for photos accepted with ms. Identification of subjects required.

Fillers: Anecdotes, facts, newsbreaks. **Buys 5/year.** Length: 500-1,500 words. **Pays $50-125.**

Tips: "We like to review manuscripts rather than queries. Artwork (photos, drawings, etc.) is a real plus. We enjoy (our readers enjoy) practical, nuts and bolts, news-you-can-use articles."

$ ARTS MANAGEMENT, 110 Riverside Dr., Suite 4E, New York NY 10024. (212)579-2039. **Contact:** A.H. Reiss, editor. **2% freelance written.** Magazine published 5 times/year for cultural institutions. Estab. 1962. Circ. 6,000. Pays on publication. Byline given. Buys all rights. Accepts queries by mail. Responds in 2 months to queries. Writer's guidelines for #10 SASE.

- *Arts Management* is almost completely staff-written and uses very little outside material.

Nonfiction: Short articles, 400-900 words, tightly written, expository, explaining how arts administrators solved problems in publicity, fund raising, and general administration; actual case histories emphasizing the how-to. Also short articles on the economics and sociology of the arts and important trends in the nonprofit cultural field. Must be fact filled, well organized, and without rhetoric. No photographs or pictures. **Pays 2-4¢/word.**

N $ DESIGN MART, Penton Media, 1300 E. 9th Street, Cleveland OH 44114-1503. (216)696-7000. Fax: (216)696-0177. Website: www.penton.com. Managing Editor: Elizabeth McAdam. Bimonthly magazine. Written for the professionals in the technology industry who are interested in new products. Circ. 112,000. Editorial lead time 6 weeks. Sample copy not available.

$ $ $ HOW, Design Ideas at Work, F&W Publications, Inc., 4700 E. Galbraith Rd., Cincinnati OH 45236. (513)531-2222. Fax: (513)531-2902. E-mail: editorial@howdesign.com. Website: www.howdesign.com. **Contact:** Bryn Mooth, editor. **75% freelance written.** Bimonthly magazine covering graphic design profession. "*HOW: Design Ideas at Work* strives to serve the business, technological and creative needs of graphic-design professionals. The magazine provides a practical mix of essential business information, up-to-date technological tips, the creative whys and hows behind noteworthy projects, and profiles of professionals who are impacting design. The ultimate goal of *HOW* is to help designers, whether they work for a design firm or for an inhouse design department, run successful, creative, profitable studios." Estab. 1985. Circ. 38,000. **Pays on acceptance.** Byline given. Buys first North American serial rights. Responds in 6 weeks to queries. Sample copy for cover price plus $1.50 (cover price varies per issue). Writer's guidelines by e-mail.

Nonfiction: Features cover noteworthy design projects, interviews with leading creative professionals, profiles of established and up-and-coming firms, business and creativity topics for graphic designers. Special issues: Self-Promotion Annual (September/October); Business Annual (November/December); International Annual of Design (March/April); Creativity/Paper/Stock Photography (May/June); Digital Design Annual (July/August). No how-to articles for beginning artists or fine-art-oriented articles. **Buys 40 mss/year.** Query with published clips and samples of subject's work, artwork or design. Length: 1,500-2,000 words. **Pays $700-900.** Sometimes pays expenses of writers on assignment.

Photos: State availability with submission. Reviews Information updated and verified. Buys one-time rights. Captions required.

Columns/Departments: Design Disciplines (focuses on lucrative fields for designers/illustrators); Digital Design (behind the scenes of electronically produced design projects); Workspace (takes an inside look at the design of creatives' studios), 1,200-1,500 words. **Buys 35 mss/year.** Query with published clips. **Pays $250-400.**

Tips: "We look for writers who can recognize graphic designers on the cutting-edge of their industry, both creatively and business-wise. Writers must have an eye for detail, and be able to relay *HOW*'s editorial style in an interesting, concise manner—without omitting any details. Showing you've done your homework on a subject—and that you can go beyond asking 'those same old questions'—will give you a big advantage."

$ $ INTERIOR BUSINESS MAGAZINE, The Lawn & Landscape Media Group, 4012 Bridge Ave., Cleveland OH 44113. (800)456-0707. Fax: (216)961-0364. Website: www.interiorbusinessonline.com. Publisher: Bob West. **Contact:** Ali Cybulski, managing editor. **5-10% freelance written.** Magazine covering interior landscaping. "*Interior Business* addresses the concerns of the professional interior landscape contractor. It's devoted to the business management needs of interior landscape professionals." Estab. 2000. Circ. 6,000. Pays on publication. Publishes ms an average of 3 months after acceptance. Editorial lead time 3 months. Submit seasonal material 5 months in advance. Responds in 1 week to queries.

Nonfiction: Interior landscaping. "No articles oriented to the consumer or homeowner." **Buys 2 mss/year.** Length: 1,000-2,500 words. **Pays $250-500.**

Tips: "Know the audience. It's the professional business person, not the consumer."

$ TEXAS ARCHITECT, Texas Society of Architects, 816 Congress Ave., Suite 970, Austin TX 78701. (512)478-7386. Fax: (512)478-0528. E-mail: editor@texasarchitect.org. Website: www.texasarchitect.org. **Contact:** Stephen Sharpe, editor. **30% freelance written.** Mostly written by unpaid members of the professional society. Bimonthly journal covering architecture and architects of Texas. "*Texas Architect* is a highly visually-oriented look at Texas architecture, design, and urban planning. Articles cover varied subtopics within architecture. Readers are mostly architects and related building professionals." Estab. 1951. Circ. 12,000. Pays on publication. Publishes ms an average of 3 months after acceptance. Byline given. Buys one-time, all rights, makes work-for-hire assignments. Submit seasonal material 4 months in advance. Accepts queries by mail, e-mail. Responds in 6 weeks to queries. Writer's guidelines online.

Nonfiction: Interview/profile, photo feature, technical, book reviews. Query with published clips. Length: 100-2,000 words. **Pays $50-100 for assigned articles.**

Photos: Send photos with submission. Reviews contact sheets, 35mm or 4×5 transparencies, 4×5 prints. Buys one-time rights. Offers no additional payment for photos accepted with ms. Identification of subjects required.

Columns/Departments: News (timely reports on architectural issues, projects and people), 100-500 words. **Buys 10 mss/year.** Query with published clips. **Pays $50-100.**

AUTO & TRUCK

These publications are geared to automobile, motorcycle, and truck dealers; professional truck drivers; service department personnel; or fleet operators. Publications for highway planners and traffic control experts are listed in the Government & Public Service category.

$ $ AUTOINC., Automotive Service Association, 1901 Airport Freeway, Bedford TX 76021. (817)283-6205. Fax: (817)685-0225. E-mail: editor@asashop.org. Website: www.autoinc.org. Managing Editor: Levy Joffrion. **Contact:** Angie Wilson, editor. **10% freelance written.** Monthly magazine covering independent automotive repair. "The mission of *AutoInc.*, ASA's official publication, is to be the informational authority for ASA and industry members nationwide. Its purpose is to enhance the professionalism of these members through management, technical and legislative articles, researched and written with the highest regard for accuracy, quality, and integrity." Estab. 1952. Circ. 15,000. Pays on publication. Publishes ms an average of 3 months after acceptance. Byline given. Buys all rights. Editorial lead time 2 months. Accepts queries by mail, e-mail, fax. Accepts simultaneous submissions. Responds in 6 weeks to queries; 2 months to mss. Sample copy for $5 or online. Writer's guidelines online.

Nonfiction: How-to (automotive repair), technical. No coverage of staff moves or financial reports. **Buys 6 mss/year.** Query with published clips. Length: 1,200 words. **Pays $250.** Sometimes pays phone expenses of writers on assignment.

Photos: State availability of or send photos with submission. Reviews 2×3 transparencies, 3×5 prints. Buys one-time and electronic rights. Negotiates payment individually. Captions, identification of subjects, model releases required.

Tips: "Learn about the automotive repair industry, specifically the independent shop segment. Understand the high-tech requirements needed to succeed today."

$ $ BUSINESS FLEET, Managing 10-50 Company Vehicles, Bobit Publishing, 21061 S. Western Ave., Torrance CA 90501-1711. (310)533-2592. Fax: (310)533-2503. E-mail: steve.elliott@bobit.com. Website: www.businessfleet.com. **Contact:** Steve Elliott, executive editor. **30% freelance written.** Bimonthly magazine covering businesses which operate 10-50 company vehicles. "While it's a trade publication aimed at a business audience, *Business Fleet* has a lively, conversational style. The best way to get a feel for our 'slant' is to read the magazine." Estab. 2000. Circ. 100,000. Pays on publication. Publishes ms an average of 3 months after acceptance. Byline given. Offers 25% kill fee. Buys first, second serial (reprint), electronic rights. Editorial lead time 2 months. Submit seasonal material 2 months in advance. Accepts queries by mail, e-mail, fax. Responds in 3 weeks to queries; 2 months to mss. Sample copy and writer's guidelines free.

Nonfiction: How-to, interview/profile, new product, personal experience, photo feature, technical. **Buys 16 mss/year.** Query with published clips. Length: 500-2,000 words. **Pays $100-400.** Pays with contributor copies or other premiums by prior arrangement. Sometimes pays expenses of writers on assignment.

Photos: State availability with submission. Reviews 3×5 prints. Buys one-time, reprint, and electronic rights. Negotiates payment individually. Captions required.

The online magazine carries original content not included in the print edition. Contact: Steve Elliott, online editor.

Tips: "Our mission is to educate our target audience on more economical and efficient ways of operating company vehicles, and to inform the audience of the latest vehicles, products, and services available to small commercial companies. Be knowledgeable about automotive and fleet-oriented subjects."

$ $ FLEET EXECUTIVE, The Magazine of Vehicle Management, The National Association of Fleet Administrators, Inc., 100 Wood Ave. S., Suite 310, Iselin NJ 08830-2716. (732)494-8100. Fax: (732)494-6789. E-mail: publications@nafa.org. Website: www.nafa.org. **Contact:** Jessica Sypniewski, managing editor. **50% freelance written.** Monthly magazine covering automotive fleet management. "*NAFA Fleet Executive* focuses on car, van and light-duty truck management in U.S. and Canadian corporations, government agencies and utilities. Editorial emphasis is on general automotive issues; improving jobs skills, productivity and professionalism; legislation and regulation; alternative fuels; safety; interviews with prominent industry personalities; technology; Association news; public service fleet management; and light-duty truck fleet management." Estab. 1957. Circ. 4,000. Pays on publication. Publishes ms an average of 4 months after acceptance. Buys all rights. Editorial lead time 2 months. Accepts queries by mail, e-mail, fax. Accepts simultaneous submissions. Responds in 1 month to queries. Sample copy online. Writer's guidelines free.

Nonfiction: "NAFA hosts its Fleet Management Institute, an educational conference and trade show, which is held in a different city in the U.S. and Canada each year. *Fleet Executive* would consider articles on regional attractions, particularly those that might be of interest to those in the automotive industry, for use in a conference preview issue of the magazine.

The preview issue is published one month prior to the conference. Information about the conference, its host city, and conference dates in a given year may be found on NAFA's website, www.nafa.org, or by calling the association at (732)494-8100." Interview/profile, technical. **Buys 24 mss/year.** Query with published clips. Length: 500-3,000 words. **Pays $500 maximum.**

Photos: State availability with submission. Reviews electronic images.

Tips: "The sample articles online at www.nafa.org/fleetexecutive should help writers get a feel of the journalistic style we require."

$ $ GLASS DIGEST, Ashlee Publishing, 18 E. 41st St., New York NY 10017. (212)376-7722. Fax: (212)376-7723. E-mail: alec@ashlee.com. Website: www.ashlee.com. **Contact:** Alec Bradford. **15-20% freelance written.** Monthly magazine covering flat glass, architectural metal, glazing, auto glass. Estab. 1921. Pays on publication. Publishes ms an average of 2 months after acceptance. Byline given. Buys first, all rights, makes work-for-hire assignments. Editorial lead time 3 months. Accepts queries by mail, e-mail, fax. Accepts simultaneous submissions.

Nonfiction: Photo feature, technical, architectural designs & trends. "No reports on stained glass hobbyists or art glass." **Buys 16-20 mss/year.** Query. Length: 1,000-2,000 words. **Pays $100-400.** Sometimes pays expenses of writers on assignment.

Photos: State availability with submission. Negotiates payment individually. Identification of subjects required.

Tips: "Architecturally interesting projects with good photography make excellent features for *Glass Digest.*"

$ NORTHWEST MOTOR, Journal for the Automotive Industry, Northwest Automotive Publishing Co., P.O. Box 46937, Seattle WA 98146-0937. (206)935-3336. Fax: (206)937-9732. E-mail: nwmotor@qwest.net. **Contact:** J.B. Smith, editor. **5% freelance written.** Monthly magazine covering the automotive industry. Estab. 1909. Circ. 11,500. Pays on publication. Byline given. Offers 10% kill fee. Buys all rights. Editorial lead time 1 month. Submit seasonal material 2 months in advance. Accepts queries by mail, e-mail. Accepts simultaneous submissions. Sample copy for $2. Writer's guidelines for #10 SASE.

O━ Break in by sending a listing of available articles.

Nonfiction: Interested in seeing automotive environmental articles. Book excerpts, general interest, how-to, new product, photo feature, technical. **Buys 6 mss/year.** Query. Length: 250-1,200 words. **Payment varies.** Sometimes pays expenses of writers on assignment.

Photos: Send photos with submission. Reviews 3×5 prints. Buys all rights. Negotiates payment individually.

Columns/Departments: Buys 4-6 mss/year. Query. **Payment varies.**

Fillers: Anecdotes, facts. **Buys 4-9/year.** Length: 15-100 words. **Pays variable amount.**

$ OLD CARS WEEKLY, News & Marketplace, Krause Publications, 700 E. State St., Iola WI 54990-0001. (715)445-4612. Fax: (715)445-4087. E-mail: mathiowetzk@krause.com. Website: www.collect.com. Editor: Keith Mathiowetz. **Contact:** Angelo Van Dogart, associate editor. **50% freelance written.** Weekly tabloid covering old cars. Estab. 1971. Circ. 65,000. Pays in the month after publication date. Publishes ms an average of 6 months after acceptance. Byline given. For sample copy call circulation department. Writer's guidelines for #10 SASE.

Nonfiction: How-to, technical, auction prices realized lists. No "Grandpa's Car," "My First Car" or "My Car" themes. **Buys 1,600 mss/year.** Send complete ms. Length: 400-1,600 words. **Payment varies.**

Photos: Send photos with submission. Pays $5/photo. Offers no additional payment for photos accepted with ms. Captions, identification of subjects required.

Tips: "Ninety percent of our material is done by a small group of regular contributors. Many new writers break in here, but we are *usually overstocked* with material and *never* seek nostalgic or historical pieces from new authors. Our big need is for well-written items that fit odd pieces in a tabloid page layout. Budding authors should try some short, catchy items that help us fill odd-ball 'news holes' with interesting writing. Authors with good skills can work up to longer stories. A weekly keeps us too busy to answer mail and phone calls. The best queries are 'checklists' where we can quickly mark a 'yes' or 'no' to article ideas."

$ $ $ OVERDRIVE, The Voice of the American Trucker, Randall Publishing Co./Overdrive, Inc., 3200 Rice Mine Rd., Tuscaloosa AL 35406. (205)349-2990. Fax: (205)750-8070. E-mail: mheine@randallpub.com. Website: www.etrucker.net. Editor: Linda Longton. **Contact:** Max Heine, editorial director. **5% freelance written.** Monthly magazine for independent truckers. Estab. 1961. Circ. 100,000. Pays on publication. Publishes ms an average of 2 months after acceptance. Byline given. Offers 10% kill fee. Buys all North American rights, including electronic rights. Responds in 2 months to queries. Sample copy for 9×12 SASE.

Nonfiction: All must be related to independent trucker interest. Essays, exposé, how-to (truck maintenance and operation), interview/profile (successful independent truckers), personal experience, photo feature, technical. Query with or without published clips or send complete ms. Length: 500-2,000 words. **Pays $200-1,000 for assigned articles.**

Photos: Send photos with submission. Reviews transparencies, prints, slides. Buys all rights. Offers $25-150/photo.

Tips: "Talk to independent truckers. Develop a good knowledge of their concerns as small-business owners, truck drivers, and individuals. We prefer articles that quote experts, people in the industry, and truckers, to first-person expositions on a subject. Get straight facts. Look for good material on truck safety, on effects of government regulations, and on rates and business relationships between independent truckers, brokers, carriers, and shippers."

$ ROAD KING MAGAZINE, For the Professional Driver, Parthenon Publishing, 3322 West End Ave., Suite 700, Nashville TN 37203. (615)627-2200. Fax: (615)690-3401. E-mail: roadking@hammock.com. Website: www.roadking.com. Editor: Tom Berg. **Contact:** Bill Hudgins, editor-in-chief. **80% freelance written.** Bimonthly magazine. "*Road King* is published bimonthly for long-haul truckers. It celebrates the lifestyle and work and profiles interesting and/or successful drivers. It also reports on subjects of interest to our audience, including outdoors, vehicles, music and trade issues." Estab. 1963. Circ. 229,900. **Pays on acceptance.** Publishes ms an average of 4 months after acceptance. Byline given. Offers negotiable kill fee. Buys first North American serial, electronic rights. Editorial lead time 3 months. Submit seasonal material 4 months in advance. Accepts queries by mail, e-mail. Responds in 2 months to queries. Sample copy for 9×12 SAE and 5 first-class stamps. Writer's guidelines online.

Nonfiction: How-to (trucking-related), humor, interview/profile, new product, personal experience, photo feature, technical, travel. Special issues: Road Gear (the latest tools, techniques and industry developments to help truckers run a smarter, more efficient trucking business); Haul of Fame (salutes drivers whose work or type of rig makes them unique); At Home on the Road ("creature comfort" products, services and information for the road life, including what's new, useful, interesting or fun for cyber-trucking drivers); Fleet Focus (asks fleet management about what their companies offer, and drivers about why they like it there); Weekend Wheels (from Harleys to Hondas, most drivers have a passion for their "other" set of wheels. This section looks at this aspect of drivers' lives). "No fiction, poetry." **Buys 20 mss/year.** Query with published clips. Length: 850-2,000 words. **Payment negotiable.** Sometimes pays expenses of writers on assignment.

Photos: State availability with submission. Reviews contact sheets. Buys negotiable rights. Negotiates payment individually. Identification of subjects, model releases required.

Columns/Departments: Lead Driver (profile of outstanding trucker), 250-500 words; Roadrunner (new products, services suited to the business of trucking or to truckers' lifestyles), 100-250 words. **Buys 6-10 mss/year.** Query. **Payment negotiable.**

Fillers: Anecdotes, facts, gags to be illustrated by cartoonist, short humor. Length: 100-250 words. **Pays $50.**

The online magazine of *Road King* carries original content not found in the print edition. Contact: Bill Hudgins.

$ $ RV TRADE DIGEST, Your Source for Management, Marketing and Production Information, Cygnus Business Media Inc., 1233 Janeville Ave., Fort Atkinson WI 53538. (301)486-3223. Fax: (920)563-1702. E-mail: editor@rvtradedigest.com. Website: www.rvtradedigest.com. **Contact:** Frank Hurteau, editor-in-chief. **25% freelance written.** Monthly magazine. "RV Trade Digest seeks to help RV dealers become more profitable and efficient. We don't want fluff and theory. We want tested and proven ideas other dealers can apply to their own businesses. We believe sharing best practices helps everyone in the industry stay strong." Estab. 1980. Circ. 17,000. Pays 30 days after publication. Publishes ms an average of 3 months after acceptance. Byline given. Buys first North American serial rights. Editorial lead time 3 months. Submit seasonal material 4 months in advance. Accepts queries by mail, e-mail. Accepts simultaneous submissions. Responds in 2 months to queries. Sample copy for free. Writer's guidelines free.

Nonfiction: How-to (install, service parts, accessories), interview/profile (of industry leaders or successful RV dealers), new product (with emphasis on how to best sell and market the product), technical, business subjects, mobile electronics. Does not want articles about RV travel experience. **Buys 8-12 mss/year.** Length: 1,000-2,000 words. **Pays $300-500.** Pays expenses of writers on assignment.

Photos: Send photos with submission. Reviews transparencies, Prints. Buys one-time rights. Negotiates payment individually. Model releases required.

Columns/Departments: Dealer Pro-File, Profit Central, Modern Manager, Shop Talk, Industry Insider.

Tips: "Send complete manuscript. Propose an idea that will have broad appeal to the RV industry in that it will be interesting and useful to RV dealers, manufacturers and suppliers. Queries must include background/experience and published clips."

$ $ TODAY'S TRUCKING, New Communications Group, 130 Belfield Rd., Toronto ON M9W 1G1, Canada. (416)614-2200. Fax: (416)614-8861. E-mail: editors@todaystrucking.com. Website: www.todaystrucking.com. Editor: Stephen Petit. **Contact:** Rolf Lockwood. **15% freelance written.** Monthly magazine covering the trucking industry in Canada. "We reach nearly 30,000 fleet owners, managers, owner-operators, shop supervisors, equipment dealers, and parts distributors across Canada. Our magazine has a strong service slant, combining useful how-to journalism with analysis of news, business issues, and heavy-duty equipment trends. Before you sit down to write, please take time to become familiar with *Today's Trucking*. Read a few recent issues." Estab. 1987. Circ. 30,000. **Pays on acceptance.** Byline given. Buys first North American serial, second serial (reprint) rights. Editorial lead time 2 months. Submit seasonal material 3 months in advance. Accepts queries by mail, e-mail, fax. Sample copy and writer's guidelines free.

Nonfiction: How-to, interview/profile, technical. **Buys 20 mss/year.** Query with published clips. Length: 500-2,000 words. **Pays 40¢/word.** Sometimes pays expenses of writers on assignment.

Photos: State availability with submission.

Columns/Departments: Pays 40¢/word.

$ $ WESTERN CANADA HIGHWAY NEWS, Craig Kelman & Associates, 3C-2020 Portage Ave., Winnipeg MB R3J 0K4, Canada. (204)985-9785. Fax: (204)985-9795. E-mail: kelmantr@videon.wave.com. **Contact:** Terry Ross, managing editor. **30% freelance written.** Quarterly magazine covering trucking. "The official magazine of the Alberta, Saskatchewan, and Manitoba trucking associations." Estab. 1995. Circ. 4,000. Pays on publication. Publishes ms an average of 2 months after acceptance. Byline given. Buys one-time rights. Editorial lead time 3 months. Submit seasonal material 3 months in advance. Accepts simultaneous submissions. Responds in 2 months to queries; 4 months to mss. Sample copy for 10×13 SAE with 1 IRC. Writer's guidelines for #10 SASE.

Nonfiction: Essays, general interest, how-to (run a trucking business), interview/profile, new product, opinion, personal experience, photo feature, technical, profiles in excellence (bios of trucking or associate firms enjoying success). **Buys 8-10 mss/year.** Query. Length: 500-3,000 words. **Pays 18-25¢/word.** Sometimes pays expenses of writers on assignment.

Reprints: Send tearsheet, photocopy or typed ms and information about when and where the material previously appeared. Pays 60% of amount paid for an original article.

Photos: State availability with submission. Reviews 4×6 prints. Buys one-time rights. Identification of subjects required.

Columns/Departments: Safety (new safety innovation/products), 500 words; Trade Talk (new products), 300 words. Query. **Pays 18-25¢/word.**

Tips: "Our publication is fairly time-sensitive re: issues affecting the trucking industry in Western Canada. Current 'hot' topics are international trucking, security, driver fatigue, health and safety, emissions control, and national/international highway systems."

AVIATION & SPACE

In this section are journals for aviation business executives, airport operators, and aviation technicians. Publications for professional and private pilots are in the Consumer Aviation section.

$ $ AIRCRAFT MAINTENANCE TECHNOLOGY, Cygnus Business Media, 1233 Janesville Ave., Fort Atkinson WI 53538. (920)563-6388. Fax: (920)563-1702. E-mail: editor@amtonline.com. Website: www.amtonline.com. Editor: Joe Escobar. **10% freelance written.** Magazine published 10 times/year covering aircraft maintenance. "*Aircraft Maintenance Technology* provides aircraft maintenance professionals worldwide with a curriculum of technical, professional, and managerial development information that enables them to more efficiently and effectively perform their jobs. Estab. 1989. Circ. 41,500 worldwide. Pays on publication. Publishes ms an average of 2 months after acceptance. Byline given. Buys all rights, makes work-for-hire assignments. Editorial lead time 3 months. Submit seasonal material 6 months in advance. Accepts queries by mail, e-mail, fax. Accepts simultaneous submissions. Responds in 2 weeks to queries; 1 month to mss. Sample copy for free. Writer's guidelines for #10 SASE or by e-mail.

Nonfiction: How-to, technical, safety; human factors. Special issues: Aviation career issue (August). No travel/pilot-oriented pieces. **Buys 10-12 mss/year.** Query with published clips. Length: 600-1,500 words, technical articles 2,000 words. **Pays $200.**

Photos: State availability with submission. Buys one-time rights. Offers no additional payment for photos accepted with ms. Captions, identification of subjects, model releases required.

Columns/Departments: Professionalism, 1,000-1,500 words; Safety Matters, 600-1,000 words; Human Factors, 600-1,000 words. **Buys 10-12 mss/year.** Query with published clips. **Pays $200.**

Tips: "This is a technical magazine, which is approved by the FAA and Transport Canada for recurrency training for technicians. Freelancers should have a strong background in aviation, particularly maintenance, to be considered for technical articles. Columns/Departments: freelancers still should have a strong knowledge of aviation to slant professionalism, safety and human factors pieces to that audience."

N $ $ AIRPORT OPERATIONS, Flight Safety Foundation, Suite 300, 601 Madison St., Alexandria VA 22314-1756. (703)739-6700. Fax: (703)739-6708. E-mail: rozelle@flightsafety.org. Website: www.flightsafety.org. **Contact:** Roger Rozelle, director of publications. **25% freelance written.** Bimonthly newsletter covering safety aspects of airport operations. "*Airport Operations* directs attention to ground operations that involve aircraft and other equipment, airport personnel and services, air traffic control (ATC), and passengers." Estab. 1974. Circ. 2,000. Pays on publication. Publishes ms an average of 3 months after acceptance. Byline given. Buys all rights. Editorial lead time 3 months. Accepts queries by mail, e-mail, fax. Accepts previously published material. Responds in 3 weeks to queries. Sample copy online. Writer's guidelines online.

Nonfiction: Technical. No argumentation, crusading, inspiration, anecdotes, or humor. **Buys 6 mss/year.** Query. Length: 2,500-8,750 words. **Pays $200/printed page, plus 6 copies of publication.**

Photos: Send photos with submission. Reviews contact sheets, negatives, 35mm or larger transparencies, 5×7 minimum prints, GIF/JPEG files. Buys all rights. Offers $25/photo. Captions, identification of subjects, model releases required.

Tips: "Study the guidelines carefully. Be concerned above all with accuracy, fairness, and objectivity, but if you have information that you believe meets those standards, do not hesitate to query even if you aren't sure of format or style. If you have the content we need, our editorial staff will work with you to put the material into shape."

$ $ AVIATION INTERNATIONAL NEWS, The Newsmagazine of Corporate, Business, and Regional Aviation, The Convention News Co., P.O. Box 277, 214 Franklin Ave., Midland Park NJ 07432. (201)444-5075. Fax: (201)444-4647. E-mail: editor@ainonline.com. Website: www.ainonline.com. Editor *AIN* Monthly Edition: Nigel Moll. **Contact:** R. Randall Padfield, editor-in-chief. **30-40% freelance written.** Monthly magazine (with onsite issues published at 3 conventions and 2 international air shows each year) covering business and commercial aviation with news features, special reports, aircraft evaluations, and surveys on business aviation worldwide, written for business pilots and industry professionals. "While the heartbeat of *AIN* is driven by the news it carries, the human touch is not neglected. We pride ourselves on our people stories about the industry's 'movers and shakers' and others in aviation who make a difference." Estab. 1972. Circ. 40,000. **Pays on acceptance and upon receipt of writer's invoice**. Publishes ms an average of 2 months after acceptance. Byline given. Offers variable kill fee. Buys first North American serial and second serial (reprint) rights and makes work-for-hire assignments. Editorial lead time 2 months. Submit seasonal material 3 months in advance. Accepts queries by mail, e-mail, fax. Responds in 6 weeks to queries; 2 months to mss. Sample copy for $10. Writer's guidelines for 9×12 SAE with 3 first-class stamps.

- Do not send mss by e-mail unless requested.

O→ Break in with "local news stories relating to business, commercial and regional airline aviation—think turbine-powered aircraft (no stories about national airlines, military aircraft, recreational aviation or history."

Nonfiction: "We hire freelancers to work on our staff at 3 aviation conventions and 2 international airshows each year. Must have strong reporting and writing skills and knowledge of aviation." How-to (aviation), interview/profile, new product, opinion, personal experience, photo feature, technical. No puff pieces. "Our readers expect serious, real news. We don't pull any punches. *AIN* is not a 'good news' publication: It tells the story, both good and bad." **Buys 150-200 mss/year.** Query with published clips. Length: 200-3,000 words. **Pays 30¢/word to first timers, higher rates to proven *AIN* freelancers**. Pays expenses of writers on assignment.

Photos: Send photos with submission. Reviews contact sheets, transparencies, prints, TIFF files (300 dpi). Buys one-time rights. Negotiates payment individually. Captions required.

"*AIN Alerts*, our online mini-newsletter, is posted on our website twice a week and carries original content not found in our print publications. It includes 10-12 news items of about 100 words each." Contact: Gordon Gilbert, ggilbert@ainonline.com.

Tips: "Our core freelancers are professional pilots with good writing skills, or good journalists and reporters with an interest in aviation (some with pilot licenses) or technical experts in the aviation industry. The ideal *AIN* writer has an intense interest in and strong knowledge of aviation, a talent for writing news stories, and journalistic cussedness. Hit me with a strong news story relating to business aviation that takes me by surprise—something from your local area or area of expertise. Make it readable, fact-filled, and in the inverted-pyramid style. Double-check facts and names. Interview the right people. Send me good, clear photos and illustrations. Send me well-written, logically ordered copy. Do this for me consistently and we may take you along on our staff to one of the conventions in the U.S. or an airshow in Paris, Singapore, London, or Dubai."

$ $ AVIATION MAINTENANCE, PBI Media LLC, 1201 Seven Locks Rd., Suite 300, Potomac MD 20854. (301)354-1831. Fax: (301)340-8741. E-mail: am@pbimedia.com. Website: www.aviationmx.com. Managing Editor: Jim McKenna. **Contact:** Matt Thurber, editor. **60% freelance written.** Monthly magazine covering aircraft maintenance from small to large aircraft. *Aviation Maintenance* delivers news and information about the aircraft maintenance business for mechanics and management at maintenance shops, airlines, and corporate flights departments. Estab. 1982. Circ. 32,000. **Pays on acceptance.** Publishes ms an average of 2 months after acceptance. Byline given. Kill fee varies. Buys all rights. Editorial lead time 3 months. Submit seasonal material 3 months in advance. Accepts queries by mail, e-mail, fax, phone. Responds in 1 week to queries; 1 month to mss. Sample copy online. Writer's guidelines free.

Nonfiction: Exposé, interview/profile, technical. No fiction, technical how-to, or poetry. **Buys 50 mss/year.** Query with or without published clips. Length: 700-1,500 words. **Pays 35¢/word.** Pays expenses of writers on assignment.

Photos: State availability with submission. Buys all rights. Negotiates payment individually. Captions, identification of subjects required.

Columns/Departments: Intelligence (news), 200-500 words; Postflight (profile of aircraft mechanic), 800 words, plus photo. **Buys 12 mss/year.** Query with or without published clips. **Pays $200-250.**

Tips: "Writer must be intimately familiar with or involved in aviation, either as a pilot or preferably a mechanic or a professional aviation writer. Best place to break in is in the Intelligence News section or with a Postflight profile of an interesting mechanic."

N $ AVIATION MECHANICS BULLETIN, Flight Safety Foundation, Suite 300, 601 Madison St., Alexandria VA 22314-1756. (703)739-6700. Fax: (703)739-6708. E-mail: rozelle@flightsafety.org. Website: www.flightsafety.org. **Contact:** Roger Rozelle, director of publications. **25% freelance written.** Bimonthly newsletter covering safety aspects of aviation maintenance (airline and corporate). Estab. 1953. Circ. 2,000. Pays on publication. Publishes ms an average of 3 months after acceptance. Byline given. Buys all rights. Editorial lead time 3 months. Accepts queries by mail, e-mail, fax. Accepts previously published material. Responds in 3 weeks to queries. Sample copy online. Writer's guidelines online.

Nonfiction: Technical. No argumentation, crusading, inspiration, anecdotes, or humor. **Buys 6 mss/year.** Query. Length: 2,000-5,500 words. **Pays $100/printed pocket-sized page, plus 6 copies of publication.**

Photos: Send photos with submission. Reviews contact sheets, negatives, 35mm or larger transparencies, 5×7 minimum prints, GIF/JPEG files. Buys all rights. Offers $25/photo. Captions, identification of subjects, model releases required.

Tips: "Study guidelines carefully. Be concerned above all with accuracy, but if you have information that you believe meets those standards, do not hesitate to query even if you aren't sure of format or style. If you have the content we need, our editorial staff will work with you to put the material into shape."

N $ $ CABIN CREW SAFETY, Flight Safety Foundation, Suite 300, 601 Madison St., Alexandria VA 22314-1756. (703)739-6700. Fax: (703)739-6708. E-mail: rozelle@flightsafety.org. Website: www.flightsafety.org. **Contact:** Roger Rozelle, director of publications. **25% freelance written.** Bimonthly newsletter covering safety aspects of aircraft cabins (airline and corporate aviation) for cabin crews and passengers. Estab. 1956. Circ. 2,000. Pays on publication. Publishes ms an average of 3 months after acceptance. Byline given. Buys all rights. Editorial lead time 3 months. Accepts queries by mail, e-mail, fax. Accepts previously published material. Responds in 3 weeks to queries. Sample copy online. Writer's guidelines online.

Nonfiction: Technical. No argumentation, crusading, inspiration, anecdotes, or humor. **Buys 6 mss/year.** Query. Length: 2,500-8,750 words. **Pays $200/printed page, plus 6 copies of publication.**

Photos: Send photos with submission. Reviews contact sheets, negatives, 35mm or larger transparencies, 5×7 minimum prints, GIF/JPEG files. Buys all rights. Offers $25/photo. Captions, identification of subjects, model releases required.

Tips: "Study guidelines carefully. Be concerned above all with accuracy, fairness, and objectivity, but if you have information that you believe meets those standards, do not hesitate to query even if you aren't sure of format or style. If you have the content we need, our editorial staff will work with you to put the material into shape."

N $ $ FLIGHT SAFETY DIGEST, Flight Safety Foundation, Suite 300, 601 Madison St., Alexandria VA 22314-1756. (703)739-6700. Fax: (703)739-6708. E-mail: rozelle@flightsafety.org. Website: www.flightsafety.org. **Contact:** Roger Rozelle, director of publications. **25% freelance written.** Monthly magazine covering significant issues in airline and corporate aviation safety. "*Flight Safety Digest* offers the page space to explore subjects in greater detail than in other Foundation periodicals." Estab. 1982. Circ. 2,000. Pays on publication. Publishes ms an average of 3 months after acceptance. Byline given. Buys all rights. Editorial lead time 3 months. Accepts queries by mail, e-mail, fax. Accepts previously published material. Responds in 3 weeks to queries. Sample copy online. Writer's guidelines online.

Nonfiction: Technical. No argumentation, crusading, inspiration, anecdotes, or humor. **Buys 6 mss/year.** Query. Length: 4,000-15,000 words. **Pays $200/printed page, plus 6 copies of publication.**

Photos: Send photos with submission. Reviews contact sheets, negatives, 35mm or larger transparencies, 5×7 minimum prints, GIF/JPEG files. Buys all rights. Offers $25/photo. Captions, identification of subjects, model releases required.

Tips: "Study guidelines carefully. Be concerned above all with accuracy, fairness, and objectivity, but if you have information that you believe meets those standards, do not hesitate to query even if you aren't sure of format or style. If you have the content we need, our editorial staff will work with you to put the material into shape."

$ $ GROUND SUPPORT MAGAZINE, (formerly *GSE Today*), Cygnus Business Media, 1233 Janesville Ave., Fort Atkinson WI 53538. (920)563-1622. Fax: (920)563-1699. E-mail: michelle.garetson@cygnuspub.com. Website: www.groundsupportmagazine.com. **Contact:** Michelle Garetson, editor. **20% freelance written.** Magazine published 10 times/year. "Our readers are those aviation professionals who are involved in ground support—the equipment manufacturers, the suppliers, the ramp operators, ground handlers, airport and airline managers. We cover issues of interest to this community—deicing, ramp safety, equipment technology, pollution, etc." Estab. 1993. Circ. 15,000. Pays on publication. Publishes ms an average of 2 months after acceptance. Buys all rights. Editorial lead time 2 months. Accepts queries by mail, e-mail, fax. Responds in 3 weeks to queries; 3 months to mss. Sample copy for 9×11 SAE and 5 first-class stamps.

Nonfiction: How-to (use or maintain certain equipment), interview/profile, new product, opinion, photo feature, technical aspects of ground support and issues, industry events, meetings, new rules and regulations. **Buys 12-20 mss/year.** Send complete ms. Length: 500-2,000 words. **Pays $100-300.**

Photos: Send photos with submission. Reviews 35mm prints, electronic preferred, slides. Buys all rights. Offers additional payment for photos accepted with ms. Identification of subjects required.

Tips: "Write about subjects that relate to ground services. Write in clear and simple terms—personal experience is always welcome. If you have an aviation background or ground support experience, let us know."

N $ $ HELICOPTER SAFETY, Flight Safety Foundation, Suite 300, 601 Madison St., Alexandria VA 22314-1756. (703)739-6700. Fax: (703)739-6708. E-mail: rozelle@flightsafety.org. Website: www.flightsafety.org. **Contact:** Roger Rozelle, director of publications. **50% freelance written.** Bimonthly newsletter covering safety aspects of helicopter operations. "*Helicopter Safety* highlights the broad spectrum of real-world helicopter operations. Topics have ranged from design principles and primary training to helicopter utilization in offshore applications and in emergency medical service (EMS)." Estab. 1956. Circ. 2,000. Pays on publication. Publishes ms an average of 3 months after acceptance. Byline given. Buys all rights. Editorial lead time 3 months. Accepts queries by mail, e-mail, fax. Accepts previously published material. Responds in 3 weeks to queries. Sample copy online. Writer's guidelines online.

Nonfiction: Technical. No argumentation, crusading, inspiration, anecdotes, or humor. **Buys 6 mss/year.** Query. Length: 2,500-8,750 words. **Pays $200/printed page, plus 6 copies of publication.**

Photos: Send photos with submission. Reviews contact sheets, negatives, 35mm or larger transparencies, 5×7 minimum prints. Buys all rights. Offers $25/photo. Captions, identification of subjects, model releases required.

Tips: "Study guidelines carefully. Be concerned above all with accuracy, fairness, and objectivity, but if you have information that you believe meets those standards, do not hesitate to query even if you aren't sure of format or style. If you have the content we need, our editorial staff will work with you to put the material into shape."

N $ $ HUMAN FACTORS & AVIATION MEDICINE, Flight Safety Foundation, Suite 300, 601 Madison St., Alexandria VA 22314-1756. (703)739-6700. Fax: (703)739-6708. E-mail: rozelle@flightsafety.org. Website: www.flightsafety.org. **Contact:** Roger Rozelle, director of publications. **50% freelance written.** Bimonthly newsletter covering medical aspects of aviation, primarily for airline and corporate aviation pilots. "*Human Factors & Aviation Medicine* allows specialists, researchers, and physicians to present information critical to the training, performance, and health of aviation professionals." Estab. 1953. Circ. 2,000. Pays on publication. Publishes ms an average of 3 months after acceptance. Byline given. Buys all rights. Editorial lead time 3 months. Accepts queries by mail, e-mail, fax. Accepts previously published material. Responds in 3 weeks to queries. Sample copy online. Writer's guidelines online.

Nonfiction: Technical. No argumentation, crusading, inspiration, anecdotes, or humor. **Buys 6 mss/year.** Query. Length: 2,500-8,750 words. **Pays $200/printed page, plus 6 copies of publication.**

Photos: Send photos with submission. Reviews contact sheets, negatives, 35mm or larger transparencies, 5×7 minimum prints, GIF/JPEG files. Buys all rights. Offers $25/photo. Captions, identification of subjects, model releases required.

Tips: "Study guidelines carefully. Be concerned above all with accuracy, fairness, and objectivity, but if you have information that you believe meets those standards, do not hesitate to query even if you aren't sure of format or style. If you have the content we need, our editorial staff will work with you to put the material into shape."

$ $ $ PROFESSIONAL PILOT, Queensmith Communications, 3014 Colvin St., Alexandria VA 22314. (703)370-0606. Fax: (703)370-7082. E-mail: editorial@propilotmag.com. Website: www.propilotmag.com. **Contact:** Paul Richfield, executive editor. **75% freelance written.** Monthly magazine covering regional airline, corporate and various other types of professional aviation. "The typical reader has a sophisticated grasp of piloting/aviation knowledge and is interested in articles that help him/her do the job better or more efficiently." Estab. 1967. Circ. 44,000. Pays on publication. Publishes ms an average of 2-3 months after acceptance. Byline given. Kill fee negotiable. Buys all rights. Accepts queries by mail, e-mail, fax, phone.

O→ "Affiliation with an active flight department, weather activity of Air Traffic Control (ATC) is helpful. Our readers want tool tech stuff from qualified writers with credentials."

Nonfiction: "Typical subjects include new aircraft design, new product reviews (especially avionics), pilot techniques, profiles of regional airlines, fixed base operations, profiles of corporate flight departments and technological advances." All issues have a theme such as regional airline operations, maintenance, avionics, helicopters, etc. **Buys 40 mss/year.** Query. Length: 750-2,500 words. **Pays $200-1,000, depending on length. A fee for the article will be established at the time of assignment.** Sometimes pays expenses of writers on assignment.

Photos: Send photos with submission. Prefers transparencies or slides. Buys all rights. Additional payment for photos negotiable. Captions, identification of subjects required.

Tips: Query first. "Freelancer should be a professional pilot or have background in aviation. Authors should indicate relevant aviation experience and pilot credentials (certificates, ratings and hours). We place a greater emphasis on corporate operations and pilot concerns."

BEAUTY & SALON

$ AMERICAN SALON, Advanstar, 1 Park Ave., 2nd Floor, New York NY 10016. (212)951-6640. Fax: (212)951-6624. E-mail: rmcclain@advanstar.com. Website: www.advanstar.com. **Contact:** Robbin McClain, editor. **5% freelance written.** Monthly magazine covering "business stories of interest to salon owners and stylists, distributors and manufacturers of professional beauty products." Estab. 1878. Circ. 132,000. **Pays on acceptance.** Publishes ms an average of 3 months after acceptance. Byline given. Buys first North American serial, first rights. Editorial lead time 3 months. Accepts queries by mail. Sample copy for free. Writer's guidelines free.

O→ Break in with "extensive experience (in writing and the beauty industry); topic of article must be relevant. Very hard to get into our mag."

$ $ BEAUTY STORE BUSINESS, Creative Age Communications, 7628 Densmore Ave., Van Nuys CA 91406-2042. (818)782-7328, ext. 353. Fax: (818)782-7450. E-mail: mbirenbaum@creativeage.com. **Contact:** Marc Birenbaum, executive editor. **50% freelance written.** Magazine published 11 times/year covering beauty store business management and news. "The primary readers of the publication are owners, managers, and buyers at open-to-the-public beauty stores, including general-market and multicultural market-oriented ones with or without salon services. Our secondary readers are those at beauty stores only open to salon industry professionals. We also go to beauty distributors." Estab. 1994. Circ. 15,000. **Pays on acceptance.** Publishes ms an average of 3 months after acceptance. Byline given. Offers negotiable kill fee. Buys all rights. Editorial lead time 3 months. Submit seasonal material 4 months in advance. Accepts queries by mail, e-mail, fax. Responds in 1 week to queries 2 weeks, if interested, to mss. Sample copy for free.

Nonfiction: "If your business-management article will help a specialty retailer, it should be of assistance to our readers. We're also always looking for writers who are fluent in Korean." How-to (business management, merchandising, e-commerce, retailing), interview/profile (industry leaders). **Buys 20-30 mss/year.** Query. Length: 1,800-2,200 words. **Pays $250-525 for assigned articles.** Sometimes pays expenses of writers on assignment.

Photos: Do not send computer art electronically. State availability with submission. Reviews transparencies, computer art (artists work on Macs, request 300 dpi, on CD or Zip Disk, saved as JPEG, TIFF, or EPS). Buys all rights. Negotiates payment individually. Captions, identification of subjects required.

$ $ COSMETICS, Canada's Business Magazine for the Cosmetics, Fragrance, Toiletry, and Personal Care Industry, Rogers, 777 Bay St., Suite 405, Toronto ON M5W 1A7, Canada. (416)596-5817. Fax: (416)596-5179. E-mail: rwood@rmpublishing.com. Website: www.cosmeticsmag.com. **Contact:** Ronald A. Wood, editor. **10% freelance written.** Bimonthly magazine. "Our main reader segment is the retail trade—department stores, drugstores, salons, estheticians—owners and cosmeticians/beauty advisors; plus manufacturers, distributors, agents, and suppliers to the industry." Estab. 1972. Circ. 13,000. **Pays on acceptance.** Publishes ms an average of 3 months after acceptance. Byline given. Offers 50% kill fee. Buys all rights. Editorial lead time 4 months. Submit seasonal material 4 months in advance. Accepts queries by mail. Responds in 1 month to queries. Sample copy for $6 (Canadian) and 8% GST.

Nonfiction: General interest, interview/profile, photo feature. **Buys 1 mss/year.** Query. Length: 250-1,200 words. **Pays 25¢/word.** Sometimes pays expenses of writers on assignment.

Photos: Send photos with submission. Reviews 2½ up to 8×10 transparencies, 4×6 up to 8×10 prints, 35mm slides, e-mail pictures in 300 dpi JPEG format. Buys all rights. Offers no additional payment for photos accepted with ms. Captions, identification of subjects, model releases required.

Columns/Departments: "All articles assigned on a regular basis from correspondents and columnists that we know personally from the industry."

The online magazine carries original content not found in the print edition. Contact: Jim Hicks, publisher/online editor.

Tips: "Must have broad knowledge of the Canadian cosmetics, fragrance, and toiletries industry and retail business. 99.9% of freelance articles are assigned by the editor to writers involved with the Canadian cosmetics business."

$ $ DAYSPA, For the Salon of the Future, Creative Age Publications, 7628 Densmore Ave., Van Nuys CA 91406. (818)782-7328. Fax: (818)782-7450. E-mail: dayspa@creativeage.com. Website: www.dayspamagazine.com. Managing Editor: Inga Hansen. **Contact:** Linda Lewis, executive editor. **50% freelance written.** Monthly magazine covering the business of day spas, skin care salons, wellness centers. "*Dayspa* includes only well-targeted business articles directed at the owners and managers of high-end, multi-service salons, day spas, resort spas, and destination spas." Estab. 1996. Circ.

31,000. **Pays on acceptance.** Publishes ms an average of 4 months after acceptance. Byline given. Buys first, one-time rights. Editorial lead time 4 months. Submit seasonal material 4 months in advance. Accepts queries by mail, e-mail, fax, phone. Responds in 2 months to queries. Sample copy for $5.

Nonfiction: Buys 40 mss/year. Query. Length: 1,200-3,000 words. **Pays $150-500.**

Photos: Send photos with submission. Buys one-time rights. Negotiates payment individually. Identification of subjects, model releases required.

Columns/Departments: Legal Pad (legal issues affecting salons/spas); Money Matters (financial issues), both 1,200-1,500 words. **Buys 20 mss/year.** Query. **Pays $150-300.**

$ $ DERMASCOPE MAGAZINE, The Encyclopedia of Aesthetics & Spa Therapy, Geneva Corp., 2611 N. Belt Line Rd., Suite 101, Sunnyvale TX 75182. (972)226-2309. Fax: (972)226-2339. E-mail: saundra@dermascope.com. Website: www.dermascope.com. **Contact:** Saundra Brown, editor-in-chief. Monthly magazine covering aesthetics (skin care) and body and spa therapy. "Our magazine is a source of practical advice and continuing education for skin care, body, and spa therapy professionals. Our main readers are salon, day spa, and destination spa owners, managers, or technicians and aesthetics students." Estab. 1976. Circ. 15,000. Pays on publication. Publishes ms an average of 6 months after acceptance. Byline given. Buys all rights. Editorial lead time 3 months. Submit seasonal material 6 months in advance. Accepts queries by mail, fax. Responds in 1 month to queries; 6 months to mss. Sample copy available by phone.

Nonfiction: Interested in seeing nonproduct specific how-to articles with photographs. Book excerpts, general interest, historical/nostalgic, how-to, inspirational, personal experience, photo feature, technical. **Buys 6 mss/year.** Query with published clips. Length: 1,500-2,500 words. **Pays $50-250.**

Photos: State availability with submission. Reviews 4×5 prints. Buys all rights. Offers no additional payment for photos accepted by ms. Captions, identification of subjects, model releases required.

Tips: "Write from the practitioner's point of view. Step-by-step how-to's that show the skin care and body and spa therapist practical methodology are a plus. Would like more business and finance ideas, applicable to the industry."

$ $ DERMATOLOGY INSIGHTS, A Patient's Guide to Healthy Skin, Hair, and Nails, American Academy of Dermatology, 930 N. Meacham Rd., Schaumburg IL 60173. (847)330-0230. E-mail: dmonti@aad.org. Website: www.aad.org. Managing Editor: Lara Lowery. **Contact:** Dean Monti, editor. **60% freelance written.** Semiannual magazine covering dermatology. *Dermatology Insights* contains "educational and informative articles for consumers about dermatological subjects." Estab. 2000. **Pays on acceptance.** Publishes ms an average of 4 months after acceptance. Byline given. Buys all rights, makes work-for-hire assignments. Editorial lead time 4 months. Submit seasonal material 4 months in advance. Accepts queries by mail, e-mail. Responds in 3 weeks to queries; 1 month to mss. Sample copy for free. Writer's guidelines not available.

Nonfiction: General interest, how-to, interview/profile, new product, personal experience, photo feature, technical. **Buys 10-15 mss/year.** Query. Length: 750 words maximum. **Pays flat rate of $40/hour.** Sometimes pays expenses of writers on assignment.

Photos: State availability with submission. Buys all rights. Negotiates payment individually. Identification of subjects required.

Columns/Departments: Patient Perspective (patient's first-hand account). **Buys 2-3 mss/year.** Query. **Pays flat rate of $40/hour.**

$ MASSAGE & BODYWORK, Associated Bodywork & Massage Professionals, 1271 Sugarbush Dr., Evergreen CO 80439-9766. (303)674-8478 or (800)458-2267. Fax: (303)674-0859. E-mail: editor@abmp.com. Website: www.massageandbodywork.com. **Contact:** Leslie A. Young, Ph.D., editor-in-chief. **85% freelance written.** Bimonthly magazine covering therapeutic massage/bodywork. "A trade publication for the massage therapist, bodyworker, and skin care professionals. An all-inclusive publication encompassing everything from traditional Swedish massage to energy work to other complementary therapies (i.e.-homeopathy, herbs, aromatherapy, etc.)." **Pays on acceptance.** Publishes ms an average of 6 months after acceptance. Buys first North American serial, one-time, electronic rights. Editorial lead time 6 months. Submit seasonal material 6 months in advance. Accepts queries by mail, e-mail, fax, phone. Responds in 1 month to queries; 5 months to mss. Writer's guidelines online.

Nonfiction: Essays, exposé, how-to (technique/modality), interview/profile, opinion, personal experience, technical, travel. No fiction. **Buys 60-75 mss/year.** Query with published clips. Length: 1,000-3,000 words.

Reprints: Accepts previously published submissions.

Photos: State availability with submission. Reviews contact sheets. Buys one-time rights. Negotiates payment individually. Captions, identification of subjects, model releases required.

Columns/Departments: Buys 20 mss/year.

Tips: "Know your topic. Offer suggestions for art to accompany your submission. *Massage & Bodywork* looks for interesting, tightly focused stories concerning a particular modality or technique of massage, bodywork, somatic and skin care therapies. The editorial staff welcomes the opportunity to review manuscripts which may be relevant to the field of massage, bodywork, and skin care practices, in addition to more general pieces pertaining to complementary and alternative medicine. This would include the widely varying modalities of massage and bodywork, (from Swedish massage to Polarity therapy), specific technical or ancillary therapies, including such topics as biomagnetics, aromatherapy, and facial rejuvenation. Reference lists relating to technical articles should include the author, title, publisher, and publication date of works cited. Word count: 1,500-4,000 words; longer articles negotiable."

$ $ MASSAGE MAGAZINE, Exploring Today's Touch Therapies, 200 7th Ave., #240, Santa Cruz CA 95062. (831)477-1176. E-mail: edit@massagemag.com. Website: www.massagemag.com. **Contact:** Karen Menehan, editor. **25%**

freelance written. Bimonthly magazine covering massage and other touch therapies. Estab. 1985. Circ. 50,000. **Pays on acceptance.** Publishes ms an average of 1 year after acceptance. Byline given. Buys first North American serial rights. Accepts queries by mail, e-mail. Responds in 2 months to queries; 3 months to mss. Sample copy and writer's guidelines free. Writer's guidelines online.

Nonfiction: Book excerpts, essays, general interest, how-to, inspirational, interview/profile, personal experience, photo feature, technical, experiential. Length: 600-2,000 words. **Pays $50-300 for assigned articles.**

Reprints: Send tearsheet of article and typed ms with rights for sale noted and information about when and where the material previously appeared. Pays 50-75% of amount paid for an original article.

Photos: Send photos with submission. Buys one-time rights. Offers $25-100/photo. Identification of subjects, identification of photographer required.

Columns/Departments: Profiles; Table Talk (news briefs); Practice Building (business); Technique; Body/Mind. Length: 800-1,200 words. **Pays $100.**

Fillers: Facts, newsbreaks. Length: 100- 800 words. **Pays $125 maximum.**

Tips: "Our readers seek practical information on how to help their clients improve their techniques and/or make their businesses more successful, as well as feature articles that place massage therapy in a positive or inspiring light. Since most of our readers are professional therapists, we do not publish articles on topics like 'How Massage Can Help You Relax.' Please study a few back issues so you know what types of topics and tone we're looking for."

$ $ NAILPRO, The Magazine for Nail Professionals, Creative Age Publications, 7628 Densmore Ave., Van Nuys CA 91406. (818)782-7328. Fax: (818)782-7450. E-mail: nailpro@aol.com. Website: www.nailpro.com. **Contact:** Jodi Mills, executive editor. **75% freelance written.** Monthly magazine written for manicurists and nail technicians working in full-service salons or nails-only salons. It covers technical and business aspects of working in and operating a nail-care service, as well as the nail-care industry in general. Estab. 1989. Circ. 65,000. **Pays on acceptance.** Publishes ms an average of 6 months after acceptance. Byline given. Buys first North American serial rights. Editorial lead time 3 months. Submit seasonal material 3 months in advance. Accepts queries by mail, e-mail, fax. Accepts simultaneous submissions. Responds in 6 weeks to queries. Sample copy for $2 and 8½×11 SASE.

Nonfiction: Book excerpts, how-to, humor, inspirational, interview/profile, personal experience, photo feature, technical. No general interest articles or business articles not geared to the nail-care industry. **Buys 50 mss/year.** Query. Length: 1,000-3,000 words. **Pays $150-450.**

Reprints: Send ms with rights for sale noted and information about when and where the material previously appeared. Pays 25-50% of amount paid for an original article.

Photos: Send photos with submission. Reviews transparencies, prints. Buys one-time rights. Negotiates payment individually. Identification of subjects, model releases required.

Columns/Departments: Building Business (articles on marketing nail services/products), 1,200-2,000 words; Shop Talk (aspects of operating a nail salon), 1,200-2,000 words. **Buys 50 mss/year.** Query. **Pays $200-300.**

The online magazine carries original content not found in the print edition. Contact: Jodi Mills.

$ $ NAILS, Bobit Publishing, 21061 S. Western Ave., Torrance CA 90501-1711. (310)533-2400. Fax: (310)533-2504. E-mail: nailsmag@bobit.com. Website: www.nailsmag.com. **Contact:** Cyndy Drummey, editor. **10% freelance written.** Monthly magazine. "*NAILS* seeks to educate its readers on new techniques and products, nail anatomy and health, customer relations, working safely with chemicals, salon sanitation, and the business aspects of running a salon." Estab. 1983. Circ. 55,000. **Pays on acceptance.** Byline given. Buys all rights. Submit seasonal material 4 months in advance. Accepts queries by mail, e-mail, fax. Responds in 3 months to queries. Sample copy for #10 SASE. Writer's guidelines for #10 SASE.

Nonfiction: Historical/nostalgic, how-to, inspirational, interview/profile, personal experience, photo feature, technical. "No articles on one particular product, company profiles or articles slanted toward a particular company or manufacturer." **Buys 20 mss/year.** Query with published clips. Length: 1,200-3,000 words. **Pays $200-500.** Sometimes pays expenses of writers on assignment.

Photos: State availability with submission. Reviews contact sheets, transparencies, prints (any standard size acceptable). Buys all rights. Offers $50-200/photo. Captions, identification of subjects, model releases required.

The online version contains material not found in the print edition. Contact: Hannah Lee.

Tips: "Send clips and query; *do not send unsolicited manscripts.* We would like to see ideas for articles on a unique salon or a business article that focuses on a specific aspect or problem encountered when working in a salon. The Modern Nail Salon section, which profiles nail salons and full-service salons, is most open to freelancers. Focus on an innovative business idea or unique point of view. Articles from experts on specific business issues—insurance, handling difficult employees, cultivating clients—are encouraged."

$ $ SKIN INC. MAGAZINE, The Complete Business Guide for Face & Body Care, Allured Publishing Corp., 362 S. Schmale Rd., Carol Stream IL 60188. (630)653-2155. Fax: (630)653-2192. E-mail: taschetta-millane@allured.com. Website: www.skininc.com. Publisher: Marian Raney. **Contact:** Melinda Taschetta-Millane, associate publisher/editor. **30% freelance written.** Magazine published 12 times/year. "Manuscripts considered for publication that contain original and new information in the general fields of skin care and makeup, dermatological and esthetician-assisted surgical techniques. The subject may cover the science of skin, the business of skin care and makeup, and plastic surgeons on healthy (i.e., nondiseased) skin. Subjects may also deal with raw materials, formulations, and regulations concerning claims for products and equipment." Estab. 1988. Circ. 16,000. Pays on publication. Publishes ms an average of 6 months after acceptance. Byline given. Buys all rights. Editorial lead time 6 months. Submit seasonal material 1 year in advance. Accepts queries by mail, e-mail, fax, phone. Responds in 2 weeks to queries; 1 month to mss. Sample copy for free. Writer's guidelines free.

Nonfiction: General interest, how-to, interview/profile, personal experience, technical. **Buys 6 mss/year.** Query with published clips. Length: 2,000 words. **Pays $100-300 for assigned articles; $50-200 for unsolicited articles.**

Photos: State availability with submission. Reviews 3×5 prints. Buys one-time rights. Offers no additional payment for photos accepted with ms. Captions, identification of subjects, model releases required.

Columns/Departments: Finance (tips and solutions for managing money), 2,000-2,500 words; Personnel (managing personnel), 2,000-2,500 words; Marketing (marketing tips for salon owners), 2,000-2,500 words; Retail (retailing products and services in the salon environment), 2,000-2,500 words. Query with published clips. **Pays $50-200.**

Fillers: Facts, newsbreaks. **Buys 6/year.** Length: 250-500 words. **Pays $50-100.**

Tips: "Have an understanding of the skin care industry."

BEVERAGES & BOTTLING

Manufacturers, distributors, and retailers of soft drinks and alcoholic beverages read these publications. Publications for bar and tavern operators and managers of restaurants are classified in the Hotels, Motels, Clubs, Resorts & Restaurants category.

$ $ ▣ BAR & BEVERAGE BUSINESS MAGAZINE, Mercury Publications Ltd., 1839 Inkster Blvd., Winnipeg MB R2X 1R3, Canada. (204)954-2085. Fax: (204)954-2057. E-mail: mp@mercury.mb.ca. Website: www.mercury.mb.ca/. Editor: Kelly Gray. **Contact:** Kristi Balon, editorial production manager. **33% freelance written.** Bimonthly magazine providing information on the latest trends, happenings, buying-selling of beverages and product merchandising. Estab. 1998. Circ. 16,077. Pays 30-45 days from receipt of invoice. Byline given. Offers 33% kill fee. Buys all rights. Submit seasonal material 3 months in advance. Accepts simultaneous submissions. Sample copy and writer's guidelines free or by e-mail.

- Does not accept queries. Assigns stories to Canadian writers.

Nonfiction: How-to (making a good drink, training staff, etc.), interview/profile. Industry reports, profiles on companies. Query with published clips. Length: 500-9,000 words. **Pays 25-35¢/word.** Sometimes pays expenses of writers on assignment.

Photos: State availability with submission. Reviews negatives, transparencies, 3×5 prints, JPEG, EPS or TIFF files. Buys all rights. Negotiates payment individually. Captions required.

Columns/Departments: Out There (bar & bev news in various parts of the country), 100-500 words. Query. **Pays $0-100.**

$ BEER, WINE & SPIRITS BEVERAGE RETAILER, The Marketing & Merchandising Magazine for Off-Premise Innovators, Oxford Publishing Co., 307 W. Jackson Ave., Oxford MS 38655-2154. (662)236-5510. Fax: (662)236-5541. E-mail: brenda@oxpub.com. Website: www.beverage-retailer.com. **Contact:** Brenda Owen, editor. **2-5% freelance written.** Magazine published 6 times a year covering alcohol beverage retail industry (off-premise). "Our readership of off-premise beverage alcohol retailers (owners and operators of package liquor stores, wine cellars, beer barns, etc.) appreciates our magazine's total focus on helping them increase their revenue and profits. We particulary emphasize stories on retailers' own ideas and efforts to market their products and their stores' images." Estab. 1997. Circ. 20,000. **Pays on acceptance.** Publishes ms an average of 7 months after acceptance. Byline given. Buys first North American serial rights. Editorial lead time 6 months. Submit seasonal material 6 months in advance. Accepts queries by mail. Responds in 2 weeks to queries; 1 month to mss. Sample copy for $5 or online at website.

- 🔑 Break in with a "successful retailer" profile or product feature that shows your grasp on moneymaking tips, marketing, and merchandising ideas.

Nonfiction: General interest, how-to, interview/profile, industry commentary. "No book reviews; no product stories narrowly focused on one manufacturer's product; no general stories on beverage categories (scotch, tequila, etc.) unless trend-oriented." **Buys 4-6 mss/year.** Query with published clips or send complete ms. Length: 350-800 words. **Pays $100 for assigned articles.** Pays phone expenses only of writers on assignment.

Photos: State availability of or send photos with submission. Reviews contact sheets, transparencies (all sizes), prints (all sizes). Buys all rights. Offers no additional payment for photos accepted with ms on most features. Negotiates payment individually on cover stories and major features. Captions, identification of subjects, model releases required.

Columns/Departments: Successful Retailers (What business practice, unique facility feature, or other quality makes this business so successful?), 350-400 words; Marketing & Merchandising (*brief* stories of innovative efforts by retailers—displays, tastings and other events, celebrity appearances, special sales, etc.) 50-350 words. Query with published clips or send complete ms. **Pays $25-100.**

Tips: "Rely solely on off-premise beverage alcohol retailers (and, in some cases, leading industry experts) as your sources. Make certain every line of your story focuses on telling the reader how to improve his business' revenue and profits. Keep your story short, and include colorful, intelligent, and concise retailer quotes. Include a few *relevant* and irresistible statistics. We particularly appreciate trend or analysis stories when we get them early enough to publish them in a timely fashion."

N $ $ THE BEVERAGE GUIDE (ILLINOIS EDITION), MI Licensed Beverage Association, 920 N. Fairview Ave., Lansing MI 48912. (518)374-9611. Fax: (517)374-1165. E-mail: ashock@mlba.org. **Contact:** Amy Shock, editor. **40-50% freelance written.** Monthly magazine covering the hospitality industry. "Magazine devoted to the beer, wine, and spirits industry in Illinois. It is dedicated to serving those who make their living serving the public and the state through the orderly and responsible sale of beverages." Estab. 2001. Circ. 3,000. Pays on publication. Buys one-time, second serial (reprint) rights, makes work-for-hire assignments. Editorial lead time 3 months. Submit seasonal material 3 months in advance. Accepts queries by mail, e-mail. Accepts previously published material. Responds in 2 weeks to queries; 1 month to mss. Sample copy for $5 or online at website.

Nonfiction: Essays, general interest, historical/nostalgic, how-to (make a drink, human resources, tips, etc.), humor, interview/profile, new product, opinion, personal experience, photo feature, technical. **Buys 24 mss/year.** Send complete ms. Length: 1,000 words. **Pays $20-200.**

Columns/Departments: Interviews (legislators, others), 750-1,000 words; Personal Experience (waitstaff, customer, bartenders), 500 words. "Open to essay content ideas." **Buys 12 mss/year.** Send complete ms. **Pays $25-100.**

Tips: "We are particularly interested in nonfiction concerning responsible consumption/serving of alcohol. We're looking for product reviews, company profiles, personal experiences, food-related articles that would benefit our audience. Our audience is a bust group of business owners and hospitality professionals striving to obtain pertinent information that is not too wordy."

N $ $ THE BEVERAGE GUIDE (WISCONSIN EDITION), MI Licensed Beverage Association, 920 N. Fairview Ave., Lansing MI 48912. (518)374-9611. Fax: (517)374-1165. E-mail: ashock@mlba.org. **Contact:** Amy Shock, editor. **40-50% freelance written.** Monthly magazine covering the hospitality industry. "Magazine devoted to the beer, wine, and spirits industry in Wisconsin. It is dedicated to serving those who make their living serving the public and the state through orderly and responsible sale of beverages." Estab. 2001. Circ. 1,500. Pays on publication. Buys one-time, second serial (reprint) rights. Editorial lead time 3 months. Submit seasonal material 3 months in advance. Accepts queries by mail, e-mail. Accepts previously published material. Responds in 2 weeks to queries; 1 month to mss. Sample copy for $5 or online at website.

Nonfiction: Essays, general interest, historical/nostalgic, how-to (make a drink, human resources, tips, etc.), humor, interview/profile, new product, opinion, personal experience, photo feature, technical. **Buys 24 mss/year.** Send complete ms. Length: 1,000 words. **Pays $20-200.**

Columns/Departments: Interviews (legislators, others), 750-1,000 words; Personal Experience (waitstaff, customer, bartenders), 500 words. Open to essay content ideas. **Buys 12 mss/year.** Send complete ms. **Pays $25-100.**

Tips: "We are particularly interested in nonfiction concerning responsible consumption/serving of alcohol. We're looking for product reviews, company profiles, personal experiences, food-related articles that would benefit our audience. Our audience is a bust group of business owners and hospitality professionals striving to obtain pertinent information that is not too wordy."

$ $ THE BEVERAGE JOURNAL, Michigan Edition, MI Licensed Beverage Association, 920 N. Fairview Ave., Lansing MI 48912. (518)374-9611. Fax: (517)374-1165. E-mail: ashock@mlba.org. Website: www.mlba.org. **Contact:** Amy Shock, editor. **40-50% freelance written.** Monthly magazine covering hospitality industry. "A monthly trade magazine devoted to the beer, wine, and spirits industry in Michigan. It is dedicated to serving those who make their living serving the public and the state through the orderly and responsible sale of beverages." Estab. 1983. Circ. 4,200. Pays on publication. Buys one-time, second serial (reprint) rights, makes work-for-hire assignments. Editorial lead time 3 months. Submit seasonal material 3 months in advance. Accepts queries by mail, e-mail. Responds in 2 weeks to queries; 1 month to mss. Sample copy for $5 or online.

Nonfiction: Essays, general interest, historical/nostalgic, how-to (make a drink, human resources, tips, etc.), humor, interview/profile, new product, opinion, personal experience, photo feature, technical. **Buys 24 mss/year.** Send complete ms. Length:1,000 words. **Pays $20-200.**

Reprints: Accepts previously published submissions.

Columns/Departments: Interviews (legislators, others), 750-1,000 words; personal experience (waitstaff, customer, bartenders), 500 words. "Open to essay content ideas." **Buys 12 mss/year.** Send complete ms. **Pays $25-100.**

Tips: "We are particularly interested in nonfiction concerning responsible consumption/serving of alcohol. We are looking for product reviews, company profiles, personal experiences, food-related articles that would benefit our audience. Our audience is a busy group of business owners and hospitality professionals striving to obtain pertinent information that is not too wordy."

$ $ PATTERSON'S CALIFORNIA BEVERAGE JOURNAL, Interactive Color, Inc., 4910 San Fernando Rd., Glendale CA 91204. (818)291-1125. Fax: (818)547-4607. E-mail: mmay@interactivecolor.com. Website: www.beveragelink.com. **Contact:** Meridith May, managing editor. **25% freelance written.** Monthly magazine covering the alcohol, beverage, and wine industries. "*Patterson's* reports on the latest news in product information, merchandising, company appointments, developments in the wine industry, and consumer trends. Our readers can be informed, up-to-date and confident in their purchasing decisions." Estab. 1962. Circ. 20,000. Byline given. Offers negotiable kill fee. Editorial lead time 1 month. Submit seasonal material 1 month in advance. Accepts queries by mail, e-mail, fax. Sample copy for free. Writer's guidelines free.

Nonfiction: Interview/profile, new product, market reports. "No consumer-oriented articles or negative slants on industry as a whole." **Buys 200 mss/year.** Query with published clips. Length: 600-1,800 words. **Pays $60-200.**

Photos: State availability with submission. Reviews transparencies. Buys all rights. Offers no additional payment for photos accepted with ms. Captions, identification of subjects required.

Columns/Departments: Query with published clips.

$ $ $ VINEYARD & WINERY MANAGEMENT, 3535 Industrial Dr., Suite A3, Santa Rosa CA 95403. (707)566-3810. Fax: (707)566-3815. E-mail: gparnell@vwm-online.com. Website: www.vwm-online.com. **Contact:** Graham Parnell, managing editor. **70% freelance written.** Bimonthly magazine of professional importance to grape growers, winemakers and winery sales and business people. Estab. 1975. Circ. 6,500. Pays on publication. Byline given. Buys first North

American serial, simultaneous rights. Accepts queries by e-mail. Responds in 3 weeks to queries; 1 month to mss. Sample copy for free. Writer's guidelines for #10 SASE.

Nonfiction: Subjects are technical in nature and explore the various methods people in these career paths use to succeed, and also the equipment and techniques they use successfully. Business articles and management topics are also featured. The audience is national with western dominance. How-to, interview/profile, new product, technical. **Buys 30 mss/year.** Query. Length: 1,800-5,000 words. **Pays $30-1,000.** Sometimes pays expenses of writers on assignment.

Photos: State availability with submission. Reviews contact sheets, negatives, transparencies, digital photos. Black & white often purchased for $20 each to accompany story material; 35mm and/or 4×5 transparencies for $50 and up; 6/year of vineyard and/or winery scene related to story. Captions, identification of subjects required.

Tips: "We're looking for long-term relationships with authors who know the business and write well. Electronic submissions required; query for formats."

N $ $ WINES & VINES MAGAZINE, The Authoritative Voice of the Grape and Wine Industry Since 1919, The Hiaring Co., 1800 Lincoln Ave., San Rafael CA 94901. (415)453-9700. E-mail: edit@winesandvines.com. Website: www.winesandvines.com. Managing Editor: Tina Caputo. **Contact:** Jane Firstenfeld, staff writer. **50% freelance written.** Monthly magazine covering the international winegrape and winemaking industry. "Since 1919 *Wines & Vines Magazine* has been the authoritative voice of the wine and grape industry—from prohibition to phylloxera, we have covered it all. Our paid circulation reaches all 50 states and foreign countries. Because we are intended for the trade—including growers, winemakers, winery owners, wholesalers, restauranteurs, and serious amateurs—we accept more technical, informative articles. We do not accept wine reviews, wine country tours, or anything of a wine consumer nature." Estab. 1919. Circ. 4,000. **Pays on acceptance.** Publishes ms an average of 3 months after acceptance. Byline given. Buys first, electronic rights. Editorial lead time 2 months. Submit seasonal material 4 months in advance. Accepts queries by e-mail. Responds in 2-3 weeks to queries. Sample copy for $5. Writer's guidelines free.

Nonfiction: Interview/profile, new product, technical. No wine reviews, wine country travelogues, 'lifestyle' pieces, or anything aimed at wine consumers. "Our readers are professionals in the field." **Buys 60 mss/year.** Query with published clips. Length: 800-1,800 words. **Pays 15-25¢/word for assigned articles.**

Photos: State availability of or send photos with submission. Reviews transparencies, prints, GIF/JPEG files (JPEG, 300 dpi minimum). Buys one-time rights. Offers $10/published original photos. Captions, identification of subjects required.

BOOK & BOOKSTORE

Publications for book trade professionals from publishers to bookstore operators are found in this section. Journals for professional writers are classified in the Journalism & Writing category.

$ THE BLOOMSBURY REVIEW, A Book Magazine, (formerly *Bloomsbury Review*), Dept. WM, Owaissa Communications Co., Inc., P.O. Box 8928, Denver CO 80201. (303)455-3123. Fax: (303)455-7039. E-mail: bloomsb@aol.com. **Contact:** Marilyn Auer, editor. **75% freelance written.** Bimonthly tabloid covering books and book-related matters. "We publish book reviews, interviews with writers and poets, literary essays and original poetry. Our audience consists of educated, literate, nonspecialized readers." Estab. 1980. Circ. 50,000. Pays on publication. Publishes ms an average of 4-6 months after acceptance. Byline given. Buys first, one-time rights. Accepts queries by mail. Responds in 4 months to queries. Sample copy for $5 and 9×12 SASE. Writer's guidelines for #10 SASE.

Nonfiction: "Summer issue features reviews, etc., about the American West. *We do not publish fiction.*" Essays, interview/profile, book reviews. **Buys 60 mss/year.** Query with published clips or send complete ms. Length: 800-1,500 words. **Pays $10-20. Sometimes pays writers with contributor copies or other premiums "if writer agrees."**

Reprints: Considered but not encouraged. Send photocopy of article and information about when and where the article previously appeared.

Photos: State availability with submission. Reviews prints. Buys one-time rights. Offers no additional payment for photos accepted with ms.

Columns/Departments: Book reviews and essays, 500-1,500 words. **Buys 6 mss/year.** Query with published clips or send complete ms. **Pays $10-20.**

Poetry: Ray Gonzalez, poetry editor. Avant-garde, free verse, haiku, traditional. **Buys 20 poems/year.** Submit maximum 5 poems. **Pays $5-10.**

Tips: "We appreciate receiving published clips and/or completed manuscripts. Please—no rough drafts. Book reviews should be of new books (within 6 months of publication)."

$ FOREWORD MAGAZINE, ForeWord Magazine Inc., 129½ E. Front St., Traverse City MI 49684. (231)933-3699. Fax: (231)933-3899. E-mail: alex@forewordmagazine.com. Website: www.forewordmagazine.com. **Contact:** Alex Moore, managing editor. **95% freelance written.** Bimonthly magazine covering independent and university presses for booksellers and librarians with articles, news, book reviews. Estab. 1998. Circ. 15,000. Pays 2 months after publication. Publishes ms an average of 2-3 months after acceptance. Byline given. Buys all rights. Editorial lead time 3-4 months. Submit seasonal material 5 months in advance. Accepts queries by mail, e-mail. Responds in 1 month to queries; 1 month to mss. Sample copy for $10 and 8½ X 11 SASE with $1.50 postage.

Nonfiction: Reviews, 85% nonfiction and 15% fiction. Special issues: Reviews, 400 words; articles, 1,500 words. Query with published clips. **Pays $40-100 for assigned articles.**

Tips: "Be knowledgeable about the needs of booksellers and librarians—remember we are an industry trade journal, not a how-to or consumer publication. We review books prior to publication, so book reviews are always assigned—but send us a note telling subjects you wish to review in as well as a résumé."

$ THE HORN BOOK MAGAZINE, The Horn Book, Inc., 56 Roland St., Suite 200, Boston MA 02129. (617)628-0225. Fax: (617)628-0882. E-mail: magazine@hbook.com. Website: www.hbook.com. **Contact:** Roger Sutton, editor-in-chief. **75% freelance written.** Prefers to work with published/established writers. Bimonthly magazine covering children's literature for librarians, booksellers, professors, teachers and students of children's literature. Estab. 1924. Circ. 21,500. Pays on publication. Publishes ms an average of 4 months after acceptance. Byline given. Submit seasonal material 6 months in advance. Accepts queries by mail, e-mail, fax. Accepts simultaneous submissions. Responds in 2 months to queries. Sample copy and writer's guidelines online.

Nonfiction: Interested in seeing strong, authoritative pieces about children's books and contemporary culture. Writers should be familiar with the magazine and its contents. Interview/profile (children's book authors and illustrators), topics of interest to the children's bookworld. **Buys 20 mss/year.** Query or send complete ms. Length: 1,000-2,800 words. **Pays honorarium upon publication.**

The online magazine carries original content not found in the print edition and includes writer's guidelines.

Tips: "Writers have a better chance of breaking into our publication with a query letter on a specific article they want to write."

BRICK, GLASS & CERAMICS

These publications are read by manufacturers, dealers, and managers of brick, glass, and ceramic retail businesses. Other publications related to glass and ceramics are listed in the Consumer Art & Architecture and Hobby & Craft sections.

$ $ GLASS MAGAZINE, For the Architectural Glass Industry, National Glass Association, 8200 Greensboro Dr., McLean VA 22102-. (703)442-4890. Fax: (703)442-0630. E-mail: charles@glass.org. Website: www.glass.org. **Contact:** Charles Cumpston, editor. **10% freelance written.** Prefers to work with published/established writers. Monthly magazine covering the architectural glass industry. Circ. 23,291. **Pays on acceptance.** Publishes ms an average of 6 months after acceptance. Byline given. Kill fee varies. Buys first rights. Accepts queries by mail, e-mail, fax. Responds in 2 months to mss. Sample copy for $5 and 9×12 SAE with 10 first-class stamps.

Nonfiction: Interview/profile (of various glass businesses; profiles of industry people or glass business owners), new product, technical (about glazing processes). **Buys 5 mss/year.** Query with published clips. Length: 1,000 words minimum. **Pays $150-300 for assigned articles.**

Photos: State availability with submission.

Tips: *Glass Magazine* is doing more inhouse writing; freelance cut by half. "Do *not* send in general glass use stories. Research the industry first, then query."

$ STAINED GLASS, Stained Glass Association of America, 10009 E. 62nd St., Raytown MO 64133. (800)438-9581. Fax: (816)737-2801. E-mail: sgaa@stainedglass.org. Website: www.stainedglass.org. **Contact:** Richard Gross, editor. **70% freelance written.** Quarterly magazine. "Since 1906, *Stained Glass* has been the official voice of the Stained Glass Association of America. As the oldest, most respected stained glass publication in North America, *Stained Glass* preserves the techniques of the past as well as illustrates the trends of the future. This vital information, of significant value to the professional stained glass studio, is also of interest to those for whom stained glass is an avocation or hobby." Estab. 1906. Circ. 8,000. Pays on publication. Publishes ms an average of 1 year after acceptance. Byline given. Buys one-time rights. Editorial lead time 6 months. Submit seasonal material 8 months in advance. Accepts queries by mail, e-mail, fax. Responds in 3 months to queries. Sample copy and writer's guideline free.

Break in with "excellent photography and in-depth stained glass architectural knowledge."

Nonfiction: Strong need for technical and how to create architectural type stained glass. Glass etching, use of etched glass in stained glass compositions, framing. How-to, humor, interview/profile, new product, opinion, photo feature, technical. **Buys 9 mss/year.** Query or send complete ms but must include photos or slides—very heavy on photos. **Pays $125/illustrated article; $75/non-illustrated.**

Reprints: Accepts previously published submissions from nonstained glass publications only. Send tearsheet of article. Payment negotiable.

Photos: Send photos with submission. Reviews 4×5 transparencies, send slides with submission. Buys one-time rights. Pays $75 for non-illustrated. Pays $125, plus 3 copies for line art or photography. Identification of subjects required.

Columns/Departments: Teknixs (technical, how-to, stained and glass art), word length varies by subject. "Columns must be illustrated." **Buys 4 mss/year.** Query or send complete ms, but must be illustrated.

Tips: "We need more technical articles. Writers should be extremely well versed in the glass arts. Photographs are extremely important and must be of very high quality. Submissions without photographs or illustrations are seldom considered unless something special and writer states that photos are available. However, prefer to see with submission."

$ $ US GLASS, METAL & GLAZING, Key Communications, Inc., P.O. Box 569, Garrisonville VA 22463. (540)720-5584. Fax: (540)720-5687. E-mail: echilcoat@glass.com. Website: www.usglassmag.com. **Contact:** Ellen Giard Chilcoat, managing editor. **25% freelance written.** Monthly magazine for companies involved in the flat glass trades. Estab. 1966. Circ. 27,000. Pays on publication. Publishes ms an average of 3 months after acceptance. Byline given. Buys all rights. Editorial lead time 3 months. Submit seasonal material 2 months in advance. Accepts queries by mail, e-mail, fax. Accepts simultaneous submissions. Responds in 1 month to queries; 2 months to mss. Sample copy and writer's guidelines on website.

Nonfiction: **Buys 12 mss/year.** Query with published clips. **Pays $300-600 for assigned articles.** Sometimes pays expenses of writers on assignment.

Photos: State availability with submission. Reviews contact sheets. Buys first North American rights. Offers no additional payment for photos accepted with ms. Captions, identification of subjects required.

The online magazine carries original content not found in the print edition. Contact: Holly Carter.

BUILDING INTERIORS

Owners, managers, and sales personnel of floor covering, wall covering, and remodeling businesses read the journals listed in this category. Interior design and architecture publications may be found in the Consumer Art & Architecture category. For journals aimed at other construction trades see the Construction & Contracting section.

$ $ PWC, Painting & Wallcovering Contractor, Finan Publishing Co., Inc., 107 W. Pacific Ave., St. Louis MO 63119-2323. (314)961-6644. Fax: (314)961-4809. E-mail: jbeckner@finan.com. Website: www.paintstore.com. **Contact:** Jeffery Beckner, editor. **90% freelance written.** Bimonthly magazine. "*PWC* provides news you can use: Information helpful to the painting and wallcovering contractor in the here and now." Estab. 1928. Circ. 30,000. Pays 1 month after acceptance. Publishes ms an average of 1 month after acceptance. Byline given. Offers variable kill fee. Buys first North American serial rights. Editorial lead time 2 months. Submit seasonal material 2 months in advance. Accepts simultaneous submissions. Responds in 2 weeks to queries. Sample copy for free.

Nonfiction: Essays, exposé, how-to (painting and wallcovering), interview/profile, new product, opinion, personal experience. **Buys 40 mss/year.** Query with published clips. Length: 1,500-2,500 words. **Pays $300 minimum.** Pays expenses of writers on assignment.

Reprints: Send photocopy and information about when and where the material previously appeared. Negotiates payment.

Photos: State availability of or send photos with submission. Reviews contact sheets, negatives, transparencies, digital prints. Buys all rights. Offers no additional payment for photos accepted with ms. Identification of subjects required.

Columns/Departments: Anything of interest to the small businessman, 1,250 words. **Buys 2 mss/year.** Query with published clips. **Pays $50-100.**

Tips: "We almost always buy on an assignment basis. The way to break in is to send good clips, and I'll try and give you work."

$ $ QUALIFIED REMODELER, The Business Management Tool for Professional Remodelers, Cygnus Business Media, 1233 Janesville Ave., Fort Atkinson WI 53538. E-mail: jonathan.sweet@cygnuspub.com. Website: www.qualifiedremodeler.com. Editor: Roger Stanley. **Contact:** Jonathan Sweet, managing editor. **15% freelance written.** Monthly magazine covering residential remodeling. Estab. 1975. Circ. 92,500. **Pays on acceptance.** Publishes ms an average of 1 month after acceptance. Byline given. Buys all rights. Editorial lead time 3 months. Submit seasonal material 2 months in advance. Accepts queries by mail, e-mail, fax, phone. Sample copy online.

Nonfiction: How-to (business management), new product, photo feature, best practices articles, innovative design. **Buys 12 mss/year.** Query with published clips. Length: 1,200-2,500 words. **Pays $300-600 for assigned articles; $200-400 for unsolicited articles.** Sometimes pays expenses of writers on assignment.

Photos: Send photos with submission. Reviews negatives, transparencies. Buys one-time rights. Negotiates payment individually.

Columns/Departments: Query with published clips. **Pays $200-400.**

The online version contains material not found in the print edition.

Tips: "We focus on business management issues faced by remodeling contractors. For example, sales, marketing, liability, taxes and just about any matter addressing small business operation."

$ $ $ REMODELING, Hanley-Wood, LLC, One Thomas Circle NW, Suite 600, Washington DC 20005. (202)452-0800. Fax: (202)785-1974. E-mail: chartman@hanley-wood.com. Website: www.remodelingmagazine.com. Editor-in-Chief: Sal Alfano. **Contact:** Christine Hartman, managing editor. **10% freelance written.** Monthly magazine covering residential and light commercial remodeling. "We cover the best new ideas in remodeling design, business, construction and products." Estab. 1985. Circ. 80,000. Pays on publication. Publishes ms an average of 3 months after acceptance. Byline given. Offers 5¢/word kill fee. Buys first North American serial rights. Accepts queries by mail, e-mail, fax. Responds in 1 month to queries. Sample copy for free.

Nonfiction: Interview/profile, new product, technical, small business trends. **Buys 6 mss/year.** Query with published clips. Length: 250-1,000 words. **Pays 50¢/word.** Sometimes pays expenses of writers on assignment.

Photos: State availability with submission. Reviews 4×5 transparencies, slides, 8×10 prints. Buys one-time rights. Offers $25-125/photo. Captions, identification of subjects, model releases required.

The online magazine carries original content not included in the print edition. Contact: John Butterfield, online editor.

Tips: "We specialize in service journalism for remodeling contractors. Knowledge of the industry is essential."

$ $ WALLS & CEILINGS, Dept. SMM, 755 W. Big Beaver Rd., Troy MI 48084. (248)244-6244. Fax: (248)362-5103. E-mail: morettin@bnp.com. Website: www.wconline.com. **Contact:** Nick Moretti, editor. **20% freelance written.** Monthly magazine for contractors involved in lathing and plastering, drywall, acoustics, fireproofing, curtain walls, movable partitions together with manufacturers, dealers, and architects. Estab. 1938. Circ. 30,000. Pays on publication. Publishes ms an average of 6 months after acceptance. Byline given. Buys all rights. Submit seasonal material 4 months in advance. Accepts queries by mail, e-mail, phone. Accepts simultaneous submissions. Responds in 6 months to queries. Sample copy for 9×12 SAE with $2 postage. Writer's guidelines for #10 SASE.

O→ Break in with technical expertise in drywall, plaster, stucco.

Nonfiction: How-to (drywall and plaster construction and business management), technical. **Buys 20 mss/year.** Query or send complete ms. Length: 1,000-1,500 words. **Pays $50-500.** Sometimes pays expenses of writers on assignment.

Reprints: Send tearsheet or photocopy with rights for sale noted and information about when and where the material previously appeared. Pays 50% of the amount paid for an original article.

Photos: Send photos with submission. Reviews contact sheets, negatives, transparencies, prints. Buys one-time rights. Captions, identification of subjects required.

The online magazine carries original content not included in the print edition.

BUSINESS MANAGEMENT

These publications cover trends, general theory, and management practices for business owners and top-level business executives. Publications that use similar material but have a less technical slant are listed in the Consumer Business & Finance section. Journals for middle management, including supervisors and office managers, appear in the Management & Supervision section. Those for industrial plant managers are listed under Industrial Operations and under sections for specific industries, such as Machinery & Metal. Publications for office supply store operators are included in the Office Environment & Equipment section.

$ $ $ $ ACROSS THE BOARD, The Conference Board Magazine, The Conference Board, 845 Third Ave., New York NY 10022-6679. (212)759-0900. Fax: (212)836-3828. E-mail: atb@conference-board.org. Website: www.acrossteboardmagazine.com. Editor: Al Vogl. Managing Editor: Matthew Budman. **Contact:** Vadim Liberman, assistant editor. **60% freelance written.** Bimonthly magazine covering business—focuses on higher management. "*Across the Board* is a nonprofit magazine of ideas and opinions for leaders in business, government, and other organizations. The editors present business perspectives on timely issues, including management practices, foreign policy, social issues, and science and technology. *Across the Board* is neither an academic business journal not a 'popular' manual. That means we aren't interested in highly technical articles about business strategy. It also means we don't publish oversimple 'how-to' articles. We are an idea magazine, but the ideas should have practical overtones. We let *Forbes, Fortune* and *Business Week* do most of the straight reporting, while we do some of the critical thinking; that is, we let writers explore the implications of the news in depth. *Across the Board* tries to provide different angles on important topics, and to bring to its readers' attention issues that they might otherwise not devote much thought to." Circ. 30,000. Pays on publication. Publishes ms an average of 4 months after acceptance. Byline given. Offers 20% kill fee. Buys first rights. Editorial lead time 6 months. Submit seasonal material 6 months in advance. Accepts queries by mail, e-mail, fax. Accepts simultaneous submissions. Responds in 3 weeks to queries. Sample copy for free. Writer's guidelines online.

Nonfiction: Book excerpts, essays, humor, opinion, personal experience. No new product information. **Buys 30 mss/year.** Query with published clips or send complete ms. Length: 500-4,000 words. **Pays $50-2,500.** Sometimes pays expenses of writers on assignment.

Photos: State availability with submission. Reviews contact sheets. Buys one-time or all rights. Negotiates payment individually. Captions, identification of subjects required.

Tips: "We emphasize the human side of organizational life at all levels. We're as concerned with helping managers who are 'lonely at the top' as with motivating workers and enhancing job satisfaction."

$ $ $ BEDTIMES, The Business Journal for the Sleep Products Industry, International Sleep Products Association, 501 Wythe St., Alexandria VA 22304-1917. (336)299-5407. E-mail: ctsmith@sleepproducts.org. Website: www.sleepproducts.org. **Contact:** Cheminne Taylor-Smith, editor. **20-40% freelance written.** Monthly magazine covering the mattress manufacturing industry. "Our news and features are straight forward—we are not a lobbying vehicle for our association. No special slant or philosophy." Estab. 1917. Circ. 4,000. **Pays on acceptance.** Publishes ms an average of 4 months after acceptance. Byline sometimes given. Buys first North American serial rights. Editorial lead time 2 months. Accepts queries by e-mail, fax. Accepts simultaneous submissions. Responds in 1 month to queries. Sample copy for $4. Writer's guidelines free for #10 SASE or by e-mail.

O→ Break in with "Headlines"—short news stories. We also use freelancers for our monthly columns on "New Products," "Newsmakers," and "Snoozebriefs." Query first.

Nonfiction: Interview/profile, photo feature. "No pieces that do not relate to business in general or mattress industry in particular." **Buys 15-25 mss/year.** Query with published clips. Length: 500-3,500 words. **Pays 25-50¢/word for short features; $1,000 for cover story.**

Photos: State availability with submission. Buys one-time rights. Negotiates payment individually. Identification of subjects required.

Columns/Departments: Millennium Milestones (companies marking anniversaries from 25-150 years), 1,000 words.

Buys 10-12 mss/year. Query with 3 published clips. **Pays $350 or more, depending on length and degree of difficulty in getting the story.**

Tips: "Cover stories are a major outlet for freelance submissions. Once a story is written and accepted, the author is encouraged to submit suggestions to the graphic designer of the magazine regarding ideas for the cover illustration as well as possible photos/graphs/charts, etc. to be used with the story itself. Topics have included annual industry forecast; physical expansion of industry facilities; e-commerce; flammability and home furnishings; the risks and rewards of marketing overseas; the evolving family business; the shifting workplace environment; and what do consumers really want?"

$ CA MAGAZINE, Canadian Institute of Chartered Accountants, 277 Wellington St. W, Toronto ON M5V 3H2, Canada. (416)977-3222. Fax: (416)204-3409. E-mail: camagazine@cica.ca. Website: www.camagazine.com. **Contact:** Christian Bellavance, editor-in-chief. **30% freelance written.** Magazine published 10 times/year covering accounting. "*CA Magazine* is the leading accounting publication in Canada and the preferred information source for chartered accountants and financial executives. It provides a forum for discussion and debate on professional, financial, and other business issues." Estab. 1911. Circ. 74,834. **Pays on acceptance.** Publishes ms an average of 3 months after acceptance. Byline given. Offers 30% kill fee. Buys all rights. Editorial lead time 4 months. Accepts queries by e-mail. Responds in 1 month to queries. Sample copy and writer's guidelines online.

Nonfiction: Book excerpts, financial/accounting business. **Buys 30 mss/year.** Query. Length: 2,500-3,500 words. **Pays honorarium for chartered accountants; freelance rate varies.**

N $ $ CBA MARKETPLACE, CBA Service Corp., P.O. Box 62000, Colorado Springs CO 80962. E-mail: publications@cbaonline.org. Website: www.cbaonline.org. **Contact:** Lora Riley, managing editor. **20% freelance written.** Monthly magazine covering the Christian retail industry. "Writers must have knowledge of and direct experience in the Christian retail industry. Subject matter must specifically pertain to the Christian retail audience." Estab. 1968. **Pays on acceptance.** Publishes ms an average of 3 months after acceptance. Byline given. Buys all rights. Editorial lead time 3 months. Submit seasonal material 6 months in advance. Accepts queries by mail, e-mail. Responds in 2 months to queries. Sample copy for $9.50 or online.

Nonfiction: Christian retail. **Buys 24 mss/year.** Query. Length: 750-1,500 words. **Pays 20-30¢/word.**

Fillers: Cartoons. **Buys 12/year. Pays $150.**

Tips: "Only experts on Christian retail industry, completely familiar with retail audience and their needs and considerations, should submit a query. Do not submit articles unless requested."

N $ $ $ CONSUMER GOODS MANUFACTURER, Improving Business Performance Using Technology, Edgell Communications, 4 Middlebury Blvd., Randolph NJ 07869. (973)252-0100. Fax: (973)252-9020. E-mail: tclark@edgellmail.com. Website: www.consumergoods.com. **Contact:** Tim Clark, senior editor. **60% freelance written.** Monthly tabloid covering suppliers to retailers. "Readers are the functional managers/executives in all types of retail and consumer goods firms. They are making major improvements in company operations and in alliances with customers/suppliers." Estab. 1991. Circ. 26,000. Pays on publication. Publishes ms an average of 2 months after acceptance. Byline sometimes given. Buys first, second serial (reprint) rights. Internet Editorial lead time 3 months. Accepts queries by mail, e-mail, phone. Sample copy for 11x15 SAE and 6 first-class stamps. Writer's guidelines for #10 SASE.

Nonfiction: How-to, interview/profile, technical. **Buys 100 mss/year.** Query with published clips. Length: 1,200-2,400 words. **Pays $900 maximum for assigned articles.** Sometimes pays contributor copies as negotiated. Sometimes pays expenses of writers on assignment.

Photos: Send photos with submission. Reviews contact sheets, negatives, transparencies, prints. Buys one-time rights plus reprint and Internet, if applicable. Offers no additional payment for photos accepted with ms. Identification of subjects required.

Tips: "Case histories about companies achieving substantial results using advanced management practices and/or advanced technology are best."

$ $ CONTRACT MANAGEMENT, National Contract Management Association, 8260 Greensboro Dr., Suite 200, McLean VA 22102. Fax: (703)448-0939. E-mail: cm@ncmahq.org. Website: www.ncmahq.org. **Contact:** Amy Miedema, editor-in-chief. **10% freelance written.** Monthly magazine covering contract and business management. "Most of the articles published in *Contract Management (CM)* are written by members, although one does not have to be an NCMA member to be published in the magazine. Articles should concern some aspect of the contract management profession, whether at the level of a beginner or that of the advanced practitioner." Estab. 1960. Circ. 23,000. Pays on publication. Publishes ms an average of 3 months after acceptance. Byline given. Buys one-time rights. Editorial lead time 10 weeks. Submit seasonal material 3 months in advance. Accepts queries by mail, e-mail, fax, phone. Accepts previously published material. Accepts simultaneous submissions. Responds in 2 weeks to queries; 1 month to mss. Sample copy and writer's guidelines free.

Nonfiction: Essays, general interest, how-to, humor, inspirational, new product, opinion, technical. No company or CEO profiles—please read a copy of publication before submitting. **Buys 6-10 mss/year.** Query with published clips. Length: 2,500-3,000 words. **Pays $300, association members paid in 3 copies.**

Reprints: Accepts previously published submissions.

Photos: State availability with submission. Buys one-time rights. Offers no additional payment for photos accepted with ms. Captions, identification of subjects required.

Columns/Departments: Professional Development (self-improvement in business), 1,000-1,500 words; Back to Basics (basic how-tos and discussions), 1,500-2,000 words. **Buys 2 mss/year.** Query with published clips. **Pays $300.**

Tips: "Query and read at least 1 issue. Visit website to better understand our audience."

$ $ CONTRACTING PROFITS, Trade Press Publishing, 2100 W. Florist Ave., Milwaukee WI 53209. (414)228-7701. E-mail: stacie.whitacre@tradepress.com. Website: www.cleanlink.com/cp. **Contact:** Stacie H. Whitacre, editor. **40% freelance written.** Magazine published 11 times/year. covering "building service contracting, business management advice." "We are the pocket MBA for this industry—focusing not only on cleaning-specific topics, but also discussing how to run businesses better and increase profits through a variety of management articles." Estab. 1995. Circ. 32,000. Pays within 30 days of acceptance. Byline given. Buys all rights. Editorial lead time 2 months. Submit seasonal material 3 months in advance. Accepts queries by mail, e-mail. Sample copy online. Writer's guidelines free.

Nonfiction: Exposé, how-to, interview/profile, technical. "No product-related reviews or testimonials." **Buys 30 mss/year.** Query with published clips. Length: 1,200-3,000 words. **Pays $100-500.** Sometimes pays expenses of writers on assignment.

Columns/Departments: Query with published clips.

Tips: "Read back issues on our website and be able to understand some of those topics prior to calling."

$ CONVENTION SOUTH, Covey Communications Corp., 2001 W. First St., P.O. Box 2267, Gulf Shores AL 36547-2267. (251)968-5300. Fax: (251)968-4532. E-mail: info@conventionsouth.com. Website: www.conventionsouth.com. Editor: J. Talty O'Connor. **Contact:** Kristen McIntosh, executive editor. **50% freelance written.** Monthly business journal for meeting planners who plan events in the South. Topics relate to the meetings industry—how-to articles, industry news, destination spotlights. Estab. 1983. Circ. 16,000. Pays on publication. Publishes ms an average of 2 months after acceptance. Byline given. Buys first, second serial (reprint) rights. Editorial lead time 3 months. Submit seasonal material 4 months in advance. Accepts queries by mail, e-mail, fax. Accepts simultaneous submissions. Responds in 2 months to queries. Sample copy for free. Writer's guidelines for #10 SASE.

Nonfiction: How-to (relative to meeting planning/travel), interview/profile, photo feature, technical, travel. **Buys 50 mss/year.** Query. Length: 750-1,250 words. **Payment negotiable.** Pays in contributor copies or other premiums if arranged in advance. Sometimes pays expenses of writers on assignment.

Reprints: Send photocopy and information about when and where the material previously appeared. Payment negotiable.

Photos: Send photos with submission. Reviews 5×7 prints. Buys one-time rights. Offers no additional payment for photos accepted with ms. Captions, identification of subjects required.

Columns/Departments: How-to (related to meetings), 700 words. **Buys 12 mss/year.** Query with published clips. **Payment negotiable.**

Tips: "Know who our audience is and make sure articles are appropriate for them."

$ $ EXECUTIVE UPDATE, Greater Washington Society of Association Executives, Reagan Building & International Trade Center, 1300 Pennsylvania Ave. NW, Washington DC 20004. Fax: (202)326-0999. E-mail: sbriscoe@gwsae.org. Website: www.executiveupdate.com. **Contact:** Scott Briscoe, editor. **60% freelance written.** Monthly magazine "exploring a broad range of association management issues and for introducing and discussing management and leadership philosophies. It is written for individuals at all levels of association management, with emphasis on senior staff and CEOs." Estab. 1979. Circ. 14,000. **Pays on acceptance.** Publishes ms an average of 6 months after acceptance. Byline given. Offers 20% kill fee. Buys first rights. Editorial lead time 3 months. Submit seasonal material 6 months in advance. Accepts queries by mail, e-mail, fax, phone. Accepts simultaneous submissions. Responds in 1 month to queries; 2 months to mss. Sample copy and writer's guidelines free. Writer's guidelines online.

Nonfiction: How-to, humor, interview/profile, opinion, personal experience, travel, management and workplace issues. **Buys 24-36 mss/year.** Query with published clips. Length: 1,750-2,250 words. **Pays $500-700.** Pays expenses of writers on assignment.

Columns/Departments: Intelligence (new ways to tackle day-to-day issues), 500-700 words; Off the Cuff (guest column for association executives). Query. **Pays $100-200.**

$ $ EXPANSION MANAGEMENT MAGAZINE, Growth Strategies for Companies On the Move, Penton Media, Inc., 1300 E. 9th St., Cleveland OH 44114. (913)338-1508. Fax: (913)338-1503. Editor: Bill King. **Contact:** Ken Krizner, managing editor. **75% freelance written.** Monthly magazine covering economic development. Estab. 1986. Circ. 45,000. **Pays on acceptance.** Publishes ms an average of 1 month after acceptance. Byline given. Buys all rights, makes work-for-hire assignments. Editorial lead time 2 months. Sample copy for $7. Writer's guidelines free.

Nonfiction: "*Expansion Management* presents articles and industry reports examining relocation trends, strategic planning, work force hiring, economic development agencies, relocation consultants and state, province and county reviews and profiles to help readers select future expansions and relocation sites." **Buys 120 mss/year.** Query with published clips. Length: 1,000-1,500 words. **Pays $200-400 for assigned articles.** Sometimes pays expenses of writers on assignment.

Photos: Send photos with submission. Buys one-time rights. Offers no additional payment for photos accepted with ms. Captions required.

Tips: "Send clips first, then call me."

$ $ $ EXPO, Atwood Publishing LLC, 11600 College Blvd., Overland Park KS 66210. (913)469-1185. Fax: (913)469-0806. E-mail: eingram@expoweb.com. Website: www.expoweb.com. Managing Editor: Janine Taylor. **Contact:** Elizabeth Ingram, editor-in-chief. **80% freelance written.** Magazine covering expositions. "*EXPO* is the information and education resource for the exposition industry. It is the only magazine dedicated exclusively to the people with direct responsibility for planning, promoting and operating trade and consumer shows. Our readers are show managers and their staff, association executives, independent show producers and industry suppliers. Every issue of *EXPO* contains in-depth, how-to features and departments that focus on the practical aspects of exposition management, including administration, promotion and operations." Pays on publication. Byline given. Offers 50% kill fee. Buys first North American serial rights. Editorial lead time 3 months. Accepts queries by mail, e-mail, fax. Responds in 3 weeks to queries. Sample copy for free. Writer's guidelines online.

Nonfiction: How-to, interview/profile. Query with published clips. Length: 600-2,400 words. **Pays 50¢/word.** Pays expenses of writers on assignment.

Photos: State availability with submission.

Columns/Departments: Profile (personality profile), 650 words; Exhibitor Matters (exhibitor issues) and EXPOTech (technology), both 600-1,300 words. **Buys 10 mss/year.** Query with published clips.

Tips: "*EXPO* now offers shorter features and departments, while continuing to offer in-depth reporting. Editorial is more concise, using synopsis, bullets and tidbits whenever possible. Every article needs sidebars, call-outs, graphs, charts, etc., to create entry points for readers. Headlines and leads are more provocative. And writers should elevate the level of shop talk, demonstrating that *EXPO* is the leader in the industry. We plan our editorial calendar about one year in advance, but we are always open to new ideas. Please query before submitting a story to *EXPO*—tell us about your idea and what our readers would learn. Include your qualifications to write about the subject and the sources you plan to contact."

N $ $ $ FAMILY BUSINESS, The Guide for Family Companies, Family Business Publishing Co., 1845 Walnut St., Philadelphia PA 19103. Fax: (215)405-6078. E-mail: bspector@familybusinessmagazine.com. Website: www.familybusinessmagazine.com. Editor: Dan Rottenberg. **Contact:** Barbara Spector, executive editor. **50% freelance written.** Quarterly magazine covering family-owned companies. "Written expressly for family company owners and advisors. Focuses on issues—business and human dynamic—special to family enterprises. Offers practical guidance and tried-and-true solutions for business stakeholders." Estab. 1989. Circ. 6,000. **Pays on acceptance.** Publishes ms an average of 3-6 months after acceptance. Byline given. Offers 30% kill fee. Buys first, electronic rights. Editorial lead time 4 months. Submit seasonal material 6 months in advance. Accepts queries by mail, e-mail, fax. Writer's guidelines online.

Nonfiction: Book excerpts, how-to (family business related only), interview/profile, personal experience. No "articles that aren't specifically related to multi-generational family companies (no general business or small business advice). No success stories—there must be an underlying family or business lesson." **Buys 12 mss/year.** Query with published clips. Length: 2,000-2,500 words. **Pays $50-1,000.** Sometimes pays expenses of writers on assignment.

Photos: State availability with submission. Buys one-time rights. Offers $50-500 maximum/shoot. Captions, identification of subjects, model releases required.

N $ HOMEBUSINESS JOURNAL, Steffen Publishing Co., 9584 Main St., Holland Patent NY 13354. Fax: (315)865-4000. E-mail: kim@homebusinessjournal.net. Website: www.homebusinessjournal.net. **Contact:** Kim Lisi, managing editor. **90% freelance written.** Bimonthly magazine covering home businesses. "*HomeBusiness Journal* publishes material pertinent to home-based entrepreneurs." Circ. 50,000. Pays on publication. Publishes ms an average of 3-4 months after acceptance. Byline given. Buys first North American serial, second serial (reprint) rights. Editorial lead time 4-6 months. Submit seasonal material 4 months in advance. Accepts queries by mail, e-mail, fax. Accepts previously published material. Accepts simultaneous submissions. Responds in 1-2 months to queries. Sample copy for 9×12 SAE and 5 first-class stamps. Writer's guidelines online.

Nonfiction: "All above article types as they apply to home business issues." Book excerpts, general interest, how-to, humor, interview/profile, tax, marketing, finance. No highly technical, "small," or "mid-size" business articles, advertorials. **Buys 50 mss/year.** Query. Length: 700-1,100 words. **Pays $75.**

Photos: State availability with submission. Reviews 3×5 prints, GIF/JPEG files. Buys one-time rights. Offers no additional payment for photos accepted with ms. Identification of subjects, model releases required.

Columns/Departments: Neighborhood CEO (profiling home-based entrepreneurs), 700 words. **Buys 24 mss/year.** Query. **Pays $75.**

Tips: "Visit our website to view articles previously published, have a good understanding of the issues home-based entrepreneurs face, and work on creative angles for queries."

$ $ IN TENTS, The Magazine for the Tent Rental and Fabric Structure Industries, Industrial Fabrics Association International, 1801 County Rd. B W., Roseville MN 55113-4061. (651)225-6970. Fax: (651)225-6966. E-mail: bktaylor@ifai.com. Website: www.ifai.com. **Contact:** Betsy Taylor, editor. **50% freelance written.** Quarterly magazine covering tent-rental and fabric structure industries. Estab. 1994. Circ. 12,000. **Pays on acceptance.** Publishes ms an average of 2 months after acceptance. Byline given. Buys all rights. Editorial lead time 3 months. Accepts queries by mail, e-mail, fax. Sample copy and writer's guidelines free.

- Break in with familiarity of tent rental, special events, tent manufacturing and fabric structure industries. Or lively, intelligent writing on technical subjects.

Nonfiction: How-to, interview/profile, new product, photo feature, technical. **Buys 10-12 mss/year.** Query. Length: 800-2,000 words. **Pays $100-500.** Sometimes pays expenses of writers on assignment.

Photos: State availability with submission. Reviews contact sheets, negatives, transparencies, prints, Digital images. Buys one-time rights. Negotiates payment individually. Captions, identification of subjects, model releases required.

Tips: "We look for lively, intelligent writing that makes technical subjects come alive."

N $ $ MAINEBIZ, Maine's Business News Source, Mainebiz Publications, Inc., 30 Milk St., 3rd Floor, Portland ME 04101. (207)761-8379. Fax: (207)761-0732. E-mail: mcavallaro@mainebiz.biz. Website: www.mainebiz.biz. Editor: Scott Sutherland. **Contact:** Michaela Cavallaro, managing editor. **50% freelance written.** Biweekly tabloid covering business in Maine. "*Mainebiz* is read by business decision makers across the state. They look to the publication for business news and analysis." Estab. 1994. Circ. 13,000. Pays on publication. Publishes ms an average of 1 month after acceptance. Byline given. Offers 10% kill fee. Buys all rights. Editorial lead time 1 month. Submit seasonal material 2 months in advance.

Accepts queries by mail, e-mail. Responds in 3 weeks to queries. Sample copy online. Writer's guidelines online.
Nonfiction: "All pieces are reported and must comply with accepted journalistic standards. We only publish stories about business in Maine. Period." Essays, exposé, interview/profile, business trends. Special issues: See website for editorial calendar. **Buys 50+ mss/year.** Query with published clips. Length: 500-2,500 words. **Pays $50-250.** Pays expenses of writers on assignment.
Photos: State availability with submission. Reviews GIF/JPEG files. Buys one-time rights. Negotiates payment individually. Identification of subjects required.
Columns/Departments: Mixed Media (covers media in Maine—broadcast, print, book reviews), 750 words. **Buys 6-8 mss/year.** Query with published clips. **Pays $75-125.**
Tips: "Stories should be well-thought-out with specific relevance to Maine. Arts and culture-related queries are welcome, as long as there is a business angle. We appreciate unusual angles on business stories, and regularly work with new freelancers. Please, no queries unless you have read the paper."

$ NORTHEAST EXPORT, A Magazine for New England Companies Engaged in International Trade, Commerce Publishing Company, Inc., P.O. Box 254, Northborough MA 01532. (508)351-2925. Fax: (508)351-6905. E-mail: editor@northeast-export.com. Website: www.northeast-export.com. **Contact:** Carlos Cunha, editor. **30% freelance written.** Bimonthly business-to-business magazine. "*Northeast Export* is the only publication directly targeted at New England's international trade community. All stories relate to issues affecting New England companies and feature only New England-based profiles and examples. Estab. 1997. Circ. 13,500. **Pays on acceptance.** Byline given. Offers 10% kill fee. Buys all rights. Editorial lead time 2 months. Accepts queries by mail, e-mail, fax. Sample copy for free.
Nonfiction: How-to, interview/profile, travel, industry trends/analysis. "We will not take unsolicited articles. Query first with clips." **Buys 10-12 mss/year.** Query with published clips and SASE. No unsolicited material. Length: 800-2,000 words. **Payment varies.**
Photos: State availability of or send photos with submission. Reviews 2¼ transparencies, 5×7 prints. Buys one-time rights. Negotiates payment individually. Captions, identification of subjects, model releases required.
Tips: "We're looking for writers with availability; the ability to write clearly about tough, sometimes very technical subjects; the fortitude to slog through industry jargon to get the story straight; a knowledge of international trade issues and/or New England transportation infrastructure. We're interested in freelancers with business writing and magazine experience, especially those with contacts in the New England manufacturing, finance and transportation communities."

$ $ PORTABLE RESTROOM OPERATOR, Rangoon Moon, Inc., P.O. Box 904, Dahlonega GA 30533. (706)864-6838. Fax: (706)864-9851. E-mail: sesails@yahoo.com. Website: www.1promag.com. Managing Editor: M.A. Watson. **Contact:** Kevin Gralton, editor. **50% freelance written.** Magazine published 9 times/year covering portable sanitation. Estab. 1998. **Pays on acceptance.** Publishes ms an average of 2 months after acceptance. Byline given. Editorial lead time 1 month. Submit seasonal material 2 months in advance. Accepts queries by mail, e-mail, fax.
Nonfiction: Quality articles that will be of interest to our readers. Studies on governmental changes, OSHA regulations, and sanitation articles that deal with portable restrooms are of strong interest. Exposé (government relations, OSHA, EPS associated, trends, public attitudes, etc.), general interest (state portable restroom associations, conventions, etc.), historical/nostalgic, humor, inspirational, new product, personal experience, technical. Query or send complete ms. Length: Length is not important. **Pays 15¢/word.**
Photos: No negatives. "We need good contrast." Send photos with submission. Buys one-time rights. Pays $15 for b&w and color prints that are used. Captions, model releases required.
Tips: "Material must pertain to portable sanitation industry."

$ PROFESSIONAL COLLECTOR, Pohly & Partners, 27 Melcher St., 2nd Floor, Boston MA 02210-1516. (617)451-1700. Fax: (617)338-7767. E-mail: procollector@pohlypartners.com. Website: www.pohlypartners.com. **Contact:** Karen English, editor. **90% freelance written.** Quarterly magazine published for Western Union's Financial Services, Inc.'s Quick Collect Service, covering debt collection business/lifestyle issues. "We gear our articles directly to the debt collectors and their managers. Each issue offers features covering the trends and players, the latest technology, and other issues affecting the collections industry. It's all designed to help collectors be more productive and improve their performance." Estab. 1993. Circ. 161,000. Pays on publication. Byline given. Buys first North American serial rights. Editorial lead time 9 months. Submit seasonal material 9 months in advance. Accepts queries by mail, e-mail, fax. Sample copy for free. Writer's guidelines online.
Nonfiction: General interest, how-to (tips on good collecting), humor, interview/profile, new product, book reviews. **Buys 10-15 mss/year.** Query with published clips. Length: 400-1,000 words. **Payment negotiable for assigned articles.** Sometimes pays expenses of writers on assignment.
Photos: State availability with submission. Reviews contact sheets, 3×5 prints. Buys one-time rights. Negotiates payment individually. Captions, identification of subjects, model releases required.
Columns/Departments: Industry Roundup (issues within industry), 500-1,000 words; Tips, 750-1,000 words; Q&A (questions & answers for collectors), 1,500 words. **Buys 15-20 mss/year.** Query with published clips. **Payment negotiable.**
Tips: "Writers should be aware that *Professional Collector* is a promotional publication, and that its content must support the overall marketing goals of Western Union. It helps to have extensive insider knowledge about the debt collection industry."

$ $ PROGRESSIVE RENTALS, The Voice of the Rental-Purchase Industry, Association of Progressive Rental Organizations, 1504 Robin Hood Trail, Austin TX 78703. (800)204-2776. Fax: (512)794-0097. E-mail: jsherrier@apro-rto.com. Website: www.apro-rto.com. **Contact:** Julie Stephen Sherrier, editor. **50% freelance written.** Bimonthly magazine covering the rent-to-own industry. "*Progressive Rentals* is the only publication representing the rent-to-own industry and members of APRO. The magazine covers timely news and features affecting the industry, association activities, and member profiles. Awarded best 4-color magazine by the American Society of Association Executives in 1999." Estab. 1980. Circ. 5,500. **Pays on acceptance.** Publishes ms an average of 2 months after acceptance. Byline given. Offers 25% kill fee. Buys first North American serial rights. Editorial lead time 2 months. Submit seasonal material 4 months in advance. Accepts queries by mail, e-mail, fax, phone. Accepts simultaneous submissions. Responds in 1 month to queries; 2 months to mss. Sample copy for free.

Nonfiction: Exposé, general interest, how-to, inspirational, interview/profile, technical, industry features. **Buys 12 mss/year.** Query with published clips. Length: 1,200-2,500 words. **Pays $150-700.** Sometimes pays expenses of writers on assignment.

$ RENTAL MANAGEMENT, American Rental Association, 1900 19th St., Moline IL 61265. (309)764-2475. Fax: (309)764-1533. E-mail: brian.alm@ararental.org. Website: www.rentalmanagementmag.com. Managing Editor: Tamera Bonnicksen. **Contact:** Brian R. Alm, editor. **30% freelance written.** Monthly magazine for the equipment rental industry worldwide (*not* property, real estate, appliances, furniture, or cars), emphasizing management topics in particular but also marketing, merchandising, technology, etc. Estab. 1970. Circ. 20,000. **Pays on acceptance.** Publishes ms an average of 3 months after acceptance. Byline sometimes given. Buys first North American serial rights. Editorial lead time 2 months. Submit seasonal material 3 months in advance. Accepts queries by mail, e-mail, fax.

Nonfiction: Business management and marketing. **Buys 20-25 mss/year.** Query with published clips. Does not respond to unsolicited work unless being considered for publication. Length: 600-1,500 words. **Payment negotiable.** Sometimes pays expenses of writers on assignment.

Reprints: Send tearsheet or typed ms with rights for sale noted and information about when and where the material previously appeared.

Photos: State availability with submission. Reviews contact sheets, negatives, 35mm or 2¼ transparencies, any size prints. Buys one-time rights. Negotiates payment individually. Identification of subjects required.

Columns/Departments: "We are adequately served by existing columnists and have a long waiting list of others to use pending need." **Buys 20 mss/year.** Query with published clips. **Payment negotiable.**

Tips: "Show me you can write maturely, cogently, and fluently on management matters of direct and compelling interest to the small-business owner or manager in a larger operation; no sloppiness, no unexamined thoughts, no stiffness or affectation—genuine, direct, and worthwhile English. Knowledge of the equipment rental industry is a distinct plus."

$ $ SBM, Pittsburgh edition, SBN Inc., 11632 Frankstown Rd., #313, Pittsburgh PA 15235. (412)371-0451. Fax: (412)371-0452. E-mail: rmarano@sbnonline.com. Website: www.sbn-online.com. **Contact:** Ray Marano, editor. **5% freelance written.** Monthly magazine. "We provide information and insight designed to help companies grow. Our focus is on local companies with 50 or more employees and their successful business strategies, with the ultimate goal of educating entrepreneurs. Our target audience is business owners and other top executives." Estab. 1994. Circ. 16,000. Pays on publication. Publishes ms an average of 2 months after acceptance. Byline given. Buys all rights, makes work-for-hire assignments. Editorial lead time 2 months. Submit seasonal material 4 months in advance. Accepts queries by mail, e-mail, fax. Responds in 1 month to queries. Sample copy for $3. Writer's guidelines free.

O→ "Right now we have very little need for freelance work."

Nonfiction: Book excerpts, how-to, interview/profile, opinion, annual energy and telecommunication supplements, among others. "No basic profiles about 'interesting' companies or stories about companies with no ties to Pittsburgh." Query with published clips. Length: 250-1,000 words. **Pays $150-300 for assigned articles.**

Reprints: Accepts reprints (mainly columns from business professionals). Send photocopy of article or short story and information about when and where the article previously appeared.

Photos: State availability with submission. Reviews negatives, transparencies, digital. Buys one-time or all rights. Negotiates payment individually. Identification of subjects required.

Tips: "Have articles localized to the Pittsburgh and surrounding areas. We look for articles that will help our readers, educate them on a business strategy that another company may be using that can help our readers' companies grow."

$ $ SECURITY DEALER, Cygnus Publishing, 445 Broad Hollow Rd., Melville NY 11747. (631)845-2700. Fax: (631)845-7109. E-mail: susan.brady@cygnuspub.com. **Contact:** Susan A. Brady, editor. **25% freelance written.** Monthly magazine for electronic alarm dealers, burglary and fire installers, with technical, business, sales and marketing information. Circ. 25,000. Pays 3 weeks after publication. Publishes ms an average of 4 months after acceptance. Byline sometimes given. Buys first North American serial rights. Accepts simultaneous submissions.

Nonfiction: How-to, interview/profile, technical. No consumer pieces. Query by mail only. Length: 1,000-3,000 words. **Pays $300 for assigned articles; $100-200 for unsolicited articles.** Sometimes pays expenses of writers on assignment.

Photos: State availability with submission. Reviews contact sheets, transparencies. Offers $25 additional payment for photos accepted with ms. Captions, identification of subjects required.

Columns/Departments: Closed Circuit TV, Access Control (both on application, installation, new products), 500-1,000 words. **Buys 25 mss/year.** Query by mail only. **Pays $100-150.**

Tips: "The areas of our publication most open to freelancers are technical innovations, trends in the alarm industry, and crime patterns as related to the business as well as business finance and management pieces."

$ $ SMART BUSINESS, (formerly *SBN Magazine*), Smart Business Network, Inc., 14725 Detroit Ave., #200, Cleveland OH 44107. (216)228-6397. Fax: (216)529-8924. E-mail: editor@sbnonline.com. Website: www.sbnonline.com. **Contact:** Dustin S. Klein, executive editor. **5% freelance written.** Monthly business magazine with an audience made up of business owners and top decision makers. "*Smart Business* is smart ideas for growing companies. Best practices, winning strategies. The pain—and joy—of running a business. Every issue delves into the minds of the most innovative executives in Northeast Ohio to report on how market leaders got to the top and what strategies they use to stay there." Estab. 1989. Pays on publication. Publishes ms an average of 2 months after acceptance. Byline given. Offers 50% kill fee. Buys first North American serial, second serial (reprint), electronic rights. Editorial lead time 3 months. Submit seasonal material 3 months in advance. Accepts queries by mail, e-mail. Responds in 2 weeks to queries; 1 month to mss. Sample copy online. Writer's guidelines by e-mail.

Nonfiction: How-to, interview/profile. No breaking news or straight personality profiles. **Buys 2-5 mss/year.** Query with published clips. Length: 300-1,500 words. **Pays $200-500.** Sometimes pays expenses of writers on assignment.

Reprints: Accepts previously published submissions.

Photos: State availability with submission. Reviews negatives, prints. Buys one-time, reprint, or Web rights. Offers no additional payment for photos accepted with ms. Identification of subjects required.

Columns/Departments: Another View (business management related), 400-500 words. **Buys 6-8 mss/year.** Query.

The online magazine carries original content not found in the print edition. Contact: Dustin S. Klein, editor.

Tips: "The best way to submit to *Smart Business* is to read us—either online or in print. Remember, our audience is made up of top level business executives and owners."

$ $ STAMATS MEETINGS MEDIA, 550 Montgomery St., #750, San Francisco CA 94111. Fax: (415)788-0301. E-mail: tyler.davidson@meetings411.com. Website: www.meetings411.com. Destinations Editor: Lori Tenny. **Contact:** Tyler Davidson, editor (columnists, cover stories). **75% freelance written.** Monthly tabloid covering meeting, event, and conference planning. Estab. 1986. Circ. *Meetings East* and *Meetings South* 22,000; *Meetings West* 26,000. Pays 1 month after publication. Publishes ms an average of 1 month after acceptance. Byline given. Buys first North American serial, electronic rights. Editorial lead time 3 months. Submit seasonal material 3 months in advance. Accepts queries by mail, e-mail, fax. Responds in 3 weeks to queries. Sample copy for 9×13 SAE and 5 first-class stamps. Editorial calendar online.

Queries and pitches are accepted on columns and cover stories only. All other assignments (Features and Site Inspections) are based exclusively on editorial calendar. Interested writers should send a résumé and 2-3 relevant clips, which must show familiarity with meetings/conventions topics, by e-mail.

Nonfiction: How-to, travel (as it pertains to meetings and conventions). "No first-person fluff. We are a business magazine." **Buys 150 mss/year.** Query with published clips. Length: 1,200-2,000 words. **Pays $500 flat rate/package.**

Photos: State availability with submission. Buys one-time rights. Offers no additional payment for photos accepted with ms. Identification of subjects required.

Tips: "We're always looking for freelance writers who are local to our destination stories. For Site Inspections, get in touch in late September or early October, when we usually have the following year's editorial calendar available."

$ THE STATE JOURNAL, West V Media Management LLC, 13 Kanawha Blvd. W., Charleston WV 25302. (304)344-1630. Fax: (304)343-6138. E-mail: dpage@statejournal.com. Website: www.statejournal.com. **Contact:** Dan Page, editor. **30% freelance written.** "We are a weekly journal dedicated to providing stories of interest to the business community in West Virginia." Estab. 1984. Circ. 10,000. Pays on publication. Publishes ms an average of 3 weeks after acceptance. Byline given. Buys first rights. Submit seasonal material 4 months in advance. Accepts queries by mail, e-mail, fax. Sample copy for #10 SASE. Writer's guidelines for #10 SASE.

Nonfiction: General interest, interview/profile, new product, (All business related). **Buys 400 mss/year.** Query. Length: 250-1,500 words. **Pays $50.** Sometimes pays expenses of writers on assignment.

Photos: State availability with submission. Reviews contact sheets. Buys one-time rights. Offers $15/photo. Captions required.

Tips: "Localize your work—mention West Virginia specifically in the article; or talk to business people in West Virginia.

N $ $ SUSTAINABLE INDUSTRIES JOURNAL NW, Sustainable Industries Media LLC, 3941 SE Hawthorne Blvd., Portland OR 97214. Fax: (503)226-7917. E-mail: brian@sijournal.com. Website: www.sijournal.com. Managing Editor: Ari Kramer (Puget Sound). **Contact:** Brian J. Back, editor. **40% freelance written.** Monthly magazine covering environmental innovation in business (Northwest focus). "We seek high quality, balanced reporting aimed at business readers. More compelling writing than is typical in standard trade journals." Estab. 2003. Circ. 4,000. Pays on publication. Publishes ms an average of 1-3 months after acceptance. Byline sometimes given. Not copyrighted. Buys all rights. Editorial lead time 1-2 months. Accepts queries by mail, e-mail, fax. Accepts simultaneous submissions. Sample copy for free.

Nonfiction: General interest, how-to, interview/profile, new product, opinion, news briefs. Special issues: Issue themes rotate on the following topics: Agriculture & Natural Resources; Green Building; Energy; Government; Manufacturing & Technology; Retail & Service; Transportation & Tourism—though all topics are covered in each issue. No prosaic essays or extra-long pieces. Query with published clips. Length: 500-1,500 words. **Pays $0-525.**

Photos: State availability with submission. Reviews prints, GIF/JPEG files. Buys all rights. Offers no additional payment for photos accepted with ms.

Columns/Departments: Business trade columns on specific industries, 500-1,000 words. Guest columns accepted, but not compensated. Query.

$ $ UDM, Upholstery Design & Management, Chartwell Communications, 380 E. Northwest Hwy., Suite 300, Des Plaines IL 60016-2208. (847)795-7690. Fax: (847)390-7100. E-mail: mchazin@chartcomm.com. Website: www.udmonline.com. **Contact:** Michael Chazin, editor/publisher. **10% freelance written.** Monthly business-to-business magazine covering upholstered furniture/industry management. "*UDM* targets suppliers, manufacturers, and retailers/resellers of upholstered furniture for the home, office, institution. Because we are highly specialized, we need writers with a knowledge of the furniture industry and familiarity and ability to identify new style trends." Estab. 1989. Circ. 8,600. Pays on publication. Publishes ms an average of 2 months after acceptance. Byline usually given. Buys first North American serial rights. Accepts queries by mail, e-mail. Responds in 2 weeks to queries; 2 months to mss. Sample copy for free.

Nonfiction: Interview/profile. **Buys 6-10 mss/year.** Query. Length: 500-2,500 words. **Pays $250-700.** Sometimes pays expenses of writers on assignment.

Photos: Reviews transparencies, prints, digital images. Offers no additional payment for photos accepted with ms. Captions, identification of subjects required.

Tips: "Writers must have inside knowledge of furniture/upholstery or be privy to knowledge. We try to stay on the leading edge of color and style trends—12-18 months before they hit retail stores."

$ $ UNFINISHEDBUSINESS, Official Voice of the Unfinished Furniture Association, Association Headquarters, Inc., 17000 Commerce Pkwy., Mount Laurel NJ 08054. (856)439-0500, ext. 3064. Fax: (856)439-0525. E-mail: jbertonazzi@ahint.com. Website: www.unfinishedfurniture.org. **Contact:** Judy Bertonazzi, editor. **17% freelance written.** Bimonthly magazine covering unfinished furniture retailing, manufacturing and selling. "*UnfinishedBUSINESS* is a bimonthly trade publication serving the unfinished furniture industry. Our main mission is to uphold the beliefs and values of the Unfinished Furniture Association (UFA) while providing our readers with information and news that is important for their daily business activities. The UFA wishes to promote the common business interests of the unfinished furniture industry, encourage the most efficient and professional organization and administration of firms in the unfinished furniture industry, and conduct meetings and educational programs. The UFA also has a goal of collecting and publishing information about the unfinished furniture industry that is relevant to their business needs in today's business world." Estab. 1996. Circ. 3,500. Pays on publication. Publishes ms an average of 4 months after acceptance. Byline given. Offers $400 kill fee. Buys second serial (reprint) rights. Editorial lead time 2 months. Submit seasonal material 2 months in advance. Accepts queries by mail, e-mail, fax. Accepts previously published material. Accepts simultaneous submissions. Responds in 2 weeks to queries; 2 months to mss. Sample copy online. Writer's guidelines by e-mail.

Nonfiction: Interview/profile. Special issues: Furniture and Design Trends (January/February issue and July/August issue every year). No fiction, personal experience essays, historical. **Buys 6-8 mss/year.** Query. Length: 1,200-3,000 words. **Pays $400 for assigned articles.**

Photos: Send photos with submission. Reviews GIF/JPEG files (300 dpi). Buys one-time rights. Offers no additional payment for photos accepted with ms. Captions, identification of subjects required.

Tips: "Get to know professionals in the industry."

$ $ $ WORLD TRADE, "For the Executive with Global Vision", BNP, 23211 S. Pointe Dr., Suite 101, Laguna Hills CA 92653. Fax: (949)830-1328. Website: www.worldtrademag.com. Editor: Patrick Burnson. **Contact:** Lara Sowinski, associate editor. **50% freelance written.** Monthly magazine covering international business. Estab. 1988. Circ. 75,000. Pays on publication. Publishes ms an average of 1 month after acceptance. Byline given. Buys all rights. Editorial lead time 3 months. Accepts queries by mail, fax.

Nonfiction: "See our editorial calendar online at wwww.worldtrademag.com." Interview/profile, technical, market reports, finance, logistics. **Buys 40-50 mss/year.** Query with published clips. Length: 450-1,500 words. **Pays 50¢/word.**

Photos: State availability with submission. Reviews transparencies, prints. Buys all rights. Negotiates payment individually. Identification of subjects required.

Columns/Departments: International Business Services, 800 words; Shipping, Supply Chain Management, Logistics, 800 words; Software & Technology, 800 words; Economic Development (US, International), 800 words. **Buys 40-50 mss/year. Pays 50¢/word.**

Tips: "We seek writers with expertise in their subject areas, as well as solid researching and writing skills. We want analysts more than reporters. We don't accept unsolicited manuscripts, and we don't want phone calls— Please read *World Trade* before sending a query."

CHURCH ADMINISTRATION & MINISTRY

Publications in this section are written for clergy members, church leaders, and teachers. Magazines for lay members and the general public are listed in the Consumer Religious section.

$ THE AFRICAN AMERICAN PULPIT, Judson Press, 588 N. Gulph Rd., King of Prussia PA 19406. (610)768-2128. Fax: (610)768-2441. E-mail: victoria.mcgoey@abc-usa.org. Website: www.judsonpress.com/taap. Editors: Martha Simmons, Frank A. Thomas. **Contact:** Victoria McGoey, project manager. **100% freelance written.** Quarterly magazine covering African-American preaching. "*The African American Pulpit* is a quarterly journal that serves as a repository for the very best of African-American preaching and provides practical and creative resources for persons in ministry." Estab. 1997. Circ. 2,000. Pays on publication. Publishes ms an average of 6 months after acceptance. Byline always given. Editorial lead time 9 months. Submit seasonal material 1 year in advance. Accepts queries by mail, e-mail, fax, phone. Accepts simultaneous submissions. Writer's guidelines online.

Nonfiction: Sermons/articles relating to African-American preaching and the African-American Church. Book excerpts, essays, how-to (craft a sermon), inspirational, interview/profile, opinion, religious. **Buys 60 mss/year.** Send complete ms. Length: 1,500-3,000 words.

$ THE CHRISTIAN COMMUNICATOR, 9731 N. Fox Glen Dr., #6F, Niles IL 60714-4222. (847)296-3964. Fax: (847)296-0754. E-mail: lin@wordprocommunications.com. **Contact:** Lin Johnson, editor. **90% freelance written.** Monthly magazine covering Christian writing and speaking. Circ. 4,000. Pays on publication. Publishes ms an average of 6-12 months after acceptance. Byline given. Buys first, second serial (reprint) rights. Editorial lead time 3 months. Submit seasonal material 9 months in advance. Accepts queries by e-mail. Responds in 4-6 weeks to queries; 4-6 weeks to mss. Sample copy free with SAE and 5 first-class stamps. Writer's guidelines free with SASE or by e-mail.

Nonfiction: Essays, how-to, inspirational, interview/profile, opinion, book reviews. **Buys 90 mss/year.** Query or send complete ms only by e-mail. Length: 300-1,000 words. **Pays $10.**

Photos: Send photos with submission. Offers no additional payment for photos accepted with ms. Identification of subjects required.

Columns/Departments: Speaking, 650-1,000 words. **Buys 11 mss/year.** Query. **Pays $10.**

Poetry: Free verse, light verse, traditional. **Buys 11 poems/year.** Submit maximum 3 poems. Contact: Gretchen Sousa, poetry editor (gretloriat@earthlink.net) Length: 4-20 lines. **Pays $5.**

Fillers: Anecdotes, short humor. **Buys 10-30/year.** Length: 50-300 words. **Pays cassette tape.**

Tips: "We primarily use 'how to' articles and personality features on experienced writers and editors. However, we're willing to look at any other pieces geared to the writing life."

$ CROSS & QUILL, The Christian Writers Newsletter, Christian Writers Fellowship International, 1624 Jefferson Davis Rd., Clinton SC 29325-6401. (864)697-6035. E-mail: cwfi@cwfi-online.org. Website: www.cwfi-online.org. **Contact:** Sandy Brooks, editor/publisher. **75% freelance written.** Bimonthly journal featuring information and encouragement for writers. "We serve Christian writers and others in Christian publishing. We like informational and how-to articles." Estab. 1976. Circ. 1,000. Pays on publication. Publishes ms an average of 6-12 months after acceptance. Byline given. Buys first, second serial (reprint) rights. Editorial lead time 6 months. Submit seasonal material 6 months in advance. Accepts queries by mail, e-mail. Responds in 2 weeks to queries; 2 months to mss. Sample copy for $2 with 9×11 SAE and 2 first-class stamps. Writer's guidelines online or for SAE.

- "Paste article submissions into an e-mail form. We do not download submissions due to the risk of viruses. Double-space between paragraphs. Please use plain text. Do not use boldface or bullets. Submit articles to cqarticles@aol.com."

O‒ Break in by writing "good informational, substantive how-to articles. Right now we're particularly looking for articles on juvenile writing and owning and operating writers groups—successes and learning experiences; also organizing and operating writers workshops and conferences."

Nonfiction: How-to, humor, inspirational, interview/profile, new product, technical, devotional. **Buys 25 mss/year.** Send complete ms. Length: 300-800 words. **Pays $10-25.** Sometimes pays in contributor copies or subscriptions for fillers, poetry.

Photos: State availability with submission.

Poetry: Free verse, haiku, light verse, traditional. **Buys 6 poems/year.** Submit maximum 3 poems. Length: 12 lines. **Pays $5.**

Tips: "Study guidelines and follow them. No philosophical, personal reflection, or personal experiences."

$ $ GROUP MAGAZINE, Group Publishing, Inc., 1515 Cascade Ave., Loveland CO 80538. (970)669-3836. Fax: (970)679-4372. E-mail: greditor@grouppublishing.com. Website: www.groupmag.com. Editor: Rick Lawrence. **Contact:** Kathy Dieterich, assistant editor. **50% freelance written.** Bimonthly magazine for Christian youth workers. "*Group* is the interdenominational magazine for leaders of Christian youth groups. *Group*'s purpose is to supply ideas, practical help, inspiration, and training for youth leaders." Estab. 1974. Circ. 55,000. **Pays on acceptance.** Byline sometimes given. Buys all rights. Editorial lead time 4 months. Submit seasonal material 5 months in advance. Accepts queries by mail, e-mail, fax. Responds in 6 weeks to queries; 2 months to mss. Sample copy for $2, plus 10×12 SAE and 3 first-class stamps. Writer's guidelines online.

Nonfiction: Inspirational, personal experience, religious. No fiction. **Buys 30 mss/year.** Query. Length: 175-2,000 words. **Pays $125-300.** Sometimes pays expenses of writers on assignment.

Columns/Departments: Try This One (short ideas for group use), 300 words; Hands-On-Help (tips for youth leaders), 175 words; Strange But True (profiles remarkable youth ministry experience), 500 words. **Pays $40.**

$ KIDS' MINISTRY IDEAS, Review and Herald Publishing Association, 55 W. Oak Ridge Dr., Hagerstown MD 21740. (301)393-4115. Fax: (301)393-4055. E-mail: kidsmin@rhpa.org. Managing Editor: Tamara Michalenko Terry. **Contact:** Editor. **95% freelance written.** "A quarterly resource for those leading children to Jesus, *Kids' Ministry Ideas* provides affirmation, pertinent and informative articles, program ideas, resource suggestions, and answers to questions from a Seventh-day Adventist Christian perspective." Estab. 1991. Circ. 5,000. **Pays on acceptance.** Publishes ms an average of 3 months after acceptance. Byline given. Offers variable kill fee. Buys first North American serial, electronic rights. Editorial lead time 3 months. Submit seasonal material 3 months in advance. Accepts queries by mail, e-mail, fax. Responds in 3 weeks to queries; 3 months to mss. Sample copy and writer's guidelines free.

Nonfiction: Inspirational, new product (related to children's ministry), articles fitting the mission of *Kids' Ministry Ideas*. **Buys 40-60 mss/year.** Send complete ms. Length: 300-1,000 words. **Pays $30-100 for assigned articles; $30-70 for unsolicited articles.**

Photos: State availability with submission. Buys one-time rights. Captions required.

Columns/Departments: Buys 20-30 mss/year. Query. **Pays $30-100.**

Tips: "Request writers' guidelines and a sample issue."

$ $ LEADERSHIP, A Practical Journal for Church Leaders, Christianity Today International, 465 Gundersen Dr., Carol Stream IL 60188. (630)260-6200. Fax: (630)260-0114. E-mail: ljeditor@leadershipjournal.net. Website: www.leadershipjournal.net. Editor: Marshall Shelley. Managing Editor: Eric Reed. **Contact:** Dawn Zemke, editorial coordinator. **75% freelance written.** Works with a small number of new/unpublished writers each year. Quarterly magazine. Writers must have a "knowledge of and sympathy for the unique expectations placed on pastors and local church leaders. Each article must support points by illustrating from real life experiences in local churches." Estab. 1980. Circ. 65,000. **Pays on acceptance.** Publishes ms an average of 6 months after acceptance. Byline given. Offers 33% kill fee. Buys first, electronic rights. Editorial lead time 6 months. Submit seasonal material 6 months in advance. Accepts queries by mail, e-mail, fax. Responds in 3 weeks to queries; 2 months to mss. Sample copy for $5 or online. Writer's guidelines online.

Nonfiction: How-to, humor, interview/profile, personal experience, sermon illustrations. "No articles from writers who have never read our journal." **Buys 60 mss/year.** Query. Length: 300-3,000 words. **Pays $35-400.** Sometimes pays expenses of writers on assignment.

Photos: Send photos with submission. Reviews contact sheets. Buys one-time rights. Offers $25-250/photo. Captions, identification of subjects, model releases required.

Columns/Departments: Eric Reed, managing editor. Growing Edge (book/software reviews); Ministry Staff (stories from church staffers), both 500 words. **Buys 8 mss/year.** Query. **Pays $100-200.**

Tips: "Every article in *Leadership* must provide practical help for problems that church leaders face. *Leadership* articles are not essays expounding a topic or editorials arguing a position or homilies explaining Biblical principles. They are how-to articles, based on first-person accounts of real-life experiences in ministry. They allow our readers to see 'over the shoulder' of a colleague in ministry who then reflects on those experiences and identifies the lessons learned. As you know, a magazine's slant is a specific personality that readers expect (and it's what they've sent us their subscription money to provide). Our style is that of friendly conversation rather than directive discourse—what I learned about local church ministry rather than what you need to do."

$ PASTORAL LIFE, Society of St. Paul, P.O. Box 595, Canfield OH 44406-0595. (330)533-5503. E-mail: plmagazine@hotmail.com. Website: www.albahouse.org. **Contact:** Rev. Matthew Roehrig, editor. **66% freelance written.** Works with new/unpublished writers. "Monthly magazine designed to focus on the current problems, needs, issues, and all important activities related to all phases of Catholic pastoral work and life." Estab. 1953. Circ. 2,000. Pays on publication. Publishes ms an average of 4 months after acceptance. Byline given. Buys first rights. Accepts queries by mail, e-mail, phone. Responds in 1 month to queries. Sample copy and writer's guidelines for 6×9 SAE and 4 first-class stamps.

Nonfiction: "*Pastoral Life* is a professional review, principally designed to focus attention on current problems, needs, issues, and important activities related to all phases of pastoral work and life." **Buys 30 unsolicited mss/year.** Query with outline before submitting ms. Length: 1,000-3,500 words. **Pays 4¢/word minimum.**

Tips: "Articles should have application for priests and Christian leadership to help them in their ministries and lives."

$ $ THE PRIEST, Our Sunday Visitor, Inc., 200 Noll Plaza, Huntington IN 46750-4304. (260)356-8400. Fax: (260)356-8472. E-mail: tpriest@osv.com. Website: www.osv.com. Editor: Msg. Owen F. Campion. **Contact:** Murray Hubley, associate editor. **55% freelance written.** Monthly magazine. "We run articles that will aid priests in their day-to-day ministry. Includes items on spirituality, counseling, administration, theology, personalities, the saints, etc." **Pays on acceptance.** Byline given. Buys first North American serial rights. Editorial lead time 3 months. Submit seasonal material 4 months in advance. Accepts queries by mail, e-mail, fax, phone. Responds in 5 weeks to queries; 3 months to mss. Sample copy and writer's guidelines free.

Nonfiction: Essays, historical/nostalgic, humor, inspirational, interview/profile, opinion, personal experience, photo feature, religious. **Buys 96 mss/year.** Send complete ms. Length: 1,500-5,000 words. **Pays $200 minimum for assigned articles; $50 minimum for unsolicited articles.**

Photos: Send photos with submission. Reviews transparencies, prints. Buys one-time rights. Negotiates payment individually. Captions, identification of subjects required.

Columns/Departments: Viewpoint (whatever applies to priests and the Church), 1,000 words. **Buys 36 mss/year.** Send complete ms. **Pays $50-100.**

Tips: "Say what you have to say in an interesting and informative manner and stop. Freelancers are most often published in 'Viewpoints.' Please do not stray from the magisterium of the Catholic Church."

$ TEACHERS INTERACTION, Concordia Publishing House 3558 S. Jefferson Ave., St. Louis MO 63118-3968. (314)268-1083. Fax: (314)268-1329. E-mail: tom.nummela@cph.org. Editorial Associate: Jean Muser. **Contact:** Tom Nummela, editor. **20% freelance written.** Quarterly magazine of practical, inspirational, theological articles for volunteer Sunday school teachers. Material must be true to the doctrines of the Lutheran Church—Missouri Synod. Estab. 1960. Circ. 12,000. Pays on publication. Publishes ms an average of 1 year after acceptance. Byline given. Buys all rights. Submit seasonal material 1 year in advance. Accepts queries by mail, e-mail, fax. Responds in 3 months to mss. Sample copy for $4.99. Writer's guidelines for #10 SASE.

Nonfiction: How-to (practical help/ideas used successfully in own classroom), inspirational, personal experience (of a Sunday School classroom nature—growth). No theological articles. **Buys 6 mss/year.** Send complete ms. Length: 1,200 words. **Pays up to $110.**

Fillers: "*Teachers Interaction* buys short Interchange items—activities and ideas planned and used successfully in a church school classroom." **Buys 48/year.** Length: 200 words maximum. **Pays $20.**

Tips: "Practical or 'it happened to me' experiences articles would have the best chance. Also short items—ideas used in classrooms; seasonal and in conjunction with our Sunday school material, Our Life in Christ. Our format emphasizes volunteer Sunday school teachers."

$ $ TODAY'S CATHOLIC TEACHER, The Voice of Catholic Education, Peter Li Education Group, 2621 Dryden Rd., Suite 300, Dayton OH 45439. (937)293-1415. Fax: (937)293-1310. E-mail: mnoschang@peterli.com. Website: www.catholicteacher.com. **Contact:** Mary C. Noschang, editor. **60% freelance written.** Magazine published 6 times/year during school year covering Catholic education for grades K-12. "We look for topics of interest and practical help to teachers in Catholic elementary schools in all curriculum areas including religion technology, discipline, motivation." Estab. 1972. Circ. 50,000. Pays on publication. Publishes ms an average of 2 months after acceptance. Byline given. first and all rights and makes work-for-hire assignments Editorial lead time 3 months. Submit seasonal material 6 months in advance. Accepts queries by mail, e-mail, fax. Accepts simultaneous submissions. Responds in 1 month to queries; 3 months to mss. Sample copy for $3 or on website. Writer's guidelines online.

Nonfiction: Interested in articles detailing ways to incorporate Catholic values into academic subjects other than religion class. Essays, how-to, humor, interview/profile, personal experience. "No articles pertaining to public education." **Buys 15 mss/year.** Query or send complete ms. Length: 1,500-3,000 words. **Pays $150-300.** Sometimes pays expenses of writers on assignment.

Photos: State availability with submission. Reviews transparencies, prints. Buys one-time rights. Offers $20-50/photo. Captions, identification of subjects, model releases required.

Tips: "Although our readership is primarily classroom teachers, *Today's Catholic Teacher* is read also by principals, supervisors, superintendents, boards of education, pastors, and parents. *Today's Catholic Teacher* aims to be for Catholic educators a source of information not available elsewhere. The focus of articles should span the interests of teachers from early childhood through junior high. Articles may be directed to just 1 age group yet have wider implications. Preference is given to material directed to teachers in grades four through eight. The desired magazine style is direct, concise, informative, and accurate. Writing should be enjoyable to read, informal rather than scholarly, lively, and free of educational jargon."

$ WORLD PULSE, Evangelism and Missions Information Service/Wheaton College, P.O. Box 794, Wheaton IL 60189. (630)752-7158. Fax: (630)752-7155. E-mail: pulsenews@aol.com. **Contact:** Managing Editor. **60% freelance written.** Semimonthly newsletter covering mission news and trends. "We provide current information about evangelical Christian missions and churches around the world. Most articles are news-oriented, although we do publish some features and interviews." Estab. 1965. Circ. 5,000. Pays on publication. Publishes ms an average of 2 months after acceptance. Byline given. Buys first, all rights. Editorial lead time 2 months. Accepts queries by mail, e-mail, fax, phone. Sample copy and writer's guidelines free.

- Break in with "coverage of the subjects requested, bringing to the task both the topic's essential components, but with a dash of style, as well."

Nonfiction: Interview/profile, photo feature, religious, technical. Does not want anything that does not cover the world of evangelical missions. **Buys 50-60 mss/year.** Query with published clips. Length: 300-1,000 words. **Pays $25-100.**

Photos: Send photos with submission. Reviews contact sheets. Buys all rights. Negotiates payment individually.

Tips: "Have a knowledge of and appreciation for the evangelical missions community, as well as for cross-cultural issues. Writing must be economical, with a judicious use of quotes and examples."

N $ $ $ WORSHIP LEADER MAGAZINE, 26311 Junipero Serra, #130, San Juan Capistrano CA 92675. (949)240-9339. Fax: (949)240-0038. E-mail: editor@wlmag.com. Website: www.worshipleader.com. Publisher/Editor-in-Chief: Chuck Fromm. **Contact:** Y. Bonesteele, editor. **80% freelance written.** Bimonthly magazine covering all aspects of Christian worship. "*Worship Leader Magazine* exists to challenge, serve, equip, and train those involved in leading the 21st century Church in worship. The intended readership is the worship team (all those who plan and lead) of the local church." Estab. 1992. Circ. 50,000. Pays on publication. Byline given. Offers 50% kill fee. Buys first North American serial, all rights. Editorial lead time 3 months. Submit seasonal material 6 months in advance. Responds in 6 weeks to queries; 3 months to mss. Sample copy for $5. Writer's guidelines online.

Nonfiction: General interest, how-to (related to purpose/audience), inspirational, interview/profile, opinion. **Buys 15-30 mss/year.** Query with published clips. Length: 1,200-2,000 words. **Pays $200-800 for assigned articles; $200-500 for unsolicited articles.** Sometimes pays expenses of writers on assignment.

Photos: State availability with submission. Buys one-time rights. Negotiate payment individually. Identification of subjects required.

Tips: "Our goal has been and is to provide the tools and information pastors, worship leaders, and ministers of music, youth, and the arts need to facilitate and enhance worship in their churches. In achieving this goal, we strive to maintain high journalistic standards, Biblical soundness, and theological neutrality. Our intent is to present the philosophical, scholarly insight on worship, as well as the day-to-day, 'putting it all together' side of worship, while celebrating our unity and diversity."

$ $ YOUR CHURCH, Helping You With the Business of Ministry, Christianity Today, Inc., 465 Gundersen Dr., Carol Stream IL 60188. (630)260-6200. Fax: (630)260-0114. E-mail: yceditor@yourchurch.net. Website: www.yourchurch.net. Managing Editor: Mike Schreiter. **90% freelance written.** Bimonthly magazine covering church administration and products. "Articles pertain to the business aspects of ministry pastors are called upon to perform: administration, purchasing, management, technology, building, etc." Estab. 1955. Circ. 85,000 (controlled). **Pays on acceptance.** Publishes ms an average of 3-4 months after acceptance. Byline given. Buys first, electronic rights. Editorial lead time 6 weeks. Submit seasonal material 5 months in advance. Accepts queries by mail, e-mail, fax. Accepts previously published material. Responds in 1 month to queries; 3 months to mss. Sample copy for 9×12 SAE and 4 first-class stamps. Writer's guidelines free.

Nonfiction: How-to, new product, technical. **Buys 50-60 mss/year.** Send complete ms. Length: 1,000-4,000 words. **Pays 15-20¢/word.** Sometimes pays expenses of writers on assignment.

Tips: "The editorial is generally geared toward brief and helpful articles dealing with some form of church business. Concise, bulleted points from experts in the field are typical for our articles."

$ YOUTH AND CHRISTIAN EDUCATION LEADERSHIP, Pathway Press, 1080 Montgomery Ave., P.O. Box 2250, Cleveland TN 37320-2250. (423)478-7599. Fax: (423)478-7616. E-mail: ann.steely@pathwaypress.org. Editor: Wanda Griffith. **Contact:** Ann Steely, editorial assistant. **25% freelance written.** Quarterly magazine covering Christian education. "*Youth and Christian Education Leadership* is written for teachers, youth pastors, children's pastors, and other local Christian education workers." Estab. 1976. Circ. 12,000. **Pays on acceptance.** Publishes ms an average of 6 months after acceptance. Buys one-time rights. Editorial lead time 6 months. Submit seasonal material 6 months in advance. Accepts queries by mail, e-mail. Accepts simultaneous submissions. Responds in 3 months to mss. Sample copy for $1 and 9×12 SASE. Writer's guidelines free.

Nonfiction: How-to, humor (in-class experience), inspirational, interview/profile, motivational, seasonal short skits. **Buys 16 mss/year.** Send complete ms; include SSN. Send SASE for return of ms. Length: 400-1,200 words. **$25-45.**

Reprints: Send typed, double-spaced ms with rights for sale noted and information about when and where the material previously appeared. Pays 80% of amount paid for an original article.

Photos: State availability with submission. Reviews contact sheets, transparencies. Buys one-time rights. Negotiates payment individually.

Columns/Departments: Sunday School Leadership; Reaching Out (creative evangelism); The Pastor and Christian Education; Preschool; Elementary; Teen; Adult; Drawing Closer; Kids Church; all 500 words. Send complete ms with SASE. **Pays $25-45.**

Tips: "Become familiar with the publication's content and submit appropriate material. We are continually looking for 'fresh ideas' that have proven to be successful."

CLOTHING

$ APPAREL, (formerly *Bobbin*), 1500 Hampton St., Suite 150, Columbia SC 29201. (803)771-7500. Fax: (803)799-1461. Website: www.apparelmag.com. Editor-in-Chief: Kathleen DesMarteau. **25% freelance written.** Monthly magazine for CEO's and top management in apparel and soft goods businesses including manufacturers and retailers. Circ. 19,000. Pays on receipt of article. Byline given. Buys all rights. Responds in 2 weeks to queries. Sample copy for free. Writer's guidelines free.

Columns/Departments: R&D; Winning Strategies; International Watch; Best Practices; Retail Strategies; Production Solutions.

Tips: "Articles should be written in a style appealing to busy top managers and should in some way foster thought or new ideas, or present solutions/alternatives to common industry problems/concerns. CEOs are most interested in quick read pieces that are also informative and substantive. Articles should not be based on opinions but should be developed through interviews with industry manufacturers, retailers, or other experts, etc. Sidebars may be included to expand upon certain aspects within the article. If available, illustrations, graphs/charts, or photographs should accompany the article."

$ $ EMB-EMBROIDERY/MONOGRAM BUSINESS, VNU Business Publications, 1115 Northmeadows Pkwy., Roswell GA 30076. (800)241-9034. Fax: (770)569-5105. E-mail: mtalkington@embmag.com. Website: www.embmag.com. **Contact:** Mario Talkington, senior editor. **30% freelance written.** Monthly magazine covering computerized embroidery and digitizing design. "Readable, practical business and/or technical articles that show our readers how to succeed in their profession." Estab. 1994. Circ. 26,000. **Pays on acceptance.** Publishes ms an average of 3 months after acceptance. Byline given. Buys all rights. Editorial lead time 3 months. Submit seasonal material 6 months in advance. Accepts queries by mail, e-mail. Accepts simultaneous submissions. Sample copy for $10. Writer's guidelines not available.

Nonfiction: How-to (embroidery, sales, marketing, design, general business info), interview/profile, new product, photo feature, technical (computerized embroidery). **Buys 4-6 mss/year.** Query. Length: 800-2,000 words. **Pays $200 and up for assigned articles.**

Photos: Send photos with submission. Reviews transparencies, prints. Negotiates payment individually.

Tips: "Show us you have specified knowledge, experience, or contacts in the embroidery industry or a related field."

$ $ MADE TO MEASURE, Halper Publishing Co., 830 Moseley Rd., Highland Park IL 60035. Fax: (847)780-2902. E-mail: mtm@halper.com. Website: www.madetomeasuremag.com. **Contact:** Rick Levine, editor/publisher. **50% freelance written.** Semiannual magazine covering uniforms and career apparel. "A semi-annual magazine/buyers' reference containing leading sources of supply, equipment and services of every description related to the Uniform, Career Apparel, and allied trades, throughout the entire U.S." Estab. 1930. Circ. 25,000. **Pays on acceptance.** Publishes ms an average of 2 months after acceptance. Byline given. Buys first North American serial rights. Editorial lead time 4 months. Submit seasonal material 4 months in advance. Accepts queries by mail, e-mail. Accepts simultaneous submissions. Responds in 3 weeks to queries. Sample copy online.

Nonfiction: "Please only consider sending queries related to stories to companies that wear or make uniforms, career apparel or identifying apparel." Historical/nostalgic, interview/profile, new product, personal experience, photo feature, technical. **Buys 6-8 mss/year.** Query with published clips. Length: 1,000-3,000 words. **Pays $400-1,200.** Sometimes pays expenses of writers on assignment.

Photos: State availability with submission. Reviews contact sheets, any prints. Buys one-time rights. Negotiates payment individually.

Tips: "We look for features about large and small companies who wear uniforms (restaurants, hotels, industrial, medical, public safety, etc.)."

$ $ TEXTILE WORLD, Billian Publishing Co., 2100 Powers Ferry Rd., Suite 300, Atlanta GA 30339. (770)955-5656. Fax: (770)952-0669. Website: www.textileindustries.com. **Contact:** Rachael Dunn, associate editor. **5% freelance written.** Monthly magazine covering "the business of textile, apparel, and fiber industries with considerable technical focus on products and processes. No puff pieces pushing a particular product." Estab. 1868. Pays on publication. Byline given. Buys first North American serial rights.

Nonfiction: Technical, business. **Buys 10 mss/year.** Query. Length: 500 words minimum. **Pays $200/published page.**

Photos: Send photos with submission. Reviews prints. Buys one-time rights. Offers no additional payment for photos accepted with ms. Captions required.

CONFECTIONERY & SNACK FOODS

These publications focus on the bakery, snack, and candy industries. Journals for grocers, wholesalers, and other food industry personnel are listed in Groceries & Food Products.

$ $ PACIFIC BAKERS NEWS, 3155 Lynde St., Oakland CA 94601. (510)532-5513. **Contact:** C.W. Soward, publisher. **30% freelance written.** Eager to work with new/unpublished writers. Monthly newsletter for commercial bakeries in the western states. Estab. 1961. Pays on publication. No byline given; uses only 1-paragraph news items.

Nonfiction: Uses bakery business reports and news about bakers. Buys only brief "boiled-down news items about bakers and bakeries operating only in Alaska, Hawaii, Pacific Coast and Rocky Mountain states. We welcome clippings. We need monthly news reports and clippings about the baking industry and the donut business." No pictures, jokes, poetry, or cartoons. Length: 10-200 words. **Pays 10¢/word for news, and 6¢/word for clips.**

CONSTRUCTION & CONTRACTING

Builders, architects, and contractors learn the latest industry news in these publications. Journals targeted to architects are also included in the Consumer Art & Architecture category. Those for specialists in the interior aspects of construction are listed under Building Interiors.

$ $ ADVANCED MATERIALS & COMPOSITES NEWS AND COMPOSITES eNEWS, International Business & Technology Intelligence on High Performance M&P, Composites Worldwide, Inc., 991C Lomas Santa Fe Dr., MC469, Solana Beach CA 92075-2141. (858)755-1372. Fax: (858)755-5271. E-mail: info@compositesnews.com. Website: www.compositesnews.com. Managing Editor: Susan Loud. **Contact:** Steve Loud, editor. **5% freelance written.** Bimonthly newsletter covering advanced materials and fiber-reinforced composites, plus a weekly electronic version called *Composite eNews*, reaching over 13,000 subscribers and many more pass-along readers. *Advanced Materials & Composites News* "covers markets, applications, materials, processes, and organizations for all sectors of the global hi-tech materials world. Audience is management, academics, government, suppliers, and fabricators. Focus on news about growth opportunities." Estab. 1978. Circ. 13,000+. Pays on publication. Publishes ms an average of 1 months after acceptance. Byline sometimes given. Buys all rights. Editorial lead time 1 week. Submit seasonal material 1 month in advance. Accepts queries by e-mail. Responds in 1 week to queries; 1 month to mss. Sample copy for #10 SASE. Editorial calendar online.

- "We target and contact the freelancers with the most industry knowledge."

Nonfiction: New product, technical, industry information. **Buys 4-6 mss/year.** Query. Length: 100-700 words. **Pays $100-400.**

Photos: State availability with submission. Reviews 4×5 transparencies, prints, 35mm slides, JPEGs. Buys all rights. Offers no additional payment for photos accepted with ms. Captions, identification of subjects, model releases required.

$ $ AUTOMATED BUILDER, CMN Associates, Inc., 1445 Donlon St., Suite 16, Ventura CA 93003. (805)642-9735. Fax: (805)642-8820. E-mail: info@automatedbuilder.com. Website: www.automatedbuilder.com. Editor-in-Chief: Don Carlson. **Contact:** Bob Mendel. **10% freelance written.** Monthly magazine specializing in management for industrialized (manufactured) housing and volume home builders. "Our material is technical in content, and concerned with new technologies or improved methods for in-plant building and components related to building. Online content is uploaded from the monthly print material." Estab. 1964. Circ. 25,000. **Pays on acceptance.** Publishes ms an average of 3 months after acceptance. Byline given. Buys first North American serial rights. Editorial lead time 2 months. Submit seasonal material 2 months in advance. Accepts queries by mail, e-mail, fax. Responds in 2 weeks to queries. Sample copy for free.

Nonfiction: Case history articles on successful home building companies which may be 1) production (big volume) home builders; 2) mobile home manufacturers; 3) modular home manufacturers; 4) prefabricated (panelized) home manufacturers; 5) house component manufacturers; or 6) special unit (in-plant commercial building) manufacturers. Also uses interviews, photo features, and technical articles. "No architect or plan 'dreams.' Housing projects must be built or under construction." **Buys 6-8 mss/year.** Query. Phone queries OK. Length: 250-500 words. **Pays $300.**

Photos: Wants 4×5, 5×7, or 8×10 glossies. State availability with submission. Reviews 35mm or larger (35mm preferred) transparencies. Offers no additional payment for photos accepted with ms. Captions, identification of subjects required.

Tips: "Stories often are too long, too loose; we prefer 500-750 words. We prefer a phone query on feature articles. If accepted on query, article usually will not be rejected later."

$ $ CAM MAGAZINE, Construction Association of Michigan, 43636 S. Woodward, Bloomfield Hills MI 48302. (248)972-1000. Fax: (248)972-1001. Website: www.cam-online.com. **Contact:** Amanda Tackett, editor. **5% freelance written.** Monthly magazine covering all facets of the construction industry. "*CAM Magazine* is devoted to the growth and progress of individuals and companies serving and servicing the industry. It provides a forum on new construction-related technology, products and services, plus publishes information on industry personnel changes and advancements." Estab. 1978. Circ. 5,000. Pays on publication. Byline given. Buys all rights. Editorial lead time 2 months. Submit seasonal material 3 months in advance. Accepts queries by mail, e-mail, fax, phone. Sample copy and editorial subject calendar with query and SASE.

Nonfiction: Construction-related only. **Buys 3 mss/year.** Query with published clips. Length: Features: 1,000-2,000 words; will also review short pieces. **Pays $250-500.**

Photos: Send photos with submission. Reviews contact sheets, negatives, transparencies, Color or b&w prints. Buys one-time rights. Offers no additional payment for photos accepted with ms.

Tips: "Anyone having *current* knowledge or expertise on trends and innovations related to construction is welcome to submit articles. Our readers are construction experts."

$ $ CONCRETE CONSTRUCTION, Hanley-Wood, LLC., 426 S. Westgate St., Addison IL 60101. (630)543-0870. Fax: (630)543-5399. E-mail: cceditor@hanley-wood.com. Website: www.worldofconcrete.com. Editor: William Palmer. **Contact:** Pat Reband, managing editor. **20% freelance written.** Monthly magazine for concrete contractors, engineers, architects, specifiers and others who design and build residential, commercial, industrial, and public works, cast-in-place concrete structures. It also covers job stories and new equipment in the industry. Estab. 1956. Circ. 80,000. **Pays on acceptance.** Publishes ms an average of 4 months after acceptance. Byline given. Editorial lead time 4 months. Submit seasonal material 4 months in advance. Accepts queries by mail, e-mail, fax. Responds in 2 weeks to queries; 1 month to mss. Sample copy for free. Writer's guidelines free.

Nonfiction: How-to, new product, personal experience, photo feature, technical, job stories. **Buys 7-10 mss/year.** Query with published clips. Length: 2,000 words maximum. **Pays $250 or more for assigned articles; $200 minimum for unsolicited articles.** Pays expenses of writers on assignment.

Photos: Send photos with submission. Reviews contact sheets, negatives, transparencies, prints. Buys one-time rights. Offers no additional payment for photos accepted with ms. Captions required.

Tips: "Have a good understanding of the concrete construction industry. How-to stories accepted only from industry experts. Job stories must cover procedures, materials, and equipment used as well as the project's scope."

$ $ $ THE CONCRETE PRODUCER, Hanley-Wood LLC, 426 S. Westgate St., Addison IL 60101. (630)543-0870. Fax: (630)543-3112. Website: www.worldofconcrete.com. **Contact:** Rick Yelton, editor. **30% freelance written.** Monthly magazine covering concrete production. "Our audience consists of producers who have succeeded in making concrete the preferred building material through management, operating, quality control, use of the latest technology, or use of superior materials." Estab. 1982. Circ. 18,000. **Pays on acceptance.** Publishes ms an average of 2 months after acceptance. Byline given. Buys second serial (reprint) rights. Editorial lead time 4 months. Accepts queries by mail, e-mail, fax, phone. Responds in 1 week to queries; 2 months to mss. Sample copy for $4. Writer's guidelines free.

Nonfiction: How-to (promote concrete), new product, technical. **Buys 10 mss/year.** Send complete ms. Length: 500-2,000 words. **Pays $200-1,000.** Sometimes pays expenses of writers on assignment.

Photos: Scan photos at 300 dpi. State availability with submission. Reviews transparencies, prints. Offers no additional payment for photos accepted with ms. Captions, identification of subjects required.

N $ EARTH, Shepherd Media Group, P.O. Box 226789, Los Angeles CA 90053. (562)692-2292. Fax: (562)692-1843. Website: www.shepherdmachinery.com. **Contact:** Pam Pounds, editor. Quarterly magazine covering equipment used by engineering and excavating contractors in the Los Angeles area. Circ. 5,000. Byline given. Accepts queries by mail. Sample copy not available.

Nonfiction: New product, industry news. Query.

$ HARD HAT NEWS, Lee Publications, Inc., 6113 State Highway 5, Palatine Bridge NY 13428. (518)673-3237. Fax: (518)673-2381. E-mail: rdecamp@leepub.com. Website: www.hardhat.com. **Contact:** Ralph DeCamp, editor. **80% freelance written.** Biweekly tabloid covering heavy construction, equipment, road, and bridge work. "Our readers are contractors and heavy construction workers involved in excavation, highways, bridges, utility construction, and underground construction." Estab. 1980. Circ. 58,000. Byline given. Editorial lead time 2 weeks. Submit seasonal material 2 weeks in advance. Accepts queries by mail, e-mail, fax, phone. Sample copy and writer's guidelines free.

- "We especially need writers with some knowledge of heavy construction, although anyone with good composition and interviewing skills is welcome. Focus on major construction in progress in your area."

Nonfiction: Also 'Job Stories,' (a brief overall description of the project, the names and addresses of the companies and contractors involved, and a description of the equipment used, including manufacturers' names and model numbers. Quotes from the people in charge, as well as photos, are important, as are the names of the dealers providing the equipment). Interview/profile, new product, opinion, photo feature, technical. Send complete ms. Length: 50-800 words. **Pays $2.50/inch.** Sometimes pays expenses of writers on assignment.

Photos: Send photos with submission. Reviews prints; slides. Offers $15/photo. Captions, identification of subjects required.

Columns/Departments: New Products; Association News; Parts and Repairs; Attachments; Trucks and Trailers; People on the Move.

Tips: "Every issue has a focus—see our editorial calender. Special consideration is given to a story that coincides with the focus. A color photo is necessary for the front page. Vertical shots work best. We need more writers in metro NY area. Also, we are expanding our distribution into the Mid-Atlantic states and need writers in Virginia, Tennessee, North Carolina, and South Carolina."

$ $ HEAVY EQUIPMENT NEWS, Cygnus Business Media, 33 Inverness Center Pkwy., Suite 200, Birmingham AL 35242. Fax: (205)380-1384. E-mail: ashley.kizzire@cygnusb2b.com. Website: www.heavyequipmentnews.com. **Contact:** Ashley Kizzire, editor-in-chief. **30-40% freelance written.** Monthly magazine covering construction equipment and construction industry. "*Heavy Equipment News* is an editorial-driven publication for the construction contractor, focusing on job sites, asphalt-road building, concrete, business management, equipment selection and material handling." Estab. 1995. Circ. 63,000. **Pays on acceptance.** Publishes ms an average of 3 months after acceptance. Byline given. Offers 10% kill fee. Buys first North American serial, second serial (reprint), electronic rights. Editorial lead time 6 months. Submit seasonal material 6 months in advance. Accepts queries by mail, e-mail, fax. Responds in 2 weeks to queries; 1 month to mss. Sample copy for #10 SASE. Writer's guidelines free.

Nonfiction: How-to, interview/profile, new product, personal experience, technical. **Buys 12 mss/year.** Query with published clips. Length: 1,200-1,500 words. **Pays $500.**

Photos: Reviews transparencies, prints. Buys all rights. Offers no additional payment for photos accepted with ms. Captions, identification of subjects required.

Columns/Departments: Asphalt Road; Concrete Batch; Point of View; Truck Stop. Query with published clips. **Pays $300.**

$ $ MC MAGAZINE, The Voice of the Manufactured Concrete Products Industry, National Precast Concrete Association, 10333 N. Meridian St., Suite 272, Indianapolis IN 46290. (317)571-9500. Fax: (317)571-0041. E-mail: rhyink @precast.org. Website: www.precast.org. **Contact:** Ron Hyink, managing editor. **75% freelance written.** Quarterly magazine covering manufactured concrete products. "*MC Magazine* is a publication for owners and managers of factory-produced concrete products used in construction. We publish business articles, technical articles, company profiles, safety articles and project profiles with the intent of educating our readers in order to increase the quality and use of precast concrete." Estab. 1995. Circ. 8,500. **Pays on acceptance.** Publishes ms an average of 6 months after acceptance. Byline given. Buys first North American serial, second serial (reprint), all rights. Editorial lead time 3 months. Accepts queries by mail, e-mail, fax. Accepts simultaneous submissions. Responds in 1 month to queries; 2 months to mss. Sample copy online. Writer's guidelines online.

Nonfiction: How-to (business), interview/profile, technical (concrete manufacturing). "No humor, essays, fiction or fillers." **Buys 8-14 mss/year.** Query or send complete ms. Length: 1,500-2,500 words. **Pays $250-750.** Sometimes pays expenses of writers on assignment.

Photos: State availability with submission. Buys all rights. Offers no additional payment for photos accepted with ms. Captions required.

Tips: "Understand the audience and the purpose of the magazine. Understanding audience interests and needs is important and expressing a willingness to tailor a subject to get the right slant is critical. Our primary freelance needs are about general business or technology topics. Of course, if you are an engineer or a writer specializing in industry, construction or manufacturing technology, other possibilities may exist. Writing style should be concise, yet lively and entertaining. Avoid clichés. We require a third-person perspective, encourage a positive tone and active voice. For stylistic matters, follow the *AP Style Book*."

$ MICHIGAN CONTRACTOR & BUILDER, 1917 Savannah Lane, Ypsilanti MI 48198-3674. (734)482-0272. Fax: (734)482-0291. E-mail: akalousdian@cahners.com. **Contact:** Aram Kalousdian. **25% freelance written.** Weekly magazine covering the commercial construction industry in Michigan (no home building). "*Michigan Contractor & Builder's* audience is contractors, equipment suppliers, engineers, and architects. The magazine reports on construction projects in Michigan. It does not cover homebuilding. Stories should focus on news or innovative techniques or materials in construction." Estab. 1907. Circ. 3,700. Pays 1 month after publication. Byline given. Buys all rights. Accepts queries by mail, e-mail, fax, phone. Sample copy for free.

Nonfiction: Michigan construction projects. **Buys 52 mss/year.** Query with published clips. Length: 1,500 words with 5-7 photos. **Payment is negotiable.**

Photos: Send photos with submission. Reviews original prints. Buys all rights. Offers no additional payment for photos accepted with ms. Captions required.

$ $ NW BUILDER MAGAZINE, Pacific NW Sales & Marketing, Inc., 500 W. 8th St., Suite 270, Vancouver WA 98660. (360)906-0793. Fax: (360)906-0794. E-mail: mgreditor@nwbuildermagazine.com. Website: www.nwbuildermagazine.com. **Contact:** Editor. **10-50% freelance written.** Monthly journal covering NW residential and commercial building. "Articles must address pressing topics for builders in our region with a special emphasis on the business aspects of construction." Estab. 1996. Circ. 25,000. Pays on acceptance of revised ms. Publishes ms an average of 1 month after acceptance. Byline given. Buys first North American serial, electronic rights. Editorial lead time 2 months. Submit seasonal material 3 months in advance. Accepts queries by mail, e-mail, fax. Responds in 1 week to queries; 1 month to mss. Sample copy for free or online. Writer's guidelines free.

Nonfiction: How-to, interview/profile, new product, technical. No personal bios unless they teach a valuable lesson to those in the building industry. **Buys 40 mss/year.** Query. Length: 500-1,500 words. **Pays $50-300.** Sometimes pays expenses of writers on assignment.

Photos: State availability with submission. Buys first North American serial and electronic rights. Offers no additional payment for photos accepted with ms. Captions, identification of subjects, model releases required.

Columns/Departments: Engineering; Construction; Architecture & Design; Tools & Materials; Heavy Equipment; Business & Economics; Legal Matters; E-build; Building Green, all 750-1,000 words. Query.

Tips: Writers should "e-mail an intro as to why he/she should write for us. A thorough knowledge of our publication is crucial. Also, must be a Northwest slant."

$ $ PENNSYLVANIA BUILDER, Pennsylvania Builders Association, 600 N. 12th St., Lemoyne PA 17043. (717)730-4380. Fax: (717)730-4396. E-mail: scornbower@pahomes.org. Website: www.pahomes.org. **Contact:** Tara Ramsey, publication specialist. **10% freelance written.** "Quarterly trade publication for builders, remodelers, subcontractors, and other affiliates of the home building industry in Pennsylvania." Estab. 1988. Circ. 12,200. Pays on publication. Publishes ms an average of 1 year after acceptance. Byline given. Buys one-time rights. Editorial lead time 3 months. Submit seasonal material 9 months in advance. Accepts queries by mail, e-mail. Accepts simultaneous submissions. Responds in 2 weeks to queries; 3 months to mss. Sample copy for free. Writer's guidelines by e-mail. Editorial calendar online.

Nonfiction: General interest, how-to, new product, technical. No personnel or company profiles. **Buys 1-2 mss/year.** Send complete ms. Length: 800-1,200 words. **Pays $250.** Sometimes pays expenses of writers on assignment.

Reprints: Accepts previously published submissions.

Photos: Send photos with submission. Reviews negatives, transparencies, prints. Buys one-time rights. Negotiates payment individually. Captions, identification of subjects required.

$ $ PERMANENT BUILDINGS & FOUNDATIONS (PBF), R.W. Nielsen Co., 350 E. Center St., Suite 201, Provo UT 84606-3262. (801)373-0013. E-mail: rnielsen@pbf.org. Website: www.permanentbuildings.com. Managing Editor: Vanessa Hoy. **Contact:** Roger W. Nielsen, editor. **15% freelance written.** Magazine published 8 times/year. "*PBF* readers are contractors who build residential and light commercial concrete buildings. Editorial focus is on materials that last: Concrete and new technologies to build solid, energy efficient structures, insulated concrete walls and tilt-up construction, waterproofing, underpinning, roofing and the business of contracting and construction." Estab. 1989. Circ. 30,000. Pays on publication. Byline given. Buys first North American serial rights. Editorial lead time 1 month. Submit seasonal material 2 months in advance. Accepts queries by mail, e-mail. Responds in 2 weeks to queries; 1 month to mss. Sample copy for 9×12 SASE or online. Writer's guidelines free or online.

Nonfiction: How-to (construction methods, management techniques), humor, interview/profile, new product, technical, book reviews, tool reviews. Special issues: Water proofing February, Insulated Concrete Forming supplement April. Special issues: Water Proofing and Repair (February); Buyer's Guide (October); Insulated Concrete Forming Report (November); Concrete Homes (January); Commercial Market (July). **Buys 5-10 mss/year.** Query. Length: 500-1,500 words. **Pays 20-40¢/word for assigned articles; $50-500 for unsolicited articles.**

Photos: State availability with submission. Reviews contact sheets. Buys one-time rights. Offers no additional payment for photos accepted with ms. Captions, identification of subjects required.

Columns/Departments: Marketing Tips, 250-500 words; Q&A (solutions to contractor problems), 200-500 words. Query.

$ $ REEVES JOURNAL, Business News Publishing Co., 23211 South Pointe Dr., Suite 101, Laguna Hills CA 92653. Fax: (949)859-7845. E-mail: john@reevesjournal.com. Website: www.reevesjournal.com. **Contact:** John Fultz, editor. **25% freelance written.** Monthly magazine covering building subcontractors—plumbers, HVAC contractors. Estab. 1920. Circ. 13,800. Pays on publication. Byline given. Buys first North American serial, electronic rights. Editorial lead time 3 months. Accepts queries by mail, e-mail, fax. Responds in 1 month to queries; 2 months to mss. Sample copy for free. Writer's guidelines for #10 SASE.

- "Knowledge of building construction, water science, engineering is extremely helpful. Even better—former plumbing, HVAC experience, and a great command of the English language."

Nonfiction: "Only articles applicable to plumbing/HVAC subcontracting trade in the western US." How-to, interview/profile, new product, technical. Query with published clips. Length: 1,500-2,000 words. **Pays $100-350.** Pays phone expenses.

Photos: State availability with submission. Buys all rights. Negotiates payment individually. Captions, identification of subjects required.

The online magazine carries original content not found in the print edition. Contact: John Fultz.

Tips: "Know the market—we're not just another builder publication. Our target audience is the plumbing, HVAC contractor—new construction, mechanical, and service and repair. We cover the western U.S. (plus Texas)."

$ $ UNDERGROUND CONSTRUCTION, Oildom Publishing Co. of Texas, Inc., P.O. Box 941669, Houston TX 77094-8669. (281)558-6930. Fax: (281)558-7029. E-mail: rcarpenter@oildompublishing.com. Website: www.oildompublishing.com. **Contact:** Robert Carpenter, editor. **35% freelance written.** Monthly magazine covering underground oil and gas pipeline, water and sewer pipeline, cable construction for contractors and owning companies. Circ. 34,500. Publishes ms an average of 6 months after acceptance. Buys first North American serial rights. Accepts queries by mail, e-mail, fax, phone. Responds in 1 month to mss.

Nonfiction: How-to, job stories. Query with published clips. Length: 1,000-2,000 words. **Pays $3-500.** Sometimes pays expenses of writers on assignment.

Photos: Send photos with submission. Reviews color prints and slides. Buys one-time rights. Captions required.

Tips: "We supply guidelines outlining information we need." The most frequent mistake made by writers in completing articles is unfamiliarity with the field.

DRUGS, HEALTHCARE & MEDICAL PRODUCTS

N **$ $ $ HOME CARE MAGAZINE, For Business Leaders in Home Health Care**, Primedia Business Magazines, 9800 Metcalf Ave., Overland Park KS 66212. (913)341-1300. Fax: (913)967-1898. E-mail: marie_blakey@intertec.com. Website: www.homecaremag.com. Managing Editor: Paula Patch. **Contact:** Editor. **20% freelance written.** Monthly journal covering the needs of home medical equipment retailers. "We provide product and business advice and market analysis to small family-held companies that offer medical equipment and related services to patients in a home setting." Estab. 1979. Circ. 17,000. Pays on publication. Publishes ms an average of 3 months after acceptance. Byline given. Buys first, second serial (reprint) rights. Editorial lead time 3 months. Accepts queries by mail, e-mail, fax. Accepts simultaneous submissions. Responds in 6 weeks to queries; 3 weeks to mss. Sample copy online.

Nonfiction: How-to (by assignment). **Buys multiple mss/year.** Query with published clips. Length: 500-2,500 words. **Pays 50¢/word.** Sometimes pays expenses of writers on assignment.

Photos: State availability with submission. Buys all rights. Captions, identification of subjects, model releases required.

Tips: "Contributors should have knowledge of health industry."

$ $ SUNWEAR VISION, Frames Data, P.O. Box 1945, Big Bear Lake CA 92315. (909)866-5590. Fax: (909)866-5577. E-mail: cwalker@framesdata.com. Website: www.framesdata.com. **Contact:** Christie Walker, editor. **20% freelance written.** Magazine published 3 times/year for the eye wear industry. "*Sunwear Vision* brings readers current information on all the latest designs and innovations available in the field of fashion and sports sunwear." Estab. 1970. Circ. 30,000. Pays 1 month prior to publication. Publishes ms an average of 3 months after acceptance. Byline given. Buys first North American serial rights. Editorial lead time 3 months. Submit seasonal material 3 months in advance. Accepts simultaneous submissions. Responds in 1 week to queries. Sample copy for 8×10 SAE and 2 first-class stamps.

Nonfiction: How-to, new product. **Buys 10 mss/year.** Query with published clips. Length: 800-1,600 words. **Pays $300-500.**

Photos: Send photos with submission. Buys one-time rights. Offers no additional payment for photos accepted with ms. Captions, identification of subjects required.

Tips: "Write for the doctor. How can doctors make more money selling sunwear?"

$ $ VALIDATION TIMES, Washington Information Source Co., 6506 Old Stage Rd., Suite 100, Rockville MD 20852-4326. (301)770-5553. Fax: (301)468-0475. E-mail: wis@fdainfo.com. Website: www.fdainfo.com. **Contact:** Kenneth Reid, publisher. Monthly newsletter covering regulation of pharmaceutical and medical devices. "We write to executives who have to keep up on changing FDA policies and regulations, and on what their competitors are doing at the agency." Estab. 1992. Pays on publication. Publishes ms an average of 1 month after acceptance. Byline given. Makes work-for-hire assignments. Editorial lead time 1 month. Submit seasonal material 1 month in advance. Accepts queries by mail. Responds in 1 month to queries. Sample copy and writer's guidelines free.

Nonfiction: How-to, technical, regulatory. No lay interest pieces. **Buys 50-100 mss/year.** Query. Length: 600-1,500 words. **Pays $100/half day; $200 full day "to cover meetings and same rate for writing."** Sometimes pays expenses of writers on assignment.

Tips: "If you're covering a conference for non-competing publications, call me with a drug or device regulatory angle."

EDUCATION & COUNSELING

Professional educators, teachers, coaches, and counselors—as well as other people involved in training and education—read the journals classified here. Many journals for educators are non-profit forums for professional advancement; writers contribute articles in return for a byline and contributor's copies. *Writer's Market* includes only educational journals that pay freelancers for articles. Education-related publications for students are included in the Consumer Career, College & Alumni, and Teen & Young Adult sections. Listings in the Childcare & Parental Guidance and Psychology & Self-Improvement sections of Consumer Magazines may also be of interest.

$ ARTS & ACTIVITIES, Publishers' Development Corporation, Dept. WM, 591 Camino de la Reina, Suite 200, San Diego CA 92108-3104. (619)819-4530. Fax: (619)297-5353. Website: www.artsandactivities.com. **Contact:** Maryellen Bridge, editor-in-chief. **95% freelance written.** Eager to work with new/unpublished writers. Monthly (except July and August) magazine covering art education at levels from preschool through college for educators and therapists engaged in arts and crafts education and training. Estab. 1932. Circ. 20,000. Pays on publication. Publishes ms an average of 1 year after acceptance. Byline given. Buys first North American serial rights. Submit seasonal material 6 months in advance. Accepts queries by mail. Responds in 3 months to queries. Sample copy for 9×12 SAE and 8 first-class stamps. Writer's guidelines online.

- Editors here are seeking more materials for upper elementary and secondary levels on printmaking, ceramics, 3-dimensional design, weaving, fiber arts (stitchery, tie-dye, batik, etc.), crafts, painting and multicultural art.

Nonfiction: Historical/nostalgic (arts, activities, history), how-to (classroom art experiences, artists' techniques), interview/profile (of artists), opinion (on arts activities curriculum, ideas of how to do things better, philosophy of art education), personal experience (this ties in with the how-to, we like it to be personal, no recipe style), articles of exceptional art programs. **Buys 80-100 mss/year.** Length: 200-2,000 words. **Pays $35-150.**

Tips: "Frequently in unsolicited manuscripts, writers obviously have not studied the magazine to see what style of articles we publish. Send for a sample copy to familiarize yourself with our style and needs. The best way to find out if his/her writing style suits our needs is for the author to submit a manuscript on speculation. We prefer an anecdotal style of writing, so that readers will feel as though they are there in the art room as the lesson/project is taking place. Also, good quality photographs of student artwork are important. We are a *visual* art magazine!"

$ THE ATA MAGAZINE, The Alberta Teachers' Association, 11010 142nd St., Edmonton AB T5N 2R1, Canada. (780)447-9400. Fax: (780)455-6481. E-mail: postmaster@teachers.ab.ca. Website: www.teachers.ab.ca. Editor: Tim Johnston. **Contact:** Raymond Gariepy, associate editor. Quarterly magazine covering education. Estab. 1920. Circ. 39,500. Pays on publication. Publishes ms an average of 4 months after acceptance. Byline given. Buys one-time rights. Editorial lead time 2 months. Submit seasonal material 2 months in advance. Accepts queries by mail, e-mail, fax, phone. Accepts simultaneous submissions. Responds in 2 months to queries. Sample copy free. Writer's guidelines online.

Nonfiction: Education-related topics. Query with published clips. Length: 500-1,250 words. **Pays $75 (Canadian).**

Photos: Send photos with submission. Reviews 4×6 prints. Negotiates rights. Negotiates payment individually. Captions required.

$ $ $ CHILDREN'S VOICE, Child Welfare League of America, 440 First St. NW, 3rd Floor, Washington DC 20001-2085. (202)638-2952. Fax: (202)638-4004. E-mail: voice@cwla.org. Website: www.cwla.org/pubs. **Contact:** Steve Boehm, editor-in-chief. **10% freelance written.** Bimonthly magazine covering "issues of importance for children, youth, and families; professionals who work with children, youth, and families at risk; and advocates and policymakers who work in their behalf. Sample topics include fostercare and adoption, child abuse and neglect, juvenile justice, pregnant and parenting teens, childcare and early child and early childhood development, troubled youth, homeless youth, etc." Estab. 1991. Circ. 20,000. Pays on publication. Publishes ms an average of 6 months after acceptance. Byline given. Buys all rights. Editorial lead time 6 months. Submit seasonal material 6 months in advance. Accepts queries by mail, e-mail, fax. Responds in 2 weeks to queries; 2 months to mss. Sample copy for 9×12 SAE and 3 first-class stamps. Writer's guidelines online.

Nonfiction: Essays, general interest, interview/profile, opinion, personal experience, successful programs. No poetry, advertisements for products or services disguised as feature articles. **Buys 6-10 mss/year.** Query. Length: 1,800-2,800 words. **Pays 25-50¢/word. Generally does not pay cash for professionals in the field of child welfare.** Sometimes pays expenses of writers on assignment.

Photos: State availability with submission. Reviews contact sheets. Buys all rights. Negotiates payment individually. Captions, identification of subjects, model releases required.

Tips: "Writers must know the field of child welfare or have intimate knowledge of an aspect that is unique, insightful, studied, and authoritative. Material that promotes a product or service is not suitable."

$ CLASS ACT, Class Act, Inc., P.O. Box 802, Henderson KY 42419. E-mail: classact@lightpower.net. Website: classactpress.com. **Contact:** Susan Thurman, editor. **50% freelance written.** Newsletter published 9 times/year covering English/language arts education. "Our writers must know English as a classroom subject and should be familiar with writing for teens. If you can't make your manuscript interesting to teenagers, we're not interested." Estab. 1993. Circ. 300. **Pays on acceptance.** Publishes ms an average of 6 months after acceptance. Byline given. Offers 100% kill fee. Buys all rights. Editorial lead time 2 months. Submit seasonal material 3 months in advance. Accepts simultaneous submissions. Responds in 1 month to queries. Sample copy for $3. Writer's guidelines online.

- Accepts queries by mail and e-mail, but no attachments.
- Break in with "an original, ready-for-classroom-use article that provides tips for writing (but geared to a teenage audience)."

Nonfiction: How-to (games, puzzles, assignments relating to English education). "No Masters theses; no esoteric articles; no poetry; no educational theory or jargon." **Buys 12 mss/year.** Send complete ms. Length: 100-2,000 words. **Pays $10-40.**

Columns/Departments: Writing Assignments (innovative, thought-provoking for teens), 500-1,500 words; Puzzles, Games (English education oriented), 200 words; Teacher Tips (bulletin boards, time-saving devices), 100 words. "E-mailed mss (not attachments) are encouraged. Articles on disk (MS Word) also are encouraged." Send complete ms. **Pays $10-40.**

Fillers: Teacher tips. **Pays $10.**

Tips: "Please know the kind of language used by junior/senior high students. Don't speak above them. Also, it helps to know what these students *don't* know, in order to explain or emphasize the concepts. Clip art is sometimes used but is not paid extra for. We like material that's slightly humorous while still being educational. We are especially open to innovative writing assignments, educational puzzles and games, and instructions on basics. Again, be familiar with this age group. Remember we are geared for English teachers."

N $ $ $ EARLYCHILDHOOD NEWS, Excelligence Learning Corp., 2 Lower Ragsdale, Suite 125, Monterey CA 93940. (831)333-2000. Fax: (831)333-5510. E-mail: mshaw@excelligencemail.com. Website: www.earlychildhoodnews.com. **Contact:** Megan Shaw, editor. **80% freelance written.** Bimonthly magazine covering early childhood education. Targets teachers and parents of young children, infants to age 8. Estab. 1988. Circ. 55,000. Pays on publication. Publishes ms an average of 2-3 months after acceptance. Byline given. Buys all rights. Editorial lead time 2-4 months. Submit seasonal material 4 months in advance. Accepts queries by mail, e-mail, fax. Responds in 4-6 weeks to queries; 2-4 months to mss. Sample copy for free. Writer's guidelines free.

Nonfiction: Essays, general interest, inspirational, interview/profile, research-based. Special issues: Social/Emotional Development (January/February); The Power of Play (March/April); Special Needs Children (May/June); Back to School (August/September); Learning Materials and Environments (October); Creativity and Literacy (November/December). No personal stories. **Buys 40-50 mss/year.** Query. Length: 500-3,000 words. **Pays $100 minimum; $800-1,000 maximum for assigned articles; $100-300 for unsolicited articles.**

Poetry: "Poems should have a teacher-directed audience." Light verse, traditional. No "poetry not related to children, teachers, or early childhood." **Buys 6 poems/year.** Length: 10-60 lines. **Pays $100-250.**

Tips: "Knowing about the publication and the types of articles we publish is greatly appreciated. Query letters are preferred over complete manuscripts."

$ $ HISPANIC OUTLOOK IN HIGHER EDUCATION, 210 Rt 4 East, Ste 310, Paramus NJ 07652. (201)587-8800, ext 100. Fax: (201)587-9105. E-mail: sloutlook@aol.com. Website: www.hispanicoutlook.com. Editor: Adalyn Hixson. **Contact:** Sue Lopez-Isa, managing editor. **50% freelance written.** Biweekly magazine. "We're looking for higher education story articles, with a focus on Hispanics and the advancements made by and for Hispanics in higher education." Circ. 28,000. Pays on publication. Publishes ms an average of 2 months after acceptance. Byline given. Editorial lead time 2 months. Submit seasonal material 3 months in advance. Accepts queries by mail, e-mail, fax. Accepts simultaneous submissions. Sample copy for free.

O-- Break with "issues articles such as new laws in higher education."

Nonfiction: Historical/nostalgic, interview/profile (of academic or scholar), opinion (on higher education), personal experience, all regarding higher education only. **Buys 20-25 mss/year.** Query with published clips. Length: 1,750-2,000 words. **Pays $400 minimum for assigned articles.** Pays expenses of writers on assignment.

Photos: Send photos with submission. Reviews b&w or color prints. Offers no additional payment for photos accepted with ms.

Tips: "Articles explore the Hispanic experience in higher education. Special theme issues address sports, law, health, corporations, heritage, women, and a wide range of similar issues; however, articles need not fall under those umbrellas."

$ $ PTO TODAY, The Magazine for Parent Group Leaders, PTO Today, Inc., 200 Stonewall Blvd., Suite 6A, Wrentham MA 02093. (508)541-9130. Fax: (508)384-6108. E-mail: editor@ptotoday.com. Website: www.ptotoday.com. **Contact:** Craig Bystrynski, editor. **65% freelance written.** Magazine published 6 times during the school year covering the work of school parent-teacher groups. "We celebrate the work of school parent volunteers and provide resources to help them do that work more effectively." Estab. 1999. Circ. 80,000. Pays on publication. Publishes ms an average of 2 months after acceptance. Byline given. Offers 40% kill fee. Buys first North American serial, electronic, all rights. Editorial lead time 4 months. Submit seasonal material 4 months in advance. Accepts queries by e-mail. Sample copy online. Writer's guidelines by e-mail.

Nonfiction: Exposé, general interest, how-to (anything related to PTO/PTA), interview/profile, new product, personal experience. **Buys 40 mss/year.** Query. Length: 800-2,500 words. **Pays 20-40¢/word for assigned articles; $50-500 for unsolicited articles.** Sometimes pays expenses of writers on assignment.

Photos: State availability with submission. Buys one-time rights. Negotiates payment individually. Identification of subjects required.

Tips: "It's difficult for us to find talented writers with strong experience with parent groups. This experience is a big plus. Also, it helps to review our writer's guidelines before querying."

$ SCHOOL ARTS MAGAZINE, 50 Portland St., Worcester MA 01608-9959. Fax: (610)683-8229. Website: www.davis-art.com. **Contact:** Eldon Katter, editor. **85% freelance written.** Monthly magazine (September-May), serving arts and craft education profession, K-12, higher education and museum education programs written by and for art teachers. Estab. 1901. Pays on publication. Publishes ms an average of 3 months after acceptance. Buys all rights. Accepts queries by mail, phone. Responds in 3 months to queries. Sample copy for free. Writer's guidelines online.

O-- Break in with "professional quality photography to illustrate art lessons."

Nonfiction: Articles on art and craft activities in schools. Should include description and photos of activity in progress, as well as examples of finished artwork. Query or send complete ms and SASE. Length: 600-1,400 words. **Pays $30-150.**

The online version contains material not found in the print edition.

Tips: "We prefer articles on actual art projects or techniques done by students in actual classroom situations. Philosophical and theoretical aspects of art and art education are usually handled by our contributing editors. Our articles are reviewed and accepted on merit and each is tailored to meet our needs. Keep in mind that art teachers want practical tips, above all—more hands-on information than academic theory. Write your article with the accompanying photographs in hand." The most frequent mistakes made by writers are "bad visual material (photographs, drawings) submitted with articles, or a lack of complete descriptions of art processes; and no rationale behind programs or activities. Familiarity with the field of art education is essential. Review recent issues of *School Arts*."

$ $ $ TEACHER MAGAZINE, Editorial Projects in Education, 6935 Arlington Rd., Bethesda MD 20814. Fax: (301)280-3150. E-mail: info@teachermagazine.org. Website: www.teachermagazine.org. Managing Editor: Samantha Stainburn. **Contact:** Rich Shea, executive editor. **40% freelance written.** Magazine published 8 times/year covering the teaching profession. "One of the major thrusts of the current school reform movement is to make teaching a true profession. *Teacher Magazine* plays a central role in that effort. It is a national communications network that provides teachers with the information they need to be better practitioners and effective leaders." Estab. 1989. Circ. 120,000. Pays on publication. Publishes ms an average of 1 month after acceptance. Byline given. Offers 25% kill fee. Buys first North American serial, electronic rights. Editorial lead time 3 months. Submit seasonal material 4 months in advance. Accepts queries by mail, e-mail, fax. Responds in 2 months to queries. Sample copy online. Writer's guidelines free.

Nonfiction: Book excerpts, essays, interview/profile, personal experience, photo feature, investigative. No "how-to" articles. **Buys 56 mss/year.** Query with published clips. Length: 1,000-5,000 words. **Pays 50¢/word.** Sometimes pays expenses of writers on assignment.

Photos: State availability with submission. Reviews contact sheets, transparencies, prints. Buys one-time rights. Negotiates payment individually. Identification of subjects, model releases required.

Columns/Departments: Current events, forum. Query with published clips. **Pays 50¢/word.**

Tips: "Sending us a well-researched query letter accompanied by clips that demonstrate you can tell a good story is the best way to break into *Teacher Magazine.* Describe the characters in your proposed article. What scenes do you hope to include in the piece?"

$ TEACHERS OF VISION, Christian Educators Association, P.O. Box 41300, Pasadena CA 91114. (626)798-1124. Fax: (626)798-2346. E-mail: judy@ceai.org. Website: www.ceai.org. Editor: Forrest L. Turpen. **Contact:** Judy Turpen, contributing editor. **50% freelance written.** Magazine published 6 times/year for Christian teachers in public education. "*Teachers of Vision*'s articles inspire, inform, and equip teachers and administrators in the educational arena. Readers look for teacher tips, integrating faith & work, and general interest education articles. Topics include union issues, religious expression and activity in public schools, and legal rights of Christian educators. Our audience is primarily public school educators. Other readers include teachers in private schools, university professors, school administrators, parents and school board members." Estab. 1953. Circ. 10,000. Pays on publication. Publishes ms an average of 6 months after acceptance. Byline given. Buys first North American serial, second serial (reprint) rights. Editorial lead time 6 months. Submit seasonal material 6 months in advance. Accepts queries by mail, e-mail, fax. Accepts simultaneous submissions. Responds in 1 month to queries; 3-4 months to mss. Sample copy for 9×12 SAE and 4 first-class stamps. Writer's guidelines online.
Nonfiction: How-to, humor, inspirational, interview/profile, opinion, personal experience, religious. "Nothing preachy." **Buys 15-20 mss/year.** Query or send complete ms if 2,000 words or less. Length: 600-2,500 words. **Pays $30-40.**
Reprints: Accepts previously published submissions.
Photos: State availability with submission. Buys one-time and reprint rights. Offers no additional payment for photos accepted with ms.
Columns/Departments: Query. **Pays $10-30.**
Fillers: Send with SASE—must relate to public education.
Tips: "We are looking for material on living out one's faith in appropriate, legal ways in the public school setting."

$ $ TEACHING THEATRE, Educational Theatre Association, 2343 Auburn Ave., Cincinnati OH 45219-2819. (513)421-3900. Fax: (513)421-7077. E-mail: jpalmarini@edta.org. Website: www.edta.org. **Contact:** James Palmarini, editor. **65% freelance written.** Quarterly magazine covering education theater K-12, primary emphasis on middle and secondary level education. "*Teaching Theatre* emphasizes the teaching, theory, philosophy issues that are of concern to teachers at the elementary, secondary, and—as they relate to teaching K-12 theater—college levels. We publish work that explains specific approaches to teaching (directing, acting, curriculum development and management, etc.); advocates curriculum reform; or offers theories of theater education." Estab. 1989. Circ. 3,500. **Pays on acceptance.** Publishes ms an average of 3 months after acceptance. Byline given. Buys one-time, electronic rights. Editorial lead time 2 months. Submit seasonal material 3 months in advance. Accepts previously published material. Accepts simultaneous submissions. Responds in 1 month to queries; 3 months to mss. Sample copy for $2. Writer's guidelines online.
Nonfiction: "*Teaching Theatre*'s audience is well educated and most have considerable experience in their field; *generalist* articles are discouraged; readers already *possess* basic skills." Book excerpts, essays, how-to, interview/profile, opinion, technical theater. **Buys 20 mss/year.** Query. **Pays $100-300.**
Photos: State availability with submission. Reviews contact sheets, 5×7 and 8×10 transparencies, prints. Offers no additional payment for photos accepted with ms.
Tips: Wants articles that address the needs of the busy but experienced high school theater educators. "Fundamental pieces, on the value of theater education are *not* of value to us—our readers already know that."

$ $ $ $ TEACHING TOLERANCE, The Southern Poverty Law Center, 400 Washington Ave., Montgomery AL 36104. (334)956-8200. Fax: (334)956-8484. Website: www.teachingtolerance.org. **Contact:** Cynthia Pon, research editor. **65% freelance written.** Semiannual magazine. "*Teaching Tolerance* is dedicated to helping K-12 teachers promote tolerance and understanding between widely diverse groups of students. Includes articles, teaching ideas, and reviews of other resources available to educators." Estab. 1991. Circ. 600,000. **Pays on acceptance.** Byline given. Buys all rights. Editorial lead time 6 months. Submit seasonal material 6 months in advance. Accepts queries by mail, fax. Sample copy and writer's guidelines free or online. Writer's guidelines online.
Nonfiction: Essays, how-to (classroom techniques), personal experience (classroom), photo feature. "No jargon, rhetoric or academic analysis. No theoretical discussions on the pros/cons of multicultural education." **Buys 6-8 mss/year.** Query with published clips. Length: 1,000-3,000 words. **Pays $500-3,000 for assigned articles.** Pays expenses of writers on assignment.
Photos: State availability with submission. Reviews contact sheets, transparencies. Buys one-time rights. Captions, identification of subjects required.
Columns/Departments: Essays (personal reflection, how-to, school program), 400-800 words; Idea Exchange (special projects, successful anti-bias activities), 250-500 words; Student Writings (short essays dealing with diversity, tolerance & justice), 300-500 words. **Buys 8-12 mss/year.** Query with published clips. **Pays $50-1,000.**

The online magazine carries original content not found in the print edition and includes writer's guidelines. Contact: Tim Walker, online editor.

Tips: "We want lively, simple, concise writing. The writing style should be descriptive and reflective, showing the strength of programs dealing successfully with diversity by employing clear descriptions of real scenes and interactions, and by using quotes from teachers and students. We ask that prospective writers study previous issues of the magazine and writer's guidelines before sending a query with ideas. Most open to articles that have a strong classroom focus. We are interested in approaches to teaching tolerance and promoting understanding that really work—approaches we might not have heard of. We want to inform our readers; we also want to inspire and encourage them. We know what's happening nationally; we want to know what's happening in your neighborhood classroom."

$ TECH DIRECTIONS, Prakken Publications, Inc., P.O. Box 8623, Ann Arbor MI 48107-8623. (734)975-2800. Fax: (734)975-2787. E-mail: tom@techdirections.com. Website: www.techdirections.com. **Contact:** Tom Bowden, managing editor. **100% freelance written.** Eager to work with new/unpublished writers. Monthly (except June and July) magazine covering issues, trends, and activities of interest to science, technical, and technology educators at the elementary through post-secondary school levels. Estab. 1934. Circ. 43,000. Pays on publication. Publishes ms an average of 1 year after acceptance. Byline given. Buys all rights. Responds in 1 month to queries. Sample copy for $5. Writer's guidelines online.

Nonfiction: Uses articles pertinent to the various teaching areas in science and technology education (woodwork, electronics, drafting, physics, graphic arts, computer training, etc.). Prefers authors who have direct connection with the field of science and/or technical education. "The outlook should be on innovation in educational programs, processes or projects that directly apply to the technical education area." Main focus: technical career and education. General interest, how-to, personal experience, technical, think pieces. **Buys 50 unsolicited mss/year.** Length: 2,000-3,000 words. **Pays $50-150.**

Photos: Send photos with submission. Reviews color prints. Payment for photos included in payment for ms. Will accept electronic art as well.

Columns/Departments: Direct from Washington (education news from Washington DC); Technology Today (new products under development); Technologies Past (profiles the inventors of last century); Mastering Computers, Technology Concepts (project orientation).

Tips: "We are most interested in articles written by science and technical educators about their class projects and their ideas about the field. We need more and more technology-related articles, especially written for the community college level."

ELECTRONICS & COMMUNICATION

These publications are edited for broadcast and telecommunications technicians and engineers, electrical engineers, and electrical contractors. Included are journals for electronic equipment designers and operators who maintain electronic and telecommunication systems. Publications for appliance dealers can be found in Home Furnishings & Household Goods.

$ $ THE ACUTA JOURNAL OF TELECOMMUNICATIONS IN HIGHER EDUCATION, ACUTA, 152 W. Zandale Dr., Suite 200, Lexington KY 40503-2486. (859)278-3338. Fax: (859)278-3268. E-mail: pscott@acuta.org. Website: www.acuta.org. **Contact:** Patricia Scott, communications manager. **20% freelance written.** Quarterly professional association journal covering telecommunications in higher education. "Our audience includes, primarily, middle to upper management in the telecommunications department on college/university campuses. They are highly skilled, technology-oriented professionals who provide data, voice, and video communications services for residential and academic purposes." Estab. 1997. Circ. 2,200. Pays on publication. Publishes ms an average of 6 months after acceptance. Byline given. Buys first rights. Editorial lead time 6 months. Accepts queries by mail, e-mail, fax, phone. Responds in 1 month to queries; 2 months to mss. Sample copy for 9×12 SAE and 6 first-class stamps. Writer's guidelines free.

- Break in with a campus study or case profile. "Contact me with your idea for a story. Convince me that you can handle the level of technical depth required."

Nonfiction: "Each issue has a focus. Available with writer's guidelines. We are only interested in articles described in article types." How-to (telecom), technical (telecom), case study, college/university application of technology. **Buys 6-8 mss/year.** Query. Length: 1,200-4,000 words. **Pays 8-10¢/word.** Sometimes pays expenses of writers on assignment.

Photos: State availability with submission. Reviews prints. Offers no additional payment for photos accepted with ms. Captions, model releases required.

Tips: "Our audience expects every article to be relevant to telecommunications on the college/university campus, whether it is related to technology, facilities, or management. Writers must read back issues to understand this focus and the level of technicality we expect."

N $ AMERICA'S NETWORK, Advanstar Communications, 100 W. Monroe, Suite 300, Chicago IL 60603. (312)553-1943. Fax: (312)553-8926. E-mail: suzanne_sanders@advanstar.com. Website: www.americasnetwork.com. **Contact:** Suzanne Sanders. Magazine published 22 times/year. Edited for telecommunications executives and professionals who are responsible for the design, construction, sales, purchase, operationsand maintenance of telephone/telecom systems. Circ. 62,780. Editorial lead time 3 months. Sample copy not available.

$ $ DIGITAL OUTPUT, The Business Guide for Electronic Publishers, The Doyle Group, 5150 Palm Valley Rd., Suite 103, Ponte Vedra Beach FL 32082. (904)285-6020. Fax: (904)285-9944. E-mail: tmurphy@digitaloutput.net. Website: www.digitaloutput.net. **Contact:** Mike McEnaney, editor. **50% freelance written.** Monthly magazine covering electronic prepress, desktop publishing, and digital imaging, with articles ranging from digital capture and design to electronic prepress and digital printing. "*Digital Output* is a national business publication for electronic publishers and digital imagers, providing monthly articles which examine the latest technologies and digital methods and discuss how to profit from them. Our readers include service bureaus, prepress and reprographic houses, designers, commercial printers, wide-format printers, ad agencies, corporate communications and others." Estab. 1994. Circ. 30,000. Pays on publication. Publishes ms an average of 2 months after acceptance. Byline given. Offers 10-20% kill fee. Buys one-time rights including electronic rights for archival posting. Editorial lead time 3 months. Submit seasonal material 3 months in advance. Accepts queries by mail, e-mail. Responds in 3 weeks to queries; 1 month to mss. Sample copy for $4.50 or online.

Nonfiction: How-to, interview/profile, technical, case studies. **Buys 36 mss/year.** Query with published clips or hyperlinks to posted clips. Length: 1,500-4,000 words. **Pays $250-600.**

Photos: State availability with submission.

Tips: "Our readers are graphic arts professionals. Freelance writers we use are deeply immersed in the technology of commercial printing, desktop publishing, digital imaging, color management, PDF workflow, inkjet printing, and similar topics."

$ $ ELECTRONIC SERVICING & TECHNOLOGY, The Professional Magazine for Electronics and Computer Servicing, P.O. Box 12487, Overland Park KS 66282-2487. (913)492-4857. Fax: (913)492-4857. E-mail: cpersedit@aol.com. **Contact:** Conrad Persson, editor. **80% freelance written.** Monthly magazine for service technicians, field service personnel, and avid servicing enthusiasts, who service audio, video, and computer equipment. Estab. 1950. Circ. 15,000. Pays on publication. Publishes ms an average of 4 months after acceptance. Byline given. Buys one-time rights. Editorial lead time 2 months. Accepts queries by mail, e-mail, fax, phone. Accepts simultaneous submissions. Responds in 1 month to queries; 2 months to mss. Sample copy for free. Writer's guidelines free.

- Break in by knowing how to service consumer electronics products and being able to explain it in writing in good English.

Nonfiction: Book excerpts, how-to (service consumer electronics), new product, technical. **Buys 40 mss/year.** Query or send complete ms. **Pays $50/page.**

Reprints: Send ms with rights for sale noted and information about when and where the material previously appeared.

Photos: Send photos with submission. Buys one-time rights. Offers no additional payment for photos accepted with ms.

Columns/Departments: Business Corner (business tips); Computer Corner (computer servicing tips); Video Corner (understanding/servicing TV and video), all 1,000-2,000 words. **Buys 30 mss/year.** Query or send complete ms. **Pays $100-300.**

Tips: "Writers should have a strong background in electronics, especially consumer electronics servicing. Understand the information needs of consumer electronics service technicians, and be able to write articles that address specific areas of those needs."

$ $ $ SOUND & VIDEO CONTRACTOR, Primedia Business, 6400 Hollis St., Suite 12, Emeryville CA 94608. (510)985-3229. Fax: (510)653-5142. E-mail: mmayfield@primediabusiness.com. **Contact:** Mark Mayfield, editor. **60% freelance written.** Monthly magazine covering "professional audio, video, security, acoustical design, sales and marketing." Estab. 1983. Circ. 24,000. **Pays on acceptance.** Publishes ms an average of 3 months after acceptance. Byline given. Buys one-time, all rights. Editorial lead time 3 months. Accepts queries by mail, e-mail, fax, phone. Accepts simultaneous submissions. Responds ASAP to queries and to mss. Sample copy and writer's guidelines free.

Nonfiction: Historical/nostalgic, how-to, photo feature, technical, professional audio/video applications, installations, product reviews. No opinion pieces, advertorial, interview/profile, exposé/gossip. **Buys 60 mss/year.** Query. Length: 1,000-2,500 words. **Pays $200-1,200 for assigned articles; $200-650 for unsolicited articles.**

Reprints: Accepts previously published submissions

Photos: Send photos with submission. Reviews transparencies, prints. Offers no additional payment for photos accepted with ms. Identification of subjects required.

Columns/Departments: Security Technology Review (technical install information); Sales & Marketing (techniques for installation industry); Video Happenings (Pro video/projection/storage technical info), all 1,500 words. **Buys 30 mss/year.** Query. **Pays $200-350.**

Tips: "We want materials and subject matter that would be of interest to audio/video/security/low-voltage product installers/contractors/designers professionals. If the piece allows our readers to save time, money and/or increases their revenues, then we have reached our goals. Highly technical is desirable."

N $ $ SQL SERVER MAGAZINE, Penton Media, 221 E. 29th St., Loveland CO 80537. (970)663-4700. E-mail: articles@sqlmag.com. Website: www.sqlmag.com. Editor: Kathy Blomstrom. **Contact:** Suzanne Cone, assistant managing editor. **35% freelance written.** Monthly magazine covering Microsoft SQL Server. "*SQL Server Magazine* is the only magazine completely devoted to helping developers and DBAs master new and emerging SQL Server technologies and issues. It provides practical advice and lots of code examples for SQL Server developers and administrators, and includes how-to articles, tips, tricks, and programming techniques offered by SQL Server experts." Estab. 1999. Circ. 47,000. Pays on publication. Publishes ms an average of 6 months after acceptance. Byline given. Offers $100 kill fee. Buys all rights. Editorial lead time 4+ months. Accepts queries by mail, e-mail. Responds in 6 weeks to queries; 2-3 months to mss. Sample copy online. Writer's guidelines online.

Nonfiction: How-to, technical, SQL Server administration and programming. Nothing promoting third-party products or companies. **Buys 25-35 mss/year.** Query with or without published clips or send complete ms. Length: 1,800-3,000 words. **Pays 40¢/word.** Pays in contributor copies if the writer requests the substitution.

Columns/Departments: R2R Editor. Reader to Reader (helpful SQL Server hints and tips from readers), 200-400 words. Send all column/department submissions to r2r@sqlmag.com. **Buys 12-20 mss/year.** Send complete ms. **Pays $50.**

Tips: "Read back issues and make sure that your proposed article doesn't overlap previous coverage. When proposing articles, state specifically how your article would contain new information compared to previously published information, and what benefit your information would be to *SQL Server Magazine*'s readership."

ENERGY & UTILITIES

People who supply power to homes, businesses, and industry read the publications in this section.

This category includes journals covering the electric power, natural gas, petroleum, solar, and alternative energy industries.

$ $ ALTERNATIVE ENERGY RETAILER, Zackin Publications, Inc., P.O. Box 2180, Waterbury CT 06722-2180. (203)755-0158. Fax: (203)755-3480. E-mail: griffin@sme-online.com. Website: www.aer-online.com/aer/. **Contact:** Michael Griffin, editor. **5% freelance written.** Prefers to work with published/established writers. Monthly magazine on selling home hearth products—chiefly solid fuel and gas-burning appliances. "We seek detailed how-to tips for retailers to improve business. Most freelance material purchased is about retailers and how they succeed." Estab. 1980. Circ. 10,000. Pays on publication. Publishes ms an average of 2 months after acceptance. Buys first North American serial rights. Submit seasonal material 4 months in advance. Accepts queries by mail, e-mail, fax, phone. Responds in 2 weeks to queries. Sample copy for 9×12 SAE and 4 first-class stamps. Writer's guidelines online.

- Submit articles that focus on hearth market trends and successful sales techniques.

Nonfiction: How-to (improve retails profits and business know-how), interview/profile (of successful retailers in this field). No "general business articles not adapted to this industry." **Buys 10 mss/year.** Query. Length: 1,000 words. **Pays $200.**

Photos: State availability with submission. Reviews color transparencies. Buys one-time rights. Pays $25-125 maximum for 5×7 b&w prints. Identification of subjects required.

Tips: "A freelancer can best break into our publication with features about readers (retailers). Stick to details about what has made this person a success."

$ $ ELECTRICAL APPARATUS, The Magazine of Electromechanical & Electronic Application & Maintenance, Barks Publications, Inc., 400 N. Michigan Ave., Chicago IL 60611-4198. (312)321-9440. Fax: (312)321-1288. Senior Editor: Kevin N. Jones. **Contact:** Elsie Dickson, editorial director. Monthly magazine for persons working in electrical and electronic maintenance, chiefly in industrial plants, who install and service electrical motors, transformers, generators, controls, and related equipment. Estab. 1967. Circ. 17,000. **Pays on acceptance.** Publishes ms an average of 3 months after acceptance. Byline given. Buys all rights unless other arrangements made. Accepts queries by mail, fax. Responds in 1 week to queries; 1 month to mss. Sample copy for $4.

Nonfiction: Technical. Length: 1,500-2,500 words. **Pays $250-500 for assigned articles.**

Tips: "All feature articles are assigned to staff and contributing editors and correspondents. Professionals interested in appointments as contributing editors and correspondents should submit résumé and article outlines, including illustration suggestions. Writers should be competent with a camera, which should be described in résumé. Technical expertise is absolutely necessary, preferably an E.E. degree, or practical experience. We are also book publishers and some of the material in *EA* is now in book form, bringing the authors royalties. Also publishes an annual directory, subtitled *ElectroMechanical Bench Reference.*"

$ NATIONAL PETROLEUM NEWS, 250 S. Wacker Dr., Suite 1150, Chicago IL 60606. (312)977-0999 or (309)689-9969. Fax: (312)980-3135. E-mail: dwight@aip.com. Website: www.npn-net.com. **Contact:** Darren Wight, editor. **15% freelance written.** Prefers to work with published/established writers. Monthly magazine for decision-makers in the petroleum marketing and convenience store industry. Estab. 1909. Circ. 38,000. Pays on acceptance if done on assignment. Publishes ms an average of 2 months after acceptance. variable rights, depending upon author and material; usually buys all rights Accepts queries by mail, e-mail, fax. Sample copy not available.

- This magazine is particularly interested in articles on national industry-related material.

Nonfiction: Material related directly to developments and issues in the petroleum marketing and convenience store industry and "how-to" and "what-with" case studies. "No unsolicited copy, especially with limited attribution regarding information in story." **Buys 9-10 mss/year.** Length: 2,500 words maximum. **Pays $50-150/printed page.** Sometimes pays expenses of writers on assignment.

Reprints: Send typed ms on disk with rights for sale noted and information about when and where the article previously appeared.

Photos: Pays $150/printed page. Payment for color and b&w photos.

$ $ PUBLIC POWER, Dept. WM, 2301 M St. NW, Washington DC 20037-1484. (202)467-2948. Fax: (202)467-2910. E-mail: jlabella@appanet.org. Website: www.appanet.org. **Contact:** Jeanne LaBella, editor. **60% freelance written.** Prefers to work with published/established writers. Bimonthly trade journal. Estab. 1942. **Pays on acceptance.** Publishes ms an average of 3 months after acceptance. Byline given. Accepts queries by mail, e-mail, fax. Responds in 6 months to queries. Sample copy and writer's guidelines free.

Nonfiction: Features on municipal and other local publicly owned electric utilities. **Pays $600 and up.**

Photos: Reviews electronic photos (minimum 300 dpi at reproduction size), transparencies, slides, and prints.

Tips: "We look for writers who are familiar with energy policy issues."

$ $ $ TEXAS CO-OP POWER, Texas Electric Cooperatives, Inc., 2550 S. IH-35, Austin TX 78704. (512)454-0311. Website: www.texascoopower.com. Editor: Kaye Northcott. Managing Editor: Carol Moczygemba. **50% freelance written.** Monthly magazine covering rural and suburban Texas life, people, and places. "*Texas Co-op Power* provides 950,000 households and businesses educational and technical information about electric cooperatives in a high-quality and entertaining format to promote the general welfare of cooperatives, their member-owners, and the areas in which they serve." Estab. 1948. Circ. 950,000. **Pays on acceptance.** Publishes ms an average of 6 months after acceptance. Byline given. Buys first, electronic rights. Editorial lead time 3 months. Submit seasonal material 6 months in advance. Accepts queries by mail, e-mail, fax. Accepts simultaneous submissions. Responds in 1 month to queries; 2 months to mss. Sample copy online. Writer's guidelines for #10 SASE.

Nonfiction: General interest, historical/nostalgic, interview/profile, photo feature, travel. **Buys 30 mss/year.** Query with published clips. Length: 1,000-2,000 words. **Pays $400-1,000.** Sometimes pays expenses of writers on assignment.

Photos: State availability with submission. Reviews transparencies, prints. Buys one-time rights. Negotiates payment individually. Identification of subjects, model releases required.

Tips: "We're looking for Texas-related, rural-based articles, often first-person, always lively and interesting."

ENGINEERING & TECHNOLOGY

Engineers and professionals with various specialties read the publications in this section. Publications for electrical, electronics, and telecommunications engineers are classified separately under Electronics & Communication. Magazines for computer professionals are in the Information Systems section.

$ $ $ CABLING SYSTEMS, Southam Inc., 1450 Don Mills Rd., Don Mills ON M3B 2X7, Canada. (416)442-2124. Fax: (416)442-2214. E-mail: pbarker@cablingsystems.com. Website: www.cablingsystems.com. **Contact:** Paul Barker. **50% freelance written.** Magazine published 8 times/year covering structured cabling/telecommunications industry. "*Cabling Systems* is written for engineers, designers, contractors, and end users who design, specify, purchase, install, test and maintain structured cabling and telecommunications products and systems." Estab. 1998. Circ. 11,000. Pays on publication. Publishes ms an average of 1 month after acceptance. Byline given. Buys all rights. Editorial lead time 3 months. Submit seasonal material 1 month in advance. Accepts queries by mail, e-mail, phone. Accepts simultaneous submissions. Sample copy online. Writer's guidelines free.

Nonfiction: Technical (case studies, features). "No reprints or previously written articles. All articles are assigned by editor based on query or need of publication." **Buys 12 mss/year.** Query with published clips. Length: 1,500-2,500 words. **Pays 40-50¢/word.** Sometimes pays expenses of writers on assignment.

Photos: State availability with submission. Reviews contact sheets, prints. Negotiates payment individually. Captions, identification of subjects required.

Columns/Departments: Focus on Engineering/Design, Focus on Installation, Focus on Maintenance/Testing, all 1,500 words. **Buys 7 mss/year.** Query with published clips. **Pays 40-50¢/word.**

Tips: "Visit our website to see back issues, and visit links on our website for background."

$ $ $ CANADIAN CONSULTING ENGINEER, Business Information Group, 1450 Don Mills Rd., Toronto ON M3B 2X7, Canada. (416)442-2266. E-mail: bparsons@corporate.southam.ca. Website: www.canadianconsultingengineer.com. **Contact:** Bronwen Parsons, editor. **20% freelance written.** Bimonthly magazine covering consulting engineering in private practice. Estab. 1958. Circ. 8,900. Pays on publication. Publishes ms an average of 4 months after acceptance. Byline given depending on length of story. Offers 50% kill fee. Buys first North American serial rights. Editorial lead time 6 months. Responds in 3 months to mss. Sample copy for free.

- "Canadian content only."

Nonfiction: Historical/nostalgic, new product, technical, engineering/construction projects, environmental/construction issues. **Buys 8-10 mss/year.** Length: 300-1,500 words. **Pays $200-1,000 (Canadian).** Sometimes pays expenses of writers on assignment.

Photos: State availability with submission. Buys one-time rights. Negotiates payment individually.

Columns/Departments: Export (selling consulting engineering services abroad); Management (managing consulting engineering businesses); On-Line (trends in CAD systems); Employment. Length: 800 words. **Buys 4 mss/year.** Query with published clips,. **Pays $250-400.**

N $ $ $ CAREER RECRUITMENT MEDIA, (formerly *CASS Recruitment Media*), 1800 Sherman Ave., Suite #300, Evanston IL 60201-3769. E-mail: valerie.anderson@careermedia.com. Website: www.careermedia.com. **50% freelance written.** "Recruitment publications for college engineering/computer science/allied health students. Our readers are smart, savvy and hip. The writing must be, too." **Pays on acceptance.** Publishes ms an average of 2 months after acceptance. Byline given. Offers $50 kill fee. Buys all rights. Editorial lead time 2 months. Submit seasonal material 6 months in advance. Accepts queries by mail, e-mail. Accepts simultaneous submissions. Responds in 2 weeks to queries; 3 months to mss. Sample copy and writer's guidelines free.

Nonfiction: Book excerpts, exposé, interview/profile, personal experience. Special issues: Minorities; Women. **Buys 40 mss/year.** Send complete ms. Length: 1,500-3,000 words. **Pays $200-800 for assigned articles; $50-300 for unsolicited articles.** Sometimes pays expenses of writers on assignment.

Photos: Send photos with submission. Reviews 3×5 prints. Buys one-time rights. Offers no additional payment for photos accepted with ms. Identification of subjects required.

Columns/Departments: Industry Focus (analysis of hiring market within particular industry), 1,500 words. **Buys 6 mss/year.** Query. **Pays $200-300.**

Tips: "Know the hiring market for entry-level professionals and be able to communicate to college students at their level."

N $ ECN ELECTRONIC COMPONENT NEWS, Reed Business Information, 301 Gibraltar Dr., P.O. Box 650, Morris Plains NJ 07950-0650. (973)292-5100. Fax: (973)292-0783. Website: www.ecnmag.com. Editor: Aimee Kalnoskas. Managing Editor: Jeam Miller. Monthly magazine. Provides design engineers and engineering management in electronics

OEM with a monthly update on new products and literature. Circ. 131,052. Editorial lead time 8-10 weeks. Sample copy not available.

$ LASER FOCUS WORLD MAGAZINE, PennWell, 98 Spit Brook Rd., Nashua NH 03062-2801. (603)891-0123. Fax: (603)891-0574. E-mail: carols@pennwell.com. Website: www.laserfocusworld.com. Publisher: Christine Shaw. Group Editorial Director: Stephen G. Anderson. **Contact:** Carol Settino, managing editor. **1% freelance written.** Monthly magazine for physicists, scientists, and engineers involved in the research and development, design, manufacturing, and applications of lasers, laser systems, and all other segments of optoelectronic technologies. Estab. 1968. Circ. 66,000. Publishes ms an average of 6 months after acceptance. Byline given unless anonymity requested. Buys all rights. Accepts queries by mail, e-mail, fax, phone. Responds in 1 month to queries. Sample copy and writer's guidelines free. Writer's guidelines online.

Nonfiction: Lasers, laser systems, fiberoptics, optics, detectors, sensors, imaging, and other optoelectronic materials, components, instrumentation, and systems. "Each article should serve our reader's need by either stimulating ideas, increasing technical competence, or improving design capabilities in the following areas: natural light and radiation sources, artificial light and radiation sources, light modulators, optical materials and components, image detectors, energy detectors, information displays, image processing, information storage and processing, subsystem and system testing, support equipment, and other related areas. No flighty prose, material not written for our readership, or irrelevant material. Query first with a clear statement and outline of why the article would be important to our readers.

Photos: Drawings: Rough drawings acceptable, are finished by staff technical illustrator. Send photos with submission. Reviews 4×5 color transparencies, 8×10 b&w glossies.

Tips: "The writer has a better chance of breaking in at our publication with short articles because shorter articles are easier to schedule, but must address more carefully our requirements for technical coverage. Most of our submitted materials come from technical experts in the areas we cover. The most frequent mistake made by writers in completing articles for us is that the articles are too commercial, i.e., emphasize a given product or technology from one company. Also articles are not the right technical depth, too thin, or too scientific."

$ $ LIGHTING DESIGN & APPLICATION, Illuminating Engineering Society of North America, 120 Wall St., 17th Floor, New York NY 10005-4001. (212)248-5000, ext. 108. Fax: (212)248-5017. E-mail: cbeardsley@iesna.org. Website: www.iesna.org. **Contact:** Paul Tarricone, editor. **20% freelance written.** Monthly magazine. "*LD&A* is geared to professionals in lighting design and the lighting field in architecture, retail, entertainment, etc. From designers to educators to sales reps, *LD&A* has a very unique, dedicated, and well-educated audience." Estab. 1971. Circ. 10,000. **Pays on acceptance.** Publishes ms an average of 4 months after acceptance. Byline given. Buys first rights. Editorial lead time 4 months. Submit seasonal material 6 months in advance. Accepts queries by mail, e-mail, fax, phone. Accepts simultaneous submissions. Responds in 2 weeks to queries. Sample copy for free.

Nonfiction: "Every year we have entertainment, outdoor, retail and arts, and exhibits issues. Historical/nostalgic, how-to, opinion, personal experience, photo feature, technical. "No articles blatantly promoting a product, company, or individual." **Buys 6-10 mss/year.** Query. Length: 1,500-2,200 words. **Pays $300-400 for assigned articles.**

Photos: Send photos with submission. Reviews 4×5 transparencies. Offers no additional payment for photos accepted with ms. Captions required.

Columns/Departments: Essay by Invitation (industry trends), 1,200 words. Query. **Does not pay for columns.**

Tips: "Most of our features detail the ins and outs of a specific lighting project. From Ricky Martin at the Grammys to the Getty Museum, *LD&A* gives its readers an in-depth look at how the designer(s) reached their goals."

N $ $ $ MINNESOTA TECHNOLOGY, Inside Technology and Manufacturing Business, Minnesota Technology, Inc., 111 Third Ave. S., Minneapolis MN 55401. (612)373-2900. Fax: (612)339-5214. E-mail: editor@mntech.org. Website: mntechnologymag.com. **Contact:** Chris Mikko, editor. **75% freelance written.** Magazine published 5 times/year. "*Minnesota Technology* is read 5 times a year by owners and top management of Minnesota's technology and manufacturing companies. The magazine covers technology trends and issues, global trade, management techniques and finance. We profile new and growing companies, new products and the innovators and entrepreneurs of Minnesota's technology sector." Estab. 1991. Circ. 20,000. **Pays on acceptance.** Publishes ms an average of 3 months after acceptance. Byline given. Offers 25% kill fee. Buys first North American serial rights. Editorial lead time 2 months. Submit seasonal material 1 year in advance. Accepts queries by mail, e-mail, fax. Responds in 1 month to queries. Sample copy for 9×12 SAE and 5 first-class stamps. Writer's guidelines online.

Nonfiction: General interest, how-to, interview/profile. **Buys 45 mss/year.** Query with published clips. Length: 500-2,000 words. **Pays $150-1,000.**

Columns/Departments: Feature Well (Q&A format, provocative ideas from busines and industry leaders), 2,000 words; Up Front (mini profiles, anecdotal news items), 250-500 words. **Buys 30 mss/year.** Query with published clips. **Pays $150-300.**

The online magazine includes writer's guidelines. Contact: Linda Ball, online editor.

Tips: "Query with ideas for short profiles of fascinating Minnesota technology people and business written to interest even the most nontechnical person."

ENTERTAINMENT & THE ARTS

The business of the entertainment/amusement industry in arts, film, dance, theater, etc., is covered by these publications. Journals that focus on the people and equipment of various music specialties are listed in the Music section, while art and design business publications can be found in Art, Design & Collectibles. Entertainment publications for the general public can be found in the Consumer Entertainment section.

$ $ $ AMERICAN CINEMATOGRAPHER, The International Journal of Film & Digital Production Techniques, American Society of Cinematographers, 1782 N. Orange Dr., Hollywood CA 90028. (323)969-4333. Fax: (323)876-4973. E-mail: stephen@theasc.com. Website: cinematographer.com. Senior Editor: Rachael Bosley. **Contact:** Stephen Pizzello, editor. **90% freelance written.** Monthly magazine covering cinematography (motion picture, TV, music video, commercial). "*American Cinematographer* is a trade publication devoted to the art and craft of cinematography. Our readers are predominantly film-industry professionals." Estab. 1919. Circ. 45,000. Pays on publication. Publishes ms an average of 2-3 months after acceptance. Byline given. Offers 50% kill fee. Buys all rights. Editorial lead time 2 months. Submit seasonal material 3 months in advance. Accepts queries by mail, e-mail, phone. Responds in 2 weeks to queries; 2 months to mss. Sample copy and writer's guidelines free.

Nonfiction: Interview/profile, new product, technical. No reviews, opinion pieces. **Buys 20-25 mss/year.** Query with published clips. Length: 1,500-4,000 words. **Pays $600-1,200.** Pays in contributor copies if the writer is promoting his/her own product or company. Sometimes pays expenses of writers on assignment.

Tips: "Familiarity with the technical side of film production and the ability to present that information in an articulate fashion to our audience are crucial."

$ $ BOXOFFICE MAGAZINE, RLD Publishing Co., 155 S. El Molino Ave., Suite 100, Pasadena CA 91101. (626)396-0250. Fax: (626)396-0248. E-mail: editorial@boxoffice.com. Website: www.boxoffice.com. Editor-in-chief: Kim Williamson. **Contact:** Christine James, managing editor. **15% freelance written.** Monthly magazine about the motion picture industry for members of the film industry: theater owners, film producers, directors, financiers, and allied industries. Estab. 1920. Circ. 8,000. Pays on publication. Publishes ms an average of 3 months after acceptance. Byline given. Buys all rights, including electronic publishing. Submit seasonal material 5 months in advance. Accepts queries by mail, e-mail, fax. Sample copy for $5.

"*Boxoffice Magazine* is particularly interested in freelance writers who can write business articles on the exhibition industry or technical writers who are familiar with projection/sound equipment and new technologies such as digital cinema."

Nonfiction: "We are a general news magazine about the motion picture and theater industry and are looking for stories about trends, developments, problems, or opportunities facing the industry. Almost any story will be considered, including corporate profiles, but we don't want gossip or celebrity coverage." Book excerpts, essays, interview/profile, new product, personal experience, photo feature, technical, investigative "all regarding movie theater business." Query with published clips. Length: 800-2,500 words. **Pays 10¢/word.**

Photos: State availability with submission. Reviews prints, slides. Pays $10 maximum. Captions required.

The online version of this magazine carries original content. Contact: Kim Williamson.

Tips: "Request a sample copy, indicating you read about *Boxoffice* in *Writer's Market*. Write a clear, comprehensive outline of the proposed story and enclose a résumé and clip samples."

$ $ CAMPUS ACTIVITIES, Cameo Publishing Group, P.O. Box 509, Prosperity SC 29127. (800)728-2950. Fax: (803)321-2049. E-mail: cameopublishing@mac.com. Website: www.campusactivitiesmagazine.com or www.cameopub.com. Editor: Lisa Lackey. Managing Editor: Kappy Griffith. **Contact:** WC Kirby, publisher. **75% freelance written.** Magazine published 8 times/year covering entertainment on college campuses. *Campus Activities* goes to entertainment buyers on every campus in the U.S. Features stories on artists (national and regional), speakers and the programs at individual schools. Estab. 1991. Circ. 5,912. Pays on publication. Publishes ms an average of 2 months after acceptance. Byline given. Offers 15% kill fee if accepted and not run. Buys first, second serial (reprint), electronic rights. Editorial lead time 2 months. Submit seasonal material 2 months in advance. Accepts queries by mail, e-mail, fax. Accepts simultaneous submissions. Responds in 1 month to queries; 2 months to mss. Sample copy for $3.50. Writer's guidelines free.

Nonfiction: Interview/profile, photo feature. Accepts no unsolicited articles. **Buys 40 mss/year.** Query. Length: 1,400-3,000 words. **Pays $250.** Sometimes pays expenses of writers on assignment.

Photos: State availability with submission. Reviews contact sheets, negatives, 3×5 transparencies, 8×10 prints, electronic media at 300 dpi or higher. Buys one-time rights. Negotiates payment individually. Identification of subjects required.

Tips: "Writers who have ideas, proposals, and special project requests should contact the publisher prior to any commitment to work on such a story. The publisher welcomes innovative and creative ideas for stories and works with writers on such proposals which have significant impact on our readers."

$ $ DANCE TEACHER, The Practical Magazine of Dance, Lifestyle Ventures, 250 W. 57th St., Suite 420, New York NY 10107. (212)265-8890, ext. 20. Fax: (212)265-8908. E-mail: csims@lifestyleventures.com. Website: www.danceteacher.com. **Contact:** Caitlin Sims, editor. **80% freelance written.** Monthly magazine. "Our readers are professional dance educators, business persons, and related professionals in all forms of dance." Estab. 1979. Circ. 8,000. Pays on publication. Publishes ms an average of 3 months after acceptance. Byline given. Negotiates rights and permission to reprint on request. Submit seasonal material 6 months in advance. Accepts queries by mail, e-mail, fax, phone. Responds in 3 months to mss. Sample copy for 9×12 SAE and 6 first-class stamps. Writer's guidelines online.

Nonfiction: How-to (teach, business), interview/profile, new product, personal experience, photo feature. Special issues: Auditions (January); Summer Programs (February); Music & More (July); Costumes and Production Preview (November); College/Training Schools (December). No PR or puff pieces. All articles must be well-researched. **Buys 50 mss/year.** Query. Length: 700-2,000 words. **Pays $100-250.**

Photos: Send photos with submission. Reviews contact sheets, negatives, transparencies, prints. Limited photo budget.

The online magazine carries original content. Contact: Caitlin Sims.

Tips: "Read several issues—particularly seasonal. Stay within writer's guidelines."

$ $ DRAMATICS MAGAZINE, Educational Theatre Association, 2343 Auburn Ave., Cincinnati OH 45219-2815. (513)421-3900. Fax: (513)421-7077. E-mail: dcorathers@edta.org. Website: www.edta.org. **Contact:** Donald Corathers, editor-in-chief. **70% freelance written.** Monthly magazine for theater arts students, teachers and others interested in theater arts education. "*Dramatics* is designed to provide serious, committed young theater students and their teachers with the skills and knowledge they need to make better theater; to be a resource that will help high school juniors and seniors make an informed decision about whether to pursue a career in theater, and about how to do so; and to prepare high school students to be knowledgeable, appreciative audience members for the rest of their lives." Estab. 1929. Circ. 37,000. **Pays on acceptance.** Publishes ms an average of 3 months after acceptance. Byline given. Buys first North American serial rights. Submit seasonal material 3 months in advance. Accepts queries by mail, e-mail, fax. Accepts previously published material. Accepts simultaneous submissions. Responds in 3 months to queries longer than 3 months on unsolicited mss to mss. Sample copy for 9×12 SAE with 5 first-class stamps. Writer's guidelines online.

"The best way to break in is to know our audience—drama students, teachers, and others interested in theater—and to write for them."

Nonfiction: How-to (technical theater, directing, acting, etc.), humor, inspirational, interview/profile, photo feature, technical. **Buys 30 mss/year.** Send complete ms. Length: 750-3,000 words. **Pays $50-400.** Sometimes pays expenses of writers on assignment.

Reprints: Send tearsheet, photocopy or typed ms with rights for sale noted and information about when and where the material previously appeared. Pays up to 75% of amount paid for original.

Photos: Query. Purchased with accompanying ms. Reviews transparencies. Total price for ms usually includes payment for photos.

Fiction: Drama (one-act and full-length plays). Prefers unpublished scripts that have been produced at least once. "No plays for children, Christmas plays, or plays written with no attention paid to the conventions of theater." **Buys 5-9 mss/year.** Send complete ms. **Pays $100-400.**

Tips: "Writers who have some practical experience in theater, especially in technical areas, have a leg-up here, but we'll work with anybody who has a good idea. Some freelancers have become regular contributors. Others ignore style suggestions included in our writer's guidelines."

$ $ $ EMMY MAGAZINE, Academy of Television Arts & Sciences, 5220 Lankershim Blvd., North Hollywood CA 91601-3109. (818)754-2800. Fax: (818)761-8524. E-mail: emmymag@emmys.org. Website: www.emmys.tv. **Contact:** Gail Polevoi, editor. **90% freelance written.** Prefers to work with published/established writers. Bimonthly magazine on television for TV professionals. Circ. 14,000. Pays on publication or within 6 months. Publishes ms an average of 4 months after acceptance. Byline given. Offers 25% kill fee. Buys first North American serial rights. Accepts queries by mail, e-mail, fax. Responds in 1 month to queries. Sample copy for 9×12 SAE and 6 first-class stamps. Writer's guidelines online.

Nonfiction: Articles on contemporary issues, trends, and VIPs (especially those behind the scenes) in broadcast and cable TV; programming and new technology. "Looking for profiles of fascinating people who work 'below the line' in television. Also, always looking for new writers who understand technology and new media and can write about it in an engaging manner. We require TV industry expertise and clear, lively writing." Query with published clips. Length: 2,000 words. **Pays $1,000-1,200.**

Columns/Departments: Most written by regular contributors, but newcomers can break in with filler items in In the Mix or short profiles in Labors of Love. Length: 300-1,500 words, depending on department. Query with published clips. **Pays $250-750.**

Tips: "Please review recent issues before querying us. Query with published, television-related clips. No fanzine, academic, or nostalgic approaches, please. Demonstrate experience in covering the business of television and your ability to write in a lively and compelling manner about programming trends and new technology. Identify fascinating people behind the scenes, not just in the executive suites but in all ranks of the industry."

$ $ RELEASE PRINT, The Magazine of Film Arts Foundation, Film Arts Foundation, 145 9th St., Suite 101, San Francisco CA 94103. (415)552-8760. Fax: (415)552-0882. E-mail: writersguidelines@filmarts.org. Website: www.filmarts.org. **Contact:** Editor. **80% freelance written.** Monthly magazine covering U.S. independent filmmaking. "We have a knowledgeable readership of film and videomakers. They are interested in the financing, production, exhibition, and distribution of independent films and videos. They are interested in practical and technical issues and, to a lesser extent, aesthetic ones." Estab. 1977. Circ. 5,000. Pays on publication. Publishes ms an average of 3 months after acceptance. Byline given. Buys all rights for commissioned works. For works submitted on spec, buys first rights and requests acknowledgement of Release Print in any subsequent publication. Editorial lead time 4 months. Accepts queries by mail. Responds in 3 weeks to queries; 2 months to mss. Sample copy for $5 (payable to Film Arts Foundation) and 9×12 SASE with $1.52 postage. Writer's guidelines by e-mail.

Break in with a proposal for an article or interview of an American experimental, documentary or very low budget feature film/video maker with ties to the San Francisco Bay area (or an upcoming screening in this area). Submit at least 4 months prior to publication date.

Nonfiction: Interview/profile, technical, book recommendations, case studies. No film criticism or reviews. **Buys 30-35 mss/year.** Query. Length: 500-2,000 words. Sometimes pays expenses of writers on assignment.

Photos: Send photos with submission. Reviews prints. Buys one-time rights. Offers no additional payment for photos accepted with ms. Identification of subjects required.

Columns/Departments: Book Reviews (independent film & video), 800-1,000 words. **Buys 4 mss/year.** Query. **Pays 10¢/word.**

$ SCREEN MAGAZINE, Screen Enterprises, Inc., 222 W. Ontario St., Suite 500, Chicago IL 60610. (312)640-0800. Fax: (312)640-1928. E-mail: editorial@screenmag.com. Website: www.screenmag.com. **Contact:** Jim Vincent, editor. **10% freelance written.** Biweekly Chicago-based trade magazine covering advertising and film production in the Midwest and national markets. "*Screen* is written for Midwest producers (and other creatives involved) of commercials, AV, features, independent corporate and multimedia." Estab. 1979. Circ. 15,000. Pays on publication. Publishes ms an average of a few weeks after acceptance. Byline given. Makes work-for-hire assignments. Accepts queries by mail, e-mail, fax. Responds in 3 weeks to queries. Sample copy online.

Nonfiction: Interview/profile, new product, technical. "No general AV; nothing specific to other markets; no-brainers and opinion." **Buys 50 mss/year.** Query with published clips. Length: 750-1,500 words. **Pays $50-150.**

Photos: Send photos with submission. Reviews prints. Offers no additional payment for photos accepted with ms. Captions required.

Tips: "Our readers want to know facts and figures. They want to know the news about a company or an individual. We provide exclusive news of this market, in as much depth as space allows without being boring, with lots of specific information and details. We write knowledgably about the market we serve. We recognize the film/video-making process is a difficult one because it 1) is often technical, 2) has implications not immediately discerned."

$ SOUTHERN THEATRE, Southeastern Theatre Conference, P.O. Box 9868, Greensboro NC 27429-0868. E-mail: publications@setc.org. Website: www.setc.org. **Contact:** Deanna Thompson, editor. **100% freelance written.** Quarterly magazine covering theatre. "*Southern Theatre* is *the* magazine covering all aspects of theater in the Southeast, from innovative theater companies to important trends to people making a difference in the region. All stories must be written in a popular magazine style but with subject matter appropriate for theater professionals (not the general public). The audience includes members of the Southeastern Theatre Conference, founded in 1949 and the nation's largest regional theater organization. These members include individuals involved in professional, community, college/university, children's and secondary school theater. The magazine also is purchased by more than 100 libraries." Estab. 1962. Circ. 3,600. **Pays on acceptance.** Publishes ms an average of 3 months after acceptance. Byline given. Buys first North American serial, first, one-time, second serial (reprint), electronic rights. Editorial lead time 3 months. Submit seasonal material 6 months in advance. Accepts queries by mail, e-mail. Responds in 6 weeks to queries; 3 months to mss. Sample copy for $6. Writer's guidelines online.

Nonfiction: Looking for stories on design/technology, playwriting, acting, directing, all with a Southeastern connection. General interest (innovative theaters and theater programs; trend stories), interview/profile (people making a difference in Southeastern theater). Special issues: Playwriting (fall issue, all stories submitted by January 1). No scholarly articles. **Buys 15-20 mss/year.** Query with or without published clips or send complete ms. Length: 1,000-3,000 words. **Pays $50 for feature stories.** Pays in contributor copies for book reviews, sidebars, and other short stories.

Photos: State availability of or send photos with submission. Reviews transparencies, prints. Offers no additional payment for photos accepted with ms. Captions, identification of subjects, model releases required.

Columns/Departments: Outside the Box (innovative solutions to problems faced by designers and technicians), 800-1,000 words; Words, Words, Words (reviews of books on theater), 400-550 words. **Buys 2-4 mss/year.** Query or send complete ms. **No payment for columns.**

Tips: "Look for a theater or theater person in your area that is doing something different or innovative that would be of interest to others in the profession, then write about that theater or person in a compelling way. We also are looking for well-written trend stories (talk to theaters in your area about trends that are affecting them), and we especially like stories that help our readers do their jobs more effectively. Send an e-mail detailing a well-developed story idea, and ask if we're interested."

FARM

The successful farm writer focuses on the business side of farming. For technical articles, editors feel writers should have a farm background or agricultural training, but there are opportunities for the general freelancer too. The following farm publications are divided into seven categories, each specializing in a different aspect of farming: agricultural equipment; crops & soil management; dairy farming; livestock; management; miscellaneous; and regional.

Agricultural Equipment

$ $ IMPLEMENT & TRACTOR, Agri USA, 2302 W. First St., Cedar Falls IA 50613. (319)277-3599. Fax: (319)277-3783. E-mail: rvanvoorhis@cfu.net. Website: www.ag-implement.com. **Contact:** Bob Van Voorhis, editor. **10% freelance written.** Bimonthly magazine covering farm equipment, light construction, commercial turf and lawn and garden equipment. "*Implement & Tractor* offers technical and business news for equipment dealers, manufacturers, consultants and others involved as suppliers to the industry. Writers must know U.S. and global machinery and the industry trends." Estab. 1895. Circ. 7,000. Pays on publication. Publishes ms an average of 3-4 months after acceptance. Byline given. Buys all rights. Editorial lead time 2 months. Accepts queries by mail, e-mail, fax. Responds in 2 months to queries. Sample copy for $6.

Nonfiction: Interview/profile (dealer or manufacturer), new product, photo feature, technical. No general farm machinery articles or farmer profiles articles. Query with published clips. Length: 600-1,200 words. **Pays $100-250.** Sometimes pays expenses of writers on assignment.

Photos: State availability with submission. Reviews contact sheets. Buys one-time rights. Offers no additional payment for photos accepted with ms. Captions, identification of subjects required.

Tips: "Know the equipment industry, have an engineer's outlook for analyzing machinery and a writer's skills to communicate that information. Technical background is helpful, as is mechanical aptitude."

Crops & Soil Management

$ $ AMERICAN FRUIT GROWER, Meister Publishing, 37733 Euclid Ave., Willoughby OH 44094. (440)942-2000. Fax: (440)942-0662. E-mail: afg_edit@meisternet.com. Website: www.fruitgrower.com. **Contact:** Brian Sparks, managing editor. **10% freelance written.** Annual magazine covering commercial fruit growing. "How-to" articles are best. Estab. 1880. Circ. 44,000. Pays on publication. Publishes ms an average of 4 months after acceptance. Byline given. Buys first rights. Editorial lead time 2 months. Submit seasonal material 4 months in advance. Accepts queries by mail, e-mail, fax, phone. Responds in 2 weeks to queries; 2 months to mss. Sample copy for free. Writer's guidelines free.

Nonfiction: How-to (better grow fruit crops). **Buys 6-10 mss/year.** Query with published clips or send complete ms. Length: 800-1,200 words. **Pays $200-250.** Sometimes pays expenses of writers on assignment.

Photos: Send photos with submission. Reviews Prints; Slides. Buys one-time rights. Negotiates payment individually.

$ $ COTTON GROWER MAGAZINE, Meister Publishing Co., 65 Germantown Court, #202, Cordova TN 38018. (901)756-8822. Fax: (901)756-8879. Editor: Bill Spencer. **Contact:** Frank Giles, senior editor. **5% freelance written.** Monthly magazine covering cotton production, cotton markets and related subjects. Readers are mostly cotton producers who seek information on production practices, equipment and products related to cotton. Estab. 1901. Circ. 43,000. **Pays on acceptance.** Publishes ms an average of 2 months after acceptance. Byline given. Buys first rights. Editorial lead time 2 months. Submit seasonal material 2 months in advance. Accepts queries by mail, e-mail, fax, phone. Accepts simultaneous submissions. Sample copy for free. Writer's guidelines not available.

Nonfiction: Interview/profile, new product, photo feature, technical. No fiction or humorous pieces. **Buys 5-10 mss/year.** Query with published clips. Length: 500-800 words. **Pays $200-400.** Sometimes pays expenses of writers on assignment.

Photos: State availability with submission. Reviews transparencies. Buys all rights. Offers no additional payment for photos accepted with ms. Captions, identification of subjects required.

$ THE FRUIT GROWERS NEWS, Great American Publishing, P.O. Box 128, Sparta MI 49345. (616)887-9008. Fax: (616)887-2666. E-mail: gentry@iserv.net. Website: www.fruitgrowersnews.com. Publisher: Matt McCallum. **Contact:** Karen Gentry, managing editor. **25% freelance written.** Monthly tabloid covering agriculture. "Our objective is to provide commercial fruit growers of all sizes with information to help them succeed." Estab. 1970. Circ. 28,000. Pays on publication. Publishes ms an average of 2 months after acceptance. Makes work-for-hire assignments. Editorial lead time 1 month. Submit seasonal material 1 month in advance. Accepts queries by mail, e-mail, fax, phone. Accepts simultaneous submissions. Responds in 2 weeks to queries; 1 month to mss. Sample copy for free.

Nonfiction: Essays, general interest, how-to, interview/profile, new product, opinion, technical. No advertorials, other "puff pieces." **Buys 72 mss/year.** Query with published clips. Length: 800-1,200 words. **Pays $100-125.** Sometimes pays expenses of writers on assignment.

Photos: Send photos with submission. Reviews prints. Buys one-time rights. Offers $15/photo. Captions required.

$ GRAIN JOURNAL, Country Publications, Inc., 3065 Pershing Ct., Decatur IL 62526. (217)877-8660. Fax: (217)877-6647. E-mail: ed@grainnet.com. Website: www.grainnet.com. **Contact:** Ed Zdrojewski, editor. **5% freelance written.** Bimonthly magazine covering grain handling and merchandising. "*Grain Journal* serves the North American grain industry, from the smallest country grain elevators and feed mills to major export terminals." Estab. 1972. Circ. 12,000. Pays on publication. Publishes ms an average of 2 months after acceptance. Byline sometimes given. Buys first rights. Editorial lead time 2 months. Submit seasonal material 2 months in advance. Accepts simultaneous submissions. Sample copy for free.

Nonfiction: How-to, interview/profile, new product, technical. Query. Length: 750 words maximum. **Pays $100.**

Photos: Send photos with submission. Reviews contact sheets, negatives, transparencies, 3×5 prints. Buys one-time rights. Offers $50-100/photo. Captions, identification of subjects required.

Tips: "Call with your idea. We'll let you know if it is suitable for our publication."

$ GRAPE GROWER MAGAZINE, Western Ag Publishing Co., 4969 E. Clinton Way #104, Fresno CA 93727. (559)252-7000. Fax: (559)252-7387. E-mail: editorial@westagpubco.com. **Contact:** Randy Bailey, associate publisher. **20% freelance written.** Monthly magazine covering viticulture and wineries. Estab. 1968. Circ. 12,000. Pays on publication. Publishes ms an average of 4 months after acceptance. Byline sometimes given. Buys all rights, makes work-for-hire assignments. Editorial lead time 2 months. Submit seasonal material 3 months in advance. Accepts queries by mail, e-mail, fax, phone. Accepts simultaneous submissions. Responds in 2 weeks to queries; 1 month to mss. Sample copy free by e-mail.

Nonfiction: How-to, interview/profile, new product, personal experience. Query or send complete ms. Length: 900-1,500 words. Sometimes pays expenses of writers on assignment.

Photos: Send photos with submission. Reviews transparencies, prints. Buys all rights.

$ ONION WORLD, Columbia Publishing, P.O. Box 9036, Yakima WA 98909-0036. (509)248-2452, ext. 152. Fax: (509)248-4056. E-mail: brent@freshcut.com. Website: www.onionworld.net. **Contact:** Brent Clement, managing editor or

Carrie Kennington, editor. **50% freelance written.** Monthly magazine covering the world of onion production and marketing for onion growers and shippers. Estab. 1985. Circ. 5,500. Pays on publication. Publishes ms an average of 1 month after acceptance. Byline given. Not copyrighted. Buys first North American serial rights. Submit seasonal material 1 month in advance. Accepts queries by mail, e-mail, fax, phone. Accepts simultaneous submissions. Responds in 1 month to queries. Sample copy for 9×12 SAE and 5 first-class stamps.

• Columbia Publishing also produces *Fresh Cut*, *The Tomato Magazine*, *Potato Country* and *Carrot Country*.

Nonfiction: General interest, historical/nostalgic, interview/profile. **Buys 30 mss/year.** Query. Length: 1,200-1,250 words. **Pays $5/column inch for assigned articles.**

Reprints: Send photocopy and information about when and where the material previously appeared. Pays 50% of amount paid for an original article.

Photos: Send photos with submission. Buys all rights. Offers no additional payment for photos accepted with ms, unless it's a cover shot. Captions, identification of subjects required.

Tips: "Writers should be familiar with growing and marketing onions. We use a lot of feature stories on growers, shippers, and others in the onion trade—what they are doing, their problems, solutions, marketing plans, etc."

$ $ RICE JOURNAL, SpecCom International, Inc., 5808 Faringdon Place, Raleigh NC 27604-1029. (919)872-5040. Fax: (919)876-6531. E-mail: editor@ricejournal.com. Website: www.ricejournal.com. Editor: Mary Ann Rood. **5% freelance written.** Monthly (January-June) magazine covering rice farming. "Articles must discuss rice production practices. Readers are rice farmers. Include on-farm interview with 1 or more farmers who use the featured agronomic practice. Must include photo of the farmer involved in a farming activity." Estab. 1897. Circ. 10,000. Pays on publication. Byline given. Buys first rights. Editorial lead time 2 months. Accepts queries by mail, e-mail, fax. Responds in 2 weeks to queries; 2 months to mss. Sample copy online. Writer's guidelines for #10 SASE.

Nonfiction: How-to, personal experience, photo feature, technical, farmer production tips. Special issues: Land Preparation (January); Water Management (February); Weed Control (March); Rice Diseases and Management (April); Insect Control, Tracked Vehicles (May); Harvest, Curing (June). No recipes, cooking. **Buys 2 mss/year.** Query. Length: 600-2,000 words. **Pays $50-400.**

Photos: State availability with submission. Buys one-time rights. Offers no additional payment for photos accepted with ms. Captions, identification of subjects required.

$ THE VEGETABLE GROWERS NEWS, Great American Publishing, P.O. Box 128, Sparta MI 49345. (616)887-9008. Fax: (616)887-2666. E-mail: gentry@iserv.net. Website: www.vegetablegrowersnews.com. Publisher: Matt McCallum. **Contact:** Karen Gentry, managing editor. **25% freelance written.** Monthly tabloid covering agriculture. "Our objective is to provide commercial vegetable growers of all sizes with information to help them succeed." Estab. 1970. Circ. 28,000. Pays on publication. Publishes ms an average of 2 months after acceptance. Makes work-for-hire assignments. Editorial lead time 1 month. Submit seasonal material 1 month in advance. Accepts queries by mail, e-mail, fax, phone. Accepts simultaneous submissions. Responds in 2 weeks to queries; 1 month to mss. Sample copy for free.

Nonfiction: Essays, general interest, how-to, interview/profile, new product, opinion, technical. No advertorials, other "puff pieces." **Buys 72 mss/year.** Query with published clips. Length: 800-1,200 words. **Pays $100-125.** Sometimes pays expenses of writers on assignment.

Photos: Send photos with submission. Reviews prints. Buys one-time rights. Offers $15/photo. Captions required.

Dairy Farming

$ $ HOARD'S DAIRYMAN, W.D. Hoard and Sons, Co., 28 Milwaukee Ave. W., Fort Atkinson WI 53538-0801. (920)563-5551. Fax: (920)563-7298. E-mail: hoards@hoards.com. Website: www.hoards.com. Editor: W.D. Knox. **Contact:** Steven A. Larson, managing editor. Tabloid published 20 times/year covering dairy industry. "We publish semi-technical information published for dairy-farm families and their advisors." Estab. 1885. Circ. 100,000. **Pays on acceptance.** Publishes ms an average of 4 months after acceptance. Byline given. Buys first rights. Editorial lead time 2 months. Submit seasonal material 3 months in advance. Accepts queries by mail, e-mail, fax. Responds in 2 weeks to queries; 1 month to mss. Sample copy for 12×15 SAE and $3. Writer's guidelines for #10 SASE.

Nonfiction: How-to, technical. **Buys 60 mss/year.** Query. Length: 800-1,500 words. **Pays $150-350.**

Photos: Send photos with submission. Reviews 2×2 transparencies. Offers no additional payment for photos accepted with ms.

N $ WESTERN DAIRY FARMER, Bowes Publishers Ltd., 4504—61 Ave., Leduc AB T9E 3Z1, Canada. (780)980-7488. Fax: (780)986-6397. E-mail: editor-wdf-caf@webcoleduc.com. Website: www.westerndairyfarmer.com. **Contact:** Lisa Wojna, editor. **70% freelance written.** Bimonthly magazine covering the dairy industry. "*Western Dairy Farmer* is a trade publication dealing with issues surrounding the dairy industry. The magazine features innovative articles on animal health, industry changes, new methods of dairying, and personal experiences. Sometimes highlights successful farmers." Estab. 1991. Circ. 5,000. Pays on publication. Publishes ms an average of 4 months after acceptance. Byline given. Buys all rights. Editorial lead time 2 months. Submit seasonal material 2 months in advance. Accepts queries by mail, e-mail, fax. Responds in 2 weeks to queries; 2 months to mss. Sample copy for 9×12 SAE.

Nonfiction: "All topics/submissions must be related to the dairy industry." General interest, how-to, interview/profile, new product, personal experience (only exceptional stories), technical. "Not interested in anything vague, trite, or not dairy related." **Buys 50 mss/year.** Query or send complete ms. Length: 900-1,200 words. **Pays $75-150.**

Photos: State availability with submission. Reviews GIF/JPEG files. Buys all rights. Offers no additional payment for photos accepted with ms. Captions, identification of subjects, model releases required.

Tips: "Know the industry inside and out. Provide contact names and phone numbers (both for writers and subjects) with submissions. Remember, this is a specialized trade publication, and our readers are well-aquainted with the issues and appreciate new up-to-date information."

$ $ WESTERN DAIRYBUSINESS, Heritage Complex, 4500 S. Laspina, Tulare CA 93274. (559)687-3160. Fax: (559)687-3166. E-mail: tfitchette@dairybusiness.com. Website: www.dairybusiness.com. **Contact:** Todd Fitchette, editor. **10% freelance written.** Prefers to work with published/established writers. Monthly magazine dealing with large-herd commercial dairy industry. Rarely publishes information about non-Western producers or dairy groups and events. Estab. 1922. Circ. 17,000. Pays on publication. Publishes ms an average of 3 months after acceptance. Byline given. Buys first North American serial rights. Submit seasonal material 3 months in advance. Accepts queries by mail, e-mail. Responds in 1 month to queries. Sample copy for 9×12 SAE and 4 first-class stamps.

Nonfiction: Special emphasis on: environmental stewardship, herd management systems, business management, facilities/equipment, forage/cropping. Interview/profile, new product, opinion, industry analysis. "No religion, nostalgia, politics, or 'mom and pop' dairies." Query or send complete ms. Length: 300-1,500 words. **Pays $25-400 for assigned articles.**

Reprints: Seldom accepts previously published submissions. Send information about when and where the article previously appeared. Pays 50% of amount paid for an original article.

Photos: Photos are a critical part of story packages. Send photos with submission. Reviews contact sheets, 35mm or 2¼×2¼ transparencies. Buys one-time rights. Pays $25 for b&w; $50-100 for color. Captions, identification of subjects required.

Tips: "Know the market and the industry, be well-versed in large-herd dairy management and business."

Livestock

$ $ ANGUS BEEF BULLETIN, Angus Productions, Inc., 3201 Frederick Ave., St. Joseph MO 64506. (816)383-5200. Fax: (816)233-6575. E-mail: shermel@angus.org. Website: www.angusebeefbulletin.com. **Contact:** Shauna Hermel, editor. **45% freelance written.** Tabloid published 4 times/year covering commercial cattle industry. "The *Bulletin* is mailed free to commercial cattlemen who have purchased an Angus bull and had the registration transferred to them within the last 3 years." Estab. 1985. Circ. 67,000. Pays on publication. Publishes ms an average of 3 months after acceptance. Byline given. Buys first, electronic rights. Editorial lead time 3 months. Submit seasonal material 3 months in advance. Accepts queries by mail, e-mail. Accepts simultaneous submissions. Responds in 3 weeks to queries; 3 months to mss. Sample copy for $5. Writer's guidelines for #10 SASE.

Nonfiction: How-to (cattle production), interview/profile, technical (cattle production). **Buys 10 mss/year.** Query with published clips. Length: 800-2,500 words. **Pays $50-600.** Pays expenses of writers on assignment.

Photos: Send photos with submission. Reviews 5×7 transparencies, 5×7 glossy prints. Buys all rights. Offers $25/photo. Identification of subjects required.

Tips: "Read the publication *Angus Journal* and have a firm grasp of the commercial cattle industry and how the Angus breeds fit in that industry."

$ $ $ ANGUS JOURNAL, Angus Productions Inc., 3201 Frederick Ave., St. Joseph MO 64506-2997. (816)383-5200. Fax: (816)233-6575. E-mail: shermel@angusjournal.com. Website: www.angusjournal.com. **Contact:** Shauna Hermel, editor. **40% freelance written.** Monthly magazine covering Angus cattle. "The *Angus Journal* is the official magazine of the American Angus Association. Its primary function as such is to report to the membership association activities and information pertinent to raising Angus cattle." Estab. 1919. Circ. 17,000. Pays on publication. Publishes ms an average of 3 months after acceptance. Byline given. Buys first, electronic rights. Editorial lead time 2 months. Submit seasonal material 3 months in advance. Accepts queries by mail, e-mail, fax. Accepts simultaneous submissions. Responds in 3 weeks to queries; 2 months to mss. Sample copy for $5. Writer's guidelines for #10 SASE.

Nonfiction: How-to (cattle production), interview/profile, technical (related to cattle). **Buys 20-30 mss/year.** Query with published clips. Length: 800-3,500 words. **Pays $50-1,000.** Pays expenses of writers on assignment.

Photos: Send photos with submission. Reviews 5×7 glossy prints. Buys all rights. Offers $25-400/photo. Identification of subjects required.

The online magazine carries original content not included in the print edition. Contact: Shauna Hermel, online editor.

Tips: "Read the magazine and have a firm grasp of the cattle industry."

N $ $ THE BRAHMAN JOURNAL, 17269 FM 1887, Hempstead TX 77445. (979)826-4347. Fax: (979)826-8352. **Contact:** Vicki Lambert, editor. **10% freelance written.** Monthly magazine covering Brahman cattle. Estab. 1971. Circ. 4,000. Pays on publication. Publishes ms an average of 2 months after acceptance. Byline given. Not copyrighted. Buys first North American serial, one-time, second serial (reprint) rights, makes work-for-hire assignments. Submit seasonal material 3 months in advance. Sample copy for 9×12 SAE and 5 first-class stamps.

Nonfiction: General interest, historical/nostalgic, interview/profile. Special issues: Herd Bull (July); Texas (October). **Buys 3-4 mss/year.** Query with published clips. Length: 1,200-3,000 words. **Pays $100-250 for assigned articles.**

Reprints: Send ms with rights for sale noted. Pays 50% of amount paid for an original article.

Photos: Photos needed for article purchase. Send photos with submission. Reviews 4×5 prints. Buys one-time rights. Offers no additional payment for photos accepted with ms. Captions required.

N $ $ THE CATTLEMAN, Texas and Southwestern Cattle Raisers Association, 1301 W. 7th St., Ft. Worth TX 76102-2660. (817)332-7064. Fax: (817)332-5446. E-mail: anita@thecattlemanmagazine.com. Website: www.thecattlemanmagazine.com. Editor: Lionel Chambers; Managing Editor: Susan Wagner. **Contact:** Anita Braddock, director. **25% freelance written.** Monthly magazine covering the Texas/Oklahoma beef cattle industry. "We specialize in in-depth, management-type articles related to range and pasture, beef cattle production, animal health, nutrition and marketing. We want 'how-to' articles." Estab. 1914. Circ. 18,000. **Pays on acceptance.** Publishes ms an average of 2 months after acceptance. Byline given. Buys exclusive and one-time rights. Editorial lead time 2 months. Submit seasonal material 6 months in advance. Accepts queries by mail, e-mail, fax. Sample copy for free. Writer's guidelines online.

O→ Break in with "clips from other cattle magazines and demonstrated knowledge of our audiences."

Nonfiction: How-to, humor, interview/profile, new product, personal experience, technical, ag research. Special issues: Editorial calendar theme issues include: Horses (January); Range and Pasture (February); Livestock Marketing (July); Hereford and Wildlife (August); Feedlots (September); Bull Buyers (October); Mexican Marketing (December). Does not want to see anything not specifically related to beef production in the Southwest. **Buys 20 mss/year.** Query with published clips. Length: 1,500-2,000 words. **Pays $200-350 for assigned articles; $100-350 for unsolicited articles.** Sometimes pays expenses of writers on assignment.

Photos: Reviews transparencies, prints. Buys one-time rights. Offers no additional payment for photos accepted with ms. Identification of subjects required.

Fiction: Humorous, slice-of-life vignettes, western. "No fiction unrelated to cattle/ranching in the Southwest." **Buys 5 mss/year.** Send complete ms. Length: 700-1,000 words. **Pays $100.**

Tips: "In our most recent readership survey, subscribers said they were most interested in the following topics in this order: range/pasture, property rights, animal health, water, new innovations and marketing. *The Cattleman* prefers to work on an assignment basis. However, prospective contributors are urged to write the editorial director of the magazine to inquire of interest on a proposed subject. Occasionally, the editor will return a manuscript to a potential contributor for cutting, polishing, checking, rewriting or condensing. Be able to demonstrate background/knowledge in this field. Include tearsheets from similar magazines."

$ $ FEED LOT MAGAZINE, Feed Lot Magazine, Inc., P.O. Box 850, Dighton KS 67839. (620)397-2838. Fax: (620)397-2839. E-mail: feedlot@st-tel.net. Website: www.feedlotmagazine.com. **Contact:** Robert A. Strong, editor (rstrong@st-tel.net). **40% freelance written.** Bimonthly magazine. "The editorial information content fits a dual role: large feedlots and their related cow/calf, operations, and large 500pl cow/calf, 100pl stocker operations. The information covers all phases of production from breeding, genetics, animal health, nutrition, equipment design, research through finishing fat cattle. *Feed Lot* publishes a mix of new information and timely articles which directly affect the cattle industry." Estab. 1993. Circ. 12,000. Pays on publication. Publishes ms an average of 2 months after acceptance. Byline given. Offers 50% kill fee. Buys all rights. Editorial lead time 2 months. Submit seasonal material 6 months in advance. Accepts queries by mail, e-mail, fax. Responds in 1 month to queries. Sample copy and writer's guidelines for $1.50.

Nonfiction: Interview/profile, new product (cattle-related), photo feature. Send complete ms. Length: 100-400 words. **Pays 20¢/word.**

Reprints: Send tearsheet or typed ms with rights for sale noted and information about when and where the material previously appeared. Pays 50% of amount paid for an original article.

Photos: State availability of or send photos with submission. Reviews contact sheets. Buys all rights. Negotiates payment individually. Captions, model releases required.

Tips: "Know what you are writing about—have a good knowledge of the subject."

Management

$ AG JOURNAL, Arkansas Valley Publishing, P.O. Box 500, La Junta CO 81050-0500. (800)748-1997. Fax: (719)384-2867. E-mail: journal@ria.net. Website: www.agjournalonline.com. **Contact:** Jeanette Larson, managing editor. **20% freelance written.** Weekly journal covering agriculture. "The Ag Journal covers people, issues and events relevant to ag producers in our seven state region (Colorado, Kansas, Oklahoma, Texas, Wyoming, Nebraska, New Mexico)." Estab. 1949. Circ. 11,000. Pays on publication. Publishes ms an average of 2 weeks after acceptance. Byline given. Buys first, one-time rights, makes work-for-hire assignments. Editorial lead time 1 month. Submit seasonal material 1 month in advance. Accepts queries by e-mail. Accepts previously published material. Responds in 2 weeks to queries. Sample copy and writer's guidelines free.

Nonfiction: How-to, interview/profile, new product, opinion, photo feature, technical. Query by e-mail only. **Pays 4¢/word.** Sometimes pays expenses of writers on assignment.

Photos: State availability with submission. Buys one-time rights. Offers $8/photo. Captions, identification of subjects required.

Tips: "Query by e-mail."

$ AGVENTURES, Schatz Publishing Group, 11950 W. Highland Ave., Blackwell OK 74631-9511. (580)628-4551. Fax: (580)628-2011. E-mail: agventures@aol.com. Website: www.agventures.com. **Contact:** Sheree Lewis, manager. **95% freelance written.** Bimonthly business-to-business magazine covering agricultural business opportunities. Estab. 1997. Circ. 2,500. Pays on publication. Publishes ms an average of 3 months after acceptance. Byline sometimes given. Offers 50% kill fee. Buys all rights. Editorial lead time 3 months. Submit seasonal material 3 months in advance. Accepts queries by mail, e-mail, fax, phone. Accepts simultaneous submissions. Responds in 2 weeks to queries; 1 month to mss. Sample copy for $4. Writer's guidelines free.

Nonfiction: Interview/profile (research). "No personal experience (nothing in the first person)." **Buys 30-40 mss/year.** Send complete ms. Length: 2,000-3,000 words. **Pays $75-150.**
Photos: Send photos with submission. Reviews 4×6 prints. Buys all rights. Pays $20/photo. Captions, model releases required.
Tips: "We want ideas on how people are making money on their small acreage and articles that tell how they do it. The best way to get accepted is to imitate the format of existing articles."

$ SMALL FARM TODAY, The How-to Magazine of Alternative and Traditional Crops, Livestock, and Direct Marketing, Missouri Farm Publishing, Inc., Ridge Top Ranch 3903 W. Ridge Trail Rd., Clark MO 65243-9525. (573)687-3525. Fax: (573)687-3148. E-mail: smallfarm@socket.net. Website: www.smallfarmtoday.com. Editor: Ron Macher. **Contact:** Paul Berg, managing editor. Bimonthly magazine "for small farmers and small-acreage landowners interested in diversification, direct marketing, alternative crops, horses, draft animals, small livestock, exotic and minor breeds, home-based businesses, gardening, vegetable and small fruit crops." Estab. 1984 as *Missouri Farm Magazine*. Circ. 12,000. Pays 60 days after publication. Publishes ms an average of 6 months after acceptance. Byline given. Buys first serial and nonexclusive reprint rights (right to reprint article in an anthology) Submit seasonal material 4 months in advance. Accepts queries by mail, e-mail, fax. Responds in 3 months to queries. Sample copy for $3. Writer's guidelines online.

O-ᴿ Break in with a detailed "how-to" story with budget information on a specific crop or animal.

Nonfiction: Practical and how-to (small farming, gardening, alternative crops/livestock). Special issues: Poultry (January); Wool & Fiber (March); Aquaculture (July); Equipment (November). Query letters recommended. Length: 1,200-2,600 words.
Reprints: Send tearsheet, photocopy or typed ms with rights for sale noted and information about when and where the material previously appeared. Pays 57% of amount paid for an original article.
Photos: Send photos with submission. Buys one-time and nonexclusive reprint rights (for anthologies). Offers $6 for inside photos and $10 for cover photos. Pays $4 for negatives or slides. Captions required.
Tips: "No poetry or humor. Your topic must apply to the small farm or acreage. It helps to provide more practical and helpful information without the fluff. We need 'how-to' articles (how-to grow, raise, market, build, etc.), as well as articles about small farmers who are experiencing success through diversification, specialty/alternative crops and livestock, and direct marketing."

Miscellaneous

N $ BEE CULTURE, P.O. Box 706, Medina OH 44256-0706. Fax: (330)725-5624. E-mail: kim@beeculture.com. Website: www.beeculture.com. **Contact:** (Mr.) Kim Flottum, editor. **50% freelance written.** Monthly magazine for beekeepers and those interested in the natural science of honey bees, with environmentally-oriented articles relating to honey bees or pollination. Estab. 1873. Pays on both publication and acceptance. Publishes ms an average of 4 months after acceptance. Buys first North American serial rights. Accepts queries by mail, e-mail, fax, phone. Responds in 1 month to mss. Sample copy for 9×12 SAE and 5 first-class stamps. Writer's guidelines online.

O-ᴿ Break in with marketing strategies, interviews of successful beekeepers or beekeeping science, making management of bees easier or less expensive.

Nonfiction: Interested in articles giving new ideas on managing bees. Also looking for articles on honey bee/environment connections or relationships. Also uses success stories about commercial beekeepers. Interview/profile, personal experience, photo feature. No "how I began beekeeping" articles. No highly advanced, technical and scientific abstracts or impractical advice. Length: 2,000 words average. **Pays $60-100/published page and up.**
Reprints: Send photocopy and information about when and where the material previously appeared. Pays 50% of amount paid for an original article, on negotiation.
Photos: "B&W or color prints, 5×7 standard, but 3×5 are OK. 35mm slides, mid-format transparencies are excellent. Electronic images accepted and encouraged." Pays $7-10 each, $50 for cover photos.
Tips: "Do an interview story on commercial beekeepers who are cooperative enough to furnish accurate, factual information on their operations. Frequent mistakes made by writers in completing articles are that they are too general in nature and lack management knowledge."

Regional

N $ CENTRAL ALBERTA FARMER, Bowes Publishers Ltd., 4504—61 Ave., Leduc AB T9E 3Z1, Canada. (780)986-2271. Fax: (780)986-6397. E-mail: editor-wdf-caf@webcoleduc.com. Website: www.albertafarmer.com. **Contact:** Lisa Wojna, editor. **10% freelance written.** Monthly tabloid covering farming issues specific to or affecting farmers in central Alberta, Canada. "*Central Alberta Farmer* is an industry magazine-type product that deals with issues in farming. It also highlights value-added efforts in agriculture, and features stories on rural lifestyles." Estab. 1993. Circ. 22,000. Pays on publication. Publishes ms an average of 3 months after acceptance. Byline given. Buys all rights. Editorial lead time 3 months. Submit seasonal material 4 months in advance. Accepts queries by mail, e-mail, fax. Accepts simultaneous submissions. Responds in 2 weeks to queries; 2 months to mss. Sample copy for 9×12 SAE.
Nonfiction: "All articles must be related to an aspect of farming in the area *Central Alberta Farmer* covers. Freelance articles must be exceptional. Not many are accepted." General interest, how-to, interview/profile, new product, personal experience, technical. "Not interested in anything trite or trivial." **Buys 5 mss/year.** Query or send complete ms. Length: 1,000-1,500 words. **Pays $20-30.**

Photos: State availability with submission. Reviews GIF/JPEG files. Buys all rights. Offers no additional payment for photos accepted with ms. Captions, identification of subjects, model releases required.

Tips: "Know the industry well. Provide names and phone numbers with submissions (both yours and the people in the article). This is a difficult publication to break into because most copy is generated in-house. So, your submission must be far above average."

$ $ FLORIDA GROWER, The Voice of Florida Agriculture for More Than 90 Years, Meister Publishing Co., 1555 Howell Branch Rd., Suite C-204, Winter Park FL 32789. (407)539-6552. E-mail: flg_edit@meisternet.com. Website: www.floridagrower.net. Editor: Michael Allen. **Contact:** Michael Allen. **10% freelance written.** Monthly magazine "edited for the Florida farmer with commercial production interest primarily in citrus, vegetables, and other ag endeavors." "Our goal is to provide articles which update and inform on such areas as production, ag financing, farm labor relations, technology, safety, education and regulation." Estab. 1907. Circ. 12,200. Pays on publication. Byline given. Buys all rights. Editorial lead time 2 months. Submit seasonal material 3 months in advance. Accepts queries by mail, e-mail, fax, phone. Responds in 1 month to queries. Sample copy for 9×12 SAE and 5 first-class stamps. Writer's guidelines free.

Nonfiction: Interview/profile, photo feature, technical. Query with published clips. Length: 700-1,000 words. **Pays $150-250.**

Photos: Send photos with submission.

$ FLORIDAGRICULTURE, Florida Farm Bureau Federation, 5700 SW 34th St., Gainesville FL 32608. (352)374-1521. Fax: (352)374-1530. E-mail: ealbanesi@sfbcic.com. Website: www.fb.com/flfb. **Contact:** Ed Albanesi, editor. **Less than 5% freelance written.** Monthly tabloid covering Florida agriculture. Promotes agriculture to its 125,000 members families. Estab. 1943. Circ. 125,000. **Pays on acceptance.** Publishes ms an average of 3 months after acceptance. Byline sometimes given. Buys all rights. Editorial lead time 3 months. Submit seasonal material 3 months in advance. Accepts queries by mail, e-mail. Responds in 1 week to queries; 1 month to mss. Sample copy for $3.

Nonfiction: Sportsmen articles with a Florida connection. **Buys fewer than 2 mss/year.** Query. Length: 500-1,500 words. **Pays $50-100 for assigned articles.**

Photos: State availability with submission. Buys up to 3 uses. Negotiates payment individually. Captions, identification of subjects required.

N $ THE LAND, Minnesota's Favorite Ag Publication, Free Press Co., P.O. Box 3169, Mankato MN 56002-3169. (507)345-4523. E-mail: kschulz@the-land.com. Website: www.the-land.com. **Contact:** Kevin Schulz, editor. **40% freelance written.** Weekly tabloid covering farming in Minnesota. "Although we're not tightly focused on any one type of farming, our articles must be of interest to farmers. In other words, will your article topic have an impact on people who live and work in rural areas?" Prefers to work with Minnesota writers. Estab. 1976. Circ. 40,000. **Pays on acceptance.** Publishes ms an average of 2 months after acceptance. Byline given. Buys first North American serial rights. Editorial lead time 2 months. Submit seasonal material 2 months in advance. Accepts queries by mail, e-mail. Responds in 3 weeks to queries; 2 months to mss. Sample copy for free. Writer's guidelines for #10 SASE.

Nonfiction: General interest (ag), how-to (crop, livestock production, marketing). "Nothing that doesn't pertain to Minnesota agricultural or rural life." **Buys 80 mss/year.** Query. Length: 500-750 words. **Pays $30-60 for assigned articles.**

Photos: Send photos with submission. Reviews contact sheets. Buys one-time rights. Negotiates payment individually.

Columns/Departments: Query. **Pays $10-50.**

Tips: "Be enthused about rural Minnesota life and agriculture and be willing to work with our editors. We try to stress relevance. When sending me a query, convince me the story belongs in a Minnesota farm publication."

$ $ MAINE ORGANIC FARMER & GARDENER, Maine Organic Farmers & Gardeners Association, 662 Slab City Rd., Lincolnville ME 04849. (207)763-3043. E-mail: jenglish@midcoast.com. Website: www.mofga.org. **Contact:** Jean English, editor. **40% freelance written.** Prefers to work with published/established local writers. Quarterly magazine. "*MOF&G* promotes and encourages sustainable agriculture and environmentally sound living. Our primary focus is organic farming, gardening, and forestry, but we also deal with local, national, and international agriculture, food, and environmental issues." Estab. 1976. Circ. 10,000. Pays on publication. Publishes ms an average of 8 months after acceptance. Byline and bio offered. Buys first North American serial, first, one-time, second serial (reprint) rights. Submit seasonal material 1 year in advance. Accepts queries by mail, e-mail. Accepts simultaneous submissions. Responds in 2 months to queries. Sample copy for $2 and SAE with 7 first-class stamps. Writer's guidelines free.

Nonfiction: Book reviews; how-to based on personal experience, research reports, interviews. Profiles of farmers, gardeners, plants. Information on renewable energy, recycling, nutrition, health, nontoxic pest control, organic farm management and marketing. "We use profiles of New England organic farmers and gardeners and news reports (500-1,000 words) dealing with U.S./international sustainable ag research and development, rural development, recycling projects, environmental and agricultural problems and solutions, organic farms with broad impact, cooperatives and community projects." **Buys 30 mss/year.** Query with published clips or send complete ms. Length: 250-3,000 words. **Pays $20-200.**

Reprints: Send ms with rights for sale noted and information about when and where the material previously appeared. Pays 50% of amount paid for an original article.

Photos: State availability of b&w photos with query; send 3×5 b&w photos with ms. State availability with submission. Buys one-time rights. Captions, identification of subjects, model releases required.

Tips: "We are a nonprofit organization. Our publication's primary mission is to inform and educate, but we also want readers to enjoy the articles."

FINANCE

These magazines deal with banking, investment, and financial management. Publications that use similar material but have a less technical slant are listed under the Consumer Business & Finance section.

N $ $ $ ADVISOR'S EDGE, Canada's Magazine for the Financial Professional, Rogers Media, Inc., 156 Front St. W., 4th Floor, Toronto, ON M5J 2L6, Canada. (416)642-4729. Fax: (416)642-4949. E-mail: dgage@rmpublishing.com. Website: www.advisorsedge.ca. **Contact:** Deanne Gage, managing editor. Monthly magazine covering the financial industry (financial advisors and investment advisors). "*Advisor's Edge* focuses on sales and marketing opportunities for the financial advisor (how they can build their business and improve relationships with clients." Estab. 1998. Circ. 36,000. Pays on publication. Publishes ms an average of 3 months after acceptance. Byline given. Offers 25% kill fee. Buys one-time, electronic rights. Editorial lead time 3 months. Accepts queries by e-mail. Sample copy online.

Nonfiction: "We are looking for articles that help advisors do their jobs better." How-to, interview/profile. No articles that aren't relevant to how a financial advisor does his/her job. **Buys 12 mss/year.** Query with published clips. Length: 1,500-2,000 words. **Pays $900 (Canadian).** Pays in contributor copies only if an industry contributor (i.e., an advisor).

$ $ $ $ BANKING STRATEGIES, Bank Administration Institute (BAI), Chicago IL. E-mail: kcline@bai.org. Website: www.bai.org/bankingstrategies. **Contact:** Kenneth Cline, senior editor. **70% freelance written.** Magazine covering banking and financial services. "Magazine covers banking from a strategic and managerial perspective for its senior financial executive audience. Each issue includes in-depth trend articles and interviews with influential executives." Offers variable kill fee. Buys all rights. Accepts queries by e-mail. Responds almost immediately to queries.

Nonfiction: How-to (articles that help institutions be more effective and competitive in the marketplace), interview/profile (executive interviews). "No topic queries, we assign stories to freelancers. I'm looking for qualifications as opposed to topic queries. I need experienced writers/reporters." **Buys 30 mss/year.** E-queries preferred. **Pays $1.25/word for assigned articles.**

Tips: "Demonstrate ability and financial services expertise. I'm looking for freelancers who can write according to our standards, which are quite high."

N $ $ $ COLLECTIONS & CREDIT RISK, The Authority for Commercial and Consumer Professionals, Thomson Media, 300 S. Wacker Dr., Suite 1800, Chicago IL 60606. (312)913-1334. Fax: (312)913-1365. E-mail: catherine.ladwig@thomsonmedia.com. Website: www.creditcollectionsworld.com. Editor: David E. Whiteside. **Contact:** Catherine (Kit) Ladwig, managing editor. **33% freelance written.** Monthly journal covering debt collections and credit risk management. "*Collections & Credit Risk* reports and analyzes events and trends affecting consumer and commercial credit practices and debt collections. The entire credit cycle is covered from setting credit policy and making loan decisions to debt recovery, collections, bankruptcy, and debt sales." Estab. 1996. Circ. 30,000. **Pays on acceptance.** Publishes ms an average of 3 months after acceptance. Byline given. Kill fee determined case by case. Buys all rights. Editorial lead time 3 months. Accepts queries by mail, e-mail, fax. to queries. Sample copy free or online.

Break in with a "a query with clips of business trend stories using 8-10 sources and demonstrating strong analysis."

Nonfiction: Interview/profile, technical, business news and analysis. "No unsolicited submissions accepted—freelancers work on assignment only." **Buys 30-40 mss/year.** Query with published clips. Length: 1,000-2,500 words. **Pays $800-1,000.** Sometimes pays expenses of writers on assignment.

The online version contains material not found in the print version.

Tips: "This is a business news and analysis magazine focused on events and trends affecting the credit-risk management and collections professions. Our editorial approach is modeled after *Business Week, Forbes, Fortune, Wall Street Journal.* No fluff accepted."

$ $ CREDIT UNION MANAGEMENT, Credit Union Executives Society, 5510 Research Park Dr., Madison WI 53711. (608)271-2664. Fax: (608)271-2303. E-mail: editors@cues.org. Website: www.cumanagement.org. **Contact:** Mary Arnold or Theresa Sweeney, editors. **44% freelance written.** Monthly magazine covering credit union, banking trends management, HR, marketing issues. "Our philosophy mirrors the credit union industry of cooperative financial services." Estab. 1978. Circ. 7,413. **Pays on acceptance.** Publishes ms an average of 2 months after acceptance. Editorial lead time 3 months. Submit seasonal material 4 months in advance. Accepts queries by mail, e-mail, fax, phone. Accepts simultaneous submissions. Responds in 2 weeks to queries; 1 month to mss. Sample copy and writer's guidelines free.

Nonfiction: Book excerpts, how-to (be a good mentor/leader, recruit, etc.), interview/profile, technical. **Buys 74 mss/year.** Query with published clips. Length: 700-2,400 words. **Pays $250-350.** Pays phone expenses only of writers on assignment.

Columns/Departments: Management Network (book/Web reviews, briefs), 300 words; Trends (marketing trends), 700 words; Point of Law, 700 words; Plugged In (new technology/operations trends), 700 words. Query with published clips. **Pays $250-350.**

Tips: "The best way is to e-mail an editor; include résumé. Follow up with mailing cover letter and clips. Knowledge of financial services is very helpful."

$ $ EQUITIES MAGAZINE LLC, P.O. Box 130H, Scarsdale NY 10583. (914)723-6702. Fax: (914)723-0176. E-mail: equitymag@aol.com. Website: www.equitiesmagazine.com. **Contact:** Robert J. Flaherty, editor. **50% freelance written.** "We are a seven-issues-a-year financial magazine covering the fastest-growing public companies in the world. We study the management of companies and act as critics reviewing their performances. We aspire to be 'The Shareholder's Friend.' We want to be a bridge between quality public companies and sophisticated investors." Estab. 1951. Circ. 18,000. Pays on publication. Publishes ms an average of 2 months after acceptance. Byline given. Buys all rights. Accepts queries by mail. Sample copy for 9×12 SAE and 5 first-class stamps.

Nonfiction: "We must know the writer first as we are careful about whom we publish. A letter of introduction with résumé and clips is the best way to introduce yourself. Financial writing requires specialized knowledge and a feel for people as well, which can be a tough combination to find." Carries guest columns by famous money managers who are not writing for cash payments, but to showcase their ideas and approach. Exposé, new product, technical. **Buys 30 mss/year.** Query with published clips. Length: 300-1,500 words. **Pays $250-750 for assigned articles, more for very difficult or investigative pieces.** Pays expenses of writers on assignment.

Photos: Send color photos with submission. Reviews contact sheets, negatives, transparencies, prints. Offers no additional payment for photos accepted with ms. Identification of subjects required.

Columns/Departments: Pays $25-75 for assigned items only.

Tips: "Give us an idea for a story on a specific publically-owned company, whose stock is traded on NASDAQ, the NYSE, or American Stock Exchange. Anyone who enjoys analyzing a business and telling the story of the people who started it, or run it today, is a potential *Equities* contributor. But to protect our readers and ourselves, we are careful about who writes for us. We do not want writers who are trading the stocks of the companies they profile. Business writing is an exciting area and our stories reflect that. If a writer relies on numbers and percentages to tell his story, rather than the individuals involved, the result will be numbingly dull."

$ $ $ THE FEDERAL CREDIT UNION, National Association of Federal Credit Unions, 3138 N. 10th St., Arlington VA 22201. (703)522-4770. Fax: (703)524-1082. E-mail: tfcu@nafcu.org. Website: www.nafcu.org. Executive Editor: Jay Morris. **Contact:** Robin Johnston, publisher/managing editor. **30% freelance written.** "Looking for writers with financial, banking, or credit union experience, but will work with inexperienced (unpublished) writers based on writing skill. Published bimonthly, *The Federal Credit Union* is the official publication of the National Association of Federal Credit Unions. The magazine is dedicated to providing credit union management, staff and volunteers with in-depth information (HR, technology, security, board management, etc.) they can use to fulfill their duties and better serve their members. The editorial focus includes coverage of management issues, operations, technology as well as volunteer-related issues." Estab. 1967. Circ. 8,000. Pays on publication. Publishes ms an average of 3 months after acceptance. Byline given. Buys first North American serial rights, rights to publish and archive online. Submit seasonal material 5 months in advance. Accepts queries by mail, e-mail, fax. Accepts simultaneous submissions. Responds in 2 months to queries. Sample copy for 10×13 SAE and 5 first-class stamps. Writer's guidelines for #10 SASE.

Break in with "pithy, informative, thought-provoking items for our 'Management Insight' section (for free or a small fee of $50-200)."

Nonfiction: Humor, inspirational, interview/profile. Query with published clips and SASE. Length: 1,200-2,000 words. **Pays $400-1,000.**

Photos: Send photos with submission. Reviews 35mm transparencies, 5×7 prints, high-resolution photos. Buys all rights. Offers no additional payment for photos accepted with ms. Pays $50-500. Identification of subjects, model releases required.

The online magazine carries original content not found in the print edition, as well as some print copy. Contact: Robin Johnston.

Tips: "We would like more articles on how credit unions are using technology to serve their members and more articles on leading-edge technologies they can use in their operations. If you can write on current trends in technology, human resources, or strategic planning, you stand a better chance of being published than if you wrote on other topics."

$ FINANCIAL PLANNING, Thomson Media, State Street Plaza, 26th Floor, New York NY 10001. (212)803-8696. Fax: (212)843-9608. E-mail: richard.koreto@thomsonmedia.com. Website: www.financial-planning.com. **Contact:** Richard Koreto, executive editor. **30-40% freelance written.** Monthly magazine covering investment strategies, estate planning, practice management and other issues facing professional financial planners and money managers. Estab. 1971. Circ. 100,000. Pays on publication. Publishes ms an average of 3 months after acceptance. Byline given. Offers 15% kill fee. Buys all rights. Editorial lead time 3 months. Submit seasonal material 4 months in advance. Accepts queries by mail, e-mail. Responds in 3 weeks to queries; 1 month to mss. Sample copy for $10. Writer's guidelines free.

Nonfiction: Book excerpts, how-to, interview/profile, new product, opinion, technical. No product endorsements. **Buys 25-30 mss/year.** Query (e-mail preferred). Length: 1,800-2,500 words. **Payment varies.** Sometimes pays expenses of writers on assignment.

Photos: State availability with submission. Reviews contact sheets, any size prints. Offers no additional payment for photos accepted with ms. Identification of subjects required.

The online magazine carries original content not included in the print edition. Contact: John Whelan, online editor.

Tips: "Avoid articles that are too general—ours is a professional readership who require thoughtful, in-depth analysis of financial issues. A submission that includes charts, graphs, and statistical data is much more likely to pique our interest than overviews of investing."

$ ILLINOIS BANKER, Illinois Bankers Association, 133 S. Fourth St., Suite 300, Springfield IL 62701. (217)789-9340. Fax: (217)789-5410. **Contact:** Debbie Jemison, editor. "Our audience is approximately 3,000 bankers and vendors related to the banking industry. The purpose of the publication is to educate and inform readers on major public policy issues affecting banking today, as well as provide new ideas that can be applied to day-to-day operations and management. Writers may not sell or promote a product or service." Estab. 1891. Circ. 2,500. Publishes ms an average of 3 months after acceptance. Byline given. Buys first North American serial rights. Editorial lead time 2 months. Accepts simultaneous submissions. Responds in 3 months to queries. Sample copy and writer's guidelines free.

Nonfiction: "It is *IBA* policy that writers do not sell or promote a particular product, service, or organization within the content of an article written for publication." Essays, historical/nostalgic, interview/profile, new product, opinion, personal experience. Query. Length: 1,000-1,500 words.

Photos: State availability with submission. Reviews contact sheets, negatives, transparencies, prints. Captions, identification of subjects required.

Tips: "Articles published in *Illinois Banker* address current issues of key importance to the banking industry in Illinois. Our intention is to keep readers informed of the latest industry news, developments, and trends, as well as provide necessary technical information. We publish articles on any topic that affects the banking industry, provided the content is in agreement with Association policy and position. Because we are a trade association, most articles need to be reviewed by an advisory committee before publication; therefore, the earlier they are submitted the better. Some recent topics include: agriculture, bank architecture, commercial and consumer credit, marketing, operations/cost control, security, and technology. In addition, articles are also considered on the topics of economic development and business/banking trends in Illinois and the Midwest region."

$ INVESTMENT NEWS, Crain Communications, 711 Third Ave., New York NY 10017-4014. (212)210-0100. Fax: (212)210-0444. E-mail: kgirard@crain.com. Website: www.investmentnews.com. Editor: Keith Girard. **10% freelance written.** Weekly magazine, newsletter, tabloid covering financial planning and investing. "It covers the business of personal finance to keep its audience of planners, brokers and other tax investment professionals informed of the latest news about their industry." Estab. 1997. Circ. 60,000. Pays on publication. Publishes ms an average of 1 month after acceptance. Byline given. Negotiate kill fee. Buys all rights, makes work-for-hire assignments. Editorial lead time 2 weeks. Submit seasonal material 1 month in advance. Sample copy for free. Writer's guidelines free.

Tips: "Come to us with a specific pitch-preferably based on a news tip. We prefer to be contacted by fax or e-mail."

$ MORTGAGE BANKING, The Magazine of Real Estate Finance, Mortgage Bankers Association of America, 1919 Pennsylvania Ave., NW, Washington DC 20006. (202)557-2853. Fax: (202)721-0245. E-mail: janet_hewitt@mbaa.org. Website: www.mbaa.org. Deputy Editor: Lesley Hall. **Contact:** Janet Reilley Hewitt, editor-in-chief. Monthly magazine covering real estate finance. "Timely examinations of major news and trends in the business of mortgage lending for both commercial and residential real estate." Estab. 1939. Circ. 8,000. **Pays on acceptance.** Publishes ms an average of 2 months after acceptance. Byline given. Negotiates kill fee. Buys one-time rights, makes work-for-hire assignments. Editorial lead time 2 months. Submit seasonal material 3 months in advance. Accepts queries by mail, e-mail, fax. Accepts simultaneous submissions. Responds in 1 month to queries; 4 months to mss. Sample copy and writer's guidelines free.

Nonfiction: Book excerpts, essays, interview/profile, opinion. Special issues: Commercial Real Estate Special Supplemental Issue (January); Internet Guide Supplemental Issue (September). **Buys 30 mss/year.** Query. Length: 3,000-4,000 words. **Writers' fees negotiable.** Sometimes pays expenses of writers on assignment.

Photos: State availability with submission. Reviews prints. Buys one-time rights. Negotiates payment individually. Identification of subjects, model releases required.

Columns/Departments: Book reviews (current, relevant material), 300 words; executive essay (industry executive's personal views on relevant topic), 750-1,000 words. **Buys 2 mss/year.** Query. **Pay negotiated.**

Tips: "Trends in technology, current and upcoming legislation that will affect the mortgage industry are good focus."

$ $ $ $ ON WALL STREET, Thomson Media, 40 W. 57th St., New York NY 10019. (212)803-8782. Fax: (212)631-9731. E-mail: evan.cooper@thomsonmedia.com. Website: www.onwallstreet.com. **Contact:** Evan Cooper, editor-in-chief. **50% freelance written.** Monthly magazine for stockbrokers. "We help 95,000 stockbrockers build their business." Estab. 1991. Circ. 95,000. Pays on publication. Publishes ms an average of 1 month after acceptance. Byline given. Offers 50% kill fee. Buys first North American serial rights. Editorial lead time 2 months. Submit seasonal material 2 months in advance. Accepts queries by mail, e-mail. Accepts simultaneous submissions. Responds in 1 week to queries; 1 month to mss. Sample copy for free. Writer's guidelines free.

Nonfiction: How-to, interview/profile. "No investment-related articles about hot stocks, nor funds or hot alternative investments." **Buys 30 mss/year.** Query. Length: 1,000-3,000 words. **Pays $1/word.**

Photos: State availability with submission. Reviews contact sheets. Buys one-time rights. Negotiates payment individually. Identification of subjects required.

Tips: "Writers should know what stockbrokers need to expand their business—industry-specific knowledge of cold-calling, selling investment ideas."

$ $ SERVICING MANAGEMENT, The Magazine for Loan Servicing Professionals, Zackin Publications, P.O. Box 2180, Waterbury CT 06722-2180. (800)325-6745 ext. 241. Fax: (203)755-3480. E-mail: bates@sm-online.com. Website: www.sm-online.com. **Contact:** Michael Bates, editor. **15% freelance written.** Monthly magazine covering residential mortgage servicing. Estab. 1989. Circ. 20,000. **Pays on acceptance.** Publishes ms an average of 2 months after acceptance. Byline given. Buys all rights. Accepts queries by mail, e-mail, fax. Responds in 2 weeks to queries. Sample copy and writer's guidelines free. Writer's guidelines online.

- Break in by "submitting a query for Servicing Reports, a monthly department featuring news and information about mortgage servicing and the industry. It should be informative, topical and include comments by industry professionals."

Nonfiction: How-to, interview/profile, new product, technical. **Buys 10 mss/year.** Query. Length: 1,500-2,500 words. Will pay industry experts with contributor copies or other premiums rather than a cash payment.

Photos: State availability with submission. Reviews contact sheets. Buys all rights. Offers no additional payment for photos accepted with ms. Identification of subjects required.

Columns/Departments: Buys 5 mss/year. Query. **Pays $200.**

$ TRADERS MAGAZINE, Thomson Media Group, 1 State St. Plaza, 17th Floor, New York NY 10001. (212)465-7124. Fax: (212)295-1725. E-mail: john.byrne@thomsonmedia.com. Website: www.tradersmagazine.com. **Contact:** John Aidan Byrne, editor. **35% freelance written.** Monthly magazine plus 2 specials covering equity trading and technology. "Provides comprehensive coverage of how institutional trading is performed on NASDAQ and the New York Stock Exchange." Pays on publication. Publishes ms an average of 2 months after acceptance. Byline given. Buys all rights. Editorial lead time 2 months. Submit seasonal material 3 months in advance. Accepts queries by mail, e-mail, phone. Sample copy free to writers on assignment.

O→ Needs more "buy-side" stories (on mutual fund, pension fund traders, etc.), "sell-side" stories on hot-button topics.

Nonfiction: Book excerpts, exposé, general interest, historical/nostalgic, how-to, humor, interview/profile, new product, opinion, personal experience, religious, technical. Special issues: Correspondent clearing (every market) and market making survey of broker dealers. No stories that are related to fixed income and other non-equity topics. **Buys 12-20 mss/year.** Query with published clips or send complete ms. Length: 750-2,800 words.

Columns/Departments: Special Features (market regulation and human interest), 1600 words; Trading & Technology, 1,600 words; Washington Watch (market regulation), 750 words. Query with published clips.

Fiction: Ethnic, historical, humorous, mystery, science fiction, slice-of-life vignettes. No erotica. **Buys 1 mss/year.** Query with or without published clips or send complete ms. Length: 2,100-2,800 words.

The online magazine carries original content not found in the print edition. "We welcome controversy in both mediums."

Tips: "Boil it all down and don't bore the hell out of readers. Advice from a distinguished scribe which we pass along. Learn to explain equity market making and institutional trading in a simple, direct manner. Don't waffle. Have a trader explain the business to you if necessary. The *Traders Magazine* is highly regarded among Wall Street insiders, trading honchos, and Washington Pundits alike."

FISHING

$ $ PACIFIC FISHING, FIS North America, 4209 21st Ave., Suite 402, Seattle WA 98199. (206)216-0111. Fax: (206)216-0222. E-mail: brad@pacificfishing.com. Website: www.pfmag.com. **Contact:** Brad Warren, editor. **75% freelance written.** Works with some new/unpublished writers. Monthly magazine for commercial fishermen and others in the commercial fishing industry throughout Alaska, the west coast, and the Pacific. "*Pacific Fishing* views the fisherman as a small businessman and covers all aspects of the industry, including harvesting, processing and marketing." Estab. 1979. Circ. 10,000. Pays on publication. Publishes ms an average of 2 months after acceptance. Byline given. Buys first North American serial rights. Accepts queries by mail, e-mail, fax, phone. Variable response time to queries. Sample copy and writer's guidelines for 9×12 SAE with 10 first-class stamps.

O→ Study the magazine before querying. "We also manage North American content for www.fis.com, the leading online provider of global news and market intelligence for the commercial fishing and seafood industry. Study the site and e-mail us for details if interested."

Nonfiction: "Articles must be concerned specifically with commercial fishing. We view fishermen as small business operators and professionals who are innovative and success-oriented. To appeal to this reader, *Pacific Fishing* offers 4 basic features: Technical, how-to articles that give fishermen hands-on tips that will make their operation more efficient and profitable; practical, well-researched business articles discussing the dollars and cents of fishing, processing and marketing; profiles of a fisherman, processor or company with emphasis on practical business and technical areas; and in-depth analysis of political, social, fisheries management and resource issues that have a direct bearing on commercial fishermen." Editors here are putting more focus on local and international seafood marketing, technical coverage of gear and vessels. Interview/profile, technical (usually with a business book or slant). **Buys 20 mss/year.** Query noting whether photos are available, and enclosing samples of previous work and SASE. Length: varies, one-paragraph news items to 3,000-word features. **Pays 20¢/word for most assignments.** Sometimes pays expenses of writers on assignment.

Reprints: Send photocopy and information about when and where the material previously appeared. Pays 100% of the amount paid for an original article.

Photos: "We need good, high-quality photography, especially color, of commercial fishing. We prefer 35mm color slides or JPEG files of at least 300 dpi." Our rates are $200 for cover; $50-100 for inside color; $25-75 for b&w and $10 for table of contents.

FLORISTS, NURSERIES & LANDSCAPERS

Readers of these publications are involved in growing, selling, or caring for plants, flowers, and trees. Magazines geared to consumers interested in gardening are listed in the Consumer Home & Garden section.

$ $ DIGGER, Oregon Association of Nurserymen, 29751 SW Town Center Loop W., Wilsonville OR 97070. (503)682-5089. Fax: (503)682-5727. E-mail: csivesind@oan.org. Website: www.oan.org. **Contact:** Cam Sivesind, manager of publications and communications. **50% freelance written.** Monthly magazine covering nursery and greenhouse industry. "Our readers are mainly nursery and greenhouse operators and owners who propagate nursery stock/crops, so we write with them in mind." Circ. 5,000. Pays on receipt of copy. Publishes ms an average of 2 months after acceptance. Byline given. Offers 100% kill fee. Buys first North American serial rights. Editorial lead time 6 weeks. Submit seasonal material 2 months in advance. Accepts queries by mail, e-mail, fax, phone. Sample copy and writer's guidelines free.

Nonfiction: General interest, how-to (propagation techniques, other crop-growing tips), interview/profile, personal experience, technical. Special issues: Farwest Magazine (August)—this is a triple-size issue that runs in tandem with our annual trade show (11,500 circulation for this issue). "No articles not related or pertinent to nursery and greenhouse industry." **Buys 20-30 mss/year.** Query. Length: 800-2,000 words. **Pays $125-400 for assigned articles; $100-300 for unsolicited articles.** Sometimes pays expenses of writers on assignment.

Photos: State availability with submission. Reviews negatives, 5×7 prints, slides. Buys one-time rights. Offers $25-150/photo. Captions, identification of subjects required.

Tips: "Our best freelancers are familiar with or have experience in the horticultural industry. Some 'green' knowledge is a definite advantage."

$ GROWERTALKS, Ball Publishing, 335 N. River St., P.O. Box 9, Batavia IL 60510. (630)208-9080. Fax: (630)208-9350. E-mail: beytes@growertalks.com. Website: www.growertalks.com. **Contact:** Chris Beytes, editor. **50% freelance written.** Monthly magazine. "*GrowerTalks* serves the commercial greenhouse grower. Editorial emphasis is on floricultural crops: bedding plants, potted floral crops, foliage and fresh cut flowers. Our readers are growers, managers, and owners. We're looking for writers who've had experience in the greenhouse industry." Estab. 1937. Circ. 9,500. Pays on publication. Publishes ms an average of 3 months after acceptance. Byline given. Buys first North American serial rights. Editorial lead time 4 months. Submit seasonal material 3 months in advance. Accepts queries by mail, e-mail, fax. Responds in 1 month to queries. Sample copy and writer's guidelines free.

Nonfiction: How-to (time- or money-saving projects for professional flower/plant growers), interview/profile (ornamental horticulture growers), personal experience (of a grower), technical (about growing process in greenhouse setting). "No articles that promote only 1 product." **Buys 36 mss/year.** Query. Length: 1,200-1,600 words. **Pays $125 minimum for assigned articles; $75 minimum for unsolicited articles.**

Photos: State availability with submission. Reviews 2½×2½ slides and 3×5 prints. Buys one-time rights. Negotiates payment individually. Captions, identification of subjects, model releases required.

The online magazine carries original content not included in the print edition. Contact: Chris Beytes, online editor.

Tips: "Discuss magazine with ornamental horticulture growers to find out what topics that have or haven't appeared in the magazine interest them."

$ $ THE GROWING EDGE, New Moon Publishing, Inc., 341 SW Second St., Corvallis OR 97333. (541)757-2511. Fax: (541)757-0028. E-mail: doug@growingedge.com. Website: www.growingedge.com. **Contact:** Doug Peckenpaugh, editor. **85% freelance written.** Bimonthly magazine covering indoor and outdoor high-tech gardening techniques and tips. Estab. 1980. Circ. 20,000. Pays on publication. Publishes ms an average of 3 months after acceptance. Byline given. first serial and reprint rights Submit seasonal material 6 months in advance. Accepts queries by mail, e-mail. Responds in 3 months to queries. Sample copy for $3. Writer's guidelines online.

Break in with "a detailed, knowledgeable e-mail story pitch."

Nonfiction: How-to, interview/profile, personal experience (must be technical), book reviews, general horticulture and agriculture. Query. Length: 500-3,500 words. **Pays 20¢/word (10¢ for first rights, 5¢ for nonexclusive reprint and nonexclusive electronic rights).**

Reprints: Send tearsheet, photocopy or typed ms with rights for sale noted and information about when and where the material previously appeared. Payment negotiable.

Photos: Buys first and reprint rights. Pays $25-175. Pays on publication. Credit line given.

Tips: Looking for more hydroponics articles and information that will give the reader/gardener/farmer the "growing edge" in high-tech gardening and farming on topics such as high intensity grow lights, water conservation, drip irrigation, advanced organic fertilizers, new seed varieties, and greenhouse cultivation.

$ $ ORNAMENTAL OUTLOOK, Your Connection To The South's Horticulture Industry, Meister Publishing Co., 1555 Howell Branch Rd., Suite C204, Winter Park FL 32789. (407)539-6552. Fax: (407)539-6544. E-mail: oo_edit@meisternet.com. Website: www.ornamentaloutlook.com. **Contact:** Michael Allen, managing editor. **50% freelance written.** Monthly magazine. "*Ornamental Outlook* is written for commercial growers of ornamental plants in the Southeast U.S. Our goal is to provide interesting and informative articles on such topics as production, legislation, safety, technology, pest control, water management and new varieties as they apply to Southeast growers." Estab. 1991. Circ. 12,500. Pays 30 days after publication. Publishes ms an average of 4 months after acceptance. Byline given. Buys all rights. Editorial lead time 2 months. Submit seasonal material 3 months in advance. Accepts queries by mail, e-mail, fax, phone. Responds in 3 months to queries. Sample copy for 9×12 SAE and 5 first-class stamps. Writer's guidelines free.

Nonfiction: Interview/profile, photo feature, technical. "No first-person articles. No word-for-word meeting transcripts or all-quote articles." Query with published clips. Length: 750-1,000 words. **Pays $250/article including photos.**

Photos: Send photos with submission. Reviews contact sheets, transparencies, prints. Buys one-time rights. Captions, identification of subjects required.

Tips: "I am most impressed by written queries that address specific subjects of interest to our audience, which is the *Southeast* grower of *commercial* horticulture. Our biggest demand is for features, about 1,000 words, that follow subjects listed on our editorial calendar (which is sent with guidelines). Please do not send articles of national or consumer interest."

$ $ TREE CARE INDUSTRY MAGAZINE, Tree Care Industry Association, 3 Perimeter Rd. Unit 1, Manchester NH 03103-3341. (800)733-2622 or (603)314-5380. E-mail: garvin@treecareindustry.org. Website: www.treecareindustry.org. Mark Garvin, editor. **50% freelance written.** Monthly magazine covering tree care and landscape maintenance. Estab. 1990. Circ. 28,500. Pays within 30 days of publication. Publishes ms an average of 3 months after acceptance. Byline given. Buys first North American serial, electronic rights. Editorial lead time 10 weeks. Submit seasonal material 3 months in advance. Accepts queries by mail, e-mail, fax, phone. Responds in 2 weeks to queries; 2 months to mss. Sample copy for 9×12 SAE and 6 first-class stamps. Writer's guidelines free.

Nonfiction: Book excerpts, historical/nostalgic, interview/profile, new product, technical. **Buys 40 mss/year.** Query with published clips. Length: 900-3,500 words. **Pays negotiable rate.**

Photos: Send photos with submission. Reviews prints. Buys one-time and web rights. Negotiate payment individually. Captions, identification of subjects required.

Columns/Departments: Management Exchange (business management-related); 1,200-1,800 words; Industry Innovations (inventions), 1,200 words; From The Field (OP/ED from practitioners), 600 words. **Buys 40 mss/year.** Send complete ms. **Pays $100 and up.**

Tips: "Preference is given to writers with background and knowledge of the tree care industry; our focus is relatively narrow."

GOVERNMENT & PUBLIC SERVICE

Listed here are journals for people who provide governmental services at the local, state, or federal level or for those who work in franchised utilities. Journals for city managers, politicians, bureaucratic decision makers, civil servants, firefighters, police officers, public administrators, urban transit managers, and utilities managers are listed in this section.

$ AMERICAN FIRE JOURNAL, Fire Publications, Inc., 9072 Artesia Blvd., Bellflower CA 90706. (562)866-1664. Fax: (562)867-6434. E-mail: afjm@accessl.net. Website: www.americanfirejournal.com. Editor: Carol Carlsen Brooks. **Contact:** John Ackerman, publisher. **90% freelance written.** Monthly magazine covering fire service. "Written by firefighters for firefighters." Estab. 1940s. Circ. 6,000. Pays on publication. Publishes ms an average of 6 months after acceptance. Byline given. Buys first rights. Editorial lead time 3 months. Submit seasonal material 3 months in advance. Accepts queries by mail, e-mail, fax, phone. Responds in 2 weeks to queries; 2 months to mss. Sample copy for $3.50. Writer's guidelines free.

Nonfiction: Historical/nostalgic, how-to, new product, opinion, photo feature, technical. **Buys 50 mss/year.** Send complete ms. Any length. **Pays $150 maximum.**

Photos: Send photos with submission. Reviews contact sheets, negatives, transparencies, prints (any size). Buys one-time rights. Offers $5-50/photo. Captions required.

Columns/Departments: Hot Flashes (news/current events), 100-300 words; Innovations (new firefighting tricks and techniques), 300-1,000 words. Also, Important Happenings. **Buys 2-4 mss/year.** Send complete ms. **Pays $10 maximum.**

Fillers: Anecdotes, facts, newsbreaks. **Buys 2-4/year.** Length: 300-1,000 words. **Pays $25 maximum.**

Tips: "Content of articles is generally technical, tactical, educational or related to fire service legislation, current events or recent emergency incidents. We do not publish fiction or people profiles. We do, however, accept manuscripts for a monthly column of fire-service-related humor. Your punctuation, grammar and spelling are not our primary concerns. We have editors to correct these. We are more interested in your expertise, knowledge and experience in fire service subjects. However, it is important to spell names, places and organizations correctly, as our editors may not be familiar with them. Do not include opinions (unless you are submitting a Guest Editorial), unsubstantiated statements or untested tactics in your article. Accuracy is essential. Be sure of your facts, and always attribute information and identify sources."

$ CHIEF OF POLICE MAGAZINE, National Association of Chiefs of Police, 3801 Biscayne Blvd., Miami FL 33137. (305)573-0070. Fax: (305)573-9819. E-mail: policeinfo@aphf.org. Website: www.aphf.org. **Contact:** Jim Gordon, executive editor. Bimonthly journal for law enforcement commanders (command ranks). Circ. 13,500. **Pays on acceptance.** Publishes ms an average of 6 months after acceptance. Byline given. Buys first rights. Submit seasonal material 6 months in advance. Accepts queries by mail, e-mail, fax. Accepts simultaneous submissions. Responds in 2 weeks to queries. Sample copy for $3 and 9×12 SAE with 5 first-class stamps. Writer's guidelines online.

O─ Break in with "a story concerning command officers or police family survivors."

Nonfiction: "We want stories about interesting police cases and stories on any law enforcement subject or program that is positive in nature." General interest, historical/nostalgic, how-to, humor, inspirational, interview/profile, new product, personal experience, photo feature, religious, technical. "No exposé types or anti-police." **Buys 50 mss/year.** Send complete ms. Length: 600-2,500 words. **Pays $25-75 for assigned articles; $25-100 for unsolicited articles.** Sometimes pays expenses of writers on assignment.

Photos: Send photos with submission. Reviews 5×6 prints. Buys one-time rights. Pays $5-10 for b&w; $10-25 for color. Captions required.

Columns/Departments: New Police (police equipment shown and tests), 200-600 words. **Buys 6 mss/year.** Send complete ms. **Pays $5-25.**

Fillers: Anecdotes, short humor, law-oriented cartoons. **Buys 100/year.** Length: 100-1,600 words. **Pays $5-25.**

Tips: "Writers need only contact law enforcement officers right in their own areas and we would be delighted. We want to recognize good commanding officers from sergeant and above who are involved with the community. Pictures of the subject or the department are essential and can be snapshots. We are looking for interviews with police chiefs and sheriffs on command level with photos."

$ $ CORRECTIONS TECHNOLOGY & MANAGEMENT, Hendon Publishing, Inc., 130 Waukegan Rd., Deerfield IL 60015. (847)444-3300. Fax: (847)444-3333. E-mail: tcaestecker@hendonpub.com. Website: www.ctmmag.com. **Contact:** Tom Caestecker, assistant editor. **40% freelance written.** Magazine covering correctional facility management. "We focus on positive stories of corrections professionals doing their job. For stories...lots of quotes, dramatic photos. Make it real. Make it useful." Estab. 1997. Circ. 15,000. Pays 1 month after publication. Publishes ms an average of 3 months after acceptance. Byline given. Buys first North American serial rights. Editorial lead time 4 months. Submit seasonal material 6 months in advance. Responds in 1 month to mss. Sample copy for 9×12 SAE and 6 first-class stamps. Writer's guidelines online.

Nonfiction: Facility design, technology, management, safety, trainings, interview/profile, photo features. "Nothing 'general market.' Must be corrections-specific." **Buys 30 mss/year.** Query with published clips. Length: 2,000-2,500 words.

Photos: Send photos with submission. Reviews transparencies, 8×10 prints. Buys all rights. Negotiates payment individually. Captions, identification of subjects, model releases required.

Columns/Departments: Corrections Profile (spotlight on one facility), 2,000 words; Tactical Profile (products in corrections tactics), 1,000 words. **Buys 3 mss/year.** Query with published clips. **Pays 10-15¢/word.**

$ $ COUNTY, Texas Association of Counties, P.O. Box 2131, Austin TX 78768. (512)478-8753. Fax: (512)481-1240. E-mail: jiml@county.org. Website: www.county.org. **Contact:** Jim Lewis, editor. **15% freelance written.** Bimonthly magazine covering county and state government in Texas. "We provide elected and appointed county officials with insights and information that helps them do their jobs and enhances communications among the independent office-holders in the courthouse." Estab. 1988. Circ. 5,500. **Pays on acceptance.** Publishes ms an average of 2 months after acceptance. Byline given. Makes work-for-hire assignments. Editorial lead time 2 months. Submit seasonal material 4 months in advance. Accepts queries by mail, e-mail, phone. Responds in 2 weeks to queries; 1 month to mss. Sample copy and writer's guidelines for 8×10 SAE with 3 first-class stamps.

Nonfiction: Historical/nostalgic, photo feature, government innovations. **Buys 5 mss/year.** Query with published clips. Length: 1,000-3,000 words. **Pays $300-500.** Sometimes pays expenses of writers on assignment.

Photos: State availability with submission. Buys all rights. Negotiates payment individually. Captions, identification of subjects, model releases required.

Columns/Departments: Safety; Human Resources; Risk Management (all directed toward education of Texas county officials), maximum length 1,000 words. **Buys 2 mss/year.** Query with published clips. **Pays $300.**

Tips: "Identify innovative practices or developing trends that affect Texas county officials and have the basic journalism skills to write a multi-sourced, informative feature."

$ $ FIRE CHIEF, Primedia Business, 330 N. Wabash, Suite 2300, Chicago IL 60611. (312)595-1080. Fax: (312)595-0295. E-mail: jwilmoth@primediabusiness.com. Website: www.firechief.com. **Contact:** Janet Wilmoth, editor. **60% freelance written.** Monthly magazine. "*Fire Chief* is the management magazine of the fire service, addressing the administrative, personnel, training, prevention/education, professional development and operational issues faced by chiefs and other fire officers, whether in paid, volunteer, or combination departments. We're potentially interested in any article that can help them do their jobs better, whether that's as incident commanders, financial managers, supervisors, leaders, trainers, planners, or ambassadors to municipal officials or the public." Estab. 1956. Circ. 53,000. Pays on publication. Publishes ms an average of 6 months after acceptance. Byline given. Kill fee negotiable. Buys first, one-time, second serial (reprint), all rights. Editorial lead time 2 months. Submit seasonal material 4 months in advance. Accepts queries by mail, e-mail, fax. Responds in 1 month to queries; 2 months to mss. Sample copy and writer's guidelines free or online.

Nonfiction: "If your department has made some changes in its structure, budget, mission, or organizational culture (or really did reinvent itself in a serious way), an account of that process, including the mistakes made and lessons learned, could be a winner. Similarly, if you've observed certain things that fire departments typically could do a lot better and you think you have the solution, let us know." How-to, technical. **Buys 50-60 mss/year.** Query with published clips. Length: 1,500-8,000 words. **Pays $50-400.** Sometimes pays expenses of writers on assignment.

Photos: State availability with submission. Reviews transparencies, prints. Buys one-time or reprint rights. Captions, identification of subjects required.

Columns/Departments: Training Perspectives; EMS Viewpoints; Sound Off; Volunteer Voice, all 1,000-1,800 words.

Tips: "Writers who are unfamiliar with the fire service are very unlikely to place anything with us. Many pieces that we reject are either too unfocused or too abstract. We want articles that help keep fire chiefs well-informed and effective at their jobs."

$ $ FIREHOUSE MAGAZINE, Cygnus Business Media, 445 Broad Hollow Rd., Suite 21, Melville NY 11747. (631)845-2700. Fax: (631)845-7109. E-mail: editors@firehouse.com. Website: www.firehouse.com. Editor-in-Chief: Harvey Eisner. **Contact:** Peter Matthews, assistant editor. **85% freelance written.** Works with a small number of new/unpublished writers each year. Monthly magazine. "*Firehouse* covers major fires nationwide, controversial issues and trends in the fire service, the latest firefighting equipment and methods of firefighting, historical fires, firefighting history and memorabilia. Fire-related books, fire safety education, hazardous materials incidents and the emergency medical services are also covered." Estab. 1976. Circ. 127,000. Pays on publication. Byline given. Accepts queries by mail, e-mail, fax. Sample copy for 9×12 SAE and 8 first-class stamps. Writer's guidelines online.

Nonfiction: Book excerpts (of recent books on fire, EMS and hazardous materials), historical/nostalgic (great fires in history, fire collectibles, the fire service of yesteryear), how-to (fight certain kinds of fires, buy and maintain equipment, run a fire department), technical (on almost any phase of firefighting, techniques, equipment, training, administration), trends in the fire service. No profiles of people or departments that are not unusual or innovative, reports of nonmajor fires, articles not slanted toward firefighters' interests. No poetry. **Buys 100 mss/year.** Query with or without published clips. Length: 500-3,000 words. **Pays $50-400 for assigned articles.**

Photos: Send photos with submission. Pays $25-200 for transparencies and color prints. Cannot accept negatives. Captions, identification of subjects required.

Columns/Departments: Training (effective methods); Book Reviews; Fire Safety (how departments teach fire safety to the public); Communicating (PR, dispatching); Arson (efforts to combat it). Length: 750-1,000. **Buys 50 mss/year.** Query or send complete ms. **Pays $100-300.**

Tips: "Have excellent fire service credentials and be able to offer our readers new information. Read the magazine to get a full understanding of the subject matter, the writing style and the readers before sending a query or manuscript. Send photos with manuscript or indicate sources for photos. Be sure to focus articles on firefighters."

$ FOREIGN SERVICE JOURNAL, 2101 E. St. NW, Washington DC 20037-2990. (202)338-4045. Fax: (202)338-6820. E-mail: dorman@afsa.org. Website: www.afsa.org. **Contact:** Shawn Dorman. **75% freelance written.** Monthly magazine for Foreign Service personnel and others interested in foreign affairs and related subjects. Estab. 1924. Pays on publication. Publishes ms an average of 3 months after acceptance. Byline given. Buys first North American serial rights. Accepts queries by mail, e-mail, fax. Responds in 1 month to queries. Sample copy for $3.50 and 10×12 SAE with 6 first-class stamps. Writer's guidelines for #10 SASE.

O→ Break in through "Postcard from Abroad—short items (600 words) on life abroad."

Nonfiction: Uses articles on "diplomacy, professional concerns of the State Department and Foreign Service, diplomatic history and articles on Foreign Service experiences. Much of our material is contributed by those working in the profession. Informed outside contributions are welcomed, however." Essays, exposé, humor, opinion, personal experience. **Buys 15-20 unsolicited mss/year.** Query. Length: 1,000-3,000 words. **Offers honoraria.**

Tips: "We're more likely to want your article if it has something to do with diplomacy or U.S. foreign policy."

$ $ THE JOURNAL OF SAFE MANAGEMENT OF DISRUPTIVE AND ASSAULTIVE BEHAVIOR, Crisis Prevention Institute, Inc., 3315-K N. 124th St., Brookfield WI 53005. Fax: (262)783-5906. E-mail: info@crisisprevention.com. Website: www.crisisprevention.com. **Contact:** Diana B. Kohn, editor/advertising manager. **20% freelance written.** Semiannual journal covering safe management of disruptive and assaultive behavior. "Our audience is human service and business professionals concerned about workplace violence issues. *CPI* is the world leader in violence prevention training." Estab. 1980. Circ. 12,000. Pays on publication. Publishes ms an average of 6 months after acceptance. Byline given. Offers 50% kill fee. Buys one-time, second serial (reprint) rights. Editorial lead time 6 months. Submit seasonal material 3 months in advance. Responds in 1 month to queries. Sample copy and writer's guidelines free.

Nonfiction: "Each issue is specifically devoted to one topic. Inquire about topics by e-mail." Interview/profile, new product, opinion, personal experience, research. Inquire for editorial calendar. **Buys 5-10 mss/year.** Query. Length: 1,500-3,000 words. **Pays $50-300 for assigned articles; $50-100 for unsolicited articles.**

Tips: "For more information on CPI, please refer to our website."

$ $ LAW AND ORDER, Hendon Co., 130 N. Waukegan Rd., Deerfield IL 60015. (847)444-3300. Fax: (847)444-3333. E-mail: esanow@hendonpub.com. Website: www.lawandordermag.com. **Contact:** Ed Sanow, editor-in-chief. **90% freelance written.** Prefers to work with published/established writers. Monthly magazine covering the administration and operation of law enforcement agencies, directed to police chiefs, sheriffs, and supervisors. Estab. 1953. Circ. 42,000. Pays on publication. Publishes ms an average of 6 months after acceptance. Byline given. Buys first North American serial rights. Submit seasonal material 3 months in advance. Accepts queries by mail, e-mail, fax, phone. Responds in 1 month to queries. Sample copy for 9×12 SAE. Writer's guidelines online.

Nonfiction: General police interest. How-to (do specific police assignments), new product (how applied in police operation), technical (specific police operation). Special issues: Weapons (January); Buyers Guide (February); S.W.A.T. (March); Community Relations (April); Science & Technology (May); Training (June); Mobile Patrol (July); Communications (August); Uniforms (September); IACP (October); Investigative (November); Computing & the Internet (December). No articles dealing with courts (legal field) or convicted prisoners. No nostalgic, financial, travel or recreational material. **Buys 150 mss/year.** Query; no simultaneous queries. Length: 2,000-3,000 words. **Pays 10-25¢/word.**

Photos: Send photos with submission. Reviews transparencies, prints. Buys all rights. Pays $25-40/photo. Identification of subjects required.

Tips: "*L&O* is a respected magazine that provides up-to-date information that police chiefs can use. Writers must know their subject as it applies to this field. Case histories are well received. We are upgrading editorial quality—stories *must* show some understanding of the law enforcement field. A frequent mistake is not getting photographs to accompany article."

$ $ LAW ENFORCEMENT TECHNOLOGY, Cygnus Business Media, P.O. Box 803, 1233 Janesville Ave., Fort Atkinson WI 53538-0803.. (920)563-1726. Fax: (920)563-1702. E-mail: ronnie.garrett@cygnuspub.com. Editor: Ronnie Garrett. **50% freelance written.** Monthly magazine covering police management and technology. Estab. 1974. Circ. 35,000. Pays on publication. Publishes ms an average of 6 months after acceptance. Byline given. Offers 25% kill fee. Buys first North American serial rights. Editorial lead time 6 months. Submit seasonal material 6 months in advance. Responds in 1 month to queries; 2 months to mss. Writer's guidelines for #10 SASE.

Nonfiction: Book excerpts, how-to, interview/profile, photo feature, police management and training. **Buys 15 mss/year.** Query. Length: 800-1,800 words. **Pays $75-400 for assigned articles.**

Reprints: Send ms with rights for sale noted and information about when and where the material previously appeared. Payment negotiable.

Photos: Send photos with submission. Reviews contact sheets, negatives, 5×7 or 8×10 prints. Buys one-time rights. Offers no additional payment for photos accepted with ms. Captions required.

Tips: "Writer should have background in police work or currently work for a police agency. Most of our articles are technical or supervisory in nature. Please query first after looking at a sample copy."

$ $ NATIONAL FIRE & RESCUE, SpecComm International, Inc., 5808 Faringdon Place, Suite 200, Raleigh NC 27609. (919)872-5040. Fax: (919)876-6531. E-mail: editor@nfrmag.com. Website: www.nfrmag.com. **Contact:** Phill Powell, editor. **80% freelance written.** "*National Fire & Rescue* is a bimonthly magazine devoted to informing the nation's fire and rescue services, with special emphasis on fire departments serving communities of less than 100,000. It is the *Popular Science* for fire and rescue with easy-to-understand information on science, technology, and training." Estab. 1980. Circ. 30,000. Pays on publication. Publishes ms an average of 5 months after acceptance. Byline given. Offers 50% kill fee. Buys first North American serial rights. Editorial lead time 2 months. Submit seasonal material 3 months in advance. Accepts simultaneous submissions. Responds in 1 month to queries. Call for writer's guidelines.

Nonfiction: Book excerpts, how-to, humor, inspirational, interview/profile, new product, personal experience, photo feature. No pieces marketing specific products or services. **Buys 40 mss/year.** Query with published clips. Length: 600-2,000 words. **Pays $100-350 for assigned articles; $100-200 for unsolicited articles.** Pays expenses of writers on assignment.

Photos: State availability with submission. Buys one-time rights. Offers $50-200/photo. Identification of subjects required.

Columns/Departments: Leadership (management); Training; Special Operations, all 800 words. **Buys 16 mss/year.** Send complete ms. **Pays $100-200.**

Tips: "Discuss your story ideas with the editor."

$ $ $ $ NFPA JOURNAL, National Fire Protection Association, P.O. Box 9101, Quincy MA 02269-9101. (617)984-7567. Fax: (617)984-7090. E-mail: nfpajournal@nfpa.org. Website: www.nfpa.org. Publisher: Kathie Robinson. **Contact:** John Nicholson, managing editor. **50% freelance written.** Bimonthly magazine covering fire safety, fire science, fire engineering. "The *NFPA Journal*, the official journal of the NFPA, reaches all of the association's various fire safety professionals. Covering major topics in fire protection and suppression, the bimonthly *Journal* carries investigation reports; special NFPA statistical studies on large-loss and multiple-death fires, fire fighter deaths and injuries, and other annual reports; articles on fire protection advances and public education; and information of interest to NFPA members. Fire fighting techniques and fire department management are also covered." Estab. 1969. Circ. 74,000. **Pays on acceptance.** Publishes ms an average of 1 year after acceptance. Byline given. Buys all rights. Editorial lead time 6 months. Accepts queries by e-mail, fax. Sample copy and writer's guidelines free. Writer's guidelines online.

Nonfiction: Technical. No fiction, product pieces or human interest. **Buys 10 mss/year.** Query. Length: 2,000-2,500 words. **Pays $1,200-2,500 for assigned articles.** Sometimes pays expenses of writers on assignment.

Photos: State availability with submission. Buys one-time rights. Negotiates payment individually. Captions, identification of subjects, model releases required.

Tips: "Query or call. Be familiar with our publication and audience. We happily send out sample issues and guidelines. Because we are a peer-reviewed journal, we can not endorse or promote particular products—no infomercials please! We appreciate and value quality writers who can provide well-written material on technical subjects related to fire and life safety."

$ $ 9-1-1 MAGAZINE, Official Publications, Inc., 18201 Weston Place, Tustin CA 92780-2251. (714)544-7776. Fax: (714)838-9233. E-mail: publisher@9-1-1magazine.com. Website: www.9-1-1magazine.com. **Contact:** Randall Larson, editor. **85% freelance written.** Bimonthly magazine for knowledgeable emergency communications professionals and those associated with this respectful profession. "Serving law enforcement, fire and emergency medical services, *9-1-1 Magazine* provides valuable information to readers in all aspects of the public safety communications and response community. Each issue contains a blending of product-related, technical, operational, and people-oriented stories, covering the skills, training, and equipment which these professionals have in common." Estab. 1989. Circ. 20,000. Pays on publication. Publishes ms an average of 4-6 months after acceptance. Byline given. Offers 20% kill fee. Buys one-time, second serial (reprint) rights. Accepts queries by mail, e-mail, fax. Responds in 1 month to queries; 2 months to mss. Sample copy for 9×12 SAE and 5 first-class stamps. Writer's guidelines online.

Nonfiction: New product, photo feature, technical, incident report. **Buys 20-30 mss/year.** Query with SASE or by e-mail. We prefer queries, but will look at manuscripts on speculation. Most positive responses to queries are considered on spec, but occasionally we will make assignments. Length: 1,000-2,500 words. **Pays 10¢/word.**

Photos: Send photos with submission. Reviews color transparencies, prints, hi-res digital (300 dpi). Buys one-time rights. Offers $50-100/interior, $300/cover. Captions, identification of subjects required.

Fillers: Cartoons. **Buys 6/year. Pays $25.**

The online version of this magazine contains material not found in the print version.

Tips: "We are looking for writers knowledgable in this field. As a trade magazine, stories should be geared for professionals in the emergency services and dispatch field, not the lay public. We seldom use poetry or fiction. Our primary considerations in selecting material are: quality, appropriateness of material, brevity, knowledge of our readership, accuracy, accompanying photography, originality, wit and humor, a clear direction and vision, and proper use of language."

$ $ $ PLANNING, American Planning Association, 122 S. Michigan Ave., Suite 1600, Chicago IL 60603. (312)431-9100. Fax: (312)431-9985. E-mail: slewis@planning.org. Website: www.planning.org. **Contact:** Sylvia Lewis, editor. **25%**

freelance written. Monthly magazine emphasizing urban planning for adult, college-educated readers who are regional and urban planners in city, state or federal agencies or in private business or university faculty or students. Estab. 1972. Circ. 35,000. Pays on publication. Publishes ms an average of 2 months after acceptance. Byline given. Buys all rights. Accepts queries by mail, e-mail, fax. Responds in 5 weeks to queries. Sample copy and writer's guidelines for 9×12 SAE with 5 first-class stamps. Writer's guidelines online.

Nonfiction: "It's best to query with a fairly detailed, 1-page letter or e-mail. We'll consider any article that's well written and relevant to our audience. Articles have a better chance if they are timely and related to planning and land use and if they appeal to a national audience. All articles should be written in magazine feature style." Exposé (on government or business, but topics related to planning, housing, land use, zoning), general interest (trend stories on cities, land use, government), how-to (successful government or citizen efforts in planning, innovations, concepts that have been applied), technical (detailed articles on the nitty-gritty of planning, zoning, transportation but no footnotes or mathematical models). Special issues: Transportation Issue (May 2003); Technology Issue (July 2003). Also needs news stories up to 500 words. **Buys 36 features and 24 news story mss/year.** Length: 500-2,000 words. **Pays $150-1,000.**

Photos: "We prefer that authors supply their own photos, but we sometimes take our own or arrange for them in other ways." State availability with submission. Buys one-time rights. Pays $100 minimum for photos used on inside pages and $300 for cover photos. Captions required.

$ $ POLICE AND SECURITY NEWS, DAYS Communications, Inc., 1208 Juniper St., Quakertown PA 18951-1520. (215)538-1240. Fax: (215)538-1208. E-mail: jdevery@policeandsecuritynews.com. **Contact:** James Devery, editor. **40% freelance written.** Bimonthly tabloid on public law enforcement and private security. "Our publication is designed to provide educational and entertaining information directed toward management level. Technical information written for the expert in a manner that the nonexpert can understand." Estab. 1984. Circ. 22,000. Pays on publication. Publishes ms an average of 2 months after acceptance. Byline given. Buys first North American serial rights. Accepts queries by mail, e-mail, fax, phone. Accepts simultaneous submissions. Sample copy and writer's guidelines for 9×12 SAE with $2.18 postage.

Nonfiction: Al Menear, articles editor. Exposé, historical/nostalgic, how-to, humor, interview/profile, opinion, personal experience, photo feature, technical. **Buys 12 mss/year.** Query. Length: 200-4,000 words. **Pays 10¢/word. Sometimes pays in trade-out of services.**

Reprints: Send tearsheet, photocopy or typed ms with rights for sale noted and information about when and where the material previously appeared.

Photos: State availability with submission. Reviews 3×5 prints. Buys one-time rights. Offers $10-50/photo.

Fillers: Facts, newsbreaks, short humor. **Buys 6/year.** Length: 200-2,000 words. **Pays 10¢/word.**

N $ TRANSACTION/SOCIETY, Bldg. 4051, Rutgers University, New Brunswick NJ 08903. (732)445-2280, ext. 83. Fax: (732)445-3138. E-mail: ihorowitz@transactionpub.com. Website: www.transactionpub.com. Publisher: Jonathan B. Imber. **Contact:** Irving Louis Horowitz, editor. **10% freelance written.** Prefers to work with published/established writers. Bimonthly magazine for social scientists (policymakers with training in sociology, political issues, and economics). Estab. 1962. Circ. 15,000. Pays on publication. Publishes ms an average of 6 months after acceptance. Byline given. Buys all rights. Responds in 3 months to queries. Sample copy and writer's guidelines for 9×12 SAE with 5 first-class stamps.

Nonfiction: Andrew McIntosh, managing editor. "Articles of wide interest in areas of specific interest to the social science community. Must have an awareness of problems and issues in education, population, and urbanization that are not widely reported. Articles on overpopulation, terrorism, international organizations." Book excerpts, essays, interview/profile, photo feature. No general think pieces. Query. **Pays for assigned articles only.**

Photos: Douglas Harper, photo editor. Pays $200 for photographic essays done on assignment or upon publication.

Tips: "Submit an article on a thoroughly unique subject, written with good literary quality. Present new ideas and research findings in a readable and useful manner. A frequent mistake is writing to satisfy a journal, rather than the intrinsic requirements of the story itself. Avoid posturing and editorializing."

GROCERIES & FOOD PRODUCTS

In this section are publications for grocers, food wholesalers, processors, warehouse owners, caterers, institutional managers, and suppliers of grocery store equipment. See the section on Confectionery & Snack Foods for bakery and candy industry magazines.

$ AUTOMATIC MERCHANDISER MAGAZINE, Cygnus Business Media, P.O. Box 803, Fort Atkinson WI 53538. (800)547-7377. Fax: (920)568-2305. E-mail: stacey.meacham@amonline.com. Website: www.amonline.com. Editor: Elliot Maras. **Contact:** Stacey Meacham, managing editor. **30% freelance written.** Monthly magazine covering vending and office coffee. Estab. 1940. Circ. 16,000. **Pays on acceptance.** Byline given. Buys first rights. Editorial lead time 1 months. Accepts queries by mail, e-mail, fax. Accepts simultaneous submissions. Sample copy online.

$ $ $ DISTRIBUTION CHANNELS, AWMA's Magazine for Candy, Tobacco, Grocery, and General Merchandise Marketers, American Wholesale Marketers Association, 1128 16th St. NW, Washington DC 20036. (202)463-2124. Fax: (202)467-0559. E-mail: tracic@awmanet.org. Website: www.awmanet.org. **Contact:** Traci Carneal, editor-in-chief. **75% freelance written.** Magazine published 10 times/year. "We cover trends in candy, tobacco, groceries, beverages, snacks and other product categories found in convenience stores, grocery stores, and drugstores, plus distribution topics. Contributors should have prior experience writing about the food, retail, and/or distribution industries. Editorial includes a mix of columns, departments, and features (2-6 pages). We also cover AWMA programs." Estab. 1948. Circ. 10,000.

Pays on acceptance. Publishes ms an average of 2 months after acceptance. Byline given. Editorial lead time 4 months. Accepts queries by mail, e-mail, fax. Writer's guidelines online.

Nonfiction: How-to, technical, industry trends; also profiles of distribution firms. No comics, jokes, poems, or other fillers. **Buys 80 mss/year.** Query with published clips. Length: 1,200-3,600 words. **Pays $200-1,200 (generally).** Sometimes pays industry members who author articles. Pays expenses of writers on assignment.

Photos: Authors must provide artwork (with captions) with articles.

Tips: "We're looking for reliable, accurate freelancers with whom we can establish a long-term working relationship. We need writers who understand this industry. We accept very few articles on speculation. Most are assigned. To consider a new writer for an assignment, we must first receive his or her résumé, at least 2 writing samples, and references. We only work with full-time freelancers."

N $ $ $ $ FOOD PRODUCT DESIGN MAGAZINE, Weeks Publishing, 3400 Dundee Rd., Suite 100, Northbrook IL 60062. (847)559-0385. Fax: (847)559-0389. E-mail: weeksfpd@aol.com. **Contact:** Lynn Kuntz, editor. **50% freelance written.** Monthly magazine covering food processing industry. "The magazine written for food technologists by food technologists. No foodservice/restaurant, consumer or recipe development." Estab. 1991. Circ. 30,000. Pays on publication. Publishes ms an average of 2 months after acceptance. Byline given. Offers 50% kill fee. Buys one-time, all rights, makes work-for-hire assignments. Editorial lead time 4 months. No queries to queries. Sample copy for 9×12 SAE and 5 first-class stamps.

Nonfiction: Technical. **Buys 30 mss/year.** Length: 1,500-7,000 words. **Pays $100-1,500.** Sometimes pays expenses of writers on assignment.

Reprints: Accepts previously published submissions depending on where it was published.

Photos: State availability with submission. Reviews transparencies, prints. Buys rights depending on photo. Offers no additional payment for photos accepted with ms. Captions required.

Columns/Departments: Pays $100-500.

Tips: "If you haven't worked in the food industry in Research & Development, or QA/QC, don't bother to call us. If you can't communicate technical information in a way that is clear, easy-to-understand and well organized, don't bother to call us. While perfect grammar is not expected, good grammar and organization is."

N $ $ FOODSERVICE DIRECTOR, VNU Business Media, 770 Broadway, New York NY 10003. (646)654-7403. Fax: (646)654-7410. Editor-In-Chief: James Pond. Feature Editor: Karen Weisberg. News Editor: Jennifer Alexis. **20% freelance written.** Monthly tabloid covering noncommercial foodservice operations for operators of kitchens and dining halls in schools, colleges, hospitals/health care, office and plant cafeterias, military, airline/transportation, correctional institutions. Estab. 1988. Circ. 45,000. Pays on publication. Byline sometimes given. Buys all rights for print and online usage. Submit seasonal material 3 months in advance. Accepts simultaneous submissions. Sample copy for free.

Nonfiction: How-to, interview/profile. **Buys 60-70 mss/year.** Query with published clips. Length: 700-900 words. **Pays $250-500.** Sometimes pays expenses of writers on assignment.

Photos: Send photos with submission. Reviews transparencies. Buys all rights. Offers no additional payment for photos accepted with ms. Identification of subjects required.

Columns/Departments: Equipment (case studies of kitchen/serving equipment in use), 700-900 words; Food (specific category studies per publication calendar), 750-900 words. **Buys 20-30 mss/year.** Query. **Pays $250-500.**

$ $ FRESH CUT MAGAZINE, The Magazine for Value-added Produce, Columbia Publishing, 417 N. 20th Ave., Yakima WA 98902. (509)248-2452. Fax: (509)248-4056. E-mail: rick@freshcut.com. **Contact:** Rick Stedman, editor. **40% freelance written.** Monthly magazine covering minimally processed fresh fruits and vegetables, packaged salads, etc. "We want informative articles about processing produce. We also want stories about how these products are sold at retail, in restaurants, etc." Estab. 1993. Circ. 18,464. Pays on publication. Publishes ms an average of 2 months after acceptance. Byline given. Buys all rights. Editorial lead time 2 months. Submit seasonal material 3 months in advance. Accepts queries by mail, e-mail, fax, phone. Responds in 1 month to queries; 2 months to mss. Sample copy for 9×12 SAE. Writer's guidelines for #10 SASE.

Nonfiction: Historical/nostalgic, new product, opinion, technical. Special issues: Retail (May); Foodservice (February, July); Packaging Technology (December). **Buys 2-4 mss/year.** Query with published clips. **Pays $5/column inch for assigned articles; $75-125 for unsolicited articles.**

Reprints: Send tearsheet with rights for sale noted and information about when and where the material previously appeared. Pays 50% of amount paid for an original article.

Photos: Send photos with submission. Reviews transparencies. Buys one-time rights. Offers no additional payment for photos accepted with ms. Identification of subjects required.

Columns/Departments: Packaging; Food Safety; Processing/Engineering. **Buys 20 mss/year.** Query. **Pays $125-200.**

Fillers: Facts. Length: 300 words maximum. **Pays $25-50.**

$ $ HEALTH PRODUCTS BUSINESS, CYGNUS Business Media, Inc., 445 Broad Hollow Rd., Suite 21, Melville NY 11747. (631)845-2700. Fax: (631)845-2723. Website: www.healthproductsbusiness.com. **Contact:** Michael Schiavetta, editor. **70% freelance written.** Monthly magazine covering natural health products. "The business magazine for natural products retailers." Estab. 1954. Circ. 18,000. Pays on publication. Publishes ms an average of 3 months after acceptance. Byline given. Buys first North American serial rights. Editorial lead time 4 months. Submit seasonal material 3 months in advance. Accepts queries by mail, fax. Sample copy for $3.

Nonfiction: Query first. **Pays $200-450 for articles on natural health retailing.**

Photos: State availability with submission.

The online version of this publication contains material not found in the print edition. Contact: Michael Schiavetta, editor.

Tips: "We are always looking for well-written features with a lot of detailed information, but new writers should always query first to receive information. We prefer writers with industry experience/interest. AP Style, a plus."

$ $ PRODUCE MERCHANDISING, Vance Publishing Corp., 10901 W. 84th Terrace, Lenexa KS 66214. (913)438-8700. Fax: (913)438-0691. E-mail: jkresin@producemerchandising.com. Website: www.producemerchandising.com. **Contact:** Janice M. Kresin, editor. **33% freelance written.** Monthly magazine. "The magazine's editorial purpose is to provide information about promotions, merchandising, and operations in the form of ideas and examples. *Produce Merchandising* is the only monthly journal on the market that is dedicated solely to produce merchandising information for retailers." Circ. 12,000. **Pays on acceptance.** Publishes ms an average of 3 months after acceptance. Byline given. Buys all rights. Editorial lead time 3 months. Accepts queries by mail. Responds in 2 weeks to queries. Sample copy for free.

Nonfiction: How-to, interview/profile, new product, photo feature, technical (contact the editor for a specific assignment). **Buys 48 mss/year.** Query with published clips. Length: 1,000-1,500 words. **Pays $200-600.** Pays expenses of writers on assignment.

Photos: State availability of or send photos with submission. Reviews color slides and 3×5 or larger prints. Buys all rights. Offers no additional payment for photos accepted with ms. Captions, identification of subjects, model releases required.

Columns/Departments: Contact editor for a specific assignment. **Buys 30 mss/year.** Query with published clips. **Pays $200-450.**

Tips: "Send in clips and contact the editor with specific story ideas. Story topics are typically outlined up to a year in advance."

$ $ WESTERN GROCER MAGAZINE, Mercury Publications Ltd., 1839 Inkster Blvd., Winnipeg MB R2X 1R3, Canada. (204)954-2085. Fax: (204)954-2057. E-mail: mp@mercury.mb.ca. Website: www.mercury.mb.ca/. Editor: Frank Yeo. **Contact:** Kristi Balon, editorial production manager. **75% freelance written.** Bimonthly magazine covering the grocery industry. Reports profiles on independent food stores, supermarkets, manufacturers and food processors, brokers, distributors and wholesalers. Estab. 1916. Circ. 15,500. Pays 30-45 days from receipt of invoice. Byline given. Offers 33% kill fee. Buys all rights. Submit seasonal material 3 months in advance. Sample copy and writer's guidelines free or by e-mail.

- Assigns stories to Canadian writers based on editorial needs of publication.

Nonfiction: How-to, interview/profile. Industry reports and profiles on companies. Query with published clips. Length: 500-9,000 words. **Pays 25-35¢/word.** Sometimes pays expenses of writers on assignment.

Photos: State availability with submission. Reviews negatives, transparencies, 3×5 prints, JPEG, EPS, or TIF files. Buys all rights. Negotiates payment individually. Captions required.

Tips: "Send an e-mailed, faxed, or mailed query outlining your experience, interests, and pay expectations. A requirement also is clippings."

HOME FURNISHINGS & HOUSEHOLD GOODS

Readers rely on these publications to learn more about new products and trends in the home furnishings and appliance trade. Magazines for consumers interested in home furnishings are listed in the Consumer Home & Garden section.

$ FINE FURNISHINGS INTERNATIONAL, G&W McNamara Publishing, 4215 White Bear Parkway, Suite 100, St. Paul MN 55110. Fax: (651)653-4308. E-mail: ffiedit@gwmcnamara.com. Website: www.ffimagazine.com. **Contact:** Esther De Hollander, managing editor. Bimonthly magazine covering the high-end furniture industry. Estab. 1997. Circ. 22,400. Pays on publication. Publishes ms an average of 3 months after acceptance. Byline given. Offers $150-250 kill fee. Buys all rights. Editorial lead time 2 months. Submit seasonal material 3 months in advance. Accepts queries by mail, e-mail. Sample copy for $6. Writer's guidelines free.

Nonfiction: Historical/nostalgic, how-to, interview/profile, technical. Query. **Pays $150.** Sometimes pays expenses of writers on assignment.

Tips: "The most helpful experience is if a writer has knowledge of interior design or, specifically, fine furniture. We already have a pool of journalists, although we welcome clips from writers who would like to be considered for assignments. Particularly if they have a profile of a high-end interior designer. Our style is professional business writing—no flowery prose. Articles tend to be to the point as our readers are busy professionals who read for information, not for leisure."

$ $ $ HOME FURNISHINGS RETAILER, National Home Furnishings Association (NHFA), P.O. Box 2396, High Point NC 27261. (336)801-6156. Fax: (336)801-6102. E-mail: tkemerly@nhfa.org. **Contact:** Trisha Kemerly, editor. **75% freelance written.** Monthly magazine published by NHFA covering the home furnishings industry. "We hope that home furnishings retailers view our magazine as a profitability tool. We want each issue to help them make money or save money." Estab. 1927. Circ. 15,000. **Pays on acceptance.** Publishes ms an average of 6 weeks after acceptance. Byline given. Buys first North American serial rights. Editorial lead time 3 months. Accepts queries by mail, e-mail. Responds in 1 month to queries. Sample copy available with proper postage. Writer's guidelines for #10 SASE.

Break in by "e-mailing queries that pertain to our market—furniture retailers. We publish articles that give our readers tangible ways to improve their business."

Nonfiction: Query with published clips. Length: 3,000-5,000 words (features). **Pays $350-500 for assigned articles.**

Photos: State availability with submission. Reviews transparencies. Buys one-time rights. Negotiates payment individually. Identification of subjects required.

Columns/Departments: Columns cover business and product trends that shape the home furnishings industry. Advertising and Marketing; Finance; Technology; Training; Creative Leadership; Law; Style and Operations. Length: 1,200-1,500 words. Query with published clips.

Tips: "Our readership includes owners of small 'ma and pa' furniture stores, executives of medium-sized chains (2-10 stores), and executives of big chains. Articles should be relevant to retailers and provide them with tangible information, ideas, and products to better their business."

$ HOME LIGHTING & ACCESSORIES, P.O. Box 2147, Clifton NJ 07015. (973)779-1600. Fax: (973)779-3242. Website: www.homelighting.com. **Contact:** Linda Longo, editor. **25% freelance written.** Prefers to work with published/established writers. Monthly magazine for lighting showrooms/department stores. Estab. 1923. Circ. 10,000. Pays on publication. Publishes ms an average of 6 months after acceptance. Buys first rights. Submit seasonal material 6 months in advance. Accepts queries by mail, e-mail. Responds in 2 months to queries. Sample copy for 9×12 SAE and 4 first-class stamps.

Nonfiction: Interview/profile (with lighting retailers), personal experience (as a businessperson involved with lighting), technical (concerning lighting or lighting design), profile (of a successful lighting retailer/lamp buyer). Special issues: Outdoor (March); Tribute To Tiffanies (August). **Buys less than 10 mss/year.** Query.

Reprints: Send tearsheet and information about when and where the material previously appeared.

Photos: State availability with submission. Offers no additional payment for 5×7 or 8×10 b&w glossy prints. Captions required.

Tips: "Have a unique perspective on retailing lamps and lighting fixtures. We often use freelancers located in a part of the country where we'd like to profile a specific business or person. Anyone who has published an article dealing with any aspect of home furnishings will have high priority."

$ WALL FASHIONS, (formerly *The Wall Paper*), G&W McNamara Publishing, 4215 White Bear Parkway, Suite 100, St. Paul MN 55110-7635. Fax: (651)653-4308. E-mail: klundquist@gwmcnamara.com. Website: www.thewallpaper.com. **Contact:** Kate Lundquist. Tabloid published 10 times/year on the wall coverings industry. Estab. 1979. Circ. 16,700. Pays on publication. Byline given. Offers $150-250 kill fee. Buys all rights. Editorial lead time 2 months. Submit seasonal material 3 months in advance. Accepts queries by mail, e-mail. Responds in 2 months to queries. Sample copy for $4. Writer's guidelines free.

Nonfiction: Historical/nostalgic, how-to, interview/profile. Query with published clips. **Pays $150.** Sometimes pays expenses of writers on assignment.

Photos: State availability with submission. Reviews 4×6 or larger transparencies, 4×6 or 8×10 prints. Buys all rights. Offers no additional payment for photos accepted with ms. Captions required.

Tips: "Most of all we need creative ideas and approaches to topics in the field of furniture and interior design. A writer needs to be knowledgeable in the field because our readers would know if information was inaccurate. We are looking mostly for features on specific topics or on installation or design."

N $ WINDOW FASHIONS, G&W McNamara Publishing, Inc., 4215 White Bear Pkwy., Suite 100, St. Paul MN 55110. Fax: (651)653-4308. E-mail: wf@gwmcnamara.com. Website: www.window-fashions.com. **Contact:** Linda Henry, senior editor. **30% freelance written.** Monthly magazine "dedicated to the advancement of the window fashions industry, *Window Fashions* Design & Education magazine provides comprehensive information on design and business principles, window fashion aesthetics and product applications. The magazine serves the window-treatment industry, including designers, retailers, dealers, specialty stores, workrooms, manufacturers, fabricators, and others associated with the field of interior design. Writers should be thoroughly knowledgable on the subject and submittals need to be comprehensive." Estab. 1981. Circ. 30,000. Pays on publication. Publishes ms an average of 3 months after acceptance. Byline given. Buys all rights. Editorial lead time 3 months. Submit seasonal material 4 months in advance. Accepts queries by mail, e-mail. Accepts simultaneous submissions. Sample copy for $5.

Nonfiction: How-to (window fashion installation), interview/profile (of designers), personal experience. "No broad topics not specific to the window fashions industry." **Buys 24 mss/year.** Query or send complete ms. Length: 800-1,000 words.

Tips: "The most helpful experience is if a writer has knowledge of interior design or, specifically, window treatments. We already have a pool of generalists, although we welcome clips from writers who would like to be considered for assignments. Our style is professional business writing—no flowery prose. Articles tend to be to the point, as our readers are busy professionals who read for information, not for leisure. Most of all we need creative ideas and approaches to topics in the field of window treatments and interior design. A writer needs to be knowledgeable in the field because our readers would know if information were inaccurate."

HOSPITALS, NURSING & NURSING HOMES

In this section are journals for medical and nonmedical nursing home personnel, clinical and hospital staffs, and medical laboratory technicians and managers. Journals publishing technical material on medical research and information for physicians in private practice are listed in the Medical category.

N $ AMERICAN JOURNAL OF NURSING, 345 Hudson St., 16th Floor, New York NY 10014. (212)886-1200. Fax: (212)886-1206. E-mail: ajn@lww.com. Website: www.nursingcenter.com. **Contact:** Diana Mason, editor-in-chief. Monthly magazine covering nursing and health care. Estab. 1900. Circ. 342,000. Pays on publication. Publishes ms an average of 6 months after acceptance. Byline given. Accepts queries by mail. Responds in 2 weeks to queries; 10 weeks to mss. Sample copy and writer's guidelines free.

Nonfiction: Practical, hands-on clinical evidence-based articles of interest to nurses in all settings; professional issues; personal experience. Now accepting commentaries, poetry, short stories, and personal essays. Opinion, personal experience.

Photos: Now accepting paintings, drawings, photos of sculpture, and other artwork. Reviews b&w and color transparencies, prints. Identification of subjects, model releases required.

Tips: "Send an outline with query letter."

$ $ $ $ HOSPITALS & HEALTH NETWORKS, Health Forum, 1 N. Franklin, 29th Floor, Chicago IL 60606. E-mail: bsantamour@healthforum.com. Website: www.hhnmag.com. **Contact:** Bill Santamour, managing editor. **25% freelance written.** Monthly magazine covering hospitals. "We are a business publication for hospital and health system executives. We use only writers who are thoroughly familiar with the hospital field. Submit résumé and up to five samples of health care-related articles. We assign all articles and do not consider manuscripts." Estab. 1926. Circ. 85,000. **Pays on acceptance.** Publishes ms an average of 3 months after acceptance. Byline given. Offers variable kill fee. Buys all rights. Editorial lead time 2-3 months. Accepts queries by e-mail. Responds in 2-4 months to queries.

Nonfiction: Interview/profile, technical. Query with published clips. Length: 350-2,000 words. **Pays $300-1,500 for assigned articles.**

Tips: "If you demonstrate via published clips that you are thoroughly familiar with the business issues facing health-care executives, and that you are a polished reporter and writer, we will consider assigning you an article for our InBox section to start out. These are generally 350 words on a specific development of interest to hospitals and health system executives. Persistence does not pay with us. Once you've sent your résumé and clips, we will review them. If we have no assignment at that time, we will keep promising freelance candidates on file for future assignments."

$ JOURNAL OF CHRISTIAN NURSING, Nurses Christian Fellowship, InterVarsity Christian Fellowship, P.O. Box 7895, Madison WI 53707-7895. (608)846-8560. E-mail: jcn.me@ivcf.org. Website: www.ncf-jcn.org. Editor: Judith Allen Shelly. **Contact:** Cathy Walker, managing editor. **30% freelance written.** Quarterly magazine covering spiritual care, ethics, crosscultural issues, etc. "Our target audience is Christian nurses in the U.S., and we are nondenominational in character. We are prolife in position. We strive to help Christian nurses view nursing practice through the eyes of faith. Articles must be relevant to Christian nursing and consistent with our statement of faith." Estab. 1984. Circ. 8,000. **Pays on acceptance.** Publishes ms an average of 1-2 years after acceptance. Byline given unless subject matter requires pseudonym. Offers 50% kill fee. Buys first, second serial (reprint) rights. Editorial lead time up to 2 years. Submit seasonal material 1 year in advance. Accepts queries by mail, e-mail. Responds in 1 month to queries; 2 months to mss. Sample copy for $5 and SAE with 4 first-class stamps. Writer's guidelines online.

Nonfiction: How-to, humor, inspirational, interview/profile, opinion, personal experience, photo feature, religious, all must be appropriate for Christian nurses. Poetry not accepted. No purely academic articles, subjects not appropriate for Christian nurses, devotionals, Bible study. **Buys 20-30 mss/year.** Send complete ms. Length: 6-12 pages (typed, double spaced). **Pays $25-80, and up to 8 complimentary copies.**

Reprints: Send tearsheet or photocopy and information about when and where the material previously appeared.

Photos: State availability of or send photos with submission. No rights purchased; all photos returned. Offers no additional payment for photos accepted with ms. Identification of subjects, model releases required.

Columns/Departments: Book Reviews (Resources). **No payment for Book Reviews.**

Tips: "Unless an author is a nurse, it will be unlikely that he/she will have an article accepted—unless it's a very interesting story about a nurse who is involved in creative ministry with a strong faith dimension."

$ $ $ LONG TERM CARE, The Ontario Long Term Care Association, 345 Renfrew Dr., Suite 102-202, Markham ON L3R 9S9, Canada. (905)470-8995. Fax: (905)470-9595. E-mail: hlrpublishing@bellnet.ca. Website: www.oltca.com. Assistant Editor: Tracey Ann Schofield. **Contact:** Heather Lang, editor. Quarterly magazine covering "practical articles of interest to staff working in a long term care setting (nursing home, retirement home); professional issues; information must be applicable to a Canadian setting; focus should be on staff and for resident well-being." Estab. 1990. Circ. 6,000. Pays on publication. Publishes ms an average of 4 months after acceptance. Byline given. Buys one-time rights. Editorial lead time 3 months. Submit seasonal material 5 months in advance. Responds in 3 months to queries. Sample copy for free. Writer's guidelines online.

Nonfiction: General interest, how-to (practical, of use to long term care practitioners), inspirational, interview/profile. No product-oriented articles. Query with published clips. Length: 800-1,500 words. **Pays up to $1,000 (Canadian).**

Reprints: Send tearsheet, photocopy or typed ms and information about when and where the material previously appeared. Pays 50% of amount paid for an original article.

Photos: Send photos with submission. Reviews contact sheets, 5×5 prints. Buys one-time rights. Offers no additional payment for photos accepted with ms. Captions, model releases required.

Columns/Departments: Resident Health (nursing, rehabilitation, food services); Resident Life (activities, volunteers, spiritual and pastoral care); Environment (housekeeping, laundry, maintenance, safety, landscape and architecture, staff health and well being), all 800 words. Query with published clips. **Pays up to $1,000 (Canadian).**

Tips: "Articles must be positive, upbeat, and contain helpful information that staff and managers working in the long term care field can use. Focus should be on staff and resident well being. Articles that highlight new ways of doing things are particularly useful. Please call the editor to discuss ideas. Must be applicable to Canadian settings."

$ NURSEWEEK, NurseWeek Publishing, 1156-C Aster Ave., Sunnyvale CA 94086. (800)859-2091. Fax: (408)249-3756. E-mail: carolb@nurseweek.com. Website: www.nurseweek.com. **Contact:** Carol Bradley, editor. *NurseWeek* is an independent biweekly news magazine supported by advertising revenue, sales of continuing education, and trade shows. Its editorial mission is to provide nurses with the latest news, resources, and opportunities to help them succeed in their lives and careers. Five regional editions: California, Mountain West, South Central, Midwest, and Great Lakes. Assigns articles. **Pays on acceptance.**

NurseWeek.com is updated daily with news content and posts new job listings on a daily basis.

$ $ $ NURSING SPECTRUM, Florida Edition, Nursing Spectrum, 1001 W. Cypress Creek Rd., Suite 330, Ft. Lauderdale FL 33309. (954)776-1455. Fax: (954)776-1456. E-mail: pclass@nursingspectrum.com. Website: www.nursingspectrum.com. **Contact:** Phyllis Class, RN, editorial director. **80% freelance written.** Biweekly magazine covering registered nursing. "We support and recognize registered nurses. All articles must have at least 1 RN in byline. We prefer articles that feature nurses in our region, but articles of interest to all nurses are welcome, too. We look for substantive, yet readable articles. Our bottom line—timely, relevant, and compelling articles that support nurses and help them excel in their clinical and professional careers." Estab. 1991. Circ. 90,000. Pays on publication. Byline given. Buys all rights. Editorial lead time 3 months. Submit seasonal material 4 months in advance. Accepts queries by mail, e-mail, fax, phone. Responds in 1 month to queries; 4 months to mss. Sample copy and writer's guidelines free. Writer's guidelines online.

"Having an original idea is paramount and the first step in writing an article. We are looking for success stories, nurses to be proud of, and progress that is helping patients. If you and your colleagues have dealt with and learned from a thorny issue, tell us how. What is new in your field? Consider your audience: all RNs, well educated, and of various specialties. Will they relate, be inspired, learn something? The best articles are both interesting and informative."

Nonfiction: General interest, how-to (career management), humor, interview/profile, personal experience, photo feature. Special issues: Critical Care; Nursing Management. "No articles that do not have at least 1 RN on the byline." **Buys 125 plus mss/year.** Length: 700-1,200 words. **Pays $50-800 for assigned articles.** Sometimes pays expenses of writers on assignment.

Photos: Buys one-time rights. Negotiates payment individually. Captions, identification of subjects, model releases required.

Columns/Departments: Perspectives in Leadership (nurse managers); Advanced Practice (advanced practice nurses); Humor Infusion (cartoon, amusing anecdotes); Career Fitness (career tips, types of careers). **Buys 75 mss/year.** Query with published clips. **Pays $50-120.**

Tips: "Write in 'magazine' style—as if talking to another RN. Use to-the-point, active language. Narrow your focus. Topics such as 'The Future of Nursing' or 'Dealing With Change' are too broad and nonspecific. Use informative but catchy titles and subheads (we can help with this). If quoting others be sure quotes are meaningful and add substance to the piece. To add vitality, you may use statistics and up-to-date references. Try to paint a complete picture, using pros and cons. Be both positive and realistic."

$ $ $ NURSING SPECTRUM, Greater Philadelphia/Tri-State edition, Nursing Spectrum, 2002 Renaissance Blvd., Suite 250, King of Prussia PA 19406. (610)292-8000. Fax: (610)292-0179. E-mail: dnovak@nursingspectrum.com. Website: www.nursingspectrum.com. **Contact:** Donna Novak, editorial director. **80% freelance written.** Biweekly magazine covering registered nursing. "We support and recognize registered nurses. All articles must have at least one RN in byline. We prefer articles that feature nurses in our region, but articles of interest to all nurses are welcome, too. We look for substantive, yet readable articles. Our bottom line—timely, relevant, and compelling articles that support nurses and help them excel in their clinical and professional careers." Estab. 1992. Circ. 74,000. Byline given. Writer's guidelines online.

$ $ $ NURSING SPECTRUM, New England edition, Nursing Spectrum, 1050 Waltham St., Suite 330, Waltham MA 02421. (781)863-2300. Fax: (781)863-6277. E-mail: jborgatti@nursingspectrum.com. Website: www.nursingspectrum.com. **Contact:** Joan Borgatti, RN, editor. **80% freelance written.** Biweekly magazine covering registered nursing. "We support and recognize registered nurses. All articles must have at least one RN in byline. We prefer articles that feature nurses in our region, but articles of interest to all nurses are welcome, too. We look for substantive, yet readable articles. Our bottom line—timely, relevant, and compelling articles that support nurses and help them excel in their clinical and professional careers." Estab. 1997. Circ. 80,000. Byline given. Accepts queries by mail, e-mail, fax, phone. Writer's guidelines online.

- See *Nursing Spectrum, Florida Edition* for article needs.

The online version carries original content not found in the print edition. Contact: Cynthia Saver, RN, editor.

$ $ $ NURSING SPECTRUM, Washington, DC/Baltimore edition, Nursing Spectrum, 803 W. Broad St., Suite 500, Falls Church VA 22046. (703)237-6515. Fax: (703)237-6299. E-mail: pmeredith@nursingspectrum.com. Website: www.nursingspectrum.com. **Contact:** Cindy Saver, RN, editor. **80% freelance written.** Biweekly journal covering registered nursing. "We support and recognize registered nurses. All articles must have at least one RN in byline. We prefer articles that feature nurses in our region, but articles of interest to all nurses are welcome, too. We look for substantive, yet readable articles. Our bottom line—timely, relevant, and compelling articles that support nurses and help them excel in their clinical and professional careers." Estab. 1990. Circ. 1 million. Writer's guidelines online.

- See *Nursing Spectrum, Florida Edition* for article needs.

$ $ NURSING2003, Lippincott Williams & Wilkins, 1111 Bethlehem Pike, P.O. Box 908, Springhouse PA 19477-0908. (215)646-8700. Fax: (215)653-0826. E-mail: nursing@lww.com. Website: www.nursing2003.com. Editor-in-Chief:

Cheryl L. Mee, RN, BC, MSN. Managing Editor: Jane Benner. **Contact:** Pat Wolf, editorial dept. **100% freelance written.** Monthly magazine "written by nurses for nurses; we look for practical advice for the direct caregiver that reflects the author's experience." "Any form acceptable, but focus must be nursing." Estab. 1971. Circ. over 300,000. Pays on publication. Publishes ms an average of 18 months after acceptance. Byline given. Offers 50% kill fee. Buys all rights. Submit seasonal material 8 months in advance. Responds in 2 weeks to queries; 3 months to mss. Sample copy for $5. Writer's guidelines online.

Nonfiction: Book excerpts, exposé, how-to (specifically as applies to nursing field), inspirational, opinion, personal experience, photo feature. No articles from patients' point of view, poetry, etc. **Buys 100 mss/year.** Query. Length: 100 words minimum. **Pays $50-400 for assigned articles.**

Reprints: Send photocopy and information about when and where the material previously appeared. Pays 50% of amount paid for an original articles.

Photos: State availability with submission. Buys all rights. Offers no additional payment for photos accepted with ms. Model releases required.

Tips: "Basically, *Nursing2003* is a how-to journal, full of hands-on, practical articles. We look for the voice of experience from authors and for articles that help our readers deal with problems they face. We're always interested in taking a look at manuscripts that fall into the following categories: clinical articles, drug articles, charting/documentation, emotional problems, legal problems, ethical dilemnas, difficult ot challenging cases."

HOTELS, MOTELS, CLUBS, RESORTS & RESTAURANTS

These publications offer trade tips and advice to hotel, club, resort, and restaurant managers, owners, and operators. Journals for manufacturers and distributors of bar and beverage supplies are listed in the Beverages & Bottling section.

$ $ BARTENDER MAGAZINE, Foley Publishing, P.O. Box 158, Liberty Corner NJ 07938. (908)766-6006. Fax: (908)766-6607. E-mail: barmag@aol.com. Website: www.bartender.com. Editor: Jaclyn M. Wilson. **Contact:** Jackie Foley, publisher. **100% freelance written.** Prefers to work with published/established writers; eager to work with new/unpublished writers. Quarterly magazine emphasizing liquor and bartending for bartenders, tavern owners, and owners of restaurants with full-service liquor licenses. Circ. 148,225. Pays on publication. Publishes ms an average of 3 months after acceptance. Byline given. Buys first North American serial, first, one-time, second serial (reprint), simultaneous, all rights. Submit seasonal material 3 months in advance. Accepts simultaneous submissions. Responds in 2 months to mss. Sample copy for 9×12 SAE and 4 first-class stamps.

Nonfiction: General interest, historical/nostalgic, how-to, humor, interview/profile (with famous bartenders or ex-bartenders), new product, opinion, personal experience, photo feature, travel, nostalgia, unique bars, new techniques, new drinking trends, bar sports, bar magic tricks. Special issues: Annual Calendar and Daily Cocktail Recipe Guide. Send complete ms and SASE. Length: 100-1,000 words.

Reprints: Send tearsheet and information about when and where the material previously appeared. Pays 25% of amount paid for an original article.

Photos: Send photos with submission. Pays $7.50-50 for 8×10 b&w glossy prints; $10-75 for 8×10 color glossy prints. Captions, model releases required.

Columns/Departments: Bar of the Month; Bartender of the Month; Drink of the Month; Creative Cocktails; Bar Sports; Quiz; Bar Art; Wine Cellar; Tips from the Top (from prominent figures in the liquor industry); One For the Road (travel); Collectors (bar or liquor-related items); Photo Essays. **Length:** 200-1,000 words. Query by mail only with SASE. **Pays $50-200.**

Fillers: Anecdotes, newsbreaks, short humor, clippings, jokes, gags. Length: 25-100 words. **Pays $5-25.**

Tips: "To break in, absolutely make sure that your work will be of interest to all bartenders across the country. Your style of writing should reflect the audience you are addressing. The most frequent mistake made by writers in completing an article for us is using the wrong subject."

$ $ CHEF, The Food Magazine for Professionals, Talcott Communications Corp., 20 W. Kinzie, 12th Floor, Chicago IL 60610. (312)849-2220. Fax: (312)849-2174. E-mail: chef@talcott.com. Website: www.chefmagazine.com. **Contact:** Editor. **40% freelance written.** Monthly magazine covering chefs in all food-service segments. "*Chef* is the one magazine that communicates food production to a commercial, professional audience in a meaningful way." Circ. 42,000. **Pays on acceptance.** Byline given. Offers 10% kill fee. Buys first North American serial, second serial (reprint) rights. Editorial lead time 2 months. Submit seasonal material 4 months in advance. Accepts queries by mail, e-mail, fax. Writer's guidelines free.

Nonfiction: Book excerpts, essays, exposé, general interest, historical/nostalgic, how-to (create a dish or perform a technique), inspirational, interview/profile, new product, opinion, personal experience, photo feature, technical. **Buys 30-50 mss/year.** Query. Length: 750-1,500 words. **Pays $250-500.** Sometimes pays expenses of writers on assignment.

Reprints: Accepts previously published submissions.

Photos: State availability with submission. Reviews transparencies. Buys one-time rights. Negotiates payment individually. Captions, identification of subjects required.

Columns/Departments: Flavor (traditional and innovative applications of a particular flavor) 1,000-1,200 words; Dish (professional chef profiles), 1,000-1,200 words; Savor (themed recipes), 1,000-1,500 words. **Buys 12-18 mss/year.** Query. **Pays $250-500.**

Tips: "Know food and apply it to the business of chefs. Always query first, *after* you've read our magazine. Tell us how your idea can be used by our readers to enhance their businesses in some way."

$ $ CHRISTIAN CAMP & CONFERENCE JOURNAL, Christian Camping International U.S.A., P.O. Box 62189, Colorado Springs CO 80962-2189. (719)260-9400. Fax: (719)260-6398. E-mail: editor@cciusa.org. Website: www.cciusa.org. **Contact:** Justin Boles, managing editor or Alison Hayhoe, editor. **75% freelance written.** Prefers to work with published/established writers. Bimonthly magazine emphasizing the broad scope of organized camping with emphasis on Christian camps and conference centers. "All who work in youth camps and adult conferences read our magazine for inspiration and to get practical help in ways to serve in their operations." Estab. 1963. Circ. 8,000. Pays on publication. Publishes ms an average of 4 months after acceptance. Byline given. Buys negotiable rights. Submit seasonal material 6 months in advance. Accepts queries by mail, e-mail. Responds in 1 month to queries. Sample copy for $2.95 plus 9×12 SASE. Writer's guidelines online.

Nonfiction: General interest (trends in organized camping in general, Christian camping in particular), how-to (anything involved with organized camping from motivating staff, to programming, to record keeping, to camper follow-up), inspirational, interview/profile (with movers and shakers in Christian camping; submit a list of basic questions first). **Buys 20-30 mss/year.** Query required. Length: 500-3,000 words. **Pays 16¢/word.**

Reprints: Send photocopy and information about when and where the material previously appeared. Pays 50% of amount paid for an original article.

Photos: Price negotiable for 35mm color transparencies.

The online version of this publication contains material not found in the print edition. Contact: Justin Boles, managing editor.

Tips: "The most frequent mistake made by writers is that they send articles unrelated to our readers. Ask for our publication guidelines first. Profiles/interviews are the best bet for freelancers."

$ CLUB MANAGEMENT, The Resource for Successful Club Operations, Finan Publishing Company, 107 W. Pacific Ave., St. Louis MO 63119-2323. (314)961-6644. Fax: (314)961-4809. E-mail: tfinan@finan.com. Website: www.club-mgmt.com. **Contact:** Tom Finan, editor. Bimonthly magazine covering club management, private club market, hospitality industry. Estab. 1925. Circ. 16,702. Pays on publication. Publishes ms an average of 2 months after acceptance. Buys first North American serial, electronic rights. Accepts queries by mail, e-mail, fax.

Nonfiction: General interest, historical/nostalgic, how-to, interview/profile, personal experience, photo feature, technical, travel. **Buys 100 mss/year.** Query with published clips. Length: 2,000-2,500 words.

Photos: State availability with submission.

Columns/Departments: Sports (private club sports: golf, tennis, yachting, fitness, etc.).

Tips: "We don't accept blind submissions. Please submit a résumé and clips of writer's work. Send copies, not originals."

$ $ EL RESTAURANTE MEXICANO, P.O. Box 2249, Oak Park IL 60303-2249. (708)445-9454. Fax: (708)445-9477. E-mail: kfurore@restmex.com. **Contact:** Kathleen Furore, editor. Bimonthly magazine covering Mexican restaurants. "*El Restaurante Mexicano* offers features and business-related articles that are geared specifically to owners and operators of Mexican, Tex-Mex, Southwestern, and Latin cuisine restaurants." Estab. 1997. Circ. 25,000. Pays on publication. Publishes ms an average of 3 months after acceptance. Byline given. Buys first North American serial rights. Responds in 2 months to queries. Sample copy for free.

Nonfiction: Looking for stories about unique Mexican restaurants and about business issues that affect Mexican restaurant owners. "No specific knowledge of food or restaurants is needed; the key qualification is to be a good reporter who knows how to slant a story toward the Mexican restaurant operator." **Buys 2-4 mss/year.** Query with published clips. Length: 800-1,500 words. **Pays $225.** Pays expenses of writers on assignment.

Tips: "Query with a story idea and tell how it pertains to Mexican restaurants."

$ $ FLORIDA HOTEL & MOTEL JOURNAL, The Official Publication of the Florida Hotel & Motel Association, Accommodations, Inc., P.O. Box 1529, Tallahassee FL 32302-1529. (850)224-2888. Fax: (850)385-5657. E-mail: journal@fhma.net. Website: www.flahotel.com. **Contact:** Lytha Page Belrose, editor. **10% freelance written.** Prefers to work with published/established writers. Monthly except combination August/September and December/January issues. Magazine acting as a reference tool for managers and owners of Florida's hotels, motels, and resorts. Estab. 1978. Circ. 8,500. Pays on publication. Publishes ms an average of 1-2 months after acceptance. Byline given. Buys first rights. Editorial lead time 1-9 months. Submit seasonal material 4-5 months in advance. Accepts queries by mail. Accepts previously published material. Responds in 2-4 months to queries. Sample copy and writer's guidelines free. Writer's guidelines online.

- Preference is given to articles that include references to member properties and general managers affiliated with the Florida Hotel and Motel Association. Since the Association acquires new members weekly, queries may be made prior to the scheduling of interviews. This does not preclude the use of materials or ideas based on non-member properties, but member property sources are preferable.

Nonfiction: How-to (pertaining to hotel management), interview/profile, new product, personal experience, technical. No travel tips or articles aimed at the traveling public, and no promotion of individual property or destination. Query with published clips. Length: 500-2,000 words. **Pays 10¢/published word.** Pays in contributor copies if the article is reprinted with persmission, or the author is a paid representative of a company which is publicized in some manner through the article. Sometimes pays expenses of writers on assignment.

Photos: State availability with submission. Buys all rights. Offers no additional payment for photos accepted with ms. Captions, identification of subjects, model releases required.

Columns/Departments: Management Monograph, 1,000 words (expert information for hotel and motel management);

Florida Scene, 700 words (Florida-specific, time-sensitive information for hotel managers or owners); National Scene, 1,000 words (USA-specific, time-sensitive information for hotel managers or owners); Fillers and Features, 1,000 words (information specific to editorial focus for the issue). Query. **Pays 10¢/word.**

Fillers: Anecdotes, facts, short humor. Length: 50-1,000 words. **Pays 10¢/word.**

Tips: "We use press releases provided to this office that fit the profile of our magazine's departments, targeting items of interest to the general managers of Florida's lodging operations. Feature articles are written based on an editorial calendar. We also publish an annual buyer's guide that provides a directory of all FH&MA member companies and allied member companies."

$ $ $ $ HOSPITALITY TECHNOLOGY, Edgell Communications, 4 Middlebury Blvd., Randolph NJ 07869. (973)252-0100. Fax: (973)252-9020. E-mail: rpaul@edgellmail.com. Website: www.htmagazine.com. **Contact:** Reid Paul, managing editor. **70% freelance written.** Magazine published 9 times/year. "We cover the technology used in foodservice and lodging. Our readers are the operators, who have significant IT responsibilities." Estab. 1996. Circ. 16,000. **Pays on acceptance.** Publishes ms an average of 1 month after acceptance. Byline given. Buys all rights, makes work-for-hire assignments. Editorial lead time 2 months. Accepts queries by mail, e-mail, fax, phone. Responds in 2 weeks to queries.

Nonfiction: How-to, interview/profile, new product, technical. Special issues: "We publish two studies each year, the Restaurant Industry Technology Study and the Lodging Industry Technology Study." No unsolicited mss. **Buys 40 mss/year.** Query with published clips. Length: 800-1,200 words. **Pays $1/word.** Sometimes pays expenses of writers on assignment.

$ $ $ PIZZA TODAY, The Monthly Professional Guide to Pizza Profits, Macfadden Protech, LLC, P.O. Box 1347, New Albany IN 47151. (812)949-0909. Fax: (812)941-9711. E-mail: jwhite@pizzatoday.com. Website: www.pizzatoday.com. **Contact:** Jeremy White, editor-in-chief. **30% freelance written.** Works only with published/established writers. Monthly magazine for the pizza industry, covering trends, features of successful pizza operators, business and management advice, etc. Estab. 1983. Circ. 40,000. **Pays on acceptance.** Publishes ms an average of 2 months after acceptance. Byline given. Offers 10-30% kill fee. Buys all rights. Submit seasonal material 3 months in advance. Accepts queries by mail, e-mail, fax. Responds in 2 months to queries; 3 weeks to mss. Sample copy for 10×13 SAE and 6 first-class stamps. Writer's guidelines for #10 SASE.

Nonfiction: Interview/profile, entrepreneurial slants, pizza production and delivery, employee training, hiring, marketing, and business management. No fillers, humor or poetry. **Buys 50 mss/year.** Length: 1,000 words. **Pays 50¢/word, occasionally more.** Sometimes pays expenses of writers on assignment.

Photos: Reviews contact sheets, negatives, transparencies, color slides, 5×7 prints. Captions required.

Tips: "We currently need articles that cover ways pizzeria operators can increase profits through the bar area."

INDUSTRIAL OPERATIONS

Industrial plant managers, executives, distributors, and buyers read these journals. Some industrial management journals are also listed under the names of specific industries. Publications for industrial supervisors are listed in Management & Supervision.

INDUSTRIAL FABRIC PRODUCTS REVIEW, Industrial Fabrics Association International, 1801 County Rd. B W., Roseville MN 55113-4061. (651)222-2508. Fax: (651)225-6966. E-mail: gdnordstrom@ifai.com. Website: www.ifai.com. **Contact:** Galynn Nordstrom, editorial director. **50% freelance written.** Monthly magazine covering industrial textiles and products made from them for company owners, salespeople, and researchers in a variety of industrial textile areas. Estab. 1915. Circ. 11,000. Pays on publication. Publishes ms an average of 2 months after acceptance. Byline given. Buys all rights. Accepts queries by mail, e-mail, phone. Responds in 1 month to queries. Editorial calendar online.

- Break in by "researching the industry/magazine audience and editorial calendar. We rarely buy material not directed specifically at our markets."

Nonfiction: Technical, marketing, and other topics related to any aspect of industrial fabric industry from fiber to finished fabric product. Special issues: New Products, New Fabrics, and Equipment. No historical or apparel-oriented articles. **Buys 50-60 mss/year.** Query with phone number. Length: 1,200-3,000 words.

Tips: "We encourage freelancers to learn our industry and make regular, solicited contributions to the magazine. We do not buy photography."

$ $ MODERN MATERIALS HANDLING, (formerly Warehousing Management), Reed Business Information, 275 Washington St., Newton MA 02458. (617)558-4569. E-mail: gforger@reedbusiness.com. Website: www.reedbusiness.com. **Contact:** Gary Forger, chief editor. **40% freelance written.** Magazine published 11 times/year covering warehousing, distribution centers, inventory. "*Warehousing Management* is an 11 times-a-year glossy national magazine read by managers of warehouses and distribution centers. We focus on lively, well-written articles telling our readers how they can achieve maximum facility productivity and efficiency. Heavy management components. We cover technology, too." Estab. 1945. Circ. 42,000. Pays on acceptance (allow 4-6 weeks for invoice processing). Publishes ms an average of 1 month after acceptance. Byline given. Editorial lead time 3 months. Accepts queries by mail, e-mail, fax. Sample copy for free. Writer's guidelines free.

- "*Warehousing Management* is now a subaddition of *Modern Materials Handling*, a magazine that has been around for 58 years."

Nonfiction: Articles must be on-point, how-to pieces for managers. How-to, new product, technical. Special issues: State-of-the-Industry Report, Peak Performer, Salary and Wage survey, Warehouse of the Year. Doesn't want to see anything that doesn't deal with our topic—warehousing. No general-interest profiles or interviews. **Buys 25 mss/year.** Query with published clips. **Pays $300-650.**

Photos: State availability with submission. Reviews negatives, transparencies, prints. Buys all rights. Offers no additional payment for photos accepted with ms. Captions, identification of subjects required.

The online magazine carries original content not found in the print edition and includes writer's guidelines.

Tips: "Learn a little about warehousing, distributors and write well. We typically don't accept specific article queries, but welcome introductory letters from journalists to whom we can assign articles. But authors are welcome to request an editorial calendar and develop article queries from it."

$ $ $ PEM PLANT ENGINEERING & MAINTENANCE, Clb Media, Inc., 3228 S. Service Rd., 2nd Floor, West Wing, Burlington ON L7N 3H8, Canada. (905)634-2100. Fax: (905)634-2238. E-mail: rrobertson@clbmedia.ca. Website: www.pem-mag.com. **Contact:** Rob Robertson, editor. **30% freelance written.** Bimonthly magazine looking for "informative articles on issues that affect plant floor operations and maintenance." Circ. 18,500. Pays on publication. Publishes ms an average of 3 months after acceptance. Byline given. Buys one-time rights. Editorial lead time 4 months. Submit seasonal material 4 months in advance. Accepts simultaneous submissions. Responds in 3 weeks to queries; 1 month to mss. Sample copy and writer's guidelines free. Writer's guidelines online.

Nonfiction: How-to (how-to keep production downtime to a minimum, how-to better operate an industrial operation), new product, technical. **Buys 6 mss/year.** Query with published clips. Length: 750-4,000 words. **Pays $500-1,400 (Canadian).** Sometimes pays expenses of writers on assignment.

Photos: State availability with submission. Reviews transparencies, prints. Buys one-time rights. Negotiates payment individually. Captions required.

Tips: "Information can be found at our website. Call us for sample issues, ideas, etc."

$ $ QUALITY DIGEST, 40 Declaration Dr., Suite 100, Chico CA 95973. (530)893-4095. Fax: (530)893-0395. E-mail: editorial@qualitydigest.com. Website: www.qualitydigest.com. **Contact:** Robert Green, managing editor. **75% freelance written.** Monthly magazine covering quality improvement. Estab. 1981. Circ. 75,000. **Pays on acceptance.** Byline given. Buys all rights. Submit seasonal material 4 months in advance. Accepts queries by mail, e-mail, fax. Accepts simultaneous submissions. Responds in 3 months to mss. Sample copy and writer's guidelines free.

Nonfiction: Book excerpts, how-to (implement quality programs and solve problems for benefits, etc.), interview/profile, opinion, personal experience, technical. **Buys 2-5 mss/year.** Query with or without published clips or send complete ms. Length: 800-3,000 words. **Pays $200-600 for assigned articles. Pays in contributor copies for unsolicited mss.** Sometimes pays expenses of writers on assignment.

Reprints: Send tearsheet and information about when and where the material previously appeared.

Photos: Send photos with submission. Reviews any size prints. Buys one-time rights. Offers no additional payment for photos accepted with ms. Captions, identification of subjects, model releases required.

The online magazine carries original content not found in the print edition and includes writer's guidelines. Contact: Dirk Dusharme.

Tips: "Please be specific in your articles. Explain what the problem was, how it was solved and what the benefits are. Tell the reader how the technique described will benefit him or her. We feature shorter, tighter, more focused articles than in the past. This means we have more articles in each issue. We're striving to present our readers with concise, how-to, easy-to-read information that makes their job easier."

$ $ WEIGHING & MEASUREMENT, WAM Publishing Co., P.O. Box 2247, Hendersonville TN 37077. (615)824-6920. Fax: (615)824-7092. E-mail: dwam34@inwave.com. Website: www.weighingandmeasurement.com. **Contact:** David M. Mathieu, editor. Bimonthly magazine for users of industrial scales. Estab. 1914. Circ. 13,900. **Pays on acceptance.** Byline given. Offers 20% kill fee. Buys all rights. Accepts queries by mail, e-mail, fax, phone. Responds in 2 weeks to queries. Sample copy for $2.

Nonfiction: Interview/profile (with presidents of companies), personal experience (guest editorials on government involvement in business, etc.), technical, Profile (about users of weighing and measurement equipment); Product reviews. **Buys 15 mss/year.** Query on technical articles; submit complete ms for general interest material. Length: 1,000-2,500 words. **Pays $175-300.**

INFORMATION SYSTEMS

These publications give computer professionals more data about their field. Consumer computer publications are listed under Personal Computers.

$ $ COMPUTER GRAPHICS WORLD, PennWell, 98 Spit Brook Rd., Nashua NH 03062-2801. (603)891-0123. Fax: (603)891-0539. E-mail: phill@pennwell.com. Website: www.cgw.com. **Contact:** Phil LoPiccolo, editor. **25% freelance written.** Monthly magazine. "*Computer Graphics World* specializes in covering computer-aided 3D modeling, animation, and visualization, and their uses in entertainment applications." Estab. 1978. Circ. 50,000. **Pays on acceptance.** Publishes ms an average of 3 months after acceptance. Byline given. Offers 20% kill fee. Buys all rights. Editorial lead time 4 months. Submit seasonal material 3 months in advance. Sample copy for free.

Nonfiction: New product, opinion, technical, user application stories, professional-user, techonology innovations. "We do not want to run articles that are geared to computer programmers. Our focus as a magazine is on users involved in specific applications." **Buys 10-20 mss/year.** Query with published clips. Length: 1,200-2,000 words. **Pays $500 minimum.**

Columns/Departments: Technology stories (describes innovation and its implication for computer graphics users), 750-

1,000 words; Reviews (offers hands-on review of important new products), 750 words. Query with published clips. **Pays $300-500.**

Tips: "Freelance writers will be most successful if they have some familiarity with computers and know how to write from a user's perspective. They do not need to be computer experts, but they do have to understand how to explain the impact of the technology and the applications in which a user is involved. Our feature section, and our application story section are open to freelancers. The trick to winning acceptance for your story is to have a well-developed idea that highlights a fascinating new trend or development in computer graphics technology or profiles a unique use of the technology by a single user or a specific class of users."

$ $ $ DESKTOP ENGINEERING, Complete Computing Resource for Engineers, Helmers Publishing, P.O. Box 874, Peterborough NH 03458. (603)924-9631. Fax: (603)924-4004. E-mail: de-editors@helmers.com. Website: www.deskeng.com. **Contact:** Jennifer M. Runyon, managing editor. **90% freelance written.** Monthly magazine covering microcomputer hardware/software for hands-on design and mechanical engineers and engineering management. Estab. 1995. Circ. 62,000. Pays on publication. Publishes ms an average of 4 months after acceptance. Byline given. Buys all rights. Editorial lead time 3 months. Accepts queries by mail, e-mail, fax, phone. Responds in 6 weeks to queries; 6 months to mss. Sample copy free; editorial calendar online. Writer's guidelines online.

Nonfiction: How-to, new product, technical, reviews. "No fluff." **Buys 120 mss/year.** Query. Length: 750-1,500 words. **Pays 60¢/word for assigned articles; negotiable for unsolicited articles.** Sometimes pays expenses of writers on assignment.

Photos: Send photos with submission. Negotiates payment individually. Captions required.

Columns/Departments: Product Briefs (new products), 50-100 words; Reviews (software, hardware), 500-1,500 words. **Buys 30 mss/year.** Query. **Payment varies.**

The online magazine carries original content not found in the print edition. Contact: Jennifer M. Runyon.

Tips: "Call the editors or e-mail them for submission tips."

$ $ $ GAME DEVELOPER, CMP Media LLC, 600 Harrison St., San Francisco CA 94107. (415)947-6000. Fax: (415)947-6090. E-mail: editors@gdmag.com. Website: www.gdmag.com. Managing Editor: Everard Strong. **Contact:** Jennifer Olsen, editor-in-chief. **90% freelance written.** Monthly magazine covering computer game development. Estab. 1994. Circ. 35,000. Pays on publication. Publishes ms an average of 3-6 months after acceptance. Byline given. Buys first North American serial, first, electronic, all rights. Editorial lead time 3 months. Submit seasonal material 4 months in advance. Accepts queries by e-mail. Sample copy for free. Writer's guidelines online.

Nonfiction: How-to, personal experience, technical. **Buys 50 mss/year.** Query. Length: 3,000-5,000 words. **Pays $150/page.**

Photos: State availability with submission.

The online magazine carries original content not found in the print edition and includes writer's guidelines. Contact: Daniel Huebner, online editor.

Tips: "We're looking for writers who are professional game developers with published game titles. We do not target the hobbyist or amateur market."

$ $ $ iSERIES NEWS, Penton Technology Media, 221 E. 29th St., Loveland CO 80538. (970)663-4700. Fax: (970)667-2321. E-mail: editors@iseriesnetwork.com. Website: www.iseriesnetwork.com. **Contact:** Sue Johnson. **40% freelance written.** Magazine published 14 times/year. "Programming, networking, IS management, technology for users of IBM AS/400 platform." Estab. 1982. Circ. 30,000 (international). Pays on publication. Publishes ms an average of 3 months after acceptance. Byline given. Offers 50% kill fee. Buys first, second serial (reprint), all rights. Editorial lead time 4 months. Submit seasonal material 4 months in advance. Accepts queries by mail, e-mail, fax, phone. Responds in 3 weeks to queries; 5 weeks to mss. Writer's guidelines online.

Nonfiction: Book excerpts, opinion, technical. **Buys 70 mss/year.** Query. Length: 1,500-2,500 words. **Pays 17-50¢/word for assigned articles.** Pays in contributor copies upon request of the author. Sometimes pays expenses of writers on assignment.

Reprints: Send photocopy. Payment negotiable.

Photos: State availability with submission. Offers no additional payment for photos accepted with ms.

Columns/Departments: Dialog Box (computer industry opinion), 1,500 words; Load'n'go (complete utility). **Buys 24 mss/year.** Query. **Pays $250-1,000.**

The online magazine carries original content not found in the print edition and includes writer's guidelines. Contact: Lori Piotrowski.

Tips: "Be familiar with IBM AS/400 computer platform."

$ JOURNAL OF INFORMATION ETHICS, McFarland & Co., Inc., Publishers, 720 Fourth Ave. S., St. Cloud State University, St. Cloud MN 56301. (320)255-4822. Fax: (320)255-4778. E-mail: hauptman@stcloudstate.edu. **Contact:** Robert Hauptman, LRTS, editor. **90% freelance written.** Semiannual scholarly journal. "Addresses ethical issues in all of the information sciences with a deliberately interdisciplinary approach. Topics range from electronic mail monitoring to library acquisition of controversial material. The *Journal*'s aim is to present thoughtful considerations of ethical dilemmas that arise in a rapidly evolving system of information exchange and dissemination." Estab. 1992. Pays on publication. Publishes ms an average of 2 years after acceptance. Byline given. Buys all rights. Submit seasonal material 8 months in advance. Accepts queries by mail, e-mail, fax, phone. Sample copy for $21. Writer's guidelines free.

Nonfiction: Essays, opinion, book reviews. **Buys 10 mss/year.** Send complete ms. Length: 500-3,500 words. **Pays $25-50 depending on length.**

Tips: "Familiarize yourself with the many areas subsumed under the rubric of information ethics, e.g., privacy, scholarly communication, errors, peer review, confidentiality, e-mail, etc. Present a well-rounded discussion of any fresh, current, or evolving ethical topic within the information sciences, or involving real-world information collection/exchange."

$ SYS ADMIN, CMP Media, LLC, 1601 W. 23rd St., Suite 200, Lawrence KS 66046. (785)838-7555. Fax: (785)841-2047. E-mail: rendsley@cmp.com. Website: www.sysadminmag.com. Editor-in-Chief: Amber Ankerholz. **Contact:** Rikki Endsley, associate managing editor. **90% freelance written.** Monthly magazine. "*Sys Admin* is written for UNIX systems administrators. Articles are practical and technical. Our authors are practicing UNIX systems administrators." Estab. 1992. Circ. 60,000. Pays on publication. Publishes ms an average of 6 months after acceptance. Byline given. Buys all rights. Editorial lead time 4 months. Accepts queries by mail, e-mail, fax, phone. Accepts simultaneous submissions. Responds in 1 month to queries. Sample copy for free. Writer's guidelines online.

Nonfiction: Technical. **Buys 40-60 mss/year.** Query. Length: 3,000 words. **Payment varies.**

$ WINDOWS DEVELOPER MAGAZINE, CMP Media LLC, 600 Harrison St., San Francisco CA 94107. (785)838-7547. Fax: (253)423-5685. E-mail: wdletter@cmp.com. Website: www.wd-mag.com. Editor: John Dorsey. **Contact:** Amy Stephens, managing editor. **90% freelance written.** Monthly magazine. "*WD* is written for advanced Windows programmers. Articles are practical, advanced, code-intensive, and not product-specific. We expect our authors to be working Windows programmers." Estab. 1990. Circ. 58,000. **Pays on acceptance.** Publishes ms an average of 6 months after acceptance. Byline given. Offers $150 kill fee. Buys all rights. Editorial lead time 3 months. Accepts simultaneous submissions. Responds in 2 weeks to queries. Sample copy for free. Writer's guidelines online.

Nonfiction: Technical. **Buys 70-80 mss/year.** Query. Length: Varies. **Payment varies.**

INSURANCE

N $ $ $ $ ADVISOR TODAY, 2901 Telestar Court, Falls Church VA 22042. (202)331-6054. Fax: (202)835-9608. Website: www.advisortoday.com. **Contact:** Ayo Mseka, editor-in-chief. **25% freelance written.** Monthly magazine covering life insurance and financial planning. "Writers must demonstrate an understanding at what insurance agents and financial advisors do to earn business and serve their clients." Estab. 1906. Circ. 110,000. Pays on acceptance or publication (by mutual agreement with editor). Publishes ms an average of 3 months after acceptance. Makes work-for-hire assignments. Editorial lead time 3 months. Submit seasonal material 6 months in advance. Accepts queries by mail, e-mail, fax, phone. Sample copy for free. Writer's guidelines online.

O→ Break in with queries for "pieces about sales techniques and product disclosure issues."

Nonfiction: Insurance. **Buys 8 mss/year.** Query. Length: 1,500-6,000 words. **Pays $800-2,000.**

Tips: Prior to January 2000, *Advisor Today* was published under the title *LAN* (Life Association News).

$ $ GEICO DIRECT, K.L. Publications, 2001 Killebrew Dr., Suite 105, Bloomington MN 55425-1879. (952)854-0155. Fax: (952)854-9440. E-mail: klpub@aol.com. **Contact:** Jan Brenny, editor. **60% freelance written.** Semiannual magazine published for the Government Employees Insurance Company (GEICO) policyholders. Estab. 1988. Circ. 4,000,000. **Pays on acceptance.** Byline given. Buys first North American serial rights. Accepts queries by mail. Responds in 3 months to queries. Writer's guidelines for #10 SASE.

O→ Break in by "submitting an idea (or editorial approach) for auto/home safety or themed regional travel—1 theme with several destinations around the country—that is unique, along with proof of research and writing ability."

Nonfiction: Americana, home and auto safety, car care, financial, lifestyle. General interest (for 50-plus audience), how-to (auto/home related only), technical (auto), travel. Query with published clips. Length: 1,000-2,200 words. **Pays $300-650.**

Photos: Reviews 35mm transparencies. Payment varies.

Columns/Departments: Moneywise; Your Car. Length: 500-600 words. Query with published clips. **Pays $175-350.**

Tips: "We prefer work from published/established writers, especially those with specialized knowledge of the insurance industry, safety issues, and automotive topics."

JEWELRY

$ $ AJM: THE AUTHORITY ON JEWELRY MANUFACTURING, Manufacturing Jewelers and Suppliers of America, 45 Royal Little Dr., Providence RI 02904. (401)274-3840. Fax: (401)274-0265. E-mail: tinaw@ajm-magazine.com. Website: www.ajm-magazine.com. **Contact:** Tina Wojtkielo, editor. **75% freelance written.** Monthly magazine. "*AJM* is a monthly magazine providing technical, marketing and business information for finished jewelry manufacturers and supporting industries." Estab. 1956. **Pays on acceptance.** Publishes ms an average of 6 months after acceptance. Byline given. all rights for limited period of 18 months Editorial lead time 1 year. Submit seasonal material 6 months in advance. Accepts queries by mail, e-mail, fax. Responds in 2 months to mss. Sample copy and writer's guidelines free.

Nonfiction: All articles should focus on jewelry manufacturing techniques, especially how-to and technical articles. How-to, new product, technical. "No generic articles for a wide variety of industries, articles for hobbyists, or articles written for a consumer audience. Our focus is professional jewelry manufacturers and designers, and articles for AJM should be carefully targeted for this audience." **Buys 40 mss/year.** Query. Length: 2,500-3,000 words. **Pays $300-500 for assigned articles.** Sometimes pays expenses of writers on assignment.

Reprints: Occasionally accepts previously published submissions. Query.

Photos: State availability with submission. Buys one-time rights. Negotiates payment individually. Captions required.

Tips: "Because our editorial content is highly focused and specific, we assign most article topics rather than relying on outside queries. We are, as a result, always seeking new writers comfortable with business and technical topics who will work with us long term and whom we can develop into 'experts' in jewelry manufacturing. We invite writers to send an introductory letter and clips highlighting business and technical writing skills if they would like to be considered for a specific assignment."

$ THE DIAMOND REGISTRY BULLETIN, 580 Fifth Ave., #806, New York NY 10036. (212)575-0444. Fax: (212)575-0722. E-mail: diamond58@aol.com. Website: www.diamondregistry.com. **Contact:** Joseph Schlussel, editor-in-chief. **50% freelance written.** Monthly newsletter. Estab. 1969. Pays on publication. Buys all rights. Submit seasonal material 1 month in advance. Accepts queries by mail, e-mail. Accepts simultaneous submissions. Responds in 3 weeks to mss. Sample copy for $5.

Nonfiction: How-to (ways to increase sales in diamonds, improve security, etc.), interview/profile (of interest to diamond dealers or jewelers), prevention advice (on crimes against jewelers). Send complete ms. Length: 50-500 words. **Pays $75-150.**

Tips: "We seek ideas to increase sales of diamonds."

$ $ THE ENGRAVERS JOURNAL, P.O. Box 318, Brighton MI 48116. (810)229-5725. Fax: (810)229-8320. E-mail: sdavis@engraversjournal.com. Website: www.engraversjournal.com. Publisher: Michael J. Davis. **Contact:** Sonja Davis, general manager. **60% freelance written.** Monthly magazine covering the recognition and identification industry (engraving, marking devices, awards, jewelry, and signage.). "We provide practical information for the education and advancement of our readers, mainly retail business owners." Estab. 1975. **Pays on acceptance.** Publishes ms an average of 1 year after acceptance. Byline given. Buys one-time rights, makes work-for-hire assignments. Accepts queries by mail, e-mail, fax. Responds in 2 weeks to mss. Sample copy for free. Writer's guidelines free.

- To break in, submit well-written, fairly in-depth general business articles. Topics and article style should focus on the small retail business owner, and should be helpful and informative.

Nonfiction: General interest (industry related), how-to (small business subjects, increase sales, develop new markets, use new sales techniques, etc.), technical. No general overviews of the industry. Length: 1,000-5,000 words. **Pays $200 and up.**

Reprints: Send tearsheet, photocopy or typed ms with rights for sale noted and information about when and where the material previously appeared. Pays 50-100% of amout paid for original article.

Photos: Send photos with submission. Pays variable rate. Captions, identification of subjects, model releases required.

Tips: "Articles should always be down to earth, practical, and thoroughly cover the subject with authority. We do not want the 'textbook' writing approach, vagueness, or theory—our readers look to us for sound practical information. We use an educational slant, publishing both trade-oriented articles and general business topics of interest to a small retail-oriented readership."

$ $ LUSTRE, The Jeweler's Magazine on Design & Style, Cygnus Publishing Co., 24 Mountain Ridge Dr., Cedar Grove NJ 07009. (631)845-2700. Fax: (631)845-7109. E-mail: lorraine.depasque@cygnuspub.com. Website: www.lustremag.com. Managing Editor: Matthew Kramer. **Contact:** Lorraine DePasque, editor-in-chief. Bimonthly trade magazine covering fine jewelry and related accessories. "*LUSTRE* is dedicated to helping the retail jeweler stock, merchandise, sell and profit from upscale, high-quality brand name and designer jewelry. Many stories are how-to. We also offer sophisticated graphics to showcase new products." Estab. 1997. Circ. 12,200. Pays on publication. Publishes ms an average of 4 months after acceptance. Byline given. Offers 50% kill fee. Buys all rights. Editorial lead time 4 months. Submit seasonal material 4 months in advance. Accepts queries by mail. Responds in 4 weeks to queries. Sample copy for free.

Nonfiction: How-to, new product. **Buys 18 mss/year.** Query with published clips. Length: 1,000-2,500 words. **Pays $500.** Sometimes pays expenses of writers on assignment.

Photos: State availability with submission. Buys one-time rights, plus usage for 1 year after publication date (but not exclusive usage). Offers no additional payment for photos accepted with ms. Captions, identification of subjects required.

Columns/Departments: Celebrity Link (tie in designer jewelry with celebrity), 500 words; Details (news about designer jewelry), 500 words; International Eye, 500 words. **Buys 8 mss/year.** Query. **Pays $500.**

Tips: "Step 1: Request an issue sent to them; call (212) 921-1091; ask for assistant. Step 2: Write a letter to Lorraine with clips. Step 3: Lorraine will call back. Background in jewelry is helpful."

N $ $ MODERN JEWELER, Cygnus Business Media, 19 W. 44th St., Suite 1405, New York NY 10036-5902. (212)921-1091. Fax: (212)921-5539. Website: www.modernjeweler.com. Managing Editor: Matthew Kramer. **Contact:** Barbara Moss, editor. **20% freelance written.** Monthly magazine covering fine jewelry and watches. Estab. 1901. Circ. 33,000. **Pays on acceptance.** Publishes ms an average of 2 months after acceptance. Byline given. Buys all rights. Editorial lead time 2 months. Submit seasonal material 2 months in advance. Accepts queries by mail, fax. Responds in 3 weeks to queries; 3 months to mss. Sample copy for SAE.

Nonfiction: Technical.

Photos: State availability with submission. Reviews transparencies, prints.

Tips: "Requires knowledge of retail business, experience in dealing with retail and manufacturing executives and analytical writing style. We don't frequently use writers who have no ties to or experience with the jewelry manufacturing industry."

JOURNALISM & WRITING

Journalism and writing magazines cover both the business and creative sides of writing. Writing publications offer inspiration and support for professional and beginning writers. Although there are many valuable writing publications that do not pay, we list those that pay for articles.

$ $ $ $ AMERICAN JOURNALISM REVIEW, 1117 Journalism Bldg., University of Maryland, College Park MD 20742. (301)405-8803. Fax: (301)405-8323. E-mail: editor@ajr.org. Website: www.ajr.org. Editor: Rem Rieder. **Contact:** Lori Robertson, managing editor. **80% freelance written.** Monthly magazine covering print, broadcast, and online journalism. "Mostly journalists subscribe. We cover ethical issues, trends in the industry, coverage that falls short." Circ. 27,000. Pays within 1 month after publication. Publishes ms an average of 2 months after acceptance. Byline given. Offers 25% kill fee. Buys first North American serial, electronic rights. Editorial lead time 1 month. Accepts queries by mail, e-mail, fax. Responds in 3 weeks to queries. Sample copy for $4.95 pre-paid or online. Writer's guidelines online.

Nonfiction: Exposé, personal experience, ethical issues. **Buys many mss/year.** Query with published clips or send complete ms. Length: 2,000-4,000 words. **Pays $1,500-2,000.** Pays expenses of writers on assignment.

Fillers: Jill Rosen, assistant managing editor. Anecdotes, facts, short humor, short pieces. Length: 150-1,000 words. **Pays $100-250.**

Tips: "Write a short story for the front-of-the-book section. We prefer queries to completed articles. Include in a page what you'd like to write about, who you'll interview, why it's important and why you should write it."

$ AUTHORSHIP, National Writers Association, 3140 S. Peoria, PMB #295, Aurora CO 80014. (303)841-0246. E-mail: sandywrter@aol.com. Website: www.nationalwriters.com. Editor: Sandy Whelchel. **Contact:** Kathe Gustafson. Quarterly magazine covering writing articles only. "Association magazine targeted to beginning and professional writers. Covers how-to, humor, marketing issues." Disk and e-mail submissions given preference. Estab. 1950s. Circ. 4,000. **Pays on acceptance.** Byline given. Buys first North American serial, second serial (reprint) rights. Editorial lead time 3 months. Submit seasonal material 6 months in advance. Accepts simultaneous submissions. Responds in 2 months to queries. Sample copy for 8½×11 envelope.

Nonfiction: Writing only. Poetry (January/February). **Buys 25 mss/year.** Query or send complete ms. Length: 900 words. **Pays $10, or discount on memberships and copies.**

Photos: State availability with submission. Reviews 5×7 prints. Buys one-time rights. Offers no additional payment for photos accepted with ms. Identification of subjects, model releases required.

Tips: "Members of National Writers Association are given preference. Writing conference in Denver every June."

$ BOOK DEALERS WORLD, North American Bookdealers Exchange, P.O. Box 606, Cottage Grove OR 97424. (561)258-2625. Fax: (561)258-2625. Website: www.bookmarketingprofits.com. **Contact:** Al Galasso, editorial director. **50% freelance written.** Quarterly magazine covering writing, self-publishing, and marketing books by mail. Circ. 20,000. Pays on publication. Publishes ms an average of 3 months after acceptance. Byline given. Buys first North American serial, second serial (reprint) rights. Accepts simultaneous submissions. Responds in 1 month to queries. Sample copy for $3.

Nonfiction: Book excerpts (writing, mail order, direct mail, publishing), how-to (home business by mail, advertising), interview/profile (of successful self-publishers), positive articles on self-publishing, new writing angles, marketing. **Buys 10 mss/year.** Send complete ms. Length: 1,000-1,500 words. **Pays $25-50.**

Reprints: Send ms with rights for sale noted and information about when and where the material previously appeared. Pays 80% of amount paid for an original article.

Columns/Departments: Print Perspective (about new magazines and newsletters); Self-Publisher (on successful self-publishers and their marketing strategy). Length: 250-1,000 words. **Buys 20 mss/year.** Send complete ms. **Pays $5-20.**

Fillers: Fillers concerning writing, publishing, or books. **Buys 6/year.** Length: 100-250 words. **Pays $3-10.**

Tips: "Query first. Get a sample copy of the magazine."

$ $ BRIDGES ROMANCE MAGAZINE, Bridges Romance Magazine, P.O. Box 150099, Denver CO 80215-0099. Fax: (303)984-0051. E-mail: web@bridgesmagazine.info. Website: www.bridgesmagazine.info. **Contact:** Becci Davis, editor-in-chief/managing editor. **65% freelance written.** Bimonthly magazine covering women's fiction reading and writing. "We are printed in a flip-format. One half of the magazine is geared toward readers of women's fiction (book reviews, author profiles, etc.) while the other half is geared toward authors. We need writing how-to's, editor/publisher profiles, researching articles, etc." Estab. 2000. Pays on publication. Publishes ms an average of 2 months after acceptance. Byline given. Buys first North American serial, one-time, second serial (reprint) rights. Editorial lead time 3 months. Submit seasonal material 4 months in advance. Accepts queries by e-mail. Accepts previously published material. Accepts simultaneous submissions. Responds in 6 weeks to queries; 3 months to mss. Sample copy for 9×12 SAE and 4 first-class stamps. Writer's guidelines online.

Nonfiction: How-to (writing technique), interview/profile, opinion. "All special projects are assigned. We don't accept freelance submissions for this purpose." Book reviews are done inhouse. **Buys 50 mss/year.** Query. Length: 500-2,000 words. **Pays 1-10¢/word for assigned articles; 1-5¢/word for unsolicited articles.**

Photos: State availability with submission. Buys one-time rights. Offers no additional payment for photos accepted with ms.

Tips: "Please make sure your topic is well researched and your ideas are clearly conveyed. Our readers don't just want to know why you think something is important, but also how your experience or expertise can benefit them. Target authors—our reader's portion is almost completely done by *Bridges* staff."

$ BYLINE, P.O. Box 5240, Edmond OK 73083-5240. (405)348-5591. E-mail: mpreston@bylinemag.com. Website: www.bylinemag.com. **Contact:** Marcia Preston, editor/publisher. **80% freelance written.** Eager to work with new/unpublished writers or experienced ones. Magazine published 11 times/year for writers and poets. Estab. 1981. **Pays on acceptance.**

Publishes ms an average of 3 months after acceptance. Byline given. Buys first North American serial rights. Editorial lead time 3-4 months. Submit seasonal material 6 months in advance. Accepts queries by mail, e-mail. Accepts simultaneous submissions. Responds in 2 months or less to queries. Sample copy for $4 postpaid. Writer's guidelines online.

- Please *do not send* complete mss by e-mail.

"First $ale is probably the easiest way to break in. Do not submit full manuscript by e-mail."

Nonfiction: "We're always searching for appropriate, well-written features on topics we haven't covered for a couple of years." Needs articles of 1,500-1,800 words connected with writing and selling. No profiles of writers. **Buys approximately 75 mss/year.** Prefers queries; will read complete mss. Send SASE. Length: 1,500-1,800 words. **Pays $75.**

Columns/Departments: End Piece (humorous, philosophical, or motivational personal essay related to writing), 700 words, **pays $35**; First Sale (account of a writer's first sale), 250-300 words, **pays $20**; Only When I Laugh (writing-related humor), 50-600 words; **pays $15-25**; Great American Bookstores (unique, independent bookstores), 500-600 words. Send complete ms. **Pays $30-40.**

Fiction: Mainstream, genre, literary. No science fiction, erotica, or extreme violence. **Buys 11 mss/year.** Send complete ms. Length: 2,000-4,000 words. **Pays $100.**

Poetry: "All poetry should connect in some way with the theme of writing or the creative process." Sandra Soli, poetry editor. Free verse, haiku, light verse, traditional. **Buys 100 poems/year.** Submit maximum 3 poems. Length: Under 30 lines. **Pays $10, plus free issue.**

Tips: "We're open to freelance submissions in all categories. We're always looking for clear, concise feature articles on topics that will help writers write better, market smarter, and be more successful. Strangely, we get many more short stories than we do features, but we buy more features. If you can write a friendly, clear, and helpful feature on some aspect of writing better or selling more work, we'd love to hear from you."

$ CANADIAN WRITER'S JOURNAL, P.O. Box 5180, New Liskeard ON P0J 1P0, Canada. (705)647-5424. Fax: (705)647-8366. E-mail: cwj@cwj.ca. Website: www.cwj.ca. **Contact:** Deborah Ranchuk, editor. **75% freelance written.** Bimonthly magazine for writers. Accepts well-written articles by all writers. Estab. 1984. Circ. 350. Pays on publication. Publishes ms an average of 9 months after acceptance. Byline given. Buys one-time rights. Accepts queries by mail, e-mail, fax, phone. Responds in 2 months to queries. Sample copy for $8, including postage. Writer's guidelines online.

Nonfiction: Looking for articles on how to break into niche markets. How-to (articles for writers). **Buys 200 mss/year.** Query optional. **Pays $5/published magazine page (approx. 450 words).**

Reprints: Send ms with rights for sale noted and information about when and where the material previously appeared.

Fiction: Requirements being met by annual contest. Send SASE for rules, or see guidelines on website.

Poetry: Short poems or extracts used as part of articles on the writing of poetry.

Tips: "We prefer short, tightly written, informative how-to articles. U.S. writers note that U.S. postage cannot be used to mail from Canada. Obtain Canadian stamps, use IRCs, or send small amounts in cash."

N $$$ E CONTENT MAGAZINE, Digital Content Strategies & Resources, Online, Inc., 213 Danbury Rd., Wilton CT 06897. Fax: (203)761-1444. E-mail: ecnews@infotoday.com. Website: www.econtentmag.com. **Contact:** Michelle Manafy, editor. **90% freelance written.** Monthly magazine covering digital content trends, strategies, etc. "*E Content* is a business publication. Readers need to stay on top of industry trends and developments." Estab. 1979. Circ. 12,000. Pays within 1 month of publication. Byline given. Offers 20-50% kill fee. Buys all rights. Editorial lead time 4 months. Accepts queries by e-mail. Responds in 3 weeks to queries; 1 month to mss. Sample copy and writer's guidelines online. Writer's guidelines online.

Nonfiction: Exposé, how-to, interview/profile, new product, opinion, technical, news features, strategic and solution-oriented features. No academic or straight Q&A. **Buys 48 mss/year.** Query with published clips. Length: 1,000-2,000 words. **Pays 40-50¢/word.** Sometimes pays expenses of writers on assignment.

Photos: State availability with submission. Buys one-time rights. Negotiates payment individually. Captions required.

Columns/Departments: Profiles (short profile of unique company, person or product), 1,200 words; New Features (breaking news of content-related topics), 500 words maximum. **Buys 40 mss/year.** Query with published clips. **Pays 30-40¢/word.**

Tips: "Take a look at the website. Most of the time, an e-mail query with specific article ideas works well. A general outline of talking points is good, too. State prior experience."

$ FELLOWSCRIPT, InScribe Christian Writers' Fellowship, 333 Hunter's Run, Edmonton AB T6R 2N9, Canada. (780)988-5622. Fax: (780)430-0139. E-mail: submissions@inscribe.org. Website: www.inscribe.org. **Contact:** Elsie Montgomery, editor. **100% freelance written.** Quarterly writers' newsletter featuring Christian writing. "Our readers are Christians with a commitment to writing. Among our readership are best-selling authors and unpublished beginning writers. Submissions to us should include practical information, something the reader can put into practice immediately." Estab. 1983. Circ. 250. Pays on publication. Publishes ms an average of 2 months after acceptance. Byline given. Buys one-time rights. Editorial lead time 3 months. Submit seasonal material 4 months in advance. Accepts queries by mail, e-mail, fax, phone. Accepts simultaneous submissions. Responds in 1 month to queries; 2 months to mss. Sample copy for $2.50, 9×12 SAE, and 2 first-class stamps or IRCs. Writer's guidelines online.

"The best bet to break in at *FellowScript* is to write something very specific that will be useful to writers. We receive far too many 'general' submissions which try to cover too much territory in 1 article. Choose your topic and keep a narrow focus."

Nonfiction: All must pertain to writing and the writing life. Essays, exposé, how-to (for writers), inspirational, interview/profile, new product, personal experience, photo feature, religious. "Does not want poetry, fiction or think piece, commentary articles." **Buys 30-45 mss/year.** Send complete ms. Length: 250-900 words. **Pays 2½¢/word (Canadian).**

Photos: State availability with submission.

Columns/Departments: Book reviews, 150-300 words; Market Updates, 50-300 words. **Buys 1-3 mss/year.** Send complete ms. **Pays 1 copy.**

Fillers: Facts, newsbreaks. **Buys 5-10/year.** Length: 25-75 words. **Pays 1 copy.**

Tips: "Send your complete manuscript by post or e-mail. E-mail is preferred. Tell us a bit about yourself. Write in a casual, first-person, anecdotal style. Be sure your article is full of practical material, something that can be applied. Most of our accepted freelance submissions fall into the 'how-to' category, and involve tasks, crafts, or procedures common to writers. Please do not swamp us with inspirational articles (e.g., 'How I sold My First Story'), as we receive too many of these already."

N $ FREELANCE MARKET NEWS, An Essential Guide for Freelance Writers, The Writers Bureau Ltd., Sevendale House, 7 Dale St., Manchester M1 1JB, England. (44) 161 228 2362. Fax: (44) 161 228 3533. E-mail: fmn@writersbureau.com. Website: www.writersbureau.com. **Contact:** Angela Cox, editor. **20% freelance written.** Monthly newsletter covering freelance writing. Estab. 1968. **Pays on acceptance.** Byline given. Buys first rights. Editorial lead time 3 months. Submit seasonal material 3 months in advance. Accepts queries by mail, e-mail, fax. Accepts simultaneous submissions. Sample copy and writer's guidelines for #10 SASE.

Nonfiction: How-to. **Buys 12 mss/year.** Query. Length: 750-1,500 words. **Pays £50/1,000 words.**

$ $ FREELANCE WRITER'S REPORT, CNW Publishing, Inc., Main St., P.O. Box A, North Stratford NH 03590-0167. (603)922-8338. Fax: (603)922-8339. E-mail: fwrwm@writers-editors.com. Website: www.writers-editors.com. **Contact:** Dana K. Cassell, editor. **25% freelance written.** Monthly newsletter. "*FWR* covers the marketing and business/office management aspects of running a freelance writing business. Articles must be of value to the established freelancer; nothing basic." Estab. 1982. Pays on publication. Publishes ms an average of 6 months after acceptance. Byline given. Buys one-time rights. Editorial lead time 2 months. Submit seasonal material 2 months in advance. Accepts queries by mail, e-mail. Accepts simultaneous submissions. Responds in 1 week to queries; 1 month to mss. Sample copy for 6×9 SAE with 2 first-class stamps (for back copy); $4 for current copy. Writer's guidelines online.

Nonfiction: Book excerpts, how-to (market, increase income or profits). No articles about the basics of freelancing. **Buys 50 mss/year.** Send complete ms. Length: Up to 900 words. **Pays 10¢/word.**

Reprints: Accepts previously published submissions.

The online magazine carries original content not found in the print edition and includes writer's guidelines.

Tips: "Write in a terse, newsletter style."

$ MAINE IN PRINT, Maine Writers and Publishers Alliance, 14 Maine St., Suite 416, Brunswick ME 04011. (207)729-8808. Fax: (207)725-1014. Website: www.mainewriters.org. Editor: Pat Sims. Bimonthly newsletter for writers, editors, teachers, librarians, etc., focusing on Maine literature and the craft of writing. Estab. 1975. Circ. 3,000. Pays on publication. Publishes ms an average of 2 months after acceptance. Byline given. Buys one-time rights. Editorial lead time 2 months. Accepts queries by mail. Accepts simultaneous submissions. Sample copy and writer's guidelines free.

Nonfiction: Essays, how-to (writing), interview/profile, technical. No creative writing, fiction, or poetry. **Buys 20 mss/year.** Query with published clips. Length: 400-1,500 words. **Pays $25-50 for assigned articles.**

Reprints: Send tearsheet and information about when and where the material previously appeared. Pays $25.

Photos: State availability with submission. Offers no additional payment for photos accepted with ms.

Columns/Departments: Front-page articles (writing related), 500-1,500 words. **Buys 20 mss/year.** Query. **Pays $25 minimum.**

Tips: "Become a member of Maine Writers & Publishers Alliance. Become familiar with Maine literary scene."

$ $ $ MASTHEAD, The Magazine About Magazines, North Island Publishing, 1606 Sedlescomb Dr., Unit 8, Mississauga ON L4X 1M6, Canada. (905)625-7070. Fax: (905)625-4856. E-mail: wshields@masthead.ca. Website: www.mastheadonline.com. **Contact:** William Shields, editor. **40% freelance written.** Journal published 10 times/year covering the Canadian magazine industry. "With its lively mix of in-depth features, news stories, service pieces, surveys, tallies, and spirited commentary, this independent journal provides detailed coverage and analysis of the events, issues, personalities, and technologies shaping Canada's magazine industry." Estab. 1987. Circ. 4,200. Pays on publication. Publishes ms an average of 2 months after acceptance. Byline given. Offers 50% kill fee. Buys first North American serial rights. Editorial lead time 1 month. Accepts queries by mail. Accepts simultaneous submissions. Responds in 2 weeks to queries; 1 month to mss. Sample copy for free. Writer's guidelines free or by e-mail.

Nonfiction: "We generally pay $600-850 for a cover story running 2,000-2,500 words, depending on the amount of research, etc., required. For the most part, *Masthead* generates feature ideas in-house and then assigns the stories to regular contributors. When space permits, we sometimes run shorter features or service pieces (1,000-1,500 words) for a flat rate of $350." Book excerpts, essays, exposé, historical/nostalgic, how-to, humor, interview/profile, new product, opinion, personal experience, technical. No articles that have nothing to do with Canadian magazines. Length: 100-3,000 words. **Pays $30-850 (Canadian).** Sometimes pays expenses of writers on assignment.

Photos: State availability with submission. Negotiates payment individually. Identification of subjects required.

Columns/Departments: Back of the Book, the guest column, pays freelancers a flat rate of $350 and runs approximately 950 words. Back of the Book columns examine and/or comment on issues or developments relating to any department: editorial, art, production, circulation, publishing, advertising, etc. **Buys 10 mss/year.** Query with published clips. **Pays $350 (Canadian).**

Fiction: Novel excerpts. No excerpts that have nothing to do with Canadian magazines. Query with published clips.

The online magazine carries original content. Contact: William Shields.

Tips: "Have a solid understanding of the Canadian magazine industry. A good way to introduce yourself is to propose small articles on new magazines."

N $ $ MSLEXIA, For Women Who Write, Mslexia Publications Ltd., P.O. Box 656, Newcastle upon Tyne NE99 1PZ, United Kingdom. (0044) 191 261 6656. E-mail: postbag@mslexia.demon.co.uk. Website: www.mslexia.co.uk. Editor: Debbie Taylor. **Contact:** Melanie Ashby, deputy editor. **60% freelance written.** Quarterly magazine offering advice and publishing opportunities for women writers, plus poetry and prose submissions on a different theme each issue. "*Mslexia* tells you all you need to know about exploring your creativity and getting into print. No other magazine provides *Mslexia*'s unique mix of advice and inspiration; news, reviews, interviews; competitions, events, grants; all served up with a challenging selection of new poetry and prose. *Mslexia* is read by authors and absolute beginners. A quarterly master class in the business and psychology of writing, it's the essential magazine for women who write." Estab. 1998. Circ. 12,000. Pays on publication. Publishes ms an average of 1 month after acceptance. Byline given. Offers 50% kill fee. Buys one-time rights. Editorial lead time 3 months. Submit seasonal material 3 months in advance. Accepts queries by mail, e-mail, phone. Accepts simultaneous submissions. Responds in 3 months to mss. Sample copy online. Writer's guidelines online or by e-mail.

- This publication does not accept e-mail submissions except from overseas writers.

Nonfiction: How-to, interview/profile, opinion, personal experience. No general items about women or academic features. "We are only interested in features (for tertiary-educated readership) about women's writing and literature." **Buys 40 mss/year.** Query with published clips. Length: 500-2,000 words. **Pays $70-400 for assigned articles; $70-300 for unsolicited articles.** Pays in contributor copies for poetry and prose submitted for the New Writing section of the magazine. Sometimes pays expenses of writers on assignment.

Columns/Departments: "We are open to suggestions, but would only commission 1 new column/year, probably from a UK-based writer." **Buys 12 mss/year.** Query with published clips.

Fiction: Sheila Mulhern, editorial assistant. "See guidelines on our website. Submissions not on one of our current themes will be returned (if submitted with a SASE) or destroyed." **Buys 30 mss/year.** Send complete ms. Length: 50-3,000 words.

Poetry: Sheila Mulhern, editorial assistant. Avant-garde, free verse, haiku, traditional. **Buys 40 poems/year.** Submit maximum 4 poems.

Tips: "Read the magazine; subscribe if you can afford it. *Mslexia* has a particular style and relationship with its readers which is hard to assess at a quick glance. The majority of our readers live in the UK, so feature pitches should be aware of this. We never commission work without seeing a written sample first. We rarely accept unsolicited manuscripts, but prefer a short letter suggesting a feature, plus a brief bio and writing sample."

$ NEW WRITER'S MAGAZINE, Sarasota Bay Publishing, P.O. Box 5976, Sarasota FL 34277-5976. (941)953-7903. E-mail: newriters@aol.com. Website: www.newriters.com. **Contact:** George S. Haborak, editor. **95% freelance written.** Bimonthly magazine. "*New Writer's Magazine* believes that *all* writers are *new* writers in that each of us can learn from one another. So, we reach pro and nonpro alike." Estab. 1986. Circ. 5,000. Pays on publication. Byline given. Buys first rights. Accepts queries by mail. Responds in 1 month to queries; 1 month to mss. Sample copy for $3. Writer's guidelines for #10 SASE.

Nonfiction: General interest, how-to (for new writers), humor, interview/profile, opinion, personal experience (with pro writer). **Buys 50 mss/year.** Send complete ms. Length: 700-1,000 words. **Pays $10-50.**

Photos: Send photos with submission. Reviews 5×7 prints. Offers no additional payment for photos accepted with ms. Captions required.

Fiction: Experimental, historical, humorous, mainstream, slice-of-life vignettes. "Again we do *not* want anything that does not have a tie-in with the writing life or writers in general." **Buys 2-6 mss/year.** Send complete ms. Length: 700-800 words. **Pays $20-40.**

Poetry: Free verse, light verse, traditional. Does not want anything *not* for writers. **Buys 10-20 poems/year.** Submit maximum 3 poems. Length: 8-20 lines. **Pays $5 minimum.**

Fillers: For cartoons, writing lifestyle slant. Buys 20-30/year. Pays $10 maximum. Anecdotes, facts, newsbreaks, short humor. **Buys 5-15/year.** Length: 20-100 words. **Pays $5 maximum.**

Tips: "Any article with photos has a good chance, especially an up close and personal interview with an established professional writer offering advice, etc. Short profile pieces on new authors also receive attention."

$ OHIO WRITER, Poets' & Writers' League of Greater Cleveland, 12200 Fairhill Rd., Cleveland OH 44120. (216)421-0403. Fax: (216)791-1727. E-mail: pwlgc@msn.com. Website: www.pwlgc.com. **Contact:** Stephen and Gail Bellamy, editors. **75% freelance written.** Bimonthly magazine covering writing and Ohio writers. Estab. 1987. Pays on publication. Publishes ms an average of 4 months after acceptance. Byline given. Buys one-time, second serial (reprint) rights. Editorial lead time 4 months. Submit seasonal material 4 months in advance. Accepts queries by mail, e-mail, fax, phone. Responds in 6 weeks to mss. Sample copy for $2.50. Writer's guidelines for #10 SASE.

Nonfiction: "All articles must related to the writing life or Ohio writers, or Ohio publishing scene." Essays, how-to, humor, inspirational, interview/profile, opinion, personal experience. **Buys 24 mss/year.** Send complete ms and SASE. Length: 2,000-2,500 words. **Pays $25 minimum, up to $50 for lead article, other payment under arrangement with writer.**

Reprints: Send ms with rights for sale noted and information about when and where the material previously appeared. Pays 50% of amount paid for an original article.

Columns/Departments: Subjectively Yours (opinions, controversial stance on writing life), 1,500 words; Reviews (Ohio writers, publishers, or publishing), 400-600 words; Focus on (Ohio publishing scene, how to write/publish certain kind of writing, e.g., travel), 1,500 words. **Buys 6 mss/year.** Send complete ms. **Pays $25-50; $5/book review.**

Tips: "We look for articles about writers and writing, with a special emphasis on activities in our state. However, we publish articles by writers throughout the country that offer something helpful about the writing life. Profiles and interviews of writers who live in Ohio are always needed. *Ohio Writer* is read by both beginning and experienced writers and hopes to create a sense of community among writers of different genres, abilities, and backgrounds. We want to hear a personal voice, one that engages the reader. We're looking for intelligent, literate prose that isn't stuffy."

N $ $ POETS & WRITERS MAGAZINE, 72 Spring St., New York NY 10012. Fax: (212)226-3963. E-mail: editor@pw.org. Website: www.pw.org. **Contact:** Therese Eiben, editor. **100% freelance written.** Bimonthly professional trade journal for poets and fiction writers and creative nonfiction writers. Estab. 1973. Circ. 70,000. Pays on acceptance of finished draft. Publishes ms an average of 4 months after acceptance. Byline given. Offers 20% kill fee. Buys first North American serial rights. Submit seasonal material 4 months in advance. Accepts queries by mail. Responds in 6 weeks to mss. Sample copy for $4.95 to Sample Copy Dept. Writer's guidelines for #10 SASE.

- No poetry or fiction.

Nonfiction: How-to (craft of poetry or fiction writing), interview/profile (with poets or fiction writers). "We do not accept submissions by fax or e-mail." **Buys 35 mss/year.** Query with published clips or send complete ms. Length: 500-2,500 depending on topic words.

Photos: State availability with submission. Reviews b&w prints. Offers no additional payment for photos accepted with ms.

Columns/Departments: Literary and Publishing News, 500-1,000 words; Profiles of Emerging and Established Poets and Fiction Writers, 2,000-3,000 words; Regional Reports (literary activity in US), 1,000-2,00 words. Query with published clips or send complete ms. **Pays $150-300.**

$ THE WIN INFORMER, The Professional Association for Christian Writers, Writers Information Network, P.O. Box 11337, Bainbridge Island WA 98110. (206)842-9103. Fax: (206)842-0536. E-mail: writersinfonetwork@juno.com. Website: www.bluejaypub.com/win. **Contact:** Elaine Wright Colvin, editor. **33⅓% freelance written.** Bimonthly magazine for this professional association for Christian writers covering the CBA and religious publishing industry. Estab. 1983. Circ. 1,000. **Pays on acceptance.** Publishes ms an average of 1-4 months after acceptance. Byline given. Buys first North American serial rights. Editorial lead time 2 months. Submit seasonal material 2 months in advance. Accepts queries by e-mail. Responds in 1 month to mss. Sample copy for $10, 9×12 SAE with 4 first-class stamps. Writer's guidelines online.

O→ Break in by "getting involved in the Christian publishing (CBA) industry; interview CBA published authors, CBA editors, or CBA bookstore managers."

Nonfiction: For advanced/professional writers only. How-to (writing), humor, inspirational, interview/profile, new product, opinion, personal experience, religious, technical. No beginners basics material used. Send complete ms. Submit material in the body of e-mail only. Length: 50-800 words. **Pays $5-50, sometimes pays other than cash.** Sometimes pays expenses of writers on assignment.

Columns/Departments: Industry News; Book Publisher News; Editor/Agent Hot News; News of the Magazines; Awards & Bestsellers; Conference Tips; Conference Schedule; New Book Alert; Bulletin Board; Computer Corner. Send complete ms in body of e-mail or as an e-mail attachment.

N $ WRITER'S APPRENTICE, For Aspiring, Beginning, and Intermediate Writers, Prairie River Publishing, 607 N. Cleveland St., Merrill WI 54452. (715)536-3167. Fax: (715)536-3167. E-mail: tina@writersapprentice.com. Website: www.writersapprentice.com. **Contact:** Tina L. Miller, editor-in-chief. **90% freelance written.** Monthly trade magazine (beginning in 2004), 3 issues in 2003. "*Writer's Apprentice* magazine offers real, practical advice for writers—whether writing for pleasure or publication. Specifics, resources, information, encouragement, and answers to the questions they have." Estab. 2002. Circ. 10,000. Pays on publication. Byline given. Not copyrighted. Buys first rights. Editorial lead time 6-9 months. Submit seasonal material 6-9 months in advance. Accepts queries by mail, e-mail, fax. Responds in 3-4 weeks to queries; 6 months to mss. Sample copy for 9×12 SAE and 4 first-class stamps. Writer's guidelines online.

Nonfiction: Essays, general interest, how-to, humor, inspirational, interview/profile, personal experience, technical. No fiction, poetry, or stories/articles that do not have a practical, take-away value. Query or send complete ms. Length: 300-900 words. **Pays $15-50.**

Photos: State availability with submission. Reviews GIF/JPEG files. Buys one-time rights. Negotiates payment individually. Identification of subjects, model releases required.

Columns/Departments: The Writing Life (back page essays), 300-600 words. Send complete ms. **Pays $10-25.**

Tips: "Pretend your best friend wants to become a writer. Think of all the questions he/she will have. What can you teach him/her that you already know? How can you share the benefit of your experience? What advice would you give? How would you help him/her get started? Become this imaginary new writer's mentor. Write it down in a concise article on a specific topic, and we're very likely to buy it. But remember: It's got to be real, practical, focused, informative, do-able, and contain resources or a how-to. No 'fluff' stories or stories that are too generic."

$ $ WRITER'S DIGEST, 4700 E. Galbraith Rd., Cincinnati OH 45236. (513)531-2690, ext. 1483. E-mail: wdsubmissions@fwpubs.com. Website: www.writersdigest.com. **Contact:** Submissions Editor. **70% freelance written.** Monthly magazine about writing and publishing. "Our readers write fiction, nonfiction, plays, and scripts. They're interested in improving writing skills and the ability to sell their work and find new outlets for their talents." Estab. 1920. Circ. 150,000. **Pays on acceptance.** Publishes ms an average of 9-12 months after acceptance. Byline given. Offers 25% kill fee. Buys first world serial rights for one-time editorial use, possible electronic posting, and magazine promotional use. Pays 25% reprint fee and 10% for electronic use in fee-charging mediums. Sample copy for $7 ($9 Canada; $11 other foreign), send check/

money order to Writer's Digest/F&W Publication Products, P.O. Box 2031, Harlan IA 51593; or call (888)419-0421. Writer's guidelines online.

- *Writer's Digest* strongly prefers e-queries and responds in 3 weeks to e-queries; 3 months to mail queries w/SASE. The magazine does not accept or read e-queries with attachments.

O-w "Break in through Markets Spotlight, or with a 1,000-word profile of a niche writing market."

Nonfiction: "What we need is the how-to article: How to write compelling leads and conclusions, how to improve your character descriptions, how to become more efficient and productive. We like plenty of examples, anecdotes, and details in our articles. On how-to technique articles, we prefer to work with writers with a proven track record of success. For example, don't pitch us an article on creating effective dialogue if you've never had a work of fiction published. Don't query about setting up a book tour if you've never done one. We like our articles to speak directly to the reader through the use of the first-person voice. We are seldom interested in author interviews, and 'evergreen' topics are not accepted unless they are timely and address industry trends. Must have fax to receive galleys. "Don't send articles today that would have fit in *WD* 5 years ago. No articles titled 'So You Want to Be a Writer,' and no first-person pieces without something readers can learn from in the sharing of the story. Avoid the 'and then I wrote' article that is a promotional vehicle for you without tips on how others can put your experience to work." **Buys 75 mss/year.** "We only accept electronic final manuscripts." Length: 1,000-2,000 words. **Pays 25-40¢/word.**

Tips: "Two-thirds of assignments are based on staff-generated ideas. Only about 25 unsolicited queries for features are assigned/year. Note that our standing columns and departments are not open to freelance submissions. Further, we buy at most 2 interviews/profiles/year; nearly all that we publish are staff-written. Candidates for First Success interviews (all of which are conducted in-house; candidates must be first-time authors) should send galleys and information about themselves at least 5 months before their book's pubilcation date to Jessica Yerega at the address above."

$ WRITER'S FORUM, Writer's Digest School, 4700 E. Galbraith Rd., Cincinnati OH 45236. (513)531-2690, ext. 1343. E-mail: wdsforum@fwpubs.com. Website: www.writersdigestschool.com. **Contact:** Maria Witte, editor. **100% freelance written.** Tri-annual newsletter covering writing techniques, marketing, and inspiration for students enrolled in fiction and nonfiction writing courses offered by Writer's Digest School. Estab. 1970. Circ. 10,000. **Pays on acceptance.** Publishes ms an average of 1-2 years after acceptance. Byline given. Buys first, second serial (reprint) rights. Accepts queries by mail, e-mail. Accepts simultaneous submissions. Sample copy for #10 SASE.

O-w Break in with something "how-to" oriented that is geared toward beginning writers and/or writers just breaking into print.

Nonfiction: How-to (write or market short stories, or articles, novels, and nonfiction books). **Buys 12 mss/year.** Prefers complete mss to queries. Length: 500-1,000 words. **Pays $25.**

N $ $ THE WRITER, Morris Publishing, 21027 Crossroads Circle, P.O. Box 1612, Waukesha WI 53187-1612. E-mail: editor@writermag.com. Website: www.writermag.com. **Contact:** Elfrieda Abbe, editor-in-chief. **20% freelance written.** Prefers to buy work of published/established writers. Estab. 1887. **Pays on acceptance.** Publishes ms an average of 8 months after acceptance. Buys first North American serial rights. Accepts queries by mail, e-mail. Sample copy for $4. Writer's guidelines online.

- "No phone queries."

Nonfiction: Practical articles for writers on how to write for publication, and how and where to market manuscripts in various fields. Considers all submissions promptly. No assignments. Length: 2,000 words maximum length.

Reprints: Send tearsheet or photocopy and information about when and where the material previously appeared.

Tips: "We are looking for articles with plenty of practical, specific advice, tips, techniques that aspiring and beginning writers can apply to their own work. New types of publications and our continually updated market listings in all fields will determine changes of focus and fact."

$ WRITERS' JOURNAL, The Complete Writer's Magazine, Val-Tech Media, P.O. Box 394, Perham MN 56573-0394. (218)346-7921. Fax: (218)346-7924. E-mail: writersjournal@lakesplus.com. Website: www.writersjournal.com. Managing Editor: John Ogroske. **Contact:** Leon Ogroske, editor. **90% freelance written.** Bimonthly trade magazine covering writing. "*Writers' Journal* is read by thousands of aspiring writers whose love of writing has taken them to the next step: Writing for money. We are an instructional manual giving writers the tools and information necessary to get their work published. We also print works by authors who have won our writing contests." Estab. 1980. Circ. 26,000. Pays on publication. Publishes ms an average of 10 months after acceptance. Byline given. Buys one-time rights. Editorial lead time 8 months. Submit seasonal material 8 months in advance. Accepts queries by mail, e-mail, fax, phone. Accepts simultaneous submissions. Responds in 6 weeks to queries; 6 months to mss. Sample copy for $5.

Nonfiction: Looking for articles on fiction writing (plot development, story composition, character development, etc.) and writing "how-to." Book excerpts, essays, exposé, general interest (to writers), humor, inspirational, interview/profile, new product, opinion, personal experience, photo feature, technical. No erotica. **Buys 45 mss/year.** Send complete ms. Length: 800-2,500 words. **Pays with a 1-year subscription, money depending on article and budget, and in contributor copies or other premiums if author agrees.**

Photos: State availability with submission. Reviews contact sheets, prints. Buys one-time rights. Negotiates payment individually. Model releases required.

Columns/Departments: For Beginners Only (helpful advice to beginners), 800-2,500 words. **Buys 30 mss/year.** Send complete ms. **Pays $20, money depending on article, and a 1-year subscription.**

Fiction: "We only publish winners of our fiction contests—16 contests/year."

Poetry: Esther Leiper-Jefferson, poetry editor. No erotica. **Buys 25 poems/year.** Submit maximum 4 poems. Length: 25 lines. **Pays $5.**

Fillers: Anecdotes, facts, short humor, cartoons. **Buys 20/year.** Length: 200 words. **Pays $10.**

Tips: "Appearance must be professional with no grammatical or spelling errors submitted on white paper, double spaced with easy-to-read font. We want articles that will help writers improve technique in writing, style, editing, publishing, and story construction. We are interested in how writers use new and fresh angles to break into the writing markets."

$ WRITING THAT WORKS, The Business Communications Report, 7481 Huntsman Blvd., #720, Springfield VA 22153-1648. E-mail: inq@writingthatworks.com. Website: www.apexawards.com. **Contact:** John De Lellis, editor/publisher. Monthly newsletter on business writing and communications. "Our readers are company writers, editors, communicators, and executives. They need specific, practical advice on how to write well as part of their job." Estab. 1983. Pays within 45 days of acceptance. Publishes ms an average of 3 months after acceptance. Byline sometimes given. Buys all rights. Editorial lead time 3 months. Accepts queries by mail, e-mail. Responds in 1 month to queries. Sample copy and writer's guidelines online. Writer's guidelines online.

Nonfiction: Practical, short, how-to articles and quick tips on business writing techniques geared to company writers, editors, publication staff and communicators. "We're always looking for shorts—how-to tips on business writing." How-to. **Buys 120 mss/year.** Accepts electronic final mss. Length: 100-500 words. **Pays $35-150.**

Columns/Departments: Writing Techniques (how-to business writing advice); Style Matters (grammar, usage, and editing); Online Publishing (writing, editing, and publishing for the Web); Managing Publications; PR & Marketing (writing).

Fillers: Short tips on writing or editing. Mini-reviews of communications websites for business writers, editors, and communicators. Length: 100-150 words. **Pays $35.**

Tips: "We do not use material on how to get published or how to conduct a freelancing business. Format your copy to follow *Writing That Works* style. Include postal and e-mail addresses, phone numbers, website URLs, and prices for products/services mentioned in articles."

LAW

While all of these publications deal with topics of interest to attorneys, each has a particular slant. Be sure that your subject is geared to a specific market—lawyers in a single region, law students, paralegals, etc. Publications for law enforcement personnel are listed under Government & Public Service.

$ $ $ $ ABA JOURNAL, The Lawyer's Magazine, American Bar Association, 750 N. Lake Shore Dr., Chicago IL 60611. (312)988-6018. Fax: (312)988-6014. E-mail: abajournal@abanet.org. Website: www.abajournal.com. Editor: Danial J. Kim. **Contact:** Debra Cassens, managing editor. **10% freelance written.** Monthly magazine covering law. "The *ABA Journal* is an independent, thoughtful and inquiring observer of the law and the legal profession. The magazine is edited for members of the American Bar Association." Circ. 389,000. **Pays on acceptance.** Byline given. Makes work-for-hire assignments. Accepts queries by mail, e-mail. Sample copy and writer's guidelines free. Writer's guidelines online.

Nonfiction: Legal features. "We don't want anything that does not have a legal theme. No poetry or fiction." **Buys 5 mss/year.** Query with published clips. Length: 700-3,500 words. **Pays $400-2,000 for assigned articles.**

Columns/Departments: Law Beat (reports on legal news and trends), 700-1,400 words; Solo Network (advice for solo practitioners), 1,000 words; In the Office (life on the job for lawyers), 700-1,400 words; In re Technology (technology for lawyers), 700-1,400 words. **Buys 25 mss/year.** Query with published clips. **Pays $350-1,200.**

N $ $ $ BENCH & BAR OF MINNESOTA, Minnesota State Bar Association, 600 Nicollet Ave., Suite 380, Minneapolis MN 55402-1641. (612)333-1183. Fax: (612)333-4927. **Contact:** Judson Haverkamp, editor. **10% freelance written.** Magazine published 11 times/year. "Audience is mostly Minnesota lawyers. *Bench & Bar* seeks reportage, analysis, and commentary on trends and issues in the law and the legal profession, especially in Minnesota. Preference to items of practical/human interest to professionals in law." Estab. 1931. Circ. 16,000. **Pays on acceptance.** Publishes ms an average of 3 months after acceptance. Byline given. Buys first North American serial rights, makes work-for-hire assignments. Responds in 1 month to queries. Writer's guidelines free.

Nonfiction: How-to (how to handle particular types of legal, ethical problems in office management, representation, etc.), humor, interview/profile, technical (/legal). "We do not want one-sided opinion pieces or advertorial." **Buys 2-3 mss/year.** Query with or without published clips or send complete ms. Length: 1,500-3,000 words. **Pays $300-800.** Sometimes pays expenses of writers on assignment.

Photos: State availability with submission. Reviews 5×7 prints. Buys one-time rights. Pays $25-100 upon publication. Identification of subjects, model releases required.

$ $ $ $ CALIFORNIA LAWYER, Daily Journal Corporation, 1145 Market St., 8th Floor, San Francisco CA 94103. (415)252-0500. Fax: (415)252-0288. E-mail: peter_allen@dailyjournal.com. Website: www.dailyjournal.com. Managing Editor: Tema Goodwin. **Contact:** Peter Allen, editor. **30% freelance written.** Monthly magazine of law-related articles and general-interest subjects of appeal to lawyers and judges. "Our primary mission is to cover the news of the world as it affects the law and lawyers, helping our readers better comprehend the issues of the day and to cover changes and trends in the legal profession. Our readers are all 140,000 California lawyers, plus judges, legislators and corporate executives. Although we focus on California and the West, we have subscribers in every state. *California Lawyer* is a general interest magazine for people interested in law. Our writers are journalists." Estab. 1981. Circ. 140,000. **Pays on acceptance.** Publishes ms an average of 3 months after acceptance. Byline given. Offers 25% kill fee. Buys first North American serial, electronic rights. Editorial lead time 3 months. Accepts queries by mail, e-mail, fax. Sample copy and writer's guidelines for #10 SASE.

O→ Break in by "showing us clips—we usually start people out on short news stories."

Nonfiction: Essays, general interest, interview/profile, News and feature articles on law-related topics. "We are interested in concise, well-written and well-researched articles on issues of current concern, as well as well-told feature narratives with a legal focus. We would like to see a description or outline of your proposed idea, including a list of possible sources." **Buys 12 mss/year.** Query with or without published clips or send complete ms. Length: 500-5,000 words. **Pays $50-2,000.** Pays expenses of writers on assignment.

Photos: Jake Flaherty, art director. State availability with submission. Reviews prints. Identification of subjects, model releases required.

Columns/Departments: California Esq. (current legal trends). 300 words. **Buys 6 mss/year.** Query with or without published clips. **Pays $50-250.**

$ $ $ $ CORPORATE LEGAL TIMES, 656 W. Randolph St., #500-E, Chicago IL 60661-2114. (312)654-3500. E-mail: rvosper@cltmag.com. Website: www.corporatelegaltimes.com. **Contact:** Robert Vosper, managing editor. **50% freelance written.** Monthly tabloid. "*Corporate Legal Times* is a monthly national magazine that gives general counsel and inhouse attorneys information on legal and business issues to help them better manage corporate law departments. It routinely addresses changes and trends in law departments, litigation management, legal technology, corporate governance and inhouse careers. Law areas covered monthly include: Intellectual property, international, technology, project finance, e-commerce and litigation. All articles need to be geared toward the inhouse attorney's perspective." Estab. 1991. Circ. 45,000. Pays on publication. Publishes ms an average of 3 months after acceptance. Byline given. Buys all rights. Editorial lead time 3 months. Submit seasonal material 3 months in advance. Accepts queries by mail, e-mail. Responds in 3 weeks to queries. Sample copy for $17. Writer's guidelines online.

Nonfiction: Interview/profile, news about legal aspects of business issues and events. **Buys 12-25 mss/year.** Query with published clips. Length: 500-3,000 words. **Pays $500-2,000.**

Photos: Freelancers should state availability of photos with submission. State availability with submission. Reviews color transparencies, b&w prints. Buys all rights. Offers $25-150/photo. Identification of subjects required.

Tips: "Our publication targets general counsel and inhouse lawyers. All articles need to speak to them—not to the general attorney population. Query with clips and a list of potential inhouse sources."

$ $ $ JOURNAL OF COURT REPORTING, National Court Reporters Association, 8224 Old Courthouse Rd., Vienna VA 22182. (703)556-6272. Fax: (703)556-6291. E-mail: jschmidt@ncrahq.org. **Contact:** Jacqueline Schmidt, editor. **20% freelance written.** Monthly (bimonthly July/August and November/December) magazine. "The *Journal of Court Reporting* has two complementary purposes: to communicate the activities, goals and mission of its publisher, the National Court Reporters Association; and, simultaneously, to seek out and publish diverse information and views on matters significantly related to the information/court reporting and captioning profession." Estab. 1905. Circ. 34,000. **Pays on acceptance.** Publishes ms an average of 3 months after acceptance. Byline given. Buys one-time rights, makes work-for-hire assignments. Editorial lead time 3 months. Accepts simultaneous submissions. Sample copy for $6. Writer's guidelines free.

Nonfiction: Essays, historical/nostalgic, how-to, interview/profile, new product, technical. **Buys 10 mss/year.** Query. Length: 1,200 words. **Pays $55-1,000.** Sometimes pays expenses of writers on assignment.

Photos: State availability with submission. Buys one-time rights. Offers no additional payment for photos accepted with ms. Captions, identification of subjects, model releases required.

$ LAW OFFICE COMPUTING, James Publishing, 3505 Cadillac Ave., Suite H, Costa Mesa CA 92626. (714)755-5450. Fax: (714)751-5508. E-mail: editorloc@jamespublishing.com. Website: www.lawofficecomputing.com. **Contact:** Amanda Clifford, executive editor. **90% freelance written.** Bimonthly magazine covering legal technology industry. "*Law Office Computing* is a magazine written for attorneys and other legal professionals. It covers the legal technology field and features software reviews, profiles of prominent figures in the industry, and 'how-to' type articles." Estab. 1991. Circ. 7,000. Pays on publication. Publishes ms an average of 2 months after acceptance. Byline given. Buys first North American serial rights. Editorial lead time 4 months. Submit seasonal material 4 months in advance. Accepts queries by mail, e-mail, fax. Sample copy for free. Writer's guidelines online.

Nonfiction: How-to, interview/profile, new product, technical. Special issues: Looking for Macintosh and Linux articles. **Buys 30 mss/year.** Query. Length: 2,000-3,500 words. **Pays on a case-by-case basis.** Sometimes pays expenses of writers on assignment.

Photos: State availability with submission.

Columns/Departments: Tech profile (profile firm using technology), 1,200 words; My Solution, 1,500 words; Software reviews: Short reviews (a single product), 400-800 words; Software Shootouts (2 or 3 products going head-to-head), 1,000-1,500 words; Round-Ups/Buyer's Guides (8-15 products), 300-500 words/product. Each type of software review article has its own specific guidelines. Request the appropriate guidelines from editor. **Buys 6 mss/year.** Query. **Pays on a case-by-case basis.**

Tips: "If you are a practicing attorney, legal MIS or computer consultant, try the first-person My Solution column or a short review. If you are a professional freelance writer, technology profiles or a news story regarding legal technology are best, since most of our other copy is written by legal technology professionals."

$ LEGAL ASSISTANT TODAY, James Publishing, Inc., P.O. Box 25202, Santa Ana CA 92799. (714)755-5468. Fax: (714)751-5508. E-mail: rhughes@jamespublishing.com. Website: www.legalassistanttoday.com. **Contact:** Rod Hughes, editor/publisher. Bimonthly magazine "geared toward all legal assistants/paralegals throughout the United States and Canada, regardless of specialty (litigation, corporate, bankruptcy, environmental law, etc.). How-to articles to help paralegals perform their jobs more effectively are most in demand, as is career and salary information, and timely news and trends pieces." Estab. 1983. Circ. 10,000. Pays on publication. Byline given. Buys first North American serial, electronic rights. non-exclusive electronic/Internet right and non-exclusive rights to use the article, author's name, image and biographical data in advertising and promotion. Editorial lead time 10 weeks. Submit seasonal material 3 months in advance. Accepts queries by mail, e-mail, fax. Accepts simultaneous submissions. Responds in 2 month to mss. Sample copy and writer's guidelines free. Writer's guidelines online.

Nonfiction: Interview/profile (unique and interesting paralegals in unique and particular work-related situations), news (brief, hard news topics regarding paralegals. Features: present information to help paralegals advance their careers).

Photos: Send photos with submission.

Tips: "Fax a detailed outline of a 3,000 to 4,500-word feature about something useful to working legal assistants. Writers *must* understand our audience. There is some opportunity for investigative journalism as well as the usual features, profiles and news. How-to articles are especially desired. If you are a great writer who can interview effectively, and really dig into the topic to grab readers' attention, we need you."

$ $ THE NATIONAL JURIST, Crittenden Magazines, P.O. Box 939039, San Diego CA 92193. (858)503-7562. Fax: (858)503-7588. **Contact:** Keith Carter, managing editor. **5% freelance written.** Bimonthly magazine covering law literature. Estab. 1991. Circ. 100,000. Pays on publication. Buys all rights. Accepts queries by mail, e-mail, fax, phone.

Nonfiction: General interest, how-to, humor, interview/profile. **Buys 4 mss/year.** Query. Length: 750-3,000 words. **Pays $100-500 for assigned articles.**

Photos: State availability with submission. Reviews contact sheets. Negotiates payment individually.

Columns/Departments: Pays $100-500.

$ $ THE PENNSYLVANIA LAWYER, Pennsylvania Bar Association, P.O. Box 186, 100 South St., Harrisburg PA 17108-0186. E-mail: editor@pabar.org. Executive Editor: Marcy Carey Mallory. Editor: Geoff Yuda. **Contact:** Donald C. Sarvey, editorial director. **25% freelance written.** Prefers to work with published/established writers. Bimonthly magazine published as a service to the legal profession and the members of the Pennsylvania Bar Association. Estab. 1979. Circ. 30,000. **Pays on acceptance.** Publishes ms an average of 6 months after acceptance. Byline given. Buys first, one-time rights. Submit seasonal material 6 months in advance. Accepts queries by mail, e-mail. Responds in 2 months to queries; 2 months to mss. Sample copy for $2. Writer's guidelines for #10 SASE or by e-mail.

Nonfiction: All features must relate in some way to Pennsylvania lawyers or the practice of law in Pennsylvania. How-to, interview/profile, law-practice management, technology. **Buys 8-10 mss/year.** Query. Length: 1,200-2,000 words. **Pays $50 for book reviews; $75-400 for assigned articles; $150 for unsolicited articles.** Sometimes pays expenses of writers on assignment.

Photos: State availability with submission. Reviews contact sheets. Buys one-time rights. Negotiates payment individually. Identification of subjects required.

$ $ $ STUDENT LAWYER, The Magazine of the Law Student Division, American Bar Association, 750 N. Lake Shore Dr., Chicago IL 60611. (312)988-6048. Fax: (312)988-6081. E-mail: abastulawyer@abanet.org. Website: www.abanet.org/lsd. **Contact:** Ira Pilchen, editor. **85% freelance written.** Works with a small number of new writers each year. Monthly magazine. "*Student Lawyer* is a legal-affairs features magazine that competes for a share of law students' limited spare time, so the articles we publish must be informative, lively, well-researched good reads." Estab. 1972. Circ. 35,000. **Pays on acceptance.** Publishes ms an average of 3 months after acceptance. Byline given. Buys first rights. Editorial lead time 5 months. Submit seasonal material 6 months in advance. Accepts queries by mail, e-mail, phone. Writer's guidelines online.

Nonfiction: Essays (on legal affairs), interview/profile (prominent person in law-related fields), opinion (on matters of current legal interest). No fiction, please. Query with published clips. Length: 2,000-2,500 words. **Pays $500-1,200 for features.** Sometimes pays expenses of writers on assignment.

Columns/Departments: Profile (profiles out-of-the-ordinary lawyers), 1,200 words; Coping (dealing with law school), 1,200 words; Online (Internet and the law), 1,200 words; Leagal-ease (language and legal writing), 1,200 words; Jobs (marketing to legal employers), 1,200 words; Opinion (opinion on legal issue), 800 words. Query with published clips. **Pays $200-500.**

Tips: "*Student Lawyer* actively seeks good, new reporters and writers eager to prove themselves. Legal training definitely not essential; writing talent is. The writer should not think we are a law review; we are a features magazine with the law (in the broadest sense) as the common denominator. Find issues of national scope and interest to write about; be aware of subjects the magazine—and other media—have already covered and propose something new. Write clearly and well. Expect to work with editor to polish manuscripts to perfection. We do not make assignments to writers whose work we are not familiar. If you're interested in writing for us, send a detailed, thought-out query with 3 previously published clips. We are always willing to look at material on spec. Sorry, we don't return manuscripts."

LUMBER

$ $ BUILDING MATERIAL DEALER, National Lumber & Building Material Dealers Association, 1405 Lilac Dr. N, Minneapolis MN 55422. Fax: (763)582-3024. Website: www.dealer.org. **Contact:** Carla Waldemar, editor. **10% freelance written.** Monthly magazine covering the lumber and building center industry. Estab. 1985. Circ. 30,000. Pays on publication.

Publishes ms an average of 2 months after acceptance. Byline given. Buys one-time rights. Editorial lead time 3 months. Submit seasonal material 3 months in advance. Accepts queries by mail, fax. Accepts simultaneous submissions. Responds in 2 months to queries; 1 month to mss. Sample copy for $5.

Nonfiction: New product, technical. No general business, interviews/profiles. **Buys 24 mss/year.** Query with published clips. Length: 600-2,500 words. **Pays $100-300.**

Reprints: Accepts previously published submissions.

Photos: State availability with submission. Buys one-time rights. Offers no additional payment for photos accepted with ms. Identification of subjects required.

$ $ PALLET ENTERPRISE, Industrial Reporting Inc., 10244 Timber Ridge Dr., Ashland VA 23005. (804)550-0323. Fax: (804)550-2181. E-mail: editor@ireporting.com. Website: www.palletenterprise.com. Managing Editor: Chaille Brindley. **Contact:** Tim Cox, editor. **40% freelance written.** Monthly magazine covering lumber and pallet operations. Articles should offer technical, solution-oriented information. Anti-forest articles are not accepted. Articles should focus on machinery and unique ways to improve profitability/make money. Estab. 1981. Circ. 14,500. Pays on publication. Buys first, one-time, electronic rights, makes work-for-hire assignments. May buy all rights. Rights purchased depends on the writer and the article. Editorial lead time 2 months. Submit seasonal material 2 months in advance. Accepts queries by mail, e-mail, fax, phone. Accepts previously published material. Accepts simultaneous submissions. Sample copy online. Writer's guidelines free.

Nonfiction: "We only want articles of interest to pallet manufacturers, pallet recyclers, and lumber companies/sawmills." Interview/profile, new product, opinion, technical, industry news; environmental; forests operation/plant features. No lifestyle, humor, general news, etc. **Buys 20 mss/year.** Query with published clips. Length: 1,000-3,000 words. **Pays $200-400 for assigned articles; $100-400 for unsolicited articles.** Call editor to discuss circumstances under which writers are paid in contributor copies. Sometimes pays expenses of writers on assignment.

Photos: State availability with submission. Reviews 3×5 prints. Buys one time rights and Web rights. Negotiates payment individually. Captions, identification of subjects required.

Columns/Departments: Green Watch (environmental news/opinion affecting U.S. forests), 1,500 words. **Buys 12 mss/year.** Query with published clips. **Pays $200-400.**

Tips: "Provide unique environmental or industry-oriented articles. Many of our freelance articles are company features of sawmills, pallet manufacturers, pallet recyclers, and wood waste processors."

$ $ SOUTHERN LUMBERMAN, Hatton-Brown Publishers, P.O. Box 681629, Franklin TN 37068-1629. (615)791-1961. Fax: (615)591-1035. E-mail: southernlumberman@forestind.com. Website: www.southernlumberman.com. **Contact:** Nanci P. Gregg, editor. **20% freelance written.** Works with a small number of new/unpublished writers each year. Monthly journal for the sawmill industry. Estab. 1881. Circ. 15,000. Pays on publication. Publishes ms an average of 3 months after acceptance. Byline given. Buys first North American serial rights. Submit seasonal material 6 months in advance. Responds in 1 month to queries; 2 months to mss. Sample copy for $3 and 9×12 SAE with 5 first-class stamps. Writer's guidelines for #10 SASE.

Nonfiction: How-to (sawmill better), technical, equipment analysis, sawmill features. **Buys 10-15 mss/year.** Query with or without published clips or send complete ms. Length: 500-2,000 words. **Pays $150-350 for assigned articles; $100-250 for unsolicited articles.** Sometimes pays expenses of writers on assignment.

Reprints: Send tearsheet or photocopy of article and information about when and where the article previously appeared. Pays 25-50% of amount paid for an original article.

Photos: Always looking for news feature types of photos featuring forest products, industry materials or people. Send photos with submission. Reviews transparencies, 4×5 color prints. Pays $10-25/photo. Captions, identification of subjects required.

Tips: "Like most, we appreciate a clearly-worded query listing merits of suggested story—what it will tell our readers they need/want to know. We want quotes, we want opinions to make others discuss the article. Best hint? Find an interesting sawmill operation owner and start asking questions—I bet a story idea develops. We need color photos too. Find a sawmill operator and ask questions—what's he doing bigger, better, different. We're interested in new facilities, better marketing, improved production."

$ $ TIMBERLINE, Timber Industry Newsline/Trading Post, Industrial Reporting Inc., 10244 Timber Ridge Dr., Ashland VA 23005. (804)550-0323. Fax: (804)550-2181. E-mail: editor@ireporting.com. Website: www.timberlinemag.com. Managing Editor: Chaille Brindley. **Contact:** Tim Cox, editor. **50% freelance written.** Monthly tabloid covering the forest products industry. Articles should offer technical, solution-oriented information. Anti-forest products, industry articles are not accepted. Articles should focus on machinery and unique ways to improve profitability and make money. Estab. 1994. Circ. 30,000. Pays on publication. Byline given. Buys first, one-time, electronic rights, makes work-for-hire assignments. May purchase all rights. Rights purchased depends on the writer and the article. Editorial lead time 2 months. Submit seasonal material 2 months in advance. Accepts queries by mail, e-mail, fax, phone. Accepts previously published material. Accepts simultaneous submissions. Sample copy online. Writer's guidelines free.

Nonfiction: "We only want articles of interest to loggers, sawmills, wood treatment facilities, etc. Readers tend to be pro-industry/conservative, and opinion pieces must be written to appeal to them." Historical/nostalgic, interview/profile, new product, opinion, technical, Industry News; Environmental Operation/Plant Features. No lifestyles, humor, general news, etc. **Buys 25 mss/year.** Query with published clips. Length: 1,000-3,000 words. **Pays $200-400 for assigned articles; $100-400 for unsolicited articles.** Call editor to discuss circumstances under which writers are paid in contributor copies. Sometimes pays expenses of writers on assignment.

Photos: State availability with submission. Reviews 3×5 prints. Buys one time rights and Web rights. Negotiates payment individually. Captions, identification of subjects required.

Columns/Departments: From the Hill (legislative news impacting the forest products industry), 1,800 words; Green Watch (environmental news/opinion affecting U.S. forests), 1,500 words. **Buys 12 mss/year.** Query with published clips. **Pays $200-400.**

Tips: "Provide unique environmental or industry-oriented articles. Many of our freelance articles are company features of logging operations or sawmills."

N $ $ TIMBERWEST, Timber/West Publications, LLC, P.O. Box 610, Edmonds WA 98020-0160. Fax: (425)771-3623. E-mail: timberwest@forestnet.com. Website: www.forestnet.com. **Contact:** Diane Mettler, managing editor. **75% freelance written.** Monthly magazine covering logging and lumber segment of the forestry industry in the Northwest. "We publish primarily profiles on loggers and their operations, with an emphasis on the machinery, in Washington, Oregon, Idaho, Montana, Northern California, and Alaska. Some timber issues are highly controversial and although we will report on the issues, this is a pro-logging publication. We don't publish articles with a negative slant on the timber industry." Estab. 1975. Circ. 10,000. **Pays on acceptance.** Byline given. Not copyrighted. Buys first North American serial, second serial (reprint) rights. Editorial lead time 3 months. Accepts queries by mail, fax. Responds in 3 weeks to queries. Sample copy for $2. Writer's guidelines for #10 SASE.

Nonfiction: Historical/nostalgic, interview/profile, new product. No articles that put the timber industry in a bad light—such as environmental articles against logging. **Buys 50 mss/year.** Query with published clips. Length: 1,100-1,500 words. **Pays $350.** Pays expenses of writers on assignment.

Photos: Send photos with submission. Reviews contact sheets, transparencies, prints, GIF/JPEG files. Buys all rights. Offers no additional payment for photos accepted with ms. Captions, identification of subjects required.

Fillers: Facts, newsbreaks. **Buys 10/year.** Length: 400-800 words. **Pays $100-250.**

Tips: "We are always interested in profiles of loggers and their operations in Alaska, Oregon, Washington, Montana, and Northern California. Also articles pertaining to current industry topics, such as fire abatement, sustainable forests, or new technology. Read an issue to get a clear idea of the type of material *TimberWest* publishes. The audience is primarily loggers and topics that focus on an 'evolving' timber industry versus a 'dying' industry will find a place in the magazine. When querying, a clear overview of the article will enhance acceptance."

MACHINERY & METAL

$ $ $ CUTTING TOOL ENGINEERING, CTE Publications, Inc., 400 Skokie Blvd., Suite 395, Northbrook IL 60062-7903.. (847)498-9100. Fax: (847)559-4444. Website: www.ctemag.com. **Contact:** Don Nelson, editorial director. **40% freelance written.** Monthly magazine covering industrial metal cutting tools and metal cutting operations. "*Cutting Tool Engineering* serves owners, managers and engineers who work in manufacturing, specifically manufacturing that involves cutting or grinding metal or other materials. Writing should be geared toward improving manufacturing processes." Circ. 35,000. Pays 1 week before publication. Publishes ms an average of 2 months after acceptance. Byline given. Offers 50% kill fee. Buys all rights. Editorial lead time 2 months. Accepts queries by mail, fax. Responds in 2 months to mss. Sample copy and writer's guidelines free.

Nonfiction: How-to, opinion, personal experience, technical. "No fiction, articles that don't relate to manufacturing." **Buys 30 mss/year.** Length: 1,500-3,000 words. **Pays $450-1,000.** Pays expenses of writers on assignment.

Photos: State availability with submission. Reviews transparencies, prints. Buys all rights. Negotiates payment individually. Captions required.

Tips: "For queries, write two clear paragraphs about how the proposed article will play out. Include sources that would be in the article."

$ $ $ THE FABRICATOR, The Croydon Group, Ltd., 833 Featherstone Rd., Rockford IL 61107. (815)399-8700. Fax: (815)484-7700. E-mail: dand@thefabricator.com. Website: www.thefabricator.com. **Contact:** Dan Davis, executive editor. **15% freelance written.** Monthly magazine covering metal forming and fabricating. Our purpose is to disseminate information about modern metal forming and fabricating techniques, machinery, tooling and management concepts for the metal fabricator. Estab. 1971. Circ. 55,000. Pays on publication. Byline given. Buys all rights. Editorial lead time 6 months. Accepts queries by mail, e-mail. Responds in 2 weeks to queries; 1 month to mss. Sample copy and writer's guidelines free. Writer's guidelines online.

Nonfiction: How-to, technical, company profile. Special issues: Forecast issue (January). No unsolicited case studies. Query with published clips. Length: 800-1,200 words. **Pays 40-80¢/word.** Sometimes pays expenses of writers on assignment.

Photos: Request guidelines for digital images. State availability with submission. Reviews transparencies, prints. Rights purchased depends on photographer requirements. Negotiates payment individually. Captions, identification of subjects required.

The online magazine carries original content not found in the print edition. Contact: Laurie Harshbarger.

$ MATERIAL HANDLING WHOLESALER, Specialty Publications International, Inc., P.O. Box 725, Dubuque IA 52004-0725. (877)638-6190 or (563)557-4495. Fax: (563)557-4499. E-mail: dmillius@mhwmag.com. Website: www.mhwmag.com. **Contact:** Cathy Murphy, editor. **100% freelance written.** Monthly magazine covering material handling industry. *MHW* is published monthly for new and used equipment dealers, equipment manufacturers, manufacturer reps, parts suppliers, and service facilities serving the material handling industry. Estab. 1979. Circ. 12,500. Pays on publication.

Publishes ms an average of 2 months after acceptance. Byline given. Buys first rights. Editorial lead time 1 month. Submit seasonal material 2 months in advance. Accepts queries by mail, e-mail, fax. Accepts simultaneous submissions. Sample copy for $29 annually-3rd class. Writer's guidelines free.

Nonfiction: General interest, how-to, inspirational, new product, opinion, personal experience, photo feature, technical, material handling news.

Photos: Send photos with submission. Reviews 3×5 prints. Buys all rights. Offers no additional payment for photos accepted with ms.

Columns/Departments: Aftermarket (aftermarket parts and service); Battery Tech (batteries for lifts-MH equipment; Marketing Matters (sales trends in MH industry); Internet at Work (internet trends), all 1,200 words. **Buys 3 mss/year.** Query. **Pays $0-50.**

The online version of this publication contains material not found in the print edition. Contact: Cathy Murphy, online editor.

$ MODERN MACHINE SHOP, Gardner Publications, Inc., 6915 Valley Ave., Cincinnati OH 45244-3029. (513)527-8800. Fax: (513)527-8801. E-mail: malbert@mmsonline.com. Website: www.mmsonline.com. **Contact:** Mark Albert, editor-in-chief. **5% freelance written.** Monthly magazine. Estab. 1928. Pays 1 month following acceptance. Publishes ms an average of 6 months after acceptance. Byline given. Accepts queries by mail, e-mail, fax, phone. Responds in 1 month to mss. Call for sample copy. Writer's guidelines online.

Advances in metalworking technology are occurring rapidly. Articles that show how this new technology, as embodied in specific products, is being implemented in shops and plants are sought after. Writers are strongly encouraged to call to discuss an idea.

Nonfiction: Uses only articles dealing with all phases of metalworking, manufacturing, and machine shop work, with photos. "Ours is an industrial publication, and contributing authors should have a working knowledge of the metalworking industry. We regularly use contributions from machine shop owners, engineers, other technical experts, and suppliers to the metalworking industry. Almost all of these contributors pursue these projects to promote their own commercial interests." **Buys 5 or fewer unsolicited mss/year.** Query. Length: 1,000-3,500 words. **Pays current market rate.**

The online magazine carries original content not found in the print edition. Contact: A.J. Sweatt (ajsweatt@mmsonline.com).

Tips: "Articles that review basic metalworking/machining processes, especially if they include a rethinking or re-evaluation of these processes in light of today's technical trends, are always welcome."

$ MSI, Reed Business Information, 2000 Clearwater Dr., Oak Brook IL 60523-8809. (630)288-8757. Fax: (630)288-8764. E-mail: rmichel@cahners.com. Website: www.manufacturingsystems.com. **Contact:** Roberto Michel, editor. Monthly magazine. "*Manufacturing Systems* is about the use of information technology to improve productivity in discrete manufacturing and process industries." Estab. 1984. Circ. 105,000. Pays on publication. Publishes ms an average of 3 months after acceptance. Byline sometimes given. Buys all rights. Editorial lead time 3 months. Submit seasonal material 4 months in advance. Accepts queries by e-mail. Sample copy for free. Writer's guidelines online.

Nonfiction: Technical, features about supply chain management software. **Buys 9 mss/year.** Query.

Photos: No additional payment for photos. Captions required.

$ $ ORNAMENTAL AND MISCELLANEOUS METAL FABRICATOR, National Ornamental And Miscellaneous Metals Association, 532 Forest Pkwy., Suite A, Forest Park GA 30297. Fax: (404)363-2857. E-mail: todd@nomma.org. **Contact:** Todd Daniel, editor. **20% freelance written.** Bimonthly magazine "to inform, educate, and inspire members of the ornamental and miscellaneous metalworking industry." Estab. 1959. Circ. 8,000. Pays when article is received. Byline given. Buys one-time rights. Editorial lead time 2 months. Accepts queries by mail, e-mail, fax. Responds in 1 month to queries. Sample copy for 9×12 SAE and 6 first-class stamps. Writer's guidelines for $1.

Nonfiction: Book excerpts, essays, exposé, general interest, historical/nostalgic, how-to, humor, inspirational, interview/profile, new product, opinion, personal experience, photo feature, technical. **Buys 5-7 mss/year.** Query. Length: 1,200-2,000 words. **Pays $300-350 for assigned articles; $150 for unsolicited articles.** Pays expenses of writers on assignment.

Reprints: Send tearsheet, photocopy or typed ms with rights for sale noted and information about when and where the material previously appeared. Pays 100% of amount paid for an original article.

Photos: State availability with submission. Reviews contact sheets, negatives, transparencies, prints. May offer additonal payment for photos accepted with ms. Model releases required.

Tips: "Make article relevant to our industry. Don't write in passive voice."

$ $ $ PRACTICAL WELDING TODAY, The Croydon Group, Ltd., 833 Featherstone Rd., Rockford IL 61107-6302. (815)227-8282. Fax: (815)484-7715. E-mail: stephaniev@thefabricator.com. Website: www.thefabricator.com. **Contact:** Stephanie Vaughan, associate editor. **15% freelance written.** Bimonthly magazine covering welding. "We generally publish how-to, educational articles that teach people about a process or how to do something better." Estab. 1997. Circ. 40,000. Pays on publication. Byline given. Buys all rights. Editorial lead time 6 months. Accepts queries by mail, e-mail. Responds in 2 weeks to queries; 2 months to mss. Sample copy and writer's guidelines free. Writer's guidelines online.

Nonfiction: How-to, technical, company profiles. Special issues: Forecast issue on trends in welding (January/February). No promotional, one-sided, persuasive articles, unsolicited case studies. **Buys 5 mss/year.** Query with published clips. Length: 800-1,200 words. **Pays 40-80¢/word.** Sometimes pays expenses of writers on assignment.

Photos: State availability with submission. Reviews contact sheets. Rights purchased depends on photographer requirements. Negotiates payment individually. Captions, identification of subjects required.

Tips: "Follow our author guidelines and editorial policies to write a how-to piece from which our readers can benefit."

$ $ SPRINGS, The Magazine of Spring Technology, Spring Manufacturing Institute, 2001 Midwest Rd., Suite 106, Oak Brook IL 60523-1335. (630)495-8588. Fax: (630)495-8595. **Contact:** Rita Schauer, editor. **10% freelance written.** Bimonthly magazine covering precision mechanical spring manufacture. Articles should be aimed at spring manufacturers. Estab. 1962. Circ. 10,800. Pays on publication. Publishes ms an average of 3-6 months after acceptance. Byline given. Buys first rights. Editorial lead time 4 months. Accepts simultaneous submissions. Sample copy and writer's guidelines free.

Nonfiction: General interest, how-to, interview/profile, opinion, personal experience, technical. **Buys 4-6 mss/year.** Length: 2,000-10,000 words. **Pays $100-600 for assigned articles; $50-300 for unsolicited articles.**

Photos: State availability with submission. Reviews transparencies, prints. Buys one-time rights. Offers no additional payment for photos accepted with ms. Captions required.

Fillers: Facts, newsbreaks. **Buys 4/year.** Length: 200-1,000 words. **Pays $25-50.**

Tips: "Call the editor. Contact springmakers and spring industry suppliers and ask about what interests them. Include interviews/quotes from people in the spring industry in the article. The editor can supply contacts."

$ $ $ STAMPING JOURNAL, The Croydon Group Ltd., 833 Featherstone Rd., Rockford IL 61107. (815)227-8285. Fax: (815)484-7783. E-mail: katm@thefabricator.com. Website: www.thefabricator.com. **Contact:** Kathleen McLaughlin, associate editor. **15% freelance written.** Bimonthly magazine covering metal stamping. "We look for how-to, educational articles—nonpromotional." Estab. 1989. Circ. 35,000. Pays on publication. Byline given. Buys all rights. Editorial lead time 6 months. Accepts queries by mail, e-mail, fax, phone. Responds in 2 weeks to queries; 2 months to mss. Sample copy and writer's guidelines free.

Nonfiction: How-to, technical, company profile. Special issues: Forecast issue (January). No unsolicited case studies. **Buys 5 mss/year.** Query with published clips. Length: 1,000 words. **Pays 40-80¢/word.** Sometimes pays expenses of writers on assignment.

Photos: State availability with submission. Reviews contact sheets. Rights purchased depends on photographer requirements. Negotiates payment individually. Captions, identification of subjects required.

The online magazine contains material not found in the print edition. Contact: Vicki Bell, online editor.

Tips: "Articles should be impartial and should not describe the benefits of certain products available from certain companies. They should not be biased toward the author's or against a competitor's products or technologies. The publisher may refuse any article that does not conform to this guideline."

$ $ $ TPJ—THE TUBE & PIPE JOURNAL, The Croydon Group, Ltd., 833 Featherstone Rd., Rockford IL 61107. (815)227-8262. Fax: (815)484-7713. E-mail: ericl@thefabricator.com. Website: www.thefabricator.com. Executive Editor: Dan Davis. **Contact:** Eric Lundin, associate editor. **15% freelance written.** Magazine published 8 times/year covering metal tube and pipe. Educational perspective—emphasis is on "how-to" articles to accomplish a particular task or how to improve on a process. New trends and technologies are also important topics. Estab. 1990. Circ. 30,000. Pays on publication. Byline given. Buys all rights. Editorial lead time 6 months. Accepts queries by mail, e-mail. Responds in 2 weeks to queries; 2 months to mss. Sample copy and writer's guidelines free. Writer's guidelines online.

Nonfiction: Any new or improved tube production or fabrication process—includes manufacturing, bending, and forming tube (metal tube only). How-to, technical. Special issues: Forecast issue (January). No unsolicited case studies. **Buys 5 mss/year.** Query with published clips. Length: 800-1,200 words. **Pays 40-80¢/word.** Sometimes pays expenses of writers on assignment.

Photos: State availability with submission. Reviews contact sheets. Rights purchased depends on photographer requirements. Negotiates payment individually. Captions, identification of subjects required.

Tips: "Submit a detailed proposal, including an article outline, to the editor."

$ $ WIRE ROPE NEWS & SLING TECHNOLOGY, VS Enterprises, P.O. Box 871, Clark NJ 07066. (908)486-3221. Fax: (732)396-4215. E-mail: vsent@aol.com. Website: www.wireropenews.com. Editor: Barbara McGrath. Managing Editor: Conrad Miller. **Contact:** Edward J. Bluvias, publisher. **100% freelance written.** Bimonthly magazine "published for manufacturers and distributors of wire rope, chain, cordage, related hardware, and sling fabricators. Content includes technical articles, news and reports describing the manufacturing and use of wire rope and related products in marine, construction, mining, aircraft and offshore drilling operations." Estab. 1979. Circ. 4,300. **Pays on acceptance.** Publishes ms an average of 6 months after acceptance. Byline sometimes given. Buys all rights. Editorial lead time 2 months. Submit seasonal material 2 months in advance. Accepts queries by mail, fax. Accepts simultaneous submissions.

Nonfiction: General interest, historical/nostalgic, interview/profile, photo feature, technical. **Buys 30 mss/year.** Send complete ms. Length: 2,500-5,000 words. **Pays $300-500.**

Photos: Send photos with submission. Reviews contact sheets, 5×7 prints, digital. Buys all rights. Offers no additional payment for photos accepted with ms. Identification of subjects required.

Tips: "We are accepting more submissions and queries by e-mail."

MAINTENANCE & SAFETY

$ $ AMERICAN WINDOW CLEANER MAGAZINE, Voice of the Professional Window Cleaner, P.O. Box 70888, Port Richmond CA 94807. (510)233-4011. Fax: (510)233-4111. E-mail: awcmag@aol.com. Website: www.awcmag.com. **Contact:** Richard Fabry, editor. **20% freelance written.** Bimonthly magazine window cleaning. "Articles to help window cleaners become more profitable, safe, professional, and feel good about what they do." Estab. 1986. Circ. 8,000. **Pays on acceptance.** Publishes ms an average of 4-8 months after acceptance. Byline given. Offers 33% kill fee. Buys first rights. Editorial lead time 2 months. Submit seasonal material 3 months in advance. Responds in 2 weeks to queries; 1 month to mss. Sample copy for free. Writer's guidelines online.

Nonfiction: How-to, humor, inspirational, interview/profile, personal experience, photo feature, technical. Special issues: Upcoming conventions to be covered will be held in Dallas, Texas (2004), and Orlando, Florida (2005). "We do not want PR-driven pieces. We want to educate not push a particular product." **Buys 20 mss/year.** Query. Length: 500-5,000 words. **Pays $50-250.**

Photos: State availability with submission. Reviews contact sheets, transparencies, 4×6 prints. Buys one-time rights. Offers $10 per photo. Captions required.

Columns/Departments: Window Cleaning Tips (tricks of the trade); 1,000-2,000 words; Humor-anecdotes-feel good-abouts (window cleaning industry); Computer High-Tech (tips on new technology), all 1,000 words. **Buys 12 mss/year.** Query. **Pays $50-100.**

Tips: "*American Window Cleaner Magazine* covers an unusual niche that gets peoples' curiosity. Articles that are technical in nature and emphasize practical tips or safety, and how to work more efficiently have the best chances of being published. Articles include: window cleaning unusual buildings, landmarks; working for well-known people/celebrities; window cleaning in resorts/casinos/unusual cities; humor or satire about our industry or the public's perception of it. At some point, we make phone contact and chat to see if our interests are compatible."

$ CANADIAN OCCUPATIONAL SAFETY, CLB Media, Inc., 3228 S. Service Rd., Suite 209, Burlington ON L7N 3H8, Canada. (905)634-2100 ext. 35. Fax: (905)634-2238. E-mail: mgault@clbmedia.ca. Website: www.cos-mag.com. **Contact:** Michelle Gault, editor. **40% freelance written.** Bimonthly magazine. "We want informative articles dealing with issues that relate to occupational health and safety in Canada." Estab. 1989. Circ. 14,000. Pays on publication. Publishes ms an average of 3 months after acceptance. Byline given. Buys one-time rights. Editorial lead time 4 months. Submit seasonal material 4 months in advance. Accepts queries by mail, e-mail, fax, phone. Responds in 3 weeks to queries; 1 month to mss. Sample copy and writer's guidelines free.

Nonfiction: How-to, interview/profile. **Buys 30 mss/year.** Query with published clips. Length: 500-2,000 words. **Payment varies.** Sometimes pays expenses of writers on assignment.

Photos: State availability with submission. Reviews transparencies. Buys one-time rights. Negotiates payment individually. Captions required.

Tips: "Present us with an idea for an article that will interest workplace health and safety professionals, with cross-Canada appeal."

$ CLEANING BUSINESS, P.O. Box 1273, Seattle WA 98111. Fax: (206)622-6876. E-mail: bills@cleaningconsultants.com. Website: www.cleaningbusiness.com. William R. Griffin, Publisher. **Contact:** Bill Sieckowski, editor. **80% freelance written.** Quarterly magazine. "We cater to those who are self-employed in any facet of the cleaning and maintenance industry and seek to be top professionals in their field. *Cleaning Business* is published for self-employed cleaning professionals, specifically carpet, upholstery and drapery cleaners; janitorial and maid services; window washers; odor, water and fire damage restoration contractors. Our readership is small but select. We seek concise, factual articles, realistic but definitely upbeat." Circ. 6,000. Pays 1 month after publication. Publishes ms an average of 3 months after acceptance. Byline given. Buys all rights, makes work-for-hire assignments. Submit seasonal material 6 months in advance. 3 months or less to mss. Sample copy for $3 and 8×10 SAE with 3 first-class stamps. Writer's guidelines for #10 SASE.

Nonfiction: Exposé (safety/health business practices), how-to (on cleaning, maintenance, small business management), humor (clean jokes, cartoons), interview/profile, new product (must be unusual to rate full article—mostly obtained from manufacturers), opinion, personal experience, technical. Special issues: "What's New?" (February). No "wordy articles written off the top of the head, obviously without research, and needing more editing time than was spent on writing." **Buys 40 mss/year.** Query with or without published clips. Length: 500-3,000 words.

Photos: "Magazine size is 8½×11—photos need to be proportionate. Also seeks full-color photos of relevant subjects for cover." State availability with submission. Buys one-time rights. Pays $5-25 for. Captions, identification of subjects, model releases required.

Columns/Departments: "Ten regular columnists now sell four columns per year to us. We are interested in adding Safety & Health and Fire Restoration columns (related to cleaning and maintenance industry). We are also open to other suggestions—send query." **Buys 36 mss/year.** Query with or without published clips. **Pays $15-85.**

Fillers: Anecdotes, gags to be illustrated by cartoonist, newsbreaks, short humor, jokes, gags, poetry. **Buys 40/year.** Length: 3-200 words. **Pays $1-20.**

Tips: "We are constantly seeking quality freelancers from all parts of the country. A freelancer can best break in to our publication with fairly technical articles on how to do specific cleaning/maintenance jobs; interviews with top professionals covering this and how they manage their business; and personal experience. Our readers demand concise, accurate information. Don't ramble. Write only about what you know and/or have researched. Editors don't have time to rewrite your rough draft. Organize and polish before submitting."

$$ EXECUTIVE HOUSEKEEPING TODAY, The International Executive Housekeepers Association, 1001 Eastwind Dr., Suite 301, Westerville OH 43081. (614)895-7166. Fax: (614)895-1248. E-mail: avance@ieha.org. Website: www.ieha.org. **Contact:** Andi Vance, editor. **95% freelance written.** Monthly magazine for "nearly 8,000 decision makers responsible for housekeeping management (cleaning, grounds maintenance, laundry, linen, pest control, waste management, regulatory compliance, training) for a variety of institutions: hospitality, healthcare, education, retail, government." Estab. 1930. Circ. 5,500. **Pays on acceptance.** Publishes ms an average of 6 months after acceptance. Byline given. Buys first North American serial rights. Editorial lead time 2 months. Submit seasonal material 3 months in advance. Accepts queries by mail, e-mail, fax, phone. Sample copy and writer's guidelines free. Writer's guidelines online.

Nonfiction: General interest, interview/profile, new product (related to magazine's scope), personal experience (in housekeeping profession), technical. **Buys 30 mss/year.** Query with published clips. Length: 500-1,500 words. **Pays $150-250.**
Photos: State availability with submission. Reviews negatives. Buys one-time rights. Offers no additional payment for photos accepted with ms. Identification of subjects required.
Columns/Departments: Federal Report (OSHA/EPA requirements), 1,000 words; Industry News; Management Perspectives (industry specific), 500-1,500 words. Query with published clips. **Pays $150-250.**
Tips: "Have a background in the industry or personal experience with any aspect of it."

$ $ PEST CONTROL MAGAZINE, 7500 Old Oak Blvd., Cleveland OH 44130. (440)243-8100. Fax: (440)891-2683. Website: www.pestcontrolmag.com. **Contact:** Susan Porter, associate publisher/executive editor. Monthly magazine for professional pest management professionals and sanitarians. Estab. 1933. Circ. 20,000. Pays on publication. Buys all rights. Submit seasonal material 3 months in advance. Accepts queries by mail, e-mail, phone. Responds in 1 month to mss. Sample copy not available. Writer's guidelines online.

Break in with "information directly relating to the field—citing sources that are either industry experts (university or otherwise) or direct quotes from pest/management professionals."

Nonfiction: Prefers contributors with pest control industry background. All articles must have trade or business orientation. How-to, humor, inspirational, interview/profile, new product, personal experience (stories about pest management operations and their problems), case histories, new technological breakthroughs. No general information type of articles desired. **Buys 3 mss/year.** Query. Length: 1,000-1,400 words. **Pays $150-400 minimum.**
Photos: Certain digital photos accepted; please query on specs. State availability with submission. Pays $50-500 for 8 × 10 color or transparencies for front cover graphics. No additional payment for photos used with ms.
Columns/Departments: Regular columns use material oriented to this profession. Length: 550 words.

The online magazine carries original material not found in the print edition. Contact: Heather Gooch.

MANAGEMENT & SUPERVISION

This category includes trade journals for middle management business and industrial managers, including supervisors and office managers. Journals for business executives and owners are classified under Business Management. Those for industrial plant managers are listed in Industrial Operations.

N $ $ CONTACT MANAGEMENT, Canada's Professional Customer Contact Solutions Forum, August Communications, 225-530 Century St., Winnipeg MB R3H 0Y4, Canada. (888)573-1136. Fax: (866)957-0217. E-mail: s.thiessen@august.ca. Website: www.contactmanagement.ca. **Contact:** Sean Thiessen, managing editor. **90% freelance written.** Bimonthly magazine covering Canadian contact centres. "*Contact Management* is the only magazine specifically targeted at Canadian contact centres. Direct mailed to managers, executives, and suppliers, the magazine explores topics important to the successful execution and planning of the day-to-day activities in a modern Canadian contact centre." Estab. 2000. Circ. 5,200. Pays 30 days after publication. Publishes ms an average of 2 months after acceptance. Byline given. Buys all rights. Editorial lead time 3 months. Submit seasonal material 3 months in advance. Accepts queries by mail, e-mail, fax. Responds in 1 week to queries. Sample copy for free. Writer's guidelines free.
Nonfiction: Exposé, how-to, interview/profile, new product, technical. **Buys 12 mss/year.** Query with published clips. Length: 700-2,250 words. **Pays 15-40¢/word for assigned articles.**
Photos: State availability with submission. Reviews GIF/JPEG files. Buys all rights. Negotiates payment individually. Identification of subjects required.
Columns/Departments: Buys 6 mss/year. Query with published clips. **Pays 15-40¢/word.**

$ HR MAGAZINE, On Human Resource Management, Society for Human Resource Management, 1800 Duke St., Alexandria VA 22314-3499. (703)548-3440. Fax: (703)535-6488. E-mail: hrmag@shrm.org. Website: www.shrm.org. Editor: Patrick Mirza. **Contact:** Karen Caldwell, editorial assistant. **70% freelance written.** Monthly magazine covering human resource management professions with special focus on business news that affects the workplace including compensation, benefits, recruiting, training and development, management trends, court decisions, legislative actions, and government regulations. Accepts queries and mss via website; responds in 45 days. Estab. 1948. Circ. 165,000. **Pays on acceptance.** Publishes ms an average of 2 months after acceptance. Byline given. Buys all rights. Editorial lead time 4 months. Sample copy for free. Writer's guidelines online.

Break in by having "relevant writing experience and a sharp, narrowly-focused article idea on something new or not well-covered elsewhere."

Nonfiction: Technical, expert advice and analysis, news features. **Buys 50 mss/year.** Query. Length: 1,800-2,500 words. Pays expenses of writers on assignment.
Photos: State availability with submission. Buys one-time rights. Identification of subjects, model releases required.
Tips: "Readers are members of the Society for Human Resource Management (SHRM), mostly HR managers with private employers."

$ $ $ HUMAN RESOURCE EXECUTIVE, LRP Publications Magazine Group, 747 Dresher Rd., P.O. Box 980, Dept. 500, Harsham PA 19044. (215)784-0910. Fax: (215)784-0275. E-mail: dshadovitz@lrp.com. Website: www.hrexecutive.com. **Contact:** David Shadovitz, editor. **30% freelance written.** "Monthly magazine serving the information needs of chief human resource professionals/executives in companies, government agencies and nonprofit institutions with 500 or more employees." Estab. 1987. Circ. 60,000. **Pays on acceptance.** Publishes ms an average of 2 months after acceptance. Byline given. Pays 50% kill fee on assigned stories. Buys first, all rights. including reprint rights Accepts queries by mail, e-mail, fax. Responds in 1 month to mss. Writer's guidelines online.

Nonfiction: Book excerpts, interview/profile. **Buys 16 mss/year.** Query with published clips. Length: 1,800 words. **Pays $200-900.** Sometimes pays expenses of writers on assignment.

Photos: State availability with submission. Reviews contact sheets. Buys first and repeat rights. Offers no additional payment for photos accepted with ms. Identification of subjects required.

$ $ INCENTIVE, VNU Business Publications, Dept. WM, 770 Broadway, New York NY 10003. (646)654-7646. Fax: (646)654-7650. E-mail: lestelle@incentivemag.com. Website: www.incentivemag.com. **Contact:** Libby Estell, managing editor. Monthly magazine covering sales promotion and employee motivation: managing and marketing through motivation. Estab. 1905. Circ. 41,000. **Pays on acceptance.** Publishes ms an average of 3 months after acceptance. Byline given. Buys all rights. Accepts queries by mail, e-mail, fax. Responds in 1 month to queries; 2 months to mss. Sample copy for 9×12 SAE.

Nonfiction: General interest (motivation, demographics), how-to (types of sales promotion, buying product categories, using destinations), interview/profile (sales promotion executives), travel (incentive-oriented), Corporate case studies. **Buys 48 mss/year.** Query with published clips. Length: 1,000-2,000 words. **Pays $250-700 for assigned articles; Does not pay for unsolicited articles.** Pays expenses of writers on assignment.

Reprints: Send tearsheet and information about when and where the material previously appeared. Pays 50% of the amount paid for an original article.

Photos: Send photos with submission. Reviews contact sheets, transparencies. Offers some additional payment for photos accepted with ms. Identification of subjects required.

Tips: "Read the publication, then query."

N $ $ SKATEPARK, Harris Publishing, 360 B St., Idaho Falls ID 83402. (208)524-7000. Fax: (208)522-5241. E-mail: john@skateparkmag.com. Website: www.skateparkmag.com. Executive Editor: Steve Smede. **Contact:** John Adams, editor. **25% freelance written.** Magazine published 8 times/year covering skatepark market. "*Skate Park* targets a park and recreation management readership. Articles should focus on the skatepark market as a whole, not the sport of skateboarding itself." Estab. 2001. Circ. 20,000. Pays on publication. Publishes ms an average of 6 months after acceptance. Byline given. Offers $50 kill fee. Buys first North American serial, electronic rights. Editorial lead time 2 months. Submit seasonal material 1 year in advance. Accepts queries by mail, e-mail. Accepts simultaneous submissions. Responds in 2 weeks to queries; 2 months to mss. Sample copy for $5. Writer's guidelines for #10 SASE.

Nonfiction: How-to, interview/profile, new product, opinion, photo feature, technical, travel. "*Skate Park* does not publish articles about skaters, X-Games, pros, etc. Writers should find interesting and informative article ideas that focus on skateparks and related issues." **Buys 4-6 mss/year.** Query with or without published clips. Length: 600-2,000 words. **Pays $50-300 for assigned articles.** Sometimes pays expenses of writers on assignment.

Photos: State availability of or send photos with submission. Reviews 35mm transparencies, GIF/JPEG files. Buys one-time rights. Offers no additional payment for photos accepted with ms. Captions, identification of subjects, model releases required.

Columns/Departments: How'd They Do That? (explores a specific challenge and how subject was able to overcome it), 800-1,200 words. **Buys 2 mss/year.** Query. **Pays $50-200.**

Tips: "We are looking for articles that managers can use as a resource when considering skatepark construction, management, or safety. We are not a traditional skateboarding magazine. We are a trade journal that offers up-to-date industry news and features that promote the skatepark industry."

$ SUPERVISION, 320 Valley, Burlington IA 52601. Publisher: Michael S. Darnall. **Contact:** Teresa Levinson, editor. **95% freelance written.** Monthly magazine for first-line foremen, supervisors, and office managers. "*Supervision*'s objective is to provide informative articles which develop the attitudes, skills, personal and professional qualities of supervisory staff, enabling them to use more of their potential to maximize productivity, minimize costs, and achieve company and personal goals." Estab. 1939. Circ. 2,620. Pays on publication. Publishes ms an average of 6 months after acceptance. Buys all rights. Accepts queries by mail. Responds in 1 month to mss. Sample copy and writer's guidelines for 9×12 SAE with 4 first-class stamps; mention *Writer's Market* in request.

Nonfiction: How-to (cope with supervisory problems, discipline, absenteeism, safety, productivity, goal setting, etc.), personal experience (unusual success story of foreman or supervisor). No sexist material written from only a male viewpoint. **Buys 12 mss/year.** Include biography and/or byline with ms submissions. Length: 1,500-1,800 words. **Pays 4¢/word.**

Tips: "Following AP stylebook would be helpful." Uses no advertising. Send correspondence to Editor.

N $ $ TODAY'S PLAYGROUND, The National Magazine for Today's Playground Design & Standards, Harris Publishing, 360 B St., Idaho Falls ID 83402. (208)524-7000. Fax: (208)522-5241. E-mail: john@todaysplayground.com. Website: www.todaysplayground.com. Executive Editor: Steve Smede. **Contact:** John Adams, editor. **25% freelance written.** Magazine published 8 times/year covering playgrounds and the play equipment market. "*Today's Playground* targets a park and recreation management readership. Articles should focus on the playground market as a whole, including aquatic play and surfacing." Estab. 2000. Circ. 35,000. Pays on publication. Publishes ms an average of 6 months after acceptance. Byline given. Buys first North American serial, electronic rights. Editorial lead time 2 months. Submit seasonal material 1 year in advance. Accepts queries by mail, e-mail. Accepts simultaneous submissions. Responds in 2 weeks to queries; 2 months to mss. Sample copy for $5. Writer's guidelines for #10 SASE.

Nonfiction: How-to, interview/profile, new product, opinion, personal experience, photo feature, technical, travel. "*To-*

day's Playground does not publish any articles that do not directly relate to the playground industry." **Buys 4-6 mss/year.** Query with or without published clips. Length: 600-2,000 words. **Pays $50-300 for assigned articles.** Sometimes pays expenses of writers on assignment.

Photos: State availability of or send photos with submission. Reviews 35mm transparencies, GIF/JPEG files. Buys one-time rights. Offers no additional payment for photos accepted with ms. Captions, identification of subjects, model releases required.

Columns/Departments: Playground Profile (an article that profiles a unique play area and focuses on community involvement, unique design, or human interest), 800-1,200 words. **Buys 2 mss/year.** Query. **Pays $50-200.**

Tips: "We are looking for articles that managers can use as a resource when considering playground construction, management, safety, etc. Writers should find unique angles to playground-related features. We are a trade journal that offers up-to-date industry news and features that promote the playground industry."

N $ $ $ $ TRAINING MAGAZINE, The Human Side of Business, Lakewood Publications, 50 S. 9th St., Minneapolis MN 55402. (612)333-0471. Fax: (612)333-6526. E-mail: edit@trainingmag.com. Website: www.trainingmag.com. **Contact:** Gail Johnson, managing editor. **10% freelance written.** Monthly magazine. "Our core readers are managers and professionals who specialize in employee training and development (e.g., corporate training directors, VP-human resource development, etc.). We have a large secondary readership among managers of all sorts who are concerned with improving human performance in their organizations. We take a businesslike approach to training and employee education." Estab. 1964. Circ. 50,000. **Pays on acceptance.** Publishes ms an average of 3 months after acceptance. Byline given. Buys first North American serial, second serial (reprint) rights. Accepts queries by mail, e-mail, fax. Responds in 2 weeks to queries; 2 months to mss. Sample copy for 10×13 SAE and 4 first-class stamps. Writer's guidelines for #10 SASE or on website.

Nonfiction: Essays, how-to (on training, management, sales, productivity improvement, etc.), humor, interview/profile, new product, opinion, photo feature, technical (use of audiovisual aids, computers, etc.). "No puff, no 'testimonials' or disguised ads in any form." **Buys 15 mss/year.** Query. Length: 200-3,000 words. **Pays $125-1,500.**

Photos: State availability with submission. Reviews transparencies, prints. Buys fist rights and limited reprint rights. Negotiates payment individually. Identification of subjects required.

Columns/Departments: Training Today (new briefs, how-to tips, reports on pertinent research, trend analysis, etc.), 400 words. **Buys 12 mss/year.** Query. **Pays $125-200.**

Tips: "Send an intriguing query that demonstrates writing ability, as well as some insight into the topic you propose to cover. Then be willing to submit the piece on spec. We accept and publish only a small fraction of the manuscripts we receive. How can you improve the chances that your submission will be accepted? Remember two things: 1. *Training* exists for its readers, not its authors. 2. *Training* is, as the name suggests, a magazine; it is not an academic or professional 'journal.' What do those statements mean? The first means that while authors may have many reasons for submitting articles to *Training*, we do not publish articles in order to publicize authors or to promote or help sell their products or services. Regardless of its form—testimonial, case history or whatever—a manuscript that trumpets the benefits of some product, program or technique without explaining how the reader can achieve those benefits (other than by hiring the author or buying the author's products) will not be accepted. 'Tell 'em what you're going to do for them but don't give 'em the recipe' is a legitimate formula for an advertisement or a client proposal, but not for an article submitted to *Training*. The second statement means that we want manuscripts written in the style of magazine articles, not formal 'papers.' Do not begin with phrases such as 'The purpose of this paper is to....' Do not use footnotes; quote sources directly, as newspapers do. Your writing should be clear, crisp,simple, informal and direct."

MARINE & MARITIME INDUSTRIES

$ $ MARINE BUSINESS JOURNAL, The Voice of the Marine Industries Nationwide, 330 N. Andrews Ave., Ft. Lauderdale FL 33301. (954)522-5515. Fax: (954)522-2260. E-mail: sboating@southernboating.com. Website: www.marinebusinessjournal.com. **Contact:** Timothy Banse, executive editor. **25% freelance written.** Bimonthly magazine that covers the recreational boating industry. "*The Marine Business Journal* is aimed at boating dealers, distributors and manufacturers, naval architects, yacht brokers, marina owners and builders, marine electronics dealers, distributors and manufacturers, and anyone involved in the U.S. marine industry. Articles cover news, new product technology, and public affairs affecting the industry." Estab. 1986. Circ. 26,000. Pays on publication. Publishes ms an average of 1 month after acceptance. Byline given. Buys first North American serial, one-time, second serial (reprint) rights. Accepts queries by mail, e-mail. Responds in 2 weeks to queries. Sample copy for $2.50, 9×12 SAE with 7 first-class stamps. Writer's guidelines for #10 SASE.

Nonfiction: Buys 20 mss/year. Query with published clips. Length: 500-2,000 words. **Pays $100-200.** Sometimes pays expenses of writers on assignment.

Photos: State availability with submission. Reviews 35mm or larger transparencies, 5×7 prints. Buys one-time rights. Offers $25-50/photo. Captions, identification of subjects, model releases required.

Tips: "Query with clips. It's a highly specialized field, written for professionals by professionals, almost all on assignment or by staff."

$ $ PROFESSIONAL MARINER, Journal of the Maritime Industry, Navigator Publishing, P.O. Box 569, Portland ME 04112. (207)822-4350. Fax: (207)772-2879. E-mail: editors@professionalmariner.com. Website: www.professionalmariner.com. **Contact:** John Gormley, editor. **75% freelance written.** Bimonthly magazine covering professional seamanship and maritime industry news. Estab. 1993. Circ. 29,000. Pays on publication. Byline given. Buys all rights. Editorial lead time 3 months. Accepts queries by mail, e-mail, fax, phone. Accepts simultaneous submissions.

Nonfiction: For professional mariners on vessels and ashore. Seeks submissions on industry news, regulations, towing, piloting, technology, engineering, business, maritime casualties, and feature stories about the maritime industry. Does accept "sea stories" and personal professional experiences as correspondence pieces. **Buys 15 mss/year.** Query. Length: Varies; short clips to long profiles/features. **Pays 20¢/word.** Sometimes pays expenses of writers on assignment.

Photos: Send photos with submission. Reviews prints, slides. Buys one-time rights. Negotiates payment individually. Captions, identification of subjects required.

Tips: "Remember that our audience is professional mariners and other marine professionals. Stories must be written at a level that will benefit this group."

MEDICAL

Through these journals, physicians, therapists, and mental health professionals learn how other professionals help their patients and manage their medical practices. Publications for nurses, laboratory technicians, and other medical personnel are listed in the Hospitals, Nursing & Nursing Home section. Publications for drug store managers and drug wholesalers and retailers, as well as hospital equipment suppliers, are listed with Drugs, Health Care & Medical Products. Publications for consumers that report trends in the medical field are found in the Consumer Health & Fitness categories.

$ $ $ AMERICA'S PHARMACIST, National Community Pharmacists Association, 205 Daingerfield Rd., Alexandria VA 22314. (703)683-8200. Fax: (703)683-3619. E-mail: mike.conlan@ncpanet.org. Website: www.ncpanet.org. **Contact:** Michael F. Conlan, editor. **10% freelance written.** Monthly magazine. "*America's Pharmacist* publishes business and management information and personal profiles of independent community pharmacists, the magazine's principal readers." Estab. 1904. Circ. 25,000. Pays on publication. Publishes ms an average of 3 months after acceptance. Byline given. Offers 20% kill fee. Buys all rights. Editorial lead time 3 months. Submit seasonal material 3 months in advance. Accepts queries by mail, e-mail, fax. Accepts simultaneous submissions. Responds in 1 week to queries; 2 weeks to mss. Sample copy for free.

Nonfiction: Interview/profile, business information. **Buys 3 mss/year.** Query. Length: 1,500-2,500 words. **Pays $500-1,000.** Sometimes pays expenses of writers on assignment.

Photos: State availability with submission. Reviews contact sheets. Buys one-time rights. Negotiates payment individually. Captions, identification of subjects, model releases required.

$ $ CONTINUING CARE, Stevens Publishing, 5151 Beltline Rd., Dallas TX 75254. (972)687-6786. Fax: (972)687-6770. E-mail: sbienkowski@stevenspublishing.com. Website: www.ccareonline.com. **Contact:** Sandra Bienkowski, editor. **10% freelance written.** Monthly journal covering care management. "*Continuing Care* provides practical information for managed care professionals in case management and discharge planning of high-risk, high-cost patient cases in home health care, rehabilitation, and long-term care settings. *Continuing Care* encourages practical articles on case management, focusing on quality outcome of patient care at a cost-effective price to the health care payer. The magazine also informs readers on professional and business news, insurance and reimbursement issues, and legal and legislative news." Estab. 1971. Circ. 22,000. Pays on publication. Byline given. Offers no kill fee. Buys all rights. Editorial lead time 4 months. Submit seasonal material 4 months in advance. Accepts queries by mail, e-mail, fax, phone. Accepts simultaneous submissions. Sample copy for free. Writer's guidelines free.

Nonfiction: Essays, exposé, general interest, new product, opinion, technical. **Buys 4 mss/year.** Query with published clips. Length: 1,500-2,000 words. **Pays $0-500.** Sometimes pays in contributor copies.

Photos: Send photos with submission. Offers $0-500/photo. Captions, identification of subjects required.

Columns/Departments: Managed Care, 2,000 words. **Buys 3 mss/year.** Query with published clips. **Pays $0-50.**

$ $ $ HEALTHPLAN, American Association of Health Plans, 1129 20th St. NW, Suite 600, Washington DC 20036. (202)778-3246. Fax: (202)331-7487. E-mail: gfauntleroy@aahp.org. Website: www.aahp.org. Editor: Louise Kertesz. **Contact:** Glenda Fauntleroy, managing editor. **75% freelance written.** Bimonthly magazine. "*Healthplan* is geared toward administrators in HMOs, PPOs, and similar health plans. Articles should inform and generate interest and discussion about topics on anything from patient care to regulatory issues." Estab. 1990. Circ. 9,000. Pays within 30 days of acceptance of article in final form. Publishes ms an average of 2 months after acceptance. Byline given. Offers 30% kill fee. Buys all rights. Editorial lead time 2 months. Submit seasonal material 4 months in advance. Accepts queries by mail, e-mail, fax. Accepts simultaneous submissions. Sample copy for free.

Nonfiction: Book excerpts, how-to (how industry professionals can better operate their health plans), opinion. "We do not accept stories that promote products." Query with published clips or send complete ms. Length: 1,800-2,500 words. **Pays 65¢/word minimum for assigned articles.** Pays phone expenses of writers on assignment. Buys all rights.

Tips: "Look for health plan success stories in your community; we like to include case studies on a variety of topics—including patient care, provider relations, regulatory issues—so that our readers can learn from their colleagues. Our readers are members of our trade association and look for advice and news. Topics relating to the quality of health plans are the ones more frequently assigned to writers, whether a feature or department. We also welcome story ideas. Just send us a letter with the details."

$ $ JEMS, The Journal of Emergency Medical Services, Jems Communications, 525 B St., Suite 1900, San Diego CA 92101. (619)687-3272. E-mail: a.j.heightman@elsevier.com. Website: www.jems.com. **Contact:** A.J. Heightman, editor. **95% freelance written.** Monthly magazine directed to personnel who serve the pre-hospital emergency medicine industry: Paramedics, EMTs, emergency physicians and nurses, administrators, EMS consultants, etc. Estab. 1980. Circ. 45,000. Pays on publication. Publishes ms an average of 6 months after acceptance. Byline given. all North American serial rights Submit seasonal material 6 months in advance. Accepts queries by mail, e-mail, fax. Responds in 2-3 months to queries. Sample copy and writer's guidelines free. Writer's guidelines online.

Nonfiction: Essays, exposé, general interest, how-to, humor, interview/profile, new product, opinion, personal experience, photo feature, technical, continuing education. **Buys 50 mss/year.** Query. **Pays $200-400.**

Photos: State availability with submission. Reviews 4×6 prints. Buys one-time rights. Offers $25 minimum per photo. Identification of subjects, model releases required.

Columns/Departments: Length: 850 words maximum. "Columns and departments are staff-written with the exception of commentary on EMS issues and practices." Query with or without published clips. **Pays $50-250.**

Tips: "Please submit a one-page query letter before you send a manuscript. Your query should answer these questions: 1) What specifically are you going to tell *JEMS* readers? 2) Why do *JEMS* readers need to know this? 3) How will you make your case (i.e., literature review, original research, interviews, personal experience, observation)? Your query should explain your qualifications, as well as include previous writing samples."

$ $ $ MANAGED CARE, 780 Township Line Rd., Yardley PA 19067-4200. (267)685-2784. Fax: (267)685-2966. E-mail: editors@managedcaremag.com. Website: www.managedcaremag.com. **Contact:** John Marcille, editor. **50% freelance written.** Monthly magazine. "We emphasize practical, usable information that helps the HMO administrator cope with the options, challenges, and hazards in the rapidly changing health care industry. Our regular readers understand that 'health care reform' isn't a piece of legislation; it's an evolutionary process that's already well under way. But we hope to help our readers also keep the faith that led them to medicine in the first place." Estab. 1992. Circ. 60,000. **Pays on acceptance.** Publishes ms an average of 6 weeks after acceptance. Byline given. Offers 20% kill fee. Buys all rights. Editorial lead time 3 months. Submit seasonal material 4 months in advance. Accepts queries by mail, e-mail, fax. Responds in 3 weeks to queries; 2 months to mss. Sample copy for free. Writer's guidelines on request.

Nonfiction: "I strongly recommend submissions via e-mail. You'll get a faster response." Book excerpts, general interest (trends in health-care delivery and financing, quality of care, and employee concerns), how-to (deal with requisites of managed care, such as contracts with health plans, affiliation arrangements, accredidation, computer needs, etc.), original research and review articles that examine the relationship between health care delivery and financing. Also considered occasionally are personal experience, opinion, interview/profile and humor pieces, but these must have a strong managed care angle and draw upon the insights of (if they are not written by) a knowledgeable MD or managed care professional. **Buys 40 mss/year.** Query with published clips. Length: 1,000-3,000 words. **Pays 60¢/word.** Pays expenses of writers on assignment.

Photos: State availability with submission. Reviews contact sheets, negatives, transparencies, prints. Buys first-time rights. Negotiates payment individually.

Tips: "Know our audience (health plan executives) and their needs. Study our website to see what we cover."

$ $ $ $ MEDICAL ECONOMICS, 5 Paragon Dr., Montvale NJ 07645-1742. (201)358-7367. Fax: (201)722-2688. E-mail: helen.mckenna@medec.com. Website: www.memag.com. **Contact:** Helen A. McKenna, outside copy editor. Semi-monthly magazine (24 times/year). "*Medical Economics* is a national business magazine read by M.D.s and D.O.s in office-based practice. Our purpose is to be informative and useful to practicing physicians in the professional and financial management of their practices. We look for contributions from writers who know—or will make the effort to learn—the nonclinical concerns of today's physician. These writers must be able to address those concerns in feature articles that are clearly written and that convey authoritative information and advice. Our articles focus very narrowly on a subject, and explore it in depth." Circ. 170,000. **Pays on acceptance.** Offers 25% kill fee. Buys first world publication rights Accepts queries by mail, e-mail, fax. Sample copy online. Writer's guidelines online.

Nonfiction: Articles about private physicians in innovative, pioneering, and/or controversial situations affecting medical care delivery, patient relations, or malpractice prevention/litigation; personal finance topics. "We do not want overviews or pieces that only skim the surface of a general topic. We address physician readers in a conversational, yet no-nonsense tone, quoting recognized experts on office management, personal finance, patient relations, and medical-legal issues." Query with published clips. Length: 1,000-1,800 words. **Pays $1,200-2,000 for assigned articles.** Pays expenses of writers on assignment.

Photos: Will negotiate an additional fee for photos accepted for publication.

Tips: "We look for articles about physicians who run high-quality, innovative practices suited to the age of managed care. We also look for how-to service articles—on practice-management and personal-finance topics—which must contain anecdotal examples to support the advice. Read the magazine carefully, noting its style and content. Then send detailed proposals or outlines on subjects that would interest our mainly primary-care physician readers."

$ MEDICAL IMAGING, 295 Promenade St., Suite 2, Providence RI 02908. (401)455-0555. Fax: (401)455-1551. E-mail: mtierney@mwc.com. Website: www.medicalimagingmag.com. **Contact:** Mary Tierney, editor. **60% freelance written.** Monthly magazine covering diagnostic imaging equipment. Estab. 1986. Circ. 20,000. Pays on publication. Publishes ms an average of 2 months after acceptance. Byline given. Buys all rights. Editorial lead time 2 months. Sample copy for $10 prepaid.

Nonfiction: Interview/profile, technical. "No general interest/human interest stories about healthcare. Articles *must* deal with our industry, diagnostic imaging." **Buys 6 mss/year.** Query with published clips. Length: 1,500-2,500 words. Sometimes pays expenses of writers on assignment.

Photos: State availability with submission. Reviews negatives. Buys all rights. Offers no additional payment for photos accepted with ms. Identification of subjects, model releases required.

Tips: "Send a letter with an interesting story idea that is applicable to our industry, diagnostic imaging. Then follow up with a phone call. Areas most open to freelancers are features and technology profiles. You don't have to be an engineer or doctor but you have to know how to talk and listen to them."

$ $ $ $ MODERN PHYSICIAN, Essential Business News for the Executive Physician, Crain Communications, 360 N. Michigan Ave., Chicago IL 60601. E-mail: jconn@crain.com. Website: www.modernphysician.com. **Contact:** Joseph Conn, editor. **10% freelance written.** Monthly magazine covering business and management news for doctors. "*Modern Physician* offers timely topical news features with lots of business information—revenues, earnings, financial data." Estab. 1997. Circ. 32, 552. **Pays on acceptance.** Publishes ms an average of 2 months after acceptance. Byline given. Buys all rights. Editorial lead time 2 months. Accepts queries by mail, e-mail. Responds in 6 weeks to queries. Sample copy for free. Writer's guidelines sent after query.

O→ Break in with a regional story involving business or physicians.

Nonfiction: Length: 750-1,000 words. **Pays 75¢-$1/word.**

The online magazine carries original content not found in the print edition. Contact: Joseph Conn.

Tips: "Read the publication, know our audience, come up with a good story idea that we haven't thought of yet."

$ $ $ THE NEW PHYSICIAN, 1902 Association Dr., Reston VA 20191. **Contact:** Rebecca Sernett, editor. **40% freelance written.** Magazine published 9 times/year for medical students, interns, residents, and educators. Circ. 38,000. **Pays on acceptance.** Publishes ms an average of 3 months after acceptance. Accepts simultaneous submissions. Responds in 3 months to mss. Sample copy for 10×13 SAE and 5 first-class stamps. Writer's guidelines for #10 SASE.

Nonfiction: Articles on social, political, economic issues in medical education/health care. **Buys 7 mss/year.** Query or send complete ms. Length: 800-3,000 words. **Pays 25-50¢/word.** Sometimes pays expenses of writers on assignment.

Reprints: Send photocopy and information about when and where the material previously appeared. Payment varies.

Tips: "Although we are published by an association (the American Medical Student Association), we are not a 'house organ.' We are a professional magazine for readers with a progressive view on health care issues and a particular interest in improving medical education and the health care system. Our readers demand sophistication on the issues we cover. Freelancers should be willing to look deeply into the issues in question and not be satisfied with a cursory review of those issues."

$ $ PHYSICIAN, Focus on the Family, 8605 Explorer Dr., Colorado Springs CO 80920. (719)531-3400. Fax: (719)531-3499. E-mail: physician@macmail.fotf.org. Website: www.family.org. Editorial Director: Charles Johnson. **Contact:** Scott Denicola, editor. **20% freelance written.** Bimonthly magazine. "The goal of our magazine is to encourage physicians in their faith, family, and medical practice. Writers should understand the medical lifestyle." Estab. 1989. Circ. 89,000. **Pays on acceptance.** Publishes ms an average of 6 months after acceptance. Byline given. Buys first North American serial, electronic rights. Editorial lead time 1 year. Accepts queries by mail, e-mail, fax. Responds in 2 months to queries. Sample copy for SASE.

Nonfiction: General interest, interview/profile, personal experience, religious, technical. "No patient's opinions of their doctor." **Buys 20-30 mss/year.** Query. Length: 900-2,400 words. **Pays $100-500 for assigned articles.** Sometimes pays expenses of writers on assignment. Accepts previously published submissions.

Photos: State availability with submission. Reviews transparencies. Buys one-time rights. Negotiates payment individually.

Tips: "Most writers are M.D.'s."

$ $ PODIATRY MANAGEMENT, Kane Communications, Inc., P.O. Box 750129, Forest Hills NY 11375. (718)897-9700. Fax: (718)896-5747. E-mail: bblock@prodigy.net. Website: www.podiatrym.com. Publisher: Scott C. Borowsky. **Contact:** Barry Block, editor. Magazine published 9 times/year for practicing podiatrists. "Aims to help the doctor of podiatric medicine to build a bigger, more successful practice, to conserve and invest his money, to keep him posted on the economic, legal and sociological changes that affect him." Estab. 1982. Circ. 13,500. Pays on publication. Byline given. Buys first North American serial, second serial (reprint) rights. Submit seasonal material 4 months in advance. Accepts queries by e-mail. Accepts simultaneous submissions. Responds in 2 weeks to queries. Sample copy for $3 and 9×12 SAE. Writer's guidelines for #10 SASE.

Nonfiction: Book excerpts, general interest (taxes, investments, estate, estate planning, recreation, hobbies), how-to (establish and collect fees, practice management, organize office routines, supervise office assistants, handle patient relations), interview/profile (about interesting or well-known podiatrists), personal experience. Special issues: "These subjects are the mainstay of the magazine, but offbeat articles and humor are always welcome." **Buys 25 mss/year.** Length: 1,000-2,500 words. **Pays $150-600.**

Reprints: Send photocopy. Pays 33% of amount paid for an original article.

Photos: State availability with submission. Buys one-time rights. Pays $15 for b&w contact sheet.

Tips: "We have been persuading writers to use e-mail for the past few years because of the speed, ease of editing, and general efficiency of the process. The tragic events of 9/11/01 along with the anthrax issue now make the policy mandatory...and the trees will also appreciate it!"

N $ $ PUBLIC SAFETY PRODUCT NEWS, Cygnus Business Media, 1233 Janesville Ave., Fort Atkinson WI 53538. (800)547-7377. Fax: (920)563-1702. E-mail: jeannine.wendorf@cygnuspub.com. Website: www.publicsafety.com. Editor: Ronnie Garrett. **Contact:** Jeannine Wendorf, managing editor. **25% freelance written.** Bimonthly tabloid covering

EMS. "*Public Safety Product News* is a bimonthly magazine reaching EMS professionals nationwide stationed in fire departments, independent and private EMS units, and disaster preparedness agencies. Editorial should be business-casual with an emphasis on improving the EMTs daily practices and the department as a whole." Circ. 25,000. Pays on publication. Publishes ms an average of 3-4 months after acceptance. Byline given. Offers 10% or $100 kill fee. Buys first North American serial, electronic rights. Editorial lead time 2 months. Submit seasonal material 4 months in advance. Accepts queries by mail, e-mail. Responds in 2-4 weeks to queries; 2 months to mss. Sample copy for $10. Writer's guidelines free.
Nonfiction: How-to, interview/profile, new product, technical. No humor, first-person experience, inspirational, or opinion pieces. **Buys 12 mss/year.** Query with or without published clips. Length: 1,800-2,200 words. **Pays $300-500 for assigned articles.**
Photos: State availability with submission. Reviews contact sheets, negatives, 4×5 transparencies, 4×5 prints, TIFF/JPEG files. Buys one-time rights. Offers no additional payment for photos accepted with ms. Captions, identification of subjects required.

N $ $ **SOUTHERN CALIFORNIA PHYSICIAN**, LACMA Services, Inc., 523 W. 6th St., 10th Floor, Los Angeles CA 90014-1210. (213)630-1147. Fax: (213)630-1152. E-mail: editor@socalphys.com. Website: www.socalphys.com. **Contact:** Barbara Feiner, editor-in-chief. **50% freelance written.** Monthly magazine covering the practice of medicine in Southern California. "*Southern California Physician* covers political, legislative, economic, and social/public health issues relevant to practicing medicine in today's challenging healthcare environment." Estab. 2001. Circ. 20,000. **Pays on acceptance.** Publishes ms an average of 6 months after acceptance. Byline given. Offers 50% kill fee. Buys first North American serial, electronic rights. Editorial lead time 6 months. Submit seasonal material 6 months in advance. Accepts queries by mail, e-mail. Accepts simultaneous submissions. Responds in 4-6 weeks to queries; 2 months to mss. Sample copy for $3.50.
Nonfiction: Book excerpts, essays, how-to, interview/profile, opinion, personal experience. No fiction, poetry, new products, or press releases masquerading as stories. **Buys 50 mss/year.** Query with published clips. Length: 1,000-2,500 words. **Pays $100-500.** Sometimes pays expenses of writers on assignment.
Photos: State availability with submission. Buys one-time rights. Offers $25-100/photo. Captions, identification of subjects, model releases required.
Columns/Departments: Politics As Unusual (California legislation), 1,500 words; Careers & Recruitment (job-related issues), 1,000 words; Hot Topics (time-sensitive news), 1,500 words; Medtropolis (profiles of physicians), 1,500 words. **Buys 25 mss/year.** Query with published clips. **Pays $100-300.**
Tips: "I genereally prefer to work on assignment, as my needs tend to be quite specific. The best way to connect with us is to let us know you're interested in receiving an assignment, describe your areas of expertise/interest, and send clips of your strongest work."

$ $ **STITCHES, The Journal of Medical Humour**, Stitches Publishing, Inc., 16787 Warden Ave., R.R. #3, Newmarket ON L3Y 4W1, Canada. (905)853-1884. Fax: (905)853-6565. **Contact:** Simon Hally, editor. **90% freelance written.** Monthly magazine covering humor for physicians. "*Stitches* is read primarily by physicians in Canada. Stories with a medical slant are particularly welcome, but we also run a lot of nonmedical material. It must be funny and, of course, brevity is the soul of wit." Estab. 1990. Circ. 37,500. Pays on publication. Publishes ms an average of 2 months after acceptance. Byline given. Buys first North American serial, electronic rights. Editorial lead time 1 month. Submit seasonal material 4 months in advance. Responds in 6 weeks to queries; 2 months to mss. Sample copy and writer's guidelines free.
Nonfiction: Humor, personal experience. **Buys 30 mss/year.** Send complete ms. Length: 200-2,000 words. **Pays 40¢/word (Canadian).**
Fiction: Humorous. **Buys 40 mss/year.** Send complete ms. Length: 200-2,000 words. **Pays 25¢/word (US) to US contributors.**
Poetry: Humorous. **Buys 5 poems/year.** Submit maximum 5 poems. Length: 2-30 lines. **Pays 35¢/word (US) to US contributors.**
Tips: "Due to the nature of humorous writing, we have to see a completed manuscript, rather than a query, to determine if it is suitable for us. Along with a short cover letter, that's all we require."

$ $ **STRATEGIC HEALTH CARE MARKETING**, Health Care Communications, 11 Heritage Lane, P.O. Box 594, Rye NY 10580. (914)967-6741. Fax: (914)967-3054. E-mail: healthcomm@aol.com. Website: www.strategichealthcare.com. **Contact:** Michele von Dambrowski, editor. **90% freelance written.** Monthly newsletter covering health care marketing and management in a wide range of settings including hospitals, medical group practices, home health services, and managed care organizations. Emphasis is on strategies and techniques employed within the health care field and relevant applications from other service industries. Works with published/established writers only. Estab. 1984. Pays on publication. Publishes ms an average of 2 months after acceptance. Byline given. Offers 25% kill fee. Buys first North American serial rights. Accepts queries by mail, e-mail. Responds in 1 month to queries. Sample copy for 9×12 SAE and 3 first-class stamps. Guidelines sent with sample copy only.

- *Strategic Health Care Marketing* is specifically seeking writers with expertise/contacts in managed care, patient satisfaction, and e-health.

Nonfiction: "Preferred format for feature articles is the case history approach to solving marketing problems. Crisp, almost telegraphic style." How-to, interview/profile, new product, technical. **Buys 50 mss/year.** *No unsolicited mss.* Length: 700-3,000 words. **Pays $100-500.** Sometimes pays expenses of writers on assignment with prior authorization.
Photos: Photos, unless necessary for subject explanation, are rarely used. State availability with submission. Reviews contact sheets. Buys one-time rights. Offers $10-30/photo. Captions, model releases required.
The online magazine carries original content not found in the print edition. Contact: Mark Gothberg.

Tips: "Writers with prior experience on business beat for newspaper or newsletter will do well. We require a sophisticated, in-depth knowledge of health care and business. This is not a consumer publication—the writer with knowledge of both health care and marketing will excel. Absolutely no unsolicited manuscripts; any received will be returned or discarded unread."

$ $ $ $UNIQUE OPPORTUNITIES, The Physician's Resource, U O, Inc., 455 S. Fourth Ave., Suite 1236, Louisville KY 40202. Fax: (502)587-0848. E-mail: bett@uoworks.com. Website: www.uoworks.com. Editor: Mollie Vento Hudson. **Contact:** Bett Coffman, associate editor. **45% freelance written.** Bimonthly magazine covering physician relocation and career development. "Published for physicians interested in a new career opportunity. It offers physicians useful information and first-hand experiences to guide them in making informed decisions concerning their first or next career opportunity. It provides regular features and columns about specific aspects of the search process." Estab. 1991. Circ. 80,000 physicians. Pays 30 days after acceptance. Publishes ms an average of 2 months after acceptance. Byline given. Offers 15-33% kill fee. Buys first North American serial, electronic rights. Editorial lead time 3 months. Submit seasonal material 6 months in advance. Responds in 2 months to queries. Sample copy for 9×12 SAE and 6 first-class stamps. Writer's guidelines online.

Nonfiction: Practice options and information of interest to physicians in career transition. **Buys 14 mss/year.** Query with published clips. Length: 1,500-3,500 words. **Pays $750-2,000.** Sometimes pays expenses of writers on assignment.

Photos: State availability with submission. Buys electronic rights. Negotiates payment individually. Identification of subjects, model releases required.

Columns/Departments: Remarks (opinion from physicians and industry experts on physician career issues), 500-1,000 words; Technology (technical articles relating to medicine or medical practice and business) 1,000-1,500 words. Query with published clips. **Payment negotiated individually.**

The online magazine carries original content not found in the print edition.

Tips: "Submit queries via letter or e-mail with ideas for articles that directly pertain to physician career issues, such as specific or unusual practice opportunities, relocation or practice establishment subjects, etc. Feature articles are most open to freelancers. Physician sources are most important, with tips and advice from both the physicians and business experts. Physicians like to know what other physicians think and do and appreciate suggestions from other business people."

MUSIC

Publications for musicians and for the recording industry are listed in this section. Other professional performing arts publications are classified under Entertainment & the Arts. Magazines featuring music industry news for the general public are listed in the Consumer Entertainment and Music sections. (Markets for songwriters can be found in *Songwriter's Market*, Writer's Digest Books.)

N **$ CLASSICAL SINGER MAGAZINE**, Classical Publications, Inc., P.O. Box 95490, South Jordan UT 84095-0490. (801)254-1025. Fax: (801)254-3139. E-mail: cjw@classicalsinger.com. Website: www.classicalsinger.com. **Contact:** Ms. CJ Williamson, editor. Monthly magazine covering classical singers. Estab. 1988. Circ. 6,000. Pays on publication. Publishes ms an average of 3 months after acceptance. Byline given. Buys second serial (reprint), all rights. Editorial lead time 3 months. Submit seasonal material 3 months in advance. Accepts queries by e-mail. Accepts previously published material. Responds in 1 month to queries. Potential writers will be given password to website version of magazine and writer's guidelines online.

E-mail, mail, or fax writing sample. If accepted, editor will give assignment. Most future correspondence is done via e-mail. All mss must be submitted electronically in Word 98 or higher.

Nonfiction: Editorial calendar available on request. "The best way to find materials for articles is to look on the General Interest forum on our website and see what singers are interested in." Book excerpts, exposé (carefully done), how-to, humor, interview/profile, new product, personal experience, photo feature, religious, technical, travel, Crossword Puzzles on opera theme. No reviews. Query with published clips. Length: 500-3,000 words. **Pays 5¢/word ($50 minimum). Writers also receive 10 copies of the magazine.** Pays telephone expenses of writers with assignments when Xerox copy of bill submitted.

Photos: Send photos with submission. Buys all rights. Captions required.

The online magazine carries original content not found in the print edition. Contact editor by e-mail.

Tips: "*Classical Singer Magazine* has a full-color, glossy cover, glossy b&w pages inside. It ranges in size from 40 pages during the summer to 92 pages in September. The mission statement is: 'Information for a classical singer's career, support for a classical singer's life, and enlightenment for a classical singer's art.'"

$ CLAVIER MAGAZINE, The Instrumentalist Publishing Co., 200 Northfield Rd., Northfield IL 60093. (847)446-5000. Fax: (847)446-6263. **Contact:** Judy Nelson, editor. **1% freelance written.** Magazine published 10 times/year. featuring practical information on teaching subjects that are of value to studio piano teachers and interviews with major artists. Estab. 1937. Circ. 14,000. Pays on publication. Publishes ms an average of 18 months after acceptance. Byline given. Buys all rights. Submit seasonal material 6 months in advance. Accepts queries by mail, fax, phone. Responds in 6 weeks to queries. Sample copy and writer's guidelines free.

Nonfiction: "Articles should be of interest and direct practical value to concert pianists, harpsichordists, and organists who are teachers of piano, organ, harpsichord, and electronic keyboards. Topics may include pedagogy, technique, performance, ensemble playing and accompanying." Historical/nostalgic, how-to, interview/profile, photo feature. Length: 10-12 double-spaced pages. **Pays small honorarium.**

Reprints: Occasionally we will reprint a chapter in a book.

Photos: Digital artwork should be sent in TIF, EPS, JPEG files for PhotoShop at 300 dpi. Send photos with submission. Reviews negatives, 2¼×2¼ transparencies, 3×5 prints. Buys all rights. Offers no additional payment for photos accepted with ms. Identification of subjects required.

N $ $ $ MIX MAGAZINE, Primedia Business Magazines, 6400 Hollis St., Suite 12, Emeryville CA 94608. Fax: (510)653-5142. E-mail: gpetersen@primediabusiness.com. Website: www.mixmag.com. **Contact:** George Petersen, editorial director. **50% freelance written.** Monthly magazine covering pro audio. "*Mix* is a trade publication geared toward professionals in the music/sound production recording and post-production industries. We include stories about music production, sound for picture, live sound, etc. We prefer in-depth technical pieces that are applications-oriented." Estab. 1977. Circ. 50,000. Pays on publication. Publishes ms an average of 3 months after acceptance. Byline given. Offers 50% kill fee. Buys first North American serial rights. Editorial lead time 10 weeks. Submit seasonal material 3 months in advance. Responds in 2 weeks to queries; 1 month to mss. Sample copy for $6. Writer's guidelines free.

Nonfiction: How-to, interview/profile, new product, technical, Project/Studio Spotlights. Special issues: Sound for picture supplement (April, September), Design issue. **Buys 60 mss/year.** Query. Length: 500-2,000 words. **Pays $300-800 for assigned articles; $300-400 for unsolicited articles.**

Photos: State availability with submission. Reviews 4×5 transparencies, prints. Buys one-time rights. Negotiates payment individually. Captions, identification of subjects required.

Tips: "Send Blair Jackson a letter outlining the article, including a description of the topic, information sources, what qualifies writers for the story, and mention of available graphics. A writing sample is also helpful."

$ MUSIC CONNECTION, The West Coast Music Trade Magazine, Music Connection, Inc., 4215 Coldwater Canyon Blvd., Studio City CA 91604. (818)755-0101. Fax: (818)755-0102. E-mail: markn@musicconnection.com. Website: www.musicconnection.com. **Contact:** Mark Nardone, senior editor. **40% freelance written.** "Biweekly magazine geared toward working musicians and/or other industry professionals, including producers/engineers/studio staff, managers, agents, publicists, music publishers, record company staff, concert promoters/bookers, etc." Estab. 1977. Circ. 75,000. Pays after publication. Publishes ms an average of 2 months after acceptance. Byline given. Kill fee varies. Buys all rights. Editorial lead time 2 months. Submit seasonal material 2 months in advance. Sample copy for $5.

Nonfiction: How-to (music industry related), interview/profile, new product, technical. Query with published clips. Length: 1,000-5,000 words. **Payment varies.** Sometimes pays expenses of writers on assignment.

Photos: State availability with submission. Reviews transparencies, prints. Buys one-time rights. Negotiates payment individually. Identification of subjects required.

Tips: "Articles must be informative music/music industry-related pieces, geared toward a trade-reading audience comprised mainly of musicians. No fluff."

N $ $ $ $ OPERA NEWS, Metropolitan Opera Guild, Inc., 70 Lincoln Center Plaza, New York NY 10023-6593. (212)769-7080. Fax: (212)769-8500. Website: www.operanews.com. Editor/Publisher: Rudolph S. Rauch. Executive Editor: F. Paul Driscoll. **Contact:** Kitty March, editor. **75% freelance written.** Monthly magazine for people interested in opera; the opera professional as well as the opera audience. Estab. 1936. Circ. 105,000. Pays on publication. Publishes ms an average of 4 months after acceptance. Byline given. first serial rights only. Editorial lead time 4 months. Sample copy for $5. Writer's guidelines not available.

- Break in by "showing incisive knowledge of opera and the opera scene. We look for knowledgeable and informed writers who are capable of discussing opera in detailed musical terms—but in an engaging way."

Nonfiction: Most articles are commissioned in advance. Monthly issues feature articles on various aspects of opera worldwide. Emphasis is on high quality writing and an intellectual interest to the opera-oriented public. Historical/nostalgic, interview/profile, informational, think pieces, opera, CD, and DVD reviews. Query. Length: 1,500-2,800 words. **Pays $450-1,200.** Sometimes pays expenses of writers on assignment.

Photos: State availability with submission. Buys one-time rights.

Columns/Departments: Buys 24 mss/year.

OFFICE ENVIRONMENT & EQUIPMENT

$ $ OFFICE DEALER, Updating the Office Products Industry, P.O. Box 1028, Mt. Airy NC 27030. (336)783-0000. Fax: (336)783-0045. E-mail: epowell@os-od.com. Website: www.os-od.com. **Contact:** Edwin T. Powell, managing editor. **80% freelance written.** Bimonthly magazine covering the office product industry. "*Office Dealer* is an industry publication serving subscribers involved in the reselling of office supplies, furniture and equipment." Estab. 1987. Circ. 11,000. Pays on publication. Byline given. Buys first North American serial rights. Editorial lead time 4 months. Submit seasonal material 6 months in advance. Accepts queries by mail, e-mail, fax. Accepts simultaneous submissions. Responds in 1 month to queries; 2 months to mss. Sample copy and writer's guidelines free.

Nonfiction: Book excerpts, interview/profile, new product, technical. "We do not publish a great deal of computer-related information—although that will continue to change as the digital age evolves." **Buys 30 mss/year.** Length: 1,500-2,200 words. **Pays $400-650.** Sometimes pays expenses of writers on assignment.

Photos: State availability with submission. Reviews contact sheets, prints. Buys one-time rights. Negotiates payment individually. Captions, identification of subjects, model releases required.

Columns/Departments: In the News; People on the Move; Product Panorama; Product Focus. **Buys 6 mss/year.** Query. **Pays $150-300.**

Tips: "Feature articles for the year are outlined in an editorial calendar published each fall. Although changes can occur, we make every effort to adhere to the published calendar. Feature articles are written by our staff or by freelance writers. We do not accept corporate 'byline' articles. We seek publishable stories written to an agreed-upon length, with text for agreed-upon components—such as sidebars. Stories should be as generic as possible, free of jargon, vague statements, unconfirmed facts and figures, and corporate superlatives. Each query should include the primary focus of the proposed article, the main points of discussion, and a list of any sources to be described or interviewed in the story. Samples of a writer's past work and clips concerning the proposed story are helpful."

$ $ OFFICE SOLUTIONS, The Magazine for Office Professionals, Office Vision Inc., P.O. Box 1028, Mt. Airy NC 27030. (336)783-0000. Fax: (336)783-0045. E-mail: epowell@os-od.com. Website: www.os-od.com. **Contact:** Edwin T. Powell, managing editor. **80% freelance written.** Bimonthly magazine covering the office environment. "*Office Solutions* subscribers are responsible for the management of their office environments." Estab. 1984. Circ. 83,000. Pays on publication. Publishes ms an average of 2 months after acceptance. Byline given. Buys first North American serial rights. Editorial lead time 3 months. Submit seasonal material 4 months in advance. Accepts queries by mail, e-mail, fax. Accepts simultaneous submissions. Responds in 3 weeks to queries; 2 months to mss. Sample copy and writer's guidelines free.

Nonfiction: "Our audience is responsible for general management of an office environment, so articles should be broad in scope and not too technical in nature." Book excerpts, interview/profile, new product, technical. **Buys 75 mss/year.** Query. Length: 1,500-2,200 words. **Pays $400-650.** Sometimes pays expenses of writers on assignment.

Photos: State availability with submission. Reviews contact sheets, prints. Buys one-time rights. Negotiates payment individually. Captions, identification of subjects, model releases required.

Columns/Departments: Inbox (news); Office Toolbox (catch all for new products); Product Focus (one product each issue); Business Computing; Trendwatch—all 700-1,000 words. **Buys 12 mss/year.** Query. **Pays $150-400.**

Fillers: Facts, short humor. **Buys 10-15 issue/year.** Length: 500-800 words. **Pays $150-250.**

Tips: "Feature articles for the year are outlined in an editorial calendar published each fall. Although changes can occur, we make every effort to adhere to the published calendar. Feature articles are written by our staff or by freelance writers. We seek publishable stories written to an agreed-upon length, with text for agreed-upon components—such as sidebars. Stories should be as generic as possible, free of jargon, vague statements, unconfirmed facts and figures, and corporate superlatives. Each query should include the primary focus of the proposed article, the main points of discussion, and a list of any sources to be described or interviewed in the story. Queries should be a single page or less and include a SASE for reply. Samples of a writer's past work and clips concerning the proposed story are helpful."

PAPER

$ $ THE PAPER STOCK REPORT, News and Trends of the Paper Recycling Markets, McEntee Media Corp., 9815 Hazelwood Ave., Cleveland OH 44149. (440)238-6603. Fax: (440)238-6712. E-mail: psr@recycle.cc. Website: www.recycle.cc. **Contact:** Ken McEntee, editor. Biweekly newsletter covering market trends, news in the paper recycling industry. "Audience is interested in new innovative markets, applications for recovered scrap paper as well as new laws and regulations impacting recycling." Estab. 1990. Circ. 2,000. Pays on publication. Publishes ms an average of 1 month after acceptance. Byline given. Buys first, all rights. Editorial lead time 2 months. Submit seasonal material 2 months in advance. Accepts queries by mail, e-mail, fax, phone. Accepts simultaneous submissions. Responds in 1 month to queries. Sample copy for #10 SAE with 55¢ postage.

Nonfiction: Book excerpts, essays, exposé, general interest, historical/nostalgic, interview/profile, new product, opinion, photo feature, technical, all related to paper recycling. **Buys 0-13 mss/year.** Send complete ms. Length: 250-1,000 words. **Pays $50-250 for assigned articles; $25-250 for unsolicited articles.** Pays expenses of writers on assignment.

Photos: State availability with submission. Reviews contact sheets. Negotiates payment individually. Identification of subjects required.

The online magazine carries original content not found in the print edition. Contact: Ken McEntee, online editor.

Tips: "Article must be valuable to readers in terms of presenting new market opportunities or cost-saving measures."

$ $ RECYCLED PAPER NEWS, Independent Coverage of Environmental Issues in the Paper Industry, McEntee Media Corp., 9815 Hazelwood Ave., Cleveland OH 44149. (440)238-6603. Fax: (440)238-6712. E-mail: rpn@recycle.cc. Website: www.recycle.cc. **Contact:** Ken McEntee, president. **10% freelance written.** Monthly newsletter. "We are interested in any news impacting the paper recycling industry as well as other environmental issues in the paper industry, i.e., water/air pollution, chlorine-free paper, forest conservation, etc., with special emphasis on new laws and regulations." Estab. 1990. Pays on publication. Publishes ms an average of 2 months after acceptance. Buys first, all rights. Editorial lead time 1 month. Submit seasonal material 1 month in advance. Accepts queries by mail, e-mail, fax, phone. Accepts simultaneous submissions. Responds in 2 months to queries. Sample copy for 9×12 SAE and 55¢ postage. Writer's guidelines for #10 SASE.

Nonfiction: Book excerpts, essays, how-to, interview/profile, new product, opinion, personal experience, photo feature, technical, new business, legislation, regulation, business expansion. **Buys 0-5 mss/year.** Query with published clips. **Pays $10-500.** Pays writers with contributor copies or other premiums by prior agreement.

Reprints: Accepts previously published submissions.

Columns/Departments: Query with published clips. **Pays $10-500.**

Tips: "We appreciate leads on local news regarding recycling or composting, i.e., new facilities or businesses, new laws and regulations, unique programs, situations that impact supply and demand for recyclables, etc. International developments are also of interest."

PETS

Listed here are publications for professionals in the pet industry—pet product wholesalers, manufacturers, suppliers, and retailers, and owners of pet specialty stores, grooming businesses, aquarium retailers, and those interested in the pet fish industry. Publications for pet owners are listed in the Consumer Animal section.

$ $ PET AGE, H.H. Backer Associates, Inc., 200 S. Michigan Ave., Suite 840, Chicago IL 60604-2383-2404. (312)663-4040. Fax: (312)663-5676. E-mail: petage@hhbacker.com. Editor-In-Chief/Associate Publisher: Karen Long MacLeod. **Contact:** Cathy Foster, senior editor. **90% freelance written.** Monthly magazine for pet/pet supplies retailers, covering the complete pet industry. Prefers to work with published/established writers. Will consider new writers. Estab. 1971. Circ. 23,022. **Pays on acceptance.** Publishes ms an average of 3 months after acceptance. Byline given. Buys first North American serial, one-time rights. Sample copy and writer's guidelines available.

Nonfiction: How-to articles on marketing/merchandising companion animals and supplies; how-to articles on retail store management; industry trends and issues; animal health care and husbandry. No profiles of industry members and/or retail establishments or consumer-oriented pet articles. **Buys 80 mss/year.** Query with published clips. Length: 1,500-2,200 words. **Pays 15¢/word for assigned articles.** Pays documented telephone expenses.

Photos: Reviews transparencies, slides, and 5×7 glossy prints. Buys one-time rights. Captions, identification of subjects required.

Tips: "This is a business publication for busy people, and must be very informative in easy-to-read, concise style. Articles about animal care or business practices should have the pet-retail angle or cover issues specific to this industry."

N $ $ PET COMMERCE, August Communications, 225-530 Century St., Winnipeg MB R3H 0Y4, Canada. (888)573-1136. Fax: (866)957-0217. E-mail: r.naud@august.ca. Website: www.petcommerce.ca. Managing Editor: Sean Thiessen. **Contact:** Rachel Naud, editor. **60% freelance written.** Bimonthly magazine covering pet retail and supply industry. Estab. 1997. Circ. 8,416. Pays 1 month after publication. Byline given. Offers 100% kill fee. Buys all rights. Editorial lead time 3 months. Submit seasonal material 3 months in advance. Accepts queries by mail, e-mail, fax. Responds in 1 week to queries. Sample copy online.

Nonfiction: General interest, how-to, interview/profile, new product. Special issues: Annual Pond issue (February/March); Pre-PIJAC Convention issue (June/July); PIJAC Trade Show issue (August/September); Post PIJAC Convention issue (October/November). No consumer-related articles. **Buys 35-40 mss/year.** Query with published clips. Length: 1,500-3,000 words. **Pays 15-30¢/word for assigned articles.**

Photos: Send photos with submission. Reviews GIF/JPEG files. Buys all rights. Negotiates payment individually. Captions, identification of subjects, model releases required.

Columns/Departments: Clinic Corner (profile of vet), 2,000 words; Company Profile (profile of pet company), 2,000 words. **Buys 12 mss/year.** Query with published clips. **Pays 15-30¢/word.**

$ $ PET PRODUCT NEWS, Fancy Publications, P.O. Box 6050, Mission Viejo CA 92690. (949)855-8822. Fax: (949)855-3045. **Contact:** Marilyn Iturri, editor. **70% freelance written.** Monthly magazine. "*Pet Product News* covers business/legal and economic issues of importance to pet product retailers, suppliers, and distributors, as well as product information and animal care issues. We're looking for straightforward articles on the proper care of dogs, cats, birds, fish, and exotics (reptiles, hamsters, etc.) as information the retailers can pass on to new pet owners." Estab. 1947. Circ. 26,000. Pays on publication. Byline given. Offers $50 kill fee. Buys first North American serial rights. Editorial lead time 3 months. Submit seasonal material 4 months in advance. Accepts queries by mail, fax. Responds in 2 weeks to queries. Sample copy for $5.50. Writer's guidelines for #10 SASE.

Nonfiction: General interest, interview/profile, new product, photo feature, technical. "No cute animal stories or those directed at the pet owner." **Buys 150 mss/year.** Query. Length: 500-1,500 words. **Pays $175-350.**

Columns/Departments: The Pet Dealer News‹ (timely news stories about business issues affecting pet retailers), 800-1,000 words; Industry News (news articles representing coverage of pet product suppliers, manufacturers, distributors, and associations), 800-1,000 words; Pet Health News‹ (pet health and articles relevant to pet retailers); Dog & Cat (products and care of), 1,000-1,500 words; Fish & Bird (products and care of), 1,000-1,500 words; Small Mammals (products and care of), 1,000-1,500 words; Pond/Water Garden (products and care of), 1,000-1,500 words. **Buys 120 mss/year.** Query. **Pays $150-300.**

Tips: "Be more than just an animal lover. You have to know about health, nutrition, and care. Product and business articles are told in both an informative and entertaining style. Talk to pet store owners and see what they need to know to be better business people in general, who have to deal with everything from balancing the books and free trade agreements to animal rights activists. All sections are open, but you have to be knowledgeable on the topic, be it taxes, management, profit building, products, nutrition, animal care, or marketing."

PLUMBING, HEATING, AIR CONDITIONING & REFRIGERATION

$ $ HEATING PLUMBING AIR CONDITIONING, One Mount Pleasant Rd., Toronto ON M4Y 2Y5, Canada. (416)704-1549. **Contact:** Kerry Turner, editor. **20% freelance written.** Monthly magazine. For a prompt reply, "enclose a sheet on which is typed a statement either approving or rejecting the suggested article which can either be checked off, or a quick answer written in and signed and returned." Estab. 1923. Circ. 16,500. Pays on publication. Publishes ms an average of 3 months after acceptance. Accepts queries by mail, e-mail, phone. Responds in 2 months to queries.

Break in with technical, "how-to," Canadian-specific applications/stories.

Nonfiction: News, business management articles that inform, educate, motivate, and help readers to be more efficient and profitable. Readers design, manufacture, install, sell, service maintain, or supply all mechanical components and systems in residential, commercial, institutional, and industrial installations across Canada. How-to, technical. Length: 1,000-1,500 words. **Pays 25¢/word.** Sometimes pays expenses of writers on assignment.

Reprints: Send tearsheet or photocopy with rights for sale noted and information about when and where the material previously appeared.

Photos: Prefers 4×5 or 5×7 glossies, high resolution JPEGS. Photos purchased with ms.

Tips: "Topics must relate directly to the day-to-day activities of *HPAC* readers in Canada. Must be detailed, with specific examples, quotes from specific people or authorities—show depth. We specifically want material from other parts of Canada besides southern Ontario. U.S. material must relate to Canadian readers' concerns. We primarily want articles that show *HPAC* readers how they can increase their sales and business step-by-step based on specific examples of what others have done."

$ $ HVACR NEWS, (formerly *Western HVACR News*), Trade News International, 4444 Riverside Dr., #202, Burbank CA 91505-4048. Fax: (818)848-1306. E-mail: news@hvacrnews.com. Website: www.hvacrnews.com. **Contact:** Gary McCarty. Monthly tabloid covering heating, ventilation, air conditioning, and refrigeration. "We are a national trade publication writing about news and trends for those in the trade." Estab. 1981. Circ. 50,000. Pays on publication. Byline sometimes given. Buys first North American serial rights. Editorial lead time 2 months. Submit seasonal material 2 months in advance. Accepts queries by mail, e-mail. Responds in 1 month to queries. Sample copy online. Writer's guidelines by e-mail.

Nonfiction: General interest, how-to, interview/profile, photo feature, technical. **Buys 25 mss/year.** Query with published clips. Length: 250-1,000 words. **Pays 25¢/word.** Sometimes pays expenses of writers on assignment.

Photos: Send photos with submission. Buys one-time rights. Offers $10 minimum. Negotiates payment individually. Identification of subjects required.

Columns/Departments: Technical only. **Buys 24 mss/year. Pays 20¢/word.**

Tips: "Writers must be knowledgeable about the HVACR industry."

$ $ SNIPS MAGAZINE, 755 W. Big Beaver Rd., Troy MI 48084-4900. (248)244-6416. Fax: (248)362-0317. E-mail: base@bnp.com. Website: www.snipsmag.com. **Contact:** Michael McConnell, managing editor. **2% freelance written.** Monthly magazine for sheet metal, warm air heating, ventilating, air conditioning, and roofing contractors. Estab. 1932. Publishes ms an average of 3 months after acceptance. Buys all rights. Accepts queries by mail, e-mail, fax, phone. Call for writer's guidelines.

Break in with a "profile of a local contractor in our industries."

Nonfiction: Material should deal with information about contractors who do sheet metal, warm air heating, airconditioning, ventilation, and metal roofing work; also about successful advertising and/or marketing campaigns conducted by these contractors and the results. Length: Under 1,000 words unless on special assignment. **Pays $200-300.**

Photos: Negotiable.

PRINTING

$ $ IN-PLANT GRAPHICS, North American Publishing Co., 401 N. Broad St., Philadelphia PA 19108. Fax: (215)238-5457. E-mail: editor.ipg@napco.com. Website: www.ipgonline.com. **Contact:** Bob Neubauer, editor. **10% freelance written.** "*In-Plant Graphics* features articles designed to help in-house printing departments increase productivity, save money, and stay competitive. *IPG* features advances in graphic arts technology and shows in-plants how to put this technology to use. Our audience consists of print shop managers working for (nonprint related) corporations (i.e., hospitals, insurance companies, publishers, nonprofits), universities, and government departments. They often oversee graphic design, prepress, printing, bindery, and mailing departments." Estab. 1951. Circ. 23,000. Pays on publication. Publishes ms an average of 5 months after acceptance. Byline given. Buys all rights. Editorial lead time 2 months. Submit seasonal material 3 months in advance. Accepts queries by mail, e-mail, fax. Writer's guidelines online.

Nonfiction: "Stories include profiles of successful in-house printing operations (not commercial or quick printers); updates on graphic arts technology (new features, uses); reviews of major graphic arts and printing conferences (seminar and new equipment reviews)." New product (graphic arts), technical (graphic arts/printing/prepress). No articles on desktop publishing software or design software. No Internet publishing articles. **Buys 5 mss/year.** Query with published clips. Length: 800-1,500 words. **Pays $300-450.** Pays writers with contributor copies or other premiums for consultants who agree to write just for exposure.

Photos: State availability with submission. Reviews transparencies, prints. Buys one-time rights. Negotiates payment individually. Captions, identification of subjects required.

The online magazine carries original content not found in the print edition. Contact: Bob Neubauer.

Tips: "To get published in *IPG*, writers must contact the editor with an idea in the form of a query letter that includes published writing samples. Writers who have covered the graphic arts in the past may be assigned stories for an agreed-upon fee. We don't want stories that tout only 1 vendor's products and serve as glorified commercials. All profiles must be well balanced, covering a variety of issues. If you can tell us about an in-house printing operation that is doing innovative things, we will be interested."

$ $ SCREEN PRINTING, 407 Gilbert Ave., Cincinnati OH 45202-2285. (513)421-2050. Fax: (513)421-5144. E-mail: screen@stmediagroup.com. Website: www.screenweb.com. **Contact:** Tom Frecska. **30% freelance written.** Monthly magazine for the screen printing industry, including screen printers (commercial, industrial, and captive shops), suppliers and manufacturers, ad agencies and allied professions. Works with a small number of new/unpublished writers each year. Estab. 1953. Circ. 17,000. Pays on publication. Publishes ms an average of 3 months after acceptance. Byline given. Buys all rights. Accepts queries by mail, e-mail, fax. Response time varies to queries. Sample copy available. Writer's guidelines for #10 SASE.

Nonfiction: "Because the screen printing industry is a specialized but diverse trade, we do not publish general interest articles with no pertinence to our readers. Subject matter is open, but should fall into 1 of 4 categories—technology, management, profile, or news. Features in all categories must identify the relevance of the subject matter to our readership. Technology articles must be informative, thorough, and objective—no promotional or 'advertorial' pieces accepted. Management articles may cover broader business or industry specific issues, but they must address the screen printer's unique needs. Profiles may cover serigraphers, outstanding shops, unique jobs and projects, or industry personalities; they should be in-depth features, not PR puff pieces, that clearly show the human interest or business relevance of the subject. News pieces should be timely (reprints from nonindustry publications will be considered) and must cover an event or topic of industry concern." Unsolicited mss not returned. **Buys 10-15 mss/year.** Query. **Pays $400 minimum for major features.**

Photos: Cover photos negotiable; b&w or color. Published material becomes the property of the magazine.

The online magazine carries information from the print edition, as well as original content not found in the print edition. Contact: John Tymoski.

Tips: "Be an expert in the screen-printing industry with supreme or special knowledge of a particular screen-printing process, or have special knowledge of a field or issue of particular interest to screen-printers. If the author has a working knowledge of screen printing, assignments are more readily available. General management articles are rarely used."

PROFESSIONAL PHOTOGRAPHY

Journals for professional photographers are listed in this section. Magazines for the general public interested in photography techniques are in the Consumer Photography section. (For listings of markets for freelance photography use *Photographer's Market*, Writer's Digest Books.)

$ $ NEWS PHOTOGRAPHER, National Press Photographers, Inc., 3200 Croasdaile Dr., #306, Durham NC 27705. (919)383-7246. Fax: (919)383-7261. E-mail: magazine@nppa.org. Website: www.nppa.org. **Contact:** Editor. Published 12 times/year. "*News Photographer* magazine is dedicated to the advancement of still and television news photography. The magazine presents articles, interviews, profiles, history, new products, electronic imaging, and news related to the practice of photojournalism." Estab. 1946. Circ. 11,000. **Pays on acceptance.** Publishes ms an average of 4 months after acceptance. Byline given. Offers 100% kill fee. Buys one-time, and archival electronic rights rights. Editorial lead time 2 months. Submit seasonal material 2 months in advance. Accepts queries by mail, e-mail, fax, phone. Accepts previously published material. Accepts simultaneous submissions. Responds in 1 month to queries. Sample copy for 9×12 SAE and 3 first-class stamps. Writer's guidelines free.

Nonfiction: Historical/nostalgic, how-to, interview/profile, new product, opinion, personal experience, photo feature, technical. **Buys 10 mss/year.** Query. Length: 1,500 words. **Pays $300.** Pays expenses of writers on assignment.

Photos: State availability with submission. Reviews negatives, 35mm transparencies, 8×10 prints. Buys one-time rights. Negotiates payment individually. Captions, identification of subjects required.

Columns/Departments: Query.

$ $ THE PHOTO REVIEW, 140 E. Richardson Ave., Suite 301, Langhorne PA 19047. (215)891-0214. Fax: (215)891-9358. E-mail: info@photoreview.org. Website: www.photoreview.org. **Contact:** Stephen Perloff, editor-in-chief. **50% freelance written.** Quarterly magazine covering art photography and criticism. "*The Photo Review* publishes critical reviews of photography exhibitions and books, critical essays, and interviews. We do not publish how-to or technical articles." Estab. 1976. Circ. 2,000. Pays on publication. Publishes ms an average of 9-12 months after acceptance. Byline given. Buys first rights. Editorial lead time 3 months. Submit seasonal material 6 months in advance. Accepts queries by mail. Accepts simultaneous submissions. Responds in 2 months to queries; 3 months to mss. Sample copy for $7. Writer's guidelines for #10 SASE.

Nonfiction: Interview/profile, photography essay, critical review. No how-to articles. **Buys 20 mss/year.** Send complete ms. Length: 2-20 typed pages. **Pays $10-250.**

Reprints: Send tearsheet, photocopy or typed ms with rights for sale noted and information about when and where the material previously appeared. Payment varies.

Photos: Send photos with submission. Reviews contact sheets, transparencies, prints. Buys all rights. Offers no additional payment for photos accepted with ms. Captions required.

N $ $ SHUTTERBUG/eDIGITALPHOTO.COM, Primedia, 5211 S. Washington Ave., Titusville FL 32780. Fax: (321)269-2025. E-mail: editorial@shutterbug.net. Website: www.shutterbug.net. Managing Editor: Bonnie Paulk. **Contact:**

George Schaub, editor. **90% freelance written.** Monthly tabloid covering photography and digial imaging. "Written for the avid amateur, part-time and fulltime professional photographers. Covers equipment techniques, profiles, technology and news in both silver-halide and digital imaging." Estab. 1972. Circ. 90,000. Pays on publication. Publishes ms an average of 90 days after acceptance. Byline given. Offers 50% kill fee. Buys first North American serial, second serial (reprint), electronic rights. Editorial lead time 3 months. Submit seasonal material 6 months in advance. Accepts queries by mail. Responds in 1 month to queries; 1 month to mss. Sample copy not available. Writer's guidelines for #10 SASE.
Nonfiction: How-to, interview/profile, new product, photo feature, technical, travel. **Buys 100 mss/year.** Query with or without published clips. Length: 1,000-2,000 words. **Payment rate depends on published length.** Sometimes pays expenses of writers on assignment.
Photos: Send photos with submission. Reviews contact sheets, transparencies, CD-ROMs. Buys one-time rights. Offers no additional payment for photos accepted with ms. Captions, model releases required.

$ TODAY'S PHOTOGRAPHER INTERNATIONAL, American Image Press, Inc., P.O. Box 777, Lewisville NC 27023. (336)945-9867. Fax: (336)945-3711. Website: www.aipress.com. **Contact:** Vonda H. Blackburn, editor. **100% freelance written.** Bimonthly magazine. "The make-money-with-your-camera magazine." Estab. 1984. Circ. 93,000. Pays on publication. Publishes ms an average of 4 months after acceptance. Byline given. Buys simultaneous rights. Editorial lead time 4 months. Submit seasonal material 8 months in advance. Accepts simultaneous submissions. Responds in 1 month to queries; 2 months to mss. Sample copy for $3. Writer's guidelines online.
Nonfiction: How freelance photographers make money. How-to (make money with your camera). Nothing outside making money with a camera. Query. Length: 800-2,000 words. **Payment negotiable.**
Photos: State availability with submission. Reviews contact sheets, transparencies, prints. Buys one-time rights. Offers no additional payment for photos accepted with ms. Captions, identification of subjects, model releases required.
Columns/Departments: Query with published clips.

REAL ESTATE

$ $ AREA DEVELOPMENT MAGAZINE, Sites and Facility Planning, Halcyon Business Publications, Inc., 400 Post Ave., Westbury NY 11590. (516)338-0900, ext. 211. Fax: (516)338-0100. E-mail: gerri@areadevelopment.com. Website: www.areadevelopment.com. **Contact:** Geraldine Gambale, editor. **80% freelance written.** Prefers to work with published/established writers. Monthly magazine covering corporate facility planning and site selection for industrial chief executives worldwide. Estab. 1965. Circ. 45,000. Pays on publication. Publishes ms an average of 2 months after acceptance. Byline given. Buys all rights. Accepts queries by mail, e-mail, fax. Responds in 3 months to queries. Sample copy for free. Writer's guidelines for #10 SASE.
Nonfiction: Related areas of site selection and facility planning such as taxes, labor, government, energy, architecture, and finance. Historical/nostalgic (if it deals with corporate facility planning), how-to (experiences in site selection and all other aspects of corporate facility planning), interview/profile (corporate executives and industrial developers). **Buys 75 mss/year.** Query. Length: 1,500-2,000 words. **Pays 30¢/word.** Sometimes pays expenses of writers on assignment.
Photos: State availability with submission. Reviews transparencies. Negotiates payment individually. Captions, identification of subjects required.

The online version of this publication contains material not found in the print edition. Contact: Geraldine Gambale, online editor.

$ $ CANADIAN PROPERTY MANAGEMENT, Mediaedge Communications Inc., 5255 Yonge St., Suite 1000, Toronto ON M2N 6P4, Canada. (416)512-8186 or (866)216-0860. Fax: (416)512-8344. E-mail: barbc@mediaedge.ca. Website: www.mediaedge.ca. **Contact:** Barb Carss, editor. **10% freelance written.** Magazine published 8 times/year covering Canadian commercial, industrial, institutional (medical and educational), residential properties. "*Canadian Property Management* magazine is a trade journal supplying building owners and property managers with Canadian industry news, case law reviews, technical updates for building operations and events listings. Feature building and professional profile articles are regular features." Estab. 1985. Circ. 14,500. Pays on publication. Publishes ms an average of 3 months after acceptance. Byline given. Buys all rights. Editorial lead time 2 months. Submit seasonal material 2 months in advance. Accepts queries by mail, e-mail, fax, phone. Accepts simultaneous submissions. Responds in 3 weeks to queries; 2 months to mss. Sample copy for $5, subject to availability. Writer's guidelines free.
Nonfiction: Interview/profile, technical. "No promotional articles (e.g., marketing a product or service geared to this industry)!" Query with published clips. Length: 700-1,200 words. **Pays 35¢/word.**
Photos: State availability with submission. Reviews transparencies, 3×5 prints, digital (at least 300 dpi). Offers no additional payment for photos accepted with ms. Captions, identification of subjects, model releases required.
Tips: "We do not accept promotional articles serving companies or their products. Freelance articles that are strong, information-based pieces that serve the interests and needs of property managers and building owners stand a better chance of being published. Proposals and inquiries with article ideas are appreciated the most. A good understanding of the real estate industry (management structure) is also helpful for the writer."

$ $ $ $ COMMERCIAL INVESTMENT REAL ESTATE, CCIM, 430 N. Michigan Ave., Suite 800, Chicago IL 60611-4092. (312)321-4460. Fax: (312)321-4530. E-mail: magazine@ccim.com. Website: www.ccim.com/magazine. **Contact:** Jennifer Norbut, editor. **10% freelance written.** Bimonthly magazine. "*CIRE* offers practical articles on current trends and business development ideas for commercial investment real estate practitioners." Estab. 1982. Circ. 12,500. **Pays on acceptance.** Publishes ms an average of 4 months after acceptance. Byline given. Buys all rights. Editorial lead time 4 months. Submit seasonal material 4 months in advance. Accepts queries by mail, e-mail, fax. Responds in 2 weeks to queries; 1 month to mss. Sample copy online. Writer's guidelines online.

O→ Break in by sending résumé and feature-length clips, "including commercial real estate-related clips if available. We keep writers' materials on file for assigning articles."

Nonfiction: How-to, technical, business strategies. **Buys 6-8 mss/year.** Query with published clips. Length: 2,000-3,500 words. **Pays $1,000-1,600.**

Photos: May ask writers to have sources. Send images to editors.

Tips: "Always query first with a detailed outline and published clips. Authors should have a background in writing on business or real estate subjects."

$ $ THE COOPERATOR, The Co-op and Condo Monthly, Yale Robbins, LLC, 31 E. 28th St., 12th Floor, New York NY 10016. (212)683-5700. Fax: (212)696-1268. E-mail: debbie@cooperator.com. Website: www.cooperator.com. **Contact:** Debra A. Stock, managing editor. **70% freelance written.** Monthly tabloid covering New York City real estate. "*The Cooperator* covers condominium and cooperative issues in New York and beyond. It is read by condo unit owners and co-op shareholders, real estate professionals, board members and managing agents, and other service professionals." Estab. 1980. Circ. 60,000. Pays on publication. Publishes ms an average of 3 months after acceptance. Byline given. Buys all rights, makes work-for-hire assignments. Submit seasonal material 3 months in advance. Accepts queries by mail, e-mail, fax. Responds in 1 month to queries. Sample copy and writer's guidelines free.

Nonfiction: All articles related to co-op and condo ownership. Interview/profile, new product, personal experience. No submissions without queries. Query with published clips. Length: 1,500-2,000 words. **Pays $200-250.** Sometimes pays expenses of writers on assignment.

Photos: State availability with submission. Reviews contact sheets, negatives, transparencies, prints, digital. Rights purchased vary. Negotiates payment individually. Captions, identification of subjects required.

Columns/Departments: Profiles of co-op/condo-related businesses with something unique; Building Finance (invesment and financing issues); Buying and Selling (market issues, etc.); Management/Board Relations and Interacting With Professionals (issues dealing with board members and the professionals that help run the building); Interior Design (architectural and interior/exterior design, lobby renovation, etc.); Building Maintenance(issues related to maintaining interior/exterior, facades, lobbies, elevators, etc.); Legal Issues Related to Co-Ops/Condos; Real Estate Trends, all 1,500 words. **Buys 55 mss/year.** Query with published clips. **Pays $200-250.**

Tips: "You must have experience doing journalistic reporting, especially real estate, business, legal or financial. Must have published clips to send in with résumé and query."

$ $ FLORIDA REALTOR MAGAZINE, Florida Association of Realtors, 7025 Augusta National Dr., Orlando FL 32822-5017. (407)438-1400. Fax: (407)438-1411. E-mail: flrealtor@far.org. Website: floridarealtormagazine.com. Assistant Editor: Leslie Stone. **Contact:** Tracey Lawton, editor-in-chief. **30% freelance written.** Journal published 11 times/year covering Florida real estate. "As the official publication of the Florida Association of Realtors, we provide helpful articles for our 85,000 members. We try to stay up on the trends and issues that affect business in Florida's real estate market." Estab. 1925. Circ. 85,000. Pays on publication. Publishes ms an average of 1 month after acceptance. Byline given. Editorial lead time 2 months. Accepts queries by mail, e-mail, fax, phone. Accepts simultaneous submissions. Sample copy online.

Nonfiction: Book excerpts, how-to, inspirational, interview/profile, new product, all with real estate angle—Florida-specific is good. "No fiction, poetry." **Buys varying number of mss/year.** Query with published clips. Length: 800-1,500 words. **Pays $300-700.** Sometimes pays expenses of writers on assignment.

Photos: State availability with submission. Buys one-time rights. Negotiates payment individually. Captions, identification of subjects, model releases required.

Columns/Departments: Written in-house. Publishes: Promotional Strategies, 900 words; Technology & You, 1,000 words; Realtor Advantage, 1,000 words. **Buys varying number of mss/year. Payment varies.**

Fillers: Short humor. **Buys varying number/year.**

Tips: "Build a solid reputation for specializing in real estate-specific writing in state/national publications. Query with specific article ideas."

$ JOURNAL OF PROPERTY MANAGEMENT, Institute of Real Estate Management, P.O. Box 109025, Chicago IL 60611-9025. (312)329-6058. Fax: (312)410-7958. E-mail: adruckman@irem.org. Website: www.irem.org. **Contact:** Amanda Druckman, associate editor. **30% freelance written.** Bimonthly magazine covering real estate management. "The *Journal* has a feature/information slant designed to educate readers in the application of new techniques and to keep them abreast of current industry trends." Circ. 20,000. **Pays on acceptance.** Publishes ms an average of 3 months after acceptance. Byline given. Buys all rights. Accepts queries by mail, e-mail, fax. Responds in 6 weeks to queries; 1 month to mss. Sample copy for free. Writer's guidelines online.

Nonfiction: Demographic shifts in business employment and buying patterns, marketing. How-to, interview/profile, technical (building systems/computers). "No non-real estate subjects, personality or company humor." **Buys 8-12 mss/year.** Query with published clips. Length: 1,200-1,500 words. Sometimes pays expenses of writers on assignment.

Reprints: Send tearsheet, photocopy or typed ms. Pays 35% of amount paid for an original article.

Photos: State availability with submission. Reviews contact sheets. Buys one-time rights. May offer additional payment for photos accepted with ms. Identification of subjects, model releases required.

Columns/Departments: Insurance; Tax Issues; Technology; Maintenance; Personal Development; Legal Issues. Length: 500 words. **Buys 6-8 mss/year.** Query.

$ NATIONAL RELOCATION & REAL ESTATE, RIS Media, 50 Water St., Norwalk CT 06854. (203)855-1234. Fax: (203)852-7208. E-mail: erin@rismedia.com. Website: rismedia.com. **Contact:** Erin Harrison, executive editor. **30-50% freelance written.** Monthly magazine covering residential real estate and corporate relocation. "Our readers are professionals within the relocation and real estate industries; therefore, we require our writers to have sufficient knowledge of the workings of these industries in order to ensure depth and accuracy in reporting." Estab. 1980. Circ. 45,000. Pays on publication. Byline sometimes given. Offers kill fee. Buys all rights. Editorial lead time 2 months. Accepts queries by mail, e-mail. Responds in 2 weeks to queries. Sample copy for free.

Nonfiction: Exposé, how-to (use the Internet to sell real estate, etc.), interview/profile, new product, opinion, technical. Query with published clips. Length: 250-1,200 words. Pays unsolicited article writers with contributor copies upon use. Sometimes pays expenses of writers on assignment.

Photos: Send photos with submission. Reviews transparencies. Offers no additional payment for photos accepted with ms. Captions required.

Columns/Departments: Query with published clips.

The online news carries original content not found in the print edition. Website features daily news service, written submissions and other information on publication. Contact: Ed Silverstein.

Tips: "All queries must be done in writing. Phone queries are unacceptable. Any clips or materials sent should indicate knowledge of the real estate and relocation industries. In general, we are open to all knowledgeable contributors."

$ $ OFFICE BUILDINGS MAGAZINE, Yale Robbins, Inc., 31 E. 28th St., New York NY 10016. (212)683-5700. Fax: (212)545-0764. E-mail: info@yrinc.com. Website: www.yrinc.com; www.mrofficespace.com. **Contact:** Debbie Estock, executive editor. **15% freelance written.** "Annual magazine covering market statistics, trends, and thinking of area professionals on the current and future state of the real estate market." Estab. 1987. Circ. 10,500. Pays half on acceptance and half on publication. Byline sometimes given. Offers kill fee. Buys all rights. Editorial lead time 2 months. Accepts queries by mail, e-mail, fax. Sample copy and writer's guidelines free.

Nonfiction: Survey of specific markets. **Buys 15-20 mss/year.** Query with published clips. Length: 1,500-2,000 words. **Pays $600-700.** Sometimes pays expenses of writers on assignment.

N $ $ PROPERTIES MAGAZINE, Properties Magazine, Inc., P.O. Box 112127, Cleveland OH 44111. (216)251-0035. Fax: (216)251-0064. E-mail: kkrych@propertiesmag.com. Editor: Kenneth C. Krych. **25% freelance written.** Monthly magazine covering real estate, residential, commerical construction. "*Properties Magazine* is published for executives in the real estate, building, banking, design, architectural, property management, tax, and law community—busy people who need the facts presented in an interesting and informative format." Estab. 1946. Circ. over 10,000. Pays on publication. Publishes ms an average of 2 months after acceptance. Byline given. Buys first rights. Editorial lead time 2 months. Submit seasonal material 2 months in advance. Accepts queries by mail, fax. Responds in 3 weeks to queries. Sample copy for $3.95.

Nonfiction: General interest, how-to, humor, new product. Special issues: Environmental issues (September); Security/Fire Protection (October); Tax Issues (November); Computers In Real Estate (December). **Buys 30 mss/year.** Send complete ms. Length: 500-2,000 words. **Pays 50¢/column line.** Sometimes pays expenses of writers on assignment.

Photos: Send photos with submission. Reviews prints. Buys one-time rights. Offers no additional payment for photos accepted with ms. Negotiates payment individually. Captions required.

Columns/Departments: Buys 25 mss/year. Query or send complete ms. **Pays 50¢/column line.**

N $ $ REM, The Real Estate Magazine, House Publications, 115 Thorncliff Park Dr., Toronto ON M4C 3E4, Canada. (416)425-3504. Fax: (416)406-0882. E-mail: jim@remonline.com. Website: www.remonline.com. **Contact:** Jim Adair, editor. **35% freelance written.** Monthly trade journal covering real estate. "*REM* provides Canadian real estate agents and brokers with news and opinion they can't get anywhere else. It is an independent publication and not affiliated with any real estate board, association, or company." Estab. 1989. Circ. 50,000. **Pays on acceptance.** Publishes ms an average of 2 months after acceptance. Offers 25% kill fee. Buys first Canadian serial rights. Editorial lead time 3 months. Submit seasonal material 3 months in advance. Accepts queries by mail, e-mail, fax. Accepts previously published material. Accepts simultaneous submissions. Sample copy for free.

Nonfiction: Book excerpts, exposé, inspirational, interview/profile, new product, personal experience. No articles geared to consumers about market conditions or how to choose a realtor. Must have Canadian content. **Buys 60 mss/year.** Query. Length: 500-1,500 words. **Pays $200-400.**

Photos: Send photos with submission. Reviews transparencies, prints, GIF/JPEG files. Buys one-time rights. Offers $25/photo. Captions, identification of subjects required.

Tips: "Stories must be of interest or practical use for Canadian realtors. Check out our website to see the types of stories we require."

RESOURCES & WASTE REDUCTION

$ $ COMPOSTING NEWS, The Latest News in Composting and Scrap Wood Management, McEntee Media Corp., 9815 Hazelwood Ave., Cleveland OH 44149. (440)238-6603. Fax: (440)238-6712. E-mail: cn@recycle.cc. **Contact:** Ken McEntee, editor. **5% freelance written.** Monthly newsletter. "We are interested in any news impacting the composting industry including new laws, regulations, new facilities/programs, end-uses, research, etc." Estab. 1992. Circ. 1,000. Pays on publication. Publishes ms an average of 1 month after acceptance. Buys first, all rights. Editorial lead time 1 month. Submit seasonal material 1 month in advance. Accepts queries by mail, e-mail, fax, phone. Accepts previously published material. Accepts simultaneous submissions. Responds in 2 months to queries. Sample copy for 9×12 SAE and 55¢ postage. Writer's guidelines for #10 SASE.

Nonfiction: Book excerpts, essays, general interest, how-to, interview/profile, new product, opinion, personal experience, photo feature, technical, new business, legislation, regulation, business expansion. **Buys 0-5 mss/year.** Query with published clips. Length: 100-5,000 words. **Pays $10-500.** Pays writers with contributor copies or other premiums by prior agreement.

Columns/Departments: Query with published clips. **Pays $10-500.**

The online magazine carries original content not found in the print edition. Contact: Ken McEntee.

Tips: "We appreciate leads on local news regarding composting, i.e., new facilities or business, new laws and regulations, unique programs, situations that impact supply and demand for composting. International developments are also of interest."

$ $ $ EROSION CONTROL, The Journal for Erosion and Sediment Control Professionals, Forester Communications, Inc., 2946 De La Vina St., Santa Barbara CA 93105. (805)682-1300. Fax: (805)682-0200. E-mail: eceditor@forester.net. Website: www.erosioncontrol.com. **Contact:** Janice Kaspersen, editor. **60% freelance written.** Magazine published 7 times/year covering all aspects of erosion prevention and sediment control. "*Erosion Control* is a practical, hands-on, 'how-to' professional journal. Our readers are civil engineers, landscape architects, builders, developers, public works officials, road and highway construction officials and engineers, soils specialists, farmers, landscape contractors and others involved with any activity that disturbs significant areas of surface vegetation." Estab. 1994. Circ. 20,000. Pays 30 days after acceptance. Publishes ms an average of 3 months after acceptance. Byline given. Buys all rights. Editorial lead time 4 months. Submit seasonal material 4 months in advance. Accepts queries by mail, e-mail, fax, phone. Responds in 3 weeks to queries. Sample copy and writer's guidelines free.

Nonfiction: Photo feature, technical. **Buys 15 mss/year.** Query with published clips. Length: 3,000-4,000 words. **Pays $700-850.** Sometimes pays expenses of writers on assignment.

Photos: Send photos with submission. Reviews transparencies, prints. Buys all rights. Offers no additional payment for photos accepted with ms. Captions, identification of subjects, model releases required.

Tips: "Writers should have a good grasp of technology involved, good writing and communication skills. Most of our freelanced articles include extensive interviews with engineers, contractors, developers, or project owners, and we often provide contact names for articles we assign."

$ $ MSW MANAGEMENT, The Journal for Municipal Solid Waste Professionals, Forester Communications, Inc., P.O. Box 3100, Santa Barbara CA 93130. (805)682-1300. Fax: (805)682-0200. E-mail: editor@forester.net. Website: www.mswmanagement.net. **Contact:** John Trotti, editor. **70% freelance written.** Bimonthly magazine. "*MSW Management* is written for public sector solid waste professionals—the people working for the local counties, cities, towns, boroughs, and provinces. They run the landfills, recycling programs, composting, incineration. They are responsible for all aspects of garbage collection and disposal; buying and maintaining the associated equipment; and designing, engineering, and building the waste processing facilities, transfer stations, and landfills." Estab. 1991. Circ. 25,000. Pays on publication. Byline given. Buys all rights. Editorial lead time 4 months. Submit seasonal material 4 months in advance. Accepts queries by mail, e-mail, fax, phone. Accepts simultaneous submissions. Responds in 6 weeks to queries; 2 months to mss. Sample copy and writer's guidelines free. Writer's guidelines online.

Nonfiction: Photo feature, technical. "No rudimentary, basic articles written for the average person on the street. Our readers are experienced professionals with years of practical, in-the-field experience. Any material submitted that we judge as too fundamental will be rejected." **Buys 15 mss/year.** Query. Length: 3,000-4,000 words. **Pays $350-750.** Sometimes pays expenses of writers on assignment.

Photos: Send photos with submission. Reviews transparencies, prints. Buys all rights. Offers no additional payment for photos accepted with ms. Captions, identification of subjects, model releases required.

The online version of *MSW Management* includes material not found in the print edition. Contact: John Trotti.

Tips: "We're a small company, easy to reach. We're open to any and all ideas as to possible editorial topics. We endeavor to provide the reader with usable material, and present it in full color with graphic embellishment whenever possible. Dry, highly technical material is edited to make it more palatable and concise. Most of our feature articles come from freelancers. Interviews and quotes should be from public sector solid waste managers and engineers—*not* PR people, *not* manufacturers. Strive to write material that is 'over the heads' of our readers. If anything, attempt to make them 'reach.' Anything submitted that is too basic, elementary, fundamental, rudimentary, etc., cannot be accepted for publication."

$ $ $ STORMWATER, The Journal for Surface Water Quality Professionals, Forester Communications, Inc., 2946 De La Vina St., Santa Barbara CA 93105. (805)682-1300. Fax: (805)682-0200. E-mail: sweditor@forester.net. Website: www.stormh2o.com. **Contact:** Janice Kaspersen, editor. **10% freelance written.** "*Stormwater* is a practical business journal for professionals involved with surface water quality issues, protection, projects, and programs. Our readers are municipal employees, regulators, engineers, and consultants concerned with stormwater management." Estab. 2000. Circ. 20,000. Publishes ms an average of 3 months after acceptance. Byline given. Editorial lead time 4 months. Submit seasonal material 4 months in advance. Accepts queries by mail, e-mail. Responds in 3 weeks to queries. Writer's guidelines free.

Nonfiction: Technical. **Buys 8-10 mss/year.** Query with published clips. Length: 3,000-4,000 words. **Pays $700-850.** Sometimes pays expenses of writers on assignment.

Photos: Send photos with submission. Buys all rights. Offers no additional payment for photos accepted with ms. Captions, identification of subjects, model releases required.

Tips: "Writers should have a good grasp of the technology and regulations involved in stormwater management and good interviewing skills. Our freelanced articles include extensive interviews with engineers, stormwater managers, and project owners, and we often provide contact names for articles we assign. See past editorial content online."

$ WASTE AGE MAGAZINE, The Business Magazine For Waste Industry Professionals, Intertec Publishing, 6151 Powers Ferry Rd. NW, Atlanta GA 30339-2941. (770)618-0112. Fax: (770)618-0349. E-mail: ptom@primediabusiness.com. Editorial Director: Bill Wolpin. **Contact:** Patti Tom, managing editor. **50% freelance written.** Monthly magazine. "*Waste Age* reaches individuals and firms engaged in the removal, collection, processing, transportation, and disposal of solid/hazardous liquid wastes. This includes: private refuse contractors; landfill operators; municipal, county and other government officials; recyclers and handlers of secondary materials; major generators of waste, such as plants and chain stores; engineers, architects and consultants; manufactures and distributors of equipment; universities, libraries and associations; and legal, insurance and financial firms allied to the field. Readers include: owners, presidents, vice-presidents, directors, superintendents, engineers, managers, supervisors, consultants, purchasing agents and commissioners." Estab. 1958. Circ. 40,000. Pays on publication. Publishes ms an average of 4 months after acceptance. Byline given. Editorial lead time 2 months. Responds in 1 week to queries; 1 month to mss. Sample copy for free. Writer's guidelines free.

Nonfiction: How-to (practical information on improving solid waste management, i.e., how to rehabilitate a transfer station, how to improve recyclable collection, how to manage a landfill, etc.), interview/profile (of prominent persons in the solid waste industry.). "No feel-good 'green' articles about recycling. Remember our readers are not the citizens but the governments and private contractors. No 'why you should recycle' articles." **Buys over 50 mss/year.** Query. Length: 500-2,000 words. Pays expenses of writers on assignment.

Photos: Send photos with submission. Reviews contact sheets, negatives, transparencies, prints, digital. Negotiates payment individually. Identification of subjects required.

Tips: "Read the magazine and understand our audience. Write useful articles with sidebars that the readers can apply to their jobs. Use the Associated Press style book. Freelancers can send in queries or manuscripts, or can fax or e-mail a letter of interest (including qualifications/résumé) in possible assignments. Writers must be deadline-oriented."

$ $ WATER WELL JOURNAL, National Ground Water Association, 601 Dempsey Rd., Westerville OH 43081. Fax: (614)898-7786. E-mail: jross@ngwa.org. Website: www.ngwa.org. **Contact:** Jill Ross, director of publications. **25% freelance written.** Monthly magazine covering the ground water industry; well drilling. "Each month the *Water Well Journal* covers the topics of drilling, rigs and heavy equipment, pumping systems, water quality, business management, water supply, on-site waste water treatment, and diversification opportunities, including geoexchange installations, environmental remediation, irrigation, dewatering and foundation installation. It also offers updates on regulatory issues that impact the ground water industry." Estab. 1948. Circ. 30,000. Pays on publication. Publishes ms an average of 3 months after acceptance. Byline given. Buys all rights. Editorial lead time 2 months. Submit seasonal material 3 months in advance. Accepts queries by mail, e-mail, fax, phone. Responds in 2 weeks to queries; 1 month to mss. Sample copy for 9×12 SAE and 2 first-class stamps. Writer's guidelines free.

Nonfiction: Essays (sometimes), historical/nostalgic (sometimes), how-to (recent examples include how to chlorinate a well; how to buy a used rig; how to do bill collections), interview/profile, new product, personal experience, photo feature, technical, business managment. No company profiles; extended product releases. **Buys up to 20 mss/year.** Query with published clips. Length: 1,000-4,000 words. **Pays $100-600.**

Photos: State availability with submission. Offers $50-250/photo. Captions, identification of subjects required.

Tips: "Some previous experience or knowledge in groundwater/drilling/construction industry helpful. Published clips a must."

SELLING & MERCHANDISING

Sales personnel and merchandisers interested in how to sell and market products successfully consult these journals. Publications in nearly every category of Trade also buy sales-related materials if they are slanted to the product or industry with which they deal.

$ $ BALLOONS AND PARTIES MAGAZINE, Partilife Publications, 65 Sussex St., Hackensack NJ 07601. (201)441-4224. Fax: (201)342-8118. E-mail: mark@balloonsandparties.com. Website: www.balloonsandparties.com. **Contact:** Mark Zettler, publisher. **10% freelance written.** International trade journal for professional party decorators and for gift delivery businesses published 6 times/year. Estab. 1986. Circ. 7,000. Pays on publication. Publishes ms an average of 3 months after acceptance. Byline given. Buys all rights. Submit seasonal material 6 months in advance. Accepts queries by mail, e-mail, fax, phone. Responds in 6 weeks to queries. Sample copy for 9×12 SAE.

Nonfiction: Essays, how-to, interview/profile, new product, personal experience, photo feature, technical, craft. **Buys 12 mss/year.** Query with or without published clips or send complete ms. Length: 500-1,500 words. **Pays $100-300 for assigned articles; $50-200 for unsolicited articles.** Sometimes pays expenses of writers on assignment.

Reprints: Send ms with rights for sale noted and information about when and where the material previously appeared Length: up to 2,500 words. Pays 10¢/word.

Photos: Send photos with submission. Reviews 2×2 transparencies, 3×5 prints. Buys all rights. Captions, identification of subjects, model releases required.

Columns/Departments: Problem Solver (small business issues); Recipes That Cook (centerpiece ideas with detailed how-to), 400-1,000 words. Send complete ms with photos.

Tips: "Show unusual, lavish, and outstanding examples of balloon sculpture, design and decorating, and other craft projects. Offer specific how-to information. Be positive and motivational in style."

$ $ $ $ CONSUMER GOODS TECHNOLOGY, Edgell Communications, 4 Middlebury Blvd., Randolph NJ 07867. (973)252-0100. Fax: (973)252-9020. Website: www.consumergoods.com. **Contact:** John Hall, managing editor (jhall@edgellmail.com) or Tim Clark, senior editor (tclark@edgellmail.com). **40% freelance written.** Monthly tabloid benchmarking business technology performance. Estab. 1987. Circ. 25,000. Pays on publication. Publishes ms an average of 2 months after acceptance. Byline given. Buys first North American serial, second serial (reprint), electronic, all rights. Editorial lead time 3 months. Accepts queries by e-mail. Sample copy online. Writer's guidelines by e-mail.

Nonfiction: "We create several supplements annually, often using freelance." Essays, exposé, interview/profile. **Buys 60 mss/year.** Query with published clips. Length: 700-1,900 words. **Pays $600-1,200.** Sometimes pays expenses of writers on assignment.

Photos: Buys all rights. Negotiates payment individually. Identification of subjects, model releases required.

Columns/Departments: Columns 400-750 words—featured columnists. **Buys 4 mss/year.** Query with published clips. **Pays 75¢-$1/word.**

Tips: "All stories in *Consumer Goods Technology* are told through the voice of the consumer goods executive. We only quote VP-level or C-level CG executives. No vendor quotes. We're always on the lookout for freelance talent. We look in particular for writers with an in-depth understanding of the business issues faced by consumer goods firms and the technologies that are used by the industry to address those issues successfully. 'Bits and bytes' tech writing is not sought; our focus is on benchmarketing the business technology performance of CG firms, CG executives, CG vendors, and CG vendor products. Our target reader is tech-savvy, CG C-level decision maker. We write to, and about, our target reader."

$ $ CONVENIENCE STORE DECISIONS, Donohue-Meehan Publishing, Two Greenwood Square, #410, Bensalem PA 19020. (215)245-4555. Fax: (215)245-4060. E-mail: bdonahue@penton.com. Website: www.c-storedecisions.com. Editor-in-Chief: Jay Gordon. **Contact:** Bill Donahue, managing editor. **15-20% freelance written.** Monthly magazine covering convenience retail/petroleum marketing. "*CSD* is received by top-level executives in the convenience retail and petroleum marketing industry. Writers should have knowledge of the industry and the subjects it encompasses." Estab. 1990. Circ. 42,000. Pays on publication. Byline given. Buys all rights, makes work-for-hire assignments. Editorial lead time 3-5 months. Submit seasonal material 3 months in advance. Accepts queries by mail, e-mail, fax. Accepts simultaneous submissions. Responds in 3 weeks to queries. Sample copy and writer's guidelines free.

O→ Break in with a "demonstrated knowledge of finance and business, with special emphasis on retail. Keen powers of observation and attention to detail are also prized."

Nonfiction: Interview/profile (retailers), photo feature, technical. No self-serving, vendor-based stories. "We need real-life, retailer-based work." **Buys 12 mss/year.** Query with published clips. Length: 1,000-2,000 words. **Pays $200-600 for assigned articles.** Sometimes pays expenses of writers on assignment.

Photos: State availability with submission. Buys all rights. Negotiates payment individually. Identification of subjects required.

Tips: Offer experience. "We get queries from freelancers daily. We are looking for writers with industry experience. Bring us a story."

[N] **$ $ COUNTRY SAMPLER'S COUNTRY BUSINESS**, Emmis Communications, 707 Kautz Rd., St. Charles IL 60174. (630)377-8000, ext. 866. Fax: (630)377-8194. E-mail: cbiz@sampler.emmis.com. Website: www.country-business.com. **Contact:** Susan Wagner, editor. **40% freelance written.** Magazine published 7 times/year covering gift and home decor retail. "*Country Business* articles are written for independent retailers of gifts and home accents. Articles should include solid business advice on the various aspects of running a retail business." Estab. 1983. Circ. 35,000. Pays 1 month after acceptance of final ms. Publishes ms an average of 6-8 months after acceptance. Byline given. Offers $50 kill fee. Buys all rights, makes work-for-hire assignments. Editorial lead time 4-6 months. Submit seasonal material 6 months in advance. Accepts queries by mail, e-mail. Accepts simultaneous submissions. Sample copy for free. Writer's guidelines by e-mail.

Nonfiction: How-to, interview/profile, technical, finance, legal, marketing, small business. No fiction, poetry, fillers, photos, artwork, profiles of businesses, unless queried and first assigned. **Buys 20-30 mss/year.** Query with published clips or send complete ms. Length: 1,000-2,500 words. **Pays $275-500 for assigned articles; $200-350 for unsolicited articles.** Sometimes pays expenses of writers on assignment.

Columns/Departments: Display & Design (store design and product display), 1,500 words; Retailer Profile (profile of retailer—assigned only), 1,800 words; Vendor Profile (profile of manufacturer—assigned only), 1,200 words; Technology (Internet, computer-related articles as applies to small retailers), 1,500 words; Marketing (marketing ideas and advice as applies to small retailers), 1,500 words; Finance (financial tips and advice as applies to small retailers), 1,500 words; Legal (legal tips and advice as applies to small retailers), 1,500 words; Employees (tips and advice on hiring, firing, and working with employees as applies to small retailers), 1,500 words. **Buys 15 mss/year.** Query with published clips or send complete ms. **Pays $250-350.**

$ $ $ GIFTWARE BUSINESS, VNU Business Media, 770 Broadway, New York NY 10003. Fax: (646)654-4977. E-mail: krood@giftwarebusiness.com. Website: www.giftwarebusiness.com. Editor: Chris Gigley. **Contact:** Kerry Rood. **10% freelance written.** Monthly magazine, newsletter and online product. "The magazine is for the serious gift retailer." Estab. 1943. Circ. 30,000. Pays on publication. Publishes ms an average of 3 months after acceptance. Byline given. Buys all rights. Editorial lead time 2 months. Submit seasonal material 6 months in advance. Accepts queries by mail, e-mail, fax. Sample copy for free. Writer's guidelines not available.

Nonfiction: How-to, interview/profile, new product, personal experience. Query with published clips. Length: 400-2,000 words. **Pays 50-75¢/word.** Sometimes pays expenses of writers on assignment.

Photos: Send photos with submission. Reviews 4×6 transparencies, 5×7 prints, digital images. Buys all rights. Offers no additional payment for photos accepted with ms. Captions required.
Columns/Departments: Pays 50¢/word.

$ $ GIFTWARE NEWS, Talcott Corp., 20 W. Kinzie, 12th Floor, Chicago IL 60610. (312)849-2220. Fax: (312)849-2174. **Contact:** John Saxtan, editor-in-chief. **20% freelance written.** Monthly magazine covering gifts, collectibles, and tabletops for giftware retailers. Estab. 1976. Circ. 35,000. Pays on publication. Publishes ms an average of 2 months after acceptance. Byline given. Buys all rights. Submit seasonal material 6 months in advance. Responds in 2 months to mss. Sample copy for $5.
Nonfiction: How-to (sell, display), new product. **Buys 50 mss/year.** Query with published clips or send complete ms. Length: 1,500-2,000 words. **Pays $400-500 for assigned articles; $200-300 for unsolicited articles.**
Photos: Send photos with submission. Reviews 4×5 transparencies, 5×7 prints, electronic images. Offers no additional payment for photos accepted with ms. Identification of subjects required.
Columns/Departments: Stationery, giftbaskets, collectibles, holiday, merchandise, tabletop, wedding market and display—all for the gift retailer. Length: 1,500-2,500 words. **Buys 10 mss/year.** Send complete ms. **Pays $100-250.**
Tips: "We are not looking so much for general journalists but rather experts in particular fields who can also write."

$ $ NEW AGE RETAILER, Continuity Publishing, 1300 N. State St., #105, Bellingham WA 98225. (800)463-9243. Fax: (360)676-0932. E-mail: luanne@newageretailer.com. Website: www.newageretailer.com. **Contact:** Luanne Napoli, editor-in-chief. **90% freelance written.** Bimonthly magazine for retailers of New Age books, music, and merchandise. "The goal of the articles in *New Age Retailer* is usefulness—we strive to give store owners and managers practical, in-depth information they can begin using immediately. We have 3 categories of articles: retail business methods that give solid information about the various aspects of running an independent store; inventory articles that discuss a particular New Age subject or trend and include lists of books, music, and products suitable for store inventory; and education articles that help storeowners and managers gain knowledge and stay current in New Age subjects." Estab. 1987. Circ. 10,000. Pays on publication. Publishes ms an average of 4 months after acceptance. Byline given. Offers 10% kill fee. Buys first North American serial, second serial (reprint), simultaneous, electronic rights. Editorial lead time 4 months. Submit seasonal material 4 months in advance. Accepts queries by mail, e-mail, fax, phone. Accepts simultaneous submissions. Responds in 1 month to queries; 2 months to mss. Sample copy for $5. Writer's guidelines online.
Nonfiction: Book excerpts, how-to, interview/profile, new product, opinion, personal experience, technical, business principles, spiritual. No self-promotion for writer's company or product. Writer must understand independent retailing and New Age subjects. **Buys approximately 50 mss/year.** Query with published clips. Length: 1,500-5,000 words. **Pays $150-450 for assigned articles; $100-300 for unsolicited articles.** Sometimes pays with advertisement space in magazine. Sometimes pays expenses of writers on assignment.
Photos: State availability of or send photos with submission. Reviews 2×3 minimum size prints, digital images at 300 dpi. Buys one-time rights. Negotiates payment individually. Captions required.
Tips: "E-mail Luanne Napoli (luanne@newageretailer.com), or phone her at (800)463-9243, ext. 3014. Describe your expertise in the New Age market and independent retailing. Have an idea for an article ready to pitch. Promise only what you can deliver."

$ $ NICHE, The Magazine For Craft Gallery Retailers, The Rosen Group, 3000 Chestnut Ave., Suite 304, Baltimore MD 21211. (410)889-3093. Fax: (410)243-7089. E-mail: hoped@rosengrp.com. **Contact:** Hope Daniels, editor. **75% freelance written.** Quarterly business-to-business magazine for the progressive craft gallery retailer. Each issue includes retail gallery profiles, store design trends, management techniques, financial information, and merchandising strategies for small business owners. Estab. 1988. Circ. 20,000. Pays on publication. Publishes ms an average of 6 months after acceptance. Byline given. Buys first North American serial rights. Editorial lead time 6 months. Submit seasonal material 9-12 months in advance. Accepts queries by mail, e-mail, fax. Responds in 6 weeks to queries; 6 weeks to mss. Sample copy for $3.
Nonfiction: *Niche* is looking for in-depth articles on store security, innovative merchandising/display, design trends, or marketing and promotion. Stories of interest to independent retailers, such as gallery owners, may be submitted. Interview/profile, photo feature, articles targeted to independent retailers and small business owners. **Buys 20-28 mss/year.** Query with published clips. **Pays $300-700.** Sometimes pays expenses of writers on assignment.
Photos: Send photos with submission. Reviews 4×5 transparencies, slides. Negotiates payment individually. Captions required.
Columns/Departments: Retail Details (short items at the front of the book, general retail information); Artist Profiles (biographies of American Craft Artists); Resources (book/video/seminar reviews/educational opportunities pertaining to retailers). Query with published clips. **Pays $25-150.**

$ O&A MARKETING NEWS, KAL Publications, Inc., 559 S. Harbor Blvd., Suite A, Anaheim CA 92805. (714)563-9300. Fax: (714)563-9310. E-mail: kathy@kalpub.com. Website: www.kalpub.com. **Contact:** Kathy Laderman, editor-in-chief. **3% freelance written.** Bimonthly tabloid. "*O&A Marketing News* is editorially directed to people engaged in the distribution, merchandising, installation, and servicing of gasoline, oil, TBA, quick lube, carwash, convenience store, alternative fuel, and automotive aftermarket products in the 13 Western states." Estab. 1966. Circ. 7,500. Pays on publication. Publishes ms an average of 2 months after acceptance. Byline sometimes given. Buys first, electronic rights. Editorial lead time 1 month. Submit seasonal material 1 month in advance. Accepts queries by mail, e-mail, fax. Accepts simultaneous submissions. Responds in 2 months to queries; 2 months to mss. Sample copy for 9×13 SAE and 10 first-class stamps. Writer's guidelines not available.
Nonfiction: Interview/profile, photo feature, industry news. Nothing that doesn't pertain to the petroleum marketing

industry in the 13 Western states. **Buys 35 mss/year.** Send complete ms. Length: 100-500 words. **Pays $1.25/column inch.**
Photos: State availability of or send photos with submission. Reviews contact sheets, 4×6 prints. electronic rights. Offers $5/photo. Captions, identification of subjects required.
Columns/Departments: Oregon News (petroleum marketing news in state of Oregon). **Buys 7 mss/year.** Send complete ms. **Pays $1.25/column inch.**
Fillers: Gags to be illustrated by cartoonist, short humor. **Buys 7/year.** Length: 1-200 words. **Pays column inch.**
Tips: "Seeking Western industry news pertaining to the petroleum marketing industry. It can be something simple—like a new gas station or quick lube opening. News from "outlying" states such as Montana, Idaho, Wyoming, New Mexico, and Hawaii is always needed—but any timely, topical news-oriented stories will be considered."

$ PARTY & PAPER RETAILER, 107 Mill Plain Rd., Suite 204, Danbury CT 06811-6100. (203)730-4090. Fax: (203)730-4094. E-mail: editor@partypaper.com. Website: www.partypaper.com. **Contact:** Jacqueline Shanley, editor-in-chief. **90% freelance written.** Monthly magazine covering "every aspect of how to do business better for owners of party and fine stationery shops. Tips and how-tos on display, marketing, success stories, merchandising, operating costs, e-commerce, retail technology, etc." Estab. 1986. Circ. 20,000. Pays on publication. Offers 15% kill fee. Buys first North American serial rights. Editorial lead time 6 months. Submit seasonal material 6 months in advance. Accepts queries by mail, e-mail, fax. Responds in 2 months to queries. Sample copy for $6.

O→ Especially interested in news items on party retail industry for our Press Pages. Also, new column on Internet retailing ("Cyberlink") which covers all www-related topics.

Nonfiction: Book excerpts, how-to (retailing related), new product. No articles written in first person. **Buys 100 mss/year.** Query with published clips. Length: 800-1,800 words. Pays phone expenses only of writers on assignment.
Reprints: Send tearsheet or photocopy of article and information about when and where the article previously appeared.
Photos: State availability with submission. Reviews transparencies. Buys one-time rights. Negotiates payment individually. Captions, identification of subjects required.
Columns/Departments: Shop Talk (successful party/stationery store profile), 1,800 words; Storekeeping (selling, employees, market, running store), 800 words; Cash Flow (anything finance related), 800 words. **Buys 30 mss/year.** Query with published clips. **Payment varies.**

$ $ SPECIALTY COFFEE RETAILER, The Coffee Business Monthly, Adams Business Media, 250 S. Wacker Dr., Suite 1150, Chicago IL 60606-5827. (630)482-9143. Fax: (630)482-9145. E-mail: sgillerlain@aip.com. Website: www.specialty-coffee.com. Sue Gillerlain, editor-in-chief. **Contact:** Managing Editor: Jenifer Everley. **60% freelance written.** Monthly magazine covering coffee—retail and roasting, tea. "*Specialty Coffee Retailer* is the business monthly for the specialty coffee industry. The magazine provides practical business information for the profitable operation of a coffeehouse, cart/kiosk/drive-through, or tea house. Featured topics include business management and finance, marketing and promotion, site selection, store design, equipment selection and maintenance, drink preparation, tea trends, new products and more." Estab. 1994. Circ. 7,500. Pays on publication. Publishes ms an average of 2 months after acceptance. Byline given. Buys first North American serial, electronic rights. Editorial lead time 2 months. Submit seasonal material 5 months in advance. Accepts queries by mail, e-mail, fax. Accepts simultaneous submissions. Sample copy by e-mail.
Nonfiction: How-to (select a roaster, blend coffees, purchse tea, market chai). No opinion, essays, book reviews, humor, personal experience. **Buys 36 mss/year.** Query with published clips. Length: 1,800-2,500 words. **Pays $300-425.** Sometimes pays expenses of writers on assignment.
Photos: Send photos with submission. Reviews transparencies, 3×5 prints. Offers no additional payment for photos accepted with ms.
Tips: "Be willing to contact industry experts for inclusion in stories."

$ $ TRAVEL GOODS SHOWCASE, The source for luggage, business cases, and accessories, Travel Goods Association, 5 Vaughn Dr., Suite 105, Princeton NJ 08540. (609)720-1200. Fax: (609)720-0620. E-mail: john@travel-goods.org. Website: www.travel-goods.org. Editor: Michele M. Pittenger. **Contact:** John Misiano, senior editor. **5-10% freelance written.** Magazine published 5 times/year covering travel goods, accessories, trends, and new products. "*Travel Goods Showcase* contains articles for retailers, dealers, manufacturers and suppliers, about luggage, business cases, personal leather goods, handbags, and accessories. Special articles report on trends in fashion, promotions, selling and marketing techniques, industry statistics, and other educational and promotional improvements and advancements." Estab. 1975. Circ. 11,500. **Pays on acceptance.** Publishes ms an average of 2 months after acceptance. Byline given. Offers $50 kill fee. Editorial lead time 3 months. Submit seasonal material 2 months in advance. Accepts queries by mail, e-mail. Responds in 2 weeks to queries; 1 month to mss. Sample copy and writer's guidelines free.
Nonfiction: Interview/profile, new product, technical, travel, retailer profiles with photos. "No manufacturer profiles." **Buys 3 mss/year.** Query with published clips. Length: 1,200-1,600 words. **Pays $200-500.**

SPORT TRADE

Retailers and wholesalers of sports equipment and operators of recreation programs read these journals. Magazines about general and specific sports are classified in the Consumer Sports section.

$ $ AQUATICS INTERNATIONAL, Hanley-Wood, LLC, 4160 Wilshire Blvd., Los Angeles CA 90010. Fax: (323)801-4986. E-mail: lhochberg@hanley-wood.com. Website: www.aquaticsintl.com. **Contact:** Len Hochberg, editor. Magazine published 10 times/year covering public swimming pools and waterparks. Estab. 1989. Circ. 30,000. Pays on publication. Publishes ms an average of 3 months after acceptance. Byline given. international rights in perpetuity and makes work-for-hire assignments. Editorial lead time 3 months. Responds in 1 month to queries. Sample copy for $10.50.

Nonfiction: How-to, interview/profile, technical. **Buys 6 mss/year.** Query with published clips. Length: 1,500-2,500 words. **Pays $525 for assigned articles.**

Columns/Departments: Pays $250.

Tips: "Query letter with samples."

N $ $ CROSSFIRE, Paintball Digest, 570 Mantus Rd., P.O. Box 690, Sewell NJ 08080. (888)834-6026. E-mail: editor@crossfiremag.com. Website: www.crossfiremag.com. **Contact:** John Amodea, executive editor. **100% freelance written.** Monthly magazine covering paintball sport. "*Crossfire* will cover all aspects of the paintball industry from tactics to safety." Pays on publication. Byline given. Makes work-for-hire assignments. Editorial lead time 1 year. Submit seasonal material 2 months in advance. Accepts queries by mail, e-mail, fax. Accepts simultaneous submissions. Responds in 2 weeks to queries. Sample copy for free.

Nonfiction: How-to, humor, interview/profile, new product, personal experience, photo feature, technical, travel, Tournament coverage, industry news. **Buys 1-3 mss/year.** Send complete ms. Length: 700-1,900 words. **Pays 7-22¢.**

Photos: Send photos with submission. Reviews negatives. Buys all rights. Negotiates payment individually. Captions, identification of subjects, model releases required.

Fillers: Facts, gags to be illustrated by cartoonist, newsbreaks. **Buys 24/year.** Length: 25-100 words. **Pays 7-22¢.**

Tips: "Paintball or extreme sport participation is a plus."

$ $ FITNESS MANAGEMENT, Issues and Solutions in Fitness Services, Leisure Publications, Inc., 4160 Wilshire Blvd., Los Angeles CA 90010. (323)964-4800. Fax: (323)964-4835. E-mail: edit@fitnessmanagement.com. Website: www.fitnessmanagement.com. Publisher: Chris Ballard. **Contact:** Ronale Tucker, editor. **50% freelance written.** Monthly magazine. "Readers are owners, managers, and program directors of physical fitness facilities. *FM* helps them run their enterprises safely, efficiently, and profitably. Ethical and professional positions in health, nutrition, sports medicine, management, etc., are consistent with those of established national bodies." Estab. 1985. Circ. 26,000. Pays on publication. Publishes ms an average of 5 months after acceptance. Byline given. Offers 50% kill fee. Buys all rights (all articles published in *FM* are also published and archived on its website). Submit seasonal material 6 months in advance. Accepts queries by mail, e-mail, fax. Responds in 3 months to queries. Sample copy for $5. Writer's guidelines for #10 SASE.

Nonfiction: How-to (manage fitness center and program), new product (no pay), photo feature (facilities/programs), technical, News of fitness research and major happenings in fitness industry. No exercise instructions or general ideas without examples of fitness businesses that have used them successfully. **Buys 50 mss/year.** Query. Length: 750-2,000 words. **Pays $60-300 for assigned articles.** Pays expenses of writers on assignment.

Photos: Send photos with submission. Reviews contact sheets, 2×2 and 4×5 transparencies, prefers glossy prints, 5×7 to 8×10. Captions, model releases required.

The online magazine carries original content not found in the print edition. Includes sample articles. Contact: Ronale Tucker.

Tips: "We seek writers who are expert in a business or science field related to the fitness-service industry or who are experienced in the industry. Be current with the state of the art/science in business and fitness and communicate it in human terms (avoid intimidating academic language; tell the story of how this was learned and/or cite examples or quotes of people who have applied the knowledge successfully)."

N $ $ GOLF COURSE MANAGEMENT, Golf Course Superintendents Association of America, 1421 Research Park Dr., Lawrence KS 66049. (785)842-2456. Fax: (785)932-3665. E-mail: shollister@gcsaa.org. Website: www.gcsaa.org. **Contact:** Scott Hollister, editor. **85% freelance written.** Monthly magazine covering the golf course superintendent. "*GCM* helps the golf course superintendent become more efficient in all aspects of their job." Estab. 1924. Circ. 40,000. **Pays on acceptance.** Publishes ms an average of 6 months after acceptance. Byline given. Buys first North American serial rights, Web rights, and makes work-for-hire assignments. Editorial lead time 6 months. Submit seasonal material 6 months in advance. Accepts simultaneous submissions. Responds in 3 weeks to queries; 1 month to mss. Sample copy and writer's guidelines free.

Nonfiction: How-to, interview/profile. No articles about playing golf. **Buys 40 mss/year.** Query. Length: 1,500-2,500 words. **Pays $300-450 for assigned articles.** Sometimes pays expenses of writers on assignment.

Photos: Send photos with submission. Buys all rights. Offers no additional payment for photos accepted with ms. Identification of subjects required.

Tips: "Writers should have prior knowledge of the golf course superintendent profession."

$ $ HOCKEY BUSINESS NEWS, Transcontinental Sports Publications, 25 Sheppard Ave. W., Suite 100, Toronto ON M2N 6S7, Canada. (416)227-8237. Fax: (416)340-2786. E-mail: wkarl@thehockeynews.com. Website: www.thehockeynews.com. **Contact:** Wayne Karl, editor. **70% freelance written.** Journal published 9 times/year covering the hockey industry. Estab. 1994. Circ. 6,000. Pays on publication. Publishes ms an average of 1 month after acceptance. Byline given. Kill fee negotiated. Buys first North American serial, electronic, all rights. Editorial lead time 2 months. Accepts queries by mail, e-mail, fax, phone. Accepts simultaneous submissions. Responds in 2 weeks to queries; 1 month to mss. Writer's guidelines by e-mail.

Nonfiction: Exposé, general interest, how-to, interview/profile, new product, opinion, technical. Query with published clips. **Pays 35¢/word.** Sometimes pays expenses of writers on assignment.

Photos: State availability with submission. Reviews transparencies, prints. Buys all rights. Negotiates payment individually. Identification of subjects required.

Columns/Departments: **Buys 9 mss/year.** Query with published clips. **Pays 35¢/word.**

$ IDEA HEALTH & FITNESS SOURCE, IDEA Inc., Dept. WM, 6190 Cornerstone Court E., Suite 204, San Diego CA 92121. (858)535-8979. Fax: (858)535-8234. E-mail: ryanp@ideafit.com. Website: www.ideafit.com. **Contact:** Pat Ryan, vice president of education. **70% freelance written.** Magazine published 10 times/year "for fitness professionals—aerobics instructors, one-to-one trainers and studio and health club owners—covering topics such as aerobics, nutrition, injury prevention, entrepreneurship in fitness, fitness-oriented research and exercise programs." Estab. 1984. Circ. 23,000. **Pays on acceptance.** Publishes ms an average of 4 months after acceptance. Byline given. Buys all rights. Accepts queries by mail, e-mail, fax. Accepts simultaneous submissions. Responds in 2 months to queries. Sample copy for $4. Writer's guidelines online.

Nonfiction: How-to, technical. No general information on fitness; our readers are pros who need detailed information. **Buys 15 mss/year.** Query. Length: 1,000-3,000 words. **Payment varies.**

Photos: State availability with submission. Buys all rights. Offers no additional payment for photos with ms. Model releases required.

Columns/Departments: Research (detailed, specific info; must be written by expert), 750-1,500 words; Industry News (short reports on research, programs and conferences), 150-300 words; Fitness Handout (exercise and nutrition info for participants), 750 words. **Buys 80 mss/year.** Query. **Payment varies.**

Tips: "We don't accept fitness information for the consumer audience on topics such as why exercise is good for you. Writers who have specific knowledge of, or experience working in, the fitness industry have an edge."

$ $ NSGA RETAIL FOCUS, National Sporting Goods Association, 1601 Feehanville Dr., Suite 300, Mt. Prospect IL 60056-6035. (847)296-6742. Fax: (847)391-9827. E-mail: info@nsga.org. Website: www.nsga.org. **Contact:** Larry N. Weindruch, editor/publisher. **20% freelance written.** Works with a small number of new/unpublished writers each year. Bimonthly magazine. "*NSGA Retail Focus* serves as a bimonthly trade journal for sporting goods retailers who are members of the association." Estab. 1948. Circ. 2,000. Pays on publication. Publishes ms an average of 1 month after acceptance. Byline given. Offers kill fee. Buys first, second serial (reprint), electronic rights. Submit seasonal material 6 months in advance. Accepts queries by mail, e-mail. Sample copy for 9×12 SAE and 5 first-class stamps.

Nonfiction: Interview/profile, photo feature. "No articles written without sporting goods retail businesspeople in mind as the audience. In other words, no generic articles sent to several industries." **Buys 12 mss/year.** Query with published clips. **Pays $75-300.** Sometimes pays expenses of writers on assignment.

Photos: State availability with submission. Reviews contact sheets, negatives, transparencies, 5×7 prints. Buys one-time rights. Payment negotiable.

Columns/Departments: Personnel Management (succinct tips on hiring, motivating, firing, etc.); Sales Management (in-depth tips to improve sales force performance); Retail Management (detailed explanation of merchandising/inventory control); Advertising (case histories of successful ad campaigns/ad critiques); Legal Advisor; Computers; Store Design; Visual Merchandising; all 1,500 words. **Buys 12 mss/year.** Query. **Pays $75-300.**

$ $ PADDLE DEALER, The Trade Magazine for Paddlesports, Paddlesport Publishing, Inc., P.O. Box 775450, Steamboat Springs CO 80477. (970)879-1450. Fax: (970)870-1404. E-mail: matt@paddlermagazine.com. Website: www.paddlermagazine.com. Editor: Eugene Buchanan. **Contact:** Matt Hansen, managing editor. **70% freelance written.** Quarterly magazine covering the canoeing, kayaking and rafting industry. Estab. 1993. Circ. 7,500. Pays on publication. Publishes ms an average of 6 months after acceptance. Byline given. first North American serial and one-time electronic rights. Editorial lead time 2 months. Submit seasonal material 6 months in advance. Accepts queries by mail, e-mail, fax. Accepts simultaneous submissions. Responds in 3 months to queries. Sample copy for 8½×11 SAE and $1.78. Writer's guidelines for #10 SASE.

Nonfiction: New product, technical, business advice. **Buys 8 mss/year.** Query or send complete ms. Length: 2,300 words. **Pays 15-20¢/word.** Sometimes pays expenses of writers on assignment.

Photos: State availability with submission. Reviews transparencies, 5×7 prints. Buys one-time rights.

Columns/Departments: Profiles, how-to, great ideas, computer corner. **Buys 12 mss/year.** Query or send complete ms. **Pays 10-20¢/word.**

$ $ POOL & SPA NEWS, Hanley-Wood, LLC, 4160 Wilshire Blvd., Los Angeles CA 90010. (323)801-4972. Fax: (323)801-4986. E-mail: etaylor@hanley-wood.com. Website: poolspanews.com. **Contact:** Pervin Lakdawalla, editor. **15% freelance written.** Semimonthly magazine covering the swimming pool and spa industry for builders, retail stores, and service firms. Estab. 1960. Circ. 16,300. Pays on publication. Publishes ms an average of 2 months after acceptance. Buys all rights. Accepts queries by mail, e-mail. Responds in 1 month to queries. Sample copy for $5 and 9×12 SAE and 11 first-class stamps.

Nonfiction: Interview/profile, technical. Send résumé with published clips. Length: 500-2,000 words. **Pays $150-500.** Pays expenses of writers on assignment.

Reprints: Send ms with rights for sale noted and information about when and where the material previously appeared. Payment varies.

Photos: Payment varies.

Columns/Departments: **Payment varies.**

The online magazine carries original content not found in the print edition. Contact: Margi Millunzi, online editor.

$ $ REFEREE, Referee Enterprises, Inc., P.O. Box 161, Franksville WI 53126. Fax: (262)632-5460. E-mail: jarehart@referee.com. Website: www.referee.com. Editor: Bill Topp. **Contact:** Jim Arehart, associate editor. **75% freelance written.**

Monthly magazine covering sports officiating. "Referee is a magazine for and read by sports officials of all kinds with a focus on baseball, basketball, football, softball and soccer officiating." Estab. 1976. Circ. 40,000. **Pays on acceptance.** Publishes ms an average of 6 months after acceptance. Byline given. Kill fee negotiable. Buys all rights. Editorial lead time 6 months. Accepts queries by mail, e-mail, fax. Responds in 2 weeks to queries; 1 month to mss. Sample copy for #10 SASE. Writer's guidelines online.

Nonfiction: Book excerpts, essays, historical/nostalgic, how-to (sports officiating related), humor, interview/profile, opinion, photo feature, technical (as it relates to sports officiating). "We don't want to see articles with themes not relating to sport officiating. General sports articles, although of interest to us, will not be published." **Buys 40 mss/year.** Query with published clips. Length: 500-2,500 words. **Pays $100-400.** Sometimes pays expenses of writers on assignment.

Photos: State availability with submission. Reviews contact sheets, negatives, transparencies, prints. Purchase of rights negotiable. Offers $35-40 per photo. Identification of subjects required.

Tips: "Query first and be persistent. We may not like your idea but that doesn't mean we won't like your next one. Professionalism pays off."

$ $ SKI AREA MANAGEMENT, Beardsley Publications, P.O. Box 644, 45 Main St. N, Woodbury CT 06798. (203)263-0888. Fax: (203)266-0452. E-mail: sam@saminfo.com. Website: www.saminfo.com. Editor: Jennifer Rowan. **Contact:** Rick Kahl, managing editor. **85% freelance written.** Bimonthly magazine covering everything involving the management and development of ski resorts. "We are the publication of record for the North American ski industry. We report on new ideas, developments, marketing, and regulations with regard to ski and snowboard resorts. Everyone from the CEO to the lift operator of winter resorts reads our magazine to stay informed about the people and procedures that make ski areas successful." Estab. 1962. Circ. 4,500. Pays on publication. Byline given. Offers kill fee. Buys all rights. Editorial lead time 2 months. Submit seasonal material 3 months in advance. Accepts queries by mail, e-mail. Responds in 2 weeks to queries. Sample copy for 9×12 SAE with $3 postage or online. Writer's guidelines for #10 SASE.

Nonfiction: Historical/nostalgic, how-to, interview/profile, new product, opinion, personal experience, technical. "We don't want anything that does not specifically pertain to resort operations, management, or financing." **Buys 25-40 mss/year.** Query. Length: 500-2,500 words. **Pays $50-400.**

Reprints: Accepts previously published submissions.

Photos: Send photos with submission. Reviews transparencies, prints. Buys one-time rights or all rights. Offers no additional payment for photos accepted with ms. Identification of subjects required.

The online magazine carries original content not found in the print edition. Contact: Olivia Rowan.

Tips: "Know what you are writing about. We are read by people dedicated to skiing and snowboarding and to making the resort experience the best possible for their customers. It is a trade publication read by professionals."

$ $ THOROUGHBRED TIMES, Thoroughbred Times Co., Inc., 496 Southland Dr., P.O. Box 8237, Lexington KY 40533. (859)260-9800. **Contact:** Mark Simon, editor. **10% freelance written.** Weekly tabloid "written for professionals who breed and/or race thoroughbreds at tracks in the U.S. Articles must help owners and breeders understand racing to help them realize a profit." Estab. 1985. Circ. 23,000. Pays on publication. Publishes ms an average of 1 month after acceptance. Byline given. Offers 50% kill fee. Buys first publication rights. Submit seasonal material 2 months in advance. Responds in 2 weeks to mss. Sample copy not available.

Nonfiction: General interest, historical/nostalgic, interview/profile, technical. **Buys 52 mss/year.** Query. Length: 500-2,500 words. **Pays 10-20¢/word.** Sometimes pays expenses of writers on assignment.

Photos: State availability with submission. Reviews prints. Buys one-time rights. Offers $25/photo. Identification of subjects required.

Columns/Departments: Vet Topics; Business of Horses; Pedigree Profiles; Bloodstock Topics; Tax Matters; Viewpoints; Guest Commentary.

Tips: "We are looking for farm stories and profiles of owners, breeders, jockeys, and trainers."

STONE, QUARRY & MINING

$ $ CANADIAN MINING JOURNAL, Business Information Group, 1450 Don Mills Rd., Toronto ON M3B 2X7, Canada. (416)510-6742. Fax: (416)442-2175. E-mail: jwerniuk@canadianminingjournal.com. **Contact:** Jane Werniuk, editor. **5% freelance written.** Magazine covering mining and mineral exploration by Canadian companies. "*Canadian Mining Journal* provides articles and information of practical use to those who work in the technical, administrative, and supervisory aspects of exploration, mining and processing in the Canadian mineral exploration and mining industry." Estab. 1879. Circ. 10,000. Pays on publication. Publishes ms an average of 3 months after acceptance. Byline given. Buys one-time, electronic rights, makes work-for-hire assignments. Submit seasonal material 3 months in advance. Accepts queries by mail, e-mail, fax, phone. Responds in 1 week to queries; 1 month to mss.

Nonfiction: Opinion, technical, operation descriptions. **Buys 6 mss/year.** Query with published clips. Length: 500-1,400 words. **Pays $100-600.** Pays expenses of writers on assignment.

Photos: State availability with submission. Reviews 4×6 prints or high resolution files. Buys one-time rights. Negotiates payment individually. Captions, identification of subjects, credits required.

Columns/Departments: Guest editorial (opinion on controversial subject related to mining industry), 600 words. **Buys 3 mss/year.** Query with published clips. **Pays $150.**

Tips: "I need articles about mine sites that it would be expensive/difficult for me to reach. I also need to know that the writer is competent to understand and describe the technology in an interesting way."

$ COAL PEOPLE MAGAZINE, Al Skinner, Inc., Dept. WM, 629 Virginia St. W, P.O. Box 6247, Charleston WV 25362. (304)342-4129. Fax: (304)343-3124. Editor/Publisher: Al Skinner. **Contact:** Christina Karawan, president. **50% freelance written.** Monthly magazine. "Most stories are about people or historical—either narrative or biographical on all levels of coal people, past and present—from coal execs down to grass roots miners. Most stories are upbeat—showing warmth of family or success from underground up!" Estab. 1976. Circ. 11,000. Pays on publication. Publishes ms an average of 3 months after acceptance. Byline given. Buys first, second serial (reprint) rights, makes work-for-hire assignments. Submit seasonal material 2 months in advance. Responds in 3 months to mss. Sample copy for 9×12 SAE and 10 first-class stamps.

Nonfiction: Book excerpts (and film if related to coal), historical/nostalgic (coal towns, people, lifestyles), humor (including anecdotes and cartoons), interview/profile (for coal personalities), personal experience (as relates to coal mining), photo feature (on old coal towns, people, past and present). Special issues: Calendar issue for more than 300 annual coal shows, association meetings, etc. (January); Surface Mining/Reclamation Award (July); Christmas in Coal Country (December). No poetry, fiction, or environmental attacks on the coal industry. **Buys 32 mss/year.** Query with published clips. Length: 5,000 words. **Pays $90 for assigned articles.**

Reprints: Send tearsheet and information about when and where the material previously appeared. Pays 50% of amount paid for an original article.

Photos: Send photos with submission. Reviews contact sheets, transparencies, 5×7 prints. Buys one-time reprint rights. Captions, identification of subjects required.

Columns/Departments: Editorials—anything to do with current coal issues (nonpaid); Mine'ing Our Business (bull pen column—gossip—humorous anecdotes); Coal Show Coverage (freelance photojournalist coverage of any coal function across the U.S.). Length: 300-500 words. **Buys 10 mss/year.** Query. **Pays $50.**

Fillers: Anecdotes. Length: 300 words. **Pays $35.**

Tips: "We are looking for good feature articles on coal people, towns, companies—past and present, color slides (for possible cover use), and b&w photos to complement stories. Could also use a few news writers to take photos and do journalistic coverage on coal events across the country. Slant stories more toward people and less on historical. More faces and names than old town, company store photos. Include more quotes from people who lived these moments!" The following geographical areas are covered: Eastern Canada; Mexico; Europe; China; Russia; Poland; Australia; as well as U.S. states: Alabama, Tennessee, Virginia, Washington, Oregon, North and South Dakota, Arizona, Colorado, Alaska, and Wyoming.

$ $ COLORED STONE, Lapidary Journal/Primedia Inc., 60 Chestnut Ave., Suite 201, Devon PA 19333-1312. (610)964-6300. Fax: (610)293-0977. E-mail: cs_editorial@primediamags.com. Website: www.colored-stone.com. **Contact:** Morgan Beard, editor-in-chief. **50% freelance written.** Bimonthly magazine covering the colored gemstone industry. "*Colored Stone* covers all aspects of the colored gemstone (i.e., no diamonds) trade. Our readers are manufacturing jewelers and jewelry designers, gemstone dealers, miners, retail jewelers and gemologists." Estab. 1987. Circ. 11,000. **Pays on acceptance.** Publishes ms an average of 2 months after acceptance. Byline given. Buys one-time, all rights. Editorial lead time 2 months. Submit seasonal material 4 months in advance. Accepts queries by mail, e-mail, fax. Accepts simultaneous submissions. Responds in 1 month to queries; 2 months to mss. Sample copy and writer's guidelines free. Writer's guidelines online.

Nonfiction: Exposé, interview/profile, new product, technical. "No articles intended for the general public." **Buys 35-45 mss/year.** Query with published clips. Length: 400-2,200 words. **Pays $200-600.**

Photos: State availability with submission. Reviews any size transparencies, 4×6 prints and up. Buys one-time rights. Offers $15-50/photo. Captions, identification of subjects, model releases required.

Tips: "A background in the industry is helpful but not necessary. Please, no recycled marketing/new technology/etc. pieces."

$ CONTEMPORARY STONE & TILE DESIGN, Business News Publishing Co., 210 Route 4 E., Suite 311, Paramus NJ 07652. (201)291-9001. Fax: (201)291-9002. E-mail: cstd@bnp.com. Website: www.stoneworld.com. Publisher: Alex Bachrach. **Contact:** Michael Reis, senior editor, or Jennifer Adams, editor. Quarterly magazine covering the full range of stone and tile design and architecture—from classic and historic spaces to current projects. Estab. 1995. Circ. 14,000. Pays on publication. Publishes ms an average of 3 months after acceptance. Byline given. Buys first rights. Submit seasonal material 6 months in advance. Responds in 3 weeks to queries. Sample copy for $10.

Nonfiction: Overall features on a certain aspect of stone design/tile work, or specific articles on individual architectural projects. Interview/profile (prominent architect/designer or firm), photo feature, technical, architectural design. **Buys 8 mss/year.** Query with published clips. Length: 1,500-3,000 words. **Pays $6/column inch.** Pays expenses of writers on assignment.

Photos: State availability with submission. Reviews transparencies, prints. Buys one-time rights. Pays $10/photo accepted with ms. Captions, identification of subjects required.

Columns/Departments: Upcoming Events (for the architecture and design community); Stone Classics (featuring historic architecture); question and answer session with a prominent architect or designer. Length: 1,500-2,000 words. **Pays $6/inch.**

Tips: "The visual aspect of the magazine is key, so architectural photography is a must for any story. Cover the entire project, but focus on the stonework or tile work and how it relates to the rest of the space. Architects are very helpful in describing their work and often provide excellent quotes. As a relatively new magazine, we are looking for freelance submissions and are open to new feature topics. This is a narrow subject, however, so it's a good idea to speak with an editor before submitting anything."

$ $ PIT & QUARRY, Advanstar Communications, 7500 Old Oak Blvd., Cleveland OH 44130. (440)891-2607. Fax: (440)891-2675. E-mail: mkuhar@advanstar.com. Website: www.pitandquarry.com. Managing Editor: Darren Constantino. **Contact:** Mark S. Kuhar, editor. **10-20% freelance written.** Monthly magazine covering nonmetallic minerals, mining, and crushed stone. Audience has "knowledge of construction-related markets, mining, minerals processing, etc." Estab. 1916. Circ. 25,000. **Pays on acceptance.** Publishes ms an average of 6 months after acceptance. Byline given. Buys first North American serial rights. Editorial lead time 6 months. Accepts queries by mail, e-mail, fax, phone. Accepts simultaneous submissions. Responds in 1 month to queries; 4 months to mss. Sample copy for 9×12 SAE and 4 first-class stamps.

Nonfiction: How-to, interview/profile, new product, technical. No humor or inspirational articles. **Buys 12-15 mss/year.** Query. Length: 1,000-1,500 words. **Pays $250-700 for assigned articles; $250-500 for unsolicited articles.** Pays writers with contributor copies or other premiums for simple news items, etc. Sometimes pays expenses of writers on assignment.

Photos: State availability with submission. Buys one-time rights. Offers no additional payment for photos accepted with ms. Identification of subjects, model releases required.

Columns/Departments: Brand New; Techwatch; E-business; Software corner; Equipment Showcase. Length: 250-750 words. **Buys 5-6 mss/year.** Query. **Pays $250-300.**

The online magazine sometimes carries original content not found in the print edition.

Tips: "Be familiar with quarry operations (crushed stone or sand and gravel), as opposed to coal or metallic minerals mining. Know construction markets. We always need equipment-focused features on specific quarry operations."

$ STONE WORLD, Business News Publishing Company, 210 Route 4 E., Suite 311, Paramus NJ 07652. (201)291-9001. Fax: (201)291-9002. E-mail: info@stoneworld.com. Website: www.stoneworld.com. **Contact:** Michael Reis, editor, or Jennifer Adams, managing editor. Monthly magazine on natural building stone for producers and users of granite, marble, limestone, slate, sandstone, onyx and other natural stone products. Estab. 1984. Circ. 21,000. Pays on publication. Publishes ms an average of 4 months after acceptance. Byline given. Buys first North American serial, second serial (reprint) rights. Submit seasonal material 6 months in advance. Responds in 2 months to queries. Sample copy for $10.

Nonfiction: How-to (fabricate and/or install natural building stone), interview/profile, photo feature, technical, architectural design, artistic stone uses, statistics, factory profile, equipment profile, trade show review. **Buys 10 mss/year.** Query with or without published clips or send complete ms. Length: 600-3,000 words. **Pays $6/column inch.** Pays expenses of writers on assignment.

Reprints: Send photocopy with rights for sale noted and information about when and where the material previously appeared. Pays 50% of amount paid for an original article.

Photos: State availability with submission. Reviews transparencies, prints, slides, digital images. Buys one-time rights. Pays $10/photo accepted with ms. Captions, identification of subjects required.

Columns/Departments: News (pertaining to stone or design community); New Literature (brochures, catalogs, books, videos, etc., about stone); New Products (stone products); New Equipment (equipment and machinery for working with stone); Calendar (dates and locations of events in stone and design communities). Query or send complete ms. Length 300-600 words. **Pays $6/inch.**

Tips: "Articles about architectural stone design accompanied by professional color photographs and quotes from designing firms are often published, especially when one unique aspect of the stone selection or installation is highlighted. We are also interested in articles about new techniques of quarrying and/or fabricating natural building stone."

TOY, NOVELTY & HOBBY

$ $ MODEL RETAILER, Resources for Successful Hobby Retailing, Kalmbach Publishing Co., 21027 Crossroads Circle, Waukesha WI 53187-1612. (262)796-8776. Fax: (262)796-1383. E-mail: staff@modelretailer.com. Website: www.modelretailer.com. **Contact:** Mark Savage, editor. **5% freelance written.** Monthly magazine. "*Model Retailer* covers the business of hobbies, from financial and shop management issues to industry trends and the latest product releases. Our goal is to provide hobby shop entrepreneurs with the tools and information they need to be successful retailers." Estab. 1987. Circ. 6,000 (controlled circulation). **Pays on acceptance.** Publishes ms an average of 3 months after acceptance. Byline given. Buys first rights. Editorial lead time 3 months. Submit seasonal material 6 months in advance. Accepts queries by mail, e-mail, fax. Sample copy and writer's guidelines free. Writer's guidelines online.

Nonfiction: How-to (business), new product. "No articles that do not have a strong hobby or small retail component." **Buys 2-3 mss/year.** Query with published clips. Length: 750-2,000 words. **Pays $250-500 for assigned articles; $100-250 for unsolicited articles.** Sometimes pays expenses of writers on assignment.

Photos: State availability with submission. Reviews 4×6 prints. Buys one-time rights. Negotiates payment individually. Captions, identification of subjects required.

Columns/Departments: Shop Management; Sales Marketing; Technology Advice; Industry Trends, all 500-750 words. **Buys 2-3 mss/year.** Query with published clips. **Pays $100-200.**

N $ PEN WORLD INTERNATIONAL, World Publications, Inc., 3946 Glade Valley Dr., Kingwood TX 77339-2059. (281)359-4363. Fax: (281)359-5748. E-mail: editor@penworld.com. Website: www.penworld.com. Editor: Marie Picon. Magazine published 7 times/year. Published for the collectors and connoiseurs of contemporary and vintage writing instruments. Circ. 105,994. Sample copy not available.

TRANSPORTATION

These publications are for professional movers and people involved in the transportation of goods. For magazines focusing on trucking see also Auto & Truck.

$ BUS CONVERSIONS, The First and Foremost Bus Converters Magazine, MAK Publishing, 7246 Garden Grove Blvd., Westminster CA 92683. (714)799-0062. Fax: (714)799-0042. E-mail: editor@busconversions.com. Website: www.busconversions.com. **Contact:** Tiffany Christian, editorial assistant. **95% freelance written.** Monthly magazine covering the bus conversion industry. Estab. 1992. Circ. 10,000. Pays on publication. Buys first North American serial rights. Accepts queries by mail, e-mail.

Nonfiction: Each month, *Bus Conversions* publishes a minimum of 2 coach reviews, usually anecdotal stories told by those who have completed their own bus conversion. Publishes some travel/destination stories (all of which are related to bus/RV travel). Looking for articles on engine swaps, exterior painting and furniture. How-to (articles on the electrical, plumbing, mechanical, decorative and structural aspects of bus conversions; buses that are converted into RVs).

Photos: Include color photos (glossy) with submission. Photos not returned unless an SASE is included.

Columns/Departments: Industry Update; Products of Interest; Ask the Experts; One For the Road; Road Fix.

Tips: "Most of our writers are our readers. Knowledge of bus conversions and the associate lifestyle is a prerequisite."

N $ ITS WORLD, Technology and Applications for Intelligent Transportation Systems, Scranton Gillette Communications, 380 E. Northwest Highway, Suite 200, Des Plaines IL 60016. (847)391-1000. Fax: (847)390-0408. Website: www.itsworld.com. **Contact:** Tim Gregorski, managing editor. **50% freelance written.** Bimonthly tabloid covering intelligent transportation systems (the application of communications and computer technologies to surface transportation). "We focus on ITS based global projects, and the logistics of these projects." Estab. 1996. Circ. 25,000. Pays on publication. Publishes ms an average of 2 months after acceptance. Byline given. Buys all rights. Editorial lead time 2 months. Submit seasonal material 2 months in advance. Accepts queries by e-mail, fax, phone. Accepts simultaneous submissions. Responds in 6 weeks to queries; 1 month to mss. Sample copy and writer's guidelines free.

Photos: Send photos with submission. Reviews negatives, 2×7 transparencies, prints. Offers no additional payment for photos accepted with ms. Captions, identification of subjects required.

Columns/Departments: World Watch (trends, activities and market opportunities in intelligent transportation systems in a country or region outside the U.S.); Washington Watch (ITS issues/Washington D.C. perspective); editorials (ITS issues/opinions), all 1,500 words. Query.

Tips: "Expertise in surface transportation and/or the application of advanced technologies (telecommunications, computers, etc.) to surface transportation is a must. Writers who demonstrate this through published works and other background information will be given highest consideration."

N $ $ LIMOUSINE DIGEST, Digest Publications, 29 Fostertown Rd., Medford NJ 08055. (609)953-4900. Fax: (609)953-4905. E-mail: info@limodigest.com. Website: www.limodigest.com. **Contact:** Susan W. Keehn, editor. **33% freelance written.** Monthly magazine covering ground transportation. "*Limousine Digest* is 'the voice of the limousine industry.' We cover all aspects of ground transportation from vehicles to operators, safety issues and political involvement." Estab. 1990. Circ. 22,000. Pays on publication. Publishes ms an average of 2 months after acceptance. Byline given. Makes work-for-hire assignments. Editorial lead time 1 year. Submit seasonal material 2 months in advance. Accepts queries by mail, e-mail, fax, phone. Accepts simultaneous submissions. Sample copy for free.

Nonfiction: Historical/nostalgic, how-to (start a company, market your product), humor, inspirational, interview/profile, new product, personal experience, photo feature, technical, travel, Industry news, business. **Buys 1-3 mss/year.** Send complete ms. Length: 700-1,900 words. **Pays 7-22¢/word. Will pay authors in advertising trade-outs.**

Reprints: Accepts previously published submissions.

Photos: Must include photos to be considered. Send photos with submission. Reviews negatives. Buys all rights. Negotiates payment individually. Captions, identification of subjects, model releases required.

Columns/Departments: New Model Showcase (new limousines, sedans, buses), 1,000 words; Player Profile (industry members profiled), 700 words; Hall of Fame (unique vehicles featured), 500-700 words; Association News (association issues), 400 words. **Buys 5 mss/year.** Query. **Pays 7-22¢/word.**

Fillers: Facts, gags to be illustrated by cartoonist, newsbreaks. **Buys 24/year.** Length: 25-100 words. **Pays 7-22¢/word.**

$ $ METRO MAGAZINE, Bobit Publishing Co., 21061 S. Western Ave., Torrance CA 90501. E-mail: info@metro-magazine.com. Website: www.metro-magazine.com. Editor: Steve Hirano. **Contact:** Leslie Davis, managing editor. **10% freelance written.** Magazine published 9 times/year covering public transportation. "*Metro Magazine* delivers business, government policy, and technology developments that are *industry specific* to public transportation." Estab. 1904. Circ. 20,500. **Pays on acceptance.** Publishes ms an average of 2 months after acceptance. Byline given. Offers 10% kill fee. Buys all rights. Editorial lead time 3 months. Submit seasonal material 3 months in advance. Accepts queries by e-mail. Responds in 2 weeks to queries; 1 month to mss. Sample copy for $8. Writer's guidelines by e-mail.

Nonfiction: How-to, interview/profile (of industry figures), new product (related to transit—bus and rail—private bus), technical. **Buys 6-10 mss/year.** Query. Length: 400-1,500 words. **Pays $80-400.**

Photos: State availability with submission. Buys all rights. Negotiates payment individually. Captions, identification of subjects, model releases required.

Columns/Departments: Query. **Pays $20¢/word.**

The online magazine carries original content not found in the print edition. Contact: Leslie Davis.

$ $ SCHOOL BUS FLEET, Bobit Publishing Co., 21061 S. Western Ave., Torrance CA 90501. (310)533-2400. Fax: (310)533-2502. E-mail: sbf@bobit.com. Website: www.schoolbusfleet.com. **Contact:** Steve Hirano, editor. **10% freelance written.** Magazine covering school transportation of K-12 population. "Most of our readers are school bus operators, public and private." Estab. 1965. Circ. 24,000. **Pays on acceptance.** Publishes ms an average of 3 months after acceptance.

Byline given. Offers 25% kill fee or $50. Buys first North American serial rights. Editorial lead time 3 months. Submit seasonal material 3 months in advance. Accepts queries by mail, e-mail, fax. Responds in 1 month to queries. Sample copy for free. Writer's guidelines free.

Nonfiction: Interview/profile, new product, technical. **Buys 6 mss/year.** Query with published clips. Length: 600-1,800 words. **Pays 20-25¢/word.** Sometimes pays expenses of writers on assignment.

Photos: State availability with submission. Reviews transparencies, 4×6 prints. Buys one-time rights. Negotiates payment individually. Captions, identification of subjects required.

Columns/Departments: Shop Talk (maintenance information for school bus mechanics), 650 words. **Buys 2 mss/year.** Query with published clips. **Pays $100-150.**

Tips: "Freelancers should submit ideas about innovations in school bus safety and operations."

TRAVEL

Travel professionals read these publications to keep up with trends, tours, and changes in transportation. Magazines about vacations and travel for the general public are listed in the Consumer Travel, Camping & Trailer section.

$ $ $ CRUISE INDUSTRY NEWS, Cruise Industry News, 441 Lexington Ave., Suite 1209, New York NY 10017. (212)986-1025. Fax: (212)986-1033. E-mail: oivind@cruiseindustrynews.com. Website: www.cruiseindustrynews.com. **Contact:** Oivind Mathisen, editor. **20% freelance written.** Quarterly magazine covering cruise shipping. "We write about the *business* of cruise shipping for the industry. That is, cruise lines, shipyards, financial analysts, etc." Estab. 1991. Circ. 10,000. Pays on acceptance or on publication. Publishes ms an average of 4 months after acceptance. Byline given. Offers 25% kill fee. Buys first rights. Editorial lead time 3 months. Accepts queries by mail. Reponse time varies to queries. Sample copy for $15. Writer's guidelines for #10 SASE.

Nonfiction: Interview/profile, new product, photo feature, travel, Business. No travel stories. **Buys more than 20 mss/year.** Query with published clips. Length: 500-1,500 words. **Pays $500-1,000 for assigned articles.** Sometimes pays expenses of writers on assignment.

Photos: State availability with submission. Buys one-time rights. Pays $25-50/photo.

$ $ LEISURE GROUP TRAVEL, Premier Tourism Marketing, 4901 Forest Ave., Downers Grove IL 60515. (630)964-1431. Fax: (630)852-0414. E-mail: info@premiertourismmarketing.com. Website: www.premiertourismmarketing.com. **Contact:** John Kloster, editor-in-chief. **15% freelance written.** Bimonthly magazine covering group travel. We cover destinations and editorial relevant to the group travel market. Estab. 1994. Circ. 15,012. Pays on publication. Byline given. Buys first rights, including online publication rights. Editorial lead time 6 months. Submit seasonal material 6 months in advance. Accepts queries by mail, e-mail. Sample copy online.

Nonfiction: Travel. **Buys 36-50 mss/year.** Query with published clips. Length: 1,200-3,000 words. **Pays $0-500.**

Tips: "Experience in writing for 50+ travel marketplace a bonus."

N $ $ MOTOR COACH EAST, The Voice of the Eastern Motor Coach Industry, August Communications, 225-530 Century St., Winnipeg MB R3H 0Y4, Canada. (888)573-1136. Fax: (866)957-0217. E-mail: c.wood@august.ca. Website: www.august.ca. Managing Editor: Sean Thiessen. **Contact:** Crystal Wood, editor. **90% freelance written.** Quarterly magazine covering the Eastern motor coach industry. "*Motor Coach East* services motor coach companies and tour operators in the eastern Canadian provinces and northeastern United States." Estab. 2002. Circ. 6,382. Pays 1 month after publication. Publishes ms an average of 2 months after acceptance. Byline given. Buys all rights. Editorial lead time 3 months. Submit seasonal material 3 months in advance. Accepts queries by mail, e-mail, fax, phone. Accepts previously published material. Responds in 2 weeks to queries; 1 month to mss. Sample copy for free. Writer's guidelines free.

Nonfiction: Interview/profile, new product, technical, travel. **Buys 15-20 mss/year.** Query with published clips. Length: 700-2,250 words. **Pays 15-30¢/word.**

Photos: State availability with submission. Reviews GIF/JPEG files. Buys all rights. Offers no additional payment for photos accepted with ms. Captions required.

N $ $ MOTOR COACH WEST, The Voice of the Western Motor Coach Industry, August Communications, 225-530 Century St., Winnipeg MB R3H 0Y4, Canada. (888)573-1136. Fax: (866)957-0217. E-mail: c.wood@august.ca. Website: www.august.ca. Managing Editor: Sean Thiessen. **Contact:** Crystal Wood, editor. **90% freelance written.** Quarterly magazine covering the Western motor coach industry. "*Motor Coach West* services motor coach companies and tour operators in the western Canadian provinces and northwestern United States." Estab. 2001. Circ. 2,925. Pays 1 month after publication. Publishes ms an average of 2 months after acceptance. Byline given. Buys all rights. Editorial lead time 3 months. Submit seasonal material 3 months in advance. Accepts queries by mail, e-mail, fax, phone. Accepts previously published material. Responds in 2 weeks to queries; 1 month to mss. Sample copy for free. Writer's guidelines free.

Nonfiction: Interview/profile, new product, technical, travel. **Buys 15-20 mss/year.** Query with published clips. Length: 700-2,250 words. **Pays 15-30¢/word.**

Photos: State availability with submission. Reviews GIF/JPEG files. Buys all rights. Offers no additional payment for photos accepted with ms. Captions required.

$ $ SPECIALTY TRAVEL INDEX, Alpine Hansen, 305 San Anselmo Ave., #313, San Anselmo CA 94960. (415)455-4900. Fax: (415)459-4974. E-mail: info@specialtytravel.com. Website: www.specialtytravel.com. Editor: C. Steen Hansen. **Contact:** Susan Kostrzewa, managing editor. **90% freelance written.** Semiannual magazine covering adventure and special interest travel. Estab. 1980. Circ. 45,000. Pays on receipt and acceptance of all materials. Byline given. Buys one-time rights. Editorial lead time 3 month. Submit seasonal material 3 months in advance. Accepts queries by mail, e-mail. Writer's guidelines on request.

Nonfiction: How-to, personal experience, photo feature, travel. **Buys 15 mss/year.** Query. Length: 1,250 words. **Pays $200 minimum.**

Reprints: Send tearsheet. Pays 100% of amount paid for an original article.

Photos: State availability with submission. Reviews 35mm transparencies, 5×7 prints. Negotiates payment individually. Captions, identification of subjects required.

Tips: "Write about group travel and be both creative and factual. The articles should relate to both the travel agent booking the tour and the client who is traveling."

$ STAR SERVICE, NORTHSTAR Travel Media, 500 Plaza Dr., Secaucus NJ 07094. (201)902-2000. Fax: (201)319-1797. E-mail: sgordon@ntmllc.com. Website: www.starserviceonline.com. **Contact:** Steven R. Gordon, editor-in-chief. "Eager to work with new/unpublished writers as well as those working from a home base abroad, planning trips that would allow time for hotel reporting, or living in major ports for cruise ships." Worldwide guide to accommodations and cruise ships sold to travel professionals on subscription basis. Estab. 1960. Pays 15 days after publication. Buys all rights. Accepts queries by mail, e-mail, fax. Responds in 1 month to queries. Writer's guidelines and list of available assignments for #10 SASE.

O→ Break in by "being willing to inspect hotels in remote parts of the world."

Nonfiction: Objective, critical evauations of hotels and cruise ships suitable for international travelers, based on personal inspections. Freelance correspondents ordinarily are assigned to update an entire state or country. "Assignment involves on-site inspections of all hotels and cruise ships we review; revising and updating published reports; and reviewing new properties. Qualities needed are thoroughness, precision, perserverance and keen judgment. Solid research skills and powers of observation are crucial. Travel writing experience is highly desirable. Reviews must be colorful, clear, and documented with hotel's brochure, rate sheet, etc. We accept no advertising or payment for listings, so reviews should dispense praise and criticism where deserved." Now accepting queries for destination assignments with deadlines through June 2003. Query should include details on writer's experience in travel and writing, clips, specific forthcoming travel plans, and how much time would be available for hotel or ship inspections. Sponsored trips are acceptable. **Buys 4,500 mss/year. Pays $25/report used.**

The online magazine carries original content not found in the print edition. Contact: Steven R. Gordon.

Tips: "We may require sample hotel or cruise reports on facilities near freelancer's hometown before giving the first assignment. No byline because of sensitive nature of reviews."

N $ $ TRAVEL TIPS, Premier Tourism Marketing, 4901 Forest Ave., Downers Grove IL 60515. (630)964-1431. Fax: (630)852-0414. E-mail: info@premiertourismmarketing.com. Website: www.premiertourismmarketing.com. **Contact:** John Kloster, editor-in-chief. **75% freelance written.** Bimonthly magazine covering group travel. "We cover destinations and editorial relevant to the group travel market." Estab. 1994. Circ. 12,500. Pays on publication. Byline given. Buys first, electronic rights. Editorial lead time 6 months. Submit seasonal material 6 months in advance. Accepts queries by mail, e-mail. Sample copy online.

Nonfiction: Travel. **Buys 36-50 mss/year.** Query with published clips. Length: 1,200-3,000 words. **Pays $0-500.**

Tips: "Experience in writing for 50+ travel marketplace a bonus."

$ $ VACATION INDUSTRY REVIEW, Interval International, 6262 Sunset Dr., Miami FL 33143. (305)666-1861, ext. 7238. Fax: (305)668-3408. E-mail: matthew.mcdaniel@intervalintl.com. **Contact:** Matthew McDaniel, editor-in-chief. **30% freelance written.** Quarterly magazine covering leisure lodgings (timeshare resorts, fractionals, and other types of vacation-ownership properties). "The international readership of *VIR* consists of people who develop, finance, market, sell, and manage timeshare resorts and mixed-use projects such as hotels, resorts, and second-home communities with a vacation-ownership component worldwide; and suppliers of products and services to the vacation-ownership industry." Prefers to work with published/established writers. Estab. 1982. Circ. 30,000. Pays on publication. Publishes ms an average of 6 months after acceptance. Byline given. all rights or makes work-for-hire assignments Submit seasonal material 6 months in advance. Accepts queries by mail, e-mail, fax. Sample copy for 9×12 SAE and 3 first-class stamps or online. Writer's guidelines for #10 SASE.

O→ Break in by writing a letter to tell us about yourself, and enclosing 2 or 3 (nonreturnable) samples of published work that show you can meet our specialized needs.

Nonfiction: How-to, interview/profile, technical. No consumer travel, hotel, or nonvacation real-estate material. **Buys 6-8 mss/year.** Query with published clips. Length: 1,000-1,500 words. **Pays 30¢/word.**

Photos: Only send photos on assignment. Reviews 35mm transparencies, 5×7 or larger prints, electronic images. Generally offers no additional payment for photos accepted with ms. Captions, identification of subjects required.

Tips: "We do not want consumer-oriented destination travel articles. We want articles about the business aspects of the vacation-ownership industry: entrepreneurship, project financing, design and construction, sales and marketing, operations, management—anything that will help our readers plan, build, sell and run a quality timeshare or vacation-ownership property that satisfies the owners/guests and earns a profit for the developer and marketer. We're also interested in owner associations at vacation-ownership resorts (not residential condos). Requires electronic submissions. Query for details."

VETERINARY

$ $ VETERINARY ECONOMICS, Business Solutions for Practicing Veterinarians, Veterinary Healthcare Communications, 8033 Flint, Lenexa KS 66214. (913)492-4300. Fax: (913)492-4157. E-mail: vmpg@vetmedpub.com. Website:

www.vetmedpub.com. Managing Editor: Portia Stewart. **Contact:** Marnette Falley, editor. **20% freelance written.** Monthly magazine covering veterinary practice management. "We address the business concerns and management needs of practicing veterinarians." Estab. 1960. Circ. 52,000. Pays on publication. Publishes ms an average of 3 months after acceptance. Byline given. Buys first rights. Editorial lead time 3 months. Submit seasonal material 3 months in advance. Accepts queries by mail, e-mail, fax. Accepts simultaneous submissions. Responds in 3 months to queries. Sample copy and writer's guidelines free. Writer's guidelines online.

Nonfiction: How-to, interview/profile, new product, personal experience. **Buys 24 mss/year.** Query with or without published clips or send complete ms. Length: 1,000-2,000 words. **Pays $50-400.**

Photos: Send photos with submission. Reviews transparencies, prints. Buys one-time rights. Offers no additional payment for photos accepted with ms. Captions, identification of subjects required.

Columns/Departments: Practice Tips (easy, unique business tips), 200-300 words. Send complete ms. **Pays $35.**

Tips: "Among the topics we cover: Veterinary hospital design, client relations, contractual and legal matters, investments, day-to-day management, marketing, personal finances, practice finances, personnel, collections, and taxes. We also cover news and issues within the veterinary profession; for example, articles might cover the effectiveness of Yellow Pages advertising, the growing number of women veterinarians, restrictive-covenant cases, and so on. Freelance writers are encouraged to submit proposals or outlines for articles on these topics. Most articles involve interviews with a nationwide sampling of veterinarians; we will provide the names and phone numbers if necessary. We accept only a small number of unsolicited manuscripts each year; however, we do assign many articles to freelance writers. All material submitted by first-time contributors is read on speculation, and the review process usually takes 12 to 16 weeks. Our style is concise yet conversational, and all manuscripts go through a fairly rigorous editing process. We encourage writers to provide specific examples to illustrate points made throughout their articles."

Scriptwriting

Scriptwriting makes some particular demands, but one thing remains the same for authors of novels, nonfiction books, and scripts: You'll learn to write by rewriting. Draft after draft your skills improve until, hopefully, someone likes your work enough to hire you.

Whether you are writing a video to train doctors in a new surgical technique, alternative theater for an Off-Broadway company, or you want to see your name on the credits of the next Harrison Ford movie, you must perfect both writing and marketing skills. A successful scriptwriter is a talented artist and a savvy business person. But marketing must always be secondary to writing. A mediocre pitch for a great script will still get you farther than a brilliant pitch for a mediocre script. The art and craft of scriptwriting lies in successfully executing inspiration.

Writing a script is a private act. Polishing it may involve more people as you ask friends and fellow writers to take a look at it. The polishing (and rewriting) is completed based on the knowledge of the entire filmmaking team (producers, directors, actors, cinematographers, etc.). The team's experience helps shape the production of a script. Scripts, unlike other forms of writing, are not just meant to be read—they are meant to be produced.

Marketing takes your script public in an effort to find the person willing to give the most of what you want, whether it's money, exposure, or control, in return for your work. There are accepted ground rules to presenting and marketing scripts. Following those guidelines will maximize your chances of getting your work before an audience.

Presenting your script professionally earns a serious consideration of its content. Certain scripts have a definite format and structure. An educational video written in a one-column format, a feature film much longer than 120 pages, or an hour-long TV show that peaks during the first 20 minutes indicates an amateur.

Submission guidelines are similar to those for other types of writing. The initial contact is a one-page query letter, a brief synopsis, and a few lines as to your credits or experience relevant to the subject of your script. Never send a complete manuscript until it's requested. Almost every script sent to a producer, studio, or agent must be accompanied by a release form. Ask the producer or agent for this form when invited to submit the complete script. Always include a SASE if you want your work returned.

Most writers break in with spec scripts, written for free, which serve as calling cards to show what they can do. These scripts plant the seeds of your professional reputation by making the rounds of influential people looking to hire writers, from advertising executives to movie moguls. Spec scripts are usually written for existing TV shows because people are most likely to be familiar with the characters and basic structure of an existing series. Also, new writers are rarely

---

For More Information

FORMATTING RESOURCES

- *Formatting & Submitting Your Manuscript*, by Jack and Glenda Neff and Don Prues (Writer's Digest Books).
- *The Complete Guide to Standard Script Formats*, by Hilis R. Cole and Judith H. Haag (CMC Publishing).

---

trusted with the launch of a new TV series. Most writers must earn their wings by writing for an existing series.

Good writing is more important than a specific plot. Have several spec scripts completed, as a producer will often decide that a story is not right for him, or a similar work is already in production, but will want to know what else you have. Be ready for that invitation.

Writing a script is a matter of learning how to refine your writing so that the work reads as a journey, not a technical manual. The best scripts have concise, visceral scenes that demand to be presented in a specific order and accomplish definite goals.

Educational videos have a message that must be expressed economically and directly, engaging the audience in an entertaining way while maintaining interest in the topic. Character and dialogue that expose a thematic core and engender enthusiasm or involvement in the conflict drive theatrical plays. Cinematic screenplays, while more visually-oriented, are a series of discontinuous scenes stacked to illuminate the characters, the obstacles confronting them, and the resolution they reach.

A script is a difficult medium—written words that sound natural when spoken, characters that are original yet resonate with the audience, believable conflicts and obstacles in tune with the end result.

BUSINESS & EDUCATIONAL WRITING

Scripts for corporate training, business management, and education videos have become as sophisticated as those designed for TV and film, and they carry the additional requirement of conveying specific content. With an audience that is increasingly media literate, anything that looks and feels like a "training film" will be dead in the water. The trick is to produce a script that engages, compels, *and* informs about the topic.

Larger companies often have in-house video production companies, but others rely on freelance writers. Your best bet would be to find work with companies that specialize in making educational and corporate videos while at the same time making yourself known to the creative directors of in-house video staffs in large corporations. Advertising agencies are also a good source of work, as they often are asked by their clients for help in creating films and use freelance writers and producers.

Business and educational videos are a market-driven industry, with material created either in response to a general need or a specific demand. The production company usually identifies a subject and finds the writer. As such, there is a perception that a spec script will not work in this media. While it is true that, as in TV and theatrical films, a writer's spec script is rarely produced, it is a good résumé of qualifications and sample of skills. Your spec script should demonstrate knowledge of this industry's specific format. For the most part, video scripts are written in two columns, video on the left, audio on the right.

Aside from the original script, another opportunity for the writer is the user's guide that often accompanies a video. If you are hired to create the auxiliary material you'll receive a copy of the finished video and write a concurrent text for the teacher or implementor to use.

Budgets are tighter for educational or corporate videos than for theatrical films. You'll want to work closely with the producer to make sure your ideas can be realized within the budget. Your fee will vary with each job, but generally a script written for a production house in a subject area with broad marketability will pay $5,000-7,000. A custom-produced video for a specific company will usually pay less. The pay does not increase exponentially with your experience; large increases come if you choose to direct and produce as well as write.

Information on business and educational script markets listed in the previous edition of *Writer's Market* but not included in this edition can be found in the General Index.

A/V CONCEPTS CORP., 30 Montauk Blvd., Oakdale NY 11769-1399. (631)567-7227. Fax: (631)567-8745. E-mail: editor@edconpublishing.com. Website: www.edconpublishing.com. **Contact:** Laura Solimene, editor. Estab. 1971. Produces supplementary materials for elementary-high school students, either on grade level or in remedial situations. **100% freelance written.** "All scripts/titles are by assignment only. Do not send manscripts." Employs video, book, and personal computer media. Buys all rights. Writing samples returned with 9×12 SAE with 5 first-class stamps. Responds in 1 month to outline, 6 weeks on final scripts. **Pays $300 and up.**

Needs: Main concentration in language arts, mathematics, and reading. "Manuscripts must be written using our lists of vocabulary words and meet our readability formula requirements. Specific guidelines are devised for each level. Student activities required. Length of manuscript and subjects will vary according to grade level for which material is prepared. Basically, we want material that will motivate people to read."

Tips: "Writers must be highly creative and disciplined. We are interested in high interest/low readability materials. Send writing samples, published or unpublished."

SAM BLATE ASSOCIATES, LLC, 10331 Watkins Mill Dr., Montgomery Village MD 20886-3950. (301)840-2248. Fax: (301)990-0707. E-mail: info@writephotopro.com. Website: www.writephotopro.com. **Contact:** Sam Blate, manager. "Produces educational and multimedia for business, education, institutions and state and federal governments." **Works with 2 local writers/year on a per-project basis—it varies as to business conditions and demand.** Buys first rights when possible. Query with writing samples and SASE for return. Responds in 1 month to queries. **Payment depends on contact with client. Pays some expenses.**

Needs: Scripts on technical, business and outdoor subjects.

Tips: "Writers must have a strong track record of technical and aesthetic excellence."

JIST PUBLISHING, 8902 Otis Ave., Indianapolis IN 46216. (317)613-4200. Fax: (317)613-4304. E-mail: info@jist.com. Website: www.jist.com. **Contact:** Constance Carlisle, video production manager. Estab. 1981. Produces career counseling, motivational materials (youth to adult) that encourage good planning and decision making for a successful future. Also produces videos on issues related to domestic violence, character education, child abuse, violence, anger management and parenting. **Buys 2-3 script(s)/year. Works with 3-4 writer(s)/year.** Buys all rights. Accepts previously produced material. Catalog online. Query with synopsis. Responds in 3 months to queries.

Needs: Videotapes, DVDs, multimedia kits. DVDs and 15-30 minute video VHS tapes on job search materials and related markets.

Tips: "We are actively acquiring more titles relevant to our subject matter and audience. We pay a royalty on finished video productions—repackaging, marketing, duplicating and taking care of all other expenses as we acquire the rights to them. Contact us, via e-mail or in writing, for details."

N **PALARDO PRODUCTIONS**, 1807 Taft Ave., Suite 4, Hollywood CA 90028. (323)469-8991. Fax: (323)469-8991. E-mail: palardopro@aol.com. **Contact:** Paul Ardolino, director. Estab. 1971. Produces material for youth ages 13-35. **Buys 3-4 script(s)/year.** Buys all rights. Query with synopsis, résumé. Responds in 2 weeks to queries; 1 month to scripts. **Pays in accordance with WGA standards.**

Needs: Videotapes, multimedia kits, tapes and cassettes. "We are seeking comedy feature scripts involving technology and coming of age; techno-shortform projects."

Tips: "Do not send a complete script—only synopsis of four pages or less *first*."

CHARLES RAPP ENTERPRISES, INC., 1650 Broadway, New York NY 10019. (212)247-6646. **Contact:** Howard Rapp, president. Estab. 1954. Produces materials for firms and buyers. **Works with 5 writers/year.** Accepts previously produced material. Submit résumé or sample of writing. Responds in 1 month to queries; 2 months to scripts. **Pays in accordance with WGA standards.**

Needs: Videotapes, treatments; scripts.

SPENCER PRODUCTIONS, INC., P.O. Box 2247, Westport CT 06880. (212)865-8829. **Contact:** Bruce Spencer, general manager; Alan Abel, creative director. Produces material for high school students, college students and adults. Occasionally uses freelance writers with considerable talent. Query. Responds in 1 month to queries. **Payment negotiable.**

Needs: Tapes and Cassettes. Satirical material only.

Tips: "For a comprehensive view of our humor requirements, we suggest viewing our feature film production, *Is There Sex After Death* (Rated R), starring Buck Henry. It is available at video stores. Or read *Don't Get Mad ... Get Even* and *How to Thrive on Rejection* by Alan Abel (published by W.W. Norton), both available from Barnes & Noble or Amazon." Also Books-on-Tape. "Send brief synopsis (one page) and outline (2-4 pages)."

TALCO PRODUCTIONS, 279 E. 44th St., New York NY 10017-4354. (212)697-4015. Fax: (212)697-4827. **Contact:** Alan Lawrence, president; Marty Holberton, vice president. Estab. 1968. Produces variety of material for TV, radio, business, trade associations, nonprofit organizations, public relations (chiefly political and current events), etc. Audiences range from young children to senior citizens. **20-40% freelance written. Buys scripts from published/produced writers only.** Buys all rights. No previously produced material. Submit résumé, production history. Responds in 3 weeks to queries. **Makes outright purchase. Pays in accordance with WGA standards. Sometimes pays the expenses of writers on assignment.**

Needs: Films, videotapes, tapes and cassettes, CDs. "We maintain a file of writers and call on those with experience in the same general category as the project in production. *We do not accept unsolicited manuscripts.* We prefer to receive a writer's résumé listing credits. If his/her background merits, we will be in touch when a project seems right." Talco reports that it is doing more public relations-oriented work: Print, videotape and radio.

Tips: "Concentration is now in TV productions. Production budgets are tighter."

N **ED TAR ASSOCIATES, INC.**, 230 Venice Way, Venice CA 90291. (310)306-2195. Fax: (310)306-0654. **Contact:** Ed Tar, president. Estab. 1972. Audience is dealers, salespeople, public. Buys all rights. No previously produced material. Submit résumé, writing samples. **Makes outright purchase.**

Needs: Films (16, 35mm), videotapes, multimedia kits, business theater; live shows; TV infomercials. "We are constantly looking for *experienced* writers of corporate, product and live show scripts."

PLAYWRITING

TV and movies are visual media where the words are often less important than the images. Writing plays uses different muscles, different techniques. Plays are built on character and dialogue—words put together to explore and examine characters.

The written word is respected in the theater by producer, cast, director, and even audience, to a degree unparalleled in other formats. While any work involving so many people to reach its final form is in essence a collaboration, it is presided over by the playwright, and changes can be made only with her approval, a power many screenwriters can only envy. If a play is worth producing, it will be produced "as is."

Counterbalancing the greater freedom of expression are the physical limitations inherent in live performance: a single stage, smaller cast, limited sets and lighting, and, most importantly, a strict, smaller budget. These conditions affect not only what, but also how, you write.

Start writing your play by reading. Reading gives you a feel for how characters are built, layer by layer, word by word, how each interaction presents another facet of a character. Exposition must mean something to the character, and the story must be worth telling for a play to be successful.

Once your play is finished you begin marketing it, which can take as long (or longer) than writing it. Before you begin you must have your script bound (three brads and a cover are fine) and copyrighted at the Copyright Office of the Library of Congress (see Minding the Details for information on obtaining a copyright) or registered with the Writers Guild of America (www.wga.org).

Your first goal will be to get at least a reading of your play. You might be lucky and get a small production. Community theaters or smaller regional houses are good places to start. Volunteer at a local theater. As prop mistress or spotlight operator you will get a sense of how a theater operates, the various elements of presenting a play, and what can and cannot be done, physically as well as dramatically. Personal contacts are important. Get to know the literary manager or artistic director of local theaters, which is the best way to get your script considered for production. Find out about any playwrights' groups in your area through local theaters or the drama departments of nearby colleges and universities. Use your creativity to connect with people that might be able to push your work higher.

Contests can be a good way to get noticed. Many playwriting contests offer a prize—at least a staged reading and often a full production. Once you've had a reading or workshop production, set your sights on a small production. Use this as a learning experience. Seeing your play on stage can help you view it more objectively and give you the chance to correct any flaws or inconsistencies. Incorporate any comments and ideas from the actors, director, or even audience, that you feel are on the mark, into revisions of your script.

You can also use a small production as a marketing tool. Keep track of all the press reviews, any interviews with you, members of the cast, or production, and put together a "press kit" for your play that can make the rounds with the script.

After you've been produced you have several directions to take your play. You can aim for a larger commercial production; you can try to get it published; you can seek artistic grants. After you have successfully pursued at least one of those avenues you can look for an agent. Choosing one direction does not rule out pursuing others at the same time.

Good reviews in a smaller production can get you noticed by larger theaters paying higher royalties and doing more ambitious productions. To submit your play to larger theaters you'll put together a submission package. This will include a one-page query letter to the literary

For More Information

RESOURCES

- *The Dramatists Sourcebook* (Theatre Communications Group).
- *Grants and Awards Available to American Writers* (PEN American Center).
- NEA Theater Program Fellowship for Playwrights (http://arts.endow.gov), 1100 Pennsylvania Ave. NW, Washington DC 20506. (202)682-5400.
- The Dramatists Guild of America, Inc. (www.dramaguild.com), 1501 Broadway, Suite 701, New York NY 10036. (212)398-9366.
- The International Women's Writing Guild (www.iwwg.com), P.O. Box 810, Gracie Station, New York NY 10028-0082. (212)737-7536.
- The Playwrights' Center (www.pwcenter.org), 2301 Franklin Ave. E., Minneapolis MN 55406-1099. (612)332-7481.
- Northwest Playwrights Guild (www.nwpg.org), P.O. Box 1728, Portland OR 97207.

manager or dramaturg briefly describing the play. Mention any reviews and give the number of cast members and sets. You will also send a two- to three-page synopsis, a ten-page sample of the most interesting section of your play, your résumé, and the press kit you've assembled. Do not send your complete manuscript until it is requested.

You can also explore publishing your play. *Writer's Market* lists many play publishers. When your script is published, your play will make money while someone else does the marketing. You'll be listed in a catalog that is sent to hundreds or thousands of potential performance spaces—high schools, experimental companies, regional and community theaters—for possible production. You'll receive royalty checks for both performance fees and book sales. In contacting publishers you'll want to send your query letter with the synopsis and reviews.

Once you have been produced on a commercial level, your play has been published, or you have won an important grant, you can start pursuing an agent. This is not always easy. Fewer agents represent playwrights alone—there's more money in movies and TV. No agent will represent an unknown playwright. Having an agent does *not* mean you can sit back and enjoy the ride. You will still need to get out and network, establishing ties with theaters, directors, literary managers, other writers, producers, state art agencies, and publishers, trying to get your work noticed.

There is always the possibility of moving from plays to TV and movies. There is a certain cachet in Hollywood surrounding successful playwrights. The writing style will be different—more visually oriented, less dependent on your words. The money is better, but you will have less command over the work once you've sold that copyright. It seems to be easier for a playwright to cross over to movies than for a screenwriter to cross over to plays.

Information on playwriting markets listed in the previous edition of *Writer's Market* but not included in this edition can be found in the General Index.

ABINGDON THEATRE CO., 312 W. 36th St., 1st Floor, New York NY 10036. (212)868-2055. Fax: (212)736-6608. E-mail: alcnyc@aol.com. Website: www.abingdon-nyc.org. **Contact:** Pamela Paul, artistic director. Estab. 1993. **Produces 2 main stage and 3 workshop plays/year.** Professional productions for a general audience. Submit full-length script. No one-act. Responds in 4 months. Buys variable rights. **Payment is negotiated.** Include SASE for return of manuscript.

Needs: All scripts should be suitable for small stages. No musicals where the story line is not very well-developed and the driving force of the piece.

ACT II PLAYHOUSE, P.O. Box 555, Ambler PA 19002. (215)654-0200. Fax: (215)654-5001. E-mail: act2playhouse@aol.com. Website: www.act2.org. **Contact:** Stephen Blumenthal, literary manager. Estab. 1998. **Produces 5 plays/year.** Query and synopsis. Responds in 1 month. **Payment negotiable.**

Needs: Contemporary comedy, drama, musicals. Full length. 6 character limitation; 1 set or unit set. Does not want period pieces. Limited number of scenes per act.

[N] **ALABAMA SHAKESPEARE FESTIVAL**, 1 Festival Dr., Montgomery AL 36117. Fax: (334)271-5353. Website: www.asf.net. Artistic Director: Kent Thompson. **Contact:** Gwen Orel, literary manager. **Produces 14 plays/year.** Inhouse productions for general and children's audience. Unsolicited scripts accepted for the Southern Writers' Project only. Responds in 1 year. **Pays royalty.**
Needs: "Through the Southern Writers' Project, ASF develops works by Southern writers, works that deal with the South and/or African-American themes, and works that deal with Southern and/or African-American history."

ALLEYWAY THEATRE, 1 Curtain Up Alley, Buffalo NY 14202-1911. (716)852-2600. Fax: (716)852-2266. E-mail: email@alleyway.com. Website: alleyway.com. **Contact:** Literary Manager. Estab. 1990. **Produces 4 full-length, 6-12 short plays/year.** Submit complete script; include tape for musicals. Responds in 6 months. Buys first production, credit rights. **Pays 7% royalty for production.**

- Alleyway Theatre also sponsors the Maxim Mazumdar New Play Competition. See the Contest & Awards section for more information.

Needs: "Theatrical" work as opposed to mainstream TV.
Tips: Sees a trend toward social issue-oriented works. Also interested in "nontraditional" children's pieces. "Plays on social issues should put action of play ahead of political message. Not interested in adapted screen plays. Theatricality and setting are central."

ALLIANCE THEATRE CO., 1280 Peachtree St. NE, Atlanta GA 30309. (404)733-4650. Fax: (404)733-4625. E-mail: ATCLiterary@woodruffcenter.org. Website: www.alliancetheatre.org. **Contact:** Freddie Ashley, literary associate. Estab. 1969. **Produces 11 plays/year.** Professional production for local audience. Query with synopsis or submit through agent. Enclose SASE. Responds in 9 months.
Needs: Full-length scripts and scripts for young audiences (max. length 60 minutes).
Tips: "As the premier theater of the southeast, the Alliance Theatre Company sets the highest artistic standards, creating the powerful experience of shared theater for diverse people. Please submit via snail mail."

APPLE TREE THEATRE, 595 Elm Pl., Suite 210, Highland Park IL 60035. (847)432-8223. Fax: (847)432-5214. E-mail: appletreetheatre@yahoo.com. Website: www.appletreetheatre.com. Artistic Director: Eileen Boevers. **Contact:** Literary Assistant. Estab. 1983. **Produces 5 plays/year.** "Professional productions intended for an adult audience mix of subscriber base and single-ticket holders. Our subscriber base is extremely theater-savvy and intellectual." Submit query and synopsis, along with tapes for musicals. Rights obtained vary. **Pays variable royalty.** Return SASE submissions only if requested.
Needs: "We produce a mixture of musicals, dramas, classical, contemporary, and comedies. Length: 90 minutes-2½ hours. Small space, unit set required. No fly space, 3¼ thrust stage. Maximum actors 15.
Tips: "No farces or large-scale musicals. Theater needs small shows with 1-unit sets due to financial concerns. Also note the desire for nonlinear pieces that break new ground. *Please do not submit unsolicited manuscripts—send letter and description*; if we want more, we will request it."

ARENA PLAYERS REPERTORY, CO., 296 Route 109, East Farmingdale NY 11735. (516)293-0674. Fax: (516)777-8688. E-mail: arena10@aol.com. Producer/Director: Frederic De Feis. **Contact:** Audrey Perry, production coordinator. Estab. 1954. **Produces 19 (at least 1 new) plays/year.** Professional production on either Arena Players' Main Stage or Second Stage Theatres. Intended for a conventional, middle-class audience. Query with synopsis or submit complete ms. Responds in 1 year. **Pays flat fee of $400-600.**
Needs: Main Stage season consists of Neil Simon-type comedies, Christie-esque mysteries and contemporary dramas. Prefers single set plays with a minimal cast (2 to 8 people). Only full-length plays will be considered.
Tips: No one-acts and musicals.

ARENA STAGE, 1101 Sixth St. SW, Washington DC 20024. (202)554-9066. Fax: (202)488-4056. E-mail: vworthington@arenastage.org. Website: www.arenastage.org. Artistic Director: Molly Smith. **Contact:** Cathy Madison, literary manager. Estab. 1950. **Plus various reading series in the Old Vat Room.** This is a professional theater. The Kreeger Theater seats 514 (modified thrust stage). The Fichandler Stage seats 827 (arena stage). The Old Vat Room seats 110 (cabaret stage). Accepts unsolicited scripts from Washington, DC, Maryland and Virginia writers only; all other writers should send synopsis, bio, 10-page diologue sample and letter of inquiry. Responds in 1 week to queries, 1 year to scripts.
Needs: Full length comedy, drama, satire, musicals, translations, adaptations, solo pieces. Special interests include unrpdocued works, plays for a multicultural company, plays by women, writers of color, physically disabled writers and other "non-mainstream" artists. We prefer cast sizes under 10, unless the play is a musical.
Tips: "Best for writer if he/she is agent-represented."

[A] **ARIZONA THEATRE, CO.**, P.O. Box 1631, Tucson AZ 85702. (520)884-8210. Fax: (520)628-9129. E-mail: swyer@aztheatreco.org. Website: www.aztheatreco.org. **Contact:** Samantha K. Wyer, associate artistic director. Estab. 1966. **Produces 6 plays/year.** Arizona Theatre Company is the State Theatre of Arizona and plans the season with the population of the state in mind. *Agented submissions only*, though Arizona writers may submit unsolicited scripts. Responds in 6 months. **Payment negotiated.**
Needs: Full length plays of a variety of genres and topics and full length musicals. No one-acts.
Tips: "Please include in the cover letter a bit about your current situation and goals. It helps in responding to plays."

ART STATION THEATRE, P.O. Box 1998, Stone Mountain GA 30086. (770)469-1105. Fax: (770)469-0355. E-mail: info@artstation.org. Website: www.artstation.org. **Contact:** Jon Goldstein, literary manager. Estab. 1986. **Produces 5 plays/**

year. "ART Station Theatre is a professional theater located in a contemporary arts center in Stone Mountain, which is part of Metro Atlanta." Audience consists of middle-aged to senior, suburban patrons. Query with synopsis and writing samples. Responds in 6-12 months. **Pays 5-7% royalty.**

Needs: Full length comedy, drama and musicals, preferably relating to the human condition in the contemporary South. Cast size no greater than 6.

ARTISTS REPERTORY THEATRE, 1516 S.W. Alder St., Portland OR 97205. E-mail: allen@artistsrep.org. Website: www.artistsrep.org. **Contact:** Allen Nause, artistic director. Estab. 1982. **Produces "5 plays on main stage, and 2 plays on our second stage."** Plays performed in professional theater with a subscriber-based audience. Send synopsis, sample, and résumé. No unsolicited mss accepted. Responds in 6 months. **Pays royalty.**

Needs: "Full-length, hard-hitting, emotional, intimate, actor-oriented shows with small casts (rarely exceeds 10-13, usually 2-7). Language and subject matter are not a problem." No one-acts or children's scripts.

ASIAN AMERICAN THEATER CO., 690 5th St., Suite 211, San Francisco CA 94107. (415)543-5738. Fax: (415)543-5638. E-mail: info@asianamericantheater.org. Website: www.asianamericantheater.org. **Contact:** Noel Madlansacay, literary associate. Estab. 1973. **Produces 3 plays/year.** Produces amateur (emerging artists) and professional productions for API audiences. Submit complete script. Responds in 3 months. **Payment varies.**

Needs: Anything by, for and about an API audience. No limitations in cast, props or staging.

Tips: Looking for plays by, for and about Asian Pacific Islander Americans. Scripts from Asian Pacific Islander American women and under-represented Asian Pacific Islander ethnic groups are especially welcome.

ASOLO THEATRE CO., 5555 N. Tamiami Trail, Sarasota FL 34234. (941)351-9010. Fax: (941)351-5796. E-mail: bruce_rodgers@asolo.org. Website: www.asolo.org. **Contact:** Bruce E. Rodgers, associate artistic director. Estab. 1960. **Produces 7-8 plays/year.** A LORT theater with 2 intimate performing spaces. No unsolicited scripts. Send a letter with 1-page synopsis, 1 page of dialogue, and SAE. Responds in 8 months. **Negotiates rights and payment.**

Needs: Play must be full length. "We operate with a resident company in rotating repertory."

BAILIWICK REPERTORY, Bailiwick Arts Center, 1229 W. Belmont Ave., Chicago IL 60657-3205. (773)883-1090. Fax: (773)883-2017. E-mail: bailiwickr@aol.com. Website: www.bailiwick.org. **Contact:** David Zak, artistic director. Estab. 1982. **Produces 5 mainstage plays (classic and newly commissioned) each year; 50 one-acts in annual Directors Festival.** Pride Performance Series (gay and lesbian), includes one-acts, poetry, workshops, and staged adaptations of prose. Submit year-round. One-act play fest runs July-August. Responds in 9 months for full-length only. **Pays 6% royalty.**

Needs: "We need daring scripts that break the mold. Large casts or musicals are OK. Creative staging solutions are a must."

Tips: "Know the rules, then break them creatively and boldly! Please send SASE for manuscript submission guidelines *before you submit* or get manuscript guidelines at our website."

BAKER'S PLAYS PUBLISHING CO., P.O. Box 699222, Quincy MA 02269-9222. (617)745-0805. Fax: (617)745-9891. E-mail: 411@bakersplays.com. Website: www.bakersplays.com. **Contact:** Kurt Gombar, chief editor. Estab. 1845. **Publishes 20-30 straight plays and musicals. Works with 2-3 unpublished/unproduced writers annually. 80% freelance written. 75% of scripts unagented submissions**. Plays performed by amateur groups, high schools, children's theater, churches and community theater groups. Submit complete script with news clippings, résumé. Submit complete cassette of music with musical submissions. Responds in 4 months. **Pay varies; negotiated royalty split of production fees; 10% book royalty.**

Needs: "We are finding strong support in our new division—plays from young authors featuring contemporary pieces for high school production."

Tips: "We are particularly interested in adaptation of lesser-known folk tales from around the world. Also of interest are plays which feature a multicultural cast and theme. Collections of one-act plays for children and young adults tend to do very well. Also, high school students: Write for guidelines for our High School Playwriting Contest."

MARY BALDWIN COLLEGE THEATRE, Mary Baldwin College, Staunton VA 24401. Fax: (540)887-7139. Website: www.mbc.edu. **Contact:** Virginia R. Francisco, professor of theater. Estab. 1842. **Produces 5 plays/year.** 75% of scripts are unagented submissions. Works with 0-1 unpublished/unproduced writers annually. An undergraduate women's college theater with an audience of students, faculty, staff and local community (adult, conservative). Query with synopsis. Responds in 1 year. Buys performance rights only. **Pays $10-50 per performance.**

Needs: Full-length and short comedies, tragedies, music plays, particularly for young women actresses, dealing with women's issues both contemporary and historical. Experimental/studio theater not suitable for heavy sets. Cast should emphasize women. No heavy sex; minimal explicit language.

Tips: "A perfect play for us has several roles for young women, few male roles, minimal production demands, a concentration on issues relevant to contemporary society, and elegant writing and structure."

BLOOMSBURG THEATRE ENSEMBLE, Box 66, Bloomsburg PA 17815. (570)784-5530. Fax: (570)784-4912. Ensemble Director: James Goode. **Contact:** Play Section Chair. Estab. 1979. **Produces 6 plays/year.** Professional productions for a non-urban audience. Query and synopsis. Responds in 9 months. Buys negotiable rights **Pays 6-9% royalty. Pays $50-70 per performance.** "Because of our non-urban location, we strive to exposé our audience to a broad range of theatre—both classical and contemporary. We are drawn to language and ideas and to plays that resonate in our community. We are most in need of articulate comedies and cast sizes under 6."

Tips: "Because of our non-urban setting we are less interested in plays that focus on dilemmas of city life in particular.

Most of the comedies we read are cynical. Many plays we read would make better film scripts; static/relationship-heavy scripts that do not use the 'theatricality' of the theatre to an advantage."

BOARSHEAD THEATER, 425 S. Grand Ave., Lansing MI 48933. Website: www.boarshead.org. **Contact:** John Peakes, founding art director. Estab. 1966. **Produces 8 plays/year (6 mainstage, 2 Young People's Theater productions inhouse), 4 or 5 staged readings.** Mainstage Actors' Equity Association company; also Youth Theater—touring to schools by our intern company. Query with one-page synopsis, cast list (with descriptions), 5-10 pages of representative dialogue, description of setting, special needs and e-mail address for our response. Responds in 1 month to queries and synopsis. Full scripts (if requested) in 8 months. **Pays royalty for mainstage productions, transport/per diem for staged readings.**
Needs: Thrust stage. Cast usually 8 or less; occasionally up to 20; no one-acts and no musicals considered. Prefer staging which depends on theatricality rather than multiple sets. "Send materials for full length plays (only) to John Peakes, founding art director. For Young People's Theater, send one-act plays (only); 4-5 characters."
Tips: Plays should not have multiple realistic sets—too many scripts read like film scripts. Focus on intelligence, theatricality, crisp, engaging humorous dialogue. "Write a good play and prove it in a precise 10 pages of great dialogue. Also, don't tape your submission so it takes 3 minutes to open. Puts me in a negative mood."

CALIFORNIA THEATER CENTER, P.O. Box 2007, Sunnyvale CA 94087. (408)245-2978. Fax: (408)245-0235. E-mail: ctc@ctcinc.org. Website: www.ctcing.org. **Contact:** Will Huddleston, literary manager/resident director. Estab. 1976. **Produces 15 plays/year.** "Plays are for young audiences in both our home theater and for tour." Query and synopsis. Responds in 6 months. **Negotiates set fee.**
Needs: All plays must be suitable for young audiences, must be around 1 hour in length. Cast sizes vary. Many shows require touring sets.
Tips: "Almost all new plays we do are for young audiences, one-acts with fairly broad appeal, not over an hour in length, with mixed casts of two to eight adult, professional actors. We read plays for all ages, though plays for kindergarten through fourth grade have the best chance of being chosen. Plays with memorable music are especially looked for, as well as plays based upon literary works or historical material young people know from school. Serious plays written in the style of psychological realism must be especially well written. Satires and parodies are difficult for our audiences unless they are based upon material familiar to children. Anything "cute" should be avoided. In the summer we seek large cast plays that can be performed entirely by children in our Summer Conservatory programs. We particularly look for plays that can do well in difficult venues, such as high school gymnasiums, multi-purpose rooms, etc."

CENTER STAGE, 700 N. Calvert St., Baltimore MD 21202-3686. (410)685-3200. **Contact:** Gavin Witt, resident dramaturg. Estab. 1963. **Produces 6-8 plays/year.** LORT 'C' and LORT 'D' theaters. Audience is both subscription and single-ticket. Wide-ranging audience profile. Query with synopsis, 10 sample pages and résumé, or submit through agent. Responds in 3 months. Rights negotiated. **Payment negotiated.**
Needs: Produces dramas, comedies, musical theater works. "Casts over 12 would give us pause. Be inventive, theatrical, not precious; we like plays with vigorous language and stage image. Domestic naturalism is discouraged; strong political or social interests are encouraged." No one-act plays. "Plays about bourgeois adultery, life in the suburbs, Amelia Earhart, Alzheimer's, mid-life crises, 'wacky southerners', fear of intimacy, Hemingway, Bible stories, backstage life, are unacceptable, as are spoofs and mysteries."
Tips: "We are interested in reading adaptations and translations as well as original work. Strong interest in plays about the African-American experience."

CHARLOTTE REPERTORY THEATRE, 129 W. Trade St., Charlotte NC 28202. (704)333-8587. Fax: (704)333-0224. E-mail: maman@charlotterepertorytheatre.com. Website: www.charlotterep.org. **Contact:** Michael Aman. Estab. 1976. "We are a not-for-profit regional theater." Submit 10-20 sample pages with SASE. Responds in 3 months. **Writers receive free plane fare and housing for festival.**
Needs: Seeking plays for staged readings at the "In the Works" New Plays Festival. No limitations in subject matter, cast, props, stage, etc.

CHILDREN'S STORY SCRIPTS, Baymax Productions, 2219 W. Olive Ave., PMB 130, Burbank CA 91506-2648. (818)787-5584. E-mail: baymax@earthlink.net. **Contact:** Deedra Bebout, editor. Estab. 1990. "Our audience consists of children, grades K-8 (5-13-year-olds)." Send complete script with SASE. Responds in 1 month. Licenses all rights to story; author retains copyright. **Pays graduated royalty based on sales.**
Needs: "We add new titles as we find appropriate stories. We look for stories which are fun for kids to read, involve a number of readers throughout, and dovetail with school subjects. This is a must! Not life lessons . . . school subjects."
Tips: "The scripts are not like theatrical scripts. They combine dialogue and prose narration, á la Readers Theatre. If a writer shows promise, we'll work with him. Our most important goal is to benefit children. We want stories that bring alive subjects studied in classrooms. Facts must be worked unobtrusively into the story—the story has to be fun for the kids to read. Send #10 SASE for guidelines with samples. We do not respond to submissions without SASE."

CHILDSPLAY, INC., P.O. Box 517, Tempe AZ 85280. (480)858-2127. Fax: (480)350-8584. E-mail: info@childsplayaz.org. Website: childsplayaz.org. **Contact:** Graham Whitehead, associate artistic director. Estab. 1978. **Produces 5-6 plays/year.** "Professional touring and in-house productions for youth and family audiences." Submit synopsis, character descriptions and 7- to 10-page dialogue sample. Responds in 6 months. **Pays royalty of $20-35/performance (touring) or pays $3,000-8,000 commission. Holds a small percentage of royalties on commissioned work for 3-5 years.**
Needs: Seeking theatrical plays on a wide range of contemporary topics. "Our biggest market is K-6. We need intelligent theatrical pieces for this age group that meet touring requirements and have the flexibility for in-house staging. The company has a reputation, built up over 25 years, of maintaining a strong aesthetic. We need scripts that respect the audience's

intelligence and support their rights to dream and to have their concerns explored. Innovative, theatrical and small is a constant need." Touring shows limited to 5-6 actors; in-house shows limited to 6-10 actors.

Tips: No traditionally-handled fairy tales. "Theater for young people is growing up and is able to speak to youth and adults. The material must respect the artistry of the theater and the intelligence of our audience. Our most important goal is to benefit children. If you wish your materials returned send SASE."

CIRCLE THEATRE, 2015 S. 60th St., Omaha NE 68106. (402)553-4715. E-mail: dlmarr@cox.net. **Contact:** Doug Marr, artistic director. Estab. 1983. **Produces 5 plays/year.** Professional productions, general audience. Query and synopsis. Responds in 2 months. **Pays $15-30 per performance.**

Needs: Comedies, dramas, musicals—original unproduced works. Full length, all styles/topics. Small casts, simple sets.

CIRCUIT PLAYHOUSE/PLAYHOUSE ON THE SQUARE, 51 S. Cooper, Memphis TN 38104. (901)725-0776. **Contact:** Jackie Nichols, artistic director. **Produces 16 plays/year. 100% of scripts unagented submissions. Works with 1 unpublished/unproduced writer/year**. Professional plays performed for the Memphis/Mid-South area. Member of the Theatre Communications Group. Contest held each fall. Submit complete script. Responds in 6 months. Buys percentage of royalty rights for 2 years. **Pays $500.**

Needs: All types; limited to single or unit sets. Casts of 20 or fewer.

Tips: "Each play is read by three readers through the extended length of time a script is kept. Preference is given to scripts for the southeastern region of the U.S."

I.E. CLARK PUBLICATIONS, P.O. Box 246, Schulenburg TX 78956-0246. Website: www.ieclark.com. **Contact:** Donna Cozzaglio, general manager. Estab. 1956. Publishes 10-15 plays/year for educational theater, children's theater, religious theater, regional professional theater and community theater. Publishes unagented submissions. Catalog for $3. Writer's guidelines for #10 SASE. Submit complete script, 1 at a time with SASE. Responds in 6 months. Buys all available rights; "We serve as an agency as well as a publisher." **Pays standard book and performance royalty, amount and percentages dependent upon type and marketability of play.**

- "One of our specialties is "Young Adult Awareness Drama"—plays for ages 13 to 25 dealing with sex, drugs, popularity, juvenile, crime, and other problems of young adults. We also need plays for children's theatre, especially dramatizations of children's classic literature."

Needs: "We are interested in plays of all types—short or long. Audiotapes of music or videotapes of a performance are requested with submissions of musicals. We require that a play has been produced (directed by someone other than the author); photos, videos and reviews of the production are helpful. No limitations in cast, props, staging, etc. Plays with only one or two characters are difficult to sell. We insist on literary quality. We like plays that give new interpretations and understanding of human nature. Correct spelling, punctuation and grammar (befitting the characters, of course) impress our editors."

Tips: Publishes plays only. "Entertainment value and a sense of moral responsibility seem to be returning as essential qualities of a good play script. The era of glorifying the negative elements of society seems to be fading rapidly. Literary quality, entertainment value and good craftsmanship rank in that order as the characteristics of a good script in our opinion. 'Literary quality' means that the play must—in beautiful, distinctive, and un-trite language—say something; preferably something new and important concerning man's relations with his fellow man or God; and these 'lessons in living' must be presented in an intelligent, believable and creative manner. Plays for children's theater are tending more toward realism and childhood problems, but fantasy and dramatization of fairy tales are also needed."

CLEVELAND PLAY HOUSE, 8500 Euclid Ave., Cleveland OH 44106. E-mail: sgordon@clevelandplayhouse.com. Website: www.clevelandplayhouse.com. Artistic Director: Peter Hackett. **Contact:** Seth Gordon, director of new play development. Estab. 1915. **Produces 10 plays/year.** "We have five theatres, 100-550 seats." 10 page sample with synopsis is best introduction. Responds in 6 months. **Payment is negotiable.**

Needs: All styles and topics of new plays.

COLONY THEATRE CO., 555 N. Third St., Burbank CA 91502-1103. Website: www.colonytheatre.org. **Contact:** Wayne Liebman, literary manager. **Produces 6 plays/year.** Professional 276-seat theater with thrust stage. Casts from resident company of professional actors. *Agented submissions only.* Negotiated rights. **Pays royalty for each performance.**

Needs: Full length (90-120 minutes) with a cast of 4-12. No musicals or experimental works.

Tips: "We seek works of theatrical imagination and emotional resonance on universal themes."

CONFRONTATION, A Literary Journal, C.W. Post of Long Island University, Brookville NY 11548-1300. (516)299-2720. Fax: (516)299-2735. E-mail: mtucker@liu.edu. **Contact:** Martin Tucker, editor. Estab. 1968. **Publishes 2 plays/year.** Submit complete script. Responds in 2 months. Obtains first serial and reprint rights. **Pays up to $50.**

Needs: "We have an annual one-act play contest, open to all forms and styles. Award is $200 and publication."

CONTEMPORARY DRAMA SERVICE, Meriwether Publishing Ltd., P.O. Box 7710, Colorado Springs CO 80933. Fax: (719)594-9916. E-mail: merpcds@aol.com. Website: www.contemporarydrama.com. Editor: Arthur Zapel. **Contact:** Theodore Zapel, associate editor. Estab. 1969. **Publishes 50-60 plays/year.** "We are specialists in theater arts books and plays for middle grades, high schools and colleges. We publish textbooks for drama courses of all types. We also publish for mainline liturgical churches—drama activities for church holidays, youth activities and fundraising entertainments. These may be plays, musicals or drama-related books." Query with synopsis or submit complete script. Responds in 6 weeks. Obtains either amateur or all rights. **Pays 10% royalty or negotiates purchase.**

- Contemporary Drama Service is now looking for play or musical adaptations of classic stories by famous authors and playwrights. Also looking for parodies of famous movies or historical and/or fictional characters, i.e. Robin Hood, Rip Van Winkle, Buffalo Bill, Huckleberry Finn.

Needs: "Most of the plays we publish are one-acts, 15-45 minutes in length. We also publish full-length two-act musicals or three-act plays 90 minutes in length. We prefer comedies. Musical plays must have name appeal either by prestige author or prestige title adaptation. Musical shows should have large casts for 20 to 25 performers. Comedy sketches, monologues and plays are welcomed. We prefer simple staging appropriate to middle school, high school, college or church performance. We like playwrights who see the world with a sense of humor. Offbeat themes and treatments are accepted if the playwright can sustain a light touch. In documentary or religious plays we look for good research and authenticity. We are publishing many scenebooks for actors (which can be anthologies of great works excerpts), scenebooks on special themes and speech and theatrical arts textbooks. We also publish many books of monologs for young performers. We are especially interested in authority-books on a variety of theater-related subjects."

Tips: Contemporary Drama Service is looking for creative books on comedy, monologs, staging amateur theatricals and Christian youth activities. "Our writers are usually highly experienced in theatre as teachers or performers. We welcome books that reflect their experience and special knowledge. Any good comedy writer of monologs and short scenes will find a home with us."

CREEDE REPERTORY THEATRE, P.O. Box 269, Creede CO 81130-0269. (719)658-2541. **Contact:** Maurice Lemee, director. Estab. 1966. **Produces 6 plays/year.** Plays performed for a smaller audience. Query and synopsis. Responds in 1 year. **Royalties negotiated with each author—paid on a per performance basis.**

Needs: One-act children's scripts. Special consideration given to plays focusing on the cultures and history of the American West and Southwest.

Tips: "We seek new adaptations of classical or older works as well as original scripts."

[N] **DALLAS CHILDREN'S THEATER**, Rosewood Center for Family Arts, 5938 Skillman, Dallas TX 75231. E-mail: family@dct.org. Website: www.dct.org. **Contact:** Robyn Flatt, executive director. Estab. 1984. **Produces 11 plays/year.** Professional theater for family and student audiences. Query with synopsis, number of actors required, any material regarding previous productions of the work, and a demo tape or lead sheets (for musicals). Responds in 8 months. Rights negotiable. **Pays negotiable royalty.** No materials will be returned without a SASE included.

Needs: Substantive material appropriate for youth and family audiences. Most consideration given to full-length, non-musical works, especially classic and contemporary adaptations of literature. Also interested in social, topical issue-oriented material. Very interested in scripts which enlighten diverse cultural experiences, particularly Hispanic and African-American experiences. Prefers scripts with no more than 15 cast members; 6-12 is ideal.

Tips: No adult experience material. "We are a family theater." Not interested in material intended for performance by children or in a classroom. Productions are performed by professional adults. Children are cast in child-appropriate roles. "We receive far too much light musical material that plays down to children and totally lacks any substance. Be patient. We receive an enormous amount of submissions. Most of the material we have historically produced has had previous production. We are not against perusing non-produced material, but it has rarely gone into our season unless we have been involved in its development."

DETROIT REPERTORY THEATRE, 13103 Woodrow Wilson, Detroit MI 48238-3686. (313)868-1347. Fax: (313)868-1705. **Contact:** Barbara Busby, literary manager. Estab. 1957. **Produces 4 plays/year.** Professional theater, 194 seats operating on A.E.A. SPT contract Detroit metropolitan area. Submit complete ms in bound folder, cast list and description with SASE. Responds in 6 months. **Pays royalty.**

Needs: Wants issue-oriented works. Cast limited to no more than 7 characters. No musicals or one-act plays.

DIVERSIONARY THEATRE, 4545 Park Blvd., San Diego CA 92116. (619)220-6830. **Contact:** Chuck Zito, executive director. Estab. 1985. **Produces 5 plays/year.** Non-professional productions of gay, lesbian, bisexual and transgender content. Not accepting unsolicited scripts at this time.

DIXON PLACE, 258 Bowery, 2nd Floor, New York NY 10012. (212)219-0736. Fax: (212)219-0761. E-mail: submissions@dixonplace.org. Website: www.dixonplace.org. **Contact:** Amanda Gutowski, artistic associate. Estab. 1986. **Produces 12 plays/year.** "We present occasional play readings at our downtown, off-off Broadway performance venue." Audience is usually made up of supporters of the writer and other artists. Submit 10-page script sample with synopsis and video of recent original performance. Does not accept submissions from outside NYC area. Responds in 6 months. **Pays flat fee.**

Needs: Musicals, one-acts, full-length plays, not already read or workshopped in New York. Particularly interested in non-traditional, either in character, content, structure and/or themes. "We almost never produce kitchen sink, soap opera-style plays about AIDS, coming out, unhappy love affairs, getting sober or lesbian parenting. We regularly present new works, plays with innovative structure, multi-ethnic content, non-naturalistic dialogue, irreverent musicals and the elegantly bizarre. We are an established performance venue with a very diverse audience. We have a reputation for bringing our audience the unexpected. Submissions accepted year-round."

[A] **DORSET THEATRE FESTIVAL**, Box 510, Dorset VT 05251-0510. (802)867-2223. Fax: (802)867-0144. E-mail: theatre@sover.net. Website: www.dorsettheatrefestival.org. **Contact:** John Nassivera, producing artistic director. Estab. 1976. **Produces 5 plays/year (1 a new work).** "Our plays will be performed in our Equity summer stock theater and are intended for a sophisticated community." Agented submissions only. Responds in 6 months. **Rights and compensation negotiated.**

Needs: "Looking for full-length contemporary American comedy or drama." Limited to a cast of 6.

Tips: "Language and subject matter appropriate to general audience."

DRAMATIC PUBLISHING, 311 Washington St., Woodstock IL 60098. (815)338-7170. Fax: (815)338-8981. E-mail: plays@dramaticpublishing.com. Website: www.dramaticpublishing.com. **Contact:** Linda Habjan, editor. **Publishes 40-50 titles/year.** Publishes paperback acting editions of original plays, musicals, adaptations, and translations. **Receives 250-500 queries and 600 mss/year.** Catalog and script guidelines free. **Pays 10% royalty on scripts; performance royalty varies.**

Needs: Interested in playscripts appropriate for children, middle and high schools, colleges, community, stock and professional theaters. Send full ms.

Tips: "We publish all kinds of plays for the professional, stock, amateur, high school, elementary and children's theater markets: full lengths, one acts, children's plays, musicals, adaptations."

[N] **THE EAST VILLAGE EXPERIMENTAL THEATRE CO.**, 3711 President St., Philadelphia PA 19114. Fax: (215)612-8597. E-mail: info@eastvillageetc.org. Website: www.eastvillageetc.org. **Contact:** Randy Lee Hartwig, executive director. Estab. 2000. **Publishes 12-15 plays/year.** Performs for a variety of artists at a variety of venues - school to performance art. Query with synopsis, résumé, writing samples and production history. Responds in 2 months. "We develop new projects of performance from radio and video to film and theatre. Once the project has reached production we are publishing manuscripts, videotapes, films, audio tapes, scores. etc." **Pays lease per performance.** Include SASE for return of materials.

Needs: "We are looking for interdisciplinary and multimedia projects in film, video, radio, theatre, performance art, dance, music and site-specific events."

Tips: "The performing arts audiences are seeking exciting and honest works that are less linear and narrative and more visual and associative. We are seeking to combine visual, media and performing arts in formats and venues that are suitable to the work and content of the project."

[N] **EAST WEST PLAYERS**, 120 Judge John Aiso St., Los Angeles CA 90012. (213)625-7000, ext. 27. Fax: (213)625-7111. E-mail: info@eastwestplayers.org. Website: www.eastwestplayers.org. Artistic Director: Tim Dang. Estab. 1965. **Produces 5 plays/year.** Professional 240-seat theater performing under LOA-BAT contract, presenting plays which explore the Asian-Pacific or Asian-American experience. Query and synopsis. **Pays royalty against percentage of box office.**

Needs: "Whether dramas, comedies, performance art or musicals, all plays must either address the Asian-American experience or have a special resonance when cast with Asian-American actors."

ELDRIDGE PUBLISHING CO., P.O. Box 14367, Tallahassee FL 32317. (850)385-2463. Fax: (850)385-7098. E-mail: info@histage.com. Website: www.histage.com. Editor: Susan Shore. Estab. 1906. **Publishes 60 new plays/year for junior high, senior high, church, and community audience.** Query with synopsis (acceptable) or submit complete ms (preferred). Please send CD with any musicals. Responds in 2 months. Buys all rights. **Pays 50% royalties and 10% copy sales in general market. Makes outright purchase of $200-600 in religious market.**

Needs: "We are most interested in full-length plays and musicals for our school and community theater market. Nothing lower than junior high level, please. We always love comedies but also look for serious, high caliber plays reflective of today's sophisticated students. We also need one-acts and plays for children's theater. In addition, in our religious market we're always searching for holiday or any time plays."

Tips: "Submissions are welcomed at any time. Authors are paid royalties twice a year. They receive complimentary copies of their published plays, the annual catalog, and 50% discount if buying additional copies."

[A] **THE EMPTY SPACE THEATRE**, 3509 Fremont Ave. N, Seattle WA 98103. (206)547-7633. Fax: (206)547-7635. E-mail: emptyspace@emptyspace.org. Website: www.emptyspace.org. **Contact:** Adam Greenfield, associate artistic director. Estab. 1970. **Produces 6 plays/year between October and July.** Professional productions. *Agented submissions only*, unless a writer is from the Northwest. Reponds to queries in 2 months, scripts in 6 months **Typically, we ask for something close to 5% of the author's royalties for 5 years. Pays 6-10% royalty or $2,500-10,000 playwright commission.**

Needs: Full-length plays, full-length musicals, solo pieces, translations, adaptations. "The Empty Space strives to make theatre an event—bold, provocative, celebratory—brings audience and artists to a common ground through an uncommon experience." Prefers small casts.

Tips: "The Empty Space produces work that specifically supports our artistic vision—generally rough and bold plays that seek to engage audiences on a visceral level; highly theatrical works."

ENCORE PERFORMANCE PUBLISHING, 450 La Have St., Unit 17, Suite 123, Bridgewater NS B4V 3T2, Canada. (902)543-6027. Fax: (902)543-6156. E-mail: encoreplay@aol.com. Website: www.encoreplay.com. **Contact:** Michael C. Perry, editor. Estab. 1979. **Produces 30 plays/year.** "Our audience consists of all ages with emphasis on the family; educational institutions from elementary through college/university, community theaters and professional theaters." No unsolicited mss. Query with synopsis, production history and SASE. Responds in 1 month to queries; 3 months to scripts. Submit from May-August. **Pays 50% performance royalty; 10% book royalty.**

Needs: "We are looking for plays with strong message about or for families, plays with young actors among cast, any length, all genres. We prefer scripts with at least close or equal male/female roles, could lean to more female roles." Plays must have had at least 2 fully staged productions. Unproduced plays can be read with letter of recommendation accompanying the query. This letter must be written and signed by someone not related to the author.

Tips: "No performance art pieces or plays with overtly sexual themes or language. Looking for adaptations of Twain and other American authors."

THE ENSEMBLE STUDIO THEATRE, 549 W. 52nd St., New York NY 10019. (212)247-4982. Fax: (212)664-0041. Website: www.ensemblestudiotheatre.org. Artistic Director: Curt Dempster. **Contact:** Tom Rowan, literary manager. Estab. 1971. **Produces 250 projects/year for off-off Broadway developmental theater in a 100-seat house, 60-seat workshop**

space. Do not fax mss or résumés. Submit complete ms. Responds in 6 months. **Standard production contract: mini contract with Actors' Equity Association or letter of agreement. Pays $80-1,000.**

Needs: Full-length plays with strong dramatic actions and situations and solid one-acts, humorous and dramatic, which can stand on their own. Musicals also accepted; send tape of music. Special programs include Going to the River Series, which workshops new plays by African-American women, and the Sloan Project, which commissions new works on the topics of science and technology. Seeks "original plays with strong dramatic action, believable characters and dynamic ideas. We are interested in writers who respect the power of language." No verse-dramas or elaborate costume dramas.

Tips: Deadline for one-act play marathon submissions is November 8. Full-length plays accepted year-round. "We are dedicated to developing new American plays."

ENSEMBLE THEATRE OF CINCINNATI, 1127 Vine St., Cincinnati OH 45248. (513)421-3555. Fax: (513)562-4104. Website: cincyetc.com. **Contact:** D. Lynn Meyers, producing artistic director. Estab. 1987. **Produces 7 plays/year, including a staged reading series.** Professional year-round theater. Query with synopsis, submit complete ms or submit through agent. Responds in 6 months. **Pays 5-10% royalty.**

Needs: Dedicated to good writing, any style for a contemporary, small cast. Small technical needs, big ideas.

[N] **THE ESSENTIAL THEATRE**, 995 Greenwood Ave. #6, Atlanta GA 30306. (404)876-8471. **Contact:** Peter Hardy, artistic director. Estab. 1987. **Produces 3 plays/year.** "Professional theatre on a small budget, for adventurous theatregoers interested in new plays." Submit complete script. Responds in 6 months. Include SASE for return of submission.

Needs: Accepts full-length, unproduced plays by Georgia residents only, to be considered for Essential Theatre Playwriting Award. Winner receives $400 and full production.

FIRST STAGE, P.O. Box 38280, Los Angeles CA 90038. (323)850-6271. Fax: (323)850-6295. E-mail: firststagela@aol.com. Website: www.firststagela.org. **Contact:** Dennis Safren, literary manager. Estab. 1983. **Produces 50 plays/year; 130 short plays (under 15 minutes) for annual fundraiser, which requires a $40 donation.** First Stage is a non-profit organization dedicated to bringing together writers, actors and directors in the development of new material for stage and screen. Submit complete script. Responds in 6 months.

Needs: Original non-produced plays in any genre. Correct play format. No longer than two hours. Produces one-act play contest, which requires a $10 donation. Deadline September 15. The deadline for "Playwright's Express" is March 19th.

Tips: No TV sitcoms. "We are a development organization."

[A] **FLORIDA STAGE**, 262 S. Ocean Blvd., Manalapan FL 33462. (561)585-3404. Fax: (561)588-4708. Website: www.floridastage.org. **Contact:** Des Gallant, literary manager. Estab. 1985. **Produces 5 plays/year.** Professional equity productions; 250 seat thrust; looking for edgy work that deals with issues and ideas; stylistically innovative. Agented submissions only. Responds in 1 year. Buys production rights only. **Pays royalty.**

Needs: "We need drama and comedy; issue-oriented plays, innovative in their use of language, structure and style." No more than 8 actors.

Tips: No kitchen sink; no Neil Simon type comedy; no TV sitcom type material. "We see a propensity for writing scripts that forget the art of the theater and that are overly influenced by TV and film. Theater's most important asset is language. It is truly refreshing to come across writers who understand this. Eric Overmyer is a great example.

THE FOOTHILL THEATRE CO., P.O. Box 1812, Nevada City CA 95959. (530)265-9320. Fax: (530)265-9325. E-mail: gary@foothilltheatre.org. Website: www.foothilltheatre.org. **Contact:** Gary Wright, literary manager. Estab. 1977. **Produces 6-9 plays/year.** "We are a professional theater company operating under an Actors' Equity Association contract for part of the year, and performing in the historic 246-seat Nevada Theatre (built in 1865) and at an outdoor amphitheatre on the north shore of Lake Tahoe. We also produce a new play development program called New Voices of the Wild West that endeavors to tell the stories of the non-urban Western United States." The audience is a mix of locals and tourists. Query by e-mail. Responds in 6 months-1 year. Buys negotiable rights. **Payment varies.**

Needs: "We are most interested in plays which speak to the region and its history, as well as to its current concerns." "No melodramas. Theatrical, above all."

Tips: "At present, we're especially interested in unproduced plays that speak to the rural and semi-rural American West for possible inclusion in our new play reading and development program, New Voices of the Wild West. History plays are okay, as long as they don't sound like you wrote them with an encyclopedia open in your lap. The best way to get our attention is to write something we haven't seen before, and write it well."

FOUNTAIN THEATRE, 5060 Fountain Ave., Los Angeles CA 90029. (323)663-2235. Fax: (323)663-1629. E-mail: ftheatre@aol.com. Website: fountaintheatre.com. Artistic Directors: Deborah Lawlor, Stephen Sachs. **Contact:** Simon Levy, dramaturg. Estab. 1990. Produces both a theater and dance season. Produced at Fountain Theatre (99-seat equity plan). *Professional recommendation only.* Query with synopsis to Simon Levy, producing director/dramaturg. Responds in 6 months. Rights acquired vary. **Pays royalty.**

Needs: Original plays, adaptations of American literature, "material that incorporates dance or language into text with unique use and vision."

THE FREELANCE PRESS, P.O. Box 548, Dover MA 02030-2207. (508)785-8250. Fax: (508)785-8291. **Contact:** Narcissa Campion, managing director. Estab. 1984. **Publishes 4 plays/year.** Submit complete ms with SASE. Responds in 4 months. **Pays 70% of performance royalties to authors. Pays 10% script and score royalty.**

Needs: "We publish original musical theater to be performed by young people, dealing with issues of importance to them. Also adapt 'classics' into musicals for 8- to 16-year-old age groups to perform." Large cast, flexible.

SAMUEL FRENCH, INC., 45 W. 25th St., New York NY 10010. (212)206-8990. Fax: (212)206-1429. E-mail: samuelfrench@earthlink.net. Website: www.samuelfrench.com. **Contact:** Submissions Editor. Estab. 1830. **Publishes 30-40 titles/year.** Publishes paperback acting editions of plays. Receives 1,500 submissions/year, mostly from unagented playwrights. 10% of publications are from first-time authors; 20% from unagented writers. **Pays 10% royalty on retail price, plus amateur and stock royalties on productions.**

Needs: Comedies, mysteries, children's plays, high school plays.

Tips: "Broadway and Off-Broadway hit plays, light comedies and mysteries have the best chance of selling to our firm. Our market is comprised of theater producers—both professional and amateur—actors and students. Read as many plays as possible of recent vintage to keep apprised of today's market; write plays with good female roles; and be one hundred percent professional in approaching publishers and producers. We recommend (not require) that submissions be in the format used by professional playwrights in the U.S., as illustrated in our playlet *Guidelines*, which sells for $4 post-paid. No plays with all-male casts, radio plays or verse plays."

WILL GEER THEATRICUM BOTANICUM, P.O. Box 1222, Topanga CA 90290. (310)455-2322. Fax: (310)455-3724. E-mail: theatricum@earthlink.net. Website: www.theatricum.com. **Contact:** Ellen Geer, artistic director. Estab. 1973. **Produces 3 classical and 1 new play if selected/year.** Professional productions for summer theater. "Botanicum Seedlings" new plays selected for readings and one play each year developed. Contact: Jennie Webb. Send synopsis, sample dialogue and tape if musical. Responds in 6 months. **Pays 6% royalty or $150 per show.**

Needs: Socially relevant plays, musicals; all full-length. Cast size of 4-10 people. "We are a large outdoor theatre—small intimate works could be difficult."

Tips: "September submissions have best turn around for main season; year-round for 'Botanicum Seedlings.'"

THE GENESIUS GUILD, 520 8th Ave., 3rd Floor, Suite 330, New York NY 10018-6507. (212)244-5404. Fax: (212)591-6503. E-mail: literary@genesiusguild.org. Website: www.genesiusguild.org. Artistic Director: Thomas Morrissey. **Contact:** Sasha Mervyn and Miri Ben-Shalom, literary liaisons. Estab. 1993. **Produces 4-6 plays/year.** "We produce professional productions under Equity showcase, LOA, TYA, and staged reading guidelines depending upon project and venue." Query with synopsis, writing sample, résumé, production history and production requirements. Responds in 6 months. **Pays $500 option fee against box office royalties of usually 5% for first year.**

Needs: "We accept and are looking for all types of plays and musicals. Our goal is to develop and produce the next new groundbreaking or impactful theatre. We also provide a range of developmental programs for new musicals and plays; inhouse readings, staged readings, workshop and showcase productions."

Tips: "As a busy NYC non-profit theatre company please be patient and understanding of our limited resources and realize that we cannot always get back to each writer as quickly or with as much feedback as we'd like."

GEORGIA REPERTORY THEATRE, c/o Department of Drama, University of Georgia, Athens GA 30602-3154. (706)542-2836. Fax: (706)542-2080. E-mail: partridg@arches.uga.edu. **Contact:** Allen Partridge, dramaturg. Estab. 1991. **Produces 1-2 plays/year.** Professional productions on university campus. Query with sample scene. Responds in 2 months. Buys rights for initial (premiere) production. **Pays honorarium, plus expenses for playwright.**

Needs: Full-length plays with moderate-sized casts.

GEVA THEATRE CENTER, 75 Woodbury Blvd., Rochester NY 14607. (585)232-1366. **Contact:** Marge Betley, literary manager. **Produces 7-11 plays/year.** Professional and regional theater, modified thrust, 552 seats; second stage, 180 seats. Subscription and single-ticket sales. Query with sample pages, synopsis and résumé. Responds in 3 months.

Needs: Full-length plays, translations and adaptations.

THE GOODMAN THEATRE, 170 N. Dearborn St., Chicago IL 60601-3205. (312)443-3811. Fax: (312)443-3821. E-mail: staff@goodman-theatre.org. Website: www.goodman-theatre.org. **Contact:** Literary Manager. Estab. 1925. **Produces 9 plays/year.** "The Goodman is a professional, not-for-profit theater producing a series in both the Albert Theatre and the Owen Theatre. The Goodman does not accept unsolicited scripts from playwrights or agents, nor will it respond to synopsis of plays submitted by playwrights, unless accompanied by a stamped, self-addressed postcard. The Goodman may request plays to be submitted for production consideration after receiving a letter of inquiry or telephone call from recognized literary agents or producing organizations." Responds in 6 months. Buys variable rights. **Pays variable royalty.**

Needs: Full-length plays, translations, musicals; special interest in social or political themes.

N A **GRETNA THEATRE**, P.O. Box 578, Mt. Gretna PA 17064. Fax: (717)964-2189. E-mail: gretnatheatre@paonline.com. Website: www.mtgretna.com/theatre. **Contact:** Will Stutts, executive director. Estab. 1923. "Plays are performed at a professional equity theater during summer." Agented submissions only. **Pays negotiable royalty (6-12%).**

Needs: "We produce full-length plays for a summer audience—subject, language and content are important." Prefer "Package" or vehicles which have "Star" role.

Tips: "No one-acts. No 'Romantic Comedy.'"

THE HARBOR THEATRE, 160 W. 71st St., 20A, New York NY 10023. (212)787-1945. Website: www.harbortheatre.org. **Contact:** Stuart Warmflash, artistic director. Estab. 1993. **Produces 1-2 plays/year.** Off-off Broadway showcase. Query and synopsis. Responds in 10 weeks. **Makes outright purchase of $500.**

Needs: Full-length and one-act festival. *"We only produce plays developed in our workshop."* .

HEUER PUBLISHING CO., 210 2nd St., Suite 301, Cedar Rapids IA 52406-0248. (319)364-6311. Fax: (319)364-1771. E-mail: editor@hitplays.com. Website: www.hitplays.com. Owner/Editor: C. Emmett McMullen. **Contact:** C.E. McMullen, editor. Estab. 1928. Publishes plays, musicals and theatre texts for junior and senior high schools and community theaters.

Query with synopsis or submit complete script. Responds in 2 months. Purchases amateur rights only. **Pays royalty or makes outright purchase.**

Needs: "One-, two- and three-act plays and musicals suitable for middle, junior and senior high school productions. Preferably comedy or mystery/comedy with a large number of characters and minimal set requirements. Please avoid controversial or offensive subject matter."

HONOLULU THEATRE FOR YOUTH, 2846 Ualena St., Honolulu HI 96819-1910. (808)839-9885, ext. 17. Fax: (808)839-7018. E-mail: mark@htyweb.org. Website: www.htyweb.org. **Contact:** Mark Lutwak, artistic director. Estab. 1955. **Produces 8 plays/year.** Professional company performing for young people and families throughout the state of Hawaii. Query and synopsis. **Pays 6-7½% royalty.** Include SASE for return of submission.

Needs: Plays that will speak to the children of Hawaii about their culture(s), history, and the world. Plays are targeted to narrow age ranges: Lower and upper elementary, middle school, high school and preschool. Six actors maximum; 75 minutes maximum. No large cast musicals.

Tips: "Avoid omniscient narrators and talking down to children."

HORIZON THEATRE CO., P.O. Box 5376, Atlanta GA 31107. (404)523-1477. E-mail: horizonco@mindspring.com. Website: www.horizontheatre.com. **Contact:** Lisa Adler, artistic director. Estab. 1983. **Produces 5 plays/year.** Professional productions. Query with synopsis and résumé. Responds in 6 months. Buys rights to produce in Atlanta area. **Pays 6-8% royalty or $50-75/performance.**

Needs: "We produce contemporary plays with a realistic base, but which utilize heightened visual or language elements. Interested in comedy, satire, plays that are entertaining and topical, but also thought provoking. Also particular interest in plays by women or with Southern themes." No more than 10 in cast.

Tips: "No plays about being in theater or film; no plays without hope; no plays that include playwrights as leading characters; no all-male casts; no plays with all older (50 plus) characters. Southern theme plays considered for New South Play Festival."

ILLINOIS THEATRE CENTRE, 371 Artists' Walk, P.O. Box 397, Park Forest IL 60466. (708)481-3510. Fax: (708)481-3693. E-mail: ilthctr@bigplanet.com. Website: www.ilthctr.org. Artistic Director: Etel Billig. Estab. 1976. **Produces 8 plays/year.** Professional Resident Theatre Company in our own space for a subscription-based audience. Query with synopsis or agented submission. Responds in 2 months. Buys casting and directing and designer selection rights. **Pays 7-10% royalty.**

Needs: All types of 2-act plays, musicals, dramas. Prefers cast size of 6-10.

Tips: Always looking for mysteries and comedies. "Make sure your play arrives between November and January when play selections are made."

IMAGINATION STAGE, 4908 Auburn Ave., Bethesda MD 20814. (301)320-2550. Fax: (301)320-1860. E-mail: info@imaginationstage.org. Website: www.imaginationstage.org. **Contact:** Janet Stanford, artistic director. Estab. 1979. **Produces 12 plays/year.** "We do 5 plays for children on our professional mainstage each season—small cast shows. We also produce shows with students in summer camps and during the year—large cast, often musical." Query and synopsis. Responds in 2 months. **Payment negotiable.**

Needs: On main stage—sophisticated, literary, innovative material for ages 4-12; for student stage—large cast ensemble pieces with good acting roles for performers ages 7-18. Does not want spoofs of fairytales. "We are interested in technically challenging, multimedia material as well as more traditional works."

INDIANA REPERTORY THEATRE, 140 W. Washington St., Indianapolis IN 46204-3465. (317)635-5277. Fax: (317)236-0767. Artistic Director: Janet Allen. **Contact:** Literary Manager. Estab. 1972. **Produces 9 plays/year.** Plays are produced and performed at the Indiana Repertory Theatre, the state's only professional, nonprofit resident theater. Audiences range from child to adult, depending on show. Query with synopsis. Responds in 2 months to synopsis; 6 months to ms. Rights and payment negotiated individually.

Needs: Full-length plays; adaptations of well-known literary works; plays about Indiana and the Midwest; African-American plays; Native-American plays; contemporary comedies; plays with compelling characters, situations, language, and theatrical appeal. Prefer casts of 5 or fewer.

Tips: No musicals or plays that would do as well in film and on TV.

INTERACT THEATRE CO., The Adrienne, 2030 Sansom St., Philadelphia PA 19103. (215)568-8077. Fax: (215)568-8095. E-mail: interact@interacttheatre.org or loebell@interacttheatre.org. Website: www.interacttheatre.org. **Contact:** Larry Loebell, literary manager/dramaturg. Estab. 1988. **Produces 3 plays/year.** Produces professional productions for adult audience. Query with synopsis and bio. No unsolicited scripts. Responds in 4 months. **Pays 2-8% royalty or $25-100/performance.**

Needs: Contemporary dramas and comedies that explore issues of political, social, cultural or historical significance. "Virtually all of our productions have political content in the foregound of the drama." Prefer plays that raise interesting questions without giving easy, predictable answers. "We are interested in new plays." Limit cast to 10. No romantic comedies, family dramas, agit-prop.

[A] **INTIMAN THEATRE**, P.O. Box 19760, Seattle WA 98119. (206)269-1901. Fax: (206)269-1928. E-mail: intiman@intiman.org. Website: www.intiman.org. **Contact:** Literary Manager. Artistic Director: Bartlett Sher. Estab. 1972. **Produces 6 plays/year.** LORT C Regional Theater in Seattle. Best submission time is November through April. *Agented submissions only* or by professional recommendation.

Needs: Well-crafted dramas and comedies by playwrights who full utilize the power of language and character relationships to explore enduring themes. Prefers nonnaturalistic plays and plays of dynamic theatricality.

JEWEL BOX THEATRE, 3700 N. Walker, Oklahoma City OK 73118-7099. (405)521-1786. Fax: (405)525-6562. **Contact:** Charles Tweed, production director. Estab. 1956. **Produces 6 plays/year.** Amateur productions. 3,000 season subscribers and general public. Submit 2 complete scripts. Responds in 4 months. **Pays $500 contest prize.**

Needs: Send SASE for entry form during September-October. "We produce dramas and comedies. Only full-length plays can be accepted. Our theater is in-the-round, so we adapt plays accordingly." Deadline: mid-January.

JEWISH ENSEMBLE THEATRE, 6600 W. Maple Rd., West Bloomfield MI 48322. (248)788-2900. E-mail: jetplay@aol.com. **Contact:** Evelyn Orbach, artistic director. Estab. 1989. **Produces 5 plays/year.** Professional productions at the Aaron DeRoy Theatre (season) and Scottish Rite Cathedral Theatre (schools), as well as tours to schools. Submit complete script. Responds in 1 year. "Obtains rights for our season productions and staged readings for festival." **Pays 6-8% royalty for full production or honorarium for staged reading—$100/full-length play.**

Needs: "We do few children's plays except original commissions; we rarely do musicals." Cast limited to a maximum of 8 actors.

Tips: "We are a theater of social conscience with the following mission: to produce work on the highest possible professional level; to deal with issues of community & humanity from a Jewish perspective; to provide a platform for new voices and a bridge for understanding to the larger community."

N **JUNETEENTH LEGACY THEATRE**, P.O. Box 3463, Louisville KY 40201-3463. **Contact:** Lorna Littleway, producing director. Estab. 1999. **Produces 15 plays/year.** Professional productions for mainstage, readers theatre tour and a festival of staged readings. General and youth audiences. Submit complete script. Responds in months. **Pays 50%/performance for mainstage; 25%/performance for readers theatre tour. No royalty for festival of staged readings.** Include SASE for return of script. Do not send synopsis or electronic script.

Needs: Any genre or length is acceptable, but plays must address one of five themes: African American 19th-century experience; pre and Harlem Renaissance; Caribbean/Native American influence on African Americans; contemporary issues and African American youth; and new images of women.

Tips: "There is a $15 script processing fee. Make checks payable to Juneteenth Legacy Theatre."

KITCHEN DOG THEATER, 3120 McKinney Ave., Dallas TX 75204. (214)953-2258. Fax: (214)953-1873. **Contact:** Dan Day, artistic director. Estab. 1990. **Produces 8 plays/year.** Kitchen Dog has two performance spaces: a 100-seat black box and a 200-seat thrust. Submit complete manuscript with SASE. Each year the deadline for submissions is March 15. Writers are notified by May 15. Buys rights to full production. **Pays $40-75 per performance; $500-1,000 for winner of New Works Festival.**

Needs: "We are interested in experimental plays, literary adaptations, historical plays, political theater, gay and lesbian work, culturally diverse work, and small musicals. Ideally, cast size would be 1-5, or more if doubling roles is a possibility." No romantic/light comedies or material that is more suited for television than the theater.

Tips: "We are interested in plays that are theatrical and that challenge the imagination—plays that are for the theater, rather than T.V. or film."

KUMU KAHUA, 46 Merchant St., Honolulu HI 96813. (808)536-4222. Fax: (808)536-4226. **Contact:** Harry Wong, artistic director. Estab. 1971. **Produces 5 productions, 3-4 public readings/year.** "Plays performed at new Kumu Kahua Theatre, flexible 120-seat theater, for community audiences." Submit complete script. Responds in 4 months. **Pays royalty of $50/performance; usually 20 performances of each production.**

Needs: "Plays must have some interest for local Hawai'i audiences."

LILLENAS PUBLISHING CO., P.O. Box 419527, Kansas City MO 64141-6527. (816)931-1900. Fax: (816)412-8390. E-mail: drama@lillenas.com. Website: www.lillenasdrama.com. **Contact:** Kim Messer, product manager. Estab. 1926. "We publish on 2 levels: (1) Program Builders—seasonal and topical collections of recitations, sketches, dialogues, and short plays; (2) Drama Resources which assume more than 1 format: (a) full-length scripts, (b) one-acts, shorter plays and sketches all by 1 author, (c) collection of short plays and sketches by various authors. All program and play resources are produced with local church and Christian school in mind. Therefore there are taboos." Queries are encouraged, but synopsis and complete scripts are read. Responds in 3 months. "First rights are purchased for Program Builders scripts. For Drama Resources, we purchase all print rights." **Drama Resources are paid on a 10% royalty, whether full-length scripts, one-acts, or sketches. No advance.**

- This publisher is interested in collections of and individual sketches. There is also a need for short pieces that are seasonal and on current events.

Needs: 98% of Program Builders materials are freelance written. Scripts selected for these publications are outright purchases; verse is minimum of 25¢/line, prose (play scripts) are minimum of $5/double-spaced page. "Lillenas Drama Resources is a line of play scripts that are, for the most part, written by professionals with experience in productions as well as writing. However, while we do read unsolicited scripts, more than half of what we publish is written by experienced authors whom we have already published."

Tips: "All plays need to be presented in standard play script format. We welcome a summary statement of each play. Purpose statements are always desirable. Approximate playing time, cast and prop lists, etc., are important to include. Contemporary settings generally have it over Biblical settings. Christmas and Easter scripts must have a bit of a twist. Secular approaches to these seasons (Santas, Easter bunnies, and so on), are not considered. We sell our product in 10,000 Christian bookstores and by catalog. We are probably in the forefront as a publisher of religious drama resources." Request a copy of our newsletter and/or catalog.

LONG WHARF THEATRE, 222 Sargent Dr., New Haven CT 06511. (203)787-4284. Fax: (203)776-2287. Website: www.longwharf.org. **Contact:** Christina D. Eger, artistic administrator. Estab. 1965. **Produces 8 plays/year.** Professional regional theater. *Agented submissions only.* Responds in approximately 2 months to queries.

Needs: Full-length plays, translations, adaptations. Special interest: Dramatic plays and comedies about human relationships, social concerns, ethical and moral dilemmas.

LOS ANGELES DESIGNERS' THEATRE, P.O. Box 1883, Studio City CA 91614-0883. E-mail: ladesigners@juno.com. **Contact:** Richard Niederberg, artistic director. Estab. 1970. **Produces 8-20 plays/year.** Professional shows/"industry" audience. Submit proposal only (i.e. 1 page in #10 SASE). Reports in 3 months (minimum) to submission Purchases rights by negotiation, first refusal for performance/synchronization rights only. **Payment varies.**

- "We want highly commercial work without liens, 'understandings,' or promises to anyone."

Needs: All types. No limitations—"We seek design challenges." No "boring" material. "Shorter plays with musical underscores are desirable, nudity and 'street' language and political themes are OK."

MAGIC THEATRE, Bldg. D, Fort Mason, San Francisco CA 94123. (415)441-8001. Fax: (415)771-5505. E-mail: magicthtre@aol.com. Website: www.magictheatre.org. Artistic Director: Larry Eilenberg. **Contact:** Mark Routhier, literary manager. Estab. 1967. **Produces 6 mainstage plays/year, plus monthly reading series and several festivals each year which contain both staged readings and workshop productions.** Regional theater. Query with synopsis, SASE, dialogue sample (10 pages). Responds in 6-8 months. **Pays royalty or per performance fee.**

Needs: "Plays that are innovative in theme and/or craft, cutting-edge political concerns, intelligent comedy. Full-length only, strong commitment to multicultural work."

Tips: "Not interested in classics, conventional approaches and cannot produce large-cast (over 10) plays. Send query to Mark Routhier, literary manager."

MANHATTAN THEATRE CLUB, 311 W. 43rd St., 8th Floor, New York NY 10036. (212)399-3000. Fax: (212)399-4329. E-mail: lit@mtc-nyc.org. Website: www.manhattantheatreclub.com. Director of Play Development: Paige Evans. **Contact:** Elizabeth Bennett, literary manager. **Produces 7-8 plays/year.** One Broadway and two Off-Broadway theatres, using professional actors. Solicited and agent submissions only. No queries. Responds within 6 months.

Needs: "We present a wide range of new work, from this country and abroad, to a subscription audience. We want plays about contemporary concerns and people. All genres are welcome. Average cast is eight. MTC also maintains an extensive play development program."

McCARTER THEATRE, 91 University Place, Princeton NJ 08540. E-mail: literary@mccarter.org. Website: www.mccarter.org. **Contact:** Literary Manager. **Produces 5 plays/year; 1 second stage play/year.** Produces professional productions for a 1,077-seat theater. Agented submissions only. Responds in 1 month; agent submissions 3 months. **Pays negotiable royalty.**

Needs: Full length plays, musicals, translations.

MERIWETHER PUBLISHING, LTD., 885 Elkton Dr., Colorado Springs CO 80907-3557. Fax: (719)594-9916. E-mail: merpcds@aol.com. Website: meriwether.com. President: Mark Zapel. Editor: Arthur L. Zapel. **Contact:** Ted Zapel, associate editor. Estab. 1969. "We publish how-to theatre materials in book and video formats. We are interested in materials for middle school, high school and college level students only." Query with synopsis/outline, résumé of credits, sample of style and SASE. Catalog available for $2 postage. Responds in 1 month to queries; 2 months to full-length mss. **Offers 10% royalty or makes outright purchase.**

Needs: Musicals for a large cast of performers. 1-act or 2-act comedy plays with large casts. Book mss on theatrical arts subjects, especially books of short scenes for amateur and professional actors. "We are now looking for scenebooks with special themes: 'scenes for young women,' 'comedy scenes for two actors,' etc. These need not be original, provided the compiler can get letters of permission from the original copyright owner. We are interested in all textbook candidates for theater arts subjects. Christian children's activity book mss also accepted. We will consider elementary level religious materials and plays, but no elementary level children's secular plays."

Tips: "We publish a wide variety of speech contest materials for high-school students. We are publishing more full length play scripts and musicals based on classic literature or popular TV shows, provided the writer includes letter of clearance from the copyright owner. Our educational books are sold to teachers and students at college and high-school levels. Our religious books are sold to youth activity directors, pastors and choir directors. Another group of buyers is the professional theater, radio and TV category. We will be especially interested in full length (two- or three-act) plays with name recognition, either the playwright or the adaptation source."

METROSTAGE, 1201 N. Royal St., Alexandria VA 22314. (703)548-9044. Fax: (703)548-9089. Website: www.metrostage.org. **Contact:** Carolyn Griffin, producing artistic director. Estab. 1984. **Produces 5-6 plays/year.** Professional productions for 130-seat theatre, general audience. Query with synopsis, 10 page dialogue sample, play workshop and production history. Responds in 3 months. **Pays royalty.**

Needs: Contemporary themes, small cast (up to 6 actors), unit set.

Tips: "Plays should have *already* had readings and workshops before being sent for our review. Do not send plays that have never had a staged reading."

MILL MOUNTAIN THEATRE, Market Square, Center in Square, Roanoke VA 24011-1437. (540)982-0596. Fax: (540)342-5745. E-mail: outreach@millmountain.org. Website: www.millmountain.org. Producing Artistic Director: Jere Lee Hodgin. **Contact:** Julianne Homokay, literary coordinator. **Produces 5-7 established plays, 5 new one-acts, 2 new full-length plays, and 2 school tours/year.** Trinkle Mainstage, 400 seats, flexible proscenium stage; Waldron Stage, 125 seats, flexible black box. Accepts unsolicited one-acts only, year-round, all styles. All other submissions for the Norfolk Southern Festival of New Works, mainstage, second stage, and touring productions by invitation only. Responds in 6-12 months.

MOVING ARTS, 514 South Spring St., Los Angeles CA 90013-2304. (213)622-8906. Fax: (213)622-8946. E-mail: treynichols@movingarts.org. Website: www.movingarts.org. Artistic Director: Kimberly Grann. **Contact:** Trey Nichols, literary director. Estab. 1992. **Produces 10 plays/year.** Professional productions produced under Actors Equity Association 99-Seat Plan. "Our audiences are eclectic, literate, diverse adults." Query with synopsis, 10-20 page dialogue sample, bio, cover letter. Responds in 9 months. Obtains 5% of future income for 5-year period. **Pays 6% of box office gross.** Include SASE for return of submissions.

Needs: Full-length and one-act plays. (One-act plays accepted *only* for our Premiere One-Act Competition. $10 entry fee, $200 1st prize. Submission period is November 1-February 28. Send SASE or e-mail for full guidelines.) "Original drama or comedy that is bold, challenging, and edgy; plays that speak to the human condition in a fresh and startling way. We are not limited to any particular style or genre; we are confined only by the inherent truth of the material." Cast limit of 8. Theatre is a 60-seat black box. Limited backstage space, no fly space, limited wing space. "No plays that are like sitcoms or showcases, or too 'well-made.' We don't do plays for children (although we welcome young audiences) and tend to stay away from period pieces, heavy dramas, and performance art." "Los Angeles has a very exciting theatre scene today. The most exhilarating work is in the smaller theatres (Circle X, Evidence Room, Zoo District, Theatre of NOTE, and Actors Gang, to name a few). The BCT (Big Cheap Theatre) ethic, its spirit and grace and sense of wonder, is the blood that pumps life into this recent shift in the American theatre aesthetic, and writers—*especially* writers—need to know what this is about."

Tips: "If you're a Southern California playwright, come see our play readings and shows. Party with us! Get to know us, our spirit and our work. If not, control the controllable. Keep your cover letter brief, polite and to the point. If you've been referred by a writer or director or seen prior productions, mention it. If you've seen prior productions, we appreciate it. When we read your work, we respond to the writing, but professionalism (or lack thereof) affects our evaluation in terms of potential artistic relationship. Three-hole punched script, 2-3 fasteners, SASE, clean copy, it all matters. Be patient with our process. Don't pester with follow-up queries. We love playwrights, so trust that your work will recieve as much time and attention as our limited but committed resources allow."

NEBRASKA THEATRE CARAVAN, 6915 Cass St., Omaha NE 68132. Fax: (402)553-6288. E-mail: caravan@omahaplayhouse.com. Website: www.omahaplayhouse.com. **Contact:** Rick Scott, director of outreach and touring. Estab. 1976. **Produces 4-5 plays/year.** "Nebraska Theatre Caravan is a touring company which produces professional productions in schools, arts centers, and small and large theaters for elementary, middle, high school and family audiences." Query and synopsis. Responds in 3 weeks. Negotiates production rights "unless the work is commissioned by us." **Pays $20-50 per performance.**

Needs: "All genres are acceptable bearing in mind the student audiences. We are truly an ensemble and like to see that in our choice of shows; curriculum ties are very important for elementary and hich school shows; 75 minutes for middle/high school shows. No sexually explicit material."

Tips: "We tour eight months of the year to a variety of locations. Flexibility is important as we work in both beautiful performing arts facilities and school multipurpose rooms."

NEW AMERICAN THEATER, 118 N. Main St., Rockford IL 61101. (815)963-9454. Fax: (815)963-7215. Website: www.newamericantheater.com. Richard Raether. **Contact:** Project Director, 'New Voices in the Heartland'. Estab. 1972. The New American Theater is a professional equity theater company performing on a thrust stage with 280-seat house. Submit synopsis and sample dialogue with SASE by October 15th—send full scripts only when requested. Unsolicited full scripts will not be considered.

Needs: New works for "New Voices in the Heartland," an annual play festival of staged readings. The works may have been workshopped, but not previously produced. Event is in August.

Tips: "More than 1 synopsis may be submitted; however, only 1 full script will be considered."

THE NEW GROUP, 154 Christopher St., Suite 2A-A, New York NY 10014. (212)691-6730. Fax: (212)691-6798. Artistic Director: Scott Elliott. **Contact:** Ian Morgan, associate artistic director. Estab. 1991. **Produces 3 plays/year.** Off-Broadway theater. Submit sample with cover letter. Responds in 9 months to submissions. **Pays royalty. Makes outright purchase.**

Needs: "We produce challenging, character-based scripts with a contemporary sensibility." Does not want to receive musicals, historical scripts or science fiction.

NEW JERSEY REPERTORY CO., Lumia Theatre, 179 Broadway, Long Branch NJ 07740. (732)229-3166. Estab. 1997. **Produces 25 script-in-hand readings.** Professional productions year round. Previously unproduced plays only. Submit complete script. Responds in 1 year. Rights negotiable.

Needs: Cast size no more than 5. Unit or simple set.

NEW PLAYS, INC., P.O. Box 5074, Charlottesville VA 22905. (434)979-2777. Fax: (434)984-2230. E-mail: patwhitton@aol.com. Website: www.newplaysforchildren.com. **Contact:** Patricia Whitton Forrest, publisher. Estab. 1964. **Publishes 3-6 plays/year.** Publishes for children's or youth theaters. Submit complete script. Attempts to respond in 2 months, sometimes longer. Buys all semi-professional and amateur rights in U.S. and Canada. **Pays 50% royalty on productions, 10% on sale of books.**

Needs: "I have eclectic taste—plays must have quality and originality in whatever genres, topics, styles or lengths the playwright chooses."

Tips: "No adaptations of stuff that has already been adapted a million times, e.g., *Tom Sawyer*, *A Christmas Carol*, or plays that sound like they've been written by the guidance counselor. There will be more interest in youth theater productions with moderate to large casts (15 people). Plays must have been produced, directed by someone other than the author or author's spouse. People keep sending us material suitable for adults—this is not our market. Read our online catalog."

NEW REPERTORY THEATRE, P.O. Box 610418, Newton Highlands MA 02161-0418. (617)332-7058. Fax: (617)527-5217. E-mail: info@newrep.org. Website: www.newrep.org. **Contact:** Rick Lombardo, producing artistic director. Estab. 1984. **Produces 5 plays/year.** Professional theater, general audience. Query with synopsis and dialogue sample. Buys production and subsidiary rights. **Pays 5-10% royalty.**
Needs: Idea laden, all styles, full-length only. Small cast, unit set.
Tips: No sit-coms like comedies. Incorporating and exploring styles other than naturalism.

NEW THEATRE, 4120 Laguna St., Coral Gables FL 33155. (305)443-5373. Fax: (305)443-1642. E-mail: rda@new-theatre.org. Website: www.new-theatre.org. **Contact:** Rafael De Acha, artistic director. Estab. 1986. **Produces 7 plays/year.** Professional productions. Query and synopsis. Responds in 2 months. Rights subject to negotiation. **Payment negotiable.**
Needs: Full-length. Interested in non-realistic, language plays. No musicals; no large casts.
Tips: "No kitchen sink realism. Send a simple query with synopsis. Be mindful of social issues."

NEW YORK STATE THEATRE INSTITUTE, 37 First St., Troy NY 12180. (518)274-3200. Fax: (518)274-3815. E-mail: nysti@capital.net. Website: www.nysti.org. **Contact:** Ed. Lange, associate artistic director. **Produces 5 plays/year.** Professional regional productions for adult and family audiences. Query and synopsis. Responds in 6 weeks. **Payment varies.**
Needs: "We are not interested in material for 'mature' audiences. Submissions must be scripts of substance and intelligence geared to family audiences."
Tips: Do not submit complete script unless invited after review of synopsis.

NEW YORK THEATRE WORKSHOP, 83 E. Fourth St., New York NY 10003. Fax: (212)460-8996. Artistic Director: James C. Nicola. **Contact:** Toni Amicarella, artistic associate/literary. Estab. 1979. **Produces 6-7 full productions and approximately 50 readings/year.** Plays are performed off-Broadway, Equity off-Broadway contract. Audience is New York theater-going audience and theater professionals. Query with synopsis, 10-page sample scene and tape/CD/video (if appropriate). Responds in 5-7 months. Buys option to produce commercially; percentage of box office gross from commercial and percentage of author's net subsidiary rights within specified time limit from our original production. **Pays fee because of limited run, with additional royalty payments for extensions; $1,500-2,000 fee range.**
Needs: Full-length plays, translations/adaptions, music theater pieces; proposals for performance projects. Socially relevant issues, innovative form and language.
Tips: "No overtly commercial and conventional musicals or plays."

NORTH SHORE MUSIC THEATRE AT DUNHAM WOODS, 62 Dunham Rd., Beverly MA 01915. (978)232-7203. Fax: (978)921-0793. E-mail: jlarock@nsmt.org. Website: www.nsmt.org. **Contact:** John La Rock, associate producer. Estab. 1955. **Produces 8 plays/year.** Plays are performed at Arena theater for 24,000 subscribers. Submit letter of interest, synopsis, production details, music tape/CD, SASE. Responds in 4 months. Rights negotiable. **Payment negotiable.**
Needs: Musicals only (adult and children's), with cast size under 15.
Tips: No straight plays, opera.

NORTHERN LIGHTS PLAYHOUSE, (formerly Michael D. Cupp), P.O. Box 256, Dept. SWV, Hazelhurst WI 54531-0256. (715)356-7173 ext. 958. Fax: (715)356-1851. E-mail: nlplays@newnorth.net. **Contact:** Artistic Director. Estab. 1976. **Produces 6 plays/year.** Professional Summer Theatre & Professional Dinner Theatre. Audience mostly senior-family oriented. Query with synopsis, cast breakdown and set requirements. Responds in 6 months. **Pays royalty, per performance or makes outright purchase.**
Needs: Comedies (2 hours), children's theatre (1 hour). Prefers cost efficient productions.
Tips: No sexy, racy or lewd productions, no dramas. "Remember you are writing for the audience. Be commercial."

NORTHERN WESTCHESTER CENTER FOR THE ARTS, 272 N. Bedford Rd., Mounr Kisco NY 10549. E-mail: paul@nwcaonline.org. Website: nwcaonline.org. **Contact:** Paul Andrew Perez, theater director. Estab. 1982. **Produces 6 plays/year.** Plays are amateur productions performed in a 300 seat black box. Send a synopsis and a writing sample. If a musical, send a CD or a cassette with at least 3 songs. Responds in 6 weeks. **Pays 5% royalty.** Submissions accompanied by a SASE will be returned.
Needs: "Up to this point, we have produced mainly children's musicals, but I am expanding into adult plays. I will be presenting a staged reading series in the fall with 6 readings as well as 2 full performances." There are no real production limitations.
Tips: "Keep costs down! Don't write too many characters."

NORTHLIGHT THEATRE, 9501 Skokie Blvd., Skokie IL 60077. (847)679-9501. Fax: (847)679-1879. Website: www.northlight.org. **Contact:** Rosanna Forrest, literary manager. Estab. 1975. **Produces 5 plays/year.** "We are a professional, equity theater, LORT D. We have a subscription base of over 8,000 and have a significant number of single ticket buyers." Query with synopsis and SASE/SASP for response. No unsolicited mss accepted. Responds in 3-4 months. Buys production rights, plus royalty on future mountings. **Pays royalty.**
Needs: "Full-length plays, translations, adaptations, musicals. Interested in plays of 'ideas'; plays that are passionate and/or hilarious; plays of occasional intelligence and complexity. Generally looking for cast size of 6 or fewer, but there are exceptions made for the right play."
Tips: "Please, do not try to do what television and film do better; preferably, we are looking for heightened realism.

However, we are a mainstream regional rep theater, so unlikely to consider anything overtly experimental or absurdist."

THE O'NEILL PLAYWRIGHTS CONFERENCE, 534 W. 42 St., New York NY 10036. (212)244-7008. Fax: (212)967-2957. Artistic Director: James Houghton. **Contact:** Beth Whitaker, artistic associate. Estab. 1965. **Produces 12-15 plays/year.** The O'Neill Center theater is located in Waterford, Connecticut, and operates under an Equity LORT contract. There are 4 theaters: Barn—250 seats, Ampitheater—300 seats, Edith Oliver Theater—150 seats, Dina Merrill—188 seats. "Please send #10 SASE for guidelines in the fall, or call to be added to our mailing list." *Do not send full scripts.* Decision by late April. We accept submissions September 1-October 1 of each year. Conference takes place during June/July each summer. Playwrights selected are in residence for one month and receive a four-day workshop and two script-in-hand readings with professional actors and directors. **Pays stipend plus room, board and transportation.**

EUGENE O'NEILL THEATER CENTER, O'NEILL MUSIC THEATER CONFERENCE, 534 W. 42nd St., New York NY 10036. Fax: (212)967-2957. Website: www.oneilltheatercenter.org. Developmental process for new music theater works creative artists in residence with artistic staff and equity company of actors/singers public and private readings, script in hand, piano only. For guidelines and application deadlines, send SASE to address above. **Pays stipend, room and board.**

ODYSSEY THEATRE ENSEMBLE, 2055 S. Sepulveda Blvd., Los Angeles CA 90025. (310)477-2055. Fax: (310)444-0455. **Contact:** Sally Essex-Lopresti, director of literary programs. Estab. 1969. **Produces 9 plays/year.** Plays performed in a 3-theater facility. "All 3 theaters are Equity 99-seat theater plan. We have a subsciption audience of 4,000 for a nine-play main season, and they are offered a discount on our rentals and co-productions. Remaining seats are sold to the general public." No unsolicited material. Query with résumé, synopsis, sample dialogue, and cassette if musical. Responds in 2 weeks. Buys negotiable rights. **Pays 5-7% royalty.** Does not return scripts without SASE.

Needs: Scripts must be securely bound. "Full-length plays only with either an innovative form and/or provocative subject matter. We desire highly theatrical pieces that explore possibilities of the live theater experience. We are not reading one-act plays or light situation comedies."

N **OMAHA THEATER COMPANY FOR YOUNG PEOPLE**, 2001 Farnam St., Omaha NE 68102. (402)345-4852. **Contact:** James Larson, artistic director. **Produces 6 plays/year.** "Our target audience is children, preschool-high school and their parents." Query and synopsis. Responds in 9 months. **Pays royalty.**

Needs: "Plays must be geared to children and parents (PG rating). Titles recognized by the general public have a stronger chance of being produced." Cast limit: 25 (8-10 adults). No adult scripts.

Tips: "Unproduced plays may be accepted only after a letter of inquiry (familiar titles only!)."

ONE ACT PLAY DEPOT, Box 335, Spiritwood SK S0J 2M0, Canada. E-mail: submissions@oneactplays.net. Website: oneactplays.net. Submit complete script by mail or via e-mail as a plaintxt file or pasted into the body of the message.

Needs: Interested only in one-act plays. Does not want musicals, farces. Do not mail originals. "Our main focus will be black comedy, along with well-written dramatic and comedic pieces."

Tips: "All non-.txt attachments will be destroyed unread."

THE OPEN EYE THEATER, P.O. Box 959, Margaretville NY 12455. (845)586-1660. Fax: (845)586-1660. E-mail: openeye@catskill.net. Website: www.theopeneye.org. **Contact:** Amie Brockway, producing artistic director. The Open Eye is a not-for-profit professional theater company working in New York City since 1972, in the rural villages of Delaware County, New York, since 1991, and on tour. The theater specializes in the development of new plays for multi-generational audiences (children ages 8 and up, and adults of all ages). Ensemble plays with music and dance, culturally diverse and historical material, myth, folklore, and stories with universal themes are of interest. Program includes readings, developmental workshops, and fully staged productions.

Tips: Send 1-page letter with 1-paragraph plot synopsis, cast breakdown and setting, résumé and SAE. "We will provide the stamp and contact you if we want to see the script."

OREGON SHAKESPEARE FESTIVAL, P.O. Box 158, Ashland OR 97520. Website: www.osfashland.org. **Contact:** Stephany Smith-Pearson, literary assistant. Estab. 1935. **Produces 11 plays/year.** The Angus Bowmer Theater has a thrust stage and seats 600. The New Theatre is an experimental space that seats 260-350. The Elizabethan Theatre seats 1,200 (stages almost exclusively Shakespearean productions). Agented submissions only. Responds in 6 months. Negotiates individually for rights with the playwright's agent. **Pays royalty.**

Needs: "A broad range of classic and contemporary scripts. One or two fairly new scripts/season. Also one play reading annually focuses on new work. Plays must fit into ten-month rotating repertory season." Small musicals OK. Submissions from women and minority writers are strongly encouraged. Submissions should include a cast list that specifies gender, age and race, plot synopsis and 10-page dialogue sample. Best time to submit is September-December. No one-acts.

Tips: "We're always looking for a good comedy which has scope. We tend to prefer plays with a literary quality. We encourage translations of foreign plays as well as adaptations of non-dramatic material."

JOSEPH PAPP PUBLIC THEATER, 425 Lafayette St., New York NY 10003. (212)539-8500. Website: www.publictheater.org. Producer: George C. Wolf. **Contact:** Michael Kenyon, literary assistant. Estab. 1964. **Produces 5 plays/year.** Professional productions. Query with synopsis and 10-page sample. Responds in 1 month.

Needs: All genres, no one-acts.

⊘ **PEGASUS THEATRE**, 3916 Main St., Dallas TX 75226-1228. (214)821-6005. Fax: (214)826-1671. E-mail: comedy@pegasustheatre.org. Website: www.pegasustheatre.com. **Contact:** Steve Erwin, new plays manager. Estab. 1985. **Produces 3 plays/year.** Produces plays under an Umbrella Agreement with AEA. "Our productions are presented for the general public to attend. Our audience is primarily in the 20-60 range with middle to high level income. We are exclusively focused on the presentation of new, original, contemporary comedies." Query with synopsis, 10 sample pages. Responds in 6 months. **Pays 5-8% royalty.**

Needs: New and original comedies with a satiric slant. Limit cast size to under 10, single set.

Tips: "No murder-mysteries, please. We'd rather not look at one-acts that don't have companion pieces or at plays that read and play like extended-length sitcoms. Neatness and proper formatting always make a better impression—even with the best of scripts. Not accepting submissions."

PERSEVERANCE THEATRE, 914 Third St., Douglas AK 99824. (907)364-2421. Fax: (907)364-2603. **Contact:** Peter DuBois, artistic director. Estab. 1979. **Produces 6 plays/year.** Semi-professional productions for the Juneau community audiences and, on tour, statewide. Responds in 6 months. Rights purchased varies. World-premiere credit most commonly. **Makes outright purchase of $2,000.**

Needs: "Great interest in Alaskana, Native Alaskan, and Alaska native work."

PHILADELPHIA THEATRE CO., 230 S. 15th St., 4th Floor, Philadelphia PA 19102. (215)985-1400. Fax: (215)985-5800. Website: www.phillytheatreco.com. **Contact:** Michele Volansky, dramaturg. Estab. 1974. **Produces 4 plays/year.** Agented submissions only. No e-mail submissions. If no agent, send 10 pages sample dialogue, short synopsis and letter.

Needs: Philadelphia Theatre Company produces contemporary American plays. No musicals or children's plays.

Tips: "Our work is challenging and risky—look to our history for guidance."

PIONEER DRAMA SERVICE, INC., P.O. Box 4267, Englewood CO 80155-4267. (303)779-4035. Fax: (303)779-4315. E-mail: playwrights@pioneerdrama.com. Website: www.pioneerdrama.com. Publisher: Steven Fendrich. **Contact:** Beth Somers, submissions editor. Estab. 1963. **Publishes 30 plays/year.** Plays are performed by schools, colleges, community theaters, recreation programs, churches and professional children's theaters for audiences of all ages. Query preferred. Responds in about 2 weeks to query; 4 months to submissions. Retains all rights. Buys All rights. **Pays royalty.**

- All submissions automatically entered in Shubert Fendrich Memorial Playwriting Contest.

Needs: "Musicals, comedies, mysteries, dramas, melodramas and children's theater. Two-acts up to 90 minutes; children's theater, 1 hour. Prefers many female roles, simple sets. Plays need to be appropriate for amateur groups." Prefers secular plays.

Tips: Interested in adaptations of classics of public domain works appropriate for children and teens. Also plays that deal with social issues for teens and preteens. "Check out the website to see what we carry and if your material would be appropriate. Make sure to include query letter, proof of productions and an SASE."

PITTSBURGH PUBLIC THEATER, 621 Penn Ave., Pittsburgh PA 15222. (412)316-8200. Fax: (412)316-8216. Website: www.ppt.org. Artistic Director: Ted Pappas. **Contact:** Kyle Brenton, resident dramaturg. Estab. 1975. **Produces 7 plays/year.** O'Reilly Theater, 650 seats, thrust seating. Query with synopsis or agented submissions year-round. Responds in 4 months.

Needs: Full-length plays, adaptations and musicals.

Tips: "We ask for a letter, character breakdown, synopsis and 10-page dialogue sample."

PLAYERS PRESS, INC., P.O. Box 1132, Studio City CA 91614-0132. **Contact:** Robert W. Gordon, editorial vice president. **Publishes 20-30 plays/year; 30 books/year.** "We deal in all entertainment areas and handle publishable works for film and television as well as theater. Performing arts books, plays and musicals. All plays must be in stage format for publication." Also produces scripts for video and material for cable television. Query with #10 SASE, reviews and proof of production. Responds in 1 month. Buys negotiable rights. "We prefer all rights." **Pays 10-75% royalty. Makes outright purchase of $100-25,000. Pays per performance royalties.**

Needs: "We prefer comedies, musicals and children's theater, but are open to all genres. We will rework the script after acceptance. We are interested in the quality, not the format. Performing Arts Books that deal with theater how-to are of strong interest."

Tips: "Send only material requested. Do not telephone."

PLAYSCRIPTS, INC., P.O. Box 237060, New York NY 10023. Phone/fax: (866)639-7529. E-mail: questions@playscripts.com. Website: www.playscripts.com. **Contact:** Douglas Rand, editor. Estab. 1998. Audience is professional, community, college, high school and children's theaters worldwide. Send complete ms, preferably electronically; see website for guidelines. Response time varies. Buys exclusive publication and performance licensing rights. **Pays negotiated book and production royalties.**

Needs: "Playscripts, Inc. publishes one-act and full-length plays for professional, community, college, high school and children's theaters. We are open to a wide diversity of writing styles and content."

Tips: "Playscripts, Inc. is a play publishing company optimized for the Internet. We provide all of the same licensing and book production services as a traditional play publisher, along with unique online features that maximize the exposure of each dramatic work."

PLAYWRIGHTS HORIZONS, 416 W. 42nd St., New York NY 10036. (212)564-1235. Fax: (212)594-0296. Website: www.playwrightshorizons.org. Artistic Director: Tim Sanford. **Contact:** Lisa Timmel, literary manager (plays); send musicals Attn: Musical Theatre Program. Estab. 1971. **Produces 6 plays/year.** Plays performed off-Broadway for a literate, urban, subscription audience. Submit complete ms with author bio; include tape or CD for musicals. Responds in 6 months. Negotiates for future rights. **Pays royalty. Makes outright purchase.**

Needs: "We are looking for new, full-length plays and musicals by American authors."

Tips: "No adaptations, children's theater, biographical or historical plays. We look for plays with a strong sense of language and a clear dramatic action that truly use the resources of the theater."

PLAYWRIGHTS THEATRE OF NEW JERSEY, P.O. Box 1295, Madison NJ 07940-1295. (973)514-1787. Fax: (973)514-2060. E-mail: playnj@aol.com. Website: www.ptnj.org. Artistic Director: John Pietrowski. **Contact:** Peter Hays, literary manager. Estab. 1986. **Produces 3 plays/year.** "We operate under a Small Professional Theatre Contract (SPT), a development theatre contract with Actors Equity Association. Readings are held under a staged reading code." Submit synopsis, first 10 pages, short bio, and production history with SASE. Responds in 1 year. "For productions we ask the playwright to sign an agreement that gives us exclusive rights to the play for the production period and for 30 days following. After the 30 days we give the rights back with no strings attached, except for commercial productions. We ask that our developmental work be acknowledged in any other professional productions." **Makes outright purchase of $750.**

- Submissions are accepted in May and June—only those two months. Write for guidelines before submitting.

Needs: Any style or length; full length, one acts, musicals.

Tips: "We are looking for American plays in the early stages of development—plays of substance, passion, and light (comedies and dramas) that raise challenging questions about ourselves and our communities. We prefer plays *that can work only on the stage* in the most theatrical way possible—plays that are not necessarily 'straight-on' realistic, but rather ones that use imagery, metaphor, poetry and musicality in new and interesting ways. Plays go through a three-step development process: A roundtable (inhouse reading), a public concert reading and then a workshop production."

THE PLAYWRIGHTS' CENTER'S PLAYLABS, 2301 Franklin Ave. E., Minneapolis MN 55406. (612)332-7481. Fax: (612)332-6037. E-mail: info@pwcenter.org. Website: www.pwcenter.org. **Contact:** Kristen Gandrow, playwrights' services director:. Estab. 1971. "Playlabs is a 2-week developmental workshop for new plays. The program is held in Minneapolis and is open by script competition. Up to 5 new plays are given reading performances. Announcements of playwrights by May 1. Playwrights receive honoraria, travel expenses, room and board.

Needs: "We are interested in playwrights with ambitions for a sustained career in theater, and scripts that could benefit from development involving professional dramaturgs, directors, and actors." US citizens or permanent residents, only. Participants must attend all of festival. Send SASE after October 15 for application. Submission deadline: December 1. Call for information on competitions. No previously produced materials.

Tips: "We are a service organization that provides programs for developmental work on scripts for members."

PLAYWRIGHTS' PLATFORM, 164 Brayton Rd., Boston MA 02135. (617)630-9704. Website: www.playwrightsplatform.org. **Contact:** George Sauer, producing director. Estab. 1972. **Produces approximately 50 readings/year.** Plays are read in staged readings at Hovey Players on Spring St. (Walthan MA). Accepts scripts on a face-to-face basis. Query and synopsis. Responds in 2 months. Include SASE for return of submission.

Needs: Any types of plays. "We will not accept scripts we think are sexist or racist." Massachusetts residents only.

PLOWSHARES THEATRE CO., 2870 E. Grand Blvd., Suite 600, Detroit MI 48202-3146. (313)872-0279. Fax: (313)872-0067. E-mail: plowshares@earthlink.net. Website: www.plowshares.org. **Contact:** Gary Anderson, producing artistic director. Estab. 1989. **Produces 5 plays/year.** Professional productions of plays by African-American writers for African-American audience and those who appreciate African-American culture. *Agented submissions only.* Responds in 8 months.

Tips: "You'll increase the chances of your submission if it is written by an African-American and with the willingness to be developed. It must also be very good, while the writer should be ready to make a commitment."

PORTLAND STAGE CO., P.O. Box 1458, Portland ME 04104. (207)774-1043. Fax: (207)774-0576. E-mail: portstage@aol.com. Artistic Director: Anita Stewart. **Contact:** A.J. McComish, literary manager. Estab. 1974. **Produces 7 plays/year.** Professional productions at the Portland Performing Arts Center. Send first 10 pages with synopsis. Responds in 3 months. Buys 3- or 4-week run in Maine. **Pays royalty.**

Needs: Developmental Staged Readings: Little Festival of the Unexpected.

Tips: "Work developed in Little Festival generally will be more strongly considered for future production."

PRIMARY STAGES CO., INC., 131 W. 45 St., 2nd Floor, New York NY 10036. (212)840-9705. Fax: (212)840-9725. **Contact:** Tyler Marchant, associate artistic director. Estab. 1985. **Produces 4 plays/year.** All plays are produced professionally off-Broadway at Primary Stages Theatre, 99 seat proscenium stage; Phil Bosakowski Theatre, 45 seat proscenium stage; Elysabeth Kleinhans Theatrical Foundation, 199 seat theatre, 150 seat theatre, 4 black box. Agented submissions or synopsis, 10 sample pages, résumé, SASE; cassette or CD for musicals. Responds in 6 months. **Pays flat fee.** Guidelines for SASE.

Needs: Full-length plays, small cast (6 or fewer) musicals. New York City or American Premiers only, written by American playwrights. Small cast (1-6), unit set or simple changes, no fly or wing space.

Tips: Best submission time: September-June. Chances: Over 1,000 scripts read, 4-5 produced. Women and minorities encouraged to submit.

PRINCE MUSIC THEATER, 100 S. Broad St., Suite 650, Philadelphia PA 19110. (215)972-1000. Fax: (215)972-1020. Website: www.princemusictheater.org. **Contact:** Majorie Samoff, producing artistic director. Estab. 1984. **Produces 4 musicals/year.** Professional musical productions. Send synopsis and sample audio tape with no more than 4 songs. Responds in 6 months. **Pays royalty.**

Needs: Song-driven music theater/opera pieces, varied musical styles. Nine in orchestra, 10-14 cast, 36x60 stage.

Tips: Innovative topics and use of media, music, technology a plus. Sees trends of arts in technology (interactive theater, virtual reality, sound design); works are shorter in length (1-1æ hours with no intermissions or two hours with intermission).

[N] PRINCETON REP CO., One Paller Square, Suite 541, Princeton NJ 08542. E-mail: prcreprap@aol.com. Website: www.princetonrep.org. Artistic Director: Victoria J. Liberatori. **Contact:** K. Pylar-Moore, assistant to the artistic director. Estab. 1984. **Produces 3 plays/year.** Plays are performed in site-specific venues, outdoor amphitheatres, and indoor theatres with approximately 199 seats. "Princeton Rep Company works under actors' equity contracts, and its directors are members of the SSDC." Query, synopsis, and 10 pages of sample dialogue. Responds in up to 18 months. Rights are negotiated on a play-by-play basis. **Payment negotiated on a play-by-play basis.**

Needs: Produces stories that are relevant to the middle and working people of all regions of the United States. "If the play demands a cast of thousands, please don't waste your time and postage." No love stories of the rich, famous, and fastuous, and no drama or comedy set in a prep school or ivy league college. "Theatre is such a marginalized art form it has all but disappeared. The power of the theatre to transform, inform, and radicalize has been co-opted by a tiny coterie of privileged brats. If you have a spirit that you think can mobilize an audience, like rap mobilized millions of young people, don't mail us, call us today."

PUERTO RICAN TRAVELING THEATRE, 141 W. 94th St., New York NY 10025. (212)354-1293. Fax: (212)307-6769. E-mail: prttny@aol.com. **Contact:** Miriam Colon Valle, founder/artistic director. Estab. 1967. **Produces 3 plays/year.** Two plays performed in our theater, one during the summer in the streets, parks, playgrounds. Professional Theatre, Actors Equity LOA contract. Query and synopsis. Retain some subsidiary rights. Fee negotiable, but we are a small theater. **Payment negotiable.**

Needs: Primarily plays by Latinos or Spaniards. Prefer strong story lines. Limit 8 characters. No fly space, little wing space. The stage is 21×19. No sitcoms or revues.

Tips: "Make certain the play is for the stage, not for TV or films. That means larger than life characters, heightened language."

PULSE ENSEMBLE THEATRE, P.O. Box 1533, Radio City Station, New York NY 10101. (212)695-1596. Fax: (212)695-1596. E-mail: pet@pulseensembletheatre.org. Website: www.pulseensembletheatre.org. **Contact:** Alexa Kelly (for full lengths); Brian Richardson (for one-acts). Estab. 1989. **Produces 6 plays/year.** Query and synopsis only. Responds in 3-6 months. Buys variable rights. **Usually pays 2% of gross.**

Needs: Meaningful theater. No production limitations. Does not want to see fluff or vanity theater.

THE PURPLE ROSE THEATRE CO., P.O. Box 220, Chelsea MI 48118. (734)433-7782. Fax: (734)475-0802. E-mail: purplerose@earthlink.net. Website: www.purplerosetheatre.org. **Contact:** Anthony Caselli, associate artistic director. Estab. 1990. **Produces 4 plays/year.** PRTC is a regional theater with an S.P.T. equity contract which produces plays intended for Midwest/Middle American audience. Query with synopsis, character breakdown, and 10-page dialogue sample. Responds in 9 months. **Pays 5-10% royalty.**

Needs: Modern, topical full length, 75-120 minutes. Prefers scripts that use comedy to deal with serious subjects. 10 cast maximum. No fly space, unit set preferable but not required. Intimate 168 seat ¾ thrust house.

[N] [⊕] RED LADDER THEATRE CO., 3 St. Peter's Buildings, York St., Leeds LS9 1AJ, United Kingdom. (0113)245-5311. E-mail: wendy@redladder.co.uk. Website: www.redladder.co.uk. **Contact:** Wendy Harris, artistic director. Estab. 1969. **Produces 2 plays/year.** "Our work tours nationally to young people, aged 13-25, in youth clubs, community venues and small scale theatres." Query and synopsis. Responds in 6 months. **Offers ITC/Equity writers contract.** "We discourage unsolicited scripts being sent to the company."

Needs: One hour in length for cast size no bigger than 5. Work that connects with a youth audience that both challenges them and offers them new insights. "We consider a range of styles and are seeking originality." Small scale touring. Does not want to commission single issue drama. The uses of new technologies in production (DVD, video projection). Young audiences are sophisticated.

Tips: "Please do not submit full length plays. Get in touch with us first. Tell us about yourself and why you would like to write for Red Ladder. We like to hear about ideas you may have in the first instance."

ROUND HOUSE THEATRE, P.O. Box 30688, Bethesda MD 20814. (301)933-9530. Fax: (301)933-2321. Website: www.roundhousetheatre.org. Artistic Director: Jerry Whiddon. **Contact:** Danisha Crosby, director of productions. **Produces 5-7 plays/year. Also produces New Voices, a play reading series of** *local* playwrights (6/year). Professional AEA Theatre. Query with synopsis; send complete scripts for New Voices. Responds in 2-12 months. **Pays negotiated percentage for productions; no payment for New Voices readings.** Include SASE for return of submission.

[A] SEATTLE CHILDREN'S THEATRE, 201 Thomas St., Seattle WA 98109. (206)443-0807. **Contact:** Madeleine Oldham, literary manager/dramaturg. Estab. 1975. **Produces 6 plays/year.** Professional (adult actors) performing for young audiences, families and school groups. Resident company—not touring. Agented submissions or submission by professional recommendation. Responds in 8 months. **Payment varies**

Needs: Full-length plays and musicals for young and family audiences.

SEATTLE REPERTORY THEATRE, P.O. Box 900923, Seattle WA 98109. Website: www.seattlerep.org. Artistic Director: Sharon Ott. **Contact:** Mervin P. Antonio, director of new project development. Estab. 1963. **Produces 9 plays/year.** 5 in the 800 seat Bagley Wright Theatre, 4 in the 300 seat Leo K Theatre. Send query, résumé, synopsis and 10 sample pages. Responds in 6 months. Buys percentage of future royalties. **Pays royalty.**

Needs: "The Seattle Repertory Theatre produces eclectic programming. We welcome a wide variety of writing."

SECOND STAGE THEATRE, 307 W. 43rd St., New York NY 10036. (212)787-8302. Fax: (212)397-7066. **Contact:** Christopher Burney, associate artistic director. Estab. 1979. **Produces 4 plays/year.** Professional off-Broadway productions.

Adult and teen audiences. Query with synopsis and 10-page writing sample or agented submission. Responds in 6 months. **Payment varies**

Needs: "We need socio-political plays, comedies, musicals, dramas—full lengths for full production, one-acts for workshops (comedies only)."

Tips: "No biographical or historical dramas. Writers are realizing that audiences can be entertained while being moved. Patience is a virtue but persistence is appreciated."

SHAW FESTIVAL THEATRE, P.O. Box 774, Niagara-on-the-Lake ON L0S 1J0, Canada. (905)468-2153. Fax: (905)468-5438. Website: www.shawfest.com. **Contact:** Jackie Maxwell, artistic director. Estab. 1962. **Produces 10 plays/year.** "Professional theater company operating 3 theaters (Festival: 861 seats; Court House: 324 seats; Royal George: 328 seats). Shaw Festival presents the work of George Bernard Shaw and his contemporaries written during his lifetime (1856-1950) and in 2000 expanded the mandate to include works written about the period of his lifetime." Query with SASE or SAE and IRC's, depending on country of origin. "We prefer to hold rights for Canada and northestern U.S., also potential to tour." **Pays 5-10% royalty.**

Needs: "We operate an acting ensemble of up to 75 actors; and we have sophisticated production facilities. During the summer season (April-November) the Academy of the Shaw Festival sometimes organizes workshops of new plays."

Tips: "We are a large acting company specializing in plays written between 1856-1950 (during Shaw's lifetime) and in plays about that period."

SOUTH COAST REPERTORY, P.O. Box 2197, Costa Mesa CA 92628-1197. (714)708-5500. Fax: (714)545-0391. E-mail: theatre@scr.org. Website: www.scr.org. Dramaturg: Jerry Patch. **Contact:** Jennifer Kiger, literary manager. Estab. 1964. **Produces 11 plays/year.** Professional nonprofit theater; a member of LORT and TCG. "We operate in our own facility which houses the 507-seat Segerstrom stage and 336-seat Julianne Argyros stage. We have a combined subscription audience of 18,000." Query with synopsis and 10 sample pages of dialogue. Scripts considered with agent. Responds in 4 months. Acquires negotiable rights. **Pays royalty.**

Needs: "We produce full lengths. We prefer plays that address contemporary concerns and are dramaturgically innovative. A play whose cast is larger than 15-20 will need to be extremely compelling, and its cast size must be justifiable."

Tips: "We don't look for a writer to write for us—he or she should write for him or herself. We look for honesty and a fresh voice. We're not likely to be interested in writers who are mindful of any trends. Originality and craftsmanship are the most important qualities we look for."

SOUTH COAST REPERTORY'S HISPANIC PLAYWRIGHT'S PROJECT, P.O. Box 2197, Costa Mesa CA 92628-2197. (714)708-5500, ext. 5405. Fax: (714)545-0391. E-mail: juliette@scr.org. Website: www.scr.org. **Contact:** Juliette Carrillo, director of HPP. Estab. 1985. **Produces at least 3 workshops/readings/year.** "The Hispanic Playwrights Project is a workshop for the development of new plays by Latina/Latino writers. While focusing on the developmental process, the Project also serves to increase the visibility of work by emerging and established Hispanic-American playwrights and to encourage production of that work in the nation's resident theaters. In the past 15 years, more than half of the plays developed have gone on to productions at theatres across the U.S. Playwrights chosen for HPP will be brought to Costa Mesa to participate in a workshop with a director, dramaturg, and cast of professional actors. Together, they will work on the script, preparing it for a presentation before a public audience." Submit complete script with a synopsis and biography by January 15. Early submissions are highly encouraged. Include SASE if script is to be returned. Responds in 2 months. Holds rights to do production for 1 month after reading. **Pays per diem, travel, and lodging for workshop.**

Needs: Writers must be of Latino heritage. No plays entirely in Spanish (must be mostly English). No musicals or solo pieces. New and unproduced plays are preferred, but previously produced plays that would benefit from further development may also be considered. Selected playwrights will be notified by April 1.

SOUTHERN APPALACHIAN REPERTORY THEATRE (SART), Mars Hill College, P.O. Box 1720, Mars Hill NC 28754. (828)689-1384. E-mail: sart@mhc.edu. Artistic Director: William Gregg. Estab. 1975. **Produces 5-6 plays/year.** "Since 1975 the Southern Appalachian Repertory Theatre has produced 47 world premieres in the 175-seat Owen Theatre on the Mars Hill College campus. The theater's goals include producing quality theatre and seeking integrity, both in artistic form and in the treatment of various aspects of the human condition. SART is a professional summer theater company whose audiences range from students to senior citizens." SART also conducts an annual Southern Appalachian Playwrights Conference in which 4-5 playwrights are invited for a weekend of public readings of their new scripts in the Owen Theatre. The conference is held in late March/early April. Submissions must be postmarked by October 31. If a script read at the 2003 conference is selected for production, it will be given a fully-staged production in the 2004 summer season. Playwrights receive honorarium and housing. Enclose SASE for return of script.

Needs: Comedies, dramas and musicals. Since 1975, one of SART's goals has been to produce at least one original play each summer season. To date, 46 original scripts have been produced. Plays by Southern Appalachian playwrights or about the history, culture or human experience of the Southern Appalachian region are preferred, but by no means exclusively. Complete scripts of full-length plays and musicals (include recording of at least 4 songs) are welcomed; new plays are defined as those that are unpublished and have not received a fully-staged production. "Workshops and other readings do not constitute a fully-staged production."

STAGE LEFT THEATRE, 3408 N. Sheffield, Chicago IL 60657. (773)883-8830. Fax: (773)472-1336. E-mail: SLTChicago@aol.com. Website: www.stagelefttheatre.com. **Contact:** Jessi D. Hill, artistic director. Estab. 1982. **Produces 4 plays/year.** Professional productions (usually in Chicago), for all audiences (usually adult). Submit query, 10-page excerpt, 1-page synopsis, author's résumé, and SASE. **Pays 6% royalty.**

Needs: "Any length, any genre, any style that fits the Stage Left mission—plays that raise the level of debate on social and political issues. We do have an emphasis on new work."
Tips: "Your play must raise debate on a political or social issue."

STAGE ONE: The Louisville Children's Theatre, 501 W. Main St., Louisville KY 40202-3300. (502)589-5946. Fax: (502)588-5910. E-mail: stageone@stageone.org. Website: www.stageone.org. **Contact:** J. Daniel Herring, artisitic director. Estab. 1946. **Produces 6-7 plays/year.** Plays performed by an equity company for young audiences ages 4-18; usually does different plays for different age groups within that range. Submit complete script. Responds in 4 months. **Pays negotiable royalty.**
Needs: "Good plays for young audiences of all types: adventure, fantasy, realism, serious problem plays about growing up or family entertainment. Ideally, cast at 12 or less. Honesty, visual potentiality, worthwhile story and characters are necessary. An awareness of children and their schooling is a plus. No campy material or anything condescending to children. Musicals accepted if they are fairly limited in orchestration."

STAGES REPERTORY THEATRE, 3201 Allen Parkway, Suite 101, Houston TX 77091. (713)527-0220. Fax: (713)527-8669. Website: www.stagestheatre.com. **Contact:** Rob Bundy, artistic director. Estab. 1975. **Produces 12-14 plays/year.** Query with synopsis and SASE. Responds in 8 months. **Pays 3-10% royalty.**
Needs: Full-length, theatrical, non-realistic work. 6-8 characters maximum. "Unit set with multiple locations is preferable." No "kitchen sink" dramas. Plays also accepted October 1-December 31 for submission into the Southwest Festival of New Plays, held every June. Categories include Women's Playwrights' Division, Texas Playwrights' Division, Children's Theatre Playwrights' Division and Latino Playwrights' Division. More information can be found on website.

STAMFORD THEATRE WORKS, 95 Atlantic St., Stamford CT 06901. (203)359-4414. Fax: (203)356-1846. E-mail: STWCT@aol.com. Website: www.stamfordtheatreworks.org. **Contact:** Steve Karp, producing director. Estab. 1988. **Produces 4-6 plays/year.** Professional productions for an adult audience. *Agented submissions* or queries with a professional recommendation. Responds in 3 months. **Pays 5-8% royalty.** Include SASE for return of submission.
Needs: Plays of social relevance; contemporary work. Limited to unit sets; maximum cast of about 8.

STATE THEATER CO., 719 Congress Ave., Austin TX 78701. (512)472-5143. Fax: (512)472-7199. E-mail: mpolgar@austintheateralliance.org. **Contact:** Michelle Polgar, associate artistic director. Estab. 1982. **Produces 5 plays/year.** "Strong commitment to and a history of producing new work." Responds in late summer. **Pays royalty.**
Needs: Full length, adaptations.
Tips: Submit first 10 pages of plays, brief synopsis, and résumé. Submission period: December 1-March 1.

STEPPENWOLF THEATRE CO., 758 W. North Ave., Chicago IL 60610. (312)335-1888. Fax: (312)335-0808. Website: www.steppenwolf.org. Artistic Director: Martha Lavey. **Contact:** Edward Sobel, literary manager. Estab. 1976. **Produces 9 plays/year.** 500-, 300- and 100-seat performance venues. Many plays produced at Steppenwolf have gone to Broadway. "We currently have 20,000 savvy subscribers." Agented submissions only with full scripts. Responds in 6-8 months. Buys commercial, film and television in addition to production rights. **Pays 6-8% royalty.**
Needs: "Actor-driven works are crucial to us, plays that explore the human condition in our time. We max at around ten characters."
Tips: No musicals or romantic/light comedies. Plays get produced at STC based on ensemble member interest.

STUDIO ARENA THEATRE, 710 Main St., Buffalo NY 14202. (716)856-8025. Website: www.studioarena.org. **Contact:** Maisha Davis, assistant to the artistic director. Estab. 1965. **Produces 6-8 plays/year.** Professional productions. Agented submissions only.
Needs: Full-length plays. No fly space.
Tips: "Do not fax or send submissions via the Internet. Submissions should appeal to a diverse audience. We do not generally produce musicals. Please send a character breakdown and 1-page synopsis for a faster reply."

TADA!, 15 W. 28th St., 3rd Floor, New York NY 10001. (212)252-1619. Fax: (212)252-8763. E-mail: ewilson@tadatheater.com. Website: www.tadatheater.com. **Contact:** Emmanuel Wilson, literary manager. Estab. 1984. **Produces 3 musical plays/year.** "TADA! produces original musicals performed by children and teens, ages 8-18. Productions are for family audiences." Submit a brief summary of the musical, 10 pages from the scripts, and a CD or cassette with songs from the score. Responds in 2-3 months. **Pays 5% royalty. Commission fee.**

- TADA! also sponsors an annual one-act playwriting contest for their Spring Staged Reading Series. Works must be original, unproduced and unpublished one-acts. Plays must be geared toward teen audiences. Call or e-mail for guidelines.

Needs: "Generally pieces run from 45-70 minutes. Must be enjoyed by children and adults and performed by a cast of children ages 8-17."
Tips: "No redone fairy tales or pieces where children are expected to play adults. Plays with animals and non-human characters are highly discouraged. Be careful not to condescend when writing for children's theater."

TEATRO VISIÓN, 1700 Alum Rock Ave., San Jose CA 95116. (408)272-9926. Fax: (408)928-5589. **Contact:** Elisa Marina Alvarado, artistic director. Estab. 1984. **Produces 3 plays/year.** Professional productions for a Latino population. Query with synopsis or submit complete ms. Responds in 6 months. **Pays 5-10% royalty. Makes outright purchase of $500-1,000. Pays $50-60 per performance.**
Needs: "We produce plays by Latino playwrights. Plays that highlight the Chicano/Latino experience."
Tips: "Prefers plays written by Latino writers."

THE TEN-MINUTE MUSICALS PROJECT, P.O. Box 461194, West Hollywood CA 90046. E-mail: info@tenminutemusicals.org. Website: www.tenminutemusicals.org. **Contact:** Michael Koppy, producer. Estab. 1987. **Produces 1-10 plays/year.** "Plays performed in Equity regional theaters in the US and Canada." Deadline August 31; notification by November 30. Submit complete script, lead sheets and cassette. Buys performance rights. **Pays $250 royalty advance upon selection, against equal share of performance royalties when produced.**

Needs: Looking for complete short stage musicals playing between 7-14 minutes. Limit cast to 10 (5 women, 5 men).

TENNESSEE STAGE CO., P.O. Box 1186, Knoxville TN 37901. (865)546-4280. Fax: (865)546-9677. **Contact:** Tom Parkhill, artistic director. Estab. 1989. Venue is a 100 seat black box theater. Professional productions (non-Equity) for a general audience in the Knoxville area. Submit complete script. Responds immediately. **Pays moderate royalty.**

Needs: Any material will be considered. Please limit submissions to one script annually. "Generally our productions run toward a simple staging. While heavily technical plays will be considered, a more simple piece will have a stronger chance of getting an opportunity here."

Tips: "Write a good light comedy with a smallish cast and a simple setting."

THEATER AT LIME KILN, 14 S. Randolph St., Lexington VA 24450. E-mail: jhlimekiln@aol.com. Website: www.theateratlimekiln.com. **Contact:** John Healey, artistic director. Estab. 1984. **Produces 3 (1 new) plays/year.** Outdoor summer theater. Query and synopsis. Responds in 3 months. Buys performance rights. **Pays $25-75 per performance.**

Needs: Plays that explore the history and heritage of the Appalachian region. Minimum set required.

Tips: "Searching for plays that can be performed in outdoor space. Prefer plays that explore the cultural and/or history of the Appalichian region."

THEATER BY THE BLIND, 306 W. 18th St., New York NY 10011. (212)243-4337. Fax: (212)243-4337. E-mail: gar@panix.com. Website: www.tbtb.org. **Contact:** Ike Schambelan, artistic director. Estab. 1979. **Produces 2 plays/year.** "Off-off Broadway, Theater Row, general audiences, seniors, students, disabled. If play transfers, we'd like a piece." Submit complete script. Responds in 3 months. **Pays $750-1,000/production.**

Needs: Genres about blindness.

THE THEATER OF NECESSITY, 11702 Webercrest, Houston TX 77048. (713)733-6042. Estab. 1981. **Produces 8 plays/year.** "We usually keep script on file unless we are certain we will never use it." Plays are produced in a small professional theater. Submit complete script. Responds in 2 years. Buys performance rights. **Pays standard royalties (average $500/run).**

Needs: "Any play in a recognizable genre must be superlative in form and intensity. Experimental plays are given an easier read. We move to larger venue if the play warrants the expense."

THEATER OF THE FIRST AMENDMENT, George Mason University, Fairfax VA 22030-4444. Website: www.gmu.edu/cfa. **Contact:** Kristin Johnsen-Neshati, artistic associate. Estab. 1990. **Produces 3 plays/year.** Professional productions performed in an Equity SPT 150-seat theater. Query and synopsis. Responds in 3 months. **Pays combination of percentage of box office gross against a guaranteed minimum royalty.**

Needs: "We are interested in cultural history made dramatic, as distinct from history dramatized; large battles joined; hard questions asked; word and image stretched."

THEATRE & CO., 36 King St. W, P.O. Box 876, Kitchener, ON N2G 4C5, Canada. (519)571-7080, ext. 223. Fax: (519)571-9051. Website: www.theatreandcompany.org. Artistic Director: Stuart Scadron-Wattles. **Contact:** Lisa O'Connell, literary manager. Estab. 1988. **Produces 6 plays/year.** Professional productions for a general audience. Query with synopsis, 10 pages of sample dialogue and SAE with IRCs. Responds in 1 year. **Pays $50-100 per performance.**

- Theatre & Company is particularly interested in work by Canadians.

Needs: Full-length; comedy or drama. Looking for small cast (less than 8) ensemble comedies. "Our emphasis is on regional writers familiar with our work. There is no 'best bet.' We want good stage writing that hits hard on a number of levels: Heart, head, gut and funnybone." No cast above 10; prefers unit staging.

Tips: Looks for "innovative writing for an audience which loves the theater. Avoid current trends toward shorter scenes. Playwrights should be aware that they are writing for the stage, not television."

THEATRE BUILDING CHICAGO, 1225 W. Belmont Ave., Chicago IL 60657. (773)929-7367 ext. 22. Fax: (773)327-1404. E-mail: tim@theatrebuildingchicago.org. Website: www.theatrebuildingchicago.org. **Contact:** John Sparks, artistic director. **Produces mostly readings of new works, 4 skeletal productions, and Stages Festival.** "Mostly developed in our workshop. Some scripts produced are unagented submissions. Plays performed in 3 small off-Loop theaters are seating 148 for a general theater audience, urban/suburban mix." Submit synopsis, sample scene, CD or cassette tape and piano/vocal score of three songs, and author bios. Responds in 3 months.

Needs: Musicals *only.* "We're interested in all forms of musical theater including more innovative styles. Our production capabilities are limited by the lack of space, but we're very creative and authors should submit anyway. The smaller the cast, the better. We are especially interested in scripts using a younger (35 and under) ensemble of actors. We mostly look for authors who are interested in developing their scripts through workshops, readings and production." No casts over 12. No one-man shows or 'single author' pieces.

Tips: "We would like to see the musical theater articulating something about the world around us, as well as diverting an audience's attention from that world." Offers Script Consultancy—A new program designed to assist authors and composers in developing new musicals through private feedback sessions with professional dramaturgs and musical directors. For further info contact (773)929-7367, ext. 222.

THEATRE DE LA JEUNE LUNE, 105 N. First St., Minneapolis MN 55401-1411. (612)332-3968. Fax: (612)332-0048. **Contact:** Barbara Berlovitz, Vincent Garcieux, Robert Rosen, Dominique Serrand, Steven Epp, artistic directors. Estab. 1979. **Produces 3-4 plays/year.** Professional nonprofit company producing September-June for general audience. Query and synopsis. Indefinite response time **Pays royalty or per performance**

Needs: "All subject matter considered, although plays with universal themes are desired; plays that concern people of today." No unsolicited scripts please. No psychological drama or plays that are written alone in a room without the input of outside vitality and life.

Tips: "We are an acting company that takes plays and makes them ours; this could mean cutting a script or not heeding a writer's stage directions. We are committed to the performance in front of the audience as the goal of all the contributing factors; therefore, the actor's voice is extremely important. Most of our plays are created by the company. We have never produced a play that was sent to us."

THEATRE IV, 114 W. Broad St., Richmond VA 23220. (804)783-1688. Fax: (804)775-2325. E-mail: bmiller@theatreiv.org. Website: www.theatreiv.org. **Contact:** Bruce Miller, artistic director. Estab. 1975. **Produces approximately 20 plays/year.** National tour of plays for young audiences—maximum cast of 5, maximum length of an hour. Mainstage plays for young audiences in 600 or 350 seat venues. Query and synopsis. Responds in 1 month. Buys standard production rights. **Payment varies.**

Needs: Touring and mainstage plays for young audiences. Touring—maximum cast of 5, length of 60 minutes.

THEATRE THREE, P.O. Box 512, 412 Main St., Port Jefferson NY 11777-0512. (631)928-9202. Fax: (631)928-9120. Website: www.theatrethree.org. **Contact:** Clayton Phillips, artistic director. Estab. 1969. "We produce an Annual Festival of One-Act Plays on our Second Stage." Deadline for submission is September 30. Send SASE for festival guidelines. Responds in 6 months. "We ask for exclusive rights up to and through the festival." **Pays $70 for the run of the festival.**

Needs: One-act plays. Maximum length: 40 minutes. "Any style, topic, etc. We require simple, suggested sets and a maximum cast of six. No adaptations, musicals or children's works." Also accepts submissions for small cast plays and musicals for development on our second stage.

Tips: "Too many plays are monologue-dominant. Please—reveal your characters through action and dialogue."

[A] **THEATRE THREE**, 2800 Routh St., Dallas TX 75201. (214)871-3300. Fax: (214)871-3139. E-mail: theatre3@airmail.net. Website: www.theater3dallas.com. **Contact:** Jac Alder, executive producer-director. Estab. 1961. **Produces 7 plays/year.** Professional regional theatre, in-the-round. Audience is college age to senior citizens. Query with synopsis; agented submissions only. Responds in 6 months. **Contractual agreements vary.**

Needs: Musicals, dramas, comedies, bills of related one-acts. Modest production requirement; prefer casts no larger than 10.

Tips: No parodies or political commentary/comedy. Most produced playwrights at Theatre Three (to show "taste" of producer) are Moliere, Sondheim, Ayckbourne, Miller, Stoppard, Durang (moralists and irony-masters).

THEATRE WEST, 3333 Cahuenga W., Los Angeles CA 90068-1365. (323)851-4839. Fax: (323)851-5286. E-mail: theatrewest@theatrewest.org. Website: www.theatrewest.org. **Contact:** Chris DiGiovanni and Doug Haverty, moderators of the Writers Workshop. Estab. 1962. "99-seat waiver productions in our theater. Audiences are primarily young urban professionals." Residence in Southern California is vital as it's a weekly workshop. Submit script, résumé and letter requesting membership. Responds in 4 months. Contracts a percentage of writer's share to other media if produced on MainStage by Theatre West. **Pays royalty based on gross box office.**

Needs: Full-length plays only, no one-acts. Uses minimalistic scenery, no fly space.

Tips: "Theatre West is a dues-paying membership company. Only members can submit plays for production. So you must first seek membership to the Writers Workshop. We accept all styles of theater writing, but theater only—no screenplays, novels, short stories or poetry will be considered for membership."

THEATRE WEST VIRGINIA, P.O. Box 1205, Beckley WV 25802-1205. (304)256-6800. Fax: (304)256-6807. E-mail: theaterwv@charter.net. Website: www.theatrewestvirginia.com. **Contact:** Marina Dolinger, artistic director. Estab. 1955. **Produces 6 plays/year.** Professional educational touring theatre—K-6 and 7-12 grade levels. Outdoor drama, musicals. Query and synopsis. Responds in 3 months. **Pays 3-6% royalty.**

Needs: Appropriate material for K through 12. Cast limited to 6 actors/van and truck tour.

Tips: Material needs to be educational, yet entertaining.

[N] **THEATREWORKS**, 1100 Hamilton Court, Menlo Park CA 94025-1425. (650)463-7126. Fax: (650)463-1963. E-mail: jeannie@theatreworks.org. Website: www.theatreworks.org. Robert Kelley. **Contact:** Jeannie Barroga, literary manager. Estab. 1970. **Produces 8 plays/year.** Plays are professional productions intended for an adult audience. Receives all methods of submission. Responds in 3 months. Buys performance rights. **Payment varies per contract.**

Needs: TheatreWorks has a high standard for excellence. "We prefer well-written, well-constructed plays that celebrate the human spirit through innovative productions and programs inspired by our exceptionally diverse community. There is no limit on the number of characters, and we favor plays with multi-ethnic casting possibilities. We have an Equity Letter of Agreement (LOA) artist contract. Plays are negotiated per playwright." Does not want one-acts, plays with togas. Plays with musical elements.

Tips: "Check our website for Submission Checklist Request and the New Works Program under About Us."

THEATREWORKS/USA, 151 W. 26th St., 7th Floor, New York NY 10001. (212)647-1100. Fax: (212)924-5377. E-mail: malltop@theatreworksusa.org. Website: www.theatreworksusa.org. **Contact:** Michael Alltop, assistant artistic director. Estab. 1961. **Produces 3-4 plays/year.** Professional equity productions for young audiences. Weekend series at Equitable

Towers, NYC. Also, national and regional tours of each show. Query and synopsis. Responds in 6 months. Obtains performing rights. **Pays 6% royalty.**

Needs: "One-hour musicals or plays with music written for K-3rd or 3rd-7th grade age groups. Subjects: Historical, biography, classic literature, fairy tales with specific point of view, contemporary literature. Also, adaptations of classic literature for high school, up to all actors." Limited to 5-6 actors (11 for high school show) and a portable set. Do not rely on lighting or special effects.

Tips: "No campy, 'fractured' fairy tales, shows specifically written to teach or preach, shows relying heavily on narrators or 'kiddy theater' filled with pratfalls, bad jokes, and audience participation. Write smart. Kids see a lot these days, and they are sophisticated. Don't write down to them. They deserve a good, well-told story. Seeing one of our shows will provide the best description. We commission almost all of our own work, so most submissions will not have a chance of being produced by us. We read submissions to gauge a playwright's style and appropriateness for possible future projects."

THEATRICAL OUTFIT, P.O. Box 1555, Atlanta GA 30301. **Contact:** Kate Warner, artistic associate. Estab. 1978. **Produces 4-5 plays/year.** Year round productions. Query with synopsis, first 10 pages, letter of reference or 1 page résumé and a SAS postcard. **Pays 5-8% royalty.**

Needs: Adaptations of classic works, new plays. Plays that focus on southern literature. Minimal sets.

N ⊕ **TRAVERSE THEATRE**, Cambridge St., Edinburgh EH1 2ED, United Kingdom. Philip Howard. **Contact:** Roxana Silbert, literary director. Estab. 1963. **Produces 4-6 plays/year.** "We are Scotland's Theatre of New Writing and have two spaces (a 100-seater and a 250-seater). We are a professional company." Submit complete script. Responds in 3 months. "We only attain rights on playtexts at the point at which we decide to produce them, unless they are commissioned scripts." Include SASE for return of submission.

Needs: "We focus on producing contemporary Scottish plays, plays by Scottish writers, plays with a strong and clear connection to Scottish culture. We do some International work, but this rarely comes to us through unsolicited sources."

TROUPE AMERICA, INC., 528 Hennepin Ave., Suite 206, Minneapolis MN 55403. (612)333-3302. Fax: (612)333-4337. E-mail: cwollan@mninter.net. Website: www.troupeamerica.com. **Contact:** Curt Wollan, president/executive director. Estab. 1987. **Produces 10-12 plays/year.** Professional production in Minneapolis or on the road. Intended for general and family audiences as well as community arts series and University Arts Series audiences. Query with sample of script, synopsis and CD or cassette tape of music. Responds in 1 year. Buys the right to perform and license the production for 10 years. **Pays 2½-5% royalty.**

Needs: Family holiday musicals—2 hours with intermission and small cast musicals; biographic musicals—2 hours with intermission; musical adaptations of famous works—2 hours with intermission; smaller contained musicals get attention and single set scripts do as well.

Tips: No heavy dramas, political plays (unless satirical) and any play dealing with sex, drugs, or violence. The size of the cast is important. The smaller the size, the more likely it will get produced. Economics is a priority. If possible, send an invitation to other productions of the script.

TRUSTUS THEATRE, P.O. BOX 11721, Columbia SC 29211-1721. (803)254-9732. Fax: (803)771-9153. **Contact:** Jon Tuttle, literary manager. Estab. 1984. **Produces 10-15 plays/year.** Trustus Mainstage Theatre—T.C.G. Professional Company. Query and synopsis. Responds in 3 months. All rights revert to author after production. **Pays standard royalty.**

Needs: Experimental, hard-hitting, off-the-wall one-act comedies or "dramadies" suitable for open-minded Late-Night series audiences; no topic taboo; no musicals or plays for young audiences. Small cast, modest production demands.

UNICORN THEATRE, 3828 Main St., Kansas City MO 64111. (816)531-7529 ext. 15. Fax: (816)531-0421. Website: www.unicorntheatre.org. Producing Artistic Director: Cynthia Levin. **Contact:** Herman Wilson, literary assistant. **Produces 6-8 plays/year.** "We are a professional Equity Theatre. Typically, we produce plays dealing with contemporary issues." Send complete script (to Herman Wilson) with brief synopsis, cover letter, bio, character breakdown and SASPC if script is to be returned. Include SASPC if acknowledgement of receipt is desired. Responds in 4-8 months.

Needs: Prefers contemporary (post-1950) scripts. Does not accept musicals, one-acts, or historical plays. A royalty/prize of $1,000 will be awarded the playwright of any play selected through this process, The New Play Development Award. This script receives production as part of the Unicorn's regular season.

URBAN STAGES, 17 E. 47th St., New York NY 10017. (212)421-1380. Fax: (212)421-1387. E-mail: urbanstage@aol.com. Website: www.urbanstages.org. Artistic Director: Frances Hill. Literary Manager: David Sheppard. **Contact:** T.L. Reilly, producing director. Estab. 1986. **Produces 2-4 plays/year.** Professional productions off Broadway—throughout the year. General audience. Submit complete script. Responds in 4 months. If produced, option for 1 year. **Pays royalty.**

Needs: Full-length; generally 1 set or styled playing dual. Good imaginative, creative writing. Cast limited to 3-7.

Tips: "We tend to reject 'living-room' plays. We look for imaginative settings. Be creative and interesting with intellectual content. All submissions should be bound. Send SASE. We are looking for plays with ethnic backgrounds. Send script with $5 processing fee."

UTAH SHAKESPEAREAN FESTIVAL, Plays in Progress, 351 W. Center St., Cedar City UT 84720-2498. (435)586-7884. Fax: (435)865-8003. Founder/Executive Producer: Fred C. Adams. **Contact:** R. Scott Phillips, managing director. Estab. 1961. **Produces 9 plays/year.** Travelling audiences ranging in ages from 6-80. Programming includes classic plays, musicals, new works. Submit complete script, no synopsis. Responds in 3-4 months. **Pays small stipend in addition to travel and hotel expenses for staged readings only.**

Needs: The USF is only interested in material that explores characters and ideas that focus on the West and our Western experience, spirit and heritage. Preference is given to writers whose primary residence is in the Western United States. Cast size is a consideration due to the limited time of rehearsal and the actors available during the USF production period. Does not want plays that do not match criteria.

Tips: "We want previously unproduced plays with western themes by western playwrights."

WALNUT STREET THEATRE, Ninth and Walnut Streets, Philadelphia PA 19107. (215)574-3550. Fax: (215)574-3598. Producing Artistic Director: Bernard Havard. **Contact:** Literary Office. Estab. 1809. **Produces 10 plays/year.** "Our plays are performed in our own space. WST has 3 theaters—a proscenium (mainstage), 1,052 seats; 2 studios, 79-99 seats. We have a subscription audience, largest in the nation." Query with synopsis, 10-20 pages of dialogue, character breakdown and bio. Responds in 5 months. Rights negotiated per project. **Pays negotiable royalty or makes outright purchase.**

Needs: "Full-length dramas and comedies, musicals, translations, adaptations and revues. The studio plays must have a cast of no more than four and use simple sets."

Tips: "Bear in mind that on the mainstage we look for plays with mass appeal, Broadway-style. The studio spaces are our off-Broadway. No children's plays. Our mainstage audience goes for work that is entertaining and light. Our studio season is where we look for plays that have bite and are more provocative." Include SASE for return of materials.

WATERLOO COMMUNITY PLAYHOUSE, P.O. Box 433, Waterloo IA 50704-0433. (319)235-0367. Fax: (319)235-7489. E-mail: wcpbhct@cedarnet.org. **Contact:** Charles Stilwill, managing artistic director. Estab. 1917. **Produces 11 plays/year.** Plays performed by Waterloo Community Playhouse with a volunteer cast. "We are one of the few theaters with a committment to new scripts. We do at least one and have done as many as four a year. We have 4,300 season members. Average attendance is 330. We do a wide variety of plays. Our public isn't going to accept nudity, too much sex, too much strong language. We don't have enough Black actors to do all-Black shows. Theater has done plays with as few as 2 characters and as many as 98. We also produce children's theater. Please, no loose pages." Submit complete script. Responds in 1 year. **Makes outright purchase of $400-500.**

Needs: "For our Children's Theater and our Adult Annual Holiday (Christmas) show, we are looking for good adaptations of name stories. Most recently: *Miracle on 34th Street*, *Best Christmas Pageant Ever*, and *It's A Wonderful Life*."

WEST COAST ENSEMBLE, P.O. Box 38728, Los Angeles CA 90038. (323)876-9337. Fax: (323)876-8916. Website: wcensemble.org. **Contact:** Les Hanson, artistic director. Estab. 1982. **Produces 6 plays/year.** Plays performed at a theater in Hollywood. Submit complete script. Responds in 9 months. Obtains exclusive rights in southern California to present the play for the period specified. Ownership and rights remain with the playwright. **Pays $25-45 per performance.**

Needs: Prefers a cast of 6-12.

Tips: "Submit the script in acceptable dramatic script format."

WILLOWS THEATRE CO., 1425 Gasoline Alley, Concord CA 94520. (925)798-1824. Fax: (925)676-5726. E-mail: willowsth@aol.com. Website: www.willowstheatre.org. Artistic Director: Richard Elliott. **Produces 6 plays/year.** "Professional productions for a suburban audience." Accepts new manuscripts in April and May only; accepts queries year-round. Responds in 6 months to scripts. **Pays standard royalty.**

Needs: "Commercially viable, small-medium size musicals or comedies that are popular, rarely produced, or new. Certain stylized plays or musicals with a contemporary edge to them (e.g., *Les Liasons Dangereuses, La Bete, Candide*)." No more than 15 actors. Unit or simple sets with no fly space, no more than 7 pieces. "We are not interested in 1-character pieces."

Tips: "Our audiences want light entertainment, comedies, and musicals. Also, have an interest in plays and musicals with a historical angle." Submission guidelines are on website.

[A] **THE WILMA THEATER**, 265 S. Broad St., Philadelphia PA 19107. (215)893-9456. Fax: (215)893-0895. E-mail: info@wilmatheater.org. Website: www.wilmatheater.org. **Contact:** Nakissa Etemad, dramaturg and literary manager. Estab. 1980. **Produces 4 plays/year.** LORT-C 300-seat theater, 7,500 subscribers. *Agented submissions only* or full ms recommended by a literary manager, dramaturg, or other theater professional. Responds in 6 months.

Needs: Full-length plays, translations, adaptations, and musicals from an international repertoire with emphasis on innovative, bold staging; world premieres; ensemble works; works with poetic dimension; plays with music; multimedia works; social issues. Prefers maximum cast size of 12. Stage 44'x46'.

Tips: "Before submitting any material to The Wilma Theater, please research our production history. Considering the types of plays we have produced in the past, honestly assess whether or not your play would suit us. In general, I believe researching the various theaters to which you send your play is important in the long and short run. Different theaters have different missions and therefore seek out material corresponding with those goals. In other words, think through what is the true potential of your play and this theater, and if it is a compatible relationship."

WOMEN'S PROJECT AND PRODUCTIONS, 55 West End Ave., New York NY 10023. (212)765-1706. Fax: (212)765-2024. Website: www.womensproject.org. **Contact:** Karen Keagle, literary manager. Estab. 1978. **Produces 3 plays/year.** Professional Off-Broadway productions. Query with synopsis and 10 sample pages of dialogue. Responds in 8 months.

Needs: "We are looking for full-length plays, written by women."

SCREENWRITING

Practically everyone you meet in Los Angeles, from your airport cabbie on, is writing a script. It might be a feature film, movie of the week, TV series, or documentary, but the sheer amount of competition can seem overwhelming. Some will never make a sale, while others make a decent living on sales and options without ever having any of their work produced. But there are those writers who make a living doing what they love and seeing their names roll by on the credits. How do they get there? How do *you* get there? Work on your writing. You'll improve with each script, so there's no way of getting around the need to write and write some more. It's a good idea to read as many scripts as you can get your hands on.

Writing for TV

To break into TV you must have spec scripts—work written for free that serves as a calling card and gets you in the door. A spec script showcases your writing abilities and gets your name in front of influential people. Whether a network has invited you in to pitch some ideas, or a movie producer has contacted you to write a first draft for a feature film, the quality of writing in your spec script got their attention and that may get you the job.

It's a good idea to have several spec scripts, perhaps one each for three of the top five shows in the format you prefer to work in, whether it's sitcom (half-hour comedies), episodic (one-hour series), or movie of the week (two-hour dramatic movies). Perhaps you want to showcase the breadth of your writing ability; your portfolio could include a few prime time sitcoms (i.e., *Friends*, *Everybody Loves Raymond*, *Will & Grace*), and one or two episodics in a particular genre (i.e., *The Sopranos*, *Law and Order*, *NYPD Blue*). These are all "hot" shows for writers and can demonstrate your abilities to create believable dialogue for characters already familiar to your intended readers. For TV and cable movies you should have completed original scripts (not sequels to existing movies) and you might also have a few for episodic TV shows.

In choosing the shows you write spec scripts for, you must remember one thing: Don't write a script for a show you want to work on. If you want to write for *Will & Grace*, for example, you'll send a *Dharma & Greg* script and vice versa. It may seem contradictory, but it's standard practice. It reduces the chances of lawsuits, and writers and producers can feel very proprietary about their show and their stories. They may not be objective enough to fairly evaluate your writing. In submitting another similar type of show you'll avoid these problems while demonstrating comparable skills.

In writing your TV script you must get *inside* the show and understand the characters' internal motivations. You must immerse yourself in how the characters speak, think, and interact. Don't introduce new characters in a spec script for an existing show—write believable dialogue for the characters as they are portrayed. Be sure to choose a show that you like—you'll be better able to demonstrate your writing ability through characters you respond to.

You must also understand the external factors. How the show is filmed bears on how you write. Most sitcoms are shot on videotape with three cameras, on a sound stage with a studio audience. Episodics are often shot with one camera and include on-location shots. Another important external influence in writing for TV is the timing of commercials in conjunction with the act structure. Generally, a sitcom has a teaser (short opening scene), two acts, and a tag (short closing scene), and an episodic has a teaser, four acts, and a tag. Each act closes with a turning point. Watching TV analytically and keeping a log of events will reveal some elements of basic structure.

Writing for the movies

An original movie script contains characters you have created, with story lines you design, allowing you more freedom than you have in TV. However, your writing must still convey believable dialogue and realistic characters, with a plausible plot and high-quality writing carried through roughly 120 pages. The characters must have a problem that involves the audience. When you go to a movie you don't want to spend time watching the *second* worst night of a character's life. You're looking for the big issue that crystallizes a character, that portrays a journey with important consequences.

At the same time you are creating, you should also be constructing. Be aware of the basic three-act structure for feature films. Scenes can be of varying lengths, but are usually no longer than three- to three-and-a-half pages. Some writers list scenes that must occur, then flesh them out from beginning to end, writing with the structure of events in mind. The beginning and climactic scenes are the easiest; it's how they get there from here that's difficult.

Many novice screenwriters tend to write too many visual cues and camera directions into their scripts. Your goal should be to write something readable, like a "compressed novella." Write succinct resonant scenes and leave the camera technique to the director and producer.

It seems to be easier for TV writers to cross over to movies. Cable movies bridge the two, and are generally less derivative and more willing to take chances with a higher quality show designed to attract an audience not interested in network offerings. Cable is also less susceptible to advertiser pullout, which means it can tackle more controversial topics.

Feature films and TV are very different and writers occupy different positions. TV is a medium for writers and producers; directors work for them. Many TV writers are also producers. In feature films the writers and producers work for the director and often have little or no say about what happens to the work once the script has been sold. For TV the writer pitches the idea; for feature films generally the producer pitches the idea and then finds a writer.

Marketing your scripts

If you do intend to make writing your profession, you must act professionally. Accepted submission practices should become second nature.

- The initial pitch is made through a query letter, which is no longer than one page with a one-paragraph synopsis and brief summary of your credits if they are relevant to the subject of your script.
- Never send a complete manuscript until it is requested.
- Almost every script sent to a producer, studio, or agent must be accompanied by a release form. Ask for that company's release form when you receive an invitation to submit the whole script. Mark your envelope "release form enclosed" to prevent it being returned unread.
- Always include a SASE if you want your work returned; a disposable copy may be accompanied by a self-addressed postcard for reply.
- Allow four to six weeks from receipt of your manuscript before writing a follow-up letter.

When your script is requested, be sure it's written in the appropriate format. Unusual binding, fancy cover letters, or illustrations mark an amateur. Three brass brads with a plain or black cover indicate a pro.

There are a limited number of ideas in the world, so it's inevitable that similar ideas occur to more than one person. Hollywood is a buyer's market and a release form states that clearly. An idea is not copyrightable, so be careful about sharing premises. The written expression of that idea, however, can be protected and it's a good idea to do so. The Writers Guild of America (see the For More Information box under Playwriting in this section) can register scripts for TV and theatrical motion pictures, series formats, story lines, and step outlines.

Information on screenwriting markets listed in the previous edition of *Writer's Market* but not included in this edition can be found in the General Index.

ALLIED ARTISTS, INC., P.O. Box 73033, Las Vegas NV 89170-3033. (702)991-9011. Fax: (248)282-0764. E-mail: alliedartistsinc@usa.net. Website: www.alliedartistsonline.com. **Contact:** John Nichols, vice president, development. Estab. 1990. Produces material for broadcast and cable television, home video and film. **Buys 3-5 script(s)/year. Works with 10-20 writer(s)/year.** Buys first or all rights. Accepts previously produced material. Submit synopsis, outline. Responds in 2 months to queries; 3 months to scripts. **Pays in accordance with WGA standards.**

Needs: Films, videotapes. Social issue TV special (30-60 minutes); special interest home video topics; positive values feature screenplays.

Tips: "We are looking for positive, up-lifting dramatic stories involving real people situations. Future trend is for more reality-based programming, as well as interactive television programs for viewer participation. Send or e-mail brief query. Do not send scripts or additional material until requested."

ANGEL FILMS, 967 Highway 40, New Franklin MO 65274-9778. (573)698-3900. Fax: (573)698-3900. E-mail: angelfilm@aol.com. **Contact:** Matthew Eastman, vice president of production. Estab. 1980. Produces material for feature films, television. **Buys 10 script(s)/year. Works with 20 writer(s)/year.** Buys all rights. Accepts previously produced material. Query with synopsis. Responds in 6-8 weeks to queries; 8-10 weeks to scripts. **Makes outright purchase.**

Needs: Films (35mm), videotapes. "We are looking for projects that can be used to produce feature film and television feature film and series work. These would be in the areas of action adventure, comedy, horror, thriller, science fiction, animation for children." Also looking for direct to video materials.

Tips: "Don't copy others. Try to be original. Don't overwork your idea. As far as trends are concerned, don't pay attention to what is 'in.' By the time it gets to us it will most likely be on the way 'out.' And if you can't let your own grandmother read it, don't send it. Slow down on western submissions. They are not selling. If you wish material returned, enclose proper postage with all submissions. Send SASE for response to queries and return of scripts."

BARNSTORM FILMS, 73 Market St., Venice CA 90291. (310)396-5937. Fax: (310)450-4988. **Contact:** Tony Bill, president. Estab. 1969. Produces feature films. **Buys 2-3 script(s)/year. Works with 4-5 writer(s)/year.**

Tips: "Looking for strong, character-based commercial strips. Not interested in science fiction or fantasy. Must send SASE with synopsis. Query first, do not send script unless we request it!"

BAUMGARTEN-MERIMS ENTERTAINMENT, 1640 S. Sepulveda Blvd., Suite 218, Los Angeles CA 90025. (310)445-1625. Fax: (310)996-1892. E-mail: baumgartenmerims@yahoo.com. **Contact:** Adam Merims, producer, or Grant Stoner, creative executive. Estab. 2000. Audience is motion picture and television viewers. **Buys 35 script(s)/year. Works with 100 writer(s)/year.** Buys motion picture and television rights. Accepts previously produced material. Query with synopsis. Responds in 1 month to queries. **Pays in accordance with WGA standards.**

Needs: Films (35 mm), videotapes. "We have feature projects in development at all the studios. We have TV projects with all the cable networks. We are always looking for good material."

Tips: Interested in original motion picture, television and cable material, movies and dramatic series.

BIG EVENT PICTURES, 11288 Ventura Blvd., #909, Studio City CA 91604. E-mail: bigevent1@hotmail.com. **Contact:** Michael Cargile, president. Produces feature films for theaters, cable TV and home video. PG, R, and G-rated films. Query by e-mail. Producers will respond if interested.

Needs: Films. All genres. Looking for good material from writers who have taken the time to learn the unique and difficult craft of scriptwriting.

Tips: "Interesting query letters intrigue us—and tell us something about the writer. Query letter should include a short 'log line' or 'pitch' encapsulating 'what this story is about' and should be no more than 1 page in length. We look for unique stories with strong characters and would like to see more action and science fiction submissions. We make movies that we would want to see. Producers are known for encouraging new (e.g. unproduced) screenwriters and giving real consideration to their scripts."

BIG STAR ENTERTAINMENT GROUP, INC., (formerly Big Star Motion Pictures, Ltd.), 13025 Yonge St., #201, Richmond Hill ON L4E 1Z5, Canada. (416)720-9825. Fax: (905)773-3153. Website: www.bigstarentertainment.tv. **Contact:** Frank A. Deluca. Estab. 1991. **Buys 1-2 script(s)/year. Works with 1-3 writer(s)/year.** Query with synopsis. Script should be submitted by agent or lawyer. Responds in 3 months to queries; 3 months to scripts.

Needs: Films (35 mm). "We are active in all medias, but are primarily looking for television projects, cable, network, etc. Family films are of special interest as well as published works."

CLARION TELEVISION, The 1929 Building, Merton Abbey Mills, Water Mill Way, London SW19 2RD, United Kingdom. +44(208)540-0110. Fax: +44(709)203-0160. E-mail: info@clariontv.com. Website: www.clariontv.com. **Contact:** Richard J. Hannah, executive producer. Estab. 1982. Clarion Television handles television, serious TV documentaries and low budget drama. **Buys 4-6 script(s)/year. Works with 4-6 writer(s)/year.** Buys all rights. Accepts previously produced material. Catalog for large enough SAE to fit A4 brochure, appropriate postage. Query with synopsis. Responds in 1 month to queries; 3 months to scripts.

Needs: Films (35mm), videotapes, multimedia kits, tapes and cassettes. Wants documentary ideas based on the rights of children and their plight in the world. Low budget drama that is not "queer as folk" or anything from that genre. Looking for stories with International appeal. New ideas for animations are also much appreciated. Our principal market is "grown up television for kids." Does not want action or U.S.A.-centric material.

Tips: "For drama, we are looking to avoid U.S.A.-centric plots, because we are low budget (e.g., less than two million dollars per movie). We are not interested in plots with strong sex and violence contents. We are interested in stories well told with developed characters and depth, preferably even a moral bent. Multi-channel TV has an appetite for reality TV and low budget TV movies. We this trend continuing for some time, unfortunately."

CLC PRODUCTIONS, 1223 Wilshire Blvd., Suite 404, Santa Monica CA 90403. (310)454-0664. Fax: (310)459-2889. **Contact:** Alison Doyle. Estab. 1994. TV and film. Has own financing. Open to co-productions with established companies or producers. "We are interested in suspense, comedy, action/adventure with a strong female role age 35-45." **Buys 4-5 script(s)/year. Works with 5-10 writer(s)/year.** Buys all rights. Responds in 1 month to scripts.

CPC ENTERTAINMENT, 353 W. 57th St., #2227, New York NY 10019. (212)554-6447. E-mail: development@cpcentertainment.com. Website: www.cpcentertainment.com. **Contact:** Peggy Chane, producer/director; Sylvie de la Riviere, vice president creative affairs; Steve Nemiroff, manager development. Feature and TV. **Buys 5 script(s)/year. Works with 10 writer(s)/year.** Buys all rights. Submit resumé, 1 sentence premise, and 3 sentence synopsis. Prefers e-mail queries. Responds in 2 weeks to queries; 3 months to scripts. **Makes outright purchase. Pays in accordance with WGA standards.**

Needs: Feature and TV movie screenplays: small independent, or any budget for thrillers, true stories, action/adventure, character driven stories of any genre.

[N] **DAYDREAM PRODS., INC.**, 5400 Aldea Ave., Encino CA 91316. (818)990-9033. Fax: (818)990-9035. E-mail: slsdaydream@aol.com. **Contact:** Sheryl Schwartz Steinman, president, or Alan Steinman, vice president of production. Estab. 1995. **Buys 2 script(s)/year. Works with 3-4 writer(s)/year.** Buys all rights. Accepts previously produced material. Query with synopsis. Responds in 4 months to queries. **Pays in accordance with WGA standards.**
Needs: Television 2-hour MOWs; family oriented, and children's programming.
Tips: "Looking for television projects, MOW's, sitcoms, and children's programming. Also looking for short films for independent production, family features, comedy or drama."

LOUIS DIGIAIMO & ASSOCIATES, 214 Sullivan St., Suite 2C, New York NY 10012. (212)253-5510. E-mail: l.digiaimo@att.net. **Contact:** Lou DiGiaimo, Jr., producer. Estab. 1970. All audiences. **Buys 4-5 script(s)/year. Works with 3-4 writer(s)/year.** Buys all rights. Accepts previously produced material. Query with synopsis. Responds in 1 month to queries; 2 months to scripts.
Needs: Films.

ENTERTAINMENT PRODUCTIONS, INC., 2118 Wilshire Blvd., #744, Santa Monica CA 90403. (310)456-3143. Fax: (310)456-8950. **Contact:** M.E. Lee, story editor; Edward Coe, producer. Estab. 1971. Produces theatrical and television productions for worldwide distribution. Query with synopsis and a Writer Submission Release. Responds to queries in 1 month only if SASE is included. **Purchases rights by negotiations.**
Needs: Scripts having the power to attract audiences worldwide. Will consider participation, co-production.
Tips: "Submit your one strongest writing."

FAST CARRIER PICTURES, INC., c/o Showtime, 10880 Wilshire Blvd., #1100, Los Angeles CA 90024. (310)234-5376. E-mail: steve@fastcarrier.com. Website: www.fastcarrier.com. **Contact:** Steve Rubin, president; Rory Aylward, vp development. Estab. 2000. Mass market motion picture/TV audience. **Buys 8-10 script(s)/year. Works with 10-20 writer(s)/year.** Buys all rights. No previously produced material. Catalog Online At Website. Query with synopsis. Responds to queries immediately; 1-2 months to scripts.
Needs: "Our bread basket is cable, broadcast and smaller theatrical films in the following genres: women in jeopardy, lower budget family movies tied to a holiday, low budget westerners, horror, romantic comedy. No teen sex comedies, serial killer movies, gross violence and humor at the expense of women, children and minorities. No large science fiction, historical epics."
Tips: "All script ideas should be pitched in paragraph form to: Rory Aylward, VP Development, at fastcarriervp@aol.com."

FEURY/GRANT ENTERTAINMENT, 441 West End Ave. #10A, New York NY 10024-5328. (212)724-9290. Fax: (212)724-9233. **Contact:** Joseph Feury, executive producer. Estab. 1982. Buys all rights. Accepts previously produced material. Query with synopsis. **Pays negotiated option.**
Needs: Films.

JACK FREEDMAN PRODUCTIONS, 1093 Braxton Ave., Suite 228, Los Angeles CA 90024. (310)208-2200. E-mail: freedmanfilms@aol.com. **Contact:** Story Department. Estab. 1988. Commercial films. **Buys 0-10 script(s)/year. Works with 10-15 writer(s)/year.** Buys all rights. Query with synopsis via e-mail preferred, or provide SASE. Responds in 1 week to queries; 2 weeks to scripts. **Payment varies.**
Needs: Films (for theatrical).

GINTY FILMS, 16255 Ventura Blvd., Suite 625, Encino CA 91436. (310)277-1408. E-mail: rwginty@aol.com. Website: www.robertginty.com. **Contact:** Cheri Williams, assistant. Estab. 1989. Commercial audience. **Buys 12-15 script(s)/year. Works with 10-20 writer(s)/year.** Buys first rights, all rights. Accepts previously produced material. Query with synopsis, production history. Responds in 1 month to queries; 1 month to scripts. **Pays in accordance with WGA standards.**
Needs: Films.

STEPHAN GRAY, 205 S. Beverly Dr., Suite 212, Los Angeles CA 90212. (310)888-0090. E-mail: bhlit@cs.com. Website: www.beverlyhillslit.com. **Contact:** Stephan Gray, CEO, Producers: Richard Harding and Joe Medwar. **Works with 4-8 writer(s)/year.** Options scripts to package scripts for production only. Accepts previously produced material. Query with synopsis.
Needs: Films (35mm). "Most writers should review my website at www.beverlyhillslit.com and grayfoxfilms.com."

BETH GROSSBARD PRODUCTIONS, 9696 Culver Blvd., Suite 208, Culver City CA 90232. Fax: (310) 841-2555 or (310)841-5934. **Contact:** K. Jacobs, development associate; Beth Grossbard, executive producer. Estab. 1994. **Buys 12 script(s)/year. Works with 20+ writer(s)/year.** Buys first rights and true-life story rights. Query with synopsis, treatment/outline. Responds in 1 month to queries; 2 months to scripts. **Pays in accordance with WGA standards.**
Needs: Films (35 mm).
Tips: "Develops material for television, cable and feature film markets. Areas of interest include: true stories, literary material, family dramas, social issues, young adult themed and children's stories, historical/biographical accounts and legal issues. Will also consider plays, book proposals, small press books, or concept pages for film development."

[A] **HBO FILMS**, 2049 Century Park E., Suite 3600, Los Angeles CA 90067. Fax: (310)201-9552. Website: www.hbo.com. **Contact:** Kandace Williams, story editor HBO Films. Query with synopsis (1 page or shorter) *through agent or lawyer only.* No unrepresented writers. Do *not* email your query. Responds in 1 month to queries. **Payment varies.**
Needs: Features for TV. Looks at all genres except family films with children as main protagonists. Focus on socially

relevant material and true stories. "HBO looks for true stories, known people, controversy, politics, etc." "Not looking for standard movie-of-the-week fare. HBO Films does not do family films, straight 'genre' movies, broad comedies or high-budget action movies."

Tips: "Make sure industry standards are adhered to. Not interested in looking at work that is unprofessionally presented. Only submit synopsis if you have a true story or fiction completed script or book. Not interested in partially completed projects. You should send a 1-page synopsis only, through your agent or lawyer. Generally, HBO Films prefers nonfiction. Stories that have a political or social angle, are controversial, edgy or interesting above and beyond are the typical TV movie."

IFM FILM ASSOCIATES, INC., 1328 E. Palmer Ave., Glendale CA 91205-3738. (818)243-4976. Fax: (818)550-9728. Website: www.ifmfilm.com. **Contact:** Brad Benjamin, executive assistant. Estab. 1994. Film and television all media world wide. **Buys 10 script(s)/year. Works with 30 writer(s)/year.** Buys all rights. Catalog for SAE with $3. Query with synopsis. Responds in 1 month to queries; 3 months to scripts. **Pays in accordance with WGA standards.**

Needs: Films (35mm). Thrillers, family, action.

INTERNATIONAL HOME ENTERTAINMENT, 1440 Veteran Ave., Suite 650, Los Angeles CA 90024. (323)663-6940. **Contact:** Jed Leland, Jr., assistant to the president. Estab. 1976. Buys first rights. Query. Responds in 2 months to queries. **Pays in accordance with WGA standards.**

O‑ Looking for material that is international in scope.

Tips: "Our response time is faster on average now (3-6 weeks), but no replies without a SASE. No unsolicited mss. We do not respond to unsolicited phone calls or e-mail."

JOADA PRODUCTIONS, INC., 1437 Rising Glen Rd., Los Angeles CA 90069. **Contact:** Joan McCall, vp development; David Sheldon, president/producer. Estab. 1980. Produces feature films as well as movies for television. Query with synopsis, 2 pages and SASE.

Needs: "We look for all types of fresh and unique material, including comedy, family, suspense, drama, horror, sci-fi, thrillers, action-adventure."

Tips: "A synopsis should tell the entire story with the entire plot—including the beginning, the middle and the end. The producers have been in business with 20th Century Fox, Orion/MGM, Columbia Pictures and currently have contracts with Montel Williams and Paramount Pictures. Do not send scripts or books unless requested."

THE KAUFMAN CO., 12400 Wilshire Blvd., Los Angeles CA 90025. E-mail: submit@thekaufmancompany.com. Website: www.thekaufmancompany.com. **Contact:** Courtney Morrison, manager of development. Estab. 1990. Intended for all audiences. **Buys 5-10 script(s)/year. Works with 10 writer(s)/year.** Buys all rights. Query with synopsis. Responds in 3 weeks to queries; 3 months to scripts. **Pays in accordance with WGA standards.**

Needs: We option screenplays and mss for television, cable and film. "Must be a truly engaging story—no personal slice-of-life melodramas."

FRED KUEHNERT PRODUCTIONS, (formerly Skyline Partners), 10550 Wilshire Blvd., #1001, Los Angeles CA 90024. (310)470-3363. Fax: (310)470-0060. E-mail: fkuehnert@earthlink.com. **Contact:** Fred Kuehnert. Estab. 1990. Produces material for theatrical, television, video audiences. **Buys 3 script(s)/year.** Buys all rights. Query with synopsis. Responds to query/synopsis within 2 weeks and if script is requested will respond within 1 month. **Payment negotiable.**

Needs: Films (35mm).

Tips: "First, send a treatment so a determination can be made if the genre or concept is something we're looking for. Secondly, we will contact writer if there is preliminary interest. Thirdly, send complete script, plus release form."

LANCASTER GATE ENTERTAINMENT, 16001 Ventura Blvd., #110, Encino CA 91436. (818)995-6000. **Contact:** Brian K. Schlichter, vice president, development and production. Estab. 1989. Theatrical and television. **Works with dozens of writer(s)/year.** Rights purchased negotiable. Query. Responds in 1 month to queries. **Pays in accordance with WGA standards.**

Needs: Films (35-70 mm). Feature and television scripts, pitches.

N **LAST MINUTE PRODUCTIONS**, 2515 Astral Dr., Los Angeles CA 90046. **Contact:** Henry Bloomstein. Last Minute Productions, the low budget/independent division of Red Hots Entertainment, favors horror, thrillers, urban culture dramas and comedies that can be filmed on a restricted economical budget, $500,000-1.5 million.

ARNOLD LEIBOVIT ENTERTAINMENT, P.O. Box 261, Cedar City UT 84721. E-mail: director@scifistation.com. Website: www.scifistation.com. **Contact:** Barbara Schimpf, vice president, production; Arnold Leibovit, director/producer. Estab. 1988. Produces material for motion pictures and television. **Works with 1 writer(s)/year.** Query with synopsis. A submission release must be included with all queries. Responds in 2 months to queries. **Pays in accordance with WGA standards.**

Needs: Films (35mm), videotapes. "Prefers high concept, mixed genres, comedy, adventure, science fiction/fantasy, as well as unusual, visually rich, character-driven smaller works with unusual twists, comic sensibility, pathos, and always the unexpected." Does not want novels, plays, poems, treatments; no submissions on disk.

Tips: "New policy: Submission of logline and synopsis for evaluation first. Do not send scripts until we ask for them. An Arnold Leibovit Entertainment release form must be completed and returned with material. Accepting loglines via e-mail."

LEO FILMS, 6249 Langdon Ave., Van Nuys CA 91411. (323)666-7140. Fax: (323)666-7414. E-mail: lustgar@pacbell.net. Website: www.leofilms.com. **Contact:** Steve Lustgarten, president. Estab. 1989. Feature/film. **Buys 2 script(s)/year. Works with 2 writer(s)/year.** Buys all rights. Accepts previously produced material. Query with synopsis. Responds in 1 month to queries; 2 months to scripts. **Payment varies—options and sales.**

Needs: Films (35 mm). "Looking for good stories-honor, urban, action."
Tips: E-mail first if available. "Will also consider novels, short stories and treatments that have true movie potential."

LOCKWOOD FILMS (LONDON), INC., 12569 Boston Dr., RR #41, London ON N6H 5L2, Canada. (519)657-3994. Fax: (519)657-3994. E-mail: nancycjohnson@hotmail.com. **Contact:** Nancy Johnson, president. Estab. 1974. Entertainment and general broadcast for kids 9-12 and family viewing. **Works with 5-6 writer(s)/year.** Query with synopsis, résumé, writing samples. Submissions will not be considered without a signed proposal agreement; we will send one upon receiving submissions. **Pays negotiated fee.**
Needs: Family entertainment: series, seasonal specials, mini-series, and MOW. Also feature films, documentaries.
Tips: "Potential contributors should have a fax machine and should be prepared to sign a 'proposal submission agreement.' We are in development with national broadcaster on live-action family drama series. Looking for international co-production opportunities. Writers from the US sending proposals with a SASE with American postage should understand we can not mad., Suite 525, Los Angeles CA 90025-3339. E-mail: rrobinson@randwell.com. Website: www.randwell.com. **Contact:** Tom Kageff, vice president. Estab. 1997. TV and features audience. **Buys 3-4 script(s)/year. Works with 2-3 writer(s)/year.** Buys all rights. Query with synopsis. Responds in 2 weeks to queries; 3 months to scripts. **Pays in accordance with WGA standards.**
Needs: Films (35mm). Good character pieces with a strong plot and/or strong concepts. No sci-fi, no westerns.
Tips: "Please keep synopsis to no more than one page. We hardly if ever request a copy of unsolicited material so don't be surprised if we pass."

MARSHAK/ZACHARY, 8840 Wilshire Blvd., 1st Floor, Beverly Hills CA 90211. Fax: (310)358-3192. E-mail: zacharyent@aol.com. **Contact:** Alan W. Mills, associate. Estab. 1981. Audience is film goers of all ages, television viewers. **Buys 3-5 script(s)/year. Works with 10 writer(s)/year.** Rights purchased vary. Query with synopsis. Responds in 2 weeks to queries; 3 months to scripts. **Payment varies.**
Needs: Films for theatrical, cable, and network television release.
Tips: "Submit logline (1-line description) and a short synopsis of storyline. Short biographical profile, focus on professional background. SASE required for all mailed inquiries. If submissions are sent via e-mail, subject must include specific information or else run the risk of being deleted as junk mail. All genres accepted, but ideas must be commercially viable, high concept, original, and marketable."

MEDIACOM DEVELOPMENT CORP., P.O. Box 73033, Las Vegas NV 89170-3033. (702)991-9011. Fax: (248)282-0764. E-mail: fgirard@mail.com. Website: www.mediacorp.org. **Contact:** Felix Girard, director/program development. Estab. 1978. **Buys 8-12 script(s)/year.** Buys all rights or first rights. Query with writing samples. Responds in 1 month to queries. **Negotiates payment depending on project.**
Needs: Films, videotapes, multimedia kits, tapes and cassettes. Publishes software ("programmed instruction training courses"). Looking for new ideas for CD-ROM and DVD titles.
Tips: "E-mail brief query before sending material. Especially interested in flexibility to meet clients' demands, creativity in treatment of precise subject matter. We are looking for good, fresh projects (both special and series) for cable and pay television markets. A trend in the audiovisual field that freelance writers should be aware of is the move toward more interactive video disc/computer CRT delivery of training materials for corporate markets."

MICHAEL MELTZER PRODUCTIONS, 12207 Riverside Dr., #208, Valley Village CA 91607. (818)766-8339. Fax: (818)766-5936. E-mail: melmax@aol.com. **Contact:** Michael Meltzer, producer. Query with synopsis. Responds in 1 month to queries; 2 months to scripts.
Needs: Films (35 mm).

MONAREX HOLLYWOOD CORP., 11605 W. Pico Blvd., Suite 200, Los Angeles CA 90064. (310)478-6666. Fax: (310)478-6866. E-mail: monarexcorp@aol.com. **Contact:** Chris D. Nebe, president. Estab. 1978. All audiences. **Buys 3-4 script(s)/year. Works with 5-10 writer(s)/year.** Buys all rights. Query with synopsis. Responds in 1 month to queries. **Pays in accordance with WGA standards.**
Needs: Films (35mm), videotapes, DVD. Needs dramatic material with strong visuals, action, horror, dance, romantic comedies, anything commercially viable. "We are only interested in screenplays. We are interested to acquire completed films of all genres."

MWG PRODUCTIONS, 8075 West 3rd St., Suite 402, Los Angeles CA 90048. (323)937-8313. Fax: (323)937-5239. E-mail: wynne9@aol.com. Website: www.alaskadq.com. **Contact:** Max Goldenson, executive producer. Estab. 1981. **Buys 3 script(s)/year. Works with 10 writer(s)/year.** Buys all rights. Accepts previously produced material. Query with synopsis, résumé. Responds in 1 month to queries; 3 months to scripts. **Pays in accordance with WGA standards.**
Needs: Films, videotapes, multimedia kits.

NHO ENTERTAINMENT, 11962 Darlington Ave., Los Angeles CA 90049. E-mail: mark.costa@nhoentertainment.com; ford.oelman@nhoentertainment.com. Website: www.nhoentertainment.com. **Contact:** Mark Costa, partner. Estab. 1999. All audiences. **Buys 5 script(s)/year. Works with 10 writer(s)/year.** Buys all rights. Accepts previously produced material. Catalog for #10 SASE. Query with synopsis, résumé, writing samples, production history. Via e-mail. Responds in 1 month to queries. **Pays in accordance with WGA standards.**
Needs: Films, videotapes, multimedia kits, tapes and cassettes. "We are currently accepting all forms of submissions and encourage all writers with material to e-mail query letters."

POP/ART FILM FACTORY, 513 Wilshire Blvd., Suite 215, Santa Monica CA 90401. E-mail: dzpff@earthlink.net. Website: www.home.earthlink.net/~dzpff. **Contact:** Daniel Zirilli, CEO/director. Estab. 1990. Produces material for "all audiences/feature films." Query with synopsis. **Pays on per project basis.**

Needs: Films (35mm), multimedia kits, documentaries. "Looking for interesting productions of all kinds. We're producing 3 feature films/year, and 15-20 music-oriented projects. Also exercise and other special interest videos."
Tips: "Send a query/pitch letter and let me know if you are willing to write on spec (for the first job only; you will be paid if the project is produced). Be original. Do not play it safe. If you don't receive a response from anyone you have ever sent your ideas to, or you continually get rejected, don't give up if you believe in yourself. Good luck and keep writing!" Will look at "reels" (3⁄4 or VHS).

PROMARK ENTERTAINMENT GROUP, 3599 Cahuenga Blvd. W., Los Angeles CA 90026. (323)878-0404. Fax: (323)878-0486. E-mail: gwishnick@promarkgroup.com. **Contact:** Gil-Adrienne Wishnick, vice president development. Promark is a foreign sales company, producing theatrical films for the foreign market. **Buys 8-10 script(s)/year. Works with 8-10 writer(s)/year.** Buys all rights. Query with synopsis (shorter is better). Responds in 1 month to queries; 2 months to scripts. **Makes outright purchase.**
Needs: "Promark is currently looking for low budget, science fiction action tales that are based on a documented event or generally accepted, supernatural lore, such as vampires. We are also looking for family film scripts for our two family lines, mostly high concept comedies for the entire family. We will still consider an action thriller, but only as a co-production or if there are strong attachments."

THE PUPPETOON STUDIOS, P.O. Box 261, Cedar City UT 84721. E-mail: director@scifistation.com. Website: www.scifistation.com. **Contact:** Arnold Leibovit, director/producer. Estab. 1987. "Broad audience." **Works with 1 writer(s)/year.** Query with synopsis. Submission release required with all queries. Do not send script unless requested. Responds in 2 month to queries. **Pays in accordance with WGA standards.**
Needs: Films (35mm). "We are seeking animation properties including presentation drawings and character designs. The more detailed drawings with animation scripts the better. Always looking for fresh broad audience material." No novels, plays, poems, treatments; no submissions on disk.

RANDWELL PRODUCTIONS, INC., 11111 Santa Monica Blvd., Suite 525, Los Angeles CA 90025-3339. E-mail: rrobinson@randwell.com. Website: www.randwell.com. **Contact:** Tom Kageff, vice president. Estab. 1997. TV and features audience. **Buys 3-4 script(s)/year. Works with 2-3 writer(s)/year.** Buys all rights. Query with synopsis. Responds in 2 weeks to queries; 3 months to scripts. **Pays in accordance with WGA standards.**
Needs: Films (35mm). Good character pieces with a strong plot and/or strong concepts. No sci-fi, no westerns.
Tips: "Please keep synopsis to no more than one page. We hardly if ever request a copy of unsolicited material so don't be surprised if we pass."

RED HOTS ENTERTAINMENT, 3105 Amigos Dr., Burbank CA 91504-1806. E-mail: chipdaniel2@excite.com. **Contact:** Kit Gleason, head story editor, Senior Vice President/Creative Director: Dan Pomeroy. Producer/Director: Chip Miller. Estab. 1990. **Buys 1 script(s)/year. Works with 1-2 writer(s)/year.** Buys first and all rights. No previously produced material. Query with synopsis, release form, personal bio, SASE. Responds in 5 months to queries; 6 months to scripts. **Pays in accordance with WGA standards. Negotiable on writer's previous credits, etc.**
Needs: Films (16 and 35mm), videotapes. "We are a feature film and television and music video production company and have no audiovisual material needs."
Tips: "Best advice possible: originality, uniqueness, write from your instincts and don't follow trends. Screenplays and T.V. scripts should be mailed to our Burbank, CA production office with a proper industry release form, a 1-page synopsis, and SASE, please. No hi-tech stories, fatal disease things. Looking for youth-driven material and solid literate material with unique premise and characters with substance. No period themes."

EDGAR J. SCHERICK ASSOCIATES, 1950 Sawtelle Blvd., Suite 282, Los Angeles CA 90025. (310)996-2376. E-mail: ejsa@msn.com. **Contact:** Stephen Abronson, director of development. Network and cable TV, theatrical audience. **Buys 3 script(s)/year. Works with 10 writer(s)/year.** Buys all rights. Accepts previously produced material. Query with synopsis.
Needs: Historical pieces and biopics. "We are looking for dramas, thrillers and mysteries."

N **SILENT SOUND FILMS, LTD.**, United Kingdom. E-mail: thj@silentsoundfilms.co.uk. Website: www.silentsoundfilms.co.uk. **Contact:** Timothy Foster, MD. Estab. 1997. Stage and fiction movies only. No TV or publishing. "We usually originate our own material, but will usually start with outside material by optioning the work." No previously produced material. Query with synopsis. Responds in 2 weeks to queries; 1-2 months to scripts. **Writers paid in accordance with WGA standards or the UK 'pact' agreement, if British production.**
Needs: Films (35mm). "We are interested in excellent writing (anything from musicals to mysteries to social dramas) with developed plot themes and original characters. So if you have a story that is nonparochial, we would be interested to see an e-mailed package that comprises: a one-page synopsis, no more than eight pages of scenario, and a brief biography. Do not send images, complete screenplays or large attachments. To put it plainly, we haven't got time to enter into correspondence on submissions that we don't want to take further. If it's something that grabs our attention, you will certainly hear from us." Does not want "U.S.-based movies, nor storylines with principally American characters set anywhere else. Nothing personal, it's just that we are involved in what is unreliably called art house films and the best American art house films are made by Americans. So why compete?"
Tips: "Firstly, if you want to make a good impression, follow the submission guidelines closely. I have often noticed that flashy headed notepaper covered with hype can precede a stereotypical and predictable scenario. And believe me a scenario is the hardest thing to write. Good writers embark upon their trade with humility. This is reflected too by a simple submission note accompanying the material. The type of writer who believes in having to 'pitch an idea' will be better off trying elsewhere. We seek material that may well include a good 'pitchable idea' but also one that goes a lot deeper. I suppose

the filmic equivalent of literature as opposed to bestseller. Great writing is rare, but we know it when we see it. Good luck to everyone!"

SILVER LION FILMS, 701 Santa Monica Blvd., Suite 240, Santa Monica CA 90401. (310)393-9177. Fax: (310)458-9372. E-mail: dkz@silverlinefilms.com. **Contact:** David Kohner Zuckerman, director of development. Estab. 1988. General audience. Query. Responds in 3 months to queries; 6 months to scripts. **Pays percentage of budget.**

Needs: Films (35mm), TV/cable mow's and TV series pitches.

ALAN SMITHEE FILMS, 7510 Sunset Blvd., #525, Hollywood CA 90046. Website: www.smithee.com/films. **Contact:** Cinjun Sinclair, story analyst; Fred Smythe, director. Estab. 1990. Mass, cable television and theatrical releases. **Buys 1 script(s)/year. Works with 5 writer(s)/year.** Buys first or all rights, or options short-term. No previously produced material. Query with synopsis. Responds in 2 months to queries. **Pays in accordance with WGA standards.**

Needs: Films (35mm), videotapes. Wants internationally marketable material. No specific needs, varies constantly with market.

Tips: "There is no 'best bet.' It's a competitive market. Our needs are slave to the ups and downs of the industry."

SOUTH FORK PRODUCTIONS, P.O. Box 1935, Santa Monica CA 90406-1935. Fax: (310)829-5029. E-mail: sullivanprods@ireland.com. **Contact:** Jim Sullivan, producer. Estab. 1980. Produces material for TV and film. **Buys 2 script(s)/year. Works with 4 writer(s)/year.** Buys all rights. Query with synopsis, résumé, SASE. **Pays in accordance with WGA standards.**

O→ South Fork is currently looking for Irish-based scripts.

Needs: Films (16, 35mm), videotapes.

Tips: "Follow established formats for treatments. SASE for return."

STARLIGHT PICTURES, 1725 S. Rainbow Blvd., #2-186, Las Vegas NV 89102. E-mail: ideamaster@aol.com. **Contact:** Brian McNeal, development executive. Estab. 1989. Audience is world-wide movie-going public. **Buys 3 script(s)/year. Works with 3 writer(s)/year.** Buys all rights. Accepts previously produced material. Query with synopsis. Responds in 3 months to queries; 4 months to scripts. **Pays in accordance with WGA standards or sometimes an option against larger purchase amounts.**

Needs: Films (35 mm). "Not necessarily looking at this time, but 'good' scripts will always get our attention. Prefer well-written dramatic scripts set in *any* genre."

Tips: "It is sad to say that Hollywood is inundated with scripts by writers that possess 7th grade writing skills. This makes it harder for the 'good' scripts by real writers to get noticed. Please learn your craft before submitting material."

STUDIO MERRYWOOD, a division of EduMedia, 125 Putnam Ave., Suite 232, Hamden CT 06517-2899. (203)407-8793. Fax: (203)407-8794. E-mail: rdsetc@att.net. Website: www.enaware.com/bardsworld/bardswb.html. **Contact:** Raúl daSilva, CEO/creative director. Estab. 1984. Produces feature films, TV series, documentaries. "We are not seeking any externally written screenplays for features but will engage produced screenwriters as consultants if they have been further recognized in the industry through leadership or international competitive festival prizes."

Needs: "Currently, no external material is sought. This may change. Thus, seasoned, professional writers may e-mail us for a status on needs. As in Tips, below, please lead your e-mail letter with a paragraph on your qualifications."

Tips: "This is not a market for novice writers. We are a small, creative shop and cannot train neophyte, unpublished or unproduced writers who would best try larger markets and media facilities. We cannot return or even acknowledge any unsolicited material and will discard such material. Those qualified please contact us first by e-mail with your qualifications and your offerings."

TOO NUTS PRODUCTIONS, L.P., A Division of Creative Hive, LLC, 1511 Sawtelle Blvd., Suite 288, Los Angeles CA 90025. (310)979-3343. E-mail: buzzus@creativehivegroup.com. Website: www.creativehivegroup.com. **Contact:** Ralph Scott, president/co-executive producer. Estab. 1994. Audience is children. **Buys 4-10 script(s)/year. Works with 4-6 writer(s)/year.** Buys both first and all rights. Query with synopsis, résumé, writing samples, production history. Responds in 3 months to queries; 6 months to scripts. **Pays royalty, makes outright purchase.**

Needs: Videotapes, multimedia kits, tapes and cassettes, CD-ROMs. Audio books and half-hour television edutation with a twist. Storylines for our current television and multimedia state, including "Toad Pizza," "The Salivating Salamander," "The Contest-Ants," "Anonymouse," etc.

Tips: "Suggestion: Use the words 'Too Nuts' at least twice in your query. If you don't know how to giggle all the way to the bank, don't contact us. If you've already exorcised your inner child, don't contact us either!"

VANGUARD PRODUCTIONS, 12111 Beatrice St., Culver City CA 90230. **Contact:** Terence M. O'Keefe, president. Estab. 1985. **Buys 1 script(s)/year.** Buys all rights. Accepts previously produced material. Query with synopsis, résumé. Responds in 3 months to queries; 6 months to scripts. **Pays in accordance with WGA standards. Negotiated option.**

Needs: Films (35mm), videotapes.

WOODBERRY PRODUCTIONS, 3410 Descanso Dr., Suite 4, Los Angeles CA 90026. (323)668-9170. E-mail: lindagrae@aol.com. **Contact:** Linda Graeme, producer. Estab. 1994. Drama producer—film and TV. **Works with 2-3 writer(s)/year.** Options film & TV rights only. Query with synopsis, writing samples. Responds in 1 month to queries; 3 months to scripts. **Pays in accordance with WGA standards.**

Needs: Drama production for film and TV. Looking for character-driven dramatic material. Usual 2-hour. No big-budget, high-action studio fare.

Tips: Break in with a "letter/email with short and concise description of project, plus brief rundown of writing history."

THE WOOFENILL WORKS, INC., 516 E. 81st St., Suite #3, New York NY 10028-2530. (212)734-2578. Fax: (212)734-3186. E-mail: woofenill@earthlink.net. Website: home.earthlink.net/~woofenill/. **Contact:** Kathy Winthrop, creative executive. Estab. 1992. Theatrical motion pictures. **Buys 2-4 script(s)/year.** Buys all rights. Query with synopsis. Responds in 1 month to queries. **Acquires option, then payment on production.**
Needs: Films (35mm). Do not send e-mail or scripts unless requested.
Tips: "We suggest that interested writers first review the company's website and in particular, the section General Business Parameters."

Contests & Awards

The contests and awards listed in this section are arranged by subject. Nonfiction writers can turn immediately to nonfiction awards listed alphabetically by the name of the contest or award. The same is true for fiction writers, poets, playwrights and screenwriters, journalists, children's writers, and translators. You'll also find general book awards, fellowships offered by arts councils and foundations, and multiple category contests.

New contests and awards are announced in various writer's publications nearly every day. However, many lose their funding or fold—and sponsoring magazines go out of business just as often. We have contacted the organizations whose contests and awards are listed here with the understanding that they are valid through 2004-2005. If you are using this section in 2006 or later, keep in mind that much of the contest information listed here will not be current. Requirements such as entry fees change, as do deadlines, addresses, and contact names. **Contact names**, **entry fees**, and **deadlines** have been highlighted and set in bold type for your convenience.

To make sure you have all the information you need about a particular contest, always send a SASE to the contact person in the listing before entering a contest. The listings in this section are brief, and many contests have lengthy, specific rules and requirements that we could not include in our limited space. Often a specific entry form must accompany your submission. A response with rules and guidelines will not only provide specific instructions, it will also confirm that the award is still being offered.

When you receive a set of guidelines, you will see that some contests are not for some writers. The writer's age, previous publication, geographic location, and length of the work are common matters of eligibility. Read the requirements carefully to ensure you don't enter a contest for which you are not qualified. You should also be aware that every year, more and more contests, especially those sponsored by "little" literary magazines, are charging entry fees.

Contest and award competition is very strong. While a literary magazine may publish ten short stories in an issue, only one will win the prize in a contest. Give yourself the best chance of winning by sending only your best work. There is always a percentage of manuscripts cast off immediately as unpolished, amateurish, or wholly unsuitable for the competition.

To avoid first-round rejection, make certain that you and your work qualify in every way for the award. Some contests are more specific than others. There are many contests and awards for a "best poem," but some award only the best lyric poem, sonnet, or haiku.

Winning a contest or award can launch a successful writing career. Take a professional ap-

For More Information

The following resources provide additional listings of contests and awards:

- *Novel & Short Story Writer's Market* (Writer's Digest Books)—fiction.
- *Poet's Market* (Writer's Digest Books)—poetry.
- *Children's Writer's & Illustrator's Market* (Writer's Digest Books)—children's.
- *The Writer's Chronicle* (The Associated Writing Programs)—literary.
- *Editor & Publisher*'s annual Journalism Awards Issue (published in the last week of December)—journalism.
- The Dramatists Guild's *Resource Directory*—playwriting.

proach by doing a little extra research. Find out who the previous winner of the award was by investing in a sample copy of the magazine in which the prize-winning article, poem, or short story appeared. Attend the staged reading of an award-winning play. Your extra effort will be to your advantage in competing with writers who simply submit blindly.

If a contest or award requires nomination by your publisher, ask your publisher to nominate you. Many welcome the opportunity to promote a work (beyond their own conventional means). Just be sure the publisher has plenty of time before the deadline to nominate your work.

Information on contests and awards listed in the previous edition of *Writer's Market* but not included in this edition can be found in the General Index.

General

THE ANISFIELD-WOLF BOOK AWARDS, The Cleveland Foundation, 1422 Euclid Ave., Suite 1300, Cleveland OH 44115. (216)861-3810. Fax: (216)861-2229. E-mail: contactus@clevefdn.org. Website: www.anisfield-wolf.org. **Contact:** Marcia Bryant. "The Anisfield-Wolf Book Award annually honors books which contribute to our understanding of racism or our appreciation of the diversity of human culture published during the year of the award." Judged by a 5-member panel chaired by Dr. Henry Louis Gates of Harvard University and including Joyce Carol Oates, Rita Dove, Steven Pinker, and Simon Schama. Any work addressing issues of racial bias or human diversity may qualify. **Deadline: January 31.** Guidelines for SASE. Prize: $20,000 divided among the winners.

ARTSLINK PROJECTS AWARD, CEC International Partners, 12 W. 31st St., New York NY 10001. (212)643-1985, ext. 22. Fax: (212)643-1996. E-mail: artslink@cecip.org. Website: www.cecip.org. **Contact:** Jennifer Gullace, ArtsLink coordinator. Offered annually to enable artists of all media to work in Central and Eastern Europe with colleagues there on collaborative projects. Check website for deadline and other information. Prize: Up to $10,000.

BANTA AWARD, Wisconsin Library Association, c/o Literary Awards Committee, 5250 E. Terrace Dr., Suite A-1, Madison WI 53718-8345. (608)245-3640. Website: www.wla.lib.wi.us. **Contact:** Chair, Literary Award Committee. Offered annually for books published during the year preceding the award. The Literary Awards Committee reviews all works by Wisconsin authors that are not edited, revised editions, textbooks, or written in foreign languages. Review copies or notification of books, along with verification of the author's ties to Wisconsin, may be submitted to the Committee, by the publisher or author. Only open to writers born, raised, or currently living in Wisconsin. **Deadline: March of calendar year following publication.** Prize: $500, a trophy given by the Banta Corporation Foundation, and presentation at the Annual Conference of the Wisconsin Library Association between late October and early November.

N **BBC WILDLIFE MAGAZINE NATURE WRITING AWARD**, *BBC Wildlife Magazine*, Broadcasting House, Whiteladies Rd., Bristol BS8 2LR, United Kingdom. +44 (0)117 973 8402. Fax: +44 (0)117 946 7075. E-mail: nina.epton@bbc.co.uk. **Contact:** Nina Epton. Offered annually for unpublished work. "We are looking for new and established writers who are able to capture their observations of and feelings about nature on paper. The main conditions are that the essay should not be pure fiction, a poem, or written from an animal's point of view. It should not exceed 800 words. There are 4 categories: adult amateur, adult professional/semi-professional, young essay writer (age 13-17), young essay writer (age 12 or under). Entrants must buy the relevant copy of *BBC Wildlife Magazine* containing the entry form and rules. This is usually our May issue, but it's best to check with the office first." Prize-winners in this competition grant, free of charge, the right for all or part of their essay to be published, broadcast, transmitted, and read in all media (now known or hereafter created), or on stage, in connection with this competition. This includes the right for the essays to be published in *BBC Wildlife* (or any resulting anthology) and syndicated, if the organizers so wish. **Deadline: Varies from year to year (usually the end of June). Best to contact the office and ask for details.** Guidelines for SASE. Prize: Varies slightly from year to year. Normally a top prize of £1,000 for the overall winner. If the winner is a professional or semi-professional writer, there will also be a £200 prize for the best essay by an amateur. Runners-up (to a maximum of 6) will each win £150. The winning essays will be published in *BBC Wildlife Magazine*. Open to any writer.

THE BOARDMAN TASKER AWARD FOR MOUNTAIN LITERATURE, The Boardman Tasker Charitable Trust, Pound House, Llangennith, Swansea Wales, UK. (00 44) 1792-386-215. Fax: (00 44) 1792-386-215. E-mail: margaretbody@lineone.net. Website: www.boardmantasker.com. **Contact:** Margaret Body. Offered annually to reward a work of nonfiction or fiction, in English or in translation, which has made an outstanding contribution to mountain literature. Books must be published in the UK between November 1 of previous year and October 31 of year of the prize. Writers may obtain information, but entry is by publishers only. "No restriction of nationality, but work must be published or distributed in the UK." **Deadline: August 1.** Guidelines for SASE. Prize: £2,000.

N **DAFOE BOOK PRIZE**, J.W. Dafoe Foundation, 359 University College, University of Manitoba, Winnipeg MB R3T 2M8, Canada. **Contact:** Dr. James Fergusson. The Dafoe Book Prize was "established to honor John Dafoe, editor of the Winnipeg Free Press from 1900 to 1944, and is awarded each year to the book that best contributes to our understanding of Canada and/or its relations abroad." Books must be previously published January-December of contest year. Co-authored books are eligible, but not edited books consisting of chapters from many different authors. Submit 4 copies of book. **Deadline: December 6.** Prize: $10,000. Judged by board members and academics.

DEBUT DAGGER, Crime Writers' Association, New Writing Competition, P.O. Box 63, Wakefield WF2 0YW, England. E-mail: debutdagger@thecwa.co.uk. Website: www.thecwa.co.uk. An annual competition for unpublished crime writers. Submit the opening 3,000 words of a crime novel, plus a 500-word synopsis of its continuence. The 2003 competition, sponsored by Orion, is open between March and September. **Charges £10/entry.** Prize: £250 cash, and silver Dagger pin to be presented at the Dagger Awards Ceremony in November.

THE RALPH WALDO EMERSON AWARD, The Phi Beta Kappa Society, 1606 New Hampshire Ave. NW, Washington DC 20009. (202)265-3808. Fax: (202)986-1601. E-mail: ccurtis@pbk.org. Website: www.pbk.org/scholarships/books. **Contact:** Ms. Cameron Curtis. Estab. 1960. "The Ralph Waldo Emerson Award is offered annually for scholarly studies that contribute significantly to interpretations of the intellectual and cultural condition of humanity. This award may recognize work in the fields of history, philosophy, and religion; these fields are conceived in sufficiently broad terms to permit the inclusion of appropriate work in related fields such as anthropology and the social sciences. Biographies of public figures may be eligible if their critical emphasis is primarily on the intellectual and cultural condition of humanity." Work must have appeared in print May 1, 2002-April 30, 2003. Entries must be submitted by the publisher. Entries must be preceded by a letter certifying that the book(s) conforms to all the conditions of eligibility and stating the publication date of each entry. If accepted, 8 copies of each entry are required for the Emerson Award. Ineligible entries will be returned by Phi Beta Kappa. Books will not be entered officially in the competition until all copies and the letter of certification have been received. **Deadline: April 30.** Prize: $2,500. Judged by a rotating panel of distinguished scholars and experts in the field. Open to US residents only.

THE MARIAN ENGEL AWARD, The Writers' Trust of Canada, 40 Wellington St. E., Suite 300, Toronto ON M5E 1C7, Canada. (416)504-8222. Fax: (416)504-9090. E-mail: info@writerstrust.com. Website: www.writerstrust.com. **Contact:** Sharon Poitras. The Engel Award is presented annually at the Great Literary Awards Event, held in Tornoto each Spring, to a female Canadian writer for a body of work in hope of continued contribution to the richness of Canadian literature. Prize: $10,000. Open to Canadian residents only.

THE TIMOTHY FINDLEY AWARD, The Writers' Trust of Canada, 40 Wellington St. E., Suite 300, Toronto ON M5E 1C7, Canada. (416)504-8222. Fax: (416)504-9090. E-mail: info@writerstrust.com. Website: www.writerstrust.com. **Contact:** Sharon Poitras. The Findley Award is presented annually at The Great Literary Awards Event held in Toronto each spring, to a male Canadian writer for a body of work in hope of continued contribution to the richness of Canadian literature. Prize: $10,000. Open to Canadian residents only.

FOREWORD MAGAZINE BOOK OF THE YEAR AWARDS, ForeWord Magazine. (231)933-3699. E-mail: karen@forewordmagazine.com. Website: www.forewordmagazine.com. **Contact:** Karen Connick. Annual. Eligibility: Must have 2002 copyright. **Deadline: January 15.** Prize: $1,500 cash prize will be awarded to a Best Fiction and Best Nonfiction choice as determined by the editors of *ForeWord Magazine*. Judged by a jury of librarians, booksellers and reviewers who are selected to judge the categories for entry and select winners and finalists based on editorial excellence and professional production as well as the originality of the narrative and the value the books adds to its genre. Open to any writer.

FRONTIERS IN WRITING, Panhandle Professional Writers, P.O. Box 19303, Amarillo TX 79114. E-mail: pcs@arn.net. Website: users.arn.net/~ppw. Offered annually for unpublished work to encourage new writers and to bring them to the attention of the publishing industry. **Deadline: March 1.** Guidelines for SASE. **Charges varying fee.** Prize: Varies, see guidelines.

THE JANE GESKE AWARD, *Prairie Schooner*, 201 Andrews Hall, P.O. Box 880334, Lincoln NE 68588-0334. (402)472-0911. Fax: (402)472-9771. E-mail: eflanagan2@unl.edu. Website: www.unl.edu/schooner/psmain.htm. **Contact:** Hilda Raz. Offered annually for work published in *Prairie Schooner* in the previous year. Prize: $250. Open to any writer.

INDEPENDENT PUBLISHER BOOK AWARDS, Jenkins Group/Independent Publisher Online, 400 W. Front St., #4A, Traverse City MI 49684. (231)933-4954, ext. 1011. Fax: (231)933-0448. E-mail: jimb@bookpublishing.com. Website: www.independentpublisher.com. **Contact:** Jim Barnes. "The Independent Publisher Book Awards were conceived as a broad-based, unaffiliated awards program open to all members of the independent publishing industry. The staff at *Independent Publisher* magazine saw the need to bring increased recognition to the thousands of exemplary independent, university, and self-published titles produced each year. The IPPY Awards reward those who exhibit the courage, innovation, and creativity to bring about change in the world of publishing. Independent spirit and expertise comes from publishers of all areas and budgets, and we judge books with that in mind. For 20 years our mission at *Independent Publisher* has been to recognize and encourage the work of publishers who exhibit the courage and creativity necessary to take chances, break new ground, and bring about changes, not only to the world of publishing, but to our society, our environment, and our collective spirit. Entries will be accepted in 52 categories, including 3 new ones this year: aging/death & dying, psychology/mental health, historical/military fiction." Offered annually for books published between January 1 and December 31. **Deadline: April 15.** Guidelines for SASE. **Charges $50 until November 15; $55 until January 15; $60 until April 15.** Prize: $500 and a trophy to 1 book in each of the following categories: Most Original Concept; Best Corporate Branding Book; Best Book Arts Craftsmanship; Most Inspirational to Youth; Best Health Book; Most Likely to Save the Planet; Most Unique Design; Story Teller of the Year; Most Life-Changing; Business Breakthrough of the Year. Judged by a panel of experts representing the fields of design, writing, bookselling, library, and reviewing. Open to any writer.

JACK KAVANAGH MEMORIAL YOUTH BASEBALL RESEARCH AWARD, Society for American Baseball Research (SABR), 812 Huron Rd. E., #719, Cleveland OH 44115. (216)575-0500. Fax: (216)575-0502. E-mail: education@sabr.org. Website: www.sabr.org. **Contact:** Rodney Johnson, contest/award director. Offered annually for unpublished work. Purpose is to stimulate interest in baseball research by youth under age of 21. Deadline is typically 1 month prior to our

National Convention, usually held in late June or early July. Guidelines for SASE. Prize: Award is $200 cash prize, publication in *SABR Journal* and/or website, 3-year SABR membership, plaque honoring award. Up to 3 finalists also receive 1-year SABR membership. Judged by the Youth/Education Awards Committee. Acquires nonexclusive rights to SABR to publish the entrants' submissions in printed and/or electronic form.

DOROTHEA LANGE—PAUL TAYLOR PRIZE, Center for Documentary Studies at Duke University, 1317 W. Pettigrew St., Durham NC 27705. (919)660-3663. Fax: (919)681-7600. E-mail: alexad@duke.edu. Website: cds.aas.duke.edu/l-t/. **Contact:** Alexa Dilworth. Offered annually to "promote the collaboration between a writer and a photographer in the formative or fieldwork stages of a documentary project. Collaborative submissions on any subject are welcome." Guidelines for SASE or on website. **Deadline: January 31.** Submissions accepted during January only. Prize: $10,000.

FENIA AND YAAKOV LEVIANT MEMORIAL PRIZE, Modern Language Association of America, 26 Broadway, 3rd Floor, New York NY 10004-1789. (646)576-5141. Fax: (646)458-0030. E-mail: awards@mla.org. Website: www.mla.org. **Contact:** Annie Reiser, coordinator of book prizes and special projects. This prize is to honor, in alternating years, an outstanding English translation of a Yiddish literary work or an outstanding scholarly work in any language in the field of Yiddish. Offered every two years. In 2004, it will be awarded to a scholarly work published between 1999 and 2003. In 2005 it will be awarded to a translation published between 2002 and 2005. Open to MLA members and nonmembers. Authors or publishers may submit titles. Guidelines for SASE or by e-mail. **Deadline: May 1, 2004.** Prize: $500, and a certificate, to be presented at the Modern Language Association's annual convention in December.

N THE GLENNA LUSCHEI PRAIRIE SCHOONER AWARD, *Prairie Schooner*, 201 Andrews Hall, P.O. Box 880334, Lincoln NE 68588-0334. (402)472-0911. Fax: (402)472-9771. E-mail: eflanagan2@unl.edu. Website: www.unl.edu/schooner/psmain.htm. **Contact:** Hilda Raz. Offered annually for work published in *Prairie Schooner* in the previous year. Prize: $1,000. Open to any writer.

N THE GRANT MACEWAN YOUNG WRITER'S SCHOLARSHIP, Alberta Community Development, 9th Floor Standard Life Centre, 10405 Jasper Ave., Edmonton AB T5J 4R7, Canada. Website: www.cd.gov.ab.ca. This annual award was created by the government of Alberta to honor the life and contributions of the late Dr. Grant MacEwan. Open to young Alberta writers (16-25) who create a literary work reflecting Alberta and/or Dr. MacEwan's interests. **Deadline: December 31.** Guidelines for SASE. Prize: 4 scholarships of $2,500 each. Judged by a panel of Alberta authors and educators.

MISSISSIPPI REVIEW PRIZE, *Mississippi Review*, U.S.M. Box 5144, Hattiesburg MS 39406. (601)266-4321. Fax: (601)266-5757. E-mail: rief@netdoor.com. Website: www.mississippireview.com. **Contact:** Rie Fortenberry, contest director. Offered annually for unpublished fiction and poetry. Guidelines available online or with SASE. **Charges $15 fee.** Prize: $1,000 each for fiction and poetry winners.

N THE W.O. MITCHELL LITERARY PRIZE, The Writers' Trust of Canada, 40 Wellington St. E., Suite 300, Toronto ON M5E 1C7, Canada. (416)504-8222. Fax: (416)504-9090. E-mail: info@writerstrust.com. Website: www.writerstrust.com. **Contact:** Sharon Poitras. Offered annually for a writer who has produced an outstanding body of work and has acted during his/her career as a "caring mentor" for other writers. They must also have published a work of fiction or had a new stage play produced during the 3-year period for each competition. Every third year the W.O. Mitchell Literary Prize will be awarded to a writer who works in French. Prize: $15,000. Open to Canadian residents only.

N MLA PRIZE IN CHICANA & CHICANO AND LATINA & LATINO LITERARY AND CULTURAL STUDIES, Modern Language Association of America, 26 Broadway, 3rd Floor, New York NY 10004-1789. (646)576-5141. Fax: (646)458-0030. E-mail: awards@mla.org. Website: www.mla.org. **Contact:** Coordinator of Book Prizes. Award for an outstanding scholarly study in any language of United States Latina & Latino and Chicana & Chicano literature or culture. *Open to current MLA members only.* Authors or publishers may submit titles. **Deadline: May 1.** Guidelines for SASE. Prize: $1,000, and a certificate to be presented at the Modern Language Association's annual convention in December.

NATIONAL OUTDOOR BOOK AWARDS, Box 8128, Idaho State University, Pocatello ID 83209. (208)282-3912. E-mail: wattron@isu.edu. Website: www.isu.edu/outdoor/books. **Contact:** Ron Watters. Eight categories: History/biography, outdoor literature, instructional texts, outdoor adventure guides, nature guides, childrens' books, design/artistic merit, and nature and the environment. Additionally, a special award, the Outdoor Classic Award, is given annually to books which, over a period of time, have proven to be exceptionally valuable works in the outdoor field. Application forms and eligibilty requirements are available online. **Deadline: September 1. Charges $65 fee.** Prize: Winning books are promoted nationally and are entitled to display the National Outdoor Book Award (NOBA) medallion.

NEW CENTURY WRITER AWARDS (NOVELS/NOVELLAS), NCWA, 32 Alfred St., Suite B, New Haven CT 06512-3927. (203)469-8824. Fax: (203)468-0333. E-mail: newcenturywriter@yahoo.com. Website: www.newcenturywriter.org. **Contact:** Jason Marchi, executive director. Offered annually to discover and encourage emerging writers of novels and novellas. Guidelines/entry fee for the asking, no SASE required. Open to all writers, both nonpublished and those with a limited publication history. Call if in doubt about your eligibility. New Century Writer also provides the annual Ray Bradbury Short Story Fellowship for 1 or 2 short story writers to attend the *Zoetrope* Short Story Writers' Workshop at Francis Ford Coppola's Blancaneaux Lodge in Belize, Central America (see the Ray Bradbury Short Story Fellowship listing for complete details). **Deadline: July 31 (postmarked). Charges $35 for 1 novella/novel; $30 each for 2 or more novellas/novels.** Prize: 1st Place: $2,000; 2nd Place: $1,000; 3rd Place: $500; 4th-10th Place: $100.

OHIOANA WALTER RUMSEY MARVIN GRANT, Ohioana Library Association, 274 E. First Ave., Suite 300, Columbus OH 43201. (614)466-3831. Fax: (614)728-6974. E-mail: ohioana@sloma.state.oh.us. Website: www.oplin.lib.oh

.us/products/ohioana/marvin.doc. **Contact:** Linda Hengst. Offered annually to encourage young writers; open to writers under age 30 who have not published a book. Entrants must have been born in Ohio or have lived in Ohio for at least 5 years. Enter 6 pieces of prose totaling 10-60 pages. **Deadline: January 31.** Prize: $1,000.

PEN CENTER USA LITERARY AWARDS, (formerly PEN Center Literary Awards), PEN Center USA, 672 S. Lafayette Park Place, #42, Los Angeles CA 90057. (213)365-8500. Fax: (213)365-9616. E-mail: awards@penusa.org. Website: www.penusa.org. **Contact:** Literary Awards Coordinator. Offered for work published or produced in the previous calendar year. Open to writers living west of the Mississippi River. Award categories: drama, screenplay, teleplay, journalism. **Deadline: 4 copies must be received by January 31.** Prize: $1,000.

N **THE PRAIRIE SCHOONER READERS' CHOICE AWARDS**, *Prairie Schooner*, 201 Andrews Hall, P.O. Box 880334, Lincoln NE 68588-0334. (402)472-0911. Fax: (402)472-9771. E-mail: eflanagan2@unl.edu. Website: www.unl.edu/schooner/psmain.htm. **Contact:** Hilda Raz. Annual awards (usually 4-6) for work published in *Prairie Schooner* in the previous year. Prize: $250. Open to any writer.

PULITZER PRIZES, The Pulitzer Prize Board, 709 Journalism, Columbia University, New York NY 10027. (212)854-3841. Website: www.pulitzer.org. **Contact:** Sig Gissler, administrator. Estab. 1917. Journalism in US newspapers (published daily or weekly), and in letters, drama, and music by Americans. **Deadline: February 1 (journalism); March 1 (music and drama); July 1 and November 1 (letters).**

N **THE HELEN PUTNAM MEMORIAL WRITERS FOR PEACE PRIZES**, Adaptive Solutions, P.O. Box 1545, Castleton VT 05735. E-mail: adaptivesolutions@icaal.com. Website: www.adaptivesolutions.net. **Contact:** Dianna C. Wuagneux, Ph.D. "This award recognizes the research and writings of men and women whose published and unpublished works may inspire the imagination and efforts necessary to help bring about peace by exploring and illuminating the value of distinct human societies and their interdependence. This semiannual award is open to all writers. Submission are limited to 6,000 words and will be assessed according to the writer's ability to deliver factual and important information in a way that is both concise and engaging—tell a story." Submissions are accepted continuously with the client for the following year's prize being December 15. Awards are made in January of even years. **Deadline: December 15.** Guidelines for SASE. **Charges $25.** Prize: $500, certificate, and consideration for inclusion in a proposed web-based "Writers for Peace Anthology." Open to any writer.

DAVID RAFFELOCK AWARD FOR PUBLISHING EXCELLENCE, National Writers Association, 3140 S. Peoria, #295, Aurora CO 80014. (303)841-0246. Fax: (303)841-2607. E-mail: sandywrter@aol.com. Website: www.nationalwriters.com. **Contact:** Sandy Whelchel. Contest is offered annually for books published the previous year. The purpose of this contest is to assist published authors in marketing their works and to reward outstanding published works. **Deadline: May 1.** Guidelines for SASE. **Charges $100 fee.** Prize: Publicity tour, including airfare, valued at $5,000.

ROCKY MOUNTAIN ARTISTS' BOOK COMPETITION, Hemingway Western Studies Center, Boise State University, 1910 University Dr., Boise ID 83725. (208)426-1999. Fax: (208)426-4373. E-mail: ttrusky@boisestate.edu. Website: www.boisestate.edu/hemingway/. **Contact:** Tom Trusky. Offered annually "to publish multiple edition artists' books of special interest to Rocky Mountain readers. Topics must be public issues (race, gender, environment, etc.). Authors may hail from Topeka or Ulan Bator, but their books must initially have regional appeal." Acquires first rights. Open to any writer. **Deadline: September 1-December 1.** Guidelines for SASE. Prize: $500, publication, standard royalties.

WILLIAM SANDERS SCARBOROUGH PRIZE, Modern Language Association of America, 26 Broadway, 3rd Floor, New York NY 10004-1789. (646)576-5141. Fax: (646)458-0030. E-mail: awards@mla.org. Website: www.mla.org. **Contact:** Annie Reiser, coordinator of book prizes and special projects. Offered annually for work published in the previous year. "Given in honor of a distinguished man of letters and the first African-American member of the Modern Language Association, this prize will be awarded to an outstanding scholarly study of black American literature or culture." Open to MLA members and nonmembers. Authors or publishers may enter titles. Guidelines for SASE or by e-mail. **Deadline: May 1.** Prize: $1,000, and a certificate, to be presented at the Modern Language Association's annual convention in December.

N **JOANNA CATHERINE SCOTT NOVEL EXCERPT PRIZE**, National League of American Pen Women, Nob Hill, San Francisco Branch, 1544 Sweetwood Dr., Colma CA 94015. E-mail: pennobhill@aol.com. Website: www.welcome.to/soulmakingcontest. **Contact:** Eileen Malone. Send first chapter or the first 20 pages, whichever comes first. Include a 1-page synopsis. Annually. **Deadline: November 30.** Guidelines for SASE. **Charges $5/entry (make checks payable to NLAPW, Nob Hill Branch).** Prize: 1st Place: $100; 2nd Place: $50; 3rd Place: $25. Open to any writer.

BYRON CALDWELL SMITH AWARD, Hall Center for the Humanities, 1540 Sunflower Rd., Lawrence KS 66045-7618. (785)864-4798. Website: www.hallcenter.ku.edu. **Contact:** Janet Crow, executive director. Offered in odd years to an individual who lives or is employed in Kansas, and who has authored an outstanding book published in the previous 2 calendar years. Translations are eligible. **Deadline: March 3.** Guidelines for SASE. Prize: $2,000.

TOWSON UNIVERSITY PRIZE FOR LITERATURE, College of Liberal Arts, Towson University, Towson MD 21252. (410)704-2128. **Contact:** Dean, College of Liberal Arts. Estab. 1979. Book or book-length ms that has been accepted for publication, written by a Maryland author who must have resided within the state of Maryland at least 3 years at the time of nomination, and must be a resident of the state of Maryland at the time the prize is awarded. **Deadline: June 15.** Guidelines for SASE. Prize: $1,000.

WORLD FANTASY AWARDS ASSOCIATION, P.O. Box 43, Mukilteo WA 98275-0043. Website: www.worldfantasy.org. **Contact:** Peter Dennis Pautz, president. Estab. 1975. Offered annually for previously published work recommended by previous convention attendees in several categories, including life achievement, novel, novella, short story, anthology, collection, artist, special award-pro, and special award nonpro. Works are recommended by attendees of current and previous 2 years' conventions, and a panel of judges. **Deadline: July 1.**

Nonfiction

ANTHEM ESSAY CONTEST, The Ayn Rand Institute, P.O. Box 6099, Dept. DB, Inglewood CA 90312. (310)306-9232. Fax: (310)306-4925. E-mail: essay@aynrand.org. Website: www.aynrand.org/contests. **Contact:** Marilee Dahl. Estab. 1992. Offered annually to encourage analytical thinking and excellence in writing, and to expose students to the philosophic ideas of Ayn Rand. "For information contact your English teacher or guidance counselor or visit our website." **Deadline: March 18.** Prize: 1st Place: $2,000; 2nd Place (10): $500; 3rd Place (20): $200; Finalist (45): $50; Semifinalist (175): $30.

RAY ALLEN BILLINGTON PRIZE, Organization of American Historians, 112 N. Bryan Ave., Bloomington IN 47408-4199. (812)855-9852. Fax: (812)855-0696. E-mail: awards@oah.org. Website: www.oah.org. **Contact:** Award and Prize Committee Coordinator. Offered in even years for the best book in American frontier history, defined broadly so as to include the pioneer periods of all geographical areas and comparison between American frontiers and others. Guidelines available on website. **Deadline: October 1.** Prize: $1,000, a certificate, and a medal.

BIOGRAPHERS' CLUB PRIZE, Biographers' Club, The Secretary, 17 Sutherland St., London, England SW1V 4JU. (020)7828 1274. Fax: (020)7828 7608. E-mail: lownie@globalnet.co.uk. Website: www.booktrust.org.uk. **Contact:** Andrew Lownie. The annual prize is sponsored by the Daily Mail, and all previous winners have gone on to secure publishing contracts—some for 6-figure sums. Entries should consist of a 15-20 page synopsis and 10 pages of a sample chapter for a biography. **Deadline: August 1.** Guidelines for SASE. Prize: £1,000. Judged by 3 distinguished biographers. Judges have included Michael Holroyd, Victoria Glendinning, Selina Hastings, Frances Spalding, Lyndall Gordon, Anne de Courcy, Nigel Hamilton, Anthony Sampson, and Mary Lovell. Judges for 2003 are Professor David Ellis, Sarah Bradford, and Lucy Moore. Open to any writer.

BIRKS FAMILY FOUNDATION AWARD FOR BIOGRAPHY, Canadian Authors Association, Box 419, 320 S. Shores Rd., Campbellford ON K0L 1L0, Canada. (705)653-0323. Fax: (705)653-0593. E-mail: canauth@redden.on.ca. Website: www.canauthors.org. **Contact:** Alec McEachern. Offered annually for a biography about a Canadian. Entry form required. Obtain entry form from contact name or download from website. **Deadline: December 15.** Guidelines for SASE. **Charges $25 (Canadian) entry fee.** Prize: $2,500, and a silver medal.

BOWLING WRITING COMPETITION, American Bowling Congress Publications, 5301 S. 76th St., Greendale WI 53129-1127. Fax: (414)321-8356. E-mail: abcpr@bowling.com. Website: www.bowl.com. **Contact:** Bill Vint, editor. Estab. 1935. Offered for feature, editorial, and news all relating to the sport of bowling. **Deadline: December 15.** Prize: 1st Place in each division: $300. In addition, News and Editorial: $225; $200; $175; $150; $75; and $50; Feature: $225; $200; $175; $150; $125; $100; $75; $50; and $50; with 5 honorable mention certificates awarded in each category.

THE BROSS PRIZE, The Bross Foundation, Lake Forest College, 555 N. Sheridan, Lake Forest IL 60045. (847)735-5175. Fax: (847)735-6192. E-mail: rmiller@lfc.edu. **Contact:** Professor Ron Miller. Offered every 10 years for unpublished work "to award the best book or treatise on the relation between any discipline or topic of investigation and the Christian religion." Next contest in 2010. Manuscripts awarded prizes become property of the college. Open to any writer. **Deadline: September 1 of contest year.** Guidelines for SASE. Prize: Award varies depending on interest earned.

JOHN BULLEN PRIZE, Canadian Historical Association, 395 Wellington, Ottawa ON K1A 0N3, Canada. (613)233-7885. Fax: (613)567-3110. E-mail: cha-shc@archives.ca. Website: www.cha-shc.ca. **Contact:** Joanne Mineault. Offered annually for an outstanding historical dissertation for a doctoral degree at a Canadian university. Open only to Canadian citizens or landed immigrants. **Deadline: November 30.** Guidelines for SASE. Prize: $500.

CANADIAN AUTHORS ASSOCIATION LELA COMMON AWARD FOR CANADIAN HISTORY, Box 419, 320 S. Shores Rd., Campbellford ON K0L 1L0, Canada. (705)653-0323. Fax: (705)653-0593. E-mail: canauth@redden.on.ca. Website: www.canauthors.org. **Contact:** Alec McEachern. Offered annually for a work of historical nonfiction on a Canadian topic by a Canadian author. Entry form required. Obtain entry form from contact name or download from website. **Deadline: December 15.** Guidelines for SASE. **Charges $25 (Canadian) entry fee.** Prize: $2,500, and a silver medal.

CANADIAN LIBRARY ASSOCIATION STUDENT ARTICLE CONTEST, Canadian Library Association, 328 Frank St., Ottawa ON K2P 0X8, Canada. (613)232-9625, ext. 318. Fax: (613)563-9895. Website: www.cla.ca. **Contact:** Brenda Shields. Offered annually to "unpublished articles discussing, analyzing, or evaluating timely issues in librarianship or information science." Open to all students registered in or recently graduated from a Canadian library school, a library techniques program, or faculty of education library program. Submissions may be in English or French. **Deadline: April 1.** Guidelines for SASE. Prize: 1st Place: $150, publication, and trip to CLA's annual conference; 1st runner-up: $150, and $75 in CLA publications; 3rd runner-up: $75, and $75 in CLA publications.

THE DOROTHY CHURCHILL CAPPON CREATIVE NONFICTION AWARD, *New Letters*, 5101 Rockhill Rd., Kansas City MO 64110. (816)235-1168. Fax: (816)235-2611. E-mail: newletters@umkc.edu. Website: www.umkc.edu/newletters. **Contact:** Aleatha Ezra. Contest is offered annually for unpublished work to discover and reward new and upcoming authors. Acquires first North American serial rights. Open to any writer. **Deadline: Third week of May.** Guidelines for SASE. **Charges $15 fee** (includes a 1-year subscription to *New Letters*). Prize: 1st Place: $1,000, and publication in a volume of *New Letters*; 2 runners-up will receive a year's subscription and will be considered for publication.

All entries will receive consideration for publication in future editions of *New Letters*.

MORTON N. COHEN AWARD, Modern Language Association of America, 26 Broadway, 3rd Floor, New York NY 10004-1789. (646)576-5141. Fax: (646)458-0030. E-mail: awards@mla.org. Website: www.mla.org. **Contact:** Coordinator of Book Prizes. Estab. 1989. Awarded in odd-numbered years for a distinguished edition of letters. At least 1 volume of the edition must have been published during the previous 2 years. Editors need not be members of the MLA. **Deadline: May 1.** Guidelines for SASE. Prize: $1,000, and a certificate.

THE THOMAS COOK TRAVEL BOOK AWARD, The Thomas Cook Group, The Thomas Cook Business Park, Peterborough, Cambs PE3 8SB, United Kingdom. (44)1733 402009. Fax: (44)1733 416688. Website: www.thetravelbookaward.com. **Contact:** The Administrator. Annual award to reward and encourage the art of travel writing and to inspire in the reader the wish to travel. Books should have been published for the first time during January 1 and December 31; should be available in the English language (but may be translations); should be a minimum of 150 pages; and must be travel narratives (i.e., not guidebooks). **Deadline: March 31.** Guidelines for SASE. Prize: £10,000. Judged by a panel of 7 or 8 judges from travel literature/media/publishing (changes annually). Open to any writer.

AVERY O. CRAVEN AWARD, Organization of American Historians, 112 N. Bryan Ave., Bloomington IN 47408-4199. (812)855-9852. Fax: (812)855-0696. E-mail: awards@oah.org. Website: www.oah.org. **Contact:** Award and Prize Committee Coordinator. Offered annually for the most original book on the coming of the Civil War, the Civil War years, or the Era of Reconstruction, with the exception of works of purely military history. Guidelines on website. **Deadline: October 1.** Prize: $500, and a certificate.

A CUP OF COMFORT, Adams Media Corp., 57 Littlefield St., Avon MA 02322. (508)427-7100. Fax: (541)424-2422. E-mail: wordsinger@aol.com. Website: www.cupofcomfort.com. **Contact:** Colleen Sell, editor. "A Cup of Comfort is the best-selling book series featuring from-the-heart, slice-of-life true stories about the relationships and experiences that deeply affect our lives. This paid and bylined publishing opportunity is open to aspiring and experienced writers as well as to people from all walks of life." Stories must be true, written in English, uplifting, positive, and/or inspiring, and appropriate for a mainstream audience. This prize includes publication in an anthology: Four anthologies are published each year, 2 in Spring and 2 in Fall; and some years an additional "niche" volume (i.e., cookbook, collection of prayers, etc.) are also compiled. Contest is offered 4 or 5 times/year. Deadline for Spring publications is usually August or September of previous year; for Fall publications January of same year. **Deadlines for upcoming anthologies: A Cup of Comfort: Inspiration, March 1; A Cup of Comfort for Teachers, August 2003; A Cup of Comfort: Courage, September 2003.** Finalists are selected throughout the submission period, so early entry is encouraged. Guidelines for SASE or by e-mail. Open to aspiring and published writers. Allow 6-9 months for response. Prize: Grand Prize: $500; $100 for each other story published in each book (50-60 stories/anthology). Judged by Colleen Sell, editor, in conjunction with publisher's review committee. The editor reviews all submissions and selects finalists. The publisher must approve the final selections. Acquires limited rights for a specified period of time; applies only to those stories selected for publication.

MERLE CURTI AWARD, Organization of American Historians, 112 N. Bryan Ave., Bloomington IN 47408-4199. (812)855-9852. Fax: (812)855-0696. E-mail: awards@oah.org. Website: www.oah.org. **Contact:** Award and Prize Committee Coordinator. Offered annually for books in the field of American social history (even-numbered years) and intellectual history (odd-numbered years). Guidelines available on website. **Deadline: October 1.** Guidelines for SASE. Prize: $1,000, a certificate, and a medal.

ANNIE DILLARD AWARD IN CREATIVE NONFICTION, *Bellingham Review,* Mail Stop 9053, Western Washington University, Bellingham WA 98225. (360)650-4863. E-mail: bhreview@cc.wwu.edu. Website: www.wwu.edu/~bhreview. **Contact:** Brenda Miller. Offered annually for unpublished essays on any subject and in any style. Guidelines for SASE or on website. **Deadline: December 1-March 15.** Prize: 1st Place: $1,000, plus publication and copies.

GORDON W. DILLON/RICHARD C. PETERSON MEMORIAL ESSAY PRIZE, American Orchid Society, Inc., 16700 AOS Lane, Delray Beach FL 33446-4351. (561)404-2043. Fax: (561)404-2045. E-mail: jmengel@aos.org. Website: www.orchidweb.org. **Contact:** Jane Mengel. Estab. 1985. "An annual contest open to all writers. The theme is announced each May in *Orchids* magazine. All themes deal with an aspect of orchids, such as repotting, growing, hybridizing, etc. Unpublished submissions only." Themes in past years have included Orchid Culture, Orchids in Nature, and Orchids in Use. Buys one-time rights. **Deadline: November 30.** Prize: Cash award, and certificate. Winning entry usually published in the May issue of *Orchids* magazine.

THE FREDERICK DOUGLASS BOOK PRIZE, Gilder Lehrman Center for the Study of Slavery, Resistance & Abolition of Yale University, P.O. Box 208206, New Haven CT 06520-8206. (203)432-3339. Fax: (203)432-6943. E-mail: gilder.lehrman.center@yale.edu. Website: www.yale.edu/glc. **Contact:** Robert P. Forbes, associate director. Write or fax, Attention: Douglass Prize. Offered annually for books published the previous year. "The annual prize of $25,000 is awarded for the most outstanding book published on the subject of slavery, resistance, and/or abolition. Works related to the American Civil War are eligble only if their primary focus is slavery, resistance, or abolition." **Deadline: March 29.** Guidelines for SASE. Prize: $25,000, and a bronze medallion.

THE DRAINIE-TAYLOR BIOGRAPHY PRIZE, The Writers' Trust of Canada, 40 Wellington St. E., Suite 300, Toronto ON M5E 1C7, Canada. (416)504-8222. Fax: (416)504-9090. E-mail: info@writerstrust.com. Website: www.writerstrust.com. **Contact:** Sharon Poitras. Awarded annually to a Canadian author for a significant work of biography, autobiography, or personal memoir. Award presented at the Great Literary Awards event held in Toronto each spring. Prize: $10,000.

DAVID W. AND BEATRICE C. EVANS BIOGRAPHY & HANDCART AWARDS, Mountain West Center for Regional Studies, Utah State University, Logan UT 84322-0735. (435)797-3630. Fax: (435)797-3899. E-mail: mwc@cc.usu.edu. Website: www.usu.edu/~pioneers/mwc.html. **Contact:** Glenda Nesbit, office manager. Estab. 1983. Offered to encourage the writing of biography about people who have played a role in Mormon Country. (Not the religion, the country: Intermountain West with parts of Southwestern Canada and Northwestern Mexico.) Publishers or authors may nominate books. Criteria for consideration: Work must be a biography or autobiography on "Mormon Country"; must be submitted for consideration for publication year's award; new editions or reprints are not eligible; mss are not accepted. Submit 5 copies. **Deadline: December 1.** Guidelines for SASE. Prize: $10,000 and $1,000.

EVENT CREATIVE NONFICTION CONTEST, *Event*, P.O. Box 2503, New Westminster BC V3L 5B2, Canada. (604)527-5293. Fax: (604)527-5095. E-mail: event@douglas.bc.ca. Website: event.douglas.bc.ca. **Contact:** Ian Cockfield, managing editor. Offered annually for unpublished creative nonfiction. Guidelines for SASE (Canadian postage/IRCs only). Acquires first North American serial rights for the 3 winning entries. Open to any writer, except Douglas College employees. **Deadline: April 15. Charges $25 entry fee, which includes 1-year subscription; US residents, pay in US funds.** Prize: 3 winners will each receive $500, plus payment for publication.

WALLACE K. FERGUSON PRIZE, Canadian Historical Association, 395 Wellington, Ottawa ON K1A 0N3, Canada. (613)233-7885. Fax: (613)567-3110. E-mail: cha-shc@archives.ca. Website: www.cha-shc.ca. **Contact:** Joanne Mineault. Offered to a Canadian who has published the outstanding scholarly book in a field of history other than Canadian history. **Deadline: December 1.** Guidelines for SASE. Prize: $1,000.

ROSALIE FLEMING MEMORIAL ESSAY AND CREATIVE NONFICTION PRIZE, National League of American Pen Women, Nob Hill, San Francisco Branch, 1544 Sweetwood Dr., Colma CA 94015. E-mail: pennobhill@aol.com. Website: www.welcome.to/soulmakingcontest. **Contact:** Eileen Malone. All prose works must be typed, page numbered, stapled, and double-spaced. One essay/entry, up to 3,000 words. Annually. **Deadline: November 30.** Guidelines for SASE. **Charges $5/entry (make checks payable to NLAPW, Nob Hill Branch).** Prize: 1st Place: $100; 2nd Place: $50; 3rd Place: $25. Open to any writer.

THE FOUNTAINHEAD ESSAY CONTEST, The Ayn Rand Institute, Dept. W, P.O. Box 57044, Irvine CA 92619-7044. E-mail: essay@aynrand.org. Website: www.aynrand.org/contests/. Estab. 1985. Offered annually to encourage analytical thinking and excellence in writing, and to expose students to the philosophic ideas of Ayn Rand. "For information contact your English teacher or guidance counselor, or visit our website." Length: 800-1,600 words. **Deadline: April 15.** Prize: 1st Place: $10,000; 2nd Place (5): $2,000; 3rd Place (10): $1,000; Finalist (35): $100; Semifinalist (200): $50.

DIXON RYAN FOX MANUSCRIPT PRIZE, New York State Historical Association, P.O. Box 800, Cooperstown NY 13326. (607)547-1491. Fax: (607)547-1405. E-mail: goodwind@nysha.org. Website: www.nysha.org. **Contact:** Daniel Goodwin, director of publications. Offered annually for the best unpublished book-length ms dealing with some aspect of the history of New York State. Open to any writer. **Deadline: January 20.** Guidelines for SASE. Prize: $3,000.

GEORGE FREEDLEY MEMORIAL AWARD, Theatre Library Association, Benjamin Rosenthal Library, Queens College, C.U.N.Y., 65-30 Kissena Blvd., Flushing NY 11367. (718)997-3672. Fax: (718)997-3753. E-mail: rlw$lib@qc1.qc.edu. Website: tla.library.unt.edu. **Contact:** Richard Wall, book awards committee chair. Estab. 1968. Offered for a book published in the US within the previous calendar year on a subject related to live theatrical performance (including cabaret, circus, pantomime, puppetry, vaudeville, etc.). Eligible books may include biography, history, theory, criticism, reference, or related fields. **Deadline: February 15 of year following eligibility.** Prize: $250, and certificate to the winner; $100, and certificate for honorable mention.

THE CHRISTIAN GAUSS AWARD, The Phi Beta Kappa Society, 1606 New Hampshire Ave. NW, Washington DC 20009. (202)265-3808. Fax: (202)986-1601. E-mail: ccurtis@pbk.org. Website: www.pbk.org/scholarships/books. **Contact:** Ms. Cameron Curtis. The Christian Gauss Award is offered annually for books published between May 1 and April 30 in the field of literary scholarship or criticism. "The prize was established in 1950 to honor the late Christian Gauss, the distinguished Princeton University scholar, teacher, and dean, who also served as President of the Phi Beta Kappa Society. To be eligible, a literary biography must have a predminantly critical emphasis." Entries must be submitted by the publisher. Entries must be preceded by a letter certifying that the book(s) conform to all conditions of eligibility and stating the publication date of each entry. If accepted, 8 copies of each entry are required for the Gauss Award. Ineligible entries will be returned by Phi Beta Kappa. Books will not be entered officially in the competition until all copies and the letter of certification have been received. **Deadline: April 30.** Prize: $2,500. Judged by a rotating panel of distinguished scholars and experts in the field. Open to US residents only.

GOVERNOR GENERAL'S LITERARY AWARD FOR LITERARY NONFICTION, Canada Council for the Arts, 350 Albert St., P.O. Box 1047, Ottawa ON K1P 5V8, Canada. (613)566-4414, ext. 5576. Fax: (613)566-4410. E-mail: joanne.larocque-poirier@canadacouncil.ca. Website: www.canadacouncil.ca/prizes/ggla. **Contact:** Joanne Larocque-Poirier. Offered for work published September 1, 2002-September 30, 2003. Given annually to the best English language and the best French language work of literary nonfiction by a Canadian. Publishers submit titles for consideration. **Deadline: April 15 or August 7, 2003, depending on the book's publication date.** Prize: Each laureate receives $15,000, and nonwinning finalists receive $1,000.

JAMES T. GRADY—JAMES H. STACK AWARD FOR INTERPRETING CHEMISTRY FOR THE PUBLIC, American Chemical Society, 1155 16th St. NW, Washington DC 20036-4800. (202)872-4408. Fax: (202)776-8211. E-mail: awards@acs.org. Website: www.acs.org/awards/grady-stack.html. **Contact:** Alicia Harris. Offered annually for previously published work to recognize, encourage, and stimulate outstanding reporting directly to the public, which materially increases the public's knowledge and understanding of chemistry, chemical engineering, and related fields. Guidelines online at website. Rules of eligibility: A nominee must have made noteworthy presentations through a medium of public communication to increase the American public's understanding of chemistry and chemical progress. This information shall have been disseminated through the press, radio, television, films, the lecture platform, books, or pamphlets for the lay public. **Deadline: February 1.** Prize: $3,000, medallion with a presentation box, and certificate, plus travel expenses to the meeting at which the award will be presented.

JOHN GUYON NONFICTION PRIZE, *Crab Orchard Review*, English Dept., Southern Illinois University Carbondale, Carbondale IL 62901-4503. Website: www.siu.edu/~crborchd. **Contact:** Jon C. Tribble, managing editor. Offered annually for unpublished work. This competition seeks to reward excellence in the writing of creative nonfiction. This is not a prize for academic essays. *Crab Orchard Review* acquires first North American serial rights to submitted works. **Deadline: February 1-March 15.** Guidelines for SASE. **Charges $15/essay (limit of 3 essays of up to 6,500 words each).** Prize: $1,500, and publication.

ALBERT J. HARRIS AWARD, International Reading Association, Division of Research and Policy, 800 Barksdale Rd., Newark DE 19714-8139. (302)731-1600, ext. 423. Fax: (302)731-1057. E-mail: research@reading.org. Website: www.reading.org. **Contact:** Marcella Moore. Offered annually to recognize outstanding published works on the topics of reading disabilities and the prevention, assessment, or instruction of learners experiencing difficulty learning to read. Open to any writer. Copies of the applications and guidelines can be downloaded in PDF format from the International Reading Association's website. **Deadline: September 15.** Guidelines for SASE. Prize: Monetary award and recognition at the International Reading Association's annual convention.

ELLIS W. HAWLEY PRIZE, Organization of American Historians, 112 N. Bryan Ave., Bloomington IN 47408-4199. (812)855-9852. Fax: (812)855-0696. E-mail: awards@oah.org. Website: www.oah.org. **Contact:** Award and Prize Committee Coordinator. Offered annually for the best book-length historical study of the political economy, politics, or institutions of the US, in its domestic or international affairs, from the Civil War to the present. Books must be written in English. Guidelines available on website. **Deadline: October 1.** Prize: $500, and a certificate.

HENDRICKS MANUSCRIPT AWARD, New Netherland Project, New York State Library, Cultural Exchange Center, 8th Floor, Madison Ave., Empire State Plaza Station, Albany NY 12220-0536. (518)474-6067. Fax: (518)473-0472. E-mail: cgehring@mail.nysed.gov. Website: www.nnp.org. **Contact:** Charles Gehring. Offered annually for the best published or unpublished ms focusing on any aspect of the Dutch colonial experience in North America. **Deadline: February 15.** Guidelines for SASE. Prize: $2,000.

THE KIRIYAMA PACIFIC RIM BOOK PRIZE, Kiriyama Pacific Rim Institute, 650 Delancey St., Suite 101, San Francisco CA 94107. (415)777-1628. Fax: (415)777-1646. E-mail: admin@kiriyamaprize.org. Website: www.kiriyamaprize.org. **Contact:** Jeannine Cuevas, prize manager. Offered for work published from October 1 of the previous year through December 31 of the current prize year to promote books that will contribute to greater mutual understanding and increased cooperation throughout all areas of the Pacific Rim and South Asia. Guidelines and entry form on request, or may be downloaded from the prize website. Books must be submitted for entry by the publisher. Proper entry forms must be submitted. Contact the administrators of the prize for complete rules and entry forms. **Deadline: October 27, 2003.** Prize: $30,000 to be divided equally between the author of 1 fiction and of 1 nonfiction book.

KATHERINE SINGER KOVACS PRIZE, Modern Language Association of America, 26 Broadway, 3rd Floor, New York NY 10004-1789. (646)576-5141. Fax: (646)458-0030. E-mail: awards@mla.org. Website: www.mla.org. **Contact:** Coordinator of Book Prizes. Estab. 1990. Offered annually for a book published during the previous year in English in the field of Latin American and Spanish literatures and cultures. Books should be broadly interpretive works that enhance understanding of the interrelations among literature, the other arts, and society. Author need not be a member of the MLA. **Deadline: May 1.** Guidelines for SASE. Prize: $1,000, and a certificate.

KRASZNA-KRAUSZ PHOTOGRAPHY & MOVING IMAGE BOOK AWARDS, Kraszna-Krausz Foundation, 122 Fawnbrake Ave., London, England SE24-0BZ. (+44)20-7738-6701. E-mail: awards@k-k.org.uk. Website: www.k-k.org.uk. **Contact:** Andrea Livingstone. These annual awards recognize outstanding achievements in the publishing and writing of books (published between June and May) on the art, history, practice, and technology of photography and the moving image (film, TV, etc.). All submissions must be made by the publisher of the title. **Deadline: July 1.** Guidelines for SASE. Prize: Main Awards (2): £5,000 UK Sterling; Finalist Awards: £1,000 UK Sterling. Judged by an international panel of 3 judges which changes annually. Open to any writer.

LERNER-SCOTT PRIZE, Organization of American Historians, 112 N. Bryan Ave., Bloomington IN 47408-4199. (812)855-9852. Fax: (812)855-0696. E-mail: awards@oah.org. Website: www.oah.org. **Contact:** Award and Prize Committee Coordinator. Offered annually for the best doctoral dissertation in US women's history. Guidelines available at website. **Deadline: November 1 for a dissertation completed in the previous academic year (July 1-June 30).** Prize: $1,000, and a certificate.

LINCOLN PRIZE AT GETTYSBURG COLLEGE, Gettysburg College and Lincoln & Soldiers Institute, 233 N. Washington St., Gettysburg PA 17325. (717)337-6590. Fax: (717)337-6596. E-mail: civilwar@gettysburg.edu. Website: www.gettysburg.edu/lincoln_prize. **Contact:** Diane Brennan. Offered annually for the finest scholarly work in English on the era of the American Civil War. The award will usually go to a book published in the previous year; however articles, essays, and works of fiction may be submitted. Guidelines for SASE or on website. **Deadline: November 1.** Prize: $50,000.

JAMES RUSSELL LOWELL PRIZE, Modern Language Association of America, 26 Broadway, 3rd Floor, New York NY 10004-1789. (646)576-5141. Fax: (646)458-0030. E-mail: awards@mla.org. Website: www.mla.org. **Contact:** Coordinator of Book Prizes. Offered annually for literary or linguistic study, or critical edition or biography published in previous year. *Open to MLA members only.* **Deadline: March 1.** Guidelines for SASE. Prize: $1,000, and a certificate.

SIR JOHN A. MACDONALD PRIZE, Canadian Historical Association, 395 Wellington, Ottawa ON K1A 0N3, Canada. (613)233-7885. Fax: (613)567-3110. E-mail: cha-shc@archives.ca. Website: www.cha-shc.ca. **Contact:** Joanne Mineault. Offered annually to award a previously published nonfiction work of Canadian history "judged to have made the most significant contribution to an understanding of the Canadian past." Open to Canadian citizens only. **Deadline: December 1.** Guidelines for SASE. Prize: $1,000.

GRANT MACEWAN AUTHOR'S AWARD, Alberta Community Development, 9th Floor Standard Life Centre, 10405 Jasper Ave., Edmonton, AB T5J 4R7, Canada. Website: www.cd.gov.ab.ca. This annual award was created by the government to honor the life and contributions of the late Dr. Grant MacEwan. Books submitted must reflect Alberta and/or Dr. MacEwan's interests and must have been published between January 1 and December 31. **Deadline: December 31.** Guidelines for SASE. Prize: $25,000. Judged by a jury of prominent Alberta authors.

HOWARD R. MARRARO PRIZE, Modern Language Association of America, 26 Broadway, 3rd Floor, New York NY 10004-1789. (646)576-5141. Fax: (646)458-0030. E-mail: awards@mla.org. Website: www.mla.org. **Contact:** Coordinator of Book Prizes. Offered in even-numbered years for a scholarly book or essay on any phase of Italian literature or comparative literature involving Italian, published in previous 2 years. Authors must be members of the MLA. **Deadline: May 1, 2004.** Guidelines for SASE. Prize: $1,000, and a certificate.

McLEMORE PRIZE, Mississippi Historical Society, P.O. Box 571, Jackson MS 39205-0571. (601)359-6850. Fax: (601)359-6975. E-mail: kblount@mdah.state.ms.us. Website: www.mdah.state.ms.us. **Contact:** Katie Blount. Offered for a scholarly book on a topic in Mississippi history/biography published in the year of competition. **Deadline: November 1.** Prize: Cash award and attendance at national meeting.

MID-LIST PRESS FIRST SERIES AWARD FOR CREATIVE NONFICTION, Mid-List Press, 4324 12th Ave. S., Minneapolis MN 55407-3218. Fax: (612)823-8387. E-mail: guide@midlist.org. Website: www.midlist.org. **Contact:** Lane Stiles, publisher. Open to any writer who has never published a book of creative nonfiction. Submit either a collection of essays or a single book-length work; minimum length 50,000 words. Accepts simultaneous submissions. Guidelines and entry form for SASE or on website. **Deadline: July 1. Charges $30 (US dollars) fee.** Prize: Awards include publication and an advance against royalties.

KENNETH W. MILDENBERGER PRIZE, Modern Language Association of America, 26 Broadway, 3rd Floor, New York NY 10004-1789. (646)576-5141. Fax: (646)458-0030. E-mail: awards@mla.org. Website: www.mla.org. **Contact:** Coordinator of Book Prizes. Offered annually for a publication (articles in odd-numbered years and books in even-numbered years) from the previous biennium in the field of teaching foreign languages and literatures. In 2003 the award will be given to an article published in 2001 or 2002. Author need not be a member. **Deadline: May 1.** Guidelines for SASE. Prize: $500 for articles, and $1,000 for books, a certificate, and a year's membership in the MLA.

MLA PRIZE FOR A DISTINGUISHED BIBLIOGRAPHY, Modern Language Association of America, 26 Broadway, 3rd Floor, New York NY 10004-1789. (646)576-5141. Fax: (646)458-0030. E-mail: awards@mla.org. Website: www.mla.o rg. **Contact:** Coordinator of Book Prizes. Offered in even-numbered years for enumerative and descriptive bibliographies published in monographic, book, or electronic format in the 2 years prior to the competition. Open to any writer or publisher. **Deadline: May 1, 2004.** Guidelines for SASE. Prize: $1,000, and a certificate.

MLA PRIZE FOR A DISTINGUISHED SCHOLARLY EDITION, Modern Language Association of America, 26 Broadway, 3rd Floor, New York NY 10004-1789. (646)576-5141. Fax: (646)458-0030. E-mail: awards@mla.org. Website: www.mla.org. **Contact:** Coordinator of Book Prizes. Offered in odd-numbered years. Work published in 2001 or 2002 qualifies for the 2003 competition. To qualify for the award, an edition should be based on an examination of all available relevant textual sources; the source texts and the edited text's deviations from them should be fully described; the edition should employ editorial principles appropriate to the materials edited, and those principles should be clearly articulated in the volume; the text should be accompanied by appropriate textual and other historical contextual information; the edition should exhibit the highest standards of accuracy in the presentation of its text and apparatus; and the text and apparatus should be presented as accessibly and elegantly as possible. Editor need not be a member of the MLA. **Deadline: May 1.** Guidelines for SASE. Prize: $1,000, and a certificate.

MLA PRIZE FOR A FIRST BOOK, Modern Language Association of America, 26 Broadway, 3rd Floor, New York NY 10004-1789. (646)576-5141. Fax: (646)458-0030. E-mail: awards@mla.org. Website: www.mla.org. **Contact:** Coordinator of Book Prizes. Offered annually for the first book-length scholarly publication by a current member of the association. To qualify, a book must be a literary or linguistic study, a critical edition of an important work, or a critical biography. Studies dealing with literary theory, media, cultural history, and interdisciplinary topics are eligible; books that are primarily translations will not be considered. **Deadline: April 1.** Guidelines for SASE. Prize: $1,000, and a certificate.

MLA PRIZE FOR INDEPENDENT SCHOLARS, Modern Language Association of America, 26 Broadway, 3rd Floor, New York NY 10004-1789. (646)576-5141. Fax: (646)458-0030. E-mail: awards@mla.org. Website: www.mla.org. **Contact:** Coordinator of Book Prizes. Offered annually for a book in the field of English, or another modern language, or literature published in the previous year. Authors who are enrolled in a program leading to an academic degree or who hold tenured or tenure-track positions in higher education are not eligible. Authors need not be members of MLA. Guidelines and application form for SASE. **Deadline: May 1.** Prize: $1,000, a certificate, and a year's membership in the MLA.

GEORGE JEAN NATHAN AWARD FOR DRAMATIC CRITICISM, Cornell University, Dept. of English, Goldwin Smith Hall, Ithaca NY 14853. (607)255-6801. Fax: (607)255-6661. E-mail: english_chair@cornell.edu. Website:

www.arts.cornell.edu/english/nathan/index.html. **Contact:** Chair, Department of English. Offered annually to the American "who has written the best piece of drama criticism during the theatrical year (July 1-June 30), whether it is an article, an essay, treatise, or book." Only published work may be submitted; author must be an American citizen. Guidelines for SASE. Prize: $10,000, and a trophy.

NATIONAL BUSINESS BOOK AWARD, PricewaterhouseCoopers and BMO Financial Group, 77 King St. W., Toronto ON M5K 1G8, Canada. (416)941-8344. Fax: (416)941-8345. E-mail: mafreedman@freedmanandassociates.com. Website: www.pwc.com. **Contact:** Faye Mattachione. Offered annually for books published January 1-December 31 to recognize excellence in business writing in Canada. Publishers nominate books. **Deadline: December 31.** Prize: $10,000.

NATIONAL WRITERS ASSOCIATION NONFICTION CONTEST, The National Writers Association, 3140 S. Peoria, #295, Aurora CO 80014. (303)841-0246. Fax: (303)841-2607. E-mail: sandywrter@aol.com. **Contact:** Sandy Whelchel, director. Annual contest "to encourage writers in this creative form and to recognize those who excel in nonfiction writing." **Deadline: December 31.** Guidelines for SASE. **Charges $18 fee.** Prize: 1st Place: $200; 2nd Place: $100; 3rd Place: $50.

THE NATURAL WORLD BOOK PRIZE, The Wildlife Trusts & Booktrust, Book House, 45 E. Hill, Wandsworth, London SW18 2QZ, England. Fax: (00 44) 8516 2978. E-mail: tarryn@booktrust.org.uk. Website: www.booktrust.org.uk. **Contact:** Amanda Spivack. "This annual award rewards the book that most imaginatively promotes the understanding and conservation of our natural environment and its wildlife in an accessible and enjoyable fashion. The books must be accessible to the general, nonspecific reader and published between June 1, 2002 and May 31, 2003. Entries must be full length, unified, and substantial new works by an author of any nationality, but the book must be published in the UK by a UK publisher." Prize: £5,000 to the author(s) or editor(s) of the winning book. The judges reserve the right to award a discretionary prize of £1,000 to a runner up.

THE FREDERIC W. NESS BOOK AWARD, Association of American Colleges and Universities, 1818 R St. NW, Washington DC 20009. (202)387-3760. Fax: (202)265-9532. E-mail: info@aacu.nw.dc.us. Website: www.aacu-edu.org. **Contact:** Bethany Sutton. Offered annually for work published in the previous year. "Each year the Frederic W. Ness Book Award Committee of the Association of American Colleges and Universities recognizes books which contribute to the understanding and improvement of liberal education." Guidelines for SASE and on website. "Writers may nominate their own work; however, we send letters of invitation to publishers to nominate qualified books." **Deadline: May 1.** Prize: $2,000, and presentation at the association's annual meeting; transportation and 1 night hotel for meeting are also provided.

NORTH AMERICAN INDIAN PROSE AWARD, University of Nebraska Press, 233 N. Eighth St., Lincoln NE 68588-0255. Fax: (402)472-0308. E-mail: gdunham1@unl.edu. **Contact:** Gary H. Dunham, editor, Native American studies. Offered for the best new nonfiction work by an American-Indian writer. **Deadline: July 1.** Prize: Publication by the University of Nebraska Press with a $1,000 advance.

C.B. OLDMAN PRIZE, International Association of Music Libraries United Kingdom and Ireland Branch, c/o Queen Mother Library, Meston Walk, Aberdeen AB24 3VE, United Kingdom. (01224) 272590. Fax: (01224) 487048. E-mail: r.turbet@abdn.ac.uk. Website: www.music.ox.ac.uk/IAML/. Annual contest for the best book of music bibliography, librarianship, or reference by an author domiciled in the United Kingdom or Ireland. **Deadline: December 31.** Prize: £150. Judged by a committee of 3 whose members spend 3 years (staggered so that there is only one newcomer annually).

OUTSTANDING DISSERTATION OF THE YEAR AWARD, International Reading Association, 800 Barksdale Rd., P.O. Box 8139, Newark DE 19714-1839. (302)731-1600, ext. 423. Fax: (302)731-1057. E-mail: research@reading.org. Website: www.reading.org. **Contact:** Marcella Moore. Offered annually to recognize dissertations in the field of reading and literacy. **Deadline: October 1.** Guidelines for SASE. Copies of the applications and guidelines can be downloaded in PDF format from International Reading Association's website. Prize: $1,000.

FRANK LAWRENCE AND HARRIET CHAPPELL OWSLEY AWARD, Southern Historical Association, Dept. of History University of Georgia, Athens GA 30602-1602. (706)542-8848. Fax: (706)542-2455. Website: www.uga.edu/~sha. **Contact:** Secretary-Treasurer. Estab. 1934. Managing Editor: John B. Boles. Offered in odd-numbered years for recognition of a distinguished book in Southern history published in even-numbered years. Publishers usually submit the books. **Deadline: March 1.**

THE PEARSON WRITERS' TRUST NONFICTION PRIZE, The Writers' Trust of Canada, 40 Wellington St. E., Suite 300, Toronto ON M5E 1C7, Canada. (416)504-8222. Fax: (416)504-9090. E-mail: info@writerstrust.com. Offered annually for a work of nonfiction published in the previous year. Award presented at the Great Literary Awards event held in Toronto each spring. Applications for SASE. **Deadline: Late July or mid-November, depending on publication date.** Prize: $10,000 (Canadian), and up to 4 runners-up prizes of $1,000 (Canadian).

LOUIS PELZER MEMORIAL AWARD, Organization of American Historians, *Journal of American History*, 1215 E. Atwater, Indiana University, Bloomington IN 47401. (812)855-9852. Fax: (812)855-0696. E-mail: awards@oah.org. Website: www.oah.org. **Contact:** Award and Prize Committee Coordinator. Offered annually for the best essay in American history by a graduate student. The essay may be about any period or topic in the history of the US, and the author must be enrolled in a graduate program at any level, in any field. Length: 7,000 words (including endnotes) maximum. Guidelines available on website. **Deadline: December 1.** Prize: $500, a medal, a certificate, and publication of the essay in the *Journal of American History.*

PEN/MARTHA ALBRAND AWARD FOR FIRST NONFICTION, PEN American Center, 568 Broadway, New York NY 10012. (212)334-1660. Fax: (212)334-2181. E-mail: jm@pen.org. **Contact:** John Morrone, coordinator. Offered annually for a first published book of general nonfiction distinguished by qualities of literary and stylistic excellence. Eligible books must have been published in the calendar year under consideration. Authors must be American citizens or permanent residents. Although there are no restrictions on the subject matter of titles submitted, nonliterary books will not be considered. Books should be of adult nonfiction for the general or academic reader. Publishers, agents, and authors themselves must submit 3 copies of each eligible title. **Deadline: December 15.** Prize: $1,000.

PEN/MARTHA ALBRAND AWARD FOR THE ART OF THE MEMOIR, Pen American Center, 568 Broadway, New York NY 10012. (212)334-1660. Fax: (212)334-2181. E-mail: jm@pen.org. **Contact:** John Morrone. Offered annually to an American author for his/her memoir published in the current calendar year, distinguished by qualities of literary and stylistic excellence. Send 3 copies of each eligible book. Open to American writers. **Deadline: December 15.** Prize: $1,000.

PEN/JERARD FUND, PEN American Center, 568 Broadway, New York NY 10012. (212)334-1660. Fax: (212)334-2181. E-mail: jm@pen.org. **Contact:** John Morrone. Estab. 1986. Biennial grant offered in odd-numbered years for an American woman writer of nonfiction for a book-length work-in-progress. **Deadline: January 3, 2005.** Prize: $5,500 grant.

PEN/SPIELVOGEL-DIAMONSTEIN AWARD, PEN American Center, 568 Broadway, New York NY 10012. (212)334-1660. Fax: (212)334-2181. E-mail: jm@pen.org. **Contact:** John Morrone. Offered for the best previously unpublished collection of essays on any subject by an American writer. "The $5,000 prize is awarded to preserve the dignity and esteem that the essay form imparts to literature." The essays included in books submitted may have been previously published in magazines, journals, or anthologies, but must not have collectively appeared before in book form. Books will be judged on literary character and distinction of the writing. Publishers, agents, or the authors must submit 4 copies of each eligible title. **Deadline: December 15.** Prize: $5,000.

THE PHI BETA KAPPA AWARD IN SCIENCE, The Phi Beta Kappa Society, 1606 New Hampshire Ave. NW, Washington DC 20009. (202)265-3808. Fax: (202)986-1601. E-mail: ccurtis@pbk.org. Website: www.pbk.org/scholarships/books. **Contact:** Ms. Cameron Curtis. Estab. 1959. "The Phi Beta Kappa Award in Science is offered annually for outstanding contributions by scientists to the literature of science. The intent of the award is to encourage literate and scholarly interpretations of the physical and biological sciences and mathematics; monographs and compendiums are not eligible. To be eligible, biographies of scientists must have a substantial critical emphasis on their scientific research." Entries must have been published May 1, 2002-April 30, 2003. Entries must be submitted by the publisher. Entries must be preceded by a letter certifying that the book(s) conforms to all the conditions of eligibility and stating the publication date of each entry. If accepted, 6 copies of each entry are required for the Science Award. Ineligible entries will be returned by Phi Beta Kappa. Books will not be entered officially in the competition until all copies and the letter of certification have been received. **Deadline: April 30.** Prize: $2,500. Open to US residents only.

PRISM INTERNATIONAL PRIZE FOR LITERARY NONFICTION, (formerly Maclean Hunter Endowment Literary Nonfiction Prize), Sponsored by Rogers, PRISM International, Buch E462—1866 Main Mall, Vancouver BC V6T 1Z1, Canada. (604)822-2514. Fax: (604)822-3616. E-mail: prism@interchange.ubc.ca. Website: prism.arts.ubc.ca. **Contact:** Mark Mallet, executive editor. Offered annually for published and unpublished writers to promote and reward excellence in literary nonfiction writing. *PRISM* buys first North American serial rights upon publication. "We also buy limited Web rights for pieces selected for website." Open to anyone except students and faculty of the Creative Writing Program at UBC or people who have taken a creative writing course at UBC in the 2 years prior to contest deadline. All entrants receive a 1-year subscription to *PRISM*. **Deadline: September 30.** Guidelines for SASE. **Charges $25, plus $5 for each additional entry (outside Canada use US funds).** Prize: $1,500 for the winning entry, plus $20/page for the publication of the winner in *PRISM*'s winter issue.

JAMES A. RAWLEY PRIZE, Organization of American Historians, 112 N. Bryan Ave., Bloomington IN 47408-4199. (812)855-9852. Fax: (812)855-0696. E-mail: awards@oah.org. Website: www.oah.org. **Contact:** Award and Prize Committee Coordinator. Offered annually for a book dealing with the history of race relations in the US. Books must have been published in the current calendar year. Before submitting a nomination, a listing of current committee members and details about individual prizes must be obtained from the OAH website. **Deadline: October 1; books to be published after October 1 of the calendar year may be submitted as page proofs.** Prize: $1,000, and a certificate.

PHILLIP D. REED MEMORIAL AWARD FOR OUTSTANDING WRITING ON THE SOUTHERN ENVIRONMENT, Southern Environmental Law Center, 201 W. Main St., Charlottesville VA 22902. (434)977-4090. Fax: (434)977-1483. E-mail: selcva@selcva.org. Website: www.SouthernEnvironment.org. **Contact:** Cathryn McCue, award director. Offered annually for nonfiction pieces that pertain to the natural resources in at least 1 of the following: Alabama, Georgia, North Carolina, South Carolina, Tennessee, Virginia. Two categories for works published in previous calendar year: books and journalism. Minimum length: 3,000 words. Prize: $1,000 each. Category for unpublished advocacy piece. Length 2,000-5,000 words. Prize: $250.

EVELYN RICHARDSON NONFICTION AWARD, Writers' Federation of Nova Scotia, 1113 Marginal Rd., Halifax NS B3H 4P7, Canada. (902)423-8116. Fax: (902)422-0881. E-mail: talk@writers.ns.ca. Website: www.writers.ns.ca. **Contact:** Jane Buss, executive director. "Nova Scotia's highest award for a book of nonfiction written by a Nova Scotian, the Evelyn Richardson Nonfiction Award is presented annually by the Writers' Federation of Nova Scotia. The Award is named for Nova Scotia writer Evelyn Richardson, whose book *We Keep a Light* won the Governor General's Literary Award for nonfiction in 1945." There is **no entry fee** or form. Full-length books of nonfiction written by Nova Scotians, and published as a whole for the first time in the previous calendar year, are eligible. Publishers: Send 4 copies and a letter attesting to the author's status as a Nova Scotian, and the author's current mailing address and telephone number. **Deadline: First Friday in December.** Prize: $1,000.

THE ROYAL SOCIETY OF LITERATURE AWARD UNDER THE W.H. HEINEMANN BEQUEST, Somerset House-Strand, London, England WC2R 1LA. (44)2078454676. Fax: (44)2078454679. E-mail: info@rslit.org. Website: www.rslit.org. Offered annually for previously published work appearing in print between January and December 2003. "W.H. Heinemann's Bequest was 'the encouragement of genuine contributions to literature.' Most often awarded to works of nonfiction, though novels, if of sufficient distinction, will not be overlooked." **Deadline: December 15.** Guidelines for SASE. Prize: £5,000. Judged by 3 Fellows of the Royal Society of Literature. Open to any writer.

THE CORNELIUS RYAN AWARD, The Overseas Press Club of America, 40 W. 45th St., New York NY 10036. (212)626-9220. Fax: (212)626-9210. **Contact:** Sonya Fry, executive director. Offered annually for excellence in a nonfiction book on foreign affairs. Generally publishers nominate the work, but writers may also submit in their own name. The work must be published and on the subject of foreign affairs. **Deadline: End of January. Charges $125 fee.** Prize: $1,000, and certificate.

SASKATCHEWAN NONFICTION AWARD, Saskatchewan Book Awards, Inc., Box 1921, Regina SK S4P 3E1, Canada. (306)569-1585. Fax: (306)569-4187. E-mail: director@bookawards.sk.ca. Website: www.bookawards.sk.ca. **Contact:** Joyce Wells, executive director. Offered annually for work published September 15, 2002-September 14, 2003. This award is presented to a Saskatchewan author for the best book of nonfiction, judged on the quality of writing. **Deadline: First deadline: July 31; Final deadline: September 14.** Guidelines for SASE. **Charges $15 (Canadian).** Prize: $1,500.

SASKATCHEWAN SCHOLARLY WRITING AWARD, Saskatchewan Book Awards, Inc., Box 1921, Regina SK S4P 3E1, Canada. (306)569-1585. Fax: (306)569-4187. E-mail: director@bookawards.sk.ca. Website: www.bookawards.sk.ca. **Contact:** Joyce Wells, executive director. Offered annually for work published September 15, 2002 to September 14, 2003 annually. This award is presented to a Saskatchewan author for the best contribution to scholarship. The work must recognize or draw on specific theoretical work within a community of scholars, and participate in the creation and transmission of knowledge. **First deadline: July 31; Final deadline: September 14.** Guidelines for SASE. **Charges $15 (Canadian).** Prize: $1,500.

THE BARBARA SAVAGE 'MILES FROM NOWHERE' MEMORIAL AWARD, The Mountaineers Books, 1001 SW Klickitat Way, Suite 201, Seattle WA 98134. (206)223-6303. Fax: (206)223-6306. E-mail: mbooks@mountaineersbooks.org. Website: www.mountaineersbooks.org. **Contact:** Mary Metz. Offered in even-numbered years for previously unpublished book-length nonfiction personal adventure narrative. Narrative must be based on an outdoor adventure involving hiking, mountain climbing, bicycling, paddle sports, skiing, snowshoeing, nature, conservation, ecology, or adventure travel not dependent upon motorized transport. Subjects *not* acceptable include hunting, fishing, or motorized or competitive sports. **Deadline: March 1, 2004.** Guidelines for SASE. Prize: $3,000 cash award, a $12,000 guaranteed advance against royalties, and publication by The Mountaineers.

ALDO AND JEANNE SCAGLIONE PRIZE FOR COMPARATIVE LITERARY STUDIES, Modern Language Association of America, 26 Broadway, 3rd Floor, New York NY 10004-1789. (646)576-5141. Fax: (646)458-0030. E-mail: awards@mla.org. Website: www.mla.org. **Contact:** Coordinator of Book Prizes. Offered annually for outstanding scholarly work published in the preceding year in the field of comparative literary studies involving at least 2 literatures. Author must be a member of the MLA. Works of scholarship, literary history, literary criticism, and literary theory are eligible; books that are primarily translations are not eligible. **Deadline: May 1.** Guidelines for SASE. Prize: $2,000, and a certificate.

ALDO AND JEANNE SCAGLIONE PRIZE FOR FRENCH AND FRANCOPHONE STUDIES, Modern Language Association of America, 26 Broadway, 3rd Floor, New York NY 10004-1789. (646)576-5141. Fax: (646)458-0030. E-mail: awards@mla.org. Website: www.mla.org. **Contact:** Coordinator of Book Prizes. Offered annually for work published in the preceding year that is an outstanding scholarly work in the field of French or francophone linguistic or literary studies. *Author must be a member of the MLA.* Works of scholarship, literary history, literary criticism, and literary theory are eligible; books that are primarily translations are not eligible. **Deadline: May 1.** Guidelines for SASE. Prize: $2,000, and a certificate.

ALDO AND JEANNE SCAGLIONE PRIZE FOR ITALIAN STUDIES, Modern Language Association of America, 26 Broadway, 3rd Floor, New York NY 10004-1789. (646)576-5141. Fax: (646)458-0030. E-mail: awards@mla.org. Website: www.mla.org. **Contact:** Coordinator of Book Prizes. Offered in odd-numbered years for a scholarly book on any phase of Italian literature or culture, or comparative literature involving Italian, including works on literary or cultural theory, science, history, art, music, society, politics, cinema, and linguistics, preferably but not necessarily relating other disciplines to literature. Books must have been published in year prior to competition. Authors must be members of the MLA. **Deadline: May 1.** Guidelines for SASE. Prize: $2,000, and a certificate.

ALDO AND JEANNE SCAGLIONE PRIZE FOR STUDIES IN GERMANIC LANGUAGES & LITERATURE, Modern Language Association of America, 26 Broadway, 3rd Floor, New York NY 10004-1789. (646)576-5141. Fax: (646)458-0030. E-mail: awards@mla.org. Website: www.mla.org. **Contact:** Coordinator of Book Prizes. Offered in even-numbered years for outstanding scholarly work appearing in print in the previous 2 years and written by a member of the MLA on the linguistics or literatures of the Germanic languages. Works of literary history, literary criticism, and literary theory are eligible; books that are primarily translations are not eligible. **Deadline: May 1.** Guidelines for SASE. Prize: $2,000, and a certificate.

ALDO AND JEANNE SCAGLIONE PRIZE FOR STUDIES IN SLAVIC LANGUAGES AND LITERATURES, Modern Language Association of America, 26 Broadway, 3rd Floor, New York NY 10004-1789. (646)576-5141. Fax: (646)458-0030. E-mail: awards@mla.org. Website: www.mla.org. **Contact:** Coordinator of Book Prizes. Offered each odd-numbered year for books published in the previous 2 years. Books published in 2001 or 2002 are eligible for the 2003 award. Membership in the MLA is not required. Works of literary history, literary criticism, philology, and literary theory are eligible; books that are primarily translations are not eligible. **Deadline: May 1.** Guidelines for SASE. Prize: $2,000, and a certificate.

SCIENCE WRITING AWARDS IN PHYSICS AND ASTRONOMY, American Institute of Physics, 1 Physics Ellipse, College Park MD 20740-3843. (301)209-3090. Fax: (301)209-0846. E-mail: pubinfo@aip.org. Website: www.aip.org/aip/writing. **Contact:** Flory Gonzalez. Offered for previously published articles, booklets, or books "that improves the general public's appreciation and understanding of physics and astronomy." Four categories: articles or books intended for children, preschool-15 years old; broadcast media involving radio or television; journalism, written by a professional journalist; and science, written by physicists, astronomers, or members of AIP or affiliated societies. Guidelines by phone, e-mail, or website. **Deadline: March 1.** Prize: $3,000, engraved Windsor chair, and certificate awarded in each category.

MINA P. SHAUGHNESSY PRIZE, Modern Language Association of America, 26 Broadway, 3rd Floor, New York NY 10004-1789. (646)576-5141. Fax: (646)458-0030. E-mail: awards@mla.org. Website: www.mla.org. **Contact:** Coordinator of Book Prizes. Offered annually for research publication (book) in the field of teaching English language, literature, rhetoric, and composition published during preceding year. Authors need not be members of the MLA. **Deadline: May 1.** Guidelines for SASE. Prize: $1,000, a certificate, and a year's membership in the MLA.

N **SOUTHERN CALIFORNIA GENEALOGICAL SOCIETY'S WRITERS CONTEST**, Southern California Genealogical Society, 417 Irving Dr., Burbank CA 91504-2408. (818)843-7247. Fax: (818)843-7262. E-mail: scgs@scgsgenealogy.com. Website: www.scgsgenealogy.com. **Contact:** Beth Maltbie Uyehara. **Category 1:** Research-oriented family, local, or ancestral history (3,000 words maximum). **Category 2:** Miscellaneous (must relate to family or local history), can include how-to articles, memoirs, accounts of ancestral events or dramas, reflections, personality sketches, humor, etc. (1,000-2,000 words). **Category 3:** Miscellaneous (must relate to family or local history), can include how-to articles, memoirs, accounts of ancestral events or dramas, reflections, personality sketches, humor, etc. (1,000 words or less). **Deadline: December 31 (must be received November 1-December 31).** Guidelines for SASE. Prize: **Categories 1 & 2**: 1st Prize: $250; 2nd Prize: $125; 3rd Prize: $75. **Category 3:** 1st Prize: $125; 2nd Prize: $75; 3rd Prize: $50. All Honorable Mentions receive a 1-year subscription to *The Searcher*. Judged by newspaper editors from Book Review sections. "We reserve one-time rights to publication of all material submitted, whether it is a prize winner or not." Open to any writer.

N **SWACKHAMER PEACE ESSAY CONTEST**, Nuclear Age Peace Foundation, PMB 121, 1187 Coastal Village Rd., Suite 1, Santa Barbara CA 93108-2794. (805)965-3443. Fax: (805)568-0466. E-mail: advocacy@napf.org. Website: www.wagingpeace.org. **Contact:** David Krieger. Offered annually for unpublished work. "The Swackhamer Peace Essay Contest seeks suggestions for constructive approaches from high school students to the problems of war and peace. The topic of the 2003 contest is: How would a peace education course in your school benefit students, the school, the community, and the world? What lessons and issues do you think should be included in such a course?" All essays become the property of the Nuclear Age Peace Foundation. The prize-winning essays will be published by the Foundation and will be sent to the Secretary General of the United Nations for transmittal to the UN General Assembly, to the President of the United States, and to other key world and national leaders. The winning essays will also be made widely available for use by newspapers, magazines, and broadcasting networks. Other essays, including honorable mentions, may be published by the Foundation and used on its website or in publications. **Deadline: June 1 (postmarked).** Guidelines for SASE. Prize: 1st Place: $1,500; 2nd Place: $1,000; 3rd Place: $500. Honorable Mentions may also be awarded. Judged by a committee of judges selected by the Nuclear Age Peace Foundation.

THE THEATRE LIBRARY ASSOCIATION AWARD, Theatre Library Association, Benjamin Rosenthal Library, Queens College, C.U.N.Y., 65-30 Kissena Blvd., Flushing NY 11367. (718)997-3672. Fax: (718)997-3753. E-mail: rlw$lib@qc1.qc.edu. Website: tla.library.unt.edu. **Contact:** Richard Wall, book awards committee chair. Estab. 1973. Offered for a book published in the US within the previous calendar year on a subject related to recorded or broadcast performance (including motion pictures, television, and radio). Eligible books may include biography, history, theory, criticism, reference, or related fields. **Deadline: February 15 of year following eligibility.** Prize: $250, and certificate to the winner; $100 and certificate for honorable mention.

HARRY S. TRUMAN BOOK AWARD, Harry S. Truman Library Institute for National & International Affairs, 500 West U.S. Hwy. 24, Independence MO 64050-1798. (816)833-0425. Fax: (816)833-2715. E-mail: lisa.sullivan@nara.gov. Website: www.trumanlibrary.org. **Contact:** Book Award Administrator. Offered in even-numbered years for a book published January 1, 2002-December 31, 2003, dealing "primarily and substantially with some aspect of the history of the United States between April 12, 1945 and January 20, 1953, or with the public career of Harry S. Truman." **Deadline: January 20, 2004.** Guidelines for SASE. Prize: $1,000.

N **FREDERICK JACKSON TURNER AWARD**, Organization of American Historians, 112 N. Bryan Ave., Bloomington IN 47408-4199. (812)855-9852. Fax: (812)855-0696. E-mail: awards@oah.org. Website: www.oah.org. **Contact:** Award and Prize Committee Coordinator. Offered annually for an author's first book on some significant phase of American history and also to the press that submits and publishes it. The entry must comply with the following rules: 1) The work must be the first book-length study of history published by the author; 2) If the author has a Ph.D., he/she must have received it no earlier than 7 years prior to submission of the ms for publication; 3) The work must be published in the calendar year before the award is given; 4) The work must deal with some significant phase of American history. Before submitting a nomination, a listing of current committee members and details about individual prizes must be obtained from the OAH website. **Deadline: October 1.** Prize: $1,000, certificate, and medal.

N **TURNING WHEEL YOUNG WRITER'S AWARD**, *Turning Wheel: The Journal of Socially Engaged Buddhism*, P.O. Box 4650, Berkeley CA 94704. (510)655-6169, ext. 303. Fax: (510)655-1369. E-mail: sue@bpf.org. Website: www.bpf.

org. **Contact:** Susan Moon, editor. Contest for "essays from a socially engaged Buddhist perspective by emerging writers (30 and under) on an aspect of each issue's theme." Contest is ongoing—1 award given each issue of quarterly. Open to writers 30 and under who have not previously published in *Turning Wheel*. **Deadline: 3 months before publication of each quarterly issue; details posted on website.** Guidelines for SASE. Prize: $500, and publication in *Turning Wheel*. Judged by *Turning Wheel* Editor Susan Moon, and the *Turning Wheel* Editorial Committee. Acquires first publication rights.

N **THE ELIE WIESEL PRIZE IN ETHICS ESSAY CONTEST**, The Elie Wiesel Foundation for Humanity, 529 Fifth Ave., Suite 1802, New York NY 10017. (212)490-7777. Fax: (212)490-6006. E-mail: info@eliewieselfoundation.org. Website: www.eliewieselfoundation.org. "Since 1989, The Elie Wiesel Foundation has sponsored the Prize in Ethics Essay Contest. This annual competition is intended to challenge undergraduate juniors and seniors in colleges and universities throughout the United States and Canada to analyze ethical questions and concerns facing them in today's complex society. All students are encouraged to write thought-provoking, personal essays." **Deadline: Early December.** Guidelines for SASE. Prize: 1st Prize: $5,000; 2nd Prize: $2,500; 3rd Prize: $1,500; Honorable Mentions (2): $500. Judged by a distinguished panel of readers who evaluate all contest entries, and a jury, including Elie Wiesel, chooses the winners.

L. KEMPER AND LEILA WILLIAMS PRIZE, The Historic New Orleans Collection and Louisiana Historical Association, 533 Royal St., New Orleans LA 70130-2179. Fax: (504)598-7108. E-mail: johnl@hnoc.org. Website: www.hnoc.org. **Contact:** Chair, Williams Prize Committee. Director: John H. Lawrence. Offered annually for the best published work on Louisiana history. **Deadline: January 15.** Prize: $1,500, and a plaque.

WRITERS' JOURNAL ANNUAL TRAVEL WRITING CONTEST, Val-Tech Media, P.O. Box 394, Perham MN 56573. (218)346-7921. Fax: (218)346-7924. E-mail: writersjournal@lakesplus.com. Website: www.writersjournal.com. **Contact:** Leon Ogroske. Offered annually for unpublished work. Buys one-time rights. Open to any writer. 2,000 word maximum. No e-mail submissions accepted. **Deadline: November 30.** Guidelines for SASE. **Charges $5 fee.** Prize: 1st Place: $50; 2nd Place: $25; 3rd Place: $15, plus honorable mentions. Prize-winning stories and selected honorable mentions will be published in *Writer's Journal* magazine.

N **THE WRITERS' TRUST OF CANADA'S SHAUGHNESSY COHEN AWARD FOR POLITICAL WRITING**, The Writers' Trust of Canada, 40 Wellington St. E., Suite 300, Toronto ON M5E 1C7, Canada. (416)504-8222. Fax: (416)504-9090. E-mail: info@writerstrust.com. Website: www.writerstrust.com. **Contact:** Sharon Poitras. Awarded annually for "a nonfiction book of outstanding literary merit that enlarges our understanding of contemporary Canadian political and social issues." Presented at the Great Literary Awards event each spring in Toronto. Prize: $10,000.

LAMAR YORK PRIZE FOR NONFICTION CONTEST, *The Chattahoochee Review*, Georgia Perimeter College, 2101 Womack Rd., Dunwoody GA 30338-4497. (770)551-3019. Website: www.chattahoochee-review.org. **Contact:** JoAnn Adkins, managing editor. Offered annually for unpublished creative nonfiction and nonscholarly essays. *The Chattahoochee Review* buys first rights only for winning essay/ms for the purpose of publication in the summer issue. **Deadline: January 15.** Guidelines for SASE. **Charges $10 fee/entry.** Prize: $1,000, and publication in the Summer issue.

Fiction

AIM MAGAZINE SHORT STORY CONTEST, P.O. Box 1174, Maywood IL 60153-8174. (708)344-4414. E-mail: apiladoone@aol.com. Website: www.aimmagazine.org. **Contact:** Myron Apilado, editor. Estab. 1974. $100 prize offered to contest winner for best unpublished short story (4,000 words maximum) "promoting brotherhood among people and cultures." **Deadline: August 15.** Open to any writer.

THE SHERWOOD ANDERSON FOUNDATION FICTION AWARD, (formerly Sherwood Anderson Writer's Grant), Sherwood Anderson Foundation, 3501 Highway 54 W., Studio C, Chapel Hill NC 27516. Annual award for short stories and chapters of novels to "encourage and support developing writers." Entrants must have published at least 1 book of fiction or have had several short stories published in major literary and/or commercial publications. Do not send your work by e-mail. Only mss in English will be accepted. **Deadline: April 1. Charges $20 application fee (payable to The Sherwood Anderson Foundation).** Award for the last 3 years has been $10,000. Judged by a committee established by the foundation. Open to any writer.

SHERWOOD ANDERSON SHORT FICTION AWARD, *Mid-American Review*, Dept. of English, Bowling Green State University, Bowling Green OH 43403. (419)372-2725. E-mail: karenka@bgnet.bgsu.edu. Website: www.bgsu.edu/midamericanreview. **Contact:** Michael Czyzniejewski, fiction editor. Offered annually for unpublished mss. Contest is open to all writers not associated with judge or *Mid-American Review*. **Deadline: October 1.** Guidelines for SASE. **Charges $10.** Prize: $500, plus publication in the spring issue of *Mid-American Review*. Judged by editors and a well-known writer, e.g. Peter Ho Davies or Melanie Rae Thon. Open to any writer.

N **ANTHOLOGY ANNUAL CONTEST**, P.O. Box 4411, Mesa AZ 85211-4411. (480)461-8200. E-mail: info@anthology.org. Website: www.anthology.org. **Contact:** Sharon Skinner, contest coordinator. Annual competition for short stories. All prize-winning stories are published in January/February of following year. Open to any writer, any genre. Erotica and graphic horror are not encouraged. **Deadline: August 31.** Guidelines for SASE. **Charges $5/short story.** Prize: $150. Judged by a panel of local writers and *Anthology* staff. Acquires one-time rights.

N **ANTIETAM REVIEW LITERARY AWARD**, *Antietam Review*, 41 S. Potomac St., Hagerstown MD 21740. (301)791-3132. Fax: (240)420-1754. **Contact:** Winnie Wagaman, managing editor. "We consider all fiction manuscripts sent to *Antietam Review* Literary Contest as entries for inclusion in each issue. We look for well-crafted, serious literary prose fiction under 5,000 words." Offered annually for unpublished work. Reading period: June 1-September 1. Guidelines for SASE. **Charges $10/story.** Prize: $100.

ANVIL PRESS INTERNATIONAL 3-DAY NOVEL WRITING CONTEST, Anvil Press, 6 W. 17th Ave., Vancouver BC V5Y 1Z4, Canada. (604)876-8710. Fax: (604)879-2667. E-mail: 3day@anvilpress.com. Website: www.anvilpress.com. **Contact:** Brian Kaufman or Lisa Sweanor. Estab. 1988. Offered annually for the best novel written in 3 days (Labor Day weekend). Entrants return finished novels to Anvil Press for judging. To register, send SASE (IRC if from outside Canada) for details, or entry form available from website. **Deadline: Friday before Labor Day weekend. Charges $35 fee.**

THE ISAAC ASIMOV AWARD, International Association for the Fantastic in the Arts and *Asimov's* magazine, School of Mass Communications, University of South Florida, 4202 E. Fowler, Tampa FL 33620. (813)974-6792. Fax: (813)974-2592. E-mail: rwilber@chuma.cas.usf.edu. **Contact:** Rick Wilber, administrator. "The annual award honors the legacy of one of science fiction's most distinguished authors through an award aimed at unpublished, undergraduate writers." **Deadline: December 15.** Guidelines for SASE. **Charges $10 for up to 3 submissions.** Prize: $500, and consideration for publication in *Asimov's*. Winner receives expense-paid trip to Ft. Lauderdale, Florida, to attend conference on the Fantastic in mid-March where award is given. Judged by *Asimov's* editors.

AUTHORMANIA.COM WRITING CONTEST, AuthorMania.com, Route 4, Box 201-A, Buna TX 77612. E-mail: TeddyBearTeam@aol.com. Website: www.authormania.com. **Contact:** Cindy Thomas, contest director. Annual contest for unpublished short stories on any topic, but no more than 5,000 words. "Enter as many times as you wish, but each entry must be mailed separately, and each must include an entry fee. No handwritten submissions." **Deadline: February 14. Charges $20 entry fee.** Prize: $1,000, and publication on AuthorMania.com. Open to any writer.

AUTHORS IN THE PARK SHORT STORY CONTEST, Authors in the Park, P.O. Box 85, Winter Park FL 32790-0085. (407)658-4520. E-mail: authorsinthepark@earthlink.net. **Contact:** David or Jennifer Foley. Estab. 1985. Offered annually to help expose fiction writers to literary journals. Length: 5,000 words maximum. Guidelines for SASE or by e-mail. Open to any writer. **Deadline: April 30. Charges $12 fee.** Prize: 1st Prize: $1,000; 2nd Prize: $500; 3rd Prize: $250.

BARD FICTION PRIZE, Bard College, P.O. Box 5000, Annandale-on-Hudson NY 12504-5000. (845)758-7087. E-mail: bfp@bard.edu. Estab. 2001. Annually. Guidelines for SASE. Prize: $30,000 cash award, and appointment as writer-in-residence at Bard College for 1 semester.

BEST PRIVATE EYE NOVEL CONTEST, Private Eye Writers of America and St. Martin's Press, 175 Fifth Ave., New York NY 11215. (212)674-5151. Fax: (212)254-4553. **Contact:** Julie Sullivan. Offered annually for unpublished, book-length mss in the "private-eye" genre. Open to authors who have not published a "private-eye" novel. **Deadline: August 1.** Guidelines for SASE. Prize: Advance against future royalties of $10,000, and publication by St. Martin's Press.

BONOMO MEMORIAL LITERATURE PRIZE, Italian Americana, URI/CCE, 80 Washington St., Providence RI 02903. (401)277-5306. Fax: (401)277-5100. E-mail: bonomoal@etal.uri.edu. Website: www.uri.edu/prov/italian/italian.html. **Contact:** Carol Bonomo Albright, editor. Offered annually for the best fiction, essay, or memoir that is published annually by an Italian-American. Acquires first North American serial rights. Guidelines for SASE. Prize: $250.

THE MAN BOOKER PRIZE, The Man Group, c/o Booktrust, Book House, 45 E. Hill, Wandsworth London SW18 2QZ, England. Fax: (00 44) 20 8516 2978. E-mail: tarryn@booktrust.org.uk. Website: www.themanbookerprize.com. **Contact:** Mr. Martyn Goff, OBE (Overall Administrator for The Man Booker Prize). "The Booker Prize for Fiction was set up in 1968 as a result of discussions between Booker plc and the Publishers Association about the need for a signifiant literary award in Britain, along the lines of the Prix Goncourt and similar awards in France. In 2002 the sponsorship of the Prize was awarded to The Man Group, and the prize is now known as The Man Booker Prize." Books are only accepted through UK publishers. However, publication outside the UK does not disqualify a book once it is published in the UK. Open to any full-length novel (published October 1, 2002-September 30, 2003) written by a citizen of the Commonwealth or the Republic of Ireland. No novellas, collections of short stories, translations, or self-published books. **Deadline: July.** Prize: The winner receives £50,000, and the short-listed authors receive £2,500. Judged by judges appointed by the Booker Prize Management Committee.

BOSTON REVIEW SHORT STORY CONTEST, *Boston Review*, E-53-407 MIT, Cambridge MA 02139. Website: bostonreview.mit.edu. Stories should not exceed 4,000 words and must be previously unpublished. **Deadline: October 1. Charges $20 fee (check or money order payable to** ***Boston Review*****).** Prize: $1,000, and publication in a later issue of *Boston Review*.

BOULEVARD SHORT FICTION CONTEST FOR EMERGING WRITERS, *Boulevard Magazine*, 6614 Clayton Rd., PMB #325, Richmond Heights MO 63117. (314)862-2643. Fax: (314)781-7250. Website: www.richardburgin.com. **Contact:** Richard Burgin, senior editor. Offered annually for unpublished short fiction to award a writer who has not yet published a book of fiction, poetry, or creative nonfiction with a nationally distributed press. "We hold first North American rights on anything not previously published." Open to any writer with no previous publication by a nationally known press. Guidelines for SASE or on website. **Deadline: December 15. Charges $15 fee/story; includes 1-year subscription to** *Boulevard*. Prize: $1,500, and publication in 1 of the next year's issues.

RAY BRADBURY SHORT STORY FELLOWSHIP, New Century Writer Awards, 32 Alfred St., Suite B, New Haven CT 06512-3927. (203)469-8824. Fax: (203)468-0333. E-mail: newcenturywriter@yahoo.com. Website: www.newcenturyw

riter.org. **Contact:** Jason Marchi, executive director. Open to all writers, both nonpublished and those with limited publication history, who enter at least 1 short story into the annual New Century Writers Award Competition (see listing for complete details). Open to all genres, not just science fiction. The first-place winner (and possibly the second-place winner) of each annual Ray Bradbury Fellowship attends the highly touted week-long *Zoetrope* Short Story Writer's Workshop at Francis Ford Coppola's Blancaneaux Lodge in Belize, Central America, during the first week of July. Special note: The remaining Top 10 short-story winners who are not awarded a Bradbury Fellowship receive cash awards. In addition, the Top 10 short stories will be considered for publication in the print magazines *Verbidice* and *Futures*, and are invited for inclusion in the annual *Top 10* short story and poetry anthology published by Scissor Press (www.scissorpress.com). See website for details on the *Zoetrope* Workshop and a list of past instructors. Guidelines/entry forms free. No SASE required. **Deadline: February 15. Charges $15 for 1 short story; $10/story for 2 or more stories.** Prize: The fellowship is worth approximately $4,500-5,000, and includes aifrare, workshop fees, a private (and beautiful) room, and all meals at Blancaneaux Lodge (excluding alcoholic beverages), and a $500 cash stipend.

SANDRA BROWN AWARD FOR OUTSTANDING SHORT FICTION, *descant*, Texas Christian University's literary journal, TCU Box 297270, Fort Worth TX 76129. (817)257-6537. Fax: (817)257-6239. E-mail: descant@tcu.edu. **Contact:** Dave Kuhne, editor. Offered annually for unpublished short stories. Publication retains copyright but will transfer it to the author upon request. **Deadline: September-April.** Guidelines for SASE. Prize: $250. Open to any writer.

THE CAINE PRIZE FOR AFRICAN WRITING, 2 Drayson Mews, London, England W8 4LY, United Kingdom. (020) 7376 0440. Fax: (020) 7938 3728. E-mail: caineprize@jftaylor.com. Website: www.caineprize.com. **Contact:** Nick Elam. Annual award for a short story (3,000-15,000 words) by an African writer. "An 'African writer' is normally taken to mean someone who was born in Africa; who is a national of an African country; or whose parents are African, and whose work has reflected African sensibilities." Entries must have appeared for the first time in the 5 years prior to the closing date for submissions, which is January 31 each year. Publishers should submit 12 copies of the published original with a brief cover note (no pro forma application). **Deadline: January 31.** Guidelines for SASE. Prize: $15,000 (£10,000). Judged by a panel of judges appointed each year. "We publish an anthology of short-listed stories with the agreement of the authors."

CANADIAN AUTHORS ASSOCIATION JUBILEE AWARD FOR SHORT STORIES, P.O. Box 419, 320 S. Shores Rd., Campbellford ON K0L 1L0, Canada. (705)653-0323. Fax: (705)653-0593. E-mail: canauth@redden.on.ca. Website: www.canauthors.org. **Contact:** Alec McEachern. Offered annually for a collection of short stories by a Canadian author. Entry form required. Obtain entry form from contact name or download from website. **Deadline: December 15.** Guidelines for SASE. **Charges $25 fee (Canadian).** Prize: $2,500, and a silver medal.

CANADIAN AUTHORS ASSOCIATION MOSAID TECHNOLOGY INC. AWARD FOR FICTION, (formerly Canadian Authors Association Award for Fiction), Box 419, 320 South Shores Rd., Campbellford ON K0L 1L0, Canada. (705)653-0323. Fax: (705)653-0593. E-mail: canauth@redden.on.ca. Website: www.canauthors.org. **Contact:** Alec McEachern. Offered annually for a full-length novel by a Canadian citizen. Entry form required. Obtain entry form from contact name or download from website. **Deadline: December 15.** Guidelines for SASE. **Charges $25 fee (Canadian).** Prize: $2,500, and a silver medal.

CAPE FEAR CRIME FESTIVAL SHORT STORY CONTEST, Atticus, Inc., 5828 Greenville Loop Rd., Wilmington NC 28409. (910)264-2101. Fax: (910)256-4770. E-mail: booklady@ec.rr.com. Website: www.galleone.com/cfcf.htm. **Contact:** Nicole Smith, contest director. "The CFCF Short Story Contest was created in concert with the annual Cape Fear Crime Festival, a mystery writer and reader's conference held in North Carolina. The purpose of the annual Story Contest is to provide a forum in which to discover, publish, and promote new writers, and to introduce readers to promising authors through the publication of the contest's annual chapbook. Contest organizers are also interested in bridging the imagined gap between genre and nongenre fiction." No specific categories, as long as the story has a strong mystery or crime theme. **Deadline: June 1.** Guidelines for SASE. **Charges $8/entry—unlimited entries.** Prize: 1st Place: $100; 2nd Place: $75; 3rd Place: $50. All winning stories will be published in the Story Contest chapbook, which is distributed to hundreds of Festival attendees. Winning authors will also receive free registration to the Cape Fear Crime Festival, and a free Saturday night dinner featuring a celebrated mystery author. Each winning story is subject to editorial review and will be copyedited for grammatical errors, spelling mistakes, and libelous language. All editorial changes will be shared with the winning authors before the chapbook goes to press. Judged by a panel of local bookstore employees, editors, and librarians, to determine the semifinalists. Semifinalist stories are then passed on to a celebrity judge who determines which stories win 1st, 2nd, and 3rd Place. 2003 celebrity judge was author Margaret Maron. Prize winning stories may be included in a Cape Fear Crime Anthology to be published at a later date. Open to any writer.

THE ALEXANDER PATTERSON CAPPON FICTION AWARD, *New Letters*, 5101 Rockhill Rd., Kansas City MO 64110. (816)235-1168. Fax: (816)235-2611. E-mail: newletters@umkc.edu. Website: www.umkc.edu/newletters. **Contact:** Aleatha Ezra. Offered annually for unpublished work to discover and reward new and upcoming writers. Buys first North American serial rights. Open to any writer. **Deadline: Third week in May.** Guidelines for SASE. **Charges $15 (includes a 1-year subscription to** *New Letters*). Prize: 1st Place: $1,000, and publication in a volume of *New Letters*; 2 runners-up will receive a year's subscription and will be considered for publication. All entries will be given consideration for publication in future issues of *New Letters*.

CAPTIVATING BEGINNINGS CONTEST, *Lynx Eye*, 542 Mitchell Dr., Los Osos CA 93402. (805)528-8146. Fax: (805)528-7876. E-mail: pamccully@aol.com. **Contact:** Pam McCully, co-editor. Annual award for unpublished stories "with engrossing beginnings, stories that will enthrall and absorb readers." **Deadline: January 31.** Guidelines for SASE.

Charges $5/story. Prize: $100, plus publication; $10 each for 4 honorable mentions, plus publication. Judged by *Lynx Eye* editors. Open to any writer.

RAYMOND CARVER SHORT STORY CONTEST, Humboldt State University, 1 Harpst St., Arcata CA 95521-8299. (707)826-5946, ext. 1. Fax: (707)826-5939. E-mail: carver@humboldt.edu. **Contact:** Brian Derr, coordiantor. Annual award for unpublished stories named in honor of award-winning writer and HSU alumnus, Raymond Carver. Open to all genres of short stories. Open to writers living in the US, or US citizens living abroad. **Deadline: January 10 (postmarked).** Guidelines for SASE. **Charges $10 entry fee.** Prize: 1st Place: $1,000, and publication in *Toyon*, HSU's literary magazine; 2nd Place: $500, and honorable mention in *Toyon*; 3rd Place: Honorable mention in *Toyon*.

G.S. SHARAT CHANDRA PRIZE FOR SHORT FICTION, BkMk Press, University of Missouri-Kansas City, 5101 Rockhill Rd., Kansas City MO 64110. (816)235-2558. Fax: (816)235-2611. E-mail: bkmk@umkc.edu. Website: www.umkc.edu/bkmk. **Contact:** Ben Furnish. Offered annually for the best book-length ms collection (unpublished) of short fiction in English by a living author. Translations are not eligible. Initial judging is done by a network of published writers. Final judging is done by a writer of national reputation. Guidelines for SASE, by e-mail, or on website. **Deadline: December 1 (postmarked). Charges $25 fee.** Prize: $1,000, plus book publication by BkMk Press.

CHILDREN'S WRITERS FICTION CONTEST, Stepping Stones, P.O. Box 8863, Springfield MO 65801-8863. (417)863-7369. E-mail: verwil@alumni.pace.edu. **Contact:** V.R. Williams, coordinator. Offered annually for unpublished fiction. **Deadline: July 31.** Guidelines for SASE. **Charges $8.** Prize: $260, and/or publication in *Hodge Podge*. Judged by Goodin, Williams, Goodwin and/or associates. "Entries are judged for clarity, grammar, punctuation, imagery, content, and suitability for children." Open to any writer.

THE ARTHUR C. CLARKE AWARD, Sir Arthur C. Clarke, 60 Bournemouth Rd., Folkestone, Kent CT19 5AZ, United Kingdom. E-mail: arthurclarkeaward@yahoo.co.uk. Website: www.clarkeaward.com. **Contact:** Paul Kincaid. Annual award presented to the best science fiction novel, published between January 1 and December 31 of the year in question, receiving its first British publication during the calendar year. **Deadline: 2nd week in December.** Prize: £2,003 (rising by £1 each year), and an engraved bookend. Judged by representatives of the British Science Fiction Association, the Science Fiction Foundation, and the Science Museum. Open to any writer.

COMMONWEALTH WRITERS PRIZE, The Commonwealth Foundation, % Booktrust, Book House, 45 E. Hill, Wandsworth London SW18 2QZ. Fax: (00 44) 20 8516 2978. E-mail: tarryn@booktrust.org.uk. Website: www.commonwealthwriters.com. **Contact:** Ms. Diana Bailey. The purpose of the annual award is "to encourage and reward the upsurge of new Commonwealth fiction and ensure that works of merit reach a wider audience outside their country of origin. The Commonwealth Foundation established the Commonwealth Writers Prize in 1987. For the purpose of the Prize, the Commonwealth is split into 4 regions—Africa, Caribbean and Canada, Eurasia, and Southeast Asia and South Pacific. Each region has 2 regional winners, 1 for the Best Book and 1 for the Best First Book. To be eligible for the Best Book Award, the author must have at least 1 work of fiction previously published between January 1 and December 1. To be eligible for the Best First Book Award, the book must be the author's first work of fiction (inluding a collection of short stories) to be published." This prize is publisher entry only, except in the case of some African and Asian countries where self-published works may be accepted at the administrator's discretion. Please contact Booktrust on this matter. All entries must be from Commonwealth citizens. All work must be written in English, translations are not eligible. **Deadline: November 15.** Prize: £10,000 to the overall best book; £3,000 to the overall best first book; £1,000 to 8 regional winners, 2 from each of the 4 regions. Judged by 4 panels of judges, 1 for each region. Each region has a chairperson and 2 judges. Once the regional winners are announced, the chairpersons read all 8 books and meet to decide which of the winners will receive the overall awards. This judging is headed by an eminent critic/author.

DAVID DORNSTEIN MEMORIAL CREATIVE WRITING CONTEST FOR YOUNG ADULT WRITERS, The Coalition for the Advancement of Jewish Education, 261 W. 35th St., Floor 12A, New York NY 10001. (212)268-4210. Fax: (212)268-4214. E-mail: cajeny@caje.org. Website: www.caje.org. **Contact:** Operations Manager. Contest offered annually for an unpublished short story based on a Jewish theme or topic. Writer must prove age of 18-35 years old. Submit only 1 story each year. Guidelines on website or available on request from CAJE office. **Deadline: December 31.** Prize: 1st Place: $700; 2nd Place: $200; 3rd Place: $100, and publication in the *Jewish Education News*.

JACK DYER FICTION PRIZE, *Crab Orchard Review*, Dept. of English, Southern Illinois University Carbondale, Carbondale IL 62901-4503. Website: www.siu.edu/~crborchd. **Contact:** Jon C. Tribble, managing editor. Offered annually for unpublished short fiction. *Crab Orchard Review* acquires first North American serial rights to all submitted work. Open to any writer. **Deadline: February 1-March 15.** Guidelines for SASE. **Charges $15/entry (can enter up to 3 stories, each story submitted requires a separate fee and can be up to 6,000 words), which includes a 1-year subscription to** *Crab Orchard Review*. Prize: $1,500, and publication.

STEPHEN EISEN MEMORIAL YOUTH PRIZES IN FICTION, National League of American Pen Women, Nob Hill, San Francisco Branch, 1544 Sweetwood Dr., Colma CA 94015. E-mail: pennobhill@aol.com. Website: www.welcome.to/soulmakingcontest. **Contact:** Eileen Malone. All prose works must be typed, page-numbered, stapled, and double-spaced. All entrants must be in grades 5-12, or equivalent. Grade or age must be indicated. One story/entry, up to 3,000 words. Annually. **Deadline: November 30.** Guidelines for SASE. **Charges $5/entry (make checks payable to NLAPW, Nob Hill Branch).** Prize: 1st Place: $50; 2nd & 3rd Place: $25.

FANTASTICAL VISIONS SHORT STORY CONTEST, Fantasist Enterprises, P.O. Box 9381, Wilmington DE 19809. E-mail: contests@fantasistent.com. Website: www.fantasistent.com. **Contact:** William H. Horner III. Offered annually for writers of quality, unpublished, short fantasy fiction. **Deadline: November 15.** Guidelines for SASE. **Charges**

There is no entry fee for 1 entry; however there is a $5 fee for 2 entries, and each additional entry is $3. Prize: 1st Prize: $200; 2nd Prize: $150; 3rd Prize: $100. Winning stories will be published in an annual anthology of fiction. Judged by William H. Horner III, editor-in-chief; Courtney Dudek; and a handful of volunteer readers. Acquires first anthology rights to winning and honorable mention stories. Copyright remains in name of authors. Open to any writer.

THE WILLIAM FAULKNER CREATIVE WRITING COMPETITION, The Pirate's Alley Faulkner Society, 624 Pirate's Alley, New Orleans LA 70116-3254. (504)586-1609. E-mail: faulkhouse@aol.com. Website: www.wordsandmusic.org. **Contact:** Rosemary James, director. Offered annually for unpublished mss to encourage publisher interest in a promising writer's novels, novellas, novels-in-progress, short stories, personal essays, poems, or short stories by high school students. The Society retains the right to publish excerpts of longer fiction; short stories, essays, poems in toto. Open to all authors working in English. Additional information on the competition and the festival is on the website. **Deadline: April 30. Charges entry fee: Novel—$35; novella—$30; novel-in-progress—$30; short story, personal essay, and individual poem—$25; high school short story—$10 (paid by school).** Prize: Novel: $7,500; novella: $2,500; novel-in-progress: $2,000; short story: $1,500; personal essay: $1,000; individual poem: $750; high school: $750 for student and $250 for sponsoring teacher. The Society also awards gold medals in William Faulkner's likeness; airfare and hotel expenses for winners to attend Words & Music: A Literary Feast in New Orleans, encompassing a major national writers' conference, and the Faulkner Society's gala annual meeting and Salute to All Great Writers: Past, Present, and Yet To Come, at which winners are presented by their judges. Note: For foreign residents the Society pays airfare only from selected US points of entry.

FISH ANNUAL SHORT STORY PRIZE, Fish Publishing, Durrus, Bantry, Co. Cork, Ireland. E-mail: info@fishpublishing.com. Website: www.fishpublishing.com. **Contact:** Prize Coordinator. Offered annually for unpublished mss. **Deadline: November 30. Charges $15 for 1st story; $10 for each additional story.** Prize: 1st Prize: $1,500; 2nd Prize: 1 week at Anam Cara Writers' Retreat in the west of Ireland. The top 15 stories will be published in Fish's anthology, which is launched at the West Cork Writers Festival in June, and will be read by literary agents, including Shirley Stewart, Merric Davidson, and Andrew Russell. Judged by a panel of international judges which changes every year. Open to any writer.

THE $5000 SHORT STORY COMPETITION, Scribendi.com, 4 Sherman St., Thamesville ON N0P 2K0, Canada. Fax: (801)469-6206. E-mail: contactus@scribendi.com. Website: www.scribendi.com. **Contact:** Chandra Clarke. Contest is offered every 6 months. "The contest is designed to give unpublished mainstream/literary short story authors a chance at 2 things they generally lack early in their careers—substantial financial reward and publication. We will have categories for genre fiction in the future." **Deadline: September 15.** Guidelines for SASE. **Charges $10.** Prize: 1st Prize: Up to $5,000, publication in the *Literati* short story anthology, and a certificate; 2nd Prize: Up to $500, free publication of a book-length work under the *Literati* imprint, publication in the *Literati* short story anthology, and a certificate; 3rd Prize: Up to $50, free sign-up for publication of a book-length work under the *Literati* imprint, publication in the *Literati* short story anthology, and a certificate; 4th-15th Place: Publication in the *Literati* short story anthology, and a certificate. Judged by the editorial staff at Scribendi.com and/or published short story authors, if they are available.

THE JOHN GARDNER FICTION BOOK AWARD, Creative Writing Program, Binghamton University-State University of New York, P.O. Box 6000, Binghamton NY 13902-6000. (607)777-6134. Fax: (607)777-2408. E-mail: mgillan@binghamton.edu. Website: www.binghamton.edu/english. **Contact:** Maria Mazziotti Gillan, director, creative writing program. Offered annually for work that appeared in print between January 1 and December 31 of year preceding award. **Deadline: April 1.** Guidelines for SASE. Prize: $1,000. Judged by a professional writer not on the Binghamton University faculty. Open to any writer.

THE JOHN GARDNER MEMORIAL PRIZE FOR FICTION, *Harpur Palate at Binghamton University*, Dept. of English, Binghamton University, P.O. Box 6000, Binghamton NY 13902-6000. (607)355-4761. Website: harpurpalate.binghamton.edu. **Contact:** Managing Editor. Contest offered annually for previously published fiction in any genre, up to 8,000 words. **Deadline: January 1-March 1.** Guidelines for SASE. **Charges $10/story.** Prize: $500, and publication in summer issue of *Harpur Palate*. All entrants receive a copy of the issue in which the winning story appears. Name and contact information should appear in the cover letter only. Acquires first North American serial rights. Open to any writer.

DANUTA GLEED LITERARY AWARD FOR FIRST BOOK OF SHORT FICTION, The Writers' Union of Canada, 40 Wellington St. E., 3rd Floor, Toronto ON M5E 1C7, Canada. (416)703-8982, ext. 223. Fax: (416)504-7656. E-mail: projects@writersunion.ca. Website: www.writersunion.ca. **Contact:** Deborah Windsor. Offered annually to Canadian writers for the best first collection of published short stories in the English language. Must have been published in the previous calendar year. Submit 4 copies. **Deadline: January 31.** Guidelines for SASE. Prize: 1st Place: $5,000; $500 to each of 2 runners-up.

GLIMMER TRAIN'S FALL SHORT-STORY AWARD FOR NEW WRITERS, Glimmer Train Press, Inc., 1211 NW Glisan St., Suite 207, Portland OR 97209. (503)221-0836. Fax: (503)221-0837. E-mail: eds@glimmertrain.com. Website: www.glimmertrain.com. **Contact:** Linda Swanson-Davies. Offered for any writer whose fiction hasn't appeared in a nationally-distributed publication with a circulation over 5,000. Word limit: 8,000 words. **Open August 1-September 30.** Follow online submission procedure on website. Notification on January 2." **Charges $12 fee/story.** Prize: Winner receives $1,200, publication in *Glimmer Train Stories*, and 20 copies of that issue. First/second runners-up receive $500/$300, respectively, and consideration for publication.

GLIMMER TRAIN'S SPRING SHORT-STORY AWARD FOR NEW WRITERS, Glimmer Train Press, Inc., 1211 NW Glisan St., Suite 207, Portland OR 97209. (503)221-0836. Fax: (503)221-0837. E-mail: eds@glimmertrain.com.

Website: www.glimmertrain.com. **Contact:** Linda Swanson-Davies. Offered for any writer whose fiction hasn't appeared in a nationally-distributed publication with a circulation over 5,000. Word limit: 8,000 words. **Contest open February 1-March 31.** Follow online submission procedure on website. Notification on July 1." **Charges $12 fee/story.** Prize: Winner receives $1,200, publication in *Glimmer Train Stories*, and 20 copies of that issue. First/second runners-up receive $500/$300, respectively, and consideration for publication.

GLIMMER TRAIN'S SUMMER FICTION OPEN, Glimmer Train Press, Inc., 1211 NW Glisan St., Suite 207, Portland OR 97209. (503)221-0836. Fax: (503)221-0837. E-mail: eds@glimmertrain.com. Website: www.glimmertrain.com. **Contact:** Linda Swanson-Davies. Offered annually for unpublished stories as "a platform for all themes, all lengths, all writers." Open to any writer. Follow online submission procedure on website. **Deadline: June 30. Charges $15 fee/story.** Prize: 1st Place: $2,000, publication in *Glimmer Train Stories*, and 20 copies of that issue; 2nd Place: $1,000, and possible publication in *Glimmer Train Stories*; 3rd Place: $600, and possible publication in *Glimmer Train Stories*.

GLIMMER TRAIN'S WINTER FICTION OPEN, Glimmer Train, Inc., 1211 NW Glisan St., Suite 207, Portland OR 97209. (503)221-0836. Fax: (503)221-0837. E-mail: eds@glimmertrain.com. Website: www.glimmertrain.com. **Contact:** Linda Swanson-Davies. Offered annually for unpublished work as "a platform for all themes, all lengths, and all writers." Follow online submission procedure on website. **Charges $15/story.** Prize: 1st Place: $2,000, publication in *Glimmer Train Stories*, and 20 copies of that issue; 2nd Place: $1,000, possible publication in *Glimmer Train Stories*; 3rd Place: $600, possible publication in *Glimmer Train Stories*. Open to any writer.

GLIMMER TRAIN'S VERY SHORT FICTION AWARD, Glimmer Train Press, Inc., 1211 NW Glisan St., #207, Portland OR 97209. (503)221-0836. Fax: (503)221-0837. E-mail: eds@glimmertrain.com. Website: glimmertrain.com. **Contact:** Linda Swanson-Davies. Offered twice yearly to encourage the art of the very short story. Word count: 2,000 maximum. Open April 1-July 31 (Summer contest) or November 1-January 31 (Winter contest). Follow online submission process on website. Results will be e-mailed to all entrants on November 1 (for Summer contest) and May 1 (for Winter contest). **Charges $10 fee/story.** Prize: 1st Place: $1,200, publication in *Glimmer Train Stories* (circulation 13,000), and 20 copies of that issue. Runners-up: $500/$300, respectively, and consideration for publication.

THE PHILLIP GOOD MEMORIAL PRIZE, *QWF Magazine*, P.O. Box 1768, Rugby CV21 42A, United Kingdom. 01788 334302. E-mail: jo@qwfmagazine.co.uk. Website: www.qwfmagazine.co.uk. **Contact:** The Competition Secretary. Estab. 1998. Annual international short story competition open to all writers over 18. **Deadline: August 21.** Guidelines for SASE. **Charges £5 for each story up to 5,000 words (checks payable to J.M. Good).** Prize: 1st Prize: £300; 2nd Prize: £150; 3rd Prize: £75. Judged by Lynne Barrett-Lee. Copyright remains with the author, but permissions will be requested to include the winning entries in the anthology or *QWF Magazine*.

GOVERNOR GENERAL'S LITERARY AWARD FOR FICTION, Canada Council for the Arts, 350 Albert St., P.O. Box 1047, Ottawa ON K1P 5V8, Canada. (613)566-4414, ext. 5576. Fax: (613)566-4410. E-mail: joanne.larocque-poirier@canadacouncil.ca. Website: www.canadacouncil.ca/prizes/ggla. **Contact:** Joanne Larocque-Poirier. Offered annually for the best English-language and the best French-language work of fiction by a Canadian published September 1, 2002-September 30, 2003. Publishers submit titles for consideration. **Deadline: April 15 or August 7, 2003, depending on the book's publication date.** Prize: Each laureate receives $15,000, and nonwinning finalists receive $1,000.

DRUE HEINZ LITERATURE PRIZE, University of Pittsburgh Press, 3400 Forbes Ave., 5th Floor, Eureka Bldg., Pittsburgh PA 15260. (412)383-2492. Fax: (412)383-2466. E-mail: susief@pitt.edu. Website: www.pitt.edu/~press. **Contact:** Sue Borello, assistant to the director. Estab. 1981. Offered annually to writers who have published a book-length collection of fiction or a minimum of 3 short stories or novellas in commercial magazines or literary journals of national distribution. Does not return mss. **Deadline: Submit in May and June only.** Guidelines for SASE. Prize: $15,000.

ERNEST HEMINGWAY FOUNDATION PEN AWARD FOR FIRST FICTION, PEN New England, P.O. Box 400725, North Cambridge MA 02140. (617)499-9550. Fax: (617)353-7134. E-mail: awards@pen-ne.org. Website: www.pen-ne.org. **Contact:** Mary Sullivan. Offered for first-published novel or short story collection by an American author. Guidelines and entry form for SASE. **Deadline: December 15.**

LORIAN HEMINGWAY SHORT STORY COMPETITION, Hemingway Days Festival, P.O. Box 993, Key West FL 33041-0993. (305)294-0320. E-mail: calico2419@aol.com. Website: www.shortstorycompetition.com. **Contact:** Carol Shaughnessy, co-coordinator. Estab. 1981. Mail for guideline requests only. Guidelines for SASE or by e-mail. Offered annually for unpublished short stories up to 3,000 words. **Deadline: May 15. Charges $10/story postmarked by May 1, $15/story postmarked by May 15; no stories accepted after May 15.** Prize: 1st Place: $1,000; 2nd and 3rd Place: $500; runners-up awards; honorable mentions will also be awarded.

THE WINIFRED HOLTBY MEMORIAL PRIZE, Somerset House-Strand, London, England, WC2R 1LA. (44) 207 845 4676. Fax: (44) 207 845 4679. E-mail: info@rslit.org. Website: www.rslit.org. This annual award is for the best regional novel published January-December of the year written in the English language. Only British, Irish, or Commonwealth writers may enter. **Deadline: December 15.** Guidelines for SASE. Prize: £1,000. Judged by 3 Fellows of the Royal Society of Literature.

L. RON HUBBARD'S WRITERS OF THE FUTURE CONTEST, P.O. Box 1630, Los Angeles CA 90078. (323)466-3310. Website: www.writersofthefuture.com. **Contact:** Contest Administrator. Offered for unpublished work "to find, reward, and publicize new speculative fiction writers so they may more easily attain professonal writing careers." Open to new and amateur writers who have not professionally published a novel or short novel, more than 1 novelette, or more than 3 short stories. Eligible entries are short stories or novelettes (under 17,000 words) of science fiction or fantasy.

Guidelines for SASE or on website. **Deadline: December 31, March 31, June 30, September 30.** Prize: Awards quarterly 1st Place: $1,000; 2nd Place: $750; and 3rd Place: $500. Annual Grand Prize: $4,000.

INDIANA REVIEW FICTION CONTEST, *Indiana Review*, BH 465/Indiana University, Bloomington IN 47405-7103. (812)855-3439. Fax: (812)855-4253. E-mail: inreview@indiana.edu. Website: www.indiana.edu/~inreview. **Contact:** Danit Brown. Maximum story length is 15,000 words (no minimum). Offered annually for unpublished work. **Deadline: Early October.** Guidelines for SASE. **Charges $15 fee (includes a year's subscription).** Prize: $1,000. Judged by guest judges. Aimee Bender judged the 2003 contest. Open to any writer.

JAPANOPHILE ANNUAL SHORT STORY CONTEST, Japanophile, P.O. Box 7977, Ann Arbor MI 48107-7977. (734)930-1553. Fax: (734)930-9968. E-mail: japanophile@aol.com. Website: www.japanophile.com. **Contact:** Susan Aitken, editor. Offered annually for unpublished work to encourage good fiction writing that contributes to the understanding of Japan and Japanese culture. **Deadline: December 31.** Guidelines for SASE. **Charges $5 fee.** Prize: $100, certificate, and publication.

N JERRY JAZZ MUSICIAN NEW SHORT FICTION AWARD, *Jerry Jazz Musician*, 2207 NE Broadway, Portland OR 97232. (503)287-5570. Fax: (801)749-9896. E-mail: jm@jerryjazzmusician.com. Website: www.jerryjazz.com. **Contact:** Joe Maita. Contest is offered 3 times/year. "We value creative writing and wish to encourage writers of short fiction to pursue their dream of being published. *Jerry Jazz Musician*, an online magazine, would like to provide another step in the career of an aspiring writer. Three times a year, *Jerry Jazz Musician* awards a writer who submits, in our opinion, the best original, previously unpublished work of approximately 3,000-5,000 words. The winner will be announced via a special mailing of our *Jerry Jazz* newsletter. Publishers, artists, musicians, and interested readers are among those who subscribe to the newsletter. Additionally, the work will be published on the home page of *Jerry Jazz Musician* and featured there for at least 4 weeks. The *Jerry Jazz Musician* reader tends to be well educated, with strong interests in music, history, literature, art, film, and theater, particularly that of the counter-culture of mid-20th century America. Writing should appeal to a reader with these characteristics." Guidelines available online. **Deadline: September 15, 2003; January 15, 2004; and May 15, 2004.** Prize: $200. Judged by the editors of *Jerry Jazz Musician*. Open to any writer.

JAMES JONES FIRST NOVEL FELLOWSHIP, Wilkes University, English Dept., Kirby Hall, Wilkes-Barre PA 18766. (570)408-4530. Fax: (570)408-7829. E-mail: english@wilkes.edu. Website: www.wilkes.edu/humanities/jones.asp. **Contact:** Jacqueline Mosher, coordinator. Offered annually for unpublished novels, novellas, and closely-linked short stories (all works in progress). "The award is intended to honor the spirit of unblinking honesty, determination, and insight into modern culture exemplified by the late James Jones." The competition is open to all American writers who have not previously published novels. **Deadline: March 1. Charges $20 fee.** Prize: $6,000; $250 honorarium (runner-up).

N JUST DESSERTS SHORT-SHORT FICTION CONTEST, *Passages North*, Dept. of English, Northern Michigan University, 1401 Presque Isle Ave., Marquette MI 49855. (906)227-1203. Fax: (906)227-1096. E-mail: passages@nmu.edu. Website: www.myweb.nmu.edu/~passages. **Contact:** Katie Hanson. Offered every 2 years to publish new voices in literary fiction. Guidelines available for SASE or download from website. **Deadline: Submit September 15-January 15. Charges $8 reading fee/story.** Prize: $1,000, and publication for the winner; 2 honorable mentions also published; all entrants receive a copy of *Passages North*.

KLOPP ANTHOLOGIST'S ANNUAL SHORT STORY AWARD FOR NEW WRITERS, Klopp Anthologist Publications, 23 Pine Grove St., Woodstock NY 12498. E-mail: kloppanthologist@hotmail.com. Website: 81x.com/kloppanthologis/kloppanthologist. **Contact:** Kenneth Bender. Offered annually for unpublished short fiction to showcase new and emerging writers. Guidelines available for SASE, by e-mail and on website. "We reserve first-time publishing rights, after which all rights revert back to the writer." Open to any writer; however, all submissions must be in English. **Deadline: January 31 (postmarked). Charges $20 for each story submitted.** Prize: 1st Place: $300; 2nd Place: $150; 3rd Place: $75. Five honorable mentions receive a free copy of publication. Judged by a panel of readers in the literary field.

THE LAWRENCE FOUNDATION AWARD, *Prairie Schooner*, 201 Andrews Hall, P.O. Box 880334, Lincoln NE 68588-0334. (402)472-0911. Fax: (402)472-9771. E-mail: eflanagan2@unl.edu. Website: www.unl.edu/schooner/psmain.htm. **Contact:** Hilda Raz. Offered annually for the best short story published in *Prairie Schooner* in the previous year. Prize: $1,000.

URSULA K. LEGUIN PRIZE FOR IMAGINATIVE FICTION, *Rosebud*, P.O. Box 459, Cambridge WI 53523. E-mail: jrodclark@smallbytes.net. Website: www.rsbd.net. **Contact:** J. Roderick Clark, editor. Biennial (odd years) contest for unpublished stories. Next contest opens April 1, 2003. Acquires first rights. Open to any writer. **Deadline: September 30. Charges $10/story fee.** Prize: $1,000, plus publication in *Rosebud*.

N LONG FICTION CONTEST, White Eagle Coffee Store Press, P.O. Box 383, Fox River Grove IL 60021. (847)639-9200. E-mail: wecspress@aol.com. Website: http://members.aol.com/wecspress. **Contact:** Frank E. Smith, publisher. Offered annually since 1993 for unpublished work to recognize and promote long short stories of 8,000-14,000 words (about 30-50 pages). Sample of previous winner: $5.95, including postage. Open to any writer, no restrictions on materials. **Deadline: December 15.** Guidelines for SASE. **Charges $15 fee, $5 for second story in same envelope.** Prize: (A.E. Coppard Prize) $500, and publication, plus 25 copies of chapbook.

MALICE DOMESTIC GRANTS FOR UNPUBLISHED WRITERS, Malice Domestic, P.O. Box 31137, Bethesda MD 20284-1137. Website: www.malicedomestic.org. **Contact:** Grants chair. Offered annually for unpublished work. Malice awards 2 grants to unpublished writers in the Malice Domestic genre at its annual convention in May. The competition is designed to help the next generation of Malice authors get their first work published and to foster quality Malice literature.

Writers who have been published previously in the mystery field, including publication of a mystery novel, short story, or nonfiction work, are ineligible to apply. Members of the Malice Domestic Board of Directors and their families are ineligible to apply. Malice encourages applications from minority candidates. Guidelines on website. **Deadline: December 15.** Prize: $1,000.

MARY MCCARTHY PRIZE IN SHORT FICTION, Sarabande Books, P.O. Box 4456, Louisville KY 40204. (502)458-4028. Fax: (502)458-4065. E-mail: sarabandeb@aol.com. Website: www.SarabandeBooks.org. **Contact:** Kirby Gann, managing editor. Offered annually to publish an outstanding collection of stories, novellas, or short novel (less than 250 pages). All finalists considered for publication. **Deadline: January 1-February 15.** Guidelines for SASE. **Charges $20 fee.** Prize: $2,000, and publication (standard royalty contract).

MID-LIST PRESS FIRST SERIES AWARD FOR SHORT FICTION, Mid-List Press, 4324 12th Ave. S., Minneapolis MN 55407-3218. Fax: (612)823-8387. E-mail: guide@midlist.org. Website: www.midlist.org. **Contact:** Lane Stiles, publisher. Open to any writer who has never published a book-length collection of short fiction (short stories, novellas); minimum 50,000 words. Accepts simultaneous submissions. Guidelines and entry form for SASE or on website. **Deadline: July 1. Charges $30 (US dollars) fee.** Prize: Awards include publication and an advance against royalties.

MID-LIST PRESS FIRST SERIES AWARD FOR THE NOVEL, Mid-List Press, 4324-12th Ave. S., Minneapolis MN 55407-3218. (612)822-3733. Fax: (612)823-8387. E-mail: guide@midlist.org. Website: www.midlist.org. **Contact:** Lane Stiles, publisher. Offered annually for unpublished novels to locate and publish quality mss by first-time writers, particularly those mid-list titles that major publishers may be rejecting. Guidelines for SASE or on website. Open to any writer who has never published a novel. **Deadline: February 1. Charges $30 (US dollars) fee.** Prize: Advance against royalties, plus publication.

MILKWEED NATIONAL FICTION PRIZE, Milkweed Editions, 1011 Washington Ave. S., Suite 300, Minneapolis MN 55415. (612)332-3192. Fax: (612)215-2550. Website: www.milkweed.org. **Contact:** Elisabeth Fitz, first reader. Estab. 1986. Annual award for unpublished works. "Milkweed is looking for a novel, novella, or a collection of short stories. Manuscripts should be of high literary quality and must be double-spaced and between 150-400 pages in length. Due to new postal regulations, writers who need their work returned must include a check for $5 rather than a SAS book mailer. Manuscripts not accompanied by a check for postage will be recycled." Winner will be chosen from the mss Milkweed accepts for publication each year. All mss submitted to Milkweed will automatically be considered for the prize. Submission directly to the contest is no longer necessary. "Must be written in English. Writers should have previously published a book of fiction or 3 short stories (or novellas) in magazines/journals with national distribution." Catalog available on request for $1.50. Guidelines for SASE or online. **Deadline: Open.** Prize: Publication by Milkweed Editions, and a cash advance of $5,000 against royalties agreed upon in the contractual arrangement negotiated at the time of acceptance.

C. WRIGHT MILLS AWARD, The Society for the Study of Social Problems, 901 McClung Tower, University of Tennessee, Knoxville TN 37996-0490. (865)689-1531. Fax: (865)689-1534. E-mail: mkoontz3@utk.edu. Website: www.it.utk.edu/sssp. **Contact:** Michele Smith Koontz, administrative officer. Offered annually for a book published the previous year that most effectively critically addresses an issue of contemporary public importance; brings to the topic a fresh, imaginative perspective; advances social scientific understanding of the topic; displays a theoretically informed view and empirical orientation; evinces quality in style of writing; and explicitly or implicitly contains implications for courses of action. **Deadline: January 15.** Prize: $500 stipend.

N **MOTA 4: INTEGRITY**, TripleTree Publishing, P.O. Box 5684, Eugene OR 97405. (541)338-3184. Fax: (541)484-5358. E-mail: Liz@TripleTreePub.com. Website: www.TripleTreePub.com. **Contact:** Liz Cratty, contest/award director. "Each MOTA contest/year/issue has a theme. The theme for MOTA 4 is Integrity. It is our intention to publish an extraordinary annual anthology of unpublished fine fiction, devoted to the challenging issues of our times as played out in fictional scenarios. It is part of the mission statement of TripleTree Publishing to publish previously unpublished writers. Nothing makes us happier than to help launch a writing career. Writers can also submit on a noncontest basis. One-time nonexclusive publication and 'best of' anthology rights are acquired for the monetary prize offered. Placing second or third does not guarantee publication, but if we choose, we may publish these entries with no further monetary consideration. We ask that a winning author not publish the piece for a year after it appears in our anthology." **Deadline: November 1.** Guidelines for SASE. **Charges $12 fee for the Emerging Writers Contest.** Prize: 1st Place: $100, plus publication; 2nd Place: $50 and possible publication; 3rd Place: $25 and possible publication. Judged by a panel of professional fiction writers, along with the year's guest editor. Open to any writer.

N **MOUNTAINLAND AWARD FOR SHORT FICTION**, Godot Enterprises and Mountainland Writers Group, P.O. Box 910, Ogden UT 84402-0910. (801)475-4387. Fax: (801)340-0084. E-mail: submissions@godot-enterprises.com. Website: www.godot-enterprises.com. **Contact:** Michael Combe. Offered quarterly to discover unpublished emerging writers and works. Open to the following genres: action/adventure, military, science fiction/fantasy, historical, humor, mainstream, mystery/suspense, western. Prizes are awarded in each genre. Entries may be submitted in more than 1 genre category. **Deadline: March 31, June 30, September 30, December 31. Charges $10.** Prize: Grand Prize: $500, plus publication in *Mountainland Magazine*; Genre Prizes: $50, plus publication in *Mountainland Magazine*. Judged by a panel of published writers and educators, plus Godot Enterprises' editorial staff (Michael Combe, executive director; Steve Ludlow, senior editor; Frank Cole, associate editor; Judy Combe, associate editor). Acquires First North American serial rights. Open to any writer.

NATIONAL WRITERS ASSOCIATION NOVEL WRITING CONTEST, The National Writers Association, 3140 S. Peoria, #295, Aurora CO 80014. (303)841-0246. Fax: (303)841-2607. **Contact:** Sandy Whelchel, director. Annual contest "to help develop creative skills, to recognize and reward outstanding ability, and to increase the opportunity for the marketing and subsequent publication of novel manuscripts." **Deadline: April 1. Charges $35 fee.** Prize: 1st Place: $500; 2nd Place: $300; 3rd Place: $200.

NATIONAL WRITERS ASSOCIATION SHORT STORY CONTEST, The National Writers Association, 3140 S. Peoria, #295, Aurora CO 80014. (303)841-0246. Fax: (303)841-2607. **Contact:** Sandy Whelchel, director. Annual contest "to encourage writers in this creative form, and to recognize those who excel in fiction writing." **Deadline: July 1.** Guidelines for SASE. **Charges $15 fee.** Prize: 1st Place: $200; 2nd Place: $100; 3rd Place: $50.

NEW CENTURY WRITER AWARDS (FICTION), 32 Alfred St., Suite B, New Haven CT 06512-3927. (203)469-8824. Fax: (203)468-0333. E-mail: newcenturywriter@yahoo.com. Website: www.newcenturywriter.org. **Contact:** Jason J. Marchi, executive director. Offered annually to discover emerging writers of short stories and novels. Guidelines/entry forms for the asking. All entrants receive 1-year subscription to *The Anvil*, an educational newsletter for writers. Open to all writers, both nonpublished and those with limited publication history. Call if you doubt your eligibility. Also provides the annual Ray Bradbury Short Story Fellowship for a short fiction writer to attend the Zoetrope Short Story Writers' Workshop at Francis Ford Coppola's Blancaneaux Lodge in Belize, Central America (see Ray Bradbury Short Story Fellowship listing for complete details). **Deadline: February 15. Charges $10-35 entry fee.** Prize: 1st Place: $2,000; 2nd Place: $1,000; 3rd Place: $500; 4th-10th Place: $100.

NEW MUSE AWARD, Broken Jaw Press, Box 596 Station A, Fredericton NB E3B 5A6, Canada. E-mail: jblades@nbnet.nb.ca. Website: www.brokenjaw.com. **Contact:** Joe Blades. Offered annually for unpublished fiction mss no less than 100 pages to encourage development of book-length mss by Canadian writers without a first fiction book published. Guidelines for SASE or go to www.brokenjaw.com/newmuse.htm. **Deadline: January 31. Charges $20 fee (all entrants receive copy of winning book upon publication).** Prize: $500 cash, and book publication on trade terms.

NEW YORK STORIES FICTION PRIZE, New York Stories, English Dept., E-103, LaGuardia Community College/CUNY, 31-10 Thomson Ave., Long Island City NY 11101. E-mail: nystories@lagcc.cuny.edu. Website: www.newyorkstories.org. **Contact:** Daniel Lynch, contest director. Offered annually for unpublished work to showcase new, quality short fiction. Stories must not exceed 6,500 words. Open to any writer. **Deadline: September 15.** Guidelines for SASE. **Charges $15 fee (payable to New York Stories).** Prize: 1st Place: $500 and publication; 2nd Place: $250, and consideration for publication.

THE FLANNERY O'CONNOR AWARD FOR SHORT FICTION, The University of Georgia Press, 330 Research Dr., Athens GA 30602-4901. (706)369-6130. Fax: (706)369-6131. Website: www.ugapress.org. **Contact:** Nicole Mitchell, director. Estab. 1981. Does not return mss. Manuscripts must be 200-275 pages long. Authors do not have to be previously published. **Submission Period: April 1-May 31.** Guidelines for SASE. **Charges $20 fee.** Prize: $1,000, and publication under standard book contract.

FRANK O'CONNOR AWARD FOR SHORT FICTION, *descant*, Texas Christian University's literary journal, TCU Box 297270, Fort Worth TX 76129. (817)257-6537. Fax: (817)257-6239. E-mail: descant@tcu.edu. **Contact:** Dave Kuhne, editor. Offered annually for unpublished short stories. Publication retains copyright but will transfer it to the author upon request. **Deadline: September-April.** Guidelines for SASE. Prize: $500.

THE OHIO STATE UNIVERSITY PRIZE IN SHORT FICTION, (formerly The Sandstone Prize in Short Fiction), The Ohio State University Press and the MFA Program in Creative Writing at The Ohio State University, 1070 Carmack Rd., Columbus OH 43210-1002. (614)292-1462. Fax: (614)292-2065. E-mail: ohiostatepress@osu.edu. Website: ohiostatepress.org. Offered annually to published and unpublished writers. Submissions may include short stories, novellas, or a combination of both. Manuscripts must be 150-300 typed pages; novellas must not exceed 125 pages. No employee or student of The Ohio State University is eligible. **Deadline: November 15. Charges $20 fee.** Prize: $1,500, publication under a standard book contract.

ORANGE PRIZE FOR FICTION, Orange PCS, c/o Booktrust, Book House, 45 E. Hill, Wandsworth, London SW18 2QZ, United Kingdom. Fax: (00 44) 20 8516 2978. E-mail: tarryn@booktrust.org.uk. Website: www.orangeprize.com. **Contact:** Ms. Becky Shaw. This annual award is for a full-length novel written by a woman which fulfills the criteria of excellence in writing, relevance to people's everyday and imaginative lives, accessibility, and originality. The award is open to any full-length novel written in English between April 1, 2002 and March 31, 2003 by a woman of any nationality. Translations are not eligible, neither are novellas or collections of short stories. Books from all genres are encouraged, but all books must be unified and substantial works written by a single author. All entries must be published in the UK between the publication dates, but may have been previously published outside the UK. Publisher entry only. **Deadline: December 2.** Prize: £30,000 and a statuette known as a "Bessie." Judged by a panel of women.

OTTAWA PUBLIC LIBRARY ANNUAL SHORT STORY CONTEST, Ottawa Public Library, 101 Centrepointe Dr., Ottawa ON K2G 5K7, Canada. (613)580-2424, ext. 41468. E-mail: esme.bailey@library.ottawa.on.ca. Website: www.library.ottawa.on.ca. **Contact:** Esme Bailey. Offered annually for unpublished short stories (written in French or English) to encourage writing in the community. Open to residents of Ottawa, Ontario, age 18 or older. Guidelines for SASE or online. **Deadline: March 3. Charges $5/story.** Prize: 1st Prize: $500; 2nd Prize: $250; 3rd Prize: $100.

PATERSON FICTION PRIZE, One College Blvd., Paterson NJ 07505-1179. (973)684-6555. Fax: (973)684-5843. E-mail: mgillan@pccc.cc.nj.us. Website: www.pccc.cc.nj.us/poetry. **Contact:** Maria Mazziotti Gillan, director. Offered annually for a novel or collection of short fiction published the previous calendar year. **Deadline: April 1.** Guidelines for SASE. Prize: $1,000.

WILLIAM PEDEN PRIZE IN FICTION, *The Missouri Review*, 1507 Hillcrest Hall, Columbia MO 65211. (573)882-4474. Fax: (573)884-4671. Website: www.missourireview.org. **Contact:** Hoa Ngo, managing editor. Offered annually "for the best story published in the past volume year of the magazine. All stories published in *The Missouri Review* are automatically considered." Prize: $1,000, and reading/reception.

PEN/FAULKNER AWARDS FOR FICTION, PEN/Faulkner Foundation, 201 E. Capitol St., Washington DC 20003. (202)675-0345. Fax: (202)608-1719. E-mail: delaney@folger.edu. Website: www.penfaulkner.org. **Contact:** Janice F. Delaney, executive director. Offered annually for best book-length work of fiction by an American citizen published in a calendar year. **Deadline: October 31.** Prize: $15,000 (one winner); $5,000 (4 nominees).

PAUL PERRY SHORT-SHORT PRIZE, National League of American Pen Women, Nob Hill, San Francisco Branch, 1544 Sweetwood Dr., Colma CA 94015. E-mail: pennobhill@aol.com. Website: www.welcome.to/soulmakingcontest. **Contact:** Eileen Malone. All prose works must be typed, page numbered, stapled, and double-spaced. One short-short/entry, under 500 words. Annually. **Deadline: November 30.** Guidelines for SASE. **Charges $5/entry (make checks payable to NLAPW, Nob Hill Branch).** Prize: 1st Place: $100; 2nd Place: $50; 3rd Place: $25. Open to any writer.

PHOEBE WINTER FICTION CONTEST, *Phoebe*, George Mason University, 4400 University Dr., Fairfax VA 22030-4444. (703)993-2915. E-mail: phoebe@gmu.edu. Website: www.gmu.edu. **Contact:** Emily Tuszynska. Offered annually for unpublished work. **Deadline: December 1.** Guidelines for SASE. **Charges $10.** Prize: $1,000, and publication in Fall issue. All entrants receive a free issue. Judged by outside judge—recognized fiction writer hired by *Phoebe*—changes each year. Acquires first serial rights, if work is accepted for publication. Open to any writer.

POCKETS FICTION-WRITING CONTEST, The Upper Room, 1908 Grand Ave., P.O. Box 340004, Nashville TN 37203-0004. (615)340-7333. E-mail: pockets@upperroom.org. Website: www.pockets.org. **Contact:** Lynn W. Gilliam. Offered annually for unpublished work to discover new writers. **Deadline: March 1-August 15.** Guidelines for SASE. Prize: $1,000, and publication in *Pockets*.

THE KATHERINE ANNE PORTER PRIZE FOR FICTION, *Nimrod International Journal*, 600 S. College Ave., Tulsa OK 74104. (918)631-3080. Fax: (918)631-3033. E-mail: nimrod@utulsa.edu. Website: www.utulsa.edu/nimrod. **Contact:** Francine Ringold. This annual award was established to discover new, unpublished writers of vigor and talent. **Deadline: April 30.** Guidelines for SASE. **Charges $20 (includes a 1-year subscription to** *Nimrod*). Prize: 1st Place: $2,000, and publication; 2nd Place: $1,000, and publication. Judged by the *Nimrod* editors (finalists) and a recognized author selects the winners. *Nimrod* retains the right to publish any submission. Open to US residents only.

PRISM INTERNATIONAL ANNUAL SHORT FICTION CONTEST, Prism International, Creative Writing Program, UBC, Buch E462, 1866 Main Mall, Vancouver BC V6T 1Z1, Canada. (604)822-2514. Fax: (604)822-3616. E-mail: prism@interchange.ubc.ca. Website: prism.arts.ubc.ca. **Contact:** Fiction Contest Manager. Offered annually for unpublished work to award the best in contemporary fiction. Works of translation are eligible. Guidelines for SASE, by e-mail, or on website. Acquires first North American serial rights upon publication, and limited Web rights for pieces selected for website. Open to any writer except students and faculty in the Creative Writing Department at UBC, or people who have taken a creative writing course at UBC with the 2 years prior to the contest deadline. **Deadline: January 31. Charges $22/story, $5 each additional story (outside Canada pay US currency); includes subscription.** Prize: 1st Place: $2,000; Runners-up(5): $200 each; winner and runners-up published.

THOMAS H. RADDALL ATLANTIC FICTION PRIZE, Writers' Federation of Nova Scotia, 1113 Marginal Rd., Halifax NS B3H 4P7, Canada. (902)423-8116. Fax: (902)422-0881. E-mail: talk@writers.ns.ca. Website: www.writers.ns.ca. **Contact:** Jane Buss, executive director. "This award was established by the Writers' Federation of Nova Scotia and the Writers' Development Trust in 1990 to honor the achievement of Thomas H. Raddall, and to recognize the best Atlantic Canadian adult fiction. Thomas Head Raddall is probably best-known for *His Majesty's Yankees* (1942), *The Governor's Lady* (1960), *The Nymph and the Lamp* (1950), and *Halifax, Warden of the North* (1948)." There is no entry fee or form. Full-length books of fiction written by Atlantic Canadians, and published as a whole for the first time in the previous calendar year, are eligible. Entrants must be native or resident Atlantic Canadians who have either been born in Newfoundland, Prince Edward Island, Nova Scotia, or New Brunswick, and spent a substantial portion of their lives living there, or who have lived in 1 or a combination of these provinces for at least 24 consecutive months prior to entry deadline date. Publishers: Send 4 copies and a letter attesting to the author's status as an Atlantic Canadian, and the author's current mailing address and telephone number. **Deadline: First Friday in December.** Prize: $10,000.

RAMBUNCTIOUS REVIEW FICTION CONTEST, *Rambunctious Review*, 1221 W. Pratt Blvd., Chicago IL 60626. Annual themed contest for unpublished stories. Acquires one-time publication rights. Open to any writer. **Deadline: December 31.** Guidelines for SASE. **Charges $3/story.** Prize: 1st Prize: $100; 2nd Prize: $75; 3rd Prize: $50; all winning stories will be published in future issues of *Rambunctious Review*. Acquires one-time publication rights.

RIVER CITY WRITING AWARDS IN FICTION, The University of Memphis/Hohenberg Foundation, Dept. of English, Memphis TN 38152. (901)678-4591. Fax: (901)678-2226. Website: www.people.memphis.edu/~rivercity. **Contact:** Mary Leader. Offered annually for unpublished short stories of 7,500 words maximum. Guidelines for SASE or on website. **Deadline: March 15. Charges $12/story, which is put toward a 1-year subscription for** *River City*. Prize: 1st Place: $1,500; 2nd Place: $350; 3rd Place: $150.

THE ROGERS WRITERS' TRUST FICTION PRIZE, The Writers' Trust of Canada, 40 Wellington St. E., Suite 300, Toronto ON M5E 1C7, Canada. (416)504-8222. Fax: (416)504-9090. E-mail: info@writerstrust.com. Website: www.writerstrust.com. **Contact:** Sharon Poitras. Awarded annually for a distinguished work of fiction, either a novel or short story collection, published within the previous year. Presented at the Great Literary Awards event held in Toronto each spring. Prize: $10,000. Open to Canadian residents only.

SASKATCHEWAN FICTION AWARD, Saskatchewan Book Awards, Inc., Box 1921, Regina SK S4P 3E1, Canada. (306)569-1585. Fax: (306)569-4187. E-mail: director@bookawards.sk.ca. Website: www.bookawards.sk.ca. **Contact:** Joyce Wells, executive director. Offered annually for work published September 15, 2002 to September 14, 2003. This award is presented to a Saskatchewan author for the best book of fiction (novel or short fiction), judged on the quality of writing. **Deadline: First deadline: July 31; Final deadline: September 14.** Guidelines for SASE. **Charges $15 (Canadian).** Prize: $1,500.

MICHAEL SHAARA AWARD FOR EXCELLENCE IN CIVIL WAR FICTION, US Civil War Center, LSU, Raphael Semmes Dr., Baton Rouge LA 70803. (225)578-3151. Fax: (225)578-4876. E-mail: lwood@lsu.edu. Website: www.cwc.lsu.edu. **Contact:** Leah Jewett, director. Offered annually for fiction published January 1-December 31 "to encourage examination of the Civil War from unique perspectives or by taking an unusual approach." All Civil War novels are eligible. Nominations should be made by publishers, but authors and critics can nominate as well. **Deadline: December 31.** Guidelines for SASE. Prize: $2,500, which includes travel stipend.

SKYLINE MAGAZINE ANNUAL SHORT STORY CONTEST, Skyline Publications/*Skyline Magazine*, P.O. Box 295, Stormville NY 12582-5417. (845)227-5171. Fax: (845)226-8392. E-mail: SkyWriterr@aol.com. Website: www.skylinepublications.com. **Contact:** Victoria Valentine. "Annual award for unpublished short stories to offer incentive and compensation for authors and their contributions, and to draw more interest to short story writing by both beginners and by young authors just starting out. Everyone stands an equal chance in our contest. We judge blind entries, with authors receving an ID number. Judges are not revealed until the end of the contest. Stories are evaluated on originality, subject interest, writing style, grammar, and punctuation. We look for storylines that grab our attention—flow smoothly—with strong, unique characterizations and imagery—powerful conclusions and/or surprise endings are a must." **Deadline: March 1-August 30.** Guidelines for SASE. **Charges $5.** Prize: 1st Prize: $100; 2nd Prize: $50; 3rd Prize: $25, along with publication in *Skyline Magazine*, and a free copy of the issue in which the winning stories appear. Judged by Victoria Valentine, H. Tomas Beck, and 3 impartial author/judges to be named. Open to any writer.

ELIZABETH SIMPSON SMITH AWARD, Charlotte Writers Club, P.O. Box 220954, Charlotte NC 28222-0954. E-mail: akalnik@carolina.rr.com. **Contact:** Blynn Field, ESS award chairperson. Offered annually for unpublished short stories by North Carolina and South Carolina residents. **Deadline: April 30.** Guidelines for SASE. **Charges $10 fee.** Prize: $500, and a plaque.

SHEILA K. SMITH SHORT STORY PRIZE, National League of American Pen Women, Nob Hill, San Francisco Branch, 1544 Sweetwood Dr., Colma CA 94015-2029. E-mail: pennobhill@aol.com. Website: www.welcome.to/soulmakingcontest. **Contact:** Eileen Malone. One story/entry, up to 5,000 words. All prose works must be typed, page numbered, stapled, and double-spaced. Annually. **Deadline: November 30.** Guidelines for SASE. **Charges $5/entry (make checks payable to NLAPW, Nob Hill Branch).** Prize: 1st Place: $100; 2nd Place: $50; 3rd Place: $25. Open to any writer.

SNAKE NATION PRESS ANNUAL AWARD FOR SHORT FICTION, Snake Nation Press, 110 W. Force St., Valdosta GA 31601. (229)244-0752. E-mail: jeana@snakenationpress.org. Website: www.snakenationpress.org. **Contact:** Jean Arambula. Contest for a collection of unpublished short stories by a new or underpublished writer. Entries accepted year round. **Deadline: June 15.** Guidelines for SASE. **Charges $20 reading fee.** Prize: $1,000, and publication. Judged by an independent judge. Open to any writer.

KAY SNOW WRITING AWARDS, Willamette Writers, 9045 SW Barbur Blvd., Suite 5A, Portland OR 97219. (503)452-1592. Fax: (503)452-0372. E-mail: wilwrite@teleport.com. Website: www.willamettewriters.com. **Contact:** Elizabeth Shannon. Contest offered annually to "offer encouragement and recognition to writers with unpublished submissions." Acquires right to publish excerpts from winning pieces 1 time in their newsletter. **Deadline: May 15.** Guidelines for SASE. **Charges $15 fee; no fee for student writers.** Prize: 1st Place: $300; 2nd Place: $150; 3rd Place: $50; excerpts published in Willamette Writers newsletter, and winners acknowledged at banquet during writing conference. Student writers win $50 in categories for grades 1-5, 6-8, and 9-12. $500 Liam Callen Memorial Award goes to best overall entry.

SOUL OF THE WRITER AWARD, Grammar Bytes, 3044 Shepherd of Hills, PMB519, Branson MO 65616. E-mail: contest@grammarbytes.com. Website: www.grammarbytes.com. **Contact:** Shane Jeffries. Offered once a year to unpublished submissions. "Soul of the Writer Award was created to aid writers in their journey toward ultimate literary goals—whatever they may be. We look at fiction of any genre, any style." Guidelines for SASE. Limit of 12,000 words/short story submission. Previous winners will select semi-finalists, then a committee of 3 prominent writers will make final decision. Writers retain all rights. Open to any writer. **Deadline: May 31 (postmarked). Charges $25.** Prize: 1st Place: $250; 2nd Place: $125; 3rd Place: $25, plus certificate.

SOUTH CAROLINA FICTION PROJECT, South Carolina Arts Commission, 1800 Gervais St., Columbia SC 29201. (803)734-8696. Fax: (803)734-8526. E-mail: goldstsa@arts.state.sc.us. Website: www.state.sc.us/arts. **Contact:** Sara June Goldstein, contest director. Offered annually for unpublished short stories of 2,500 words or less. *The Post and Courier* newspaper (Charleston, South Carolina) purchases first publication rights. Open to any writer who is a legal resident of South Carolina and 18 years of age or older. Twelve stories are selected for publication. **Deadline: January 15.** Guidelines for SASE. Prize: $500.

THE SOUTHERN REVIEW/LOUISIANA STATE UNIVERSITY SHORT FICTION AWARD, Louisiana State University, 43 Allen Hall, Baton Rouge LA 70803. (225)578-5108. Fax: (225)578-5098. E-mail: bmacon@LSU.edu or jeaster@LSU.edu. Offered for first collections of short stories by Americans published in the US during the previous year. Publisher or author may enter by mailing 2 copies of the collection. **Deadline: January 31.**

SPOKANE PRIZE FOR SHORT FICTION, Eastern Washington University Press, 705 W. First Ave., Spokane WA 99201. (800)508-9095. Fax: (509)623-4283. E-mail: ewupress@ewu.edu. Website: www.ewupress.ewu.edu. **Contact:** Christopher Howell. "Annual award to publish the finest work the literary world has to offer." **Deadline: May 15.** Guidelines for SASE. **Charges $25.** Prize: $1,500, and publication. Judged by EWU Press staff. Open to any writer.

THE STORYCOVE FLASH FICTION CONTEST, Word Smitten, LLP, P.O. Box 5067, St. Petersburg FL 33737. E-mail: editor@wordsmitten.com. Website: www.wordsmitten.com. **Contact:** Susan Johnson. Offered annually for unpublished, original fiction with memorable characters and interesting consequences with 500 or fewer words. Submit story embedded in an e-mail (no attachments) with your name at the top of the e-mail. Guidelines for SASE, by e-mail, and on website. **Deadline: May 1. Charges $10/entry.** Prize: $150, and publication in Native Shore Fiction/Word Smitten Summer edition. Judged by recognized authors. In last year's major fiction competition, Peter Meinke, winner of The Flannery O'Connor Award, was judge. Acquires one-time rights for publication, then all rights revert to author. Open to any writer.

THE SUNDAY STAR SHORT STORY CONTEST, *The Toronto Star*, 1 Yonge St., 5th Floor, Toronto ON M5A 4L1, Canada. Website: www.thestar.com. Annual contest for unpublished work offered "to encourage good, quality short story writing." Must be a Canadian citizen if living outside Canada, or a resident of Canada and at least 16 years or older. Guidelines on website or on "StarPhone (416)350-3000, ext. 2747." **Deadline: December 31. Charges $5.** Prize: 1st Place: $10,000, plus tuition fee for the Humber School of Writers Creative Correspondence Program; 2nd Place: $3,000; 3rd Place: $1,000; 7 runners-up receive $200 each. Judged by Ryerson Writing Centre (initial judging). Final judging by panel of writers and editors from *The Star*.

THE PETER TAYLOR PRIZE FOR THE NOVEL, Knoxville Writers' Guild and University of Tennessee Press, P.O. Box 2565, Knoxville TN 37901-2565. Website: www.knoxvillewritersguild.org. **Contact:** Brian Griffin. Offered annually for unpublished work to discover and publish novels of high literary quality. Guidelines for SASE or on website. Open to US residents writing in English. Members of the Knoxville Writers' Guild do the initial screening. A widely published novelist chooses the winner from a pool of finalists. 2003 judge: John Casey. 2002 judge: Alan Cheuse. **Deadline: February 1-April 30. Charges $20 fee.** Prize: $1,000, publication by University of Tennessee Press a (standard royalty contract).

THREE OAKS PRIZE FOR FICTION, Story Line Press, P.O. Box 1240, Ashland OR 97520-0055. (541)512-8792. Fax: (541)512-8793. E-mail: mail@storylinepress.com. Website: www.storylinepress.com. Offered annually to find and publish the best work of fiction. Open to any writer. **Deadline: April 30.** Guidelines for SASE. **Charges $25.** Prize: $1,500 advance, and book publication.

WAASMODE FICTION CONTEST, *Passages North*, Dept. of English, Northern Michigan University, 1401 Presque Isle Ave., Marquette MI 49855. (906)227-1203. Fax: (906)227-1096. E-mail: passages@nmu.edu. Website: www.myweb.nmu.edu/~passages. **Contact:** Katie Hanson. Offered every 2 years to publish new voices in literary fiction. Guidelines for SASE or download from website. **Deadline: Submit September 15-January 15.** Guidelines for SASE. **Charges $8 reading fee/story.** Prize: $1,000, and publication for winner; 2 honorable mentions also published; all entrants receive a copy of *Passages North*.

WHIM'S PLACE CHANGING OF THE SEASONS FLASH FICTION WRITING CONTEST, WhimsPlace.com, 14207 W. 94th St., Lenexa KS 66215. E-mail: hyashar@whimsplace.com. Website: www.whimsplace.com/contest/contest.asp. **Contact:** Hdar Yashar. Offered quarterly for flash fiction. "We love flash fiction! That's why we're having a contest. We also feel that contests are a great way to boost an ego, enhance a résumé, and to just have some plain old fashion fun with your writing. We expect good writing, however. It must be tightly written, organized, and proofread." Submissions are accepted only through Whim's Place online submission form. Entries over 500 words will automatically be disqualified. **Deadline: March 21; June 21; September 21; December 21. Charges $5.** Prize: 1st Place: $250; 2nd Place: $200; 3rd Place: $150; Honorable Mentions (8): $50. "Also, part of the proceeds from the contest will be awarded to charity in the name of our special judge. The charity will also be chosen by him/her." Judged by Whim's Place staff members, and an appointed guest judge each season. The special judge will be a published author or an editor. "All rights remain with the author; however, we do reserve the right to publish the top winning entries on our website." Open to any writer.

TOBIAS WOLFF AWARD IN FICTION, *Bellingham Review*, Mail Stop 9053, Western Washington University, Bellingham WA 98225. (360)650-4863. E-mail: bhreview@cc.wwu.edu. Website: www.wwu.edu/~bhreview/. **Contact:** Brenda Miller. Offered annually for unpublished work. Guidelines for SASE or online. **Deadline: December 1-March 15. Charges $15 entry fee for 1st entry, and $10 for each additional entry.** Prize: $1,000, plus publication and subscription.

WORD SMITTEN'S TENTEN FICTION COMPETITION, Word Smitten, LLP, P.O. Box 5067, St. Petersburg FL 33737-5067. E-mail: editor@wordsmitten.com. Website: www.wordsmitten.com. **Contact:** Susan Johnson. Contest offered annually for unpublished short stories that require exactly 1,010 words. "The word count does not include the story title, but we recommend you keep it short. Excise those adverbs! Cut those adjectives. Make us laugh or make us weep. Above all, pay rigorous attention to the word count. It's why we call it the TenTen. It's a challenge to be precise, be witty, be short!" For more details visit website. Guidelines by e-mail or on website. **Deadline: July 1. Charges $15/entry.** Prize: $1,010, and publication in *Native Shore Fiction/Word Smitten* Summer edition. Judged by recognized authors. "In last year's major competition, Peter Meinke, winner of The Flannery O'Connor Award was our judge." Buys one-time rights for publication, and then all rights revert to author. Open to any writer.

N **WORLD'S BEST SHORT SHORT STORY FICTION CONTEST**, English Dept., Writing Program, Florida State University, Tallahassee FL 32306. (850)644-2773. E-mail: southeastreview@english.fsu.edu. Website: www.english.fsu.edu/southeastreview. **Contact:** James Kimbrell, editor, *The Southeast Review*. Estab. 1986. Annual award for unpublished short short stories (no more than 500 words). **Deadline: February 15. Charges $10 fee/story.** Prize: $500, an all-expense-paid-trip to read at FSU, and a box of Florida oranges.

N **WRITER'S REPERTORY SHORT FICTION LITERARY AWARD**, Center for Teaching and Learning, University of Illinois at Springfield, One University Plaza, MS BRK 461, Springfield IL 62703. (217)206-6503. E-mail: writersrepertory@hotmail.com. Website: www.uis.edu/ctl. **Contact:** Penny Pennell. "We are seeking unpublished short fiction (1,500 words maximum). Writer's Repertory is a student-run organization seeking exposure for both the organization and the Center for Teaching and Learning. The contest grew out of a graduate assistant's yearlong project." Entries are limited to the first 200 entries, after 200, entries will be returned unread. **Deadline: December 14.** Guidelines for SASE. **Charges $5 entry fee.** Prize: 1st Place: $300, and publication in *The Alchemist Review* (the student-run literary journal produced by the English Department at the University of Illinois at Springfield), and 2 copies of the journal; 2nd Place: $100, and 1 copy of *The Alchemist Review*; 3rd Place: 1 copy of *The Alchemist Review*. Judged by graduate students in the English Department with a primary focus on creative writing. Open to any writer.

WRITERS' JOURNAL ANNUAL FICTION CONTEST, Val-Tech Media, P.O. Box 394, Perham MN 56573. (218)346-7921. Fax: (218)346-7924. E-mail: writersjournal@lakesplus.com. Website: www.writersjournal.com. **Contact:** Leon Ogroske. Offered annually for previously unpublished fiction. Open to any writer. **Deadline: January 30.** Guidelines for SASE. **Charges $5 reading fee.** Prize: 1st Place: $50; 2nd Place: $25; 3rd Place: $15, plus honorable mentions. Prize-winning stories and selected honorable mentions published in *Writers' Journal*.

WRITERS' JOURNAL ANNUAL HORROR/GHOST CONTEST, Val-Tech Media, P.O. Box 394, Perham MN 56573. (218)346-7921. Fax: (218)346-7924. E-mail: writersjournal@lakesplus.com. Website: www.writersjournal.com. **Contact:** Leon Ogroske. Offered annually for previously unpublished works. Open to any writer. **Deadline: March 30.** Guidelines for SASE. **Charges $5 fee.** Prize: 1st Place: $50; 2nd Place: $25; 3rd Place: $15, plus honorable mentions. Prize-winning stories and selected honorable mentions published in *Writers' Journal* .

WRITERS' JOURNAL ANNUAL ROMANCE CONTEST, Val-Tech Media, P.O. Box 394, Perham MN 56573. (218)346-7921. Fax: (218)346-7924. E-mail: writersjournal@lakesplus.com. Website: www.writersjournal.com. **Contact:** Leon Ogroske. Offered annually for previously unpublished works. Open to any writer. **Deadline: July 30.** Guidelines for SASE. **Charges $5 fee.** Prize: 1st Place: $50; 2nd Place: $25; 3rd Place: $15, plus honorable mentions. Prize-winning stories and selected honorable mentions published in *Writers' Journal*.

WRITERS' JOURNAL ANNUAL SHORT STORY CONTEST, Val-Tech Media, P.O. Box 394, Perham MN 56573. (218)346-7921. Fax: (218)346-7924. E-mail: writersjournal@lakesplus.com. Website: www.writersjournal.com. **Contact:** Leon Ogroske. Offered annually for previously unpublished short stories. Open to any writer. **Deadline: May 30.** Guidelines for SASE. **Charges $7 reading fee.** Prize: 1st Place: $300; 2nd Place: $100; 3rd Place: $50, plus honorable mentions. Prize-winning stories and selected honorable mentions published in *Writers' Journal*.

ZOETROPE SHORT STORY CONTEST, *Zoetrope: All-Story*, 916 Kearny St., San Francisco CA 94133. (415)788-7500. Fax: (415)989-7910. Website: www.all-story.com. **Contact:** Francis Ford Coppola, publisher. Annual contest for unpublished short stories. Guidelines for SASE or on website. Open to any writer. **Deadline: October 1. Charges $15 fee.** Prize: 1st Plsce: $1,000; 2nd Place: $500, 3rd Place: $250, plus 10 honorable mentions.

Poetry

N **ACADEMI CARDIFF INTERNATIONAL POETRY COMPETITION**, Academi (The Welsh Academy) and the City of Cardiff, P.O. Box 438, Cardiff, Wales CF10 5 YA, United Kingdom. E-mail: competitions@academi.org. Website: www.academi.org. **Contact:** Peter Finch, contest/award director. "This annual competition is open to everyone—the only criteria being that poems submitted must be of 50 lines or less, written in English, and previously unpublished. All entries must be accompanied by payment and an entry form, which may be downloaded from the Academi website." **Deadline: January 6.** Guidelines for SASE. **Charges £5/poem.** Prize: 1st Prize: £5,000; 2nd Prize: £700; 3rd Prize: £300; 4th-8th Prize: £200. All cash awards include publication in the *New Welsh Review*, Wales' leading literary journal, and on the Academi website. Judged by Carol Ann Duffy and Roger Garfitt.

N **AKRON POETRY PRIZE**, University of Akron Press, 374B Bierce Library, Akron OH 44325-1703. (330)972-5342. Fax: (330)972-8364. E-mail: uapress@uakron.edu. Website: www.uakron.edu/uapress/poetry.html. **Contact:** Elton Glaser, poetry editor. Annual book contest for unpublished poetry. "The Akron Poetry Prize brings to the public writers with original and compelling voices. Books must exhibit three essential qualities: mastery of language, maturity of feeling, and complexity of thought." Guidelines available online or for SASE. The final selection will be made by a nationally prominent poet. The University of Akron Press has the right to publish the winning ms, inherent with winning the Poetry Prize. Open to all poets writing in English. **Deadline: May 15-June 30. Charges $25 fee.** Prize: Winning poet receives $1,000, and publication of book.

ANHINGA PRIZE FOR POETRY, Anhinga Press, P.O. Box 10595, Tallahassee FL 32302. (850)521-9920. Fax: (850)442-6363. E-mail: info@anhinga.org. Website: www.anhinga.org. **Contact:** Rick Campbell. Offered annually for a book-length collection of poetry by an author who has not published more than 1 book of poetry. Guidelines for SASE or on website. Open to any writer writing in English. **Deadline: February 15-May 1. Charges $20 fee.** Prize: $2,000, and publication.

ANNUAL GIVAL PRESS OSCAR WILDE AWARD, Gival Press, LLC, P.O. Box 3812, Arlington VA 22203. (703)351-0079. Fax: (703)351-0079. E-mail: givalpress@yahoo.com. Website: www.givalpress.com. **Contact:** Robert L. Giron. Award given to the best previously unpublished original poem written in English of any length, in any style, typed, double-spaced on 1 side only, which best relates alternative lifestyles, often referred to as gay/lesbian/bisexual/transgendered life, by a poet who is 18 or older. Entrants are asked to submit their poems in the following manner: (1) without any kind of identification, with the exception of titles, and (2) with a separate cover page with the following information: name, address (street, city, and state with zip code), telephone number, e-mail address (if available) and a list of poems by title. Checks drawn on American banks should be made out to Gival Press, LLC, and mailed to: Gival Press, LLC, P.O. Box 3812, Arlington VA, 22203. **Deadline: June 27 (postmarked). Charges $5 reading fee (USD).** Prize: $100 (USD), and the poem, along with information about the poet, will be published on the website of Gival Press. Open to any writer.

ANNUAL GIVAL PRESS POETRY CONTEST, Gival Press, LLC, P.O. Box 3812, Arlington VA 22203. (703)351-0079. Fax: (703)351-0079. E-mail: givalpress@yahoo.com. Website: www.givalpress.com. **Contact:** Robert L. Giron. Offered annually for a previously unpublished poetry collection of at least 45 pages, which may include previously published poems. The competition seeks to award well-written, original poetry in English on any topic, in any style. Guidelines for SASE, by e-mail, or on website. Entrants are asked to submit their poems in the following manner: (1) without any kind of identification, with the exception of the titles, and (2) with a separate cover page with the following information: name, address (street, city, state, and zip code), telephone number, e-mail address (if available), and a list of the poems by title. Checks drawn on American banks should be made out to Gival Press, LLC, and mailed to: Gival Press, LLC, P.O. Box 3812, Arlington VA 22203. **Deadline: December 15 (postmarked). Charges $20 reading fee (USD).** Prize: $1,000, plus publication, standard contract, and 20 author's copies. Open to any writer.

ANNUAL GIVAL PRESS TRI-LANGUAGE POEM CONTEST, Gival Press, LLC, P.O. Box 3812, Arlington VA 22203. (703)351-0079. Fax: (703)351-0079. E-mail: givalpress@yahoo.com. Website: www.givalpress.com. **Contact:** Robert L. Giron. Previously unpublished original poems written in English, French, or Spanish, of 20 lines or less, typed and double-spaced, on any topic, in any style, are eligible. Poets may submit up to 3 poems. Entrants are asked to submit their poems in the following manner: (1) without any kind of identification, with the exception of the titles, and (2) with a separate cover page with the following information: name, address (street, city, state and zip code), telephone number, e-mail address (if available), and a list of the poems by title. Checks drawn on American banks should be made out to Gival Press, LLC, and mailed to: Gival Press, LLC, P.O. Box 3812, Arlington VA 22203. **Deadline: October 12 (postmarked). Charges $5 reading fee.** Prize: $75 for the winning poems written in English, French, or Spanish, and the poems, along with the information about the poets, will be published on the website of Gival Press. Open to any writer.

THE ANNUAL PRAIRIE SCHOONER STROUSSE AWARD, *Prairie Schooner*, 201 Andrews Hall, P.O. Box 880334, Lincoln NE 68588-0334. (402)472-0911. Fax: (402)472-9771. E-mail: eflanagan2@unl.edu. Website: www.unl.edu/schooner/psmain.htm. **Contact:** Hilda Raz. Offered annually for the best poem or group of poems published in *Prairie Schooner* in the previous year. Prize: $500.

APR/HONICKMAN FIRST BOOK PRIZE, (formerly Honickman/APR First Book Prize), *The American Poetry Review*, 117 S. 17th St., Suite 910, Philadelphia PA 19103-5009. (215)496-0439. Fax: (215)569-0808. Website: www.aprweb.org. Offered annually for a poet's first unpublished book-length ms. Judging is by a different distinguished poet each year. Past judges include Gerald Stern, Louise Glück, Robert Creeley, Adrienne Rich, Derek Walcott, and Jorie Graham. Open to US citizens. **Deadline: October 31.** Guidelines for SASE. **Charges $25 fee.** Prize: Publication by *APR* (distrubution by Copper Canyon Press through Consortium), $3,000 cash prize, plus $1,000 to support a book tour.

ART COOPERATIVE POETRY FELLOWSHIP, (formerly Art Coop Poetry Fellowship), Cottonwood Art Co-operative, 1124 Columbia NE, Albuquerque NM 87106. E-mail: art_coop@yahoo.com. Website: www.geocities.com/art_coop. **Contact:** Editor-in-Chief. Contest offered annually. For most recent information, please visit website or write for guidelines with SASE. Submit with cover sheet, bio, and publications list. Open to any writer. **Deadline: December 1. Charges $15 for up to 3 poems, $2 each thereafter.** For additional flat $15 fee and SASE, feedback provided on poems. Prize: Cash award to be determined, not less than $250, and publication to support serious, aspiring poets. Open to any writer.

ATLANTIC POETRY PRIZE, Writers' Federation of Nova Scotia, 1113 Marginal Rd., Halifax NS B3H 4P7, Canada. (902)423-8116. Fax: (902)422-0881. E-mail: talk@writers.ns.ca. Website: www.writers.ns.ca. **Contact:** Jane Buss, executive director. Full-length books of adult poetry written by Atlantic Canadians, and published as a whole for the first time in the previous calendar year, are eligible. Entrants must be native or resident Atlantic Canadians who have either been born in Newfoundland, Prince Edward Island, Nova Scotia, or New Brunswick, and spent a susbstantial portion of their lives living there, or who have lived in one or a combination of these provinces for at least 24 consecutive months prior to entry deadline date. Publishers: Send 4 copies and a letter attesting to the author's status as an Atlantic Canadian and the author's current mailing address and telephone number. **Deadline: First Friday in December.** Prize: $1,000.

THE BACKWATERS PRIZE, The Backwaters Press, 3502 N. 52nd St., Omaha NE 68104-3506. (402)451-4052. E-mail: gkosm62735@aol.com. Website: www.thebackwaterspress.homestead.com. **Contact:** Greg Kosmicki. Offered annually to find the best collection of poems, or single long poem, no collaborations, to publish and help further the poet's career. Collections must be unpublished, however parts of the ms may have been published as a chapbook, or individual poems may have been previously published in magazines. **Deadline: June 4. Charges $25 fee.** Prize: $1,000, and publication of the winning ms in an edition of at least 500 copies in perfect bound format.

THE BASKERVILLE PUBLISHERS POETRY AWARD, *decant*, Texas Christian University's literary journal, TCU Box 297270, Fort Worth TX 76129. (817)257-6537. Fax: (817)257-6239. E-mail: descant@tcu.edu. **Contact:** Dave Kuhne, editor. Annual award for an outstanding poem published in an issue of *descant*. **Deadline: September-April.** Guidelines for SASE. Prize: $250. Publication retains copyright, but will transfer it to the author upon request. Open to any writer.

SHAUNT BASMAJIAN CHAPBOOK AWARD, The Canadian Poetry Association, POB 22571, St. George Postal Outlet, 264 Bloor St. W., Toronto ON M5S 1V8, Canada. E-mail: writers@sympatico.ca. Website: www.mirror.org/cpa/shaunt.html. Annual award to honor Shaunt Basmajian, a founding member of The Canadian Poetry Association. Submissions can be published or unpublished and up to 24 pages in length. **Deadline: April 30. Charges $15 (check/money order payable to The Canadian Poetry Association).** Prize: $100 (Canadian), publication, and 50 copies of the resulting chapbook. Judged by a CPA committee of 3 judges. Open to any writer.

BBC WILDLIFE MAGAZINE POET OF THE YEAR AWARD, *BBC WIldlife Magazine*, Broadcasting House, Whiteladies Rd., Bristol BS8 2LR, United Kingdom. +44 (0)117 973 8402. Fax: +44 (0)117 946 7075. E-mail: nina.epton@bbc.co.uk. **Contact:** Nina Epton. Offered annually for unpublished poetry. "The poem (no longer than 50 lines) must be on the subject of the natural world and/or our relationship with it. There are no restrictions on the form the poem takes—it can be a song of praise, an ode, or a lament, in rhyme, free or blank verse. There are 5 categories: adult, age 15-17, age 12-14, age 8-11, age 7 and under. Entrants must buy the relevant copy of *BBC Wildlife Magazine* containing the entry form and rules. This is usually our April issue, but it's best to check with the office first. By entering the competition, entrants grant, free of charge, the right for all or part of their poem to be published, broadcast, transmitted, and read in all media (now known or hereafter created), or on stage, including the right for the poems to be published in *BBC Wildlife Magazine* and any resulting anthology, if the organizers wish." **Deadline: Varies from year to year. Best to contact the office, and ask for details.** Guidelines for SASE. Prize: £500 to the overall winner; £100 for the runners-up; £50 for young poets. Open to any writer.

BC CHAPTER INTERNATIONAL POETRY CONTEST, British Columbia Chapter of The Canadian Poetry Association, P.O. Box 3, Clinton, BC V0K 1K0, Canada. E-mail: charlotte@artvilla.com. Website: www.artvilla.com/mair/contest.htm. **Contact:** Charlotte Mair. Send any number of poems, any style, any theme, and any length. Annually. **Deadline: September 15. Charges $10 for 3 poems (check payable to Charlotte Mair).** Prize: 1st Place: $50; 2nd Place: $40; 3rd Place: $30; 4th Place: $20; 5th Place: $10; 6th Place: $5; up to 10 Honorable Mentions. All 6 cash-prize winners and honorable mentions will be published in the 2nd edition of *Dogwood Express* (Little Red Hen Publishing Co.). Open to any writer.

THE BINGHAMTON UNIVERSITY MILT KESSLER POETRY BOOK AWARD, Binghamton University Creative Writing Program, Dept. of English, General Literature & Rhetoric, P.O. Box 6000, Binghamton NY 13902-6000. (607)777-2713. E-mail: cwpro@binghamton.edu. Website: english.binghamton.edu/cwpro/BookAwards/BookAwards.htm. **Contact:** Maria Mazziotti Gillan, creative writing program director. Estab. 2001. Offered annually for previously published work. Open to any writer over 40. Book must be published, be 48 pages or more with a press run of 500 copies or more. "Please explain any special criteria (such as residency) or nominating process that must be met before a writer's entry will be considered." Each book submitted must be accompanied by an application form. Publisher may submit more than 1 book for prize consideration. Send 3 copies of each book. Guidelines available online or for SASE. Must have appeared in print between January 1 and December 31 of year preceding award. **Deadline: March 1.** Prize: $1,000. Judged by professional poet not on Binghamton University faculty.

BLACK WARRIOR REVIEW CHAPBOOK CONTEST, *Black Warrior Review*, Box 862936, Tuscaloosa AL 35486. (205)348-4518. Website: www.webdelsol.com/bwr. **Contact:** Dan Kaplan, editor. Submit 10-25 pages of unpublished poetry, and SASE for contest results. All entrants receive a 1-year subscription. All poems also considered for general publication. Check website or current issue for guidelines and postmark dates. Guidelines for SASE. **Charges $10 entry fee.** Prize: $1,500. Open to any writer.

BLUESTEM POETRY AWARD, Dept. of English, Emporia State University 1200, Emporia KS 66801. (620)341-5216. Fax: (620)341-5547. E-mail: bluestem@emporia.edu. Website: www.emporia.edu/bluestem. **Contact:** Philip Heldrich, director. Offered annually "to recognize outstanding poetry." Full-length, single-author collections, at least 48 pages long. **Deadline: March 1. Charges $20 fee.** Prize: $1,000, and a published book.

THE BORDIGHERA ITALIAN-AMERICAN POETRY PRIZE, (formerly The Bordighera Bilingual Italian-American Poetry Prize), Sonia Raiziss-Giop Foundation, 57 Montague St. #8G, Brooklyn NY 11201-3356. E-mail: daniela@garden.net. Website: www.ItalianAmericanWriters.com. **Contact:** Daniela Gioseffi. Offered annually "to find the best unpublished manuscripts of poetry in English, by an American of Italian descent, to be translated into quality Italian and published bilingually." **Deadline: May 31.** Guidelines for SASE. Prize: $2,000, and bilingual book publication to be divided between poet and translator.

BOSTON REVIEW POETRY CONTEST, *Boston Review*, E-53-407 MIT, Cambridge MA 02139. Website: bostonreview.mit.edu. Submit up to 5 unpublished poems, no more than 10 pages total. **Deadline: June 1. Charges $15 fee (check or money order payable to** ***Boston Review*****).** Prize: $1,000, and publication in the October/November issue of *Boston Review*.

bp NICHOL CHAPBOOK AWARD, Phoenix Community Works Foundation, 316 Dupont St., Toronto ON M5R 1V9, Canada. (416)964-7919. Fax: (416)964-6941. E-mail: info@pcwf.ca. Website: www.pcwf.ca. **Contact:** Philip McKenna, award director. Offered annually to a chapbook (10-48 pages) of poetry in English, published in Canada in the previous year. **Deadline: March 30.** Guidelines for SASE. Prize: $1,000 (Canadian).

[N] BRIGHT HILL PRESS ANNUAL POETRY CHAPBOOK COMPETITION, Bright Hill Press, P.O. Box 193, Treadwell NY 13846. E-mail: wordthur@catskill.net. **Contact:** Bertha Rogers. Poetry in odd-numbered years, fiction even years, 16-24 pages, including bio, contents, acknowledgment, and title. Two title pages, 1 with name, address, etc., 1 with title only. Guidelines for SASE or by e-mail. **Deadline: July 31. Charges $10 fee.** Prize: $250, and 25 chapbooks and publication.

BRITTINGHAM PRIZE IN POETRY/FELIX POLLAK PRIZE IN POETRY, University of Wisconsin Press, Dept. of English, 600 N. Park St., University of Wisconsin, Madison WI 53706. Website: www.wisc.edu/wisconsinpress/poetryguide.html. **Contact:** Ronald Wallace, contest director. Estab. 1985. Offered for unpublished book-length mss of original poetry. Submissions must be *received* by the press *during* the month of September, accompanied by a SASE for contest results. Does *not* return mss. One entry fee covers both prizes. Guidelines for SASE or online. **Charges $20 fee (payable to University of Wisconsin Press).** Prize: $1,000, and publication of the 2 winning mss.

[N] THE DOROTHY BRUNSMAN POETRY PRIZE, Bear Star Press, 185 Hollow Oak Dr., Cohasset CA 95973. (530)891-0360. E-mail: bspencer@bearstarpress.com. Website: www.bearstarpress.com. **Contact:** Beth Spencer. Offered annually to support the publication of 1 volume of poetry. Guidelines on website. Open to poets living in the Western States (those in Mountain or Pacific Time Zones, plus Alaska and Hawaii). **Deadline: November 30. Charges $16 fee.** Prize: $1,000, and publication.

[Canadian] CAA JACK CHALMERS POETRY AWARD, Box 419, 320 S. Shores Rd., Campbellford ON K0L 1L0, Canada. (705)653-0323. Fax: (705)653-0593. E-mail: canauth@redden.on.ca. Website: www.canauthors.org. **Contact:** Alec McEachern. Offered annually for a volume of poetry by a Canadian citizen. Entry form required. Obtain form from contact name or download from website. **Deadline: December 15.** Guidelines for SASE. **Charges $25 fee (Canadian).** Prize: $2,500, and a silver medal.

[N] GERALD CABLE BOOK AWARD, Silverfish Review Press, P.O. Box 3541, Eugene OR 97403. (541)344-5060. E-mail: sfrpress@earthlink.net. **Contact:** Rodger Moody, series editor. Purpose is to publish a poetry book by a deserving author who has yet to publish a full-length book collection. Open to any writer. Guidelines for SASE or by e-mail. **Deadline: December 1. Charges $20 reading fee.** Prize: $1,000, and publication by the Press for a book-length ms of original poetry.

[N] CAMPBELL CORNER POETRY CONTEST, Graduate Studies/Sarah Lawrence College, One Meadway, Bronxville NY 10708. (914)395-2371. Fax: (914)395-2664. **Contact:** Dean of Graduate Studies. **Deadline: March 15.** Guidelines for SASE. **Charges $20.** Prize: $2,500. The work will also be published on Campbell Corner's Language Exchange. Judged by Phyllis Levin, Beth Ann Fennelly, and David Baker. Open to any writer.

HAYDEN CARRUTH AWARD, Copper Canyon Press, P.O. Box 271, Port Townsend WA 98368. (360)385-4925. Fax: (360)385-4985. E-mail: poetry@coppercanyonpress.org. Website: www.coppercanyonpress.org. **Contact:** Office Manager. Offered annually for unpublished work. Contest is for new and emerging poets who have published no more than 2 full-length books of poetry. Chapbooks of 32 pages or less are not considered to be full length, and books published in other genres do not count toward the 2-book limit. **Deadline: November 1-30 (reading period).** Guidelines for SASE. **Charges $20 fee.** Prize: $1,000 advance, and book publication by Copper Canyon Press.

THE CENTER FOR BOOK ARTS POETRY CHAPBOOK COMPETITION, (formerly Poetry Chapbook Competition), The Center for Book Arts, 28 W. 27th St., 3rd Floor, New York NY 10001. (212)481-0295. Fax: (212)481-9853. E-mail: info@centerforbookarts.org. Website: www.centerforbookarts.org. **Contact:** Rory Golden. Offered annually for unpublished collections of poetry. Individual poems may have been previously published. Collection must not exceed 500 lines or 24 pages. **Deadline: December 1 (postmarked).** Guidelines for SASE. **Charges $15 fee.** Prize: $500 award, $500 honorarium for a reading, publication, and 10 copies of chapbook. Judged by Sharon Dolin and C.K. Williams (2004 judges). Open to any writer.

JOHN CIARDI POETRY AWARD FOR LIFETIME ACHIEVEMENT, Italian Americana, URI/CCE, 80 Washington St., Providence RI 02903-1803. Fax: (401)277-5100. E-mail: bonomoal@etal.uri.edu. Website: www.uri.edu/prov/italian/italian.html. **Contact:** Carol Bonomo Albright, editor. Offered annually for lifetime achievement in all aspects of poetry: creative, critical, etc. Applicants should have at least 2 books published. Open to Italian-Americans only. Guidelines for SASE. Prize: $1,000.

JOHN CIARDI PRIZE FOR POETRY, BkMk Press, University of Missouri-Kansas City, 5101 Rockhill Rd., Kansas City MO 64110. (816)235-2558. Fax: (816)235-2611. E-mail: bkmk@umkc.edu. Website: www.umkc.edu/bkmk. **Contact:** Ben Furnish. Offered annually for the best book-length collection (unpublished) of poetry in English by a living author. Translations are not eligible. Initial judging is done by a network of published writers. Final judging is done by a writer of national reputation. Guidelines for SASE, by e-mail, or on website. **Deadline: December 1 (postmarked). Charges $25 fee.** Prize: $1,000, plus book publication by BkMk Press.

CLEVELAND STATE UNIVERSITY POETRY CENTER PRIZES, Cleveland State University Poetry Center, 2121 Euclid Ave., Cleveland OH 44115-2214. (216)687-3986. Fax: (216)687-6943. E-mail: poetrycenter@csuohio.edu. Website: www.csuohio.edu/poetrycenter. **Contact:** Rita Grabowski, poetry center coordinator. Estab. 1962. Offered annually to identify, reward, and publish the best unpublished book-length poetry ms submitted (40 pages of poetry, minimum) in 2 categories: First Book and Open Competition (for poets who have published a collection at least 48 pages long, with a press run of 500). "Submission implies willingness to sign standard contract for publication if manuscript wins." One or more of the other finalist mss may also be published for standard contract (no prize). Does not return mss. **Deadline:**

Submissions accepted November-January only (postmarked February 1). Guidelines for SASE. **Charges $20 fee.** Prize: $1,000, and publication.

THE COLORADO PRIZE FOR POETRY, *Colorado Review*/Center for Literary Publishing, Dept. of English, Colorado State University, Ft. Collins CO 80523. (970)491-5449. E-mail: creview@colostate.edu. Website: www.coloradoreview.com. **Contact:** Stephanie G'Schwind, managing editor. Offered annually to an unpublished collection of poetry. **Deadline: January 12. Charges $25 fee.** Prize: $1,500, and publication of book.

BETSY COLQUITT AWARD FOR POETRY, *descant*, Texas Christian University's literary journal, TCU Box 297270, Fort Worth TX 76129. (817)257-6537. Fax: (817)257-6239. E-mail: descant@tcu.edu. **Contact:** Dave Kuhne, editor. Offered annually for unpublished poems or series of poems. Publication retains copyright but will transfer it to the author upon request. **Deadline: September-April.** Guidelines for SASE. Prize: $500.

CONTEMPORARY POETRY SERIES, University of Georgia Press, 330 Research Dr., Suite B100, Athens GA 30602-4901. (706)369-6135. Fax: (706)369-6131. Website: www.ugapress.org. Offered 2 times/year. Two awards: 1 for poets who have not had a full-length book of poems published **(deadline in September),** and 1 for poets with at least 1 full-length publication **(deadline in January).** Guidelines for SASE. **Charges $20 fee.**

CORNER AWARD, (formerly Poet's Corner Award), Broken Jaw Press, Box 596 Stn. A, Fredericton NB E3B 5A6, Canada. (506)454-5127. Fax: (506)454-5127. E-mail: jblades@nbnet.nb.ca. Website: www.brokenjaw.com. Offered annually to recognize the best book-length ms by a Canadian poet. Guidelines for SASE or on website at www.brokenjaw.com/poetscorner.htm. **Deadline: December 31. Charges $20 fee (which includes copy of winning book upon publication).** Prize: $500, plus trade publication of poetry ms.

CPA ANNUAL POETRY CONTEST, The Canadian Poetry Association, Box 22571, St. George Postal Outlet, 264 Bloor St. W., Toronto, ON M5S 1V8, Canada. E-mail: writers@sympatico.ca. Website: www.mirror.org/cpa/annual.html. Send any number of poems, any style, any theme, and any length. Annually. **Deadline: June 30. Charges $5/poem.** Prize: 1st Place: $50; 2nd Place: $40; 3rd Place: $30; 4th Place: $20; 5th Place: $10; 6th Place: $5; up to 10 Honorable Mentions. All 6 cash prize winners will be published in *Poemata*, the CPA's newsletter. All winning poems, including honorable mentions, will be published on the CPA website. Open to any writer.

CRAB ORCHARD AWARD SERIES IN POETRY, *Crab Orchard Review* and Southern Illinois University Press, Dept. of English, Carbondale IL 62901-4503. Website: www.siu.edu/~crborchd. **Contact:** Jon C. Tribble, series editor. Offered annually for collections of unpublished poetry. Visit website for current deadlines. Guidelines for SASE. **Charges $25 fee.** Prize: 1st Place: $3,500, and publication; 2nd Place: $1,500, and publication.

ALICE FAY DI CASTAGNOLA AWARD, Poetry Society of America, 15 Gramercy Park S., New York NY 10003. (212)254-9628. Fax: (212)673-2352. Website: www.poetrysociety.org. **Contact:** Brett Lauer, programs associate. Offered annually for a manuscript-in-progress of poetry or verse-drama. Guidelines for SASE or on website. **Deadline: October 1-December 21.** Prize: $1,000.

EMILY DICKINSON AWARD IN POETRY, Universities West Press, (928)774-9574. Fax: (928)774-9574. E-mail: glenn@usa.net. Website: popularpicks.com. **Contact:** Glenn Reed. Offered annually for unpublished poetry in any form or style, and on any subject. Winner and finalists grants UWP rights to publish the winning poems on the popularpicks.com website and in its anthology. "A submission should include: no more than 3 poems, total entry not to exceed 6 pages, short biographical statement, **reading fee of $12,** and a SASE or e-mail address (preferred) for results. Awards are open to all writers except those who are currently students or employees of Northern Arizona University." Visit the website, or send a SASE for guidelines. **Deadline: August 31. Charges $12 reading fee.** Prize: 1st Award: $1,200; 2nd Award: $750; 3rd Award: $500. All award-winning poems, as well as finalists' poems, approximately 50-60 poems, will be featured in an anthology of poems annually published by Universities West Press. Award winners and finalists will each receive, without charge, a copy of the anthology. Final judging of submitted poems will be done by a poet of national/international reputation.

DISCOVERY/*THE NATION*, The Joan Leiman Jacobson Poetry Prizes, The Unterberg Poetry Center of the 92nd Street YM-YWHA, 1395 Lexington Ave., New York NY 10128. (212)415-5759. Website: www.92y.org. Open to poets who have not published a book of poems (chapbooks, self-published books included). Must have guidelines; send SASE, call, or see website. **Deadline: January. Charges $5 fee.**

STEPHEN EISEN MEMORIAL YOUTH PRIZES IN POETRY, National League of American Pen Women, Nob Hill, San Francisco Branch, 1544 Sweetwood Dr., Colma CA 94015. E-mail: pennobhill@aol.com. Website: www.welcome.to/soulmakingcontest. **Contact:** Eileen Malone. Poetry may be double or single spaced. One-page poems only and oly 1 poem/page. All entrants must be in grades 5-12, or equivalent. Grade or age must be indicated. Three poems/entry. Annually. **Deadline: November 30.** Guidelines for SASE. **Charges $5/entry (make checks payable to NLAPW, Nob Hill Branch).** Prize: 1st Place: $50; 2nd & 3rd Place: $25.

T.S. ELIOT PRIZE FOR POETRY, Truman State University Press, New Odyssey Series, 100 E. Normal St., Kirksville MO 63501-4221. (660)785-7336. Fax: (660)785-4480. E-mail: tsup@truman.edu. Website: tsup.truman.edu. **Contact:** Nancy Rediger. Annual competition for unpublished poetry collection. Guidelines for SASE, on website, or by e-mail. **Deadline: October 31 (postmarked). Charges $25 fee.** Prize: $2,000, and publication.

MAURICE ENGLISH POETRY AWARD, 2222 Rittenhouse Square, Philadelphia PA 19103-5505. Fax: (215)732-1382. **Contact:** Helen W. Drutt English. Offered annually for a distinguished book of poems published in the previous calendar year. Poets must be over 50 years of age to enter the contest. "No entry forms; no telephone calls, please." **Deadline: April 1.** Prize: $3,000, plus a public reading in Philadelphia. Judged by a sole judge.

ROBERT G. ENGLISH/POETRY IN PRINT, P.O. Box 30981, Albuquerque NM 87190-0981. (505)888-3937. Fax: (505)888-3937. Website: www.poets.com/RobertEnglish.html. **Contact:** Robert G. English, owner. Offered annually "to help a poetry writer accomplish their own personal endeavors. Hopefully the prize amount of the Poetry in Print award will grow to a higher significance. The contest is open to any writer of any age. Hopefully to prepare writers other than just journalists with a stronger desire to always tell the truth." No limit to number of entries; 60-line limit/poem. "Please enclose SASE." **Deadline: August 1. Charges $10/poem.** Prize: $1,000.

N **JANICE FARRELL POETRY PRIZE**, National League of American Pen Women, Nob Hill, San Francisco Branch, 1544 Sweetwood Dr., Colma CA 94015. E-mail: pennobhill@aol.com. Website: www.welcome.to/soulmakingcontest. **Contact:** Eileen Malone. Poetry may be double- or single-spaced. One-page poems only and only 1 poem/page. All poems must be titled. Three poems/entry. Annually. **Deadline: November 30.** Guidelines for SASE. **Charges $5/entry (make checks payable to NLAPW, Nob Hill Branch).** Prize: 1st Place: $100; 2nd Place: $50; 3rd Place: $25. Judged by a local San Francisco successfully published poet. Open to any writer.

FIELD POETRY PRIZE, Oberlin College Press/FIELD, 10 N. Professor St., Oberlin OH 44074-1095. (440)775-8408. Fax: (440)775-8124. E-mail: noc.press@oberlin.edu. Website: www.oberlin.edu/~nocpress. **Contact:** Linda Slocum, managing editor. Offered annually for unpublished work. "The FIELD Poetry Prize contest seeks to encourage the finest in contemporary poetry writing." No simultaneous submissions. Open to any writer. **Deadline: Submit in May only.** Guidelines for SASE. **Charges $22 fee, which includes a 1-year subscription.** Prize: $1,000, and book published in Oberlin College Press's FIELD Poetry Series.

FIVE POINTS JAMES DICKEY PRIZE FOR POETRY, Five Points, Georgia State University University Plaza, Atlanta GA 30303-3083. (404)651-0071. Fax: (404)651-3167. E-mail: msexton@gsu.edu. Website: www.webdelsol.com/Five_Points. **Contact:** Megan Sexton. Offered annually for unpublished poetry. **Deadline: November 30.** Guidelines for SASE. **Charges $15 fee (includes 1-year subscription).** Prize: $1,000, plus publication.

FOLEY POETRY CONTEST, America Press, 106 W. 56th St., New York NY 10019. (212)581-4640. Fax: (212)399-3596. Website: www.americamagazine.org. **Contact:** Paul Mariani, poetry editor. Estab. 1909. Offered annually for unpublished works between January and April. **Deadline: April.** Guidelines for SASE. Prize: Prize consists of $1,000, usually awarded in June. Open to any writer.

THE 49th PARALLEL POETRY AWARD, *Bellingham Review*, Mail Stop 9053, Western Washington University, Bellingham WA 98225. (360)650-4863. E-mail: bhreview@cc.wwu.edu. Website: www.wwu.edu/~bhreview/. **Contact:** Brenda Miller. Estab. 1977. Offered annually for unpublished poetry. Guidelines available on website or for SASE. **Deadline: December 1-March 15. Charges $15 for first entry (up to 3 poems), $10 each additional entry (including each additional poem).** Prize: 1st Place: $1,000, and publication. All finalists considered for publication, all entrants receive subscription.

FOUR WAY BOOKS POETRY PRIZES, Four Way Books, P.O. Box 535, Village Station, New York NY 10014. (212)619-1105. Fax: (212)406-1352. E-mail: four_way_editors@yahoo.com. Website: www.fourwaybooks.com. **Contact:** K. Clarke, contest coordinator. Four Way Books runs different prizes annually. For guidelines send a SASE or download from website. **Deadline: March 31.** Prize: Cash honorarium, and book publication.

ROBERT FROST POETRY AWARD, The Robert Frost Foundation, Heritage Place, 439 S. Union, Lawrence MA 01843. (978)725-8828. Fax: (978)725-8828. E-mail: mejaneiro@aol.com. Website: www.frostfoundation.org. **Contact:** Mary Ellen Janeiro. Offered annually for unpublished work "to recognize poets writing today in the tradition of Frost and other American greats. Poems should be written in the spirit of Frost, as interpreted by the poet's knowledge of Frost's poetry, life, persona, etc." More than 1 poem may be entered. Open to any writer. **Deadline: September 1.** Guidelines for SASE. **Charges $10 fee/poem.** Prize: $1,000.

ALLEN GINSBERG POETRY AWARDS, The Poetry Center at Passaic County Community College, One College Blvd., Paterson NJ 07505-1179. (973)684-6555. Fax: (973)684-5843. E-mail: mgillan@pccc.cc.nj.us. Website: www.pccc.cc.nj.us/poetry. **Contact:** Maria Mazziotti Gillan, executive director. Offered annually for unpublished poetry "to honor Allen Ginsberg's contribution to American literature." The college retains first publication rights. Open to any writer. **Deadline: April 1.** Guidelines for SASE. **Charges $13, which covers the cost of a subscription to *The Paterson Literary Review*.** Prize: $1,000.

GOVERNOR GENERAL'S LITERARY AWARD FOR POETRY, Canada Council for the Arts, 350 Albert St., P.O. Box 1047, Ottawa ON K1P 5V8, Canada. (613)566-4414, ext. 5576. Fax: (613)566-4410. E-mail: joanne.larocque-poirier@canadacouncil.ca. Website: www.canadacouncil.ca/prizes/ggla. **Contact:** Joanne Larocque-Poirier. Offered for the best English-language and the best French-language work of poetry by a Canadian published September 1, 2002-September 30, 2003. Publishers submit titles for consideration. **Deadline: April 15 or August 7, 2003, depending on the book's publication date.** Prize: Each laureate receives $15,000, and nonwinning finalists receive $1,000.

GREEN ROSE PRIZE IN POETRY, *New Issues Poetry & Prose*, Dept. of English, Western Michigan University, 1903 W. Michigan Ave., Kalamazoo MI 49008-5331. (269)387-8185. Fax: (269)387-2562. E-mail: herbert.scott@wmich.edu. Website: www.wmich.edu/newissues. **Contact:** Herbert Scott, editor. Offered annually for unpublished poetry. The university will publish a book of poems by a poet writing in English who has published 1 or more full-length books of poetry. Guidelines for SASE or on website. *New Issues Poetry & Prose* obtains rights for first publication. Book is copyrighted in author's name. **Deadline: September 30. Charges $20 fee.** Prize: $1,000, and publication of book. Author also receives 10% of the printed edition.

THE GRIFFIN POETRY PRIZE, The Griffin Trust for Excellence in Poetry, 6610 Edwards Blvd., Mississauga, ON L5T 2V6, Canada. (905)565-5993. E-mail: info@griffinpoetryprize.com. Website: www.griffinpoetryprize.com. **Contact:** Ruth Smith. Offered annually for work published between January 1 and December 31. **Deadline: December 31.** Prize: 2 $40,000 (Canadian) prizes. One prize will go to a living Canadian poet or translator, the other to a living poet or translator from any country, which may include Canada. Judged by a panel of qualified English-speaking judges of stature. Judges are chosen by the Trustees of The Griffin Trust For Excellence in Poetry. Open to any writer.

GREG GUMMER POETRY AWARD, *Phoebe*, George Mason University, 4400 University Dr., Fairfax VA 22030-4444. (703)993-2915. E-mail: phoebe@gmu.edu. Website: www.gmu.edu/pups/phoebe. **Contact:** Emily Tuszynska. Offered annually for unpublished work. **Deadline: December 1.** Guidelines for SASE. **Charges $10 fee.** Prize: $1,000, and publication in Fall 2002 issue. All entrants receive free Fall 2002 issue. Judged by outside judge—a recognized poet hired by *Phoebe* each year. Acquires first serial rights, if work is to be published. Open to any writer.

VIOLET REED HAAS POETRY CONTEST, Snake Nation Press, 110 W. Force St., Valdosta GA 31601. (229)244-0752. E-mail: jeana@snakenationpress.org. Website: www.snakenationpress.org. **Contact:** Jean Arambula. Offered annually for poetry mss of 50-75 pages. **Deadline: June 15. Charges $10 reading fee.** Prize: $500, and publication. Judged by an independent judge.

KATHRYN HANDLEY PROSE-POEM PRIZE, National League of American Pen Women, Nob Hill, San Francisco Branch, 1544 Sweetwood Dr., Colma CA 94015. E-mail: pennobhill@aol.com. Website: www.welcome.to/soulmaking contest. **Contact:** Eileen Malone. Poetry may be double- or single-spaced. One-page poems only, and only 1 poem/page. Three poems/entry. Annually. **Deadline: November 30.** Guidelines for SASE. **Charges $5/entry (make checks payable to NLAPW, Nob Hill Branch).** Prize: 1st Place: $100; 2nd Place: $50; 3rd Place: $25. Open to any writer.

HOW DO I LOVE THEE? OPEN COMPETITION FOR LOVE POETRY, *How Do I Love Thee? Magazine*/Poetry for Life Publishing, No. 1, Blue Ball Corner, Water Lane, Winchester, Hampshire SO23 0ER, United Kingdom. E-mail: adrian.abishop@virgin.net. **Contact:** Adrian Bishop, editor. Annually, Must Be Unpublished. **Deadline: January 31. Charges £3/poem (make checks payable to Poetry Life).** Prize: 1st Prize: £500; 2nd Prize: £100; 3rd & 4th Prize: £50; Special Commendations (20): £10 Book Token. All winning entries and special commendations will be published in *How Do I Love Thee? Magazine*. Judged by Adrian Bishop. Open to any writer.

INDIANA REVIEW POETRY CONTEST, *Indiana Review*, BH 465/Indiana University, Bloomington IN 47405-7103. (812)855-3439. Fax: (812)855-4253. E-mail: inreview@indiana.edu. Website: www.indiana.edu/~inreview. **Contact:** Danit Brown. Offered annually for unpublished work. Judged by guest judges; Denise Duhamel judged the 2003 contest. Open to any writer. Send no more than 4 poems, 15-page maximum (no minimum). **Deadline: Early April.** Guidelines for SASE. **Charges $15 fee (includes a year's subscription).** Prize: $1,000. Judged by guest judges. David St. John judged the 2001 contest.

IOWA POETRY PRIZES, University of Iowa Press, 119 W. Park Rd., Iowa City IA 52242. (319)335-2000. Fax: (319)335-2055. E-mail: rhonda-wetjen@uiowa.edu. Website: www.uiowapress.org. **Contact:** Rhonda Wetjen. Offered annually to encourage poets and their work. Submit mss in April; put name on title page only. Open to writers of English (US citizens or not). Manuscripts will not be returned. Previous winners are not eligible. **Deadline: April. Charges $20 fee.**

IRA LEE BENNETT HOPKINS PROMISING POET AWARD, International Reading Association, P.O. Box 8139, Newark DE 19714-8139. (302)731-1600. Fax: (302)731-1051. E-mail: exec@reading.org. Website: www.reading.org. Offered every 3 years to a promising new poet of children's poetry (for children and young adults up to grade 12) who has published no more than 2 books. **Deadline: December 1.** Guidelines for SASE. Prize: $500.

RANDALL JARRELL/HARPERPRINTS POETRY CHAPBOOK COMPETITION, (formerly Randall Jarrell Poetry Prize), North Carolina Writers' Network, 3501 Highway 54 W., Studio C, Chapel Hill NC 27516. E-mail: mail@ncwriters.org. Website: www.ncwriters.org. **Contact:** Lisa Robinson Bailey, production coordinator. Offered annually for unpublished work "to honor Randall Jarrell and his life at UNC-Greensboro by recognizing the best poetry submitted." Competition is open to North Carolina residents who have not published a full-length collection of poems. **Deadline: January 31. Charges $10 (NCWN members), $15 (nonmembers) entry fee.** Prize: $200, chapbook publication, and a reading and reception.

ROBINSON JEFFERS TOR HOUSE PRIZE FOR POETRY, Robinson Jeffers Tor House Foundation, P.O. Box 2713, Carmel CA 93921. (831)624-1813. Fax: (831)624-3696. E-mail: thf@torhouse.org. Website: www.torhouse.org. **Contact:** Elliot Ruchowitz-Roberts. "The Prize for Poetry is an annual living memorial to American poet Robinson Jeffers (1887-1962). It honors well-crafted, unpublished poetry in all styles, ranging from experimental work to traditional forms including short narrative poems." **Deadline: March 15.** Guidelines for SASE. **Charges $10 for first 3 poems; $15 for up to 6 poems; $2.50 for each additional poem.** Prize: $1,000; $200 for Honorable Mention. Judged by a distinguished panel of published poets and editors (preliminary judging). Final judging by a poet nationally known. Past judges have been Mary Oliver, Donald Hall, Dana Giola, Sherod Santos, Jane Hirshfield, and John Haines. Open to any writer.

THE JUNIPER PRIZE, University of Massachusetts, Amherst MA 01003. (413)545-2217. Fax: (413)545-1226. E-mail: info@umpress.umass.edu. Website: www.umass.edu/umpress/juniper.html. **Contact:** Alice I. Maldonado, assistant editor/Web manager. Estab. 1964. Awarded annually for an original ms of poems. In alternating years, the program is open to poets either with or without previously published books. **Deadline: September 30. Charges $15 fee.** Prize: The University of Massachusetts Press publishes the winning ms, and a $1,000 prize is awarded in lieu of royalties on the first print run.

KALLIOPE'S ANNUAL SUE SANIEL ELKIND POETRY CONTEST, *Kalliope, a journal of women's literature and art*, 11901 Beach Blvd., Jacksonville FL 32246. (904)646-2081. Website: www.fccj.org/kalliope. **Contact:** Mary Sue

Koeppel, editor. Offered annually for unpublished work. "Poetry may be in any style and on any subject. Maximum poem length is 50 lines. Only unpublished poems are eligible." No limit on number of poems entered by any 1 poet. The winning poem is published as are the finalists' poems. Copyright then returns to the authors. Guidelines for SASE and on website. **Deadline: November 1. Charges $4/poem, or $10 for 3 poems.** Prize: $1,000, publication of poem in *Kalliope*.

BARBARA MANDIGO KELLY PEACE POETRY AWARDS, Nuclear Age Peace Foundation, PMB 121, 1187 Coast Village Rd., Suite 1, Santa Barbara CA 93108-2794. (805)965-3443. Fax: (805)568-0466. E-mail: advocacy@napf.org. Website: www.wagingpeace.org. **Contact:** David Krieger. "The Barbara Mandigo Kelly Peace Poetry Contest was created to encourage poets to explore and illuminate positive visions of peace and the human spirit. The contest honors the late Barbara Kelly, a Santa Barbara poet and longtime supporter of peace issues. Awards are given in three categories: adult (over 18 years), youth between 12 and 18 years, and youth under 12." Contest is offered annually. All submitted articles should be unpublished. **Deadline: July 1 (postmarked).** Guidelines for SASE. **Charges $12 for up to 3 poems; no fee for youth entries.** Prize: Adult: $1,000; Youth (13-18): $200; Youth (12 and under): $200. Honorable Mentions may also be awarded. Judged by a committee of poets selected by the Nuclear Age Peace Foundation. The Foundation reserves the right to publish and distribute the award-winning poems, including honorable mentions. Open to any writer.

THE MILTON KESSLER MEMORIAL PRIZE FOR POETRY, *Harpur Palate* at Binghamton University, Dept. of English, Binghamton University, P.O. Box 6000, Binghamton NY 13902-6000. (607)355-4761. Website: harpurpalate.binghamton.edu. **Contact:** Managing Editor. Contest offered annually for previously unpublished poems in any style, form, or genre of no more than 3 pages. **Deadline: July 1-October 1.** Guidelines for SASE. **Charges $10/5 poems.** Prize: $500, and publication in Winter issue of *Harpur Palate*. All entrants receive a copy of the issue in which the winning poem appears. Name and contact information should appear in the cover letter only. Acquires first North American serial rights. Open to any writer.

THE LADY MACDUFF POETRY CONTEST, P.O. Box 563, Hackensack NJ 07602-0563. (877)816-3129. Fax: (201)342-7396. E-mail: rexdalepublishco@cs.com. Website: www.rexdalepublishing.com. **Contact:** Elaine Rexdale. Offered annually for poetry written in English. Open to any writer. **Deadline: November 30.** Guidelines for SASE. **Charges $25 fee.** Prize: Grand Prize: $500, publication, and 10 copies; 1st Place: $100.

GERALD LAMPERT MEMORIAL AWARD, The League of Canadian Poets, 54 Wolseley St., Suite 204, Toronto ON M5T 1A5, Canada. (416)504-1657. Fax: (416)504-0096. E-mail: league@poets.ca. Website: www.poets.ca. **Contact:** Edita Page. **"We are moving in July (we don't know the address yet). Entrants should check our website for an up-to-date address."** Offered annually for a first book of poetry by a Canadian poet published in the preceding year. Guidelines for SASE and on website. **Deadline: November 1. Charges $15 fee.** Prize: $1,000.

THE LEDGE ANNUAL POETRY CHAPBOOK CONTEST, *The Ledge Magazine*, 78-44 80th St., Glendale NY 11385. **Contact:** Timothy Monaghan. Offered annually to publish an outstanding collection of poems. Open to any writer. **Deadline: October 31.** Guidelines for SASE. **Charges $15 fee.** Prize: $1,000, publication of chapbook, and 50 copies; all entrants receive a copy of winning chapbook.

THE LEDGE POETRY AWARDS, *The Ledge Magazine*, 78-44 80th St., Glendale NY 11385. **Contact:** Timothy Monaghan. Offered annually for unpublished poems of exceptional quality and significance. All poems considered for publication in the magazine. Open to any writer. **Deadline: April 30.** Guidelines for SASE. **Charges $10 for 3 poems; $3/additional poem ($15 subscription gains free entry for the first 3 poems).** Prize: 1st Place: $1,000, and publication in *The Ledge Magazine*; 2nd Place: $250, and publication in *The Ledge Magazine*; 3rd Place: $100, and publication in *The Ledge Magazine*.

LENA-MILES WEVER TODD POETRY SERIES, Pleiades Press & Winthrop University, Dept. of English, Central Missouri State University, Warrensburg MO 64093. (660)543-8106. Fax: (660)543-8544. E-mail: kdp8106@cmsu2.cmsu.edu. Website: www.cmsu.edu/englphil/pleiades.html. **Contact:** Kevin Prufer. Offered annually for an unpublished book of poetry by an American or Canadian poet. Guidelines for SASE or by e-mail. The winning book is copyrighted by the author and Pleiades Press. **Deadline: Generally September 30; e-mail for firm deadline. Charges $15, which includes a copy of the winning book.** Prize: $1,000, and publication of winning book in paperback edition. Distribution through Louisiana State University Press.

THE LARRY LEVIS PRIZE FOR POETRY, *Prairie Schooner*, 201 Andrews Hall, P.O. Box 880334, Lincoln NE 68588-0334. (402)472-0911. Fax: (402)472-9771. E-mail: eflanagan2@unl.edu. Website: www.unl.edu/schooner/psmain.htm. **Contact:** Hilda Raz. Offered annually for poetry published in *Prairie Schooner* in the previous year. Prize: $1,000.

FRANCES LOCKE MEMORIAL POETRY AWARD, The Bitter Oleander Press, 4983 Tall Oaks Dr., Fayetteville NY 13066-9776. (315)637-3047. Fax: (315)637-5056. E-mail: bones44@ix.netcom.com. Website: www.bitteroleander.com. **Contact:** Paul B. Roth. Offered annually for unpublished, imaginative poetry. Open to any writer. **Deadline: June 15.** Guidelines for SASE. **Charges $10 for 5 poems, $2 for each additional poem.** Prize: $1,000, and 5 copies of issue.

LOUISIANA LITERATURE PRIZE FOR POETRY, Louisiana Literature, SLU—Box 792, Southeastern Louisiana University, Hammond LA 70402. (504)549-5022. Fax: (504)549-5021. E-mail: lalit@selu.edu. Website: www.selu.edu/orgs/lalit/. **Contact:** Jack Bedell, contest director. Estab. 1984. Offered annually for unpublished poetry. All entries considered for publication. **Deadline: April 1.** Guidelines for SASE. **Charges $12 fee.** Prize: $400.

LOUISE LOUIS/EMILY F. BOURNE STUDENT POETRY AWARD, Poetry Society of America, 15 Gramercy Park S., New York NY 10003. (212)254-9628. Fax: (212)673-2352. Website: www.poetrysociety.org. **Contact:** Brett Lauer, programs associate. Offered annually for unpublished work to promote excellence in student poetry. Open to American high school or preparatory school students (grades 9-12). Guidelines for SASE and on website. Judged by prominent American poets. **Deadline: October 1-December 21. Charges $5 for a student submitting a single entry; $20 for a high school submitting unlimited number of its students' poems.** Prize: $250.

PAT LOWTHER MEMORIAL AWARD, 54 Wolseley St., Toronto ON M5T 1A5, Canada. (416)504-1657. Fax: (416)504-0096. E-mail: league@poets.ca. Website: www.poets.ca. **Contact:** Edita Page. Estab. 1966. **"We are moving in July (new address is not yet known). Entrants should check our website for an up-to-date address."** Offered annually to promote new Canadian poetry/poets and also to recognize exceptional work in each category. Submissions to be published in the preceding year. Enquiries from publishers welcome. Open to Canadians living at home and abroad. The candidate must be a Canadian citizen or landed imigrant, though the publisher need not be Canadian. Call, write, fax, or e-mail for rules. **Deadline: November 1. Charges $15 fee/title.** Prize: $1,000.

LULLWATER PRIZE FOR POETRY, *Lullwater Review*, Emory University, P.O. Box 22036, Atlanta GA 30322. (404)727-6184. **Contact:** Laurel DeCou; Gwyneth Driskill. Offered annually for unpublished submissions. **Deadline: November 1.** Guidelines for SASE. **Charges $8 entry fee.** Prize: $500, plus publication in *The Lullwater Review*. Judged by a professor of English at Emory University. Open to any writer.

LUMINA NATIONAL POETRY CONTEST, Sarah Lawrence College, Attn: Poetry Contest, 1 Mead Way, Bronxville NY 10708. **Contact:** Hanne Winarsky. "*Lumina*, Sarah Lawrence's graduate literary magazine, welcomes all work of the highest standard, in any style or form. Previous issue included work by Tom Lux, Vijay Seshadri, Suzanne Gardinier, and Stephen Dobyns." Submitted poems must be unpublished, in English; translations are not considered. Three poems of up to 40 lines each/entry. Please submit 2 copies of each poem, 1 with name, address, and contact information, 1 with no identifying information. Students currently enrolled in Sarah Lawrence's MFA program are not eligible. **Deadline: February 1.** Guidelines for SASE. **Charges $5 (make checks payable to *Lumina*, Sarah Lawrence College).** Prize: 1st Place: $150; 2nd Place: $75: 3rd Place: $50. All winners receive a complementary copy of *Lumina*. Acquires First North American serial rights upon acceptance (revert to author after publication).

THE MACGUFFIN NATIONAL POET HUNT, *The MacGuffin*, 18600 Haggerty, Livonia MI 48152. E-mail: macguffin@schoolcraft.cc.mi.us. Website: www.macguffin.org. **Contact:** Managing Editor. "The purpose of the National Poet Hunt contest is to judge each piece blindly in its own right. It is not judged against another poet, only on the merits of the piece of itself. By sponsoring this contest, we've been able to publish new poets and give confidence to those who've entered by assuring those writers that the pieces would be judged on their own merits and that that work would be read by a renowned published poet." Offered annually for unpublished work. **Deadline: End of May.** Guidelines for SASE. **Charges $15 for a 5-poem entry.** Prize: First Prize: $500; 2nd Prize: $250; 3rd Prize: $100, and up to 3 Honorable Mentions. All winning poems published in the fall issue of *The MacGuffin*. Judged by a well-known poet. Past judges include Molly Peacock, Gary Gildner, and Richard Tillinghast. Acquires First rights (if piece is published). Once published, all rights revert to the author. Open to any writer.

NAOMI LONG MADGETT POETRY AWARD, Lotus Press, Inc., P.O. Box 21607, Detroit MI 48221. (313)861-1280. Fax: (313)861-4740. E-mail: lotuspress@aol.com. **Contact:** Constance Withers. Offered annually to recognize an outstanding unpublished poetry ms by an African-American. Guidelines for SASE or by e-mail. **Deadline: April 1-June 1.** Prize: $500, and publication by Lotus Press.

THE MALAHAT REVIEW LONG POEM PRIZE, *The Malahat Review*, Box 1700 STNCSC, Victoria BC V8W 2Y2, Canada. E-mail: malahat@uvic.ca (queries only). Website: malahatreview.ca. **Contact:** Marlene Cookshaw. Offered every 2 years to unpublished long poems. Preliminary reading by editorial board; final judging by the editor and 2 recognized poets. Obtains first world rights. After publication rights revert to the author. Open to any writer. **Deadline: March 1.** Guidelines for SASE. **Charges $30 fee (includes a 1-year subscription to the** *Malahat*, published quarterly). Prize: $400, plus payment for publication ($30/page).

MORTON MARR POETRY PRIZE, *Southwest Review*, P.O. Box 750374, Dallas TX 75275-0374. (214)768-1037. Fax: (214)768-1408. E-mail: swr@mail.smu.edu. Website: www.southwestreview.org. **Contact:** Willard Spiegelman. Annual award given to a poem by a writer who has not yet published a first book. Contestants may submit no more than 6 poems in a "traditional" form (i.e., sonnet, sestina, villanelle, rhymed stanzas, blank verse, etc.). A cover letter with name, address, and other relevant information may accompany the poems which must be printed without any identifying information. **Deadline: November 30.** Guidelines for SASE. **Charges $5/poem.** Prize: $1,000, and publication in *The Southwest Review*. Open to any writer.

THE LENORE MARSHALL POETRY PRIZE, The Nation and The Academy of American Poets, 588 Broadway, Suite 604, New York NY 10012-3210. (212)274-0343. Fax: (212)274-9427. E-mail: rmurphy@poets.org. Website: www.poets.org. **Contact:** Ryan Murphy, awards coordinator. Offered annually for book of poems published in US during previous year and nominated by the publisher. Self-published books are not eligible. **Deadline: April 1-June 15 (postmarked).** Prize: $25,000.

MID-LIST PRESS FIRST SERIES AWARD FOR POETRY, Mid-List Press, 4324 12th Ave. S., Minneapolis MN 55407-3218. Fax: (612)823-8387. E-mail: guide@midlist.org. Website: www.midlist.org. **Contact:** Lane Stiles, publisher. Estab. 1990. Offered annually for unpublished book of poetry to encourage new poets. Guidelines for SASE or on website. Contest is open to any writer who has never published a book of poetry. "We do not consider a chapbook to be a book of poetry." **Deadline: February 1. Charges $30 (US dollars) fee.** Prize: Publication, and an advance against royalties.

MISSISSIPPI VALLEY NON-PROFIT POETRY CONTEST, Midwest Writing Center, P.O. Box 3188, Rock Island IL 61204-3188. (309)359-1057. **Contact:** Max Molleston, chairman. Estab. 1972. Offered annually for unpublished poetry:

adult general, student division, Mississippi Valley, senior citizen, religious, rhyming, jazz, humorous, haiku, history, and ethnic. Up to 5 poems may be submitted with a limit of 50 lines/poem. **Deadline: April 1. Charges $5 fee, $3 for students.** Prize: Cash prizes.

MORSE POETRY PRIZE, Northeastern University English Dept., 406 Holmes Hall, Boston MA 02115. (617)437-2512. E-mail: g.rotella@neu.edu. Website: www.casdn.neu.edu/~english. **Contact:** Guy Rotella. Offered annually for previously published poetry book-length mss of first or second books. **Deadline: September 15. Charges $15 fee.** Prize: $1,000, and publication by Northeastern University Press.

KATHRYN A. MORTON PRIZE IN POETRY, Sarabande Books, P.O. Box 4456, Louisville KY 40204. (502)458-4028. Fax: (502)458-4065. E-mail: sarabanden@aol.com. Website: www.SarabandeBooks.org. **Contact:** Kirby Gann, managing editor. Offered annually to publish an outstanding collection of poetry. All finalists considered for publication. **Deadline: January 1-February 15.** Guidelines for SASE. **Charges $20 fee.** Prize: $2,000 and publication under standard royalty contract.

SHEILA MOTTON AWARD, New England Poetry Club, 16 Cornell St., Apt. 2, Arlington MA 02476-7710. **Contact:** Elizabeth Crowell. For a poetry book published in the last 2 years. Send 2 copies of the book and **$10 entry fee.** Prize: $500.

ERIKA MUMFORD PRIZE, 16 Cornell St., Apt. 2, Arlington MA 02476-7710. **Contact:** Elizabeth Crowell. Offered annually for a poem in any form about foreign culture or travel. **Deadline: June 30.** Guidelines for SASE. **Charges $10 for up to 3 entries in NEPC contests.** Prize: $250.

NATIONAL WRITERS ASSOCIATION POETRY CONTEST, The National Writers Association, 3140 S. Peoria, #295, Aurora CO 80014. (303)841-0246. Fax: Fax:(303)841-2607. **Contact:** Sandy Whelchel, director. Annual contest "to encourage the writing of poetry, an important form of individual expression but with a limited commercial market." Guidelines for SASE. **Charges $10 fee.** Prize: 1st Place: $100; 2nd Place: $50; 3rd Place: $25.

HOWARD NEMEROV SONNET AWARD, *The Formalist: A Journal of Metrical Poetry*, 320 Hunter Dr., Evansville IN 47711. **Contact:** Mona Baer. Offered annually for an unpublished sonnet to encourage poetic craftsmanship, and to honor the memory of the late Howard Nemerov, third US Poet Laureate. Final judge for year 2003: Dana Gioia. Acquires first North American serial rights for those sonnets chosen for publication. Upon publication all rights revert to the author. Open to the international community of writers. **Deadline: June 15.** Guidelines for SASE. **Charges $3 entry fee/sonnet.** Prize: $1,000, and publication in *The Formalist*; 11 other finalists also published.

N **THE PABLO NERUDA PRIZE FOR POETRY**, *Nimrod International Journal*, 600 S. College Ave., Tulsa OK 74104. (918)631-3080. Fax: (918)631-3033. E-mail: nimrod@utulsa.edu. Website: www.utulsa.edu/nimrod. **Contact:** Francine Ringold. Annual award to discover new writers of vigor and talent. **Deadline: April 30.** Guidelines for SASE. **Charges $20 (includes a 1-year subscription to *Nimrod*).** Prize: 1st Place: $2,000, and publication; 2nd Place: $1,000, and publication. Judged by the *Nimrod* editors (finalists), and a recognized author selects the winners. *Nimrod* retains the right to publish any submission. Open to US residents only.

NEW CENTURY WRITER AWARDS (POETRY), New Century Writer, 32 Alfred St., Suite B, New Haven CT 06512-3927. (203)469-8824. Fax: (203)468-0333. E-mail: newcenturywriter@yahoo.com. Website: www.newcenturywriter.org. **Contact:** Jason Marchi, executive director. Offered annually to discover and encourage emerging writers of poetry. All genres. Winners announced on website in December. Guidelines/entry fee for the asking, no SASE required. All entrants receive a 1-year susbcription to *The Anvil*, an educational newsletter for writers. Open to all poets, both unpublished and those with a limited history of publishing their poetry. Call if in doubt about your eligibility. New Century Writer also provides the annual Ray Bradbury Short Story Fellowship for 1 or 2 short story writers to attend the *Zoetrope* Short Story Writers' Workshop at Francis Ford Coppola's Blancaneaux Lodge in Belize, Central America (see the Ray Bradbury Short Story Fellowship listing for complete details). **Deadline: May 31. Charges $4/poem.** Prize: 1st Place: $250; 2nd Place: $150; 3rd Place: $75; 4th-10th Place: $25. Open to any writer.

NEW ISSUES FIRST BOOK OF POETRY PRIZE, *New Issues Poetry & Prose*, Dept. of English, Western Michigan University, 1903 W. Michigan Ave., Kalamazoo MI 49008-5331. (269)387-8185. Fax: (269)387-2562. E-mail: herbert.scott@wmich.edu. Website: www.wmich.edu/newissues. **Contact:** Herbert Scott, editor. Offered annually for publication of a first book of poems by a poet writing in English who has not previously published a full-length collection of poems in an edition of 500 or more copies. *New Issues Poetry & Prose* obtains rights for first publication. Book is copyrighted in author's name. Guidelines for SASE or on website. **Deadline: November 30. Charges $15.** Prize: $2,000, and publication of book. Author also receives 10% of the printed edition.

THE NEW LETTERS POETRY AWARD, *New Letters*, 5101 Rockhill Rd., Kansas City MO 64110. (816)235-1168. Fax: (816)235-2611. E-mail: newletters@umkc.edu. Website: www.umkc.edu/newletters. **Contact:** Aleatha Ezra. Offered annually for unpublished work to discover and reward new and upcoming writers. Buys first North American serial rights. Open to any writer. **Deadline: Third week of May.** Guidelines for SASE. **Charges $15 fee (includes a year's subscription to *New Letters*).** Prize: 1st Place: $1,000, and publication in *New Letters*; Runners-up (2) will receive a 1-year subscription, and will be considered for publication. All entries will be given consideration for publication in future issues of *New Letters*.

NEW RIVER POETS QUARTERLY POETRY AWARDS, New River Poets, a chapter of Florida State Poets Association, Inc., 5545 Meadowbrook St., Zephyrhills FL 33541-2715. **Contact:** June Owens, awards coordinator. Offered quarterly (February, May, August, and November) for previously published and unpublished work to acknowledge and reward outstanding poetic efforts. Previous winners have been Glenna Holloway, Maureen Tolman Flannery, and Virginia H. McKinnie. **Deadline: February 15, May 15, August 15, and November 15.** Guidelines for SASE. **Charges $4 fee for 1-3 poems, $1 each additional poem (no limit).** Prize: Awarded each quarter. 1st Prize: $60; 2nd Prize: $40; 3rd Prize: $30. Judged by the 1st-Place winning authors in each quarterly competition who judge the unscreened entries in a subsequent competition. Open to any writer.

NLAPW INTERNATIONAL HAIKU CONTEST, (formerly NLAPW International Poetry Contest), The Palomar Branch of The National League of American Pen Women, 11929 Caminito Corriente, San Diego CA 92128. **Contact:** Helen J. Sherry. Annual contest for unpublished haiku (any form). All proceeds from this contest provide an annual scholarship for a student entering college in the fields of art, letters, or music. Open to the public. Categories: Haiku (any style). Open to any writer. Please do not call. Send SASE for information. **Deadline: First Friday in March. Charges $5 for 2 haiku.** Prize: 1st Prize: $100; 2nd Prize: $40; 3rd Prize: $20, and honorable mentions. Winning poems will be published in a chapbook.

NO LOVE LOST III, Hidden Brook Press, 412-701 King St. W., Toronto ON M5V 2W7, Canada. (416)504-3966. Fax: (801)751-1837. E-mail: writers@hiddenbrookpress.com. Website: www.hiddenbrookpress.com/an-NLL.htm. No Love Lost III is an annual international poetry anthology contest. "Love, hate, lust, desire, passion, jealousy, and ambivalence. Including brotherly, sisterly, parental love, love of country, city." Send 3 unpublished poems with SASE. Electronic and hard copy submissions required. **Deadline: October 31. Charges $15 for 3 poems (includes purchase of book).** Prize: 1st Prize: $100; 2nd Prize: $75; 3rd Prize: $50; 4th Prize: $40; 5th Prize: $30; 6th Prize: $25; 7th Prize: $20; 8th-10th Prize: $10, plus up to 12 Honorable Mentions. Up to 300 poems published. Open to any writer.

THE OHIO STATE UNIVERSITY PRESS/*THE JOURNAL* AWARD IN POETRY, The Ohio State University Press and *The Journal*, 1070 Carmack, Columbus OH 43210. (614)292-6930. Fax: (614)292-2065. E-mail: ohiostatepress@osu.edu. Website: www.ohiostatepress.org. **Contact:** David Citino, poetry editor. Offered annually for unpublished work, minimum of 48 pages of original poetry. **Deadline: Entries accepted September 1-30. Charges $25 fee.** Prize: $2,000, and publication.

THE OPEN WINDOW IV, Hidden Brook Press, 412-701 King St. W., Toronto ON M5V 2W7, Canada. (416)504-3966. Fax: (801)751-1837. E-mail: writers@hiddenbrookpress.com. Website: www.hiddenbrookpress.com/an-OW.htm. An annual poetry anthology contest. "A wide open window theme including family, nature, death, rhyming, city, country, war and peace, social...long, short haiku, or any other genre." Send sets of 3 poems with short bio (35-40 words) and a SASE. Electronic and hard copy submissions required. **Deadline: February 2. Charges $15 for 3 poems.** Prize: 1st Prize: $100; 2nd Prize: $75; 3rd Prize: $50; 4th Prize: $40; 5th Prize: $30; 6th Prize: $25; 7th Prize: $20; 8th-10th Prize: $10, plus up to 12 honorable mentions. All winners, honorable mentions, and runners up receive 1 copy of the book for each published poem. Open to any writer.

GUY OWEN AWARD, *Southern Poetry Review*, Dept. of Languages, Literature, and Philosophy, Armstrong Atlantic State University, Savannah GA 31419-1997. (912)927-5289. Fax: (912)927-5399. E-mail: parhamro@mail.armstrong.edu. Website: www.spr.armstrong.edu. **Contact:** Robert Parham. This annual contest was established to "honor the founder of *Southern Poetry Review* and to sustain its ongoing publication." **Deadline: See website.** Guidelines for SASE. **Charges $15 entry fee (includes 1-year subscription to *Southern Poetry Review*).** Prize: $1,000, and publication of winning poem in *Southern Poetry Review*. Judged by a different established poet each year. Open to any writer.

THE PATERSON POETRY PRIZE, The Poetry Center at Passaic County Community College, One College Blvd., Paterson NJ 07505-6555. (973)684-6555. Fax: (973)684-5843. E-mail: mgillan@pccc.cc.nj.us. Website: www.pccc.cc.nj.us/poetry. **Contact:** Maria Mazziotti Gillan, director. Offered annually for a book of poetry published in the previous year. **Deadline: February 1.** Guidelines for SASE. Prize: $1,000.

PEARL POETRY PRIZE, Pearl Editions, 3030 E. Second St., Long Beach CA 90803. (562)434-4523. Fax: (562)434-4523. E-mail: mjohn5150@aol.com. Website: www.pearlmag.com. **Contact:** Marilyn Johnson, editor/publisher. Offered annually "to provide poets with further opportunity to publish their poetry in book-form and find a larger audience for their work." Manuscripts must be original works written in English. Guidelines for SASE or on website. **Deadline: July 15. Charges $20.** Prize: $1,000, and publication by Pearl Editions.

PEN/JOYCE OSTERWEIL AWARD FOR POETRY, PEN American Center, 568 Broadway, Suite 401, New York NY 10012. (212)334-1660, ext. 108. E-mail: jm@pen.org. Website: www.pen.org. **Contact:** John Morrone, literary awards manager. *Candidates may only be nominated by members of PEN.* This award "recognizes the high literary character of the published work to date of a new and emerging American poet of any age, and the promise of further literary achievement." Nominated may not have published more than 1 book of poetry. Offered every 2 years (odd years). **Deadline: January 3.** Prize: $5,000. Judged by a panel of 3 judges selected by the PEN Awards Committee.

PEN/VOELCKER AWARD FOR POETRY, PEN American Center, 568 Broadway, Suite 401, New York NY 10012. (212)334-1600, ext. 108. E-mail: jm@pen.org. Website: www.pen.org. **Contact:** John Morrone, literary awards manager. *Candidates can be nominated for Award only by members of PEN.* Award given to an American poet "whose distinguished and growing body of work to date represents a notable and accomplished presence in American literature." Offered every 2 years (even years). **Deadline: January 1 (nominations).** Prize: $5,000 stipend. Judged by a panel of 3-5 poets or other writers.

THE PHI BETA KAPPA POETRY AWARD, The Phi Beta Kappa Society, 1606 New Hampshire Ave. NW, Washington DC 20009. (202)265-3808. Fax: (202)986-1601. E-mail: ccurtis@pbk.org. Website: www.pbk.org/scholarships/

poetry.htm. **Contact:** Ms. Cameron Curtis. "The Phi Beta Kappa Poetry Award was established in the spirit of the missions of both Phi Beta Kappa and the Winston Foundation to foster excellence in the liberal arts. The annual award is intended to recognize the best book of poetry published in the United States during the previous year." The work can be nominated by its author or, with the poet's consent, by a publisher, agent, or other representative. The submission should include 1 copy of the book, and a cover letter including the date of publication and contact information for the author and publisher. The winning poets are required to grant permission to reproduce portions of the book in publicizing the award and/or in Phi Beta Kappa publications; attend the public awards presentation in Washington, DC, in Fall, and read from their work; produce a commissioned original piece for *The American Scholar*; and grant permission to have The Phi Beta Kappa Poetry Award medal on the book cover. **Deadline: June 30.** Guidelines for SASE. Prize: $10,000, and bronze medal for the Award recipient; $2,500 for 4 finalists; stickers noting PBK Poetry Award honoree status for the winning book covers. Judged by a different eminent poet each year. Previous judges were Yusef Komunyakaa and John Ashberry. Open to US residents only.

PHILBRICK POETRY AWARD, Providence Athenaeum, 251 Benefit St., Providence RI 02903. (401)421-6970. Fax: (401)421-2860. E-mail: rgilpin@providenceathenaeum.org. Website: www.providenceathenaeum.org. **Contact:** Risa Gilpin. Offered annually for New England poets who have not yet published a book. Previous publication of individual poems in journals or anthologies is allowed. Judged by nationally-known poets. Mei-Mei Berssenbrugge is the 2003 judge. Guidelines for SASE or on website. **Deadline: June 15-October 15. Charges $8 fee (includes copy of previously published chapbook).** Prize: $500, publication of winning ms as a chapbook, and a public reading at Providence Athenaeum with the final judge/award presenter.

POETIC LICENCE CONTEST FOR CANADIAN YOUTH, League of Canadian Poets, 54 Wolseley St., Toronto ON M5T 1A5, Canada. (416)504-1657. Fax: (416)504-0096. E-mail: league@poets.ca. Website: www.poets.ca or www.youngpoets.ca. **"We are moving in July (new address is not yet known). Entrants should check our website for an up-to-date address."** Offered annually for unpublished work to seek and encourage new poetic talent in two categories: grades 7-9 and 10-12. Entry is by e-mail only. Open to Canadian citizens and landed immigrants only. Guidelines for SASE or on website. For more information about the contest see website. **Deadline: December 1.** Prize: 1st Place: $150; 2nd Place: $100; 3rd Place: $50.

THE POETRY BUSINESS BOOK & PAMPHLET COMPETITION, The Poetry Business, The Studio, Byram Arcade, Westgate, Huddersfield HD1 1ND, United Kingdom. (00 44) 1484 434840. Fax: (00 44) 1484 426566. E-mail: edit@poetrybusiness.co.uk. Website: www.poetrybusiness.co.uk. **Contact:** Peter Sansom and Janet Fisher. "The purpose of this annual contest is to find and publish new or less-well-known poets. Entrants should submit a short manuscript. The winners will have a chapbook published; these winners can then submit an extended manuscript. The overall winner will have a full-length book published under our own imprint (Smith/Doorstop Books)." No poetry by or for children. Work must be in English. **Deadline: October 31.** Guidelines for SASE. **Charges £18.** Prize: Book publication, plus share of a cash prize. Judged by the directors of The Poetry Business, who are experienced editors, plus a well-known poet. Open to any writer.

THE POETRY CENTER BOOK AWARD, The Poetry Center, San Francisco State University, 1600 Holloway Ave., San Francisco CA 94132-9901. (415)338-2227. Fax: (415)338-0966. E-mail: newlit@sfsu.edu. Website: www.sfsu.edu/~newlit/welcome.htm. **Contact:** Steve Dickison, director. Estab. 1980. Offered annually for books of poetry and chapbooks, published in year of the prize. "Prize given for an extraordinary book of American poetry." Please include a cover letter noting author name, book title(s), name of person issuing check, and check number. Will not consider anthologies or translations. **Deadline: December 31. Charges $10 reading fee/entry.** Prize: $500, and an invitation to read in the Poetry Center Reading Series.

POETRY IN PRINT POETRY CONTEST, Poetry in Print, P.O. Box 30981, Albuquerque NM 87190-0981. Phone/fax: (505)888-3937. **Contact:** Robert G. English. No limit to the number of entries; 60 lines of poetry accepted. **Deadline: August 1. Charges $10.** Prize: $1,000. Open to any writer.

POETS OUT LOUD PRIZE, Poets Out Loud, Fordham University at Lincoln Center, 113 W. 60th St., Room 924, New York NY 10023. (212)636-6792. Fax: (212)636-7153. E-mail: pol@fordham.edu. Website: www.fordham.edu/english/pol. **Contact:** Elisabeth Frost. Annual competition for an unpublished, full-length poetry ms (50-80 pages). Winning volume is published each fall by Fordham University Press in paper and cloth editions. **Deadline: October 15.** Guidelines for SASE. **Charges $25 entry fee.** Prize: $1,000, book publication, and a gala reading with prize judge. Judged by a group of judges of national reputation. Open to any writer.

THE HELEN PUTNAM MEMORIAL POETS FOR PEACE PRIZE, Adaptive Solutions, P.O. Box 1545, Castleton VT 05735. E-mail: adaptivesolutions@icaal.com. Website: www.adaptivesolutions.net. **Contact:** Dianna C. Wuagneux, Ph.D. "This award recognizes the poetic works of men and women whose published and unpublished poems may inspire the imagination and efforts necessary to help bring about peace by exploring and illuminating the value of distinct human societies and their interdependence. This semiannual award is open to all writers. Submissions are open to any style and will be assessed according to the writer's ability to deliver this important message in a way that is both evocative and engaging—tell a story." Submissions are accepted continuously with the client for the following year's prize being December 15. Awards are made in January of even years. **Deadline: December 15.** Guidelines for SASE. **Charges $25.** Prize: $300, certificate, and consideration for inclusion in a proposed web-based, *Writer's For Peace Anthology.*

RAINMAKER AWARDS IN POETRY, ZONE 3, Austin Peay State University, P.O. Box 4565, Clarksville TN 37044. (931)221-7031. Fax: (931)221-7393. E-mail: zone3@apsu01.apsu.edu. **Contact:** Susan Wallace, managing editor.

Offered annually for unpublished poetry. Previous judges include Carolyn Forché, Marge Piercy, Howard Nemerov, and William Stafford. Open to any poet. Guidelines for SASE. **Charges $8 fee (includes 1-year subscription).** Prize: 1st Place: $500, 2nd Place: $300, 3rd Place: $100.

N **RAMBUNCTIOUS REVIEW POETRY CONTEST**, *Rambunctious Review*, 1221 W. Pratt Blvd., Chicago IL 60626. Annual themed contest for unpublished poems. Acquires one-time publication rights. Open to any writer. **Deadline: December 31.** Guidelines for SASE. **Charges $2/poem.** Prize: 1st Prize: $100; 2nd Prize: $75; 3rd Prize: $50; all winning entries will be published in future issues of *Rambunctious Review*.

LEVIS READING PRIZE, Virginia Commonwealth University, Dept. of English, P.O. Box 842005, Richmond VA 23284-2005. (804)828-1329. Fax: (804)828-8684. E-mail: eng_grad@vcu.edu. Website: www.has.vcu.edu/eng/grad/Levis_Prize.htm. **Contact:** Jeff Lodge. Offered annually for books of poetry published in the previous year to encourage poets early in their careers. The entry must be the writer's first or second published book of poetry. Previously published books in other genres, or previously published chapbooks, do not count as books for this purpose. **Deadline: January 15.** Guidelines for SASE. Prize: $1,000 honorarium, and an expense-paid trip to Richmond to present a public reading.

RED ROCK POETRY AWARD, *Red Rock Review*, Community College of Southern Nevada, English Dept., 3200 E. Cheyenne Ave., North Las Vegas NV 89030. (702)651-4094. Fax: (702)651-4639. E-mail: rich_logsdon@ccsn.nevada.edu. Website: www.ccsn.nevada.edu/english/redrockreview/contest.htm. **Contact:** Rich Logsdon. Offered annually for unpublished poetry. Open to any writer. **Deadline: October 31.** Guidelines for SASE. **Charges $6 for 3 poems.** Prize: $500.

RIVER CITY WRITING AWARDS IN POETRY, The University of Memphis/Hohenberg Foundation, Dept. of English, Memphis TN 38152. (901)678-4591. Fax: (901)678-2226. Website: www.people.memphis.edu/~rivercity. **Contact:** Mary Leader. Offered annually for unpublished poems of 2 pages maximum. Guidelines for SASE or on website. **Deadline: March 15. Charges $5 fee/poem.** Prize: 1st Place: $1,000; 2nd and 3rd Place: Publication, and 1-year subscription. Open to any writer.

N **RIVER STYX 2003 INTERNATIONAL POETRY CONTEST**, *River Styx* Magazine, 634 N. Grand Blvd., 12th Floor, St. Louis MO 63103. (314)533-4541. Fax: (314)533-3345. Website: www.riverstyx.org. **Contact:** Richard Newman, editor; Melissa Gurley Banks, managing editor. Offered annually for unpublished poetry. Poets may send up to 3 poems, not more than 14 pages. Open to any writer. 2003 judge: Miller Williams. Past judges include Billy Collins, Marylin Hacker, Mark Doty, Molly Peacock, and Philip Levine. **Deadline: May 31.** Guidelines for SASE. **Charges $20 reading fee (which includes a 1-year subscription).** Prize: $1,000, and publication in August issue.

NICHOLAS ROERICH POETRY PRIZE, Story Line Press, Three Oaks Farm, P.O. Box 1240, Ashland OR 97520-0055. (541)512-8792. Fax: (541)512-8793. E-mail: mail@storylinepress.com. Website: www.storylinepress.com. **Contact:** Roerich Prize Coordinator. Estab. 1988. Offered annually for full-length book of poetry. Any writer who has not previously published a full-length collection of poetry (48 pages or more) in English is eligible to apply. Guidelines for SASE or on website. **Deadline: May 1-October 31. Charges $20 fee.** Prize: $1,000, publication, and reading at the Nicholas Roerich Museum in New York.

N **THE RUNES AWARD**, *RUNES, A Review of Poetry*/Arctos Press, P.O. Box 401, Sausalito CA 94966. Fax: (415)331-3092. E-mail: RunesRev@aol.com. Website: http://members.aol.com/Runes. **Contact:** C.B. Follett or Susan Terris. No poems longer than 100 lines. Offered annually for unpublished poems. **Deadline: June 1 (submissions accepted to contest accepted in April and May only).** Guidelines for SASE. **Charges $15 for 3 poems (includes a 1-year subscription to *RUNES, A Review of Poetry*)**; additional poems $3 each. Prize: $1,000, plus publication in *RUNES, A Review of Poetry*. Judged by Li-Young Lee (2003 competition); Jane Hirshfield (2004 competition). Acquires one-time publication rights. Open to any writer.

N **SALMON RUN PRESS NATIONAL POETRY BOOK AWARD**, Salmon Run Press, P.O. Box 672130, Chugiak AK 99567-2130. (907)688-4268. Fax: (907)688-4268. E-mail: salmonrp@aol.com. **Contact:** John Smelcer. Offered annually to previously published or unpublished poetry. "Each year we invite poets nationwide to send their 68-96 page poetry manuscript. Individual poems may have been previously published, but the manuscript must be unpublished." Poems may be on any subject/style. Acquires one-time rights. Open to any writer. **Deadline: December 31.** Guidelines for SASE. **Charges $10 fee.** Prize: $1,000, publication of ms (minimum 500 copies), advertising in national literary magazines (*Poets & Writers*, etc.); arrangements for national reviews with approximately 50-100 promotional copies sent.

BENJAMIN SALTMAN POETRY AWARD, Red Hen Press, P.O. Box 3537, Granada Hills CA 91394. (818)831-0649. Fax: (818)831-6659. E-mail: editors@redhen.org. Website: www.redhen.org. **Contact:** Kate Gale. Offered annually for unpublished work "to publish a winning book of poetry." Open to any writer. **Deadline: October 31.** Guidelines for SASE. **Charges $15 fee.** Prize: $1,000, and publication.

SASKATCHEWAN POETRY AWARD, Saskatchewan Book Awards, Inc., Box 1921, Regina SK S4P 3E1, Canada. (306)569-1585. Fax: (306)569-4187. E-mail: director@bookawards.sk.ca. Website: www.bookawards.sk.ca. **Contact:** Joyce Wells, executive director. Offered annually for work published September 15, 2002-September 14, 2003 annually. This award is presented to a Saskatchewan author for the best book of poetry, judged on the quality of writing. **Deadline: First deadline: July 31; Final deadline: September 14.** Guidelines for SASE. **Charges $15 (Canadian).** Prize: $1,500.

THE HELEN SCHAIBLE INTERNATIONAL SHAKESPEAREAN/PETRARCHAN SONNET CONTEST, Poets' Club of Chicago, 1212 S. Michigan Ave., #2702, Chicago IL 60605. **Contact:** Tom Roby, chair. Offered annually for original and unpublished Shakespearean or Petrarchan sonnets. One entry/author. Submit 2 copies, typed and double-spaced; 1 with name and address, 1 without. All rules printed here. Send SASE for winners list. **Deadline: September 1.** Prize: 1st Place: $50; 2nd Place: $35; 3rd Place: $15; 3 Honorable Mentions.

SEEDS 6, Hidden Brook Press, 412-701 King St. W., Toronto ON M5V 2W7, Canada. (416)504-3966. Fax: (801)751-1837. E-mail: writers@hiddenbrookpress.com. Website: www.hiddenbrookpress.com/contest1.htm. "The *SEEDS* International Poetry Chapbook Anthology Contest is interested in all types and styles of poetry. See the *SEEDS* website for examples of the type of poetry we have published in the past." Annually. **Deadline: April 1 and November 30. Charges $12 for 3 poems.** Prize: 1st Prize: $50; 2nd Prize: $25; 3rd Prize: $15; 4th-9th Prize: $10, plus 15-25 Honorable Mentions. Winning poems published in the *SEEDS International Poetry Chapbook Anthology.* All winning and honorable mention submissions receive 1 copy of the book for each published poem. Open to any writer.

SLAPERING HOL PRESS CHAPBOOK COMPETITION, The Hudson Valley Writers' Center, 300 Riverside Dr., Sleepy Hollow NY 10591. (914)332-5953. Fax: (914)332-4825. E-mail: info@writerscenter.org. Website: www.writerscenter.org. **Contact:** Stephanie Strickland or Margo Stever, co-editors. The annual competition is open to poets who have not published a book or chapbook, though individual poems may have already appeared. Limit: 16-20 pages. The press was created in 1990 to provide publishing opportunities for emerging poets. **Deadline: May 15.** Guidelines for SASE. **Charges $10 fee.** Prize: $500, publication of chapbook, 10 copies of chapbook, and a reading at The Hudson Valley Writers' Center.

SLIPSTREAM ANNUAL POETRY CHAPBOOK COMPETITION, Slipstream, Box 2071, Niagara Falls NY 14301. (716)282-2616 (after 5 p.m. EST). E-mail: editors@slipstreampress.org. Website: www.slipstreampress.org. **Contact:** Dan Sicoli, co-editor. Offered annually to help promote a poet whose work is often overlooked or ignored. Open to any writer. **Deadline: December 1.** Guidelines for SASE. **Charges $15.** Prize: $1,000, and 50 copies of published chapbook.

THE SOW'S EAR CHAPBOOK PRIZE, *The Sow's Ear Poetry Review*, 355 Mount Lebanon Rd., Donalds SC 29638-9115. (864)379-8061. E-mail: errol@kitenet.net. **Contact:** Errol Hess, managing editor. Estab. 1988. Offered for poetry mss of 22-26 pages. Guidelines for SASE or by e-mail. **Deadline: Submit March-April. Charges $10 fee.** Prize: 1st Place: $1,000, 25 copies, and distribution to subscribers; 2nd Place: $200; 3rd Place: $100.

THE SOW'S EAR POETRY PRIZE, *The Sow's Ear Poetry Review*, 355 Mount Lebanon Rd., Donalds SC 29638-9115. (864)379-8061. E-mail: errol@kitenet.net. **Contact:** Errol Hess, managing editor. Estab. 1988. Offered for previously unpublished poetry. Guidelines for SASE or by e-mail. All submissions considered for publication. **Deadline: Submit September-October. Charges $2 fee/poem.** Prize: 1st Place: $1,000; 2nd Place: $250; 3rd Place: $100; publication, plus option of publication for 20-25 finalists.

SPOKANE PRIZE FOR POETRY, Eastern Washington University Press, 705 W. First Ave., Spokane WA 99201. (800)508-9095. Fax: (509)623-4283. E-mail: ewupress@ewu.edu. Website: www.ewupress.ewu.edu. **Contact:** Christopher Howell. "Annual award to publish the finest work the literary world has to offer." **Deadline: May 15.** Guidelines for SASE. **Charges $25.** Prize: $1,500, and publication. Judged by EWU Press staff. Open to any writer.

SPOON RIVER POETRY REVIEW EDITORS' PRIZE, (formerly Editors' Prize), *Spoon River Poetry Review*, Campus Box 4241, English Dept., Illinois State University, Normal IL 61790-4241. (309)438-7906. Website: www.litline.org/spoon. **Contact:** Lucia Cordell Getsi, editor. Offered annually for unpublished poetry "to identify and reward excellence." Guidelines on website. Open to all writers. **Deadline: April 15. Charges $16 (entitles entrant to a year's subscription valued at $15).** Prize: 1st Place: $1,000; Runners-Up prizes (2): $100 each; publication of 1st Place, runners-up, and selected honorable mentions.

SPS STUDIOS POETRY CARD CONTEST, SPS Studios, Inc., publishers of Blue Mountain Arts®, P.O. Box 1007, Boulder CO 80306. (303)449-0536. Fax: (303)447-0939. E-mail: editorial@spsstudios.com. Website: www.sps.com. "We're looking for original poetry, which can be rhyming or nonrhyming, although we find nonrhyming poetry reads better. Poems may also be considered for possible publication on greeting cards or in book anthologies, but that is separate from the contest." Contest is offered biannually. **Deadline: December 31 and June 30.** Guidelines for SASE. Prize: 1st Prize: $300; 2nd Prize: $150; 3rd Prize: $50. Judged by SPS Studios editorial staff. Open to any writer.

ANN STANFORD POETRY PRIZE, *The Southern California Anthology*, c/o Master of Professional Writing Program, WPH 404, U.S.C., Los Angeles CA 90089-4034. (213)740-3252. Website: www.usc.edu/dept/LAS/mpw. **Contact:** James Ragan, contest director. Estab. 1988. Offered annually for previously unpublished poetry to honor excellence in poetry in memory of poet and teacher Ann Stanford. Submit cover sheet with name, address, phone number, and titles of the 5 poems entered. **Deadline: April 15.** Guidelines for SASE. **Charges $10 fee.** Prize: 1st Place: $1,000; 2nd Place: $200; 3rd Place: $100. Winning poems are published in *The Southern California Anthology*, and all entrants receive a free issue.

THE EDWARD STANLEY AWARD, *Prairie Schooner*, 201 Andrews Hall, P.O. Box 880334, Lincoln NE 68588-0334. (402)472-0911. Fax: (402)472-9771. E-mail: eflanagan2@unl.edu. Website: www.unl.edu/schooner/psmain.htm. **Contact:** Hilda Raz. Offered annually for poetry published in *Prairie Schooner* in the previous year. Prize: $1,000.

THE AGNES LYNCH STARRETT POETRY PRIZE, University of Pittsburgh Press, 3400 Forbes Ave., Pittsburgh PA 15261. Website: www.pitt.edu/~press. **Contact:** Susan Borello. Estab. 1980. Series Editor: Ed Ochester. Offered annually for first book of poetry for poets who have not had a full-length book published. Mandatory guidelines for SASE. **Deadline: March and April only. Charges $20 fee.** Prize: $5,000.

THE ELIZABETH MATCHETT STOVER MEMORIAL AWARD, *Southwest Review*, P.O. Box 750374, Dallas TX 75275-0374. (214)768-1037. Fax: (214)768-1408. E-mail: swr@mail.smu.edu. Website: www.southwestreview.org. **Contact:** Elizabeth Mills and Willard Spiegelman. Offered annually for unpublished poems or group of poems. Please note that mss are submitted for publication, not for the prizes themselves. Guidelines for SASE and on website. Prize: $250. Judged by Elizabeth Mills, senior editor, and Willard Spiegelman, editor-in-chief. Open to any writer.

STROKESTOWN INTERNATIONAL POETRY COMPETITION, Strokestown International Poetry Festival, Bawn St., Strokestown, County Roscommon, Ireland. (+353) 78 33759. E-mail: twiggezvous@eircom.net. Website: www.strokestownpoetryprize.com. **Contact:** M.J.C. Harpur. This annual competition was established "to promote excellence in poetry, and participation in the reading and writing of it." **Deadline: February 19.** Guidelines for SASE. **Charges $5 (4 Euros, £3).** Prize: 1st Prize: 4,000 euros (approximately $3,900) for a poem in English of up to 70 lines; 2nd Prize: 1,000 euros; 3rd Prize: 500 euros. All 10 shortlisted poets are invited to read at the Strokestown International Poetry Festival for a fee and travel expenses. Acquires first publication rights. Open to any writer.

HOLLIS SUMMERS POETRY PRIZE, Ohio University Press, Scott Quadrangle, Athens OH 45701. (740)593-1155. Fax: (740)593-4536. Website: www.ohio.edu/oupress. **Contact:** David Sanders. Offered annually for unpublished poetry books. Books will be eligible if individual poems or sections have been published previously. Open to any writer. **Deadline: October 31.** Guidelines for SASE. **Charges $15.** Prize: $500, and publication of the ms in book form.

MAY SWENSON POETRY AWARD, Utah State University Press, 7800 Old Main Hill, Logan UT 84322-7800. (435)797-1362. Fax: (435)797-0313. E-mail: michael.spooner@usu.edu. Website: www.usu.edu/usupress. **Contact:** Michael Spooner. Offered annually in honor of May Swenson, one of America's major poets. Contest for unpublished mss in English, 50-100 pages; not only a "first book" competition. Entries are screened by 6 professional writers and teachers. The finalists are judged by a nationally known poet. Former judges include: Alicia Ostriker, Mark Doty, John Hollander, and Mary Oliver. Open to any writer. **Deadline: September 30.** Guidelines for SASE. **Charges $25 fee.** Prize: $1,000, publication of ms, and royalties.

TRANSCONTINENTAL POETRY AWARD, Pavement Saw Press, P.O. Box 6291, Columbus OH 43206. (614)445-0534. E-mail: info@pavementsaw.org. Website: pavementsaw.org. **Contact:** David Baratier, editor. Offered annually for a first book of poetry. Judged by Editor David Baratier and a guest judge (2001 judge David Bromige). Guidelines on website. **Deadline: August 15. Charges $15 fee.** Prize: $1,500, 30 copies for judge's choice, standard royalty contract for editor's choice. Open to any writer.

KATE TUFTS DISCOVERY AWARD, Claremont Graduate University, 160 E. 10th St., Harper B7, Claremont CA 91711-6165. (909)621-8974. Fax: (909)607-8438. Website: www.cgu.edu/tufts. **Contact:** Betty Terrell, awards coordinator. Estab. 1993. Offered annually for a first book by a poet of genuine promise. Entries must be a published book completed September 15, 2002-September 15, 2003. Open to US residents only. Guidelines for SASE or on website. **Deadline: September 15.** Prize: $10,000.

KINGSLEY TUFTS POETRY AWARD, Claremont Graduate University, 160 E. 10th St., Harper B7, Claremont CA 91711-6165. (909)621-8974. Fax: (909)607-8438. Website: www.cgu.edu/tufts. **Contact:** Betty Terrell, awards coordinator. Estab. 1992. Offered annually "for a work by an emerging poet, one who is past the very beginning but who has not yet reached the acknowledged pinnacle of his or her career." Guidelines for SASE or on website. **Deadline: September 15.** Prize: $100,000.

DANIEL VAROUJAN AWARD, New England Poetry Club, 16 Cornell St., #2, Arlington MA 02476-7710. **Contact:** Elizabeth Crowell. Offered annually for "an unpublished poem worthy of Daniel Varoujan, a poet killed by the Turks at the onset of the first genocide of this century which decimated three-fourths of the Armenian population." Send poems in duplicate. Open to any writer. **Deadline: June 30.** Guidelines for SASE. **Charges $10 for 3 entries in NEPC contests paying $3,000 in prizes.** Prize: $1,000.

CHAD WALSH POETRY AWARD, (formerly Chad Walsh Poetry Prize), *Beloit Poetry Journal*, P.O. Box 151, Farmington ME 04938. (207)778-0020. Website: www.bpj.org. **Contact:** Lee Sharkey and John Rosenwald, editors. Offered annually to honor the memory of poet Chad Walsh, a founder of the *Beloit Poetry Journal*. The editors select a strong poem or group of poems from the poems published in the journal that year. Prize: $3,000.

WAR POETRY CONTEST, Winning Writers, 39 Avenue A, Dept. 111, New York NY 10009. (866)946-9748. Fax: (212)254-8198. E-mail: warcontest@winningwriters.com. Website: www.winningwriters.com/annualcontest.htm. **Contact:** Adam Cohen. "This annual contest seeks outstanding unpublished poetry on the theme of war. 1-3 poems should be submitted, up to a maximum total of 500 lines. English language. No translations, please." **Deadline: May 31.** Guidelines for SASE. **Charges $10.** Prize: 1st Prize: $1,000, and publication on WinningWriters.com; 2nd Prize: $500, and publication on WinningWriters.com; 3rd Prize: $250, and publication on WinningWriters.com; Honorable Mentions (5): $50. Judged by award-winning poet Jendi Reiter. Acquires nonexclusive right to publish submissions on WinningWriters.com. Open to any writer.

THE WASHINGTON PRIZE, The Word Works, Inc., P.O. Box 42164, Washington DC 20015. E-mail: editor@wordworksdc.com. Website: www.wordworksdc.com. **Contact:** Miles David Moore. Offered annually "for the best full-length poetry manuscript (48-64 pp.) submitted to The Word Works each year. The Washington Prize contest is the only forum in which we consider unsolicited manuscripts." Submissions accepted in the month of February. Acquires first publication rights. Open to any American writer. **Deadline: March 1 (postmarked).** Guidelines for SASE. **Charges $20 fee.** Prize: $1,500, and book publication; all entrants receive a copy of the winning book.

WERGLE FLOMP POETRY CONTEST, Winning Writers, 39 Avenue A, Dept. 111, New York NY 10009. (866)946-9748. Fax: (212)254-8198. E-mail: flompcontest@winningwriters.com. Website: www.winningwriters.com/contestflomp.htm. **Contact:** Adam Cohen. "This annual contest seeks the best unpublished parody poem that has been sent to a 'vanity poetry contest' as a joke. Vanity contests are those whose main purpose is to appeal to poets' egos and get them to buy expensive products like anthologies, chapbooks, CDs, plaques, and silver bowls. The Wergle Flomp Prize will be awarded for the best bad poem. One poem of any length should be submitted, along with the name of the vanity contest that was spoofed. The poem should be in English. Inspired gibberish is also accepted. Online submission at WinningWriters.com is preferred." **Deadline: April 1.** Guidelines for SASE. Prize: $817.70, and publication on WinningWriters.com. Honorable Mentions will also be published on WinningWriters.com. Judged by award-winning poet Jendi Reiter. Acquires nonexclusive right to publish submissions on WinningWriters.com. Open to any writer.

WHITE PINE PRESS POETRY PRIZE, White Pine Press, P.O. Box 236, Buffalo NY 14201. E-mail: wpine@whitepine.org. Website: www.whitepine.org. **Contact:** Elaine LaMattina, managing editor. Offered annually for previously published or unpublished poets. Manuscript: Up to 80 pages of original work; translations are not eligible. Poems may have appeared in magazines or limited-edition chapbooks. Open to any US citizen. **Deadline: November 30 (postmarked). Charges $20 fee.** Prize: $1,000, and publication. Judged by a poet of national reputation. All entries are screened by the editorial staff of White Pine Press.

WICK POETRY CHAPBOOK SERIES 'OPEN' COMPETITION, Wick Poetry Program, Dept. of English, Kent State University, P.O. Box 5190, Kent OH 44242-0001. (330)672-2067. Fax: (330)672-2567. E-mail: wickpoet@kent.edu. Website: dept.kent.edu/wick. **Contact:** Maggie Anderson, director. Offered annually for a chapbook of poems by a poet currently living in Ohio. **Deadline: October 31.** Guidelines for SASE. Prize: Publication of the chapbook by the Kent State University Press.

WICK POETRY CHAPBOOK SERIES 'STUDENT' COMPETITION, Wick Poetry Program, Dept. of English, Kent State University, P.O. Box 5190, Kent OH 44242-0001. (330)672-2067. Fax: (330)672-2567. E-mail: wickpoet@kent.edu. Website: dept.kent.edu/wick. **Contact:** Maggie Anderson, coordinator. Offered annually for publication of a chapbook of poems by a poet currently enrolled in an Ohio college or university. **Deadline: October 31.** Guidelines for SASE. Prize: Publication of the chapbook by the Kent State University Press.

STAN AND TOM WICK POETRY PRIZE, Wick Poetry Program, Dept. of English, Kent State University, P.O. Box 5190, Kent OH 44242-0001. (330)672-2067. Fax: (330)672-2567. E-mail: wickpoet@kent.edu. Website: dept.kent.edu/wick. **Contact:** Maggie Anderson, coordinator. Open to anyone writing in English who has not previously published a full-length book of poems (a volume of 48 pages or more published in an edition of 500 or more copies). **Deadline: May 1.** Guidelines for SASE. **Charges $20 fee.** Prize: $2,000, and publication by the Kent State University Press.

THE RICHARD WILBUR AWARD, The University of Evansville Press, University of Evansville, Evansville IN 47722. **Contact:** The Editors. Offered in even-numbered years for an unpublished poetry collection. Guidelines for SASE and online at http://english.evansville.edu/english/WilburAwardGuidelines.htm. **Deadline: December 1, 2004. Charges $25 fee.** Prize: $1,000, and publication by the University of Evansville Press.

WILLIAM CARLOS WILLIAMS AWARD, Poetry Society of America, 15 Gramercy Park S., New York NY 10003. (212)254-9628. Fax: (212)673-2352. Website: www.poetrysociety.org. **Contact:** Brett Lauer, programs associate. Offered annually for a book of poetry published by a small press, nonprofit, or university press. Winning books are distributed to PSA members upon request and while supplies last. **Deadline: October 1-December 21.** Guidelines for SASE. **Charges $20 fee.** Prize: $500-1,000.

N **JAMES WRIGHT POETRY AWARD**, *Mid-American Review*, Dept. of English, Bowling Green State University, Bowling Green OH 43403. (419)372-2725. Fax: (419)372-6805. E-mail: karenka@bgnet.bgsu.edu. Website: www.bgsu.edu/midamericanreview. **Contact:** Karen Craigo, poetry editor. Offered annually for unpublished poetry. Open to all writers not associated with *Mid-American Review* or judge. **Deadline: October 1.** Guidelines for SASE. **Charges $10.** Prize: $500, publication in Spring issue of *Mid-American Review*. Judged by editors and a well known writer, e.g., Kathy Fagan, Bob Hicok.

WRITERS' JOURNAL POETRY CONTEST, Val-Tech Media, P.O. Box 394, Perham MN 56573. (218)346-7921. Fax: (218)346-7924. E-mail: writersjournal@lakesplus.com. Website: www.writersjournal.com. **Contact:** Esther M. Leiper. Offered for previously unpublished poetry. **Deadline: April 30, August 30, December 30.** Guidelines for SASE. **Charges $3/each poem entered.** Prize: 1st Place: $50; 2nd Place: $25; 3rd Place: $15; 1st, 2nd, 3rd Place, and selected honorable mention winners will be published in *Writers' Journal* magazine.

Playwriting & Scriptwriting

ALBERTA PLAYWRITING COMPETITION, Alberta Playwrights' Network, 2633 Hochwald Ave. SW, Calgary AB T3E 7K2, Canada. (403)269-8564; (800)268-8564. Fax: (403)265-6773. E-mail: apn@nucleus.com. Website: www.nucleus.com/~apn. Offered annually for unproduced plays with full-length and Discovery categories. Discovery is open only to previously unproduced playwrights. Open only to residents of Alberta. **Deadline: January 15. Charges $40 fee (Canadian).** Prize: Full length: $3,500 (Canadian); Discovery: $1,500 (Canadian); written critique, workshop of winning play, reading of winning plays at a Showcase Conference.

N **AMERICAN CINEMA FOUNDATION SCREENWRITING COMPETITION**, American Cinema Foundation, 9911 W. Pico Blvd., #510, Los Angeles CA 90035. (310)286-9420. Fax: (310)286-7914. E-mail: acinema@cinemafoundation.com. Website: www.cinemafoundation.com. **Contact:** Gary McVey. Annual contest "to elicit theatrical or TV scripts which tell a positive story about specific fundamental values and their importance to society." **Deadline: March 31.**

Guidelines for SASE. **Charges $30.** Prize: $5,000. Judged by members of the entertainment industry. Open to any writer.

ANNUAL INTERNATIONAL ONE-PAGE PLAY COMPETITION, Lamia Ink!, P.O. Box 202, Prince Street Station, New York NY 10012. **Contact:** Cortland Jessup, founder/artistic director. Offered annually for previously published or unpublished 1-page plays. Acquires "the rights to publish in our magazine and to be read or performed at the prize awarding festival." Playwright retains copyright. **Deadline: March 15.** Guidelines for SASE. **Charges $2/play or $5/3 plays.** Prize: $200, staged reading, and publication of 12 finalists.

N **ANNUAL ONE-ACT PLAYWRITING CONTEST**, TADA!, 15 W. 28th St., 3rd Floor, New York NY 10001. (212)252-1619. Fax: (212)252-8763. E-mail: playcontest@tadatheater.com. Website: www.tadatheater.com. **Contact:** Emmanuel Wilson, literary manager. Offered annually to encourage playwrights to develop new plays for teen audiences ages 12-18. Call or e-mail for guidelines. Must address teen subjects and issues. Predominantly teen cast. **Deadline: January 20.** Prize: Staged readings and honorarium for winners.

BAKER'S PLAYS HIGH SCHOOL PLAYWRITING CONTEST, Baker's Plays, P.O. Box 699222, Quincy MA 02269-9222. (617)745-0805. Fax: (617)745-9891. Website: www.bakersplays.com. **Contact:** Kurt Gombar, general manager. Offered annually for unpublished work about the "high school experience," but can be about any subject, so long as the play can be reasonably produced on the high school stage. Plays may be of any length. Plays must be accompanied by the signature of a sponsoring high school drama or English teacher, and it is recommended that the play receive a production or a public reading prior to the submission. Multiple submissions and co-authored scripts are welcome. Teachers may not submit a student's work. The ms must be firmly bound, typed, and come with SASE that includes enough postage to cover the return of the ms. Plays that do not come with a SASE will not be returned. Do not send originals; copies only. **Deadline: January 31.** Guidelines for SASE. Prize: 1st Place: $500, and publication; 2nd Place: $250; 3rd Place: $100.

BAY AREA PLAYWRIGHTS FESTIVAL, Produced by The Playwrights Foundation, 131 10th St., 3rd Floor, San Francisco CA 94103. (415)263-3986. E-mail: literary@playwrightsfoundation.org. Website: www.playwrightsfoundation.org. **Contact:** Amy Mueller, artistic director; Christine Young, literary manager. Offered annually for unpublished plays by established and emerging theater writers nationally to support and encourage development of a new work. Unproduced full-length plays only. Open to all writers. Guidelines for SASE and on website. **Deadline: January 31 (postmarked).** Prize: Small stipend and in-depth development process with dramaturg and director, and a professionally staged reading in San Francisco.

N **BIENNIAL PROMISING PLAYWRIGHT AWARD**, Colonial Players, Inc., Box 2167, Annapolis MD 21404. (410)268-7373. **Contact:** Vice President. Offered every 2 years for unpublished full-length plays and adaptations. Open to any aspiring playwright residing in any of the states descendant from the original 13 colonies (Connecticut, Delaware, Georgia, Maryland, Massachusetts, New Hampshire, New Jersey, New York, North Carolina, Pennsylvania, Rhode Island, South Carolina, and Virginia), West Virginia, or Washington, DC. Next contest runs September 1-December 31, 2004. Guidelines for SASE. Prize: Production, and $750 cash award. Colonial Players, Inc., reserves the right to premiere the play on a royalty-free basis within 2 years after the cash award is presented.

N **BIG BREAK INTERNATIONAL SCREENWRITING COMPETITION**, Final Draft, Inc., 16000 Ventura Blvd., Suite 800, Encino CA 91436. (800)231-4055. Fax: (818)995-4422. E-mail: bigbreak@finaldraft.com. Website: www.finaldraft.com. **Contact:** Eric Cohen. **Deadline: March 15.** Guidelines for SASE. **Charges $50.** Prize: 1st Prize: $10,000; 2nd Prize: $3,000; 3rd Prize: $1,000. Judged by industry professionals. Open to any writer.

CAA CAROL BOLT AWARD FOR DRAMA, Canadian Authors Association with the support of the Playwrights Union of Canada and Playwrights Canada Press, 320 S. Shores Rd., P.O. Box 419, Campbellford ON K0L 1L0, Canada. (705)653-0323. Fax: (705)653-0593. E-mail: canauth@redden.on.ca. Website: www.CanAuthors.org. **Contact:** Alec McEachern. Annual contest for the best English-language play for adults by an author who is Canadian or landed immigrant. Submissions should be previously published or performed in the year prior to the giving of the award. For instance, in 2002 for this year's award to be given in July 2003. Open to Canadian citizens or landed immigrants. **Deadline: December 15, except for plays published or performed in December, in which case the deadline is January 15.** Guidelines for SASE. **Charges $25 (Canadian funds) fee.** Prize: $1,000, and a silver medal. Judged by a trustee for the award (appointed by the CAA). The trustee appoints up to 3 judges. The identities of the trustee and judges are confidential. Short lists are not made public. Decisions of the trustee and judges are final, and they may choose not to award a prize.

CALIFORNIA YOUNG PLAYWRIGHTS CONTEST, Playwrights Project, 450 B St., Suite 1020, San Diego CA 92101-8093. (619)239-8222. Fax: (619)239-8225. E-mail: write@playwrightsproject.com. Website: www.playwrightsproject.com. **Contact:** Cecelia Kouma, managing director. Offered annually for previously unpublished plays by young writers to stimulate young people to create dramatic works, and to nurture promising writers. Scripts must be a minimum of 10 standard typewritten pages; send 2 copies. Scripts will *not* be returned. All entrants receive detailed evaluation letter. Writers must be California residents under age 19 as of the deadline date. **Deadline: April 1.** Guidelines for SASE. Prize: Professional production of 3-5 winning plays at the Old Globe Theatre in San Diego, plus royalty.

COE COLLEGE PLAYWRITING FESTIVAL, Coe College, 1220 First Ave. NE, Cedar Rapids IA 52402-5092. (319)399-8624. Fax: (319)399-8557. E-mail: swolvert@coe.edu. Website: www.public.coe.edu/departments/theatre/. **Contact:** Susan Wolverton. Estab. 1993. Offered biennially for unpublished work to provide a venue for new works for the stage. "There is usually a theme for the festival. We are interested in full-length productions, *not* one acts or musicals. There are no specific criteria although a current résumé and synopsis is requested." Open to any writer. **Deadline: Before June 1.** Notified by September 1. Guidelines for SASE. Prize: $325, plus 1-week residency as guest artist with airfare, room and board provided.

THE CUNNINGHAM COMMISSION FOR YOUTH THEATRE, The Theatre School, DePaul University, 2135 N. Kenmore, Chicago IL 60614. (773)325-7938. Fax: (773)325-7920. E-mail: lgoetsch@depaul.edu. Website: theatreschool.depaul.edu/programs/prize.htm. **Contact:** Lara Goetsch. Chicago-area playwrights only. Commission will result in a play for younger audiences that "affirms the centrality of religion, broadly defined, and the human quest for meaning, truth, and community." **Deadline: December 1.** Guidelines for SASE. Prize: $5,000 ($2,000 when commission is contracted, $1,000 if script moves to workshop, $2,000 as royalty if script is produced by the Theatre School). Open to any writer.

DRURY UNIVERSITY ONE-ACT PLAY CONTEST, Drury University, 900 N. Benton Ave., Springfield MO 65802-3344. E-mail: msokol@drury.edu. **Contact:** Mick Sokol. Offered in even-numbered years for unpublished and professionally unproduced plays. One play/playwright. Guidelines for SASE or by e-mail. **Deadline: December 1.**

N DUBUQUE FINE ARTS PLAYERS ANNUAL ONE-ACT PLAY CONTEST, Dubuque Fine Arts Players, 1686 Lawndale, Dubuque IA 52001. E-mail: garms@clarke.edu. **Contact:** Gary Arms. "We select 3 one-act plays each year. We award cash prizes of up to $600 for a winning entry. We produce the winning plays in August." Offered annually for unpublished work. **Deadline: January 31.** Guidelines for SASE. **Charges $10.** Prize: 1st Prize: $600; 2nd Prize: $300; 3rd Prize: $200. Judged by 3 groups who read all the plays; each play is read at least twice. Plays that score high enough enter the second round. The top 10 plays are read by a panel consisting of 3 directors and 2 other final judges. Open to any writer.

N EMERGING PLAYWRIGHT'S AWARD, Urban Stages, 17 E. 47th St., New York NY 10017-1920. (212)421-1380. Fax: (212)421-1387. E-mail: tlreilly@urbanstages.org. Website: www.urbanstages.org. **Contact:** T.L. Reilly, producing director. Estab. 1986. Submissions required to be unproduced in New York City. Send script, letter of introduction, production history, author's name, résumé, and SASE. Submissions accepted year-round. Plays selected in August and January for award consideration. One submission/person. **Deadline: Ongoing. Charges $5.** Prize: $500 (in lieu of royalties), and a staged production of winning play in New York City. Open to US residents only.

ESSENTIAL THEATRE PLAYWRITING AWARD, The Essential Theatre, 995 Greenwood Ave. #6, Atlanta GA 30306. (404)876-8471. E-mail: pmhardy@aol.com. **Contact:** Peter Hardy. Offered annually for unproduced, full-length plays by Georgia writers. No limitations as to style or subject matter. **Deadline: April 15.** Prize: $400, and full production.

SHUBERT FENDRICH MEMORIAL PLAYWRITING CONTEST, Pioneer Drama Service, Inc., P.O. Box 4267, Englewood CO 80155. (303)779-4035. Fax: (303)779-4315. E-mail: playwrights@pioneerdrama.com. Website: www.pioneerdrama.com. **Contact:** Lori Conary, assistant editor. Offered annually for unpublished, but previously produced, submissions to encourage the development of quality theatrical material for educational and community theater. Rights acquired only if published. Authors already published by Pioneer Drama are not eligible. **Deadline: March 1.** Guidelines for SASE. Prize: $1,000 royalty advance, publication.

FIREHOUSE THEATRE PROJECT NEW PLAY COMPETITION, The Firehouse Theatre Project, P.O. Box 5165, Richmond VA 23220. (804)355-2001. E-mail: newplays@firehousetheatre.org. Website: www.firehousetheatre.org. **Contact:** Literary Manager FTP. "This annual award is intended to encourage American playwrights to continue to produce new scripts for the theater; thereby maintaining a fertile base for American voices in the dramatic literature of current times and the years to come. The scripts must be full-length theatrical scripts in English on any topic. All scripts must be submitted by an agent or accompanied by a professional letter of recommendation from a director, literary manager, or dramaturg. Translations, adaptations, musicals, one-acts, film and television screenplays are ineligible and will not be considered." Open to US residents only. Submissions must be unpublished. Visit website for complete submission guidelines. **Deadline: August 31.** Prize: 1st Prize: $1,000 with a production or a fully produced staged reading at the 2004 FTP Festival of New American Plays (January 2004); 2nd Prize: $500 with a staged reading at the 2004 FTP Festival; 3rd Prize: $250 with a possible staged reading at the 2004 FTP Festival. Judged by a committee selected by the executive board of the Firehouse Theatre Project. Acquires the right to produce the winning scripts for the 2004 FTP Festival of New American Plays. Following the Festival production dates, all rights are relinquished to the author.

FULL-LENGTH PLAY COMPETITION, West Coast Ensemble, P.O. Box 38728, Los Angeles CA 90038. (323)876-9337. Fax: (323)876-8916. Website: www.wcensemble.org. **Contact:** Les Hanson, artistic director. Offered annually "to nurture, support, and encourage" unpublished playwrights. Permission to present the play is granted if work is selected as finalist. **Deadline: December 31.** Guidelines for SASE. Prize: $500, and presentation of play.

GILMAN & GONZALEZ-FALLA THEATER FOUNDATION AWARD, 109 E. 64th St., New York NY 10021. (212)734-8011. Fax: (212)734-9606. E-mail: soncel@aol.com. Website: www.ggftheater.org. **Contact:** C.M. Gonzalez-Falla, vice president. Offered annually for body of work to encourage the creative elements in the American musical theater. The lyricist, book writer, or composer should have a work produced in the US in either a commercial theater or a professional not-for-profit theater. Two letters of recommendation from professionals involved in the theater are required. Open to US residents and American citizens. **Deadline: December 31.** Guidelines for SASE. Prize: $25,000.

GOVERNOR GENERAL'S LITERARY AWARD FOR DRAMA, Canada Council for the Arts, 350 Albert St., P.O. Box 1047, Ottawa ON K1P 5V8, Canada. (613)566-4414, ext. 5576. Fax: (613)566-4410. E-mail: joanne.larocque-poirier@canadacouncil.ca. Website: www.canadacouncil.ca/prizes/ggla. **Contact:** Joanne Larocque-Poirier. Offered for the best English-language and the best French-language work of drama by a Canadian published September 1, 2002-September 30, 2003. Publishers submit titles for consideration. **Deadline: April 15 or August 7, depending on the book's publication date.** Prize: Each laureate receives $15,000, and nonwinning finalists receive $1,000.

HENRICO THEATRE CO. ONE-ACT PLAYWRITING COMPETITION, Henrico Recreation & Parks, P.O. Box 27032, Richmond VA 23273. (804)501-5138. Fax: (804)501-5284. E-mail: per22@co.henrico.va.us. Website: www.co.henri

co.va.us/rec. **Contact:** Amy A. Perdue. Offered annually for previously unpublished or unproduced plays or musicals to produce new dramatic works in one-act form. "Scripts with small casts and simpler sets given preference. Controversial themes and excessive language should be avoided." **Deadline: July 1.** Guidelines for SASE. Prize: $300; Runner-up: $200. Winning entries may be produced; videotape sent to author.

HOLLYWOOD SCREENPLAY AWARDS, (formerly The Columbus Screenplay Discovery Awards), 433 N. Camden Dr., #600, Beverly Hills CA 90210. (310)288-1882. Fax: (310)475-0193. E-mail: awards@hollywoodawards.com. Website: www.HollywoodAwards.com. **Contact:** Carlos de Abreu. Annual contest "to discover new screenplay writers." Judged by reputable industry professionals (producers, development executives, story analysts). Open to any writer. **Deadline: May 31.** Guidelines for SASE. **Charges $55 fee.** Prize: Cash prizes, plus professional development guidance, and access to agents, producers, and studios.

JEWEL BOX THEATRE PLAYWRIGHTING COMPETITION, Jewel Box Theatre, 3700 N. Walker, Oklahoma City OK 73118-7099. (405)521-1786. **Contact:** Charles Tweed, production director. Estab. 1982. Offered annually for full-length plays. Send SASE in October for guidelines. **Deadline: January 15.** Prize: $500.

THE KENNEDY CENTER FUND FOR NEW AMERICAN PLAYS, J.F. Kennedy Center for the Performing Arts, Washington DC 20566. (202)416-8024. Fax: (202)416-8205. E-mail: rsfoster@kennedy-center.org. Website: kennedy-center.org/fnap. **Contact:** Rebecca Foster, manager, theater programming. Estab. 1988. Offered for previously unproduced work. "Program objectives: To stimulate and foster the development of new plays, ensuring the continued vitality of the nation's theatrical heritage; to nurture American playwrights and support the creation of new works; to provide nonprofit professional theater organizations with additional resources to mount enhanced productions of new plays; to encourage playwrights to write, and nonprofit professional theaters to produce new American plays; to ease the financial burdens of nonprofit professional theater organizations producing new plays; to provide a playwright with a better production of the play than the producing theater would normally be able to accomplish." Nonprofit professional theater organizations can mail in name and address to be placed on the mailing list or check website. Submissions and funding proposals only through the producing theater. Production grants are given to theaters to underwrite specific or extraordinary expenses relating to: Creative support, actor support, and production support. Development grants are given to theaters to underwrite expenses for a reading and workshop of a new play in development. **Deadline: Early May.** Prize: Production grant: Playwright receives $10,000 (theater receives an amount determined by budget submitted). Development grant: Playwright receives $2,500 (theater receives an amount determined by budget submitted); a few encouragement grants of $2,500 may be given to promising playwrights chosen from the submitted proposals.

MARC A. KLEIN PLAYWRITING AWARD FOR STUDENTS, Dept. of Theater Arts, Case Western Reserve University, 10900 Euclid Ave., Cleveland OH 44106-7077. (216)368-4868. Fax: (216)368-5184. E-mail: ksg@po.cwru.edu. Website: www.cwru.edu/artsci/thtr. **Contact:** Ron Wilson, reading committee chair. Estab. 1975. Offered annually for an unpublished, professionally unproduced full-length play, or evening of related short plays, by a student at an American college or university. **Deadline: May 15.** Prize: $1,000, which includes $500 to cover residency expenses; production.

KUMU KAHUA/UHM THEATRE DEPARTMENT PLAYWRITING CONTEST, Kumu Kahua Theatre, Inc./University of Hawaii at Manoa, Dept. of Theatre and Dance, 46 Merchant St., Honolulu HI 96813. (808)536-4222. Fax: (808)536-4226. E-mail: kkt@pixi.com. Website: www.kumukahua.com. **Contact:** Harry Wong III, artistic director. Offered annually for unpublished work to honor full-length and short plays. Guidelines available every September. First 2 categories open to residents and nonresidents. For Hawaii Prize, plays must be set in Hawaii or deal with some aspect of the Hawaiian experience. For Pacific Rim prize, plays must deal with the Pacific Islands, Pacific Rim, or Pacific/Asian-American experience—short plays only considered in 3rd category. **Deadline: January 2.** Prize: $500 (Hawaii Prize); $400 (Pacific Rim); $200 (Resident).

L.A. DESIGNERS' THEATRE-COMMISSIONS, L.A. Designers' Theatre, P.O. Box 1883, Studio City CA 91614-0883. (323)650-9600 or (323)654-2700 T.D.D. Fax: (323)654-3210. E-mail: ladesigners@juno.com. **Contact:** Richard Niederberg, artistic director. Quarterly contest "to promote new work and push it onto the conveyor belt to filmed or videotaped entertainment." All submissions must be registered with copyright office and be unpublished. Material will *not* be returned. "Do not submit anything that will not fit in a #10 envelope. No rules, guidelines, fees, or entry forms. Just present an *idea* that can be commissioned into a full work." Proposals for uncompleted works are encouraged. Unpopular political, religious, social, or other themes are encouraged; 'street' language and nudity are acceptable. Open to any writer. **Deadline: March 15, June 15, September 15, December 15.** Prize: Production or publication of the work in the Los Angeles market. "We only want 'first refusal.'"

[N] LOVE CREEK ANNUAL SHORT PLAY FESTIVAL, Love Creek Productions, % Granville, 162 Nesbit St., Weehawken NJ 07086-6817. E-mail: creekread@aol.com. **Contact:** Cynthia Granville-Callahan, festival manager. Estab. 1985. *E-mail address is for information only.* Annual festival for unpublished plays, unproduced in New York in the previous year, under 40 minutes, at least 2 characters, larger casts preferred. "We established the Festival as a playwriting competition in which scripts are judged on their merits in performance." All entries must specify "festival" on envelope and must include letter giving permission to produce script, if chosen, and stating whether equity showcase is acceptable. "We are giving strong preference to scripts featuring females in major roles in casts which are predominantly female." **Deadline: Ongoing.** Guidelines for SASE. Prize: Cash prize awarded to overall winner.

[N] LOVE CREEK MINI FESTIVALS, Love Creek Productions, co Granville, 162 Nesbit St., Weehawken NJ 07086-6817. E-mail: creekread@aol.com. **Contact:** Cynthia Granville-Callahan, festival literary manager. *E-mail address is for information only.* "The Mini Festivals are an outgrowth of our annual Short Play Festival in which we produce scripts concerning a particular issue or theme which our artistic staff selects according to current needs, interests and concerns of our members, audiences and playwrights submitting to our Short Play Festival throughout the year." Considers scripts unpublished, unproduced in New York City in the past year, under 40 minutes, at least 2 characters, larger casts preferred. Submissions must list name of festival on envelope and must include letter giving permission to produce script, if chosen, and stating whether equity showcase is acceptable. Finalists receive a mini-showcase production in New York City. Write for upcoming themes. "We are giving strong preference to scripts featuring females in major roles in casts which are predominantly female." **Deadline: Ongoing.** Guidelines for SASE. Prize: Winner of overall festival series receives a cash prize.

MAXIM MAZUMDAR NEW PLAY COMPETITION, Alleyway Theatre, One Curtain Up Alley, Buffalo NY 14202-1911. (716)852-2600. Fax: (716)852-2266. E-mail: email@alleyway.com. Website: alleyway.com. **Contact:** Literary Manager. Estab. 1990. Annual competition. Full Length: Not less than 90 minutes, no more than 10 performers. One-Act: Less than 20 minutes, no more than 6 performers. Children's plays. Musicals must be accompanied by audio tape. Finalists announced October 1. "Playwrights may submit work directly. There is no entry form. Annual playwright's fee $5; may submit 1 in each category, but pay only 1 fee. Please specify if submission is to be included in competition." "Alleyway Theatre must receive first production credit in subsequent printings and productions." **Deadline: July 1.** Prize: Full length: $400, production, and royalties; One-act: $100, production, plus royalties.

MOVING ARTS PREMIERE ONE-ACT COMPETITION, Moving Arts, 514 S. Spring St., Los Angeles CA 90013-2304. (213)622-8906. Fax: (213)622-8946. E-mail: treynichols@movingarts.org. Website: www.movingarts.org. **Contact:** Trey Nichols, literary director. Offered annually for unproduced one-act plays in the Los Angeles area and "is designed to foster the continued development of one-act plays." All playwrights are eligible except Moving Arts resident artists. Guidelines for SASE or by e-mail. **Deadline: February 28 (postmarked). Charges $10 fee/script.** Prize: 1st Place: $200, plus a full production with a 4-8 week run; 2nd and 3rd Place: Program mention and possible production.

MUSICAL STAIRS, West Coast Ensemble, P.O. Box 38728, Los Angeles CA 90038. (323)876-9337. Fax: (323)876-8916. **Contact:** Les Hanson. Offered annually for unpublished writers "to nurture, support, and encourage musical creators." Permission to present the musical is granted if work is selected as finalist. **Deadline: June 30.** Prize: $500, and presentation of musical.

NANTUCKET SHORT PLAY COMPETITION AND FESTIVAL, Nantucket Theatrical Productions, Box 2177, Nantucket MA 02584. (508)228-5002. **Contact:** Jim Patrick, artistic director. Offered annually for unpublished plays to "seek the highest quality of playwriting distilled into a short-play format." Selected plays receive staged readings. Plays must be less than 40 pages. **Deadline: January 1. Charges $10 fee.** Prize: $200, plus staged readings.

NATIONAL AUDIO DRAMA SCRIPT COMPETITION, National Audio Theatre Festivals, 115 Dikeman St., Hempstead NY 11150. (516)483-8321. Fax: (516)538-7583. Website: www.natf.org. **Contact:** Sue Zizza. Offered annually for unpublished radio scripts. "NATF is particularly interested in stories that deserve to be told because they enlighten, intrigue, or simply make us laugh out loud. Contemporary scripts with strong female roles, multi-cultural casting, and diverse viewpoints will be favorably received." Preferred length is 25 minutes. Guidelines on website. Open to any writer. NATF will have the right to produce the scripts for the NATF Live Performance Workshop; however, NATF makes no commitment to produce any script. The authors will retain all other rights to their work. **Deadline: November 15. Charges $25 fee (US currency only).** Prize: $800 split between 2-4 authors, and free workshop production participation.

NATIONAL CANADIAN ONE-ACT PLAYWRITING COMPETITION, Ottawa Little Theatre, 400 King Edward Ave., Ottawa ON K1N 7M7, Canada. (613)233-8948. Fax: (613)233-8027. E-mail: olt@on-aibn.com. Website: www.o-l-t.com. **Contact:** Elizabeth Holden, office manager. Estab. 1913. Purpose is "to encourage literary and dramatic talent in Canada." Guidelines for #10 SASE with Canadian postage or #10 SAE with 1 IRC. **Deadline: August 31.** Prize: 1st Place: $1,000; 2nd Place: $700; 3rd Place: $500.

NATIONAL CHILDREN'S THEATRE FESTIVAL, Actors' Playhouse at the Miracle Theatre, 280 Miracle Mile, Coral Gables FL 33134. (305)444-9293. Fax: (305)444-4181. Website: www.actorsplayhouse.org. **Contact:** Earl Maulding. Offered annually for unpublished musicals for young audiences. Target age is between 5-12. Script length should be 45-60 minutes. Maximum of 8 actors to play any number of roles. Settings which lend themselves to simplified scenery. Bilingual (English/Spanish) scripts are welcomed. Call or visit website for guidelines. Open to any writer. **Deadline: June 1. Charges $10 fee.** Prize: 1st Place: $500, full production.

NATIONAL LATINO PLAYWRIGHTS AWARD, (formerly National Latino Playwriting Award), Arizona Theatre Co. in affiliation with Centro Cultural Mexicano, 40 E. 14th St., Tucson AZ 85701. (520)884-8210. Fax: (520)628-9129. E-mail: ERomero@aztheatreco.org. Website: www.aztheatreco.org. **Contact:** Elaine Romero, playwright-in-residence. Offered annually for unproduced (professionally), unpublished plays over 50 pages in length. "The plays may be in English, bilingual, or in Spanish (with English translation). The award recognizes exceptional full-length plays by Latino playwrights on any subject." Open to Latino playwrights currently residing in the US, its territories, and/or Mexico. **Deadline: December 30.** Guidelines for SASE. Prize: $1,000.

NATIONAL ONE-ACT PLAYWRITING COMPETITION, Little Theatre of Alexandria, 600 Wolfe St., Alexandria VA 22314. Website: www.thelittletheatre.com/oneact. Estab. 1978. Offered annually to encourage original writing for theater. Submissions must be original, unpublished, unproduced one-act stage plays. "We usually produce top 2 or 3 winners." Guidelines for SASE or on website. **Deadline: Submit scripts for contest from January 1-May 31. Charges $20/play; 2 play limit.** Prize: 1st Place: $350; 2nd Place: $250; 3rd Place: $150.

NATIONAL TEN-MINUTE PLAY CONTEST, Actors Theatre of Louisville, 316 W. Main St., Louisville KY 40202-4218. (502)584-1265. E-mail: tpalmer@actorstheatre.org. Website: www.actorstheatre.org. **Contact:** Tanya Palmer, literary manager. Offered annually for previously (professionally) unproduced 10-minute plays (10 pages or less). "Entries must *not* have had an Equity or Equity-waiver production." One submission/playwright. Scripts are not returned. Please write or call for submission guidelines. Open to US residents. **Deadline: December 1 (postmarked).** Prize: $1,000.

[N] **NEW WORKS FOR THE STAGE**, COE College Theatre Arts Dept., 1220 First Ave. NE, Cedar Rapids IA 52402. (319)399-8624. Fax: (319)399-8557. E-mail: swolvert@coe.edu. Website: www.public.coe.edu/departments/theatre. **Contact:** Susan Wolverton. Offered every 2 years (odd years) "to encourage new work, to provide an interdisciplinary forum for the discussion of issues found in new work, to offer playwright contact with theater professionals who can provide response to new work." Full-length, original unpublished and unproduced scripts only. No musicals, adaptations, translations, or collaborations. Submit 1-page synopsis, résumé, and SASE if the script is to be returned. **Deadline: June 1, 2004.** Prize: $325, plus travel, room and board for residency at the college.

'THE NEXT STAGE' NEW PLAY READING FESTIVAL, The Cleveland Play House, P.O. Box 1989, Cleveland OH 44106-0189. Fax: (216)795-7005. E-mail: sgordon@clevelandplayhouse.com. Website: www.clevelandplayhouse.com. **Contact:** Seth Gordon, director of new play development. Offered annually for unpublished/unproduced submissions. "'The Next Stage' is our annual new play reading series. Up to 6 writers are brought to our theater for 1 week of rehearsal/development. The plays are then given public staged readings, and at least 1 is chosen for a full production in the upcoming season." **Deadline: Ongoing.** Guidelines for SASE. Prize: Staged reading of play, fee, travel, and housing, consideration for full production. Writers sign a 3-month option for production of script.

DON AND GEE NICHOLL FELLOWSHIPS IN SCREENWRITING, Academy of Motion Picture Arts & Sciences, 8949 Wilshire Blvd., Beverly Hills CA 90211-1972. (310)247-3059. E-mail: nicholl@oscars.org. Website: www.oscars.org/nicholl. **Contact:** Greg Beal, program coordinator. Estab. 1985. Offered annually for unproduced screenplays to identify talented new screenwriters. Guidelines for SASE, available January 1-April 30. Recipients announced late October. Open to writers who have not earned more than $5,000 writing for films or TV. **Deadline: May 1. Charges $30 fee.** Prize: $30,000 in fellowships (up to 5/year).

OGLEBAY INSTITUTE TOWNGATE THEATRE PLAYWRITING CONTEST, Oglebay Institute, Stifel Fine Arts Center, 1330 National Rd., Wheeling WV 26003. (304)242-7700. Fax: (304)242-7747. Website: www.oionline.com. **Contact:** Kate H. Crosbie, director of performing arts. Estab. 1976. Offered annually for unpublished works. "All full-length nonmusical plays that have never been professionally produced or published are eligible." Open to any writer. **Deadline: January 1; winner announced May 31.** Guidelines for SASE. Prize: Run of play and cash award.

ONE ACT MARATHON, Attic Theatre, 5429 W. Washington Blvd., Los Angeles CA 90016. (323)734-8977. E-mail: AtticTheatre1@aol.com. Website: www.AtticTheatre.org. **Contact:** Literary Manager. Offered annually for unpublished work. **Deadline: September 30.** Guidelines for SASE. **Charges $15.** Prize: 1st Place: $250; 2nd Place: $100; 1st-3rd Place scripts will be produced. Acquires 6-month window for 1st-6th Place entries for exclusive option.

MILDRED & ALBERT PANOWSKI PLAYWRITING AWARD, Forest Roberts Theatre, Northern Michigan University, Marquette MI 49855-5364. (906)227-2559. Fax: (906)227-2567. Website: www.nmu.edu/theatre. **Contact:** Megan Marcellini, award coordinator. Estab. 1977. Offered annually for unpublished, unproduced, full-length plays. Guidelines and application for SASE. **Deadline: August 15-November 15 (due at office on the 15th).** Prize: $2,000, a fully-mounted production, and transportation to Marquette to serve as Artist-in-Residence the week of the show.

PERISHABLE THEATRE'S WOMEN'S PLAYWRITING FESTIVAL, P.O. Box 23132, Providence RI 02903. (401)331-2695. Fax: (401)331-7811. E-mail: info@perishable.org. Website: www.perishable.org. **Contact:** Maythinee Washington, festival cooordinator. Offered annually for unproduced, one-act plays (up to 30 minutes in length when fully produced) to encourage women playwrights. Judged by reading committee, the festival director, and the artistic director of the theater. Open to women playwrights exclusively. **Deadline: October 15 (postmarked).** Guidelines for SASE. **Charges $5 fee/playwright (limit 2 plays/playwright).** Prize: $500, and travel to Providence.

PETERSON EMERGING PLAYWRIGHT COMPETITION, Catawba College Theatre Arts Dept., 2300 W. Innes St., Salisbury NC 28144. (704)637-4440. Fax: (704)637-4207. E-mail: lfkesler@catawba.edu. Website: www.catawba.edu. **Contact:** Linda Kesler, theatre arts department staff. Offered annually for full-length unpublished work "to assist emerging playwrights in the development of new scripts, hopefully leading to professional production. Competition is open to all subject matter except children's plays. Playwrights may submit more than 1 entry." Open to any writer. Guidelines for SASE or by e-mail. **Deadline: February 15.** Prize: Production of the winning play at Catawba College; $2,000 cash award; transportation to and from Catawba College for workshop and performance; lodging and food while in residence; professional response to the performance of the play.

ROBERT J. PICKERING AWARD FOR PLAYWRIGHTING EXCELLENCE, Coldwater Community Theater, % 89 Division, Coldwater MI 49036. (517)279-7963. Fax: (517)279-8095. **Contact:** J. Richard Colbeck, committee chairperson. Estab. 1982. Previously unproduced monetarily. "To encourage playwrights to submit their work, to present a previously unproduced play in full production." Submit script with SASE. "We reserve the right to produce winning script." **Deadline: December 15.** Guidelines for SASE. Prize: 1st Place: $300; 2nd Place: $100; 3rd Place: $50.

PILGRIM PROJECT GRANTS, 156 Fifth, #400, New York NY 10010. (212)627-2288. Fax: (212)627-2184. E-mail: davida@firstthings.com. **Contact:** Davida Goldman. Grants for a reading, workshop production, or full production of plays that deal with questions of moral significance. **Deadline: Ongoing.** Guidelines for SASE. Prize: Grants of $1,000-7,000.

PLAYHOUSE ON THE SQUARE NEW PLAY COMPETITION, Playhouse on the Square, 51 S. Cooper, Memphis TN 38104. **Contact:** Jackie Nichols. Submissions required to be unproduced. **Deadline: April 1.** Guidelines for SASE. Prize: $500, and production.

PLAYWRIGHT DISCOVERY AWARD, VSA Arts Connection, 1300 Connecticut Ave. NW, Suite 700, Washington DC 20036. (202)628-2800. Fax: (202)737-0725. E-mail: playwright@vsarts.org. Website: www.vsarts.org. **Contact:** Johanna Bentwood, information specialist. Invites students with and without disabilities (grades 6-12) to submit a one-act play that documents the experience of living with a disability. Two plays will be selected for production at the John F. Kennedy Center for the Performing Arts. **Deadline: March 15.** Guidelines for SASE. Prize: Monetary award, and a trip to Washington DC to view the production or staged reading.

PRIME TIME TELEVISION COMPETITION, Austin Film Festival, 1604 Nueces, Austin TX 78701. (512)478-4795. E-mail: austinfilm@aol.com. Website: www.austinfilmfestival.com. **Contact:** BJ Burrow. Offered annually for unpublished work to discover talented television writers, and introduce their work to production companies. Categories: drama and sitcom. Contest open to writers who do not earn a living writing for television or film. **Deadline: June 15.** Guidelines for SASE. **Charges $30.** Prize: $1,000 in each category.

PRINCESS GRACE AWARDS PLAYWRIGHT FELLOWSHIP, Princess Grace Foundation—USA, 150 E. 58th St., 21st Floor, New York NY 10155. (212)317-1470. Fax: (212)317-1473. E-mail: pgfusa@pgfusa.com. Website: www.pgfusa.com. **Contact:** Ms. Toby E. Boshak, executive director. Offered annually for unpublished, unproduced submissions to support playwright-through-residency program with New Dramatists, Inc., located in New York City. Entrants must be US citizens or have US status. Guidelines for SASE or on website. **Deadline: March 31.** Prize: $7,500, plus residency with New Dramatists, Inc., in New York City, and representation/publication by Samuel French, Inc.

THE LOIS AND RICHARD ROSENTHAL NEW PLAY PRIZE, Cincinnati Playhouse in the Park, Box 6537, Cincinnati OH 45206-0537. (513)345-2242. Website: www.cincyplay.com. **Contact:** Literary Associate. Annual award for playwrights and musical playwrights. "The Lois and Richard Rosenthal New Play Prize was established in 1987 to encourage the development of new plays that are original, theatrical, strong in character and dialogue, and make a significant contribution to the literature of American theater. Residents of Cincinnati, the Rosenthals are committed to supporting arts organizations and social agencies that are innovative and that foster social change." Plays must be full-length in any style: comedy, drama, musical, etc. Translations, adaptations, individual one-acts, and any play previously submitted for the Rosenthal Prize, are not eligible. Collaborations are welcome, in which case prize benefits are shared. Plays must be unpublished prior to submission and may not have received a full-scale, professional production. Plays that have had a workshop, reading, or nonprofessional production are still eligible. Playwrights with past production experience are especially encouraged to submit new work. Submit a 2-page maximum abstract of the play including title, character breakdown, story synopsis, and playwright information (bio or résumé). Also include up to 5 pages of sample dialogue. If submitting a musical, please include a tape or CD of selections from the score. All abstracts and dialogue samples will be read. From these, selected mss will be solicited. Do not send a ms with, or instead of, the abstract. Unsolicited mss will not be read. Submitted materials, including tapes and CDs, will be returned only if a SASE with adequate postage is provided. Only 1 submission/playwright each year. **Deadline: July 1-December 31.** Prize: A full production at Cincinnati Playhouse in the Park as part of the annual season and regional and national promotion; and $12,500 award, plus travel and residency expenses for the Cincinnati rehearsal period.

THE SCREENWRITER'S PROJECT, Indifest: Film Festival & Market, P.O. Box 148849, Chicago IL 60614-8849. (773)665-7600. E-mail: info@indifestchicago.com. Website: www.indifestchicago.com. Offered annually to give both experienced and first-time writers the opportunity to begin a career as a screenwriter. **Deadline: May 1; June 1; July 1.** Guidelines for SASE. **Charges $40 fee for May 1 deadline; $50 fee for June 1 deadline; $60 fee for July 1 deadline.** Prize: Various cash awards and prizes.

N **SCRIPTAPALOOZA SCREENWRITING COMPETITION**, Write Brothers, Inc., Scriptmag.com, & WritersScriptNetwork.com, 7775 Sunset Blvd., PMB #200, Hollywood CA 90046. (323)654-5809. E-mail: info@scriptapalooza.com. Website: www.scriptapalooza.com. Annual contest open to unpublished scripts from any genre. Open to any writer, 18 or older, without produced feature film credits. Submit 1 copy of a 90-130-page screenplay with 2 title pages. Body pages must be numbered and scripts must be in industry standard format and bound with 2 or 3 brads. **Deadline: Early Deadline: January 7; Deadline: March 3; Late Deadline: April 15.** Guidelines for SASE. **Charges Early Deadline Fee: $40; Fee: $45; Late Deadline Fee: $50.** Prize: 1st Place: $10,000 and software package from Write Brothers, Inc.; 2nd and 3rd Place, plus 10 Runners up: Software package from Write Brothers, Inc. 1st-3rd Place has script submitted to Scriptapalooza participants, literary reps, and production companies listed on website.

SIENA COLLEGE INTERNATIONAL PLAYWRIGHTS COMPETITION, Siena College Theatre Program, 515 Loudon Rd., Loudonville NY 12211-1462. (518)783-2381. Fax: (518)783-2381. E-mail: maciag@siena.edu. Website: www.siena.edu/theatre. **Contact:** Gary Maciag, director. Offered every 2 years for unpublished plays "to allow students to explore production collaboration with the playwright. In addition, it provides the playwright an important development opportunity. Plays should be previously unproduced, unpublished, full-length, nonmusicals, and free of copyright and royalty restrictions. Plays should require unit set or minimal changes and be suitable for a college-age cast of 3-10. There is a required 4-6 week residency." Guidelines for SASE. Guidelines are available after November 1 in odd-numbered years. Winning playwright must agree that the Siena production will be the world premiere of the play. **Deadline: February 1-June 30 in even-numbered years.** Prize: $2,000 honorarium; up to $2,000 to cover expenses for required residency; full production of winning script.

DOROTHY SILVER PLAYWRITING COMPETITION, The Eugene S. & Blanche R. Halle Theatre of the Jewish Community Center of Cleveland, 3505 Mayfield Rd., Cleveland Heights OH 44118. (216)382-4000, ext. 274. Fax: (216)382-5401. E-mail: halletheatre@clevejcc.org. Website: www.clevejcc.org. **Contact:** Kris Barnes, box office manager. Estab. 1948. All entries must be original works, not previously produced, suitable for a full-length presentation; directly concerned with the Jewish experience. **Deadline: May 1.** Prize: Cash award, plus staged reading.

SOUTHEASTERN THEATRE CONFERENCE NEW PLAY PROJECT, P.O. Box 9868, Greensboro NC 27429. (336)272-3645. Fax: (336)272-8810. E-mail: setc@mindspring.com. Website: www.setc.org. **Contact:** Susan Sharp. Offered annually for the discovery, development, and publicizing of worthy new unproduced plays and playwrights. Eligibility limited to members of 10 state SETC Region: Alabama, Florida, Georgia, Kentucky, Mississippi, North Carolina, South Carolina, Tennessee, Virginia, or West Virginia. Submissions accepted on disk only, in Microsoft Word format only. Check the SETC website for full submission details. No musicals or children's plays. **Deadline: March 1-June 1.** Guidelines for SASE. Prize: $1,000, staged reading at SETC Convention, and expenses paid trip to convention.

SOUTHERN APPALACHIAN PLAYWRIGHTS CONFERENCE, Southern Appalachian Repertory Theatre, P.O. Box 1720, Mars Hill NC 28754. (828)689-1384. Fax: (828)689-1272. E-mail: SART@mhc.edu. Website: www.sart.mhc.edu. **Contact:** Managing Director. Offered annually for unpublished, unproduced, full-length plays to promote the development of new plays. All plays are considered for later production with honorarium provided for the playwright. **Deadline: October 31 (postmarked).** Guidelines for SASE. Prize: 4-5 playwrights are invited for staged readings in March or April, room and board provided.

SOUTHERN PLAYWRIGHTS COMPETITION, Jacksonville State University, 700 Pelham Rd. N., Jacksonville AL 36265-1602. (256)782-5414. Fax: (256)782-5441. E-mail: swhitton@jsucc.jsu.edu. Website: www.jsu.edu/depart/english/southpla.htm. **Contact:** Steven J. Whitton. Estab. 1988. Offered annually to identify and encourage the best of Southern playwriting. Playwrights must be a native or resident of Alabama, Arkansas, Florida, Georgia, Kentucky, Louisiana, Missouri, North Carolina, South Carolina, Tennessee, Texas, Virginia, or West Virginia. **Deadline: February 15.** Guidelines for SASE. Prize: $1,000, and production of the play.

[N] **SOUTHWEST THEATRE ASSOCIATION NATIONAL NEW PLAY CONTEST**, Southwest Theatre Association, % David H. Fennema, Dept. of Music and Theatre Arts, Cameron University, Lawton OK 73505-6377. E-mail: davidf@cameron.edu. Website: www.southwest-theater.com. **Contact:** David H. Fennema, co-chair. Annual contest for unpublished, unproduced work to promote the writing and production of new one-act or full-length plays. No musicals, translations, adaptations of previously produced or published work, or children's plays. Guidelines for SASE or by e-mail. Open to writers who reside in the US. One entry/writer. **Deadline: March 15. Charges $10 (make check payable to SWTA).** Prize: $200 honorarium, a reading at the annual SWTA conference, complimentary registration at conference, 1-year membership in SWTA, award plaque, and possibility of excerpt publication in the professional journal of SWTA.

STANLEY DRAMA AWARD, Dept. of Theatre Wagner College, One Campus Rd., Staten Island NY 10301. (718)390-3157. Fax: (718)390-3323. **Contact:** Dr. Felicia J. Ruff, director. Offered for original full-length stage plays, musicals, or one-act play sequences that have not been professionally produced or received trade book publication. **Deadline: October 1.** Guidelines for SASE. **Charges $20 submission fee.** Prize: $2,000.

THEATRE BC'S ANNUAL CANADIAN NATIONAL PLAYWRITING COMPETITION, Theatre BC, P.O. Box 2031, Nanaimo BC V9R 6X6, Canada. (250)714-0203. Fax: (250)714-0213. E-mail: pwc@theatrebc.org. Website: www.theatrebc.org. **Contact:** Robb Mowbray, executive director. Offered annually to unpublished plays "to promote the development and production of previously unproduced new plays (no musicals) at all levels of theater. Categories: Full Length (2 acts or longer); One Act (less than 60 minutes); and an open Special Merit (juror's discretion). Guidelines for SASE or on website. Winners are also invited to New Play Festival: Up to 18 hours with a professional dramaturg, registrant actors, and a public reading in Kamloops (every spring). Production and publishing rights remain with the playwright. Open to Canadian residents. All submissions are made under pseudonyms. E-mail inquiries welcome. **Deadline: Fourth Monday in July. Charges $35/entry, and optional $25 for written critique.** Prize: Full Length: $1,000; One Act: $750; Special Merit: $500.

THEATRE CONSPIRACY ANNUAL NEW PLAY CONTEST, Theatre Conspiracy, 10091 McGregor Blvd., Ft. Myers FL 33919. (239)936-3239. Fax: (239)936-0510. E-mail: info@theatreconspiracy.org. **Contact:** Bill Taylor, award director. Offered annually for unproduced full-length plays with 8 or less characters and simple production demands. Open to any writer. **Deadline: November 30.** Guidelines for SASE. **Charges $5 fee.** Prize: $700, and full production.

[N] **THEATRE IN THE RAW ONE-ACT PLAY WRITING CONTEST**, Theatre In the Raw, 3521 Marshall St., Vancouver BC V5N 4S2, Canada. (604)708-5448. E-mail: titraw@vcn.bc.ca. **Contact:** Artistic Director. Annual contest for an original one-act play, presented in proper stage-play format, that is unpublished and unproduced. The play (with no more than 6 characters) cannot be longer than 25 double-spaced, typed pages equal to 30 minutes. **Deadline: September 30. Charges $25 entry fee, $40 for 2 plays (payable to Theatre In the Raw).** Prize: 1st Prize: $150, at least 1 dramatic reading or staging of the play at a Theatre In the Raw Cafe/Venue, or as part of a mini-tour program for the One-Act Play Series Nights; 2nd Prize: $50; 3rd Prize: $40.

THEATREFEST REGIONAL PLAYWRITING CONTEST, TheatreFest, Montclair State University, Upper Montclair NJ 07043. (973)655-7071. Fax: (973)655-5335. E-mail: surowitzj@mail.montclair.edu. Website: www.montclair.edu. **Contact:** John Wooten, artistic director. Offered annually for unpublished work to encourage and nurture the work of American dramatists. Open to any writer in the tri-state area (New Jersey, New York, Connecticut). Guidelines are available September-

January, send a SASE for guidelines. **Deadline: January 7.** Prize: 1st Place: $1,500, and equity production; Runners-up (2): $500. TheatreFest has option to re-option play after production at TheatreFest.

THEATREPEI NEW VOICES PLAYWRITING COMPETITION, P.O. Box 1573, Charlottetown PE C1A 7N3, Canada. (902)894-3558. Fax: (902)368-4418. E-mail: theatre@isn.net. **Contact:** Dawn Binkley, general manager. Offered annually. Open to individuals who have been residents of Prince Edward Island for 6 months preceding the deadline for entries. **Deadline: February 14.** Guidelines for SASE. **Charges $5 fee.** Prize: Monetary.

THUNDERBIRD FILMS SCREENPLAY COMPETITION, Thunderbird Films, 214 Riverside Dr. #112, New York NY 10025. (212)352-4498. Website: home.att.net/thunderbirdfilms. **Contact:** Eric Stannard. Offered annually for unpublished work to encourage, promote, and reward writers of original, well-crafted screenplays. Open to any writer. **Deadline: Varies.** Guidelines for SASE. **Charges $40 fee.** Prize: $2,000 and possible option by Thunderbird Films.

TRUSTUS PLAYWRIGHTS' FESTIVAL, Trustus Theatre, Box 11721, Columbia SC 29211-1721. (803)254-9732. Fax: (803)771-9153. E-mail: trustus@trustus.org. Website: www.trustus.org. **Contact:** Jon Tuttle, literary manager. Offered annually for professionally unproduced full-length plays; cast limit of 8; prefer challenging, innovative dramas and comedies; no musicals, plays for young audiences, or "hillbilly" southern shows. Guidelines and application for SASE. **Deadline: Applications received between December 1, 2002 and February 27, 2004 only.** Prize: Public staged-reading and $250, followed after a 1-year development period by full production, $500, plus travel/accommodations to attend opening.

UBC'S CREATIVE WRITING RESIDENCY PRIZE IN STAGEPLAY, *PRISM International* and the Dept. of Theatre, Film, and Creative Writing at the University of British Columbia, c/o *PRISM International*, Creative Writing Program, UBC, Buch. E462-1866 Main Mall, Vancouver BC V6T 1Z1, Canada. Website: www.creativewriting.ubc.ca/resprize. UBC's Creative Writing Residency Prize in Stageplay is the result of a cooperative venture between the literary magazine *PRISM International* and the Dept. of Theatre, Film, and Creative Writing at the University of British Columbia. The prize will be awarded tri-annually. Plays should be original, previously unproduced, with 2 or more acts, and have a running time of at least 75, and no more than 120, minutes. Scripts should be in stageplay format and in English. Entries (with entry fee) will be accepted beginning October 1; the **postmarked deadline for entries is March 31.** The winner will be announced October 1. For complete rules and entry guidelines, visit the official website. Prize: $10,000 (Canadian), plus expenses for a 1-month residency at the University, during which time, the winning playwright will be available for consultation with students. The winning play will be published as part of *PRISM*'s regular volume year. The theater program at UBC has an option to produce the winning play as part of their regular season at the Freddie Wood Theatre, The Chan Centre for the Performing Arts, or in co-production with a local theater company.

UNICORN THEATRE NEW PLAY DEVELOPMENT, Unicorn Theatre, 3828 Main St., Kansas City MO 64111. (816)531-7529, ext. 18. Fax: (816)531-0421. Website: www.unicorntheatre.org. **Contact:** Herman Wilson, literary assistant. Offered annually to encourage and assist the development of an unpublished and unproduced play. Acquires 2% subsidiary rights of future productions for a 5-year period. **Deadline: Ongoing.** Guidelines for SASE. Prize: $1,000, and production.

VERMONT PLAYWRIGHT'S AWARD, The Valley Players, P.O. Box 441, Waitsfield VT 05673. (802)496-3751. E-mail: valleyplayers@madriver.com. Website: www.valleyplayers.com. **Contact:** Jennifer Howard, chair. Offered annually for unpublished, nonmusical, full-length play suitable for production by a community theater group to encourage development of playwrights in Vermont, New Hampshire, and Maine. **Deadline: February 1.** Prize: $1,000.

VSA ARTS PLAYWRIGHT DISCOVERY AWARD, VSA Arts, John F. Kennedy Center for the Performing Arts, 1300 Connecticut Ave. NW, Suite 700, Washington DC 20036. (202)628-2800. Fax: (202)737-0725. E-mail: playwright@vsarts.org. Website: www.vsarts.org. **Contact:** Elena Widder, director of performing arts. Offered annually for unpublished work. "Students grades 6-12 are invited to submit an original one-act script that examines the experience of living with a disability. The award challenges student writers with and without disabilities to create a one-act script about their own life, or about experiences in the life of another person or fictional character." Authors must be US citizens or permanent residents of the US. Guidelines for SASE, by e-mail, or on website. **Deadline: April 15.** Prize: Monetary award along with an expense-paid trip to the Kennedy Center in Washington DC to see their scripts performed live.

JACKIE WHITE MEMORIAL NATIONAL CHILDREN'S PLAYWRITING CONTEST, Columbia Entertainment Co., 309 Parkade, Columbia MO 65202. (573)874-5628. **Contact:** Betsy Phillips, director. Offered annually for unpublished plays. "Searching for good scripts, either adaptations or plays with original story lines, suitable for audiences of all ages." Script must include at least 7 well-developed roles. **Deadline: June 1.** Guidelines for SASE. **Charges $10 fee.** Prize: $500. Company reserves the right to grant prize money without production. All entrants receive written evaluation.

WRITE A PLAY! NYC, (formerly New York City Public School Playwriting Contest), Young Playwrights, Inc., 306 W. 38th St., Suite 300, New York NY 10018. (212)594-5440. Fax: (212)594-5441. E-mail: writeaplay@aol.com. Website: youngplaywrights.org. **Contact:** Literary Department. Offered annually for plays by NYC public school students only. **Deadline: April 1.** Prize: Varies.

YEAR END SERIES (YES) NEW PLAY FESTIVAL, Dept. of Theatre, Nunn Dr., Northern Kentucky University, Highland Heights KY 41099-1007. (859)572-6362. Fax: (859)572-6057. E-mail: forman@nku.edu. **Contact:** Sandra Forman, project director. Receives submissions from May 1-October 31 in even-numbered years for the Festivals which occur in April of odd-numbered years. Open to all writers. **Deadline: October 31.** Guidelines for SASE. Prize: $500, and an expense-paid visit to Northern Kentucky University to see the play produced.

ANNA ZORNIO MEMORIAL CHILDREN'S THEATRE PLAYWRITING COMPETITION, University of New Hampshire, Dept. of Theatre and Dance, PCAC, 30 College Rd., Durham NH 03824-3538. (603)862-2919. Fax: (603)862-

0298. E-mail: mike.wood@unh.edu. Website: www.unh.edu/theatre-dance. **Contact:** Michael Wood. Offered every 4 years for unpublished well-written plays or musicals appropriate for young audiences with a maximum length of 60 minutes. Guidelines and entry forms for SASE. May submit more than 1 play, but not more than 3. Open to all playwrights in US and Canada. All ages are invited to participate. **Deadline: September 1, 2004.** Prize: $1,000, and play produced and underwritten as part of the season by the UNH Department of Theatre and Dance. Winner will be notified in November 2004.

Journalism

AAAS SCIENCE JOURNALISM AWARDS, American Association for the Advancement of Science, Office of News and Information, 1200 New York Ave. NW, Washington DC 20005. (202)326-6440. E-mail: media@aaas.org. Website: www.aaas.org. Offered annually for previously published work July 1-June 30 to reward excellence in reporting on science and its applications in daily newspapers with circulation over 100,000; newspapers with circulation under 100,000; general circulation magazines; radio; television and online." Sponsored by the Whitaker Foundation. **Deadline: August 1.** Prize: $2,500, plaque, trip to AAAS Annual Meeting.

THE AMERICAN LEGION FOURTH ESTATE AWARD, The American Legion, 700 N. Pennsylvania, Indianapolis IN 46206. (317)630-1253. Fax: (317)630-1368. E-mail: PR@legion.org. Website: www.legion.org. Offered annually for journalistic works published the previous calendar year. "Subject matter must deal with a topic or issue of national interest or concern. Entry must include cover letter explaining entry, and any documention or evidence of the entry's impact on the community, state, or nation. No printed entry form." Guidelines for SASE or on website. Judged by a volunteer panel of 4 practicing print or broadcast journalists and/or educators. Judges submit their recommendation to the National Public Relations Commission for final approval. **Deadline: January 31.** Prize: $2,000 stipend to defray expenses of recipient accepting the award at The American Legion National Convention in September.

AMY WRITING AWARDS, The Amy Foundation, P.O. Box 16091, Lansing MI 48901. (517)323-6233. Fax: (517)323-7293. E-mail: amyfoundtn@aol.com. Website: www.amyfound.org. **Contact:** James Russell, president. Estab. 1985. Offered annually for nonfiction articles containing scripture published in the previous calendar year in the secular media. **Deadline: January 31.** 1st Prize: $10,000; 2nd Prize: $5,000; 3rd Prize: $4,000; 4th Prize: $3,000; 5th Prize: $2,000; and 10 prizes of $1,000.

AVENTIS PASTEUR MEDAL FOR EXCELLENCE IN HEALTH RESEARCH JOURNALISM, Canadians for Health Research, P.O. Box 126, Westmount QC H3Z 2T1, Canada. (514)398-7478. Fax: (514)398-8361. E-mail: info@chrcrm.org. Website: www.chrcrm.org. **Contact:** Linda Bazinet. Offered annually for work published the previous calendar year in Canadian newspapers or magazines. Applicants must have demonstrated an interest and effort in reporting health research issues within Canada. Guidelines available from CHR or on website. **Deadline: February.** Prize: $2,500, and a medal. The winner's name also appears on a permanent plaque at the Canadian Medical Hall of Fame in London, Ontario.

ERIK BARNOUW AWARD, Organization of American Historians, 112 N. Bryan Ave., Bloomington IN 47408-4199. (812)855-9852. Fax: (812)855-0696. E-mail: awards@oah.org. Website: www.oah.org. **Contact:** Award & Prize Committee Coordinator. One or 2 awards are given annually in recognition of outstanding reporting or programming on network or cable television, or in documentary film, concerned with American history, the study of American history, and/or the promotion of history. Entries must have been released the year of the contest. Guidelines available on website. **Deadline: December 1.** Prize: $500, and a certificate.

THE WHITMAN BASSOW AWARD, Overseas Press Club of America, 40 W. 45th St., New York NY 10036. (212)626-9220. Fax: (212)626-9210. Website: www.opcofamerica.org. **Contact:** Sonya Fry, executive director. Offered annually for best reporting in any medium on international environmental issues. Work must be published by US-based publications or broadcast. **Deadline: End of January. Charges $125 fee.** Prize: $1,000, and certificate.

MIKE BERGER AWARD, Columbia University Graduate School of Journalism, 2950 Broadway, MC 3800, New York NY 10027-7004. (212)854-5974. Fax: (212)854-3148. E-mail: jf680@columbia.edu. Website: www.jrn.columbia.edu. **Contact:** Jane M. Folpe, program coordinator. Offered annually honoring "human-interest reporting about daily life in New York City in the tradition of the late Meyer 'Mike' Berger. All newspaper reporters whose beat is New York City, whether they report for dailies, weeklies, or monthlies, are eligible." **Deadline: March 15.** Prize: Cash prize.

THE WORTH BINGHAM PRIZE, The Worth Bingham Memorial Fund, 1616 H St. NW, 3rd Floor, Washington DC 20006. (202)737-3700. Fax: (202)737-0530. E-mail: susan@icfj.org. **Contact:** Susan Talaly, project director. Offered annually to articles published during the year of the award. "The Prize honors newspaper or magazine investigative reporting of stories of national significance where the public interest is being ill-served. Entries may include a single story, a related series of stories, or up to 3 unrelated stories. Please contact us for guidelines and entry form." **Deadline: January 2.** Guidelines for SASE. Prize: $10,000.

NICHOLAS BLAKE FOREIGN FREE-LANCE REPORTING GRANT, Family of Nicholas Blake, Nicholas Blake Grant Program, 1500A Lafayette Rd., Box 320, Portsmouth NH 03801. Estab. 2001. Contest offered annually for material published between January 1, 2002-December 31, 2003. The purpose of the grant program is to support current freelance print journalists who specialize in foreign reporting on national (or significant regional) political or armed conflicts within foreign countries. The grant program was created in honor of Nicholas C. Blake, an American freelance journalist who died in 1985 while pursuing a story on the Guatemalan civil war. The grant program seeks to recognize that freelance foreign reporting is an important but under-emphasized branch of print journalism and to reward high-quality, innovative foreign reporting by these journalists. The program is intended to recognize the difficult conditions under which many freelance foreign print reporters work, and to foster their important role in foreign reporting by providing them needed financial support. An additional goal is to assist in the career development of these individuals, whether it is freelance reporting or as foreign correspondents with news organizations. Complete grant submission guidelines can be obtained by sending an e-mail request to nblakegrant@aol.com. **Deadline: September 1-December 31, 2003.** Prize: $5,000 grant.

HEYWOOD BROUN AWARD, The Newspaper Guild-CWA, 501 Third St. NW, Washington DC 20001-2797. (202)434-7173. Fax: (202)434-1472. E-mail: azipser@cwa-union.org. Website: www.newsguild.org. **Contact:** Andy Zipser. Offered annually for works published the previous year. "This annual competition is intended to encourage and recognize individual journalistic achievement by members of the working media, particularly if it helps right a wrong or correct an injustice. First consideration will be given to entries on behalf of individuals or teams of no more than 2." **Deadline: Last Friday in January.** Guidelines for SASE. Prize: $5,000, and plaque.

HARRY CHAPIN MEDIA AWARDS, World Hunger Year, 505 Eighth Ave., Suite 2100, New York NY 10018-6582. (212)629-8850, ext. 122. Fax: (212)465-9274. E-mail: media@worldhungeryear.org. Website: www.worldhungeryear.org. **Contact:** Lisa Ann Batitto. Estab. 1982. Open to works published the previous calendar year. Critical issues of domestic and world hunger, poverty and development (newspaper, periodical, TV, radio, photojournalism, books). **Deadline: Mid-January.** Guidelines for SASE. **Charges $25 for 1 entry, $40 for 2 entries, or $50 for 3-5 entries.** Prize: Several prizes from $1,000-2,500.

CONGRESSIONAL FELLOWSHIP PROGRAM, American Political Science Association, 1527 New Hampshire Ave. NW, Washington DC 20036-1206. (202)483-2512. Fax: (202)483-2657. E-mail: cfp@apsanet.org. Website: www.apsanet.org/about/cfp. **Contact:** Program Coordinator. Offered annually for professional journalists who have 2-10 years of full-time professional experience in newspaper, magazine, radio, or television reporting at time of application to learn more about the legislative process through direct participation. Visit our website for deadlines. Open to journalists and scholars. Prize: $38,000, and travel allowance for 3 weeks' orientation and legislation aide assignments December-August.

[N] THE JANE CUNNINGHAM CROLY PRINT JOURNALISM AWARD FOR EXCELLENCE IN COVERING ISSUES OF CONCERN TO WOMEN, The General Federation of Women's Clubs, 1734 N St. NW, Washington DC 20036. (202)347-3168. Fax: (202)835-0246. E-mail: gfwc@gfwc.org. Website: www.gfwc.org. **Contact:** Sally Kranz. An annual award "to honor the print journalist whose writing demonstrates a concern for the rights and the advancement of women in our society and/or an awareness of women's sensitivity, strength, and courage, and/or an attempt to counteract existing sexism." Open to women and men who write for newspapers, magazines, Internet publications, or news services in the United States—either on staff or in a freelance capacity. Three articles must be submitted by each person. Articles must have been published between January 1 and December 31, 2003. **Deadline: March 3.** Guidelines for SASE. **Charges $50 (the fee is reduced by $10 for subsequent entries from other writers at the same news organization).** Prize: $1,000 presented at GFWC's annual International Convention. GFWC pays airfare and expenses. The winner is asked to deliver an address on some aspect of the media and issues of concern to women. Judged by 2 prominent journalists, and 1 leader of a major woman's organization.

FREEDOM OF THE PRESS AWARD, National Press Club, General Manager's Office, National Press Club, National Press Bldg., Washington DC 20045. (202)662-7532. Fax: (202)662-7512. E-mail: jbooze@npcpress.org. Website: npc.press.org. **Contact:** Joann Booze. Offered annually "to recognize members of the news media who have, through the publishing or broadcasting of news, promoted or helped to protect the freedom of the press" during the previous calendar year. Categories: A US journalist or team for work published or broadcast in the US; a foreign journalist or team for work published or broadcast in their home country. Guidelines on website. Open to professional journalists. **Deadline: April 1.** Prize: $1,000 in each category.

ROBIN GOLDSTEIN AWARD FOR WASHINGTON REGIONAL REPORTING, National Press Club, Administered by the National Press Foundation, General Manager's Office, National Press Club, National Press Bldg., Washington DC 20045. (202)662-8744. E-mail: jbooze@npcpress.org. Website: npc.press.org. **Contact:** Joann Booze. Offered annually for a Washington newspaper correspondent "who best exemplifies the standards set by the late Robin Goldstein, who established the Washington bureaus of the Asbury Park (NJ) Press and the Orange County (CA) Register. Working alone in each bureau, Goldstein proved that one dedicated reporter can do it all for the hometown readers—news, features, enterprise, analysis and columns. This contest honors reporters who demonstrate excellence and versatility in covering Washington from a local angle." Guidelines on website. **Deadline: April 1.** Prize: $1,000.

[N] EDWIN M. HOOD AWARD FOR DIPLOMATIC CORRESPONDENCE, National Press Club, General Manager's Office, National Press Club, National Press Bldg., Washington DC 20045. (202)662-8744. E-mail: jbooze@npcpress.org. Website: npc.press.org. **Contact:** Joann Booze. Offered annually to recognize excellence in reporting on diplomatic and foreign policy issues. Categories: newspaper and broadcast. Guidelines on website. **Deadline: April 1.** Prize: $500 in each category.

ICIJ AWARD FOR OUTSTANDING INTERNATIONAL INVESTIGATIVE REPORTING, International Consortium of Investigative Journalists, A Project of the Center for Public Integrity, 910 17th St. NW, 7th Floor, Washington DC 20006. (202)466-1300. Fax: (202)466-1101. E-mail: info@icij.org. Website: www.icij.org. **Contact:** Laura Peterson or Andre Verloy. Offered annually for works produced in print, broadcast, and online media between June 1, 2002, and June 1, 2003, are eligible. Work must be on a transnational, investigative topic. Guidelines for SASE or on website. **Deadline: July 15.** Prize: 1st Place: $20,000; up to 5 finalist awards of $1,000 each.

N INVESTIGATIVE JOURNALISM GRANT, Fund For Investigative Journalism, P.O. Box 60184, Washington DC 20039-0184. (202)362-0260. Fax: (301)422-7449. E-mail: fundfij@aol.com. Website: www.fij.org. **Contact:** John Hyde. Offered 3 times/year for original investigative newspaper and magazine stories, radio and TV documentaries, books and media criticism. Guidelines on website or by e-mail. The Fund also offers an annual $25,000 FIJ Book Prize in November for the best book chosen by the board during the year. **Deadline: February 1, June 1, and October 1.** Prize: Grants of $500-10,000.

THE IOWA AWARD/THE TIM McGINNIS AWARD, *The Iowa Review*, 308 EPB, University of Iowa, Iowa City IA 52242. (319)335-0462. E-mail: iowa-review@uiowa.edu. Website: www.uiowa.edu/~iareview. **Contact:** David Hamilton. "Offered annually for work already published in our magazine, usually within the previous year. The Iowa Award is a judge's choice of the best work of the year. The McGinnis Award is the editors' choice of a work that usually expresses an off-beat and (we hope) sophisticated sense of humor." Guidelines for SASE or on website. No entry form. Prize: $1,000 for Iowa Award; $500 for McGinnis Award.

N ANSON JONES, M.D. AWARD, Texas Medical Association, 401 W. 15th St., Austin TX 78701-1680. (512)370-1381. Fax: (512)370-1629. E-mail: brent.annear@texmed.org. Website: www.texmed.org. **Contact:** Brent Annear, media relations manager. Offered annually "to the media of Texas for excellence in communicating health information to the public." Open only to Texas media or writers published in Texas. Guidelines posted online. **Deadline: January 15.** Prize: $1,000 for winners of each of the categories.

N ROBERT L. KOZIK AWARD FOR ENVIRONMENTAL REPORTING, National Press Foundation, General Manager's Office, National Press Club, National Press Bldg., Washington DC 20045. (202)662-8744. E-mail: jbooze@npcpress.org. Website: npc.press.org. **Contact:** Joann Booze. Offered annually to recognize excellence in environmental reporting at the local, national, or international level that impacted or prompted action to remedy an environmental situation. Categories: print and broadcast. Guidelines on website. **Deadline: April 1.** Prize: $500, and Kozik medal in each category.

LIVINGSTON AWARDS FOR YOUNG JOURNALISTS, Mollie Parnis Livingston Foundation, Wallace House, 620 Oxford, Ann Arbor MI 48104. (734)998-7575. Fax: (734)998-7979. E-mail: LivingstonAwards@umich.edu. Website: www.livawards.org. **Contact:** Charles Eisendrath. Offered annually for journalism published January 1-December 31 the previous year to recognize and further develop the abilities of young journalists. Includes print, online, and broadcast. Guidelines on website. Judges include Mike Wallace, Ellen Goodman, and Tom Brokaw. Open to journalists who are 34 years or younger as of December 31 of previous year and whose work appears in US-controlled print or broadcast media. **Deadline: February 1.** Prize: (3)$10,000: 1 each for local reporting, national reporting, and international reporting.

FELIX MORLEY JOURNALISM COMPETITION, Institute for Humane Studies, 3301 N. Fairfax Dr., Suite 440, Arlington VA 22201. (800)697-8799. Fax: (703)993-4890. E-mail: dalban@gmu.edu. Website: www.theihs.org/morley. **Contact:** Dan Alban. Offered annually for nonfiction published July 1, 2002-November 29, 2003, to reward young journalists who effectively address individual rights and free markets in their work. Writers must be either full-time students or be 25 years old as of the December 1 deadline. Prize: 1st Place: $2,500; 2nd Place: $1,000; 3rd Place: $750; and $250 to several runners-up.

N NATIONAL PRESS CLUB CONSUMER JOURNALISM AWARDS, National Press Club, National Press Bldg., Washington DC 20045. (202)662-8744. E-mail: jbooze@npcpress.org. Website: npc.press.org. **Contact:** Joann Booze. Offered annually to recognize excellence in reporting on consumer topics in the following categories: newspapers, periodicals, television, and radio. Entries must have been published/broadcast in the previous calendar year. Include a letter detailing how the piece or series resulted in action by consumers, the government, the community or an individual. Guidelines on website. **Deadline: April 1.** Prize: $500 for each category.

NATIONAL PRESS CLUB JOSEPH D. RYLE AWARD FOR EXCELLENCE IN WRITING ON THE PROBLEMS OF GERIATRICS, National Press Club, General Manager's Office, National Press Club, National Press Bldg., Washington DC 20045. (202)662-7532. Fax: (202)662-7512. Website: npc.press.org. **Contact:** Joann Booze. Offered annually for work published in the previous year. This award emphasizes excellence and objectivity in coverage of the problems faced by the elderly. Guidelines on website. Open to professional print journalists. **Deadline: April 1.** Prize: $2,000.

N NATIONAL PRESS CLUB ONLINE JOURNALISM AWARD, National Press Club, General Manager's Office, National Press Club, National Press Bldg., Washington DC 20045. (202)662-8744. E-mail: jbooze@npcpress.org. Website: npc.press.org. **Contact:** Joanne Booze. Offered annually to recognize the most significant contributions to journalism by the online media in 2 categories: Best Journalism Site (this award honors the best journalistic use of the online medium); and Distinguished Online Contribution (this award goes to the best individual contribution to public service using online technology). Guidelines on website. **Deadline: April 1.** Prize: $1,000 in each category.

NATIONAL PRESS CLUB SANDY HUME MEMORIAL AWARD FOR EXCELLENCE IN POLITICAL JOURNALISM, National Press Club, General Manager's Office, National Press Club, National Press Bldg., Washington DC 20045. (202)662-8744. Fax: (202)662-7512. E-mail: jbooze@npcpress.org. Website: npc.press.org. **Contact:** Joann Booze. Offered annually for work published in the previous calendar year. "This award honors excellence and objectivity in political coverage by reporters 34 years old or younger. Named in memory of Sandy Hume, the reporter for *The Hill* who broke the story of the aborted 1997 coup against House Speaker Newt Gingrich, this prize can be awarded for a single story of great distinction or for continuing coverage of 1 political topic." Guidelines on website. Open to professional journalists 34 or younger. **Deadline: April 1.** Prize: $1,000.

N NATIONAL PRESS CLUB WASHINGTON CORRESPONDENCE AWARDS, National Press Club, National Press Bldg., Washington DC 20045. (202)662-8744. E-mail: jbooze@npcpress.org. Website: npc.press.org. **Contact:** Joann

Booze. Offered annually to honor the work of reporters who cover Washington for the benefit of the hometown audience. "This award is for a single report or series on one topic, not for national reporting, nor for a body of work. Entrants must demonstrate a clear knowledge of how Washington works and what it means to the folks back home." Guidelines on webiste. **Deadline: April 1.** Prize: $1,000.

NEWSLETTER JOURNALISM AWARD, National Press Club, National Press Bldg., Washington DC 20045. (202)662-8744. E-mail: jbooze@npcpress.org. Website: npc.press.org. **Contact:** Joann Booze. Offered annually to acknowledge excellence in newsletter journalism in 2 categories: Best analytical or interpretive reporting piece or best exclusive story. Entries must be published by an independent newsletter and serve the audience and mission of the newsletter. Guidelines on website. **Deadline: April 1.** Prize: $2,000 for each category.

ALICIA PATTERSON JOURNALISM FELLOWSHIP, Alicia Patterson Foundation, 1730 Pennsylvania Ave. NW, Suite 850, Washington DC 20006. (202)393-5995. Fax: (301)951-8512. E-mail: info@aliciapatterson.org. Website: www.aliciapatterson.org. **Contact:** Margaret Engel. Offered annually for previously published submissions to give 8-10 full-time print journalists or photojournalists a year of in-depth research and reporting. Applicants must have 5 years of professional print journalism experience and be US citizens. Fellows write 4 magazine-length pieces for the *Alicia Patterson Reporter*, a quarterly magazine, during their fellowship year. Fellows must take a year's leave from their jobs, but may do other freelance articles during the year. Write, call, fax, or check website for applications. **Deadline: October 1.** Prize: $35,000 stipend for calendar year.

THE PULLIAM JOURNALISM FELLOWSHIPS, *The Indianapolis Star*, a Gannett Co. publication, P.O. Box 145, Indianapolis IN 46206-0145. (317)444-6001 or (800)669-7827. Fax: (317)444-6750. E-mail: russell.pulliam@indystar.com. Website: www.indystar.com/pjf. **Contact:** Russell B. Pulliam. Offered annually as an intensive 10-week summer "training school" for college students with firm commitments to, and solid training in, newspaper journalism. "Call or e-mail us in September 2004, and we'll send an application packet." **Deadline: March 1.** Prize: $6,600 for 10-week session, June-August 2004.

THE MADELINE DANE ROSS AWARD, Overseas Press Club of America, 40 W. 45th St., New York NY 10036. (212)626-9220. Fax: (212)626-9210. E-mail: sonya@opcofamerica.org. Website: www.opcofamerica.org. **Contact:** Sonya Fry, executive director. Offered annually for best international reporting in any medium showing a concern for the human condition. Work must be published by US-based publications or broadcast. Printable application available on website. **Deadline: Late January; date changes each year. Charges $125 fee.** Prize: $1,000, and certificate.

ARTHUR ROWSE AWARD FOR PRESS CRITICISM, General Manager's Office, National Press Club, National Press Bldg., Washington DC 20045. (202)662-8744. E-mail: jbooze@npcpress.org. Website: npc.press.org. **Contact:** Joann Booze. Offered annually for work published or broadcast the previous calendar year. "This award, sponsored by former *US News & World Report* reporter Arthur Rowse, honors excellence in examining the role and work of the news media. Categories: Single Entry (3 categories) and Body of Work (2 categories). Single Entry: newspapers, magazines, newsletters, and online; TV and radio; books. Body of Work: newspapers, magazines, newsletters, and online; TV and radio. Guidelines on website. Open to professional journalists (with the exception of those entering as book authors). **Deadline: April 1.** Prize: $1,000 in each category.

SCIENCE IN SOCIETY AWARD, National Association of Science Writers, Inc., P.O. Box 890, Hedgesville WV 25427. (304)754-5077. E-mail: diane@nasw.org. Website: www.nasw.org. **Contact:** Diane McGurgan. Offered annually for investigative or interpretive reporting about the sciences and their impact for good and bad. Six categories: newspaper, magazine, television, radio, book, and Internet. Material may be a single article or broadcast or a series. Works must have been first published or broadcast in North America between June 1, 2001, and May 31, 2002; books must have a 2001 copyright date and may have been published any time that year. **Deadline: July 1.** Guidelines for SASE. Prize: $1,000, and a certificate of recognition.

THE TEN BEST 'CENSORED' STORIES OF 2003, (formerly The Ten Best 'Censored' Stories of 2001), Project Censored—Sonoma State University, Rohnert Park CA 94928. (707)664-2500. Fax: (707)664-2108. E-mail: censored@sonoma.edu. Website: www.projectcensored.org. **Contact:** Peter Phillips, director. Offered for current published, nonfiction stories of national social significance that have been overlooked or under-reported by the news media. Peter Phillips and Project Censored choose 25 stories that have been underreported to make up *Censored 2003: The News That Didn't Make the News and Why*, published by Seven Stories Press. **Deadline: October 1.**

THE LAWRENCE WADE JOURNALISM FELLOWSHIP, The Heritage Foundation, 214 Massachusetts Ave. NE, Washington DC 20002. (202)546-4400. Fax: (202)546-8328. E-mail: info@heritage.org. Offered annually to award a journalism student who best exemplifies the high ideals and standards of the late Lawrence Wade. Applicants must be enrolled full-time in an accredited college or university. Guidelines for SASE. Prize: $1,000, and 10-week salaried internship at the Heritage Foundation.

Writing for Children & Young Adults

THE GEOFFREY BILSON AWARD FOR HISTORICAL FICTION FOR YOUNG PEOPLE, The Canadian Children's Book Centre, 40 Orchard View Blvd., Suite 101, Toronto ON M4R 1B9, Canada. (416)975-0010. Fax: (416)975-8970. E-mail: brenda@bookcentre.ca. Website: www.bookcentre.ca. **Contact:** (Ms.) Brenda Halliday, librarian. Created in Geoffrey Bilson's memory in 1988. Offered annually for a previously published "outstanding work of historical fiction for young people by a Canadian author." Open to Canadian citizens and residents of Canada for at least 2 years. **Deadline:**

December 31. Prize: $1,000. Judged by a jury selected by the Canadian Children's Book Centre.

N **BOSTON GLOBE-HORN BOOK AWARDS**, *The Boston Globe*, Horn Book, Inc., 56 Roland St., Suite 200, Boston MA 02129. (617)628-0225. Website: www.hbook.com. **Contact:** Roger Sutton. Offered annually for excellence in literature for children and young adults (published June 1, 2002-May 31, 2003). Categories: picture book, fiction and poetry, nonfiction. Judges may also name several honor books in each category. Books must be published in the United States. **Deadline: Approximately May 15.** Guidelines for SASE. Prize: Winners receive $500, and engraved silver bowl; honor book recipients receive an engraved silver plate. Judged by a panel of 3 judges selected each year.

MARGUERITE DE ANGELI PRIZE, Delacorte Press Books for Young Readers, Random House, Inc., 1745 Broadway, New York NY 10019. (212)782-9000. Fax: (212)782-9452. Website: www.randomhouse.com/kids. Estab. 1992. Offered annually for an unpublished fiction ms suitable for readers 8-12 years of age, set in North America, either contemporary or historical. Guidelines on website. **Deadline: April 1-June 30.** Prize: $1,500 in cash, publication, and $7,500 advance against royalties; world rights acquired.

DELACORTE PRESS CONTEST FOR A FIRST YOUNG ADULT NOVEL, (formerly Delacorte Press Prize for a First Young Adult Novel), Random House, Inc., 1540 Broadway, 19th Floor, New York NY 10036. Website: www.randomhouse.com/kids/games/delacorte.html. Offered annually "to encourage the writing of contemporary young adult fiction." Open to US and Canadian writers who have not previously published a young adult novel. Guidelines on website. **Deadline: October 1-December 31 (postmarked).** Prize: $1,500 cash, publication, and $6,000 advance against royalties. Judged by the editors of Delacorte Press Books for Young Readers.

THE NORMA FLECK AWARD FOR A CANADIAN CHILDREN'S NONFICTION BOOK, The Canadian Children's Book Centre, 40 Orchard View Blvd., Suite 101, Toronto ON M4R 1B9, Canada. (416)975-0010. Fax: (416)975-8970. E-mail: info@bookcentre.ca. Website: www.bookcentre.ca. **Contact:** Shannon Howe, program coordinator. The Norma Fleck Award was established by the Fleck Family Foundation in May 1999 to honor the life of Norma Marie Fleck, and to recognize exceptional Canadian nonfiction books for young people. Publishers are welcome to nominate books using the online form found at www.bookcentre.ca. Offered annually for books published between May 1, 2002 and April 30, 2003. Open to Canadian citizens or landed immigrants. **Deadline: March 31.** Schedule decided upon annually. Prize: $10,000 goes to the author (unless 40% or more of the text area is composed of original illustrations, in which case the award will be divided equally between the author and the artist). $5,000 in matching funding will be made available for promotional purposes to all of the shortlisted titles. Judged by a minimum of 3 jury members and the total number, if more, will be an uneven number. The jury will always include at least 3 of the following: a teacher, a librarian, a bookseller, and a reviewer. There should be at least 1 new jury member each year. A juror will have a deep understanding of, and some involvement with, Canadian children's books. The Canadian Children's Book Centre will select the jury members.

GOVERNOR GENERAL'S LITERARY AWARD FOR CHILDREN'S LITERATURE, Canada Council for the Arts, 350 Albert St., P.O. Box 1047, Ottawa ON K1P 5V8, Canada. (613)566-4414, ext. 5576. Fax: (613)566-4410. E-mail: joanne.larocque-poirier@canadacouncil.ca. Website: www.canadacouncil.ca/prizes/ggla. **Contact:** Joanne Larocque-Poirier. Offered for the best English-language and the best French-language works of children's literature by a Canadian in 2 categories: text and illustration. Books must have been published between September 1, 2002 and September 30, 2003. Publishers submit titles for consideration. **Deadline: April 15 or August 7, 2003, depending on the book's publication date.** Prize: Each laureate receives $15,000, and nonwinning finalists receive $1,000.

GUIDEPOSTS YOUNG WRITERS CONTEST, *Guideposts*, 16 E. 34th St., New York NY 10016. (212)251-8100. Website: gp4teens.com. **Contact:** Kathryn Slattery. Offered annually for unpublished high school juniors and seniors. Stories "needn't be about a highly dramatic situation, but it should record an experience that affected you and deeply changed you. Remember, *Guideposts* stories are true, not fiction, and they show how faith in God has made a specific difference in a person's life. We accept submissions after announcement is placed in the October issue each year. If the manuscript is placed, we require all rights to the story in that version." Open only to high school juniors or seniors. **Deadline: November 24.** Prize: 1st Place: $10,000; 2nd Place: $8,000; 3rd Place: $6,000; 4th Place: $4,000; 5th Place: $3,000; 6th-10th Place: $1,000; 11th-20th Place: $250 gift certificate for college supplies.

HIGHLIGHTS FOR CHILDREN FICTION CONTEST, *Highlights for Children*, 803 Church St., Honesdale PA 18431-1824. (570)253-1080. Website: www.highlights.com. **Contact:** Marileta Robinson, senior editor. Offered for stories for children ages 2-12; category varies each year. Stories should be limited to 800 words for older readers, 400 words for younger readers. No crime or violence, please. Specify that ms is a contest entry. **Deadline: January 1-February 28 (postmarked).** Guidelines for SASE. Prize: $1,000 to 3 winners.

INTERNATIONAL READING ASSOCIATION CHILDREN'S BOOK AWARDS, International Reading Association, P.O. Box 8139, Newark DE 19714-8139. (302)731-1600, ext. 293. Fax: (302)731-1057. Website: www.reading.org. **Contact:** Janet Butler. Offered annually for an author's first or second published book in fiction and nonfiction in 3 categories: primary (preschool-age 8), intermediate (ages 9-13), and young adult (ages 14-17). Recognizes newly published authors who show unusual promise in the children's book field. Guidelines and deadlines for SASE. Prize: $500, and a medal for each category.

CORETTA SCOTT KING BOOK AWARD, Coretta Scott King Task Force, American Library Association, 50 E. Huron St., Chicago IL 60611. (800)545-2433. Fax: (312)280-3256. E-mail: olos@ala.org. Website: www.ala.org. **Contact:** Tanga Morris. Offered annually for children's books by African-American authors and/or illustrators published the previous year. Three categories: preschool-grade 4; grades 5-8; grades 9-12. **Deadline: December 1.** Guidelines for SASE. Prize: Honorarium, framed citation, and a set of *Encyclopedia Britannica* or *World Book Encyclopedias*.

ANNE SPENCER LINDBERGH PRIZE IN CHILDREN'S LITERATURE, The Charles A. & Anne Morrow Lindbergh Foundation, 2150 Third Ave. N., Suite 310, Anoka MN 55303. (763)576-1596. Fax: (763)576-1664. E-mail: info@lindberghfoundation.org. Website: www.lindberghfoundation.org. **Contact:** Executive Director. Offered every 2 years in even years for a children's fantasy novel published in the English language in that or the preceding year. Entries must include 4 copies of the book and an application fee of $25 (payable to the Lindbergh Foundation) for each title submitted. Open to any writer. **Deadline: November 1.**

THE VICKY METCALF AWARD FOR CHILDREN'S LITERATURE, The Writers' Trust of Canada, 40 Wellington St. E., Suite 300, Toronto ON M5E 1C7, Canada. (416)504-8222. Fax: (416)504-9090. E-mail: info@writerstrust.com. Website: www.writerstrust.com. **Contact:** Sharon Poitras. The Metcalf Award is presented annually at The Great Literary Awards Event held in Toronto each spring, to a Canadian writer for a body of work in children's literature. Prize: $15,000. Open to Canadian residents only.

MILKWEED PRIZE FOR CHILDREN'S LITERATURE, Milkweed Editions, 1011 Washington Ave. S., Suite 300, Minneapolis MN 55415. (612)332-3192. Fax: (612)215-2550. Website: www.milkweed.org. **Contact:** Elisabeth Fitz, first reader. Estab. 1993. Annual prize for unpublished works. "Milkweed is looking for a novel intended for readers aged 8-13. Manuscripts should be of high literary quality and must be double-spaced, 90-200 pages in length. The Milkweed Prize for Children's Literature will be awarded to the best manuscript for children ages 8-13 that Milkweed accepts for publication during each calendar year by a writer not previously published by Milkweed Editions." All mss submitted to Milkweed will automatically be considered for the prize. Submission directly to the contest is not necessary. Must review guidelines, available at website or for SASE. Catalog for $1.50 postage. Prize: $5,000 advance on royalties agreed upon at the time of acceptance.

THE NATIONAL CHAPTER OF CANADA IODE VIOLET DOWNEY BOOK AWARD, National Chapter of Canada IODE, 40 Orchard View Blvd., Suite 254, Toronto ON M4R 1B9, Canada. (416)487-4416. Fax: (416)487-4417. E-mail: iodecanada@sympatico.ca. Website: www.iodecanada.ca. Offered annually for children's books of at least 500 words. Entries must have appeared in print January 1-December 31. Open to Canadian citizens only. **Deadline: December 31.** Guidelines for SASE. Prize: $3,000 (Canadian funds).

NESTLÉ SMARTIES BOOK PRIZE, Nestlé Smarties, c/o Booktrust, Book House, 45 E. Hill, Wandsworth, London SW18 2QZ, United Kingdom. Fax: (00 44) 20 8516 2978. E-mail: tarryn@booktrust.org.uk. Website: www.booktrusted.com. **Contact:** Kate Mervyn Jones. "The Nestlé Smarties Book Prize was established in 1985 to encourage high standards and stimulate interest in children's books. The prize is split into 3 age categories: 5 and under, 6-8, and 9-11. Within the last couple of years, a new category, the Kids' Club Network Special Award has been introduced. The books are judged by our adult panel, who shortlist 3 outstanding books in each category, and the final decision of who gets Gold, Silver, Bronze, and the KCN Special Award is left to our young judges. The young judges are chosen from classes of school children who complete a task for their age category, the best 50 from each category go on to judge the 3 books in their age category. The KCN children judge the 6-8 books. From the 200 classes who judge the books, 1 class from each category is invited to present the award at the ceremony in London. The children are chosen from projects they submit with their votes." Open to works of fiction or poetry for children written in English by a citizen of the UK, or an author resident in the UK. All work must be submitted by a UK publisher. **Deadline: July.** Prize: Gold Award winners in each age category: £2,500; Silver Award winners in each age category: £1,500; Bronze Award winners in each age category: £500; certificate for the KCN Special Award winner.

(ALICE WOOD MEMORIAL) OHIOANA AWARD FOR CHILDREN'S LITERATURE, Ohioana Library Association, 274 E. First Ave., Suite 300, Columbus OH 43201. (614)466-3831. Fax: (614)728-6974. E-mail: ohioana@sloma.state.oh.us. Website: www.oplin.lib.oh.us/OHIOANA/. **Contact:** Linda R. Hengst. Offered to an author whose body of work has made, and continues to make, a significant contribution to literature for children or young adults and through their work as a writer, teacher, administrator, or through community service, interest in children's literature has been encouraged and children have become involved with reading. Nomination forms for SASE. Recipient must have been born in Ohio or lived in Ohio at least 5 years. **Deadline: December 31.** Prize: $1,000.

PATERSON PRIZE FOR BOOKS FOR YOUNG PEOPLE, The Poetry Center at Passaic County Community College, One College Blvd., Paterson NJ 07505-1179. (973)684-6555. Fax: (973)684-5843. E-mail: mgillan@pccc.cc.nj.us. Website: www.pccc.cc.nj.us/poetry. **Contact:** Maria Mazziotti Gillan, director. Offered annually for books published the previous calendar year. Three categories: pre-kindergarten-grade 3; grades 4-6; and grades 7-12. Open to any writer. **Deadline: April 1.** Guidelines for SASE. Prize: $500 in each category.

PEN/PHYLLIS NAYLOR WORKING WRITER FELLOWSHIP, PEN American Center, 568 Broadway, New York NY 10012. (212)334-1660. Fax: (212)334-2181. E-mail: jm@pen.org. **Contact:** John Morrone. Offered annually to a "writer of children's or young-adult fiction in financial need, who has published at least 2 books, and no more than 3, in the past 10 years, which may have been well reviewed and warmly received by literary critics, but which have not generated sufficient income to support the author." Writers must be nominated by an editor or fellow writer. **Deadline: January 15.** Prize: $5,000.

PRIX ALVINE-BELISLE, Association pour L'avancement des sciences et des techniques de la documentation, ASTED, Inc., 3414 av. Parc #202, Montreal QC H2X 2H5, Canada. (514)281-5012. Fax: (514)281-8219. E-mail: lcabral@asted.org. Website: www.asted.org. **Contact:** Louis Cabral, executive director. Offered annually for work published the previous year before the award to promote authors of French youth literature in Canada. **Deadline: April 1.** Prize: $1,000.

SAINSBURY'S BABY BOOK AWARD, J. Sainsbury's plc, c/o Booktrust, Book House, 45 E. Hill, Wandsworth, London SW18 2QZ, United Kingdom. Fax: (00 44) 20 8516 2978. E-mail: tarryn@booktrust.org.uk. Website: www.booktrusted.com. **Contact:** Ms. Yvonne Hook. The Sainsbury's Baby Book Award was established in 1999 and is awarded annually. The award is given to the best book, published between September 1, 2002 and August 31, 2003, in the opinion of the judges for a baby under 1 year of age. Authors and illustrators must be of British nationality, or other nationals who have been residents in the British Isles for at least 10 years. Books can be any format. **Deadline: June.** Prize: £2,000, and a crystal award. In addition, the publisher receives a crystal award naming them as "The Sainsbury's Baby Book Award Publisher of the Year."

SASKATCHEWAN CHILDREN'S LITERATURE AWARD, Saskatchewan Book Awards, Inc., Box 1921, Regina SK S4P 3E1, Canada. (306)569-1585. Fax: (306)569-4187. E-mail: director@bookawards.sk.ca. Website: www.bookawards.sk.ca. **Contact:** Joyce Wells, executive director. Offered annually for work published September 15, 2002-September 14, 2003. This award is presented to a Saskatchewan author for the best book of children's or young adult's literature, judged on the quality of writing. **Deadline: First Deadline: July 31; Final Deadline: September 14.** Guidelines for SASE. **Charges $15 (Canadian).** Prize: $1,500.

SYDNEY TAYLOR BOOK AWARD, Association of Jewish Libraries, 15 E. 26th St., 10th Floor, New York NY 10010. (212)725-5359. E-mail: llibbylib@aol.com. Website: www.jewishlibraries.org. **Contact:** Libby White, chair. Offered annually for work published in the year of the award. "Given to distinguished contributions to Jewish literature for children. One award for older readers, 1 for younger." Publishers submit books. **Deadline: December 31.** Guidelines for SASE. Prize: Certificate, cash award, and gold seal for cover of winning book.

TEDDY AWARD FOR BEST CHILDREN'S BOOK, Writers' League of Texas, 1501 W. Fifth St., Suite E-2, Austin TX 78703. (512)499-8914. Fax: (512)499-0441. E-mail: wlt@writersleague.org. Website: www.writersleague.org. **Contact:** Stephanie Sheppard, director. Offered annually for work published June 1, 2002-May 31, 2003. Honors an outstanding book for children published by a member of the Writers' League of Texas. Writer's League of Texas dues may accompany entry fee. **Deadline: May 31.** Guidelines for SASE. **Charges $10 fee.** Prize: $1,000, and trophy.

TORONTO MUNICIPAL CHAPTER IODE BOOK AWARD, Toronto Municipal Chapter IODE, 40 St. Clair Ave. E., Toronto ON M4T 1M9, Canada. (416)925-5078. Fax: (416)925-5127. **Contact:** IODE Education Committee. Offered annually for childrens' books published by a Canadian publisher. Author and illustrator must be Canadian citizens residing in or around Toronto. **Deadline: Late November.** Prize: $1,000.

PAUL A. WITTY SHORT STORY AWARD, Executive Office, International Reading Association, P.O. Box 8139, Newark DE 19714-8139. (302)731-1600, ext. 293. Fax: (302)731-1057. E-mail: exec@reading.org. Website: www.reading.org. **Contact:** Janet Butler, public information associate. Offered to reward author of an original short story published in a children's periodical during 2002 which serves as a literary standard that encourages young readers to read periodicals. Write for guidelines. **Deadline: December 1.** Prize: $1,000.

WORK-IN-PROGRESS GRANT, Society of Children's Book Writers and Illustrators (SCBWI) and Judy Blume, 8271 Beverly Blvd., Los Angeles CA 90048. (323)782-1010. E-mail: scbwi@scbwi.org. Website: www.scbwi.org. Two grants—1 designated specifically for a contemporary novel for young people—to assist SCBWI members in the completion of a specific project. Open to SCBWI members only. **Deadline: March 1.** Guidelines for SASE.

WRITING FOR CHILDREN COMPETITION, No Noun-Sense, 147-2211 No. 4 Rd., Richmond BC V6X 3X1, Canada. (604)825-8861. Fax: (604)214-1306. E-mail: editor@webprospects.com. Website: www.nonounsense.com. **Contact:** Project Coordinator. Offered annually for unpublished work to promote the art or writing for children. Guidelines on website. Open to any writer. **Deadline: April 24. Charges $10.** Prize: 1st Prize: $200; 2nd Prize: $50; 3rd Prize: $25. Winner and 4 honorable mentions will be published on the No Noun-Sense website, along with their bios.

WRITING FOR CHILDREN COMPETITION, The Writers' Union of Canada, 40 Wellington St. E., 3rd Floor, Toronto ON M5E 1C7. (416)703-8982, ext. 223. Fax: (416)504-7656. E-mail: projects@writersunion.ca. Website: www.writersunion.ca. **Contact:** Projects Coordinator. Offered annually "to discover developing Canadian writers of unpublished children's/young adult fiction or nonfiction." Open to Canadian citizens or landed immigrants who have not been published in book format, and who do not currently have a contract with a publisher. **Deadline: April 24. Charges $15 entry fee.** Prize: $1,500; the winner and 11 finalists' pieces will be submitted to 3 Canadian publishers of children's books.

Translation

AMERICAN TRANSLATORS ASSOCIATION STUDENT TRANSLATION PRIZE, (formerly Student Translation Prize), American Translators Association, 225 Reinekers Lane, Suite 590, Alexandria VA 22314. (703)683-6100. Fax: (703)683-6122. E-mail: ata@atanet.org. Website: www.atanet.org. Support is granted for a promising project to an unpublished student enrolled in a translation program at a US college or university. Must be sponsored by a faculty member. **Deadline: April 15.** Prize: $500, and up to $500 toward expenses for attending the ATA Annual Conference.

ASF TRANSLATION PRIZE, The American-Scandinavian Foundation, 58 Park Ave., New York NY 10016-3007. (212)879-9779. Fax: (212)686-2115. E-mail: ahenkin@amscan.org. Website: www.amscan.org. **Contact:** Andrey Henkin. Offered annually to a translation of Scandinavian literature into English of a Nordic author born within the last 200 years. "The Prize is for an outstanding English translation of poetry, fiction, drama, or literary prose originally written in Danish, Finnish, Icelandic, Norwegian, or Swedish that has not been previously published in the English language." **Deadline:**

June 1. Guidelines for SASE. Prize: $2,000, publication of an excerpt in an issue of *Scandinavian Review*, and a commemorative bronze medallion. Runner-up receives the Leif and Inger Sjöberg Prize: $1,000, publication of an excerpt in an issue of *Scandinavian Review*, and a commemorative bronze medallion.

FAF TRANSLATION PRIZE, French-American Foundation, 509 Madison Ave., New York NY 10022. (212)829-8800. Fax: (212)829-8810. E-mail: info@frenchamerican.org. Website: www.frenchamerican.org. **Contact:** Veronique Lemire. Offered annually for previously published work that appeared in print between January 1-December 1 of the calendar year. "The FAF Translation Prize aims at promoting the translation of French-language books into English (on the American book market). The award goes to the translator." The publisher should send 2 copies of the English translation and the French text. **Deadline: December 1.** Prize: 2 prizes (fiction and nonfiction) of $7,500 each. Judged by a panel of publishers, translators, and academics. Open to any writer.

GERMAN PRIZE FOR LITERARY TRANSLATION, American Translators Association, 225 Reinekers Lane, Suite 590, Alexandria VA 22314. (703)683-6100. Fax: (703)683-6122. E-mail: ata@atanet.org. Website: www.atanet.org. Offered in odd-numbered years for a previously published book translated from German to English. In even-numbered years, the Lewis Galentiere Prize is awarded for translations other than German to English. **Deadline: May 15.** Prize: $1,000, a certificate of recognition, and up to $500 toward expenses for attending the ATA Annual Conference.

JOHN GLASSCO TRANSLATION PRIZE, Literary Translators' Association of Canada, c/o 272 Heneker, Sherbrooke QC J1J 3G4, Canada. (819)820-1244. E-mail: patricia.godbout@courrier.usherb.ca. Website: www.attlc-ltac.org/glasscoe.htm. Estab. 1981. Offered annually for a translator's first book-length literary translation into French or English, published in Canada during the previous calendar year. The translator must be a Canadian citizen or landed immigrant. Eligible genres include fiction, creative nonfiction, poetry, and children's books. **Deadline: June 30.** Prize: $1,000.

GOVERNOR GENERAL'S LITERARY AWARD FOR TRANSLATION, Canada Council for the Arts, 350 Albert St., P.O. Box 1047, Ottawa ON K1P 5V8, Canada. (613)566-4414, ext. 5576. Fax: (613)566-4410. E-mail: joanne.larocque-poirier@canadacouncil.ca. Website: www.canadacouncil.ca/prizes/ggla. **Contact:** Joanne Larocque-Poirier. Offered for the best English-language and the best French-language work of translation by a Canadian published September 1, 2002-September 30, 2003. Publishers submit titles for consideration. **Deadline: April 15 or August 7, 2003, depending on the book's publication date.** Prize: Each laureate receives $15,000, and nonwinning finalists receive $1,000.

JAPAN-U.S. FRIENDSHIP COMMISSION PRIZE FOR THE TRANSLATION OF JAPANESE LITERATURE, Donald Keene Center of Japanese Culture at Columbia University, 507 Kent Hall, MC 3920, Columbia University, New York NY 10027. (212)854-5036. Fax: (212)854-4019. E-mail: donald-keene-center@columbia.edu. Website: www.columbia.edu/cu/ealac/dkc. "The Donald Keene Center of Japanese Culture at Columbia University annually awards $5,000 in Japan-U.S. Friendship Commission Prizes for the Translation of Japanese Literature. A prize is given for the best translation of a modern work of literature or for the best classical literary translation, or the prize is divided between a classical and modern work. Translators of any nationality are welcome to apply. To qualify, works must be book-length translations of Japanese literary works: novels, collections of short stories, literary essays, memoirs, drama or poetry. Submissions will be judged on the literary merit of the translation and the accuracy with which it reflects the spirit of the Japanese original. Eligible works include unpublished manuscripts, works in press, or books published during the 2 years prior to the prize year." **Deadline: February 1.** Guidelines for SASE. Judged by a panel of distinguished writers, editors, translators, and scholars.

THE HAROLD MORTON LANDON TRANSLATION AWARD, The Academy of American Poets, 584 Broadway, Suite 604, New York NY 10012-3210. (212)274-0343, ext. 17. Fax: (212)274-9427. E-mail: murphy@poets.org. Website: www.poets.org. **Contact:** Ryan Murphy, awards coordinator. Offered annually to recognize a published translation of poetry from any language into English. Open to living US citizens. Anthologies by a number of translators are ineligible. **Deadline: December 31.** Guidelines for SASE. Prize: $1,000.

THE MARSH AWARD FOR CHILDREN'S LITERATURE IN TRANSLATION, The Marsh Christian Trust/Administered by NCRCL, University of Surrey Roehampton, Digby Stuart College, Roehampton Lane, London, England SW15 5PH. 020 8392 3014. Fax: 020 3892 3819. **Contact:** Dr. Gillian Lathey. Offered every two years to raise awareness in the UK of the quality of children's books written in other languages and of the work of their translators. Entries must be submitted by British publishing companies and published between June 30, 2002 and June 30, 2004. No translations first published in the USA or Australia are eligible for this award. **Deadline: June 30, 2004.** Guidelines for SASE. Prize: £1,000. Judged by critics and translators of children's books.

PEN AWARD FOR POETRY IN TRANSLATION, PEN American Center, 568 Broadway, New York NY 10012. (212)334-1660, ext. 108. E-mail: jm@pen.org. Website: www.pen.org. **Contact:** John Morrone, literary awards manager. This award "recognizes book-length translations of poetry from any language into English, published during the current calendar year. All books must have been published in the U.S. Translators may be of any nationality. U.S. residency/citizenship not required." **Deadline: December 16.** Prize: $3,000. Judged by a single translator of poetry appointed by the PEN Translation Committee.

PEN/BOOK-OF-THE-MONTH CLUB TRANSLATION PRIZE, PEN American Center, 568 Broadway, New York NY 10012. (212)334-1660. Fax: (212)334-2181. E-mail: jm@pen.org. **Contact:** John Morrone. Offered for a literary book-length translation into English published in the calendar year. No technical, scientific, or reference books. Publishers, agents, or translators may submit 3 copies of each eligible title. **Deadline: December 15.** Prize: $3,000.

THE RAIZISS/DE PALCHI TRANSLATION FELLOWSHIP, The Academy of American Poets, 584 Broadway, Suite 604, New York NY 10012-3210. (212)274-0343. Fax: (212)274-9427. Website: www.poets.org. **Contact:** Awards

Director. Offered in even-numbered years to recognize outstanding unpublished translations of modern Italian poetry into English. Applicants must verify permission to translate the poems or that the poems are in the public domain. Open to any US citizen. **Deadline: September 1-November 1.** Guidelines for SASE. Prize: $20,000, and a 6-week residency at the American Academy in Rome.

LOIS ROTH AWARD FOR A TRANSLATION OF A LITERARY WORK, Modern Language Association, 26 Broadway, 3rd Floor, New York NY 10004-1789. (646)576-5141. Fax: (646)458-0030. E-mail: awards@mla.org. Website: www.mla.org. **Contact:** Coordinator of Book Prizes. Offered every 2 years (odd years) for an outstanding translation into English of a book-length literary work published the previous year. Translators need not be members of the MLA. **Deadline: May 1.** Guidelines for SASE. Prize: $1,000, and a certificate.

ALDO AND JEANNE SCAGLIONE PRIZE FOR A TRANSLATION OF A LITERARY WORK, Modern Language Association of America, 26 Broadway, 3rd Floor, New York NY 10004-1789. (646)576-5141. Fax: (646)458-0030. E-mail: awards@mla.org. Website: www.mla.org. **Contact:** Coordinator of Book Prizes. Offered in even-numbered years for the translation of a book-length literary work appearing in print during the previous year. Translators need not be members of the MLA. **Deadline: April 1.** Guidelines for SASE. Prize: $2,000, and a certificate.

ALDO AND JEANNE SCAGLIONE PRIZE FOR A TRANSLATION OF A SCHOLARLY STUDY OF LITERATURE, Modern Language Association of America, 26 Broadway, 3rd Floor, New York NY 10004-1789. (646)576-5141. Fax: (646)458-0030. E-mail: awards@mla.org. Website: www.mla.org. **Contact:** Coordinator of Book Prizes. Offered in odd-numbered years "for an outstanding translation into English of a book-length work of literary history, literary criticism, philology, or literary theory published during the previous biennium." Translators need not be members of the MLA. **Deadline: May 1.** Guidelines for SASE. Prize: $2,000, and a certificate.

Multiple Writing Areas

ALLIGATOR JUNIPER AWARD, *Alligator Juniper*/Prescott College, 220 Grove Ave., Prescott AZ 86301. (928)778-2090, ext. 2012. E-mail: aj@prescott.edu. Website: www.prescott.edu. **Contact:** Miles Waggener, managing editor. Offered annually for unpublished work. Guidelines on website. All entrants receive a copy of the next issue of *Alligator Juniper*, a $7.50 value. **Deadline: October 1. Charges $10.** Prize: $500, plus publication. Judged by the staff and occasional guest judges. Acquires first North American rights. Open to any writer.

AMERICAN LITERARY REVIEW CONTEST, *American Literary Review*, P.O. Box 311307, University of North Texas, Denton TX 76203-1307. (940)565-2755. E-mail: americanliteraryreview@yahoo.com. Website: www.engl.unt.edu/alr. **Contact:** Managing Editor. Offered annually for unpublished work. This contest alternates annually between poetry and fiction. Open to any writer. **Deadline: Varies each year.** Guidelines for SASE. **Charges $10 entry fee.** Prize: $1,000, and publication.

AMERICAN MARKETS NEWSLETTER COMPETITION, *American Markets Newsletter*, 1974 46th Ave., San Francisco CA 94116. E-mail: sheila.oconnor@juno.com. **Contact:** Sheila O'Connor. "Accepts fiction and nonfiction up to 2,000 words. Entries are eligible for cash prizes and all entries are eligible for worldwide syndication whether they win or not. Here's how it works. Send us your double-spaced manuscripts with your story/article title, byline, word count, and address on the first page above your article/story's first paragraph (no need for separate cover page). There is no limit to the number of entries you may send." Annually. **Deadline: December 31.** Guidelines for SASE. **Charges $10 for 1 entry; $15 for 2 entries; $20 for 3 entries; and $25 for 4 or 5 entries.** Prize: 1st Place: $300; 2nd Place: $100; 3rd Place: $50. Judged by a panel of independent judges. Open to any writer.

ARIZONA AUTHORS' ASSOCIATION ANNUAL NATIONAL LITERARY CONTEST, Arizona Authors' Association, P.O. Box 87857, Phoenix AZ 85080-7857. (602)769-2066. Fax: (623)780-0468. E-mail: info@azauthors.com. Website: www.azauthors.com. **Contact:** Toby Heathcotte, contest coordinator. Offered annually for previously unpublished poetry, short stories, essays, and articles. New awards for published books in fiction, anthology, nonfiction, and children's. Winners announced at an award banquet in Phoenix in November, and short pieces published in *Arizona Literary Magazine*. **Deadline: July 1. Charges $10 fee for poetry; $15 for short stories and essays, and $30 for books.** Prize: $100.

ART COOPERATIVE TRAVELING FELLOWSHIP, (formerly Art Coop Traveling Fellowship), Cottonwood Art Cooperative, 1124 Columbia NE, Albuquerque NM 87106. E-mail: art_coop@yahoo.com. Website: www.geocities.com/art_coop. **Contact:** Editor-in-Chief. For most recent information, please visit website or write for guidelines with SASE. Submit cover letter explaining project and location, anticipated budget, bio, and publications list. Submit 3-50 page portfolio of fiction or creative nonfiction, 10-20 pages of poetry, or slides of visual artwork with SASE. **Deadline: December 1. Charges $20 fee.** For an additional flat $15 fee and SASE, feedback is provided. Prize: Cash award to be determined, and publication to support serious, aspiring poets, essayists, fiction writers, and visual artists in completing a project that requires travel. Open to any writer/artist.

ARTS & LETTERS PRIZES, *Arts & Letters Journal of Contemporary Culture*, Campus Box 89, GC&SU, Milledgeville GA 31061. (478)445-1289. E-mail: al@gcsu.edu. Website: al.gcsu.edu. **Contact:** The Editors. Offered annually for unpublished work. **Deadline: April 30 (postmarked). Charges $15/entry (payable to GC&SU), which includes a 1-year subscription to the journal.** Prize: $1,000 for winners in fiction, poetry, and drama (one-act play). Fiction and poetry winners will attend a weekend program in October, and the drama winner will attend a Spring festival that includes a production of the prize-winning play. Judged by editors (initial screening); 2003 final judges: Bret Lott (fiction), Gerald Stern (poetry), Arthur Kopit (drama). Open to any writer.

ASTED/GRAND PRIX DE LITTERATURE JEUNESSE DU QUEBEC-ALVINE-BELISLE, Association pour l'avancement des sciences et des techniques de la documentation, 3414 Avenue du Parc, Bureau 202, Montreal QC H2X 2H5, Canada. (514)281-5012. Fax: (514)281-8219. E-mail: info@asted.org. Website: www.asted.org. **Contact:** Micheline Patton, president. "Prize granted for the best work in youth literature edited in French in the Quebec Province. Authors and editors can participate in the contest." Offered annually for books published during the preceding year. **Deadline: June 1.** Prize: $1,000.

ATLANTIC WRITING COMPETITION FOR UNPUBLISHED MANUSCRIPTS, Writers' Federation of Nova Scotia, 1113 Marginal Rd., Halifax NS B3H 4P7. (902)423-8116. Fax: (902)422-0881. E-mail: talk@writers.ns.ca. Website: www.writers.ns.ca. **Contact:** Monika Sormova, executive assistant. "Established in 1975 under the auspices of the Nova Scotia Branch of the Canadian Authors' Association, the Atlantic Writing Competition has been sponsored by the Writers' Federation of Nova Scotia since 1976. We encouarge all writers in Atlantic Canada to explore and celebrate their talents by sending in their new, untried work. Manuscripts are read by a team of 2 or 3 judges. WFNS chooses judges carefully, trying to balance skills, points of view, and taste. Judges are professionals who work as writers, editors, booksellers, librarians, or teachers. Because our aim is to help Atlantic Canadian writers grow, judges return written comments when the competition is concluded. Anyone resident in the Atlantic Provinces for at least 6 months prior to the contest deadline is eligible to enter. Only 1 entry/category is allowed. Writers whose work has been professionally published in book form, or frequently in periodical or media production, may not enter in the genre in which they have been published or produced. Entries must be the original, unpublished work of the writer, and must not have been accepted for publication or submitted elsewhere. The same work may not be submitted again. Entry forms will be available on the WFNS website in April, or contact the office for a copy of the form. For more information on the Atlantic Writing Competition, visit our website at www.writers.ns.ca/competitions." **Deadline: First Friday in August. Charges $15 fee ($10 for WFNS members); $25 for novel ($20 for WFNS members).** Prize: **Novel**, 1st Place: $200; 2nd Place: $150; 3rd Place: $100. **Writing for Children**, 1st Place: $150; 2nd Place: $75; 3rd Place: $50. **Poetry**, 1st Place: $100; 2nd Place: $75; 3rd Place: $50. **Short Story**, 1st Place: $100; 2nd Place: $75; 3rd Place: $50. **Essay/Magazine Article**, 1st Place: $150; 2nd Place: $75; 3rd Place: $50.

AWP AWARD SERIES, Associated Writing Programs, Carty House, Mail Stop 1E3, George Mason University, Fairfax VA 22030. (703)993-4301. Fax: (703)993-4302. E-mail: awp@gmu.edu. Website: awpwriter.org. **Contact:** Supriya Bhatnagar. Offered annually to foster new literary talent. Categories: poetry (Donald Hall Poetry Prize), short fiction, and creative nonfiction. Guidelines for SASE and on website. Open to any writer. **Deadline: Must be postmarked January 1-February 28. Charges $20 for nonmembers, $10 for members.** Prize: Cash honorarium ($4,000 for Donald Hall Prize for Poetry, and $2,000 each for short fiction and creative nonfiction), and publication by a participating press.

EMILY CLARK BALCH AWARD, *Virginia Quarterly Review*, 1 West Range, P.O. Box 400223, Charlottesville VA 22904-4233. (434)924-3124. Fax: (434)924-1397. Website: www.virginia.edu/vqr. **Contact:** Staige D. Blackford, editor. Annual award for the best short story/poetry accepted and published by the *Virginia Quarterly Review* during a calendar year. No deadline. Prize: $500.

BEACON STREET REVIEW EDITOR'S CHOICE AWARD, *Beacon Street Review*, Emerson College, 120 Boylston St., Boston MA 02116. E-mail: beaconstreetreview@hotmail.com. **Contact:** Prose or Poetry Editor. Annual award for unpublished prose and poetry. **Deadline: "Please e-mail or send a SASE for guidelines and upcoming submission deadlines."** Guidelines for SASE. Prize: $100. Judged by an established local author. Open to any writer.

BERTELSMANN FOUNDATION'S WORLD OF EXPRESSION SCHOLARSHIP PROGRAM, Bertelsmann, 1540 Broadway, New York NY 10036. (212)782-0316. Fax: (212)782-0349. E-mail: bwoesp@bmge.com. Website: www.worldofexpression.org. **Contact:** Veronica Valerio. Offered annually for unpublished work to NYC public high school seniors. Three categories: poetry, fiction/drama, and personal essay. **Deadline: February 1.** Guidelines for SASE. Prize: 72 awards given in literary (3) and nonliterary (2) categories. Awards range from $500-10,000.

THE BOSTON AUTHORS CLUB BOOK AWARDS, The Boston Authors Club, 121 Follen Rd., Lexington MA 02421. **Contact:** Andrew McAleer. Julia Ward Howe Prize offered annually for books published the previous year. Two awards are given, 1 for trade books of fiction, nonfiction, or poetry, and the second for children's books. Authors must live or have lived within 100 miles of Boston. **Deadline: January 1.** Prize: Certificate and honorarioum of $500 in each category.

THE BRIAR CLIFF POETRY & FICTION COMPETITION, *The Briar Cliff Review*, Briar Cliff University, 3303 Rebecca St., Sioux City IA 51104-0100. (712)279-5321. Fax: (712)279-5410. E-mail: currans@briarcliff.edu. Website: www.briarcliff.edu/bcreview. **Contact:** Tricia Currans-Sheehan, editor. Offered annually for unpublished poetry and fiction. **Deadline: Submissions between August 1 and November 1.** No mss returned. Guidelines for SASE. **Charges $15.** Prize: $500, and publication in Spring issue. Judged by editors. "We guarantee a considerate reading." Open to any writer.

ARCH & BRUCE BROWN FOUNDATION, The Arch & Bruce Brown Foundation, PMB 503, 31855 Date Palm Dr., Suite 3, Cathedral City CA 92234. E-mail: archwrite@aol.com. Website: www.aabbfoundation.org. **Contact:** Arch Brown, president. Annual contest for unpublished, "gay-positive works based on history." Type of contest changes each year: novel (2003), short fiction (2004). **Deadline: November 30.** Guidelines for SASE. Prize: $1,000 (not limited to a single winner). Open to any writer.

CECIL A. BROWNLOW PUBLICATION AWARD, IHS Aviation Information, administered by Flight Safety Foundation, Suite 300, 601 Madison St., Alexandria VA 22314. (703)739-6700. Fax: (703)739-6708. E-mail: rozelle@flightsafety.org. Website: www.flightsafety.org. **Contact:** Roger Rozelle, director of publications. Offered annually for work published July 1, 2002-June 30, 2003. Nominees should represent standards of excellence in reporting/writing accurately and objectively about commercial aviation safety or business/corporate aviation safety through outstanding articles, books, or other communication media. Nominations may be made on behalf of individuals, print or electronic media, or organizations. The contributions of individuals during a lifetime are eligible, as are long-term achievements of publications. **Deadline: August 1.** Guidelines for SASE. Prize: $1,000, travel to the FSF International Air Safety Seminar (IASS), held annually in a different international location (where the award will be presented), and a wood-framed, hand-lettered citation. Judged by a panel of aviation safety specialist editors. Open to any writer.

BURNABY WRITERS' SOCIETY CONTEST, Burnaby Writers' Society, 6584 Deer Lake Ave., Burnaby BC V5G 3T7, Canada. E-mail: lonewolf@portal.ca. Website: www.bws.bc.ca. **Contact:** Eileen Kernaghan. Offered annually for unpublished work. Open to all residents of British Columbia. Categories vary from year-to-year. Send SASE for current rules. Purpose is to encourage talented writers in all genres. **Deadline: May 31.** Guidelines for SASE. **Charges $5 fee.** Prize: 1st Place: $200; 2nd Place: $100; 3rd Place: $50; and public reading.

BYLINE MAGAZINE AWARDS, P.O. Box 5240, Edmond OK 73083-5240. (405)348-5591. E-mail: MPreston@bylinemag.com. Website: www.bylinemag.com. **Contact:** Marcia Preston, award director. Contest includes several monthly contests, open to anyone, in various categories that include fiction, nonfiction, poetry, and children's literature; an annual poetry chapbook award which is open to any poet; and an annual *ByLine* Short Fiction and Poetry Award open only to our subscribers. For chapbook award and subscriber awards, publication constitutes part of the prize, and winners grant first North American rights to *ByLine*. **Deadline: Varies. Charges $3-5 for monthly contests, and $15 for chapbook contest.** Prize: **Monthly contests:** Cash and listing in magazine; **Chapbook Award:** Publication of chapbook, 50 copies and $200; ***ByLine* Short Fiction and Poetry Award:** $250 in each category, plus publication in the magazine.

CANADIAN AUTHORS ASSOCIATION AWARDS PROGRAM, P.O. Box 419, Campbellford ON K0L 1L0, Canada. (705)653-0323. Fax: (705)653-0593. E-mail: canauth@redden.on.ca. Website: www.canauthors.org. **Contact:** Alec McEachern. Offered annually for short stories, fiction, poetry, history, and biography. Entrants must be Canadians by birth, naturalized Canadians, or landed immigrants. Entry form required for all awards. Obtain entry form from contact name or download from website. **Deadline: December 15.** Guidelines for SASE. **Charges $25 (Canadian) fee/title entered.** Prize: $2,500, and a silver medal.

N **CANADIAN HISTORICAL ASSOCIATION AWARDS**, Canadian Historical Association, 395 Wellington, Ottawa ON K1A 0N3, Canada. (613)233-7885. Fax: (613)567-3110. E-mail: cha-shc@archives.ca. Website: www.cha-shc.ca. **Contact:** Joanne Mineault. Offered annually. Categories: Regional history, Canadian history, history (not Canadian), women's history (published articles, English or French), doctoral dissertations. Open to Canadian writers. **Deadline: Varies.** Guidelines for SASE. Prize: $1,000.

CELTIC VOICE WRITING CONTEST, Bardsong Press, P.O. Box 775396, Steamboat Springs CO 80477-5396. (970)870-1401. Fax: (970)879-2657. E-mail: celts@bardsongpress.com. Website: www.bardsongpress.com. Offered annually for unpublished work to encourage and celebrate Celtic heritage and culture through poetry, short stories, essays, and creative nonfiction. Guidelines for SASE or on website. **Deadline: September 30. Charges $10 fee.** Prize: Cash award for category winners. Publication for winners and honorable mentions.

N **CHAUTAUQUA LITERARY JOURNAL ANNUAL CONTESTS**, *Chautauqua Literary Journal*, a publication of the Writers Center at Chautauqua, Inc., P.O. Box 2039, York Beach ME 03910. E-mail: CLJEditor@aol.com. **Contact:** Richard Foerster, editor. Offered annually for unpublished work to award literary excellence in the categories of poetry and prose (short stories and/or creative nonfiction). Guidelines for SASE or by e-mail. **Deadline: September 30 (postmarked). Charges $15/entry.** Prize: $1,500 in each of the 2 categories or poetry and prose, plus publication in *Chautauqua Literary Journal*. Judged by the editor and editorial staff of the *Chautauqua Literary Journal*. Acquires first North American serial rights, and one-time nonexclusive reprint rights. Open to any writer.

CHICAGO LITERARY AWARD, Left Field Press/*Another Chicago Magazine*, 3709 N. Kenmore, Chicago IL 60613-2905. E-mail: editors@anotherchicagomag.com. Website: www.anotherchicagomag.com. **Contact:** Editors. Offered annually for unpublished works to recognize excellence in poetry and fiction. Guidelines for SASE and on website. Buys first North American serial rights. Open to any writer. **Deadline: December 15. Charges $12 fee.** Prize: $1,000, and publication.

N **CHICANO/LATINO LITERARY CONTEST**, Dept. of Spanish and Portuguese, University of California-Irvine, Irvine CA 92697. (949)824-5443. Fax: (949)824-2803. E-mail: cllp@uci.edu. Website: www.hnet.uci.edu/spanishandportuguese./contest.html. **Contact:** Faye Hirsty. Estab. 1974. Offered annually "to promote the dissemination of unpublished Chicano/Latino literature in Spanish or English, and to encourage its development. The call for entries will be genre specific, rotating through four categories: novel (2003), short story (2004), poetry (2005), drama (2006)." The contest is open to all citizens or permanent residents of the US. **Deadline: June 1.** Guidelines for SASE. Prize: 1st Place: $1,000, and publication, transportation to receive the award; 2nd Place: $500; 3rd Place: $250.

N **CLEVERKITTY CATERWAULING CONTEST**, Cleverkitty.com, 8600 W. Charleston Blvd., Las Vegas NV 89117-5416. (702)240-1938. E-mail: caterwauling@cleverkitty.com. Website: www.cleverkitty.com. **Contact:** Kim Cady, contest director. "Our website celebrates all things feline. Our annual contest is for writers of all kinds of short literature, fiction or nonfiction (stories concerning real-life experiences are accepted) relating to "The Cat." There are no separate categories at this time. The pieces will be judged for impact and overall excellence." **Deadline: August 31.** Prize: 1st Place: $100; 2nd Place: $50; 3rd Place: $20 to winning author's favorite animal charity. Also, all winners will receive a membership at "Best Friends Animal Sanctuary" in Kanab, Utah (1 of the premier animal sanctuaries in the USA). Open to any writer.

CNW/FFWA ANNUAL FLORIDA STATE WRITING COMPETITION, Florida Freelance Writers Association, P.O. Box A, North Stratford NH 03590-0167. E-mail: contest@writers-editors.com. Website: www.writers-editors.com. **Contact:** Dana K. Cassell, executive director. Annual award "to recognize publishable talent." Divisions & Categories: Nonfiction (previously published article/essay/column/nonfiction book chapter; unpublished or self-published article/essay/column/nonfiction book chapter); Fiction (unpublished or self-published short story or novel chapter); Children's Literature (unpublished or self-published short story/nonfiction article/book chapter/poem); Poetry (unpublished or self-published free verse/traditional). **Deadline: March 15.** Guidelines for SASE. **Charges $5 (active or new CNW/FFWA members) or $10 (nonmembers) for each fiction/nonfiction entry under 3,000 words; $10 (members) or $20 (nonmembers) for each entry of 3,000 words or longer; and $3 (members) or $5 (nonmembers) for each poem.** Prize: 1st Place: $100, plus certificate; 2nd Place: $75, plus certificate; 3rd Place: $50, plus certificate. Honorable Mention certificates will be awarded in each category as warranted. Judged by editors, librarians, and writers. Open to any writer.

COLORADO BOOK AWARDS, Colorado Center for the Book, 2123 Downing, Denver CO 80205. (303)839-8320. Fax: (303)839-8319. E-mail: ccftb@compuserve.com. Website: www.ColoradoBook.org. **Contact:** Christiane H. Citron, executive director. Offered annually for work published by December of previous year or current calendar year. The purpose is to champion all Colorado authors and in particular to honor the award winners and a reputation for Colorado as a state whose people promote and support reading, writing, and literacy through books. The categories are children, young adult, fiction, nonfiction, and poetry, and other categories as determined each year. Open to authors who reside or have resided in Colorado. Guidelines for SASE. **Charges $45 fee.** Prize: $250 in each category, and an annual gala event where winners are honored.

COMPACT FICTION/SHORT POEM COMPETITION, *Pottersfield Portfolio*, P.O. Box 40, Station A, Sydney NS B1P 6G9, Canada. Website: www.pportfolio.com. **Contact:** Lars Willum. Offered annually for unpublished work: Stories of 1,500 words or less and poems of 20 lines or less. Maximum of 2 stories or 3 poems per author. Buys first Canadian serial rights; copyright remains with author. Guidelines for SASE or on website. **Deadline: May 1. Charges $20 for the first entry, $5 for each subsequent entry in the same category.** Prize: $200 for the best story and the best poem, publication, and a 1-year subscription to *Pottersfield Portfolio*.

VIOLET CROWN BOOK AWARDS, Writers' League of Texas, 1501 W. Fifth St., Suite E-2, Austin TX 78703. (512)499-8914. Fax: (512)499-0441. E-mail: wlt@writersleague.org. Website: www.writersleague.org. **Contact:** Stephanie Sheppard, director. Offered annually for work published June 1, 2002-May 31, 2003. Honors 3 outstanding books published in fiction, nonfiction, and literary categories by Writers' League of Texas members. Membership dues may accompany entry fee. **Deadline: May 31.** Guidelines for SASE. **Charges $10 fee.** Prize: $1,000 prizes (3), and trophies.

THE CRUCIBLE POETRY AND FICTION COMPETITION, *Crucible*, Barton College, College Station, Wilson NC 27893. (252)399-6456. E-mail: tgrimes@barton.edu. **Contact:** Terrence L. Grimes, editor. Offered annually for unpublished mss. **Deadline: Late April.** Guidelines for SASE. Prize: $150 (1st Prize); $100 (2nd Prize) and publication in *Crucible*. Judged by in-house editorial board. Open to any writer.

CUNARD FIRST BOOK AWARD, Writers' Federation of Nova Scotia, 1113 Marginal Rd., Halifax NS B3H 4P7. (902)423-8116. Fax: (902)422-0881. E-mail: talk@writers.ns.ca. Website: www.writers.ns.ca. **Contact:** Jane Buss, executive director. This award was established by the Atlantic Book Week Steering Committee to honor the first published book by an Atlantic-Canadian author. Full-length books of fiction, nonfiction, or poetry written by Atlantic Canadians, and published as a whole for the first time in the previous calendar year, are eligible. Entrants must be native or resident Atlantic Canadians who have either been born in Newfoundland, Prince Edward Island, Nova Scotia, or New Brunswick, and spent a susbstantial portion of their lives living there, or who have lived in 1 or a combination of these provinces for at least 24 consecutive months prior to entry deadline date. Entries submitted to the Atlantic Poetry Prize, Evelyn Richardson Nonfiction Award, Thomas Head Raddall Atlantic Fiction Award, Dartmouth Book Award, and/or Ann Connor Brimer Award are automatically entered in the competition. Publishers: Send 4 copies and a letter attesting to the author's status as an Atlantic Canadian and the author's current mailing address and telephone number. **Deadline: First Friday in December.** Prize: $500.

DANA AWARDS IN THE NOVEL, SHORT FICTION AND POETRY, 7207 Townsend Forest Court, Browns Summit NC 27214-9634. (336)656-7009. E-mail: danaawards@pipeline.com. Website: www.danaawards.com. **Contact:** Mary Elizabeth Parker, chair. Three awards offered annually for unpublished work written in English. Purpose is monetary award for work that has not been previously published or received monetary award, but will accept work published simply for friends and family. Works previously published online are not eligible. No work accepted by or for persons under 16 for any of the 3 awards. Awards: **Novel:** For the first 50 pages of a novel completed or in progress. **Short fiction:** Short fiction (no memoirs) up to 10,000 words. **Poetry:** For best group of 5 poems based on excellence of all 5 (no light verse, no single poem over 100 lines). **Deadline: October 31 (postmarked). Charges $20 fee/novel entry, $15 fee/short fiction or poetry entry.** Prize: $1,000 in each category.

E.F.S. ANNUAL WRITING COMPETITION, E.F.S. Online Publishing, 2844 Eighth Ave., Suite 6E, New York NY 10039-2171. (800)835-3957. Website: www.efs-enterprises.com. **Contact:** Rita Baxter. Offered annually for unpublished work in the following categories: fiction, nonfiction, poetry, screenplays, and plays. **Deadline: September 15.** Guidelines for SASE. **Charges $20/ms.** Prize: $50, and electronic publishing contract. Open to any writer.

E.F.S. RELIGIOUS FICTION & NONFICTION WRITING COMPETITION, E.F.S. Online Publishing, 2844 Eighth Ave., Suite 6E, New York NY 10039-2171. (800)835-3957. Website: www.efs-enterprises.com. **Contact:** Rita Baxter. Offered annually for unblished work in the following categories: inspirational/religious fiction, inspirational/

religious nonfiction. **Deadline: July 15.** Guidelines for SASE. **Charges $20/ms.** Prize: $50, electronic publishing contract. Open to any writer.

N EATON LITERARY AGENCY'S ANNUAL AWARDS PROGRAM, Eaton Literary Agency, P.O. Box 49795, Sarasota FL 34230. (941)366-6589. Fax: (941)365-4679. E-mail: eatonlit@aol.com. **Contact:** Richard Lawrence, vice president. Offered annually for unpublished mss. **Deadline: March 31 (mss under 10,000 words); August 31 (mss over 10,000 words).** Guidelines for SASE. Prize: $2,500 (over 10,000 words); $500 (under 10,000 words). Judged by an independent agency in conjunction with some members of Eaton's staff. Open to any writer.

THE VIRGINIA FAULKNER AWARD FOR EXCELLENCE IN WRITING, *Prairie Schooner*, 201 Andrews Hall, P.O. Box 880334, Lincoln NE 68588-0334. (402)472-0911. Fax: (402)472-9771. E-mail: eflanagan2@unl.edu. Website: www.unl.edu/schooner/psmain.htm. **Contact:** Hilda Raz. Offered annually for work published in *Prairie Schooner* in the previous year. Prize: $1,000.

FINELINE COMPETITION FOR PROSE POEMS, SHORT SHORTS, AND ANYTHING IN BETWEEN, *Mid-American Review*, Dept. of English, Bowling Green State University, Bowling Green OH 43403. (419)372-2725. E-mail: karenka@bgnet.bgsu.edu. Website: www.bgsu.edu/midamericanreview. **Contact:** Michael Czyzniejewski, editor-in-chief. Offered annually for previously unpublished submissions. Contest open to all writers not associated with current judge or *Mid-American Review*. **Deadline: October 1.** Guidelines for SASE. **Charges $10/group of 3 pieces or $5 each.** All $10-and-over participants receive prize issue. Prize: $500, plus publication in spring issue of *Mid-American Review*; 10 finalists receive notation plus possible publication. Judged by well-known writer, e.g., Michael Martone, Alberto Rios, Stephen Dunn. Open to any writer.

N THE FLORIDA REVIEW EDITOR'S AWARD, Dept. of English, University of Central Florida, Orlando FL 32816. (407)823-2038. E-mail: FloridaReview@mail.ucf.edu. Website: www.flreview.com. **Contact:** Patrick Rushin. Annual awards for the best unpublished fiction, poetry, and memoir. **Deadline: April 4.** Guidelines for SASE. **Charges $15.** Prize: $1,000 (in each genre) and publication in *The Florida Review*. Judged by the editors in each genre. Acquires first rights. Open to any writer.

THE GREENSBORO REVIEW LITERARY AWARD IN FICTION AND POETRY, *The Greensboro Review*, English Dept., 134 McIver Bldg., P.O. Box 6170, Greensboro NC 27402-6170. (336)334-5459. E-mail: jlclark@uncg.edu. Website: www.uncg.edu/eng/mfa. **Contact:** Jim Clark, editor. Offered annually for fiction (7,500 word limit) and poetry recognizing the best work published in the spring issue of *The Greensboro Review*. Sample issue for $5. **Deadline: September 15.** Guidelines for SASE. Prize: $500 each for best short story and poem. Rights revert to author upon publication. Open to any writer.

GSU REVIEW WRITING CONTEST, *GSU Review*, Attn: Annual Contest, Georgia State University Plaza, Campus Box 1894, Atlanta GA 30303-3083. (404)651-4804. E-mail: kchaple@emory.edu. **Contact:** Katie Chaple, editor. Offered annually "to publish the most promising work of up-and-coming writers of poetry (3-5 poems, none over 50 lines) and fiction (8,000 word limit)." Rights revert to writer upon publication. **Deadline: January 31.** Guidelines for SASE. **Charges $10 fee.** Prize: $1,000 to winner of each category, plus a copy of winning issue to each paid submission.

N INDIANA REVIEW ½ K (SHORT-SHORT/PROSE-POEM) CONTEST, *Indiana Review*, BH 465/Indiana University, Bloomington IN 47405-7103. (812)855-3439. Fax: (812)855-4253. E-mail: inreview@indiana.edu. Website: www.indiana.edu/~inreview. **Contact:** Danit Brown. Maximum story/poem length is 500 words. Offered annually for unpublished work. **Deadline: Early June.** Guidelines for SASE. **Charges $15 fee for no more than 3 pieces (includes a year's subscription).** Prize: $500. Judged by guest judges. Ray Gonzalez was 2003 judge. Open to any writer.

N IOWA AWARD IN POETRY, FICTION, & ESSAY, *The Iowa Review*, 308 EPB, The University of Iowa, Iowa City IA 52242. (319)335-0462. Fax: (319)335-2535. E-mail: iareview@blue.weeg.uiowa.edu. Website: www.uiowa.edu/~iareview. **Deadline: February 1. Charges $15 entry fee.** Prize: $1,000, and publication.

N THE IOWA REVIEW STAFF AWARD, *The Iowa Review*, 308 EPB, The University of Iowa, Iowa City IA 52242. (319)335-0462. Fax: (319)335-2535. E-mail: iareview@blue.weeg.uiowa.edu. Website: www.uiowa.edu/~iareview. "Award given to a former contributor who returns to our pages, in any genre, and whose work is most admired by our student staff members." Prize: $1,000.

N ROBERT F. KENNEDY BOOK AWARDS, 1367 Connecticut Ave., NW, Suite 200, Washington DC 20036. (202)463-7575. Fax: (202)463-6606. E-mail: info@rfkmemorial.org. Website: www.rfkmemorial.org. **Contact:** Book Award Director. Offered annually for work published the previous year "which most faithfully and forcefully reflects Robert Kennedy's purposes—his concern for the poor and the powerless, his struggle for honest and even-handed justice, his conviction that a decent society must assure all young people a fair chance, and his faith that a free democracy can act to remedy disparities of power and opportunity." **Deadline: January 31. Charges $25 fee.** Prize: $2,500, and a bust of Robert F. Kennedy.

LARRY LEVIS EDITORS' PRIZE IN POETRY/THE MISSOURI REVIEW EDITOR'S PRIZE IN FICTION & ESSAY, *The Missouri Review*, 1507 Hillcrest Hall, Columbia MO 65211. (573)882-4474. Fax: (573)884-4671. Website: www.missourireview.org. **Contact:** Hoa Ngo. Offered annually for unpublished work in 3 categories: fiction, essay, and poetry. Guidelines for SASE after June. **Deadline: October 15. Charges $15 fee (includes a 1-year subscription).** Prize: $2,000 in each genre, plus publication; 3 finalists in each category receive a minimum of $100.

THE HUGH J. LUKE AWARD, *Prairie Schooner*, 201 Andrews Hall, P.O. Box 880334, Lincoln NE 68588-0334. (402)472-0911. Fax: (402)472-9771. E-mail: eflanagan2@unl.edu. Website: www.unl.edu/schooner/psmain.htm. **Contact:**

Hilda Raz. Offered annually for work published in *Prairie Schooner* in the previous year. Prize: $250.

THE LUSH TRIUMPHANT, *subTerrain Magazine*, P.O. Box 3008, MPO, Vancouver BC V6B 3X5, Canada. E-mail: subter@portal.ca. Website: www.subterrain.ca. The Lsuh Triumphant is a combination of the *subTerrain* Poetry Awards, *subTerrain Magazine* Awards, and the *subTerrain* Short Story Contest. Annual contest for fiction, poetry, and creative nonfiction. All entries must be previously unpublished and not currently under consideration in any other contest or competition. Entries will not be returned. Results of the competition will be announced in the Summer issue of *subTerrain*. All entrants receive a complimentary 1-year subscription to *subTerrain*. **Deadline: May 15. Charges $20/entry (entrants may submit as many entries in as many categories as they like).** Prize: The winning entries in each category will receive $500 and will be published in the Fall issue of *subTerrain*. The 1st runner-up in each category will be published in a future issue of *subTerrain*. Open to any writer.

BRENDA MACDONALD RICHES FIRST BOOK AWARD, Saskatchewan Book Awards, Inc., Box 1921, Regina SK S4P 3E1, Canada. (306)569-1585. Fax: (306)569-4187. E-mail: director@bookawards.sk.ca. Website: www.bookawards.sk.ca. **Contact:** Joyce Wells, executive director. Offered annually for work published September 15, 2002-September 14, 2003. This award is presented to a Saskatchewan author for the best first book, judged on the quality of writing. Books from the following categories will be considered: children's; drama; fiction (short fiction by a single author, novellas, novels); nonfiction (all categories of nonfiction writing except cookbooks, directories, how-to books, or bibliographies of minimal critical content); poetry. **Deadline: First deadline: July 31; Final deadline: September 14.** Guidelines for SASE. **Charges $15 (Canadian).** Prize: $1,500.

MAMMOTH PRESS AWARDS, 7 S. Juniata St., DuBois PA 15801. E-mail: info@mammothbooks.com. Website: www.mammothbooks.com. **Contact:** Antonio Vallone. Offered annually for unpublished works. Prose mss may be a collection of essays or a single long work of creative nonfiction, a collection of stories or novellas or a novel. Poetry mss may be a collection of poems or a single long poem. Translations are acceptable. "Manuscripts as a whole must not have been previously published. Some or all of each manuscript may have appeared in periodicals, chapbooks, anthologies or other venues. These must be identified. Authors are responsible for securing permissions." Guidelines for SASE or by e-mail. **Deadline: March 1-August 31 (prose); September 1-February 28 (poetry). Charges $20 fee.** Prize: $750 advance against royalties, standard royalty contract and publication.

MANITOBA WRITING AND PUBLISHING AWARDS, c/o Manitoba Writers' Guild, 206-100 Arthur St., Winnipeg MB R3B 1H3, Canada. (888)637-5802. Fax: (204)942-5754. E-mail: mbwriter@mts.net. Website: www.mbwriter.mb.ca. **Contact:** Robyn Maharaj. Offered annually: The McNally Robinson Book of Year Award (adult); The McNally Robinson Book for Young People Awards (8 and under and 9 and older); The John Hirsch Award for Most Promising Manitoba Writer; The Mary Scorer Award for Best Book by a Manitoba Publisher; The Carol Shields Winnipeg Book Award; The Eileen McTavish Sykes Award for Best First Book; The Margaret Laurence Award for Fiction; The Alexander Kennedy Isbister Award for Non-Fiction; The Manuela Dias Book Design of the Year Award; The Best Illustrated Book of the Year Award; and the biennial Le Prix Littéraire Rue-Deschambault. Guidelines and submission forms available on website at www.mbwriter.mb.ca/mwapa.html. Open to Manitoba writers only. **Deadline: December 1 (books published December 1-31 will be accepted until mid-January).** Prize: Several prizes up to $5,000 (Canadian).

MASTERS LITERARY AWARDS, Titan Press, P.O. Box 17897, Encino CA 91416-7897. **Contact:** Contest Coordinator. Offered annually and quarterly for work published within 2 years (preferred) and unpublished work (accepted). Fiction, 15-page maximum; poetry, 5 pages or 150-lines maximum; and nonfiction, 10-pages maximum. "A selection of winning entries may appear in our national literary publication." Winners may also appear on the Internet. Titan Press retains one-time publishing rights to selected winners. **Deadline: Ongoing (nominations made March 15, June 15, September 15, December 15).** Guidelines for SASE. **Charges $15.** Prize: $1,000, and possible publication in the *Titan Press Internet* journal.

THE MCGINNIS-RITCHIE MEMORIAL AWARD, *Southwest Review*, P.O. Box 750374, Dallas TX 75275-0374. (214)768-1037. Fax: (214)768-1408. E-mail: swr@mail.smu.edu. Website: www.southwestreview.org. **Contact:** Elizabeth Mills & Willard Spiegelman. The McGinnis-Ritchie Memorial Award is given annually to the best works of fiction and nonfiction that appeared in the magazine in the previous year. Manuscripts are submitted for publication, not for the prizes themselves. Guidelines for SASE or on website. Prize: 2 cash prizes of $500 each. Judged by Elizabeth Mills, senior editor, and Willard Spiegelman, editor-in-chief. Open to any writer.

MID-LIST PRESS FIRST SERIES AWARDS, Mid-List Press, 4324 12th Ave. S., Minneapolis MN 55407-3218. (612)822-3733. Fax: (612)823-8387. E-mail: guide@midlist.org. Website: www.midlist.org. **Contact:** Lane Stiles. Offered annually for authors who have yet to publish books in any of 4 categories: creative nonfiction, short fiction, poetry, and novels. Guidelines for SASE or online at website. **Deadline: Varies. Charges $30 fee (US dollars).** Prize: An advance against royalties and publication.

MIDLAND AUTHORS AWARD, Society of Midland Authors, P.O. Box 10419, Chicago IL 60610-0419. E-mail: writercc@aol.com. Website: www.midlandauthors.org. **Contact:** Carol Jean Carlson. Offered annually for published fiction, nonfiction, poetry, biography, children's fiction and children's nonfiction. Authors must reside in the states of Illinois, Indiana, Iowa, Kansas, Michigan, Minnesota, Mississippi, Nebraska, North Dakota, South Dakota, Wisconsin, or Ohio. Guidelines and submission at website. **Deadline: March 1.** Prize: Monetary award given to winner in each category.

MOUNTAINS & PLAINS BOOKSELLERS ASSOCIATION REGIONAL BOOK AWARD, Mountains & Plains Booksellers Association, 19 Old Town Square, Suite 238, Fort Collins CO 80525. (970)484-5856. Fax: (970)407-1479. E-mail: lisa@mountainsplains.org. Website: www.mountainsplains.org. **Contact:** Lisa D. Knudsen. The purpose of these annual awards is to honor outstanding books published between November 2002 and October 2003 which are set in our region. The Mountains & Plains region includes Colorado, Wyoming, New Mexico, Utah, Idaho, Texas, Montana, Kansas, Arizona, Nebraska, Oklahoma, North Dakota, and South Dakota. **Deadline: October 1.** Guidelines for SASE. **Charges $50.** Prize: Each award includes a $500 prize and a framed copy of the poster. Press releases are sent out nationally and regionally, MPBA's 250 bookstores receive free posters, and the winning titles are featured on the back of the MPBA regional catalog, *Reading the West*. The prizes are awarded at a banquet in Santa Fe in March. Judged by 3 panels of judges, 1 each for adult fiction, adult nonfiction and the arts, and children's. Each panel consists of 3 persons selected by the Awards Committee. The panelists represent a cross-section of the book community in our region, including, at various times, members of the media, librarians, and booksellers. Open to any writer.

NATIONAL LOOKING GLASS CHAPBOOK COMPETITION, Pudding House Publications, 60 N. Main St., Johnstown OH 43031. (740)967-6060. E-mail: pudding@johnstown.net. Website: www.puddinghouse.com. **Contact:** Jennifer Bosveld. Offered twice/year for "a collection of poems, short-short stories, or other creative writing that represents our editorial slant: popular culture, social justice, psychological, sociological, travel, political, environmental. Submissions might be themed or not." Guidelines on website. Past winners include Roy Bentley, David Hernandez, Rebecca Baggett, Willie Abraham Howard Jr., Michael Day, Bill Noble, William Keener, Mark Taksa, Ron Moran, and many others. **Deadline: June 30, September 30. Charges $10 fee.** Prize: $100, publication of chapbook, 20 free books.

THE NEBRASKA REVIEW AWARDS IN FICTION, POETRY AND CREATIVE NONFICTION, *The Nebraska Review*, FAB 212, University of Nebraska-Omaha, Omaha NE 68182-0324. (402)554-3159. E-mail: jreed@unomaha.edu. **Contact:** Coreen Wees (poetry), James Reed (fiction), or John Price (creative nonfiction). Estab. 1973. Offered annually for previously unpublished fiction, creative nonfiction, and a poem or group of poems. **Deadline: November 30. Charges $15 fee (includes a subscription to *The Nebraska Review*).** Prize: $500 for each category.

N **NEW ENGLAND WRITERS FREE VERSE AND FICTION CONTESTS**, New England Writers, P.O. Box 5, Windsor VT 05089-0005. (802)674-2315. E-mail: newvtpoet@aol.com. **Contact:** Dr. Frank and Susan Anthony. Poetry line limit: 30 lines. Fiction word limit: 1,000 words. **Deadline: June 15.** Guidelines for SASE. **Charges $6 for 3 poems or 1 fiction; $5 for 2 or more entries of 3 poems or 1 fiction.** Prize: The winning poems are published in *The Anthology of New England Writers*. The free verse contest has Robert Penn Warren Awards of $300, $200, and $100, with 10 Honorable Mentions of $20. The short fiction contest has 1 Marjory Bartlett Sanger Award of $300, with 5 Honorable Mentions of $30. Judged by published, working university professor of the genre. Open to any writer.

NEW LETTERS LITERARY AWARDS, *New Letters*, 5101 Rockhill Rd., Kansas City MO 64110-2499. (816)235-1168. Fax: (816)235-2611. E-mail: newletters@umkc.edu. Website: www.umkc.edu/newletters. **Contact:** Aleatha Ezra. Award has 3 categories (fiction, poetry, and creative nonfiction) with 1 winner in each. Offered annually for previously unpublished work. **Deadline: May 20.** Deadline is always the closest Friday to May 15. Guidelines for SASE. **Charges $20 fee (includes a year's subscription).** Prize: 1st Place: $1,000, plus publication; Runners-Up: A year's subscription to *New Letters* and consideration for publication. Judged by 2 rounds of regional writers (preliminary judging). Winners picked by an anonymous judge of national repute. Acquires first North American serial rights. Open to any writer.

N **NEW MILLENNIUM WRITING AWARDS**, New Millennium Writings, Room M2, P.O. Box 2463, Knoxville TN 37901. E-mail: mark@mach2.com. Website: www.newmillenniumwritings.com/awards.html. **Contact:** Contest Coordinator. Offered twice annually for unpublished fiction, poetry, essays or nonfiction prose, to encourage new fiction writers, poets and essayists, and bring them to attention of publishing industry. Entrants receive an issue of *NMW* in which winners appear. **Deadline: November 17 and June 17.** Guidelines for SASE. **Charges $17 entry fee for each submission.** Prize: Fiction: $1,000; Poetry: $1,000; Nonfiction: $1,000; winners published in *NMW* and on website.

NEW WRITERS AWARDS, Great Lakes Colleges Association New Writers Awards, English Dept., The College of Wooster, Wooster OH 44691. (330)263-2575. Fax: (330)263-2693. E-mail: dbourne@mail.wooster.edu. **Contact:** Prof. Daniel Bourne, award director. Offered annually to the best first book of poetry and the best first book of fiction among those submitted by publishers. An honorarium of at least $300 will be guaranteed the author by each of the colleges visited. Open to any first book of poetry or fiction submitted by a publisher. **Deadline: February 28.** Guidelines for SASE. Prize: Winning authors tour the GLCA colleges, where they will participate in whatever activities they and the college deem appropriate.

N **THE NOMA AWARD FOR PUBLISHING IN AFRICA**, Kodansha Ltd., Japan, P.O. Box 128, Witney, Oxon OX8 6LU, United Kingdom. (+44) (0)1993-775235. Fax: (+44) (0)1993-709265. E-mail: maryljay@aol.com. Website: www.nomaaward.org. **Contact:** Mary Jay, secretary to the Noma Award Managing Committee. "The Noma Award is open to African writers and scholars whose work is published in Africa, rather than outside. The spirit within which the Award is given is to encourage and reward genuinely autonomous African publishers, and African writers. The annual award is given for an outstanding new book in any of these 3 categories: scholarly or academic; books for children; and literature and creative writing (including fiction, drama, poetry, and essays on African literature)." Entries must be submitted by publishers in Africa, who are limited to 3 entries (in any combination of the eligible categories). The Award is open to any author who is indigenous to Africa (a national, irrespective of place of domicile). **Deadline: February 28.** Guidelines for SASE. Prize: $10,000 (U.S.). Judged by an impartial committee chaired by Mr. Walter Bgoya, comprising African scholars and book experts, and representatives of the international book community, is entrusted with the selection of the annual prize. This Managing Committee is the Jury. The Jury is assisted by independent opinion and assessment from a large and distinguished pool of subject specialists from throughout the world, including many in Africa.

N **OREGON BOOK AWARDS**, Literary Arts, 219 NW 12th Ave., #219, Portland OR 97203. (503)227-2583. E-mail: la@literary-arts.org. Website: www.literary-arts.org. **Contact:** Kristy Athens, award coordinator. The annual Oregon Book

Awards celebrate Oregon authors in the areas of poetry, fiction, nonfiction, drama, and young readers' literature published between April 1, 2002 and March 31, 2003. Annually, Must Be Previously Published, Date Eligibility Between April 1, 2002 and March 31, 2003. **Deadline: May 30.** Guidelines for SASE. Prize: Finalists are invited on a statewide reading tour and are promoted in bookstores and libraries across the state. Winners receive a cash prize. Judged by judges who are selected from Oregon for their expertise in a genre. Past judges include Dorothy Allison, Chris Offutt, and Maxine Kumin.

THE ORWELL PRIZE, *The Political Quarterly* and the George Orwell Memorial Fund, c/o Simage Communications, Fulton House, Fulton Rd., Wembley Park, Middlesex HA9 0TF, United Kingdom. (020) 8584 0444. Fax: (020) 8584 0443. E-mail: orwell@simage-comms.co.uk. **Contact:** Sir Bernard Crick. Annual contest for books, pamphlets, newspaper and/or periodical articles, features or columns, or sustained reportage on a theme, published in the English language in Great Britain or Ireland during the calendar year 2002. "The prizes are to encourage good writing about politics, political thinking, or public policy construed in the broadest sense (whether political, economic, social, or cultural, and including fiction) of a kind that is aimed at, or accessible to, the reading public, rather than specialist or academic audiences, giving equal value to style and content." Open to residents of Great Britain or Ireland only. **Deadline: January 10.** Guidelines for SASE. Prize: £1,000 for the journalist entry, and £1,000 for the book or pamphlet author. Judged by Sir Bernard Crick, Carmen Callil, and David Hare.

PEACE WRITING INTERNATIONAL WRITING AWARDS, Peace and Justice Studies Association, 2582 Jimmie, Fayetteville AR 72703-3420. (479)442-4600. E-mail: jbennet@uark.edu. Website: comp.uark.edu/~jbennet/OMNI. **Contact:** Dick Bennett. Offered annually for unpublished books. "PeaceWriting encourages writing about war and international nonviolent peacemaking and peacemakers. PeaceWriting seeks book manuscripts about the causes, consequences, and solutions to violence and war, and about the ideas and practices of nonviolent peacemaking and the lives of nonviolent peacemakers." Three categories: Nonfiction Prose (history, political science, memoirs); Imaginative Literature (novels, plays, collections of short stories, collections of poetry, collections of short plays); and Works for Young People. Open to any writer. Enclose SASE for ms return. **Deadline: December 1.** Guidelines for SASE. Prize: $500 for best nonfiction; $500 for best imaginative work; and $500 for best work for young people.

PEN CENTER USA WEST ANNUAL LITERARY AWARDS, PEN Center USA West, 672 S. Lafayette Park Place, #42, Los Angeles CA 90057. (213)365-8500. Fax: (213)365-9616. E-mail: awards@penusa.org. Website: www.penusa.org. **Contact:** Literary Awards Cooridnator. Offered annually for fiction, nonfiction, poetry, children's literature, or translation published January 1-December 31 of the current year. Open to authors west of the Mississippi River. **Deadline: December 19.** Guidelines for SASE. **Charges $25 fee.** Prize: $1,000.

POSTCARD STORY COMPETITION, The Writers' Union of Canada, 40 Wellington St. E., 3rd Floor, Toronto ON M5E 1C7, Canada. (416)703-8982, ext. 223. Fax: (416)504-7656. E-mail: projects@writersunion.ca. Website: www.writersunion.ca. **Contact:** Project Coordinator. Offered annually for original and unpublished fiction, nonfiction, prose, verse, dialogue, etc. with a maximum 250 words in length. Open to Canadian citizens or landed immigrants only. **Deadline: February 14.** Guidelines for SASE. **Charges $5 entry fee.** Prize: $500.

THE PRESIDIO LA BAHIA AWARD, Sons of the Republic of Texas, 1717 Eighth St., Bay City TX 77414. (979)245-6644. Fax: (979)244-3819. E-mail: srttexas@srttexas.org. Website: www.srttexas.org. **Contact:** Janet Hickl. Offered annually "to promote suitable preservation of relics, appropriate dissemination of data, and research into our Texas heritage, with particular attention to the Spanish Colonial period." **Deadline: June 1-September 30.** Guidelines for SASE. Prize: $2,000 total; 1st Place: Minimum of $1,200, 2nd and 3rd prizes at the discretion of the judges.

QWF LITERARY AWARDS, Quebec Writers' Federation, 1200 Atwater Ave., Montreal QC H3Z 1X4, Canada. (514)933-0878. Fax: (514)934-2485. E-mail: qspell@total.net. Website: www.qwf.org. **Contact:** Diana McNeill. Offered annually for a book published October 1-September 30 to honor excellence in English-language writing in Quebec. Categories: fiction, nonfiction, poetry and first book, and translation. Author must have resided in Quebec for 3 of the past 5 years. **Deadline: May 31 for books, and August 15 for books and finished proofs.** Guidelines for SASE. **Charges $10/title.** Prize: $2,000 in each category; $1,000 for first book.

REGINA BOOK AWARD, Saskatchewan Book Awards, Inc., Box 1921, Regina SK S4P 3E1, Canada. (306)569-1585. Fax: (306)569-4187. E-mail: director@bookawards.sk.ca. Website: www.bookawards.sk.ca. **Contact:** Joyce Wells, executive director. Offered annually for work published September 15, 2002-September 14, 2003. In recognition of the vitality of the literary community in Regina, this award is presented to a Regina author for the best book, judged on the quality of writing. Books from the following categories will be considered: children's; drama; fiction (short fiction by a single author, novellas, novels); nonfiction (all categories of nonfiction writing except cookbooks, directories, how-to books, or bibliographies of minimal critical content); poetry. **Deadline: First deadline: July 31; Final deadline: September 14.** Guidelines for SASE. **Charges $15 (Canadian).** Prize: $1,500.

JOHN LLEWELLYN RHYS PRIZE, *The Mail on Sunday*, % Book House, 45 E. Hill, Wandsworth, London SW18 2QZ, United Kingdom. Fax: (00 44) 20 8516 2978. E-mail: tarryn@booktrust.org.uk. Website: www.booktrust.org.uk. **Contact:** Ms. Paula Johnson. "The Prize was founded in 1942 by Jane Oliver, the widow of John Llewellyn Rhys, a young writer killed in action in World War II. This is one of Britain's oldest and most prestigious literary awards, with an unequalled reputation of singling out the fine young writers—from poets to novelists, biographers and travel writers—early in their careers." Entries can be any work of literature written by a British Commonwealth writer aged 35 or under at the time of publication. Books must be written in English, published between January 1, 2002 and December 31, 2002, and translations are not eligible. **Deadline: August 2003.** Prize: £5,000 to the winner and "500 to shortlisted authors.

SUMMERFIELD G. ROBERTS AWARD, Sons of the Republic of Texas, 1717 Eighth St., Bay City TX 77414. (979)245-6644. Fax: (979)244-3819. E-mail: srttexas@srttexas.org. Website: www.srttexas.org. **Contact:** Janet Hickl. Offered annually for submissions published during the previous calendar year "to encourage literary effort and research about historical events and personalities during the days of the Republic of Texas, 1836-1846, and to stimulate interest in the period." **Deadline: January 15.** Prize: $2,500.

SASKATCHEWAN BOOK OF THE YEAR AWARD, Saskatchewan Book Awards, Inc., Box 1921, Regina SK S4P 3E1, Canada. (306)569-1585. Fax: (306)569-4187. E-mail: director@bookawards.sk.ca. Website: www.bookawards.sk.ca. **Contact:** Joyce Wells, executive director. Offered annually for work published September 15-September 14 annually. This award is presented to a Saskatchewan author for the best book, judged on the quality of writing. Books from the following categories will be considered: children's; drama; fiction (short fiction by a single author, novellas, novels); nonfiction (all categories of nonfiction writing except cookbooks, directories, how-to books, or bibliographies of minimal critical content); poetry. Visit website for more details. **Deadline: First deadline: July 31; Final deadline: September 14.** Guidelines for SASE. **Charges $15 (Canadian).** Prize: $1,500.

N **SASKATOON BOOK AWARD**, Saskatchewan Book Awards, Inc., Box 1921, Regina SK S4P 3E1, Canada. (306)569-1585. Fax: (306)569-4187. E-mail: director@bookawards.sk.ca. Website: www.bookawards.sk.ca. **Contact:** Joyce Wells, executive director. Offered annually for work published September 15, 2002-September 14, 2002. In recognition of the vitality of the literary community in Saskatoon, this award is presented to a Saskatoon author for the best book, judged on the quality of writing. Books from the following categories will be considered: children's; drama; fiction (short fiction by a single author, novellas, novels); nonfiction (all categories of nonfiction writing except cookbooks, directories, how-to books, or bibliographies of minimal critical content); poetry. **Deadline: First deadline: July 31; Final deadline: September 14.** Guidelines for SASE. **Charges $15 (Canadian).** Prize: $1,500.

N **THE MONA SCHREIBER PRIZE FOR HUMOROUS FICTION & NONFICTION**, 11362 Homedale St., Los Angeles CA 90049. E-mail: brashcyber@pcmagic.net. Website: home.pcmagic.net/brashcyber/mona.htm. **Contact:** Brad Schreiber. **Deadline: December 1. Charges $5 fee (payable to Mona Schreiber Prize).** Prize: 1st Place: $500; 2nd Place: $250; 3rd Place: $100. Judged by Brad Schreiber, author, journalist, consultant, instructor at UCLA Extension Writers' Program, "Writing Humorous Fiction and Nonfiction." Open to any writer.

N **SHOCK YOUR MAMA HUMOR COMPETITION**, Abbott Productions, P.O. Box 188, Reno OH 45773-0188. E-mail: info@shockyourmama.com. Website: www.shockyourmama.com. **Contact:** Mary Ann Abbott, editor. Contest offered in the spring and fall to "help discover and publish budding humorists as well as provide an outlet for previously published authors. The contest includes 2 categories: poetry and prose. Poetry: 100 lines or less and can be a parody of a popular poem. Fiction or nonfiction prose: 1,000 words or less. Prizes will be awarded based on merit, not the style of the entry." **Deadline: October 1 and April 1.** Guidelines for SASE. **Charges $5 entry fee.** Prize: 1 "Editor's Choice" winner from each 6-month period will receive $50. 4 runners-up will also be selected each period. All 10 winners will have their work published in a Summer anthology, and all 10 will receive a copy of the publication. Judged by editor and staff. Acquires one-time publication rights. Open to any writer.

SHORT GRAIN WRITING CONTEST, *Grain* Magazine, Box 67, Saskatoon SK S7K 3K1, Canada. (306)244-2828. Fax: (306)244-0255. E-mail: grainmag@sasktel.net. Website: www.grainmagazine.ca. **Contact:** Jennifer Still. Contest Director: Elizabeth Philips. Offered annually for unpublished dramatic monologues, postcard stories (narrative fiction) and prose (lyric) poetry, and nonfiction creative prose. Maximum length for short entries, 500 words; Long Grain of Truth (nonfiction), 5,000 words or less. Guidelines for SAE and IRC or Canadian stamps. All entrants receive a 1-year subscription to *Grain*. *Grain* purchases first Canadian serial rights only; copyright remains with the author. Open to any writer. No fax or e-mail submissions. **Deadline: January 31. Charges $25 fee for 2 entries, plus $5 for additional entries; US and international entries $25, plus $4 postage in US funds (non-Canadian).** Prize: Three prizes of $500 in each category.

SHORT PROSE COMPETITION FOR DEVELOPING WRITERS, The Writers' Union of Canada, 40 Wellington St. E., 3rd Floor, Toronto ON M5E 1C7, Canada. (416)703-8982, ext. 223. Fax: (416)504-7656. E-mail: projects@writersunion.ca. Website: www.writersunion.ca. **Contact:** Project Coordinator. Offered annually "to discover developing Canadian writers of unpublished prose fiction and nonfiction." Length: 2,500 words maximum. Open to Canadian citizens or landed immigrants who have not been published in book format, and who do not currently have a contract with a publisher. **Deadline: November 3.** Guidelines for SASE. **Charges $25 entry fee.** Prize: $2,500, and possible publication in a literary journal.

THE BERNICE SLOTE AWARD, *Prairie Schooner*, 201 Andrews Hall, PO Box 880334, Lincoln NE 68588-0334. (402)472-0911. Fax: (402)472-9771. E-mail: eflanagan2@unl.edu. Website: www.unl.edu/schooner/psmain.htm. **Contact:** Hilda Raz. Offered annually for the best work by a beginning writer published in *Prairie Schooner* in the previous year. Prize: $500.

SOUTHWEST REVIEW AWARDS, Southern Methodist University, 307 Fondren Library W., P.O. Box 750374, Dallas TX 75275-0374. (214)768-1036. Fax: (214)768-1408. E-mail: swr@mail.smu.edu. Website: www.southwestreview.org. **Contact:** Elizabeth Mills. "The $500 John H. McGinnis Memorial Award is given each year for fiction and nonfiction that has been published in the *Southwest Review* in the previous year. Stories or articles are not submitted directly for the award, but simply for publication in the magazine. The Elizabeth Matchett Stover Award, an annual prize of $250, is awarded to the author of the best poem or group of poems published in the *Southwest Review* during the preceding year. Stories or articles are not submitted directly for the award, but simply for publication in the magazine. Morton Marr Poetry Prize gives an annual award of $1,000 to a poem by a writer who has not yet published a first book. Contest entry fee is $5/poem. Entry deadline is November 30."

WALLACE STEGNER FELLOWSHIPS, Creative Writing Program, Stanford University, Dept. of English, Stanford CA 94305-2087. (650)723-2637. Fax: (650)723-3679. E-mail: gay.pierce@leland.stanford.edu. Website: www.stanford.edu/dept/english/cw/. **Contact:** Gay Pierce, program administrator. Offered annually for a 2-year residency at Stanford for emerging writers to attend the Stegner workshop to practice and perfect their craft under the guidance of the creative writing faculty. Guidelines available. **Deadline: December 1. Charges $50 fee.** Prize: Living stipend (currently $22,000/year) and required workshop tuition of $6,500/year.

TENNESSEE WRITERS ALLIANCE LITERARY COMPETITION, Tennessee Writers Alliance, P.O. Box 120396, Nashville TN 37212. Website: www.tn-writers.org. **Contact:** Jane Hicks, competition director. Offered annually for unpublished short fiction and poetry. Membership open to all, regardless of residence, for $25/year; $15/year for students. "For more information and guidelines visit our website or send a SASE." **Deadline: July 1. Charges $10 fee for members, $15 fee for nonmembers.** Prize: 1st Place: $500; 2nd Place: $250; 3rd Place: $100.

THOUGHT MAGAZINE WRITER'S CONTEST, *Thought Magazine*, P.O. Box 117098, Burlingame CA 94011-7098. E-mail: ThoughtMagazine@yahoo.com. Website: www.thoughtmagazine.org. **Contact:** Kevin J. Feeney. Offered twice a year "to recognize and publish quality writing in the areas of short fiction, poetry, and short nonfiction, and to identify and give exposure to writers who have not yet been published." Fiction and nonfiction maximum of 3,000 words; poetry maximum of 100 lines. Include name, address, phone number, and/or e-mail. Buys one-time publication rights for winning entries. **Deadline: August 15 and April 15.** Guidelines for SASE. **Charges $5/story or essay or 3 poems.** Prize: 1st Place: $75, plus publication; 2nd Place: $50, plus publication; all submissions considered for publication.

TORONTO BOOK AWARDS, City of Toronto c/o Toronto Protocol, 100 Queen St. W., 10th Floor, West Tower, City Hall, Toronto ON M5H 2N2, Canada. (416)392-8191. Fax: (416)392-1247. E-mail: bkurmey@toronto.ca. Website: www.toronto.ca/book_awards. **Contact:** Bev Kurmey, protocol consultant. Offered annually for previously published fiction, nonfiction, or juvenile books that are "evocative of Toronto." 2003 marks the 30th anniversary of these awards. Previously published entries must have appeared in print between January 1 and December 31 the year prior to the contest year. **Deadline: February 28.** Guidelines for SASE. Prize: Awards total $15,000. $1,000 to shortlist finalists (usually 4-6) with remainder to the winner. Judged by independent judging committee of 5 people chosen through an application and selection process.

MARK TWAIN AWARD FOR SHORT FICTION, *Red Rock Review*/Community College of Southern Nevada, English Dept., 3200 E. Cheyenne Ave., N. Las Vegas NV 89030. (702)651-4094. Fax: (702)651-4639. E-mail: richard_logsdon@ccsn.nevada.edu. Website: www.ccsn.nevada.edu/english/redrockreview/contest.html. **Contact:** Rich Logsdon, editor. Offered annually for unpublished fiction to emerging writers of fiction and poetry. **Deadline: October 31. Charges $10 fee.** Prize: $1,000.

WESTERN HERITAGE AWARDS, National Cowboy & Western Heritage Museum, 1700 NE 63rd, Oklahoma City OK 73111. (405)478-6404. Fax: (405)478-4714. E-mail: editor@nationalcowboymuseum.org. Website: www.nationalcowboymuseum.org. **Contact:** M.J. VanDeventer, publications director. Offered annually for excellence in representation of great stories of the American West published November 30-December 1. Competition includes 7 literary categories: nonfiction, western novel, juvenile book, art book, short story, poetry book, and magazine article.

WESTERN MAGAZINE AWARDS, Western Magazine Awards Foundation, Main Post Office, Box 2131, Vancouver BC V6B 3T8, Canada. (604)669-3717. Fax: (604)669-3701. E-mail: wma@direct.ca. Website: www.westernmagazineawards.com. **Contact:** Bryan Pike. Offered annually for magazine work published January 1-December 31 of previous calendar year. Entry categories include business, culture, science, technology and medicine, entertainment, fiction, political issues, and much more. Guidelines for SASE or on website. Applicant must be Canadian citizen, landed immigrant, or full-time resident. The work must have been published in a magazine whose main editorial office is in Western Canada, the Northwest Territories, and Yukon. **Deadline: February 23. Charges $27 for work in magazines with circulation under 20,000; $35 for work in magazines with circulation over 20,000.** Prize: $500.

WESTMORELAND POETRY & SHORT STORY CONTEST, (formerly Westmoreland Short Story & Poetry Contest), Westmoreland Arts & Heritage Festival, RR 2, Box 355A, Latrobe PA 15650-9415. (724)834-7474. Fax: (724)850-7474. E-mail: info@artsandheritage.com. **Contact:** Donnie A. Gutherie. Offered annually for unpublished work. Writers are encouraged to submit short stories from all genres. The purpose of the contest is to provide writers varied competition in 2 categories: short story and poetry. Entries must be 4,000 words or less. No erotica or pornography. **Deadline: March.** Guidelines for SASE. **Charges $10 fee/story, $10 fee/2 poems.** Prize: Up to $200 in prizes.

WILLA LITERARY AWARD, Women Writing the West, 8547 E. Arapahoe Rd., #J541, Greenwood Village CO 80112-1436. (210)695-5328. Fax: (210)695-5227. E-mail: CMass22@aol.com. Website: www.womenwritingthewest.org. **Contact:** Cynthia Massey, contest director. "The WILLA Literary Award honors the best in literature featuring women's stories set in the West published each year. Women Writing the West (WWW), a nonprofit association of writers and other professionals writing and promoting the Women's West, underwrites and presents the nationally recognized award annually (for work published between January 1 and December 31). The award is named in honor of Pulitzer Prize winner Willa Cather, one of the country's foremost novelists. The award is given in 7 categories: historical fiction, contemporary fiction, original softcover, nonfiction, memoir/essay nonfiction, poetry, and children's/young adult fiction/nonfiction." **Deadline: March 1, 2004.** Guidelines for SASE. **Charges $50 entry fee.** Prize: Each winner receives $100, and a trophy award. Each finalist receives a plaque. Award announcement is in early August, and awards are presented to the winners and finalists at the annual WWW Fall Conference. Judged by professional librarians, not affiliated with WWW. Open to any writer.

N **WILLAMETTE AWARD FOR FICTION AND POETRY**, *Clackamas Literary Review*, 19600 S. Molalla Ave., Oregon City OR 97045. (503)657-6958. E-mail: clr@clackamasliteraryreview.com. Website: www.clackamasliteraryreview.com. **Contact:** Kate Gray or Amanda Coffey. Annual award to "celebrate and reward the best fiction and poetry written by established or emerging writers." **Deadline: June 1.** Guidelines for SASE. **Charges $10.** Prize: $500 for each winner (1 in poetry, 1 in fiction). Judged by a prominent writer. Open to any writer.

WIND CONTESTS, (formerly Wind Magazine Contests), *Wind*, P.O. Box 24548, Lexington KY 40524. (859)277-6849. Website: www.wind.wind.org. **Contact:** Chris Green, editor. Offered annually for unpublished poems, chapbooks, and short stories. Consult website or send SASE for guidelines. **Deadline: March 1 for poems; July 30 for short stories; October 31 for chapbooks.** Guidelines for SASE. **Charges $3/poem, $10/short story, and $15/chapbook.** Prize: $500, and publication in *Wind* for winning poem and short story; $100 plus 25 copies of winning chapbook; chapbook is published as summer issue of *Wind*. All entries receive copy of chapbook. All finalists receive a 1-year subscription to the magazine. Enclose SASE for results.

N **L.L. WINSHIP/PEN NEW ENGLAND AWARD**, PEN New England, P.O. Box 400725, Cambridge MA 02140. (617)499-9550. E-mail: awards@pen-ne.org. Website: www.pen-ne.org. **Contact:** Mary Sullivan, coordinator. Offered annually for work published in the previous calendar year. This annual prize is offered for the best book by a New England author or with a New England topic or setting. Open to fiction, nonfiction, and poetry. **Deadline: December 15.** Guidelines for SASE.

N **WOMEN IN THE ARTS ANNUAL FICTION CONTEST**, Women In the Arts, P.O. Box 2907, Decatur IL 62524. (217)872-0811. **Contact:** Vice President. Annual competition for essays, fiction, fiction for children, plays, rhymed poetry, and unrhymed poetry. **Deadline: November 1.** Guidelines for SASE. **Charges $2/submission.** Prize: 1st Prize: $50; 2nd Prize: $35; 3rd Prize: $15. Judged by professional writers. Open to any writer.

N **WOMEN'S EMPOWERMENT AWARDS WRITING COMPETITION**, E.F.S Online Publishing, 2844 Eighth Ave., Suite 6E, New York NY 10039-2171. (800)835-3957. Website: www.efs-enterprises.com. **Contact:** Rita Baxter. Offered annually, for unpublished work, to both empower women and to provide writers the opportunity to publish their work in the following categories: fiction, playwriting, and essays. **Deadline: November 15.** Guidelines for SASE. **Charges $20/ms.** Prize: $50, and electronic publishing contract. Open to any writer.

JOHN WOOD COMMUNITY COLLEGE ADULT CREATIVE WRITING CONTEST, (formerly Quincy Writer's Guild Annual Creative Writing Contest), 1301 S. 48th St., Quincy IL 62305. Website: www.jwcc.edu. **Contact:** Sherry L. Sparks, contest coordinator. Categories include serious poetry, light poetry, nonfiction, fiction. "No identification should appear on manuscripts, but send a separate 3×5 card for each entry with name, address, phone number, e-mail address, word count, title of work, and category in which each work should be entered." Only for previously unpublished work: serious or light poetry (2 page/poem maximum), fiction (2,000 words maximum), nonfiction (2,000 words maximum). Guidelines for SASE or online. Period of Contest: January 1-April 1. Contest in conjunction with Mid Mississippi Review Writer's Conference. **Charges $3/poem; $5/fiction or nonfiction.** Prize: Cash prizes dictated by the number of entries received.

N **THE WORD GUILD CANADIAN WRITING AWARDS**, (*formerly the God Uses Ink Awards*), The Word Guild, Box 487, Markham, ON L3P 3R1. E-mail: info@thewordguild.com. Website: www.thewordguild.com. **Contact:** Audrey Dorsch. This contest is offered "to encourage writers who are Christian by giving recognition to excellence." Open to Canadian citizens only. The Castle Quay Award is open to Canadian citizens only and someone who has never had a book published. The Youth! Write Award is open to Canadian citizens only ages 15-25. **Categories for work published in 2002:** Nonfiction Books (life stories, personal growth, relationships, culture, leadership and philosophy, and special—books of poetry, anthology, etc.); Novels (literary/mainstream); Children & Young Adult Books (novels and nonfiction); Self-Published Books; Articles (news, feature, column/editorial/opinion, personal experience, devotional/inspirational, humor); Letter to the Editor; Short Story (fiction); Children & Young Adult (articles and short stories); Poetry (rhymed or free verse; maximum of 40 lines). **Categories for unpublished work:** Castle Quay Books Unpublished Mss 1st-Time Author Award (must send entire mss—see guidelines on website); Youth! Write Award (specific details on website). Annually. **Deadline: January 10 for published work; April 1 for unpublished work.** Guidelines for SASE. **Charges $40 (Canadian)/$30 (US) for books; $20 (Canadian)/$15 (US) for short items.** Prize: Book Awards: $200; Short Items: $100; Castle Quay Books Award: Ms published; Youth! Write Award: Registration at the God Uses Ink conference, plus runners-up awards. Judged by writers, editors, etc.

Arts Councils & Foundations

ALABAMA STATE COUNCIL ON THE ARTS FELLOWSHIP-LITERATURE, (formerly Fellowship-Literature), Alabama State Council on the Arts, 201 Monroe St., Montgomery AL 36130. (334)242-4076, ext. 224. Fax: (334)240-3269. E-mail: randy@arts.state.al.us. Website: www.arts.state.al.us. **Contact:** Randy Shoults. Literature fellowship offered every year, for previously published or unpublished work to set aside time to create and to improve skills. Two-year Alabama residency required. Guidelines available. **Deadline: March 1.** Prize: $10,000 or $5,000.

N **AMERICAN PRINTING HISTORY ASSOCIATION FELLOWSHIP IN PRINTING HISTORY**, American Printing History Association, P.O. Box 4519, Grand Central Station, New York NY 10163. E-mail: programs@printinghistor y.org. Website: www.printinghistory.org. **Contact:** Mark Samuels Lasner, VP for programs. Annual award for research in any area of the history of printing in all its forms, including all the arts and technologies relevant to printing, the book arts, and letter forms. Applications are especially welcome from those working in the area of American printing history, but the subject of research has no geographical or chronological limitations, and may be national or regional in scope, biographical, analytical, technical, or bibliographic in nature. Printing history-related study with a recognized printer or book artist may also be supported. The fellowship can be used to pay for travel, living, and other expenses. Applicants are asked to submit an application form, a curriculum vitae, and a 1-page proposal. Two confidential letters of recommendation specific to this fellowship should be sent separately by the recommenders. **Deadline: December 1.** Guidelines for SASE. Prize: Up to $2,000. Judged by a committee. Open to any writer.

ART COOPERATIVE FICTION FELLOWSHIP, (formerly Art Coop Fiction Fellowship), Cottonwood Art Co-operative, 1124 Columbia NE, Albuquerque NM 87106. E-mail: art_coop@yahoo.com. Website: www.geocities.com/art_coop. **Contact:** Editor-in-Chief. Offered annually. For most recent information, please visit website or write for guidelines with SASE. Submit with cover sheet, bio, and publications list. Open to any writer. **Deadline: December 1 (postmark). Charges $15 for 3-50 page portfolio.** For additional flat fee of $15 and SASE, feedback provided on fiction. Prize: Cash award to be determined, not less than $250, and publication to support serious, aspiring authors. Open to any writer.

N **ARTIST TRUST/WASHINGTON STATE ARTS COMMISSION FELLOWSHIP AWARDS**, Artist Trust, 1835 12th Ave., Seattle WA 98122-2437. (206)467-8734. E-mail: info@artisttrust.org. Website: www.artisttrust.org. **Contact:** Susan Myers, program director. "The fellowship is a merit-based award of $6,000 to practicing professional Washington State artists of exceptional talent and demonstrated ability." Applicants must be individual artists; Washington State residents; not matriculated students; and generative artists. Offered every 2 years in odd years. **Deadline: June 20.** Guidelines for SASE. Judged by a selection panel of artists and/or arts professionals in the field chosen by the Artist Trust staff. Prize: $6,000.

ARTS RECOGNITION AND TALENT SEARCH, National Foundation for Advancement in the Arts, 800 Brickell Ave., Suite 500, Miami FL 33131. (305)377-1140 or (800)970-ARTS. Fax: (305)377-1149. E-mail: info@nfaa.org. Website: www.ARTSawards.org. **Contact:** Christopher Schram, programs officer. Estab. 1981. For high school seniors in dance, music, jazz, photography, theater, film & videos, visual art, voice, and writing. Applications available on website or by phone request. **Deadline: Early-June 1 ($30 fee); regular-October 1 ($40 fee).** Prize: Individual awards range from $100-10,000 in an awards package totalling $900,000—$3 million in scholarship opportunities and the chance to be named Presidential Scholars in the Arts.

GEORGE BENNETT FELLOWSHIP, Phillips Exeter Academy, 20 Main St., Exeter NH 03833-2460. Website: www.exeter.edu. **Contact:** Charles Pratt, coordinator, selection committee. Estab. 1968. Annual award for Fellow and family "to provide time and freedom from material considerations to a person seriously contemplating or pursuing a career as a writer. Applicants should have a manuscript in progress which they intend to complete during the fellowship period." Duties: To be in residency for the academic year; to make oneself available informally to students interested in writing. Guidelines for SASE or on website. The committee favors writers who have not yet published a book with a major publisher. Residence at the Academy during the Fellowship period required. **Deadline: December 1.** Prize: $10,000 stipend, room and board.

BUSH ARTIST FELLOWS PROGRAM, The Bush Foundation, E-900 First National Bank Bldg., 332 Minnesota St., St. Paul MN 55101. (651)227-0891. Fax: (651)297-6485. Website: www.bushfoundation.org. **Contact:** Kathi Polley, program assistant. Estab. 1976. Award for Minnesota, North Dakota, South Dakota, and western Wisconsin residents 25 years or older (students are not eligible) "to buy 12-18 months of time for the applicant to further his/her own work." All application categories rotate on a 2-year cycle. Publishing, performance, and/or option requirements for eligibility. Applications available August 2004. **Deadline: October.** Prize: Up to 15 fellowships/year, $44,000 each.

N **CHESTERFIELD WRITERS FILM PROJECT FELLOWSHIP**, The Chesterfield Writers Film Project, 1158 26th St., PMB 544, Santa Monica CA 90403. (213)683-3977. E-mail: info@chesterfield-co.com. Website: www.chesterfield-co.com. **Contact:** Edward Rugoff. This annual contest is offered "to nurture the talent of aspiring screenwriters." **Deadline: May 15.** Guidelines for SASE. **Charges $39.50.** Prize: "We award up to 5 $20,000 fellowships. In addition, each fellow participates in a 10-month screenwriting workshop under the guidance of a professional screenwriter and a Paramount Studio executive." Judged by Chesterfield staff. Open to any writer.

N **CITYARTISTS PROGRAM**, Office of Arts & Cultural Affairs, 700—5th Ave., Suite 1766, Seattle WA 98104. (206)684-7171. Fax: (206)684-7172. Website: www.cityofseattle.gov/arts/. **Contact:** Irene Gomez, project manager. The CityArtists Program funds new or remounted work by Seattle-based artists. The project-based application is available every year for clusters of disciplines in alternate years. Next program deadline in 2004 will be open to the following primary disciplines: literary, visual, and film new media. Interdisciplinary and Traditional/Living Arts that include the primary disciplines can apply every year. Decided through an open, competitive, peer-panel review process, and subject to approval by the full Commission. Applicants must have 1 year residence or permanent work space in the city of Seattle, Washington. Guidelines available 2 months prior to deadline. Prize: Awards range from $1,000-10,000.

N **CONNECTICUT COMMISSION ON THE ARTS ARTIST FELLOWSHIPS**, One Financial Plaza, Hartford CT 06103-2601. (860)566-4770. Fax: (860)566-6462. Website: www.ctarts.org/artfellow.htm. **Contact:** Linda Dente, program manager. **Deadline: September 2004.** Prize: $5,000, and $2,500. Judged by peer professionals (writers, editors).

N **CREATIVE SCOTLAND AWARD**, Scottish Arts Council, 12 Manor Place, Edinburgh Scotland EH3 7DD, United Kingdom. E-mail: help.desk@scottisharts.org.uk. Website: www.scottisharts.org.uk. The purpose of the award is to create a dynamic arts environment which enhances the quality of life for the people of Scotland. The annual award provides a unique opportunity to experiment and realize imaginative ideas in a major project. Guidelines for SASE. Prize: Cash prize. Judged by an independent final panel.

[N] **DELAWARE DIVISION OF THE ARTS**, 820 N. French St., Wilmington DE 19801. (302)577-8284. Fax: (302)577-6561. E-mail: kpleasanton@state.de.us. Website: www.artsdel.org. **Contact:** Kristin Pleasanton, coordinator. Award offered annually "to help further careers of Delaware's emerging and established professional artists." Annually. **Deadline: August 1.** Guidelines for SASE. Prize: $10,000 for masters, $5,000 for established professionals; $2,000 for emerging professionals. Judged by out-of-state professionals in each division.

[N] **DOCTORAL DISSERTATION FELLOWSHIPS IN JEWISH STUDIES**, National Foundation for Jewish Culture, 330 7th Ave., 21st Floor, New York NY 10001. (212)629-0500. Fax: (212)629-0508. E-mail: grants@jewishculture.org. Website: www.jewishculture.org/grants. Offered annually to students. Deadline varies, usually early January. Open to students who have completed their course work and need funding for research in order to write their dissertation thesis or a Ph.D. in a Jewish field of study. Guidelines for SASE. Prize: $7,000-$10,000 grant.

[N] **GAP (GRANTS FOR ARTIST PROJECTS) PROGRAM**, Artist Trust, 1835 12th Ave., Seattle WA 98122. (206)467-8734. Fax: (206)467-9633. E-mail: info@artisttrust.org. Website: www.artisttrust.org. **Contact:** Program Director. "The GAP is awarded annually to approximately 50 artists, including writers, per year. The award is meant to help finance a specific project, which can be in very early stages or near completion. Literature fellowships are offered every other year, and approximately 6 $6,000 literature fellowships are awarded. The award is made on the basis of work of the past 5 years." Full-time students are not eligible. Open to Washington state residents only. **Deadline: The last Friday of February.** Guidelines for SASE. Prize: Up to $1,400 for artist-generated projects.

GEILFUSS, HUNTER & SMITH FELLOWSHIPS, Wisconsin Historical Society, 816 State St., Madison WI 53706-1482. (608)264-6461. Fax: (608)264-6486. E-mail: jkcalder@whs.wisc.edu. Website: www.wisconsinhistory.org. **Contact:** Kent Calder. Offered quarterly for unpublished writing on Wisconsin history. Guidelines for SASE or on website at: www.wisconsinhistory.org/research/fellowships.html. Rights acquired if award is accepted. Prize: $500-3,000.

GIFT OF FREEDOM, A Room of Her Own Foundation, P.O. Box 778, Placitas NM 87043. E-mail: info@aroomofherownfoundation.org. Website: www.aroomofherownfoundation.org. **Contact:** Darlene Chandler Bassett. Award offered every other year to provide very practical help both materially and in professional guidance and moral support, to women who need assistance in making their creative contribution to the world. Guidelines available on website. **Deadline: February 1. Charges $25.** Prize: Up to $50,000 over two years, also a mentor for advice and dialogue, and access to the Advisory Council for professional and business consultation. Judged by members of AROHO's Board of Directors, Advisory Council, and volunteers from a wide variety of backgrounds.

[N] **HAWAI'I AWARD FOR LITERATURE**, State Foundation on Culture and the Arts, 250 S. Hotel St., 2nd Floor, Honolulu HI 96813. (808)586-0303. Fax: (808)586-0308. E-mail: sfca@sfca.state.hi.us. Website: www.state.hi.us/sfca. **Contact:** Hawai'i Literary Arts Council (Box 11213, Honolulu HI 96828-0213). "The annual award honors the lifetime achievement of a writer whose work is important to Hawai'i and/or Hawai'i's people." Nominations are a public process; inquiries should be directed to the Hawai'i Literary Arts Council at address listed. "Cumulative work is considered. Self nominations are allowed, but not usual. Fiction, poetry, drama, certain types of nonfiction, screenwriting and song lyrics are considered. The award is not intended to recognize conventional academic writing and reportage, nor is it intended to recognize more commercial types of writing, e.g., advertising copy, tourist guides, and how-to manuals." **Deadline: November.** Prize: Governor's reception and cash award.

THE HODDER FELLOWSHIP, The Council of the Humanities, Joseph Henry House, Princeton University, Princeton NJ 08544. (609)258-4717. Fax: (609)258-2783. E-mail: humcounc@princeton.edu. Website: www.princeton.edu/~humcounc/. **Contact:** Cass Garner. The Hodder Fellowship is awarded to a humanist in the early stages of a career for the pursuit of independent work at Princeton in the humanities. The recipient has usually written 1 book and is working on a second. Preference is given to applicants outside of academia. "The Fellowship is designed specifically to identify and nurture extraordinary potential rather than to honor distinguished achievement." Candidates for the Ph.D. are not eligible. Submit résumé, sample of work (up to 10 pages), proposal, and SASE. **Deadline: November 1.** Prize: Approximately $51,000 stipend.

[N] **ILLINOIS ART COUNCIL ARTISTS FELLOWSHIP PROGRAM IN POETRY & PROSE**, Illinois Art Council, 100 W. Randolph, Suite 10-500, Chicago IL 60601. (312)814-6740. Fax: (312)814-1471. E-mail: susan@arts.state.il.us. Website: www.state.il.us/agency/iac. **Contact:** Susan Eleuterio, director, literature. Offered biannually for Illinois writers of exceptional talent to enable them to pursue their artistic goals. Applicant must have been a resident of Illinois for at least 1 year prior to the deadline. Guidlines for SASE. **Deadline: September 1, 2003 (prose); September 1, 2004 (poetry).** Prize: Nonmatching award of $7,000; finalist award of $700.

CHRISTOPHER ISHERWOOD FELLOWSHIPS, Christopher Isherwood Foundation, Box 650, Montrose AL 36559. E-mail: james@americanartists.org. Website: www.isherwoodfoundation.org. **Contact:** James P. White, executive director. Awards are given annually to selected novelists who have published a novel. **Deadline: October 1.** Prize: Fellowship consists of $3,000. Judged by advisory board.

[N] **KANSAS ARTS COMMISSION INDIVIDUAL ARTIST FELLOWSHIPS/MINI-FELLOWSHIPS**, Kansas Arts Commission, 700 SW Jackson St., Suite 1004, Topeka KS 66603-3761. (785)296-3335. Fax: (785)296-4989. E-mail: kac@arts.state.ks.us. Website: arts.state.ks.us. **Contact:** Karen Brady. Offered annually for Kansas artists, both published and unpublished. Fellowships are offered in 10 artistic disciplines, rotating 5 disciplines every other year, and are awarded based on artistic merit. The fellowship disciplines are: music composition, choreography, film/video, interdisciplinary/ performance art, playwriting, fiction, poetry, 2-dimensional visual art, 3-dimensional visual art, and crafts. Mini-fellowships (up to 12) are awarded annually to emerging artists in the same 10 disciplines. Guidelines on website. **Deadline: Varies.** Prize: Fellowship: $5,000. Mini-fellowship: $500.

EZRA JACK KEATS MEMORIAL FELLOWSHIP, Ezra Jack Keats Foundation (funding) awarded through Kerlan Collection, University of Minnesota, 113 Andersen Library, 222 21st Ave. S., Minneapolis MN 55455. (612)624-4576. Fax: (612)625-5525. E-mail: CLRC@tc.umn.edu. Website: special.lib.umn.edu/clrc/. **Contact:** Library Assistant. Purpose is "to award a talented writer and/or illustrator of children's books who wishes to use Kerlan Collection for the furtherance of his or her artistic development. Special consideration will be given to someone who would find it difficult to finance the visit to the Kerlan Collection." Open to any writer and illustrator. **Deadline: May 1.** Guidelines for SASE. Prize: $1,500 for travel to study at Kerlan Collection.

N **MASSACHUSETTS CULTURAL COUNCIL ARTISTS GRANTS PROGRAM**, Massachusetts Cultural Council, 10 St. James Ave., Boston MA 02116-3803. (617)727-3668. Fax: (617)727-0044. E-mail: mcc@art.state.ma.us. Website: www.massculturalcouncil.org. **Contact:** Elaine Mariner, director of programs. Awards in poetry, fiction, and playwriting/ new theater works (among other discipline categories) are $5,000 each in recognition of exceptional original work. Criteria: Artistic excellence and creative ability, based on work submitted for review. Judged by independent peer panels composed of artists and art professionals.

N **MINNESOTA STATE ARTS BOARD ARTIST ASSISTANCE FELLOWSHIP**, Minnesota State Arts Board, Park Square Court, 400 Sibley St., Suite 200, St. Paul MN 55101-1928. (651)215-1600 or (800)866-2787. Fax: (651)215-1602. E-mail: amy.frimpong@arts.state.mn.us. Website: www.arts.state.mn.us. **Contact:** Amy Frimpong. Literary categories include prose, poetry, playwriting, and screenwriting. Open to Minnesota residents. Prize: Annual fellowships of $8,000 to be used for time, materials, living expenses.

MONEY FOR WOMEN, Barbara Deming Memorial Fund, Inc., P.O. Box 630125, The Bronx NY 10463. **Contact:** Susan Pliner. "Small grants to individual feminists in fiction, nonfiction, and poetry, whose work addresses women's concerns and/or speaks for peace and justice from a feminist perspective." Guidelines and required entry forms for SASE. "The Fund does not give educational assistance, monies for personal study or loans, monies for dissertation, research projects, or self-publication, grants for group projects, business ventures, or emergency funds for hardships." Open to citizens of the US or Canada. The fund also offers 2 awards, the Gertrude Stein Award for outstanding works by a lesbian and the Fannie Lou Hamer Award for work which combats racism and celebrates women of color. No special application necessary for these 2 awards. Recipients will be chosen from all the proposals. **Deadline: December 31 (fiction) and June 30 (nonfiction and poetry).** Prize: Grants up to $1,500.

JENNY McKEAN/MOORE VISITING WRITER, English Dept., George Washington University, Washington DC 20052. (202)994-6180. Fax: (202)994-7915. E-mail: dmca@gwu.edu. Website: www.gwu.edu/~english. **Contact:** David McAleavey. Offered annually to provide 1-year visiting writers to teach 1 George Washington course and 1 free community workshop each semester. Guidelines for SASE or on website. This contest seeks someone specializing in a different genre each year; in 2004-2005, a fiction writer. **Deadline: November 15.** Prize: Annual stipend approximately $50,000, plus reduced-rent townhouse (not guaranteed).

N **WILLIAM MORRIS SOCIETY IN THE US FELLOWSHIP**, William Morris Society in the US, P.O. Box 53263, Washington DC 20009. E-mail: us@morrissociety.org. Website: www.morrissociety.org. **Contact:** Mark Samuels Lasner. Offered annually "to promote study of the life and work of William Morris (1834-96), British poet, designer, and socialist. Award may be for research or a creative project." Curriculum vitae, 1-page proposal, and 2 letters of recommendation required for application. Applicants must be US citizens or permanent residents. **Deadline: December 1.** Prize: Up to $1,000, multiple, partial awards possible.

N **NEBRASKA ARTS COUNCIL INDIVIDUAL ARTISTS FELLOWSHIPS**, Nebraska Arts Council, 3838 Davenport St., Omaha NE 68131-2329. (402)595-2122. Fax: (402)595-2334. E-mail: swise@nebraskaartscouncil.org. Website: www.nebraskaartscouncil.org. **Contact:** Suzanne Wise. Estab. 1991. Offered every 3 years (literature alternates with other disciplines) to recognize exemplary achievements by originating artists in their fields of endeavor and support the contributions made by Nebraska artists to the quality of life in this state. "Generally, distinguished achievement awards are $5,000 and merit awards are $1,000-2,000. Funds available are announced in September prior to the deadline." Must be a resident of Nebraska for at least 2 years prior to submission date; 18 years of age; not enrolled in an undergraduate, graduate, or certificate-granting program in English, creative writing, literature, or related field. **Deadline: November 15, 2005.** Prize: $5,000, and merit awards are $1,000-2,000.

N **NEW JERSEY STATE COUNCIL ON THE ARTS FELLOWSHIP PROGRAM**, New Jersey State Council on the Arts, 225 W. State St., P.O. Box 306, Trenton NJ 08625. (609)292-6130. Fax: (609)989-1440. E-mail: njsca@njartscouncil.org. Website: www.njartscouncil.org. **Contact:** Beth A. Vogel, program officer. Offered every other year. Writers may apply in either poetry, playwriting, or prose. Fellowship awards are intended to provide support for the artist during the year to enable him or her to continue producing new work. Send for guidelines and application, or visit website. Must be New Jersey residents; may *not* be undergraduate or graduate matriculating students. **Deadline: July 15.** Prize: $5,000-12,000.

N **NEW WRITERS' BURSARIES**, Scottish Arts Council, 12 Manor Place, Edinburgh EH3 7DD, Scotland. (0131) 2266051. Fax: (0131) 225 9833. E-mail: help.desk@scottisharts.org.uk. Website: www.scottisharts.org.uk. Offered annually to assist new writers with little or no previous publication based in Scotland who need finance for a period of concentrated work on their writing or to buy equipment. A portfolio of writing, which should include work-in-progress amounting to 20 pages. Work in progress must be typed. Statement from a "referee" who should have special knowledge of the writer's work (such as a writer, publisher, editor, or literary agent). Open to writers who have their principal residence in Scotland. Full-time students are not eligible to apply. **Deadline: April 4.** Guidelines for SASE. Prize: 10 grants of £2,000 are available. Judged by the New Writers' Bursaries Group.

OREGON LITERARY FELLOWSHIPS, Literary Arts, Inc., 219 NW 12th Ave., #219, Portland OR 97203. (503)227-2583. E-mail: la@literary-arts.org. Website: www.literary-arts.org. **Contact:** Kristy Athens, award coordinator. The annual Oregon Literary Fellowships support Oregon writers with a monetary award. **Deadline: June 27.** Guidelines for SASE. Prize: $500-2,000. Fellows are also offered residencies at Caldera, a writers' retreat in Central Oregon. Judged by judges who are selected from Oregon for their expertise in a genre.

PEW FELLOWSHIPS IN THE ARTS, 230 S. Broad St., Suite 1003, Philadelphia PA 19102. (215)875-2285. Fax: (215)875-2276. Website: www.pewarts.org. **Contact:** Melissa Franklin, director. Offered annually to provide financial support directly to artists so that they may have the opportunity to dedicate themselves wholly to the development of their artwork for up to 2 years. Areas of interest have included fiction, creative nonfiction, poetry, playwriting, and screenwriting. Call for guidelines or view from the website. Entrants must be Pennsylvania residents of Bucks, Chester, Delaware, Montgomery, or Philadelphia counties for 2 years or longer. Current students are not eligible. **Deadline: December.** Prize: $50,000 fellowship.

THE CHARLES PICK FELLOWSHIP, School of English and American Studies, University of East Anglia, Norwich NR4 7TJ, United Kingdom. "The Charles Pick Fellowship is dedicated to the memory of the distinguished publisher and literary agent, Charles Pick. Applicants must be writers of fictional or nonfictional prose (no more than 2,500 words) in English who have not yet published a book." All applicants must provide reference from an editor, agent, or accredited teacher of creative writing. **Deadline: January 31.** Guidelines for SASE. Prize: £10,000. Judged by a distinguished panel of writers. Open to any writer.

RHODE ISLAND STATE COUNCIL ON THE ARTS FELLOWSHIPS (LITERATURE), RI State Council on the Arts, 83 Park St., 6th Floor, Providence RI 02903. (401)222-3880. Fax: (401)222-3018. E-mail: info@risca.state.ri.us. Website: www.risca.state.ri.us. **Contact:** Fellowship Coordinator. Offered every year for previously published or unpublished works in the categories of poetry, fiction, and playwriting/screenwriting. Open to Rhode Island residents only. Guidelines available on website. **Deadline: April 1.** Prize: $5,000 fellowship; $1,000 runner-up.

THE SASKATCHEWAN ARTS BOARD INDIVIDUAL ASSISTANCE GRANT PROGRAM, The Saskatchewan Arts Board, 2135 Broad St., Regina SK S4P 3V7, Canada. (306)787-4056. Fax: (306)787-4199. E-mail: grants@artsboard.sk.ca. Website: www.artsboard.ck.ca. **Contact:** Dianne Warren, literary arts consultant. "The Individual Assistance Grant Program assists the Saskatchewan Arts Board in fulfilling its mandate by providing grants to Saskatchewan artists and individuals active in the arts in the province. These grants support the creation of new work in any art form or development and performance of work; study in a formal or informal setting; research in the arts; or travel to attend events or participate in eligible activities." Applicants must be residents of Saskatchewan and at minimum must have achieved a level of emerging professional in their field. **Deadline: October 1 and March 15.** Prize: **A Grants**: $4,000 (maximum) to artists or individuals working in the arts who have achieved a senior level of accomplishment, and who have made a sustained and progressive nationally or internationally recognized contribution to their discipline or to the arts in general. **B Grants**: $12,000 (maximum) to artists or individuals working in the arts who have been practicing professionally in their discipline or in the arts for a sustained period of time, and are able to demonstrate a regionally or nationally recognized contribution to their discipline or to the arts in general. **C Grants**: $20,000 (maximum) to artists or individuals working in the arts striving to achieve a professional level in their discipline and who can demonstrate their commitment to the achievement of a professional level in their discipline through training, mentorships, or peer recognition and are producing a growing repertoire of work. Judged by a panel of adjudicators consisting of a jury of professionals in each artistic discipline.

THE SOCIETY FOR THE SCIENTIFIC STUDY OF SEXUALITY STUDENT RESEARCH GRANT, The Society for the Scientific Study of Sexuality, P.O. Box 416, Allentown PA 18105-0416. (610)530-2483. Fax: (610)530-2485. E-mail: thesociety@inetmail.att.net. Website: www.sexscience.org. **Contact:** Ilsa Lottes. Offered twice a year for unpublished works. "The student research grant award is granted twice yearly to help support graduate student research on a variety of sexually related topics." Guidelines and entry forms for SASE. Open to students pursuing graduate study. **Deadline: February 1 and September 1.** Prize: $1,000.

TENNESSEE ARTS COMMISSION LITERARY FELLOWSHIP, Tennessee Arts Commission, 401 Charlotte Ave., Nashville TN 37243-0780. (615)741-2093. Website: www.arts.state.tn.us. **Contact:** M. Flint Clouse, director of arts programs. Offered annually. Applicant must have some history of publication, but not specifically this work submitted. "This award is designed to recognize Tennessee professional artists, i.e., those individuals who either by education, experience, or natural talent engage in a particular art form or discipline. Because of this participation, they are financially compensated for such, and this compensation provides the major source of support for their livelihood." Provides 1 fellowship to "an outstanding literary artist who lives and works in Tennessee. This year, applicants must be writers of prose and must be able to show a history of publication other than vanity press. A journalist whose only publication has been through the media for which he or she works is not eligible." **Deadline: January 21.** Guidelines for SASE. Prize: $5,000. Judged by a professional chosen by the staff.

TRILLIUM BOOK AWARD/PRIX TRILLIUM/TRILLIUM BOOK AWARD FOR POETRY, (formerly Trillium Book Award/Prix Trillium), Ontario Media Development Corp., 175 Bloor St. E., North Tower, Suite 300, Toronto ON

M4W 3R8, Canada. (416)314-6568. Fax: (416)314-2495. E-mail: gthomson@omdc.on.ca. Estab. 1994. Offered annually for titles published for the first time in 2002 that will remain in print that year and be available for sale in Spring 2003. Publishers submit titles on behalf of authors. Authors must have been Ontario residents 3 of the last 5 years. **Deadline: November for titles published between January and October; December for books published in November and December.** Guidelines for SASE. Prize: **Trillium Book Award/Priz Trillium:** The winning author in each category (English and French) receives $20,000; the winning publisher in each category receives $2,500. **Trillium Book Award for Poetry:** The winning author in each category (English and French) receives, $10,000; the winning publisher in each category receives $2,000. Judged by a jury of writers, poets, and other members of the literary community.

VERMONT ARTS COUNCIL, 136 State St., Drawer 33, Montpelier VT 05633-6001. (802)828-3291. Fax: (802)828-3363. E-mail: mbailey@vermontartscouncil.org. Website: www.vermontartscouncil.org. **Contact:** Michele Bailey. Offered quarterly for previously published or unpublished works. Opportunity Grants are for specific projects of writers (poetry, playwriters, fiction, nonfiction) as well as not-for-profit presses. Also available are Artist Development funds to provide technical assistance for Vermont writers. Write or call for entry information. Open to Vermont residents only. Prize: $250-5,000.

N **WISCONSIN ARTS BOARD ARTIST FELLOWSHIP AWARDS**, Wisconsin Arts Board, 101 E. Wilson St., 1st Floor, Madison WI 53702. (608)266-0190. Fax: (608)267-0380. E-mail: artsboard@arts.state.wi.us. Website: www.arts.state.wi.us. **Contact:** Mark Fraire, grant programs and services specialist. Offered every 2 years (even years), rewarding outstanding, professionally active Wisconsin artists by supporting their continued development, enabling them to create new work, complete work in progress, or pursue activities which contribute to their artistic growth. If the deadline falls on a weekend, the deadline is extended to the following Monday. Application is found on the Wisconsin Arts Board website at www.arts.state.wi.us on August 2, 2002. The Arts Board requires permission to use the work sample, or a portion thereof, for publicity or educational purposes. Contest open to professionally active artists who have resided in Wisconsin 1 year prior to application. Artists who are full-time students pursuing a degree in the fine arts at the time of application are not eligible. **Deadline: September 17, 2002.** Prize: $8,000 fellowship awarded to 7 Wisconsin writers.

N **DAVID T.K. WONG FELLOWSHIP**, School of English and American Studies, University of East Anglia, Norwich NR4 7TJ, United Kingdom. Offered annually for mss of no more than 5,000 words (in English). The purpose of the award is to promote "excellence in the writing of literature." The Fellowship is awarded to a writer planning to produce a work of prose fiction in English which deals seriously with some aspect of life in the Far East. **Deadline: October 31.** Guidelines for SASE. **Charges £5.** Prize: £25,000. Judged by a distinguished international panel. Open to any writer.

N **WRITER & PLAYWRIGHTS BURSARIES**, Scottish Arts Council, 12 Manor Place, Edinburgh Scotland EH3 7DD, United Kingdom. E-mail: help.desk@scottisharts.org.uk. Website: www.scottisharts.org.uk. Offered twice a year for practicing writers based in Scotland who need finance for a period of concentrated work on their next book. "The bursary may be used to a quiet period of writing at home or elsewhere, or it may be used for necessary travel and research." Submission of a portfolio of writing, which should include work in progress amounting to 20 pages, is required. Work in progress must be typed. A statement from a "referee" who should have specialized knowledge of the writer's work (such as a writer, publisher, editor, or literary agent) is also required. **Deadline: July 26 and December 20.** Guidelines for SASE. Prize: Grants ranging anywhere from £3,000 to £10,000. Judged by Writer's Bursaries Group.

Resources

Publications

In addition to newsletters and publications from local and national organizations, there are trade publications, books, and directories which offer valuable information about writing and about marketing your manuscripts and understanding the business side of publishing. Some also list employment agencies that specialize in placing publishing professionals, and some announce freelance opportunities.

TRADE MAGAZINES

ADVERTISING AGE, Crain Communications, Inc., 711 Third Ave., New York NY 10017-4036. (212)210-0100. Website: www.adage.com. *Weekly magazine covering advertising in magazines, trade journals, and business.*

AMERICAN JOURNALISM REVIEW, University of Maryland, 1117 Journalism Bldg. University of Maryland, College Park MD 20742-7111. (301)405-8803. Website: www.ajr.org. *10 issues/year magazine for journalists and communications professionals.*

DAILY VARIETY, Reed Business Info, 5700 Wilshire Blvd., Suite 120, Los Angeles CA 90036. (323)857-6600. Website: www.variety.com. *Trade publication on the entertainment industry with helpful information for screenwriters.*

EDITOR & PUBLISHER, Adweek Magazines, 770 Broadway, New York NY 10003-9595. (800)562-2706. Website: www.editorandpublisher.com. *Weekly magazine covering the newspaper industry in North America.*

FOLIO: The Magazine for Magazine Management, Primedia Business Magazines & Media, 11 Riverbend Dr. S., P.O. Box 4272, Stamford CT 06907-0272. (203)358-9900. Website: www.foliomag.com. *Monthly magazine covering the magazine publishing industry.*

GIFTS & DECORATIVE ACCESSORIES, Reed Business Information, 360 Park Ave. S., New York NY 10010. (646)746-6400. Website: www.giftsanddec.com. *Monthly magazine covering greeting cards among other subjects, with an annual buyer's directory in September.*

HORN BOOK MAGAZINE, The Horn Book, Inc., 56 Roland St., Suite 200, Boston MA 02129. (617)628-0225. Website: www.hbook.com. *Bimonthly magazine covering children's literature.*

PARTY & PAPER RETAILER, 107 Mill Plain Rd., Danbury CT 06811. (203)730-4090. Website: www.partypaper.com. *Monthly magazine covering the greeting card and gift industry.*

PUBLISHERS WEEKLY, Reed Business Information, 360 Park Ave. S.,, New York NY 10010. (646)746-6758. Website: www.publishersweekly.com. *Weekly magazine covering the book publishing industry.*

TRAVELWRITER MARKETLETTER, P.O. 1782, Springfield VA 22151. (253)399-6270. Website: www.travelwriterml.com. *Monthly newsletter for travel writers with market listings as well as trip information.*

WRITER'S DIGEST, 4700 E. Galbraith Rd., Cincinnati OH 45236. (800)333-0133. Website: www.writersdigest.com. *Monthly writers' magazine.*

BOOKS AND DIRECTORIES

AGENTS, EDITORS, AND YOU, edited by Michelle Howry, Writer's Digest Books, 4700 E. Galbraith Rd., Cincinnati OH 45236. (800)448-0915. Website: www.writersdigest.com.

AV MARKET PLACE, R.R. Bowker, 630 Central Ave., New Providence NJ 07974. (888)269-5372. Website: www.bowker.com.

BACON'S NEWSPAPER/MAGAZINE DIRECTORY, Bacon's Information, Inc., 332 S. Michigan Ave., Chicago IL 60604. (312)922-2400. Website: www.bacons.com.

THE COMPLETE BOOK OF SCRIPTWRITING, by J. Michael Straczynski, Writer's Digest Books, 4700 E. Galbraith Rd., Cincinnati OH 45236. (800)448-0915. Website: www.writersdigest.com.

THE COMPLETE GUIDE TO LITERARY CONTESTS, compiled by Literary Fountain, Prometheus Books, 59 John Glenn Dr., Amherst NY 14228-2197. (800)421-0351. Website: www.prometheusbooks.com.

THE COMPLETE GUIDE TO SELF-PUBLISHING, by Marilyn and Tom Ross, Writer's Digest Books, 4700 E. Galbraith Rd., Cincinnati OH 45236. (800)448-0915. Website: www.writersdigest.com.

DRAMATISTS SOURCEBOOK, edited by Kathy Sova, Theatre Communications Group, Inc., 520 Eighth Ave., 24th Floor, New York NY 10018-4156. (212)609-9100. Website: www.tcg.org.

FORMATTING & SUBMITTING YOUR MANUSCRIPT, by Jack and Glenda Neff, Don Prues and the editors of *Writer's Market*, Writer's Digest Books, 4700 E. Galbraith Rd., Cincinnati OH 45236. (800)448-0915. Website: www.writersdigest.com.

GRANTS AND AWARDS AVAILABLE TO AMERICAN WRITERS, PEN American Center, 568 Broadway, 4th Floor, New York NY 10012. (212)334-1660. Website: www.pen.org.

GUERRILLA MARKETING FOR WRITERS, by Jay Conrad Levinson, Rick Frishman & Michael Larsen, Writer's Digest Books, 4700 E. Galbraith Rd., Cincinnati OH 45236. (800)448-0915. Website: www.writersdigest.com.

HOW TO WRITE IRRESISTIBLE QUERY LETTERS, by Lisa Collier Cool, Writer's Digest Books, 4700 E. Galbraith Rd., Cincinnati OH 45236. (800)448-0915. Website: www.writersdigest.com.

INTERNATIONAL DIRECTORY OF LITTLE MAGAZINES & SMALL PRESSES, edited by Len Fulton, Dustbooks, P.O. Box 100, Paradise CA 95967. (530)877-6110. Website: www.dustbooks.com.

JUMP START YOUR BOOK SALES, by Marilyn & Tom Ross, Writer's Digest Books, 4700 E. Galbraith Rd., Cincinnati OH 45236. (800)448-0915. Website: www.writersdigest.com.

LITERARY MARKET PLACE and INTERNATIONAL LITERARY MARKET PLACE, R.R. Bowker, 630 Central Ave., New Providence NJ 07974. (888)269-9372. Website: www.bowker.com.

MY BIG SOURCEBOOK, EEI Communications, 66 Canal Center Plaza, Suite 200, Alexandria VA 22314. (703)683-0683. Website: www.eeicommunications.com.

ONLINE MARKETS FOR WRITERS: How and Where to Make Money By Selling Your Writing On the Internet, by Anthony and Paul Tedesco, MarketsForWriters.com Press. Website: www.marketsforwriters.com.

ROGET'S DESCRIPTIVE WORD FINDER, by Barbara Ann Kipfer, Writer's Digest Books, 4700 E. Galbraith Rd., Cincinnati OH 45236. (800)448-0915. Website: www.writersdigest.com.

WRITER'S ONLINE MARKETPLACE, by Debbie Ridpath Ohi, Writer's Digest Books, 4700 E. Galbraith Rd., Cincinnati OH 45236. (800)448-0915. Website: www.writersdigest.com.

Websites

The Internet provides a wealth of information for writers. The number of websites devoted to writing and publishing is vast and continues to expand. Below is a short—and thus incomplete—list of websites that offer information and hypertext links to other pertinent sites relating to writing and publishing. Because the Internet is such an amorphous, evolving, mutable entity with website addresses launching, crashing, and changing daily, some of these addresses may be obsolete by the time this book goes to print. But this list does give you a few starting points for your online journey.

Agents

WritersNet: www.writers.net
This site includes a bulletin board where writers can discuss their experiences with agents.

Agent Research and Evaluation: www.agentresearch.com
This is the websiteof AR&E, a company that specializes in keeping tabs on literary agents. For a fee you can order their varied services to learn more about a specific agents.

The Query Guild: www.queryguild.com
A working tool where writers can post queries for samples or receive feedback from other authors.

Writer Beware: www.sfwa.org/beware
The Science Fiction Writers of America's page of warnings about agents and subsidy publishers.

Writer's Market: www.writersmarket.com
This giant, searchable database includes agents and publishers, and offers daily updates tailored to your individual needs.

Link sites

Books A to Z: www.booksatoz.com
Information on publications, services, and leads to other useful websites, including areas for book research, production services, self-publishing, bookstores, organizations, and publishers.

Dictionary.com: www.dictionary.com
If you're not sure about what the word "meticulous" means, then use this searchable site. The site also provides links to Roget's Thesaurus, *international dictionaries, and translator tools.*

Encyclopedia.com: www.encyclopedia.com
This free encyclopedia offers more than 50,000 articles, plus links to more.

Freelance Writers: www.freelancewrite.about.com
Links to resources relating to jobs, business writing, contracts, and grantwriting.

Publishers' Catalogues Home Page: www.lights.com/publisher
A mammoth link collection of publishers around the world arranged geographically. This site is one of the most comprehensive directories of publishers on the Internet.

Thesaurus.com: www.thesaurus.com
Need to find another word for "super"? Then use this searchable thesaurus to find synonyms for words as well as links to international dictionaries and translator tools.

Writing for Dollars: www.awoc.com
Besides the free newsletter, freelance writers will find money-making tips.

Zuzu's Petals Literary Resource: www.zuzu.com
Contains more than 10,000 organized links to helpful resources for writers, researchers, and others. Zuzu's Petals also publishes an electronic quarterly.

Marketing and Publicists

BookTalk: www.booktalk.com
This site "offers authors an opportunity to announce and market new releases to millions of viewers across the globe."

Book Marketing Update: http://bookmarket.com
This website by John Kremer, author of 1001 Ways to Market Your Books *(Open Horizons), offers helpful tips for marketing books and many useful links to publishing websites. Also offers an e-newsletter so writers may share their marketing success stories.*

Guerrilla Marketing: www.gmarketing.com
The authors of Guerrilla Marketing for Writers *(Writer's Digest Books) provide many helpful resources to help you successfully market your book.*

About Publishing: http://publishing.about.com
This website provides a wide range of information about publishing, including several articles on independent publicists.

Authorlink: www.authorlink.com
"The news, information, and marketing community for editors, literary agents, and writers." Showcases manuscripts of experienced and beginning writers.

BookWire: www.bookwire.com
BookWire bills itself as the book industry's most comprehensive online information source. The site includes industry news, features, reviews, fiction, events, interviews, and links to other book sites.

Publishers Lunch: www.publisherslunch.com
This site allows you to sign up for the free newsletter, which offers daily updates on what's going on in the world of publishing. It's a good way to keep on top of the market.

Miscellaneous

Delphi Forums: www.delphiforums.com
This site hosts forums on many topics including writing and publishing. Just type "writing" in the search bar, and you'll find 100 pages where you can talk about your craft.

Freelance Online: www.freelanceonline.com
A directory of, and resource center for, freelancers in the field of communications. Jobs, message boards, a searchable directory of over 700 freelancers, frequently asked questions, resources, and networking for beginning freelancers. The FAQ for freelancers has lots of useful information catalogued and linked especially for freelancing beginners.

Hollywood Network: http://hollywoodnetwork.com
This site covers everything in Hollywood whether it's dealmaking, music, screenwriting, or profiles of agents and Hollywood executives.

Mr. Magazine: www.mrmagazine.com
Find the latest information on consumer magazines. Look for the "30 Most Notable Launches" of the previous year and the monthly titles page—a comprehensive list of every new magazine launched each month.

Novel Advice: www.noveladvice.com
A cyber-journal devoted to the craft of writing. This site offers advice, online courses on the craft of writing (for a fee), and an extensive list of research resources.

ShawGuides: www.shawguides.com
Searchable database of writers' conferences.

United States Postal Service: www.usps.com
Domestic and international postage rate calculator, stamp ordering, zip code look-up, express mail tracking, etc.

Multiple services

Book Zone: www.bookzone.com
A catalog source for books, audio books, and more, with links to other publishing opportunities, diversions and distractions such as news, classifieds, contests, magazines, and trade groups.

BookWeb: www.ambook.org
This site of the American Booksellers Association offers book news, markets, discussion groups, events, resources, and other book-related information.

Creative Freelancers: www.freelancers.com
A meeting spot for freelancers and employers. Writers post their résumés for free, and employers post job listings in writing, editing, proofreading, etc.

Editor & Publisher: www.editorandpublisher.com
The Internet source for Editor & Publisher, *this site provides up-to-date industry news, with other opportunities such as a research area and bookstore, a calendar of events, and classifieds.*

MarketsForWriters.com: www.marketsforwriters.com
Site rooted in groundbreaking book, Online Markets for Writers: How to Make Money By Selling Your Writing on the Internet *(Owl Books/Henry Holt & Co.), offering online market information, interviews, extensive resources, and advice from expert contributors including the National Writers Union (NWU) and the American Society of Journalists and Authors (ASJA).*

RoseDog.com: www.rosedog.com
This site is for readers, writers, agents, and publishers. Post excerpts from your unpublished work at no cost, to be reviewed by agents and publishers.

Small Publisher Association of North America (SPAN): www.SPANnet.org
This site includes membership information, publishing events and calendar, links, book sales, and other services.

Write4Kids.com: www.write4kids.com
Presented by Children's Book Insider, The Newsletter for Children's Writers. *Offers information on numerous aspects of publishing and children's literature, such as an InfoCenter, a Research Center, results of various surveys, and secrets on getting published.*

Writers Write: www.writerswrite.com
Offers current writing and publishing news, message boards, and job listings.

Research

AcqWeb: http://acqweb.library.vanderbilt.edu
Although geared toward librarians and researchers, AcqWeb provides reference information useful to writers, such as library catalogs, bibliographic services, Books in Print, *and other Web reference resources.*

CopyLaw.com: www.copylaw.com
Confused about copyrights? Many beginning writers may find the task of copyright searches daunting, but this site helps plan permission requests and locate copyrights.

FindLaw: www.findlaw.com
Contains information on landmark legal decisions, and includes legal publishers and state and local bar association information.

InfoNation: www.un.org/Pubs/CyberSchoolBus/infonation/e_infonation.htm
A two-step database that allows you to view and compare the most up-to-date statistical data for the Member States of the United Nations.

Information Please: www.infoplease.com
General reference.

International Trademark Association: www.inta.org
Check the correct spelling of nearly 4,000 trademarks and service marks, and get the correct generic term.

Library of Congress: http://lcweb.loc.gov/
Provides access to Library of Congress catalogs and other research vehicles, including full access to bills under consideration in the U.S. House of Representatives and Senate.

Literary Market Place: www.literarymarketplace.com
Provides contact information for U.S., Canadian, and international publishers (small and large), and agents. Focused searches available.

Media Resource Service: www.mediaresource.org
This service provided by the Scientific Research Society helps writers find reputable sources of scientific information at no charge.

Mediafinder: www.oxbridge.com
Contains basic facts about 75,000 publications.

Newswise: www.newswise.com
A comprehensive database of news releases from top institutions engaged in scientific, medical, liberal arts, and business research.

OANDA, The Currency Site: www.oanda.com
Find current names for the world's currencies and exchange rates.

PollingReport.com: www.pollingreport.com
Includes recent public opinion poll results from leading U.S. polling firms on politics, business, social issues, news events, sports, and entertainment.

ProfNet: www.profnet.com
Contains names of more than 4,000 news and information officers at colleges and universities, corporations, think tanks, national labs, medical centers, nonprofits, and PR agencies courtesy of this PR Newswire service.

The Publishing Law Center: www.publaw.com
Links and articles about intellectual property and other legal issues.

Refdesk: www.refdesk.com
Provides an easy-to-navigate, searchable index of websites that provide facts, figures, and interesting information.

SharpWriter.com: www.sharpwriter.com
Dictionaries, encyclopedic references, grammar tips.

U.S. Copyright Office: www.loc.gov/copyright/search
Locate the copyright status of millions of books, music recordings, movies, and software.

The World Factbook: www.odci.gov/cia/publications/factbook/index.html
Includes facts on every country in the world, on subjects from population to exports.

Writer's Digest: www.writersdigest.com
This site includes information about writing magazine pieces from Writer's Digest, *and writers' conferences.*

Organizations

Whether you write nonfiction or science fiction, self-help or short stories, there are national organizations representing your field as a whole or representing their members in court. Hundreds more smaller, local groups are providing assistance from paragraph to paragraph. There is an organization—probably several—to suit your needs.

THE ACADEMY OF AMERICAN POETS, 588 Broadway, Suite 604, New York NY 10012-3210. (212)274-0343. Fax: (212)274-9427. E-mail: academy@poets.org. Website: www.poets.org. Executive Director: Tree Swenson.

AMERICAN BOOK PRODUCERS ASSOCIATION, 156 Fifth Ave., New York NY 10010. (212)645-2368. Fax: (212)645-8769. E-mail: office@ABPAonline.org. Website: www.abpaonline.org. President: Susan Knopf.

AMERICAN MEDICAL WRITERS ASSOCIATION, 40 W. Gude Dr., Suite 101, Rockville MD 20850-1192. (301)294-5303. Fax: (301)294-9006. E-mail: info@amwa.org. Website: www.amwa.org. Executive Director: Donna Munari.

AMERICAN SOCIETY OF JOURNALISTS AND AUTHORS, 1501 Broadway, Suite 302, New York NY 10036. (212)997-0947. Fax: (212)768-7414. E-mail: info@asja.org. Website: www.asja.org. Executive Director: Brett Harvey.

AMERICAN TRANSLATORS ASSOCIATION, 225 Reinekers Lane, Suite 590, Alexandria VA 22314. (703)683-6100. Fax: (703)683-6122. E-mail: ata@atanet.org. Website: www.atanet.org. President: Thomas L. West III.

THE ASIAN AMERICAN WRITERS' WORKSHOP, 16 W. 32nd St., Suite 10A, New York NY 10001. (212)494-0061. Fax: (212)494-0062. E-mail: desk@aaww.org. Website: www.aaww.org. Executive Director: Quang Bao.

THE ASSOCIATED WRITING PROGRAMS, George Mason University, Mailstop 1E3, Fairfax VA 22030. (703)993-4301. E-mail: awp@gmu.edu. Website: www.awpwriter.org. Executive Director: David Fenza.

ASSOCIATION OF AMERICAN PUBLISHERS, INC., 71 Fifth Ave., 2nd Floor, New York NY 10003. (212)255-0200. Fax: (212)255-7007. Website: www.publishers.org. President and CEO: Patricia S. Schroeder.

THE ASSOCIATION OF AUTHORS' REPRESENTATIVES, INC., P.O. Box 237201 Ansonia Station, New York NY 10003. Website: www.aar-online.org.

ASSOCIATION OF DESK-TOP PUBLISHERS, 3401-A800 Adams Ave., San Diego CA 92116-3245. (619)563-9714.

THE AUTHORS GUILD, 31 E. 28th St., 10th Floor, New York NY 10016-7923. (212)563-5904. Fax: (212)564-5363. E-mail: staff@authorsguild.org. Website: www.authorsguild.org. President: Letty Cottin Pogrebin.

THE AUTHORS LEAGUE OF AMERICA, INC., 31 E. 28th St., 10th Floor, New York NY 10016. (212)564-8350. Executive Director: Paul Aiken.

CANADIAN AUTHORS ASSOCIATION, Box 419, Campbellford, ON K0L 1L0, Canada. (705)653-0323. Fax: (705)653-0593. E-mail: canauth@redden.on.ca. Website: www.canauthors.org. Contact: Alec McEachern.

THE DRAMATISTS GUILD OF AMERICA, INC., 1501 Broadway, Suite 701, New York NY 10036. (212)398-9366. Fax: (212)944-0420. E-mail: Igor@Dramaguild.com. Website: www.dramatistsguild.com. President: John Weidman.

EDITORIAL FREELANCERS ASSOCIATION, 71 W. 23rd St., Suite 1910, New York NY 10010-4102. (212)929-5400. Fax: (212)929-5439. E-mail: info@the-efa.org. Website: www.the-efa.org.

THE EDUCATION WRITERS ASSOCIATION, 2122 P St. NW, Suite 201, Washington DC 20037. (202)452-9830. Fax: (202)452-9837. E-mail: ewa@ewa.org. Website: www.ewa.org. President: Robin Farmer.

INTERNATIONAL WOMEN'S WRITING GUILD, Box 810, Gracie Station, New York NY 10028-0082. (212)737-7536. Fax: (212)737-9469. Website: www.iwwg.com. Executive Director: Hannelore Hahn.

MYSTERY WRITERS OF AMERICA, INC., 17 E. 47th St., 6th Floor, New York NY 10017. (212)888-8171. Fax: (212)888-8107. E-mail: mwa@mysterywriters.org. Website: www.mysterywriters.org. President: Michael Connelly.

NATIONAL ASSOCIATION OF SCIENCE WRITERS, INC., P.O. Box 890, Hedgesville WV 25427. (304)754-5077. Fax: (304)754-5076. E-mail: DBlum@facstaff.wisc.edu. President: Deborah Blum.

THE NATIONAL WRITERS ASSOCIATION, 3140 S. Peoria St., #295PMB, Aurora CO 80014. (303)841-0246. Fax: (303)841-2607. E-mail: ExecDirSandyWhelchel@nationalwriters.com. Website: www.nationalwriters.com. Executive Director: Sandy Whelchel.

NATIONAL WRITERS UNION, 113 University Place, 6th Floor, New York NY 10003. (212) 254-0279. Fax: (212) 254-0673. E-mail: nwu@nwu.org. Website: www.nwu.org. President: Jonathan Tasini.

NEW DRAMATISTS, 424 W. 44th St., New York NY 10036. (212)757-6960. Fax: (212)265-4738. E-mail: newdramatists@newdramatists.org. Website: www.newdramatists.org. Executive Director: Joel K. Ruark.

NOVELISTS, INC., P.O. Box 1166, Mission KS 66222-0166. E-mail: info@ninc.com. Website: www.ninc.com. President: Patricia Rice.

PEN AMERICAN CENTER, 568 Broadway, 4th Floor, New York NY 10012. (212)334-1660. Fax: (212)334-2181. E-mail: pen@pen.org. Website: www.pen.org.

POETRY SOCIETY OF AMERICA, 15 Gramercy Park, New York NY 10003. (212)254-9628. Website: www.poetrysociety.org. Executive Director: Alice Quinn.

PUBLIC RELATIONS SOCIETY OF AMERICA, 33 Irving Place, New York NY 10003-2376. (212)995-2230. Fax: (212)995-0757. Website: www.prsa.org. President and CEO: Reed B. Byrum.

ROMANCE WRITERS OF AMERICA, 3707 FM 1960 W., Suite 555, Houston TX 77068. (281)440-6885. Fax: (281)440-7510. E-mail: info@rwanational.org. Website: www.rwanational.com. President: Shirley Hailstock.

SCIENCE FICTION AND FANTASY WRITERS OF AMERICA, INC., P.O. Box 877, Chestertown MD 21620. E-mail: execdir@sfwa.org. Website: www.sfwa.org. Executive Director: Jane Jewell.

SOCIETY OF AMERICAN TRAVEL WRITERS, 1500 Sunday Dr., Suite 102, Raleigh NC 27607. (919)861-5586. Fax: (919)787-4916. E-mail: satw@satw.org. Website: www.satw.org.

SOCIETY OF CHILDREN'S BOOK WRITERS AND ILLUSTRATORS, 8271 Beverly Blvd., Los Angeles CA 90048. (323)782-1010. Fax: (323)782-1892. E-mail: scbwi@scbwi.org. Website: www.scbwi.org. President: Stephen Mooser. Executive Director: Lin Oliver.

SOCIETY OF PROFESSIONAL JOURNALISTS, Eugene S. Pulliam National Journalism Center, 3909 N. Meridian St., Indianapolis IN 46208. (317)927-8000. Fax: (317)920-4789. E-mail: questions@spj.org. Website: www.spj.org.

VOLUNTEER LAWYERS FOR THE ARTS, 1 E. 53rd St., 6th Floor, New York NY 10022
4201. (212)319-2787, ext. 1. Fax: (212)752-6575. Website: www.vlany.org. Executive Director: Elena M. Paul.

WESTERN WRITERS OF AMERICA, % Larry K. Brown, 209 E. Iowa, Cheyenne WY 82009. E-mail: membership@westernwriters.org. Website: www.westernwriters.org. President: Paul Andrew Hutton.

WOMEN WRITING THE WEST, 8547 E. Arapahoe Rd., J541, Greenwood CO 80112-1436. (303)674-5450. Website: www.womenwritingthewest.org. President: Cynthia Leal Massey.

WRITERS GUILD OF ALBERTA, Percy Page Centre, 11759 Groat Rd., Edmonton AB T5M 3K6, Canada. (780)422-8174. Fax: (780)422-2663. E-mail: mail@writersguild.ab.ca. Website: www.writersguild.ab.ca. President: Christina Grant.

WRITERS GUILD OF AMERICA, EAST, 555 W. 57th St., Suite 1230, New York NY 10019, (212)767-7800. Fax: (212)582-1909. Website: www.wgaeast.org. Executive Director: Mona Mangan.

WRITERS GUILD OF AMERICA, WEST, 7000 W. Third St., Los Angeles CA 90048, (323)951-4000. Fax: (323)782-4000. Website: www.wga.org. President: Victoria Riskin.

Glossary

Key to symbols and abbreviations appears on the front and back inside covers.

Advance. A sum of money a publisher pays a writer prior to the publication of a book. It is usually paid in installments, such as one-half on signing the contract; one-half on delivery of a complete and satisfactory manuscript. The advance is paid against the royalty money that will be earned by the book.

Agent. A liaison between a writer and editor or publisher. An agent shops a manuscript around, receiving a commission when the manuscript is accepted. Agents usually take a 10-15% fee from the advance and royalties, 10-20% if a co-agent is involved, such as in the sale of dramatic rights.

All rights. See Rights and the Writer in the Minding the Details section.

Anthology. A collection of selected writings by various authors or a gathering of works by one author.

Assignment. Editor asks a writer to produce a specific article for an agreed-upon fee.

Auction. Publishers sometimes bid for the acquisition of a book manuscript that has excellent sales prospects. The bids are for the amount of the author's advance, advertising and promotional expenses, royalty percentage, etc. Auctions are conducted by agents.

Avant-garde. Writing that is innovative in form, style, or subject, often considered difficult and challenging.

B&W. Abbreviation for black and white photographs.

Backlist. A publisher's list of its books that were not published during the current season, but that are still in print.

Bimonthly. Every two months.

Bio. A sentence or brief paragraph about the writer. It can appear at the bottom of the first or last page of a writer's article or short story or on a contributor's page.

Biweekly. Every two weeks.

Boilerplate. A standardized contract. When an editor says "our standard contract," he means the boilerplate with no changes. Writers should be aware that most authors and/or agents make many changes on the boilerplate.

Book packager. Draws all elements of a book together, from the initial concept to writing and marketing strategies, then sells the book package to a book publisher. Also known as book producer or book developer.

Business-size envelope. Also known as a #10 envelope, it is the standard size used in sending business correspondence.

Byline. Name of the author appearing with the published piece.

Category fiction. A term used to include all various labels attached to types of fiction. See also *genre*.

Chapbook. A small booklet, usually paperback, of poetry, ballads, or tales.

Circulation. The number of subscribers to a magazine.

Clean copy. A manuscript free of errors, cross-outs, wrinkles, or smudges.

Clips. Samples, usually from newspapers or magazines, of your *published* work.

Coffee-table book. An oversize book, heavily illustrated.

Column inch. The amount of space contained in one inch of a typeset column.

Commercial novels. Novels designed to appeal to a broad audience. These are often broken down into categories such as western, mystery, and romance. See also *genre*.

Commissioned work. See *assignment.*

Concept. A statement that summarizes a screenplay or teleplay—before the outline or treatment is written.

Confessional. Genre of fiction essay in which the author or first-person narrator confesses something shocking or embarassing.

Contact sheet. A sheet of photographic paper on which negatives are transferred so you can see the entire roll of shots placed together on one sheet of paper without making separate, individual prints.

Contributor's copies. Copies of the issues of magazines sent to the author in which the author's work appears.

Cooperative publishing. See *co-publishing.*

Co-publishing. Arrangement where author and publisher share publication costs and profits of a book. Also known as *cooperative publishing*. See also *subsidy publisher.*

Copyediting. Editing a manuscript for grammar, punctuation, and printing style, not subject content.

Copyright. A means to protect an author's work. See Copyright in the Minding the Details section.

Cover letter. A brief letter, accompanying a complete manuscript, especially useful if responding to an editor's request for a manuscript. A cover letter may also accompany a book proposal. A cover letter is *not* a query letter; see Targeting Your Ideas in the Getting Published section.

Creative nonfiction. Nonfictional writing that uses an innovative approach to the subject and creative language.

CV. Curriculum vita. A brief listing of qualifications and career accomplishments.

Derivative works. A work that has been translated, adapted, abridged, condensed, annotated, or otherwise produced by altering a previously created work. Before producing a derivative work, it is necessary to secure the written permission of the copyright owner of the original piece.

Desktop publishing. A publishing system designed for a personal computer. The system is capable of typesetting, some illustration, layout, design, and printing—so that the final piece can be distributed and/or sold.

Docudrama. A fictional film rendition of recent newsmaking events and people.

Eclectic. Publication features a variety of different writing styles of genres.

Electronic submission. A submission made by modem or on computer disk.

El-hi. Elementary to high school.

E-mail. Electronic mail. Mail generated on a computer and delivered over a computer network to a specific individual or group of individuals. To send or receive e-mail, a user must have an account with an online service, which provides an e-mail address and electronic mailbox.

Erotica. Fiction or art that is sexually oriented.

Experimental. See *avant-garde.*

Fair use. A provision of the copyright law that says short passages from copyrighted material may be used without infringing on the owner's rights.

Feature. An article giving the reader information of human interest rather than news. Also used by magazines to indicate a lead article or distinctive department.

Filler. A short item used by an editor to "fill" out a newspaper column or magazine page. It could be a timeless news item, a joke, an anecdote, some light verse or short humor, puzzle, etc.

First North American serial rights. See Rights and the Writer in the Minding the Details section.

First-person point of view. In nonfiction, the author reports from his or her own perspective; in fiction, the narrator tells the story from his or her point of view. This viewpoint makes frequent use of "I," or occasionally, "we."

Formula story. Familiar theme treated in a predictable plot structure—such as boy meets girl, boy loses girl, boy gets girl.

Frontlist. A publisher's list of its books that are new to the current season.

Galleys. The first typeset version of a manuscript that has not yet been divided into pages.

Genre. Refers either to a general classification of writing, such as the novel or the poem, or to the categories within those classifications, such as the problem novel or the sonnet. Genre fiction describes commercial novels, such as mysteries, romances, and science fiction. Also called category fiction.

Ghostwriter. A writer who puts into literary form an article, speech, story, or book based on another person's ideas or knowledge.

Gift book. A book designed as a gift item. Often small in size with few illustrations and placed close to a bookstore's checkout as an "impulse" buy, gift books tend to be written to a specific niche, such as golfers, mothers, etc.

Glossy. A black and white photograph with a shiny surface as opposed to one with a nonshiny matte finish.

Gothic novel. A fiction category or genre in which the central character is usually a beautiful young girl, the setting an old mansion or castle, and there is a handsome hero and a real menace, either natural or supernatural.

Graphic novel. An adaptation of a novel in graphic form, long comic strip, or heavily illustrated story, of 40 pages or more, produced in paperback form.

Hard copy. The printed copy of a computer's output.

Hardware. All the mechanically-integrated components of a computer that are not software. Circuit boards, transistors, and the machines that are the actual computer are the hardware.

High-lo. Material written for newer readers, generally adults, with a *high* interest level and *low* reading ability.

Home page. The first page of a World Wide Web document.

Honorarium. Token payment—small amount of money, or a byline and copies of the publication.

How-to. Books and magazine articles offering a combination of information and advice in describing how something can be accomplished. Subjects range widely from hobbies to psychology.

Hypertext. Words or groups of words in an electronic document that are linked to other text, such as a definition or a related document. Hypertext can also be linked to illustrations.

Illustrations. May be photographs, old engravings, artwork. Usually paid for separately from the manuscript. See also *package sale*.

Imprint. Name applied to a publisher's specific line or lines of books (e.g., Eos is an imprint of HarperCollins).

Interactive. A type of computer interface that takes user input, such as answers to computer-generated questions, and then acts upon that input.

Interactive fiction. Works of fiction in book or computer software format in which the reader determines the path the story will take. The reader chooses from several alternatives at the end of a "chapter," and thus determines the structure of the story. Interactive fiction features multiple plots and endings.

Internet. A worldwide network of computers that offers access to a wide variety of electronic resources.

Kill fee. Fee for a complete article that was assigned but which was subsequently cancelled.

Lead time. The time between the acquisition of a manuscript by an editor and its actual publication.

Libel. A false accusation or any published statement or presentation that tends to expose another to public contempt, ridicule, etc.

List royalty. A royalty payment based on a percentage of a book's retail (or "list") price.

Literary fiction. The general category of serious, nonformulaic, intelligent fiction.

Little magazine. Publications of limited circulation, usually on literary or political subject matter.

LORT. An acronym for League of Resident Theatres. Letters from A to D follow LORT and designate the size of the theater.

Mainstream fiction. Fiction that transcends popular novel categories such as mystery, romance, and science fiction. Using conventional methods, this kind of fiction tells stories about people and their conflicts with greater depth of characterization, background, etc., than the more narrowly focused genre novels.

Mass market. Nonspecialized books of wide appeal directed toward a large audience. Smaller and more cheaply produced than trade paperbacks, they are found in many nonbookstore outlets, such as drugstores or supermarkets.

Memoir. A narrative recounting a writer's (or fictional narrator's) personal or family history.

Midlist. Those titles on a publisher's list that are not expected to be big sellers, but are expected to have limited sales. Midlist books are mainstream, not literary, scholarly, or genre, and are usually written by new or unknown writers.

Model release. A paper signed by the subject of a photograph (or the subject's guardian, if a juvenile) giving the photographer permission to use the photograph editorially or for advertising purposes or for some specific purpose as stated.

Modem. A device used to transmit data from one computer to another via telephone lines.

Monograph. A detailed and documented scholarly study concerning a single subject.

MOW. Movie of the week.

Multimedia. Computers and software capable of integrating text, sound, photographic-quality images, animation, and video.

Multiple submissions. Sending more than one poem, gag, or greeting card idea at the same time. This term is often used synonymously with *simultaneous submission*.

Narrative nonfiction. A narrative presentation of actual events.

Narrative poem. Poetry that tells a story. One of the three main genres of poetry (the others being dramatic poetry and lyric poetry).

Net royalty. A royalty payment based on the amount of money a book publisher receives on the sale of a book after booksellers' discounts, special sales discounts, and returns.

Network. A group of computers electronically linked to share information and resources.

New Age. A "fringe" topic that has become increasingly mainstream. Formerly New Age included UFOs and occult phenomena. The term has evolved to include more general topics such as psychology, religion, and health, but emphasizing the mystical, spiritual, or alternative aspects.

Newsbreak. A brief, late-breaking news story added to the front page of a newspaper at press time or a magazine news item of importance to readers.

Nostalgia. A genre of reminiscence, recalling sentimental events or products of the past.

Novella. A short novel, or a long short story; 7,000 to 15,000 words approximately. Also known as a novelette.

Novelization. A novel created from the script of a popular movie, usually called a movie "tie-in" and published in paperback.

On spec. An editor expresses an interest in a proposed article idea and agrees to consider the finished piece for publication "on speculation." The editor is under no obligation to buy the finished manuscript.

One-time rights. See Rights and the Writer in the Minding the Details section.

Outline. A summary of a book's contents in five to 15 double-spaced pages; often in the form of chapter headings with a descriptive sentence or two under each one to show the scope of the book. A screenplay's or teleplay's outline is a scene-by-scene narrative description of the story (ten-15 pages for a ½-hour teleplay; 15-25 pages for a one-hour teleplay; 25-40 pages for a 90-minute teleplay; 40-60 pages for a two-hour feature film or teleplay).

Over-the-transom. Describes the submission of unsolicited material by a freelance writer.

Package sale. The editor buys manuscript and photos as a "package" and pays for them with one check.

Page rate. Some magazines pay for material at a fixed rate per published page, rather than per word.

Parody. The conscious imitation of a work, usually with the intent to ridicule or make fun of the work.

Payment on acceptance. The editor sends you a check for your article, story, or poem as soon as he decides to publish it.

Payment on publication. The editor doesn't send you a check for your material until it is published.

Pen name. The use of a name other than your legal name on articles, stories, or books when you wish to remain anonymous. Simply notify your post office and bank that you are using the name so that you'll receive mail and/or checks in that name. Also called a *pseudonym*.

Photo feature. Feature in which the emphasis is on the photographs rather than on accompanying written material.

Plagiarism. Passing off as one's own the expression of ideas and words of another writer.

Proofreading. Close reading and correction of a manuscript's typographical errors.

Proposal. A summary of a proposed book submitted to a publisher, particularly used for nonfiction manuscripts. A proposal often contains an individualized cover letter, one-page overview of the book, marketing information, competitive books, author information, chapter-by-chapter outline, two to three sample chapters and attachments (if relevant) such as magazine articles about the topic and articles you have written (particularly on the proposed topic).

Proscenium. The area of the stage in front of the curtain.

Prospectus. A preliminary written description of a book or article, usually one page in length.

Pseudonym. See *pen name*.

Public domain. Material that was either never copyrighted or whose copyright term has expired.

Query. A letter that sells an idea to an editor. Usually a query is brief (no more than one page) and uses attention-getting prose.

Release. A statement that your idea is original, has never been sold to anyone else, and that you are selling the negotiated rights to the idea upon payment.

Remainders. Copies of a book that are slow to sell and can be purchased from the publisher at a reduced price. Depending on the author's book contract, a reduced royalty or no royalty is paid on remainder books.

Reporting time. The time it takes for an editor to report to the author on his/her query or manuscript.

Reprint rights. See Rights and the Writer in the Minding the Details section.

Round-up article. Comments from, or interviews with, a number of celebrities or experts on a single theme.

Royalties, standard hardcover book. 10% of the retail price on the first 5,000 copies sold; 12½% on the next 5,000; 15% thereafter.

Royalties, standard mass paperback book. 4 to 8% of the retail price on the first 150,000 copies sold.

Royalties, standard trade paperback book. No less than 6% of list price on the first 20,000 copies; 7½% thereafter.

Scanning. A process through which letter-quality printed text or artwork is read by a computer scanner and converted into workable data.

Screenplay. Script for a film intended to be shown in theaters.

Self-publishing. In this arrangement, the author keeps all income derived from the book, but he pays for its manufacturing, production, and marketing.

Semimonthly. Twice per month.

Semiweekly. Twice per week.

Serial. Published periodically, such as a newspaper or magazine.

Serial fiction. Fiction published in a magazine in installments, often broken off at a suspenseful spot.

Series fiction. A sequence of novels featuring the same characters.

Short-short. A complete short story of 1,500 words maximum, and around 250 words minimum.

Sidebar. A feature presented as a companion to a straight news report (or main magazine article) giving sidelights on human-interest aspects or sometimes elucidating just one aspect of the story.

Simultaneous submissions. Sending the same article, story, or poem to several publishers at the same time. Some publishers refuse to consider such submissions.

Slant. The approach or style of a story or article that will appeal to readers of a specific magazine. For example, a magazine may always use stories with an upbeat ending.

Slice-of-life vignette. A short fiction piece intended to realistically depict an interesting moment of everyday living.

Slides. Usually called transparencies by editors looking for color photographs.

Slush pile. The stack of unsolicited or misdirected manuscripts received by an editor or book publisher.

Software. The computer programs that control computer hardware, usually run from a disk drive of some sort. Computers need software in order to run.

Style. The way in which something is written—for example, short, punchy sentences or flowing narrative.

Subsidiary rights. All those rights, other than book publishing rights included in a book contract—such as paperback, book club, movie rights, etc.

Subsidy publisher. A book publisher who charges the author for the cost to typeset and print his book, the jacket, etc., as opposed to a royalty publisher who pays the author.

Synopsis. A brief summary of a story, novel, or play. As part of a book proposal, it is a comprehensive summary condensed in a page or page and a half, single-spaced.

Tabloid. Newspaper format publication on about half the size of the regular newspaper page, such as *The Star*.

Tagline. A caption for a photo or a comment added to a filler.

Tearsheet. Page from a magazine or newspaper containing your printed story, article, poem, or ad.

Teleplay. A play written for or performed on television.

TOC. Table of Contents.

Trade. Either a hardcover or paperback book; subject matter frequently concerns a special interest. Books are directed toward the layperson rather than the professional.

Transparencies. Positive color slides; not color prints.

Treatment. Synopsis of a TV or film script (40-60 pages for a two-hour feature film or teleplay).

Unsolicited manuscript. A story, article, poem, or book that an editor did not specifically ask to see.

Vanity publisher. See *subsidy publisher.*

World Wide Web (WWW). An Internet resource that utilizes hypertext to access information. It also supports formatted text, illustrations, and sounds, depending on the user's computer capabilities.

Work-for-hire. See Copyright in the Minding the Details section.

YA. Young adult books.

Book Publishers Subject Index

This index will help you find publishers that consider books on specific subjects—the subjects you choose to write about. Remember that a publisher may be listed here only under a general subject category such as Art and Architecture, while the company publishes *only* art history or how-to books. Be sure to consult each company's detailed individual listing, its book catalog, and several of its books before you send your query or proposal. The page number of the detailed listing is provided for your convenience.

FICTION

Adventure

Comic Books

Confession

Erotica

Ethnic

Experimental

Fantasy

Feminist

Gay/Lesbian

Gothic

Historical

Horror

Humor

Juvenile

More Great Books to Help You Sell Your Work!

Latest Edition!

2004 Novel & Short Story Writer's Market

edited by Anne Bowling

Discover buyers hungry for your work! You'll find the names, addresses, pay rates, and editorial needs of thousands of fiction publishers. Plus, loads of helpful articles and informative interviews with professionals who know what it takes to get published!

#10855-K/$24.99/690 p/pb *Available December 2003*

Grammatically Correct

by Anne Stilman

Make sure your writing is smooth, clear, graceful — and correct. With this easy-to-use reference, you can quickly master the building blocks that make up good writing — including punctuation, spelling, style, usage and more. Complete with exercises and examples!

#10529-K/$19.99/352 p/hc

New Markets!

2004 Children's Writer's & Illustrator's Market

edited by Alice Pope

As a writer, illustrator, or photographer in the children's and young adult markets, this is your single-most important resource! Inside, you'll find up-to-date listings of agents and representatives, magazine and book publishers, contests and awards, game and puzzle manufacturers, script buyers, toy companies, and more! And, you'll get advice on using the Internet to your best advantage, examples of great query letters, and interviews with industry experts.

#10853-K/$23.99/400 p/pb *Available December 2003*

The Marshall Plan for Getting Your Novel Published

by Evan Marshall

In the third book of the popular *Marshall Plan* series, noted author and agent Evan Marshall offers 87 no-nonsense tips for writing professional quality fiction, plus detailed advice on submitting your work, selecting and working with a publisher, and promoting your finished novel.

#10858-K/$21.99/240 p/hc

Snoopy's Guide to the Writing Life

edited by Barnaby Conrad with a forward by Monte Schulz

Thirty famous writers, including Ray Bradbury, Sue Grafton and Fannie Flagg, respond to their favorite "Snoopy-at-the-typewriter" strips. Each strip inspires a reflection on some aspect of the writing life — from getting rejected to the search for new ideas. The essays are light and sometimes humorous, but they all reveal the wisdom behind the world's most literary beagle.

#10856-K/$19.99/192 p/hc

Pick up these helpful references today at your local bookstore, use the handy Order Card on the reverse side, or visit the Web site: www.writersdigest.com/store/books.asp.

Literary

Mainstream/ Contemporary

Military/War

Multicultural

Multimedia

Mystery

Occult

Picture Books

Plays

Poetry (Including Chapbooks)

Poetry In Translation

Regional

Religious

Romance

Science Fiction

Short Story Collections

Spiritual (New Age, etc.)

Sports

Suspense

Translation

Western

Young Adult

NONFICTION

Agriculture/Horticulture

Americana

Animals

Anthropology/ Archaeology

Art/Architecture

Astrology/Psychic/New Age

Biography

Business/Economics

Child Guidance/Parenting

Coffeetable Book

Computers/Electronic

Contemporary Culture

Cookbooks

Cooking/Foods/Nutrition

Creative Nonfiction

Educational

Ethnic

Fashion/Beauty

Film/Cinema/Stage

Gardening

Gay/Lesbian

General Nonfiction

Gift Books

Government/Politics

Health/Medicine

History

Hobby

How-To

Humor

Illustrated Book

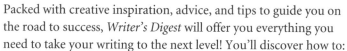

Juvenile Books

Language and Literature

Memoirs

Military/War

Money/Finance

Multicultural

Multimedia

Music/Dance

Nature/Environment

Philosophy

Photography

Psychology

Recreation

Reference

Regional

Religion

Science/Technology

Self-Help

Sex

Sociology

Software

Spiritual

Sports

Technical

Textbook

Translation

Travel

True Crime

Women's Issues/Studies

World Affairs

General Index

This index lists every market appearing in the book; use it to find specific companies you wish to approach. Markets that appeared in the 2003 edition of *Writer's Market*, but are not included in this edition are identified by a two-letter code explaining why the market was omitted: (**ED**)—Editorial Decision, (**NS**)—Not Accepting Submissions, (**NR**)—No or Late Response to Listing Request, (**OB**)—Out of Business, (**RR**)—Removed by Market's Request, (**UC**)—Unable to Contact, (**RP**)—Business Restructured or Purchased, (**NP**)—No Longer Pays or Pays in Copies Only, (**SR**)—Subsidy/Royalty Publisher, (**UF**)—Uncertain Future, (**Web**)—a listing that appears on our website at www.WritersMarket.com

A

B

D

E

F

H

M

GENERAL INDEX